Platter's
by
Diners Club
INTERNATIONAL

2019
SOUTH AFRICAN

WINE
GUIDE

39TH EDITION

Available on the
App Store

GET IT ON
Google play

John Platter SA Wine Guide (Pty) Ltd
www.wineonaplatter.com

PUBLISHER

Jean-Pierre Rossouw

EDITOR

Philip van Zyl

ASSOCIATE EDITORS

Tim James & Cathy van Zyl

TASTERS

Winnie Bowman, Hennie Coetzee, Greg de Bruyn, Joanne Gibson, Tim James, Angela Lloyd, Cathy Marston, Fiona McDonald, Gregory Mutambe, Christine Rudman, Dave Swingler, Cathy van Zyl & Meryl Weaver. Previous editions: David Biggs, David Clarke, Christian Eedes, Higgo Jacobs, Ingrid Motteux, Khuselo Mputa, Jörg Pfützner, James Pietersen & Samarie Smith

COPYWRITERS

Hennie Coetzee, Joanne Gibson, Tim James, Angela Lloyd, Cathy Marston, Fiona McDonald, Christine Rudman, Wendy Toerien, Cathy van Zyl & Meryl Weaver

COORDINATORS

Ina de Villiers (information); MF Schoeman & Christina Harvett (wine & tasting)

DATABASE & QR CODES

Sean de Kock, Ben van Rensburg (Modern Web Presence)

TYPESETTING & MAPS

Gawie du Toit

ADVERTISING, SALES & ADMINISTRATION

Christine Bishop ▪ T +27 (0)28-316-3049 ▪ F +27 (0)86-602-9679 ▪ office@wineonaplatter.com

© John Platter SA Wine Guide (Pty) Ltd 2019
PO Box 537, Hermanus 7200
T +27 (0)28-316-3049 ▪ F +27 (0)86-602-9679 ▪ office@wineonaplatter.com

Wineonaplatter.com
Facebook.com/wineonaplatter
Twitter.com/wineonaplatter ▪ @wineonaplatter

ISBN 978-0-9870046-8-0

Printed and bound in the Republic of South Africa by ABC Press, Cape Town

Contents

A WARM WELCOME FROM DINERS CLUB   5

SOME TRENDS IN SOUTH AFRICAN WINE   6

EDITOR'S NOTE   9

OUR METHOD & THE ACCOLADES WE AWARD   11

WINERIES OF THE YEAR   12

    Top Performing Winery of the Year 2019   12

    Newcomer Winery of the Year 2019   12

    Editor's Award 2019   12

WINES OF THE YEAR   13

FIVE STARS   14

HIGHLY RECOMMENDED   16

TASTERS FOR THIS EDITION   19

HOW TO USE THIS GUIDE   22

A–Z OF SOUTH AFRICAN PRODUCERS   41

THIS YEAR'S RATINGS SUMMARISED   597

THE INDUSTRY   625

    Overview   625

    Industry Organisations   627

    Winegrowing Areas   630

    Grape Varieties   635

    Competitions, Challenges & Awards   640

    Wine & Brandy Education   642

    Make Your Own Wine or Brandy   643

    A-Code Numbers & Certification Codes   644

STYLES & VINTAGES   645

    Recent South African Vintages   645

    Older Vintages   645

    South African Wine Styles   646

    South African Brandy, Husk Spirit & Sherry-Style Wines   648

WORDS & PHRASES   649

    Winetasting Terms   649

    Winemaking Terms   651

TOURING WINE COUNTRY   655

    Wine Routes, Trusts & Associations   655

    Winelands Tourism Offices   655

    Specialist Wine Tours   656

    Restaurants in the Winelands and Cape Town   658

    Accommodation in the Winelands and Cape Town   666

    Disabled Access in SA Wineries   671

    Winelands Maps   673

A Warm Welcome from Diners Club

It is with great pleasure that I welcome you, on behalf of Diners Club, to this 39th edition of the Platter's by Diners Club South African Wine Guide.

We are proud to support the wonderful world of South African wine through Platter's; our Diners Club Winemaker of the Year and Young Winemaker of the Year awards; and also our Winelist Awards.

Platter's is the keystone in celebrating South African wine excellence as this unique guide assesses thousands of wines a year — a monumental project of vital importance — and the wines that are judged best-of-best in these pages have really had to prove themselves. It's not only about the top achievers of course, and the pages of this guide are packed with indispensable knowledge for all wine lovers, including background facts and figures, and information on touring our beautiful winelands. We also encourage you to download the companion app for iPhone or Android.

For more on how Diners Club can enhance your wine, food and travel experiences, please visit www.dinersclub.co.za

Here's to a sparkling 2019!

Lesego Chauke-Motshwane
Director, Diners Club South Africa

Some Trends in South African Wine

It gets better and better at the top end of Cape wine. The revolution in winemaking, now increasingly marked by attention to site and viticulture, continues to develop, and to attract the admiration of the wine-drinking world.

But the split between the two ends of the South African wine industry continues to widen: at one extreme is a tiny (though expanding) elite producing fine wine to great local and international applause; at the other, bulk-producers selling at rock-bottom prices that contribute to worries about the financial viability of swathes of the industry. For some years, many grapegrowers have endured costs rising much more rapidly than their income. It is notable, however, that some farmers oriented to providing fruit to the co-ops, big merchants and occasional private cellars are seeking other ways out. Some are working with producers who can pay high prices for special parcels of grapes; others are bottling their own wines from specially tended vineyards; some are doing all of this and also working collaboratively to raise their game and their income. Breedekloof Makers is a good example: various wineries from that mostly bulk-producing region are lifting their collective image through premium bottlings of chenin blanc - a grape which the industry rockstars have made ever more fashionable.

Less focused, but also proliferating, are groupings of established wineries aiming to share costs and widen their impact in marketing their products, especially overseas. Generally they are not regional, but based on a shared stylistic approach, or a perceived shared market. Further, going beyond the wine routes, some areas are combining an enrichment of the local wine culture with marketing via festivals. These could be based on a signature grape variety — like pinot noir in the Hemel-en-Aarde, chardonnay in Elgin. There are also producer groups based on style (port and MCC sparkling for example) or grape variety (chenin blanc, sauvignon blanc, pinotage), working to advance both technical capacity as well as image — the latter primarily via competitions. Stellenbosch producers of cabernet sauvignon wines have recently combined varietal and regional criteria for the Stellenbosch Cabernet Collective. Various strategies, then, based on an increasingly important recognition: that working together to achieve common goals is vital.

There's still plenty of good value on local shelves. But buyers of South African wine at the top end will have noted that the cost of the most admired bottles (and of many ambitious new entrants, of which there never seems to be a shortage) has been rising implacably in recent years. The sustainability of parts of that trend must also be questionable: just how many beautifully and fascinatingly made chenin blancs and cinsauts off lovingly nurtured old vines can the market absorb at R200 and more (often much more)?

The 'ultra-premium' category identified by the leading industry analyst Nielsen is of red wines selling for R125 or more, and whites over R96. It represents less than 2% of the local wine market; well over 50% of bottled wine sells to wine-drinkers for under R40 per bottle. We must remember when admiring the wines rating highest in this Guide that (it's surely safe to hazard) they are generally in that top 2%, and quite possibly most are in the top 1% by price.

Declining vineyard – rising production

The drought that afflicted many parts of the Cape winelands for 3 years was broken last winter (definitively - for now — we hope), but its legacy, despite including the generally excellent 2017 vintage, will add momentum to various disturbing trends in the wine industry. A reduced 2018 crop will affect the incomes of many growers. A consequence of that, exacerbated by drought damage to some vineyards, is likely to be an acceleration in the decline of the total vineyard, as uneconomic vineyards are simply abandoned or, where possible, replaced by a more financially viable crop.

In fact, doubtless connected to the economics, there's a continuing reduction in the number of grape farmers: 3029 of them in 2017, compared with 3 839 ten years back. Consolidation seems to be the immediate explanation.

The decline in the size of the South African national vineyard has been steadily continuing since 2006. At the end of 2017, wine-grapes covered just under 95 000 hectares; at the end of 2006 the figure had been over 102 000.

Counter-intuitively, however, the volume of wine produced has been growing fairly steadily over that period: that is, fewer vines, but more wine. The total wine crop in 2017 was over 1 118 million litres – 100 million litres more than in 2006. The apparent anomaly is explained by the trend of producers faced with low and stagnant grape prices finding that the only way to maintain their income is by increasing the yield that a vineyard bears. Unfortunately (though not inevitably) this is generally a very short-term strategy that can lead to lower quality wine, and can also damage a vineyard and shorten its lifespan.

Planting vines

If the total South African vineyard is shrinking, it is also slightly changing its shape, and this is a more encouraging trend. The number of different varieties planted has been rising steadily this century from around 80 to over 100 now. We can now find wines made from such grapes as marsanne, roussanne, durif (petite sirah) and alvarinho, and they should soon be joined by the likes of nero d'Avola and agiorgitiko.

The dominance of traditional varieties is little affected by such upstarts, however. Over 65% of South African wine produced in 2017 was white, and grape plantings reflect this, with chenin blanc consolidating its lead at 18.6%, followed by colombard (like chenin, also much used for brandy) at 11.9%. Then come cabernet sauvignon (11%) and shiraz (10.3%). Then back to white varieties for sauvignon blanc (9.8%), then something of a drop to pinotage (7.4%), chardonnay (7.1) and merlot (5.8%).

An exciting development, one somewhat connected to the interest in newer varieties, is the increase in co-planting projects between established grape-farmers and younger winemakers without their own land. Costs are shared, and medium-term contracts promise the farmers committed sales, while the winemakers are assured of supplies of desirable grapes – something that is becoming increasingly important as more and more ambitious young winemakers seek out fine vineyards. Sometimes, of course, they're seeking old vines, a category growing in marketing and, arguably, quality significance: the Old Vines Project is doing excellent work in not only bringing farmers and winemakers together in arrangements that keep good older, lower-yielding vineyards viable, but in helping farmers get the best out of their older vineyards – and to farm their younger vineyards in such a way as to ensure their future viability as old ones. In a world first, members of the Project can display a Certified *Heritage* Vineyards seal on qualifying bottles, including the planting date of the vineyard from which the grapes came.

As interesting aspect of some newer plantings that might more frequently be noticed by visitors to the winelands is the use of the 'echalas' method, leading to what might seem at first sight to be densely planted fields of poles. The Afrikaans name 'stok-by-paaltjie' is more frequently used than the French one, and graphically describes its essence: instead of being conventionally trellised on wires, or planted as a low-growing bush, each vine has its own pole, to which shoots may be tied. It's a very expensive, labour-intensive method, but particularly useful in steep or windy sites. And, like the concern with older vines, evidence of how attention to vineyard practice is becoming the single most important element of the drive to ever-improved wines at the top of the South African industry.

In the cellar

It can't be forgotten that the winelover's willingness to learn to appreciate new aromas, flavours and textures is vital to the success of the winemaker's willingness to experiment. The export market has been crucial for many local makers of 'natural' wines, skin-fermented whites, and the like (the avant garde is international, after all) but the local market has also become more open. So there's more of such wines about.

It undoubtedly makes categorisation of wine more complicated. Previously, if a wine was listed as 'an unwooded white', that usually implied that it had been fermented in stainless steel tanks and bottled without much maturation in any other vessel – apart from the bottle of course – before hitting the shelves. But now there are some decidedly superior white wines technically in the 'unwooded' category that had previously been matured in oak (new barrels if some oak flavour was wanted to add complexity, previously used barrels if neutrality was wanted in the oxidative process of barrel-ageing). Now they might be lengthily and complexly matured in concrete or plastic egg-shaped containers or in clay pots (often called amphoras). Such maturation helps preserve the wine's fruit purity, freshness and vitality – as does stainless steel, but there are added benefits from concrete and clay, especially in mouthfeel, texture. It is certainly not unusual to step into the working end of a winery these days and find such containers.

Larger oak casks (generally oval shaped, containing a few thousand litres or more, and referred to as foudres) are also being used increasingly for storage and maturation – the larger the volume of liquid in relation to the oak surface, the less influence the oak has on the wine, especially as the foudre ages (and they are, anyway, vastly too expensive to replace). As with many of the practices of new-wave winemakers, this is all thoroughly traditional: before the 1960s saw the start of an influx of new 225-litre barrels for maturing red wine, this is how much South African red wine was matured. And the fashionability of cement tanks (starting to effectively replace stainless steel in some cellars) has a long precedent here, both for fermentation and shorter-term storage.

Even where maturation in small barrels is still desired, the trend is still slowly away from a high proportion of new wood, for both red wines and oak-matured whites. The blockbuster (suavely soft and sweetish, ultra-ripe, alcoholic, redolent of expensive oak) is certainly not defeated, but losing ground, as sheer drinkability and the charms of pure fruit and freshness become clearer.

Another traditional practice adopted by many new-wave vintners, but of a much older and latterly much more neglected tradition, is fermenting white wines on their skins. Generally white wines are fermented from juice with the

grapeskins removed; including the skins adds colour – even to the point of the wine being orange (often the word used to describe this kind of wine). Frequently these skin-contact white wines are blended with more conventionally made wines, to add complexity of a savoury kind, as well as a little tannic 'grip'.

'Orange' wines tend to be associated with the larger 'natural wine' movement, which is continuing to spread its influence in Cape winemaking. The precise meaning of the term is disputed, but should involve, firstly, wine made from organically grown grapes (that is, the naturalness starts in the vineyard); secondly, an avoidance of processes like fining and filtration, and of all additives (including commercial yeasts and acid) in the winemaking process – except (unless you're a real fundamentalist winemaker) for sulphur, that vital preservative. But more and more fairly conventional winemakers, not only in South Africa, are reducing their active interventions of this kind in the cellar.

Drinking the stuff

South African wine is being drunk more than ever, fortunately for the industry – even if most concerned observers would prefer a smaller proportion of exported wine to be travelling in bulk (it's now a hefty 61% that is not packaged at home). Exports account for a little under half of South African wine production: nearly 450 million litres in 2017 – the highest figure yet except for one anomalous year (2013).

Back home, per capita consumption of wine was a meagre 7.6 litres in 2017 – down on the previous year, but still up on the year before that. Now there's a set of statistics we could all do our part in improving.

Editor's Note

Ten years ago, for our 29th edition, I spent many hours compiling the set of GPS coordinates which appears in the A-Z directory of producers in this hardcover version of our guide, and underpins the map functionality in our apps and website.

I well recall how complicated it all seemed, and how tricky it was — and still is — to correctly enter a coordinate into one's phone or other device. Which is why I was interested in a TED talk by Chris Sheldrick, originally from the music industry, where bands and equipment keep getting lost, outlining his idea for a simpler and better addressing system.

That concept is now What3Words, an app and back-end which divides the world into 3m × 3m squares, each with a unique 3-word address. Which means that via the app (or W3W website), it is possible to precisely locate any person or thing on the planet using just three words.

I'm very pleased that for this edition Platter's has teamed with W3W to allow wine-loving visitors and locals to more easily navigate the winelands. Look for the 🔤 icon among the contact details of the producer listing in the A-Z. And if you type (or say, the system allows voice input) these three words, mediating.offered.inclusive, you'll find us!

Also new in 2019

Another way we're looking to add value this year is by introducing a new icon, highlighting wines certified as having been produced from vines that are officially 'old', i.e. 35 years or more. It's thought that SA has the most surviving old vines of any wine-growing country in the world, a total of some 3,200 ha, and much good work is being to revive and extend the lives of the old-timers. For winelovers, one of the newest and increasingly visible evidence of this is the Certified Heritage Vineyard seal ('sticker') appearing on bottles of wine officially certified by the Old Vine Project, more details about which appear on page 628. We have partnered with OVP to flag the wines certified under this initiative by means of the 🏵 icon.

Long-time readers will notice another new icon, intended to draw attention to wines that we believe will repay extended cellaring: at least

8-10 years for reds and fortifieds, and 4-6 years for whites. We feel there's enough interest locally and worldwide in collecting SA wine, and optimally cellaring it, to merit special focus on ageability. Look for the 🏛 symbol in the A-Z.

Contextualising our ratings

Another new, and much more plentiful icon this edition is the score for wines according to the 100-point system, alongside the familiar 0-5 star ratings. American critic Robert Parker invented the 100-point scoring system in the 1970s, and today it's the global standard. Therefore we feel that by combining this notation with our own long-standing star-rating system, our international readers will better understand and contextualise our judging team's pronouncements.

Important to note is that we see the two systems coexisting in Platter's in the future. There are no plans to phase out the star ratings, which have been integral to the guide since its inception. Also to note that we introduced judging on the 100-point scale internally only in 2015, and thus 100-point equivalents for vintages tasted prior to that date are not displayed in the A-Z.

As many loyal readers know, a compendium of all the year's tasting results appears in a separate section of the guide under the heading This Year's Ratings Summarised (see page 597). For the sake of clarity, in a part of the guide that's already dense with detail, we've not included the 100-point scores for now. Look for them in the A-Z.

I've left probably the most important and obvious innovation for last. Historically, the guide's highest distinctions have been (a) the Five Star rating for wines which emerge from a stringent, multi-stage process with a rating of 95 points or more and (b) the Winery of the Year, a prestigious accolade given, chiefly, to the producer who was the top achiever in that year's guide.

Recognising depth in the industry

This year, in addition to the above, we're publishing the list of wines which not only achieved the maximum Five Stars but also the highest score in their category, under the banner of Wines of the Year. On the winery accolades side, we're expand-ing our recognition and giving awards to a trio of stellar producers, namely the top performer of the year in terms of the number of Five Star wines in this edition, the newcomer of the year, which is the producer debuting with the highest scores, and thirdly my Editor's Award for the individual or team whose performance on and off the track sets a benchmark for the industry.

These new awards by no means diminish the esteem in which we hold our 'traditional' summit wines and wineries. On the contrary, they serve to acknowledge what is recognised around the world as the much-increased depth in our industry in recent years. See page 11 for a more detailed description of our rating methodology and the awards that flow from it.

It's worth pointing out that there has been no change in our long-standing goal of tasting, rating and describing as many as possible SA-made wines available during the currency of the book, both locally and overseas. Tasting notes for the wines in the A–Z section are accompanied by news about the wineries and winemakers (and distilleries and distillers), general information about products, vinification facilities, vineyards, and amenities available to visitors.

For those setting out on wineland rambles, the maps have again been fully updated, along with the quick-lookup tables which furnish key visitor information about the wineries of a particular area.

Special thanks

I'd like to recognise and thank the members of our tasting team, whose professionalism, enthusiasm and willingness to go the extra 100 miles never cease to amaze. Their initials appear below the wines they tasted, as follows: Winnie Bowman (WB), Hennie Coetzee (HC), Greg de Bruyn (GdB), Joanne Gibson (JG), Tim James (TJ), Angela Lloyd (AL), Cathy Marston (CM), Fiona McDonald (FM), Gregory Mutambe (GM), Christine Rudman (CR), Dave Swingler (DS), Cathy van Zyl (CvZ) and Meryl Weaver (MW). For more about these stalwarts, see page 19.

I'd also like to give special thanks to associate editors Cathy van Zyl (also copywriter) and Tim James (also copywriter and proofreader); copywriters Hennie Coetzee, Joanne Gibson, Angela Lloyd, Cathy Marston, Fiona McDonald, Christine Rudman, Wendy Toerien and Meryl Weaver; information coordinator Ina de Villiers; wine coordinator MF Schoeman and Wines of the Year tasting coordinator Christina Harvett, both assisted by Kirschni Adams, Monique Africa, Tiffany Andrews, Candice Franken, Lucy Hopkins, Robyn-Leigh Rhode, Junaid Suliman, Andrew Sutherland, SiphokaziTaliwe and Marinda Visagie; map and typesetting guru Gawie du Toit; Christine Parent for book sales, administration and advertising coordination; Lara Philp and Johan Rademan of Vineyard Connection for the use of their excellent facilities; Lauren de Kock for fact-checking; Mark Whyte and XtraSmile Couriers; Christelle Reade-Jahn and the Brandy Foundation; Ben van Rensburg (Modern Web Presence) for the QR code; and the ever-helpful SAWIS and VinPro. Special thanks to Sean de Kock for 24 × 7 help with the database, intranet and website.

Those who read my Note from year to year will know that son Luke has always dreamed of being a pilot, and these days is working towards his commercial aviation licence. The rest of the family has wings, too: mine are mostly folded, while directing Platter's traffic from the 'comfort' of my PC; wife Cathy, respected Master of Wine and Platter's taster, whose further, behind-the-scenes contribution as associate editor is enormous, vital and much appreciated, takes off many times a year to judge, lecture and generically promote wine (and occasionally dance on tables) around the word; and new family member Cessna, personality-packed Staffie who's flown straight into our hearts.

Sincere thanks to SA's wineries, without whose support the book could not be produced.

And, as always, an invitation to join us on the web, Facebook and Twitter (see page 2 for details), and to look for our apps in the on-line stores.

Finally, our ratings are the considered opinion of wine experts who understand the responsibility of adducing a star rating to a product as changeable as wine. However, because of the subjective element associated with wine assessment, we strongly recommend you view our rankings as adjuncts to the tasting notes rather than as oracular pronouncements. And we continue to urge you, in the words of a local winery's marketing slogan, to 'trust your taste'.

Philip van Zyl

Our Method & The Accolades We Award

Platter's is one of the few wine guides in the world that aims to taste and rate every wine from every South African vintage — and it's been doing so since 1980. In this endeavour, Platter's uses two judging methods: label-sighted assessment as well as blind tasting (with no label showing).

As Platter's is primarily a wine guide and not a wine competition, our expert tasters initially assess the wines sighted to have access to vital contextual details such as site, climate and style. Since Platter's not only rates wines, but also provides rich editorial content, this information enables our team to understand (and editorialise) the intent of the producer and the wine's backstory.

Then, when it comes to the highest ratings and the pinnacle awards, we shift to a blind tasting format as we now compare the top-rated wines against each other and within their categories to assess the wines solely in terms of organoleptic quality.

Annually Platter's assesses a potential 9,000 wines. Those rated 93 points or more by the sighted judges are all entered into this second round of blind tasting. Small panels, including expert palates from outside the Platter's team, now assess the wines without sight of the label to reach a panel consensus score. The wines that the panels regard as superlative in both a South African and international context are awarded the guide's highest rating, namely Five Stars, which equates to 95-100 points.

The highest-scoring Five Star wine within each tasting category is further acknowledged as a Wine of the Year. In instances where a number of wines were tied at equal points, we asked the panel to identify their favourite and this became the Wine of the Year.

Other important wines are those which rated 94 points, i.e. did not make the Five Star selection but are extremely fine and collectable in their own right. They are listed under the heading Highly Recommended.

Implicit in both the Five Star and Highly Recommended categories is the potential that the wines will improve with further bottle-maturation: 8-10 years, perhaps more in the case of reds and fortified wines, and around 4-6 years for the whites. (Proper storage is, of course, vital for sound maturation.)

During the sighted tasting cycle, our team identified a number of bottlings, over and above the Five Stars and Highly Recommended, which show particular potential for cellaring. All ageworthy wines are highlighted in the A-Z directory with this new symbol: (🐝)

Tasters also identified wines which they felt particularly worthy of note — interesting, attractive, unusual, unique, representative of an important trend, etc. You'll find these Hidden Gems in the A-Z, flagged with this icon: (💎)

Finally, there are the Top Performing Winery, Newcomer Winery and the Editor's Award for the year.

The Editor's Award is an accolade that recognises a winegrowing team (or teams) who, based on performance in the current edition as well as their track record, are ambassadors par excellence for South African wine.

The Newcomer Winery of the Year is awarded to a producer whose wine portfolio has been assessed by Platter's for the first time and achieved the highest ratings at the Five Star tasting, or the highest scores (should the wines not have reached the Five Star round).

The Top Performing Winery of the Year is awarded to the winery that achieves the most Five Star results after the annual final tasting round. In the case of an overall Five Star tie, this award goes to the winery that then has the most 94-point wines, and so on, until the year's Top Performer is identified.

Further details about all releases listed in the Wines of the Year section will be found under the names of the relevant producers in the A-Z. The blind tasting is audited by Grant Thornton South Africa.

Wineries of the Year

Top Performing Winery of the Year 2019

MULLINEUX

This is not the first time that the winery that Andrea and Chris Mullineux founded over a decade back has been here: they triumphed in achieving more Five Star wines than anyone else in both 2014 and 2016, an unmatched record. This edition they have five top ratings and a Wine of the Year, for their renowned Straw Wine – which has one of the most remarkable track records in the Guide, having only once (somehow!) in 9 years failed to achieve Five Stars. It's a Swartland wine, like all from the Mullineux winery, which helped pioneer

a new and exciting reputation for this region. Chris and Andrea now have a permanent winemaking and vineyard base there, on their Roundstone farm, though grapes are also brought in from other parts of the Swartland. Leeu Passant in Franschhoek is another part of their winemaking for Mullineux & Leeu Family Wines (the joint venture with Indian businessman Analjit Singh), and the Leeu Passant Stellenbosch Chardonnay was our chardonnay Wine of the Year this year.

Newcomer Winery of the Year 2019

ERIKA OBERMEYER WINES

Erika Obermeyer says: 'if it excites you and scares you at the same time, it probably means you should do it!'. She did it. After many years of making the still wines at Graham Beck, she 'took a leap of faith' and set out to produce her own range of wines. She seeks out older vines across the Western Cape and vinifies the grapes in rented space for now – she hopes to have her own facility 'in the near future'. The essential ingredients for Erika in the art of crafting a fine wine are 'true

terroir, balance, honesty and a light touch'. Such wines can, she says, 'tell a rich and deeply fascinating story of a time, a place, and a maker'. Two of the maiden vintages in her top range – the Cabernet Sauvignon and Syrah-Grenache Noir-Cinsault – achieved our highest rating; the Sauvignon Blanc was just one point away from it. A remarkable achievement, promising even greater ones in the future from this greatly welcome new label.

Editor's Award 2019

NEWTON JOHNSON VINEYARDS

This family winery in Upper Hemel-en-Aarde is widely held in as much affection as in high esteem, and is a fitting first personal selection by the guide's editor of a producer to be singled out for especial praise. The winery was founded by Dave Johnson and Felicity (née Newton) in the mid-1990s in what was still an unproven winegrowing area. The (enlarged) farm is now home to them and the families of their sons – Bevan (marketing manager) and Gordon (winemaker with wife Nadia). The winery has been both innovative and

ever-striving to raise its already high standard of excellence. Numerous Five Star wines over the years have included a near-perfect run for their Family Vineyards Pinot Noir, which made it again in 2019. But there's a remarkably wide range of wines, all combining precision, respect for terroir and joyfulness. Nadia and Gordon also make the stunning range of Shannon wines, and the L'Illa from Nadia's home farm. It could all be grounds for arrogance and assertiveness – but the Newton Johnsons remain as unassuming as they are successful.

Wines of the Year

These are the highest-scoring Five Star wines within each tasting category. In instances where there were a number of wines tied at equal points, we asked the panel to identify their favourite.

Cabernet Franc
☐ Raats Dolomite 2016

Cabernet Sauvignon
☐ Le Riche Reserve 2015

Grenache Noir
☐ Sadie Soldaat 2017

Merlot
☐ Shannon The Shannon Black 2013

Petit Verdot
☐ Thelema Sutherland Reserve 2015

Pinotage
☐ Kanonkop Black Label 2016

Pinot Noir
☐ Crystallum Cuvée Cinema 2017

Shiraz/Syrah
☐ Leeuwenkuil Syrah 2015

Tinta Barocca
☐ Elemental Bob Cosmic Flower Graveyard 2017

Red Blends, Cape Bordeaux
☐ Plasir de Merle Signature 2012

Red Blends, with Pinotage
☐ Beyerskloof Faith 2014

Red blends, with Shiraz/Syrah
☐ Saronsberg Full Circle 2016

Red Blends, Other
☐ Ernie Els Proprietor's Blend 2016

Chardonnay
☐ Leeu Passant Stellenbosch 2016

Chenin Blanc
☐ DeMorgenzon The Divas 2017

Sauvignon Blanc, Unwooded
☐ Steenberg The Black Swan 2017

Sauvignon Blanc, Wooded
☐ Bartho Eksteen Houtskool 2017

Semillon
☐ Rickety Bridge Road to Santiago 2016

White Blends, Cape Bordeaux
☐ Vergelegen GVB 2015

White Blends, Other
☐ Thorne & Daughters Rocking Horse 2017

Méthode Cap Classique
☐ Villiera Monro Brut 2012

Natural Sweet
☐ Klein Constantia Vin de Constance 2014

Noble Late Harvest
☐ Paul Cluver Riesling 2017

Vin de Paille
☐ Mullineux Straw Wine 2017

Port-style
☐ Overgaauw Cape Vintage 1998

Five Stars

These are wines achieving the guide's highest distinction, a Five Star rating, or 95 and above points. Please refer to the A-Z section for the points for each wine.

Cabernet Franc
☐ Raats 2016
☐ Raats Dolomite 2016
☐ Van Loggerenberg Breton 2017

Cabernet Sauvignon
☐ Bartinney 2015
☐ Erika Obermeyer Erika O 2015
☐ Le Riche Reserve 2015
☐ Reyneke Biodynamic Reserve 2015
☐ Stellenbosch Reserve Ou Hoofgebou 2016
☐ Warwick The Blue Lady 2015

Grenache Noir
☐ Sadie Soldaat 2017

Merlot
☐ Oldenburg 2015
☐ Shannon The Shannon Black 2013
☐ Thelema Reserve 2015

Petit Verdot
☐ Thelema Sutherland Reserve 2015

Pinotage
☐ Beeslaar 2016
☐ Beyerskloof Diesel 2016
☐ Kanonkop Black Label 2016

Pinot Noir
☐ Crystallum Cuvée Cinéma 2017
☐ Newton Johnson Family Vineyards 2017

Shiraz/Syrah
☐ Dorrance Syrah Cuvée Ameena 2016
☐ Hartenberg CWG Auction Reserve Shiraz 2015
☐ Leeuwenkuil Heritage Syrah 2015
☐ Luddite Shiraz 2014
☐ Mullineux Iron Syrah 2016
☐ Mullineux Schist Roundstone Syrah 2016
☐ Porseleinberg Syrah 2016
☐ Rall Ava Syrah 2017
☐ Rhebokskloof Black Marble Hill Syrah 2015
☐ Rust en Vrede Single Vineyard Syrah 2015

Tinta Barocca
☐ Elemental Bob Cosmic Flower Graveyard 2017

Red Blends, Cape Bordeaux
☐ Allée Bleue L'Amour Toujours 2014
☐ Kanonkop Paul Sauer 2015
☐ Muratie Ansela van de Caab 2015
☐ Plaisir de Merle Signature 2012

☐ Ridgeback Signature C 2016

Red Blends, with Pinotage
☐ Beyerskloof Faith 2014

Red blends, with Shiraz/Syrah
☐ Boekenhoutskloof The Chocolate Block 2017
☐ Erika Obermeyer Erika O Syrah-Grenache Noir-Cinsault 2016
☐ Saronsberg Full Circle 2016

Red Blends, Other
☐ Ernie Els Proprietor's Blend 2016
☐ Rust en Vrede Estate 2015
☐ Waterford The Jem 2014

Chardonnay
☐ Haskell Anvil 2017
☐ Leeu Passant Stellenbosch 2016
☐ Oak Valley Groenlandberg 2017
☐ Restless River Ava Marie 2016
☐ Warwick The White Lady 2017

Chenin Blanc
☐ Beaumont Hope Marguerite 2017
☐ Botanica Mary Delany 2017
☐ Cederberg Five Generations 2016
☐ City on a Hill 2017
☐ David & Nadia 2017
☐ David & Nadia Hoë-Steen 2017
☐ David & Nadia Skaliekop 2017
☐ DeMorgenzon Reserve 2017
☐ DeMorgenzon The Divas 2017
☐ Metzer Montane 2017
☐ Rall Ava 2017
☐ Sadie Skurfberg 2017
☐ Savage Never Been Asked To Dance 2017
☐ Spier 21 Gables 2017
☐ Spier Farm House Organic 2016
☐ Spioenkop Sarah Raal 2017
☐ Stellenrust 53 Barrel Fermented 2017
☐ Thistle & Weed Duwweltjie 2017

Sauvignon Blanc, Unwooded
☐ Steenberg The Black Swan 2017

Sauvignon Blanc, Wooded
☐ Bartho Eksteen Houtskool 2017

Semillon
☐ Alheit La Colline 2017
☐ Benguela Cove Catalina 2017
☐ Rickety Bridge Road to Santiago 2016

Five Stars *(continued)*

White Blends, Cape Bordeaux
- ☐ Cape Point Isliedh 2017
- ☐ Shannon Capall Bán 2015
- ☐ Vergelegen GVB 2015
- ☐ Warwick Professor Black 2017

White Blends, Other
- ☐ B Vintners Vine Exploration Co Harlem to Hope 2017
- ☐ Lourens Lindi Carien 2017
- ☐ Mullineux Old Vines 2017
- ☐ Rall 2017
- ☐ Sadie Palladius 2016
- ☐ Savage 2017
- ☐ Stark-Condé The Field Blend 2017
- ☐ Thorne & Daughters Rocking Horse 2017

Méthode Cap Classique
- ☐ Colmant Absolu Zero Dosage NV
- ☐ Villiera Monro Brut 2012
- ☐ Woolworths Vintage Reserve Brut 2012

Natural Sweet
- ☐ Klein Constantia Vin de Constance 2014

Noble Late Harvest
- ☐ Paul Cluver Riesling 2017

Vin de Paille
- ☐ Mullineux Straw Wine 2017

Port-style
- ☐ De Krans Cape Vintage Reserve 2016
- ☐ Overgaauw Cape Vintage 1998

Brandy/Husk Spirit
- ☐ Boplaas Potstill 20 Years Reserve
- ☐ Dalla Cia 10 Year Old Celebration Cabernet Sauvignon-Merlot Husk Spirit
- ☐ KWV 10 Year Old Vintage
- ☐ KWV 12 Year Old Barrel Select
- ☐ KWV 15 Year Old Alambic
- ☐ KWV 20 Year Old
- ☐ KWV Nexus
- ☐ Oude Meester Souverein
- ☐ Van Ryn 12 Year Distillers Reserve
- ☐ Van Ryn 15 Year Fine Cask Reserve
- ☐ Van Ryn 20 Year Collectors Reserve

Highly Recommended

These are wines of exceptional merit, scoring 94 points.

Cabernet Franc
- [ ] Mulderbosch 2016
- [ ] Raats Eden High Density Single Vineyard 2016
- [ ] Warwick 2015

Cabernet Sauvignon
- [ ] Boekenhoutskloof Franschhoek 2016
- [ ] Edgebaston 'GS' 2015
- [ ] Grangehurst The Reward 2011
- [ ] Kanonkop 2014
- [ ] Kleine Zalze Vineyard Selection 2016
- [ ] Le Riche CWG Auction Reserve 2015
- [ ] Muratie Martin Melck Family Reserve 2015
- [ ] Nederburg Two Centuries 2015
- [ ] Rainbow's End 2016
- [ ] Rust en Vrede Single Vineyard 2015
- [ ] Rustenberg Peter Barlow 2015
- [ ] Schultz 2015
- [ ] Spier 21 Gables 2015
- [ ] Thelema 2015
- [ ] Tokara Reserve 2015

Cinsaut
- [ ] Artisanal The Apprentice (white) 2017
- [ ] Bosman Twyfeling 2016
- [ ] Kaapzicht Skuinsberg 2017
- [ ] Savage Follow The Line 2017
- [ ] Terracura Silwervis 2016

Grenache Noir
- [ ] Anysbos 2016

Merlot
- [ ] Creation Reserve 2016
- [ ] Groot Constantia 2016
- [ ] Shannon Mount Bullet 2015

Pinotage
- [ ] Allée Bleue Platinum 2016
- [ ] Alvi's Drift Verreaux 2015
- [ ] Diemersdal Reserve 2017
- [ ] Môreson MKM 2015

Pinot Noir
- [ ] B Vintners Black Bream 2017
- [ ] Botanica Mary Delany 2017
- [ ] Cape Chamonix Reserve 2017
- [ ] Creation Emma 2017
- [ ] Crystallum Bona Fide 2017
- [ ] Newton Johnson Windansea 2017
- [ ] Radford Dale AD 2017
- [ ] Richard Kershaw Elgin Clonal Selection 2017
- [ ] Storm Ignis 2016

Shiraz/Syrah
- [ ] Blackwater Cultellus Syrah 2016
- [ ] Boschkloof Epilogue Syrah 2016
- [ ] Cirrus Syrah 2015
- [ ] De Grendel Shiraz 2016
- [ ] De Grendel Elim Shiraz 2016
- [ ] De Trafford Syrah 393 2016
- [ ] GlenWood Grand Duc Syrah 2015
- [ ] Hartenberg The Stork Shiraz 2015
- [ ] La Motte Pierneef Syrah-Viognier 2016
- [ ] Lomond Cat's Tail Syrah 2015
- [ ] Remhoogte Reserve Syrah 2016
- [ ] Reyneke Biodynamic Reserve Red 2016
- [ ] Richard Kershaw Deconstructed Groenland Bokkeveld Shale SH9C Syrah 2016
- [ ] Ron Burgundy Sons of Sugarland Syrah 2017
- [ ] Savage The Girl Next Door Syrah 2017
- [ ] Stark-Condé Syrah 2016
- [ ] Uva Mira DW Syrah 2015

Red Blends, Cape Bordeaux
- [ ] Cape Chamonix Troika 2016
- [ ] Constantia Glen Five 2014
- [ ] De Toren Fusion V 2016
- [ ] De Trafford The Drawing Board 2016
- [ ] Diemersdal Private Collection 2016
- [ ] Glen Carlou The Curator's Collection 2017
- [ ] Jean Daneel Directors Signature 2015
- [ ] Jordan CWG Auction Reserve Sophia 2015
- [ ] Lourensford Chrysalis 2015
- [ ] Morgenster Estate Reserve 2015
- [ ] Oldenburg Rhodium 2015
- [ ] Rainbow's End Family Reserve 2015
- [ ] Spier CWG Auction Reserve Frans K Smit 20 Year Celebration 2015
- [ ] Stellenbosch Vineyards Right Bank 2015
- [ ] Strydom CWG Auction Reserve The Game Changer 2015
- [ ] The High Road Director's Reserve 2015
- [ ] Tokara Director's Reserve 2014
- [ ] Uva Mira OTV 2015
- [ ] Vilafonté Series C 2015
- [ ] Vondeling Philosophie 2015
- [ ] Warwick Three Cape Ladies 2015
- [ ] Warwick Trilogy 2015

Red Blends, with Pinotage
- [ ] Alvi's Drift Albertus Viljoen Bismarck 2015
- [ ] Bosman Erfenis 2015

Highly recommended (continued)

□ Hughes Nativo 2015

Red Blends, with Shiraz/Syrah

□ Anwilka 2015
□ Artisanal JJ Handmade Eight Pillars 2015
□ Cape Rock 2017
□ De Grendel Sir David Graaff First Baronet of Cape Town 2015
□ Flagstone Red Velvet 2014
□ KWV The Mentors Canvas 2016
□ Migliarina Parquet 2016
□ Ridgeback Signature S 2016
□ Rust en Vrede 1694 Classification 2015
□ Sadie Columella 2016
□ Spice Route Chakalaka 2015
□ The Butcher Shop & Grill Limited Editions Niels Verburg 2015
□ Waterkloof Circle of Life 2015

Red Blends, Other

□ Glenelly 2013
□ Hogan Divergent 2017
□ JC Wickens Swerver Swartland Red 2017
□ Leeu Passant 2016
□ Lourens Howard John 2017
□ Paserene Marathon 2016
□ Villiera The Clan 2016
□ Vuurberg Reserve 2015

Chardonnay

□ B Vintners Fire Heath 2017
□ Cape Chamonix Reserve 2017
□ Crystallum The Agnes 2017
□ Eikendal Infused by Earth 2016
□ Julien Schaal Confluence 2017
□ Lanzerac Mrs English 2017
□ Longridge Clos du Ciel 2016
□ Newton Johnson Family Vineyards 2017
□ Oak Valley Beneath The Clouds 2017
□ Paul Cluver Chardonnay 2017
□ Paul Cluver Seven Flags 2017
□ Radford Dale 2017
□ Richard Kershaw Clonal Selection Elgin 2017
□ Richard Kershaw Lower Duivenhoks River 2017
□ Tokara Reserve 2017

Chenin Blanc

□ Alheit Fire By Night 2017
□ Alheit Huilkrans 2017
□ Alheit Nautical Dawn 2017
□ Bellingham The Bernard Series Old Vine 2017
□ Blackwater Picquet 2017
□ Botanica Mary Delany Untitled #1 2017
□ Carinus Rooidraai 2017

□ Catherine Marshall Fermented in Clay 2017
□ Dornier Moordenaarskloof 2017
□ Jordan Inspector Péringuey 2017
□ Kaapzicht The 1947 2017
□ Keermont Riverside 2017
□ Kleine Zalze Family Reserve 2017
□ Lourens Blouklip Steen 2017
□ Lourens Skuinskap Steen 2017
□ Michaella 2017
□ Perdeberg Dry Land Courageous Barrel Fermented 2017
□ Raats Original 2017
□ Raats Old Vine 2017
□ Raats Eden High Density Single Vineyard 2016
□ Sadie Mev. Kirsten 2017
□ Spioenkop Johanna Brandt 2017
□ Van Loggerenberg Kameradarie 2017
□ Van Loggerenberg Trust Your Gut 2017
□ Waterford Antique NV

Grenache Blanc

□ Rall 2017
□ The Foundry 2017

Pinot Blanc

□ Stofberg Mariëtte 2017

Sauvignon Blanc, Unwooded

□ Diemersdal 8 Rows 2018
□ Groot Constantia 2017
□ Groote Post Kapokberg 2017
□ Nicky Versfeld 2017
□ Seven Springs 2016
□ Thelema 2018

Sauvignon Blanc, Wooded

□ Bartho Eksteen CWG Auction Reserve Vloekskoot 2017
□ Erika Obermeyer Erika O 2017
□ Iona Barrel Fermented 2017
□ Klein Constantia Block 382 2017
□ Nederburg Two Centuries 2017
□ Neil Ellis Amica 2017
□ Stellenrust Barrel Fermented 2017

Semillon

□ Anthonij Rupert Laing Groendruif 2015
□ Arcangeli 2017
□ Botanica Mary Delany 2017
□ Cederberg Ghost Corner 2017

Semillon Gris

□ Mullineux CWG Auction Reserve The Gris 2017

Viognier

□ Ridgeback 2017

Highly recommended *(continued)*

White Blends, Cape Bordeaux
☐ Cederberg Ghost Corner The Bowline 2017
☐ Constantia Glen Two 2017
☐ Flying Cloud Witch of the Wave 2016
☐ Highlands Road Sine Cera 2016
☐ Iona One Man Band 2016
☐ Newton Johnson Resonance 2017
☐ Spier Frans K. Smit 2016
☐ Steenberg Magna Carta 2017
☐ Tokara Director's Reserve 2016
☐ Trizanne Reserve Semillon-Sauvignon Blanc 2017

White Blends, Other
☐ Backsberg Family Reserve 2017
☐ Cape Rock 2017
☐ City on a Hill 2017
☐ David & Nadia Aristargos 2017
☐ DeMorgenzon Maestro 2016
☐ Luddite Saboteur 2017
☐ Olifantsberg 2017
☐ Opstal Carl Everson 2017
☐ Painted Wolf VI 2017
☐ Sijnn 2017
☐ Thelema Sutherland Viognier-Roussanne 2015
☐ Waterkloof Circle of Life 2015

Méthode Cap Classique
☐ Bartho Eksteen Dom NV
☐ Cederberg Blanc de Blancs Brut 2013
☐ Graham Beck Blanc de Blancs Brut 2013
☐ Graham Beck Cuvée Clive 2012

☐ Klein Constantia Brut 2011
☐ Pongrácz Desiderius 2011
☐ Saltare Brut Reserve NV
☐ Silverthorn CWG Auction Reserve Big Dog IV 2013
☐ Taillefert Brut 2012

Dessert Wine, Fortified
☐ Daschbosch Hanepoot 2016
☐ Orange River White Muscadel 2017
☐ Rietvallei 1908 Red Muscadel 2015

Late Harvest
☐ Gabriëlskloof Broken Stem 2016

Natural Sweet
☐ Groot Constantia Grand Constance 2015

Noble Late Harvest
☐ Boekenhoutskloof 2015
☐ Buitenverwachting 1769 2016
☐ Ken Forrester T' 2017
☐ Lomond 2017
☐ Miles Mossop Kika 2017

Vin de Paille/Straw Wine
☐ Donkiesbaai Hooiwijn 2017
☐ Fairview La Beryl Blanc 2017
☐ Orange River 2017
☐ Stellar Heaven on Earth NV

Port-style
☐ Boplaas Cape Vintage Reserve 2016

Tasters for this Edition

Winifred Bowman

Introduced to wine at a young age, through a thimbleful of sweet muscadel with Sunday lunch, Winnie's immersion in the fruit of the vine deepened during her student days at Stellenbosch University and later through frequent travels to international winegrowing areas, and widened to include brandy and husk spirit. A qualified physiotherapist and biomedical scientist, and holder of a PhD in Education, she is a Cape Wine Master, and regular judge at several local and international wine and spirit competitions. Winnie also loves books, opera and experimenting with cocktails with her wannabe mixologist son.

Hennie Coetzee

Raised in the industrial town of Sasolburg, northern Free State, Hennie was a stranger to wine culture until he first set foot on a winefarm as a Stellenbosch University student. The wine passion culminated in several local and international wine qualifications and a mild obsession to taste as many different wines as humanly possible. When he's not nose deep in a glass of wine, he enjoys running in the beautiful mountains of the Cape – often with a celebratory bottle of grenache, baguette and smelly cheese in his backpack. He judges occasionally for various local competitions and publications.

Greg de Bruyn

Greg is an architect by day, and a wine devotee after hours. A casual interest in wine tasting at a social club snowballed, leading him to qualify as a wine judge in 1996 and a Cape Wine Master in 2000. He was runner-up in Wine magazine's inaugural New Wine Writer competition, after which he contributed regularly to that and other wine publications. In 1999, Greg settled in the Cape, first to establish a new wine estate in Hermanus, and later as a specialist consultant in winery construction. He has judged for Veritas, Diners Club Winemaker of the Year, Nederburg Auction and several magazine panels, and has been a taster for this guide since 2010. Greg doesn't like pretentious wine or arrogant wine-people, or arrogant wine or pretentious wine-people for that matter.

Joanne Gibson

Joanne has been a journalist, specialising in wine, for over two decades. She received her Level 4 Diploma from the Wine & Spirit Education Trust in 2003 while working as a feature writer for Harpers Wine & Spirit magazine in London. After returning to South Africa in 2004, she worked as deputy editor at Good Taste and then Wine magazine before going freelance in 2009. Winner of both the Du Toitskloof Wine and Franschhoek Literary Festival Wine Writer of the Year awards, she has also been shortlisted no fewer than four times in the Louis Roederer International Wine Writers' Awards. As a sought-after freelance writer and copy editor, her passion is digging up nuggets of SA wine history, from legendary Constantia to Oom Koos Mostertpotjiewyn.

Tim James

Tim, a Cape Wine Master, is an established and multiple award-winning winewriter, contributing freelance to local and international publications and websites, most frequently nowadays to Winemag.co.za but also a regular column to the London-based World of Fine Wine magazine. He is also SA consultant to the World Atlas of Wine. Tim's book, Wines of the New South Africa: Tradition and Revolution, was published in 2013. He has been a taster (and associate editor) for this guide for many years.

Angela Lloyd

Serendipity led to Angela's interest in wine. She met her husband, Mark, within three weeks of arriving in South Africa in 1970 and shortly after attended tastings organised by the Wine Tasters' Guild, of which Mark was a member. Her enjoyment began with SA semi-sweet whites, soon joined by reds. Today, her enthusiasm for wine extends worldwide; orange wines are a current fascination. Angela, with 33 editions our longest-serving tasting team member, believes keeping an open mind can lead to many exciting wine discoveries.

Cathy Marston

Cathy hails from Yorkshire, UK, and after completing her degree in English at Cambridge University, she joined Adnams Wine Merchants, passing all the Wine & Spirit Education Trust (WSET) exams, culminating in the Level 4 Diploma. She came to South Africa in 2001, and opened and ran The Nose Restaurant & Wine Bar, selling it after seven successful years. Cathy now concentrates on tasting, writing for local and international publications, and, increasingly, on wine education and edutainment events. She was the first WSET Approved Programme Provider in Africa, and was named WSET Educator of the Year 2015. She started studying for her Master of Wine qualification last year.

Fiona McDonald

Travel is said to broaden the mind, and Fiona, former editor of Wine magazine for eight years, has had her wine mind broadened by having been a long-serving jury president of several international wine competitions: International Wine Challenge, International Wine & Spirit Competition, Concours Mondial de Bruxelles and, now, Decanter World Wine Awards' regional panel chair for South Africa. Initially trained as a news journalist, she got into wine by happy accident, helping to organise The Mercury Wine Week in between reportage and newsroom management as the night news editor on that Durban broadsheet. Currently freelancing, Fiona edits Cheers magazine, and contributes to a range of publications and websites.

Gregory Mutambe

Encouraged to follow his father into accounting, Gregory instead found himself on a journey into wine and food, first as a winemaking assistant at Mukuyu, one of the handful of wineries in his home country, Zimbabwe, and later as a Cape Wine Academy student in Gauteng. Currently he heads the sommelier team at Cape Town's 12 Apostles Hotel & Spa, oversees an awarded winelist, and judges for several local competitions. Holder of the Wine Judging Academy and UCT Wine Business Management qualifications, Gregory is enrolled in the Court of Master Sommelier and University of South Africa BComm programmes, his aim being to become a wine economist. He is also founding chair of BLACC, a new organisation reaching out to black Africans interested in furthering their wine knowledge.

Christine Rudman

Christine's love affair with wine started when she joined the then Stellenbosch Farmers' Winery after a Johannesburg FMCG marketing career. Enrolling in the Cape Wine Academy, she achieved her Cape Wine Master qualification in 1986; left SFW to run the CWA for seven years; and has since been occupied with consultancy work, wine-judging, -lecturing and -writing. She has been a taster for this guide since the 2003 edition. Christine has a wine column in Die Burger newspaper, writes freelance for other publications, and has published two editions of A Guide to the Winelands of the Cape. Technical director of Michelangelo International Wine Awards, she travels widely, serves on various local and international juries (including panel chair at Veritas and International Wine & Spirit Competition), and looks forward to working with wine for years to come.

Dave Swingler

A taster for this guide for two decades, Dave has over the years consulted to restaurants, game lodges and convention centres, taught wine courses and contributed to radio, print and other media. He is co-author of One Hundred Wines – An Insider's Guide to South African Wine, and drinks contributor to Posh Nosh. Dave is a long-standing member of the International Wine & Food Society, the South African consultant for its Annual Vintage Chart, and cellarmaster of the Cape Town branch. A psychiatrist by day, he's intrigued by language in general, and the lexicon of wine in particular.

Cathy van Zyl

Cathy started her wine journey on a bicycle: she asked her husband to ride SA's famed Cape Town Cycle Tour with her; he accepted if she attended a wine course with him. She has since notched up more than 21 tours - and passed the prestigious Master of Wine examination. Previously chair of the Institute of Masters of Wine's education committee, she is now a member of its Council. Cathy judges locally and internationally, and is the SA contributor to Le Grand Tasting app by Bettane+Desseauve. She occasionally contributes to wine journals and websites around the world, but spends most of her wine-time as associate editor of this guide.

Meryl Weaver

The Cape winelands lured Meryl away from her legal career and, more than 20 years later, she remains firmly under their spell. She has conducted wine presentations abroad on SA wine on behalf of Wines of South Africa, lectures for the Cape Wine Academy, tastes and writes about wine, and judges for various wine competitions and magazines. Meryl qualified as a Cape Wine Master and has graduated with distinction from the Wine Judging Academy. She ensures, however, that the vinous learning curve continues by visiting wine-producing countries, combining some of her other passions, food and travel.

How to use this Guide

Note: The example text used here is illustrative and not complete or up to date. See A–Z for full details.

Producer's name

Our track-record-based rating system
See next page for an explanation

Listings of wines available during the currency of the book

Wine name, vintage, colour & style

Location: nearest major centre to winery, vineyard, head office

Map & grid reference: see Maps section for winery's position

WO: Wine of Origin geographical unit, region, district or ward; wines described/rated bear the first-mentioned WO certification unless noted

Unless noted, red wines wooded; whites unoaked

Symbols
See next page for a complete list

Other attractions or activities available on the property

Bartinney Private Cellar

Perched high on the slopes of the Helshoogte Pa
owned by Michael and Rose Jordaan who are in
plantings interspersed with native fynbos on ste

★★★★ **Cabernet Sauvignon** Elegant & und
fruit tempered by savoury Marmite hints, olive ta
lengthy finish. 12-18 months French oak, 50% n

★★★★☆ **Elevage** Poised & polished **10** ooze
Stellenbosch fruit shows minty notes on nose giv
balanced grippy tannins. Shades of dark chocola

★★★★☆ **Chardonnay** Classically styled **13** c
citrus on nose before palate glides delicately into
ity & lengthy finish.

★★★★☆ **Sauvignon Blanc** Peaches & cream
green figs & quinces below. Good depth & lengtl

Location/map: Stellenbosch ▪ WO: Banghoek/Stell
10-4 ▪ Closed all pub hols ▪ Cellar tours by appt ▪ B
Stellenbosch) ▪ Owner(s) Rose & Michael Jordaan ▪
Ryno Maree (Oct 2010) ▪ 27ha/±17ha (cab, chard,
BWI champion ▪ Postnet Suite 231 Private Bag X5G
bartinney.co.za ▪ S 33° 55' 34.66" E 018° 55' 56.79

Barton Vineyards

Barton is a 200-ha working farm in the hills over
offering a range of activities, farm produce and lu
stylish wines is still boutique in scale, critical acc
having to expand the cellar facilities to vinify oth

★★★★☆ **Winemakers Reserve** Maiden **11**
elegance & balance than barrel sample. Understa
nuance. So tailored & sleek, belies its youthful int

★★★★ **Shiraz-Cabernet Sauvignon** Youthf
with garrigue scrub, pepper & a touch of cab's cle

Rouge (NEW) ⊘ ★★★★ 4-way blend **12**, shiraz
ture, & merlot & malbec plump out fruit-filled in

Blanc 13 ★★★★ **Sauvignon Blanc 13** ★★★

Location: Bot River ▪ Map: Elgin, Walker Bay & Bc
ing, sales & cellar tours Mon-Fri 9—5 Sat 10—4 ▪
olive oil, marinated olives & proteas ▪ Barton Vill
winemaker(s)/viticulturist(s) PJ Geyer (Oct 2010)
raz, chenin, sauv, sem) ▪ 120t/20,000cs own labe
River 7185 ▪ info@bartonvineyards.co.za ▪ www.
2" ▪ F +27 (0)28-284-9776 ▪ **T +27 (0)28-284**

Symbols
See next page for a complete list

☐ Brief introduction/news update

All wines dry unless noted

Abbreviations
See next page for a list of abbreviations

Taster/s initials

Tastings, sales & cellar tour times (closed Saturdays & Sundays but open public holidays unless noted)

Names of owner, winemaker, viticulturist & consultant/s; year/month of appointment in brackets

Production, in tons and/or 6-bottle cases (cs) and red:white ratio

Postal & email address, website (see www.wineonaplatter.com for social media details)

T = Telephone number
F= Fax number

Date established

Total hectares/hectares under vine (not necessarily in production); main varieties planted

GPS coordinates, based on Datum WGS 84

...inney Private Cellars, a boutique wine estate ...heir bio-diversity credentials with new ...aced slopes.

...1 (★★★★☆) improves on **10** with refined black ...anilla & spice. Delightfully gritty texture & clean

...stinction. Cab-led Bordeaux blend from ...o plushy black fruit with herbal hints & nicely ...hy finish.

...orm of **12** showing oatmeal, cream & yellow ... pineapples & tropical fruit, balancing oak/acid-

...★★) preview moves on to flinty minerality with ... concentrated appeal of **13**. — CM

...Est 2006 ▪ 1stB 2008 ▪ Tasting & sales Mon-Fri ...Wine Bar Mon-Sat 11.30-9 (cnr Church & Bird Str, ...ker(s) Ronell Wid (consultant) ▪ Viticulturist(s) ...8t/4,000cs own label 70% red 30% white ▪ ...bosch 7599 ▪ info@bartinney.co.za ▪ www. ...(0)21-885-2852 ▪ **T +27 (0)21-885-1013**

...e Bot River Valley, rich in biodiversity and ...mmodation. Though the own portfolio of ...ulting in French-trained winemaker PJ Geyer ...ers' wines on contract.

...d Bordeaux blend, now bottled, shows more ...ed core of inky red fruit & violets with cedary ...l age with distinction.

...hious **11 blend** has a sappy texture, infused ...teousness. Supple structure enhanced by oak. ...es though equal part cab adds pliable struc- ...o tasted: **Shiraz Rosé 13 ★★★ Chenin** **13 ★★★★** — MW

...WO: Walker Bay ▪ Est 2001 ▪ 1stB 2003 ▪ Tast- ...ster Sun, Dec 25 & Jan 1 ▪ Lavender products, ...er(s) Peter J Neill ▪ Cellarmaster(s)/ ...30ha (cab, malbec, merlot, mourv, pinot, shi- ...d 50% white 10% rosé ▪ IPW ▪ PO Box 100 Bot ...eyards.co.za ▪ S 34° 15' 43.8" E 019° 10' 29.

How To Use This Guide

Our Track-Record-Based Rating System

General rating   ★★★★ **Caldera**
For wines rated 4-star or better wines, we give the 'track-record rating' over two or more vintages in the margin. Wines rated 4½ stars or more are set in red type

Vintage-specific rating   06 (★★★★)
Any differences from the general rating are noted in brackets beside the particular vintage

★★★★★	95–100 / 18–20 pts	Superlative. A South African classic
★★★★☆	90–94 / 17–17.5 pts	Outstanding
★★★★	86–89 / 16–16.5 pts	Excellent
★★★★	83–85 / 15.5 pts	Very good/promising
★★★	80–82 / 15 pts	Good, for early drinking
★★★	77–79 / 14.5 pts	Average, with some appeal
★★	73–76 / 14 pts	Pleasant enough
★★	70–72 / 13 pts	Plain and simple
★	65–69 / 12 pts	Unexciting
★	60–64 / 11 pts	Very ordinary
No star	50–59 / 10 pts	Somewhat less than ordinary

Symbols

Winery symbols

- ⓠ Open for tasting (no fee unless noted)
- 🍴 Restaurant/refreshments
- ⌂ Accommodation
- ◎ Other tourist attractions/amenities on the property
- ⌂ Bring your own (BYO) picnic
- ⓐ Child friendly
- ⓑ Wheelchair friendly
- (NEW) New winery
- /// What3Words address*

*See Editor's Note

Wine symbols

- (88) Rating on 100-point scale (see above)
- ⊘ Good value
- (NEW) New wine
- (X) Wine still selling, not retasted
- ⊘ Organic
- ◎ Biodynamic
- ⑦ Hidden gem
- ✸ From vines officially 35 years or older*
- ✿ Worth cellaring 8-10 years (reds, fortifieds), 4-6 years (whites)*

Abbreviations

% alc	Percentage alcohol by volume	NLH	Noble Late Harvest
1stB	First bottled vintage	NV	Non-vintage. Year of harvest not
BEE	Black Economic Empowerment		stated on label
BYO	Bring your own (wine, picnic)	RS	Residual sugar
Cs	Cases	SAA	Selected to fly with SAA
CWG	Cape Winemakers Guild	SLH	Special Late Harvest
CWM	Cape Wine Master	Veritas	SA National Bottled Wine Show
Est	Date established	WIETA	Wine & Agricultural Ethical Trade
g/l	Grams per litre		Association
IPW	Integrated Production of Wine	WO	Wine of Origin
IWC	International Wine Challenge		
IWSC	International Wine & Spirit Competition	cabernet/cab	cabernet sauvignon
		pinot	pinot noir
LBV	Late Bottled Vintage	chenin	chenin blanc
Malo	Malolactic fermentation	sauvignon/sauv	sauvignon blanc
MCC	Méthode cap classique	touriga	touriga nacional
MW	Master of Wine	tinta	tinta barocca

WINE VILLAGE

HERMANUS

Offering the largest selection of premium South African Wines

Available for shipping world wide - door to door

CELEBRATING 20 YEARS

VOTED ONE OF *South Africa's Best* WINE SHOPS

OPEN 7 DAYS A WEEK	Mon-Fri: **09:00 - 18:00**
	Sat: **09:00 - 17:00**
	Sun: **10:00 - 15:00**

The most unique South African wine experience

TEL: +27 (0) 28 316 3988

Hemel-en-Aarde Village, Hermanus, South Africa
wine@hermanus.co.za | www.winevillage.co.za
GPS Coordinates: S34°24'40.7" E019°12'1.9"

The Wine Show
tops! at SPAR

Platter's Diners Club INTERNATIONAL
RECOMMENDED

DURBAN

JOHANNESBURG

CAPE TOWN

PORT ELIZABETH

NELSPRUIT

WINEDERLAND IS WAITING

f TheWineShow   @ThewineshowZA

Quality, Design and Innovation

Liebherr built-in Wine and Beverage Coolers, provide a compact storage solution, unique to Liebherr. Whether in a large kitchen or part of a bar, the pair integrate perfectly into your furnishings. Your wine and beverage collections can be magnificently presented with soft lighting, and at the perfect temperatures.

www.liebherr-appliances.co.za

Distributed in Southern Africa by Liebherr-Africa (Pty) Limited
Vlakfontein Road, Fulcrum Industrial, Springs, Gauteng
Tel: 011 365 2561/2/3
Fax: 086 674 9628

LIEBHERR
Quality, Design and Innovation

DELVE INTO THE **FINER THINGS**

The Table Bay

With unrivalled views of the Atlantic Ocean and one of the world's natural wonders, The Table Bay invites you to take full advantage of the hotel's unmatched facilities and all that Cape Town has to offer. It is the best address in Cape Town.

   | 33°54'11.15"S 18°22'24.48"E

TABLE BAY BREAKWATER BOULEVARD, VICTORIA & ALFRED WATERFRONT, 8001
TELEPHONE +27 (0)21 406 5000 FACSIMILE +27 (0)21 406 5686 FOR MORE
INFORMATION VISIT SUNINTERNATIONAL.COM

You don't have to travel the country to find the **BEST WINES.**

THE *wine route* IS CLOSER THAN YOU THINK.
Choose from over 100 leading estates at Checkers & Checkers Hyper.

Checkers
better and better

CitySightseeing Cape Town

All Day - Every Day!

- Easy access to Table Mountain,
- Red City Tour, Mini Peninsula, Downtown, Wine and Sunset Bus
- Walking Tours of the City and Bo-Kaap
- Harbour and Canal Cruises

OFFICIAL TOUR

Cape Explorer

WINE TOUR & TASTINGS
FRANSCHHOEK & STELLENBOSCH

The best way to see the Winelands, with 2 hours at leisure to explore the historic town of Franschhoek and a scenic drive through Stellenbosch.

FULL DAY TOUR
INCLUDES
2 wine tastings
Cheese pairing
Cellar tour
Duck parade

FRANSCHHOEK WINE TRAM

DEPARTS: Tuesday - Thursday - Saturday

NEW TOUR!

Relax and let the Cape Explorer luxury coach drive you to join the Franschhoek Wine Tram for this unique wine experience.

CAPE POINT
& PENGUINS

Complete your visit to Cape Town by joining us on this live guided (in English) tour to Cape Point, Cape of Good Hope with a stop at Boulders Beach to view the penguins.

THE ART OF LOGISTICS

BEEN THERE, DONE THAT?

GET A FRIEND THAT ALWAYS HAS
NEW DISCOVERIES TO SHARE:

- ✓ View the trophies won by South Africa's first-ever Grand Prix racing driver
- Play 3-D glow-in-the-dark golf
- Discover the new (and only) museum dedicated to the San people
- Get into the Gangster Museum
- Swim with crocodiles in the winelands
- Gape at the tallest species of tree in the world
- Devour deep-fried prawn bao
- Get a fresh perspective from the rooftop of a six-star coworking space
- Treat yourself to a helicopter clay pigeon shooting tour

CapeTownMagazine.com

EXCITING DISCOVERIES. ALWAYS.

SELECTED WINE FROM SOUTH AFRICA
CAPREO

Door-to-Door Wine Delivery

to Europe, UK and Switzerland

Taste and order directly at the CAPREO partner wineries. **Free delivery for 18 bottles or more.**

- **Over 50 top wineries**
- **More than 500 selected premium wines**
- **Fast & secure shipping**
- **Affordable prices**

www.capreo.com

BIG 5 SAFARI & SPA

**Real Africa. Real Close To Cape Town.
Over 10 000-hectares of Big 5 conservancy.**

4-STAR ACCOMMODATION | SPA
GAME DRIVE | HORSEBACK & QUAD BIKE SAFARI

At the award-winning Aquila Private Game Reserve and Spa, guests will get the opportunity to experience a Big 5 safari, together with outstanding service; it just does not get any better than this. With game drives, quad bike and horseback safaris situated just 2 hours' drive from Cape Town, it's the closest you will get to real Africa, in the lap of luxury.

The world-class spa at Aquila adds to the already exceptional facilities and services on offer. It is a masterpiece of luxury, defined by its serenity and creative use of natural elements.

FACILITIES & ACTIVITIES
4-STAR ESTABLISHMENT | PREMIER, FAMILY & LUXURY COTTAGES | LODGE ROOMS | DAY TRIP SAFARI | HORSEBACK SAFARI | QUAD BIKE SAFARI | STAR SAFARI | OVERNIGHT SAFARI | FLY-IN SAFARI | WINE TASTING | INDOOR & OUTDOOR RESTAURANTS | OUTDOOR POOL | WET BAR CIGAR LOUNGE | CONFERENCE CENTRE | SPA | CURIO SHOP | CHILDREN'S FACILITIES & JUNIOR RANGER PROGRAMME

www.aquilasafari.com   **f** AquilaSafari   **○ ○** AquilaSafaris

+27 (0)21 430 7260 or RES@AQUILASAFARI.COM

ANNO 1945

THE FRANSCHHOEK
CELLAR

Coffee Bar | Alfresco Restaurant | Wine Pairings
Children's Play Area | Accommodation | Selection of Event Spaces

Main Road Franschhoek   Tel: 021 876 2086
www.thefranschhoekcellar.co.za   email: fhccellardoor@dgb.co.za

UNLOCK THE

BECOME

RT OF DINING

MEMBER

64 to unlock our global village
Entertainment experiences.

ub.co.za

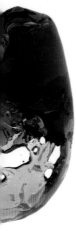

Find South Africa's best wineries with what3words

Every winery in Platter's Wine Guide is listed with its 3 word address. This refers to the precise location of the winery entrance. Enter the 3 word address into the free what3words app to make sure you arrive at the right place, relaxed and ready to enjoy South Africa's finest wines.

///dream.stardom.chart

Stellenbosch, Western Cape

A–Z of South African Producers

AA Badenhorst Family Wines

Ⓟ Ⓗ Ⓞ

Internationally acclaimed winecrafting, multifarious creativity - and witty banter - continue apace at Adi Badenhorst's Swartland property, which he co-owns with cousin Hein, with new wines, styles and projects all continuously bubbling up and keeping things interesting. The winemaking focus is shifting more towards single-vineyard expressions of old vines including a tinta barocca, though none of the latest vintages of Adi's complex, intriguing and sometimes profound wines were ready to taste this edition. Meanwhile the Caperitif Cape Vermouth is now in its eighth incarnation, while the Swaan Cape Tonic Water may soon be joined by matching spirit with the arrival of a potstill at the farm.

Location: Malmesbury ▪ Map: Swartland ▪ Map grid reference: C8 ▪ Est 2007 ▪ 1stB 2006 ▪ Tasting, sales & tours by appt ▪ Closed all pub hols & weekends ▪ Conferences ▪ Function venue for 130 people ▪ Conservation area ▪ Guest cottages ▪ Owner(s) Adi & Hein Badenhorst ▪ Winemaker(s) Adi Badenhorst (2006), with Jasper Wickens (2008) ▪ Viticulturist(s) Pierre Rossouw (Jan 1975) ▪ 100ha/43ha (cinsaut, grenache, shiraz, chard, chenin, rouss) ▪ 40,000cs own label 60% red 40% white ▪ PO Box 1177 Malmesbury 7299 ▪ adi@iafrica.com ▪ www.aabadenhorst.com ▪ S 33° 32' 38.01" E 018° 49' 7.42" ▪ ⌨ uprooting.feed.pollsters ▪ F +27 (0)21-794-5196 ▪ T +27 (0)82-373-5038

Aan de Doorns Cellar

Ⓟ Ⓖ

Grower-owned Aan de Doorns is mainly a supplier to, and shareholder in, export powerhouse FirstCape. But 25,000 cases of appealing, affordable wines are made for the house labels, available for tasting at the visitor venue near Worcester. Frost damage and reduced volumes were concerns in harvest 2018 but cellar chief Johan Morkel, in his 25th season here, is delighted with the quality, chenin and colombard in particular.

Vintage range

★★★★ **Muscat d'Alexandrie** Ⓩ Fortified dessert **15** (87), ex tank, heady grape & floral perfume harbinger of delights to come: glacé fruit & honeycomb flavours yet uncloying, refined. 375 ml. No **14**.

★★★★ **Red Muscadel** Ⓩ 375 ml of delicious, sweet fortified muscat in **15** (87). Full muscat fragrance, sumptuous but uncloying; lingering smooth fruity glow. Improves on **13** ★★★★ (84). **14** untasted.

Cabernet Sauvignon Ⓩ ★★★ Previewed **16** (78) has blackcurrants throughout, savoury ripe tannin, nice juicy drinkability. **Pinotage** Ⓩ ★★★ Salty liquorice, dark berries, **16** (81)'s new-oak staves show in savoury toastiness, enough tannin for some ageing. Already drinking well. **Shiraz** Ⓩ ★★★ Tank sample **16** (78) similar styling to maiden **15** ★★ (74): vanilla, deep dark fruit, curvaceous lines, easy-drinking pleasure. **Doornroodt** Ⓩ ★★★ Ruby cab & merlot designed to enjoy at youthful best. **16** (78) succulent red berries, touch oak adding stiffening. **Chenin Blanc** ⊘ ★★★ Shows fresh apple & pear vibrancy, ends crisply dry in **18** (79). **Sauvignon Blanc** ★★ Gently fruity style, ex-tank **18** (74) the perfect summertime quaffer. **Sweet William Vonkelwyn** Ⓩ ★★ Pink bubbly from colombard & pinotage, **NV** (74) fruit gum scented, sweet & convivial, a party goer. **Cape Ruby** Ⓩ ★★★★ Tank sample **15** (84) shows sound fruity profile. Very smooth, drinkable.

Route 43 range

Deep Red ⊘ ★★★ Shiraz-led with pinotage, giving **16** (78) dark-toned fruit, even hints of mocha, though wine is unwooded. Juicy, smooth, oh so easy to drink. Also in 3L, like Crisp White. **Fruity White** ⊘ ★★★ From colombard, pre-bottling **18** (78) is exuberantly fruity in perfume & flavour, the semi-sweet styling fitting in perfectly. **Crisp White** ⊘ ★★★ Dry sauvignon/colombard blend & name says it all, **18** (78) ex tank is appealingly fruity-fresh. — CR

Location/map/WO: Worcester ▪ Map grid reference: B4 ▪ Est 1954 ▪ Tasting & sales Mon–Fri 8–5 Sat 9-1 ▪ Olive/olive oil & wine pairing by appt ▪ Closed all pub hols ▪ Tours during harvest by appt ▪ Owner(s) 27 shareholders ▪ Cellarmaster(s) Johan Morkel (Nov 1993) ▪ Winemaker(s) Gert van Deventer (Sep 1997) & Chris Geldenhuys (Sep 2016) ▪ Viticulturist(s) Pierre Snyman ▪ 1,600ha (cab, ptage, chard, chenin, cbard) ▪ 32,700t/25,000cs own label ▪ PO Box 235 Worcester 6849 ▪ info@aandedoorns.co.za ▪ www.aandedoorns.co.za ▪ S 33° 41' 47.0" E 019° 29' 26.2" ▪ ⌨ lookout.sprouts.expensively ▪ F +27 (0)23-347-4629 ▪ T +27 (0)23-347-2301

☐ **Abalone** *see* Whalehaven Wines

Abingdon Wine Estate ⓠ ⑪ ⓐ

A pioneering family-run estate at Lions River in the KwaZulu-Natal Midlands, its 1,150m altitude offsetting inland humidity and cooling the vines. Co-owner Ian Smorthwaite and daughter Laurie make the wine and tend the vineyard, which includes nebbiolo first planted in 2003, then added to in 2013, and now bottled for commercial release. Mother Jane welcomes visitors and wedding parties, while Laurie also offers personalised wine education through her KZN School of Wine, based at the estate.

Location: Lions River ▪ Map: KwaZulu-Natal ▪ Map grid reference: B2 ▪ Est 2004 ▪ 1stB 2007 ▪ Tasting room & restaurant open Fri-Sun & pub hols 10-4 for personalised tastings & fresh country meals ▪ Weekday visits strictly by appt ▪ Weddings & corporate functions ▪ Owner(s) Ian & Jane Smorthwaite ▪ Winemaker(s)/viticulturist(s) Ian & Laurie Smorthwaite ▪ 7ha/3ha (cab, nebbiolo, shiraz, chard, sauv, viog) ▪ Lions River KZN Midlands ▪ jane@abingdonestate.co.za, ian@abingdonestate.co.za ▪ www.abingdonestate.co.za ▪ S 29° 26' 36.71" E 030° 09' 14.18" ▪ 🌐 ensnared.sealable.cowboys ▪ F +27 (0)86-572-6877 ▪ **T +27 (0)83-463-8503 (Jane)**

☐ **Abraham Perold Heritage Collection** *see* KWV Wines

Accolade Wines South Africa

A scion of Accolade Wines, one of the big five international wine businesses, Accolade Wines South Africa produces globally represented brand Kumala, fast-growing varietal range Fish Hoek, and highly regarded pinnacle label Flagstone, all listed separately.

Location: Somerset West ▪ Winemaker(s) Gerhard Swart (head winemaker), Juan Slabbert & Chandré Petersen ▪ 6.4m cs own label ▪ PO Box 769 Stellenbosch 7599 ▪ info@flagstonewines.com ▪ www.acco-lade-wines.com ▪ F +27 (0)21-852-5085 ▪ **T +27 (0)21-852-5052**

☐ **Adama** *see* Bosman Family Vineyards

Aden's Star

This is the vintage-dated portfolio made by a consultant for Jason Neal, CEO of Johannesburg drinks company Nicholson Smith. Jason's non-vintage labels, Pandora's Box and Bella Vino, are listed separately.

The Golden Fleece Red Blend ⓠ ★★★★ Smooth, characterful **14** ⑧⑤, cab-led 5-way Bordeaux red, offers good body, firm core of ripe fruit & dry tail. Occasional release: **Sauvignon Blanc**. — FM

Location: Johannesburg ▪ WO: Western Cape ▪ Est 1997 ▪ 1stB 2012 ▪ Closed to public ▪ Owner(s) Jason Neal ▪ Winemaker(s)/viticulturist(s) James McKenzie ▪ 6,000cs own label 100% red ▪ PO Box 1659 Jukskei Park 2153 ▪ jason@nicholsonsmith.co.za ▪ www.nicholsonsmith.co.za ▪ F +27 (0)11-496-2952 ▪ **T +27 (0)11-496-2947**

☐ **Admiral's Choice** *see* La Couronne Wines
☐ **Adoro Wines** *see* Naudé Wines

AD Wines ⓠ

Despite the success of his first ('14) Skylark – 'a gloriously enjoyable cinsault' – Adrian Dommisse had decided to focus on his fast-growing Cape Town law firm and fatherhood. 'But the spirit of wine wouldn't let me go.' Winemaker friend Justin van Wyk (Constantia Glen) helped him find three vineyards and they made separate batches in the same way, with minimal intervention, ultimately choosing a Darling wine (with a splash of Elgin) for bottling. An 'overjoyed' Adrian promises his journey will continue next year.

★★★★ **Skylark** Exciting new-wave cinsaut, **17** ⑧⑨ even better than debut **14** ⑧⑧, as pretty yet serious too. Mostly Darling grapes bunch fermented, 8 months old oak, scented strawberries, cured meat & fynbos, fine, gently gripping texture. Endlessly beguiling & delightful. — TJ, CvZ

Location: Cape Town ▪ WO: Western Cape ▪ Est 2013 ▪ 1stB 2014 ▪ Tasting by appt only ▪ Owner(s) Dommisse Holdings Pty Ltd, shareholder Adrian Dommisse ▪ Winemaker(s) Adrian Dommisse ▪ 2t/150cs own label 100% red ▪ PO Box 711 Hermanus 7200 ▪ adriandommisse@gmail.com ▪ www.adwines.co.za ▪ **T +27 (0)71-674-4316**

☐ **Africa Five** *see* Stellenview Premium Wines
☐ **African Dawn** *see* Rooiberg Winery

☐ **African King** see Zidela Wines
☐ **African Roots** see Seven Sisters Vineyards
☐ **African Tribe** see Baratok Wines
☐ **Agaat** see Truter Family Wines
☐ **Ahrens Family** see The Ahrens Family

Akkerdal Wine Estate ⓠ ⌂

The reality for Western Cape winegrowers the past drought years is highlighted by Pieter Hanekom, who says his Akkerdal estate 'occasionally had no water at all'. What saw the vines through this nightmare was 'healthy soil', which is why he continues to farm biodynamically (without certification at this stage), as it will 'ultimately benefit the land, the crop and the wine, all with the added advantage of taking care of Mother Earth'. With Franschhoek family roots dating back to 1741, his words have a particular resonance.

Limited Releases

★★★★ **Malbec** ⓠ **15** ⑧⑦ intense sour cherry & spice appeal, skilfully reins in fruit generosity to finish with elegance & focus. Attractive dinner companion, with sufficient heft to partner hearty food.

★★★★ **Kallie's Dream** ⓠ Rhône-style **15** ★★★★★ ⑨① engages on many levels, not least the unusual co-ferment of all components: shiraz (48%), mourvèdre, grenache, carignan & viognier. Fruit rich, yet plenty of tannic oomph & freshening acidity; lingering pure-fruited farewell. Worth waiting since **10** ⑧⑦.

★★★★ **TDT** ⓠ **12** ⑧⑦ creative blend tempranillo, durif & tannat has intriguing dark perfumed fruit & supple tannins. Succulent, balanced but still youthful, with potential. Step up previous.

★★★★ **Wild Boar** ⓠ **15** ⑧⑦ first since **09** ⑧⑦, 'wild' in its daredevil mix of petit verdot, cab franc, petite sirah & roobernet (20% each) with shiraz & tannat (10% apiece). Dry & firm, myriad red berry fruits to contemplate, dissect or simply enjoy.

Not tasted: **SG Rose**. Discontinued: **Merlot, Petit Noir, SG Blush**.

Akkerdal range

★★★★ **Shiraz** ⓠ With dash mourvèdre, **12** ⑧⑦ mid-2013 still tight but dry tannins & oak (18 months) revealed underlying seriousness. Needed cellar time to reveal all its charms.

★★★★ **Sauvignon Blanc** ⓠ Accomplished **15** ⑧⑦, plenty green fig & lime, steely acidity adds backbone with farewell of tropical fruit; perfect balance. Ticks the boxes & raises bar on last-tasted **10** ★★.

Discontinued: **Passion Reserve**. — HC

Location/map/WO: Franschhoek ▪ Map grid reference: C4 ▪ Est 2000 ▪ 1stB 2001 ▪ Tasting & sales Mon-Fri 10-4 by appt only ▪ Closed all pub hols ▪ Self-catering chalet ▪ Owner(s)/cellarmaster(s)/winemaker(s) Pieter Hanekom ▪ Viticulturist(s) Pieter Hanekom, advised by Eben Archer ▪ 18ha (barbera, cab f, carignan, durif, grenache, malbec, merlot, mourv, p verdot, roobernet, shiraz, tannat, tempranillo, chard, nouvelle, sauv, sem, viog) ▪ 6,000cs own label 95% red 4% white 1% rosé ▪ IPW, WIETA ▪ PO Box 36 La Motte 7691 ▪ wine@akkerdal.co.za ▪ www.akkerdal.co.za ▪ S 33° 52′ 50.9″ E 019° 3′ 3.8″ ▪ 🖳 surges.telegraphs.campsites ▪ F +27 (0)21-876-3189 ▪ **T +27 (0)21-876-3481/+27 (0)82-442-1746**

Akkerdraai ⓠ ⌖

Wine had long been a hobby of Salie de Swardt and, post retirement from international enterprise Media24, making wine (with consultants) in the Helderberg took that interest to a new level. Cabernet remains his focus, with Ronell Wiid, a Diners Club Winemaker of the Year, advising.

Cabernet Sauvignon ⓠ ★★★★ Well-priced **14** ⑧③ satisfying glassful of sweet cassis fruit, fresh acidity & form-giving tannins. Deft oak (10% new) for complexity, structure, not flavour. Not tasted: **Cabernet Sauvignon-Merlot**. — CvZ

Location/map: Stellenbosch ▪ Map grid reference: E8 ▪ WO: Western Cape ▪ Est 1956 ▪ 1stB 2007 ▪ Tasting by appt only ▪ Fee R25, waived on purchase ▪ Closed Easter Fri-Mon, Dec 25 & Jan 1 ▪ Walks/hikes ▪ Owner(s)/cellarmaster(s) Salie de Swardt ▪ Winemaker(s) Ronell Wiid (consultant), with Salie de Swardt (Jan 2013) ▪ Viticulturist(s) Ronell Wiid (consultant) ▪ 1.5ha (cab) ▪ 12t 100% red ▪ PO Box 22 Lynedoch 7603 ▪ saliedes@mweb.co.za ▪ S 33° 59′ 53.52″ E 018° 49′ 50.94″ ▪ 🖳 crossing.bossy.name ▪ **T +27 (0)21-881-3861/+27 (0)83-264-1463**

☐ **Alchemy** see Hartenberg Estate

Alexanderfontein

Viticulturist and winemaker Theo Basson produces these wines as a separate range for Ormonde Private Cellar, the sizeable family business in Darling. The screwcapped bottlings are designed to be unpretentious - enhancing 'enjoyment of the simpler aspects of life'.

Cabernet Sauvignon ⊘ ★★★ Where previous was slightly confected, cloying, pre-bottling **15** ⑧① is the opposite: fresh cherries & blueberries on nose, quite lean & tangy on palate. Coastal WO unless noted. **Merlot** ★★★ **16** ⑦⑨ offers ripely fruity aromas, but the palate is rather light & ungenerous. **Shiraz** ⊘ ★★★ Lithe **15** ⑧② preview has spice-studded black plum fruit, slightly metallic on finish but pleasant overall. **Chardonnay** ★★★ Shyly fruity aromas on unoaked **17** ⑦⑨, with a creamy texture, firm acidity & a sweet-sour finish. **Chenin Blanc** ★★★ Rounded, fresh & tasty **18** ⑧⓪ has an easy balance & dry finish, making for pleasant current drinking. Tasted ex tank, as next. **Sauvignon Blanc** ★★★ Forward, enticing passionfruit aromas & green-tinged flavours on lively, tasty & dry **18** ⑧②. WO W Cape. — TJ

☐ **AlexKia** see Rooiberg Winery

Alheit Vineyards ⓠ

Chris and Suzaan Alheit recorded their seventh harvest in 2017 (the vintage of the current releases), a milestone they feel represents the end of chapter one of Alheit Vineyards and the beginning of a new phase. 'We learned a great deal in the first seven years,' they declare, admitting to 'many highs and lows, some mistakes and some good victories.' The three new chenin blancs, from Stellenbosch, Swartland and Citrusdal Mountain, reflect their new strong focus on origin. 'In the Cape context, old-vine chenin provides a terrific opportunity to explore the effect of origin on wine' - an effect so eloquently expressed not only in the chenins but throughout the range. The evocative labels, a collaboration between the Alheits and Fanakalo design studio, 'with much back and forth discussion', only enhance the masterly wines.

★★★★☆ **Cartology** ⓐ ⓦ The original Alheit wine, from far-flung sites; 87/13 blend chenin/semillon in **17** ⑨③. Great purity, lifted freshness lends delicacy to creamy texture, white peach concentration. Lightly spiced, precise conclusion completes satisfaction. 100% oak, 27% new 2,000L foudre.

★★★★☆ **Fire By Night** ⓃⒺⓌ ⓐ ⓦ Evocative label paying homage to the Paardeberg. Chenin from 3 dryland vineyards, youngest 38 years old. **17** ⑨④ austere, resolutely dry, its grainy texture reflecting weathered granite soils, but also rich in flavour. Unadorned, complete; has a great future. Older oak & 17% concrete 'egg'.

★★★★☆ **Huilkrans** ⓃⒺⓌ ⓐ ⓦ Citrusdal Mountain's Skurfberg vineyard responsible for some of SA's most renowned chenins; this majestic **17** ⑨④ joins them. Power, richness, with resonating length to its bracing finish. A grand wine, deserving time & contemplation. Spontaneous ferment, older oak. Unfined, unfiltered, as all.

★★★★☆ **Magnetic North** ⓐ Previously with 'Mountain Makstok' suffix. No change in quality of this extraordinary Citrusdal Mountain chenin. **17** ⑨③ exudes lemon peel, pebbly intensity. Ripe flavours, full body contained by bracing acidity; uncompromisingly dry. Fermented, aged in old 300L oak.

★★★★☆ **Nautical Dawn** ⓃⒺⓌ ⓐ ⓦ From 2 Stellenbosch maritime chenin vineyards 30 & 40 years old. Much floral, white peach charm in **17** ⑨④; youthful approachability in its ripe-fruited succulence, length, but doesn't lack steely backbone necessary for interesting development.

★★★★☆ **Radio Lazarus** ⓐ ⓦ Swansong for this label: old Bottelary vines no longer viable. **17** ⑨③ great aromatic breadth but also mineral tension, vigour in its concentrated, reverberating flavours. Lovely textural quality from ferment/ageing in 100% (Bottelary) clay pots - only unoaked wine in range.

★★★★★ **La Colline Vineyard** ⓐ ⓦ Wonderfully expressive of 80+ year Franschhoek vineyard. **17** ⑨⑤ exuberant, ripely scented lemon rind, spices; richness, full body invigorated by sheer concentration of flavour, firm dry finish. Excellent potential. Fermented/aged in 'youngest' old oak (4-5 years) 'as it needs to breathe.'

★★★★☆ **Hemelrand Vine Garden** ⓐ Sophisticated **17** ⑨③ near-equal chenin, chardonnay, roussanne, verdelho with subtle 4% muscat de Frontignan; from mixed Hemel-en-Aarde Ridge vineyard. Seductively silky; plenty underlying energy to focus floral, stonefruit. Whole greater than sum of parts. — AL

Location: Hermanus ▪ Map: Walker Bay & Bot River ▪ Map grid reference: B4 ▪ WO: Citrusdal Mountain/
Stellenbosch/Swartland/Franschhoek/Bottelary/Western Cape/Hemel-en-Aarde Ridge ▪ Est 2010 ▪ 1stB 2011
▪ Closed to public; tasting by special arrangement only ▪ Owner(s) Chris & Suzaan Alheit ▪ Cellarmaster(s)
Chris Alheit ▪ Winemaker(s) Chris & Suzaan Alheit, with Franco Lourens (Jan 2016) ▪ 60t/3,000cs own label
100% white ▪ PO Box 711 Hermanus 7200 ▪ chris@alheitvineyards.co.za ▪ www.alheitvineyards.co.za ▪ S 34°
20'35.56" E 019° 18'11.30" ▪ ⌖ zones.italics.gathering ▪ **T +27 (0)83-274-6860**

Alkmaar Boutique Vineyard

Energy and activity are transforming this Wellington boutique winery as recent owners Juan Möller and
Charmaine Olivier plan a wedding/conference venue, serviced and self-catering accommodation, and
mountain biking facilities. Eminent independent vintner Johan Joubert consults on an expanding range,
soon to include a pinotage-based Cape Blend.

★★★★ **Pinotage** ⓥ Elegant expression of variety showing judicious oak, vibrant ripe berry fruit,
supple palate & focused finish. **12** ⑧⑦ rung above **11** ★★★★.

★★★★ **Shiraz-Mourvèdre-Viognier** ⓥ Ripe & robust, shiraz-dominated **13** ⑧⑥ has dense black
cherry fruit with tobacco aromas, mouthcoating tannins. Fuller, more focused than **12** ★★★★ ⑧④.

Cabernet Sauvignon-Merlot-Petit Verdot ⓥ ★★★★ Was 'Master'. Bigger than previous, with
savoury-tarry undertones & black fruit, **13** ⑧⑤ sleek & smooth, full bodied & very ripe. **Chardonnay-
Pinot Noir** ★★★★ Just-dry, palest pink rosé, **18** ⑧⑤ vibrant & fruity with raspberries-&-cream flavours,
gentle zip of lemon on finish. **Viognier** ★★★★ Summery fresh peach & spice appeal on unoaked **18** ⑧④,
balanced & rounded. **Chardonnay-Viognier** ⓥ ★★★★ Zesty **18** ⑧⑤ in lightly aromatic style, lively &
fresh for al fresco lunches & patio parties. **Méthode Cap Classique Brut** ⑭ ★★★ Deep gold-hued **11**
⑧⓪ dry sparkler from undisclosed variety/ies, evolved bruised apple, toast flavours & creamy mousse on
broad palate, best enjoyed soon. — WB

Location/map/WO: Wellington ▪ Map grid reference: C4 ▪ Est 2001 ▪ 1stB 2005 ▪ Tasting & sales Mon-Fri 10-4
Sat 10-2 pub hols by appt ▪ Cellar tours by appt ▪ Walks (part of Wellington Wine Walk) ▪ Owner(s) Juan
Möller & Charmaine Olivier ▪ Winemaker(s) Johan Joubert (Feb 2017, consultant), with Dawid Futhwa (Jan
2010) ▪ Viticulturist(s) Dawid Futhwa (Jan 2003) ▪ 9.9ha (cab, merlot, mourv, p verdot, ptage, shiraz, chard,
viog) ▪ 50t/900cs own label 83% red 17% white + 12,000L bulk ▪ PO Box 1273 Blouvlei Rd Wellington 7654
▪ alkmaarwines@mweb.co.za ▪ www.alkmaarwines.co.za ▪ S 33° 39'37.98" E 019° 1'55.14" ▪ ⌖ bells.fires.
flushes ▪ **T +27 (0)21-873-0191**

Allée Bleue Wines

Two red wines aimed at collectors and connoisseurs debut this edition from German-owned Franschhoek
estate Allée Bleue. The Black Series limited releases are intended to 'shine the spotlight on the standout barrels of particular cultivars in each vintage', according to their maker, Van Zyl du Toit. His creations (including
the separately listed Blue Owl range) are part of a diverse offering, from agri-products like fruit and herbs to
conference and wedding venues, bistro, picnics and luxury accommodation in the manor, dating from 1690.

Black Series ⑭

★★★★ **Old Vine Pinotage** ⊛ Best 3 barrels from ungrafted Piekenierskloof bushvines planted 1964
deliver profusion of ripe berries in **16** ⑧⑧, vanilla & spice from 70% new French oak, 16 months, big
tannins & a bit of heat from 14.6% alcohol.

★★★★ **The Lemon Grove Syrah** Single low-cropped vineyard on home-farm, **14** ⑧⑧ rich, ripe & dark
hued, blackberry fruit & spice ex oaking regime as for sibling. Handles same alcohol better.

Platinum range

★★★★★ **Pinotage** ⓥ ⊛ Plenty of tannic backbone on **16** ⑨④ to support the plush blackberry &
cherry fruit. Generous, but careful oaking (95% French, rest American, 14 months) helps elevate it a notch,
give more polish, refinement than in **15** ⑨①. Piekenierskloof & Franschhoek grapes. Also in 1.5L.

★★★★★ **L'Amour Toujours** ⓥ ⊛ Flagship red, led by the 2 cabs, merlot & petit verdot supporting.
Quintessential Cape Bordeaux flavours of cassis, cedarwood & a freshening herbal top note. Intriguing &
rewarding **14** ★★★★★ ⑨⑤ manages power with finesse, like **13** ⑨③. WO Banghoek.

★★★★ **Isabeau** ② Alluring mix of citrus, tropical & stonefruit on **14** ⑧⑥, mostly chardonnay, plus semillon, dab viognier. Deft 25% new wood adds caramel & oaky notes. Dual Walker Bay-Coastal WO.

Premium range

★★★★ **Cabernet Sauvignon-Merlot** ② Minty blackcurrant fruit & plenty of firm tannin on well-structured **14** ⑧⑦, with drop petit verdot, judiciously oaked. Back to form after **13** ★★★ ⑧①, also from Banhoek grapes. Magnums available.

★★★★ **Chenin Blanc** ⊘ Tropical fruit flavours abound on vibrant **17** ⑧⑧, tiny splash viognier adds spice. Barrel-fermented (15% new, 6 months) Walker Bay & Franschhoek fruit.

★★★★ **Sauvignon Blanc** ⊘ 4 months on lees & dash semillon give **17** ⑧⑦ ex Walker Bay a creamy texture to the abundant gooseberry, Granny Smith apple & greenpepper fruit.

★★★★ **Méthode Cap Classique Brut** Delicious **14** ⑧⑨ sparkling, perfectly dry with lemony bubbles & biscuit nuance from 36 months on lees. Equal pinot noir & chardonnay, latter oaked. Walker Bay WO. **Shiraz** ★★★★ Deep & dark, full body to match the colour. Powerful tannins supported by perfume & ripe red fruit. **15** ⑧④ lacks finesse perhaps, but compensates by making a steak more enjoyable. **Méthode Cap Classique Brut Rosé** ② ★★★★ A little pinker & a bit more pinot noir (58%) than sibling, rest pinotage, 18 months on lees. Ex-Franschhoek **14** ⑧⑤ perfect summer bubbly. Not tasted: **Cape Ruby**.

Starlette range

Pinotage ⊘ ⑨ ★★★★ Berry surge with touch of coffee, **16** ⑧⑤ drinks easily with ample tannic oomph to hold your attention. **Blanc** ⊘ ⑨ ★★★★ Pungent lime & gooseberry on **18** ⑧④, underpinned by a vibrant acidity from majority sauvignon, partnered by chenin & semillon. Deliciously priced too.

Rouge ★★★ Fruity & easy, just enough backbone to be interesting & fun. **17** ⑧① mostly cab (50%) with merlot & shiraz. Coastal WO. **Shiraz Rosé** ⊘ ★★★★ Now an all-Franschhoek dry pink. **18** ⑧④ easy poolside quaffing, strawberries & raspberries in abundance. — HC

Location/map: Franschhoek • Map grid reference: C6 • WO: Franschhoek/Walker Bay/Banghoek/Coastal/ Piekenierskloof/Piekenierskloof-Franschhoek/Walker Bay-Franschhoek/Walker Bay-Coastal • Est 1690 • 1stB 2001 • Tasting & sales Mon-Fri 9-5 Sat 10-5 Sun/pub hols 10-4 • Tasting fee R45/4 wines • Cellar tours by appt • Bistro Allée Bleue • Picnics (booking required) • Jungle gym • Tour groups by appt • Farm produce • Conferences • Weddings • Allée Bleue accommodation - Kendall Cottage & Manor House • Owner(s) DAUPHIN Entwicklungs-und Beteiligungs GMH (Germany) • Winemaker(s) Van Zyl du Toit (Jul 2009), with Clayton Christians (Aug 2017) • Viticulturist(s) Douw Willemse (Sep 2008) • 210ha/31ha (cab, merlot, ptage, pinot, shiraz, chard, chenin, sauv, sem, viog) • 450t/30,000c 45% red 50% white 5% MCC • IPW • PO Box 100 Groot Drakenstein 7680 • info@alleebleue.com • www.alleebleue.co.za • S 33° 51' 29.0" E 018° 59' 12.9" • ⓦ havens.livelihoods.unbuckle • F +27 (0)21-874-1850 • **T +27 (0)21-874-1021**

Allesverloren ② ⑪ ◎ ⑧ ⑤

The name of the 18th-century Malan family estate on the slopes of Swartland's Kasteelberg means 'all is lost', but in fact something is gained this edition: a chenin blanc, which we're flagging as a 'Hidden Gem' on its own merits as well as for diversifying the previously red/pink portfolio with one of Swartland's signature white varieties. Shiraz and, particularly, Portuguese grapes remain the focus though, with varietals, blends, fortified and rosé (the latter another nugget worth seeking out) all on offer.

★★★★ **Tinta Barocca** ⓐ Cassis & crushed herb notes, deep but refined tannin grip, white pepper & dark spice persistence. **16** ⑧⑧ handsome, complex, & savoury partner for venison.

★★★★ **Red Muscadel** Generously perfumed fruit & sweet spice in fresh, delicious **18** ⑧⑨ fortified, tangy acidity & alcohol slimming down hefty sugar (242 g/l) into svelte mouthful of candyfloss & cherry.

★★★★ **Fine Old Vintage** ② Enduring label, accessible 'port' from traditional varieties. **11** ⑧⑦ preview jammy dark fruit notes & cedar spice, fine tannins ably mask the sweetness, keep alcohol in check.

Tinta Rosé ⊘ ⑨ ★★★★ Very few SA rosés from Portuguese grapes (here tinta & touriga, with others). **18** ⑧⑤ merges exuberant fruit, sweet spice & exotic tobacco note; fresh & dry, with food-welcoming racy acidity. **Chenin Blanc** ⑯ ⑨ ★★★★ Charming debut. Deep & forthcoming ripe nectarine, pear &

pineapple in elegantly shaped **18** (83). Unoaked yet has interest, complexity & structure - might surprise you 5 years hence.

Cabernet Sauvignon ★★★★ Blackcurrant & menthol notes in variety-true **16** (85) matched by firm tannins, fresh acidity. Well balanced & delicious now & for good few years. 18 months French oak, 5% new, as all reds unless noted. **Shiraz ★★★★** Forest fruit notes of **16** (85) give way to black pepper & spice. Silky & savoury, spiciness recurring in aftertaste. **1704 Red** (②) **★★★** Unwooded mix tinta & shiraz, **15** (82) restrained dark fruit & spice notes, silky tannins, some leather & plum on finish. Not tasted: **Touriga Nacional, Três Vermelhos**. — GM

Location: Riebeek West ▪ Map/WO: Swartland ▪ Map grid reference: D6 ▪ Est 1704 ▪ Tasting & sales Mon-Fri 9-5 Sat 9-2 ▪ Tasting R35/5 wines or R50/10 wines ▪ Closed Good Fri, Dec 25 & Jan 1 ▪ Cellar tours by appt ▪ Pleasant Pheasant Restaurant T +27 (0)22-461-2170 Tue 10.30-3 Wed-Sat 9-3 & 6-10 Sun 9-4 ▪ Facilities for children ▪ Conferences/functions T +27 (0)22-461-2253 ▪ Owner(s) Malan Boerdery Trust ▪ Cellarmaster(s) Danie Malan (Nov 1987) ▪ Winemaker(s) Wilhelm de Vries (Jan 2016) ▪ 227ha/187ha (cab, shiraz & various port varieties) ▪ 100,000c own label 90% red 10% white ▪ PO Box 23 Riebeek West 7306 ▪ info@allesver-loren.co.za ▪ www.allesverloren.co.za ▪ S 33° 21'32.5" E 018° 52'24.1" ▪ ⓦ newness.attracts.reflects ▪ F +27 (0)22-461-2444 ▪ **T +27 (0)22-461-2589**

☐ **Almara** see Southern Sky Wines

Almenkerk Wine Estate

The Belgian/Dutch Van Almenkerk family's showpiece estate in Elgin, converted from apples to vines from 2002, is 'coming of age', says cellarmaster Joris van Almenkerk. Progressive viticulture, a modern, built-to-spec cellar and 'confident' team have given them detailed insight into the flavour profiles and stylistic possibilities of the different vineyard sites. Now the focus is on fine-tuning trellising systems, picking times and fermentation/maceration methods et al in support of their goal of natural, minimalist, authentic wines.

★★★★☆ Merlot (🐝) New to the guide, understated & perfectly poised **15** (93). Leafy, tomato, graphite & savoury elements vie with rich fruitcake & spice. Like other reds, fermented with native yeasts. Rounded & plush, but reined in by 18 months French oak.

★★★★ Syrah Seductive yet restrained **14 ★★★★★** (90) shows serious intent of natural ferment & subsequent skin maceration. Deep, savoury, rich & nuanced with a layered palate. Elegant & refined with a long aftertaste. 18 months in French oak. Notch up on last-tasted **11** (87).

★★★★ Chardonnay (🐝) Subtle vanilla & orange blossom on **16 ★★★★★** (93) nose & palate shows careful oaking (25% new). Natural ferment & lees contact add texture to refined, elegant & restrained mouthful. Compelling freshness & taut core set against creamy richness. First tasted since **12**. Also in 1.5L.

★★★★☆ Sauvignon Blanc Bright elderflower & granadilla appeal on **17** (91) single vineyard wine. Beautiful balance of acid & fruit. Extended lees contact & stirring adds body & texture. Long & rewarding, will age with distinction. Different league to last-reviewed **12**. — WB, FM

Location/map/WO: Elgin ▪ Map grid reference: B2 ▪ Est 2004 ▪ 1stB 2009 ▪ Tasting, sales & cellar tours Tue-Sun 10-4 (Sep-May) & Tue-Sat 10-4 (May-Sep) ▪ Open pub lunch except on Mon ▪ Meals/picnics by prior booking (min 20 pax), or BYO picnic ▪ Walks/hikes ▪ Conservation area ▪ Heliport ▪ Boule court ▪ Owner(s) Van Almenkerk family ▪ Cellarmaster(s) Joris van Almenkerk ▪ Winemaker(s) Joris van Almenkerk, with Danver van Wyk (Feb 2009) ▪ Viticulturist(s) Michael Keown (Jan 2014) ▪ 104.2ha/15ha (cabs s/f, malbec, merlot, mourv, p verdot, shiraz, chard, sauv, viog) ▪ 100t/5,000c own label 65% red 30% white 5% rosé ▪ Brands for clients: De Mikke Patron, Pot Luck Club ▪ CVC member, WWF-SA Conservation Champion ▪ PO Box 1129 Grabouw 7160 ▪ info@almenkerk.co.za ▪ www.almenkerk.co.za ▪ S 34° 12'55" E 019° 01'57" ▪ ⓦ bookmark.prefigures.unvarying ▪ **T +27 (0)21-848-9844**

Alphabetical

David Cope, wine distributor and owner of Cape Town wine bar Publik, has lost one partner in this, his own label, but gained another – his wife, Donné. They work with different winemakers in rented cellar space. Drinkability is always a prime aim, but so is showcasing some lesser-known, under-appreciated varieties.

Vin Ordinaire ⊘ ★★★★ Multi-varietal red blend has a rather more Bordeauxish look in **16** ⑧④, making for a good, serious structure to carry the pleasing ripe berry flavours to a satisfying conclusion. From Swartland & Stellenbosch grapes. **Vin Rosé** (NEW) ★★★ Light coppery pink **17** ⑧② from Darling mourvèdre & cinsaut, matured in old oak. Plenty of fruit; rounded, fresh & bone-dry. **Vin Blanc** ★★★★ Very drinkable **17** ⑧④ mostly from Swartland roussanne with some oak-matured chardonnay ex Stellenbosch. Full flavoured, with crisp, green-edged acidity. Occasional release: **Dirty Julie Dry White**. — TJ

Location: Stellenbosch ▪ WO: Western Cape ▪ Est 2010 ▪ 1stB 2008 ▪ Closed to public ▪ Owner(s) David Cope & Donné Bullivant Cope ▪ 8,500cs own label 45% red 45% white 10% rosé ▪ drink@alphabetical.co.za ▪ www. alphabetical.co.za

---

Alte Neffen Wines

Amarone-style vine-drying of grapes, leading to extra concentration of flavours and tannins, is the approach preferred by Hilko Hegewisch, Stellenbosch boutique winemaker and brand co-owner with Europe-based nephew Helmut Peters. Their 'method kaperone' is represented here by a slow-evolving Shiraz; for earlier gratification, see their partly desiccated merlot blend under Black Door.

★★★★ **Shiraz Method Kaperone** Deep & dense **15** ⑧⑦'s on-vine drying produces concentrated inky & tarry overtones, thick tannins, brooding weight, suggesting extended cellaring, like **14** ★★★★ ⑧④.— GdB

Location/WO: Stellenbosch ▪ Est/1stB 2013 ▪ Closed to public ▪ Owner(s) Hilko Hegewisch & Helmut Peters ▪ Winemaker(s) Hilko Hegewisch ▪ 55t/1,400cs own label 100% red ▪ 22 Van Coppenhagen Str Rozendal Stellenbosch 7600 ▪ hilko@hegewisch.co.za ▪ www.alteneffen.co.za ▪ F +27 (0)86-614-5993 ▪ **T +27 (0)21-887-9544/+27 (0)82-788-9505**

☐ **Altitude Collection** see The Bald Ibis

Alto Wine Estate   ⓠ ⓒ

On the steep northern slopes of the Helderberg, red-wines-only Alto is one of the top Stellenbosch estates in the Distell wine portfolio. It is also one of few in the Cape where just five winemakers have crafted the wines over eight decades: Manie Malan, who originally planted the vines, Piet du Toit and son Hempies, and Schalk van der Westhuizen and now his son Bertho, whose tenure will doubtless merit adding 'B' to the name of the MPHS tribute blend.

★★★★ **Cabernet Sauvignon** Sweet cassis fruit, subtle meaty tones & deftly handled oak (18 months, 70% new, French & American). **15** ⑧⑨ vibrant & lithe, back on form after more muscular **14** ★★★★ ⑧④.

★★★★☆ **Shiraz** Tastily combines old-Cape savouriness with modern dark berries & black pepper flourish. **15** ⑨① touch drier than also-tasted **16** ⑨⓪; both well structured, hint vanilla in farewell courtesy 30-40% American oak.

★★★★ **MPHS** ⊘ Appropriately priced & packaged Bordeaux flagship, **12** ⑧⑨ equal cab, cab franc blend, classic French barrique ageing yet attractive Italianate sour cherry fruit profile. Approachable, but styled for decade minimum.

★★★★ **Alto Rouge** A Cape institution, made for more than half a century. Near-equal cab franc, cab, shiraz & merlot with drop petit verdot in **16** ★★★★ ⑧⑤. Like **15** ⑧⑧, less savoury, more sweet vanilla, detracting from dense fruit body. Also in larger bottles, as all above.

Fine Old Vintage ⊘ ★★★★ Fruitcake richness & marked sweetness on **08** ⑧⑤ 'port' from undisclosed varieties. — CvZ

Location/map/WO: Stellenbosch ▪ Map grid reference: E8 ▪ Est 1693 ▪ 1stB 1921 ▪ Tasting & sales Mon-Fri 9-5 Sat/Sun 10-4 ▪ Fee R40/wine tasting ▪ Closed Good Fri & Dec 25 ▪ Biltong & wine pairing R110pp, advance booking required ▪ Hiking trail ▪ MTB track ▪ Owner(s) Distell ▪ Cellarmaster(s) Bertho van der Westhuizen (May 2015) ▪ Viticulturist(s) Bertho van der Westhuizen & Danie van Zyl ▪ 191ha/83ha (cabs s/f, merlot, shiraz) ▪ 800t/100,000cs own label 100% red ▪ PO Box 104 Stellenbosch 7599 ▪ info@alto.co.za ▪ www. alto.co.za ▪ S 34° 0' 10.4" E 018° 50' 49.4" ▪ 🖉 hoses.bookmakers.sweetly ▪ F +27 (0)21-881-3894 ▪ **T +27 (0)21-881-3884**

Altydgedacht Estate

It's all action at Altydgedacht, as this Durbanville family estate has teamed up with outside partners to offer paintballing, obstacle courses and a zipline for visitor groups to the farm. New and exciting activities are balanced by time and tradition when it comes to the wines, with Oliver Parker and Etienne Louw producing their pure-fruited varietal classics and innovative popular blends in one of SA's oldest working cellars.

★★★★ **Pinotage** Traditionally styled **16** (86), sweet black berry fruit mingled with fresh herbs & baking spices. French & American oak adds vanilla & toasted coconut to well-managed tannins.

★★★★ **Tintoretto** ② Unique, top-drawer Cape Blend of pinotage (50%), barbera, shiraz, **15** (86) floral tones to brambly fruit in spicy core, lovely pliable tannin support.

★★★★ **Gewürztraminer** Beautifully balanced **17** (89), technically off-dry but lively natural acidity offsets, litchi & lime mingle with ginger, star anise in satisfying mouthful, made for Thai food. No **16**.

★★★★ **Sauvignon Blanc** ⊘ Classic Durbanville sauvignon, **18** (88) preview crackles with feisty green-pepper, guava & signature dustiness. Excellent acidity, already integrated, leads to satisfying conclusion.

★★★★ **The Ollo** ② Viognier leads white blend named for longtime cellarmaster; chardonnay, semillon & chenin in support in **15** (87). Pungent aromas, fleshy oak-tinged body freshened by fine, crunchy acidity.

Barbera ② ★★★☆ Still one of only handful of SA varietal bottlings of this north Italian variety. Individual, slightly wild **15** (84), savoury-spicy & meaty touches, food-inviting tart edge. **Pinotage Blanc de Noir** ② ★★★ Strawberry fruit & a cranberry twist on **17** (81), fresh & gently dry. Savoury **16** (81) was from cab franc. **Muskarade** ★★★★ Attractive, aromatic blend muscat, gewürztraminer, riesling, ex-tank **17** (83) bright & breezy, lots of flowers (lilies, rosepetals, blossoms) & good limy acid providing balance to off-dry sweetness. Not tasted: **Méthode Cap Classique Blanc de Blancs**. — CM

Location/WO: Durbanville ▪ Map: Durbanville, Philadelphia & Darling ▪ Map grid reference: C7 ▪ Est 1698 ▪ 1stB 1981 ▪ Tasting & sales Mon-Fri 8–5 Sat 9–4 Sun 11-3 ▪ Tasting R40/5 wines ▪ Closed Easter weekend, Dec 25/26 & Jan 1 ▪ Cellar tours by appt ▪ Breakfast & light lunches Mon-Sat 9-3.30 Sun 11-3 (T +27 (0)21-975-7815/eat@altydgedacht.co.za) ▪ Facilities for children ▪ Weddings/functions ▪ Conservation area ▪ Zip Zoom (zipline & obstacle course) T +27 (0)82-562-3615 ▪ Lockdown Paintball T +27 (0)72-989-7383 ▪ Owner(s) Parker family ▪ Cellarmaster(s) Oliver Parker (1981) ▪ Winemaker(s) Etienne Louw (Jan 2006) ▪ Viticulturist(s) John Parker (1981), Gerrit Visser (Aug 2014, farm manager) ▪ 175ha/78ha (14 varieties, r/w) ▪ 800t total 152t own label 30% red 65% white 5% rosé ▪ PO Box 213 Durbanville 7551 ▪ info@altydgedacht.co.za ▪ www.altydgedacht.co.za ▪ S 33° 50' 50.2" E 018° 37' 29" ▪ [sat] unforgettable.quiche.magnitudes ▪ F +27 (0)86-218-5637 ▪ **T +27 (0)21-976-1295**

Alvi's Drift Private Cellar

Part of a diverse agribusiness on the 6,000-ha Worcester farm owned and run by Bertie van der Merwe and sons, lawyer Johan and doctor Alvi, the eponymous wine brand launched in 2004 continues to up quality and variety. Alvi is part of a winemaking trio led by cellarmaster Riaan Marais, with internationally trained and experienced Linley Schultz as consultant. Joining the portfolio is the premium '221' range, comprising a fascinating 'multicultural' red and a chenin, Alvi's favourite variety, and the dominant planting along with pinotage, chardonnay and shiraz.

Reserve range

★★★★☆ **Verreaux Pinotage** ⓐ Prestige bottling named for resident majestic Black Eagle. Vanilla overlay to plum fruit gives **16** (93) a plush feel, though not quite as intensely flavoured as brilliant, svelte **15** (94). All-new oak, half each French & American for 22 months. Needs 3-5 years to settle, integrate.

★★★★☆ **Albertus Viljoen Bismarck** One of 2 big, bold (but not alcoholic, at ±13.5%) Cape Blends, this shiraz dominated - 44% in **16** (92), with pinotage & cab, showing fine interplay of ripe plum fruit & deft oaking, 22 months, 30% new, combo French, American. Similar regime for also-reviewed **15** (94), with petit verdot, dashes grenache, viognier, petite sirah; more complex, sleek & svelte, though presently dense tannins invite few years cellaring.

★★★★☆ **Drift Fusion** ⊘ Sumptuous Cape Blend, **16** (90) abundant primary fruit & excellent vinosity. Pinotage with cab & shiraz, dashes petit verdot, grenache. Cab leads, loses grenache in also-tasted **15** (93), superior integration of structural elements; smooth & sensual - a wine for contemplation. **14** untasted.

★★★★☆ **Chardonnay** ⊘ Peach & nectarine fruit ripeness in **17** ⑨⓪ lifted by citrus, all well-woven with the wood (mostly older French, 11 months) in a textured structure, attractive salinity on finish.

★★★★☆ **Albertus Viljoen Chenin Blanc** Generous, oak-fermented, slightly oxidative styling for this prestige label. **16** ⑨① & also-tasted **17** ⑨⓪ see very ripe melon fruit & few grams sugar well contained by 30% new wood & balanced alcohol. Both excellent, true to form, but miss the restraint of **15** ★★★★★ ⑨⑤.

★★★★☆ **CVC** ⊘ Chenin (72%) blend with viognier & chardonnay; sympathetic partial oaking creates creamy showcase for ripe peach, apricot & guava fruit in **17** ⑨⓪. Opulent but more measured than last.

★★★★☆ **Muscat de Frontignan White** ② Exceptional fortified dessert, 18 months matured in small oak. Like last-tasted, copper-hued **10** ★★★★★ ⑨⑦, old gold **14** ⑨③ an endless, unctuous mouthful, with bright marmalade acidity energising decadent sweetness (348 g/l sugar). No **11**, **13**; **12** untasted. 375 ml.

221 range (NEW)

★★★★ **Special Cuvée** Intriguing, harmonious union of 7 SA, Bordeaux & Rhône red/white varieties. **17** ⑧⑦ ample red-berry fruit & supportive tannin, seamlessly melded by year 30% new oak. WO W Cape.

★★★★ **Chenin Blanc** Shows house-style ripe-fruitedness, generous oaking, lees richness, but steel/ concrete tank component & effective natural acidity (no malo) keep **18** ⑧⑨ fresh, lively.

Alvi's Drift Signature range

★★★★ **Viognier** Soft peach & apricot flavours swirl amongst hefty wood vanilla features. Chill **17** ★★★ ⑧⓪ for summer sipping. Not as balanced as **16** ⑧⑥.

Chenin Blanc ⊘ ⑨ ★★★ Kiddies' sherbet aromas announce fruitily fresh, softly dry **17** ⑧①, fun & easy to drink.

Cabernet Sauvignon ★★★ **17** ⑧⓪'s juicy bramble fruit given a dark choc seam by 8 months oaking (as for red siblings), mix of French & American wood. **Merlot** ★★★ Juice drawn off skins to concentrate flavours of **17** ⑧②, succulent blueberries & plums buffed by French oak. **Pinotage** ★★★ With its raspberry & vanilla aromas, juicy mulberry & mocha flavours, **17** ⑦⑦ will win many fans. **Shiraz** ★★★ Violet perfume, twist black pepper & hint of sweet BBQ spice seasoning for **17** ⑧⓪'s raspberry fruit intensity. All-new oak, American only. **Pinotage Rosé** ★★ Candyfloss aroma & red berry/watermelon flavours, **18** ⑦⑤'s barely dry finish calls for chilling to ensure real refreshment. **Chardonnay** ★★★ Tangy citrus fruit lavished with all-new French oak (3 months) yet **17** ⑧① is balanced &, in fact, delicious. **Chardonnay-Pinot Noir** ★★★ Light yet tasty **17** ⑧⓪, 70/30 unoaked blend bunch-pressed for delicacy, avoids any sharp edges. Not tasted: **Sauvignon Blanc**.

Sparkling range

Not tasted: **Thornlands Méthode Cap Classique**. Discontinued: **Sparkling Rosé**, **Sparkling Sahara**, **Sparkling Nude**. — DS

Location/map: Worcester ▪ Map grid reference: B5 ▪ WO: Worcester/Western Cape ▪ Est 1928 ▪ 1stB 2004 ▪ Tasting, sales & tours by appt ▪ Closed all pub hols ▪ Farm produce ▪ Owner(s) Bertie, Alvi & Johan van der Merwe ▪ Cellarmaster(s) Riaan Marais ▪ Winemaker(s) Alvi van der Merwe & Linley Schultz (consultant) ▪ Viticulturist(s) Jan du Toit ▪ 6,000ha/420ha (22 varieties, mostly ptage, shiraz, chard, chenin) ▪ ±7,500t/280,000cs own label ▪ IPW ▪ PO Box 126 Worcester 6849 ▪ info@alvisdrift.co.za ▪ www.alvisdrift. co.za ▪ S 33° 46′ 25.8″ E 019° 31′ 53.7″ ▪ ⬚ grits.exulting.turnings ▪ **T +27 (0)23-340-4121**

☐ **Amatra** *see* Catherine Marshall Wines
☐ **Ama Ulibo** *see* Goedverwacht Wine Estate

Ambeloui Wine Cellar
⑨ ◎

For the first time, MCC specialists Nick Christodoulou and son Alexis have named their Brut sparkling after a non-family member. Luvuyo, meaning 'love' in Xhosa, was chosen by colleagues Alfred Mlata and Nowetu Ndaba, part of the Hout Bay boutique cellar team for over 15 years. Viticulturist Alexis hopes the two rows of meunier at their ambeloui ('little vineyard' in Cypriot) will be ready for their first crop this year.

★★★★☆ **Méthode Cap Classique Brut Rosé Rosanna** Delicious NV ⑨② bubbly from pinot noir & chardonnay (60/40) shimmers with bright red-berried fruit (cranberry, pomegranate) backed by fresh savoury & yeasty notes (36 months on lees). Elegant & refined, for contemplative sipping.

★★★★☆ **Méthode Cap Classique Brut Luvuyo** 'Love' in Xhosa, **16** ★★★★ ⑧⑧ 60/40 pinot noir/ chardonnay sparkler, on lees 2 years. Fruity & fresh, with racy acidity & strawberries-&-cream whiffs, clean & precise. Next tranche will have 3 years lees ageing. **15** ⑨② ('Ashley') also available ex cellardoor.— CM

Location: Hout Bay ▪ Map: Cape Peninsula ▪ Map grid reference: B3 ▪ WO: Western Cape ▪ Est 1994 ▪ 1stB 1998 ▪ Tasting by appt ▪ Open for sales on 1st weekend of Nov annually ▪ Annual harvest festival (mid-March) ▪ Owner(s) Nick & Ann Christodoulou ▪ Cellarmaster(s) Nick Christodoulou (1994) ▪ Winemaker(s) Nick Christodoulou (1994), with Alexis Christodoulou (2009) ▪ Viticulturist(s) Alexis Christodoulou (2009) ▪ 1ha/0.5ha (pinot noir/meunier, chard) ▪ 15t/3,000cs own label 100% MCC ▪ PO Box 26800 Hout Bay 7872 ▪ wine@ ambeloui.co.za ▪ www.ambeloui.co.za ▪ S 34° 0' 49.5" E 018° 22' 55.4" ▪ 🖃 sturdiness.receiving.roasted ▪ F +27 (0)88-021-790-7386 ▪ **T +27 (0)21-790-7386/+27 (0)82-460-8399/+27 (0)82-880-1715**

Ameera   ⓦ

Cape Town businessman Marc Machtelinckx and family over the past seven years have transformed a Cinderella vine and olive property on Stellenbosch's Annandale Road into an ameera ('princess'). With tender loving care and organic farming practices, they nursed the vineyard back to health and today produce a flagship Ameera and early/easy-drinking Duel range, offered for tasting/sale at the farm by appointment.

Ameera range
Cabernet Sauvignon ★★★★ Same oaking as Syrah, here giving savoury, meaty character to the dark plummy fruit; similar dry, firm tannins but **15** ⑧③ accessible, not harsh. Pair with rich dishes. **Syrah** ★★★★ Opulent, lovely dark fruit, prosciutto notes from 16 months in barrel (French & Hungarian, half new). Palate is dry, **15** ⑧④'s tannins adding a serious note for cellaring, making it food friendly. **Envie Sauvignon Blanc** ★★★ Admirable green notes in **17** ⑧② , grassy, green pepper, with lime zest, the palate showing some stonefruit. Nice flavour/perfume contrast, makes it interesting. Not tasted: **Blanc de Noir**.

Duel by Ameera range
Not tasted: **Cabernet Sauvignon-Shiraz**. — CR

Location/map/WO: Stellenbosch ▪ Map grid reference: D7 ▪ Est/1stB 2012 ▪ Tasting & sales Mon-Sat by appt ▪ Fee R30 ▪ Owner(s) Marc Machtelinckx & Kathleen Raemdonck ▪ Winemaker(s) Philip Costandius, Marius Roux (2012/13 vintages, both consultants) & Marc Machtelinckx ▪ 12.5ha/4.5ha (cab, shiraz) ▪ ±30t/2,000cs own label 80% red 10% white 10% rosé + 20,000L bulk ▪ PO Box 3949 Somerset West 7129 ▪ wine@ ameera.co.za ▪ www.ameera.co.za ▪ S 33° 59' 42.62" E 018° 48' 40.08" ▪ 🖃 toolbar.hunches.often ▪ F +27 (0)21-448-8611 ▪ **T +27 (0)21-881-3146**

☐ **Amy** see VinGlo Wines

☐ **Anchor Drift** see Viljoensdrift Fine Wines & Cruises

Andreas Wines   ⓦ ⓖ

Developments continue apace at the 18th-century Wellington home-farm of premium shiraz label Andreas, owned since 2015 by a group of British winelovers and friends of David Croft, former MD of Yorkshire Television. Following the opening of luxury poolside accommodation, the first full-time winemaker has been appointed - Shaun Meyeridricks, ex Boekenhoutskloof - along with a new sales manager, Lawrence White, 'injecting fresh passion into the Andreas brand'.

★★★★ **Shiraz** ⓧ Big, ripe & generous **14** ⑧⑦ bursts with sweetly spicy black fruit on silky tannin struc-ture. Bright aromas linger to satisfying finish. Ready, & should cellar well. Also in 1.5L.— GdB

Location/map/WO: Wellington ▪ Map grid reference: C3 ▪ Est 2003 ▪ 1stB 2004 ▪ Tasting & sales by appt Mon-Fri 9—5 ▪ Closed all pub hols ▪ Cellar tours by appt ▪ Luxury accommodation ▪ Owner(s) Andreas Wine Trading Incorporated (England) ▪ Cellarmaster(s)/winemaker(s) Shaun Meyeridricks (Dec 2017) ▪ 6ha/4.5ha (mourv, shiraz) ▪ 43t/4,688cs own label 100% red ▪ PO Box 892 Wellington 7654 ▪ info@andreas.co.za ▪ www.andreas.co.za ▪ S 33° 37' 54.87" E 019° 2' 33.55" ▪ 🖃 absolves.repudiates.skiffs ▪ F +27 (0)86-664-5087 ▪ **T +27 (0)21-873-2286**

Andy Mitchell Wines

Greyton family farm Heuningkloof is home to the Andy Mitchell Wines brand, owned by Vikki Mitchell. A new boutique cellar on the hill is slowly taking shape, while the garage-cellar remains the creative centre for daughter Olivia Mitchell Legavre and husband Stefan Legavre's wines, some produced occasionally. The pinot noir tasted this edition was sourced from Elgin; however the family team are very excited about the imminent launch of their home-grown shiraz and unwooded chardonnay.

Elgin Pinot Noir ★★★☆ Good core of earthy-smoky red fruit, fresh acidity, firm tannins, **16** ⑧⑤ shows Elgin's cooler provenance but is still tightly buttoned, needs some time to show full potential. **Décolletage** ⑨ ★★★★ Merlot brings some plummy generosity & flesh to promising **13** ⑧④ Bordeaux red. Cab, cab franc important structural players, need time to temper youthful astringency. Elgin & Stanford grapes, older French oak. Not tasted: **Heuningkloof Shiraz Rosé, Swartland Chenin Blanc, Méthode Cap Classique**. Occasional release: **Crooked Path Pinot Noir, Crooked Path Shiraz, Syrah-Grenache-Mourvèdre**. — MW

Location: Greyton • Map: Southern Cape • Map grid reference: A1 • WO: Elgin/Elgin-Walker Bay • Est/1stB 2003 • Tasting, sales & cellar tours by appt • Closed Easter Fri/Sun & Dec 25 • Owner(s) Vikki Mitchell • Winemaker(s) Olivia Mitchell Legavre (Jan 2008), with Stefan Legavre (2016) • 1st own label 42% red 21% white 13% rosé 24% MCC + 200cs for clients • PO Box 543 Paarden Eiland 7420 • olivia@andymitchellwines.com • www.andymitchellwines.com • **T +27 (0)28-254-9045/+27 (0)84-588-1309**

☐ **Angels Tears** see Grande Provence Heritage Wine Estate

Annandale Wines

Owner, winemaker and viticulturist Hempies du Toit was a strong proponent of traditional winegrowing long before it became fashionable. His charmingly rustic estate on Annandale Road in the Helderberg is noteworthy, too, for extended barrelling (up to 8 years!) and releasing vintages only when deemed ready, hence the venerable but still lively wines listed here.

★★★★ Cabernet Sauvignon Rounded yet fresh, remarkably youthful **12** ★★★★ ⑧③, concentrated & fruit driven, overtly spicy from 5 years in oak, a high-toned element too. Follows more elegant **06** ⑧⑨.

★★★★ Shiraz ⑨ Improving on **04** ⑧⑦, **05** ★★★★★ ⑨⓪ shows vintage quality. Dark creamy plums, savoury cured meat, fragrant fynbos & fine exotic spice. Oak vanilla rounds the seamless mouthful.

★★★★ Cavalier ⑨ Three-way blend (shiraz, cab, merlot), 7 years barrelled; **07** ⑧⑧ rich & spicy, bold black cherry & plum, flick of pepper & cranberry on finish. **05, 06** not made.

CVP ⑨ **★★★★** Fireside warming 'port', shiraz mellowed 8 years in old brandy vats. **06** ⑧④ rich dark chocolate & smoky plum pudding, fiery spirit bite. Not tasted: **Cabernet Franc, Merlot, Nostalgia**. — GdB

Location/map/WO: Stellenbosch • Map grid reference: E8 • Est/1stB 1996 • Tasting & sales Mon-Sat 9–5 • Closed Easter Fri-Mon, Ascension day & Dec 25 • Farm produce • BYO picnic • Owner(s) Hempies du Toit • Winemaker(s)/viticulturist(s) Hempies du Toit (1996) • 72ha/45ha (cabs s/f, merlot, shiraz) • 250t/10,000cs own label 100% red • PO Box 12681 Stellenbosch 7613 • info@annandale.co.za • www.annandale.co.za • S 33° 59' 49.2" E 018° 49' 50.9" • ⌨ dreaming.divide.puzzles • F +27 (0)21-881-3562 • **T +27 (0)21-881-3560**

Annex Kloof Wines

Grape-growing Basson brothers - Thys, Tobie and Hugo - harvest 8,000 tons annually from extensive vineyards first planted on Swartland's Paardeberg by their grandfather more than a century ago. Most of the crop is sold, but winemaker Hugo vinifies a select portion for their Annex Kloof label. Red wine is the focus, and the Rhône blend is the star of the show on recent performance, but the malbec is Hugo's real pride and joy.

Annex Kloof range
★★★★ Malbec Enticing blueberries, apricots & orange peel on **16** ⑧⑨'s nose & palate, slick use of oak for support & flavour. Approachable & fruity but not frivolous, with commendable dry finish.

★★★★★ Tulu ⊘ ⑯ Another thoroughly enjoyable vintage, **16** ⑨③ easy to drink (& incredibly good value) but serious, deserves contemplation. Syrah (86%), grenache, mourvèdre, giving pure black fruit accented by white pepper, hint oak spice from 18 months 1st/2nd fill barrels (as Malbec).

Xenna range

Shiraz ★★★ Older-oak-matured **17** ⑦⑨ tad rustic, just a hint of blackberry fruit & noticeable 14.9% alcohol. **Chenin Blanc** ⊘ ★★★★ Stock the fridge for summer! Wave of guava & tropical fruit, invigorating freshness on **18** ⑧④, dry yet not austere. Discontinued: **Pinotage**. — HC

Location: Malmesbury ▪ Map/WO: Swartland ▪ Map grid reference: C7 ▪ Est/1stB 2006 ▪ Tasting & cellar tours by appt only; sales daily 8-1.30 ▪ Closed Easter Fri-Mon, Ascension day, Pentecost, Dec 16/25/26 & Jan 1 ▪ Walks/hikes ▪ Conservation area ▪ Accommodation ▪ Owner(s) Hugo Basson, with brothers Thys & Tobie ▪ Winemaker(s) Hugo Basson (Jan 2006) ▪ 600ha (cab, grenache, malbec, merlot, mourv, p verdot, ptage, shiraz, tinta barocca, chard, chenin, cbard, irsai oliver, sauv) ▪ 150t own label 95% red 5% white ▪ PO Box 772 Malmesbury 7299 ▪ info@annexkloofwines.co.za ▪ www.annexkloofwines.co.za ▪ S 33° 30' 39.1" E 018° 48' 22.5" ▪ codified.surprises.olives ▪ F +27 (0)86-569-3957 ▪ **T +27 (0)22-487-3870**

☐ **Another World Wines** see Bruce Jack Wines

AntHill Wines   ⓠ

The chameleonic portfolio of wine industry supplier Mark Howell and construction project manager Hylton Schwenk reflects their varying grape sources and fondness for giving each new batch a different name. Amid the flux is one constant: their favourite grape varieties - cabernet, pinot noir and sauvignon blanc. See under Entre Nous for parcels made by boutique vintner Mark 'with others'.

Location: Somerset West ▪ Est 1999 ▪ 1stB 2000 ▪ Tasting by appt ▪ Owner(s) Mark Howell & Hylton Schwenk ▪ Winemaker(s) Mark Howell (Feb 2000) ▪ 1,200cs own label 60% red 40% white ▪ 19 Immelman Rd Somerset West 7130 ▪ www@telkomsa.net ▪ S 34° 4' 30.8" E 018° 52' 37.6" ▪ starting.dispose.fades ▪ F +27 (0)86-668-4566 ▪ **T +27 (0)82-895-9008**

Anthology Wines

Cape-born and -bred Johannesburg banking business analyst Christian Naudé makes his artisan wines on Stellenbosch's De Goede Sukses estate, home of Marklew Family Wines and the single-site blocks from which he sources his grapes. His '15 vintage recently made the Top 6 in the Cabernet Franc Challenge, and it and the '16 Chardonnay have new labels to celebrate.

★★★★☆ **Cabernet Franc** Heavyweight **16** ⑨⓪'s big 15.4% alcohol, bold plum & blackberry body held in check by sizeable tannins. Shade less refinement this vintage than **15** ⑨③, more raw power, but could mellow into something very special given 3-5 years in the cellar.

★★★★☆ **Chardonnay** Half barrel-fermented/aged 12 months, 50% new French, rest in (neutral) Flexcube. Self-assured **17** ⑨② less fruity than **16** ⑨②, which had a citrus enlivenment, but similar well-judged oak, savoury dryness & salinity, satisfying richness.

Not tasted: **Cabernet Sauvignon**. — CvZ

Location: Stellenbosch ▪ WO: Simonsberg–Stellenbosch ▪ Est/1stB 2014 ▪ Closed to public ▪ Sales online ▪ Owner(s) Christian Naudé ▪ Winemaker(s) Christian Naudé (Feb 2014) ▪ 55ha/±40ha (cabs s/f, merlot, ptage, shiraz, chard, sauv) ▪ 2,250cs own label 66% red 34% white ▪ De Goede Sukses, R44 Muldersvlei Stellenbosch 7600 ▪ info@anthologywines.co.za ▪ www.anthologywines.co.za ▪ **T +27 (0)83-238-5887**

Anthonij Rupert Wyne

International businessman Johann Rupert's model wine enterprise, named after his late brother, has 18th-century Franschhoek estate L'Ormarins as its exquisite, mountain-silhouetted home. The venture encompasses an internationally awarded quintet of brands, and upscale visitor attractions such as the remarkable, 100+ year retrospective Franschhoek Motor Museum, linked to the two tasting venues by specially built trams. Grapes are sourced from own prime vineyards in Darling, Swartland, Elandskloof and the home farm, as well as significant sites, including old-vine parcels around the winelands. Vinification is by specialist winemakers in custom facilities, such as the new Cape of Good Hope cellar, devoted to the eponymous range, with on-trend, Italian amphora-shaped concrete tanks which 'make a huge statement'.

Anthonij Rupert range

★★★★☆ **Cabernet Sauvignon** (ⓐ) Natural ferment, 18-24 months oaking, 90% new. Cassis, lead pencil, cigarbox & forest floor with sweet-fruit finish (yet dry), **12** ⑨③ quintessential ripe SA cab: modern but not forced. Ready now but structured to reward 10 years. WO Franschhoek.

★★★★★ **Cabernet Franc** All-new French barriques, 18-24 months, only 20 barrels produced. **12** ⑨⓪ ripest, darkest in the portfolio with brooding black fruit, cocoa-rich chocolate, lead pencils, none of cab franc's leafiness. Fresh & linear, tannins firm & dry, needs time. WO W Cape.

★★★★★ **Merlot** Opulent plum fruit, smart oak sheen, ripe & statuesque tannins (barrel 18-24 months, 80% new, as next): **13** ⑨⓪'s Parker-esque modernity very well done. Already 5 years old, will show more complexity in another 5, crafted to improve decade+. WO Coastal.

★★★★★ **Syrah** (ⓐ) Sculptured & toned **13** ⑨③, integrated & confident. Arresting aromatics, fruit density & intensity, liquorice detail. Reined-in power, elements mesh in a seamless way.

★★★★ **Anthonij Rupert** Stately, elegant marriage both cabs plus 5% merlot, 3% petit verdot, 24 months all-new oak. **11** ⑧⑧ coconut & nutmeg detail, less fruit-sweet than single-variety bottlings with drying tannins controlling ripe plums & prunes, cassis on finish. Not quite as well-knit, though.

★★★★ **Optima** Cab franc, merlot, cab (41/30/25) & petit verdot: **14** ⑧⑨ modern & vibrant. Packed with red/black fruit, violet nuance, tightly coiled tannins, liquorice & lead pencil finish. Also in magnum, 3L.

Cape of Good Hope range

★★★★ **Parel Vallei Merlot** Banana bread, plum & prune aromas, some forest floor development on elegant **13** ⑧⑧ from Helderberg fruit. Rich, not overwhelming, freshness from crisp acidity.

★★★★ **Sneeuwkrans Pinot Noir** From ±700m elevation Elandskloof site, **15** ⑧⑧ high-toned cherry fruit, leafy top notes & vibrant tension thanks to variety's signature acidity. Finely textured, silky, enough grip to extend the palate.

★★★★ **Basson Pinotage** (ⓦ) From challenging dryland bushvine Basson-family Swartland site. **15** ⑧⑨ dark & opulent, variety-true mulberry nuance, smooth & succulent but acid/fruit/tannin structure to age.

★★★★☆ **Riebeeksrivier Southern Slopes** (ⓐ) Intention of 'Slopes' pair to show aspect/soil influence. **14** ⑨③ higher clay content in Malmesbury shale. Bone-dry, deep & rich, fruit-filled but not fruity, supple tannins & peppery conclusion. Melange durif, cinsaut, mourvèdre & viognier but mostly shiraz (60%).

★★★★☆ **Riebeeksrivier Western Slopes** (ⓐ) Shiraz (80%) with seasoning grenache, cinsaut, mourvèdre & carignan. Soil shale/schist, less opulent but thrilling fruit intensity, **14** ⑨③ tannins giving greater form, structure, some smoky notes. Older oak for this & S. Slopes for ±year.

★★★★☆ **Serruria Chardonnay** From acclaimed Elandskloof vineyard. Lemon-infused charm: ~grass, ~Cream biscuit, ~thyme, & beautifully integrated vanilla oak on **16** ⑨⓪. Lacks profundity but very smart. Part barrel-fermented/aged, 32% new, 31% on lees in tank.

★★★★☆ **Riebeeksrivier Chenin Blanc** (✓) Exquisite balance, umami savouriness delivered by **17** ⑨⓪ from Rupert Swartland farm, Riebeeksrivier. Khaki bush, fynbos, salt & earth, spirited acidity, satisfying dryness & length. To cellar 5-10 years.

★★★★☆ **Van Lill & Visser Chenin Blanc** (✓) (ⓐ) (ⓦ) Citrusdal Mountain bushvines, 54 years old, **17** ⑨③ extremely complex, unfruity wet earth, nuts, cream nuances; leesy smoothness yet bold seam of acidity. Stately & reserved with sense of weight (small portion oak) & profundity. Will age decade+.

★★★★ **Altima Sauvignon Blanc** Different picking dates, various yeast strains give **17** ⑧⑧'s range from white asparagus & grapefruit to green fig & tropical fruit. Good palate weight. WO Elandskloof.

★★★★☆ **Laing Groendruif Semillon** (✓) (ⓐ) (ⓦ) Citrusdal Mountain dryland bushvines from an old-vine hero, Henk Laing. **15** ⑨④ semillon, 54% oaked, hay/straw aromas, long & reined-in lemon-toned palate. Precise, mineral with beautiful crystalline structure for ageing 10+ years.

★★★★☆ **Riebeeksrivier Caroline** Assured, personality-packed white blend, **15** ⑨⓪ tangerine & orange zest vibrancy, harmonious palate with marzipan, nougat & quinine nuances. 40% chenin, with roussanne, marsanne, viognier.

Jean Roi range

★★★★ **Rosé** Beautiful bespoke bottle for pale glassful inspired by Provence. Enticing strawberries-&-cream bouquet & -palate, **17** ⑧⑧ suave & dry; not serious but very grown-up. Cinsaut with grenache, dash shiraz.

L'Ormarins range

★★★★ **Méthode Cap Classique Brut Classique Rosé** ⊘ Chardonnay & pinot noir sparkling, 60/40, 24 months on lees. **NV** ⑧⑦ deep sunset hue, red fruit/boiled sweet note to the bouquet; lemon & strawberry candyfloss tastes & lovely dry zesty finish.

★★★★☆ **Méthode Cap Classique Brut Rosé** Pale copper/pink, 76/24 pinot noir & chardonnay sparkler pressed together, a rare technique worldwide; 24 months on lees. **15** ⑨⓪ tiny bubbles, sherbet tastes, berries-&-cream nuance. Fresh palate & lively, some minerality.

★★★★ **Méthode Cap Classique Blanc de Blancs** Chardonnay sparkle, 20% barrel ferment, 4 years on lees in bottle. Myriad tiny bubbles, fresh lemon-toned finish, some creamy notes, Granny Smith apple, **13** ⑧⑨ unashamedly New World in style.

★★★★ **Méthode Cap Classique Brut** ⊘ Chardonnay & pinot noir bubbles, 66:34 ratio, 24 months on lees. Pale **NV** ⑧⑦, slow tantalising bubbles & floral nose followed by full & creamy palate, enlivened by Granny Smith acidity. Smooth & sophisticated.

Late Bottled Vintage ★★★ From touriga, natural ferment, older oak 36 months. **14** ⑧① raisiny, richly sweet, not showing much age. Firm tannins & low fortification, for easy sipping. Not tasted: **Sagnac**.

Terra del Capo range

Sangiovese ⑨ ★★★☆ As in Italy, a variety designed for food. Attractive clean leather, slight smoky notes on cherry-toned **15** ⑧⑤. Fresh tannic & acid bite, generously fruited end. WO Coastal. **Pinot Grigio** ⑨ ★★★ One of only a handful on the market, from older vineyards. **18** ⑧② nut, whiteflower & pear, satisfying vinosity, rounder & sleeker than most.

Protea range

Cabernet Sauvignon ⊘ ⑨ ★★★★ Standout in this good-value range, **16** ⑧⑤ complexity, freshness, cassis & inky tones, oak spice & pleasant grip from lovely ripe tannins. WO W Cape unless noted. **Rosé** ⊘ ⑨ ★★★ Striking pale pink in clear patterned bottle. **18** ⑧② mostly mourvèdre, few months lees contact; lovely wild berry scents, lightish 12.5% alcohol, mineral finish. WO Coastal. **Sauvignon Blanc** ⑨ ★★★ Green grass & fig plus slight smoky note, zippy acidity, **18** ⑧① adds touch more interest, sophistication even, to the usual easy drinkability.

Merlot ★★★ Distinctive, eye-catching bottles, each a different design, twist-off cork. Generous & easy **16** ⑧⓪, commendable plum varietal character, clean leather detail. WO Coastal. **Shiraz** ⊘ ★★★★ Deep red & black fruit, loads of spice, even hint of leather: **17** ⑧④ succulent, streamlined & handsome, exceptionally good everyday drinking. **Chardonnay** ★★★ Sleek & welcoming lemon drop & Lemon Cream notes, creamy mouthfeel & lovely weight from oaked portion. **18** ⑧② friendly acidity for food or solo sipping. **Chenin Blanc** ★★★ Tropical & flowery, zesty fruity refreshment in **18** ⑧①, just chill & enjoy. **Pinot Grigio** ★★★ Water-white **18** ⑧⓪, peardrop & blackcurrant, misses nuttiness of Italian offerings but brisk & characterful. — CR, CvZ

Location/map: Franschhoek ▪ Map grid reference: C5 ▪ WO: Western Cape/Coastal/Swartland/Elandskloof/ Citrusdal Mountain/Franschhoek/Stellenbosch ▪ Est 1714 ▪ 1stB 1982 ▪ Two tasting rooms: Anthonij Rupert & Terra del Capo, both by appt only ▪ Fee R25-R70 per flight of 3-4 wines ▪ Closed Good Fri & Dec 25 ▪ Antipasti Bar serving local artisanal produce ▪ Cheese, olive oil & honey ▪ Franschhoek Motor Museum by appt only T +27 (0)21-874-9002; admittance R80pp, seniors R60pp & children (3-12 yrs) R50pp ▪ Two specially built trams travel between the motor museum & tasting rooms ▪ Owner(s) Johann Rupert ▪ Winemaker(s) Dawie Botha (Jan 2005), Zanie Viljoen (Jan 2007), Vernon van der Hoven (2012) & Mark van Buuren (2013) ▪ 4 farms: total ±1,100ha/±210ha (cabs s/f, carignan, cinsaut, grenache, marsanne, merlot, mourv, pinot, sangio, shiraz, chard, chenin, pinot grigio, rouss) ▪ ISO 14001:2009 ▪ PO Box 435 Franschhoek 7690 ▪ tasting@ rupertwines.com ▪ www.rupertwines.com ▪ S 33° 53' 16.77" E 019° 0' 17.70" (Anthonij Rupert/Cape of Good

Hope/L'Ormarins), S 33° 52' 47.36" E 019° 0' 10.91" (Terra Del Capo/Protea) ▪ ⟨☞⟩ wildebeest.tapping.filmy ▪
F +27 (0)21-874-9111 ▪ **T +27 (0)21-874-9004/+27 (0)21-874-9041 (tasting)**

Anura Vineyards

Consolidation and fresh focus have seen Anura, the frog-themed Simonsberg-Paarl estate owned by Tymen
Bouma and family, rationalise the wine portfolio into Estate, Reserve and Signature tiers, the latter being
high-end and red-wine focused, with small volumes and special packaging. The popular and beautiful
Cooperage events space has hosted wine awards and even a chocolate festival in the past year, while the
Wagon Trail microbrewery, Forest Hill cheesery and Trading Post deli all have loyal followings.

Signature Series

★★★★ **Cabernet Sauvignon** (NEW) Deep, ripe cassis abundance contrasting with dry spice & prominent
all-new oak backing (2 years, French). **14** (86) needs time for elements to marry harmoniously.

★★★★ **Nebbiolo** (NEW) Gymnastic litheness apparent on red fruit- & cinnamon-toned **14** (87), dry & lean,
with leashed power. Polished 2 years in barrel, 20% new, same in bottle.

★★★★ **Syrah** (NEW) Subtle dried herb & oregano appeal to deep red- & black-fruited **15** (86), quite
muscular & spicy from combo French/American oak, 20 months, long dry aftertaste.

★★★★ **Cape Cuvée** Many-layered **15** (87) pinotage (40%), cab & syrah blend; generous, persistent
fruitcake, cocoa & plum flavour, structure from 70% new oak, some American, 2 years. 15% alcohol part of
a forthright personality.

Carignan (NEW) ★★★ Herb & fynbos overlie vibrant red cherry fruit on **14** (80). Serious intent evident in 2
years French wooding, 20% new, further 2 years bottle conditioning. **Grenache** ★★★★ Appealing fynbos
& herb mingle with gentle black fruit, **14** (85) supple, light bodied & fresh despite year in older oak & 2
in bottle. **Pinotage** (NEW) ★★★★ Upfront cherry & plum vivacity on **15** (83). Bright, succulent & spicy, it's
backed by dry, fine tannin from new oak, 50% American, 20 months. Not tasted: **Sangiovese**.

Reserve range

★★★★ **Cabernet Sauvignon** (Ⓥ) Dark & brooding, **14** (89) cassis & violets leading to fresh black berry
flavours. Velvety & rich yet not heavy, with baking spice adding interest. **13** untasted.

★★★★ **Petit Verdot** Still-rare solo bottling, black pastille succulence & focused tautness. Dry, with light
spice nuance, **13** (86) was oaked 28 months, half new. No **12**, **11** untasted.

★★★★ **Pinotage** Supple & generous **16** (88), smooth, with ample ripe red-berry fruit. Oak, just one third
new, provides harmonious support & savouriness. Good length. **15** not reviewed.

★★★★ **Syrah** (Ⓥ) Continues boldness of **08** (87) & standout **10** ★★★★★ (91), but **12** ★★★ (80) is
powerfully earthy & dry, lean framed. Oak, 60% new, dominates plum fruit. No **11**.

★★★★ **Syrah-Mourvèdre-Grenache** Smoky overlay to vibrant, spicy **15** (86), first tasted since **09** (89).
Shiraz still leads but mourvèdre upped notably to 35%, grenache to 15%. Broad, textured plum-rich palate
framed by oak, third new. Alcohol 15%.

★★★★ **Chardonnay** Vanilla, citrus & pineapple on bold, naturally fermented **17** (86). Acid is lively &
fresh but all-new French oak speaks loudest, in broad, reverberating tones. **16** ★★★★ (84) less intense.

★★★★ **Sauvignon Blanc Unfiltered** (Ⓥ) From Darling, **15** (86) very herbaceous floral/fynbos nose
leading to mouthful of luscious tropical fruit, refreshing grapefruit finish.

★★★★ **Méthode Cap Classique Brut** Crisp, dry & vivid **13** (87) sparkling with lemon sherbet zip,
portion older-oaked before second ferment, aiding light biscuit note. **12** untasted. **11** ★★★★★ (95) was
exceptional. WOW Cape.

Merlot (Ⓥ) ★★★★ **15** (83) has tannin grip & bitter-cocoa edge to spicy mulberry fruit. Less impressive
than plush, soft **14** ★★★★ (89). **Chenin Blanc** (Ⓥ) ★★★★ Stonefruit tang to **16** (83) is framed by nutty
oak notes. Soft & spicy. **Viognier** (Ⓥ) ★★★★ Nectarine & spice typicity on **16** (83), creamy breadth from
4 months on lees & 10% oaked portion. Nice body & length. Not tasted: **Malbec**. Discontinued: **Cape
Vintage Reserve**.

Anura range

Grenache Noir (Ⓥ) ★★★ Spicy tealeaf tannic dryness on **14** (77), muted red fruit dominated by oak,
despite use of older barrels only. **Merlot** (Ⓥ) ★★★ Banana nuance to bright red-fruit flavour on **16** (81).

Medium bodied & unfussy. **Pinotage** ② ★★★★ Sweet vanilla edge to ultra-ripe blueberry appeal of **16** ⑧③ courtesy 40% American oak. Slightly bitter tail. **Pinotage-Syrah** ★★★ Peppery plum & pomegranate on improved **16** ⑧② 60/40 mix, supple & juicy, with nice frame of oak. **Arpeggio** ★★★ Light-bodied & easy blend of shiraz, mourvèdre & dab viognier, **16** ⑧① appealing spicy overlay from judicious 20% new French oak. **Rosé** ★★★ Raspberry & cherry brightness to dry **18** ⑧⓪ from pinot noir. Succulent & effortless, it's a poolside pink. **Chardonnay** ★★★ A tropical tack taken in **18** ⑧②, with pineapple more than than typical citrus. Medium body, lively acidity & spice from oak staves. **Pinot Gris** ★★★ Dusty lemon tang on unfussy **18** ⑧①. Light, fresh & perfect for summertime enjoyment. Not tasted: **Tempranillo**, **Legato**, **Sauvignon Blanc**. — FM

Location/map: Paarl ▪ Map grid reference: C7 ▪ WO: Simonsberg-Paarl/Darling/Western Cape ▪ Est 1990 ▪ 1stB 2001 ▪ Tasting, sales & cellar tours daily 9–5 ▪ Closed Good Fri, Dec 25 & Jan 1 ▪ Fee R60/cheese & wine, R35/wine only ▪ Trading Post Deli ▪ Farm produce & Forest Hill cheese ▪ Tour groups ▪ The Cooperage events venue (40-300 guests seated & up to 850 cocktail style) ▪ Wagon Trail Brewery & Restaurant open Tue-Sun 9-4; with craft beer tasting at R36/flight (4x100ml) ▪ Owner(s) Bouma family ▪ Cellarmaster(s) Tymen Bouma (1990) ▪ Winemaker(s) Stander Maass (2017) & Lance Bouma (Jan 2007) ▪ Viticulturist(s) Tymen Bouma & Stephen Elliot (Jan 2007) ▪ 240ha/120ha (cab, carignan, grenache, malbec, merlot, mourv, nebbiolo, p verdot, ptage, pinot, sangio, shiraz, tempranillo, chard, chenin, nouvelle, pinot gris, sauv, verdelho) ▪ 750t/60,000cs own label 80% red 17% white 2% rosé 1% fortified ▪ PO Box 244 Klapmuts 7625 ▪ info@anura.co.za, wine@anura.co.za ▪ www.anura.co.za ▪ S 33° 48' 41.4" E 018° 53' 19.8" ▪ 🌐 spinning. heiress.duplicity ▪ **T +27 (0)21-875-5360**

Anwilka ⓠ

Low-profile red-wine specialist Anwilka's Helderberg vineyard is planted with classic Bordeaux and Rhône varieties and sustainably farmed to the exacting standards of its owners, including eminent French wine men Bruno Prats and Hubert de Boüard. Anwilka was developed in collaboration with Klein Constantia (sharing owners, outlets and tasting locale), but has its own cellar and winemaker.

★★★★★ **Anwilka** 🍷 Brooding, powerful & measured, **15** ⑨④ shiraz-cab (with dash of petit verdot) shows pedigree. Intricate detail in spicy fruit core follows to gracious peacock-tail finish. Noble & assured, with weight & fragrance in perfect balance. Even better than fine **14** ⑨③. Also in magnum.

★★★★ **Petit Frère** ⊘ Moreish, approachable **16** ⑧⑨ syrah, cab, petit verdot worthy foil to august sibling. Cheerfully plush red cherry fruit has plenty of heft, elegant shape. Only 30% oaked, all new.— GdB

Location/WO: Stellenbosch ▪ Est 1997 ▪ 1stB 2005 ▪ Tasting & sales by appt at Klein Constantia ▪ Owner(s) Zdenek Bakala, Charles Harman, Bruno Prats & Hubert de Boüard ▪ MD Hans Aström ▪ Winemaker(s) Jean du Plessis (Aug 2008) ▪ Viticulturist(s) Piet Neethling, with Johan Wiese (consultant, both 1997) ▪ 48ha/±39ha (cab, malbec, p verdot, shiraz) ▪ 200t/±28,000cs own label 100% red ▪ PO Box 5298 Helderberg 7135 ▪ info@kleinconstantia.com ▪ www.kleinconstantia.com ▪ F +27 (0)21-794-2464 ▪ **T +27 (0)21-794-5188**

Anysbos ⓠ 🖐 📷 🆕

Johan and Sue Heyns' farm in Bot River is named for an aromatic plant of the Overberg. Since their arrival nearly a decade ago, wheatfields have been turned into olive groves and vines grow where canola and barley were before — the first dryland-farmed grenache bushvines were planted in 2012. The 2019 harvest was destined to be the first vinified in their own cellar; till now the wines have been made (in hands-off fashion) at neighbouring Gabriëlskloof, by Marelise Niemann of Momento Wines.

★★★★★ **Grenache Noir** 🍷 Cured meat & strawberry enticements on **16** ⑨④, joining a welcome wave of medium-bodied, lightly wooded SA reds. Refined, with superbly judged tannin grip, fresh seam of acid accentuating fruit purity. Some wholebunch; naturally vinified, matured in older oak. Young bushvine fruit.

★★★★★ **White Blend** Like the label, elegantly understated. **17** ⑨② lemon & white peach tones, smoky & fruit-rich but not sweet, lovely vibrant acidity, long dry finish. Foot crushed, basket pressed & barrel fermented, chenin (61%) & roussanne (21%) co-vinified, with grenache blanc. Older oak.— TJ, CvZ

Location/WO: Bot River ▪ Map: Walker Bay & Bot River ▪ Map grid reference: C3 ▪ Est 2010 ▪ 1stB 2018 ▪ Tasting, sales & cellar tours by appt ▪ Farm produce ▪ BYO picnic by appt ▪ Owner(s) Anysbos Olywe BK ▪ Winemaker(s) Marelise Niemann (2016) ▪ Viticulturist(s) Quintus le Roux (2012) ▪ 320ha/15ha (grenache n/b, shiraz, chenin) ▪ PO Box 550 Bot River 1785 ▪ info@anysbos.co.za ▪ S 34° 15′ 23.96″E 019° 15′ 37.84″ ▪ F +27 (0)86-552-1763 ▪ **T +27 (0)82-601-1067**

☐ **Aphaea** *see* Val du Charron
☐ **Apogée** *see* La Vierge Private Cellar
☐ **Arboretum** *see* Botanica Wines

Arcangeli Vineyards

This Bot River wine venture owned by construction businessman Sandro Arcangeli and his family has an international feel: Italian, via the proprietors, reflected in the new restaurant, Adventura, serving Italian dishes under a pergola eventually to be covered by nebbiolo vines; Portuguese, through the farm's previous owners and their beloved verdelho - 'a problematic variety to market and sell, as it is unknown', admits winemaker Krige Visser, a South African who is fond of French varieties, especially semillon. Intuitive and non-interventionist winemaking drive this singular range.

★★★★ **Romulus Nebbiolo** Krige Visser's understanding of tannins evident in **17** ⑧⑦, if lower-key than traditional in this Italian variety. Poise, freshness & flavoursome earthy/cherry tones well set off by unintimidating grip, bone-dry finish. Rawsonville fruit.

★★★★ **Syrah-Mourvèdre** ② Syrah's (72%) dark fruit the backdrop to spice, scrub, meaty complexity, firm tannic grasp in **16** ⑧⑦. Tight, brooding, mid-2017 but promising, will reward cellaring.

★★★★☆ **Semillon** ⓢ Texture, structure & ageability rather than fruit main focus of individual **17** ⑨⑭. Intriguing almost rustic earthy, hay character, resistant grip juxtaposed with creamy weight, which age should resolve. Spontaneous ferment, portion on skins/some stalks.

★★★★☆ **Feiteiras Verdelho** Riveting acidity, sweet baked apple & even whiff of caramel are echoes of variety's alter ego as Madeira but no hint of maderisation in **17** ⑨⑪. Bigger than **16** ⑨⓪ (14% alcohol vs 12.5%), similar lean, firm frame, appetising saline length. Portion skin-fermented; 100% older oaked.

Merlot-Petit Verdot-Cabernet Sauvignon ② ★★★★ Cigarbox, cassis & plum, **16** ⑧④ led by merlot (42%) but exhibits little of that variety's fruit generosity, needs few years to develop. — AL

Location: Bot River ▪ Map: Walker Bay & Bot River ▪ Map grid reference: C3 ▪ WO: Bot River/Western Cape ▪ Est/1stB 2015 ▪ Tasting & sales by appt ▪ Restaurant ▪ Luxury guest cottages ▪ Owner(s) Roodeheuvel Boerdery cc (Directors Allesandro & Fabio Arcangeli) ▪ Winemaker(s) Krige Visser ▪ 16.2ha/4.2ha (cab, merlot, mourv, p verdot, shiraz, verdelho) ▪ 3,500cs own label 70% red 30% white ▪ PO Box 234 Bot River 7185 ▪ info@arcangeliwines.com ▪ www.arcangeliwines.com ▪ S 34° 14′ 3.6″ E 019° 12′ 33.3″ ▪ ⓦ thesis.freely. reassuring ▪ **T +27 (0)82-412-7795**

☐ **Arco Laarman** *see* Laarman Wines

Arendsig Handcrafted Wines

Arendsig co-owner and cellarmaster Lourens van der Westhuizen focuses exclusively on 'top quality single-vineyard wines' in a boutique cellar on the Robertson family farm.

Location/map: Robertson ▪ Map grid reference: C4 ▪ Est/1stB 2004 ▪ Tasting & cellar tours by appt ▪ Tour groups ▪ Pre-booked picnic baskets or BYO picnic ▪ Wedding/function venue ▪ Accommodation available ▪ Owner(s) Lourens van der Westhuizen ▪ Cellarmaster(s)/viticulturist(s) Lourens van der Westhuizen (2004) ▪ 95ha/12ha (cab, shiraz, chard, sauv, viog) ▪ 100t/5,000cs own label 50% red 50% white ▪ PO Box 170 Robertson 6705 ▪ info@arendsig.co.za ▪ www.arendsig.co.za ▪ S 33° 55′ 37.9″ E 020° 0′ 47.6″ ▪ ⓦ hence.uninterrupted.enlarging ▪ F +27 (0)86-535-0693/+27 (0)23-616-2090 ▪ **T +27 (0)84-200-2163/+27(0)23 616-2835**

Arendskloof-New Cape Wines

These are the prestige wines of Christiaan Groenewald, twice Diners Club Winemaker of the Year and owner/winemaker at separately listed Eagle's Cliff Wines-New Cape Wines. Intended to complement good food, Arendskloof labels are 'made in a way to try and keep nature in the wines'. The promised rare varietal bottling of petite sirah, promised last time, is here - and exceptional.

Voetspore range

★★★★ **Merlot** ⊘ Lightly spiced red berries in **15** (87), full of flavour & character, complexity. Silky & rounded, harmonious tannins & dried herb finish. WO W Cape, as all.

★★★★☆ **Petit Sirah** (NEW) ⊘ (🐝) Delicate but ripe bramble & hedgerow fruit, violet perfume & hints of fynbos on svelte **16** (90), deep flavours & long savoury finish. 50% new oak, year, well meshed with firm but fine structure. No track record, but all set for a fine future.

★★★★ **Pinotage** Intense yet elegant **15** ★★★★★ (90) has a delicious coolness about it, pristine plum & spice flavours in harmony with the structure & 50% new French oak. Also-tasted **17** (88) similar pleasing attributes but tannins more prominent, best kept for later. No **16**.

★★★★ **Tannat** (🐝) One of fewer than 10 varietal bottlings in our guide, **16** (86) expectedly big & bold, ageworthy, but welcome & appealing berry succulence too, exotic spice & dark-fruit pastille finish.

★★★★ **Shiraz-Tannat** Sweet fruited, with depth & length, **16** (87) reveals a juicy spice-infused black cherry & plum character, tempered by supple tannins. Fine partner for hearty meat stews.

★★★★ **Tannat-Syrah** (⊘) Unusual & ambitious blend. **12** ★★★★★ (92) trumps last-tasted **09**. Spicy black plum & prune, firm but noble tannin (as expected from tannat).

★★★★ **Pinot Grigio** (⊘) Lighter-styled **16** ★★★★☆ (84) shows floral wafts, gentle orchard fruit with a spicy edge. Not the complexity of **15** (87).

★★★★ **Witkruisarend** (⊘) From sauvignon, chardonnay & roussanne, **14** (86) creamy, rounded, with yellow peach & nougat attractions; sufficient lemon lift to enliven vanilla finish from 40% oaked portion.

Cabernet Sauvignon ⊘ ★★★★ Judicious oak backing (30% new) for fresh black & red fruit in **17** (84), medium bodied, balanced & smooth enough for current drinking. **Pinot Noir** (⊘) ★★★★ Misses the mark of **15** ★★★★ (87), mashed sweet strawberries & spice, **16** (84) gentle, soft, but not the length & depth of previous. **Shiraz** (⊘) ★★★★ Exuding black cherry & black pepper, **13** (85) is commendably dry but still tight, with lively acidity. **Chenin Blanc** (⊘) ★★★ Gentle tropical fruit on **16** (81) with hint of oak; easygoing, bonus of moderate 12% alcohol. **Sauvignon Blanc** (⊘) ★★★★ Fragrant white flowers, apple & capsicum flavours on **16** (84). Light & gentle for easy sipping. **Brut Rosé MCC** (⊘) ★★★☆ Classic & engaging pink sparkling, **12** (84) dry, fresh & crisp, lemon sherbet notes from chardonnay, delicate red berry flavours from pinot noir. Year/2 cellaring should add complexity. Not tasted: **Pinot Noir Rosé, Chardonnay**. — WB

☐ **Are We Having Fun Yet?** *see* Wine Village-Hermanus

Arra Vineyards ⓘ

'At Arra Vineyards, we are dedicated to ensuring that our wines reach maturity in bottle before we release them for sale,' says Chris van Reenen, viticulturist and winemaker on these Paarl slopes on Klapmuts Hill, planted with red varieties and viognier. 'It's an ideal location with magnificent views.'

Reserve range

★★★★ **Shiraz** ⊘ Leather, tobacco & fruitcake spice to the fore on nicely evolved **08** (88). Still packed with ripe almost jammy fruit but with balancing savoury/meaty nuances. Drinks well now.

Not tasted: **Cabernet Sauvignon, Nobility, Viognier**.

Barrel Select range

★★★★☆ **Shiraz** ⊘ With splashes mourvèdre & carignan, **09** (91) still remarkably fresh, showing abundant red fruit & fine tannins, though evolution deliciously evident in savoury spice & leather notes. A very harmonious older wine.

Not tasted: **Cabernet Sauvignon, Mourvèdre, Pinotage, Shiraz-Mourvèdre-Viognier**.

Arra Vineyards range

Cape Blend ⊘ (🍷) ★★★★ Pinotage with 20% merlot & petit verdot, splash mourvèdre, **12** (85) well-knit, still fruity-fresh after 4 years in bottle. **Shiraz-Cabernet Sauvignon** ⊘ (🍷) ★★★ Equal blend shows some evolution in leather, coriander, meaty notes but there's ample red & black fruit to support great-value **14** (82).

Cabernet Sauvignon ★★★★ Opens up on palate, pleasant earthiness adding to **15** (83)'s ripe black berry charm, smooth for easy drinking. **Mourvèdre** (⊘) ★★★★ Exotic **10** (84) with dark fruit & fynbos plus attractive hint of vanilla. Good concentration, smooth texture. **Pinotage ★★★** Sweet, ripe, juicy mulberries & raspberries on soft, suave **16** ⑧②, enticing, with hints of lavender & vanilla. **Shiraz** ⊘ **★★★★** Svelte **15** ⑧④ has lively red fruit seasoned with white pepper & star anise; polished in 500L oak, 2 years. **Shiraz-Mourvèdre ★★★** Macerated dark fruit, fennel & liquorice on nose of **12** ⑧① but palate somewhat muted, probably best enjoyed soon. 26% mourvèdre. **Blanc de Noir** ⊘ **★★★** Dry, creamy, pearl pink **18** ⑧②, mostly ptage, 19% shiraz, has rosepetal & Turkish delight aroma, piquant red fruit. **Viognier** ⊘ **★★★★** Offering astonishing value, like last-tasted **14 ★★★★** ⑧⑦, silky **16** ⑧⑤ has hints of marzipan & ginger (third wooded) elevating peachy freshness, finishing dry. **Natural Sweet Red Blend ★★★** Pleasantly sweet **16** ⑦⑨ is mostly pinotage & cab, leaves caramelised berry impression. **Natural Sweet Viognier** ⊘ **★★★** More verve in **13** ⑧⓪ than previous; honeyed sweetness of ripe peach & sultana balanced by good acidity for a nice clean finish. **Cape Vintage** (NEW) **★★★★** 'Port' from ruby cab, decade in French oak, **08** ⑧③ soft, yielding, with flavours of boozy berries & chocolate orange. 500 ml. Coastal WO. Not tasted: **Merlot, Cabernet Sauvignon-Petit Verdot-Merlot, Chenin Blanc.** — JG

Location/map: Paarl ▪ Map grid reference: C8 ▪ WO: Paarl/Coastal ▪ Est 1998 ▪ 1stB 2001 ▪ Tasting & sales Wed-Sun 10-4.30 ▪ Owner(s) Arra Vineyards (Pty) Ltd ▪ Winemaker(s)/viticulturist(s) Chris van Reenen ▪ 72ha/28ha (cab, merlot, ptage, ruby cab, shiraz, viog) ▪ 20,000cs ▪ PO Box 298 Klapmuts 7625 ▪ sales@arrawines.com, orders@arrawines.com ▪ www.arrawines.com ▪ S 33° 49' 25.9" E 018° 51' 47.7" ▪ ▦ integrate. recycle.splashing ▪ **T +27 (0)21-875-5363**

Artisanal Boutique Winery ⓠ

Tertius Boshoff and Kobie van der Westhuizen are, respectively, winemaker and viticulturist at substantial Stellenbosch producer Stellenrust. This is a more personal project for the pair, with its own vineyard sources and its own home in an old cellar elsewhere in Stellenbosch. The Artisanal portfolio has an experimental, off-centre flavour to it, with a few small batches of pretty special wine being made - and more current experiments which, Tertius says, will hopefully one day successfully get into bottle.

Artisanal Boutique Winery range

★★★★☆ JJ Handmade Eight Pillars (醸) From Stellenbosch, Swartland & 30 year old Piekenierskloof vines, **15** ㊙④ is powerful but shows restraint too, floral delicacy to spicy fruit & peppery oak, impressive persistence. From shiraz (56%) & 7 others.

SeriesRARE range

★★★★☆ Villain Vines Carignan (NEW) (醸) Old-vine intensity evident in **16** ㊙③ from venerable dryland block in Voor Paardeberg: vivid blue & black berry aromas, dense but lithe & harmonious palate courtesy 16 months older oak.

★★★★☆ The Phantom Grenache (NEW) (醸) 42 year old dry-farmed Piekenierskloof origins evident in **16** ㊙③'s mouthfilling red cherry fruit, earthy spice & cured meat complexities. Brooding, introverted mid-2018, decanting or preferably cellaring recommended to reveal full charm.

★★★★☆ After Eight Shiraz (醸) Bottelary Hills vines fringed by eucalyptus trees, **15** ㊙③ selected & vinified to maximise expression of site's overt mint chocolate character. Sleek & very seductive, pepper, violet & blue berry notes in an elegant tannin structure.

★★★★☆ The Apprentice White Cinsault (NEW) (醸) A real collector's item - minuscule 100 cases made by harvest interns from Bottelary cinsaut block with mutated vines producing 'white' & light pink bunches, pressing halted before juice colouration. **17** ㊙④ brims with orchard fruit, hay, honey & exotic spice, subtle oak vanilla from spontaneous ferment in older barrels.— WB

Location/map: Stellenbosch ▪ Map grid reference: C3 ▪ WO: Stellenbosch/Coastal/Voor Paardeberg/Piekenierskloof ▪ Est/1stB 2013 ▪ Tasting, sales & cellar tours by appt only ▪ Closed all pub hols ▪ Owner(s) Tertius Boshoff & Kobie van der Westhuizen ▪ Cellarmaster(s) Tertius Boshoff (Jan 2005) ▪ Winemaker(s) Tertius Boshoff (Jan 2005) & Herman du Preez (Jan 2016) ▪ Viticulturist(s) Kobie van der Westhuizen (Jan 2000) ▪ 20ha/4ha (cabs s/f, carignan, cinsaut, grenache, merlot, ptage, shiraz, chenin) ▪ 10t/600cs own label 70% red 30% white ▪ PO Box 26 Koelenhof 7605 ▪ artisanswinery@gmail.com ▪ S 33° 51' 44.41" E 018° 46' 34.11" ▪ ▦ corkscrews.installs.confetti ▪ **T +27 (0)82-455-6431**

☐ **Artisan Collection** see Snow Mountain Wines

☐ **Artist Series** *see* Véraison Vineyards
☐ **Art Series** *see* Seven Springs Vineyards

Arumdale Cool Climate Wines ⓠ

Mark Simpson's Huguenot ancestors were from a renowned wine region, the Loire, so it's appropriate that he's invested in wine as both a brand owner – of these more serious Arumdale bottlings and the separately listed meal mates, Robin Hood Legendary Wine Series – and a merchant, via his outlet in Grabouw town.

★★★★ **St Andrew's Blend** ⓠ Cab (60%), merlot & shiraz **14** ⑧⑦ improves on last-tasted **12** ★★★★ ⑧④ in texture, depth & concentration of black fruit, supple, silky integrated tannin. Long rich finish.

Pink Shiraz ⓠ ★★★ Pomegranate pink hue to bright, tangy dry **15** ⑧① rosé. Fun, light bodied & easy.

Special LYC Sauvignon Blanc ⓠ ★★★ Maintains form with nectarine, white pepper & rich lees breadth, **15** ⑧① pleasant acid tang & dry finish. Not tasted: **Shiraz**. — FM

Location/map/WO: Elgin ▪ Map grid reference: B1 ▪ Est 1962 ▪ 1stB 2003 ▪ Tasting & sales Mon-Fri 10-4 Sat/Sun & pub hols by appt only ▪ No tasting fee if purchasing ▪ Closed Easter Fri-Mon, Dec 25/26 & Jan 1 ▪ Owner(s) Mark Simpson ▪ Cellarmaster(s)/winemaker(s) Christo Versfeld (Villiersdorp Cellar) ▪ (cab, merlot, shiraz, sauv) ▪ PO Box 2 Elgin 7180 ▪ royalwine@arumdale.co.za ▪ www.arumdale.co.za, www. robinhoodlegendarywines.co.za ▪ S 34° 9' 14.51" E 019° 1' 48.22" ▪ 🅰 trap.approach.hiking ▪ F +27 (0)21-859-3430 ▪ **T +27 (0)21-859-3430**

Asara Wine Estate & Hotel

This historic Stellenbosch property, completely transformed this century, has a five-star hotel, complete with various dining options and arguably the largest selection of craft gin in the southern hemisphere, but 'making magnificent wine is at the heart of what Asara is all about'. To this end, its winemaking consultant in recent years, Johan Joubert, has been appointed cellarmaster. The CWG member, who put Kleine Zalze on the map, will support Janette van Lill and Christiaan Nigrini in the cellar while working with viticulturist Allan Cockcroft to drive forward a vineyard plan involving new plantings and removal of alien vegetation.

Speciality Collection

★★★★ **Bell Tower Estate Wine** ⓐ Consistently good Bordeaux-style flagship, fleshy 5-way blend in **15** ⑧⑦, cab & cab franc (32/23) leading the cassis & foliage aromas, black fruit flavours, savoury spice & minerality. Also in magnum, as next. No **14**.

★★★★ **Avalon** One of few SA Amarone-style wines, **13** ⑧⑥ red & dark fruit, violet & cinnamon notes, sweetness from alcohol & some American oak artfully masked by solid tannins, freshened by acidity. Vine-dried pinotage & shiraz, lengthy 3 years in oak, 30% new.

★★★★ **Carillon** ⓠ Noble Late Harvest from chenin, old oak aged. Deep gold **14** ⑧⑦ attractive stonefruit & rooibos aromas, bracing acidity to balance the apricot richness, uncloying orange marmalade conclusion.

The Red Cab ★★★ 'Noir de noir' partner for White Cab, **17** ⑧② 's mulberry & cassis tones mingle with attractive spices & herbs. Judicious 10% new-oak support, soft tannins, accessible medium body. **Passione Pinotage** ⓝⓔⓦ ★★★★ Full bodied & savoury, brambleberry, molasses & cinnamon complexity, **16** ⑧⑤ 's fruitiness neatly channelled by firm tannin grip, aided by year barrels & staves. **The White Cab** ★★★ Unusual white from cabernet, ripe red-fruit notes, melon & citrus tang. Dry & brisk **18** ⑦⑧ to chill & enjoy. **Méthode Cap Classique** ⓥ ★★★★ Zesty dry sparkling from 62% chardonnay & pinot noir, **15** ⑧④ creamy brioche from year on lees, lemon meringue whiffs & freshness from the white grape. **Vine Dried Sauvignon Blanc** ★★★★ Was 'Sundried', still is from sauvignon. Intricate vinification for **16** ⑧④ vin de paille, concentrated & packed with personality. Desiccated fruit flavours, vanilla tinge from oak.

Vineyard Collection

★★★★ **Cabernet Sauvignon** Youthful **15** ★★★★ ⑧③ 's sweetness noticeable but balanced by tannin & acid. Stewed red fruit, molasses note a shade off more primary, **14** ⑧⑦. Also in magnum, as Merlot & Shiraz.

★★★★ **Pinotage** ⓝⓔⓦ Plum & mulberry fragrance, vanilla touches on voluptuous **17** ⑧⑥. Plush dark fruit given form by lovely broad tannins. Will reward few years patience.

Cape Fusion ⊛ ★★★★ Generously scented **16** ⑧④ trio shiraz, pinotage & malbec has red & black fruit, buchu & spice complexity. Downy tannins for immediate pleasure, sufficient padding for few years. Also in 375ml & 1.5L. **Chenin Blanc** ⊛ ★★★★ Friendly & satisfying **17** ⑧④, interesting & different aromas of ripe fig, mango & honeysuckle, fresh tropical flavours supported by subtle oak (5% new).

Merlot ★★★★ Get together with friends type red. **15** ⑧③ lightly oaked, approachable, succulent fruit laced with thyme & dark chocolate, spicy end. **Shiraz** ★★★★ Vibrant dark berries pave way for black pepper & salami notes, **15** ⑧③ supple tannin structure & savoury-smoky persistence. **Pinotage Rosé** ★★★ Attractive copper glints, spiced cherries & pomegranate, dry & zesty finish, **18** ⑧① perfect sunset sipper. **Chardonnay Lightly Wooded** ★★★ Carefully oaked (just 10% new) to preserve citrus, white peach & almond flavours on **17** ⑧① yet add appealing nuttiness to stonefruit finish. **Sauvignon Blanc** ⊘ ★★★★ Alluring tropical fruit nuances in **17** ⑧③ followed by crisp acidity, citrus whiffs & Granny Smith apple. 30% from Bot River; dash semillon in the mix too. Discontinued: **Petit Verdot**.

Discontinued: **Cape Vinelands Collection**. — GM

Location/map: Stellenbosch ▪ Map grid reference: D6 ▪ WO: Stellenbosch/Coastal ▪ Est/1stB 2001 ▪ Tasting Mon-Sat 10-6 Sun 10-4 ▪ Fee R60/3 wines, R85/5 wines ▪ Sales 10-6 (summer)/10-4 (winter) ▪ Closed Dec 25 ▪ Tasting centre ▪ Cellar tours by appt Mon-Fri at 11 & 3 ▪ Tour groups ▪ 5-star TGCSA hotel ▪ Raphael's ▪ Mise en Place restaurant ▪ Sansibar bistro & gin lounge ▪ Deli ▪ Gift shop ▪ Function & banqueting facilities ▪ Conferences ▪ Weddings ▪ Vineyard walks ▪ Bikes & Wines tasting tours ▪ Cookery school ▪ Cellarmaster(s) Johan Joubert (2018) ▪ Winemaker(s) Janette van Lill (Oct 2016) & Christiaan Nigrini (Nov 2016) ▪ Viticulturist(s) Allan Cockcroft (2013) ▪ 180ha/102ha (cabs s/f, malbec, merlot, p verdot, ptage, shiraz, chard, chenin, sauv) ▪ 1,000t/125,000cs own label 70% red 30% white ▪ IPW, WIETA ▪ PO Box 882 Stellenbosch 7599 ▪ winery-info@asara.co.za ▪ www.asara.co.za ▪ S 33° 56'.35.00" E 018° 48'.31.00" ▪ 🖪 also.behaving. keener ▪ **T +27 (0)21-888-8000**

Ashbourne ⊘

Business is booming at Anthony Hamilton Russell's top-flight, pinotage-championing venture, and this means not only new wines added to the brand but also new sources of grapes to meet growing demand. Their quest for quality pinotage led them to the Swartland, under the expert guidance of acclaimed viticulturist Rosa Kruger. With her help, winemaker Emul Ross identified a 1972 bushvine vineyard, considered the perfect partner to an equally exciting block of Swartland cinsaut, to produce the new wines in the range. Back in Hemel-en-Aarde, they are expanding their own pinotage plantings, continuing to believe in the variety's future, locally and around the world.

★★★★☆ **Pinotage** 🍇 From single Hemel-en-Aarde Valley parcel, **16** ⑨③ confidently launches forth with elegant black-berried fruit in heady mix with vanilla, leather, perfume & tar. Destemmed fruit adds silky texture & soft tannins, leading to lengthy finish with aromas of fresh herbs. 40% new oak, barrel & foudre.

★★★★ **Pinotage-Cinsault** ⑭⑮ Leaps from glass trailing black & red berry fruit with great verve & joy, **18** ⑧⑦ silky texture, bouncy acidity & low tannins (no oak) all make summer chilling a great option. **Rosé** ⑭⑮ ★★★★ Partner pink to white blend in same attractive 'belle époque' packaging. **18** ⑧③, fashionably from cinsaut, dry, zippy & fresh, with pomegranates & watermelons - lovely summer sipper. **Sauvignon Blanc-Chardonnay** ★★★★ Leads with lemon & lime, giving way to guava & granadilla in fruit-packed **18** ⑧③ mouthful. 80/20 ratio, 4 months lees contact adds richness. Walker Bay WO. — CM

Location: Hermanus ▪ WO: Swartland/Walker Bay/Hemel-en-Aarde Valley ▪ Est 1996 ▪ 1stB 2001 ▪ Tasting & sales at Hamilton Russell Vineyards ▪ Owner(s) Anthony Hamilton Russell ▪ Winemaker(s) Emul Ross (2014) ▪ Viticulturist(s) Johan Montgomery (2005) ▪ 64ha/24.35ha (ptage, sauv, sem) ▪ 23t/12,000cs own label 50% red 50% white ▪ PO Box 158 Hermanus 7200 ▪ info@ashbournewines.com ▪ www.ashbournewines.com ▪ F +27 (0)28-312-1797 ▪ **T +27 (0)28-312-3595**

Ashton Winery ⊘ ⑪ 🍇 ⑤

Robertson Valley sunshine is transformed into 15 million litres of wine and sweet grape concentrate at the grower-owned winery on the hill above Ashton town. An important 3% is bottled under the own label which, regional sales representative Michelle Brown says, has benefited recently from 'many positive changes' including a new red-wine cellar and full branding overhaul. The plan is to 'grow locally and abroad while applying our new philosophy of simply enjoying wine and life with all the beauty it has to offer'.

Reserve range

Roodewal ★★★★ Shiraz, cab, merlot named after red slopes of Langeberg mountains. Spiced fruitcake richness yet **17** ⑧④ remains smoothly elegant, the oaking, (14 months, half new) well integrated.
Chardonnay Limited Release ★★★ Portion barrel aged, giving **17** ⑧① lemon cream flavours, zesty citrus finish. Friendly 12.5% alcohol.

Ashton range

Red Muscadel ⑦ **★★★** Powerful **17** ⑧② fortified has seductive richness & perfume, toffee & dried fruit, Turkish delight, finishes long & spicy. 500 ml.

Merlot ⓃⓊ **★★★** Herbaceous notes in red-fruited **17** ⑦⑧, fresh & juicy drinkability. **Pinotage ★★★** Hint of scrub in **16** ⑦⑧'s mulberry styling, has juicy accessibility. **Shiraz** ⊘ **★★★** Dark fruited & savoury, **16** ⑧① is smoothly appealing. **Cabernet Sauvignon-Merlot ★★★** Blackcurrants, hint of eucalyptus in 50/50 medium-bodied **16** ⑦⑧ blend. **Satynrosé ★★** From pinotage, **17** ⑦⑤ strawberry-hued & styled semi-sweet. **Chardonnay Unwooded ★★** Citrus & tropical tones, **18** ⑦⑥ ends softly fruity, fresh. **Chenin Blanc ★★★** Granny Smith apple & guava in **18** ⑦⑧, tangy fresh flavours. **Satynwit ★★** Gently fruity dry chenin, **17** ⑦⑤ crisp & light (12% alcohol). Well-priced range. **Satynperlé ★★ 17** chenin-based apple & pear semi-sweet, refreshed by perlé bubbles. **Sauvignon Blanc ★★★** Gooseberry & lime, **18** ⑦⑨ crackles with freshness. **Bonica Rosé Vin Doux ★★** Gently fruity sweet bubbly from pinotage in **17** ⑦②, a pink party pleaser. **Sauvignon Blanc Sparkling Brut** Ⓩ **★★** With sauvignon's summer fruit freshness, dry **17** ⑦④ perfect for everyday celebrations. Not tasted: **Cabernet Sauvignon, Satynrooi.** — CR

Location: Ashton ▪ Map/WO: Robertson ▪ Map grid reference: B4 ▪ Est 1962 ▪ 1stB 1970 ▪ Tasting & sales Mon-Fri 8-5 Sat 10-2 ▪ Closed Good Fri & Dec 25/26 ▪ Cellar tours by appt ▪ Facilities for children ▪ Tour groups ▪ Picnic baskets by appt ▪ Owner(s) 45 shareholders ▪ Cellarmaster(s) Sterik de Wet (Oct 2009) ▪ Winemaker(s) Heinrich Coetzee (Sep 2013) & Prieur du Plessis (Oct 2017) ▪ Viticulturist(s) Hennie Visser (VinPro) ▪ 1,280ha (cab, merlot, ptage, ruby cab, shiraz, chard, chenin, sauv) ▪ 24,041t/15m L total: 3% under own label 56% bulk & 41% grape juice concentrate ▪ Other export brands: Berryfields, Joy, Khoi Klaas, Nine Fields ▪ ISO 22000, HACCP, IPW, WIETA ▪ PO Box 40 Ashton 6715 ▪ info@ashtonwinery.com ▪ www.ashtonwinery.com ▪ S 33° 50' 12.1" E 020° 1' 48.3" ▪ ⌨ theories.platinum.partakes ▪ F +27 (0)23-615-1284 ▪ **T +27 (0)23-615-1135**

Aslina Wines

Award-winning Ntsiki Biyela, formerly with Stellekaya, continues building a global market for her quartet of wines under the Aslina label (in homage to the grandmother who raised her in a small KwaZulu-Natal village, prior to her studies in oenology/viticulture at Stellenbosch University). Production is now equally divided between whites (Sauvignon, Chardonnay) and reds (Cabernet, red blend Umsasane). She also markets a blended wine, Suo Red Collection No 2, made with California vintner Helen Keplinger.

Location: Somerset West ▪ 1stB 2013 ▪ Closed to public ▪ Owner(s)/winemaker(s) Ntsiki Biyela ▪ 2,000cs own label 50% red 50% white ▪ ntsiki@aslinawines.com ▪ www.aslinawines.co.za

☐ **Astraeus** see Waterkloof

Ataraxia Wines

Kevin and Hanli Grant ('and a few friends') bought the Ataraxia home-farm, spectacularly situated in Hemel-en-Aarde Ridge, in 2004. The vineyards are on elevated, mostly south-facing slopes (14 ha already, another 10 planned). Kevin's aim is for the wines he makes to be 'a pure expression of the soil in which they grow'. There are now 4: Chardonnay, Sauvignon Blanc, Serenity (red blend), and a long-gestated Pinot Noir.

Location: Hermanus ▪ Map: Walker Bay & Bot River ▪ Map grid reference: C4 ▪ Est 2004 ▪ 1stB 2005 ▪ Wine Lounge: tasting & sales Mon-Fri 9-4 Sat 10-4 Sun in season only ▪ Fee R50pp, refunded with individual purchase ▪ Closed Easter Fri/Sun, Dec 25 & Jan 1 ▪ Art exhibition ▪ Owner(s) Kevin Grant Wines (Pty) Ltd ▪ Cellarmaster(s)/winemaker(s) Kevin Grant (Sep 2004) ▪ Viticulturist(s) Eddie Boucher (2017) ▪ 47ha/14ha (pinot, chard) ▪ 83t/12,000cs own label 40% red 60% white ▪ PO Box 603 Hermanus 7200 ▪ info@ataraxiawines.co.za ▪ www.ataraxiawines.co.za ▪ S 34° 20' 27.0" E 019° 18' 30.8" ▪ ⬚ inherent.dumbbells.intervene ▪ F +27 (0)28-212-1921 ▪ T +27 (0)28-212-2007

☐ **Athena** *see* Thor Vintners
☐ **Aubergine Restaurant** *see* Migliarina Wines

Auction Crossing Private Cellar ⓠ

Vinified using traditional methods by winemaker/co-owner Leon Dippenaar, the Syrah is now the only wine in the portfolio of tiny (wonderfully scenic) Hex River Valley winery Auction Crossing, sourced from many climates and terroirs, and bottled on demand exclusively for export.

Location: De Doorns ▪ Map: Worcester ▪ Map grid reference: C1 ▪ Est 2003 ▪ 1stB 2004 ▪ Tasting & cellar tours by appt ▪ Closed all pub hols ▪ Tour groups by appt only ▪ Owner(s) De Villiers Graaff, AJ Reyneke & Leon Dippenaar ▪ Cellarmaster(s)/winemaker(s)/viticulturist(s) Leon Dippenaar (Aug 2004) ▪ ±41ha/2ha (mourv, shiraz, viog) ▪ 10t/4,000cs own label 75% red 25% white ▪ The Pines PO Box 5 Hex River 6855 ▪ auctioncrossing@hexvalley.co.za ▪ www.auctioncrossing.co.za ▪ S 33° 29' 42.8" E 019° 34' 32.7" ▪ F +27 (0)23-357-9255 ▪ T +27 (0)83-455-5194

Audacia Wines ⓠ ⑪ ⊚ ⑧ ⑤

The Strydom and Harris family owners of Stellenbosch's Audacia want their wines to be innovative and reflect global health and wellness trends. Hence the emphasis in their red-only portfolio on 'free from' (gluten, vegan-unfriendly animal products, added preservatives - the latter achieved by replacing sulphur with antioxidant-rich rooibos and honeybush wood) and 'low in' (alcohol and kilojoules). Sample these 'great-tasting natural wines' by appointment or at the popular Root44 weekend market on the estate.

Audacia range

Cabernet Sauvignon ⓠ ★★★★ Attractive, well-rounded **14** ⑭'s spicy fruit tucked in with deft tannin & harmonious French oak (33% new); hints of leather, violet & fynbos add complexity & up the appeal. **Cape Candy** ⓠ ★★★ Sweetness implied in wine's name comes from exposure to rooibos & honeybush chips in tank, yet NV ⑦ from merlot finishes dry with tannin flick. **Merlot** ★★★★ Toasted & charred notes prevail on **14** ⑧, dark fruit cake with hint of alcohol on strong tannin backbone. **Rouge Noble** ⓠ ★★★ 70% malbec in improved NV ⑧ 3-way Bordeaux blend. Ripe & red-fruited, light & pleasant sipper. **Jeté** ⓠ ★★★ Lightly oaked NV ⑧ blend, 4 Bordeaux red grapes plus shiraz & roobernet. Fruity, with a spicy twist, accessibility ensured by few grams sugar. Not tasted: **Cabernet Franc, Shiraz**.

No Sulphur Added range

★★★★ **Code Breaker** ⓠ Characterful & unusual merlot, **13** ⑧ has rooibos & honeybush as natural preservative yet more mint & lavender notes than expected fynbos. Succulent mulberry fruit, fresh finish. **Cabernet Sauvignon** ⓠ ★★ Decidedly different, **15** ⑭ Xmas pudding, tealeaf, marzipan & liquorice aromas; deliciously fruity, soft & fresh; attractive wine though lacks classic cab characteristics. **Merlot** ★★★ Two months on rooibos wood lend a tangy character to **15** ⑱. Not for the purist, but has some quirky appeal. **Shiraz** ⓠ ★★★ Dried buchu/rooibos notes, slight smokiness on **14** ⑧, plum & cherry hints, slides down effortlessly. **Premium Red Blend** ⓠ ★★ Characterful NV ⑭ from merlot & shiraz, forest berries dominated by tealeaf & buchu. Sweet hint & nutmeg spice make for interesting drink. Occasional release: **Natural Red Blend**.

Lower Kilojoules range

Lower Kilojoules ⓠ ★★ Rooibos/honeybush seasoning used on low-alcohol (7.5%) NV ⑦ from shiraz pervades in same way as pine tones of Greek retsina. Nutritional info on back label. — GdB

Location/map/WO: Stellenbosch ▪ Map grid reference: E8 ▪ Est 1930 ▪ Tasting by appt; closed pub hols ▪ On-consumption & sales at Audacia-Root44 Market Sat/Sun 11-4 ▪ Root44 Market (wine, food, arts, crafts, jewellery, kiddies area & live music from 1pm) ▪ Owner(s) Strydom & Harris families ▪ Cellarmaster(s)/winemaker(s)/viticulturist(s) Michael van Niekerk (Aug 2009) ▪ 32ha/20ha (cabs s/f, malbec, merlot, p verdot, roobernet, shiraz) ▪ 120t/18,000cs own label 100% red ▪ IPW ▪ PO Box 12679 Die Boord 7613 ▪ info@audacia. co.za ▪ www.audacia.co.za ▪ S 33° 59' 45.7" E 018° 50' 2.9" ▪ ⬚ fury.decks.qualified ▪ F +27 (0)21-881-3137 ▪ T +27 (0)21-881-3052

Aufwaerts Co-operative

Breedekloof family enterprise Aufwaerts produces mostly bulk wine but also markets a limited-release 5-year-old brandy, Twee Eeue, named for the original production process which straddled the 20th and 21st centuries. The distillery has been a national monument since the 1940s.

Location: Rawsonville • Map: Breedekloof • Map grid reference: B6 • Tasting by appt • Winemaker(s) Hennie de Villiers • PO Box 51 Rawsonville 6845 • hanepoot39@gmail.com • S 33° 41' 42.4" E 019° 17' 33.7" • deserve.prefigured.dolly • F +27 (0)23-349-1202 • **T +27 (0)23-349-1202**

Aurelia Wines

Groote Post winemaker Lukas Wentzel feels his own-label MCC bubbly brand is hitting its stride, as he expands production in response to growing demand and seeks to extend the time on lees. New 'cellar assistants' are sons Wian and Dewald, keen to earn extra pocket money, something dad is happy to encourage.

Brut Rosé ★★★ Pinot noir portion upped to 40% (rest chardonnay) in light, pleasurable MCC sparkler, with hints of spice, strawberry & yeast. **16** (82) an easier-drinking version of previous. **Brut ★★★★** Fresh, fruity, frothy crowd-pleasing **16** (84) MCC from chardonnay & pinot noir (70/30). Short lees time (14 months) adds some yeasty intensity to bouncy citrus & apple fruit. — CM

Location/WO: Darling • Est 2010 • 1stB 2008 • Closed to public • Owner(s)/cellarmaster(s)/winemaker(s) Lukas Wentzel • 3t/600cs own label • WIETA • PO Box 102 Darling 7345 • lukas@grootepost.co.za • **T +27 (0)22-492-2825/+27 (0)82-306-7373**

Autumn Harvest Crackling

These long-established, lightly sparkling, lower-alcohol wines are made by Distell, and also sold in 1L & 1.5L. **Crisp Perlé Rosé ★★** Party-starting NV (76) pink with faint berry tone, gentle fizz, echoing sweetness. **Crisp Perlé White ★★** More 'chilled-out' than 'crackling', NV (72) barely manages a bubble, few grams sugar perk up drinkability. **Crisp Perlé Red** ⊘ **★★★** Berry-toned NV (77) satisfies with prickle of tiny bubbles, friendly bite of tannin. — CvZ

Avondale

'The circle of life' is a key concept at this Paarl farm where the Grieve family is committed to sustainable winegrowing based on organic and biodynamic as well as scientific principles. They're thought to be the first in SA to import clay qvevri from Georgia, the former Soviet republic that winemaker Corné Marais visited in 2017, finding himself amazed by the quality of wine produced. 'These ancient vessels are a progression from the locally handcrafted clay amphorae we've been utilising for years,' says co-owner Johnathan Grieve.

Location/map: Paarl • Map grid reference: F6 • Est 1996 • 1stB 1999 • Tasting & sales Mon-Sun 10-4 • Fee R70pp • Closed Dec 25 & Jan 1 • Cellar tours by appt only • FABER restaurant • Eco Wine Safari Tue-Fri at 10am by appt: R300pp incl MCC on arrival, tour & tasting in vyds, cellar tour • Child friendly • Owner(s) Grieve family/The Avondale Trust • Winemaker(s) Corné Marais (Oct 2008), with Ivan September (Jan 2012) • Viticulturist(s) Johnathan Grieve (Jul 1999) • 300ha/70ha (cabs s/f, grenache, merlot, mourv, shiraz, chard, chenin, rouss, sem, viog) • 500t/50,000cs own label 50% red 38% white 2% rosé 10% MCC • EU Organic & USDA NOP organic • PO Box 602 Paarl South 7624 • wine@avondalewine.co.za • www.avondalewine.co.za • S 33° 45' 52.9" E 019° 0' 4.7" • nitrate.loaded.salt • **T +27 (0)21-863-1976**

Avontuur Estate

Late founder Tony Taberer's sons Michael and Philip have fine-tuned what he began in the 1980s, focusing as much on growing quality wine from prime Helderberg vineyards as on breeding champion racehorses. Add delights both indoor (a restaurant) and out (farm walks), all against a scenic backdrop of mountain, ocean, vineyards and paddocks, and you have a winning formula.

Premiere range

★★★★ Dominion Royale Shiraz Reserve Dark-berried **14** (87) has complex flavours including cured meats, less herbaceous than **12** (87). Good balance & presence. Now only seasoned casks. No **13**.

★★★★ Baccarat Tomato & bramble notes mingle with toasty vanilla oak & cigarbox on **12** (86) cab franc-led Bordeaux blend. Supple tannins & structure, medium body with grip for food. No **11**.

★★★★ Luna de Miel Chardonnay Reserve Gorgeous **17** ⑧⑦ extends uptick of last-tasted **15** ★★★★ ⑧④, crunchy apple freshens the glossy butterscotch tones & dash viognier. 50% new wood well contained.

★★★★ Sarabande Sauvignon Blanc Reserve ⓧ **15** ⑧⑦ improves on **14** ★★★ ⑧⓪ with crisp apple, stonefruit & full creamy palate. 15% oaked chardonnay adds to harmony, complexity & texture.

Minelli Pinot Noir Reserve ⓧ ★★★ Spicy, dense strawberry compote flavours with a medicinal edge in retasted **12** ⑧①. Misses variety's ethereality, finesse. **Natural Sweet Viognier** ★★★★ Ripe peach & nectarine fruit; sweet, full & charming but **18** ⑧⑤ needs more complexity for higher rating. 375 ml.

Estate range

★★★★ Cabernet Sauvignon Focused, elegant **14** ⑧⑥ in style of previous with dried herb & lead pencil profile. Balanced, integrated oak & tannin, long savoury finish.

Cabernet Franc ⓧ ★★★ Herbal edge on **14** ⑧②, rustic, with big tannins. **Pinotage** ⓧ ★★★ Voluptuous **14** ⑧①, smoother than previous, ripe sweet plums & spice, good balance, just a tad unlingering. **Cabernet Sauvignon-Merlot** ★★★ Juicy fresh berries on **15** ⑧⓪ equal blend, with savoury, meaty extras. Light the barbecue fire! Also in magnum. **Sauvignon Blanc** ★★★ Unwooded & brisk, **18** ⑦⑨ with crisp, grassy green notes. **Brut Cap Classique** ⓧ ★★★ Onion skin hue on **NV** ⑧① (**10**) tradition-al-method sparkling from chardonnay & pinot noir. Faint apple & black olive flavours with coarse bubbles, uncomplicated & light. Not tasted: **Pinot Noir-Chardonnay**.

Brandy range

★★★★ Private Collection 10 Year Old Potstill New bottling of estate potstill from chenin as luxuriously rich & flavourful as previous. Rather high residual sugar (20 g/l) enhances silkiness as well as sweetness.— DS, TJ

Location/WO: Stellenbosch ▪ Map: Helderberg ▪ Map grid reference: C2 ▪ Est 1850 ▪ 1stB 1984 ▪ Tasting & sales Mon-Fri 8.30–5 Sat/Sun 9–4 ▪ Fee R50/5 wines ▪ Closed Good Fri, Dec 25 & Jan 1 ▪ Cellar tours by appt ▪ Tour groups ▪ Avontuur Estate Restaurant ▪ Function venue ▪ Thoroughbred stud ▪ Self-guided farm walks ▪ Seasonal events ▪ Owner(s) Taberer family ▪ Winemaker(s) / brandy master(s) Jan van Rooyen (Jan 2011) ▪ Viticulturist(s) Pippa Mickleburgh (Sep 1999) & Paul Wallace (consultant) ▪ 110ha/40ha (cabs s/f, merlot, p verdot, ptage, pinot, shiraz, chard, sauv, viog) ▪ 300t ▪ 60% red 40% white ▪ PO Box 1128 Somerset West 7129 ▪ info@avontuurestate.co.za ▪ www.avontuurestate.co.za ▪ S 34° 1′ 33.2″ E 018° 49′ 23.8″ ▪ ✉ pens. stronger.aground ▪ F +27 (0)21-855-4600 ▪ **T +27 (0)21-855-3450**

Axe Hill ⓨ

A substantial drop in yields, as Calitzdorp experienced its fourth year of drought, must have brought at least a bit of benefit for self-trained winemaker and owner Mike Neebe. Inspired by a visit to the Douro, he has over the years crafted a range of 'ports' and unfortified reds from Portuguese varieties, and expanded the ranges to include Rhône grapes and a chenin – all in boutique-sized premises. But if cellar space remains constrained, Mike's enthusiasm and talent certainly aren't. The '15 reds promised last time are here, and show fine potential, deserving of many years' ageing.

Axe Hill range

★★★★ Touriga Nacional Deep spiced plum/prune flavours tempered by firm but svelte tannins, **15** ⑧⑥ concentrated, brooding, typical of variety, needs time to develop. Old French oak, 16 months.

★★★★ Machado ⊘ Like **14** ⑧⑦ (& the other reds here), **15** ★★★★★ ⑨⓪ riper styled but with more balance, polish, potential to develop. Rich, dark fruit & chocolate, souzão & touriga (35/30), dashes shiraz & tinta in supple tannin framework. Combo old/new French & American oak, 18 months.

★★★★ Cape Late Bottled Vintage ⓧ Dark fruitcake tones on foot-pressed **10** ⑧⑥ 'port' from touriga (60%), tinta, souzão, made in a crossover style - both high alcohol & sugar. Better than **09** ★★★ ⑧① though strictly too tannic & peppery for LBV style, cellaring recommended.

★★★★★ Cape Vintage ⓧ From touriga (60%) with souzão & tinta, as was equally delicious **12** ⑨② plenty of ripe flavour in **13** ★★★★ ⑧⑦, lightly & elegantly rich, with pleasing near-dry finish, but lacks the tannic depth & intensity for Vintage style.

Distinta ★★★★ Port-grape blend is ripe & rounded, though **15** ⑧④ also has good structure, freshness, offsetting 14.5% alcohol warmth. Touriga, tinta, souzão, with tad more substance, longevity than Lenie's 2-way mix. **Ambientem** ★★★ Curvy & approachable chenin, **17** ⑧② baked apple & almond, dry but rich, the viscous texture aided by old French oak & lees. Good with Thai food & curries. **Cape Ruby** ⓥ ★★★ Same varieties as Vintage, latest NV ⑧⓵ shows notably ripe character & dark, smoky flavours. Some easy charm, but the acidity standing a bit apart, & tending to the insubstantial. **Cape White** ⓥ ★★★☆ 'White port' from chenin, solera aged. NV ⑧④ tastes like the entire pudding course (apple crumble, cream plus the dessert wine) in one delicious mouthful, but uncloying, in fact almost dry on taste. Occasional release: **Shiraz**.

Lenie's Hof range

Red ⓝⒺⓌ ★★★ Older-oaked touriga & tempranillo, **16** ⑧② supple & succulent, delivers mouthfilling spiced plums & liquorice at moderate 13.5% alcohol. Affable fireside quaffer, also hearty-food mate. **Tant Lenie** ★★★ Single-block, oak-fermented viognier, **17** ⑧⓵ dried peach & apricot, some pithiness from skin contact, perhaps too generous & warm for solo, needs - & will complement - a meal. — MW

Location/WO: Calitzdorp ▪ Map: Klein Karoo & Garden Route ▪ Map grid reference: B5 ▪ Est 1993 ▪ 1stB 1997 ▪ Tasting, sales & cellar tours Mon-Sat by appt ▪ Owner(s) Axe Hill Winery (Pty) Ltd ▪ Cellarmaster(s)/winemaker(s) Mike Neebe (Oct 2007) ▪ Viticulturist(s) Johannes Mellet (Aug 2009, consultant) ▪ ±60ha/1.5ha (grenache, souzão, tinta barocca, tinta roriz, touriga nacional, viog) ▪ ±5t/±1,000cs own label 70% red 30% white ▪ Wesoewer Rd Calitzdorp 6660 ▪ info@axehill.co.za ▪ www.axehill.co.za ▪ S 33° 30' 54.6" E 021° 41' 23.0" ▪ ⓦ succeeds.guided.crewmen ▪ **T +27 (0)11-447-3900/+27 (0)44-213-3585/+27 (0)83-676-3000**

Ayama Wines   ⓠ ⓟ ⊙ ⌂ ◎ ⓑ

'We are proudly South Africans now, but still Italians!' say Michela and Attilio Dalpiaz, explaining why they can't 'take it easy' on Slent, the Voor Paardeberg farm they and friends from the old country bought in the mid-2000s, restoring the old farmstead, establishing an olive grove and over time introducing different grape varieties, including SA's first vermentino. From the new and brilliant Ayamateca farm store to their guest house and Perdjie school project, they're constantly 'working on more and more to share and offer'.

Ayama range

Pinotage ★★★ Unoaked, so there's a fresh berry riot on the nose of **17** ⑧⓵, spice on the palate & a firm redcurrant handshake. WO W Cape. **Chenin Blanc** ★★★ Packed with nectarine, yellow peach & apple, **17** ⑧⓵ deliciously dry with long lime twist on the finish. **Vermentino** ★★★☆ SA's first commercial bottling, featuring fruit from young vines. Older-oaked **17** ⑧⑤, too young to rate last time, has settled in bottle. Light of foot, with delicate lemon & dried herb flavours. Also in 1.5, 3 & 5L for the large/extended famiglia. Not tasted: **Cabernet Sauvignon, Merlot, Shiraz**.

Baboon Selection

Baboon's Back Petite Sirah ★★★☆ Ruby-hued **17** ⑧③ is now bottled, offers lively bramble & hedgerow fruit, subtle spice from older oak, crushed green herbs & hint of smoke. **Baboon's Cuddle Pinotage** ★★★☆ Chocolate-dipped plums mingle with coffee & caramel on full & inviting palate, **17** ⑧⑤ concludes with a fresh, lifted acidity. Only 33% oaked. WO W Cape. **Baboon's Cheek Viognier** ★★★ Now bottled, **17** ⑧⓵ a voluptuous melange of peaches & cream, apricot kernel & exotic spice. Delicious solo, works well with food too. Not tasted: **Baboon's Back Shiraz, Baboon's Swing Chenin Blanc**.

Leopard Spot range

Red ★★★ Occasional sightings of the big cats on Paardeberg inspire this unwooded range. Cape Blend pinotage (52%), shiraz, grenache, dark berries & spice on still-fresh, mouthfilling **15** ⑧② **White** ★★★☆ Good intensity on **17** ⑧⑤ chenin, fresh orchard fruit perfumes, lovely depth & length turning savoury in conclusion.

Méthode Cap Classiques

Not tasted: **Rosé, Blanc de Blancs, Brut**. — WB

Location/map: Paarl ▪ Map grid reference: B2 ▪ WO: Voor Paardeberg/Western Cape ▪ Est 2005 ▪ 1stB 2006 ▪ Tasting & sales Mon-Sun 10-4.30 ▪ Meals/refreshments by appt; or BYO picnic ▪ Deli with fresh farm produce, olive oil, wines & much more ▪ Walks/hikes ▪ Child friendly ▪ Conservation area ▪ Ayama Rock guest house ▪ Owner(s) Slent Farms (Pty) Ltd (5 partners) ▪ Cellarmaster(s)/winemaker(s) Michela Sfiligoi (2005) ▪ Viticulturist(s) Attilio Dalpiaz (2005) ▪ 210ha/65ha (cab, carignan, grenache n/b, merlot, petite sirah, ptage, shiraz, chenin, sauv, vermentino, viog) ▪ 300t/40,000cs own label 40% red 58% white 2% rosé ▪ WIETA ▪

Suite 106 Private Bag X3041 Paarl 7620 ▪ info@slentfarms.com ▪ www.ayama.co.za ▪ S 33° 37′ 22.5″ E 018° 49′ 19″ ▪ ⬜ downloads.marigolds.swam ▪ F +27 (0)86-662-2765 ▪ **T +27 (0)21-869-8313**

☐ **Azania** *see* Jacques Germanier
☐ **Baboon Selection** *see* Ayama Wines

Babylon's Peak Private Cellar

Ⓠ ⌂ ◎ Ⓑ

Prompted by an increased demand for their wines, the Basson family spent much of 2017/8 focused on establishing new vineyards in the Paardeberg, expanding the cellar and other facilities and enhancing their range, with two new premium reds maturing in barrel when the guide went to print. Mature vineyards, including 46-year-old chenin, underpin Stephan Basson's fine-fruited, well-priced line-up.

★★★★ Pinotage ⊘ Deliciously intense **17** ㉘'s pure black pastille & plum fruit merges nicely with firm tannic grip, helps extend the finish. Attractive mocha nuance from year older barrels.

★★★★ Cabernet Sauvignon-Malbec ⊘ Harmonious **16** ㉘ 70/30 blend improves on **15 ★★★★** ㉔ in very good fruit expression & structure, deft use of older oak, greater mulberry, cassis, mineral complexity.

★★★★ SMG Ⓠ First tasted since velvety **10** ㉘, **16 ★★★★★** ㉙ worth the wait. Enticingly spicy red fruit rolls onto the palate in waves; lingering fynbos, white pepper aromas, bright red-berry flavours, melded oak. 65% shiraz, 30% mourvèdre, dash grenache.

★★★★ Viognier-Roussanne ⊘ Older-barrel-fermented, lees-aged **17** ㉙, persistent & pervasive spiced grapefruit character, white flower & peach complexity. Gram sugar smooths, doesn't unbalance food-friendly 73/37 blend.

Shiraz-Carignan ⊘ **★★★★** Thrilling tannin lift on attractive **17** ㉔ duo shiraz (60%) & dryland carignan. Year older oak allows pristine red & black berry fruit to shine, adds subtle spice. **Chenin Blanc** ⊘ **★★★★** From old dryland vineyard, **18** ㉔'s richness ex extended lees contact & smidgen sugar enlivened by vibrant acidity for fresh, engaging glassful. — HC

Location: Malmesbury ▪ Map/WO: Swartland ▪ Map grid reference: C8 ▪ Est/1stB 2003 ▪ Tasting & sales by appt only ▪ Conservation area ▪ Dams for fishing ▪ Self-catering cottage ▪ Owner(s) Stephan Basson ▪ Cellarmaster(s)/winemaker(s)/viticulturist(s) Stephan Basson (Jan 2003) ▪ 580ha/230ha (carignan, grenache, mourv, ptage, shiraz, chenin, rouss, viog) ▪ 30,000cs own label 65% red 35% white + 500,000L bulk ▪ PO Box 161 Malmesbury 7299 ▪ info@babylonspeak.co.za ▪ www.babylonspeak.co.za ▪ S 33° 33′ 40.8″ E 018° 48′ 38.6″ ▪ ⬜ glider.starstruck.convert ▪ F +27 (0)86-518-3773 ▪ **T +27 (0)21-300-1052**

Babylonstoren

Ⓠ ⑪ ⌂ ◎ Ⓑ

This historic farm on the slopes of the Simonsberg was first granted to a free burgher in 1692, and buildings on the property date back to the mid-18th century. But the splendid garden (with more than 300 varieties of edible and medicinal plants) was laid out in 2007, under the aegis of the current owner, Karen Roos, as the focus of an offering of accommodation, food and wine. The vineyards are more extensive, of course, and all four varieties of white grapes planted are reflected in the new blend, Candide.

★★★★ Shiraz Ripe, sweet dark fruit on **16** ㉖, with smokiness & plenty of oak influence (60% new). Firm tannins. Less blockbusterish than previous, but lingering sweetness will be a problem for some.

★★★★★ Nebukadnesar Blend of 49% cab with 4 other Bordeaux varieties. **16** ㉚ big, impressive wine in a massive bottle, but with a subtle fragrance, the generous fruit complemented by dried herbs, cedar & tobacco. Sweet red fruit not outweighed by the mighty tannins or the all-new oak, but needs time to harmonise & soften.

★★★★ Babel Shiraz & cab lead **17** ㉖ with 5 other varieties. Nicely structured but designed for earlier drinking than Nebukadnesar. Juicy & fleshy, if a bit sweet. Better balanced than **16 ★★★★** ㉔.

★★★★ Chardonnay Toasty aromas dominate nuts & lemon-lime on **17** ㉘. Full bodied; plenty of fruit, good easygoing acidity. Oak flavours (50% new) might integrate in time, but now too obvious for balance.

★★★★ Candide Ⓝⓔⓦ Nearly half chenin, viognier adding aromatic, apricot notes, chardonnay & semillon adding citrus, weight & further interest. Flavourful, satiny **18** ㉘ partly bunch fermented, partly oaked.

★★★★ **Sprankel 13** ★★★★☆ ㉒ the best yet of this MCC sparkling from chardonnay. As with **12** ㉘, also matured 4 years before disgorgement, there's an elegant fresh austerity as well as flavour intensity, a coupling that gives great satisfaction. Bone-dry, something unusual here. WO W Cape.

Mourvèdre Rosé ★★★ Well-flavoured, pale salmon-coloured **18** ㉛ pleasantly fruity, easygoing, fresh & dry. WO W Cape, as next. **Chenin Blanc** ★★★★ Fresh, green-tinged **18** ㉞ with tropical notes, some yellow peach. Softly rounded & balanced, but little intensity or length of flavour. WO W Cape. **Viognier** ★★★★ Restrained apricot aroma & flavour on **17** ㉟, with savoury oak element (50% new) well integrated - & adding a little tannic bite. Understated varietal charm abetted by some sweetness. — TJ

Location: Paarl ▪ Map: Franschhoek ▪ Map grid reference: B8 ▪ WO: Simonsberg-Paarl/Western Cape ▪ Est 1692 ▪ 1stB 2011 ▪ Tasting & sales daily 10–5 in winter/10–6 in summer ▪ Hosted wine tasting, cellar tours daily 11–3 ▪ Tour groups by appt ▪ Farm shop & online shop ▪ Guided garden tours at 10 daily ▪ Babylonstoren Farm Hotel ▪ Bakery dinners Wed & Fri from 7 ▪ Babel Restaurant: breakfast Mon–Sun 8–9.30, lunch Wed–Sun from 12, dinner Mon–Sun from 7; The Greenhouse Restaurant Mon–Sun 10–4 ▪ Garden Spa 8-7 ▪ Healing Garden Tue 9.30 ▪ Olive oil press ▪ Mampoer distillery ▪ Cellarmaster(s) Charl Coetzee ▪ Winemaker(s) Klaas Stofberg, with Marina Laubser ▪ Viticulturist(s) Ian de Villiers ▪ Babylonstoren Farm, Franschhoek ▪ cellar@babylonstoren.com ▪ www.babylonstoren.com ▪ S 33° 49′ 26.73″ E 018° 55′ 39.08″ ▪ 🎧 squeamish.cyclist.engrossed ▪ **T +27 (0)21-863-3852**

Backsberg Estate Cellars ⓥ ⑪ ⊚ ⑤ ⑤

A major focus at the Back family estate in Paarl over the past decade or so has been on environmentally and socially responsible initiatives, with patriarch Michael Back's continuing inspiration and work, and son and co-owner Simon latterly running the business. A keen eye has also been kept on the vineyards, with recent plantings of chardonnay, roussanne and pinotage, and lesser-known durif and marselan. A block of malbec, in conversion for three years, will deliver a fully organic harvest this year. Some 15 years since the last refresh, packaging is being modernised across the ranges. Such ongoing tweaks, plus steadfast quality and value, will doubtless see the 103-year-old venture flourish over its next century.

Flagship - Backsberg Family Reserve range

★★★★☆ **Red Blend** ⓐ The carefully crafted pinnacle, Bordeaux red mostly cab (50%), merlot & malbec in fine **16** ㉓. Generous fruit tightly packed & well-contained in harmonious oak/tannin structure. Always one of the best in this extensive range. Ageworthy.

★★★★☆ **White Blend** ⓐ Unusual & impressive roussanne-led blend with sauvignon & chardonnay. **17** ㉔ better integrated than weighty **16** ㉒; stem ginger nuance, sauvignon's elevated acidity perfectly judged to counter others' fullness. Brief oaking, 100% new. WO Coastal.

Black Label range

★★★★ **Pumphouse Shiraz** ⓐ Round & full, sweet red & black fruit dusted with pepper & aromatic baking spices. Lithe tannins accessible now & will carry **16** ㉙ for many years, like **15** ★★★★☆ ㉒.

★★★★☆ **Klein Babylons Toren** ⊘ⓐ Stalwart Cape Bordeaux blend from cab (52%), merlot & malbec in **16** ㉓. Less opulent than last, sterner, more tightly wound tannins, more classic lead pencil & tobacco notes. Various larger bottle formats.

★★★★☆ **Sonop Chardonnay** High-end version, shows serious intent in all-new barrel ferment. **17** ★★★★ ㉖ still unsettled mid-2018, smoky whiffs, sweet oaky notes somewhat at odds with bone-dry finish. **16** ㉑'s substantial & convincing citrus fruit handled similar woody overlay better in youth.

★★★★ **John Martin Reserve Sauvignon Blanc** Pleasing smoky whiff from 50% barrel-fermented (not -aged) portion accentuates **18** ㉙'s fig & gooseberry tones, softens variety's acidity. Subtle, suave & smooth. Dash roussanne.

★★★★ **Hillside Viognier** Returns after a break with **18** ㉗, pale & gently peachy, dry, with brief (2 months) oak adding suggestion of sweet baking spices to commendably restrained wine.

★★★★ **Méthode Cap Classique Brut** Ready to celebrate, **16** ★★★★ ㉕ dry sparkler frothy & rich, ample green, red & candied apple tones, caramel nuance from ±year on lees. Pinot noir & chardonnay, like shade more impressive **15** ㉘.

Premium range

★★★★ **Cabernet Sauvignon** ⊘ Assured if tad brash, **17** ⑧⑥'s big tannins padded by dense fruit, needs year/2 to settle. Also-tasted **16** ⑧⑥ equally bold & robust, with floral note & lemony acid backbone.

Pinotage ⑰ ★★★★ If a wine could wear a smiley face, **17** ⑧③ would: bountiful strawberry & mulberry fruit, refreshing acidity & friendly tannins. From happy Wellington vines.

Merlot ★★★ Bright plummy fruit, supple tannins for easy, early enjoyment in **16** ⑧②. **Dry Red** ⑨ ★★★ Reliable, user-friendly **NV** ⑧⓪ (**16**) of undisclosed composition. Generous fruit, firm structure. Also in 1.5L. WO W Cape. **Pinotage Rosé** ★★★ Impressively long, with modest 12.5% alcohol, dry **18** ⑧② has attractive raspberry tang. **Rosé** ⊘ ★★★ Two Italian, two French & a South African grapes walk into the cellar... & out pops a lovely pink, lightish (12% alcohol) & off-dry **18** ⑦⑧. **Chardonnay** ★★★★ Repeats successful formula in **17** ⑧③: partial, brief oak exposure delivers lemon butter fruit, gentle spice dusting. Some Wellington fruit. **Chenin Blanc** ⊘ ★★★ Pretty & perky **18** ⑧⓪, peaches & pears with touch sugar & splash chardonnay to enjoy anytime. WO Coastal. **Sauvignon Blanc** ★★★ **18** ⑦⑧ brief but bright & fruity for everyday quaffing. WO Coastal. **Special Late Harvest** ★★★★ Equal roussanne, viognier & gewürztraminer in engaging, ginger beer-nuanced **18** ⑧③. Moderately sweet, slips down easily.

Kosher range

Merlot ★★★ **17** ⑦⑨ plummy on entry & at the end, charry in between. **Pinotage** ★★★ Glides down without fuss thanks to gram sugar, fruity sweetness in **17** ⑧⓪. **Chardonnay** ★★★ Beguiling sweet hint, variety-true lemon/lime aromas & good mouthfeel make for satisfying **18** ⑧② glassful. **Méthode Cap Classique Brut** ★★★ Bubbly from chardonnay with dash pinot noir for pale pink tint, **17** ⑧⓪ lemon sherbet flavours, frothy mousse. WO Coastal. **Kiddush Sacramental Wine** ⑨ ★★ Sacramental wine from shiraz **17** ⑦④, rather blandly sweet.

Fortified range

★★★★ **Pinneau** ⑮ Pineau des Charentes-style dessert, gewürztraminer & roussanne juice fortified with 10 year old house brandy. **17** ⑧⑧ elegant marzipan, lemon & vanilla fusion with staying power. First since **10** ★★★★ ⑧④ oak-matured chenin.

Cape Vintage Reserve ★★★★ Obvious fortification (10 year old brandy) on nose & palate of full-bore **17** ⑧③ 'port' from barbera & zinfandel. Long & firm, tannin for keeping few years, not over-sweet.

Brandy range

★★★★ **Sydney Back 1st Distillation** ⑨ Dark amber on this 20 year old, rich texture, round & well matured, with marmalade, dark chocolate flavours. Loads of oaky vanilla & mature character, but touch less fresh than the younger brandies. 100% potstill from chenin, as all.

★★★★ **Sydney Back Finest Matured (10 Year Old)** ⑨ Inviting honey, dried apricot & marzipan aromas on the nose. Effortlessly elegant & light footed, with vanilla, toasty nuts, sweet tobacco & caramel.

★★★★ **Sydney Back Special Release (15 Year Old)** ⑨ Complex nose of dried fruit & toasty nuts, hint of anise. Astounding intensity of apricot, peach & touch of sweet vanilla on the palate. Floral notes all the way & hint of orange peel.— CvZ, WB, TJ

Location: Paarl • Map: Franschhoek • Map grid reference: B8 • WO: Paarl/Coastal/Western Cape • Est 1916 • 1stB 1970 • Tasting & sales Mon-Fri 9—5 Sat/Sun 10—4 • Fee R30 • Open 365 days a year • Cellar tours by appt • Self-guided tours of the cellar, brandy cellar, winery & historic corridors • Wine pairings: chocolate & wine; cheese & wine • Backsberg Restaurant • Facilities for children • Tour groups • Conferences • Weddings & functions • Pre-ordered picnics • Environmental talks (by appt only) • Sunday picnic concerts (in summer) • Brandy & Blues evenings (in winter) • Sydney Back potstill brandy • Owner(s) Michael & Simon Back • Winemaker(s) Alicia Rechner (Jun 2012) • Viticulturist(s) Talitha Venter (Jul 2016) • 70ha (cab, merlot, ptage, shiraz, chard, sauv) • 900t/160,000cs own label 65% red 30% white 5% rosé • WWF-SA Conservation Champion • PO Box 537 Suider-Paarl 7624 • info@backsberg.co.za • www.backsberg.co.za • S 33° 49' 42.9" E 018° 54' 56.9" • 🖃 leaven.juror.merrily • **T** +27 (0)21-875-5141

☐ **Badenhorst Family Wines** *see* AA Badenhorst Family Wines
☐ **Bader & Walters** *see* Viva Africa Wines

Badsberg Wine Cellar

Breedekloof's burgeoning reputation is being driven by unfortified/table wines, and this large, long-established grower-owned winery has added to the lustre through many successes in competitions and professional tastings, not least the Young Wine Show best-wine-overall trophy for the Pinotage Generaal Smuts. That said, Badsberg thankfully also remains a treasure trove of fortifieds and other sweet treats.

★★★★ **Pinotage Generaal Smuts** ⓥ Seriously conceived & modern, **16** ⑧⑦ vibrant ruby colour follows through with red fruit profile, firm tannin structure & length. Elegant, shows fine complexity.

★★★★ **Chardonnay Sur Lie** Big mouthful aimed at fans of oaky style - 8 months mix French/Hungarian wood. **17** ★★★★ ⑧③ citrus lightness lifts it gently. **15** ⑧⑦ better balanced. No **16**.

★★★★★ **Badslese** ⓥ Unwooded Natural Sweet dessert from chenin & muscat d'Alexandrie; only in best years (no **10**, **11**). With muscat portion upped to 30%, **12** ★★★★★ ⑨② is pure indulgence: melting quince, melon & grape flavours, as scintillating & precise as **09**, our 2012 White Wine of the Year.

★★★★ **Noble Late Harvest** Ample jasmine allure on **17** ★★★★★ ⑨⓪ botrytis dessert, judged Young Wine Show champion. Penetrating sweetness (196 g/l sugar) balanced by harmonious acidity; good intensity, body & length with clean dry finish. Low alcohol. Unwooded chenin & muscat d'Alexandrie (80/20), like last-tasted **09** ⑧⑦. 375 ml.

★★★★ **Red Muscadel** Seductive florality of copper-hued **17** ⑧⑦ fortified dessert balances smooth sweetness, perfumed muscat typicity, spice & puréed plum flavour with defined, dry-seeming finish.

★★★★ **Red Jerepigo** Lively red cherry & caramel sweetness on **16** ★★★★☆ ⑧⑤ from pinotage leavened by fiery fortification. Clean, dry tail but tad shorter than last **14** ⑧⑦, ex ruby cab.

Pinotage ★★★☆ Improves on previous with twist of tannin from 6 months oaking. **17** ⑧③ charming & bright-fruited yet with smoky depth & length. **Belladonna** ★★★ Soft & fleshy **16** ⑧② blend of cab & 4 others. Spicy oak a tad firm. **Perlé Moscato** ★★ Perfumed **18** ⑦④ rosé from muscat de Frontignan balances berry sweetness with acid tang. Low alcohol. **Barrel Fermented Chenin Blanc** ⓥ ★★★☆ Youthful **16** ⑧④ rich & rounded, generous apricot, baked apple & clove aromas & flavours from 5 months oak ageing. **Chenin Blanc** ⊘ ★★★ Unfussy, bright tropical fruit on easy-drinking **18** ⑧⓪. Balanced zesty acid makes for al fresco enjoyment. **Sauvignon Blanc** ★★★ Piquant lemon & granadilla appeal on just-dry **18** ⑦⑧. Also in 3L cask. **Vin Doux** ⓥ ★★★ Sweet, frothy & grapey **15** ⑦⑧ sparkling from muscat d'Alexandrie, with low alcohol. **Hanepoot Jerepigo** ★★★☆ Vibrant spirit fortification tempers raisined sweetness of **17** ⑧④ dessert. Lovely dulcet muscat notes. **Cape Vintage** ⓥ Sweet, soft & dusty - more like 'fortified red wine' than 'port', needs more zip & grip. **13** ⑦⑧ from undisclosed varieties. Not tasted: **Merlot**. Discontinued: **Noble Late Harvest Limited Edition**. — FM

Location: Rawsonville ▪ Map/WO: Breedekloof ▪ Map grid reference: B5 ▪ Est 1951 ▪ 1stB 1958 ▪ Tasting & sales Mon-Fri 9—5 Sat 10—1 ▪ Fee R20pp for groups of 10+ ▪ Closed all pub hols ▪ Cellar tours by appt ▪ BYO picnic ▪ Facilities for children ▪ Farm produce ▪ Conferences (40 pax) ▪ Conservation area ▪ Soetes & Soup (Jul) ▪ Owner(s) 26 members ▪ Cellarmaster(s) Willie Burger (1998) ▪ Winemaker(s) Henri Swiegers (2002), with Stian Victor (2017) & Jaco Booysen (Jan 2007) ▪ Viticulturist(s) Shazell van den Berg (2017) ▪ ±1,500ha/±1,300ha (ptage, shiraz, chenin, cbard) ▪ ±30,000t ▪ 20% red 65% white 10% rosé 5% fortified ▪ ISO 22000:2009, IPW, WIETA ▪ PO Box 72 Rawsonville 6845 ▪ maritza@badsberg.co.za ▪ www.badsberg.co.za ▪ S 33° 39' 40.1" E 019° 16' 9.2" ▪ ⌨ overlaying.layout.nettle ▪ F +27 (0)86-574-6091 ▪ **T +27 (0)23-344-3021**

☐ **Bag-in-Box Collection** *see* Jacques Germanier
☐ **Bainskloof** *see* Bergsig Estate
☐ **Balance** *see* Overhex Wines International
☐ **Bald Ibis** *see* The Bald Ibis

Baleia Wines

The Joubert family has farmed near Riversdale in the southern Cape since the 1900s, initially with grain and sheep but, descended from French Huguenots, with 'viticulture in our blood', vines have been a feature of each property added to the landholding. The propitious farm Dassieklip was acquired in 2001 by Fanie Joubert and, since 2009/10, the planting of vineyards and olive groves has been overseen by son Jan-Hendrik. The range is enhanced by terracotta amphora maturation, and will soon feature MCC sparkling and a fortified. The cellar is in Riversdale town, next to the tasting venue, conveniently near the N2 highway.

Baleia Wines range

★★★★ **Erhard Pinot Noir** ⓩ Worthy effort from this cool region, **14** ⑧⑨ bears out promise of **13** ★★★☆ ⑧④. Charming floral notes & convincing red berry fruit, hints of rosewater & fertile earth.

★★★★ **Tempranillo** ⓩ Among handful of varietal bottlings of this great Spanish variety. **15** ⑧⑦ makes no attempt to emulate Rioja, but shows the succulent delicacy & noble structure in New World context.

Inge Chardonnay ⓩ ★★★★ Packed with tropical fruit, expressive **14** ⑧⑤ has a butterscotch richness from the oaking, requisite freshness in a nicely rounded body. More controlled, less showy than **13** ★★★★ ⑧⑥. Not tasted: **Syrah**, **Rosé**, **Sauvignon Blanc**.

Director's Reserve range

Not tasted: **Sebastian**. — GdB

Location: Riversdale ▪ Map: Klein Karoo & Garden Route ▪ Map grid reference: C6 ▪ WO: Cape South Coast ▪ Est 2010 ▪ 1stB 2011 ▪ Tasting, sales & cellar tours Mon-Fri 9–5 Sat/pub hols 10-3 ▪ Olive oil ▪ Facilities for children ▪ Deli for refreshments/meals; or BYO picnic ▪ Pet friendly area ▪ Videira Country House, luxury self-catering accommodation ▪ Hiking, biking & bird watching ▪ Owner(s) Fanie & Jan-Hendrik Joubert ▪ Winemaker(s) Abraham de Klerk ▪ 1,000ha/9.5ha (pinot, shiraz, tempranillo, chard, sauv) ▪ 80t/600cs own label 60% red 40% white ▪ PO Box 268 Riversdale 6670 ▪ info@baleiawines.com ▪ www.baleiawines. com ▪ S 34° 6′ 36.89″ E 021° 15′ 18.48″ ▪ 🖭 ponytailed.accent.request ▪ F +27 (0)86-560-0367 ▪ **T +27 (0)28-713-1214**

☐ **Bales Choice** *see* Wade Bales Fine Wines & Spirits
☐ **Balthazar** *see* Roodezandt Wines
☐ **Bandana** *see* Klein Roosboom

Baratok Wines ⓠ ⓞ

Operating from Paarl's Mooi Bly farm, Baratok owner Alex Boraine's mostly export wine business includes an innovative venture, BuytheBarrel, which affords aspirant vintners the means to vinify, bottle, package and optionally market their own wine brand. See the Make Your Own Wine section for details.

Location/map: Paarl ▪ Map grid reference: F3 ▪ Est 2012 ▪ Tasting by appt ▪ Closed all pub hols ▪ Tour groups ▪ Olive oil ▪ Conferences ▪ Owner(s)/winemaker(s) Alex Boraine ▪ (cab, cinsaut, malbec, merlot, ptage, shiraz, chard, chenin, sauv, sem, viog) ▪ 27t/200,000L own label 60% red 40% white; 90,000L for clients + 480,000L bulk ▪ Brands for clients: African Tribe, Belle Vallee, Kipepeo, Terre de Papillon ▪ PO Box 668 Wellington 7654 ▪ alex@baratokwines.co.za ▪ S 33° 41′7.0″ E 019° 1′21.9″ ▪ 🖭 mullet.boggle.shortness ▪ **T +27 (0)84-582-6376**

☐ **Barber's Wood** *see* Celestina

Barista

Owned by Vinimark, Barista is made by Bertus Fourie, nicknamed 'Starbucks' after his 'magical recipe' for overtly mocha-toned pinotage (selected grapes, specific yeasts, special oak treatment) spawned an entire 'coffee' genre. An ace in the kitchen, he creates dishes to pair with his wine, sometimes on camera.

Pinotage ★★★☆ **18** ⑧③ will no doubt prove as popular as its predecessors (**17** sold out untasted) with its mocha, toffee & cherry liqueur aromas, juicy plum & mulberry flavours. Freshness, moderate alcohol ensure food compatibility. Discontinued: **Chardonnay**. — JG

Location/WO: Robertson ▪ Est/1stB 2009 ▪ Closed to public ▪ Owner(s) Vinimark ▪ Winemaker(s) Bertus Fourie ▪ 750t/100,000cs own label ▪ PO Box 6223 Paarl 7620 ▪ info@vinimark.co.za ▪ www.baristawine.co.za ▪ F +27 (0)21-886-4708 ▪ **T +27 (0)21-883-8043**

Barnardt Boyes Wines

Stellenbosch-based global wine distribution business Barnardt Boyes is part of a diverse group, including luxury goods manufacturer Carrol Boyes Functional Art and citrus exporter FruitOne. More specifically, it is a collaboration between two university friends: John Boyes, FruitOne director (and Carrol's brother), and Neels Barnardt, wine industry veteran. Carrol's own wine brand, Carrol Boyes Collection, is listed separately.

Dorp Street range (NEW)

Cabernet Sauvignon ⊘ ★★★ Appealing **16** (81), quite serious dark-fruit aromas, yet flavours are easy-going, fruity, with smoky twirl. Range celebrates 'historic, oak-hugged' Stellenbosch avenue. **Sauvignon Blanc** ★★ Naturally fermented **17** (76), no mistaking the variety: grassy & zippy, brush of oak gives some palate weight for food pairing. — WB, CvZ

Location/WO: Stellenbosch ▪ Est 2012 ▪ 1stB 2009 ▪ Closed to public ▪ Owner(s) N Barnardt & J Boyes ▪ Winemaker(s) Hendrik Snyman (Jun 2013) ▪ 50,000cs own label 50% red 50% white ▪ Other export brands: Carrol Boyes Collection, Dorp Street Wine ▪ neels@barnardtboyes.com ▪ www.barnardtboyes.com ▪ F +27 (0)21-883-3491 ▪ **T +27 (0)21-883-3447**

☐ **Baron Diego** see Govert Wines
☐ **Barony** see Rosendal Wines
☐ **Barrel Selection 008** see Imbuko Wines

Barrydale Winery & Distillery (Ⓠ) (Ⓨ) (ⓞ)

Owned by Southern Cape Vineyards, Barrydale Winery & Distillery has become a popular stop on sight-seer-friendly Route 62 at Barrydale town. Here winemaker Jandre Human has diversified into craft brewing, noting that the Barry Ale and Lady Lager 'partner perfectly with the home-made pizza from our restaurant'.

Southern Cape Vineyards range

Shiraz (Ⓩ) ★★★ Brims with berries & cherries, **16** (80) soft & juicy for easy drinking (easy on the wallet, too). **Ruby Cabernet-Merlot** (Ⓩ) ★★ Plummy merlot (20%) apparent on **17** (74)'s nose, not so much on the palate, which is rather stern, with sour cherry character. **Chardonnay** ⊘ ★★★ Unoaked **18** (82) is very smooth, subtle ginger & turmeric adding spice to zesty tangerine & citrus. **Chenin Blanc** ⊘ ★★★ White peach, guava & tangy tangerine on **18** (80), with modest alcohol for uncomplicated summer refreshment. **Sauvignon Blanc** ⊘ ★★★ Easy-drinking **18** (81) shows textbook greenpepper on nose, lime on palate, zesty & balanced at 12.5% alcohol.

Cape Brandy range

★★★★ **Joseph Barry VSOP** (Ⓩ) Deep gold colour & more power than VS: deeper, richer flavours of dried fruit, caramel & hazelnuts, the palate full & rounded. 5 year old potstill. From colombard & ugni blanc, as all in the range.

★★★★☆ **Joseph Barry XO** (Ⓩ) Special blend from a single batch of 10 year old potstill, especially handsomely packaged. Rich & dark, characterful & rounded, showing lovely complexity. Notes of plum compote, spicy nuts & vanilla linger on the long & pliable finish. 40% alcohol, as all.

★★★★ **Ladismith Klein Karoo 8 Year Old** (Ⓩ) Light gold in colour, mellow flavours of baked fruit, dusty Karoo scrub, pot-pourri & dried herbs. Smooth & delicate to the last chocolaty drop. 100% potstill.

Joseph Barry VS (Ⓩ) ★★★☆ Produced in locally traditional Woudberg copper stills, as all in the range, lightest amber colour, light footed, fresh & fruity, with pear drop, hints of nuts & chocolate. 100% potstill, oak aged 3 years. — JG, WB

Location: Barrydale ▪ Map: Klein Karoo & Garden Route ▪ Map grid reference: C7 ▪ WO: Klein Karoo ▪ Est 1941 ▪ 1stB 1976 ▪ Tasting & sales Tue-Fri 9—5 Sat 9—4 Sun 9-3 ▪ Fee R25 for groups of 5+ ▪ Closed Easter Fri-Mon, Dec 25/26 & Jan 1 ▪ Restaurant ▪ Craft beer brewery ▪ Owner(s) Southern Cape Vineyards (SCV) ▪ Winemaker(s) Jandre Human ▪ ±110ha (cab, merlot, shiraz, chard, cbard, sauv) ▪ 28% red 72% white ▪ PO Box 56 Ladismith 6655 ▪ accounts@scv.co.za ▪ www.barrydalewines.co.za ▪ S 33° 54' 35.83" E 020° 42' 45.20" ▪ ⟐ unlock.playground.subscriptions ▪ **T +27 (0)28-572-1012**

Barry Gould Family Wines (Ⓠ) (Ⓨ) (ⓐ) (ⓞ) (ⓐ)

'Natural' has been the approach of architect Barry Gould and family since they began growing wine on a small scale sixteen years ago, and the tempo of releases from their Elgin base has been unhurried to say the least - '08 is the current vintage, and '09 is due only on its 10th birthday. Visitor facilities, as might be expected, are rooted in farm life, and include a country house, walking trails and fresh produce.

A Simple Red (Ⓩ) ★★★ Wild-yeast-fermented cab & merlot (50/50), **08** (81) perfumed blackcurrant & soft vanilla; finishes tad warm (15% alcohol) but overall is appealing, simple in a good way. — WB

Location/map/WO: Elgin ▪ Map grid reference: D2 ▪ Est 2003 ▪ 1stB 2004 ▪ Tasting & sales by appt ▪ Closed
Good Fri, Dec 25 & Jan 1 ▪ Meals/functions by arrangement (up to 20 pax) ▪ Wildekrans Country House
(B&B) + self-catering cottage ▪ Child-friendly ▪ Gifts ▪ Farm produce ▪ Conference venue (20 pax) ▪ 4-day
fully guided slack-packing trail ▪ Owner(s) Barry Gould & Alison Green ▪ Cellarmaster(s) Barry Gould (2003)
▪ Winemaker(s) Barry Gould (2003), with family (2004) ▪ Viticulturist(s) Grapes bought in ▪ 50cs own
label 100% red ▪ PO Box 7 Elgin 7180 ▪ barry@barrygould.co.za ▪ S 34° 12' 12.7" E 019° 8' 53.6" ▪ 🚗 reduce.
explicated.conclude ▪ F +27 (0)21-848-9788 ▪ **T +27 (0)21-848-9788/+27 (0)82-901-4896**

Bartho Eksteen

At Attaquaskloof, the Eksteen family farm in Hemel-en-Aarde Valley near Hermanus, veteran winemaker
Bartho Eksteen has a two-tier business model: crafting wines of the best possible quality (assisted by
son Pieter Willem) and running an academy for young winemakers and distillers (see Wijnskool, listed
separately), which explains why most wines have a 'school' theme. Proud member of the prestigious Cape
Winemakers Guild since 2011, and even prouder ambassador of Afrikaans (hence all labels printed in his
mother tongue), Bartho's favoured cultivar is sauvignon blanc but his 'big love' is blending. A new cellar,
exclusively for grapes from the farm and Wijnskool projects, was on track for harvest 2019 at print time.

CWG Auction Reserves

★★★★ **Professore** (NEW) Probable world first: Cape Blend of 3 SA crosses, pinotage, roobernet & white
grape nouvelle (70/20/10) honouring the pair of academics, Abraham Perold & Chris Orffer, who created
them. **16** (88) ripe plum & cherry core with forest floor & green herbal notes.

★★★★☆ **Vloekskoot** (🍷) Sauvignon blanc, dry yet evocative of syrupy pineapple rings in cream, **17**
(94) with 14% semillon, fermented/10 months old 500L oak, dense mouthfeel balanced by bright acidity,
grapefruit lingering on finish.

Flagship range

★★★★☆ **Groepsdruk** The best barrel (new French) of **16** (91) Ouskool has 13% each mourvèdre &
grenache plus dash viognier to spice up syrah's intense black & red cherry/berry fruit. Floral, herbal &
meaty notes, fresh acidity balancing 14.5% alcohol. WO W Cape.

★★★★☆ **Houtskool** (🍷) Elegant wooded sauvignon, **17 ★★★★★** (95) less alcohol (under 13%) than
CWG sibling, splash semillon contributing to orange/lime citrus verve, 10 months older oak providing
lemon curd creaminess. Gorgeous concentration, great balance, persistent finish. Follows fine **16** (93).

Signature range

★★★★ **Ouskool** Rhône-style red has violet & pepper aromas leading to tangy red fruit on palate, **16** (89)
nicely rounded, with subtle baking spices after 21 months new French oak. WO W Cape, as Blom & Dom.

★★★★☆ **Blom** (🍷) Raises bar for SA pink wine, deliciously dry, fresh, Provence-inspired **18** (93) from
46% grenache with syrah, mourvèdre, viognier. Fynbos, pepper & savoury edge to apricot, strawberry &
crunchy red-apple fruit. Also in magnum, as Ouskool.

★★★★ **Meester** A less forthright sauvignon than Houtskool, **17** (88) intense lime, gooseberry & passionfruit flavours, 7% wooded semillon smoothing the palate, toning down mouthwatering acidity.

★★★★☆ **Dom** (🍷) Latest NV (94) méthode cap classique sparkling, equal pinot noir & chardonnay plus
4% meunier, elegant & complex, apple Danish & marzipan richness balancing fresh citrus fruit, pinpoint
bubbles persisting as long as steely-clean finish.

★★★★☆ **Soetmuis** (🍷) Natural Sweet from old-vine Paarl chenin, unwooded. **15** (90) like a walk in a
spring meadow: delicate, sweet-scented, the perfumes turning mineral on complex palate with underlying
creaminess to the rich bouquet of flavours. Minuscule 50-case production.— JG

Location: Hermanus ▪ Map: Walker Bay & Bot River ▪ Map grid reference: A3 ▪ WO: Upper Hemel-en-Aarde
Valley/Western Cape/Paarl ▪ Est/1stB 2015 ▪ Tasting & sales Mon-Sat 10-4 (subject to change) ▪ Closed Good
Fri, Dec 16/25 & Jan 1 ▪ Cellar tours by appt ▪ Meals by prior arrangement ▪ Conferences ▪ Functions & events
▪ MTB ▪ Historic building ▪ Owner(s) Eksteen family ▪ Winemaker(s) Bartho Eksteen (Jan 2015), with Pieter
Willem Eksteen (Jan 2015, assistant) ▪ Viticulturist(s) various ▪ 5ha total ▪ 4,540cs own label 34% red 37%
white 19% rosé 10% MCC ▪ PO Box 1999 Hermanus 7200 ▪ bartho@hermanus.co.za, sune@hermanus.co.za ▪

www.wijnskool-academy.co.za ▪ S 34° 23' 57.31" E 019° 13' 1.17" ▪ ⌨ founds.siding.evicted ▪ F +27 (0)86-554-0896 ▪ T +27 (0)82-920-7108 (Bartho), +27 (0)72-323-5060 (Suné)

Bartinney Private Cellar

The visitor offering at Michael and Rose Jordaan's vertiginous patch of heaven, high in Banhoek Valley just over the brow of the Helshoogte Pass outside Stellenbosch, continues to improve, with luxury vineyard guest cottages recently added. The trail-running and MTB tracks are personally scoped (and often maintained) by Rose herself, and she simultaneously collects indigenous fynbos for the aromatic component of her latest project, a 'seasonal' craft gin named The Tempest. The fynbos and botanical theme continues at the tasting venue, where visitors are encouraged to crush and smell plant cuttings as they sample the wines of widely experienced consultant Ronell Wiid, who's delighted to be involved in both distilling and winemaking.

Reserve range

★★★★☆ **Skyfall Cabernet Sauvignon** ⓐ Bolder than Bartinney sibling yet **14** ⑨③ elegant, refined, perhaps even tad demure on finish. Seductive Xmas pudding, cherry & tobacco on structured, firm & complex palate, fruit well-framed by oak, 18 months, 80% new French. Needs time.

★★★★☆ **Hourglass Chardonnay** ⓐ Special fruit selection from favoured high vineyard. Firm & svelte, **17** ⑨③ has yet to show its true colours, the vibrant lime flavours & creamy French oak (half new, 11 months) still at the tango-dancing stage, marriage & blissful harmony inevitable but a way off.

Bartinney range

★★★★★ **Cabernet Sauvignon** ⊘ ⓐ Inky, graphite-toned black fruit on **15** ⑨⑤ shows deep intensity & refinement, tiny berry size contributing to exceptional concentration. Oak, 18 months, half new French, just one of many complex layers, all wonderfully defined & persistent.

★★★★☆ **Elevage** Cab & petit verdot share near-equal billing in spicy, dry mouthful with merlot. **12** ⑨② blackcurrant notes temper firm grip from 50% new French oak, 12- 18 months. Certain to age well for years. Stellenbosch WO.

★★★★☆ **Chardonnay** ⓐ Mandarin brightness with butter & caramel oak notes on **17** ⑨③. Vivid, vibrant & fresh, with spice highlights & rounded richness from 11 months in French wood, ramped to 50% new from 33% on **16** ⑨④. Approachable, but so much better in a few years.

★★★★ **Sauvignon Blanc** Trademark vivacity & pineapple-citrus appeal in **18** ★★★★ ⑧⑤. Balanced & lively, with broad lees appeal. Tasted pre-bottling, like **17** ⑧⑦.— FM

Location/map: Stellenbosch ▪ Map grid reference: H5 ▪ WO: Banghoek/Stellenbosch ▪ Est 2006 ▪ 1stB 2008 ▪ Tasting & sales Mon-Thu 12-5 Fri 12-8 ▪ Wine & tapas Fri 12-8 Sat 10-3 ▪ Closed Dec 25/26 & Jan 1 ▪ Cellar tours by appt ▪ Bartinney Wine & Champagne Bar Mon-Sat 11.30-9 (T +27 (0)76-348-5374, 5 Bird Str Stellenbosch) ▪ MTB trails ▪ Annual trail run events ▪ Monthly live music events ▪ Vineyard guest cottages ▪ Craft beer & gin ▪ Owner(s) Rose & Michael Jordaan ▪ Winemaker(s) Ronell Wiid (consultant) ▪ Viticulturist(s) Logan Jooste (Jun 2017) ▪ 27ha/±17ha (cab, chard, sauv) ▪ 100t/4,000cs own label 70% red 30% white ▪ WWF-SA Conservation Champion ▪ Postnet Suite 231 Private Bag X5061 Stellenbosch 7599 ▪ info@bartinney.co.za, tastingshed@bartinney.co.za ▪ www.bartinney.co.za ▪ S 33° 55' 34.66" E 018° 55' 56.79" ▪ ⌨ logs.twisting.unscrew ▪ F +27 (0)86-298-0447 ▪ T +27 (0)21-885-1013

Barton Vineyards

The hectares of vineyard on this family estate in the Walker Bay district, between the towns of Bot River and Hermanus, are outnumbered by those conserving the region's biodiversity. There are also many devoted to olives and lavender, as well as guest accommodation. From 2018, the restrained, elegant styling of the wines is in the experienced hands of Villion Family Wines' Kobie Viljoen, who's leasing the cellar and acting as consultant winemaker for Barton.

★★★★ **Merlot** ⓠ Typical fruitcake, chocolate aromas & dry herbal twist on **15** ⑧⑧. Light-fruited sweetness (but dry enough finish). Oaking supportive (30% new). Tannins assertive, but a pleasing whole.

★★★★ **Winemakers Reserve** ⓠ Cedar, cigarbox, berry fruit on **14** ⑧⑦ blend 57% merlot with cab, malbec. Complete, balanced, even rather elegant. Should mature good few years. Walker Bay WO.

★★★★ **Shiraz-Cabernet Sauvignon** ⓠ With 70% shiraz, **12** ★★★★ ⑧④ combines sweet, juicy fruit with spicy savoury notes & same herbal edge as **11** ⑧⑥. Time to go, but big tannins won't go away.

Rouge ★★★ Blend shift for **16** (82), now merlot-led with cab & mourvèdre. But ripe, restrained & deftly structured as usual. Drinking well, but no hurry. Walker Bay WO, as next. **Pinot Noir Rosé ★★★** Customary notes of raspberry with earthy hint on dry, salmon pink **18** (82). Soft texture, but a good acid bite for freshness. **Chenin Blanc** (Ⓠ) **★★★★** Forward, fruity & friendly aromas & flavours (mostly tending to the tropical side of things) on **17** (84). It's juicy & impeccably balanced, with some real substance to it. Drinkable as ever. **Sauvignon Blanc** (Ⓠ) **★★★** Easygoing, dry, fresh & lively **17** (80) with light tropical flavours & aromas that are forthcoming but not gushing. Discontinued: **Sauvignon Blanc-Semillon.** — TJ

Location: Bot River ▪ Map: Walker Bay & Bot River ▪ Map grid reference: B2 ▪ WO: Bot River/Walker Bay ▪ Est 2001 ▪ 1stB 2003 ▪ Tasting, sales & cellar tours Mon-Fri 9–5 Sat 10–4 ▪ Closed Easter Fri/Mon, Dec 25/26 & Jan 1 ▪ Lavender products, olive oil ▪ Barton Villas ▪ Owner(s) Annie & Suzy Neill ▪ Cellarmaster(s)/winemaker(s) Kobie Viljoen (Jan 2018, consultant) ▪ Viticulturist(s) consultants ▪ 200ha/30ha (cab, malbec, merlot, mourv, pinot, shiraz, chenin, sauv, sem) ▪ 120t/20,000cs own label 40% red 50% white 10% rosé ▪ IPW ▪ PO Box 100 Bot River 7185 ▪ info@bartonvineyards.co.za ▪ www.bartonvineyards.co.za ▪ S 34° 15' 43.8" E 019° 10' 29.2" ▪ ⓕ bracing.pick.ogled ▪ F +27 (0)28-284-9776 ▪ **T +27 (0)28-284-9283**

Bayede!   (Ⓠ)

Bayede! is the traditional greeting reserved for the Zulu king. The bead-adorned wines, sourced from top producers, are integral to what's believed to be one of Africa's first royal-signature 'by appointment' brands. It's focused on enterprise development, job creation and promotion of various industry sectors. Recent successes include further SAA listings and a Nederburg Auction selection for the 7 Icon Chardonnay.

7 Icon Wines

★★★★ Cabernet Sauvignon (Ⓠ) Shows great composure & elegance it its restrained lines, persistent length. **11 ★★★★★** (92) ready, but no rush. Follows cedar-scented **09** (86). WO Stellenbosch, as next two.

★★★★ Merlot (Ⓠ) Lively dark fruit, rich fruitcake & spice on mellow, made-for-food **15** (88). Well structured, silky, with savoury farewell from French oaking, quarter new.

★★★★ Pinotage Reserve (Ⓠ) Vibrant plum & mulberry, earthy nuance on **15** (87). Juicy, abundant fruit mingles with supple tannins & oak spice (33% new). Drinking well, could age few years.

★★★★ Shiraz (Ⓠ) A step up from **11 ★★★** (81), offering bramble fruit, spicy cured meat flavours & fragrant pot-pourri. **14** (87) good balance & typicity, long, dry savoury finish. WO Coastal. No **13**.

★★★★ Chardonnay (Ⓠ) Well-judged & -crafted **16** (87) baked apple & crème brûlée richness & subtle vanilla (just 10% new oak). Palate smooth & broad, balanced, a delicate sweet spice in farewell.

★★★★ Chenin Blanc (Ⓠ) Wonderful expression of white stonefruit with balanced acidity, judicious old oak. **15** (87) markedly dry & precise, persistent & savoury. **14** untasted. Stellenbosch WO.

Sauvignon Blanc (Ⓠ) **★★★★** Fruit-filled **13** (84) has pleasant pithy texture, satisfying weight & good length. Decant, so brimstone whiffs can blow off.

King Shaka-Zulu range (NEW)

Pinotage ★★★ Spirited berries, cocoa & gently firm tannins in quaffable unoaked **16** (79). **Chenin Blanc ★★★** Playful & effortless **17** (80), lively pineapple, crunchy apple & granadilla on a creamy palate.

King & Queen range

King Goodwill Shiraz ★★★ Aromas of blackberry & mulberry, notes of liquorice, leather, **15** (81) mellow & smooth, drinks well now. **King Goodwill Jubilee ★★★** Fruit forward, juicy & succulent Bordeaux blend from cab, merlot, petit verdot, **16** (81) smoky, savoury aftertaste. **Queen Nandi Méthode Cap Classique Brut Rosé ★★★★** Vibrant pink dry sparkling, **16** (84) fragrant strawberry & baked apple, smooth & persistent mousse, lifted citrus finale to generous flavours. Darling WO.

Prince range

Cabernet Sauvignon ★★★ Ups the quality in **17** (81), crunchy cranberry exit after rounded black fruit flavours, brush of oak, touch of mocha. **Merlot ★★★** Mellow, for easy drinking, **17** (78) also has a gentle plum & spice piquancy. **Pinotage** (Ⓠ) **★★★** Dark, dusty chocolate-dipped plums with mocha notes for smooth everyday sipping in **16** (81). **Sauvignon Blanc ★★★** Greengage, cut grass & capsicum flavours, pleasantly light **18** (81)'s sippability assisted by few grams sugar. Discontinued: **Red.**

Princess range

Chardonnay-Pinot Noir ★★★ Dry rosé with delicate pink hue, the colour & red berries courtesy **18** ⑧①'s 6% pinot noir component, the citrus finish from chardonnay. — WB

Location/map: Paarl ▪ Map grid reference: E6 ▪ WO: Robertson/Stellenbosch/Western Cape/Coastal/Darling ▪ Est 2009 ▪ Tasting & sales in showroom/office at 5 Stasie Str Southern Paarl Mon-Fri or by appt ▪ Fee R30 ▪ Private VIP tastings at Villa Beanto Winelands Estate by appt only ▪ Closed all pub hols ▪ Tour groups by appt ▪ 60% red 30% white 10% rosé ▪ PO Box 7362 Northern Paarl 7623 ▪ anto@bayede.co.za ▪ www.bayede.co.za ▪ S 33° 45' 54.77" E 018° 57' 41.03" ▪ ⌘ internal.avocado.reserved ▪ F +27 (0)86-610-0479 ▪ T +27 (0)21-863-3406/+27 (0)83-650-3585

☐ **Bayten** see Buitenverwachting
☐ **BC Wines** see Brandvlei Cellar
☐ **Beachhouse** see Douglas Green

Beau Constantia ⓆⓋ◎

The success of on-site restaurant Chef's Warehouse at Beau Constantia has seen an increase in visitors to the Du Preez-family-owned boutique winery atop Constantia Nek Pass. While production of the handcrafted, estate-grown wines remains 'modest', the Pas De Nom lifestyle range (exclusively available from the cellar-door and not reviewed this edition) has expanded to cater for rising demand. Visitors can now also taste a range of spirits made with Guy Munton Private Artisanal Distiller. Like the wines, the Gin, Amber Vodka and Cape Vodka are named for family members.

★★★★☆ **Stella** ⓐ Heady floral, berry & white pepper aromas, dark, concentrated, succulent fruit from best 4 barrels of syrah (50% new, mostly 2nd-fill French), 25% bunch-fermented, in cellarworthy **16** ⑨②.

★★★★ **Lucca** Luscious plum fruit, hints of dark mint chocolate & aniseed in **15** ⑧⑧, 70/30 blend of merlot & cab franc, well knit after 18 months 35% new oak, alcohol slightly warming though.

★★★★ **Aidan** 49% shiraz asserts dominance over petit verdot, malbec & cab in **15** ⑧⑨ with floral perfume (lavender, violet) & white pepper lifting black cherry & mulberry fruit. Same oak as Lucca.

★★★★ **Cecily** Viognier, aptly named for 'graceful' Du Preez matriarch, **17** ⑧⑨ smooth, rich, refined, orange blossom & orange stonefruit framed by delicate spice of creamy oak (8 months, 20% new).

★★★★☆ **Pierre** Naturally vinified from minuscule yields of sauvignon & 11% semillon, vibrant **17** ⑨⓪ redolent of Granny Smith apple, passionfruit & lime, piercing 8 g/l acidity offset by rich lanolin smoothness from 8 months in oak (22% new).— JG

Location/WO: Constantia ▪ Map: Cape Peninsula ▪ Map grid reference: B3 ▪ Est 2003 ▪ 1stB 2010 ▪ Tasting & sales Tue-Sun 11-6 ▪ Fee R55, waved according to purchase ▪ Closed Good Fri, Dec 25/26 & Jan 1 ▪ Amphitheatre for concerts & outdoor events ▪ Chef's Warehouse ▪ Beau Constantia spirits (gin & vodka) available in tasting room ▪ Owner(s) Apostax (Pty) Ltd ▪ Winemaker(s) Justin van Wyk (Sep 2010) ▪ Viticulturist(s) Ewald Heyns (May 2015, farm manager) ▪ 22ha/±11ha (cabs s/f, malbec, merlot, p verdot, shiraz, sauv, sem, viog) ▪ 40t/4,000cs own label 80% red 20% white ▪ 1043 Constantia Main Rd Constantia 7806 ▪ winesales@beauconstantia.com ▪ www.beauconstantia.com ▪ S 34° 0' 48.57" E 018° 24' 21.67" ▪ ⌘ praises.wheeze.uninvolved ▪ F +27 (0)21-794-0534 ▪ T +27 (0)21-794-8632

Beau Joubert Wines Ⓠ

One of few US-SA ventures locally, Beau Joubert is owned by longtime MD Andrew Hilliard, joined by Christian Kuun, equally stalwart winemaker and Robert Carter, heading global sales. Grapes are sourced around home base in Stellenbosch's Polkadraai Hills and Breedekloof, and while the focus is on international markets, local winelovers are welcome for a tasting by appointment.

Beau Joubert range

★★★★ **Cabernet Sauvignon** Ⓠ First reviewed since **10** ★★★★ ⑧③, **13** ⑧⑦ reaps reward of time in bottle. Intense cassis, cedar & graphite notes, dark fruit backed up by firm but rounded tannin structure.

★★★★ **Shiraz** Ⓠ Coconut & vanilla on entry with generous sour cherry, bramble & spice, **13** ⑧⑦'s powdery tannins supported by oak (25% new). Step up on last-tasted **11** ★★★ ⑧②.

★★★★ **Ambassador** ⓐ Cab franc (61%), merlot & splash cab in fine **13** ⑧⑦ Stellenbosch ambassador, with taut tannic backbone supporting bright blackberry fruit, which soaks up 2 years in new oak.

Old Vine Chenin Blanc ⓐ ★★★★ Delicate honeysuckle & peach, lipsmacking freshness, hint oak, beautiful fantail finish make for satisfying, elegant sipping in **16** ⑧④ ex Breedekloof. **Fat Pig** ⓐ ★★★★ Nimble & relatively light-bodied 'port' from shiraz at just 16.5% alcohol, **12** ⑧③ savoury clove spice notes & sweet red fruit, pleasant tannic farewell. Not tasted: **Christmas Cabernet**, **Sauvignon Blanc**, **Vintage Méthode Cap Classique Pinot Noir Brut**.

Oak Lane range

Merlot-Cabernet Sauvignon ⓐ ★★★ Eminently drinkable blend, dry tannin supporting big, ripe black fruit flavours; **15** ⑧① easy & likeable. **Shiraz-Cabernet Sauvignon** ⓐ ★★★ Spicy, ripe-fruited sipper with enough substance for food & character for solo; brush older oak on bargain-priced **15** ⑧①. **Chenin Blanc-Sauvignon Blanc** ⓐ ★★★ Tropical melange thanks to chenin taking lead (85%) in easy-drinking **17** ⑦⑧. Bouncy acidity, lively finish; ready for summer. — HC

Location: Stellenbosch ▪ WO: Stellenbosch/Breedekloof ▪ Est 1695 ▪ 1stB 2000 ▪ Tasting by appt only ▪ Owner(s) Andrew Hilliard (MD), Robert Carter (global sales) & Christian Kuun ▪ Cellarmaster(s)/winemaker(s) Christian Kuun (Dec 2006) ▪ PO Box 1114 Stellenbosch 7599 ▪ andrew@beaujoubert.com ▪ www.beaujoubert.com ▪ ⬚ bounded.insect.standard ▪ F +27 (0)21-881-3377 ▪ **T +27 (0)21-881-3103**

Beaumont Family Wines   ⓐ ⑪ ⌂ ◎ ⓑ

The Beaumont's farm in Bot River was established around 1750. Wine featured from the 1940s but had been discontinued by the time Jayne and Raoul Beaumont bought Compagnes Drift in 1974. They replanted the vineyards, but only in 1994 did Jayne produce the first wine under the family name in the refurbished old cellar. It's a welcoming, friendly family farm, where innovation coexists with the consistency that prime mover Sebastian Beaumont insists on. Most recently, a new tasting room has been opened, 'in the heart of the winery'. Outside, amongst other plantings, is a new dryland bushvine vineyard of mourvèdre, syrah and grenache, prompted by threats of climate change. 'The Kin' wineclub (see the website) allows fans access to 'very limited bottlings of niche wines'.

★★★★☆ **CWG Auction Reserve Whole Bunch Mourvèdre** ⓃⒺⓌ ⓐ First - successful! - experiment with 100% bunch ferment on variety, single barrel destined for 2018 auction. Rich **16** ⑨③, full-fruited but sappy freshness energises & keeps it crisply focused. 16 months seasoned wood. Unusual; will secure rarity prices.

★★★★ **Mourvèdre** A favourite grape here, deliciously different. Toned athletic body of terrific **15** ★★★★☆ ⑨⓪ supports polished black berry fruit with layers of allure. 3 years in oak (10% new) vs 2 for **14** ⑧⑧, yet latter is the more savoury.

★★★★ **Pinotage** Understated, carries the gravitas of old vines with a light touch. Previewed **16** ⑧⑥'s fragrant plummy features calmed by 15% new oak; crunchy tannins call for food.

★★★★ **Dangerfield Syrah** Dark fruit in velvety tannins but **16** ★★★★☆ ⑨⓪ more supple, not as overtly peppery as **15** ⑧⑨. 'A new style': 30% wholebunch in open vats, then less oak (15% new, 16 months). Also in 1.5 & 3L.

★★★★☆ **Ariane** Bordeaux blend named for founders Jayne & Raoul Beaumont's daughter. Brother Sebastian's self-declared 'best-yet' vintage is elegantly styled, has a 'cool' cabernet linearity, the antithesis of plush. **16** ⑨⓪ demands & deserves time in your cellar to meld. 20 months oak, 22% new.

★★★★☆ **Vitruvian** ⓐ Eclectic mourvèdre-led (30%) harmonious blend with cab franc, pinotage, syrah & petit verdot in beautiful **15** ⑨③. Fragrant red berry fruit intensity is leavened by savoury & spicy flavours with sleek, well-tailored tannins; the different components ensure a unique experience.

★★★★★ **Hope Marguerite** ⓐ ⓦ Serial accolades for scintillating rendition of chenin ex 40 year old vines. **17** ⑨⑤ retains accustomed classic style; layered with tropical fruit, fleshed out by creamy oatmeal from deft oaking (year in 20% new barrels), yet wonderfully restrained & elegant. Also in magnum, like New Baby.

★★★★ **Chenin Blanc** 'Baby' of cellar's chenins, but **18** ⑧⑦ packed with pure melon & peach flavours given zip by crisp green-apple acid. Unoaked & full of zest, will delight with peri-peri chicken.

★★★★☆ **New Baby** (&) New-wave chenin-based white (with sauvignon, semillon, chardonnay & colombard). **17** (93) bouncy summer-salad fruit tempered by grassy herb interest & stony minerality, fine texture.

★★★★ **Goutte d'Or** Noble Late Harvest chenin, old-barrel fermented/matured. Second consecutive tiny drought harvest, yet **17** (89) preview rich & opulent as ever, botrytis-brushed pineapple with tangerine twist, tad more sugar (103 g/l) than tighter **16** ★★★★☆ (92) (86 g/l). 375 ml, as next 2.

★★★★☆ **Cape Vintage Foot Stomped** 'Port' from equal tinta & pinotage. Rich **16** (90) ex tank mid-2018 laden with moist fruitcake supported by clean spirit. Very youthful & primary still. In delightfully drier spectrum (71 g/l sugar) like **15** (91) (65 g/l).

★★★★★ **Starboard Dessert Wine** (Ⓥ) 5 vintages of Cape Vintage become a **NV** (99) named thus, absent an official SA 'port' category for a multi-vintage bottling. The result - our magnificent, inaugural Fortified Wine of the Year. Leftovers of wines between 2005 & 2011 blended in a delicious, mature tipple redolent of dried fruit & nuts, drawing rooms & leather couches.

Constable House ★★★☆ Aims at easy drinking, succeeds in over-delivering. Pre-bottled **16** (83) shiraz, cab & tinta blends fruit & charm with enough grip & older oak to add gravitas. Magnums a sure-fire party pack. In abeyance: **R&B, Leo's Whole Bunch Chenin Blanc, Chenin Blanc Demi-Sec.** — DS

Location/WO: Bot River • Map: Walker Bay & Bot River • Map grid reference: C2 • Est 1750 • 1stB 1994 • Tasting & sales Mon-Fri 9.30–4.30 Sat 10–3 • Tasting fee R4opp • Closed Dec 25/26 & Jan 1 • Platters & pre-booked picnic baskets • Farm produce • Walking/hiking trails • Conservation area • 250 year old watermill • Art/jewellery exhibits • 2 historic self-catering guest cottages • Owner(s) Beaumont family • Winemaker(s) Sebastian Beaumont (Jun 2003) • Viticulturist(s) Sebastian Beaumont (Jun 1999) • 500ha/31ha (mourv, ptage, shiraz, chenin) • 150t/20,000cs own label 40% red 60% white • IPW • PO Box 3 Bot River 7185 • info@beaumont.co.za • www.beaumont.co.za • S 34° 13' 27.2" E 019° 12' 24.9" • 🌐 advanced.textiles.telegrams • **T +27 (0)28-284-9194**

Beeslaar Wines

Few are doing more for the international reputation and prestige of pinotage than Abrie Beeslaar. Well-known British critic Tim Atkin thinks that the variety's current claim to make great wines is 'largely based on the achievements of one man' – Beeslaar - for this, his own label, and for the top pinotages from Kanonkop, where Abrie is winemaker. Stellenbosch is the source for all these wines, with the eponymous one coming from a single vineyard with shale soils, unlike the decomposed granite of Kanonkop.

★★★★★ **Pinotage** (&) Ripe & rich, but **16** (95) refined enough to make the 14.5% alcohol a surprise, so balanced it is. Plenty of sweet fruit (dark cherries, raspberries) & velvet texture, with tannins molten & soft, though informing, & good acidity. 50% new oak well integrated. **15** ★★★★★ (93) as ageworthy.— TJ

Location/WO: Stellenbosch • Est 2011 • 1stB 2012 • Closed to public • Owner(s) Abrie & Jeanne Beeslaar • Cellarmaster(s)/winemaker(s) Abrie Beeslaar (Jul 2011) • Viticulturist(s) Abrie Beeslaar • 8t/750cs own label 100% red • PO Box 93 Elsenburg 7607 • info@beeslaar.co.za • www.beeslaar.co.za • F +27 (0)86-595-9424 • **T +27 (0)83-663-3256/+27 (0)84-255-8686**

Bein Wine Cellar   (Ⓥ)

Luca and Ingrid Bein farm their thumbnail merlot vineyard in Stellenbosch's Polkadraai Hills with Swiss precision. Qualified oenologists, they employ the latest technology (satellite data, drone monitoring, hi-tech irrigation). Former veterinarians, they also embrace the natural in both viti- and viniculture (including runner ducks on pest patrol).

★★★★☆ **Merlot** Flagship wine a blend of vineyard parcels. Drought concentrated **16** (90) but 30% new oak ensures lovely balance & supports the focused flavours & elegant structure. Smooth & tempting, like **15** (94), but will age. Heft from splash petit verdot ex neighbours, as other reds. Also in 375 ml.

★★★★☆ **Merlot Reserve** Only best vintages, from vines identified by aerial imaging as part of 'precision viticulture'. **16** (92) more intense & tannic than siblings but well structured & managed, deserves cellaring 6-8 years. All-new oak 22 months.

Little Merlot ★★★ From the more vigorous vines, emphasising fruitiness - mulberry & cranberry in **17** (82). Easy to like, though 14.3% alcohol not so 'little'. Year old oak. **Pink Merlot** ★★★☆ Rosé from lusher parts of block picked early to capture strawberry fruit without sweetness. **18** ⟨84⟩ gutsy, dry & spicy, with usual - unconventional - dash hanepoot. Not tasted: **Merlot Forte**. — DS

Location/map/WO: Stellenbosch ▪ Map grid reference: B6 ▪ Est/1stB 2002 ▪ Tasting, sales & cellar tours Mon-Sat by appt only ▪ Owner(s)/cellarmaster(s)/winemaker(s) Luca & Ingrid Bein ▪ Viticulturist(s) Luca Bein ▪ 3ha/2ha (merlot) ▪ 16t/2,400cs own label 80% red 20% rosé ▪ IPW ▪ PO Box 3408 Matieland 7602 ▪ lib@beinwine.com ▪ www.beinwine.com ▪ S 33° 57′ 40.10″ E 018° 44′ 13.30 ▪ ⌖ obsession.plumbed.southward ▪ **T +27 (0)21-881-3025**

Belfield Wines

A sad year at Belfield, with the sudden passing of co-owner/founder Mike Kreft, his family expressing gratitude for 'the incredible love and support' of the Elgin community. Mike and wife Mel transformed an old pear orchard into a reputed boutique vineyard and cellar, with accommodation in a verdant setting. The 2018 vintage is gestating under the wing of winemaker Gavin Patterson, while the wine brand is in the hands of Mike's son and daughter, Allister and Jenna, and Mel looks after the cottages.

★★★★ **Magnifica** ⟨Ⓩ⟩ Cab with dashes cab franc & merlot, **15** ⟨86⟩ commanding tannins, primary dark fruit & tapenade savouriness that merge well with graphite minerality, cigarbox & spice ex 22% new oak.

★★★★ **Aristata** ⟨Ⓩ⟩ Merlot with dabs of the two cabs, **14** ⟨87⟩ luscious berry, violet & nutmeg spice. Generous & soft tannins, dark fruits & cocoa conclusion. Gentle oak, 14 % new.

Not tasted: **Syrah, Rosé Cabernet Sauvignon**. — GM

Location/map/WO: Elgin ▪ Map grid reference: B2 ▪ Est 2000 ▪ 1stB 2005 ▪ Tasting, sales & tours by appt ▪ 4 self-catering cottages, cottages@belfield.co.za ▪ Owner(s) Mel Kreft ▪ Cellarmaster(s) Allister Kreft ▪ Winemaker(s) Gavin Patterson ▪ Viticulturist(s) Paul Wallace ▪ 5.5ha/2.5ha (cabs s/f, merlot, shiraz) ▪ 17t/2,000cs own label 100% red ▪ PO Box 191 Elgin 7180 ▪ allister@undertheinfluence.co.za ▪ www.belfield.co.za ▪ S 34° 10′ 20″ E 019° 01′ 43″ ▪ ⌖ exclaim.settles.pleadingly ▪ **T +27 (0)82-228-9568**

☐ **Bella Vino** *see* Nicholson Smith
☐ **Bellemore** *see* Bellevue Estate Stellenbosch
☐ **Belle Vallee** *see* Baratok Wines

Bellevue Estate Stellenbosch

Recent 'moving and shaking' continues at the Morkel-family-owned estate in Stellenbosch's Bottelary Hills. Abreast of the heirloom variety trend, there's a superb new old-vine pinotage - Bellevue a 1950s pioneer of the variety - and a dry hanepoot (with barrel-fermented chardonnay and bottle-fermented bubbly to come), and the farm's oldest building (early 1700s) is morphing into a modern conference venue.

PK Morkel Collection

★★★★ **Pinotage** ⟨Ⓩ⟩ Opulent & concentrated **10** ⟨87⟩, plum & blackberry fruit, vanilla & spice appeal. Full bodied yet nimble, ripe, mouthfilling tannins.

Not tasted: **Petit Verdot, Tumara**.

Estate range

★★★★ **Malbec** ⟨Ⓩ⟩ Expressive **14** ⟨87⟩ is elegant & smooth, with dried herb & plum flavours, dusty tannins, & fresh dark-berry twist on the finish. Perfect for roast meats.

★★★★★ **1953 Single Vineyard Pinotage** ⟨NEW⟩ ⟨Ⓐ⟩ ⟨Ⓦ⟩ Low-yield, single-vineyard bottling makes a bold statement in its brooding plum & mulberry fruit, firm tannin backbone & serious musculature of oak (70% new, 18 months). But there's also elegance & finesse in **16** ⟨93⟩, a leavening savouriness & superb length. Will go decade plus.

Cinsaut ⟨Ⓥ⟩ ★★★★ In-demand variety shows lovely fruit abundance in **17** ⟨85⟩ - dark berries & cherries - plus earthy creaminess & hint of vanilla from year in large, older oak. **Muscat d'Alexandrie** ⟨NEW⟩ ⟨Ⓥ⟩ ★★★ Rare dry/unfortified bottling of yesteryear variety. Delightful **18** ⟨80⟩ delicately perfumed with grape, litchi & rosepetal, fruity & fragrant yet the dryness also makes it a good lighter-food partner.

Pinotage ★★★★ Forthright yet polished, **15** ⟨84⟩ sweet plum fruit with wild herbs & toasty notes on supple texture & structure, American oak, 50% new, in sync. **Shiraz** ★★★ Savoury dark fruit of **17** ⟨79⟩

somewhat overshadowed by overt oak character, robust finish. **Atticus Cape Blend** ★★★ Unusual blend of cab, pinotage (30%) & petit verdot, **16** ⑧ fleshy & accessible, the juicy ripe fruit in harmony with French & American wood. **Chardonnay** ⑨ ★★★ Bright tropical wafts on straightforwardly pleasant unwooded **16** ⑧ tank sample. **Sauvignon Blanc** ★★★ Oozes tropical fruit salad & lemon freshness in **18** ⑧, easy sipping for summer. Not tasted: **Pinot Noir, Eselgraf Single Vineyard Chenin Blanc.** — WB

Location/map: Stellenbosch ▪ Map grid reference: C3 ▪ WO: Bottelary ▪ Est 1701 ▪ 1stB 1999 ▪ Tasting & sales Mon–Sun 9–5 Fri 9–7 ▪ Closed Good Fri, Dec 25 & Jan 1 ▪ Pizza & wine tasting ▪ Kiddies play area ▪ Restaurant Tue–Sun 9–5 Fri 9–7 ▪ Weddings & functions ▪ Conferences ▪ Owner(s) Dirkie Morkel ▪ Winemaker(s) Wilhelm Kritzinger (Feb 2002) & Anneke Potgieter (Feb 2003) ▪ Viticulturist(s) Dirkie Morkel (Jan 1979) ▪ 291ha/151ha (cabs s/f, cinsaut, malbec, merlot, p verdot, ptage, pinot, shiraz, chenin, sauv) ▪ ±750t/±20,000cs own label 97% red 3% white; ±20,000cs for clients; balance in bulk wine & grapes ▪ Export brands: Bellemore, Houdamond, Morkel ▪ Labels for clients: Direct Wines/Laithwaites (UK), Marks & Spencer (UK), Woolworths ▪ IPW, WIETA ▪ PO Box 33 Koelenhof 7605 ▪ info@bellevue.co.za ▪ www.bellevue.co.za ▪ S 33° 52' 48.48" E 018° 45' 50.40" ▪ ✉ cherry.treaties.lively ▪ **T** +27 (0)21-865-2055/4

Bellingham ⑨ ⑪ ⑩ ⑧

Exciting changes at this iconic DGB-owned venture, as winemaker Richard Duckitt moves here from sibling winery Boschendal. Richard will focus on The Bernard Series, named for the pioneering Bernard Podlashuk who established the Bellingham brand in the 1940s; longtime incumbent Mario Damon will continue to make the region-specific Homestead range. Despite the dry conditions of recent years, both winemakers remain positive about the quality of the grapes, and the cellar is investing in new foudres to increase production of their premium wines. Which can be tasted and enjoyed at the multi-amenity visitor venue in Franschhoek town, where wine pairings, events and al fresco dining are the order of the day.

The Bernard Series

★★★★☆ **Bush Vine Pinotage** ⓐ Exotic & mysterious **16** ㉝ mingles smoky, dark, black-berried fruit with intriguing whiffs of biltong, spice & perfume. Firm tannins (helped by 50% new oak) support the many layers, leading to a bright red-fruit finish.

★★★★☆ **Small Basket Press Syrah** Impressive **16** ㉑ preview, with 2% viognier, looks set for great things, with a rich mouthful of plums & cherries, elegant tannins & lipsmacking liquorice & aniseed finish. Gritty texture provides interest through to lengthy finish.

★★★★☆ **Small Barrel SMV** ⓐ Multi-faceted **15** ㉝ shiraz blend with mourvèdre & dash viognier follows style of exceptional **14** ★★★★★ ㉗. Upfront oak gives way to rich black fruit, hints of milk chocolate, eucalyptus, coffee & spice, pretty perfumed notes linger at the finish.

★★★★☆ **Old Vine Chenin Blanc** ⓐ ⓦ From 3 selected plots of old bushvines, **17** ㉞ oozes complexity & interest. Plenty of tropical fruit (pineapple, mango) with creamy spicy oak (portion new) & delicious aged notes of wet wool & lanolin, focused by pure, clean acidity - this wine is on a lovely path to good times.

★★★★☆ **Whole Bunch Grenache Blanc-Viognier** 10% viognier shows its character on generally understated **17** ㉚ with subtle peach & ginger notes vying with stewed pear & cream. Good palate weight & soft, lingering finish make for excellent food partner. Paarl WO. **16** not made.

★★★★☆ **Whole Bunch Roussanne** Unwooded **18** ㉛ shows interesting combination of citrus (lemon, lime) mixed with white peach, cooked pear & spicy aniseed kick at the tail. Lovely texture & pithy notes throughout, delicious pairing for roast chicken.

★★★★ **Hand Picked Viognier** ⑨ Floral bouquet, quirky lime sherbet flavour & brush of oak spice on New World-style **17** ㉚. Buoyed by nippy acidity & chalky finish, will improve with time.

Homestead Series

★★★★ **Pinotage** ⊘ Fragrant **17** ㊏ adds black fruit (plum, cherry) to spicy oak & meaty palate in very drinkable sip for superior mid-week suppers. Stellenbosch WO, as next.

★★★★ **Chardonnay** ⑨ Aromatic **16** ★★★★ ㊐, array of ripe kumquat, marmalade & blossom, subtle oak adds to balanced salt-sprinkled palate. Attractive, if not as lingering as **15** ㊙.

★★★★☆ **Chenin Blanc** ⊘ Nicely handled fruit-oak balance on **17** ★★★★ ㊙. Creamy peaches with nutty muesli notes & refreshing lime finish. 40% wood, none new. Standout debut **16** ㉝ also from Paarl.

★★★★ Sauvignon Blanc Pungent & pronounced **18 ★★★★** ⑧⑤ has all the g's - grapefruit, gooseberry & poached guava - in abundance, making for very enjoyable drinking. WO Cape Town. **17** ⑧⑦ racy & mouthwatering.

Shiraz ★★★★ Shy fruit **17** ⑧③ hiding behind rather forthright oak, needs time to settle but already showing pleasing peppery, cured meat notes with soft tannins & acidity. — CM

Location/map: Franschhoek ▪ Map grid reference: C2 ▪ WO: Coastal/Paarl/Stellenbosch/Cape Town ▪ Est 1693 ▪ 1stB 1947 ▪ Tasting & sales at Bellingham cellardoor, located at Franschhoek Cellar: Mon-Thu 10-6 Fri/Sat 10-9 Sun 10-5 ▪ Closed Easter Fri/Sun, Dec 25/26 & Jan 1 ▪ Al fresco-style food & kiddies play area daily ▪ Farm produce ▪ Events venue (seat 300 pax) ▪ Owner(s) DGB (Pty) Ltd ▪ Winemaker(s) Richard Duckitt (Nov 2017), with Mario Damon (Jan 2002) ▪ Viticulturist(s) Heinie Nel (Jul 2018) ▪ 4,000t/560,000cs own label 50% red 49% white 1% rosé ▪ ISO 9001:2000, HACCP, IPW, WIETA ▪ PO Box 52 Franschhoek 7690 ▪ bellingham@dgb.co.za ▪ www.bellinghamwines.com ▪ S 33° 54'16.4" E 019° 6'40.7" ▪ ⊠ receives.scoured.dumping ▪ F +27 (0)21-876-4107 ▪ **T +27 (0)21-876-2086**

Bellpost ⓠ

West Coast family farms Bellevue and Buitepos each contribute to the name of the Thiart father-and-sons winery, where owner Lollies and siblings Nico (viticulturist) and Koos (winemaker) vinify a smidgen of their crop - further reduced by water deficits in 2017/18. Notwithstanding, groundwork has been completed for replanting unproductive and virused blocks when the rains return.

Merlot ★★★ Fruitcake & marinated cherry flavours with gentle spice, supple tannins in **15** ⑧⓪, slightly gritty on finish. 40-50% new oak, year, for the reds. **Ruby Cabernet ★★★** Dark wild berries & earthy herb touch in delightful **14** ⑧①, balanced & moreish, with sour cherry grip. **Shiraz ★★★** Cured meat & hedgerow fruit on smooth, easy-drinking **15** ⑧⓪, good match for robust pastas. **Chardonnay ★★★** Bright orchard fruit combines with leesy creaminess on unoaked, bunch-pressed **16** ⑧①. Fresh, with lively lemon rind exit. **C'est La Vie ★★★** Delicate floral, baked apple & peachy scents on **14** ⑧⓪, partly oaked chardonnay, viognier & nouvelle. Gentle acid invites drinking now. — WB

Location: Vredendal ▪ Map: Olifants River ▪ Map grid reference: B3 ▪ WO: Western Cape ▪ Est/1stB 2005 ▪ Tasting, sales & cellar tours by appt; tasting & sales also at Thi Art Restaurant, Vredendal ▪ Owner(s) Lollies Thiart ▪ Winemaker(s) Koos Thiart (Jan 2005) ▪ Viticulturist(s) Nico Thiart (Jan 2005) ▪ 5ha/2ha (merlot, ruby cab, shiraz, chard, viog) ▪ 12t/1,800cs own label 80% red 20% white ▪ PO Box 39 Vredendal 8160 ▪ bellpost@starmail.co.za ▪ www.bellpost.co.za ▪ S 31° 36'24.1" E 018° 25'0.6" ▪ ⊠ swaps.gibbering.handset ▪ F +27 (0)27-213-2562 ▪ **T +27 (0)27-213-2562/+27 (0)82-619-2428 (cellar); +27 (0)76-792-0806 (Thi Art restaurant)**

Bemind Wyne deur Ilse Schutte ⓠ ⑾ ⊚

Raised in upcountry Potchefstroom, Ilse Schutte is happily ensconced in tucked-away, proudly unbusy McGregor, sourcing locally and elsewhere in Breede River Valley, and making soupçons of wine 'from the heart' (hence her brand name, which translates as Beloved Wines). Her must-visit venue on the main street now hosts convivial pairings of wine and food made by Ilse and family, served on the cellar stoep.

Langstraat ⒩⒠⒲ ⑰ **★★★★** Tiny (40-case) parcel of merlot from garden vineyard in McGregor town. **17** ⑧④ mint chocolate & cherries, silky texture, 14 months oaking in balance.

Cinsault ★★★ 18 ⑧① preview captures variety's elegant charm. Light oaking for half lets the red cherry flavours shine, a juicy mouthful from Breedekloof grapes. **Shiraz ★★★** Handsome **16** ⑧② boldly styled, dark plums/prunes well spiced, nicely rounded body. **Méthode Cap Classique Brut ★★★** Zero-dosage **NV** ⑧① bubbly from chardonnay & pinot noir is lemon toned, with the palate-cleansing dryness you'd expect. Nice mineral finish. Not tasted: **Sauvignon Blanc**. — CR

Location: McGregor ▪ Map: Robertson ▪ Map grid reference: D6 ▪ WO: McGregor/Breedekloof ▪ Est 2015 ▪ Tasting, sales & cellar tours Wed-Fri 10-5 Sat 10-2 ▪ Fee R30/3 wines, waived on purchase ▪ Closed Easter Fri-Sun, Pentecost, Dec 25/26 & Jan 1 ▪ Food & wine pairing on request ▪ Deli products ▪ Owner(s) Ilse Schutte ▪ Cellarmaster(s)/winemaker Ilse Schutte (Jan 2015) ▪ 10-15t/±850cs own label 50% red 30% white 20% MCC ▪ IPW ▪ PO Box 446 McGregor 6708 ▪ ilse@bemindwyne.co.za ▪ www.bemindwyne.co.za ▪ S 33° 56'49" E 019° 49'44" ▪ ⊠ motors.coupler.stations ▪ F +27 (0)86-550-5999 ▪ **T +27 (0)83-380-1648**

Benguela Cove Lagoon Wine Estate

The modern, 400-ton gravity-fed cellar complete, an impressive array of attractions for families and winelovers have followed at entrepreneur Penny Streeter OBE's wine estate on Bot River Lagoon in cool-climate Walker Bay: various food-and-wine tastings, cellar and vineyard tours; pontoon cruises on the lagoon and Pirate Adventure Golf Course; fine-dining at Moody Lagoon Restaurant and more casual options at Blackbeards Diner and the Tea Room; a shop and conferencing/wedding facilities. Wine remains the focal point under awarded winemaker Johann Fourie, with new ranges including an Icon intended as 'an ode to the environment', and an experimental line-up 'celebrating diversity and the artistry of winemaking'. New on the team is brand and business manager Samarie Smith, respected winewriter and judge.

Icon range (NEW)

★★★★★ **Catalina Semillon** Stellar debut for confident, layered & profound **17** (95), showing smoke & oystershell minerality, bone-dry fantail finish. High barrel-fermented portion (80%, 20% new oak) & rapier-like acidity from eschewed malo create prospect of long, rewarding future.

Vinography range (NEW)

★★★★☆ **Chardonnay** Barrel-fermented **17** (93), taut, unyielding, with tightly wound acidity, trenchant dryness & compact lemon/lime fruit supported by detailed oaking. Lots of potential, needs year/2 to unwind.

★★★★☆ **Sauvignon Blanc** Racier & drier than Estate version, more polished & with greater poise. **17** (93) reminiscent of iconic fumé blancs from California. Starts fermentation in tank, transferred midway to all-new barrels, smidgen acacia wood. Very special.

Estate range

★★★★ **Pinot Noir** Unforced, lightly oaked **17** (86), easy cherry fruit, icing sugar nuance, satisfying grip & acidity for rich meals. 15% wholebunch, 85% wholeberry. Notch up on last-tasted **15** ★★★ (82).

★★★★ **Syrah** Was 'Shiraz'. **16** (86) modern but not overdone. Pure fruit shows black pepper & fynbos, combines well with reined-in oak, 50% new. Less mineral than **15** (87), with subtle pleasant bitter edge.

★★★★ **Estate Collage** Cab & malbec (52%, 32%) drive this forceful Bordeaux blend with petit verdot & merlot. **15** (87)'s plump fruit, athletic tannins & compact body impress, need few years to mellow.

★★★★ **Chardonnay** More expressive in youth than Vinography sibling, **17** (89)'s shapely citrus curves plump out lean 1.7 g/l sugar frame, as do vanilla flavours & satin texture ex oak ferment/ageing.

★★★★ **Sauvignon Blanc** Now bottled, **17** (87)'s passionfruit & gooseberry tones given body & length by 40% barrel-fermented portion, freshness from tank, hint sweetness ups approachability.

★★★★☆ **Semillon-Sauvignon Blanc** Blend of three different terroirs, 80% in oak 5 months, **16** ★★★★ (88) has semillon's (54%) lemon character in its zesty acidity, piquant curd flavours, matched with sauvignon's high-toned pyrazine. Follows exceptional **15** (94).

★★★★ **Joie de Vivre Brut** Sparkler from chardonnay (57%) & pinot, with 2 years on lees, **14** (86) full spectrum of apple aromas & flavours, some red berries, too, especially in the finish.

★★★★☆ **Noble Late Harvest** Botrytis dessert from sauvignon blanc. **15** (91) vivacious & beautifully balanced by vibrant acidity. Opulent smooth texture with delicious piquancy & length.

Cabernet Sauvignon ★★★☆ Intense blackcurrant tones & raspberry piquancy, **15** (85)'s oak (40% new French) gives cedary nuance nicely seamed with fruit, sappy grape tannin for balanced structure. Not tasted: **Cabernet Franc**.

Lighthouse range (NEW)

Rosé ★★★ Co-fermented shiraz, mourvèdre & viognier in pretty coral pink **18** (82), faint aromas but well-composed & textured dry palate for food. **Sauvignon Blanc** ★★★ Heady Granny Smith apple, pear drop & guava bouquet on just-bottled **18** (82); texture & weight from 20% oaked portion. — CvZ

Location: Hermanus ▪ Map: Walker Bay & Bot River ▪ Map grid reference: B2 ▪ WO: Walker Bay ▪ Est 2004 ▪ 1stB 2007 ▪ Tasting room hours: Mon-Sun 8-8 (summer)/8-6 (winter) ▪ Tasting fee R8opp ▪ Chocolate/cheese/oyster & wine pairing R110pp ▪ Millionaires tasting R40/R55pp ▪ Cheese & charcuterie platter R220 ▪ Moody Lagoon Restaurant (fine dining); Blackbeards Diner; Tea Room; Deli ▪ Shops ▪ Facilities for children ▪ Tour groups ▪ Pirate Adventure Golf course ▪ Vineyard safaris, winery tours and pontoon cruise on the lagoon ▪ Conferencing & wedding facilities ▪ Owner(s) Benguela Cove Investments (Pty) Ltd (Penny Streeter OBE)

▪Winemaker(s) Johann Fourie (Sep 2016), with Michelle Waldeck (Feb 2017) ▪ Viticulturist(s) Jaco Mouton ▪ 206ha/66ha (cabs s/f, malbec, merlot, p verdot, pinot, shiraz, chard, sauv, sem, viog) ▪ 600t/4,400cs own label 50% red 50% white ▪ PO Box 327 Bellville 7535 ▪ info@benguelacove.co.za ▪ www.benguelacove.co.za ▪ S 34° 20' 45.0" E 019° 8' 15.7" ▪ ⊞ cove.minerals.dismantles ▪ T +27 (0)21-944-1041 (head office)/+27 (0)83-645-6198 (wine sales)

☐ **Berg en Dal** see Wine-of-the-Month Club

Bergheim

General practitioner Edwin Jordaan, enthused by food and cooking, music and wine, vinifies small batches with minimum intervention in rented cellar space on Paarl Mountain. His Shiraz and Mignon dry white (both '16) were due at the bottling line at press time.

Location/map: Paarl ▪ Map grid reference: E6 ▪ Est/1stB 2000 ▪ Tasting by appt ▪ Owner(s) Edwin Jordaan ▪ Cellarmaster(s)/winemaker(s) Edwin Jordaan (Jan 2000) ▪ 4-6t/1,000cs own label 66% red 34% white ▪ PO Box 6020 Paarl 7622 ▪ drjordaan@gmail.com ▪ S 33° 45' 20.2" E 018° 57' 42.5" ▪ F +27 (0)21-862-7852 ▪ T +27 (0)82-923-3115, +27 (0)21-863-1529

☐ **Bergkelder Selection** see Fleur du Cap

Bergsig Estate

The low-key, sixth-generation Lategan brothers, bottling under the family label since the 1970s, are planting more touriga nacional on their Breedekloof estate (for the Cape Vintage), harvesting rare-in-SA furmint (for the Icarus White), rejuvenating old riesling vines and releasing the first Noble Late Harvest since 2004.

Limited Editions

★★★★ **Tant Anna Chardonnay** ⑭ Year in new French oak leaves an imprint, but big-bodied **17** ⑧⑥ is generously laced with citrus, smoothly textured & lengthy on finish, & should settle with time.

★★★★ **Chenin Blanc Reserve** Prominent wood (50% new) on **17** ⑧⑨, but reined in from **16** ⑧⑦, allowing luscious stonefruit & melon to show. Vibrant acid & leesy notes yet to marry, but promising well. Not tasted: **Cabernet Sauvignon Reserve**.

Bergsig Estate range

★★★★ **Icarus Red** ⑫ Ripe, substantial **14** ⑧⑧ barrel selection of cab & touriga individual & appealing, with Xmas pudding dark fruits, spiciness from new oak. No **13**. **12** ★★★★★ ⑨④ was exceptional.

★★★★☆ **Icarus White** ⑫ Oak (older) still dominant in stylish **16** ⑨③ chardonnay, chenin, riesling blend, but fruit beginning to assert itself mid-2017. Appealing mix of orange marmalade & yellow stonefruit, spiced with vanilla & cloves. Body & freshness to match; should settle & improve.

★★★★ **Gewürztraminer Edel Laatoes** Beguiling rosewater scents show on restrained, well-judged **17** ⑧⑨ botrytis dessert, with delicate spices, tangy dried apricots filling the (unoaked) palate. 375 ml.

★★★★ **Cape Vintage** ⑫ Succulent, smooth & spicy 'port' from tinta. **04** ⑧⑦ generously flavoured but not sweet, sufficient fire to warm a winter night.

Cabernet Sauvignon ⑫ ★★★ Savoury tones to **14** ⑦⑧'s cherry & plum fruit, thinnish body. Also in magnum. WO W Cape. **Pinotage** ★★★ Traditionally styled **16** ⑧⓪, ripe & high-toned, with wild plummy fruit & prominent tannins. **Touriga Nacional** ⑫ ★★★ Unfortified bottling of traditional 'port' grape. Plummy baked fruit on **13** ⑧②, juicier than previous, with spicy black cherries. **The Family Friend** ★★★ Shiraz-led unwooded Cape Blend **17** ⑧② makes for pleasant anytime drinking. Fruit driven, fresh & lightish, with ripe plum flavour. **Rose Gold Rosé** ★★★ Was 'Shiraz Rosé', still made from that variety. Lively strawberry fruit on **18** ⑦⑦, pretty silvery pink, just-dry, light & refreshing. **Chardonnay** ★★★★ Dominant oak spices mask **17** ⑧③'s marmalade-tinged fruit; fresh, clean palate with decent body, clean finish. **Chenin Blanc** ★★★ Light-bodied, fruit-driven **17** ⑧② is tasty & pleasant, offers juicy pear & pineapple. **Gewürztraminer** ★★★★ Typically fragrant **18** ⑧③ has a touch of sweetness, lots of Turkish delight & personality, soft acidity. **Weisser Riesling** ⑫ ★★★★ Unquestionably riesling on nose, hint of kerosene development but also lots of steely dryness, apple & stonefruit still on **12** ⑧④, light & crisp. **Sauvignon Blanc** ⊘ ★★★ Spicy, fruity **18** ⑧② is light & refreshingly crisp, interesting nutmeg hint on granadilla & gooseberry. 1.5L. Also in 750ml. **Weisser Riesling Late Harvest** ⑫ ★★★★ Ample terpene notes show more development than fresher, dry sibling; generous sweetness from late-harvested fruit, raisined sultanas, honey & lanolin on **13** ⑧③. **Cape Ruby** ⓠ ★★★★ Unoaked **NV** ⑧④ port-style from tinta, delicious, approachable as this style should be. Not tasted: **Cape LBV**. Discontinued: **Bouquet Light, Special Late Harvest**.

Bainskloof range

Black Frost Pinotage ⓠ ★★★★ 'Lost' component of **13** ⑧④ spent 40 months in French & American barrels; rich & mellow, the heavy oak spices well integrated into wild berry fruit. — GdB

Location: Wolseley ▪ Map: Breedekloof ▪ Map grid reference: A3 ▪ WO: Breedekloof/Western Cape ▪ Est 1843 ▪ 1stB 1977 ▪ Tasting & sales Mon-Fri 8–5 Sat/pub hols 9–4 ▪ Fee R20 for groups of 10+ ▪ Closed Good Fri, Dec 25 & Jan 1 ▪ Cellar tours by appt ▪ Bergsig Bistro ▪ Facilities for children ▪ Farm produce ▪ Conferences ▪ Self-guided birdwatching route ▪ MTB ▪ Conservation area, visits by appt ▪ Lategan family history & historical artefacts on display ▪ Soetes & Soup (Jul) ▪ Owner(s) Lategan family ▪ Cellarmaster(s) De Wet Lategan (Jan 1989) ▪ Winemaker(s) Chris du Toit (Jul 2003) ▪ Viticulturist(s) Louis & Plum Lategan (1991) ▪ 253ha (cab, ptage, shiraz, touriga, chard, chenin, sauv) ▪ 3,200t/100,000cs own label 35% red 60% white 4% rosé 1% other + 140,000cs for clients ▪ Other export brands: White River, Bulldozer Pinotage ▪ Brands for clients: Woolworths ▪ BRC, IPW, WIETA ▪ PO Box 15 Breërivier 6858 ▪ wine@bergsig.co.za ▪ www.bergsig.co.za ▪ S 33° 31' 7.78" E 019° 11' 37.14" ▪ 🌐 lighting.elastic.punch ▪ F +27 (0)23-355-1658 ▪ **T +27 (0)23-355-1603**

☐ **Bernard Series** *see* Bellingham
☐ **Berrio Wines** *see* The Berrio Wines
☐ **Berryfields** *see* Ashton Winery

Bester Family Wines

Zakkie Bester's roots are in the Swartland: he can trace his local ancestry back to the 1700s but he also built up in-depth experience of the area as cellarmaster/CEO of Riebeek Cellars and a 'retirement' marketing the winery's bulk wine. Who better qualified, therefore, to source grapes for a personal project. Just two wines, so far, available online and for tasting/sale at select outlets (see below).

Barbera ⓠ ★★★★ Fruit-driven **16** ⑧④ richly layered, sweet spicy & dried herb notes, a red berry succulence giving delicious drinkability enhanced by approachable tannins, suggestion of sweetness. **Chenin Blanc** ★★★★ From 30 year old bushvines, no oak but long lees contact, giving **17** ⑧④ palate fullness, length. Honeysuckle scents, apple & pear fruitiness, zesty-fresh. Ticks many boxes, lots to like here. — CR

Location: Riebeek-Kasteel ▪ WO: Swartland ▪ Est/1stB 2016 ▪ Closed to public ▪ Wines available for tasting & sales at Enjoy Liquors, Riebeek-Kasteel, and Toast Restaurant on Delsma Farm near Hermon ▪ Owner(s) Zakkie Bester ▪ Winemaker(s) Zakkie Bester (2016) ▪ 1,400cs own label 50% red 50% white ▪ PO Box 292 Riebeek-Kasteel 7307 ▪ zakkie@ijbester.co.za ▪ www.besterwines.com ▪ **T +27 (0)82-805-5586**

☐ **Bethani** *see* Cathedral Peak Wine Estate

Beyerskloof

ⓠ 🍴 ⊚ ♿

In 1988, after two decades at Kanonkop, industry legend Beyers Truter (partnered by four Johannesburg winelovers) purchased Koelenhof farm Nooitgedacht which, coincidentally, had belonged to his ancestors, the Beyers family, for five generations until 1895. 'That's why it could only have one name – Beyerskloof.' The next generation is taking over, with son Anri in charge of winemaking and daughter Corné running the on-site bistro. They share their father's unwavering devotion to pinotage as well as his dedication to social responsibility through the Beyers Truter Fetal Alcohol-Syndrome and Interrelated Treatment Help (FAITH) fund. And, of course, to the winelover: 'Our constant desire to be innovative, forward thinking and ultimately ahead of the pack is driven by a yearning to please the everyday consumer.'

★★★★★ **Diesel Pinotage** 🐾 Aged 18 months in 100% new French oak, kingpin pinotage memorialising founder Beyers Truter's beloved canine companion has enough structure & balance in **16** ★★★★★ ⑨⑤ to last a (dog's) lifetime. More refined than **15** ⑨④, with toned-down alcohol (14.5%).

★★★★ **Pinotage Reserve** Ribena-like black berry intensity in **16** ⑧⑨ from mature bushvines, rich & full bodied yet lifted by fresh acidity, 15 months mostly 2nd-fill French oak give sweet spicing.

★★★★☆ Winemakers Reserve Pinotage (NEW) (🌿) Best 10 barrels of Pinotage Reserve, & offering all the luscious fruit of Diesel with less wood influence (only 15 months, 50% new, for aniseed interest), **16** (92) delivers standout character, flavour & longevity for attractive price.

★★★★ Field Blend Richly textured **14** ★★★★☆ (91) from co-grown, -fermented, -matured cab (85%) & merlot planted ca 1988 beside the cellar, plenty of black berry & plum fruit, hints of nutmeg & mocha from 2 years new French oak. Beautifully integrated, more complex than **13** (89).

★★★★ Faith (🌿) Always-impressive flagship Cape Blend of 34% pinotage with equal cab & merlot, best barrels of vintage, **14** ★★★★★ (95) goes up a notch on statuesque **13** (91), shows both power & poise, dense forest fruits well-integrated with subtle mocha after 20 months new French oak, 2 years bottle.

★★★★ Synergy Cape Blend (⊘) Juicy, fruity & rounded **16** (88), pinotage only 50% of blend with 18% each cab/merlot plus 3 others, 14 months French oak, 10% new. Shade less focused than **15** ★★★★☆ (90).

★★★★ Traildust Glossy **16** (89) sees pinotage reunited with parents cinsaut (35%) & pinot noir (33%) over 14 months in 3rd-fill French barrels. Red fruit with hints of spice, leather.

★★★★ Lagare Cape Vintage Pinotage's plum pudding richness lifted by the savoury spice & black pepper of 20% shiraz in port-style **16** (87), foot-crushed the traditional way, fortified with pinotage brandy.

Pinotage (⊘) ★★★★ Latest vintage of 'SA's most popular pinotage' is, as ever, smooth, fruity, soft & juicy. Mostly bushvine **17** (83) for drinking young, with vibrant red fruit & baking spice. WO W Cape, as next 2.

Cabernet Sauvignon-Merlot (⊘) ★★★ 50/50 blend from **15** (82) flew off the shelves & **16** (82) should prove equally popular: soft & smooth, with choc/plum pudding richness & alcohol below 14%. Also in magnum. **Pinotage Dry Rosé** ★★★ Red berry fruit (some sweet, some piquant) on cheery pink, **17** (80) dry, medium bodied from 3 months on lees but very refreshing. **Chenin Blanc-Pinotage** ★★★ Pinotage versatility evident in this 'white Cape Blend' with 78% chenin in unwooded **17** (80), dry, smooth & full of tropical fruit. Coastal WO. — JG

Location/map: Stellenbosch ▪ Map grid reference: E3 ▪ WO: Stellenbosch/Western Cape/Coastal ▪ Est 1988 ▪ 1stB 1989 ▪ Tasting & sales Mon-Fri 9–4 Sat 9.30–4 Sun 10-3.30 ▪ Closed Easter Fri-Mon, Dec 25/26 & Jan 1 ▪ Cellar tours by appt ▪ Red Leaf Restaurant ▪ Conferences (30 pax) ▪ Owner(s) Beyers Truter, Jan Morgan & Barnie van Straten ▪ Cellarmaster(s) Beyers Truter (Jan 1988) ▪ Winemaker(s) Anri Truter (Jan 2004), with Buddy Hendricks (Jan 2010) & Elsa du Plessis (Aug 2017) ▪ Viticulturist(s) Johan Pienaar (2000, consultant) ▪ 130ha/90ha (cab, cinsaut, merlot, ptage, pinot, shiraz) ▪ 700t/350,000cs own label 96% red 2% white 2% rosé + 10,000cs for clients ▪ Brands for clients: Pick's Pick, Woolworths ▪ IPW, WIETA, WWF ▪ PO Box 107 Koelenhof 7605 ▪ reception@beyerskloof.co.za ▪ www.beyerskloof.co.za ▪ S 33° 53' 28.0" E 018° 49' 23.6" ▪ (♿) planting. purses.living ▪ **T** +27 (0)21-865-2135

Bezalel Wine & Brandy Estate   (♀) (🍴) (🏠) (📷) (👤)

At this Northern Cape estate on the Kokerboom Food & Wine Route, the Bezuidenhout family offers 'authentic Green Kalahari hospitality', whether you're after a meal at their Garden Café, an overnight stay in their Country House, or simply a taste of their wines, oak-matured fortifieds, potstill brandies or infusions.

Bezalel Estate range

★★★★ Fortified Cape Tawny From 4 port grapes including rare cornifesto, 66 months older oak, **NV** (87) luscious sweetness yet acidity to balance richness of brandied orange, caramelised nut & baking spice.

Sangiovese ★★☆ Piquant red berries on lightly wooded **18** (78), with firm tannins & racy acidity to cut through creamy pasta & cheesy pizza. **Merlot Blanc de Noir** (NEW) ★★☆ Off-dry **17** (77) has candied orange peel as well as red cherry notes, smooth after 6 weeks on lees. **Suikerbekkie Sweet Rosé** ★★ Deeper colour this time, hence name change from 'Blush'. Full-sweet **18** (75) ripe cherry fruit from 68% sangiovese co-fermented with gewürztraminer for rosepetal & litchi notes. **Colombard** ★★★ From single block picked over 5 weeks, **18** (79) dry & very fresh, mouthcoating pear & guava fruit, subtle citrus too. **Zandland Viognier** (👤) ★★ Only 2nd crop from this Zandland block, basket-pressed **17** (74) unusual buchu aroma & more typical peach, oak-derived sweetness & spice on palate. Not tasted: **Pinot Noir**, **Shiraz**, **Sauvignon Blanc**, **Gewürztraminer Jerepigo**.

Brandy range

★★★★ **VSOP Cape Brandy** New packaging for this potstill brandy, double distilled from mostly colombard (with sauvignon, tinta, cab & shiraz), 5 years in Cape Tawny barrels. Smooth & rich, gentle dried fruit, nut & creamy marzipan flavours.

Not tasted: **XO Cape Brandy**. — JG, WB

Location: Upington • Map: Northern Cape, Free State & North West • Map grid reference: B8 • WO: Northern Cape • Est 1949 (farm)/1997 (cellar) • 1stB 1998 • Tasting, sales & cellar tours Mon-Fri 8.30–5.30 Sat 8.30–3 • Fee R50–R100pp • Large groups by appt • Closed Easter Fri/Mon & Dec 25 • Garden Café: breakfast, lunch & platters • Venue for conferences & weddings • Accommodation • Craft beer • Owner(s) Bezuidenhout family • Winemaker(s) Martiens Bezuidenhout (2015) • Viticulturist(s) Inus Bezuidenhout (1989) • 60ha/44ha (cab, cornifesto, merlot, pinot, sangio, shiraz, touriga, cbard, gewürz, sauv, viog) • ±1,000cs own label 40% red 60% white • IPW • PO Dyasonsklip 8805 • info@bezalel.co.za • www.bezalel.co.za • S 28° 36' 28.69" E 021° 6' 19.01" • ⌂ earthen.subpart.plugs • F +27 (0)54-491-1141 • **T +27 (0)54-491-1325/+27 (0)83-257-4736**

Bezuidenhout Family Wines

Paarl-based Cape Wine Master Francois Bezuidenhout says his long dreamed of boutique label honours 17th-century ancestor Wijnand Leenders, a farmer from the town Bezuidenhout who, as head gardener for the Dutch East India Company, was one of the Cape's first vinegrowers and winemakers. Regionality is a focus, and the wines are 'southern Rhône influenced, with a South African flair'.

Leenders range

★★★★ **Baviaan** Harmonious chenin (72%), viognier, roussanne & grenache blanc, **18** ㊆ suave creaminess from partial oaking combines attractively with vivacious pineapple & fig flavours. WO W Cape.

Sielverkoper ★★★★ Lightly oaked shiraz (71%) seasoned with mourvèdre, carignan, grenache, **17** ㊄ carefully extracted for good, unheavy concentration, firm but approachable tannins. **Armosyn** ★★★☆ Premium-priced dry rosé, palest pearly pink **18** ㊂ smooth, clean guava flavour & mineral undertone, mouthfilling despite slender 12.5% alcohol, lifted leafy farewell. From Robertson mourvèdre. — JG, CvZ

Location/map: Paarl • Map grid reference: E6 • WO: Breedekloof/Robertson/Western Cape • Est/1stB 2018 • Tasting & sales Mon-Fri 8.30–6.30 Sat 8.30–3.30 Sun 8.30–12 • Closed Good Fri, Dec 25 & Jan 1 • Facilities for children • Walks • Owner(s) Francois Bezuidenhout • Winemaker(s) Francois Bezuidenhout (Apr 2018) • 1,000cs own label 60% red 40% white • Taillerfer Str Paarl 7646 • francois@bezfamily.com • www. bezfamily.com • S 33° 45' 55.2" E 018° 57' 27.6" • **T +27 (0)21-863-0872**

☐ **Big Bill** see KWV Wines

☐ **Big Easy** see Ernie Els Wines

☐ **Big Flower** see Botanica Wines

Biodynamix

The Frater brothers have several projects on the go in Paarl, Biodynamix being a joint venture between winemaker Dan and viticulturist Gerard, with grapes from the latter's Paarl Mountain farm Houmoed. Though not certified biodynamic, there's much emphasis on the farming on naturalness, and in the cellar at family seat De Zoete Inval, the wines are pampered with classical music. See under Frater Family Wines for the wines of third sibling John Robert.

★★★★ **Max 1** ㉘ Shiraz (70%) with merlot & dash cab, naturally co-fermented & older oaked, **15** ㊇ has earthy scrub nuances in its hedgerow fruit, grainy tannins which should soften over time.— CR, CvZ

Location/WO: Paarl • Est/1stB 2015 • Closed to public • Owner(s) Joint venture members: Dan & Gerard Frater • Cellarmaster(s)/winemaker(s) Dan Frater (2015) • Viticulturist(s) Gerard Frater (2001) • 12ha/2ha (cab, merlot, shiraz) • 12t/500cs own label 100% red • PO Box 591 Paarl 7646 • biodynamix.sales@gmail.com • www.biodynamix.co.za • **T +27 (0)82-328-1807**

☐ **Birkenhead Estate & Brewery** see Walker Bay Estate

Bitou Vineyards

Red-wine varieties, including rare durif/petite sirah, as well as chenin have joined the vines planted a decade ago in an old polo field on the Bitou River bank on the Cape's Garden Route for boutique vintner and property developer Ronald Leacy. Nearing completion is the cellar, restaurant and tasting venue alongside the N2 highway, welcome news for holidaymakers and sun-seekers who flock to nearby Plettenberg Bay.

Location: Plettenberg Bay ▪ Map: Klein Karoo & Garden Route ▪ Map grid reference: C1 ▪ Est 2009 ▪ Tasting Mon-Fri by appt ▪ Closed all pub hols ▪ Owner(s) Ronald Leacy - Leacy Property (Pty) Ltd ▪ Winemaker(s) Anton Smal (Feb 2015, consultant) ▪ 15ha/9.5ha (chard, sauv, sem) ▪ 56t/5,000cs ▪ info@bitouvineyards.co.za ▪ www.bitouvineyards.co.za ▪ S 34° 0′ 59″ E 023° 23′ 22″ ▪ 🖃 dentist.charades.gnat ▪ **T +27 (0)82-922-0809**

Bizoe Wines

Taking its name from the French word for kiss, Somerset West-based Rikus Neethling's boutique wine venture has once more expanded, adding two easy-drinking wines. Having started on a wing and a prayer, Bizoe is now in its second decade, with an ever-increasing fan following of its original white blend and syrah, the latter from a singular Wolseley vineyard which Rikus would marry if he weren't already!

Bizoe Wines range

★★★★☆ **Estalét Syrah** Beloved Wolseley block features in supple, subtle **15** (91). Rounded, ripe & plush, with understated plum & spice from integrated oak (10% American). Silky, complex & textured.

★★★★ **Idioglossia Chardonnay** Lime tang on **17** (86) leads to rich, honeyed caramelised orange, ripe & appealing. Franschhoek grapes 40% fermented naturally in amphora, rest in old French oak, 9 months.

★★★★☆ **Henriëtta** Tautly wound **17** (92) Franschhoek semillon (70%) & sauvignon maintains precision & focus of previous. Textured, chalky mouthfeel tempered by vivid lemon twist. Half oak-fermented portion adds body. Subtle & refined with long aftertaste.

Idioglossia Malbec (NEW) ★★★★ Deeply perfumed violet **16** (85) is soft textured & juicy. Black fruit ex Swartland shows a saline nuance & spicy note from 15 months in old oak. Not tasted: **Tiny Noble Late Harvest**.

RNW range (NEW)

Cabernet Sauvignon ★★★ Light-bodied red cherry ease on **17** (79) fireside quaffer from Robertson & Elgin. **Sauvignon Blanc** ★★★ Smokey mandarin flavour, **18** (78) juicy & bright, lemon zest exit. — FM

Location: Somerset West ▪ WO: Western Cape ▪ Est/1stB 2008 ▪ Closed to public ▪ Owner(s)/cellarmaster(s)/winemaker(s) Rikus Neethling ▪ Viticulturist(s) Org Viljoen ▪ 2,000cs ▪ Unit 189 Croydon Vineyard Estate Somerset West 7130 ▪ info@bizoe.co.za ▪ www.bizoe.co.za ▪ F +27 (0)86-653-8186 ▪ **T +27 (0)21-843-3307**

Blaauwklippen Vineyards

New ownership promises to bring plenty of positive change for one of Stellenbosch's original estates, latterly redeveloped into a popular destination farm with many allures. Renovation of the Manor House and Jonkershuis will take place this year, and new accommodation is on the cards, while the ever-popular Family Market continues to draw the crowds each week. In her third season here, winemaker Narina Cloete is hitting her stride, crafting multiple variants of Blaauwklippen's signature zinfandel grape while overseeing a wide-ranging portfolio rationalisation. Meanwhile, their boutique brandy and gin tastings are also proving popular with visitors.

Blaauwklippen range

★★★★ **Estate Blend** (NEW) Promising barrel sample of **17** (86) 5-way Bordeaux red, mainly cabernet with merlot. Wonderful colour, then classic notes of blackcurrant pastille, tobacco, cassis, tar with attractive freshness & excellent weight.

★★★★ **Zinfandel Blanc de Noir** Was 'White Zinfandel'. Perky, fresh & bone-dry **18** ★★★☆ (83) has whispers of red fruit with some biscuity lees adding depth & interest. Summer sipper, shade less convincing as **17** (87). Coastal WO.

Zinfandel ★★★ Mix of bold black fruit on **17** (80) lashed with raisins, greenpepper & earthy overtones, lots of acid & tannins may need time to resolve. **Winning Blend** ★★★★ Long-running Blaauwklippen Blending Competition champion mixes mainly shiraz with malbec, petit verdot & merlot. Previewed **17**

⑮ ripe, chunky black fruit, robust tannins & pleasing vanilla cream finish (16 months oak, 23% new). Magnums only. **Sauvignon Blanc** ⓝ ★★★★ From mostly cool-climate fruit (Constantia, Lambert's Bay), 18 ⑧ zippy & lively, citrus plus tweaks of peachy tropical fruit. Soft, pleasant acidity & length.

Specialities

★★★★ **Zinfandel Noble Late Harvest** ② Very sweet & raisined 13 ★★★ ⑧ botrytis dessert, older oak fermented/aged. Subtle spice & tobacco notes, not the precision or freshness of 12 ⑧. 375 ml.

★★★★★ **10 Year Potstill Brandy** ② Light amber-gold glints entice, as do floral & tropical aromas. Nutty, rich & rounded on palate, with cinnamon spice, elegant balance & subtle texture. From colombard, sauvignon & chenin, 38% alcohol.

Viva Zinfandel Méthode Cap Classique ★★★ Unique-in-SA champagne-method dry sparkler from zinfandel, 16 ⑧ light & fresh, soft red fruit & salty tang courtesy 21 months on lees. Unpretentious & fun: take it to a party. **Before & After Aperitif** ★★★ Unusual NV ⑧ Noble Late Harvest zinfandel & malbec fortified with potstill brandy. Spice notes abound plus cocoa, raisins & dustiness on finish, tad unbalanced now, may come round in time. Add it to ice cream or sip with strong cheese. Not tasted: **Ons Sprankel**. — CM, WB

Location/map: Stellenbosch ▪ Map grid reference: E7 ▪ WO: Stellenbosch/Coastal/Western Cape ▪ Est 1682 ▪ 1stB 1974 ▪ Tasting & sales Mon-Sat 10–6 (summer)/10-5 (winter) Sun/pub hols 10–5 ▪ Wine tasting; chocolate & wine pairing; macaron & wine pairing; canapé & wine pairing ▪ Closed Dec 25 & Jan 1 ▪ Wine blending on request ▪ Cellar tours daily, booking advised ▪ Family market every Sun 10-3 ▪ Bistro ▪ Facilities for children ▪ Gift shop ▪ Weddings/functions ▪ Walks/hikes & MTB ▪ Gin & brandy (tastings only) R85/tasting ▪ Owner(s) Blaauwklippen Agricultural Estates (Pty) Ltd ▪ Winemaker(s) Narina Cloete (Jun 2016) ▪ Viticulturist(s) Christo Hamman (Jan 2009) & Jeremy Arries (Aug 2015) ▪ 160ha ▪ 500t/60,000cs wine & 650cs (x4-btl) brandy ▪ IPW ▪ PO Box 54 Stellenbosch 7599 ▪ nanette@blaauwklippen.com ▪ www.blaauwklippen.com ▪ S 33° 58′ 23.3″ E 018° 50′ 51.0″ ▪ ⊡ pillow.bank.pictures ▪ F +27 (0)21-880-0136 ▪ T +27 (0)21-880-0133

Black Block Wines

The minimalist, severely elegant yet sensual label (square, black, textured, with the variety in silver and vintage in blue) of this one-wine venture reveals the design interest of architects Derick Henstra and Peter Fehrsen. Their Pinot is off high-lying Tulbagh/Durbanville vines, made with the aid of James McKenzie.

★★★★ **Pinot Noir** Forthright, fragrant, sweetly ripe fruit on 17 ⑧. Dark cherry flavours with savoury edge on slightly rustic palate; plenty of acid & light tannic grip. Last was chunkier 14 ★★★★ ⑧. — TJ

Location: Cape Town ▪ WO: Coastal ▪ Est/1stB 2012 ▪ Closed to public ▪ Owner(s) Derick Henstra & Peter Fehrsen ▪ Winemaker(s) Derick Henstra & Peter Fehrsen, advised by James McKenzie ▪ 100% red ▪ jacqui@blackblockwines.co.za ▪ www.blackblockwines.co.za ▪ T +27 (0)21-421-6803

☐ **Black Box** see Wineways Marketing

Black Door

Drying of grape bunches on the vine to concentrate flavours is relatively rare in modern SA winemaking but familiar (via the likes of Amarone) to the clientele of Helmut Peters, Europe-based wine-partner of Stellenbosch boutique vintner Hilko Hegewisch. Method kaperone, their preferred term for this desiccated style, is on full display under the Alte Neffen entry; this newer red is the 'baby' version, for earlier drinking.

Black Door ★★★★ Merlot, cab & shiraz blend NV ⑧ has 20% vine-dried grapes, light oaking, satisfying fruit concentration, supple tannins. WO W Cape. — GdB

Black Elephant Vintners ⓠ

This boutique Franschhoek winery continues its path of change and improvement, though timings dictate that sadly this means no new wines for us to taste this year. Production takes place at nearby Haut Espoir, where winemaker Jacques Wentzel, with co-owners Kevin Swart and Raymond Ndlovu create unusual and quirky names for the ranges, much appreciated by audiences at home and overseas.

Black Elephant range

★★★★ **Chardonnay-Pinot Noir Brut MCC** ⓐ Plenty of lees contact (30 months) on zesty **NV** ㊆ sparkling, giving salty mineral edge. Crisp Granny Smith apples with lemon-almond notes. 75/25 ratio.

Amistad Syrah ⓐ ★★★ Lots of cinnamon spice on **14** ㊀ shade less balanced than previous, with chocolate, plum & raisin all vying for top spot with spice. **The Fox & The Flamingo Full Bodied Rosé** ⓐ ★★★★ Interesting dry pink **17** ㊇ from cab, 6 months in old oak. Cherry & soft cheese flavours with menthol edge, before creamy blackcurrant finish. **Timothy White** ⓐ ★★★ Mainly chenin & sauvignon with semillon & viognier, **16** ㊀ less intense than previous. Quiet yellow & green fruit with herbal hints with crisp acidity. Not tasted: **Three Men in a Tub with a Rubberduck Pinotage, Nicholas Red, Two Dogs, a Peacock & a Horse Sauvignon Blanc, The Dark Side of the Vine Semillon, The Honey Thief Natural Sweet.**

The Back Roads range

★★★★ **Matoppie Petite Sirah** ⓐ Deep, deep hued **15** ㊉ shows similar intensity of flavour - violet, raspberry, dark chocolate. Lovely soft tannins & clean acidic freshness, great example of this rare grape & worth keeping for more excitement to come.

Bo Lamotte Viognier ⓐ ★★★★ Single-block **15** ㊇ mixes apples & spice with citrus fruit, wrapped up with liquorice & aniseed. Nice texture from softening old oak, will do well with Cape Malay food. Not tasted **Bakenshoek Grenache Noir, Die Middagkrans Malbec.** — CM

Location/map/WO: Franschhoek ▪ Map grid reference: C1 ▪ Est 2013 ▪ 1stB 2012 ▪ Tasting, sales & cellar tours by appt ▪ Owner(s) Kevin Swart, Raymond Ndlovu & Jacques Wentzel ▪ Winemaker(s) Jacques Wentzel (Jan 2013) ▪ 140t/18,000cs own label 30% red 70% white ▪ IPW ▪ PO Box 686 Franschhoek 7690 ▪ sales@bevintners.co.za, jacques@bevintners.co.za, kevin@bevintners.co.za ▪ www.bevintners.co.za ▪ S 33° 54' 9.00 E 019° 7' 14.00", S 33° 54' 20.47" E 019° 6' 52.75" (Ryan's Kitchen) ▪ 🖼 wildly.mulling.firming ▪ T +27 (0)21-876-2903

☐ **Black Forest** *see* Louis
☐ **Black Granite** *see* Darling Cellars
☐ **Black Label** *see* Backsberg Estate Cellars

Black Oystercatcher Wines ⓐ ⓟ ⌂ ◎ ⓐ ⓑ

By the end of last century, the Humans were well established on their Moddervlei farm on the windy Agulhas plain, near the tip of Africa, so Dirk Human knew well 'the unique geology and cool climate' which was to shape the character of his wines. In 1998, he and his family 'decided to live their dream' and planted vines, becoming a pioneer of the Elim ward. It's now expanded to be a major destination in the area for everyone from brides to cyclists to diners. For beer drinkers too, with a resident craft beer producer.

★★★★ **Triton** ⓐ Silky smooth trio of mostly shiraz, splashes cab, mourvèdre. Mulberry & plum fruit of **14** ㊅ mingles with spicy/peppery tapenade notes over dark berries. Year old oak a subtle support.

★★★★ **Blanc Fumé** Selection within top-performing block for this sauvignon, intended for ageing. **14** ㊇ star-bright golden hue, passionfruit & winter melon nuances, bracing acidity countered by creamy lees from ferment in old barrels. **13** untasted.

★★★★☆ **White Pearl** ⊘ Exceptional Bordeaux blend of barrel fermented-semillon (60%), unoaked sauvignon. **16** ㊒ generosity & richness harmonised by mineral edge, reined in by brisk acidity. Dried herb & almond complexity, lengthy farewell.

Sauvignon Blanc ⓦ ★★★★ Vivid demo of complexity achieved through phased picking: nettles & capsicum from early fraction, kiwi fruit & gooseberry ex later 2 triages. Clean-cut acidity & minerality on **17** ㊄.

Cabernet Sauvignon-Merlot ★★★★ Elegant & well-integrated **15** ㊃ benefits from 3 years ageing in bottle. Redcurrants & cassis perfume from cab (54%) dusted with thyme & dark spices. Dry, commendably modest 13% alcohol. **Rosé** ★★★★ Sunset pink **17** ㊂ from merlot (67%) & cab, distinctive pomegranate, cherry & dried herb allures. Equally attractive dryness & svelte 11.5% alcohol. **Méthode Cap Classique Brut Rosé** ★★★ From merlot, **15** ㊀ dry sparkling a celebration of apple, brioche & citrus; unfiltered. Not tasted: **Sauvignon Blanc Reserve, Noble Late Harvest.** — GM

ocation/WO: Elim ▪ Map: Southern Cape ▪ Map grid reference: B3 ▪ Est 1998 ▪ 1stB 2003 ▪ Tasting, sales & ellar tours Mon–Fri 9–5 Sat 10–2.30 ▪ Sauvignon blanc vertical tasting by appt ▪ Closed Good Fri, Dec 24/25 & Jan 1 ▪ Restaurant, function & wedding venue: kitchen open Tue–Sun 11–2.30, booking essential (venue@ blackoystercatcher.co.za) ▪ Facilities for children ▪ Tour groups ▪ Conferences ▪ Conservation area ▪ Cycling oute ▪ Annual Sauvignon Blanc & Oyster Festival (Dec); peak season programme and other activities throughout the year ▪ Accommodation (stay@blackoystercatcher.co.za) ▪ Fraser's Folly craft beer R30/tasting Owner(s)/cellarmaster(s)/viticulturist(s) Dirk Human ▪ Winemaker(s) Dirk Human, with Willem Pietersen ▪ ,550ha/18.5ha (cab, merlot, shiraz, sauv, sem) ▪ ±110t/±15,000cs own label 20% red 60% white 20% rosé ▪ IPW, WIETA ▪ PO Box 199 Bredasdorp 7280 ▪ wine@blackoystercatcher.co.za, orders@blackoystercatcher. o.za ▪ www.blackoystercatcher.co.za ▪ S 34° 37' 58.0" E 019° 49' 39.9" ▪ ⟦∰⟧ posse.clergy.lifesavers ▪ F +27 0)86-666-7954 ▪ **T +27 (0)28-482-1618**

☐ **Black Pack** *see* Painted Wolf Wines

Black Pearl Vineyards ⓥ ⌂ ◎ ♿

From berry to bottle, self-taught winegrower and Cape Wine Master Mary-Lou Nash runs this boutique Paarl winery while her father, Lance, manages 'the least commercial tasting room in SA' - his kitchen! 'You could mistake Dr Nash for Dr Dolittle - both former medical doctors, English, eccentric, living with an extended menagerie...' Theirs may be a self-described 'madcap outfit', but they take their mostly exported wines very seriously, and the whole range offer seriously good value for money.

★★★★ **The Mischief Maker** ⊘ Silky blend of syrah (77%) & mourvèdre gets first grenache addition in **16** ★★★★★ ⑨⓪; enticing, with rose & violet perfume, cassis & black cherry fruit, black pepper, tobacco & vanilla from year in French oak. Less earthy than **15** ⑧⑨.

★★★★★ **Oro** ⊘ ⓐ Offering remarkable value, complex **16** ⑨③ cab-shiraz (78/22) seduces with hints of cinnamon, aniseed, pepper & fresh sage, melange of bright red fruit. Well knit after year French oak, with filigree tannins.

★★★★ **Chenin Blanc** ⊘ Dry, crisp & fresh, unwooded **18** ⑧⑨ from Swartland hugely over-delivers, its peach & chamomile perfume leading to citrus & stonefruit flavours in abundance, lingering on finish.

Not tasted: **Cabernet Sauvignon, Mourvèdre, Grenache-Mourvèdre.** — JG

Location/map: Paarl ▪ Map grid reference: D5 ▪ WO: Coastal/Swartland ▪ Est 1998 ▪ 1stB 2001 ▪ Tasting, sales & tours just about anytime but phone ahead ▪ Closed Dec 25 ▪ Walks ▪ Lapa & camping facilities ▪ Self-catering cottage ▪ Conservation area ▪ Owner(s) Lance & Mary-Lou Nash ▪ Winemaker(s)/viticulturist(s) Mary-Lou Nash CWM ▪ 240ha/7.2ha (cab, shiraz) ▪ ±5,000cs own label 90% red 10% white ▪ IPW ▪ PO Box 609 Suider-Paarl 7624 ▪ info@blackpearlwines.com ▪ www.blackpearlwines.com ▪ S 33° 44' 10.5" E 018° 53' 40.8" ▪ ⟦∰⟧ craziness.distinct.forgotten ▪ **T +27 (0)83-297-9796/+27 (0)83-395-6999**

☐ **Blacksmith** *see* The Blacksmith
☐ **Black Swan** *see* Hout Bay Vineyards
☐ **Black Tie** *see* Wineways Marketing

Blackwater Wine ⓥ

The past year has seen artisan winemaker Francois Haasbroek add new wines to his range from three vineyards he believes worthy of attention. Daniel Grenache is from Bot River and named for the youngest member of the Haasbroek family, the 10th generation, as indicated by the faint X on the label. More immediately recognisable is Picquet, a variant of the original spelling of Swartland town Piket(berg), origin of the chenin blanc. Vinification methods are as carefully considered as the names. Francois likes skin ferment on whites (including, unusually, riesling, his third new wine) for the 'structure and depth' it brings; whole bunches in red ferments 'add a pithy dry feel without drying out the wine.' Production of this fine, thoughtful and delicious range has moved to De Meye in Stellenbosch, where tastings are offered by appointment.

★★★★★ **Omerta** ⓧ One of few varietal carigans in SA, **15** ⑨③ follows trend for lighter, fresher reds. Part bunch-ferment lends vibrancy, precision, to gently persuasive & lengthy cranberry flavours.

★★★★ **Zeitgeist Cinsault** Apt new name: cinsau(l)t very much part of 'spirit of the age'. Deft, unoaked **17** (89) from Darling, pure varietal character, rich substance balanced by lightness of vibrant structure; bone-dry. 40% bunch ferment, aged in concrete 'egg'. Unfined.

★★★★☆ **Daniel Grenache** (NEW) (ᴁ) From Bot River, **17** (93) rich in flavour & body, the generous red cherries & spice are concentrated & long. Perfectly managed lively & juicy grape tannins provide energy & lightness to the ripe fruit. 50% wholebunch, old oak 11 months.

★★★★ **Cuvee Terra Lux Pinot Noir** (ᴅ) **15** ★★★★ (84) more robust than Elgin stablemate but not lacking dark-fruited richness in its soft core. May benefit with year/2. **14** (88) elegant & silky.

★★★★☆ **Prodigium Pinot Noir** (ᴅ) Dark fruit, spicy fragrance highlighted by Elgin's trademark natural vibrancy on **16** (90); there's substance & fine tannin too, with overall balance for current drinking, promising future. Older French barriques, 16 months. No **14**, **15**.

★★★★☆ **Cultellus Syrah** (ᴁ) As with all these reds, **16** (94) has freshness & purity but also textural depth & finest of tannins. Darker fruit, bit more muscle than **15** (93) but still harmonious & elegant. Spontaneous ferment, 40% wholebunch; French oak, none new.

★★★★ **Noir** Ripest, biggest feel of reds but no loss of balance, bright flavours from wholebunch portion on **15** (89), syrah (89%), splashes co-fermented carignan, cinsaut. Supple, well-integrated tannins & lingering savouriness for current & future enjoyment.

★★★★☆ **Picquet Chenin Blanc** (NEW) (ᴁ) Grown-up chenin from mature Piketberg vineyard. **17** (94) easy poise, natural freshness lifts, lightens lees creaminess, focuses subtle yet deep earthy, bruised apple flavours. Bone-dry, very long. Spontaneous ferment old, larger oak, 10 months lees ageing.

★★★★ **The Underdog Chenin Blanc** (⊘) Usual Swartland fruit for previewed **18** (89), though unwooded vs **15** (87) oaked. Gorgeous pear, apple fragrance, pure flavours weighted but with no loss of edge by 6 months on lees. Promises easy yet satisfying drinking. No **16**; **17** untasted.

★★★★ **Pleasure Garden Palomino** From Robertson single block, **17** (86) fruitier than **16** (86); some terpene, spice aromas, plump juiciness controlled by textured grip, savoury, dry conclusion. Pleasureable individual. Natural ferment in concrete 'egg'.

★★★★☆ **Blanc** Mainly chenin, barrel fermented, with clairette & palomino both skin-fermented, then oak-aged 10 months. **17** (90) attractive pale orange glow, more vinous than fruity with savoury acid backbone, rumble of tannin. Very tasty; happy partner to richer fish or poultry dishes. Occasional release, last was **14** ★★★★ (88) chenin, semillon. WO W Cape.

Riesling (NEW) ★★★☆ In more sombre, austere mood. **17** (84) steely, bone-dry, with finely spiced tannin tail from 8 days ferment on skins. Old-oak ageing on lees injects slight textural padding, but probably shows at best with food. 10.5% alcohol, WO Elgin. Not tasted: **Highroller Sauvignon Blanc**. — AL

Location/map: Stellenbosch ▪ Map grid reference: E1 ▪ WO: Swartland/Elgin/Western Cape/Robertson/ Darling/Bot River ▪ Est/1stB 2010 ▪ Tasting by appt only ▪ Owner(s) Blackwater Wines & Vines ▪ Cellarmaster(s)/winemaker(s)/viticulturist(s) Francois Haasbroek (Feb 2010) ▪ (carignan, cinsaut, pinot, shiraz, chenin, palomino, sauv) ▪ 30t/5,000cs own label 70% red 30% white ▪ Rose Str Paarl 7646 ▪ info@ blackwaterwine.com ▪ www.blackwaterwine.com ▪ S 33° 49′ 0.7″ E 018° 49′ 48.8″ ▪ [AW] movable.wisp. simulator ▪ T +27 (0)82-329-8849

Blake Family Wines (ᴘ)

Husband-and-wife team Andries and Marinda Blake source most grapes for their boutique label from dryland bushvines in Swartland, Andries having a nose for finding the best blocks after working in the area for many of his more than 25 years as winemaker. 'Blending,' Andries believes, 'is an art where a winemaker can show flair and skill.' Hence the pair of 'gems' in the top range, recently joined by varietal wines. All may be tasted at their new venue on the West Coast Road (R27).

Blake's range

★★★★ **Amethyst** Pinotage, cab, shiraz plus dash petit verdot in spicy, dark-fruited **16** (86). Rich, full bodied, with still youthfully assertive tannins & oak (80% new French).

★★★★ **Tourmaline** Chenin-based **17** (89) follows in flavoursome footsteps of **16** (87) with fresh limy tang & nutty richness from new-oaked partners chardonnay & viognier. Worth keeping few years.

Blake's Boys range

Malbec ★★★★ Fruit for juicy, plummy **16** (83) highlighted by gentle rounded tannins & freshness. Exuberance of 100% new French oak will benefit from year/2. WOW Cape for both. **Chenin Blanc** ★★★★ Full of sun-filled juicy flavours enhanced by 30% oaking, all new, **17** (85) is characterful & satisfying. — AL

Location: Malmesbury ▪ Map: Durbanville, Philadelphia & Darling ▪ Map grid reference: A1 ▪ WO: Swartland/Western Cape ▪ Est 2013 ▪ 1stB 2011 Tasting & sales Tue-Sun 8-4 at cellardoor facility on R27 before Yzerfontein turn-off ▪ Closed Good Fri, Dec 25 & Jan 1 ▪ Sales also via website & selected wine shops ▪ Owner(s) Andries & Marinda Blake ▪ Cellarmaster(s)/winemaker(s) Andries Blake ▪ 5t/2,000cs own label 40% red 60% white ▪ PO Box 1121 Malmesbury 7299 ▪ info@blakefamilywines.com ▪ www.blakefamily-wines.com ▪ S 33° 20′ 17.93″ E 018° 14′ 24.08″ ▪ **T +27 (0)82-922-6162**

☐ **Blake's Boys** see Blake Family Wines
☐ **Bloemcool** see Fairview

Bloemendal Wine Estate ⟨♀⟩ ⟨♍⟩ ⟨◎⟩ ⟨⟨&⟩

Bloemendal was established in 1702 to provide fresh produce for Dutch East India Company ships as they passed through Cape Town. Today customers of the 239-hectare Durbanville farm would expect a different sort of product - still fresh, but made from vines planted on many different aspects and elevations. The standout among the mostly classic French varieties is sauvignon blanc, which thrives thanks to the Atlantic's cooling influence. The celebrated Suider Terras sauvignon vineyard turned 35 and officially 'old' in 2017. This status will be reflected on the wine's label, as will its registration with the Old Vine Project. Visitors to the estate can sample Suider Terras and the rest of the range at the recently expanded tasting venue.

Estate range

★★★★ **Tierberg Single Vineyard Syrah** ⟨♀⟩ Riper dark spice on **14** (89) than previous, richer, more immediately approachable but also sufficient structure to warrant ageing. Older French oak.

★★★★ **Single Vineyard Chardonnay** ⟨♀⟩ Poised **14** (89) combines weight & breadth with freshness. Toasty oak yet to integrate with limy oatmeal flavours. Uncompromisingly dry finish also needs to settle.

★★★★☆ **Suider Terras Sauvignon Blanc** ⟨♀⟩ Off windswept southerly terrace, **15** ★★★★★ (96) gripping intensity, fantastic concentration. Superbly balanced, both weight & agility with endless length. Older French oak matured. Will reward cellaring. **14** (93) also exceptional.

★★★★☆ **Semillon** ⟨♀⟩ Promises to be up with best of this variety. **14** (94) smart oaking (used 500L French) enhances naturally silky texture & citrus peel, lemongrass concentration, though there is still a sense of tightness, linearity. All suggest lengthy lifespan.

★★★★☆ **Kanonberg** ⟨♀⟩ Excellent follow up to **14** ★★★★★ (95), **15** (93) sauvignon/semillon 70/30 partnership enhanced by careful oaking (50% barrel fermented, 100% oaked as blend). Dense silk texture energised by bracing acidity & 12.5% alcohol for a balanced whole, with great future.

Méthode Cap Classique ⟨♀⟩ ★★★ For those who like some real pizazz in their sauvignon/semillon, **15** (81) displays pairing's typical fruit plus a little leesy extra dimension & refreshing bubble. Not tasted: **Semillon Noble Late Harvest**.

Waterlily range

★★★★ **Shiraz** ⟨♀⟩ Most serious of range, still youthfully accessible. **15** (87) shows medium-bodied elegance in its dark berries & spice, suppleness, well-rounded dryness. Older oak, 17 months; 40% unoaked.

Cabernet Sauvignon ⟨♀⟩ ★★★ Carefully structured to be in tune with light blackberry features, **14** (81) rounded in older oak. **Malbec** ★★★★ In pure, fruit-forward mode as range dictates. **16** (85) ripe & vibrantly fresh dark berry flavours; nip of tannin lends form without disturbing early-drinking satisfaction. Older oak. **Merlot** ★★★ Sweet-fruited **16** (80) has juicy flesh, balanced freshness & hint toasty oak to counteract sweetish conclusion. **Pinotage** ⟨♀⟩ ★★★★ Big, luscious & fruit driven, **15** (83)'s mulberry exuberance barely contained by fine tannins. Year older French oak. **Sauvignon Blanc** ★★★ Now bottled, **17** (82) full of juicy tropical fruit, lively acidity & few grams sugar for drinkability. Tiny portion oaked for greater harmony. Not tasted: **Shiraz Rosé**. — AL

Location/WO: Durbanville ▪ Map: Durbanville, Philadelphia & Darling ▪ Map grid reference: C7 ▪ Est 1702 ▪ 1stB 1987 ▪ Tasting & sales Mon-Sat 10-5 Sun/pub hols 11-3; larger groups by appt ▪ Fee R40pp/Waterlily range & R6opp/Estate range ▪ Closed Dec 25/26 & Jan 1 ▪ Bon Amis @ Bloemendal ▪ MTB ▪ Owner(s) Spirito Trade 82 (Pty) Ltd ▪ Cellarmaster(s)/viticulturist(s) Andri Hanekom (2017) ▪ Winemaker(s) Boetman Langevelt (2006) ▪ (cab, malbec, merlot, ptage, shiraz, chard, sauv, sem) ▪ 100t ▪ PO Box 466 Durbanville 7551 ▪ info@bloemendalwines.co.za ▪ www.bloemendalwines.co.za ▪ S 33° 50′ 22.1″ E 018° 36′ 1.4″ ▪ 🌐 patterned.upward.perspective ▪ T +27 (0)21-975-9591

☐ **Blouvlei Wyne** *see* Mont du Toit Kelder
☐ **Blue Bottle** *see* Rooiberg Winery

Blue Crane Vineyards

A breeding pair of SA's endangered national bird inspired the name of this Tulbagh property, bought by Johannesburg-based mining businessman and racehorse owner (It's My Turn the 2018 Gold Cup winner) Fred Crabbia in 2009. Husband-and-wife duo Chris and Zia Fox handle the vines and wines respectively, along with the olive groves.

★★★★ Pinotage Subtle soft plum fruit of **15 ★★★★** ⑧⑤ shaded by spicy oak (40% new, some American, as for Shiraz) mid-2018. Needs time to meld. **14** ⑧⑦ better balanced in youth.

★★★★ Viognier ⊘ Oak cradles typically peachy fruit on barrel-fermented **16 ★★★★** ⑧⑤. Fresh, piquant & balanced, with judicious 30% new wood used, down from 50% in **15** ⑧⑦.

Shiraz ⊘ **★★★★** Rich, spicy **14** ⑧④ is fresh, bright & supple, with good fruit/oak balance (touch less American wood than Pinotage). **Chenin Blanc ★★★☆** Honeyed stonefruit on **16** ⑦⑧ again swamped by racy acidity though oaking toned down from previous. Light & uncomplicated. **Sauvignon Blanc** ⊘ **★★★★** Produced intermittently. Signature grapefruit & lemon pith tang on **17** ⑧④. Good body & length with lasting fruit on leesy tail. **First Flight** ⊘ **★★★★** Was 'Sauvignon Blanc-Chenin Blanc-Viognier'. Same blend in **16** ⑧③, ripe honeyed stonefruit matched by fresh acid, oak & lees. Not tasted: **Cabernet Sauvignon, SMV, Full Flight**. — FM

Location/WO: Tulbagh ▪ Est 2001 ▪ 1stB 2004 ▪ Closed to public ▪ Sales via website ▪ Owner(s) Fred & Manuela Crabbia ▪ Cellarmaster(s)/winemaker(s) Zia Fox ▪ Viticulturist(s) Chris Fox ▪ 138ha/9ha (cab, mourv, ptage, pinot, shiraz, chard, chenin, sauv, viog) ▪ 4,000cs own label 75% red 25% white ▪ PO Box 306 Tulbagh 6820 ▪ info@bluecrane.co.za ▪ www.bluecrane.co.za ▪ F +27 (0)23-230-0825 ▪ **T +27 (0)23-230-0823/+27 (0)60-980-0384/+27 (0)82-495-8512**

☐ **Blue Moose** *see* The Grape Grinder

Blue Owl Wines ⊕

This standalone label is produced in Franschhoek by Allée Bleue, whose team says it is 'really starting to take flight', with several export markets opening and the range possibly being extended with a Rosé '18.
Merlot ⊘ **★★★★** Structured & juicy **17** ⑧⑤, ample sour cherry & blackcurrant flavour but shade less finesse than in last-tasted **15 ★★★★** ⑧⑦. **Chardonnay** ⊘ **★★★★** Fresh, uncomplicated **17** ⑧④ has no wood, so lemon & melon fruit the focus, texture & body from 4 months on lees. — HC

Location: Franschhoek ▪ WO: Coastal ▪ 1stB 2015 ▪ Tasting at Allée Bleue Wines ▪ Winemaker(s) Van Zyl du Toit, with Clayton Christians (Aug 2017) ▪ PO Box 100 Groot Drakenstein 7680 ▪ info@alleebleue.com ▪ www.alleebleue.com ▪ F +27(0) 21-874-1850 ▪ **T +27(0) 21-874-1021**

☐ **Bob's Your Uncle** *see* Boer & Brit

Boekenhoutskloof Winery ⊕ ♿

The estate is tucked into the mountains at the southern end of the lovely Franschhoek Valley, but reaches far: not only to associated brands Wolftrap and Porcupine Ridge (listed elsewhere), but to properties in Stellenbosch, the Hemel-en-Aarde (see Cap Maritime entry) and the Swartland — which includes Porseleinberg, with its own highly reputed label but now also growing much of the fruit for the famous Boekenhoutskloof Syrah. That wine, and the others under the prestigious estate label, are the prime focus of chief winemaker, Gottfried Mocke, whose first vinifications here, from vintage 2016, feature below. Boekenhoutskloof's original winemaker, Marc Kent, remains the prime force and visionary, however, and he's overseen remarkable developments, the most recent and noticeable of which is a spectacular semi-underground maturation cellar, replete with a remarkable array of oak casks and barrels.

★★★★☆ **Franschhoek Cabernet Sauvignon** ⊛ Combines ripeness & intensity with purity & finesse. **16** ⑨④ complex black fruit, dab cab franc in play, authoritative tannin structure from 18 months new oak. As with **15** ⑨②, not for the impatient: decant in youth but ideally keep 6+ years.

★★★★☆ **Stellenbosch Cabernet Sauvignon** ⊛ From Helderberg fruit, typically leaner than Franschhoek sibling yet always an exceptional glassful, with pinpoint balance & staying power. **16** ⑨③ precise blue/black fruit, cigar smoke, plush leather & fragrant fynbos notes. 60% new oak, 18 months.

★★★★☆ **CWG Auction Reserve Syrah** ⊛ Fragrant **16** ⑨③ full-throttle hedgerow fruit, smoked meat & sweet tobacco encased in supple tannin. 50/50 Swartland (Porseleinberg)/Stellenbosch fruit, 40% wholebunch ferment in concrete, matured in older barriques. Like **15** ⑨②, made to last decade or more.

★★★★☆ **Syrah** ⊛ Inky-crimson **16** ⑨③ beautifully structured & understated. Ripe plum, mulberry, cured meat aromas & flavours accented by a smoky minerality. Mostly larger Austrian oak, none new; natural ferment & portion wholebunch. **15** ★★★★★ ⑨⑤ was the first from all-Swartland vineyards.

★★★★☆ **The Chocolate Block** ✓ ⊛ Remarkable quality & consistency from sizeable production, 2,057 barrels in **17** ★★★★★ ⑨⑤. Mainly syrah (64%) with grenache (14%) from own vineyards; bought-in cab (new barriques, rest older oak), cinsaut & viognier, as in **16** ⑨④. Plush & generous but serious, with structure & underlying power for good few years cellaring. Swartland WO. Also in 1.5L & 3L.

★★★★☆ **Semillon** ⊛ ⊛ Old vines (planted 1902, 1936 & 1942) for **16** ⑨③, with dash muscat d'Alexandrie, effusive spring blossom, orchard fruit, lanolin & citrus aromas. Seamless & richly textured, long elegant finish. 90% natural ferment in new oak, rest in concrete 'eggs'.

★★★★☆ **Noble Late Harvest** ⊛ Semillon botrytis dessert from single certified-organic riverside block stuns with intense stonefruit, honey, frangipane & preserved ginger. **15** ⑨④ luscious, with impressive concentration, 153 g/l sugar balanced by pinpoint acid. 30 months in new oak. 375 ml. — WB

Location/map: Franschhoek ▪ Map grid reference: D1 ▪ WO: Franschhoek/Swartland/Coastal/Stellenbosch ▪ Est 1994 ▪ 1stB 1996 ▪ Tasting by appt only ▪ Closed all pub hols ▪ Owner(s) Boekenhoutskloof Winery (Pty) Ltd ▪ Cellarmaster(s) Marc Kent (1994) ▪ Winemaker(s) Gottfried Mocke, Johan Nesenberend, Heinrich Hugo & Eben Meiring ▪ Viticulturist(s) Takkies Cloete ▪ Boekenhoutskloof: 71ha/9ha (cabs s/f, merlot, sem); Porseleinberg: 135ha/90ha (cinsaut, grenache, shiraz); Goldmine: 65ha/40ha (cinsaut, grenache, shiraz, chenin) ▪ 60% red 39% white 1% rosé ▪ BRC, HACCP, IPW ▪ PO Box 433 Franschhoek 7690 ▪ info@boekenhoutskloof.co.za ▪ www.boekenhoutskloof.co.za ▪ S 33° 56' 33.0" E 019° 6' 28.0" ▪ 🖾 franchiser.dipper. reduce ▪ **T +27 (0)21-876-3320**

Boer & Brit   ⓠ

Founded just under a decade ago by Stefan Gerber and Alex Milner, direct descendants of two major Anglo-Boer War protagonists, this cleverly branded export label, with wines styled to be 'as intense and genuine as the battle their ancestors fought long ago', is now wholly owned by Stefan and offered for tasting at a farm stall in the heart of wildflower country on the West Coast.

Location: Bitterfontein ▪ Map: Olifants River ▪ Map grid reference: A1 ▪ Est 2010 ▪ 1stB 2008 ▪ Tasting at Gerber & Co farmstall at Bitterfontein on N7, open daily 8-5 ▪ Owner(s) Stefan Gerber ▪ Winemaker(s) Stefan Gerber & Alex Milner (both Jul 2010) ▪ 30t/±10,000cs own label 60% red 40% white ▪ Other export label: Bob's Your Uncle ▪ PO Box 3384 Matieland 7602 ▪ stefan@boerandbrit.com ▪ www.boerandbrit.com ▪ S 31° 2' 27.73" E 018° 16' 6.96" ▪ **T +27 (0)84-515-6677**

☐ **Boland Cellar** see Boland Kelder

Boland Kelder   ⓠ ⑪ ⊚

Significant and awarded Paarl-based grower-owned Boland Kelder continues to execute and refine the strategy set in 2016, its 75th anniversary. With 1,900 ha of vineyards to choose from, the focus is admirable: blends with the winery's three flagship varieties for the One Formation range, Talent & Terroir tapping into popular tastes, Five Climates drawing from a quintet of regions, and the Reserve collection putting the best foot forward. Note the particular showcasing of chenin: five varietals and blends across the ranges.

Reserve No. 1 range

★★★★ Cabernet Sauvignon ⊘ Concentration & intensity the hallmarks of **16** ⑧⑧ barrel sample, cassis & cedar, silky tannins, sleek but with hidden power. Back on track after **14 ★★★** ⑧②; no **15**.

★★★★ Shiraz ⊘ Sampled before bottling, black fruit & cigarbox, cocoa notes from mainly new oak. **16** ⑧⑧ supple, harmonious, noteworthy.

★★★★ Chenin Blanc ⊘ Partial barrel ferment for previewed **17** ⑧⑧, total 14 months oak, long lees contact. Has intense stonefruit, good palate weight; fruit is the hero, savoury spicing subtle.

★★★★ Chenin Blanc Unwooded ⊘ **18** ⑧⑦ ex tank already showing quince & melon styling, zesty limy freshness, satisfying length. Nice contrast to oaked sibling.

Not tasted: **Merlot**, **Pinotage**, **Chardonnay**.

One Formation range

★★★★ Pinotage-Shiraz-Grenache ⊘ New name (was 'Red Blend'), same components. Blueberry pinotage typicity, espresso savouriness, **16** ⑧⑧'s tannin stiffening promising good ageing.

★★★★ Shiraz-Grenache-Viognier 🆕 ⊘ 85% shiraz, **16** ⑧⑨ has black plums at core, cinnamon & nutmeg highlights, silky liquorice flavours. Delicious. WO W Cape for both reds.

★★★★ Chenin Blanc-Sauvignon Blanc-Grenache Blanc ⊘ Dab of oak in previewed **18** ⑧⑨, same varieties as **17** ⑧⑥'s 'White Blend'. Quince & melon from chenin dominance but other nuances add interest, complexity. Sleek & stylish, lovely mineral finish.

Five Climates Single Varietal range

Chardonnay ★★★ Citrus styled, unoaked, svelte (13% alcohol) but lees contact has added creaminess to **18** ⑧①'s texture. **Chenin Blanc** ⊘ **★★★☆** Quince & bruised apple, there's no mistaking the variety in unwooded **18** ⑧④. Not tasted: **Sauvignon Blanc**.

Talent & Terroir range

Shiraz ⊘ 🍷 **★★★☆** Richly fruity, **17** ⑧⑤ barrel sample is packed with flavour & spice, full, round & satisfying. **Chenin Blanc** ⊘ 🍷 **★★★☆** Citrus & greengage, zesty **18** ⑧④ unoaked tank sample remains variety true, as all Boland chenins, but has own charming & delicious personality.

Sauvignon Blanc 🆕 ⊘ **★★★☆** Pre-bottling, **18** ⑧⑤ crackles with freshness, gooseberry & lime. Persistent finish. — CR

Location/map: Paarl ▪ Map grid reference: E4 ▪ WO: Coastal/Western Cape ▪ Est/1stB 1941 ▪ Tasting & sales Mon-Fri 9–5 Sat/pub hols 10-3 ▪ Closed Easter weekend, Dec 25/26 & Jan 1 ▪ Cellar tours by appt ▪ Meals/refreshments ▪ Owner(s) 57 producing shareholders ▪ Winemaker(s) Handré Barkhuizen (2009) & Bernard Smuts (2001), with Monique de Villiers (2015) & Rosco Lewis (2016) ▪ Viticulturist(s) Spekkies van Breda (2016) ▪ 1,900ha (cab, merlot, ptage, shiraz, chard, chenin, nouvelle, sauv, viog) ▪ 21,881t/240,000cs own label 48% red 50% white 2% rosé + 330,300cs for clients ▪ Other export brands: Lindenhof, Lionsway, Montestell ▪ WIETA ▪ PO Box 7007 Noorder-Paarl 7623 ▪ info@bolandkelder.co.za ▪ www.bolandkelder.co.za, www.bolandcellar.co.za ▪ S 33° 48' 47.21" E 018° 48' 31.70" (farm), S 33° 41' 19.6" E 018° 57' 20.1" (deli) ▪ 🖽 though.contributed.quotable ▪ F +27 (0)21-862-5379 ▪ **T +27 (0)21-872-1766**

Bon Courage Estate   ⓠ ⑪ ⓐ ⓑ

A Breede River-side property in Robertson, Bruwer family-owned for three generations, each contributing to the range, the quality and especially to the estate's ongoing market relevance. A large range suits all tastes and prices, from popular to sophisticated. Patriarch Willie planted chenin and muscats in the 1920s, his son André established the classic labels, and incumbent cellarmaster Jacques produces acclaimed MCC bubblies and upmarket reds. Celebrating renewal and tradition, there's a new tasting locale, and the Cape Dutch manor was 200 years old in 2018.

Inkará range

★★★★ Cabernet Sauvignon Sample tasted previously, **15 ★★★★★** ⑨⓪ year later showing same admirable styling but with more depth, better tannin integration, a step up. Lots of care: whole-berry ferment, new French/American oak 18-24 months. Handsome, muscular, will reward cellaring, like **14** ⑧⑦.

★★★★ **Merlot** Ⓖ Now bottled, **15** ⑧⑧ has settled into a well-formed dark berry & chocolate beauty. Tannins more melded, still promising a long life ahead: made with serious intent.

★★★★ **Shiraz** Previewed last time, **15** ⑧⑨ shows same mocha-chocolate savoury richness, now more in harmony with dark berry opulence. Packed with flavour & interest, new-oak tannins promising a future.

Pinot Noir ★★★★ Now bottled & showing better, **15** ⑧④ a bold varietal expression, with flesh & power: wild dark fruit, earthy notes, well oaked (24 months), giving flavour, firm dry tannin.

Jacques Bruére Méthode Cap Classique sparkling range

★★★★★ **Cuvée Brut Rosé** Ⓐ Palest of pinks, but don't be fooled by **11** ⑨③'s prettiness; longest on lees of these, 48 months, 80% pinot noir for red berries, faintest hint of forest floor, chardonnay's role is freshness, some citrus flavour. Nothing overt, just harmony & grace.

★★★★★ **Blanc de Blancs** Ⓐ Chardonnay, bone-dry, elegant & refined, **11** ⑨③ is all about lemon, nicely capturing the preserved version in its perfume, zest in the flavours. Gentle brioche notes from oak & 24 months on lees fit the character. Great focus & finesse. Also in 3L.

★★★★★ **Brut Reserve** Ⓕ 60/40 pinot noir, chardonnay; 10% oaked, as rest; **11** ⑨③ spent 36-48 months on its lees, & it shows in the flavour richness. Baked apple & lemon preserve, crushed almonds, elegantly structured & crisply fresh. Classic styling, but offers more.

Bon Courage range

★★★★ **Cabernet Sauvignon** ⓥ Now bottled, better-integrated **15** ⑧⑧ shows classic cab cassis, new oak well-judged for cedar spicing, tannin backbone, no barrier to current enjoyment. Has elegance & style.

★★★★ **Le Terroir Chardonnay** Ⓖ Same winemaking as Prestige Cuvée, **16** ⑧⑦ takes it to another level. Forthcoming citrus preserve perfume & flavours, laced with brightening acidity, vanilla notes an underpin. Intense, vibrant.

★★★★ **Gewürztraminer Special Late Harvest** Expressive honeysuckle & rosewater perfumes, **18** ⑧⑨'s flavours as compelling, sweet stonefruit & pineapple. Both elegant (11% alcohol) & rich, acidity giving great length. Improves on **17** ★★★★ ⑧④.

★★★★☆ **Noble Late Harvest** Ⓖ From riesling, unoaked, fully botrytised grapes account for **16** ⑨②'s richness (202 g/l sugar) & honeyed flavours. Tangy stonefruit & pineapple pierced through by limy acidity; shows admirable tension & vibrancy. 375 ml.

★★★★ **White Muscadel** Weaves its complexity & concentration like a well-fitting cloak, everything in place. **18** ★★★★☆ ⑨① sultanas & dried stonefruit, citrus peel, especially tangerine, sweeter than red version but shot through with revitalising acidity. Improves on **17** ⑧⑥.

Estate Blend Red ⓥ ⓦ ★★★★ Consistent style, cab-led with shiraz, both important to **16** ⑧④. Cassis core, with shiraz giving smoky, dry scrub savoury interest. Supple tannins add to the pleasure. **André's Fame Colombard** ⓦ ★★★ Ex tank already promises enjoyment, an enlivening leafy top note to the litchi/guava styling, zinging fresh. **18** ⑧② admirably slender (11.5% alcohol), not a shy bone in its body. **Gewürztraminer Dry** ⓦ ★★★ Previewed **18** ⑧① delightfully expressive, Turkish delight/rosewater perfume, becoming more linear on the palate, aromatically spiced but with restraint, focus. Dry styling unusual in SA. **The Gooseberry Bush Sauvignon Blanc** ⓦ ★★★ Yes, gooseberries but also capsicum & nettles, **18** ⑧① is taut, intense, with invigorating freshness & length. Quite cool-climate styling, admirable.

The Mulberry Bush Merlot ★★★ Cassis & dark plums, there's a creaminess to **17** ⑧①'s fruit, light oaking aiding the enjoyment. Different, improved style to more tannic **16** ★★ ⑦④. **Pinotage** ★★★ Satisfyingly opulent, now-bottled **15** ⑧① showcases dark fruit ripeness & vanilla from 50% wooded component (some American barrels). Curvaceous & ultra-smooth. **The Pepper Tree Shiraz** ★★★★ Savoury seasoning an equal partner with berry/plum fruit in **16** ⑧⑤, intriguing whiffs of fynbos, dry scrub. Smooth texture, with enough tannin backing for food matching. **Chardonnay Prestige Cuvée** ★★★★ Harmonious fruit/oak partnership, butterscotch seam through **17** ⑧④'s white peach & citrus flavours. Lots on offer without excess; has personality, quiet confidence. **Chardonnay Unwooded** ★★★ Pre-bottled sample **18** ⑧① shows stonefruit & citrus, perked up by limy acidity. Good example of the variety unadorned. **Estate Blend White** ★★★ From 71% colombard with chardonnay, **18** ⑧① shows litchi & pineapple styling from the dominant partner, no hardship. Vibrantly fresh, sleek (12% alcohol) & tasty. **Blush Vin Doux** ⓥ ★★★ This has party written all over it, elegantly structured **NV** ⑦⑦ from muscadel. Pale pink bubbly with a grapey, dried fruit character, suiting the sweetness. **Red Muscadel** ★★★★ Raisins & dried stonefruit, fortified **18** ⑧④ has admirable flavour concentration, is full-sweet without being cloying. **Cape Vintage** ★★★ Equal blend touriga, tinta & souzão - you can't go more port-classic than that. **17** ⑧① spent year in oak, has sweet dark-toned opulence, fruit & liquorice, the faintest whiff of scrub.

Like Father Like Son range

Merlot-Cabernet Sauvignon ⊘ ★★★ Ex-tank **18** ⑦⑧ unoaked to supply fruit-driven, honest, uncomplicated drinking pleasure. **Pinotage Rosé** ★★ Heaps of fruit in **18** ⑦④, reflecting the variety; sweet, with moderate alcohol. **Chenin Blanc** ★★★ Budget priced & made for sharing with friends, as all these. Apple & green plum, trim-figured **18** ⑦⑧ is dry & zesty. — CR

Location/map/WO: Robertson ▪ Map grid reference: B5 ▪ Est 1927 ▪ 1stB 1983 ▪ Tasting & sales Mon-Fri 8–5 Sat 9–3 ▪ Fee R20pp for groups of 10+ ▪ Closed Good Fri, Dec 25 & Jan 1 ▪ Café Maude T +27 (0)23-626-6806 ▪ Facilities for children ▪ Olive oil ▪ Owner(s) André & Jacques Bruwer ▪ Winemaker(s) Jacques Bruwer, with Phillip Viljoen (Jan 2015) ▪ Viticulturist(s) André Bruwer ▪ 150ha (cab, pinot, shiraz, chard) ▪ 40% red 50% white 10% rosé ▪ Export brand: Three Rivers ▪ PO Box 589 Robertson 6705 ▪ wine@boncourage.co.za ▪ www.boncourage.co.za ▪ S 33° 50' 43.8" E 019° 57' 38.0" ▪ ⌗ lushly.widgets.forgave ▪ F +27 (0)23-626-3581 ▪ T +27 (0)23-626-4178

☐ **Bonfire Hill Extreme Vineyards** see Bruce Jack Wines
☐ **Bonne Esperance** see KWV Wines

Bonnievale Wines
⑨ ⓐ ⓑ ⓒ

Near the namesake Breede River town, Bonnievale Wines says it has made significant strides in efficiencies and fruit quality, not to mention consumer awareness of its premium value proposition, thanks to rebranding (a new logo, most obviously, and the mid-tier repositioned as River Collection). Crediting the 'invaluable' contribution made by strategic brand advisor Carina Gouws, CEO John Barnardt believes these changes 'will have a significant impact on our market presence'.

Barrel Select range
★★★★ **Shiraz** ⊘ A real fireside comforter, **15** ⑧⑧ liquidised dark fruit & dried prunes in a generous spice-sprinkled body; balanced, with cappuccino on the finish.

Cabernet Sauvignon ★★★★ Ripe blackcurrant in a supple structure, **15** ⑧⑤ medium body, dry, chocolate & vanilla notes adding depth to tasty mouthful.

River Collection
....
Cinsault Rosé ⓃⒺⓌ ⑨ ★★★ Delightful sunset hue & rosepetal perfume - **18** ⑧① is pretty & charming, the flavours crisply dry & zesty to the end. Attractive addition to burgeoning category. **Chenin Blanc** ⓃⒺⓌ ⊘ ⑨ ★★★★ Lovely expression of the grape, there being no wood to complicate the bright, pure & fresh pineapple, passionfruit & zingy lime. **18** ⑧③ simply delicious.
....
Merlot ★★★ No-worries **17** ⑧② will welcome you home, offer Christmas cake & plum pudding with mulled wine spices. **Pinotage** ★★★ Chocolate-dipped plums, wild heather & wafts of coffee, **17** ⑧② just-dry & easy to sip. **Shiraz** ★★ Dark sweet fruit mixed with toffee, **17** ⑦⑤ is juicy if tad less generous than last. **Cabernet Sauvignon-Merlot** ★★★ Sweet black fruit, spicecake & mocha touch make **17** ⑦⑨ slip down easily. **Chardonnay** ⊘ ★★★★ Unadorned by oak, lemon & crunchy apple have free rein on **18** ⑧④'s fleshy palate, finishing clean & bright. **Sauvignon Blanc** ★★★ Crisp **18** ⑦⑦, sun-ripe tropical flavours which exit quite hastily. **Natural Sweet Shiraz** ★★ Fragrant & markedly sweet **NV** ⑦④, wild berry aromas/flavours & a dusty edge. Serve chilled. Not tasted: **Sauvignon Blanc Brut**. Discontinued: **Cabernet Sauvignon-Shiraz**.

Perlé range
Dusk ⑫ ★ Low-alcohol rosé from ruby cab, **NV** ⑥⑦ with teeny soft bubbles, charming sweetness. Not tasted: **Dawn**, **Sushi**.

Discontinued: **Riggton range**. — WB

Location/WO: Bonnievale ▪ Map: Robertson ▪ Map grid reference: D3 ▪ Est 1950 ▪ 1stB 1977 ▪ Tasting & sales Mon-Fri 9–5 Sat 10–1 ▪ Closed Easter Fri-Mon, Dec 25/26 & Jan 1 ▪ Cheese straws, biltong/droëwors

▪ Facilities for children ▪ Tour groups ▪ Conferences (12 pax) ▪ Christmas Market ▪ Owner(s) 110 members ▪ Winemaker(s) Marthinus Rademeyer (Dec 2009), Edwin Mathambo (Dec 2012) & Jean Slabber (Jun 2017) ▪ Viticulturist(s) Sakkie Bosman (Nov 2006) ▪ 1,697ha (cab, merlot, ptage, shiraz, chard, chenin, cbard, sauv) ▪ ISO 22 000, IPW, WIETA ▪ PO Box 206 Bonnievale 6730 ▪ info@bonnievalewines.co.za ▪ www.bonnievalewines.co.za ▪ S 33° 57' 27" E 020° 06' 06" ▪ article.traumas.responded ▪ F +27 (0)23-616-2332 ▪ **T +27 (0)23-616-2795**

Bonview Wines

Carel and Teuns Keuzenkamp, owners of negociant business Bonview, have long-term contracts with various Cape cellars, and target mainly West Africa and China with 'quality wines that are affordable and attuned to the tastes of everyday wine consumers'.

Location: Stellenbosch ▪ Est 2011 ▪ 1stB 2012 ▪ Closed to public ▪ Owner(s) Carel & Teuns Keuzenkamp ▪ 7,000cs own label 95% red 5% white ▪ PO Box 1977 Somerset West 7129 ▪ bonview@telkomsa.net ▪ F +27 (0)86-224-9348 ▪ **T +27 (0)21-887-5812**

Boplaas Family Vineyards   Ⓡ ⓜ ⓐ ⓐ

Another member of the family joins the team at this powerhouse of Portuguese-style wines in Klein Karoo's Calitzdorp. Cellarmaster Carel Nel and daughters Margaux and Rozanne (winemaker and marketer respectively) will now work alongside son/brother Daniel, who will be responsible for innovation and expansion of the farm's range of award-winning potstill brandies. To help him on his way, a new still (named Falcon) was installed last year. 2018 was full of academic success for Margaux, who completed her MBA to go with her MSc on touriga nacional as a table wine. To top it all, she married long-term partner Leon Coetzee, also her wine-partner in The Fledge & Co, listed separately.

Heritage Reserve range

★★★★★ **White Muscadel** Ⓡ Limited bottling in exceptional years to honour Nel family association with fortified muscat de Frontignan since mid 1800s. **14** ⑨③ oozes marmalade, honey, candied ginger. Mouthfilling, complex & rich with a cleansing fresh finish. Will reward ageing.

Discontinued: **Red Muscadel**.

Family Reserve range

★★★★ **Cabernet Sauvignon** Dense & concentrated **15** ⑧⑦ from Stellenbosch mixes intriguing raspberry & cherry notes with dark chocolate & mint, vanilla & cream from year new/2nd-fill oak.

★★★★ **Touriga Francesa** Ⓡ From Stellenbosch, scarce grape (4 ha in SA!), **12** ⑧⑦ enchants with black fruit pastille flavours, hint of dark chocolate, rounded mouthfeel & fragrant mint finish.

★★★★★ **Touriga Nacional** Ⓡ 'King of Portuguese grapes' sourced from 3 old Stellenbosch blocks. **14** ⑨⓪ has plum, blackberry & savoury meat flavours wrapped in supple tannins, leading to a lengthy farewell. Great for rich grilled meat dishes. 14 months French oak.

★★★★ **Gamka** Ⓡ In **15** ★★★★★ ⑨②, Stellenbosch shiraz (39%) ramps up the blend with Calitzdorp touriga & tinta, year in new oak. Perfumed ripe wild berries, scrub, cured meat flavours & lifted floral finish. Big & bold, made to last decade or more. Last tasted was **13** ⑧⑥.

★★★★★ **Ring of Rocks** ⓥ ⓐ Rich & warming blend of Portuguese grapes (tintas barocca & francesa, touriga), **15** ⑨② styled for the long term, with firm ripe tannins, lively acidity & delicious chewy black fruit. Some new oak adds vanilla, spice & overall complexity.

★★★★ **Bobbejaanberg Sauvignon Blanc Reserve** Plenty of sappy green fruit on **18** ⑧⑨ - figs, peppers, limes - held together with lively acidity, leading to flinty finish. Outeniqua vines. Most enjoyable though shade less intense than stellar **17** ★★★★★ ⑨③.

★★★★★ **Gamka Branca** ⓐ Very accomplished **17** ⑨③ mixes old-vine chenin with chardonnay, grenache blanc, viognier & verdelho into seamless mouthful of peach, pith & peel, with cream & spice. Delicious texture from old oak & lees, endless finish. WO W Cape.

Discontinued: **Pinot Noir Méthode Cap Classique**.

Boplaas range

★★★★ Ouma Cloete Straw Wine ⓦ From air-dried viognier & muscat de Frontignan, **15** (87) oozes bright orchard fruit, honey & candied pineapple. Full, with balanced sweetness. Serve well-chilled.

★★★★★ The 1932 Block Hanepoot ⓦ Exceptional fortified from small, very low-yielding single block planted along the Gamka River in 1932. **15** (92) wonderful freshness balancing the intense, opulent fruit & floral flavours. Concentrated, with a lemon zest finish. 500 ml.

★★★★ Red Muscadel Intense & aromatic **17** (87) shows layers of flavour - jasmine, apricot, raisin & honey - in luscious mouthful with well-integrated alcohol & excellent length.

★★★★ Cape Ruby ⓦ Super expression of this 'port' style. NV (86) red fruited, vanilla nuanced. Sweet & delicious, ends with a fresh berry tang. Tinta (70%), touriga, souzão, 6 months in port 'pipes'.

★★★★★ Cape Tawny ⓦ 'Port' from tinta (70%), touriga, souzão. Toasted nuts & dried fig aromas followed by mellow caramel richness from 10-12 years in barrel (500L). NV (94) elegant & seamless, with savoury hints. Match with mature hard cheese. WO W Cape.

★★★★★ Cape Tawny Vintners Reserve Bin 1880 ⓦ Concentrated 'port' with many flavour layers, raisined fruit, wonderful oak/alcohol integration & unflagging finish. NV (94) from tinta (85%) & touriga, aged minimum 10 years. 375 ml.

★★★★☆ Cape Vintage (🍇) Classic 'port' **16** (93) exudes a beguiling warmth, with raisins, fruitcake, dark chocolate & baking spices, year oak adds delicious aniseed finish. From 80% touriga with tinta barocca & tiny tweak of souzão, all from Calitzdorp, prepped for the long haul. 18% alcohol.

★★★★☆ Cape Vintage Reserve (🍇) So much going on in **16** (94) 'port'! Raisins, damsons, Xmas cake, orange peel added to chocolate, leather & spice. Styled for long ageing - warm, well-managed alcohol, firm tannins & delicious gritty texture all confirm. Mainly touriga nacional with dashes tinta barocca, souzão & touriga franca from Stellenbosch & Calitzdorp. 19% alcohol. Year Portuguese 'pipes'.

★★★★ Cape Vintage The Chocolate Choc-cherry notes on lively **16** ★★★★ (85) 'port' from tinta & 30% touriga. Interesting spice notes & cocoa powder tail, shade less intense than **15** (87). Year barrelled. 375 ml. WO W Cape.

- - - - - - - - - -

Cabernet Sauvignon (✓) (🍷) ★★★★ A mouthwatering fruit bomb, **16** (84) shimmers with lively red & black cherries; moderate alcohol adds to appeal of delightfully appetising summer red. **Touriga Nacional** (✓) (🍷) ★★★★ Characterful **17** (84) showing good typicity - dense black fruit with orange peel twists - chunky but smooth tannins & bright finish.

- - - - - - - - - -

Pinotage ★★★ Moreish red fruit on just-dry **17** (81) makes for easy-drinking fun. 9 months older French oak adds touch of coffee/toffee at finish. **Tinta Barocca** ★★★ Old oak adds spicy, earthy notes to juicy, black-fruit-packed **16** (82). Lovely braai wine. **Eerste Water Sauvignon Blanc** (NEW) ★★★★ Floral, fresh & fruity **18** (85) mixes tropical fruit & citrus with crunchy acidity & touch of cream. Grapes from Calitzdorp area's Groenfontein Valley. **Pinot Noir Brut Sparkling** ★★★ Dry, playful & frothy, **18** (82) cranberry & cherry fruit whizzed up with lively acidity for the perfect Sunday brunch fizz. **Hanepoot** ⓦ ★★★ Fortified muscat shimmers gold in the glass, offers grapey melon flavours, lovely clean spirity grip on the finish of **17** (81). **White Muscadel** ⓦ ★★★★ A festival of candied fruit & citrus rind, sweet yet bouncy, spirity & delightful. **17** (84) a fortified to brighten your everyday. Not tasted: **Merlot, Stoepsit Sauvignon Blanc, Cape Portuguese White Blend.** Occasional release: **Cape Tawny, Cape Tawny Reserve.** Discontinued: **Tinta Chocolat, Red Muscadel Reserve, Muscadel Reserve.**

Brandy range

★★★★ Carel Nel Reserve 5 Years ⓦ Leafy fresh notes over dried apricot & pear. Fine depth of flavour, delicate & velvety, with a floral dry finish. 40% potstill. From colombard, as all.

★★★★★ Potstill Reserve 15 Years (NEW) Lovely depth of colour, a limpid amber, soft aromas of dried peach, roast hazelnut, marmalade & herbs - wonderful complexity & dimension, mirrored on a palate which is full & round, harmonious & elegant. Old Limousin cask aged, as all.

★★★★★ Potstill Reserve 20 Years ⓦ Gold coloured with hint of olive green on rim. Fruitcake, dried apricots, marzipan, sweet prune flavours, mingling with smooth vanilla. Super-complex, elegant & silky palate - both delicate & penetrating - leads to a gorgeous long finish. Just 500 bottles made.

★★★★☆ **Potstill Reserve 8 Years** ⓥ Serious, effortlessly elegant 100% potstill (as are 15 & 20 Years) shows caramel, sweet & smoky oak, fuller body with chocolate & dried fruit. Silky & complex, still youthful, with clean vanilla finish.

Occasional release: **Potstill Reserve 12 Years**. — CM, WB

Location: Calitzdorp ▪ Map: Klein Karoo & Garden Route ▪ Map grid reference: B5 C4 ▪ WO: Calitzdorp/ Western Cape/Stellenbosch/Calitzdorp-Stellenbosch ▪ Est 1880 ▪ 1stB 1982 ▪ Tasting & sales Mon-Fri 9-5 Sat 9-4 Sun 10-3 ▪ Fee R35pp ▪ Closed Good Fri & Dec 25 ▪ Cellar tours by appt ▪ Facilities for children ▪ Gifts ▪ Farm produce ▪ Walks/hikes ▪ Conservation area ▪ Ring of Rocks ▪ Boplaas Stoepsit Bistro ▪ Spirits tasting incl brandy, gin & whiskey ▪ Owner(s) Carel Nel ▪ Cellarmaster(s) Carel Nel (1982) ▪ Winemaker(s) Margaux Nel (Dec 2006) ▪ Viticulturist(s) Danie Strydom ▪ 2,300ha/70ha (cab, ptage, shiraz, tinta, touriga, chard, cbard, sauv) ▪ 55% red 45% white ▪ IPW ▪ PO Box 156 Calitzdorp 6660 ▪ info@boplaas.co.za ▪ www.boplaas. co.za ▪ S 33° 32' 8.0" E 021° 41' 1.9" (Boplaas), S 34° 4' 45.40" E 022° 8' 25.22" (Boplaas on Garden Route) ▪ 🄰🄳 traditional.external.theatrics ▪ F +27 (0)44-213-3750 ▪ **T +27 (0)44-213-3326**

Boschendal Wines ⓥ ⓜ ⓐ ⓞ ⓐ ⓑ

The splendid, extensive and historic Boschendal estate is on the Franschhoek edge of Stellenbosch, with its iconic white-gabled Manor House (recently refurbished) seen across vineyards and against the backdrop of towering Groot Drakenstein mountains. Joining the great array of visitor attractions, which includes a 'historic tasting' of 5 wines representing Boschendal's history, is the Heritage Rose Garden – 'the largest such rose garden in the southern hemisphere', they proudly claim. It is also home to Boschendal Wines, owned by major producer DGB. Last year saw the arrival of widely experienced Jacques Viljoen as new cellarmaster. He'll be working alongside Lizelle Gerber, responsible for white and sparkling wines – and DGB's new group winemaker, Stephan Joubert – whose former position as viticulturist has been taken over by Heinie Nel .

Reserve Collection

★★★★ **Méthode Cap Classique Brut** Latest NV ⑧⑦ bubbly near-equal blend chardonnay & pinot noir. Brioche, ripe apple, subtle berries on the aroma, with more citrus on the crisp, sufficiently dry but lightly rich palate.

★★★★☆ **Méthode Cap Classique Grande Cuvée Brut** ⓥ Classic pinot noir & chardonnay (61/39) bubbly, former's gentle raspberry notes dominating **13** ★★★★ ⑧⑦. Lively & refreshing, if yet to gain lees complexity of **12** ⑨②. Elgin grapes.

★★★★☆ **Vin d'Or** ⓥ Noble Late Harvest **15** ⑨③ from riesling replicates **13** ⑨④ exactly: gorgeous scented spice elaborated by botrytis. Luscious flavours, cleansed by a riveting acid, culminate in explosive tangy tail. Just 12% alcohol adds to the any-time-of-day drinking pleasure. No **14**.

★★★★ **10 Year Old Potstill Brandy** ⓥ Quite deep-coloured, suggesting richness to come. Heady dried fruit, spice & sandalwood; the palate a touch too sweet & fiery for elegance, but very sippable.

Méthode Cap Classique Brut Rosé ★★★★ Latest apricot-gold **NV** ⑧⑤ sparkling mostly from pinot noir (& a little pinotage, chardonnay), step up from previous. Crisp & dry, with fresh red apple, strawberry & cranberry notes. **Méthode Cap Classique Jean Le Long** ⓥ ★★★★ New disgorgement of **07** ⑧④ from chardonnay with 5 years on-cork ageing, shows signs of tiring, shorter flavours, though bubble remains bright enough. Best drink up. Coastal WO. **Méthode Cap Classique Demi Sec** 🄽🄴🅆 ★★★ Easygoing pleasure on **NV** ⑧② from chardonnay & pinot noir. Uncomplicated & decent, with fruity off-dry charm. Not tasted: **Grande Reserve**.

1685 range

Cabernet Sauvignon ⓥ ★★★ Fruit the main focus in this range. Fresh ripe blackberries in **15** ⑧① with hint spicy oak. Tannins tempered for current drinking by gram sugar; can age few years too. Stellenbosch WO. **Merlot** ★★★ Offers fruitcake & tobacco notes, & definite herbal twist. **16** ⑧② firmly structured & hint of sweetness. This range WO W Cape or Coastal unless noted. **Shiraz** ★★★★ Pleasing ripe, dark fruit on **16** ⑧④; juicy but well structured, with bright acidity & gentle tannic underpinning. 30% new oak. **S&M** ★★★ Usual 70/30 shiraz/mourvèdre blend in **16** ⑧②. Firmer structure than Shiraz, bolder & a little rustic. A few enriching grams of sugar, like most in range - here a bit more evident. **Chardonnay-Pinot Noir** ★★★★ Pink-tinged gold **17** ⑧④ rosé (61% chardonnay) has delicious berried charm, with a well-balanced freshness & gratifying hint of sweetness. **Chardonnay** ★★★★ Forward citrus, buttered toast notes introduce partly oaked **17** (83). Rich, with lemon-lime acidity, rounded, with usual deftly managed flattering sweetness (4 g/l sugar). **Chenin Blanc** (NEW) ★★★★ Dried peach, melon, thatch on **17** (83). The sweet element (5 g/l sugar) more obvious here than on other whites, but with nice acid lift, for unpretentious, undemanding pleasure. **Sauvignon Blanc Grande Cuvée** ★★★★ Tropical fruit on **17** (84) with green grassy notes. Passionfruit dominates silky-soft palate - plumped out by splash unoaked semillon & a sweet note, but shot through with fresh acidity.

Pavillion range
Pavillion Blanc (②) ★★☆ Ripe fig tones daubed with muscat & fruit-lifting 7 grams sugar, juicy **15** (78) from chenin, sauvignon & hanepoot. Not tasted: **Shiraz-Cabernet Sauvignon**.

Sommelier Selection
Pinotage (②) ★★★ Just 50% oak-aged to promote ripe mulberry fruit to fore, **15** (81) substance to allow lively, firm tannins time to round with time. Also in 1.5L. **Chenin Blanc** (②) ★★★ Softer, more juicy peachy flavours in **16** (79) than **15** (78); few grams sugar diminish some heat in tail.

Boschendal Classics
Not tasted: **Lanoy, Larone, Blanc de Noir, Rose Garden Rosé, Rachel's Chenin Blanc, Boschen Blanc, Le Bouquet**.

Elgin Series
Not tasted: **Pinot Noir, Chardonnay, Sauvignon Blanc**. — TJ

Location/map: Franschhoek ▪ Map grid reference: D6 ▪ WO: Western Cape/Coastal/Stellenbosch/Elgin ▪ Est 1685 ▪ 1stB 1975 ▪ Tasting & sales daily 10-6 (Oct-Mar) & 10-5 (Apr-Sep) ▪ Chocolate & wine pairing ▪ Brandy tasting ▪ Signature experiences, presented from a private room, include a Historic tasting of 5 wines representing the history of Boschendal; Connoisseur tasting of 5 limited release wines; MCC & Canapé pairing; MCC & Oyster pairing; Shiraz & Angus Beef pairing ▪ Closed Good Fri & Dec 25 ▪ Cellar tours daily 10.30, 12, 1.30 & 3 R6opp ▪ Vineyard tours 11.30 R15opp ▪ Cheese platters on request R125ea ▪ The Werf Restaurant ▪ Farmshop & deli ▪ Weddings & functions ▪ Facilities for children ▪ Tour groups ▪ Gifts ▪ The Werf Cottages & Orchards Cottages (23 luxury cottages) ▪ Owner(s) DGB (Pty) Ltd ▪ Group winemaker Stephan Joubert ▪ Cellarmaster(s) Jacques Viljoen (Aug 2018) ▪ Winemaker(s) Lizelle Gerber (whites & MCC, 2006) & Jacques Viljoen (reds & rosé, 2018) ▪ Viticulturist(s) Heinie Nel (Jul 2018) ▪ 2,240ha/200ha (shiraz, sauv) ▪ 3,100t/500,000cs own label 32% red 43% white 14% rosé 11% sparkling ▪ WIETA, WWF-SA Conservation Champion ▪ Private Bag X03 Groot Drakenstein 7680 ▪ cellardoor@boschendal.co.za ▪ www.boschendal-wines.com ▪ S 33° 52′ 27.5″ E 018° 58′ 34.4″ ▪ ⊠ nooks.electronic.sweetening ▪ F +27 (0)21-874-1531 ▪ **T +27 (0)21-870-4200**

☐ **Boschenheuwel** see Wine-of-the-Month Club

Boschheim (②)
Polymer scientist and boutique vintner Andy Roediger vinifies for his own labels, Boschheim and Muse, whenever time allows. The Stellenbosch Cape Wine Master works with black grapes only, currently Bordeaux and Rhône, and looks to progress from 'a social winemaking facility to a fully functional small winery' through ongoing purchases of cellar equipment.

Location/map: Stellenbosch ▪ Map grid reference: E5 ▪ 1stB 2003 ▪ Tasting & sales by appt ▪ Owner(s) Andy Roediger ▪ Winemaker(s) Andy Roediger & Mark Philp ▪ 1,800cs own label 100% red ▪ PO Box 3202 Matieland 7602 ▪ andy@roedigeragencies.co.za ▪ S 33° 55′ 54.9″ E 018° 50′ 10.5″ ▪ ⊠ goes.cheat.sliders ▪ F +27 (0)21-886-4731 ▪ **T +27 (0)21-887-0010**

☐ **Boschheuvel** see Zidela Wines

Boschkloof Wines (②) (⑪)
Shiraz continues to be an important focus at this family farm on Stellenbosch's Polkadraai Hills, and young Reenen Borman, together with father Jacques, Boschkloof's owner and cellarmaster, is 'working on another top-end syrah', parallel to the much-praised Epilogue. The increased focus on single-vineyard wines is inherent to the quest to best reflect the soil and soul of the area. Using concrete 'eggs' is part of experimentation to achieve more vinous building-blocks at the blending stage. While here respecting the traditions and

terroir of Boschkloof, Reenen's experimental 'new wave' bent gets expression in the Kottabos range and, even more exuberantly, in his own Ron Burgundy wines - both labels listed separately.

★★★★☆ **Epilogue** (🍇) Single-vineyard shiraz, like **15** (90). More expressive & fascinating than the Syrah. A floral note (lilies) is part of the dark fruit complexity & finesse of **16** (94), lifted by 25% bunch ferment, supported by judicious oaking (20% new). Firmly built. Long-lingering dry finish.

★★★★☆ **Syrah** Spicy perfume with mix of red & darker fruit on **16** (90) - though it's understated & far from simply fruity, with a savoury depth. Tannin, acidity & oak (just 10% new) all in balance for a wine that should develop further complexity but is already approachable.

★★★★ **Cabernet Sauvignon-Merlot** (✓) **16** (86) same 60:40 partnership as **15** ★★★★ (84). Berry fruit, with spicy notes of tobacco & cedar. Controlled ripeness, with the 14.5% alcohol in balance, the whole even rather elegant. Good now, but will grow.

★★★★☆ **Conclusion** (🍇) A barrel selection of nearly equal cab franc & cab with merlot; always serious, with depth & concentration. **15** (91)'s tannins firm but ripe, built for the longer haul, sheathed by glossy fruit for immediate enjoyment but the best lies ahead.

★★★★ **Chardonnay** Offers harmony & thrill, with a fresh, refined lightness, **17** (89) a good step-up on **16** ★★★ (81). 20% tank-matured portion adds to fruit purity; rest in older oak. Fine acid thread. WO W Cape.

Merlot (🍇) ★★★☆ Floral notes in **16** (84)'s perfume, lovely plummy fruit but the structure is quite 'masculine'; firm dry tannins from 18 months oaking. Drink from **19** till 2025. **Sauvignon Blanc** (🍇) ★★★☆ Gooseberries & passionfruit throughout **17** ★★★★ (84), salty acidity making it a perfect food companion, but also track record for further development. WO W Cape. Not tasted: **Cabernet Sauvignon**. — TJ

Location/map: Stellenbosch ▪ Map grid reference: C6 ▪ WO: Stellenbosch/Western Cape ▪ Est/1stB 1996 ▪ Tasting, sales & cellar tours Mon-Fri 9-5 Sat 10-3 ▪ Fee R30 ▪ Closed Easter Fri-Sun, Dec 25 & Jan 1 ▪ Cheese & charcuterie platters ▪ BYO picnic ▪ Owner(s)/cellarmaster(s) Jacques Borman ▪ Winemaker(s) Reenen Borman (Jun 2010) ▪ Viticulturist(s) Jacques Borman, with Reenen Borman ▪ 30ha/19ha (cabs s/f, merlot, shiraz, chard) ▪ ±100-150t/6-8,000cs own label 90% red 10% white ▪ PO Box 1340 Stellenbosch 7599 ▪ boschkloof@adept.co.za, info@boschkloofwines.com ▪ www.boschkloofwines.com ▪ S 33° 57' 37.0" E 018° 46' 11.8" ▪ 📍 mission.rates.rating ▪ F +27 (0)21-881-3032 ▪ **T +27 (0)21-881-3293 (office)/+27 (0)21-881-3268 (cellar)**

Boschrivier Wines: NJT de Villiers   (🍷)(🍴)(☕)(🏠)(📷)(♿)

A pioneer in the Stanford area, Theo de Villiers followed in his great-grandfather's footsteps and established vines on inherited farmland in 1998. His firstborn Shiraz since has gained siblings, and the visitor facilities on his property have grown and diversified, but Theo's day job as paediatrician in Worcester continues and his passion for wine, lived out on weekends, is as strong as ever.

Cabernet Sauvignon ★★★ Retasted, **14** (81) improved by extra year in bottle. Cassis & black plums seem richer, creamier, tannins still a presence but without edges, there to ensure a future. **Shiraz** ★★★★ Well-made example of variety, **16** (84)'s dark fruit given year oaking backbone, portion new; savoury, meaty finish. **Rosé** ★★ Ex-tank **18** (75) from shiraz & cab is a dry easy-drinker, shows berries & candyfloss. **Sauvignon Blanc** (🍇) ★★★☆ Forthcoming passionfruit perfume & flavours proclaim the cooler growing conditions of **17** (84), nice limy acidity at the end. Has personality, vibrancy. Elgin grapes. — CR

Location: Stanford ▪ Map: Walker Bay & Bot River ▪ Map grid reference: C8 ▪ WO: Overberg/Cape South Coast ▪ Est 1998 ▪ 1stB 2002 ▪ Tasting & sales Mon-Fri 8-5 Sat 9-5 ▪ Closed Dec 25 ▪ Restaurant ▪ BYO picnic ▪ Gift shop ▪ Farm produce ▪ Conferences/functions (60 pax) ▪ Walking/hiking & 4x4 trails ▪ 3 self-catering farmhouses ▪ Owner(s)/viticulturist(s) Theodore de Villiers ▪ Winemaker(s) Mike Dobrovic ▪ 14ha (cab, shiraz) ▪ 7t/ha ±1,950cs own label 68.5% red 21% white 10.5% rosé ▪ Remhoogte Caledon 7230 ▪ drnjtdevilliers@ mweb.co.za ▪ www.boschrivierwines.co.za ▪ S 34° 23' 19.4" E 019° 37' 51.0" ▪ 📍 tandem.deems.unescorted ▪ F +27 (0)23-342-2215 ▪ **T +27 (0)23-347-3313/2 ext 3; +27 (0)76-736-0351; +27 (0)28-008-5031 (tasting)**

Bosman Family Vineyards ⓟ ⓟⓟ ◎

Nurturing one of SA's pre-eminent vine nurseries, the Bosman family returned to handcrafted winegrowing in the mid-2000s when 8th-generation Petrus Bosman put Corlea Fourie in charge of their renovated centuries-old Wellington cellar. Since recognised internationally for sustainability and ethical initiatives (the Adama Trust, formed in 2008, raised the bar for transformation), the family produce a portfolio which includes SA's first nero d'avola, a trendy skin-fermented white and novelties like sweet zinfandel. 'While respecting the past, they have the courage to try new things,' explains brand manager Neil Büchner. The vineholding ranges across Wellington and Hermon, as well as Upper Hemel-en-Aarde, where their second visitor venue, The Frame House, has now opened in a tranquil vine-and-forest setting.

Adama range

★★★★ **Red** Cinnamon-spiced whole greater than sum of parts (8 cultivars, various oak treatments over 9 months) in shiraz-led **17** ⑧⑦, fresh & food friendly, with choc-cherry appeal. WO W Cape.

★★★★ **White** Slightly less elegant, nuanced than **16** ★★★★☆ ⑨①, chenin-based **17** ⑧⑨ with 6 other varieties (2 regions) deftly oaked for smooth vanilla tones to complement cardamom-spiced citrus fruit.

Creative Space range

★★★★★ **Twyfeling Cinsaut** ⓐ Adds variety to name in stylish **16** ★★★★★ ⑨④. From Bovlei bushvines, year French oak (third new) imparting tobacco & spice nuances to vivid red cherry & raspberry fruit. Luscious, with fine-grained tannins, pleasant earthiness. **15** ⑨⑥ was maiden vintage.

★★★★☆ **Optenhorst Chenin Blanc** ⓐ ⓨ Naturally barrel-fermented/aged on lees 6 months, rich yet lemon-fresh **16** ⑨③ from SA's 4th-oldest chenin vineyard has elegantly creamy texture & clean minerality as backdrop to concentrated, subtly spiced pear & apricot fruit. Just 9% new oak vs 20% previously.

★★★★☆ **Fides Grenache Blanc** Fermented naturally on skins 3 weeks then basket-pressed (20% into Russian oak barrels for 9 months), **17** ⑨① 'orange wine' finely textured tannin backbone supporting marmalade & marzipan intensity. Robust enough to handle very rich dishes.

Dolce Primitivo ★★★☆ Sweet, textured **17** ⑧④ dessert from zinfandel, sun-dried then bunch fermented in older oak for stewed fruit, choc-caramel richness. At 10% alcohol, more charming than previous. 500 ml.

Nero range

★★★★ **Nero d'Avola** After 2 years in oak (20% new, 40% American), **16** ⑧⑨ has Italianate savoury edge to ripe cherry fruit. Full bodied but moderate acidity keeps it fresh. Greater complexity & ageing potential than **15** ★★★★ ⑧④.

Signature range

★★★★ **Cabernet Sauvignon** From 3 Wellington sites, **14** ⑧⑨ intense cassis & black cherry fruit, well integrated after 18 months in French oak (third new), enhancing dark chocolate & cedar spice.

★★★★ **Pinotage** ⓠ Ripe mulberry fruit somewhat shaded by toasty vanilla oak (50% new, some American), savoury spice & leather notes. But **15** ⑧⑦'s potential shows in vibrant acidity, edgy tannins; improves on last-tasted **13** ★★★★ ⑧④ - just needs time.

★★★★ **Erfenis** ⓐ Conceived as an 'ode to the vintage', only the best barrels in the cellar - mostly French, 20% new in **15** ★★★★★ ⑨④, 38% pinotage & 23% nero d'avola plus cab, cab franc, cinsaut & merlot. Vibrant berry fruit, full body with firm but fine tannins, fresh acid. Step up on **14** ⑧⑦.

Discontinued: **Méthode Cap Classique Steen**.

Upper Hemel-en-Aarde range

★★★★ **Chardonnay** More mineral, elegant than **16** ★★★ ⑧①, **17** ⑧⑥ lemon-fresh yet rounded from 9 months on lees (20% in 2nd-fill French oak).

★★★★☆ **Sauvignon Blanc** ⓥ ⓐ Floral, herbal, fynbos aromas invite sips of tangy passionfruit & lime in crisp, lively **17** ⑨③, showing maritime terroir with flinty undertone & lingering, slightly saline finish.

★★★★ **Loose Cannon Méthode Cap Classique** ⓝ Mostly chardonnay with 25% pinot & 0.5% meunier, zero-dosage **14** ⑧⑥ sparkling bone-dry yet full of peach & red berry flavours, fine mousse & creamy texture from 18 months on lees.

Pinot Noir ★★★☆ Violet perfume on sleek, lightly oaked **16** ⑧④, showing red fruit of the forest (forest floor too) with hint of tobacco.

Generation 8 range

★★★★ Chenin Blanc ⊘ Unoaked **17** (86) seduces with yellow pear & cling peach, luscious mouthfeel (from skin-macerated component) & 12.5% alcohol. Youthful **18** (86) promises more of the same.

Cabernet Sauvignon (NEW) ⊘ **★★★★** Cassis & black cherry richness in **17** (85), very much fruit driven, only 20% wooded in French oak for subtle cedar spice. **Merlot** ⊘ **★★★★** Redolent of plum pudding & dark chocolate, **17** (84) full bodied yet smooth & approachable, deftly oaked (as for Cab). **Shiraz** (NEW) ⊘ **★★★★** Oak plays 2nd fiddle to mulberry & black plum fruit, pinch black pepper in **17** (83). Easy-drinking food match at 13% alcohol. **Rosé** (NEW) **★★★★** From the Bosmans' Hermanus vine garden (47 varieties) comes fresh & fruity **17** (83), packed with red berries, also peach & melon, & lovely coral hue. — JG

Location: Wellington/Hermanus ▪ Map: Wellington/Walker Bay & Bot River ▪ Map grid reference: C3 B3 ▪ WO: Wellington/Upper Hemel-en-Aarde Valley/Western Cape ▪ Est 1699 ▪ 1stB 2004 ▪ Wellington: Tasting & cellar tours by appt T +27 (0)63-052-5352/taste@bosmanwines.com ▪ Tasting fee R50pp ▪ Sales Mon-Thu 9-5 Fri 9-4.30 Sat by appt ▪ Closed Sun, Easter Fri-Mon & Dec 25 ▪ Upper Hemel-en-Aarde (De Bos Farm, Karwyderskraal Rd, Upper Hemel-en-Aarde, Hermanus 7200): Tasting & picnics, book at taste@bosman-hermanus.com/T +27 (0)63-083-5571 ▪ Tasting fee R50pp ▪ Sales Tue-Sat 9-5 Sun 10-4 ▪ Closed Mon, Easter Fri-Mon & Dec 25 ▪ Picnics, food & wine pairings, nature trails & coffee available ▪ Owner(s) Bosman Adama (Pty) Ltd ▪ Cellarmaster(s) Corlea Fourie (Nov 2006) ▪ Winemaker(s) Natasha Williams (Mar 2018) ▪ Viticulturist(s) Johan Viljoen (Mar 2014) ▪ 300ha (47 varieties r/w) ▪ 5,000t/20,000cs own label 70% red 25% white 5% rosé ▪ Brands for clients: Sainsbury Supermarkets, The Cooperative ▪ BBBEE certificate (level 4), Fairtrade accredited ▪ PO Box 9 Wellington 7654 ▪ taste@bosmanwines.com ▪ www.bosmanwines.com, www.bosmanhermanus.com ▪ S 33°37'34.7" E019°01'28.9" (Wellington) S 34°21'53.28" E 019°13'46.15" (Hermanus) ▪ 🖃 ordering.fell.pump ▪ F +27 (0)21-873-2517 ▪ **T +27 (0)21-873-3170**

Botanica Wines

After two years of farming organically, vintage 2019 will see all of Botanica's grapes certified organic. 'Not much other news,' says owner/winemaker Ginny Povall, which is good news considering the former New York corporate consultant's wines have gone from strength to strength since 2009 when she established vineyards on her flower farm, Protea Heights, in Stellenbosch's Devon Valley. Her flowers continue to be as sought after in European export markets as her wines, and all things floral are celebrated in her wine labels, most notably those for the Mary Delany flagships which are named after (and feature the work of) the artist who crafted intricate botanical collages out of thousands of pieces of cut paper in the late 1700s.

Mary Delany Collection

★★★★★ Pinot Noir ⊘ (🏵) Subtle smoke adds to the floral (wild rose, violet) & forest-fruit allure of **17** (94), which sees Hemel-en-Aarde Ridge & Stellenbosch grapes brought together over 8 months in older French oak. Delicate yet by no means lightweight.

★★★★★ Chenin Blanc (🏵) With 7 maximum ratings since debut in **09**, this now richly deserves SA icon status. Once again sourced from venerable high-altitude Citrusdal vines, 50% old-oaked for silky smoothness, **17** (95) abounds with pear, guava, citrus & stonefruit, yet for all its concentrated complexity, remains pure, focused, supremely elegant.

★★★★☆ Chenin Blanc Untitled No. 1 (🏵) Like its stellar sibling, **17** (94) from Citrusdal Mountain but 100% oaked with slightly lower alcohol (13%) & touch more sugar (3.3 g/l). Redolent of blossoms & white peach, with layers of citrus & stonefruit, leaves more spicy, savoury impression. Occasional release.

★★★★☆ Semillon (🏵) Whiffs of fresh straw & ginger spice introduce beautifully poised **17** (94) from Elgin. There's racy lime & orange citrus, some subtle salinity too, but mostly it's all about texture (smooth viscosity from 8 months in old French oak) & balance.

★★★★☆ Fire Lily Straw Wine (②) (🏵) Deep, iridescent amber hue, piercing sweetness & acid, luscious honeyed stonefruit, combine in harmonious work of art. **NV** (94) Stellenbosch viognier is dedicated to the Urban Caracal Project, with 100% of revenue donated to this preservation cause.

Not tasted: **Three Barrels Pinot Noir**.

Arboretum range

★★★★ Arboretum Cab's cassis richness to the fore in smooth Bordeaux-style **16** (89), seamlessly knitted with cab franc, merlot & petit verdot. 12 months in old oak, as all reds below.

Big Flower range

★★★★ **Cabernet Sauvignon** Dense, dark, delicious **16** ⑧⑦ is enjoyable now but has enough structure (chalky tannins, balancing acidity) to improve over 5 years.

★★★★ **Cabernet Franc** Approachable **16** ⑧⑥ less lean & leafy than **15** ★★★★ ⑧③, sweet ripe berry & cherry fruit upfront & tangy, peppery finish. Balanced at 14.5% alcohol.

★★★★ **Merlot** Nothing green about voluptuous **16** ⑧⑥, packed with ripe black plum & cherry fruit. Richly flavoured with lingering finish, step up on **15** ★★★★ ⑧④.

Rosé ★★★★ Very dry but soft & accessible **18** ⑧⑤ from petit verdot redolent of honeysuckle & capsicum, refreshes at modest 12.5% alcohol. Not tasted: **Petit Verdot**. — JG

Location/map: Stellenbosch ▪ Map grid reference: D4 ▪ WO: Stellenbosch/Citrusdal Mountain/Elgin/Western Cape ▪ Est/1stB 2008 ▪ Tasting Fri & Sat 11-3 during summer season, or by appt ▪ Wine sales Mon-Fri 8-5 ▪ Farm produce ▪ Conferences ▪ Walks/hikes ▪ MTB trail ▪ Refreshments offered at Sugarbird Manor guest house ▪ Owner(s) Virginia C Povall ▪ Winemaker(s) Virginia Povall (Jan 2008) ▪ Viticulturist(s) Francois Viljoen ▪ 21.6ha/5ha (cabs s/f, merlot, p verdot, pinot) ▪ PO Box 12523 Die Boord 7613 ▪ ginny@botanicawines. com ▪ www.botanicawines.com ▪ S 33° 54' 18.5" E 018° 49' 25.4" ▪ ⊞ tabloid.simply.mountain ▪ **T +27 (0)76-340-8296**

Botha Wine Cellar   ⓋⒶⒸⓈ

Breedekloof's Botha Wine Cellar, one of several grower-owned wineries established mid-20th century, turns 70 this year. The mostly bulk-wine-focused venture has seen steady growth in production (from a modest ±3,000 tons), technological advancement and many changes, but also enviable continuity: only five people have headed the cellar. It was during the tenure of JC 'Dassie' Smith that the Veritas-lauded Hanepoot Jerepigo '00 was produced. It's now been re-released as a premium-priced limited edition (just 50 bottles) – of special note to collectors of rare parcels and fans of wines from old vines.

Reserve range

Merlot ⓥ ★★★ Typical choc & fruit notes somewhat masked by dry spicy oak (75% new) on **14** ⑧①, though ripe sweet fruit returns at end. **Shiraz** ⓥ ★★★★ Spicy mocha & sweet plum vibrancy on **14** ⑧④. Oak & alcohol (15.3%) are prominent. **Bush Vine Barrel Fermented Chenin Blanc** ★★★★ From ±30 year old dryland vines. 11 months oaking, portion natural ferment, giving **17** ⑧④ toast & stonefruit flavours, acidity refreshed. **Late Bottled Vintage** ⓥ ★★★ Typical raisins, nuts, spice & dried plum on **10** ⑧① port-style offering from shiraz. Smooth & silky, with noticeable oak. Not tasted: **Cabernet Sauvignon**, **Barrel Fermented Chardonnay**.

Dassie's Reserve range

Dassie's Rood ⓥ ★★★ Spot on blend for fruity easy drinking, 50% cinsaut with cab & ruby cab in **16** ⑦⑧. Also in 3L cask, as rest. **Dassie's Rosé** ⓥ ★★ From chenin, colombard & 2 others, the colour from ruby cab. Candied fruit aroma but **16** ⑦④ tastes drier than you'd expect from a semi-sweet; light textured, fresh. **Dassie's Blanc** ★★ Light-textured (12% alcohol) fruity **18** ⑦⑤ quaffer from chenin.

Botha range

Cabernet Sauvignon ★★★ Combo French/American oak adds spice to **15** ⑧①'s cassis flavours, smooth & round. **Merlot** ★★★ Red berries & vanilla, juicy & streamlined **17** ⑦⑧ drinks well. **Pinotage** ⓥ ★★★ Plush dark fruit, with just a hint of tannin on the finish, lightly oaked **16** ★★★ ⑦⑨ made to be enjoyed at youthful best. **Shiraz** ★★★ Savoury black cherries, **16** ⑦⑧ is smooth & succulent. **Chenin Blanc** ⓥ ★★ Apple & pear flavours in **17** ⑦④, has elegant, fruity-fresh appeal. **Sauvignon Blanc** ⓥ ★★★ Green fig & litchi in crisply dry **18** ⑧① nice mineral touch at the end. **Chardonnay Brut** ⓥ ★★★ Straightforward **NV** ⑦⑦ dry carbonated fizz with tangy peach & nectarine fruitiness. **Red Jerepigo** ⓥ ★★★ Fortified shiraz, **16** ⑦⑧ preview salty liquorice scented, wild berries, a minty note, but palate has power-packed fruit, almost jammy sweetness. **Hanepoot Jerepigo** ⓥ ★★★★ Heady sultana on richly sweet **15** ⑧③ fortified dessert. Pure muscat fruit, well balanced & clean finishing. Less intense than last **13** ★★★★ ⑧⑦. — CR

Location: Worcester ▪ Map/WO: Breedekloof ▪ Map grid reference: B3 ▪ Est 1949 ▪ 1stB 1974 ▪ Tasting & sales Mon-Fri 9–5 Sat 10–1 ▪ Closed Easter Fri-Sun, Dec 25/26 & Jan 1 ▪ Cellar tours by appt ▪ BYO picnic ▪ Conservation area ▪ Breedekloof Soetes & Soup festival ▪ Owner(s) Botha Wynkelder (Edms) Bpk ▪ Production manager Johan Linde (Nov 1996) ▪ Cellarmaster(s) Gerrit van Zyl (Nov 2007) ▪ Winemaker(s)

Michiel Visser (Nov 1999) & Annamarie van Niekerk (Dec 2008), with Stefan Joubert (Nov 2016) ▪ Viticulturist(s) Jan-Carel Coetzee (Nov 2010) ▪ 1,969ha (cab, merlot, ptage, shiraz, chard, chenin, cbard, sauv) ▪ 38,711t/15,000cs own label 61% red 25% white 14% fortified ▪ ISO 22000:2009 ▪ IPW, WIETA ▪ PO Box 30 PK Botha 6857 ▪ admin@bothakelder.co.za ▪ www.bothakelder.co.za ▪ S 33° 34′ 1.5″ E 019° 15′ 27.5″ ▪ ▥ saved.ultrahigh.gentler ▪ F +27 (0)23-355-1615 ▪ **T +27 (0)23-355-1740**

☐ **Bottega Family Wines** see Idiom Collection

Bouchard Finlayson ⓠ ⓜ ⊖ ⊚ ⓑ

The devil's in the details, according to winemaker Chris Albrecht, as he approaches a decade in the cellar at this impressive Hemel-en-Aarde Valley property. In the vineyards, this means any new plantings carefully consider the perfect match of scion, rootstock and terroir (this includes the young estate shiraz vines which should be producing their first crop this year). In the cellar Chris is experimenting with wholebunch ferments and carbonic maceration, all in line with the mantra of continuous improvement. He's backed and guided in his quest for perfection by cellarmaster and co-founder Peter Finlayson, whose knowledge of Hemel-en-Aarde is second to none.

★★★★★ Galpin Peak Pinot Noir ⊘ ⓐ Powerful & muscular **16 ★★★★★** ⑨③, complex mix red cherry fruit, perfume, burnt sugar & toast. 31% new oak adds nutmeg & cinnamon while portion wholebunch gives freshness, helped by lively acidity. Like **15** ⑨⑤, styled for long haul, especially in 1.5 & 3L formats.

★★★★☆ Tête de Cuvée Galpin Peak Pinot Noir ⓠ Selection of 9 new barrels of only the best vintages, then bottle-matured before release. **13** ⑨④ benefits from time under cork: less primary cherry fruit, more complex, developed, nutty mushroom depth. Retains supple polish of the variety at its best.

★★★★☆ Hannibal Unusual but very effective blend of Italian & French grapes led by sangiovese, **16** ⑨② appetising & meaty, savoury notes of earth, tar & smoke, charred oak marrying nicely with red & black cherry fruit. Year oak (21% new). Magnums too. Walker Bay WO.

★★★★☆ Kaaimansgat Crocodile's Lair Chardonnay ⓐ Confident **17** ⑨③ shines with fresh mandarin orange, pink grapefruit, given breadth by barrel ferment (19% new) & 70% malo, both adding delicious custard-cream notes, honey & spice. Plenty of length augurs bright future. Overberg WO.

★★★★☆ Missionvale Chardonnay ⓐ Superb **16** ⑨③ shows layer upon layer of flavour - mandarin orange, melon, cooked apple, toffee, toast & butter. Barrel fermented, slightly less new oak this year (29%), & 80% malo for texture, complexity & weight. Could drink now, but so much more ahead.

★★★★ Sans Barrique Chardonnay Surprisingly spicy unoaked **17** ⑧⑥ bounces up a notch on **16 ★★★★** ⑧⑤ with fresh citrus & cream, given length & weight by salty lees & limy acidity. Own & Elandskloof fruit.

★★★★ Sauvignon Blanc Floral & fruity **18** ⑧⑥ has ripe peachy notes with lemon zest & salty leesy tang (4 months). Lively acidity, fuller than previous, helped by 9% semillon.

★★★★ Sauvignon Blanc Reserve ⓠ Block selection, & only in best years; extended skin contact & fruit intensity of 15% semillon distinguishes **17 ★★★★☆** ⑨④ from sibling, gunsmoke & deep minerality accompany tropical tones in flinty finish, like **16** ⑧⑧.

★★★★ Blanc de Mer Just-dry **17 ★★★★** ⑧⑤ cries out for seafood platter to complement soft lime cordial flavours & snappy acidity. Mostly riesling with viognier, chardonnay & others. Unwooded, like **16** ⑧⑥. Cape South Coast WO.

Walker Bay Pinot Noir (ⓝⓔⓦ) **★★★★** Declassified Galpin Peak **14** ⑧⑤ offers good value, with nicely developed notes of toast, coffee & savoury to light red fruit. To be enjoyed early, also in its 1.5 & 3L formats. Discontinued: **Kaaimansgat Limited Edition Chardonnay**. — CM

Location: Hermanus ▪ Map: Walker Bay & Bot River ▪ Map grid reference: B4 ▪ WO: Hemel-en-Aarde Valley/ Cape South Coast/Overberg/Walker Bay ▪ Est 1989 ▪ 1stB 1991 ▪ Tasting, sales & cellar tours Mon-Fri 9–5 Sat 10–1 ▪ Fee R30pp/3 wines, R50pp/6 wines ▪ Closed all pub hols ▪ Deli platter ▪ Gift shop ▪ BYO picnic ▪ Conservation area ▪ Nature walks by appt (guided & self-guided) ▪ Owner(s) The Tollman Family Trust ▪ Cellarmaster(s) Peter Finlayson (1989) ▪ Winemaker(s) Chris Albrecht (Nov 2010) with Neliss Uys (Jun 2017) ▪ Viticulturist(s) Mortimer Lee (Dec 2009) ▪ 125ha/22ha (barbera, nebbiolo, pinot, sangio, chard, riesling, sauv) ▪ 280t/35,000cs own label 30% red 70% white ▪ IPW, WWF-SA Conservation Champion ▪ PO Box 303

Hermanus 7200 ▪ info@bouchardfinlayson.co.za ▪ www.bouchardfinlayson.co.za ▪ S 34° 22′ 54.0″ E 019° 14′ 30.9″ ▪ ⌨ freeway.nostalgia.laughing ▪ F +27 (0)28-312-2317 ▪ **T +27 (0)28-312-3515**

Boucheron Wines $\textcircled{Q}$

Headquartered in Gauteng's Randburg area, Boucheron has expanded from a boutique-wine merchant founded by Fredy Pummer in 1996 to a producer of own-label wine, including a rare white merlot.

Location: Randburg ▪ Est 1996 ▪ 1stB 2012 ▪ Tasting & sales Mon-Thu 8-4 Fri 8-3 ▪ Owner(s)/cellarmaster(s) Fredy Pummer ▪ 5,200cs ▪ PO Box 870 Strathavon 2031 ▪ info@boucheron.co.za ▪ www.boucheron.co.za ▪ F +27 (0)86-218-6913 ▪ **T +27 (0)11-708-3444**

☐ **Boutinot** *see* Wildeberg Wines
☐ **Brahms** *see* Domaine Brahms Wineries

Bramon Wines

Not much changes on this bubbly-focused family farm outside Plettenberg Bay, with wines crafted by Anton Smal. The on-site restaurant, now under new management, drives most of their sales, with visitors flocking to enjoy food, wine and magnificent views of Formosa Peak and the Tsitsikamma mountains.

Bramon Méthode Cap Classique range
★★★★ **Blanc de Blancs** Elegant **16** ⑧⑨ from chardonnay mixes creamy lemon fruit with attractive bready, yeasty notes. A little longer lees-time would add richness to pleasant, light & enjoyable bubbly.
★★★★ **Sauvignon Blanc** Plenty of varietal flavours on **15** ⑧⑨ - herb, pepper & crunchy apple. 26 months on lees takes the edge off & rounds out a zippy, fresh & unusual fizz.

The Crags range
★★★★ **Rosé** Serious pink from pinot, 10% chardonnay. **17** ⑧⑥, now bottled, ripe, soft, red-berried fruit, salty note & pleasing earthy/spicy finish add up to excellent food partner. On track after **16** ★★★★ ⑧⑷.
★★★★☆ **Sauvignon Blanc** ⊘ Back on form after **16** ★★★★ ⑧⑦, **17** ⑨⓪ swirls a glassful of grass, grapefruit & pepper, good palate weight from 5 months on lees, clean & zippy acidity, excellent length.
Not tasted: **Anton's Selection**. — CM

Location/WO: Plettenberg Bay ▪ Map: Klein Karoo & Garden Route ▪ Map grid reference: C1 ▪ Est 2000 ▪ 1stB 2004 ▪ Tasting & sales daily 9-5.30 ▪ Fee R10/tasting glass, waived on wine purchase ▪ Closed Dec 25 ▪ Cellar tours by appt ▪ Restaurant ▪ Facilities for children ▪ Southern Crags Conservancy ▪ Waterfall Cottage (4 pax, self-catering) ▪ Owner(s) Private company ▪ Cellarmaster(s)/winemaker(s) Anton Smal (Feb 2010) ▪ Viticulturist(s) Peter Thorpe (2000) ▪ 10ha/6ha (chard, sauv) ▪ 50t/6,400cs own label 100% white ▪ PO Box 1606 Plettenberg Bay 6602 ▪ accounts@bramonwines.co.za ▪ www.bramonwines.co.za ▪ S 33° 57′ 20.30″ E 023° 28′ 45.02″ ▪ ⌨ bushes.roundup.predominant ▪ F +27 (0)86-589-6816 ▪ **T +27 (0)44-534-8007**

Brampton $\textcircled{Q}$ $\textcircled{¶}$

DGB's Brampton delights the crowds in central Stellenbosch with approachable, easy-drinking wines sampled at one of SA's first urban wine studios, slotting in perfectly into the café culture of trendy Church Street. Multiple awards from international competitions show that good wines and good times go together well.
Cabernet Sauvignon ★★★ Cheery & pleasant **16** ⑧②, tweak of new American oak adds sweetness to ripe black fruit. Soft tannins, juicy texture. Stellenbosch WO, like Shiraz. **Pinotage** ⑨ ★★★★ Accessible, with personality aplenty, **15** ⑧④ bright fruit & touches meat spice & coriander, 20% new oak tannin nudge. Versatile crowd pleaser. Coastal WO, as Roxton. **Shiraz** ★★★ Peppery black-berried fruit with hints of leather & spice, **16** ⑧② delicious everyday glugger. **Roxton** ★★★★ Named after pedigree bull (like Brampton, the range's 'sire'), aptly powerful yet well-structured **15** ⑧⑤ mostly shiraz, dashes petit verdot, malbec. Ripe black plums & cherries mingled with coffee & spice. **OVR** ⑨ ★★★★ Undisclosed varieties in **15** ⑧④, old vines deliver melange of fruits with spice & solid core, firm yet accessible tannin. **Unoaked Chardonnay** ★★★ Flowery, peachy **17** ⑦⑧ needs tad more acid to freshen fairly warm alcohol of 14%. **Sauvignon Blanc** ★★★ Rounded, soft & easy-drinking **17** ⑦⑨ sure to win friends with tropical fruit melange. Not tasted: **Rosé**. — CM

Location/map: Stellenbosch ▪ Map grid reference: F5 ▪ WO: Western Cape/Coastal/Stellenbosch ▪ Est/1stB 1996 ▪ Opening hours Mon–Sun 10-9 pub hols 11-9, with wine tasting from 11-4 ▪ Fee R25/3 wines R50/6 wines ▪ Closed Good Fri, Dec 25/26 & Jan 1 ▪ Light lunches/dinner 12-8pm; refreshments all day ▪ Craft beer ▪ Owner(s) DGB (Pty) Ltd ▪ Winemaker(s) Boschendal Cellar ▪ Viticulturist(s) Heinie Nel (Jul 2018) ▪ 500t/80,000cs own label 40% red 55% white 5% rosé ▪ WIETA ▪ 11 Church Str Stellenbosch 7600 ▪ brampton@dgb.co.za ▪ www.brampton.co.za ▪ S 33° 56′17.42″ E 018° 51′38.08″ ▪ ▥ trainer.blocks.coach ▪ **T +27 (0)21-883-9097**

Brandvlei Cellar ⓠ ⓞ ⓑ

The grower-owned winery in the shadow of Jonaskop peak started out in 1955 on premises beside Brandvlei Dam and moved to the current location between Worcester and Villiersdorp 19 years later when the dam was enlarged. 'Quality wines that everyone can enjoy and afford' is the aim, and the small fraction of output that appears under the BC Wines label certainly hits that target.

BC Wines range

Cabernet Sauvignon ⊘ ★★★ Juicy-fruity **17** ⑦⑨ is youthful & fresh for early drinking. **Pinotage** ⊘ ★★★ Unwooded **17** ⑧⓪, light bodied, easy on the palate, with high-toned wild berry jam flavours. **Shiraz** ⊘ ★★★ Appealingly fruity & supple, unoaked **17** ⑧⓪ has hints of fynbos & pepper, sufficient weight & finish. **Ruby Cabernet-Merlot** ★★ Lacking component varieties' ebullience & plumminess, **17** ⑦⑥ instead offers mixed red fruit, rather heavy tannins. **Chardonnay** ⊘ ★★★ Light but poised **18** ⑧⓪ has a pinch of wood, convincing lemon-lime fruit, satisfying acid lift. **Chenin Blanc** ⊘ ★★★ Fresh, light, friendly **18** ⑧⓪ offers generous fruit, guava & pear to the fore. **Sauvignon Blanc** ★★ Light bodied, with pungent aromas, **18** ⑦② is austere, thin & brief. **Bacchanté** ⊘ ★★★ Chenin blend with colombard, dash viognier, **18** ⑦⑨ is off-dry, generously fruity. **Sauvignon Blanc Brut** (ⓝⓔⓦ) ⊘ ★★★ Carbonated dry **NV** ⑦⑧ sparkler shows varietal dusty-grassy notes, foamy mousse, piquant acidity. Not tasted: **Hanepoot Jerepigo**. — GdB

Location/map: Worcester ▪ Map grid reference: B5 ▪ Est 1955 ▪ Tasting & sales Mon–Thu 8—5 Fri 8—4.30 Sat 9-1 ▪ Closed all pub hols ▪ Cellar tours by appt only ▪ Conferences ▪ Owner(s) 19 members ▪ Cellarmaster(s) Jean le Roux (Aug 1995) ▪ Winemaker(s) Willie Biggs (Sep 2009) & Daneel Jacobs (Sep 2007) ▪ Viticulturist(s) Danie Conradie (Sep 2004) ▪ 1,630ha (cab, ptage, chard, chenin, cbard, sauv) ▪ 28,500t 20% red 80% white ▪ PO Box 595 Worcester 6849 ▪ sales@bcwines.co.za ▪ www.bcwines.co.za ▪ S 33° 48′19.5″ E 019° 28′8.1″ ▪ ▥ pleasant.comical.quad ▪ F +27 (0)23-340-4332 ▪ **T +27 (0)23-340-4215**

☐ **Bredell's** see JP Bredell Wines

Breëland Winery ⓠ ⓙ ⓐ ⓖ ⓞ

Blessed with immense unspoilt beauty, Lizelle Marais' farm in Slanghoek Valley is a nature-, sport- and wine-lover's paradise, offering game viewing, bird watching, rock climbing, fishing, mountain biking, hiking and more, plus tastings of the Breëland label, part of a much bigger production from 100 hectares of vines.

Cabernet Sauvignon ⓧ ★★★ Primary blackcurrant & mulberry with nutty twist on super-ripe **15** ⑧② fruit bomb. **Pinotage** ⓧ ★★ Brambleberry fruit on **15** ⑦③, chewy, leathery tannins, short finish. **Chenin Blanc Royal** ⓧ ★★★★ Fruit is the star of barrel-fermented **14** ⑧③. White peaches, lemons & flowers, appealing viscosity & crisp finish. **Sauvignon Blanc** ⓧ ★★★★ Sound & cheerfully ripe **17** ⑧③ shows melon & papaya fruit on crackling acidity. Summer delight. Not tasted: **Pinotage Rosé**. — GdB

Location: Rawsonville ▪ Map: Breedekloof ▪ Map grid reference: A5 ▪ WO: Slanghoek/Western Cape ▪ Est 1825 ▪ 1stB 2010 ▪ Tasting, sales & cellar tours Mon–Sat by appt ▪ Fee R20pp tour & tasting ▪ Closed Ash Wed, Easter Fri-Mon, Ascension day, Dec 25 & Jan 1 ▪ Pre-booked lunches (5 days prior notice) ▪ BYO picnic ▪ Walks/hikes ▪ MTB & 4x4 trails ▪ Conservation area ▪ Wedding/function venue ▪ Self-catering guest accommodation (mountain hut/farm house) ▪ Owner(s) Lizelle Marais ▪ Cellarmaster(s)/winemaker(s) Wickus Erasmus (Dec 2008) ▪ Viticulturist(s) Wickus Erasmus ▪ 1,500ha/100ha (cab, cinsaut, nebbiolo, ptage, shiraz, tannat, chenin, cbard, hanepoot, pinot gris, sauv, sem) ▪ 3,200t/500cs own label 20% red 80% white + 500cs for clients ▪ Brands for clients: Kaap Agri, Wine Village-Hermanus, Wine Boutique l'Aghulhas ▪ PO Box 26 Rawsonville 6845 ▪ lizelle@boegoekloof.co.za ▪ www.buchukloof.co.za, www.maraiswines.co.za ▪ S 33° 39′2.87″ E 019° 13′40.08″ ▪ ▥ undergrad.rookies.snared ▪ F +27 (0)86-562-6056 ▪ **T +27 (0)23-344-3129/+27 (0)78-575-2365**

Brenaissance

In the hands of entrepreneurial couple Tom and Hayley Breytenbach, formerly anonymous Devon Valley grape-growing property High Mead has been transformed into a winery (the grapes assigned to specialists for vinification), multi-amenity visitor venue and Boran cattle stud.

★★★★ **King of Clubs Cabernet Sauvignon** ⓩ Focused **09** ⑧⑦ shows complexity: mint, cedar, cassis, black olive, tobacco, cigarbox; ripe & supple tannins.

Not tasted: **Queen of Hearts Merlot, Lord T Secret Blend, Ace of Spades Blanc de Noir, Knight of White Chardonnay, Lady H Sauvignon Blanc**. — AL

Location/map/WO: Stellenbosch • Map grid reference: D4 • 1stB 2009 • Tasting & sales Mon-Sun 11-5 (Oct-Apr)/Wed-Sun 11-5 (Mar-Sep) • Pizza & wine pairing • Café Blanc de Noir restaurant • Child friendly • Conferences/functions • Wedding venue & chapel • Accommodation • Boran cattle stud • Owner(s) Tom & Hayley Breytenbach • Winemaker(s) various • 58.23ha/31.65ha (cabs s/f, malbec, merlot, p verdot, shiraz, chard) • 5,058cs own label 70% red 30% white • Suite 3 Private Bag X4 Die Boord Stellenbosch 7613 • info@brenaissance.co.za • www.brenaissance.co.za • S 33° 55' 4.31" E 018° 49' 7.82" • ⓦ file.cages.soda • **T +27 (0)21-200-2537**

☐ **Brendel Collection** *see* Le Manoir de Brendel

Brenthurst Winery

New vintages from Paarl-based advocate José Jordaan's 'hobby that got out of hand' were still incubating at press time but previous releases have included Bordeaux varietal bottlings and blends from his own vines, and a pinot noir and shiraz from bought-in grapes.

Location: Paarl • Est 1993 • 1stB 1994 • Open to public only by special appt • Owner(s) José Jordaan • Winemaker(s) José Jordaan, with Martin Fourie (consultant) • Viticulturist(s) Johan Wiese (1991, consultant) • 5ha (cabs s/f, merlot, p verdot) • 15t • PO Box 6091 Paarl 7622 • suite1105@absamail.co.za • F +27 (0)21-424-5666 • **T +27 (0)21-863-1154/1375, +27 (0)83-418-4110**

☐ **Bridge Wines** *see* The Bridge of Hope Wines
☐ **Brink Family Vineyards** *see* Pulpit Rock Winery
☐ **Britz Brothers** *see* Under Oaks
☐ **Broken Stone** *see* Slaley

Brookdale Estate

The development of this Paarl property, owned by UK-based Tim Rudd, proceeds apace. Nearly 20ha of vines have been planted in the last two years on Brookdale's granitic slopes, while 3 ha of salvaged old bushvine chenin gave the estate's first release, vinified by Duncan Savage in his Savage Wines facility. Brookdale's own cellar will follow when the vineyards mature.

Brookdale Estate range ⓝⓔⓦ

Chenin Blanc ★★★★ Barrel-fermented/aged **17** ⑧⑤ oxidatively handled, hence more funky nut aromatic features but brighter pear, tangerine appeal on palate, with creamy oak note. Brisk & commendably dry; needs time to fully harmonise. 50% new French wood. — AL, CvZ

Location/WO: Paarl • Est 2016 • Closed to public • Owner(s) Rudd Farms Limited (Tim Rudd) • GM Schalk Pienaar (Apr 2016), with Anne Hawley • Winemaker(s) Duncan Savage (Oct 2016, consultant) • Viticulturist(s) Kevin Watt (Feb 2016, consultant), with Adam Dirkse (Oct 2016) • 57ha/12ha under vine • 50% red 50% white • Hawequa Forest Rd Klein-Drakenstein Paarl 7646 • enquire@brookdale-estate.com • www.brookdale-estate.com • **T +27 (0)76-400-0229**

Brothers Wines

After years of tasting the wines of the world, and studying winemaking at Stellenbosch, Cape Town corporate executive Greg Castle realised his dream of an own boutique brand in 2005, naming it for sons Dylan and Alex. The wines, from top Constantia, Swartland and Stellenbosch vineyards, are available in specialist wine shops and select eateries, as well as overseas.

Location: Cape Town ▪ Est/1stB 2005 ▪ Closed to public ▪ Owner(s) Greg Castle ▪ Cellarmaster(s)/winemaker(s) Greg Castle (2005) ▪ 10t/1,666cs own label 55% red 45% white ▪ PO Box 21681 Kloof Str Cape Town 8008 ▪ info@brotherswines.co.za ▪ www.brotherswines.com ▪ F +27 (0)86-528-6081 ▪ **T +27 (0)82-600-2555**

Bruce Jack Wines   ⓠ

Bruce Jack, who helped place SA in the international spotlight with innovative Flagstone Winery, over the years has been involved with making and marketing many different styles of wine, with varying tiers of quality and price, locally and overseas. This new 'combi' listing brings together his South Africa-based ventures: wholly-owned The Drift Estate, centred on his family's Appelsdrift Farm near Napier, and Bonfire Hill Extreme Vineyards, previously listed under 'Another World Wines'; his newly launched partnership brand named Bruce Jack Wine with Breedekloof's uniWines/Daschbosch (not tasted by us); and Mary Le Bow, a limited-release occasional label which Bruce makes for the Frater family of Ashton.

The Drift Estate range

★★★★☆ **There Are Still Mysteries Single Vineyard Pinot Noir** ⓠ Intriguing **15** ㉒ from steep wind-buffeted slope defies categories, delivers savoury depth & length, fine stemmy grip, knife-edge acidity & lightest touch of French oak, just 10% new. No **14**.

★★★★☆ **Moveable Feast Red Blend** ⓐ Vibrant & creative union of partly co-fermented malbec, shiraz, tannat, touriga nacional & pinot noir, latter back in action in **15** ㉓ after **14** ㉒'s barbera. Unfettered by new oak, shows tight-packed black fruit, fynbos & pot-pourri. Suave & absolutely captivating.

★★★★☆ **Over The Moon Red Blend** ⓝⓔⓦ ⓐ Only older oak for well-conceived & -composed **17** ㉓ from mostly touriga franca & tinta barocca (52/28), splash shiraz. Mandarin, orange zest & pot-pourri aromas are beguiling, perhaps more so are the lively fruitiness, deliciously dry finish & lithe tannin form.

★★★★ **Year of the Rooster Rosé** Per back label, 'Seriously dry 007-type of wine from vineyard planted on the side of a windswept, fynbos-festooned mountain.' **17** ㉘ from cinsaut & touriga nacional.

Penelope Méthode Cap Classique ⓝⓔⓦ ★★★★ Dedicated to Bruce Jack's 'bubbly' wife, creator of the range's unique & inspired packaging. From touriga franca & syrah (2%), characterful if unclassic sparkler, **15** ㉘ unashamedly fruity with good weight from old-barrel ferment of base wine. Not tasted: **Gift Horse Single Vineyard Barbera**.

Bonfire Hill Extreme Vineyards range

Red ★★★★ Shiraz (64%), grenache (22%), smidgens malbec & touriga nacional in lively **16** ㉘. Savoury & smoky, touch vanilla ex brief sojourn in oak, approachable tannins. WO W Cape. **White** ★★★★ Forthcoming white peach, fresh apricot & lemon on partly oaked **17** ㉘ chenin (70%) with equal grenache blanc, roussanne. Friendly & not too serious, yet full of verve & persistence. WO Coastal.

Mary Le Bow Trust range

★★★★ **Mary le Bow** ⓠ ⓐ Scintillating colour, cherry-violet & cassis perfume elevate **14** ★★★★☆ ㉓ blend (shiraz, cab & merlot). Cool, velvety palate with chalky tannin. Sweet-spice gloss from mostly American oak (15% new). Shows restraint of **09**, rather than power of **11** ★★★★ ㉘. No **12**, **13**.— CvZ

Location: Napier ▪ Map: Southern Cape ▪ Map grid reference: B2 ▪ WO: Overberg/Western Cape/Coastal/Robertson ▪ 1stB 2005 ▪ Tasting by appt only ▪ Wine sales via website ▪ Owner(s)/winemaker(s) Bruce Jack ▪ Viticulturist(s) Andre Purdy ▪ Ecocert (not vyds), WIETA ▪ PO Box 55 Napier 72720 ▪ orders@thedrift.co.za ▪ www.brucejack.com ▪ S 34° 23' 50.94" E 019° 42' 37.01" ▪ F +27 (0)86-563-9533 ▪ **T +27 (0)86-150-2025**

Brugman Wines

The boutique wines of the Brugman family are named after co-owner Sandie and her daughters Lisa and twins Ilse and Karla, and include cabernets sauvignon and franc, sauvignon blanc and straw wine.

Location: Stellenbosch ▪ Est 2002 ▪ 1stB 2005 ▪ Closed to public ▪ Wines available via website or by email; also available from Die Boord Spar/Tops in Stellenbosch ▪ Owner(s) Brugman family ▪ PO Box 6365 Uniedal 7612 ▪ acquire@brugmanwine.com ▪ www.brugmanwine.com

Brunia Wines

The family owners of Cold Mountain, the large Stanford-area home-farm of the Brunia label (named for a rare fynbos species), are committed to sustainability, noting that 'organic cultivation is now embedded'. The promised inaugural pinot noir under their stewardship, vinified by young Wade Sander, has been released, with new vintages of the white wines and cool-climate shiraz/syrah to follow in the course of this year.

★★★★ **Pinot Noir** Gentle strawberry aromas & juicy red-berry character ably supported by supple, well-structured tannins & 10 months older oak in naturally fermented **17** (88). Sunday's Glen WO.

★★★★ **Shiraz** ⓥ Violet & lavender perfume on **12** ★★★★☆ (93). Excellent cool-climate expression, elegant, with long peppery mineral finish. Distinct improvement on last-tasted **10** ★★★ (81) & **09**.

Not tasted: **Chardonnay**, **Sauvignon Blanc**, **Semillon**. — WB

Location: Stanford ▪ Map: Southern Cape ▪ Map grid reference: B2 ▪ WO: Walker Bay/Sundays Glen ▪ Est 2005 ▪ 1stB 2009 ▪ Tasting & sales by appt only ▪ Tasting R50pp ▪ Closed all pub hols ▪ Self-guided hiking trails ▪ Mountain biking ▪ Conservation area ▪ Owner(s) Sander family ▪ Winemaker(s) Wade Sander ▪ Viticulturist(s) Conrad Schutte (consultant) ▪ 417ha/17ha (pinot, shiraz, chard, sauv, sem) ▪ 75t own label 26% red 10% white, balance sold ▪ Sandies Glen Rd Sondagskloof Stanford 7210 ▪ info@bruniawines.co.za ▪ www.bruniawines.co.za ▪ S 34° 28' 9.25" E 019° 39' 42.60" ▪ ⌖ gridded.hauntings.cubicles ▪ **T +27 (0)28-341-0432**

☐ **Brutus Family Reserve** see Seven Sisters Vineyards
☐ **Buckleberry** see Louis

Buffalo Creek Wines ⓥ

Father-and-son growers Leroy and Mark Tolmay aim to produce affordably priced and easily drinkable wines, profits from which are distributed among the staff on their McGregor farm. Current releases are Merlot and Pinotage '16, Sunset Red NV, and Rosé, Chardonnay and Sauvignon Blanc '18.

Location: McGregor ▪ Map: Robertson ▪ Map grid reference: D6 ▪ Est/1stB 2005 ▪ Tasting, sales & cellar tours Mon-Fri 9-6 Sat 9-12.30 Sun by appt only ▪ Closed Easter Sun, Dec 25 & Jan 1 ▪ Owner(s) Leroy & Mark Tolmay ▪ Cellarmaster(s)/winemaker(s) Mark Tolmay (Jun 2005) ▪ 1,328ha/30ha (p verdot, ptage, pinot, merlot, chard, chenin, cbard, sauv) ▪ ±350-380t/500-600cs own label 65% red 25% white 10% rosé ▪ PO Box 124 McGregor 6708 ▪ info@buffalocreek.co.za ▪ S 34° 0' 2.97" E 019° 53' 11.94" ▪ ⌖ outwitting.pebble. stretchy ▪ F +27 (0)23-625-1727 ▪ **T +27 (0)23-625-1727**

Buitenverwachting ⓥ ⑪ ◎ ♿

Simon van der Stel is the father of winemaking in South Africa, and this land formed part of his original Constantia holding. Its ancient soils have been home to vines since the 1700s but its modern renaissance has been under the ownership of Richard and Christine Mueller since the 1980s. Christine's son (and co-proprietor) Lars Maack has consistently ratcheted up quality, updated plantings and refined the visitor offering at this showpiece property. A strong Cape Dutch heritage is skilfully melded with contemporary design in the recent upgrade of the tasting area (housed in the original wine cellar) and restaurant. After a decade as deputy to now-retired veteran vintner Hermann Kirschbaum, cellar chief Brad Paton maintains the renowned quality and classic styling.

Buitenverwachting range

★★★★☆ **Cabernet Sauvignon** ⓥ Elegant **14** (90) returns to stellar form with velvety texture & ripe Xmas cake notes; stately, with all-French oak seamlessly integrated, lovely silky-smooth length. Improves on **13** ★★★★ (89) which had a light herbal edge.

★★★★ **Merlot** ⓥ Fynbos & graphite temper fruitcake notes of **13** (89). Enticing ripeness & succulence cradled by oak (20-24 months). Lovely body, concentration & length.

★★★★☆ **Christine** ⓐ Harmonious **13** (93) adds to lustre of flagship Bordeaux blend, near-equal cab & cab franc with dabs malbec & petit verdot. Merlot (19%) added this vintage, showing deep, smooth, sexy dark fruitcake & tobacco appeal. Seamless & polished from 23 months in 90% new oak.

★★★★ **Meifort** ⊘ Bright, spicy & juicy **15** (89) merlot-led 4-way Bordeaux red forgoes the malbec of exceptional **14** ★★★★☆ (92). Gentle frame supports pliable, approachable wine, with high 15.7% alcohol not obvious.

★★★★☆ **Chardonnay** Elegant, creamy & rich **17** ⑨ lives up to reputation of previous in structure, citrus vivacity & spicy refinement. Silky, rich & supported by barrel ferment/11 months in quarter-new French oak.

★★★★☆ **Husseys Vlei Sauvignon Blanc** ⊛ Displays vibrant acidity typical of the grape but also the rounded fruit expression it delivers. **17** ⑨ taut, crisp yet smooth & broad. No semillon as in **16** ⑨ & previous. Lively, zesty but understated. Will age well.

★★★★☆ **1769** ⊛ Ambrosial barley sugar & jasmine sweetness of Noble Late Harvest from muscat de Frontignan checked by cleansing acidity. Poised, structured & rich, it finishes clean & seemingly dry. Partial skin ferment on **16** ⑨, then year in older oak & 18 months in bottle. 500 ml.

Blanc de Noir ⊘ ★★★★ Vivid strawberry attraction on light-bodied, semi-dry **18** ⑧ preview. Lovely fresh acidity on merlot, cab & cab franc mix. **Sauvignon Blanc** ★★★★ Tropical fruit on vivacious **18** ⑧ tank sample. Succulent & fresh, with broad mid-palate & long finish. **Buiten Blanc** ⊘ ★★★★ Ever-reliable summer 'must have', **18** ⑧ is mainly sauvignon with dabs chenin, semillon & gewürztraminer. Citrus zip & zest galore. WO W Cape. **Méthode Cap Classique Brut** ★★★★ Toast & citrus marmalade flavours on **NV** ⑧ bubble from chardonnay & pinot noir. Crisp yet full, rich & long.

Limited Release range

★★★★☆ **Cabernet Franc** ⊗ Tautly focused, reined-in inky black fruit & cocoa depths with satiny oak sheen from nearly 2 years in barrel. **13** ⑨ layered, rich & concentrated. Shows what the grape can deliver.

★★★★☆ **Maximus** Broad, creamy **16** ⑨ sauvignon balances honeyed apple tart & spice with fresh acid lift. Structured, smooth & svelte from barrel ferment & 18 months in French oak, 40% new. No **15**.

Rough Diamond ⊗ ★★★★ Big-boned **12** ⑧, black fruit & graphite depth from malbec & petit verdot in 60/40 blend. Dry tannin squeeze from 80% new oak. Cellardoor only. **G** ⊛ ★★★★ Freshness of palate belies overt, typical pot-pourri perfume of gewürztraminer. Barrel-aged (unusually) **17** ⑧ from Durbanville is fresh, with spicy nectarine lift, confident & uncloying, lovely lime & lees tail. Occasional release: **3rd Time Lucky**. In abeyance: **Malbec, Pinot Noir Block 8**. — FM

Location: Constantia ▪ Map: Cape Peninsula ▪ Map grid reference: B3 ▪ WO: Constantia/Western Cape ▪ Est 1796 ▪ 1stB 1985 ▪ Tasting & sales Mon-Fri 9-5 Sat 10-5 ▪ Closed all pub hols ▪ Cellar tours by appt ▪ Selection of platters available in tasting room ▪ Buitenverwachting Restaurant ▪ Deli & coffee shop ▪ Conferences ▪ Owner(s) Richard & Sieglinde (Christine) Mueller, Lars Maack ▪ Estate manager Hermann Kirschbaum (Jan 1993) ▪ Cellarmaster(s) Brad Paton (Jan 2005) ▪ Winemaker(s) Brad Paton (Jan 2005), with Stephan Steyn ▪ Viticulturist(s) Peter Reynolds (Jan 2001) ▪ 147ha/105ha (cabs s/f, merlot, chard, sauv) ▪ 800t/320,000cs own label 20% red 80% white ▪ PO Box 281 Constantia 7848 ▪ info@buitenverwachting.com ▪ www.buitenverwachting.com ▪ S 34° 2′ 30.4″ E 018° 25′ 1.5″ ▪ 🖷 riddles.merely.washcloths ▪ F +27 (0)21-794-1351 ▪ **T +27 (0)21-794-5190/1**

☐ **Bulldozer** see Bergsig Estate
☐ **Burger Family Vineyards** see Rietvallei Wine Estate

Burgershof

One of the area's original farms, Burgershof is in the Klaasvoogds ward of Robertson. Latterly the Reynecke family have focused on modern, in-demand varietal and blended wines but their heritage and biggest strength is fortified muscat. The quality's in the soil – viticulturally and according to local lore: the blood of early colonist Clas Vogt, horribly killed by an elephant, said to give the grape its special beauty in these parts.

★★★★ **Red Muscadel** ⊗ Premium-priced & -packaged **16** ⑧ is complex, light footed, near-perfect balance of sugar & alcohol even topped by fine persistent finish. Gorgeous flavour array - peach through tealeaf to ginger. 375 ml intended as a gift for someone special.

Merlot ⊗ ★★★ Winemaking process 'a secret :)' but result is remarkably soft tannin pillow for **16** ⑦'s plummy fruit, charmingly fresh, juicy, yet satisfyingly vinous. **Pinotage** ★★★ With dark berries, tapenade & meaty complexity, dry finish despite sweet fruit core, **16** ⑦ ticks all the boxes. **Cabernet Sauvignon-Shiraz** ⊗ ★★ Uncomplex but pleasant **16** ⑦ braai companion, near-equal blend has intense fruit backing its big, burly tannins. **Chardonnay** ⊗ ★★★ Belle of the unfortified ball, **17** ⑧ citrus plus almond note from oak, vivacious acidity in support, moreish dry finish. **Sauvignon Blanc** ⊗ ★★★ **17** ⑦'s tropical fruit salad perfume & flavours, rounded acidity & bone-dry tail make a refreshing patio sipper or al fresco lunch partner. — WB, CvZ

Location/WO: Robertson ▪ Est 1864 ▪ 1stB 2000 ▪ Closed to public ▪ Sales at La Verne Wine Boutique & Ashton Wine Boutique ▪ Owner(s) Hennie Reynecke ▪ Cellarmaster(s)/winemaker(s)/viticulturist(s) Hennie Reynecke (Jan 1979) ▪ 70ha (cab, merlot, muscadel r/w, ptage, ruby cab, shiraz, chard, chenin, cbard, sauv) ▪ IPW, WIETA ▪ PO Box 72 Klaasvoogds River 6707 ▪ burgershof@barvallei.co.za ▪ www.burgershof.com ▪ F +27 (0)23-626-5433 ▪ **T +27 (0)23-626-5433**

Bushmanspad Estate

In the latest move in a career spanning several Cape wine regions, young Aldert Nieuwoudt has swapped one beautiful 'berg' with another: the Helderberg, where he worked three vintages at Haskell Vineyards, and now the Langeberg, joining Menno Schaafsma's Bushmanspad as winemaker and farm manager. The estates have guest accommodation in common, the facilities here being ideally situated mid-slope to take advantage of the tremendous view over Robertson Valley.

★★★★ Grand Reserve Merlot ⓥ 2-barrel limited release, **15** ⑧⑥ still has chewy tannins, taut black cherry centre. Finesse rather than power, with delicately fragrant threads, should develop with cellaring.

★★★★ The Menno ⓥ 6-way blend led by shiraz & malbec, **15** ⑧⑨ fine black fruit, dense but supple & sleek, with hints of smoked meat & cherries. Drink or keep several years. No **13**, **14**.

Cabernet Sauvignon ★★★ Oak-spiced mulberry fruit prevails on juicy, lightweight **16** ⑧② showing appealing aromatic profile. **Cabernet Franc** ⓥ **★★★** Toffee & plummy fruit a bit off-target for variety, but medium-bodied **15** ⑧② is pleasant sipping with no rough edges. **Malbec ★★★★** Plummy black fruit, tending to jammy, with spicy aromas, **16** ⑧⑤ ripe, gentle tannins, medium body. **Shiraz ★★★★** Lush, ripe & perfumed black fruit on **16** ⑧⑤ with tarry, savoury notes & suede tannins. **Cabernet Sauvignon-Merlot** (NEW) **★★★** Harmonious blend with dashes malbec, mourvèdre, **17** ⑧⓪ plush red & black fruit, chewy tannins, rather brief farewell. **Red Gold Blend ★★★** 6-way **17** ⑧② Bordeaux/Rhône mix displays very youthful/grapey fruit, unresolved sticky tannins. Though sturdy (14.8% alcohol), lighter than last. **Pink Gold Rosé** ⓥ **★★★** Upfront strawberry flavours on **18** ⑧① from malbec, lightish textured, with lean body tangy acid. **Sauvignon Blanc ★★★** Unwooded in **18** ⑧② showing pungent nettle & khaki bush aromas, tad less effusive on palate, tangy acid. — GdB

Location: Bonnievale ▪ Map/WO: Robertson ▪ Map grid reference: C1 ▪ Est 2000 ▪ 1stB 2006 ▪ Tasting & sales Mon-Fri 8.30–5 ▪ Fee R40/5 wines ▪ Cheese platters by appt ▪ BYO picnic ▪ Walks/hikes ▪ Self-catering cottages ▪ Owner(s) Menno Schaafsma ▪ Cellarmaster(s)/winemaker(s)/viticulturist(s) Aldert Nieuwoudt (Jan 2018) ▪ 52ha (cabs s/f, malbec, merlot, mourv, shiraz, sauv) ▪ 400t own label 80% red 15% white 5% rosé ▪ PO Box 227 Bonnievale 6730 ▪ info@bushmanspad.co.za ▪ www.bushmanspad.co.za ▪ S 33° 53' 55.0" E 020° 11' 46.7" ▪ [w] swooped.oilfield.pollsters ▪ **T +27 (0)23-616-2961**

☐ **Butcher Shop & Grill** *see* The Butcher Shop & Grill

B Vintners Vine Exploration Co

Cousins Bruwer Raats and Gavin Bruwer Slabbert, both of Raats Family Wines, wanted to also explore wider than their specialty in cabernet franc and chenin blanc — with historically significant varieties like hanepoot and pinotage, for example — and to feel free to cross the Stellenbosch border. So in 2014 they jointly created their Vine Exploration Co (with not much imagination needed to explain the B Vintners bit). As they say: 'By honouring the heritage of the Cape and incorporating innovative and minimal intervention winemaking techniques, B Vintners allows the vineyard to tell the tale.'

★★★★☆ Black Bream Pinot Noir ⓥ ⓦ From Walker Bay vines near the ocean, **17** ⑨④ fragrant, elegant & complex, layers of succulent cherry, strawberry, raspberry wrapped by taut tannin. Like **16** ⑨② approachable & well-judged oak (16 months, 15% new). Named for SA's national fish (aka 'galjoen').

★★★★☆ Liberté Pinotage ⓦ Pure & subtle **17** ⑨③ like **16 ★★★★★** ⑨⑤ skilfully constructed & precise, showcasing variety's positive attributes. Floral, medium bodied & fresh, clever oaking (16 months, 10% new) allows black cherry fruit to take centre stage.

★★★★☆ Fire Heath Chardonnay ⓦ Bunch-pressed, naturally fermented **17** ⑨④ ex Walker Bay, expressive but showcasing producer's light touch, as in **16** ⑨① Overt citrus & honey accented by lively acidity, gentle wooding (older barrels, 10 months).

★★★★ **De Alexandria** Rare-in-SA bone-dry muscat d'Alexandrie from 0.3ha Helderberg vineyard. **17** ★★★★★ ⑨⓪ more refined than **16** ⑧⑦, shows greater typicity in grapey litchi, spice & lemon pith nuances.

★★★★★ **Harlem to Hope** ⓐ Poised & charming blend celebrating heirloom varieties chenin & semillon (64/28), muscats de Frontignan & d'Alexandrie. **17** ⑨⑤ expressive pear & ginger, ripe fruit giving the impression of sweetness though bone-dry, savouriness from older oak, as in equally stellar **16** ⑨⑤.— HC

Location/map: Stellenbosch ▪ Map grid reference: B6 ▪ WO: Stellenbosch/Walker Bay ▪ Est/1stB 2014 ▪ Tasting Mon-Fri 9-5 by appt ▪ Fee R500 (2-10 pax) ▪ Closed all pub hols ▪ Owner(s)/cellarmaster(s) Bruwer Raats & Gavin Bruwer Slabbert ▪ own label 50% red 50% white ▪ PO Box 2068 Dennesig 7601 ▪ braats@mweb.co.za ▪ www.bvintners.com ▪ S 33° 58′ 16.6″ E 018° 44′ 55.3″ ▪ warps.picnic.apparent ▪ F +27 (0)86-647-8500 ▪ T +27 (0)21-881-3078

☐ **Cabrière** see Haute Cabrière

Cadequin Vineyard

Helderberg small-scale wine and olive growers Robbie and Tarina Terheijden are undaunted by drought-induced lower yields in 2018, emphasising instead how excited they are about prospects for their current pinotage ('16, by consultant winemaker Riaan Oosthuizen) to shine at competitions, and for new chenin vines to take root in their tiny vineyard. The first crop for their artisan olive oil is further reason for optimism.

Location: Sir Lowry's Pass ▪ Map: Helderberg ▪ Map grid reference: H8 ▪ Est 2008 ▪ 1stB 2014 ▪ Tasting & sales by appt Mon-Fri 9-4 Sat/Sun 9-1 ▪ R50/tasting ▪ Closed Ash Wednesday, Easter Fri-Mon, Ascension day, Dec 25 & Jan 1 ▪ Playground ▪ Olives ▪ Airbnb Cadequin Vineyard Cottage (self-catering) ▪ Owner(s) Robbie & Tarina Terheijden ▪ Winemaker(s) Riaan Oosthuizen (Jan 2013, Nomada Wines) ▪ Viticulturist(s) Jaco Mouton (Jan 2010, consultant) ▪ 1ha (ptage, chenin) ▪ 1,6t ▪ 13 High Riding Estate, 54 Old Sir Lowry's Pass Rd Somerset West 7130 ▪ moon@vodamail.co.za ▪ S 34° 7′ 20.89″ E 018° 55′ 30.26″ ▪ seminal.snacks. habituated ▪ T +27 (0)71-673-5552

☐ **Café Culture** see KWV Wines

Calais Wine Estate

Calais is a farm founded in 1692 by Huguenot Jean Manje, who named it after his home town. The current owners are represented by estate manager Melt van der Spuy, who oversees a portfolio of vines, wines and guest accommodation with attractive views over Paarl's bucolic Dal Josaphat area.

Klein Valley range

St Mikhail Cabernet Sauvignon ⓥ ★★★ Country-style **11** ⑦⑧ with earthy & savoury notes to plum pudding flavours, 2nd fill oak contributing to the tannic dryness. **Applause** ⓥ ★★★ **11** ⑧⑴ cab/shiraz blend has clean oak & blackberry wafts, juicy berry sweetness anchored by firm tannins. Could age few years. **Bel Canto** ⓥ ★★★★ Mature **11** ⑧⑤ cab, shiraz, merlot is a hearty winter stew red, with earth, spice from older oak & red fruit, robust tannins. **St Katerina Barrel Fermented Viognier** ⓥ ★★★ Attractive, peachy **13** ⑧⑴ has some richness & texture, sufficient acidity to refresh the creamy finish.

Calais range

Chardonnay ⓥ ★★ Unoaked **13** ⑦⑷ straightforward easy-drinker with ripe pineapple flavour. Wellington WO. **Sauvignon Blanc** ⓥ ★★ Lightly tropical **13** ⑦⑷ for uncomplicated quaffing. — JG

Location/map: Paarl ▪ Map grid reference: G4 ▪ WO: Paarl/Wellington ▪ Est/1stB 2000 ▪ Tasting by appt ▪ Sales daily 8-4 ▪ Guest accommodation ▪ Owner(s) Calais Wine Estate shareholders ▪ Farm manager Melt van der Spuy (Dec 2015) ▪ 23ha (cab, merlot, p verdot, ptage, ruby cab, shiraz, chard, chenin, sauv) ▪ 150t/3,000cs own label 70% red 30% white ▪ PO Box 9006 Klein Drakenstein 7628 ▪ info@calais.co.za ▪ www.calais.co.za ▪ S 33° 42′ 32.1″ E 019° 1′ 24.6″ ▪ expect.entire.fizzy ▪ T +27 (0)21-868-3888

Calitzdorp Cellar

Fresh energy and excitement at Calitzdorp Cellar on tourist-friendly Route 62, with young incoming winemaker Danie van der Westhuizen promising new table wines, MCC sparkling and brandy, and a tasting room update completed to showcase the beautiful views over the Klein Karoo landscape. Danie intends to focus on terroir, noting that the 40 owner-grower farms, spread over 300 ha, encompass many terrains and soil types, and this diversity 'infuses complex flavours into the various cultivars'.

★★★★ **Hanepoot** Driest of the fortifieds, now **NV** ⑧⑥. Less ebullient fruit aromas than previous but pleasing savoury notes add complexity. Honeyed palate enlivened by seamless spirit & zesty acidity.

★★★★ **Red Muscadel** Beautiful garnet hue, vivid sultana flavours with lavender nuance, fine balance o' sweetness, alcohol & acidity for uncloying finish, **17** ⑧⑥ fortified well worth seeking out.

★★★★☆ **White Muscadel** 🍇 Gorgeous pear & white peach aromas touched with honey & fynbos, all repeated on palate with freshness & purity, delicate persistence. Like sibling fortifieds, **17** ⑨⓪ will reward lengthy cellaring.

★★★★ **Golden Jerepigo** Golden by name, golden by colour & plenty of Golden Syrup goodness to entice & delight. Latest fortified **NV** ⑧⑤ usual hanepoot & white muscadel combo, touch drier than normal.

Tinto 🍇 ★★★ Unfettered by obvious oak, **NV** ⑧② shows pot-pourri & orange zest exuberance, generous fruit, brisk cranberry finish. Lovely summer red from mostly touriga, equal merlot & petit verdot.

Cabernet Sauvignon ★★★ Plums & cassis with vanilla oak overlay, big but well-handled 15% alcohol, **16** ⑦⑨ nicely dry so it remains food-friendly. **Merlot** 🍇 ★★★ Plum & chocolate on ripe, forthcoming **16** ⑦⑧, just enough tannin grip for Karoo lamb & other red meats. **Pinotage** ★★★ Bright acidity, supple tannins & earthy note in **16** ⑦⑨. **Shiraz** ★★★ Vibrant red berries & plums, crisp acidity, **16** ⑧⓪ year in oak, like the other vintage-dated reds, 12% new versus older barrels for the rest. **Pinotage Blanc de Noir** ★★★ Returns after extended break with pretty pink **18** ⑦⑨, abundant berries & cherries, hint grassiness & dab sugar for drinkability. **Rosé** 🍇 ★★★ Attractive **NV** ⑧⓪ from merlot, cab & shiraz showing fresh berry flavours; good off-dry styling with balancing savoury notes & acidity. **Limited Edition Chenin Blanc-Muscat d'Alexandrie Delight** ★★★ Now vintage dated, varietally labelled. 50/50 blend but shows more muscat character in ginger spice & effusive grapiness. Enjoy slightly fizzy, just-sweet **18** ⑦⑨ well-chilled. **Cape Ruby** ⊘ ★★★★ Fruitcake & tangerine-toned 50/50 **NV** ⑧③ mix tinta & touriga, rich & round for solo sipping (though at 18% alcohol small sips probably in order). **Cape Vintage** 🍇 ★★★★ Equal tinta & touriga in attractive savoury-toned **16** ⑧④ 'port'. Unshowy mid-2017 yet good depth & weight, harmonious 20% alcohol & authentic tight finish. Not tasted: **Touriga Nacional**, **Chardonnay**, **Chenin Blanc**, **Sauvignon Blanc**, **Hanepoot Muskadel Reserve**. — CvZ

Location/WO: Calitzdorp ▪ Map: Klein Karoo & Garden Route ▪ Map grid reference: B5 ▪ Est 1928 ▪ 1stB 1976 ▪ Tasting & sales Mon-Fri 9-5 Sat 9-1 ▪ Closed Good Fri & Dec 25 ▪ Cellar tours by appt ▪ Tour groups ▪ BYO picnic ▪ Conferences ▪ Owner(s) 40 members ▪ Cellarmaster(s)/viticulturist(s) Danie van der Westhuizen (Dec 2017) ▪ Winemaker(s) Danie van der Westhuizen (Dec 2017), with Abraham Pretorius ▪ 300ha (13 varieties, r/w) ▪ 5,000t/7,000cs own label ▪ IPW ▪ PO Box 193 Calitzdorp 6660 ▪ info@calitzdorpwine.co.za ▪ www.calitzdorpwine.co.za ▪ S 33° 32' 18.9" E 021° 41' 10.6" ▪ 🖬 faltering.pianists.highlights ▪ F +27 (0)44-213-3328 ▪ **T +27 (0)44-213-3301**

Camberley Wines

🍷 🍴 🏠 📷

John and Gaël Nel, welcoming visitors to their scenic Banhoek Valley spot for over two decades with an eclectic mix of stylish attractions mirroring their passions (he wine and sport, she food and gardening), add to their boutique offering of appealing reds this year. The seamless Celebration is for all comers, as is the guest cottage, now conveniently self-catering.

Camberley range

★★★★ **Cabernet Franc** 🍇 Quiet **14** ★★★ ⑦⑧ with dark fruit & spice, soft, uncomplicated & easy. Style departure from plush, powerful **10** ⑧⑦, which needed decanting or time.

★★★★ **Shiraz** Ripe & ready to drink, **15** ⑧⑥ smooth tannins cosseting cherry & red plum fruit, smoky & spicy nuances, rooibos-tinged persistence. **14** sold out untasted.

★★★★ **Cabernet Sauvignon-Merlot** 🍇 Cedarwood & tobacco notes are foils for ebullient Camberley ripeness (15.5% alcohol) on **14** ⑧⑥, now bottled. Pristine red fruit in sync with polished tannins.

Illusion ★★★★ Was 'Pinotage' & vintage dated. Variety's bramble- & mulberry fruit, clean leather undertones on **NV** ⑧③. Savoury, with well-polished tannins, like the red siblings, from 14 months in barrel, 25% new; perfect with venison. **Celebration** (NEW) ★★★ For early enjoyment, **NV** (80) cinnamon & redcurrant fruit, soft tannins, easy to drink but before celebrating, note the high 16.2% alcohol. Mostly shiraz, splash cab. **Philosophers' Stone** ★★★ Bordeaux red blend, previously vintage dated. Cab franc-led **NV** (82) farmyard tones, satisfying savoury finish but less gravitas than **14** ★★★★ (86) from merlot & both cabs. **Sparkling Shiraz** ★★★★ New disgorgement of **15** (84) fizz. Luscious mulberry & cherry notes & few grams sugar brightened by fine bubbles & acidity for clean, enjoyable & unusual drink. Not tasted: **Cabernet Sauvignon Reserve**, **The 5th Element**, **Elixir Fortified Red**. Occasional release: **Elm Tree Merlot**, **Charisma**.

Prohibition range

Red ★★★ Unchallenging easy-sipping **NV** (78), red fruit, oak spice & rhubarb nuance from 60/40 cab/merlot. Not tasted: **White**. — GM

Location/map/WO: Stellenbosch ▪ Map grid reference: H4 ▪ Est 1990 ▪ 1stB 1996 ▪ Tasting & sales Mon-Sat & pub hols 9–5 Sun 9-3 ▪ Tasting fee depending on wine of choice ▪ Closed Dec 25 & Jan 1 ▪ Cellar tours by appt ▪ Café Pavè open Fri-Sun from 8 for breakfast & light lunch; during high season it will probably be open daily ▪ Cycle showroom ▪ Self-catering guest cottage ▪ Owner(s) John & Gaël Nel ▪ Winemaker(s) John Nel ▪ Viticulturist(s) Bennie Booysen ▪ 7ha (cabs s/f, merlot, p verdot, ptage, shiraz, touriga) ▪ ±35t/6,400cs own label 100% red ▪ PO Box 6120 Uniedal 7612 ▪ john@camberley.co.za ▪ www.camberley.co.za ▪ S 33° 55'8.9" E 018° 55'58.3" ▪ adopting.possible.exactly ▪ F +27 (0)21-885-1822 ▪ **T +27 (0)21-885-1176**

☐ **Camino Africana** see Edgebaston

Canto Wines   (wine) (restaurant) (photo) (accommodation)

This young boutique venture in Durbanville, emphasising MCC sparkling, has had a busy year. Owner Marinus Neethling has opened a deli, catering for picnics, functions and weddings, and launched Yoga Saturdays where very sensibly your morning stretch is followed by bubbly and a macaroon. Winemaker Anneke Potgieter has added to the range, offered at the tasting room along with endless mountain views.

Canto Wines range

★★★★ **Merlot** ⊘ Plenty of oak influence (18 months in barrel) on lively **16** (86), adding smoke, tar, leather & chocolate to bright red cherry fruit. Soft tannins & balancing acidity add to overall appeal.

★★★★ **Pinotage** (NEW) ⊘ Firmly styled **16** (86) mixes ripe black plummy fruit with hints of coffee, smoke & tar. Tannins & zippy acidity suggest further development - certainly benefits from decanting now.

★★★★ **Chardonnay** (NEW) 100% new French oak makes presence felt on showy **17** (87) but plenty of fruit - apple, peach, mango - backs it up, zesty acidity & interesting oatmeal, caramel & spice notes all suggest a keeper.

Unwooded Chardonnay (NEW) ★★★★ Refreshing mouthful of tropical & citrus fruit, **16** (84) full flavoured, richly textured, with enlivening acidity. **Sauvignon Blanc** (NEW) ★★★★ Variety-true **17** (84) explodes with greenpepper, guava & granadilla, underpinned by typical Durbanville dusty notes at finish.

Méthode Cap Classique range

★★★★ **Pinot Noir** (NEW) Delightful concentration of fruit on impressive **13** (88) rosé sparkling, showing elegant savoury notes of yeast, brioche, bright red-cherry & strawberry with saline tang. Excellent balanced acidity & length. Stellenbosch grapes, like Shiraz.

★★★★ **Brut** (NEW) Fine mousse on **15** (87) sparkler from chardonnay, lime sherbet perfume, candy apple flavour, zinging acidity keeps it focused, dry. Drink now as aperitif, can age.

Shiraz (NEW) ★★★★ Unusual bubbles from shiraz, **13** (85) pale onion skin colour with earthy, plummy notes. Fresh & spicy palate with decent length. Year on lees. **Pinot Noir-Chardonnay** (NEW) ★★★★ Floral & pretty **14** (85) a 50/50 blend aged on lees for 12 months. Fresh acidity, crisp apple & tangy lemon make for enjoyable everyday fizz. WO W Cape. — CM

Location: Durbanville ▪ Map: Durbanville, Philadelphia & Darling ▪ Map grid reference: C7 ▪ WO: Durbanville/Stellenbosch/Western Cape ▪ Est/1stB 2015 ▪ Tasting & sales Tue-Thu 9-5 Fri 9-6 Sat 9-3 ▪ Wine & MCC tasting R55pp; macaron & MCC pairing R95pp ▪ Closed Good Fri, Dec 25 & Jan 1 ▪ Deli products available from tasting room ▪ Picnics ▪ Play area for children ▪ Functions & weddings ▪ MTB trail ▪ Owner(s) Marinus Neethling ▪ Winemaker(s) Anneke Potgieter (Sep 2015, consultant) ▪ 22ha/18ha (merlot, chard) ▪ 8-10t/3,500cs own

label 40% red 30% white 30% MCC ▪ info@cantowines.co.za ▪ www.cantowines.co.za ▪ S 33° 48'19.56"E
018° 37'27.41" ▪ ⌨ antihero.many.upon ▪ **T +27 (0)21-492-2821**

Capaia Wine Estate ⓠ ⑪ ⊚ ⓐ

Ingrid von Essen and Stephan von Neipperg's showpiece on the Philadelphia Hills is going 'more green' with
the addition of solar panels providing part of the electric power requirements. The estate has also entered
into an agreement with CapeNature for the long-term conservation of the property's biodiversity. Newly
established mountain bike and trail-running routes are drawcards for outdoor enthusiasts, and athletes and
sedentary types alike can now also sample the delights of Olivia, the new deli, open on weekend mornings.

★★★★ ONE Herbal & savoury introduction to **12** ⑧⑦, led by the 2 cabs plus merlot & splash petit verdot.
Intense & grippy, with abundant black fruit. Also-tasted **13** ⑧⑦, syrah replacing merlot, meatier, softer
fruited & lacking some finesse of sibling. **11** untasted. Various bottle formats available.

Cabernet Sauvignon-Merlot ★★★★ Sweet-fruited **16** ⑧⑤ has dashes cab franc & shiraz in support,
ample black fruit & enough tannic grip, but not quite as refined as **15 ★★★★** ⑧⑦. **Rosé ★★★★** Previewed
18 ⑧③, beautiful pale salmon hue from merlot (92%) with sauvignon, array of fresh, dry red-berry flavours
- a real crowd pleaser & big step up. **Sauvignon Blanc ★★★★** Succulent tropical notes with gooseberry
on ex-tank **18** ⑧④, typical cool-climate zip underpinned by wet stone minerality, nice tautness & focus.
Occasional release: **Shiraz.** In abeyance: **Mariella's.** — HC

Location/WO: Philadelphia ▪ Map: Durbanville, Philadelphia & Darling ▪ Map grid reference: C5 ▪ Est 1997
▪ 1stB 2003 ▪ Tasting, sales & cellar tours Mon-Fri 8-5; Sat/Sun tasting & sales at Mariella's ▪ Tour groups
▪ Mariella's Restaurant T +27 (0)21-972-1103/+27 (0)72-770-9695, mariellas@capaia.co.za ▪ Deli Olivia ▪
Facilities for children ▪ Picnic baskets in summer ▪ MTB & trail running routes ▪ Owner(s) Ingrid von Essen &
Stephan von Neipperg ▪ Cellarmaster(s) Bernabé Strydom (Oct 2006), assisted by Stephan von Neipperg ▪
Winemaker(s) Gerhard Augustyn (Oct 2015) ▪ Viticulturist(s) Schalk du Toit (2009, consultant) ▪ 140ha/60ha
(cabs s/f, merlot, p verdot, shiraz, sauv) ▪ 260t/26,000cs own label 85% red 15% white ▪ IPW ▪ PO Box 25
Philadelphia 7304 ▪ info@capaia.co.za ▪ www.capaia.com ▪ E 018° 34'7.82" S 33° 42'
47.60" ▪ ⌨ unbuckle.revisit.intelligent ▪ F +27 (0)21-972-1894 ▪ **T +27 (0)21-972-1081 (winery); +27
(0)21-972-1103 (restaurant)**

☐ **Cape Bay** see FirstCape Vineyards

Cape Chamonix Wine Farm ⓠ ⑪ ⓐ ⊚

Cape Chamonix in Franschhoek has a history going back to the 17th century, but the modern farm (and
name) are thanks to German owner Chris Hellinger, here for more than a quarter century. Blessed by its
mountain slope site and clay-rich soils, the property is capable of producing top-class whites and reds, in
the confident hands of winemaker Thinus Neethling, as the line-up and awards track record shows. The
vines are largely unirrigated, the beneficiary of Franschhoek's high rainfall, which leads to another advantage here, Cape Chamonix's own water from an underground spring. Geared for visitors, there is a restaurant,
conservation area and range of accommodation, all taking advantage of the breathtaking views.

Reserve range

★★★★★ Cabernet Franc ⑳ Consistently among SA's best, variety-true **16** ⑨③ shows vivid cassis,
whiffs of graphite, crushed herbs, body silky & succulent, tannins harmonious. Has fruit purity & presence,
wonderful style, a cab franc template.

★★★★★ Pinot Noir ⑳ Best older vineyards, 60% new French oak, **17** ⑨④ has classic varietal elegance
yet packed with fruit & interest; sour cherry intensity, savoury spice, backing freshness. Tannins masterly,
firm without edges, show tensile strength.

★★★★★ Greywacke Pinotage ⑳ **16** ⑨③ half grapes normal harvest, rest vine dried, foot crushed,
frequently pumped-over, 18 months oaked, 30% new. Fruit is Xmas cake & prunes, layered complexity,
mocha chocolate, sweet spice yet black pepper; juicy, elegant, streamlined. Individual, impressive.

★★★★ Marco Polo ⑳ As expected from a cab-led Bordeaux blend, barrel-selected **13** ⑧⑧ has firm
tannin & acid backbone, mulberry fruit & cedar - all supported by well-judged 18 months oak, 60% new.

★★★★★ **Troika** ⓐ Best vineyards/barrels for polished **16** ★★★★★ ⑨⑷ Bordeaux red, cab franc-led with cab, 10% each merlot, petit verdot. Plush berries, crushed herbs, lead pencils & oak-influenced cigarbox. Like **15** ⑨⑸, deep & involving, master crafted, tannins supple, promise cellaring.

★★★★☆ **Chardonnay** ⓐ Older vineyards, barrel selection, **17** ⑨⑷ lavished with care, wild ferment, 70% new oak. Toasted brioche, lemon preserve, a suggestion of richness but nothing overt, it's all seamless, shows good breeding. Minerality on the finish, just more to admire.

★★★★☆ **White** Classic sauvignon, semillon 80/20 blend, wholebunch, barrel fermented/aged portion. Sampled before bottling, **17** ⑨⓪ powerfully scented: vanilla biscuit & tropical tones, whiff of citrus, refreshing acidity anchors the flavours, giving vitality, food-friendly grip.

Cape Chamonix range

★★★★☆ **Feldspar Pinot Noir** ⊘ Younger vineyards, less new oak than sibling, **17** ⑨② tasted ex barrel designed for earlier drinking but no lesser for that. Bright red berries, succulent, 16 months in barrel a harmonious addition for appealing spice array, supple tannins. Delicious.

★★★★☆ **Chardonnay** ⓐ Younger vineyards than reserve, less oak, less new, still well-crafted, wild ferment, barrelled 12 months. **17** ⑨③ a delight, oozes personality: lemon/lime intensity, melba toast, a brightly fresh finish, almost tangy in its fruit/acid juxtaposition.

★★★★ **Chardonnay Unoaked** Grapefruit & lemon in **18** ⑧⑧ ex-tank sample, admirable fruit purity, with enough deep flavour to handle food. Elegant, bone-dry & zinging fresh, a fine-boned example of the variety.

★★★★ **Sauvignon Blanc** Tiny portion oaked; preview **18** ⑧⑧'s most distinguishing feature is invigorating freshness, makes the fruit spark with life & vitality, giving length & excellent cellaring potential.

Rouge ★★★★ Merlot/cab with malbec, dash petit verdot in **16** ⑧③ work-in-progress. Dark fruited, 18 months seasoned barrels, initial impression of being smoky, tarry, but perked up by palate's juicy freshness. Charming colourful label. Not tasted: **MCC Blanc de Blancs**. — CR

Location/map/WO: Franschhoek ▪ Map grid reference: C1 ▪ Est 1991 ▪ 1stB 1992 ▪ Tasting & sales Mon-Sun 8.30–5 ▪ Fee R60 (non reserve)/R100 (reserve tasting) ▪ Closed Dec 25 & Jan 1 ▪ Cellar tours by appt ▪ Conservation area ▪ Marco Polo Lodge, Waterfall Lodge, Forest Suites & fully equipped self-catering cottages ▪ Owner(s) Chris Hellinger ▪ Cellarmaster(s)/winemaker(s)/viticulturist(s) Thinus Neethling (2015) ▪ 300ha/50ha (cabs s/f, malbec, merlot, p verdot, ptage, pinot, chard, chenin, sauv, sem) ▪ 180-220t/30,000cs own label 60% red 40% white ▪ IPW ▪ PO Box 28 Franschhoek 7690 ▪ marketing@chamonix.co.za, winemaker@chamonix.co.za ▪ www.chamonix.co.za ▪ S 33° 53' 60.0" E 019° 7' 34.0" ▪ ⌖ matchbox.blameless.breathes ▪ F +27 (0)21-876-3237 ▪ **T +27 (0)21-876-8400**

☐ **Cape Classic** *see* Kumala

Cape Classics　　　　　　　ⓠ

The largest importer of SA wines into the US, Cape Classics is responsible for 30% of all locally produced wine sold there. The Somerset West-based company's own brands - listed below - are represented in over 15 countries. The original Indaba line made by celebrated winemaker Bruwer Raats (see Raats Family Wines) now boasts sales of over 10 million bottles, while the more recent Jam Jar just posted four years of double-digit sales growth. Investment in education remains a priority for Cape Classics, a highlight being the first class of teachers trained under the aegis of the Indaba Foundation graduating in August 2018.

Cape Classics range

Braai ★★★ Delicious homage to the barbecue, beloved by most South Africans (& not just them). Cab does the cooking, cab franc, petit verdot in bonhomous support. **17** ⑧⓪ abundance of black fruit & broad tannins.

Indaba range

★★★★ **Chenin Blanc** ⊘ Deliciously fruity & friendly but enough gravitas to command attention. **17** ⑧⑦ gains texture & body from touch oak, 5 months on lees & few grams sugar.

Merlot ⊘ ★★★ With cherry, plum & touch of oak, **17** ⑧② is fresh & affable, but also touch more serious than generous price suggests. **Mosaic** ⊘ ★★★★ Bountiful mulberry & blueberry fruit on solid tannic backbone, toothsome **17** ⑧③ a step-up, 4-way Bordeaux blend, mainly cab. Also 3L casks in some markets, as next 2. **Chardonnay** ⊘ ★★★★ Praiseworthily poised & elegant given the price, **17** ⑧④ generous citrus

& lime with tiny (3%) but telling new-wood component. **Sauvignon Blanc ★★★** Forthcoming & incisive multi-region **17** ⑧①, ample fresh, tasty grapefruit & lime. Punches above its price, as all these.

Jam Jar range

Sweet White ★★★ Perfumed muscat d'Alexandrie from Olifants River. Low-alcohol **17** ⑦⑧ not too complex, but balanced & not over-sweet, huge fun to drink. **Sweet Shiraz ★★** Paarl-sourced **17** ⑦① straightforward but likeable - if sweet red wine is your thing. — HC

Location: Somerset West ▪ Map: Helderberg ▪ Map grid reference: F4 ▪ WO: Western Cape ▪ Est 1991 ▪ 1stB 1996 ▪ Tasting by appt only ▪ Owner(s) André Shearer ▪ Winemaker(s) Bruwer Raats (Indaba & Cape Classics ranges, May 2010) ▪ 270,000cs own label 35% red 65% white ▪ PO Box 1695 Somerset West 7129 ▪ info@capeclassics.com ▪ www.capeclassics.com, www.indabawines.com, www.jamjarwines.com ▪ S 34° 4′ 5.9″ E 018° 53′ 38.2″ ▪ 📷 city.leotard.trek ▪ **T +27 (0)21-847-2400**

☐ **Cape Collection** see Kumala
☐ **Cape Cult** see Darling Cellars
☐ **Cape Discovery** see Stellenview Premium Wines

Cape Dreams
⬚

Time flies when chasing your dream! Bunty Khan bottled her first vintage exactly a decade ago, with a vision of marketing quality wine overseas at competitive prices, and furthering enfranchisement and development at home. Now a Wines of South Africa board member, and with a growing footprint in 20 countries, Bunty says 'substantial progress has been made in making Cape Dreams an internationally recognised brand... thanks to strong collaborations with strategic partners', including the go-head Rooiberg Wines team.

Cape Dreams range

Cabernet Sauvignon ★★★ Blackcurrant & cherry fruit on **17** ⑧②, a little cedar spice & graphite, too, from older oak/tanks with staves (as most of these reds). **Merlot ★★★** Mediumweight **17** ⑧⓪ has dark chocolate notes offsetting tangy berry/cherry flavours, less green than previous. **Pinotage ★★★** Lightly wooded **17** ⑧①'s medium body is smooth, with juicy red berry fruit, slightly acerbic finish. **Shiraz ★★★★** Smoke & BBQ spices enliven dark fruit of **17** ⑧③, very smooth for easy drinking. **Selected Red** ⊘ **★★★** Super braai wine, **17** ⑦⑦ fruity unwooded blend of cab/shiraz (25% each), pinotage & others. **Pinotage Rosé ★★★** Rosy **18** ⑧① a semi-dry foil for Asian spice with white peach & ripe strawberry fruit, smoothly dry. **Chardonnay ★★★★** Unwooded **18** ⑧③, fresh citrus & ripe pear fruit, tangy but smooth from time on lees. **Chenin Blanc ★★★** Refreshing **18** ⑧⓪ offers tropical fruit salad flavours, month on lees provides textural enhancement. **Colombar ★★★** Honey-drizzled melons & pears on semi-sweet **18** ⑧⓪, uncloying thanks to balancing acidity. **Sauvignon Blanc ★★★** Refreshing at 12.5% alcohol, just-dry **18** ⑧① has tropical flavours galore, from passionfruit to pineapple. **Natural Sweet Red ★★★** Made for serving chilled with mature cheeses, not-too-sweet **17** ⑦⑧ blends 50% shiraz/cab, pinotage/merlot & others. Not tasted: **Cabernet Sauvignon-Merlot, Natural Sweet Blanc.**

Reserve range

Not tasted: **Cabernet Sauvignon, Pinotage, Shiraz.** — JG

Location/map/WO: Robertson ▪ Map grid reference: A6 ▪ Tasting & cellar tours by appt ▪ Owner(s) Bunty Khan ▪ Cellarmaster(s) André van Dyk ▪ Winemaker(s) Andre Schriven ▪ (cab, merlot, ptage, shiraz, chard, chenin, cbard, sauv) ▪ 60% red 40% white ▪ BEE, HACCP, IPW, ISO 9001, WIETA ▪ sales@capedreamswine.co.za ▪ www.capedreamswine.co.za ▪ S 33° 46′ 35.3″ E 019° 45′ 42.9″ ▪ 📷 highrise.hideaways.flickered ▪ **T +27 (0)21-531-2016/+27 (0)83-792-7638/+27 (0)83-780-9428**

☐ **Cape Elements** see Nico van der Merwe Wines

Cape Elevation Vineyards

Mark Dendy Young, with a background in winemaking as well as Franschhoek's hospitality industry has, he says, long wanted to craft wines 'from cool high lying vineyards'. Which he's now doing, alongside deeply experienced Cathy Marshall (Catherine Marshall Wines), sourcing fruit from various 'elevated' Elgin sites and vinifying it in Stellenbosch for his limited bottlings.

Trig Beacon Pinot Noir ② ★★★★ Partial wholeberry ferment, long skin contact shows in **16** ⑧④ preview's colour, sweet cherry aromas & flavours, more New World in style than Old. Chewy tannins need time. Not tasted: **Contour Path Sauvignon Blanc**. — WB, CvZ

Location: Stellenbosch • WO: Elgin • Est/1stB 2015 • Closed to public • Owner(s) Mark Dendy Young • Winemaker(s) Cathy Marshall & Mark Dendy Young (both 2015) • Viticulturist(s) various Elgin growers • Eikendal Rd, Stellenbosch 7600 • mark@elevationvineyards.co.za • www.elevationvineyards.co.za • **T +27 (0)72-665-5338**

☐ **Cape Fern** see Truter Family Wines
☐ **Cape Five** see Stellenview Premium Wines
☐ **Cape Fynbos** see The Grape Grinder
☐ **Cape Haven** see Pulpit Rock Winery

Capelands Estate   ② ⑪ ⓐ

The Somerset West boutique estate of Italian-born Johann Innerhofer and Laura Mauri boasts not only a rare-in-SA walled vineyard, but also accommodation and a restaurant with views of False Bay. Their flagship Redstone label features paintings by Laura, expressive of the vineyard and the vintage. The wine is made by consultants Louis Nel and Rocco de Villiers.

★★★★ **CR1 Redstone Reserve** ⓐ Was just 'Redstone', from tiny 3 ha parcel. **15** ★★★★☆ ⑨③ harvested early, shows in freshness & tight tannins, beautifully pure fruit - cassis, sour cherries, blueberries abound. 77% cabernet, rest malbec; only 7,000 bottles. Follows sumptuous **14** ⑧⑦.

Not tasted: **Klein Redstone, Whitestone Chardonnay, Whitestone Chenin Blanc**. — HC

Location: Somerset West • Map: Helderberg • Map grid reference: F7 • WO: Stellenbosch • Est 2004 • 1stB 2010 • Tasting available at Capelands Restaurant during operating times only - see website for trading hours • Guest house • Owner(s) Capelands Resort Estate (Pty) Ltd • Winemaker(s) Louis Nel, with Rocco de Villiers (both consultants) • Viticulturist(s) Francois Hanekom (Feb 2009, consultant) • 12.5ha/3ha (cab) • 6t/2,500cs own label 100% red • 3 Old Sir Lowry's Pass Rd Somerset West 7130 • restaurant@capelands.com • www. capelands.com • S 34° 6' 29.57" E 018° 53' 4.42" • ✉ swear.postage.decency • F +27 (0)86-299-3905 • **T +27 (0)21-858-1477**

☐ **The Capeman** see Darling Cellars

Capenheimer

SA's original perlé wine, inspired by Italian Lambrusco. Launched by Monis in 1962, now made by Distell.
Capenheimer ② ★★ Light (11% alcohol) spritzy semi-sweet from undisclosed white grapes, **NV** ⑦④ has tangy freshness, nice fruity flavours. — CR

Capensis

A joint venture between Antony Beck, America-based director of Graham Beck, and Barbara Banke, owner of Jackson Family Wines in California, Capensis is intended to express wines 'from the Cape'. To this end, they and winemaker Graham Weerts, Jackson's locally born and trained winemaster, chose chardonnay, believing the world's truly great vineyard sites are revealed by only a few noble grape varieties. Their focus has fallen on the Fijnbosch Capensis Vineyard in Banhoek Valley near Stellenbosch, which is being replanted incrementally with different clones on various trellises.

★★★★ **Chardonnay** ② Less reliance on new oak in **15** ★★★★☆ ⑨③ (30% versus 50% in **14** ⑧⑧), 100% in maiden **13**) translates into less rich but more satisfying, complex glassful. Regal, with pure seam of citrus, characteristic saline acidity & taut form, superb now & for good few years.— CvZ

Location: Stellenbosch • WO: Western Cape • 1stB 2013 • Closed to public • Owner(s) Barbara Banke (owner of Jackson Beck, Jackson Family Wines US) & Antony Beck (director of Graham Beck Wines SA) • Winemaker(s) Graham Weerts • Viticulturist(s) Rosa Kruger (consultant) • 4st/2,000cs own label 100% white • info@capensiswines.com • www.capensiswines.com • **T +1 884-889-7365**

☐ **Cape of Good Hope** see Anthonij Rupert Wyne

Cape Point Vineyards ⓠ 🍴 ⓞ 🅰 ♿

Accolades continue to stream in for what was our inaugural (2008) Winery of the Year, founded by businessman Sybrand van der Spuy in 1996 and still the only winefarm on the Cape Peninsula's cool, narrow, southern tip. Situated high up in an idyllic lakeside setting, the tasting area and restaurant are home to a popular Thursday Community Market, and winemaker Riandri Visser says a new conservatory room will allow visitors to enjoy the 'phenomenal views' in all weather. She is now able to source grapes (70% red) from WO Cape Town-designated vineyards to produce a range of wines for Sybrand's new Cape Town Wine Company, listed separately.

★★★★☆ **Cape Town Chardonnay** Ⓐ Adds 'Cape Town' to name. Own & Durbanville fruit, bunch pressed, wild fermented & barrel matured 10 months in French oak, 20% new. **17** ⑨③ impresses with intense citrus & stonefruit, creamy mouthfeel, subtle oak spice & lingering mineral finish.

★★★★☆ **Sauvignon Blanc Reserve** Ⓐ Fermented/matured in 600L French oak barrels, elegant **17** ⑨③ has mere smidgen semillon to enhance rich, honeyed, lanolin texture providing backdrop to concentrated lime, tangerine & gooseberry flavours, underscored by flinty minerality. Own fruit only.

★★★★☆ **Cape Town Sauvignon Blanc** ⓥ Own & Durbanville grapes; **18** ⑨① waxy mouthfeel from 11% semillon, 3 months on lees in tank. Floral/fynbos aromas, racy acidity & salty finish framing fresh lime, white peach & grapefruit flavours.

★★★★ **Marks & Spencer Sauvignon Blanc** Ⓝⓔⓦ Made exclusively for the UK retailer, **18** ⑧⑨ with 4% semillon quite steely (especially on finish) with taut acidity, fresh lime, white peach & grapefruit flavours.

★★★★ **Noordhoek Sauvignon Blanc** Adds vineyard location to name. Unwooded yet nicely mouthcoating from 8 months lees stirring, tautly knit even after 8 months in bottle pre-release, **17** ★★★★☆ ⑨② with 3% semillon (all own fruit) improves on **16** ⑧⑨, packed with fruit, ginger nuance on finish.

★★★★★ **Isliedh** Ⓐ Richly textured yet almost ethereally fresh **17** ⑨⑤ blends barrel-fermented sauvignon & 23% semillon vinified in clay amphoras, 10 months on lees, resulting in many layers of flavour: white peach, citrus, vanilla, subtle honey & baking spice, all remarkably poised & ageworthy.

Occasional release: **Semillon**, **Noble Late Harvest**. In abeyance: **Cabernet Sauvignon**. — JG

Location: Noordhoek ▪ Map: Cape Peninsula ▪ Map grid reference: A4 ▪ WO: Cape Town ▪ Est 1996 ▪ 1stB 2000 ▪ Tasting & sales Mon-Sun 11-6 ▪ Fee R50-R125 ▪ Cheese platters available during tasting hours ▪ Restaurant, picnics, breakfast, deli & sundowners ▪ Weddings & events ▪ Weekly Thu evening food markets ▪ Child friendly ▪ Conservation area ▪ Owner(s) Sybrand van der Spuy ▪ Winemaker(s) Riandri Visser (Jul 2014), with Adriaan Jacobs (Jun 2017) ▪ Viticulturist(s) Steffan Lochner (May 2016) ▪ 22ha (sauv, sem) ▪ 25,000cs own label 100% white; Stonehaven ±150,000cs ▪ Brands for clients: Marks & Spencer, Woolworths ▪ IPW, Farming for the Future ▪ PO Box 100 Noordhoek 7979 ▪ info@cape-point.com ▪ www.capepointvineyards.co.za ▪ S 34° 5′ 41.82″ E 018° 22′ 17.28″ ▪ Ⓜ lapped.elected.accord ▪ F +27 (0)21-789-0614 ▪ **T +27 (0)21-789-0900**

Cape Rock Wines ⓠ 🍷

Willie Brand and landscape architect son Gavin's excellent boutique-wine venture is based on a property between Vredendal and Klawer on the West Coast, and its focus is on Rhône grapes from mostly own vines, grown and vinified with minimal intervention. The Cabernet persists in the portfolio because Willie likes it, though it too is naturally fermented, additive free, aged in old oak and bottled with low sulphur. Like so many colleagues, the Brands were impacted by the drought, with yields down between 25 and 30%.

★★★★ **Amnesty** Juicy **17** ⑧⑨, equal syrah, grenache & mourvèdre, improves on **16** ★★★★ ⑧⑤ with vivacious mulberry, cranberry & redcurrant fruit, delicate spice from year old oak. WO W Cape.

★★★★☆ **Red** Ⓐ A hedonistic but serious blend of mostly syrah (86%), drops mourvèdre & viognier, naturally co-fermented before year older French barrels. **17** ⑨④ spice, plum & pomegranate tones, more complex than last-tasted **14** ★★★★ ⑧⑧.

★★★★☆ **White** Ⓐ Mostly viognier, trio grenache blanc, rousanne & marsanne in support. **17** ⑨④ enticing bouquet cinnamon spice & white flowers herald full-bodied palate, attractive saline note. Satisfyingly dry (just 1.2 g/l sugar), beautifully textured from 6 months on fine lees in older barrels.

Cabernet Sauvignon ★★★★☆ Succulent & expressive **17** ⑧⑤ showcases variety's blackberry & cassis fruit, gets chocolate nuance from year older oak (as for all the reds). Much improved from previous. **Capa Roca**

Ⓐ ★★★★ Happy, drinkable assemblage touriga & souzão with cab, shiraz & 3 other bit players. **15** (84) juicy, creamy texture & balanced freshness, full body. In abeyance: **Carignan, Rosé.** — HC

Location: Vredendal ▪ Map: Olifants River ▪ Map grid reference: B4 ▪ WO: Olifants River/Western Cape ▪ Est 2001 ▪ 1stB 2002 ▪ Tasting, sales & cellar tours by appt ▪ Closed Good Fri, Dec 25 & Jan 1 ▪ BYO picnic ▪ Owner(s) Willie Brand ▪ Cellarmaster(s) Willie Brand (Jan 2001) ▪ Winemaker(s) Willie Brand (Jan 2001) & Gavin Brand ▪ 13ha/11ha (cab, carignan, grenache, mourv, shiraz, chenin, cbard, marsanne, rouss, viog) ▪ 40t/2,100cs own label 60% red 40% white ▪ PO Box 261 Vredendal 8160 ▪ caperockwines@gmail.com ▪ www.caperockwines.co.za ▪ S 31° 43' 3.12" E 018° 31' 26.37" ▪ 📷 thigh.authenticity.freshness ▪ F +27 (0)27-213-5567 ▪ **T +27 (0)27-213-2567**

☐ **Cape Soleil** see Jacques Germanier
☐ **Cape to Cairo** see Rogge Cloof
☐ **Cape to Cape** see Nordic Wines

Cape Town Wine Company (NEW)

This is the brainchild of Cape Point Vineyards owner Sybrand van der Spuy, whose Dutch ancestor Meldt van der Spuy, arrived at the Cape in 1707, acquired one of only four liquor licences, and made his fortune trading in the Cape's finest wines. Sourcing grapes from WO Cape Town vineyards only, Sybrand intends to honour his forefather through wines that 'stand tall alongside the internationally recognised Cape Town brand.'

★★★★ **Sauvignon Blanc** ⊘ Green apple & lime to the fore in zesty **17** (86), very aromatic with vibrant acidity, smooth mouthfeel from 3 months on lees, clean flinty finish.

Cabernet Sauvignon ⊘ ★★★★ Intended for early drinking, **17** (84) is medium bodied, fresh, with sweet dark-berry fruit, lightly brushed with vanilla/mocha oak spice. **Méthode Cap Classique** ★★★★ Salmon pink **15** (85) dry sparkling is 100% pinot noir, frothily exuberant, with tangy red-berry fruit & cinnamon oatmeal biscuit spice/leesiness. — JG

Location/WO: Cape Town ▪ Est/1stB 2017 ▪ Closed to public ▪ Owner(s) Sybrand van der Spuy ▪ Winemaker(s) Riandri Visser (Jul 2014), with Adriaan Jacobs (Jun 2017) ▪ Viticulturist(s) Steffan Lochner (May 2016) ▪ own label 70% red 29% white 1% rosé ▪ PO Box 100 Noordhoek 7979 ▪ marketing@capetownwine.com ▪ www.capetownwinecompany.com ▪ **T +27 (0)21-789-0900**

☐ **Cape Tranquility** see Pulpit Rock Winery

Cape Venture Wine Co.

As youngsters, Americans Charles Brain and Walker Brown hiked six days and 100 kilometers along SA's Wild Coast, and the dog that accompanied them is remembered in the name of their wine range, now with fans in 25 US states. Charles and Walker are 'working on a few new secret projects' but mostly focused on 'growing our two current wines', Rhône Red Blend and Chenin Blanc, 'and telling the story of Lubanzi'.

Est 2016 ▪ 1stB 2017 ▪ Closed to public ▪ Owner(s) Charles Brain, Cathi & David Brain, Walker Brown ▪ Winemaker(s) Trizanne Barnard & Bruce Jack (Sep 2017, both consultants) ▪ 3,800cs own label 50% red 50% white ▪ Fair for Life, WIETA ▪ 1342 Florida Ave NW Washington DC 20009 ▪ hello@capeventurewine.com ▪ www.lubanziwines.com ▪ **T +1 816 560 6149**

☐ **Cape View** see Kaapzicht Wine Estate
☐ **Capeville** see Cronier Wines
☐ **Cape Vinelands** see Asara Wine Estate & Hotel
☐ **Cape West** see Namaqua Wines
☐ **Cape Wine Company** see Erasmus Family Wines

Cap Maritime (NEW)

This project in Upper Hemel-en-Aarde is Boekenhoutskloof's latest terroir adventure. At press time, the Franschhoek-based producer was sealing a purchase of land for what will be an independent label (like Porseleinberg in Swartland). Plans to plant chardonnay and pinot noir on a substantial scale are already advanced. A new cellar is coming 'sooner rather than later'; meanwhile Gottfried Mocke will make the wines at Boekenhoutskloof, as he did with these maiden releases, from grapes off leased land in the same ward.

★★★★☆ **Pinot Noir** ⓐ Poised & elegant **17** ⑨③ from pristine Upper Hemel-en-Aarde fruit (as next). Precision winemaking preserves delicate fresh redcurrant & wild strawberry fragrance & flavour, adds smooth & good frame of tannin for further ageing.

★★★★☆ **Chardonnay** ⓐ Like sibling, spontaneously fermented but in 70% new oak & concrete 'eggs' versus Pinot's 100% open concrete. **17** ⑨③ polished & powerful, with orchard fruit, yellow peach & lemon curd sumptuousness which belies its bone-dry finish, echoing preserved lemon aftertaste. — WB

☐ **Cappupino Ccinotage** see Boland Kelder
☐ **Cap Vino** see Winkelshoek Wine Cellar
☐ **Caresse Marine** see Wildekrans Wine Estate

Carinus Family Vineyards

This project brings together distant vineyards and distantly related Carinus men, wine-loving scions of their grape-farming families. The chenins come off the huge, mostly irrigated Swartland farm of Hugo's family, the syrah from Danie's holdings on the Polkadraai Hills in Stellenbosch. In a modest shed, Lukas van Loggerenberg makes the wines (as well as his own - see Van Loggerenberg Wines) in hands-off manner. More old French barrels have been acquired to allow for greater volumes and new bottlings.

★★★★ **Syrah** Still fruit-forward, fresh & charming, **17** ⑧⑨ touch more serious than previous, with a good grip & bone-dry, but still committed to delightful drinkability. Bunch-pressed, matured in old oak.

★★★★☆ **Chenin Blanc** Established now as a fine bargain, only a little less impressive than Rooidraai. **17** ⑨① lovely but not showy, with stonefruit, straw & earthy tinge. Full but subtle flavours - a succulent green note to layers of lingering ripe flavour. Decent acid, good balance, ingratiating few grams of sugar.

★★★★★ **Rooidraai Chenin Blanc** ⓐ Off dryland bushvines on the red-soiled Swartland farm whose name it uses. **17** ★★★★★ ⑨④ less ripely fruit-forward than its partner, & drier; more savoury, complex, earthy, the acid more penetrating, giving a very fine structure. Good successor to maiden **16** ⑨⑤. Both chenins matured in neutral old oak.— TJ

Location: Stellenbosch • WO: Swartland/Stellenbosch • Est 2016 (cellar) • 1stB 2011 • Closed to public • Owner(s) Johan Georg Carinus • Winemaker(s) Lukas van Loggerenberg (Dec 2015) • Viticulturist(s) Danie & Hugo Carinus • 10t/810cs own label • Fransmanskraal Farm Devon Valley Stellenbosch 7600 • danie@carinusvineyards.co.za, hugo@carinusvineyards.co.za • www.carinusvineyards.co.za • **T +27 (0)72-249-3599**

Carmen Stevens Wines ⓠ

Catoria is the mostly UK- and US-exported label of awarded Carmen Stevens, latterly of Amani, in which cellar she now makes her wines from contracted fruit. Since 2011, Carmen has been one of the top names in the portfolio of customer-funded online retailer Naked Wines, and her association with the UK-based organisation and its member 'angels' has also provided support for her charitable trust's school feeding initiative.

Catoria range

Pinotage ⓠ ★★★ Soft, friendly plum, choc & vanilla aromas, followed by unexpectedly firm palate, **15** ⑧① invites a food accompaniment. **Shiraz** ⓠ ★★★★ Plush & rich **15** ⑧④ shows its 15% alcohol but retains freshness, verve, thanks to white pepper seasoning & crisp acidity. **Many Hands** ⓠ ★★★★ Bordeaux blend has leafy cab franc in ascendancy with merlot & petit verdot. **16** ⑧④ ripe & juicy black fruit with herbaceous nuance on palate. Stellenbosch vines. **Little Angel White** ⓠ ★★★ Dash sauvignon adds papaya & passionfruit notes, & some freshness to lightly wooded chardonnay in **16** ⑦⑧, creamy & very soft. **Sauvignon Blanc** ⓠ ★★★★ Very dry & fresh, **17** ⑧④ zesty lime & passionfruit, oaked fraction lends palate weight to cool Elgin & Tygerberg fruit. Not tasted: **Coastal Blend**. — JG, CvZ

Location: Somerset West • Map: Stellenbosch • Map grid reference: B6 • WO: Western Cape/Stellenbosch • Est/1stB 2014 • Tasting & cellar tours by appt • Owner(s) Carmen Stevens • Cellarmaster(s) Carmen Stevens (Nov 2013) • Winemaker(s) Carmen Stevens (Nov 2013), with Bevan Kruger (Oct 2014) • Viticulturist(s) Jaco Engelbrecht (2016) • 160t/19,500cs own label 70% red 30% white + 19,500cs for clients • WIETA • 9 Panorama Str Somerset West 7130 • nakedwine1@gmail.com • S 33° 57' 54.3" E 018° 43' 59.5" • ⒲ mistook. silver.approaching • **T +27 (0)82-857-0641**

☐ **Carpe Diem** see Diemersfontein Wines

Carrol Boyes Collection

Internationally hailed SA designer Carrol Boyes partners with her brother, farmer and financier, John Boyes, in this range of limited-edition wines, featuring Carrol's bold and striking designs in the packaging. See Barnardt Boyes Wines for contact details. Fans of the Iconic Collection sparkling to note this is now sourced from Champagne and thus not featured here.

Carrol Boyes Collection

Shiraz ★★★ Natural fermentation & serious new-oaking for **15** ⑦, but 'green walnut' tannins have the upper hand mid-2018, demand a hearty meal. WO W Cape for all unless noted. **Cape Blend** ★★★ Cabled trio, French-oak aged 18 months. Cab's bold tannins to the fore in **15** ⑧, pinotage contributes the lively acidity, merlot the plummy fruit. **Méthode Cap Classique Brut Rosé** ⑭ ★★★ Sunset pink **13** ⑧ sparkler from pinot noir, oaked, then 28 months on lees. Low-key strawberries followed by a demanding savoury dryness - no hardship: stick to canapés, forgo the desserts. WO Stellenbosch. Not tasted: **Méthode Cap Classique Gold, Méthode Cap Classique Silver.**

Private Collection

★★★★ **Shiraz** ⑫ Like **12** ⑧, **13** ★★★★ ⑧ voluptuous aromas of vanilla & sweet spice from new oak, palate more savoury, with house's strong tannins. Stellenbosch WO.

Sketchbook range

Cabernet Sauvignon ⑫ ★★★ Plum fruit & leafy note, **14** ⑧ grippy tannins with slight astringency, good dry finish for food partnering. **Merlot** ★★★ Dusty plum nuance, **16** ⑦ lightly flavoured & easy for summer entertaining. **Fine Red Blend** ★★★ Bordeaux-style **16** ⑧, juicy & fresh, firm tannins supporting plump black fruit. From Stellenbosch, mostly cab, with merlot & equal cab franc & petit verdot. **Chardonnay** ★★★ Barrel fermented **17** ⑧, ample palate appeal, salad of citrus flavours (lemon, lime, tangerine) melding with vanilla, genuine dryness making it a versatile table companion. **Chenin Blanc** ★★★★ Charming wine (& label, as all), **17** ⑧ gains creamy texture from three months on lees in tank (previous in barrel), white peach & flowers, soft mouthfeel. Not tasted: **Rosé.** — CvZ

Casa Mori   ⑨ ⑩ ⑩

At their brand-home in the hills above Stellenbosch, father and son duo Eugene and Bruno Mori aim to offer visitors a taste of Italy, from small parcels of handcrafted sangiovese, among other wines, to home-grown artichokes and barrel-aged vinegar, to Tuscan-style farmhouse accommodation.

Location/map: Stellenbosch ▪ Map grid reference: D3 ▪ Est 1995 ▪ 1stB 2009 ▪ Tasting, sales & tours by appt ▪ Farm produce ▪ Conferences/functions ▪ Artichoke feast ▪ B&B facilities (4 rooms) ▪ Owner(s) Eugene Mori ▪ Winemaker(s) Bruno Julian Mori (1997, consultant), with Eugene Mori ▪ Viticulturist(s) Bruno Julian Mori (1997, consultant) ▪ 4.4ha/2.3ha (cab, malbec, sangio, shiraz, viog) ▪ 1st/2,000cs own label 97% red 1% white 2% rosé ▪ PO Box 71 Koelenhof 7605 ▪ dumori@mweb.co.za ▪ www.casamori.co.za ▪ S 33° 53′ 15.28″ E 018° 48′ 27.64″ ▪ ⓦ visual.thankful.goods ▪ F +27 (0)21-949-8524 ▪ **T +27 (0)21-948-8348/+27 (0)83-620-0016 (Eugene)**

☐ **Casa Simelia** see Simelia Wines
☐ **Cathedral Cellar** see KWV Wines

Cathedral Peak Wine Estate   ⑨ ⑩ ⑭

Mauritz Koster and Justin Vermaak's winery is not just the only winery in the central Drakensberg (hence the name), but also, they say, the largest in KwaZulu-Natal. Flip Smith, in charge of the high-lying vineyards (1,100 m above sea level) and the cellar, deals with challenges that might shock his Western Cape counterparts: heavy summer rainfall and extreme weather conditions, including hail. But awards have started arriving. Also welcome are tasters, brides and grooms, conference-goers, and those in search of lunch.

Bethani range

Merlot ★★★ Expressive fruit, red berries, cherries, underpinned by dry, firm but not harsh tannins, for further cellaring but **14** ⑦ already drinking well. **Barrel Pinotage** ★★★ Riper than sibling, some new oak, **15** ⑧ has vibrant fruit, berries, plums, similar liquorice tones, appealing vanilla spicing. Tannin backbone but no barrier to enjoyment. **Pinotage** ★★★ From first pinotage planted in KZN, no lack of attention for

14 ⑧⓪, 24 months oaking giving prosciutto, salty liquorice savouriness, dark fruit in harmony with tannins, smooth texture. **Cellar Door ★★★** Wood char, smoky notes on **13** ⑦⑦ pinotage & merlot blend, elegantly structured & good freshness but a bit short on fruit. — CR, CvZ

Location: Winterton ▪ Map/WO: KwaZulu-Natal ▪ Map grid reference: B2 ▪ Est 2007 ▪ 1stB 2012 ▪ Tasting & sales Mon-Fri 9.30-4 Sat/Sun 9.30-4 to be pre-booked ▪ Tasting R10pp/wine ▪ Closed Dec 25/26 & Jan 1; or when booked for weddings ▪ Light meals 9.30-3 daily ▪ Conference facility ▪ Wedding venue & chapel ▪ Christmas market ▪ Owner(s) Mauritz Koster & Justin Vermaak ▪ Winemaker(s) Flip Smith (Jan 2015), with Carel Smith (Jan 2015) ▪ Viticulturist(s) Flip Smith (Jan 2015) ▪ 11ha (cab, merlot, ptage, pinot, sauv) ▪ 25t/±4,200cs own label 77% red 8% white 5% rosé 5% MCC 5% jerepigo ▪ PO Box 345 Winterton KwaZulu-Natal 3340 ▪ caren@cathpeakwines.com ▪ www.cathpeakwines.com ▪ S 28° 50′ 24.88″ E 029° 27′ 10.29″ ▪ **T +27 (0)63-075-1123**

Catherine Marshall Wines ⓠ

Cathy Marshall must count as one of SA wine's most respected (somewhat) elder states(wo)men, though her vitality is undiminished – as is her passion for pinot noir. But while it remains an important focus, and what she's probably best known for, pinot is not the only variety that she crafts in her small Stellenbosch winery. The grapes mostly originate in Elgin, whose cooler climate, she says 'best suits the style of wines that we like to make', with 'finesse, purity and vibrancy'. Cathy's son, Jonathan Oxenham, is now listed as a winemaker as well as part owner, and is, says Cathy, 'more involved in the business now'.

Fine Art Collection

★★★★☆ Pinot Noir Finite Elements ⓐ Barrels from clay & sandstone sites chosen to 'harmonise well & produce a seamless wine'. Refined, with depth & breadth, & real purchase on the palate. The 'grunt' on **16** ⑨① persists in striking **17** ⑨③, also a drought year. Now less new oak (10%). Tiny production.

★★★★☆ Peter's Vision ⓐ Striking, art-adorned wine named for mentor Peter Oxenham, from cab franc & merlot. **16** ⑨③ smoked meat, violets & mulberry fruit woven into savoury, textured tannin lattice. Persistent finish keeps 14.5% alcohol in check. Now only seasoned oak, 18 months.

★★★★☆ Chenin Blanc Fermented in Clay ⓐ Traditional approach to hand-sorted cool-climate grapes: gentle press to clay amphoras (& 20% seasoned oak), natural ferment. **17** ⑨④ elegant, finessed, with an extraordinary variety-transcending vinosity.

Catherine Marshall range

★★★★☆ Pinot Noir On Clay Soils ⓥ ⓐ Iron-rich clay soils confer depth & power, harnessed by Marshall restraint. Sumptuous **17** ⑨③ has savoury fruit in a textured structure with fine grip, tactile & very elegant. 10% new oak, 9 months. **16** sold out untasted.

★★★★ Pinot Noir On Sandstone Soils ⓥ Balanced, lacy elegance reflects the soil; understated intensity reflects cellar handling. **17** ⑧⑨ weaves pomegranate crispness with perfumed black cherry profile, well-synced 5% new oak.

★★★★ Riesling ⓥ Aiming for 'Mosel style' via cool-climate grapes grown on red slate soils in Elgin's Kogelberg Biosphere. **17** ⑨⓪ slightly sweeter than **16** ⑨②, higher 12% alcohol too, but same riverstone flinty nuance to juicy fruit, long-lingering, delightfully tart finish. Perfect for Asian food.

★★★★☆ Sauvignon Blanc ⓥ Punchy flavours - lime, passionfruit & mango - on very fresh **17** ⑨⓪, with stony mineral grip of **16** ⑨②; tiny oaked portion contributes to outstanding, satisfyingly balanced wine. 4 different clones fermented separately - they ripen at different times.

★★★★ Myriad ⓠ Jerepiko-style dessert mostly ex grenache, **09** ⑧⑨ yards ahead of merlot **08 ★★★** ⑧①. Delicate, deluxe medley of prunes, nuts & smoke. Beautifully balanced. 375 ml. WO W Cape.

Amatra range

★★★★ The Oreads Red Merlot from French clone, named for caves above Marshall's seaside home. Graceful **17** ⑧⑦, supple & fresh; lovely now & for good few years. 12 months older oak.

★★★★ Jono's Wave Chenin Blanc Elgin & Stellenbosch grapes vinified in cask & amphora, wild yeast ferment. Slightly edgy **17** ⑧⑧ yet balanced by generous succulent fruit. No longer with semillon.— DS

Location: Stellenbosch ▪ Map: Helderberg ▪ Map grid reference: D1 ▪ WO: Elgin/Western Cape ▪ Est/1stB 1997 ▪ Tasting, sales & cellar tours by appt ▪ Closed Easter Fri-Sun, Dec 25 & Jan 1 ▪ Owner(s) Cathy Marshall, Greg

Mitchell, Jonathan Oxenham & Jeff Jolly ▪ Cellarmaster(s) Catherine Marshall (Oct 1996) ▪ Winemaker(s) Shawn Fortuin (Jan 2010) & Jonathan Oxenham (2017) ▪ Viticulturist(s) various ▪ 50t/8,000cs own label 60% red 37% white 3% fortified ▪ IPW ▪ PO Box 13404 Mowbray 7705 ▪ cathy@cmwines.co.za ▪ www.cmwines.co.za ▪ S 34° 1' 10.47" E 018° 50' 41.02" ▪ [wifi] flows.habitats.recliners ▪ F +27 (0)86-523-7479 ▪ **T +27 (0)83-258-1307**

☐ **Catoria** see Carmen Stevens Wines

Cavalli Wine & Stud Farm (♀) (†↑) (◎) (♿)

Having reviewed the current and likely future form of its planted cultivars, the Smith family's equine-themed Helderberg wine and lifestyle estate has decided to back the two thoroughbreds, cabernet and chenin, as both lead blend components and varietals, for the pinnacle labels going forward. The other grapes on the manicured property will continue to feature in small parcels sold only at the cellardoor. All are worth seeking out, as much for quality and interest as the beautiful individualised labels.

Flagship Collection

★★★★ **Cremello** Judicious oaking (barrel fermented/aged year, 30% new) for **16** ⑧⑥ sophisticated chenin, chardonnay & verdelho. Satisfyingly rich & rounded, enlivened by welcome seam of acidity.

Warlord ★★★☆ Melange black & red fruit on **16** ⑧③ cab-led blend with malbec & petit verdot. Fruit-filled, with fair grip. WO W Cape. Also in magnum.

Premium Collection

Colt Cabernet Sauvignon ★★★★ Don't mistake **16** ⑧③'s translucence for lighter styling: true-to-variety blue/black fruit, firm acidity, densely packed tannins for now or ±3 years. **Filly Chenin Blanc** (NEW) ★★★ Pretty peach tones to vanilla/nut aromas & flavours on **17** ⑧⓪ bone-dry table companion, old-oak-fermented/aged 9 months. Discontinued: **Valkyrie, Night Mare, Vendetta**.

Estate Collection

★★★★ **The Foal Verdelho** Rare-in-SA white grape. Though bone-dry, **16** ★★★ ⑧② has a satin texture, vanilla conclusion. Similar vinification to **15** ⑧⑦ (partial barrel ferment/ageing) but not as vibrant or linear.

The Foal Chardonnay ★★★ Ripe orange & tangerine on **16** ⑧② overlaid with creamy oak, which contributes to sweet impression despite being technically dry. **Capriole Méthode Cap Classique** (NEW) ★★★★ Exquisite label - as all from this stable - for lively & engaging **15** ⑧⑤ sparkling from chardonnay. Enticing orange blossom & subtle biscuit fragrance, nicely dry & smooth. — CvZ

Location: Stellenbosch ▪ Map: Helderberg ▪ Map grid reference: C1 ▪ WO: Stellenbosch/Western Cape ▪ Est/1stB 2008 ▪ Wine tasting & sales Wed-Sun 10-6 ▪ Closed Dec 26 & Jan 1 ▪ Cavalli Restaurant Wed-Sun lunch & dinner ▪ Sport & music memorabilia ▪ Art gallery ▪ Fashion boutique ▪ Conferences ▪ Banqueting facility (350 seater) ▪ Conservation area ▪ Equestrian centre: stable tours & out-rides by appt ▪ Owner(s) Smith family ▪ Winemaker(s) Craig Barnard (Nov 2014), with Kerrylea Alborough (Sep 2017) ▪ Viticulturist(s) Craig Barnard (Nov 2014) ▪ 110ha/29ha (cab, malbec, p verdot, shiraz, chard, chenin, verdelho, viog) ▪ 100t/6,500cs own label 45% red 40% white 15% rosé ▪ IPW, WIETA ▪ PO Box 102 Somerset West 7129 ▪ wines@cavalliestate.com ▪ www.cavalliestate.com ▪ S 34° 0' 35.91" E 018° 48' 47.06" ▪ [wifi] keyboards.barometers.activates ▪ F +27 (0)86-766-6556 ▪ **T +27 (0)21-855-3218**

Cecilia Wines (♀)

The Van Niekerk family - Cerina, owner and creator of Cecilia boutique wines, her husband Jaco and their first little bundle of joy, Cecile - have moved from the Klawer area to Citrusdal, where Jaco is joining Piekenierskloof Wine Company as cellarmaster and Cerina continuing with her handcrafted Pinotage (the Shiraz-Mourvèdre still in abeyance). A trained concert pianist, Cerina is also looking to sustain a second passion project: furthering music appreciation among the children of the local community.

★★★★ **Pinotage** (❋) Old Citrusdal Mountain bushvines, natural ferment, older oak, **16** ⑧⑨ has lovely deep notes, mulberries, liquorice, campfire smokiness. Tannins firm, not hard, but best lies ahead. — CR

Location: Citrusdal ▪ Map: Olifants River ▪ Map grid reference: D7 ▪ WO: Citrusdal Mountain ▪ Est 2010 ▪ 1stB 2013 ▪ Tasting & sales Mon-Sat 10-5 at Hebron, Piekenierskloof Pass, N7 ▪ Owner(s) Cerina van Niekerk ▪ Cellarmaster(s)/winemaker(s) Cerina van Niekerk (2007) ▪ 2t/100cs own label 100% red ▪ cerina@

cecilliawines.co.za ▪ www.ceciliawines.co.za ▪ S 32° 37' 4.15" E 018° 57' 20.98" ▪ firestorm.jolts.meaty ▪
T +27 (0)82-334-9422

Cederberg Private Cellar

There can't be many local wine estates investing in frost prevention, but after big losses in 2016, that's exactly what owner and cellarmaster David Nieuwoudt is doing. His high-altitude vineyards (at 1,000 metres in the remote Cederberg Mountains, among the highest in SA) are now prepped for aspersion - spraying water onto the buds, which then freezes around them and radiates latent heat - though last vintage had no need, being dubbed 'excellent' for aromatic wines in particular. David's other project, Cederberg Brewery, is up and running under the guidance of Namibian-born assistant winemaker and now brewer, Alex Nel, with interesting brews — one using rainwater, another barley ground at the farm's restored 1924 watermill.

Five Generations range

★★★★☆ **Cabernet Sauvignon** Ⓐ Plenty of charry, smoky oak (100% new French) on **16** ⑨③ flagship but plenty of concentrated, deep & dark fruit to handle it. Flavours of blackcurrant pastilles, liquorice & dark chocolate follow in weighty mouthful, with sturdy tannins & endless length. Needs & deserves time.

★★★★☆ **Chenin Blanc** Ⓘ In stellar **16** ★★★★★ ⑨⑤, as in **15** ⑨④, 10% viognier adds delicious perfume to concentrated peach, pineapple & cooked apple, delicate spice, cream & muesli hints from 100% barrel ferment, third in new oak. Excellent vein of lime acidity keeps things snappy & fresh right through to finish.

David Nieuwoudt Ghost Corner range

★★★★★ **Pinot Noir** ⊘ Ⓐ From Elim fruit - as all this range - **17** ⑨⓪ shimmers with soft red fruit (raspberry & strawberry) with underlying hints of fresh herbs & soft spice from gentle oaking. Needs time to mesh, expect more to come.

★★★★★ **Wild Ferment Sauvignon Blanc** Lengthy spontaneous ferment in old oak gives **17** ⑨① interesting layers of flavour & texture. Subtle hints of lemon, quince & yellow apple combined with cream, oatmeal & grainy pear texture. Excellent food partner, interesting future.

★★★★☆ **Sauvignon Blanc** Ⓐ Vibrant & racy **17** ⑨③ all thrilling excitement in the mouth with sappy green figs & peppers backed by strong flinty mineral backbone with just a hint of cream. Acidity beautifully integrated, adding fresh citrus notes & finish is pure & lipsmackingly fresh. Last year **16** ★★★★★ ⑨⑤ tasted, incorrectly vintaged.

★★★★☆ **Semillon** Ⓐ Stand-out **17** ⑨④ is all you'd expect from cooler-climate semillon, mixing pungent grassy, stalky green-edged fruit with lovely oaking (only 30%, third new) bringing just a touch of smoke & cream. Waxy interest starting to show on lengthy citrus tail.

★★★★★ **The Bowline** Ⓐ Reduced oak (only 37%) on expertly done **17** ⑨④ allows sauvignon & semillon (61/39) to shine, with fresh citrus, some tropical hints of melon & mango. Classic pairing produces silky & assured combination of cream, spice & hint of soft cheese on interesting & ageworthy wine.

Cederberg Private Cellar range

★★★★ **Cabernet Sauvignon** Big wine with lots to like: bright black cherries & plummy fruit, well-integrated tannins & bouncy acidity all handling weighty alcohol (14.5%) nicely. **16** ★★★★★ ⑨①'s oaking, 60% new, adds delicious vanilla lick at tail. Improves on **15** ⑧⑨.

★★★★★ **Shiraz** Ⓐ Out-there **16** ⑨③ shows off with vibrant colour, blackberries, chocolate & charred meat with creamy black pepper sauce hints crying out for a good steak. 100% new oak, 60% new French, small portion American add layers of interest & elegance, carrying fruit through to solid ending. Magnums available, as for exceptional **15** ★★★★★ ⑨⑧.

★★★★ **Merlot-Shiraz** ⊘ Cherry-berry fruit bomb nose on **16** ⑧⑥ 67/33 blend relaxes into chocolate & toffee notes with touch of green freshness. Only old oak. Cut above **15** ★★★★ ⑧④ everyday drinker.

★★★★ **Chenin Blanc** ⊘ Unoaked **18** ⑧⑨ needs little more than this concentrated mouthful of fresh, crunchy apple, pear & pineapple to delight. Lipsmacking salty tang from 4 months on lees, lengthy finish.

★★★★ **Sauvignon Blanc** Long hang-time in cooler climate gives **18** ⑧⑧ intense aromas & flavours of tropical fruit (guava & litchi) along with tinned grapefruit & pear. Zesty & fresh - most enjoyable.

★★★★☆ **Blanc de Blancs Brut** ⓐ Chardonnay MCC **13** ⑨④ rested 52 months on lees adding generous amounts of cream, yeast, salty notes to soft yellow fruit, with strong notes of mixed peel & spice. Excellent acidity & great length add up to an individual & exciting sparkling.

Sustainable Rosé ⓥ ★★★★ Dry pink from shiraz **18** ⑧③ is lively & fresh, with all the flavours of Provence - strawberry, soft cheese & herb - attractive pithy finish. **Bukettraube** ⓥ ★★★★ Balances ripe stonefruit & touch of pleasing confection with delicate sweetness (23.5 g/l sugar) & bouncy acidity. **18** ⑧⑤ excellent with Thai green curry. — CM

Location: Citrusdal ▪ Map: Olifants River ▪ Map grid reference: D7 ▪ WO: Cederberg/Elim ▪ Est 1973 ▪ 1stB 1977 ▪ Tasting Mon-Sat 9-12 & 2-4.30; pub hols 9-11.30 & 4-5.30 ▪ Fee R40 ▪ Closed Good Fri & Dec 25 ▪ Sales Mon-Sat 8-12.30 & 2-5; Sun/pub hols 9-12 & 4-6 ▪ BYO picnic ▪ Sanddrif Holiday Resort self-catering cottages; camping ▪ Walks/hikes ▪ MTB ▪ Conservation area ▪ Rock climbing ▪ Sport climbing ▪ Observatory ▪ Craft beer brewery ▪ Owner(s) Nieuwoudt family ▪ Cellarmaster(s) David Nieuwoudt (Jan 1997) ▪ Winemaker(s) Alex Nel (whites, Aug 2011) & Tammy Turck-Nel (reds, Aug 2011) ▪ Viticulturist(s) Oubaas Laubscher (Oct 2015) ▪ 5,500ha/74ha (cab, shiraz, bukettraube, chenin, sauv) ▪ 900t/90,000cs own label 40% red 60% white ▪ WWF-SA Conservation Champion ▪ PO Box 84 Clanwilliam 8135 ▪ info@cederberg-wine.com ▪ www.cederbergwine.com ▪ S 32° 30'12.8" E 019° 15'27.7" ▪ ⓦ withdrawn.reptile.plods ▪ F +27 (0)86-531-0491 ▪ **T +27 (0)27-482-2827**

Celestina

Celestina means 'little celestial one' and was chosen one starry night, no doubt over something delicious and rare, by respected Cape Town wine merchant Caroline Kilian and her husband Ray. Situated in Baardskeerdersbos near Elim, their vineyard is small enough to allow for weekend viticulture and Dirk Human from nearby Black Oystercatcher to vinify the harvest.

★★★★☆ **Sauvignon Blanc-Semillon** ⓥ Older-oak-fermented/aged white Bordeaux blend, equal partners sauvignon, semillon in **17** ⑨② Intense greenpepper & grass notes, vibrant cool-climate acidity, mineral conclusion with Granny Smith apple & citrus nuances. Advances fine form of **16** ⑨①. — HC

Location: Baardskeerdersbos ▪ WO: Cape Agulhas ▪ Est 2004 ▪ 1stB 2009 ▪ Closed to public ▪ Owner(s) Caroline Kilian ▪ Winemaker(s) Dirk Human (Black Oystercatcher) ▪ Viticulturist(s) Caroline & Ray Kilian ▪ 3.4ha/1.85ha (sauv, sem) ▪ 6t/600cs own label 100% white ▪ c/o Caroline's Fine Wine Cellar, Shop 44 Matador Centre 62 Strand Str Cape Town 8001 ▪ carowine2@mweb.co.za ▪ www.carolineswine.com ▪ **T +27 (0)21-419-8984**

Cellar Cask

South Africa's first bag-in-box, launched in 1979, styled by Distell to meet rising demand for Natural Sweet wines with lower alcohol levels. Today in 750ml glass, 2L and 5L packs.

Select Johannisberger Red ★★ Semi-sweet **NV** ⑦⑤ has plummy fruit, juicy freshness, lightish body. **Select Johannisberger Rosé** ★★ Neutral, full-sweet **NV** ⑦③, with confectionery fruitiness. **Select Johannisberger White** ★★ Uncomplicated, modestly sweet **NV** ⑦③. Lightish body & alcohol. Fresh, fruity. — GdB

☐ **Cellar Door** see Namaqua Wines

Chabivin Champagne & MCC House ⓠ

Chabivin is a boutique venture by local bubbly specialist Hendrik Snyman and the Charbaut family, producers of fine champagne near Epernay. Their visitor venue on the Stellenbosch outskirts offers tastings of the Chabivin sparklers in a charming and tranquil setting.

Location/map: Stellenbosch ▪ Map grid reference: E7 ▪ Est 2008 ▪ Tasting & sales Tue-Fri 9-5 Sat/Sun 10-4; in winter by appt only ▪ Fee R30/3 MCC ▪ Owner(s) Hendrik Snyman & Charbaut family ▪ Winemaker(s)/viticulturist(s) Hendrik Snyman ▪ 3ha/0.4ha (pinot, chard) ▪ ±8t/1,500cs own label 100% MCC ▪ PO Box 12456 Die Boord Stellenbosch 7613 ▪ info@chabivin.co.za ▪ www.chabivin.co.za ▪ S 33° 58'24.27" E 018° 51'8.17" ▪ ⓦ pitchers.roaming.desk ▪ F +27 (0)86-540-6237 ▪ **T +27 (0)21-880-1643**

☐ **Chameleon** *see* Jordan Wine Estate
☐ **Chamonix** *see* Cape Chamonix Wine Farm
☐ **Chapel** *see* Robertson Winery
☐ **Chapel Cellar** *see* Zanddrift Vineyards - Chapel Cellar

Charla Haasbroek Wines

Radical, new-wave winemaking from the own label of Charla Haasbroek, who's the winemaker at Sijnn, has so far produced three fascinating wines in small quantities — nothing new to taste this year, however. The grapes all come off the extreme, stony soils of the Sijnn farm near the mouth of the Breede River.

★★★★☆ **Threads** ⓧ Chenin off a specific shale site, **17** ⑨① spontaneous ferment, unfiltered (like all these). 9 months older oak. Medley of generous flavours, but oxidative handling means no simple fruitiness. Full, pure, rich, but elegant, precise - with a stony quality in the exciting harmony.

Not tasted: **Colourblind, Tapestry**. — TJ

Location/WO: Malgas ▪ Est/1stB 2016 ▪ Closed to public ▪ Winemaker(s) Charla Haasbroek (Sijnn) ▪ Lemoentuin Farm 342 Malgas ▪ charlahaasbroek@gmail.com ▪ **T +27 (0)82-782-5875**

☐ **Charles Borro** *see* Govert Wines

Charles Fox Cap Classique Wines ⓧ Ⓐ

An 'avid Francophile', who shares the French belief that terroir is all-important for quality wine, businessman Charles Fox with wife Zelda purchased Furneaux, an Elgin fruit farm, in 2005 with the express purpose of making champagne-style sparkling. With top advisers, they planted selected clones of traditional varieties, and haven't looked back since 2010 when a cellar with underground storage for 200,000 bottles was built. Handcrafted with input from Reims consultant Nicolas Follet, the Vintage and Prestige Cuvée MCC sparklers were released to instant acclaim, and are now joined by two non-vintage wines 'in response to requests from both the export and local market'.

★★★★☆ **Reserve Rosé** ⓝⒺⓦ Copper-hued **NV** ⑨⓪ bubbly from pinot noir, 15% chardonnay & 9% meunier has intense red berry & pomegranate fruit & fine mousse. Richly biscuity from minimum 2 years on lees, yet taut, dry & refreshing.

★★★★☆ **Vintage Brut Rosé** ⓧ With 40 months lees ageing, **12** ⑨③ clean & savoury, delicious brioche notes edged with soft crushed berries & oyster saltiness. 50% pinot noir. Portion oaked, as all.

★★★★☆ **Prestige Cuvée Blanc de Blancs** ⓧ Stunning 100% chardonnay offering, **13** ⑨③ superfine bubbles bursting with Granny Smith apple against a buttered brioche backdrop, some seabreeze savouriness too. Very rich (30% oaked) yet fresh. On lees 3 years.

★★★★☆ **Prestige Cuvée Cipher** ⓧ Accomplished flagship only in outstanding years, tangy **12** ⑨② is equal pinot noir/chardonnay, with lively citrus & pear fruit, oystershell minerality, creamy texture & spicy ginger on lingering finish. 33% wooded, 4.5 years on lees.

★★★★ **Reserve Brut** ⓝⒺⓦ Toasty from minimum 2 years on lees, 28% wooded **NV** ⑧⑨ also has fresh apple & ginger enhanced by persistent bubble. Chardonnay with 31% pinot noir, 14% meunier.

★★★★☆ **Vintage Brut** ⓧ Equal pinot noir & meunier, chardonnay, on stellar **13** ⑨④, 30 months on lees. Savoury sparkler, with glorious mid-palate richness & fine bead. — JG

Location/map/WO: Elgin ▪ Map grid reference: C3 ▪ Est 2007 ▪ 1stB 2010 ▪ Tasting, sales & cellar tours Mon-Sun 10-4 ▪ Fee applicable ▪ Closed Dec 25 & Jan 1 ▪ Play area for children ▪ Owner(s) Charles & Zelda Fox ▪ Cellarmaster(s) Charles Fox (2010) ▪ Winemaker(s) Nicolas Follet (2010, consultant) ▪ Viticulturist(s) Kevin Watt (2008, consultant) ▪ 33.4ha/9ha (pinot noir/meunier, chard) ▪ 5,000cs own label 100% MCC ▪ PO Box 105 Elgin 7180 ▪ charlesfoxmcc@gmail.com ▪ www.charlesfox.co.za ▪ S 34° 14' 14.38" E 019° 04' 41.99" ▪ 🌐 when.dives.commending ▪ F +27 (0)86-536-2924 ▪ **T +27 (0)21-300-1065/+27 (0)82-569-2965/+27 (0)82-471-3444**

Chateau Libertas

The grandfather of SA's reds, available since 1932 and still a paragon of value & drinkability. By Distell.

Chateau Libertas ⊘ ★★★ In its 85th vintage, ever-amiable & ready-on-release blend offers abundance of red & dark fruit, juicy & fine-grained tannins leading up to fragrant cherry farewell on **17** ⑦⑧. — GM

Chateau Naudé Wine Creation

One-time pharmacist Francois Naudé came to winemaking later in life as the self-taught architect of Stellenbosch property L'Avenir's rise to fame. He now focuses on one wine, Le Vin de François, master-blending it from carefully selected parcels of some of the country's finest pinotage exponents. Sought after by collectors in some 11 countries, who rate it as 'one of, if not the best pinotage in the world', the wine celebrated its 10th anniversary bottling in 2018. The vintner, who also consults widely, is supported by son Francois jnr and daughter Melissa in their family 'château' venture.

Location: Stellenbosch ▪ Est 2006 ▪ 1stB 2007 ▪ Closed to public ▪ Owner(s) Francois Naudé snr, Francois Naudé jnr & Melissa Naudé ▪ Cellarmaster(s) Francois Naudé (Jul 2007) ▪ 400cs own label 100% red ▪ 11 Weidenhof Str Stellenbosch 7600 ▪ naude@levindefrancois.co.za ▪ www.levindefrancois.com ▪ F +27 (0)86-651-3192 ▪ **T +27 (0)21-883-8469**

Chennells Wines ⓥ

'While we live, let us truly live' is the credo of Jeremy and Colleen Chennells, landowners and boutique vintners in prime Helderberg, who converted the trees on their fruit estate to vines in 2003, allowing for 'personal care and total family involvement'. They strive to farm responsibly and holistically.

Cabernet Sauvignon ⓥ ★★★★ Bold & robust **10** ⑧④ aims for seriousness in riper vintage, achieves good concentration of savoury dark berry fruit; supportive tannins & acid but 15% alcohol obvious in youth. **Shiraz** ⓥ ★★★ Ripe black berries & spice, some earthiness & tobacco on **10** ⑧①, otherwise attractive wine somewhat unbalanced by 15% alcohol. WO W Cape. **The Journey** ⓥ ★★★ Named for this family's life voyage, equal cab/shiraz in **13** ⑧②, bold & ripe dark fruit, oaked 19 months but tannins amenable. **A Handful of Summers** ⓥ ★★★★ Oak-enriched **13** ⑧④ viognier shows ripe apricot compote features; fresher flavours, dry rather grippy conclusion. **Viognier** ⓥ ★★★★ **14** ⑧④ is something different. Fermented in barrel, savoury oatmeal & peach flavours, variety's usual aromas tamed. Lovely! — CR

Location: Stellenbosch ▪ Map: Helderberg ▪ Map grid reference: C2 ▪ WO: Stellenbosch/Western Cape ▪ Est 2004 ▪ 1stB 2008 ▪ Tasting, sales & cellar tours Mon-Sun 9-5 by appt ▪ Closed all pub hols ▪ Owner(s) Jeremy & Colleen Chennells ▪ Cellarmaster(s)/winemaker(s) Jeremy Chennells & Chris Keet (Jul 2009, consultant) ▪ Viticulturist(s) Colleen Chennells & Chris Keet (Jul 2009, consultant) ▪ 5ha/3.2ha (cab, shiraz, viog) ▪ 26t/330cs own label 85% red 15% white ▪ Romond Vineyards Klein Helderberg Rd Somerset West 7130 ▪ chennell@iafrica.com ▪ www.chennellswines.com ▪ S 34° 1′ 52.61″ E 018° 49′ 59.67″ ▪ ⊠ oscillated.tingly. lions ▪ **T +27 (0)21-855-3905**

☐ **Chip Off The Old Block** see Ormonde Private Cellar
☐ **Chocoholic** see Darling Cellars
☐ **Chouette!** see New Beginnings Wines
☐ **Chris Keet** see Keet Wines
☐ **Christina Van Loveren** see Van Loveren Family Vineyards
☐ **Christine-Marié** see Niel Joubert Estate
☐ **Chrysalis** see Loursford Wine Estate
☐ **Cilliers Cellars** see Stellendrift - SHZ Cilliers/Kuün Wyne

Cilmor Winery ⓥ

This 10,000-ton Worcester winery, vinifying six to eight million litres of Fairtrade-certified bulk wine annually from surrounding vineyards, is the legacy of early 20th-century vegetable and poultry farmer Cecil Morgan. The Cilmor Trust's urban development of his Kuils River farms underpins the winegrowing endeavours, including an extensive range of bottled wines available for on-site tasting.

Premium Collection ⑩

Cabernet Sauvignon ★★★ Cured beef, some underlying plummy fruit, **18** ⑧① is succulent, has nice elegance & drinkability. Doesn't speak in a loud voice but is very likeable. Gently extracted, briefly oaked (staves), as all the reds. **Pinotage** ★★★ Vanilla & blueberries, **18** ⑦⑨ aims to be friendly, appealing.

Enough grip to handle food, the ideal braai wine, as back label puts it. **Shiraz** ★★★ Fynbos & scrub notes in **18** ⑦⑧, some floral nuances & black pepper, red berries; sleek, the tannins in support. Early-picked style, has appealing drinkability. **Chardonnay** ★★★ Oak's toastiness well partnered by **18** ⑦⑨'s orange & tangerine styling. Good mouthfeel, tangy & fresh, if not very complex. **Chenin Blanc** ★★★ Cool-fruit styling for **18** ⑦⑧, crunchy pear & touch of lemon, which deepens in the flavours. Also-tasted **15** ★★★★ ⑧③ quince & melon preserve, a strong seam of citrus, lovely pine nut richness though unwooded, it's the bottle age. No **17**, **16**. **Sauvignon Blanc** ★★★ Gooseberry & lime, some green asparagus but it's **18** ⑧②'s nervous tension that impresses, vibrates with freshness. Also-reviewed **15** ★★★★ ⑧④ proves variety can age, thanks to good acid backbone. Melon & salted limes, an attractive pungency, long finish. At its best now. No **17**, **16**. Not tasted: **Merlot, Merlot Rosé**.

Popular range (NEW)

Berry Juicy Red ★★ Shiraz, ruby cab & merlot contribute to **NV** ⑦④'s claim to name accuracy, though also a confected element in the fruit spectrum, pastilles & pink sweets. Juicy but quite light, textured. WO W Cape for both. **Fruity Bouquet White** ⊘ ★★★ Different front labels here to Collection, very colourful. Equal chenin & sauvignon in bouncy **NV** ⑧②, passionfruit & litchi, name is spot-on. Great drinkability, well priced. Not tasted: **Candy Floss Rosé**. — CR, CvZ

Location/map: Worcester ▪ Map grid reference: B4 ▪ WO: Worcester/Western Cape ▪ Est 1997 ▪ 1stB 2015 ▪ Tasting & sales Mon-Fri 9-4.30 Sat/Sun by appt ▪ Fee R50 ▪ Closed all pub hols ▪ Owner(s) Cilmor Trust ▪ Cellarmaster(s) Quintin van der Westhuizen (Dec 2012) ▪ Winemaker(s) Marioline Matthee (Nov 2015) ▪ Viticulturist(s) Rudi du Toit (July 2008) ▪ ±2,000ha/452.21ha (cab, merlot, ptage, roobernet, ruby cab, shiraz, chard, chenin, cbard, hanepoot, nouvelle, pinot gris, sauv, viog) ▪ 8,500t/±3,100cs own label 28% red 44% white 28% rosé ▪ Fairtrade, IPW, WIETA ▪ PO Box 5628 Worcester West 6862 ▪ info@cilmorwines.com ▪ www.cilmorwines.com ▪ S 33° 44'30.02" E 019° 28'49.02" ▪ ⟨trim.thesis.lamps⟩ ▪ F +27 (0)86-732-3875 ▪ **T +27 (0)23-340-4141**

☐ **Circle of Life** see Waterkloof
☐ **Circumstance** see Waterkloof

Cirrus Wines   ⓥ

A mutual love of wine brought together the Duncan family, owners of California's Silver Oak Cellars, and Jean Engelbrecht of Stellenbosch's Rust en Vrede, first as friends, then in 2003 as partners in Cirrus Wines. They still believe that wine, above all else, should bring people together, and they're looking forward to producing a Cirrus in the US in the future.

★★★★☆ **Cirrus Syrah** ⊛ Evocative **15** ⑨④, with splash viognier, has poise & subtlety, hints of peppery scrub. Lithe, supple, focused on detail & finesse above raw power. 16 months French oak, 30% new, lend roundness without intruding.— GdB

Location/WO: Stellenbosch ▪ Est 2002 ▪ 1stB 2003 ▪ Tasting & sales at Guardian Peak (see entry) ▪ Owner(s) Jean Engelbrecht & Duncan family (Napa, CA) ▪ Winemaker(s) Roelof Lotriet (Sep 2014) ▪ ±7.5t/1,200cs own label 100% red ▪ IPW ▪ PO Box 473 Stellenbosch 7599 ▪ info@cirruswines.com ▪ www.cirruswines.com ▪ **T +27 (0)21-881-3881**

City on a Hill Wine Company   ⓥ

André Bruyns assists heavyweight winemakers David and Nadia Sadie in their Paardeberg cellar but is also nurturing his own brand — making his wine in similarly subtle, hands-off way, from Swartland fruit. The established white comes off Paardeberg granite, while the forthcoming red (first vintage 2018) is from shale soils in the Kasteelberg area. The name and label richly evoke for André biblical and hillside vineyard themes.

★★★★★ **Chenin Blanc** (NEW) ⊛ Exhilarating **17** ⑨⑥ from shy-yielding dryland vines, harmonious compendium of complex textures & flavours. Limpid & assured, with a whisper of scrub & enduring elegant conclusion, balanced 12.5% alcohol. 'Natural' winemaking of the highest order.

★★★★ **Muscat d'Alexandrie** (NEW) Intense tropical aromas announce **17** ⑧⑧, which delights even more on palate with lipsmacking dryness & low (11%) alcohol. 10 months in seasoned casks add oomph. For al fresco dining.

★★★★☆ **White** ⊛ Stellar expression of old-vine Swartland chenin, bunchpressed & naturally made. **17** ⑨④ has dashes viognier & muscat d'Alexandrie, but not fruity: like previous (without muscat), has a spicy, dusty-earth profile, elegant, dry stony finish. Some weight from 10 months old oak. — DS

Location: Malmesbury ▪ Map/WO: Swartland ▪ Map grid reference: C8 ▪ Est/1stB 2015 ▪ Tasting by appt ▪ Owner(s) André Bruyns ▪ Winemaker(s) André Bruyns (2015) ▪ 600cs own label 100% white ▪ andre@cityonahillwine.co.za ▪ www.cityonahillwine.co.za ▪ S 33° 32′ 41.41″ E 018° 49′ 36.14″ ▪ ⟦ᴍ⟧ illogical.funds.virulently

CK Wines

Beau Joubert winemaker (and petrolhead) Christian Kuun has driven this solo vehicle for a decade now, sourcing grapes mostly from his home range of Stellenbosch, with a string of unreleased vintages attesting to his high standards. His Bare Facts wines, as we noted last time, are paragons of value and drinkability.

CK Signature series

★★★★ **Sincera** Elegant & expectedly aromatic cab franc, **16** ⑧⑨ black plum, tealeaf & fynbos fragrances, structure supplied by 50% new oak, 18 months. Tight in youth, give it time. No **14**. **15** untasted.

★★★★☆ **Eccentrica** Bone-dry MCC sparkler from pinot noir. **15** ⑨① subtle red apple, strawberry & pleasant savoury backbone from 3 years lees ageing. Persistent, fresh & more characterful than **13** ★★★★ ⑧⑦. No **14**.

Cape Vintage ⓝⓔⓦ ★★★★ Interesting 'port' from shiraz, **12** ⑧⑤ oxidative but very drinkable, good uplifting acidity & sprinkle sugar for balance. Not tasted: **Integra**. Discontinued: **Altruista**.

The Bare Facts range

Cabernet Sauvignon ⊘ ⓖⓟ ★★★★ Fresh, herbal **17** ⑧④, ample cassis fruit & prominent but amiable grip, nicely rounded in 25% new oak. Great T-bone partner. **Merlot** ⊘ ⓖⓟ ★★★★ Enticing plums, violets & chocolate wrapped in velour tannin, **17** ⑧④ classic & delicious. Deliciously priced also.

Not tasted: **Cabernet Franc, Chenin Blanc, Sauvignon Blanc.** — HC

Location/WO: Stellenbosch ▪ Est 2009 ▪ 1stB 2010 ▪ Closed to public ▪ Owner(s)/cellarmaster(s)/winemaker(s) Christian Kuun ▪ 12,000cs own label 70% red 25% white 5% MCC ▪ winemaker@ckwines.co.za, sales@ckwines.co.za ▪ www.ckwines.co.za ▪ F +27 (0)86-504-6209 ▪ **T +27 (0)82-615-8105**

Claime d'Or ⓠ

Wine-loving couple Bernardo Rapoport and Magriet de Wet became vintners just over a decade ago after acquiring a portion of Robertson farm Goudmyn ('Gold Mine') from the Burger family of Rietvallei. Kobus Burger still vinifies the handsomely labelled bottlings, with gold as leitmotif and in some cases, hue.

Location: Robertson ▪ Est/1stB 2008 ▪ Tasting & sales at Rietvallei Wine Estate ▪ Owner(s) Magriet de Wet & Bernardo Rapoport ▪ Cellarmaster(s)/winemaker(s) Kobus Burger (2002, Rietvallei) ▪ Viticulturist(s) Kobus Burger (Rietvallei) ▪ 10ha (cabs s/f, sauv) ▪ 30% red 60% white 10% rosé ▪ PO Box 2040 Parklands 2121 ▪ lezaan@rietvallei.co.za ▪ www.claimedorwines.co.za ▪ F +27 (0)23-626-4514 ▪ **T +27 (0)23-626-3596**

Clairvaux Family Wines ⓠ ⊖ ⓫

Situated on Robertson town's doorstep, Clairvaux's De Wet family owners absolutely nailed the first principle of real estate. Their winemaker/manager, Jaco van der Merwe, gets the wine side of things right, too, even in a dry year like 2018, where Jaco says the whites show good aromas and the reds fine structures and colours. Bulk wine is the focus, but the small parcels under this label are eminently drinkable and affordably priced.

★★★★ **Red Muscadel** ⓠ Fortified dessert for winter nights, summer days over ice. **16** ⑧⑥ improves on last-tasted **12** ★★★★ ⑧④, sweet berry flavours lifted by zesty lemon tang & well-integrated spirit.

Cabernet Sauvignon ⓖⓟ ★★★ Partly oaked **16** ⑧⓪, vibrant ruby hue with berry flavours to match; soft, with gentle tannins. A delightful any-occasions red.

Shiraz ★★★ Spice & savoury notes on swiggable **16** ⑧⓪, succulent berry finish, good tannin handshake. **Sauvignon Blanc** ★★★ Shade less extroverted than previous, **18** ⑦⑨'s tropical flavours more modest, the acid bite a little sharper. **Good Night Irene** ★★★ Sweet, fragrant **18** ⑧②, fortified hanepoot with grapey flavours, good spirituous grip on departure. **Madonna's Kisses** ★★★ Fortified white muscadel **18**

⑧⓪ pleasant enough but still unmeshed mid-2018, boiled sweet & spicy flavours standing apart from the alcohol. **Cape Vintage ★★★☆** As ever, **16** ⑦⑦ from shiraz more 'fortified dessert wine' than Vintage 'port'. Easy & rather sweet plum compote flavours, low-for-style 16.5% alcohol. — WB

Location/map/WO: Robertson ▪ Map grid reference: B6 ▪ Est/1stB 2000 ▪ Tasting & sales Mon-Fri 8-5 ▪ Closed all pub hols ▪ Cellar tours by appt ▪ BYO picnic ▪ Sales (at cellar price) also from La Verne Wine Boutique T +27 (0)23-626-4314 Mon-Fri 9-5.30 Sat 9-3 ▪ Owner(s) Wouter J de Wet snr & jnr ▪ Winemaker(s) / manager Jaco van der Merwe (Oct 2011) ▪ 200ha (cab, merlot, ptage, shiraz, chard, chenin, cbard, hanepoot, muscadel, sauv) ▪ 4,000t/3.2m L bulk ▪ PO Box 179 Robertson 6705 ▪ info@clairvauxcellar. co.za ▪ www.clairvauxcellar.co.za ▪ S 33° 48' 13.8" E 019° 52' 21.1" ▪ ⊡ lively.unknowns.natures ▪ F +27 (0)23-626-1925 ▪ **T +27 (0)23-626-3842**

☐ **Clarington** see Normandie Est. 1693
☐ **Clearsprings** see Trizanne Signature Wines

Cloof Wine Estate

Ⓠ Ⓐ Ⓑ Ⓕ

Foreign owned the past two decades, the Cloof home-farm near Darling has 135 ha under vine (including venerable bushvines planted in 1966, 1976 and 1987) and a very large tract of highly endangered veld which, as a WWF-SA Conservation Champion, the estate actively protects. The team report 'a plethora of exciting developments' since last edition, including a range refresh (retaining the ever-popular Very Sexy Shiraz) and a brand-new tasting area. They're planning 'an invigorating revolution' to the on-farm events calendar for 2019 and beyond, and unsurprisingly the natural environment will feature strongly, as will their centrepiece gig – the Rocking the Daisies music festival, which annually attracts 10,000 (thirsty!) music lovers.

Iconic range

★★★★☆ Crucible Shiraz Ⓖ Standard bearer, made (in tiny quantities) only in exceptional vintages. Full-bodied yet refined **14** ㉝ has concentrated black plum & berry fruit with white pepper & baking spice. Stablemate may be Very Sexy but this is for a long-term relationship. Last tasted was **06 ★★★★**.

The Winemakers Selection

★★★★ Limited Release Cabernet Sauvignon Ⓖ Intense **14** ㊏ concentrated dark berry fruit, firm oak frame (well-judged 15% new French, 2 years), dry integrated tannins & long liquorice tail.

★★★★ Cloof Pinotage Ⓖ Alluring deep black & blue fruit on **15** ㊏ improves on **13 ★★★★** ㊏. Backbone of oak (30% new) & light tannin squeeze support soft-textured palate. No **14**.

★★★★ Cloof Syrah Ⓖ Soft & seamlessly integrated after 15 months in 90% new French oak, **13** ㊏ is jam-like in its black & red cherry/berry intensity, yet balanced by fresh acidity & peppery spice.

Merlot Ⓖ **★★★☆** Ripe plums on nose of **12** ㊋, sweet prunes, milk chocolate & fruitcake sweetness on palate balanced by mouthwatering prickle of acidity. **Cloof Lynchpin** Ⓖ **★★★☆** Cabernet franc leads merlot (30%) in **14** ㊃, ample juicy blue fruit shaded by oak (60% new) & 15% alcohol; somewhat ponderous compared with **13 ★★★★** ㊇. **CvD Méthode Cap Classique Blanc de Blancs** Ⓖ **★★★** Chardonnay bubbly has typical apple & brioche notes with zippy lime freshness in **14** ㊁.

The Signature range

★★★★ The Very Sexy Shiraz ⊘ Firm yet supple **16** ㊏ is spicy & rich, with signature plum & brush of dried herbs. Good intensity, concentration & depth. Oak is well knit after year in barrel. **15** untasted.

Cloof Cab Cult Cabernet Sauvignon Ⓖ **★★★★** Friendly appeal to bright, blue-fruited **15** ㊐, medium body & light tannic grip from 14 months in French barrels. **Inkspot** Ⓖ **★★★★** Cab added to pinotage-led blend of shiraz & dab cinsaut in **14** ㊒. Vibrant, light & supple, with spicy berry fruit to end. **The Dark Side** Ⓖ **★★★★** Cassis & vanilla lift on **15** ㊏ blend of near-equal cab & shiraz, chalky grip from year in 15% new French barrels.

The Duckitt Collection

Cabernet Sauvignon ⊘ **★★★★** Light bodied, approachable **17** ㊐ has trademark cassis notes. 50/50 split of tank & barrel maturation makes for a fresh & pleasant wine. **Merlot** ⒩Ⓔ⒲ **★★★** Leafy sheen to fruitcake & cocoa notes on **16** ㊋. Structured & firm with 50/50 tank & barrel components. Good integration of oak & fruit. **Pinotage** ⒩Ⓔ⒲ **★★★** Unpretentious blue & black berry brightness on savoury **16** ㊓. Portion had year in older oak, adding dry grip of tannin. **Shiraz** ⒩Ⓔ⒲ ⊘ **★★★★** Deep black fruit & earthiness to

14 (83). Like cab, gains freshness from tank portion blended with the oaked fraction, gentle tannin grip. **Cabernet Sauvignon-Merlot-Cabernet Franc** (Ⓥ) ★★★☆ Offers light, bright cassis with soft tannin grip from 10 months oaking. 16 (83) not as bold as last-tasted 14 ★★★★ (86). **Chardonnay** (ⓃⒺⓌ) ★★★ Packs a bold nectarine wallop! Uncomplicated & unoaked, 18 (80) is fresh & easy. **Chenin Blanc** (ⓃⒺⓌ) ★★☆ Gentle melon & quince on no-worries 18 (79), succulent & light. **Sauvignon Blanc** (Ⓥ) ★★★ Fynbos brush to 17 ★★★ (80) tank sample. Typical lemon/lime twang, unfussy & easy to drink, lowish 12% alcohol.

The Bush Vines range
Merlot (ⓃⒺⓌ) (⊘) ★★★★ Rounded & softly fruited, 17 (83) spicy tobacco notes, some structure & grip from quarter oaked portion. **Pinotage-Shiraz** (⊘) ★★★ Meaty prune notes on 85/15 blend. 16 (80)'s gentle concentration makes for easy drinking. **Pinotage Rosé** (Ⓥ) ★★★ Brimming with raspberry, guava, watermelon & ruby grapefruit, 16 (77) is dry & refreshing at 12.5% alcohol. **Rosé** (ⓃⒺⓌ) (⊘) ★★★ Coral hue to 18 (78), gently juicy poolside pink with cherry/strawberry appeal. **Chenin Blanc** ★★★ A veritable fruit bowl with melon & granadilla zip, 18 (79) appealing casual quaffer. **Sauvignon Blanc** (ⓃⒺⓌ) (⊘) ★★★ Taut, bright & appealing, with lemon vibrancy & flint on 17 (80), succulent summertime sipper. — FM

Location: Darling ▪ Map: Durbanville, Philadelphia & Darling ▪ Map grid reference: B3 ▪ WO: Darling/Western Cape ▪ Est/1stB 1998 ▪ Tasting & sales Tue-Sat 10-4 ▪ Closed pub hols (TBC) ▪ Cellar tours by appt ▪ Conservation area ▪ Game & eco drives by appt ▪ Child friendly ▪ Owner(s) Cloof Wine Estate (Pty) Ltd ▪ Winemaker(s) Hennie Huskisson (Sep 2017) ▪ Viticulturist(s) Peter Duckitt (May 2004) ▪ 1,300ha/135ha (cabs s/f, merlot, ptage, shiraz, chard, chenin, viog) ▪ 600t/100,000cs own label 88% red 12% white ▪ WWF-SA Conservation Champion ▪ PO Box 269 Darling 7345 ▪ info@cloof.co.za ▪ www.cloof.co.za ▪ S 33° 28' 58.1" E 018° 31' 23.4" ▪ (Ⓜ) overly.realtime.violets ▪ F +27 (0)22-492-3261 ▪ **T +27 (0)22-492-2839**

Clos Malverne   (Ⓥ) (🍴) (🏠) (📷) (♿)

Truly a family business, with owner Seymour Pritchard directing operations, wife Sophia aiding in developing the export market (now 70% of sales) and daughter Belinda looking after visitors. Besides a production facility, they have geared their Devon Valley estate to be a tourist magnet, with diverse wine range and craft beer, accommodation that's been increased, a spa, and restaurant which grows its own organic produce. Winecrafting remains traditional, using tried-and-tested methods and equipment such as basket pressing.

Clos Malverne range
★★★★ **Merlot** (Ⓥ) Vibrant ripe plums & warm, comforting spice on more complex 15 (87), harmonious, not overripe, with integrated tannins & long berry liqueur farewell. Improves on 14 ★★★★ (84).

★★★★ **Le Café Pinotage** Popular 'coffee' style, 16 (86) is dry but gives an impression of sweetness from the toasted French/American new oak. Dark fruit at core, smoothly curvaceous.

★★★★ **Pinotage Reserve** (Ⓥ) Opulent berry & dark choc aromas, followed by 14 (86) palate that is bright & densely packed. Dash cab for complexity. Deserves time to reveal full charm. 50% new oak.

★★★★☆ **Auret** (Ⓥ) Flagship Cape Blend does not disappoint in 14 (93). Deep core of black fruit, creamy & layered; broad, rich with fine tannins & impressive length. Mostly cab, with 30% pinotage & 10% merlot. Approachable in youth, but will reward the patient.

★★★★ **Spirit of Malverne Limited Release** (Ⓥ) Previewed & provisionally rated 15 ★★★★ (87) Cape Blend is highly aromatic - scented violets over hedgerow & bramble fruit - shows lovely freshness if not (yet) the complexity of 13 (93), alcohol & tannins need more time to integrate. No 14.

★★★★ **Ellie Méthode Cap Classique Shiraz Rosé** (Ⓥ) Whisper of pink on 13 (86) delightful traditional-method bubbly. Mouthfilling savoury wild berry flavours, baked biscuits & smooth, creamy mousse.

....

Cabernet Sauvignon-Shiraz (🍇) ★★★ Deep, dark plums in 14 (81), vanilla-spiced opulence, some chocolate tones. A generous, smooth-textured wine.

....

Cabernet Sauvignon-Merlot ★★★★ In this 60/40 blend, cab plays a bigger role than you'd expect; vivid cassis leading to 15 (84)'s well-structured body, firm but accessible tannins. **Chardonnay** ★★★★ Lightly oaked, French/American yet a strong presence. Adds oatmeal biscuit scents/flavours, leaves 17 (83)'s palate savoury & dry, not as amenable as 15 ★★★★ (87). 16 untasted. WO W Cape. **Sauvignon Blanc** ★★★★ Tighter focus than its Devonet sibling, 17 (84) has more varietal purity: lime & minerality, the expected freshness, finishing long. **Sauvignon Blanc Brut Reserve ★★★** Apple & pear styling in perky **NV** ⑧⓪, as refreshing as you'd expect a brut bubbly to be. In abeyance: **Auret Limited Release**.

Devonet range
Merlot-Pinotage ★★★ Ripe black plums/prunes & a definite mocha chocolate overtone, smooth, round, **17** ⑧① is easy to like. **Rosé ★★★** Attractive berry/cherry scents, **17** ⑦⑧'s palate dry & crisp. WO W Cape, as next. **Sauvignon Blanc ★★★** Crisp styling for **17** ⑧①, apple/pear fruit salad, a leafy top note, good brightening acidity. — CR

Location/map: Stellenbosch ▪ Map grid reference: D4 ▪ WO: Stellenbosch/Western Cape ▪ Est/1stB 1986 ▪ Tasting & sales Mon-Fri 10-4.30 Sat/Sun 10-1 pub hols 12-5 ▪ Fee R30/4 wines or R50/6 wines ▪ Closed Dec 25 & Jan 1 ▪ Cellar tours Mon-Fri (booking essential) ▪ The Restaurant @ Clos Malverne ▪ Tour groups ▪ Weddings/functions ▪ Wellness Day Spa ▪ Accommodation: 9 x 4-star rooms & 1 self-catering unit ▪ Owner(s) Seymour & Sophia Pritchard ▪ Cellarmaster(s) IP Smit (Jul 1997) ▪ Winemaker(s) IP Smit (Jul 1997), with Mynardt Hitchcock (1999) ▪ Viticulturist(s) IP Smit (Jul 2015) ▪ 7ha (merlot, ptage, shiraz, sauv) ▪ ±200t/80,000cs own label 50% red 50% white ▪ PO Box 187 Stellenbosch 7599 ▪ info@closmalverne.co.za ▪ www.closmalverne.co.za ▪ S 33° 54′ 38.0″ E 018° 48′ 49.2″ ▪ ⌨ clipped.call.bikes ▪ **T +27 (0)21-865-2022**

Clouds Wine Estate   ⓠ ⓣ ⓐ ⓞ

Establishing 'a modern winery and luxurious accommodation' was the ambition of Paul Burema and Jolanda van Haperen when they acquired this small estate on Stellenbosch's Helshoogte Pass. They are Dutch, and the striking orange-dominated branding no doubt alludes to their origin. The wine is eminently local, of course, with Donovan Rall (also making for Vuurberg and under his own name) as cellarmaster. An estate-grown red blend joins the range, and the Chenin returns in fascinating guise, matured in concrete and clay.

★★★★☆ Pinot Noir ⊘ Forward combo cherries, earthy, savoury notes on pleasing **17** ⑨② - now just 20% of grapes brought in from Hemel-en-Aarde. Full flavour well balanced by acid & light tannic grip, with unobtrusive oaking.

★★★★ Shiraz Pure, sweet red fruit gives enticing perfume to wholebunch, natural ferment **16 ★★★★☆** ⑨②. Molten tannins - big but smoothly round, with enough fruit flavour to ensure harmony in a few years. Older oak only. 14.5% alcohol doesn't show. From Swartland grapes, like less expressive **15** ⑧⑧.

★★★★☆ Red Blend (NEW) Cab-based **16** ⑨② blend with 30% merlot & a splash of petit verdot. Ripe, engaging fruitcake & tobacco aromas, no obvious oakiness to obscure the purity. Rich & flavourful, with sweet fruit supported by firm tannic structure, leading to dry finish. 14.3% alcohol.

★★★★ Pink From sauvignon with 2% shiraz for onion skin colour & to divert from obvious varietalism. Refreshing, serious **17** ⑧⑥, with stony minerality. More dry & elegant than **16 ★★★★** ⑧③.

★★★★ Chardonnay Clean freshness on lightish, well-structured **17** ⑧⑨, with more lime than lemon notes. Matured in oak, concrete & clay pots, giving dry delicacy. **16 ★★★★☆** ⑨③ included some Ceres grapes.

★★★★ Chenin Blanc From ripe old-vine Wellington fruit. **17 ★★★★☆** ⑨② matured in concrete 'egg' & amphora, enhancing purity of aroma & flavour & vibrant freshness - although quite rich & silky. Last-made **14** ⑧⑧ ex Swartland. Really delightful drinking.

★★★★☆ Sauvignon Blanc ⊘ Citrus, gooseberry & passionfruit prominent on **17** ⑨②. Crisp & fresh, but with some texture & weight, a core of sweet fruit & smooth dry, grapefruity finish. WO W Cape, like Pink.

★★★★ Méthode Cap Classique Previously from chardonnay alone, **15** ⑧⑦ sparkling is 50% pinot. An elegant, crisp, bone-dry austerity to the balanced, apple-citrus palate, following on from yeasty aromas. — TJ

Location/map: Stellenbosch ▪ Map grid reference: H5 ▪ WO: Stellenbosch/Western Cape/Swartland/Wellington ▪ Est/1stB 1993 ▪ Tasting & sales Mon-Sun 10-5 ▪ Breakfast ▪ Hotel & villas ▪ Conferences ▪ Owner(s) Paul Burema & Jolanda van Haperen ▪ Cellarmaster(s) Donovan Rall (Jan 2014, Vuurberg) ▪ Winemaker(s) Donovan Rall (Jan 2014, Vuurberg), with Paul Burema (Jan 2012) ▪ Viticulturist(s) Wynand Pienaar (Aug 2009, consultant) ▪ 4.5ha/2.7ha (cab, merlot, p verdot, pinot, chard, sauv) ▪ 24t/2,500cs own label 40% red 60% white ▪ PO Box 540 Stellenbosch 7599 ▪ info@cloudsestate.co.za ▪ www.cloudsestate.co.za ▪ S 33° 55′ 23.9″ E 018° 55′ 29.7″ ▪ ⌨ tracks.keys.swells ▪ F +27 (0)21-885-2829 ▪ **T +27 (0)21-885-1819**

Cloverfield Wines

Pioneers in traditionally sheep- and ostrich-rearing Robertson Valley, the Marais family made their first wines in 1945. In 1978, third-generation Pietie Marais married Irish-born Liz, an event which brought three sons as well as hope, love and luck to the farm. No wonder their slogan is 'Wines of Good Fortune'.

Location/map: Robertson ▪ Map grid reference: B5 ▪ Est 1945 ▪ 1stB 2002 ▪ Tasting & sales Mon-Fri 9-4 ▪ Closed Easter Fri-Mon, Dec 25 & Jan 1 ▪ Owner(s) Henry, Cobus & Pieter Marais ▪ Cellarmaster(s)/winemaker(s) Cobus Marais (2002) ▪ Viticulturist(s) Pieter Marais ▪ ±120ha total ▪ (merlot, shiraz, chard, chenin, sauv) ▪ 40% red 60% white ▪ PO Box 429 Robertson 6705 ▪ info@cloverfield.co.za ▪ www.cloverfield.co.za ▪ S 33° 49'57.3" E 019° 55'34.1" ▪ ⌖ cuter.wagging.defrosting ▪ F +27 (0)23-626-3203 ▪ **T +27 (0)23-626-4118**

☐ **Cluster Series** see Laarman Wines
☐ **Cocoa Hill** see Dornier Wines
☐ **Coetzee Family** see Matzikama Organic Cellar
☐ **Cold Mountain** see Brunia Wines

Collatio Wines

Wessel du Toit, associate professor at Stellenbosch's Viticulture & Oenology school, has been involved with wine education and research for almost two decades, so it's unsurprising his own boutique range sets out to teach as well as delight. With wine geeks, tasting clubs and educators in mind, and collatio ('bringing together and comparing') as the organising principle, Wessel seasonally sources from high-end vineyards to produce pairs of barrels, adjusting a single element of the vinification for one of them to demonstrate 'the effect that one simple intervention can have on a wine'.

★★★★ **Cabernet Sauvignon 7 Dae** One of a pair, **16** ⑧⑧ fermented on skins just 7 days, same oak regime as partner. Almost blackcurrant jam intensity, but there's lively & very appealing natural grip on the palate. WO Stellenbosch for both.

★★★★ **Shiraz Nuwe Hout** Like sibling, 4 years in barrel, but this **15** ⑧⑧ in new, lightly toasted. Spice & char complement red fruits, tannins gruffer & less supple, yet structure more pleasing. Longer future.

★★★★ **Chenin Blanc Een Gisting** Part of pair to show influence of malolactic fermentation on same wine. **17** ⑧⑦ white peach & nuts, smooth & succulent enlivened by bright lemon/lime acidity courtesy no MLF. One 225L barrel, just 280 bottles made, as all.

Cabernet Sauvignon 35 Dae ★★★★ Should be tasted with its sibling, to highlight differences; this **16** ⑧④ fermented, macerated 35 days on skins. Savoury gloss on ripe, similar fruit profile, grippier tannin & sterner profile. **Shiraz Ou Hout** ★★★★ Again, one of a pair. **15** ⑧④ spent 18 months in 4 year old oak; initially dark-toned & meaty, yet has lip-smacking acidity, bright & fresh, with restrained grip. WO Paarl for both. **Chenin Blanc Twee Gisting** ★★★★ This **17** ⑧⑤ completed MLF, secondary fermentation which converts the 'harsh' malic acid into 'soft' lactic acid. Similary smooth & long with an almost aloe lift on the finish, attractive peachiness. — CR, CvZ

Location: Stellenbosch ▪ Map: Helderberg ▪ Map grid reference: A3 ▪ WO: Coastal/Paarl/Stellenbosch ▪ Est 2015 ▪ 1stB 2016 ▪ Tasting by appt only ▪ Closed all pub hols ▪ Owner(s) Wessel du Toit ▪ Cellarmaster(s)/ winemaker(s) Wessel du Toit (Jan 2015) ▪ 2t/180cs own label 50% red 50% white ▪ PO Box 986 Stellenbosch 7599 ▪ wessel@collatiowines.co.za ▪ www.collatiowines.co.za ▪ S 34° 2'23.3" E 018° 45'5.5" ▪ **T +27 (0)82-563-4418**

☐ **Collection** see Roos Family Vineyards

Colmant Cap Classique & Champagne

Belgium émigrés Jean-Philippe and Isabelle Colmant's bijou estate in Franschhoek Valley is the inspiration for their 2001 move to SA and heart of their burgeoning sparkling wine venture – the cap classiques handcrafted in the on-site cellar, the champagnes from select houses. New to the MCC range is a long-gestated, wonderfully svelte brut nature bubbly, bone-dry and so sushi compatible, there's nori embedded in the aroma. A greater part of the farm is occupied by chardonnay and pinot noir, supplemented with fruit from Elgin and Robertson. There's also a cellardoor, with private chef-led pairings, vegetable gardens and free-ranging chickens, all living in harmony with nature.

★★★★ **Brut Rosé** Citrus tang from chardonnay, strawberry nuance & seriousness from 77% pinot on expressive, dry NV (88) sparkler. No reserve wine or oaked portion, but 30 months on lees give extra body. Franschhoek, Elgin & Robertson vines unless noted.

★★★★★ **Absolu Zero Dosage** (NEW) (⊛) Ultra-fine NV (95) bubbly from chardonnay, steely & uncompromising, breathtakingly dry after seven years on lees. Immensely sophisticated, with umami & rock pool scents, satisfying lemon body to which small oaked & reserve-wine fractions add an elegant, weightless backbone, inviting further ageing. No Elgin fruit.

★★★★☆ **Brut Chardonnay** (⊛) Assured & beautifully crafted blanc de blancs dry sparkler, latest NV (93) with increased oaked portion (34%), reserve-wine component (14.5%) & time on lees (48 months) over previous, creating a perfect foil for the ethereal, delicate mousse & bouquet.

★★★★☆ **Brut Reserve** (⊛) Near-equal pinot noir & chardonnay bubbly, NV (93) most New World in style of this handsome celebratory line-up. Forthright lemon & apple, piercing acid seam, small oaked portion, some reserve wine & 30 months on lees for weight & length.

★★★★ **Sec Reserve** Beguiling NV (87) bubbles from pinot noir (52%) & chardonnay, unabashedly fruit focused yet dry- & light-seeming, no discernible sweetness despite 23 g/l sugar. 24 months on lees, small oaked component, some reserve wine deftly woven into the vivacious personality.— CvZ

Location/map: Franschhoek ▪ Map grid reference: C1 ▪ WO: Western Cape ▪ Est 2005 ▪ 1stB 2006 ▪ Tasting & sales Mon-Fri 11-1; or by appt ▪ Fee R20 per ½ glass MCC ▪ Cellar tours on request ▪ Private bubbly & food pairing experiences hosted by chef Duncan Doherty ▪ Owner(s) Jean-Philippe Colmant ▪ Cellarmaster(s) Jean-Philippe Colmant ▪ Wine consultants Nicolas Follet & Pieter Ferreira ▪ 5ha/3ha (pinot, chard) ▪ 8,800cs own label 100% MCC ▪ PO Box 602 Franschhoek 7690 ▪ info@colmant.co.za ▪ www.colmant.co.za ▪ S 33° 55′ 22.4″ E 019° 7′ 37.3″ ▪ enhances.sumptuous.herds ▪ F +27 (0)21-876-3732 ▪ **T +27 (0)21-876-4348/+27 (0)83-778-8874**

☐ **Commander Selection** see La Couronne Wines
☐ **Commando** see Distell

Compagniesdrift (Ⓥ)

Compagniesdrift is primarily a wine storage, bottling and labelling services company in Stellenbosch – a successful empowerment venture owned by Myburgh Family Trust and Meerlust Workers' Trust. Its wine range (maiden vintage 2015, but this is our first taste) is made in the Meerlust cellar, just down the road. **Cabernet Sauvignon-Merlot** ★★★ Plenty of ripe fruity aromas & flavours on **17** (80), with very bright acid & dry tannin force. **Chardonnay-Pinot Noir** ★★★ Pinot just 2% on **17** (82) - for colour & some berry flavour, following the nutty, smoky, faintly lemon aromas. Light & friendly rosé. **Chardonnay Unwooded** ★★★ Shy but fresh & clean aromas on **17** (80). Acidity a touch aggressive for the mild fruit. Probably best with food. — TJ, CvZ

Location/WO: Stellenbosch ▪ Est 2010 ▪ 1stB 2015 ▪ Tasting by appt only ▪ Sales Mon-Thu 8-5 Fri 8-3 ▪ Closed all pub hols ▪ Owner(s) Myburgh Family Trust & Meerlust Workers' Trust ▪ Winemaker(s) Chris Williams (consultant) ▪ 10% red 90% white ▪ PO Box 7121 Stellenbosch 7599 ▪ info@compagniesdrift.com ▪ www.compagniesdrift.com ▪ F +27 (0)21-843-3691 ▪ **T +27 (0)21-843-3902/913/916**

Conceito Vinhos (Ⓥ)

This cross-continental wine venture is based at a winery in Portugal's Douro Valley, established in 2005 by winemaker and CEO Rita Marques, whose family has owned vineyards there since the 1940s. Having 'fallen in love' with SA, since 2011 she's regularly visited, sourced local grapes and made small parcels of own-label wine. The Syrah listed here was produced at Boekenhoutskloof in Franschhoek.

★★★★ **Conceito Syrah** (Ⓥ) From Swartland, older oaked, **16** (87) preview has inky depths, plum/cherry fruit, dark chocolate, tobacco & traces of mocha. Full but not robust, tannins a bit chalky. Youthful, will integrate over time.— GdB, CR

WO: Swartland ▪ Est/1stB 2005 ▪ Tastings only in Douro, Portugal, by prior arrangement ▪ Owner(s) Conceito Vinhos Lda ▪ Winemaker(s) / CEO Rita Marques ▪ conceito@conceito.com.pt ▪ www.conceito.com.pt ▪ N 41° 02′ 23″W 7° 18′ 05″ ▪ padding.deems.incisive ▪ **T +351 279 778 059**

☐ **Condé** see Stark-Condé Wines

Conradie Penhill Artisanal Wines

Nuy Valley in the Langeberg Mountain foothills is home to the Conradie family and their partners in this venture, Gareth and Kate Penny. Much has happened since joining forces in 2015, including renovations and extensions to the cellar and tasting room. Here visitors may sample the two ranges made by fifth-generation cellarmaster, CP Conradie, Breedekloof/Worcester Winemaker of the Year in 2017, and Ronwan Griffiths.

Conradie Family Vineyards range

Pinotage-Cabernet Sauvignon ★★★ Juicy **18** ⑦⑧ mix pinotage with 40% cab, some oak spice in tail. Few grams sugar for early drinkability. **Sweet Rosaline Perlé Rosé ★★** Fruitily sweet, with grapey hints from muscat de Frontignan & low 9.5% alcohol, **NV** ⑦④ lightly sparkling pink is an any-occasion celebrator. **Sauvignon Blanc ★★★** Ripe figs, wild herbs inviting introduction to **18** ⑧②. Pure fruited, vivacious, 2 months on lees with lees stirring enhances balance, length. Nuy, Elim & Darling grapes. Not tasted: **Barrel Selection Reserve Cabernet Sauvignon**, **Barrel Selection Reserve Pinotage**. Occasional release: **Friederich Conradÿ Méthode Cap Classique Brut**, **Red Muscadel Limited Release**.

Penhill range

Saw Edge Peak ★★★ Cabernet & 4 other Bordeaux varieties, **15** ⑧② is rich, full-bodied but also has pleasing freshness & well-managed tannins. Noticeable oak spice (French & American) may better meld with year/2. Not tasted: **Premium Sauvignon Blanc**. Discontinued: **The Staging Post**, **Peddlars' Rest**, **Two Palms**. — AL

Location/map: Worcester ▪ Map grid reference: C3 ▪ WO: Western Cape ▪ Est/1stB 2004 ▪ Tasting, sales & cellar tours Mon-Fri 9–4.30 Sat 9-3; after-hours by appt ▪ Closed Easter Fri/Mon, Ascension day, Dec 25 & Jan 1/2 ▪ Nuy Valley Guest House ▪ Facilities for children ▪ Tour groups ▪ Conferences ▪ Walks/hikes ▪ MTB & 4x4 trails ▪ Conservation area ▪ Annual Nuy Valley Feast (May) ▪ Owner(s) CP Conradie & Gareth Penny ▪ Cellarmaster(s) CP Conradie (Jan 2004) ▪ Winemaker(s) CP Conradie (Jan 2004), with Ronwan Griffiths (Sep 2009) ▪ Viticulturist(s) CP Conradie ▪ 4,500ha/83ha (cab, ptage, red muscadel, shiraz, chard, chenin, cbard, pinot gris, sauv) ▪ 1,840t total 80t/17,000cs own label 84% red 12% white 4% rosé ▪ PO Box 5298 Worcester 6851 ▪ wine@conradiepenhill.com ▪ www.conradiepenhill.com ▪ S 33° 39' 28.0" E 019° 37' 59.6" ▪ redevelop.aerosol.wealthiest ▪ F +27 (0)86-509-4911 ▪ T +27 (0)23-342-7025

☐ **Conservation Coast** see Whalehaven Wines

Constantia Glen

This Waibel-family-owned boutique estate lies on Constantia Nek Pass at the northern end of Constantia Valley, which exposes the mostly north-east facing vineyards to afternoon sun and enables the grapes for the Bordeaux-style blends, a major focus, to achieve full ripeness. Always with an eye on the future, how to improve wine quality, they target particular areas that require attention. For example, an improved vine training system for a high-lying sauvignon vineyard; new sauvignon plantings; trials with soil management to offset drought conditions; and, not forgetting visitor experiences, expanding the tasting room offering.

★★★★☆ Constantia Glen Five ⑧ Classic 5-part Bordeaux-style red. French barriques 18 months, 80% new, for a rich chocolate seam throughout. Black cherries, cassis, crystallised violets, seductively complex layers. **14** ⑨④ is full-ripe without excess: this is a keeper. Also in larger formats.

★★★★☆ Constantia Glen Three ⑧ Merlot leads in **15** ⑨③, with cab franc, cab. Highly perfumed delight, cassis & violets, cocoa-rich chocolate, plush & streamlined. Already tempting because of its polish & style but a distinguished future lies ahead. A triumph. Also in magnum.

★★★★☆ Sauvignon Blanc ⑧ Different clones, some high-elevation vineyards, gave **18** ⑨③'s 3-week harvest, accounting for the layering here (as does splash unoaked semillon). Greengage & lime on a bed of minerals, finishes zesty & long, with almost saline acidity. Worthy successor to **17 ★★★★★** ⑨⑤.

★★★★☆ Constantia Glen Two ⑧ Cellar care included different provenance barrels (including acacia), clay amphora, 7 months on lees, so expect something special in **17** ⑨④ sauvignon/semillon blend. Both tropical fruit & minerality, a creamy texture, without losing the signature freshness.— CR

Location/WO: Constantia ▪ Map: Cape Peninsula ▪ Map grid reference: B3 ▪ Est 2000 ▪ 1stB 2005 ▪ Tasting & sales: in season Mon–Sun 10–8; out of season Sun–Fri 10–5 & Sat 10–8 ▪ Tasting fees from R60, waived according to purchase ▪ Closed Dec 25 & Jan 1 ▪ Brunch; various platters; gourmet flammkuchen; wine & chocolate pairing; salads; desserts; various soups during winter ▪ Owner(s) Tumado Investments (Pty) Ltd ▪ Winemaker(s) Justin van Wyk (Dec 2011), with Megan van der Merwe (May 2015) ▪ Viticulturist(s) Etienne Southey (Sep 2012, farm manager) & Andrew Teubes (consultant) ▪ 60ha/28.5ha (cabs s/f, malbec, merlot, p verdot, sauv, sem) ▪ 200t/25,000cs own label 70% red 30% white ▪ PO Box 780 Constantia 7848 ▪ wine@ constantiaglen.com ▪ www.constantiaglen.com ▪ S 34° 0' 54.51" E 018° 24' 53.64" ▪ ⬚ tags.replace.retires ▪ F +27 (0)21-795-6101 ▪ **T +27 (0)21-795-6100**

Constantia Mist

Boutique farm Constantia Mist is now officially certified as organic, crowning owner and property developer John Schooling's endeavour to 'keep any intervention to a minimum, thereby enhancing the natural beauty of Constantia Valley'. He's looking into establishing shiraz soon. The current plantings, all sauvignon, are managed, and their fruit vinified, by nearby organic estate Silvermist.

★★★★ Sauvignon Blanc ⊘ Feisty & brisk, with pungent wild herb, gooseberry flavours. **17** ⑧⑦ quite intense, hint of grapefruit pith making it a food partner rather than solo entertainer.— MW

Location/WO: Constantia ▪ Est 2004 ▪ 1stB 2009 ▪ 4-star guest house (self-catering) ▪ Owner(s) Eagles Nest Property Investments (Pty) Ltd ▪ Cellarmaster(s) John Schooling (2009) ▪ Winemaker(s)/viticulturist(s) Gregory Louw (Silvermist Organic Wine Estate) ▪ 6.6ha/2.8ha (sauv) ▪ 5.4t/ha 250cs own label 100% white ▪ Postnet Suite 96 Private Bag X16 Constantia 7848 ▪ johns@stagprop.com ▪ www.constantiamist.co.za ▪ F +27 (0)21-794-4123 ▪ **T +27 (0)21-794-0904**

Constantia Nectar

Another recreation of the old Constantia dessert wines from muscat de Frontignan must be welcome. This one comes from the few hectares of vines at Peter Rawbone-Viljoen's Huis-in-Bos property in that famous area, tended by acclaimed Kevin Watt. Two vintages – '09 and '10 – were made, and then for five years all the grapes were sold, but Constantia Nectar has been vinified each year from '16. Made off-site by Teddy Hall, the wine comes in stylish ceramic bottles.

★★★★☆ Natural Sweet White muscat de Frontignan aged 2 years in old oak, minimum 2 years in showstopping 375ml bottle. **09** ⑨⓪ nectarine, apricot & fynbos honey notes, complex flavours & nicely judged 114 g/l sugar lifted by bright acidity. Charming, & amazingly fresh for age.— DS, CvZ

Location/WO: Constantia ▪ Est 2007 ▪ 1stB 2011 ▪ Closed to public ▪ Owner(s) Peter Rawbone-Viljoen Trust ▪ Winemaker(s) Teddy Hall (Jan 2009, consultant) ▪ Viticulturist(s) Kevin Watt (Aug 2006, consultant) ▪ 4.5ha/2.5ha (muscat de F) ▪ 9t/1,600cs own label 100% natural sweet ▪ Huis-in-Bos Klein Constantia Rd Constantia 7806 ▪ info@constantianectar.co.za ▪ www.constantianectar.co.za ▪ **T +27 (0)21-794-3382**

Constantia Royale

There have been exciting developments at this small, family-owned winery. Previously listed as Nova Zonnestraal, the new name, Constantia Royale, proclaims its provenance in the world-renowned Constantia appellation on the Cape Peninsula. More sauvignon vines have been planted for the wine, now made at the new, state-of-the-art Constantia Uitsig cellar.

★★★★ Sauvignon Blanc Following house style of elegantly balanced but ripe & velvety sauvignons, **18** ⑧⑧ sees some semillon plumping starfruit, nectarine & herbaceous flavours. Engaging & ready for the table.— MW

Location/WO: Constantia ▪ Map: Cape Peninsula ▪ Map grid reference: B3 ▪ Est 1997 ▪ 1stB 2015 ▪ Tasting by appt only ▪ Closed all pub hols ▪ Owner(s) Lynn Marais Rowand ▪ Cellarmaster(s) Jacques du Plessis (Jan 2018, consultant) ▪ Winemaker(s) Roger Burton (Oct 2013, consultant) ▪ Viticulturist(s) Joseph van Wyk Contractors (Nov 2013) ▪ 16ha/7.5ha (sauv, sem) ▪ 3st/3,750cs own label 100% white ▪ Suite 193 Private Bag X16 Constantia 7848 ▪ wine@constantiaroyale.co.za ▪ www.constantiaroyale.co.za ▪ S 34° 0' 18.00" E 018° 26' 60.00" ▪ ⬚ postgraduate.radiology.trombone ▪ F +27 (0)21-794-4642 ▪ **T +27 (0)21-794-4841**

Constantia Uitsig

In tandem with vine improvement and replanting, a new on-site cellar has taken shape, and 2018 saw the first Constantia Uitsig wines made in the state-of-the-art facility. It's now the domain of Geisenheim University graduate Danna de Jongh, who took over as winemaker from Jacques du Plessis just after the harvest. This property has an auspicious history, originally being part of the 17th-century estate of the first Cape governor, Simon van der Stel. Markets being very much part of the early Cape's commerce, it's perhaps fitting that there's now a Heritage Market on the estate too, offering a decadent array of artisan food and beverages. The Constantia Uitsig wines tasted this edition continue to show the elegant balance and restraint for which this label has become renowned.

★★★★ **Red Horizon** ⓥ Like **12** ⑧, **14** ⑧ a merlot-led blend with cab & cab franc (58/37/5). Bright, lovely fruit purity undiminished by 18 months oak ageing, 60% new. Restrained, elegant, will reward a few years in the cellar. Cab more dominant on richer **13** ★★★★★ ⑨.

★★★★ **Chardonnay Reserve** ⓥ Toasted nuts, lime & butterscotch on curvaceous, succulent **16** ⑧. Oak (30% new) in harmony, adds to ripe impression. No **15**.

★★★★ **Chardonnay Unwooded** Good example of this style, shows fruit purity & length. **17** ⑧ step up on **16** ★★★ ⑧, with fresh pear & lime. Elegant & light (13% alcohol) yet engaging & earnest.

★★★★ **Sauvignon Blanc** ⊘ Like **16** ⑧, step-up **17** ★★★★★ ⑨ has touch semillon & lees-ageing creating a silky texture. Shows a pervasive zesty intensity that celebrates its cool-maritime provenance.

★★★★★ **Semillon** Vintage warmth reflected in rounder, plusher style. Barrel-fermented (15% new) **16** ★★★★ ⑧ no shortage of waxy opulence & rich honeyed quince flavour, just less vibrancy & focus than scintillating **15** ⑨.

★★★★ **Natura Vista** Semillon & unwooded sauvignon (72/28) blend in **16** ⑧. Rich lanolin & herbaceous notes, less vibrant than **15** ⑧ (despite no malo/bâtonnage) but enough structure & substance for fine dining.

★★★★ **Méthode Cap Classique** Brut sparkling from chardonnay, **15** ⑧ some creaminess (36 months on lees, 10% oaked portion), with fresh apple & honeycomb flavours. Elegant, if shade less expressive than **14** ★★★★★ ⑨.

★★★★ **Red Muscat d'Alexandrie** ⓥ Sweet & moreish **NV** ⑧ (blend of 3 vintages) fortified dessert from very old vines, aged in seasoned oak. Aromatic & grapey, rich & warming, with a spirity twist.— MW

Location/WO: Constantia • Map: Cape Peninsula • Map grid reference: B3 • Est 1980 • 1stB 1988 • Tastings at the Heritage Market Tue-Sun 11-7; sales Tue-Sun 11-5 • Closed Good Fri, Dec 25/26 & Jan 1 • Fee R60pp/3 wines; artisanal cheese & charcuterie platters R225 • Hanepoot grapes sold annually • Open Door Restaurant • Chris Nixon Cycling Academy • Heritage Market: Aegir Beer, Alexander Avery Fine Chocolates, Constantia Uitsig Wine Shop, Kristen's Kick-Ass Ice Cream, Nest Deli, Sushi Box • Owner(s) Constantia Uitsig Holdings (Pty) Ltd • Winemaker(s)/viticulturist(s) Danna de Jongh (Aug 2018) • 60ha/20ha (cabs s/f, chard, muscat d'A, sauv, sem) • 100t/20,000cs own label 10% red 90% white • PO Box 32 Constantia 7848 • info@uitsig. co.za • www.uitsig.co.za • S 34° 2' 51.9" E 018° 25' 27.5" • tiles.entering.snoot • **T +27 (0)21-794-6500**

☐ **Constitution Road** see Robertson Winery
☐ **Contours Collection** see Swartland Winery
☐ **Cool Climate Collection** see Corder Family Wines
☐ **Cooperative** see Bosman Family Vineyards

Copeland Spirits (NEW)

James Copeland, electronic musician and DJ, now makes 'pisco' at his craft distillery on Cape Town's Peninsula (also home of Copeland Rum). Aromatic grape varieties from winemaker brother Matthew at Vondeling in Voor Paardeberg are cold-fermented on their skins, half then single-distilled 'for character and body', the rest double-distilled 'for finesse and aroma'. You'll find it at pop-up bars at events and locations around Cape Town and Johannesburg.

★★★★ **Pisco** Delightfully smooth & fragrant brandy, notes of passionfruit, melon, wax & just-husked almonds. Juice & skins of same grapes as Vondeling Babiana (chenin, chardonnay, viognier, grenache blanc), 50/50 single/double distilled, rested year in tank (not oak) for fruit purity. 43% alcohol.— WB

Location: Cape Town ▪ Est/1stB 2018 ▪ Closed to public ▪ Owner(s) James Copeland ▪ Cellarmaster(s)/wine-maker(s) James Copeland (Jan 2018) ▪ Postnet Suite 416 Private Bag X4 Sun Valley Cape Town 7985 ▪ james@copelandrum.com ▪ www.copelandrum.com ▪ T +27 (0)76-481-9302

☐ **Copper Collection** see Oneiric Wines
☐ **Coral Reef** see Wineways Marketing

Corder Family Wines

The brand belongs to Ian and Anette Corder, he an advertising and marketing man, she a former wine tourism practitioner. The grapes for the listed vintages are from an Elgin farm, vinified by a local consultant.

Cool Climate Collection

★★★★ **Chardonnay** (②) Fine, balanced **15** (86) richly layered with butterscotch & peach/pear flavour, well enlivened by lovely vein of fresh acid. Gloss of 10% new oak adds to satisfaction.

★★★★ **Sauvignon Blanc** (②) Super **15** (89) shows classic cool-climate cut grass & fig notes in a textured body; a seam of drying minerality gives a slight edge on **14** (87), which finished a tad sweet.

Not tasted: **Pinot Noir**, **Syrah**. — DS

Location/WO: Elgin ▪ Est 2003 ▪ 1stB 2007 ▪ Closed to public ▪ Owner(s) Ian & Anette Corder ▪ 90t ▪ own label 20% red 80% white ▪ PO Box 169 Elgin 7180 ▪ ian@corderwines.co.za ▪ www.corderwines.co.za ▪ T +27 (0)21-846-8081

☐ **Coutelier** see Domaine Coutelier
☐ **Covenant** see Croydon Vineyard Residential Estate

Cranefields Wine   (②)

Focused on exports (Hamburg-based merchant Siegfried Greve is co-owner), Cranefields' wines are pro-duced at Villiersdorp Cellar and named for SA's national bird, the Blue Crane. Both their brands, Cranefields and Little Brown Job, are now solely blended wines, and both help raise funds for birdlife conservation.

Location/map: Villiersdorp ▪ Map grid reference: B2 ▪ Est/1stB 1995 ▪ Tasting by appt only ▪ Owner(s) SJ Greve & CJ Roux ▪ Winemaker(s) Christo Versfeld (Villiersdorp Cellar) ▪ Viticulturist(s) Charl Roux (Feb 1998) ▪ 35ha (cab, merlot, shiraz) ▪ 220t/6,000cs own label 100% red ▪ PO Box 417 Villiersdorp 6846 ▪ cranefields@telkomsa.net ▪ www.cranefields.com ▪ S 34° 2' 45.99" E 019° 13' 59.64" ▪ 🖾 seminar.ruses.digit ▪ F +27 (0)28-840-0440 ▪ T +27 (0)28-840-2565

Craven Wines   (②)

The Cravens (Australian Mick and local Jeanine) focus on early picking of single-vineyard, single-variety Stellenbosch sites, freshness being a central aim for their light, interesting and delightfully drinkable wines. Bunch- and skin-ferment on white grapes aids in giving the textural and savoury characters they seek.

Location: Stellenbosch ▪ Est 2013 ▪ 1stB 2014 ▪ Tasting & sales by appt only ▪ Owner(s) Jeanine & Mick Craven ▪ Winemaker(s) Jeanine & Mick Craven (Jan 2013) ▪ 38t own label 60% red 40% white ▪ PO Box 972 Somerset Mall 7137 ▪ www.cravenwines.com ▪ T +27 (0)72-701-2723

Creation Wines   (②) (🍴) (🛇) (♿)

Swiss viti-vini man Jean-Claude Martin and wife Carolyn (scion of the respected Finlayson winegrowing clan) embody their brand, spoiling visitors to their Hemel-en-Aarde estate with many delights, regularly garnering international 'innovative wine tourism' accolades. Recent additions include assistant winemaker Gerhard Smith, the 'area's first' chenin and new varieties from maturing vines to expand the Reserve wines (and charm new markets South Korea, Mauritius and Kenya). Gourmet food-and-wine pairings, sommelier internships and artist showcases happily co-exist with grassroots community projects.

Premium range

★★★★ **Sumac Grenache** Rich yet elegant, fresh **16** ★★★★★ (92), mellow oak flavours from 18 months large older barrels. Advertised lemon/sumac notes along with exotic pomegranate & sour cherry make for a brilliant food wine, as in **15** (87).

★★★★ **Merlot** ⓥ Immensely likeable mouthful of chocolate/mocha & zesty berry fruit harmonising with oak's vanilla. **16** ⑧⑥ balanced & round, finishes with lingering fruit sweetness & lift. **15** untasted.

★★★★☆ **Reserve Merlot** ⓐ Liqueur-like texture on **16** ⑨④ palate, with velvet tannins, good balance & smoky grip from 25% new oak. Will age well & deepen the complex flavour array, including spice cake, cherry, violet, dark chocolate & roasted hazelnut.

★★★★☆ **Emma Pinot Noir** 🆕 ⓐ Occasional release named for owners' daughter, only 2 special barrels which got 50% new oak & 30% whole bunches. **17** ⑨④ spicy, fragrant, hint of rose in the structured cherry & plum fruit, firm texture sets up long rewarding future.

★★★★ **Pinot Noir** ⊘ ⓐ Most light-footed of the pinot siblings, balanced, gentle savoury grip from 20% new oak, year. **17** ★★★★★ ⑨① purer & more precise than **16** ⑧⑨, lush red berry fruit, fynbos & attractive pomegranate piquancy.

★★★★☆ **Reserve Pinot Noir** ⊘ ⓐ Vineyard-selected **17** ⑨③ substantial, full, without being weighty, lively berry fruit, sour cherry & forest floor aromas. Long exotic spice farewell before fine palate intensity & spice from well-judged barrelling, 25% new, 14 months).

★★★★☆ **The Art of Pinot Noir** ⓐ A further selection - in the cellar - & 60% new oak result in this complex pinnacle wine. **17** ⑨③ kaleidoscope of concentrated red & black fruit, Asian spice, vanilla & waft of sea air. Plushness in harmony with wood, will give many years pleasure. Follows dark & brooding **16** ★★★★★ ⑨⑤.

★★★★ **Merlot-Cabernet Sauvignon-Petit Verdot** ⓐ Needs time to fully reveal the charms currently veiled by 33% new oak. **16** ⑧⑨ 45/40/15 blend abundantly fruity, full & harmonious, notes of blueberry in the rich & powerful body.

★★★★ **Syrah-Grenache** ⓐ Another candidate for the cellar, commanding tannin structure needing time to resolve. 80/20 blend in **16** ⑧⑨, luscious hedgerow fruit, dark plums, sprinkling of pepper & whiff of smoke in savoury conclusion.

★★★★☆ **Chardonnay** ⓐ Plenty going on in vibrant **17** ⑨⓪, persistent & expressive nose & palate, with lemon curd, vanilla & caramel notes from 25% new oak. Opulent, & on track after **16** ★★★★ ⑧⑦.

★★★★☆ **Reserve Chardonnay** ⓐ Single parcel, barrel-fermented, combines impressive depth with elegance, wet stone minerality & grapefruit pithiness. Very svelte, **17** ⑨③ delicious lemony poached-apple fruit, cinnamon & vanilla on bed of oak, 40% new.

★★★★☆ **The Art of Chardonnay** ⓐ Specific site within a single vineyard for this standout bottling. Barrel-fermented **17** ⑨③ unfolds to reveal voluptuous preserved lemon, honeysuckle, orchard fruit & a buttery underlay from 60% new oak.

★★★★☆ **Cool Climate Chenin Blanc** 🆕 ⓐ Great fruit purity & clarity in **17** ⑨①, maturation in older oak (& regular lees stirring) add complexity & tempered mouthfeel. Seductive floral fragrance matched by ample concentration of stonefruit & citrus.

★★★★ **Viognier** ⊘ More focus & complexity in **17** ★★★★★ ⑨⓪, cooler climate evident in brightness of the fruit flavours & stony mineral core. Unoaked, like **16** ⑧⑥, accentuating white blossom fragrance & fresh-picked orchard fruit. Cape South Coast WO.

★★★★ **Sauvignon Blanc-Semillon** Creamy & harmonious **17** ⑧⑧ appeals with citrus, lemon meringue & beeswax flavours, delicate salty tang. Generous 80/20 blend, barrel fermented.

Sauvignon Blanc ⓥ ★★★★ Nettles & greengage on bright, tightly wound **17** ⑧⑤. Bone-dry lunch companion with zesty citrus tail. Not tasted: **Syrah**. — WB

Location: Hermanus ▪ Map: Walker Bay & Bot River ▪ Map grid reference: C4 ▪ WO: Walker Bay/Cape South Coast ▪ Est 2002 ▪ 1stB 2006 ▪ Tasting, sales & cellar tours daily 10-5 ▪ Closed Dec 25 & Jan 1 ▪ The Story of Creation Pairing; small plate pairing; brunch pairing; wine & chocolate pairing; tea pairing ▪ Kiddies' beverages & snack pairing menu ▪ Owner(s) Jean-Claude & Carolyn Martin, Jonathan Drake ▪ Cellarmaster(s) Jean-Claude Martin (Jan 2006) ▪ Winemaker(s) Jean-Claude Martin (Jan 2006), with Gerhard Smith (Dec 2017) ▪ Viticulturist(s) Jean-Claude Martin & Peter Davison (consultant), advised by Johan Pienaar (all 2002) ▪ 50ha (cab, grenache, merlot, p verdot, pinot, shiraz, chard, sauv, sem, viog) ▪ 350t/50,000cs own label 65% red 35% white ▪ EnviroWines, IPW ▪ PO Box 1772 Hermanus 7200 ▪ info@creationwines.com ▪ www.creationwines.com ▪ S 34° 19' 51.90" E 019° 19' 35.53" ▪ ✉ rectifying.awaiting.aware ▪ F +27 (0)28-212-1127 ▪ T +27 (0)28-212-1107

☐ **Creative Block** see Spier

☐ **Credo** see Stellenbosch Vineyards

Cronier Wines

Brand owner Johan Cronje, whose ancestors 300 years ago farmed the two original Wellington estates, celebrates the area's rich winegrowing tradition in a portfolio of export brands such as Capeville, Cronier, Driebergen Reserve, Heritage, Le Mieux and Maison de Vin.

Location: Wellington/Paarl ▪ Est 1698 ▪ 1stB 2006 ▪ Tasting by appt only ▪ Owner(s) Johan Cronje ▪ First Floor, FFG Building, Zomerlust Estate, Bergriver Boulevard, Paarl 7646 ▪ pr@cronierwines.com ▪ www. cronierwines.com ▪ F +27 (0)21-872-3673 ▪ **T +27 (0)21-872-2643**

Croydon Vineyard Residential Estate

Croydon was one of the first upmarket vineyard lifestyle property developments between Cape Town and Somerset West. Ownership includes a stake in the estate's cellar and vineyards and, better, supplies of appropriately named wines. Vinification is in the hands of Rikus Neethling of Bizoe Wines, who lives on site.

Covenant range

★★★★ **Cabernet Sauvignon** ⊘ Cassis, spice & liquorice on nicely contained **17** ⑧⑥, which improves on **16** ★★★★ ⑧④. Rich & gentle, yet with firm frame of older oak. Layered & smooth, long rewarding tail.

★★★★ **Shiraz** ⊘ Maintains form in **17** ⑧⑥ with generous dark fruit core, defined firm structure from 15 months in older oak, which adds spice & grip. Long rewarding aftertaste.

Merlot ⑧Ⓔ ★★★★ Typical fruitcake & leafy blackcurrant on **17** ⑧④. Deep, inky & concentrated, with firm frame. 15 months oaking, none new. **Pinotage** ★★★★ Deep, inky blue & black fruit on compact **17** ⑧③. Sturdy yet succulent, with bright spice lift. Improves on previous. **Chenin Blanc** ⑧Ⓔ ★★★★ Ripe honeyed edge to melon & stonefruit vivacity on poised **17** ⑧④. Textured yet pure, fresh & light. Fermented & aged in concrete 'egg'. **Sauvignon Blanc** ⑧Ⓔ ★★★ Gently rounded, tropical-toned & succulent **17** ⑧②. Lemon drop delicacy with bright acid highlights on naturally fermented Elgin fruit. **Méthode Cap Classique Brut** ⑧Ⓔ ★★★ Sourdough vies with apple on **16** ⑧⓪ dry bubbly from Franschhoek chardonnay. Freshness makes way for broad, creamy, oxidative tail.

Title Deed range

Cape Blend ⊘ ★★★★ Medium-bodied, slightly grippy **17** ⑧④ shows more shiraz character than pinotage in 5-way mix. Spice mingles with blue & black fruit. Good braai partner. **Rosé** ★★★ Union of pinotage & cab franc produces bright, juicy, berry-toned dry pink pleaser. **18** ⑧⓪ light, fresh & easy-drinking. **Chenin Blanc** ★★★ Nectarine & pithy citrus mingle with lees breadth on light, juicy **18** ⑧⓪. Ideal summer sipper.

Croydon range

In abeyance: **Portion 20**. — FM

Location: Stellenbosch ▪ Map: Helderberg ▪ Map grid reference: A3 ▪ WO: Stellenbosch/Coastal/Western Cape ▪ Est/1stB 2004 ▪ Tasting & sales Mon-Fri 8-5 ▪ Closed all pub hols ▪ Cellar tours by appt ▪ Facilities for children ▪ Tour groups ▪ Conferences ▪ Events ▪ Owner(s) Croydon Vineyard Estate ▪ Winemaker(s) Rikus Neethling (consultant), with Jannie Alexander ▪ Vineyard manager Ben van Zyl ▪ 8ha (cabs s/f, malbec, merlot, ptage, shiraz, chenin) ▪ 65t/4,000cs own label 95% red 5% white ▪ Unit 1 Croydon Vineyard Estate Somerset West 7130 ▪ admin@croydon-estate.co.za ▪ www.croydon-estate.co.za ▪ S 34° 2′ 23.3″ E 018° 45′ 5.5″ ▪ ⬚ lakefront.bowstring.marry ▪ F +27 (0)21-843-3609 ▪ **T +27 (0)21-843-3610**

Crystallum

Having bought their own 8-ha property a few kilometres beyond Hemel-en-Aarde Ridge ward in 2017, to supplement grapes brought in for their acclaimed boutique venture, winemaker Peter-Allan Finlayson and architect brother Andrew are now planting a further 2 ha of chardonnay, with more pinot noir to follow, all from hand-picked classic clones: chardonnay chosen for high acids, pinot for performing well in the clay-rich soils. Potential sites are always being sought, and one outside Stanford looks particularly promising. Believing that farming must be spot-on to accurately reflect each wine's terroir in the bottle, Andrew is now playing an active role in managing some of the vineyards they source from, learning much about organic and sustainable farming in the process.

★★★★☆ **Bona Fide Pinot Noir** 🌿 From vineyard in lowest, warmest ward, Hemel-en-Aarde Valley. **17** ⑨④ reflects origin in its ripe, dark-scented succulence, delivered with poise & restraint. Gentle wild herbal note adds interest to overall graceful, elegant profile. 60% whole bunch, 20% new French barriques.

★★★★☆ **Cuvée Cinéma Pinot Noir** 🌿 Tension & vibrancy clues to cool elevated Hemel-en-Aarde Ridge source. **17** ★★★★★ ⑨⑤ has mouthwatering fruit purity & depth, silky texture complemented by secure structure, auguring well for long ageing. 50% whole bunches (40% in **16** ⑨③) & 30% new oak augment superb quality.

★★★★☆ **Mabalel Pinot Noir** Most youthfully unrevealing, delicate of these pinots, **17** ⑨②'s ripe 14% alcohol well-shielded by fresh fruity acids, more red than black fruit & fine, vibrant tannins. Just 5% whole bunch, native ferment as is whole range. From 700 metre high Elandskloof vineyard.

★★★★☆ **Peter Max Pinot Noir** ⊘ Full bodied & with density to its dark-berry, undergrowth fruit, 2017s also refined & supple. Balanced structure & freshness of fine tannins allow for current & future drinking pleasure. **16** ★★★★ ⑧⑦ more easygoing. 30% wholebunch, 10% new oak. From 4 vineyards, WO W Cape.

★★★★☆ **Clay Shales Chardonnay** 🌿 Youthfully & classically compact, brief glimpses of intense lime pith, hazelnut purity, carried lengthily by freshness, tingling acid from its cool-climate origin. All anchored by 10 months on lees. **17** ⑨③ from Hemel-en-Aarde Ridge. Bunchpressed, older oak.

★★★★☆ **The Agnes Chardonnay** 🌿 More youthfully approachable than Clay Shales, **17** ⑨④ has elegant breadth of ripe citrus, oatmeal, supple feel; restraining resolute line of acidity suggests future promise. From 5 Hemel-en-Aarde & Overberg sites, varying soils. Wholebunch, 10% new oak.

Not tasted: **Whole Bunch Pinot Noir**. — AL

Location: Bot River ▪ WO: Western Cape/Hemel-en-Aarde Ridge/Elandskloof/Hemel-en-Aarde Valley ▪ Est 2006 ▪ 1stB 2007 ▪ Closed to public ▪ Owner(s) Crystallum Coastal Vineyards (Pty) Ltd ▪ Winemaker(s) Peter-Allan Finlayson (2006) ▪ 60t/7,000cs own label 60% red 40% white ▪ PO Box 857 Hermanus 7200 ▪ info@crystallumwines.com ▪ www.crystallumwines.com

☐ **Culemborg** see DGB (Pty) Ltd

☐ **Culinaria Collection** see Leopard's Leap Family Vineyards

☐ **Cutters Cove** see Robert Stanford Estate

Dâbar

The Hebrew name means 'promise', and judging from the bountiful produce grown on Jannie Gutter's Vierfontein farm near Napier, it could be said to mean 'the promise of fruitfulness'. While some crops are destined for export, the growing line-up of wines is available within the immediate local area, with plans to have them available online by press time. The wines, which reflect their cool-climate origin, are crafted in Stellenbosch by experienced Rianie Strydom (Strydom Vintners).

★★★★ **Shiraz** ⊘ White pepper, pimento & cinnamon carry through to smooth, silky mouthful in **15** ⑧⑧, yard ahead of firm & dry **14** ★★★★ ⑧④. Both for solo sipping, with enough weight for food.

Pinot Noir ⊘ ★★★★ Enjoys aromatic breadth, concentration of forest floor, dark cherry flavours in its supple feel; **16** ⑧⑤ notable astringency needs time to round, reveal extent of sweet-fruited conclusion. French oak, 25% new. **Chardonnay** ★★★★ Cool feel in bracingly fresh **17** ⑧⑤. Medium body, with concentration of pickled lime fruity acids which linger on the tangy, dry tail. Current edginess, toasty oak (25% new) flavours should harmonise over next year. **Cuveé Brut** ★★★ Méthode cap classique bubbly from chardonnay (60%) & pinot noir, old-oak fermented, 4 years on lees. **13** ⑧⓪ some citrus & red fruits; a little coarse, less convincing than last. Not tasted: **Sauvignon Blanc**. — AL

Location/WO: Napier ▪ 1stB 2010 ▪ Closed to public ▪ Owner(s) Jannie Gutter ▪ Winemaker(s) Rianie Strydom (Haskell Vineyards) ▪ Viticulturist(s) Conrad Schutte (consultant) ▪ 25ha (pinot, shiraz, chard, sauv) ▪ 50% red 50% white ▪ rani@atwine.co.za ▪ **T +27 (0)84-506-8024**

☐ **Da Capo Vineyards** see Idiom Collection

Dagbreek

Third-generation Peet Smith's boutique winery on the Breede River near Rawsonville is quietly gaining a following with a portfolio of Cape rarities, mostly black grapes from Portugal and Italy, and more recently French variety carmenère. His wines are packed with character, the straw wine, with a nudge of grape tannin, being just one example.

Dagbreek range

★★★★ **Nebbiolo** Floral **14** ⑧⑦, well integrated & still fruity after lengthy sojourn (52 months) in older French oak, strong tannins as might be expected from the grape.

Touriga Nacional ★★★★ Full bodied & intense **14** ⑧④, good padding of black fruit on athletic tannin frame. Flavoursome, just a hint of sweetness & alcohol warmth. Oak as for Nebbiolo. Not tasted: **Pinotage, Tinta Barocca, Tinta Amarela, Chenin Blanc Barrel Selection, Chenin Blanc**. Occasional release: **Cape Vintage**.

Family Editions

★★★★ **Red Muscadel** Fruitcake, orange peel & savoury spice on enticing **16** ⑧⑧ fortified dessert. Unctuous raisin & sultana richness, sweetness ably balanced by lively acidity.

Special Editions

Straw Wine ★★★★ From chenin, now-bottled **16** ⑧④ something of a maverick, quite dry for the style, nutty & oxidative, backbone of tannin also unusual for vin de paille. Not tasted: **Carma**. — HC

Location: Rawsonville ▪ Map/WO: Breedekloof ▪ Map grid reference: C5 ▪ Est/1stB 2009 ▪ Tasting, sales & cellar tours Mon-Sat by appt ▪ Closed all pub hols ▪ BYO picnic ▪ Walking/hiking trails ▪ Owner(s) Peet Smith ▪ Cellarmaster(s)/winemaker(s) Peet Smith (2009) ▪ Viticulturist(s) Leon Dippenaar (2009, consultant) ▪ 108ha/48ha under vine ▪ 7t/1,000cs own label 70% red 30% white ▪ WIETA ▪ PO Box 237 Rawsonville 6845 ▪ dagbreek@compnet.co.za ▪ www.dagbreek.co.za ▪ S 33° 39′ 56.20″ E 019° 18′ 26.99″ ▪ ⑭ undaunted. lambing.twig ▪ F +27 (0)86-529-2865 ▪ **T +27 (0)82-820-2256**

DA Hanekom Familie Wyne

The names of vineyardist/winemaker Andri and wife Yvette Hanekom's debut wines recall shared holidays on a Karoo family farm and memories of a local landmark mountain. Vinification and tasting are at Durbanville's Bloemendal, where Andri is resident winemaker after stints at Delheim, Marianne and Cathedral Peak in KwaZulu-Natal.

Putfontein ★★★★ Bright, polished & poised **16** ⑧④ Stellenbosch pinotage, plentiful raspberry & red-currant flavours, clean leather nuance, uplifting tannin bite. Very drinkable but, at 15% alcohol, no quaffer.

Witteberg ★★★ Bone-dry **17** ⑧① faint white peach & tropical tones, welcome steely chenin acidity for food; 14.5% alcohol warms the finish. — AL, CvZ

Location: Durbanville ▪ Map: Durbanville, Philadelphia & Darling ▪ Map grid reference: C7 ▪ WO: Paarl/Stellenbosch ▪ Est/1stB 2016 ▪ Tasting by appt only ▪ Closed all pub hols ▪ Owner(s) Andri & Yvette Hanekom ▪ Cellarmaster(s) Andri Hanekom (Jan 2016) ▪ 4t/580cs own label 50% red 50% white ▪ WIETA ▪ andri@dahfamiliewyne.com ▪ www.dahfamiliewyne.com ▪ S 33° 50′ 22.1″ E 018° 36′ 1.4″ ▪ **T +27 (0)66-189-3371**

Dainty Bess

A family affair, this: some of the fruit for Jane Ferreira-Eedes' bubbly comes from a tiny parcel of Wellington pinot noir planted by her father in the 1990s, the name from a favourite creamy pink rose in her mother's garden. The wine is being well received, says Jane, who plans to lift production over the next 5 years.

★★★★ **Pinot Noir Méthode Cap Classique** Delectable dry sparkler, dainty in name, appearance & taste: ballerina pink **15** ⑧⑧, gentle strawberry, cherry & spice, soft creamy mousse from 34 months on lees. Elgin & Wellington fruit.— WB

Location: Cape Town ▪ WO: Western Cape ▪ Est/1stB 2016 ▪ Tasting by appt only ▪ Owner(s) Jane Ferreira-Eedes ▪ Winemaker(s) Corné Marais (consultant) ▪ 2t from Klein Optenhorst (0.25ha pinot), Wellington; additional fruit from Shannon Vineyards, Elgin ▪ 4t ▪ 100% MCC ▪ 44 Liesbeek Rd Rosebank Cape Town 7700 ▪ daintybesswine@gmail.com ▪ www.daintybess.co.za ▪ **T +27 (0)83-324-6855**

Dalla Cia Wine & Spirit Company

This family-run venture in Stellenbosch keeps their Italian heritage alive, in both their range of wines and spirits, and ever-popular Pane E Vino Food & Wine Bar in Bosman's Crossing on the outskirts of town. Availability of their red and white wines is on the increase domestically, co-owner George Dalla Cia notes, and their attention is turning to the spirit portfolio. Sales and listings of innovative Dalla Cia Corretto, 'grappa' in a sachet, convenient for 'correcting' your espresso as per the old-country custom, are growing. And a handsomely packaged 9-year-old potstill joins the single- and dual-cultivar grappas in sharing la dolce vita.

Dalla Cia Wine range

★★★★ Classico Cabernet Sauvignon Rich & ripe **16** ★★★★☆ ⑨⓪ loses splash petit verdot of **15** ⑧⑦, now 100% cab showing advertised classic flavours of blackcurrant, cedar & pleasing spice notes of cinnamon & aniseed. Well-integrated, chewy tannins (helped by 70% new oak) & light, elegant finish.

★★★★ Pinot Noir ⓧ Modern & ripe **15** ⑧⑦ blends perfumed rosepetals & spicy earth with red fruit & a savoury, meaty core. Plenty of sweet spice & soft tannins throughout, may improve further with time. No **14**. Also in magnum, as Teano.

★★★★☆ Giorgio ⓐ Cabernet with merlot & petit verdot, Bordeaux blend **15** ⑨③ is weighty & serious. Velvety black-fruit aromas/flavours of cherry, currant, perfume & polish wrapped in silky tannins. Handles hefty alcohol (15%) & 80% new oak with ease, only going to improve over next decade. No **14**.

★★★★☆ Teano ⓧ Mostly French varieties plus nod to Italian ancestry with 15% sangiovese. **14** ⑨②, first since **11** ⑨⓪, shows power in firm tannins & lively acidity running through ripe melange of red & black fruit. Good length, intensity & new-oak backbone suggest a good future. WO W Cape, as next.

★★★★ Chardonnay ⓧ Subtle vanilla oak (a mere 10%) adds interest & length to quiet **16** ⑧⑨. Ripe yellow stonefruit & creamy oatmeal texture from 6 months lees, fresher than previous.

Sauvignon Blanc ★★★★ Tank sample **18** ⑧③ very unformed - grapefruit, guava & grass - still on lees, rating tentative.

Dalla Cia Husk Spirit range

★★★★★ 10 Year Old Celebration Cabernet Sauvignon-Merlot ⓧ ⓐ Limited release marks distillery's 10th anniversary. Rich, with a velvet texture, delightfully mellow. Long-lasting sipper to be savoured. 500 ml, stylishly packaged.

★★★★ Cabernet Sauvignon-Merlot Premium Selection ⓧ Slight straw tinge to this more refined, less aggressive Premium (lightly barrelled) version of the standard Husk Spirit from these varieties. Supple, gently unctuous palate, lingering finish.

★★★★ Pinot Noir-Chardonnay ⓧ Fresh aromas of fruit & nuts; some delicacy, focus & refinement evident on a delightfully textured, smooth & balanced palate.

★★★★ Single Cultivar Organic Merlot ⓧ ⓨ High-toned note gives magnificent lift to red berry & floral aromas; sweet spice & some citrus buoy spirity finish (43% alcohol). Smooth & elegant.

Cabernet Sauvignon-Merlot ⓧ **★★★★** Robust aromas & flavours, husk-y, quiet berry hint. Smooth enough, but with some rusticity. Not tasted: **Limited Edition Pinot Noir**.

Brandy range ⓑ

★★★★ H&G Fine & Rare Potstill Brandy Evocatively packaged potstill aged 9 years. Rich & rounded, with waxy plum & orchard fruit flavours, roasted nuts all in harmony with supportive oak. Smooth & long. From semillon & shiraz.— CM, WB

Location/map: Stellenbosch ▪ Map grid reference: E5 ▪ WO: Stellenbosch/Western Cape ▪ Est 2004 ▪ Tasting, sales & traditional Italian meals at Pane E Vino Food & Wine Bar, Mon-Fri 10-6 Sat 10-5 ▪ Grappa Distillery by appt Mon-Fri 10-4 ▪ Owner(s) George Dalla Cia ▪ Winemaker(s) Giorgio Dalla Cia ▪ 18,000cs ▪ 7A Lower Dorp Str Bosman's Crossing Stellenbosch 7600 ▪ info@dallacia.com ▪ www.dallacia.com ▪ S 33° 56' 25.8" E018° 50' 50.1" ▪ 🖷 agents.tigers.tripped ▪ F +27 (0)21-887-2621 ▪ **T +27 (0)21-888-4120**

Damarakloof

The vineyard on family farm Damarakloof near Paarl was once was a racetrack, deemed too gravelly for cultivation. The organically tended chenin vines have seen more than 60 seasons, and current custodian

Agnes de Vos is very aware of their worth, entrusting the old-timers to only 'highly trained vineyard staff' and equally capable consultant vinifier Carla Pauw of Saltare.

Racetrack range

Regale ⓥ ★★★★ Clean black fruit on soft, juicy **15** ⑧④ Bordeaux red blend, supple tannins & fragrant spicy whiffs. Very pleasant drinking though tad shorter than last-made **08** ★★★★ ⑧⑦. Enjoy soon. **Chenin Blanc** ⓥ ★★★ Soft yellow apple, almond & marzipan on **15** ⑧① shaded by lots of toffee & vanilla. Would suit a nice pork roast. — CM

Location/map/WO: Paarl ▪ Map grid reference: A7 ▪ Est/1stB 2006 ▪ Tasting, sales & function venue by appt - contact Peter Gary T +27 (0)82-766-9095 ▪ Owner(s) Agnes de Vos ▪ Winemaker(s) Carla Pauw (Jan 2006) ▪ Farm manager Jürgen Sutherland ▪ 19ha (cabs s/f, merlot, chenin) ▪ 10t/1,300cs own label 50% red 50% white ▪ PO Box 38 Elsenburg 7607 ▪ agnesdev@telkomsa.net ▪ www.damarakloof.co.za ▪ S 33° 48' 41.79" E 018° 47' 21.19" ▪ ✉ beckoning.tectonic.retinal ▪ F +27 (0)21-884-4304 ▪ **T +27 (0)21-884-4304**

☐ **Daniel Collection** *see* La Petite Vigne
☐ **Daredevils' Drums** *see* Springfontein Wine Estate

D'Aria Winery

ⓠ ⓜ ⓐ ⓘ ⓢ

The music leitmotif continues at family-owned D'Aria Winery on the slopes of Durbanville's cool-climate Tygerberg Hills. To celebrate a decade in their cellar (first-vintage '07 made off-site), Rudi von Waltsleben, guitarist and winemaker, has composed and released a song entitled Kaapstad (Cape Town) to complement the Cape Minstrel Pinotage, honouring the rich local wine heritage and music. The wine ranges and labels are being revamped to reflect the growing number of Wine of Origin Cape Town certifications, and a new assistant winemaker, Lutske Doubell, joins the ensemble.

Reserve range

★★★★☆ **The Soprano Shiraz** Drier, more structured & serious than SV version. Some white pepper & piquant red fruit, quite compact & complex, with a warm, dense fruit centre but much fresher, more balanced intensity in **16** ⑨① than opulent **15** ★★★★ ⑧⑥. Durbanville WO.

★★★★☆ **The Songbird Sauvignon Blanc** Characteristic Durbanville dusty nuance interwoven with crisp grapefruit flavours, textural pithy grip leavened by leesy richness; **17** ⑨① tighter & trimmer than previous, but equally melodious.

Artisan range

★★★★★ **The Following Sauvignon Blanc** ⓥ Mostly fermented & aged in concrete 'eggs', 20% in new oak. **16** ⑨② flavours develop in intensity: flint, greengage, herb & starfruit; freshening grapefruit thread with oak a creamy platform. Persistent, confident & entertaining.

Cape Minstrel Pinotage ⓥ ★★★★ Celebrating Cape Town's famous annual Minstrel Carnival with a Mardi Gras of dark berry flavours, piquant dry freshness, approachable lithe structure in **15** ⑧④.

Cape range

★★★★ **SV Shiraz** Beguiling **16** ⑧⑦ is rounded, rich & ready, with sweet spicy coconut notes, red fruit & creamy-juicy texture. Like shade more impressive **15** ⑧⑧, has splash viognier. WO Cape Town, like Merlot.

★★★★ **Lullaby Noble Late Harvest** ⓥ From botrytised semillon, unctuous **15** ⑧⑦ dessert has honey-drizzled papaya, caramelised pineapple & toffee apple complexity (40% oaked). Excellent with cheese.

Merlot ★★★ A wine of contrasts: rich dark berries curtailed by dry chalky tannins, finishing with a ripe warmth (14.5% alcohol). **16** ⑦⑨ needs more time to knit. **Blush** ★★★ Attractive, easy-drinking **18** ⑧⓪ rosé from merlot & sauvignon blanc, juicy ripe red-berry flavours, few grams sugar taste dry thanks to tangy twist of acidity. **Sauvignon Blanc** ⓥ ★★★★ Yellow peach, asparagus & hint of guava, lees contact gives nice breadth on **17** ⑧④. Sugar-acid balance lends appealing drinkability. Not tasted: **Cabernet Sauvignon-Merlot**.

Music range

Shiraz-Cabernet Sauvignon-Merlot ★★★★ For cosy campfires, **17** ⑧③ is warming (15% alcohol) with ripe dark-fruit compote flavours, spicy black pepper & dusting of cocoa. **Sauvignon Blanc** ★★★ Fresh tropical flavours & clean crisp acidity, lightish & fresh, **18** ⑧⓪ is ready for the summer soirée. Discontinued: **Pinotage-Shiraz**.

Sparkling range

Rock Song Sparkling Shiraz ★★★ More in the heavy metal spectrum, **17** ⑦ dry fizz has a dark brooding colour, ripe berry compote flavours & savoury finish with slight tannic kick. **Love Song Sparkling Pinot Noir** ★★★ Antithesis of Rock Song, **18** ⑧ delicate sunset-pink bubbly with floral & savoury flavours, crisp balance. Very quaffable. **Pop Song Sparkling Sauvignon Blanc** ★★★ Though dry, **18** ⑦ sparkler has distinct & pleasant fruit sweetness, refreshing sherbetty citrus tang. Pure summer fun.

Brandy range

★★★★ **The Piccolo 5 Year Potstill Brandy** ⓥ Amber-hued **12** ⑧ vintage potstill from colombard with rich caramel, roasted hazelnut & marmalade flavours, smooth, well-integrated spirit. Light footed & flavoursome, handsomely packaged, too. 500 ml, 40% alcohol.— MW, WB

Location: Durbanville ▪ Map: Durbanville, Philadelphia & Darling ▪ Map grid reference: C7 ▪ WO: Western Cape/Durbanville/Cape Town ▪ Est/1stB 2007 ▪ Tasting & sales Mon-Sat 10-6 Sun 11-5 ▪ Fee R20 ▪ Closed Dec 24/25 & Jan 1 ▪ Cheese platters, gourmet burgers, oysters, kiddies cookie tasting ▪ Kiddies play area ▪ Venue @ D'Aria T +27 (0)21-975-0421: conferences/events/weddings ▪ Trail running & MTB ▪ 3-star guest cottages ▪ Craft gin ▪ Owner(s) Barinor Holdings ▪ Brandy master Rudi von Waltsleben (2008) ▪ Winemaker(s) Rudi von Waltsleben (Nov 2007), with Lutske Doubell (2017) ▪ Viticulturist(s) Johan von Waltsleben (1998) ▪ 80ha/63ha (cab, merlot, shiraz, sauv) ▪ M13 Tyger Valley Rd Durbanville 7550 ▪ info@daria.co.za ▪ www.dariawinery.co.za ▪ S 33° 50′ 28.6″ E 018° 36′ 36.2″ ▪ ⌨ steady.dices.seperators ▪ F +27 (0)86-539-4519 ▪ **T +27 (0)21-801-6772**

Darling Cellars

ⓥ ⑪ ⒪ ⓐ ⓖ

This large and dynamic West Coast winery appears to be in perpetual motion, constantly innovating in all areas of the business. In the vineyards, there are new plantings of sauvignon and chenin, and the first harvest of durif; in the cellar upgrades to the off-loading and cooling systems; and a new labelling machine and much additional storage space in the bottling department. All no doubt helping fine-tune its portfolio, especially the Heritage Collection which is inspired by locally significant personalities and landmarks.

Darling Heritage Collection

★★★★ **Sir Charles Darling** Plush & polished flagship, **16** ⑧ Bordeaux blend 70% cab with merlot, dry & judiciously oaked, precise tannin the backdrop for ripe & generous dark fruit.

★★★★ **The Old Grain Silo Darling** Previous shiraz-based 5-way blend labelled 'Kroon' is renamed, switches to shiraz (55%) & pinotage in two vintages reviewed. **15** ★★★★ ⑧ modern styling, with agile tannins, vanilla oak sheen (French/American) & sweet-fruit finish; **16** ⑧ slightly more savoury.

★★★★ **Lime Kilns Darling** Accomplished melange mostly chenin, viognier, splash chardonnay in **17** ⑧. Intense, floral & voluptuous, with well-judged brush of oak. Skilfully handles higher-than-usual 13.8% alcohol.

★★★★☆ **Lady Ann Darling** ⊘ ⓐ Sophisticated 50/50 white blend marrying semillon's smoke & straw with sauvignon's fig & florals. **17** ⑨ rich & finely textured, saline top note & oak in support. For now or 5+ years.

Ultra Premium range

★★★★ **Old Bush Vine Cinsaut** ⓦ From 30+ year old vines, **16** ★★★★★ ⑨ enticing cherry hue, icing sugar & raspberry aromas, well-constructed tannin lattice. Light-seeming even at 14% alcohol. Improves on **15** ⑧.

★★★★ **Old Bush Vine Chenin Blanc** ⓐ ⓦ Deft juxtaposition of white orchard fruit with floral & earth nuances, subtle wooding (**16** ⑧ unoaked), vibrant seam of tangerine acidity. **17** ★★★★★ ⑨ for contemplative sipping.

Gustus range

★★★★ **Skattie** ⓥ Afrikaans for 'darling'. Deliciously uncloying **16** ⑧ Natural Sweet dessert from pinotage, with variety's mulberry charm & fresh-fruit fragrance (no raisins). Delightful 375 ml packaging.

Pinotage ⓥ ★★★★ Lots to like about **15** ⑧: not over-extracted or exaggerated; creamy mulberry fruit, freshening tannin. Some would even celebrate slight acetone lift & rubber nudge as quintessential pinotage.

Shiraz ⓥ ★★★★ Promising wholeberry-fermented **15** ⑧, alluring coconut aroma (10% American oak), fruit-packed & approachable, with structure to meld & grow. **Sauvignon Blanc** (NEW) ★★★ Uncomplicated **17** (80), round, smooth & nicely dry for seafood. WO W Cape, as next. **Noble Late Harvest** (NEW) ⊘ ★★★☆ From chenin, **16** (83) has enough tangy acidity to enliven caramel & dried apricot sweetness, good form from 30% oak-aged portion. Enjoy well-chilled, soon.

Reserve range

Old Blocks Pinotage ⊘ (ⓣ) ★★★★ Most mature & generous of these, **15** (85)'s mulberry & raspberry appeal heightened by creamy vanilla oak (mix French/American), characteristic lively acidity. **Black Granite Shiraz** ⊘ (ⓣ) ★★★★ Intensely aromatic **16** (84), very attractive black pepper overlay to dark, brooding fruit. Tannins pliable enough for early drinking, also allow cellaring a few years. Touch American oak, like Old Blocks. Also in 1.5L, like Chocoholic. **Arum Fields Chenin Blanc** (ⓣ) ★★★ More about structure & texture in **18** (79) but still plenty of appeal, especially the balance between lightish alcohol, few grams sugar, gentle acidity & grip from 3 months on lees.

Terra Hutton Cabernet Sauvignon ★★★ Satisfyingly dry & lightly oaked **16** (82) has variety's cassis & blueberry but not its firm tannins, so it drinks easily now. **Cinful Cinsault** (ⓩ) ★★★ Playful, off-dry, quaffable **15** (81) cinsaut; splashes pinotage & barbera give extra berry appeal, structure & length. **Six Tonner Merlot** ★★★ Plummy **16** (82), bright & zesty everyday red. **Chocoholic Pinotage** ⊘ ★★★ Two vintages tasted of this slightly decadent off-dry sipper. **17** (82) packed with promised choc-mocha, mulberry & red fruit, slightly sweeter yet more vivacious than similarly styled **16** (81). **The Capeman SMG** ⊘ ★★★ Honest, unforced **17** (79) is mostly shiraz, with dashes mourvèdre & grenache; nice red berry fruit, fynbos nuance, just a hint of oak. **Pyjama Bush Rosé** ★★ Sauvignon with 1% grenache for whisper of pink, **18** (73) dry, grassy & only just vinous. **Quercus Gold Chardonnay** (ⓩ) ★★ Unwooded **17** (74) fresh & dry but varietal citrus still shaded by fermentation bubblegum character mid-2017. **Bush Vine Sauvignon Blanc** ★★★ Soft acidity, faint grassy passionfruit aromas, briefish farewell in **18** (78).

Cellarmaster Signature Selection (NEW)

No. 6 ★★★★ Mostly shiraz (61%) with six others in **15** (85), attractive freshness & vivacious red & black fruit, integrated tannin so it's accessible on release. **No. 8** ★★★★ Rhône blend of mostly shiraz & 3 others, red fruit nicely shaped by tannin, peppery, savoury & some raisin nuances, sturdy 14.9% alcohol. **15** (85) ready to drink now.

Darling Cellars range

Cabernet Sauvignon-Merlot ⊘ ★★★ Unoaked **17** (77) fruit-packed with good tannin bite, dry finish for food; handles 13.8% alcohol with aplomb. WO W Cape for all except Sweet Darling. **Merlot Rosé** ★★ Undemanding pink, **18** (74) with faint strawberry tones, gentle dry & easy to sip. **Sweet Rosé** ★★ Very demure NV (72) from pinotage, muscat & shiraz, fleeting semi-sweet flavours. **Chenin Blanc-Sauvignon Blanc** ⊘ ★★★ Gets spicy-floral lift from dab bukettraube. **18** (78) wallet-pleasing & characterful picnic partner also in 500 ml. **Sweet White** ★★ Muscat & chenin are the partners in light, sweet NV (75), with tropical flavours & aromas. **Sweet Darling Red** ⊘ ★★★ Cab, merlot & cinsaut with plenty to say in latest NV (79): plum, coffee, choc & enlivening tannic grip.

Méthode Cap Classique range

★★★★ **Blanc de Blancs Brut** ⊘ Two vintages of well-priced dry chardonnay bubbly tasted. Both creamy & rich, shot through with lemon acidity, persistent dry finish. Honey & nougat complexity on **16** (86) from extra year in bottle; **17** (86) equally impressive.

Brut Rosé (NEW) ⊘ ★★★ Gutsy dry **16** (82) from seldom-sparkling grenache delivers interesting glassful of red berries with old leather aromas, tannic tug. **Demi-Sec** (NEW) ⊘ ★★★ Frothy & pleasantly sweet celebrator from chenin, low-alcohol **16** (82) with unusual aroma combo of pear drop & khaki bush.

Wildflower range

Muskadel ★★★ Fortified dessert with rooibos & honey tones, fresh (not raisined) fruit. NV (82) uncomplex but pleasing fire & tug of tannin. WO W Cape for both. **Cape Ruby** ★★★ Fruity NV (78) from Portuguese varieties with decent warmth & grip for firesides or with ice & lime zest, as winemakers suggest. — CvZ

Location: Darling ▪ Map: Durbanville, Philadelphia & Darling ▪ Map grid reference: B2 ▪ WO: Darling/Western Cape ▪ Est 1948 ▪ 1stB 1981 ▪ Tasting & sales Mon-Fri 9—5 Sat 10—2 ▪ Closed Good Fri, Dec 25 & Jan 1 ▪ Cellar tours by appt ▪ Cheese platters ▪ Facilities for children ▪ Bottling services offered ▪ Owner(s) 20 shareholders

• Winemaker(s) Pieter-Niel Rossouw (Sep 2014), with Carel Hugo (Jun 2009), Anthony Meduna (Oct 2011) & Maggie Venter (Jun 2014) ▪ 1,000ha (barbera, cab, carignan, cinsaut, durif, grenache, malbec, merlot, mourv, ptage, shiraz, chard, chenin, riesling, sauv, sem) ▪ 6,500–7,500t/450,000cs own label 60% red 30% white 10% rosé • Other export brands: Black Granite, Cape Cult, Capeman, Chocoholic ▪ PO Box 114 Darling 7345 ▪ info@darlingcellars.co.za ▪ www.darlingcellars.co.za ▪ S 33° 26′ 25.7″ E 018° 31′ 25.1″ ▪ climber.overruling. knotting ▪ **T** +27 (0)22-492-2276/+27 (0)74-683-4454

☐ **Darlington** see Withington

Daschbosch

A large wine business by any definition, Daschbosch's 50 shareholders control 2,050 ha of vineyards in Breedekloof, and cellarmaster Nicolaas Rust and team annually vinify around 45,000 tons, from which some 100,000 cases are selected for the various own labels. Diversity, ethical trade and innovation are key values, and these are likely to continue post the merger with Goudini Wines underway while we wrote this guide.

Daschbosch range

★★★★★ **Hanepoot** ⓐ ⓦ Outstanding fortified from ancient muscat d'Alexandrie bushvines. Like 15 ⑨⑤, 16 ★★★★★ ⑨④ shows sultanas & dried stonefruit in a highly concentrated form, full-sweet & luscious, hedonistic texture, mouthcoating richness. Will age beautifully. 9 months small oak. 375 ml.

Daschbosch Premium range

★★★★ **Cape Blend** 🆕 Two-thirds pinotage with petit verdot, cab & petite sirah, an unusual blend & it works. Liquorice & black plums, scrub, 16 ⑧⑥ layered & involving, sweetly oak-spiced, succulent texture.
★★★★ **Steen** Oaked version of 3 chenins across the ranges, long lees contact for 17 ⑧⑥'s creamy texture. Orange, tangerine & vanilla, makes an impression; not a shy bone in this body, nor woodier 16 ★★★ ⑧②.

Daschbosch Popular Premium range 🆕

Cabernet Sauvignon ★★★ As other reds, previewed 17 ⑧① is barrel-aged 9–12 months for both flavour & tannin backbone. Fruit still core, glossy blackcurrants, a hint of fynbos. Nicely balances ageability & access.
Merlot ★★★ Oak use positions 17 ⑧① barrel sample up the scale from Palesa sibling. Meaty, peppery, with cushion of vibrant cassis, tannins a presence but fine grained. **Sauvignon Blanc** ★★★☆ Tank sample 18 ⑧③ promises well: green pea typicity, a mineral thread through the flavours, zinging fresh. WO W Cape.

Meander range

Moscato ⓦ ★★★ Like drinking hanepoot grape juice, except for the tiny bubbles & alcohol (just 5.5%). NV ⑦⑧ aromatic, sweet & delicious. Serve well chilled.

Pinotage 🆕 ⓥ ★★★ Gentle mocha, liquorice tones fit well with 17 ⑧①'s dark fruit; tannins in harmony, enjoyment assured. More approachable than Palesa version. **Shiraz** ★★ Now some light oaking & 17 ⑦⑥'s red fruit gains savoury notes, but essentially still a smooth early-drinker. **Chenin Blanc** ★★ Green apple & pear, 18 ⑦⑥ is crisp & light, a good quaffer. **Moscato Pink** ⓩ ★★ Naturally sweet perlé wine (as is the white version), latest NV ⑦④'s low 5.5% alcohol & grapey flavours bound to be a party hit.

Palesa Fairtrade range

Merlot ★★ Blackcurrants sprinkled with spice, 17 ⑦⑤ is satisfyingly smooth, made for early enjoyment.
Pinotage ★★★ Dark toned, cocoa & campfire smoke, black plums, 17 ⑦⑧'s whole effect is savoury, the tannins firm, ending dry. Could do with more time. **Chenin Blanc** ★★★ Different styling to the other chenins, mineral & fynbos, 18 ⑧① has precision & focus. Also in 3L cask. **Sauvignon Blanc** ★★ Consistent style, lime with a touch of fynbos in 18 ⑦⑤, light & fresh. — CR

Location: Rawsonville ▪ Map: Breedekloof ▪ Map grid reference: C6 ▪ WO: Breedekloof/Western Cape ▪ Est/1stB 2007 ▪ Tasting & sales at Goudini Wines ▪ Owner(s) 50 shareholders ▪ Cellarmaster(s) Nicolaas Rust (Oct 2008) ▪ Senior winemaker(s) WS Visagie (Nov 2010), Schalk van der Merwe (Dec 2007) & Christo Smit (Jan 2001) ▪ Viticulturist(s) Nicholas Bruyns (Jul 2013) ▪ 2,050ha (cab, cinsaut, merlot, ptage, shiraz, chard, chenin, cbard, sauv) ▪ 45,000t/100,000cs own label 50% red 50% white + 50,000cs for clients ▪ ISO 22000:2008, Fairtrade, IPW, WIETA ▪ PO Box 174 Rawsonville 6845 ▪ info@uniwines.co.za ▪ www.uniwines.co.za ▪ S 33° 41′ 37.8″ E 019° 19′ 9.5″ ▪ rowing.step.insisting ▪ **F** +27 (0)86-529-1392 ▪ **T** +27 (0)23-349-1110

☐ **Dassie's Reserve** see Botha Wine Cellar

David & Nadia ⓪

It's a fine team: David Sadie is based in the historic cellar on Paardebosch farm, on the slopes of the Paardeberg, while Nadia, viticulturist and soil scientist, takes prime responsibility for the vineyards they draw grapes from, on the home-farm or elsewhere in the Swartland. Their signature varieties are chenin blanc and grenache noir, and they admit to a dream of producing single-vineyard grenache wines to parallel their highly regarded chenins. When those wines happen, no doubt they will reflect the Sadies' aesthetic of fresh, elegant and delicate but substantial wines, made in hands-off fashion. The current range are now available at Bill & Co in Malmesbury, a venue they have an interest in and that's clearly much more than a wine bar.

David & Nadia range

★★★★☆ **Grenache** Flavour without heaviness is the refrain throughout these ranges, **17** ⑩ is also fruit-filled without being fruity. Strawberry profile with a hint of earthiness from 3 Swartland blocks; 30-50% bunch pressed, 4 weeks on skins, 11 months older oak. Seamless, & charming in its lightness.

★★★★★ **Elpidios** ⓐ Pace-setting Rhône-style red blend from schist & granite sites, some whole bunches used in savoury & earthy **16** ⑬, mostly carignan (34%) & shiraz (33%) with pinotage, cinsaut & grenache, shows linear purity, Swartland's lacy tannins, & steely presence.

★★★★★ **Chenin Blanc** ⓐ ⓦ A leader of the minimal intervention/oxidative pack. From old (1968) Paardeberg block, **17** ⑮ has trademark ethereal white peach & pear tones. Like **16** ★★★★★ ⑬, hallmark dryness & profundity.

★★★★☆ **Aristargos** ⓐ Authoritative white blend off mostly dryland bushvine blocks, some 50+ years. Persistent **17** ⑭'s earth & umami tones have evocative power. Chenin with viognier, clairette, semillon, roussanne & marsanne. Old oak, native yeasts, no additives, low sulphur; no fining/filtration, as for all.

Discontinued: **Perdekamp Semillon**.

Topography range

★★★★☆ **Pinotage** Herb & scrub, strawberry & ash, a singular interpretation from dryland Paardeberg vineyard shifting the pinotage paradigm. Replete with fine fruit, **17** ⑩ entices with lighter styling. As usual, there's no shortage of endearing - or enduring - class. Year in large seasoned vats.

★★★★☆ **Semillon** ⓦ From 50 year old dryland bushvines in granite soils. Singular **17** ⑪ enjoys 7-10 days skin contact in oxidative 'orange wine' genre. Lean & earthy, with hint of khaki bush, it shows precision & freshness, echoing persistence. Just 11% alcohol.

Single Vineyard range

★★★★★ **Hoë-Steen Chenin Blanc** ⓐ ⓦ Ex 50 year old bushvines with roots in clay & unusually tall shoots, hence 'High Chenin', this typically more powerful than Skaliekop sibling. Refined **17** ⑯ customary pear & wet wool aromas, intense bruised apple flavours, with harmonious length & an extraordinary presence.

★★★★★ **Skaliekop Chenin Blanc** ⓐ From shale ('skalie') site planted in 1985; as Hoë-Steen sibling, bunch pressing, minimal intervention, older oak. Individual, wild 'dissident' profile in steely, mineral **17** ⑮, with khaki bush & scrub features. A tense, ferrous character with an exquisite saline conclusion. — DS

Location: Malmesbury ▪ Map/WO: Swartland ▪ Map grid reference: C8 ▪ Est/1stB 2010 ▪ Tasting by appt ▪ Owner(s)/winemaker(s)/viticulturist(s) David & Nadia Sadie ▪ (carignan, cinsaut, grenache, ptage, shiraz, chenin, clairette, marsanne, rouss, sem, viog) ▪ 75t/9,000cs own label 35% red 65% white ▪ Swartland Independent Producers (2011) ▪ info@davidnadia.com ▪ www.davidnadia.com ▪ S 33° 32' 41.41" E 018° 49' 36.14" ▪ ⅿ illogical.funds.virulently ▪ F +27 (0)86-512-4903 ▪ **T +27 (0)72-375-4336**

David Frost Wines ⓪

An elegant new sauvignon dedicated to SA champion golfer and vintner David Frost's wife, Colene, joins the line-up of this edition. A pinotage/pinot noir blend is also to be released, featuring a newly designed label. The wines are made at D'Aria by Rudi von Waltsleben, with fruit from cooler Cape winegrowing regions.

Par Excellence range

★★★★ **Cape Blend** Big-hitting **16** ⑧⑥, pinotage (80%) the driver, shiraz & cab the wedge & putter. Ripe & brooding, unabashedly New World - with matching 14.8% alcohol. Too powerful perhaps for solo, but good with robust fare at the 19th. Durbanville WO. Also in magnum.

The Colene range 🆕

★★★★ **Sauvignon Blanc** Limited release ex Elim, **17** ⑧⑦ flinty & herbaceous notes on a cool-fruit backdrop, crisp & well balanced. Vivacious cultivar expression & fine food partner.

Grand Slam range

Cabernet Sauvignon ⓧ ★★★ Vague melange of black fruits, **15** ⑦⑦ drinkable if undistinguished. **Pinotage** ⓧ ★★★ Sappy, ripe & rich **16** ⑧⓪, with mulled wine, spicy undertone. Good winter warmer. **Shiraz** ⓧ ★★★ Less knit than previous, with sweet fruits, hammy notes & bitter coffee all jostling mid-2016. **15** ⑦⑧ may harmonise given time. **Sauvignon Blanc** ★★★ Colene's younger, coastal-vine sibling is light, fresh & crisp, with green herb & grapefruit flavours. **18** ⑧⓪ easy summer quaffing. Not tasted: **Shiraz-Cabernet Sauvignon-Pinotage, Rosé**. — MW

Location: Durbanville ▪ Map: Durbanville, Philadelphia & Darling ▪ Map grid reference: C7 ▪ WO: Western Cape/Durbanville/Elim ▪ Est 1994 ▪ Tasting by appt ▪ Owner(s) David Frost ▪ Winemaker(s)/viticulturist(s) Rudi von Waltsleben (D'Aria Winery) ▪ 30,000cs 40% red 60% white ▪ PO Box 3556 Tyger Valley 7536 ▪ info@ frostwines.com ▪ www.frostwine.com ▪ S 33° 50' 28.6" E 018° 36' 36.2" ▪ 🗺 combo.claimants.cloudlike ▪ **T +27 (0)82-686-6854**

☐ **David Nieuwoudt** *see* Cederberg Private Cellar
☐ **Dawn Patrol** *see* Trizanne Signature Wines

De Breede Organic Vineyards ⓠ

Boutique-scale Harteebesterivier estate just outside Worcester, its organic vines and 200-year-old cellar are the source of these personality-packed wines, overseen and made by owner Debbie Alcock-Bousfield as a complement to her internationally awarded Gourmet Africa condiment range.

★★★★ **Syrah** ⓧ ⓥ Appealing freshness on bright-fruited **11** ⑧⑦ - a bit lighter, suppler, less extracted than the others, but still powerful & just as characterful.

Cabernet Sauvignon ⓧ ⓥ ★★ Stewed, porty notes on über-ripe **12** ⑦④ mask both varietal character & origin; misses structure & refinement of previous. For early drinking. **1st XI Merlot** ⓧ ⓥ ★★★★ Violets & crème de cassis abundance on **10** ⑧③. Like Cab, touch jammy but more structure-giving tannins & finesse; good juicy acidity, too. **Little Red Rooster** ⓧ ⓥ ★★ Porty black fruit with green undertones on **13** ⑦① Bordeaux blend led by merlot. Drink soon. **The Rooster** ⓧ ⓥ ★★★ Like sibling, **12** ⑦⑦ has concentrated, sweet & ripe dark fruit in rustic, porty frame. More structure here, but still very evolved for **12** ⑦⑦. **The Rooster Reserve** ⓧ ⓥ ★★★ Savoury notes to ripe black fruit on smoky **10** ⑦⑦ Bordeaux red. Firm tannin profile gives drying effect to otherwise well-expressed, mature fruit flavours. — HJ

Location: Worcester ▪ Map/WO: Breedekloof ▪ Map grid reference: D4 ▪ Est 2006 ▪ 1stB 2009 ▪ Tasting by appt ▪ Owner(s)/viticulturist(s) Debbie Alcock-Bousfield ▪ Winemaker(s) Debbie Alcock-Bousfield & Isaac Mabeta (2009) ▪ 26ha/2.5ha (cabs s/f, malbec, merlot, p verdot) ▪ ±20t/2,000cs own label 99% red 1% rosé ▪ Certified organic by BCS ▪ PO Box 511 Worcester 6849 ▪ info@burchells.co.za ▪ www.gourmet-africa.com ▪ S 33° 37' 10.69" E 019° 22' 44.79" ▪ 🗺 speeded.decorate.backboard ▪ **T +27 (0)23-342-5388**

De Doorns Wynkelder (Koöp) Bpk ⓠ ♿

Grower-owned De Doorns winery produces mostly in bulk for customers in the wine and spirit trade, but also bottles a limited range of proprietary wines, available for sampling at the Wine House in De Doorns village, fringed by vines and bounded by the soaring Hex River Mountain chain.

Roodehof ★★ Very lightly oaked, **17** ⑦④ is intended for early enjoyment, vivid cassis from cab-led blend, partnered with ruby cab, pinotage. Smooth & juicy. **Sauvignon Blanc** ★★★ Green figs, some citrus notes, **18** ⑦⑧ friendly alcohol (12%) for summertime sipping, crisply dry. **Demi-Sec Sparkling** ★★ Bubbly from sauvignon, **17** ⑦⑤ with pear flavours & grapey hints, charming sweetness. Not tasted: **Cabernet Sauvignon, Muscadel**. — CR, CvZ

Location: De Doorns ▪ Map/WO: Worcester ▪ Map grid reference: D1 ▪ Est 1968 ▪ Tasting & sales Mon-Fri 8–5 Sat 8–2 ▪ Cellarmaster(s) Danie Koen ▪ Winemaker(s) Danie Koen, with Peter James Thomson ▪ PO Box 129 De Doorns 6875 ▪ ddwk@hexvallei.co.za ▪ www.dedoornscellar.co.za ▪ S 33° 29' 10.3" E 019° 39' 43.2" ▪ 🗺 exactitude.brave.dandelion ▪ F +27 (0)86-579-1310 ▪ **T +27 (0)23-356-2100**

Definitum Wines

A decade ago, Helderberg negociants Fritz van der Merwe and De Wet Schreiber set out to be the definitive producer of whatever variety or blend they market (hence the brand name), and offer something novel or offbeat. Their fan base has grown significantly and production has increased to keep up.

★★★★ **Petit Verdot Reserve** ⓥ Good example of the grape, would do well at dinner table. **15** ⑧⑦ more serious than last-tasted **11**★★★ ⑦⑧, juicy, with ripe black fruit, pleasant dryness & subtle oak.

Arbalest ⓥ ★★★★ Cab-led 5-way Bordeaux blend, **16** ⑧④'s succulent red fruit underpinned by fine, gripping tannins; long & luscious. **Benevolence** ⓥ ★★★ Inky & dark, generous black berry fruit & managed tannins. **16** ⑧①, from pinotage, malbec, shiraz & 2 others, improves on previous. — HC

Location: Strand ▪ WO: Stellenbosch ▪ Est/1stB 2009 ▪ Closed to public ▪ Owner(s) Fritz van der Merwe & De Wet Schreiber ▪ 1,580cs own label 100% red ▪ PO Box 917 Strand 7139 ▪ info@definitum.co.za ▪ www. definitum.co.za

De Grendel Wines ⓥ ⑪ ⓞ ⓛ

A large (800-ha) Durbanville farm within close proximity to Cape Town, belonging to fourth baronet Sir De Villiers Graaff, schooled in agriculture, De Grendel is a multifaceted agribusiness encompassing a cattle and sheep stud, horses, game, blueberries and — oh yes! — wine. The venture also offers impeccable tourist attractions like indigenous gardens and a restaurant using home-grown produce, and an eco-responsible focus for the farm and staff. Central to the operation is cellarmaster Charles Hopkins, who shares the farm's values and vision. There are other Graaff-owned properties in the winelands, like cool-climate Ceres Plateau (Op Die Berg wines), Firgrove in Stellenbosch, plus other areas sourced when needed. Like Elgin, for a new shiraz bottled only in magnum, available to Loyalty Club members.

★★★★☆ **Op Die Berg Pinot Noir** ⊘ 'Op Die Berg' a reference to their Ceres Plateau property. Long skin contact, 13 months older barrels, handsome **16** ⑨① has power & concentration. Good typicity, raspberries & cherries, gentle forest floor, but oak savouriness takes it to another level.

★★★★☆ **Elim Shiraz** ⑯ⓝ ⓐ Special release, only in magnums, numbered bottles. Distinctive black pepper notes in **16** ⑨④, morello cherries & scrub. Plush, the tannins supple; sleekly powerful, stylish.

★★★★★ **Shiraz** ⓐ Never fails to impress; velvety, curvaceous, packed with flavour, deep & involving: dark fruit, savoury spice, mocha chocolate from French/American barrels. Only at the end do you get the grip revealing **16** ⑨④'s musculature. WO Coastal, as next.

★★★★☆ **Rubáiyát** 4-part Bordeaux blend, cab- & petit verdot-led, 80% new barriques 18 months, **16** ⑧⑧'s mixed berry fruit easily match. Complex scents, dry scrub, lovely cedar notes, compact tannins.

★★★★☆ **Sir David Graaff** ⓐ Honours the late founder. **15** ⑨④, now bottled, equal shiraz/cab from own Firgrove vines. Better melded, overall effect remains a powerhouse of scents & flavours. Oak influence (barriques 22 months, 80% new) is bed of fine-grained tannins, a future.

★★★★☆ **Op Die Berg Chardonnay** Cool growing conditions give elegance, intensify **17** ⑨②'s flavours, provide signature freshness. Only 60% of wine oaked but plays an important role, toasted brioche seam to the citrus. Plenty to admire.

★★★★★ **Koetshuis Sauvignon Blanc** ⓐ Previewed **18** ⑨① has a classic mineral/wet slate profile, very focused & intense. Whiff of green peas adds interest. Third of wine oaked but minimal influence, a gentle savoury note on finish. Perfect seafood fare & will age well. WO W Cape.

★★★★ **Viognier** ⓥ Floral, peachy aromas the variety can do so well; with just 15% oaking, **17** ⑧⑦ allows the fruit to shine. No shortage of flavour but has an admirable delicacy, finesse.

★★★★★ **Winifred** Same varieties, **17** ⑨② blend change: usual viognier lead, supported by semillon, chardonnay. Creative, & it works, viognier tamed, given palate breadth without losing the aromatics. French/Romanian barriques provide a smoky/almond seam, grip at the end.

★★★★ **Méthode Cap Classique Brut** ⓥ Chardonnay (64%) & pinot noir give citrus freshness to **15** ⑧⑧ sparkler. Elegantly dry, 20 months on lees & pinot noir's influence felt in the biscuit, red berry tones.

★★★★ **Sauvignon Blanc Noble Late Harvest** Scant indication of what's ahead, **17** ⑧⑥ gooseberries/ passionfruit, then an explosion of sweetness. But in a svelte body (9% alcohol), given vibrancy by the acidity. More intense than **15** ★★★★ ⑧⑤, which also unwooded. 375 ml.

Merlot ★★★★ Now bottled, **16** ⑧④'s tannins better integrated. Same styling, vivid cassis, violets, tobacco, lots to like, 13 months French barriques for ageing, structure, but already accessible. **Amandelboord Pinotage** ★★★★ Bold & ripe, with black plums, spicy/smoky depths, **17** ⑧④'s tannins well-judged for grip & backbone but fruit ensures plush drinkability. High alcohol not discernible. **Rosé** ★★★ Equal pinotage & cab in **18** ⑧①, red berry/cherry vivacity; elegant, dry, tasty. WO Coastal. **Sauvignon Blanc** ★★★★ Unwooded but 100 days on lees, so **18** ⑧⑤ offers palate weight & creaminess to bolster the intense grapefruit/gooseberry character, signature freshness. Touch of semillon. — CR

Location: Durbanville ▪ Map: Durbanville, Philadelphia & Darling ▪ Map grid reference: C8 ▪ WO: Durbanville/ Coastal/Ceres Plateau/Elim/Cape Town/Western Cape ▪ Est 1720 ▪ 1stB 2004 ▪ Tasting & sales Mon-Sat 9–5 Sun 10–4 ▪ Closed Dec 25 ▪ Cellar tours by appt ▪ Conferences ▪ De Grendel Restaurant ▪ Three Spades Cider ▪ Owner(s) De Villiers Graaff ▪ Cellarmaster(s) Charles Hopkins (Oct 2005) ▪ Viticulturist(s) Kudzai Mwerenga (2009) ▪ 800ha/75ha (cab f, merlot, p verdot, ptage, pinot noir/gris, shiraz, chard, sauv, sem, viog) ▪ 80,000cs own label 35% red 50% white 15% rosé ▪ Plattekloof Rd Panorama 7500 ▪ info@degrendel. co.za ▪ www.degrendel.co.za ▪ S 33° 51' 2.5" E 018° 34' 18.4" ▪ �📱 walked.approximates.doings ▪ T +27 (0)21-558-6280

☐ **Dekker's Valley** see Mellasat Vineyards
☐ **De Kleine Leeuwen** see Leeuwenberg

De Kleine Wijn Koöp

De Kleine Wijn Koöp is a Stellenbosch collective of 'okes who dig and produce niche wines with cool packaging. Every harvest brings a fresh set of eye-, palate- and intellect-tickling releases, and most sell out in less time than it takes these 'flip-flops and boardshorts' vintners to pen the witty notes for their labels.

★★★★ **Knapse Kêrel Cabernet Franc** Ready-to-drink **16** ⑧⑧ fresh & involving, herbal & spicy nuances to full spectrum of red fruit. As previous, & all these, untrammelled by new oak, beautifully dry & lightish (12.8% alcohol).

★★★★ **Kreatuur Synachin** ⑬ From syrah (57%), grenache (27%) & cinsaut, as name suggests. Perfumed **17** ⑧⑧'s raspberry & cranberry succulence supported by a fine tannic backbone. Well crafted but doesn't take itself too seriously. WO Coastal.

Ou Treffer Cinsaut ★★★★ Juicy **17** ⑧④, abundant red berry fruit, mildly gripping tannins for early drinking; rides the wave of light, fresh Cape cinsauts. Not tasted: **Heimwee Cabernet Sauvignon**, **Hoendertande Grenache**. — HC

Location: Stellenbosch ▪ WO: Stellenbosch/Coastal ▪ Est/1stB 2011 ▪ Closed to public ▪ Sales via website ▪ Owner(s) Hendrik Stephanus Opperman Rabie, Rohan CY Etsebeth, Pieter van der Byl Smuts van Niekerk & Jan Georg Solms ▪ 5,000cs own label ▪ kantoor@dekleinewijnkoop.co.za ▪ www.dekleinewijnkoop.co.za

☐ **De Knolle Fonteyn** see Rogge Cloof

De Krans Wines   ⑨ ⑪ ⓐ ⑧ ⑤

Boets Nel, MD of this family winery near the Klein Karoo town of Calitzdorp, compares the drought leading up to the 2018 harvest with a famously terrible one of exactly a century earlier. This time, production was severely down, but the quality is 'superb', he says. Fortunately, they 'managed to save most of the vines' (fellow-owner and viticulturist brother Stroebel deserving credit there). Focus remains 'on what we're doing well already': apart from the bistro and deli and other visitor attractions, that includes being among the local leaders of fortified winemaking, but also their table wines from classic and, more recently, 'port' varieties. See also the entries for Garden Route, where Boets sources from contracted vineyards, and Le Sueur, the label of De Krans cellarmaster Louis van der Riet. The large offering has been usefully organised into ranges.

Terroir range
★★★★ **Tinta Roriz** ⊘ Rather delicious **16** ⑧⑥, with spice, cherries & more leathery notes, but structure more formidable than usual, big tannins needing time - lingering flavour suggests enough fruit for that.

★★★★ **Touriga Nacional** Another unfortified port grape bottling. Previewed **17** ⑧⑦ has blackberry, cocoa & nutmeg notes - & much more tannic-acid structure than **16** ★★★★ ⑧④. Depth of flavour supported by modest oaking, like all these.

★★★★☆ **Tritonia Red** Touriga (70%) blended with 3 tintas as usual on **16** ⑨⓪. Dark fruit & tobacco on aromas & flavours more complex than the varietal port-grape table reds. Like them, ripe & a touch sweet. Velvety texture - a glove for an iron fist of tannin. Lingering flavours. Should develop well.

★★★★ **Tritonia White** From malvasia rei (palomino) & verdelho - 12% in rather rustic **16** ⑧⑦. Attractive pear drop aromas, an earthy hint. Broad flavours, balanced, firm acidity for freshness. 11.7% alcohol.

A Twist of Fate ★★★★ Blend tintas barroca & amarela; red fruit, a touch earthy. **16** ⑧⑤ more structured than previous, but the most easygoing of these reds; approachable & pretty delicious. **Zero Dosage Méthode Cap Classique** Ⓥ ★★★★ Unique, characterful bubbly: tinta & chenin with 60% chardonnay, all oaked. **14** ⑧⑤ yeasty Marmite & dark-fruit hint. Clean, tasty & grippy-dry. WO Klein Karoo

Classic range

Basket Press Cabernet Sauvignon Ⓥ ★★★☆ Good typical aromas of berry fruit with cedar & tobacco on **17** ⑧③. Dry tannins & bright acidity neatly balance the nearly off-dry level of sweetness, without much fruit intensity. **Pinotage Rosé** ★★ Bubblegum fragrance & modest fruit on **18** ⑦⑥, the 4.7 g/l sweetness offset by a whack of acid. Klein Karoo WO. **Wild Ferment Unwooded Chardonnay** ★★ Usual pleasant limy aromas & insubstantial flavours on rather acid **17** ⑦⑥. **Free-Run Unwooded Chenin Blanc** ★★★ Less fruity than usual, **18** ⑦⑧ has green boiled sweet notes & citrus. Tasty, but rather tart. **Premium Moscato Perlé White** Ⓥ ★★ 'White' added to name. **17** ⑥⑦ insipidly pretty, sweetish, with low 8% alcohol. WO W Cape, as next. **Premium Moscato Perlé Red** (NEW) ★★ Muscadel gives grapey fragrance, pinotage adds colour & fruit on sweet **17** ⑦⑥.

Fortified range

★★★★☆ **Muscat de Frontignan** Ⓥ Very sweet, very softly smooth but not too unctuous fortified grape juice - **17** ⑨⓪ at 15.6% alcohol. There's a real complexity of flavours, beyond the muscat grapiness, & a gorgeous, sumptuous harmony. Should develop interestingly. Great value.

★★★★☆ **Cape Tawny Limited Release** Elegantly rich fortified blended from wines 5-15 years in oak. Chocolate orange leads the complexity of aroma & flavour on latest **NV** ⑨② Remarkably light, lively & fresh effect: there's no heaviness here. Mostly tinta, with tinta amarela, touriga. WO W Cape.

★★★★ **Cape Vintage** Attractive blend of 5 port varieties, touriga in the lead at 50%. **17** ⑧⑧ barrel sample more focused, complex & lively than Ruby & a touch more powerful; less structured & intense than Reserve. Will keep, but good now.

★★★★☆ **Cape Vintage Reserve** ⓐ Renowned 'port'. **16** ★★★★★ ⑨⑤ has 74% touriga with tintas barocca & roriz - similar to **15** ⑨②. Complex aromas (nuts, fruit, dark choc) emerge from inky depths. Plenty of flavour balanced by noble spirit fire & proud tannin. Long prospects, but approachable now.

★★★★ **Original Espresso** Deliciously decadent as ever, latest **NV** ⑧⑦ fortified dessert from 5 port varieties; toasted oak adds coffee, choc & burnt nutshell character to the fruit. Beautifully balanced. 375 ml. **Premium Cape Ruby** Ⓥ ★★★★ Delicious **NV** ⑧④ fortified, pre-bottling rich & dark, mostly tinta (50%) & touriga. No great depth, offering lighter, simpler pleasure than the other 'ports'. **Original Cape Pink** ★★ From four port varieties. Some charm but latest **NV** ⑦④, as before, more of a sweet, spirity rosé than a 'port'. — TJ

Location: Calitzdorp ▪ Map: Klein Karoo & Garden Route ▪ Map grid reference: B5 ▪ WO: Calitzdorp/Western Cape/Klein Karoo ▪ Est 1964 ▪ 1stB 1977 ▪ Wine tasting, sales & deli Mon-Sun 9-5 ▪ Tasting fee R40pp ▪ Bistro (indoor/outdoor seating) Mon-Sun 10-4.30 ▪ Biscotti & wine tasting daily (booking advised) ▪ Closed Good Fri & Dec 25 ▪ Pick your own: apricots last week Nov-1st week Dec; peaches 16-28 Dec; hanepoot grapes 2nd week Feb-1st week Mar ▪ Children's playground ▪ Walking trail ▪ Hand-crafted beer ▪ Owner(s) De Krans Wines (MD Boets Nel & directors Stroebel Nel, René Oosthuizen & Louis van der Riet) ▪ Winemaker(s) Louis van der Riet (Aug 2012) ▪ Viticulturist(s) Stroebel Nel (Jan 1988) ▪ 78ha/45ha (cab, tinta barocca/roriz, touriga nacional, chard, chenin & muscats) ▪ 600t/40—50,000cs own label 50% red 10% white 3% rosé 37% fortifieds ▪ IPW ▪ PO Box 28 Calitzdorp 6660 ▪ dekrans@mweb.co.za ▪ www.dekrans.co.za ▪ S 33° 32' 6.3" E 021° 41' 9.0" ▪ 〰 keyholes.strolling.precise ▪ F +27 (0)44-213-3562 ▪ **T +27 (0)44-213-3314/64**

Delaire Graff Estate

There's much that glitters at this luxurious property on the Helshoogte Pass outside Stellenbosch town. When the first Delaire bottling was made 35 years back it was a much smaller affair (John Platter, co-founder of this guide was also the estate's father). Many new owners followed, but stability and transformation arrived with London-based diamantaire Laurence Graff a few decades later. Delaire Graff is now an art-rich locus of smart dining and accommodation - the lodges were being expanded in 2018, and a luxury villa on the way — with, of course, a diamond centre. And one of SA's pricier wine portfolios: even the third tier is branded as Luxury. The more unassuming Morné Vrey is the winemaker, bringing in grapes from elsewhere, when necessary, to supplement the home vineyards.

Icon range

★★★★☆ **Laurence Graff Reserve** ⓦ Big, powerful cab (14.9% alcohol), but the quality of dark-bright fruit, suppleness of ripe & forceful tannins, well absorbed 80% new oak, & overall excellent balance mean that **15** ⑨③'s rippling musculature has some grace & is not flashily showy. Superb example of the style.

★★★★ **Merlot** Moves to this range with quality leap in **16** ★★★★☆ ⑨② - no green rasp like **15** ★★★★ ⑧④, closer to **14** ⑧⑧. Enticing aromas fruitcake, dry spice & tobacco lead to big, concentrated but balanced palate, also mixing fruity & savoury. Strong tannins complement juiciness. 14.7% alcohol; 80% new oak.

★★★★☆ **Terraced Block Reserve** ⓦ In established style, **16** ⑨③ is harmoniously poised between restraint & exuberance, the most complex of the chardonnays. 40% new oak supportive only, as in **15** ⑨①; the vivid acidity carries the flavours to a lingering finish. Banghoek WO, like others in range unless noted.

★★★★☆ **White Reserve** ⓦ Semillon (62%) & sauvignon beautifully bound: **16** ⑨③ blended, matured in tank after 5 months in oak (mostly older). Semillon dominant in youth with lemon & wax, but hints of blackcurrant in the complex whole. Fresh; long lemony finish. WO Coastal, as splendid **15** ★★★★★ ⑨⑧.

★★★★ **Sunrise Brut Méthode Cap Classique** Characterful, idiosyncratic **NV** ⑧⑦ bubbly from 58% chenin with chardonnay & cab franc. More earthy than classic brioche; flavourful & appley, with good fresh citric bite; nicely dry. WO W Cape.

★★★★ **Sunburst Noble Late Harvest** ② Honeyed, marmalade aromas on oaked sauvignon **15** ⑧⑦. Lightly sumptuous, more charming than complex or intense; sweetness exposed by modest acid.

★★★★☆ **Cape Vintage** ⓦ **16** ⑨③ blends touriga with tinta barocca, like **15** ★★★★★ ⑨⑤. Alarmingly delicious in youth but serious, with fruit depth & tannic structure to mature well a decade or more. In classic style, sweet richness yields almost dry finish - impressively more so than most local 'ports'. Stellenbosch WO.

Not tasted: **Cabernet Sauvignon Reserve**.

Premium range

★★★★☆ **Botmaskop** ⓦ 69% cab in 5-way Bordeaux-style blend. Dark-berried **16** ⑨③ is undeniably big: in structure, alcohol (14.8%), sweetly full-fruited flavour. But the balance, & even harmony, keeps its impressiveness short of blockbusterdom. Supportive 45% new oak. Like **15** ⑨④, in magnum too.

★★★★☆ **Chardonnay Banghoek Reserve** ⓦ Like Terraced Block, a subtle green glint on **17** ⑨③ - but this version shows its 40% new oaking more. Ripe, but not too showy. Early complexity of toast, stonefruit, oatmeal, lemony citrus. Rich texture with finesse-giving good vein of lemony acid, as on **16** ⑨④.

★★★★ **Chenin Blanc Swartland Reserve** As usual, toasty oak (25% new) dominates quiet dried peach & thatch aromas & palate of **17** ⑧⑥, though flavourful fruit lurks. Slightly sweet-sour finish.

★★★★☆ **Coastal Cuvée Sauvignon Blanc** Vivid, lively **18** ⑨② from widely sourced vineyards. More intense tropicality than in other version - blackcurrant, grassy & grapefruit notes too. A splash of semillon & oaked fraction add some weight & depth. Fine acidic grip.

Luxury range

★★★★ **Summercourt Chardonnay** Forward aromas of tropical fruit, ⑧⑥, & plenty of flavour too - more intense than **16** ★★★☆ ⑧④. Fresh len

★★★★ **Sauvignon Blanc** Balance of tropical & greener fruit on **18** ⑧⑧. ing, fresh, dry & succulent, with a touch of semillon for added breadth. Fron

Shiraz-Cabe.
black fruit & pep
mai.
& mola.

★★★★ **Banghoek Chardonnay Eau de Vie** Supple potstill husk spirit digestif, with aromatic 'husky' nuttiness & sweet fruit reminiscences on quite fiery palate. 500 ml.

Shiraz ★★★ Sweet-fruited, lightly oaked **17** ⑧② Flavourful, with moderate tannic grip & prominent acid to lift the heavy ripeness. **Cabernet Franc Rosé** ★★★☆ Fine fragrance on **18** ⑧⑤, with varietal dried leaf note. Fresh, flavourful & dry, with more character & elegance than most rosés. — TJ

Location/map: Stellenbosch ▪ Map grid reference: H5 ▪ WO: Stellenbosch/Banghoek/Western Cape/Coastal/Swartland ▪ Est 1983 ▪ 1stB 1984 ▪ Tasting & sales Mon-Sat 10-5 Sun 10-4 ▪ Fee R60/3 wines, R95/5 wines, R350/5 Icon range wines ▪ Cellar tours by appt (no tours during harvest) ▪ Gifts ▪ Farm produce ▪ Walks/hikes ▪ Art collection ▪ Delaire Graff & Indochine Restaurants ▪ 5-star Lodges & Spa ▪ Owner(s) Laurence Graff ▪ Winemaker(s) Morné Vrey (Jul 2009) ▪ Viticulturist(s) Kallie Fernhout (Jun 2010) ▪ 42ha/20ha (cabs s/f, malbec, merlot, p verdot, chard, sauv) ▪ 480t/30,000cs own label 36% red 48% white 16% rosé ▪ WIETA ▪ PO Box 3058 Stellenbosch 7602 ▪ info@delaire.co.za ▪ www.delaire.co.za ▪ S 33° 55′ 17.70″ E 018° 55′ 22.08″ ▪ ⓦ warmers.rise.easy ▪ F +27 (0)86-775-1720 ▪ **T +27 (0)21-885-8160**

Delheim Wines   ⓠ ⑪ ⓐ ⓖ

A sad time for all at this family-owned winery, as well as their many fans and supporters around the world, with the passing of founder Michael 'Spatz' Sperling, one of the legends of the SA wine industry, local pioneer of wine tourism and co-founder of the Stellenbosch Wine Route. In his memory, the new Iconoclast Cape Blend is now available (not tasted by us) in small quantities from the cellardoor, which continues to charm guests with unusual pairing options, family-friendly events and homely restaurant. Winemaker Altus Treurnicht further improves the wines, while the replanting and rejuvenation programme in the vineyards takes place under the watchful eye of director and viticulturist Victor Sperling. His sister Nora, meanwhile, shares the Delheim story with markets in numerous countries.

★★★★☆ **Grand Reserve** ⓐ The flagship, always cab, **15** ⑨③ with dashes merlot & cab franc, latter prominent in smoky perfume & warm herbaceous aromas, giving way to rich black-berried fruit, tobacco & classic cedar twist. Positive tannins, lively acidity. 30% new oak. Keep, if possible.

★★★★☆ **Vera Cruz Pinotage** ⓥ Fine example of the variety; **15** ⑨⓪ follows form with dense, concentrated wild berry fruit, dark chocolate on big, bold structure, seamless texture & pure, lingering finish. Cellarworthy classic from prized 21 year old 'Protea' bushvine block.

★★★★ **Shiraz** Everything present & correct in **16** ★★★★ ⑧⑤ - black plums & mulberries, dark chocolate & spicy peppery tannins. Some wholebunch adds silky texture. **14** ⑧⑥ supple & juicy. **15** untasted.

★★★★☆ **Vera Cruz Shiraz** ⓐ Premium label showing classic northern Rhône violets, cloves & pepper on elegant **15** ⑨③. Picked over 4 occasions to give layers of smoked meat, sweet spice, fresh ripe plum & cherry. Silky tannins & texture, firm positive finish. From a single site, like **14** ⑨⓪. Simonsberg–Stellenbosch WO.

★★★★☆ **Chardonnay Sur Lie** Delicious integration already showing on **16** ⑨⓪ combining toast & butter with soft fresh peaches. 9 months in oak & on lees add creamy oatmeal notes & salty nuance on finish. Already very satisfying now, should improve.

★★★★ **Chenin Blanc Wild Ferment** Crunchy apples & pears on fresh **17** ⑧⑨, gains weight mid-palate from smidge old French oak (30% for 8 months). Zippy acidity & subtle spice keep interest going through to lengthy tail. Simonsberg–Stellenbosch WO, as next three.

★★★★ **Blanc de Blancs Brut** MCC sparkling from chardonnay, **15** ⑧⑦ spent 2 years on lees gaining attractive brioche notes & good, persistent bubbles. Soft yellow apple throughout & pleasing salty finish.

★★★★ **Spatzendreck** ⓐ Afternoon tea in a glass: honey, apricot jam, hints of sweet spice & butter from old oak. Delightful acidity balances **16** ⑧⑥ Natural Sweet from muscat de Frontignan, chenin & riesling. 500 ml.

★★★★☆ **Edelspatz Noble Late Harvest** ⓐ Glorious melange of ripe tropical fruit (pineapple, ⬤, peach), unwooded **18** ⑨③ from riesling beguiles with added botrytis notes of honey, marmalade ⬤es. Elegant & balanced, excellent depth & lively acidity. 375 ml.

⬤et Sauvignon ⓥ ★★★★ Eminently gluggable **16** ⑧③ gives silky-smooth mouthful of ⬤ with refreshing herbal top notes. Better than your average braai wine. WO Coastal.

Merlot ⊘ ★★★ Chewy tannins under leafy mulberry fruit, black cherry highlights. **15** ⑧² muted & introverted, might open with time. **Pinotage** ★★★★ Forthright & sturdy **16** ⑧⁵ mixes black fruit, eucalyptus & tweak of coffee into enjoyable everyday red, partner for steak. **Pinotage Rosé** ★★★ Tiny amount of muscat adds delightful perfume to fresh-fruited, just-dry **18** ⑧¹. Happy summer quaffing all-round. Coastal WO, like Sauvignon. **Gewürztraminer** ★★★★ Absolutely classic flavours of Turkish delight & litchi on off-dry **17** ⑧³. Decent acidity offsets sugar nicely, making great food partner. **Sauvignon Blanc** ★★★ Plenty of flavour in peach- & tropical-fruited **18** ⑧², with fresh acidity & interesting almond note on finish. — CM

Location/map: Stellenbosch ▪ Map grid reference: F2 ▪ WO: Stellenbosch/Simonsberg–Stellenbosch/Coastal ▪ Est 1971 ▪ 1stB 1961 ▪ Tasting & sales Mon-Sun 9-5 ▪ Wine & cupcake pairing daily ▪ Closed Easter Fri/Sun, Dec 25 & Jan 1 ▪ Cellar tours daily at 10.30 & 2.30 ▪ Delheim Restaurant ▪ Tour groups ▪ Gifts ▪ MTB trails ▪ Conferences ▪ Conservation area ▪ Events: see website for schedule ▪ Owner(s) Delheim Trust ▪ Winemaker(s) Altus Treurnicht (Jul 2015) ▪ 375ha/118ha (cab, merlot, ptage, shiraz, chard, chenin, gewürz, riesling, sauv) ▪ 980t/120,000cs own label 50% red 30% white 20% rosé ▪ Brands for clients: Woolworths ▪ Level 8 BBEE, WIETA, WWF-SA Conservation Champion ▪ PO Box 210 Stellenbosch 7599 ▪ info@delheim.com ▪ www.delheim.com ▪ S 33° 52' 10.1" E 018° 53' 9.8" ▪ ⌖ pointed.developer.palace ▪ F +27 (0)21-888-4601 ▪ **T +27 (0)21-888-4600**

☐ **De Liefde** see Mountain Ridge Wines
☐ **Delush** see Orange River Cellars

De Meye Wines   ⓠ ⑪ ⓐ ⓖ

There have been five generations of Myburghs on this Stellenbosch family farm, which celebrates 20 years of winegrowing under the De Meye label just as winemaker since inception, Marcus Milner, takes his leave. He retains his friendship with the family, and a track record of consistently crafted, elegant wines. Boutique vintner Francois Haasbroek, a long-time friend of Philip Myburgh and current head of operations, is moving his Blackwater Wine venture here and will vinify both portfolios in the De Meye cellar.

★★★★ **Cabernet Sauvignon** ⓐ Includes drop merlot in **15** ⑧⁹. Meaty-savoury & earthy core, tightly coiled in youth; shows classic cab restraint & serious intent, slower evolving than last **13** ⑧⁸. Deserves ageing. Combo new/2nd-fill oak, as other reds.

★★★★ **Trutina** Flagship red blend mostly merlot in **13** ⑧⁷, with cab franc, shiraz, cab. Earth, sweet tobacco, dark fruit & cocoa complexity; suppler than siblings & also restrained. Balance renders 14.8% alcohol unobtrusive.

Merlot ⊘ ★★★ Christmas pudding, dried fruit compote, savoury & sweet tobacco aromas, **13** ⑧² somewhat subdued on palate, with dry chalky tannins & fresh acidity. Enjoy now with a warming casserole. **Shiraz** ★★★★ Splashes merlot & cab franc in **15** ⑧⁵, better than last but needing time. Appealing smoky bacon & black pepper nuances in tight dry tannin framework. **Shiraz Rosé** ★★★ Perfumed red berry tone to dry, piquant **18** ⑦⁹, pithy twist shade less elegant than last but still tasty sunset/al fresco sipper. **Chardonnay Unwooded** ★★★ Dew-fresh citrus & early picked stonefruit, dry, crisp & tangy at pleasing 11.8% alcohol in **17** ⑧¹. **Chenin Blanc** ★★★★ Fresh tropical tone on single-block **17** ⑧⁴, honeyed nuance from 20% oaked component. Some grip & brisk acidity, tad feistier than last, thus better with food. — MW

Location/map/WO: Stellenbosch ▪ Map grid reference: E1 ▪ Est/1stB 1998 ▪ Tasting & sales Wed-Fri 12-5 Sat/Sun & pub hols 11-4 ▪ Fee R30/5 wines ▪ Closed Good Fri, Dec 25/26 & Jan 1 ▪ Cellar tours Mon-Fri by appt ▪ 'The Table at De Meye' open for lunch Thu-Sun, booking essential T +27 (0)72-696-0530, www.thetablerestaurant.co.za ▪ The Shed function venue (up to 120 pax) ▪ Farm produce ▪ Owner(s) Jan Myburgh Family Trust ▪ Winemaker(s) Francois Haasbroek (Oct 2018, consultant) ▪ Viticulturist(s) Philip Myburgh & Johan Pienaar (Jan 2006, consultant) ▪ 100ha/65ha (cabs s/f, merlot, shiraz, chard, chenin) ▪ 300t/36,000cs own label 65% red 25% white 10% rosé ▪ IPW ▪ PO Box 20 Elsenburg 7607 ▪ info@demeye.co.za ▪ www.demeye.co.za ▪ S 33° 49' 0.7" E 018° 49' 48.8" ▪ ⌖ movable.wisp.simulator ▪ **T +27 (0)21-884-4131**

☐ **De Mikke Patron** see Almenkerk Wine Estate

DeMorgenzon   ⓠ ⓐ

This fine, seriously ambitious estate in Stellenboschkloof does not remain content with the plaudits it increasingly gathers. Says GM and cellarmaster Carl van der Merwe: 'Focus, and continuous improvement are the main drivers at DeMorgenzon.' Supportive evidence comes from the recent major replanting programme, and he adds that 'the new plantings of chardonnay, chenin blanc, roussanne, marsanne and syrah are looking fabulous, with the maiden crop of 2018 looking beautiful in the winery'. The oldest chenin vineyard, planted in 1972, last year provided varied clonal material to be multiplied and banked for future estate plantings. In the cellar, there's also movement, with experimentation involving, for example, skin contact and wholebunch pressing. The orientation remains to 'minimum influence winemaking', including wild ferments, minimal or no filtration, and reduced sulphur additions.

Reserve range

★★★★☆ **Syrah** ⓥ Rich, opulently impressive **15** ⑨③. Unfolding intense, ripe fruit flavours controlled mostly by big but yielding grape tannins. Restrained oaking (15% new) in supportive role. Deserves good few years in bottle before broaching, will develop much longer.

★★★★★ **Chardonnay** ⓐ As always has equipoise of richness & restraint, forcefulness & elegance. **17** ★★★★☆ ⑨③ a little toasty oak (20% new) evident, but should soon integrate. Deep, concentrated, complex flavours with lively balancing acidity. Like **16** ⑨⑤, should acquire even greater character over a decade.

★★★★☆ **Chenin Blanc** ⓐ ⓦ Internationally acclaimed **17** ★★★★★ ⑨⑤ the finest yet of a great example of SA chenin in richer, oaked style. If there's silky opulence, with a core of sweet peach fruit, there's also fine, complex detail & elegance. A thrilling wine to delight for a decade & more. Like **16** ⑨④, gorgeous but subtle.

★★★★★ **The Divas Chenin Blanc** ⓐ ⓦ From section of oldest vineyard, made when Reserve Chenin can do without. Previously a **13** listed as 'Special Cuvée'. **17** ⑨⑦ as fine as the Chenin, but more stony & savoury (a hint of liquorice), the concentrated ripe fruit balanced by a thrilling acidity. A splendid future awaits.

★★★★ **Méthode Cap Classique Chenin Blanc** Warm apple tart aromas with some toasted brioche too on latest, partly oaked **NV** ⑧⑦ sparkling. Lots of apple-peach flavour, fresh & dry.

★★★★☆ **Vinedried Chenin Blanc** ⓥ Complex aromas & flavours on **11** ⑨③ include typical notes of decadent grape maturity from desiccated grapes – also marmalade, marzipan, dried fruit. Would need more piercing acid to be really thrilling, but delicious & soft textured; clean finish. Only older oak. 375 ml.

Maestro range

★★★★☆ **Red** ⓐ Led by cab & merlot, with cab franc & malbec, **16** ⑨① a little less bold & exuberant than previous. Ripe, dark berry aromas overlaid with cedar & tobacco. Ripe, rounded palate also blends fruit & savoury. 14.4% alcohol & 20% new oak in balance. Will benefit from time.

★★★★ **Blue** ⓥ Grenache 44%, with mourvèdre, syrah, petite sirah. **15** ⑧⑨ open knit, powerfully built, with kernel of sweetness playing with dry tannins. Not quite in harmony - time might resolve.

★★★★☆ **White** ⓐ Roussanne leads understatedly expressive **16** ⑨④ blend with chardonnay, chenin, viognier & grenache. Rich & broad flavours, controlled by firm balanced acidity, supported by light oaking. Subtle, complex fruitiness, also herbal & savoury notes.

CWG Auction Reserve range

★★★★☆ **Grenache Blanc** ⓝⓔⓦ ⓐ White-flower charm & delicate peachy fruitiness on youthful, fresh **17** ⑨③. Fine balance of flavour, acidic structure & textural breadth, of forwardness & restraint. Intensity of fruit well revealed on lingering dry finish. On lees 14 months in older oak.

★★★★☆ **Roussanne** Floral, citrus, spice & herbs on **17** ⑨② with honey & dried peach on the palate too. Generous, ripe-fruited breadth; gently sweet (4.4 g/l sugar) but with balancing natural acidity. Wholebunch, natural ferment. Quite easygoing, but should develop even further interest.

Special Release range ⓝⓔⓦ

★★★★☆ **Sauvignon Blanc-Semillon** Sauvignon (87%) gives great freshness & subtle blackcurrant, tropical-tinted character - but simple fruitiness not of the essence of balanced **16** ⑨② despite core of sweet ripeness. Semillon adds breadth & waxy-lemon notes. Unobtrusive light oaking.

DMZ range

★★★★ **Grenache Noir** Most attractive drinking already, **16** ⑧⑦ has ripe, spicy, expressive fragrance, generous flavours. Deftly balanced & lively, with a good grip. Matured in older oak of various formats.

★★★★ **Syrah** Another happily drinkable but not-unserious offering, typical of this range. Peppery spice, bright & dark fruit; gently firm grip on **16** ⑧⑨. Matured in barrels & foudres. Keep for a good few years.

★★★★ **Chardonnay** Portion matured in tank to preserve the pure fruit character, rest lightly oaked on **17** ⑧⑨. Bright & fresh; not intensely flavoured but satisfying & lingering.

★★★★ **Chenin Blanc** Mildly exuberant aromas, full flavours on **18** ⑧⑥; light oaking adds breadth & texture. Undemanding but very satisfying. In awe of its senior siblings - but what chenin wouldn't be?

★★★★ **Sauvignon Blanc** Passionfruit & citrus on not overly extrovert **17** ⑧⑦. Good bite of grapefruity acid well balanced by a little sugar to give an unaggressive tasty, dry conclusion.

Garden Vineyards range

Rosé ⊘ ★★★★ Appealing, copper-pink **17** ⑧④ from shiraz with 4 other varieties. Intriguing dusky, musky aromas lead to elegant & restrained bone-dry palate. Good case for rosé as more than frivolous. — TJ

Location/map/WO: Stellenbosch ▪ Map grid reference: C5 ▪ Est 2003 ▪ 1stB 2005 ▪ Tasting & sales daily 10-5 ▪ Fee R30-R125 ▪ Closed Good Fri, Dec 25/26 & Jan 1 ▪ Cellar tours on request ▪ Conservation area ▪ Owner(s) Wendy & Hylton Appelbaum ▪ Cellarmaster(s) / Chief executive Carl van der Merwe (Jul 2010), with junior winemaker Dirk van Zyl (Jun 2017) ▪ Viticulturist(s) Danie de Waal (Dec 2014) ▪ 91ha/55ha (cabs s/f, durif, grenache n/b, malbec, merlot, mourv, p verdot, pinot, shiraz, chard, chenin, rouss, sauv, sem, viog) ▪ 500t/40,000cs own label 40% red 50% white 10% rosé ▪ IPW ▪ PO Box 1388 Stellenbosch 7599 ▪ info@demorgenzon.co.za ▪ www.demorgenzon.co.za ▪ S 33° 56' 22.99" E 018° 45' 0.17" ▪ ⟨m⟩ dreaming.lobster.faces ▪ F +27 (0)21-881-3773 ▪ **T** +27 (0)21-881-3030

☐ **Den** see Painted Wolf Wines
☐ **Denneboom** see Oude Denneboom
☐ **De Oude Opstal** see Stellendrift - SHZ Cilliers/Kuün Wyne

Desert Rose Wines

Rose-like gypsum crystal formations found in their area of the West Coast, and a favourite Sting song, gave Vredendal nurseryman Alan van Niekerk and Namaqua Wines grower Herman Nel the name for their boutique wine collaboration. To note that public tasting facilities have been closed, hopefully to reopen soon.

Cabernet Sauvignon ⊘ ★★★ Food-inviting **09** ⑦⑧ has walnut piquancy, sour cherry flavours, & cool vintage's pleasant grip. Also-available **18** untasted. **Alex's Rose** ⊘ ★★★ **12** ⑧⓪ equal parts shiraz, merlot, cab, offers charred oaky aromas with rhubarb-laced fruit. Hint of cassis, then waves of chalky tannin. **Magda's Rose** ⊘ ★★★★ Cab-led (60%) **11** ⑧③ with merlot, shiraz; bright, convincing blackcurrant fruit on lightish body. Well knit, but still fresh & youthful. **Nicola's Rose** ⊘ ★★★★ Succulent mulberry, savoury nuances on silky **10** ⑧④ dry rose from cab, merlot & shiraz. Not tasted: **Shiraz**. — GdB

Location: Vredendal ▪ WO: Western Cape ▪ Owner(s) Alan van Niekerk & Herman Nel ▪ Winemaker(s) Herman Nel ▪ desertrose@nashuaisp.co.za ▪ ⟨m⟩ dorms.landowning.dicey ▪ F +27 (0)27-213-2858 ▪ **T** +27 (0)82-809-2040/+27 (0)82-800-2270

☐ **Destiny** see Mont Destin Wines/Destiny Shiraz

De Toren Private Cellar   ⊘

Precision informs everything at this boutique winery in Stellenbosch's Polkadraai Hills overlooking False Bay. Precision viticulture means picking segments of vine rows days apart, precise berry (not just bunch) selections, and meticulous attention to detail in the cellar, a converted chicken abattoir with the tower housing its unique gravity drainage system for all tanks. Co-owner Emil den Dulk is the custodian of the 'winecrafting roadmap', an exhaustively detailed spreadsheet of options & proportions for the flagship quintuple red blend Fusion V, annually taste-tested locally and abroad by regular clients, critics and sommeliers. 2019 marks year three of the move towards a greener way of doing things, with organic certification the eventual aim.

★★★★ **Délicate** Cherry & blueberry vivacity to improved **NV** ⑧⑧ blend malbec, merlot, cab & cab franc. Lively & fresh, notable vanilla & spice from 60% of wine in combo French/American oak, 12 months.

★★★★☆ **Fusion V** ⊛ Latest blend of stellar 5-way Bordeaux red has cab down to 52%, **16** ⑨④ elegant & sophisticated, with fruitcake generosity, tobacco & spice highlights framed by well-judged oak, 50% new. Seamless, it will age well. Also in larger, small bottle formats.

★★★★☆ **Z** Bright plum, spice & cedar on **16** ⑨2 'little brother'. Merlot (54%) leads cab & cab franc, malbec & petit verdot. Muscular but refined, with integrated French oak (30% new). Layered, rich & long. Also in 1.5L & 3L. — FM

Location/map/WO: Stellenbosch ▪ Map grid reference: B6 ▪ Est 1994 ▪ 1stB 1999 ▪ Tasting, sales & cellar tours Mon-Fri 9-4 by appt only ▪ Tours ±1½ hr at R180pp, waived on purchase ▪ Closed all pub hols ▪ Owner(s) Edenhall Trust ▪ Winemaker(s) Charles Williams (Dec 2008), with Martin Fourie (Dec 2015) ▪ Viticulturist(s) John Kotzé (Sep 2017) ▪ 25ha/±21ha (cabs s/f, malbec, merlot, p verdot) ▪ 15ot/10,000cs own label 100% red ▪ PO Box 48 Vlottenburg 7604 ▪ info@de-toren.com ▪ www.de-toren.com ▪ S 33° 57' 34.5" E 018° 45' 7.5" ▪ 📱 pleads.sportier.plunger ▪ F +27 (0)21-881-3335 ▪ **T +27 (0)21-881-3119**

De Trafford Wines ⑨

David Trafford can scarcely believe 2018 marked his 27th vintage on secluded Stellenbosch Mountain family farm Mont Fleur, where he made his first wines as a young architect exploring a new creative outlet. Typically unassuming, this thoughtful vintner hails time as evidence of what he considers a distinguishing factor of his acclaimed portfolio of predominantly red wines: ageability. He's showcasing this with a 10-year 'library' release of his '09 wines, a vintage he rates as one of his best (despite a harvest spent defending vineyards and buildings against raging wildfires). Weekday tastings remain by appointment; the Saturday 'open days' now have new tasting options (including 'library' wines and his Sijnn bottlings, listed separately) and a mountain vineyard walk.

★★★★☆ **Cabernet Sauvignon** ⓐ Brilliant expression of exceptional vintage, regal **15** ⑨3 pure ripe blackcurrant, dried herbs & cigarbox underpinned by suave tannins, impeccable balance & sophistication, concentration from minuscule yield, just 1kg per vine. Natural-yeast fermentation, as all. Also in 1.5 & 3L.

★★★★ **Merlot** ⓐ Complex & well-crafted **14** ★★★★☆ ⑨0 steps up on **13** ⑧8 with bouquet of violets, dark fruit & spice; svelte, balanced, with creamy oak (35% new), refined tannins & lifted berry finish.

★★★★☆ **Blueprint Syrah** ⓐ Consistently excellent & charcterful, a **16** ⑨3 doesn't disappoint. Liqueur-like plum, mulberry & sweet cherry flavours, hints of white pepper & cured meat, wonderful tannin structure, built to give years of drinking pleasure. Like **15** ★★★★★ ⑨7 & previous, grapes mostly from neighbour Keermont.

★★★★☆ **Syrah 393** ⓐ Deep, intense purple colour on home-grown **16** ⑨4, with classic crushed pepper notes on nose & palate overlying rich fruit. Complex leather & savoury spice add to luscious texture & body. Also in magnum, as is Drawing Board.

★★★★☆ **Syrah CSC** ⑨ Wind-reduced (by 50%) home shiraz crop supplemented in **13** ⑨1 with fruit from select Cape South Coast (Malgas, Upper Hemel-en-Aarde, Stanford) sites. Perfumed with mulberry & white pepper, concentrated & sleek, 14.7% alcohol unnoticeable.

★★★★☆ **The Drawing Board** ⓝⓔⓦ ⓐ Standout once-off Bordeaux blend, best barrels of near-equal cab franc, merlot & cab from own high-lying sites. **16** ⑨4 opulent yet vibrates with energy, the fine tannin structure in harmony with the pure fruit. Year new oak, further 9 months 2nd-fill casks as blend.

★★★★☆ **Chenin Blanc** ⓐ Barrel-fermented **17** ⑨3, textured & layered with fragrant baked apricot & hazelnut pie, lemon curd & quince flavours. Rich yet vivacious, citrus zest brightening the finish. 15% new oak for 9 months. Also in 1.5 & 3L.

★★★★☆ **Old Vine Chenin Blanc** ⓝⓔⓦ A gem from 54 year old Paarl bushvines, **17** ⑨2 soft floral & honey aromas with delicate apple & orchard fruit flavours, rounded & mouthfilling through to the mineral finish. Label by daughter Rosalyn Trafford.

★★★★☆ **Straw Wine** SA's first air-dried, naturally fermented, oak-aged chenin dessert. **15** ⑨1 steps up with wave upon wave of exotic dried tropical fruit, roasted nuts, honey & hints of vanilla, balanced by a swish of fresh lemon on the finish. 375 ml.

Not tasted: Cabernet Franc, Elevation 393. — WB

Location/map: Stellenbosch ▪ Map grid reference: G8 ▪ WO: Stellenbosch/Coastal/Cape South Coast ▪ Est/1stB 1992 ▪ Tasting, sales & tours Mon-Fri by appt only; Sat 10-1 ▪ Private tasting (current releases) R200pp to the CWG Trust weekdays / Sat R100pp, waived on purchase; Vintage tasting (6 wines from library selection) R450pp; The Sijnn Experience R200pp; Vineyard Walk R200pp – all to be booked in advance ▪ Closed all pub hols ▪ Owner(s) David & Rita Trafford ▪ Winemaker(s) David Trafford & Hendry Hess ▪

Viticulturist(s) Schalk du Toit (consultant) ▪ 200ha/5ha (cabs s/f, merlot, shiraz) ▪ 71t/7,000cs own label 70% red 30% white ▪ PO Box 495 Stellenbosch 7599 ▪ info@detrafford.co.za ▪ www.detrafford.co.za ▪ S 34° 0′ 45.1″ E 018° 53′ 57.8″ ▪ ⌖ unworldly.crackle.sweeping ▪ **T +27 (0)21-880-1611**

Deux Frères Wines   ⓠ ⑪

The French name means 'two brothers', here Stephan and Retief du Toit, who own and run this boutique winery in Stellenbosch near L'Avenir, where the wine was vinified before they recently got an on-site production facility. Two of the wine names, and most of the grape varieties, follow the French theme, including the chenin joining the range this edition, along with a limited-edition mourvèdre in numbered magnums.

★★★★ **Mourvèdre** ⓝⒺⓦ ⊛ Only 500 hand-numbered magnums, older barrels 30 months. **14** ⑧⑥ deep & dense, dark-fruited plums/prunes, scrub & maraschino cherries. Palate also serious, foundation of compact tannins for definition, ageing.

★★★★ **Fraternité** Shiraz, 25% mourvèdre, **15** ⑧⑦ dark toned, plush & ripe, generously spiced, prosciutto savouriness. Curvaceous, yet tannins a dry, firm presence. 2 years French/American oak, 30% new.

Chenin Blanc ⓝⒺⓦ ⓥ ★★★★ Barrel fermented/aged year, all new. Quince & tropical notes in **17** ⑧⑤, lovely ginger biscuit spicing; elegant, zesty & vibrant. The nervous tension of a racehorse.

Liberté ★★★★ Now 100% cabernet, previewed **15** ⑧③ mostly Hungarian barrels, 26 months, 70% new. Dusty spice & white pepper overlay to dark plummy fruit. Nice grip for food, cellaring, already accessible.

Blanc de Noir ★★★ From grenache, coral pink & bone-dry **17** ⑦⑧, perky red berries; light enough (12% alcohol) for everyday imbibing. WO Durbanville. — CR

Location/map: Stellenbosch ▪ Map grid reference: E3 ▪ WO: Stellenbosch/Durbanville ▪ Est 2008 ▪ 1stB 2012 ▪ Tasting, sales & cellar tours Tue-Fri 11-4 Sat 10-2; tasting by appt 1 May to 31 Aug ▪ Closed Sun/Mon, Easter Fri-Mon, Dec 25 & Jan 1 ▪ Wine & food pairing available on request ▪ Tasting platters & picnics to be pre-booked ▪ Owner(s) Stephan & Retief du Toit ▪ Cellarmaster(s)/viticulturist(s) Stephan du Toit (Jan 2008) ▪ 2.1ha (cab, malbec, mourv, p verdot, shiraz) ▪ 1,700cs own label 80% red 20% rosé ▪ PO Box 209 Koelenhof 7605 ▪ stephan@dfwines.co.za ▪ www.dfwines.co.za ▪ S 33° 52′ 51.16″ E 18° 50′ 44.93″ ▪ ⌖ molars.goat.offer ▪ F +27 (0)86-621-2425 ▪ **T +27 (0)21-889-9865/+27 (0)82-371-4770**

De Villiers Wines   ⓠ

Cellarmaster on the eponymous Paarl family farm, Villiers de Villiers makes wine under own labels and for export brands, under contract to buyers in China and a variety of other markets.

Location/map: Paarl ▪ Map grid reference: E6 ▪ Est/1stB 1688 ▪ Tasting & sales by appt ▪ Owner(s) De Villiers Family Trust ▪ Cellarmaster(s)/winemaker(s)/viticulturist(s) Villiers de Villiers (1980) ▪ 50,000cs own label 80% red 20% white ▪ Brands for clients: Huangtai Wines ▪ PO Box 659 Suider-Paarl 7624 ▪ info@devillier-swines.com ▪ www.devillierswines.com ▪ S 33° 45′ 43.3″ E 018° 57′ 40.8″ ▪ ⌖ table.pancake.purple ▪ F +27 (0)86-653-8988 ▪ **T +27 (0)21-863-2175**

☐ **Devonet** see Clos Malverne

Devonvale Golf & Wine Estate   ⓠ ⑪ ⌂ ◎ ♿

The wine brand made from vines on Stellenbosch's luxe Devonvale Golf & Wine Estate is focused since 2015 on the Friends Forever label, says longtime general manager Ryno Bernardo, and on reducing volumes to ±10,000 bottles (50/50 white/red) to simplify logistics (vinification is off-site), reduce cost and improve margins. The wines are sold mainly through the restaurant, functions and events on the estate.

Friends Forever range

Shiraz ★★★ **15** ⑧② offers mocha notes & black cherries, with commendable body & texture. Tangy acid edge, but an improvement on previous years. **Sauvignon Blanc** ★★ Rather insubstantial **17** ⑦⑥, chalky-mineral texture, fleeting muted fruit.

Provoyeur range

Shiraz ⓠ ★★★ **13** ⑦⑦ a step up on previous, with nutty, toasty notes over ripe jammy fruit. Not tasted: **Cabernet Sauvignon**, **Special Reserve Shiraz**. — GdB

Location/map/WO: Stellenbosch ▪ Map grid reference: D3 ▪ Est 1997 ▪ 1stB 2004 ▪ Tasting by appt ▪ Fee R45pp ▪ Sales Mon-Sat 11-6 ▪ Chez Shiraz restaurant ▪ Tour groups ▪ Golf ▪ Pro shop ▪ Conferences ▪ Devonvale Golf Lodge ▪ Owner(s) Devonmust (Pty) Ltd ▪ Winemaker(s) Riaan Wassüng (Stellenbosch University Welgevallen Cellar) ▪ Viticulturist(s) Southern Turf Management (2015) ▪ 117ha/1.2ha (shiraz) ▪ 5t/±800cs own label 50% red 50% white ▪ PO Box 77 Koelenhof 7605 ▪ info@devonvale.co.za ▪ www.devonvale.co.za ▪ S 33° 52' 59.6" E 018° 48' 15.0" ▪ ⌨ smile.paving.drones ▪ F +27 (0)21-865-2601 ▪ T +27 (0)21-865-2080

DeWaal Wines   ⚲ 🍴 ◎

Pieter de Waal is current owner of the Uiterwyk ('Outskirts') farm in Stellenbosch, one of the oldest in the area, having been settled in 1682; the lovely Cape Dutch homestead dates from 1791. It's been in the family since 1864, and the wines are made by two other De Waals: whites by Chris, reds by Daniël. Pinotage remains a focus, with one of the three versions named for CT de Waal, the first person to produce a wine from the variety, in 1941. The flagship bottling is off the Cape's oldest pinotage vines, planted in 1950.

DeWaal range

★★★★ **Cabernet Sauvignon** Intense dark-berry aromas, concentrated flavours in excellent vintage, **15** ★★★★☆ (90) textured, layered, with good supporting tannin structure, long savoury bite on the finish. 25% new oak 18 months. More focused than **14** (87).

★★★★☆ **CT de Waal Pinotage** (🖉) Brooding plum, fine herbs & supple tannin backbone, **15** (90) characterful, juicy & harmonious, layered chocolate & savoury notes. More accessible now than TOTH sibling yet built to last. Last-tasted **13** ★★★★ (89) also had 60% new-oak support, adding allspice complexity.

★★★★☆ **Top Of The Hill Pinotage** (🐝) Flagship & pride of the estate - only the best fruit for this new-oak-matured (18 months) label, only 400 cases produced. **15** (93) ripe plum & mulberry fruit mingle with vanilla notes on superbly structured & -layered palate - textbook pinotage, to cellar decade plus.

★★★★ **Signal Rock** Merlot, cab & pinotage combine in delightful **15** (89), Christmas pudding, dried herbs & gentle vanilla flavours (33% new oak, 18 months), succulent, with enduring savoury farewell.

Merlot ★★★★ Rich fruitcake & red berry flavours on **15** (84). Fresh & succulent, good balance & dried herb lift on finish. Drinking well now. **Pinotage** (🖉) ★★★★ A pinotage to turn non-fans into aficionados. Versatile & balanced, a fresh lift offsetting tight tannin & keeping **15** (84) twinkle-toed.

Young Vines range

Merlot ★★★ Vibrant red fruit & spice from older oak, 3 months, on easy, everyday **17** (81) sipper. Serve slightly chilled. **Shiraz** ★★★ Tasty mouthful of savoury, meaty & dark mulberry flavours in **16** (82); juicy, with upfront fruit for zero-effort sipping. **Chenin Blanc** ★★★ Unoaked & water-white, tropical fruit bounding out the glass, **18** (81) lovely fruit purity & ringing citrus freshness. **Sauvignon Blanc** ★★★ Tad less complex than last, **18** (82) green grass & citrus flavours; lean, brisk lemon zest aftertaste. — WB

Location/map/WO: Stellenbosch ▪ Map grid reference: C5 ▪ Est 1682 ▪ 1stB 1972 ▪ Tasting & sales Mon-Sat & pub hols 10-4.30 ▪ Tasting R50/standard & R70/premium ▪ Closed Sun, Easter weekend, Dec 25/26 & Jan 1 ▪ Cheese platters in season (pre-bookings only) ▪ Top of the Hill walks in season (monthly on a Sat from Sep-Apr) ▪ Owner(s) Pieter de Waal ▪ Winemaker(s)/viticulturist(s) Chris de Waal & Daniël de Waal (whites/reds, consultants) ▪ 800t ▪ 50% red 50% white ▪ IPW ▪ PO Box 15 Vlottenburg 7604 ▪ admin@dewaal.co.za ▪ www.dewaal.co.za ▪ S 33° 56' 29.3" E 018° 45' 59.9" ▪ ⌨ sampling.think.waxes ▪ T +27 (0)21-881-3711

Dewaldt Heyns Family Wines   ⚲

These wines are made by Dewaldt Heyns (and may be sampled) at the winery with which he is more famously associated — Saronsberg in Tulbagh. But the grapes are off the family farm in the Swartland, and the name of the range is offered as a tribute to the hard work of his father among the vines.

Weathered Hands range

★★★★ **Pinotage** From old bushvines; very fine, silky **14** (88) harmoniously melds ripe plum fruit with vanilla oak (55% new, 22 months), gears up on less structured, sweet-tasting **13** ★★★★ (85).

★★★★ **Shiraz** (🖉) Stunning **15** ★★★★★ (93) deep, dark & brooding, spicy bramble fruit toned by earthy elements, folded with wonderfully fine tannins. Serious wine, delicious in youth, will reward patience. Raises the bar on **14** (87), surprisingly poised given 14.7% alcohol. 60% new French oak.

★★★★☆ **Chenin Blanc** ⊛ From ±40 year old bushvines on weathered granite, limpid **17** ⑨③ is sumptuous but refined, vinous rather than fruity. Perfumed, with big, rich structure, quickened by minerality. French oak, 40% new. First made since **13** ⑨③.— DS

Location: Tulbagh/Swartland ▪ WO: Swartland ▪ Est/1stB 2006 ▪ Tasting by appt at Saronsberg Cellar ▪ Owner(s) Dewaldt Heyns Family Wines ▪ Cellarmaster(s)/winemaker(s)/viticulturist(s) Dewaldt Heyns ▪ (ptage, shiraz, chenin) ▪ 15t/1,100cs own label 60% red 40% white ▪ dewaldt@dewaldtheyns.com ▪ **T +27 (0)82-441-4117**

De Wet Cellar ⓆⓎⒺⓄⓏ

Much of this go-ahead grower-owned winery's cellar near Worcester is devoted to export giant and partner FirstCape, but the De Wet label gets equal love and attention. Cases in point are the new packaging for the MCC, greater focus on classic varieties, and new tasting venue manager. A new post has been created to enhance client service, and priority is given to automation and technology 'to ensure and protect quality'.

★★★★ **Chardonnay** ⊘ Packs lot of character into svelte body. **17** ⑧⑧ preserved lime, vanilla biscuit & lovely palate weight; fuller, more concentrated than you'd expect at 12% alcohol. Ends savoury.

★★★★ **Chenin Blanc Wood Matured** ⊘ From single block, **17** ⑧⑥ 8 months in barrel, good chenin fruit typicity, intriguing ginger savoury underpin. Individual, tasty. Up a notch on **16** ★★★★ ⑧⑤.

★★★★ **Cravate** ⓆⓏ Serious-minded **11** ⑧⑦ brut MCC bubbly from chardonnay, 4 years on lees. Yeasty biscuit nose & mouthfilling mousse, elegant ripe peach & citrus notes, clean lemon finish.

★★★★ **Red Muscadel** ⊘ Fortified muscat an area talent, & **17** ⑧⑨ confirms it: raisins & dried stone-fruit scents, but the taste is the real pleasure, richly sweet, like drinking raisins. Well priced, as Hanepoot.

★★★★ **White Muscadel** ⓆⓏ Honey & lemon, some dried apricot on **16** ⑧⑦ fortified, even floral notes — many layers of interest here including flavours of liquidised sultanas. Serve chilled with really good cheese.

Hanepoot ⊘ ⊛ ★★★ One sniff & memories surface of fat, juicy muscat grapes, but fortified **17** ⑧① offers more: mouthcoating sweet opulence, dried fruit flavours, barley sugar. Serve well-chilled.

Shiraz ★★★ Older barrels allow **17** ⑧⓪ fruit expression, cherries & hedgerow berries, nicely spiced, enough tannin grip for ageing few years. **Merlot-Cabernet Sauvignon** ⊘ ★★★ Cellar calls it the 'braai wine', fitting description for **17** ⑧⓪; berries & plums, a toasty nuance, grip at the end. **Cape Blend** ⓆⓏ ★★★ Petit verdot-led, with pinotage & shiraz, **16** ⑧① is dark toned, fruit the main player. With oak adding some spicing, definition, designed for early enjoyment. **Petillant Rosé** ⓆⓏ ★★★ From pinotage, **NV** ⑦⑧ with a fresh-picked grapiness, lively bubbles & touch of sweetness adding to the appeal. **Chenin Blanc** ⊘ ★★★ Smells & tastes like just-sliced apple & pear, **18** ⑧① wonderfully fruity, zesty lime-acid grip. **Petillant Fronté** ⓆⓏ ★★ Semi-sweet perlé from white muscadel, **NV** ⑦④ ⑦ prominent muscat & sultana aromas, comes across fresher on palate, acidity adding lift. Low 8% alcohol. **Sauvignon Blanc** ⊘ ★★★ Passionfruit & guava speak of youth & vitality, **18** ⑧① ends crisply fresh, appetising. **Special Late Harvest** ⓆⓏ ★★★ Forthcoming sultana richness is the first impression of **16** ⑦⑧'s bouquet, but there's enough acidity to balance the sweetness, give tasty enjoyment. **Cape Ruby** ⓆⓏ ★★★★ For drinking rather than cellaring, **NV** ⑧④ 'port' a fruitcake delight, enough spicing to add to attraction, smooth & satisfyingly round. Not tasted: **Cabernet Sauvignon**. — CR

Location/map/WO: Worcester ▪ Map grid reference: B3 ▪ Est 1946 ▪ 1stB 1964 ▪ Tasting Mon-Fri 9-5 Sat 9-2 ▪ Closed all pub hols ▪ Cellar tours by appt ▪ Cheese platters ▪ BYO picnic ▪ Wedding/function venue for hire ▪ Owner(s) 25 members ▪ Manager Tertius Jonck ▪ Winemaker(s) Tertius Jonck (Sep 2007) & Phillip Vercuiel (Dec 2007) ▪ Viticulturist(s) Hennie Visser (Jul 2008, VinPro) ▪ 1,000ha (cab, shiraz, chard, chenin, sauv) ▪ 19,000t/30,000cs own label 29% red 36% white 5% rosé 30% fortified + 10m L bulk ▪ ISO 22000, SGS ▪ PO Box 16 De Wet 6853 ▪ admin@dewetcellar.co.za ▪ www.dewetcellar.co.za ▪ S 33° 36'24.2" E 019° 30'36.5" ▪ ⓔ ecology.network.moderate ▪ F +27 (0)23-341-2762 ▪ **T +27 (0)23-341-2710**

De Wetshof Estate ⓆⓄⓏ

The third generation of the De Wet wine dynasty are doing parents and industry veterans, Danie and Lesca, proud. Johann, viticulture-savvy CEO and international marketer of their Robertson 'house of chardonnay', was 2018 Western Cape Young Farmer of the Year, for his work on new clones and virgin sites. Sibling Peter makes the acclaimed wine, alongside his father, stalwart Mervyn Williams and recent arrival Danie Morkel, and finesses the finances. Their annual Chardonnay Celebration is a SA winelands highlight, most recently hosting renowned UK wine expert Steven Spurrier, a man with a singular connection with chardonnay.

★★★★ Naissance Cabernet Sauvignon Plush plum fruit, graphite, subtle oak & choc-mocha on **16** (88). Excellent balance & velvety tannins from 18-24 months 40% new French barrels. Will reward patience.

★★★★ Thibault (ℚ) Impressive Bordeaux-style red, one of handful made over the years. **10** (87) merlot (88%) & cab; plush, harmonious plum & vanilla. Elegant, with a supple tannin structure.

★★★★ Nature In Concert Pinot Noir Heady violet perfume leads out silky red berry fruit on **17** (87), first since **13** (88). Svelte & savoury in youth; on past form, will gain satisfying earthiness with age. Older oak. Also in magnum.

★★★★☆ Bateleur Chardonnay Majestic flagship from same single-vineyard since **91**. Aromatic **16** (91) has abundant citrus fruit layered with vanilla oak (year, 100% new) in firm, crafted body. Regal, harmonious, built to last. **15** sold out untasted. Also in 1.5, 3 & 5L.

★★★★ Finesse Chardonnay Best balanced of the chardonnay quintet, mix of clones in variety of limestone blocks. Elegant **17** (89)'s citrus enriched by butterscotch from lees ageing in 10% new wood, lifted by fresh tail.

★★★★☆ The Site Chardonnay (ℚ) Fine new-barrel-fermented version from estate's oldest single block, 17B, planted in 1986. **15** (93) shows steely lemon zest freshness supported by creamy vanilla; breadth & texture with a touch of chalky mineral chiming in on the finish. Ageworthy & a real gem.

★★★★ Bon Vallon Chardonnay Pure expression untrammelled by oak, tank sample **18** (87) also mouthfillingly rich from weekly lees stirring, adding butteriness to fresh granadilla fruit. Fuller body than Limestone sibling.

★★★★ Limestone Hill Chardonnay (⊘) Flavourful unoaked, lees-aged rendition of the variety. Fresh lemon notes on **18** (86), crisp depth of flavour from lime-rich clay soils, just-dry lipsmacking sweet-sour tang. Improves on **17 ★★★★** (84).

★★★★ Riesling A preview last time, **17** (87)'s perfumed orange blossom & stonefruit underpinned by riverstone minerality, technically semi-sweet yet crisp, food-friendly tail now gaining breadth in bottle.

★★★★ Sauvignon Blanc Charming **18** (86) fresh & floral, good mix of lemon & lime flavours backed by ripe tropicality & roundness from 3 months lees ageing. Broad rather than bracing, as sauvignon can be.

★★★★ Méthode Cap Classique Pinot Noir Brut Elegant bottle-fermented sparkling, from the fine languid bead through rich, warm bakery aromas to chiselled, complex finish. **11 ★★★★☆** (90) steps up on copper-tinged **10** (87). 5+ years on lees, zero dosage. Rich, deep & expansive; very satisfying.

★★★★ Méthode Cap Classique Cuvée Brut (ℚ) Champagne-method sparkler from chardonnay & pinot noir; **09** (87) exotic bouquet of leesy yellow fruit, apple cake & honey. Super focus & length.

★★★★☆ Edeloes (ℚ) Exceptional botrytised riesling dessert wine, occasional release. **06** (92) is voluptuous, complex & rich, with bright pineapple & apricot flavours complemented by pristine acid backbone for a clean lifted finish. Terrific length. 500 ml. — DS

Location/map/WO: Robertson ▪ Map grid reference: C4 ▪ Est 1949 ▪ 1stB 1972 ▪ Tasting & sales Mon-Fri 8.30–4.30 Sat 9.30–12.30 ▪ Closed Easter Fri/Sun/Mon, May 1, Dec 25/26 & Jan 1 ▪ Cellar tours by appt Mon-Fri 8.30-4.30 ▪ Conservation area ▪ Owner(s) Danie, Peter & Johann de Wet ▪ Cellarmaster(s) Danie de Wet (Jan 1973) ▪ Winemaker(s) Danie de Wet (Jan 1973), Mervyn Williams (2001), Peter de Wet (2007) & Danie Morkel (2017) ▪ Viticulturist(s) Rudolf Kriel (2012), advised by Phil Freese & Francois Viljoen (both 1997) ▪ 600ha/180ha (cab, merlot, pinot, chard, riesling, sauv) ▪ 1,800t 8% red 90% white 1% rosé 1% MCC ▪ ISO 9001:2015, ISO 22000:2005, BBBEE Grade 6, CVC, Enviro Scientific, Integrity & Sustainability, IPW, WWF-SA Conservation Champion ▪ PO Box 31 Robertson 6705 ▪ info@dewetshof.com ▪ www.dewetshof.com ▪ S 33° 52'38.0" E 020° 0'35.1" ▪ ⌖ unspecified.trapped.fence ▪ **T +27 (0)23-615-1853**

☐ **De Wit Family** *see Signal Gun Wines*

DGB (Pty) Ltd

Well-established producer with a strong portfolio of premium wine brands including Bellingham, Boschendal, Brampton, Douglas Green, Franschhoek Cellar, Old Road Wine Company, Tall Horse, The

Beachhouse, The Bernard Series and The Saints, and international labels such as Culemborg, Millstream and Oude Kaap, some listed separately.

Location: Wellington ▪ Est 1942 ▪ Closed to public ▪ Owner(s) DGB Brait SE ▪ Winemaker(s)/viticulturist(s) see under Bellingham, Boschendal, Brampton & Franschhoek Cellar ▪ Private Bag X03 Groot Drakenstein 7680 ▪ info@dgb.co.za ▪ www.dgb.co.za ▪ T +27 (0)21-001-3150

☐ **Diamond Collection** *see* Lutzville Vineyards

Die Bergkelder Wine Centre

Literally 'Mountain Cellar', after the maturation facilities deep within Stellenbosch's Papegaaiberg, Die Bergkelder is the home of Fleur du Cap, listed separately. FdC wines can be tasted during a cellar tour and monthly salt pairing dinners, while other premium and super-premium wines in the Distell portfolio can be tasted and purchased at Die Bergkelder Wine Centre. The Vinotèque, now in its 35th year, markets fine wines with the option of having purchases stored in perfect cellar conditions. T +27 (0)21-809-8281 ▪ info@ vinoteque.co.za ▪ www.vinoteque.co.za.

Location: Stellenbosch ▪ All day tasting & sales Mon-Fri 8–5 Sat 9–2 ▪ Tour fee R60pp ▪ Open non-religious pub hols ▪ Tours Mon-Fri 10, 11, 2 & 3; Sat 10, 11 & 12; incl AV presentation; bookings: info@bergkelder. co.za ▪ T +27 (0)21-809-8025 ▪ Special group tours, private tastings by appt ▪ Owner(s) Distell ▪ PO Box 184 Stellenbosch 7599 ▪ info@bergkelder.co.za ▪ www.bergkelder.co.za ▪ S 33° 56'8.8" E 018° 50'54.7" ▪ ▦ staring.gliders.apples ▪ F +27 (0)21-883-9533 ▪ T +27 (0)21-809-8025

Die Kat se Snor

The cat's whiskers are more like a moustache (the primary Afrikaans meaning of 'snor') on the label of Gerhard Smith's own project – so there's humour as well as high ambition involved. Gerhard's 'day job' is making wine for Creation Wines in the Hemel-en-Aarde (where he was previously winemaker at La Vierge). His focus here will be on pinot noir, made with minimal intervention – 'with other projects where opportunity and fantastic grapes make themselves available'.

★★★★ **Cinsaut** Cherry & strawberry fruit-sweetness on delicious **17** ⑧⑨ expertly wrapped by lithe grape tannins, buoyed by tangy acidity. Unforced, moderate 13.6% alcohol, quietly confident. Just 750 bottles. Only older oak, 10 months, for these.

★★★★ **Pinot Noir** Overberg vines, **15** ⑧⑧ quintessential pinot with bright cherry & raspberry fruit, attractive goût de terroir earthiness, shape-giving acid backbone. 20% wholebunch, 100% for siblings.

★★★★☆ **Chardonnay** Exceptionally fine, well-considered offering. Energised cool-climate lemons & limes, Indian spice nuances, harmonious structure. **17** ⑨⓪ from Hemel-en-Aarde Valley grapes.— WB, CvZ

Location: Hermanus ▪ WO: Stellenbosch/Overberg/Hemel-en-Aarde Valley ▪ Est/1stB 2014 ▪ Closed to public ▪ Owner(s) Gerhard Smith ▪ Winemaker(s)/viticulturist(s) Gerhard Smith (Jan 2014) ▪ Own label 70% red 30% white ▪ katsesnorwines@gmail.com ▪ T +27 (0)76-254-0294

☐ **Die Laan** *see* Stellenbosch University Welgevallen Cellar

Die Mas van Kakamas

The family-owned business of ex-teachers Vlok and Welna Hanekom continues to evolve and grow. Their 1,400-ha estate on the Orange River near Kakamas in the Northern Cape produces table grapes, dried fruit as well as wines and distilled products, the latter now joined by a handcrafted dry gin, a first for the region.

Brandy range
Die Kalahari Truffel ⑫ ★★★★ 5 year old 100% potstill from chenin delights with soft, svelte flavours of dried fruit, hints of vanilla oak with dark chocolate & roasted almonds on the finish. **Vêr In Die Ou Kalahari** ⑫ ★★★ 3 year old blended brandy from chenin is robust, fresh & vibrant, brims with ripeness & sweet fruit. Has fiery Kalahari sunsets deeply embedded in it.

Die Mas range
Not tasted: **Cabernet Sauvignon**, **Merlot**, **Pinotage**, **Shiraz**, **Chardonnay**, **Sauvignon Blanc**.
Discontinued: **Petit Verdot**.

Rooi Kalahari range
Not tasted: **Rooi Muskadel, Cape Vintage**.

Goue Kalahari range
Not tasted: **Hanepoot, Wit Muskadel**. — WB

Location: Kakamas ▪ Map: Northern Cape, Free State & North West ▪ Map grid reference: B8 ▪ WO: Northern Cape ▪ Est/1stB 2005 ▪ Tasting, sales & cellar tours Mon-Fri 8-5 Sat/pub hols 9-2 ▪ Closed Dec 25 ▪ Meals/refreshments by appt; or BYO picnic ▪ Facilities for children ▪ Tour groups ▪ Gift shop ▪ Farm produce ▪ Conferences ▪ Walks/hikes ▪ MTB trail ▪ Conservation area ▪ Camping facilities, 3 self-catering chalets & large lapa/bush pub ▪ Owner(s) Die Mas Boerdery (Pty) Ltd ▪ Cellarmaster(s)/winemaker(s) André Landman (Apr 2016) ▪ 1,400ha/80ha (cab, merlot, muscadel r/w, p verdot, pinot, ptage, sangio, shiraz, souzão, tinta, touriga, chard, chenin, cbard, sauv, viog) ▪ 700t/4,000cs own label 30% red 20% white 50% brandy ▪ PO Box 193 Kakamas 8870 ▪ wine@diemas.co.za ▪ www.diemas.co.za ▪ S 28° 45′ 48.59″ E 020° 38′ 26.45″ ▪ [*w*] culturing.potting.room ▪ F +27 (0)86-531-9243 ▪ **T +27 (0)54-431-0245/+27 (0)71-015-7131**

Diemersdal Estate

Dating back to 1698, with records showing that wine has been made here since 1702, this landmark property on the slopes of Durbanville's Dorstberg has been home to the Louw family since 1885. The palm trees planted by oupa Matthys may now be as tall as the whitewashed gables but sixth-generation winemaker Thys is mostly focused on the extensive plantings of sauvignon blanc. He and his estimable team make nine sauvignons (including dry, sweet and even a rosé with a splash of cab) for the estate portfolio alone (see Sir Lambert Wines and Sauvignon Wines entries for variations on the theme). And they're planting more, and expanding the cellar production area accordingly.

MM Louw range

★★★★☆ **Cabernet Sauvignon** ⓐ Classic Durbanville elegance & grace yet a firm structure too, **16** ⑨③ with herbal nuance. 100% new oak beautifully balanced by deep red & black fruit, the cigarbox, polished leather nuances well integrated.

★★★★☆ **Pinotage** ⓝⒺⓦ Voluptuous plums, exotic spice & dark chocolate, **16** ⑨⓪'s boldness underpinned by good tension between fruit, acid & tannin, negating the big alcohol (15.3%). Durbanville WO.

★★★★☆ **Sauvignon Blanc** ⓐ Flagship white from estate's oldest sauvignon vines. **17** ⑨③ serious, understated, vanilla from 40% new oak tempering vivacious & exceptionally persistent grape- & stonefruit flavours.

Reserve range

★★★★☆ **Pinotage** ⓐ As previous, shows brasher side of variety's personality - **17** ⑨④ spicy & rich plum, mulberry fruit, substantial 14.8% alcohol. All under control of velvety but effective tannins & 16 months in French oak, adding gravity & a future for the patient. WO Durbanville, as next.

★★★★☆ **Private Collection** ⓐ Seamless 5-way Bordeaux blend led by cab & merlot (54/25) in **16** ⑨④. Pure fruited, with polished tannins & impressive intensity. Continues higher standard set by **15** ⑨②.

★★★★☆ **Wild Horseshoe Sauvignon Blanc** This more recent skin-fermented (4 days) version of estate's signature grape gets yet more textural richness from extended lees contact & 11 months in oak, 20% new. **17** ⑨① ripe apple, light honey & citrus flavours. Natural ferment, no filtration.

★★★★☆ **8 Rows Sauvignon Blanc** ⓐ Row selection from old block, dry farmed (as all estate's vines). Unwooded **18** ⑨④ luminous purity, aromatic intensity & flinty minerality, gains a textural element from lees stirring. A big presence which will age with distinction.

★★★★☆ **Sauvignon Blanc** ⓐ Ample concentration & intensity in this unoaked bottling. Complexity, too: lime, quince, nettle & smoky hint in a full body toned by 4 months sur lie. Impressive balance between **18** ⑨①'s richness & fruit acidity sets up a fine future. Decant in youth to get all the nuances.

★★★★☆ **Noble Late Harvest Sauvignon Blanc** ⓧ Thrilling & moreish **16** ⑨③ botrytis dessert entices those seeking luscious sweetness with zesty sauvignon kick. Dried fruit in a savoury mantle with nuts & caramel from older oak; beautifully balanced & persistent. Last tasted was **03**.

Discontinued: **Grenache**.

Diemersdal Estate range

★★★★ **Pinotage** Less restrained than Reserve, 17 (88) also less reliant on oak than 16 ★★★★ (84), better structured & with variety's fresh acid lift. Succulent plums, savoury nuance & dried herbs to enjoy.

★★★★ **Chardonnay Unwooded** Most attractive fruit-centric styling, 18 (87)'s lemon zest, crisp apple & delicate spring blossom notes get bit more serious on palate via mineral & grapefruit pith nuances.

★★★★☆ **Grüner Veltliner** ⓥ Exotic alternative to sauvignon, complex, lean & mineral Austrian variety lures with pepper, greengage & citrus fruit, trailed by sweet gush of stonefruit. 17 (93) youthfully tight, with racy acidity & flinty finish.

★★★★ **Sauvignon Blanc** Abundant tropicality in 18 (86), with lime zest juiciness, brisk acidity checked by few grams sugar, moderate 13% alcohol. Perfect solo, but many food options too. Try goat's cheese crostini. Now also in magnum.

★★★★ **Winter Ferment Sauvignon Blanc** ⓦ Intricate vinification: grape must kept frozen pre-ferment (in tank) till until onset of winter, ±4 months, to increase flavour intensity. Fragrant 18 ★★★★☆ (93) more intense, complex, than 17 (87), same delicious balance & varietal flavours.

Sauvignon Rosé ⓣ ★★★☆ Flirty luminous pink, rosepetal perfume, dry red-berry crunch & lemon peel conclusion. 18 (84) usual combo cabernet & sauvignon blanc (93%), latter's acidity balanced by gram sugar for delicious everyday drinking.

Malbec ★★★☆ Brooding mulberry, pot-pourri & earthy spices on broad & textured 17 (85). French & smidgen American oak for support, satisfying dryness for food. **Merlot** ★★★☆ Rich & fruity 17 (84) appeals with dark plum, fruitcake & warm spice wrapped in vanilla. Nicely dry, though, thus food-friendly too. Durbanville WO. **Shiraz** ★★★☆ Durbanville & Swartland serve up savoury mouthful of cured meat, smoke & thatch, pleasantly sweetened with fruit pastille notes. 17 (85) fleshy, with balancing cranberry zip.

Matys range

Sauvignon Blanc ⓣ ★★★☆ Just the ticket for an uncomplicated summer libation: 18 (83) white & yellow stonefruit, citrus zing, smooth & friendly to the end.

Cabernet Sauvignon-Merlot ★★★ 74/26 blend in 17 (78) slips down easily, tasty red & black berries, vanilla hint from 14 months older oak, light brush of tannin. WO W Cape for these. — WB

Location: Durbanville ▪ Map: Durbanville, Philadelphia & Darling ▪ Map grid reference: D7 ▪ WO: Cape Town/Durbanville/Western Cape/Coastal ▪ Est 1698 ▪ 1stB 1976 ▪ Tasting & sales Mon-Sat/pub hols 9–5 Sun 10–3 ▪ Closed Good Fri, Dec 25 & Jan 1 ▪ Cellar tours by appt ▪ Diemersdal Farm Eatery ▪ Owner(s) Tienie Louw ▪ Winemaker(s) Thys Louw & Mari Branders, with Juandré Bruwer ▪ Viticulturist(s) Div van Niekerk (1980) ▪ (cab, grenache, malbec, merlot, p verdot, ptage, shiraz, chard, grüner veltliner, sauv) ▪ 50% red 50% white ▪ BRC, HACCIP ▪ PO Box 27 Durbanville 7551 ▪ info@diemersdal.co.za ▪ www.diemersdal.co.za ▪ S 33° 48' 6.3" E 018° 38' 25.1" ▪ ⓦ reductive.poppy.loincloths ▪ **T +27 (0)21-976-3361**

Diemersfontein Wines   ⓠ ⓨ ⓐ ⓞ

Entrepreneurial owners David and Susan Sonnenberg hoped to plant more of their vineyard with its signature variety, pinotage, if rains during winter 2018 broke the Cape's three-year drought - good news for devotees of Diemersfontein's trendsetting coffee-toned pinotage and its always-impressive Carpe Diem sibling. New is the pairing of wines with biltong and artisanal sweets, and a tasting deck (also offering the portfolio from empowerment venture Thokozani, listed separately) overlooking mountains and horse paddocks - a pleasing backdrop to the many attractions on the picture-perfect Wellington estate.

Carpe Diem Reserve range

★★★★ **Malbec** Brawny, muscular 16 (88) has intense mulberry fruit with puckering tannins, promising good development in bottle. Fruit from Bot River. 14 months 70% new French barriques.

★★★★☆ **Pinotage** Accomplished flagship label sets perennially high standard. 16 (91) follows form, with unintrusive oak spices fleshing out dense, honest berry fruit. Ripe yet balanced, finishes elegantly. 16 months in French/American barrel mix, 70% new.

★★★★ **Viognier** ⓥ Layered peach, brûlée & cream on svelte 16 (89). Complex blend of tank & 30% oak-fermented/aged portions ensure freshness. Structured & refined. Follows standout 15 ★★★★☆ (93).

Not tasted: **Chenin Blanc**.

Diemersfontein range

★★★★ **Cabernet Sauvignon** Sweetly ripe, supple **16** ★★★★ ⑧⑤ misses focus & grunt of **15** ⑧⑧ but offers satisfying drinking. Plum pudding fruit with hints of liquorice, gentle tannins.

★★★★ **Shiraz** Solid, meaty **17** ⑧⑦ has plum pudding fruit with fragrant cinnamon spicing, plenty of body & presence. Slightly chewy tannins should settle with time. Improves on **16** ★★★★ ⑧⑤.

★★★★ **Summer's Lease** Mainly shiraz in **16** ⑧⑥, offering cheerful red berries with satisfying structure & acid. Appealing & characterful, fuller, more focused than **15** ★★★ ⑧②.

Merlot ★★★★ Elegantly structured **17** ⑧⑤ has convincing black fruit, firm tannins & good varietal focus. Robertson fruit. **Pinotage** ★★★★ House's signature mocha style persists in **17** ⑧④, lending exaggerated toffee/caramel flavours to basically fine fruit. Also in magnum. **Harlequin Shiraz-Pinotage** ⑫ ★★★ Dusty blueberry & smoky coffee appeal to pre-bottling **16** ⑧① 70/30 blend. Soft & approachable, with light cocoa tail. **Rosé** ★★★ Rosepetal-scented dry **18** ⑧⓪ from grenache is pure summer pleasure. Undemanding, appealing, for early drinking. **Chenin Blanc** ★★★★ Tank sample shows appealing cling peach & dried apricot. **18** ⑧③ light, fresh & friendly. **Sauvignon Blanc** ★★★ Pre-bottling sample **18** ⑧① shows bubblegum fermentation character & green figs. Bracingly fresh acidity, likeable. WO W Cape. Discontinued: **For The Birds Red**, **For The Birds White**, **Maiden's Prayer White**.

Brandy range

★★★★☆ **10 Year Old Potstill** A serious & special crafted brandy in attractive modern packaging, hand labelled & wax sealed. Dark plum, chocolate & roasted nut aromas; seamless & mellow on palate, elegant, long & fresh finish. New blend from chenin & crouchen, 39% alcohol. 1,400 500-ml bottles.— GdB, WB

Location/map: Wellington ▪ Map grid reference: B4 ▪ WO: Wellington/Western Cape ▪ Est 2000 ▪ 1stB 2001 ▪ Tasting & sales daily 10—5 ▪ Closed Dec 25 ▪ Cellar tours by appt ▪ Wine & biltong/artisanal sweets pairings ▪ Snack platters ▪ Seasons Restaurant ▪ Tour groups ▪ Conferences ▪ Weddings ▪ Amphitheatre, contact them for upcoming events ▪ Walks/hikes ▪ 3-star Diemersfontein Country House ▪ Owner(s) David & Susan Sonnenberg ▪ Winemaker(s) Francois Roode (Sep 2003), with Lauren Hulsman (Nov 2011) ▪ Viticulturist(s) Waldo Kellerman (Aug 2007) ▪ 180ha/45ha (cabs s/f, grenache, malbec, mourv, p verdot, ptage, roobernet, shiraz, chenin, viog) ▪ 600t/80,000cs own label 88% red 10% white 2% rosé ▪ HACCP, IPW, WIETA ▪ PO Box 41 Wellington 7654 ▪ tastingroom@diemersfontein.co.za ▪ www.diemersfontein.co.za ▪ S 33° 39' 41.1" E 019° 0' 31.1" ▪ ⫿ tracks.runner.rooting ▪ F +27 (0)21-864-2095 ▪ **T +27 (0)21-864-5050**

□ **Die Tweede Droom** *see* Groot Parys Estate

Dieu Donné Vineyards ⑫ ⑪ ⓒ

This mountainside winery is a popular stop on the Franschhoek Wine Tram route courtesy of its sweeping valley views, fine food and vaunted wines, standouts being The Cross Collection reds blends and MCC blanc de blancs sparkling, benefiting from the farm's vini-viti duo's combined 50 years here.

Location/map: Franschhoek ▪ Map grid reference: C1 ▪ Est 1984 ▪ 1stB 1986 ▪ Tasting & sales Mon-Fri 9—5 Sat/Sun 10.30—5 ▪ Fee R30 ▪ Closed Dec 25 & Jan 1 ▪ Cellar tours Mon-Fri by appt ▪ Cheese platters ▪ Roca Restaurant ▪ Owner(s) Robert Maingard ▪ Cellarmaster(s)/winemaker(s) Stephan du Toit (May 1996) ▪ Viticulturist(s) Hennie du Toit (Apr 1988) ▪ 40ha (cab, merlot, shiraz, chard, sauv) ▪ ±280t/33,000cs own label 60% red 32% white 3% rosé 5% MCC ▪ PO Box 94 Franschhoek 7690 ▪ info@dieudonnevineyards. com ▪ www.dieudonnevineyards.com ▪ S 33° 53' 46.9" E 019° 7' 45.0" ▪ ⫿ vying.printers.dauntingly ▪ F +27 (0)21-876-2102 ▪ **T +27 (0)21-876-2493**

□ **Dig This!** *see* Stellar Winery
□ **Discovery Series** *see* FirstCape Vineyards

Distell

Helmed by CEO Richard Rushton, Distell Group Holdings Limited is Africa's largest producer of wines, spirits, ciders and other ready-to-drink (RTD) beverages, and the SA leader with annual turnover of more than R21-billion and customers in more than 100 countries. From its Stellenbosch HQ, Distell produces some of SA's most successful and enduring brands. After recent rationalisation, the portfolio includes the following wine brands: Alto, Autumn Harvest Crackling, Capenheimer, Cellar Cask, Chateau Libertas, Drostdy-Hof, Durbanville Hills (with local partners), Flat Roof Manor, Fleur du Cap, 4th Street, Graça, Kellerprinz, Monis (also producing sherry-style wines), Nederburg, Oom Tas, Overmeer, Paarl Perlé, Plaisir de Merle, Pongrácz, Sedgwick's, Tassenberg, The House of JC le Roux, Two Oceans and Zonnebloem. The group's brandy labels include Commando, Flight of the Fish Eagle, Klipdrift, Mellow-Wood, Olof Bergh Solera, Oude Meester, Richelieu, Van Ryn and Viceroy. Distell also provides independent Allesverloren with a range of services. See Die Bergkelder for details about the Vinoteque Wine Bank, and separate entries for most of the above.

Location: Stellenbosch ▪ PO Box 184 Stellenbosch 7599 ▪ info@distell.co.za ▪ www.distell.co.za ▪ **T +27 (0)21-809-7000**

☐ **DMZ** *see* DeMorgenzon

Domaine Brahms Wineries ⓘ ⑪ ⊚

Co-owner Gesie van Deventer's name translates as 'little spirit' but there's nothing small about her thinking or work ethic. She's less involved with the small-scale winegrowing and antiques business on the Paarl home-farm due to her role as executive mayor of Stellenbosch, but son Jacques Lategan has ably stepped into her shoes and is taking care of both vineyard and cellar.

★★★★ **Shiraz** ⓩ **10** ⑧⑦ improves on **08** ★★★★ with lots of concentrated dark-berried fruit & hints of sweaty leather. Silky tannins, lower alcohol make for thoroughly enjoyable wine. **09** untasted.

Cabernet Sauvignon ⓩ ★★★★ Creamy-rich tannin platform for pleasant & improved **14** ⑧④, alluring balance with just a touch of forest floor. Very youthful, will improve with time. **Pinotage** ⓩ ★★★ Dry, bold, even austere tannin underpin for **13** ⑧①, with raspberry fruitcake & resinous finish, touch of oak (none new). Challenging, needs time. **Quartet** ⓩ ★★★★ **12** ⑧⑤ merlot-dominated Bordeaux blend, brightly fruited, soft & enticing. **Sonato** ⓩ ★★ **11** ⑦⑥ mixes shiraz/merlot 72/28, jammy & foursquare. **Unwooded Chenin Blanc** ⓩ ★★★ Preserved figs, melon & pineapple in **16** ⑧①, vibrant & engaging. Not tasted: **Chenin Blanc**. — HC

Location/map/WO: Paarl ▪ Map grid reference: C3 ▪ Est 1998 ▪ 1stB 1999 ▪ Tasting & tours (vyd/cellar/wine) by appt ▪ Fee R5/wine ▪ Chapel & wedding/function venue ▪ Toeka store for antiques, vintage tractors & cars, light lunches & traditional fare ▪ Gift shop ▪ Owner(s) Johan & Gesie van Deventer ▪ Winemaker(s)/viticulturist(s) Jacques Lategan ▪ 12ha (cab, merlot, ptage, shiraz, chenin) ▪ 50,000L 90% red 10% white ▪ PO Box 2136 Windmeul 7630 ▪ brahms@iafrica.com, toeka@mweb.co.za ▪ www.domainebrahms.co.za ▪ S 33° 40′ 27.28″ E 18° 53′ 29.24″ ▪ ⓕ flannels.rarity.steamboats ▪ F +27 (0)86-614-9445 ▪ **T +27 (0)21-869-8555/+27 (0)76-914-5714 (Toeka)**

Domaine Coutelier ⓘ ⌂ ⊚

Briton Quint Cutler and French wife Floriane swapped aviation and humanitarian aid for wine production on a boutique parcel of 17th-century farmland atop the Devon Valley ridge. The 'Home of Cutler' offers estate reds, whites from off-site grapes, personal tastings, cottage accommodation and '270°' views.

Reserve range

★★★★ **Merlot** ⓩ Excellent varietal expression on **12** ⑧⑧: depth, silky tannins, ripe blackcurrant & plum fruit, earthy/meaty forest floor aromas. Elegantly poised, youthful & ambitious.

Coutelier range

★★★★ **Cabernet Sauvignon** ⓩ Primary blackcurrant & plum on big, muscular **14** ⑧⑧ showing youthful exuberance, backed by robust tannins & tarry/spicy notes. Improving label, one to watch.

★★★★ **Merlot** ⓩ Deep, brooding **14** ⑧⑨ has focused black fruit core, impressive weight & length. 18 months in 60% new French oak lend subtle spicy note, silky tannin texture. Improves on **13** ★★★★ ⑧⑤.

★★★★ **Chardonnay** ⓩ Generous, barrel fermented **14** leesy, solid oak, edgy acid & nutty-lemon flavours; **15** ⑧⑧ similar but richer, riper, more nuanced wood. Durbanville vines.

Méthode Cap Classique ⓩ Await new vintage.

Festin range

Red Blend ⓩ ★★★★ Merlot & cab show prominent mulberry fruit with meaty substance, **14** ⑧⑤ appealingly plump & rounded, with ripe tannins & savoury notes. — GdB

Location/map: Stellenbosch ▪ Map grid reference: D4 ▪ WO: Stellenbosch/Coastal ▪ Est/1stB 2012 ▪ Tasting, sales & cellar tours by appt ▪ Closed all pub hols ▪ Weddings/functions ▪ Two self-catering cottages ▪ Owner(s)/winemaker(s) Quint Cutler – 4ha/3.5ha (cab, carmenère, merlot) ▪ ±21t/2,300cs own label 70% red 10% white 10% rosé 10% MCC ▪ 45 Blumberg Dr Devon Vale Stellenbosch 7600 ▪ quint.cutler@domainecoutelier.com ▪ www.domainecoutelier.com ▪ S 33° 54′ 2.80″ E 018° 47′ 58.46″ ▪ ⌧ drainage.region.october ▪ T +27 (0)21-300-0649/+27 (0)79-498-0772

Domaine des Dieux   ⓠ ⓟ ⓐ

The 'Home of the Gods' is unusual in that there's no cellar — vinification happens off-site, which simply means nothing gets in the way of the fine view from the visitor venue of the vineyards (some with Italian varieties, still quite rare in SA) and Mount Babylonstoren piercing the Hemel-en-Aarde sky. Sparkling is the main emphasis (there's even a monthly Bubbly Friday) but white and red drinkers aren't neglected, and the seriously conceived rosé is the perfect foil for the platters served here (or anywhere, for that matter).

★★★★ **Josephine Pinot Noir** ⓥ Complex, spicy/aromatic mix of tobacco, roasted nuts & anise, layered with bright cherry & violets, **13** ⑧⑥ is more expressive & substantial than **12** ★★★ ⑧①.

Syrah-Mourvèdre ⓥ ★★★★ Pungently savoury **13** ⑧④ has distinct Rhône-like scrub aroma, with fruit-drop cherry on quite robust tannins. Pulling in several directions, but may knit in time. **Sauvignon Blanc** ⓥ ★★★★ Newly bottled **16** ⑧③ shows edgy gunsmoke note over sweet granadilla fruit, elegant acid. Unknit, but should settle with time. Not tasted: **Petit Rose, Chardonnay, Rose of Sharon Méthode Cap Classique Brut Rosé, Claudia Méthode Cap Classique Brut.** — GdB

Location: Hermanus ▪ Map: Walker Bay & Bot River ▪ Map grid reference: C4 ▪ WO: Hemel-en-Aarde Ridge ▪ Est 2002 ▪ 1stB 2006 ▪ Tasting & sales at the vineyards: summer Mon-Sat 11-5 Sun 11-4; winter Mon-Sun 11-4 ▪ Closed Easter Fri/Sun, Dec 25/26 & Jan 1 ▪ Cheese & meat platters; refreshments ▪ Child-friendly ▪ Bubbly Friday (last Friday of every month) ▪ Owner(s) Domaine des Dieux (Pty) Ltd ▪ Winemaker(s) consultants ▪ Vineyard manager(s) Shane Mullis & Leonore Kroukamp ▪ Viticulturist(s) Johan Pienaar ▪ 28ha/20ha under vine (pinot, mourv, shiraz & other Bordeaux and Italian red varieties, chard, sauv) ▪ 15,000cs own label 30% red 25% white 45% MCC ▪ PO Box 2082 Hermanus 7200 ▪ info@domainedesdieux.co.za ▪ www.domainedesdieux.co.za ▪ S 34° 19′ 35.81″ E 019° 19′ 50.71″ ▪ ⌧ remixing.fishers.privy ▪ F +27 (0)87-230-6286 ▪ T +27 (0)28-313-2126/+27 (0)83-536-5916

☐ **Dombeya** *see* Haskell Vineyards

Domein Doornkraal   ⓠ ⓟ ⓐ ⓞ

With virtually all their wines being sold to locals and passing trade at their roadside farm stall near De Rust, co-owner and viticulturist Celia le Roux and her winemaker father, Swepie, hit the spot with styles suitable for the hot sunny days as well as the chilly nights of the Klein Karoo.

Domein Doornkraal range

★★★★ **Kaptein** Deep brown NV ⑧⑨ fortified from red muscadel thrills with toasty, coffee, caramel, raisin notes. Xmas spices & roasted nuts round off delicious mouthful to warm the cockles in winter.

Tickled Pink ★★★ Light, fun rosé fizz (bottle comes with an ostrich feather!), NV ⑦⑧ from muscadel is fresh & floral, with pretty strawberry fruit. **Kuierwyn** ★★★ Low-alcohol NV ⑦⑧ Natural Sweet white is softly fruity for easy drinking, with hints of talc & perfume. Variety/ies undisclosed, as most here. **Majoor** ★★★★ Plenty of lemon on NV ⑧③ fortified muscat d'Alexandrie - dried, glacé & spiced. Nice balance between sweetness & acid, good length. **Jerepigo** ★★★ Clean grapey aromas on NV ⑧① fortified, with raisins & coffee adding depth & interest. Warming alcohol suggests enjoying with food. **Luitenant** ★★★★ Oxidative toffee, coffee, nutty aromas & flavours on NV ⑧③ red jerepiko. Try with baked camembert cheese. **Pinta** ★★★ Raisins & coffee on NV ⑧⓪ 'port' followed by lashings of blackberry jam & hint toffee. Tad more acid would improve. Not tasted: **Pinotage Rosé, Tanige Port.**

Swepie Selection

Kannaland Rooi Merlot ⓥ ★★★ Pleasantly fruity **16** ⑧① has plenty of interest - red & black berries, tweak of spice - soft tannins & clean finish. Lovely everyday quaffer.

Kannaland Wit Chenin Blanc ★★ Style change on **17** (74), now drier, grapefruit & lemon replacing tropical fruit, still with easy 12.5% alcohol. Not tasted: **Kannaland Wit Sauvignon Blanc**. — CM

Location: De Rust ▪ Map: Klein Karoo & Garden Route ▪ Map grid reference: B3 ▪ WO: Western Cape ▪ Est 1880 ▪ 1stB 1973 ▪ Tasting & sales at Doornkraal Padstal Mon-Fri & pub hols 8-5 Sat 8-3 Sun 10-2 ▪ Closed Dec 25 & Sun (mid term) ▪ Light refreshments ▪ Farm & regional produce ▪ Gifts ▪ Function venue on farm ▪ Self-catering farm cottage & lodge ▪ Owner(s) Swepie le Roux & family ▪ Cellarmaster(s) Swepie le Roux (Apr 2011) ▪ Winemaker(s) Swepie le Roux ▪ Viticulturist(s) Celia le Roux ▪ 2,000ha/10ha (cab, merlot, muscadel, ptage, tinta b, chenin) ▪ 110t/4,500cs own label 15% red 15% white 70% fortified ▪ PO Box 14 De Rust 6650 ▪ wyn@doornkraal.co.za ▪ www.doornkraal.co.za ▪ S 33° 32′ 43.5″ E 022° 26′ 42.6″ ▪ 🖵 saucepan.chuckle.fixed ▪ F +27 (0)86-528-5633 ▪ **T +27 (0)44-251-6715, +27 (0)82-763-5296 (farm stall)**

☐ **Donatus** see Dornier Wines

Donkiesbaai   ⓛ

The West Coast holiday resort of Donkin Bay, known affectionately as 'Donkey' Bay, and favoured by the family of owner Jean Engelbrecht (of Rust en Vrede), lends its name to this high-end label, which debuted in our 2013 edition with an exceptional chenin blanc named 'Steen'. Elements from the early days - stressing Afrikaans on labels and sourcing fruit from montane West Coast ward Piekenierskloof - continue in the excellent new pair of wines vinified by Roelof Lotriet.

★★★★ Grenache Noir (NEW) From Piekenierskloof vines, **16** (89) shows great promise, juicy berry fruit, commendable heft & charming silky texture. 22 months French oak, 50% new.

★★★★ Pinot Noir Tends towards savoury, with muted fruit highlights, convincing tannin texture, elegant finish & salty twist. **17** (86) still taut, should open up with time in bottle. Ceres Plateau fruit.

★★★★☆ Rooiwijn (NEW) Rhône blend equal 47% grenache & cinsaut, splash syrah, **17** (90) delightful floral scents, bracing raspberry fruit, subtle sweet spices. Juicy & light bodied yet precise & intense, with fragrant finale. WO Piekenierskloof.

★★★★☆ Steen (🏅) Muscular & expressive yet subtly nuanced chenin from Piekenierskloof & Stellenbosch vines. **17** (92)'s 70% oaked component offers spicing without intruding on ripe stonefruit with appealing roundness & texture. Built to last.

★★★★★ Hooiwijn (🏅) **17** ★★★★★ (94) standout straw wine from chenin, like **16** (96). Heavenly wafts of honey & dried apricots, intensely sweet, tempered by piercing acidity, achieving perfect poise & balance. 8 months in seasoned French oak. WO W. Cape. 375 ml. — GdB

Location: Stellenbosch ▪ WO: Piekenierskloof/Ceres Plateau/Western Cape ▪ Est 2010 ▪ 1stB 2011 ▪ Tasting & sales at Guardian Peak ▪ Owner(s) Jean Engelbrecht ▪ Winemaker(s) Roelof Lotriet (Sep 2014) ▪ ±35t/5,600cs own label 25% red 75% white ▪ IPW ▪ PO Box 473 Stellenbosch 7599 ▪ info@donkiesbaai.com ▪ www.donkiesbaai.com ▪ **T +27 (0)21-881-3881**

☐ **Don King** see Govert Wines
☐ **Don Morris** see Govert Wines

Doolhof Wine Estate   ⓛ 🍴 🏠 ◎ ♿

Tucked between Bain's Kloof Pass and Groenberg Mountain high above Wellington, this estate was named 'Labyrinth' by early settlers who found only one way in and out. Today visitors can safely explore parts of the 380 ha of vineyard, forest and fynbos on a walk along a 10-km stretch of river, home to abundant wildlife. 'Who knows, you might even come across the Minotaur!' quip the Kerrison family owners, whose winemaker/viticulturist Gielie Beukes aims to express the many distinct microclimates in his wines.

Location/map: Wellington ▪ Map grid reference: D3 ▪ Est 1712 ▪ 1stB 2003 ▪ Tasting & sales Mon-Sat 10—5 Sun 10-4 ▪ Fee R30/5 wines ▪ Closed Good Fri, Dec 25/26 & Jan 1 ▪ Cellar tours by appt ▪ Light lunches Tue-Sun 11-3; picnics by appt ▪ Walks/hikes ▪ MTB & 4x4 trails ▪ 5-star Grand Dédale Country House ▪ Craft gin distillery ▪ Owner(s) Dennis Kerrison ▪ Winemaker(s) Gielie Beukes (Aug 2014), with Natasha Pretorius (Oct 2016) ▪ Viticulturist(s) Gielie Beukes (Aug 2014) ▪ 380ha/38ha (cabs s/f, malbec, merlot, p verdot, ptage, shiraz, chard, sauv) ▪ 250t/25,000cs own label 70% red 28% white 2% blanc de noir ▪ IPW, WIETA ▪ PO Box

157 Wellington 7654 ▪ wine@doolhof.com ▪ www.doolhof.com ▪ S 33° 37' 35.6" E 019° 4' 58.7" ▪ restates.
reclassify.sharpens ▪ F +27 (0)21-864-2321 ▪ **T +27 (0)21-873-6911**

Doran Vineyards

André Badenhorst, veteran viticultural revitaliser of top Constantia estates, says his Elsenburg College tutors
were right: it takes 10 years to know a specific terroir. He and old Irish friend Edwin Doran acquired Voor
Paardeberg farm Far Horizons in 2010, resolving to develop it into a premium wine property. Now, nine
years on (call it an 'Irish decade'), they're confident enough to name (and plant) chenin and Rhône varieties
(roussanne, grenache noir/blanc, shiraz) as most suited to the terrain and Doran wine style. By their own
account the venture has become more serious, but essentially they're still 'two old buggers having fun'.

Doran Vineyards range

★★★★ Shiraz ⊘ Seductive **15** ⑧⑧'s plum, blackberry fragrance dusted with clove & violet, fruit
encased in fine tannin lattice. Year older oak.

★★★★☆ Chenin Blanc ⊘ Pure drinking pleasure. Quince & pineapple allure on characterful, old-barrel-fermented **15** ⑨②, apple pie richness nicely offset by tangy acidity, mineral freshness. Punches above its
price, as all these wines. WO Swartland.

★★★★☆ L'Alliance ⊘ Temporarily 'No Name Yet' last time, actual moniker does much better job of
identifying this as a (delicious & serious) field blend. Chenin, grenache blanc & roussanne, co-fermented/
year older oak. **17** ⑨① sleek & effortless, almond, honey & pear flavours, persistent mineral finish.

Arya ⊘ ⑨ **★★★☆** 2nd field blend, same varieties as L'Alliance, this stainless steel fermented. **17** ⑧④ tad
less gravity but as delightful, pear, honey & thatch, racy acidity, bone-dry finish. WO W Cape.

Pinotage ⑨ **★★★** Dark fruit, spice & roasted chicory tones, **15** ⑧① grippy tannins, savoury end. Not
tasted: **Rosie D.** In abeyance: **The Romy D, Incipio.** Discontinued: **Rosie D Pinotage Rosé.**

Horse Mountain range

No bottlings under this good-value label in 2017 and 2018.— GM

Location/map: Paarl ▪ Map grid reference: C1 ▪ WO: Voor Paardeberg/Swartland ▪ Est 2010 ▪ 1stB 2012
▪ Tasting Mon-Fri by appt Sat/Sun & pub hols 10-4 ▪ Closed Good Fri, Dec 25/26 & Jan 1 ▪ Owner(s)
Edwin Doran & André Badenhorst ▪ Winemaker(s) Martin Lamprecht ▪ Viticulturist(s) Basson Potgieter ▪
170ha/55ha (cabs s/f, merlot, ptage, shiraz, chenin, grenache blanc/noir, rouss) ▪ 450t/30,000cs own label ▪
PO Box 2143 Windmeul 7630 ▪ andrebad@iafrica.com ▪ www.doranvineyards.co.za ▪ S 33° 34' 56.12" E018° 51'
59.15" ▪ smock.debating.lavishes ▪ **T +27 (0)74-165-4028**

☐ **Doreen** see Teddy Hall Wines

Dormershire Estate

Paul and Sunette Frost's boutique estate in Stellenbosch is said to be named with an anagram for the previous owner's wife and daughters: Doris, Merle and Shirley. The wines are made by Sunette with long-time
advisor Kowie du Toit, from cabernet, shiraz and sauvignon vines with glorious views of Table Mountain.

Cabernet Sauvignon ⑨ **★★★★** As expected, juicier & earlier accessible than the Reserve, a savoury
note makes **07** ⑧④ a good food match. **Reserve Cabernet Sauvignon** ⑨ **★★★★** Selection of best
barrels, 18 months oak. Despite big alcohol, **07** ⑧④ shows balance & restraint. **Shiraz** ⊘ **★★★** First
tasted since **07** ⑧①, well-priced & ready-now **15** ⑧⓪ reflects estate's Old World styling: red plums lightly
dusted with wood spices, lithe & dry tannins. **Shiraz-Cabernet Sauvignon** ⊘ **★★★** Equal partnership
delivers red & black fruit, faint floral & tapenade nuances in **15** ⑧⓪. Cab's firm (not hard) tannins evident,
thus age or pair with food. **Fudge Hammer Rosé ★★** Smoked meat, soft red & black berries - no fudge
character except noticeable sweetness on **17** ⑦⑥, best served well-chilled. From shiraz, with pleasing light
11% alcohol. **Sweet Red** ⑨ **★★★★** Jerepiko-style fireside snuggler from shiraz, **NV** ⑧④ with intriguing
savoury overlay. Not tasted: **Stoep Shiraz, Sauvignon Blanc.** — CvZ

Location: Kuils River ▪ Map/WO: Stellenbosch ▪ Map grid reference: A5 ▪ Est 1996 ▪ 1stB 2001 ▪ Tasting & sales
Mon-Fri 8-2 by appt only T +27 (0)21-801-4991 ▪ Owner(s) SPF Family Trust ▪ Winemaker(s) Sunette Frost
& Kowie du Toit ▪ Viticulturist(s) Johan Pienaar (consultant) ▪ 8ha/5ha (cab, shiraz, sauv) ▪ ±50t/8,000cs

own label 85% red 10% white 5% rosé ▪ PO Box 491 Bellville 7535 ▪ wine@dormershire.co.za ▪ www. dormershire.co.za ▪ S 33° 56′ 27.0″ E 018° 42′ 54.7″ ▪ ⌕ clumsy.goad.annuals ▪ F +27 (0)21-945-1174 ▪ **T +27 (0)21-801-4677**

Dornier Wines   ⓦ ⑪ ⌂ ⊚ ⓰

Picturesque family-owned Dornier Wines comprises four different farms in the foothills of Stellenbosch Mountain, giving new viticulturist Arjen Rijpstra and winemaker Philip van Staden a range of terroirs to work with. They are fine-tuning their vineyard and cellar techniques to ensure full phenolic ripeness and greater fruit intensity, with more pump-overs for the red wines. The focus on identifying and separately vinifying standout blocks and clones is paying dividends, as is evident in their debuting old-vines chenin.

Founders range

★★★★☆ **CMD** ⓨ Smoky, savoury dark-berried allure on **14** ⑭ flagship blend. Still malbec-led, but now with petit verdot & cab in the (75/20/5) mix. Handsome, velvet textured, suave rather than powerful, with 60% new oak in harmony. No **13**.

Donatus range

★★★★ **Red** ⓨ Continues 4-way Bordeaux blend formula with cab in lead. Youthful **12** ⑧⑨ has large petit verdot component showing in brooding, concentrated dark fruit with solid oak support (30% new).

★★★★ **White** ⓨ Barrel-fermented/aged chenin & semillon (80/20, no Swartland component this time). Assertive & ripe, but **16** ⑧⑦ not as harmonious or intense as **15** ★★★★☆ ⑨③. Warming farewell.

Dornier range

★★★★ **Equanimity Cabernet Sauvignon** ⊘ Rich cassis on **16** ★★★★☆ ⑨⓪ & tailored ripe tannins (hallmark of all the 2016 reds), after a change in winemaking technique. Good extraction & oak spicy platform for opulent fruit. Appealing step up on **15** ⑧⑦, will continue to develop.

★★★★ **Merlot** Ample juicy appeal on **16** ⑧⑨, lithe tannins ensure structure while allowing fruit to shine. Oak & 14.5 % alcohol in balance. Even better than **15** ★★★★ ⑧④.

★★★★ **Siren Syrah** Similar fynbos notes to previous, riper in warmer **16** ⑧⑨ vintage but well managed, balanced, with ample spicy, smoky fruit in modern, approachable style. Respectable dry finish.

★★★★ **Cabernet Sauvignon-Merlot** Different ratio (59/41) in **16** ⑧⑦. Touch reticent, not as rich as the Cab but similar dark-fruit profile & bright acidity. Will evolve gracefully over 3-4 years.

★★★★ **Bush Vine Chenin Blanc** Bold, concentrated & silky **17** ⑧⑧ exudes mouthfilling apple, dried peach & preserved quince from Swartland bushvines. Both tank & oak ferment, 8 months lees ageing.

★★★★☆ **Moordenaarskloof** ⓝⒺⓦ ⊛ From block of 32 year old vines, **17** ⑨④ intense yet delicate chenin showing beautiful fruit purity, freshness & length. Fermented & matured entirely in old oak, with 9 months on lees complementing its vibrancy & distinction.

★★★★ **Semillon** Low-yield vines deliver lovely honey & lemon flavours with clean, fresh vein of acidity. Subtle, mostly older oak allows fruit purity to shine. **17** ⑧⑨ zestier than **16** ⑧⑨, but as accomplished.

★★★★☆ **Froschkönig Natural Sweet** ⓨ Preserved quince & pineapple on **16** ⑨③ 'Frog Prince', first since **13** ⑨② , also from vine-dried chenin. Decadently sweet & tangy; delightful intensity for 11.5% alcohol; a liquid dessert! 375 ml.

Malbec ⓨ ★★★ A hearty meal wine. Like previous, **15** ⑧⓪ has dry chalky tannins but more fruit, flavour, to balance. **Petit Verdot** ⓝⒺⓦ ★★★★ Core of inky blueberry fruit still encased in firm tannins mid-2018, but **15** ⑧③ should blossom with time in the cellar. **Pinotage** ★★★★ Cooler vintage & leaner tannins factor in on **15** ⑧③, showing a tighter profile than usual. Has pinotage's spicy fruit with dry food-friendly finish. **Tempranillo** ⓨ ★★★ Rare varietal bottling, offering smoke & spice with clean ripe black fruit. Like previous, **13** ⑧②'s tannins are chewy, with dry grip; best cellared or decanted.

Cocoa Hill range

Red ⊘ ⓦ ★★★★ Bottled version of **16** ⑧④, 6-way blend led by merlot & shiraz, fulfils preview's promise. Billows sweet fruit in a supple frame that exudes drinkability. A steal at the price too! **Merlot Rosé** ⓦ ★★★ Bright & tangy red fruit on **17** ⑧② pink, with lees contact adding heft. Dry, well-crafted aperitif/ summer al fresco partner.

Chenin Blanc ★★★ Includes outsourced fruit & 5 months on lees, as for Sauvignon. Dry **17** ⑧⓪ fits the clean, balanced & amiable quaffing brief. **Sauvignon Blanc ★★★** Easy-drinking **17** ⑧⓪ shows hints of stonefruit & grass. Dry, light, with waxy note.
WO W Cape, like Chenin. — MW

Location/map: Stellenbosch ▪ Map grid reference: F7 ▪ WO: Stellenbosch/Western Cape/Swartland ▪ Est 1995 ▪ 1stB 2002 ▪ Tasting & sales daily 9-5 ▪ Cellar tours by appt ▪ Dornier Bodega Restaurant: (Sep-Apr) Mon-Sun lunch 12-6.30; (May-Aug) Wed-Sun lunch 11.30-4.30 ▪ Art ▪ Conference & function venues ▪ Conservation area ▪ Homestead with 6 bedrooms & large entertainment areas ▪ Owner(s) Dornier family ▪ Winemaker(s) Philip van Staden (Oct 2015) ▪ Viticulturist(s) Arjen Rijpstra (Nov 2017) ▪ 180ha/48ha (cabs s/f, malbec, merlot, p verdot, ptage, shiraz, tempranillo, chenin, sauv, sem) ▪ 380t 78% red 16% white 6% rosé ▪ PO Box 7518 Stellenbosch 7599 ▪ info@dornier.co.za ▪ www.dornier.co.za ▪ S 33° 59′ 31.00″ E 018° 52′ 19.00″ ▪ ⌗ crib.shadows.mulled ▪ F +27 (0)21-880-1499 ▪ **T +27 (0)21-880-0557**

☐ **Dorp Street** *see* Barnardt Boyes Wines

Dorrance Wines

Christophe Durand moved from France to Cape Town in 1995, supplying wine barrels to the local industry. But, as well as meeting his wife-to-be, Sabrina, he got completely drawn into Cape wine to the extent of making his own – a first Syrah in 2001. After many years working in rented space, he established his own cellar in a heritage building in the heart of Cape Town, bringing grapes sourced from around the winelands through the city streets. The wines are made in increasingly non-interventionist manner, Christophe having 'made the choice to work with natural acidities as well as natural yeasts'.

★★★★★ Syrah Cuvée Ameena ⊘ ⊛ Thrilling perfumed spice pervades & focuses **16** ★★★★★ ⑨⑤'s cool, peppery red-fruit bouquet & warmer, richer flavours in a refined structure master-crafted from Swartland/Elgin fruit & older French oak, 24 months. Echoing finish, as in **15** ⑨③.

★★★★☆ Chardonnay Cuvée Anaïs ⊛ True to house style, **17** ⑨③ shows restraint, a classic fruit profile & natural acidity to carry its full, rich body. Elegance & poise enhanced by use of older oak only (previous had 10% new). Elgin, Franschhoek grapes.

★★★★★ Chenin Blanc Cuvée Kama ⊛ Svelte, satisfying **17** ⑨③ from Swartland. Enticing mix of ripe fruit (pear, apple) & minerals unfettered by any new oak; classic & invigorating. Coiled in youth, but depth & complexity wait to unleash the 'sensual gratification' of its name. Old barrels & concrete 'eggs'.

∙∙

Rouge ⊘ ⊛ **★★★★** Super-value **17** ⑧⑤ from trendy cinsaut, fabulous concentration of fresh flavours, ample substance & interest, punches well above its weight. **Rosé** ⊛ **★★★☆** From cinsaut, like Rouge, delivering crisply dry, spiced cranberry flavour in thoroughly enjoyable **18** ⑧④. **Blanc** ⊛ **★★★★** Fragrant **18** ⑧⑤ viognier traverses jasmine & white peach on its way to engagingly bone-dry conclusion. — DS

∙∙

Location: Cape Town ▪ Map: Cape Peninsula ▪ Map grid reference: B1 ▪ WO: Swartland/Western Cape ▪ Est/1stB 2000 ▪ Tasting, sales & cellar tours Mon-Fri 11-6 or by appt ▪ Wine shop ▪ Bouchon bistro & wine bar Mon-Fri from 4-11, www.bouchon.co.za ▪ Owner(s) Christophe & Sabrina Durand ▪ Cellarmaster(s)/winemaker(s) Christophe Durand ▪ 11ha ▪ 30t/4,666cs own label ▪ 95 Hout Str Cape Town 8001 ▪ christophe@dorrancewines.com ▪ www.dorrancewines.com ▪ S 33° 55′ 12.93″ E 018° 25′ 5.99″ ▪ ⌗ mimosas.oiliness. unprovable ▪ F +27 (0)86-588-2989 ▪ **T +27 (0)21-422-0695/+27 (0)83-409-7071**

☐ **Double Door** *see* La Bri Estate

Douglas Green

Consistent, good-quality and -value wines is the proposition from DGB-owned Douglas Green, a local wine institution launched in Paarl by the namesake negociant 77 years ago and still making friends around the world. The easy-drinking bottlings have especial resonance with young local chefs, as food partners in an annual inter-hotel competition.

Vineyard Creations

Pinotage ⊚ ★★★ Nice balance on **17** ⑳ between black fruit & charry coffee & chicory notes, finishes sweet. Appetising drinking. **Chardonnay** ⊚ ★★★★ Delicious & hugely enjoyable **17** ㉝ has lashings of fruit (pineapple, apple, mango) & tiniest lick of cream from small dash oak. Absolute crowd pleaser, perfect with or without food.

Cabernet Sauvignon ★★★ Black fruit & hints of leafy stalkiness on **17** ㉙, uncomplicated glugger, just-dry, with soft oak stave notes (same treatment for all reds). **Merlot** ★★★ Red cherry-berry fruit **17** ㉗ with smooth tannins & bitter chocolate finish. **Shiraz** ★★★ Red berries & savoury roast meat notes combine on **17** ⑳ to make pleasant braai partner to steak & chops. **Chenin Blanc** ⊘ ★★★ Forthcoming & lively **17** ㉛, deliciously sweet stonefruit taste & textured palate to partner spicy curries. Unoaked & light, lingering salty aftertaste. **Sauvignon Blanc** ⊘ ★★★ Surprisingly rich, fleshy & poised **17** ㉘, tropical fruit, musky aromas & fresh acidity. Comfortably dry for summer aperitifs. Could even age a bit. — CM

Location: Wellington ▪ WO: Western Cape ▪ Est 1942 ▪ Closed to public ▪ Owner(s) DGB (Pty) Ltd ▪ Blending manager Dico du Toit (2012) ▪ Oenologist Jaco Potgieter (2000) ▪ Viticulturist(s) Heinie Nel (Jul 2018) ▪ 50% red 49% white 1% rosé ▪ ISO 9001:2000, Fairtrade, HACCP, IPW, WIETA ▪ PO Box 246 Wellington 7654 ▪ douglasgreen@dgb.co.za ▪ www.douglasgreenwines.com ▪ F +27 (0)21-864-1287 ▪ **T +27 (0)21-864-5300**

Douglas Wine Cellar - Landzicht Wyn ⓠ ⊚

Far-flung, but no less dynamic than its colleagues in the south, Douglas Cellar is planting a significant 100 ha of vines over the next four years to supply its portfolio, which forms part of the much larger Northern Cape agribusiness GWK. An updated tasting venue awaits visitors to the premises in the town of Douglas, where the house brandy and on-trend new gin can also be sampled.

Winemakers Reserve range

Sauvignon Blanc ★★★ Very pleasant mouthful of grapefruit & gooseberry, **18** ㉛ slightly confected but no harm done, all set for summer sunshine. WO W Cape. Not tasted: **Cabernet Sauvignon Reserve**, **Merlot Reserve**, **Petit Verdot**.

Landzicht range

Red Muscadel ⊚ ★★★ Now vintage dated, **17** ⑳ fortified steps up on previous with touch more acidity nicely balancing flowery flavours with luscious oxidative notes (toffee, nuts).

Cabernet Sauvignon ★★ Ripe blackcurrant-toned **17** ㉖ has attractive green edge to fruit, soft tannins & appealing freshness. **Merlot** ★★ Ripe, fat, plummy fruit on **17** ㉔ backed by sturdy tannins & hints of black fruit jam. **Nagmaalwyn** ★★★ Pronounced & pleasing grape & raisin aromas on **NV** ⑳ sacramental wine, lashings of sugar & nice, balancing acidity. **Chenin Blanc** ★★★ Off-dry **18** ㉗ has plenty of aromatics (pineapple, litchi, waxy notes) but tails off a little at the finish. Pleasant if unexciting. **Rosenblümchen** ★★ Candyfloss pink **NV** ㉓ Natural Sweet rosé shows soft, sherbet sweetness with spiced litchi tail. **Blümchen** ★★ Subdued aromas on **NV** ㉓ Natural Sweet white, enjoyable but lacks strong character. **Hanepoot** ★★★ Bright **17** ㉘ fortified shows litchi, peach & rosepetal notes with still-fiery alcohol - needs time to settle. **White Muscadel** ⊘ ★★★★ Aromas of raisins, grapes, honey & flowers on **16** ㉝. Nice balancing acidity with warm finish; perfumed & pleasing though shade less thrilling than standout **15** ★★★★ ㉗. **Red Jerepigo** ★★★ From touriga & souzão, fortified **17** ㉘ mixes raisins & black cherry jam with warm alcohol. Needs to go with a good winter pud. **Cape Ruby** ⊘ ★★★ Deep, intense colour of **15** ㉘ 'port' matched by deep, intense flavours of liquorice, aniseed & spice, hints of mint & herbs. Touriga & souzão. **Oak Matured Full Cream** ⊘ ★★★ Raisin character, **11** ㉘ is more 'fortified muscadel' than 'full cream sherry' but will make lots of friends: rich & sweet, with toffee flavours. **Brandy** ⊘ ★★★ Potstill brandy from chenin & colombard aged 3-5 years in oak. Less fruity than nutty & leathery, with a caramel hint. Fiery 43% alcohol, best for blending; a bitter tinge & a pleasing dryness if one samples it solo. 350 & 750 ml. — CM, TJ

Location: Douglas ▪ Map: Northern Cape, Free State & North West ▪ Map grid reference: C5 ▪ WO: Northern Cape/Prieska/Western Cape ▪ Est 1968 ▪ 1stB 1977 ▪ Tasting & sales Mon-Fri 8-1 & 2-5 ▪ Closed all pub hols ▪ Cellar tours by appt ▪ Function/lapa venue (up to 60 pax) ▪ Owner(s) GWK Ltd ▪ Cellarmaster(s) Ian Sieg

▪ Winemaker(s) Ian Sieg, with Sanmari Snyman ▪ Douglas + Landzicht GWK: 350ha (cab, ruby cab, shiraz, chard, chenin, cbard, muscadels r/w) ▪ 40,000cs own label 20% red 40% white 5% rosé 35% fortified ▪ PO Box 47 Douglas 8730 ▪ wynkelder@gwk.co.za ▪ www.gwk.co.za, www.landzicht.co.za ▪ S 29° 3′ 57.0″ E 023° 46′ 7.8″ ▪ 🖅 hardy.streams.inhibitor ▪ F +27 (0)53-298-1845 ▪ **T +27 (0)53-298-8314/5**

☐ **Down to Earth** see Villiera Wines

Dragonridge

Johan and Diana Simons' lovely 320-ha Fynbos Estate on the Swartland's Paardeberg has a peak reminiscent of a sleeping dragon (the likeness grows, apparently, after a few good glassfuls). Eco-tourism, weddings and more, with a wide range (occasionally quirky) of wines made by Johan totally naturally in his old cellar, with truly minimal sulphur, off organic vineyards — a rare combination in the Cape. An MCC from chardonnay is maturing in bottle. Probably its name will continue the night-sky theme already prominent.

★★★★ Aquila ⓥ These reds share an unusual aromatic note, **16** ⑧⑥ sangiovese & cab adds tomato leaf & red berries. Balances fresh lightness, vinosity, lingering fruit, tannic grip. Good dry finish.

★★★★ Supernova Méthode ancestrale sparkler from pinotage/chenin, a lovely light apricot-gold in **17** ⑧⑥. Notes of yeast, apple, berry. Cranberry freshness, flavourful yet delicate. Dry; 10.5% alcohol. Last was **15 ★★★** ⑧①.

Cabernet Sauvignon Wooded ⓥ ★★★ Ripe, sweet & alcoholic (15.4%) **15** ⑧①, but oak (none new) is supportive of black berry fruits. Natural vinification, as all these. **Mourvèdre** ⓥ ★★★ Very ripe in this context, **15** ⑧① with rustic dark-fruit notes - the aromas rather beguiling, but not enough substance to balance burning 14.5% alcohol, despite a sweet fruit core. **Pinotage Wooded** ⓥ ★★★★ Remarkably, only 11% alcohol on **16** ⑧③, but enough fruit & weight, the tannic grip & acid in balance with the lightness. Dry, satisfying. **Sangiovese** ⓥ ★★★ Cherry typicity to **15** ⑦⑧ but more austere, grippy than previous. Acidity is high at 7.7 g/l. **Shiraz** ⓥ ★★★★ Idiosyncratic **15** ⑧④ is juicy & ripe with a spicy, meaty edge; pliable & light bodied. Fermented with viognier skins. **Dark Star** ⓥ ★★★ Smooth, silky & spicy **11** ⑧①, equal mix pinotage, sangiovese, shiraz & mourvèdre. Juicy fruit compote with oak sheen. **Jack's Red** ★★★ Light, sweet-fruited (but firmly dry) **12** ⑧②, idiosyncratic, rustic, bright & fresh. Mostly shiraz & pinotage, lightly oaked. **Orion** ★★★ Previously 'Chardonnay' - which remains the variety in old-oaked **17** ⑧②, expressed in typical citrus notes & a very fresh lemony acid. Bone-dry, just 11.5% alcohol. **Cygnus Chenin Blanc** ⓥ ★★★ Tarte tatin character on ripe, appealing **15** ⑧①. Natural ferment & extended skin contact, along with year in older oak add texture & cashew nut nuance. **Capella** ★★★★ Extended skin contact on unoaked **17** ⑧③ gives deeper gold colour & a touch of tannic grip. Richly textured, bone-dry, serious acidic structure & intriguing character - not for all tastes, but fascinating for some. **Galaxy** ★★★☆ Yellow-gold colour, bruised apple notes speak of long skin contact & oxidative winemaking on **17** ⑧③ chenin & viognier. Plenty of (atypical) flavour with firm enlivening acidity. **Rigel Straw Wine** ⓥ ★★★ Faint marzipan, apricot & honeycomb notes on wooded **15** ⑧① from chenin. Oxidative & rich, broad textured, with high acid countering huge sugar level. Clean dry finish. Not tasted: **Cosmos**. — TJ

Location: Malmesbury ▪ Map/WO: Swartland ▪ Map grid reference: C8 ▪ Est 2004 ▪ 1stB 2006 ▪ Tasting, sales & cellar tours by appt ▪ Fee R90, waived on purchase ▪ Closed Good Fri, Dec 25/26 & Jan 1 ▪ Country meals by arrangement for groups of 10+ ▪ Facilities for children ▪ Farm produce ▪ Weddings/functions ▪ Conferences ▪ Walks/hikes ▪ Simson-Simons Contract Nature Reserve ▪ Guest houses: 6-bedroom, 2 x 4-bedroom & 2 x 2-bedroom cottages ▪ De Perdestal Restaurant open for Sunday lunch (bookings only) ▪ Owner(s) Fynbos Estate (3 partners) ▪ Cellarmaster(s) Johan Simons (Jan 2004) ▪ Winemaker(s) Johan Simons (Jan 2004), Andy Kershaw (2015, consultant) ▪ Viticulturist(s) Johan Simons (Jun 1997) ▪ 32oha/13ha (cab, mourv, ptage, sangio, shiraz, chard, chenin, viog) ▪ 35t/1,400cs own label 40% red 45% white 5% rosé 10% méthode ancestrale ▪ Swartland Independent Producers ▪ P O Box 526 Malmesbury 7299 ▪ info@fynbosestate.co.za, info@dragonridge.co.za ▪ www.dragonridge.co.za, www.fynbosestate.co.za ▪ S 33° 33′ 28.9″ E 018° 47′ 5.6″ ▪ 🖅 newsprint.bitumen.zipping ▪ F +27 (0)86-611-5125 ▪ **T +27 (0)22-487-1153**

☐ **Dragon's Back** see Kumala
☐ **Driebergen** see Cronier Wines

riehoek Wines

igh-altitude vines are proving increasingly exciting for the Du Toit family at their tucked-away vineyard nd tourist destination in the rugged Cederberg Conservancy, beloved by ecophiles and outdoor enthusiasts round the world. Vinifier and neighbour, David Nieuwoudt of Cederberg Private Cellar, is equally enthusias- c, as these 5 hectares, at over 1,000 m above sea level, start to show their full potential.

★★★★☆ **Mieke Pinot Noir** ⊘ 🐝 Classically styled **17** ⑨1 redolent of raspberries, tealeaves & sweet aking spice, obvious oak (though only 20%) needs time to settle & harmonise - will be worth the wait.

★★★★☆ **Shiraz** 🐝 Lots to love in **16** ⑨3: black fruit, sweet spice, coffee & dark chocolate, pleasing floral aromas too. Elegantly weighted on palate, ripe tannins sturdily supporting fruit & oak, helped by fresh appetising acidity. 60% new French oak.

★★★★☆ **Ludic Sauvignon Blanc** ⊘ Previewed **18** ⑨2 looks promising, lashings of ripe tropical fruit - guava & papaya - lapped up with salty acidity. Surely more to come here. Give it time.— CM

ocation: Citrusdal ▪ Map: Olifants River ▪ Map grid reference: D6 ▪ WO: Cederberg ▪ Est/1stB 2009 ▪ Sales Mon-Sat ▪ Closed Good Fri & Dec 25 ▪ Facilities for children ▪ Gift shop ▪ Walking/hiking & MTB trails ▪ Horse ding ▪ Bird watching ▪ Fishing ▪ Bushman paintings ▪ Conservation area ▪ Self-catering cottages & camping Beauty treatments ▪ Owner(s) Du Toit family ▪ Cellarmaster(s)/winemaker(s) David Nieuwoudt (Jan 2008, ederberg) ▪ Viticulturist(s) Dawie Burger (Jun 2006), advised by David Nieuwoudt ▪ 375ha/5ha (pinot, hiraz, sauv) ▪ 3,500cs own label 40% red 60% white ▪ PO Box 89 Clanwilliam 8135 ▪ driehoekcederberg@ mail.com ▪ www.cederberg-accommodation.co.za ▪ S 32° 26′ 34.40″ E 019° 11′ 24.32″ ▪ ✍ gleeful.rudder. ehash ▪ F +27 (0)86-720-2474 ▪ **T +27 (0)27-482-2828**

☐ **Drie Papen Fontein** see Fairview
☐ **Drift** see Bruce Jack Wines

---

rostdy-Hof Wines

aunched in 1973, Drostdy-Hof is another Distell label with roots in SA history: the name recalls De Oude rostdy, Tulbagh's magistracy, a national monument and for a time the brand's cellardoor. Early accessibility as remained the focus, with low-alcohol and naturally sweet wines keeping the styling current.

Core range

Claret Select ⊘ ★★★ Versatile & compatible **NV** ⑦7, with soft tannins, medium body & ripe red-berry flavours for any get-together. Other bottle/pack sizes available to suit the occasion, as all the ranges. **Premier Grand Cru** ⊘ ★★★ Chenin-led **NV** ⑦8 is dry & tangy, with tropical fruit salad flavours, restrained 11.5% alcohol. **Adelpracht** ⊘ ★★★ Dried apple & peach flavours, honey-smooth mouthfeel, fresh finish, late-harvested **NV** ⑦9 a good partner for spicy Asian fare. Not tasted: **Cabernet Sauvignon, Merlot, Pinotage, Reserve Shiraz, Shiraz-Pinotage, Shiraz-Merlot, Rosé, Chardonnay, Chenin Blanc/Steen, Sauvignon Blanc, Chardonnay-Viognier, Stein Select, Late Harvest.**

Light range

Extra Light Rosé ★★ Copper-hued **NV** ⑦4 'sipping or snacking wine'. Aromas of ripe berry & musk candy are sweet yet palate is bone-dry, with low 9% alcohol (like next). **Extra Light** ★★ Delicately zesty **NV** ⑦3 has lime on nose, lemon on palate, is crisp & clean.

Natural Sweet range

Red ★★ Ruby-red **NV** ⑦3 packed with ripe cherries & berries, very sweet but not too cloying thanks to bal- ancing acidity. Low 8% alcohol, as all these. **Rosé** ★★ Pink **NV** ⑦5, exuberant ripe strawberries, decadently sweet but light & fresh. **White** ★★ Sweet, grapey **NV** ⑦4, crisp & clean despite high sugar. Serve all these well-chilled. WO W Cape for all ranges. — JG

Druk My Niet Wine Estate

A phoenix has risen from the ashes of January 2017's devastating fire, and the Kirchner and Stein families threw the cellar doors wide in April, holding an open day for clients and friends. The owners are well on the way to getting over the trauma of seeing the 1692 wine cellar, staff cottages and manor house razed after meticulous renovation. The small but perfectly formed winery is now in the capable hands of Marcus Milner.

Icon Collection

★★★★ Invictus (Ⓥ) Merlot leads the 2 cabs on **13** ⑧⑥ Bordeaux blend flagship. Firm core of dark fruit well integrated with oak, 25% new. Long tail, with hint of cracked pepper. Also in 1.5 & 3L, as next.

★★★★ T3 (Ⓥ) Spicy plum vivacity to bold **13** ⑧⑧, unusual & interesting blend tannat, tempranillo & tinta amarela. Leaner than last, with nutty notes from oak, 30% new. WO W Cape.

★★★★ C68 Chenin Blanc (Ⓥ) Bright & fresh **17** ⑧⑧ ups the bar on **16 ★★★☆** ⑧④. Leesy breadth & oak platform (24% new) matched by ripe tropical flavour. Structured & long.

★★★★☆ C68 Puella (Ⓥ) Intensely sweet **15 ★★★★** ⑧⑦ dessert from air-dried chenin not as impressive as **13** ⑨②, which somewhat more structured. Ample apricot, sun-dried pineapple & honey flavours b a tad shorter. **14** untasted.

Mirus (Ⓥ) **★★★★** From a shiraz single-vineyard. **14** ⑧③ dry spice from third new oak & chunky ripe black fruit off unirrigated vines.

Estate Collection

★★★★ Cabernet Franc (Ⓥ) **13** ⑧⑥ maintains inky cocoa depths & Xmas pudding styling of previous but somewhat leaner, more reined-in. Sleek oak integration, 25% new.

Cabernet Sauvignon (Ⓥ) **★★★★** Ample dark fruits & nutty spice on **13** ⑧⑤ but acidity is apparent in juicy tang. **Malbec** (Ⓥ) **★★★★** Herb brush to plum & cherry notes on **13** ⑧④, lithe & touch lean. — FM

Location/map: Paarl ▪ Map grid reference: G4 ▪ WO: Paarl/Western Cape ▪ Est 2003 ▪ 1stB 2009 ▪ Tasting, sales & cellar tours by appt ▪ Closed all pub hols ▪ Meals/refreshments on request ▪ BYO picnic ▪ Tour groups ▪ Walks/hikes ▪ Conservation area ▪ Tasting of handcrafted goat and cow's milk cheeses by prior arrangement ▪ Owner(s) Georg & Dorothee Kirchner, Jens-Peter Stein ▪ Winemaker(s) Marcus Milner (Aug 2018) ▪ 24.5ha/9ha (cabs s/f, malbec, merlot, shiraz, tannat, tempranillo, tinta amarela, viog) ▪ 110t cellar, 60t/3,500cs own label 80% red 20% white ▪ IPW ▪ PO Box 7383 Paarl 7620 ▪ georg.kirchner@dmnwines. co.za ▪ www.dmnwines.co.za ▪ S 33° 41′ 23.26″ E 019° 1′ 40.23″ ▪ [✉] cleanings.boathouse.frog ▪ **T +27 (0)82-758-4106**

☐ **Duckitt** *see* Cloof Wine Estate
☐ **Duel** *see* Ameera
☐ **Duke of Wellington** *see* Wellington Wines

Dunstone Winery (Ⓥ)(🍴)(🏠)(◎)(👤)(♿)

Lee and Abbi Wallis' beautiful estate is home to a country house, bistro and boutique cellar, the latter successfully moved to a different part of the Wellington property to create space for extra tanks, and recommissioned in time for the 2018 crush. Rhône varieties predominate, notably shiraz, it being the focus (with grenache) of current plantings, as well as the name of the Weimaraner in the winery logo.

Dunstone range

★★★★ Merlot (✓) Fruit-driven **16** ⑧⑦ is muscular yet supple, showing dark heart of plums & blackcurrants. 14 months in well-seasoned barrels fills out body, softens tannins.

★★★★ Shiraz Less dense & focused than **15** ⑧⑧, with dusty-leafy notes creeping in, **16 ★★★☆** ⑧④ pleasantly ripe black fruit & gentle tannins, brief farewell.

Shiraz Rosé ★★★ Very pleasing, light & bright **18** ⑧② has tempered strawberry fruit, nice dry lime-mineral finish. Pretty pale salmon hue. **Viognier ★★★** Appealing body & texture, but little varietal character in **17** ⑧②, muted fruit, gentle acidity. Fermented/6 months in older barrels. Not tasted: **Sauvignon Blanc.**

Stones in the Sun range

Not tasted: **Syrah.** — GdB

Location/map/WO: Wellington ▪ Map grid reference: C3 ▪ Est/1stB 2006 ▪ Tasting, sales & cellar tours Wed-Sun 8-4, Mon-Tue by appt ▪ Fee R30pp, waived on purchase ▪ Closed Dec 25 ▪ The Stone Kitchen ▪ Facilities for children ▪ Conferences ▪ Dunstone Country House luxury B&B guest house, self-catering cottage & self-catering house ▪ Owner(s) Abbi & Lee Wallis ▪ Winemaker(s) Danie de Bruyn (2018) ▪ Viticulturist(s) Johan Viljoen (Icon Vines & Wines) ▪ 6ha (grenache, merlot, mourv, shiraz, viog) ▪ 30t/3,300cs own label 65% red 25% white 10% rosé ▪ PO Box 901 Wellington 7654 ▪ wine@dunstone.co.za ▪ www.dunstone.co.za

▪ S 33° 38′ 5.3″ E 019° 3′ 36.8″ ▪ ⌨ evading.prevail.weirdness ▪ F +27 (0)21-873-6770 ▪ **T +27 (0)21-873-6770**

☐ **Du Plevaux** *see Imbuko Wines*

Du Preez Estate ⓘⓓ

Hendrik Lodewyk du Preez put down roots here in Breedekloof early last century, and the third generation today owns and runs the estate. Widely seasoned Francois Joubert, winemaker since 2016, says a strategy change has seen the multi-tiered portfolio substantially trimmed, enabling the team to focus on raising the quality of the two ranges featured below. Attention is also being given to the planting of additional blocks.

Hendrik Lodewyk range

★★★★ **Petit Verdot** ⓐ Inky **12** ㊥ brooding dark berries, mouthfilling liqueur-like viscosity. Smooth & complex, with freshness & savoury, gentle grip. No **11**. Goudini WO.

Cabernet Sauvignon ⓐ ★★★★ Vibrant cassis, dried herbs on **15** ㊙, focused & light footed, showing good depth of flavour & length. WO W Cape, like Du Preez sibling. **Méthode Cap Classique** ⓥ ★★★★ Lively & focused dry sparkling with creamy mousse, crunchy apple & citrus flavours, very appealing freshness & zest. **NV** ㊙ from chardonnay (85%) & pinot noir. Well priced too.

Du Preez Private Cellar range

★★★★☆ **Hanepoot** ⓐ Lemon-gold colour on **15** ㊙ fortified entices, seduction continues on palate with voluptuous grapey barley sweets & bitter marmalade. Unctuous & super-sweet yet balanced by fiery alcohol for wonderfully clean, bright conclusion. Different league to last **11** ★★★★ ㊙.

Sauvignon Blanc ⓥ ⓣ ★★★ A celebration of ripe tropical fruit, **18** ㊙ gets some creaminess from lees ageing before a zippy crunchy-apple conclusion. Has summer written all over it.

Cabernet Sauvignon ⓐ ★★★ Dusty dark fruit with gripping tannins in **15** ㊙. **Merlot** ⓥ ★★★ Plum & spice aromas, **17** ㊙ easy palate, partial oaking aids the friendly & well-rounded personality. Great with barbecued lamb chops. **Polla's Red** ⓐ ★★★ Undemanding crowd favourite, **16** ㊙ perky red fruit, chocolate overlay, soft smooth tannin. Pinotage & 3 others, mostly unoaked; also in magnum. WO W Cape. Not tasted: **Shiraz.** — WB

Location: Rawsonville ▪ Map: Breedekloof ▪ Map grid reference: B6 ▪ WO: Breedekloof/Western Cape/Goudini ▪ Est 1916 ▪ 1stB 1998 ▪ Tasting & sales Mon-Fri 8–5 Sat 10–1 ▪ Closed all pub hols ▪ Cellar tours by appt, 1-day prior notice required ▪ Tour groups (max 40 pax), 1-day prior notice required ▪ Owner(s) Du Preez family ▪ Winemaker(s) Francois Joubert (Jan 2016) ▪ Viticulturist(s) Jean du Preez ▪ 350ha (cab, merlot, p verdot, ptage, shiraz, chard, chenin, cbard, nouvelle, sauv) ▪ 6,000t ▪ IPW ▪ PO Box 12 Route 101 Rawsonville 6845 ▪ info@dupreezestate.co.za ▪ www.dupreezestate.co.za ▪ S 33° 41′ 37.1″ E 019° 16′ 59.6″ ▪ ⌨ thankful.slouches.conflate ▪ F +27 (0)23-349-1923 ▪ **T +27 (0)23-349-1995**

Durbanville Hills ⓘ⑪ⓞⓓⓓ

Local artist Theo Vorster was commissioned to create the authentically Cape Town look and feel of Durbanville Hills' new Collector's Reserve range of wines. The idea of linking landmarks and natural phenomena like the noon gun, cableway and Castle of Good Hope is to tie up with the recent demarcation, Wine of Origin Cape Town, which includes Durbanville. It also underlines the fact that this large hillside venture - a successful collaboration between local growers, a staff trust and industry giant Distell - overlooks the chilly waters of Table Bay, and is near the city centre. There is a host of micro- and meso-climates and terroirs in Durbanville to draw upon each harvest, ensuring fans of the large-volume wines (and the collector's items) are well satisfied, which of course is the main focus of the tight-knit production and management team.

Durbanville Hills range

★★★★ **Cabernet Sauvignon** ⓥ Supple, textured **17** ㊙ has inky cocoa depth to succulent blue- & black-fruited palate. Structured & long, the oak - all French staves - seamlessly integrated & gentle.

★★★★☆ **Tangram** ⓐ Cabs franc & sauvignon share equal billing in powerful yet nuanced **15** ㊙ 5-way Bordeaux blend. Supple, lithe & velvety, nothing is out of place. All-new French oak (2 years) is well knit. Elegant, refined, with long rich aftertaste. No **14**.

★★★★☆ **Tangram Sauvignon Blanc-Semillon** ⓦ Sauvignon still leads in refined & elegant **17** ⑨③ Bordeaux white. Trademark lemon curd, almond & spice layers with nettle note of 12% semillon adding complexity. Oak, third new French, used for ferment & 10-month maturation supports fruit well.

★★★★ **Méthode Cap Classique Blanc de Blancs** Marmalade & toast of all-chardonnay **15** ⑧⑥ sparkler shows influence of 10% oaked portion & 3 years on lees. Broad & complex, with flavour fantail at end. **Merlot** ⓥ ★★★★ Lives up to previous in fynbos-tinged, juicy dark-fruit appeal, **17** ⑧⑤ light textural tannin grip from French oak staves, 12 months. **Pinotage** ★★★ Subtle coffee bean note to red & blue fruit vivacity of **16** ⑧②, engaging & light bodied. **Shiraz** ★★★★ Deep spicy black-fruit attractions on **16** ⑧⑤, subtle tannin squeeze from combo French & American oak staves, 12 months. Appealing & tasty. **Merlot Rosé** ★★★ Ideal for summer sipping, dry **18** ⑧① is tangy, with soft red-berry vibrancy. **Chardonnay** ⓥ ★★★★ Small portion fermented with French oak staves, adding interest, body & length in **17** ⑧⑤, peach, citrus & cream breadth complete a reliably flavoursome wine. **Chenin Blanc** ★★★ Vivid gooseberry & stonefruit zip on light, bright & juicy **18** ⑧⓪, lightly oaked. **Sauvignon Blanc** ⓥ ★★★★ Dependable drinkability & flavour. Refreshing & bright, with lees note adding breadth & length, **18** ⑧③ has cool-climate passionfruit & grapefruit vigour. **Sparkling Sauvignon Blanc** ★★★ Tropical/pineapple notes & few grams sugar lighten typically zesty carbonated **18** ⑧⓪ sparkler. Easy & bright.

Collectors Reserve range ⓝⒺⓌ

★★★★☆ **Cabernet Sauvignon** ⓥ Lovely interplay of violet, tobacco, cassis & chocolate, **16** ⑨⓪ silky & supple, with layered palate. Richly fruited & concentrated but restrained, with oak, half new, well integrated.

★★★★ **Merlot** Firm fleshed, dark & brambly **16** ⑧⑦. Assured, poised, structured & long, with tomato nuance & liquorice too. Well-meshed oak, 50% new French. Rich, concentrated & lingering.

★★★★ **Pinotage** Vibrant bright cranberry & plum fruit tempered by gentle squeeze of tannin from year in 50% new oak. **16** ⑧⑥ plush, soft & succulent, light backbone & alcohol (12.4%).

★★★★ **Shiraz** Perky **16** ⑧⑥ makes a peppery entry until plum & spice step in. Bright, with oak (50% new, 14 months) a touch dry & firm but blue berry succulence rounds out the long tail.

★★★★ **Chardonnay** Subtle tarte tatin & spice allure on **17** ⑧⑥. Taut, focused, with lively cleansing acid to counter richer creamy notes from partial barrel ferment/10 months, 50% new. Balanced & persistent.

★★★★ **Chenin Blanc** Melange of fruit on platform of polished oak (French & American, 50% new; portion unwooded). **17** ⑧⑧ vivacious & rich, with freshness & creamy breadth & length.

★★★★ **Sauvignon Blanc** Lovely cohesion & vivacity on taut, mineral & pithy **17** ⑧⑥. Cool-grown fruit expresses granadilla & lime with lovely tension of opposites, good concentration & length.

Rhinofields range

★★★★ **Merlot** Lithe, focused **15** ⑧⑥ has firm frame fleshed out with Xmas cake & spice. Succulent, rich & balanced, fruit offset by well-knit new French oak.

★★★★ **Chardonnay** ⓧ Vivacious citrus fruit given centre stage by carefully scripted oak (only half in barrel, half new), **16** ⑧⑨ balanced, elegant & broad, zesty lime twist in the tail.

★★★★ **Sauvignon Blanc** ⓧ Grapefruit vies with tropical fruit on **17** ⑧⑨ tank sample, a step beyond **16** ★★★★☆ ⑧④. Juicy yet structured, with mineral contrast at end.

★★★★ **Noble Late Harvest** ⓥ Beautiful balance of fresh acidity & overt ripe, honeyed botrytis sweetness on **15** ⑧⑦ unoaked sauvignon blanc. Nuanced & focused, enduring flavours & complexity, low 9.9% alcohol. 375 ml.

Pinotage ★★★★ Downy ease to light-bodied, approachable **16** ⑧⑤. Bright blueberry fruit has cocoa edge & depth. Not tasted: **Shiraz**. — FM

Location/WO: Durbanville ▪ Map: Durbanville, Philadelphia & Darling ▪ Map grid reference: C7 ▪ Est 1998 ▪ 1stB 1999 ▪ Tasting & sales Mon 12-6 Tue-Fri 10-6 Sat 10-4 Sun 11-4 (bar & kitchen close 1hr earlier) ▪ Fee R70/8 wines incl crystal glass ▪ Closed Dec 25 & Jan 1/2 ▪ Chocolate/biltong/cheese & wine pairings ▪ Tasting room menu available daily ▪ Cellar tours by appt ▪ Restaurant: breakfast 8.30-11 & lunch 12-3 Tue-Sun; dinner 6-10 Tue-Sat ▪ Facilities for children ▪ Conferences ▪ Weddings/functions ▪ Owner(s) Distell, 9 farmers & staff trust ▪ Cellarmaster(s) Martin Moore (Nov 1998) ▪ Winemaker(s) Wilhelm Coetzee (reds, Sep 2008) & Kobus Gerber (whites, Jul 2015) ▪ Viticulturist(s) Henk van Graan (consultant) ▪ 770ha ▪ 6,000t/300,000cs wn label 40% red 58% white 2% rosé ▪ ISO 9000-1, ISO 14000-1, BRC, HACCP, IPW, WIETA ▪ PO Box 3276 Durbanville 7551 ▪ info@durbanvillehills.co.za ▪ www.durbanvillehills.co.za ▪ S 33° 49′ 29.9″ E 018° 33′ 56.7″ ▪ Ⓜ narrowing.uppermost.incidentally ▪ T +27 (0)21-558-1300

Du'SwaRoo ⓆⓄ

Du'SwaRoo boutique winery in Calitzdorp is now aptly owned and helmed by a Calitz - Kallie - with wife Pat at the tiller of the range of branded farm produce. Former proprietor Tony Bailey, who named the venture after significant places in his life (Durban, South West Africa/Namibia and Klein Karoo), remains involved and, as co-winemaker, is benefiting from the recent cellar expansion and equipment upgrade. A 'small but beautiful' tasting venue has been added and is open at regular hours (visits previously by appointment).

Sirocco Bin 5 ⓃⒶ ⓥ ⓣ ★★★ Elegant (13% alcohol) & tasty 'Calitzdorp Blend' touriga, tinta & shiraz. **NV** ⑧⓪ (uncertified) dark plums & prunes, vanilla overlay from 36 months oaking.

Petit Verdot ⓃⒶ ⓥ ★★★ Lots of concentration in **17** ⑧①, dark & berry rich, full bodied, with youthful tannins for ageing. **JMC Pinotage** ⓠ ★★★ Heady berry perfume & flavours, full-ripe & curvy, **16** ⑧①'s juicy fruit is star of the show, tannins well integrated. **Khamsin** ⓠ ★★★ Fruitcake & vanilla-rich **NV** ⑧① shiraz is well spiced from 30 months in older oak, ends nicely dry. For those who like big, flavourful reds. **Shiraz** ★★★ Long barrel fermentation (36 months) but amenable tannins in **15** ⑧①, bold Xmas cake & vanilla styling. **Tannat** ⓃⒶ ★★★ One of only a handful on the market. Light-textured (12.5% alcohol) **17** ⑦⑨ offers piquant blackcurrants, juicy smooth appeal. **Bailey** ⓃⒶ ★★★ Mulberry & plum, well spiced by 2 years in barrel. Smooth-textured **NV** ⑦⑧ uncertified tinta, best enjoyed young. **Touriga Nacional** ⓃⒶ ★★★ Spiced fruitcake, hint of scrub in **15** ⑧②, sleek & streamlined but with enough grip for ageing. **Ubique** ⓃⒶ ★★★ Uncertified **NV** ⑦⑧ touriga, mulberry & plum, sleek with livening acidity for early drinking. **Sirocco Bin 4** ⓠ ★★★ Touriga 50%, tinta 30% with shiraz; **NV** ⑧① almost plum pudding ripeness, vanilla spiced, smooth & round, just enough grip for cellaring. **Shiraz Rosé** ⓃⒶ ★★★ Berry fruit offset by **18** ⑦⑧'s crisp dryness. **Chardonnay** ⓠ ★★★ Peach & buttered toast, **17** ⑦⑧ has a rounded mouthfeel, good appetite appeal. **Chenin Blanc** ★★★ Unoaked in **18** ⑧①, crunchy apple & quince, has verve, freshness. **Cape Vintage** ⓠ ★★★★ Vibrant nutty spice & raisin notes on **11** ⑧⑤ port-style fortified, which retains 66/34 mix of touriga & tinta. Fiery core with good spirit integration. **Cape Vintage Reserve** ⓃⒶ ⓥ ★★★★ Touriga with tinta in **14** ⑧③ port-syle fortified, 3 years in barrel giving smoky, savoury tones to the dark plum/prune fruit. Also-tasted **12** ★★★ ⑧①, 60 months oaked, a coffee ground, liquorice character, treacly flavours. Not tasted: **Sharki, Tessa, Mistral**. — CR

Location/WO: Calitzdorp ▪ Map: Klein Karoo & Garden Route ▪ Map grid reference: B5 ▪ Est/1stB 2008 ▪ Tasting, sales & cellar tours Mon-Sat 10-4 ▪ Closed Good Fri & Dec 25 ▪ Farm produce & deli products ▪ Owner(s)/cellarmaster(s) Kallie Calitz ▪ Winemaker(s) Kallie Calitz & Tony Bailey ▪ Viticulturist(s) Tony Bailey (2008) ▪ 0.6ha (shiraz, tinta, touriga); 1.5ha/20t hanepoot also grown but delivered to Calitzdorp Cellar ▪ 200cs own label 80% red 10% white 10% port ▪ PO Box 279 Calitzdorp 6660 ▪ sales@duswaroo. co.za ▪ www.duswaroo.co.za ▪ S 33° 30′ 57.9″ E 021° 41′ 38.3″ ▪ Ⓜ devout.vies.restorer ▪ T +27 (0)44-213-3137/+27 (0)44-213-3055/+27 (0)82-826-2419

Du Toitskloof Winery ⓆⓅⓄ⑤

From small beginnings - six farmers started this winery on 18 ha of land in the Rawsonville area in 1962 - through expansion to more farmers, with a business of supplying bulk wine to larger producers, to where they are today, a large and successful enterprise. Still grower-owned, all 22 members are Fairtrade accredited, and Du Toitskloof has become the largest Fairtrade venture in the world, with more than 1,600 staff and families benefiting from the social enfranchisement and training programmes. Expansion continues: production increased by 2,500t since last edition, and there are now six diverse ranges of bottled wines.

Quest range

★★★★☆ **Heroes Journey 1 Bordeaux Blend** ⓠ Inky, deep **12** ⑨② cab (44%), merlot, petit verdot is pliable, layered & elegant, with spicy cassis in abundance. Cedar & tobacco sheen from two years oaking.

★★★★ **Heroes Journey 2 Rhône Blend** ⓠ **12** ⑧⑥ mimics **11** ⑧⑦ in dark-berried savoury appeal. Spicy hit from higher (38%) mourvèdre portion (rest syrah). Rich, ripe with firm dry tannin squeeze.

Méthode Cap Classique ⊘ ★★★ Blanc de blancs dry sparkling from chardonnay boasts grapefruit & Lemon Cream scents/flavours, good freshness. NV ⑧ attractively packaged.

Land's End range
★★★★ **Syrah** ⓥ Appealing black cherry, plum & scrub notes on **15** ★★★★ ⑧ enhanced by black pepper spicing, savoury beetroot finish. Fresh & vibrant, like last-tasted **12** ⑧.

Sauvignon Blanc ⓦ ★★★★ Lovely cool-climate notes in **17** ⑧, herbs & fynbos, suggestion of salt spray, a piquant gooseberry core adding vibrancy. Cape South Coast WO for these.

Selected Vineyard range

Nebbiolo ⊘ ⓦ ★★★★ Few on the market, **15** ⑧ has trademark violets perfume & tannin backbone, dry finish, without sacrificing red cherry fruit, supple texture. **Dimension Red** ⓦ ★★★★ Creative blend cab, merlot, shiraz, dash petit verdot, 25 months French barriques. **15** ⑧ integrated tannins, well-spiced dark fruit, chocolate, white pepper, lovely plush drinkability.

Cabernet Sauvignon ★★★ Shows blackcurrants, especially expressive in the flavours, but **16** ⑦ also has a savoury side, well spiced from 10 months oaking. **Merlot** ★★★ Mulberries shot through with herbaceous notes, slight touch of mint, **17** ⑦ has merlot typicity & drinks so easily. **Pinotage** ★★★ Blueberries & spice, almost mocha chocolate savouriness, **16** ⑧'s oak giving a nice dry food-friendly finish. **Shiraz** ★★★ Smoky tones from oak in **15** ⑦, fruit dark & ripe, the palate pleasingly smooth, round & juicy. **Pinotage Rosé** ★★★ Delightfully fruity **18** ⑦, red berries in a slender dry body (12.5% alcohol), perky & fresh.

Heritage range

Pinotage-Merlot-Ruby Cabernet ⓥ ★★★ Earthy note on juicy, sweet-fruited **16** ⑧. Dry, gentle tannin grip. Also in 3L. **Cabernet Sauvignon-Shiraz** ⓥ ★★★ Fruitcake spice appeal to pliant **16** ⑧ 60/40 blend with sweetish tail. Also in 3L. **Chardonnay** ★★★ Half the wine oaked, gives **17** ⑦ Lemon Cream flavours, ends zesty-fresh. **Chenin Blanc** ⊘ ★★★ There's tropical fruit, but light-textured **18** ⑧ also has vibrantly fresh appeal. Also in 3L pack. Not tasted: **Sauvignon Blanc**.

Tunnel range

Robust Red ★★ Was 'Red'. From pinotage & ruby cab, unwooded NV ⑦ designed for early drinking, & fits the bill with character. **Sweet Rosé** ★★ Muscat & chenin, with sauvignon & pinotage (for colour), NV ⑦'s dominant flavour is muscat, aromatic & tangy-sweet. Low 9% alcohol. **Crisp White** ★★ Was 'White'. Mainly sauvignon, third colombard, fittingly named; NV ⑦ light (12.5% alcohol) & apple-fresh. **Sweet White** ★★ Was 'Moscato'. Delicate floral perfume in NV ⑦ from muscat & colombard combo, grapey flavours, drier than you'd expect, more 'semi' than sweet. **Sweet Red** ★★ Pinotage & chenin with ruby cab, only 8% alcohol, no guessing NV ⑦'s intention here: fruity, uncomplicated enjoyment.

Fairtrade range ⓕ

Zola Cape Cuvée ⓦ ★★★ No oaking for **17** ⑧ cab/pinotage blend, but fruit makes up for it, a berry parade, expressive & succulent. Even hints of dark chocolate.

Zola Pinotage Rosé ★★★ Attractively packaged, this & rest of range. Expressive red berries & strawberries throughout **18** ⑦, light, fresh, eminently quaffable. **Dimension Chardonnay** ★★★ Exuberantly fruity, unoaked **18** ⑧ boasts citrus & pear, tangy freshness.

Sparkling Wine range
Vin Doux Red Sparkling Wine ★★ From pinotage in all its berry glory, NV ⑦ is for parties: light (8% alcohol), sweet & lively. **Sparkling Brut** ★★★ Lemon drop flavours in NV ⑦ from sauvignon, light, dry & zinging fresh.

Dessert Wines
Hanepoot Jerepigo ⓥ ★★★★ Ambrosial honeyed seduction of balanced **14** ⑧ fortified from muscat d'Alexandrie. Richly sweet but with a clean finish. Drink now, say the team, or up to 50 years! **Red Muscadel** ★★★★ Scents of raisins, dried fruit leap out of the glass, **15** ⑧ fortified is powerful, unashamedly sweet, the texture silky, mouthcoating. Worth cellaring, a long life ahead. 500 ml. **Cape Ruby**

★★★ Tinta with souzão, **13** ⑧¹ 'port' fits the Ruby style: fruit is the hero, rich & mellow, oak adding flavour, no firmness. 500 ml. — CR

Location: Rawsonville ▪ Map: Breedekloof ▪ Map grid reference: B6 ▪ WO: Western Cape/Cape South Coast ▪ Est 1962 ▪ Tasting & sales Mon-Fri 8–5 Sat/pub hols 9-4 ▪ Closed Good Fri, Dec 25 & Jan 1 ▪ Cellar tours by appt ▪ Ou Meul Bakery ▪ Owner(s) 22 members ▪ Cellarmaster(s) Shawn Thomson (Oct 1999) ▪ Winemaker(s) Tiaan Loubser (Nov 2016), Willie Stofberg (Feb 2011) & Mathilda Viljoen (Nov 2016), with Derrick Cupido (Jan 1993) ▪ Viticulturist(s) Leon Dippenaar (Jan 2005, consultant) ▪ 900ha (cab, merlot, ptage, shiraz, chard, chenin, cbard, sauv) ▪ 16,500t/±800,000cs own label 40% red 60% white ▪ Fairtrade ▪ PO Box 55 Rawsonville 6845 ▪ info@dutoitskloof.co.za ▪ www.dutoitskloof.co.za ▪ S 33° 42' 9.2" E 019° 16' 8.9" ▪ ⬛ passer.crewmen.reaming ▪ F +27 (0)23-349-1581 ▪ **T +27 (0)23-349-1601**

DuVon Private Cellar ⓠ ⌂ ⓒ

When not growing grapes for bigger brands, Armand du Toit and his uncle, Alex von Klopmann, vinify small batches in the restored 1940s cellar on Little Italy farm in Robertson's De Goree district. Latest releases are Cab and Shiraz '17, and Chenin Blanc and Sauvignon Blanc '18.

Location/map: Robertson ▪ Map grid reference: B7 ▪ Est/1stB 2003 ▪ Tasting, sales & cellar tours by appt ▪ Conferences ▪ Weddings ▪ Guest house ▪ Owner(s) Armand du Toit & Alex von Klopmann ▪ Cellarmaster(s)/winemaker(s)/viticulturist(s) Armand du Toit ▪ 29.5ha/27ha (cab, ruby cab, shiraz, chenin, cbard, sauv) ▪ 400t/1,200cs own label 60% red 40% white ▪ PO Box 348 Robertson 6705 ▪ info@duvon.co.za ▪ www.duvon.co.za ▪ S 33° 48' 46.8" E 019° 47' 4.1" ▪ ⬛ nifty.report.hilltops ▪ F +27 (0)86-626-1490 ▪ **T +27 (0)72-514-4204**

☐ **D'Vine** see Swartland Winery
☐ **Dwyka Hills** see Eagle's Cliff Wines-New Cape Wines
☐ **Dyasonsklip** see Bezalel Wine & Brandy Estate

Eagle's Cliff Wines-New Cape Wines ⓠ ⑪ ⓒ ⑧ ⓹

A pair of rare Black Eagles, which made their nest in the cliffs overlooking the vineyards near Worcester, served as inspiration for the packaging for these entry-level bottlings made by Christiaan Groenewald, increasingly assisted by young sons Jacques and Nicholas. The two-time Diners Club Winemaker of the Year's top label, Arendskloof/Voetspore, is listed separately.

Eagle's Cliff range

Pinotage ⊘ ⑲ ★★★★ Delicious & moreish **17** ⑧⑤, rounded & fruity, spiced plum & hint of liquorice, brush of oak (20%) for complexity. All but lights the braai fire.

Shiraz-Pinotage ⑫ ★★★ Invariably vibrant & engaging blend. Another successful 80/20 marriage in **14** ⑧¹, with coffee, smoke & strawberry attractions. Well priced, too. **Chenin Blanc** ⑫ ★★★ Water-white **17** ⑦⑧ is light of foot, offers tropical fruit flavours for effortless sipping. **Sauvignon Blanc** ★★★ Sunshiney orchard fruit & ripe apples on vibrant **18** ⑦⑧. Not tasted: **Cabernet Sauvignon-Merlot**, **Shiraz Rosé**.

Dwyka Hills range

Shiraz ⑫ ★★★★ Characterful olive tapenade nuances, balanced finish (even with 14.7% alcohol), unfettered by oak. **14** ⑧④ worth seeking out. WO W Cape. — WB

Location/map: Worcester ▪ Map grid reference: A6 ▪ WO: Breede River Valley/Western Cape ▪ Est 2000 ▪ Tasting & sales Mon-Thu 10-3 Fri 10-2 ▪ Closed all pub hols ▪ Cheese & meat platters daily ▪ Bistro ▪ Facilities for children ▪ Tour groups ▪ Wedding & function venue ▪ Owner(s)/winemaker(s) Christiaan Groenewald ▪ 600ha/8oha ▪ 40% red 60% white ▪ PO Box 898 Worcester 6849 ▪ christiaan@ncw.co.za ▪ www.eaglescliff.co.za ▪ S 33° 50' 25.4" E 019° 25' 7.4" ▪ ⬛ marbles.convinces.tiled ▪ F +27 (0)86-236-4959 ▪ **T +27 (0)23-340-4112**

Eagles' Nest ⓠ ⑪ ⓒ ⓹

The Mylrea family's eyrie overlooking False Bay continues to attract visitors in droves, not just because it is one of the stops on the popular Constantia wine loop visited by double-decker sightseeing tour buses.

The top-tier producer has established a stellar reputation in just two decades after a devastating wild fire in 2000 destroyed commercial forestry plantations on its steep slopes, and forced the switch to vines and wines. Consultants had carte blanche with regard to winemaking here — terraced - vineyards and advised the planting of shiraz and viognier. Drawing on their continued sage counsel, as well as personal experience gained in New Zealand and Bordeaux, winemaker Duran Cornhill has charted a steady course in his year at the helm.

★★★★★ **Merlot** Due care & consideration given to restrained, elegantly sensual, mulberry-fruited **14** ⑨⓪, including 2 years in bottle at cellar. Supple, gentle, balanced oak (just 33% new), delicious velvety, long & spicy finish. Also in 1.5L, as all except Sauvignon.

★★★★★ **Shiraz** ⓐ Trademark blue & black fruit on **15** ㊟, with spicy dried herb nuances from elevated cool site. Integrated, refined & elegant, if tad sweeter than stellar **14** ★★★★★ ㊡. Firm oak (40% new for 18 months) cradles fruit to lengthy conclusion.

★★★★ **Sauvignon Blanc** Bright tangy grapefruit & lime zest vivacity on **17** ★★★★ ⑧⑤. Rounded & juicy. As with **16** ⑧⑥, grapes from Darling & Durbanville.

★★★★★ **Viognier** ⓐ Textured **17** ㊟ reveals layers of stonefruit, acid freshness & creamy oak support (20% new, 6 months). Broad yet focused & balanced, a pithy crunch & defined finish.— FM

Location: Constantia ▪ Map: Cape Peninsula ▪ Map grid reference: B3 ▪ WO: Constantia/Coastal ▪ Est 2001 ▪ 1stB 2005 ▪ Tasting & sales daily 10-4.30 ▪ Fee R65pp, waived on purchase of R500+ ▪ Closed Good Fri, Dec 25/26 & Jan 1 ▪ Cheese & charcuterie platters ▪ 4x4 farm tour & tasting - booking essential ▪ Owner(s) Mylrea family ▪ Winemaker(s) Duran Cornhill (Aug 2017), with Martin Meinert (2001, consultant) ▪ Viticulturist(s) Kobus Jordaan (2008) ▪ 38ha/12ha (merlot, shiraz, viog) ▪ 100t/15,000cs own label 85% red 15% white ▪ PO Box 535 Constantia 7848 ▪ info@eaglesnestwines.com ▪ www.eaglesnestwines.com ▪ S 34° 0' 54.2" E 018° 24' 54.3" ▪ ✉ graduate.shiniest.grownup ▪ F +27 (0)21-794-7113 ▪ **T +27 (0)21-794-4095**

☐ **Earth's Essence** see KWV Wines

☐ **Ecology** see PaardenKloof

☐ **Edenhof** see Schalkenbosch Wines

Edgebaston
⑨

David Finlayson — owner and cellarmaster here — is from one of modern SA wine's most noteworthy families. He learnt winemaking with his father, Walter, at the family's Glen Carlou property (and no doubt also much from uncle Peter at Bouchard Finlayson). When Walter's estate was sold, David in 2004 acquired this one on the slopes of the Simonsberg near Stellenbosch town, with its deep clay topsoil and shale subsoils — unique to this part of Stellenbosch, he says. The original name of the farm was revived, as Edgebaston was, happily, also the name of the part of England where David's mother was born and raised. He now oversees both vineyards and cellar. See also the Van der Merwe & Finlayson entry.

Camino Africana range

★★★★☆ **David Finlayson Cabernet Franc** ⑨ ⓐ Combines elegance with underlying power. **15** ㊉ classic leafy, spicy aromas, & seamless integration of rich dark fruit with a firm tannin spine.

★★★★☆ **David Finlayson Chenin Blanc** ⓐ Fragrant stonefruit, ripe apple, citrus fruit aromas & flavours reined in by deft oaking, **17** ㊟ mouthfilling & creamy with fresh, lengthy lemon finish. Wild-yeast fermented in concrete 'eggs', then older wood, 10 months.

Not tasted: **David Finlayson Pinot Noir Reserve**.

Edgebaston range

★★★★★ **'GS' Cabernet Sauvignon** ⓐ Honours George Spies & his legendary 1960s cabs. Strict barrel selection from single clone, **15** ㊉ vibrant & opulent with deep blackcurrant & mulberry, crushed green herb, dusting of cocoa. Intense, smooth & ageworthy, like **14** ★★★★★ ㊡.

★★★★ **Cabernet Sauvignon** Step-up 15 ★★★★★ ⑨⓪ has bright & generous cassis, cigarbox & leather tones, balanced & concentration, long dark-chocolate farewell. Also-tasted **16** ⑧⑧ longer oaked, 24 months vs 18, similar attractions but shade less intensity.

★★★★ **Pinot Noir** ⊘ Strawberry & raspberry tones are precise & vibrant yet delicate, **17** ⑧⑦'s wooding (all older, 18 months) cleverly cossets the fruit, creates creamy platform for it to shine. WO W Cape.

★★★★ **Syrah** Full-throttle **17** ⑧⑨ needs time for ample hedgerow fruit, coriander-cured meat aromas & flavours, firm tannins & 30% new oak to coalesce.

★★★★ **Chardonnay** Naturally fermented in barrel, **17** ⑧⑧ vibrant & on point. Aromatic, too, with blossom perfume & cinnamon-dusted apple tart swathed in vanilla.

....

The Berry Box Red ⑦ ★★★★ Merlot (58%) & petit verdot in harmonious & delectable mouthful of fruity fun. **16** ⑧④ lightly oaked, juicy & spicy. No rush to uncork, there's muscle in them berries. **Sauvignon Blanc** ⑦ ★★★★ Sprightly **18** ⑧⑤ packed with vivacious tropical fruit & citrus, creamy mouthfeel from 2 months lees-ageing/stirring. **The Berry Box White** ⑦ ★★★★ Easy just-dry sipper offering a salad of fruit flavours gently brushed with oak. Sauvignon, semillon, viognier & chenin do the drinkability box-ticking in **18** ⑧③.

....

The Pepper Pot ⑧ ★★★★ Syrah & 4 others in step-up **16** ⑧④. True to name: bursts with peppery, savoury flavours, soft & approachable. WO Coastal. Not tasted: **Reserve Cabernet Sauvignon**. — WB
Location/map: Stellenbosch ▪ Map grid reference: E3 ▪ WO: Stellenbosch/Coastal/Western Cape ▪ Est/1stB 2004 ▪ Tasting by appt only ▪ Owner(s) David Finlayson ▪ Cellarmaster(s) David Finlayson (Jan 2004) ▪ Winemaker(s) Pieter van der Merwe (Jan 2016) ▪ 30ha/24ha (cab, shiraz, chard, sauv) ▪ 300t/60,000cs own label 60% red 40% white ▪ PO Box 2033 Dennesig 7601 ▪ david@edgebaston.co.za ▪ www.edgebaston.co.za ▪ S 33° 53′ 33.82″ E 018° 51′ 17.61″ ▪ ⓜ bolt.audible.massive ▪ **T +27 (0)21-889-9572/+27 (0)83-263-4353**

☐ **Edward Snell & Co** *see* Wellington VO

☐ **Eendevanger** *see* illimis Wines

Eenzaamheid   ⓠ ⓒ

The Briers-Louw family cultivate some 400 hectares of dryland vineyard on their 17th-century farm near Paarl. Janno, the winemaker, notes that though drought saw the total 2018 crop down 35%, the fruit 'was very healthy with surprisingly good analysis', adding 'the past three vintages again highlight the importance of soil in the viticultural/winemaking equation'. More positive news is that volumes of this boutique own-brand are increasing; heavier reds, like pinotage and shiraz, are especially popular in China, while the chenin has almost doubled in quantity thanks mostly to local demand.

★★★★ **Cinsaut** ⊘ Introduced by gorgeous spice, red berry fragrance, **17** ★★★★★ ⑨⓪ pure, concentrated flavours lifted by usual freshness, tangy dryness. Lightish body for lunchtime drinking. Unwooded, where **16** ⑧⑦ was older-oaked.

★★★★ **Pinotage** Pinotage in bright-fruited, juicy mode; **16** ⑧⑨ also has neat tannin trim. Nicely balanced for current enjoyment & keeping few years. **15** ★★★★★ ⑨③ also tasted; riper, more complex with smoothly integrated tannin. Big but balanced. Excellent potential. Both deftly French oaked, 5% new.

★★★★★ **Shiraz** ⊘ Satisfyingly rich, with sweet black berries & spice, not over-ripe or heavy. **16** ⑨② gently firm conclusion; good potential. Also-reviewed **15** ⑨③ intense, powerful, with more roast meat, mushroom savouriness; vibrant yet unharsh tannins. Both will benefit from several more years. Oaking supportive, as always: 10% new French.

★★★★ **Cuvée** Like **15** ⑧⑥, satisfying pocket pleaser. **16** ★★★★ ⑧⑤, shiraz-led sextet, delivers generosity of dark berry flavours, savouriness in its gently rounded form.

★★★★★ **Chenin Blanc** From vines well into third decade, **16** ★★★★ ⑧⑧ unshowy concentration & some honeyed evolution. Nicely fleshed with yellow peach tastiness but less vitality, length, than **15** ⑨②. Fermented/aged in older 300L French oak.

Vin Blanc ★★★ Juicy melange chenin with semillon, viognier, clairette. Unoaked **17** ⑧② plentiful ripe melon, apricot flavours lifted by bright acid, dry finish. — AL
Location/map/WO: Paarl ▪ Map grid reference: B5 ▪ Est 1693 ▪ 1stB 2010 ▪ Tasting by appt only ▪ Conferences ▪ Owner(s) Christo & Karina Briers-Louw ▪ Winemaker(s) Janno Briers-Louw (Apr 2008) ▪ Viticulturist(s) André Coetzee (Sep 2003) ▪ 1,185ha/400ha (cinsaut, ptage, shiraz, chenin) ▪ 3,000t/6,000cs own label 70% red 30% white ▪ Fairtrade, WIETA ▪ PO Box 22 Klapmuts 7625 ▪ wine@eenzaamheid1.co.za ▪ www.eenzaamheidwines.co.za ▪ S 33° 44′ 52.67″ E 018° 50′ 12.06″ ▪ ⓜ blank.officers.captivates ▪ F +27 (0)86-583-5741 ▪ **T +27 (0)82-493-9930**

Eerste Hoop Wine Cellar ⓠ

Diané Wentzel has been appointed viticulturist and winemaker at Belgian-owned Eerste Hoop boutique winery, named for 17th century Cape governor Willem Adriaan van der Stel's hunting lodge in the mountains between Bot River and Villiersdorp. Diané is excited about the opportunity to work with cooler-climate fruit, and plans to utilise more traditional methods of allowing fruit expression, with minimum intervention.

Lemahieu range

★★★★ **Red Blend Lady Brigitte** Shiraz, grenache & mourvèdre (53/32/15) seamlessly interwoven in **16** ⑧⑦, spicy & savoury flavours in supple, dry tannin framework, with ripeness well contained & crafted.

White Blend Lodewijkx ★★★★ Chenin, viognier & chardonnay melange billows spice, stonefruit, florals & lime, **17** ⑧⑤'s palate equally outspoken, ripe fruit, pithiness & tannin grip freshened somewhat by acidity but perhaps too bold for solo.

Eerste Hoop range

★★★★ **Cabernet Sauvignon** Latest release switches to NV ⑧⑥. Very ripe berry jam aromas but more balanced, juicier & less overt on palate. Smooth, supple tannins, ends respectably dry, ready to drink.

★★★★ **Shiraz** Big, bold & very concentrated yet balanced, despite 15% alcohol thanks to bright fruit, leavening acid thread. **15** ⑧⑥ does need a robust meal though. **14** ★★★★ ⑧⑤ softer, less emphatic.

Pinot Noir ★★★ Also now NV ⑧①. High-toned strawberry & savoury nuances, dry dusty tannins; tad rustic, unlingering, but pleasant enough for a braai, even lightly chilled with game fish. **Blushing Bride Pinot Noir Rosé** ⓠ ★★★ Bright cherry pink **14** ⑦⑦ redolent of mixed berries, very dry, with pinot's earthiness coming to fore & ending warm, detracting from freshness. **Wooded Chardonnay** ★★★★ Catnip to fans of heavily oaked styles, **16** ⑧③'s overt barrel character saved - just - by ripe, abundant lime fruit, fresh farewell. Even so, less balanced than **15** ★★★★ ⑧⑥. Not tasted: **Viognier**.

Witklip range

Shiraz ★★★ Aiming to please & ready to pour, like its range siblings. **17** ⑧① supple, spicy, balanced & friendly. **Rosé** ⓝⓔⓦ ★★★ Pale onion-skin-hued **18** ⑦⑨ is dry, clean, piquantly red berried for lively sunset/aperitif sipping. **Chardonnay** ★★★ Smooth-textured poached pear with a twist of lime, **18** ⑧⓪ a little riper & richer than previous but nicely poised, not heavy. — MW

Location/map: Villiersdorp ▪ Map grid reference: A2 ▪ WO: Cape South Coast/Western Cape ▪ 1stB 2009 ▪ Tasting, sales & cellar tours by appt only ▪ Owner(s) Lodewijk Lemahieu (Belgium) ▪ Winemaker(s)/viticulturist(s) Diané Wentzel (Dec 2017) ▪ 24.5ha/11ha (cab, grenache, mourv, pinot, shiraz, chard, chenin, viog) ▪ 85t/14,000cs 55% red 42% white 3% rosé ▪ Brands for clients: Oggendau, Skoon Vallei, Stilfontein ▪ PO Box 89 Elgin 7180 ▪ admin@eerstehoop.co.za ▪ www.eerstehoop.co.za ▪ S 34° 5′ 23.7″ E 019° 11′ 50.7″ ▪ 🚲 biker. reconciles.playdate ▪ **T +27 (0)28-841-4190/+27 (0)82-754-4408**

☐ **Eighth Wonder Wines** *see* VinGlo Wines

Eikehof Wines ⓠ ⓜ ⓞ

One of the stops on Franschhoek's Wine Tram, oak-shaded family farm Eikehof offers visitors a 'relaxed and intimate atmosphere', and a glimpse into the history of winegrowing in the valley, owner Francois Malherbe saying the character of the 1903 cellar where his great-grandfather made wine is unchanged. Moreover, vines from that era supply the grapes for a semillon which has returned to Francois' line-up after some years.

Location/map: Franschhoek ▪ Map grid reference: C3 ▪ Est 1903 ▪ 1stB 1992 ▪ Tasting & sales Mon-Sun 10.30-4 ▪ Closed Dec 24/25/31 & Jan 1 ▪ Cheese platters ▪ Weddings & functions ▪ Franschhoek Wine Tram ▪ Owner(s)/cellarmaster(s)/winemaker(s) Francois Malherbe ▪ 29ha/24ha (cab, merlot, shiraz, chard, sauv, sem) ▪ 28t/3,000cs own label 80% red 20% white ▪ PO Box 222 Franschhoek 7690 ▪ eikehof@mweb.co.za ▪ www.eikehof.com ▪ S 33° 52′ 53.3″ E 019° 3′ 52.0″ ▪ 🚲 kilos.preservation.rosewater ▪ F +27 (0)21-876-2469 ▪ **T +27 (0)21-876-2469**

Eikendal Vineyards ⓠ ⓜ ⓐ ⓞ ⓐ ⓑ

This welcoming Swiss-owned Helderberg estate, with popular restaurant, lodge and distinctive barrel-vaulted cellar, has cemented its reputation as a 'house of chardonnay' with the new Infused by Earth bottling, a striking estate-grown addition to a range that already includes an Elgin chardonnay as well as two combining Stellenbosch and Elgin fruit, including the ever-popular unwooded Janina. However, there's more to Eikendal than chardonnay, insists cellarmaster Nico Grobler, pointing out that, inter alia, the ultra-premium Infused range also includes the 'extremely limited release' Cabernet Franc, while the Charisma blend of shiraz, petit verdot and sangiovese will benefit from new plantings of the latter.

Infused by Earth range

★★★★☆ **Cabernet Franc** Returns to guide with **15** (94) after exactly a decade's break. From small, unirrigated section of Classique block, a sumptuous wine of plush dark fruit & soft tannins, beautifully integrated after year older French oak, with mint chocolate & freshly ground pepper lift.

★★★★☆ **Chardonnay** (NEW) Concentrated citrus & nutty undertones in remarkable **16** (94), from bushvines on poor decomposed granite at wind-exposed top of farm, bunch-pressed into tank for wild ferment, then 60% new barrels, rest granite amphoras. Unfined/filtered.

Eikendal Vineyards range

★★★★☆ **Cabernet Sauvignon** Cellar chief Nico Grobler 'absolutely obsessed' with showcasing estate's koffieklip (ferricrete) soils in this wine. Impressive **16** (93) naturally fermented, new oak now below 20% for maximum expression of red & black fruit, a little cedar spice. Tightly structured for lengthy cellaring.

★★★★ **Merlot** With its floral perfume & voluptuous texture, **16** ★★★★☆ (90) equally poised but more 'feminine' than Cab, adds lovely choc-plum typicity & tangy freshness to its charms. 500L barrels, mostly untoasted, 10% new. More elegant than **15** (89).

★★★★☆ **Pinotage** Perfume, freshness & tightness are what the team wants (& gets) in **17** (91), ex mature Stellenbosch bushvines. Old oak, 15% concrete 'eggs' for vivacious red-fruit flavour, intriguing hints of baking spice & orange chocolate. WO W Cape.

★★★★☆ **Classique** With year in bottle still to come pre-release, **16** (93) Bordeaux blend already shows harmony between near-equal cab & merlot (38/35), cab franc, petit verdot, components vinified separately with maximum 20% new oak to show ripe black fruit, preserve tight, chalky texture.

★★★★☆ **Charisma** Eclectic red continues upward path in youthful **17** (93), mostly shiraz, 16% petit verdot for black-fruit depth & aniseed (both varieties year old wood), plus 5% unoaked 2018 sangiovese for freshness. Near-identical blend to stellar **15** ★★★★★ (95). **16** untasted.

★★★★☆ **Chardonnay** Remarkable balance between sweet & savoury, citrus & oak, richness & flinty freshness in **17** (93), huge complexity from diverse blocks, clones, farms, areas, plus year in French oak (15% new) on lees of up to 4 previous vintages.

★★★★☆ **Mon Désir Chardonnay** (NEW) 'The Chanel No. 5 of Elgin' is team's take on delicate **17** (93), only 10% malo allowed over 14 months older oak to retain floral notes (jasmine, orange blossom) & lingering citrus freshness. Single clone (CY277) & block, natural ferment. Just 11.5% alcohol.

★★★★☆ **Janina Unwooded Chardonnay** Beautiful minerality, focused fruit purity & intensity on **17** (92) from own & Elgin grapes, naturally fermented in combo stainless steel tanks & cement/polyethylene 'eggs' for abundant citrus fruit/zest, green apple freshness. Lovely length.

★★★★ **Sauvignon Blanc** Loire meets New World in **17** (89) from Elgin, gooseberry, granadilla & guava notes carrying through to palate, textured from 6 months on lees, some in plastic/concrete 'eggs'.— JG

Location: Stellenbosch ▪ Map: Helderberg ▪ Map grid reference: C1 ▪ WO: Stellenbosch/Western Cape/Elgin ▪ Est 1981 ▪ 1stB 1984 ▪ Tasting & sales Mon-Sat 9.30-5 (Sep-May)/10-4 (Jun-Aug) Sun 10-5 ▪ Fee R60/5 wines; pizza & wine pairing R100 (winter); cheesecake pairing R100; kiddies cookie tasting R60 ▪ Closed Good Fri, Dec 25/26 & Jan 1 ▪ Cucina di Giovanni @ Eikendal Tue-Sat lunch & dinner Sun lunch only ▪ Facilities for children ▪ Tour groups ▪ Tractor rides (weekends) ▪ Walks/hikes ▪ Flyfishing ▪ Cheetah Outreach (seasonal) ▪ Eikendal Lodge ▪ Owner(s) Substantia AG ▪ Cellarmaster(s) Nico Grobler (2007) ▪ Winemaker(s) Christo Hanse (2012) ▪ Farm manager Willem van Kerwel (2012) ▪ 78ha/±41ha (cabs s/f, cinsaut, grenache, malbec, merlot, mourv, p verdot, chard) ▪ 250t/40,000cs own label 50% red 50% white ▪ IPW ▪ PO Box 2261 Stellenbosch 7601 ▪ marketing@eikendal.co.za ▪ www.eikendal.com ▪ S 34° 0' 46.7" E 018° 49' 24.5" ▪ tripling.photons.installed ▪ F +27 (0)21-855-1027 ▪ **T +27 (0)21-855-1422, +27 (0)21-855-5033 (Restaurant)**

☐ **Eksteen Family Vineyards** *see* Stone Ridge Wines

☐ **Elandsberg** *see* Viljoensdrift Fine Wines & Cruises

Elemental Bob

You don't get a winemaker much more passionately devoted to hands-off winemaking than Somerset West-based boutique vintner Craig Sheard, whose focus is on fresh, personality-driven wines that 'take you on a sensory and spiritual journey'. During his own journey — around SA's winelands — Craig has come across inspiring old vines, prompting him to do something he doesn't ordinarily like to do: 'organise'. The new Cosmic Flower line-up will comprise wines from single, old-vine vineyards; the Cosmic Hands range a red and a white blend, and the Retro Series wines from younger vineyards in a more easygoing style.

Cosmic Flower (NEW)

★★★★★ **Graveyard Tinta Barocca** (ORG) Lithe & feisty **17** (95), animated pot-pourri & orange zest bouquet with sweet baking spice dusting, sour plum fruit curtailed, licked into shape by dry tail. Shows that SA reds can be serious at just 12.3% alcohol. From 46 year old vines.

★★★★★ **The Rupert Chenin Blanc** (ORG) From venerable 66 year old vines, **17** (93) perfectly poised & satisfying without reliance on oak. Rounded, with subtle heft (13.9% alcohol), delicate white peach & earth aromas, marzipan & wild honey flavours. Natural ferment on lees in older barrels, full malo, as other whites in range.

★★★★ **My Darling Chenin Blanc** More fruit-filled, less mineral than The Rupert. **17** (88) ex 35 year old vineyard, generous yellow cling peach & tangerine, fresh orange tang; serious & well-composed but not dour.

★★★★☆ **Farmer Red Beard Palomino** (ORG) Just 1.5 g/l sugar, 12.2% alcohol for **17** (93) from 90 year old Robertson vineyard. Savoury, saline & fine-boned with refined umami & white floral nuances.

Rest Your Head Chardonnay ★★★☆ Toasty & nutty **17** (85) gains almost too much texture from 11 months on lees. Bone-dry end (1.08 g/l sugar) almost unnerving after rich & broad middle. From 'young' - in this line-up - 33 year old vineyard.

My Cosmic Hand range

★★★★☆ **Somersault Cinsault** (NEW) From 25 year old vines, **17** (91) energetic & savoury, reminiscent of France's Arbois in its light-seeming concentration & complexity without being 'worked'. Smidgen shiraz, fermented/aged 11 months older oak.

★★★★★ **White** (V) Intense **15** (91) from viognier, chenin, verdelho & semillon, exuding complex lemon zest, peach & apricot aromas with distinctive white pepper spicing. Fresh & juicy, but savoury & saline, not fruit-sweet. Pithy grip from 40% whole bunches, 7 days skin contact, 10 months old oak.

Not tasted: **Red**.

Retro Series

★★★★ **The Sandman Grenache** (NEW) Unforced & pleasantly rustic **17** (86), high-toned maraschino cherry note, bone-dry with present but approachable tannins, wild strawberry finish. Some whole bunches & 11 months older oak, as next.

★★★★☆ **Over There Pinot Noir** Ex Overberg, hence 'Over There' inserted into name for **17** ★★★★ (85). Same gently gruff tannins, lovely dryness as **16** (90); distinct high-toned eau de cologne character but drinks really well. These reds to open now or in a few years.

★★★★☆ **Chenin Blanc** (V) (ORG) Skin-macerated **16** (94) commands attention from start to finish: deep yellow hue, unexpected smoky overlay, marked dryness, exceptional presence at just 12% alcohol. Edgy, as intended. Widely sourced fruit.

In abeyance: **Red Blend**, **Grenache Blanc**, **White Blend**. — CvZ

Location: Somerset West ▪ WO: Stellenbosch/Western Cape/Robertson/Overberg ▪ Est/1stB 2004 ▪ Closed to public ▪ Owner(s)/winemaker(s) Craig Sheard ▪ 1,200cs own label 40% red 60% white ▪ elementalbob@gmail.com ▪ www.elementalbob.co.za ▪ **T +27 (0)82-265-1071**

Elgin Heights

Smarag, the Joubert family's Elgin holding, is the grape source of a variety of vinous gems including their own Elgin Heights Shiraz, Chardonnay, Sauvignon Blanc and pair of MCC sparklings, vinified by contracted winemakers. Public tastings at Rozendal, their Stellenboschkloof home-farm, are no longer offered but the wines are available directly and in select outlets. On-farm conference facilities are still available.

Location: Stellenbosch ▪ 1stB 2007 ▪ Closed to public ▪ Conference facilities at Rozendal ▪ Owner(s) Ryk Joubert ▪ Winemaker(s) Kobie Viljoen & Corné Marais (consultants) ▪ Viticulturist(s) DD Joubert ▪ 111ha/70ha (cab, merlot, shiraz, chard, sauv, viog) ▪ PO Box 52 Vlottenburg 7604 ▪ admin@401rozendal.co.za ▪ www. elginheights.co.za ▪ F +27 (0)86-648-1704

Elgin Ridge   ⓥ ⓐ ⓘ

According to winemaker Kosie van der Merwe, two factors have allowed Brian and Marion Smith's wine-growing venture in Elgin survive a halving of the average annual rainfall with sustainable yields and quality intact. First, the clay underlying the surface shales has encouraged the vines' roots to reach deeper into the subsoil and survive the summer without irrigation. Second, and more important, is the humus levels in the soils built up over 10 years at the certified-biodynamic farm. Complementing the biodynamics-inspired holistic approach is a variety of farm animals, which feature prominently in the gallery of evocative photos on the Elgin Ridge website, taken by professional photographer Marion, also chair of Elgin Wine Valley.

★★★★ **282 Pinot Noir** ⓥ ⓘ Tender, balanced structure harmonised with **16** ⑧⑨'s ripe dark cherries, undergrowth notes. Deliciously drinkable, will keep if you can resist. Older French oak. **15** held back for further ageing. Also in 1.5L, like Chardonnay.

★★★★ **282 Chardonnay** ⓘ ⓑ Enjoys benefit of great vintage; **17** ★★★★★ ⑨③ generous citrus, peach charm, natural ferment enhance subtle complexity. Elgin's trademark taut acid knits wine, lends length to bone-dry finish; will reward cellaring. Sensitively oaked; 20% new French.

★★★★ **282 Sauvignon Blanc** ⓥ ⓘ **16** ★★★★ ⑧④ fuller-bodied, softer than pebbly-fresh **15** ⑧⑧. Natural ferment & lees ageing add palate weight but probably not as long-lived as previous.

★★★★☆ **Chaos White** ⓘ ⓑ **17** ⑨③ individual & intriguing. Sauvignon & semillon (55/45), natural ferment, portion on skins, mainly barrelled. Striking freshness reflects strong vintage but also the harmony in its silky texture, distinctive earthy, spicy citrus tones. Firm, dry & ageworthy. 500 ml. Chill lightly.

Marion's Vineyards ★★★★ Méthode cap classique sparkling from chardonnay. **13** ⑧③ two years in barrel yields light gold hue, toasty/biscuity character. Bone-dry (no dosage), arresting sparkle offset by 30 months on lees. **12** sold out untasted. — AL

Location/map/WO: Elgin ▪ Map grid reference: B3 ▪ Est 2007 ▪ 1stB 2009 ▪ Tasting, sales & tours Mon-Sat & pub hols 10-4 Sun 10-2 ▪ Farm produce ▪ BYO picnic ▪ Owner(s) Brian & Marion Smith ▪ Winemaker(s) Kosie van der Merwe ▪ Viticulturist(s) Kevin Watt (Apr 2007, consultant), with Taurai Mutumbwa ▪ 20.2ha/6.5ha (cab f, pinot, chard, sauv, sem) ▪ 45t/4,000cs own label 20% red 80% white ▪ Organic & biodynamic certification ▪ PO Box 143 Elgin 7180 ▪ info@elginridge.com ▪ www.elginridge.com ▪ S 34° 12' 10.68" E 019° 0' 14.34" ▪ ⓦ encounters.soloists.unflagging ▪ F +27 (0)21-846-8060 ▪ **T +27 (0)21-846-8060**

Elgin Vintners   ⓥ ⓐ ⓘ

There's been a change in logo and packaging of the wines from this unique Elgin enterprise — six dedicated grape-growers, and six winemakers charged with crafting individual wines. Orange remains the signature colour, but more subtly so, and there's now plentiful reference to the richness of the flora surrounding the vineyards. The large Elgin Orchards farm is at the centre of the project, and there a new 3 ha of pinot vines are being planted, to feed increased production

★★★★ **Merlot** ⓥ Attractive Xmas cake aromas & flavours on **15** ★★★★ ⑧④ joined by herbal character. Good fruit with a friendly acid/tannin grip, but a touch of leanness; less rich than last-tasted **13** ⑧⑧.

★★★★ **Pinot Noir** ⓥ Ripe dark cherry & strawberry undertones on **16** ⑧⑨ but the effect is deliciously savoury. Good oaking (22% new); serious tannin-acid structure. Like **15** ★★★★ ⑧④, will benefit from year or 2 in bottle.

★★★★ **Syrah** Benefits of maturer wine show in added complexity, harmony. Riper fruit on **15** ⑧⑥ but fresher & lighter-feeling than also-tasted, shallower **13** ★★★★ ⑧⑤ which drinks well now. Both balanced & fairly easygoing despite good structure & 25% new oak. No **14**.

★★★★ **Chardonnay** Two vintages tasted, both with green cool-climate gleams. **16** ⑧⑧ rounded & well-balanced, oaking (20% new) supportive of the good citrus fruit, acidity lively. **14** ⑧⑥ touch too oaky & less elegant, but succulent. Drink soonish. **15** untasted.

★★★★ **The Century** Well-knit & pleasing blend in 17 (88) is 65% sauvignon, rest semillon, giving tropical & lemon notes. Unoaked as usual. Balanced, fresh & bone-dry, with some weight & length. No hurry to drink up.

Merlot Rosé ★★★ Attractive berry aromas & flavours & a herbal note on dry, rounded 18 (82), with a hint of tannic tug. **Sauvignon Blanc** ★★★★ Pleasing mix of tropical, floral & blackcurrant notes on 17 (85), with fresh green ones coming through on the crisp palate. **Viognier** ⦵ ★★★ Advanced, slightly honeyed aromas on 13 (81), the fruit having faded somewhat, though the spiciness of oak (50% new) remains. Nice roundness, smooth texture - but drink soon. Discontinued: **Agama**. — TJ

Location/map/WO: Elgin ▪ Map grid reference: B2 ▪ Est 2003 ▪ 1stB 2004 ▪ Tasting & sales Mon-Fri 10-4 & weekends by appt ▪ Function facility ▪ MTB route ▪ Fynbos walks ▪ Birding ▪ Vineyard tours ▪ Homestead to rent for getaway weekends ▪ Owner(s) Derek Corder, Max Hahn, Alastair Moodie, James Rawbone-Viljoen, Rob Semple & Paul Wallace ▪ Cellarmaster(s)/winemaker(s) Kevin Grant, Gavin Patterson, Nico Grobler, Martin Meinert, Niels Verburg, Joris van Almenkerk ▪ Viticulturist(s) Paul Wallace ▪ ±75ha (cab, malbec, merlot, pinot, shiraz, chard, riesling, sauv, sem, viog) ▪ 750t/14,500cs own label ▪ IPW ▪ PO Box 121 Elgin 7180 ▪ info@elginvintners.co.za ▪ www.elginvintners.co.za ▪ S 34°10'52.18" E 019° 0'42.54" ▪ 🌐 snarl.crosses. conferred ▪ F +27 (0)86-646-3693 ▪ T +27 (0)21-848-9587

☐ **Embrace** see Stellenrust
☐ **Emineo** see Rogge Cloof

Enfin Wines ⦵

Garagiste and attorney Susan van Aswegen sources her grapes from various areas but home base is Huguenot Street in Franschhoek. Her focus is on syrah, with ageing in different oak types reflected in some of the wine names. Minimal intervention and a sense of fun are paramount.

★★★★ **Sebastian Unfiltered Cinsaut** A 'comeback kid' variety in SA, 17 (87) from Paarl shows why: delicious raspberry fruit, depth, caramel complexity & ageing potential from 8 months new oak.

★★★★ **Alice Unfiltered Malbec** Fruit-driven 17 (87) has variety-true blackberry tone & big tannins underpinned by fresh acidity, fantail finish. WO Durbanville.

★★★★ **Ouma Rachel Syrah** ⦵ Opulent & smooth, inky hued; baking spice bouquet & black bramble fruits lingering lengthily, 15 (87) comfortable in its French oak cloak.

★★★★ **The American Syrah** Elim's cool-climate white pepper, obvious vanilla from American oak, redberry fruit on 16 (87) given form, extra appeal by fine line of acidity, well-judged tannic grip.

Strawberry Lane Pinot Noir ★★★★ New name particularly apt: ample strawberry fruit on juicy 16 (85), 20% wholebunch adds tannin backbone, appealing grip to lift the bar on previous. **The Romanian Syrah** ★★★★ Like American sibling, named for oak used, here all-new, which threatens to dominate the sweet fruit of 15 ★★★★ (87). Bold, with plush dark opulence, but lacking stature of 15 ★★★★ (87). **Casablanca Fumé Blanc** ★★★★ Brief sojourn (4 months) in new wood for 17 (84) sauvignon, giving intense herbal aroma, lemon, sage & cream flavours; succulent, but misses depth, intensity of 16 ★★★★ (87). WO W Cape. — HC

Location/map: Franschhoek ▪ Map grid reference: C1 ▪ WO: Elim/Paarl/Durbanville/Western Cape ▪ Est/1stB 2014 ▪ Tasting by appt ▪ Owner(s)/winemaker(s) Susan van Aswegen ▪ 6t 90% red 10% white ▪ 4 Huguenot Str Franschhoek 7690 ▪ info@enfinwines.co.za ▪ S 33° 54' 49.85" E 019° 7' 18.68" ▪ 🌐 sighing.freshening. geeky ▪ T +27 (0)83-310-1679

☐ **Enon** see Zandvliet Wine Estate

Entre Nous ⦵ 🍷

The five friends who 'between us' (hence the brand name) vinify bought-in grapes in Stellenbosch are excited about a cracker '15 Cabernet which they've been nurturing and plan to unleash sometime this year. The three lawyers, quantity surveyor and wine barrel expert invite winelovers to join them (by appointment) for tours, tastings, or bottling/labelling sessions followed by 'a long slow braai'.

Viognier (NEW) ★★★ Shows less of variety's peachy appeal & more of robust barrel ageing (18 months, 20% new), warm alcohol, tangy farewell. 16 (79) for fans of big, bold wines. Not tasted: **Chardonnay**. In abeyance: **Cabernet Sauvignon**, **Starboard**. — MW

Location/map: Stellenbosch ▪ Map grid reference: H5 ▪ WO: Western Cape ▪ Est/1stB 2000 ▪ Tasting, sales & cellar tours by appt ▪ BYO picnic ▪ Owner(s) Geoff Brooker, Mark Howell, Steve Kirk-Cohen, Andre Smalberger & Terry Winstanley ▪ Cellarmaster(s)/winemaker(s) Steve Kirk-Cohen, Andre Smalberger & Terry Winstanley (2000), Mark Howell & Geoff Brooker (2005) ▪ ±1,176cs own label 85% red 15% white ▪ c/o Terry Winstanley PO Box 695 Cape Town 8000 ▪ terry.winstanley@gmail.com ▪ S 33° 55' 25.96" E 018° 57' 03.12" ▪ assist.moment.hillside ▪ **T +27 (0)82-574-5173**

Epicurean Wines

Three people eminent in high finance or high politics are behind this label. Just one wine is made, the proportions within the Bordeaux-style blend varying substantially in response to vintage. The Rupert & Rothschild team sources and vinifies the grapes, but the owners have their say at blending time.

★★★★☆ **Epicurean** (🏅) Merlot dominant last year; **12** (93) half cab, with merlot & petit verdot. A little more alcoholic power at 13.7%, same impressive fruit density & concentration; well-absorbed 80% new oaking. Still youthful, the savoury sombreness starting to open, strong tannins to integrate. — TJ

WO: Stellenbosch ▪ Est 2001 ▪ 1stB 2003 ▪ Closed to public ▪ Owner(s) Epicurean Wine (Pty) Ltd ▪ Cellarmaster(s) Mutle Mogase, Mbhazima Shilowa, Moss Ngoasheng ▪ Winemaker(s) Yvonne Lester (consultant) ▪ 1,000cs own label 100% red ▪ WIETA ▪ 55 Curson Str Hyde Park 2196 ▪ info@epicureanwine. co.za ▪ www.epicureanwine.co.za ▪ **T +27 (0)11-568-3100**

Equitania

Formerly a luxurious private homestead, Equitania is now the Institute of Mine Seismology's Helderberg HQ, welcoming visitors since 2018. Its blocks of cab and cab franc are registered single-vineyard, but currently vinified as a blend in striking new livery by top-rated Ronell Wiid. We look forward to tasting it next edition.

Location: Stellenbosch ▪ Map: Helderberg ▪ Map grid reference: C3 ▪ Est 2000 ▪ 1stB 2008 ▪ Tasting & sales by appt; see website for details ▪ Closed all pub hols ▪ BYO picnic ▪ Walking/hiking trails ▪ Owner(s) Institute of Mine Seismology ▪ Winemaker(s) Ronell Wiid (consultant) ▪ Viticulturist(s) Francois Hanekom (consultant) ▪ 4.65ha/1.38ha (cabs s/f) ▪ 10.54t/12,000cs own label 100% red ▪ Postnet Suite #854 Private Bag X15 Somerset West 7130 ▪ kobus@equitania.co.za ▪ www.equitania.co.za ▪ S 34° 2' 26.15" E 018° 49' 5.51" ▪ encounter.piano.plotting ▪ **F +27 (0)21-809-2061 ▪ T +27 (0)21-809-2070**

Erasmus Family Wines

(♀)

Previously listed under Cape Wine Company, vintner Erlank Erasmus' creations mostly head off to markets overseas, but last year's five star success helped prompt him to establish a brand home and tasting outlet in the manor of Laborie estate in Paarl. The wines featured here are made in boutique quantities from mainly older bushvines in two prime areas. See Taillefert Wines for a different facet of Erlank's winecrafting.

Erasmus Family range

★★★★ **Grenache** (♀) Fresh & lively **15** (87) perfectly balances cherry & strawberry with spice & iodine. Loses jamminess of **14** ★★★★☆ (84), benefits from clean fruit & precise flavours. Piekenierskloof grapes.

★★★★☆ **Shiraz** (✓)(🏅) Delicious & satisfying **16** (93) continues good form of previous with multiple layers of blackberry, liquorice, leather & clove. Silky texture & velvet tannins (helped by 30% new French oak) harmonise with clean acidity in a lengthy finish.

★★★★☆ **Family Reserve** Was 'Erasmus Family'. Like **15** ★★★★★ (95), **16** (90) a 4-way blend (mostly carignan with mourvèdre, grenache & shiraz) delivers spice bomb notes - nutmeg, cloves, allspice - mixed with ripe red plums. Elegant & restrained, with lengthy complex finish. 14 months French oak, 30% new.

Chenin Blanc (NEW) ★★★ Nicely balanced **17** (80) gains creamy spice from 50% oak (10% new) to brighten up honeyed pineapple & soft appley fruit.

Nieuwe Haarlem

★★★★ **Cinsaut** (♀) Moreish **16** (87) from 40 year old bushvines, rustic, earthy notes overlie ripe red cherries & berries. Gentle oaking (20% new) adds spice & smoke. Piekenierskloof WO for these.

Pinotage (NEW) ★★★★ Classic pinotage aroma of warm red fruit (cherries & plums), toasty spices & distinctive 'metallic' mid-palate. **17** (85) hints of coffee, nice supple tannins & clean acidic finish. — CM

Location/map: Paarl ▪ Map grid reference: E6 ▪ WO: Swartland/Piekenierskloof ▪ Est/1stB 2010 ▪ Tasting & sales Wed-Thu 11-4 Fri/Sat 11-5 Sun/pub hols 11-2.30 ▪ Closed Good Fri, Dec 25 & Jan 1 ▪ Owner(s)/winemaker(s) Erlank Erasmus ▪ 1,500cs own label 80% red 20% white ▪ BEE, Fairtrade, WIETA ▪ Taillerfer Str Paarl 7646 ▪ erlank@capewinecompany.co.za ▪ S 33° 45′ 55.2″ E 018° 57′ 27.6″ ▪ ⌨ deserved.eminent.edit ▪ **T +27 (0)21-863-0872**

☐ **Erasmus Wines** *see* Erasmus Family Wines
☐ **Erica O** *see* Erika Obermeyer Wines

Erika Obermeyer Wines

Former long-time Graham Beck white-wine maker Erika Obermeyer relishes the hands-on nature of own-label creation: liaising with growers, nurturing old, mostly dryland-farmed, sometimes bushvine sauvignon, chenin, cabernet and cinsaut, and vinifying in rented space with assistant Hans Johannes at her side. The 'fun and engaging' marketing through direct channels and social media should not detract from 'serious, quality-driven' wines – as the ratings below make abundantly clear. This fine debut makes Erika Obermeyer Wines our well-deserved Newcomer Winery of the Year, the first such award we have made.

Erica O range

★★★★★ **Cabernet Sauvignon** ⊛ Inky colour already cues you in on what's to come; **15** ⑨⑤ is deep & rich, plums & cassis, tobacco & savoury spice from 22 months French oak, 85% new, is a big personality. Textured body, as befits the fruit, the tannins giving a good foundation, definition & a future.

★★★★★ **Syrah-Grenache Noir-Cinsault** ⊛ Syrah at 53% dictates the styling, but other varieties have their say. Veil of fynbos honey & scrub on **16** ⑨⑤'s tightly packed fruit, supple tannins, stemmy lift yet ultimately light & smooth, a mineral thread thanks to granite soils. Firgrove & Voor Paardeberg fruit. 10% new oak.

★★★★☆ **Sauvignon Blanc** ⊛ Older Groenekloof vines than Meticulous. **17** ⑨④ more restrained, less fruit-forward, has fynbos & minerality, tighter acidity yet with distinct richness from 30% barrel ferment/5 months ageing. Complex, sophisticated & poised. No rush to open: should show best in 3+ years.

Premium range

★★★★ **Meticulous Sauvignon Blanc** From Groenekloof, **17** ⑧⑧ exudes green-scented notes, asparagus, fresh peas, with lovely piquant passionfruit seaming the flavours. Zesty, limy, stimulates the taste buds, very long finish.

Flabbergast Cinsault ★★★★ Dryland, old Firgrove vines; **16** ⑧⑤ savoury leather pouch appeal (partly oaked), palate soft fresh fruits, supple, bright acidity extends the finish. — CR, CvZ

Location: Stellenbosch ▪ WO: Stellenbosch/Groenekloof/Coastal ▪ Est 2016 ▪ 1stB 2015 ▪ Tasting by appt only ▪ Owner(s)/winemaker(s) Erika Obermeyer ▪ 30t/4,000cs own label 55% red 45% white ▪ IPW ▪ PO Box 2706 Paarl 7620 ▪ erika@erikaobermeyerwines.co.za ▪ www.erikaobermeyerwines.co.za ▪ **T +27 (0)82-940-3499**

Ernie Els Wines

Harvest 2018 was a watershed for this Helderberg mountain property, co-owned by sweet-swinging SA-born golfer Ernie Els. After bringing in the crop from vineyards refined to extract the prime terroir's potential for bold yet sophisticated reds (emphasising cabernet from 11 site-suited clones), long-term winemaker and MD Louis Strydom and team turned to the cellar. A size reduction allows focus on the Signature and Proprietor's flagship labels and micro-batch vinification from pockets of vines, precision farmed down to the last row. The project includes a tasting room overhaul (with vinotèque) and 120-seat fine-dining restaurant (with menu to match both star-studded wines and spectacular views). The farm is closed to visitors until spring 2019, but it'll be worth the wait.

Ernie Els range

★★★★☆ **Cabernet Sauvignon** ⊛ Aristocratic **16** ⑨③ a multi-layered classic with dark fruit & cigarbox, cedar & dark spice, graphite edge. As in **15** ⑨②, dense tannins need few years or decanting. Dashes petit verdot & shiraz.

★★★★☆ **Proprietor's Cabernet Sauvignon** ② Quintessential Stellenbosch cab, brooding **15** ⑨ with dark fruit & backbone of leather, graphite & violet. Still settling but 60% new oak, good extraction & solid mid-palate fruit will serve it well over the next decade.

★★★★ **Merlot** ⑥ Well-crafted **16** ⑧ with smidgens cab franc & malbec, prune, cocoa & crushed herb complexity, nimble tannins. Full bodied & serious enough for good few years cellaring.

★★★★ **Proprietor's Syrah** ② Engaging **15** ★★★★☆ ⑨, with dash of viognier, entices with perfumed aromas & gentle play of dark fruit & pepper spice. A luminosity carries through to the palate; medium body, well-judged oak & stately tannin. Outperforms **14** ⑧.

★★★★☆ **Ernie Els Signature** ② Stately, beautifully modulated flagship, **14** ⑨ a 5-way Bordeaux blend with cab & merlot (60/25) adding a spark of freshness to the big (15%) alcohol via cool herbaceous notes & succulent red fruit. Serious 85% new French oak sets up long, fruitful future. Also in 1.5, 3 & 5L.

★★★★☆ **CWG Auction Reserve** ② ⑥ Second parcel of **15** ⑨ from 2018 auction, not retasted. Regal blend, cab & shiraz with cinsaut fashionably replacing **14** ⑨'s merlot; drapes a mantle of intense fruit over backbone of taut tannin & judicious French & American oak (60% new), fruit purity persists on palate, auguring well for extended cellaring.

★★★★☆ **Proprietor's Blend** ⑥ Magnificent 5-way Bordeaux blend with 20% shiraz. **16** ★★★★★ ⑨ improves on **15** ⑨ with mulberry, blackcurrant in harmony with dark spice, savoury conclusion, finely grained tannin support. Somewhat formidable in youth, with hefty alcohol, 25% new oak. Give it plenty of time.

Sauvignon Blanc ★★★★ Ripe gooseberries & limes, crunchy acidity & bone-dry finish, **18** ⑧ refreshes & whets the appetite.

Big Easy range

★★★★ **Red** Satisfying shiraz-led 6-way combo, **17** ⑧ steps up on already handsome **16** ★★★ ⑧ with expressive violet bouquet, polished tannins, savoury tail seasoned with older oak. Also in 1.5, 3 & 5L.

Cabernet Sauvignon ★★★★ Has a dash of suave cinsaut to make it as effortless as the co-proprietor's swing, **17** ⑧ given subtle form by 40% old-oaked portion. **Rosé** ★★★ Bone-dry, food-styled **18** ⑧, lively pomegranates & strawberries, lightish 11.6% alcohol. Shiraz with splash viognier. **Chenin Blanc** ★★★★ Ripe quince, pineapple & mango appeal on generous **18** ⑧, bright acidity & juicy tropical tail for fruity enjoyment. WO W Cape, as all these. — GM

Location/map: Stellenbosch ▪ Map grid reference: E8 ▪ WO: Stellenbosch/Western Cape ▪ Est 1999 ▪ 1stB 2000 ▪ Closed for renovations, please phone ahead ▪ Owner(s) Ernie Els & Baron Hans von Staff-Reitzenstein ▪ Cellarmaster(s)/winemaker(s) Louis Strydom (Dec 1999) ▪ Viticulturist(s) Leander Koekemoer (2015) ▪ 72ha/45ha (cab, merlot, shiraz) ▪ 400t/30,000cs own label 80% red 20% white + 1,500cs for clients ▪ PO Box 7595 Stellenbosch 7599 ▪ info@ernieelswines.com ▪ www.ernieelswines.com ▪ S 34° 0' 52.8" E 018° 50' 53.5" ▪ ☞ rinsing.resources.inhabits ▪ F +27 (0)21-881-3688 ▪ **T +27 (0)21-881-3588**

Ernst Gouws & Co Wines   ② ③ ⑤

Winemaker and Huguenot scion Ernst Gouws and wife Gwenda started their own Stellenbosch wine company 15 years ago, buying and vinifying grapes. Daughter Ezanne Gouws-du Toit, also a qualified winemaker, handles marketing, sales and exports besides raising two toddlers.

★★★★ **Merlot** ② Brawny **15** ⑧ shows super-ripe red berry fruit with robust tannins. Aromatic & savoury notes need time to knit, suggest promising future.

★★★★ **Chardonnay** ② Leaner, mineral-driven **16** ⑧ is tank fermented, older barrel aged 7 months, bringing fresh lime fruit into foreground. Appealing texture & richness, lingering finish.

★★★★ **Nineteenfiftytwo** ② Seriously conceived semillon (75%) & sauvignon blend, all-new barrel fermented, **16** ⑧ showing typical wild nettle & wool aromas, restrained oak, abundant body & texture.

Pinot Noir ② ★★★ Tarry notes on **16** ⑧ but fragrant berry fruit too. WO W Cape. **Pinotage** ② ★★★★ Subdued but generous **16** ⑧ has ripe plum & bramble fruit, robust but smooth tannins, no rough edges. **Shiraz** ★★★★ Livelier & more defined, **16** ⑧ from Stellenbosch also touch more streamlined, less ripe than ex-Swartland **15** ⑧ with its stewed fruit. In magnum, too. **Chenin Blanc** ★★★★ Fresh-&-fruity Stellenbosch character, **18** ⑧'s crunchy apple lends crispness to lightish body, decent length of flavour.

Sauvignon Blanc ★★★ Tank sample **18** ⑧ tingles with freshness, cut grass aromas & flavours add to the racy green character. — DS

Location/map: Stellenbosch ▪ Map grid reference: D1 ▪ WO: Stellenbosch/Western Cape ▪ Est/1stB 2003 ▪ Tasting & sales at Koelenhof Winery Mon-Thu 9-5 Fri 9-4 Sat 10-2 ▪ Closed Easter Fri/Sun, Ascension day, Dec 25/26 ▪ Jan 1 ▪ Facilities for children ▪ Owner(s) Gouws family ▪ Cellarmaster(s) Ernst Gouws snr ▪ 40,000cs own label 40% red 60% white ▪ IPW ▪ PO Box 7450 Stellenbosch 7599 ▪ ernst@ernstgouws.co.za ▪ www.ernstgouws.co.za ▪ S 33° 50′ 3.4″ E 018° 47′ 52.7″ ▪ ⌨ climate.helpers.spades ▪ F +27 (0)21-865-2894 ▪ **T +27 (0)21-865-2895**

Escapades Winery

The range of Escapades wines, not ready for this edition, is being expanded to include a white and red, and undergoing a facelift, with new labels and packaging. This is a multinational venture, owned by Sweden-based Greek national Takis Soldatos, working with Kiwi-born, SA-stationed winemaker Chris Kelly, who also spends three months of the year making Takis' Italian wines in Puglia. Though Escapades wines were exclusively for export, there are plans to enter the local market.

Location/map: Stellenbosch ▪ Map grid reference: B4 ▪ Est/1stB 2006 ▪ Tasting by appt ▪ Owner(s) Takis Soldatos ▪ Winemaker(s) Chris Kelly (Oct 2010, consultant) ▪ (cab, malbec, ptage, shiraz, sauv, sem) ▪ 100t/10,000cs own label 40% red 50% white 10% rosé ▪ PO Box 99 Somerset Mall 7129 ▪ info@escapadewinery.com ▪ www.escapadewinery.com ▪ S 33° 54′ 47.7″ E 018° 44′ 7.7″ ▪ ⌨ carpenters.zing.sentence ▪ F +27 (0)86-585-6549 ▪ **T +27 (0)82-569-3371**

☐ **Eskdale** see Frater Family Wines

Esona Boutique Wine

Robertson's Esona ('The Very One') specialises in varietal wines from registered single-vineyards, produced in a recently inaugurated on-site cellar. Owners Rowan and Caryl Beattie retain stocks of multiple vintages, enabling winelovers to experience the differences between the harvests (special candle-lit tastings available by appointment). The visitor venue overlooks the Breede River, and includes Caryl's Deli and refurbished open fermentation 'kuipe' dating back 100 years.

Single Vineyard range

★★★★ **Shiraz** ⓐ Lithe but structured **16** ⑧ has deep dark berry fruit, good concentration & bright tang on long finish. Follows form of **15** ⑧, **14** ⑧ & **13** ⑧, all still selling.

★★★★ **Chardonnay** ⓐ Ripe, rich mouthfeel with leesy breadth & strudel appeal on **16** ⑧. **15** ⑧ crisper, with higher acidity, like **14** ⑧. All still available.

★★★★ **Chenin Blanc** ⓝ Bright, bold & luscious **17** ⑧, sunshine-in-a-bottle styling but firm oak structure to control it, good acid to balance vibrant orchard & apple fruit. Will age well.

Frankly My Dear Pinot Noir Blanc de Noir ⓐ ★★★ Crushed strawberry appeal to nose & palate on nicely dry **17** ⑧. **Sauvignon Blanc** ⓐ ★★★★ **16** ⑧ offers lemon verbena zip & flinty tautness. **13** ★★★ ⑧ is fresh courtesy high acid yet showing evolution. Modest alcohol on these vintages still selling at cellardoor. Not tasted: **Pinot Noir, Méthode Cap Classique.** — WB

Location/map/WO: Robertson ▪ Map grid reference: C4 ▪ Est 2002 ▪ 1stB 2010 ▪ Tasting & sales Mon-Fri 9-5 Sat/pub hols 10-4 ▪ Closed Dec 25 & Jan 1 ▪ Std tasting; Taste-the-Difference tasting (2 vintages/3 cultivars); fruit preserve/chocolate/music & wine pairing ±55 min, essential to book ▪ Taste-of-Africa ▪ Caryl's Deli ▪ Owner(s) Rowan & Caryl Beattie ▪ Winemaker(s) Charmaine Arendse (Jan 2017), mentored by Lourens van der Westhuizen (Jan 2010) ▪ 17ha/9.83ha (grenache, mourv, pinot, shiraz, chard, chenin, cbard, sauv) ▪ ±250t/6,000cs own label 34% red 66% white ▪ PO Box 2619 Clareinch 7400 ▪ info@esona.co.za ▪ www.esona.co.za ▪ S 33° 54′ 16.14″ E 020° 0′ 38.66″ ▪ ⌨ kayaks.glee.databank ▪ F +27 (0)21-787-3792 ▪ **T +27 (0)76-343-5833**

☐ **Essay** see MAN Family Wines
☐ **Essence du Cap** see Fleur du Cap
☐ **Eternal** see Kumala

Euphoria

Chandré Petersen crafted a lovely pinot noir at De Grendel as a Cape Winemakers Guild protégé. She's since graduated from that programme and taken up a prestigious winemaking position at Accolade Wines, leaving little time for the own-label. However, the wine is still available by arrangement.

★★★★☆ **Pinot Noir** Ⓥ Sleek **13** ⑨① shows exceptional fruit purity: cherries & raspberries melded with dark earth & judicious 33% new oak. Seamless & delicious now but has depth for cellaring.— WB, CvZ

Location: Somerset West ▪ WO: Ceres Plateau ▪ Est 2013 ▪ 1stB 2014 ▪ Tasting by appt ▪ Owner(s)/wine-maker(s) Chandré Petersen ▪ 35cs own label 100% red ▪ chandre.petersen@accolade-wines.com ▪ **T** +27 (0)21-850-5885

Excelsior Estate

With a manor house (converted into luxury accommodation) dating back to the 'era of the ostriches in Robertson', and the rooms named after the on-site thoroughbred stud's most famous racehorses over the last 145 years, Old World charm resonates throughout this Robertson family estate. The wines, though, are unabashedly New World - fruity and generous - and hugely successful, locally and overseas. Plantings of malbec, to blend with the cab, are in progress. And Ernest Reyneke has come on board as marketing manager to help keep it all on a winning track.

Excelsior Reserve range

★★★★ **Evanthuis Cabernet Sauvignon** Ⓥ Off farm's oldest vines, fruitcake & cassis richness yet still streamlined, **13** ⑧⑧ already has palate appeal, plus good oak foundation for cellaring.

★★★★ **Gondolier Merlot** Durban July winner no shrinking violet, **15** ⑧⑥ abundant black fruit & some earthiness on bales of velvet tannin, deft oaking (20% new, year) completes delicious wine which improves on last **13** ★★★★ ⑧④.

★★★★ **San Louis Shiraz** Ripe tannins firmly control **15** ⑧⑥'s galloping red & black berries, spicing from fruit & year French/American oak, 20% new add to more finessed performance than last **13** ★★★★ ⑧⑤.

Excelsior Classic range

Chardonnay Ⓥ ★★★ Tangy & fresh **18** ⑧⓪ preview maximises drinkability by merging citrus & pear fruit, dash sugar & clever winemaking (25% new French oak, 3 months).

Cabernet Sauvignon ★★★ Rich, ripe & dense **17** ⑧⓪ preview. Ample cassis & top note of coffee from 9 months French & American oak, 30% new. **Merlot** ★★★ What merlot fans want: a juicy wine with velvet tannin, touch of chocolate & violet fragrance. **17** ⑧⓪ part oaked, 50% new, 9 months. **Paddock Shiraz** ★★★ Generous tannin & perfume on **16** ⑧⓪ with splash petit verdot. Oak spice supporting succulent fruit draws you in for a second sip. **Caitlyn Rosé** ★★★ Friendly, easy & dry **18** ⑦⑦, exuberant raspberry coulis flavours from shiraz. **Sauvignon Blanc** ★★★ Bracingly fresh & intense **18** ⑧② with loads of gooseberry & lime, long mineral farewell. **Viognier** ★★★ Charming just-dry **18** ⑧⓪ tank sample, generous spice, peach & apricot undimmed by oak, perfect for Tuesday night curry.

Purebred range

Red Ⓥ ★★★ Unoaked shiraz & merlot, **16** ⑦⑧ spicy, juicy & friendly, equally amicable price. **Sauvignon Blanc** ★★★ Easy **18** ⑦⑧, perfectly fresh, lovely palate texture thanks to a gram of sugar. — HC

Location/map/WO: Robertson ▪ Map grid reference: C4 ▪ Est 1859 ▪ 1stB 1990 ▪ Tasting & sales Mon-Fri 10-4 Sat 10-3 ▪ Deli serving light lunches ▪ Picnics available on request ▪ Facilities for children ▪ Conferences ▪ 4-star Excelsior Manor Guest House ▪ Owner(s) Freddie & Peter de Wet ▪ Cellarmaster(s) Johan Stemmet (Aug 2003) ▪ Winemaker(s) Johan Stemmet (Aug 2003), with Kelly Gova (2005) ▪ Viticulturist(s) Freddie de Wet (1970) ▪ 320ha/220ha (cab, merlot, p verdot, shiraz, chard, sauv) ▪ 2,200t/320,000cs own label 75% red 25% white ▪ Other export brand: Stablemate ▪ BRC ▪ PO Box 17 Ashton 6715 ▪ info@excelsior.co.za ▪ www.excelsior.co.za ▪ S 33° 51′ 15.1″ E 020° 0′ 25.6″ ▪ welder.honed.machin ▪ **F** +27 (0)23-615-2019 ▪ **T** +27 (0)23-615-1980

Excelsior Vlakteplaas

Danie Schoeman's family have grown grapes on their Klein Karoo farm since the 1930s, but the recent drought has been very difficult and no premium fortifieds were made last year. Happily Danie has stock of the '15 sweet desserts featured below to offer by-appointment visitors to the cellardoor near De Rust.

His Master's Choice range

Red Muscadel ② ★★★★ Rich dried peach & honey on **15** ⑧④ sweet charmer. Nicely balanced acidity gives a clean, lingering finish. **White Muscadel** ② ★★★ Dusty peach & fig fruit notes on a rustic spirit base, **15** ★★★ ⑧⓪ slightly cloying but that's ok when winter's clawing at the door. — DB

Location: De Rust ▪ Map: Klein Karoo & Garden Route ▪ Map grid reference: B3 ▪ WO: Klein Karoo ▪ Est 1934 ▪ 1stB 1998 ▪ Tasting & sales by appt only ▪ Closed Easter Fri-Mon, Ascension day, Dec 16/25/26 & Jan 1 ▪ Owner(s)/winemaker(s) Danie Schoeman ▪ 31ha (merlot, ptage, ruby cab, chenin, muscadel r/w) ▪ 490t/2,000cs own label 50% red 50% white ▪ PO Box 112 De Rust 6650 ▪ jjschoeman@telkomsa.net ▪ S 33° 29'16.74" E 022° 35'25.50" ▪ ✉ solar.resettling.prompting ▪ F +27 (0)44-241-2569 ▪ **T +27 (0)82-821-3556**

Fable Mountain Vineyards

This Tulbagh boutique producer, sibling to Mulderbosch, benefits from a unique location high on the slopes of the Witzenberg mountains, on the boundary of a wilderness nature reserve. The elevation, aspect, cool nights and mainly schist/clay soils, with pockets of quartz, impart a naturally high acidity in the grapes, giving a freshness and longevity to the wines. Winemaker Tremayne Smith is identifying special vineyards for the newly launched Small Batch range of mostly syrahs, made in exceptional vintages only. These and the new Raptor Post wines (the only ones from outsourced grapes) will now be distributed in the US by Pascal Schildt, an importer who specialises in showcasing smaller, niche producers.

Fable Mountain Vineyards range

★★★★★ **Syrah** ② Sophisticated & focused **15** ⑨③. White pepper & sweet spice streamlined by fine dry tannins. Structured for the longer term, with innate balance, showing fine pedigree of these Tulbagh vineyards, consistent source of top-quality syrah. Ripe **14** ★★★★★ ⑨⑤ had great precision.

★★★★★ **Night Sky** ② Intricately woven **15** ⑨③ is mainly grenache & syrah, with mourvèdre. Firm but elegant structure for rich core of perfumed berry fruit; deserves time to shine. Some Swartland grapes. Native yeasts, 10% whole bunch, larger mostly older French oak 10 months, as for Syrah.

★★★★ **Belle Flower** A food-pairing rosé, now from mourvèdre, naturally fermented/aged in old 500L oak. **17** ★★★★ ⑧④ savoury red fruit, silky yet fresh, clean farewell. Moderate 12.6% alcohol. Less intense than **15** ⑧⑦. No **16**.

★★★★★ **Jackal Bird** ② Standout white blend shows delicate vitality & purity, youthful harmony in the intricate weave of its chenin, grenache, roussanne, chardonnay & viognier make-up. **14** ⑨③ satin texture, concluding pithy grip add dimension. Natural ferment in oak (15% new), concrete 'eggs'. WO W Cape.

Small Batch Series ⓃⒺⓌ

★★★★ **Grenache** Variety's scented, sweet tobacco profile on **17** ⑧⑦. Same winemaking as Mourvèdre, old oak & concrete 'eggs'. Ripe & concentrated, warm-hearted despite measured 13.7% alcohol. Silky, approachable tannins, but potential to improve.

★★★★ **Syrah SYB7** This trio of Tulbagh syrahs, from 3 different vineyard elevations, identically made: natural ferment in open concrete tanks, aged 14 months in old 500L oak. **17** ⑧⑥, ex lowest-lying block, ripe & more savoury, quite dense & muscular. Youthful, needs time to develop & show full potential.

★★★★★ **Syrah SYB8** Alluring, scented white pepper on **17** ⑨②, from higher vineyard than B7. Distinctly more elegant than siblings, also lowest sugar & alcohol (13.8%), highest acidity. Dry & sappy, lovely fruit purity & balance; will continue to unfurl beautifully with time.

★★★★ **Syrah SYB9** Has both the highest alcohol (14.6%) & vineyard elevation of the trio, latter giving fresher impression than B7. **17** ⑧⑨ ripe but bright fruit; supple but structured to age.

Mourvèdre ★★★★ Rather closed & unknit mid-2018. Dark fruit, quite fresh, not revealing enough earnest intent in youth. Feels warmer than 12.9% alcohol. **17** ⑧③ may blossom with time.

The Raptor Post range

Red ★★★ Juicy & spicy melange of grenache, syrah & mourvèdre. **16** ⑧② dry, supple & balanced, lots of accessible flavour. WO Coastal. **Rosé ★★★** From mourvèdre & syrah, **17** ⑧⓪ savoury & dry, with subtle red fruit & brisk acidity. Modest 12.8% alcohol but quite forthright, for food rather than solo. — MW

Location: Tulbagh ▪ WO: Tulbagh/Coastal/Western Cape ▪ Est 1989 ▪ 1stB 2009 ▪ Tasting at Mulderbosch Vineyards ▪ Conservation area ▪ Owner(s) Tulbagh Holdings MRU Limited ▪ Winemaker(s) Tremayne Smith (Aug 2016) ▪ Farm manager Werner Wessels (2013) ▪ 179ha/28ha (grenache, mourv, shiraz) ▪ PO Box 12817 Die Board 7613 ▪ tremayne@fablewines.com ▪ www.fablewines.com ▪ **T +27 (0)21-881-8140**

☐ **Fabulous!** see Wineways Marketing
☐ **Fairhills** see Origin Wine
☐ **Fair Karoo** see Rogge Cloof
☐ **Fairtrade Original** see Piekenierskloof Wine Company

Fairvalley Wines ⓠ

This friendly, affordable range with Fairtrade accreditation was established in 1998 to benefit winefarm employees in Paarl. Latterly it thrived as a joint venture between Fairvalley Farmworkers Association and Piekenierskloof Wine Company but from the 2018 vintage, has returned — both as regards location and partnership — to its roots on Fairview.

Pinotage ⓥ **★★★** Vibrant **17** ⑧② inky hue, matching deep raspberry & mulberry notes, juicy acidity & friendly grip. WO W Cape & Fairtrade certified, as all unless noted.

Chardonnay ⓠ **★★★** Youthful **17** ⑧⓪ preview needs time to develop tangerine & pineapple of predecessor, very little oak influence from older 500L French & American barrels. **Chenin Blanc ★★★** White peach & pear aromas, appley flavours, cheery freshness, **18** ⑦⑧ from Paarl has summer fun written all over it. **Sauvignon Blanc** ⓠ **★★★** Previewed last edition, **17** ⑧② exuberant lime & grapefruit, very crisp & dry, flinty finish & reined-in 12% alcohol. Not tasted: **Chardonnay Reserve**. Discontinued: **Cabernet Sauvignon**. — CvZ

Location: Paarl ▪ WO: Western Cape/Paarl ▪ Est 1997 ▪ 1stB 1998 ▪ Tasting by appt only ▪ Fee R25 ▪ Closed Good Fri, Dec 25 & Jan 1 ▪ Sales at Fairview ▪ Owner(s) Fairvalley Farmworkers Association ▪ Cellarmaster(s)/winemaker(s) Awie Adolf (2018) ▪ 30,000cs own label 50% red 50% white ▪ Fairtrade ▪ PO Box 6219 Paarl 7620 ▪ wine@fairvalley.co.za ▪ F +27 (0)21-863-2591 ▪ **T +27 (0)21-863-2450**

Fairview

Multi-tasker Charles Back (see also Spice Route) oversees one of the winelands' busiest cellardoors at this, his Paarl home-farm, complemented by a thriving cheesery (the resident roaming goat herd inspiring their own wine brand, Goats do Roam, also listed separately) and artisan deli. Winemaker since 1996, Anthony de Jager, and assistants produce wines neatly assigned to five ranges. These include wines of particular interest and excellence, some from varieties relatively new to Fairview's hillsides, such as grenache, tempranillo, marsanne and verdelho. Other ranges cover Fairview's trademark stellar shirazes, off-farm single-vineyard parcels, sweet wines and a long list of popular favourites, something for every taste and budget. Fifth range La Capra being trimmed and will continue with just four wines: a merlot, pinotage, chenin and sauvignon.

Regional Revival range

★★★★☆ Caldera Grenache (83%) with mourvèdre & shiraz, expressive, delicious ripe berry fruit to the fore in **16** ⑨② Lithe & supple, with silky tannins, showing finesse, fragrance & length. Seasoned oak, 16 months. Coastal WO, as next.

★★★★☆ Extraño Spanish-inspired blend led by tempranillo (75%), the extraño ('stranger') in Fairview's vineyards, with grenache & carignan. **15** ⑨① dark, weighty fruit structure laced with pretty floral & aromatic notes, smooth tannins & satisfyingly fragrant finish. 20% new oak.

★★★★☆ Homtini ⓐ Beautifully poised & stylish **16** ⑨③ sangiovese blend with cab, merlot & shiraz. Darling dryland vines yield dense, richly ripe fruit with intensity & structure, boldly confident tannins & seductively fragrant finish.

★★★★☆ **Drie Papen Fontein** Terroir-expressive Bordeaux-style **17** ⑨② blend of tank-fermented sauvignon & barrel-fermented (third new) semillon, showing enticingly complex nuances of seagrass, oystershell, fennel & lime. From dry-farmed vineyards near Darling.

★★★★ **Méthode Cap Classique Brut** ⓥ Unique sparkling from 50% viognier, equal grenache blanc & noir, 18 months on lees, **15** ⑧⑥ refreshes with lemon, green apple & cream cracker notes.
Not tasted: **Nurok**.

Limited Releases

★★★★☆ **Stok by Paaltjie Grenache** Referring to 'staked vine' (echalas) trellising system on Paarl home-farm, **16** ⑨② has style & panache. Remarkably full body is packed with red berry fruit, laced with floral scents & savoury aromatics, herbal fynbos & smoky oak spices from 15 months in older wood.

★★★★ **Primo Pinotage** Muscular yet well-mannered **16** ⑧⑦ has concentrated black fruit with smoky-spicy embellishments, thick tannic texture. Serious oaking: 60% new, 20 months. Needs time. **15** untasted.

★★★★☆ **Eenzaamheid Shiraz** ⓐ From shale site in Agter Paarl, **16** ⑨③ is terroir-revealing & intense, shows power as well as finesse. Subtle herbaceous threads in dense black cherry fruit, aromatic tobacco & subdued barrel spicing (some new). Cellarworthy, but accessible now.

★★★★☆ **Jakkalsfontein Shiraz** ⓥ Back on track after subdued **14** ★★★★ ⑧⑧, **15** ⑨⓪ packed with black cherry & blackberry; hints of baking spice & liquorice from 20 months in French oak, 40% new. Rich & full bodied, bold but soft tannins.

★★★★☆ **The Beacon Shiraz** ⓥ Full-bodied **15** ⑨③ sees 10% less new oak than Eenzaamheid, allowing ripe, concentrated dark fruit to shine against complex aromatic backdrop (florals, fynbos, herbs, smoke, leather & intense pepper). Tannins firm but fine.

★★★★ **Pegleg Carignan** ⊛ Laudable rendition of notoriously tricky variety, **16** ⑧⑧ from 1981 Swartland block (SA's oldest) reveals luscious cherry fruit centre & brightly aromatic spices, finishing with white pepper twist. Older oak.
Not tasted: **Cyril Back**.

Sweet Wines range

★★★★☆ **La Beryl Blanc** ⓐ Fragrant floral-tinged honey with 'moskonfyt' (grape syrup) note on stunning **17** ⑨④ chenin (73%) & muscat de Frontignan straw wine. Intense sweetness is tempered by racy acidity, lingering to long, elegant finish. Honours Back matriarch. Unoaked, like **16** ⑨③.

★★★★ **La Beryl Rouge** Quirky full-sweet wooded shiraz straw wine, **17** ⑧⑥ has character & appeal. Robust tannins, fresh ripe fruit & pretty floral hues suggest match with strong cheeses. 500 ml, as Blanc.

Sweet Red ⓥ ★★★★ A fortified blue cheese match of note, **16** ⑧⑤ from petite sirah with 10% each tempranillo & souzão, has very rich, boozy Christmas cake flavours: dried fruit, mixed spice & nuts.

Fairview range

★★★★ **Stellenbosch Cabernet Sauvignon** ⓐ Brawny yet poised & vibrant, **16** ⑧⑦ shows aromatic tea with leafy-earthy notes, sweet-salty liquorice & cassis. 18 months in barrels, 20% new. Unknit tannins suggest cellaring.

★★★★ **Barbera** Typically tangy, with crushed red berry fruit, **16** ⑧⑥ is plush & juicy, with mild tannins. Very appealing, food friendly. Year in barrels, mostly French.

★★★★ **Bushvine Cinsault** Was 'Paarl Cinsault', still is from there. Fragrantly sweet red fruit dominates elegant **17** ⑧⑦: fresh cherries & plums spiced with twist of white pepper. Worthy example of variety's resurrection, from 30+ year old vines.

★★★★ **Piekenierskloof Grenache** ⓥ Ex high-lying bushvines planted 1973, silky **16** ⑧⑥ delicate in terms of both fruit & spice. Fresh acidity, therefore a versatile food wine.

★★★★ **Mourvèdre** Meaty, savoury **16** ⑧⑥ has sweetly ripe fruit with mixed spices, aromatic tobacco & dusty-earthy notes. Rather rigid tannins should soften & knit with time. Coastal WO.

★★★★☆ **Petite Sirah** ⓐ Variety also known as durif; like **14** ⑨① rugged, foursquare **15** ⑨⓪ is anything but 'petite'. Angular, with concentrated black fruit blanketed in tannin, 2 years in oak (partly new, some American) add to the forceful personality. Lay down for 3-4 years.

★★★★ **Pinotage** Familiar face in a sea of foreigners, **17** ⑧⑥ has welcoming rush of wild-berry fruit on firm tannins. Expressive & well gauged, with appealing floral notes.

★★★★ **Shiraz** Convincing scrub & pepper on medium-bodied, Rhône-styled **16** ⑧⑥, with spicy red fruit, ripe tannins & fine balance. Paarl & Darling vines.

★★★★ **Tannat** Robust variety from s-w France, one of still only handful in SA, **15** ⑧⑦ admirably plush & approachable despite hefty tannins; characterful & different.

★★★★ **Chardonnay** Elegantly restrained oak characters add breadth to appealing citrus fruit on **17** ⑧⑦ from Darling & Paarl. Thickly rich leesiness, tempered acid, gratifying finish.

★★★★ **Paarl Chenin Blanc 17** ★★★★ ⑧④ gets more oak (50%, of which 40% new) than fruitier **15** ⑧⑦. Tangy apricot & pineapple with toasty-nutty undertones, prominent acid. **16** untasted.

★★★★ **Darling Riesling** Off-dry at 12 g/l sugar, **18** ⑧⑥ has delicious floral/citrus tone with typical West Coast minerality. Hints of litchi & rosewater, tingling acidity suggest spicy food matches.

★★★★ **Roussanne** Rhône variety shows well in Paarl vineyards, **17** ⑧⑧ offering subtle aromatics, honeyed peach & citrus with satisfyingly rich, leesy texture. 40% barrel fermented.

★★★★ **Darling Sauvignon Blanc** Commendable fruit purity on **18** ⑧⑥ from dryland vineyards, backed up by striking lime-mineral tones. Full & generous, with satisfyingly crisp acidity. **17** untasted.

★★★★ **Verdelho** Madeira's signature variety gaining traction with New World producers; unwooded **17** ⑧⑥ terpene hints with crisp, salty minerality, supported by papaya & melon fruit layers. Paarl & Swartland vines.

★★★★ **Viognier** Somewhat heavy-handed, with savoury flavours overshadowing white peach fruit. Half-oaked **16** ★★★★ ⑧④ satisfyingly fat & textural, but a shade off **15** ⑧⑥.

......

Darling Chenin Blanc ⑦ ★★★★ The unwooded sibling; full & generous **18** ⑧④ has cling peach & melon fruit on creamy mineral texture. Richness from lees contact, typical salty-bitter twist on finish.

......

Stellenbosch Merlot ⑦ ★★★★ Aromas promise plum & mocha richness, but **15** ⑧③'s palate doesn't deliver much ripe fruit; tannins tad green, some liquorice on exit.

La Capra range

Not tasted: **Merlot, Pinotage, Chenin Blanc, Sauvignon Blanc**. Discontinued: **Cabernet Sauvignon, Malbec, Sangiovese, Shiraz, Chardonnay, Pinot Grigio, Bouquet Fair, Muscadel**. — GdB

Location/map: Paarl ▪ Map grid reference: D6 ▪ WO: Paarl/Coastal/Darling/Swartland/Stellenbosch/Piekenierskloof ▪ Est 1693 ▪ 1stB 1974 ▪ Tasting & sales Mon-Sun 9–5, last tasting 30min before closing ▪ Standard/master tasting (applicable fees apply) ▪ Closed Dec 25 & Jan 1 ▪ The Goatshed Restaurant ▪ Deli: artisanal cheeses & fresh farm breads ▪ Owner(s) Charles Back ▪ Winemaker(s) Anthony de Jager (Dec 1996), with Stephanie Wiid (2010) & Annette van Zyl (2014) ▪ 500ha/300ha (cab, carignan, grenache, merlot, mourv, petite sirah, ptage, shiraz, tannat, tempranillo, chenin, sauv, viog) ▪ 2,100t/260cs own label 80% red 15% white 5% rosé ▪ ISO 9001:2001, BRC, Fairtrade, HACCP, IPW, WIETA ▪ PO Box 583 Suider-Paarl 7624 ▪ info@fairview.co.za ▪ www.fairview.co.za ▪ S 33° 46′19.16″ E 018° 55′25.26″ ▪ ▥ breezes.sting.result ▪ F +27 (0)21-863-2591 ▪ **T +27 (0)21-863-2450**

False Bay Vineyards
⑦

Though pocket friendly and intended as 'everyday enjoyment', these wines by Waterkloof are treated seriously, with old vines, wild-yeast ferments and large-oak ageing the norm. The new Revenant label is a tribute to a sauvignon/chenin blend named Cuvée Jean Paul, which launched the wine career of Waterkloof owner Paul Boutinot in 1984.

False Bay range

......

Slow Chenin Blanc ⊘ ⑦ ★★★★ Older Swartland & Wellington bushvines for **17** ⑧④, fresher than previous though quite plush brioche & yellow peach flavours. More rounded & fruity than Peacock. For - slow - sipping with a meal. Very good value too!

......

Bushvine Pinotage ★★★ Low-yield, 30 year old Paarl bushvines show savoury smokiness, with spiced berry, liquorice flavours. **16** ⑧① supple & amiable (13% alcohol) barbecue & hearty meal mate. **Old School Syrah** ⊘ ★★★★ Ex Helderberg, Stellenbosch & Swartland, different source & less (old) oaking than Peacock sibling, suppler, touch friendlier. **17** ⑧③ smoky bacon & some white pepper, juicy. **Whole Bunch Cinsault-Mourvèdre** ★★★ Rosé off Swartland & Stellenbosch vines, **18** ⑦⑨ strawberry & savoury nuances, dry, delicate & fruity but fresh. At modest 12% alcohol, delightful sunset sipper. **Crystalline Chardonnay** ② ★★★ Part natural ferment for **17** ⑧②, lees ageing adds creaminess to ripe pear & lime flavours; gentle, balanced acidity, enough substance for food. Not tasted: **Windswept Sauvignon Blanc**.

Revenant range ⒩

Revenant ★★★★ Old-oaked sauvignon (80%) & chenin, **17** ⑧⑤ celebrates blend that launched owner Paul Boutinot's career in 1980s. Lovely freshness, green herbs & apples, creamy succulence & gentle, lingering farewell. Stylish solo sipper or table companion.

Peacock Wild Ferment range

★★★★ **Chardonnay** Ripe pear & lime on unoaked **18** ★★★★ ⑧④, bright & fresh, plenty of pure chardonnay flavour for the modest 12.6 alcohol. Shade off **16** ⑧⑥, though; now more in summer sipping style. **17** untasted.

Merlot ★★★★ Dapper step up on last, **17** ⑧⑤ tangy berry fruit & fresh herb nuance, juicier, with pliable, friendlier tannins. Solo or with tomato-based food. Schapenberg Hill vines, as most of these. **Syrah** ★★★ Smoky dark fruit & fynbos scrub, **16** ⑧① quite piquant & dry, feistier than False Bay stablemate. For food partnering rather than solo. **Chenin Blanc** ★★★★ Old Helderberg bushvines, **18** ⑧③ partly wooded (vs no oak for False Bay version), floral, ripe apple flavours, gentle creaminess, plump but fresh. Some nice purity but gentler, more demure than last. **Sauvignon Blanc** ★★★★ Appealing fig, tropical notes on **18** ⑧④, a creamy plump undertone from lees contact. Plusher, riper, than last vintage yet balanced, fresh & quaffable. Not tasted: **Cabernet Sauvignon**. — MW

Location: Somerset West ▪ WO: Stellenbosch/Coastal/Swartland ▪ Est/1stB 2000 ▪ Tasting at Waterkloof ▪ Owner(s) Paul Boutinot ▪ Cellarmaster(s) Nadia Barnard (Jan 2013) ▪ 160,000cs own label 30% red 65% white 5% rosé ▪ IPW, WIETA ▪ PO Box 2093 Somerset West 7129 ▪ info@waterkloofwines.co.za ▪ www. falsebayvineyards.co.za ▪ F +27 (0)21-858-1293 ▪ **T +27 (0)21-858-1292**

☐ **Family Tree** see Stamboom

☐ **Fantail** see Morgenhof Wine Estate

☐ **Far & Near** see L'Avenir Vineyards

☐ **Farm Animals** see Osbloed Wines

☐ **Farm House** see Spier

☐ **Fat Barrel** see Imbuko Wines

Fat Bastard

As we put together this edition, the team at Robertson Winery was celebrating 21 years since linking with Franco-British venture Thierry & Guy to produce these 'full-bodied wines to be enjoyed with bellyfuls of laughs'. Brand creator Guy Anderson and vigneron Thierry Boudinaud made an experimental chardonnay in the late 1990s and pronounced a 'fat bastard', launching a happy hippo-logoed international success story. **Cabernet Sauvignon** ★★★★ 16 months on French & American oak add chocolate sweetness to dense black fruit, chewy tannins of **16** ⑧③. WO Robertson, as all. **Merlot** ★★★ Plummy **17** ⑧② with chalky tannins, hints of dark chocolate & liquorice, touch less plush, generous than last. **Pinotage** ★★★ **17** ⑧⓪ shows juicier black & blue berry fruit than also-tasted **16** ⑧①, the latter more mocha-toned from slightly longer (16 vs 14 months) in combo old/new French/American oak. **Shiraz** ★★★ Ripe, jammy, extracted **16** ⑧⓪, some cinnamon & pepper intrigue but acidity & oak less well integrated than previous. **Rosé** ★★★ Now from cinsaut, zippy **18** ⑦⑨ packed with tart red berries. Comfortable 10.5% alcohol. **Chardonnay** ② ★★★★ Four months in tank with oak chips, **17** ⑧③ as fat as predecessor, with its vanilla cream texture & ripe peachy tangerine fruit. **Sauvignon Blanc** ★★★ Ripe tropical pungency to **18** ⑦⑨, smooth, with layers of white peach & lime. **The Golden Reserve** ⒩ ★★★ Oozing soft, ultra-ripe black fruit, velvety **17** ⑧⓪ cab/ merlot has 12.6 g/l sugar & 16 months oak enhancing the velvet texture. Discontinued: **Pinot Noir**. — JG

Felicité

A sea of sickly sweet rosés encouraged the Newton Johnson family in the late 90s to introduce a 'classy' version, described in these pages as 'unashamedly dry rosé for grown-ups'. Now a standalone, extended label, Felicité - with Stettyn Family Vineyards as winegrowing partner - still aims for drinkability with panache.

inot Noir ⊘ ★★★ Older oak for **17** ⑧, to let the fruit speak: glossy red berries, some floral notes, ele-
ant, with a tailored tannin backbone. Subtle earthy thread fits right in. Cape South Coast WO. **Rosé ★★★**
uminous coral hue, **18** ⑧ celebrates shiraz's red berry & strawberry fruitiness. Slender & dry, and
haracter to match food, share with friends. With 5% sauvignon. WO W Cape, as next. **Chardonnay ★★★**
alate- & wallet-pleasing unwooded **18** ⑧, nothing fancy here, just lovely fruit purity; fresh grapefruit,
ngerine scents & flavours, elegant & zesty. — CR

ernskloof Wines

ⓆⓀⓂⓄⓈ

ided by Prince Albert Valley's relative isolation and warm climate, Diederik le Grange and family make cer-
fied-organic wine in small batches. They've uprooted all the chardonnay to focus on red wine and, with a
onstantly evolving portfolio, invite winelovers to come to the tasting locale and see what's available. Other
nticements for visiting include stay-overs, running trails and a property steeped in character and history.

ocation: Prince Albert ▪ Map: Klein Karoo & Garden Route ▪ Map grid reference: A3 ▪ Est 2009 ▪ 1stB
010 ▪ Tasting, sales & cellar tours Mon-Fri 9-5 Sat 10-5 Sun by appt 10-2 ▪ Closed Good Fri, Ascension
ay & Dec 25 ▪ Facilities for children ▪ BYO picnic ▪ Walks/hikes ▪ Mountain running trails (7, 10 & 16km) ▪
onservation area ▪ Angeliersbosch guest house (up to 8 guests), no pets allowed ▪ Owner(s) Le Grange
amily ▪ Cellarmaster(s)/winemaker(s) Diederik le Grange (2010) ▪ Viticulturist(s) Diederik le Grange (2009)
▪ 1,026ha/7ha (cab, merlot, ptage, shiraz) ▪ 40t/1,900cs own label 42% red 29% white 29% rosé ▪ Lacon
rganic ▪ PO Box 41 Prince Albert 6930 ▪ info@fernskloof.co.za ▪ www.fernskloof.co.za ▪ S 33° 16' 23.77" E
22° 10' 55.60" ▪ ✉ arch.vitally.celebration ▪ **T +27 (0)23-541-1702**

☐ **Festin** see Domaine Coutelier
☐ **56Hundred** see Nederburg Wines

Fijndraai Estate

ⓆⓂⓄ

ines were removed from the Fijndraai estate in the 1980s, giving Laurel van Coller, who took ownership
n the early 2000s, the opportunity to select and plant 'boutique' cultivars — chiefly Mediterranean ones
which are well-suited to this Lynedoch area of Stellenbosch, originally part of Meerlust. Only small parcels
are vinified under the guidance of Ken Forrester, most grapes being sold to nearby farms. Some produce
award-winning wines, much to the delight of Laurel and brand co-owner Veronique Kritzinger.

Van Coller Family Reserve range

Viognier-Chenin Blanc-Roussanne ★★★★ Zesty, fresh **17** ⑧ blend has delicate apricot features from
the viognier component, nice balance if shorter on interest than **16 ★★★★** ⑧. Not tasted: **Shiraz-
Grenache-Durif**. — AL

Location/WO: Stellenbosch ▪ Est 2007 ▪ 1stB 2011 ▪ Tasting at Ken Forrester Wines (see entry) ▪ Olive oil ▪
Walks/hikes ▪ MTB trail ▪ Self-catering accommodation ▪ Equestrian centre ▪ Owner(s) Laurel van Coller &
Veronique Kritzinger ▪ Winemaker(s) Ken Forrester (Jan 2010, consultant) ▪ Viticulturist(s) Pieter Rossouw
(Feb 2011, consultant) ▪ 93ha/11.11ha (durif, grenache, sangio, shiraz, pinot grigio, rouss, viog) ▪ 178t/1,094cs
own label 77% red 23% white ▪ WIETA ▪ PO Box 24 Lynedoch Stellenbosch 7603 ▪ info@fijndraai.com ▪
www.fijndraai.com ▪ **T +27 (0)82-817-6372**

☐ **Finch Mountain** see Rooiberg Winery
☐ **Fine Art Collection** see Catherine Marshall Wines
☐ **Firefly** see Stellar Winery

FirstCape Vineyards

Powerhouse export-only brand FirstCape was formed in 2002 as a joint venture between five Breede River
Valley cellars and British marketer Brand Phoenix. Currently all bottling is in the UK. The wines featured
below are a subset of a larger portfolio, which includes light (5.5% alcohol) wines and sparkling. Newer
markets in China (Five Cellars, Discovery) and Canada (Cape Bay) keep growing the footprint.

Discovery Series Gold range

★★★★ **Tannat** ⑫ Fully oaked, 20% new in **14** ⑧, giving spice dusting to earthy, scrub, wild berry
tones. Nice freshness, tannins firm & dry enough for food, cellaring. Satisfying example of the variety.

Cabernet Sauvignon ⨂ ★★★ Appealing cassis in **14** ⑦⑧ cloaks the tannins, making them approachable but, with 30% new oak (as next), the wine was created with some ageing in mind. **Pinot Noir** ⨂ ★★★★ Bigger structure than most, **12** ⑧④ forest floor typicity, dark fruit, forceful tannins from year oaking.

Discovery Series Cream range

Classique ⨂ ★★★ 60/40 merlot/cab in **15** ⑦⑧, year in barrel, 20% new, spice & fruitcake aromas, structure more serious; firm but ripe tannins, savoury length. **Grand Reserve** ⨂ ★★★★ Cab, shiraz & merlot, **12** ⑧④ shows cassis & spice, vanilla notes, appetising freshness in the ultra-smooth body/texture. 1 months oak fully integrated.

Discovery Series Silver range

Cabernet Sauvignon ⨂ ★★★ Like Gold Series, 30% new oak, & it shows in **15** ⑧①, mixed spice, perfume & grainy tannins. Sufficient plum & blackberry fruit to balance, but this cab can age. **Pinotage** ⨂ ★★★ Small portion wooded, **14** ⑧① is fruit driven, plums & cherries, smooth & streamlined. Not for keeping.

Discovery Series Black range

Shiraz ⨂ ★★ No oaking for **15** ⑦④ showcases the plush appeal shiraz can have, smooth & round, to be enjoyed at youthful best. Not tasted: **Cabernet Sauvignon**, **Merlot**, **Pinotage**.

FirstCape range

Not tasted: **Cabernet Sauvignon**, **Malbec**, **Pinotage**.

Five Cellars range

Not tasted: **Cabernet Sauvignon**, **Merlot**, **Pinotage**, **Shiraz**. — CR, CvZ

Location: Paarl ▪ WO: Western Cape ▪ Est 2002 ▪ Closed to public ▪ Owner(s) Aan de Doorns, Badsberg, De Wet, Goudini & Stettyn wineries ▪ Winemaker(s) David Smit ▪ WIETA ▪ PO Box 62 Simondium 7670 ▪ david@firstcape.com ▪ www.firstcape.com ▪ F +27 (0)21-874-8344 ▪ **T +27 (0)21-874-8340**

☐ **First Sighting** see Strandveld Wines

Fish Hoek Wines ⓠ

The middle child of Accolade Wines South Africa, and sibling to unfussy Kumala and sophisticated Flagstone (both listed separately), Fish Hoek is a 'lifestyle' label featuring only single grape varieties 'to allow the purity of taste to speak for itself'. It's also the only Fairtrade brand in global parent Accolade Wines' portfolio.

Cinsaut Rosé ⊘ ⑲ ★★★★ Tasty, well-made pink from trendy variety, **17** ⑧③ watermelon, cranberry & lemon thyme flavours, tangy, dry & sushi friendly.

Merlot ⊘ ★★★ Easygoing **18** ⑧② has a sweet mixed berry feel, while also-tasted **17** ⑧② has slightly higher alcohol. Sprinkles pepper & cocoa from American & French oak. Both good for pasta night.
Pinotage ⊘ ★★★ Forthcoming **17** ⑦⑨'s plummy fruit touched with peppery nuances, oak staves add some structure. **Shiraz** ⊘ ★★★ Fireside companion has a bright gleam, **17** ⑧② offers mulberries, black figs & plums, fresh acidity & brush oak to balance the ripe fruit. **Chenin Blanc** ⨂ ★★★ Less savoury & piquant than last, **17** ⑦⑧ upfront tropical fruit, easy to sip. **Sauvignon Blanc** ★★★ Quaffable & fun, **17** ⑦⑧'s tropical tones leap out the glass, subtler fynbos & lime keep the exuberance in check. Not tasted: **Malbec**. — DS

Location: Somerset West ▪ WO: Western Cape ▪ Tasting & sales at Flagstone Winery (see entry) ▪ Owner(s) Accolade Wines South Africa ▪ Winemaker(s) Gerhard Swart (head, Sep 2007) & Chandré Petersen (2018) ▪ 50% red 50% white ▪ Fairtrade ▪ PO Box 769 Stellenbosch 7599 ▪ info@flagstonewines.com ▪ www.fishhoekwines.com ▪ F +27 (0)21-852-5085 ▪ **T +27 (0)21-852-5052**

☐ **Five Cellars** see FirstCape Vineyards
☐ **Five Climates** see Boland Kelder
☐ **Five Generations** see Cederberg Private Cellar
☐ **Five's Reserve** see Van Loveren Family Vineyards
☐ **Flagship** see Stellenbosch Vineyards

Flagstone Winery

Quirkily (aptly?) housed in a converted dynamite factory, one of SA's early 'wineries without a vineyard' was founded in 1998 by SA-schooled, Aussie-trained Bruce Jack. Group winemaker for subsequent owners (global players Constellation from 2008 and Accolade since 2011), Bruce has weighed anchor for new adventures. But his vision and creativity still infuse the team, now led by veteran Gerhard Swart. With its awarded, mostly high-end wines, Somerset West-based Flagstone is the pinnacle of Accolade SA's trio of internationally regarded brands, with separately listed Fish Hoek and Kumala as siblings.

Super Premium range

★★★★★ **Time Manner Place Pinotage** ⓐ Heaps of sex-appeal from Breedekloof single-vineyard, limited-release **16** ⑨③ a union of plush fruit with cool minty edge & authoritative oak (50% new, mostly American). Savoury undertone, mineral freshness & compact tannins. Deliciously persistent, like **14** ★★★★★ ⑨⑤. No **15**.

★★★★☆ **Velvet Red Blend** ⓝⓔⓦ ⓐ Luxury packaging (& price) for sumptuous wine from 85% shiraz with mourvèdre & splash viognier, widely sourced. **14** ⑨④ ripe mulberry fruit laced with American oak vanilla (25% new) encased in pliable tannic frame, sweet feel from 15% alcohol in the farewell.

Flagstone range

★★★★☆ **Music Room Cabernet Sauvignon** Somewhat more classic in style, **16** ⑨⓪ melds fruit from 3 regions into harmonious melange of rich cassis, cooler cranberry & nuances of wild mint & fynbos. Clever use of oak & attention to detail create a tour de force with good cellaring prospects.

★★★★☆ **Writer's Block Pinotage** ⓐ Single Breedekloof vineyard delivers again, **16** ⑨③ both sophisticated & modern, with a touch of spicy American oak, the richness & concentration also seen in **15** ★★★★★ ⑨⑤ under tight control, firm tannin in place to aid longevity.

★★★★ **Dark Horse Shiraz** Going up a notch on **14** ⑧⑨, **15** ★★★★★ ⑨⓪ from combo warm- & cool-area fruit delivers a full-bodied, ripe-berried style with leavening whiffs of white pepper spice. very smooth, American oak dominance fully assimilated. Simply moreish.

★★★★ **Treaty Tree Reserve Red** ⓥ Alluring Bordeaux-style **16** ⑧⑧, sweet, scented dark fruit, powerful tannin & toasty trio American, French & Hungarian oak creating a smart, focused wine that lingers.

★★★★ **Dragon Tree** ⓥ Multi-source Cape Blend, bold-fruited **16** ⑧⑦ dominated by pinotage & shiraz, cab adding vibrancy. Tannins equally forthright in youth, demand food partners or a cellar. **15** untasted.

★★★★ **Two Roads Chardonnay** Two roads, 2 fruit sources (Wellington, Stellenbosch) lead to a celebration of lime fruit, rich yet delicately spiced. **17** ⑧⑥'s deft use of oak (6 months) & lively acidity suit al fresco dining.

★★★★☆ **Tributary Chenin Blanc** ⓥ Oozing tropical charm, **17** ⑨⓪ from sunny Wellington, Paarl & Stellenbosch delivers ample peach & apricot, a limy edge adds freshness to palate, French & Hungarian oak accentuates creamy texture of persistent fruit. A show pony perhaps, but individual.

★★★★☆ **Free Run Sauvignon Blanc** ⓥ Captures essence of cool-climate Elgin & Elim. Bright, steely grass & greenpepper fruit, tense acidity & suggestions of oystershell minerality in both aroma & texture. All aided by 10% semillon & reductive winemaking. **17** ⑨⓪ flinty, chalky & mouthwatering.

★★★★ **Word of Mouth Viognier** Bunch-pressed **17** ⑧⑧ billows peach, apricot & spice; stonefruit leads on palate too, while French & Hungarian oak adds structure to mineral-toned finish.

★★★★☆ **Treaty Tree Reserve White** ⓥ Captivating sauvignon & semillon (65/35) blend. Showing cool provenance, **17** ⑨① vibrates with grapefruit & tense acidity, flinty minerality spotlit by finessed oaking (just 17% wooded, all French, rest tank). Food wine par excellence from WO Elim.

Noon Gun ⓣ ★★★ Gentle, fresh appetiser, **17** ⑧⓪ delightful unoaked chenin, sauvignon, viognier & semillon offering fruity picnic fun.

Fiona Pinot Noir ⓧ ★★★★ French, American & Hungarian oak tempers the Elgin fruit of **16** ⑧⑤, adds spice to strawberry, cherry & blackcurrant flavours. Delicate & delicious everyday pinot. **Truth Tree Pinotage** ★★★★ Again with dash pinot noir, **17** ⑧④ as interesting & delicious as previous, red berries brushed with mocha, sweet spicy oak to savour in the finish. **Longitude** ★★★ Crowd-pleasing **17** ⑧① packed with red berries, spiced with smoked meats, seamed with tealeaf & mocha. Shiraz, cab, malbec &

merlot showing nimble tannins, fresh dry finish. **Last Word** ⒢ ★★★★ Made for the meal's end, port-style **13** ⑻⑷ from Breedekloof pinotage calls for creamy gorgonzola. French/American oak spices the sweet, plummy/dark chocolate core; good chalky finish.

Poetry range

Cinsaut Rosé ⊘ ⒯ ★★★ From in-vogue grape, in fashionable drier, lighter style, crimson **18** ⑻② pretty & tasty, sweet-fruited red berries & limes, brisk finish.

....

Cabernet Sauvignon ★★★ Brooding **17** ⑺⑻ somewhat austere, the robust tannins calling for hearty food. **Merlot** ★★★ Plummy, moreish **17** ⑺⑻ spiced by French & American oak, a minty edge freshens. Splashes cab & malbec. **Chardonnay** ★★ A go-to chardonnay, brushed with oak in **18** ⑺⑹. Not too big, not too simple, hits a sweet spot especially with chicken on the braai. **Sauvignon Blanc** ★★★ Melon & granadilla perked up with zesty acid in light, tangy **17** ⑺⑺. — DS

Location: Somerset West ▪ Map: Helderberg ▪ Map grid reference: B6 ▪ WO: Western Cape/Breedekloof/Coastal/Cape South Coast/Elim/Elgin ▪ Est 1998 ▪ 1stB 1999 ▪ Tasting & sales Mon-Fri 10-4 Sat 10-3 ▪ Fee R40pp ▪ Cheese & wine pairing, popcorn & wine pairing - please phone to book ▪ Closed Sundays, Good Fri, Dec 25/26 & Jan 1 ▪ Cellar tours by appt ▪ Owner(s) Accolade Wines South Africa ▪ Winemaker(s) Gerhard Swart (head, Sep 2007), with Mia Boonzaier (Jan 2008), Willene Bester (Jun 2014) & Gerald Cakijana (Jan 2000) ▪ 60% red 40% white ▪ W.R. Quinan Blvd Paardevlei Somerset West 7130 ▪ info@flagstonewines.com ▪ www.flagstonewines.com ▪ S 34° 5' 26.38" E 018° 48' 30.04" ▪ ⒨ smiled.common.balance ▪ F +27 (0)21-852-5085 ▪ **T +27 (0)21-852-5052**

☐ **Flash Series** see The Blacksmith

Flat Roof Manor

Named for the elegant double-story Georgian homestead — one of only three left in the Cape - on Stellenbosch's Uitkyk, this good-value label remains in the Distell portfolio after the sale of the estate to US investors. Further streamlining means only the Pinot Grigio (vintage '18) is being marketed, untasted by us.

☐ **Fledge & Co** see The Fledge & Co
☐ **Fleur de Vie** see Fleur du Cap

Fleur du Cap ⒬

The Distell-owned Fleur du Cap brand has been revitalised and repackaged, with stylish new labels reflecting tweaked names and tiers. The flagship wine is Laszlo, honouring Julius Laszlo, pioneer of barrel ageing in SA. Series Privée Unfiltered is the new name for the much-decorated Unfiltered range, while the Bergkelder Selection (temporarily excluding the Noble Late Harvest) is now styled Essence du Cap, and Fleur de Vie denotes their lighter-style wines. Grapes are still sourced from a diversity of prime locations throughout the Cape, each contributing its own terroir and flavour profile to an enduring portfolio, turning 50 this edition.

Flagship range

★★★★★ **Laszlo** ⒶⒷ Sumptuous & velvety, **15** ⑼③ aligns classic & New World styles into structured sophistication. Prestige blend now cab-led (33%) with other 4 Bordeaux reds. Less new oak (40%, previously 100%) perfectly synchronised with the dark fruit ex Stellenbosch & Paarl.

Series Privée Unfiltered

★★★★★ **Cabernet Sauvignon** ⒶⒷ Classic pencil shavings & cassis on **15** ⑼② fine dry tannins in elegant restraint, oak integrated with fruit & structure to age with confidence. Raises bar on **14** ★★★★ ⑻⑺. Stellenbosch WO, as Merlot. 30-40% new barrels for these reds, varying ratios French & American.

★★★★ **Merlot** ⒶⒷ Youthful beauty **15** ★★★★★ ⑼② a class above **14** ⑻⑺, with future rewards in store. Herbaceous nuance to ripe & rich red-fruited flavours, lovely intensity & freshness, dry chalky tannins rein in concentrated fruit. Only 10% American. Clarified by gravity, as all these.

★★★★ **Pinotage** Riper **16** ⑻⑼ is rich & rounded, lacks elegance of **15** ★★★★★ ⑼② though structure & freshness do fine job of tempering opulent mocha-tinged fruit & alcohol. 40% American oak.

★★★★☆ **Chardonnay** Change from refined & fresh **16** ⑬ to bold, ripe & prominently oaked **17** ★★★★ ⑧. Like Chenin, barrel fermented/8 months, 80% new oak (vs 35% for previous), requiring some time for pear & lime fruit to assert & restore balance.

★★★★ **Chenin Blanc** Generous & warm-hearted **17** ⑧ shows warmer Paarl provenance in ample dried yellow peach & lime. Oak quite dominant (40% new), less balanced & vibrant than **16** ★★★★☆ ⑭, which included Stellenbosch grapes.

★★★★ **Sauvignon Blanc** Darling grapes give characteristic dusty tone to more vegetal & stonefruit flavours, **17** ⑧ not as ripe as **16** ⑧ but shows some warmth despite modest 13% alcohol. Not as scintillating as **15** ★★★★★ ⑮.

Bergkelder Selection

★★★★☆ **Noble Late Harvest** ⑫ From botrytised viognier, unwooded, **16** ⑬ sublime dried pineapple & yellow peach, unctuously ripe & viscous with tangy acidity to balance, Cape Agulhas coolness shows its merit in a warmer year, capturing the essence of viognier in a decadently delightful way. **15** ★★★★★ ⑰ was a chenin from Darling. 375 ml.

Essence du Cap range

★★★★ **Cabernet Sauvignon** Ripe & rich, but **16** ★★★★ ⑧'s firm structure with herbaceous nuance appears fresher & the most balanced of these similarly made reds. This cab not as fine as **15** ⑧.

Chardonnay ⑰ ★★★★ Fresh pear & brush of butterscotch well balanced by acidity, flavoursome **17** ⑧ less plump & oaky than previous, just as bright & ready to enjoy for a few years.

Merlot ★★★★ Lively herbaceous tone to fruit & structure assimilates **16** ⑧ warmth better than Shiraz & Pinotage. For earlier enjoyment than previous. **Pinotage** ★★★ Plenty of ripe mulberry fruit on **16** ⑧, rounded but perhaps tad fresher than Shiraz, more substantial. Will peak earlier than last. **Shiraz** ★★★ A big mouth-warming spicy presence, **16** ⑲ less fruit & substance than previous, tad gawky too without braaied chop in hand. **Chenin Blanc** ★★★ Some baked apple & twist of lemon, **18** ⑧ muted version of last year's vibrant & flavour-packed preview. **Sauvignon Blanc** ★★★ Dried vegetable tone, some tropical fruit & warm heart (despite modest 13.15% alcohol), **18** ⑧ different character to previous vintage's vivacious piquancy.

Fleur de Vie range

Natural Light Rosé ★★ Mostly chenin, splash pinotage to give crunchy quaffer a blush & savoury hint. **18** ⑯ tangy, technically dry despite some sugar, light 9.5% alcohol (as next) a bonus. **Natural Light Chenin Blanc** ★★ Now bottled, **17** ⑮ is crisp despite few grams sugar, feather-light & friendly, with hint of scented fruit. — MW

Location: Stellenbosch ▪ WO: Western Cape/Coastal/Stellenbosch/Darling/Paarl/Cape Agulhas ▪ Est 1968 ▪ 1stB 1969 ▪ Tasting, sales & tours at Die Bergkelder Wine Centre (see entry) ▪ Owner(s) Distell ▪ Cellarmaster(s) Elunda Basson (Sep 2016) ▪ Winemaker(s) Pieter Badenhorst (Dec 2006) ▪ Viticulturist(s) Bennie Liebenberg ▪ ±17,000t/±290,000cs own label 47% red 53% white ▪ ISO 14001, ISO 9001, BRC, HACCP, IFS ▪ info@fleurducap.co.za ▪ www.fleurducap.co.za ▪ **T** +27 (0)21-809-8025

Flight of the Fish Eagle

Among Distell's most popular pure potstill brandies, Flight of the Fish Eagle celebrates the graceful raptor whose distinctive call, to many, is the essence of the African wild. The brandy's age is undisclosed, but its smoothness makes it perfect for first-time drinkers, Distell says, and recommends it be enjoyed on the rocks.

★★★★ **Natural Potstill Brandy** ⑫ Pale gold colour belies intensity of aroma (red berry fruit, orange, honey). Refined, with a long finish. Modern style; 100% potstill from chenin & colombard. — WB, TJ

☐ **Flippenice** *see* Tulbagh Winery

Flotsam & Jetsam

Increased sales, especially in foreign markets, and fruit availability have seen growth in this second label of Chris and Suzaan Alheit, the pair behind the stellar Alheit Vineyards range, with the original cinsaut being joined by a chenin. Both, Chris modestly says, are the result of 'fantastic vineyards' and 'simple' winemaking.

'Sometimes wine just needs to be wine,' he insists; 'for normal levels of enjoyment, pour it in your glass and drink it.' Excellent advice for this eminently drinkable pair.

★★★★☆ **Cinsault Stalwart** ⓦ Packed with red summer fruits, zingy freshness & a spicy tangy conclusion, 17 ★★★★ ⑧⑨ offers immediate pleasure, more so with light chilling. Tad less serious than 15 ⑨①, 'it's supposed to be fun!' advises winemaker, but no less delicious.

★★★★ **Chenin Blanc Heirloom** ⓦ Usual Alheit quality delivered in more approachable style. 17 ⑧⑧ has old-vine concentration, texture augmented by lees ageing; mainly barrel-ferment, portion in new 2,000L foudre, 10% concrete 'egg'.— AL

Location: Hermanus • WO: Western Cape • Est/1stB 2015 • Closed to public • Owner(s) Chris & Suzaan Alheit • Winemaker(s) Chris & Suzaan Alheit (both Jan 2015), with Franco Lourens (Jan 2016) • Viticulturist(s) Chris Alheit • (cinsaut, chenin) • 60t/6,000cs own label 50% red 50% white • PO Box 711 Hermanus 7200 • www.flotsamandjetsam.co.za • **T +27 (0)28-312-2083**

☐ **Flower Collection** *see* River Garden
☐ **Flutterby** *see* Boland Kelder

Flying Cloud Ⓠ

Cape Town advocate Donald Ackerman opening a second practice in George, and moving the address of his boutique wine venture there, indicates future strategy: he's discovered a pinot noir vineyard in the vicinity which meets his very meticulous standards, grapes already harvested, and is even contemplating the eventual building of a cellar. What remains unchanged is his passion for excellence.

★★★★ **Sea Serpent** Two barrels of sleek & intensely fruity syrah, thanks to Elim terroir. 16 ⑧⑨ gets its polish & charcuterie savouriness from 19 months French oaking, half new. Delicious.

★★★★ **Witch of the Wave** ⓐ Sauvignon & semillon (60/40) for the discerning palate. 16 ★★★★☆ ⑨④'s svelte body packs more interest than 15 ⑧⑧, orange blossom & tangerine, a fine thread of almond spicing, longer mineral finish. Just one 500L barrel.— CR

Location: George • Map: Klein Karoo & Garden Route • Map grid reference: C3 • WO: Elim • Est 2013 • 1stB 2014 • Tasting by appt only • Owner(s)/winemaker(s) Donald Ackerman • 200cs own label 66% red 34% white • 62 Cathedral Str George 6529 • flyingcloudwines@icloud.com • S 33° 57' 27.52" E 022° 27' 34.07" • **T +27 (0)82-610-2422, +27 (0)44-050-0033**

Foothills Vineyards Ⓠ ⑪ ⓐ ⊚

Glenn Hesse and Tim Featherby's boutique venture in the Helderberg foothills has entered its second decade. Their Klein Welmoed property on Raithby Road was in bad shape when they bought it, but with high-calibre consultants and much TLC they established new vineyards (and a luxury guest house), and the potential is now revealing itself more fully, especially in the expanding Monogram Collection.

Monogram Collection

★★★★ **Shiraz** ⓝⓔⓦ Perhaps 'Syrah' a more apropos name, given the Old World savouriness of wild herbs, dried meat & liquorice seaming the hedgerow fruit of mouthfilling but balanced 16 ⑧⑧.

★★★★ **Semillon** ⓝⓔⓦ Older oak contributes texture, creaminess & savoury dimension to 17 ⑧⑨'s fresh orchard fruit. Variety's lanolin & waxy nuances add complexity on harmonious, mineral-edged palate.

★★★★ **Méthode Cap Classique** ⓝⓔⓦ Delicate floral & baked apple fragrances reverberate in the full, creamy mousse of 16 ⑧⑧ dry sparkling from chardonnay (65%) & pinot noir, the sleekness aided by barrel fermentation/15 months on lees.

★★★★☆ **Straw Wine** ⓐ Air-dried & barrel-fermented viognier, 15 ⑨⓪ seduces with vibrant gold appearance, peach, honey, marmalade & toasted hazelnut richness, good viscosity & long lemon rind finish. Older oak, 2 years. 375 ml.

Foothills range

Pinot Noir ⓥ ★★★★ Pulpy strawberries & dried herbs mingle attractively with spice from older oak on broad 17 ⑧③, smooth, silky, lifted dry finish. **Syrah** ★★★★ Wild berries, leather & Asian spice in generous 16 ⑧④, lovely cranberry grip on the farewell. 10% new oak nicely judged. **Dry Rosé** ★★★★ Delightful, palest pink 17 ⑧⑤, delicate & fragrant, dry tropical flavours & tangy conclusion from mostly shiraz, splashes semillon & viognier. **Sauvignon Blanc ★★★★** With dab (unoaked) semillon, **17** ⑧⑤ steps up with perfumed white flower, greengage & tropical notes, zippy acid that refreshes. **Viognier** ⓃⒺⓌ **★★★** Appealing peaches-&-cream styling for **17** ⑧② complete with aromatic spice & roasted nut topping; voluptuous & rounded. **The Partners** ⓋⒼ **★★★★** Peach blossom appeal on unoaked **16** ⑧④ from sauvignon, viognier & semillon. Mouthfilling & textured, with plenty of personality. Not tasted: **Chardonnay**. — WB

Location/WO: Stellenbosch ▪ Map: Helderberg ▪ Map grid reference: B1 ▪ Est 2008 ▪ 1stB 2012 ▪ Tasting & sales by appt ▪ Fee R50pp ▪ Meals/refreshments by appt ▪ Olive oil ▪ Conferences ▪ 4-star luxury guesthouse (B&B), info@kleinwelmoed.co.za ▪ Owner(s) Glenn Hesse & Tim Featherby ▪ Winemaker(s) Bernard le Roux ▪ Viticulturist(s) Bennie Booysen ▪ 39ha/19ha (pinot, shiraz, chard, sauv, sem, viog) ▪ 8,000cs own label 25% red 70% white 5% rosé ▪ IPW ▪ PO Box 647 Somerset Mall 7137 ▪ info@foothillsvineyards.co.za ▪ www. kleinwelmoed.co.za ▪ S 34° 0' 58.86" E 018° 47' 43.08" ▪ ℳ armbands.busy.horizon ▪ F +27 (0)21-842-2775 ▪ **T +27 (0)21-842-0045**

☐ **Foot of Africa** see Kleine Zalze Wines
☐ **Force Majeure** see Mother Rock Wines
☐ **Forresters** see Ken Forrester Wines

Fortes Family Wines Ⓥ 🍷 ⓃⒺⓌ

Neil Fortes, after decades travelling the world for his Wine Guru company, returned to SA in 2005 and bought land in Napier Valley — a 'special terroir', with the rare advantage of a natural spring water supply. Initial plantings of 2 ha of sauvignon produced a 2016 maiden vintage which Neil makes a little further south, in Elim, working with Conrad Vlok of Strandveld. The coming years will see expansion 'to a full range vineyard'.
Sauvignon Blanc ★★★★ Addition to growing wooded category has personality, distinctiveness. **16** ⑧⑤ & **17** ⑧⑤ tasted, former the soulful introvert, latter forthcoming with floral, lemongrass, pea green notes. Both also smoky 'fumé' accents from older oak, bite of passionfruit acidity which works well with food. — TJ, CvZ

Location/WO: Napier ▪ Map: Southern Cape ▪ Map grid reference: B2 ▪ Est 2005 ▪ 1stB 2016 ▪ Tasting, sales & cellar tours by appt only ▪ Closed all pub hols ▪ BYO picnic ▪ Owner(s) The Trojan Trust ▪ Cellarmaster(s)/winemaker(s) Neil Fortes & Conrad Vlok (Jun 2006, consultants) ▪ Viticulturist(s) Neil Fortes (Jun 2006, consultant) ▪ 3.5ha/2ha (sauv) ▪ 5t/600cs own label 100% white ▪ PO Box 208 Napier 7270 ▪ info@wineguru.ca ▪ www.forteswines.com ▪ S34° 27' 50.0" E 019° 53' 56.0" ▪ **T +27 (0)71-223-9927**

☐ **Fortress Hill** see Fort Simon Wine Estate

Fort Simon Wine Estate Ⓥ ⓞ 🏃

The Uys-family-owned and -run winery sits on the scenic upper reaches of the Bottelary Hills, the vineyards forming an arc around the eponymous turreted 'fortress' (inspired by Duwisib Castle in Namibia) which houses the cellar and visitor facilities. It's a warmly welcoming stronghold, with functions venue and a wedding chapel, as well as place to taste Dirk Tredoux's 'bold, New World-style' wines.

Platinum Collection
★★★★ Viognier Noble Late Harvest Unencumbered by oak, **17** ⑧⑥ has muscat-like grapey fruit; unctuously rich & intensely sweet (258 g/l sugar) but well focused & appealing. 375 ml.

Viognier ★★★ Heavy oak (60% new) on **17** ⑧② masks varietal fragrance, presents charred, toasty notes on thick, textured body.

Fort Simon range
★★★★ Shiraz Sweetly ripe fruit to the fore on **15 ★★★★** ⑧⑤, with perhaps more oak spicing than **14** ⑧⑥ from 18 months in barrel, 20% new. Accessible medium body.

Cabernet Sauvignon ⓋⒼ **★★★** Forward ripe dark fruit on **13** ⑧① with tobacco notes. Flavourful & almost off-dry, softly approachable. **Merlot ★★★★** Dark, tarry core with sombre black berries & salty liquorice notes. **16** ⑧⑤ pleasant in an austere sort of way. **Pinotage ★★★★** Oaky mocha style, **16** ⑧③ has juicy plum fruit, chewy tannins, hints of iodine & iron. **Chardonnay** ⓋⒼ **★★★★** Toasty oak more dominant on the aromas of **14** ⑧④, but better integrated on the palate, where succulent, zesty citrus orchestrates a pleasing conclusion. **Chenin Blanc ★★★** Barrel-fermented (40% new) **17** ⑧② has prominent oak, subdued fruit, slender body; hints of lees texture, brief farewell. **Sauvignon Blanc** ★★★ Tastily ripe tropical fruit on **18** ⑧②, with reined-in acidity. Mild mannered if unlingering. Not tasted: **Barrel Select Merlot-Malbec**.

Fortress Hill range

Merlot ★★★ Fresh, undemanding **16** ⑦⑧ is light, with modest black fruit & prominent tannins. **Shiraz** ⊘ ★★★ Generous fruit, soft roundness & gentle tannins make **16** ⑧③ a satisfying everyday drink. **Merlot-Cabernet Sauvignon** ⓧ ★★★ Generously fruity **16** ⑧②, gentle tannins, appealing weight & finish. Good-natured braai companion. **Sauvignon Blanc** ★★★ Easygoing, nicely poised **18** ⑧⓪, pungent nettle notes over crisp passionfruit.

Michelle d'Or range

Shiraz ⓦ ★★★ Touch of herbal scrub lends appeal to juicy, fruit-packed **16** ⑧②. Smooth tannins, rounded body.

Merlot ★★★ Chewy tannins, stewed fruit on **16** ⑦⑦; touch of toffee, mocha from toasted barrels. WO W Cape for these. **Merlot-Cabernet Sauvignon** ⓧ ★★ Attractive & undemanding **14** ⑦④, with a tussle of sweetness & acid, & a little grip. **Sauvignon Blanc** ★★★ Unpretentious **18** ⑦⑧ shows typical grassy gooseberry flavours with edgy acid finish. — GdB

Location/map: Stellenbosch ▪ Map grid reference: C4 ▪ WO: Stellenbosch/Western Cape ▪ Est 1997 ▪ 1stB 1998 ▪ Tasting & sales Mon-Fri 9.30–5 Sat 10–2 ▪ Tasting R75/5 wines ▪ Closed all pub hols & long weekends ▪ Cellar tours by appt ▪ Venue for after-hours functions/weddings & conferences (120-140 guests) ▪ Wedding chapel ▪ Owner(s) Renier, Petrus & Michéle Uys ▪ Winemaker(s) Dirk Tredoux (Oct 2016) ▪ Viticulturist(s) Renier Uys ▪ 80ha (cabs s/f, malbec, merlot, p verdot, ptage, shiraz, chard, chenin, sauv, viog) ▪ 800t/80,000cs own label 70% red 30% white ▪ PO Box 43 Sanlamhof 7532 ▪ accounts@fortsimon.com ▪ www.fortsimon.com ▪ S 33° 55' 9.5" E 018° 45' 19.4" ▪ ⓜ candy.evidence.patting ▪ **T +27 (0)21-906-0304**

☐ **Foundation Stone** *see* Rickety Bridge Winery
☐ **Foundry** *see* The Foundry
☐ **Four Cousins** *see* Van Loveren Family Vineyards

4G Wine Estate

Conceived a decade ago by luminaries including late Bordeaux oenologist-educator Denis Dubourdieu and local legend Giorgio Dalla Cia, this Stellenbosch cross-cultural venture is chasing 'first growth' status. Helanie Olivier works with French consultant Valérie Lavigne on reds from quality sites around the Western Cape for global distribution under directorship of Philipp Axt. Current releases are G '12 and Echo of G '14.

Location: Stellenbosch ▪ Est 2009 ▪ 1stB 2010 ▪ Closed to public ▪ Owner(s) Private shareholders ▪ Winemaker(s) Valérie Lavigne & Helanie Olivier ▪ 20t own label 100% red ▪ Other export brands: G., The Echo of G. ▪ info@4g-wines.com ▪ www.4g-wines.com

Four Paws Wines

ⓠ

Value-for-money wines with the elegance and balance of a cat ambling along a garden wall were the founding aims of Rob Meihuizen, Anne Jakubiec and Gerda Willers, who launched this feline-themed boutique brand 14 years ago. They're currently based at La Vigne in Franschhoek, where the previous releases listed below, along with untasted newer vintages of Shiraz, Pablo, Rosé, Chardonnay, Sauvignon Blanc, Calico and the canine member of the family, Vincent van Dogh, are available to taste by appointment.

★★★★ **Pinotage** ⓧ Brambleberry notes on full-bodied **11** ⑧⑦ from Piekenierskloof, showing vanilla tone from year 30% new oak. Drinks easily & well but underlying seriousness invites cellaring ±5 years.
★★★★ **Picatso** ⓧ Generous floral, tropical & grapey notes contrast nicely with delicate oak (2nd fill) on **15** ⑧⑥ viognier & muscat d'Alexandrie dessert. Crackling acidity adds to enjoyment, vibrancy. 375 ml.
Grenache ⓧ ★★★★ Elegant glassful, **14** ⑧④ with fine-grained tannins, intense red- & dark-fruit bouquet spiced with cherry tobacco & nutmeg. — GdB

Location/map: Franschhoek ▪ Map grid reference: C3 ▪ WO: Piekenierskloof/Western Cape ▪ Est 2005 ▪ 1stB 2006 ▪ Tasting by appt at La Vigne, R45 Franschhoek ▪ Closed weekends & pub hols ▪ Owner(s) Rob Meihuizen, Gerda Willers & Anne Jakubiec ▪ Winemaker(s) Gerda Willers (2005) ▪ Viticulturist(s) Gerda

Willers ▪ 2ha (shiraz, chenin, grenache b, rouss) ▪ 20t/3,000cs own label 70% red 30% white ▪ PO Box 69 Simondium 7670 ▪ anne@southerntrade.co.za ▪ www.fourpawswines.com ▪ S 33° 53′ 28.0″ E 019° 5′ 0.5″ ▪ ⌨ rejoices.engrave.whisker ▪ **T +27 (0)83-447-1376 (Anne)**

4th Street

An unchallenging flavour profile, low alcohol and 'urban lifestyle' positioning (slogan: 'Go 4th & connect') have helped propel this Distell label to the position of SA's top seller.

Natural Sweet range

Red ★★ Uncomplicated sweet berries on **NV** ⑦. Serve well chilled, as all. **Rosé ★** Demure pink **NV** ⑥⑧, whiffs of cherry, needs tad more zip. **White ★★** Low alcohol (±7.5%), as all, **NV** ⑦② light floral aromas, easy as can be. These also in 1.5, 3 & 5L packs. — WB

Fraai Uitzicht 1798 ⓧ ⑪ ⑭

Karl Uwe Papesch's centuries-old hillside property in Robertson's hilly Klaasvoogds ward has a tasting area, restaurant and guest house, all offering the perfect vantage to take in the eponymous 'Pretty View'. The wines are equally attractive, especially the grenache, originally intended as a foretaste of Karl Uwe's beloved Châteauneuf-du-Pape blend but happily now a fixture.

★★★★ Grenache Steps up in **16** ⑧⑥ with jasmine & fynbos fragrance, vibrant fruit, judicious oaking (20% new, 20% unwooded). As delicious as **15 ★★★★** ⑧⑤, more generous & spicy.

★★★★ Le Neuf Papesch ⓧ Flagship blend mostly mourvèdre with grenache, shiraz. **14** ⑧⑦ fragrant & fruit filled, refreshing tannic grip. As successful, poised, as **13** ⑧⑥ but fresher.

Merlot ★★★ Very ripe **14** ⑦⑨'s stewed plum aromas & flavours are consistent with its warming 15% alcohol but at odds with its gruff tannins. Perhaps time will soften. **Syrah ★★★★** Soft red fruits, subtle cardamom & nutmeg spice, **15** ⑧④ is decently dry, lithe & supple. For now & ±3 years. **Viognier ★★★★** Unshowy version of sometimes blowsy variety. Part-new-oaked **17** ⑧③ appealing peach, apricot nuances, creamy yet lively & persistent. — CvZ

Location/map/WO: Robertson ▪ Map grid reference: B4 ▪ 1stB 2000 ▪ Tasting by appt ▪ Sales Mon-Fri 10-4 ▪ Closed Dec 24/25/26 ▪ Restaurant ▪ 4-star guest house ▪ Owner(s) Karl Uwe Papesch ▪ Winemaker(s) Karl Uwe Papesch (2005) ▪ Viticulturist(s) Michael Marson ▪ 175ha/15ha (grenache, merlot, mourv, shiraz, viog) ▪ 3,000cs own label 95% red 5% white ▪ PO Box 97 Robertson 6705 ▪ info@fraaiuitzicht.com ▪ www. fraaiuitzicht.com ▪ S 33° 47′ 43.0″ E 020° 0′ 18.2″ ▪ ⌨ replace.reaching.allergies ▪ F +27 (0)86-662-5265 ▪ **T +27 (0)23-626-6156**

Fram Wines ⓧ

Thinus Krüger's orientation to new-wave, light (or lightish) wines, made with minimal intervention is indicated by his membership of the Swartland Independent Producers. No new oak, of course — except for the large vat his '17 Pinotage matured in. He ranges beyond the Swartland, however, in search of vineyards for his 'fine wines of exploration', most notably to dry slopes in the Citrusdal Mountain ward. Unusually for such a winemaker, he's even ventured to Robertson for chardonnay, and is also determined to make a cabernet sauvignon that pleases him - 2019 his third attempt, he says with rueful good humour.

★★★★ Cinsault Youthful, fresh, unwooded **17** ⑧⑨ with perfumed charm, but more than simply fruity. There's vinosity (13% alcohol) & some flavour intensity supported by acidity & subtle tannins.

★★★★ Pinotage New-waveish styling on **16 ★★★★★** ⑨②, stressing freshness, yet also rich & weighty (14.3% alcohol), with sweet, spicy fruit & a firm but unobtrusive tannic underpinning. 18 months in older oak doesn't obscure the pure flavours. Less austere in youth than **15** ⑧⑦.

★★★★ Shiraz Light-feeling, pure-fruited **17** ⑧⑨ has delicious charm - but also hint of austerity, though the tannins have typical Swartland subtly firm softness. Older oak, like **16 ★★★★** ⑧⑤. 13% alcohol.

★★★★★ Chenin Blanc ⓧ Ex Piekenierskloof & Swartland, **16** ⑨④ in same delicate yet compelling mode as **15 ★★★★★** ⑨⑦. Especially light, fresh, yet packs a wealth of flavour: hay, earthy tones with nudge of dried peach. All harmonised via natural ferment, old oak. Pithily dry.

★★★★ Dry White Latest NV ⑧⑧ from palomino & chenin; half oaked 2016, half unoaked 2017. Unusual & very appealing; less fruity than packed with dry herbs, especially fennel. Great sense of light, fresh purity. 12.1% alcohol. Improves on previous, which included other varieties.

Chardonnay ★★★★ Unoaked **17** ⑧⑤ from Robertson has attractive aromas & light flavours of citrus & white peach, enlivened by fine acidity. Balanced 12.3% alcohol. **Grenache Gris ★★★** Wholebunch ferment of light-red-skinned variety gives coppery pink colour & a touch of tannic grip. Savoury & steely **17** ⑧②, little generosity from 10.6% alcohol. WO Voor Paardeberg. — TJ

Location: Riebeek West ▪ WO: Citrusdal Mountain/Robertson/Swartland/Voor Paardeberg/Western Cape ▪ Est/1stB 2012 ▪ Tasting by appt only ▪ Owner(s) Thinus Krüger ▪ Cellarmaster(s)/winemaker(s) Thinus Krüger (Dec 2012) ▪ Viticulturist(s) Henk Laing ▪ 30t/2,500cs own label 45% red 55% white ▪ PO Box 2272 Dennesig Stellenbosch 7601 ▪ thinus@framwines.co.za ▪ www.framwines.co.za ▪ **T +27 (0)72-545-4959**

Francois La Garde ⓠ

Piet Matthée runs a specialist Stellenbosch mobile bottling and labelling company, and occasionally finds some time in the moonlight to make his small range of MCC bubblies, fulfilling 'a lifelong dream' of one of his ancestors — whose name was adopted for his project. But nothing new this year.

Location/map: Stellenbosch ▪ Map grid reference: E5 ▪ Est 2004 ▪ Tasting by appt ▪ Owner(s) PL Matthée ▪ Cellarmaster(s)/winemaker(s) Piet Matthée (Jan 2009) ▪ 1st/2,000cs own label 100% MCC ▪ PO Box 12366 Die Boord 7613 ▪ admin@technofill.co.za ▪ www.francois-lagarde.com, www.technofill.co.za ▪ S 33° 55' 25.45" E 018° 51' 6.25" ▪ 🖾 patio.beamed.rainy ▪ F +27 (0)21-887-5274 ▪ **T +27 (0)21-887-3674**

☐ **Francois le Vaillant** *see* Lutzville Vineyards

Franki's Vineyards ⓠ 🖾 🏠

'Boutique' doesn't get much smaller than the 4 tons of grapes processed in 2018 for the Franki's Vineyards label. But that's a ton more than last time, allowing winemaker Erica Joubert to double the volume of her rosé and viognier. Minimal intervention is Erica's mantra, with a focus on freshness and elegance. Swartland home-farm Eenboom also accommodates a large guest house for 'conferences, celebrations and getaways'.

★★★★ Grenache ⓥ Shy cranberry scent on **16** ⑧⑨ gives way to intense, fresh palate showing fine structure & red-berry fruit, improving on **15 ★★★★** ⑧④. Year old French oak.

★★★★ Viognier Barrel Fermented Slowly fermented in seasoned wood, **18** ⑧⑥ peaches-&-cream flavours with a spicy farewell. Minuscule production, as all these.

Joubert Red Blend ★★★★ Characterful, well-balanced & enjoyable **15** ◯84 blend mourvèdre (50%) with shiraz & grenache. Has rustic charm & flavour power, but modest 13% alcohol. **Mourvèdre Rosé ★★★** Pleasant, dry **18** ◯82, enticing summer fruits led by strawberry & just a touch of spice. Discontinued: **Viognier.** — HC

Location: Malmesbury ▪ Map/WO: Swartland ▪ Map grid reference: A6 ▪ Est 2004 ▪ 1stB 2007 ▪ Tasting, sales & cellar tours Mon-Fri 8-5 by appt ▪ Closed all pub hols ▪ BYO picnic ▪ Franki's Guest Lodge ▪ Owner(s) Franco Afrique Technologies (Pty) Ltd ▪ Winemaker(s) Erica Joubert (Jan 2004) ▪ 700ha/22ha (grenache, mourv, viog) ▪ ±160t/400cs own label 50% red 50% white/rosé ▪ PO Box 972 Malmesbury 7299 ▪ erica. joubert@cropspec.co.za ▪ www.frankisvineyards.co.za ▪ S 33° 20' 59.5" E 018° 32' 12.4" ▪ 🖾 repress.mono. reprising ▪ F +27 (0)86-660-3677 ▪ **T +27 (0)82-888-3702**

Franschhoek Cellar ⓠ 🍴 🏠 📷 🅐 🅖

Winemaker Ryan Puttick celebrated his first vintage at the Cellar last year and is full of enthusiasm for the quality of fruit harvested for this DGB-owned brand. Their elegant Franschhoek cellardoor is also a one-stop shop for tourists and locals, incorporating wine tastings, pairing options, al fresco dining and more.

Franschhoek Cellar range 🆕

★★★★☆ The Last Elephant 🏆 Statement wine evoking Franschhoek's original name, 'Elephant's Corner'. **15** ⑨⓪ 4-way merlot-led Bordeaux blend pulls out all the stops: plenty of oak (22 months, 100% new French) but enough concentrated cherry/berry fruit to handle, making for complex mouthful with elegant tannins & good length. WO Stellenbosch.

Méthode Cap Classique Sparkling range

Brut Rosé ⊘ ★★★ Subtle, vibrant touch of coral on **NV** ⑧② bubbly from pinotage & splash gamay. Bright berry fruit with refreshing biscuity lime, uncomplex yet delicious. **Brut Royale** ⊘ ★★★☆ Flavourful **NV** ⑧④ bubbly; chardonnay & pinot noir create mouthfilling combo of lime brioche & summer berries, finishing slatey-dry. WO W Cape.

Village Walk range

Not tasted: **The Churchyard Cabernet Sauvignon, Old Museum Merlot, Stone Bridge Pinotage, Baker Station Shiraz, Clubhouse Rosé, Our Town Hall Chardonnay, La Cotte Mill Chenin Blanc, Statue de Femme Sauvignon Blanc.** — CM

Location/map: Franschhoek ▪ Map grid reference: C2 ▪ WO: Coastal/Stellenbosch/Western Cape ▪ Est 1945 ▪ Tasting & sales Mon-Sat 10–6 Sun 10–5 ▪ Wine pairing: 6 wines with 6 cheeses, or with assorted chocolates ▪ Closed Easter Fri/Sun, Dec 25/26 & Jan 1 ▪ Al fresco dining daily ▪ Play area for children ▪ Farm produce ▪ Weddings ▪ Conferences ▪ Events venue (seat 300 pax) ▪ Owner(s) DGB (Pty) Ltd ▪ Winemaker(s) Ryan Puttick (Nov 2017) ▪ Viticulturist(s) Heinie Nel (Jul 2018) ▪ 300ha (cab, merlot, shiraz, chard, chenin, sauv, sem) ▪ 30,000t 49% red 50% white 1% rosé ▪ ISO 9001:2001, IPW ▪ PO Box 52 Franschhoek 7690 ▪ fhcellardoor@dgb.co.za ▪ www.thefranschhoekcellar.co.za, www.franschhoek-cellar.co.za ▪ S 33° 54' 16.4" E 019° 6' 40.7" ▪ ⚏ ironed.canyon.trifle ▪ F +27 (0)21-876-4107 ▪ **T +27 (0)21-876-2086**

☐ **Frans K Smit** *see* Spier

Frater Family Wines

On Paarl farm De Zoete Inval, fifth-generation winemaker John Robert Frater combines 'sound winemaking principles with artistry and family pride' to make 'wines with old world charm' named in honour of family members. The only exception is the Shiraz made in memory of my late great old mate David 'Shifty' Finch.'

★★★★ **Connor Cabernet Sauvignon-Petit Verdot-Malbec** Attractive melange of black & red fruit show classic Bordeaux nuances of cassis & graphite. **14** ⑧⑥ mostly cab (49%) with firm but approachable tannins. French & 25% American oak staves for extra vanilla/dried herb appeal, as for Adrian.

Adrian SMG ⊛ ★★★★ Shiraz-led with equal 14% portions mourvèdre & grenache, **14** ⑧④ swirls of spice, scrub & fresh herbs, ripe cassis fruit notes. Friendly, with latent power.

Oupa Bull Pinotage Reserve ★★★★ Rum & raisin-toned **16** ⑧③ from Paarl grapes similar lighter styling as **15** ★★★ ⑧① ex Simonsberg–Stellenbosch despite different oaking & alcohol. Fruity & lively, pleasant tannic farewell. **David Arthur Shiraz Reserve** ⑭⑬ ★★★ Ripe, almost raisined **16** ⑧⓪'s 14.8% alcohol lassoed by dry tannins, fresh acidity. Obviously powerful yet with structure/intent to improve few years. **Elizabeth Viognier-Chardonnay** ★★★ Barrel-fermented viognier (80%) leads **16** ⑧①, unoaked chardonnay gives freshness & lift. Big-boned & attractively dry with apricot & dried peach flavours. — CR, CvZ

Location/WO: Paarl ▪ Est 1878 ▪ 1stB 1976 ▪ Closed to public ▪ Owner(s) DZI Agricultural Investments cc (John Robert & Eulalia Frater) ▪ Cellarmaster(s)/winemaker(s) John Robert Frater (1999) ▪ Viticulturist(s) Robert Frater ▪ 80ha/20ha (cab, grenache, malbec, mourv, p verdot, shiraz, chard) ▪ 200t/16,000cs own label 50% red 50% white ▪ Other export brands: Eskdale, Safari ▪ PO Box 591 Suider-Paarl 7624 ▪ info@dezoeteinval. co.za, sales@fraterfamilywines.co.za ▪ www.fraterfamilywines.co.za ▪ F +27 (0)86-297-6981 ▪ **T +27 (0)21-863-1535/+27 (0)82-731-3898**

Freedom Hill Wines   ⊘ ⊚ ⊛ ♿

Civil engineer Francois Klomp is the driver behind this boutique property, a subdivision of the original Paarl farm, La Paris, on a Wemmershoek Mountain slope. Francois established the vineyards in the late 1990s, and he's since added a cellar and visitor locale which hosts, besides winelovers, weddings and various functions.

Freedom Hill range

★★★★ **Merlot** Second bottling of **14** ⑧⑥ as good as first. Blackcurrant & plum fruit in noble structure; has bedded down & developed well, smooth & ready to enjoy. WO Stellenbosch.

Pinotage ⊘ ★★★★ Somewhat untamed aromas on **13** ⑧③ follow to supple, fruit-rich palate. Slightly confected but appealing. **Cape Blend** ★★★ Compatible union of pinotage & cab, **15** ⑧② mild-mannered with bramble fruit, light oak spices & chunky tannin underpinning. **Pinotage Rosé** Ⓥ ★★★ Refreshingly dry **16** ⑲ is crisp & light-seeming, despite ±14% alcohol. WO W Cape, as next. **Chardonnay** Ⓥ ★★★★ Ripe citrus fruit & beeswax, with muted oak & medium body. **15** ⑧⑤ thoroughly pleasant, well focused & convincing. **Chenin Blanc** Ⓥ ★★★ Hint of terpene over bright stonefruit on dry, unoaked **16** ⑧②. Brightly fruity, with candied edge, modest 12.5% alcohol. **Sauvignon Blanc** ★★★ Tropical/litchi fruit of **16** ⑧① is tiring, a dusty edge developing, enjoy soon. Second bottling of this vintage. WO W Cape. Not tasted: **Premium Sauvignon Blanc**. Discontinued: **Shiraz-Cabernet Sauvignon**.

Freedom Walk 1335/88 range

Pinotage ★★★ Earthy expression of the variety, with forest floor & musk nuances to plum fruit on **15** ⑧②. French oak support is well judged. **Shiraz** Ⓥ ★★★ Liquorice & cocoa depth to juicy black fruit, **10** ⑧① straightforward but ripe & approachable. **Cape Blend** ★★★ From pinotage & cab, understated **15** ⑧② has black berry & currant fruit, light oak spicing & earthy tannin foundation. — DS

Location: Paarl ▪ Map: Franschhoek ▪ Map grid reference: B5 ▪ WO: Paarl/Western Cape/Stellenbosch ▪ Est 1997 ▪ 1stB 2000 ▪ Tasting & sales Mon-Fri 8.30-5 ▪ Fee R45pp ▪ Closed all pub hols ▪ Child friendly ▪ Wedding & function venue ▪ Owner(s) Francois Klomp ▪ Winemaker(s) Kowie du Toit (Feb 2007) ▪ 82ha/19ha (cab, ptage, shiraz) ▪ ±70t/12,000cs own label 100% red ▪ PO Box 6126 Paarl 7620 ▪ info@freedomhill.co.za ▪ www.freedomhillwines.com ▪ S 33° 49' 48.33" E 019° 0' 35.90" ▪ 📠 bottles.obediently.intermodal ▪ F +27 (0)86-244-9748 ▪ **T +27 (0)21-867-0085**

- ☐ **Freedom Walk** see Freedom Hill Wines
- ☐ **Free to Be** see Remhoogte Wine Estate
- ☐ **Friends Forever** see Devonvale Golf & Wine Estate
- ☐ **Friesland** see Kaapzicht Wine Estate
- ☐ **Frisky Zebras** see United Nations of Wine
- ☐ **Frogner** see Nordic Wines

Fryer's Cove Vineyards   Ⓨ ⑪ ⓞ ⓐ ⓖ

'Forged of the earth and tempered by the sea' is the slogan of Fryer's Cove Vineyards, owned by two family trusts and Wynand Hamman, also cellarmaster since inception, and uniquely sited in a refurbished crayfish factory in Doring Bay village on the West Coast. Sauvignon is the focus, and having vines a stone's throw from the cold Atlantic has distinct benefits. Sea mists bring not only salt-laden moisture, enhancing the inherent character of their sauvignons, but also alkalinity which helps prevent disease. The cool conditions also promote slow ripening and high natural acidity, perfect for quality and longevity in their chosen variety.

★★★★ **Bamboes Bay Hollebakstrandfontein** Was 'Blanc Fumé'. Attractive toasted hazelnut & lime, combo oak & clay pot ferment enhances silky texture & gentler, riper fruit profile of **16** ⑧⑨. Suave, polished & very seductively balanced, will have many fans. Lowest alcohol of the sauvignons tasted.

★★★★ **Bamboes Bay Sauvignon Blanc** Vivacious, balanced & tangy **17** ★★★★★ ⑨① pungent green herb & passionfruit, gooseberry flavours, creamy undertone & clean citrus farewell. Unoaked, like Doring Bay, but more substance & verve than it & wooded sibling. Step up on **16** ⑧⑨.

Doring Bay Sauvignon Blanc Ⓥ ★★★★ Dust & flint, bright acidity, some creamy lees make **17** ★★★★ ⑧⑤ very balanced, lively & quaffable. Still driest of the tasted sauvignons, less succulence & weight than last but equally appealing. WO W Cape, as next.

Pinot Noir ★★★★ Pale, almost translucent red, alluring perfume, supple palate with gentle red forest fruits & earth flavours, **15** ⑧⑤ revisited, even subtler than last edition, ready to drink. Not tasted: **Doring Bay Shiraz, Sandberg Rosé, The Jetty Sauvignon Blanc, Noble Late Harvest**. — MW

Location: Doring Bay ▪ Map: Olifants River ▪ Map grid reference: A4 ▪ WO: Bamboes Bay/Western Cape ▪ Est 1999 ▪ 1stB 2002 ▪ Tasting, sales & cellar tours Mon-Fri 9-5 Sat 10-5 ▪ Tasting fee, donations for public school ▪ Closed Sun & Christian hols ▪ Child friendly ▪ The Jetty restaurant open 10-4, bookings on weekends & pub hols ▪ West Coast walking trail ▪ Owner(s) Jan Ponk Trust, JH Laubscher Family Trust & Wynand Hamman ▪ Cellarmaster(s) Wynand Hamman (Apr 1999) ▪ Winemaker(s) Derick Koegelenberg (Apr 2017) ▪ Viticulturist(s) Jan van Zyl (Apr 1999) ▪ 6ha (pinot, sauv) ▪ 70t/5,000cs own label 20% red 80% white ▪ PO Box 93 Vredendal 8160 ▪ admin@fryerscove.co.za ▪ www.fryerscove.co.za ▪ S 31° 45' 53.1" E 018° 13'

55.8" ▪ ⌨ welded.legendary.complying ▪ F +27 (0)86-636-3295 ▪ T +27 (0)27-213-2312 (office)/+27 (0)27-215-1092 (tasting)

☐ **Future Eternal** *see* L'Avenir Vineyards

Gabriëlskloof   ⓠ ⑪ ⊚ ⊛ ⑤

Having completed his fourth harvest at Bernhard Heyns and partners' Bot River estate, cellarmaster (and Bernhard's son-in-law) Peter-Allan Finlayson confirms he's 'finally settling into my new roles and loving the different challenges presented'. The past year has seen the on-site chapel repurposed and filled with barrels and locally made amphoras dedicated to the Landscape Series; membership in the Old Vine Project secured, allowing the Elodie chenin to carry the Certified Heritage Vineyard seal; and the first home-grown chenin harvested; more is being planted, while a 2-ha block is being prepared 'for more world-class cab franc'. The most personal development in Peter-Allan and wife Nicolene's life was the birth of their first child, Theodore.

Landscape Series

★★★★ **Cabernet Franc** ⓐ Cab franc in hedonistic mode, **16** ★★★★☆ ⑨③ rich in aromatics - tobacco, woodsmoke & forest floor - & flavour; plush but controlled by fine acid line, assured structure. Oak, 50% new, carefully tuned enhancement. **15** ⑧⑨ looser-knit.

★★★★☆ **Syrah on Sandstone** ⓐ Lilting red fruit aromas, fluid freshness - **16** ⑨③ initially has a deceptive lightness. But there is fine-toned muscle in the savoury concentration, steadfastness in structure & concluding surge of delicious truffle & spice. Touch more new oak (30%) than previous, as next.

★★★★☆ **Syrah on Shale** ⓐ The weightier, richer of the Syrah pair. **16** ⑨③ has deep dark-fruit, herbal aromas, broad reach of flavour in its full body, resonating savoury tail; all delivered with refinement & balance. Subtly oaked, 30% new.

★★★★☆ **Elodie** ⓐ ⓦ Swartland & Durbanville fruit happy partners in elegant **17** ⑨③ chenin. Quietly confident pear, green apple & fresh earth flavours; lovely length emerges from still tight-knit, minerally palate. Naturally fermented, aged 10 months in large, old oak.

★★★★☆ **Magdalena** ⓐ Semillon's smooth silkiness sets the pace, 42% sauvignon adds focus & drive on **17** ⑨③. Elegantly harmonious, waxy lemon flavours seamlessly interlinked with cool blackcurrant & extended on zestily dry tail. Natural ferment, older oak. Semillon ex Franschhoek.

Special Collection

★★★★☆ **Broken Stem Late Harvest** ⓝⓔⓦ ⓐ Name refers to breaking bunch stems & leaving grapes to desiccate on vine. Naturally made & aged in old oak, **16** ⑨④ semillon is 375 ml of silky opulence, its intense raisin & lemon tang, acid backbone tempering richness of both 14.5% alcohol & 123 g/l RS.

Not tasted: **Madame Lucy**, **Noble Late Harvest**.

Estate range

★★★★ **Syrah** ⊘ Balances youthful approachability of syrah's comfortable breadth, focused dark soft berries & spice, with firm structural support. **16** ⑧⑧ a satisfying whole at a more than satisfying price.

★★★★ **The Blend** ⊘ Generous in its dark-fruit medley, creamy texture, allowing for youthful enjoyment, but **16** ⑧⑦ has the telling firm structure of a cab-led Bordeaux-style red in classic mould.

★★★★ **Chenin Blanc** ⓝⓔⓦ From Swartland & Franschhoek fruit, **17** ⑧⑥ comfortable, satisfying styling. Gentle freshness, red apple tones fleshed out by 15% semillon, harmonised in older, large oak. Spontaneous ferment.

★★★★ **Sauvignon Blanc** Just after bottling, **18** ⑧⑥ briskly fresh, its rapier acidity tempered by tropical flavours, weight from lees ageing, 11% semillon. Should settle after few months. Cape South Coast WO.

Rosebud ★★★ Attractive spiced peach scents, juiciness on **18** ⑧① rosé from co-fermented syrah & viognier. Versatile as refreshing aperitif & flavoursome, dry food wine.

Reserve range

Not tasted: **Swartriver Shiraz**. Discontinued: **Five Arches**. — AL

Location: Bot River ▪ Map: Walker Bay & Bot River ▪ Map grid reference: C3 ▪ WO: Bot River/Western Cape/Cape South Coast ▪ Est 2002 ▪ 1stB 2007 ▪ Tasting & sales Mon-Fri 9—5 Sat 11-3 ▪ Fee R60/6 wines (Estate/Reserve) or R150/6 wines (Landscape/Broken Stem), waived on purchase ▪ Closed Dec 24/25 ▪ Cellar tours by appt ▪

Restaurant ▪ Deli ▪ Child friendly; dogs welcome ▪ Weddings (very limited availability) ▪ Annual market: see website for details ▪ Owner(s) Bernhard Heyns & shareholders Johan Heyns, Barry Anderson, Wally Clarke, Peter-Allan Finlayson & Nicolene Finlayson ▪ Cellarmaster(s) Peter-Allan Finlayson (Jul 2014) ▪ Winemaker(s) Donovan Ackermann (Sep 2016) ▪ Viticulturist(s) Barry Anderson (2001) & Adriaan Davids (Jan 2003) ▪ 66ha (cabs s/f, malbec, merlot, mourv, p verdot, pinot, shiraz, chenin, sauv, sem, viog) ▪ IPW, WIETA, WWF-SA Conservation Champion ▪ PO Box 499 Kleinmond 7195 ▪ info@gabrielskloof.co.za ▪ www.gabrielskloof.co.za ▪ S 34° 14' 19.89" E 019° 14' 58.68" ▪ paradoxical.roused.reactors ▪ F +27 (0)28-284-9864 ▪ **T +27 (0)28-284-9865**

☐ **Game Reserve** *see* Rooiberg Winery
☐ **Garajeest** *see* The Garajeest

Garden Route Wines ⓠ ⓰

These vineyards are in the cool Waboomskraal Valley on the Garden Route (which lends its name), their grapes vinified by Louis van der Riet for De Krans in warmer Calitzdorp. Drought in 2018 ravaged the Klein Karoo, but not here: conditions helped sauvignon, but not pinot - none came into the cellar.

★★★★ **Pinot Noir** ⊘ As usual, fresh red-cherry, raspberry aromas & flavours on previewed **17** (88) tell of cool origins, as does firm acidity - but fully ripe. Light-feeling, elegant, silky & properly dry. Only old oak.

★★★★ **Sauvignon Blanc** Only tasted as pre-bottling samples for some years. Very young **18** ★★★★ (83) exuberantly fruity & showy, with a green bite, but shorter on substance than **17** (86).

In abeyance: **Shiraz**. — TJ

Location: Calitzdorp-Waboomskraal ▪ Map: Klein Karoo & Garden Route ▪ Map grid reference: C3 B5 ▪ WO: Outeniqua ▪ Est/1stB 2008 ▪ Tasting & sales at De Krans, Calitzdorp (see entry) ▪ Wines also available at Outeniqua Wine Emporium, Waboomskraal on N12 between George & Oudtshoorn ▪ Owner(s) Boets Nel ▪ Cellarmaster(s) Louis van der Riet (2012) ▪ Viticulturist(s) Boets Nel (2008) ▪ 9ha (pinot, sauv) ▪ 80t/±3,000cs own label 50% red 50% white ▪ PO Box 28 Calitzdorp 6660 ▪ dekrans@mweb.co.za ▪ S 33° 50' 57.60" E 022° 21' 20.00" (Waboomskraal) S 33° 32' 6.3" E 021° 41' 9.0" (Calitzdorp) ▪ F +27 (0)44-213-3562 ▪ **T +27 (0)44-213-3314**

☐ **Garden Vineyards** *see* DeMorgenzon
☐ **Gecko Ridge** *see* Thor Vintners
☐ **Genade Water** *see* JMA Louw Familie Wyn
☐ **Generation 8** *see* Bosman Family Vineyards

Genevieve Méthode Cap Classique ⓠ

Melissa Nelsen's middle name is Genevieve, making for an eminently suitable brand name for her champagne-method sparkling wines from chardonnay. Long based in Bot River, she more recently bought a farm there. Her address in Karwyderskraal Road is somewhat less French but arguably no less appropriate.

Blanc de Blancs Zero Dosage ⓠ ★★★★ Leaner, food-styled **12** ◯84 chardonnay bubbly, 4 years on lees, bone-dry & mineral with subtle toasty brioche & apple flavours. Not tasted: **Blanc de Blancs Brut**. — MW

Location: Bot River ▪ Map: Walker Bay & Bot River ▪ Map grid reference: C2 ▪ WO: Overberg ▪ Est 2009 ▪ 1stB 2008 ▪ Tasting by appt ▪ Owner(s) Melissa Nelsen ▪ Viticulturist(s) Leon Engelke (2008) ▪ 16t/1,650cs own label 100% MCC ▪ Klein Botrivier Farm Karwyderskraal Rd Bot River ▪ melissa@genevievemcc.co.za ▪ www.genevievemcc.co.za ▪ S 34° 16' 35.95" E 019° 11' 9.19" ▪ victors.inductions.member ▪ **T +27 (0)83-302-6562**

Gentleman Spirits ⓠ

With Swiss partner Urs Gmuer, master distiller Rolf Zeitvogel oversees the crafting of a very fine and handsomely packaged portfolio of husk spirits (and gins). Stellenbosch's Blaauwklippen estate is where it all happens (tasting, too), so it's no surprise to see 'grappa' from zinfandel, the locally very rare variety which has long been a Blaauwklippen speciality.

Husk Spirit range

★★★★ **Marc de Shiraz** ⓠ Violet & lavender scents, black berries & exotic spice. Smooth, elegant, with lovely depth & leafy freshness. 43% alcohol, as all these.

★★★★ **Marc de Zinfandel** ⓩ Wild flowers, dried herbs & warm spice introduce the silky palate & delicate fire. Clean, bright, with subtle nut, mocha & red berry perfume. Balanced, well-integrated spirit.

★★★★☆ **Zinfandel Distiller's Reserve** New distillation every bit as delightful as last, smooth & silky with a long Asian spice finish from 4 years older brandy barrels. Wild berries, cherries, preserved ginger & smoke: satisfying complexity on nose, ample flavours, too. Limited edition of just 600 bottles.

In abeyance: **Marc de Merlot**, **Marc de Zinfandel Noble Late Harvest**. — WB

Location/map: Stellenbosch ▪ Map grid reference: E7 ▪ Est/1stB 2012 ▪ Tasting & sales at Blaauwklippen (see entry for opening hours) ▪ Closed Dec 25 & Jan 1 ▪ Distillery tours by appt only ▪ Owner(s) Urs Gmuer, Rolf Zeitvogel ▪ Master distiller/MD Rolf Zeitvogel ▪ Distillery manager Pierre du Toit, with Tiaan Langenegger ▪ 2,000cs ▪ info@triplethree.co.za ▪ www.triplethree.co.za ▪ S 33° 58' 23.3" E 018° 50' 51.0" ▪ 🌐 strengthens. mooring.register ▪ F +27 (0)21-880-0136 ▪ **T +27 (0)82-907-9787**

Gentleman's Reserve Boutique Wines   ⓩ 🍴 🏠 📷

Things are going nicely for the young Stellenbosch- and, in particular, Simonsberg-focused boutique venture of Duan and Ilze Brits, whose handcrafted '14 and '15 wines, made at Simonsberg estate Marklew where Duan is a former winemaker, have sold out. The '16 vintages of Time Will Tell (cabernet franc), Tide is Turning (shiraz blend) and Shiraz MCC, and the non-vintage Chardonnay sparkling will be released later this year.

Location/map: Stellenbosch ▪ Map grid reference: E4 ▪ Est/1stB 2012 ▪ Tasting by appt ▪ Meals/refreshments by appt ▪ Guest house ▪ Wedding venue ▪ Owner(s) Duan & Ilze Brits ▪ Cellarmaster(s)/winemaker(s) Duan Brits (Jan 2011) ▪ 500cs own label 25% red 25% white 50% MCC ▪ PO Box 64 Elsenburg 7607 ▪ phbrits@gmail.com, ilzewasy@gmail.com ▪ S 33° 53' 42.90" E 018° 49' 60.00" ▪ 🌐 strengthens.mooring.register ▪ **T +27 (0)78-475-5188/+27 (0)72-343-7210**

Gerakaris Family Wines   ⓩ 🍴 📷 🏠 NEW

Kath and Minos Gerakaris have something unique: not just an urban winery, but one in suburban Johannesburg (the barcodes on the bottles wittily suggest the city skyline, Hillbrow Tower and all), allowing Joburgers 'to see and smell the fermentations, to taste wine straight out of the press'. From the outset, they've welcomed visitors to taste in their garden. It's Mina who vinifies the grapes brought all the way from Swartland. Her winemaking is 'simple, traditional, minimalist', including natural ferments for all.

Thomas ★★★ Similar winemaking to Tom but 10% new oak, higher alcohol (13%); **15** ⑧⑴ shiraz delicate cherry & mulberry fruit just balancing firm tannins; zesty, for food. **Tom** ★★★ Plum & prune intensity, **15** ⑧② leafiness & admirable elegance (12% alcohol), lovely savoury conclusion. From shiraz, 18 months seasoned barrels. **Elli** ★★ Wild-yeast, barrel-fermented **17** ⑺④ chenin will have its fans: idiosyncratic umami & seaweed characters, bone-dry & sherry-like nuttiness. **Ellaki** ★★ Tank fermented with wild yeast, several months on lees. Dry **17** ⑺④ chenin very demure, with nutty, sherry-like palate. — CR, CvZ

Location: Johannesburg ▪ WO: Swartland ▪ Tasting, sales & cellar tours Wed-Fri 12-5 Sat 10-3 Sun 11-2 ▪ Fee R30pp ▪ Closed Easter Fri/Sun, Dec 25-Jan 1 ▪ Snacks/cheese platters ▪ Children welcome ▪ Winery available for small functions ▪ Owner(s) Kath & Minos Gerakaris ▪ Winemaker(s) Kath Gerakaris ▪ 57% red 43% white ▪ 20 Marlborough Ave Craighall Park Johannesburg 2196 ▪ kath@gerakaris.co.za ▪ www.gerakaris.co.za ▪ S 26° 7' 40.76" E 028° 0' 59.92" ▪ **T +27 (0)72-638-7636**

☐ **Geyser** *see* Withoek
☐ **Ghost Corner** *see* Cederberg Private Cellar
☐ **Ghost Tree** *see* SylvanVale Vineyards
☐ **Giant Periwinkle** *see* The Giant Periwinkle

Gilga Wines   ⓩ 🏠

Cellarmaster Stefan Gerber (also of Boer & Brit) partners with John Rowan in this Stellenboschkloof boutique winery, whose untasted line-up includes varietal Syrah and blend Amurabi. A spacious self-catering guest house on the property can be booked via the website.

Location/map: Stellenbosch ▪ Map grid reference: D5 ▪ Est/1stB 2002 ▪ Tasting & sales by appt ▪ Guest house ▪ Owner(s) John Rowan & Stefan Gerber ▪ Cellarmaster(s)/viticulturist(s) Stefan Gerber (Jun 2010) ▪ 4ha/3.5ha (grenache, mourv, shiraz, tempranillo) ▪ 10t/1,100cs own label 100% red ▪ PO Box 871

Stellenbosch 7599 ▪ info@gilga.co.za ▪ www.gilga.co.za ▪ S 33° 56′ 46.1″ E 018° 47′ 20.6″ ▪ ⌨ mankind. impaired.raced ▪ T +27 (0)84-515-6677

☐ **Glass Collection** *see* Glenelly Estate

Glen Carlou

It's hard to miss the silverware taking pride of place in Glen Carlou's tasting room: two huge trophies for performance in the 2018 Young Wine Show. Fittingly, it was chardonnay which took the honours, a variety this Paarl winery has specialised in over the past 30 years. Founders, the Finlayson family, established the reputation, burnished during the Hess Collection tenure and now continued in its third year of ownership by the Pactolus consortium of three wine-loving cousins. Cellar chief Johnnie Calitz has crushed only two harvests at the cellar - the attached cellardoor boasts a cracking view of Paarl's granite dome from its shaded deck and popular restaurant - and anticipates making greater strides during his third in 2019.

The Prestige Collection

★★★★☆ **Gravel Quarry Cabernet Sauvignon** Ⓐ Red flagship, **15** ⑨ first since **11** ⑨, velvety smooth, regal & rich, with fruitcake & cedar spice. Beautiful integration of fruit & oak (new, 18 months). Svelte, subtle & harmonious. A classic.

★★★★☆ **Quartz Stone Chardonnay** Single-vineyard **17** ⑨ is broad & opulent, long-lingering succulent citrus & spicy cream, restrained yet immensely rewarding. Mostly naturally fermented (10% in Nomblot tank), 90% in all-new French oak. Simonsberg-Paarl WO.

★★★★ **The Welder** Ⓩ After-dinner treat returns to Natural Sweet in **16** ⑧ after Noble Late Harvest **15** ★★★☆ ⑧. All chenin, all sweetness & ethereal beauty, with apricot & nectarine tang. Unoaked.

The Curator's Collection

★★★★ **Malbec** Occasional release, last was **11** ★★★☆ ⑧. Plush suppleness on **17** ⑧, rich plum & cherry vivacity, creamy oak (half new) supports the fruit without dominating. Lovely lightness & texture.

★★★★ **Mourvèdre** Ⓩ Savoury earthy spice & solid core of blue fruit on **14** ⑧, grip & backbone provided by 2 years older French oak. Available only ex cellar, as all these.

★★★★ **Syrah** Ⓩ Confident herb-brushed **15** ⑧, succulent plum & sour cherry with liquorice nuance at end; fruit well-framed by older French oak, 18 months.

★★★★☆ **Red Blend** Ⓝⓔⓦ Ⓐ Equal parts cab & cab franc join 20% merlot in **17** ⑨ debut. Turned earth, mocha swarthiness is refined, rich & rewarding. Muscular but smooth & layered. Needs time but will reward patience. Simonsberg-Paarl, as Malbec.

★★★★ **Chardonnay** Ⓩ Orange blossom perfume to light-bodied **15** ⑧ special barrel selection; marmalade tang dances on creamy oak platform from year in 50% new casks; broad but restrained.

★★★★ **Chenin Blanc** Remains vivid & zesty in **18** ⑧, stonefruit life matches creamy breadth from natural ferment, ageing in old oak. Tribute to venerable 50 year old Swartland bushvines, like **17** ★★★★ ⑧.

★★★★ **Semillon-Sauvignon Blanc** Ⓝⓔⓦ Broad, rich palate melds attractively with tauter nettle & lemon typical of cool-climate Groenekloof grapes. Creamy underpinning from natural ferment & ageing in 50% new oak. **18** ⑧ 50/50 mix.

Sauvignon Blanc Ⓩ ★★★★ Expressive lemon leaf, fynbos & flint tussle on **17** ⑧, nice dryness & acidity from Darling single-vineyard grapes.

The Pactolus Collection Ⓝⓔⓦ

★★★★ **Chardonnay** Opulent, plush **17** ⑧ offers up caramel, butterscotch & vanilla but could do with more freshness. 90% natural ferment in new oak, rest in concrete 'egg'. WO Simonsberg-Paarl.

The Classic Collection

★★★★ **Cabernet Sauvignon** Yielding & generous **17** ⑧ is ripe in its plum, cassis abundance, with well-knit oak. **16** ⑧ leaner, more restrained. Identical winemaking & maturation (15 months, all old).

★★★★ **Grand Classique** Smooth-textured approachability on **15** ⑧ Bordeaux red quintet. Signature Xmas cake & spice with platform of oak, 30% new, harmoniously supporting fruit. No **14**.

★★★★ **Petit Verdot-Tannat** Ⓩ Shows influence of 44% tannat in its dry, spicy tannic grip which shades the succulent red fruit. **12** ★★★★ ⑧ less impressive than **11** ⑧.

★★★★ **Chardonnay** Vivacious orange cream breadth to **17** ⑧⑥. Structured but svelte, reined-in, with well-meshed 30% new oak applied for 10 months. Textured & long, retains freshness to end.

Merlot ★★★☆ Smoke overlays black berry fruit on **17** ⑧④. Medium bodied & soft, light grip courtesy of oaking mainly in large (6,000L) vats. Simonsberg-Paarl WO, as Rosé & chardonnays. **Pinot Noir** ⊘ ★★★★ Perky & spicy **16** ⑧⑤ is nimble & sprightly. Light bodied & red fruited, soft tannin squeeze from 11 months French oak, just 20% new. **Syrah** ⓧ ★★★★ Pepper seasons rich plum notes of **15** ⑧⑤, oak (30% new) frames fruit beautifully; velvety smooth with a defined end. **Pinot Noir Rosé** ★★★ Dry subtlety to succulent, strawberry-toned summertime pink. **18** ⑧⓪ charmingly light & tangily juicy. **Unwooded Chardonnay** ★★★ Bright, zesty citrus on focused **18** ⑧②. Palate weight comes from ferment in concrete 'egg' & lees contact. Crisp & clean. **Sauvignon Blanc** ★★★ Lemon verbena & grapefruit zip & zest on **18** ⑧⓪. Light, gentle but juicy. Cape Town WO.

The Haven Collection

★★★★ **Shiraz** ⑯④ ⊘ Lithe **16** ⑧⑥, ample cherry succulence & vivid spice but rumble of leashed power too. Ripe fruit checked by year in large-format (6,000L) old oak vats.

Cabernet Sauvignon ⊘ ★★★★ Generous berry compote with spice & gentle grip on **17** ⑧③ from year oaking in older 6,000L vats. WO Coastal, as all these. **Chardonnay** ⊘ ★★★★ Orange verve & zip on light, easy-drinking **18** ⑧③. Just a third oaked, none new for 3 months, adding subtle cream nuance. — FM

Location/map: Paarl ▪ Map grid reference: D7 ▪ WO: Paarl/Simonsberg-Paarl/Coastal/Darling/Swartland/Groenekloof/Cape Town ▪ Est 1985 ▪ 1stB 1988 ▪ Tasting & sales Mon-Fri 9–5 Sat/Sun 10–4 ▪ Fee R50-R150 ▪ Closed Good Fri, Dec 25 & Jan 1 ▪ Cellar tours by appt ▪ Restaurant ▪ Facilities for children ▪ Tour groups ▪ Gifts ▪ Weddings ▪ Conferences ▪ Conservation area ▪ Gallery @ Glen Carlou ▪ Owner(s) Pactolus Consortium (chair Wayne Pitout) ▪ Cellarmaster(s)/winemaker(s) Johnnie Calitz (Oct 2016) ▪ Viticulturist(s) Marius Cloete (2000) ▪ 130ha/68ha (cabs s/f, malbec, mourv, p verdot, pinot, shiraz, chard) ▪ ±700t/100,000cs own label ▪ PO Box 23 Klapmuts 7625 ▪ welcome@glencarlou.co.za ▪ www.glencarlou.co.za ▪ S 33° 48' 44.85" E 018° 54' 12.88" ▪ 🖵 consoled.restorer.swirl ▪ F +27 (0)86-215-8157 ▪ **T +27 (0)21-875-5528**

Glenelly Estate

⚲ 🍴 ◎ ⑤

When May de Lencquesaing bought this Stellenbosch estate in 2003 (at the age of 78), she brought to the Cape, with her vision of 'a new adventure' and faith in Cape terroir, not only her personal history as the owner of a great estate in Bordeaux, but that of the 250-year involvement of her family with wine. She had the manor house restored, a large cellar built, and a major vineyard-planting programme begun. Some of her magnificent collection of glass is housed in the museum on the estate, reflecting another lifelong passion. Luke O'Cuinneagain has been cellarmaster here for a decade now, making natural-ferment wines that combine warm-country power with classic finesse. May's grandchildren, Nicolas Bureau and Arthur de Lencquesaing are now also involved at Glenelly.

Lady May range

★★★★★ **Lady May** ⓧ Cab-based, **13** ⑨④ adds 15% mix of cab franc, petit verdot & malbec. Though still young, the big but classic structure offers alluring invitation to dark-fruited, richly tannined depths. Quite tough now, though lively, but promises real harmony in 5-10 years. Long, genuinely dry finish.

Estate Reserve range

★★★★★ **Red** 🍂 Cab continues its rise - to 47% in **13** ⑨④, with merlot, cab franc, shiraz & petit verdot. Developing aromas & flavours add savoury complexity to the usual sweet fruity charm & tobacco notes. More ripeness & power (14.5% alcohol) than previously, with firm tannic backbone, but elegance too.

★★★★☆ **Chardonnay** 🍂 There's ripe sweet fruit & richness on **17** ⑨③, with complex notes of oatmeal, nuts, stonefruit, citrus, toasty oak & earth. All finely & unshowily balanced with a good acid to elegant effect. Silky & supple now, but will benefit from a good few years in bottle.

Glass Collection

★★★★ **Cabernet Sauvignon** ⓧ Perhaps the most easygoing of the reds. **16** ⑧⑧ has serious structure, but plush & loose-knit. Modest 13% alcohol helps approachability. Like all, integrated oak, good dry finish.

★★★★ **Cabernet Franc** ⊘ More herbal than previous (dark cherry too, but more savoury than fruity), with a quite stern tannic structure. Good dry finish. **16** ⑧⑦ impressive, but needs time to gain generosity.

★★★★ **Merlot** ⊘ Mild, fresh & pure notes of red & darker fruits on **16** (88), spice & herbal edge. Firm acid & tannin, & oak support for the full, ripe flavours. Young but approachable. 14.5% alcohol in balance.

★★★★ **Syrah** ⊘ As usual, charming & generous, light-hearted (though not unserious) - no new oak, lower alcohol, no great intensity of fruit. **16** (88) pleasing harmony & balance, gently informing tannins.

★★★★ **Chardonnay Unwooded** Fine example of the style. Forward clean freshness on substantial **18** (87). As usual, purity compensates for the oaked version's complexity. Will age & develop. **17** untasted. Stellenbosch WO.— TJ

Location/map: Stellenbosch ▪ Map grid reference: F4 ▪ WO: Simonsberg–Stellenbosch/Stellenbosch ▪ Est/1stB 2003 ▪ Tasting Tue & Wed 10-6 Thu-Sat 10-7 Sun 10-3 ▪ Closed Easter Fri/Sun, Dec 25 & Jan 1 ▪ Cellar tours by appt ▪ Glass museum ▪ Restaurant: lunch Tue-Sun 12-3; dinner Thu-Sat 6.30-8.30 (last order) ▪ Owner(s) May-Eliane de Lencquesaing ▪ Cellarmaster(s) Luke O'Cuinneagain (Jan 2008) ▪ Winemaker(s) Luke O'Cuinneagain (Jan 2008), with Jerome Likwa (Jan 2008) ▪ Viticulturist(s) Heinrich Louw (2003) ▪ 123ha/57ha (cabs s/f, merlot, p verdot, shiraz, chard) ▪ 500t/55,334cs own label 90% red 10% white ▪ PO Box 1079 Stellenbosch 7599 ▪ wine@glenelly.co.za ▪ www.glenellyestate.com ▪ S 33° 55' 6.1" E 018° 52' 45.1" ▪ ⌨ quiz.ticked.hails ▪ F +27 (0)21-809-6448 ▪ **T +27 (0)21-809-6440**

Glen Heatlie Wines ⓠ

Joan-Marie Heatlie last year joined the Mullineux winemaking team, but will resume her own venture after making no wines in 2017 and 2018, focusing on old vineyards. Joan's label is named for the family farm near Worcester where her Scottish great-grandfather distilled Heatlie's Prized Brandy in the 1880s.

★★★★ **Agnes** ⓥ Old, dryland & organically farmed Paarl chenin, **15** (89) made with minimal intervention in old oak. Elegantly flavoursome & balanced, with light-stepping, easy charm.

Ruptura ⓥ ★★★★ Equal blend Worcester shiraz & Piekenierskloof grenache. Old-oaked **15** (84)'s very ripe character dulls the freshness a little, despite good flavour, a bright acidity & firm build. — TJ

Location: Worcester ▪ WO: Paarl/Worcester-Piekenierskloof ▪ Est 2006 ▪ Tasting by appt only ▪ Owner(s)/winemaker(s) Joan Heatlie ▪ 3,100ha/45ha (cab, merlot, shiraz, chenin, chard, cbard, sauv, sem) ▪ joan@glenheatlie.co.za ▪ **T +27 (0)82-364-4702**

Glenview Wines

Vintner and surfer Robin Marks continues to do steady online business, locally and abroad, by sourcing wines from coastal vineyards for his own label (the brand name a reference to Glen Beach near Robin's Camps Bay home). His selling point remains quality wines for everyday drinking at affordable prices.

Merlot ★★★ Red berries, savoury spicing, which particularly shows in the flavours. Despite only half the wine being oaked, **17** (82) would be a good partner for meat dishes, rich pasta. **Sauvignon Blanc** ★★★ Melon & gooseberries in **18** (81), light textured, ends dry, zesty. Tentatively rated preview. — CR, CvZ

Location: Cape Town ▪ WO: Stellenbosch ▪ Est/1stB 1998 ▪ Closed to public ▪ Owner(s) Robin Marks ▪ Winemaker(s) Danie Steytler jnr (consultant) ▪ 14,000cs own label 50% red 50% white ▪ PO Box 32234 Camps Bay 8040 ▪ bayexport@kingsley.co.za ▪ www.glenviewwine.com ▪ F +27 (0)21-511-2545 ▪ **T +27 (0)21-438-1080**

GlenWood ⓠ ⓥⓥ ◎ ⓖ

This family-owned Franschhoek estate was bought in 1984, allowing Alastair Wood 'to pursue his dream of farming and producing wine'. Involved from the outset in developing the property (which had been a general farm) was Dawid 'DP' Burger, who became winemaker when the cellar was built at the turn of the century. The vineyard block, planted by him, providing grapes for the Grand Duc Chardonnay he makes has now just turned 30. While the 'quest for the perfect wine and food match or experience' continues, the estate's motto of 'simple, natural, quality' goes wider: for example, 10 ha are dedicated to regenerating indigenous Cape fynbos, and only environmentally-friendly farming is practised. Witness too the involvement in a programme to transform the education landscape in the valley.

Grand Duc range

★★★★☆ **Syrah** Floral & red-fruit fragranced **15** (94) plush but not sacrificing freshness, perfectly judged oak (2 years, all new) helps make it delicious now, but will reward patience, like luscious **14** (91). WO Coastal.

★★★★☆ **Chardonnay** From low-yielding (3 t/ha) vineyard. Always impressive, & curvaceous **16** (93) continues the enviable track record with beguiling buttered toast & lime preserve flavours. Naturally fermented, then 2 years in all-new French oak.

★★★★☆ **Semillon-Sauvignon Blanc** Light, yet profoundly focused & penetrating **17** (93) from 73% semillon & sauvignon, wild-yeast fermented & aged 12 months 50% new French oak. Flavours of thatch, butterscotch, lime & citrus in a delicious yet serious body.

★★★★☆ **Noblesse** Previously **NV** (93), now vintage dated. Enchanting **14** (93) from naturally fermented botrytised semillon cosseted in oak, 50% new, 3 years. Pure, balanced, with candied apricot & orange peel. Not as sweet as many (just 92 g/l sugar) & light-footed (13% alcohol). 375 ml.

Vigneron's Selection

★★★★ **Shiraz** Smoky & darkly spiced **16** (87), ample liquorice & plump blackberry fruit. Oak spice, well integrated tannin grip from 2nd-fill French oak, 18 months.

★★★★☆ **Chardonnay** A larger-than-life personality, wild-yeast-fermented **16** (92) even fuller-bodied & -flavoured than previous, intense lemon & lime backbone, prominent spice & oak detail from 80% new barrels, 12 months.

GlenWood range

★★★★ **Merlot** Expressive chocolate & plum notes on **17** (87) supported by velvety tannins, flavours equally smooth & seamless, with rich savoury undertones. Ideal fireside companion, in magnum too.

★★★★ **Unwooded Chardonnay** Segues from orange blossoms, to nuts & tropical fruits, to green apple flavours & acidity in **17** (88), bone-dry but not austere thanks to creaminess from 5 months on lees.

★★★★ **Sauvignon Blanc-Semillon** Unwooded little brother of the Grand Duc. **17** (87) precise & linear equal partnership, sauvignon's rapier acidity providing perfect foil for semillon's breadth & weight.— HC

Location/map: Franschhoek ▪ Map grid reference: C2 ▪ WO: Franschhoek/Coastal ▪ Est/1stB 2002 ▪ Tasting & sales Mon-Fri 10–5 Sat/Sun (Aug-Jun only) 11-4 ▪ Closed Easter Fri/Sun, Dec 25 & Jan 1 ▪ Tasting R60 ▪ Cellar tours daily at 11; cellar tour with owner/winemaker available by prior arrangement, min 2 persons ▪ Restaurant ▪ Owner(s) Alastair G Wood ▪ Cellarmaster(s)/viticulturist(s) DP Burger (Apr 1991) ▪ Winemaker(s) Zinaschke Steyn (Jan 2015) ▪ 49ha/30ha (merlot, shiraz, chard, sauv, sem) ▪ 150t/16,000cs own label 50% red 50% white ▪ IPW, WIETA ▪ PO Box 204 Franschhoek 7690 ▪ info@glenwoodvineyards.co.za ▪ www.glenwoodvineyards.co.za ▪ S 33° 54' 56.7" E 019° 4' 57.0" ▪ visited.increment.tapas ▪ **T +27 (0)21-876-2044**

☐ **Glorious** *see* Stellenbosch Family Wines

Goats do Roam Wine Company

Born in 1998 in Paarl, this 'kid' is Charles Back of Fairview's fun range of highly drinkable, good-value wines from mostly southern French varieties (hence the wordplay on Côtes du Rhône and Côte Rôtie) as well as Italian grapes (plus cabernet) for The Goatfather. See Fairview entry for tasting hours.

★★★★ **Goat Roti** Silky **14** (88) from Elim, Stellenbosch & Darling syrah, the latter co-fermented with splash Paarl viognier, oak (20% new) adding cinnamon spice to rich plum fruit.

Goats do Roam Red ★★★★ Reliably cheerful 5-way Rhône blend led by syrah, **17** (85) gushes with ripe, juicy fruit. Punches above its weight. **The Goatfather** ★★★★ Italian blend, sangiovese-led with dash of cab, **16** (85) should please the Don with happy, juicy red-berry fruit. Characterful & likeable. Coastal WO, rest W Cape.

Goats do Roam Rosé ★★★★ Strawberries & boiled sweets with pithy/salty dry finish on **18** (83), from grenache, shiraz, mourvèdre. Refreshing poolside companion. **Goats do Roam White** ★★★★ Well-balanced **17** ★★★★ (84) from free-run juice of roussanne, viognier, grenache blanc & chenin, unwooded. Floral notes & concentrated citrus, stonefruit & tropical flavours. — GdB

Goede Hoop Estate ⓠ ⑪ ⑩

The Bestbier family have laid down deep roots in the granitic soils of this 120-ha estate in Stellenbosch's Bottelary Hills. Current custodian Pieter is the third generation to farm the property, purchased by his grandfather in 1928. Now there is a fourth generation, with son Johan having joined 'the family firm' handling marketing.

Estate range

Merlot ★★★ Lean, taut **14** ⑧⓪ sets blue & black fruit against cocoa earthiness. **Pinotage ★★★☆** Ripe prune & berry brightness of **13** ⑧③ checked by grip of tannin from year in older oak. **Chardonnay ★★☆** Citrus notes on **14** ⑦⑨ are fleshed out by creamy vanilla. Gentle & soft. **Sauvignon Blanc ★★★** Gentle lemon zest & light acidity on **17** ⑦⑦. **PJ Bestbier Méthode Cap Classique Brut** ⓃⒺⓌ **★★★** Crisp, dry orange & stonefruit appeal to uncomplicated **12** ⑧⓪ dry sparkler from chardonnay & pinot noir, showing well-judged ripeness. WO W Cape. Not tasted: **Cabernet Sauvignon, Shiraz**.

Domaine range

Merlot ★★★ Improves on previous in sheer gluggability. **17** ⑧⓪ cheery red fruit with soft plum & spice on light body. In abeyance: **Chenin Blanc**.

Heritage Wines

Not tasted: **Estate Wine**. In abeyance: **Estate Straw Wine**. — FM

Location/map: Stellenbosch ▪ Map grid reference: C3 ▪ WO: Bottelary/Western Cape ▪ Est 1928 ▪ 1stB 1974 ▪ Tasting, sales & cellar tours Mon-Fri 9–4 Sat 10–1 ▪ Closed Easter Fri-Sun, Dec 24/25/26/31 & Jan 1 ▪ Pieter's private cellar: monthly 4-course gourmet meal with wine R440pp (subject to change), booking essential (12 seats only) ▪ MTB trail ▪ Owner/s Pieter Bestbier ▪ 122ha/71ha (cab, cinsaut, malbec, merlot, ptage, shiraz, chard, chenin, sauv) ▪ ±600t/10,000cs own label 80% red 20% white & ±200,000L bulk ▪ PO Box 25 Kuils River 7579 ▪ goede@adept.co.za ▪ www.goedehoop.co.za ▪ S 33° 54′ 32.0″ E 018° 45′ 14.0″ ▪ Ⓜ neon.raced. compiled ▪ F +27 (0)21-906-1553 ▪ **T +27 (0)81-283-1618**

☐ **Goederust** see Rooiberg Winery

Goedvertrouw Estate ⓠ ⑪ ⌂ ⑩ Ⓐ

There's been nothing tasted from Bot River's Goedvertrouw for some years now, but estate owner Elreda Pillmann does have 'very limited stock' of past releases (sauvignon, chardonnay and pinot noir) available. Two decades back, Elreda and late husband Arthur were among the avant garde, farming sustainably and hand-crafting, so a visit here is an homage of sorts but even non-winegeeks should find tannie Elreda's pre-booked 'boeremeals' and the bucolic setting worth the trip.

Location: Bot River ▪ Map: Walker Bay & Bot River ▪ Map grid reference: D2 ▪ Est 1990 ▪ 1stB 1991 ▪ Tasting & sales by appt ▪ Home-cooked meals & accommodation by appt ▪ Play area for children ▪ Walks ▪ Farm produce ▪ Small conferences ▪ Conservation area ▪ Owner/s/winemaker/s/viticulturist/s Elreda Pillmann ▪ 8ha (cab, pinot, chard, sauv) ▪ 70% red 30% white ▪ PO Box 37 Bot River 7185 ▪ goedvertrouw@breede.co.za ▪ S 34° 9′ 56.7″ E 019° 13′ 24.1″ ▪ Ⓜ dynamic.marine.earthiness ▪ **T +27 (0)28-284-9769**

Goedverwacht Wine Estate ⓠ ⑪ ⌂ ⑩

Across their eight Bonnievale farms, acquired over decades, Jan du Toit and son Gawie continue to live the dream of grandfather Gabriël, who turned from civil engineering to winegrowing in the 1960s. SA's national bird, the Blue Crane, features on their labels, and several export brands have taken flight from their cellar and Cape vernacular-style visitor locale nested on the Breede River bank.

Maxim range

★★★★ Cabernet Sauvignon ⓠ From a single parcel on weathered shale, **15** ⑧⑥ elegant & sleek, modern; for earlier enjoyment courtesy less new oak than previous (40% versus 100%).

Chardonnay ⓠ **★★★★** Previewed **17** ⑧③ has creamy texture from 10 months in mostly older oak but refreshes with lemon-lime flavours, plenty of acidity.

Great Expectations range

Crane White Colombar ⊕ ★★★ Poolside quaffing doesn't get much better than bright, crisp **18** ⑧⓪, with tropical fruit salad flavours & unboozy 11.5% alcohol.

Crane Red Merlot ★★★ Soft, mediumweight **17** ⑦⑨ is plummy, with chocolate nuances from year in oak (50% new). **Shiraz** ⊗ ★★★ Floral aromas, viscous texture & ripe, spiced red berry/cherry fruit on unwooded **16** ⑧② preview, clean food-friendly finish. **Triangle** ★★★ Easy-drinking **16** ⑧② with plums, berries & dark chocolate from new oak staves blends cab with 28% cab franc, 14% merlot. **Shiraz Rosé** ★★★ Dry but fruity **18** ⑧⓪ with friendly 11.5% alcohol offers red cherries, cranberries & guava. Smooth, with spicy ginger & pepper finish. **Chardonnay** ★★★ Previewed **18** ⑦⑨ promises crisp citrus refreshment, lightly oaked for smoothness. **Sauvignon Blanc** ★★★ Water-white appearance belies solid flavour (fig & granadilla) & character of **18** ⑧① rounded yet zesty. **Sparkling Rosé Demi-Sec** ★★ Fun fizz **18** ⑦⑤ packed with sweet berry & banana flavours, alcohol only 11.5%. — JG

Location: Bonnievale ▪ Map/WO: Robertson ▪ Map grid reference: C4 ▪ Est 1960s ▪ 1stB 1994 ▪ Tasting, sales & cellar tours Mon-Fri 8.30-4.30 Sat 10-1 ▪ Closed Easter Fri/Sun, Dec 25/26 & Jan 1 ▪ Mediterranean or quiche & salad platter; picnic basket for 2 (incl sparkling wine) - 2 days prior booking essential ▪ BYO picnic ▪ Tour groups ▪ Conservation area ▪ Owner(s) Jan du Toit & Sons (Pty) Ltd ▪ Winemaker(s) Christiaan van Tonder (Sep 2016) ▪ Viticulturist(s) Jan du Toit, advised by Francois Viljoen ▪ 220ha/150ha (cabs s/f, merlot, p verdot, shiraz, chard, chenin, cbard, sauv) ▪ 3,000t/2.1M L 30% red 65% white 5% rosé ▪ Other export brands: Ama Ulibo, Kaapse Droom, Misty Kloof's, Soek die Geluk ▪ BEE, IPW, WIETA ▪ PO Box 128 Bonnievale 6730 ▪ goedverwachtestate@lando.co.za, winemaker@goedverwacht.co.za ▪ www.goedverwacht.co.za ▪ S 33° 55' 11.3" E 020° 0' 19.1" ▪ ⊞ cosponsors.specify.violinist ▪ F +27 (0)23-616-2073 ▪ **T +27 (0)23-616-3430**

☐ **Gôiya** see Namaqua Wines
☐ **Golden Seahorse** see Govert Wines
☐ **Goose Wines** see The Goose Wines

Goudini Wines   ⓠ ⓞ

Selected from the 20,000+ tons produced in the Breedekloof district by its 40 grower-owners, Goudini Wines' own substantial brand is now focused on easy-drinkers (the Reserve wines having sold out) — and a happy collection they are too! More smiley-faced news comes with the recent merger of Goudini and down-the-road Daschbosch, and consolidation of all tasting at these premises, meaning visitors now have three times the number of wines to try and buy.

Goudini range

Merlot ★★☆ Juicy, bouncy, fruit-forward **17** ⑦⑧, ex tank is gluggable & pocket friendly. **Shiraz** ★★☆ Coffee, mocha & spice on pre-bottling **17** ⑦⑨, gentle tannins, soft & easy. **Unwooded Chardonnay** ★★★ Vibrant apple & floral flavours with lifted acidity on affable **18** ⑧②. **Chenin Blanc** ★★★ Tank sample **18** ⑧② oozes sunshine fruit, just-dry & perfect for summer enjoyment. **Sauvignon Blanc** ★★ Dry, lean **18** ⑦③ preview has a stern acid backbone. Serve well chilled. **Brut Sparkling** ⊗ ★★★ From sauvignon, **NV** ⑧① light, balanced & moreish, green herb & lemon seaming the frothy bubbles. Discontinued: **Cabernet Sauvignon**. — WB

Location: Rawsonville ▪ Map: Breedekloof ▪ Map grid reference: C6 ▪ WO: Breedekloof/Goudini ▪ Est 1948 ▪ Tasting & sales Mon-Thu 8—5 Fri 8-4 Sat/pub hols 10—2 ▪ Closed Good Fri, Dec 25/26 & Jan 1 ▪ Cellar tours by appt ▪ Fully licensed bar ▪ Conferences ▪ Wild Clover craft beer ▪ Owner(s) 40 members ▪ Cellarmaster(s) Nicolaas Rust ▪ Assistant winemaker(s) Nicolaas du Toit (2017) & Godknows Chiringamutambo (2017) ▪ 1,000ha (merlot, ruby cab, shiraz, chard, chenin, sauv) ▪ 22,000t/66,000cs own label 45% red 45% white 10% rosé ▪ PO Box 132 Rawsonville 6845 ▪ info@goudiniwine.co.za ▪ www.goudiniwine.co.za ▪ S 33° 41' 37.8" E 019° 19' 9.5" ▪ ⊞ summer.canoe.guesses ▪ F +27 (0)23-349-1988 ▪ **T +27 (0)23-349-1090**

☐ **Goue Kalahari** see Die Mas van Kakamas
☐ **Gouverneurs** see Groot Constantia Estate

Govert Wines

The Stellenbosch-based Keuzenkamp family source export wines from around the Cape winelands for clients and their own labels Baron Diego, Charles Borro, Don King/Morris, Golden Seahorse, Loyal Brothers, Pegalle, Rocco Bay and Ruby Ridge.

Location: Stellenbosch ▪ Est 2002 ▪ 1stB 2007 ▪ Closed to public ▪ Owner(s) Teuns Keuzenkamp ▪ 180,000cs own label 80% red 5% white 15% rosé ▪ PO Box 1977 Somerset West 7129 ▪ info@govertwines.com ▪ www. govertwines.com ▪ F +27 (0)86-224-9348 ▪ **T +27 (0)21-887-5812**

☐ **GPS Series** *see* Richard Kershaw Wines

Graça

In Portuguese-inspired packaging since launch in 1983, these hugely successful Distell-owned wines are unabashed crowd pleasers, intended for 'talking, eating, drinking, laughing, singing, sharing'.

Graça ★★ No-worry **NV** ⑦④ with muted floral & orchard fruit, slightly sweet lemon-toned farewell. **Rosé ★★** Sunset hue, subtle berry tone, hint of sweetness, laid-back & easily quaffable **NV** ⑦③. — CvZ

Graceland Vineyards ⑨

Situated in Stellenbosch's 'golden triangle', renowned particularly for reds from Bordeaux varieties and shiraz, family boutique venture Graceland has grown steadily in reputation, locally and abroad. Volumes, too, have risen as Paul McNaughton and winemaker/viticulturist wife Susan added a varietal shiraz, rosé and trio of blends to the original merlot and cabernet sauvignon, all elegantly packaged with beautiful label art.

★★★★ Cabernet Sauvignon ⑨ Unapologetically big, bold & plush, **16** ⑧⑦ exudes cassis, cedar & graphite, yet fine, dense tannins supply necessary freshness & form. Approachable, will reward few years.

★★★★ Merlot ⑨ Appealing blueberry fruit, plums & herbs on entry, tight-grained tannins & a sappy farewell; **16** ⑧⑦ is food friendly & polished after ageing in 30% new French oak.

★★★★ Strawberry Fields ⑨ Shiraz-cab mix; **14** ⑧⑧ has expressive spice, black berry fragrance & rich, mouthcoating flavours, tasty savoury length. Subtle French oak embellishment. **13** not tasted.

Shiraz ⑨ **★★★** Ripe & opulent **15** ⑧① shows good spice & sweet black fruit, harmonious tannins ahead of a luscious farewell. Not tasted: **Colour Field, Three Graces, Rosé**. — HC

Location/map/WO: Stellenbosch ▪ Map grid reference: E7 ▪ Est/1stB 1998 ▪ Tasting & sales Mon-Fri by appt ▪ Fee R50 ▪ Closed all pub hols ▪ Owner(s) Paul & Susan McNaughton ▪ Cellarmaster(s)/winemaker(s)/viticulturist(s) Susan McNaughton (2001) ▪ 18ha/10ha (cab, merlot, shiraz) ▪ 55t/8,333cs own label 100% red ▪ Suite 144 Private Bag X4 Die Boord 7613 ▪ graceland@iafrica.com ▪ www.gracelandvineyards.com ▪ S 33° 59' 37.5" E 018° 50' 3.1" ▪ ⌑ nurture.legs.dating ▪ F +27 (0)86-556-4600 ▪ **T +27 (0)21-881-3121**

Graham Beck ⑨ ⑤

The decision that the Graham Beck winery (founded by the late mining magnate who gave it its name, and now owned by his family) should concentrate only on high-end sparkling wines was accompanied by substantial investment at the Madeba estate in Robertson. A new era as an MCC specialist was begun in 2018, the team says, with a great deal of new cellar equipment enabling them 'to increase production without sacrificing any of the important attention to detail'. A new ageing cellar crucially ensures enough space for extended time on lees for all the MCCs. The vineyards are vital: those for the discontinued still wines have been replanted with chardonnay and pinot noir – some 40 ha over the past half-decade. It's hard not to agree that this is all 'truly exciting!'.

Icon Collection

★★★★☆ Cuvée Clive ⑧ 100% Robertson chardonnay for the superb flagship sparkler, always showing presence & poise; **12** ⑨④ dry, with intense citrus & buttered toast palate from 5 years lees ageing. The mousse is velvety, mouthfilling & never-ending. For really special occasions.

Vintage Collection

★★★★☆ Brut Rosé ⑧ Coral-hued dry sparkling gains palate weight, savouriness & biscuit overlay to spiced strawberry flavours from 5 years on lees. The creamy bubbles melt in the mouth, making **13** ⑨③ a perfect accompaniment for seafood. 96% pinot noir, splash chardonnay. **12** untasted.

★★★★☆ **Blanc de Blancs Brut** ⓐ Lime, lemon, apple cake, warm spice on 50% barrel-fermented **13** ⑨④ bubbly from Robertson chardonnay. With 3 years lees-ageing, the palate is well-rounded, creamy, enveloping the fruit. Rich & satisfying, long savoury twist on the finish.

★★★★☆ **Brut Zero** Ⓩ Unlike all-chardonnay **11** ⑨③, **12** ⑨① mostly pinot noir (77%), 60 months on lees, no dosage (added sugar) for bone-dry palate, almost austere finish. Taut, mineral & linear, with red berry tang, exceptionally food friendly.

Non-Vintage Collection

★★★★ **Brut Rosé** Refreshing & bright **NV** ⑧⑦ sparkle from pinot noir (54%) & chardonnay is packed with fresh berry fruit & oatmeal cookie undertones ex 15-18 months lees maturation. Zesty, & touch drier than vintage-dated sibling.

★★★★ **Brut** Consistent mainstay fizz from chardonnay & pinot noir (51/49) lives up to its reputation in latest **NV** ⑧⑦. Fresh tropical & citrus fruit, gentle beads of mousse in perfect harmony. Also in 375ml & 1.5L.

★★★★ **Bliss Demi Sec** A crisp semi-sweet delight from chardonnay & pinot noir (51/49), **NV** ⑧⑧ bouncy red berries-&-cream, caramelised nuts & silky mousse. Excellent with chicken liver parfait.— WB

Location/map: Robertson ▪ Map grid reference: B6 ▪ WO: Western Cape/Robertson ▪ Est 1983 ▪ 1stB 1991 ▪ Tasting & sales Mon-Fri 9–5 Sat/Sun 10–4 ▪ Cellar tours by appt only ▪ Closed on selected public holidays ▪ Tasting options: A Gorgeous Duo complementary; Classic R50; Vintage Méthode Cap Classique R75; Deluxe Méthode Cap Classique tasting 'A Glass Act' R125; Proprietors Collection R150/3 wines or R50/wine ▪ Owner(s) Graham Beck Enterprises ▪ Cellarmaster(s) Pieter Ferreira (Aug 1990) ▪ Winemaker(s) Pierre de Klerk (Oct 2010) ▪ Viticulturist(s) Pieter Fouché ▪ Robertson 140ha ▪ 2,450t/140,000cs MCC ▪ ISO 14001, IPW, SABS 1841, WIETA, WWF-SA Conservation Champion ▪ PO Box 724 Robertson 6705 ▪ cellar@grahambeck. co.za, market@grahambeck.co.za ▪ www.grahambeck.com ▪ S 33° 48'14.95" E 019° 48'1.41" ▪ ✏ upfront. renaming.inkjet ▪ F +27 (0)23-626-5164/+27 (0)21-874-1712 (marketing) ▪ **T +27 (0)23-626-1214/+27 (0)21-874-1258 (marketing)**

Grand Domaine ⓆⓃᴱᵂ

Owned by Origin Wines founder Bernard Fontannaz, the Grand Domaine home-farm at the crest of Stellenbosch's Devon Valley is planted with all five red Bordeaux varieties, though it's a white grape from that famed French region, sauvignon blanc, which headlines these ranges. GM/and winemaker Monique Fourie is committed to producing a sauvignon 'like no other', and for The Pledge, she sources 10 parcels of grapes from 10 regions, vinifies them all separately, and ultimately selects only 'the best of the best'.

The Pledge range

★★★★ **Sauvignon Blanc** Succulent yet pithy grapefruit vivacity to **17** ⑧⑦, approachable & refreshing. Grapes from 10 different parcels, Lutzville to Walker Bay.

Grand Vin de Stellenbosch range

★★★★ **Sauvignon Blanc** Pepper & flint pungency to **17** ⑧⑥ from Devon Valley fruit. Bright lemony fruit with good acidity & signature verve, lengthy conclusion.

Cabernet Sauvignon-Merlot ★★★ Dusty red & blue fruit on light-bodied **16** ⑧⓪ Bordeaux blend. 2nd-fill oak vs some new wood for Rhône sibling. **Shiraz-Mourvèdre** ★★★★ Smoky blue & black fruit, with herb nuance in conclusion of vegan-friendly **17** ⑧③. **Chardonnay-Viognier** ★★★ Perfumed, juicy **17** ⑧①, peach fruit from 20% viognier & light vanilla from partial oak ferment, food-inviting taut acidity. — WB, FM, CvZ

Location/map: Stellenbosch ▪ Map grid reference: D4 ▪ WO: Stellenbosch/Western Cape ▪ Est/1stB 2014 ▪ Tasting strictly by appt ▪ Owner(s) Bernard Fontannaz ▪ Winemaker(s) / GM Monique Fourie (2018), with Skye Nolan (2016) ▪ 40% red 60% white ▪ PO Box 7177 Stellenbosch 7599 ▪ info@granddomaine.co.za ▪ www.granddomaine.co.za ▪ S 33° 54'0.61" E 018° 48'23.49"

☐ **Grand Duc** see GlenWood

Grande Provence Heritage Wine Estate ⓆⓎⓀⓄⓈⓀ

A visit to this historic Franschhoek estate, owned by a Dutch-Belgian consortium, is a multi-sensorial adventure. Wine is the main focus, with 22 ha under vine, and the visitor offering is rich and varied: there's a fabulous art gallery; exclusive public sculpture display of renowned local artist Anton Smit; acclaimed restaurant; and upmarket accommodation. Weddings, conferences and corporate events are all catered for. The wine offering has been tweaked and new labels launched, and Thys Smit is the new man in the cellar.

Grande Provence range

★★★★ Shiraz Refined, elegant & rich **15** ⑧⑧ shows good concentration. Deep layers of black fruit, spice & earth supported by harmonious oak, 30% new. Trademark peppery tail.

★★★★ Zinfandel Lithe, supple **17 ★★★★** ⑧⑤ offers signature ripe red cherry vibrancy. Succulent & structured from French & American oak, all old. Wellington grapes, like **15** ⑧⑦. **16** untasted.

★★★★☆ Red Flagship Bordeaux blend is alluring, complex & nuanced on **15 ★★★★** ⑧⑨, merlot (60%) leads cab & malbec. All-new oak a tad dominant mid-2018, giving cocoa powder sheen to fruitcake generosity. Needs time. Cab-led **14** ⑨② better balanced.

★★★★ Chardonnay ⊘ Big butterscotch, vanilla & citrus on **17** ⑧⑦, ripe orange fruit successfully countering the bold oak (11 months, 50% new French) so elegance is retained. Layered & complex, it needs time to fully mesh. No **16**.

★★★★☆ Amphora ⓘ Pithy citrus texture, apple spice cake & dried thyme notes, **16** ⑨① from old (30+ years) Franschhoek chenin plus 5% muscat for fragrance, unusual yet immensely satisfying. Dry & seamless, naturally fermented/matured 7 months on skins in Italian clay amphoras.

★★★★ Sauvignon Blanc Cool-climate typicity on **17 ★★★★** ⑧⑤ ex Durbanville & Stellenbosch. Lively fig, gooseberry & citrus, with good length & body. Follows **16** ⑧⑦, more subdued than **15 ★★★★★** ⑨②.

★★★★☆ White Restrained yet complex blend chenin, viognier & chardonnay in **16** ⑨⓪. Vivacious orchard fruit, spice & subtle biscuit from half oaked portion, all older wood. Taut & reined-in. Needs time.

★★★★ Méthode Cap Classique Vintage Reserve Brut Tangy lime zip of 50/50 chardonnay & pinot noir on long-gestated **11** ⑧⑥ sparkling. 60 months on lees impart rich biscuit notes yet ample lemon zest vivacity too. No **10**.

Cabernet Sauvignon ⓘ **★★★★** Ripe cassis fruit, dinner companion **15** ⑧④ in a lighter style than last, creamy mouthfeel & fresh berry finish. **Rosé ★★★☆** Candyfloss pink hue to dry 50/50 blend of cab & merlot on firm & succulent **17** ⑧⑤. Good concentration & depth. **Chenin Blanc** (NEW) **★★★★** Attractive vivid granadilla & peach on maiden **17** ⑧④, mid-palate breadth from 4 months on lees, ripe long tail. Coastal WO. **Méthode Cap Classique Rosé Brut** (NEW) **★★★★** Frothy berry brightness to pink **NV** ⑧④ dry sparkler. Equal chardonnay & pinot noir with 2% pinotage. Like non-vintage Brut, 15 months on lees in bottle. **Méthode Cap Classique Brut** (NEW) **★★★** Lively fizz on **NV** ⑧② dry sparkler. Green apple & gingerbread appeal, with leesy note from 15 months in bottle before disgorgement. Discontinued: **Chenin Blanc-Viognier**, **Muscat d'Alexandrie**.

Angels Tears range

La Chocolat (NEW) **★★★** Bold chocolate styling on **17** ⑦⑧ pinotage, with raspberry & smoky oak from staving in tank. Will have its fans. WO W Cape, as all these. **Merlot-Cabernet Sauvignon** ⊘ **★★★★** Goes up a notch in **17** ⑧③ with easy-drinking blend, oak staved for additional body. Bright-berried fruit appeal remains. **Rosé ★★★** Raspberry succulence of mainly pinotage, dab shiraz on **18** ⑦⑨ everyday dry pink. **Sauvignon Blanc ★★★** Dusty gravel edge to taut grapefruit tang on **18** ⑧⓪. Uncomplicated, bright & refreshing. **Moscato ★★★** Was 'Muscat d'Alexandrie-Chenin Blanc', **18** ⑧⓪ Natural Sweet still from those varieties, & retains aromatic grape sweetness & appeal. Fresh & fun, light 10.5% alcohol.

Discontinued: **Vignerons Reserve 4 Barrel Selection.** — FM

Location/map: Franschhoek ▪ Map grid reference: C2 ▪ WO: Franschhoek/Western Cape/Coastal/ Stellenbosch/Wellington ▪ Est 1694 ▪ 1stB 2004 ▪ Tasting & sales Mon-Sun 10–6 (winter) & 10-7 (summer) ▪ Fee R50-R60/4 wines, R120/food & wine pairing ▪ Group tastings under oak tree in summer and during winter in cathedral extension of art gallery (seat up to 80 pax) ▪ Cellar & gallery tours Mon-Fri 11 & 3 Sat/Sun by appt ▪ Wine blending sessions by appt ▪ Kiddies grape juice tastings ▪ Picnics ▪ The Restaurant at Grande Provence ▪ Tour groups ▪ Gift shop ▪ Conferences & weddings ▪ Art gallery ▪ Harvest festival ▪ The Owner's Cottage & La Provençale Villa in the Vineyard at Grande Provence ▪ On Franschhoek Wine Tram route, express wine tram tasting option for R50/4 wines ▪ Owner(s) Dutch & Belgium consortium ▪ Winemaker(s) Thys Smit (Jun 2015) ▪ 32ha/22ha (cab, merlot, chard, sauv) ▪ Grande Provence: 120t/10,000cs own label 60% red 40% white; Angels Tears: 300t/60,000cs own label 30% red 60% white 10% rosé ▪ PO Box 102 Franschhoek

7690 ▪ reservations@grandeprovence.co.za ▪ www.grandeprovence.co.za ▪ S 33° 53′ 57.6″ E 19° 06′ 10.5″ ▪ ⌂ bowhead.surfaced.mothership ▪ F +27 (0)21-876-8601 ▪ T +27 (0)21-876-8600

☐ **Grand Slam** *see* David Frost Wines
☐ **Grand Vin de Stellenbosch** *see* Grand Domaine

Grangehurst ⓠ ⌂

Ten years after his first harvest (in the converted squash court that initially served as the cellar) Jeremy Walker was joined by freshly matriculated Gladys Brown, who worked the 2002 harvest 'to get an idea of what winemaking is all about'. Fast forward 17 years and she's a fixture at this quality-focused Helderberg boutique venture, which still basket-presses its grapes in classic fashion. To recognise and reward Gladys' significant contribution, along with that of the other team members, a new wine has been added to the range. In typical Grangehurst fashion, it's a long-gestated project and the current vintage is '11. Nothing is hurried, and wines are released at their prime, something loyal fans admire.

★★★★☆ **Cabernet Sauvignon Reserve** ⓠ Everything a mature cab should be: smooth, velvety, beautifully evolved with gentle spice & ripe black fruits. **08** ⑨① textured, refined, bright & fresh, it's at its peak. Includes splash merlot. No **07**. 28 months in wood, rest 22–26 unless noted.

★★★★☆ **The Reward** 🆕 🍃 Profits go to cellar team, hence name. 100% cabernet is broad, refined, mature & smooth, brambly hedgerow generosity framed by older French oak, 18 months. **11** ⑨④ statuesque but sexy, drinks beautifully now. In magnum too, as all reds below except The Point.

★★★★☆ **350 Pinotage Reserve** ⓠ Picked 350 years to the day from first harvest at the Cape - 2 Feb 1659, **09** ⑧⑨ pure hedgerow fruit & spice verve with supportive oak from 35 months ageing. Pliable, textured & harmoniously long.

★★★★☆ **Pinotage** ⓠ Shy red fruits & raspberry succulence on a plush palate. **08** ⑨① elegant, with structured body & good length. Splashes cab & merlot in the mix, as is dab (13%) American oak.

★★★★ **Cabernet Sauvignon-Merlot** ⓠ Cab leads in **08** ⑧⑧ but merlot adds leafy tomato nuance to the reined-in, black fruit compote-packed palate. Svelte & glossy, with cocoa richness lurking. Like **07** ★★★★☆ ⑨①, delightfully youthful.

★★★★☆ **CWG Auction Reserve Blend** 🍃 Rich Xmas pudding & spice on **14** ⑨⓪ Bordeaux blend cab, petit verdot & merlot. Tense & a touch nervy, fruit is bright & vivid. Light tannin grip supported by third French & American oak (80/20) for 33 months.

★★★★ **Grangehurst** ⓠ Voluptuous mouthful of fruitcake & spice on mature **08** ⑧⑨ cab-led 3-way Bordeaux blend. Integrated & refined, with dry tannin squeeze from 32 months oaking.

★★★★ **Nikela** ⓠ Pliable, plush & rounded **08** ⑧⑨ from near-equal cab & pinotage, dabs shiraz, merlot & mourvèdre. Ripe, & lighter bodied than **07** ★★★★☆ ⑨② yet rewarding & smooth.

★★★★ **The Point** 🆕 ⊘ Confident **14** ⑧⑦ Cape Blend of cab, pinotage & shiraz, basket pressed. Silky smooth, effortless refinement of cassis, spice, plum & reined-in cedar from 18 months French oak.

Daylea Red ⓠ ★★★★ Rich & rounded spicy mouthful of Christmas cake on **07** ⑧④ shiraz blend. Silky, integrated & sexily mature. **Cape Rosé Blend** ★★★☆ Previewed **17** ⑧④ again blends cab, pinotage, shiraz & merlot with chenin for attractive, juicy, berry-toned dry easy-drinker. — FM

Location/WO: Stellenbosch ▪ Map: Helderberg ▪ Map grid reference: C1 ▪ Est/1stB 1992 ▪ Tasting & sales Mon-Fri 10–3 Sat/Sun/pub hols plse phone to enquire ▪ Tasting R50pp, refundable with purchase ▪ Closed Easter Fri-Mon, Dec 25/26 & Jan 1 ▪ Self-catering guest cottages ▪ Owner(s) Grangehurst Winery (Pty) Ltd ▪ Cellarmaster(s) Jeremy Walker (Jan 1992) ▪ Winemaker(s) Jeremy Walker (Jan 1992), with Gladys Brown (Jan 2002) ▪ ±13ha/6ha own (cab) + 8ha bought in grapes (merlot, p verdot, ptage, shiraz) ▪ 8ot/8,000cs own label 90% red 10% rosé + 2,000cs for clients ▪ Brands for clients: Woolworths ▪ PO Box 206 Stellenbosch 7599 ▪ winery@grangehurst.co.za ▪ www.grangehurst.co.za ▪ S 34° 01′ 02.9″ E 018° 49′ 50.5″ ▪ ⌂ centenary. pottery.smudge ▪ F +27 (0)86-710-6070 ▪ T +27 (0)21-855-3625

☐ **Granger Bay** *see* Sauvignon Wines
☐ **Grinder** *see* The Grape Grinder
☐ **Great Expectations** *see* Goedverwacht Wine Estate
☐ **Great Five** *see* Stellenview Premium Wines

☐ **Great South African Wine Company** *see* The Great South African Wine Company
☐ **Griffin** *see* Stettyn Family Vineyards
☐ **Groblershoop** *see* Orange River Cellars

Groenland   Ⓠ Ⓖ

Consistent quality, ungreedy prices and a warm cellardoor welcome are hallmarks of the Steenkamp family venture in Stellenbosch's Bottelary Hills. Last edition we anticipated a cellardoor-only tribute blend by winemaker Piet for his father, winery owner and co-vinifier Kosie. Simply named Steenkamp, the stellar wine celebrates the remarkable 45th vintage of this 'legend in own right'.

Premium range

★★★★ **Cabernet Sauvignon** Rich cassis & leather nuance on bold yet polished **16** ⑧⑦. Complex & full, with dense tannins for balance, finishes beautifully dry. New French oak, year, for this range.

★★★★ **Merlot** Red-fruit compote with mulled-wine spice & vanilla, **16** ⑧⑧'s vibrant fruit is tempered by oak, the palate weight & depth finely judged, long flavoursome finish.

★★★★ **Shiraz** Kaleidoscope of exotic spice, cured meat, hedgerow fruit & white pepper, **16** ⑧⑨ hearty & extrovert - a wine with personality & balance, appealing savoury farewell. Some American oak.

★★★★☆ **Steenkamp** (NEW) (🍇) Sophisticated new flagship from cab & merlot (66/33), handsomely packaged **14** ⑨⓪ blackcurrant, pencil shavings & fruitcake, the fruit in harmony with vanilla oak. Layered, elegant & complex, lingering finish.

★★★★ **Antoinette Marié** Third each merlot, cab & shiraz in fruit-forward **16** ⑧⑨. Abundant dark flavours, creamy chocolate, violets & hint of sweet coconut shaped by firm oak. **15** untasted.

Classic range

Shiraz ★★★ Similar to sibling but older oak only. **17** ⑧② more accessible, too, juicy & food friendly. Also in 1.5, 3 & 5L, as next. **Antoinette Marié** ⊘ ★★★★ Merlot based with shiraz & drop cab, **16** ⑧⑤ dark fruited, spicy & succulent, shows good balance & smooth tannin structure. **Sauvignon Blanc** Ⓠ ★★★ Fragrant herbs & greenpepper on light, fun-to-drink **17** ⑧① lemon zip on finish. Not tasted: **Cabernet Sauvignon**.

Landskap range

Shiraz-Merlot ⊘ ★★☆ Pleasing & fruity equal shiraz & merlot is easy & gluggable in **17** ⑦⑧. **Chenin Blanc** ★★★ Unoaked **18** ⑦⑨ is just-dry & offers bright orchard fruit & zingy citrus aftertaste. — WB

Location/map: Stellenbosch ▪ Map grid reference: B3 ▪ WO: Bottelary ▪ Est 1932 ▪ 1stB 1997 ▪ Tasting & sales Mon-Fri 10—4 Sat 10—1 ▪ Fee R30pp ▪ Closed Easter Fri/Sun & Dec 25 ▪ Cellar tours by appt ▪ Owner(s) Kosie Steenkamp ▪ Winemaker(s) Kosie Steenkamp (Feb 1975), with Piet Steenkamp (Jan 2001) ▪ Viticulturist(s) Piet Steenkamp (Jan 2001) ▪ 192ha/154ha (cab, merlot, ptage, shiraz, chard, chenin, sauv) ▪ 1,500t/±13,000cs own label 75% red 25% white ▪ BEE level 3, IPW ▪ PO Box 4 Kuils River 7579 ▪ steenkamp@groenland. co.za ▪ www.groenland.co.za ▪ S 33° 53′ 48.9″ E 018° 44′ 5.3″ ▪ 🖾 standouts.curtails.immaculately ▪ **T +27 (0)21-903-8203**

☐ **Groenlandberg** *see* Oak Valley Estate

Groot Constantia Estate   Ⓠ Ⓜ Ⓞ Ⓐ Ⓖ

History and modernity continue to combine every day at this iconic Constantia property, which just celebrated its 333rd birthday. A bottle of 1858 Pontac has returned home and is now displayed in the Cloete Cellar Museum (alongside a 195-year-old bottle of Grand Constance) where it was made, and can be seen by the almost half a million people who visit the estate each year. Using a combination of different downloadable apps, visitors enjoy tours of the Cape Dutch buildings and vineyards, often ending up in one of the tasting rooms or restaurants. Winemaker Boela Gerber ensures that he combines traditional practices with new tweaks ('you can't change a brand like Groot Constantia overnight!') aimed at improving ripeness at lower alcohol levels and increasing freshness in his exceptional range of cool-climate wines.

Gouverneurs Reserve range

★★★★☆ **Red** ⌖ Accomplished cab-led Bordeaux blend **15** ⑨③ shows ripe, elegant black-berried fruit lifted by fresh herbal notes, wrapped up with sturdy tannins & cedar hints from 73% new oak. Positive acidity adds delicious length to multi-layered finish.

★★★★☆ **White** ⌖ Plenty of interest on **16** ⑨② from semillon & 25% sauvignon. 50% new oak adds toffee & caramel notes to orange marmalade fruit with baked apple spice. Pleasing complexity & interest though tad less intense than stellar **15** ★★★★★ ⑨⑤.

Groot Constantia range

★★★★☆ **Cabernet Sauvignon** ⌖ Classic cool-climate cab **16** ⑨① balances restrained blackcurrant fruit with a delicious tweak of mint & herbs. Solid tannins & fresh acidity plus 33% new French oak add cedar & vanilla notes. All suggest it's a keeper.

★★★★☆ **Merlot** ⌖ Exciting & excellent **16** ⑨④ improves on previous with elegant layers of plummy/cherry fruit, coffee, leather & perfumed spice, with pleasing lick of vanilla on lengthy finish (61% new French oak). Delicious drinking now but plenty of ageing potential as well.

★★★★ **Pinotage** ⌖ WO Constantia's only pinotage **16** ⑧⑨ is a confident mouthful of jammy red fruit given definition by roasted coffee, nuts & leather overtones. Sturdy tannins need time to settle, worth the wait.

★★★★☆ **Shiraz** ⌖ Fine, peppery **16** ⑨③ gives layers of aromatic black fruit - plums, cherries - with lovely silky texture courtesy 40% wholebunch ferment. Hints of smoke, leather & juicy tannins carry through to superb ripe finish.

★★★★ **Constantia Rood** Cut-above everyday drinking **16** ⑧⑨ offers value & flavour with silky tannins wrapping up ripe, black-berried fruit. Mainly merlot with pinotage & others, aged in mostly older oak, also available (& strongly recommended) in magnums.

★★★★☆ **Chardonnay** ⌖ Oak (35% new) dominates nose of **17** ⑨② bringing vanilla, toast & popcorn notes before ripe yellow fruit asserts - baked stonefruit, pineapple & pear. Lingering finish suggests plenty more to come, so keep it if you can.

★★★★ **Sauvignon Blanc** ⌖ Back on form after quieter **16** ★★★★ ⑧⑦. **17** ⑨④ shimmers with fresh, crunchy green apple, grass & pepper, mouthwatering acidity & sappy touches of salinity from 4 months on lees. Beautifully integrated throughout, tiny amount of oak just adds breadth & interest at the finish.

★★★★ **Méthode Cap Classique Brut Rosé** Slightly less lees-ageing (15 months) on **15** ⑧⑨ leads to fruitier mouthful - strawberries & cranberries - edged by delightful salty/savoury notes, crisp dry bubbles. 90/10 pinot noir/chardonnay.

★★★★☆ **Grand Constance** ⌖ Exciting & enticing aromas of exotic spices, flowers, honey & perfume **15** ⑨④ explodes into memorable mouthful of honey-roasted pears, ripe peaches with a touch of tropical fruits. Some skin contact & 24 months in old small-oak adds texture & richness. Natural Sweet from red & white muscat de Frontignan, like **14** ★★★★★ ⑨⑤. 375 ml.

····························

Rosé 🆕 ⍉ ★★★★ Estate's pink changes from blanc de noir to bone-dry rosé in **18** ⑧④, component varieties make the complete 'Bordeaux blend': cab, merlot, semillon & sauvignon! Delightful floral notes mingle with strawberry & cherry, leading to lipsmacking finish.

····························

Cape Ruby ★★★★ Winter-warming **16** ⑧③ fortified from touriga gives lots of chocolate, Xmas cake & spice notes to raisined black fruit. Fiery alcohol lingers to satisfying finish.

Cape Brandy range

★★★★ **VSOP** ⍉ Vivid pear drop scents entice on 6 year old 100% potstill from sauvignon, pinotage. Smooth, with subtle caramel & vanilla oak creaminess on palate. Exquisite packaging. 375 ml.— CM, WB

Location/WO: Constantia ▪ Map: Cape Peninsula ▪ Map grid reference: B3 ▪ Est 1685 ▪ 1stB 1688 ▪ Tasting & sales daily 9–6 ▪ Fee R90 tasting & tour ▪ Closed Good Fri & Dec 25 ▪ Cellar tours 10-4 on the hour, every hour ▪ Simon's at Groot Constantia Restaurant; Jonkershuis Constantia Restaurant ▪ Facilities for children ▪ Tour groups ▪ Gifts ▪ Conferences ▪ Walks/hikes ▪ Conservation area ▪ Iziko Museum, manor house, historic buildings ▪ Owner(s) Groot Constantia Trust NPC RF ▪ Winemaker(s) Boela Gerber (Jan 2001), with Louise van der Westhuizen ▪ Vineyard manager Floricius Beukes ▪ Viticulturist(s) Andrew Teubes (2009) ▪ 170ha/±90ha (cab, merlot, ptage, pinot, shiraz, chard, muscat, sauv, sem) ▪ 650t/450,000cs ▪ WWF-SA Conservation Champion ▪ Private Bag X1 Constantia 7848 ▪ enquiries@grootconstantia.co.za ▪ www.grootconstantia. co.za ▪ S 34° 1′ 37.44″ E 018° 25′ 27.39″ ▪ anatomic.doctoral.marigolds ▪ F +27 (0)21-794-1999 ▪ **T +27 (0)21-794-5128**

☐ **Grootdrink** *see* Orange River Cellars
☐ **Groot Eiland** *see* Daschbosch

Groote Post Vineyards

With views over Table Bay in one direction and across lush acres of Spring flowers (at the right time of year) in the other, a monthly family market, game drives and bird-watching walks, the Pentz family's Darling Hills farm offers plenty of reasons to visit all year round. Winemaker Lukas Wentzel celebrates his 19th vintage at the farm with as much enthusiasm as ever. His newer blends - Sea Salter and Salt of the Earth - have been well received, so much so that the original plan to keep them solely for the wine club has been shelved.

Kapokberg range

★★★★ Pinot Noir ⓐ Fresh & fragrant **15** ⑧⑥, from elevated single block, classic pinot notes of red berries, tealeaves & herbal whiffs. Skilfully oaked (20% new) for long term, would benefit from keeping.

★★★★ Chardonnay ⓐ Vibrant, exciting **17** ★★★★☆ ⑨⓪ steps up on **16** ⑧⑧ with more new oak (now 40%) adding subtle creamy undertones to peaches-&-cream mouthful, salty backbone gives interest & length. Should improve over time.

★★★★☆ Sauvignon Blanc ⓐ Effortlessly elegant **17** ⑨④ starting to gain complexity, melding creamy orange & lemon fruit with saline hints, stonefruit & flowers into a delicious mouthful. As in **15** ⑨③, appetising acidity ensures still more to come - if you can bear to wait. No **16**.

Varietal range

★★★★ Shiraz ⓐ Friendly **16** ⑧⑨ softer than **15** ⑧⑨, with plushy, plummy notes topped off with whiffs of chocolate & sweet spice. Excellent partner for game meats. Good future too.

★★★★☆ Salt of the Earth ⓝⓔⓦ Accomplished blend of shiraz & cinsaut (60/40), **15** ⑨① mixes sweet black cherry/berry fruit with delightful perfume, leather & game. Good grip from tannins, helped by 60% new French oak, excellent concentration & balance. Very promising debut.

★★★★ Unwooded Chardonnay Lipsmacking lime marmalade vies with crunchy green apple on **18** ★★★★ ⑧⑤. Crisp, lively acidity, touch of warmth at finish, just a shade less thrilling than **17** ⑧⑥.

★★★★ Riesling Brilliantly balanced **18** ⑧⑦ treads delicate line between edgy acidity & drop softening sugar (8.7 g/l), both wonderful backdrop to blossoms, litchis & limes. Good potential, & great with food.

★★★★ Sauvignon Blanc Fruit-forward **18** ⑧⑨, slightly less stellar than **17** ★★★★☆ ⑨③, but bountiful grapefruit, lemon, lime, exotic spice notes add interest. 50% skin contact 6-12 hours, 2 months on lees.

★★★★ Semillon ⓐ Refreshing, nuanced **15** ⑧⑦'s fruit wraps around judicious oak structure, extends to the finish where it shows in lime & red apple complexity.

Merlot ★★★★ Restrained notes of black cherries, blackberries on **16** ⑧⑤ backed up by ripe tannins & lively acidity, pleasing savoury finish. **Pinot Noir Rosé Limited Release ★★★** Pretty, pale pink **18** ⑧⓪ packs in plenty of strawberries with hints of soft cheese. Drier this year & better for it. **Chenin Blanc ★★★** Easy-drinking **18** ⑧① offers soft yellow apple edged with gentle aromas of talcum powder & flowers. Pleasant drinking. WO W Cape. **Riesling Barrique ★★★** Unusual **17** ⑧② 35% aged in new 500L acacia wood adding soft texture & smoky toast to slight flavours of lime & lily. Not tasted: **Sea Salter.**

The Old Man's Blend range

The Old Man's Blend Red ⓥ ⓣ **★★★★** Eminently gluggable, always enjoyable merlot-led 4-way blend, **17** ⑧④ delivers juicy black fruit, pepper & spice in spades. The large bottle formats (1.5 & 3L) highly recommended. **The Old Man's Blend White** ⓣ **★★★★** Summer-fruit heaven in a glass, **18** ⑧④ gives crowd-pleasing flavours of pineapple, apple & citrus with a lipsmacking finish. Mainly sauvignon with chenin & semillon. WO Coastal for this pair.

Méthode Cap Classique range
Brut Rosé ★★★★ Pleasing improvement on latest **NV** ⑧③ sparkler, delicious red fruit now happily joined by tweak of tealeaf, aniseed & salt. Chardonnay & pinot noir (70/30%), 9 months on lees. — CM

Location: Darling ▪ Map: Durbanville, Philadelphia & Darling ▪ Map grid reference: A3 ▪ WO: Darling/ Coastal/Western Cape ▪ 1stB 1999 ▪ Tasting, sales & cellar tours Mon-Fri 9—4 Sat/Sun & pub hols 10—4 ▪ Fee R25 for groups of 10+ ▪ Closed Good Fri, Dec 25/26 & Jan 1 ▪ Hilda's Kitchen open for lunch Wed-Sun, booking essential ▪ Facilities for children ▪ Conferences ▪ Walks/hikes ▪ Game drives to be pre-booked; fee on request ▪ Conservation area & bird hide ▪ Groote Post country market last Sunday of the month Aug-Apr only ▪ Owner(s) Peter & Nicholas Pentz ▪ Winemaker(s) Lukas Wentzel (Nov 2000) ▪ Viticulturist(s) Jannie de Clerk (1999), advised by Johan Pienaar ▪ 3,000ha/100ha (cabs s/f, merlot, pinot, shiraz, chard, chenin, riesling, sauv, sem) ▪ 580t/64,000cs own label ▪ PO Box 103 Darling 7345 ▪ wine@grootepost.co.za ▪ www. grootepost.com ▪ S 33° 29' 0.5" E 018° 24' 35.0" ▪ ⌖ heron.blanketed.saddles ▪ **T +27 (0)22-492-2825**

Groot Parys Estate
Die Tweede Droom ('Second Dream'), the range name chosen by Dutch partners Mariëtte Ras and Eric Verhaak, is their way of expressing empathy with Huguenot Jean le Roux, who fled 17th-century France and received a dreamed-of lifeline in the form of Paarl farmland. On a part of his estate, Mariëtte and Eric farm sustainably and vinify naturally, as they've done since their winegrowing imaginings became real in 2002.

Die Tweede Droom range
★★★★ Chenin Blanc Vatgegis Zippy lightness to 17 ★★★ ⑧① in spite of (old) oak ferment, gentle stonefruit appeal with cream backing. Charming, if touch less substance, interest than **15** ⑧⑦. **16** untasted.
Chardonnay Vatgegis ★★★★ Bright citrus marmalade & creaminess from 10 months older French oak, **17** ⑧③ good structure & enduring flavour. **Chenin Blanc Spontane Gisting ★★★** Unwooded & naturally fermented. Sweet/sour tension on **17** ⑧②, ripe tropical notes & decent mid-palate weight. — WB, FM

Location/map/WO: Paarl ▪ Map grid reference: E5 ▪ Est 1699 ▪ 1stB 1709 ▪ Tasting & sales by appt ▪ Owner(s) Eric Verhaak & Mariëtte Ras ▪ Viticulturist(s) Donovan Boois ▪ 81ha/22ha (ptage, ruby cab, chard, chenin, cbard) ▪ 100t 90% white 10% rosé ▪ PO Box 82 Huguenot 7645 ▪ grootparys@wam.co.za ▪ www.grootparys. co.za ▪ S 33° 44' 48.0" E 018° 58' 41.6" ▪ ⌖ pressing.official.airbag ▪ **T +27 (0)76-567-8082**

Groot Phesantekraal   ⓠ ⑨¶
Fourth-generation owner André Brink and wife Ronelle's Durbanville wine venture is the realisation of a lifelong dream. It was registered as 'Groot Phesantekraal', name of the original estate, granted in 1698 and in family hands since 1897, and the range is being re-branded accordingly (only the Shiraz still 'Phizante Kraal'). Also re-named is the 'Pinotage' we liked last time, 'Berliet' being the 1927 car owned by André's late father. Continuing the 're-' theme, Etienne Louw of Altydgedacht has re-placed Thys Louw as winemaker.

Flagship range
★★★★ Anna De Koning Best-years pinnacle wine shows fine complexity, baked apple & crème brûlée on rich texture, creamy oak supports bold fruit, adds hints of spice to lifted finish. **17** ⑧⑨ from chenin, barrel-fermented, 10% new French, rung up from last **14 ★★★★** ⑧③.

Groot Phesantekraal range
★★★★ Cabernet Sauvignon ⓠ Blueberry fruit merges with cassis in seamless, supple tannin framework of fine **15** ⑧⑥. Super balance gears up on generous but oaky **14 ★★★★** ⑧④. Durbanville WO.
★★★★ Berliet ⓠ Renamed since tasted last time, **16** ⑧⑦ pinotage priciest of the reds but still good value. Just enough spiced plum fruit tucked into lithe tannins to ensure beautiful balance. Most promising.
★★★★ Sauvignon Blanc ⓥ Taut & lean **18** ⑧⑥ trumpets cool-climate greenpepper & greengage. Firm, with stern acid backbone but in harmony with bright fruit flavours. Long, some minerality showing.
★★★★ Méthode Cap Classique Blanc de Blancs ⓠ Satisfying **15** ⑧⑦ sparkling from chardonnay, on lees 17 months. Elegant, quite fruity in youth but great grip in the bone-dry finish. WO Durbanville.

Chenin Blanc ⓥ ⑨ **★★★★** The usual pocket-friendly summer delight, **18** ⑧⑤ oozes fresh tropical fruit salad flavours with a zingy citrus tail.

Phizante Kraal range

Shiraz ⓥ ★★★★ Wild, brambly aromas on **15** ⑧⑤, but conducive vintage shows in elegant & accessible structure, with balanced tannins & acidity, focused intensity. Third new oak. Durbanville WO. — WB

Location: Durbanville ▪ Map: Durbanville, Philadelphia & Darling ▪ Map grid reference: D7 ▪ WO: Cape Town/Durbanville ▪ 1stB 2005 ▪ Tasting & sales Tue-Fri 8-4 Sat 9-2.30 ▪ Fee R30 ▪ Restaurant Tue-Fri b'fast 8-11 lunch 12-3 Sat brunch 9-2.30 ▪ Closed Easter weekend, Dec 25 to early Jan ▪ Owner(s) André & Ronelle Brink ▪ Winemaker(s) Etienne Louw (Jan 2017, Altydgedacht) ▪ Viticulturist(s) André Brink ▪ 50ha (cab, ptage, shiraz, chenin, sauv) ▪ 5,100cs own label ▪ PO Box 8 Durbanville 7551 ▪ wines@phesantekraal.co.za ▪ www.grootphesantekraal.co.za ▪ S 33° 47' 46.73" E 018° 40' 12.96" ▪ ⌖ calmest.sneezed.obtains ▪ F +27 (0)21-975-3589 ▪ **T +27 (0)21-825-0060**

Group CDV

The initials stand for Cape Dutch Vignerons, a Netherlands-owned business supplying wines especially to European supermarkets, packaged locally or at their facilities in France. 'If we can't supply it... it is simply not there!' is the proud claim - bulk wines, buyers own brands, bag-in-box, etc, as well as their own portfolio, with labels such as Klein Centennial, Klein Kasteelberg, Nuwe Wynplaas and Vry Burger.

Location: Somerset West ▪ Est/1stB 2006 ▪ Closed to public ▪ Owner(s) Groupe LFE South Africa ▪ Cellarmaster(s) Nicky Versfeld (consultant) ▪ 1.2m cs own label 60% red 35% white 5% rosé ▪ Fairtrade ▪ PO Box 88 Somerset Mall 7137 ▪ rob@groupcdv.co.za ▪ www.groupcdv.co.za ▪ F +27 (0)21-851-3578 ▪ **T +27 (0)21-850-0160**

Grundheim Wines   ⓥ ♿

Lingering drought has prompted the Grundling family, stalwarts of Klein Karoo grape/winegrowing and distilling, to focus less on the former and more on the latter. With their distributor, Brand Republic, they've produced a pair of craft gins under the Black Mountain label, and a third, Naakte Naartjie, under the family brand. Other new spirits are expected to flow from the father and son's antique wood-fired copper kettle.

Fortified range

★★★★ **Late Bottled Vintage** ⓥ Commendable & complex 'port' from touriga & tinta. **09** ★★★★ ⑧④, first since **05** (only touriga) richly fruity & textured.

White Port ⓥ ★★★ Fortified chenin aged year in old brandy barrels. **10** ⑧① fynbos & almond notes, lovely sweet/savoury contrast in the tail. Not tasted: **Red Muscadel, White Muscadel, Rosyntjiewyn, Cape Ruby Port, Cape Vintage Port**.

Brandy range

Boegoe ⓥ ★★ Blended 9 year old potstill with natural buchu, giving a minty, herbal character, dusty palate. For medicinal purposes or with a mixer for a refreshing drink. 375 ml. **Gemmer** ⓥ ★★★★ Blended 9 year old potstill, natural fresh ginger for a delightful balanced drink with spicy kick. Enjoy on its own or with ginger ale for a cocktail. **Kuipers** ⓥ ★★★ 5 year old blended brandy (43% alcohol) from colombard & chenin. Nuts, fynbos & dried apricot flavours; sweet, fragrant & spicy finish. **Potstill 12 Year Old** ⓥ ★★★★ Ginger, spice & sherry-like notes; light, refined feeling, though the 40% alcohol does add more pale fire than might be expected from this level of maturation.

Grundheim range

Not tasted: **Stasiemeester Shiraz**. — CR, TJ

Location: Oudtshoorn ▪ Map: Klein Karoo & Garden Route ▪ Map grid reference: B4 ▪ WO: Western Cape ▪ Est/1stB 1995 ▪ Tasting & sales Mon-Fri 9-5 Sat 9-1 ▪ Fee R40pp ▪ Closed Easter Fri/Sun, Dec 25 & Jan 1 ▪ Craft gin distillery ▪ Owner(s) Danie Grundling ▪ Winemaker(s) Dys Grundling (1997) ▪ 25ha (muscadel r/w, ruby cab, tinta, touriga, cbard, hanepoot) ▪ 360t/10,000L own label ▪ PO Box 400 Oudtshoorn 6620 ▪ grundheim@absamail.co.za ▪ www.grundheim.co.za ▪ S 33° 37' 40.1" E 022° 3' 54.6" ▪ ⌖ circulating.copier.reabsorbed ▪ F +27 (0)86-616-6311 ▪ **T +27 (0)44-272-6927/+27 (0)71-657-4851**

Guardian Peak Wines   ⓥ ♙ ◎ ♿

Owned by Jean Engelbrecht, headquartered at Rust en Vrede nearby, Guardian Peak and its team are assured of a steady supply of fruit from long-term-contracted winegrowers beyond its prime Helderberg mountainside location. This frees them to trial cellar techniques, from wholebunch (for red) to clay pot (for white) fermentation in pursuit of quality with accessibility.

★★★★ **Cabernet Sauvignon** ⊘ Satisfying black fruit core on **17** ⑧⑥ shows improvement over **16** ★★★★ ⑧⑤, with refined tannins, appealing earthy notes. Still taut, should open in bottle.

★★★★☆ **Lapa Cabernet Sauvignon** ⓐ Bold, dense & imposing **16** ⑨② from Stellenbosch has nervous tension, plush tannins, precise blackcurrant fruit. Fine varietal definition, with earthy liquorice thread, showing great ageing potential. 18 months small French oak, 30% new.

★★★★ **Shiraz** ⊘ Better structure & focus in **17** ⑧⑥ than **16** ★★★★ ⑧④, showing herbal fynbos aromas & solid black cherry/plum fruit. Supple tannins, good depth & length.

★★★★ **Summit** Delicious, juicy syrah, mourvèdre, grenache **16** ⑧⑨ gushes red berry aromas, dense spicy compote gets a gentle tannin caress threaded with herbal scrub.

Merlot ★★★★ Savoury notes on riper, fuller **17** ⑧③, with cassis & plum fruit, same chalky tannins as last.
Sauvignon Blanc ★★★ Hints of pungent khaki bush & edgy acidity on rather austere **18** ⑦⑧, tending towards greenness. — GdB

Location/map: Stellenbosch ▪ Map grid reference: E8 ▪ WO: Western Cape/Stellenbosch ▪ Est 1997 ▪ 1stB 1998 ▪ Tasting & sales Mon-Sun 9–5 ▪ Closed Easter Fri/Sun & Dec 25 & Jan 1 ▪ Guardian Peak Grill ▪ Merchandise available ▪ Owner(s) Jean Engelbrecht ▪ Winemaker(s) Roelof Lotriet (Sep 2015), with Jorrie du Plessis (Jan 2018) ▪ ±400t/62,000cs own label 90% red 10% white ▪ IPW ▪ PO Box 473 Stellenbosch 7599 ▪ info@guardianpeak.com ▪ www.guardianpeak.com ▪ S 34° 0' 40.19" E 018° 50' 31.99" ▪ ⬛ converses.birdies.complications ▪ **T +27 (0)21-881-3899**

☐ **Guinea Fowl** see Saxenburg Wine Farm
☐ **Guru** see Hoopenburg Wines
☐ **Gustus** see Darling Cellars
☐ **Habata** see Le Grand Chasseur Estate
☐ **Hagelsberg** see Middelvlei Estate

Hamilton Russell Vineyards ⓠ ⓘ

Exciting times ahead for this renowned Hemel-en-Aarde Valley estate - and not all of them on these shores. With demand for his wines always exceeding supply, owner Anthony Hamilton Russell has decided to take his SA expertise to the Willamette Valley in Oregon, US, a region noted for premium pinot noir and chardonnay. He and winemaker Emul Ross will be making pinot from two celebrated vineyards, hoping to satisfy the growing demand for their brand stateside. Back home, the programme to isolate and cultivate their own yeast has come to fruition, and Sauvage yeast is now commercially available around the world. And the replanting programme continues apace, as they look forward to the first local Dijon pinot noir clone 943 coming online in a few years' time.

★★★★☆ **Pinot Noir** ⓐ Classically styled **17** ⑨③ eases onto the palate with poise & grace, revealing layers of flavours - cooked red berries, leather, truffles, tobacco - all bound together by restrained, supportive oak (37% new). Combo of wholebunch & destemmed fruit gives crunchy texture to lengthy finish.

★★★★☆ **Chardonnay** ⓐ Subtle & seamless **17** ⑨③ melds toasty, creamy oak (31% new) with melange of citrus & peach; 10% unwooded portion keeps freshness, aided by zesty acidity. Delightful development - oatmeal, popcorn & honey hints - but plenty more to come. Both wines in magnum too.— CM

Location: Hermanus ▪ Map: Walker Bay & Bot River ▪ Map grid reference: B4 ▪ WO: Hemel-en-Aarde Valley ▪ Est 1975 ▪ 1stB 1981 ▪ Tasting & sales Mon-Fri 9–5 Sat 10–2 ▪ Closed Easter Fri/Mon, Dec 25/26 & Jan 1 ▪ Tours by appt ▪ Fynbos reserve & 2 wetlands ▪ Owner(s) Anthony Hamilton Russell ▪ Winemaker(s) Emul Ross (2014) ▪ Viticulturist(s) Johan Montgomery (2005) ▪ 170ha/52ha (pinot, chard) ▪ 12,900cs own label 50% red 50% white ▪ WWF-SA Conservation Champion ▪ PO Box 158 Hermanus 7200 ▪ info@hamiltonrussellvineyards.com ▪ www.hamiltonrussellvineyards.com ▪ S 34° 23' 23.0" E 019° 14' 30.6" ▪ ⬛ uncork.weathermen.exception ▪ F +27 (0)28-312-1797 ▪ **T +27 (0)28-312-3595**

Hannay Wines

The Hannay winery in Elgin's picturesque Valley Green has 'settled into a smooth-running facility' as a custom crush centre – with a sparkling-wine client now added to the portfolio. Meanwhile, winemaking consultants Richard Kershaw and Dudley Wilson continue to craft the cool-climate wines of brand owner Malcolm Dicey, off vineyards tended by another acclaimed guru, Kevin Watt.

★★★★ Cabernet Franc Dark fruit & dry leaf on smart **16** ⑧⑨. Oak supportive (10% new), but lightish palate a touch tannic & powerful for the flavour intensity. 14.7% alcohol adds sweet note to the dry finish.

★★★★☆ Chardonnay Complex aromas on natural ferment **17** ⑨②- toasted biscuit, herbs, stonefruit, citrus. Expressive fruit on palate too, with fine acidity (no malolactic ferment) & light oak support (11% new, 10 months). Modestly lingering.

★★★★☆ Sauvignon Blanc ⊘ ⊛ Blackcurrant leaf the dominant note on distinctive **17** ⑨③, though tropical fruit has its say too. Refined, elegant structure, with succulent, unaggressive but serious acidity, also some weight & texture. Fine example of cooler-climate sauvignon.— TJ

Location/map/WO: Elgin ▪ Map grid reference: B2 ▪ Est/1stB 2011 ▪ Tasting, sales & cellar tours by appt ▪ Fee R100 for groups of 10+ ▪ BYO picnic ▪ Light/buffet lunches by appt only ▪ Owner(s) Malcolm J Dicey ▪ Winemaker(s) Richard Kershaw (2012, consultant) & Dudley Wilson (2016, consultant) ▪ Viticulturist(s) Kevin Watt (2012, consultant) ▪ 72ha/11.3ha under vine ▪ 220t majority custom crush ▪ 50% red 50% white ▪ IPW, SIZA, WIETA ▪ PO Box 36 Elgin 7680 ▪ winemaker@hannaywines.co.za, info@valleygreen.co.za ▪ www.hannay.co.za ▪ S 34° 12′ 12.07″ E 19° 02′ 35.10″ ▪ rebranded.bareness.goal ▪ F +27 (0)86-718-2203 ▪ **T +27 (0)21-848-9770/+27 (0)71-676-9588**

Hartenberg Estate

Family-owned Hartenberg is recognised for its quality wines across a spectrum of varieties and ranges. From the top tiers, paying homage to the people who shaped the Bottelary estate, through to the premium level. Though Carl Schultz, winemaker here for more than 25 years, has become a celebrated shiraz maestro (no fewer than 5 distinct varietal versions and 4 blends this edition), his true love, and only wine he collects, is riesling, plantings of which have doubled at Hartenberg. One of his two current CWG wines is a riesling, only the third (and first this decade) in the auction's history. Carl pays tribute to his long-serving, dedicated farm team, including viticulturist Wilhelm Joubert, who again won the VinPro Stellenbosch Vineyard Block of the Year competition, this time with a merlot parcel.

Ultra Premium range
★★★★☆ Gravel Hill Shiraz ⊛ Muscular flagship has most new oak (80%, previously 50%) of all the shirazes. Earthy, savoury & liquorice flavours from namesake soils. Quite closed in **14** ⑨①, fine-grained tannin structure enveloping dark fruit core. Ageworthy, but less gravitas than **13** ★★★★★ ⑨⑤.

Super Premium range
★★★★☆ The Stork ⊛ Deeply perfumed, with white pepper nuance on **15** ⑨④ shiraz from clay-rich soils. Less oak & longer skin contact than flagship imparts supple tannins & elegant restraint. Lovely fruit purity & similar refinement in this fine vintage to **14** ⑨③, but even more potential.

★★★★☆ The Mackenzie ⊛ Cab, merlot, cab franc, malbec, petit verdot blend (66/14/7/7/7), **15** ⑨① similar deep flavours & dark fruit to **14** ⑨②, framed by dry chalky tannins. More New World than classic - assertive & concentrated. Touch more new oak (70%), but as before, has pedigree to age a decade.

★★★★ The Megan Full-bodied, more opulent style in shiraz-led **15** ⑧⑦, with mourvèdre & grenache (10/2). Initially quite forthcoming, savoury, ripe & spicy, then restrained by fine dry tannins. Less new oak & ageing than previous, also a shade off **14** ⑧⑧.

★★★★☆ The Eleanor Flagship chardonnay from single Burgundy CY95 clone. **16** ⑨① focused citrus & herb flavours with toasted hazelnut from oak (50% new). Zesty & tightly knit, still elegant & sleek (courtesy 13 months on lees). Not as fine as **15** ⑨③, though more intense than Premium sibling.

CWG Auction Reserves
★★★★☆ Shiraz ⊛ Consummate blend of the two illustrious Gravel Hill & Stork vineyard parcels. **15** ★★★★★ ⑨⑤ refined, scented fruit & white pepper with a polished, lithe structure. Oak just 50% new, as in **14** ⑨③. All elements in harmony. A worthy investment, long, rewarding life ahead.

★★★★☆ **Riesling** (NEW) (🏅) Honeyed terpene nuance from botrytis & some pre-ferment skin contact in old oak. **16** (91) still tightly coiled, tensile acidity streamlines richer fruit & 13.7% alcohol. Revealing just a glimpse of charm that will unfold over 6-10 years.

Premium range

★★★★ **Cabernet Sauvignon** More structure & concentration in **15** ★★★★☆ (90) (despite bigger yield) than also-tasted **16** (87). Firm tannins tightly woven into dark fruit, augurs well for a long life. Winemaking differs in the younger vintage, from lower yields. More open-textured & approachable, will peak earlier.

★★★★ **Merlot** Richer & riper **15** ★★★★☆ (93), with more new oak & longer in barrel than also-reviewed **16** ★★★★ (85). Still an infant, fine tannins cosseting the fruit. Elegant restraint with definite potential to improve. Both include 30% whole berries, but younger vintage highly strung, with tart red fruit, needs time & a meal. **14** (89) was better balanced than latest vintage.

★★★★ **Shiraz** Two vintages tasted, similarly made, with 15-20% juice bled off & more new, but less time in oak than previous. **16** (86) more savoury & spicy than **15** (89); structured, but doesn't have the brightness, substance or longevity.

★★★★ **Chardonnay** Like more intense Eleanor, **17** (88) gets full oak treatment (& barrels rolled, not stirred) but less new wood & bottle maturation. Poached pears trimmed into form by tangy citrus. Clean piquancy with toasty nuance, pleasing food partner.

★★★★ **Riesling** Touch botrytis gives apple blossom & honeyed tone to **17** (87). Richer & more body than the norm, courtesy 6 months sur lie, pleasing freshness & balance. More approachable than CWG sibling. Improves on **16** ★★★★ (85). WO W Cape.

Doorkeeper Shiraz ★★★☆ From estate's younger vineyards, year old-oak aged. **16** (83) ripe, supple & amiable, for earlier drinking than the other shirazes. Less structure, though, than previous. **Cabernet Sauvignon-Shiraz** ★★★★ Cab's firmer structure dominates shiraz spicy ripeness in **16** (84). Tad less harmonious than more-exuberant & -balanced **15** ★★★★ (88). Time may resolve, mid-2018 still melding. WO Coastal. **Sauvignon Blanc** ★★★☆ Dried grass, gooseberry & some minerality on **17** (85). Different ripeness levels give piquantly fresh, food-styled wine, the brisk acidity tempered by riper-picked parcels. Raises bar on previous. Occasional release: **Occasional Chardonnay, Occasional Riesling, Riesling Noble Late Harvest**.

Alchemy range

Merlot-Cabernet Franc-Malbec ★★★ Merlot from estate leads (82%) **16** (81), showing cultivar's red piquant fruit & firm tannins, other partners add warm liquorice nuance. Different ratios & less amiable & balanced than last. WO Coastal for the reds. **Syrah-Cabernet Sauvignon** (✓) ★★★★ Most balanced & lowest alcohol of this range. Cab is 49% but dominates the dark berry & herbaceous flavours. **16** (84)'s supple structure makes for satisfying, approachable quaffer or meal mate though not as polished as **15** ★★★★ (86). **Syrah-Mourvèdre-Grenache** ★★★ Estate syrah for **16** (80) with outsourced fruit. Piquant, savoury blend with dry chalky tannins just offset by fruit. Least balanced of this range, needs a barbecue. **Chenin Blanc-Semillon-Sauvignon Blanc** ★★★ Light **17** (80) a tangy, crisp summer blend. Ripe Golden Delicious apples turn Granny Smith green on palate. Estate sauvignon & bought-in chenin, semillon. Tart citrus tone super with seafood. — MW

Location/map: Stellenbosch ▪ Map grid reference: C4 ▪ WO: Stellenbosch/Coastal/Western Cape ▪ Est/1stB 1978 ▪ Tasting & sales summer: Mon-Fri 9-5 Sat 9-4 Sun 10-4; winter: Wed-Fri 9-5 Sat 9-4 Sun 10-4 ▪ Closed Good Fri, Dec 25 & Jan 1 ▪ Tasting fee refunded with purchase ▪ Cellar tours by appt ▪ Picnics & lunches 12-3 Tue-Sun (summer); lazy lunches Wed-Sun (winter) ▪ Light snacks, charcuterie & cheese platters served throughout the day ▪ Facilities for children ▪ Walks/hikes ▪ Bird watching ▪ Bottelary Renosterveld Conservancy ▪ Owner(s) Hartenberg Holdings ▪ Cellarmaster(s) Carl Schultz (Nov 1993) ▪ Winemaker(s) Patrick Ngamane (Jan 2001), with Oscar Robyn (Nov 2003) ▪ Viticulturist(s) Wilhelm Joubert (May 2006) ▪ 187ha/85ha (cab, merlot, shiraz, chard, riesling, sauv) ▪ 55ot/60,000cs own label 80% red 20% white ▪ IPW ▪ PO Box 12756 Die Boord 7613 ▪ info@hartenbergestate.com ▪ www.hartenbergestate.com ▪ S 33° 53′ 52.5″ E 018° 47′ 30.4″ ▪ 📷 uptake.website.showdown ▪ F +27 (0)21-865-2153 ▪ **T +27 (0)21-865-2541**

☐ **Hartswater** see Orange River Cellars

Haskell Vineyards

This 25-ha Helderberg mountainside property with 14 ha under vine, owned since 2002 by American-born international real estate magnate Preston Haskell IV, grows a limited selection of classic varieties across many soils, aspects and elevations. Even after reducing irrigation to strengthen the vines, the drought of the past three years has had an impact. Of the three single-site Syrahs, Aeon was worst hit and hasn't been made for the last two years; Hades and Pillars have produced less fruit. The team, now led by Rudolph Steenkamp (winemaker since inception Rianie Strydom focusing on the Strydom Vintners family venture), hope ongoing experiments with organic farming will help yield more positive results. Charles Joubert joins as head chef, as major renovations are completed to the Longtable restaurant, a glassed patio providing guests views across the vineyards.

Haskell range

★★★★☆ **Aeon Syrah** A masterclass in shiraz, Haskell provides 3 from different sites to showcase differences. Expressive red berries in **14** (92), svelte & streamlined till the end, when the firm dry finish reminds you the wine is built to last.

★★★★ **Hades Syrah** From older oak, changed to 30% new in **15** (88), adding flavours & structure. Hedgerow fruit, whiff of violets, campfire smoke; fresh, smooth textured, finishing firmly dry, savoury.

★★★★☆ **Pillars Syrah** Range flagship, **14** (92) similar oaking to Aeon but open fermenters, long skin contact, natural yeast. Most textbook of the 3 shirazes, wild dark berries, scrub, cloves & pepper. Sleek & compact, enough fine-grained tannins for ageing.

★★★★☆ **Haskell IV** Well-considered cab-led blend with 3 other Bordeaux varieties. **13** (92) shows some evolution in its ripe, savoury fruit, if slightly less concentration than usual to balance prominent acid, firm grape tannins. Monitoring advisable. Oaking, 70% new, remains polished accessory.

★★★★☆ **Haskell II** Syrah & cab an underrated combination in SA, 60/40 in **14** (90) illustrates its merit both in accessibility & ageworthiness. Syrah's suave dark-fruited richness leads, companion cab providing necessary tannin restraint. Partners in pleasure now & for future.

★★★★★ **Anvil Chardonnay** From one of Stellenbosch's oldest chardonnay vineyards (1988), giving wines of great power yet no heaviness. **17** (95) expansive nutty lime complexity enlivened & carried with memorable length by the urgent acidity. Masterly balance, as for **16** ★★★★★ (93), allows for rewarding ageing.

Dombeya range

★★★★ **Fenix Cabernet Sauvignon** Strength of vintage evident in **15** (89); rich blackberry, cedar-spiced layers, firm yet unforbidding build. Freshness & juicy, ripe tannins enhance current accessibility, promote future promise. 18 months French oak, 20% new.

★★★★ **Merlot** In sprightly, upbeat mode. **16** (88) forward, bright red berries & chocolate breeze across palate with freshness & succulent grip. Good now; pity to over-age, lose fruit.

★★★★ **Boulder Road Shiraz** Silky & fresh, **15** (89)'s comfortable grip, pure peppery & dark berry flavours provide ready satisfaction. Ripe yet unheavy & dry make this a versatile food partner.

★★★★ **Chardonnay** Clean limy zest fused with roast hazelnut savouriness offer plenty of interest in **17** (89). Accessibility isn't at expense of structure allowing few years' ageing. **16** untasted. WO W Cape, as next.

Sauvignon Blanc ★★★★ Previewed **18** (84) offers plenty juicy vibrancy in its herb-edged tropical flavours & zestily clean finish. — AL

Location/map: Stellenbosch ▪ Map grid reference: F8 ▪ WO: Stellenbosch/Western Cape ▪ Est 2002 ▪ 1stB 2008 ▪ Tasting & sales Tue-Fri 9–5 Sat/Sun & pub hols 10-5 ▪ Tasting fee applies ▪ Closed Mon, Easter Fri-Mon, Dec 25 & Jan 1 ▪ Cellar tours on special request only ▪ Facilities for children ▪ Long Table Restaurant Tue-Sun 11.30-6 ▪ Picnics (Oct-Mar), booking essential ▪ Self-catering accommodation in The Residence and Cottage ▪ Owner(s) Preston Haskell ▪ Winemaker(s)/viticulturist(s) Rudolph Steenkamp (Oct 2018) ▪ 25ha/14ha (cabs s/f, merlot, shiraz, chard) ▪ ±80t/3,600cs own label 80% red 20% white ▪ PO Box 12766 Die Boord 7613 ▪ info@haskellvineyards.com ▪ www.haskellvineyards.com ▪ S 34° 0′ 13.9″ E 018° 51′ 38.4″ ▪ lampshades.toughening.wheat ▪ F +27 (0)21-881-3986 ▪ **T +27 (0)21-881-3895**

Haute Cabrière

From their Franschhoek base, boundlessly passionate and energetic Achim and Hildegard von Arnim in the 1980s helped pioneer terroir-based varietal specialisation - chardonnay and pinot noir specifically - as well as bottle-fermented sparkling wine in SA. Their premium bubblies, varietal and blended still wines and Champagne-inspired fortified, now crafted by son Takuan, are expertly matched with dishes in mountain-recessed Haute Cabrière Restaurant that, again, led the way in wine-and-food pairing.

Haute Cabrière range

★★★★ Pinot Noir Reserve ⓥ Convincingly fragrant **15** ⑧⑥ offers sweetly ripe red berry fruit with rustic, earthy core; silky texture, persistent finish. WO Franschhoek.

★★★★ Chardonnay-Pinot Noir Trend-setting chard/pinot dry rosé. Pre-bottling, **18** ⑧⑥ fat & generous peach & pear fruit, gently cosseting acid & gratifying finish.

Unwooded Pinot Noir ★★ Light Ribena fruit & prominent tannins on previewed **18** ⑦⑤, misses depth & length of previous. Not tasted: **Chardonnay Reserve**.

Pierre Jourdan range

★★★★ Belle Rose ⓥ Switch to 100% pinot noir for latest **NV** ⑧⑦ MCC rosé dry sparkling, showing pretty salmon hue, subtle berry fruit, creamy lees texture, vibrant bubble. Improves on previous chard/pinot release. 18 months on lees, like Brut.

★★★★☆ Blanc de Blancs Svelte **NV** ⑨⓪ MCC brut bubbles from chardonnay, 40% wooded; rich, leesy body from 7 years on lees. Buttery toasted shortbread with yeasty highlights, threads of citrus marmalade & zest, fine, steady bead, crisply tart finish.

★★★★ Brut ⓥ Well-judged & -rounded chardonnay (80%) & pinot noir **NV** ⑧⑥ MCC bubbly is consistently pleasant, with silky mousse, delicate shortbread & tangy green apple fruit.

★★★★ Ratafia Chardonnay juice fortified with cask-aged brandy, perennially popular **NV** ⑧⑥ aperitif is rich & warming. Lipsmacking nutty citrus fruit with mellow spirit (18.5%).

Tranquille ★★★★ Reliable, likeable dry rosé from pinot noir & chardonnay. **NV** ⑧⑤ packed with berry fruit, finishing with a salty-mineral twist. — GdB

Location/map: Franschhoek ▪ Map grid reference: C1 ▪ WO: Western Cape/Franschhoek ▪ Est 1982 ▪ 1stB 1984 ▪ Tasting & sales: (Nov-Apr) Mon-Sat/pub hols 10-6 Sun 11-5; (May-Oct) Mon-Sat/pub hols 10-5 Sun 11-4 ▪ Cellar tours Mon-Sat at 11; private tasting/tour to be pre-booked ▪ Haute Cabrière Restaurant ▪ Owner(s) Clos Cabrière (Pty) Ltd ▪ Cellarmaster(s) Takuan von Arnim (2005), with Tim Hoek (Dec 2014) ▪ Viticulturist(s) Tim Hoek (Dec 2014) ▪ 30ha (pinot, chard) ▪ 40% red 60% white ▪ PO Box 245 Franschhoek 7690 ▪ info@ cabriere.co.za ▪ www.cabriere.co.za, www.pierrejourdan.co.za ▪ S 33° 54′ 51.8″ E 019° 8′ 8.2″ ▪ 📖 contingent. chairlifts.bushy ▪ **T +27 (0)21-876-8500**

Haut Espoir ⓥ ◎ ⓑ

Sustainability underpins every activity at the Armstrong family farm, set in the mountainous beauty of the Franschhoek Conservancy. They've added a new wetland trail to their popular fynbos walks, while assistant winemaker Bradley Ewerts spent time in Burgundy, brushing up on his biodynamics to further improve farming practices back home.

★★★★ Cabernet Sauvignon 5 years in old barrels gives **10** ⑧⑥ soft tannins to wrap round dense, dark cooked fruit - some blackberries & currants - & forthright alcohol of 15%. Not classic, but very appealing.

★★★★ Shiraz Plenty of dried fruit, leather, earthy notes & touch portiness, **12** ⑧⑥ carries off hefty 15.4% alcohol with style. Lovely tannin integration & really delicious red fruit/vanilla combo at finish. Steps up on **11 ★★★★☆** ⑧⑤ but, like Cab, is ready, needs broaching in next year/2.

★★★★ Gentle Giant ⓥ Mainly merlot with petit verdot & cab, **14** ⑧⑨ delivers complex mix of ripe blackcurrant, dried herbs, liquorice & toffee. 2 years old oak give supple tannins & coffee hints before ripe red-fruit finish. No **13**.

★★★★ Chardonnay ⓑ Better-judged than **16 ★★★★☆** ⑧⑤, **17** ⑧⑥ displays layers of yellow stonefruit mingled with spice & vanilla oak (none new). Lively acidic backbone allows development of burnt caramel & toffee notes - keep few years if you can.

★★★★ **Semillon** Rich, developed **17** ★★★★ (85) shows plenty (old) oak - butterscotch & toffee - creamy edge to apple & pear from full malo. Lacks fruit of **16** (87) but enjoyable food wine nonetheless.

Shiraz Rosé ★★★ Rich & quite serious, gaining weight from barrel ageing & warm alcohol, balancing acid brings it all together. Enjoy **17** (81) with charcuterie or terrines. **Cloudfall** (🍷) ★★★★ 5-way blend dominated by sauvignon & semillon. **16** (84) mere brush of oak lets luscious stonefruit prevail, with balancing citrus edge, greengage freshness & creamy mouthfeel. **White Port** (🍷) ★★★ Amber-gold **NV** (81) solera-style 'port' from semillon, trailing honeysuckle & caramel as it glides over noticeably sweet, soft palate. In abeyance: **Cabernet Franc**. — CM

Location/map/WO: Franschhoek ▪ Map grid reference: D1 ▪ Est 1999 ▪ 1stB 2004 ▪ Tasting & sales Mon-Fri 11-5 Sat/Sun by appt ▪ Closed all pub hols ▪ Cellar tours by appt ▪ Fynbos walks by appt ▪ Wetland trail ▪ Conservation area ▪ Craft beer & gin ▪ Owner(s) Armstrong family ▪ Winemaker(s) Marozanne Bieldt, with Bradley Ewerts (Jan 2018) ▪ Viticulturist(s) Rob Armstrong ▪ ±23ha/12ha (cab, merlot, p verdot, shiraz) ▪ 70t/10,000cs own label 70% red 30% white ▪ PO Box 681 Franschhoek 7690 ▪ wine@hautespoir.com ▪ www.hautespoir.com ▪ S 33° 56'23.6" E 019° 6'20.9" ▪ [✉] feed.honed.strolling ▪ F +27 (0)21-876-4038 ▪ **T +27 (0)21-876-4000**

Havana Hills

Exciting signs of revival and expansion at this maritime winery in Philadelphia ward just north of Cape Town. Owner Xinxing Pang's recent investments have breathed new life into the venture, clearly evident in the range of quality, good-value wines reviewed this year. Winemaker Piet Kleinhans and colleagues Joseph Gertse and Rudi Benn — with near 5 decades' combined service here — now have the wherewithal to realise the potential of the property established by entrepreneur Kobus du Plessis and winemaker Nico Vermeulen late last century. Most of the wines are exported to China, but local and European markets are also targeted.

Kobus range

★★★★★ **Red** (🍎) Youthful **15** (91) Bordeaux blend cab, merlot & cab franc (49/42/9) confidently raises bar on last-tasted **12** ★★★★ (84). More elegant than powerful, clean lines & fresh dark fruit interwoven with fine, chalky tannins. Ageworthy, deserves cellar time. WO W Cape.

★★★★ **Chardonnay** Flint, minerality & lime on **17** (88), wild fermented in mostly older oak, 8 months on lees. Clean & sleek, with racy, cool elegance. Stylish return after **14** ★★★★ (84). No **15**, **16** untasted.

Havana Hills range

★★★★ **Cabernet Sauvignon** (✓) Flavourful savoury dark plum still encased in firm dry fruit/oak tannins (18 months, 30% new), **15** (86) quite restrained mid-2018, best cellared few years. Last **12** (87) was suppler on release.

★★★★ **Shiraz** (✓) Good extract & 100% new oak create stable foundation for rich red fruit & pepper. **15** (89) already tempting, deserves & will reward ageing. Improves on last **11** ★★★★ (84).

. . . .

Sangiovese (✓) (🍷) ★★★★ A bright step up, **14** (83) laden with fresh cherry & sweet tobacco appeal. Deftly hides few grams sugar for balanced, light & juicy feel. Equally pleasing solo or with food.

. . . .

Merlot (✓) ★★★★ Generous & warm-hearted **15** (85), smoky black cherry intensity, touch of sugar, supple tannins & a freshness that tempers. **Pinot Noir** (✓) ★★★★ Returns to guide after extended break with cooler-vintage **15** (85). Initially savoury & mushroomy, with piquant nuance, reveals more fragrant charm & balance with decanting. **Chardonnay-Pinot Noir** (🍷) ★★★ Just 15% pinot noir on pale salmon-hued **14** (81) rosé. Forward aromas hinting at ripe strawberry. Flavourful, lightly fresh & neatly balanced. WO Coastal. **Sauvignon Blanc Sparkling** (NEW) ★★★ Fruity carbonated summer fizz, **17** (77) technically dry but plenty of stonefruit sweetness, so best served well chilled. In abeyance: **Cabernet Sauvignon-Barbera**.

Lime Road range

Cabernet Sauvignon-Merlot-Cabernet Franc (✓) (🍷) ★★★★ Bordeaux blend - effectively 'mini Kobus' - majorly over-delivers: fruit driven & friendly, spiced dark fruit & juicy supple tannin. **14** (85) delicious & huge bargain. **Sauvignon Blanc** (✓) (🍷) ★★★ Lively fig & herb flavours, savoury acidity, some lees creaminess, mild 12.5% alcohol - **17** (82) ticks those summer sipping & light food partnering boxes.

. . . .

Shiraz-Mourvèdre-Viognier ⓥ ★★★ Rich & full-flavoured **13** ⑧⓪, gently structured, well & unobtrusively oaked. Savoury element mingles nicely with the sweet dark fruit. WO W Cape. Not tasted: **Shiraz**, **Cabernet Sauvignon Rosé**. — MW

Location: Philadelphia ▪ WO: Philadelphia/Western Cape/Coastal ▪ Est 1999 ▪ 1stB 2000 ▪ Closed to public ▪ Owner(s) Xinxing Pang ▪ Winemaker(s) Piet Kleinhans (Sep 2008), Joseph Gertse (Jan 2000) & Mike Dobrovic (consultant) ▪ Viticulturist(s) Rudi Benn (Jan 2001) ▪ 260ha/60ha (barbera, cabs s/f, merlot, mourv, sangio, shiraz, sauv) ▪ 70,000cs own label 70% red 30% white ▪ IPW ▪ PO Box 451 Melkbosstrand 7437 ▪ sales@havanahills.co.za ▪ www.havanahills.co.za ▪ F +27 (0)21-972-1105 ▪ **T +27 (0)21-972-1110**

☐ **Hawk's Head** *see* Southern Sky Wines

Hawksmoor at Matjieskuil ⓥ ⑴ ⌂ ⌾

Ironically, Hawksmoor's old vines fared well in 2018's drought, returning heavier tonnage than usual! Word of the relaxed tastings under the oaks at the historic, Rhône- and chenin-focused southern Paarl boutique property is out and guest numbers are up. The annual Hawksmoor lot at the Cape Wine Auction has raised R1.4 million for charity (Pebbles Project being their favourite) over the past three years.

Signature range

★★★★ **Algernon Stitch** ⊘ Mourvèdre & shiraz share equal billing in **14** ⑧⑥, spicy black fruit is succulent yet the whole is leaner than **12** ⑧⑧, with dry tannin from 2 years in old oak, further 2 in bottle. No **13**.

★★★★ **Saint Alfege's** ⊘ Gentle, juicy mouthful of plum & smoke on **14** ⑧⑥ shiraz & mourvèdre, which improves on **12** ★★★★ ⑧④. Supple & restrained. Oak, 2 years older French, seamless & integrated. No **13**.

Cabernet Franc ★★★ Earth-, coffee- & cocoa-tinged blackcurrant fruit on chunky **15** ⑧② Bold & powerful, it cries out for food. **Mourvèdre** ★★★★ Fruit carries the day on unoaked **15** ⑧④ Spice, herbs, black & blue berries with a graphite nuance, balanced & deep. Not tasted: **Edward Goodge**.

Limited Releases

Shiraz ⓥ ★★★ Hint of scrub, hedgerow fruit in **14** ⑦⑧, less plush than previous, lithe body, good freshness. **Triginta** ⓥ ★★★★ Triginta is Latin for 30, which is the months **14** ⑧④ shiraz spent in older barrels. Shows bright red fruit, the tannins savoury, harmonious. Drinking well, can age further. **Magdalen** ★★★★ Light berry notes of **17** ⑧③ rosé belie the mid-palate presence of gentle grip. Dry, succulent, with hint of flint. Not tasted: **Cape Blend**, **French Blend With A Cape Twist**.

Classic range

Pinotage ⓥ ★★★ Unoaked **14** ⑦⑧, plummy, with variety's trademark juicy smoothness. **Pinotage Lightly Oaked** ★★★ Subtle old oak frames sour cherry & brambly black fruit compote on succulent **14** ⑧⓪. **Serliana** ⊘ ★★★★ Vivid apricot & nectarine on zesty, fresh **17** ⑧③ chenin. Light & zippy, with easy charm. From 35 year old bushvines, unoaked. — FM

Location/map/WO: Paarl ▪ Map grid reference: A7 ▪ Est 1692 ▪ 1stB 2005 ▪ Tasting by appt 10-4 daily ▪ Fee dependent on number of people/wines tasted ▪ Sales by appt daily ▪ Specialise in group tastings (8-20 pax), with option of lunch in the Cape Dutch manor house - prior arrangement essential ▪ Closed Easter Fri-Sun, Dec 25/31 & Jan 1 ▪ Luxury guest house ▪ Wedding & function venue ▪ Owner(s) Brameld Haigh ▪ Winemaker(s) various ▪ Viticulturist(s) Paul Wallace (2004) ▪ Farm manager Jan Lategan ▪ ±23ha (cab f, mourv, ptage, shiraz, chenin) ▪ ±130t/1,000cs own label 65% red 25% white 10% rosé ▪ PO Box 9 Elsenburg 7607 ▪ wines@hawksmoor.co.za ▪ www.hawksmoor.co.za ▪ S 33° 48' 47.4" E 018° 46' 14.1" ▪ ▱ beckoning. tectonic.retinal ▪ F +27 (0)86-605-9008 ▪ **T +27 (0)21-884-4587**

Hazendal Wine Estate ⓥ ⑴ ⌾ ⑧ ⑤

Historic Hazendal, founded in 1699 and owned since 1994 by Mark Voloshin, offers guests a dynamic destination and experience, influenced by Russian traditions, which are expressed in, among others, the vodka handcrafted from premium grapes, Russian tea experience and the owner's private Russian art collection. Attractions at the flourishing family-run enterprise in Stellenbosch include an upgraded fine-dining restaurant, deli, smart conference facilities, art gallery, MTB park and interactive edutainment centre for children.

Location/map: Stellenbosch ▪ Map grid reference: B3 ▪ Est 1699 ▪ 1stB 1996 ▪ Wine tasting Tue-Sun 9-5 ▪ Sales online ▪ Cellar tours to be pre-booked ▪ Restaurant ▪ Babushka Deli Mon-Sun 8-5 ▪ Tapas Tue-Sat 4-7 ▪ Picnics ▪ Facilities for children ▪ Conferences, weddings & functions: functions@hazendal.co.za ▪ Russian tea ceremonies ▪ Art gallery ▪ Bike park & MTB trail ▪ Craft beer available from deli ▪ Craft vodka distillery ▪ Owner(s) Mark Voloshin ▪ Cellarmaster(s)/winemaker(s) Clarise Sciocatti-Langeveldt (Jul 2016) ▪ Viticulturist(s) Clarise Sciocatti-Langeveldt (Jun 2016) ▪ 145ha/12ha (cab, carignan, carménère, ptage, pinot, shiraz, albarinho, chard, chenin, marsanne, rouss, sauv, sem) ▪ 100t/26,000cs own label 50% red 50% white ▪ Bottelary Rd Stellenbosch 7600 ▪ reception@hazendal.co.za ▪ www.hazendal.co.za ▪ S 33° 54'2.7" E 018° 43'9.1" ▪ 🗺 coyote.shortness.drifts ▪ **T +27 (0)21-903-5034**

☐ **HB Vineyards** *see* Hout Bay Vineyards

☐ **Headbutt** *see* Rooiberg Winery

☐ **Heaven on Earth** *see* Stellar Winery

☐ **Heeren van Oranje Nassau** *see* De Villiers Wines

☐ **Hendrik Lodewyk** *see* Du Preez Estate

☐ **Hercules Paragon** *see* Simonsvlei International

☐ **Heritage Heroes** *see* Nederburg Wines

Hermanuspietersfontein Wynkelder   Ⓨ Ⓜ ⌂ ⊚ ♿

There's a whole lotta punning going on in the branding at proudly Afrikaans winery Hermanuspietersfontein, aka HPF, and if you don't speak the lingo, the references to families and their inevitable black sheep probably won't resonate. But that's just the sauce. The wines are the meat, and they're expertly prepared by winemaker/GM Wilhelm Pienaar mostly from HPF-owned, maritime-influenced Sunday's Glen vines nearby, and served with plenty of panache - and freshly made tapas, if you're visiting the now more comfortably appointed Hermanus tasting venue at The Village, a lifestyle hub at Hemel-en-Aarde Valley's entrance.

Flagship Wines

★★★★☆ **Die Arnoldus** Ⓥ Pinnacle of an imposing range impresses with subtlety & balance rather than weight. **13** ⑨② complex, finely detailed fruit interwoven with sweet spice & floral notes. 5-way Bordeaux blend (60% cab) spent 26 months in 100% new oak. Also in magnum.

★★★★☆ **Die Martha** Shiraz-led 4-way Rhône blend, **14** ⑨② has both power & elegance, richly ripe plum pudding fruit, delightful herb & spice threads, aromatic tobacco on finish. Plush & silky, polished by 2 years in French oak foudre.

Classic Wines

★★★★☆ **Swartskaap** ⓐ Ripe, opulent fruit of fine **15** ⑨② vintage almost obscures cab franc's minerality & freshness, producing succulent blackcurrant essence on silky tannins. Rich & generous, promising even better things with cellaring.

★★★★ **Kleinboet** ⓐ Classic 5-way Bordeaux red, **15** ⑧⑨ has form & focus, ripe black fruit, herbal & steely mineral notes, well-rounded body. Fresh & youthful, with ageing potential.

★★★★ **Skoonma** Ⓥ Very appealing mostly shiraz blend from Somerset West, **15** ⑧⑧ brightly fruit-driven with delicious sweet spices, satisfyingly full & long. **14** ★★★★ ⑧④ from Walker Bay, as next.

★★★★ **Bloos** Subtle & poised dry rosé from the 5 Bordeaux red varieties, lightly oaked in **18** ⑧⑥, displaying appealingly ripe berry fruit on rich, leesy texture.

★★★★★ **Kat Met Die Houtbeen** ⓐ Barrel-fermented sauvignon, with more semillon (25%) in **16** ★★★★☆ ⑨③ than sublime **15** ⑨⑤. Dense, aromatic & finely detailed, more lithe than previous. Herbs & spices layered with baked apple & green fig fruit. Should improve over at least 2-3 years.

★★★★ **Kaalvoet Meisie** The 'unshod' (tank-fermented) sauvignon, splashes semillon & nouvelle in **17** ⑧⑥. Strident nettle & khaki bush aromas, bracing gooseberry fruit on lees creaminess, crisp acidity.

★★★★☆ **Witbroodjie** ⓐ Barrel-fermented **17** ⑨② semillon has a lot of style. Heady dusty & nettle aromas woven into lean, mineral palate, focused varietal wool/lanolin core. Seriously crafted to last but approachable now.

★★★★ **Stertswaai** Semillon with chardonnay & sauvignon, barrel- & foudre-fermented **16** ⑧⑧ maintains impressive form. Ripe fig & subtle oak on rich, broad palate.

Posmeester ★★★★ Pippy, coffee-toned merlot-shiraz blend, **17** ⑧③ fresh & juicy with sweetly ripe fruit, caramel toffee & mouthcoating tannin. — GdB

Location: Hermanus • Map: Walker Bay & Bot River • Map grid reference: A3 • WO: Sunday's Glen/Walker Bay/Western Cape • Est 2005 • 1stB 2006 • Tasting & sales Mon-Fri 9-5 Sat 9-4 Sun (15 Dec-15 Jan) 10.30-3 • Closed Easter Fri/Sun, Dec 25/26 & Jan 1 • Cellar tours on request • Food & wine market Sat 9-1 • Self-catering cottages • Owner(s) The Pretorius Family Trust, Gerrie Heyneke • Winemaker(s) / GM Wilhelm Pienaar (Dec 2015) • Viticulturist(s) Lochner Bester (Nov 2012) • 320ha/±65ha (cabs s/f, grenache, malbec, merlot, mourv, p verdot, shiraz, nouvelle, sauv, sem, viog) • 350t/25,000cs own label 50% red 40% white 10% rosé • WWF-SA Conservation Champion • Hemel-en-Aarde Village Suite 47 Private Bag X15 Hermanus 7200 • kelder@hpf1855.co.za • www.hpf1855.co.za • S 34° 24′ 38.7″ E 019° 11′ 51.7″ • 🖳 mutterings.alongside. huffs • F +27 (0)28-316-1293 • **T +27 (0)28-316-1875**

Hermit on the Hill Wines   ⓠ

Paradigm-shifting wines are the norm at this boutique family venture, and now owners Pieter and Lohra de Waal are set to explore what this means outside of SA. They've bought half a hectare, 1,200 lazki rizling and gelber muskateller vines, and a small house and cellar in Globoka, Slovenia, in the hills near the border with Croatia. It's very much a side project, and Pieter is determined his southern hemisphere wines will be his priority. In addition to Hermit on the Hill, he has a stake in Mount Abora Vineyards.

★★★★ **Stellenbosch Syrah** ⓠ **15** ★★★★ ⑧④ opens in glass to sweet black cherry fruit, meaty notes, medium body & freshening acidity. Last-tasted **13** ⑧⑧ also needed time to unfold. 18 months in older oak.

★★★★ **Skermunkel Semillon** ⓠ Aptly named 'Rascal' in **16** ⑧⑦ flouts convention with oxidative, sherry-like bouquet, bruised apple & barley sugar palate. Rich, smooth, saline, intriguing.

★★★★ **The Starry Knight** New disgorgement of **15** ⑧⑦ unusual sparkling from grenache blanc & roussanne. Characterful & honeyed, long appley/pithy finish. Voor Paardeberg grapes, small portion oaked. Also in magnum.

The Red Knight ★★★ Laudably dry, light (12% alcohol) & succulent **16** ⑧②. Lightly chill & enjoy this summer. Mourvèdre (35%), grenache, shiraz & cinsaut from Swartland. Misreported previously as discontinued, like next. **The White Knight** ★★★★ Smoky & light-footed (just 12.5% alcohol) **17** ⑧⑤, attractive floral & lemongrass tones, earthy natural winemaking nuance & pleasant tannic tug. From semillon, older oaked. Not tasted: **Knights in Tights Mourvèdre Luminoir**, **The Second Crusade Chenin Blanc**, **Grenache Blanc**, **The Round Table Roussanne**. Discontinued: **Paarl Syrah**, **Stellenbosch Syrah Reserve**, **The Souvenir Viognier**. — CvZ

Location: Bellville/Stellenbosch • WO: Stellenbosch/Swartland/Voor Paardeberg • Est/1stB 2000 • Tasting & sales by appt • Owner(s)/cellarmaster(s) Pieter de Waal • Winemaker(s) Pieter & Lohra de Waal • mourv, shiraz, chenin, grenache b, rouss, sem, viog • 10t/1,000cs own label 40% red 60% white • PO Box 995 Bellville 7535 • pieter@dw.co.za • www.hermitonthehill.co.za • **T +27 (0)83-357-3864**

Herold Wines   ⓠ ⑪ ⌂ ◎ ⑧ ⑥

Cool conditions in Nico and Maureen Fourie's farm at the foot of Cradock Peak in Outeniqua Ward prompted the first planting of pinot noir two decades ago — the vineyard almost surrounded by a nature reserve that unhelpfully harbours baboons, bush pigs and fruit-eating birds. Pinot remains the focus of the now wide-ranging plantings and of Nico's wines, with a new but mature, special bottling this year.

★★★★ **Pinot Noir** Elegant **15** ⑧⑦ more depth & character than 'Screwcap', & less herbal. Textured & well structured by acid & mild tannin, nothing overt. Well oaked, a little new. **14** ★★★★ ⑧③ earlier.

★★★★☆ **Private Collection Pinot Noir Reserve** (NEW) ⊘ From a weighty bottle, **13** ⑨⓪ shows good savoury development - mushroom, forest floor - plus signature red-fruited fragrance. Silky softness, the gentlest tannic grip, but firm integrated acid, modest oak. Plenty of flavour, with a future yet.

★★★★ **Sauvignon Blanc** ⊘ More blackcurrant & floral notes, tinged with green, on **17** ⑧⑥ than ripely tropical **16** ★★★★ ⑧③, & racier. Not greatly intense, but fairly lingering. Steely, with a lively acidity.

Pinot Noir 'Screwcap' ★★★★ Bright red fruit & wild herbal element on aromatic **15** (83). Lively & fresh, rather simple & unlingering, but a wholly delightful drink. **Syrah** (✓) ★★★★ Appealing **16** (84) has red & darker fruit & spice introduction. Ripe & quite powerful but also a feeling of freshness. Modestly oaked. **Red Men** (✓) ★★★★ **16** (84) half merlot with shiraz & cab - fruitcake, spice & blackcurrant all there. At just 13% alcohol, it's lightish & supple, easygoing but not trivial, with a pleasing grip. **Schaam Schaap** (✓) ★★★★ Rosé from pinot & chardonnay, **17** (84) well defined, not the usual vague fruitiness, with savoury note, fresh acidity & earthy grip on surprisingly rich palate - just 12% alcohol. **Riesling** ★★★ Early kerosene notes on rather rustic **17** (80). Unlike stony-dry previous, this oily & sweet (31 g/l sugar), with not quite enough balancing acidity, but peachy-flavourful. Not tasted: **Pinot Noir Reserve**, **John Segon Red Blend**, **Laatlammetjie Natural Sweet**. — TJ

Location: George ▪ Map: Klein Karoo & Garden Route ▪ Map grid reference: C3 ▪ WO: Outeniqua ▪ Est 1999 ▪ 1stB 2003 ▪ Tasting, sales & cellar tours Mon-Sat 10-4 ▪ Fee R20, waived on purchase ▪ Closed Easter Sun & Dec 25 ▪ Light refreshments/cheese platters during opening hours ▪ Picnic baskets/farm lunches with 2 days prior notice ▪ Facilities for children ▪ Tour groups ▪ Gifts ▪ Farm produce ▪ Conferences ▪ Walks/hikes ▪ MTB ▪ Conservation area ▪ Self-catering cottages ▪ Owner(s) Nico & Maureen Fourie ▪ Winemaker(s)/viticulturist(s) Nico Fourie (Jul 2011) ▪ 324ha/8ha (cab, merlot, pinot, shiraz, chard, riesling, sauv, sem) ▪ 45t/5,400cs own label 55% red 25% white 20% rosé ▪ PO Box 10 Herold 6615 ▪ info@heroldwines.co.za ▪ www.heroldwines. co.za ▪ S 33° 51' 49.4" E 022° 28' 9.9" ▪ 🗺 alleviates.taller.notions ▪ F +27 (0)86-698-6607 ▪ **T +27 (0)72-833-8223**

Hidden Valley Wines

(✓) (🍴) (🏠) (📷) (♿)

'The greatest location imaginable' enthuses winemaker Annalie van Dyk about this 'hidden gem of a place' in the upper reaches of Helderberg Mountain, with steep-angled vineyards, imposing cellar, awarded Overture restaurant (recently extensively renovated) and luxury Bush Lodge, among many allures. Locally still rare red-wine grape tannat being key to her Hidden Secret blend, Annalie is nurturing a limited-release varietal bottling which will be available exclusively at the tasting centre, affording visitors 'a truly unique experience'.

★★★★☆ **Hidden Gems** (✓) Cab-led **15** (92) with 36% petit verdot, 14% merlot, rich & velvety with sweetly succulent black fruit, subtle oak spice (18 months in French barrels, 20% new) & slightly minty herbal lift on dry, lingering finish.

★★★★ **Hidden Secret** (✓) Choc-nut spiced **15** ★★★★★ (93) even more harmonious & well structured than **14** (89), with fresh acid balancing very rich mulberry, plum & cherry fruit. 70% shiraz, 25% tannat, rest cab, aged in French oak (20% new) 18 months.

★★★★ **Sauvignon Blanc** Has many layers of tropical fruit: passion-, pineapple, grape- & lime, **17** (89) intensely zesty yet also sleek & succulent, ripe yet refreshing.

Hidden Treasure ★★★★ Unwooded merlot-led **17** (85) rosé offers good refreshment at under 13% alcohol, dry, with red berry, guava & kiwi fruit flavours. **Sauvignon Blanc-Viognier** ★★★ With viognier at 35%, 10% of blend oaked for smoothness, peachy **17** (82) is dry & fresh, with spicy finish. Discontinued: **Pinotage**, **Viognier**. — JG

Location/map/WO: Stellenbosch ▪ Map grid reference: E8 ▪ Est/1stB 1995 ▪ Tasting & sales: summer Mon-Thu 9-6 Fri 9-8 (sundowners at wine tasting centre) Sat/Sun 9-6; winter Mon-Sun 9-5 ▪ Fee R60pp ▪ Open pub hols, but closed Dec 25 & Jan 1 ▪ Cellar tours by appt ▪ Overture Restaurant ▪ The Deck at Hidden Valley ▪ Charcuterie & cheese/winter/chocolate platters ▪ Picnics, to be pre-booked ▪ Table olives & olive oil ▪ Tour groups by appt ▪ Boardroom & conference facilities ▪ Functions ▪ Sculpture studio ▪ Bush Lodge luxury accommodation ▪ Nature trail ▪ Conservation area ▪ Owner(s) Riaan Stassen ▪ Winemaker(s) Annalie van Dyk (Nov 2014) ▪ Viticulturist(s) Daniel Roux (Nov 2013) ▪ 40ha/21ha (cab, merlot, p verdot, shiraz, tannat, sauv, viog) & 3ha olives ▪ 150t/24,000cs own label 70% red 30% white ▪ WWF-SA Conservation Champion ▪ PO Box 12334 Die Boord 7613 ▪ info@hiddenvalleywines.co.za ▪ www.hiddenvalleywines.co.za ▪ S 34° 1' 14.72" E 018° 51' 10.06" ▪ 🗺 sparkly.captivated.redeems ▪ F +27 (0)21-880-2645 ▪ **T +27 (0)21-880-2646**

Highberry Wines

(✓) (📷)

Late last century a cult bottling of sauvignon blanc placed Somerset West's Schapenberg on the map of top SA terroir, and the opening of the Highberry tasting/function venue lets winelovers experience the False

Bay-facing hill in all its windblown glory. Ex Waterkloof winemaker Werner Engelbrecht here partners with local vinegrower Andre Parker and entrepreneur Jabulani Ntshangase, latterly a New York resident.

★★★★ Sauvignon Blanc Vibrant gooseberry, apple & lime fruit, buchu & mineral notes, 17 ⑧⑦'s acidity cleansing counterpoint to richness from barrelled component, 10% semillon (oaked) & 8 months on lees.

Cabernet Sauvignon ★★★☆ Attractive crossover styling, 16 ⑧④ fruit-filled yet with classic cedarwood, spice & dried herb notes, firm tannin grip underpinned by 20% new oak, 16 months. — GM

Location: Sir Lowry's Pass ▪ Map: Helderberg ▪ Map grid reference: F6 ▪ WO: Stellenbosch ▪ 1stB 2014 ▪ Tasting by appt only ▪ Function venue ▪ Owner(s) Andre Parker, Werner Engelbrecht & Jabulani Ntshangase ▪ Winemaker(s) Werner Engelbrecht (Jan 2014) ▪ Viticulturist(s) Edward Etson (Jul 2003) ▪ 65ha/49ha (cabs s/f, malbec, merlot, p verdot, shiraz, chard, sauv, sem) ▪ 350t/3,000cs own label 50% red 50% white ▪ werner@highberry.co.za ▪ www.highberry.co.za ▪ S 34° 6' 3.29" E 018° 54' 8.92" ▪ 🖳 exhaled.tenacious. noodles ▪ **T +27 (0)21-852-3754**

High Constantia Wine Cellar   Ⓠ ⑪ ☺

David van Niekerk's winery lies on a small portion of the original, 17th-century Constantia estate, internationally renowned for dessert wine. Here, high-quality fruit is produced and vinified by David and his long-time assistant Roger Arendse in a cellar 'reminiscent of High Constantia's original home of wine'. Still and sparkling wines from classic French varieties appear under the High Constantia and Silverhurst labels.

Location: Constantia ▪ Map: Cape Peninsula ▪ Map grid reference: B3 ▪ Est 1693 ▪ 1stB 2000 ▪ Tasting, sales & cellar tours Mon-Fri 8–5 Sat 10-3 ▪ Fee R70 ▪ Closed Easter Sun, Dec 25 & Jan 1 ▪ BYO picnic ▪ Meals pre-arranged with private chef Marc Wassung ▪ Owner(s) David van Niekerk ▪ Cellarmaster(s)/viticulturist(s) David van Niekerk (Jan 1999) ▪ Winemaker(s) David van Niekerk (Jan 1999) & Roger Arendse (Jan 2001) ▪ 10ha (cabs s/f, malbec, merlot, pinots noir/meunier, chard, sauv) ▪ 70t/11,000cs own label 52% red 15% white 3% rosé 30% MCC + 3,800cs for clients ▪ Brands for clients: Terra Madre ▪ Groot Constantia Rd Constantia 7800 ▪ david@highconstantia.co.za, info@highconstantia.co.za ▪ www.highconstantia.co.za ▪ S 34° 1' 31.3" E 018° 25' 36.1" ▪ 🖳 nightshade.surging.spaceship ▪ F +27 (0)21-794-7999 ▪ **T +27 (0)21-794-7171/+27 (0)83-300-2064**

Highgate Wine Estate   Ⓠ ⑪ ◎ ⑧

Welcome revitalisation continues at the KwaZulu-Natal boutique estate owned by Rudi and Cindy Kassier, with a purpose-designed and -built (using reclaimed red clay bricks) cellar and wine room opening to the public. Three young colleagues, Thomas Herselman, Cathryn Kassier and winemaker Thornton Pillay, with Stellenbosch study and work experience in common, are the driving force, offering tastings, tours and wine etiquette courses. With a new restaurant also open, the aim is to 'offer the best service and create a wine experience showcasing the uniqueness of KZN-certified wines'.

Black Edition Cabernet Sauvignon (ⁿᵉʷ) **★★★** Dark plummy fruit in 17 ⑦⑦, gentle savoury tone from 15 months oak, sleek & perky-fresh. Displays more ripeness than you'd expect from 12% alcohol. Acidity bit high, stands out. **Cabernet Sauvignon** (ⁿᵉʷ) **★★★** Blackcurrant & liquorice, hint of fennel, 17 ⑦⑧ is streamlined, elegant, with house-style freshness aiding drinkability. **Merlot** (ⁿᵉʷ) **★★★** Bright cherries & plums in trim-figured 17 ⑦⑧, 15 months in barrel but fruit is the hero, fresh & lively. **Pinotage ★★★** Piquant blueberries, oak not really in evidence, 17 ⑧① has variety's trademark succulent freshness, drinkability. Youthful, fruit driven, appealing. **Tomcat Pinotage** (ⁿᵉʷ) **★★★** Dark berries to the fore, some gentle background spice but 17 ⑧①'s palate is what appeals most, juicy, fresh, loads of fruit flavour. **Syrah** (ⁿᵉʷ) **★★★** Light alcohol, as all (here 11%), 17 ⑧⓪ juicy & sleek mulberry flavours, white pepper from year oak. Early picking gives herbaceous seam, not unattractive. **Rosé** (ⁿᵉʷ) **★★** Mainly cab with pinotage, showing in 18 ⑦③'s herbaceous tone, gentle berry fruit. Dry, light textured; highish acidity makes this a good palate cleanser. **Chardonnay ★★★** Fresher style than last, more citrus showing, elegant (just 12% alcohol) 17 ⑦⑧ has a melon core, zesty acidity adding vibrancy. — CR

Location: Lions River ▪ Map/WO: KwaZulu-Natal ▪ Map grid reference: B2 ▪ Est/1stB 2010 ▪ Tasting, sales & cellar tours Wed-Sun 10-3; cellar tours available by appt Mon/Tue ▪ Closed Dec 25 ▪ Menu Restaurant open for lunch & dinner, www.menuathighgate.com ▪ Wine etiquette courses ▪ Events & weddings ▪ Country shops catering for all ages adjacent to cellar (Piggly Wiggly) ▪ Owner(s) Rudi & Cindy Kassier ▪ Winemaker(s) Thornton Pillay ▪ 57ha/4ha (cab, merlot, ptage, shiraz, chard) ▪ 12t/1,250cs own label 75% red 25% white

▪ PO Box 1025 Howick 3290 ▪ wine@highgatewineestate.co.za ▪ www.highgatewineestate.co.za ▪ S 29° 27' 29.92" E 030° 8' 8.66" ▪ consistency.looses.vigilantly ▪ T +27 (0)82-345-5706/+27 (0)82-895-1667/+27 (0)33-234-2002

Highlands Road Estate ⓣ ⑪ ⓞ ⓑ ⓦ

Highlands Road, Port Elizabeth attorney Michael White's estate in cool-climate Elgin, has been garnering award after award for their Bordeaux-inspired white wines, and now the wooded Sauvignon Reserve and blended Sine Cera (an Italian sculpting term for perfection) are joined by a varietal Semillon, so all eyes must be on that groaning medal cabinet. On the red-wine side, Michael notes, syrah is the star of the 2018 vintage, while their various styles of pinot noir continue to appeal to winelovers at home and abroad.

★★★★ **Pinot Noir** ⊘ Well-balanced **15** ⑧⑨ starting to show pleasing development (game, earth, leather) to fresh strawberries & sweet spice. Nicely handled oak (25% new) supports good structure & tannins through to just-dry finish. Rung above **14** ★★★★ ⑧⑤.

★★★★ **Syrah** ⓐ Stately **15** ★★★★☆ ⑨① oozes Old World charm, generous tobacco, leather notes supporting stewed black plums & cherries, spice accents from 30% new oak & nice textural finish. Set to improve over next 5 years. Confident step up on **14** ⑧⑨.

★★★★☆ **Chardonnay** ⓐ Youthful **17** ⑨③ shows plenty of promise, warm peach & melon already knitting nicely with creamy oatmeal & touches of spice from 33% new oak. Zesty acidity carries through to citrus finish. Expect lots more enjoyment as it matures.

★★★★★ **Sauvignon Blanc White Reserve** ⓠ Taut flinty entry to **15** ⑨⑦ reveals fantail of leesy cream on palate, courtesy of subtle old-oak barrel ferment. Confident, structured & persistent, the texture & palate weight set it apart.

★★★★☆ **Sauvignon Blanc** ⊘ Elegantly structured unwooded **15** ⑨⓪ improves on last year's provisional rating (& on **14** ★★★ ⑧①). 8 months on lees add creaminess to multiple layers of tropical/stone fruit, bottle age adds hints of orange marmalade & attractive notes of lanolin & lime to lengthy finish.

★★★★ **Semillon** ⓝⓔⓦ Somewhat shy but with great potential, flowers, herbs & citrus combine well with prominent oak (40% new-oak fermented) while drop sugar (5.5 g/l) offsets lively acidity. Keep **17** ⑧⑨ if you can - promising debut.

★★★★ **Sine Cera** ⓐ Serious & weighty blend semillon & sauvignon (50/50) uses judicious oak (17%, 40% new) to add nuance & interest to heady mix of peaches, limes, fresh herbs. Lovely texture combines richness with zesty acidity, all carried through to endless finish. **16** ★★★★☆ ⑨④ continues steady improvement on **15** ⑧⑧ & previous.

★★★★☆ **Noble Late Harvest** ⓠ Dried pineapple vies with tangy lime zest on barrel-fermented botrytis dessert. Beautiful poise of sweetness matched by lively acid. Balanced, dry-seeming finish with lingering brûlée flavour memory. **15** ⑨④ from sauvignon blanc, like **14** ★★★★ ⑧④.

Pinot Noir Rosé ⓠ ★★★★ Firm-bodied, dry **16** ⑧③ shows ample tangy berry charm, lees contact adds texture & heft to palate. **Pinot Noir Late Harvest** ⓠ ★★★ Unusual barrel-aged dessert. **15** ⑧① offers fruit compote & spice but alcohol (16%) is prominent, as is dry tannin grip. — CM

Location/map/WO: Elgin ▪ Map grid reference: C3 ▪ Est 2005 ▪ 1stB 2007 ▪ Tasting, sales & cellar tours Mon-Sun 10–4 ▪ Cheese & charcuterie platters ▪ Facilities for children ▪ Boule court ▪ Owner(s) Michael White ▪ Winemaker(s) Vanessa Simkiss ▪ Viticulturist(s) Paul Wallace ▪ 28ha/10ha (pinot, shiraz, chard, sauv, sem) ▪ 70t/4,500cs own label 35% red 65% white ▪ PO Box 94 Elgin 7180 ▪ info@highlandsroadestate.co.za ▪ www.highlandsroadestate.co.za ▪ S 34° 14' 4.4" E 019° 4' 14.3" ▪ ⓦ deemed.kitchen.tigers ▪ T +27 (0)71-271-0161/+27 (0)78-332-5782

☐ **High Road** see The High Road

Hildenbrand Wine & Olive Estate ⓣ ⑪ ⓖ ⓦ

Reni Hildenbrand is the live wire behind this characterful Wellington boutique estate, where wine is handcrafted, extra virgin olive oil produced, feet put up (by guests of the country house) and time somehow found to rescue animals - and name wines after them: Justi & Semi the shiraz-malbec being the latest.

Estate Single Vineyard range

Chardonnay Barrique ⓐ ★★★ Big mouthful of orange citrus fruit, white blossoms & creamy vanilla. **13** (82) carries oak nicely, alcohol not so much. **Chenin Blanc** ⓐ ★★★ Better balance on previewed **15** (79), with restrained fruit, measured acidity. Pleasant sipper. **Semillon** ⓐ ★★★ Honeyed nose of **13** (81) followed by cooked stonefruit & yellow citrus. Not tasted: **Cabernet Sauvignon, Malbec, Shiraz, Shiraz Rosé, Orange Wine, Chardonnay, Chenin Blanc Barrel Fermented**. Occasional release: **Sleepless Nights NLH Semillon**.

Estate Animal range

Emma & Asa ⓐ ★★★ Named for farm's two goats, **09** (81) chenin, semillon & chardonnay, all barrel fermented. Rich honey/muesli notes, fresh acidity, good match for goats' cheese! Not tasted: **Roikat Shiraz, Cuvée Justi & Semi**. Occasional release: **Wild Style Méthode Cap Classique**.

Hildenbrand Wines range

Not tasted: **Crouchen Blanc, Cuvée Hilda**. — GdB

Location/map/WO: Wellington ▪ Map grid reference: B4 ▪ Est 1991 ▪ 1stB 1999 ▪ Tasting & sales Mon-Fri 10-4 Sat/Sun 9-12 by appt ▪ Wine tasting R50pp; olive & oil tasting R15pp ▪ Closed Easter Sat/Sun, Dec 24/25 & Jan 1 ▪ Food & wine evenings/lunch by appt ▪ Klein Rheboskloof Country & Guest House ▪ Owner(s)/cellarmaster(s)/winemaker(s) Reni Hildenbrand ▪ ±4,500cs ▪ PO Box 270 Wellington 7654 ▪ info@wine-estate-hildenbrand.co.za ▪ www.wine-estate-hildenbrand.co.za ▪ S 33° 39' 33.3" E 019° 1' 46.3" ▪ 🄼 limit. tickles.fevered ▪ **T +27 (0)82-656-6007**

Hill & Dale Wines

Winemaker since inception Guy Webber is understandably proud of Hill & Dale, launched in 2003 and today, with volumes of well over 100,000 cases a year, still delivering on its original promise of 'estate'-quality wines at supermarket prices. Latterly owned by the Schreiber family, the brand is sibling to Neethlingshof and mostly made there from the estate's grapes. 'Exciting' new packaging is due soon.

Merlot ★★★ Leafy cassis varietal character, **17** (80) with tarry edge & prominent tannins. **Pinotage** ★★★ Sweetly ripe berry compote on **17** (82), with slight steely edge & chalky tannins. **Cabernet Sauvignon-Shiraz** ★★★ Pleasantly quaffable **17** (82) has blackcurrant & cherry fruitiness, medium body, chewy tannins on finish. **Dry Rosé Merlot** ⊘ ★★★ Well-mannered, dry & fruity **18** (80) is easygoing summer sipping. **Chardonnay** ⊘ ★★★ Primary orange squash flavours on unwooded **18** (80), with satisfying substance & fresh acidity. Likeable & easy to drink. **Sauvignon Blanc** ⊘ ★★★ Bright, fresh **18** (80) has ripe pear & gooseberry fruit, subdued acidity, clean finish. Discontinued: **Shiraz**. — GdB

Location/WO: Stellenbosch ▪ Est 2003 ▪ 1stB 2001 ▪ Closed to public ▪ Owner(s) Schreiber family ▪ Winemaker(s) Guy Webber (Oct 1998) ▪ 112,000cs own label 30% red 35% white 35% rosé ▪ WIETA ▪ PO Box 104 Stellenbosch 7599 ▪ info@hillanddale.co.za ▪ www.hillanddale.co.za ▪ F +27 (0)21-883-8941 ▪ **T +27 (0)21-883-8988**

Hillcrest Estate   ⓐ 🍴 ◎

This Durbanville hilltop farm's ancient soils were quarried before the owners, in construction, were persuaded to plant vines and convert a storeroom into a small cellar for self-taught winemaker Graeme Reed. Today, a dynamic duo has taken up where he left off. GM Arno Smith, vineyardist and winemaker, is devoted to the established, classic Bordeaux blends but particularly proud, too, of his single-vineyard wines (named for his loyal little Jack Russell). Mike Crafford, managing the olive orchards and hip outdoor Quarry events venue, is now also in charge of the casual eatery.

Metamorphic Collection

★★★★ **Quarry** ⓐ From merlot, **15** (89) cherry, plum & berry notes, thyme & oak spice accents (50% new). Plush yet vibrant courtesy enlivening cool-climate acidity.

★★★★☆ **Hornfels** ⓐ Noble Bordeaux red, **14** (93) not very expressive mid-2018 yet a commanding presence, with striking dark-fruit complexity, insistent tannins. Allow 5+ years before broaching. 30% each cab franc, merlot & petit verdot plus cab. **13** (91) approachable in youth, despite similar power.

Not tasted: **Atlantic Slopes**.

Saartjie Single Vineyard Selections

★★★★ **Cabernet Franc** Unshowy yet multifaceted **17** ⑧⑦'s rich black fruit nuanced with crushed herb & tealeaf, accessible tannins, spiced cassis farewell. 20% new oak in support, as all reds this range.

★★★★ **Malbec** Textbook **17** ⑧⑧ forthcoming fruit, Christmas spices, cocoa aromas & flavours. Rounded & laid-back to drink now or in a few years.

★★★★ **Petit Verdot** ⓐ Violets, jasmine, cassis, mulberry & blackberry: a spectrum of complex nuances in **17** ⑧⑥ raise the bar on **16** ★★★★ ⑧⑤). Well-handled if still stern tannins, pleasing minerality. Not tasted: **Semillon**.

Hillcrest Estate range

Red Shale Blend ★★★ Was 'Red Shale Merlot', now a Bordeaux quartet, merlot uppermost in **17** ⑧①. Juicy, with plump tannins, comfortable braai wine. **Robbenzicht** ★★★★ Merlot-cab duo with redcurrants & mint chocolate from the former, cassis & dark spice the latter. Well-integrated **16** ⑧④ fireside companion. Just 10% new oak, as for sibling. Not tasted: **Cabernet Sauvignon Rosé, Sauvignon Blanc**. — GM

Location: Durbanville ▪ Map: Durbanville, Philadelphia & Darling ▪ Map grid reference: C7 ▪ WO: Cape Town ▪ Est/1stB 2002 ▪ Tasting & sales daily 10–5 ▪ Fee R30/estate range, R75/full range ▪ Olive platter ▪ Closed Dec 25/26 & Jan 1 ▪ Cellar tours by appt ▪ Restaurant T +27 (0)21-975-2346 open daily for b'fast & lunch ▪ Outdoor beer garden ▪ Wedding/function venue ▪ Farm produce ▪ MTB ▪ Conservation area ▪ Craft beer brewery: Tasting & sales Tue-Sun 11–4; tasting fee R60pp ▪ Owner(s) PD Inglis, R Haw, G du Toit & E Menegablo ▪ Winemaker(s) Arno Smith (Jan 2014) ▪ Viticulturist(s) Arno Smith ▪ 25ha (cabs s/f, malbec, merlot, p verdot, sauv) ▪ 60t/±6,000cs own label 45% red 55% white ▪ Private Bag X3 Durbanville 7551 ▪ info@hillcrestfarm.co.za ▪ www.hillcrestfarm.co.za ▪ S 33° 49′ 38.2″ E 018° 35′ 25.9″ ▪ ⓦ flog.worthier. transistor ▪ **T +27 (0)21-970-5800**

Hillock Wines   ⓠ ⓜ ⓐ ⓞ

Below winter-snow-tipped mountain peak Towerkop, Andy and Penny Hillock's Klein Karoo grape-growing guest farm Mymering, with its cosy accommodation, homemade meals, handcrafted wines and various outdoor pursuits, is ideal for a country getaway or intimate wedding, the latter made even more special by the former surgeon's deft touch with his recent MCC bubblies.

Location: Ladismith ▪ Map: Klein Karoo & Garden Route ▪ Map grid reference: B6 ▪ Est 2010 ▪ 1stB 2011 ▪ Tasting, sales & cellar tours daily 10–5 ▪ Closed Dec 25 ▪ Light lunches 12–3 daily ▪ Tour groups ▪ Gifts ▪ Farm produce ▪ Guided hikes & vineyard tours ▪ Mountain biking ▪ 4-star guest house (sleeps 20), Mymering Estate www.mymering.com ▪ Owner(s) Andy & Penny Hillock ▪ Winemaker(s) Andy Hillock ▪ Viticulturist(s) Riaan Steyn ▪ 400ha/5oha (shiraz, chard, chenin) ▪ 24t/3,600cs own label 50% red 50% white ▪ PO Box 278 Ladismith 6655 ▪ penny@mymering.com ▪ www.hillockwines.com, www.mymering.com ▪ S 33° 29′ 55.24″ E 021° 10′ 18.65″ ▪ ⓦ quantifies.superstore.feathered ▪ F +27 (0)28-551-1313 ▪ **T +27 (0)28-551-1548**

☐ **Hill of Enon** see Zandvliet Wine Estate

☐ **Hills** see The Hills

☐ **Hilton Vineyards** see Richard Hilton Vineyards

Hirst Wines

Yorkshireman and entrepreneur Luke Hirst's Vino Pronto wine shop in Cape Town is well-known for its hard-to-find, young-gun and fine-wine selection. But there's another good reason to pop in: Luke's own-label bottlings from Stellenbosch and Swartland, satisfying high-quality wines at friendly prices.

Hirst Wines range

★★★★ **Riverhorse** ⓥ Equal cab & merlot in fascinating red from Stellenbosch. Savoury & salty, **16** ⑧⑦ supported by a pure black fruit core & long velvety chocolate farewell.

The Front Row range

★★★★ **Shiraz** ⓥ Quintessential Swartland shiraz. **14** ⑧⑦ white pepper, baking spice in pure red fruit, finely integrated tannin rounds off a pleasantly fresh offering. Old oak & hands-off approach, as all.

★★★★ **Chenin Blanc** ⓥ Lightish, gentle & charming **14** ⑧⑦ surprisingly intense flavour for just 12% alcohol. Oxidative winemaking shows in bruised apple finish.— HC

ocation: Cape Town ▪ WO: Swartland/Stellenbosch ▪ Est/1stB 2013 ▪ See website for sales hours ▪ Owner(s)
uke Hirst ▪ Own label 50% red 50% white ▪ PO Box 12066 Hout Bay 7872 ▪ hirstluke1@gmail.com ▪ www.
inopronto.co.za ▪ **T +27 (0)82-751-8169**

❒ **His Master's Choice** see Ridgeback
❒ **His Master's Choice** see Excelsior Vlakteplaas

Hofstraat Kelder   ⓠ ⓨ ⓐ

ofstraat is named for the Malmesbury street where friends Wim Smit and Jerry Finley's wine journey
egan. Vinification subsequently moved to a smallholding nearby, but the principles of boutique handcraft-
ng and hands-off winemaking continued. Beside by-appointment sampling, sales and tours, Wim and Jerry
resent monthly 'first Thursday' tastings at the cellar, which doubles as a rentable function facility. They also
ffer to mentor aspirant winemakers by arrangement, facilitating grape sourcing through to labelling.

Renosterbos range

Barbera ★★ Savoury & farmyard notes plus some high tones on naturally bunch-fermented 16 ⑬.
Heavyset, but softer tannins than other reds. Older oak, as all. **Nebbiolo ★★★** From Breedekloof, 16 ⑳
ints of varietal tomato concentrate, smoother texture, better structure than previous though rather oxida-
ive prune juice character. **Shiraz ★★★★** Loads of dense black fruit, raw meat & pepper, all nicely balanced
n 16 ⑱. Unknit oak & tannins intrude somewhat. **Tinta Barocca ⓝⓔⓦ ★★★** Savoury spices & porty black
ruit on wild but characterful 16 ⑫. Still-integrating wood (11 months French, as all) makes for rough
annins and chalky finish. Not tasted: **Merlot, Pinotage, Chenin Blanc, Die Solder, Cape Vintage.**

Oesland range

Cabernet Sauvignon ★★★ Savoury barnyard whiff on middleweight 16 ⑱, bright red-berry fruit which
ends abruptly with tannic edge. — GdB

Location: Malmesbury ▪ Map: Swartland ▪ Map grid reference: C7 ▪ WO: Swartland/Breedekloof ▪ Est 2002 ▪
1stB 2003 ▪ Tasting, sales & tours by appt ▪ Scheduled tasting evenings every first Thu of the month ▪ Dine at
the cellar on Fri evenings ▪ Functions (up to 80 pax) ▪ Owner(s)/cellarmaster(s)/winemaker(s) Wim Smit &
Jerry Finley ▪ 4t/505cs own label 100% red ▪ PO Box 1172 Malmesbury 7299 ▪ renosterbos@cornergate.com ▪
S 33° 26' 56.1" E 018° 44' 1.8" ▪ 🗺 activity.awaiting.pans ▪ F +27 (0)22-487-3202 ▪ **T +27 (0)83-270-2352**

Hogan Wines

Jocelyn Hogan Wilson, who's as elegant and quietly expressive as her wines, has expanded her production a
little — and her exports quite substantially. Even better news is that earlier hints about introducing another
white and another red are getting more concrete expression and should result in a larger range as from the
2019 harvest. 'I am experimenting with chardonnay from three incredible sites,' she says, 'and 'also working
with some Helderberg cabernet franc'. Her vinification is at Zorgvliet in Stellenbosch, alongside some other
space-renting winemakers, where she enjoys 'sharing philosophies, ideas and techniques'.

★★★★☆ Divergent ⓐ Near-equal blend cab, partly bunch-ferment cinsaut (both Stellenbosch) &
carignan (Wellington). **17** ⑭ pure-fruited, energetic gorgeousness from fragrant start to lingering dry
finish. Firm tannic structure but juicy & fresh; core of sweet red fruit, with wild cherry note. Older oak only,
as **16** ⑬.

★★★★☆ Chenin Blanc ⓐ **17** ⑬ typically combines an elegantly understated subtlety of varietal
character with a real depth of flavour & confidence of structure, a thoroughly enlivening acidity & dry
finish. These wines both spontaneous ferment, no additives.— TJ

Location: Stellenbosch ▪ WO: Coastal/Swartland ▪ Est 2013 ▪ 1stB 2014 ▪ Closed to public ▪ Owner(s) Jocelyn
Hogan Wilson ▪ Winemaker(s) Jocelyn Hogan Wilson (Nov 2013) ▪ 20t/2,200cs own label 50% red 50%
white ▪ PO Box 2226 Dennesig 7601 ▪ jocelyn@mweb.co.za ▪ www.hoganwines.co.za ▪ **T +27 (0)21-885-
1275**

Holden Manz Wine Estate   ⓠ ⓨ ⓐ ⓐ ⓐ

Situated in the southernmost corner of Franschhoek Valley, 'sustainable family farm' Holden Manz, with
luxury guesthouse, spa, restaurant and impressive contemporary African art collection curated by owners

Gerard Holden and Migo Manz, is going increasingly green. 'Our solar panel capacity has risen from 50 to 65 kWp,' notes Bordeaux University-trained winemaker Thierry Haberer, whose 'intimate' approach to winemaking includes small-batch ferments of fruit from a variety of terroirs. Getting to know these parcels well is key. 'Your work in the cellar becomes very simple when you understand your vineyard.'

Reserve range

★★★★☆ **Cabernet Franc** At over 15% alcohol, **15** ⑨⓪ undeniably powerful with dense black fruit, also liquorice & dark chocolate from 22 months in 50% new oak, but overall impression is one of polish, balance & persistence.

★★★★ **Merlot** ⓃⒺⓦ Plenty of choc-vanilla appeal in full-bodied **15** ⑧⑨, 22 months in new French oak. Voluptuously soft with sweet blueberry, plum, damson jam flavours. Alcohol also +15%.

★★★★☆ **Syrah** Maximum density, weight & ripe plum succulence in **15** ⑨⓪, calling for a T-bone & an Uber at over 15.5% alcohol. Richly smooth from 22 months in new 500L French oak with hints of smoke & leather adding interest. Rich yet vibrant.

Avant Garde range

★★★★ **Big G** ⓥ Velvety **14** ⑧⑧ blends 52% cab, 30% cab franc & merlot, 22 months in French oak (30% new). Ripe fruit concentration, tannic grip & cocoa on finish - also warmth from 15% alcohol.

★★★★ **Visionaire** Packed with forest fruits, more elegant than stablemates, **14** ⑧⑨ 22 months in barriques has cab in ascendancy (37%) with merlot, shiraz, splashes cab franc & malbec.

★★★★ **Chardonnay** French oak (50% new, 8 months) well integrated in **17** ⑧⑧, imparting creamy oatmeal softness to fresh & caramelised citrus fruit flavours. Includes Stellenbosch grapes.

Good Sport Cape Vintage ⓥ ★★★ Christmas pudding, spice & raisin nuttiness on all-shiraz **11** ⑧⓪ 'port'. Pleasantly rich & ripe, with dry tannin grip & fiery but well-knit spirit.

Modern range

★★★★ **Vernissage** ⊘ Juicy red fruit to the fore in lightly oaked **15** ⑧⑥, blending spicy shiraz with ±30% merlot & cab, dash cab franc. At 14% alcohol, more approachable & refreshing than **14** ★★★★ ⑧③

★★★★ **Chenin Blanc** ⓥ Fresh, elegant **17** ⑧⑨, just 5% aged 4 months in 20% new French oak, alive with stonefruit flavours, natural acidity balancing soft, round, rich texture. Promising debut.

Rosé ⓥ ★★★ Crisply dry pink for summer lunchtimes, **17** ⑦⑧ from syrah & 4 others has cranberry & red cherry fruit, fresh, spicy finish. WO W Cape.

Contemporary range

★★★★ **Cabernet Sauvignon** Graphite edge to rich cassis fruit in **16** ⑧⑦, first in 3 years, mediumweight with soft tannins & tobacco/mocha notes from 22 months 20% new oak.— JG

Location/map: Franschhoek ▪ Map grid reference: D1 ▪ WO: Franschhoek/Western Cape ▪ Est 2010 ▪ 1stB 2009 ▪ Tasting & sales daily 10-5 ▪ Fee R30 ▪ Cellar tours by appt ▪ Franschhoek Kitchen ▪ Spa ▪ Picnic area ▪ Holden Manz Country House ▪ Owner(s) Gerard Holden & Migo Manz ▪ Winemaker(s) Thierry Haberer (Dec 2014), with Annamarie Fourie (Apr 2015) ▪ Viticulturist(s) Tertius Oosthuizen (Sep 2010) & Marko Roux (Oct 2016, consultant) ▪ 20ha/16ha (cabs s/f, merlot, shiraz) ▪ 110t/13,332cs own label 85% red 3.85% white 6.65% rosé 4.5% port ▪ IPW ▪ PO Box 620 Franschhoek 7690 ▪ info@holdenmanz.com ▪ www.holdenmanz.com ▪ 33°56'6.3" E 019°7'8.3" ▪ ⌨ yodel.parody.prefaces ▪ F +27 (0)21-876-4624 ▪ **T +27 (0)21-876-2738**

☐ **Home of Erasmus** *see* Erasmus Family Wines
☐ **Homestead Series** *see* Bellingham

Hoopenburg Wines

⓪ ⌂ ⌂ ⌂

Like the famous old car-industry advertising slogan, 'everything keeps going right' at Gregor Schmitz's estate on the northern edge of Stellenbosch. Production volumes continue to rise (allowing for more stringent selection for the various ranges), new markets to open (US the latest) and existing outlets to expand (notably in southern Africa). The portfolio is also growing: the Bordeaux blend debuting this edition is to be joined by, inter alia, a vine-dried shiraz and pink sparkling. As GM Anton Beukes says: 'Exciting times!'

Integer range

★★★★ **Merlot-Cabernet Sauvignon-Petit Verdot** (NEW) Cape Bordeaux offering with heft & substance, **16** (89) shows succulent blackcurrant fruit & solid tannins, deft 18 months mostly older French barriques. WO Coastal, as next.

★★★★☆ **Syrah-Mourvèdre-Carignan** ⊘ Impressive **16** (91) Rhône blend (71% syrah) is complex, layered & rich. Savoury overtones laced with spicy red fruit, meaty-savoury core & silky tannins combine into very appealing whole.

★★★★☆ **Chardonnay** ⊘ Accomplished, refined **17** (92) follows form of previous, with succulent melon & citrus fruit centre stage, judiciously handled oak (30% new) in wings. Fine poise & balance, with zesty acid lending shape to creamy, rounded body.

★★★★ **Méthode Cap Classique Brut** Bone-dry **16** (88) (zero dosage) chardonnay sparkler has creamy mousse, tangy baked apple fruit, spicy ginger snap notes, all charmingly integrated. New disgorgement of **14** ★★★★★ (90), with 20% pinot noir, also tasted: richer, fuller brioche, same apple & ginger highlights.

Cabernet Sauvignon (②) ★★★ **14** (81) has distinct green edge to black & red fruit, less ripe & resolved than previous.

Hoopenburg Bush Vine range

★★★★ **Pinot Noir** ⊘ Appealing floral scents & ripe red berries on **16** (86), with well-judged tannins, convincing heft, impressive finish. Punches above its weight, improves on **15** ★★★★ (84). WO W Cape.

Cabernet Sauvignon ★★★ **16** (81) has slightly wild but intense blackcurrant fruit with charred notes & high-toned acidity. Needs more time for edges to smooth. **Merlot** ★★★ Malty notes on earthy, savoury **16** (80). Substantial body, muted blackcurrant fruit. WO W Cape. **Pinotage** ★★★ High-toned berry fruit on **16** (80), with juicy body, toasty oak spices. Mild mannered, quaffable. **Shiraz** ★★★★ **16** (84) is likeable, easygoing, shows sweetly ripe black fruit with restrained oak. Last-tasted **14** also available. Coastal WO. **Rosé** (②) ★★★ Palest of pinks on **17** (81) from cabernet, fresh red berries & hint of spice, few grams sugar perfectly balance zippy acidity. **Chardonnay** (②) ★★★ Unwooded **17** (81), nice fresh yellow fruit flavours with hints of marzipan & pear. Improves on previous. Coastal WO, as next. **Chenin Blanc** ⊘ ★★★ Cheerful, fresh & fruity **18** (81) offers satisfying early drinking. Hints of pineapple & pear drops. **Sauvignon Blanc** (②) ★★★ Shy confected green fruit on **17** (81), touches of lemon & lime with sherbet finish.

Guru range

Merlot ★★★ Light, fresh **17** (78) has primary fruit & chocolate flavours, though rather rough oak from 3 months on staves. WO W. Cape, like next. **Cabernet Sauvignon-Merlot** ★★★ Forward, primary plum fruit on light, juicy **16** (80). Touch of oak (staves) lends spice. Easygoing quaffer. **Sauvignon Blanc** (②) ★★★ Bright **17** (78) more concentrated than previous but still an uncomplicated everyday white. — GdB

Location/map: Stellenbosch ▪ Map grid reference: E1 ▪ WO: Stellenbosch/Coastal/Western Cape ▪ Est/1stB 1992 ▪ Tasting, sales & cellar tours Mon-Fri 8.30-4 ▪ Fee R30/6-8 wines ▪ Closed all pub hols ▪ BYO picnic ▪ Conferences ▪ Guest house T +27 (0)21-884-4534 ▪ Owner(s) Gregor Schmitz ▪ GM Anton Beukes (Aug 2009) ▪ Winemaker(s) Anton Bothma (Jan 2017) ▪ Viticulturist(s) Gert Snyders ▪ 70ha/30ha (cab, merlot, ptage, pinot, shiraz, chard, chenin) ▪ 180t/40,000cs own label 80% red 18% white 2% MCC ▪ PO Box 1233 Stellenbosch 7599 ▪ info@hoopenburg.com ▪ www.hoopenburgwines.co.za ▪ S 33° 49′33.4″ E 018° 49′9.3″ ▪ 🔲 narrations.monuments.reconnect ▪ T +27 (0)21-884-4221

Hornbill Garagiste Winery   (②) (🍴) (🏠) (📷)

Architect John Dry and his artist wife Erna moved from Pretoria to Hermanus in 1998. 'The fresh air, sea, mountains, fynbos and Cape wines did the rest,' they say modestly of their successful ceramic studio, gallery and garagiste winery at Hemel-en-Aarde Village, where they also offer luxury self-catering accommodation.

★★★★ **Cape Blend** Whole greater than sum of parts (50/50 pinotage/shiraz), **17** (86) smooth & supple with tangy berry fruit. Year older French oak, as all reds. Range fermented naturally without additives.

★★★★ **Chenin Blanc** Rich texture & layers of pear, white peach & green melon fruit in **17** (87), 9 months lees contact in old French oak showing on savoury, subtly spiced finish. Alcohol well under 12%.

Pinotage ★★★ Rich, velvety **17** (82) packed with sweet, ripe, dark berry/cherry fruit, unashamedly big & bold at almost 15.5% alcohol. **Shiraz** (NEW) ★★★★ Fragrant, floral **17** (85) rich in red berry fruit, seasoned with pepper & subtle spice, medium body for easy drinking. Occasional release: **Merlot**. — JG

Location: Hermanus ▪ Map: Walker Bay & Bot River ▪ Map grid reference: A3 ▪ WO: Cape South Coast ▪ Est 2004 ▪ 1stB 2005 ▪ Tasting, sales & tours Mon-Fri 9-5 Sat 9-2 ▪ Closed Easter Fri/Sun, Dec 25 & Jan 1 ▪ Gifts ▪ Art gallery & ceramic studio ▪ Self-catering accommodation ▪ Artisan bakery & restaurant ▪ Owner(s) John Dry ▪ Winemaker(s) John Dry (2004) ▪ 6t/800cs own label 100% red ▪ PO Box 4 Hermanus 7200 ▪ hornbill@intekom.co.za ▪ www.hornbillhouse.co.za ▪ S 34° 24' 46.3" E 019° 11' 54.4" ▪ 🔲 twinkly.wedges.pedestals ▪ F +27 (0)28-316-3794 ▪ T +27 (0)28-316-2696

☐ **Horse Mountain** *see Doran Vineyards*
☐ **Houdamond** *see Bellevue Estate Stellenbosch*
☐ **House of GM & Ahrens** *see The House of GM&AHRENS*
☐ **House of JC le Roux** *see The House of JC le Roux*
☐ **House of Krone** *see Krone*

House of Mandela   ⓠ

The owners of this negociant business, Makaziwe and Tukwini Mandela, are 'the proud progeny of the Royal House of Mandela'. The wines commemorate, they say, 'the life and spirit of a great African soul', Nelson Mandela. Makaziwe and Tukwini now collaborate with D'Aria on their locally sourced wines, and tastings are available by arrangement at that Durbanville winery's premises pending a dedicated tasting venue.

King Vusani range
★★★★ Shiraz Perfumed & bright **16** (86) shows influence of oak (as for Cab) but it's well meshed with concentrated blueberry & spicy plum fruit, deep inky nuances. Good length of flavour.

★★★★ Chardonnay (NEW) Creamy, rounded & rich **15** (86) is balanced, with fruit & oak, third new French, in harmony. Appealing citrus & cinnamon spice on structured palate.

Cabernet Sauvignon ★★★★ Firmly structured & spicy from 15 months in French oak, 40% new, but **17** (83)'s black cherry fruit livens the palate. Discontinued: **Pinotage**.

Phumla range (NEW)
Pinotage ★★★ Subtle coffee/mocha note to vivid blueberry vitality of **16** (81), chalky grip courtesy 10 months on French oak staves. **Chenin Blanc ★★★** Mandarin vibrancy to naturally fermented **16** (81), creamy breadth from half the wine spending 8 months in oak.

Thembu Tribute range
Cabernet Sauvignon ★★ Honest, appealing bright raspberry notes on **16** (75), fruity & succulent.
Shiraz ★★★ Fynbos & plum tones with light succulence make **16** (77) a crowd pleaser. **Sauvignon Blanc ★★** Tropical passionfruit ease on light **17** (73). Fairtrade certified. Discontinued: **Merlot, Pinotage, Chardonnay, Chenin Blanc.**

Discontinued: **Royal Reserve range.** — WB, FM

Location: Durbanville ▪ Map: Durbanville, Philadelphia & Darling ▪ Map grid reference: C7 ▪ WO: Western Cape ▪ Est 2009 ▪ Tasting by appt ▪ Owner(s) Makaziwe & Tukwini Mandela ▪ Winemaker(s)/viticulturist(s) Rudi von Waltsleben (D'Aria Winery) ▪ 50% red 50% white ▪ capewinematch@gmail.com ▪ www.houseof-mandela.com ▪ S 33° 50' 28.6" E 018° 36' 2.7" ▪ 🔲 steady.dices.seperators ▪ T +27 (0)82-686-6854

Hout Bay Vineyards   ⓠ ⓐ

Peter and Catharine Roeloffze swapped their careers in 2001 for 18 years' hard labour! Rightly proud they are of it too, having had to literally carve out the slopes of Hout Bay's Skoorsteenkop peak to establish 1.1 ha of vines, a cellar and a home. This indefatigable, self-taught couple produces a wide range of wine styles, with every facet of growing and production handcrafted with dedication and passion.

Hout Bay Vineyards range
★★★★ Shiraz Lovely white pepper, sweet spice & red fruit on **15** (86), restrained in youth by tangy acidity. A food wine with dry finish, best decanted if broaching now but ideally given time to settle.

★★★★ Petrus Attractive 5-way Rhône blend, shiraz (46%) in lead in **14** (88), with convincing pepper & scrub notes. Still touch unknit & feisty, shade off dark & handsome **13 ★★★★★** (92) but better than warmer **12 ★★★★** (85). Half new oak. WO W Cape. Also in 1.5 & 3L.

★★★★ **Klasiek by Catherine** Well-crafted chardonnay-led sparkling with equal pinot noir & meunier. **15** (87) mostly savoury, cranberry flavours, bone-dry, 3 years on lees providing subtle creamy brioche base & freshness. No **14**.

Merlot ★★★ Dark, ripe fruit conserve flavours on **16** (81), with slightly stalky dry tannin counterpoint, char nuance from 50% new oak, 2 years. Mid-2018 less balanced than previous, though cellaring might resolve. **Blush** ★★★ Light, sunset pink **18** (78) rosé mostly chardonnay, pinot noir; brisker style, drier & less aromatic than previous in absence of viognier but pleasingly light, clean & crisp. **Sauvignon Blanc** ★★★★ Two different vintages & styles tasted: **17** ★★★ (81) tighter, more piquant greengage & lime, bone-dry & food styled. **18** (84) better balanced & friendlier, riper yellow peach flavours, ready to enjoy solo.

Black Swan range
★★★★ **Cape Vintage** Tasty modern-style 'port', **13** (89) lovely pepperiness on deep, brooding core of dark fruit & molasses, dry pliable tannins, 19% alcohol nicely integrated. Equal parts 5 traditional varieties. No **11**, **12**. WO W Cape.— MW

Location: Hout Bay • Map: Cape Peninsula • Map grid reference: A3 • WO: Hout Bay/Western Cape • Est 2001 • 1stB 2004 • Tasting, sales & cellar tours by appt • Fee R50pp (min R300) • Facilities for children • Owner(s) Peter & Catharine Roeloffze • Cellarmaster(s)/winemaker(s)/viticulturist(s) Peter & Catharine Roeloffze (both Jan 2004) • 3.5ha/1.1ha (pinots meunier/noir, merlot, shiraz, chard, sauv, viog) • 24t/2,800cs own label 40% red 20% white 20% rosé 20% MCC • Other brand: HB Vineyards • PO Box 26659 Hout Bay 7872 • cathy@4mb.co.za • www.houtbayvineyards.co.za • S 34° 1′ 31.0″ E 018° 22′ 31.0″ • ⓘ hatches.invariably. shrugged • F +27 (0)86-514-9861 • **T +27 (0)83-790-3303**

Houw Hoek Vineyards
(ⓞ) (🍴) (📷) (👤)

Clive Heward's Houw Hoek Farm Stall on Elgin's Houw Hoek pass is much larger in size and scope than 'farm stall' usually indicates. A few hectares of chardonnay have been yielding grapes for a wine vinified by Kevin Grant of Ataraxia, and now Kevin is also making an Elgin shiraz for the brand.

★★★★ **Chardonnay** Expressive fruit, intense citrus dusted with sweet spice, **15** (87) still in prime of health. Racy acidity is an appealing underpin, the whole effect lively, vibrant, packed with flavour.

Shiraz (NEW) ★★★ Opaque colour, deep & dense, smoky liquorice tones, some prosciutto, **15** (82) generous flavours, dark fruit & streamlined body. — GdB, CR

Location/map/WO: Elgin • Map grid reference: D3 • Est 2004 • 1stB 2012 • Tasting & sales Mon-Sat 9.30-5 • Closed Dec 25 • Farm stall • Coffee shop Mon-Sun 7.30-5 b'fast & lunch • Gift shop • Facilities for children • Tour groups • Walking/hiking trails • Craft beer • Owner(s) Clive Heward • Cellarmaster(s)/winemaker(s) Kevin Grant (Jan 2013, consultant) • Viticulturist(s) Braam Gericke (consultant) • 10ha/2ha (chard) • 8t/800cs own label • houwhoekfarmstall@gmail.com • www.houwhoekfarmstall.co.za • S 34° 12′ 24.62″ E 019° 8′ 55.19″ • ⓘ incident.survive.clans • **T +27 (0)28-284-9015 (farm stall)**

☐ **Huangtai Wines** see De Villiers Wines

Hughes Family Wines
(ⓞ)

While quantities of Billy Hughes' Swartland-origin wines are down — no '16s, only smidgens of '17 and '18 — the Argentina-born, SA-naturalised marine and mineral projects engineer says the drought gave winemaker Lieze Norval 'the wonderful opportunity to experiment with the making of white wines and try different lengths of skin contact and maceration', the results to be released 'in small batches with alternative labels'. The approach to growing and vinifying the mostly Mediterranean varieties remains organic and non-interventionist, with creative touches like the underground cellar made from recycled shipping containers, topped with a view-rich tasting area.

Nativo range
★★★★☆ **Red Blend** ⊘ (🐝) Rich yet light of foot - the essence of Swartland. Supple **15** (94) has depth & resonance, less fruit sweetness & more grip than sumptuous **14** (90). Maverick blend of shiraz, mourvèdre, grenache, tempranillo, pinotage (at 6%, less than previous). Half in old oak. **13** untasted.

★★★★☆ **White Blend** ⓧ ♡ Singular **15** ⑨② melange chenin, grenache blanc & roussanne led by 70% viognier in new-wave Swartland style: minimal intervention & just a lick of old oak allow fruit to shine. Viognier component pleasingly restrained; balanced, poised & bone-dry.— DS

Location: Malmesbury ▪ Map/WO: Swartland ▪ Map grid reference: C6 ▪ Est 2000 ▪ 1stB 2004 ▪ Tasting by appt ▪ Owner(s)/cellarmaster(s) Billy Hughes ▪ Winemaker(s) Lieze Norval ▪ Viticulturist(s) Kevin Watt (Jul 2005, consultant) ▪ 52ha/27ha (grenache n/b, mourv, ptage, tempranillo, shiraz, chenin, rouss, viog) ▪ 180t total 25t/3,600cs own label 50% red 50% white ▪ Organic ▪ 6 Riverstone Rd Tierboskloof Hout Bay 7806 ▪ billy@nativo.co.za ▪ www.nativo.co.za ▪ S 33° 20' 37.71" E 018° 43' 45.09" ▪ ⧆ erase.stylings.guesses ▪ **T +27 (0)21-790-4824/+27 (0)83-270-2457**

☐ **Huguenac** see Huguenot Wine Farmers

Huguenot Wine Farmers

Privately owned wholesalers in Wellington, blending, marketing and distributing a range of liqueurs; spirits such as Huguenac Brandy and Buchu Brandy; Huguenot wine brands (Cabernet, Smooth Red, Nagmaalwyn, Jeripico, Hanepoot) and Zellerhof 5L Vats (Smooth Red, Premier Grand Cru, Late Harvest); and Huguenot sherry-style wines Ship Fortified and Old Brown.

Location: Wellington ▪ Closed to public ▪ Owner(s) JC Botha (Pty) Ltd ▪ Cellarmaster(s) Johan Goosen (Jul 2016) ▪ Trade enquiries Gert Brynard ▪ PO Box 275 Wellington 7654 ▪ gmbrynard@jcbotha.co.za ▪ F +27 (0)21-873-2075 ▪ **T +27 (0)21-864-1277**

Huis van Chevallerie   ⓠ ◎

Christa von La Chevallerie's family farm on the Paardeberg in Swartland (bought by her father in 1956) supplies grapes to some great names in modern Cape wine – but also increasingly to her own label. The chenin named for the farm, Nuwedam, was the first to be released bearing the Certified Heritage Vineyard logo of the Old Vines Project – whose inspirational founder, Rosa Kruger, was the viticulturist who helped the equally ardent Christa to rehabilitate the old bushvines on the farm.

★★★★☆ **Nuwedam Old Vine Chenin Blanc** ⑲ ⓐ ⓦ Naturally made, old-oaked **17** ⑨③ off bush-vines planted in 1974. Good varietal aromas, hinting at oxidative styling; deliciously flavourful too (earthy & saline more than fruity), but the main excitement is in the balanced, thrilling acidity.

★★★★ **Filia** ⓦ MCC bubbly from old-vine chenin. Oxidative bruised apple aromas on intriguing **15** ⑧⑦. Persistent varietal flavours but no typical development from 18 months on lees. Zero dosage, bone-dry. **14** ⑧⑦ also available.

The Hummingbird Colibri ⑲ ★★★★ Most unusual smoked meat notes mix with floral ones on characterful **17** ⑧⑤ bubbly from rare-in-SA Spanish grape maccabeo/viura with 30% chenin. Dry, stony & austere, with piquant appley acidity. WO Voor Paardeberg. **Circa** ★★★★ Lightly sparkling **NV** ⑧⑤ take on Italy's Prosecco; pinotage with 15% colombard. Charming pale partridge-eye colour & berry-rich notes. Lively, fresh & dry, with tart, tannin element. Like Filia, also 1.5L. — TJ, CvZ

Location: Malmesbury ▪ Map: Swartland ▪ Map grid reference: C8 ▪ WO: Swartland/Voor Paardeberg ▪ Est 1956 ▪ 1stB 2011 ▪ Tasting by appt only ▪ Closed most pub hols ▪ Fynbos & vineyard tours by appt ▪ Owner(s) Chevallerie (Pty) Ltd ▪ Cellarmaster(s)/winemaker(s) Christa von La Chevallerie ▪ Viticulturist(s) Christa von La Chevallerie, Rosa Kruger ▪ 20ha (ptage, chenin) ▪ 90% sparkling 10% other ▪ Nuwedam Paardeberg PO Box 185 Malmesbury 7299 ▪ info@huisvanchevallerie.com ▪ www.huisvanchevallerie.com ▪ S 33° 31' 31.15" E 018° 47' 15.06 ▪ ⧆ tinged.deciding.foreseeing ▪ **T +27 (0)87-550-1637**

Hunneyball Wines   ⓠ ⓗ ◎

Swedish transplants Jim Hunneyball and wife Marie own and run a luxury guest house in Stellenbosch town, make boutique quantities of wine from local grapes, and provide guided winetasting and cultural tours with a particular emphasis on promoting the top echelons of SA wine to visiting tourists.

Location/map: Stellenbosch ▪ Map grid reference: F5 ▪ Est 2012 ▪ 1stB 2011 ▪ Tasting by appt ▪ Guided wine/regional tours ▪ Hunneyball House 32 Herold Str Stellenbosch ▪ Winemaker(s) Jim & Marie Hunneyball ▪ 5t ▪ 100% red ▪ PO Box 795 Stellenbosch 7599 ▪ jim@africaninvite.com, marie@hunneyballhouse.com ▪ www.

africaninvite.com, www.hunneyballhouse.com ▪ S 33° 56′ 13.99″ E 018° 51′ 7.58″ ▪ ⌖ craft.shades.belonged
▪ T +27 (0)71-674-9379

☐ **Hunterspeak** *see* Niel Joubert Estate
☐ **Huntersville** *see* Valley Vineyards Wine Company
☐ **Hunting Family** *see* Slaley
☐ **Hutton Ridge** *see* Valley Vineyards Wine Company
☐ **Hypocrite** *see* Wazu Wine Merchants
☐ **Idelia** *see* Swartland Winery
☐ **Ideology** *see* Spier

Idiom Collection
ⓆⓎ◎

The Italian Bottega family continue to fine-tune their Helderberg mountainside winery, vineyards and visitor centre, home to the Idiom Collection and main grape source for sibling venture Whalehaven in Hermanus. They're introducing three new Idiom wines (including a locally unusual blend of Spanish grapes), marking the 10th anniversary of the 900 Series Cabernet exclusively for loyalty club members, and importing Italian expertise to update local vineyard staff on pruning techniques.

Idiom Collection

★★★★ **Malbec** ⓃⒺⓌ 2 vintages tasted, both big, ripe, full bodied. **14** ★★★ ⑧② overt mintiness with vanilla spicing, decidedly medicinal palate, big, unpolished tannins. **15** ⑧⑥ better modulated, with fresh mulberry & cherry fruit, strong oak spice, riper tannins.

★★★★ **Sangiovese** Opulent cherry fruit with tealeaf & sweet spices on impressive **15** ⑧⑨, reflecting fine vintage. Plush & supple, lithe & silky, showing good varietal definition.

★★★★ **Cabernet Sauvignon-Merlot-Cabernet Franc-Petit Verdot** Compelling Bordeaux blend, **14** ★★★★★ ⑨① shows balance, intensity & silky texture. Subtle, with earthy nuances, generous blackcurrant fruit. 14 months French oak, 40% new. Elegant step up on **13** ⑧⑦.

★★★★★ **Cape Blend** Bold & forthright **14** ★★★★ ⑧⑧, pinotage, cab & merlot with dash shiraz is fruit-led, with meaty-leathery aromatic tones. Red & black berries, maraschino cherries, borne on pervasive tannin base. Less knit than **13** ⑨②.

★★★★ **Semillon** ⓃⒺⓌ Accomplished barrel-fermented **15** ⑧⑧ has enticing varietal lanolin & wet pebbles; also-reviewed **16** ★★★★ ⑧⑤ lighter, still showing oak aromas. Both are mineral & crisp.

★★★★ **Viognier** Barrel-fermented & aged **16** ⑧⑨ shows aromatic oak spices with solid, intact peach-fruit core touched by ginger. Leesy & textural, with elegant lengthy finish.

Shiraz-Mourvèdre-Viognier ★★★★ Sweet aromatic tobacco & oak spices to the fore in **14** ⑧④, with ripe plummy fruit somewhat overwhelmed. **Grenache-Tempranillo** ⓃⒺⓌ ★★★★ Strident minty-medicinal tones detract somewhat on **15** ⑧③ Spanish pairing. Fresh & juicy, with reined-in tannins. Alcohol a bold 15.5%. Not tasted: **Barbera, Nebbiolo, Zinfandel**.

900 Series

★★★★ **Barbera** Meaty, aromatic **15** ⑧⑦ shows opulently ripe fruit, brawny body, but less varietal definition. Rich oak spices, supple & juicy, with firm tannin grip.

★★★★☆ **Nebbiolo** Persuasive, elegant interpretation of the great Piedmont variety, **15** ⑨① still shows heavy oak influence (50% new), but refined red fruit spiced with tomato essence, shines through. Thick tannin mantle needs time to knit & soften. Also-tasted **14** ⑨⓪ similar but less bright, more integrated.

Not tasted: **Cabernet Franc, Mourvèdre, Sangiovese**.

Heritage Series

Rosso di Stellenbosch ★★★★ Rhubarb & tomato paste notes on cheerful, juicy **16** ⑧④. Sangiovese with 3% barbera. **Bianco di Stellenbosch** ★★★★ Stellenbosch pinot gris provides light & refreshing sipping in **17** ⑧③, showing tinned pears with a hint of anise. — GdB

Location: Sir Lowry's Pass ▪ Map: Helderberg ▪ Map grid reference: H7 ▪ WO: Stellenbosch ▪ Est 1999/1stB 2003/4 ▪ Tasting & sales Tue-Sun 10-5 and Restaurant Tue-Sun 11-5 (see website for extended hours in summer) ▪ Wine tasting & canapés; food & wine experience; deli & restaurant ▪ Fynbos perfumery & imported Vinotria Italian wine library ▪ 'Italia in Campagna' harvest festival (Feb/Mar) ▪ Owner(s) Bottega family ▪ Winemaker(s) Reino Thiart ▪ 35ha (barbera, cabs s/f, merlot, mourv, nebbiolo, p verdot, ptage, sangio, shiraz, zin, sauv, sem, viog) ▪ 85% red 15% white ▪ PO Box 3802 Somerset West 7129 ▪ info@bottegafamilywine.co.za ▪ www.idiom.co.za, www.bottegafamilywine.co.za ▪ S 34° 6' 17.25" E 018° 56' 26.11" ▪ coolest.operate.reclassify ▪ F +27 (0)21-851-5891 (sales) ▪ **T +27 (0)21-858-1088 (tasting/restaurant)/+27 (0)21-852-3590 (distribution/sales)**

Idun (NEW)

Idun is the Norse goddess of eternal youth, which is why Albert Rousset, a Mauritian of French-Danish descent, named his Elgin farm after her. He says a late midlife crisis at 50, after he'd had a successful career in apparel, pushed him to embark on his dream journey, winemaking. 'Idun allows me to express myself through every bottle created. She is my personal renaissance and she will guide you on your quest for yours.'

Sauvignon Blanc ★★★ Gooseberry & passionfruit in expressive **17** (82), shows good typicity, fresh & lively, exactly what you'd expect from sauvignon, some minerality on the finish. Not tasted: **Merlot**, **Syrah**, **Chardonnay**. — CR, CvZ

Location: Elgin ▪ WO: Cape South Coast ▪ Closed to public ▪ Owner(s) Albert & Joanne Rousset ▪ Winemaker(s) Kobie Viljoen (consultant) ▪ info@idunwines.co.za ▪ www.idun.co.za

illimis Wines (Q)

In the four years of producing her illimis wines, brand owner and winemaker Lucinda Heyns has sourced fruit from the same single parcels. 'It's a privilege to work with the same vines year-in, year-out,' she says, noting that with each vintage she not only gains a better understanding of each site but appreciates better the impact of the varied characteristics of each growing cycle on the wines. Her intention to make wines that are a window to the vineyard is resonating, and production is up 50%.

★★★★ Cinsault Serious wine despite light colour & alcohol (12.5%), **17** (89) bone-dry with vibrant cherry fruit, supple tannins from 60% carbonic maceration, 40% bunch ferment.

★★★★ Chenin Blanc Repeats successful formula of subtly savoury **16** (86) with effective but gentle acidity, **17 ★★★★★** (90) reined-in alcohol (13.5%) for better balance, bone-dryness without austerity. Neutral oak fermentation, WO Elgin.

★★★★ Riesling Tight & taut **17** (89), a wine requiring hand-selling given it departs from the norm with more texture, breadth & weight. Bunch press, spontaneous ferment in old barrels, giving wonderful umami appeal.— CvZ

Location: Somerset West ▪ WO: Darling/Elgin ▪ Est/1stB 2015 ▪ Tasting by appt ▪ Owner(s)/winemaker(s) Lucinda Heyns ▪ 940cs ▪ lucinda@illimiswines.com ▪ www.illimiswines.com ▪ **T +27 (0)84-370-4282**

Imbuko Wines (Q)(¶¶)(◎)

Winemakers and entrepreneurs don't necessarily inhabit the same body, but Imbuko Wines' Theunis van Zyl is an exception. He and his family in the past 15 years have built a dynamic, hugely successful wine business (see production figures below), with numerous export brands and markets, on the principle of listening to customers and adjusting styles, packaging etc accordingly. At deceptively tranquil Wellington home-farm Uitkyk, they're expanding warehouse space to accommodate growth, and planning to continue with their winning recipe, which includes 'making wine fun'.

Du Plevaux Private Collection

Jean Prieur Pinotage ★★★ Soft, 'creamy' aromas of dark fruit & mocha contrast with still-firm tannins in **15** (82), needing more time to fully integrate. WO Wellington, as all this range. **Daniël Johannes Shiraz ★★★★** Dense dark berries on a savoury backbone, delicious spicy note on the finish of improved **15** (84). Barrel ageing for these reds, all others oak staving unless noted. **Madeleine Menanteau Sauvignon Blanc ★★★** Shy tropical aromas joined by more extrovert flavours of citrus peel, **18** (81) concludes on snappy, zesty note. Preview tasted, as next. **Elizabeth Albertha Chenin Blanc-Viognier ★★★** High-toned perfume & fresh orchard-fruit flavours, **18** (82) tasty if somewhat subdued version of the Hidden Gem we sampled last time.

Van Zijl Family Vintners range

★★★★ **Reserve Blue Ink Cabernet Sauvignon** ⓥ Full-bodied, fruit-forward **15** ⑧⑦'s cassis & violet attractions are well supported by serious oaking; drinks well now, will reward few years ageing.

Chardonnay-Viognier ⓟ ★★★ Creamy baked apple, vibrant fresh stonefruit & sprinkle of spice (though unwooded), **18** ⑧① delightful, softly dry summer white.

Cabernet Sauvignon ★★★ Easy **16** ⑧⓪, gentle berry fruit flavours & touch of vanilla. Few grams sugar aid drinkability, as reds in all ranges. **Coffee Pinotage** ★★★ Advertised espresso aromas waft from the **17** ⑧① glass, joined on palate by plummy fruit flavours. **Pinotage** ★★★ Gluggable bright berries, cocoa & pleasantly grippy tannins in **16** ⑦⑨. **Shiraz-Mourvèdre** ★★★ Just a smidgen of mourvèdre this time, giving earthy, spicy nuances to juicy mulberry fruit. **16** ⑦⑨ smooth everyday red - in magnum too. **Bushvine Chenin Blanc** ★★★ Fragrant tropical fruit salad before guava-toned flavours, **18** ⑦⑨ lighter (12% alcohol) & leaner than last. **Sauvignon Blanc** ★★ Trim-figured **18** ⑦⑤, demure greengage & green plum notes, lemon/lime goodbye.

Imbuko range

Cabernet Sauvignon ⓥ ★★★ Bright red berries in harmony with gentle vanilla oak in **16** ⑦⑦. **Merlot** ⓥ ★★★ Soft & easy **17** ⑦⑦, crunchy cranberry flavours & warm Xmas spices courtesy combo French/ American oak. **Iswithi Pinotage** ⓥ ★★★ Sweet, plump, ripe plums, suggestions of coffee & nutmeg in lightish, unoaked **16** ⑦⑧, to serve lightly chilled. **Chenin Blanc** ★★ Playful & easy **18** ⑦④ offers lively pineapple & passionfruit flavours. **Sauvignon Blanc** ★★ Firm acid on light, reticent, citrus-toned **18** ⑦④.

Pomüla range

Moscato Spumante ⓥ ★★★ Perlé low-alcohol **NV** ⑦⑧ from muscats d'Alexandrie & de Frontignan with funky label. Grapey froth to get the party started. — WB

Location/map: Wellington ▪ Map grid reference: B4 ▪ WO: Western Cape/Wellington ▪ Est/1stB 2004 ▪ Tasting Mon-Fri 9-5 Sat/pub hols 9-2 ▪ Fee R30/5 wines ▪ Sales 8-5 ▪ Closed Easter weekend, Dec 25 & Jan 1 ▪ Cellar tours by appt only ▪ Food & wine pairing by appt ▪ Farm produce ▪ Owner(s) Imbuko Wines (Pty) Ltd ▪ Cellarmaster(s) Theunis van Zyl (2004) ▪ Viticulturist(s) Jan-Louw du Plessis ▪ 60ha (cab, cinsaut, merlot, ptage, shiraz, chenin, sauv, viog) ▪ 570,000cs own label 60% red 40% white ▪ Other export brands: Barrel Selection 008, Fat Barrel, King Shaka, Kleine Kaap, Makulu, Rebourne Fairtrade & Releaf Organic ▪ Fairtrade, IPW, ISO, Organic ▪ PO Box 810 Wellington 7654 ▪ wines@imbuko.co.za ▪ www.imbuko.co.za ▪ S 33° 40′ 30.84′ E 019° 01′ 18.87′ ▪ ⏏ bonanza.conceding.clinch ▪ **T +27 (0)21-873-7350**

☐ **Imoya** see KWV Brandies
☐ **Indaba** see Cape Classics
☐ **Indwe** see Trizanne Signature Wines
☐ **Infiniti** see Stellenbosch Vineyards
☐ **Infused by Earth** see Eikendal Vineyards
☐ **Ingenuity** see Nederburg Wines
☐ **Inkará** see Bon Courage Estate
☐ **Integer** see Hoopenburg Wines

Intellego Wines

ⓥ

Among the cohort of Swartland vintners pushing the envelope on non-interventionist winemaking is Jurgen Gouws, ex Lammershoek, building his Intellego ('Understanding') brand since 2014. He collaborates with growers of select vineyards, renting space in a Perdeberg cellar. His collection, with labels as fun and funky as his website, is growing and 2019 will deliver an as yet unnamed skin-contact viognier.

Location: Malmesbury ▪ Est/1stB 2009 ▪ Tasting by appt ▪ Owner(s)/winemaker(s) Jurgen Gouws ▪ 2,000cs own label 40% red 60% white ▪ jurgen@intellegowines.co.za ▪ **T +27 (0)82-392-3258**

☐ **Intulo** see Kumala

Iona Vineyards

Back in 1997, when there was still comparatively little wine-life in Elgin, Andrew Gunn farsightedly bought an old apple property and planted vineyards. The home farm is on Elgin's coolest ridge, and there are two others, including Brocha, belonging to Andrew's wife, Rozy. There's been much development in the last two decades and, as Andrew says, 'Iona continues to improve, refine and re-invent' – including significant new equipment for Werner Muller's cellar, and working with viticulturist Jaco Engelbrecht. And the next generation advances, as Andrew's son Richard joins the marketing team. Meanwhile Brad Gold comes in as general manager, with Andrew moving to a supportive 'chairman' role. The philosophy remains simple: 'Maximum care by hand in the vineyard, minimum manipulation and additives in the cellar.'

Iona Vineyards range

★★★★ Pinot Noir ⊘ Forward, generous aromas on **15** ★★★★☆ ⑨1 (dark cherry, some forest floor, even a touch of dark chocolate). Similarly rich, flavourful palate with sweet, even bold fruit, given form by slight tannin & fresh acidity, supported by judicious oaking (15% new). **14** ⑧8 was a touch awkward.

★★★★ One Man Band Ripely fruity, spicy aromas on **13** ★★★★☆ ⑨1, with added complexity from bottle age. Two thirds shiraz plus 5 other varieties. Big wine, but 14.5% alcohol in balance with savoury-sweet fullness. Dry finish comes with reprise of aroma's berry notes. Better constructed than **12** ⑧7.

★★★★☆ Chardonnay ☆ Rich, intense aromas & flavours on **17** ⑨3 yet not without characteristic elegance, thanks to the convincing balance between fruit & structure - notably the fine acidity off cool Iona vineyards. Oak support vital for complexity, but invisible.

★★★★☆ 8+8 Riesling ⒩ The numbers in the name refer to sugar & acid in g/l on **17** ⑨0 - & the thrill of that poised balance is at the vinous core here, with the spicy peach fruit as flesh. Natural ferment in mix steel & older oak. Youthful; should benefit from a good few years harmonising in bottle.

★★★★☆ Barrel Fermented Sauvignon Blanc ⒩ ☆ The fruitiness more muted, the savoury complexity increased on **17** ⑨4 compared with unoaked version. Oak (20% new) not directly obvious but adding breadth & deeper interest. Citric acidity carries the flavours to a lingering, bone-dry conclusion.

★★★★☆ Sauvignon Blanc ☆ Exuberant aromas introduce **17** ⑨3 - blackcurrant & citrus notes with a savoury green element complement the tropical ripeness on the palate. A dollop (unoaked) semillon adds to breadth & complexity, while a vibrant acid enlivens the whole.

★★★★☆ One Man Band White ☆ Cool-climate sauvignon's aromatic blackcurrant apparent on **16** ⑨4) blend with 48% semillon (less than previously) hinting at beeswax & lemon. Typical lively, succulent freshness. Natural ferment in old oak contributes to breadth & texture.

Not tasted: **Solace Syrah**.

Husk Spirit range

Corretto ⓠ **★★★** From cab & merlot; light amber hue, playful label, fragrant black-fruit perfume; alcohol quite prominent - perhaps better to 'correct' your shot with an espresso. — TJ, WB

Location/map/WO: Elgin ▪ Map grid reference: C4 ▪ Est 1997 ▪ 1stB 2001 ▪ Tasting, sales & tours Mon-Fri 8–5 Sat by appt ▪ Closed all pub hols ▪ Walks/hikes ▪ MTB ▪ Conservation area ▪ Owner(s) Andrew & Rozanne Gunn, Workers Trust ▪ Winemaker(s) Werner Muller (May 2011), with Thapelo Hlasa (Jun 1997) & Bobby Wallace (May 2017) ▪ Vineyard manager(s) Joseph Sebulawa & Bobby Wallace (May 2017) ▪ Viticulturist(s) Jaco Engelbrecht (consultant) ▪ 100ha/40ha (cab, merlot, mourv, p verdot, pinot, shiraz, chard, sauv) ▪ 250t/24,000cs own label 25% red 75% white ▪ PO Box 527 Grabouw 7160 ▪ orders@iona.co.za ▪ www.iona. co.za ▪ S 34° 16' 42.2" E 019° 4' 58.2" ▪ ⓦ refills.hikers.androids ▪ F +27 (0)86-627-8960 ▪ **T +27 (0)28-284-9678**

☐ **Italian Collection** *see* Morgenster Estate
☐ **Iwayini** *see* Maiden Wine Cellars
☐ **Ixia** *see* Theuniskraal

Izak van der Vyver Wines

Approaching a third decade of boutique winemaking, local general practitioner Izak van der Vyver's passion for Elgin sauvignon is undimmed, his new vintage sourced from a mountain block behind the home of his friend Paul Cluver, in whose cellar he vinifies.

★★★★ **Limited Release Sauvignon Blanc** ⊘ Gorgeously fragrant tropical & green herb aromas & flavour on elegant **17** (89). Rounded, full, courtesy long lees ageing. Balanced racy-fresh finish.— WB

Location/WO: Elgin ▪ 1stB 2002 ▪ Closed to public ▪ Owner(s) Izak van der Vyver ▪ Cellarmaster(s) Andries Burger (Paul Cluver Wines) ▪ Winemaker(s) Izak van der Vyver (Jan 2002) ▪ 1.4t/±166cs own label ▪ PO Box 42 Grabouw 7160 ▪ drs@telkomsa.net ▪ F +27 (0)21-859-3607 ▪ **T +27 (0)21-859-2508**

J9 Wine   ⓺ ⓴ 🆕

'The J9 challenge is for everyone to go out and live their 9 lives and do the 9 things they have always wanted to do,' says CEO/founder Janine Petersen, a single mother who believes 'anything is possible through hard work and perseverance'. Having gained experience in wine-making, -marketing and -distribution alongside several 'big names', who continue to support her, she sources from across the winelands.

Merlot ★★★ Welcomely modest alcohol on ready-now & cheerful **15** (82), chocolate, black plum & some cured meat savouriness. **Merlot-Cabernet Sauvignon** ★★★ Less fruit-rich than Merlot, but **14** (80) convincing blackcurrant & oak spice notes, firmer tannins from 22% cab component. WO W Cape. **Chenin Blanc** ⊘ ★★★★ Pleasing, slightly salty dry white for lunchtimes, **16** (83) understated stonefruit & thatch contrasting with exuberant palate. WO Coastal. **Sauvignon Blanc** ★★★ Dusty & stony flavours, **17** (81) easygoing & refreshing, rounded acidity & faint grassy aromas. — GdB, CvZ

Location/map: Stellenbosch ▪ Map grid reference: E1 ▪ WO: Stellenbosch/Coastal/Western Cape ▪ Est 2016 ▪ 1stB 2017 ▪ Tasting Mon-Fri 9-5 Sat 9-2 ▪ Fee R45pp ▪ Closed Easter Sat/Sun, Dec 25 & Jan 1 ▪ Food pairing, chocolate & biltong pairing ▪ Owner(s) Janine Petersen ▪ info@j9wine.com ▪ www.j9wine.com ▪ S 33° 49' 33.4" E 018° 49' 9.3" ▪ **T +27 (0)21-884-4221/+27 (0)74-701-0000**

☐ **Jack Parow Brandy** see Parow Brandy

Jacobsdal   ⓺

This family-owned Stellenbosch property sees third-generation Cornelis Dumas (winemaker for over half a century) and son Hannes vinifying just two wines themselves off their substantial vineyards. The two enduring reds, from dryland bushvines, are fermented in traditional open concrete tanks, using wild yeasts. The results are modest in the best sense: lightish, elegant and eminently drinkable. From 2019, the home team are taking over their own marketing, which had been handled by Distell for some time.

★★★★ **Cabernet Sauvignon** Unshowy, quietly classic. Blackcurrant & cigarbox on well & restrainedly structured **15** (87). Naturally & traditionally made. Will mature yet.

Pinotage ⓺ ★★★ Unusually light-coloured **14** (81) has charming red-fruited perfume over darker notes. Lightness of fruit is rather elegant, but substantial dry tannins a little unbalanced. — TJ

Location/map/WO: Stellenbosch ▪ Map grid reference: B6 ▪ Est 1916 ▪ 1stB 1974 ▪ Tasting on the farm by appt only ▪ Owner(s) Dumas Ondernemings (Pty) Ltd ▪ Cellarmaster(s) Cornelis Dumas ▪ Winemaker(s)/viticul-turist(s) Cornelis Dumas, with Hannes Dumas ▪ 73ha (cab, merlot, ptage, chenin, sauv) ▪ 300t/10,000cs own label 100% red ▪ PO Box 11 Kuils River 7579 ▪ info@jacobsdal.co.za ▪ www.jacobsdal.co.za ▪ S 33° 58' 4.9" E 018° 43' 34.6" ▪ 🖭 coupler.triumphing.palatial ▪ **T +27 (0)21-881-3336**

☐ **Jacoline Haasbroek Wines** see My Wyn
☐ **Jacques Bruére** see Bon Courage Estate

Jacques Germanier   ⓺ ⓴ 🏠 ◎

A pioneer (as 'African Terroir') of sustainable farming in SA, Swiss-owned Jacques Germanier aims to 'delight people with our wines while sharing the important concerns of organic and Fairtrade standards'. The awarded wines, in bespoke packaging, are offered for tasting at the brand home, Sonop Farm near Paarl, along with conference and function facilities, accommodation and cinematic views.

Organic range
Sonop Cabernet Sauvignon-Merlot ⓺ ⊘ ★★★ Cherries, raisins & dark chocolate on **15** (82). Dense & forthright, with chalky texture, rather abrupt finish. **Sonop Chardonnay-Sauvignon Blanc** ⓺ ⊘ ★★★ Unoaked, early-drinking **16** (80) shows barley sugar with honey melon, soft acidity. Pleasing lees

texture. Not tasted: **Winds of Change Cabernet Sauvignon-Merlot-Shiraz, Winds of Change Chardonnay-Sauvignon Blanc-Viognier**. — GdB

Location/map: Paarl ▪ Map grid reference: C1 ▪ WO: Western Cape ▪ Est/1stB 1991 ▪ Tasting & cellar tours by appt ▪ Lunch available for larger groups on request - to book ahead ▪ Conferences ▪ Functions ▪ Conservation area ▪ Guest house ▪ Owner(s) Sophie Germanier ▪ Winemaker(s) Jaco Marais (Nov 2012) ▪ Viticulturist(s) AJ de Beers (Jan 2017) ▪ 75ha organic vineyards (cab, merlot, ptage, shiraz, chard, sauv, viog) ▪ Brands for clients: Azania, Bag in Box Collection, Cape Soleil, Jacques Germanier (Organic), Landela, Milton Grove, Out of Africa, Sonop (Organic), The Big 5, Tribal, Winds of Change (Organic) ▪ IPW, Organic ▪ PO Box 2029 Windmeul Paarl 7630 ▪ admin@germanier.co.za ▪ www.germanier.co.za ▪ S 33° 37' 1.8" E 018° 50' 38.4" ▪ ⟨m⟩ ultimate.dimension.consults ▪ **T +27 (0)21-869-8103**

Jacques Smit Wines ⓆⓂⒶ

Only two wines tasted this edition, but they are of particular importance to Wellington-based vine nursery-man and vintner Jacques Smit. Both from rare red-fleshed local variety roobernet, a 1950s crossing by prof Chris Orffer of cabernet and alicante bouschet, but released onto the market only four decades later. Jacques loves port-style wines, and he rates the LBV over the Vintage, saying the latter is best served with ice.

Limited Releases

Cabernet Sauvignon Ⓠ ★★★★ Juicy & appealing **07** (84) easygoing mealtime companion. **Vine Valley** Ⓠ ★★★★ Boldly fruited **06** (84) blend cab (67%) & shiraz nicely integrated, pleasing firm handshake. **Cape Late Bottled Vintage Roobernet** ★★★★ 'Port' from uncommon red variety, **08** (84) forthcoming, almost pruney fruitcake intensity, cinnamon & nutmeg dusting from different size barrels. Full-sweet & curvy, scarcely showing its age. Retasted, as next. **Cape Vintage Roobernet** ★★★ Unoaked, dark-fruited **11** (77) shows some maturity year later. Smoky, treacly flavours, not as layered as LBV. Serve on crushed ice as winemaker suggests. 375 ml for these fortifieds. Not tasted: **Shiraz**. — CR

Location/map/WO: Wellington ▪ Map grid reference: B3 ▪ Est/1stB 2003 ▪ Tasting, sales & tours by appt ▪ Closed Easter Fri/Sun/Mon, Ascension day, Dec 25/26 & Jan 1 ▪ Facilities for children ▪ Wellington Wine Walk ▪ Owner(s) Jacques & Marina Smit ▪ Cellarmaster(s)/winemaker(s)/viticulturist(s) Jacques Smit ▪ 60ha/32ha (cab, roobernet, shiraz, Cape riesling, chenin) ▪ 300t total 100% red ▪ Welvanpas PO Box 137 Wellington 7654 ▪ info@vines2wine.com ▪ www.vines2wine.com ▪ S 33° 39' 2.2" E 019° 1' 9.0" ▪ ⟨m⟩ teachers.submits.lipstick ▪ F +27 (0)21-873-2143 ▪ **T +27 (0)21-873-1265**

☐ **Jailbreak** *see* Mountain Ridge Wines
☐ **Jakkalskloof** *see* Wine-of-the-Month Club

Jakkalsvlei Private Cellar ⓆⓇⒶⒶ

Jantjie Jonker's 25,000 cases of own-label wine take the name of the family farm and the many foxes and jackal in these Langeberg foothills near Herbertsdale village on the Garden Route. Lord Jackal is a limited-release label sold only at the multi-attraction cellardoor, while Jackal Lager and Wolf Ale fashionably extend the theme and brand presence into the craft beer arena.

Location: Herbertsdale ▪ Map: Klein Karoo & Garden Route ▪ Map grid reference: C5 ▪ Est 1987 ▪ 1stB 2008 ▪ Tasting & sales Mon-Sun 10-4 ▪ Restaurant ▪ Deli ▪ Conferences ▪ Facilities for children ▪ Walks/hikes ▪ Pick your own hanepoot ▪ Music festival ▪ MTB & trail run event ▪ Craft beer: Jackal Lager & Wolf Ale ▪ Owner(s)/viticulturist(s) Jantjie Jonker ▪ Cellarmaster(s) Jantjie & Andrew Jonker ▪ 80ha/26ha (cab, merlot, muscadel r, ptage, chenin, hanepoot, sauv) ▪ 350t/25,000cs ▪ PO Box 79 Herbertsdale 6505 ▪ info@jakkalsvlei.co.za ▪ www.jakkalsvlei.co.za ▪ S 33° 59' 15.31" E 021° 43' 9.33" ▪ ⟨m⟩ outcomes.smiles.married ▪ F +27 (0)86-593-0123 ▪ **T +27 (0)44-333-0222**

Jakob's Vineyards Ⓠ

In 2001, Johannesburgers André and Yvonne de Lange fell in love with and bought this small farm in the Hemel-en-Aarde. They planted a hectare of cabernet (a rare variety in this cooler area) but are also re-establishing renosterveld vegetation. Nothing new to taste this edition, but André promises wine for next year.

★★★★ **Cabernet Sauvignon** Ⓠ Tobacco notes on ripe, dark-berried aromas of maturing but still youthful **12** (88). Serious wine, firm tannic structure but some juiciness too. Doesn't show 14.5% alcohol.

★★★★ **Cabernet Franc** ② Deep-coloured, ripe **12** (88) has refined berry aromas & hints of varietal spice & dried leaf. More complex & supple than the Cab, but less harmonious, with warming finish.— TJ

Location: Hermanus ▪ Map: Walker Bay & Bot River ▪ Map grid reference: C4 ▪ WO: Hemel-en-Aarde Ridge ▪ Est 2002 ▪ 1stB 2006 ▪ Tasting by appt ▪ Wine & olive products available via online shop ▪ Owner(s) André & Yvonne de Lange ▪ Farm manager Peter Davison ▪ Winemaker(s) Peter-Allan Finlayson (2010, consultant) ▪ Viticulturist(s) Johan Pienaar (Jun 2003, consultant) ▪ 5ha/1ha (cab) ▪ 5t/±500cs own label 100% red ▪ PO Box 15885 Vlaeberg 8018 ▪ wine@jakobsvineyards.co.za ▪ www.jakobsvineyards.co.za ▪ S 34° 19' 43.48" E 019° 19' 46.41" ▪ ⬚ tones.unplugging.accruing ▪ F +27 (0)86-589-4619 ▪ **T +27 (0)82-371-5686**

☐ **Jam Jar** *see* Cape Classics

Jan Harmsgat ⓆⓎⓐ◎

The unusual name of this large Robertson farm on the Langeberg foothills seems to be a corruption of the original (1723) 'Jan Harmansz Schat', meaning the 'treasure' of its founding owner. Wine (made by Lourens van der Westhuizen of Arendsig) is a small part of agricultural production here, and there are also luxury accommodation, functions facilities and a restaurant.

JHG Wine Collection

★★★★ **Chardonnay** Characterful **16** (86) offers pleasing ripe yellow peach notes. Very well balanced, good acid thread & light oaking contributing to rich velvet texture. More intensity than **15** ★★★★ (84).

★★★★ **Chenin Blanc** Rich & flavourful, light gold **17** (87) has notes of ripe, bruised apple along with apricot. Good natural acid beautifully poised. Usual modest, unobtrusive oaking.

★★★★ **Sauvignon Blanc** Beguiling, harmonious **17** (87) delivers passionfruit aromas & plenty of flavour. Good texture, grippy but unaggressive succulence. Natural ferment, minimal intervention, as all.

Cabernet Sauvignon ★★★★ Fresh, pure, ripe fruit aromas & flavours on **16** (85), old oak playing just a supportive role. Lightly but effectively structured to allow for easy, early drinkability. **Pinotage** ★★★★ Attractive, lifted varietal aromas on **16** (85) lead to rich, flavourful palate & sweetly lingering finish. Generous & friendly, with the gentlest of tannic grips. **Shiraz** ★★★★ Fresh varietal aromas & delicious sweet fruit on **16** (83). Very light in feel, though tasty, & with prominent acidity. — TJ

Location: Bonnievale ▪ Map/WO: Robertson ▪ Map grid reference: C2 ▪ Est 1723 ▪ Tasting & sales Mon-Sun 8-5 ▪ Fee R30 ▪ Open all year round ▪ 5-star Country Guest Lodge & Restaurant ▪ Gift shop ▪ Farm produce ▪ Conferences ▪ Walks/hikes ▪ MTB trail ▪ Heritage property ▪ Vineyard tours; farm & nature 4x4 tour ▪ Owner(s) XH Mkhwanazi/AH Kleinhans-Curd ▪ Winemaker(s) Lourens van der Westhuizen (Jan 2011, consultant) ▪ Viticulturist(s) Kowie Smit (Dec 2012, consultant) ▪ 625.05ha/16.35ha (cab, ptage, pinot, shiraz, chard, sauv, viog) ▪ 260t/3,300cs own label 65% red 35% white ▪ IPW, Global Gap, Siza, WIETA ▪ PO Box 161 Swellendam 6740 ▪ wine@janharmsgat.com ▪ www.janharmsgat.com ▪ S 33° 56' 48" E 020° 12' 58" ▪ ⬚ validates.understudy.ungraded ▪ F +27 (0)86-523-9284 ▪ **T +27 (0)23-616-3407**

JAN Wines Ⓠ

SA's culinary pride, and proud South African Jan Hendrik van der Westhuizen, of Michelin-starred establishment JAN in Nice, collaborates with vintner Frank Meaker at Swartland's organic Org de Rac winery on a select 6,000 bottles of each of two Mediterranean blends. To be found through his website, at JAN itself and its adjoining new dining-room MARIA, honouring maternal forebears.

★★★★☆ **Syrah-Grenache-Mourvèdre-Verdelho** ⓥ A barrel selection, as next, excellent **16** (90) fynbos-tinged red fruit, black spices & firm tannin. Oak (50% new, 12 months) obvious in vanilla, cinnamon & clove tones. Majority shiraz (66%) gets freshness via unexpected dash white grape verdelho.

Verdelho-Roussanne-Chenin Blanc ⓥ ★★★★ Verdelho at 51% in **17** (85), perfumed white flowers, peach & vanilla from 20% new oak, which tad dominant mid-2018. Rich & broad yet salinity & acid enliven the whole. — HC, CvZ

WO: Swartland ▪ Tasting for groups & sales at Org de Rac (see entry) ▪ Wines also available online ▪ Owner(s) Jan Hendrik van der Westhuizen ▪ Cellarmaster(s) Frank Meaker (Org de Rac) ▪ Winemaker(s) Jurgen Siebritz (Org de Rac) ▪ pro@orgderac.co.za ▪ www.janhendrik.com ▪ **T +27 (0)22-913-2397**

☐ **Jardin** *see* Jordan Wine Estate

☐ **Jason's Creek** *see* Jason's Hill Private Cellar

Jason's Hill Private Cellar

⊘ ⑪ ◎ ⑤ ♿

For five generations the Du Toit family were grape farmers on this 100-ha Rawsonville property - until the sixth generation: daughter Ivy showed an expertise in winemaking, so a cellar was built. There's now enough going on, both wine and other attractions, not least of which is spectacular Slanghoek mountain scenery, for a steady stream of visitors.

Jason's Hill range

★★★★ Cabernet Sauvignon ⊘ Pristine cassis, lead pencil & polished leather on supple tannin frame. **15** ⑧⑦ complex & savoury, ageworthy. Improves on **13 ★★★** ⑧②. No **14**.

★★★★ Izak Reserve All 5 Bordeaux red varieties, but unusually **15** ⑧⑦ equal petit verdot/cab franc-led. Graphite, scrub, earthiness the fruit, 18 months oak (80% new) showing serious intent. Needs time.

★★★★ Beatrix Chenin Blanc ⑯④ Named after 19th-century pioneering woman farmer. Hungarian oak 14 months gives ginger biscuit tones to the citrus, **16** ⑧⑨ ends dry, taut, almost austere but in a sophisticated way.

Merlot ★★★ Vanilla & bright red berries, **16** ⑦⑧'s perfume draws you in, but firm dry tannins need more time, will reward bottle ageing. Or match with rich dishes. **Shiraz ★★★** Nice combo vivid fruit & oak seasoning in **15** ⑧① vanilla & sweet spice, tannins end dry, no barrier to enjoyment.

Jason's Creek range

Not tasted: **Classic Red**. — CR

Location: Rawsonville ▪ Map/WO: Breedekloof ▪ Map grid reference: A5 ▪ Est/1stB 2001 ▪ Tasting & sales Mon-Fri 8–5 Sat 10-3 ▪ Bistro Mon-Sat 10–3 (also available for functions) ▪ Shop ▪ Facilities for children ▪ Weddings/functions ▪ 6.5km hiking trail ▪ Owner(s) Du Toit family ▪ Cellarmaster(s) Ivy du Toit (Jan 2001) ▪ Viticulturist(s) Alister Oates (Jan 2004) ▪ 100ha ▪ 45% red 55% white ▪ PO Box 14 Rawsonville 6845 ▪ info@jasonshill.co.za ▪ www.jasonshill.co.za ▪ S 33° 39' 52.3" E 019° 13' 40.6" ▪ ⌨ chilled.armbands.wiper ▪ **T +27 (0)23-344-3256**

Jasper Raats Single Vineyard Wines

⊘

Longridge cellarmaster Jasper Raats, who spent seven years in New Zealand working with sauvignon blanc and pinot noir from various origins, believes that the fruit of a single vineyard planted with a single variety and vinified naturally produces the purest expression of terroir. Accordingly, he invested considerable time on his return to SA identifying suitable sites. With the exception of the pinot noir, his wines reflect the name of the vineyards where they are grown.

★★★★☆ Die Plek Cinsault ⊘ From 40+ year old Helderberg vines, naturally fermented (as all these wines), older oak 13 months. **16** ⑨② wonderfully poised & delicate, with considerable presence - at just 12.3% alcohol - courtesy regal tannin frame, acid backbone. Less fragrant than **15** ⑨① but just as fine.

★★★★ Cuvée Rika Pinot Noir From Elgin, **16** ⑧⑥ at first appears simply fruity but there's presence, too, courtesy fine tannins, bright seam of acidity & lifted 14.8% alcohol. Beautifully dry, for food, with modest oak support. 1.5L.

★★★★ Driefontein Syrah ⑯ Masterly, if uncompromising mid-2018, tannins, well-judged acidity, compact cassis & liquorice-toned blue fruit, **15 ★★★★★** ⑨③ has power & structure to reward the patient. Savoury toned, despite fruitiness & 15% (well-managed) alcohol, unlike vanilla-laced **14** ⑧⑨.

★★★★ Driefontein Sauvignon Blanc ⊘ Single-vineyard fruit bunch-pressed, old barrel fermented/10 months, which tempers acidity, adds signature creamy texture. **16** ⑧⑦ back on track after **15 ★★★★☆** ⑧④, with Loire-like yellow fruit tones. Also in 1.5L. — CvZ

Location: Stellenbosch ▪ Map: Helderberg ▪ Map grid reference: C1 ▪ WO: Stellenbosch/Elgin ▪ Est 2010 ▪ 1stB 2011 ▪ Tasting & sales Mon-Sat 10-5 (last tasting at 4.30) ▪ Closed Easter Fri/Mon, Dec 25/26 & Jan 1 ▪ Owner(s) Vigneron Consulting Ltd ▪ Winemaker(s)/viticulturist(s) Jasper Raats (2010) ▪ 2ha (pinot, sauv) ▪ 13t/1,700cs own label 60% red 40% white ▪ info@jasperraats.co.za ▪ www.jasperraats.co.za ▪ S 34° 0' 55.2" E 018° 49' 60.0" ▪ ⌨ flows.habitats.recliners ▪ F +27 (0)21-855-4083 ▪ **T +27 (0)76-752-5270**

☐ **Jasper Wickens** *see* JC Wickens Wines

☐ **JC le Roux** *see* The House of JC le Roux

JC Wickens Wines

The youthful Wickens pair, Jasper (winemaker, as he is also at AA Badenhorst) and Franziska (viticulturist), have renovated a century-old cellar on Waterval, the Paardeberg farm of Franziska's family: 'The first time in 70 years with wine inside!' Not much yet, but volumes (and exports) are growing, and the quality is superb, all in accordance with the hands-off principles and precepts of Swartland Independent Producers. The real focus is the vineyards, and they've been planting varieties like carignan, tinta barocca and palomino. No Shiraz was made in 2017 but, despite the drought, there should be a 2018.

Swerwer range

★★★★☆ **Swartland Red Blend** ⓐ Tinta barocca as usual in **17** ⑨④, with cinsaut (52%) & grenache (40%). Scrubby herbal lift, olivaceous savouriness; full & vinous but light-feeling & fresh (13% alcohol). Textured, well balanced, with good tannic grip. 80% wholebunch fruit; older oak. **16** ★★★★★ ⑨⑤ especially fine.

★★★★☆ **Chenin Blanc** Typically understated fruitiness on **17** ⑨② but there's peach lingering among the aromatic echoes of a sun-warmed hillside. Good flavour depth & length, with fine acidity adding austere element to the seductiveness. Like red, natural yeast ferment in old barrels.

Not tasted: **Shiraz.** — TJ

Location: Malmesbury ▪ Map/WO: Swartland ▪ Map grid reference: C8 ▪ Est 2012 ▪ Tasting strictly by appt only ▪ Owner(s)/winemaker(s) Jasper Wickens ▪ Viticulturist(s) Franziska Wickens ▪ 1,000cs ▪ jcwickens@gmail.com ▪ S 33° 33′ 44″ E 018° 49′ 9″ ▪ **T +27 (0)72-461-4249**

☐ **JD Initial Series** *see* Jean Daneel Wines

Jean Daneel Wines

The new website address (see below) reflects the shared passions of veteran vintner Jean Daneel and his family in bucolic Napier. After an illustrious career at top-rated Buitenverwachting and Morgenhof, Jean helped pioneer winegrowing in ancient, off-the-beaten-track southern Cape soils in the late 1990s. Son Jean-Pierre continues the winecrafting in their village cellar, with tastings by appointment at nearby country-chic JD Bistro, the preserve of chef brother Marchand and foodie mum Renée.

Directors Signature Series

★★★★ **Red** ⓐ Clean black berry fruit in a fine structure, remarkably measured considering all-new wood, 28 months, & 15% alcohol. Cab, cab franc & merlot, **15** ★★★★★ ⑨④ a pleasure now but will amply reward patience. First tasted since **05**.

Not tasted: **Chenin Blanc, Sauvignon Blanc.**

Signature Series

★★★★☆ **Red** Its succulent fruit sequestered by fairly austere tannins mid-2018, **15** ★★★★ ⑧⑧ Bordeaux/shiraz blend needs a meal accompaniment or, preferably, cellaring to harmonise the serious vinification: ferment in 500L barrel, then 2 years smaller oak, half new. First rated since **11** ⑨⓪.

★★★★☆ **Chenin Blanc** Old bushvines supply the apple, pear & stewed quince fruit, & the fresh acidity, 20% new oak the rich oatmeal texture, peanut brittle & almond features. All harmoniously melded in **16** ⑨⓪ with enough verve for food pairing.

Not tasted: **Méthode Cap Classique.**

JD Initial Series

Red ⓩ ★★★★ Svelte, with iodine & white pepper, berry fruit ably supported by 2 years old oak. **14** ⑧⑤ is 94% shiraz, dash merlot. Napier grapes but WO Overberg. — DS

Location: Napier ▪ Map: Southern Cape ▪ Map grid reference: B2 ▪ WO: Western Cape/Overberg ▪ Est/1stB 1997 ▪ Tasting, sales & cellar tours by appt ▪ Closed Dec 25 & Jan 1 ▪ JD Bistro ▪ Owner(s) Jean & Renée Daneel ▪ Winemaker(s) Jean-Pierre Daneel ▪ 70t 40% red 60% white ▪ PO Box 200 Napier 7270 ▪ info@jdwines.co.za ▪ www.jdwinesandbistro.co.za ▪ S 34° 28′ 37.82″ E 019° 54′ 17.09″ ▪ bowling.exiled.stapling ▪ **T +27 (0)28-423-3724**

☐ **Jean Roi** *see* Anthonij Rupert Wyne
☐ **Jemma** *see* Painted Wolf Wines
☐ **JHG Wine Collection** *see* Jan Harmsgat

JH Meyer Signature Wines Ⓠ

Energetic Johan Meyer — he also collaborates with two fellow young guns on stellar Mount Abora Vineyards, and partners a UK importer on ultra-au naturel Mother Rock Wines — reserves his solo 'signature' venture for special parcels of pinot noir and chardonnay, from Elgin to Elandskloof to the Cape South Coast. He's true throughout to the tenets of non-interventionist winemaking, spending time with growers, advancing sustainable and organic farming methods.

Single Vineyards range

★★★★☆ **Elands River Pinot Noir** ⊘ From Elandskloof fruit, **17** ⑨⓪ more fruit-filled than Elgin sibling, with caramel & baked strawberry tones, crushed sage note. Broader, too, with more tannic grip. Last-tasted was **14** ★★★★ ⑧⑤.

★★★★ **Palmiet Pinot Noir** ⊘ ⑯ Effortless **17** ★★★★★ ⑨③ an ethereal beauty from Elgin with delicate raspberry & cherry fruit, tealeaf & seagrass nuances. Modest 12.5% alcohol but convincing grip & focus. Wholebunch fermentation, 8 weeks on skins, no new oak or additives; as for Elands River. Last tasted was **15** ⑧⑦.

★★★★ **Pinot Noir NSA** ⑯⑷ ⊘ No sulphur added to **17** ⑧⑧, from Cape South Coast. Very pretty musk & sugared strawberry fruit, dainty earthiness, spicy whiffs, variety's hallmark acidity: ticks all the pinot boxes. Like rest of range, not only for fans of the 'natural' wave.

★★★★ **Palmiet Chardonnay** ⑯ Adds Elgin origin to name. **17** ★★★★★ ⑨③ no shrinking violet; intense citrus, white pear & lime underpinned by wet stone minerality. Precise, linear & very dry. Minute portion oaked, naturally fermented. Last-tasted was **14** ⑧⑥.

Not tasted: **Cradock Peak Pinot Noir**.

JH Meyer Signature Wines range

Not tasted: **Carbonic Pinot Noir**. — HC, CvZ

Location: Hermon ▪ WO: Elgin/Cape South Coast/Elandskloof ▪ Est/1stB 2011 ▪ Private tastings on request ▪ Owner(s) Johan Meyer ▪ Cellarmaster(s)/winemaker(s)/viticulturist(s) Johan Meyer (2011) ▪ 25t ▪ Own label 80% red 20% white ▪ 1 Main Rd Hermon 7308 ▪ jhmeyerwines1984@gmail.com ▪ www.jhmeyerwines.co.za ▪ T +27 (0)79-280-0237

☐ **Jikken Bareru Experimental Barrels** *see* The Fledge & Co

JMA Louw Familie Wyn Ⓠ ⑾ ◎ Ⓐ Ⓛ

Malmesbury winegrower Juan Louw named his boutique fortified brand after his son, Johannes Michiel Adriaan, as well as his namesake and ancestor who was one of the first farmers in Swartland. A family member still owns the original farm, Tweekuil, and Juan believes his wines are 'a tribute to all JMA Louws'.

Genade Water range

Hanepoot ★★★ Nine years in old oak gives deep brown colour to **NV** ⑧① fortified muscat d'Alexandrie, along with savoury, umami notes & finish. Swartland grapes, like next. **Rooi Jeripigo** ★★★ Unusual fortified from mourvèdre & cabernet, aged 3 years in very old oak. **NV** ⑦⑦ earthy flavours with raisins & coffee. **Muskadel** ★★★ Plenty of raisins & dark chocolate on very sweet & concentrated fortified **NV** ⑧④ from white & red muscat de Frontignan ex Breedekloof vines. 375 ml, as all these. — CM

Location: Malmesbury ▪ Map: Durbanville, Philadelphia & Darling ▪ Map grid reference: A3 ▪ WO: Worcester ▪ Est 2007 ▪ 1stB 2008 ▪ Vygevallei farmstall (R27): Tasting & sales Mon-Sat 10-5 Sun 10-4 ▪ Closed Dec 25 & Jan 1 ▪ Cellar tours ▪ Restaurant ▪ Facilities for children ▪ Gifts ▪ Farm produce ▪ Owner(s) Juan Louw ▪ Winemaker(s)/viticulturist(s) Juan Louw (Jan 2007) ▪ 560t/1,500cs own label 30% red 70% dessert ▪ PO Box 283 Malmesbury 7299 ▪ vygevallei@nuweland.za.net ▪ www.nuweland.za.net ▪ S 33° 24' 03.87" E 018° 16' 41.73" ▪ ⌨ cyclone.rereading.visuals ▪ T +27 (0)78-111-7913

☐ **Joachim Scholtz** *see* Rogge Cloof

Johan Joubert Wines

An independent venture by vintner Johan Joubert after a sojourn at Stellenbosch star Kleine Zalze and stint at Paarl stalwart Boland, it allows expression of the effect of Helderberg and Stellenbosch mountain soils on his favourite varieties, chenin and cabernet. This CWG member mid-2018 was appointed cellarmaster for Stellenbosch's Asara (for whom he'd been consulting). He also advises Wellington boutique winery Alkmaar.

★★★★ CWG Auction Reserve Granite Selection Cabernet Sauvignon (⊛) This second parcel of classic Stellenbosch cab is for 2018 auction. Another year has benefited understated **15** ★★★★★ (93): lovely depth of blackcurrant flavour, in harmony with polished tannin structure, subtle cedar & cigarbox from 100% new French oak, 27 months. Elegant & rich, concludes with fine herbal lift. — WB

Location/WO: Stellenbosch ▪ Est 2016 ▪ 1stB 2015 ▪ Closed to public ▪ Owner(s) Johan Joubert ▪ Cellarmaster(s)/winemaker(s)/viticulturist(s) Johan Joubert (Aug 2016) ▪ 8t total/600cs own label 70% red 30% white + 15,111cs for clients ▪ WIETA ▪ 18 Santa Rosa Str Die Boord Stellenbosch 7600 ▪ info@johanjoubertwines.com ▪ www.johanjoubertwines.com ▪ T +27 (0)21-887-4425

☐ **John B** *see* Rietvallei Wine Estate

Joostenberg Wines

(⊕)(⊕)(⌂)(◉)(⊕)

With its charming cluster of old oak-shaded buildings, the Myburghs' Paarl estate (in the family since 1879) has the warmly authentic atmosphere of a working farm. It embraces both tradition and modern developments. Since winemaking was revived here in 2000, quality and style have developed along with the Cape wine revolution. Tyrrel Myburgh is in charge of vineyard and cellar; his pleasing and unpretentious wines, always properly dry, are made with minimal intervention (reflecting both old and avant-garde concerns), as fine, honest expressions of his organic vineyards. For the new label established with Philip, his brother and joint owner of Joostenberg, see Myburgh Bros.

Estate range

★★★★ Philip Albert Cabernet Sauvignon (⊘) Tobacco notes mingle with dark berries on seriously styled **16** (88) - savoury rather than fruity. Pleasing in youth, but with firm structure & good balance to develop.

★★★★ Klippe Kou Syrah (⊘) Restrained aromas on **16** (88), dusty spice note. Less generous than **15** ★★★★★ (94), with brighter acidity, but also understated & pleasing; firmly built, nicely dry finish. Older oak.

★★★★☆ Bakermat (⊘) Syrah (43%) leads cab in **16** (92), with mourvèdre, touriga - clever, successful blend, the spicy berry fruit with an edge of wildness. Balanced, succulent acid, firm but unaggressive tannins, some fruit-rich power to carry it to maturity, but already appealing. Properly dry.

★★★★ Die Agteros Chenin Blanc (⊘)(⊛) Sweet fruit aromas & flavours on very pleasing (bone-dry) **17** (87), though not much intensity. Usual soft texture, enough acid for a little grip, showing more on finish. Partly oaked.

★★★★ Fairhead (⊘) Roussanne up to 62% on **17** (87), for dried herb notes, with chenin & 10% subtly peachy viognier adding perfume. Lovely silky texture, soft but with a little fresh acid bite. Just 13% alcohol. Old oak & concrete 'eggs'.

★★★★☆ Chenin Blanc Noble Late Harvest Very much in Sauternes style, but all from chenin. **17** (92) old-oaked dessert wine offers subtle coconut, marmalade, with botrytis honey adding to complexity. Finely balanced & elegant, more light-feeling than overtly rich or intense (114 g/l RS), despite power of 14.5% alcohol. 375 ml.

Discontinued: **The Piano Man Viognier**.

Family Wines range

The Family Blend (⊘) ★★★☆ Mostly shiraz in blend. **17** (83) quite light coloured; mildly fruity & easygoing, with a respectable grip. Modestly oaked. **Chenin Blanc** (⊘) ★★★☆ Ever-reliable pleasure & satisfaction here, & **17** (84), with notes of thatch, dried peach & spice, no exception: full flavoured but unshowy, balanced & ripely rounded.

Small Batch Collection

★★★★ **No. 7 Lightweight Syrah** ⊘ Bright, red-fruited **17** ⑧ a touch leaner & tarter, more serious than previous **15** ★★★★ ⑧, though still very tasty. Moderately grippy. Just 12.5% alcohol.

★★★★ **No. 10 Touriga Nacional** ⓥ ⊘ Most appealing **15** ⑧, naturally made. Packed with delicious flavour, but not showy - harmonious & airy, rather. Some grip, but light extraction & usual modest oaking.

★★★★ **Early Bird Chenin Blanc** ⑳ ⊘ Less alcohol (11%), more succulent acid & freshness on **16** ⑧ than on other whites. Lovely aromas & flavours, though not fruity - stony, mineral, savoury, even a green note. Old oak.

Not tasted: **No. 11 Mourvèdre**. Discontinued: **No. 9 Long & Late**.

Little J range

Not tasted: **Shiraz, Chenin Blanc**. — TJ

Location/map/WO: Paarl ▪ Map grid reference: A7 ▪ Est/1stB 1999 ▪ Tasting & cellar tours by appt at Joostenberg Wines ▪ Sales daily 10—5 at the Joostenberg Deli & Bistro on Klein Joostenberg Farm ▪ Closed Dec 25 & Jan 1 ▪ Joostenberg Bistro ▪ Facilities for children ▪ Tour groups ▪ Gifts ▪ Farm produce ▪ Conferences ▪ Ludwig's rose nursery & Van den Berg garden centre ▪ Guest accommodation (3 double rooms), contact anette@joostenberg.co.za ▪ Owner(s) Philip & Tyrrel Myburgh ▪ Cellarmaster(s)/viticulturist(s) Tyrrel Myburgh (1999) ▪ Winemaker(s) Tyrrel Myburgh (1999), with Elmerie Joubert (2017) ▪ 29.53ha (cab, merlot, mourv, shiraz, touriga nacional, alvarinho, chenin, rouss, viog) ▪ 120t/6,000cs own label 35% red 50% white 15% NLH ▪ PO Box 82 Elsenburg 7607 ▪ winery@joostenberg.co.za ▪ www.joostenberg.co.za ▪ S 33° 48' 47.21" E 018° 48' 31.70 (Joostenberg Wines), S 33° 49' 34.8" E 018° 47' 45.5" (Joostenberg Deli & Bistro) ▪ ⟪⟫ centipedes.bridesmaids.dinners ▪ **T +27 (0)21-200-9903 (Joostenberg Wines)/+27 (0)21-884-4141 (Joostenberg Deli & Bistro)**

Jordan Wine Estate   ⓥ ⑪ ⌂ ⊚ ⓹

Redeveloped with terroir-matched classic varieties by Ted and Sheelagh Jordan after they bought it in 1982, this internationally acclaimed Stellenboschkloof estate has been in the hands of trained geologist son Gary and economist wife Kathy since 1993. Having consistently improved on its reputation, the pair are shifting a bit more of their focus offshore (having established High Timber restaurant on the Thames a decade ago and helped its reputation soar) by investing in a small country estate an hour south of London. The plan for Mousehall is to plant pinot noir and chardonnay for bubbly, as well as botanicals for gin. And, once the manor and oast house have been refurbished, use the existing agricultural buildings for a small distillery, wine cellar and honey house. Auspicious, then, that Wade Roger-Lund, on the Jordanwinemaking team, was 2018 Diners Club Young Winemaker of the Year with a new MCC sparkling.

CWG Auction Reserve range

★★★★☆ **Sophia** ⓐ Selection of best Cobblers Hill new barrels plus 'reserve' cabernet. Firm & composed **15** ⑨ primary cassis with leafy, lead pencil notes, beautiful dryness backed by sweet fruit, tannins more open than **14** ⑨. Will reward patience a decade-plus.

★★★★☆ **Chardonnay** ⓐ Purpose-crafted fruit from Nine Yards vineyard for elite auction. 100% new oak in **16** ⑨ down to 80% for **17** ⑨, showing thrilling integration of wood, compact citrus fruit & rapier acidity. A class act.

Reserve range

★★★★☆ **Sophia** ⓐ Assured & noble Bordeaux blend; mostly cab with 29% merlot, 13% cab franc in **14** ⑨. Sweet plum fruit in masterly tannin structure, claret-like elegance, dryness. Like CWG sibling, selection of Cobblers Hill barrels but larger older-oak portion.

★★★★☆ **Nine Yards Chardonnay** ⓐ Poised **17** ⑨ as alluring & accomplished as **16** ⑨, showing uncompromising purity, minerality & chalkiness of respected vineyard. Similarly irresistible now but structured for the long haul. Takes 70% new oak, more than last, in its stride.

★★★★ **Méthode Cap Classique Blanc de Blancs** ⑳ Jordans limbering up ahead of launching English sparkling from their new Sussex estate? **15** ⑧ from chardonnay, extra-dry, creamy & smooth from 2 years on lees, persistent freshness for solo sipping or celebratory meals.

★★★★☆ **Mellifera Natural Sweet** ⓧ Understated presence, finesse & grace always the intention with this Natural Sweet from raisined riesling. On paper, **16** (92) an anomaly with 12% alcohol & 125 g/l sugar versus **14** (92)'s 9% & 97 g/l, yet retains light touch, sophistication.

Not tasted: **Cobblers Hill**.

Jordan Estate range

★★★★☆ **The Long Fuse Cabernet Sauvignon** Sweet cassis & lead pencil appeal, **15** (90)'s curves given form by tight tannins & acidity. Also-tasted **14** (90) similar tautness, both show why variety always the keystone of Jordan's superb Bordeaux blends.

★★★★ **Black Magic Merlot** Lively acidity, silky depth, confident **15** (86) more settled & drier than Chameleon sibling, lithe & fruity.

★★★★ **The Prospector Syrah** Now-bottled, **16** ★★★★☆ (90) more distinguished & engaging than **15** (89), black pepper & fynbos fragrance, supple red fruit, friendly tannins & beautiful fantail finish.

★★★★★ **Barrel Fermented Chardonnay** ⓧ Generous, proudly New World style. Like **16** (95), **17** ★★★★★ (93)'s precise fruit & vivacious acidity provide perfect counterweight to robust oak regime: 91% of wine wooded, 23% new barriques, occasional barrel rolling; tank-fermented portion also through malo.

★★★★ **Unoaked Chardonnay** Accomplished Chablis-inspired version relies on varietal fruit & lees ageing for flavour, shape & quality. **17** (88) intense lemon infusion, subtly savoury lemongrass nuance, refreshing citrus lift on finish.

★★★★☆ **Inspector Péringuey Chenin Blanc** ⓧ ⓧ Standout attribute of **17** (94) is tightly wound, long finish that evokes all that went before: peach fruit, rich wood character (older, ferment/ageing on lees), pinpoint balance between weight, finesse & power, as in exceptional **16** ★★★★★ (95).

★★★★ **The Real McCoy Riesling** Two vintages assessed. Previewed **18** (88) ginger beer, lime & lemon sherbet nuances, near-perfect balance between sweetness & acidity, like **17** (87) which has still-youthful hue & floral/citrus aromas, nascent terpene complexity. WO W Cape.

★★★★ **The Outlier Sauvignon Blanc** ⓧ ⓧ Totally captivating **17** ★★★★☆ (93), partly oak-fermented/aged with occasional lees stirring. Gentle gunflint/smoke whiffs, cool & fresh, bone-dry, discreetly rich. Like **16** (89), more textural than aromatic.

★★★★ **The Cold Fact Sauvignon Blanc** Two vintages of the unwooded sauvignon reviewed, both show blackcurrant notes on tropical fruit, specifically granadilla. **17** (89)'s well-judged weight, body, augur well for **18** (89) tank sample.

Chameleon range

No Added Sulphur Merlot ⓧ ★★★☆ Whimsical illustrations by Linda Kathryn Wright of Cape Dwarf Chameleon for this range. **17** (83) vivacious & fruity, oak (70% American) in support. Flavoursome, laudable dryness, as for all. Ready now for everyday enjoyment. **Rosé** ⓧ ★★★☆ Sunset pink **17** (83) has grown-up body (13.5% alcohol, bone-dry 1.7 g/l sugar), fruity but not 'tutti'. Mostly merlot (65%), only free-run juice off vines dedicated to rosé.

Cabernet Sauvignon-Merlot ★★★ Stern but not unapproachable **15** (82), more savoury spices than younger red siblings, satisfying dry finish for food. **No Added Sulphur Cabernet Franc-Cabernet Sauvignon-Merlot** (NEW) ★★★ Cassis & plum **16** (81) lifted by 41% cab franc leafiness, grippier than siblings courtesy both cabs' firmer tannins. **Chenin Blanc** (NEW) ★★★☆ Two vintages tasted. Characterful weekday drinking delivered by tropical- & whiteflower-toned **17** with exuberant green & yellow apple palate. Previewed **18** (83) similar nuances but more intense. **Sauvignon Blanc-Chardonnay** ★★★ Marriage 67% sauvignon, chardonnay & chenin strikes all the happy sipping notes in **17** (81). — CvZ

Location/map: Stellenbosch ▪ Map grid reference: C5 ▪ WO: Stellenbosch/Western Cape ▪ Est 1982 ▪ 1stB 1993 ▪ Tasting & sales daily 9.30–4.30 ▪ Tasting fee R50pp, waived on purchase ▪ Cellar tours by appt Mon-Fri 11 & 1.30 ▪ Pre-booking required for: tasting & cellar tour R150pp; speciality tasting from R220pp; exclusive vineyard & cellar wine safari from R450pp ▪ Jordan Restaurant ▪ Jordan Bakery ▪ Conferences (50 pax) ▪ Mountain biking ▪ Conservation area ▪ Jordan Luxury Suites ▪ Owner(s) Jordan family ▪ Cellarmaster(s) Gary & Kathy Jordan (1993) ▪ Winemaker(s) Sjaak Nelson (Jan 2002), with Wade Roger-Lund (2014) ▪ Viticulturist(s) Gary Jordan (1983), with Hilton Phipson (2014) ▪ 160ha/105ha (cab, merlot, shiraz, chard, chenin, riesling, sauv) ▪ 850t/100,000cs own label 45% red 54% white 1% rosé ▪ Other export brand: Jardin

▪ Brands for clients: Pick's Pick, Woolworths ▪ PO Box 12592 Die Board Stellenbosch 7613 ▪ info@jordanwines.com ▪ www.jordanwines.com ▪ S 33° 56'33.7" E 018° 44'41.3" ▪ ⌨ birdcalls.thereby.shivered ▪ F +27 (0)21-881-3426 ▪ **T +27 (0)21-881-3441**

☐ **Joseph Barry** see Barrydale Winery & Distillery

Joubert-Tradauw Wingerde & Kelder   ⓠ ⑪ ⌂ ◎ ⑧ ⑤

'Life around here is mainly about two things: the fruit of the vine and the work of human hands,' says Meyer Joubert, 3rd-generation owner of this boutique cellar and vineyards near Barrydale on the R62 tourist route. Complementing his wines are Klein Karoo tapas created by his wife, award-winning cookbook author Beate.

★★★★ **R62** Cedar spice complements wild black berry/forest fruit flavours in medium-bodied **14** ⑧⑦, tangy, with fresh acidity, savoury spices on finish. 100% cab (**13** ★★★★ ⑧④ a blend), 30% new oak.

★★★★ **Reserve Cabernet Franc** Step up on **15** ★★★★ ⑧④, **16** ⑧⑨ preview velvety smooth after 2 years in 50% new French oak, with ripe, tangy dark fruit, pepper, some mocha & liquorice.

★★★★ **Redfin Pinot Noir** ⓠ Distinctive spice with usual cherry, undergrowth nuances, **13** ⑧⑥ nip of bitterness only detraction to overall silky, fresh feel. Unfiltered, as all.

★★★★ **Syrah** Barrel sample **16** ⑧⑥ takes time to unfurl, showing fynbos/eucalyptus aromas leading to ripe dark cherry, prune & apricot fruit, fresh & juicy, with soft tannins. 2 years French oak, as R62.

★★★★ **Chardonnay Barrel Fermented** Pre-bottling, **16** ⑧⑧ already rich, concentrated & creamy, fresh citrus layered with lemon tart, toasted nuts & baking spice from year 50% new French oak.— JG

Location: Barrydale ▪ Map: Klein Karoo & Garden Route ▪ Map grid reference: C7 ▪ WO: Tradouw ▪ Est/1stB 1999 ▪ Tasting, sales & cellar tours Mon-Fri 9—5 Sat 10—2 ▪ Closed Easter Fri/Sun & Dec 25 ▪ R62 Deli Mon-Fri 9-3 Sat 10-1 breakfasts, lunches & Klein Karoo tapas ▪ Walks/hikes ▪ MTB ▪ Conservation area ▪ Lentelus B&B (www.lentelus.co.za) ▪ Owner(s) Lentelus Family Trust ▪ Cellarmaster(s)/winemaker(s)/viticulturist(s) Meyer Joubert (1999) ▪ 1,100ha/20ha (cab, merlot, shiraz, chard) ▪ 8,000cs own label 70% red 30% white ▪ PO Box 15 Barrydale 6750 ▪ info@joubert-tradauw.co.za ▪ www.joubert-tradauw.co.za ▪ S 33° 55'26.4" E 020° 35'40.6" ▪ ⌨ fine.cowbirds.installs ▪ F +27 (0)86-555-3558 ▪ **T +27 (0)28-125-0086/+27 (0)82-815-3737/+27 (0)71-656-1230**

☐ **Journeymaker** see Valley Vineyards Wine Company

Journey's End Vineyards   ⓠ ⑪ ⌂ ◎

False Bay's proximity to Sir Lowry's Pass village provides both beautiful vistas and cool breezes, gifts of nature appreciated by keen mountain bikers and horse riders but perhaps even more by Leon Esterhuizen, long-time cellar chief at the Gabb family's gently sloping property, acquired in 1995. Care for the environment - natural and social - is important here, hence WIETA accreditation, and a shift to a 'hands off' approach in the winemaking, which Leon credits to the more recent team member, Mike Dawson.

Reserve range

★★★★☆ **Cape Doctor Cabernet Sauvignon** ⓠ Brambly tobacco, ink & cocoa depth on rich **12** ⑨② from cab. Structured, nuanced & layered palate, long spicy finish. Fruit stands up to 70% new oak & will reward patience.

★★★★ **Griffin Shiraz** ⓠ Overt spice & plum on **15** ⑧⑧, firm body partly from combo American & French oak, 30% new. Textured & long. **14** not made.

★★★★ **Destination Chardonnay** Naturally fermented **17** ⑧⑨ tauter, brighter than also-tasted **16** ⑧⑦. Rich, full-bodied but restrained. Deft, well-knit oak (80% new, 10 months) adds nuance & complexity but fruit speaks loudest. Magnums available, as next.

Journey's End range

★★★★ **Cabernet Sauvignon** Supple, generous black-fruited mouthful of **15** ⑧⑨ goes up a notch on **14** ★★★★ ⑧⑤. Plush, smooth, dry & savoury, with gentle tannin grip (35% new oak, 18 months).

★★★★ **Merlot** Trademark cocoa & herb nuance to mulberry-hued **15** ⑧⑥, which improves on **14** ★★★★ ⑧⑤. Silky & generous, ripe fruit framed by seamless oak, all French, just 30% new.

★★★★ **Shiraz** Step up on **13** ★★★★ ⑧⑤ in **14** ⑧⑥ with carbonic portion, free run & mix French/American oak ageing. Fresh, inky blue fruit with good body & length.

★★★★ **Chardonnay** Vivid mandarin tang & cream breadth on **17** ⑧⑥ matches previous, though marginally lighter bodied. Bright & fresh, with half natural ferment, 30% new oak & weekly lees stirring.

Cellar range
The Pastor's Blend ★★★ Spicy Christmas appeal of four-way Bordeaux red in **16** ⑧③. Medium bodied, but with noticeable tannin grip at end. **The Huntsman Shiraz-Mourvèdre-Viognier** ⓥ ★★★★ Shiraz characters in lead on floral-tinged **16** ⑧③ blend. Tangy succulence somewhat at odds with spicy oak. **Haystack Chardonnay** ★★★ Honeyed peach appeal to fresh, pure, unaffected **17** ⑧②, made with mix older oak, staves & tank portion. WO Coastal. **The Weather Station Sauvignon Blanc** ⓥ ★★★★ Focused flint & lemon purity to zippy **17** ⑧③ tank sample; energetic, with defined dry tail. — FM

Location: Sir Lowry's Pass ▪ Map: Helderberg ▪ Map grid reference: G7 ▪ WO: Stellenbosch/Coastal ▪ Est 1995 ▪ 1stB 2001 ▪ Tasting only by appt Mon-Fri 9-5 ▪ Fee R50pp ▪ Closed Easter Fri-Mon, Dec 25 & Jan 1 ▪ Cheese platters & snacks by appt; or BYO picnic ▪ Walks/hikes ▪ Horse riding ▪ MTB ▪ Conservation area ▪ Owner(s) Gabb family ▪ Cellarmaster(s) Leon Esterhuizen (Jun 2006) ▪ Winemaker(s) Leon Esterhuizen (Jun 2006) & Mike Dawson (Jun 2015) ▪ Viticulturist(s) Lodewyk Retief (Jun 2011) ▪ 50ha/30ha (cabs s/f, malbec, merlot, mourv, p verdot, shiraz, chard, sauv, sem, viog) ▪ 300t/30,000cs own label 60% red 40% white ▪ HACCP, IPW, WIETA ▪ PO Box 3040 Somerset West 7129 ▪ info@journeysend.co.za ▪ www.journeysend.co.za ▪ S 34° 6' 35.11" E 018° 54' 54.06" ▪ ⌨ payouts.unbolted.overlays ▪ F +27 (0)86-540-1929 ▪ **T +27 (0)21-858-1929**

☐ **Joy** see Ashton Winery

JP Bredell Wines ⓥ

With Anton Bredell at the helm, the JP Bredell brand in the 1990s became synonymous with quality red wines and, perhaps more so, port-style wines standing shoulder to shoulder with those grown in the Douro. With the sale of the Stellenbosch farm and cellar, the venture is now based in the Langeberg-Garcia ward near Riversdale. Boutique production is contemplated 'but nothing concrete yet'. Meanwhile well-matured limited releases of the table wines and famed fortifieds are available for tasting/sale by appointment.

Bredell's range
★★★★ **Shiraz** ⓥ Featured in our 2007 edition, **03** ⑧⑦ was noted as improvement on previous **01**, with oak cosseting berry fruit, attractive spice on finish.

★★★★ **De Rigueur** ⓥ Cab-led Bordeaux blend, **08** ⑧⑦ bramble & cedar aromas, ripe (but just 13% alcohol), earthy & fruity palate absorbs 14 months oak. Smooth, rich texture, good dry finish.

★★★★★ **Cape Vintage Reserve** ⓥ Long-admired benchmark Cape 'port', splendid blend tinta, touriga, souzão, showing refined power, tremendous length. 60 cases of **00** held back to monitor development, now available. **03** (without 'Reserve' in name) 400 cases of never-before-available 375 ml on offer. **07** ⑨⑦ is the current, more plentiful release.

★★★★ **Late Bottled Vintage** ⓥ 'Port' now released for 1st time in 375 ml, **99** rich, silky, fragranced; also available is a further parcel of seductive, plushly ripe **04** ⑧⑦ in 375 ml. Tinta, souzão, tourigas nacional & franca; 3-4 years older barrels.

Merlot ⓥ ★★★★ Intended as Auction Reserve when Anton Bredell was CWG member, & never released, this parcel of **99** ⑧⑤ shows lovely tertiary earth, leather & undergrowth whiffs, silken sweet-fruited palate. Delicious, enjoy soon. — CM, CvZ

Location: Riversdale ▪ Map: Klein Karoo & Garden Route ▪ Map grid reference: C5 ▪ WO: Stellenbosch ▪ 1stB 1991 ▪ Tasting & sales by appt only ▪ Owner(s) Helderzicht Trust ▪ Winemaker(s)/viticulturist(s) Anton Bredell (1988) ▪ 2ha (port cultivars & some other experimentals) ▪ 500cs own label 20% red 80% port ▪ PO Box 275 Riversdal 6670 ▪ bernhard@bredellwines.co.za ▪ www.bredellwines.co.za ▪ S 33° 55' 13.58" E 021° 30' 52.13" ▪ ⌨ tabloid.enchants.headlock ▪ **T +27 (0)82-550-0684**

Julien Schaal ⓥ

Itinerant winemaker Julien Schaal has moved his winemaking home from Bot River's Gabriëlskloof cellar back to where it began: Paul Cluver Wines in Elgin. The Alsace-based former sommelier and winemaker wife

Sophie shuttle between seasons, juggling their pursuit for best expressing site differences between Upper Hemel-en-Aarde and Elgin, by making wines with careful Old World styling and nuance, with their northern hemisphere life producing grand cru riesling. Sticking to their vow to do so, should it eventuate, the duo last year flew in from France to gratefully (and ecstatically!) receive their first Platter's 5-star certificate.

★★★★☆ **Confluence Chardonnay** ⓐ Recalling stellar **16** ★★★★★ ⑨⑤ in complexity, harmony & stature, **17** ⑨④'s fruit richness & creamy oak (25% new) toned by sinewy, nervy line of acidity. Layered, with lovely mouthfeel, presence & length. Superbly gratifying. Upper Hemel-en-Aarde fruit.

★★★★☆ **Evidence Chardonnay** ⓐ Nothing overplayed on **17** ⑨③. Lively citrus fruit from cool-climate Elgin supported by cradle of integrated oak (25% new). Refined & poised, with elegance vying with succulence.

★★★★☆ **Mountain Vineyards Chardonnay** Compelling fruit, oak & lees interplay on subtle yet fresh **17** ⑨⓪. Stylish, with just 40% oaked, only 10% new. Gentle & elegant yet sprightly, with acid tang on long, rewarding finish. Mostly Elgin & Upper Hemel-en-Aarde grapes. Balanced 13% alcohol, as all.— FM

Location: Elgin ▪ WO: Cape South Coast/Elgin/Upper Hemel-en-Aarde Valley ▪ Est 2004 ▪ 1stB 2005 ▪ Tasting by appt only ▪ Owner(s) Julien Schaal ▪ Winemaker(s) Sophie & Julien Schaal ▪ 28t/4,000cs own label 100% white ▪ c/o PO Box 48 Grabouw 7160 ▪ julien@vins-schaal.com ▪ www.julienschaal.com ▪ T +33 (0)6-10-89-72-14

☐ **Juno** *see* Erasmus Family Wines
☐ **Kaap Agri** *see* Breëland Winery
☐ **Kaapse Droom** *see* Goedverwacht Wine Estate

Kaapse Familie Wingerde   ⓠ

The Cape families alluded to in the name of this joint venture have a combined 30 generations' winegrowing nous: the De Waals in Paarl's Voor Paardeberg ward, marketing as Oude Denneboom, the Loubsers near Philadelphia (Kuyperskraal) and the Le Rouxs in Paarl (Vendôme). See separate entries. The cabernet, pinotage rosé and sauvignon under this collective label untasted.

Location: Paarl ▪ Est 1688 ▪ 1stB 2014 ▪ Tasting & sales at Vendôme (see entry) ▪ Owner(s) Loubser, Le Roux & De Waal families ▪ Winemaker(s) Jannie le Roux & Altus le Roux (consultant) ▪ Viticulturist(s) Viljee Loubser ▪ WIETA ▪ Arboretum Ave Paarl 7620 ▪ info@kaapsefamiliewingerde.com ▪ www.kaapsefamiliewingerde.com ▪ T +27 (0)21-863-3905

Kaapzicht Wine Estate   ⓠ ⌂ ◎

Danie Steytler jnr had big shoes to fill after assuming winemaking duties at this large Bottelary Hills estate from his father Danie snr in 2009, after a few years gaining experience in New Zealand, France, California and locally. Aware of his heritage (Kaapzicht has been family owned since 1946), the 4th-generation winemaker has modernised the winery while respecting the venerable vines his uncle George has nurtured for decades. Prime among the gnarled vines on special sites is SA's second-oldest chenin blanc, bottled as '1947', but there are old pinotage and cinsaut vines too. Matriarch Yngvild is as dynamic as ever, celebrating 40 years of marriage in 2019 and juggling grandchildren with marketing and exports with aplomb.

Steytler range

★★★★☆ **Pinotage** ⓐ Selection of vintage's best pinotage, French oak matured 2 years. **15** ⑨② sleek & ripe, with core of pure blue & black fruit. Good concentration & density though still supple & pliable. Refined & elegant, with long aftertaste. First since **12** ⑨②. Bottelary WO.

★★★★☆ **Pentagon** ⓐ Cab (50%) leads the way in **15** ⑨① harmonious, nuanced 5-part Bordeaux blend. Svelte, with expressive cassis brushed with herb. Dark & complex, the oak (28 months) is seamlessly knit with fruit. No **13** or **14**.

★★★★☆ **Vision** ⓐ Brooding, swarthy Cape Blend of half pinotage, cab & 10% merlot in **15** ⑨③. Powerfully dark fruited, concentrated & complex yet nuanced & poised. Rich, spicy & fresh, oak is well melded after 28 months maturation. First since exceptional **12** ★★★★★ ⑨⑤. Bottelary WO, as next 2.

★★★★☆ **The 1947 Chenin Blanc** ⓐ ⓦ Impeccably crafted **17** ⑨④ from SA's 2nd-oldest chenin vines. Usual low-key winemaking: bunch pressing, natural ferment & selection of French/Hungarian barrels. Pear & quince on creamy palate, understated, elegant & complex, like **16 ★★★★★** ⑨⑤. Minuscule 150 cases.

Discontinued: **1952 Cinsaut**.

Kaapzicht range

★★★★ Cabernet Sauvignon ⓐ Shows both power & restraint in **15** ⑧⑨. Ripe, spicy hedgerow fruit with fine dry grip & silky texture from 2 years oak, half new. Layered & intricate. Will age well. No **14**.

★★★★★ Skuinsberg Cinsaut ⓥ ⓐ Single-vineyard bottling from estate's steepest slope. Light, tensile & nervy, with signature bright red-cherry & -berry fruit - all bushvine. **17 ★★★★★** ⑨④ spicy & plush yet sinewy & lithe. Old large-format casks check oak character. **15** ⑨⑦ generously structured for cinsaut. No **16**.

★★★★ Merlot Savoury, concentrated **15** ⑧⑨ balances succulence, hedgerow berries & oak tannin well. Ripe, rounded & layered, it had 18 months in French oak, a third new. No **13** or **14**. Bottelary WO.

★★★★ Pinot Noir ⓥ Seductive subtlety of **17** ⑧⑧ charms with sour cherry & forest floor vibrancy. Core of red fruit with sheen of oak from 18 months in older barrels.

★★★★ Pinotage Lives up to previous in cedar spice edge to lively red cherry fruit. **16** ⑧⑨ dark, inky depth & good concentration. 18 months in third new French oak. Dab of cab (15%).

★★★★ Shiraz Dried herb brush to spicy plum notes on New World-styled **15** ⑧⑥. Fruit & oak (2 years, half new) in harmony. Restrained & fresh with a long tail. Improves on **14 ★★★★** ⑧⑤.

★★★★ Kliprug Chenin Blanc ⓦ Tropical ease of **17** ⑧⑨ bottling of single-vineyard bushvines (1982) belies serious winemaking: bunch pressing, natural ferment in barrel, lees stirring & year in oak. Fresh acidity vies with broad, leesy, nectarine & peach palate.

★★★★ Hanepoot Jerepigo Signature floral jasmine & honeysuckle sweetness on **16** ⑧⑦ fortified dessert. Rich sultana flavour is prevented from cloying by judicious acidity. Lovely precision & focus. No **15**.

Bin 3 ★★★★ Approachable blend of merlot & cab is a crowd pleaser that over-delivers again in **15** ⑧④. Cedar spice mingles with red & blue fruit, nice oak squeeze on tail. Bottelary WO, as Estate Red, Kaleidoscope White & Hanepoot Jerepigo. **Kaleidoscope Red** ⓥ **★★★★** Soft, supple & plush 6-way blend is approachable, ripe & succulent with gentle oak-staved frame in **17** ⑧④. **Estate Red ★★★★** Dab petit verdot added to **15** ⑧⑤ mix of shiraz & cab. Chunky yet succulent & easy-drinking, gentle grip from nearly 2 years in oak. **Chenin Blanc** ⓥ **★★★★** Light **18** ⑧③ maintains form of previous in easy quaffability & stonefruit ripeness. Fresh & textured. Some old-vine fruit used. **Sauvignon Blanc** ⓥ **★★★★** Typical grapefruit tang & pepper brightness of textured **18** ⑧③, taut & focused. **Kaleidoscope White** ⓥ **★★★★** Semillon added to **18** ⑧④ mix of chardonnay, roussanne & verdelho. Melon & peach vivacity & flesh, light & juicy. Not tasted: **Pinotage Rosé**. Discontinued: **Cabernet Franc, The Glimpse, Ice, Cape Vintage**.

Brandy & Husk Spirit range

★★★★ 15 Year Potstill ⓨ As the brandy matured, it kept harmony & texture, gained in flavour complexity (the almond note particularly attractive), but perhaps lost some brightness, freshness.

Grape Husk Spirit ⓨ **★★★★** From aromatic varieties gewürztraminer & riesling, giving a gentle fragrant quality, the nuttiness touched with grape & raisin notes. Fresh & persistent. 375 ml. —— FM, TJ

Location/map: Stellenbosch ▪ Map grid reference: B4 ▪ WO: Stellenbosch/Bottelary ▪ Est 1946 ▪ 1stB 1984 ▪ Tasting & sales Mon-Fri 9–4 Sat/pub hols 10–1 ▪ Closed Good Fri, Dec 24/25/26 & Jan 1 ▪ Conference/ function/wedding & braai venues ▪ MTB trail ▪ Conservation area ▪ Self-catering cottage ▪ Potstill brandy & grappa ▪ Owner(s) Steytdal Farm (Pty) Ltd/Steytler Family Trusts ▪ Cellarmaster(s) Danie Steytler jnr (Jan 2009) ▪ Viticulturist(s) George Steytler (Jan 1984) & Robert Stolk (Jan 2016) ▪ 190ha/162ha (cabs s/f, cinsaut, malbec, merlot, p verdot, ptage, shiraz, chard, chenin, hanepoot, rouss, sauv, sem, verdelho) ▪ 1,100t/60,000cs own label 70% red 30% white + 20,000cs for clients ▪ Other export brands: Cape View, Friesland, Vet Rooi Olifant ▪ PO Box 35 Koelenhof 7605 ▪ carin@kaapzicht.co.za ▪ www.kaapzicht.co.za ▪ S 33° 54′ 47.7″ E 018° 44′ 7.7″ ▪ ⓜ hideout.binders.relation ▪ **T +27 (0)21-906-1620/1**

☐ **Kadette** *see* Kanonkop Estate

☐ **Kakamas** *see* Orange River Cellars

☐ **Kalkveld** *see* Zandvliet Wine Estate

☐ **Kanah Winery** *see* Twelve Apostles Winery

Kanonkop Estate

(symbols)

The fact that a producer's viticulture team is larger than that vinifying the wine could mean there's true commitment to bringing in quality fruit. Or, distances between vineyards are such that responsibility (and travel) need to be shared. Or, the harvest is physically just 'big'. For this celebrated and much-loved 4th-generation family estate on Stellenbosch's Simonsberg, it's all three. Current owners and brothers Paul and Johann Krige have always demanded the best quality fruit. Combined with exceptional skill in the cellar - Abri Beeslaar named International Winemaker of the Year for the 3rd time in 2018 by the International Wine & Spirit Competition — Kanonkop is widely regarded as a local 'first growth'. Plus, mostly to fuel growth in the Kadette label, they are sourcing fruit from far-flung vineyards that meet the vinous demands of their classically styled portfolio, which meant they crushed 3,000 tons for the first time in 2018.

Kanonkop Estate range

★★★★☆ Cabernet Sauvignon ⓐ Masterly **14** (94)'s immediate sensual appeal of tobacco-seamed cassis deepens into more cerebral, tightly packed dark & subtly spiced fruit, finely honed form from seamless marriage of ripe grape tannins & 50% new oak. Will reward decade-plus cellaring.

★★★★☆ Black Label ⓐ Paterfamilias of estate's pinotages, from venerable 63 year old vines, gets all-new oak essential to solidify the tannin structure & create decades-long future. Tremendous presence & personality, **16** ★★★★★ (96) also trademark freshness seen in **15** (92), compact but wonderfully deep dark fruit, exotic jasmine top note.

★★★★☆ Pinotage Serious expression of SA's home-bred grape, **16** (91) darker toned mulberry & black plum fragrance, concentrated but not forced, richness enlivened by perfectly judged acidity & expertly managed tannins. Delicious now & for 10+ years. Like many in range, also in formats up to 18L.

★★★★★ Paul Sauer ⓐ Rightly regarded as SA 'first growth' Bordeaux blend, traditionally cab-based with merlot, cab franc; 70/15/15 in **15** (95) which, though less plush than **14** (95) in cooler summer, exudes a controlled opulence thanks to satisfying dry finish & firm tannic foundation for extended ageing.

Kadette range

★★★★ Pinotage Previewed **17** (88) touch less complex, earlier-ready than senior wines but an icon in its own right given the large volumes produced. Variety-true mulberry/banana scents, fresh acid/tannin balance & supple older oak. **15** (87) as lithe & bright. **16** untasted.

★★★★ Cape Blend ⊘ Hugely popular pinotage blend gains splash cab franc to go with cab & merlot, goes a step up in **17** (89), satisfies even more than last-tasted **15** ★★★★ (84), with spiced dark fruits, smooth tannins from older oak. Like Pinotage, also in larger bottle formats.

Pinotage Dry Rosé ★★★★ Now combo Stellenbosch & Malmesbury grapes, **18** (84) beautifully dry, as full-bodied (14.3% alcohol) & fruity as before. — CvZ

Location/map: Stellenbosch ▪ Map grid reference: F2 ▪ WO: Simonsberg–Stellenbosch/Stellenbosch/Coastal ▪ Est 1910 ▪ 1stB 1973 ▪ Tasting & sales Mon-Fri 9-5 Sat 9-2 pub hols 10-4 ▪ Fee R30 ▪ Closed Good Fri, Dec 25 & Jan 1 ▪ Cheese platters in summer; traditional snoek barbecues by appt (min 15 people); or BYO picnic ▪ Conservation area ▪ Art gallery ▪ Owner(s) Johann & Paul Krige ▪ Cellarmaster(s) Abrie Beeslaar (Jan 2002) ▪ Winemaker(s) Alet de Wet (Dec 2014) ▪ Viticulturist(s) Koos du Toit (Jan 2004), Ryno Maree (May 2016) & Annelie Viljoen (2017) ▪ 120ha/100ha (cabs s/f, merlot, ptage) ▪ 3,000t/500,000cs own label 98% red 2% rosé ▪ WIETA ▪ PO Box 19 Elsenburg 7607 ▪ wine@kanonkop.co.za ▪ www.kanonkop.co.za ▪ S 33° 51'18.4" E 018° 51'36.1" ▪ ⓐ boggles.could.piglet ▪ F +27 (0)21-884-4719 ▪ **T +27 (0)21-884-4656**

Kanu Wines

(symbols)

Kanu, which bears the name of a mythical African bird of promise, has been sold by the Ben Truter Trust to private Canadian vehicle parts maker ABC Group and Botswana textile company Caratex. In addition to vine renewal under longtime viti-vini man Johan Grimbeek, renovation and expansion are underway on the Koelenhof hillside home-farm, and visitors will find a restaurant, upgraded tasting area with viewdeck, deli, curio shop, hiking trails and other attractions.

Ultra Premium range

Pinotage ⓃⒺⓌ ★★★★ Vibrant seam of tangy brambles runs through elegant **17** ⑧③, accentuating its fruitiness. Easy, soft tannin grip for current drinking, fynbos & berry farewell. Discontinued: **'Maiden White Blend'**.

Premium range

★★★★ **Keystone** Mostly cab & malbec seasoned with 14% petit verdot, 12% merlot & year older oak. **15** ⑧⑦ intense cassis, cedar & fynbos perfume; harmonious tannins, admirably dry.

★★★★ **Nu Era** ⓃⒺⓌ Near-equal shiraz & mourvèdre, **16** ⑧⑦ ripe & fruit-filled, savoury spice undertones. Reined-in tannins, few grams sugar, year older oak all aid drinkability. WO W Cape.

★★★★ **KCB Chenin Blanc** Lively & multi-layered **16** ⑧⑦'s pear tart, peach & vanilla nuances courtesy Piekenierskloof fruit, clever oaking (11 months, 15% new, French/Hungarian). Off-dry but balanced & fresh.

★★★★ **Viognier** Ⓥ Unsubtle but delicious **14** ⑧⑥. Intense ripe nectarine & apricot, saffron, flowers & honey - that's just the bouquet! Creamy mid-palate ex French & Hungarian oak, charming kumquat lift.

Merlot ★★★ Attractive cherry, cranberry tones, clove & cocoa seasoning on medium-bodied, moderately tannic **17** ⑧②. **Chenin Blanc** Ⓥ ★★★ Delicious ripe melon, pineapple & pear fruit on fresh & zesty **17** ⑧⓪. Perfect sunset sipper. WO W Cape. **Sauvignon Blanc** Ⓥ ★★★ Satisfying tropical & citrus notes; easy sipper **17** ⑦⑧ is light & vivacious. **Giselle Méthode Cap Classique** ★★★★ Crisp, dry **NV** ⑧③ sparkler marries 72% chardonnay & pinot noir for citrus & pear appeal. 18 months on lees add gentle brioche & biscuit. Not tasted: **Shiraz**. Discontinued: **Rockwood, Kia-Ora Noble Late Harvest**.

Black Label range

Rifle Range Red Ⓥ ★★★ Mainly cab with pinot noir & splash merlot in early-drinking **NV** ⑦⑦, red fruit, soft tannins & plumping gram sugar. WO W Cape, as next. **Rifle Range White** Ⓥ ★★ Brief delight from tropical sauvignon, chenin **NV** ⑦① blend. **Natural Sweet Shiraz** Ⓥ ★★ Maraschino cherry & cinnamon spicing on Glühwein-like **14** ⑦①. Sweet & uncomplicated. Discontinued: **Merlot Rosé, Semi-Sweet Rosé, Semi-Sweet White**. — GM

Location/map: Stellenbosch ▪ Map grid reference: E3 ▪ WO: Stellenbosch/Western Cape ▪ Est/1stB 1998 ▪ Tasting & sales Mon-Fri 10–4.30 Sat/Sun 10-3 ▪ Fee R60pp ▪ Restaurant ▪ Deli ▪ Curio shop ▪ Hiking trails ▪ Owner(s) ABC Group & Caratex (Pty) Ltd ▪ Cellarmaster(s)/winemaker(s) Johan Grimbeek (Jan 2002) ▪ 48ha/20ha (cab, merlot, chard, sauv) ▪ 200t/60,000cs own label 50% red 45% white 5% rosé ▪ WIETA ▪ PO Box 548 Stellenbosch 7599 ▪ info@kanu.co.za ▪ www.kanu.co.za ▪ S 33° 53' 23.35" E 018° 49' 8.44" ▪ �🖳 scooter.mimic.tins ▪ T +27 (0)21-865-2488

☐ **Kap Hase** see Migliarina Wines
☐ **Kapokberg** see Groote Post Vineyards
☐ **Kap Vino Estate** see Kunjani Wines
☐ **Karate Water** see Parow Brandy
☐ **Karoobossie** see Teubes Family Wines

Karusa Premium Wines & Craft Brewery Ⓥ 🍽 ◎ ♿

Visitors exploring the Klein Karoo will find a smorgasbord of attractions at Karusa near Oudtshoorn: small-parcel wines, from still to bubbly to fortified, a microbrewery, tapas restaurant and deli and, at road's end in the Swartberg mountain foothills, the famous Cango Caves.

Location: Oudtshoorn ▪ Map: Klein Karoo & Garden Route ▪ Map grid reference: B3 ▪ Est/1stB 2004 ▪ Tasting & sales Mon-Fri 9.30–4 Sat 10-2.30 ▪ Closed Sun, Good Fri & Dec 25 ▪ Karoo Tapas Restaurant & Deli ▪ Conferences (30-40 pax) ▪ Microbrewery ▪ Owner(s) Karusa Partnership ▪ Cellarmaster(s) Jacques Conradie (2004) ▪ 8ha (grenache, mourv, muscadel r, ptage, shiraz, touriga nacional, chard, sauv, viog) ▪ 50-70t/5,000cs own label 30% red 50% white 5% rosé 15% other ▪ PO Box 1061 Oudtshoorn 6620 ▪ info@karusa.co.za ▪ www.karusa.co.za ▪ S 33° 28' 36.0" E 022° 14' 33.2" ▪ �🖳 zoologists.concepts.prequel ▪ F +27 (0)86-600-3167 ▪ T +27 (0)44-272-8717

☐ **Kasteelberg** see Riebeek Cellars

Katbakkies Wine

Stellenbosch 'green' architect, winemaker and distiller Andries van der Walt vinifies small parcels for his Katbakkies label (and others) from his Devon Valley farm's trio of red varieties (muscadel plantings for husk spirit on hold pending better rainfall), having left sauvignon, pinot noir and petit verdot on the eponymous Cederberg farm to neighbours. All '18 wines are sold out, but the older vintages below are still available.

★★★★ Cabernet Sauvignon ⓐ Classically styled **11** ⑧⑦, built around its crunchy ripe fruit & form-giving grape tannins; well proportioned for current enjoyment & further few years.

Syrah ⓐ **★★★★** Last sampled was suave, spicy & unshowily fruity **08** ⑧④. Not tasted: **Syrah Reserve, Chenin Blanc, Perpendiculum Viognier, Viognier.** — AL

Location/map/WO: Stellenbosch ▪ Map grid reference: D5 ▪ Est/1stB 1999 ▪ Tasting & sales Mon-Sat by appt ▪ Closed all pub hols ▪ Owner(s) Andries van der Walt ▪ Cellarmaster(s) Andries van der Walt (1999) ▪ Winemaker(s) Teddy Hall (2002, consultant) & Andries van der Walt (1999) ▪ 29ha/10ha (cab, merlot, shiraz) ▪ 500cs own label 50% red 50% white ▪ PO Box 305 Stellenbosch 7599 ▪ info@katbakkies.co.za ▪ www.katbakkies.co.za ▪ S 33° 55' 37.4" E 018° 49' 14.6" ▪ 🖭 pink.primed.oval ▪ **T +27 (0)82-882-9022**

Kay & Monty Vineyards

The sauvignon blanc, pair of MCC bubblies and red blend from John Legh's polo and wine estate, also a scenic wedding and lunching spot, are named SAV, Champu and Big Red respectively. They come from a handful of hectares, among the first to be planted in the Plettenberg Bay area. Today tended by farm manager Lloyd Kasimbi, and the grapes vinified by consultant Anton Smal. Kay and Monty? They're the Legh grandparents, who loved their glass of chilled 'champu' at sundown.

Location: Plettenberg Bay ▪ Map: Klein Karoo & Garden Route ▪ Map grid reference: C1 ▪ Est 2009 ▪ 1stB 2012 ▪ Tasting Tue-Sun 10-4 ▪ Restaurant ▪ Weddings & events (200 seater venue) ▪ Guest house ▪ Owner(s) John Legh ▪ Cellarmaster(s)/winemaker(s) Anton Smal (2012, consultant) ▪ Viticulturist(s) Lloyd Kasimbi ▪ 163ha/3.99ha (pinot, chard, sauv) ▪ PO Box 295 The Crags 6602 ▪ hello@kayandmonty.com ▪ www.kayand-monty.com ▪ S 33° 55' 51.84" E 023° 26' 0.91" ▪ 🖭 kebab.variant.turnings ▪ **T +27 (0)44-534-8387/+27 (0)79-965-9779**

☐ **KC** see Klein Constantia Estate

Keermont Vineyards

There's increasing attention at Keermont to the expression of specific vineyard sites, involving both careful selection of site and rigorously non-interventionist winemaking in the cellar – both the responsibility of Alex Starey, here since the redevelopment of the Blaauwklippen Valley estate began in 2005, after it was bought in 2003 by Mark Wraith and his family. It looks as if the two single-vineyard syrahs (made only in the best years) might eventually be supplemented by a third: a new hectare is being planted at the top of the Steepside block – 'a fantastic vineyard location at about 400m above sea level'. And visitors to the estate (Fridays or by appointment) can look forward to more attention, with 'a top end tour and tasting experience'.

Single Vineyard Series

★★★★ Pondok Rug Cabernet Franc Bright berry fragrance on **15** ★★★★★ ⑨①, with dry leafy edge. A pleasing mix of austerity & fruit-rich flavour depth, firm tannins in control. Powerful, but 14.5% alcohol is in balance, & the totality even quite elegant, thanks to good balance & dry finish. Impresses more than **14** ⑧⑨. Also in magnum, as all these.

★★★★☆ Steepside Syrah ⓐ Impressive **15** ⑨③ denser in colour than Topside, notably riper & darker-fruited. The palate broader & softer, with intense flavours & supple tannins; everything in balance, including 14.8% alcohol. All reds no added yeast, fining or filtration; mostly older oak.

★★★★☆ Topside Syrah In **15** ⑨② this has the lighter colour & brighter, redder spicy fruit of the pair of single-vineyard syrahs, as in **14** ★★★★★ ⑨⑤ - though also with darker aspects. Well structured & elegant, with lovely juicy acidity & firm tannins; sweet fruit lurks in the depths, before a good dry finish.

★★★★☆ Riverside Chenin Blanc ⓐ Aromas of subtly oaked **17** ⑨④ offer early complexity, with dried peach & earthy undertone. Fine integration of acid with fruit for lively & compelling full, sweet flavour (but bone-dry) & silky texture. No **16**. **15** ★★★★ ⑧⑨ closed & quiet in youth. **14** ★★★★★ ⑨⑦ a standout.

Annual Release range

★★★★ **Cabernet Sauvignon** (NEW) Ripe dark berries & tobacco on **15** (88). Drinking well now (no hurry), with balanced structure & modest fruit intensity. 15% alcohol shows only in a little sweetness.

★★★★☆ **Merlot** ⊘ Sweet fruitcake aromas plus choc & tobacco notes on **16** (90), with dashes of malbec & cab. Delicious now, but youthful & with serious tannin-acid underpinning. Balanced, & should gain more harmony in a few years. Old-oaked, like **15** ★★★★ (87) (with different varietal support).

★★★★ **Syrah** ⊘ 100% syrah/shiraz in **14** (87), unlike previous. Attractive aromas invite to balanced palate - lighter, more elegant than 14.5% alcohol suggests. Sweet fruit, easy tannic grip, restrained oak.

★★★★ **Estate Reserve** ⊘ **13** ★★★★★ (93) a refined Bordeaux quintet with dash syrah/shiraz, as was **12** (87). Certainly ripe, yet on classic, elegant & savoury side, with restrained oaking (20% new) & good tannins well integrated with core of fruit. Pleasing dry finish. Also in magnums, like Cab & Syrah.

★★★★☆ **Terrasse** Old-oaked **16** (92) another successful blend of chenin with viognier (some peachy perfume), sauvignon (green-tinged freshness), chardonnay (lemon notes). Has weight, intensity & seductive charm without overt fruitiness, & succulent acid verve. **15** ★★★★ (87) fell a fraction short.

★★★★ **Fleurfontein** Pre-bottling **17** ★★★★★ (90) from vine-dried sauvignon is velvet-soft, but shot through with fair acidity. Range of aromas & flavours - marmalade to raisins. Low 11% alcohol, high 268 g/l sugar. Absorbs half-new oak effortlessly. A touch more lively than last-tasted **15** (87). — TJ

Location/map/WO: Stellenbosch ▪ Map grid reference: G8 ▪ Est 2003 ▪ 1stB 2007 ▪ Tasting & sales Fri 10.30-1.30 or by appt ▪ Tasting fees apply ▪ Cellar tours by appt ▪ Luxury self-catering accommodation ▪ Owner(s) Wraith family ▪ Winemaker(s)/viticulturist(s) Alex Starey (Jan 2005) ▪ 156ha/29ha (cab, merlot, shiraz, chenin) ▪ ±90t/10,000cs own label 65% red 33% white 2% dessert ▪ IPW ▪ PO Box 21739 Kloof Str Cape Town 8008 ▪ info@keermont.co.za ▪ www.keermont.co.za ▪ S 34° 0' 27.0" E 018° 53' 39.0" ▪ ▥ mellow. creased.drum ▪ F +27 (0)21-880-0566 ▪ **T +27 (0)21-880-0397**

Keet Wines ⓠ

The proportions of the varieties change slightly each year, as highly regarded Stellenbosch winemaker and consultant Chris Keet continues to refine and perfect his First Verse Bordeaux blend (there will never be a Second, Third etc, he promises). The wine will however always be true to his mantra of 'refined, focused, honest and classic'. Though his is a boutique venture, Chris' fans will be heartened to hear that production has grown by 30% as the brand gains traction both locally and in some exciting destinations abroad.

★★★★☆ **First Verse** ⊛ Merlot-led 5-way Bordeaux blend **14** (92) raises the bar on riper, cab-based **13** ★★★★ (88). More refined elegance than power, subtle berry fruit & pencil shavings threaded with fine-grained tannins. Understated, all components in place for graceful development.— MW

Location/WO: Stellenbosch ▪ Est 2008 ▪ 1stB 2009 ▪ Tasting by appt ▪ Owner(s) Christopher Keet ▪ Cellarmaster(s)/winemaker(s)/viticulturist(s) Christopher Keet (Oct 2008) ▪ 10t/1,500cs own label 100% red ▪ PO Box 5508 Helderberg 7135 ▪ chris@keetwines.co.za ▪ www.keetwines.co.za ▪ **T +27 (0)82-853-1707**

☐ **Keimoes** see Orange River Cellars
☐ **Keizer's Creek** see Roodezandt Wines
☐ **Keldermeester Versameling** see Lanzerac Wine Estate

Kellerprinz

Since 1977, a budget-priced, light-bodied braai buddy for the sweeter toothed. In a 2L pack, by Distell.
Late Harvest ⊘ ★★ Unpretentious **NV** (71) full of sweet ripe fruit & enough balancing acidity. — JG

☐ **Kelvin Grove** see Simonsvlei International

Ken Forrester Wines ⓠ ⓘ ⓐ

A serious mountain biking accident slowed the irrepressible 'Mr Chenin' Ken Forrester for a short period - but he's back in the saddle, both biking and marketing his wines worldwide with customary enthusiasm. The investment by French giant AdVini has seen construction of a new cellar on the Scholtzenhof home-farm, which nowadays is a far cry from the neglected property Ken and wife Teresa (aka 'T') bought in 1994 after decamping from Johannesburg. The zeal in resurrecting old vines on the Helderberg spread and promoting the cause of chenin blanc generally has borne fruit, with Ken Forrester Wines boasting a fine reputation locally and abroad, both for chenin and Rhône-style reds.

Icon range

★★★★☆ **The Gypsy** Seductive plush plum & spice with firm grip of harmonious oak on **14** ⑨² mix of grenache, syrah & mourvèdre. Balanced & long, lovely density & concentration. A serious but supple mouthful.

★★★★★ **The FMC** ⓐ ⓦ A leader of the Cape chenin renaissance since early 2000s. **16** ⑨³ is concise, refreshing & yet rich with its signature apricot & honeyed nuance from botrytised fraction. Natural ferment & 400L French oaking add structure. Expressive & lengthy. Stellenbosch fruit, mostly off old bushvines (1974).

★★★★★ **'T' Noble Late Harvest** ⓐ Perfectly poised **17** ⑨⁴ botrytis chenin has brûlée richness, marmalade & jasmine sweetness with vivid acid to counter & cleanse. Ambrosial, refined & elegant. New-barrel fermented. First since **13** ⑨². 375 ml.

Occasional release: **FMC Première Sélection Moelleux**.

Cellar Exclusives range

★★★★★ **Three Halves** ⓐ Vibrantly spicy, dry mourvèdre, shiraz & grenache is swarthy & brooding; **15** ⑨³ structured & firm after 18 months in older French oak, yet also generous & rich. Layered & complex with long, rewarding finish. Better balanced than **13** ★★★★ ⑧⁹, which had 15% alcohol. No **14**.

★★★★☆ **Roussanne** Richly textured, **16** ⑨¹ has trademark stonefruit & tarte tatin spice. Restrained but fresh, fruit supported by subtle frame of oak from large older barrels. Elegant & subtle, the unusual (for SA) Rhône grape is well expressed. Stellenbosch WO, as Sparklehorse & Old Vine Chenin.

Sparklehorse ⓦ ★★★★ Chenin MCC sparkling is as cheery & full of fun as its carousel label. **15** ⑧⁵ tangy apple, pear & lees (18 months) notes, fizzes to the long, dry end.

Ken Forrester range

★★★★★ **Renegade** Brambles & hedgerow fruits prominent on shiraz-led **14** ⑨⁰ Rhône blend with grenache & dab mourvèdre. Muscular but cheerful, with light cedar note from older French oak, 18 months. Solid core & concentration.

★★★★☆ **Old Vine Reserve Chenin Blanc** Ripe pear & quince fruit on polished stage of oak (20% new), **17** ⑨¹ complex, layered yet fresh, with cleansing acid. Rounded & rich, protracted nuanced finish.

★★★★ **Sauvignon Blanc Reserve** Tangy sweet-sour lemon verbena & capsicum vivacity on **17** ★★★★ ⑧⁵. Extended lees contact adds breadth & palate weight. Includes Elim & Darling fruit, like **16** ⑧⁶.

Not tasted: **Merlot Reserve Pat's Garden**.

Petit range

Cabernet Sauvignon ★★★ Easy, uncomplicated cassis ripeness on light-bodied & juicy **17** ⑧¹, with splash merlot. **Pinotage** ★★★★ Mulberry & raspberry brightness on succulent **17** ⑧³. Light spice brush on unfussy easy-drinker. **Rosé** ★★★ Cherry- & berry-toned dry **18** ⑧⁰ matches previous in its gluggability. Mix of grenache & viognier. Ideal summertime sipper. **Chardonnay** ★★★ Citrus typicity on light, bright & easy **18** ⑧¹. Unoaked, with refreshing acidity. **Chenin Blanc** ★★★ Melon, guava & pear on **18** ⑧¹. Fresh & tasty as usual, dry & bright. **Sauvignon Blanc** ★★★ Grapefruit twist on **18** ⑧⁰ livened by subtle white pepper & kiwi nuance. Perfect patio fare in summer. **Natural Sweet** ★★★ Was 'Semi-Sweet' & vintage-dated, now **NV** ⑧⁰, still chenin based. Subtly sweet fruit-salad appeal, ripe pineapple & honey countered by lively acid. — FM

Location: Stellenbosch ▪ Map: Helderberg ▪ Map grid reference: C2 B2 ▪ WO: Western Cape/Stellenbosch ▪ Est/1stB 1994 ▪ Tasting & sales on home farm, cnr R44 & Winery Rd: Mon-Fri 9-5 Sat 9.30-3.30 ▪ Tasting options: Petit R60/5 wines; Chenin 101 & Connoisseur R100/5 wines or R150/7 wines; Best of Both Worlds R100/4 wines; Rhône Connoisseur R150/5 wines - tasting fee deductable with purchases over R400pp ▪ Closed Good Fri, Dec 25 & Jan 1 ▪ Sundays & after hours tasting available at 96 Winery Rd Restaurant ▪ Owner(s) Forrester Vineyards Pty Ltd ▪ Cellarmaster(s)/winemaker(s) Ken Forrester (1994) ▪ Viticulturist(s) Pieter Rossouw (Oct 2009) ▪ (grenache, merlot, mourv, shiraz, chenin) ▪ 1,100t/185,000cs own label 45% red 55% white ▪ Other export brand: Workhorse (Marks & Spencer) ▪ Brands for clients: Woolworths ▪ ISO 9001:2000, HACCP, SEDEX, WIETA ▪ PO Box 1253 Stellenbosch 7599 ▪ info@kenforresterwines.com ▪ www.

kenforresterwines.com ▪ S 34° 1' 31.06" E 018° 49' 05.92" (home farm) S 34° 1' 38.30" E 018° 48' 31.99" (96 Winery Rd Restaurant) ▪ ⌨ airships.plums.braves ▪ F +27 (0)21-855-2373 ▪ **T +27 (0)21-855-2374**

☐ **Kershaw** *see* Richard Kershaw Wines
☐ **Kevin Arnold** *see* Waterford Estate
☐ **Kevin King** *see* South Hill Vineyards
☐ **KFK Reserve** *see* Stellenview Premium Wines
☐ **Khoi Klaas** *see* Ashton Winery

Kingna Distillery   ⓛ ⓒ

Besides wedding celebrants and conference delegates, Norbert Engel's farm at Montagu accommodates brandy lovers with his boutique distillery. Since 2007, brandy master Ruan Hunlun has been crafting colombard grapes into pure potstill: first a 5 Year Old, then an 8, probably followed by 10 and 12 as the 2,000L still and French/American oak barrels yield their riches over time.

★★★★ **Potstill Brandy 8 Year Old** ⓛ Karoo sunshine in a bottle! Gorgeous notes of violet & orange blossom leading to smooth enveloping candied fruit, entwined with gentle cinnamon spice & chocolate.

Potstill Brandy 5 Year Old ⓛ ★★★ Smooth textured, light, 'feminine' & elegant, with fresh apricot, fynbos, clove & floral perfume; oak rather obvious. From colombard, like sibling. — WB, TJ

Location/WO: Montagu ▪ Map: Klein Karoo & Garden Route ▪ Map grid reference: C8 ▪ Est 2007 ▪ 1stB 2012 ▪ Tasting, sales & distillery tours Mon-Fri 10-5 Sat/Sun by appt ▪ Closed Easter Sat/Sun, Dec 25/26 & Jan 1 ▪ Tour groups ▪ Conferences ▪ Weddings/functions ▪ Owner(s) Norbert Engel ▪ Brandy master Ruan Hunlun (Jan 2005, consultant) ▪ 1,000ha/8ha (chenin, cbard) ▪ 140t/9,000L ▪ PO Box 395 Montagu 6720 ▪ ruan@kingna.co.za ▪ www.kingna.co.za ▪ S 33° 49' 45.87" E 20° 15' 39.10" ▪ ⌨ singled.bliss.chores ▪ **T +27 (0)71-637-3958**

☐ **King & Queen** *see* Bayede!
☐ **King Shaka** *see* Imbuko Wines
☐ **King Shaka-Zulu** *see* Bayede!

Kings Kloof Vineyards   ⓛ

The Newton-King family farm high on Helderberg Mountain has long supplied fruit for some of Spier's top brands, and now the Spier team is vinifying small parcels for an own-label. Tastings are offered by appointment, with dedicated visitor facilities in progress.

Family Reserve range

★★★★ **Merlot** ⊘ ⓐ Vibrant **16** ⑧⑧ shows distinct bluegum/mint leafiness over appealing blackcurrant fruit, earth-dusty minerality. Concentrated, inky & taut, begging time in cellar. No **15**, as next.

★★★★ **Syrah** Silky **16** ⑧⑦ has dominant ripe black cherry fruit laced with sweet oak spices, hints of fynbos. Medium bodied, elegant, but still unsettled. Needs time in bottle.

★★★★ **Sauvignon Blanc** ⓛ Crisp & soundly structured, **16** ⑧⑧ ticks the boxes. Bright passionfruit with distinct mineral undertones, finishing with a salty twist.

★★★★ **Semillon** Emphatic dusty stone minerality, wet wool note on lean, racy **17** ⑧⑦. Unoaked, leesy, with shapely elegance, lingering finish. — GdB

Location: Somerset West ▪ Map: Helderberg ▪ Map grid reference: E4 ▪ WO: Stellenbosch ▪ Est 1939 ▪ 1stB 1986 ▪ Tasting by appt ▪ Owner(s) Newton-King family ▪ Cellarmaster(s) Frans Smit (1995, Spier) ▪ Winemaker(s) Frans Smit & Spier winemaking team ▪ Viticulturist(s) Johann Smit (Spier) ▪ 73ha/12ha (merlot, shiraz, sauv, sem) ▪ 120t/600cs own label 30% red 70% white ▪ WIETA ▪ PO Box 2 Somerset West 7129 ▪ richardnk@kingskloof.co.za ▪ www.kingskloof.co.za ▪ S 34° 3' 12.68" E 018°51'49.34" ▪ ⌨ served.evening.hush ▪ **T +27 (0)21-851-9080**

☐ **Kipepeo** *see* Baratok Wines

Kirabo Private Cellar

Pieter le Roux, sixth-generation winegrower on Watervalkloof, sells off most of his production. But since 2003, he and wife Karen have vinified small parcels of red under the label Kirabo ('Gift from God'), available to private clients and visitors enjoying this expansive Breedekloof estate's facilities and activities.

Location: Rawsonville ▪ Map: Breedekloof ▪ Map grid reference: C6 ▪ Est 2002 ▪ 1stB 2003 ▪ Tasting, sales & cellar/vineyard tours Mon-Fri 8.30-5 Sat by appt ▪ Closed all pub hols ▪ Meals by appt only; picnic baskets ▪ Facilities for children ▪ Tour groups ▪ Farm produce ▪ Walking/hiking trails ▪ Weddings/functions ▪ Conservation area ▪ Owner(s) Pieter & Karen le Roux ▪ Cellarmaster(s) Pieter le Roux (2002) ▪ Winemaker(s) Pieter & Karen le Roux (2002) ▪ Viticulturist(s) Pieter le Roux ▪ 1,000t/10,000L total ▪ 15t/2,500cs own label 100% red ▪ IPW ▪ PO Box 96 Rawsonville 6845 ▪ info@kirabocellar.co.za ▪ www.kirabocellar.co.za ▪ S 33° 42′ 36.68″ E 019° 21′ 27.55″ ▪ ⬛ transitive.part.reprinted ▪ T +27 (0)71-681-9019/+27 (0)83-228-5191

☐ **Kitchen Sink** see The Kitchen Sink
☐ **Klaasenbosch** see Wine-of-the-Month Club

Klawer Wine Cellars

Being overwhelmingly bulk-wine producers is no impediment to West Coast-based Andries Blake and his team from thinking outside the box when it comes to the Klawer proprietary labels. The new Vino Sacci wine pouches are a response to the many tourists, including trail walkers and campers, stopping by the cellardoor en route to the Matzikama region further to the north. Easy to pack and carry, the dinky 375-ml 'sakkies' also chill, pour and seal easily. At the other end of the scale, the Villa Esposto wines continue to impress and deliver value. All originate in 2,000+ widely scattered hectares, vinified in dual cellars at Klawer and Trawal.

Villa Esposto range

★★★★ **Chenin Blanc** Tangerine & sweet almond notes, plenty of acid zip but creamy, broad mouthfeel too, owing to balancing 6 months 2nd-fill French oak. Previewed **18** ⑧⑦ delicious & rewarding. No **17**.

★★★★☆ **Straw Wine** ② 375 ml of sweet seduction from 50 year old muscat d'Alexandrie, hand harvested & air dried 2 weeks on bed of straw. Grape & apricot enticements on rich & unctuous **16** ⑨②.

Pinotage (NEW) ★★★★ A plum, mulberry & caramel welcome to **16** ⑧⑤, fruit supported by sturdy scaffold of wood tannin thanks to generous use of oak staves, 12 months. **Pinotage Rosé** ★★★ Dry pink from pinotage, light & easy strawberry flavours, **18** ⑦⑧ pleasantly fruity farewell.

Klawer range

★★★★ **Hanepoot** ⊘ Variety's litchi & rosepetal signatures in abundance, **17** ⑧⑨ fortified dessert supported by an alluring, long-lingering sweetness. Delicious ice cold. First since **14** ⑧⑨.

★★★★ **White Muscadel** ⊘ Spicy & floral fortified oozes charm. **16** ⑧⑥ marriage of fruity sweetness, zippy acidity & integrated spirit. Rosepetal, litchi typicity with more finesse than last **13** ★★★★ ⑧③.

Cabernet Sauvignon ⊘ ★★★ Youthful exuberance held in check by firm tannins, deft, variety-true **17** ⑧① offers the expected cassis, blackberry & cigarbox. **Merlot** ★★ Red-fruited, no-frills expression of the variety, **17** ⑦⑥ a crowd pleaser helped by few grams sugar, as most of the reds. **Pinotage** ② ★★★ Quaffable example of SA's own grape, **16** ⑧① fruitcake, sour cherry & lovely dry finish. Step up on previous. **Shiraz** ★★ Spice & mulberry notes, fruit is ripe but very dry tannin makes **17** ⑦④ quite austere - a juicy steak will fix. **Shiraz-Malbec** (NEW) ⊘ ★★★ Unusual blend is plump & succulent, ample blackberry goodness sure to be an instant hit. **17** ⑧⓪ good braai red. **Chardonnay** ★★★ Friendly & easy, delicious citrus entry & marzipan finish. **18** ⑦⑧ fruit driven & fresh. **Chenin Blanc** ⊘ ★★★ Unoaked sibling to Villa Esposto is super-easy to quaff, generous tropical flavour & racy freshness. Hot December holidays beckon. **18** ⑧① previewed, as next two. **Sauvignon Blanc** ★★ Brisk acidity, tropical fruit & moderate 12% alcohol on **18** ⑦④. **Viognier** ⊘ ★★★ Highly aromatic & perfumed, peach, apricot & baking spice nuance, oaked **18** ⑧① expresses the variety with aplomb. **Michelle Vin Doux Sparkling** ⊘ ★★★ Congenial, somewhat foamy, sweet rosé bubbles from muscat. Low-alcohol NV ⑦⑧ ready for your next pool party. **African Ruby Rooibos** ★★★★ Fortified red muscadel infused with rooibos & buchu, aromatic & rich but perfectly fresh. NV ⑧④ will reward a bit of patience. **Red Muscadel** ⊘ ★★★★ Seductive sweet fortified, **17** ⑧④ with beautiful light pink hue. Pairs perfectly with vanilla ice cream to delight & impress dinner party guests.

Cape Vintage ⓃⒺⓌ ⊘ ★★★★ Darkly rich 'port' from souzão, quite serious, modern, ample fruit & tannic grip. Try **15** ⑧④ with block of dark chocolate, thank us later. Discontinued: **Shiraz-Merlot**.

Vino Sacci range ⓃⒺⓌ

Merlot ★ Piquant red fruit & tannin, **17** ⑥⑨ not too complex but cleverly packaged in spill-resistant, go-anywhere 375-ml pouch, as sibling. **Chenin Blanc** ★★ Straightforward **18** ⑦⓪ preview offers a light body of tropical fruit.

Travino range

Shiraz-Merlot ⓐ ★★ Plump & juicy **15** ⑦① spicy fruit & soft tannin. **Rosé** ⓐ ★ Brief berry fruit flavours in sweet **16** ⑥⑦, with contrasting racy-sour acidity. **Chenin Blanc-Sauvignon Blanc** ⓐ ★★ Fresh & uncomplicated **16** ⑦④, touch of guava fruit before a dry goodbye. Discontinued: **Matador**. — HC

Location: Klawer ▪ Map/WO: Olifants River ▪ Map grid reference: B4 ▪ Est 1956 ▪ Tasting & sales Mon-Fri 8–5 Sat 9–1 ▪ Facilities for children ▪ BYO picnic ▪ Owner(s) 87 members ▪ Manager Andries Blake ▪ Cellarmaster(s) Pieter van Aarde (Nov 2011) ▪ Winemaker(s) Roelof van Schalkwyk, Tiaan van Zyl, Neill Gellatly & Christo Beukes ▪ Viticulturist(s) Johannes Mellet ▪ 2,095ha (cab, merlot, ptage, ruby cab, shiraz, chard, chenin, cbard, hanepoot, muscadel, sauv, viog) ▪ 34,000t/50,000cs own label 40% red 40% white 5% rosé 15% other ▪ ISO 22000:2009, Organic, DLG, IPW ▪ PO Box 8 Klawer 8145 ▪ info@klawerwyn.co.za ▪ www.klawerwine.co.za ▪ S 31° 47' 34.9" E 018° 37' 36.1" ▪ 🖂 primly.netball.handsomest ▪ F +27 (0)27-216-1561 ▪ **T +27 (0)27-216-1530**

☐ **Klein Centennial** *see* Group CDV

Klein Constantia Estate ⓐ 🍴 📷 ♿

One of the core farms behind the modern-day wine renaissance in what was the nexus of 17th-century Cape winegrowing has been revitalised by its current custodians (including Bordeaux luminaries Bruno Prats and Hubert de Boüard). Replanting is rooted in detailed analysis of cool-climate Constantia mountainside sites and deep-seated beliefs in sustainable viticulture (such as high-density bushvines). The newer wines reflect the strategic decision to focus on sauvignon, with several bottlings expressing special vineyard blocks. Brand-new is a Reserve version of their fine sparkling. But it's the delectable dessert Vin de Constance that ultimately seduces, enticing a global audience to the chic tasting room and The Bistro @ Klein Constantia.

Estate Wines

★★★★☆ **Glen Dirk Sauvignon Blanc** Captivating fragrances on **17** ⑨② selection of top blocks on newer Constantia site: anise, jasmine & hints of nettle. Unique & characterful, presenting pure passionfruit with subtle herbaceousness. Rounded 9 months in acacia & French oak barrels.

★★★★☆ **Metis Sauvignon Blanc** ⓐ In collaboration with Pascal Jolivet, **17** ⑨③ from high-lying estate vines expresses Sancerre character: intense aromatics, oyster juice & flint. Sublime weight, focus & balance, enriched by year on fine lees & 20% neutral oak component. Also-available magnum especially worth laying down.

★★★★☆ **Perdeblokke Sauvignon Blanc** Prestige blend from premium high-lying blocks, single-vineyard **17** ⑨② has forceful aromas, flint & spices. Precise, intense & finely structured, combining ripe fruit with detailed minerality. 9 months French oak & acacia barrels.

★★★★☆ **Sauvignon Blanc Block 382** ⓐ Very special single-vineyard **17** ⑨④, made with no additives, 8 months on lees in old 500L barrels. Intensely aromatic, pure & focused, but bold & confident, with succulently ripe granadilla & gooseberry fruit.

★★★★ **Sauvignon Blanc** Unoaked version a champion of variety since mid-1980s, showing distinctive style with generous fruit, precise acid & enviable ageability record. Big aromas & grippy mouthfeel on **17** ⑧⑥.

★★★★ **Brut Méthode Cap Classique** Quite austere **14** ★★★★ ⑧⑤ sparkler from chardonnay has muted floral scents, lime-mineral notes. No wood this vintage, but lees ageing increased to 33 months. Less yeasty fullness than **13** ⑧⑥.

★★★★☆ **Brut Méthode Cap Classique Reserve** ⓃⒺⓌ ⓐ Exceptionally fine blanc de blancs sparkling, **11** ⑨④ has panache in abundance, 60 months on lees yet youthful & vibrant. Rich brioche, crisp acid & spicy apple fruit from optimally harvested chardonnay & 100% barrel fermentation in older oak.

★★★★★ **Vin de Constance** ⊛ Arguably the Cape's most famous wine, crafted to emulate the great Constantia sweet desserts of the 18th century. **14** ⑨⑤ from raisined muscat de Frontignan, as always, impossibly complex & detailed, with seductive perfume, opulent fruit & finely modulated acidity. Intricate vinification, 3 years 500L barrels of various wood types. 500 ml, magnums too.

Not tasted: **Estate Red Blend, Chardonnay, Riesling, Organic Sauvignon Blanc**. Occasional release: **Sauvignon Blanc Block 361/372, Sauvignon Blanc Block 371, Sauvignon Blanc Block 381.**

KC range

Cabernet Sauvignon-Merlot ⊘ ⑨ ★★★☆ Quaffable **16** ⑧③ Bordeaux red has savoury, meaty notes, gently smooth tannin, dark berry fruit. WO W Cape, as all these.

Pinot Noir ⊘ ★★★★ Remarkably well-priced **16** ⑧④ from Elgin & Hemel-en-Aarde vines has delicious cherry fruit, silky texture. **Rosé** ★★★★ Previewed **18** ⑧③ bone-dry pink from cab franc offers earthy notes with appealing floral scents. Crisp acidity, silky texture. **Sauvignon Blanc** ★★★★ Substantial fruit weight & body, **18** ⑧④ shows good poise & focus, Constantia & Stellenbosch vines deliver more than a quaffer. Discontinued: **Husk Spirit range.** — GdB

Location: Constantia ▪ Map: Cape Peninsula ▪ Map grid reference: B3 ▪ WO: Constantia/Western Cape ▪ Est 1823 ▪ 1stB 1824 ▪ Tasting & sales Mon-Sat 10—5 Sun & pub hols 10-4 ▪ Fee R50 ▪ Closed Good Fri & Dec 25 ▪ The Bistro @ Klein Constantia Tue-Sun 12-4 ▪ Gift shop ▪ Estate honey for sale ▪ Collection of original Constantia bottles on display ▪ Owner(s) Zdenek Bakala, Charles Harman, Bruno Prats & Hubert de Boüard ▪ MD Hans Aström ▪ Winemaker(s) Matthew Day (2009) ▪ Brandy masters Matthew Day & Giorgio Dalla Cia (Dalla Cia) ▪ Viticulturist(s) Craig Harris (Oct 2013) ▪ 146ha/64ha (cab, malbec, p verdot, shiraz, chard, muscat de F, riesling, sauv, sem) ▪ 500t/80,000cs own label 30% red 70% white ▪ WWF-SA Conservation Champion ▪ PO Box 375 Constantia 7848 ▪ info@kleinconstantia.com ▪ www.kleinconstantia.com ▪ S 34° 2′ 19.0″ E 018° 24′ 46.5″ ▪ ⬛ flattest.recyclers.herewith ▪ F +27 (0)21-794-2464 ▪ **T +27 (0)21-794-5188**

Klein DasBosch   ⓠ ⑪

Label vinified at Vriesenhof by Jan Coetzee for neighbour James 'Whitey' Basson, CEO of retailing empire Shoprite/Checkers. The wines can be tasted and purchased at Mont Marie Restaurant on Blaauwklippen Road, Stellenbosch. A selection also appears on a few other local restaurant lists and in Checkers stores.

Location/map: Stellenbosch ▪ Map grid reference: F7 ▪ Tasting & sales at Mont Marie Restaurant, Stellenbosch T +27 (0)21-880-0777 ▪ phone ahead as tasting hours are subject to change ▪ Owner(s) James Wellwood Basson ▪ Viti/vini consultant Jan Coetzee (1997) ▪ Winemaker(s) Jan Coetzee (1994) & Nicky Claasens ▪ Viticulturist(s) Eben Archer ▪ ±25ha ▪ 90% red 10% white ▪ PO Box 12320 Stellenbosch 7613 ▪ annalette@kleindasbosch.com ▪ www.kleindasbosch.co.za, www.montmarie.co.za ▪ S 33° 58′ 56.0″ E 018° 51′ 44.5″ ▪ ⬛ feasts.luring.however ▪ F +27 (0)21-880-0999 ▪ **T +27 (0)21-880-0128/+27 (0)71-859-1773 (office)/+27 (0)21-880-0777 (tasting/sales)**

☐ **Kleine Draken** *see* Zandwijk
☐ **Kleine Kaap** *see* Imbuko Wines
☐ **Kleine Parys** *see* Klein Parys Vineyards
☐ **Kleine Rust** *see* Stellenrust

Kleine Schuur Estate

When it comes to a wine estate, you don't get smaller than Danie Louw and Liezel Falck's quarter-hectare of wines in Durbanville. But as they discovered, the smallness of their dryland shiraz vineyard didn't preclude their hobby becoming a passion, and now they 'micro-manage every step of the process'. The recent drought affected small vineyards as well as large, however, and there was no 2018 Kleine Schuur harvest.

Kleine Schuur range ⑭

Shiraz ⊘ ⑨ ★★★★ Friendly single-vineyard **16** ⑧④ offers exceptional value & character: seagrass & scrub savouriness, plump fruit balanced by bright acidity, amenable tannins. — TJ, CvZ

Location/WO: Durbanville ▪ Est 2005 ▪ Closed to public ▪ Owner(s) Danie Louw & Liezel Falck ▪ Winemaker(s) Danie Louw ▪ 0.9ha/0.25ha (shiraz) ▪ 2.4t/241cs own label 100% red ▪ PO Box 2603 Durbanville 7551 ▪ info@ kleineschuur.co.za ▪ **T +27 (0)83-231-4346**

Kleine Zalze Wines

Arisen from a run-down cellar and vineyards in the 1990s under hands-on stewardship of Stellenbosch attorney-businessman Kobus Basson, Kleine Zalze winery today forms part of the De Zalze luxury residential and golf estate, and represents Kobus' vision of a quality-wine venture using fruit from rejuvenated home vines and selected partner-vineyards around the Cape. With a well-defined, multi-tier portfolio selling in over 20 countries, the team led by cellarmaster Alastair Rimmer and viticulturist Henning Retief bring in-depth international experience and a thoroughly modern mindset to their roles. Not that it's needed, but on-site top-notch restaurant Terroir reminds all involved that simple enjoyment is what it's really about.

Family Reserve range

★★★★☆ **Cabernet Sauvignon** ⓐ Superb expression of exceptional **15** ⑨③ vintage: deep blackcurrant, polished leather, intense violet on firm, well-structured backbone of fine tannin, 75% new oak in support. Generosity of texture & depth, made for the long haul. WO Stellenbosch for these unless noted.

★★★★ **Pinotage** ⓐ Hand-sorted grapes for **16** ★★★★☆ ⑨③, opulent styling with red berry fruit, plum pudding, vanilla, cedar & exotic spice. Firm but supple tannins & luscious palate weight, plus complexity & breadth, promise many years drinking pleasure. First since **09** ⑧⑦. Coastal WO.

★★★★☆ **Shiraz** ⓐ Full bodied, with brooding intensity & power, **15** ⑨③ is ripe (15.4% alcohol) but stylish, delivers a lasting taste sensation. Seriously oaked (19 months) for the long haul, deserves 6+ years to unfurl. No **14**.

★★★★☆ **Chenin Blanc** ⓐ White flagship from 3 different sites in Stellenbosch, **17** ⑨④ sublime expression of weighty, luscious quince & tropical flavours underpinned by creamy vanilla oak. Lively, integrated freshness bodes well for the future. Barrel fermented/8 months, all older wood.

★★★★☆ **Sauvignon Blanc** ⓐ Minerality, fine lemon & lime flavours with burst of ripe pineapple on **17** ⑨③'s rich palate. The key here is focus, freshness & purity - all in harmony. Stellenbosch, Durbanville & Darling grapes, 7 months on lees. Don't rush to drink.

Vineyard Selection

★★★★☆ **Cabernet Sauvignon** ⊘ ⓐ Lovely depth of blackcurrant, cedar & chocolate flavour, mingled with hints of spring flowers. **16** ⑨④ great combination of elegance & concentration on well-structured tannin backbone aided by 20 months in 40% new oak. Ageworthy.

★★★★ **Pinot Noir** ⊘ Pulpy strawberry & forest floor aromas & flavours on **17** ⑧⑥ from Elim, gentle tannins underpin creamy fruit through to savoury finish. Older barrels for 12 months create a future - well worth holding back a few years.

★★★★ **Shiraz** ⊘ Voluptuous, with sweet-savoury finish of black pepper & tapenade, **16** ⑧⑦ inherently a food partner. Ripe & full-flavoured, mulberry, exotic spice & cured meat undertones. Stellenbosch WO.

★★★★ **Shiraz-Mourvèdre-Viognier** Older-oak maturation adds chocolate & spice to **16** ⑧⑥'s delightful succulent blackberries, red plums & earth, mourvèdre (15%) aids complexity & splash viognier lifts the finish.

★★★★☆ **Chardonnay** ⊘ ⓐ Aromas of blossoms & stonefruit lead to rounded, fresh flavours of baked apple, crème brûlée & caramelised nuts on elegant, well-integrated palate. Beguiling, but 60% new-oak ageing means **17** ⑨③ is no pushover, will reward cellaring. Stellenbosch, Robertson grapes.

★★★★ **Chenin Blanc** ⊘ ⓐ Like **16** ⑧⑧, older oak to preserve fruit, briefer sojourn than Family Reserve. Fermented & aged in barrel 6 months, **17** ★★★★☆ ⑨③ textbook Kleine Zalze chenin. Tropical fruit on silky vanilla oak, exhilarating lemon freshness & length. Stellenbosch WO.

★★★★☆ **Sauvignon Blanc** ⊘ Now bottled, **17** ⑨⓪ from Stellenbosch, Darling & Durbanville fruit matches last year's promise of layered complexity, with steely minerality, pristine citrus fruit, pithy texture & long saline finish.

Cellar Selection

Cabernet Sauvignon ⑦ ★★★ One of four cabs across the ranges, this for earlier drinking. **17** ⑧② fleshy dark berries & plums, juicy, with succulent tannins in support. **Pinotage** ⊘ ⑦ ★★★★ Gluggable multi-region **17** ⑧⑤ over-delivers, velvety, ripe, dark-berry fruit & smooth, balanced tannin. **Cabernet Sauvignon-Merlot** ⑦ ★★★ Wholeberry-fermented **17** ⑧① showcases pristine fruit, freshness & rounded texture. **Cinsault Rosé** ⑭⑤ ⊘ ⑦ ★★★ A floral delight, mouthwatering acidity, wild strawberry flavours & dry earthy finish in **18** ⑧①. **Chardonnay Unwooded** ⊘ ⑦ ★★★★ Citrus, orchard fruit & dried herb notes on inviting unoaked **18** ⑧⑤, extended lees contact adds to mouthfeel & accessibility. **Chenin Blanc Bush Vines** ⊘ ⑦ ★★★★ Always exceptional value, & **18** ⑧⑤ no exception. Delights with fresh fruity flavours, smooth texture & zingy conclusion. **Sauvignon Blanc** ⊘ ⑦ ★★★★ Vibrant green grass & gooseberry aromas, broad palate, intense lively mineral finish on **18** ⑧③.

Cinsault ⑦ ★★★ Bright, berry-rich **16** ⑧① shows why cinsaut is resurgent in SA: light textured, vibrantly juicy, fresh & tasty. No wood, this is about the fruit. Coastal WO, as most of these. **Merlot** ★★★ Good typicity, with Xmas cake, plum compote & winter spice in **17** ⑧⓪. Easy, for everyday sipping. Discontinued: **Cinsault-Gamay Noir Rosé**.

Méthode Cap Classique Sparkling range

★★★★ **Brut Rosé** ⑦ Elegant & stylish 60/40 pinot noir/chardonnay bubbly. **NV** ⑧⑧'s red berries get a citrus underpin from the white grape; all come together nicely in an acid-brightened palate.

★★★★ **Brut** ⑦ Impressively consistent styling for these sparklers. Expected elegance & finesse in latest **NV** ⑧⑧; zesty, fresh berry/citrus flavours courtesy 60/40 chardonnay/pinot noir.

Not tasted: **Vintage Brut**.

Zalze range

Vineyard Reserve Cabernet Sauvignon ★★★ Fairtrade-certified **17** ⑧①, sweet blackcurrants & blackberries, hints of cedar, lively tannins on sleek body. For export, as all this & next range. **Shiraz-Grenache-Viognier** ⑦ ★★★★ Older barrels for suave tannins, Old World flavours in improved **16** ⑧④; tapenade, scrub, black pepper, plush hedgerow fruit. **Shiraz-Mourvèdre-Viognier** ★★★ Clever blend, **17** ⑧② juicy & succulent red fruit in harmonious, spicy mouthful, gentle tannin grip on farewell. **Vineyard Reserve Bush Vine Chenin Blanc** ★★★★ Fermented/aged in older barrels to preserve fruit, **17** ⑧⑤ creamy baked apple with refreshing citrus finish. Coastal WO, as Cabernet. **Bush Vine Chenin Blanc** ★★★ Bouncy, vibrant & tropical-toned **18** ⑧② is unoaked, so it's the skin/lees contact that adds textured mouthfeel & long finish. In abeyance: **Pinotage**. Discontinued: **Cabernet Sauvignon-Shiraz Rosé**.

Foot of Africa range

Shiraz Reserve ⑦ ★★★ No tank, **15** ⑧① all oaked, a charry, mocha effect which sits nicely with the dark fruit tones. **Chenin Blanc Reserve** ★★★ Freshly sliced Golden Delicious apple, hint of spice & squeeze of lime on **18** ⑧⓪. — WB

Location/map: Stellenbosch ▪ Map grid reference: E7 ▪ WO: Western Cape/Coastal/Stellenbosch ▪ Est 1695 ▪ 1stB 1997 ▪ Tasting & sales Mon-Sat 9–6 Sun 11–6 ▪ Fee R25/5 wines or R15/3 wines ▪ Closed Good Fri, Dec 25 & Jan 1 ▪ Terroir Restaurant ▪ De Zalze Golf Course ▪ Owner(s) Kobus Basson ▪ Cellarmaster(s) Alastair Rimmer (Sep 2014) ▪ Winemaker(s) RJ Botha (Dec 2012) ▪ Viticulturist(s) Henning Retief (May 2006) ▪ 130ha/80ha under vine ▪ 2,300t/400,000cs own label 40% red 50% white 10% rosé ▪ PO Box 12837 Die Boord 7613 ▪ quality@kleinezalze.co.za ▪ www.kleinezalze.co.za ▪ S 33° 58′ 14.1″ E 018° 50′ 8.9″ ▪ ⓦ cave.rally. lifelong ▪ F +27 (0)21-880-0716 ▪ **T +27 (0)21-880-0717**

Kleinhoekkloof ⑦

Former international steel man Theunis de Jongh fell in love with a farm in the folds of the Langeberg mountains near Ashton, where altitude and aspect help him and daughter Danielle produce small parcels from French varieties, harvest olives and produce their own charcuterie.

Location: Ashton ▪ Map: Robertson ▪ Map grid reference: B4 ▪ Est 2004 ▪ 1stB 2006 ▪ Phone ahead for opening hours ▪ Owner(s) Raudan Trust ▪ Cellarmaster(s)/viticulturist(s) Theunis de Jongh (2011) ▪ Winemaker(s) Theunis de Jongh (2011), with Danielle de Jongh ▪ 114ha/11.8ha (merlot, mourv, p verdot, pinot, shiraz, sauv, viog) ▪ 110t/2,400cs own label 45% red 40% white 15% rosé ▪ Other export brand: Mountain Eye ▪ PO Box

244 Ashton 6715 ▪ theunis@khk.co.za ▪ www.kleinhoekkloof.co.za ▪ S 33° 46′ 51.87″ E 020° 03′ 17.30″ ▪ ⌧
rhinos.attributions.cultivates ▪ F +27 (0)86-677-5399 ▪ **T +27 (0)82-332-5474**

☐ **Klein Kasteelberg** *see* Group CDV
☐ **Kleinood** *see* Tamboerskloof Wine – Kleinood Farm
☐ **Klein Optenhorst** *see* Dainty Bess

Klein Parys Vineyards ⓐ ⑪ ⓒ ⓑ ⓔ

Entrepreneurial winemaker Kosie Möller launched what's become a very substantial venture in the early 2000s on Klein Parys, one of Paarl's original farms (circa 1692), with an emphasis on value-for-money wines, unusual varieties and understanding consumer tastes. A pioneer of the 'lifestyle' cellardoor, Klein Parys still offers a variety of guest amenities, including on-trend craft beer and restaurant featured on a TV chat show.

Family Selection

★★★★ **Jacob** ⓥ Cape Blend of pinotage, shiraz & merlot. Rhubarb fruit with aromatic notes on **11** ★★★★ ⑧⑧, solid, four-square body & tannins, briefer finish than last-made **09** ⑧⑦.

★★★★ **Niclas** ⓥ Impressive **11** ⑧⑥ shiraz, merlot, cab blend has fine fruit purity though oak tannins from 28 months new Hungarian barriques intrude somewhat. Should resolve over the long haul wine is designed for. Major improvement on last-tasted **08** ★★★ ⑦⑧.

Beatrix ⓥ ★★★★ Evolved malty oxidative notes on **11** ⑧⑤ cab, merlot, shiraz blend. Solid but angular fruit structure, heavy oak presence which time might resolve. **Charl Sias** ⓥ ★★★★ Full-bodied & ripe **10** ⑧⑭, exotic méthode cap classique sparkling from chardonnay, nouvelle, viognier & sauvignon.

Kleine Parys Selection

Cabernet Sauvignon ★★★ Unoaked **16** ⑧① 's perfume is pure Ribena - intense, jumps out of the glass, then becomes more serious on the palate. Has definition, grip, finishes dry. WO W Cape for most of these.

Merlot ⓥ ★★★ Generous blackberry jam fruit on mild-mannered **16** ⑧⓪, lightish body, brief finish.

Shiraz ⓥ ★★★★ Solid, meaty **15** ⑧⑤ shows savoury side, with hints of plum pudding & pepper, hefty tannins invite a hearty meal. **Chenin Blanc** ★★★ With 15% chardonnay, melon-toned **18** ⑦⑧ feels fuller, riper than 12.5% alcohol suggests. **Sauvignon Blanc** ★★★ Attractive green note throughout **18** ⑧⓪, gooseberries at core, ends zesty-fresh. **Charmat Selection** ⓥ ★★★ Undisclosed varieties ex Durbanville, dry **NV** ⑦⑧ sparkling is crisp & foamy, rather light on fruit, with terpene note. Not tasted: **Chardonnay**. In abeyance: **Pinotage**, **Red Muscadel**.

Tooverberg range

Contour Merlot ⓥ ★★ Rather primary juicy plum fruit on **16** ⑦⑥, uncomplicated early drinking. Coastal WO, as next. **Merlot** ★★★ Unwooded **16** ⑦⑧ shows upfront bright berries, appealing juicy drinkability. **Chardonnay** ★★★ Tangerine & melon perfume & flavours, unwooded, sleek, & with friendly alcohol, **18** ⑦⑧ drinks easily & well. WO W Cape. Not tasted: **Pinotage Rosé**. — CR

Location/map: Paarl ▪ Map grid reference: E5 ▪ WO: Paarl/Western Cape/Coastal ▪ Est 1692 ▪ 1stB 2002 ▪ Tasting, sales & cellar tours Mon-Fri 10-5 Sat 10-3 ▪ Fee R30/4 wines, R40/6 wines ▪ Closed Good Fri, Dec 25 & Jan 1 ▪ Facilities for children ▪ Conferences ▪ Weddings/functions ▪ Oppiestoep Restaurant Mon & Tue 8-5 Wed-Sat 8-9pm Sun 8-3 ▪ Craft beer ▪ Owner(s) Kosie Möller ▪ Cellarmaster(s)/winemaker(s) Kosie Möller (2002) ▪ 56ha/45ha (cab, shiraz, chard, chenin) ▪ 1,800t/500,000cs own label 48% red 48% white 4% sparkling + 1m cs for clients ▪ Brands for clients: Kleine Parys, Miller's Mile, Tooverberg, Tooverberg Contour ▪ PO Box 1362 Suider-Paarl 7624 ▪ logistics@kparys.co.za ▪ www.kleinparysvineyards.co.za ▪ S 33° 45′ 0.2″ E 018° 58′ 48.6″ ▪ ⌧ tempting.registry.taps ▪ **T +27 (0)21-201-2494**

Klein Roosboom ⓐ ⑪ ⓒ ⓑ ⓔ

Undimmed by the sad passing of Jéan de Villiers, grape-grower for Durbanville Hills winery whose passion for the vine inspired his wife Karin to venture into boutique vintning, his family are 'brimming with excitement' over a number of developments, including the appointment of Piti Coetzee as co-winemaker, release of a new sauvignon, planting of more chenin, and opening of the refurbished eatery, doubtless to prove as popular as the 'winetasting caves' innovatively nested in old concrete fermenters.

Reserve range (NEW)

Sauvignon Blanc ★★★★ Best-years-only release. From single 22 year old block, deeper minerality, more grapefruit than KR sibling, **18** (83) ideal food wine, especially with seafood. Some ageing potential too.

Klein Roosboom range

Johan Cabernet Sauvignon ★★ Aptly recognises a 'strong & robust' son. Prosciutto & white pepper, the oak's influence prominent in **17** (76)'s character, firm foundation for cellaring, the berry fruit muted, not yet holding its own. **Nicol Merlot** ★★★ Red berries at core of **17** (80), some chocolate, savoury spice, tannin still youthful, firm & dry, needing a year/2 to soften. **Janét Shiraz** ★★★ Oaking 12 months, some new barrels, as all the varietal reds, giving toasty, sweet spice tones to **17** (81)'s dark fruit, the body smooth & round, ready to enjoy. **My Way** (❡) ★★★ Merlot/cab & 75% new oak, 16 months for **15** (78). Dark-toned in fruit, hint salinity, firm finish; a bit dry & grainy. **Marianna Rosé** ★★★ Bright pink, **18** (82) blend of merlot (60%) & sauvignon blanc, prominent red-berry scents, sauvignon lending a citrus freshness in the flavours. Tasty, solo or with food. **Dear Diary Chardonnay** ★★★ Unwooded, **18** (82) has fresh pear & apple styling, crisply dry, appetising. **Jéan Sauvignon Blanc** ★★★ From blocks 8-30 years old. Fruity-fresh, green melon & grapefruit, **18** (78) has some mineral notes one expects from Durbanville, dry finish. Not tasted: **Marné Brut Méthode Cap Classique**.

Bandana range

Not tasted: **Blanc**. — CR, CvZ

Location/WO: Durbanville ▪ Map: Durbanville, Philadelphia & Darling ▪ Map grid reference: C7 ▪ Est 1984 ▪ 1stB 2007 ▪ Tasting, sales & cellar tours Tue-Sun 10-4.30 ▪ Fee R50pp, waived on purchase (6 wines) ▪ Wine tasting in a 'cave' ▪ Closed Good Fri, Dec 25/26 & Jan 1 ▪ Cheese & charcuterie platters ▪ Facilities for children ▪ Tour groups ▪ Owner(s) Jéan de Villiers Trust ▪ Cellarmaster(s) Karin de Villiers (2007) ▪ Winemaker(s) Karin de Villiers (2007) & Piti Coetzee (2016) ▪ Viticulturist(s) Nicol de Villiers (2017) ▪ 260ha/150ha (cab, merlot, shiraz, chard, sauv) ▪ 6,000cs own label 40% red 60% white ▪ Postnet Suite #3 Private Bag X19 Durbanville 7551 ▪ info@kleinroosboom.co.za ▪ www.kleinroosboom.co.za ▪ S 33° 49' 6.24" E 018° 34' 25.86" ▪ [❢] unmatched.blabbed.alleviates ▪ F +27 (0)21-975-7417 ▪ **T +27 (0)60-877-2678**

Klein Sering (❡) (❡❡) (NEW)

When a top cardiac surgeon says he's 'a farmer at heart', and he's listed as viticulturist for a boutique wine venture, you pretty much know everything will be fine. Willie Koen's tiny block of sauvignon and semillon was planted in 2013 alongside the new family home in Cape Town's coastal Noordhoek — home to viticultural goldmine Cape Point Vineyards — and, matched with the skills of winemaker Harold Versfeld (ex Val de Vie, now partner in Dromer Wines), the trio of whites, hopefully ready for our next edition, promises to set a certain organ aflutter.

Location: Cape Town ▪ Est 2013 ▪ 1stB 2016 ▪ Tasting & vineyard tours by private pre-arrangement only ▪ Sales online ▪ Closed all pub hols ▪ Meals/refreshments by pre-booking ▪ Owner(s) Willie Koen family ▪ Winemaker(s) Harold Versfeld (Feb 2017, consultant) ▪ Viticulturist(s) Willie Koen (2013) ▪ 2ha/1.2ha (sauv, sem) ▪ 10t/±1,000cs own label ▪ PO Box 10 Noordhoek 7979 ▪ info@kleinsering.co.za ▪ www.kleinsering.co.za ▪ **T +27 (0)60-687-0875/+27 (0)82-925-5922**

☐ **Klein Simonsvlei** see Niel Joubert Estate
☐ **Klein Tulbagh Reserve** see Tulbagh Winery
☐ **Klein Valley** see Calais Wine Estate
☐ **Klein Welmoed** see Foothills Vineyards

Klipdrift (❡) (❡❡) (◎)

Distell-owned brandy range Klipdrift started life more than 80 years ago as the home brew of Robertson winegrower and distiller JP Marais, whose experiments — eagerly shared with friends — grew into a cultural icon and one of SA's best-loved brands. Over the years the portfolio expanded from the original Export to the longer-aged Premium and much-awarded Gold potstill.

★★★★★ **Gold** (❡) Seduces with complex aromas of dried apricot, raisin, orange peel & sweet spice. Finely textured, well rounded, much greater complexity than others. Vanilla & cinnamon come into greater focus just before long, fruit-filled finish. 100% potstill brandies of between 3 & 21 years age.

Export ⓧ ★★★★ A standard blended brandy (30% potstill), but arguably the best of its type. Remarkable quality at the price. A pleasure to sniff those dried apricot, fynbos & toasty nut aromas, & so smooth & balanced you could just about treat it as a liqueur brandy. From chenin & colombard, as all these.

Premium ⓧ ★★★★ Blend 5-year-matured potstill & 70% unmatured spirit. Richer, fuller than Export, greater maturity bringing sweet tobacco & spice from oak. Powerful, not too harsh to sip neat. — WB, TJ

☐ **Kloof Street** see Mullineux

Kloovenburg Wine & Olives

Vines and hardy olive trees share almost equal prominence on the Du Toit family's Riebeek-Kasteel estate on the slopes of the Bothmanskloof Pass. While matriarch Annalene turns the latter into oil, preserves and an expanding range of cosmetics, husband and owner Pieter du Toit welcomes the burgeoning interest in their spicy reds, built on the success of their signature Shiraz, first bottled two decades ago.

★★★★ **Grenache Noir** Matching 16 (88) in deep, structured mouthful, 17 (87) supple yet concentrated, with gentle grip of integrated oak, all old, 10 months. Lively & succulent to end.

★★★★ **Merlot** Elegant & poised 16 (86) improves on 15 ★★★★ (83). Spicy lift to bright hedgerow fruit but with lithe tannin & judicious oak (20% new, 14 months). Long, rich & rewarding.

★★★★ **Riebeekberg Syrah** Supple, ethereal lightness to inky black palate of naturally fermented 17 ★★★★☆ (90). Plush yet dense & nuanced, with spicy pliability, long satisfying aftertaste. Third bunch-pressed, no new oak. Step up on debut 16 (89).

★★★★ **Shiraz** Retains form in textured, peppery palate. Oak - 20% new French - frames black fruit beautifully. 16 (86), as previous, 15% wholebunch. Also in 375 ml & 1.5L.

★★★★ **Eight Feet Red** Shiraz leads grenache, carignan & mourvèdre on solid 16 (89). Dried-herb-dusted black fruit is bright &, like 15 ★★★★★ (93), complex, with natural ferment & whole-berry/-bunch portion.

★★★★ **Barrel Fermented Chardonnay** ⊘ Maintains bold rich form of 16 (87). Spicy creaminess from half natural ferment, 20% new French oak & regular lees stirring. 17 (86) fresh citrus vibrancy retained on long conclusion.

★★★★☆ **Eight Feet White** Citrus succulence to interesting 17 ★★★★ (89) mix of chenin, grenache blanc, roussanne & splash verdelho. Vanilla oak breadth from old oak, 10 months. Textured & enduring, though debut 16 (92) shade more exciting.

Carignan ★★★★ Sprightly red-fruited 17 (83) improves on 16 ★★★ (80) but retains juicy appeal & softness. **Sauvignon Blanc** ★★★ Zesty grapefruit tang on lively 18 (82), unfussy & refreshing. **Shiraz Blanc de Noir Brut Sparkling** ⊘ ★★★★ Strawberry & cherry vivacity on coral pink NV (83) carbonated fizz. Tangily tasty, dry & easy to enjoy. Not tasted: **Unwooded Chardonnay**, **Cape Vintage Shiraz**. Discontinued: **Cabernet Sauvignon**. — FM

Location: Riebeek-Kasteel ▪ Map/WO: Swartland ▪ Map grid reference: D6 ▪ Est 1704 ▪ 1stB 1998 ▪ Tasting & sales Mon-Fri 9–4.30 Sat 9–2 ▪ Fee R30 wine/olive tasting ▪ Closed Good Fri, Dec 25/26 & Jan 1 ▪ Gift shop ▪ Farm produce/olive products ▪ BYO picnic ▪ Walks/hikes ▪ Conservation area ▪ Owner(s) Pieter du Toit ▪ Cellarmaster(s) Pieter du Toit (Jan 1998) ▪ Winemaker(s) Jolandie Fouché (Dec 2014) ▪ 300ha/130ha (carignan, grenache n/b, merlot, mourv, shiraz, chard, chenin, rouss, sauv, verdelho) ▪ 200t/12,000cs own label 55% red 40% white 4% rosé 1% sparkling ▪ PO Box 2 Riebeek-Kasteel 7307 ▪ info@kloovenburg.com ▪ www.kloovenburg.com ▪ S 33° 23' 36.3" E 018° 53' 27.5" ▪ ⌖ barbers.spirals.robes ▪ F +27 (0)22-448-1035 ▪ T +27 (0)22-448-1635

☐ **Knor** see Knorhoek Wines

Knorhoek Wines

Knorhoek, on the high Simonsberg slopes, has been in the Van Niekerk family since 1887, and though the farm no longer is De Plaats Waar De Leeuwen Knorren (the place where lions growl) as in the 1600s, a strong conservation emphasis under current custodians Hansie and James means that leopard and caracal are still occasionally spotted here. Fifth-generation Barry is in his 5th year of making full-fruited, well-structured wines, while other family members look after the hospitality elements, including popular wedding venue.

Pantére range

★★★★☆ **Cabernet Sauvignon** ② Rich, velvety **15** ⑨⓪ improves on **12** ★★★★ ⑧⑧, recalls impressively crafted **11** ⑨②, with 20 months French oak (10% new) adding spice to generous ripe black fruit.

★★★★ **Bordeaux Blend** ② Less new oak this time & only French, cab-led **14** ⑧⑨ redolent of cassis & tealeaf, fruitcake richness & balancing freshness from 24% each merlot & cab franc. Stellenbosch WO.

★★★★ **Chenin Blanc** Abundant Golden Delicious apple & yellow cling peach flavours in **17** ⑧⑧, dry & fresh, with textured, subtly honeyed mouthfeel from 3 months older French oak. No **15**, **16**.

Knorhoek range

★★★★ **Cabernet Sauvignon** Aged 2 years in older French barrique, **16** ⑧⑥ is smooth, with cassis & tangy black berry fruit, fresh acidity, moderate 13.5% alcohol, good balance & length.

★★★★ **Cabernet Franc** ⊘ Rich in forest fruit, showing velvet texture from 2 years older wood, **16** ⑧⑨ nudges higher rating with toned-down alcohol (14.5%), smoke & tealeaf complexity.

Pinotage ★★★ Banana & milk chocolate aromas, **16** ⑧② fresh red berry fruit on palate, juicy but a little crisper, leaner than last. **Shiraz** ★★★★ After 22 months seasoning in French oak, **16** ⑧⑤ mixed spice & subtle BBQ smoke to complement tangy red-berry freshness. **Chenin Blanc** ⊘ ★★★★ From single dryland block planted 1980, smooth yet zesty **18** ⑧④ has intense white peach flavour, pithy grapefruit finish. Not tasted: **Merlot**, **Sauvignon Blanc**. Discontinued: **Konfetti Rosé Sparkling**.

Two Cubs range

Red Blend ⑦ ★★★ Drops barrel-aged cab & cab franc from previous vintage add to cassis richness of **17** ⑧②, 90% shiraz with pleasing pepper spice.

Pinotage ★★★ Ample berry fruit, smooth mouthfeel & mocha tone from 14 months oaking, **17** ⑦⑨ warm finish from 14.8% alcohol. **Rosé** ⊘ ★★★ Onion skin hue & gingernut spice, fresh apricot & red berry fruit, **18** ⑧⓪ ex shiraz dry & rounded from 3 months on lees. **Chenin Blanc** ★★★ Tropical fruit salad flavours in aromatic **17** ⑦⑨, drier than also-tasted **18** ⑦⑧, with higher acidity to compensate, both very drinkable. **Sauvignon Blanc** ② ★★★ Fresh ripe pear, white peach on **17** ⑦⑨, fruity & uncomplicated for easy drinking.

Discontinued: **Knor range.** — JG

Location/map: Stellenbosch ▪ Map grid reference: F3 ▪ WO: Simonsberg–Stellenbosch/Stellenbosch ▪ Est 1827 ▪ 1stB 1997 ▪ Tasting, sales & cellar tours daily 10–5 ▪ Fee R20/5 wines ▪ Closed Dec 25 ▪ Towerbosch Restaurant Wed–Sun 11.30-3.30 (Sat/Sun booking essential T +27 (0)21-865-2958) ▪ Facilities for children ▪ Tour groups ▪ Gift shop ▪ Weddings/conferences ▪ Hiking trail ▪ Horse riding ▪ Conservation area ▪ 3-star guesthouse & self-catering cottages ▪ Owner(s) Hansie & James van Niekerk ▪ Cellarmaster(s)/winemaker(s) Barry van Niekerk (Jan 2014) ▪ Viticulturist(s) James van Niekerk (1977) ▪ ±8oha (cabs s/f, merlot, ptage, shiraz, chenin, sauv) ▪ 640t/40,000cs own label 55% red 39% white 6% rosé & 184,500L bulk ▪ PO Box 2 Koelenhof 7605 ▪ office@knorhoek.co.za, cellar@knorhoek.co.za, towerbosch@knorhoek.co.za ▪ www. knorhoek.co.za ▪ S 33° 52′ 44.8″ E 018° 52′ 19.1″ ▪ loosens.having.animated ▪ F +27 (0)21-865-2627 ▪ **T +27 (0)21-865-2114**

☐ **Kobus** see Havana Hills
☐ **Koelenbosch** see Koelenhof Winery

Koelenhof Winery

② ⑪ ◎ ⑧ ⑤

A new winemaking team takes over at this grower-owned winery in Stellenbosch, the change coinciding with a drive by marketer Eugene Kinghorn to put the 'cool' into Koelenhof and make it more consumer friendly while emphasising their track record for quality, consistency and affordability. Launching this year will be the flagship '1679' range which, like their other bottled wines, will be available in new livery at the revamped tasting venue, conveniently near the N1 motorway.

Koelenbosch range

Pinotage ⑦ ★★★ Fruity **16** ⑧② ticks all the boxes for a great braai wine: bags of berries, soft tannins, juicy, fresh finish. **Sauvignon Blanc** ⑦ ★★★ Perkily pleasant **18** ⑦⑧ does very capable job of crowd pleasing with fresh summer fruit melange.

Merlot ★★★ Green edges add a refreshing tweak to soft red & black berry fruit, though **16** ⑧ shade less amenable than previous. **Shiraz** ★★★ Tobacco & smoke a little overwhelming for the shy black fruit of **16** ⑦. **Nineteenfortyone** ★★★★ Eminently drinkable blend cab, pinotage & shiraz, **16** ⑧ ripe black fruit & pleasing sweeter notes from 18 months French/American oak. **Dry Pinotage Rosé** ★★ Soft red fruit **18** ⑦ follows less-than-pleasing nose. **Chenin Blanc** ★★ Neutral **18** ⑦ offers vague appley notes & light acidity. **Pinotage Rosé Méthode Cap Classique** ⊘ ★★★ Fresh & appetising **13** ⑧ bubbly adds pleasant salty edge to crunchy cranberry & apple fruit. 24 months on lees add good richness to mid-palate before bone-dry finish. **Chardonnay Méthode Cap Classique** ⊘ ★★★★ Lemony fruit loses its way slightly amongst oxidative notes of almond, toffee & marshmallow. **12** ⑧ sparkler's acidity brightens & tangy-dry finish pleases but drink up soon. Not tasted: **Sangiovese, Koelenhof 1941 Limited Release.** Occasional release: **Chenin Blanc Wooded.** Discontinued: **Cabernet Sauvignon.**

Koelenhof range

Koelnektar ⑰ ★★★ Bursting with character, **18** ⑦ is Turkish delight in a glass. Full-sweet but crisp, gewürztraminer & hanepoot combo pretty partner for light fruity desserts.

Koelenhoffer ★★ Off-dry sauvignon **18** ⑦ mixes greenpepper & grass with ripe guava for easy-drinking enjoyment. **Sauvignon Blanc Vin Sec** ★★★ Party-popping light, semi-sweet bubbles **17** ⑦ has good balance of sugar, fruit & acidity. **Pinorto** ⊘ ★★★★ Delicious light (15.5% alcohol) pinotage 'port', **15** ⑧ packed with ripe black & red fruit, raisins & Christmas cake, fresh tarry finish. Not tasted: **Pinotage, Koelenberg, Pinotage Rosé Vin Sec.** Discontinued: **Pinotage Rosé, Hanepoot.** — CM

Location/map/WO: Stellenbosch ▪ Map grid reference: D1 ▪ Est 1941 ▪ 1stB 1970's ▪ Tasting & sales Mon-Thu 9–5 Fri 9–4 Sat/pub hols 10–2 ▪ Guided cellar tours daily ▪ Closed Easter Fri/Sun, Ascension day & Dec 25 ▪ Facilities for children ▪ Picnics to be pre-booked ▪ Conference/function venue ▪ Distillique training courses available at Koelenhof ▪ Owner(s) 67 shareholders ▪ GM Andrew de Vries (2006) ▪ Winemaker(s) Nicholas Husselman (Oct 2017), with Handré Visagie & Estian Matthee (both Jan 2018) ▪ 16,500t/22,000cs own label 45% red 45% white 8% rosé 2% fortified + 2,000cs for clients & 100,000L bulk ▪ Other export brand: Simonsbosch ▪ IPW ▪ PO Box 1 Koelenhof 7605 ▪ koelwyn@mweb.co.za ▪ www.koelenhof.co.za ▪ S 33° 50' 5.2" E 018° 47' 52.7" ▪ ⬜ toolkit.sounds.junction ▪ F +27 (0)21-865-2796 ▪ T +27 (0)21-865-2020/1

Koelenfontein   ⚲ ⌂ ◎

This Ceres mountainside family farm suffered from both drought and a devastating fire this past year. Part of the chardonnay vineyard was destroyed and sadly will not be replaced. The shiraz was saved, though yields were reduced, and the wine made, as before, by Dewaldt Heyns at Saronsberg. Good rain has since fallen and the team is optimistic about the new vintage.

★★★★ **Shiraz** Concentrated sweet fruit from low-yield (4 t/ha) vines, complemented by spice-laden oak (90% new), fine tannins. Balanced & bright, modern. **14** ⑧ already appealing, with potential to age. **Chardonnay** ★★★ Ever-riper styling, with oak & alcohol (14.8%) dominating dried-fruit flavours on **16** ⑧, warm farewell. For fans of bold wooded chardonnay. — MW

Location/WO: Ceres ▪ Map: Tulbagh ▪ Map grid reference: H5 ▪ Est 1832 ▪ 1stB 2002 ▪ Tasting & sales Mon-Fri 11–4 Sat 11–2 ▪ Closed all pub hols ▪ Farm produce ▪ Hikes ▪ Conservation area ▪ Die Kloof self-catering historic house (sleeps 6) ▪ Owner(s) Handri Conradie ▪ Winemaker(s) Dewaldt Heyns (2004) ▪ Viticulturist(s) Hennie van Noordwyk ▪ 950ha/±6ha (shiraz, chard) ▪ ±24t/2,400cs own label 50% red 50% white ▪ WWF-SA Conservation Champion ▪ PO Box 4 Prince Alfred's Hamlet 6840 ▪ wine@koelfontein.co.za ▪ www.koel-fontein.co.za ▪ S 33° 15' 54.70" E 019° 19' 29.28" ▪ ⬜ narrator.repaint.ducts ▪ F +27 (0)23-313-3137 ▪ T +27 (0)23-313-3304/+27 (0)71-413-3869

☐ **Koen Family Wines** see Klein Sering

Koni Wines   ⚲ ⑱

After a successful career in human resources management, Soweto-born, Cape Town-based Koni Maliehe decided to pursue her passion for wine while simultaneously adding value to the economy through job creation. The result is this range of 'premium quality wines at a reasonable price' that she aims to export throughout Africa and Asia. 'There are major opportunities in the smaller countries.' Next step is a formal distribution service in Johannesburg 'to reach our market in the north more quickly'.

Shiraz ★★★★ Lively coffee-toned **16** ⑧④ easy to drink, pleasant food-friendly grip from tannins & light oaking (just 10% new), ripe-fruited centre. **Cabernet Sauvignon-Merlot ★★★** Creamy oak, farmyard nuance on blackberry & plum fruit, **16 ★★★** ⑧⓪ fresh, with cab's firm tannins for food. **Sauvignon Blanc ★★** Modest **17** ⑦⑤ faintly floral aromas & flavours, tad brief. — GdB, CvZ

Location/map: Stellenbosch ▪ Map grid reference: E1 ▪ WO: Western Cape ▪ Est 2015 ▪ 1stB 2014 ▪ Tasting & cellar tours Mon-Fri 11-3 Sat/pub hols on request ▪ Fee R50pp ▪ Sales Mon-Fri 8-5 ▪ Owner(s) Koni Maliehe ▪ maliehe@live.com ▪ www.konempire.com ▪ S 33° 49' 33.4" E 018° 49' 9.3" ▪ T +27 (0)74-112-6769

Konkelberg

Intended to provide 'premium yet accessible wines for a younger wine-drinking public', Konkelberg takes its name from a rumoured 'connivance corner' in the crook of the Stellenbosch and Helderberg mountains, where early settlers rendezvoused secretly with local traders in defiance of a Dutch East India Company ban.

Rouge ⊘ ⑱ **★★★★** As usual, this charming, versatile red (varieties undisclosed) over-delivers. Previewed **17** ⑧⑤ vivacious & fruit-packed but dry enough for food, tannins just right to drink solo. Light-toned for warmer weather, too. **Sauvignon Blanc** ⊘ ⑱ **★★★★** If you prefer creamier, tropical sauvignon to racy & green, **17** ⑧⑤ from Stellenbosch vines is your go-to tipple. Also-tasted **18** ⑧⑤ tank sample (WO W Cape) similarly styled, with winemaker's signature zesty rather than sharp acidity.

Discontinued: **Shiraz, Rosé, Blanc Reserve**. — CvZ

Location: Stellenbosch ▪ Map: Helderberg ▪ Map grid reference: C1 ▪ WO: Western Cape/Stellenbosch ▪ Est 2011 ▪ 1stB 2012 ▪ Tasting & sales Mon-Sat 10-5 ▪ Closed Easter Fri/Mon, Dec 25/26 & Jan 1 ▪ Owner(s) Konkelberg Eiendoms Beperk ▪ Cellarmaster(s)/viticulturist(s) Jasper Raats (Jul 2011) ▪ Winemaker(s) Hendrien de Munck (2015) ▪ 20ha/18ha (cab f, shiraz, chenin, sauv) ▪ 180t/25,000cs own label 48% red 48% white 4% rosé plus 1,000cs for clients ▪ Suite 116 Private Bag X4 Die Boord 7613 ▪ info@konkelberg. co.za ▪ www.konkelberg.co.za ▪ S 34° 0' 55.2" E 018° 49' 60.0" ▪ ▦ promptness.anatomy.quotes ▪ T +27 (0)21-855-2005

Koopmanskloof Vineyards

The historic Koopmanskloof property (land granted in 1777) in Stellenbosch's Bottelary Hills received its conservation focus from late owner Stevie Smit, who created a 98-ha fynbos nature reserve and walking trails, a particular passion of his. The vision continues, with the venture now broadly sustainability accredited and drawing grapes from six properties, one staff-owned and -managed. The new state-of-the-art cellar, featuring automated red-wine fermenters, has been completed and ancillary buildings upgraded.

Cabernet Sauvignon ⊘ **★★★** Cassis & dark plums given a toasty overlay by oak treatment; **17** ⑧② already drinking well, the tannins supple. Fairtrade certified, as the rest. **Merlot ★★★** Red berries, hint of mint/herbs in plush-textured **17** ⑦⑧, smooth drinkability; oak gives savoury tones. **Mocha Pinotage** (NEW) **★★★** Different label to rest of range, more colourful. Definite mocha flavours in **17** ⑦⑧, combining with dark-toned fruit, plus a smooth body, will appeal widely. **Pinotage** ⊘ **★★★** Strikes a good balance between smoky spice & dark fruit, **17** ⑧①'s texture supple, smoothly rounded to give drinking pleasure. **Shiraz ★★★** Quite spicy, mocha & dark-fruit-toned **17** ⑦⑧ has a smooth, easy texture, a good match for hearty stews, braais. **Pinotage Rosé** ⊘ **★★★** Tank sample **18** ⑧⓪ already showing its potential, dry, bright berry-fruited, deepening on the palate, zesty vibrancy. **Chardonnay** ⊘ **★★★** Melon- & grape-fruit-styled, unwooded **18** ⑦⑧ has good drinkability. **Chenin Blanc** ⊘ **★★★** Apple & pear crispness, **18** ⑦⑧ is a pure, honest rendition of the variety, eminently quaffable. **Sauvignon Blanc** ⊘ **★★★** Appealing green notes in **18** ⑧①, has typicity: capsicum, lime, nettles, tangy-fresh, finishing long. — CR

Location/WO: Stellenbosch ▪ Est 1801 ▪ 1stB 1970 ▪ Closed to public ▪ Private Nature Reserve ▪ Owner(s) Managed by Koopmanskloof Wingerde (Pty) Ltd ▪ MD Rydal Jeftha ▪ Winemaker(s) Stephan Smit ▪ Viticulturist(s) Japie de Villiers ▪ 456ha (cab, carignan, merlot, ptage, roobernet, ruby cab, shiraz, chard, chenin, sauv, sem) ▪ ±3,700t/±2.5m L 50% red 50% white ▪ Other brand: The Fair Trade ▪ Fairtrade, IPW, WIETA ▪ PO Box 19 Koelenhof 7605 ▪ info@koopmanskloof.co.za ▪ www.koopmanskloof.co.za ▪ T +27 (0)21-842-0810

Kottabos

These wines are made at Boschkloof by Reenen Borman, but are more 'new wave' than the estate's (closer to Reenen's Ron Burgundy label). Nor do the grapes come off home vineyards, but others on the granitic soils of the Polkadraai Hills. The name is from an Ancient Greek game of skill, Reenen says, in which leftover wine lees was flung at targets. It fitted well with his idea of 'playing with and exploring' these vineyards.

★★★★ **Grenache-Syrah** Brightly fragrant, pure-fruited 17 ★★★★★ ⑨① combines ripe, vinous generosity with light-feeling freshness for a whole that is both serious & delicious. More complexity after a few years. Only the syrah (28%) destemmed & unoaked; grenache in old barrels. 16 ⑧⑦ had just 13% syrah.

★★★★ **Chenin Blanc** (NEW) Pleasing, balanced & bright 17 ⑧⑦ not overtly fruity, though there's dried peach & even a little ripe pineapple with the earthy, straw notes. Fresh acidity. 10 months old oak. — TJ

Kranskop Wines

'Hands-on and traditional' is the essence of the Marais family's winegrowing approach, extending from owner/cellarmaster Néwald's use of time-honoured basket pressing to the personal welcome given to visitors to the boutique cellar on the slope of the distinctive rock formation that gives the venture its name. Not that they're mired in the past — see the innovative, fashionable dry rosé debuting this edition, and the trendy emphasis on regionality in certifying their wines as 'Klaasvoogds' instead of generic 'Robertson'.

★★★★ **Viognier Noble Late Harvest** Fresh stonefruit with honey, roasted nuts (though unoaked) & cleansing citrus acidity. 17 ⑧⑨ good botrytis character, balance, enduring finish. 10% alcohol. 375 ml.

Merlot ⑦ ★★★★ Ex tank, vibrant 16 ⑧③ chock-full of fruitcake & plum, light in texture so it's oh so easy to drink. **Petite Sirah-Viognier Rosé Sec** (NEW) ⑦ ★★★ Creative varietal combo in candyfloss pink 18 ⑧① preview. Perfumed floral & peach wafts, gentle, light & dry fruit flavours. **Chenin Blanc** (NEW) ⊘ ⑦ ★★★★ Delightful 17 ⑧④ newcomer from 30 year old vines, lovely & lively interplay of citrus & tropical, touch oak adding complexity & creamy texture.

Cabernet Sauvignon ★★★ Previewed 16 ⑧⓪ soft & juicy, squishy black fruit & graphite nuance from 25% new French oak, savoury farewell. **Pinot Noir** ⊘ ★★★ Strawberry-toned, earthy flavours on food-styled 15 ⑦⑧, lean, peppery finish. **Shiraz** ★★★ Going a rung up, 15 ⑧⓪ succulent dark-fruited flavour sprinkled with warm spice. Balanced & moreish. **Tannat** ★★★★ Rarity, only handful on market. This Kranskop version becoming juicier, earlier-drinkable by the vintage. 16 ⑧③ vibrant, fruity, yet some complexity, ageability. **Chardonnay** ★★★ Half barrel fermented, 18 ⑧② preview ripe Golden Delicious apple flavours, floral tones & cream, freshness boosted by unoaked portion. **Sauvignon Blanc** ★★★ Sampled from tank, 18 ⑧② tropical aromas, lemon & lime leanness on palate. **Viognier** ★★★ Missing zip of previous, 17 ⑧② fresh orchard fruit flavours, hints of vanilla (20% oaked) & a soft acidity. — WB

Location/map: Robertson ▪ Map grid reference: B4 ▪ WO: Klaasvoogds ▪ Est 2001 ▪ 1stB 2003 ▪ Tasting, sales & tours Mon-Fri 10-4.30 Sat/pub hols 10-2 ▪ Closed Easter Sun & Dec 25 ▪ BYO picnic ▪ Owner(s) Néwald Marais ▪ Cellarmaster(s)/winemaker(s) Néwald Marais (2008) ▪ Viticulturist(s) Néwald Marais & Alrich Viljoen (Aug 2017) ▪ 43ha/30ha (cab, merlot, pinot, shiraz, tannat, chard, sauv, viog) ▪ 240t/3,000cs own label 75% red 25% white ▪ IPW ▪ PO Box 49 Klaasvoogds 6707 ▪ newald@kranskopwines.co.za ▪ www.kranskopwines.co.za ▪ S 33° 47' 53.1" E 019° 59' 56.6" ▪ purest.touted.mapmaking ▪ F +27 (0)23-626-3200 ▪ T +27 (0)23-626-3200

Krone

Home to this collection, mostly vintage-dated MCC sparkling wines, is historic Twee Jonge Gezellen in Tulbagh (the name Krone being that of its long-time owners). The farm dates back to 1710, and is not only the site of Africa's first underground cellar but also a local pioneer in cold fermentation in the 1950s, while night harvesting was introduced to SA here in the 1980s. Since being bought by wine business giant Vinimark in 2012, the estate has seen major new vineyard plantings and extensive restoration 'to reflect its impressive heritage and contemporary renaissance'.

★★★★ **Rosé Vintage Cuvée Brut** Rosy blush on dry, fresh 17 ⑧⑥ sparkling hints at vibrant red-berry notes from 80% pinot (with chardonnay), year on lees adding creaminess. Also in 375ml & 1.5L, as Borealis & Night Nectar.

★★★★ **Night Nectar Rosé** Sugar-sprinkled strawberries with cream in semi-sweet **17** ⑧⑥ bubbly, delicately blushing thanks to 80% pinot noir, rest chardonnay. Frothily charming at 11% alcohol.

★★★★ **Borealis Vintage Cuvée Brut** Nudging higher rating, with pinot noir component up to 30% (with chardonnay) in **17** ⑧⑨. Dry but rich, rounded & lemon-tart creamy, fine & persistent stream of bubbles & clean, lingering, mineral aftertaste.

★★★★ **RD 2002** ⊛ Prestige sparkler matured extraordinary 14 years, **02** ★★★★ ⑨③ seduces with lemon meringue, apple Danish, marzipan & salted caramel notes. Dry & vibrant yet rich & concentrated, even more so than maiden **01** ⑧⑨. Mostly pinot blanc, 18% chardonnay & 15% pinot noir. Tulbagh WO.

★★★★ **Night Nectar** Semi-sweet **17** ⑧⑧ bubbles, 70% chardonnay, pinot noir, heady jasmine & baked apple aromas, fine mousse, bright acidity & green apple tang ensure freshness at 43 g/l sugar.

Chardonnay-Pinot Noir ⊘ ★★★ The non-sparkling cousin, but no poor relation. **17** ⑧② very dry & fresh rosé, lemon & cranberry notes, citrus pith finish. Modest 12.5% alcohol. Discontinued: **The Phoenix**. — JG

Location/map: Tulbagh ▪ Map grid reference: F4 ▪ WO: Western Cape/Tulbagh ▪ Est 1710 ▪ 1stB 1937 ▪ Tasting & sales Mon-Sat 10—4 ▪ Closed all pub hols ▪ Cellar tours Mon-Sat at 11 ▪ Annual festival: Christmas in Winter (Jun) ▪ Art gallery ▪ Owner(s) TJG Estate (Pty) Ltd ▪ Winemaker(s) Stephan de Beer (2008), with Tanya Fourie (Jan 2018) ▪ Viticulturist(s) Rosa Kruger ▪ PO Box 16 Tulbagh 6820 ▪ info@tjg.co.za ▪ www.tweejongegezellen.co.za ▪ S 33° 14' 18.1" E 019° 6' 51.8" ▪ 🖃 sightseers.headgear.brilliance ▪ F +27 (0)23-230-0686 ▪ **T +27 (0)23-230-0680**

Kronendal Boutique Winery   ⊘ ⑪ ♿

Insufficient water prompted Pieter and Magdaleen Kroon to switch from growing fynbos (for an indigenous nursery) to vines on their Durbanville boutique property. In the past year the couple simplified the design of their Rhône blend's label 'to support and emphasise the naturalness and handcrafting' which underlie the venture. They also upgraded the website and added the convenience of online shopping.

★★★★ **Mirari** Latin for 'to wonder at'. As one does this naturally fermented blend of shiraz, mourvèdre & viognier. Plush **15** ★★★★★ ⑨⓪, ripe berry fruit supported by generous oak (50% new), more hedonistic than spicy **14** ⑧⑨.— DS

Location: Durbanville ▪ Map: Durbanville, Philadelphia & Darling ▪ Map grid reference: C7 ▪ WO: Cape Town ▪ Est 2003 ▪ 1stB 2006 ▪ Tasting, sales & cellar tours by appt ▪ Seasonal 'langtafel' lunches ▪ Owner(s) Pieter & Magdaleen Kroon ▪ Winemaker(s) Magdaleen Kroon ▪ 2ha/0.6ha (mourv, shiraz, tempranillo, viog) ▪ 4t/520cs own label 100% red ▪ PO Box 4433 Durbanville 7551 ▪ info@kronendalwine.co.za ▪ www.kronendalwine.co.za ▪ S 33° 48' 30.78" E 018° 36' 50.82" ▪ 🖃 deliverer.breadth.milkshakes ▪ F +27 (0)86-603-1170 ▪ **T +27 (0)82-499-0198**

☐ **Kruger Family** *see* Stellenview Premium Wines

Kruger Family Wines   ⊘

Both Kruger 'families' grew significantly in 2018, exults tenant winemaker Johan Kruger (ex Sterhuis). His and Belgian wife Sofie's second son Maxime lent his name to a 'sibling' bottling for UK customer-funded Naked Wines. There are three new chardonnays: two barrel-fermented, a third unwooded under the Sans Chêne (without wood/chains) label. Meanwhile, membership of the Old Vine Project spawns another three wines soon, including a Wellington 'rescue' chenin. One word: impressed.

★★★★ **Old Vines Cinsault** ⊘ ⓕ From 64 year old Piekenierskloof vines, Old World-styled **17** ⑧⑦ earthy, peppery, lipsmacking acidity & tannin. Individual, interesting terroir expression; worth seeking out.

★★★★☆ **Klipkop Chardonnay** 🆕 Natural fermentation, 25% new oak, **17** ⑨⓪ from old Piekenierskloof vineyard at 700m altitude. Smoky whiff on cool lemon & lime nose, umami palate, chalky mineral finish. Distinctly dry & closed, takes time to unfold.

★★★★ **Naked Wines Chardonnay** 🆕 Like most of the chard siblings, **17** ⑧⑥ natural ferment/ageing in oak, here 25% new. Alluring vanilla, honey & oatmeal notes & distinctive nutty-mineral finish. Bone-dry but fuller bodied than others thanks to reined-in acidity, higher 14% alcohol.

★★★★☆ **Walker Bay Chardonnay** (NEW) Old-barrel-fermented/aged **17** (90) from vines with ocean views. Attractive & complex glassful of nectarine, kumquat, honey & almond, underlying the richness are minerality & a nervous freshness that adds welcome tension & length.

Naked Wines Pinotage (🍷) ★★★☆ Delicious **17** (84) packed with mulberry, plum & forest fruit, lightly seasoned with spice. Soft tannins add to easy & immediate drinkability. WO Stellenbosch.

Merlot (🔲) ★★★ Plush red berries, some oak spicing, succulent **14** (81) is already drinking well, can age for a few years. WO Stellenbosch. **Pearly Gates Pinot Noir** ★★★★ Was 'Pinot Noir'. Charming **17** (84) from Upper Hemel-en-Aarde, elegant & composed, lovely balance between variety's characteristic bright acidity, well-formed tannins & fruit. **Elements** (🔲) ★★★★ Classic 5-part Bordeaux blend led by cab, accounting for **14** (84)'s cassis-dominant flavours. Silky smooth, the tannins a hidden support. Nice fresh finish adds to the attraction. **Naked Wines Matteo Reserve** ★★★★ Spicy & savoury shiraz-led blend, **16** (83) tannic grip from cab (26%), bright acidity from pinotage (18%), faint plummy hint from merlot (4%). **Naked Wines Maxime Reserve** (NEW) ★★★★ Dark fruit & clove scent, fine tannic grip & blueberry persistence. Shiraz (50%) leads grenache (30%) with drops cinsaut & mourvèdre in unoaked **16** (84). WO W Cape. **The Forgotten Vineyards Chardonnay** (NEW) ★★★★ Tight & taut, naturally fermented & unoaked **17** (84) just 13% alcohol, distinctly dry with faint lemon, apple & white pear. WO Citrusdal Mountain. **Sans Chêne Chardonnay** (🔲) ★★★★ Natural ferment for unwooded **17** ★★★★ (84), partly in concrete 'egg'. Earthy lemon curd perfumes & flavours, saline edge & vibrant acidity. Not very expressive but could open up over time. WO Piekenierskloof. **Angels Selection** (🔲) ★★★★ Tasty unoaked chenin blend, **16** (85) apple/pear freshness, palate weight & tropical notes from chardonnay & older-vine colombard. WO W Cape. — GM

Location: Somerset West ▪ WO: Coastal/Piekenierskloof/Stellenbosch/Western Cape/Citrusdal Mountain/Walker Bay/Upper Hemel-en-Aarde Valley ▪ Est/1stB 2015 ▪ Tasting by appt only ▪ Owner(s) Johan & Sofie Kruger ▪ Cellarmaster(s)/winemaker(s) Johan Kruger (Sep 2015) ▪ 100t/25,000cs own label 50% red 50% white + 20,000cs for clients ▪ Brands for clients: Naked Wines (UK) ▪ WIETA ▪ johan@krugerfamilywines. co.za ▪ www.krugerfamilywines.co.za ▪ **T +27 (0)83-411-0757**

Kumala   (♀)

Accolade Wines SA's export powerhouse Kumala is the top-selling SA wine brand in the UK and the largest by volume globally. Building on more than 20 years' success, and vinifying grapes from eight diverse areas, head winemaker Gerhard Swart and his team aim for 'a versatile range of everyday wines, full of life'. The wines below are only the ones available locally; the numerous export labels untasted.

Reserve range
Shiraz ★★★ A handsome rustic, **17** (80) dark plummy fruit & florals layered with fragrant mocha. Perky tannin & lively acidity balance few grams sugar & 14.5% alcohol. **Chenin Blanc** ★★★ Bold pear & melon flavours, hints of blossoms, lightly buffed by French oak. Refreshing **17** (78) to chill & enjoy. **Sauvignon Blanc** ★★ Some American oak moderates racy fruit from Olifants River, gives a litheness to **17** (76). Not tasted: **Chardonnay**.

Zenith range
Shiraz-Cabernet Sauvignon-Merlot ★★ Shiraz (79%) now leads the friendly blend. **17** (74) plump red berries & twist of pepper, simple yet enjoyable. Also in magnum. WO W Cape. Discontinued: **Rosé**, **Chenin Blanc-Chardonnay**. — DS

Location: Somerset West ▪ WO: Swartland/Olifants River/Western Cape ▪ Tasting & sales at Flagstone Winery (see entry) ▪ Owner(s) Accolade Wines South Africa ▪ Winemaker(s) Gerhard Swart (head, Sep 2007) & Juan Slabbert (Jan 2018) ▪ 50% red 50% white ▪ PO Box 769 Stellenbosch 7599 ▪ info@flagstonewines.com ▪ www.kumala.co.za ▪ **F** +27 (0)21-852-5085 ▪ **T +27 (0)21-852-5052**

Kunjani Wines   (♀) (🍴) (🏠) (📷) (NEW)

This multicultural partnership between German entrepreneur Paul Barth and SA businesswoman Pia Watermeyer involves a small Devon Valley vineyard, where Pia is learning the winemaking ropes on a handful of wines including a poignantly labelled rosé, recalling the antics of Pia's late young son James. An industrial-chic tasting area, eatery and stylish cottages share lovely valley views.

Shiraz ★★★ Pleasing **15** ⑱, ripe red & black berries, freshening burst of acidity. **Red Blend ★★★** Sweet, ripe red cherries & plums, hints oak spice & cinnamon on lively **15** ⑰ easy-drinker from cab franc, merlot & malbec. **Stolen Chicken Rosé ★★** Deep salmon hue on **17** ⑯, Ribena & candyfloss whiffs, tastes semi-dry but fairly fresh still. From cab, shiraz & merlot. **Chenin Blanc ★★** Ripe tropical, lime & oatmeal biscuit nuances on **17** ⑯. Peaking, drink soon. **Sauvignon Blanc ★★★** Peach & granadilla notes, zesty acidity, **17** ⑱ ticks the boxes with lingering summery flavours. WO W Cape. — JG, CvZ

Location/map: Stellenbosch ▪ Map grid reference: D3 ▪ WO: Stellenbosch/Western Cape ▪ Est 2017 ▪ 1stB 2011 ▪ Tasting & sales Mon-Sun 9-5 ▪ Fee R55pp ▪ Restaurant open daily ▪ 4 self-catering cottages ▪ Conference/ function venue ▪ Farm produce ▪ Walks/hikes ▪ Owner(s) Kap Vino Estate (Paul Barth & Pia Watermeyer) ▪ Farm 90, 20 Blumberg Dr Devonvale Stellenbosch 7600 ▪ info@kunjaniwines.co.za ▪ www.kunjaniwines. co.za ▪ S 33° 53′ 40.98″ E 018° 48′ 21.46″ ▪ **T +27 (0)87-630-0409**

Kuyperskraal ⓥ

Sibling to dairy products brand Fair Cape, Kuyperskraal originates in the Philadelphia area, where the Loubser family has been farming for 150 years. The current generation, five brothers, is part of collaborative marketing venture Kaapse Familie Wingerde, with Oude Denneboom and Vendôme, the latter also the tasting venue for the wines below.

Sauvignon Blanc ⓥ **★★★★** Tiny production but worth seeking out, **18** ⑱ dry, crisp, delightful spectrum of tropical & citrus flavours, good palate weight & fresh finish. WO Durbanville.

Pinotage ⓥ **★★★** Vanilla caramel-laced mulberry fruit will take fans of old-school pinotage back to the halcyon days. Previewed **16** ⑱ wholesome if somewhat chunky. — WB

Location: Philadelphia ▪ WO: Coastal/Durbanville ▪ Est 1991 ▪ 1stB 2014 ▪ Tasting & sales at Vendôme (see entry) ▪ Owner(s) Loubser brothers ▪ Cellarmaster(s) Altus le Roux (consultant) ▪ Viticulturist(s) Viljee Loubser ▪ 1,500ha/100ha (cab, ptage, sauv) ▪ 1,000t/400cs own label 30% red 70% white ▪ WIETA ▪ Malanshoogte Rd Durbanville 7550 ▪ viljee@faircape.com ▪ www.faircape.com, www.kaapsefamiliewing-erde.com ▪ F +27 (0)21-972-1973 ▪ **T +27 (0)86-169-6455**

KWV

Founded in 1918, KWV has evolved into a producer of over 100 products represented in more than 100 markets globally. The company's century-long reputation for quality is reflected in its long-standing global status for fine wines, fortifieds and brandies (see separate listings). Visitors to HQ in Paarl are greeted by venerable production facilities transformed into modern and memorable tourist spaces: the House of Fire, originally the distilling cellar for KWV's brandies, and the imposing, vaulted Cathedral Cellar, built in 1930 and now lovingly refurbished.

Location/map: Paarl ▪ Map grid reference: E6 ▪ KWV Wine Emporium: Kohler Str, T +27 (0)21-807-3007/8 F +27 (0)21-807-3119, wineemporium@kwv.co.za, www.kwvwineemporium.co.za ▪ Tasting & sales Mon-Sat 9–4.30 Sun 10-3 ▪ Several food & wine pairings available ▪ Cellar tours: Eng Mon-Sat 10, 10.30 & 2.15; Ger 10.15; Sun Eng 11 ▪ Tour groups by appt ▪ Closed Good Fri, Dec 25 & Jan 1 ▪ KWV House of Fire: Kohler Str, contact details same as for KWV Wine Emporium, or houseoffire@kwv.co.za ▪ House of Fire tour & brandy tasting: Eng Mon-Fri 11.30 & 2.30 reservations essential (max 14 persons per tour), regret no under 18s allowed ▪ KWV Sensorium: 57 Main Rd, T +27 (0)21-807-3094, sensorium@kwv.co.za, www.kwvsensorium. co.za ▪ Tasting & art museum Mon-Fri 9-4.30 ▪ Art & wine pairing ▪ Owner(s) Warshay Investment (Pty) Ltd ta KWV ▪ Chief winemaker Wim Truter ▪ Winemaker(s) Izelle van Blerk, Louwritz Louw, Andri le Roux, Kobus van der Merwe & Sacha Muller ▪ Viticulturist(s) Marco Ventrella & Oursula Lenee ▪ PO Box 528 Suider-Paarl 7624 ▪ customer@kwv.co.za ▪ www.kwv.co.za ▪ S 33° 45′ 46.87″ E 018° 57′ 59.92″ (Emporium/House of Fire), S 33° 45′ 43.26″ E 018° 57′ 44.06″ (Sensorium) ▪ F +27 (0)21-807-3000 ▪ **T +27 (0)21-807-3911 (office)**

KWV Brandies

Since 1918, KWV has been crafting world-class spirits - potstill brandy in particular - garnering an international reputation and many prestigious awards including World's Best Brandy & Cognac Producer at the International Spirit Challenge in 2018. The portfolio is crafted by master distiller Pieter de Bod and a team who are also responsible for Imoya VSOP Cognac, a collaboration with Cognac house Maison Charpentier.

The House of Fire at KWV Wine Emporium in Paarl (see KWV 'corporate' listing) provides a multifaceted showcase for these fine brandies.

★★★★★ **Nexus** ⓦ Superb packaging featuring individually crafted bottle & wooden case sets the scene for this 30 year old: fine floral notes, wafts of soft spice, dried pears & apple follow on to intense fruit on the palate. Elegant, regal & oh so smooth, with a dry lingering citrus bite. Astounding quality.

★★★★★ **20 Year Old** ⓦ Exquisite aromas - sandalwood, apricot, scented flowers, hints spice & oxidative maturity. Rich & full, yet super-refined & delicate. A touch less forceful than 15YO, but more grace. Beautifully balanced, with supreme oak support. Long, mellow, mature notes carry to slightly sweet finish.

★★★★★ **15 Year Old Alambic** ⓦ Attractive honey, soft spice & dried fruit with floral backing & some fine oak. Smooth, fine texture & good balance; great complexity from a range of citrus & rich fruitcake flavours. Mellow & mature, with everlasting finish.

★★★★★ **12 Year Old Barrel Select** ⓦ Rich, robust with caramelised nuts, sun-dried peaches, pear drop on the nose. The palate is that & more. Layers of cashew nut flavours melt in the mouth, honey, dark chocolate & fine sprinkling of spice. A triumph.

★★★★★ **10 Year Old Vintage** ⓦ Jewel bright & delicate, with citrus aromas, dried apple, spice & dark chocolate on the palate. Rounded & full bodied, with a long mellow finish. Exquisite. 100% potstill.

★★★★ **Imoya Fine Potstill** ⓦ Modern, beautifully presented brandy. Fresh fruity aromas & flavours; elegant, rich balance, subtle texture with nutty, spicy oak in support, lifted with a fresh spirity finish. 100% potstill of up to 20 years.

★★★★ **5 Year Old Superior** ⓦ Notes of sweet caramel, fruit, nuts & vanilla. Excellent balance, clean & lightly fiery on sweet-tinged finish. Blended; could compete with pure potstills on their turf!

3 Year Old Finest Blend ⓦ ★★★☆ Less aggressive than many young blended brandies - sippable neat. Fruity nose with caramel, dark molasses, tealeaves. Sufficiently complex, balanced. — WB, TJ

KWV Sherry-Style Wines

KWV's awarded fortified range consists of a Red Muscadel, Ruby and Tawny 'ports' (see KWV Wines), plus these three sherry-style wines. The trio is made from chenin blanc and colombard, and aged in small barrels for the first year. They are then transferred to a solera for a further 3–6 years' maturation.

★★★★ **Cape Pale Dry** ⓦ **NV** ⑧⑦ shows typical flor character of tealeaf & pear, almond, hints of dried fruit simmering under. Bone-dry, good freshness & spirit lift.

★★★★ **Cape Medium Cream** ⓦ Amber **NV** ⑧⑦ trademark stewed fruit & caramelised apples, the flavours rich & sweet yet uncloying. Finish is savoury, brightened by alcohol.

★★★★ **Cape Full Cream** ⓦ Golden brown **NV** ⑧⑦ shows the candied fruit profile, velvety sweetness & gentle spirity lift that proclaims the KWV's expertise with fortified wine. — CR

KWV Wines

Now in its second century of production, KWV is a globally recognised, award-winning wine and spirits company, and the highest-ranking SA wine brand in a Drinks International magazine Top 50 Most Admired Wine Brands in the World listing. The phenomenally successful ranges featured below are created under the leadership of chief winemaker Wim Truter, with 'drinkability first' as mantra and the goal of 'elegant, balanced and fresh wines of high quality'. Tastings and sales of the wines and separately listed brandies and sherry-style wines are at KWV's well-appointed Wine Emporium in Paarl (see KWV 'corporate' entry).

Abraham Perold Heritage Collection

★★★★☆ **Tributum** ⓦ Very fine Cape Blend mostly cab & pinotage, dashes shiraz & malbec. **13** ⑨② opulent & seriously oaked (70% new, 18 months, French/American) for cellaring decade or longer. This Coastal WO, but all below WO W Cape unless noted.

The Mentors range

★★★★☆ **Cabernet Sauvignon Darling** ⓦ Elegant expression of Darling's cool maritime climate: **14** ⑨② generous but reined-in blackberry fruit, hint of mint, firm but ripe tannins. 18 months, 70% new oak, as most reds this range.

★★★★ **Cabernet Sauvignon Stellenbosch** ⨂ Deep & dark but not extracted, with fresh acidity & vibrant fruit, oak-driven finish. **14** ⑧⑦ needs year/2 to show at best.

★★★★☆ **Petit Verdot** ⓐ Variety-true **16** ⑨① rich & concentrated, notes of blueberry, lavender, dark chocolate & toasty oak. Polished, firm tannins provide backbone & balance, & bode well for the future.

★★★★☆ **Pinotage** ⓐ Switching from Stellenbosch to Darling origin, **16** ⑨⓪'s fruit is dark & plummy, the body full & rounded, hints of vanilla & coconut from French & American barrels. Will reward ageing.

★★★★ **Shiraz** ⨂ Like last-tasted **09, 14** ★★★★★ ⑨⓪ ripe & expressive but not unrestrained. Violet & cassis notes, well-judged oak (some American), long spicy finish. Coastal WO, as next 2.

★★★★ **Orchestra** ⓐ Best barrels selection for this cab-led, 5-way Bordeaux blend. **16** ⑧⑧ a symphony of black & red berry fruit, vivacious & succulent yet structured by cocoa-tinged oak & fresh finish.

★★★★☆ **Canvas** ⓐ Shiraz (39%) with grenache, tempranillo, petite sirah, cinsaut & tannat colours the **16** ⑨④ canvas in bright aromas & flavours. Lipsmacking & complex, with a savoury freshness. A masterclass in blending. 50% new oak.

★★★★ **Chardonnay** ⨂ Barrel fermented/9 months, 17% wild yeast for enhanced texture & mouthfeel in intensely toasty, nutty **15** ⑧⑥. Rich, buttery yet laced with enlivening acidity. From Walker Bay vines.

★★★★☆ **Chenin Blanc** ⨂ Attention paid in its creation, different yeasts & oaking, including tank-fermented portion, shows in **15** ⑨③'s complexity: buttery richness, apple & stonefruit tones, enlivening lemon seam. Delicious now & for 5+ years. WO Paarl, as next.

★★★★☆ **Grenache Blanc** ⨂ Complex vinification - wild-yeast, lees-aged (in old oak) & tank-fermented portions. **15** ⑨③ very modern, sleek, with layers of flavour & minerality, engaging freshness.

★★★★ **Sauvignon Blanc Darling** ⨂ Bursts with flavour, gooseberries & lime, **15** ⑧⑦ intense & pure, with a zesty freshness that lasts & lasts, courtesy Darling's cooler climate.

★★★★☆ **Sauvignon Blanc Elim** ⨂ ⓐ Attractively austere **14** ⑨③ from ocean-cooled vines, mineral expression with salty hints; interesting contrast to sibling's tropical generosity. Well-judged acidity, herbal length with just enough grip from 2 months on lees. Will reward few years cellaring.

★★★★ **Semillon** ⨂ Quintessential semillon notes of hay, smoke plus variety's signature acid tension in impressive **15** ⑧⑦ from Darling. Partial barrel ferment adds subtle creaminess.

★★★★ **Sauvignon Blanc-Semillon** ⨂ Accomplished barrelled version with 2 months on lees for extra texture & weight. **15** ⑧⑦'s toastiness gives way to forthcoming capsicum & passionfruit. Delicious now, should improve year/2. WO Coastal.

Cathedral Cellar range

★★★★ **Shiraz** Previewed **16** ⑧⑧ is spicy, with robust black hedgerow fruit, meaty undertone, long finish & savouriness from 40% new oak, 6% American. Delightful wine - very lively & youthful.

★★★★☆ **Triptych** ⊘ Well-structured vintage blend, mostly cab & shiraz in **16** ⑨⓪, plus merlot & pinotage. Full bodied, amply layered with berry, spice & cured meat. Tasted pre-bottling, rating provisional, but everything set for usual pleasurable drinking.

★★★★ **Chardonnay** Harmonious assembly of oaked & 4% tank-fermented components, giving lovely freshness & crunch to **17** ⑧⑥'s rich citrus & apple flavours, extended lees contact adds complexity.

Cabernet Sauvignon ★★★★ Plush fruit, rounded mouthfeel & friendly tannins in satisfying **16** ⑧③, only 35% new oak 14-16 months. **Sauvignon Blanc** ★★★★ Beautifully balanced **17** ⑧③, lingering & generous ripe/green flavours of tropical fruit, greenpepper & herbs, cleansing lemon peel farewell.

Roodeberg range

★★★★ **Dr Charles Niehaus** ⓐ Roodeberg an iconic name in SA wine, this wine honours its father. 'Dr Charles' also early proponent of shiraz, hence variety's lead in **16** ★★★★★ ⑨⓪ characterful blend with cab, merlot & malbec. Sweet, intense black cherry flavours, deepening earthy herb notes, savoury finish. Dab American oak, as in **15** ⑧⑦. Coastal WO.

Red ★★★ Enduring & much-loved label. **17** ⑧① easy, fruity, good freshness & structure, gentle notes of vanilla & smoke. Mostly cab & shiraz. **Rosé** ★★★ Fun, fruity & just-dry **18** ⑧⓪, grapefruit & ripe strawberry flavours for easy sipping.

Laborie range

★★★★ **Méthode Cap Classique Brut Rosé** ⊘ Now NV ⑧⑧, dry sparkling from pinot noir, chardonnay, dab pinotage is all about berry liveliness, creamy bubbles & fresh, upbeat finish. Will make you smile.

★★★★ **Méthode Cap Classique Blanc de Blancs** ⊘ ⓐ For extra-special celebrations, standout **11** ★★★★☆ ⑨⓪ dry chardonnay sparkler fulfils the promise of 3 years maturation: soft smooth mousse, mouthfilling & round brioche, lemon curd & baked apple flavours, complex lees & nutty toastiness. Superb now & worth ageing, vs earlier-drinking **10**.

★★★★ **Méthode Cap Classique Brut** ⊘ Vibrant & tasty dry bubbles with plentiful berry & vanilla shortcake, good acidity reining in fruit flavours for a satisfying, lengthy finish. NV ⑧⑧ chardonnay, pinot noir & meunier, 24 months on lees vs 18 for Rosé.

Cabernet Sauvignon ★★★ Medium-bodied **17** ⑦⑧ is lightly fruited, crisp, a green bite on the finish. **Merlot** ★★★ Firm, stern & lean **17** ⑦⑦ needs robust food. **Shiraz** ★★★ Gluggable **17** ⑧②, spicy sweet fruit for everyday enjoyment. Gentle tannins here. **Merlot-Cabernet Sauvignon** ★★★ Dryish **17** ⑦⑦ shows good balance of blackcurrant fruit, earthy notes & chunky tannins. **Rosé** (NEW) ★★★ Softly dry pink, **18** ⑦⑨ offers gentle fragrant fruit & spice. **Chardonnay** ★★★ Partial oaking for **17** ⑦⑧, light bodied & apple/citrus toned. Serve well-chilled. **Sauvignon Blanc** ★★★ Delicate floral aromas, gentle green herb flavours on water-white **18** ⑦⑦. **Pineau de Laborie** ★★★★ Dessert wine in attractive packaging from unoaked pinotage, fortification bringing warmth to the ripe, luscious spicy plum fruit. NV ⑧④ in 375 ml.

Classic Collection

★★★★☆ **Cape Tawny** ⊘ ⓐ This NV ⑨③ 'port' a classic example of the style, & always-impressive performer. Melange of roasted nuts, marzipan, marmalade & rich chocolate on harmonious & perfectly integrated spirit bed. Tinta, cinsaut, souzão, touriga & shiraz aged 8-10 years in older barrels.

⋯⋯⋯

Petit Verdot ⓥ ★★★ Variety still rarely bottled on its own, sets **17** ⑧① apart from its siblings. Ripe, friendly & succulent, as good with food as solo. **Pinotage** ⓥ ★★★ Brims with plum & dark cherry fruit, **17** ⑧② hint of spice from light oaking, very gluggable. **Chardonnay** ⓥ ★★★ Touch of oak, butter-baked apple add texture & character in **17** ⑧②, nice weight & length. **Grenache Blanc** ⊘ ⓐ ★★★★ Standout among the whites here: oak-brushed **18** ⑧④ pleasingly intense & flavourful, excellent value for money. **Moscato** ⓥ ★★★ Sweet & gentle muscat d'Alexandrie, **18** ⑧① uncloying grape & floral tones, charming & summery. **Cape Ruby** ⊘ ⓐ ★★★★ Generous & rounded mouthful of sweet plum & spice, some complexity, delightful spirit kick. NV ⑧③ from tinta, shiraz & pinotage ticks all boxes for Ruby 'port'.

⋯⋯⋯

Cabernet Sauvignon ★★★ Minted dark berry fruit for everyday enjoyment in **17** ⑦⑦. **Merlot** ★★★ Light-hearted, plummy **17** ⑦⑧ is juicy, with gentle grip to finish. **Shiraz** ★★★ Dark chocolate, berries, dried herbs & friendly tannin, **17** ⑦⑧ perfect for saucy fare. **Shiraz Rosé** ★★ Pretty pink **18** ⑦③, just-dry & gentle, understated & soft flavours. **Chenin Blanc** ★★★ Appealing, crisp Granny Smith apple flavours, **18** ⑦⑧ tasty & effortless fun. **Sauvignon Blanc** ★★★ A beach wine, cool-toned **18** ⑦⑦ cucumber & green herb character, good balance. **Sparkling Cuvée Brut** ★★★ Frothy, grassy NV ⑦⑧ with a fruity finish for everyday popping. **Sparkling Demi-Sec** ★★ Fruity semi-sweet NV ⑦⑤ has good acidity to balance the sugar; creamy & gentle bubbles. **Red Muscadel** ⓧ ★★★★ High-toned cherry notes, mouthwatering raisin richness, long & fiery finish, NV ⑧④ fortified ticks all the winter-warming boxes.

Earth's Essence No Sulphur Added range

Shiraz ★★ Bright-fruited but lean, **18** ⑦⑥ with savoury spice farewell. **Chenin Blanc** (NEW) ★★ Previewed **18** ⑦③ very demure, some bruised apple flavour, lick of lemon. — WB

Kyburg Wine Estate ⓠ ⓐ

Viticulture is the focus on Fred and Rosmarie Ruest's Devon Valley estate: 90% of the grapes are sold to local producers, and 20 tons are shipped to the US to be vinified there. Recent fine-tuning is reducing labour input and green harvesting, and promoting longer, more equal ripening, Fred says. His own-brand wines, honouring a medieval castle back in Switzerland, can be tasted in a renovated century-old barn.

★★★★ **33 Latitude** More precision on cab (60%) mix with merlot & shiraz in **11** ⑧⑥ than **10** ★★★★ ⑧⑤. Generous fruit expression, with density & concentration. Oak (20% new) well knit, adding to lengthy, rewarding aftertaste.

★★★★ **Chenin Blanc** Peach & pineapple zip to bright, unwooded **17** (87), good acid/fruit balance, long fresh finish with interesting saline nuance. Last tasted **15** ★★★★ (84) from Swartland.

Cabernet Sauvignon ★★★★ Gentle & soft **11** (83), supple, generous & still-fresh fruit, 20% new French oaking is nicely integrated. Good for further 3-5 years, like 33 Latitude. **Merlot** ★★★★ Graphite & ripe berry on mature **11** (85), a step up on previous. Leaner style but pleasing spicy, dried herb notes & fine, dry tannin, light & pliable texture. **Shiraz** ★★★★ Retains form in **11** (85), ripe plum & spice flavours with firm, dry tannins & balanced acidity. Good length. Not tasted: **33 Latitude Select**. — FM, CvZ

Location/map: Stellenbosch ▪ Map grid reference: D4 ▪ WO: Devon Valley/Stellenbosch ▪ Est 1998 ▪ 1stB 2006 ▪ Tasting by appt ▪ Self-catering guesthouse (exclusive use, rental min 2 weeks) ▪ Owner(s) Fred & Rosmarie Ruest ▪ Winemaker(s) Jacques Fourie (Jan 2006, consultant) ▪ Viticulturist(s) Frans Snyman (Jul 2006, consultant) ▪ 28ha/16ha (cab, merlot, shiraz) ▪ 160t/4,000cs own label 90% red 10% white ▪ PO Box 12799 Die Boord 7613 ▪ info@kyburgwine.com ▪ www.kyburgwine.com ▪ S 33° 54′59.3″ E 018° 49′28.4″ ▪ 〰 impulses.huddled.hush ▪ **T +27 (0)21-865-2876/+27 (0)82-651-5688**

Laarman Wines   ⓠ

Having achieved local and international acclaim at Kaapzicht and Glen Carlou, veteran Arco Laarman went solo with his maiden '17 Cluster Series Chardonnay and Cabernet. Now comes his premium collection, Focal Point, featuring chardonnay, his favourite variety, and cinsaut, a heritage grape he's championing. Sources are cool-climate, single-vineyard sites in, among others, trending Piekenierskloof and Vermaaklikheid.

Focal Point range (NEW)

★★★★☆ **Cinsault** Innovative resealing cork stopper (as Chardonnay) for exceptional **17** (90), variety-true, with attractive strawberry, raspberry fruit, lithe body, lovely grip. Full, flavoursome yet unforced; easy to drink but not at all simple. Cinsaut as a stylish template.

★★★★ **Chardonnay** Cool-climate vineyard at Vermaaklikheid on South Coast, **17** (88) barrel fermented/matured with various yeasts & barrel provenance, 48% new. Fruit intensity, preserved lemon & tangerine, ginger biscuit savoury tones, supported by brisk acidity. Lovely focus & length, & a good future— CR, CvZ

Location: Paarl ▪ WO: Stellenbosch/Cape South Coast ▪ Est 2016 ▪ 1stB 2017 ▪ Tasting by appt only ▪ Owner(s)/winemaker(s) Arco Laarman ▪ 5,000cs own label 40% red 60% white ▪ 84 Wilderbosh Str Paryskloof Estate Paarl 7646 ▪ arco@laarmanwines.com ▪ www.laarmanwines.com ▪ F +27 (0)21-862-0286 ▪ **T +27 (0)83-546-1146**

☐ **Labeye** see Radford Dale
☐ **La Bonne Vigne** see Wonderfontein
☐ **Laborie** see KWV Wines

La Bourgogne Farm   ⓠ ⑪ ⌂ ⊙ Ⓐ

The passing of paterfamilias George Mayer in February 2018 left an enormous void at this boutique Franschhoek property, but new owners, his children Sophie, Dominique, Charles and Virginia, and the La Bourgogne team are determined to grow his legacy of boutique winecrafting and a welcoming cellardoor.

Flagship range

★★★★ **Progeny Semillon** Returns to line-up with **17** (88), stonefruit, citrus & lanolin allures, richness neatly balanced by seam of acidity, modest 12.5% alcohol. Obvious oak (50% new) needs time to settle.

★★★★ **Family Reserve White 1694** Just 1,100 bottles of **17** (89) produced from sauvignon, barrel-fermented semillon, aged year in 50% new oak as blend. Delicate lemon & marzipan notes, lighter (12.3% alcohol) & more balanced than **16** ★★★★ (84).

★★★★ **Progeny White Honey** (NEW) Well-crafted & harmonious Natural Sweet from semillon. **17** (88) satiny & smooth, attractive pear drop aroma, gentle freshness & light 12% alcohol.

Progeny Malbec 1694 ★★★ Luscious & ripe, with inky hue & ripe, broad tannins. **16** (80) big-boned, seasoned with 40% new French/American oak; not quite as accomplished as previous. **Progeny Syrah 1694** ★★★ Juicy **16** (81), caramel & plum tones, ripe but welcomely restrained alcohol (14.3%) & oak (40% new) compared with previous.

Premium range

Red (NEW) ★★★ Ripe-fruited & intense 16 (81) from shiraz & malbec (80/20), bold & satisfying mouthful with fair length, vanilla & spice from older French & American oak. **Rosé** ★★★★ Copper-hued, food-styled 17 (84) from shiraz, dry & full-bodied, almost bracingly fresh with crunchy red apple fruit & hint of grape tannin. **Unwooded Chardonnay** ★★★★ Jasmine- & citrus-scented 17 (84) is bright & long-lingering, gains generous mouthfeel from 3 months lees ageing. — HC

Location/map/WO: Franschhoek ▪ Map grid reference: D1 ▪ Est 1694 ▪ 1stB 1902 ▪ Tasting & sales Mon-Sun 10-5 ▪ Fee R30-R150 ▪ Closed Easter Fri-Sun, Ascension day, Dec 25/26 & Jan 1 ▪ Facilities for children ▪ Farm shop/deli ▪ Al fresco lunch; olive & olive oil tasting; infused caramel & wine pairing ▪ Walks ▪ Conservation area ▪ On Franschhoek wine tram route ▪ 6 self-catering Riverside cottages ▪ Owner(s) Mayer family, La Bourgogne Farm (Pty) Ltd ▪ Estate manager Loesje Kock (2007) ▪ Winemaker(s) DP Burger & Zinaschke Steyn (2008/2015, GlenWood) ▪ Viticulturist(s) Gappie le Roux (2003) & Erhard le Roux (2012) ▪ 22ha/4ha (malbec, shiraz, chard, sem, viog) ▪ PO Box 96 Franschhoek 7690 ▪ info@labourgogne.co.za ▪ www.labourgogne.co.za ▪ S 33° 55' 28.0" E 019° 7' 15.0" ▪ (w) compromising.fashioned.telescope ▪ **T +27 (0)21-876-3245/+27 (0)83-441-8272**

La Bri Estate
(symbols: glass / cutlery / camera)

Robin Hamilton's elegant farm, one of the original properties granted to Huguenots in Franschhoek, this edition looks back on 325 years since inception. History and tradition are no encumbrance, however, to the wine brand whose home it is: there's a modern cellar on-site and a dynamic team in charge - GM/winemaker Irene (Waller) de Fleuriot and right hand Glen Isaacs - and, with the new Double Door range, a vehicle for extending the repertoire with grapes selected from other Valley vineyards.

Estate range

★★★★ **Cabernet Sauvignon Limited Release** (glass) Floral whiff precedes wonderful smooth fruitcake flavour of 15 ★★★★☆ (93), framed by seamless French oak (new, 2 years). Lithe, restrained, elegant, as befits oldest red-wine vineyard (1999) & exceptional-years-only release. Last was 12 (88).

★★★★ **Merlot** Elegant tealeaf & black fruit on restrained 16 (87). Leashed power vies with mulberry vibrancy & piquant acidity. Complex, nuanced, with integrated & well-judged oak, just 18% new.

★★★★ **Syrah** Subtle floral edge to plum-toned 16 (88). Firm core of ripe fruit cradled by oak, 39% new, 2 years. Refined, with good complexity & length. Dash co-fermented viognier, like 15 ★★★★ (83).

★★★★☆ **Syrah 1045** (glass) Statuesque & regal 13 (93), a vineyard selection long bottle-aged at cellar. Structured yet supple, with violet- & pepper-tinged plum fruit, oak (new, 2 years) adding fine dry tannins that cosset the palate.

★★★★ **Affinity** (glass) Cab leads in 15 (87) appealing 4-way Bordeaux blend. Complex, cohesive, soft-textured & rich mouthful that tapers off on cocoa note. Poised, with deft oaking, mainly old French.

★★★★☆ **Barrel Select Chardonnay** (symbol) 2nd, riper picking of 26 year old block & cask selection result in refined & elegant 17 (93), showing cashew, orange & spice subtlety. Integrated & complex, many layers of flavour on rich palate, creaminess ex all-new French oak.

★★★★ **Chardonnay** Vivacious marmalade & mandarin fruit in lovely interplay with gentle oak (year, 50% new), creamy yet fresh. 17 (88) focused & precise, with honeyed richness on long tail.

★★★★☆ **Sauvage La Bri Blanc de Blancs** Sourdough, lime & seabreeze aromas impress on crisp, dry & intense MCC sparkling from chardonnay. 12 (92) primary ferment in old oak, then zero dosage & 48 months on lees for broad, rich & creamy texture with good minerality.

Not tasted: **Viognier Limited Release**.

Double Door range (NEW)

★★★★ **Semillon** Beeswax & honey notes of 17 (86) layered with spice & citrus. Light & juicy but with creamy breadth. Half oaked, all-new French oak aids both richness & definition/focus; long aftertaste. Neighbours' grapes, as next.

★★★★ **White** Complexity & balance on 17 (87) roussanne, chardonnay, viognier & semillon. Rounded but taut, defined & succulent. Bright stonefruit mingles with spice & nutty breadth from 50% oaking.

Merlot Rosé ★★★★ Fine debut in pink-hued 18 (84). Crisp, juicy strawberry tones with lively acid & toned body from oak ageing. Good definition & dryness. These available from cellardoor only. — FM

Location/map/WO: Franschhoek ▪ Map grid reference: C1 ▪ Est 1694 ▪ Tasting, sales & cellar tours Mon-Fri 9.30-5 Sat/Sun & pub hols 10-4 ▪ Fee varies ▪ Closed Good Fri, Dec 25 & Jan 1 ▪ Chocolate & wine pairing; biltong & wine experience; Turkish delight & wine pairing ▪ Cheese platters; bespoke picnics ▪ Bicycle friendly ▪ Weddings & functions ▪ Part of Franschhoek Tram route ▪ Owner(s) Robin Hamilton ▪ Winemaker(s) Irene Waller (Oct 2010), with Glen Isaacs (Jun 2009) ▪ Viticulturist(s) Gerard Olivier (Oct 2010) ▪ ±20ha/±15ha (cabs s/f, merlot, p verdot, shiraz, chard, viog) ▪ 100t/10,000cs own label 80% red 20% white ▪ WIETA ▪ PO Box 180 Franschhoek 7690 ▪ info@labri.co.za ▪ www.labri.co.za ▪ S 33° 55' 18.3" E 019° 7' 1.5" ▪ ⓦ resource. tweaked.implicit ▪ F +27 (0)86-275-9753 ▪ **T +27 (0)21-876-2593**

☐ **La Capra** see Fairview
☐ **La Cave** see Wellington Wines
☐ **Lace** see Almenkerk Wine Estate

La Chataigne   ⓠ ⌂ ♿

A small property in Franschhoek that is both winefarm (with access to 63-75 year-old vines) and accommodation venue, with five guest cottages. Swedish owners Richard and Julie Parkfelt give new meaning to 'hands on': each bottle of their limited production is handwritten directly onto the glass with the wine's name and details. The content is now co-crafted by neighbour and winemaker Martin Smith of Paserene.

Kastanje ⓠ ★★★ From chenin bushvines, giving expressive citrus- & apple-toned fruit to **17** ⑧②. Light textured, crisply dry, tasty. **Sauvignon Blanc** ⓠ ★★★ **17** ⑧① nice sauvignon styling, leafy, capsicum, with lime-fresh flavours & finish. Just the thing to perk up your taste buds. **18** also available but untasted by us. Not tasted: **Marron**, **Rosé**, **Semillon**. — CR

Location/map/WO: Franschhoek ▪ Map grid reference: C4 ▪ Est 1972 ▪ 1stB 2003 ▪ Tasting & sales Mon-Fri 10-4 Sat/Sun & pub hols by appt ▪ 5 guest cottages ▪ Owner(s) Parkfelt family ▪ Winemaker(s) Gerda Willers (2003, consultant) & Martin Smith ▪ 17ha/10ha (merlot, ptage, sauv, sem) ▪ 120t/1,500cs own label 25% red 65% white 10% rosé ▪ PO Box 301 Franschhoek 7690 ▪ info@lachat.co.za ▪ www.lachat.co.za ▪ S 33° 52' 59.77" E 019° 3' 11.29" ▪ ⓦ admire.rosters.grappling ▪ F +27 (0)86-545-1039 ▪ **T +27 (0)21-876-3220**

La Chaumiere Estate   ⓠ

Michael and Kristina Pawlowski came for a visit to Franschhoek, and decided to stay and make wine. The name of their 'true working farm' means, roughly, cottage in French. No new vintages were tasted this year.

Location/map: Franschhoek ▪ Map grid reference: C2 ▪ Est 2001 ▪ 1stB 2003 ▪ Tasting & cellar tours by appt ▪ Sales from local outlets, restaurants, hotels & wine bars ▪ Owner(s) Michael Pawlowski ▪ 5ha (cab, pinot, shiraz, chard) ▪ 24t/3,400cs own label ▪ PO Box 601 Franschhoek 7690 ▪ nevlotz@gmail.com ▪ www. lachaumierewines.co.za ▪ S 33° 54' 34.0" E 019° 6' 54.9" ▪ ⓦ motored.gastronomy.printable ▪ F +27 (0)21-876-2135 ▪ **T +27 (0)21-876-4830/31, +27 (0)61-311-5369**

La Couronne Wines   ⓠ ⑪ ⌂ ⓞ ⓐ

Owner Francois Smith's rejuvenation of this nautical-themed boutique winery and lifestyle estate continues with a renewed focus - in both the wine portfolio and the vine planting programme - on the varieties best suited to the terroir. The diverse, child-friendly visitor attractions, accessible via the popular Franschhoek Wine Tram, now include a third fun wine pairing, barbecued foods, joining pizza and chocolate.

Vins de Balise range

★★★★☆ **Pinotage Limited Edition** ⓠ With gravitas to match the weighty bottle, **15** ⑨① is full, firm & dry, with plum, smoke & piquant meatiness in an elegant structure. Far more refined than many of the genre. 21 months seasoned oak, some American. WO Stellenbosch.

★★★★ **Barrel Fermented Viognier** ⑯Ⓐ Brims with ripe peachy fruit swaddled in sweet oak vanilla; **16** ⑧⑦ honeyed notes & nutmeg spicing, dry conclusion. Year older oak. For Asian cuisine.

Shiraz ⑯Ⓐ ★★★★ Preview of ambitious **16** ⑧⑤ shows plump, ripe mulberry fruit shot through with coconut & mocha tones of dominant American oak; a riot of sweet-tasting flavours. 2 years 100% new oak.

Admiral's Choice

★★★★ **Malbec** Super **15** ⑧⑦ ups the ante on jammy **13** ★★★ ⑧①, rich choc & plum notes lifted by spice; balanced, with enough fruit to smooth over tannic grip. Year older wood. **14** untasted.

★★★★ **Barrel Fermented Chardonnay** Full & broad but with a bright core, juicy freshness & nutty tail of crafted **16** ⑧⑨ is alluring & rich; pure varietal fruit framed by seasoned oak. **15** sold out before tasting.

Commander Selection

Le Petite Malbec (NEW) ★★★ Spiced plum tones in midweight **15** ⑧① with splash petit verdot, glides down easily. **Merlot** ⑦ ★★★★ **15** ⑧⑤ gears up on previous with violet, bacon & mulberry features on supple oak tannins; has grip but isn't severe. 20% new wood. **Portside Red** ★★★ Malbec-led quintet of Bordeaux varieties delivers winter fireside enjoyment. **15** ⑦⑧ firmer than previous, allow year to soften. **Sauvignon Blanc** ★★★ Pleasantly fruity **17** ⑦⑧, tropical toned rather than green/bracing. WO W Cape. Not tasted: **Muscadel**. Discontinued: **Pinotage, Shiraz, Chardonnay Unwooded.**

Sailor's Selection

Upper Deck Red ★★★ Earthy, gamey notes lifted by savoury spice; **16** ⑦⑨ fleshy grenache, mourvèdre & shiraz with dollop cab franc, polished a few months in seasoned barrels. WO W Cape, like Chenin. **Merlot Rosé** ⑦ ★★★ Salmon glints to sleek **17** ⑧① with candyfloss flavour & dry rosewater finish. **Upper Deck Chenin Blanc** ★★ Crunchy green apple interest of **17** ⑦⑤ has a dry, dusty tail. — DS

Location/map: Franschhoek ▪ Map grid reference: C1 ▪ WO: Franschhoek/Western Cape/Stellenbosch ▪ Tasting & sales Mon-Sun 11-4; closed some Sundays during winter ▪ Chocolate & wine tasting; pizza & wine pairing; braai & wine pairing ▪ Closed Christian religious hols ▪ Wood-fired pizza restaurant ▪ Wine tram ▪ Traditional braai & picnics to be booked in advance ▪ Facilities for children ▪ Tour groups ▪ Weddings & functions ▪ Le Chais Villa (6 en-suite rooms) ▪ Winemaker(s) Henk Swart (May 2015) ▪ 21ha (cabs s/f, malbec, merlot, p verdot, ptage, shiraz, chard, sauv, viog) ▪ 180t/±25,000cs own label 70% red 30% white ▪ info@ lacouronnewines.co.za ▪ www.lacouronnewines.co.za ▪ S 33° 55' 8.9" E 019° 6' 40.9" ▪ 📍 ballads.currency. thumbnail ▪ **T +27 (0)21-876-3939/+27 (0)82-495-8579**

☐ **Ladismith Winery & Distillery** see Barrydale Winery & Distillery
☐ **Ladybird** see Laibach Vineyards
☐ **Lady May** see Glenelly Estate
☐ **Lady Somerset** see Somerset Wines
☐ **La Famille** see Mischa Estate

Laibach Vineyards   ⑦ 🏠

German-family-owned Laibach outside Stellenbosch is fully organic (certified in 2012), so everything here is designed to be as natural as possible. The Ladybird range, which makes up most of production, is more than a marketing construct: there really has been a significant increase in the cute little critters' numbers, allowing the vineyard scourge of mealy bug to be kept under control – the reward of nature in balance. The only change planned is installing irrigation in younger vineyards, in case of future dry conditions. Francois van Zyl, winemaker for 19 years, follows the vision, practising minimum intervention in the cellar.

Reserve range

★★★★★ **Widow's Block Cabernet Sauvignon** ⑦ Rich, dark & brooding **14** ⑨③ has more new oak (75%) than previous, masking the tight, concentrated fruit core; very firm cedary tannins. Appeals less on release than **12** ⑨③. Has pedigree to age harmoniously, though, just needs time. No **13**.

★★★★★ **Claypot Merlot** ⑦ ⑦ Long skin contact, accounting for deep colour, concentration of **15** ⑨③. Cassis, maraschino cherries, 60% new barrels giving spice flavouring, firm ageing foundation. Serious & impressive, worthy successor to understated **14** ★★★★★ ⑨⑦.

★★★★ **Pinotage RR** (NEW) ⑦ 🍷 Wild ferment, mainly new oak, **16** ⑧⑧ different to its Classic sibling. Loads of savoury spice/salty liquorice, glossy blueberry fruit; tannin structure more evident, firm but ripe, geared for cellaring. Also in 1.5, 3 & 5L.

★★★★★ **Friedrich Laibach** 🍷 Honours founder. Merlot, with cab, dash cab franc, **16** ⑨⓪ new oak 14 months, vintage's 18 best barrels: shows spicy meat extract, almost toasty, but red fruit equal to it. Sleek texture & appealing freshness, ready but built for the long haul. No **15**.

★★★★ Chenin Blanc Sur Lie (NEW) ⊘ Different vinification to Ladybird: 25% carbonic maceration, 30 days skin contact, wild ferment, half oaked/concrete 'eggs'. **17** (88) admirable result, blanched almonds, quince & melon preserve, curvaceous.

Ladybird range

★★★★★ White ⊘ ⊗ ⊛ Naturally made, combo older barrels, concrete 'eggs' & stainless steel, chardonnay plus 15% chenin. Similar to **16** (93)'s profile, **17** (93) individual & striking, sophisticated: lemon preserve, wax, an oatmeal/almond seam focusing the elements, giving length. WO W Cape, as Chenin.

Red ⊘ **★★★★** Attractive 5-part Bordeaux blend, mainly merlot with cab, cab franc; plump, red-fruited **16** (83) is juicy & smooth, tannins harmonious, can already be enjoyed. Also in magnum. **Chenin Blanc ★★★** Melon & apple in **18** (81), fresh & lively, shows good typicity, fruity all the way through. Not tasted: **Méthode Cap Classique**. Discontinued: **Sauvignon Blanc**.

Classic range

★★★★ Merlot ⊘ Less oaking than Claypot, same great vineyards: **17** (87) expressive fruit, cassis & plums, spice overlay. Suave tannins, polished & succulent for immediate pleasure but can age.

★★★★★ Natural Sweet ⊘ ⊛ 'Modern day German/Mosel-style winemaking' applied to Bottelary chenin, with low alcohol (7.5%) & piercing acidity. The effect is thrilling vibrancy, nervy tension, making **18** (93)'s baked apple/melon preserve sweetness even more delicious. 375 ml.

Cabernet Sauvignon ★★★★ A lot going on in **16** (83), plumply ripe dark fruit, a dried meat/biltong nuance, toasty oak & dry, firm tannins; accessible but will improve with ageing. **Pinotage ★★★★** Some carbonic maceration, aiding **16** (83)'s dark plum fruit focus, oaking giving liquorice savouriness. Nice grip at the end for food, but body is smoothly round, engaging. Stellenbosch WO as all these.

Discontinued: **Limited Release range**. — CR

Location/map: Stellenbosch ▪ Map grid reference: F1 ▪ WO: Simonsberg–Stellenbosch/Stellenbosch/Western Cape ▪ Est 1994 ▪ 1stB 1997 ▪ Tasting & sales Mon-Fri 10–5 Sat (Nov-Apr)/pub hols 10–1 ▪ Fee R40/4 wines ▪ Closed Easter Fri/Sun, Dec 25/26 & Jan 1 ▪ Cellar tours by appt ▪ Laibach Vineyards Lodge ▪ Owner(s) Petra Laibach-Kühner & Rudolf Kühner ▪ Cellarmaster(s)/winemaker(s) Francois van Zyl (Jan 2000) ▪ Viticulturist(s) / MD Michael Malherbe (Jun 1994) ▪ 50ha/37ha (cabs s/f, malbec, merlot, p verdot, ptage, chard, chenin) ▪ 380t/48,000cs own label 70% red 30% white + 20,000cs for Woolworths ▪ Organic ▪ PO Box 7109 Stellenbosch 7599 ▪ info@laibachwines.com ▪ www.laibachwines.com ▪ S 33° 50' 43.3" E 018° 51' 44.2" ▪ [w] records.pool.premises ▪ F +27 (0)86-665-2839 ▪ **T +27 (0)21-884-4511**

La Kavayan

Meaning 'Jan's Cellar', recalling previous Stellenbosch farm owner prof Jan Sadie, La Kavayan wine is produced by brand owner Theo Beukes with winemaker PG Slabbert but released only intermittently. As Theo says: 'We drink it, we give it away, and now and again we sell it.' Current release is Cabernet Sauvignon-Shiraz '13; follow-ups '16 and '17 still in barrel.

Location: Stellenbosch ▪ Est 1999 ▪ 1stB 2001 ▪ Closed to public ▪ Owner(s) Theo Beukes ▪ Winemaker(s) PG Slabbert (2001, consultant) ▪ Viticulturist(s) Gabriël Kriel ▪ 2ha (cab) ▪ ±10,000L own label 100% red ▪ PO Box 321 Stellenbosch 7599 ▪ diana@lakavayan.co.za, theo@minpro.co.za ▪ **T +27 (0)83-601-9030**

☐ **Lakehurst** see Wine-of-the-Month Club
☐ **Lambert's Bay's Finest** see Teubes Family Wines

Lammershoek Winery ⓛ

To appreciate the eagle on the Reserve label, and the name and curly lambshead of the fine value Innocent range, one must know the old story: that in nearby forests ewes and lambs sought shelter from black eagles. Lammershoek ('lamb's corner') was proclaimed in 1718 and vines planted soon after – though the cellar dates to the mid 1800s. It hadn't been used for 50 years when a new owner started keeping grapes back from the cooperative this century. The Paardeberg, Swartland estate was acquired in 2013 by a German consortium with soccer legend Franz Beckenbauer as the main investor. Major upgrades in vineyards, cellar and visitor facilities followed. The unshowy and fresh wines are made with minimal intervention, by Schalk Opperman, a member of the Swartland Independent Producers.

The Mysteries range

★★★★ **Die Duiker** ⓐ Impressive grenache from two dryland blocks. **16** ⑧⑧ fruit-filled & complex, cherry tobacco & violet nuances, fine dry tannins & grip from partly destemmed component.

★★★★ **Die Ou Man** ⓨ Among oldest tinta in SA, planted 1969, 1973. **16** ⑧⑨ perfumed & spiced with prune, cherry & leather, ripe tannin structure. Entirely destemmed, unlike Duiker, yet similar good dryness. Same 12-month older vat/barrel fermentation/ageing. Improves on chunky **15** ★★★★ ⑧⑤.

★★★★ **Die Harde Blaar** ⓨ ⓨ From hárslevelü, bunch pressed, portion with skin contact, showing white flower & savoury spice in **16** ⑧⑦. Untrammeled by oak, like **15** ★★★★ ⑧⑤. Just 360 bottles.

Not tasted: **Die Oranje, Die Swart Strooi**.

The Innocent range

★★★★★ **CVS** ⑭ⓔⓦ ⓥ Sleek & vibrant **17** ⑨⓪ led by 44 year old chenin with 17% sauvignon, 7% viognier. Bracingly dry & just 13% alcohol, unusual but appealing quince, melon & nectarine bouquet, subtle oak detail, mineral persistence.

Pinotage ★★★★ Unoaked **17** ⑧③, fruit-filled & bright, courtesy variety's natural acidity & semi-carbonic winemaking. Profusion of mulberry, raspberry & sour cherry, playful nudge tannin. **Syrah** ★★★★ Complex vinification/ageing for 3 bushvine parcels. Youthful & vibrant **17** ⑧③, juicy, with violet & nutmeg spicing, perfect for lamb or venison. **SMG** ⑭ⓔⓦ ★★★★ Handsome **17** ⑧④, 50% syrah, equal grenache, mourvèdre fermented separately & aged, like most in this range, in mix concrete, old foudres & used barrels. Packed with dark fruit, accented by cloves & black pepper. Coastal WO. **Rosé** ★★★ Touch of oak (4 months, older) adds breadth to **18** ⑧① pale pink, cherry toned, nicely dry, just 12.5% alcohol. From shiraz, mourvèdre & grenache. Not tasted: **Red Blend, White Blend**.

The Reserve range

Not tasted: **Syrah, Terravinum Red Blend, Chenin Blanc, Terravinum White**. — GM

Location: Malmesbury ▪ Map: Swartland ▪ Map grid reference: C8 ▪ WO: Swartland/Coastal ▪ Est 1999 ▪ 1stB 2000 ▪ Tasting, sales & cellar tours by appt ▪ Owner(s) Lammershoek Farms & Winery (Pty) Ltd ▪ Winemaker(s) Schalk Opperman (Jan 2015) ▪ Viticulturist(s) Charl van Reenen (Jan 2015) ▪ 80ha (carignan, grenache, merlot, mourv, ptage, shiraz, tinta barocca, zin, chard, chenin, hárslevelü, marsanne, sauv, viog) ▪ PO Box 597 Malmesbury 7299 ▪ info@lammershoek.co.za ▪ www.lammershoek.co.za ▪ S 33° 31'30.2" E 018° 48'21.1" ▪ 🗺 escapes.boasted.handset ▪ F +27 (0)22-487-2702 ▪ **T +27 (0)22-482-2835**

La Motte ⓨ ⓟ ⓐ ⓐ ⓐ

Its location on the slopes of the Wemmershoek mountain range in Franschhoek, a traditionally high rainfall area, has not spared richly diverse La Motte from the travails of the Western Cape drought. It's why CEO Hein Koegelenberg and estate owner and wife Hanneli Rupert-Koegelenberg are focused on sustainability and conservation of both water supply and the environment. Both elements are crucial to cellar chief Edmund Terblanche's long-term plans for site-specific syrah and chardonnay. A winelands jewel, La Motte's visitor offerings include Pierneef à La Motte Restaurant, art gallery, fynbos walks and well-stocked shop selling products from the staff empowerment venture. Little wonder the property is consistently acclaimed in the global Great Wine Capitals' Best of Wine Tourism awards.

The Pierneef Collection

★★★★☆ **Syrah-Viognier** ⓐ Alluring deep black fruit on Rhône-like **16** ⑨④. Silky yet powerful, with integrated oak (50% new, 18 months) & lovely freshness from 5% viognier. Cooler Elim & Walker Bay fruit part of the blend again. Also in magnum.

★★★★ **Sauvignon Blanc** Blackcurrant & flint typicity from Cape South Coast fruit & dab (8%) semillon. **17** ⑧⑥ vivid grapefruit zest & vibrant succulence on focused palate.

La Motte Collection

★★★★ **Syrah** Pepper & herb edge to rich plum fruit on **16** ⑧⑥. Petite sirah upped to 15% while restrained oak (30% new) keeps it harmonious, pliable & engaging. Also in magnum.

★★★★ **Méthode Cap Classique Brut** Taut **15** ⑧⑧ sparkler offers apple & lime zip from 55/45 chardonnay/pinot noir split. Complexity added by small oaked portion (15%) & 29 months on lees. Fresh, clean & enduring.

Chardonnay ★★★☆ Heady whiffs lead to subtle orange cream on light-bodied **17** (84). Like **16** (84), shows oak (25% new) but retains acid freshness, persistence. Franschhoek WO for these.

Classic Collection

★★★★ **Cabernet Sauvignon** Blue & black berry vibrancy on **16** (88). Supple & smooth yet well-framed by French oak, third new. Spicy sheen adds interest, as does 8% cinsaut. Long, rich finish.

★★★★ **Millennium** ⊘ Cocoa richness to **16** (86) merlot-led 4-way Bordeaux blend. Ripe, balanced & soft textured, approachable courtesy well-knit older oak, year. Magnums too.

★★★★☆ **Straw Wine** ② Thatch nuance to peach praline & spice on **NV** (93) dessert from air-dried viognier. Resolute sweetness (245 g/l) balanced by taut acid & oak, none new. Rich brûlée flavour memory but clean finish. 375 ml.

Sauvignon Blanc ★★★☆ Tangy tropical styling on light, easy **18** (83) using fruit from multiple areas. 10% splash of semillon. Refreshing. — FM

Location/map: Franschhoek ▪ Map grid reference: C3 ▪ WO: Western Cape/Franschhoek/Cape South Coast ▪ Est 1969 ▪ 1stB 1984 ▪ Tasting & sales Mon-Sat 9–5 ▪ Fee R60pp ▪ Booking essential for: group tastings 8-16 R70pp; themed tastings R250pp; food & wine pairing Fri 10 R250pp by appt only ▪ Closed Good Fri & Dec 25 ▪ Pierneef à La Motte Restaurant ▪ Facilities for children ▪ Tour groups (max 16), booking essential ▪ Farm shop: seasonal flowers, bread, confectionery, gifts ▪ Booking essential for: hiking trail Mon-Sat 9-2 R60pp (duration 1.5-2.5hrs, not recommended for children under 10); guided hike Mon 9 R120pp; historic walk Wed 10-11 R60pp; sculpture walk Thu 10-11 R60pp ▪ 35ha conservation area ▪ Museum Tue-Sun 9-5: Rupert family, history of La Motte, Cape Dutch architecture, life/art of JH Pierneef & other SA artists ▪ Monthly classical music concerts ▪ Owner(s) Hanneli Rupert-Koegelenberg ▪ CEO Hein Koegelenberg ▪ Cellarmaster(s) Edmund Terblanche (Dec 2000) ▪ Winemaker(s) Michael Langenhoven (Dec 2006) ▪ Viticulturist(s) Pietie le Roux (May 1986) ▪ 170ha/75ha (merlot, pinot, shiraz, chard, sauv, sem) ▪ 2,000/240,000cs own label 38.2% red 61.5% white 0.3% sparkling + 38,000cs for clients ▪ Brands for clients: Woolworths ▪ ISO 14001:2004, EnviroWines, Farming for the Future, HACCP, IPW, WIETA, WWF-SA Conservation Champion ▪ PO Box 685 Franschhoek 7690 ▪ info@la-motte.co.za ▪ www.la-motte.com ▪ S 33° 52' 52.20" E 019° 4' 25.76" ▪ ⊞ industrious.entrance.prolongs ▪ **T +27 (0)21-876-8000**

Landau du Val   ②

Basil and Jane Landau's Franschhoek property, one of the earliest in the valley, can trace its history back to 1689. Their renowned 4-ha semillon vineyard is a little younger, planted in 1905, but well over the Old Vine Project's minimum 35 years to claim 'old' status. As demand for fruit from these ancients increases, so the effort to keep them healthy intensifies. Wynand Grobler of Rickety Bridge remains in charge of winemaking.

Location/map: Franschhoek ▪ Map grid reference: D2 ▪ Tasting by appt only ▪ Sales at Rickety Bridge Winery, Franschhoek ▪ Owner(s) Basil & Jane Landau ▪ Winemaker(s) Wynand Grobler ▪ Viticulturist(s) Martin du Plessis & Pietie le Roux (consultant) ▪ 15ha under vine ▪ La Brie Robertsvlei Rd Franschhoek 7690 ▪ basillandau@mweb.co.za ▪ S 33° 55' 34.3" E 019° 6' 34.1" ▪ ⊞ feast.cloves.lodges ▪ F +27 (0)21-876-3369 ▪ **T +27 (0)82-410-1130**

☐ **Landela** see Jacques Germanier
☐ **Land of Hope** see Radford Dale
☐ **Landscape Series** see Gabriëlskloof
☐ **Land's End** see Du Toitskloof Winery
☐ **Landskap** see Groenland

Landskroon Wines   ② ⊖ ⌂ ◎ ⊙

Fifth-generation De Villiers brothers, Paul (winemaker/cellarmaster for almost 40 years) and Hugo (long-standing viticulturist), meld 17th-century Huguenot winegrowing heritage with modern production approaches. In their branch of the family since 1874, bottling since 1974, regularly renewing vineyards (shiraz the latest), Landskroon on Paarl Mountain continues doing what it does best: well-priced wines, mostly red, led by a fine Bordeaux blend and Cape Vintage fortified.

Paul de Villiers range

★★★★ **Cabernet Sauvignon** Generous oaking (French & American, 63% new) masks the fruit of **16** ⑧⑦ mid-2018. Should settle with 2-3 years cellaring, reveal more of the piquant black berries among the layers of mocha.

★★★★ **Merlot** Excellent expression of this unforgiving variety, the oak (100% French, 50% new) creating a lovely supple, supportive structure for **16** ⑧⑨'s bramble fruits. Elegant & refined, will develop.

★★★★ **Shiraz** Plump berries overlaid with coffee-choc, **16** ⑧⑥'s combo of ripe fruit, full body & 18 months in 87% new American oak makes it almost a meal in itself!

★★★★ **Reserve** Graceful flagship blend of cabs sauvignon (52%) & franc plus merlot, **16** ⑧⑨ with appealing graphite & cedar aromas from partly new French oak. Cassis & sappy red berry fruit still tightly wound - allow few years to develop.

Chenin Blanc Barrel Fermented ★★★☆ Expansive vanilla overlay to cling peach & pear fruit of **17** ⑧⑤, 10 months in barrel give attractive oak-sweet finish. A big wine despite its modest 12.4% alcohol.

Landskroon range

★★★★ **Cape Vintage** ⊘ Awarded 'port' from tintas barocca & amarela, souzão & touriga, **13** ★★★★★ ⑨⓪ 34 months old oak. Exuberantly fruity, with finely integrated spirit. For green leather armchairs, dried fruit & nuts over the next five years. Improves on softer **12** ★★★★ ⑧④ & perfumed **11** ⑧⑦.

. . . .

Cabernet Franc-Merlot ⑦ ★★★ A standout 'housewine', easy, likeable. **16** ⑧② teams unwooded cab franc with French-oak-seasoned merlot & splash shiraz for flavourful quaffing.

Cabernet Sauvignon ⊘ ★★★★ Hints of cassis & cedar herald athletic **16** ⑧③, accessible, pliable, for enjoyment now. French oak (5% new) well assimilated. **Cinsaut** ⑫ ★★★ **15** ⑦⑧'s more concentrated styling continues in **16** ⑦⑦, with similar perky tealeaf tweak to strawberry fruit. **Merlot** ★★★ Vibrant everyday sipper, **16** ⑧① offers plump mulberry flavours & mocha note from mix French & American barrels. **Pinotage** ★★ Lipsmacking **16** ⑦⑥ a robust mix of plum fruit & oak vanilla; palate-cleansing dryness for matching with food. **Shiraz** ★★★ Sweet redcurrant fruit wrapped in supple tannins, **16** ⑧① glides down easily but has enough charry grip for food. **Cinsaut-Shiraz** ⑫ ★★★ **16** ⑧② 57/43 combo more complex & spicy than varietal cinsaut. Savoury, tasty & affordable anytime red. WO W Cape. **Paul Hugo Red** ★★ Blend cab franc, shiraz & merlot, **16** ⑦⑤ is fruit filled but firmed by oak tannins mid-2018. Pair with heartier food. **Blanc de Noir Pinotage Off-Dry** ⑫ ★★★ Cranberry acidity lifts gently sweet **17** ⑧⓪. Understated, with vinous appeal. **Chardonnay** ★★★ Unoaked **17** ⑦⑨ shows some nutty complexity in its perky citrus finish. **Chenin Blanc Dry** ⊘ ★★★ Ripe fruit salad flavours of **18** ⑧① enlivened by tangy tail. Crisp, easy, refreshing. **Chenin Blanc Off-Dry** ⊘ ★★★ Hint of sweetness amplifies freshly sliced summer fruit profile of gluggable **18** ⑧②. **Sauvignon Blanc** ⑫ ★★★ Zesty acidity & friendly 13% alcohol, **17** ⑦⑧ perfect for al fresco lunches. WO W Cape. **Paul Hugo White** ⑫ ★★☆ 80% chenin buoyed by sauvignon in unchallenging yet flavoursome **17** ⑦⑦. Stock up for summer. WO W Cape. — DS

Location/map: Paarl ▪ Map grid reference: D6 ▪ WO: Paarl/Western Cape ▪ Est 1874 ▪ 1stB 1974 ▪ Tasting & sales Mon-Fri 8.30–5 Sat (Sep-Apr) 9.30-1 ▪ Closed Sun, Easter weekend, Dec 25 & Jan 1 ▪ Fee R35/5 wines, waived on purchase of 6btls ▪ Heritage food & wine pairing R85 ▪ 5 Paul's food & wine pairing R125 ▪ Cellar tours by appt Mon-Fri 9-4 ▪ BYO picnic ▪ Play area for children ▪ Permanent display of stone age artefacts ▪ Self-catering cottage ▪ Owner(s) Paul & Hugo de Villiers Family Trusts ▪ Cellarmaster(s) Paul de Villiers (Jan 1980) ▪ Winemaker(s) Michiel du Toit (Nov 2014), with Danielle du Toit (Jul 2018) ▪ Viticulturist(s) Hugo de Villiers (1995) ▪ 330ha/190ha (cab, cinsaut, merlot, ptage, shiraz, souzão, tinta amarela/barocca, touriga nacional, chenin, chard, sauv, viog) ▪ 80% red (include port) 20% white ▪ IPW, WIETA ▪ PO Box 519 Suider-Paarl 7624 ▪ huguette@landskroonwines.com ▪ www.landskroonwines.com ▪ S 33° 45' 38.34" E 018° 54' 58.38" ▪ ✉ wagging.gooseberry.discussions ▪ F +27 (0)21-863-2810 ▪ **T +27 (0)21-863-1039**

☐ **Landzicht Wyn** see Douglas Wine Cellar - Landzicht Wyn
☐ **Langeberg Wineries** see Wonderfontein
☐ **Langtafel** see Mooiplaas Estate & Private Nature Reserve

Langverwacht Wynkelder

Founded in 1954 as Boesmansrivier Wine Cellar, Bonnievale's Langverwacht is owned by a relatively small group of growers and produces mostly bulk wine. Shiraz, chardonnay and colombard are specialities under the own limited-release label, available from the cellar and a few local wine shops.

Location: Bonnievale ▪ Map: Robertson ▪ Map grid reference: D4 ▪ Est 1954 ▪ Tasting, sales & tours Mon-Fri 8-5 ▪ Closed all pub hols ▪ Owner(s) 25 members ▪ Cellarmaster(s) Johan Gerber (Dec 1986) ▪ Winemaker(s) Theunis Botha (Dec 2005) ▪ Viticulturist(s) Hennie Visser (Jul 2008) ▪ 640ha (cab, ruby cab, shiraz, chenin, chard, cbard, sauv) ▪ 14,500t/4,500cs own label 50% red 50% white ▪ IPW, WIETA ▪ PO Box 87 Bonnievale 6730 ▪ info@langverwachtwines.co.za ▪ www.langverwachtwines.co.za ▪ S 33° 57′ 32.8″ E 020° 1′ 35.3″ ▪ prevail.rehearsed.fervently ▪ F +27 (0)23-616-3059 ▪ **T +27 (0)23-616-2815**

Lanzerac Wine Estate

Uniquely situated on the outskirts of Stellenbosch suburbia, near the entrance of Jonkershoek Valley Nature Reserve, Lanzerac is advantaged by its history, setting, beautiful buildings plus the many different aspects of its vineyards, allowing for different sites, wine styles and varieties, including uncommon pinot blanc. Not resting on his laurels, long-serving winemaker Wynand Lategan is expanding the wine range, and his recently introduced Keldermeester collection honours Cape personalities and wine styles (beyond the existing Heritage range). A devastating fire which destroyed the manor house, since restored, revealed an earlier, unknown history, which now features in some exposed walls of the building.

Heritage range

★★★★☆ Pionier Pinotage Honours SA's first commercial pinotage released 1961. Single high-altitude (400 m) single-vineyard, ±20 years old, naturally fermented. **16** ⑨₃ deep glossy fruit dominates despite 21 months oak, half new. Handsome, with power & presence.

★★★★ Le Général ⑨ 4-way Bordeaux blend in **15** ⑧⑨, cab (79%) the leader in fruit & tannin. Vintage's finer stamp evident in classical styling, intensity & balance. Potential to age with distinction.

★★★★☆ Mrs English Single-vineyard chardonnay, natural ferment/ageing, year, in half-new barrels, so lots of care shown in **17** ⑨₄. Citrus, especially on palate, raw almond savoury notes, everything fits beautifully together, exuding quiet confidence, breeding.

Premium range

★★★★ Cabernet Sauvignon Cassis & sweet spice, even vanilla in **16** ⑧₇ barrel sample, all very seductive, the serious note shows on the palate, with firm dry tannins. No harshness, just indicating cellaring potential. Follows standout **15** ★★★★★ ⑨₂.

★★★★ Merlot Pre-bottled **16** ⑧⑨ impresses with vivid cassis/cherry flavours, succulent & silky smooth, tannins a hidden strength but there to ensure a future.

★★★★ Pinotage Mulberries, black plums, fruit concentration & richness in previewed **16** ⑧₈, worthy partner for the smoky oak spicing & supple tannins. Earlier drinking, but don't mistake the hidden power. Also in magnum. Stellenbosch WO.

★★★★ Syrah Expressive fruit in **16** ⑧₈, rich & deep. Only half the wine oaked but still has smoky, savoury notes, especially in the flavours. New World style, handsome, big & bold.

★★★★ Cabernet Sauvignon-Merlot-Petit Verdot Prosciutto & scrub top notes for pre-bottling **16** ⑧₈'s dark plum character, savouriness a feature here. There's depth & interest, tannins finely judged to provide definition, ageability.

★★★★ Chardonnay Citrus styling for **17** ⑧₇, grapefruit & tangerine, biscuit-shaded from partial oaking. Lovely acid grip creates flavour vibrancy, giving length & lift. Back on track after **16** ★★★★ ⑧₄.

★★★★ Sauvignon Blanc Lemongrass & grapefruit in **18** ⑧₈ preview, zinging fresh, full of life & vigour. Exactly how sauvignon should be, thanks to high-altitude, mountain-slope vines. Stellenbosch WO.

Pinotage Rosé ★★★ Bright-fruited **18** ⑧₁ tank sample has cranberry piquancy, a stylishly svelte body, refreshing dryness. **Chenin Blanc ★★★** Lightly oaked **17** ⑧₂ has beguiling flavours, stonefruit & winter melon, fruity-fresh & with good palate weight. **Blanc de Blancs Brut** ⑨ **★★★★** Refreshing **NV** ⑧₅ sparkling from chardonnay continues clean, elegant styling. Enough substance for both mealtimes & solo.

Keldermeester Versameling

★★★★ Dok (🎗) Honours doyen of SA rugby 'Doc' Danie Craven. Single-vineyard malbec, tiny crop (3 t/ha), wild ferment. Inky colour, **16** ★★★★☆ ⑨③ packed with fruit, has variety's distinctive herbaceous seam. Older oak to support the plush texture. Improves on **15** ⑧⑦.

★★★★ Prof (🎗) Blend cinsaut (60%) & pinot noir dedicated to prof Abraham Perold, who created pinotage from these varieties. **16** ⑧⑧ delicate, understated, intriguing, worthy of contemplation. WO W Cape.

★★★★ Bergpad Pinot blanc, rare in SA. **17** ⑧⑦ fermented/aged year older oak, shows starfruit & pineapple perfume/flavours, refreshed by tangy acidity. Faint biscuit note but fruit the hero here.

Bergstroom (🆕) **★★★★** Sauvignon with a third semillon from Elgin, **17** ⑧④ combines green melon & citrus, has oatmeal tones from 9 months in seasoned barrels. Taut, crisp finish. — CR

Location/map: Stellenbosch ▪ Map grid reference: G5 ▪ WO: Jonkershoek Valley/Stellenbosch/Western Cape ▪ Est 1692 ▪ 1stB 1957 ▪ Tasting & sales daily 9–5 ▪ Cellar tours on request ▪ Open all pub hols ▪ Deli platters; wine & chocolate tasting ▪ 5-star Lanzerac Hotel, Spa & Restaurants ▪ Conferences ▪ Weddings/functions ▪ Owner(s) Lanzerac Estate Investments ▪ Cellarmaster(s) Wynand Lategan (Jan 2005) ▪ Viticulturist(s) Danie Malherbe (2008) ▪ 163ha/63ha (cab, malbec, merlot, ptage, shiraz, chard, chenin, pinot blanc, sauv) ▪ 500t/24-26,000cs own label 55% red 30% white 15% rosé ▪ PO Box 6233 Uniedal 7612 ▪ wine@lanzerac. co.za, winetasting@lanzerac.co.za ▪ www.lanzeracwines.co.za ▪ S 33° 56′14.7″ E 018° 53′35.5″ ▪ 📷 slices. slowly.nuance ▪ F +27 (0)21-887-6998 ▪ **T +27 (0)21-886-5641**

La Petite Ferme Winery   (🍷)(🍽)(🏠)(◎)

Five-year upgrades and expansions launched in 2016 after the sale of La Petite Ferme by the Dendy-Young family continue, the current owners promising to release a new Rhône-style red and Bordeaux white in fresh livery soon. Winemaker/viticulturist Wikus Pretorius' fine bottlings, produced in the boutique cellar, are but one attraction on this mountainside property. There's also good food, luxury lodgings and panoramic views of Franschhoek Valley.

★★★★☆ Cabernet Sauvignon (🎗) Excellent **16** ⑨① has firm ripe tannins on guard for now, but heady violets & cassis leading to dense ripe black berry & plum fruit will offer much pleasure in years to come - tuck this one away. Simonsberg & local vines. 20% new wood, year.

★★★★ Merlot (🎗) Christmas pudding in a bottle, rich & full **16** ⑧⑧ has ripe plums, black berry & cherry deftly spiced with cinnamon, vanilla & nutmeg from year oak (15% new). Includes Helderberg grapes.

★★★★ Shiraz (🎗) With pimento & white pepper spirals, elegant **16** ⑧⑥ more Old World than New with reined-in red berry fruit & hints of charcuterie lingering on savoury finish. WO W Cape.

★★★★ The Verdict The 2 cabs lead **16** ⑧⑧ Cape Blend, with 23% pinotage & merlot. Violet, plum & cherry perfumes, lively cassis fruit & still-firm tannins needing time or robust food partners. 25% new oak.

★★★★ Barrel Fermented Chardonnay Orange blossom aroma & lingering marmalade finish attract, but **17** ⑧⑥, like **16** ★★★★ ⑧④, is all about texture: smooth, creamy & beautifully balanced. WO W Cape.

Rosé (🎗) **★★★** From merlot, briskly fresh & racy **17** ⑦⑧ pink is bone-dry & perfect for sipping on the patio. **Sauvignon Blanc** (🎗) **★★★★** Super-fresh **17** ⑧⑤ is a great pick-me-up, with hints of green apple in the zingy, zesty mix. **Viognier** (🎗) **★★★★** Unwooded **17** ⑧⑤ bursts with variety's apricot & peach, shows some restraint in crisp dry finish which reins in the smooth viscosity & breadth. Not tasted: **Baboon Rock Unwooded Chardonnay Wild Yeast Fermented**. — DS

Location/map: Franschhoek ▪ Map grid reference: C1 ▪ WO: Franschhoek/Western Cape ▪ Est 1972 ▪ 1stB 1996 ▪ Tasting daily at 10.30 by appt ▪ Fee R100pp ▪ Sales daily 8.30-5 ▪ Restaurant ▪ Guest suites ▪ Tour groups ▪ Gift shop ▪ Owner(s) The Nest Estate South Africa (Pty) Ltd, t/a La Petite Ferme ▪ GM Riaan Kruger ▪ Winemaker(s) Wikus Pretorius (Oct 2015) ▪ Viticulturist(s) Wikus Pretorius (Oct 2015) ▪ Farm manager Frans Malies ▪ 16ha/14ha (cabs s/f, merlot, shiraz, chard, sauv, viog) ▪ 60-70t/10,000cs own label 40% red 50% white 10% rosé ▪ PO Box 683 Franschhoek 7690 ▪ info@lapetiteferme.co.za ▪ www.lapetiteferme.co.za ▪ S 33° 55′6.43″ E 019° 8′10.32″ ▪ 📷 posturing.foil.softly ▪ F +27 (0)86-720-6284 ▪ **T +27 (0)21-876-3016**

La Petite Provence Wine Company

This small business is essentially a wine club, with wines now made by Simonsvlei International from on-site vines mostly for the owners of residences in Franschhoek's La Petite Provence Estate. Some of the production is exported, to Europe (from where many residents hail) as well as China and potentially Korea. **Cabernet Sauvignon** ★★★★ Cigarbox & spice nuances, ripe black & red fruit, firm tannins & well-managed oak staving. Tasted pre-bottling, **17** ⑧⑤ looks promising. **Merlot** ★★★★ Engaging blueberry, plum & cocoa tones on **17** ⑧③ preview. Like sibling, few grams sugar aid approachability, brief wooding gives form to the fruit. **Mélange** ⓧ ★★★★ Cab & merlot are the blend in **13** ⑧⑤, vivid dark fruit & spice, full body with tight but undaunting tannins for now & next few years. — GM

Location/WO: Franschhoek ▪ Est 2001 ▪ 1stB 2005 ▪ Tasting & sales Wed/Sat by appt ▪ Owner(s) La Petite Provence Wine Trust ▪ Winemaker(s) Helena Senekal (2017, Simonsvlei) ▪ 3.5ha (cab, merlot) ▪ 30t/900cs own label 100% red ▪ 2 Cabernet Dr La Petite Provence Franschhoek 7690 ▪ info@lapetiteprovence.co.za ▪ www.lapetiteprovence.co.za ▪ **T +27 (0)21-876-4178/+27 (0)21-876-4554**

La Petite Vigne

Kevin Swart, also a partner in Black Elephant Vintners, here involves his family in producing a cabernet from their boutique vineyard in Franschhoek. The wine is dedicated to Kevin's father, who passed away during their first vintage, with a moving tribute on the back label to the man and a favourite hymn.

Daniel Collection

Amazing Grace ⓧ ★★★★ Forthcoming blackcurrant perfume & flavours, **14** ⑧④'s 24-month oaking (half new) gives a lovely savoury thread, the tannins plush & approachable, the finish fruit-sweet brushed with sweet vanilla, too. Has concentration & typicity, curvaceous lines - a crowd pleaser. — CR, CvZ

Location/map/WO: Franschhoek ▪ Map grid reference: C1 ▪ 1stB 2012 ▪ Tasting & tours by appt only ▪ Owner(s) Kema Consulting (Kevin & Mandie Swart) ▪ Cellarmaster(s) Kevin Swart (Jan 2012) ▪ Winemaker(s) Kevin Swart (Jan 2012), with Gary Swart & Jospeh Ratabana (both Jan 2012) ▪ Viticulturist(s) Jacques Wentzel (Jan 2012, consultant) ▪ 3.3ha/2.5ha (cab) ▪ 3t/450cs own label 100% red ▪ PO Box 686 Franschhoek 7690 ▪ kevin@lapetitevigne.co.za ▪ S 33° 54' 9.00 E 019° 7' 14.00" ▪ ⅲ tolerably.casings.barman ▪ **T +27 (0)21-876-2903**

La RicMal

When Ricardo, eldest son of entrepreneur Malcolm Green, joined the family business in 2001 it led to their venture into the wine industry in 2007 - the business name reflecting their partnership. There are two brands, La RicMal Suprême and Lerato, with wines made from Darling grapes, and the rest of Africa a significant market.

Location/map: Stellenbosch ▪ Map grid reference: C3 ▪ Est 2007 ▪ 1stB 2008 ▪ Tasting by appt only ▪ Sales Mon-Fri ▪ Olive oil ▪ Hiking by appt only ▪ Cycling through vineyards by arrangement ▪ Owner(s) Green family ▪ Winemaker(s)/viticulturist(s) various ▪ 58.9ha/±40ha in production ▪ ±550t/±10,000cs own label 90% red 10% white ▪ WIETA ▪ rgreen@laricmal.com ▪ www.laricmal.com ▪ S 33° 52' 18.22" E 018° 46' 4.37" ▪ F +27 (0)86-624-3593 ▪ **T +27 (0)21-865-1005**

Lateganskop Winery

The Lategan family have been vinegrowing in the Wolseley area for more than 100 years. Oupa Willie, who reached a remarkable 102, built a cellar in 1969, founding a legacy that continues today. Most of the wine is sold in bulk but a small portion is bottled under the own labels.

The Zahir range

★★★★ **Red** ⓧ Previewed **13** ⑧⑦ cab, pinotage, cinsaut aged extraordinary 4 years in old oak, adding nuance & complexity. Lighter in style but packs a savoury berry punch, improves on **12** ★★★★ ⑧④.
White ⓧ ★★★★ From chenin, seriously conceived (13-16 months old oak), **16** ⑧④ tropical fruit & spice, nice pineapple bite.

Lateganskop range

Livia's Laughter Méthode Cap Classique ★★★★ Delightful dry bubbles from chardonnay & pinot noir, **13** ⑧⑤ baked apple, ginger & biscuit notes, full & smooth, long-lingering lemon curd aftertaste. **Muscat d'Alexandrie '102'** ★★★★ Attractively packaged solera-style **NV** ⑧⑤ fortified dessert honours centenarian patriarch. **13** sweet grape & boiled sweet flavours, good viscosity, whistle-clean conclusion. 500 ml.

Twins range

Not tasted: **Sauvignon Blanc**. — WB

Location: Wolseley ▪ Map: Breedekloof ▪ Map grid reference: A2 ▪ WO: Breedekloof/Western Cape ▪ Est 1969 ▪ 1stB 2004 ▪ Tasting & sales Mon-Fri 8–12 & 1–5 ▪ Closed Easter Fri-Mon, Dec 25/26 & Jan 1 ▪ Cellar tours by appt ▪ Owner(s) 5 members ▪ Cellarmaster(s) Heinrich Lategan (Oct 2008) ▪ Winemaker(s) Heinrich Lategan, with Kéan Oosthuizen (May 2011) ▪ 238ha (cab, ptage, chard, chenin, sauv, sem) ▪ 2,900t/600cs own label 30% red 70% white & ±2m L bulk ▪ PO Box 44 Breërivier 6858 ▪ lateganskop@breede.co.za ▪ www.lateganskop.co.za ▪ S 33° 30′ 57.27″ E 019° 11′ 13.65″ ▪ 🗺 prim.quarries.conflating ▪ F +27 (0)86-637-6603 ▪ T +27 (0)23-355-1719

La Terre La Mer ⓥ

Established just over a decade ago by East London winelovers, the cellar overlooks Quinera Lagoon and the Indian Ocean (La Mer) and sources grapes from the Western Cape winelands (La Terre), latterly Swartland. There are now four partners, and the vision of collegiality, handcrafting and quality remains.

Shiraz ⓥ ★★★ Plums & red berries in older-oaked **14** ⑧① retasted, shows some liquorice notes, softly fruity appeal, satisfying palate weight. — CR

Location: East London ▪ Map: Eastern Cape ▪ Map grid reference: B2 ▪ WO: Swartland ▪ Est/1stB 2008 ▪ Tasting & cellar tours by appt ▪ Owner(s)/winemaker(s) Mark Wiehahn, Jon Liesching, Nicholas Cooke & Nelanie Kaiser ▪ 2.5t shiraz ▪ 30 Plymouth Dr Nahoon Mouth East London 5241 ▪ mw-assoc@mweb.co.za ▪ T +27 (0)83-701-3148

L'Avenir Vineyards ⓥ 🍴 🏠 📷 🛏 ♿

For this fine-wine estate in the Simonsberg foothills of Stellenbosch, the French connection has been a reoccurring theme since 1992, when it was bought by French-Mauritian Marc Wiehe, through to today, with France-based AdVini as current owner. The very name, meaning 'The Future', is French. Yet the focus is local, on chenin and pinotage, from single vineyards to a beautifully packaged rosé. Bushvine pinotage plantings continue, while every care is taken to preserve the vine heritage. Stylishly designed buildings cater for visitors, and a new helipad allows partner Cape Town Helicopters to fly-in groups for exclusive tastings.

Single Block range

★★★★☆ **Pinotage** 🍇 Unlike its Provenance sibling, **16** ⑨② is 100% oaked, 18 months & all new, but the fruit easily handles it. Dark plums & piquant blueberries layered with espresso notes, hint of scrub, all on a bed of compact tannins. Built to age, this is a keeper.

★★★★ **Chenin Blanc** 🍇 All-new oak, fittingly so for wine from 45+ year old single-vineyard. There's stonefruit in **17** ★★★★★ ⑨③ accompanying almond tones, becoming more citrus towards the end, briskly fresh. Complex, tautly structured, good ageing potential. Improves on **16** ⑧⑨.

....

Glenrosé ⓥ ★★★★ Lovely packaging, glass stopper, bevelled punt gives jewel-like effect to flint bottle. What's inside is noteworthy too: pinotage provides the berry perfume, **17** ⑧④'s palate becoming more mineral, dry & fresh.

....

Provenance range

★★★★ **Cabernet Sauvignon** Long skin contact, new oak 18 months, deep-coloured & -fruited **16** ⑧⑨ has power, concentration & typicity, even a gentle herbaceous whiff. Compact, worthy tannin foundation for a future.

★★★★ **Pinotage** Riper fruit than **15** ⑧⑥, plums/prunes in partially oaked **16** ⑧⑧, nicely cocoa spiced. Verging on hedonistic but for restraint imposed by firm, ripe tannins giving definition, ageability.

★★★★ **Chenin Blanc** 85% of **17** ⑧⑧ spent time in new barrel, showing in almond seaming of the pear/melon flavours. Zesty, limy acidity brightens everything, extends the finish. Has focus, sinewy strength.

Stellenbosch Classic ★★★★ Cab-dominant Bordeaux-style blend with cab franc & merlot, **16** ⑧④ is dark fruited, with meaty notes, smoky savoury underpin, some fynbos. Main attraction remains the juicy smoothness. Not tasted: **Merlot**.

Future Eternal range

★★★★ Méthode Cap Classique Brut Blend change in **14** ⑧⑧, pinot noir & chardonnay, with gamay, pinotage, 2 years on lees. Not as refined as **13** ★★★★★ ⑨①, honey & preserved citrus notes, appears more developed. Still delicious.

Méthode Cap Classique Brut Rosé ★★★★ Red fruit dominates **16** ⑧④, made up of 6 varieties, including 31% chardonnay. Spent 14 months on the lees; vibrant berries, a strawberry note, sleekly built, ends fruity-fresh. — CR

Location/map/WO: Stellenbosch ▪ Map grid reference: E3 ▪ Est/1stB 1992 ▪ Tasting & sales: Mon-Sat 10-7 (Oct-Apr)/10-5 (May-Sep) Sun/pub hols 10-4 ▪ Fee based on tasting option selected ▪ Closed Good Fri, Dec 25 & Jan 1 ▪ Cellar tours by appt ▪ Light meals ▪ Child friendly ▪ Function venue ▪ Luxury 4-star Country Lodge ▪ Owner(s) AdVini ▪ Winemaker(s) Dirk Coetzee (Aug 2009), with Mattheus Thabo (Jan 2007) & Francois Conradie (Jan 2014) ▪ Viticulturist(s) Leigh Diedericks, with Johan Pienaar ▪ 64.9ha/34.05ha (cabs s/f, merlot, ptage, chenin, sauv) ▪ 300t/41,000cs own label 44% red 38% white 18% rosé ▪ IPW, WIETA ▪ PO Box 7267 Stellenbosch 7599 ▪ info@lavenir.co.za ▪ www.lavenirestate.co.za ▪ S 33° 53′ 7.78″ E 018° 50′ 37.12″ ▪ 🗺 padding.march.steps ▪ **T +27 (0)21-889-5001**

La Vierge Private Cellar ⓠ ⑪ ⑤

One of the wineries tilling virgin (hence 'La Vierge'), high-lying, Hemel-en-Aarde Ridge shale soils for stellar expressions of local varietal stars, La Vierge has a varied line-up: Burgundy classics chardonnay and pinot noir; Rhône stalwart shiraz; Bordeaux whites sauvignon and semillon; traditional Italians like sangiovese; plus Bordeaux components combined with bought-in grapes for their red blend. New management augurs continued excitement: winemaker Christo Kotze (ex top specialist Napa Valley, Hunter Valley and Helderberg cellars), farm manager Juan Louw (ex Swartland) and GM Tania Theron-Joubert (winemaker/marketer).

Apogée range

★★★★★ Pinot Noir ⓠ ⑧ Pinotphile winemaker held back for a wine good enough to present as his acme. **14** ⑨③ two clones (115 for bright fruit, 777 darker depth) ex farm's most elevated vines; individual, suave & textured, a lingering savoury sensation. All-new oak 10 months, then 6 months seasoned barrels.

★★★★★ Royal Nymphomane ⓠ Best barrels of cab, merlot, cab franc & malbec, made naturally. **14** ⑨① laden with blackcurrant & meaty spice, polished in all-new oak & powered by alcohol an inch shy of 15%. Demands cellar time to tame. Cape South Coast WO.

Not tasted: **Chardonnay**.

La Vierge Collection

★★★★ La Vierge Noir ⓥ ⑧ The 'noir' is 'pinot' in sleek & judiciously oaked **15** ⑧⑨. Symphony of fruits, florals & spices; satisfying & very charming, elegant glassful.

★★★★ The Affair ⓥ Sexy & generous expression of pinot noir with nimble tannins, smooth & silky texture. **17** ⑧⑦ 9 months in oak, just 20% new, for fruit support, touch of spice.

★★★★ Satyricon Handsome **16** ⑧⑦ sangiovese improves on **15** ★★★★ ⑧⑤ with tealeaf, tar & earthy undertones, floral top notes. Athletic tannins give form to supple fruit, savoury & pleasantly rustic finish.

★★★★ Anthelia Unshowy **16** ⑧⑧ shiraz's red & black fruit seasoned with cloves & black pepper, supported by densely packed tannin, augmented by 10 months in mix mostly French/America oak, 20% new.

★★★★ Nymphomane ⑧ Bordeaux quartet with cab in lead, **16** ⑧⑧ dark & savoury with tapenade & dried herb nuances, compact tannins. Exceptionally dry, satisfying meal companion. WO Walker Bay.

★★★★ Jezebelle Complex vinification shows in multifaceted **17** ⑧⑧ chardonnay: nectarine, honey, pistachio concentration, mineral persistence. 80% barrel fermented, 20% in new oak & 50% natural; remainder on lees in tank, 30% malo.

★★★★ Original Sin Kiwi, lime & grass with hint waxy apple from addition of 12% semillon to majority sauvignon. Striking cool-climate acidity & minerality on **17** ⑧⑦, engrossing & uncompromising sipper.

Seduction Pinot Noir ⊘ ⊛ ★★★★ Unwooded entry-level member of cellar's pinot quartet. **16** ⑧④ perfumed with cherry & raspberry, light grape tannins entwine with vibrant acidity, spiced berry palate.

The Last Temptation ★★★★ Riesling with floral & terpene aromas, lime & tropical flavours. **16** ⑧⑤ dry, with bracing acidity. — GM

Location: Hermanus ▪ Map: Walker Bay & Bot River ▪ Map grid reference: B4 ▪ WO: Hemel-en-Aarde Ridge/Walker Bay/Cape South Coast ▪ Est 1997 ▪ 1stB 2006 ▪ Tasting & sales Mon–Sun 10–5 ▪ Closed Good Fri & Dec 25 ▪ La Vierge Restaurant & Champagne Verandah ▪ Tour groups by appt ▪ Owner(s) La Vierge Wines (Pty) Ltd & Viking Pony Properties 355 (Pty) Ltd ▪ Winemaker(s) Christo Kotze (Jul 2017) ▪ Viticulturist(s) Juan Louw (Jul 2017) ▪ 44ha (cab f, p verdot, pinot, sangio, shiraz, chard, riesling, sauv, sem) ▪ 200t 60% red 40% white ▪ PO Box 1580 Hermanus 7200 ▪ info@lavierge.co.za ▪ www.lavierge.co.za ▪ S 34° 22' 22.3" E 019° 14' 29.4" ▪ ⫐ referees.newness.timeliness ▪ F +27 (0)28-312-1388 ▪ **T +27 (0)28-313-0130**

☐ **Lavine & Mackenzie** *see* The Wine Thief

Lazanou Organic Vineyards ⓆⓎⓌⓄ

When Josef Lazarus and Candice Stephanou bought this tiny Wellington farm in 2002, there was just one block of chenin. The vineyards have grown — all are certified organic — but there are also olives and livestock, as well as biodiversity zones. As the owners say, it's more than a wine farm, it's 'a way of life' for their family.

Location/map/WO: Wellington ▪ Map grid reference: B2 ▪ Est 2002 ▪ 1stB 2006 ▪ Tasting & sales by appt ▪ Open days with wine & food pairing - booking required ▪ Tour groups ▪ Farm produce ▪ Cow Shed Cottage ▪ Owner(s) Josef Lazarus & Candice Stephanou ▪ Winemaker(s) Rolanie Lotz (Jan 2011, consultant) ▪ Viticulturist(s) Johan Wiese (Jan 2006, consultant) ▪ 8.48ha/5.54ha (mourv, shiraz, chard, chenin, viog) ▪ 50t/6,000cs own label 50% red 50% white ▪ Certified organic by Ecocert ▪ PO Box 834 Wellington 7654 ▪ wine@lazanou.co.za ▪ www.lazanou.co.za ▪ S 33° 35' 59.58" E 018° 59' 36.12" ▪ ⫐ countdown.sandbags. tabulated ▪ F +27 (0)86-670-9213 ▪ **T +27 (0)83-265-6341**

Le Bonheur Wine Estate Ⓠ

This 18th-century estate is undergoing a revival under international wine specialist AdVini, and the French group's strategy of first rejuvenating the vineyards — which boast some of Stellenbosch's oldest sauvignon and cabernet — would have been music to the years of Michael Woodhead, the vine- and soil-loving prime mover who established Le Bonheur's reputation in the 1970s and 80s. Not neglected, the cellar has now also been refurbished and a new winemaker enlisted to revive some of the classics, including the Blanc Fumé and top-end Cabernet Sauvignon.

★★★★ **Cabernet Sauvignon** Tasty cassis of fruit-driven **15** ⑧⑥ has wood in good support (30% new, 18 months); juicy & flavourful, without leafy nuance of earlier bottlings. WO Stellenbosch.

★★★★ **Prima** Merlot-led Bordeaux blend with cab, cab franc & splash petit verdot. Last-tasted **13** ⑧⑨'s minty character becomes more herbaceous in yard-off **16** ★★★★ ⑧④. **14** & **15** untasted.

Cinsault ⑭ ★★★★ Piquant red fruit - cranberry, pomegranate - give sweet-sour twist to light & deft **17** ⑧④ from Swartland, one third briefly aged in barrel. **Chardonnay** ★★★★ Previewed **18** ⑧④ is generous, limy peach fruit seamed with clove, framed by just the right amount of oak (20% new). **Sauvignon Blanc** ★★★★ Quintessential Stellenbosch sauvignon, tank sample **18** ⑧③'s ample fruit with lick of oak nicely balanced by zesty acid for delicious dry drinkability. — DS

Location/map: Stellenbosch ▪ Map grid reference: F1 ▪ WO: Simonsberg–Stellenbosch/Stellenbosch/Swartland ▪ Est 1790s ▪ 1stB 1972 ▪ Tasting by appt only ▪ Owner(s) AdVini South Africa ▪ Winemaker(s) William Wilkinson (May 2017) ▪ 163ha/75ha (cab, merlot, chard, sauv) ▪ 600t/60,000cs own label 30% red 70% white ▪ cellar@lebonheur.co.za ▪ www.lebonheur.co.za ▪ S 33° 50' 1.0" E 018° 52' 21.4" ▪ ⫐ droplet. necks.loaders ▪ **T +27 (0)21-889-5001/+27 (0)21-875-5478**

☐ **Leenders** *see* Bezuidenhout Family Wines
☐ **Leeumasker** *see* Maske Wines

Leeu Passant ⓠ

A Franschhoek-based venture between star winegrowing couple Chris and Andrea Mullineux, Indian businessman Analjit Singh and Peter Dart, Leeu Passant, meaning 'walking or roaming lion' is an apt name for the approach here. The carefully crafted small range honours old vines and terroir, and the search is ongoing, with the able assistance of consultant viticulturist and old-vine specialist Rosa Kruger. What's included is Franschhoek cinsaut planted in 1932, and wine made from 118-year-old vines in the Dry Red. A celebration of history. Dividing their time between two properties, the Mullineux' bigger wine venture is in the Swartland, where winemaker Andrea makes completely different wines, while Chris oversees the vineyards, but all as impeccably made, as thoughtfully conceived as here. See Mullineux entry.

★★★★☆ **Dry Red Wine** Ⓐ From venerable dryland vineyards up to 118 years old, **16** ⑭ honours historical red blends by including cinsaut, here with cab, cab franc. Herbaceous, scrub notes, a berry/plum core, & the tensile strength to age. 30% new oak. Also in magnum, as white. WO W Cape.

★★★★★ **Lotter Cinsault** Ⓐ Ⓔ Ex Franschhoek, SA's second-oldest red-wine block (1932), dryland bushvines yielding minuscule 0.3 t/ha. **16** ⑬ minimal handling for site expression: piquant berries, violets, scrub/dry earth, peppery tannins for ageability. Among first to carry Old Vine Project's Certified Heritage Vineyards bottle seal.

★★★★☆ **Stellenbosch Chardonnay** Ⓐ Whole bunch, barrel fermented/matured year (30% new), unfiltered. **16** ★★★★★ ⑯ shows expected complexity, citrus to the fore, white-fleshed stonefruit, gentle savoury thread. In perfect health, beautifully crafted. **15** ⑨ was maiden vintage

Not tasted: Elandskloof Chardonnay. — CR

Location/map: Franschhoek ▪ Map grid reference: C2 ▪ WO: Stellenbosch/Franschhoek/Western Cape ▪ Est 2013 ▪ 1stB 2015 ▪ Tasting & sales Mon-Sun 10-5 at the Wine Studio, Leeu Estates, Franschhoek (booking recommended) ▪ Fee R110-R300 depending on tasting ▪ Closed Good Fri, Dec 25 & Jan 1 ▪ Owner(s) Chris & Andrea Mullineux, Analjit Singh, Peter Dart ▪ Cellarmaster(s) Andrea Mullineux ▪ Winemaker(s) Andrea Mullineux, with Wade Sander (Dec 2015) ▪ Viticulturist(s) Chris Mullineux & Rosa Kruger (consultant) ▪ 25t/1,684cs own label 55% red 45% white ▪ WIETA ▪ info@mlfwines.com ▪ www.mlfwines.com ▪ S 33° 54′33.43″ E 019° 6′14.85″ ▪ ⌖ prospects.versions.cigar ▪ F +27 (0)86-720-1541 ▪ **T +27 (0)21-492-2455 (office)/+27 (0)21-492-2224 (Wine Studio)**

Leeurivier Wyn & Olyf ⓠ

Extremely rocky soils, once quarried, in relatively new viticultural land in the hills between Bot River and Hermanus are now home to olive orchards and a small vineyard. Here Overberger Ewald Groenewald, formerly in the truck and transport business, vinifies a handful of reds in a stone cellar for long-time friends and co-owners Jakobus du Plessis and Leo Pistorius.

Leo Wyn range 🆕

Mourvèdre ★★★ Almost porty in its ripeness, deep & dense, black fruited, oak not much in evidence. **13** ⑱ big & bold, for those who like swashbuckling wines. **Pinot Noir** ★★ Full-ripe style, shows in perfume despite Walker Bay origin. **13** ⑫ toasted oak, savoury spice threaded through, tannins still firm, ending dry. Less fresh than expected, could have offset the oaking. **Petit Verdot** ★★★★ Dark plum fruit, mocha overlay, intense & somewhat extracted **13** ★★★ ⑫'s tannins needing year/2 more to knit. More vibrant & herbaceous **14** ⑭ has savoury, umami notes but also firm tannins & needs few years. **Sangiovese** ★★★ Dusty nose, cherries as an underpin, the ripeness (15.5% alcohol) shows in opulence, curvaceous body. **13** ⑳ has enough juiciness to counterbalance the dry tannins. Big but tasty. **Shiraz** ★★★ Two vintages, different origins & styles. **13** ⑱ ex Walker Bay the riper, black plus/prunes, gentle savoury notes, body smooth & round. **12** ⑱ from Klein Karoo showing more complexity, hedgerow fruit, brambleberries, touch of eucalyptus/scrub & liquorice. Streamlined, sleek, nice grip on the end. — CR, CvZ

Location: Bot River ▪ Map: Walker Bay & Bot River ▪ Map grid reference: C3 ▪ WO: Walker Bay/Klein Karoo ▪ Est 2005 ▪ 1stB 2008 ▪ Tasting & sales by appt ▪ Closed Easter Fri-Mon, Ascension day & Dec 25 ▪ Owner(s) Leeurivier Wyn & Olyf (Pty) Ltd ▪ Winemaker(s) Ewald Groenewald ▪ 70ha/4ha (malbec, mourv, p verdot, pinot, sangio) ▪ PO Box 345 Kleinmond 7195 ▪ ewald@leeurivier.co.za ▪ S 34° 16′39.99″ E 019° 13′36.22″ ▪ ⌖ response.ally.work ▪ **T +27 (0)82-883-3329**

Leeuwenberg

A brief hiatus after the passing of brand founder Tanja Kastien-Hilka ended in 2018, with the release by husband Frank Kastien of a white merlot, which just missed this edition. More to follow, promises the father of three young sons, who collectively feature as 'De Kleine Leeuwen' in one of Leeuwenberg's range names.

Est/1stB 2010 ▪ Tasting only in Wiesbaden, Germany Mon-Fri 11-7 Sat 10-6 ▪ Closed all pub hols ▪ Owner(s) Procellar Wines ▪ Winemaker(s) Frank Kastien & Kobie Viljoen ▪ 6,000cs own label 60% red 40% white ▪ PO Box 422 Franschhoek 7690 ▪ info@procellarwines.com ▪ www.procellarwines.com ▪ **T +49 (0) 611-30-86-778**

Leeuwenkuil Family Vineyards

Willie Dreyer and his wife Emma over 30 years have built Leeuwenkuil into one of the Cape's largest vine-holdings, with 1,250 hectares planted. Cellarmaster Pieter Carstens hopes the numerous varieties cultivated will all eventually become part of the new Reserve collection, where the aim is to create the best blend for each vintage, and deliver on quantity as well as quality. 'South Africa has lots of great wine, most in tiny volume,' he notes, adding: 'Blending is my game.' Smaller in quantity but celebrated for its stellar quality, the Heritage Syrah comes from two vineyards on schist soils, which Pieter describes as providing 'the truest expression of syrah in the Swartland'. The pinnacle of a portfolio of purity and understated elegance.

Heritage series

★★★★★ **Syrah** ⊘ ⊛ A Swartland standard-bearer. Multi-awarded **15** ⑰ reflects stellar vintage. Layers of scented dark spice, berry complexity gently brushed with older oak announce class. Supple silkiness merges with fine tannin, lending energy, reverberating length; all delivered with effortless elegance. Discerningly drinkable; long-term prospects too, like **14** ★★★★★ ㉔.

★★★★ **Chenin Blanc** ⊘ Has richness, but **14** ㉗'s pleasing light fruitiness is subtle rather than notably intense or lingering. Spontaneous ferment, older-oak aged. Tight now, might grow with few years.

Reserve range ⑭

★★★★ **Red** ⊘ Previewed **17** ㉘ from 4 Rhône varieties led by shiraz. Delicious, fresh & flavour-rich: savoury spice, black & blue berries. Squeeze tannin for form but offers early-drinking pleasure. Older oak rounded. Great value, as next.

★★★★☆ **White** ⊘ Hands-off approach on ex-tank **17** ㉒ unoaked chenin: natural ferment, minimal sulphur. Expressive, pure fresh-earth & floral notes, creamy undertones from 6 months on lees, bone-dry & very promising.

Rosé ★★★☆ Unusual, most attractive cinsaut/mourvèdre partnership. Pearly pink **18** ㉝, blueberry & spice flavours gain interest from natural ferment, further weight ex lees ageing. Savoury & long. Tentatively rated ex tank.

Varietal range

★★★★ **Grenache Noir** ⊘ Focus on juicy berries, gentle spice in succulent **16** ㉘. Already offers pleasurable drinking; nip freshening fine tannin, sympathetic (older) oaking encourage further ageing.

★★★★ **Grenache Blanc** ⊘ Broad, leesy **16** ★★★★ ㉔ unlike lightly floral **15** ㉗ but still charming. Structured oak texture from old barrels. Voor Paardeberg fruit, as next.

★★★★ **Marsanne** ⊘ Shows harmony of rich stonefruit, acid & palate weight from skin contact & natural ferment, ageing in older oak. **16** ㉘ dab roussanne added to seldom-seen variety.

Cinsault ⊘ ★★★★ Bright, lively berry abundance of **16** ㉝ less concentrated than **15** ★★★★ ㉗. Light bodied & easy to drink.

Leeuwenkuil range

Shiraz ⊘ ★★★★ Barrel sample **17** ㉝ full bodied, supple; promises dark-fruited, early-drinking satisfaction once bottled; has structure to age few years too. **Chenin Blanc** ⊘ ★★★ Sunny-hued **18** ㉜, generous dried peach, apricot concentration, dry & lingering. Satisfying easy-drinker. Occasional release: **Cinsaut Rosé**. — AL

Location: Stellenbosch ▪ WO: Swartland/Voor Paardeberg ▪ Est 2008 ▪ 1stB 2011 ▪ Closed to public ▪ Owner(s) Willie & Emma Dreyer ▪ Cellarmaster(s) Pieter Carstens (Aug 2008) ▪ Winemaker(s) Riaan van der Spuy (Dec 2016), Corrien Geleijnse (Jan 2012), Bernard Allison (Jan 2012), Jean Aubrey (Aug 2017) & Madré van der Walt

(Sep 2013), with Jehan de Jongh (Aug 2008) ▪ Viticulturist(s) Koos van der Merwe (Dec 2008) & Claude Uren (Jan 2012) ▪ 4,550ha ▪ 36,500t/27m L 70% red 30% white ▪ Fairtrade, WIETA ▪ PO Box 249 Koelenhof 7605 ▪ kobus@leeuwenkuilfv.co.za ▪ www.leeuwenkuilfv.co.za ▪ F +27 (0)21-865-2780 ▪ **T +27 (0)21-865-2455**

☐ **Legends** see Slanghoek Winery
☐ **Legends of the Labyrinth** see Doolhof Wine Estate

Le Grand Chasseur Estate ⓘ ♿

Owned by successful Eastern Cape fresh produce enterprise Habata, Le Grand Chasseur is planted with wine- as well as table-grape vines. The former are about 220 ha in extent and yield around 4,500 tons a season, vinified since 2011 by Carel Botha. Tastings are in Robertson town, but the vineyards are a few kilometres distant, beside the Breede River, where the namesake majestic hunter, the African Fish Eagle, makes its home.

Habata Reserve Selection 🆕

Pinotage ★★★★ Oak-spice-dusted maraschino cherry flavours, reined-in 13.5% alcohol attractive & welcome but **17** ⑧④'s firm tannins (abetted by new oak) need time to resolve. **Shiraz** ★★★★ Just-dry, very ripe (15% alcohol) **16** ⑧③'s raisin fruit freshened by firm tannins. Seriously oaked: 100% new, 15 months (vs 12 for red sibling). **Chardonnay** ★★★ Intense joiner's workshop fragrance (year 2nd-fill oak) suffuses ripe tangerine fruit, **16** ⑧② drier than Habata sibling but richer, fuller, the wood notes returning on finish.

Habata range

★★★★ **Sauvignon Blanc Mineral** ⓥ Advertised wet stone & gravel notes barely there but **16** ⑧⑦ does have plenty weight & breadth, pleasing dryness. The real allure, though, is the fine, tense acidity.
Cabernet Sauvignon-Merlot 🆕 ★★★ Unoaked, juicy **18** ⑧⓪, with cab at 70%, is light-footed (12.6% alcohol) & supple for early/easy sipping. **Chardonnay Unwooded** ★★★ Lemon & peach tones accented by subtle salinity, **18** ⑧② has smidgen sugar to smooth & extend the finish. **Sauvignon Blanc Tropical** ★★★ Trust the label: granadilla, papaya & mango all present on **18** ⑧①, bone-dry & lightish for lingering lunches. **Muscat de Frontignan** 🆕 ★★★★ Appealing **17** ⑧⑤ fortified, lemon, white peach, dried apricot & pear complexity; silky 204 g/l sweetness perhaps needs dash more acidity. 500 ml. Not tasted: **Chardonnay Wooded**. — CvZ

Location/map/WO: Robertson ▪ Map grid reference: B6 ▪ Est 1881 ▪ 1stB 1999 ▪ Tasting by appt ▪ Closed all pub hols ▪ Owner(s) Hannes Joubert (Habata Boerdery) ▪ Cellarmaster(s)/winemaker(s) Carel Botha (Jan 2011) ▪ Viticulturist(s) Jan Rabie (Sep 2015) ▪ ±1,300ha/220ha (cab, merlot, ptage, ruby cab, shiraz, chard, chenin, cbard, muscadel w, nouvelle, sauv) ▪ ±4,500t ▪ IPW ▪ PO Box 439 Robertson 6705 ▪ cellar@lgc.co.za, sales@lgc.co.za ▪ www.habata.co.za ▪ S 33° 48′ 26.8″ E 019° 52′ 40.1″ ▪ 🖼 cropping.pavements.woodcutting ▪ F +27 (0)86-734-7013 ▪ **T +27 (0)23-626-1048**

☐ **Leipoldt 1880** see Wineways Marketing

Leipzig Winery ⓘ 🍴 🏠 📷 🧑

Francois and Lida Smit's successful revival of 19th-century winefarm Leipzig in Worcester's Nuy Valley sees production increasing (and veering towards reds), and exports (to Germany) warranting two new experienced consulting winemakers. Amenities and attractions strongly suggest staying over.

★★★★☆ **Grand Master** ⓥ Superior Bordeaux-style red, gently crafted in medium-bodied, elegant style; demure cassis & mulberry, subtle spice, very supple tannins & gentle 13% alcohol. Merlot-led, 5-way **17** ⑨⓪ delicious in youth. Also-tasted **16** ⑨⓪, Coastal WO, cab uppermost, loses petit verdot without compromise. Both 9 months in old oak.
★★★★ **Master Blend** Cape Blend of mostly pinotage plus merlot, 3 others. Grippy **17** ⑧⑧ in mould of **15** ⑧⑥, plum fruit constrained by brusque tannins mid-2018, needs year/2 to relax. **16** not tasted.
★★★★ **White Leipzig** Trio chenin, chardonnay, viognier brushed with old oak. **17** ⑧⑧'s generous peach & melon flesh, nutty nuance already satisfy, but to note: last-tasted **14** ⑧⑥ gained complexity in bottle.
Pinotage ★★★★ Typical berry & banana tinges on **15** ⑧③, flies variety's flag with fine flavours & full body. Stellenbosch grapes, as next. **Shiraz** ★★★★ Scrub, smoked bacon & freshly ground black pepper notes on ready-to-enjoy **17** ⑧④. **Shiraz-Mourvèdre-Viognier** ★★★★ Spice & forest floor tones, **16** ⑧⑤ in house style of measured fruit, soft oaking & moderate alcohol; very pleasant drinking. **Chenin Blanc** ★★★★

Was 'Lida', **16** (84) still from old Durbanville bushvines. Used oak gives chalky, earthy veneer to tropical fruit. Ready to enjoy. **Pinot Gris** ★★★ Gold-glinting **18** (80) ex Stellenbosch, pear & melon, slight grip for interest & food. **Sauvignon Blanc** ★★★★ Light toned, with moderate alcohol, uncomplicated **18** (83) summer sipper with fresh nettle profile. Elim & Durbanville grapes. **Viognier** ★★★ Fantail of flavour, ripe peach & apricot fruit imply sweetness but **18** (81) splendidly dry, clean. Nuy grapes. Not tasted: **Cabernet Sauvignon**. In abeyance: **Chardonnay**. — DS

Location/map: Worcester ▪ Map grid reference: C3 ▪ WO: Western Cape/Stellenbosch/Coastal/Tygerberg/Nuy ▪ Est/1stB 2013 ▪ Tasting, sales & cellar tours Tue-Fri 10-4 Sat 10-2; or by appt ▪ Closed Ash Wednesday, Easter Mon, Dec 25 & Jan 1 ▪ Cheese & charcuterie platters by appt ▪ Facilities for children ▪ Tour groups ▪ Conferences ▪ Weddings/functions ▪ Walks/hikes ▪ MTB trail ▪ Guided tours by appt: historic buildings & art ▪ Leipzig Country House ▪ Owner(s) Francois & Lida Smit ▪ Winery manager Vian Bester ▪ Winemaker(s) Jacques Fourie & Wynand Pienaar (May 2018, consultants) ▪ 10ha/4.5ha (sauv) ▪ 49,798t own label 75% red 25% white ▪ PO Box 5104 Worcester 6849 ▪ winery@leipzigcountryhouse.co.za ▪ www.leipzigcountryhouse.co.za ▪ S33° 38' 29.90" E 019° 38' 9.44" ▪ ⬛ winery.inundate.utensil ▪ F +27 (0)86-295-5116 ▪ **T +27 (0)23-347-8422**

Le Lude Méthode Cap Classique   ⓠ ⑪ ⌂

Charming Le Lude winery in Franschhoek, owned by Nic and Ferda Barrow, specialises in méthode cap classique bubbles. The expanding range, made since inception by experienced winemaker and bubbly enthusiast Paul Gerber, includes SA's first agrafe sparkling. The production method involves a second fermentation under cork rather than crown cap, before disgorgement and further ageing under a new cork. At Orangerie restaurant on the premises, chef Nicolene Barrow crafts classic dishes to pair with the elegant bubbles.

Location/map: Franschhoek ▪ Map grid reference: C1 ▪ Est 2009 ▪ 1stB 2012 ▪ Tasting, sales & cellar tours Mon-Sun & pub hols 10-6 ▪ Orangerie restaurant ▪ Guest house ▪ Owner(s) Nic & Ferda Barrow ▪ Winemaker(s) Paul Gerber (May 2010) ▪ Viticulturist(s) Etienne Terblanche (consultant) ▪ 6.2ha/3.4ha (pinot noir/meunier, chard) ▪ 210t/120,000 btls plus magnums own label 100% MCC ▪ PO Box 578 Franschhoek 7690 ▪ info@lelude.co.za ▪ www.lelude.co.za ▪ S 33° 54' 49.24" E 019° 7' 32.78" ▪ ⬛ index.depended. wholeness ▪ **T +27 (0)21-100-3464/3465**

Le Manoir de Brendel   ⓠ ⌂ ⓞ ⓑ

Consultants are employed by Christian and Maren Brendel, German proprietors of this exclusive Franschhoek guest house and winelands function venue, to vinify house wines from the small vineyard.

Brendel Collection
Cabernet Sauvignon ⓠ ★★★ Mature **07** (81) rhubarb & prune notes, firm tannin structure for food pairing. **Merlot** ⓠ ★★★ Tobacco, dried tomato & fruit-sweet edge to **06** (78), was nearing drink-by date when last reviewed. **Pinotage** ⓠ ★★★ Sweet fruit, spicy aromas & typical acetone whiffs on ready **08** (78); handles 15% alcohol with aplomb. **Shiraz** ⓠ ★★★ Engaging sweet-sour tang on meaty **06** (78); soft textured, slips down easily. **Chardonnay** ⓠ ★★ Ripe yellow citrus & light nutty aromas on **16** (74), creamily soft, with hint of spice in tail. WO W Cape. **Sauvignon Blanc** ⓠ ★★★ Quiet tropical ripeness on **15** (78) offset by invigorating freshness. **Sauvignon Blanc-Viognier** ⓠ ★★ Bone-dry **16** (71), very soft, short on verve & fruit.

Le Manoir de Brendel Collection
Shiraz ⓠ ★★★ Stewed fruit & bottle-age nutty character, drink **05** (81) soon. — AL

Location/map: Franschhoek ▪ Map grid reference: C3 ▪ WO: Franschhoek/Western Cape ▪ Est/1stB 2003 ▪ Tasting daily 12-4 ▪ Fee R40pp, waived on purchase ▪ Sales daily 7.30-4 ▪ Open daily, closed when booked for weddings/conferences ▪ Facilities for children ▪ Gift shop ▪ Conferences: day package (60 pax)/overnight package incl 10 rooms & 2 private cottages ▪ Walks ▪ Weddings (up to 60 pax) with chapel ▪ 5-star guest house (10 suites) ▪ Owner(s) Christian & Maren Brendel ▪ Winemaker(s) Cerina de Jongh & Gerda Willers ▪ Viticulturist(s) Paul Wallace (consultant) ▪ 30ha/±23ha (cab, merlot, ptage, shiraz, chard, chenin, sauv, sem) ▪ ±150t ▪ PO Box 117 La Motte Franschhoek 7691 ▪ lmb@brendel.co.za ▪ www.le-manoir-de-brendel. com ▪ S 33° 52' 52.8" E 019° 3' 42.2" ▪ ⬛ suburbs.dominantly.fruitfully ▪ F +27 (0)21-876-4524 ▪ **T +27 (0)21-876-4525**

Lemberg Wine Estate

In addition to 'creative energy', newcomer Anri Botha brings a Masters degree in Oenology, with oak maturation as specialisation, to the winemaker/viticulturist role at Tulbagh boutique estate Lemberg. She and owner Henk du Bruyn intend to plant an additional block of hárslevelü, the Hungarian variety introduced to the SA repertoire by Lemberg's former owner, Janey Muller. 'Hárslevelü is part of our history,' Henk notes, 'and remains a unique and exciting wine in our portfolio, alongside our premium reds which are named after our lovable English Bulldogs.'

Yellow Label range

★★★★☆ **Spencer** 60% new oak apparent in milk chocolate & vanilla notes of **14** (92) pinotage; not so the 15% alcohol, in balance with juicy red fruit & smooth tannins for seamless drinkability. WO W Cape. Also in magnum, like Nelson.

★★★★ **Louis** 56% syrah plus mourvèdre & grenache (no carignan), **16** (88) is fuller-bodied than **15** (89), plush, ripe & smoky, with long finish & a structure suggesting it will grow in complexity over time.

★★★★ **Nelson** Big, bold **14** (89) intense plum, prune & dark fruit concentration yet still manages to be lively, with some smoky/cured meat notes on persistent finish. Shiraz & drop carignan.

★★★★☆ **Lady** Hárslevelü plays second fiddle to viognier (53%) in harmony with 11% each sauvignon & semillon in unusual, nutty, oxidatively made **15** (93) blend. Succulent & spicy, fragrant & fresh, with tangy stonefruit, zesty grapefruit finish.

Pinot Noir ★★★★ Light-bodied **15** (84) has chalky texture, savoury finish, attractive red fruit centre. Not tasted: **Hárslevelü**.

White Label range

Pinotage ★★★ Characterful early-drinking **14** (81) mixes berries with slight leathery note, sweet-sour palate. Older oak, wholeberry ferment. WO W Cape. **Blanc de Noir** ★★★★ Watermelon pink **18** (83) is dry, fresh, with ruby grapefruit & cranberry tang, peppery finish. Syrah & grenache. **Sauvignon Blanc** ★★★☆ Water-white **18** (84), floral, peachy aromas turning lemon-lime on palate, grapefruit conclusion, easy 12% alcohol. Not tasted: **Syrah**, **Cape Blend**. — JG

Location/map: Tulbagh ▪ Map grid reference: F5 ▪ WO: Tulbagh/Western Cape ▪ Est 1978 ▪ Tasting, sales & cellar tours Mon-Fri 9-5 Sat 10-3.30 Sun 10–3 ▪ Fee R50, waived on purchase ▪ Closed Dec 25 ▪ Meals, cheese platters & picnics by appt - book prior to visit ▪ BYO picnic ▪ Table olives & olive oil ▪ Function venue (40-60 pax) ▪ Self-catering guest cottage (sleeps 4) ▪ Owner(s) Henk du Bruyn ▪ Winemaker(s) Henk du Bruyn & Anri Botha (May 2018) ▪ Viticulturist(s) Lemberg team, advised by consultant Bennie Diedericks ▪ 21ha/9ha (grenache, ptage, pinot, shiraz, hárslevelü, sauv, viog) ▪ 70t/10,000cs own label 53% red 36% white 11% blanc de noir ▪ IPW ▪ PO Box 221 Tulbagh 6820 ▪ suzette@lemberg.co.za ▪ www.lemberg.co.za ▪ S 33° 18' 8.27" E 019° 6' 23.06" ▪ ✉ footfalls.venue.ponytail ▪ F +27 (0)21-300-1131 ▪ **T +27 (0)21-300-1130**

☐ **Le Mieux** see Cronier Wines
☐ **Lenie's Hof** see Axe Hill

Leopard Frog Vineyards

Canadian-born vigneron David John Bate uses this Fairtrade- and WIETA-accredited label as a showcase for interesting, sometimes radical vinifications such as a white blend of 13 varieties, MCC bubbly from pinotage, and a pinot noir aged an extraordinary 5 years in new oak. See also United Nations of Wine.

Location: Stellenbosch ▪ Closed to public ▪ Owner(s) Dogwood Trust ▪ Cellarmaster(s)/winemaker(s) David John Bate (Jun 2005) ▪ 300cs own label 60% red 40% white ▪ Fairtrade, WIETA ▪ 8 Royal Ascot Lane Sandown Sandton 2196 ▪ info@leopard-frog.com ▪ www.leopard-frog.com ▪ F +27 (0)11-883-0426 ▪ **T +27 (0)11-884-3304**

Leopard's Leap Family Vineyards

Food and wine are central to this growing global brand, whose name and emblem reflect admiration and care for the Cape Leopard, and in the past year owners Hanneli Rupert-Koegelenberg and Hein Koegelenberg have refined the rich, food-themed cellardoor offering yet again. In the purpose-built venue at the base of the Franschhoek mountains, where the eponymous wild cats are occasionally spotted, culinary culture is shared, along with a uniquely local meal, at the South African Table on Wednesdays, Thursdays and Saturdays. Social interaction and various causes, human and environmental, remain priorities.

Culinaria Collection

★★★★ **Pinot Noir** ⊘ Once again from Elgin fruit; **16** ⑧⑥ maintains form & style of previous: elegant & light, poised & assured. Third new oak adds frame to generous but powerful juicy berry & spice palate.

★★★★ **Grand Vin** ⊘ Serious but supple, **16** ⑧⑧ cab-led 4-way Bordeaux blend offers ripe fruitcake appeal. Ferment finished in barrel, half new, but oak is well knit with Darling & Stellenbosch fruit.

★★★★ **Chenin Blanc** ⊘ Happy trifecta of dryland, Paardeberg bushvines & partial barrel ferment make **17** ⑧⑦ complex & rich. Lovely interplay of ripe fruit, polished oak & vivid acid from 30% tank portion.

Pinot Noir-Chardonnay ★★★ Subtle floral brush to gentle cranberry & nectarine flavours on **18** ⑧④ dry rosé. Juicy, light & vivid, good body & length. **Brut Méthode Cap Classique** ★★★★ Green apple & lime crunch vies with yeasty bread notes on dry **NV** ⑧⑤ bubbly. Chardonnay leads pinot noir & meunier on balanced, fresh palate. Not tasted: **Muscat de Frontignan**.

Special Editions ⑨

★★★★ **Red Blend** ⊘ Spicy Xmas cake & hedgerow fruit richness to **16** ⑧⑧ merlot-led Bordeaux blend ex Stellenbosch. Bold yet elegant, the power leashed. Oak, all-new French, well knit after 24 months.

Pinotage ⊘ ★★★★ Blue & purple fruits abound on succulent, broad **16** ⑧⑤. Fleshy & plush but quite straightforward despite 18 months oaking, 30% new French.

Family Collection

★★★★ **Cabernet Sauvignon** ⊘ Dark-berried **16** ⑧⑥ improves on **15** ★★★★ ⑧④ with concentration & depth. Refined, velvety & plush without being overripe. Only older oak used for 15 months maturation.

Classic range

Cabernet Sauvignon ★★★ Lighter-styled **17** ⑧② is approachable & appealing in its floral, red-berry simplicity. Perdeberg & Swartland fruit, combo barrel & oak staves. **Merlot** ★★★ Cocoa edge to blue/black fruit on light-bodied **17** ⑧② touch grippy & tannic from combo oak barrels (20%) & staves. **Shiraz** ⊘ ★★★★ Step up in soft-textured, pliable spicy plum/blueberry fruit, **16** ⑧③ supple yet structured from year oaking with 50/50 barrel & staves, all French. **Cabernet Sauvignon-Merlot** ★★★ Light-bodied, fynbos-brushed berry compote is eminently sippable in **17** ⑧②. Like also-tasted **16** ★★★★ ⑧④, near-equal billing for cab & merlot, ex Swartland & Stellenbosch. **Chardonnay-Pinot Noir** ⊘ ★★★ Pale hue to citrus- & stonefruit-toned **18** ⑧① dry rosé, fresh, light & unfussy, ideal for summer lunches. **Unwooded Chardonnay** ★★★ Citrus zip of improved **18** ⑧① is fleshed out by leesy note. Uncomplicated, juicy & pleasant, nice length too. **Chenin Blanc** ★★★ Fruit salad succulence to easy **18** ⑧⓪, pineapple, melon & stonefruit softness & appeal is balanced by bright acid. **Sauvignon Blanc** ★★★ Grapefruit zest & vigour on light, unfussy **18** ⑦⑧ from Villiersdorp & Robertson fruit, dusty tail. **Sparkling Chardonnay-Pinot Noir** ⑨ ★★★ Vigorous lemon sherbet, raspberry & caramel notes on **NV** ⑧⓪ sparkler. Approachable, easy & light, subtle creamy dry finish.

Lookout range

Not tasted: **Cabernet Sauvignon-Shiraz, Pinotage Rosé, Chenin Blanc-Chardonnay, Semi Sweet**. — FM

Location/map: Franschhoek ▪ Map grid reference: C3 ▪ WO: Western Cape ▪ Est 2000 ▪ Tasting & sales Tue-Sat 9-5 Sun 11-5 ▪ Standard tasting R40/5 wines; Culinaria tasting R55/6 wines; Group tasting R65, booking essential ▪ Rotisserie lunches Wed-Sun 11.30-3.30 ▪ South African Table Wed, Thu & Sat from 12-1 ▪ Culinaria Food & Wine pairing Fri 12-1.30 only, booking essential ▪ Family Table Sun 12-3.30 ▪ Cooking demonstrations ▪ Shop: lifestyle gifts, wine accessories, tableware, linen ware, kitchen utensils & equipment, food literature ▪ Child friendly ▪ Owner(s) Hanneli Rupert-Koegelenberg & Hein Koegelenberg ▪ Winemaker(s) Renier van Deventer (Nov 2014) ▪ 600,000cs own label 60% red 39% white 1% rosé ▪ PO Box 1 La Motte 7691 ▪ info@leopardsleap.co.za ▪ www.leopardsleap.co.za ▪ S 33° 53′ 08.7″ E 019° 04′ 49.1″ ▪ 🚗 unstrapped.global.zone ▪ T +27 (0)21-876-8002

☐ **Leopard Spot** *see* Ayama Wines

☐ **Leo Wyn** *see* Leeurivier Wyn & Olyf

☐ **Le Piquet** *see* Org de Rac

Le Pommier Wines   ⓨ ⑪ ⌂ ⊙ ⑧

Like many other properties at the top of Stellenbosch's Helshoogte this was originally an apple farm, hence the name. Today it has a country-style vineyard lodge, restaurant and many other family-friendly amenities. The updated venue for tasting the wines, made by Zorgvliet, now overlooks the majestic Simonsberg.

★★★★ **Red Blend** ⊘ Merlot-led 4-way Bordeaux red, impressive solid tannin structure, luscious red & dark fruit padding. **16** (88) satisfying depth & length, as previous, which had all 5 varieties.

★★★★ **Sauvignon Blanc** ⊘ Same intense lemon & stonefruit aromas as before, **18** (88) cool green-gage fruit & wet pebble minerality, tangy but balanced palate. Complex fig, lime & gooseberry conclusion.

Cabernet Sauvignon Reserve (⚲) ★★★☆ Bright cassis, lead pencil & cigarbox on improved & more serious **16** (85). Well structured, with broad palate, clean savoury finish. WO Stellenbosch. **Jonathan's Malbec** ★★★★ For the bull that once decimated the grape harvest. **14** (83) less beefy than last, greater poise & perfumed allure even at 14.9% alcohol. Slight herbal whiff on plum & mulberry fruit, fine tannin. **Rosé** ★★★ Mostly sauvignon with dash cab for colour & red berry, cherry nuances. **18** (80) dry, flavour-some, soft acidity for easy enjoyment. **Olivia** (⚲) ★★★★ Semillon & sauvignon give **14** (85) its wet pebble flintiness, 9 months in barrel add a biscuit tone. Finishes clean, fresh & long. — GM

Location/map: Stellenbosch ▪ Map grid reference: H4 ▪ WO: Banghoek/Stellenbosch ▪ Est/1stB 2003 ▪ Wine tasting Mon-Sun 11-5 ▪ Facilities for children ▪ Picnics ▪ Le Pommier Restaurant ▪ Accommodation ▪ Owner(s) Melanie & Johan van Schalkwyk ▪ Winemaker(s) Bernard le Roux (Zorgvliet) ▪ Viticulturist(s) Hannes Jansen van Vuuren ▪ 16ha/4.8ha (cab f, malbec, sauv) ▪ 4,000cs own label 45% red 55% white ▪ PO Box 1595 Stellenbosch 7599 ▪ gm@lepommier.co.za ▪ www.lepommier.co.za ▪ S 33° 55' 8.58" E 018° 55' 43.14" ▪ ✉ mashing.port.rise ▪ T +27 (0)21-885-1269/+27 (0)74-115-3344

☐ **Lerato** *see* La RicMal

Le Riche Wines   ⓨ ⊙

'King cabernet' has been the speciality since inception of this family-owned and -run winery near Raithby. Christo le Riche, with a BSc Honours in Agriculture (and recently married), has taken over as cellarmaster and winemaker, and he's co-founded and currently chairs the Stellenbosch Cabernet Collective — sources of great pride, no doubt, for now-retired father and red-wine maestro Etienne, who's also stepping down from active CWG membership. The Le Riche wine style remains classic, with grapes continuing to be sourced entirely from the Stellenbosch area. Daughter Yvonne, a Cape Wine Master, runs all other aspects of the business with aplomb, viz sales growing locally and 35% of output exported to the US, Europe and Asia.

★★★★ **Cabernet Sauvignon** (☒) Revisited, **15** ★★★★★ (92) shows more of its rich berry fruit, elegantly framed by fine cedary tannins (from both grape & oak, 20 months, 25% new). There's inherent freshness too, bodes well for long rewarding life. 5 different Stellenbosch sites. **14** (88) for earlier drinking.

★★★★☆ **Cabernet Sauvignon Reserve** (☒) From Raithby & Firgrove sites, with longer oak ageing (2 years, 67% new) than standard version. Classic cab in fine **15** ★★★★★ (95) vintage shows pure elegance, more refinement than **14** (93). Fine-grained tannins, cool core of cassis fruit. Inherent balance, poise, to evolve well. Also in 1.5, 3 & 5L.

★★★★★ **CWG Auction Reserve Cabernet Sauvignon** (☒) Ex single low-yield (4.5t/ha) Firgrove block. All-new oak creates a plushness, temporarily veiling some of the fruit intensity, but **15** (94) has concentration & structure to grow in stature over 6-10 years. Worthy swansong for this CWG bottling.

★★★★ **Richesse** Flavoursome six-way ensemble led & streamlined by cab's fruit & structure. **16** (87) well crafted & matured in old oak, balanced & attractive staple to enjoy over the next few years.

★★★★ **Chardonnay** ⊘ Alluring citrus & toasted nut flavours from bunch pressing & equal parts tank/oak ferment (latter natural). Suppressed malo enhances zesty character, anchors confident Polkadraai fruit. **17** ★★★★★ (90) tangy & vivacious step up on **16** ★★★★ (85) & **15** (87). — MW

Location/WO: Stellenbosch ▪ Map: Helderberg ▪ Map grid reference: B1 ▪ Est 1996 ▪ 1stB 1997 ▪ Tasting, sales & cellar tours Mon-Fri 8.30-4.30 Sat by appt ▪ Closed all pub hols ▪ Hanepoot grapes (Feb & Mar) ▪ Owner(s) Le Riche Wines (Pty) Ltd ▪ Cellarmaster(s) Christo le Riche ▪ Winemaker(s) Christo le Riche (Jan 2010), with Mark Daniels (Sep 2000) ▪ 70t/9,000cs own label 90% red 10% white ▪ PO Box 5274 Helderberg 7135 ▪

wine@leriche.co.za ▪ www.leriche.co.za ▪ S 34° 0'52.87" E 018° 48'9.06" ▪ ⟨ⁱⁱⁱ⟩ cleverest.promenades.thirst ▪ F +27 (0)21-842-3472 ▪ **T +27 (0)21-842-3472**

☐ **Les Coteaux** see Mont du Toit Kelder

Le Sueur Wines ⓥ

Louis van der Riet (Le Sueur is an old family name) is cellarmaster at De Krans in Calitzdorp. His own brave label aims to strengthen perceptions of Klein Karoo dry table wines. So, for example, a chenin from the Swartberg, an area where most grapes get 'lost into bulk blends'. The new Wild Card range includes varieties even less usually associated with the Klein Karoo: first up a sauvignon blanc; a merlot's on its way.

Le Sueur range

★★★★ **Paradoks** ⓥ A 50:50 blend of pinotage's paradoxically lighter parents. On **16** ★★★★★ ⑨⑤ Calitzdorp cinsaut's bright red fruit, Outeniqua pinot noir's deeper berry, cherry & earthy notes - & the perfumed charm & elegance of both. Dry, fresh, lightish, harmonious. Older oak, as for **15** ⑧⑧.

★★★★ **Kluisenaar** Was 'Natural Barrel Fermented Chenin Blanc' - still a good summary for **17** ⑧⑨. Ripe peach & melon notes; bright acidity balancing the fruity-sweet note. Charming & rather elegant.

Wild Card range ⟨NEW⟩

★★★★ **Sauvignon Blanc** ⊘ Fig, gooseberry & tropical aromas on individual & expressive **17** ⑧⑥, passionfruit dominating the palate. Rounded, lively - not lengthy, but satisfying.

Not tasted: **Merlot**. — TJ

Location: Calitzdorp ▪ WO: Klein Karoo/Calitzdorp-Outeniqua ▪ Est 1987 ▪ 1stB 2014 ▪ Tasting & sales at De Krans, booking essential ▪ Old Boot Brew craft beer only available at De Krans bistro ▪ Owner(s)/winemaker(s) Louis van der Riet ▪ 8t/800cs own label 40% red 60% white ▪ PO Box 28 Calitzdorp 6660 ▪ louis@ lesueurwines.co.za ▪ www.lesueurwines.co.za ▪ F +27 (0)44-213-3562 ▪ **T +27 (0)44-213-3314**

☐ **L'Huguenot** see Val de Vie & Polo Club Wines

Libby's Pride Wines ⓥ

With star sign Leo, which she associates with strength and pride, Elizabeth Petersen is an entrepreneurial vintner focused on developing her good-value Libby's Pride label, available for tasting and purchase by appointment at Wellington's Linton Park Wines.

Cabernet Sauvignon ⊘ ★★★ Bouncy berry-laden **17** ⑧⓪, juicy & sappy, revelling in unwooded freshness & appeal, tweaks of pine needle & lavender at the finish. **Merlot** ⊘ ★★★ Dollop sugar rounds out bold **16** ⑧⓪, adding weight to punchy 15.2% alcohol & jammy blackcurrant fruit. **Sweet Rosé** ⓥ ★★★ Caramel & candyfloss sweetness on raspberry-hued, light-bodied **NV** ⑦⑧ pink from chardonnay & splash shiraz. **Chardonnay** ⓥ ★★★ Crisp unoaked **17** ⑦⑦ is easy-drinking in a lemon-&-lime style. **Sauvignon Blanc** ⓥ ★★★ Friendly **17** ⑦⑨ with nettly nuance & crisp acidity matching the tangy grapefruit flavours. **Sweet Lullaby** ⓥ ★★★ Plummy breadth to choc-mocha appeal of silky smooth **NV** ⑦⑦ Natural Sweet red from merlot, shiraz & ruby cab. Not tasted: **Shiraz**. — CM

Location: Wellington ▪ WO: Western Cape ▪ Tasting & sales by appt at Linton Park Wines ▪ Owner(s) Elizabeth Petersen ▪ Winemaker(s) JG Auret (2007, Linton Park) ▪ Viticulturist(s) Rudolf Jansen van Vuuren (2012, Linton Park) ▪ 550t/5,000cs own label 65% red 25% white 10% rosé ▪ info@libbyspridewines.com ▪ www. libbyspridewines.com ▪ F +27 (0)86-215-1811 ▪ **T +27 (0)82-745-5550**

☐ **Liberator** see The Liberator
☐ **Liberty** see Piekenierskloof Wine Company

Lievland Vineyards ⓥ ⓰

A trailblazer in the 1990s with its focus on shiraz, Lievland has been under the radar the past few years but rejuvenation is underway under the ownership of the fine MAN Family Wines team, now also based here. The large (110-ha), bucolic property has an excellent address - the Stellenbosch foothills of Simonsberg, Kanonkop and Warwick being neighbours - with many aspects and elevations, and the potential is huge. The historic buildings are being renovated, vines resurrected and the cellar, delightfully retro looking but perfectly functional, tweaked. Winemaker Riaan Möller calls Lievland 'an absolute sleeping beauty' and has big plans for its signature variety.

Location/map: Stellenbosch ▪ Map grid reference: F1 ▪ Tasting & sales Mon-Sun 10-4 ▪ Owner(s) MAN Vintners (Pty) Ltd ▪ Cellarmaster(s) Tyrrel Myburgh ▪ Winemaker(s) Riaan Möller ▪ 3,500cs own label ▪ PO Box 37 Klapmuts 7625 ▪ info@lievland.co.za ▪ www.lievland.co.za ▪ S 33° 50′ 29.5″ E 018° 52′ 34.8″ ▪ 🔲 kindest.quieter.hedge ▪ **T +27 (0)21-875-3079**

☐ **Lighthouse Series** see Benguela Cove Lagoon Wine Estate
☐ **Like Father Like Son** see Bon Courage Estate

L'illa ⓟ

The Catalan name (pronounced leeya) means 'island', alluding to the farm in Eilandia, Robertson, where the family of Nadia Cilliers has been for 6 generations. It produces the grapes for a Noble Late Harvest, made by Nadia and husband Gordon Newton Johnson in the Newton Johnson cellar in Hemel-en-Aarde.

★★★★☆ **Noble Late Harvest** Chenin planted 1976, wild ferment 3 months older barrels, then 7 months matured, yet **15** ⑨②'s fruit centre stage. Intense citrus with apricot, honey/barley sugar, plenty to admire, including the sugar/acid balance. Full-sweet, with lifting freshness. 375 ml.— CR

Location: Hermanus ▪ WO: Eilandia ▪ Est/1stB 2006 ▪ Tasting & sales at Newton Johnson Vineyards ▪ Owner(s)/winemaker(s) Gordon & Nadia Newton Johnson ▪ Viticulturist(s) AA Cilliers (Jan 1973) ▪ (chenin) ▪ 220cs own label 100% white ▪ PO Box 225 Hermanus 7200 ▪ gordon@newtonjohnson.com, nadia@newtonjohnson.com ▪ www.newtonjohnson.com ▪ F +27 (0)86-638-9673 ▪ **T +27 (0)28-312-3862**

☐ **Lime Road** see Havana Hills
☐ **Limestone Rocks** see Springfontein Wine Estate
☐ **Limietberg Site Exclusive** see Doolhof Wine Estate
☐ **Lindenhof** see Boland Kelder

Lingen ⓟ

At the feet of the towering, jagged Jonkershoek crags outside Stellenbosch, the Krige family's postage stamp vineyard, just 2 ha in extent, yields a special red blend. Neighbour and cellarmaster José Conde of Stark-Condé and winemaker Rudger van Wyk report that the additional plantings of mourvèdre and grenache have yet to reach maturity and make it into the assemblage.

★★★★☆ **Lingen** ⓐ Alluring **16** ⑨② shiraz, cab & petit verdot, dubbed 'braai wine for billionaires'! Textural, generous blue & black fruit with a tinge of coffee & smoke. Seamless & silky, with effortless restraint, aged in mainly French oak (30% new) it will last for ages.— FM

Location: Stellenbosch ▪ WO: Jonkershoek Valley ▪ Est 2003 ▪ 1stB 2008 ▪ Tasting & sales at Stark-Condé Wines ▪ Owner(s) JD Krige Family Trust ▪ Cellarmaster(s) José Conde (2003) ▪ Winemaker(s) Rudger van Wyk (2017) ▪ Viticulturist(s) Andrew Klinck, with Kevin Watt ▪ 7ha/2ha (cab, p verdot, shiraz) ▪ 14t/508cs own label 100% red ▪ PO Box 389 Stellenbosch 7599 ▪ info@stark-conde.co.za ▪ www.stark-conde.co.za ▪ **T +27 (0)21-861-7700**

Linton Park Wines ⓟ ⑪

On the slopes of Groenberg Mountain, Linton Park crafts a range of premium estate wines as well as the characterful Rhino ranges whose profits help support these threatened animals. Owned by London-based multinational Camellia, Linton Park also makes wines for The Bridge of Hope at their Wellington cellar.

Linton Park Estate range
★★★★ **Malbec** 🆕 ⓐ From single block, **17** ⑧⑨ shows plenty of promise. Big structure & flavours (black plums, vanilla, lavender & violets), smoky oak spices & fresh acidity. Should improve.

★★★★ **Merlot** ⊘ Sweetly fruited **16** ⑧⑦ is plump & appetising, offering soft pudding spices, plum-cake, prunes, chocolate & smoke. Ripe but firm tannins (helped by year French oak), good acid & length.

★★★★ **Pinotage** 🆕 Lots going on in **16** ⑧⑦, from black cherries, sweet spices, leather & smoke, with over-arching coffee/mocha highlights. Nicely balanced palate, with good tannins & structure.

★★★★ **Shiraz** ⓧ Spicy facets lift vibrant black cherry/berry features of **15** ⑧⑦, a yard ahead of **14** ★★★★ ⑧③ with dominant tannins needing year/2 to soften. Year in wood, 40% American.

★★★★ **De Slange Rivier** ⓧ **15** ⑧⑦ ex cab & merlot back on form after last **11** ★★★★ ⑧⑤ from merlot & shiraz; complex interplay of rich black berry fruit & pliable oaking in fresh structure.

★★★★ **Wild Ferment Chardonnay** ⑭ Rich & creamy **17** ⑧⑥ spreads lavish oak-derived flavours - butter, toast & spice - over tinned mango & melon. Interesting notes of nuts, muesli & smoke developing, suggesting more to come.

Cabernet Sauvignon ★★★☆ Layers of flavour on **16** ⑧④ developing nicely, blackcurrant pastille, leather & biltong combining with attractive spice & vanilla from year French oak. WO W Cape. **Café Cabernet** ★★★★ Generous black-fruit jam, coffee & creamy notes, **17** ⑧③ is high tea in a glass! Touch sugar makes for easy drinking. Well-executed 'cuppa java' style. **Café Malbec** ⑭ ★★★ Drier than cab sibling, **17** ⑧② all present & correct, with black fruit, coffee & chocolate all showing quite powerfully. **Chardonnay** ⓧ ★★★★ Unabashed & generous **16** ⑧⑤, oodles of tropical fruit plus oatmeal, caramel & plush vanilla oak for a rich, smooth finish. **Unwooded Chardonnay** ⑭ ★★★ Plenty of tinned & cooked fruit on **17** ⑦⑨, weighty on palate, needs drop more acid to balance. **Sauvignon Blanc** ⓧ ★★★ Grassy greengage interest of **17** ⑦⑧ needs fresh acid fillip. WO W Cape. **Méthode Cap Classique Rosé** ⑭ ★★★ Equal pinot noir & chardonnay **NV** ⑧② dry fizz spent 36 months on lees acquiring its pretty onion skin hue, full body & bubbles showing plenty of salty tang. **Méthode Cap Classique Brut** ⑭ ★★★ Fizzer from 50/50 pinot noir & chardonnay, **NV** ⑧② had 36 months on lees giving rich flavours of nuts, toffee, salty yeast.

Red Rhino range
Cabernet Sauvignon ⓥ ★★★ Plenty of herbs & spices on easy-drinking **17** ⑧⓪. Unwooded, as all reds in this range. WO W Cape, like Shiraz. **Merlot** ⓥ ★★★ Gram sugar rounds out soft black fruit flavours on **16** ⑧⓪. Coffee & leather add interest though finish doesn't linger. **Pinotage** ★★ Overwhelming spice notes a detraction in just-dry **17** ⑦③. **Shiraz** ⓥ ★★★ Shows pleasing & typical flavours of red-berried fruit, smoked salami & herbs in **16** ⑧⓪.

White Rhino range
Chardonnay ⓧ ★★★ Peach & orange profile of modest, unwooded **17** ⑦⑨ has a clean, bright finish. WO W Cape, as all these. **Chenin Blanc** ⓧ ★★★ Tropical fruit tones in light **17** ⑦⑨, clean & dry. **Sauvignon Blanc** ⓧ ★★★ Floral, tropical **17** ⑦⑦ has zippy finish, but lacks varietal punch.

The Rhino range
Not tasted: **Rosé**, **Sweet Rosé**. — CM

Location/map: Wellington ▪ Map grid reference: C2 ▪ WO: Wellington/Western Cape ▪ Est 1995 ▪ 1stB 1998 ▪ Tasting & sales Mon-Fri 9-4.30 Sat/pub hols 10-3 ▪ Cellar tours by appt ▪ Uncorked Restaurant Tue-Sat 11-3 ▪ Owner(s) Camellia PLC UK ▪ Winemaker(s) JG Auret (2007) ▪ Viticulturist(s) Rudolf Jansen van Vuuren (2012) ▪ 294ha/75ha (cabs s/f, malbec, merlot, ptage, shiraz, chard, sauv) ▪ 550t/80,000cs own label 60% red 40% white ▪ IPW, WIETA ▪ PO Box 1234 Wellington 7654 ▪ tasting@lintonparkwines.co.za ▪ www.lintonparkwines. co.za ▪ S 33° 36' 40.1" E 019° 2' 15.0" ▪ ⬚ types.mountainous.powers ▪ F +27 (0)21-873-0851 ▪ **T +27 (0)21-873-1625**

☐ **Lion Creek** *see* Napier Vineyards
☐ **Lion Ridge** *see* Valley Vineyards Wine Company
☐ **Lion's Drift** *see* Silkbush Mountain Vineyards
☐ **Lion's Pride** *see* Stellenrust
☐ **Lions River Vineyards** *see* Highgate Wine Estate
☐ **Lionsway** *see* Boland Kelder
☐ **Lisha Nelson Signature Wines** *see* Nelson Family Vineyards

Lismore Estate Vineyards ⓧ

Samantha O'Keefe arrived in the Cape from California armed with a remarkable spirit and determination, but less experience in winemaking. Since she's settled into her cool-climate estate near Greyton, only the last of these factors has changed, and she has a growing international reputation for her wines — untasted by us.

Location: Greyton ▪ Map: Southern Cape ▪ Map grid reference: A1 ▪ Est 2003 ▪ 1stB 2006 ▪ Tasting & sales by appt ▪ Owner(s)/winemaker(s) Samantha O'Keefe ▪ 232ha/14ha (shiraz, chard, sauv, viog) ▪ 105t/10,000cs own label 40% red 60% white ▪ PO Box 76 Greyton 7233 ▪ wine@lismore.co.za ▪ www.lismore.co.za ▪ S 34° 4'25.23" E 019° 41'16.83" ▪ ⌨ treasury.stuffing.tectonic ▪ T +27 (0)82-343-7913

☐ **Literature Wine** see Nordic Wines

Lithos Wines   ⓟ

Wedderwill Country Estate near Sir Lowry's Pass village in the Helderberg is where venture capitalist Sean Emery and wife Lorraine tend 2 ha of shiraz and pinotage in rocky terroir (hence the brand reference to the lithosphere). Visitors are welcome (by appointment) to taste the shiraz and Cape Blend in a stylish basement cellar adorned with art by Wim Botha, whose charcoal drawings of the Cape Eagle Owl appear on the labels.

Location: Sir Lowry's Pass ▪ Map: Helderberg ▪ Map grid reference: H6 ▪ Est/1stB 2012 ▪ Tasting, sales & cellar tours Mon-Fri 8-5 by appt Sat/Sun by appt ▪ Closed all pub hols ▪ Owner(s) Sean & Lorraine Emery ▪ Cellarmaster(s) Sean Emery, with consultant ▪ 16ha/2ha (ptage, shiraz) ▪ 20t/2,600cs own label 90% red 10% blanc de noir ▪ Postal Suite 346 Private Bag X15 Somerset West 7129 ▪ winemaker@lithos.co.za ▪ www. lithos.co.za ▪ S 34° 6'12.66" E 018° 55'15.28" ▪ ⌨ graduate.sofa.trickle ▪ F +27 (0)860-552-5521 ▪ T +27 (0)83-611-9955

Litigo Wines

Vintage 2018 hit this boutique winery's production; just 1,080 bottles were made (1,000-1,200 is the norm), leaving vintner Eben van Wyk to acknowledge 'winemaking will unfortunately continue to remain only an expensive but fulfilling hobby'. Funding 'this amazing venture' comes from his day job as a trademark lawyer. The journey continues, with planting of chardonnay on the Overberg farm acquired in 2016 with Peter-Allan Finlayson of Crystallum, who also helps craft this pinot. The plan is to ultimately produce only from their own vines and, hopefully, have a demarcated ward named for nearby landmark Shaw's Mountain.

★★★★☆ **Pinot Noir** ⊘ Enticingly ripe & generous 17 ⑨2, concentrated dark fruit layered across buxom, supple flesh, firm tannin grip, dry conclusion ensure balance, longevity. Spontaneous ferment, 30% wholebunch; 15% new oak, 11 months.— AL

Location: Hermanus ▪ WO: Overberg ▪ Est 2011 ▪ 1stB 2012 ▪ Closed to public ▪ Owner(s) Eben van Wyk ▪ Winemaker(s) Eben van Wyk & Peter-Allan Finlayson (both 2011) ▪ 2t/200cs own label 100% red ▪ Postnet Suite 134 Private Bag X1005 Claremont 7735 ▪ info@litigowines.com ▪ www.litigowines.com ▪ F +27 (0)21-683-5952 ▪ T +27 (0)82-803-4503

☐ **Little Brown Job** see Cranefields Wine
☐ **Little J** see Joostenberg Wines
☐ **Little Rock** see Mont Rochelle Hotel & Vineyard
☐ **Live-A-Little** see Stellar Winery
☐ **Lobola** see Taillard Family Wines

Lodestone Wines & Olives   ⓟ ⑪ ⓒ

With the completion of their cellar, owners of this boutique property in cool-climate Plettenberg Bay, Ingrid and Jon Tonkin, are looking forward to greater control over their harvest dates and batch sizes. Certain the investment will reflect positively in the style and complexity of future vintages, they've appointed Mark Stephens as consultant winemaker, and 'me as his assistant', quips Jon. The wines reviewed below are, therefore, among the last vinified by Anton Smal at neighbour Bramon.

Pinot Noir ⑲ ★★★★☆ Off to good start, 17 ⑧4 tiny first vintage off young vines (3 years old). Judiciously oaked & raspberry toned, with sage & tapenade nuances, brisk acidity tempered by pure fruit & powdery tannins. **Strandloper Sauvignon Blanc** ★★★ Slightly riper feel than bone-dry previous, 17 ⑧0 granadilla & papaya notes, smidgen sugar to take the edge off racy-fresh acidity. **Stonechat Méthode Cap Classique Brut Rosé** ★★★★ Characterful sunset pink dry sparkler with cured meat & strawberry notes from pinot noir (70%), Granny Smith apple acidity from chardonnay. 16 ⑧5 15 months on less, so no bread/

brioche whiffs yet, but impressively fine bubbles, creamy mousse. Not tasted: **The Jimdog**, **Stoepsit Rosé**, **Chardonnay**, **Sauvignon Blanc-Semillon**. — CvZ

Location/WO: Plettenberg Bay ▪ Map: Klein Karoo & Garden Route ▪ Map grid reference: C1 ▪ Est 2012 ▪ 1stB 2014 ▪ Tasting & sales Tue-Sun 11-4 in high season, with reduced opening times in quieter seasons (see Facebook for details) ▪ Fee R10/tasting per wine, R20/tasting for MCC & pinot noir ▪ Closed Good Fri, mid-May to mid-Jun, Dec 25 & Jan 1 ▪ Light seasonal meals; cheese & charcuterie platters ▪ Farm produce ▪ MTB trail ▪ Owner(s) Tonkin family ▪ Winemaker(s) Mark Stephens (2018, consultant) & Jon Tonkin ▪ 4.3ha (pinot, chard, sauv, sem) ▪ 28t/3,000cs own label 15% red 35% white 15% rosé 35% MCC ▪ PO Box 2747 Plettenberg Bay 6600 ▪ info@lodestonewines.com ▪ www.lodestonewines.co.za ▪ S 33° 56′ 27.70″ E 023° 26′ 4.20″ ▪ insulated.invitingly.complexion ▪ **T +27 (0)44-534-8015/+27 (0)82-600-7835**

Lomond   (P) (M) (co)

Located near shark-diving capital Gansbaai, and part of the Walker Bay Fynbos Conservancy, this pioneer winery in the cool-climate Cape Agulhas appellation has 18 different soil types, making it a biodiversity hotspot and springboard for a number of distinctive single-vineyard wines, each named for an indigenous floral species. Now entrusted to medalled ex-Simonsig winemaker Hannes Meyer, the range is available for tasting in two 'chic but relaxed' on-site visitor venues.

Icon range

★★★★ Snowbush ⓥ Unoaked sauvignon, nouvelle balanced by oaked semillon, viognier, in **13** ⑧⑥. Good weight, zestily clean conclusion - if a bit light on fruit intensity compared to **12 ★★★★☆**.

Single Vineyard range

★★★★☆ Cat's Tail Syrah ⓐ Voluptuous **15** ⑨④ has rich dark fruit at under 14% alcohol, floral aromatics giving way to pepper, tobacco, leather & Asian spices that linger on the fresh finish. 18 months French oak, 30% new, like Conebush sibling.

★★★★☆ Conebush Syrah ⓐ Continuing upward trajectory, **15** ⑨① has pure, bright, concentrated red & black berry fruit, plenty of black pepper & allspice typicity, dark chocolate too. Well integrated & balanced even at 14.5% alcohol. Also in magnum.

★★★★ Pincushion Sauvignon Blanc Alcohol toned down in **16** ⑧⑥, even more so in vibrant also-tasted **17** ⑧⑨ to offer far greater elegance than **15 ★★★★** ⑧③. Floral aromas & salad of green tropical fruit, including lime, honeydew melon & greengage.

★★★★ Sugarbush Sauvignon Blanc While blowsy **16 ★★★★** ⑧③ has 14.8% alcohol & asparagus/tinned pea notes, **17** ⑧⑦, also tasted, returns to form with fresh fig, guava & gooseberry fruit, stony minerality, clean finish.

Phantom Pinot Noir ⓥ **★★★☆** Was just 'Pinot Noir'. Silky **16** ⑧⑤ more expressive than previous, with rosepetal aromas & subtle earthiness underpinning red cherry, wild berry fruit.

Ultra Premium range

★★★★ Candelabra Cabernet Sauvignon (NEW) ⓐ Estate's first cab, ex single-vineyard, seriously oaked (18 months new French), giving dark chocolate & vanilla overlay to ripe black fruit. **16** ⑧⑧ rich yet elegant thanks to fresh acidity.

★★★★ Belladonna SMV ⓥ Adds shrubland lily to name, & is suitably fynbos scented in **16 ★★★★☆** ⑨⓪, with cedarwood & potpourri aromas leading to ripe red fruit on palate. Syrah, with 15% mourvèdre, 6% viognier, more fragrant, smooth, seamless than **15** ⑧⑨ after 14 months oaking, 25% new.

Estate range

★★★★ Syrah ⓥ Less fruity than intensely plummy nose suggests, **15** ⑧⑥ has a seam of black pepper & star anise carrying through to spicy, savoury finish.

★★★★ Sauvignon Blanc ⓥ Intensely aromatic, green herbal as well as riper lime & fig notes, **17** ⑧⑦ more youthfully harmonious than **16 ★★★★** ⑧④, with pleasing balance between being racy & rounded.

★★★★ SSV ⓥ Sauvignon combines with old-barrel-fermented semillon (20%) & viognier (5%) in **16** ⑧⑥, full in body yet fresh with white peach & green apple fruit. More focused than **15 ★★★★** ⑧③.

★★★★☆ **Noble Late Harvest** (NEW) (🏅) From botrytised viognier, 9 months in barrel, liquid gold **17** (94) syrupy sweet yet uncloying thanks to racy acidity, tangy apricot & pineapple fruit, ginger preserve-like bite & clean finish. Just 7.4% alcohol. Only 900 bottles of 500 ml.

Merlot ★★★★ Medium-bodied & juicy **16** (84) lightly wooded for maximum expression of red plum & strawberry fruit. **Merlot Rosé** (NEW) ★★★ Coral pink **17** (81) is dry & smooth, with strawberry & cranberry fruit; also-tasted **18** (82) serves cantaloupe & tangy berry flavours with pinch of spice. — JG

Location: Gansbaai ▪ Map: Southern Cape ▪ Map grid reference: A3 ▪ WO: Cape Agulhas ▪ Est 1999 ▪ 1stB 2005 ▪ Tasting & sales Mon-Sun 10-4 ▪ Food platters ▪ Craft beer ▪ Part of Walker Bay Conservancy ▪ Winemaker(s) Hannes Meyer (Jun 2018) ▪ 1,100ha/120ha (merlot, mourv, shiraz, nouvelle, sauv, sem) ▪ 850t 60% red 40% white ▪ PO Box 1269 Gansbaai 7200 ▪ info@lomond.co.za ▪ www.lomond.co.za ▪ S 34° 34' 12" E 019° 26' 24.00" ▪ whittle.shrubbery.joyriding ▪ **T +27 (0)28-388-0095/+27 (0)82-908-0099**

☐ **Longmarket** *see* Woolworths
☐ **Long Mountain** *see* Thor Vintners

Longridge Wine Estate
(🍷) (🍴) (📷) (♿)

This Netherlands-family-owned property on the slopes of the Helderberg has a simple philosophy: 'We want to make enjoyable wines, which are healthy to drink and of a world-class standard'. Cellarmaster and managing director Jasper Raats and his team therefore forgo herbicides, pesticides and chemical sprays in the vineyard, and commercial yeasts, enzymes, fining agents, stabilisers etc in the cellar. The farm is also home to free-roaming geese on insect control patrol, and cattle that provide manure for compost. This 'natural first' approach extends to the award-winning restaurant, which uses seasonal produce from its organic garden, SASSI-approved fish, beef from the farm and other produce sourced from like-minded neighbours.

Ultra Premium range

★★★★★ **Clos du Ciel** (♻️) (🏅) Suave barrel-fermented chardonnay from organic, low-crop, single-vineyard on the Helderberg. Hallmark white peach, honey & almond nuances overlay refined citrus. Present oak nudge (30% new) in **16** (94), but remains a poised & respectworthy glassful. Also in magnum.

★★★★☆ **Ou Steen Enkel Wingerd Chenin Blanc** (♻️) (🏆) Oxidatively styled, boldly flavoured with quince & bruised apple, **16** (92) cordial-like intensity & viscosity, 15 g/l sweetness heightened by oak sheen from year in 40% new barrels. Less acidity & more wood than **15** (90), nonetheless vividly portrays the beauty of small 37 year old Stellenbosch single-vineyard.

Not tasted: **Ekliptika**.

Premium range

★★★★ **Merlot** Long fruit-packed finish extended by generous 15% alcohol, **16** (86) smooth & mouthfilling, with intense chocolate & plum flavour, good grip for food. Also in magnum, as all these reds.

★★★★ **Pinotage** Exciting **17** (88)'s mulberry attraction, raspberry acidity, fresh tannic grip showcase winemaker's deft minimalist winemaking. Delicious now, with few years to go.

★★★★ **Chardonnay** (♻️) (♻️) **16** (89) pared-back version of complex & concentrated **15** ★★★★☆ (93). Faint nut & lemon-lime bouquet, subtle oak (20% new, 12 months), moderate 13% alcohol.

★★★★ **Chenin Blanc** (♻️) Last year **15** (86) tasted, incorrectly vintaged. Follow-up **16** (86) not as markedly dry but same sympathetic oaking for palate breadth rather than flavour. White peach, floral appeal overlaid with wet stone minerality & umami notes.

★★★★ **Edelgoud** (♻️) (♻️) Unwooded botrytis dessert from sauvignon, **15** (87) reined-in intensity yet intriguingly complex. Like last-tasted **12** (89), effortless, with sense of weightlessness on the palate. 375 ml.

Cabernet Sauvignon ★★★★ Departs from **14** (84)'s juicy & supple styling with impressively stern backbone & vibrant acidity. Best cellared few years to mesh with ripe cassis fruit. **The Emily** ★★★★ Delicate dry rosé dedicated to 'brave women fighting for what is right, all over the world'. **17** (84) berries-&-cream character from chardonnay, soupçon pinot noir. WO W Cape. Also in 1.5L.

Méthode Cap Classique range

★★★★ **Brut Rosé** Energetic chardonnay-led **NV** (87) dry bubbly improves on previous with higher pinot noir portion (40% versus 25%). This & 36+ months on lees add gravitas, greater weight & palate breadth. Also in magnum.

★★★★ **Brut** Any-occasion, high-spirited **NV** ⑧⑥ dry sparkler from chardonnay & pinot noir (20%), youthful Granny Smith apple tone, less rich without toffee apple nuance of previous (less time on lees - 36 months versus 60) but no less fine.

★★★★☆ **Brut Vintage Reserve** ⑨ ⑧ In best years only. New disgorgement of elegant **09** ⑨⑨ sparkler from chardonnay & pinot noir had extra year on lees, is as beautifully persistent, restrained as previous. In keeping with house style, almost bone-dry but with satisfying weight, richness.

Discontinued: **Brut Blanc de Blancs**. — CvZ

Location: Stellenbosch ▪ Map: Helderberg ▪ Map grid reference: C1 ▪ WO: Stellenbosch/Western Cape ▪ Est 1841 ▪ 1stB 1992 ▪ Tasting & sales Mon-Sat 10-5 (last tasting at 4.30) - booking essential for groups of 8+ ▪ Closed Easter Fri/Mon, Dec 25/26 & Jan 1 ▪ Cellar tours by appt ▪ Longridge Restaurant T +27 (0)21-855-4082, restaurant@longridge.co.za ▪ Tour groups ▪ Gift shop ▪ Owner(s) Van der Laan family ▪ Cellarmaster(s)/ viticulturist(s) Jasper Raats ▪ Winemaker(s) Jasper Raats & Hendrien de Munck ▪ 38ha (cab, merlot, pinot, chard, chenin) ▪ 255t/30,000cs own label 45% red 50% white 5% MCC ▪ Suite 116 Private Bag X4 Die Board 7613 ▪ info@longridge.co.za ▪ www.longridge.co.za ▪ S 34° 0' 55.2" E 018° 49' 60.0" ▪ ▦ flows.habitats. recliners ▪ F +27 (0)21-855-4083 ▪ **T +27 (0)21-855-2005**

☐ **Lookout** see Leopard's Leap Family Vineyards
☐ **Lord Somerset** see Somerset Wines
☐ **Lord Jackal** see Jakkalsvlei Private Cellar

Lord's Wines ⑨ ⑪ ◎

This family venture in the cool mountains near McGregor is expanding in more ways than one, with new tasting and function venues opening and new GM Louwrens Rademeyer welcoming his first son with wife (and sales manager) Melané. Wine-wise, her father (and owner) Jacie Oosthuizen is doubling production of their MCC sparkling to meet ever-growing demand locally and overseas.

Limited Releases

★★★★ **Three Barrel Shiraz** ⑨ Despite 3 years mainly new oak, **12** ⑧⑧ has lovely plush fruit with subtler savoury notes. Streamlined, supple tannins, dark chocolate at the end. Also in magnum, as Brut.

Lord's Wines range

★★★★ **Chardonnay** ⑨ Oak flavours part of **16** ⑧⑥'s character, nuts & buttered toast, a dry savoury finish. Supported by grapefruit tones, less showy than **15** ⑧⑥, more food friendly, still delicious.

★★★★ **Méthode Cap Classique Brut** Stylish **NV** ⑧⑦ bubbles from 70/30 chardonnay/pinot noir fizzes with freshness, shows attractive creamy-salty notes from year on lees, positive nutty finish.

Pinot Noir The Legend ★★★ Sweetly fruited **17** ⑧⓪ adds tweak of spice & hint of jam to perfectly drinkable wine. **Shiraz** ⑨ ★★★ Dark fruit, meaty nuances, vanilla spicing to the fore in the flavours; **15** ⑧① smooth & round appeal. **Pinot Noir Rosé** ★★★ Delightful aromas of earthy red berries on soft, fruity **18** ⑧⓪ with crisply appetising dry tail. Ideal summer sipper. **Sauvignon Blanc** ★★★ Soft **17** ⑦⑨ billows tropical granadilla & exotic lilies, gentle acid suggests early drinking. **Méthode Cap Classique Brut Rosé** ★★★ From pinot noir, 12 months on lees, **NV** ⑧② showing strong toffee notes along with red berry fruit, lacks elegance of previous. Discontinued: **Craft Pinot Noir**. — CM

Location/WO: McGregor ▪ Map: Robertson ▪ Map grid reference: D7 ▪ Est 2005 ▪ 1stB 2006 ▪ Tasting, sales & cellar tours Mon-Fri 9-4 Sat 10-4 Sun/pub hols by appt ▪ Cheese platters ▪ Function venue ▪ Owner(s) Jacie Oosthuizen ▪ GM Louwrens Rademeyer (Mar 2018) ▪ Cellarmaster(s) Jacie Oosthuizen (2006) ▪ Winemaker(s) Jacie Oosthuizen (2006), with Samuel Lekay (2006) ▪ Viticulturist(s) Jacie Oosthuizen (Jan 2003) ▪ 33ha/13ha (pinot, shiraz, chard, sauv) ▪ 90t/13,200cs own label 50% red 45% white 5% rosé ▪ PO Box 165 McGregor 6708 ▪ lordswinery@breede.co.za, sales@lordswinery.com ▪ www.lordswinery.com ▪ S 33° 59' 20.98" E 019° 44' 28.39" ▪ ▦ swerved.jointly.nettle ▪ **T +27 (0)23-625-1265**

☐ **Lorelei** see Rooiberg Winery
☐ **L'Ormarins** see Anthonij Rupert Wyne

Lothian Vineyards　　　　　　　　　　　　　　Ⓥ Ⓗ ⓞ

A barrel store and bonded warehouse have been built on the Wilson family's farm on the banks of the Palmiet River and a private lake in Elgin. There's sufficient space to make their wines too, at some future date; meanwhile they're made in the local Valley Green winery by the eminent Richard Kershaw, Master of Wine and Elgin-based vinifier of his own eponymous range, aided by Dudley Wilson. Richard's elegant touch is increasingly apparent in the wines. Another bit of star involvement is that of Kevin Watt in the vineyards.

Vineyard Selections

★★★★ **Pinot Noir** Fresh dark berry & note of forest floor on **17** ⑧⑧, the main accent on clean sweetish fruit rather than savoury. Light-feeling charm; good acid & a bit of soft tannin. Unobtrusive oaking.

★★★★ **Chardonnay** Ripe, clean typical varietal aromas & fairly intense flavours on **17** ⑧⑨, supported by sensitive oaking. Well balanced, with flesh, texture & good vein of enlivening lemony acidity.

★★★★☆ **Noble Late Harvest** ⑭ Old-gold **17** ⑨⓪ has sultana-raisin notes from dried grapes as well as honeyed hints of botrytis. Beautifully poised palate, with soft texture but firm underpinning of acid & vinous alcohol (12.9%) giving elegance & dry finish - subtle apricot signalling the variety, viognier. 375 ml.

Isobel Mourvèdre Rosé ★★★☆ Usual copper-pink hue on pleasingly aromatic **17** ⑧⑤. Bone-dry, with soft texture & refreshing acidity. More substance & interest than many rosés, & good step up on previous.

Weisser Riesling ★★★☆ Tasty, fresh & lightish **17** ⑧⑤ with an earthy peachiness. Succulently acidic & bright, with reasonable persistence of flavour. Another ever-improving wine. — TJ

Location/map/WO: Elgin ▪ Map grid reference: A2 ▪ Est 2004 ▪ 1stB 2010 ▪ Tasting by appt only ▪ Honey ▪ Conferences ▪ Weddings/functions ▪ Conservation area ▪ Luxury guest house (8 double en-suite rooms) ▪ Open for Elgin Open Gardens (Nov) ▪ Owner(s) Wilson family ▪ Winemaker(s) Richard Kershaw & Dudley Wilson (Jan 2016) ▪ Viticulturist(s) Kevin Watt (Mar 2009) ▪ 46ha/13ha (mourv, pinot, chard, riesling, sauv, viog) ▪ 60t 25% red 75% white ▪ IPW ▪ 68 Reservoir Rd Somerset West 7130 ▪ info@lothianvineyards.com ▪ www.lothianvineyards.com ▪ S 34° 11′ 31.49″ E 018° 58′ 57.78″ ▪ 🚗 rearranges.shaker.scrabbled ▪ **T +27 (0)21-859-9901/+27 (0)82-565-7869**

Louiesenhof Wines　　　　　　　　　　　　　Ⓥ Ⓗ ⓞ Ⓐ ⓑ

'Wine produced in harmony with nature' is the slogan at Louiesenhof, a reminder that Stefan Smit, the prime mover here, made a 'bio-organic wine' back in 1991, before eco-concern was a thing. Brandy has been a feature here for many years, and the bottlings featured below were created in association with Jos le Roux, a legend in his field. Distillation was in a kettle made in Germany, where Stefan studied.

Louiesenhof range

Premier Collection Shiraz Ⓥ ★★★☆ **11** ⑧④ lovely dark-fruited nose has a green edge, following to rich full-bodied end. **Premier Collection Cabernet Sauvignon-Cabernet Franc** Ⓥ ★★★ **11** ⑧① has fresh cab franc appeal balancing liquorice, smoke & Xmas cake aromas. Full bodied, with grippy tannin to finish. **Perroquet Pinot Duo Pétillant Rosé** Ⓥ ★★★ The 'pinot duo' are pinotage & pinot grigio/gris, made off-dry in rosepetal pink **14** ⑧①, showing savoury notes & cured meat finish. **Sauvignon Blanc** Ⓥ ★★★ **14** ⑦⑧ is barely there, with racy lemon acidity & a salty edge. Not tasted: **Free Run Pinotage**, **Cape Blend**, **Chardonnay Sur-Lie**.

Dessert Wine range

Perroquet Cape Tawny Ⓥ ★★★★ NV ⑧④ rustic glow-inducing port-style from tinta, with savoury touches. **Roobernet Cape Ruby** Ⓥ ★★★ Youthful **10** ⑧① fortified has spicy, medicinal notes. Pleasantly dry, dusty, with typical sweetness. Discontinued: **Sweet Red**.

Brandy range

★★★★ **14 Year Old** Ⓥ Blended brandy from colombard, chenin & cab, potstill component aged 14 years. Exudes dried peach, pear, fudge & marzipan flavours. Good balance, with mature fruit flavours lifted by fresh spirit on the finish. 30% potstill & 43% alcohol.

Marbonne 16 Year Old Potstill Ⓥ ★★★ Earthy, oaky notes along with fruit & spice. Fairly rich & smooth, if not harmonious. From colombard & cab. Not tasted: **7 Year Old**. Discontinued: **3 Year Old Brandy**. — WB

Location/map/WO: Stellenbosch ▪ Map grid reference: E4 ▪ Est 1991 ▪ 1stB 1995 ▪ Tasting & sales Mon-Fri 9-5 Sat/Sun 10-5 ▪ Closed Good Fri, Ascension day & Dec 25 ▪ Play area for children ▪ Tour groups ▪ Gift shop ▪ Farm produce ▪ Conferences (20 pax) ▪ Conservation area ▪ Hiking & MTB trails ▪ Antique brandy kettle on display ▪ B&B guesthouse ▪ Owner(s) WS Smit Watergang Trust ▪ Cellarmaster(s) WS Smit ▪ Brandy master(s) Stefan Smit & Jos le Roux (both 1991) ▪ Viticulturist(s) Stefan Smit (1991) ▪ 135ha (cabs s/f, merlot, ptage, shiraz, chard, chenin, pinot grigio, sauv) ▪ 900-1,000t/675,000L ▪ IPW, WIETA ▪ Koelenhof Rd (R304) Stellenbosch 7601 ▪ info@louiesenhof.co.za ▪ www.louiesenhof.co.za ▪ S 33° 53′34.7″ E 018° 49′35.3″ ▪ 〣 seated.outsiders.limbs ▪ F +27 (0)21-865-2613 ▪ **T +27 (0)21-865-2632 (office)/+27 (0)21-889-5550 (cellar)**

Louis

Cape Winemakers Guild member Louis Nel endeavours not to be 'tied down to a certain style or category'. His wines, both in terms of style and price, therefore appeal to a diverse market. Aside from vinifying for this boutique portfolio, Louis also advises various other small wineries.

Black Forest range

Shiraz-Mourvèdre ⓖ ★★★★ A real crowd pleaser. With shiraz at 85%, **16** ⑧④ Xmas cake & baking spice, wonderfully dry yet with a plushness that begs another sip. Not tasted: **Shiraz-Merlot**.

Titanic range

Cabernet Sauvignon ★★★ Modestly oaked **16** ⑦⑧, blackcurrant fruit on a bed of bone-dry tannins & sharp, lingering freshness.

Buckleberry range

Not tasted: **Cold Fermented Sauvignon Blanc**.

Louis range

Not tasted: **Cabernet Sauvignon**, **Sauvignon Blanc**. — HC

Location: Stellenbosch ▪ WO: Western Cape ▪ Est/1stB 2007 ▪ Closed to public ▪ Owner(s) Louis Nel ▪ Cellarmaster(s)/winemaker(s) Louis Nel (Jan 2007) ▪ 1st/3,000cs own label 50% red 50% white ▪ 9 Forest Str Stellenbosch 7600 ▪ louies@louiswines.com ▪ www.louiswines.com ▪ **T +27 (0)82-775-8726**

Louis 57 Wines ⓠ

If a golf buff knows the Louis involved here is international golfer Louis Oosthuizen, the '57' bit will be clear: his record-breaking low score on the Mossel Bay Golf Course. So too how the Open Champion Syrah came to be so called. The wines are made by Jacques and Reenen Borman at Boschkloof in Stellenbosch.

★★★★ **Jasoma Conclusion** Cab with cab franc, merlot, petit verdot. **16** ⑧⑥ classic berry & cigarbox aromas. Dry tannic firmness, big acidity & plenty of sweet fruit balance 15% alcohol. No **15**. WO W Cape. **Merlot** ⓝⓔⓦ ★★★ Herbal edge to typical fruitcake aromas on **16** ⑧⓪. Big acidity deals with soft ripe fruitiness. **Pinotage** ⓖ ★★★★ Expressive red fruit, maraschino cherries & plums, widely sourced **15** ⑧④ has variety's typical succulence for immediate enjoyment, the tannin backbone ensures ageing ability. **Open Champion Syrah** ★★★★ Dark, spiced plummy ripeness on **16** ⑧⑤. Big 14.5% alcohol, but balanced by plenty of flavour. Easygoing but form-giving tannins. **Shiraz** ⓖ ★★★★ Sappy hedgerow fruit, some peppery notes, ends savoury & dry. **15** ⑧④ ideal casserole companion now & for few years. **Fifty Seven Red Blend** ★★★ Softly fruity, chocolatey **16** ⑧⓪ from cab & shiraz. Big but easy. WO W Cape, as Sauvignon. **Rosé** ⓖ ★★ Mainly shiraz; 20% merlot accounts for **17** ⑦④'s strawberry tones, easy dry drinkability. **Sauvignon Blanc** ⓖ ★★★★ Quintessential sauvignon ex Somerset West & Wellington fruit. Nice intensity, gooseberries & capsicum, **17** ⑧④ becomes more mineral in the flavours. — TJ

Location: Mossel Bay ▪ Map: Klein Karoo & Garden Route ▪ Map grid reference: C4 ▪ WO: Stellenbosch/ Western Cape ▪ Est/1stB 2009 ▪ Tasting & sales Mon-Sat 10-8 at 14 Marsh Str Mossel Bay ▪ Closed Good Fri & Dec 25 ▪ Sales also via online shop ▪ Owner(s) Louis 57 Group (Pty) Ltd ▪ Winemaker(s) Jacques & Reenen Borman (Boschkloof) ▪ bertu@louis57.co.za ▪ www.louis57wines.com ▪ S 34° 10′59.46″ E 022° 9′10.78″ ▪ 〣 worker.quieter.message ▪ **T +27 (0)82-893-6848**

☐ **Louisa** see Pulpit Rock Winery

Louisvale Wines

Farm-grown chardonnay remains central, in the still wines and the pair of MCC sparklers, to this stalwart Devon Valley estate's portfolio. This edition, however, it's a pair of home-grown reds that stand out: a shiraz in the Stone Road budget range and ambitious new pinnacle cabernet sauvignon. Both should find favour in Louisvale's refurbished tasting area and recently completed wedding venue.

Louisvale range

★★★★☆ **Five Barrels Cabernet Sauvignon** ⊛ ⊛ Powerful but unintimidating, polished, **15** ⑨⓪'s 15% alcohol contained by sweet cassis fruit; both are reined in by well-managed tannin & oak (20 months, all new), commendable dryness. Suitably upscale packaging sets it apart from producer's purple livery.

★★★★ **Dominique** ⊘ ⊛ Poised **16** ⑧⑥ Bordeaux blend with similar firm backbone to **15** ★★★★ ⑧④, satisfying tannic form from cab, cab franc; merlot's fruitiness better contained. WO Coastal.

★★★★ **Chardonnay** Typically most accomplished of the chardonnays. Bright lemon & lime, deftly handled spicy oak (50% new) & restrained persistence; **17** ⑧⑧ improves on last-tasted **14** ★★★★ ⑧④.

Chavant ★★★☆ **17** ⑧③ has invigorating acidity of previous but combo of 20% new oak, inherent fruitiness & few grams sugar make for slightly sweet finish. **Chardonnay Unwooded** ★★★ For early enjoyment, **17** ⑧② has icing sugar aroma, mouthfilling ripe orange flavours. **Méthode Cap Classique Rosé Brut** ★★★ Frothy **NV** ⑧②'s 48% pinot noir adds coppery pink hue, faint savoury & strawberry scents, chardonnay the vibrant acidity. Also in magnum. **Méthode Cap Classique Brut** ★★★☆ Attractive **NV** ⑧④ bubbly tad brief but charming, with lemon sherbet & nutty aromatic appeal, lively fruit-filled palate.

Stone Road range

. . . .

Shiraz ⑨ ★★★ Ripe but bright, with gentle pepper notes, supple tannins & fresh dry finish, **16** ⑧② ticks all the boxes & shines in notably good-value range.

Cabernet Sauvignon ★★★ As previous, **15** ⑧① offers good varietal character, juicy succulence & some grassiness in balance with the modest oaking & light tannic grip. WO Coastal. **Merlot** ★★★ Plummy **16** ⑦⑨ choc & clean leather, woody conclusion (though just 10% new barrels). **Cinsault Rosé** ★★ Subtle strawberries-&-cream character, **18** ⑦⑥ light & dry. **Sauvignon Blanc** ★★★ Creamier, rounder than previous vintages, with more peach & tropical tones, less cool green notes in **18** ⑧②. — CvZ

Location/map: Stellenbosch ▪ Map grid reference: D4 ▪ **WO:** Stellenbosch/Coastal ▪ Est/1stB 1989 ▪ Tasting & sales Mon-Sat 10-4 ▪ Fee R40 ▪ Closed on selected pub hols ▪ Wedding/function venue (150 pax) ▪ Owner(s) Louisvale Wines (Pty) Ltd ▪ Directors Altmann Allers, Hendrik Kluever, Johann Kirsten & Zane Meyer ▪ Winemaker(s)/viticulturist(s) Simon Smith (Jul 1997) ▪ 34ha/23ha (cab, merlot, chard) ▪ 220t/16,000cs own label 50% red 50% white ▪ PO Box 542 Stellenbosch 7599 ▪ winery@louisvale.com ▪ www.louisvale.com ▪ S 33° 54' 32.3" E 018° 48' 24.3" ▪ ⬛ snapper.guardian.earliest ▪ F +27 (0)21-865-2633 ▪ **T +27 (0)21-865-2422**

Lourens Family Wines

Franco Lourens is 'owner, winemaker, wax-dipper (for the capsules) and delivery guy' for the own-label he began in 2016, when he joined Alheit Vineyards as assistant winemaker - 'working with Chris Alheit is by far the most important and biggest highlight of my career'. He makes his own wines in that Hemel-en-Aarde cellar, from widely sourced grapes, with a 'hands-off' philosophy: old-oak maturation, no additives other than a little sulphur. His aim, with his single-site wines, is 'to tell the story about the place, soil and farmer'.

★★★★☆ **Howard John** ⊛ Named for Franco's dad, a multi-origin blend of cinsaut, grenache, syrah, carignan. Fragrant, bright wildness on elegantly fresh **17** ⑨④. Charming & tangy but more serious than many light-styled reds of this type of blend (13% alcohol). Somewhat raw in youth, though seductive; needs time. Like others, only old oak used, & no additives.

★★★★☆ **Blouklip Steen** ⊛ From Durbanville chenin with notably pure fruit aromas, including some floral notes. A subtle, understated complexity opens up (the wine very tight in its youth). **17** ⑨④ fresh & vital, with succulent, green-tinged acidity, but also a hint of richness of effect than Skuinskap.

★★★★☆ **Skuinskap Steen** ⊛ 40+ year old Piekenierskloof chenin; name reflects the unusual pergola vine trellising. Pale gold **17** ⑨④ offers so many hints: peach, earth, honey, herbs, fennel... Taut, intense & lingering; a penetrating vibrant acidity & sense of ethereal lightness.

★★★★★ **Lindi Carien** ⓐ A tenderly drawn young woman pictured on the label - Franco's wife. **17** ⑨⑤ as lovely: widely sourced verdelho & chenin, plus 3 others. Expressive, fresh, light & refined, well structured with a tannic touch. Quietly, confidently flavourful & persistent. Many years ahead of it.— AL, TJ

Location: Hermanus ▪ WO: Western Cape/Piekenierskloof/Cape Town ▪ Est/1stB 2016 ▪ Closed to public ▪ Owner(s) Franco Lourens ▪ Winemaker(s) Franco Lourens (Jan 2016) ▪ ±14t/±1,600cs own label 35% red 65% white ▪ Private Bag X15 Suite 189 Hermanus 7200 ▪ info@lourensfamilywines.co.za ▪ www.lourensfamilywines.co.za ▪ **T +27 (0)84-919-4206**

Lourensford Wine Estate ⓟ ⓟ ⓐ ⓑ

Following on from the culling of underperforming vineyards on businessman Christo Wiese's 4,000-ha estate in the bowl of the Hottentots Holland and Helderberg mountains in Somerset West comes a renewed range focus. The Estate collection has been discontinued, and only the Limited Release, MCC sparkling and River Garden range retained (see separate listing for the latter). Flagship Chrysalis White and Red blends have been introduced, while a first-ever Pinot Noir under the Dome label (previously only in the US) has been added. The emphasis on green energy continues, as does the welcoming of guests, with a rich offering that includes a restaurant, market, craft beer and coffee roastery.

Chrysalis range ⓝⓔⓦ
★★★★☆ **Red** ⓐ Flagship Bordeaux blend of cab, merlot & cabernet franc, **15** ⑨④ impresses with poise, beautifully interwoven fruit & oak (70% new). Nuanced, layered & complex, with rich reward for patience.
★★★★☆ **White** ⓐ Taut focus on **15** ⑨③ mix of sauvignon (65%), chardonnay & dab viognier. Signature crisp citrus vibrancy but also broad mid-palate from use of acacia heads on old French barrels & natural ferment of chardonnay component. Restrained, elegant & enduring.

Limited Releases
★★★★☆ **Merlot** Agile mouthful of cocoa-tinged cherry fruitcake, **16** ⑨② dark & intense yet refined. Generously layered, with lovely integration of spicy cedar oak, 73% new. Also-tasted **15** ⑨⓪ equally deep but a tad peppery.
★★★★ **Shiraz-Mourvèdre-Viognier** Two vintages tasted: **16** ⑧⑧ more nervy than spicy **15** ★★★★★ ⑨⓪, which had more mourvèdre. Deceptively light-bodied, rich in its blueberry & plum fruit appeal. Savoury & dry. Just a third new oak used.
★★★★ **Chardonnay** Creamy breadth & brightness to **17** ⑧⑨ courtesy of complex winemaking: parts natural & barrel ferment, barrel rolling & lees contact. Rich yet vivacious. Also-reviewed **16** ★★★★★ ⑨⓪ shade tangier & more succulent. Both balanced & long.
★★★★ **Viognier** Complex yet tangy **17** ⑧⑨ improves on **16** ⑧⑧ in its refinement. Smooth, supple & spicy, with French & Hungarian oak well-knit & not obtrusive. Long lees contact adds broad dimension to both vintages tasted.
★★★★☆ **Noble Late Harvest** ⓝⓔⓦ Lively sun-dried pineapple & apricot opulence on botrytised **14** ⑨① semillon, lightly wooded. Vivid acid checks ripe honeyed sweetness. Long but clean & focused, with precise, pure tail. Light 10.5% alcohol. 375 ml.

The Dome range
★★★★ **Pinot Noir** ⓝⓔⓦ ⓥ Core of tangy, vibrant red berry fruit lightly cradled by silky oak (none new) on **17** ⑧⑧. Supple & lithe, as is also-tasted **16** ⑧⑨. Textured, cohesive & restrained mouthful.
★★★★ **Chardonnay** Cashew & apple tarte tatin notes vie with citrus zip on **17** ⑧⑨, which follows form of vibrant yet balanced also-sampled **16** ⑧⑨. Both are smooth & elegant from toned, integrated oak (third new) & complex winemaking.

Méthode Cap Classiques
★★★★ **Brut Rosé** Coral blush on **14** ⑧⑥ pinot noir-led dry sparkling. Taut, tangy strawberry zestiness & creamy fullness on mid-palate from 28 months on lees. **13** ★★★★ ⑧⑤, also reviewed, more vibrant, with green apple crunch & zip.
★★★★ **Brut** Dry sparkler from mostly chardonnay juggles fresh oystershell character with grapefruit zest & creamy, baked notes. **12** ⑧⑧ characterful, complex & rich yet crisp. 61 months on lees. Poised & pure, like also-sampled **11** ⑧⑨.

Not tasted: **Brut Zero Cuvée 89**. — FM

Location: Somerset West ▪ Map: Helderberg ▪ Map grid reference: F4 ▪ WO: Stellenbosch/Cape South Coast ▪ Est 1999 ▪ 1stB 2003 ▪ Tasting, sales & cellar tours daily 9-5 ▪ Fee R30-R60 ▪ Closed Good Fri & Dec 25 ▪ Millhouse Kitchen ▪ Tour groups ▪ Market ▪ Coffee Roastery ▪ Function hall ▪ Conservation area ▪ Craft beer: sales at market ▪ Owner(s) Christo Wiese ▪ Winemaker(s) Hannes Nel (Nov 2002), with Timothy Witbooi (May 2005) ▪ Viticulturist(s) Piet Uys ▪ 4,000ha/100ha (cab, merlot, pinot, shiraz, chard, sauv, viog) ▪ 1,200t/240,000cs own label 40% red 58% white 2% rosé ▪ BRC, CVC, HACCP, WIETA, WWF-SA Conservation Champion ▪ PO Box 16 Somerset West 7129 ▪ info@lourensford.co.za ▪ www.lourensford.co.za ▪ S 34° 4' 3.7" E 018° 53' 44.2" ▪ [map] spirit.dairy.anchors ▪ F +27 (0)21-847-0910 ▪ **T +27 (0)21-847-2333**

Lovane Boutique Wine Estate & Guest House ⓠ ⌂ ◎

Strategically located at the entrance to Stellenboschkloof, the old wagon road between Cape Town and Stellenbosch, is Theresa and Hennie Visser's 2.5-ha boutique vineyard and luxury guest house. It's a popular conference venue, and a great stepping off point for wine-routing weekenders and holidaymakers. **Cabernet Sauvignon ★★★★** Blackberry compote ripeness on **15** (83) tempered by juicy freshness. Subtle support from third new oak gives friendly & approachable mien. **Petit Verdot ★★★★** Improves on previous. Spicy & rich, **15** (83) too is big & bold, with firm tannic grip of all-new oak & 15.7% alcohol. **Shiraz ★★★** Typical ripe plum spice of **16** (82) shaded by dominant oak (all-new French, 2 years) as well as big 15.7% alcohol. Hot & tad dry, grippy. **Isikhati ★★★★** Lightly supple **15** (85), 3-way cab-led Bordeaux blend, ample red- & black-fruited appeal, with good oak surround (25% new, 24 months). Smooth, & most refined of the reds. **Theresa Blanc de Noir ★★★** Unfussy **18** (77) pink shows smoky edge to red fruit brightness. Juicy, dry & light, a summertime sipper from cab. **Chenin Blanc** (NEW) **★★★** Stonefruit vivacity & ripeness on honest, tropical-styled **17** (82), crisp acid to support fruit. **Méthode Cap Classique ★★★** Apple & lime tang on coral pink **NV** (80) fizz, sherbet zip vies with creamy yeast note on chardonnay/pinot noir blend. **Cape Vintage ★★★** Typical raisin, prune & spice richness on **16** (79) all-cab fortified 'port'. Sweet & tasty but lacks density & concentration for higher honours. 375 ml. Not tasted: **Cabernet Franc**, **Sauvignon Blanc**. — FM

Location/map/WO: Stellenbosch ▪ Map grid reference: D6 ▪ Tasting, sales & cellar tours Mon-Sun 10-5 ▪ Tasting fee R35, waived on purchase ▪ Conferences ▪ 4-star guest house (16 rooms) ▪ Owner(s) Hennie & Theresa Visser ▪ Winemaker(s)/viticulturist(s) Hennie Visser ▪ 3.6ha/2.5ha (cabs s/f, p verdot) ▪ PO Box 91 Vlottenburg 7604 ▪ info@lovane.co.za ▪ www.lovane.co.za ▪ S 33° 57' 09.74" E 018° 48' 02.38" ▪ [map] bachelor.drip.fairly ▪ **T +27 (0)21-881-3827**

☐ **Love Boat** see The Love Boat Wines

Lowerland ⓠ

Hennie Coetzee and son Bertie produce a wide range of high-quality organic produce from their varied agri-business in the Northern Cape, including this award-winning range of wines vinified by some of the Cape's most talented young winemakers. Cultivating in Prieska, one of SA's newest and furthest-flung wine wards, Lowerland is unusual in specialising in tannat and colombard, made with minimal intervention, plenty of whole bunches in the ferments and no new oak, offering a fresh and fascinating take on these varieties.

Lowerland range

★★★★ Tolbos Tannat ⓠ ♥ Style change from **15 ★★★★** (85) to fresher **16** (87), 100% bunch ferment giving fragrant red & black fruit & soft tannins. Elegantly oaked, deftly finished. One to watch.

★★★★ Vaalkameel Colombard (NEW) ♥ Contender for SA's most serious colombard. **17** (88) concentrated & creamy layers of flavour combining citrus, fresh almonds & nutmeg spice in intriguing mouthful.

★★★★ Witgat Viognier Fresh & vibrant **17** (86) mouthful of flowers, peaches & ginger spice, aided by soft kiss of oak (none new, as all), make for lovely refreshing summer drinking. No **16**. Organically grown (but wine not certified such), like MCC.

★★★★ Méthode Cap Classique (NEW) Interesting & unusual **16** (88) dry sparkling from colombard spent time in wood before 14 months on lees, adding delicious cinnamon spice to apple Danish pastry flavours & savoury finish. Zero dosage gives appetising freshness & appeal.

Occasional release: **Herd Sire Reserve**.

#WOPrieska range

Not tasted: **Die Verlore Bokooi Rooi**. — CM

Location/WO: Prieska ▪ Map: Northern Cape, Free State & North West ▪ Map grid reference: C6 ▪ Est 2000 ▪ 1stB 2006 ▪ Tasting & cellar tours by appt ▪ Owner(s) Lowerland (Pty) Ltd ▪ Winemaker(s) Johnnie Calitz (Glen Carlou), JD Pretorius (Steenberg), Lukas van Loggerenberg (Van Loggerenberg Wines) ▪ Viticulturist(s) Terblanche Viticulture, Bertie Coetzee (May 2013) ▪ 12,000ha/9ha (cab, merlot, p verdot, shiraz, tannat, chard, cbard, viog) ▪ 90t/1,300cs own label 60% red 40% white ▪ Organic vyd (Ecocert), GlobalGap, Siza ▪ PO Box 292 Lowerland Prieska 8940 ▪ bertie@lowerland.co.za, alette@lowerland.co.za ▪ www.lowerland.co.za ▪ S 29°29'15.28" E 023°0'28.41" ▪ ⌸ seat.monument.reissuing ▪ **T +27 (0)83-349-9559/+27 (0)82-854-9109**

☐ **Loyal Brothers** see Govert Wines

Lozärn Wines ⓠ ⓝⓔⓦ

Land in Robertson Valley where granny Kay's ducks once flocked has since been planted with vines, and the current Smuts family custodians are remembering their beloved relative in a wine named Kay's Legacy, one of five created by winemaker Salóme Buys-Vermeulen for this new venture. Having fallen in love 'at first sip' with carmenère back in 2012, Salóme vinified a rosé from this rare-in-SA grape, along with a rarer-still — perhaps unique — single-block version. There's also a Shiraz and Sauvignon Blanc.

Location: Bonnievale ▪ Map: Robertson ▪ Map grid reference: D3 ▪ Est/1stB 2017 ▪ Tasting, sales & cellar tours by appt ▪ Owner(s) Smuts Brothers Agri (Pty) Ltd (Directors Grant Smuts & Juan Ivan Smuts) ▪ Winemaker(s) Salóme Buys-Vermeulen (Jun 2017) ▪ 18ha under vine (carmenère) ▪ 30t/1,400cs own label 75% red 8% white 16% rosé ▪ PO Box 6 Robertson 6707 ▪ winemaker@lozarn.co.za ▪ www.lozarn.co.za ▪ S 33°58'1.49" E 020°8'12.01" ▪ ⌸ contravene.movie.blend ▪ **T +27 (0)23-616-2972**

☐ **Lubanzi** see Cape Venture Wine Co.
☐ **Luca & Ingrid Bein** see Bein Wine Cellar

Luddite Wines ⓠ ⓜ ⓞ ⓖ

With long winecrafting experience prior to going solo, Niels Verburg knew what he was looking for in his own project: a focus on shiraz, latterly chenin, and blends thereof. Luddite, on the eastern slopes of the Houw Hoek mountains overlooking Bot River village, is where he settled as boutique winemaker, with wife Penny as viticulturist. His winemaking, labels (especially the design-award-winning 'revolutionary' Saboteur) and philosophy are best summed up by his claim that 'Technology and mechanisation will never be a substitute for passion'. It's truly a family business, with daughter Alice having joined him in the cellar.

★★★★☆ **Shiraz** ⓐ Always a ripe style, boldly handsome, but gets the balance right. Morello cherries & black plums savoury spice, smoky notes, scrub, powerful **14** ★★★★★ ⑨⑤ ticks all the shiraz boxes. Oaked 2 years, has sturdy tannins for ageing. Various bottle formats. **13** ⑨③ also bold & ripe. WO Bot River.

★★★★☆ **Saboteur Red** Blend change, shiraz-led with cab, mourvèdre, less oaking than Shiraz (year), **16** ⑨② for earlier drinking. No less impressive for that: vivid dark fruit & tobacco, juicy texture & a backbone for ageing.

★★★★☆ **Saboteur White** ⓐ Closed with crown cap, tag-like neck label lauding saboteurs, as Red. Mainly chenin, with viognier, sauvignon blanc, **17** ⑨④ packs huge flavour & complexity into a trim body (12.5% alcohol). Stonefruit, thatch, minerality, ends savoury-fresh. Natural ferment, like Shiraz. Old oak.

Not tasted: **Chenin Blanc**. — CR

Location: Bot River ▪ Map: Walker Bay & Bot River ▪ Map grid reference: D2 ▪ WO: Cape South Coast/Bot River ▪ Est/1stB 2000 ▪ Tasting & sales Mon-Fri 9-3 Sat/Sun by appt ▪ Cellar tours by appt ▪ Food & wine pairing by appt ▪ Closed Dec 25 & Jan 1 ▪ Farm produce ▪ Walks/hikes ▪ Conservation area ▪ Owner(s) Niels Verburg & Hillie Meyer ▪ Cellarmaster(s) Niels Verburg (2000) ▪ Winemaker(s) Niels Verburg (2000), with cellar assistant Alice Verburg (Jan 2018) ▪ Viticulturist(s) Penny Verburg (2000) ▪ 17ha/5.8ha (cab, grenache, mourv, shiraz, chenin) ▪ 60t ▪ Own label 70% red 30% white + 1,000cs for clients ▪ PO Box 656 Bot River 7185 ▪ info@luddite.co.za, niels@luddite.co.za ▪ www.luddite.co.za ▪ S 34°12'50.5" E 019°12'24.1" ▪ ⌸ piecing.opener.embalmer ▪ **F** +27 (0)28-284-9045 ▪ **T +27 (0)28-284-9308/+27 (0)83-444-3537**

LuKa Wine Estate

Owners since 2014/5, Mark and Anneke Barnard's 'baby' is recognised as a pioneer of boutique winegrowing in Plettenberg Bay, and its sauvignon blanc has received wide acclaim and many awards. Now the Barnards' firstborn has a sibling, a pink from grapes sourced in the Riversdale area, and there's much excitement about a future bubbly. 'Watch this space!'

Rosé (NEW) ★★★ Unassuming but tasty **17** (82), mostly sauvignon, splash shiraz, partly oaked. Pinch of herbs on the generous, dry red-berry palate. WO W Cape. **Sauvignon Blanc** ★★★★ Delicate but fragrant gooseberry & passionfruit aromas, **17** (84) rounded mouthfeel without sacrificing freshness, moderate 13% alcohol allows for a 2nd glass/bottle. — HC

Location: Plettenberg Bay ▪ Map: Klein Karoo & Garden Route ▪ Map grid reference: C1 ▪ WO: Plettenberg Bay/Western Cape ▪ Est 2008 ▪ 1stB 2011 ▪ Tasting Mon-Sat 11-3.30 ▪ Owner(s) Mark & Anneke Barnard ▪ Cellarmaster(s)/winemaker(s) Anton Smal (Bramon Wines) ▪ Viticulturist(s) Mark Barnard ▪ ±7ha/2.5ha (pinot, chard, sauv) ▪ 8t/1,122cs own label 100% white ▪ PO Box 92 Knysna 6570 ▪ info@lukawines.co.za ▪ www.lukawines.co.za ▪ S 34° 2′ 28.14″ E 023° 15′ 57.56″ ▪ [map] mediating.buffets.landings ▪ F +27 (0)44-533-6782 ▪ T +27 (0)83-767-6218/+27 (0)82-498-7112

☐ **Luscious Hippos** *see United Nations of Wine*

Lutzville Vineyards (symbols)

One of SA's largest wineries, Lutzville Vineyards on the West Coast has appointed the first new cellarmaster in almost 15 years - Hendrik Myburgh - whose debut coincides with that of winemaker Christoff de Wet and viticulturist in Hugo Lambprecht. The latter joins Gideon Engelbrecht in overseeing the 2,100 hectares supplying fruit for 400,000 cases of own-label wines sold internationally. Most of the vineyards are near the Atlantic, allowing fresh morning breezes to cool the vineyards, slow ripening and protect acidities.

Francois le Vaillant range

★★★★ **Cabernet Sauvignon** (symbol) Strikes a fine balance between intense cassis fruit & enlivening tannins, **15** (87) easily soaks up 100% new oak.

★★★★ **Pinotage** (symbol) Supple & juicy black fruit on **16** (86), sweetly ripe & dense, with smooth tannins, noticeable acidity. New oak adds char hint but also structure for year/2 cellaring. No **15**.

★★★★☆ **Noble Late Harvest** (symbol) Worthy addition to botrytis dessert category. From chenin, hedonistic **12** (92) distinctive dried apricot & citrus peel flavour, lovely freshening acidity.

Diamond Collection

★★★★ **Cabernet Sauvignon** (symbol) Undaunting tannin structure the attraction in **15** (87), with voluptuous fruit, dusty & leathery nuances. Only 10-20% oak for these reds vs 100% for Le Vaillant. **14** untasted.

★★★★ **Ebenaezer** (symbol) Flagship mostly cab & shiraz, ruby cab for extra fruitiness. **15** (87) initially oaky, opens to black berry & clove; reined-in tannin & salty finish. Distinct tapenade savoury nuance, like Shiraz.

★★★★ **Oaked Chenin Blanc** (symbol) Full, rich & fruity **15** ★★★★ (84), judiciously wooded to preserve fine mineral notes. Succeeds **15** (87) from cooler Koekenaap & warmer Lutzville blocks. No **14**.

★★★★☆ **White Muscadel** (symbol) Delicate, yet no pushover, **16** (90) fortified muscat de Frontignan intoxicating bouquet of jasmine, litchi, pear & white peach. Silky, seductive, with just enough fortification to blush the cheek, let fruit shine.

Shiraz (symbol) ★★★★ Savoury & sweet vanilla overtones on **15** (84)'s sweet cherry fruit. Decent dryness, overt acidity; lacks varietal character but is appealing. **Sauvignon Blanc** (symbol) ★★★★ Round & soft **17** (84) tank sample, restrained cool green aromas; fruit-sweet entry with 14% alcohol padding out crisp acidity, adding body, texture. Not tasted: **Chardonnay**.

Lutzville range

Shiraz Rosé (symbol) ★★★ The star here. **18** (79) attractive spice & scrub hints, savoury overtones, satisfying vinosity & friendly alcohol. Driest of all these at 2.5 g/l sugar.

Cabernet Sauvignon ★★ Similar terse tannins as last vintage but less cushioning juiciness in **17** (72). **Merlot** (symbol) ★★★ Amicable **16** (78) offers black cherry fruit, bright acidity & malleable tannins. **Pinotage** ★★ Red fruit with Marmite toast overlay, **17** (73) just misses the mark of characterful previous. **Shiraz** ★★

Spice & fynbos nuances, tart red fruit, **17** (75) to drink now with a meal. Lightly oak-staved, combo French/American wood, as for all reds. **Chardonnay** ★★★ Won't disappoint fans of the unwooded style. **18** (77) rounded, with just enough lemony charm. **Chenin Blanc** ★★ Bouncy, peach-toned **18** (76) is smooth & soft courtesy few grams sugar. **Sauvignon Blanc** ★★★ No doubting the variety in **18** (77): trenchant grassy tones throughout, flavours not that persistent though. **Natural Sweet Red** ★★★ Berry-packed **NV** (77) sipper from chenin & pinotage, refreshing & light, with low ±8.5% alcohol, as all the Natural Sweets. **Natural Sweet Rosé** ★★ Loses the hanepoot & its grapey, musky attraction, so latest **NV** (73) from chenin & pinotage tad vapid by comparison. **Natural Sweet White** ★★★ Attractive **NV** (78) from chenin commendably intense tropical aromas & flavours. — CvZ

Location: Lutzville ▪ Map: Olifants River ▪ Map grid reference: B3 ▪ WO: Lutzville Valley ▪ Est 1961 ▪ 1stB 1980 ▪ Tasting & sales Mon-Fri 9-5 Sat 10-2 ▪ Closed Sun, Easter Sat, Dec 25 & Jan 1 ▪ Cellar tours by appt only ▪ Coffee shop & restaurant Mon-Fri 9-5 Sat 10-2 (kitchen closes 1hr earlier) ▪ Function/conference venue ▪ Owner(s) Lutzville Wingerde Beperk ▪ Cellarmaster(s) Hendrik Myburgh (Jan 2018) ▪ Winemaker(s) Brenda Thiart (Nov 2011), Andries Eygelaar (Jan 2014) & Christoff de Wet (Jan 2018) ▪ Viticulturist(s) Gideon Engelbrecht (Sep 2009) & Hugo Lampbrecht ▪ 2,100ha (cab, merlot, ptage, pinot, ruby cab, shiraz, chard, chenin, cbard, nouvelle, sauv, sem, viog) ▪ ±48,000t/400,000cs own label 15% red 85% white ▪ BRC, Fairtrade, IPW, WIETA ▪ PO Box 50 Lutzville 8165 ▪ catherine@lutzvillevineyards.com ▪ www.lutzville-vineyards.com ▪ S 31° 33' 35.9" E 018° 21' 0.2" ▪ 🖾 supreme.laced.tributary ▪ F +27 (0)27-217-1435 ▪ **T +27 (0)27-217-1516**

Lyngrove

Lyngrove 5-star country house and conference centre in the Helderberg overlooks close to 80 ha of vines, part of a palette from which the cellar/vineyard team of Danie van Tonder and André van den Berg produce four defined tiers - Platinum: best barrels for structure and ageing; Reserve: full, complex, bold oak; Lyngrove Collection: fruit forward, easy drinking; Lyngrove: méthode cap classique and other sparkling.

Platinum range

★★★★ **Pinotage** Deep rich fruit in **16** (88), plums/prunes, & vanilla/sweet spice, thanks to a combo French/American barrels. Voluptuous, already delicious, but there's enough structure for ageing.

★★★★ **Shiraz** Handsome big brother to Collection version in packaging & style. Loads of spice, 16 months in barrel, 40% new (as next), **16** (88)'s dark fruit an equal partner. Also scrub, violets, a curvy body.

★★★★ **Latitude** Cab with pinotage & shiraz, such berry intensity, that's your first impression. But oak-driven & compact **16** (88)'s tannins still firm, promising a long future. Still an infant.

★★★★ **Old Bush Vine Chenin Blanc** From 1980 block. Barrel fermented/aged in contrast to its sibling, **17** (88) shows nice combo of fruit & savoury: ginger & preserved melon, oatmeal, finishing long.

Reserve range

Shiraz-Pinotage ⓥ ★★★★ Using some American oak sweetens the spice array in **16** (85), cinnamon & nutmeg, adding to the blueberry/plum succulent appeal.

Cabernet Sauvignon (NEW) ★★★ Older barrels for **16** (79), lead pencils & blackcurrants, fruity freshness on the palate, & enough grip for food matching. **Chardonnay** ★★★ Partial oaking in **17** (83) gives gentle biscuit tones to the tangy-fresh peach/melon flavours.

Lyngrove Collection

Merlot ⓥ ⓥ ★★★★ Attractively perfumed **17** (84), raspberries & blackcurrants, violets, proudly show-casing merlot's unwooded attributes, the body streamlined, succulent. **Shiraz** ⓥ ★★★ Fruit-forward, unwooded **16** (82) celebrates shiraz in its dark plum, smoothly rounded, juicy approachability.

Pinotage ★★★ Lightly oaked, berry-rich **17** (78) is made for early drinking, offering a juicy, smooth texture. **Chenin Blanc** ★★★ Chenin reduced to its essence: apple & pear vibrancy in sleek **18** (81), a mineral note throughout. **Sauvignon Blanc** ★★★ Passionfruit underpinned by citrus, **18** (80) has fresh-fruity appeal. Discontinued: **Cabernet Sauvignon**.

Lyngrove range

Not tasted: **Pinot Noir Brut**, **Sparkling Brut**. — CR

Location/WO: Stellenbosch ▪ Map: Helderberg ▪ Map grid reference: B1 ▪ Est/1stB 2000 ▪ Tasting & sales by appt only ▪ Guest house ▪ Conferences (12 pax) ▪ Winemaker(s) Danie van Tonder (2015) ▪ Viticulturist(s) André van den Berg ▪ 76ha (cab, merlot, p verdot, ptage, shiraz, chard, chenin, sauv) ▪ 100,000cs own label 70% red 20% white 10% rosé ▪ WIETA ▪ PO Box 7275 Stellenbosch 7599 ▪ wine@lyngrove.co.za ▪ www.lyngrove.co.za ▪ S 34° 1′ 8.7″ E 018° 48′ 10.2″ ▪ ⓜ pomegranates.botch.faxed ▪ F +27 (0)21-880-0851 ▪ **T +27 (0)21-880-1221**

Lynx Wines ⓠ

Continuity comes from manager/winemaker Helgard van Schalkwyk after the change in ownership of this Franschhoek boutique winery in 2018 from one international family (Spanish-born Dieter Sellmeyer's) to another (Germans Manuel and Brigitte Konen). The style stays 'intimate and hands-on' across the mostly red range, including the tweaked Rhône blend and the pinnacle wine, showcasing the cellar's two best barrels.

Ultra Premium range

★★★★☆ **The Lynx** Chameleon flagship switches from 100% cab to equal cab, cab franc, splash merlot in **16** ⑨②. Bold, forthcoming & brawny, a gush of super-ripe blackcurrant fruit borne on sturdy tannins. Year new barrels, further year 2nd fill. Needs time to unfurl.

Premium range

★★★★ **Cabernet Sauvignon** Steely varietal edginess back in **17** ⑧⑦ after jammy **16** ★★★★☆ ⑧④, with subtle leafy, earthy tones spicing up rich cassis fruit. Solid tannin backbone, well-defined shape & structure. Also in magnum.

★★★★ **Cabernet Franc** Exudes varietal earthiness, iodine & pencil shavings, with a satisfying black fruit core. **17** ⑧⑧ focused & lean, promising benefits from ageing.

★★★★ **Shiraz** As in **16** ★★★★ ⑧⑤, toasted mocha flavours to the fore but **17** ⑧⑦'s cherry & plum fruit more than a match. Silky tannins & supple body; spicy & herbal scrub threads add interest.

★★★★ **Xanache** 4-way Cape Bordeaux blend, cab franc-led **17** ⑧⑦ has enticing blackcurrant fruitiness with dusty, earthy backdrop. Medium bodied, smooth textured & balanced.

★★★★ **SMG** Shiraz & mourvèdre drop viognier, embrace grenache in **17** ⑧⑥. Plush & supple, with charming spicy fruit, hints of tobacco & caramel from year oak, 30% new. **16** ⑧⑥ 'SMV' still available.

★★★★ **Viognier** Oak-driven **17** ⑧⑥ has typical white peach aromas, with vanilla & cinnamon spicing. Full bodied, with pleasing rounded shape, creamy texture, lengthy finish. 50% barrel fermented.

Grenache ★★★★☆ Jammy berry fruit on silky texture, highlighted with glacé cherries. **17** ⑧④ Ribena juiciness & focused acidity. **Pinot Noir** ★★★★ Rosepetals & raspberries on light-bodied **17** ⑧⑤, followed by salty-savoury notes. Juicy & appealing, but lacking intensity of **16** ★★★★ ⑧⑧. In abeyance: **Golden Lynx**.

Classic range

Vino Tinto ★★★☆ Bits of everything, mostly shiraz & cab, in **17** ⑦⑧. Quirky quince-rhubarb fruit profile, light & juicy if unlingering. **Blanc de Noir** ★★★ Pretty salmon-hued **18** ⑧⓪ from merlot, rosepetal scent & juicy berry fruit, acid prominent on dry palate. **Tardio** ★★★ Sweetness from 51 g/l sugar is well tempered by tingling acidity. **18** ⑦⑧ late harvested viognier rather light & brief, for casual quaffing. Modest 11.3 % alcohol. **Vino Blanco** ★★★★ Pleasantly oak-free **18** ⑧③ rousanne-viognier-grenache blanc blend shows lively fruit, perky acidity. Fresh & light-hearted. — GdB

Location/map/WO: Franschhoek ▪ Map grid reference: C4 ▪ Est/1stB 2002 ▪ Tasting, sales & cellar tours Mon-Thu 10—5 Fri/Sat 10-3 Sun/pub hols by appt ▪ Fee R50 (tasting & tour) ▪ Owner(s) Brigitte & Manuel Konen ▪ Winemaker(s) Helgard van Schalkwyk (Nov 2010) & Pierre Louw (Apr 2018) ▪ Viticulturist(s) Quinton Daniels ▪ 26ha/11ha (cabs s/f, grenache, merlot, mourv, p verdot, pinot, shiraz, viog) ▪ 130t/8,000cs own label 46% red 13% white 41% rosé ▪ IPW ▪ PO Box 566 Franschhoek 7690 ▪ winemaker@lynxwines.co.za ▪ www.lynxwines.co.za ▪ S 33° 51′ 46.1″ E 019° 2′ 14.6″ ▪ ⓜ jive.diction.degenerate ▪ F +27 (0)21-867-0397 ▪ **T +27 (0)21-867-0406**

☐ **Maankloof** see Mountain River Wines

Maanschijn

Paul Hoogwerf and Doug Mylrea are self-styled 'young-buck winemakers, seeking to craft epicurean wines from stunning Cape vineyards'. The fresh, minimal-intervention wines are made in a renovated barn between Hermanus and Stanford, beneath a peak called Maanschynkop, which gives the brand its 'moonshine' name. Production is steadily increasing. The first wines all came from Voor Paardeberg fruit, but they found two Stellenbosch vineyards to work with and plan to release three new wines based on muscat.

★★★★☆ **Kolonel Mostert en die Twee Souties** Cinsaut, shiraz & grenache, partly destemmed, on **17** ⑨②; more convincing now than as an infant sample. Gorgeous pure fruit fragrance, supple, easy tannins & fresh acid. Not intense, but more vinous than many lightish wines (13% alcohol).

★★★★ **Easy, Tiger** Light apricot-gold hue on **17** ★★★★☆ ⑨⓪ (sampled last year; benefiting from time) from grenache gris, as was previewed **16** ⑧⑦. Not about primary fruit, but subtly intense flavours: precise, elegant, fresh & dry, flirting with both charm & austerity. 12% alcohol. Natural winemaking, as for all.

★★★★ **Spin Cycle** Gold hue & oxidative bruised apple notes on **17** ⑧⑦ from verdelho, but fresh & lively. Tannic touch from skin contact. Expresses early picking & style more than variety or origin. 12% alcohol.

Not tasted: **Goldmember**. — TJ

Location: Hermanus ▪ WO: Voor Paardeberg ▪ Est 2016 ▪ Closed to public ▪ Winemaker(s) Douglas Mylrea & Paul Hoogwerf ▪ info@maanschijn.co.za ▪ www.maanschijn.co.za

Maastricht Estate

On their Durbanville farm dating back to 1702, Wheaty Louw and son Thys are happy with how their dryland vineyards coped under drought conditions, noting '2018 grape quality was outstanding'. With Etienne Louw (Altydgedacht) consulting, wine production is increasing and so they're planning a tasting venue, having found 'the perfect spot'.

★★★★ **Sauvignon Blanc** ⊘ A real summer celebrator, vibrantly fruity & exuberant - nettles, white peaches, crunchy green apples, capsicum & crushed green herbs all leap out of the glass in **18** ⑧⑦.

Cabernet Sauvignon ★★★★ More concentrated **17** ⑧⑤, red & blue berries join cigar smoke & coffee on smooth palate with tannins & well-integrated 50% new oak. **Merlot** ⑨ ★★★★ Forthright savoury aromas - meat, smoked bacon, sawdust - with good tannin grip, **16** ⑧④'s 75% new oak well absorbed.

Pinot Noir ⊘ ★★★★ Fresh fruit (cherry, strawberry) made more complex by forest floor nuance, **17** ⑧③ toastiness from 40% new oak but in harmony with fruit & lingering savoury note. **Pinotage** ★★★★ Plum, dark cherry & fragrant wild herbs in a generously fruited body, **17** ⑧⑤ creamy chocolate from 75% new wood. In abeyance: **Shiraz**. — WB

Location: Durbanville ▪ Map: Durbanville, Philadelphia & Darling ▪ Map grid reference: C7 ▪ WO: Cape Town ▪ Est 1702 ▪ 1stB 2009 ▪ Tasting by appt only, for groups of 4-8 people - contact Annelize Louw T +27 (0)82-570-9933 to arrange ▪ Owner(s) Johannes Beyers Louw ▪ Cellarmaster(s) Thys Louw jnr (Jan 2009) ▪ Winemaker(s) Etienne Louw (Feb 2017) ▪ Viticulturist(s) Johannes Beyers Louw (1986) & Thys Louw jnr ▪ 90ha (cab, ptage, pinot, shiraz, sauv) ▪ ±1,000t/3,000cs own label 40% red 60% white ▪ wine@maastricht. co.za ▪ www.maastricht.co.za ▪ S 33° 50' 22.86" E 018° 35' 26.79" ▪ 🖅 whisker.eared.moisten ▪ F +27 (0)86-521-9062 ▪ T +27 (0)21-976-1995

☐ **Maestro** see DeMorgenzon

Maiden Wine Cellars

Helderberg negociant Danie Hattingh's export business was founded in the mid-1990s with America and Europe as focuses, gradually expanding to Asia. His current release is a red blend, Private Reserve '16.

Location: Gordon's Bay ▪ Est 1995 ▪ 1stB 1999 ▪ Tasting/tours by appt; also tailor-made wine tours (max 6 people) ▪ Owner(s) Danie Hattingh ▪ 5,700cs own label 100% red ▪ Other export label: Iwayini ▪ PO Box 185 Gordon's Bay 7151 ▪ mwines@mweb.co.za ▪ www.maidenwines.co.za ▪ F +27 (0)86-688-1177 ▪ T +27 (0)82-554-9395

Maison

Leading SA homeware/furniture guru Chris Weylandt invites you to 'make yourself at home' at his casual-contemporary Franschhoek boutique estate, now boasting one of chef Liam Tomlin's popular Chefs Warehouse restaurants. A key consideration is that the 'global tapas' on offer here should pair well with the characterful wines made by self-described 'wine process facilitator, viticulturist, foreman, plaasboer' Antwan Bondesio, who is happiest wandering through the vineyards with his four-legged assistant, Eames.

★★★★ **Shiraz** Aged 16 months in French oak (third new), **15** ⑧⑧ lusciously full bodied, vanilla-licked dark fruit lifted by pepper spice & fresh acidity, in balance despite 15% alcohol.

★★★★☆ **Chardonnay** Three fruit parcels, vinified separately in French oak (30% new, 9 months, partial malo), combine seamlessly in elegant **17** ⑨② (13.7% alcohol), redolent of citrus, pear & melon with honey-nut richness & creamy texture balanced by tangy freshness.

★★★★ **Single Vineyard Chenin Blanc** Unwooded yet richly textured from 4 months on lees, imparting very pleasant yeasty undertone to fresh citrus fruit in **18** ⑧⑦. From registered single block.

★★★★ **Viognier** Very fragrant & dry, **17** ⑧⑦ improves on **16** ★★★★ ⑧⑤ in its tangy stonefruit, silky mouthfeel (from 6 months mostly older oak), fresh acidity & long finish.

★★★★ **Straw Wine** From air-dried chenin, fermented in older oak, **16** ⑧⑨ intensely sweet but uncloying thanks to tangy apricot & citrus fruit, acidic lift & dry-seeming finish with savoury hint. 500 ml.

Blanc de Noir ★★★★ Pink-gold **17** ⑧④'s barrel ferment creates creamy backdrop to tart red-berry fruit. Dry, fresh & food friendly, like also-tasted **18** ⑧⑤, with ruby grapefruit finish. Both from shiraz. **Méthode Cap Classique** ★★★ Chardonnay sparkling, bone-dry (zero dosage), **11** ⑧② fresh & steely with Cream Cracker biscuit note. Occasional release: **Single Vineyard Chenin Blanc Reserve**. — JG

Location/map/WO: Franschhoek ▪ Map grid reference: C3 ▪ Est 2005 ▪ 1stB 2008 ▪ Tasting & sales Mon-Sun 10-5 ▪ Chefs Warehouse @ Maison ▪ Owner(s) Chris Weylandt & Kim Smith ▪ Winemaker(s)/viticulturist(s) Antwan Bondesio ▪ 11ha/4.5ha (malbec, shiraz, chard, chenin, viog) ▪ 50% red 50% white ▪ PO Box 587 Franschhoek 7690 ▪ jacobus.lochner@maisonestate.co.za ▪ www.maisonestate.co.za ▪ S 33° 53' 09.7" E 019° 4' 39.80" ▪ ⓦ unanimously.unforgettable.goods ▪ F +27 (0)21-876-2116 ▪ **T +27 (0)21-876-2116**

Maison de Teijger ⓠ

Durbanville anaesthetist and small-batch vintner Charl van Teijlingen and wife Danél since 2004 have vinified classic varieties in their De Tyger Street home's double-garage for marketing off-site through wine clubs, among others. In addition to the regulars listed below, Charl and Danél make wines according to a chosen theme: chardonnay this time, bushvine reds and MCC sparkling to follow.

Chardonnay range ⓝⓔⓦ

Chardonnay Wooded ★★★☆ Broad peach & orange fullness on **17** ⑧③, nuanced palate with oak (none new) well knit. Fresh, juicy & pleasant, with long tail. **Chardonnay Unwooded** ★★★ Shows trademark orange blossom & spice, nice lees richness & breadth; **17** ⑧② tangy & vibrant.

Malbec range

Malbec Reserve ⓠ ★★★ Exotic **15** ⑧① , with rum-&-raisin spicing, mandarin & plum notes; salty, zesty & mouthfilling. Love it or hate it - it definitely makes a statement!

Petit Verdot range

Petit Verdot ⓠ ★★★★ Plummy, vanilla-dusted **15** ⑧④ takes step up with fresher acid-tannin structure; despite ripeness, remarkably unheavy & sippable. Also in magnum, like Malbec.

Sauvignon Blanc range

Sauvignon Blanc Unwooded ★★★ Cool-climate Durbanville fruit makes **18** ⑧⓪ leaner, zestier than previous. Bright, tangy & succulent. — FM

Location/WO: Durbanville ▪ Map: Durbanville, Philadelphia & Darling ▪ Map grid reference: D7 ▪ Est/1stB 2004 ▪ Tasting Sat by appt only ▪ Owner(s) Charl van Teijlingen ▪ Cellarmaster(s) Charl van Teijlingen (2004) ▪ Winemaker(s) Charl van Teijlingen, with Danél van Teijlingen (both 2004) & Matthew van Teijlingen (2016) ▪ 5-9t/±300cs own label 80% red 20% white ▪ PO Box 2703 Durbanville 7551 ▪ cteijlingen@gmail.com ▪ S 33° 49' 02.20" E 018° 39' 01.56" ▪ ⓦ handover.stoically.piercingly ▪ F +27 (0)21-975-0806 ▪ **T +27 (0)21-975-0806/+27 (0)83-456-9410**

☐ **Maison de Vin** see Cronier Wines

Major's Hill Estate ⓠ ⑪ ⓐ ⓞ ⓐ

Dewald Louw and his team were deeply saddened the past year by the passing of their 'great and exceptional winemaker', Alkie van der Mewe. Alkie was on board from inception of the Major's Hill venture in the

early 2000s on Robertson's Klipdrift farm. The brand home (and tasting venue) has since moved to Karoo1 Farm Estate near De Doorns. Juhan Hunlun, Alkie's successor, 'will be making delectable new wines soon'.

Selected Vineyards range

Cabernet Sauvignon ★★★ Earthy nuance to brambly black fruit on spicy **15** ⑧, medium bodied & uncomplicatedly pleasant. Also in magnum. **Merlot** ★★★ Loamy mulberry & cherry spice on touch unknit **13** ⑧, oak (all old) & fruit needing more time to harmonise. **Pinotage** ★★★ Approachable **14** ⑧ neatly balances spicy succulence of raspberry fruit & light squeeze of dry tannin from 24 months in old oak. **Shiraz** ★★★★ Cranberry & plum appeal on pliable, ripe & rewarding **13** ⑧, light tannin structure from same oaking as other reds. Not tasted: **Chardonnay**, **Sauvignon Blanc**. — WB, FM

Location: De Doorns • Map: Worcester • Map grid reference: D1 • WO: Robertson • 1stB 2002 • Tasting & sales Mon-Fri 9.30–1 & 2–5 Sat 10–4 • Closed Good Fri, Dec 25/26 • Facilities for children • Karoo1 Farm Estate: hotel, restaurant, conferences, weddings/functions, walking & MTB trails • Owner(s) Dewald Louw • Winemaker(s) Juhan Hunlun (Jun 2018) • 52ha (cab, merlot, ptage, shiraz, chard, sauv) • 15,000cs own label 60% red 40% white + 15,000cs for customers & 100,000L bulk • Karoo1 Farm Estate, N1 – R318, De Doorns 6875 • info@majorshill.co.za • www.majorshill.co.za • S 33° 23' 10.49" E 019° 50' 2.62" • ⌖ flaunted.achiever. yellowed • **T** +27 (0)23-358-2131

☐ **Makulu** see Imbuko Wines
☐ **Malan de Versailles** see Versailles

Malanot Wines   ⓛ ⓖ

His grandfather and father having been grape farmers in Paardeberg, it was written in the stars that Marius Malan would be involved with vines too. His journey to date has included making wine, consulting and qualifying as a Cape Wine Master and judge. This boutique vigneron ranges far and wide sourcing grapes for clients and his own range, which is also available for tasting at Oppie Dorp wine bar in Stellenbosch.

Family Reserve range

★★★★ **Triton Syrah** ⓛ Handsome **16** ⑧ has personality. Black plums, pepper & scrub, savoury spice; broad shouldered & muscular, everything beautifully in place for a long future. WO Paarl.

★★★★☆ **Chardonnay** ⓛ Bunch fermented/aged in barrel, natural yeasts. Restrained elegance in **16** ㉒ from Elgin & Franschhoek, nothing showy, citrus & toasted almonds seamlessly meshed. Lovely poise, assurance. Last tasted was **14** ㉑ from Stellenbosch.

Malanot range

★★★★ **Cherry Blossom** ⓛ Red blend, merlot rules. Cherry tobacco, plummy fruit, some chocolate, tannins firm but ripe, **13** ★★★★ ⑧ characterful but doesn't quite match last-tasted **11** ⑧. WO W Cape. **Vino Café Pinotage** ⓛ ★★★ With pronounced mocha styling, **16** ⑧ preview has smooth appeal, ends dry with a gentle grip. Wellington WO. **Rosé** ⓛ ★★★ Dry **17** ⑧ ex tank shows shiraz's red berries but is more than just fruity, there's a herbal touch, will be a nice food companion. **Bush Pig Chenin Blanc** ⓛ ★★★★ Pre-bottled **17** ⑧ delivers variety's trademark thatch & quince, some savoury notes though unoaked. Curvy, flavourful. **Sauvignon Blanc** ★★★★ Pineapple & gooseberry typicity on tangy **18** ⑧, balanced & long. Perfect poolsider. **Flower Pot** ⓛ ★★★★ Partly oaked chenin/grenache blanc & 4 others, **14** ⑧ melon & stonefruit, touch vanilla. Some bottle-age honey, but in a good way. WO W Cape. — FM

Location/map: Stellenbosch • Map grid reference: E3 • WO: Stellenbosch/Western Cape/Paarl/Wellington • Est/1stB 2006 • Tasting & sales by appt • Cellar tours by appt & during harvest only • Owner(s) Malanot Wine Projects cc • Cellarmaster(s)/winemaker(s)/viticulturist(s) Marius Malan (Jan 2006) • 500t/40,000cs own label 80% red 20% white + 2,000cs for clients • PO Box 592 Strand 7139 • marius@malanot.com • www. malanotwines.co.za • S 33° 52' 57.71" E 018° 50' 49.39" • ⌖ shears.yards.seat • **T** +27 (0)72-124-7462

☐ **Malkopbaai** see Teubes Family Wines
☐ **Mandela** see House of Mandela

MAN Family Wines   ⓛ

Reborn Stellenbosch farm Lievland is the new home of MAN Family Wines, founded in 2001 by José Conde of Stark-Condé and brothers Tyrrel and Philip Myburgh of Joostenberg to 'make wines we'd like to drink'. A signal success by any measure, MAN has since effectively added three noughts to its initial tally of 300 cases, and currently ships to 27 countries. The emphasis remains on quality and excellent value, and supportive wives Marie, Anette and Nicky kindly continue to lend the brand their initials.

MAN Family Wines range

★★★★ **Skaapveld Shiraz** ⊘ Improving on **15** ★★★☆ ⑧⑤, **16** ⑧⑥'s bold plum & spice is tempered by savoury succulence & good concentration. Layered & medium bodied. Cradle of oak from year in older American barrels.

Méthode Cap Classique Brut ⊘ ⑦ ★★★★ Oystershell & lemon tang counter richer cream, biscuit & sourdough notes on **NV** ⑧⑤ dry sparkler from chenin. Quite complex, structured & rich from 13 months on lees & dab oaked wine added with dosage.

Ou Kalant Cabernet Sauvignon ⊘ ★★★☆ Ripe softness & buxom appeal on plummy **17** ⑧⑤. Light fynbos & spice nuance from oak (30% wooded, 5% new American, rest older). Dryland Agter Paarl vines unless noted. **Jan Fiskaal Merlot** ⊘ ★★★★ Easy-drinking **16** ⑧④ appeals with its blueberry, tobacco & sweet spice flavours. Well structured & approachable. Dabs cab & tempranillo. **Bosstok Pinotage** ★★★ Light coffee note to raspberry-toned **16** ⑧②, off younger bushvines. Gentle squeeze of dry tannin from quarter American oak, 20% new. **Padstal Chardonnay** ★★★★ Stonefruit & citrus on fresh **17** ⑧③, which marries tank- & barrel-matured portions well. Good lees breadth & length. **Free-Run Steen Chenin Blanc** ★★★★ Pear & elderflower brightness to broad, leesy **18** ⑧③ from bushvines. Unoaked, succulent & fresh, with long aftertaste. **Warrelwind Sauvignon Blanc** ★★★★ Granadilla tropicality mingles with taut flint & lemon zest on structured, dry **18** ⑧③. Lees ageing & 15% semillon add texture & palate weight. Fruit widely sourced.

Essay range

Syrah-Mourvèdre-Grenache-Cinsault ⊘ ★★★★ Toned blue & black fruit on supple, spicy **16** ⑧⑤ blend of Agter Paarl grapes. Lithe & ripe, gentle oak frame supports fruit. **Chenin Blanc-Viognier-Roussanne** ★★★★ Subtle lily & elderflower delicacy on fresh & bright **18** ⑧③, unoaked. Pineapple & peach tropicality, lively acidity & long finish. — FM

Location: Stellenbosch/Paarl = WO: Coastal/Western Cape = Est 2001 = Tasting & sales at Lievland Vineyards = Owner(s) MAN Vintners (Pty) Ltd = Cellarmaster(s) Tyrrel Myburgh (2001) = Winemaker(s) Riaan Möller (Dec 2016) = 280,000cs own label 60% red 40% white = PO Box 37 Klapmuts 7625 = info@manwines.com = www. manwines.com = **T +27 (0)21-875-3026**

Manley Private Cellar ⑨ ⑪ ⑩ ⑩

One of the farms that make beautiful, mountain-encircled Tulbagh a must for the wine traveller, Manley offers accommodation, meals, function venues and outdoor attractions. The small wine range mostly travels to export markets with Trevor, Manley's resident owl, watching from some of the front labels. Current (untasted) releases are Cabernet Sauvignon '15, Pinotage and Shiraz '14, and Thatch House Red NV.

Location/map: Tulbagh = Map grid reference: F5 = Est/1stB 2002 = Tasting Mon-Fri by appt, Sat/Sun 10-3 = Fee R30, waived on purchase = Cellar tours by appt = Closed Good Fri, Dec 25 & Jan 1 = Luxury B&B = Restaurant Wed-Fri 12—9 Sat/Sun 9-9 = Wedding & conference facilities = Chapel = Owner(s) Manley Wine Lodge (Pty) Ltd = Winemaker(s)/viticulturist(s) Werner Barkhuizen = 38ha/8ha (cab, merlot, ptage, shiraz) = PO Box 318 Tulbagh 6820 = werner@manleywinelodge.co.za = www.manleywinelodge.co.za = S 33° 16' 15.8" E 019° 8' 43.8" = ◻ modifying.escapees.glistened = **F** +27 (0)23-230-0057 = **T +27 (0)23-230-0582**

☐ **Manor House** *see* Nederburg Wines
☐ **Marais Family** *see* Wonderfontein

Marianne Wine Estate ⑨ ⑪ ⑩ ⑩ ⑧ ⑥

The multifaceted property on the Simonsberg slopes between Stellenbosch and Paarl, named for a French national emblem and owned by Bordeaux's Dauriac family, is always abustle. Four hectares of virgin land are being planted with classic red varieties, and on the visitor experience side an old residence on the estate has been converted into luxury guest accommodation. In the cellar, winemaker Jos van Wyk has introduced acacia wood for some of the white-wine maturation.

Marianne range

★★★★ **Cabernet Sauvignon** ⊛ A rich body with finesse & intensity. **15** ★★★★★ (93)'s complex palate shows good purity of spicy blackberry fruit, notes of vanilla & hints of salty liquorice. Dab shiraz adds complexity & breadth. 40% new oak. Ageworthy. **14** (87) first since **09** (87).

★★★★ **Pinotage** Sumptuous **16** (88), wild heather & savoury undertones to dense plum & spicecake flavours. Careful oaking (30% new, 18 months) & inherent freshness ensure balance & vibrancy.

★★★★ **Desirade** Bordeaux blend **14** (89), 60/40 merlot & cab, more serious than **13** ★★★★ (85), shows excellent concentration of dark berry fruit around supple core of ripe tannin. Drinks very well now.

★★★★ **Sauvignon Blanc** Gains richness & vanilla from barrelled portion in **17** (88). Intriguing herbal & floral notes, a peach nuance, long waxy-savoury finish partly from drop semillon. Could age interestingly.

Merlot ② ★★★★ Plum & prune fruit, candyfloss sweetness & faint spiciness very appealing, though **14** (84)'s firm tannins & 14.7% alcohol need food. Simonsberg–Stellenbosch WO, as next 2. **Shiraz** ② ★★★★ Attractive dinner companion with black pepper & cassis notes, supple tannins & 60% new oak in **14** (84).

Cape Blend ② ★★★★ Merlot, cab & shiraz, **14** (84) shy on nose, slightly astringent on finish. Seems more 'worked' than other reds. **Rosé** ⊘ ★★★ Pretty-in-pink **17** (82) is floral & fragrant, offers delicate berry flavours & mouthwatering dry finish. From 2 white & 2 black grapes. Not tasted: **Floreal**. — WB

Location/map: Stellenbosch ▪ Map grid reference: G1 ▪ WO: Western Cape/Simonsberg–Paarl ▪ Est/1stB 2004 ▪ Tasting, sales & cellar tours Mon–Sun & pub hols 10-7 (summer)/10-6 (winter) ▪ Fee R70/5 wines; R115/wine & biltong pairing ▪ Cellar tour, barrel tasting & vertical tasting of flagship wines ▪ Meat & cheese platters ▪ Picnics ▪ The Floreal Brasserie, www.floreal.co.za ▪ Panoramic tasting deck ▪ Gift shop ▪ 4-star accommodation ▪ Owner(s) Dauriac family ▪ Winemaker(s) Jos van Wyk (Mar 2016), with Thierry Haberer (consultant) ▪ Viticulturist(s) Ernest Manuel (Sep 2017) ▪ 36ha/±26ha (cabs s/f, cinsaut, grenache, merlot, mourv, ptage, shiraz, sauv, viog) ▪ 100t/16,000cs own label 90% red 5% white 5% rosé ▪ PO Box 7300 Stellenbosch 7599 ▪ info@mariannewinefarm.co.za, hospitality@mariannewinefarm.co.za ▪ www.marian-newines.com ▪ S 33° 49' 57.6" E 018° 53' 37.4" ▪ ⬚ busting.waffle.retracing ▪ **T +27 (0)21-875-5040**

☐ **Marimba** see Southern Sky Wines

Marklew Family Wines ⓟ ⓒ

Siblings Bill and Haidee Marklew produce their wines on De Goede Sukses estate's prime Simonsberg slopes, where formerly their parents grew grapes sold to top labels. Winemaker Neil Strydom works in a 180-year-old cellar (renovations in the early 2000s included innovative combi-concrete tanks) and assists Bill in the vineyards. Untasted, but due at press time, was their first blanc de blancs sparkling.

★★★★ **Cabernet Sauvignon** Ripe mulberry & blackcurrant aromas dusted with cedar, **17** (87) persistent, with deep blueberry palate, dense tannin structure. No **16**.

★★★★ **Cape Flora Pinotage** ⊘ Perfumed **17** (88) same generous fruit as last. Primary berry & violet notes, ripe juicy core & supple tannins for now or keeping a few years. WO Coastal. **16** untasted.

★★★★ **Shiraz Reserve** Widely sourced **17** (87), plum & Xmas cake spicing, youthful & firm with taut tannin grip, heady 15% alcohol, yet enough savoury appeal for food pairing.

★★★★ **Family Reserve** ⊛ Bordeaux red with cab (52%), dashes merlot, cab franc. Laudable **16** (88) authentic forest fruit, oak spice & minerality. Poised & full, dark berry persistence. Worth keeping.

★★★★ **Chardonnay** Svelte **16** (88)'s alluring nectarine & pear interwoven with almond & vanilla ex 13 months French oak. Creamy & mouthfilling but fresh, too, with judicious 13% alcohol, enlivening acidity.

Merlot ★★★★ Enticing red & dark fruit aromas accented by dark chocolate & herbal notes. **16** (85) approachable, with malleable tannins, like previous, but more complex. **Sauvignon Blanc** ★★★ Pick-me-up **18** (81) zesty & bright, packed with ripe tropical fruit, lifted grassy finish. Occasional release: **Capensis**. — GM

Location/map: Stellenbosch ▪ Map grid reference: F1 ▪ WO: Simonsberg–Stellenbosch/Coastal/Western Cape ▪ Est 1970 ▪ 1stB 2003 ▪ Tasting, sales & tours by appt ▪ Tour groups (max 20) ▪ Private/business functions for small groups ▪ Walks ▪ Mountain biking ▪ Conservation area ▪ Owner(s) Marklew family (Edward Dudley, Edward William, Lyn & Haidee) ▪ Winemaker(s) Neil Strydom (Oct 2015) ▪ Viticulturist(s) Billy Marklew (Jun 2001), with Neil Strydom (Oct 2015) ▪ 58ha/45ha (cabs s/f, merlot, ptage, shiraz, chard, sauv) ▪

±300t/5,000cs own label 65% red 30% white 5% MCC ▪ IPW ▪ PO Box 17 Elsenburg 7607 ▪ wine@marklew.co.za ▪ www.marklew.co.za ▪ S 33° 50' 35.7" E 018° 51' 50.3" ▪ ⌑ item.puzzles.charge ▪ F +27 (0)21-884-4412 ▪ T +27 (0)21-884-4412

☐ **Martindale** see Wine-of-the-Month Club
☐ **Marvelous** see Yardstick Wines
☐ **Mary Delany** see Botanica Wines
☐ **Mary Le Bow Trust** see Bruce Jack Wines

Maske Wines ⓠ

Erich and Janine Maske contract with various winemakers and viticulturists to produce a line-up of wines for export. No newer vintages tasted this year; the '11s, reviewed a while back, are still available for tasting/sale at the Wellington home-farm by appointment.

Leeumasker range

Cape Blend ⓠ ★★★★ Pinotage with cab, shiraz & minor others, previewed **11** ⑷84 offers flowers & black cherries, ripe but balanced fruity flavours.

Maske range

Tattoo ⓠ ★★★ Named for a memorable tattoo parlour visit, **11** ⑺78 very ripe & fruit-sweet, easy to drink shiraz & cab combo. WO W Cape. Not tasted: **Cabernet Sauvignon, Merlot, Chenin Blanc.** — CvZ

Location/map: Wellington ▪ Map grid reference: C4 ▪ WO: Coastal/Western Cape ▪ Est/1stB 2000 ▪ Tasting & sales by appt only ▪ Closed Ash Wed, Easter Fri/Sun & Dec 25 ▪ Owner(s) Erich & Janine Maske ▪ Winemaker(s)/viticulturist(s) outsourced ▪ 7ha/5ha (cab, merlot, shiraz, chenin) ▪ 80% red 20% white ▪ Klein Waterval PO Box 206 Wellington 7654 ▪ laureat@iafrica.com ▪ www.maskewines.co.za ▪ S 33° 40' 4.2" E 019° 2' 37.3" ▪ ⌑ clutches.pocket.triathlete ▪ F +27 (0)21-873-3408 ▪ T +27 (0)21-873-3407

☐ **Mason's Hill** see Mason's Winery

Mason's Winery ⓠ ⑪

Derek Clift tends small parcels of vines on his stonemason family's Paarl Mountain farm (and quarry) for vinifying in shared cellar space in town. The current vintage of Derek's speciality, a low-sulphur Shiraz, is '18, available for tasting/purchase by arrangement at local steakhouse Hussar Grill.

Location/map: Paarl ▪ Map grid reference: E6 ▪ Est/1stB 2001 ▪ Tasting & sales by appt at Hussar Grill, Paarl, adjacent to cellar ▪ Owner(s) JA Clift (Pty) Ltd - Clift family ▪ Cellarmaster(s)/winemaker(s)/viticulturist(s) Derek Clift (2001) ▪ 47ha/4ha (shiraz) ▪ 30t/2,000cs own label 100% red ▪ Main Str Suider-Paarl 7646 ▪ masons@cliftgranite.co.za ▪ www.cliftgranite.co.za ▪ S 33° 45' 20.5" E 018° 57' 42.6" ▪ ⌑ touchy.dampen.dwelled ▪ F +27 (0)21-863-1601 ▪ T +27 (0)83-228-7855

☐ **Maties** see Stellenbosch University Welgevallen Cellar
☐ **Matilda's Secret** see Benguela Cove Lagoon Wine Estate
☐ **Matys** see Diemersdal Estate

Matzikama Organic Cellar

Joining the standout chenin blanc from this boutique family venture helmed by Klaas Coetzee is a still-rare varietal bottling of petite sirah (durif). Both the wines are from parcels in maritime Koekenaap ward on the West Coast, and certified organic, as are the almost 220 hectares of vines Klaas nurtures for organic and no-sulphur-added powerhouse, Stellar Winery, where he has also been winemaker since 2010.

Coetzee Family Wines range

★★★★★ **Blomveld se Vlei Chenin Blanc** ⓥ Intra-block selection, as last, impressive **17** ⑼92 rich & mouthfilling from regular bâtonnage, usual generous white peach & pear enlivened by acidity & wine's characteristic saline element. Longer oaking (18 months, all old) is judicious. WO Koekenaap.

Blomveld se Vlei Petite Sirah (NEW) ⓥ ★★★★ From Koekenaap vines, fresh & quietly confident **16** ⑻85 deep plum & prune fruit, fresh herb nuance. Still tight, terse, but promising, allow few years to settle & show at best. 18 months 2nd fill oak. Discontinued: **Blomveld se Vlei Pinot Noir.** — CvZ

Location: Vredendal ▪ WO: Olifants River/Koekenaap ▪ Est/1stB 2001 ▪ Owner(s)/winemaker(s)/viticulturist(s) Klaas Coetzee ▪ 12ha/2.5ha (cab, shiraz, tannat) ▪ 24t 100% red ▪ PO Box 387 Vredendal 8160 ▪ klaas@ matzikamawyn.co.za ▪ www.matzikamawyn.co.za ▪ 🖂 crisply.broadened.dimly ▪ **T +27 (0)82-801-3737**

☐ **Maxim** see Goedverwacht Wine Estate
☐ **Mbali** see Zidela Wines

McGregor Wines ⓠ ♿

The industrious producer-owned winery near famously sleepy McGregor village has turned 70, having been founded in 1948 and crushed the first berries a short time later, on 21 February 1950. They've come a long way, the delighted and proud team say, and their vision for the next seven decades is to produce innovative wines that excite and inspire their growers, the community and of course lovers of wine.

Winemaker's Reserve range

★★★★ **Cabernet Sauvignon** ⓠ Good varietal expression in **15** ㉇: cassis, lead pencil & smoky oak flavours, firm tannin structure with depth & length, delicious dried herb, fynbos aftertaste.

McGregor range

Colombard ✓ ⓟ ★★★ Delectable **18** ㉜ is a fragrant orchard of ripe guavas, made moreish by hint of sweetness & intriguing waft of sweet spice. **The Delicious Monster** ✓ ⓟ ★★★ Ripe, tropical fragrance on expressive **18** ㉚ from mostly chenin, splashes chardonnay & muscat. Delicious indeed.

Pinotage ★★★ Unwooded, **17** ㉙'s fresh red-berry fruit comes with hint of spice & pleasing grip. **Shiraz** ★★ Sweet red fruit on **16** ⑦, contrasting stern dusty oak. **Cabernet Sauvignon-Merlot** ★★ Oak char aromatic overlay on **17** ㉓, fleeting dark-berry fruit. **Chardonnay** ★★★ Unoaked, friendly **18** ㉙, ripe apple flavours & a lemon twist. **Chenin Blanc** ★★ Water-white **18** ㉓, piquant green apple, nice crunchy texture, uncomplicated but pleasant. **Sauvignon Blanc** ★★ Light & shy **18** ㉓, lemon peel & candied pineapple notes. **Red Muscadel** ★★★ Brick-red jerepiko is grapey, fragrant, with caramel aftertaste. **16** ㉙ appeals but could use more zip. WO W Cape. **White Muscadel** ⓠ ★★★ Dried peach & boiled sweet notes on **16** ㉛ fortified dessert. Very sweet despite spirity bite. — WB

Location: McGregor ▪ Map: Robertson ▪ Map grid reference: D6 ▪ WO: McGregor/Western Cape ▪ Est 1948 ▪ 1stB 1978 ▪ Tasting & sales Mon-Fri 8—5 Sat 9-1 ▪ Closed Good Fri, Dec 25/26 & Jan 1 ▪ Owner(s) 27 members ▪ Winemaker(s) Elmo du Plessis (Jan 2009) ▪ 14,000t 22% red 78% white ▪ IPW, WIETA ▪ PO Box 519 McGregor 6708 ▪ info@mcgregorwinery.co.za ▪ www.mcgregorwinery.co.za ▪ S 33° 56' 5.4" E 019° 50' 56.3" ▪ 🖂 limousines.promptness.phenomenal ▪ **F** +27 (0)23-625-1829 ▪ **T +27 (0)23-625-1741/1109**

☐ **Meander** see Daschbosch

Meerendal Wine Estate ⓠ 🍴 🏠 📷 🛏 ♿

Historic Durbanville estate Meerendal over the past few years has had one of the biggest upgrades since inception in 1702, from the cellar and tasting area to secure parking for 1,000 cars. Visitors come in their droves for the Parkrun and Saturday Farmers Market, not to mention the gallery, restaurant, deli, boutique hotel and distillery. Winelovers come for hands-on knowledge through the Wine Academy, and of course for wines (new vintages all labelled Wine of Origin Cape Town), among them the Heritage Block Pinotage, from a vineyard planted in 1955, securing Meerendal's status as a founding member of the Old Vine Project.

Prestige range

★★★★☆ **Intensio** 15 months French oak, 10% new, add to the luxurious texture of **17** ㉙ pinotage, made Amarone-style from vine-dried bunches in collaboration with Italian vintner Stefano Contini. Rich & full as expected, barely dry, yet under 14% alcohol. No **16**.

★★★★★ **Heritage Block Pinotage** 🛏 🍷 Restrained power on **16** ㉝, from Durbanville's oldest block, single-vineyard bushvines planted 1955, showing vibrant, tangy red berries & plums, some floral & earthy notes, subtle oak spice (vanilla, mocha) from 16 months new French oak. Good for decade plus.

Heritage Reserve ⓠ ★★★★ Unusual Cape Blend from equal pinot noir & pinotage, 2 others. **13** ㉘ supple body shows development, integrated red berry fruit, brief farewell. Not tasted: **Bin159 Shiraz**. Occasional release: **Merlot Prestige**, **Merlot Reserve**, **Liza**.

Standard range

★★★★ **Merlot** Undoubtedly complex, with plum pudding, cherry liqueur, mocha & masala notes after year in oak (10% new), but **15** ⑧⑨ not quite as smooth, rich, seamless as **14** ★★★★★ ⑨③.

★★★★ **Chardonnay Unwooded** All the citrus of **17** ★★★★ ⑧④ but 5 months on lees add toasted sesame seed & mosbolletjie bread nuances in **18** ⑧⑥. Remarkable mebos intensity/viscosity on palate, but dry & unheavy at modest 12% alcohol.

★★★★ **Sauvignon Blanc** Good weight on the mid-palate of previewed **18** ⑧⑥, soft, with litchi & gooseberry notes, finishing crisp & dry.

Pinotage ⑨ ★★★ Juicy red & black berry fruit to the fore in **15** ⑧①, aged in older French oak, with soft tannins & subtle spice. **Shiraz** ⑨ ★★★★ Characterised by red berries & tobacco spice, **15** ⑧④ seems less approachable & poised than last. **Pinotage Blanc de Noir** ★★★ Bright berry-cordial pink **18** ⑧⓪ has rosepetal aroma, strawberries-&-cream on palate, off-dry with ample acidity to balance. Occasional release: **Cabernet Sauvignon, Pinot Noir, Méthode Cap Classique**. — JG

Location: Durbanville ▪ Map: Durbanville, Philadelphia & Darling ▪ Map grid reference: C7 ▪ WO: Cape Town/Durbanville ▪ Est 1702 ▪ 1stB 1969 ▪ Tasting & sales Mon-Sat 10-6 Sun 11-6 ▪ Closed Good Fri, Dec 25 & Jan 1 ▪ Cellar tours by appt ▪ Crown Restaurant & Wine Bar at Meerendal T +27 (0)21-975-0383, Mon-Sun 7am-10pm ▪ Carlucci's Deli T +27 (0)21-612-0015, Sun-Mon 7-5 Tue-Sat 7am-8.30pm ▪ Facilities for children ▪ Tour groups ▪ Farmers Market every Sat 8-5 ▪ Weddings/functions ▪ Walking/running trials ▪ MTB trails ▪ Renosterveld conservation area ▪ Meerendal Art Gallery ▪ Meerendal Wine Academy ▪ The Meerendal Boutique Hotel ▪ Owner(s) Coertze family ▪ Cellarmaster(s)/winemaker(s) Liza Goodwin (Sep 2006) ▪ Viticulturist(s) Altus van Lill (Jun 2018) ▪ 227ha/54ha (cab, merlot, ptage, pinot, shiraz, chard, sauv) ▪ 500t/50,000cs own label 75% red 20% white 5% rosé ▪ IPW ▪ Private Bag X1702 Durbanville 7551 ▪ info@meerendal.co.za ▪ www.meerendal.co.za ▪ S 33° 47′ 55.8″ E 018° 37′ 26.2″ ▪ 🖭 fiery.kettles.funnier ▪ F +27 (0)21-975-1657 ▪ **T +27 (0)21-975-1655**

Meerhof Wines   ⑨ ⑪ ⓒ

Previously owned by the Redelinghuys family, these high-lying vineyards and cellar near Riebeek-Kasteel have been bought by Koos and Hestia Jansen van Rensburg, who have big plans for them. The aim is to significantly increase production, using these vines and more numerous ones at another farm, Rheeboksfontein. The team to oversee the growth over the next few years involves newly appointed viticulturist Johan Kellerman and cellarmaster Jaco Brand, whose personal focus includes 'full, oaked' wines. Watch this space.

Meerhof Wines range 🆕

Grenache Rosé 🍇 ★★★★ Pale pink but the rest is far from wan, wild red berries, notes of dry scrub in **18** ⑧④, the voice of grenache speaks clearly. Dry, with a mineral finish. Lovely. Fairtrade, as all except Shiraz. **Chenin Blanc** 🍇 🍷 ★★★★ Stonefruit, granadilla & a mineral top note, **18** ⑧③ has lots to offer. No oaking, a flinty savouriness at the end. Great food wine. **White Blend** 🍇 ★★★★ Creative Swartland blend of roussanne, viognier, grenache blanc. **18** ⑧④'s light oaking only evident in the flavours, white-fleshed nectarines, some lemon zest. Complex & involving.

Shiraz ★★★ Combo French/American barrels for **17** ⑧① adds vanilla, sweet spice notes to the glossy dark fruit, savoury dryness to the palate. Approachable but still youthful, will improve with age. **Chardonnay** ★★★ Lightly oaked **18** ⑦⑧ is citrus-styled, fruity-fresh, delicate biscuit shading adds interest. **Sauvignon Blanc** ★★★ Variety-true **18** ⑦⑧ has appealing drinkability, melon & citrus flavours, fresh & dry. — CR

Location: Riebeek-Kasteel ▪ Map/WO: Swartland ▪ Map grid reference: D6 ▪ 1stB 2017 ▪ Tasting, sales & cellar tours Mon-Fri 9-5 Sat/Sun 9-3 ▪ Fee R35pp ▪ Closed Dec 25 ▪ Restaurant Wed-Fri 9-5 Sat/Sun 9-3 ▪ Farm produce ▪ Conferences ▪ Walking/hiking trails ▪ Conservation area ▪ Owner(s) Koos & Hestia Jansen van Rensburg ▪ Cellarmaster(s)/winemaker(s) Jaco Brand (Oct 2017) ▪ Viticulturist(s) Johan Kellerman (Oct 2017) ▪ 230ha/130ha (cab, merlot, pinot noir/gris, shiraz, chard, chenin, grenache b, rouss, sauv, verdelho, viog) ▪ 1,000t/65,000L own label 40% red 40% white 20% rosé ▪ Fairtrade ▪ PO Box 148 Riebeek-Kasteel 7307 ▪ admin@meerhofwines.co.za ▪ www.meerhofwines.co.za ▪ S 33° 24′ 19.8″ E 018° 52′ 15.0″ ▪ 🖭 emancipate.diplomacy.determining ▪ **T +27 (0)22-125-0422/3**

☐ **Meerkat Wines** *see* Welbedacht Wine Estate

Meerlust Estate

Johannes Myburgh acquired this grand Stellenbosch estate in 1757 and developed the land and charming complex of buildings, just 5 km from False Bay. His descendants have farmed it ever since. Tradition provides an impulse to improve. Cellarmaster Chris Williams, who's established a reputation for wines blending classicism and a riper, fruitier modernism, has been researching the impressive, still lively Meerlust wines from the 1970s, especially the cabernet. He found they tended to have low alcohols and acidities, and were matured in large-format oak. So, foudres (of 4,000 and 2,400 litres) were imported from France for the cellar (itself dating to 1776, when it was built as the estate's wagon house), and Chris has been experimenting with maturing Rubicon components in them — with 'very promising results'.

★★★★☆ **Cabernet Sauvignon** Classic aromas of dark berry fruit & cigarbox on **15** ⑨⓪, with a herbal element coming through more on the slightly severe, firmly structured palate. **14** ★★★★ ⑧⑦ was a little weaker in concentration.

★★★★☆ **Merlot** ⓐ Both sombre & lively notes of spicy tobacco along with dark fruit on **16** ⑨②- with dollops of cab franc & petit verdot adding as usual to complexity. Serious, richly flavoured, more generous than the Cab, with sweeter, brighter fruit. Many years to go.

★★★★☆ **Pinot Noir** ⊘ As usual, **17** ⑨① stresses the savoury - forest floor, fungal - side of the variety, though there's depth of fruit yielding some fragrance. More forceful tannic structure than most local pinots; serious dry finish to a satisfying varietal expression.

★★★★☆ **Rubicon** ⓐ Cab-based flagship - 61% in **15** ⑨③ - with merlot, cab franc & petit verdot. The finest, most elegant of the reds, refined & intense, full of subtle flavour, with cigarbox overtones & classic dry herbal element. Tannin & acid fully involved in the whole, promising harmony. 14.1% alcohol; 66% new oak. **14** ⑨⓪, with 67% cab, equally classic in style.

★★★★☆ **Chardonnay** Still showing some new oak influence in youth, as did **16** ⑨②, **17** ★★★★ ⑧⑦ also replete with other notes: oatmeal, citrus, stonefruit. Texture tends to the heavy, though, & 4 g/l sugar is not quite balanced by the lemony acid, giving a detracting sweet-sour effect.

Occasional release: **Red**. — TJ

Location/map/WO: Stellenbosch ▪ Map grid reference: C8 ▪ Est 1693 ▪ 1stB 1975 ▪ Tasting & sales Mon-Fri 9–5 Sat 10–2 ▪ Fee R30 ▪ Closed all pub hols ▪ Cellar tours by appt ▪ Quarters self-contained cottage ▪ Owner(s) Hannes Myburgh ▪ Cellarmaster(s) Chris Williams (Jan 2004) ▪ Viticulturist(s) Roelie Joubert (2001) ▪ 400ha/110ha (cabs s/f, merlot, p verdot, pinot, chard) ▪ 500t/60,000cs own label 90% red 10% white ▪ PO Box 7121 Stellenbosch 7599 ▪ info@meerlust.co.za ▪ www.meerlust.co.za ▪ S 34° 1' 1.7" E 018° 45' 24.7" ▪ ⓜ gold.hits.chilled ▪ F +27 (0)21-843-3274 ▪ **T +27 (0)21-843-3587**

Meinert Wines

Martin Meinert is enjoying his role as 'éminence grise' after selling his eponymous wine business and label to a trio of Johannesburg partners. His watching brief officially expires this year but no doubt his knowledge and wise counsel, built up over three decades, will be generously offered if needed. Filling his large boots is Cape Wine Master Brendan Butler who parlayed his interest in wine into the role of GM/winemaker/co-viticulturist at this Devon Valley venture. Brendan's had a busy year, supervising the extension of the cellar, travelling and — a special highlight — hand-bottling a bespoke blend for London's Vivat Bacchus Restaurant.

Meinert Wines range

★★★★ **Cabernet Sauvignon** Restrained elegance on **15** ⑧⑦. Classic cassis fruit tempered by integrated French oak, just third new. Layered palate that benefits from dabs merlot, cab franc & petit verdot.

★★★★ **Merlot** Supple, plush & rounded, the ripe fruit of **15** ⑧⑥ is checked by bright, juicy acidity. Good frame of integrated oak, only 20% new. Overall, improves on **14** ★★★★ ⑧⑤.

★★★★☆ **Synchronicity** Sleek **15** ⑨⓪ blend of equal cab & merlot with dabs pinotage, petit verdot & cab franc. Firm core of rich, dark fruit, well-balanced by oak frame (40% new French, 2 years). Elegant & refined. Also in 1.5L. No **14**.

★★★★ **The German Job Riesling** ⓐ Zippy taut signature wax & green apple on dry, flinty **16** ⑧⑧ from Elgin. Lipsmackingly fresh & vibrant, with great fruit/acid tension. Will last well.

★★★★☆ **Semillon Straw Wine** ② ★★★★ Richly sweet apple & honey with subtle wax nuance on **15**
★★★★ ⑧⑥. Balanced acidity ensures clean, dry finish, as with memorable **14** ⑨③. Mostly in 375 ml.

Printer's Ink Pinotage ② ★★★★ Typical pinotage fruit vivacity on **15** ⑧③, has gentle dry tannins
but lacks its drop of merlot. **La Barry Red** ★★★★ Bold, bright & cheerful blend of merlot, cabs franc &
sauvignon. Light-bodied, easy charmer which would partner a braai or pasta equally well. Now NV ⑧③.
Coastal WO. **Sauvignon Blanc** ⑯ ★★★★ Lemon verbena softness to rounded, balanced & succulent **17**
⑧⑤ with 5% semillon portion. Light & seductive, it has good concentration. WO W Cape.

Limited Editions

★★★★ **The Italian Job White Merlot** Stonefruit vivacity plays off against berry nuance on **17** ⑧⑥.
Savoury yet tangy, dry & zesty, with creamy oak backing, third new. Slender 12% alcohol, as **15** ★★★★
⑧④. Coastal WO. No **16**.

The Graduate Syrah ⑯ ★★★★ Smoky green coffee bean on **16** ⑧④ from Upper Hemel-en-Aarde
grapes, soft, juicy, but needs more flesh & fruit. **Semillon** ② ★★★★ Only 10% oaked but 5 months on
the lees, giving **15** ⑧④ fruit focus & good palate weight, brightening freshness calls for a second glass. Not
tasted: **Pinot Noir, Chardonnay**. — FM

Location/map: Stellenbosch ▪ Map grid reference: D4 ▪ WO: Devon Valley/Coastal/Elgin/Upper Hemel-en-
Aarde Valley/Western Cape ▪ Est 1987 ▪ 1stB 1997 ▪ Tasting Mon-Sat strictly by appt only ▪ Closed all pub hols
▪ Owner(s) Hesticap (Pty) Ltd ▪ Cellarmaster(s) /winemaker/GM Brendan Butler CWM (Aug 2017), advised
by Martin Meinert (1997, consultant) ▪ Viticulturist(s) Brendan Butler CWM (Aug 2017) & Henk Marconi (Jan
1991) ▪ 19ha (cabs s/f, merlot, p verdot, ptage, shiraz, sem) ▪ 90t/8,000cs own label 67% red 33% white ▪ PO
Box 375 Stellenbosch 7599 ▪ info@meinertwines.com ▪ www.meinertwines.com ▪ S 33° 54' 1.8" E 018° 48'
50.2" ▪ 🖳 evidence.thus.improve ▪ F +27 (0)86-662-7728 ▪ **T +27 (0)21-865-2363**

Mellasat Vineyards   ② ⑪ ◎ ⓖ

Stephen Richardson, sometime Norfolk grain farmer and Paarl winegrower the past two decades, chef wife
Janet and winemaker Gizelle Coetzee provide a full palette of flavour experiences: interactive underground
cellar tastings, themed food-and-wine pairings (including a new gourmet burger offering), seasonal
pop-up eatery and more. In the vineyard, tempranillo and viognier yields actually increased in the drought,
and Stephen suggests Mediterranean varieties 'may be the way forward if these conditions continue'.

Premium Exclusives

★★★★ **'M' Cabernet Sauvignon** Elevated from Mellasat range in **13** ⑧⑦, more malleable than **12**
★★★★ ⑧④ but equally robust. Menthol & cedar accents on dark-fruit bouquet & palate.

★★★★ **Tempranillo** Less artisanal than last, **16** ⑧⑦ tannins more polished, appealing cherry, dried fig &
cranberry, sweet & moderate grip aided by 40% new oak, 50% American.

★★★★ **Viognier** Sensitively barrel-fermented in old French & Romanian oak, **17** ⑧⑥ retains varietal
apricot, gains vanilla & pecan nut; enlivening acidity & good dry finish. Worth seeking out.

Mellasat range

★★★★ **'Sigma' White Pinotage** Unusual blanc de noir, **17** ⑧⑦ star-bright gold, enticing stonefruit &
citrus, vibrant acidity & lingering tropical finish. Fermented/aged in Romanian oak, 13% new.

Chardonnay ★★★★ Apple & almond aromas & flavours mingle in appetising, lightly oaked **14** ⑧④.
Attractive creamy texture, bone-dry lemon & pistachio farewell. Not tasted: **Tuin Wyn**.

Dekker's Valley range

Shiraz ★★★★ No new oak, so there's immediate pure-fruit attraction in **15** ⑧③, along with savoury &
spicy/floral lift. Satisfying sipper now & for a few years. **Shiraz Rosé** ★★★ Watermelon, strawberry & some
spice, **17** ⑧① ticks al fresco boxes with good flavour, lightish 13% alcohol, acid zip & bone-dry farewell.
Seraphic ★★★ Light (12.3% alcohol) & zesty, perfect for sunset sipping, **17** ⑧① apple, winter melon &
lemon peel on 3-way unoaked mix chardonnay, chenin & splash viognier. Not tasted: **Revelation**. — GM

Location/map/WO: Paarl ▪ Map grid reference: G5 ▪ Est 1996 ▪ 1stB 1999 ▪ Tasting & sales Mon-Sat 9.30-5.30
Sun/pub hols 10-4 ▪ Closed Good Fri, Dec 25 & Jan 1 ▪ Cellar tours by appt ▪ Cellarmaster's reserve tasting
▪ Light lunches for groups/tours or private dinner functions by appt; picnics in summer; cheese platters;
pop-up seasonal restaurant & other food-based events ▪ Tour groups ▪ Paarl Ommiberg festival ▪ Owner(s)

Stephen Richardson ▪ Cellarmaster(s) Stephen Richardson (Jan 1999) ▪ Winemaker(s) Gizelle Coetzee (2016) ▪ Viticulturist(s) Poena Malherbe (Sep 1996) ▪ 13ha/8ha (cab, ptage, shiraz, tempranillo, chard, chenin, viog) ▪ 50t/3,500cs own label 40% red 50% white 10% rosé ▪ IPW ▪ PO Box 7169 Paarl 7623 ▪ tastingroom@mellasat.com ▪ www.mellasat.com ▪ S 33° 44' 30.0" E 019° 2' 31.0" ▪ 🖩 presses.pits.supply ▪ T +27 (0)21-862-4525

☐ **Mellow-Wood** see Distell
☐ **Mensa** see Overhex Wines International
☐ **Mentors** see KWV Wines
☐ **Mercia Collection** see Mooiplaas Estate & Private Nature Reserve

Merwida Winery 🍷 🏠 ♿

The Merwida cellar takes in grapes from several Breedekloof properties owned by the Van der Merwe family, here for over 170 years. Cousins Schalk and Pierre are eco passionate, hence their elite status as WWF-SA Conservation Champions. In conjunction with WWF-SA, they're helping preserve 800 ha of untouched wetland on their farms, 'a rare ecosystem with incredible fauna and flora'. Support for the Breedekloof Makers initiative, crafting boutique parcels of chenin, sees another brilliant release this edition.

Family Vintners range

★★★★ **Reserve Chenin Blanc** Smooth & creamy from part oaking (57%, mostly older), **17** ⑧⑦ very well-made/judged, plays to variety's strengths with opulence from baked apple, lemon brûlée flavours in perfect harmony with inherent freshness that lingers.

Merwida Winery range

★★★★ **Barbera** ⓧ Invariably excellent example of rare-in-SA variety. **15** ⑧⑦ earthy brambles & espresso, firm & bold structure, with deep savoury complexity - perfect for Italian fare.

★★★★ **Sauvignon Blanc** ⊘ Dependable label on-song in previewed **18** ⑧⑦, zingy pineapple, papaya & candied lemon gaining texture due in part to lees stirring. Delicious lemon uplift on finish.

- - - - - - - -

Pinotage Rosé 🍷 ★★★ Pretty-in-pink **18** ⑧① , amiable dry al fresco partner with alluring red berries, citrus & spice. **Chenin Blanc** ⊘ 🍷 ★★★★ The unwooded version is a little gem that will make you smile. **18** ⑧④ fruity & lively, & perfectly poised between ripe tropical fruit character & freshness. **Pinot Grigio** 🍷 ★★★ Another flavourful outdoorsy wine from this estate. **18** ⑧① spring flowers & gentle spice, a light body, effortless, for early drinking.

Cabernet Sauvignon ★★★ Dark, dusty berries & the grape's firm grip evident on leaner, structured **16** ⑧②. **Pinotage** ⓧ ★★★ Tutti-frutti **15** ⑧② is soft & supple, an easy sip. **Chardonnay** ★★★★ Rounded & smooth thanks to lees stirring, ex-tank **18** ⑧④ creamy baked apple flavour & sprinkling of spice on long finish. **Cuvée Brut** ★★ Frothy & fruity **NV** ⑦⑤ fizzer from sauvignon, dry & zesty, a party starter. **White Muscadel** ★★★★ Jerepiko **18** ⑧③ ex tank delivers the expected sunshine-in-a-bottle richness, adding boiled sweet, honeysuckle, raisin & spice to the seduction. — WB

Location: Rawsonville ▪ Map: Breedekloof ▪ Map grid reference: C6 ▪ WO: Western Cape/Breedekloof ▪ Est 1963 ▪ 1stB 1975 ▪ Tasting & sales Mon-Fri 9-12.30 & 1.30-5 Sat 9-1 ▪ Closed Easter Fri-Mon, Dec 25-Jan 1 ▪ Merwida Country Lodge T +27 (0)23-349-1435 ▪ Owner(s) Schalk & Pierre van der Merwe ▪ Cellarmaster(s)/viticulturist(s) Magnus Kriel ▪ Winemaker(s) Magnus Kriel (Dec 2000), with Sarel van Staden (Aug 1982) & Lieza van der Merwe (Jan 2015) ▪ 700ha (cab, merlot, shiraz, chard, chenin, sauv, sem, viog) ▪ 17,500t/10,000cs own label 40% red 60% white ▪ ISO 22000, Fairtrade, IPW, WIETA, WWF-SA Conservation Champion ▪ PO Box 4 Rawsonville 6845 ▪ wines@merwida.com ▪ www.merwida.com ▪ S 33° 41' 24.9" E 019° 20' 31.1" ▪ 🖩 pizzerias.applicants.reconsidered ▪ F +27 (0)23-349-1953/+27 (0)86-557-5686 ▪ T +27 (0)23-349-1144

☐ **Metafisika** see Osbloed Wines
☐ **Metamorphic** see Hillcrest Estate

Metzer Family Wines

Now a member of the Old Vine Project, Helderberg-based winemaker Wade Metzer continues 'the quest to keep as many heritage vineyard blocks in the ground' by nurturing and bottling these 'national treasures' as mono-vineyard expressions. A second venerable-vines chenin joins the portfolio, along with hot-ticket variety cinsaut, while another new label, 3 Miles to Milk Bay, accommodates 'new and interesting parcels which we come across'. The Kitchen Sink has evolved into a standalone brand and is now listed separately.

★★★★ **Cinsault** (NEW) In the vanguard of rediscovery of SA cinsaut, **17** ⑧⑨ from Helderberg vines planted 1992 has strawberry fruit & rosewater perfume; full flavoured yet light of foot, despite 14.4% alcohol.

★★★★☆ **Shiraz** White pepper introduction to savoury, spicy **17** ⑨②, like **16** ⑨②, less burly than previous; plum/blackberry fruit in rich yet elegant package. Single Helderberg block on 3 soil types, minimalist winemaking with 30% bunch ferment, year French barrels, now 10% new.

★★★★ **3 Miles to Milk Bay** (NEW) Untamed scrub, red berry & savoury notes jostle in **17** ⑧⑦ shiraz combo with cinsaut, mourvèdre, cab & splash viognier. 20% whole bunch ferment, 14 months old cask.

★★★★☆ **Maritime Chenin Blanc** (NEW) 🍃 🍂 Ex single 36 year old bushvine parcel just 4.5 km from the sea. **17** ⑨③ as svelte as sibling, same natural winemaking but tighter, more athletic - saline? - profile (abetted by no lees stirring). Seasoned oak only, 8 months.

★★★★☆ **Montane Chenin Blanc** 🍃 🍂 'Chenin Blanc' gets a prefix to highlight Helderberg foothills location of 50+ year old single vineyard site. Sensual **17** ★★★★★ ⑨⑤ has mouthfilling ripe tropical fruit in a supple, richly textured frame. As for striking **16** ⑨②, lowish 13% alcohol, 10% new oak.— DS

Location: Somerset West • WO: Stellenbosch • Est/1stB 2006 • Tasting by appt • Owner(s) Wade Metzer & Barry Holfeld • Winemaker(s) Wade Metzer • 26t/4,000cs 70% red 30% white • info@metzerwines.com • www.metzerwines.com • T +27 (0)72-279-7645

M'hudi Wines

The Rangaka family, led by matriarch Malmsey, have rebranded their Stellenbosch winegrowing venture as a boutique family concern. Current wines, made by various winemakers, include a barrel-fermented chenin, cabernet, pinotage, shiraz and Rhône-Bordeaux blend called Foro's Legacy. Sparkling wines are bottled under the Say Lovey label.

Location: Stellenbosch • Est 2005 • Tasting closed to public • Conferences (up to 70 pax) • Events (up to 200 pax) • Owner(s) Rangaka family • Winemaker(s) various • 6,000cs own label 90% red 10% rosé & white sparkling • WIETA • PO Box 30 Koelenhof 7605 • malmsey@mhudi.com • www.mhudi.com • T +27 (0)61-476-9365

☐ **Mia** see Nordic Wines

Michaella Wines

(NEW)

Five years ago, using colombard grapes grown in a back garden in Montagu, aluminium manufacturer Adrian Dix made his first wine in a shed. Today he has a 'very basic' cellar in Stellenbosch's Devon Valley for which he sources small batches of hand-picked grapes, with acclaimed young gun Lukas van Loggerenberg overseeing the minimal-intervention winemaking. Says Adrian: 'I would like to create a business that my children, Michael and Ella, can grow and develop.'

★★★★☆ **Shiraz** 🍃 Lighter in colour, extraction & body than most Stellenbosch examples, yet no lack of intensity or personality. **17** ⑨③ scrub, pepper nuances to pure & succulent fruit, real grip & structure, serious intent. Bunch ferment, old oak ageing, minuscule quantities for both.

★★★★☆ **Chenin Blanc** 🍃 Unfurls in glass to gorgeous fennel, earth & thatch perfumes, impresses with clever juxtaposition of silky ripeness & mineral salinity. **17** ⑨④ elegant & engaging, with persistent, tapering conclusion. Native yeasts, no additions, like sibling. Stellenbosch & Paarl fruit.— TJ, CvZ

Location: Stellenbosch • WO: Stellenbosch/Stellenbosch-Paarl • Est/1stB 2016 • Closed to public • Owner(s) Adrian Dix • Cellarmaster(s)/winemaker(s) Lukas van Loggerenberg (Jan 2016, consultant) • 2t/140cs own label 70% red 30% white • adrian@dixaluminium.co.za • www.michaella.co.za • F +27 (0)21-712-2978 • T +27 (0)21-712-2978/+27 (0)83-230-1634

☐ **Michelle d'Or** *see* Fort Simon Wine Estate

Micu Narunsky Wines ⓠ

No longer full-timing for another winery means Micu Narunsky has more time to market his own boutique label and plan for future vintages. Next for the jazz-piano-playing winemaker is to bottle some of the barrels resting in the Romond cellar on the Helderberg, and release the Iemanjá '11 and La Complicité '16 which we reviewed pre-labelling last year.

★★★★ **Iemanjá** Mix touriga (83%), tinta & souzão, polished & ripe **12** ⑧⑥ improves on raisiny **11** ★★★ ⑧①, perfumed dark fruit, tobacco & spicy undertones, fair tannic grip nicely augmented by lengthy 36 month sojourn mostly older oak.

★★★★☆ **La Complicité** ⓠ Successful reinvention of this wine, now 100% colombard from Stellenbosch, **16** ⑨⓪ layers of fruit (peach, papaya), creamy oatmeal notes from 50% (old) oak underpinned by a salty minerality. Exciting & unusual, step up on last **13** ★★★★ ⑧⑤ colombard blend.

Olodum ⓠ ★★★★ From 50 year old Swartland tinta, intense **11** ⑧③ handles extraordinary 4.5 years in oak nicely, adding leathery tannins & medicinal notes to slightly raisined black fruit. — GM

Location: Somerset West ▪ WO: Coastal/Stellenbosch/Swartland ▪ Est 2005 ▪ 1stB 2006 ▪ Tasting by appt ▪ Owner(s)/cellarmaster(s)/viticulturist(s) Micu Narunsky ▪ Winemaker(s) Micu Narunsky, advised by Francois Naudé ▪ 4.8t/450cs own label 85% red 15% white ▪ 3 De Hoop Cres Somerset West 7130 ▪ micunarunsky@gmail.com ▪ www.micunarunsky.com ▪ T +27 (0)73-600-3031

Middelvlei Estate ⓠ ⑪ ⌂ ◎ ⓑ ♿

It's 100 years since current custodians Ben and Tinnie Momberg's grandfather, also Tinnie, bought Middelvlei farm with his brother Niels. Their outlay of £3,000 was money well spent, given the prime location in today's Papegaaiberg ward of Stellenbosch, suited particularly to cabernet. Ben and Tinnie's belief in this noble variety saw them plant a further 10 ha in 2017. The recently extended cellardoor, 'boerebraai' (outdoor BBQ) and blend-your-own-wine experience are among many attractions maintaining the estate's popularity.

Middelvlei Estate range

★★★★ **Cabernet Sauvignon** Honest Stellenbosch cab, **16** ⑧⑥ nicely proportioned ripe fruit, cedar oak accessory. No great complexity but freshness, neat tannins should ensure several years pleasurable drinking. **15** ★★★★ ⑧⑤ was sturdier, with less freshness.

★★★★ **Shiraz** Well fleshed, with ripe, savoury olive flavours & effective, rounded tannins. **17** ⑧⑥ portion new oak, some American, adds to overall satisfaction. More harmonious than **15** ★★★★ ⑧⑤. **16** untasted.

★★★★ **Momberg** Compatible shiraz, cab, pinotage partnership; **16** ⑧⑧ fusion of dark berries, black olives, hint of oak spice in savoury whole. Sound infrastructure & freshness offer future potential. 50% new oak, portion American.

Free-Run Pinotage ★★★☆ Pure fruit, clean lines & fine integrated tannins see **17** ⑧⑤ well reflect the 'free-run' moniker. Modern, fresh style, youthfully accessible, can also age few years. **Pinotage-Merlot** ★★★ The Mombergs among first to produce this blend; **16** ⑧② continues in fruit-driven tradition, the ripe juicy mulberries contained by lively tannins. Straightforward & tasty. **Chardonnay Unoaked** ★★★ Generous lemon & orange aromas; **18** ⑧① zesty, but a little residual sugar maintains youthful approachability. WO W Cape, as all below.

Rooster range

Merlot ★★★ Crowd-pleaser style, **17** ⑦⑧ offers plenty dark berry, choc sweetness, juicy flavours & nip of rounded tannin for early enjoyment. **Shiraz** ★★ **17** ⑦③ ripe, though sweet rather than fruity, with an easy freshness that could benefit from light chilling. **Chardonnay** ★★★ Easy yet satisfying, **17** ⑧① has lightly oak-spiced citrus fruit lifted by bright, balanced acidity. Firm yet rounded build, dry & clean, fruity memory. — AL

Location/map: Stellenbosch ▪ Map grid reference: E4 ▪ WO: Stellenbosch/Western Cape ▪ Est 1941 ▪ 1stB 1973 ▪ Tasting & sales daily 10–4.30 ▪ Fee R25pp ▪ Closed Good Fri, Dec 25 & Jan 1 ▪ Cellar tours by appt ▪ Traditional lunchtime braai 7 days a week; evenings by prior arrangement for groups of 35 pax ▪ The Wine Barn function venue (150 pax) ▪ Facilities for children ▪ Conferences ▪ Walking/hiking & MTB trails ▪ Cottage (2 pax) ▪ Owner(s) Momberg family ▪ Cellarmaster(s)/winemaker(s)/viticulturist(s) Tinnie Momberg (Feb

1992) ▪ 160ha/110ha (cab, merlot, ptage, shiraz, chard, sauv) ▪ 650t/60,000cs own label 95% red 5% white ▪ Other export brands: Hagelsberg, Red Falcon ▪ IPW, WIETA ▪ PO Box 66 Stellenbosch 7599 ▪ info@middelvlei. co.za ▪ www.middelvlei.co.za ▪ S 33° 55' 41.2" E 018° 49' 55.9" ▪ ⌨ charmingly.butter.resolved ▪ F +27 (0)21-883-9546 ▪ **T +27 (0)21-883-2565**

Midgard

Now in its seventh year, this worthy private venture supports the Elkana Hostel at the Alta du Toit Aftercare Centre in Cape Town, where adults with special care needs from all Western Cape communities live and work. Quality grapes are bought in from the Durbanville area, and Nomada Wines' Riaan Oosthuizen donates his skill and knowledge to vinify the wine. All profits from sales are donated to the hostel.

Sauvignon Blanc ⊘ ⑦ ★★★★ Remarkably well priced, **18** ⑧⑤ showcases Durbanville terroir, sleek (12.5% alcohol), fynbos & zesty lime. A delight. — CR

Location/WO: Durbanville ▪ Est/1stB 2012 ▪ Closed to public ▪ Winemaker(s) Riaan Oosthuizen (Nomada Wines) ▪ 2-3t/±300cs own label 100% white ▪ PO Box 2703 Durbanville 7551 ▪ cteijlingen@gmail.com ▪ **T +27 (0)83-456-9410**

Migliarina Wines ⓠ

An experienced sommelier and winemaker, Somerset West-based Carsten Migliarina appreciates wines that have freshness, elegance and excitement, wines he enjoys drinking and that partner well with food. His annual endeavour to 'see what's possible with lesser-known grape varieties' has produced an Alsace-style pinot gris. Parquet, an extra in the range, recalls the three pieces of wood flooring making a perfect square, like the 'seamless fit' of the varietal trio.

Migliarina range

★★★★☆ **Grenache** Usual ruby luminescent eye-appeal; **17** ⑨① from Wellington slightly fuller than **16** ⑨④ (which also had some Stellenbosch fruit), more crushed raspberry substance than spice, herbs. Still refreshingly dry, with appetising savoury conclusion.

★★★★ **Syrah** ⓠ Ex Stellenbosch has perfectly pitched fresh ripe fruit, supple core currently held by imposing grape tannin (2 months on skins). **15** ⑧⑨ deserves benefit of time. 14 months older oak.

★★★★ **Syrah-Cabernet Sauvignon** ⓠ Blends spicy syrah with 25% dark-berried cab. **15** ⑧⑧ velvet mouthfeel balanced by natural freshness, tannin, harmonised in older oak. Can age.

★★★★ **Chardonnay** ⓠ Elgin's vibrancy, steeliness, hallmarks of **15** ⑧⑧, as is house's understatement, including oak - just 10% new. Bright citrus, creamy breadth satisfy now, even more after few years.

★★★★ **Chardonnay Single Vineyard** Has trademark Elgin intensity, taut acid but also richness from oak (35% new); **16** ⑧⑧ needs time to integrate with more familiar pickled-lime zest, lingering tail.

★★★★ **Chenin Blanc** Light-of-foot but depth, intensity of flavour in **17** ⑧⑨. Lees ageing adds creamy dimension, balances bone-dry conclusion. Spicy lift from 50% natural ferment, older oak. **16** untasted.

Creative range

★★★★☆ **Parquet** ⑭ ⑧ Shiraz & splashes interest from carignan, grenache, **16** ⑨④ delivers Migliarina's usual unshowy precision. Cool feel in its flavoursome, gently spiced red fruit; lithe, supple, light tannin squeeze allow for early enjoyment. Year older oak. Stellenbosch, Swartland, Wellington fruit.

★★★★ **Grey Matters Pinot Gris** ⑭ These once-offs allow for 'exploration, creativity & fun'. Punning name a mind-changing wine, **17** ⑧⑨ substantial, for food rather than aperitif; deep smoky peach flavours, 50% old oak enriched. Emphatically dry.

★★★★ **Seitensprung Riesling** ⓠ Old-oaked **16** ⑧⑧ ex Elgin offers plenty drinking fun in snappy citrus, spicy fruity acids, lowish 12% alcohol, mouthwatering bone-dry tail.— AL

Location: Somerset West ▪ WO: Stellenbosch/Elgin/Coastal/Wellington/Bottelary ▪ Est 2001 ▪ 1stB 2002 ▪ Tasting by appt only ▪ Owner(s)/winemaker(s) Carsten Migliarina ▪ 4,000cs own label 40% red 60% white + 900cs for clients ▪ Brands for clients: Kap Hase, Aubergine Restaurant ▪ PO Box 673 Stellenbosch 7599 ▪ carsten@migliarina.co.za ▪ www.migliarina.co.za ▪ **T +27 (0)72-233-4138**

☐ **Miko** *see* Mont Rochelle Hotel & Vineyard

Miles Mossop Wines

Miles Mossop is, fairly leisurely, seeking a proper home for his eponymous brand, which has been based from the start at the prestigious address of Tokara in Stellenbosch, where Miles was winemaker. He's now left, to become '100% focused' on his own wines, but has been continuing to make them there for the time being. The range isn't likely to grow substantially but, he says, 'there is a possibility of one more wine coming out in the future as part of the family range' – the wines that so far have been named for his children. He adds intriguingly: 'As well as some interesting odds and ends...' For which we can only wait, with interest.

The Family range

★★★★★ **Max** ⓐ Gorgeous & highly perfumed cab-led Bordeaux-style **15** ⑨③ (merlot 24%, petit verdot 22%) in perfect balance: no edges, just pristine black fruit, whiffs of tobacco & polished leather, firm but integrated tannin structure & assimilated 35% new French wood. Also in smaller & larger bottle formats.

★★★★★ **Saskia** ⓐ Aromatic chenin-led blend (also clairette, verdelho, viognier) from Swartland & Voor Paardeberg continues to impress. **16** ⑨③ seamless, structured, with complex flavours in harmony. Magnums too.

★★★★★ **Kika** ⓐ Poised & elegant chenin Noble Late Harvest, barrel fermented. **17** ⑨④ voluptuous & unctuous, oozing honey, crème brûlée & sweet vanilla. An enduring fresh citrus finish follows a velvet rush of tropical fruit. 375ml.

The Introduction range

★★★★ **Red** Cab (86%) & merlot in **16** ⑧⑨, dark fruited, juicy & succulent, silky tannins & older oak, 20 months, subtly supportive. Good depth & persistence.

★★★★ **Chenin Blanc** Balance & freshness are key in **17** ⑧⑨, Stellenbosch & Swartland fruit delivering dewy orchard fruit, aromatic apple pie & sprinkles of cinnamon & clove. Coastal WO.— WB

Location: Stellenbosch ▪ WO: Stellenbosch/Coastal ▪ Est/1stB 2004 ▪ Closed to public ▪ Owner(s)/winemaker(s)/viticulturist(s) Miles Mossop ▪ 6ot/3,000c own label 60% red 35% white 5% NLH ▪ PO Box 7339 Stellenbosch 7599 ▪ miles@milesmossopwines.com ▪ www.milesmossopwines.com ▪ **T +27 (0)82-413-4335**

☐ **Milkwood** see The Grape Grinder
☐ **Mill** see Windmeul Cellar
☐ **Miller's Mile** see Klein Parys Vineyards
☐ **Millstone** see Stettyn Family Vineyards
☐ **Millstream** see DGB (Pty) Ltd
☐ **Milton Grove** see Jacques Germanier

Mimosa Boutique Wines   ⓠ ⓜ ⓐ ⓞ ⓑ

Lourens van der Westhuizen of Arendsig in Robertson tends the vines and makes the wines for Mimosa Lodge in Montagu, complementing the seasonal dishes of its owner-chef, Bernhard Hess. The packaging is no less attractive than the wines, with elegant black or white labels touched by gold and silver.

Reserve range

★★★★ **Pinotage** A full-throttle version: **16** ⑧⑥ ripely powerful, with plenty of fruit flavour, strong tannic structure, obvious toasty oak & finishing rather sweet. Also in magnum, as for Natus & Chenin.

★★★★☆ **Chenin Blanc** Richly coloured, richly textured **17** ⑨⓪ has spicy oak influence slightly obscuring the good fruit, but this should integrate in a few years, given the flavour depth, with the bottle age an ambitious wine deserves. Oaking also adds to the grip. **16** not tasted.

★★★★ **Weisser Riesling Natural Sweet** ⓨ **16** ⑧⑦ same fragrance-billowing deliciousness as previous - true to the variety. Well-balanced acid means no cloy to the clean finish. 500 ml.

★★★★ **Alambic 5 Year Old Potstill** ⓨ Dark amber, with complex nose of dried pears, candied lemon peel, roasted nuts. Long, satisfying flavours; fine, smooth intensity & touch caramel on finish.

Natus MMX ★★★★ Bordeaux-style blend, led by cab in **15** ⑧⑤ with 3 others. In big, ripe house style but with notable herbaceous element & perhaps more tannin-acid structure than fruit. **14** ★★★★ ⑧⑦

something of a standout. Not tasted: **Méthode Cap Classique Blanc de Blancs Brut**, **Méthode Cap Classique Special Cuvée**.

Mimosa range

★★★★ **Cabernet Sauvignon** ⓥ Good varietal expression on **16** ⑧⑦. Shows pleasingly restrained sweet fruit, with harmonious balance & gentle grip, ensuring approachability in youth. Also magnum.

★★★★ **Shiraz** Back on track after too-sweet **15** ★★★★ ⑧④, though **16** ⑧⑥ hardly bone-dry. Rich, fruit-forward & generous, good balance & firm warm handshake from tannin. Robertson WO, as next.

★★★★ **Chardonnay** Ripe, full-fruited aromas & flavours on **17** ⑧⑥, citrus with a bruised-apple, slightly oxidative edge. Acidity balances the velvety rich ripeness, but is not entirely integrated.

Sauvignon Blanc ★★★★ Lots of luscious tropical aromas & flavours (especially passionfruit) on fresh, easygoing & enjoyable **17** ⑧③. First tasted since **14** ⑧④. Discontinued: **3 Year Old Blended Brandy**. — TJ

Location: Montagu ▪ Map: Klein Karoo & Garden Route ▪ Map grid reference: B8 ▪ WO: Western Cape/ Robertson ▪ Est 2004 ▪ 1stB 2003 ▪ Tasting & sales daily 9-5 ▪ Tour groups ▪ Conservation area ▪ 4-star Mimosa Lodge: 23 rooms, conference centre, pool, boule pitch, wine cellar, tasting room & Ma Cuisine restaurant ▪ Owner(s) Bernhard Hess ▪ Cellarmaster(s)/winemaker(s)/viticulturist(s) Lourens van der Westhuizen (consultant) ▪ 5ha/3ha (cab, shiraz, chard, sauv) ▪ 20t/2,480cs own label 70% red 30% white ▪ PO Box 323 Montagu 6720 ▪ bernhard@mimosa.co.za ▪ www.mimosawines.co.za ▪ S 33° 47′ 27.59″ E 020° 6′ 44.55″ ▪ ⓦ precarious.test.penetrator ▪ F +27 (0)86-535-0720 ▪ **T +27 (0)23-614-2351**

☐ **Miner** *see* Taillard Family Wines

Miravel   ⓥ ⑪

Maarten and Janine van Beuningen sold their vineyard in 2014 but still live on the Helderberg property and continue with the Miravel brand, named for children Mark, Michael, Melanie and David. The former Zimbabwe fruit and livestock farmers offer pre-booked meals/platters, as well as tastings of their boutique wines, produced by contracted winemakers from grapes grown by the farm's new owner and neighbours.

Sauvignon Blanc ⓥ ★★★★ Quintessential sauvignon, mineral & leafy, **17** ⑧④ crackles with freshness, finishes long.

Cabernet Sauvignon ⓥ ★★★ **13** ⑧⓪ ample cassis aromas though palate less rich, flavoursome; feisty acidity & very dry tannins create a lean, almost austere profile which needs food, time or decanting. **Ella Family Reserve Cabernet Sauvignon** ★★★★ Intense cassis, cedar-spiced by mainly new French oak in **15** ⑧④; succulent & harmonious but good backbone for ageing. **Merlot** ⓥ ★★★ Powerful cassis on very ripe **NV** ⑧⓪, with 2 years oaking giving savoury flavours, structure for maturation. **Petit Verdot** ★★★★ Full-ripe style, as all the reds (15%+ alcohol), but **15** ⑧④ has enough fruit/oak balance to be both interesting & delicious. Hint of scrub adds to the appeal. **Pinotage** ★★★★ Misreported last time as discontinued. Dark toned, plum compote, **15** ⑧③ backed by 2 years in wood for appealing savoury flavours, ageing potential. **1952 Family Blend** ★★★★ Cab-dominant Bordeaux-style red, **15** ⑧③ shows cocoa & plush dark fruit, a firm tannin foundation for further ageing. **Nigma** ⓥ ★★★★ Sauvignon blanc barrel fermented/ aged, & nicely done. Nutty overlay but **16** ⑧⑤'s limy fruit remains, gives freshness, length. — CR

Location/WO: Stellenbosch ▪ Map: Helderberg ▪ Map grid reference: A3 ▪ Est 2002 ▪ 1stB 2005 ▪ Tasting & sales Mon-Sat & pub hols by appt ▪ Closed Ash Wed, Easter Fri-Mon, Ascension day, Pentecost, Dec 25/26 & Jan 1 ▪ Meals & cheese platters by prior arrangement ▪ Owner(s) Maarten & Janine van Beuningen ▪ Winemaker(s) Gerda Willers (whites, 2007) & André Liebenberg (reds, 2012) ▪ 1,120cs own label 50% red 50% white ▪ PO Box 5144 Helderberg 7135 ▪ maarten@miravel.co.za ▪ www.miravel.co.za ▪ S 34° 1′ 58.7″ E 018° 46′ 46.9″ ▪ ⓦ no adress or information ▪ **T +27 (0)21-842-3154/+27 (0)72-212-4668**

Mischa Estate   ⓥ ⑪ ◎

This 3rd-generation estate was purchased after WWII by John Barns, who chose it for its Table Mountain view (unusual for Wellington) and named it after his grandmother's Russian ballet partner. For Andrew Barns, grandson, winemaker and co-owner with brother Gary, it all starts with improved soil and plant health, and the best use of natural resources available to them - elements on which they focus in their successful vine nursery, regenerative farming business NutraFarm, established boutique wine venture Mischa (emphasising wine purity), as well as new wine range, The Vine Guys, borrowing the siblings' nickname.

Mischa Estate range

★★★★ Cabernet Sauvignon Newly bottled after 15 months in 30% new oak (mostly French, some American, Hungarian, as all these), **17** ⑧⑥ more persistence & promise than last-tasted **14 ★★★★** ⑧④, bright fruit (blackcurrants, ripe cherries) & pinch cinnamon.

★★★★☆ Grenache Limited Edition ⑩ ⓶ Sheer drinking pleasure offered by **17** ⑨③, with its ripe, juicy, red berry fruit, also some ruby grapefruit along with cinnamon spice & pepper. 15 months oak, 20% new, medium bodied & fresh, soft chalky tannins.

★★★★ Merlot 15 ⑧⑥ (WO Wellington) smoother & more savoury/smoky than also-tasted **16** ⑧⑧ (WO Groenberg), which is fresh, aromatic (black wine gums, aniseed), with ripe plum & black berry intensity. Same oak for both (2 years, 20% new).

★★★★ Merlot-Cabernet Sauvignon Reserve ⑩ Slight prickle on **17** ⑧⑥, just bottled after 15 months in oak, 5% cabernet adding to intensity of black berry & plum fruit with dark chocolate richness.

★★★★ Créer Limited Edition ⑩ Mourvèdre (40%) adds violet & smoke aromatics, black fruit, also a little meatiness to grenache's red fruit & cinnamon in full-bodied but soft **17** ⑧⑨, year in oak, 20% new.

★★★★ Roussanne Fresh **18** ⑧⑦ steps up on viscous **17 ★★★★** ⑧⑤ thanks to lower alcohol (under 12.5%), intriguing sweet melon & Toff-o-Luxe richness despite being very dry, with underlying minerality.

Shiraz ★★★★ Ripe dark fruit & velvety mouthfeel, **15** ⑧⑤ succulent, white spice & vanilla from 3 years oak, 25% new, alcohol high (15%) but not hot.

The Vine Guys range ⑩

★★★★ Sauvignon Blanc ⊘ Herbaceous green hint on nose of otherwise tropical **17** ⑧⑥, palate pops with pink grapefruit & passionfruit, dry & fresh.

La Famille range

Cabernet Sauvignon ⓠ **★★★☆** Packed with ripe black cherries & berries, **16** ⑧⑤ nicely balanced, smooth tannins making it youthfully approachable. WO W Cape. Not tasted: **Merlot**. — JG

Location/map: Wellington ▪ Map grid reference: B2 ▪ WO: Groenberg/Wellington/Western Cape ▪ Est/1stB 1999 ▪ Tasting, sales & tours (vine nursery in winter & cellar in summer) by appt ▪ Fee R125pp, waived if purchase equals/exceed it ▪ Open pub hols by appt ▪ Snacks & meals by appt ▪ Walks ▪ MTB ▪ Owner(s) Andrew & Gary Barns ▪ Cellarmaster(s)/winemaker(s) Andrew Barns (Jan 1999) ▪ Viticulturist(s) Ruiter Smit (Jun 1960) & Eben Archer ▪ 40ha (cabs s/f, malbec, merlot, mourv, p verdot, petite sirah, shiraz, rouss, sauv, viog) ▪ 97t/4,000cs own label 75% red 25% white ▪ Oakdene Road Wellington 7654 ▪ sales@mischaestate. com ▪ www.mischaestate.com ▪ S 33° 36' 13.1" E 019° 01' 46.8" ▪ ⌧ asteroids.brandishes.newsstands ▪ **T +27 (0)21-864-1016/19/20**

☐ **Mischief Maker** *see* Valley Vineyards Wine Company

Miss Molly

Miss Molly is the focus of an effort by winemaker Clayton Reabow and the Môreson team in Franschhoek to up the quality and 'move the brand out of the entry-level wine stigma'. The inspiration for the label's name and logo is Môreson's naughty but loveable Weimaraner.

★★★★ The Huntress Pinot Noir ⊘ From single, very low-crop block, **16** ⑧⑦ ripe redcurrant & strawberry fruit, hints exotic spice & forest floor, balanced & moreish. Can age. Franschhoek WO, like next.

★★★★ Manor Born Chardonnay-Semillon Elegant **16** ⑧⑧ gets vanilla biscuit nuance to tangy citrus fruit from 40% new oak; complex, lengthy flavours with waxy overlay. Very attractive 78/22 blend. No **15**.

★★★★ Petit Rosé ⊘ MCC bubbly from chardonnay & pinot noir, **NV** ⑧⑥. Pretty pink hue & matching fruit flavours (strawberry, watermelon), soft, mouthfilling mousse & lemon biscuit nuance ex year on lees.

★★★★ Bubbly ⊘ MCC sparkling unites chardonnay & 17% chenin in bright, refreshing **NV** ⑧⑥. Crunchy apple & nectarine flavours, fresh & delicious bubbles after 12 months sur lie. WO W Cape, as Rosé.

Not tasted: **In My Bed Red Blend, Kitchen Thief Sauvignon Blanc**. — WB

☐ **Misty Kloof's** *see* Goedverwacht Wine Estate

Misty Mountains Estate

In the Klein River hills near Stanford, Misty Mountains has evolved from a natural spring to a vineyard to a winery with cellar and visitor attractions. The latter keep multiplying, and now include a restaurant and farm stall. The portfolio, too, is expanding, with the sparkling promised last edition materialising along with an unannounced rosé, joining a small but growing number of SA pinks from Spanish grape mourvèdre.

Rosé (NEW) ★★★ Deep pink **18** ⑦ from mourvèdre, subtle, somewhat fruity & fresh. **Sauvignon Blanc** ★★★★ Typical varietal freshness on textured green-apple palate, touches flint, bellpepper & green fig add complexity to cool-grown, focused **18** ⑧④. **Méthode Cap Classique** (NEW) ★★★ Extra-dry rosé sparkling from chardonnay, pinotage (30%). Pretty onion skin hue, lively strawberry, cherry notes & persistent saline finish on **15** ⑧⓪. Not tasted: **Shiraz**, **Family Reserve Sauvignon Blanc**. — HC

Location: Stanford ▪ Map: Walker Bay & Bot River ▪ Map grid reference: B5 ▪ WO: Walker Bay ▪ Est 2004 ▪ 1stB 2008 ▪ Tasting & sales Mon-Sun 9-5 ▪ Closed Good Fri, Dec 25 & Jan 1 ▪ Cellar tours by appt ▪ Conferences (±60 pax) ▪ Self-catering cottages ▪ Restaurant & farm stall ▪ Craft beer, gin & cider ▪ Owner(s) Misty Mountains Estates (director A van Vuuren) ▪ Winemaker(s) Neil Patterson ▪ Vineyard manager(s) Robert Davis ▪ 46ha/16ha (mourv, shiraz, sauv, sem) ▪ PO Box 26 Stanford 7201 ▪ info@mistymountains.co.za ▪ www.mistymountains.co.za ▪ S 34° 25′ 04″ E 019° 25′ 35″ ▪ encoded.crosswords.retry ▪ **T +27 (0)82-973-5943**

Mitre's Edge

Bernard and Lola Nicholls took over this estate on the Stellenbosch edge of Paarl in 1999, from Lola's father. Bernard the mechanical engineer became a farmer, Lola a winemaker. Some of the crop is sold off, but Lola crafts a full range of wines, focusing on the red Bordeaux varieties, in big, ripe and bold (but well-balanced) style. It's clearly working well, as exports, visitor numbers and production are satisfactorily up.

Flagship range

★★★★ **Cabernet Sauvignon** Classic blackcurrant with cedar & tobacco on **15** ⑧⑦, as usual, combined with less-classic power - 15% alcohol a touch hot on dry finish but matched by big ripe flavours & macho tannins. Just 5% new oak, as on all these.

★★★★☆ **Cabernet Franc** (🍇) The closest to elegantly balanced of these big reds. **15** ⑨① fragrant aromas - ripe dark berries, spicy dry leaf - lead to firm, fruit-filled & not overly structured palate (though a good firm grip), with a little chocolate on the dry finish. A good future ahead of it.

★★★★☆ **Malbec** Good loganberry fruit on **16** ★★★★ ⑧⑨. With Sholto, lowest alcohol (14.6%) in the range; well built but less density & structure than others, more sweet & easy charm in youth. **15** ⑨⓪ was fuller-flavoured.

★★★★☆ **Merlot** Varietal fruitcake & chocolate on aromas & flavours of **15** ★★★★ ⑧⑦, with herbal note. Strong tannin-acid skeleton to fleshy fruit; 15% alcohol adds glow to the dry conclusion. First since **12** ⑨③.

★★★★ **Petit Verdot** Dark fruit character on bold, richly textured **15** ⑧⑥, 15.1% alcohol adding warmth. Big dry tannins ideally need years to soften but the fruit concentration perhaps not there. Last made was **12** ⑧⑦.

★★★★☆ **Sholto** (🍇) Cab, merlot, cab franc & petit verdot on **14** ⑨③. More subtle & understated, & more intense, than Mitre version, though similarities of aroma & flavour. Restrained extraction, firm & pleasingly succulent. 14.3% alcohol doesn't affect lingering, properly dry finish.

Mitre's Edge range

★★★★ **The Mitre** (🍇) Cab franc (73%) rules dark-fruited, tobacco-tinged **14** ⑧⑦ blend with merlot & cab. Same character as flagships - no dumbing down. Ripeness supported by structure. Also wants time.

Shiraz ★★★★☆ Spicy, smoky aromas on big, flavourful **15** ⑧⑤ with pleasing savoury edge; surprisingly well balanced given 15.3% alcohol. Also-tasted **16** ⑧③ less big & ripe, with redder fruit & herbal notes. Not tasted: **Rosé**, **Chenin Blanc**, **Viognier**. In abeyance: **Cabernet Sauvignon**.

ME range

Classic Red (🍇) ★★★ Crunchy red fruit & leafy tannins in cab-led **NV** ⑦⑧, billed as 'braai aperitif'. **nvME** (🍇) ★★★★ Bordeaux/shiraz blend **14** ⑧⑤'s attractions bound up in dry tannins mid-2016, might since have softened & opened. — TJ

Location/map: Paarl ▪ Map grid reference: C8 ▪ WO: Simonsberg-Paarl ▪ Est 1999 ▪ 1stB 2004 ▪ Tasting & sales by appt Mon-Fri 9-5 Sat 9-1 ▪ Cellar tours by appt ▪ Guest house B&B ▪ Olive oil ▪ Owner(s) Bernard & Lola Nicholls ▪ Winemaker(s) Lola Nicholls (2004), with Bernard Nicholls ▪ Viticulturist(s) Danie Kritzinger (consultant) ▪ Vineyard manager Bertus de Clerk ▪ 58ha/18ha (cabs s/f, malbec, merlot, p verdot, shiraz, chenin, viog) ▪ 29t/3,100cs own label 90% red 9% white 1% rosé ▪ WIETA ▪ PO Box 12290 Die Boord 7613 ▪ info@mitres-edge.co.za ▪ www.mitres-edge.co.za ▪ S 33° 49' 47.3" E 018° 52' 34.4" ▪ 𝄞 embedded.shifting. apron ▪ **T +27 (0)21-875-5960**

☐ **MM Louw** see Diemersdal Estate

MolenVliet Oosthuizen Family Vineyards   ⓥ ⓐ ⓞ

These Stellenbosch reds, joined this edition by a sauvignon and made by Knorhoek's Barry van Niekerk, emanate from Banhoek Valley vines owned, together with exclusive wedding, conference and accommodation facilities, by former Springbok rugby prop Ockie Oosthuizen and wife Susan.

Private Collection
Cabernet Sauvignon ★★★★ Variety's firm tannins, prominent acidity, modest oaking (10% new) give form to **14** ⑧④'s sweet berry fruitiness. Should reward few years cellaring. **Merlot** ★★★ Appealing confectionery sugar & black plum aromas, **14** ⑧⓪ drinks easily & well courtesy very soft tannins. **Duet** ⓥ ★★★ Marries 60% cab, merlot in milk- & berry-infused mouthful, **13** ⑧① good food partner now & for the next year/2. WO Stellenbosch, like Quartet. **Proprietors Selection** ★★★★ Two vintages reviewed: **13** ⑧⑤ cab franc, cab & merlot combo, very ripe rum-&-raisin profile lifted by cab franc's leafiness. Briefer, sweeter impression than 50/50 cab/merlot **14** ⑧④. Rich & plummy, with nutmeg note, vibrant fantail conclusion. Both judicious 10% new oak. **Quartet** ⓥ ★★★★ Cab, merlot with splashes petit verdot, cab franc in **13** ⑧③ successful, if somewhat stern, nod to Bordeaux. **Sauvignon Blanc** ⓝⓔⓦ ★★★ Subdued acacia aroma, **17** ⑧② smooth & easy, variety's brisk acidity smoothed by few grams sugar. — GM, CvZ

Location/map: Stellenbosch ▪ Map grid reference: H4 ▪ WO: Simonsberg—Stellenbosch/Stellenbosch ▪ Est/1stB 2005 ▪ Tasting only available to in-house guests ▪ Wedding/conference venue ▪ 5-star luxury accommodation ▪ Owner(s) Ockie & Susan Oosthuizen ▪ Winemaker(s) Barry van Niekerk ▪ 14ha/8ha (cab, merlot, shiraz) ▪ 13t/±2,500cs own label 100% red ▪ PO Box 6288 Uniedal 7612 ▪ info@molenvliet.co.za ▪ www. molenvliet.co.za ▪ S 33° 54' 52.9" E 018° 56' 30.6" ▪ 𝄞 kitchen.dream.truth ▪ **T +27 (0)21-885-1597**

Momento Wines   ⓥ

Marelise Niemann is part of the growing circle of dynamic, creative young SA producers who, with joie de vivre, indulge in winemaking unfettered by convention. She seeks out old/unusual vineyard parcels, and vinifies these in the Gabriëlskloof cellar, allowing full expression of the terroir and fruit character with minimal intervention. A visit to Spain inspired her to focus on grenache and its mutations, and this would be her chosen variety, were she to plant her own vines.

★★★★ **Tinta Barocca** From 3 old (40+ years) parcels in Bot River, Stellenbosch & Swartland. Lighter, delicate version of variety, wild red berries, bright acidity, lively dry tannins, smoky polished leather undertone. **17** ★★★★ ⑧⑤ appealing, if shade less fruit than **16** ⑧⑥, ex single block. Natural ferment, as all.

★★★★★ **Chenin Blanc-Verdelho** Lime, baked apple & nutty, waxy flavours & clean acidity from 81% Bot River & Swartland chenin, Paardeberg verdelho. Finely nuanced wine, understated but quietly persistent & engaging. **17** ⑨⓪ less rich than **16** ⑨③, fresher, appealing now & potential to age.

Grenache Gris ⓝⓔⓦ ★★★★ Contemplative, unusual **17** ⑧⑤ from young (4 years) Voor Paardeberg vines, both subtle & delicate in flavour (some starfruit & almond) yet quite feisty in texture & acidity; skin contact adds pithy nuance, 10 months old oak rounds the edges. One to watch. Not tasted: **Grenache**. — MW

Location: Bot River ▪ WO: Western Cape ▪ 1stB 2012 ▪ Private tastings on request ▪ Owner(s)/winemaker(s) Marelise Niemann ▪ 2,300cs own label 50% red 50% white ▪ marelise@momentowines.co.za ▪ www. momentowines.co.za ▪ **T +27 (0)82-968-8588**

☐ **Moments Collection** see Teddy Hall Wines

Monis Wines

Tuscan brothers Giuseppe and Roberto Moni's cheese, olive oil, pasta and wine trading company today is a fortifieds-only business based in Paarl. Cellarmaster Michael Bucholz and his team source locally and from Breede River, Calitzdorp and Stellenbosch for their muscadel, port- and sherry-style wines. The fortifying brandy spirit is from parent Distell's own distilleries.

Monis Wines range

★★★★☆ **Wood Matured Muscadel** ⓖ 500 ml of irresistible dried orange zest, spice, muscat complexity. **04** ⑨② 's rich, silky sweetness disciplined by 5 years older oak, tangy acid. Breede River fruit.

★★★★ **Tawny Port** ⓖ Gorgeous **96** ⑧⑦ complex bouquet of spice, burnt caramel, nuts & dried fruit; slippery tail. Paarlberg tinta & cinsaut.

Vintage Port ⓖ ★★★★ Touriga's fragrance enhances ex-Calitzdorp **06** ⑧④, with warming spirity tail.

Monis Sherry-Style Wines range

★★★★ **Full Cream** ⓖ Richest, sweetest of the range, **NV** ⑧⑧ multi-layered. Honey cake, nuts, dried fruit yet somehow still savoury, which is what makes it so drinkable. Tastes drier than it is.

Medium Cream ⓖ ★★★★ A flor note in **NV** ⑧④'s perfume, nicely coupled with candied fruit, nutty richness. Semi-sweet in style, the alcohol providing enough lift for this to be a delicious aperitif. **Pale Dry** ⓖ ★★★★ From chenin, matured under flor for 3 years, then to solera for a further 3, like all these. Tealeaf & rock salt savoury thread, **NV** ⑧④ ends dry. Ideal aperitif, serve chilled. — CR

Location: Paarl ▪ WO: Breede River Valley/Paarl/Calitzdorp ▪ Est 1906 ▪ Closed to public ▪ Owner(s) Distell ▪ Cellarmaster(s) Michael Bucholz (Jul 2017) ▪ 52,000cs 100% fortified ▪ PO Box 266 Paarl 7620 ▪ mbucholz@distell.co.za ▪ www.moniswines.co.za ▪ F +27 (0)21-872-2790 ▪ **T +27 (0)21-860-1601**

☐ **Monogram Collection** *see* Foothills Vineyards

Montagu Wine Cellar ⓥ ⓒ ♿

Unsung vines in outlying areas are in the sights of young Turks from out of town. Against this backdrop, the team at grower-owned Montagu Wine Cellar this year is focusing attention on two special blocks from their extensive vineholding for a premium release: '16 Cabernet and '17 fortified red Muscat de Frontignan, latter innovatively matured in bourbon barrels. Neither available to taste this edition; looking forward to next time.

★★★★ **Red Muscadel** Pronounced grape aromas with caramel, mixed peel & floral tones on **17** ⑧⑧ fortified. Well structured, with balance between acid, sugar & alcohol leading to concentrated, positive finish.

Cabernet Sauvignon ⓖ ★★ Slight black fruit on shy but perfectly drinkable **16** ⑦④, touch sweetness on finish. **Merlot-Ruby Cabernet** ⓖ ★★★ Cheery glugger **16** ⑦⑧ is juicy & fresh, with plenty of black & red berries, charry notes on the finish. **White Muscadel** ⓖ ★★★ Pretty **16** ⑧① fortified is clean, satisfying, offers flavours of grapes, flowers & honey. Less complex than red version but still perfectly pleasant. Both WO W Cape. Not tasted: **Chenin Blanc**. — CM

Location: Montagu ▪ Map: Klein Karoo & Garden Route ▪ Map grid reference: B8 ▪ WO: Montagu/Western Cape ▪ Est 1941 ▪ 1stB 1975 ▪ Tasting & sales Mon-Fri 8–5 ▪ Closed all pub hols ▪ Farm produce ▪ Owner(s) 54 members ▪ Executive manager Jacques Jordaan (2013) ▪ Winemaker(s) Hermias Vollgraaff (Aug 2013), with Chris de Villiers (Aug 2017) ▪ 620ha (11 varieties r/w) ▪ 16,000t/11,000cs own label 12% red 82% white 6% muscadel ▪ IPW, WIETA ▪ PO Box 29 Montagu 6720 ▪ sales@montaguwines.co.za ▪ www.montaguwines.co.za ▪ S 33° 46' 37.3" E 020° 7' 58.4" ▪ ⌖ suborbital.typewriter.untying ▪ F +27 (0)23-614-1793 ▪ **T +27 (0)23-614-1125**

Mont Blois Wynlandgoed ⓥ ⓒ

Nina-Mari Bruwer's revival of the winemaking tradition at this large Robertson estate is expanding from her successful 2016-vintage debut, with the addition of a delicious grenache blanc. It comes from the first harvest off a block of bushvines — something extremely rare in Robertson, as is the variety — and was vinified in Nina-Marie's corner of the old (1884) cellar. Husband Ernst is the 6th generation of his family to own Mont Blois. Most of the grapes are sold to the big merchants, as well as to some prestigious private labels.

★★★★ **Hoog & Laag Chardonnay** Deeper gold than Kweekkamp, **17** ⑧⑦ off red Karoo clay much riper, pineapple-oriented aromas & flavours, & sweeter. Some intensity, with good acid striving to give balance.

★★★★☆ **Kweekkamp Chardonnay** From a single-vineyard on limestone, **17** ⑨② the more focused of the pair of chardonnays, with citrus, floral, tropical & liquorice notes. Serious acidic balance for the richness of the lingering fruit. As with sibling, only unobtrusive older oak.

★★★★☆ **Groot Steen Chenin Blanc** Forthcoming aromas announce the generous, rich, sweet-fruited ripeness of flavourful **17** ⑨⓪ off 32-year-old single-vineyard. Decent acidic balance maintains freshness. Natural ferment - the general rule here, as is older oak maturation.

★★★★ **Grenache Blanc** ⑭ Delightfully fruity, floral charm on light-feeling **18** ⑧⑥ off young bush-vines. Unpretentious but revealing quality of grapes & winemaking. Fresh, well balanced & delicious.

★★★★☆ **Harpie Muscadel** ⑭ Second single-vineyard fortified, matured in oak. **16** ⑨② packed with multitudinous flavours, from raisin to marmalade & beyond. Silky texture, good, balanced acid keeping from cloy, the 16% alcohol not fiery. More refined than many examples.

★★★★☆ **Pomphuis Muscadel** ⓧ Single-vineyard **16** ⑨② harks back to 1988 White Muscadel in **93** guide. Panoply of aromas & flavours, redolent of grapes, flowers, marmalade, mint humbug. Very sweet & viscous, but nicely balanced for seductiveness. Year in old oak. 500 ml. Should develop for ages.— TJ

Location/map/WO: Robertson ▪ Map grid reference: A5 ▪ Est 1869/1884 (farm/cellar) ▪ Tasting, sales & cellar tours by appt Mon-Fri 9-6 Sat 9-5 ▪ Closed Easter Fri-Mon & Dec 25 ▪ Conservation area ▪ MTB trail ▪ Owner(s) Ernst Bruwer ▪ Cellarmaster(s) Raymond Kirby (Jun 1984) ▪ Winemaker(s) Nina-Mari Bruwer (Apr 2008) ▪ Viticulturist(s) Andries Colyn (Mar 1999), Dean Kriel (Jul 2013) & John Zeeman (Jun 2017) ▪ 297ha (cbard, chard, chenin, muscadel w) ▪ Own label 100% white ▪ IPW, WIETA ▪ PO Box 181 Robertson 6705 ▪ info@montblois.co.za ▪ www.montblois.co.za ▪ S 33° 46' 4.00" E 019° 55' 35.06" ▪ Ⓦ admirably.attended. ranked ▪ **T +27 (0)23-626-4052**

Mont Destin Wines/Destiny Shiraz

Now in its third decade as a boutique winery at the foot of the Simonsberg, Mon Destin sees the beginning of a new chapter, with winemaker-owner Samantha Bürgin closing the cellardoor and trimming the range to focus on her flagship Destiny Shiraz.

★★★★☆ **Destiny Shiraz** ⓧ A barrel selection, released only when ready. **11** ⑨④ a tour de force. Big & bold, with enough concentration, tannin, for longevity. Also in 1.5L. Paarl WO.

Discontinued: **Passioné, 11 Barrels**. — JPf

Location: Stellenbosch ▪ WO: Paarl ▪ Est/1stB 1998 ▪ Closed to public; sales by email/phone ▪ Owner(s) Samantha Bürgin ▪ Winemaker(s) Samantha Bürgin (May 1996) ▪ Own label 100% red ▪ PO Box 1237 Stellenbosch 7599 ▪ info@montdestin.co.za ▪ www.montdestin.co.za ▪ F +27 (0)21-875-5870 ▪ **T +27 (0)83-288-4985**

Mont du Toit Kelder

ⓧ ⓐ ⓑ

'Winefarming is a Du Toit tradition,' says Stephan du Toit, Johannesburg senior advocate and, since 1996, owner of this farm at the foot of Wellington's Hawequa range, originally granted to his Huguenot ancestors in 1691. 'We keep going, despite the drought,' he says, his wine labels featuring French names to honour his heritage, a silhouette of the mountain, and a Khoi figure representing 'our bond with Africa and its sun'.

Mont du Toit range

★★★★☆ **Mont du Toit** Rich, velvety, harmonious after nearly year in oak, 20% American, further few in bottle, **12** ⑨①'s ripe dark fruit still fresh, tangy, with mint-choc lift on finish. Cab-led, with 17% cab franc, 11% each merlot & petit verdot. No **11**.

★★★★☆ **Le Sommet** ⓐ 'The Pinnacle' made only in exceptional years, cab-led **16** ⑨② has 22% merlot, 8% cab franc & dash tinta adding to succulent dark fruit. Sleek, silky & elegant at 13.5% alcohol, with spice & tobacco nuances from 15-20 months in barrique, some American.

★★★★ **La Colline** ⑭ From dryland vines in Paarl, **16** ⑧⑧ chenin has intense tropical flavours, ranging from guava to tangy pineapple, creamy vanilla softness & spice after 9 months in barrel.

Hawequas ★★★★ Intended for everyday drinking, smooth **14** ⑧⑤ 6-way blend led by merlot, 16 months oaked, has savoury edge to black & blue berry fruit after time in bottle.

Les Coteaux range

★★★★ **Cabernet Franc** ⊘ Fruitcake & minty dark chocolate aromas of **14** (87) carry through to palate, packed with forest fruits, elegant at 13.5% alcohol, returning to form after brisk **13** ★★★★ (85).

★★★★ **Sélection** ⊘ Merlot-led **14** (87) with cab franc & 4 others is ripely, deeply, darkly plummy, very smooth, with pinch of dried herbs lifting the aromas.

. . . .

Merlot ⊛ ★★★★ Plum pudding richness, berry freshness too, & chai spice nuances, velvet tannins from 18 months mostly French oak, 20% new. **16** (84) less leafy than last.

Cabernet Sauvignon ★★★★ Ripe cassis, plum, black cherries on **15** (85), notes of mocha & cedar spice from nicely integrated oak, 20% new. **Shiraz** ★★★★ Very ripe, dense dark fruit in **15** (85) with nuances of black pepper, cocoa & smoke, smooth, with powdery tannins.

Blouvlei range

. . . .

Selection ⊘ ⊛ ★★★★ Range previously listed separately. **15** (85) balanced 7-way blend, 71% cab gives tangy black berry succulence.

. . . .

In abeyance: **Sauvignon Blanc**. — JG

Location/map: Wellington ▪ Map grid reference: C4 ▪ WO: Wellington/Paarl ▪ Est 1996 ▪ 1stB 1998 ▪ Tasting, sales & cellar tours by appt only ▪ Closed all pub hols ▪ Hiking trails ▪ Owner(s) Stephan du Toit ▪ Cellarmaster(s) Bernd Philippi (1997) ▪ Winemaker(s) Chris Roux (2012), with Abraham Cloete (Jan 2005) ▪ ±40ha/±28ha (alicante bouschet, cabs s/f, merlot, mourv, p verdot, shiraz, tinta barocca) ▪ ±165t/±1,200cs own label 100% red ▪ IPW ▪ PO Box 704 Wellington 7654 ▪ kelder@montdutoit.co.za, marketing@mont-dutoit.co.za ▪ www.montdutoit.co.za ▪ S 33° 39′ 27.72″ E 019° 1′ 45.81″ ▪ ⌨ rummage.super.talker ▪ F +27 (0)21-864-2737 ▪ **T +27 (0)21-873-7745**

Montegray Vineyards   ⊕ ⊛ (NEW)

Montegray is the latest venture from irrepressibly energetic Rose Jordaan of Bartinney Private Cellar. It centres on a beautiful little syrah vineyard in her beloved Banhoek Valley outside Stellenbosch, purchased in 2017 because it dovetailed with her plan to produce small batches of special or interesting terroir-driven wines. (Grapes for the other wines are selected around Stellenbosch.) Pronouncing herself 'chuffed to bits' to be making shiraz again is consultant winemaker Ronell Wiid, to date the only female Diners Club Winemaker of the Year, which she won in 1999 with a shiraz blend.

★★★★ **Petit Verdot** Muscular but refined **15** (86) shows chunky blue & black fruit abundance. Succulent & bright, with light tannic grip from just 8 months in older French oak, none new.

★★★★ **Syrah** Fynbos overlay on rich, concentrated dark berry fruit on **15** (89). Oregano & smoke add interest to nuanced, layered palate which is fresh yet firm from years in older oak, further year in bottle.

★★★★ **Grenache Blanc-Roussanne** Rich, broad stonefruit appeal in 50/50 **16** (86) blend. Honeyed nectarine countered by supportive, well-knit oak (all old). Lively acid keeps whole fresh & focused.— FM

Location/map/WO: Stellenbosch ▪ Map grid reference: F5 ▪ Est 2014 ▪ 1stB 2015 ▪ Tasting & sales Mon–Sat 11-9 at Montegray & Independents Wine Bar T +27 (0)63-677-7928, 6 Bird Str Stellenbosch ▪ Closed Dec 25 & Jan 1 ▪ Wine, craft beer, gin & sharing plates ▪ Owner(s) Rose & Michael Jordaan ▪ Winemaker(s) Ronell Wiid (consultant) ▪ Viticulturist(s) Logan Jooste (Jun 2017) ▪ 3.5ha ▪ Postnet Suite 231 Private Bag X5061 Stellenbosch 7599 ▪ info@bartinney.co.za ▪ www.bartinney.co.za ▪ S 33° 56′ 18.85″ E 018° 51′ 36.89″ ▪ F +27 (0)86-298-0447 ▪ **T +27 (0)21-885-1013**

☐ **Montestell** *see* Boland Kelder
☐ **Monte Vista** *see* Mooiuitsig Wine Cellars
☐ **Montino** *see* Riebeek Cellars

Montpellier   ⊕ ⊛ ⌂ ◎ ⊗

Johannesburg lawman Lucas van Tonder has styled his historic Tulbagh Cape-Dutch farm, with landmark hillside vineyard chapel and portfolio of classic whites, reds, rosé and MCCs sparklings, as a country destination for weekends, weddings and functions. In the cellar, Danie van der Westhuizen has been joined by Reinhard Odendaal, seasoned at Beyerskloof, Barton and Walker Bay Estate.

Location/map: Tulbagh ▪ Map grid reference: F5 ▪ Est 1714 ▪ Tasting, sales & tours Mon-Fri 9-5 Sat/Sun & pub hols 10-3 ▪ Pre-booked cheese platters & light meals available during tasting hours ▪ Tour groups: gazebo with pizza oven to be pre-booked ▪ Olives ▪ Walking/hiking trails ▪ Renosterbos conservation area ▪ Guest house/B&B/self-catering ▪ Weddings: Dome & Cathedral venues ▪ Events ▪ Owner(s) Lucas J van Tonder ▪ Winemaker(s) Danie van der Westhuizen (Dec 2015) & Reinhard Odendaal ▪ 482ha/60ha (cab, merlot, p verdot, pinot, shiraz, chard, chenin, cbard, gewürz, riesling, sauv, viog) ▪ PO Box 79 Tulbagh 6820 ▪ info@montpellier.co.za ▪ www.montpellier.co.za ▪ S 33° 16' 30.4" E 019° 6' 40.0" ▪ ⊠ chops.persons.reprint ▪ F +27 (0)23-230-1574 ▪ **T +27 (0)23-230-0656**

Mont Rochelle Hotel & Vineyard   ⓆⓎⓖⓞ

Franschhoek mountainside estate Mont Rochelle, part of UK entrepreneur Richard Branson's Virgin Limited Edition portfolio since 2014, has entered phase two of a vineyard redevelopment programme, with the first vines planted as we prepared this edition. Focus has been on matching varieties, clones and rootstocks to the correct soils through GIS mapping, inter alia, to produce terroir-specific wines. In the cellar, Dustin Osborne continues his winecrafting, and at the luxury hotel and cellardoor, many attractions await.

Miko range

★★★★☆ **Syrah** Ⓐ Was 'Red'. Plush & ripe but well-balanced **10** ⑼⑶, forthright but fine tannin structure & generous plum fruit, expected spice & pepper follows through to finish. A fine example buttressed by 25% new oak, 24 months.

★★★★☆ **Chardonnay** Was 'White', still mostly chardonnay (94%) in **16** ⑼⑴, dash viognier adding pithy & floral components. Alluring aromas of citrus, minerality on palate with assertive freshness & light spicy note. Fermented/12 months in 94% new French oak.

Mont Rochelle range

★★★★ **Syrah** Mouthfillingly juicy plum fruit, but **15** ⑻⑼ has enough punchy tannins to restore balance, 15% new oak, 18 months, enhances variety's inherent spice.

Chardonnay ★★★★ Just 10% new oak on **17** ⑻⑷ yet its toasty tone is prominent, more so than last; however ample fruit (varietal & splash viognier) & minerality ensure delicious drinkability. **Sauvignon Blanc** ★★★★ More refined than previous, **17** ⑻⑶ delicious & clean fruited, abundant passionfruit & nettle, splash oaked semillon adds to mouthfeel & body. Not tasted: **Cabernet Sauvignon**. Discontinued: **Merlot**.

Little Rock range

Rouge ⊘ ★★★★ Adds syrah to previous release's Bordeaux-only grapes in **16** ⑻⑶, fruity & delicious fireside drinker. **Blanc** Ⓩ ★★★ Semillon-driven **16** ⑻⑵ with chardonnay, sauvignon & viognier, unoaked. Light & zesty picnic fare. — HC

Location/map/WO: Franschhoek ▪ Map grid reference: C2 ▪ Est 1994 ▪ 1stB 1996 ▪ Tasting & sales 10–7 daily ▪ Fee available on request ▪ Wine tasting closed Dec 25 ▪ Cellar tours Mon, Wed, Fri at 11 (pre-booking required) ▪ Winemaker tutored tastings by appt only ▪ Miko Restaurant & The Country Kitchen ▪ Mont Rochelle Hotel & Vineyard ▪ Picnics ▪ Owner(s) Virgin Limited Edition ▪ Cellarmaster(s)/winemaker(s)/viticulturist(s) Dustin Osborne ▪ 33ha/12.5ha (cabs s/f, shiraz, chard, sauv, sem) ▪ 90–120t/12,000cs own label 60% red 40% white ▪ PO Box 448 Franschhoek 7690 ▪ wine@montrochelle.virgin.com ▪ www.montrochelle.virgin.com ▪ S 33° 54' 52.1" E 019° 6' 21.9" ▪ ⊠ rusting.nudged.crept ▪ F +27 (0)21-876-3788 ▪ **T +27 (0)21-876-2770**

☐ **Mooiberg** *see* Zidela Wines

Mooi Bly Winery   Ⓠⓔⓖⓞ

Erik Schouteden nurtures the vines and wines at this boutique property owned by his Belgian in-laws, the Wouters. The small selection of classic-variety wines is supplemented by uncommon solo bottlings of malbec and tannat. Accommodation is offered in self-catering cottages overlooking Paarl's Dal Josafat area.

Location/map: Paarl ▪ Map grid reference: F4 ▪ Est/1stB 2005 ▪ Tasting, sales & cellar tours by appt ▪ Fee R75pp ▪ Closed Dec 25 & Jan 1 ▪ BYO picnic ▪ Walks ▪ 6 self-catering cottages ▪ Owner(s) Wouters family ▪

Cellarmaster(s)/winemaker(s) Erik Schouteden (Jan 2005) ▪ Viticulturist(s) Erik Schouteden (Feb 2001) ▪ 32ha/18ha (cab, malbec, shiraz, tannat, chard, chenin) ▪ 70t/6,000cs own label 50% red 50% white ▪ PO Box 801 Huguenot 7645 ▪ wine@mooibly.com ▪ www.mooibly.com ▪ S 33° 41' 7.0" E 019° 1' 21.9" ▪ ⬚ anyone. cleared.sneaker ▪ F +27 (0)21-868-2808 ▪ **T +27 (0)21-868-2808**

Mooiplaas Estate & Private Nature Reserve ⓠ ⑪ ⓐ ⓑ

This historic farm in Stellenbosch's Bottelary Hills is family owned and run but by no means a small homespun affair. International sales have grown to 85% of production, exported to 27 countries, keeping cellarmaster Louis Roos busy enough with this marketing portfolio to warrant recently appointing winemaker Bertus Basson to run the cellar. Louis' brother Tielman and his namesake son are respectively responsible for viticulture and local sales, and their new warehouse logistics, while daughter-in-law Kirsten handles administration. Mother Nature's involved too, as the fynbos reserve, popular with cyclists and hikers, helps curtail vineyard pests. See also Roos Family Vineyards entry.

Mercia Collection

★★★★ **Tabakland Cabernet Sauvignon Reserve** ⓐ Occasional release. **15** ★★★★★ ⑨⓪ first since **10** ⑧⑨, from 26 year old vines. Well structured, more concentrated & streamlined than Roos sibling, dark fruit intensity in sync with the alcohol (14.5%). Worth ageing a decade, though already balanced.

★★★★ **Watershed Syrah** ⓠ Premium label from elevated Bottelary site 'Rooirug'. **12** ⑧⑧, retasted, shows elegant development, with fruit more prominent, receding spiciness.

★★★★ **Rosalind** ⓐ Cab (50%) with cab franc & merlot, **15** ⑧⑨ still an infant, dark & red berry fruit still enveloped in firm dry tannins, structured for graceful evolution.

★★★★ **Houmoed Bushvine Chenin Blanc** ⓠ Special dryland single-vineyard reserve, barrel-fermented **15** ⑧⑧ rich & elegant, with high-toned peach & apricot. Intense fruitiness lingers long. No **14**.

★★★★ **Duel Méthode Cap Classique** ⓠ Rich, creamy & very satisfying sparkling from pinot noir & chardonnay, 36 months on lees. **NV** ⑧⑦ more classic: baked apples mingle with warm brioche aromas.

★★★★ **Laatlam Noble Late Harvest** ⓠ Intensely aromatic, syrupy sweet **13** ⑧⑨ from botrytised sauvignon blanc, showing edgy wood spices & development from 30 months in used barrels.

Roos Family range

★★★★ **Cabernet Sauvignon** Rich & big-boned **15** ⑧⑥, quite dense, chalky dry tannins anchor the dark fruit & liquorice; needs time & likely a Sunday roast, nonetheless better than **13** ★★★★ ⑧⑤. No **14**.

Pinotage ⓠ ★★★ Warm, ripe & high-toned strawberry & tobacco on unoaked **16** ⑦⑧, dash cab supporting. Fireside sipper, softer structure & touch rustic. **Chenin Blanc Bush Vine** ★★★★ Ripe Golden Delicious apple with spice dusting, **18** ⑧⑤ drier than last, crunchy but some plumpness on palate, lingering dried peach farewell. Satisfying at mealtime or solo. **Sauvignon Blanc** ★★★★ Zesty step up in **17** ⑧⑷, clean-cut gooseberry & nettle from elevated hillside vines, 6 months lees ageing add plump, silky texture.

Langtafel range

Red ⓠ ★★ Equal cab & shiraz with 10% merlot. **16** ⑦① sweet berry fruit, light, unoaked & undemanding. **Rosé** ★★ From pinotage, **18** ⑦⑥ strawberry & candyfloss aromas, dry, light & tangy, slight stalky nuance less appealing than previous. WO W Cape, as next. **White** ★★★ Dry, easy-drinking **17** ⑦⑧ colombard & chenin has more tropical & crunchy apple fruit than last, friendly 12.5% alcohol. Not tasted: **Vino Baruzzo Novella**. — MW

Location/map: Stellenbosch ▪ Map grid reference: B4 ▪ WO: Stellenbosch/Western Cape ▪ Est 1806 ▪ 1stB 1995 ▪ Tasting & sales: summer Mon-Fri 9-4.30 Sat 10-4 Sun 10.30-3.30; winter Mon-Fri 9-4.30 Sat 11-3 ▪ Fee R50/5 Family range & R85 Mercia range, waived on purchase ▪ Closed Easter weekend, Dec 24 to Jan 3 ▪ Gourmet picnic hampers & cheese platters, booking essential ▪ Private dinners/luncheons or tutored tastings in the manor house (a national monument), by appt ▪ Walks/hikes ▪ MTB ▪ Horse riding, riding lessons & trail rides ▪ Child friendly ▪ 70ha private nature reserve ▪ Owner(s) Roos Family Vineyards (Pty) Ltd ▪ Winemaker(s) Louis Roos (1983) & Bertus Basson (2017) ▪ Viticulturist(s) Tielman Roos (1981) ▪ 240ha/90ha (cabs s/f, merlot, p verdot, ptage, pinot, shiraz, chard, chenin, sauv, viog) ▪ 650t/25,000cs own label 57% red 41% white 2% rosé ▪ IPW ▪ PO Box 104 Koelenhof 7605 ▪ info@mooiplaas.co.za ▪ www.mooiplaas.co.za ▪ S 33° 55' 16.3" E 018° 44' 21.4" ▪ ⬚ reunion.capping.museums ▪ F +27 (0)86-425-7151 ▪ **T +27 (0)21-200-7493**

Mooiuitsig Wine Cellars

Mooiuitsig, the Jonker family's drinks enterprise, has a substantial portfolio (including mostly sweet wines, sherry-style wines and brandies under the Monte Vista, Mooiuitsig, Mooiuitzicht, Oude Rust, Oulap, Overberg, Potjie, Rusthof and Spes Bona labels), an own distribution network and even retail outlets. Accommodation is offered near their Bonnievale HQ.

Location: Bonnievale ▪ Est 1947 ▪ Closed to public ▪ Stay-overs at De Rust Lodge info@outdoorarena.co.za; T +27 (0)23-616-2444 ▪ Owner(s) Jonker family ▪ Winemaker(s) Nico van der Westhuizen, with Lazarus Kholomba ▪ Viticulturist(s) Casper Matthee ▪ 150ha total ▪ 2,900t ▪ PO Box 15 Bonnievale 6730 ▪ info@mooiuitsig.co.za ▪ www.mooiuitsig.co.za ▪ F +27 (0)23-616-2675 ▪ **T +27 (0)23-616-2143**

☐ **Mooiuitzicht** *see* Mooiuitsig Wine Cellars
☐ **Moonlight Organics** *see* Stellar Winery

Môrelig Vineyards

Grapes off the dryland granitic vineyards on Andrew Wightman's Paardeberg farm went into the bottles of some well-known producers before going into his own too. It was initially 'just as a hobby', but has moved well beyond that, as confirmed again by a new chenin. The wines are all firmly in the 'natural', non-interventionist mode. For Andrew's collaborative wine, see Wightman, Gouws & Clarke.

★★★★ **Syrah** Lightly fragrant **17** ⑧⑧ with red fruit, salt-&-pepper seasoning of previous. Gentle, fine tannins, fresh & altogether delicious without great intensity. Bunches pressed by foot for natural ferment.

★★★★☆ **The Hedge** ⊘ Previewed last year, **17** ⑨⓪ has burst forth with gorgeous red fruit aromas mingling with spice & lilies - the latter becoming more herbaceous on the finish. 75% syrah, with carignan & cinsaut adding lightness & easy charm. Understated but informing tannins.

Chenin Blanc (NEW) ★★★★ Golden colour, bruised apple note & savoury rather than fruity characters on richly textured, old-oaked **17** ⑧⑤ suggest oxidative winemaking - rather deliciously so, but not for everyone. — TJ

Location: Malmesbury ▪ Map/WO: Swartland ▪ Map grid reference: C8 ▪ Est/1stB 2015 ▪ Tasting by appt only ▪ Owner(s) Andrew Wightman ▪ Winemaker(s) Andrew & Brandon Wightman ▪ 42ha/24ha (carignan, ptage, shiraz, tinta barocca, chenin, clairette) ▪ 90-100t/1,000cs own label 30% red 65% white 5% rosé ▪ WIETA ▪ PO Box 1133 Malmesbury 7299 ▪ moreligvineyards@paarlonline.co.za ▪ www.moreligvineyards.co.za ▪ S 33° 31'12.73" E 018° 48' 49.40" ▪ swirly.database.timepieces ▪ **T +27 (0)82-658-1101**

Môreson

Acquired in the early 1980s by Richard Friedman, active in Franschhoek's renaissance as a wine-and-food mecca, now co-owned and run by effervescent daughter Nikki, Môreson continues to draw visitors with an on-site eatery, charcutier and small-batch distillery. Nikki is devoted to her childhood idyll, driving sustainable farming and organic production of the increasingly impressive wines. Her team includes characterful Weimaraner Miss Molly, whose name marks a range (separately listed) also aiming for a quality uptick.

★★★★ **Magia** ⓥ Refined despite fruit concentration, **13** ★★★★★ ⑨② fragrant cassis & fynbos leading to red & black berry fruit, fresh acidity, grippy but smooth tannins. 100% cabernet; some Stellenbosch fruit but will be WO Franschhoek in future. First tasted since **07**.

★★★★★ **Mata Mata** (⊛) Mostly cabernet, **16** ⑨③ has impressive presence: intense blackcurrant, cedar, polished leather & leafy coolness ex smidgen cab franc. Complex & regal, with great staying power. Own & Stellenbosch grapes, only 3 barrels, 90% new, 18 months.

★★★★☆ **Cabernet Franc** (⊛) Latterly one of SA's top bottlings, **16** ⑨③ from single block is both lush & refined, with floral perfume, ripe blackberries & delicate crushed herbs. Well structured, finish lifted by vibrant spice. 18 months, 35% new oak, as for stellar **15** ★★★★★ ⑨⑤.

★★★★★ **MKM** (⊛) Vineyard & cellar selection of Stellenbosch pinotage. Rich plum, exotic spice in harmony with well-judged savoury wood. **15** ⑨④ fermented in amphoras, some wholebunch, then 18 months in 80% new oak. Worth seeking out (& cellaring). No **14**.

★★★★☆ **The Widow Maker Pinotage** ⓥ ⓐ From dryland Stellenbosch vines planted 1994, **15** ⑨③ multidimensional & sleek, blackberry, plum & spice matched by ripe tannins, smooth cocoa-dusted tail, rich yet light footed. Includes splash 2016 vintage.

★★★★☆ **Pi Not Age** ⓥ Conceived as a lighter Cape Blend & tweaked over several harvests, **15** ⑨② pinotage plus old-vine cinsaut (60/40) anything but: densely packed fruit, exotic & earthy spices, broad & deep with suave tannin conclusion. Coastal WO.

★★★★☆ **FYM** ⓐ Tiny chardonnay single-vineyard planted 1994 with rare CY18 clone. **15** ⑨③ is creamy, leesy, elegant with a gentle richness, honeysuckle perfume & concentrated orchard fruit flavours. Barrel fermented/aged 11 months, 80% new. For luxurious seafood treats.

★★★★☆ **Mercator Chardonnay** ⓐ 'Premium' dropped from name. Melange of candied tropical fruit, crème brûlée, citrus peel balanced by sensitive oak treatment (50% new, 11 months) in **16** ⑨③. Smooth, with bright freshness & stony mineral lift.

★★★★ **Dr Reason Why** Bunch pressed & unadorned by oak, **17** ⑧⑧ chardonnay from 2 vineyards fermented in 'eggs' & amphoras. Lime, lemon, stonefruit riot on the palate, grapefruit pithiness to finish.

★★★★ **Pink Brut Rosé Méthode Cap Classique** Equal pinot noir & chardonnay, **NV** ⑧⑦ bubbly oozes fresh strawberry & cinnamon-dusted vanilla biscuit, 24 months on the lees showing in mouthfilling, creamy & persistent mousse.

★★★★ **Solitaire Blanc de Blancs Méthode Cap Classique** A joyful celebrator, **NV** ⑧⑨ sparkler brims with citrus, crunchy apple & lemon rind flavours. Full bodied, touch sweeter than last but beautifully balanced. Chardonnay, 24 months lees-aged.

★★★★ **The Fudge** ⓥ Vine-desiccated chardonnay, delicious **13** ⑧⑧ dessert spent year in oak, adding vanilla & baking spice complexity to buttery, fudgy, tropical fruits & golden sultanas.— WB

Location/map: Franschhoek ▪ Map grid reference: C3 ▪ WO: Franschhoek/Coastal/Stellenbosch ▪ Est 1983 ▪ 1stB 1994 ▪ Tasting, sales & cellar tours daily 9.30-5 ▪ Fee R60 ▪ Closed Dec 25 ▪ Bread & Wines Restaurant daily 12-3 ▪ Charcuterie by Neil Jewell ▪ Breadmaking ▪ Function venue (150-200 pax) ▪ Craft gin distillery: tasting by appt only ▪ Owner(s) Richard Friedman & The Lady Fizz ▪ Winemaker(s) Clayton Reabow (May 2007) ▪ Viticulturist(s) Ferdi Coetsee ▪ 35ha/±18ha (chard) ▪ ±120t 10% red 20% white 70% MCC ▪ EuroGAP, IPW ▪ PO Box 114 Franschhoek 7690 ▪ sales@moreson.co.za ▪ www.moreson.co.za ▪ S 33° 53' 11.9" E 019° 3' 30.6" ▪ 🖼 inductions.vacancy.photographs ▪ F +27 (0)21-876-8864 ▪ **T +27 (0)21-876-3055**

Morgenhof Wine Estate

ⓥ ⓝ ⓐ ⓞ ⓑ ⓛ

All 78 ha of vineyard on historic French-owned Morgenhof in the Simonsberg foothills are dry farmed. This practice, not common in Stellenbosch, has paid dividends by enabling the vines to adjust naturally to the drought, and though their yields have been lower they have remained in good health. This is as beneficial as the welcome rains last winter for new viticulturist Rohan Breytenbach. Wines are held back until deemed ready for release, and the latest elegant and impressive reds demonstrate the wisdom of that approach.

Morgenhof Estate range

★★★★ **Cabernet Sauvignon** ⓥ Low-cropped **13** ★★★★ ⑧④ in restrained mode, as befits variety, with herbaceous tone, firm chalky tannins that envelop dark fruit. Less balanced than **12** ⑧⑥.

★★★★☆ **Malbec Vintage Select** ⓝⓔⓦ Varietal characteristics well expressed on **14** ⑨②. Older oak showcases dark, ripe & spicy fruit-laden profile. Modern, compact style, with smooth dry tannins. Already tempting but plenty of potential.

★★★★ **Merlot-Cabernet Franc** ⓥ Elegant Bordeaux blend shows classic berry, cherry flavours with hint of pencil shaving, **12** ★★★★☆ ⑨①'s dry, fine, cedary tannins in balanced support, good complexity & length. Ageworthy, sophisticated step up on **11** ⑧⑥.

★★★★ **The Morgenhof Estate** ⓥ All five red Bordeaux varieties, led by cab & merlot (41/39) in slow-evolving **12** ★★★ ⑧⓪. Very dry & firm still, fruit held in tight tannin embrace. May benefit from further cellaring but currently best paired with robust food. Last tasted was **06** ⑧⑦.

★★★★ **Brut Reserve** ⓥ Full, persistent mousse carries red pear flavours of bone-dry **10** ⑧⑥ chardonnay, pinot noir MCC sparkling. Couple of years on lees imparts freshness & complexity to lean, focused style.

★★★★ **Cape LBV** ⓥ Late Bottled Vintage **04** ⑧⑦ spent 6 years in oak barrels. Rich, full & intensely flavoured, with grippy tannins to balance the sweetness. From touriga.

Cabernet Franc ⓥ ★★★★ Variety's piquant walnut tone on **13** ⑧④, taut & youthful with hint of perfume emerging. Not austere, but would certainly benefit from few years cellaring. **Merlot** ⓥ ★★★★ Retains merlot's minty red-fruit profile but in tighter, spicier tannin framework. **12** ⑧⑤ even leafier than previous - needs a hearty meal & cellar time to show its potential. **Pinotage** ⓥ ★★★★ Dark mulberry fruit & nice savoury tone, **13** ⑧④ drier than Fantail, similar cedary tannins, supple balance, with oak well integrated. **Chardonnay** ⓥ ★★★★ Part natural fermentation in older oak, subtle lime & ripe pear aromas, more prominent in flavour, freshening acid thread throughout. **15** ⑧⑤ good now & for a few years. **Chenin Blanc** ★★★★ Solo or meal partner (for next few years), **17** ⑧⑤ marries richer baked apple & quince flavours with fresh crunchy acidity. Medium body, brush of old oak & less overt ripe fruit than on **16** ⑧③. **Sauvignon Blanc** ⓥ ★★★ Asparagus & stonefruit plumped by ageing on lees, **17** ⑧① friendly, balanced style with dry pithy finish. Equally good solo or with a meal. Discontinued: **Noble Late Harvest**.

Fantail range

Pinotage ⓥ ★★★ Bright, bouncy **14** ⑧②, spiced berry fruit framed by clean, dry tannin structure. Offers sappy drinkability with a meal. Stellenbosch WO for these. **Pinotage Rosé** ⓥ ★★★ Sunset pink **16** ⑦⑦ is dry, with generous splash of variety's sweet red-berry flavour. Chill for delectable summer drink. Discontinued: **Cabernet Franc-Cabernet Sauvignon, Sauvignon Blanc-Chenin Blanc**. — MW

Location/map: Stellenbosch ▪ Map grid reference: F3 ▪ WO: Simonsberg–Stellenbosch/Stellenbosch ▪ Est 1692 ▪ 1stB 1984 ▪ Tasting & sales Mon-Fri 9-5.30 (Nov-Apr) & 9-4.30 (May-Oct); Sat/Sun 10-5 (Nov-Apr) & 10-3 (May-Oct) ▪ Fee R35pp ▪ Closed Good Fri, Dec 25 & Jan 1 ▪ Cellar tours/viewing of underground barrel cellar on request ▪ Cheese platters ▪ Morgenhof Restaurant ▪ Facilities for children ▪ Conferences ▪ Weddings/functions ▪ Helipad ▪ Conservation area ▪ Morgenhof Manor House ▪ Owner(s) Anne Cointreau ▪ Winemaker(s) Andries de Klerk (Jan 2012) ▪ Viticulturist(s) Rohan Breytenbach (Dec 2017) ▪ 212ha/78ha (cabs s/f, malbec, merlot, chenin, chard) ▪ 410t/70,000cs own label 60% red 38% white 2% rosé ▪ IPW ▪ PO Box 365 Stellenbosch 7599 ▪ info@morgenhof.com ▪ www.morgenhof.com ▪ S 33° 53' 38.5" E 018° 51' 39.2" ▪ ⓦ chatting.reminder.letter ▪ **T +27 (0)21-889-2000**

Morgenster Estate ⓥ ⑪ ⊚

A beautiful and storied property on the slopes of Somerset West's famous Schapenberg, Morgenster was bought by Italian businessman Giulio Bertrand in the early 1990s and transformed into a model olive and wine estate. The olive groves were planted with Italian plant material and have won countless awards over the years, locally and overseas, while on the wine side Giulio not only introduced Italian varieties (see below for the Italian Collection, with its operatic names) but persuaded Pierre Lurton of Bordeaux icon Cheval Blanc to become a consultant, latterly to winemaker Henry Kotzé. On Giulio's passing in May 2018, his two daughters inherited the venture. Further Italian varietal plantings are going ahead: his vision continues.

Morgenster Estate range

★★★★★ **Lourens River Valley** Same varieties as Reserve, different mix: merlot/cab franc (38/34) take lead in **15** ⑨①. Perfumed, plush berries, violets, spice array, hint of herbs, bolstered by firm but ripe tannins. 20% new oak vs 60% for Reserve, both 18 months. Less extracted than **14** ★★★★ ⑧⑦. Also in magnum.

★★★★★ **Reserve** ⓐ Cab/merlot (43/35), cab franc, dab petit verdot, different profile to Lourens River. Layered, cassis & plum fruit density, **15** ⑨④ balances succulence & tannin structure. Built for the future but offers earlier pleasure. Sleekly powerful, classic. Various larger bottle formats.

★★★★★ **White** Sauvignon & semillon (47%), co-fermented, barrel aged 14 months. Buttered toast, tobacco, strong oak influence but **16** ⑨②'s fruit comes into its own in the flavours, grapefruit, some graphite. Tightly knit, still youthful, will evolve over time.

Cuvée Alessandra ★★★ Prosecco-style bubbly from cab franc: neutral oak 12 months, 21 months on lees in bottle. Pale gold, energetic mousse, **16** ⑧② mixture pear & grapes; elegant, bone-dry.

Italian Collection

★★★★ **Nabucco** ⓐ Now bottled, **15** ⑧⑧ lovely fruit expression, plums, dark berries, better able to handle the tannins. Some melding, but still firm; varietal character, as in Italy, nebbiolo is long-lived, needs time. But can be enjoyed now.

★★★★ **Tosca** ⊛ Previewed last time, **15** ⑧⑥ 80% sangiovese with both cabs; glossy cherries, rich & ripe, year later better tannins, still dry but compact rather than forceful. For food, ageing.

★★★★☆ **Vespri** ⑭ⓔⓐ ⊘ Vermentino, very rare in SA. Mixed fresh/dried herbs & mustard leaf on unoaked **18** ⑨①, ruby grapefruit especially on the palate. Quite different to other white varieties, in a good way. Lithe, invigoratingly fresh, cries out for food. WO W Cape.

. . . .

Caruso ⑰ ★★★★ Pale coral rosé, cherry styling from sangiovese, **18** ⑧④ has gorgeous drinkability, sleek, bone-dry, just enough freshness to reach for the second glass.

. . . .

Single Varietal range

★★★★ **Cabernet Franc** ⊘ Glossy fruit, cassis/cherries, whiffs fynbos, graphite, promise of richness yet **16** ⑧⑧'s structure elegant, tannins compact, finishing dry, accessible. Well made, brings out more good points than **15** ★★★★ ⑧⑤.

★★★★ **Sauvignon Blanc** ⊘ Attractively layered, **18** ⑧⑧ shows some tropical notes, melon, then goes green, fennel & lime, especially on the finish. Tangy-fresh, complex, involving & rewarding.

Cabernet Sauvignon ⑫ ★★★★ Attractive, subtle fruitiness with herbal edge on restrained, lightly oaked & firmly structured **14** ⑧③, but no great concentration of flavour. **Merlot** ★★★★ Red & dark berries in **15** ⑧④, some cassis notes, all expressive & forthcoming. Bed of tannins well-judged, giving grip, structure & accessibility. Always elegant, well put-together. **Sangiovese** ★★★★ Unwooded, much lighter in structure than Tosca, **18** ⑧④ made for drinking earlier, no hardship. Fresh cherries, touch of chopped herbs, smooth & juicy, bit of grip from grape tannin. — CR

Location: Somerset West ▪ Map: Helderberg ▪ Map grid reference: F5 ▪ WO: Stellenbosch/Western Cape ▪ Est 1993 ▪ 1stB 1998 ▪ Tasting & sales Mon-Sun 10-5 ▪ Tasting fee R50-R95 wine/R55 olive oil & olive products ▪ Closed Good Fri & Dec 25 ▪ Restaurant 95@morgenster ▪ Owner(s) Bertrand family ▪ Cellarmaster(s) Henry Kotzé (Oct 2009) ▪ Winemaker(s) Henry Kotzé (Oct 2009), with consultant Pierre Lurton (Nov 1997, Château Cheval Blanc) ▪ Viticulturist(s) Corius Visser (Apr 2014) ▪ 200ha/40ha (cabs s/f, merlot, nebbiolo, p verdot, sangio, sauv, sem, vermentino) ▪ 80% red 15% white 5% rosé ▪ IPW, SIZA ▪ PO Box 1616 Somerset West 7129 ▪ info@morgenster.co.za ▪ www.morgenster.co.za ▪ S 34° 5′2.9″ E 018° 53′7.8″ ▪ 🔳 shelters.braked.sock ▪ F +27 (0)21-852-1141 ▪ **T +27 (0)21-852-1738**

☐ **Morkel** *see* Bellevue Estate Stellenbosch
☐ **Mortons** *see* Wine-of-the-Month Club

Mostertsdrift Noble Wines ⑫ ⑪ ◎ ⑧

Stellenbosch siblings and owners André Mostert and Anna-Mareè Uys nowadays sell most of their grapes but do have own boutique wines for tasting/sale, by appointment, at their welcoming cellardoor.

Cabernet Sauvignon ⑫ ★★★ More accessible than previous, **07** ⑧① with nutty complexity & creamy mouthfeel. **AnéRouge** ⑫ ★★★ Mainly cab, rest merlot. **07** ⑧①'s well-managed ripe fruit delivers balance & soft appeal. — IM

Location/map/WO: Stellenbosch ▪ Map grid reference: E4 ▪ Est/1stB 2001 ▪ Tasting, sales & cellar tours by appt ▪ Meals for groups by prior arrangement ▪ Facilities for children ▪ Conference venue ▪ Owner(s) André Mostert & Anna-Mareè Uys (Mostert) ▪ Cellarmaster(s)/winemaker(s) Anna-Mareè Uys (Jan 2001) ▪ 13ha/±8ha (cab, merlot, pinot, chard, hanepoot) ▪ ±80-100t/3,986cs own label 70% red 10% white 20% rosé + 15,000L bulk ▪ PO Box 2061 Dennesig Stellenbosch 7601 ▪ winemaker@mostertsdrift.co.za ▪ www.mostertsdrift.co.za ▪ S 33° 53′31.7″ E 018° 50′17.6″ ▪ 🔳 steered.tone.painting ▪ F +27 (0)86-516-1730 ▪ **T +27 (0)73-194-9221**

Mother Rock Wines

Johan Meyer, winemaker for Mount Abora and his own JH Meyer Signature, takes his most radical stance in terms of 'natural' winemaking with these ranges, co-owned with UK importer Ben Henshaw. Both seek to express Swartland's soils, slopes and climate. Practices like early picking and skin contact for whites, and old-oak maturation make for idiosyncratically delicious, cerebral and 'geeky' wines.

Mother Rock range

★★★★☆ **Grenache** While not from one of the permitted red grapes of France's Jura, **17** ⑨⓪ reminiscent of that area's crystalline fruit purity (raspberry/strawberry) & delicacy that belie considerable depth, complexity. Also well-judged grip & dryness; altogether a captivating glassful.

★★★★ **Syrah** Bunch ferment, minimal interference, no new oak & minuscule production, as all these. Velvet-textured **15** ⑧⑦ followed by edgier & dark **17** ★★★★ ⑧⑤, with black & red berries, peppery whiff. **16** untasted.

★★★★ **Holocene** ⓝⓔⓦ Mediterranean-style red blend with cinsaut (50%) & equal carignan & mourvèdre, exceptionally pure red fruit in **17** ⑨⓪ supported by lively acidity, given form by powder-fine tannin.

★★★★ **Kweperfontein Chenin Blanc** ⓝⓔⓦ More about site expression than fruit, **17** ⑧⑦ textured & vibrant, with lemon zest, green melon & a citrus pithiness; satisfying mouthful at just 12.5% alcohol. Not for everyone, but a clever take on natural winemaking.

★★★★☆ **Liquid Skin** Utterly thrilling 'orange wine' from chenin, **17** ⑨⓪ 8 weeks on skins & showing prominent tannins along with the peach, pear & lemon fruit. Well integrated, lifted by fine acidity. Like **15** ⑨③, non-mainstream but so carefully done, you might not notice! **16** untasted.

★★★★ **White** Partly skin-fermented creative blend chenin with viognier, semillon, grenache blanc & hárslevelü, **17** ⑧⑨ beautifully subtle statement of white pear & lemon, pleasing grainy tannins, touch pithy bitterness in very good example of style.

Discontinued: **Mourvèdre**, **Carignan-Cinsaut**.

Force Majeure range

Not tasted: **Red Blend**, **Cinsault Rosé**, **Chenin Blanc**. — HC, CvZ

Location: Hermon ▪ WO: Swartland ▪ Est/1stB 2014 ▪ Closed to public ▪ Owner(s) Johan Meyer & Ben Henshaw ▪ Winemaker(s) Johan Meyer ▪ 75t/12,500cs own label ▪ 1 Main Rd Hermon 7308 ▪ motherrockwines@gmail.com ▪ www.motherrockwines.com ▪ **T +27 (0)79-280-0237**

Mount Abora Vineyards　⑨

The trio behind in this Swartland boutique label, Pieter de Waal, Krige Visser and Johan Meyer, are also involved with separate wine ventures; Johan, producer of JH Meyer Signature and Mother Rock, found his business expanding dramatically (and adding a cellar), and had to hand over more of the Mount Abora winemaking to Krige in 2017. After skipping the 2016 vintage, drought one reason, their chenin and red blend are back on track (we'll taste them next time), the chenin fermented in a new concrete 'egg'. The design and local manufacture of a 600-litre plastic 'egg' is Pieter and Krige's latest project; first trials in 2018 yielded positive results.

★★★★ **Saffraan** A pioneer of modern, fresh & light cinsauts. Unoaked **17** ⑧⑨ a charmer; gorgeous breadth of ripe raspberry perfume; good substance, fruit intensity & length at a light but convincing 11.2% alcohol. **16** ★★★☆ ⑧④ shade less satisfying.

★★★★☆ **The Abyssinian** ⑫ Another varietal tweak in light-coloured, fresh & elegant **15** ⑨⓪: mourvèdre & grenache with less cinsaut & shiraz. Just 12.1% alcohol but with balanced weight, tannic structure & fine integrated acidity, & a savoury succulence whose harmony will only improve with a few years.

Not tasted: **Koggelbos**. — AL

Location: Hermon ▪ WO: Swartland ▪ Est/1stB 2012 ▪ Tasting & sales at The Wine Kollective in Riebeek-Kasteel ▪ Owner(s) Vinotage CC ▪ Winemaker(s) Johan Meyer & Krige Visser ▪ 3,000cs own label 60% red 40% white ▪ PO Box 995 Bellville 7535 ▪ wine@abora.co.za ▪ www.abora.co.za ▪ **T +27 (0)82-413-6719/+27 (0)83-357-3864**

☐ **Mountain Eye** *see* Kleinhoekkloof

Mountain Ridge Wines　⑨ 😊 ◎ ♿

Though their cellar (and visitor locale) is in Wolseley — on what translates as 'Love Street'! — Mountain Ridge's 17 shareholders are spread over four districts and regions, and the current focus is ensure the sustainability of all the farms involved by 'unlocking their full potential'. This entails producing 'premiumised', site-specific wines for both their own labels and bulk customers' and, via a new entity, Mountain Ridge Beverage Co, boosting local/international sales and developing new lines like the Jailbreak range.

Mountain Ridge range

★★★★ Shiraz ⊘ Packs a juicy punch! Raspberry, violets & spice, subtle oak (only 10% new) enhances the enjoyment. **14** ⑧⑦ step above **11 ★★★** ⑧⓪. **12** & **13** unreviewed.

Cabernet Sauvignon ⊘ **★★★★** Velvety tannin underpinning for attractive cassis, eucalyptus & subtle vanilla on **14** ⑧④, which improves on previous. **Merlot** ⊘ **★★** After-dinner choc-mint notes on a herbal undercarriage. **14** ⑦④ has big, bold tannins. **Sauvignon Blanc ★★** Unchallenging **18** ⑦④, forthcoming grassy & tropical notes, light & bright. Breedekloof WO.

Romansrivier range

Cabernet Sauvignon Reserve ⊘ **★★★★** Big & juicy **14** ⑧④, bold tannins offset by pleasant herbal note, nicely rounded off by a sweet farewell. **Shiraz Reserve** ⊘ **★★★★** Perfumed with generous charry oak, juicy **14** ⑧④ has fine floral palate & still-firm tannin - will reward a bit of patience.

Jailbreak range (NEW)

Shiraz ⊘ ⑦ **★★★★** Ripe plum fruit, violets & light spicing, **16** ⑧⑤ full bodied with enough tannic grip to hold your attention while sipping fireside.

Chenin Blanc ★★★ Summer fruits, tropical notes & citrus on lightly oaked **17** ⑦⑧, characterful, unpretentious & fun.

De Liefde range

Aanstap Rooies Dry Red ★★ Straightforwardly fruity **NV** ⑦④, subtly firm tannins & smoky top note. From cab & merlot in winsome packaging. **The Long & Wine'ing Road Dry White ★★** Light & breezy **NV** ⑦④ chenin showing lovely purity of fruit & tangy acidity. Serve chilled. Not tasted: **Smooch Vonkelwyn**. — HC

Location: Wolseley ▪ Map: Breedekloof ▪ Map grid reference: A2 ▪ WO: Western Cape/Breedekloof ▪ Est 1949 ▪ 1stB 1976 ▪ Tasting & sales Mon-Thu 8–5 Fri 8-4 Sat 8-12.30 ▪ Closed all pub hols ▪ Cellar tours by appt only ▪ BYO picnic ▪ Ramkiekie farmer's market (monthly) ▪ Wedding & function venue (140-160 pax) ▪ Queen B spritzer ▪ Owner(s) 17 members ▪ Cellarmaster(s) / CEO Justin Corrans (May 2017) ▪ Winemaker(s) Christo Stemmet (Jan 2010) ▪ 400ha (cab, merlot, shiraz, chenin, sauv) ▪ 8,000t/10,000cs own label 37% red 48% white 15% rosé ▪ IPW, WIETA ▪ PO Box 108 Wolseley 6830 ▪ sales@mountainridge.co.za ▪ www.mountainridge.co.za ▪ S 33° 28′ 26.04″ E 019° 12′ 10.44″ ▪ ⎙ wealthier.restrictions.wafting ▪ **T +27 (0)74-185-3780/+27 (0)74-125-8096**

Mountain River Wines

Run from one of historic Paarl Main Street's elegantly restored homes, De Villiers Brits' negociant business, founded in the early 1990s when newly democratic SA's wine exports took off, has carved a place for both its bulk and bottled wines in markets as diverse as the UK, India, China and Russia.

Mountain River range

Pinotage ⊘ **★★★★** Tropical/plum features of **16** ⑧④ lavished with new French oak, sweet fruited, with firm tannins for good food partnering. **Chardonnay** ⊘ **★★★★** Medium-bodied **12** ⑧④, zesty lime a tad overshadowed by spicy oak but enough flavour & life to knit & drink well for few years.

Maankloof range

Shiraz ⊘ **★★★** Slightly baked **16** ⑦⑧, lots of sweet spice & redcurrants in ripe, fruity style. No wood, as all this range & next. **Sauvignon Blanc ★★** Racy **18** ⑦⑤ tank sample offers cut grass flavour & zingy freshness. Not tasted: **Cabernet Sauvignon, Pinotage**. Occasional release: **Chenin Blanc**.

Zaràfa range

Cabernet Sauvignon ⊘ **★★★** Brambly forest-floor aromas & waxy nuance attract, but firm tannins need to relax, allowing **16** ⑧⓪'s fruit to shine. **Sauvignon Blanc ★★** Steely **18** ⑦⑤ preview bristles with fresh acidity & green/grassy flavours. Not tasted: **Pinotage, Shiraz, Rosé, Chardonnay**.

Ukuzala range

Occasional release: **Dry Red, Dry White**. — DS

Location: Paarl ▪ WO: Western Cape ▪ Est 1993 ▪ 1stB 1998 ▪ Closed to public ▪ Owner(s) De Villiers Brits ▪ Cellarmaster(s) De Villiers Brits, with consultants ▪ 1.2ha (shiraz) ▪ 80,000cs own label 60% red 40% white ▪ 146 Main Rd Paarl 7646 ▪ dev@mountainriverwines.co.za, mattie@mountainriverwines.co.za ▪ www. mountainriverwines.co.za ▪ F +27 (0)21-872-3255 ▪ **T +27 (0)21-872-3256**

☐ **Mountain Shadows** *see* Wineways Marketing

Mount Babylon Vineyards

Johan and Yolanda Holzhausen's Hemel-en-Aarde Ridge vines, with local landmark Babylonstoren Peak in their sight, produce fruit for specialist méthode cap classique production, currently a classic pinot/chardonnay and New World-style sparkling shiraz, made with neighbour Jean-Claude Martin of Creation Wines.

Location: Hermanus ▪ Map: Walker Bay & Bot River ▪ Map grid reference: C4 ▪ Est 2002 ▪ 1stB 2007 ▪ By invitation only ▪ Owner(s) Johan Holtzhausen ▪ Winemaker(s) Jean-Claude Martin (2008, consultant) & Johan Holtzhausen ▪ Viticulturist(s) Johan Pienaar (2002, consultant) ▪ 65ha/7ha (pinot, shiraz, viog) ▪ ±38t/±400cs own label 90% red 10% white ▪ PO Box 7370 Stellenbosch 7599 ▪ info@mountbabylon. co.za ▪ www.mountbabylon.co.za ▪ S 34° 19′ 44.0″ E 019° 19′ 34.3″ ▪ 🖾 unplug.poem.matured ▪ **T +27 (0)84-511-8180**

Mount Pleasant Vineyards

Former London banker, now active music patron in arty Darling, Alfred Legner also tends a tiny walled shiraz block in this West Coast town. The grapes are vinified in Malmesbury by Wim Smit of Hofstraat Kelder.

Location: Darling ▪ Est 2009 ▪ 1stB 2011 ▪ Closed to public ▪ Owner(s) Legner family ▪ Winemaker(s) Wim Smit (Dec 2010, Hofstraat) ▪ Viticulturist(s) Alfred Legner (Jun 2006) ▪ 0.2ha/0.1ha (shiraz) ▪ 2t/ha 66cs own label 100% red ▪ 11 High Str Darling 7345 ▪ info@darlingmusic.org ▪ **T +27 (0)72-015-1653**

☐ **Mount Sutherland Continental** *see* Super Single Vineyards

Mount Vernon Estate

Simonsberg-Paarl family estate Mount Vernon is owned by David Hooper, chair of liquor distributor Edward Snell, and wife Debbie, and produces a boutique range under the labels Mount Vernon (Vernon a family name), Three Peaks and conservation-supporting Rhino Tears. The wines are vinified by Debbie and young winemaker and Cape Wine Master Brendan Butler.

Location: Paarl ▪ Est 1996 ▪ 1stB 2005 ▪ Closed to public ▪ Owner(s) David & Debbie Hooper ▪ Cellarmaster(s) Debbie Hooper (Jan 2003) ▪ Winemaker(s) Brendan Butler (Jan 2015) ▪ Viticulturist(s) Philip du Toit (Jun 1997) ▪ 160ha/57.5ha (cab, malbec, merlot, p verdot, ptage, shiraz, chard) ▪ 210-225t/5,300cs own label 80% red 15% white 5% rosé ▪ PO Box 348 Klapmuts 7625 ▪ john@mountvernon.co.za ▪ www.mountvernon.co.za ▪ F +27 (0)86-618-9821 ▪ **T +27 (0)21-875-5073**

Moya's Vineyards   ⓘ 🅐

These wines come — in boutique quantities - from a sustainably farmed hillside property in Upper Hemel-en-Aarde Valley. They benefit from the contributions of an eminent local pair: winemaker Hannes Storm (with his eponymous range from the same area), and Johan Montgomery, viticulturist at Hamilton Russell Vineyards. After an initial stutter, the inherent quality of the vineyards is now coming through.

★★★★☆ **Pinot Noir** ⊘ ⓐ Two vintages tasted, both marked improvements on maiden release. House style establishing itself as serious, with more savoury than upfront fruit, subtly oaked & with understated tannic basis, fine enlivening acidity. Earthy, sombre notes on **16** (90), with dark cherry & berries; especially elegant **17** ⑨③ purer & lovelier. Both needing time. Decant in youth.

★★★★☆ **Sauvignon Blanc** ⊘ Complex aromas of stonefruit, tropical fruit & blackcurrant on **17** ⑨⓪ introduce a rounded, well-balanced & softly elegant palate with good informing acidity. Bone-dry & fresh too, unlike last-tasted **15** ★★★★ (84). **16** sold out before we could try it.— TJ

Location: Hermanus ▪ Map: Walker Bay & Bot River ▪ Map grid reference: B4 ▪ WO: Upper Hemel-en-Aarde Valley ▪ Est 2008 ▪ 1stB 2013 ▪ Tasting Sat/Sun by appt ▪ Closed Good Fri, Dec 25/26 & Jan 1 ▪ Part of the greater Hemel & Aarde MTB trails ▪ Owner(s) Hemel & Aarde Country Retreat (Pty) Ltd ▪ Winemaker(s)

Hannes Storm (Jan 2013, consultant) ▪ Viticulturist(s) Johan Montgomery (Jul 2008, consultant) ▪ 46ha/8.93ha (pinot, sauv) ▪ 28t/3,000cs own label 50% red 50% white ▪ IPW (vineyards) ▪ PO Box 6367 Uniedal 7612 ▪ collin@bishopcf.co.za ▪ S 34° 21′ 51.48″ E 019° 15′ 32.63″ ▪ ✉ quizzed.channels.graduate ▪ T +27 (0)82-551-0088

Mulderbosch Vineyards

Based in Stellenboschkloof, and sourcing grapes locally and from selected parcels around the Western Cape, Mulderbosch has a long and deserved reputation for consistently producing top-quality wines that deliver (as the team put it, based on loyal customer feedback) 'affordable luxury', at a time when premium wine prices keep rising. They maintain standards despite vintage vagaries by, inter alia, sound viticultural practices and early harvesting to retain fresh, natural acidity. Market share continues to grow, with new outlets in the US, where their rosé is the top-selling SA pink in its price class (and a Hidden Gem in our book, for the second year running). Other important focuses include further greening the home-farm by planting 1,000 indigenous trees, and establishing an 'entrepreneurial' vegetable garden for employees.

1000 Miles range

★★★★☆ **Sauvignon Blanc** From 3 Stellenbosch sites, **17** ⑨⓪ vivacious & zesty, with rich stonefruit & tinge of lime. Enriched by 10 months lees ageing in old oak, though less intensity & flinty verve than scintillating **15** ★★★★★ ⑨⑤, from wider range of vineyard sources. No **16**.

Single Vineyards range

★★★★ **Chenin Blanc Block A** One of trio of identically vinified chenins from registered single-vineyards, now matured 11 months in large (1,600L) vessels (previously old barriques). **17** ⑧⑨ ex sandy Polkadraai soils, gentle red apple & almond profile with some crunchy freshness. Better than **16** ★★★★ ⑧⑤, though shyest of these.

★★★★☆ **Chenin Blanc Block S2** Koelenhof shale-based block shows more elegance, fruit & substance than siblings. Lemony notes whet the appetite, crisp apple flavours & tangy finish fulfil the promise. **17** ⑨② shows real verve, follows **16** ⑨② 's graceful line.

★★★★☆ **Chenin Blanc Block W** Firgrove parcel on decomposed granite, **17** ⑨⓪ has more acidity & sugar but lowest alcohol (11.9%) of the trio. Similar earthy note, more stewed impression than **16** ★★★★ ⑧⑦, but enough fruit to achieve finer balance with the acidity.

Mulderbosch Vineyards range

★★★★☆ **Cabernet Franc** 🐾 Exciting prospects for **16** ⑨④ from special block 9B on Stellenboschkloof home-farm. Plush layers of scented fruit, lithe structure, velvety tannins & fresh, sappy farewell. Already tempting but time will bring handsome rewards.

★★★★☆ **Faithful Hound** Cab sauvignon leads the pack in **16** ⑨⓪, cab franc shifts from co-leader to second-in-command, followed by merlot, malbec & petit verdot. Succulent & rounded, with plummy dark fruit. For earlier enjoyment than more structured **15** ⑨③.

★★★★ **Chardonnay** Rich toasted nut, lime & honey on **17** ⑧⑥ from sites across Stellenbosch. Ripe & concentrated flavours from dry, windy conditions. Touch less zesty & fresh than cooler **15** ⑧⑧. No **16**.

★★★★ **Chenin Blanc Steen op Hout** ⊘ More impressive **17** ⑧⑦ from widely sourced older (20-30+ years) vines. Smooth, clean & lemony, with ripe baked-apple notes. More oak than **16** ★★★★ ⑧③ (28%, none new) but in sync with concentrated fruit.

....

Cabernet Sauvignon Rosé 🏆 ★★★★ Always-charming pink from vineyards dedicated to this style, dry **18** ⑧⑤ tangy red fruit with early picked herbaceous nuance, modest 12.7% alcohol. Also in 1.5 & (Scandinavia only) 3L pack. Coastal WO.

....

Sauvignon Blanc ⑨ ★★★★ Generous & ripe, with interesting contrast between rounded mouthfeel (partly from 12% oak) & burst of very tangy acidity. **17** ⑧③ food wine rather than solo sipper. **Méthode Cap Classique** ⑨ ★★★★ Bone-dry, food-styled sparkling, preview of **14** ⑧④ shows subtle oystershell minerality & tart freshness. Mostly pinot noir, with oaked chardonnay & meunier, 27 months on lees. Not tasted: **Chardonnay Barrel Fermented**. Discontinued: **Faithful Hound White**, **Sauvignon Blanc Noble Late Harvest**. — MW

Location/map: Stellenbosch ▪ Map grid reference: C5 ▪ WO: Stellenbosch/Western Cape/Coastal ▪ Est 1989
▪ 1stB 1991 ▪ Tasting & sales Tue-Sun & pub hols 10-6 ▪ Fee R50-R75 ▪ Closed Mon, Easter Fri & Mon, July
(annual winter break), Dec 25 & Jan 1 ▪ Pizzas & cheese boards, gourmet burgers, cappuccinos, artisanal
beer, juice ▪ Olive oil ▪ Bocce ball courts (Italian boule) ▪ Conservation area ▪ Devil's Peak and The Italian Job
craft beer on tasting destination menu ▪ Owner(s) MKV Holdings ▪ Winemaker(s) Adam Mason (Dec 2011),
with Mick Craven (Jan 2013) ▪ Viticulturist(s) Adam Mason (Jun 2013) ▪ 80ha/45.2ha (cabs s/f, merlot, p
verdot, shiraz, chard, chenin, sauv, viog) ▪ IPW, WIETA ▪ PO Box 12817 Die Boord Stellenbosch 7613 ▪ info@
mulderbosch.co.za ▪ www.mulderbosch.co.za ▪ S 33° 56' 56.00" E 018° 45' 57.00" ▪ *stadium.bridge.*
hunches ▪ F +27 (0)21-881-3514 ▪ **T +27 (0)21-881-8140**

Mullineux

Two-time recipients of this guide's coveted Winery of the Year accolade (2014, 2016), husband-and-wife
Andrea (cellar) and Chris Mullineux (vineyards, aided by consultant Rosa Kruger), have again made it to the
honours roll, this time as Top Performing Winery of the Year 2019 alongside our Newcomer Winery of the
Year and the recipient of the Editor's Award. They are in partnership with Indian businessman Analjit Singh
here in Swartland and in Franschhoek with Leeu Passant (see separate entry). The focus of this range, which
is a chenin and shiraz masterclass for wine-lovers (and -geeks), is to reflect the diverse terroir of the area,
in particular respecting the soil and vine age, while keeping cellar practices as natural as possible, with
spontaneous ferments, only older oak, no fining or filtration - and no hurry: the Essence Straw wine took
four years to ferment! Production has moved to their farm Roundstone on Kasteelberg, and new plantings
of chenin, grenache, clairette and cinsaut are now bearing fruit. New to the range is a unique white blend,
impeccably made, of course.

Single Terroir range

★★★★☆ **Granite Syrah** 🔒 Same winemaking for 3 syrahs to highlight terroir: wholebunch, natural
ferment, older 500L barrels/large foudres, unfined/filtered. Dryland Paardeberg vineyard, granite soils, give
16 ⑨③ perfume, sleek succulence, a mineral core; syrah reined in, taut & stylish. Magnums too, as for most.

★★★★★ **Iron Syrah** 🔒 Dryland Malmesbury hills vineyard with iron-rich koffieklip (ferricrete) soil, for
distinctive ferrous/savoury nuance. Other layers include scrub, wild berries, seamed black pepper; **16** ⑨⑤
'masculine', with excellent muscle tone. Long life ahead, as **15** ★★★★★ ⑨③.

★★★★☆ **Schist Syrah Roundstone** 🔒 Vineyard on Kasteelberg home-farm. Soil deeper, denser,
little water-holding capacity, vines/bunches smaller. Black plums in **16** ★★★★★ ⑨⑤, smoky, espresso
savouriness, especially on the palate. Smoothly elegant, latent power for ageing. Follows fine **15** ⑨④.

★★★★☆ **Granite Chenin Blanc** 🔒 🌱 Amongst oldest vineyards in Paardeberg, deep soils allow
dryland farming, minimal stress. Complex layers, grapefruit & almond in **17** ⑨③, more minerality & saline
acidity than **16** ⑨③, shows unwavering refinement, assurance; chenin excellence.

★★★★☆ **Quartz Chenin Blanc Leliefontein** 🔒 Quartz-rich single Kasteelberg block, stones reflect
sunlight into the canopy, aiding ripeness without sugar increase. All whites except Kloof Street made the
same natural way for site to speak. **17** ⑨③ wonderful fruit purity, sleek, poised, seamless.

Occasional release: **Schist Chenin Blanc**.

CWG Auction Reserve range

★★★★☆ **The Gris Semillon** 🔒 From granite soil, 1955 dryland Paardeberg vineyard, rare red-skinned
semillon. Last was **14**, elegant, mineral, while fuller, weightier **17** ⑨④ has beeswax, ripe yellow plums,
underpinned by vibrant, freshening acidity. Great ageability.

Signature range

★★★★☆ **Syrah** 🔒 Blend of 3 soil types specified in terroir range, half the barrel time, **16** ⑨① earlier
drinking but appearances deceive, still sleekly powered for ageing. Classic shiraz styling, scrub & hedgerow
fruit, white pepper, plush texture, sinuous elegance.

★★★★☆ **Old Vines White** 🔒 🌱 Older vines, some 80 years, 4 main Swartland soils. Chenin-led with
4 others, carefully chosen. Unchanging style & complexity, stonefruit & mineral, beeswax, almonds, **17**
★★★★★ ⑨⑤ brightened by saline acidity. Wonderful focus, intensity. Follows complex **16** ⑨②.

★★★★☆ **Radicales Libres** (NEW) (🏵) Inspired by a Rioja winemaker, hence the Spanish name, **12** (93) fits into the 'extended barrel age' category. Mullineux White of that vintage (chenin, some viognier, clairette) given 5 years oaking. Heady, class of its own, just 2 barrels. Superb.

★★★★★ **Straw Wine** (🏵) Unbeaten 5-star track record, 8 of 9 vintages. Intense & concentrated, 310 g/L sugar for **17** (96) chenin, beguiling complexity, sweet, fruity & savoury layers. Apricots, barley sugar, almond oak seam, the piercing acidity keeps it pure, vibrant. 375 ml.

Occasional release: **Essence Straw Wine**, **Olerasay Straw Wine**.

Kloof Street range

★★★★ **Swartland Rouge** Mainly syrah with 5 others (for area history), earlier drinking than other reds, but in no way lesser. **17** (89) is a perfumed, succulent, fruity-fresh delight, tannins a hidden strength.

★★★★ **Old Vine Chenin Blanc** From 45 year old vines on 2 Swartland sites, different soil types, only quarter oaked to allow fruit expression. Thatch & melon in **17** (89), has sleek power & concentration, ends mineral.— CR

Location: Riebeek-Kasteel/Franschhoek ▪ Map: Swartland/Franschhoek ▪ Map grid reference: D6 C2 ▪ WO: Swartland ▪ Est 2007 ▪ 1stB 2008 ▪ Tasting & sales Mon-Sun 10-5 at the Wine Studio, Leeu Estates, Franschhoek (booking recommended); Roundstone Farm, Riebeek-Kasteel by appt only ▪ Owner(s) Mullineux & Leeu Family Wines (Pty) Ltd ▪ Cellarmaster(s) Chris & Andrea Mullineux (May 2007) ▪ Winemaker(s) Andrea Mullineux (May 2007), with Wade Sander (2016) & Joan Heatlie (2018) ▪ Viticulturist(s) Chris Mullineux (May 2007), with Rosa Kruger ▪ 28ha (carignan, cinsaut, mourv, shiraz, chenin, clairette, viog) ▪ 160t/16,000cs own label 58% red 40% white 2% dessert ▪ PO Box 369 Riebeek-Kasteel 7307 ▪ info@mlfwines.com ▪ www.mlfwines.com ▪ S 33° 22′ 34.13″ E 018°50′ 23.74″ (Riebeek-Kasteel) S 33° 54′ 33.43″ E 019° 6′ 14.85″ (Franschhoek) ▪ 🌐 lotions.concretely.pitting ▪ **T +27 (0)21-492-2455 (office)/+27 (0)21-492-2224 (Wine Studio)**

Muratie Wine Estate   (♀) (🍴) (◎)

Take time, when you visit this beautiful old Stellenbosch estate, in the folds of the Simonsberg, to absorb the rich, 300-year heritage woven into the fabric of the place, the people and the wines. Learn how Alberta Annemarie Canitz and her father George 'discovered' the farm, and how this feisty woman became one of the first female wine estate owners in the Cape. Ansela van de Caab, Laurens Campher, the Melcks... all have a story to tell. Rijk Melck, the current owner, will recount the challenges of the current vintage, the latest and longest harvest yet. The barrels are filled and the cellar 'looks, smells and feels awesome', he enthuses, so linger a while, there is fine wine, food and entertainment to ensure that this is a memorable visit.

Premium range

★★★★ **Martin Melck Cabernet Sauvignon** Similar style to previous, but **14** (88) only 10% new oak. Cab's signature herbaceous nuance to darker core of fruit underpinned by firm but lithe tannins.

★★★★☆ **Martin Melck Cabernet Sauvignon Family Reserve** (🏵) Premium grapes & all-new oak (previously 60%) for this label. Streamlined & muscular **14** (92), fine texture, riper liquorice tone to fruit & higher alcohol (14.8%) than also-tasted **15** (94). Latter is concentrated, intense, yet more elegant & fresh, with touch of mint. Complex & layered, already enticing, but will handsomely reward ageing. Both are a level above sibling. Simonsberg—Stellenbosch WO, as Ansela.

★★★★ **Alberta Annemarie Merlot** Rich & flavoursome **15** (89), bouquet of bright berry fruit, supple tannin, real depth & intensity in fine vintage, fruit centre stage (only 10% new oak). Good potential, already tempting. Raises bar on **14 ★★★★** (85). Also in magnum, as Shiraz, Ansela.

★★★★ **George Paul Canitz Pinot Noir** Smoky, perfumed red fruit, lithe dry tannins, all enveloped in creamy oak & alcohol embrace. **16** (86) engaging dinner partner, with structure for 3-5 years, though shade off **15** (87).

★★★★☆ **Ronnie Melck Shiraz** (✓) Ample ripe & smoky, earthy profile on bold & modern **15** (92). Smooth tannins & enough freshness to handle deep core of fruit. Less time in oak, & less new, than previous but more intense fruit needs no extra embellishment.

★★★★★ **Ansela van de Caab** (🏵) Remains cab-led Bordeaux blend in **15** (95), different ratios & with petit verdot, more new oak (60%) than **14 ★★★★★** (93). Complex layers of cassis, sweet tobacco & cedar.

Fine, dry & confident tannins, all elegantly restrained, emerging with time in the glass. Like **13** ⑨⑦, lovely intensity & polish, will unfurl beautifully in your cellar.

★★★★ **Isabella Chardonnay** Toasty lime impression, brisk, tangy acidity (despite full malo) makes **17** ★★★★ ⑧⑤ appear lighter than 14% alcohol. Tad less oak, fruit & substance than **16** ⑧⑨, nonetheless a bright & zesty food wine.

★★★★ **Isabella Chardonnay Reserve** Barrel selection from **17** ⑧⑧ vintage. All-new oak tempers acidity, adds silky texture but also masks the more delicate lemon/starfruit profile. Finer than sibling but rung below more complex **14**. **16** & **15** not made. Simonsberg-Stellenbosch WO.

★★★★ **Laurens Campher Blended White** Chenin-led 4-way blend in **17** ⑧⑦, like **16** ⑧⑦, equally pleasing, but more refined & light footed. Floral, starfruit nuances, gently crisp & creamy.

★★★★ **Lady Alice Méthode Cap Classique Rosé** Brut sparkler from pinot noir honours ex owner & perennial celebrant Lady Alice Sarah Stanford. **15** ★★★★ ⑧⑤ engaging, light-hearted & tangy, but reduced lees time (20 months) less impressive than **14** ★★★★★ ⑨① & **13** ⑧⑧.

Johanna Dry Rosé ★★★ Bright, scented berry/cherry aromas & flavour on 100% pinot noir **18** ⑧⓪. Dry, light & brisk, piquant al fresco wine with pleasing balance. **Muratie Melck's Sauvignon Blanc** ★★★ Herbaceous, tinned asparagus pungency, turning tropical on palate. **18** ⑧② friendly, light quaffing style, ready to enjoy. WO W Cape. Not tasted: **Muratie Melck's Blended Red**.

Fortified Wines

★★★★☆ **Amber Forever** Perfumed raisin flavours on oak-matured fortified hanepoot, creamy, warming centre with thread of citrus peel freshness. **16** ★★★★ ⑧⑦ more delicate version of heady **15** ⑨②. 375 ml. WO W Cape.

★★★★ **Ben Prins Cape Vintage** Modern, delicious 'port' from traditional varieties. **15** ★★★★★ ⑨② concentrated black fruit, firm, dry & peppery tannins, sweetness well contained, finishes with a fiery twist. An infant, deserves decade ageing. Also-tasted **16** ⑧⑦ riper & rounder, appealing but less structured, will peak much earlier. Simonsberg-Stellenbosch WO.

★★★★ **Cape Ruby** ⑦ Deep rich fruitcake & brandy, this port-style **NV** ⑧⑦'s perfume is seductive & the flavours don't disappoint either, finishes with enlivening alcohol grip.— MW

Location/map: Stellenbosch ▪ Map grid reference: F3 ▪ WO: Stellenbosch/Simonsberg-Stellenbosch/ Western Cape ▪ Est 1685 ▪ 1stB ca 1920 ▪ Tasting & sales daily 10-5 ▪ Tasting fees: R45/standard, R80/premium, R65/chocolate pairing ▪ Closed Good Fri, Dec 25 & Jan 1 ▪ Farm Kitchen Wed-Sun 9-3 ▪ Cellar tours by appt ▪ Cheese platters ▪ Function venue ▪ MOK art gallery/exhibit ▪ Harvest festival ▪ Live music ▪ MTB ▪ Trail running ▪ Owner(s) Melck Family Trust ▪ Winemaker(s) Hattingh de Villiers (Jul 2014) ▪ Viticulturist(s) Conrad Schutte ▪ 110ha/42ha (cab, grenache, merlot, mourv, p verdot, pinot, shiraz, chard, chenin, hanepoot, port, verdelho) ▪ 300t/40,000cs own label 60% red 18% white 1% rosé 21% other ▪ IPW ▪ PO Box 133 Koelenhof 7605 ▪ info@muratie.co.za ▪ www.muratie.co.za ▪ S 33° 52′ 14.8″ E 018° 52′ 35.1″ ▪ 🗺 include.trailer.drove ▪ **T** +27 (0)21-865-2330/2336

☐ **Muse** see Boschheim

Mvemve Raats   ⑨

An enduring and rather glittering achievement and partnership is alluded to in the conjoined name of two old friends: Mzokhona Mvevme, qualified oenologist and agribusiness investment portfolio manager, and Bruwer Raats, of Raats Family Wines. They seem never to have been tempted to go beyond the partnership's one, highly successful, wine. That wine is invariably a blend of the five Bordeaux red varieties, though the proportions tend to differ with the vintage. Each variety is sourced from top sites around Stellenbosch and vinified separately. Then the blend is composed – hence part of the wine's name – from the best barrels.

★★★★★ **MR de Compostella** ⑧ Classic Cape claret now in its 12th vintage. **16** ★★★★★ ⑨③ lives up to name ('Compilation of Stars'). Precision, focus & detail remain hallmarks, as in **15** ⑨⑤, plus astonishing array of black fruit flavours on 63/17/12/6/2 blend cab, cab franc, malbec, petit verdot, merlot.— HC

Location/map/WO: Stellenbosch ▪ Map grid reference: B6 ▪ Est/1stB 2004 ▪ Tasting & sales Mon-Fri 9-5 by appt only ▪ Closed all pub hols ▪ Owner(s) Bruwer Raats & Mzokhona Mvemve ▪ Cellarmaster(s)/viticulturist(s) Bruwer Raats & Mzokhona Mvemve (both Jan 2004) ▪ Winemaker(s) Bruwer Raats & Mzokhona

Mvemve (both Jan 2004), with Gavin Bruwer Slabbert (Feb 2010) ▪ (cabs s/f, malbec, merlot, p verdot) ▪ 10t/900cs own label 100% red ▪ PO Box 2068 Dennesig Stellenbosch 7601 ▪ braats@mweb.co.za ▪ www. raats.co.za ▪ S 33° 58' 16.6" E 018° 44' 55.3" ▪ tinged.guzzle.newness ▪ F +27 (0)86-647-8500 ▪ T +27 (0)21-881-3078

MVH Signature Wines

Carefully and thoughtfully is how Matthew van Heerden makes his boutique wines, and trying to capture terroir as authentically as possible is his mantra. The onetime Diners Club Young Winemaker of the Year has used the same parcels of fruit from Elgin and Stellenbosch for six years now and knows precisely what to expect when fermenting them naturally.

★★★★☆ **Pinot Noir** ② Supple, subtle **16** ⑨⑨ shows benefit of careful sorting & pressing, & natural ferment. Light, refined & spicy, with juicy red fruit in ample core. Just 30% new oak. Elgin fruit as previous.

★★★★☆ **Chardonnay** ② Elegant & effortless **16** ⑨④ once again from Elgin & Stellenbosch grapes, naturally fermented. Lively citrus notes cradled by balancing oak, 50% new, 10 months, giving an understated creaminess to the fresh, long palate.— FM

Location: Stellenbosch ▪ WO: Elgin/Western Cape ▪ Est/1stB 2013 ▪ Tasting by appt only ▪ Owner(s) Matthew van Heerden ▪ Winemaker(s)/viticulturist(s) Matthew van Heerden (Jan 2013) ▪ 5t/400cs own label 50% red 50% white ▪ IPW ▪ PO Box 2134 Dennesig Stellenbosch 7601 ▪ mvhwines@gmail.com ▪ T +27 (0)82-771-7969/+27 (0)82-520-9338

☐ **My Best Friend** *see* Zandvliet Wine Estate

Myburgh Bros

Two sets of Myburgh brothers are invoked here: Tyrrel and Philip, current farmers at Joostenberg in Paarl (see entry), and their great grandfather Johannes and his brother Jacobus. The historical pair owned many farms and pooled resources to make wine at Joostenberg. This venture draws inspiration from the old partnership (as the retro wine label evokes) — not only old-style winemaking varieties like cinsaut and bushvines, but also the entrepreneurial spirit of embracing newer varieties like viognier.

★★★★ **Cinsaut** ⊘ Charmingly light & fresh **17** ⑧⑧ has 14% shiraz to help it attain some seriousness too, though there's no great intensity. A decent tannin grip & genuinely dry finish.

★★★★ **Viognier** ☺ Aromatic peach & floral notes on **17** ⑧⑧, & a hint of spice, but restrained rather than blowsy. Altogether well balanced - as with its partner, there's charm & a bit more than that, for untrivial pleasure.— TJ

Location/map/WO: Paarl ▪ Map grid reference: A7 ▪ Est/1stB 2017 ▪ Tasting, sales & cellar tours by appt ▪ Owner(s) Tyrrel & Philip Myburgh ▪ Cellarmaster(s)/viticulturist(s) Tyrrel Myburgh (2017) ▪ Winemaker(s) Tyrrel Myburgh (2017), with Elmerie Joubert (2017) ▪ ±8,000cs own label 50% red 50% white ▪ Control Union (Organic), IPW ▪ PO Box 82 Elsenburg 7607 ▪ tyrrel@joostenberg.co.za, winery@joostenberg.co.za ▪ S 33° 48' 47.21" E 018° 48' 31.70 ▪ centipedes.bridesmaids.dinners ▪ F +27 (0)21-884-4135 ▪ T +27 (0)21-200-9903

☐ **My Cosmic Hand** *see* Elemental Bob

My Wyn

This Franschhoek mountain vineyard and tiny cellar offers a truly personal experience, from tastings led by vini-viti couple Johan and Jacoline Haasbroek, pair of friendly Dobermanns in attendance, to view-rich walks, armed with a BYO picnic and something from their range of bubblies, whites or reds, to tailor-made visits for small groups, to food-and-wine pairings for wine clubs.

Location/map: Franschhoek ▪ Map grid reference: B1 ▪ Est/1stB 2001 ▪ Tasting, sales & cellar tours by appt, or as indicated on the gate ▪ Open pub hols by appt ▪ Tasting R75pp ▪ Cheese platters by prior arrangement, or BYO picnic ▪ Wine clubs, team building groups welcome for intimate food & wine pairing - various options available, to be pre-booked ▪ Owner(s) Jacoline Haasbroek ▪ Winemaker(s) Jacoline Haasbroek (2001) ▪ 1,250cs own label 40% red 20% white 20% port 20% MCC ▪ IPW ▪ PO Box 112 Franschhoek 7690

■ tastewine@telkomsa.net ▪ www.mywynfranschhoek.co.za ▪ S 33° 53' 29.3" E 019° 8' 3.6" ▪ �🌐 witticism. mouthparts.placebos ▪ **T** +27 (0)21-876-2518/+27 (0)83-302-5556

Nabygelegen Private Cellar   Ⓠ ⌂ ◎

Thick stone walls and firing slots are an indication of Nabygelegen's frontier past. Granted in the early 1700s, the property in Wellington's Bovlei Valley last produced wine in 1934. That was until James McKenzie called time on his international banking career in the early 2000s and settled down to farm grapes, renovate the cellar, make wine and add luxury self-catering cottages.

★★★★ **Scaramanga Red** Ⓖ Spicy plum- & berry-toned **16** ⑧⑥, unusual tempranillo blend from Coastal vines, toned, trim, with graphite, herb nuances on long, dry finish. Also in magnum. No **14** ⑧⑥.

★★★★ **Scaramanga White** Ⓖ Blossoms over citrus & stonefruit on textured, spicy chenin, chardonnay & verdelho. **16** ⑧⑥ gets length, stature & complexity from lees & oak, 20% new. Wellington WO.

Not tasted: **Cabernet Sauvignon**, **Merlot**, **Seventeen Twelve**, **Chenin Blanc**, **Sauvignon Blanc**, **Lady Anna**. — FM

Location/map: Wellington ▪ Map grid reference: C3 ▪ WO: Coastal/Wellington ▪ Est 2001 ▪ 1stB 2002 ▪ Tasting & cellar tours by appt; sales Mon-Fri 10-4 Sat by appt ▪ Closed all pub hols ▪ Tour groups ▪ Walks/hikes ▪ MTB trail ▪ Self-catering luxury accommodation ▪ Owner(s) Avalon Vineyards (Pty) Ltd ▪ Cellarmaster(s) James McKenzie (Jan 2002) ▪ Viticulturist(s) Johan Wiese (May 2001, consultant) ▪ 35ha/17ha (cab, merlot, p verdot, tempranillo, chenin, sauv) ▪ 180t/24,000cs own label 50% red 50% white ▪ PO Box 302 Wellington 7654 ▪ marketing@nabygelegen.co.za ▪ www.nabygelegen.co.za ▪ S 33° 37' 54.7" E 019° 3' 51.2" ▪ �🌐 inspired. shifters.unbuckle ▪ **T** +27 (0)21-873-7534

☐ **Naked Truth** see Picardi ReBEL

☐ **Naked Wines** see Richard Kershaw Wines

Namaqua Wines   Ⓠ ⑪ ◎ Ⓐ

Among SA's biggest and most successful producers, Namaqua is taking its slogan 'Boxing the Best' a stage further by adding three varietal wines to the West Coast winery's popular 3L-pack range. Quality, the 200 owner-growers assure, is equal to that of the bottled versions. On which subject, the winegrowing team is delighted and proud of their recent performance at the Young Wine Show, raking in the General Smuts trophy for top wine and the Pietman Hugo trophy for quality and consistency overall. Production chief Len Knoetze and crew's fine-wine making skills are further showcased in the new Doornkraal chenin, from a block using the rare-in-SA 'staked vine' training method, colloquially known as 'stok-by-paaltjie'. Namaqua's extensive portfolio can be sampled at Die Keldery, its modern visitor centre and restaurant in Vredendal.

Doornkraal range ⓃⒺⓌ

★★★★☆ **Chenin Blanc** ⓥ From low-yield Lutzville grapes handled minimally in the cellar. **17** ⑨⓪ wonderfully refined & restrained, delicate white peach & floral notes untrammelled by oak, positive earthy touch, exhilarating acidity to balance.

Spencer Bay Winemakers Reserve range

★★★★ **The Blend** ⓥ Cab-led, 5-way Bordeaux red. **14** ⑧⑥ repeats pleasing **11** ⑧⑥ formula: dark fruit, mint accent, oak (70% new, 75% American, 12-18 months, as for all) adding complexity & structure, hint sweetness. No **13**, **12**.

Cabernet Sauvignon ★★★☆ Polished **13** ⑧③ has generous black fruit & freshness that lifts the sweet vanilla-oak conclusion. For now & ±3 years. From selected top-performing blocks, as all these. **Pinot Noir** ⓥ ★★★★ Improving on previous, **13** ⑧③ is less stewed, more vibrant, with well-managed tannin/acid balance; similar red berry aromas & smoky overlay. **Pinotage** ★★★★ On-form, modern **12** ⑧④ shows succulent mulberry & plum fruit, vivacious acidity, lingering dry finish; oak less 'sweet' than siblings. **Shiraz** ★★★★ Still-youthful **12** ⑧③, with bright acidity, firm tannins as counterpoint to vanilla overlay.

Cellar Door range

★★★★ **Sauvignon Blanc** ⓃⒺⓌ ⓥ Intense pyrazine & nettle character a recognised style in SA (though perhaps less favoured in other countries). It's well done in **16** ⑧⑥, with added depth & texture from old-oak-matured portion, lees ageing for remainder.

Merlot (NEW) ⊘ ★★★★ Much commendable about **14** (83): most variety-true aroma of all producer's reds, enviable palate concentration. Overt oak sweetness a slight detraction. **Pinotage-Malbec** ★★★ Tight tannins, brisk acidity contrast with **14** (82)'s appealing strawberry jam & blue/black fruit aromas. Unusual blend, year 70% new oak, equal French/American, as for Merlot. Not tasted: **Pinotage**.

Cape West Limited Releases

Shiraz-Pinotage (🍇) ★★★ Attractively spicy, smoky & savoury 67/33 blend, **17** (82) soaks up 70% new wood (50/50 French/American, as for all), so it's less oak-sweet than siblings.

Cabernet Sauvignon-Malbec-Pinotage ★★★ Smooth & easy **17** (82) with attractive spiciness, charry finish. Good everyday drinking, as all these (but note big 14.5% alcohol here). **Cabernet Sauvignon-Pinotage** ★★★ Bright acidity for food pairing, firm tannins but no rough edges on fruity **17** (82).

Chardonnay (🍇) ★★★★ Youthful **15** (83) barrel sample ample ripe pear & creamy oatmeal, complementary part-oaking (20% new). Riper, rounder style; clean acidity for food compatibility. WO W Cape, as next. **Sauvignon Blanc** (🍇) ★★★ Ripe & juicy peach flavours, older oak for some plump succulence but overall **16** (81)'s pithy-dry tone better with a meal than solo.

Namaqua range

Cabernet Sauvignon ⊘ ★★★ Packed with black & red berries, lifted by racy acidity, **15** (77) slips down easily. Few grams sugar, high portion American oak aid drinkability, as all these reds. **Merlot** ⊘ ★★★ Sweetness well balanced by brisk acidity, **17** (77) slight leafiness & hint of clove. **Pinotage** ★★ Olive tapenade nuance on brief, uncomplicated **17** (75). **Shiraz** ⊘ ★★★ **16** (78)'s succulent fruit overlaid with smoke, refreshed by nudge tannin, vein of acidity. **Guinevere Méthode Cap Classique** ★★★★ First since **07** ★★★ (79), **10** (85) celebratory sparkling from 60% pinot noir with chardonnay has rather unorthodox orange hue, impresses with fine bead, creamy mousse, savoury/umami finish from 5 years on lees. **Noble Late Harvest** (🍇) ★★★ Unusual but pleasant **14** (82) botrytis dessert from pinotage, unoaked, & delightful savouriness, giving strawberries in balsamic vinegar effect. Would work well with soft cheeses or fresh fruit desserts. 375 ml. **Red Muscadel** ⊘ ★★★★ Partly oaked **17** (85) fortified, with exotic allure of tangerine, tealeaf & cardamom. Persistent, sweet but uncloying flavours. **White Muscadel** ⊘ ★★★★ Well-integrated alcohol, tangy acidity, intense citrus & honeysuckle aromas & flavours: **17** (83) part-oaked fortified dessert ticks all the boxes. **Hanepoot Jerepigo** (🍇) ★★★ Abundant tropical fruit rounded by touch old oak, fortified **15** (79) big-hearted & unctuous comforter for cold rainy nights. **Cape Vintage** (NEW) ★★ From shiraz, **17** (74) more jerepigo than 'port' in style, with lower alcohol (17%) & more sugar (130 g/l) than purists would expect. Not tasted: **Chenin Blanc**, **Sauvignon Blanc**. Discontinued: **Beach Braai**, **Cape Ruby**.

Gôiya range

Not tasted: **Sauvignon Blanc-Chardonnay**.

3L Box range

Cabernet Sauvignon (NEW) ★★ Friendly **16** (75) slips down easily. **Merlot** (NEW) ★★ Juicy & bright **17** (75) brushed with American oak - like Cab - for early enjoyment. **Sauvignon Blanc** (NEW) ⊘ ★★★ Figgy & grassy, with racy acidity, **18** (77) gets the party started. — CvZ

Location: Vredendal ▪ Map: Olifants River ▪ Map grid reference: B4 ▪ WO: Olifants River/Western Cape/ Lutzville ▪ Est/1stB 1947 ▪ Tasting & sales Mon-Sat 8–5 ▪ Closed Easter Fri-Mon, Ascension day & Dec 25/26 ▪ Cellar tours Mon-Fri 10 & 3, book ahead ▪ Die Keldery Restaurant T +27 (0)27-213-3699/8 Mon-Fri 8-5 Sat 9-5 & dinner Thu 7-10 ▪ Facilities for children ▪ Conferences ▪ Owner(s) 200 members ▪ Production manager Len Knoetze ▪ Winemaker(s) Driaan van der Merwe, Rudi de Wet, Koos Thiart, Johan Weideman & Reinier van Greunen ▪ Viticulturist(s) Dirk de Bruyn ▪ 4,990ha ▪ 113,692t/9.3m cs 20% red 80% white ▪ PO Box 75 Vredendal 8160 ▪ info@namaquawines.com ▪ www.namaquawines.com ▪ S 31° 42' 34.9" E 018° 30' 15.6" ▪ 📍 scattered.overactive.centenary ▪ F +27 (0)27-213-3476 ▪ **T +27 (0)27-213-1080**

Napier Vineyards   (🍷) (♿)

Scenic Napier Winery in the Groenberg hills takes its name from Cape governor Sir George Napier, who in 1840 oversaw the naming of the local town after the Duke of Wellington, vanquisher of Napoleon. Latterly connections have shifted eastward, to Bingen am Rhein, home of Reh Kendermann GmbH winery, which acquired Napier in 2017 and today sells its wines along with Black Tower and other German and international wine brands in its orbit into markets around the world.

Napier range

★★★★ Red Medallion Bordeaux-style flagship, cab (55%) plus cab franc & merlot in a generous red- & black-fruit medley. **14** ⑧⑦ similar luxurious styling, well-composed tannins as **13** ⑧⑨ but 15% alcohol noticeably warm.

★★★★ St Catherine Follows **15** ⑧⑥'s less opulent path in **17** ⑧⑧. Elegant spice from modest (older) oaking to pure citrus perfume & palate, pleasingly dry, lovely acidity extending the finish. **16** untasted.

Petite Marie Grenache Rosé ⑥ ★★★ Deep pink hue from grenache, cured meat & strawberry combo, dry, but well-hidden gram sugar makes **18** ⑦⑨ smooth & easy. Not tasted: **Cabernet Sauvignon**. Discontinued: **Greenstone**.

Lion Creek range

Cabernet Sauvignon ★★★ Berry-toned **16** ⑧⓪, unchallenging, friendly, with staying power for few years. No new oak, so the fruit really shines. **Cabernet Sauvignon-Shiraz** ★★★ With smidgen sugar for drinkability, **16** ⑧⓪ equal partnership has meaty nuance, tannins firm for food but ample fruit padding for solo. Tiny 5% new oak. **Chenin Blanc-Sauvignon Blanc** ⑧ ★★★ Bright blackberry-toned fruit on **17** ⑧①, characterful summer glassful. WO W Cape.

Brandy range

★★★★ Sir George Potstill Brandy ⑧ From 100% chenin, vibrant gold potstill, matured 5 years. Well structured, smooth & elegant; appropriately sophisticated packaging.— CvZ, WB

Location/map: Wellington ▪ Map grid reference: C3 ▪ WO: Wellington/Western Cape ▪ Est 1989/1stB 1999 ▪ Tasting & sales Mon-Thu 8-5 Fri 8–3 ▪ Fee R30/R60/R100 ▪ Cellar tours by appt ▪ Closed all pub hols ▪ Owner(s) Reh Kendermann GmbH Weinkellerei ▪ Cellarmaster(s) Leon Bester (Apr 2000) ▪ Winemaker(s) Leon Bester (Apr 2000), with Hanlie Schönborn (Sep 2012) ▪ Viticulturist(s) JP van der Merwe (Aug 2017) ▪ 135ha/89ha (cab, chenin) ▪ 650t/30,000cs own label 78% red 20% white 2% rosé ▪ WIETA ▪ PO Box 638 Wellington 7654 ▪ info@napierwinery.co.za ▪ www.napier-vineyards.co.za ▪ S 33° 38' 37.0" E 019° 2' 24.8" ▪ 🌐 shopper.internet.phones ▪ F +27 (0)86-608-5424 ▪ **T +27 (0)21-873-7829**

☐ **Natana** see Marianne Wine Estate
☐ **Nativo** see Hughes Family Wines

Natte Valleij Wines　　　　　　　　　　　　　 ⓆⓀⓄⒶ

Milner brothers Alex and Marcus (also Druk My Niet winemaker) collaborate in the family's 300-year-old Stellenbosch cellar, fairly unchanged over the centuries, on a boutique range which includes a critically acclaimed 'four pack' of cinsaut varietal bottlings, each from a different area.

Location/map: Stellenbosch ▪ Map grid reference: F1 ▪ Est 1715 ▪ Tasting, sales & cellar tours Mon-Sat by appt ▪ Closed all pub hols ▪ Facilities for children ▪ Conference/indaba venue ▪ Art gallery & art classes ▪ Artifacts & various paintings ▪ Natte Valleij B&B/self-catering cottages ▪ Owner(s)/winemaker(s) Milner family ▪ 28ha total ▪ 40t/5,000cs own label 90% red 10% white ▪ PO Box 4 Klapmuts 7625 ▪ wine@nattevalleij.co.za ▪ www.nattevalleij.co.za ▪ S 33° 50' 3.6" E 018° 52' 43.2" ▪ 🌐 sofa.cardinal.same ▪ **T +27 (0)21-875-5171**

☐ **Natural Star** see Stellar Winery
☐ **Naudé Old Vines** see Naudé Wines

Naudé Wines

Previously in a partnership with others, seasoned vintner Ian Naudé is back on his own, hence the listing change from Adoro. His focus remains the same: making wines from venerable old vines in Swartland and elsewhere. Why old vines particularly? 'It's about respect.' That the vines have been in the soil for between 30 and 50 years, and have an authenticity and character no younger vines can offer. A great believer that SA makes wines no other country can emulate, he proves it in his range. Both single-site and multi-terroir, his wines are individual, lauded locally and abroad, and have great ageing potential (see Naudé White).

Naudé Old Vines range

★★★★☆ **Cinsault** ② ⊛ Single Darling vineyard, **15** ⑨③ follows maiden **14** ⑨④ in red fruit intensity, yet also earthy, scrubby, with textured savouriness. Elegant (12% alcohol) but nothing missing, has sleek musculature. As winemaker Naudé says: 'Young at heart with an old soul.'

★★★★☆ **Grenache** ② ⊛ Naturally fermented **14** ⑨④ is light, understated, almost austere - but undeniably complex, with red cherry, pot-pourri & a pinch of pepper. Silky, with a fresh, bright finish. Swartland vines; only older oak.

★★★★☆ **Chenin Blanc** ② ⊛ Noteworthy **15** ⑨② from old Swartland/Durbanville bushvines, barrel fermented/aged, oxidatively made. Complex perfume - quince, tangerine, floral notes - but flavour is pure mineral, almost saline, with focused freshness. No **14**.

★★★★☆ **Semillon** ⊛ ⊛ Wild ferment, 10 months oak, 25% new, **16** ⑨③ melon & ginger preserve richness but not overt, in a restrained, quietly assured way, deep rather than flashy. Lovely brightening acidity, almost saline, keeps it in perfect health. No **15**.

★★★★☆ **Naudé White** ② Stylishly packaged, authoritative multi-terroir blend; part-barrel-fermented chenin & semillon, smidgen zingy sauvignon, intense, ageworthy & complex. Small parcels of older vintages re-released this edition: debut **06**, vibrant tropical, thatch, fynbos, honeyed/waxy hints, balanced 13% alcohol. **07** ⑨② similar flavour profile, richness & poise - at only 11.5% alcohol.— CR

Location: Stellenbosch ▪ WO: Western Cape/Swartland ▪ Est 2017 ▪ 1stB 2000 ▪ Closed to public ▪ Owner(s)/winemaker(s) Ian Naudé ▪ 50% red 50% white ▪ PO Box 982 Stellenbosch 7599 ▪ naudewines@gmail.com, iannaude7@gmail.com ▪ www.naudewines.co.za ▪ **T +27 (0)83-630-3794**

Naughton's Flight

Following his 'flight' from his native Ireland, Constantia-based Francis Naughton worked for many years for drinks giant SFW (precursor of Distell) before venturing into own-label winemaking, at the opposite end of the volume scale, with a top consultant oenologist in the early 2000s.

Shiraz ② ★★★☆ Nicely maturing **08** ⑧④ in the customary style, stressing the leathery, savoury side rather than the fruity - but there's a good touch of red berry succulence on the lean but balanced, structured palate. Not tasted: **Tribua**, **Délice**. — TJ

Location: Constantia ▪ WO: Stellenbosch ▪ 1stB 2003 ▪ Closed to public ▪ Owner(s) Francis Naughton ▪ (carignan, mourv, shiraz, viog) ▪ ±20,000 btls ▪ 25 Willow Rd Constantia 7806 ▪ naughts@mweb.co.za ▪ F +27 (0)21-794-3928 ▪ **T +27 (0)21-794-3928**

Nederburg Wines ② ⑪ ⊚ ⑤

Nothing stands still at dynamic Nederburg, among SA's biggest and best-known wine brands and this guide's prestigious Winery of the Year in 2011 and 2017. The Paarl-based, Distell-owned powerhouse continues to build its profile internationally as well as maintain a leading market position back at home. Cellarmaster Andrea Freeborough has been joined by two new winemakers, and together they continue to experiment with different techniques (watch out for chenin blanc aged in amphoras) as well as new-wave varieties - the maiden albariño going exclusively to Waitrose in the UK. Nederburg's partnership with SA's leading cycling team and Qhubeka, a nonprofit organisation which builds and distributes bicycles to the local community, enters its final year, generating awareness of the wines, but more importantly, creating employment as well as helping people get around more easily.

Two Centuries range

★★★★☆ **Cabernet Sauvignon** ⊛ Dense & dark **15** ⑨④ continues effortlessly in similar spectacular vein as **14** ★★★★★ ⑨⑨, our 2018 Red Wine of the Year, with extra elegance & restraint. 22 months new French oak adds layers of spice - cinnamon & nutmeg - along with smoky overtones to ripe black-berried fruit. Solid tannins & fresh acid build to long finish. Paarl grapes.

★★★★☆ **Sauvignon Blanc** ⊛ Everything is green & cream on nose of exceptional **17** ⑨④ - limes, peppers, pine needles, vanilla, touch of wax. 9 months barrel ferment/ageing add lick of spice & salt as well as weight & texture on palate, & a bright, lengthy finish. Classic example, like **16** ⑨③.

Ingenuity range

★★★★☆ **Red Italian Blend** ⓐ Shy nose takes time to shine on unusual **15** ⑨③ blend, mostly sangiovese with barbera & 10% nebbiolo. Palate more forthcoming with cherries, tar, tobacco, plenty of big ripe tannins & lively acidity. Definitely needs keeping but good times ahead. New oak, some American, 30 months. Worthy successor to **14** ⑨③.

★★★★☆ **White Blend** ⓐ Sauvignon-led 8-way blend **17** ⑨① is intriguing melange of peachstones, apples, guavas & flowers. Oak touch on chardonnay component adds almonds, cream & spice while slightly bitter note at finish adds to conviction that this is a great food wine.

Not tasted: **Red Spanish Blend.**

Manor House range

★★★★ **Cabernet Sauvignon** Mixes herbaceous notes with ripe black fruit (plums & cherries) enlivened by sweet vanilla courtesy 18 months French & American oak. **16** ⑧⑨ soft but present tannins support fruit through to pleasing conclusion.

★★★★ **Shiraz** Big & bold **15** ⑧⑨ shows pleasing development - leather, polish, chocolate & spice - enrobing black cherries & currants. Also-tasted **16** ⑧⑨ lighter, fresher, with red fruit profile; easier drinking now, should develop nicely.

★★★★ **Sauvignon Blanc** Bright, fruit-forward **18** ⑧⑨ from Darling packed with grapefruit, granadilla & plenty classic blackcurrant & leafy notes. Shade less interesting than standout **17** ★★★★★ ⑨② but totally worthwhile sipper.

Heritage Heroes range

★★★★☆ **The Brew Master** Blackcurrant pastille & cream bursting forth on **16** ⑨② cabernet-led 5-way Bordeaux blend. 2 years French & tiny tweak Americab oak softens & rounds through to more restrained finish. Elegant example, should improve.

★★★★ **The Motorcycle Marvel** ⓐ Delicious improvement over **15** ⑧⑦ in **16** ★★★★★ ⑨③ Rhône blend. Mostly carignan & shiraz with grenache, cinsaut, mourvèdre, mixing fresh cranberry, raspberry & perfume with oodles of spice & leather from French, Romanian, American oak. Fresh acidity, juicy tannins, excellent length.

★★★★ **The Anchorman** Peachy, creamy complexity on **17** ⑧⑦ chenin uses different winemaking options including (unusually) carbonic maceration. Drop sugar does no harm at all, adding to richness of mid-palate before freshening tail.

★★★★ **The Beautiful Lady** Nothing subtle about this lady but **18** ⑧⑨ gewürztraminer does show beautiful elegance & refinement after outburst of litchi, flowers & Turkish delight. Off-dry & well balanced between sugar & acidity. Perfect for pavlova. No **17**.

★★★★☆ **The Young Airhawk** Back on form in **17** ⑨① after quieter **16** ★★★★ ⑧⑦. Sauvignon, part barrel-fermented in mix of 1st/2nd/3rd-fill oak mixes flinty gunsmoke aromas with greenpepper, fig & cream. Juicy acidity carries through to lengthy limy tail.

Private Bin range for Nederburg Auction

★★★★☆ **Cabernet Sauvignon Private Bin R163** ⓐ Powerful & muscular **15** ⑨② takes itself seriously - & why not, when it packs this much blackcurrant fruit, smoky, charry oak (18 months), ripe velvety tannins & appetising acidity into one glass? Definitely one for the cellar. Paarl fruit.

★★★★ **Sauvignon Blanc Private Bin D234** ⓐ Elegant & lean, showing plenty of green (pepper, fig, lime, grass) unoaked **17** ⑧⑨ needs more time to settle & soothe rather spiky flavours. Plenty of concentration & good acidity suggest wait will be rewarded.

Not tasted: **Cinsaut, Grenache Private Bin, Merlot Private Bin R181, Pinot Noir, Petit Verdot Private Bin R104, Pinotage Private Bin R172, Shiraz Private Bin R121, Cabernet Sauvignon-Merlot Private Bin R109, Cabernet Sauvignon-Shiraz Private Bin R103, Chardonnay Private Bin D270, Gewürztraminer Private Bin D259, Riesling, Sauvignon Blanc-Semillon Private Bin D252, Eminence, Edelkeur.**

Winemaster's Reserve range

★★★★ **Merlot** Elegant & excellent example of cut-above everyday drinking pleasure, **17** ⑧⑦ mixes warming cherry-choc notes with vanilla, coffee & cream. French oak staves, as all reds this range.

★★★★ **Shiraz** Abundant oak & spice (some American staves) on peppery **16** ★★★★ ⑧⑤, with rather shier fruit than **15** ⑧⑦, needing to settle & shine. Velvety tannins & appealing vanilla finish.

★★★★ **Edelrood** No-holds-barred, full-on flavours from **16** ⑧⑨ cabernet/merlot blend (60/40). Sweetly fruited blackcurrant pastille & jam, lots of vanilla & cream given edge by lively acidity.

★★★★ **Special Late Harvest** Perfectly balanced **17** ⑧⑦ from chenin with 38% viognier walks the line between sweetness, freshening acidity & a tropical fruit explosion - melon, mango & papaya - with enjoyable bitter peel finish. **16** ★★★ ⑧① less poised.

Carignan-Grenache Rosé ⑦ ★★★ Charming dry pink **18** ⑧② from near-equal Paarl carignan & grenache packed with strawberry, hints of bubblegum & gummy bear, brisk acidic finish. Delicious! **Albariño** ⑭ⓔⓦ ⑦ ★★★ Interesting debut for this trendy Spanish grape, **18** ⑧② pretty floral notes with hints of tinned peach & pear. **Pinot Grigio** ⑦ ★★★★ Characterful **18** ⑧③ has 13% colombard; presents strong showing of pear, apple, yellow melon in off-dry summer sipper.

Cabernet Sauvignon ★★★☆ Appealing soft black-berried fruit **16** ⑧⑤ with tweaks of red cherries, sweet new leather & attractive stalky finish. Eminently enjoyable tipple. **Pinotage** ★★★ Very decent drop **16** ⑧① has oodles of ripe raspberry & plum, with soft tannins & good acidity. **Chardonnay** ★★★ Mix old & new barrels brings creamy notes to well-balanced, just-dry **17** ⑧②. Ripe orange & peach with hints of vanilla. **Sauvignon Blanc** ★★★ Bouncy & lively **18** ⑧① has 5% semillon & short lees-contact to add interest & weight to lashings of gooseberry fruit, with tropical finish. Not tasted: **Malbec, Riesling, Noble Late Harvest**.

56Hundred range

Cabernet Sauvignon ⑦ ★★★ Black cherry/berry on **17** ⑧①, just-dry, with soft tannins & choc/coffee finish. French/American staves, as all these reds. **Merlot** ⑦ ★★★ Cracking braai wine **17** ⑧⓪ is super-drinkable, spicy oak complementing blackberry fruit. Touch sugar adds to easy-drinking appeal.

Pinot Noir ★★★ Lively, light, easy-drinking **17** ⑧⓪ mixes spice, biltong & berries. Chill in summer. **Chenin Blanc** ★★★ Light fruit salad notes on just-dry **18** ⑦⑨, with apple, pear & crisp finish. **Pinot Grigio** ★★ Light, just-dry & neutral **18** ⑦⑥ lacks definitive fruit or character. **Sauvignon Blanc** ★★★ Snappy & fresh, now dry & the better for it. **18** ⑦⑧ tropical fruit mouthful with clean finish. Not tasted: **Pinotage, Shiraz, Cabernet Sauvignon-Shiraz**.

1791 range

Pinotage ⑦ ★★★ Juicy red- & black-fruit-toned **17** ⑧⓪ helped by few grams of sugar for pleasant weekday drinking.

Shiraz ★★ Smoked ham & meat notes on **17** ⑦⑥, simple & fruity. **Rosé** ★★★ Mainly shiraz with pinotage & others, **18** ⑦⑧ off-dry with sweet berries & sprightly acidity. Not tasted: **Cabernet Sauvignon, Merlot, Shiraz-Viognier, Chardonnay, Chenin Blanc, Sauvignon Blanc, Chardonnay-Viognier**.

Nederburg range

Baronne ⑦ ★★★☆ Steakhouses everywhere can rejoice in ever-reliable meaty partner delivering the goods yet again in **17** ⑧③. Mainly cab with shiraz & more, sweet-savoury notes from American oak adding to plummy black fruit. At 78,000 cases, hardly 'hidden' but undoubtedly a gem.

Duet ★★★ Shiraz & pinotage combine in off-dry **17** ⑦⑦ to deliver soft black berries & tannins. **Lyric** ★★★ Gooseberry & grapefruit on cheerful **18** ⑦⑧, from sauvignon & chenin with tweak chardonnay. Just-dry, balanced by lively acidity. **Stein** ★★★ Semi-sweet **18** ⑦⑧ chenin provides ripe mouthful of pear, pineapple & cooked apple. **Première Cuvée Brut** ★★★ Fresh, fruity & frothy **NV** ⑧① sparkling from chenin & sauvignon, great for Sunday brunch. — CM

Location/map: Paarl ▪ Map grid reference: F5 ▪ WO: Western Cape/Paarl/Darling ▪ Est 1791 ▪ 1stB ca 1940 ▪ Tasting & sales May-Sep: Mon-Fri 9-5 Sat/Sun 10-4; Oct-Apr: Mon-Fri 9-6 Sat/Sun 10-4 ▪ Various tasting fees, waived on purchase of R300+ ▪ Closed Good Fri, Dec 25 & Jan 1 ▪ Cellar tours Mon-Fri 10.30 & 3 Sat 11 Sun 11 (Oct-Apr) ▪ Large groups/foreign language tours by appt only ▪ Visitors' centre: wine tasting, cheese & wine pairing ▪ Historic Manor House (national monument) featuring The Red Table restaurant, open Tue-Sun

T +27 (0)21-877-5155 ▪ Tour groups ▪ Gifts ▪ Conferences ▪ Museum ▪ Conservation area ▪ Owner(s) Distell ▪ Cellarmaster(s) Andrea Freeborough (Jul 2015) ▪ Winemaker(s) Samuel Viljoen (reds, Oct 2014) & Elmarie Botes (whites, Dec 2017), with Heinrich Kulsen (reds, Oct 2014) & Jamie Fredericks (whites, May 2018) ▪ Viticulturist(s) Bennie Liebenberg & Henk van Graan ▪ 1,680ha (cab, carignan, grenache, malbec, merlot, p verdot, ptage, shiraz, tannat, tempranillo, chard, chenin, riesling, sauv, sem) ▪ 13,000t/2m cs own label ▪ ISO 0001:2008, ISO 14001:2004, HACCP, IPW, BRC, SGS organic ▪ Private Bag X3006 Paarl 7620 ▪ nedwines@ distell.co.za ▪ www.nederburg.co.za ▪ S 33° 43′ 15.4″ E 019° 0′ 9.4″ ▪ ⌖ steeped.fighters.playful ▪ F +27 (0)21-862-4887 ▪ T +27 (0)21-862-3104

Neethlingshof Estate ⓥ ⑪ ◎ ⑧ ⑤

Past and present entwine like the canopy of the stone pines that line the entrance to this Stellenbosch estate, once home to one of SA's first woman winemakers, the widow Maria Marais, whose son-in-law Johannes Neethling became joint owner in 1828 and renamed it Neethlingshof. The German Schreiber family are the current custodians, and they are focused equally on preserving the farm's heritage, which dates back further still, to 1692, and on farming for the future, hence being one of few WWF-SA Conservation Champions. The family's interlinked concerns are reflected in the names of the pinnacle wines.

Short Story Collection

★★★★☆ **Owl Post** Single-vineyard pinotage recognises wild owls' role in reducing pesticide use on estate. Dark ripe cherry, berry & plum fruit in balance with plush & rich structure of **17** ⑨⓪, dry penetrating finish. 15 months mainly Hungarian oak, 70% new. **16** untasted.

★★★★☆ **Caracal** Bordeaux quartet of cab (45%), merlot, malbec & cab franc, mostly French oak, 70% new. **16** ⑨⓪ is well fruited but remains sleek & muscular, with focused ripe vanilla-tinged tannins & 14.6% alcohol under control. Lingering flavours suggest patience will bring more pleasure. 1.5 & 3L available.

★★★★☆ **Jackals Dance** ⊘ Superb single-vineyard sauvignon spotlit in this prestige range. Meagre 4 t/ha crop of **18** ⑨⓪ preview carefully handled to preserve flinty green (grass/nettle) aromas; contrasting ripe fruit (fig & gooseberry) fills out balanced, softly dry palate. Lovely tension in sync with 14% alcohol.

★★★★☆ **Six Flowers** ⊘ Unusual 6-way blend in homage to Maria Marais & her five children; bold melange of creamy chardonnay & opulent viognier, aromatic riesling & gewürztraminer, a body of chenin & steely spine of sauvignon. New oak fills already ample frame of **17** ⑨⓪ & adds to exotic decadence.

★★★★☆ **Maria Magdalena Noble Late Harvest** ⓩ Unoaked botrytis dessert from riesling. **17** ⑨② billows honeyed apricot, then tangy melon & Golden Delicious apple kick in, & wonderful sugar-acid balance focuses the rich crème brûlée texture. A low-alcohol (10%) beauty with great prospects. 375 ml.

Neethlingshof range

★★★★ **Chenin Blanc** ⊘ Pear drop aroma, tropical fruit flavour & zesty, just-dry finish lift creamy oatmeal texture of **18** ⑧⑥, which saw weekly lees stirring but no wood contact.

★★★★ **Gewürztraminer** ⊘ Redolent of litchi, rosewater & Turkish delight, fresh & tangy with lime & ginger nuance on finish. **18** ⑧⑥ with whisper of sweetness, ideal partner for spicy food.

⋯

Cabernet Sauvignon ⑰ ★★★☆ Pliable, sweet tannins try to tether the cool brambly fruit of **15** ⑧⑤ but the delicious, moreish juiciness wins the day! 18 months oak, some American, down to 30% new. Magnums too for the inevitable parties. **Malbec** ⑰ ★★★☆ Something to perk up your taste buds: earthy mineral tones offset by a bright cranberry tang; velvety tannins & whiff American oak vanilla up the appeal. **17** ⑧④ also in 3, 5 & 9L, as next. **Merlot** ⑰ ★★★ Mulberry & smoked bacon features, **16** ⑧② more generous than previous thanks to padding of ripe fruit. Mostly French oak, 30% new.

⋯

Pinotage ★★★★ Quintessential pinotage plums & banana made more piquant, tasty, by cinnamon spice from French & American oak, 40% new. **17** ⑧③ full & gentle enough for solo sipping. **Shiraz** ★★★★ Brooding **15** ⑧④ has red berry & smoked meat profile with sweet mocha overlay & chewy tannins, brawny 14.7% alcohol. 15% American oak. **Cabernet Sauvignon-Merlot** ★★★★ Ample black berry fruit of **16** ⑧⑤ amplified by American oak (10%), generous but not as measured, balanced as previous, which better absorbed the wooding. **Chardonnay Unwooded** ★★★☆ Young & vibrant **18** ⑧⑤'s punchy citrus & pear profile a good bet on winelists. **Sauvignon Blanc** ★★★ Light & refreshing, has Stellenbosch's signature riper fruit flavours, granadilla & grapefruit in **18** ⑧②. — DS

Location/map/WO: Stellenbosch ▪ Map grid reference: D5 ▪ Est 1692 ▪ 1stB 1880 ▪ Tasting & sales Mon-Fri 9–5 Sat/Sun 10-4 ▪ Tasting fees: R50/5 Estate wines; R80/5 Short Story Collection wines; R65/5 Selection wines ▪ Closed Good Fri & Dec 25 ▪ Cellar tours by appt ▪ 'Flash Food & Slow Wine' pairing R110pp, booking recommended for 6+ ▪ 'Truffle & Wine' pairing R65pp ▪ Kiddies pairing R60pp ▪ Pizzas & platters available in winegarden ▪ Jungle gym ▪ Tour groups ▪ Conferences ▪ Conservation area ▪ Wednesday night live music (summer & winter) ▪ The Restaurant at Neethlingshof & Palm Terrace ▪ Owner(s) Schreiber family ▪ Cellarmaster(s) De Wet Viljoen (Jun 2003) ▪ Winemaker(s) Jacobus van Zyl ▪ Viticulturist(s) Hannes van Zyl ▪ 273ha/95ha (cabs s/f, malbec, merlot, p verdot, ptage, shiraz, chard, chenin, gewürz, riesling, sauv, viog) ▪ 500t/70,000cs own label 55% red 45% white ▪ WIETA, WWF-SA Conservation Champion ▪ PO Box 104 Stellenbosch 7599 ▪ info@neethlingshof.co.za ▪ www.neethlingshof.co.za ▪ S 33° 56' 28.2" E 018° 48' 6.7" ▪ ⬚ unwind.trailers.trail ▪ F +27 (0)21-883-8941 ▪ T +27 (0)21-883-8988

Neil Ellis Wines ⓛ ⁘ ⅙

Neil Ellis was, in the 1980s, the Cape's first real negociant winemaker, seeking widely for interesting vineyards and bottling the wines under his name. He did so very successfully, and eventually the business acquired its present handsome premises just outside Stellenbosch town. Here the next Ellis generation takes ever more of a leading role: Charl heads the financial team, Margot is brand manager, and Warren rules the cellar. Warren became a member of the prestigious Cape Winemakers Guild at the end of 2017, not long after Neil had stepped back to become a non-producing member. Warren's impact on the house tradition of rather grand, substantial wines has largely been one of 'ongoing refinement of style', but the new white blend signals the incorporation of new-wave techniques and styles into his repertoire.

Terrain Specific range

★★★★☆ Jonkershoek Valley Cabernet Sauvignon ⓐ SA classic from prime Stellenbosch terroir, aged 18 months in all-new oak. **15** ⑬'s pristine cassis & black plum fruit wraps around fine tannin spine. Full bodied & dense, like **14** ⑫, equally ageworthy.

★★★★ Groenekloof Cinsaut ⓛ Appealing Mediterranean herbs & touch pepper on improved **15** ★★★★★ ⑨⓪, red fruit freshened with oak spice, bright acidity; same fruit-sweet finish noted in **14** ⑧⑦.

★★★★☆ Piekenierskloof Grenache ⓐ Dried herb & forest floor perfume, rich fruit & warm spice in harmony with well-judged oak. **15** ⑨⓪ textured & layered, vibrant & engaging now, will reward cellaring good few years. 25% new oak, 18 months.

★★★★☆ Bottelary Hills Pinotage ⓐ Worthy **16** ⑬ successor to stellar **15** ★★★★★ ⑨⑤. Elegant & modern, sweet plum & mulberry fruit, super-fine tannins & lush farewell with perfume from 16 months in barrel, 30% new. WO Stellenbosch.

★★★★ Rodanos ⓐ Rhône blend shiraz (70%), cinsaut & grenache in **14** ★★★★☆ ⑨⓪ more complex & deep than **13** ⑧⑦. Dark berry compote & lashings of warm spice, satisfying bone-dry savoury finish. 25% new oak, 16 months. WO W Cape.

★★★★☆ Whitehall Chardonnay ⓐ Elgin fruit bunch-pressed on champagne cycle (as next) for gentle extraction, fruit purity in **17** ⑬. Natural ferment in new French oak (25%) gives creamy, characterful honeysuckle, baked Granny Smith apple richness neatly offset by perky lemon conclusion.

★★★★☆ Amica ⓐ Elegant & excellent **17** ⑭ sauvignon, naturally fermented/aged in barrel. Melange blackcurrant & gooseberry fruit with smoky note, mineral tang to finish. Concentration for cellaring several years. WO Jonkershoek Valley.

★★★★☆ Op Sy Moer ⓝⓔⓦ ⓐ Afrikaans name tells you to expect cloudiness & sediment in very attractive, minimally handled **17** ⑬, certified as 'Alternative white'. Weighty, concentrated, with apple freshness & lemon peel zing, tannic nudge. 40/30/30 combo Piekenierskloof palomino, grenache & chenin, bunch-pressed/fermented in decade-old oak.

★★★★☆ Semillon Noble Late Harvest ⓐ Lovely light-footed **16** ⑨⓪ botrytis dessert from bunch-pressed, barrel-fermented Elgin fruit. Delicate floral & roasted nut flavours & aromas, fine structure & 'cool' balancing acidity. First since **11**, untasted by us. 375 ml.

Regional range

★★★★ Stellenbosch Cabernet Sauvignon ⓐ Succulent **15** ⑧⑨, blackcurrants, smoky leather & herb nuance, taut, polished grape tannins from exceptional vintage ably supported by quarter new oak.

★★★★ **Groenekloof Syrah** ⊛ Changes from 'Shiraz' to 'Syrah' to better reflect peppery & spicy character of **16** ⑧. Lovely youthful purple hue, vibrant hedgerow fruit (aided by dash cinsaut) is the hero, 5% new oak adds form but no flavour.

★★★★ **Cabernet Sauvignon-Merlot** ⊛ Cassis, lead pencil, dried tea & fine green herb perfume (courtesy 10% cab franc), followed by luscious fruit, smooth tannin backbone & mouthfilling palate in 51/39 **16** ⑧ combo. WO Stellenbosch.

★★★★☆ **Groenekloof Sauvignon Blanc** ⊘ ⊛ SA sauvignon icon & producer's calling card. **18** ⑨ same intense greenpepper fruit, lemon/lime acidity, stony minerality as ever. Well built (for cellaring, too), expressive, bright & zesty to the last drop.

....

Aenigma ⊕ ★★★☆ Always easy-to-enjoy red from enigmatic variety/ies. **16** ⑧ for al fresco dining, just enough tannin bite to balance the rich fruit flavours.

....

Discontinued: **Stellenbosch Pinotage, Elgin Chardonnay**. — WB

Location/map: Stellenbosch ▪ Map grid reference: G5 ▪ WO: Groenekloof/Stellenbosch/Jonkershoek Valley/ Piekenierskloof/Elgin/Western Cape/Bottelary ▪ Est 1986 ▪ 1stB 1984 ▪ Tasting & sales Mon-Fri 9.30-4.30 Sat/ pub hols 10–5 ▪ Fee R40 regional range/R60 terrain specific range ▪ Closed Good Fri, Dec 25/26 & Jan 1 ▪ Antipasto platters ▪ Pesto & wine pairing ▪ Tour groups ▪ Owner(s) Neil Ellis Wines (Pty) Ltd ▪ Winemaker(s) Warren Ellis (2006) & Christiaan van der Merwe (2016) ▪ Viticulturist(s) Warren Ellis (2006) ▪ 50,000cs own label 50% red 50% white ▪ Brands for clients: Woolworths ▪ PO Box 917 Stellenbosch 7599 ▪ info@neilellis. com ▪ www.neilellis.com ▪ S 33° 55' 34.92" E 018° 53' 32.46" ▪ ⊞ blows.imposes.briskly ▪ F +27 (0)21-887- 0647 ▪ **T +27 (0)21-887-0649**

Nelson Family Vineyards Ⓠ Ⓗ Ⓒ Ⓐ Ⓖ

The Nelson winery, between Paarl and Wellington, has been producing wine for almost a quarter-century, having commenced in a purpose-built cellar under the banner of Nelson's Creek Estate in 1995. It is family owned and run, patriarch Alan Nelson's Stellenbosch-trained daughter Lisha fulfilling the winemaking role. She oversees a range of wines to delight the many visitors to the picturesque home-farm, which has become a popular venue for weddings and a variety of other functions and events.

Lisha Nelson Signature Wines

★★★★☆ **Cabernet Franc** ⊘ Eschewing the 20% American oak component of **13** ★★★★ ⑧, all-French **14** ⑨ achieves similar intensity, fruit generosity without the extra sweetness. Fine leafy plum tones, tannin grip & pinpoint acid balance bode well for cellaring.

★★★★ **Dad`s Blend** ⊘ Cab franc-dominated **12** ⑧ Bordeaux blend has sweet oak (new, 20% American) overlaying bright blackberry melange, subtle savoury lift. Deserves 3+ years to show at best.

Family Vineyards range

Rosé ★★★ Bright flamingo pink **18** ⑦, equal cab franc & shiraz, dry, candyfloss & floral tones, tart twist on finish. **Sauvignon Blanc** ★★★ Stanford grapes for **18** ⑧, appealing ripe yellow peach & herbaceous flavours, bright & crisp, ready to enjoy. WO W Cape.

Nelson Estate range

★★★★ **Shiraz** Bold, full-bodied **13** ⑧, high-toned red fruit & spiced cedar tone from 80% new oak, latter still centre stage, will need time for fruit to shine & show more harmony.

★★★★ **Cabernet Sauvignon-Merlot** Scented & opulent dark-berry compote restrained by very dry chalky tannins in **14** ⑧, cellaring will bring more poise, already better than **12** ★★★ ⑧. **13** untasted.

Chardonnay ⊘ ★★★ With 80% new oak, unashamedly bold **16** ⑧ shows more toast, nut & butter characters than fruit. Has structure & acidity, just needs year/2 to harmonise. **Noble Late Harvest** ⊘ ★★★★ Faint apricot botrytis notes with ginger accents on **15** ⑧ dessert from semillon. Charming delicacy from 12.5% alcohol, exact sugar-acid balance. Caramel nuance on conclusion from 80% new oak.

Nelson's Creek range

Shiraz ★★★ Now bottled, **17** ⑧ interesting spread of dark smoked meat & sweet-spicy florals, supple but quite robust. A barbecue & country cooking partner. **Chenin Blanc** ⊘ ★★★ Pear & white peach aromas,

17 (78) easy sipping courtesy few grams sugar. **Rosé** (NEW) ★★ From cab franc, a Natural Sweet pink with floral, cranberry flavours, **18** (73) almost cloying but light 10% alcohol just lifts it. — MW

Location/map: Paarl ▪ Map grid reference: D3 ▪ WO: Paarl/Western Cape ▪ Tasting, sales & cellar tours by appt only ▪ Closed all pub hols ▪ Facilities for children ▪ Tour groups ▪ Conferences ▪ Weddings ▪ Walks/hikes ▪ MTB trails ▪ Guest accommodation ▪ Owner(s) Alan Nelson ▪ Cellarmaster(s) Lisha Nelson (Nov 2007) ▪ Winemaker(s) Lisha Nelson (Nov 2007), with Solly Hendriks (Apr 2011) ▪ Viticulturist(s) Petrus de Villiers ▪ 142ha/41ha (cabs s/f, merlot, p verdot, ptage, shiraz, chard, chenin, sauv, sem) ▪ 210t/9,340cs own label 30% red 60% white 10% rosé ▪ IPW ▪ PO Box 2009 Windmeul 7630 ▪ lisha@nelsonscreek.co.za ▪ www. nelsonscreek.co.za ▪ S 33° 39′ 31.2″ E 018° 56′ 17.3″ ▪ ⌖ named.unchanged.bridesmaid ▪ F +27 (0)21-869-8424 ▪ **T +27 (0)21-869-8453**

☐ **Nelson's Creek** *see* Nelson Family Vineyards
☐ **Nest Egg** *see* The Fledge & Co

New Beginnings Wines ⓥ

Owned by vineyard staff, and guided by Cape Town mentors and wine exporters FMS Food & Beverages, this export-focused venture continues to grow its own range – an MCC bubbly debuts this edition – as well as its private label business. Here, Japan is a major market, with listings with two supermarket groups. The Cape Town tasting venue recently moved to a new location in Sea Point on the Atlantic seaboard.

Family Collection

Merlot ★★★★ Vivacious **15** (85) from Stellenbosch, intense plum perfume, pure black fruit & balanced grip (no new oak), light-seeming despite 14.5% alcohol. Companionable sipper solo or at mealtimes.
Chardonnay ★★ Slightly earthy **17** (73), with faint fennel & apple notes. Though lightly wooded, oak still tad obvious mid-2018, perhaps just needs time to settle. Not tasted: **Cabernet Sauvignon**, **Pinotage**, **Shiraz**, **Chenin Blanc**. Discontinued: **Pinotage Rosé**, **Shiraz Rosé**.

Renaissance Collection (NEW)

Méthode Cap Classique Demi-Sec ⊘ ★★★★ Assured & well-made semi-sweet sparkling. **14** (85) strawberry appeal, good depth & weight from 52% pinot noir/meunier & an oaked component; chardonnay's lively acidity & length balance the sugar for pleasing clean effect.

Chouette! Collection

Not tasted: **Gewürztraminer**.

Skipper's Collection

Not tasted: **Classic Dry Red**, **Classic Dry White**. — CvZ

Location: Cape Town ▪ Map: Cape Peninsula ▪ Map grid reference: B1 ▪ WO: Paarl/Stellenbosch/Western Cape ▪ Est 1996 ▪ 1stB 1999 ▪ Tasting by appt only ▪ Owner(s) Klein Begin Farming Association ▪ Brand manager FMS Food & Beverages SA cc ▪ 13ha/10ha (cab, merlot, ptage, shiraz, chard, chenin) ▪ 20,000cs own label 80% red 20% white ▪ 292 Beach Rd Unit 106 Rapallo Sea Point Cape Town 8005 ▪ info@fms-wine-marketing.co.za ▪ www.fms-wine-marketing.co.za ▪ S 33° 55′ 11.1″ E 018° 22′ 57.8″ ▪ ⌖ lifestyles.salivary.heptathlon ▪ F +27 (0)21-413-0825 ▪ **T +27 (0)21-426-5037**

☐ **New Cape Wines** *see* Eagle's Cliff Wines-New Cape Wines

Newstead Lund Family Vineyards ⓥ ⑪ ⌂ ◎

Things are moving at Doug and Sue Lund's Plettenberg Bay boutique winery, notably their MCC, made by bubbly specialist Anton Smal. So quickly does their Rosé sell out, Sue notes, 'we already have a waiting list for the next release'. The farm, increasingly popular for weddings, now has a bubbly and gin bar in the vineyards, while the tasting venue was voted among the Western Cape's top 14 by a leading magazine.

★★★★ **Méthode Cap Classique Rosé** Soft pink dry bubbles from pinot noir (with 16% chardonnay). **15** ★★★★★ (92), revisited after further year on lees, has gained some biscuity complexity to original raspberry features, more savoury interest in its great length. Maintains delicacy, fine bead & delicious sophistication. **14** (86) also accomplished.

★★★★ **Méthode Cap Classique Brut** Sparkling from chardonnay shows benefit of extra year on lees. **14** ⑧⑧ greater nutty depth, creamy texture & fine, long bead. Incisively clean, dry. Room for further improvement.

Chardonnay ★★★★ Generous lemon/lime zest attractions on unoaked **17** ⑧④. Lightish body, full of flavour for aperitif sipping or with summer dishes. **Sauvignon Blanc** ★★★ Pure, unshowy blackcurrant, tropical aromas, **17** ⑧① delicate & fresh if lacking sprightliness of previous. In abeyance: **Pinot Noir**. — AL

Location/WO: Plettenberg Bay ▪ Map: Klein Karoo & Garden Route ▪ Map grid reference: C1 ▪ Est 2008 ▪ 1stB 2012 ▪ Tasting & sales Tue-Sat 10-4 ▪ Closed Dec 25 ▪ Farm-to-fork lunches, booking required ▪ Tour groups ▪ Gift shop ▪ Farm produce ▪ Walks ▪ MTB/guided cycle tours ▪ Accommodation ▪ Craft beer & gin ▪ Owner(s) Doug & Sue Lund ▪ Cellarmaster(s)/winemaker(s) Anton Smal (Jan 2011, consultant) ▪ Viticulturist(s) Doug Lund & Gift Lwazi ▪ 11ha/6.5ha (pinot, chard, sauv) ▪ 24t/4,500cs own label white & MCC ▪ PO Box 295 The Crags 6602 ▪ info@newsteadwines.com ▪ www.newsteadwines.com ▪ S 33° 57' 7.24" E 023° 28' 18.66" ▪ ⫴ tins.goals.centenary ▪ **T +27 (0)76-300-9740 (office)**

Newton Johnson Vineyards ⓠ ⓟ ⓖ

Anyone wishing to understand the spectrum of styles and intricacies of pinot noir (five here) could do far worse than visiting Newton Johnson Vineyards in Upper Hemel-en-Aarde Valley. A family business started by Dave and Felicity Johnson (née Newton) in the mid-1990s, it's now run with flair and dedication by their sons, Bevan as marketer and Gordon as winemaker with wife Nadia. A range of soils and sites, including challenging rocky slopes, allow them to produce wines with real differences, all handled with sensitivity and minimal intervention (spontaneous fermentation, older oak, no fining, filtration) in the gravity-fed cellar. The focus is on purity of expression, no pandering to the marketplace. The family's integrity and humility, and commitment to SA and its winelands, is respected locally and abroad. As such, there surely can be no producer more deserving of the first personal selection by the guide's editor; we are delighted to name Newton Johnson Vineyards as recipient of the inaugural Editor's Award.

Family Vineyards range

★★★★☆ **CWG Auction Reserve Windansea Pinot Noir** ⓐ Same vineyard as twin but bunch-selected in stoniest, most clay-rich part. **17** ⑨③ long skin contact, most oaking - 40% new, 17 months. Svelte yet power-packed berry density, savoury; more spice than mineral, some fresh earth. Long life ahead.

★★★★★ **Pinot Noir** ⊘ ⓐ From all soils of farm's sites, **17** ⑨⑤ resumes remarkable 5-star track record after blip in **16** ★★★★★ ⑨④. Perfumed by cranberries & violets; denser fruit substrata from clay-rich vineyards; then firm structure from higher-lying gravel, with Burgundian oak boost. Finesse, elegance, complexity.

★★★★☆ **Chardonnay** ⓐ From 3 granite vineyards, different aspects, giving **17** ⑨④ its layers. Wild ferment (as all), barrelled 11 months adds oatmeal biscuit shading to brightly fresh citrus/stonefruit. Lots going on, held together by resonating acidity, for edge, vitality, great length.

Not tasted: **Granum**.

Newton Johnson range

★★★★☆ **Seadragon Pinot Noir** ⓐ Farm's oldest pinot noir block & richest-fruit wine. Vivid cherries, raspberries, violets, touch of lavender, house-style earthiness, **17** ⑨③'s perfume beguiles. What follows is a perfect reflection in texture, succulent, sleekly curvaceous, ending savoury.

★★★★ **Walker Bay Pinot Noir** ⊘ Younger, lower-elevation vineyards but winemakers call **16** ⑧⑨ 'flirtatious, fruit assertive'. Varietal-true red/dark cherry & earthy notes, alongside truffles. Lithe & silky, oak well-judged.

★★★★ **Windansea Pinot Noir** ⓐ Single 2.5 ha, high vineyard, one of 2 best 'cru' bottlings (CWG other). Aptly named site. **17** ⑨④ granite/clay's more muscular structure, denser fruit: morello cherries, berry compote alongside earth, mineral notes. Palate savoury, tannins promise long future.

★★★★ **Full Stop Rock** Named for jagged vineyard landscape; syrah with grenache, dab mourvèdre, **17** ⑧⑨ a symphony of fruits & flavours. Mulberries sweetly spiced, palate succulent, luscious fruit holding sway, tannins polished.

★★★★ **Albariño** First in SA, Iberian grape imported by Newton Johnsons. Wild ferment/aged combo concrete 'eggs', older barrels, **17** ★★★★★ ⑨⑴ about fragrance & purity: apple blossom & honeysuckle, fresh apple & white peach. Essence of fruit in linear, polished way, more focused than **16** ⑧⑻.

★★★★ **Southend Chardonnay** ⑱ Mountain slope single vineyard, combo tank/barrel, everything done to reflect **17** ★★★★★ ⑨⑶'s terroir. Jasmine top note, underlying grapefruit & lime, morphing into tangerine in the flavours, all shot through with racy acidity. Better than **16** ⑧⑼.

★★★★ **Sauvignon Blanc** Combo higher/lower mountain vineyards & 10% oaked semillon give **18** ⑧⑼ its character: some citrus, essentially mineral, but most impressive is palate weight, textured & full, carrying flavours to a long finish. Cape South Coast WO.

★★★★☆ **Resonance** ⑱ Mountain/maritime cool-climate gives **17** ⑨⑷'s styling. Sauvignon with 27% new-oak-aged semillon, minerality tinged with Lemon Cream, some gooseberries in the flavours, semillon more vocal on palate, adding breadth, beeswax richness. Complex & complete.

Discontinued: **Mrs. M Pinot Noir.** — CR

Location: Hermanus ▪ Map: Walker Bay & Bot River ▪ Map grid reference: B4 ▪ WO: Upper Hemel-en-Aarde Valley/Cape South Coast ▪ Est 1996 ▪ 1stB 1997 ▪ Tasting & sales Mon-Fri 9-4 Sat 10-2 ▪ Closed all pub hols ▪ 'Restaurant @ Newton Johnson' lunch 12-3 Wed-Sun (Apr-Nov)/Tue-Mon (Dec-Mar) ▪ Owner(s) Newton Johnson family ▪ Winemaker(s) Gordon Newton Johnson (Jan 2001) & Nadia Newton Johnson (Aug 2006) ▪ Viticulturist(s) Dean Leppan (Sep 2010) ▪ 140ha/18ha (grenache, mourv, pinot, shiraz, albariño, chard, sauv) ▪ 240t/20,000cs own label 50% red 50% white ▪ PO Box 225 Hermanus 7200 ▪ wine@newtonjohnson.com ▪ www.newtonjohnson.com ▪ S 34° 22' 9.7" E 019° 15' 33.3" ▪ ⓐⓕ royalties.conception.tripods ▪ F +27 (0)86-638-9673 ▪ **T +27 (0)28-312-3862**

Nicholson Smith

Easy-drinking and good-value wines is the brief Jason Neal, CEO of Johannesburg drinks company Nicholson Smith, delivers on. He's added four new wines (one not tasted by us) to this, his non-vintage portfolio. His vintage-dated bottlings are listed separately under Aden's Star.

Pandora's Box range
Bell Pepper Cabernet Sauvignon ★★ Sweet, juicy & confected **NV** ⑦⑸ red, a bit like vinous cooldrink. **The Black Bird Merlot** ★★ Smoky edge to **NV** ⑦⑹, ripe blue- & black-fruited mouthful. **The Professor's Pinotage** ⓃⒺⓌ ★★ Boiled sweet & strawberry notes on **NV** ⑦⑸ red. **The Persian Connection Shiraz** ⊘ ★★☆ Overtly commercial, the simplicity of light-bodied **NV** ⑦⑺ will have its fans. **Lock 1855 Merlot-Cabernet Sauvignon** ⊘ ★★☆ Floral nuance to juicy plum ease on **NV** ⑦⑼ Bordeaux blend. **The Gooseberry Sauvignon Blanc** ★★ Light, succulent & unchallenging **NV** ⑦⑸, vaguely citrus toned. **La Dolce Vita Semi-Sweet White** ⓃⒺⓌ ★★ Slight pear & melon on **NV** ⑦⑸, with modest 11.5% alcohol. **The Honeysuckle Sweet Red** ⓃⒺⓌ ★★ Sweet berry notes on easy, low-alcohol **NV** ⑦⑷. Not tasted: **The Italian Job.**

Bella Vino range
Sultry Red ★★ Uncomplicated **NV** ⑦⑶ offers easy everyday drinking in a light body, mostly from merlot. **Sublime White** ★★ Light-bodied, juicy & uncomplicated **NV** ⑦⑹ from sauvignon. **Sassy Sweet Red** ★★ Natural Sweet **NV** ⑦⑷ ticks the boxes in approachability, berry brightness & modest 10.5% alcohol. **Perky Pink** ★★ Faintest blush on **NV** ⑦⑷ Natural Sweet with floral nuances & light 10% alcohol. **Seductively Sweet White** ★★ In-your-face grapiness on light **NV** ⑦⑷ Natural Sweet. Like previous, low in alcohol. — FM

Location: Johannesburg ▪ WO: Western Cape ▪ Est 1997 ▪ 1stB 2012 ▪ Closed to public ▪ Owner(s) Jason Neal ▪ Winemaker(s)/viticulturist(s) James McKenzie (2012) ▪ 150,000cs own label 70% red 20% white 10% other ▪ PO Box 1659 Jukskei Park 2153 ▪ jason@nicholsonsmith.co.za ▪ www.nicholsonsmith.co.za ▪ F +27 (0)11-496-2952 ▪ **T +27 (0)11-496-2947**

Nick & Forti's Wines   Ⓠ

'Nick' is Nick van Huyssteen, owner of Saronsberg in Tulbagh (where the wines are made), 'Forti' is restaurateur Fortunato Mazzone - and this is their joint venture. The range is available at the winery and at Forti's restaurants and stores as well as selected outlets and eateries.

Shiraz ⓥ ★★★★ Delicious **16** ⑧⑤ is savoury, medium bodied & well balanced, with freshness & modest tannic grip. Utterly moreish. Ready, but will keep a few years. 30% new oak. WO Coastal. **Epicentre** ⓥ ★★★★ Bordeaux red from all 5 varieties; unpretentious **15** ⑧⑤ is bang for your buck. Cassis fruit on a good tannic structure, the burly 14.7% alcohol not too obvious.

....

Artspace White ★★★★ Unwooded chenin **18** ⑧⑤ offers peach & tropical fruit in a zesty, versatile food partner. — DS

Location: Tulbagh/Pretoria ▪ WO: Tulbagh/Coastal ▪ Est/1stB 2004 ▪ Tasting at Saronsberg Cellar ▪ Owner(s) Fortunato Mazzone & Saronsberg ▪ Winemaker(s) Dewaldt Heyns (2004) ▪ 4,000cs own label 85% red 15% white ▪ Box 25032 Monument Park Pretoria 0105 ▪ ritrovo@mweb.co.za ▪ www.saronsberg.com ▪ F +27 (0)12-460-5173 ▪ **T +27 (0)12-460-4367**

Nicky Versfeld Wines

CWG member Nicky Versfeld has worn just one hat during his career, namely that of winemaker, and been involved with wineries of varying sizes and types, latterly also as a consultant. This personal boutique project focuses on sauvignon blanc and semillon, the varieties that drew him to harvests in Sancerre and Bordeaux.

★★★★☆ **Sauvignon Blanc** ⊘ ⊛ After **15** ⑨③'s quintessential Darling bouquet - capsicum, dust & white pepper - next-up **17** ⑨④ perhaps less typical but no less arresting: white asparagus & tinned pea, cool, composed, with Nicky Versfeld's signature reined-in acidity & compact, finely honed body.

★★★★★ **CWG Auction Reserve Mia Semillon** Name change from 'Double Barrel' but same (14 year old Darling) vines, bunch ferment with wild yeast, 8 months older 500L barrels, then 9 in bottle. Different, riper profile though so taut **16** ⑨① , **17** ★★★★ ⑧⑧ nutty & broad tangerine nuances.— CvZ

Location: Somerset West ▪ WO: Darling ▪ Est 2016 ▪ 1stB 2015 ▪ Closed to public ▪ Winemaker(s) Nicky Versfeld ▪ 1,000cs own label 100% white ▪ Building No. 8, Fairways Office Park, 5 Niblick Way, Somerset West 7130 ▪ ncversfeld@gmail.com ▪ F +27 (0)21-851-3578 ▪ **T +27 (0)21-850-0160/1, +27 (0)83-675-8436**

Nico van der Merwe Wines ⓠ

Star winemaker and industry doyen Nico van der Merwe's dream of owning his own boutique winery was realised incrementally on land in Stellenbosch's Polkadraai Hills not far from Saxenburg, whose wine he crafted for almost 30 years. The tiny Mas Nicolas cellar he, wife Petra and family are now based at and focused on is full of red-wine vintages still maturing in barrel, and the newest white-wine vintages were unbottled as we prepared this edition. Thus nothing to taste this time, but as with all Nico's classically styled and exceptionally fine wines, they are sure to be worth the wait.

Flagship range

★★★★★ **Mas Nicolas Cape** ⓠ Gentle giant **15** ⑨③ , usual cabernet & shiraz pairing (50/50) shows beguiling dark tarry layers on fine, integrated palate. Plum, coriander, meat & mocha part of the intricate flavour profile. Last **13** ★★★★★ ⑨⑥ also had great depth, complexity. Half new wood 16 months.

Nicolas van der Merwe range

★★★★★ **Syrah** ⓠ Style change from big & muscular to polished, buffed **13** ⑨② & current **15** ★★★★★ ⑨⑤ , which is sumptuous, packed with berry & spice yet refined, beautifully balanced, persistent; lovely to drink. Also in magnum, like Mas Nicolas. No **14**.

★★★★ **Red** ⓠ Merlot back in the lead (64%, with cab & cab franc) in **15** ⑧⑨ , chunky fruit tied up in rather stern tannins mid-2017, needing time to soften. **13** ⑧⑧ was cab-based. No **14**.

★★★★☆ **White** ⓠ Unwooded Stellenbosch sauvignon (68%) & new-oak-fermented Somerset West semillon intertwine in saline **17** ⑨① , with an intense, tingling oystershell minerality. Yard ahead of mostly Robertson-sourced **15** ★★★★ ⑧⑧. No **16**.

★★★★ **Méthode Cap Classique Brut** ⓠ Latest **NV** ⑧⑥ sparkler from chardonnay, 2 years on lees (previous 5 years). Well measured & elegant, refreshing rather than rich & weighty. WO W Cape.

Five to Nine Sauvignon Blanc ⓠ ★★★ Harvested between 5 & 9 am. Racy style of **17** ⑧② tank sample shows a steeliness cushioned by few grams sugar & touch semillon. No **16**.

Robert Alexander range

★★★★ **Shiraz** ⓩ Spicy **15** ⑧⑧ offers complexity in ripe black fruit, dried herbs, cured meat, along with a tarry richness & depth; firm but accessible. 15 months mature oak. Super value too. No **14**.

Not tasted: **Merlot**.

Cape Elements range

Cape Elements ⓩ ★★★☆ Mostly shiraz, with cinsaut & grenache, ex-tank **15** ⑧⑤ rustic but juicy, with dusty oak, good anytime drinking. WO W Cape. — DS

Location/map: Stellenbosch ▪ Map grid reference: B6 ▪ WO: Stellenbosch/Western Cape ▪ Est/1stB 1999 ▪ Tasting & sales Wed 12–5 Fri 10–5 Sat 10–2, otherwise by appt ▪ Owner(s) Nico & Petra van der Merwe ▪ Cellarmaster(s)/winemaker(s) Nico van der Merwe ▪ 50t/4,000cs own label 80% red 20% white ▪ PO Box 12200 Stellenbosch 7613 ▪ nvdmwines@vodamail.co.za ▪ www.nvdmwines.co.za ▪ S 33° 57' 48.2" E 018° 43' 51.8" ▪ ▨ fishmonger.monthly.trudges ▪ F +27 (0)21-881-3063 ▪ **T +27 (0)21-881-3063**

Nico Vermeulen Wines

As a wine consultant and bulk trader for the past three decades, Nico Vermeulen is well placed to source vinous gems for his own small but growing family brand. The wines, made in rented space, offer good value for money and sport refreshingly clear, simple labels, depicting the grape berry/ies used.

★★★★ **The Right Red** ⓩ From shiraz, **14** ★★★☆ ⑧④ spicy, piquant red fruit, brisk acidity & tannins that are supple but need a meal or time to settle. Misses elegance of **13** ⑧⑥.

★★★★ **The Right White** ⓥ Two vintages, different expressions of sauvignon character & terroir. **18** ⑧⑥ mostly ex Langeberg-Garcia, cool purity of green fruit, smooth, almost delicate. **17** ⑧⑦ Darling & Lambert's Bay, signature dusty minerality & freshness, some depth & gravelly substance.

★★★★ **The Right Two Whites** ⓥ Complementary blend sauvignon (75%) & semillon in **17** ⑧⑦. Delicately scented cool green fruit, elegant & fine with partial oaking (50% new) seamlessly integrated. Well-crafted step above **15** ★★★☆ ⑧④. No **16**.

The Right Two Reds ⓥ ★★★★ Dark-fruited equal cab & merlot blend. **14** ⑧⑤ quite juicy, with sprinkling of cocoa & fresh, balanced acidity, sound but supple tannins. Well constructed, but touch off sophisticated **13** ★★★★ ⑧⑦. **Life From Old Wood** ⓃⒺⓌ ★★★★ Chenin from old Paardeberg & Malmesbury bushvines. Straw-gold **17** ⑧⑤ subtle preserved quince & baked apple underscored by toasty hazelnut & clove from part oaking (2nd-fill barrels). Understated flavours but zestily fresh, good food pairer. **Wit Muskadel** ⓃⒺⓌ ★★★★ Jerepiko-style white muscat de Frontignan, aged in older oak. Brassy-gold **16** ⑧④ grapey, barley sugar flavours, clean & light-tripping, 16.5% spirit well-integrated. Good with crushed ice as an aperitif or with curries. WO Robertson. — MW

Location: Paarl ▪ WO: Western Cape/Coastal/Robertson ▪ Est/1stB 2003 ▪ Tasting by appt at Ruitersvlei Wines ▪ Owner(s)/viticulturist(s) Nico Vermeulen ▪ Winemaker(s) Nico Vermeulen, with Judy & Izelle Vermeulen ▪ 3,000cs own label & 240,000L bulk export ▪ 3 Pieter Hugo Str Courtrai Suider-Paarl 7646 ▪ nicovermeulen@webmail.co.za ▪ F +27 (0)21-863-2048 ▪ **T +27 (0)21-863-2048/+27 (0)82-553-2024**

Niel Joubert Estate

Four generations of Jouberts have built up a solid reputation for consistent quality - of wines as well as grapes - at their estate on the Simonsberg slopes outside Paarl. Ernst Leicht, winemaker for almost 20 years, uses one third of the crop for the family label, selling the remainder to some of the Cape's top producers. Some newer vines coming online (and into bottle, 'filled with pride for your enjoyment', per their slogan) include grüner veltliner, prompting the team to say there will be 'so much more to explore' going forward.

Proprietor range

★★★★ **Malbec** ⓩ Welcome entry to this small but growing category. **14** ⑧⑦ interesting dried apricot & meat aromas; cranberries, red cherries & dried herbs on firm tannic base. Could develop well.

Christine-Marié range

★★★★ **Cabernet Sauvignon** ⓩ Full expression of warm-climate fruit & 100% new oak, **14** ⑧⑥ unashamedly New World in style, with matching alcohol (15.7%). No **10**, **12 13**.

★★★★ **Shiraz** ⓩ More freshness, balance than other red, all-new oak in harmony with persistent spice & perfumed fruit. **12** ⑧⑧ inviting now & over next few years.

★★★★ **Méthode Cap Classique** ⓥ 14 ★★★ ⑧ chardonnay bubbly follows **09** ⑧ though lacks its freshness, creamy texture, despite 36 months on lees. Quite ripe, with apple cider nuance. **12, 13** untasted.

Chardonnay ★★★★ Extra toasted dimension to clean pear & lime flavours, **17** ⑧ lower alcohol, richer & more oak (100%, 10% new) than Estate sibling. Tad less poised than partly wooded **15** ★★★★ ⑧. **16** untasted. **First Kiss Fortified Chenin Blanc** ⓥ ★★★★ Creamy honey & ginger flavours on oak-matured (9 months) **12** ⑧, warming, delightful nightcap & alternative to 'port'. Occasional release: **Merlot**.

Niel Joubert Estate range

Cabernet Sauvignon ★★★ Herbaceous note to dark berry fruit, dry lithe tannins, nice freshness in **16** ⑧. Most oak in this range though still well-judged (22%, 8% new), allowing more fruit to the fore. Paarl WO. **Merlot** ★★★ Pungent wild herb nuances, judiciously part-oaked **16** ⑦ leaner, tangier fruit profile than last, quite tightly bound in dry tannin framework. **Pinotage** ★★★ Unoaked **16** ⑧ leaner than last though ample earthy-spicy berry flavours, good freshness, finishes with dry, piquant twist which works well with tomato-based dishes & BBQ meat. **Shiraz** ⊘ ★★★★ Vibrantly fresh red fruit & black pepper on **15** ⑧. Mostly older oak well-integrated with spicy, lithe framework. Juicy, appealing, with life for a few years. **Blanc de Noir** ★★ From pinotage, **18** ⑦ delicate blush of orange, equally light cranberry flavour, dry, short fresh farewell. **Chardonnay** ★★★ Ripe, fresh citrus & pear on **17** ⑧, smooth & balanced. Only 12% old-oaked, giving pleasingly subtle, honeyed nuance. **Chenin Blanc** ★★★ Amiable, easy-drinking **18** ⑦, gentle ripe apple & poached fruit, soft acidity. **Sauvignon Blanc** ★★★ Some stonefruit & dry grass, gentle acid, less crunchy than last, **18** ⑦ rounded & ripe for laid-back quaffing. **Herr Leicht** ★★★ Unoaked **17** ⑦ blend changes to nouvelle, sauvignon, chenin. Crunchy green apples & herbs, trips lightly. — MW

Location/map: Paarl ▪ **Map** grid reference: C8 ▪ WO: Western Cape/Paarl ▪ Est 1898 ▪ 1stB 1996 ▪ Tasting & sales Mon-Fri 9-4 by appt ▪ Closed all pub hols ▪ Owner(s) Joubert family ▪ Cellarmaster(s) Ernst Leicht (Oct 2000) ▪ Winemaker(s) Ernst Leicht, with Niel Joubert jnr (May 2011) ▪ Viticulturist(s) Daan Joubert ▪ 1,000ha/300ha (cab, cinsaut, grenache n/b, malbec, merlot, ptage, shiraz, tempranillo, touriga nacional, chard, chenin, grüner veltliner, sauv) ▪ 1,953t/±160,000cs own label 49% red 50% white 1% rosé ▪ Other export brand: Hunterspeak ▪ GlobalGAP, IPW ▪ PO Box 17 Klapmuts 7625 ▪ wine@nieljoubert.co.za ▪ www. nieljoubert.co.za ▪ S 33° 49′ 54.7″ E 018° 54′ 3.2″ ▪ 🖵 alchemy.dazzled.seated ▪ F +27 (0)86-599-0725 ▪ **T +27 (0)21-875-5936**

☐ **Niels Verburg** *see* Luddite Wines

Niemandsrivier

This small property in Elgin, with 3 hectares of shiraz established by previous owner Lawrence Hyslop on uncultivated land, has been sold to retired businessman Johan Vosloo. Luddite's Niels Verburg vinified the 2016 and 2017 vintages, aiming at wine that reflects the cool climate and geology of the area.

Petra Shiraz ★★★★ Well-constructed tannic frame, zesty acidity temper & add freshness to brooding, peppery black & red fruit of **16** ⑧. Intended as a longer-term wine; give it time. Not tasted: **Rosé**. — CvZ

Location/WO: Elgin ▪ Est 2006 ▪ 1stB 2009 ▪ Closed to public ▪ Owner(s) Johan Vosloo ▪ Cellarmaster(s)/winemaker(s) Niels Verburg (Jan 2015, consultant) ▪ Viticulturist(s) Rob Semple (Jun 2006, consultant) ▪ 17.4ha/3.2ha (shiraz) ▪ 35t/200cs own label 100% red ▪ WIETA (farm) ▪ Niemandsrivier Farm PO Box 157 Elgin 7180 ▪ niemandsrivier@mweb.co.za ▪ **T +27 (0)83-440-5581**

Nietgegund

Jan Dreyer, owner of this small vineyard in Stellenbosch's Blaauwklippen Valley, is eagerly awaiting the first crop from a young cabernet franc block, to join already-established cabernet and merlot for a future Bordeaux red. His current wine, 'For a Friend', made with consultants, is a blend of merlot and shiraz.

★★★★ **Pro Amico** ⓥ Harmonious **11** ⑧ shows cured meat flavours lifted by fresh dark berries. Merlot & shiraz (90/10), latter upped to 20% on **13** ★★★★ ⑧. These & **10** ⑧ still selling. No **12** made.— WB

Location/WO: Stellenbosch ▪ Est 2004 ▪ 1stB 2008 ▪ Closed to public ▪ Owner(s) Nietgegund Boerdery (Edms) Bpk ▪ Winemaker(s) Ronell Wiid (Jan 2013, consultant) ▪ Viticulturist(s) Francois Hanekom (Sep 2006, consultant) ▪ 3.4ha/1ha (cabs s/f, merlot) ▪ 4t/100cs own label 100% red ▪ IPW ▪ PO Box 12684 Die Boord 7613 ▪ jan@nietgegund.com ▪ www.proamico.co.za ▪ **T +27 (0)21-880-0738**

Nietvoorbij Wine Cellar

Nietvoorbij's Craig Paulsen is a winemaker unlike any other. During harvest he vinifies 1,000 (!) tiny experimental batches for clients of the cellar's owner, the Agricultural Research Council. Knowledge gained is used to develop a range of good-quality, often good-value wines for Nietvoorbij's commercial label.

Location/map: Stellenbosch ▪ Map grid reference: F4 ▪ Est 1963 ▪ 1stB 1992 ▪ Tasting & sales Mon-Fri 9–4, please call ahead to book ▪ Closed Sat/Sun & all pub hols ▪ Owner(s) Agricultural Research Council ▪ Winemaker(s) Craig Paulsen ▪ Viticulturist(s) Guillaume Kotze ▪ 32ha (cabs s/f, malbec, merlot, ptage, shiraz, chard, sauv, viog) ▪ 75t/6,000cs own label 56% red 40% white 4% port ▪ Private Bag X5026 Stellenbosch 7599 ▪ cellar@arc.agric.za ▪ www.arc.agric.za ▪ S 33° 54′ 43.5″ E 018° 51′ 48.9″ ▪ ⓦ succeed.cheese.grant ▪ **T +27 (0)21-809-3091/3100**

Nieuwedrift Vineyards

The addition of a weekend restaurant to this large, 7th-generation Piketberg wheat and vine farm has boosted wine sales, obliging Johan Mostert to expand his boutique production and further diversify the portfolio, hence the wooded chardonnay in the offing. Meantime visitors happily tuck into the delicious pizzas and cheese/meat platters — and order wine...

★★★★ **Méthode Cap Classique** ⊘ Delicious **17** ⑧⑥ chardonnay sparkling more accomplished than **15** ★★★★ ⑧④. Ripe but perfectly dry, Granny Smith apple zing paired with creaminess from light oak & 11 months on lees. No **16**.

Shiraz ★★★ Seriously conceived (2 years oak) but actually fruity & fun to drink, **16** ⑧① light earthy note, spice & red berries, touch of alcohol heat no biggie. **Blanc de Noir** ★★★ Pale onion skin hue on bone-dry **18** ⑦⑧ from shiraz, fruity, easy & honest. **Chenin Blanc** ⊘ ★★★★ Improving on previous, unassuming **18** ⑧③ is textured, very fresh & dry, abundant guava, melon & gooseberry on offer. — HC

Location: Piketberg ▪ Map/WO: Swartland ▪ Map grid reference: C2 ▪ Est/1stB 2002 ▪ Tasting, sales & cellar tours Mon-Fri 9–1 & 2–6 Sat 9–2 ▪ Closed Easter Fri/Sun, Dec 25/26 & Jan 1 ▪ Nieuwedrift Wine Estate Restaurant: dinner Fri 6-9; lunch Sat & 1st Sun of the month 11-6; meals by prior arrangement Mon-Thu ▪ Facilities for children ▪ Tour groups ▪ Conferences ▪ Owner(s)/viticulturist(s) Johan Mostert ▪ Cellarmaster(s) Johan Mostert (Jan 2002) ▪ 15 1ha/15ha (shiraz, chard, chenin) ▪ 200t total 10t/1,316cs own label 28% red 40% white 16% rosé 16% MCC ▪ PO Box 492 Piketberg 7320 ▪ nieuwedrift@patat.co.za ▪ S 32° 58′ 28.1″ E 018° 45′ 10.6″ ▪ ⓦ chatty.porcupines.surnames ▪ **T +27 (0)22-913-1966/+27 (0)82-824-8104**

☐ **Nieuwe Haarlem** *see* Erasmus Family Wines
☐ **Nine Fields** *see* Ashton Winery
☐ **1900** *see* Spioenkop Wines

Nitida Cellars

Durbanville is blessed with gentle granitic slopes cooled by maritime breezes, ideal for sauvignon and semillon. Engineer Bernhard Veller and wife Peta have maximised this vinous potential since buying a sheep farm more than 20 years ago and transforming it into an acclaimed winery with many visitor offerings, including mountain bike trails, conservation areas, restaurant and function/conference venue. Conservation and sustainability are key, and Bernhard notes that solar energy provides 50% of power during harvest. Waterwise, they are self-sufficient.

★★★★☆ **Cabernet Sauvignon** ⊘ Seamless **16** ⑨② lives up to form of previous in its refined, Xmas cake, inky elegance. Poised, with subtle oak squeeze (third new) & balanced succulence. Layered, complex & rich. A cool-climate delight.

★★★★ **Merlot** ⑯ Effortless-seeming **16** ⑧⑥, plush, soft yet poised, with lovely spice, fruitcake & fine, integrated oak, just 20% new. Structured, rich & persistent.

★★★★☆ **Pinot Noir** ⊘ Supple & subtle **16** ⑨①'s fruit, spice & restrained oak (all old) harmoniously meshed. Follows form of previous. Demure, layered & focused, lightness belying its power.

★★★★ **Shiraz** Marries dark fruit, earth & cedar spice effortlessly. **16** ⑧⑦ fresh, juicy & elegant, with leashed power & concentration. Older oak used to best effect. Long, rewarding finish.

★★★★☆ **Calligraphy** ⓥ Powerfully seductive, succulent yet taut **15** ⑨② merlot-led blend with cabs sauvignon & franc plus petit verdot, offers ripe berry fruit nuanced by deep earthy cocoa notes. Integrated oak & superb length of flavour.

★★★★ **Chardonnay** ⓥ Generous creamy citrus mouthful of **16** ⑧⑧ improves on last-tasted **14** ★★★★ ⑧⑤. Fresh & tangy but shows restraint & focus on supportive oaking (40% new).

★★★★ **Riesling** Poached stonefruit with flashes of lime & spicy cinnamon, **17** ⑧⑦ lovely interplay of tangy acidity & ripeness (12.9 g/l sugar). Succulent & vivid but with good focus.

★★★★☆ **Wild Child** Oaked portion smooths edges & adds persistence to **17** ★★★★ ⑧⑧ sauvignon blanc. Broad & creamy, with lemon typicity & bright granadilla notes indicative of cool origin. Ripe yet succulent. **16** ⑨② seamless & serious.

★★★★☆ **Golden Orb** Unoaked single block of sauvignon picked in three tranches & lengthily lees aged 10 months for best terroir expression. **17** ⑨② light flinty grapefruit zip with effortless, broad-textured palate. Elegant & long.

★★★★ **Sauvignon Blanc** ⓥ Pineapple verve tussles with fynbos & flint on **17** ⑧⑦; zippy & juicy, with rounded body & good length.

★★★★ **Semillon** Combo tank- & oak-fermented portions (latter 80% new French, with lees stirring) make for complex, intriguing **17** ⑧⑦. Vivid citrus vies with dustiness & creamy breadth. Nuanced & subtle.

★★★★ **The Tinkery** Experimental label. **17** ★★★★ ⑧⑤ barrel-fermented viognier. Signature nectarine & peach, simultaneously tangy & spicy with creamy palate. **16** ⑧⑦ lower-alcohol, higher-sugar riesling.

The Dracks Méthode Cap Classique ★★★★ Was 'Matriarch'. **16** ⑧⑤ pinot noir/chardonnay sparkling offers ripe apple strudel livened by succulence & crisp, dry tail. Not tasted: **Coronata Integration**. Occasional release: **Modjadji Semillon Noble Late Harvest**. — FM

Location/WO: Durbanville ▪ Map: Durbanville, Philadelphia & Darling ▪ Map grid reference: C7 ▪ Est/1stB 1995 ▪ Tasting & sales Mon-Fri 9—5 Sat 11—4 Sun 11-3 ▪ Fee R20/4 wines R50/range ▪ Closed Good Fri, Dec 25/26 & Jan 1 ▪ Cassia Restaurant T +27 (0)21-976-0640; conference & function venue at Cassia (200 pax) ▪ Tables at Nitida T +27 (0)21-975-9357, www.tablesatnitida.co.za ▪ Facilities for children ▪ MTB, part of Hillcrest/Majik forest trail (www.tygerbergmtb.co.za) ▪ Conservation area ▪ Annual festivals: Season of Sauvignon (Oct); Feast of the Grape (Mar); Cellarbake (Mar); Soup, Sip & Bread (Jun) ▪ Owner(s) Bernhard & Peta Veller ▪ Cellarmaster(s) Bernhard Veller ▪ Winemaker(s)/viticulturist(s) Daniel Keulder (Jan 2015) ▪ 35ha/16ha (cabs s/f, p verdot, riesling, sauv, sem) ▪ 220t/18,000cs own label 30% red 70% white + 3,000cs for clients ▪ Brands for clients: Woolworths, Checkers ▪ PO Box 1423 Durbanville 7551 ▪ info@nitida.co.za ▪ www.nitida.co.za ▪ S 33° 50'3.8" E 018° 35'37.0" ▪ 🖳 predictable.march.telephoto ▪ F +27 (0)21-976-5631 ▪ **T +27 (0)21-976-1467**

Noble Hill Wine Estate ⓥ 🍴 📷 🛏 ♿

Family-owned Noble Hill stretches up the Paarl side of the Simonsberg, with a cellar, family-welcoming visitor venue and range of terroir-specific wines crafted with minimal intervention by co-owner and winemaker Kristopher Tillery. The mostly red-wine portfolio will soon be joined by a Reserve White featuring the first crops of estate chenin and grenache blanc. Preparations are underway to expand the viognier and cabernet (sauvignon and franc) plantings, having recently completed the establishment of a new olive grove.

Noble Hill range

★★★★ **Cabernet Sauvignon** Riper & warmer, with smoky cassis & tannins quite supple for cab, already approachable. **14** ⑧⑥ touch less structure, ageability, than **13** ⑧⑨. Natural ferment in tank, then French oak, 15% new, 18 months, then bottle 24 months, as all the reds.

★★★★ **Merlot** Some wild red-berry pungency in concentrated **15** ★★★★ ⑧④, quite edgy & unknit in youth, tannins on the austere side, time should resolve though less ripe fruit & balance than **14** ⑧⑥.

★★★★ **Syrah** Splashes mourvèdre & viognier in ripe & succulent **16** ⑧⑥, smoky bacon flavours, smooth tannins & warm-hearted 14% alcohol. Drink before more structured, elegant **15** ⑧⑨.

★★★★ **Estate Reserve** Continues as cab-led Bordeaux quartet in **15** ⑧⑥. Quite compact & closed in youth, some cassis fruit but merlot's piquancy shows, dry chalky tannin conceals charm, needs time. Also 200 magnums.

★★★★ **Blanc de Blancs** New to the guide, versatile brut nature bubbly from chardonnay. **15** ⑧⑧ plush & rich, ripe apple & stonefruit, sweet brioche too, freshening thread of acidity. Subtle creaminess from 2 years on lees.

Viognier ★★★★ Alluring peach & floral tones, **17** ⑧⑤ natural ferment & oak (10% new) give creamy, toasty underpinning, fresh acidity provides balance. Well crafted, ticks all varietal boxes. Not tasted: **Mourvèdre Rosé, Sauvignon Blanc**. — MW

Location: Paarl ▪ Map: Franschhoek ▪ Map grid reference: B7 ▪ WO: Simonsberg-Paarl ▪ Est/1stB 2001 ▪ Tasting & sales daily 10–5 ▪ Fee R40, waived on purchase ▪ Cellar tours by appt only ▪ Food & wine pairing option ▪ cosecha Restaurant ▪ Picnic baskets ▪ Facilities for children ▪ Farm-produced extra virgin olive oil ▪ Conservation area ▪ Hitachino Nest Japanese craft beer available at winery ▪ Owner(s) Noble Hill Trust ▪ Winemaker(s) Kristopher Tillery ▪ Viticulturist(s) Kristopher Tillery, Rodney Zimba & Johan Viljoen (consultant) ▪ 62ha/40ha (cabs s/f, merlot, mourv, p verdot, shiraz, chard, chenin, grenache blanc, marsanne, sauv, viog) ▪ PO Box 111 Simondium 7670 ▪ info@noblehill.com ▪ www.noblehill.com ▪ S 33° 49'38.0" E 018° 56' 12.1" ▪ 🌐 circulates.reaping.picket ▪ **T +27 (0)21-874-3844**

☐ **Noble Nomad** see Rosendal Wines

Noble Savage

'The untamable, adventurous, authentic, never take yourself too seriously Noble Savage' – is what the website states. And that's the brand ethos in a nutshell. Not-unserious wine for good times with friends, family or just because. Made at Bartinney Private Cellar, the wines can be found at the Bartinney Wine & Champagne Bar in central Stellenbosch.

★★★★ **Cabernet Sauvignon-Merlot** ⊘ Subtle violet scents tempt on fruitcake-rich **14** ⑧⑥, 80/20 blend of Banhoek grapes which improves on **13** ★★★ ⑧①. Rounded, concentrated & broad, light grip of fine tannin from 18 months older oak.

★★★★ **Chenin Blanc** ⊘ Vivacious **17** ⑧⑥ is zippy & fresh with pineapple & peach character typical of the grape. Medium bodied & rounded with oodles of refreshment on offer. WO W Cape, like next.

★★★★ **Sauvignon Blanc** ⊘ Preserved lemon, white pepper & flint nuances. **18** ★★★★ ⑧⑤ structured & broad from long lees contact, lengthy tapered tail. Tasted ex tank, as **17** ⑧⑨.

Cabernet Sauvignon Rosé ⊘ ★★★ Cranberry & pomegranate appeal on tangy & juicy **17** ⑧② dry pink. Ideal for summertime enjoyment. — FM

Location/map: Stellenbosch ▪ Map grid reference: F5 ▪ WO: Western Cape/Stellenbosch/Banghoek ▪ Est 2006 ▪ 1stB 2008 ▪ Sales Mon–Sat 11.30-9 at Bartinney Wine & Champagne Bar T +27 (0)76-348-5374, 5 Bird Str Stellenbosch ▪ Gin ▪ Owner(s) Rose & Michael Jordaan ▪ Winemaker(s) Ronell Wiid (2012, consultant) ▪ 13,000cs own label 50% red 50% white ▪ Postnet Suite 231 Private Bag X5061 Stellenbosch 7599 ▪ info@ bartinney.co.za ▪ www.noblesavage.co.za, www.bartinney.co.za ▪ S 33° 56'18.36"E 018° 51'36.81" ▪ 🌐 scuba.pictures.sunshine ▪ F +27 (0)21-885-2852 ▪ **T +27 (0)21-885-1013**

☐ **No House Wine** see Stellar Winery

Nomada Wines

No longer nomadic, Riaan Oosthuizen and wife Gina's own-label project has a home in Durbanville and rented cellar space on the Helderberg. Between contract winemaking and consulting, Riaan sources and vinifies grapes while Gina handles the marketing. New packaging has been introduced, of which Gina is particularly proud, and there are plans to expand the line-up.

Location: Durbanville/Stellenbosch ▪ Map: Helderberg ▪ Map grid reference: D2 ▪ Est/1stB 2007 ▪ Tasting by appt only ▪ Owner(s) Riaan & Gina Oosthuizen ▪ Winemaker(s)/viticulturist(s) Riaan Oosthuizen (2007) ▪ 66ha/7ha (cabs s/f, merlot, chenin, sauv) ▪ 55t total 10t/2,000cs own label 40% red 60% white + 6,000cs for clients ▪ Brands for clients: Cadequin, Skaap (Netherlands), Signal Gun ▪ PO Box 5145 Tygervalley 7536 ▪ nomadawines@gmail.com ▪ S 34° 1'18.4" E 018° 50'54.6" ▪ 🌐 scruff.unbridled.eclipse ▪ **T +27 (0)83-280-7690**

Nordic Wines

No prizes for guessing that negociants Peter Tillman and Wiggo Andersen have Scandinavia's imbibers in their sights, with wine selected and sourced locally for export under a variety of labels.

Location: Robertson ▪ Est 2007 ▪ 1stB 2010 ▪ Closed to public ▪ Wine orders Mon-Fri 9-5 from export offices: Nordic Wines, Robertson ▪ Owner(s) Wiggo Andersen & Peter Tillman ▪ Winemaker(s)/viticulturist(s) consultants ▪ Other export brands: Cape to Cape, Frogner, Literature Wine, Mia, Selma, Wedgewood ▪ PO Box 896 Robertson 6705 ▪ info@nordicwines.co.za, peter@nordicwines.co.za, alison@nordicwines.co.za ▪ www.nordicwines.co.za ▪ F +27 (0)23-626-1031 ▪ T +27 (0)23-626-1413/+27 (0)83-283-5354

Normandie Est. 1693

Mature vines on 17th-century Franschhoek farm Normandie contribute to an internationally acclaimed portfolio of high-end wines crafted by Johan Viljoen for SA-born international designer Mark Eisen and wife Karen. The wines are: Eisen & Viljoen and Anno 1693 (Bordeaux-style reds), karen. (merlot rosé) and Clarington (Merlot, Cabernet Sauvignon-Merlot, Rosé, Chardonnay, Chenin Blanc and Sauvignon Blanc). As might be expected, each is sumptuously yet elegantly packaged, the high-gloss, ink-coated Clarington bottle design being several years in development and patented internationally.

Location: Franschhoek ▪ Est 2008 ▪ 1stB 2009 ▪ Closed to public ▪ Owner(s) Mark & Karen Eisen ▪ Cellarmaster(s)/winemaker(s) Johan Viljoen (Feb 2008) ▪ Viticulturist(s) Johan Viljoen & Bennie Booysen (both Feb 2008) ▪ 47ha/17ha (cab, merlot, p verdot) ▪ ±130t/12,000cs own label 50% red 30% white 20% rosé ▪ WIETA ▪ PO Box 398 Pniel 7681 ▪ info@normandie1693.com ▪ www.normandie1693.com, www.claringtonwines.com ▪ T +27 (0)21-874-1039

☐ **Nova Zonnestraal** see Constantia Royale
☐ **Ntsiki Biyela Wines** see Aslina Wines

Nuiba Wines

Owner/winemaker Suzanne Coetzee, former Clos Malverne winemaker, grew up on a cattle ranch near Gobabis in Namibia, and the memory of that happy time has never left her. Hence the farm name for her Nuiba brand, and the 'post' theme, referring to a cattle staging/drinking station. The range and success continue to grow, a fourth Post joining this edition, and the first export order received.

★★★★☆ **Third Post** ⊛ Half pinotage, with cab & grenache, **16** ⑨③ is a perfumed delight, an array of vivid fruit, cinnamon- & nutmeg-spiced from 18 months in old oak. Sleek musculature, succulent, yet enough grip for a future. Doesn't put a foot wrong.

★★★★ **First Post** ⓥ Semillon, sauvignon (60/40) fermented/matured in older barrels to give **16** ⑧⑦ an oatmeal layer throughout the leafy perfume, flavours. Has admirable purity, true to the varieties.

Second Post ⓥ ★★★★ Plush red fruit, **16** ⑧④'s oaking in support, adds savoury notes, doesn't detract from the fruit-driven shiraz styling. Just enough grip at the end for definition. Simonsberg-Paarl WO.

Fourth Post ⓝⓔⓦ ★★★★ Salmon-hued, wooded dry rosé from semillon, 3% malbec, **17** ⑧③ has a white grape profile: leafy, kiwi fruit, the red component showing as a gentle berry tone in the flavours. — CR

Location: Stellenbosch ▪ WO: Piekenierskloof/Stellenbosch/Simonsberg-Paarl ▪ Est/1stB 2016 ▪ Closed to public ▪ Owner(s) Suzanne Coetzee ▪ Winemaker(s) Suzanne Coetzee (Jan 2016) ▪ 350cs own label 85% red 15% white ▪ suzanne@nuibawines.co.za ▪ www.nuibawines.co.za ▪ T +27 (0)21-881-3097

☐ **Nuwehoop** see Daschbosch
☐ **Nuweland Wynkelder** see JMA Louw Familie Wyn
☐ **Nuwe Wynplaas** see Group CDV

Nuy Wine Cellar   ⓥ ⑪ ⓐ ⓑ

Few realise that only 5% of the vast output of wine from this grower-owned cellar in Worcester's Nuy Valley is bottled under their own brand. The recently revamped ranges are the crème de la crème, representing both quality and good value, and produced from carefully selected vineyards, separately vinified. Tastings happen at the popular Nuy on the Hill visitor centre a short distance from the cellar, where one can sample the new range of gins – or skip that and tuck right into the real stars: the ambrosial fortified muscats!

Legacy range

★★★★ **Argilla** ② Named for area's soils, **15** ⑧⑥ New World-styled blend mostly pinotage & cab, with shiraz & merlot. Spicy dark fruit, warm hearted but a touch brooding, needs more time. No **14**.

★★★★ **Calcareo** ⊘ Switches from chenin blend to varietal chenin off limestone soils. **17** ★★★★☆ ⑨① layers of dried peach & lime, deliciously fresh & flavoursome, enhanced by ferment/8 months new French & American oak. Sumptuous step up on **15** ⑧⑦. **16** untasted.

★★★★ **Celine Méthode Cap Classique** Brut sparkling from chardonnay, pinot noir, **NV** ⑧⑥, distinct smoky tone to apple, shortbread flavours from extended lees time (60 months, previous 30). Balanced, appealing, if tad less verve & substance than last. WO W Cape.

★★★★☆ **Barbieri Idro** ② Stellar debut for **13** ⑨③ fortified muscat de Frontignan. 3 years in old oak has honed it into a finely polished cross between tawny 'port' & muscadel, the raisin character interleaved with citrus rind & dried apricot, tempered by tangy acidity.

Mastery range

★★★★ **Cabernet Sauvignon** ⊘ Variety's firmer tannin structure evident, **16** ⑧⑥ drier, more serious than other Mastery reds, yet balanced with potential to age. 18 months oak, 50% new, some American, as all these reds.

★★★★ **Pinotage** Billows pinotage's sweet spice, ripe banana, mulberry in **16** ★★★★ ⑧⑤, poised & rounded, 30% American oak adds smooth approachability, but riper, less fresh, structured, than **15** ⑧⑥.

★★★★ **Shiraz** Reprises previous sweet spice & pepper in **16** ⑧⑥, gets more (50%) American oak but retains upfront ripe, succulent fruit. Supple structure, good clean, dry farewell.

Chardonnay ⑦ ★★★★ Open-textured & appealing **17** ⑧⑤, gentle poached pear & subtle brush of sweet toasty oak. Silky, balanced, with gentle freshness. A serial crowd pleaser.

Sauvignon Blanc ② ★★★★ **17** ⑧④ fleshier, riper, more concentrated than Inspiration. Darling fruit adds characteristic dusty, flinty nuance to mouthfilling succulence. Ready to enjoy solo or with a meal.

Inspiration range

★★★★☆ **Red Muscadel** Vivid burnt orange hue on **17** ⑨①, unfurls with rosepetal jam & Turkish delight flavours, uncloying despite huge 256 g/l sugar. Balanced, delicate yet intense, more vitality & elegance than **16** ★★★★ ⑧⑨. Classic example of this unoaked fortified style.

★★★★☆ **White Muscadel** ② More barley sugar, with hint of orange blossom in warmer **16** ★★★★ ⑧⑥. Less vibrant acidity & poise than stellar **15** ⑨③ vintage, still fine & well priced, from this renowned fortified muscat producer.

Cabernet Sauvignon ② ★★★ Tank sample **16** ⑧① shows amiable side of variety: smooth, sappy & approachable, generous ripe cassis flavours on offer. **Koffiepit Pinotage** ★★★ As per name, **17** ⑧② has fashionable mocha-accented tone to plummy red fruit. Balanced, though, makes attractive easy drinking. **Shiraz** ② ★★★★ Spiced fruit pastille character, **16** ⑧③ fresh & pliable structure, medium body with juicy appeal. **Rouge de Nuy** ★★★ Cab & equal shiraz & pinotage, latter's ripe mulberry tones dominant, some sweet new-oak too. **NV** ⑧② supple & juicy, accessible. **Chenin Blanc** ★★★ A smooth-textured charmer, **18** ⑦⑨ crunchy Golden Delicious apple & pear, light & gentle. **Colombar Semi-Sweet** ★★ Easygoing semi-sweet quaffer, **18** ⑦⑤ uncloying, with scented green fruit & lowish 12.6% alcohol. **Sauvignon Blanc** ⊘ ★★★ Plenty of tropical fruit crisply presented, **18** ⑧② tailor-made for summer, more appealing than last. **Chant de Nuit** ★★★ More charming, summer-sippable **NV** ⑦⑧ than last, mostly chenin, dash colombard, splash rare Ferdinand de Lesseps, latter giving pineapple nuance to gently crisp apple flavours. **Muscat Sparkling Wine** ⊘ ★★★ Grapey & fresh **18** ⑦⑨ rosé sparkling, scented sweetness, uncloying & delightful with a light curry. Touch more verve than previous. **Sauvignon Blanc Sparkling Wine** ⊘ ★★★ Quaffable al fresco sparkler, **17** ⑦⑦ dry, fresh, sherbet & herbaceous twists, touch of sweetness on the tail.

Brandy range

★★★★ **Copper Potstilled** ② The 10% component aged 20 years makes all the difference (the rest 3-year & 5-year). It adds smoothness, complexity, depth, & tempers the fire. A little sweet; very sippable. — MW, TJ

Location/map: Worcester ▪ Map grid reference: C4 ▪ WO: Nuy/Western Cape ▪ Est 1963 ▪ Tasting & sales Mon-Fri 9–5 Sat/Sun 9–4 ▪ Closed Good Fri & Dec 25 ▪ Bistro & deli ▪ MTB ▪ Craft beer & non alcoholic gin ▪ Owner(s) 19 members ▪ Cellarmaster(s) Christo Pienaar (Sep 2003) ▪ Winemaker(s) Paul Burger (Nov 2016, senior) ▪ Viticulturist(s) Pierre Snyman (VinPro) ▪ 770ha (cab, merlot, muscadel, ptage, shiraz, chard, chenin, cbard, nouvelle, sauv) ▪ 18,200t/20,000cs own label ▪ PO Box 5225 Worcester 6849 ▪ wines@nuywinery.co.za ▪ www.nuywinery.co.za ▪ S 33° 41' 8.77" E 019° 35' 17.96" ▪ ⌘ chive.bitter.transitive ▪ F +27 (0)86-520-1782 ▪ **T +27 (0)23-347-0272**

☐ **Oak Lane** see Beau Joubert Wines

Oak Valley Estate   ⓠ ⑰ ⌂ ⊚ ⑤

Harvest 2018 was crushed in the Rawbone-Viljoen family's new cellar, 'an historic moment cementing our wine-estate status', says CEO Christopher, whose grandfather Sir Antonie started farming beneath Groenland Mountain in elevated Elgin in the late 1800s. A century later, Christopher's father Anthony introduced wine to the quality agribusiness (including fruit, flowers, free-range cattle and acorn-fed pigs). Now new winemaker Jacques du Plessis focuses on cool-climate pinot noir and chardonnay, spread across three tiers: Groenlandberg, Elgin and future Tabula Rasa ('Clean Slate') for small single-variety, single-clone batches. An added attraction is the new Elgin Railway Market at the farm gates.

Groenlandberg range

★★★★★ **Pinot Noir** ⊘ ⊛ Top-drawer expression of Elgin pinot, worthy successor to stellar **16** ⑨⑤. Perfumed **17** ★★★★☆ ⑨③ elegant & refined but also succulent; intense red fruit supported by well-composed oak, yielding to echoing silky length.

★★★★☆ **Chardonnay** ⊛ From high-lying vineyard on Groenlandberg, **17** ★★★★★ ⑨⑤ stylish example of cool-climate fruit with oatmeal, lemon peel & honeysuckle nuances. Serious-minded, ageworthy & showing understated elegance, & less oak than **16** ⑨④.

Elgin range

★★★★ **Sounds of Silence Pinot Noir** ⊘ Raspberry-toned **17** ⑧⑥ has soft caramel nudge from only older oak, pleasing supple grip, smooth texture & sweet-fruit finish.

★★★★☆ **Beneath The Clouds Chardonnay** ⊘ ⊛ Stylish **17** ⑨④ is exceptionally pure & fresh, evocative of place (cool) & vintage (excellent). Upfront hazelnut & lemon peel, judicious oaking ensure harmony of **16** ⑨① repeated here.

★★★★☆ **Stone & Steel Riesling** ⊘ Attractively packaged **18** ⑨② in similar vein to discreetly perfumed **17** ⑨②. Lemon zest, limy acidity & pebbly minerality, bracingly fresh but avoids austerity with well-judged few grams sugar. Captivating dinner companion.

★★★★☆ **Fountain of Youth Sauvignon Blanc** ⊘ ⊛ Everything one would expect in an Elgin sauvignon: neither lean nor overtly tropical, saline minerality & granadilla fruit. **18** ⑨③'s smidgen old-oak-fermented semillon gives extra weight, breadth. Impressive follow-up to standout **17** ★★★★★ ⑨⑤.

Discontinued: **Elgin Shiraz**, **The Oak Valley Blend**. — HC

Location/map/WO: Elgin ▪ Map grid reference: B1 ▪ Est 1898 ▪ 1stB 2003 ▪ Tasting & sales Mon-Fri 9–5 Sat/Sun 10-4 ▪ Closed Easter Mon, Dec 25/26 & Jan 1 ▪ The Pool Room Restaurant ▪ Deli: artisanal breads, homegrown free-range meats & charcuterie ▪ Self-catering 1-bedroom cottage ▪ Walks/hikes ▪ MTB trail ▪ Conservation area ▪ Owner(s) AG Rawbone-Viljoen Trust ▪ Winemaker(s) Jacques du Plessis (Oct 2018) ▪ Viticulturist(s) Jacques du Plessis (Oct 2018), assisted by Kevin Watt ▪ 32ha (pinot, chard, riesling, sauv) ▪ ±250t/±35,000cs own label 20% red 80% white ▪ GlobalGAP, IPW, WIETA, WWF-SA Conservation Champion ▪ PO Box 30 Elgin 7180 ▪ wines@oak-valley.co.za ▪ www.oakvalley.co.za ▪ S 34° 9' 24.4" E 019° 2' 55.5" ▪ ⌘ inspectors.soon.sunscreen ▪ F +27 (0)21-859-3405 ▪ **T +27 (0)21-859-4110**

☐ **Oesland** see Hofstraat Kelder
☐ **Oggendau** see Eerste Hoop Wine Cellar
☐ **Oh!** see Oneiric Wines
☐ **Old Brown** see Sedgwick's Old Brown

Oldenburg Vineyards

Adrian and Vanessa Vanderspuy had an inkling when they acquired this land high in Stellenbosch's Banhoek area in 2003 that it was special. Yet the farm and its wines, especially the latest '15s, have exceeded their expectations. There has been an intensive and continuing programme of rejuvenation and replanting of the vineyards, and the team has identified the confluence of 8 natural elements, including some specific to the property, that contribute to the quality of the wines. The stylish new labels feature these elements for the Oldenburg range, while the new top tier, Rondekop, depicts the round hill that stands out from the mountain amphitheatre that surrounds the farm. Winemaker Nic van Aarde will celebrate a double maiden in 2019: his first harvest here, in the estate's brand new, state-of-the-art cellar.

Rondekop range

★★★★☆ **Per Se Cabernet Sauvignon** (NEW) Stellar maiden release of **15** (93). Effortless elegance, luxuriant texture streamlines pure cab cassis flavours, 100% new oak, 24 months, melts into fruit concentration. Very polished presentation, already so tempting but will continue to evolve with distinction.

★★★★ **Stone Axe Syrah** (NEW) Fresh red fruit & hint of pepper, restrained but clean lines, **16** (89) more new oak (50%) than Oldenburg sibling, also the brighter, more elegant & balanced of the pair.

★★★★ **Rhodium** Merlot (70%) & cab franc duo, **15** ★★★★☆ (94) takes elegant step up on **14** (87). Scented red berry fruit in fine, dry but lithe tannin structure, 100% new oak effortlessly integrated. Already appealing but with rich future rewards in store.

Oldenburg range

★★★★☆ **Cabernet Sauvignon** Estate's more classic style aided by judicious skin contact, soft extraction, sensitive oak management. Cab's signature cassis & brushes herb & cedar from 40% new wood. Youthful, elegant restraint, yet even more concentration in **15** (93) than **14** (92), underpinned by confident, balanced tannins. Augurs well for longevity. All reds also in magnum except Grenache, other Cab.

★★★★ **Cabernet Sauvignon Barrel Selection** Restrained & perfumed **09** (87), with delicacy rather than intensity the hallmark of this selection. Big alcohol (15%) & all-new oak well managed.

★★★★☆ **Cabernet Franc Barrel Select** Standout **15** (90) vintage adds muscle tone & intensity to ripe & rich berry compote flavours, taming cultivar's firmer, piquant tannins. 25% new oak well-integrated, less restrained & more concentrated than **14** ★★★★ (84). Deserves cellar time to show true potential.

★★★★ **Merlot** A youthful, concentrated beauty in fine **15** ★★★★★ (95) vintage, rung up on **14** (88). Appealing dark cherry/berry flavours, richly textured & balanced with complementary 35% new oak.

★★★★ **Syrah** Powerhouse **15** (87) develops in intensity. Earthy, savoury tone with a warm heart, broad flavoured & robust, has the concentration of **14** (87) though less of the elegance.

★★★★ **Chardonnay** A charming table companion, **17** (89) delicious poached pear zested with lime, toasted hazelnut nuance from well-judged oaking. Similar style, but even snappier than **16** (87).

★★★★ **Chenin Blanc** Fresh apple, almond flavours & bright acidity from part tank, part oak ferment/8 months, latter adding creamy layer & richness. Notch up from demure **16** ★★★ (82), showing more fruit despite high yield.

★★★★ **Viognier** 100% ferment/ageing in French & Hungarian oak, 50% new, yet **17** (87) emerges with delicate scented peach & floral tones, balancing acidity. Fresher than **15** (87) & as appealing. **16** untasted.

Grenache Noir ★★★★ Identically made **17** (85) darker in colour & flavour profile than also-tasted **16** (83). More of everything, in fact, including vibrant freshness & succulence that lifts it above more rounded, lighter-bodied & smoother predecessor. Both have charm, but different personalities. — MW

Location/map/WO: Stellenbosch ▪ Map grid reference: H5 ▪ Est 1960s ▪ 1stB 2007 ▪ Tasting & sales Mon-Fri 10-4.30 Sat & pub hols 10-4 ▪ Reservations recommended for The Ultimate tasting experience ▪ Closed Good Fri, Dec 25/26 & Jan 1 ▪ Luxury accommodation in The Homestead (exclusive use, sleeps up to 12 in 6 bedrooms) ▪ Owner(s) Adrian & Vanessa Vanderspuy ▪ MD Judi Dyer (Apr 2017) ▪ Winemaker(s) Nic van Aarde (Nov 2018) ▪ Viticulturist(s) Zelda Shaik (Jun 2018), with Etienne Terblanche (consultant) ▪ 50ha/30ha (cabs s/f, merlot, shiraz, chard, chenin) ▪ 136t/7,400cs own label 57% red 43% white ▪ PO Box 2246 Dennesig 7601 ▪ tastingroom@oldenburgvineyards.com ▪ www.oldenburgvineyards.com ▪ S 33° 55' 7.61" E 018° 56' 8.75" ▪ chickens.splits.teaspoons ▪ F +27 (0)21-885-2665 ▪ **T +27 (0)21-885-1618 (winery), +27 (0)87-057-4515 (homestead reservations)**

☐ **Old Harbour** see Whalehaven Wines
☐ **Old Man's Blend** see Groote Post Vineyards

Old Road Wine Company

This DGB boutique standalone brand, with its own home on Franschhoek town's main road, pays tribute to the area's 'magnificent old vines that have helped forge a reputation for quality spanning generations' in three (untasted) wines: Anemos, Grand Mére and 12 Mile.'

Location/map: Franschhoek ▪ Map grid reference: C2 ▪ 1stB 2015 ▪ Tasting Tue-Sat 11-10 Sun 11-9 ▪ Sales Tue-Sat 11-5 ▪ Closed Easter Sun & Dec 25 ▪ Restaurant open for lunch & dinner ▪ Tour groups ▪ Gift shop ▪ Farm produce ▪ Owner(s) DGB (Pty) Ltd ▪ Winemaker(s) Ryan Puttick (Sep 2017) ▪ Viticulturist(s) Heinie Nel (Jul 2018) ▪ 7ha/14ha (shiraz, chenin, sem) ▪ 40% red 60% white ▪ info@orwc.co.za ▪ www.oldroadwine-company.com ▪ S 33° 54' 16.4" E 019° 6' 40.7"

Old Vines Cellars

The current preoccupation with old vines and chenin is nothing new for the owner of this Cape Town boutique venture, Irina von Holdt, a passionate advocate of her favoured variety and heirloom vineyards for more than 20 years now: 'Why do you think we named our winery as we did?!' Whether making appetising everyday tipples or serious bottlings intended for long ageing, Irina believes SA produces the finest chenins in the world, and continues to substantiate her conviction with her own range of carefully crafted wines.

Springvalley range

Shiraz-Merlot ⊘ ⊛ ★★★★ Previewed **17** ⑧⑤ set to be a little cracker: loads of spicy, floral notes, ripe black plums & soft juicy tannins. 55/45 blend. **Chenin Blanc-Sauvignon Blanc** ⊘ ⊛ ★★★★ Delicious everyday quaffing in store from ex-tank **18** ⑧⑤, packed with zippy sherbet lemons & touch of fresh herbs. Almost equal chenin/sauvignon this year.

Occasional release: **Merlot, Pinotage, Sauvignon Blanc.**

Old Vines range

Not tasted: **Chenin Blanc.** In abeyance: **Baron von Holdt, Vintage Brut.** — CM

Location: Cape Town ▪ WO: Western Cape ▪ Est/1stB 1995 ▪ Closed to public ▪ Owner(s) Irina von Holdt ▪ Winemaker(s) Irina von Holdt & Rocco de Villiers ▪ 12,000cs own label 20% red 80% white ▪ 50 Liesbeek Rd Rosebank 7700 ▪ info@oldvines.co.za ▪ www.oldvines.co.za ▪ F +27 (0)21-685-6446 ▪ **T +27 (0)21-685-6428**

☐ **Old Vine Series** see Sadie Family Wines

Olifantsberg Family Vineyards

Paul and Corine Leeuwerik's property on the slopes of Brandwacht Mountain enjoys spectacular views over the Breedekloof vineyards. Its schist and slate soils are proving ideal for the mainly Rhône varieties grown there. Cooling breezes in summer, with marked diurnal temperature changes provide slow ripening, which encourages freshness and purity in the wines. Investment in the sustainability of the vines and soil health is paramount for vineyard manager, Elizma Visser. In the cellar, where she's also in charge, experiments continue with new techniques to aid complexity, including skin ferments and German breathable plastic 'eggs' for the white wines. Across the range, there's clear evidence of greater confidence and individuality.

★★★★ **Grenache Noir** ⑭ Youthful **17** ⑧⑥ has verve & freshness. Ripe, juicy red fruits & spice need few months to resolve with vibrant grape tannin. Tasty summer drinking; can take light chilling.

★★★★ **Pinotage** Strikes modern note with plentiful bright cherry & raspberry juiciness. **17** ⑧⑦'s medium body, zesty yet unharsh grip, add to uncomplicated yet satisfying drinking.

★★★★ **Syrah** ⑫ Youthful, but shows much promise in its clean leather, red fruit notes, rich yet unheavy concentration. **16** ⑧⑨ roundly dry. Barrel fermented, 225-2,000L French, 5% new.

★★★★☆ **Silhouette** ⑭ Shiraz-based with trio southern Rhône varieties, **15** ⑨③ as distinguished as fine **14** ★★★★★ ⑨⑤. Its supple, rich texture bound by comfortable frame holds as much allure as layers of dark berries, spice & complexity-giving gamey note. Sustained appeal for all senses.

★★★★ **Blanc de Noir** One of best in genre, **17** ⑧⑨ from shiraz deserves serious attention. Warm cinnamon hue echoed in the emphatic spicy, savoury flavours. Firm, bone-dry & food friendly. 20% natural ferment in oak. No **16**.

★★★★ **Chenin Blanc** ⊘ Widely sourced fruit melds into subtle, supple whole. **15** ⑧⑨ tropical notes gain earthy, spicy nuances from native ferment in large old oak. Elegantly understated, ageworthy.

★★★★ **Lark Chenin Blanc** ⓃⒺⓌ Honours the owners (their Dutch surname translates as 'lark'), **17** ⑧⑨ elegant & harmonious, like the bird's song, gentle creaminess from lees-ageing complemented by trill of spice adding energy to the pure flavours. Oaked, 20% new.

★★★★☆ **Grenache Blanc** ⓃⒺⓌ Increasingly popular both in blends & as varietal wine. **17** ⑨② full of personality; dried grass/hay aromas, lime/herby flavours, long savoury conclusion; all underpinned by weight/breadth from 10 months on lees. Spontaneous ferment, older oak only. Debut **16** untasted.

★★★★☆ **Blanc** ⊛ Generous **17** ⑨④, mostly roussanne, grenache blanc, splash chenin, reflective of sunny climes, the dried fruit medley rich & concentrated, structure broad, textured & dry, the memory long; a poised, distinctive whole. 500L French/Hungarian oak ferment, 9% new. — AL

Location: Worcester ▪ Map: Breedekloof ▪ Map grid reference: C4 ▪ WO: Breedekloof/Western Cape ▪ Est 2003 ▪ 1stB 2005 ▪ Tasting & sales Mon-Sat by appt ▪ Owner(s) Paul J Leeuwerik ▪ Winemaker(s)/viticulturist(s) Elizma Visser (Jun 2015) ▪ 95ha/17ha (carignan, grenache n/b, mourv, ptage, shiraz, chard, chenin, rouss) ▪ 100t/±13,000cs own label 60% red 40% white ▪ PO Box 942 Worcester 6849 ▪ winemaker@olifantsberg.com ▪ www.olifantsberg.com ▪ S 33° 35′ 42.76″ E 019° 21′ 42.39″ ▪ ⒶⒿ oscillates.tribune.cuddled ▪ **T +27 (0)71-301-9440**

Olivedale Private Vineyards ⓠ

Twenty hectares, 18 varieties, soils ranging from stony clay to — just metres distant — free-draining Breede riversand: Belgian-owned Olivedale near Swellendam is a challenge - and viticulturist Carl van Wyk and consultants Abé Beukes and Jolene le Roux are so up for it! Working naturally, and experimenting with de rigueur techniques, one of their latest projects involves a custom tank enabling more precise control over skin ferments, their goal being 'a white wine with a tannin structure specifically to complement food'.

Olivedale range

★★★★ **Wild Olive Semillon** ⓃⒺⓌ Natural ferment, 40 days on skins, 6 months ageing, all in older oak. **17** ⑧⑥ full & rich, in contrast to semillon's usual racier profile; challenges convention.

★★★★ **Red Muscadel** ⓃⒺⓌ New wave fortified muscat de Frontignan with higher alcohol, reined-in sweetness, greater focus on fresh rather than dried fruit character, **17** ⑧⑥ still satisfyingly grapey, with uplifting bitter hint. Year in oak, some new. 500 ml.

Syrah ⓃⒺⓌ ★★★★ Oak-forward **17** ⑧⑤ is opaque, with faint black pepper, black/red berry scents & core of dark fruit. Very young, needs few more years to harmonise. **Tempranillo** ★★★☆ Barrel sample **17** ⑧③ atypically dark hued, like previous, with similar pleasing dry tannic grip & bracing acidity. Perfect osso bucco companion. **Shiraz-Mourvèdre-Grenache** ⊘ ★★★ Well-crafted, part-oaked **NV** ⑧① Fruit intensity, vibrant colour from shiraz's long skin contact; supple, smooth, tannins amenable for satisfying easy sipping. WO W Cape. **Chardonnay** ★★★ Riper, bolder than previous, **17** ⑧② has tangerine aromas & flavours, 13.8% alcohol, subtle oak nudge on finish. Not tasted: **Rosé**.

Queen of Africa range

Not tasted: **Edel Laat Oes**. — CvZ

Location: Swellendam ▪ Map: Southern Cape ▪ Map grid reference: D1 ▪ WO: Swellendam/Western Cape ▪ 1stB 2016 ▪ Tasting by appt only ▪ Closed all pub hols ▪ Owner(s) 8 shareholders ▪ Cellarmaster(s) Abé Beukes (2014, consultant) ▪ Winemaker(s) Jolene le Roux (Jan 2016, consultant) ▪ Viticulturist(s) Carl van Wyk ▪ 20ha (carignan, grenache, malbec, mourv, p verdot, red muscadel, roobernet, shiraz, tannat, tempranillo, touriga, chard, riesling, rouss, sauv, sem, verdelho, viog) ▪ 8st own labels 70% red 30% white ▪ Buffeljagsrivier Olivedale Swellendam 6740 ▪ jolene@olivedalewines.co.za ▪ www.olivedaleprivatevineyards.co.za ▪ S 34° 05′ 08.2″ E 020° 30′ 00.8″ ▪ ⒶⒿ acquisition.entrusts.quips ▪ **T +27 (0)28-007-0087**

Olof Bergh Solera

A rarity in the local brandy arena, Distell's Olof Bergh is matured in a dedicated cellar at Goudini in the Breede River Valley using a solera, where different batches are racked down tiers of barrels for a final product with a greater percentage of cask-aged distillate than the usual blended brandy.

Olof Bergh Solera ⊗ ★★★ Blended brandy, sippable but best for cocktails & mixers. Straightforward, with nice fruity fragrance to sniff & some caramel & oak vanilla coming through. — WB, TJ

Olsen Wines ⊗ ◎

This boutique Paarl farm on the Klein Drakenstein mountain foothills was acquired in 2002 by Greg Olsen, American physicist and the third civilian in space, latterly with daughters Kimberly and Krista as co-owners. Local point man Armand Botha tends both the vines and the cellar, and crushes just a few tons of the six varieties planted for the strikingly packaged own-label wines.

Pinotage ★★★☆ Passion for pinotage prompted Greg Olsen's farm acquisition 17 years ago. Deliciously old-style **15** ⑧⑷ with freshness, bright red fruit, smoky & high-toned notes. Integrated oak tannins courtesy all-new barrels, some American. **Cape Blend** ★★★☆ Commendably dry & balanced despite 14.9% alcohol, **15** ⑧③ dark fruit & charry nuance from new French oak. Barrel selection; equal pinotage & shiraz, 18% merlot. **Chardonnay** ★★★☆ Typical warm-climate chardonnay with ripe tangerine overtone, saturated fruit. **16** ⑧④ attractive toast & butter notes ex year in new barrels, 10% American. Quite extravagant - but it works. **Chenin Blanc** ⊘ ★★★☆ Peach & apricot tones, **17** ⑧④ nice richness & creamy texture from brief lees ageing, bone-dry finish helps contain 14.3% alcohol for 'calm & collected' overall effect. Not tasted: **Cabernet Sauvignon, Merlot, Shiraz.** — CvZ

Location/map/WO: Paarl ▪ Map grid reference: G5 ▪ Est/1stB 2002 ▪ Tasting by appt only ▪ Fee R50pp depending on sales ▪ Farm-style jams & olive oil ▪ Owner(s) Greg Olsen & daughters ▪ Cellarmaster(s)/ viticulturist(s) Armand Botha (2000) ▪ Winemaker(s) Armand Botha (2007) & Loftie Ellis (consultant) ▪ 15ha ▪ 1,500cs own label 80% red 20% white ▪ PO Box 9052 Huguenot 7645 ▪ olsenwines@mweb.co.za ▪ www. olsenprivatevineyards.co.za ▪ S 33° 44' 4.7" E 019° 3' 5.0" ▪ ⫶ parables.backdrops.pulsations ▪ F +27 (0)21-862-2589 ▪ **T +27 (0)21-862-3653**

☐ **Ondine** *see* Ormonde Private Cellar
☐ **One Formation** *see* Boland Kelder

100 Reserve

Produced in the reputed Oude Molen distillery, 100 Reserve's name suggests that all components are aged in oak, going a step above what's legally required in the blended brandy category.

Premium Brandy ⊗ ★★★☆ A sherry-like nuttiness accompanies the dried peach notes. At 43% alcohol, with a sweetish finish, it works best as a mixer but is smooth enough for the brave to try solo. Potstill component averages 4-5 years. — TJ

Oneiric Wines ⊗ ⑪ ◎

Prime mover Shan Pascall and her family's winery in Elgin now has a dedicated winemaker, Mark Wallace, son of veteran viticultural consultant Paul, who's been looking after the Oneiric vines since inception. Wallace junior takes the reins from Niels Verburg, of Luddite repute, who stays on as an adviser. New is the '18 Copper Rosé, in line with the ranges' names and creative insignia marking Shan's father's mining career.

Location/map: Elgin ▪ Map grid reference: C4 ▪ Est 2007 ▪ 1stB 2009 ▪ Tasting & sales by appt only; except in December when open most weekends ▪ Gift shop ▪ Walks/hikes ▪ Picnics to be ordered 3 days prior ▪ Conservation area ▪ Owner(s) Pascall family ▪ Winemaker(s) Mark Wallace, assisted by Niels Verburg ▪ Viticulturist(s) Paul Wallace (Aug 2007, consultant) ▪ 64ha/8ha (cab, merlot, shiraz, chard, sauv) ▪ ±18ot/10,000cs own label 65% red 35% white ▪ 76 Highlands Rd Elgin 7180 ▪ shan@oneiric.co.za ▪ www. oneiric.co.za ▪ S 34° 14' 31.0" E 019° 03' 05.8" ▪ ⫶ valuable.phenomenally.poking ▪ **T +27 (0)71-481-9560**

Oom Tas

Distell big-volume white depicts winefarmer 'Uncle Tas' beaming from retro label. In 1, 2 & 5L bottles. **Oom Tas** ⊗ ★ Eclectic notes of ginger beer, liquorice & some baked apple on dry & brief **NV** ⑥④. — CvZ

☐ **Openers** *see* Stellenview Premium Wines

Opstal Estate   ⓆⓎ🏠◎ⓈⓅ

Progressive winegrowing continues on the Louw family's visitor-friendly Slanghoek Valley farm under the leadership of 7th-generation Attie. The can-do winemaker and marketer, with longtime vine man Gerhard Theron and more recent colleague Zak Louw, has positioned Opstal as a leader in SA's New Wave by focusing on minimum-intervention winemaking, old (and mature) vines, storytelling (via the Heritage range, featuring Attie's grandfather and great-grandfather), and heritage varieties and styles, chiefly chenin but also semillon and cinsaut, the latter co-starring in a delightful new blend. Non-traditional grapes are not neglected, hence the newly cropped roussanne component in the Cape White debuting this edition.

Heritage range

★★★★☆ **Carl Everson Cape Blend** Assured, well-judged pinotage, cab, cinsaut, carignan shows nuanced fruit in favour of raw power. **16** ⑨② is supple & juicy with intricate aromas, gentle silky tannins & tantalising floral finish. An example worth following.

★★★★☆ **Carl Everson Chenin Blanc** ⓐ ⓦ Intense, expressive single-vineyard **17** ⑨③ maintains lofty standard, with layers of ripe stonefruit borne on leesy fatness, creamy texture, great palate breadth & precise lingering finish. 35 year old vines, unusually long (4 month) wild yeast ferment in large old barrels.

★★★★☆ **The Barber Semillon** Named for doyen Attie Louw's sojourn as a barber after service in WW2, stylish **17** ⑨② follows form: waxy lanolin woven with citrus zest, richly textural & weighty. Wild yeast, old-barrel fermented.

★★★★☆ **Carl Everson Cape White Blend** ⓝⓔⓦ ⓐ Deftly crafted chenin-roussanne blend with smaller parts semillon, viognier & colombard, **17** ⑨④ is robust but refined, eliciting the best of each variety. Spontaneous barrel ferment lends creamy texture, heady lees richness & precise balance.

Opstal Estate range

★★★★ **Hanepoot** Headily aromatic muscat fruit on overtly sweet **16** ⑧⑦. Ginger toned, honeyed melon preserve, subtle spirit tang & ripe figs on finish.

....

Cabernet Sauvignon-Cinsault ⓝⓔⓦ Ⓨ ★★★★ Deliciously supple, fruity **17** ⑧⑤ evokes memories of classic Cape reds. Solid cab core spiced & highlighted with lacy fragrant notes. 50% wholebunch. **Chenin Blanc** Ⓨ ★★★★ Cheerful, expressive **17** ⑧⑤ has loads of fruity charm, decent heft & lingering finish with appealing bitter twist. 8 months in foudre, 25% unoaked.

Syrah-Viognier Blush ★★★★ Near-equal blend, co-fermented, lends floral fragrance to generous fruit in **18** ⑧④ dry rosé. Light & characterful. **Sauvignon Blanc Sparkling Sec** ★★★ Light, fruit-forward, crisply tart **18** ⑦⑧ carbonated fizz shows typical sauvignon character. Discontinued: **Cabernet Sauvignon, The Mill Iron, Chardonnay Barrel Dessert**.

Sixpence range

Cabernet Sauvignon-Merlot ⊘ ★★★ Rather one-dimensional but competent **17** ⑧⓪ delivers juicy berry fruit with gentle tannins. Light & quaffable. **Sauvignon Blanc-Semillon** ⊘ ★★★ Pleasant, characterful & easy-sipping **18** ⑧① has bright fruit notes, gentle acidity. — GdB

Location: Rawsonville ▪ Map: Breedekloof ▪ Map grid reference: A5 ▪ WO: Slanghoek ▪ Est 1847 ▪ 1stB 1978 ▪ Tasting, sales & cellar tours Mon-Fri 9—5 Sat 11—3 Sun by appt ▪ Closed Easter Fri-Mon, Dec 25/26 & Jan 1 ▪ Cheese platters ▪ Restaurant Wed-Sun 9—5 ▪ Facilities for children ▪ Tour groups ▪ Gift shop ▪ Farm produce ▪ Conferences ▪ Conservation area ▪ MTB trail ▪ Accommodation ▪ Owner(s) Stanley Louw ▪ Winemaker(s) Attie Louw (Sep 2010) ▪ Viticulturist(s) Gerhard Theron (Jan 2002) & Zak Louw (Jan 2016) ▪ 419ha/101ha (cab, cinsaut, ptage, shiraz, chard, chenin, muscat d'A, sauv, sem, viog) ▪ 1,600t/25,000cs own label 30% red 55% white 10% rosé 5% dessert ▪ IPW, WIETA ▪ PO Box 27 Rawsonville 6845 ▪ wine@opstal.co.za ▪ www.opstal. co.za ▪ S 33° 38' 19.8" E 019° 13' 40.8" ▪ ⊞ bloomed.summons.finished ▪ F +27 (0)23-344-3002 ▪ **T +27 (0)23-344-3001**

Orange River Cellars   Ⓠ Ⓑ

Though the Northern Cape has a semiarid to arid climate, fine harvest conditions are never a given for the more than 800 owner-growers who cultivate some 4,000 ha of vines along the Orange River to feed this large and dynamic producer's five production cellars at Kakamas, Keimoes, Upington, Grootdrink and Groblershoop. While 2017 delivered one of the wettest seasons, 2018 brought 'perfect weather', according to Rianco van Rooyen, spokesperson for the teams who produce well over 50 million litres of wine for the own label, buyers' brands and bulk. The 2018 wines have 'amazing aromatics in whites, deep colour and soft tannins in reds', Rianco enthuses. There's an upbeat mood for orders, too, both bulk and bottled, and their new Delush brand has been well received. New CEO Charl du Plessis, with experience in the export fruit and ostrich meat markets, believes the acquisition of Farmers Pride Raisins will complement and grow the revenue stream beyond the wine production Orange River Cellars has become known for since founding in 1965.

Reserve range

Straw Wine ⊘ ⊛ Sleek & silky **17** ⑨④ from sun-dried chenin, its honeyed richness laced with complementary vanilla oak tones. Brilliant acidity carries the lush tropical flavours through to a prolonged finish. 375 ml. **Lyra Shiraz Reserve** ⓧ ★★★★ From shiraz & dash petit verdot, **14** ⑧⑤ combines 50/50 oaked & unwooded components for a delicious fruity red with vibrant black berry flavours. **Lyra Vega** ★★★★ Shiraz-based, splash petit verdot adds fresh backbone to **15** ⑧③. Forward plummy, cassis juiciness clipped by strong, toasty oak (73% new), drying tannins.

Orange River Cellars range

★★★★ **Soet Hanepoot** ⓧ Delightful, pristine expression of muscat d'Alexandrie in **16** ⑧⑦ fortified. Luscious sweet-ripe peach buoyed by a burst of spice & fire on long finish. Excellent value.

★★★★ **Red Muscadel** Flame-licked hue inviting introduction to lush **17** ⑧⑨. Generous, delicious mix raisins, dried citrus peel, spice enriched with warming fortification. Sweetly persistent.

★★★★☆ **White Muscadel** ⊛ Fortified (unoaked) muscat de Frontignan. In footsteps of stellar **16** ★★★★★ ⑨⑤, **17** ⑨④ so elegant, such fresh, cool spiced citrus peel flavours beautifully merged with warming, not overly fiery spirit (17% alc). Great balance between typical grapey sweetness & clean finish.

Cabernet Sauvignon ★★★ Strawberry & leafy tomato notes on medium-bodied **16** ⑦⑨. Straightforward, for early drinking. **Pinotage** ⊘ ★★★ **17** ⑧② with dashes petit verdot, ruby cab delivers plenty juicy, dark berry fruit framed by balanced tannins, dusting oak. **Ruby Cabernet** ⊘ ★★★ Deep ruby hue, compatible rich spice & berry flavours on smooth, quaffable **16** ⑧⓪. **Shiraz** ★★★ Light spice & plums in zippily fresh **16** ⑦⑨. Also in 3L. **Chardonnay** ⊘ ★★★ Quiet lemon, spice touches on **17** ⑧⓪; drop chenin, 8 months older oak add extra interest, satisfaction. **Chenin Blanc** ⊘ ★★★ Bright tropical fruit on **18** ⑦⑨, lipsmackingly fresh, dry. **Colombard** ⊘ ★★★ Real guava fruit bomb; juicy **18** ⑧⓪ lifted by gentle sweetness for refreshing summer sipping. **Sauvignon Blanc** ⊘ ★★★ Sweet, freshly mown grass appeal throughout **18** ⑧⓪. Brisk but not aggressive acidity. **Sparkling Rosé** ⓧ ★★★ Candyfloss pink low-alcohol bubbly from morio muscat, colombard & pinotage. **16** ⑦⑨ sweet & soft, with gentle mousse. **Sparkling Brut** ⊘ ★★★ **17** ⑧① just-dry fizzer from chenin. Fruity, with zesty bubble to brighten any occasion. **Sparkling Doux** ⓧ ★★★ Floral bubbles from morio muscat & colombard, litchi flavours on sweet & light (10% alcohol) **17** ⑦⑧. Musky finish. **Rosé Natural Sweet** ⓧ ★★★ Sweet, floral pink **17** ⑦⑧ from morio muscat, colombard & pinotage needs more zip. **Nouveau Blanc** ★★ Fruity Natural Sweet from chenin. **18** ⑦④'s lively acid & low alcohol (10.3%) make an appealing summer white. **Red Jerepigo** ⓧ ★★★★ **16** ⑧③ fortified takes ruby cab & shiraz to extremes of ripeness, yet the ultra-sweetness has a dried herb counterbalance so there's no cloy. **White Jerepigo** ⓧ ★★★ Cold tealeaves & nutty tones on attractive **16** ⑧③ fortified chenin. Smoothly warming, with lingering fruity sweetness. **Cape Ruby** ⓧ ★★★ Fruitcake, spicy plum & dusty finish on sweet **15** ⑦⑧ from ruby cab, shiraz & tannat. Light body & alcohol, more 'sweet red wine' than 'port.' — AL

Location: Upington ▪ Map: Northern Cape, Free State & North West ▪ Map grid reference: B8 ▪ WO: Northern Cape ▪ Est 1965 ▪ 1stB 1968 ▪ Tasting & sales at Upington visitor centre Mon-Fri 10–6 Sat 10-3 & at Kakamas, Keimoes & Grootdrink cellars Mon-Fri 8–5 Sat 8.30–12; closed Sun, Good Fri, Dec 25 & Jan 1 ▪ Also at Upington visitor centre: virtual cellar tours, sales of Kalahari craft beer ▪ Owner(s) ±800 shareholders ▪ CEO Charl du Plessis ▪ Cellarmaster(s) Gert Visser ▪ Cellar managers Bolla Louw (Kakamas), Johan Dippenaar (Keimoes), Johan Esterhuizen (Upington), Jim de Kock (Grootdrink), Riaan Liebenberg (Groblershoop), with winemakers (in same cellar order) George Kruger, Marko Pentz, Stefan Steenkamp; Rianco van Rooyen, Wouter Loubser; Jopie Faul, Jodie Johannes, Philani Gumede; Ferdi Laubscher; Mynhardt van der Merwe ▪ Viticulturist(s) Henning Burger (viticultural services manager), with Francois Ozrovech & AJ Jansen van Vuuren ▪ 4,000ha (ptage, ruby cab, shiraz, chard, chenin, cbard, muscat varieties) ▪ 117,000t/24m L own

label 10% red 50% white 25% rosé 15% other + 30m L for clients/bulk ▪ PO Box 544 Upington 8800 ▪ info@
orangeriverwines.com ▪ www.orangeriverwines.com ▪ S 28° 26′ 26.30″ E 021° 16′ 27.66″ ▪ 🗺 palace.mimed.
heeding ▪ F +27 (0)54-332-4408 ▪ **T +27 (0)54-337-8800**

☐ **Oranjerivier Wynkelders** *see* Orange River Cellars
☐ **Oranjezicht** *see* Rogge Cloof

Org de Rac
⊗ 🍴 ◎ ⊗ ⚙

Once a Swartland grain farm, Org de Rac over 18 years has grown into a significant producer of organic wine (and husk spirit). The family-owned venture is now taking the significant step of eschewing animal products in the production of their wines. 'Being a producer of vegan wines comes at the right time for us, as there is a growing generation of everyday consumers avoiding animal products totally,' notes cellarmaster Frank Meaker. Developments aimed at maintaining year-on-year quality improvements continue, including new plantings of shiraz and tempranillo.

Waghuis range

★★★★☆ **Rooi** ⊗ ⊗ High spirited, eclectic mix shiraz (62%), splashes grenache, mourvèdre & surprise white grape verdelho. **16** ⑨1 complex, juicy, expressive bramble fruit, baking spice & sour cherry nicely offset by not-overdone oak, 80% new, 20% American.

★★★★ **Blanc** ⊗ Verdelho (51%), roussanne (28%) & chenin trio exudes white flowers, peach & vanilla from 20% new oak. **17** ★★★★ ⑧5 rich, with saline nuance, acid lift. Oak tad more dominant mid-2018 than **16** ⑧7 at same stage.

Reserve range

★★★★☆ **Cabernet Sauvignon** ⊘ ⊗ Charming as **15** ⑨2, impressive, too, **16** ⑨2 admirable concentration, serious oak backbone (year, new French & American), lavish cassis fruit. Drinks well now, will reward cellaring few years.

★★★★ **Shiraz** ⊗ White pepper & vanilla welcome, appealing powdery tannin & satisfying dry finish. **16** ⑧6 nicely spiced, sculptured by year 90% new French/American oak.

★★★★ **Chardonnay** ⊗ Oatmeal, hazelnut & lime, **17** ⑧8's buttery richness & breadth comes from deft touch 50% new oak (not from alcohol, just 13%, or sugar, a bone-dry 1.8 g/l). Like **15** ⑧7, enlivened by bright acidity. No **16**.

Merlot ⊗ ★★★★ Plum, bramble fruit & blueberry, soupçon mint for freshness, with limber tannins, **15** ⑧4 for now or few years.

Org de Rac range

★★★★ **Cabernet Sauvignon** ⊘ ⊗ Now-bottled, **16** ⑧7 has hit its stride: more opulent than **15** ★★★ ⑧2, intense blackberry & cherry fruit, serious cab tannins & backbone to pair with a succulent steak.

★★★★ **Shiraz** ⊘ ⊗ Previously a tank sample, **16** ⑧7 delicious fruity attack, spicy follow up. Lean & tight with commendably dry farewell. 12–13 months French/American oak, like all these red single-variety bottlings. **15** ★★★ ⑧1 an approachable crowd pleaser.

★★★★ **Roussanne** (NEW) ⊘ ⊗ In-vogue variety for the budget conscious. Subtly floral & fragrant **17** ⑧8, attractive dry pineapple-like pithy texture, good presence at just 13% alcohol thanks to 15% briefly wooded portion.

★★★★ **Sauvignon Blanc** (NEW) ⊘ ⊗ From Constantia vines, **17** ⑧8 typical cool-climate expression of gooseberry, granadilla & herbs, crisp acidity. Brief skin contact & 15% wooded portion add texture.

★★★★ **La Verne Méthode Cap Classique** ⊗ ⊗ Dry sparkler from chardonnay shade less opulent than last but as satisfying. **14** ⑧7 lingering lemony mousse & aftertaste have nice summery feel for picnics.

Verdelho (NEW) ⊘ ⊗ ⊗ ★★★★ Rare-in-SA variety & welcome alternative to usual white-wine suspects. Welcomely priced, too. Oak-brushed **17** ⑧5 fresh, lively & pleasantly lean, apple, pear & spice appeal.

Merlot ⊗ ★★★★ Provisionally rated preview last time, extra year has stood **16** ⑧4 in good stead. More expressive fruit, velvety texture & less tight tannin; herbal top note still adds freshness. **Shiraz-Cabernet Sauvignon-Merlot** ⊘ ⊗ ★★★★ Spicy berries entice on near-equal partnership, **17** ⑧4 preview gets grip & structure from grape tannin & 80% oak-staved portion. Well-priced everyday red. **Chardonnay** ⊘

★★★★ Light 20% new-oak touch supports expressive fruit salad tones, lifted by brisk citrus acidity. **18** (83) step up on new-oaked previous. **The Old Pumphouse Cape Ruby Port** ★★★ **NV** (81) from cab & shiraz pleasingly sweet, cooked plum fruit & raisins, sufficient tannic grip & lively acidity.

Le Piquet range
Cabernet Sauvignon-Merlot ★★★ Savoury notes & juicy fruit, all balanced by pleasantly firm tannins. Previewed **15** (80) perfect fireside companion. **Blanc** ★★★★ Laid-back poolside sipper, **17** (83) fruity, fresh & uncomplicated trio chenin, roussanne & verdelho.

Husk Spirit range
★★★★ **Le Genio** Water-white **17** (87) from merlot, great balance & complexity, delicious length & spicy spirit bite; strawberries & cream on the nose, smooth & husk-y on palate. 43% alcohol.— HC, WB

Location: Piketberg ▪ Map: Swartland ▪ Map grid reference: C2 ▪ WO: Swartland/Constantia ▪ Est 2001 ▪ 1stB 2005 ▪ Tasting, sales & tours Mon-Fri 9—5 Sat/pub hols 9.30—2 ▪ Closed Good Fri, Dec 25 & Jan 1 ▪ Meals/refreshments/cheese platters by prior arrangement ▪ Facilities for children ▪ Tour groups ▪ Farm produce ▪ Weddings/functions (100 pax) ▪ Conferences ▪ Conservation area ▪ Owner(s) Nico Bacon ▪ Cellarmaster/GM Frank Meaker (Jul 2013) ▪ Winemaker(s) Jurgen Siebritz (Sep 2014) ▪ 220ha/54ha (cab, grenache, merlot, mourv, shiraz, chard, chenin, rouss, verdelho) ▪ 650t/62,500cs own label 85% red 10% white 5% rosé ▪ BSCI, Control Union (Organic), IPW, WIETA ▪ PO Box 268 Piketberg 7320 ▪ wine@orgderac.co.za ▪ www.orgderac. co.za ▪ S 32° 57´44.3˝ E 018° 44´57.4˝ ▪ bathhouses.teardrop.hybrid ▪ F +27 (0)22-125-0269 ▪ **T +27 (0)22-913-2397/3924**

Origin Wine Ⓠ

Restructuring in 2018 to 'drive efficiency and sustainability' at this large Stellenbosch producer, owner of global Fairtrade brand Fairhills, sees Jac Lourens (ex SA Breweries) as new COO, and an expanded winemaking team upping premium-wine production, including a new 'craft wine' range to 'simplify wine for consumers overwhelmed by choice'.

Location/map: Stellenbosch ▪ Map grid reference: D3 ▪ Est/1stB 2002 ▪ Tasting strictly by appt ▪ Owner(s) Bernard Fontannaz ▪ COO Jac Lourens (2018) ▪ Production director Grant Michaels (2004) ▪ Wine sourcing manager Johan Gerber (2016) ▪ Winemaker(s) Seugné Rossouw (2007), with Christiaan Visser, Helienne van Zyl & Justin Jacobs ▪ 7m cs ▪ 50% red 40% white 10% rosé ▪ BRC, DLG, Fairtrade, HACCP, IFS, WIETA ▪ PO Box 7177 Stellenbosch 7599 ▪ info@originwine.co.za ▪ www.originwine.co.za ▪ S 33° 52´39.07˝ E 018° 48´35.50˝ ▪ travel.explains.instant ▪ **T +27 (0)21-865-8100**

Ormonde Private Cellar

The latest offering from this substantial Darling family estate is 'specially crafted nougat', for tasting with the wines, along with chocolate. It's exactly 20 years since the first bottling here (initially as Alexanderfontein) – though Nico Basson bought the farm in 1970, primarily to start what became an acclaimed dairy stud. But he also planted vines; now there are over 300 hectares. Two thirds of the grapes are sold; the remainder go into the different Ormonde ranges, including easy-drinking Alexanderfontein (listed separately).

Ormonde Barrel Selected range
★★★★ **Cabernet Sauvignon** Good berry aromas & flavours mingle with tobacco-oaky layer on **15** (87). Succulent acid balanced by sweet element & firm but integrated dry tannin. Juicy & very drinkable now, but will keep.

★★★★ **Shiraz** Plush, ripe **15** (86) has tobacco, spice & more expressive fruit, with chocolate note on the palate, than the Old Block version. Softly textured, lingering & not too challenging.

★★★★ **Chardonnay** Forward citrus aromas on **15** (86) preview lead to tangy palate with pleasing texture, lemon acidity & plenty of flavour supported by good oak (25% new), considerable finish.

★★★★ **Sauvignon Blanc** Less exuberant, more subtle since previewed last year; **17** (88) more weight, balanced with delicious acidity. Tropical fruit, but also prominent greenpepper & some dustiness.

Pinot Noir ★★★★ Needs time; **15** (83) unusually dark with intense black berry flavours (versus red fruit of Ondine version). Soft tannins & some earthy mushroom notes.

Ondine Specialities

★★★★ Cabernet Franc ⓧ Lightly perfumed aromas of red berries touched with vanilla the main delight in **14** ⑧⑥, but tasty ripeness extends to balanced, gently gripping palate. Good now, should keep.

★★★★ Chardonnay Tasted ex tank last year, **15** ⑧⑥ has liquorice gracenote to varietal oats, nuts, citrus. Rich texture but restrained in effect & drinking well. Supportively oaked (25% new), as **14 ★★★★** ⑧⑤.

★★★★ Sauvignon Blanc More forthcoming tropical fruit on previewed **17** ⑧⑧ than Old Block version & greener edges; also not too overt. Crisp, succulent & refreshing acidity well integrated into delightful whole. No **16**.

Grenache ⓧ **★★★☆** Pre-bottling **15** ⑧⑤ not big & powerful but layered & complex, from spicy perfumed nose to ripe red berry & plum fruit. Fine, powdery tannins. **Malbec** ⓧ **★★★★** Soft & smooth, **15** ⑧③ with mocha & liquorice complementing & giving depth to primarily red fruit. **Merlot** ⓧ **★★★★** With ripe plums & dark berries, **14** ⑧④ is less fruitcakey than Chip counterpart, with quite grippy tannins. **Pinot Noir** ⓧ **★★★★** Opening up slowly, **15** ⑧③ light & lithe with earthy strawberries & warm spice, slight rusty metal tang on finish. **Chenin Blanc ★★★★** Purer fruit on **17** ⑧⑤ than Old Block version though some similar aromas & flavours. Riper, richer, though. Sweet fruit but good dry finish.

Single-Vineyard Chip Off The Old Block range

★★★★ Sauvignon Blanc ⊘ Previewed last year, **17** ⑧⑥ now less severe, more elegantly restrained. Earthy & green notes to tropical & citrus fruit. Balanced & bone-dry. Impresses more than **16 ★★★★** ⑧④.

Cabernet Sauvignon ★★★★ Previewed last year, **14** ⑧⑤ has pleasing ripe fruit flavours with a herbal element. Sappy tannins, bright acidity, supportive oaking (15% new, 9 months). **Merlot** ⓧ **★★★☆ 14** ⑧④ appeals with dark plum & blackberry nose, fruitcake richness, hints of milk chocolate & vanilla. **Shiraz ★★★** Ripe, spicy aromas on fleshy, flavourful **15** ⑧②, with easygoing tannins & very bright acidity giving sweet-sour finish. **Chenin Blanc** ⓃⒺⓦ **★★★★** Peach & melon on **17** ⑧⑤, with a more savoury element of straw & earth too. Nothing too overt. Fresh, balanced.

Ormond Heritage Collection

Not tasted: **Vernon Basson, Theodore Eksteen**. — TJ

Location/WO: Darling ▪ Map: Durbanville, Philadelphia & Darling ▪ Map grid reference: A1 ▪ 1stB 1999 ▪ Tasting & sales Mon–Fri 9–4 Sat/pub hols 9–3 ▪ Closed Good Fri, Dec 25/26 & Jan 1 ▪ Chocolate & wine and Nougat & wine pairings by appt @ R60pp ▪ Facilities for children ▪ Walks ▪ Owner(s) Basson family ▪ Winemaker(s)/viticulturist(s) Theo Basson ▪ ±300ha (cabs s/f, merlot, mourv, p verdot, pinot, shiraz, chard, chenin, sauv, sem) ▪ 1,000t/70,000c own label 40% red 60% white ▪ PO Box 201 Darling 7345 ▪ info@ormonde.co.za ▪ www.ormonde.co.za ▪ S 33° 22′ 20.2″ E 018° 21′ 23.6″ ▪ 🖵 refereed.resembled.handlebars ▪ F +27 (0)22-492-3470 ▪ **T +27 (0)22-492-3540**

☐ **Orpheus & The Raven** *see* The Vinoneers

Osbloed Wines   ⓥ

A boutique venture based in Somerset West, owner Bertus van Niekerk vinifying with qualified winemaker son Hendrik. A very personal range, which makes it interesting because it harks back to Bertus' clerical past. Most wines have biblical references attached, with individual colourful labels designed by Bertus' late wife Selma Albasini. Minimal interference is their motto, and the characterful, on-trend wines reflect that.

Metafisika range

Rooiperd ⓃⒺⓦ ⓥ **★★★★** Light crimson (matches label art), **17** ⑧④ cinsaut, redcurrants & scrub, full ripeness but a svelte body, in the nature of the variety. Palate-pleasing juicy freshness; could be template for cinsaut. Stellenbosch grapes, as all. **Wonderbare Raadsman** ⓥ **★★★★** Pinotage & parents, cinsaut & pinot noir, equal proportions, co-fermented, wild yeast, a real family affair, which works amazingly well. **17** ⑧④ vivid fruit, sleekly curvy succulence, supple tannins. **Buiteperd** ⓥ **★★★★** Rare crouchen blanc (Cape riesling). Early picked (just 11% alcohol), **17** ⑧③ some older oak; similar styling to previous, winter melon & bruised apple, dry earth/tobacco nuance, zinging freshness.

Swartperd ⓃⒺⓦ **★★★** From cab; deep, dense, cassis & black plum character, smoky spice. **17** ⑧① house-style juicy texture, a tasty mouthful. Grip at end for food, some ageing. **Kultus ★★★** Cab-led **NV** ⑧①, with cinsaut, grenache, lots of ripeness here, dark plums/prunes mixed in with cassis, good enough tannin grip for food/cellaring.

Farm Animals range

Osbloed ★★★ Shiraz & 4 Bordeaux varieties, **17** ⑧ spicy, dark-fruited, berries & cassis, balancing acidity tempers the ripeness. Juicy, tannins supple, good drinking appeal. — CR

Location: Somerset West ▪ Map: Helderberg ▪ Map grid reference: E6 ▪ Est 2009 ▪ 1stB 2010 ▪ Tasting, sales & cellar tours daily - please call ahead ▪ Owner(s) Bertus van Niekerk ▪ Cellarmaster(s) Bertus van Niekerk (Jan 2010) ▪ Winemaker(s) Bertus van Niekerk (Jan 2010), with Hendrik van Niekerk (2011) ▪ 50% red 50% white ▪ 33 Eagle Cres Somerset West 7130 ▪ bertus@osbloed.co.za ▪ www.osbloed.co.za ▪ S 34° 5' 26.22" E 018° 51' 55.87" ▪ 🌐 invented.preoccupied.deliver ▪ **T +27 (0)83-400-2999**

Oude Compagnies Post Private Cellar

Owners Jerry and Henriette Swanepoel both practised law in Cape Town, but 23 years ago decided to raise their children in the country. Great must their pride and delight be now that youngest son and qualified winemaker Dirk has taken the reins of the boutique cellar on the family estate near Tulbagh. Their philosophy is to 'put the grape in the bottle' as naturally as possible, and Sonoma-seasoned Dirk is focusing on handcrafted wines with a sense of origin. A tasting area is being set up in the old stone cellar, and hiking trails built to join already-available guest accommodation.

Compagnies Wijn range

Cabernet Sauvignon ★★★ Now bottled, **15** ⑧ true-to-type blackberry & cassis, firm tannins tempered by rich fruit padding, good dry finish. **Grenache** ★★★ Warm & ripe styling, dark plums/prunes, **16** ⑦ tannins giving backbone for ageing, food-friendly grip at the end. **Mourvèdre** ★★★ Brooding black plum fruit, meaty nuance on **17** ⑧ preview; obvious tannins need time to mesh, ease into plush fruit core. **Pinotage** ★★ Very ripe & needing freshening, **17** ⑦ shows variety's sometimes high-toned aromas. **Shiraz** ★★★ Easy to drink, with just enough black pepper interest & grip for food, **16** ⑧ bodes well for also-tasted **17** ⑧ preview, with juicy black fruit, attractive spice nuance. **Cabernet Sauvignon-Merlot** ★★ Pre-bottled NV ⑦ equal portions 2016 cab & 2015 merlot, bright cassis but tight tannins need time to relax. **The Buchu Trail** ★★★ Shiraz & mourvèdre mix has the advertised fynbos character in **16** ⑧, plus dark fruit, savoury spice, dried herbs, supple tannins. Occasional release. Discontinued: **Merlot**, **Pinotage Grand Reserve**, **Caap Ensemble**, **Buchu Berg**, **The Homestead**, **Merlot-Mourvèdre**, **Ruby Blanc**.

Swanepoel range 🆕

Syrah Rosé ★★ Bright, breezy & trim-figured (12.5% alcohol) **18** ⑦ pretty pink, dry & perfect for hot summer afternoons. From shiraz. — CR, CvZ

Location/map/WO: Tulbagh ▪ Map grid reference: F4 ▪ Est 1995 ▪ 1stB 2003 ▪ Tasting, sales & cellar tours by appt ▪ Guest accommodation ▪ Hiking trails ▪ Owner(s) Jerry Swanepoel Family Trust ▪ Cellarmaster(s)/winemaker(s)/viticulturist(s) Dirk Swanepoel (2018) ▪ 235ha/10ha (cab, grenache, mourv, ptage, shiraz) ▪ 50t/5,000cs own label 85% red 15% rosé ▪ Other export brands: Buchu Trail ▪ PO Box 11 Tulbagh 6820 ▪ swanepoel@compagnies.co.za ▪ S 33° 14' 56.9" E 019° 6' 49.1" ▪ 🌐 markers.souk.wrecked ▪ **T +27 (0)76-013-8613**

Oude Denneboom

Members of the Kaapse Familie Wingerde collaboration (with Vendôme and Kuyperskraal), the eco-minded De Waal family add 'Black Harrier' to the name of their shiraz in exceptional years, and current '16 is such a vintage. Luxury accommodation is available in self-catering cottages, and there is a small tasting venue for guests on the Voor Paardeberg estate, where De Waals have farmed for 140 years.

★★★★ **Black Harrier Shiraz** Ripe, fruity, **16** ⑧ spicy berries, clove, fynbos & hedgerow fruit on nose & palate; well balanced, smooth; the lovely fresh grip begs to be paired with grilled meat. WO Paarl. No **15**.

Chenin Blanc ⊘ 🍷 ★★★★ Unoaked **18** ⑧ preview is all apple & stonefruit deliciousness, the flavours vivacious & bright, the farewell citrus-laced & zingy, the price a bargain. — WB

Location/map: Paarl ▪ Map grid reference: C2 ▪ WO: Coastal/Paarl ▪ 1stB 2003 ▪ Tasting by appt; also available at Vendôme ▪ 4-star self-catering cottages ▪ Private game reserve ▪ Owner(s) De Waal family ▪ GM Willem de Waal ▪ Winemaker(s) Altus le Roux (consultant) ▪ Viticulturist(s) Willem de Waal ▪ 199ha/±62ha (cab, mourv, ptage, shiraz, chenin, nouvelle, viog) ▪ 600t/1,000cs own label 60% red 40% white ▪ WIETA ▪ PO Box 2087 Windmeul 7630 ▪ info@oudedenneboom.co.za ▪ www.oudedenneboom.co.za, www.kaapsefami-liewingerde.com ▪ S 33° 37′ 47.28″ E 018° 51′ 55.08″ ▪ 🖾 granules.hawking.remainder ▪ F +27 (0)86-552-2695 ▪ T +27 (0)21-869-8072/+27 (0)83-357-9756

☐ **Oude Kaap** *see* DGB (Pty) Ltd

Oudekloof Winery

History, arts and local culture are celebrated at mountainside winery Oudekloof - the very name a reference to a ravine that first gave access to Tulbagh Valley. Also on the property are some 17 ha of vines, including very old chenin, which are the source of a range of 'serious wines by not so serious people' - the latter being Andrew Jaeger and his wife Christine - transplants from the Free State who, in fact, are serious - about protecting a substantial 200 ha of indigenous vegetation and bringing the old farm and its spirit back to life.

Map: Tulbagh ▪ Map grid reference: F5 ▪ Est/1stB 2005 ▪ Tasting & sales Mon-Sun 10-3, or by arrange-ment ▪ Tasting fee R45, waived on purchase of 3 or more bottles ▪ Closed Easter Fri/Sun, Dec 25 & Jan 1 ▪ Refreshments available; meals on arrangement for tour groups & special occasions ▪ Facilities for children ▪ Tour groups ▪ Gift shop ▪ Farm produce ▪ Conference facility ▪ Hiking & MTB trails ▪ Tractor rides & historic tours ▪ Art/cultural exhibition ▪ Self-catering cottages ▪ Owner(s) 2 shareholders ▪ Cellarmaster(s) Andrew & Christine Jaeger (Jun 2015) ▪ Winemaker(s) Andrew & Christine Jaeger (Dec 2013) ▪ 420ha/17ha (cab, shiraz, chard, chenin) ▪ 400t/6,000cs own label 50% red 50% white ▪ PO Box 191 Tulbagh 6820 ▪ info@oudekloofwineestate.co.za ▪ www.oudekloofwineestate.co.za ▪ S 33° 16′ 5.72″ E 019° 4′ 29.21″ ▪ 🖾 surgeons.neutrals.draping ▪ T +27 (0)82-440-9459

Oude Meester

Venerable Oude Meester brandy was launched over 70 years ago, heralding the arrival of Distillers Corp (now Distell) as one of SA's leading producer-wholesalers. The four current bottlings, to be discontinued as stocks run out, showcase the array of styles a master distiller achieves through blending and barrel maturing over different timespans.

★★★★★ **Souverein** Ⓐ A fairly recent label & amongst the elite of the Cape's older potstill brandies - minimum 18 years in oak. Lightish amber colour to yellow rim. Thrilling floral & spice notes, more delicate than Reserve, even more complex. Not a roughness or jagged edge. Serene, silken, very long.

★★★★★ **Demant** Ⓐ Fine value offered with this 3-10 year matured potstill brandy, introduced in 2006 to celebrate Distell's diamond jubilee. Stressing a fresh, lighter elegance rather than full richness, like all in this range. Satisfying blend of maturing floral notes along with fruitier youthful ones.

★★★★☆ **Reserve 12 Year Old** Ⓐ Molten gold colour. Aromas suggest some development - nutty & spicy along with fruit & honeysuckle. Fuller, richer than Demant, as elegant & dry, with restrained oak backing. Complex, lingering, mellow finish.

VSOB Ⓐ ★★★☆ Standard blended brandy, first step of a ladder of quality in this range. Good fruity nose & palate, some dry oak & sweet forcefulness. Great for mixing, but possible to sip solo. — WB, TJ

Oude Molen Distillery

This famous distillery was founded over a century back in Stellenbosch but is now based in Elgin — where visitors can now enjoy an interactive distillery tour. Oude Molen's founding distiller, French-born René Santhagens, played a crucial role in the history of Cape spirits, encouraging superior brandy-making based on double distillation in copper potstills. The French connection has been reinforced by Oude Molen using the traditional Cognac labels VS, VSOP and XO to distinguish quality for their potstill brandies.

★★★★ **VSOP Cape Brandy** Ⓐ 5 years minimum barrel ageing adds refinement to the aromas & flavours of candied orange-peel & nuts - even a choc hint on the subtle caramel sweetness. Intense, lingering fruitiness.

★★★★☆ **XO Cape Brandy** Ⓐ Hints of floral aromatic gracefulness over more typical peach, dried pear & coconut - but in fact a range of ripe fruit discernible. From brandies aged 10-16 years, it shows added elegance & lifted refinement, with a gratifying soft, sweet-tinged smoothness.

VS Cape Brandy ⊘ ★★★★ Minimum 3 years aged in a solera system. More complex & subtle than blended brandy of this age, more elegantly refined, with a creamy sweetness. Smooth & interesting enough for solo sipping. Pushes higher rating. 40% alcohol. — TJ

Location/map: Elgin ▪ Map grid reference: B1 ▪ Tastings Mon-Fri 11-4 (booking advisable) ▪ Fee R85pp ▪ Sales Mon-Fri 11-5 ▪ Closed all pub hols ▪ Interactive distillery tour ▪ Tour groups ▪ MD Andre Simonis ▪ Brandy master(s) Kobus Gelderblom (Jun 2013, consultant), with Andy Neil & Lara Patrick ▪ PO Box 494 Grabouw 7160 ▪ info@oudemolen.co.za ▪ www.oudemolen.co.za ▪ S 34° 8' 27.77" E 019° 1' 15.64" ▪ ⌕ fines.moisture. passport ▪ F +27 (0)21-859-3192 ▪ **T +27 (0)21-859-2517**

☐ **Oude Rust** see Mooiuitsig Wine Cellars
☐ **Oulap** see Mooiuitsig Wine Cellars
☐ **Out of Africa** see Jacques Germanier
☐ **Ovation** see Thokozani Wines
☐ **Overberg** see Mooiuitsig Wine Cellars

Overgaauw Wine Estate ⓥ ⑪ ⑤

Quoted in the 1995 edition of this guide, Braam van Velden said: 'In the end the vineyard, not fashion, dictates the variety.' Patriarch and winemaker for several decades at this Stellenboschkloof property, in the family for more than 100 years, Braam knows a thing or two about starting fashions, Overgaauw having bottled the Cape's first varietal merlot, some of the first chardonnay and still the only sylvaner, and pioneered the use of Portuguese grapes for its 'port' (especially significant given the 5-star rating this edition for the Cape Vintage, made by Braam). Now the path-breaking is done, and the 'foreign' varieties have a home on the estate, his son and current winemaker David is charting a steady course.

★★★★☆ **Tria Corda** ⊘ Serious **14** ⑼ echoes **13** ⑼ in needing time to show full beauty of cab, merlot & cab franc blend. Nuanced, savoury cherry/cassis generosity on elegant, balanced frame of oak, 60% new. Long, rich & rewarding.

★★★★☆ **Cape Vintage** ⑱ Classic, superbly dry, vibrantly spicy & rich **98** ★★★★★ ⑼'port' calls on touriga nacional & equal tintas barocca & roriz, touriga franca, souzão & cornifesto for complexity. Bold & nutty, it's structured from 30 months in 1,300L vats. Good for further half-decade. Last tasted was **96** ⑼.

Touriga Nacional ⊘ ★★★★ Bright cherry verve on **15** ⑻, noticeable grape tannin grip & spice, yet smooth, succulent. **Shepherd's Cottage Cabernet Sauvignon-Merlot** ★★★★ Light-bodied but cassis-packed **17** ⑻, 60/40 mix has ample appeal, oaked third (all old) frames fruit well. **Shepherd's Cottage Sauvignon Blanc** ★★★ Light, bright & zesty **18** ⑻ tank sample shows grapefruit & melon zip, lean & focused. **Sylvaner** ⊘ ★★★★ Unique varietal bottling in SA. Unoaked **16** ⑻ lightly floral, dry, with apple vibrancy, flinty-mineral tail. — FM

Location/map/WO: Stellenbosch ▪ Map grid reference: D5 ▪ Est 1905 ▪ 1stB 1970 ▪ Tasting by appt only Wed & Fri at 11 ▪ Closed Easter Fri-Mon, Dec 25/26 & Jan 1 ▪ Restaurant open for lunch Fri-Sun from 12.30 (Sep-Apr only) T +27 (0)83-651-4003, booking essential ▪ Owner(s) Braam & David van Velden ▪ Winemaker(s) David van Velden (Jan 2003) ▪ Viticulturist(s) David van Velden ▪ 100ha/60ha (cabs s/f, merlot, ptage, touriga, chard, sauv, sylvaner) ▪ 60% red 40% white ▪ Other export brand: Sandrivier ▪ HACCP, IPW ▪ PO Box 3 Vlottenburg 7604 ▪ info@overgaauw.co.za, restaurant@overgaauw.co.za, venue@overgaauw.co.za ▪ www. overgaauw.co.za ▪ S 33° 56' 52.1" E 018° 47' 33.4" ▪ ⌕ passport.groomed.suitcase ▪ **T +27 (0)21-881-3815**

Overhex Wines International ⓥ ⑪ ⓸ ⑤ ⑤

There are some seriously creative marketing minds and winemakers at this globally operating, Worcester-based wine business. Without taking their eye off the serious quality ball, clearly evident in their Survivor range, the team continue to be on top of their game. Their new Mensa line-up of pocket-friendly, engaging wines sees technology at work in both the Helix cork closures and augmented reality app which brings the wines' intriguing labels and backstory to life. Their other ranges, spanning the full spectrum of varieties and styles, are all well-priced and balanced, for friendly drinkability.

Survivor range

★★★★ **Cabernet Sauvignon** Appealing smoky cassis & spice introduction. Dry, supple creamy tannins, **17** ⑧⑨ full bodied, bold & spicy but fresh. Well-crafted step up on **16** ★★★★ ⑧⑤. Similarly made to Pinotage & aged 15 months, but 10% new oak. These WO Swartland unless noted.

★★★★ **Pinotage** Some high-toned berry flavours & spicy oak nuances on **17** ⑧⑥ despite less new wood than **16** ⑧⑥ (now 20%, 15 months). Appears brisker, with herbaceous nuance & dry farewell. Needs some time to harmonise.

★★★★ **Wild Yeast Chardonnay** Fermented in 100% new oak, aged 11 months in barrel, thus wood dominates more demure **17** ⑧⑥ fruit profile. Fresh lime & pear with butterscotch underpinning. Time will resolve, but will always be for fans of oaky styles. WO W Cape.

★★★★ **Chenin Blanc** ⊘ Infused with ripe yellow peach flavours, **18** ⑧⑨ good fruit/oak harmony (70% fermented/aged in new wood). Dry & tangy, well crafted though shade less impressive than **17** ★★★★☆ ⑨④.

★★★★ **Sauvignon Blanc** ⊘ Colour & dried fruit/grass profile on **18** ⑧⑥ reflect drier vintage. Dry, smooth textured, touch of grapefruit on feisty, pithy, food-inclined finish. Part oak-fermented & -matured. Not tasted: **Méthode Cap Classique Brut**. Discontinued: **Merlot-Cabernet Sauvignon**.

Survivor Offspring range

Cape White Blend ⑪ ★★★☆ Ripe apple & stonefruit flavours from mix chenin, sauvignon, viognier. **17** ⑧⑤ quite rich but lovely crunchy texture too, vivacious balance.

Cape Red Blend ★★★ Similar blend & styling to previous, **17** ⑧⓪ pinotage/shiraz & 20% cab with earthy & savoury notes, some pinotage high tones. Tannins firm, acidity brisk, spicy-toasty overlay from oak staves.

Limited Edition range

Cinsault ② ★★★ Unoaked **16** ⑧① 's translucent ruby hue foreshadows lightish body, juicy, tangy cranberry & sweet tobacco notes; delightful quaffing, also lightly chilled. **Malbec** ⊘ ★★★☆ Showing good varietal character - spiced wild berry fruit - in a lithe tannin structure. **17** ⑧⑤ quite debonair, good with food, also satisfying solo. WO Swartland, as next. **Pinot Grigio** ★★★ Ultra-light, delicately flavoured **18** ⑧⓪, sherbet, starfruit & hint jasmine notes, smooth but crisp, modest 12.5% alcohol.

Balance Winemaker's Selection

Pinot Noir ⊘ ⑪ ★★★ Juicy step up, & poster child for the 'balance' in the range branding, **17** ⑧② 's perfumed red berry fruit in lovely harmony with the supple structure. Fresh, very appealing summer quaffer.

Cabernet Sauvignon ⊘ ★★★ Distinct cocoa flavour with touch tannin to structure juicy dark fruit, nice freshness too. **17** ⑧① good barbecue/campfire partner. **Merlot** ⊘ ★★★ Spiced berry tones on **17** ⑧①, fresh & friendly for early drinking. Like Pinot, more substance & balance than others in this range. **Shiraz** ⊘ ★★★ Uncomplicated laid-back drinkability in **17** ⑧⓪, spicy-sweet tobacco & earth notes, dry but juicy. **Chardonnay** ⊘ ★★★ Stewed apple & almond on unoaked **18** ⑧②, smooth, plump & creamy, twist of lime helps freshen the finish. **Chenin Blanc** ⊘ ★★★☆ Crunchy ripe apple & yellow peach flavours on **18** ⑧③, smooth texture from lees ageing, dry & flavoursome, slips down easily. **Sauvignon Blanc** ★★★ Bright tropical aromas on **18** ⑦⑨, less intense & flavoursome on palate than previous but pleasantly light & crisp. Not tasted: **Pinotage**. Discontinued: **Pinot Grigio**.

Mensa range ⑭

Chenin Blanc-Pinot Grigio ⑪ ★★★★ Bright start to this new range. Unusual blend, **18** ⑧④ crisp, tangy, dried yellow peach flavours & creaminess from lees contact. Balancing drop sugar (as most here) enhances juicy appeal.

Cabernet Sauvignon ★★★ Balanced & juicy **17** ⑧②, ready to enjoy in an armchair with a good book. **Shiraz-Malbec** ★★★ Another uncommon blend, leads with juicy, savoury & spicy fruit compote notes, **17** ⑧② sleek & rounded, comforting & flavoursome for immediate enjoyment. **Chardonnay-Pinot Noir** ★★★ Delicate orange blush on **18** ⑧① rosé (80/20 blend), stonefruit & cranberry flavours, dry but succulent, with balancing fresh twist of lime. **Sauvignon Blanc** ★★★ Friendly, tropical & creamy style. **18** ⑦⑨ similar flavours to Winemaker's sibling though this has lower alcohol & sugar (in fact, the driest in this range).

Balance Classic range

Cabernet Sauvignon-Merlot ⊘ ★★★ Fresh & cheery **17** ⑦ deftly juggles tannins & savoury red berries, tad lighter fruit intensity than last, & unoaked (as all these). **Shiraz Rosé** ⊘ ★★★ Spicy rosepetal flavours, crisp & dry, hint of cranberry tartness to freshen the tail. **18** ⑦ sunset special at lowish 12.5% alcohol. **Semi-Sweet Muscat** ⊘ ★★★ Gentle, fragrant semi-sweet from muscat d'Alexandrie. **17** ⑦ smooth, uncloying & sippable at modest 12% alcohol. Good with spicy Asian dishes/curries too. **Sauvignon Blanc-Semillon** ★★ Dried grass & waxy nuance on **18** ⑦, with lightish 12.5% alcohol. Amiable summer sipping from crisp 80/20 blend. Not tasted: **Pinotage-Shiraz, Shiraz-Merlot, Chenin Blanc-Colombar.** Discontinued: **Chardonnay-Pinot Noir.**

Balance Sparklings

Sweet Temptation Sparkling ★★ Sweet strawberry pink fizz from pinotage, **NV** ⑦ friendly fun for the sweeter toothed, at a low 8% alcohol. **Boldly Brut Sparkling** ★★★ From sauvignon, dry styled, but plenty sweet green herb/starfruit flavour & fizz to ensure **NV** ⑦ will have many fans this summer. — MW

Location/map: Worcester ▪ Map grid reference: B3 ▪ WO: Western Cape/Swartland ▪ Est/1stB 2006 ▪ Tasting & sales Mon-Thu 8–5 Fri 8-4 Sat/Sun 9-4 ▪ Closed Easter Fri-Tue & Dec 22-Jan 3 ▪ Cellar tours by appt ▪ Overhex Winery & Bistro Wed-Sun 10-4 ▪ Facilities for children ▪ Tour groups ▪ Conferences (30 pax) ▪ Weddings & functions ▪ Owner(s) G van der Wath ▪ GM Gert van Wyk ▪ Winemaker(s) Willie Malan (2002) & Ben Snyman (Dec 2010), with Dirk Rust (Jan 2012) & Heinrich Carstens (Jan 2014) ▪ Viticulturist(s) Dirk Bosman & Hennie Visser ▪ 12,500t 36% red 61% white 3% rosé ▪ ISO 22000, Fairtrade, IPW, WIETA ▪ PO Box 139 Worcester 6849 ▪ marketing@overhex.com ▪ www.overhex.com ▪ S 33° 39' 28.6" E 019° 30' 55.8" ▪ ⌨ patrol.cross.surfed ▪ F +27 (0)23-347-1057 ▪ **T +27 (0)23-347-5012**

Overmeer Cellars

Enduring (since 1986) no-frills range by Distell, with modest alcohol levels. In 3L & 5L packs.

Red ⓥ ★★ Mixed red berries, **NV** ⑦ smooth & round, easy. **Sweet Rosé** ⓥ ★★ Bright pink, berry-scented & -flavoured **NV** ⑦ satisfyingly sweet. **Grand Cru** ⓥ ★★ Summer fruit salad flavours, dry, easy-drinking **NV** ⑦ **Stein** ⓥ ★★ Apples & pears, curvy body, fruity-sweet **NV** ⑦. **Late Harvest** ⓥ ★★ Soft-textured & sweet **NV** ⑦, general fruit salad flavours. — CR

☐ **Over the Mountain** see Seven Springs Vineyards

☐ **Owl & Vine** see Alphabetical

PaardenKloof ⓥ ⑪ ◎ ⓐ

Three rivers form the borders of the large PaardenKloof home-farm in Walker Bay, and within those bounds, the owners say they allow nature to run its course. Only a fraction of the 1,430 hectares is planted with vines, so there's room aplenty for the additional five hectares established recently. The wines, by top consultants, are available at a nearby venue on the R43 Hermanus-Bot River road, with many family-friendly amenities.

PaardenKloof Private Collection

★★★★☆ **Die Fynboshuis Cabernet Sauvignon** ⓥ Sumptuous & concentrated red berry fruit, exotic dried flower aromas & flavours on **10** ⑨②, with outstanding structure & dimension.

Springtide Sauvignon Blanc ⓝⒺⓦ ★★★★ Vivid & tangy grapefruit, fynbos & granadilla, **17** ⑧④ broad on palate with long flinty tail.

Peter Clarke Collection

★★★★ **The Kiss Pinot Noir** ⓝⒺⓦ Eight months in 20% new French oak & further 50 months in bottle result in seamless integration of bright acidity, spicy cherry fruit & deeper oak notes on **13** ⑧⑦.

★★★★ **The Long Road Shiraz** ⓥ Aromatic plum, fynbos & white pepper aromas on **10** ⑧⑦. Perfectly judged oak provides framework for lush, bright fruit, rounded mouthfeel & restraint.

★★★★ **Bend In The Road Sauvignon Blanc** ⓥ Cool-climate expression, **14** ⑧⑧ with lime & grapefruit; bright & focused flavours, refreshing orchard & fynbos notes with piquant conclusion.

Gaiety Sauvignon Blanc ⓥ ★★★ Gunsmoke whiffs, attractive gravelly minerality, **10** ⑧① lightly flavoured so acidity is apparent.

Ecology range

★★★★ **Cabernet Sauvignon** ⓥ Fynbos nuances to structured, gentle succulence on **14** ⑧⑥; shows good intensity; long, fruity, tobacco-tinged tail.

Shiraz ⓥ ★★★★ Blueberry ease & plushness on **14** ⑧⑤, juicy black fruit framed by soft squeeze of tannin from 25% new oak. **Sauvignon Blanc** ⓥ ★★★ Tropical fruit balances bright lime zest styling on **15** ⑧⓪ single vineyard newcomer. — FM

Location/WO: Bot River ▪ Map: Walker Bay & Bot River ▪ Map grid reference: C3 C2 ▪ Est 2003 ▪ 1stB 2007 ▪ PaardenKloof & Ecology wines: tasting & sales at Ecology Lifestyle Farm Mon-Sun 9-5; PaardenKloof estate visits by appt ▪ Garden Restaurant Wed-Sun 9-5 ▪ Farmyard animals & jungle gym ▪ Wedding venue ▪ Day conference venue ▪ Tour groups ▪ Protea & fynbos nursery ▪ Decor service ▪ Farmstall ▪ Craft beer ▪ Winemaker(s) Kobie Viljoen, Niels Verburg & Adam Mason ▪ Viticulturist(s) Kevin Watt (Dec 2006) ▪ 23.6ha (cab, pinot, shiraz, sauv) ▪ IPW, WIETA ▪ PO Box 381 Bot River 7185 ▪ info@paardenkloof.co.za, info@ ecologylifestyle.co.za ▪ www.paardenkloof.co.za, www.ecologylifestyle.co.za ▪ S 34° 17' 44.1" E 019° 14' 5.4" (PaardenKloof), S 34° 15' 39.98" E 019° 11' 04.96" (Ecology Lifestyle Farm) ▪ ⌖ strongholds.sparrows.rumpled ▪ **T +27 (0)28-284-9824 (PaardenKloof)/+27 (0)28-284-9809 (Ecology Lifestyle Farm)**

☐ **Paarl Families** *see* Kaapse Familie Wingerde

Paarl Perlé

Fifty years ago, when lightly fizzy wines were the thing, Distillers Corporation's Paarl Perlé was the much-emulated star. The brand retains its dulcet palate-prickling character under Distillers' successor, Distell.

Paarl Perlé ★★ Unchanging style, blend of white varieties. Uncomplicated, grapey & gently sweet, **NV** ⑦③ a softly bubbly party starter. Also in 1 & 2L. — CR, CvZ

Packwood Wines   ⓥ ⑪ ⌂ ⓞ

Owned by UK émigrés Peter and Vicky Gent, Packwood country estate on the cool-climate Garden Route has luxury accommodation, an informal restaurant serving cheese-and-wine lunches and a small vineyard, tended by Vicky herself. She also makes the wines, and this edition the chardonnay grapes, previously vinified for her MCC sparkling, get a solo turn in the limelight.

★★★★ **Sauvignon Blanc** Intense maritime-climate green aromas, including tinned pea, zesty acidity softened by grain sugar, modest 12% alcohol: **17** ⑧⑥ hits the spot for summer lunches. **16** untasted.

Chardonnay ⓝⓔⓦ ★★★ Lightly wooded **17** ⑧① has nut & marzipan nuances, cool-grown acidic bounce to leaven the creamy texture & hint of sweetness. Not tasted: **Pinot Noir, Blanc de Noir, Pinot Noir Rosé, Gent Méthode Cap Classique**. — CvZ

Location/WO: Plettenberg Bay ▪ Map: Klein Karoo & Garden Route ▪ Map grid reference: C1 ▪ Est 2006 ▪ 1stB 2009 ▪ Tasting & sales Mon-Fri 11-3 Sat/Sun 10-3 pub hols by prior arrangement ▪ Cheese & wine lunch - book ahead ▪ Small tour groups by appt ▪ Farm produce ▪ Hikes ▪ MTB trail ▪ 4-star country house & self-catering cottages ▪ Owner(s) Peter & Vicky Gent ▪ Winemaker(s) Vicky Gent ▪ Viticulturist(s) Vicky Gent (Jan 2006) ▪ 380ha/3.5ha (pinot, chard, sauv) ▪ 5t/10,000cs own label 30% red 70% white ▪ PO Box 622 Knysna 6570 ▪ vicky@packwood.co.za ▪ www.packwood.co.za ▪ S 34° 0' 18.77" E 023° 13' 43.33" ▪ ⌖ signposts.visiting.zing ▪ **T +27 (0)82-253-9621**

☐ **Pactolus Collection** *see* Glen Carlou
☐ **Paddagang** *see* Tulbagh Winery
☐ **Painted Dog** *see* Painted Wolf Wines

Painted Wolf Wines   ⓥ ⑪

This 'pack' dedicated to helping conserve the Painted Wolf (African Wild Dog) while producing 'wines with character that offer fair value across the board' has a new tasting 'den' on Paarl's Main Road. But Jeremy and Emma Borg continue to roam widely, in 2018 sourcing grapes from Walker Bay and Franschhoek to supplement fruit from their drought-affected Swartland business partner, not to mention spreading their global brand pawprint as far as Russia and Holland - great news for conservation partners including SA's Endangered Wildlife Trust, Britain's TUSK and Children in the Wilderness, who receive up to 5% of turnover.

Pictus range

★★★★☆ IV ⓥ Flagship blend of Swartland shiraz, grenache & mourvèdre. 12 ⑧⑦ combines power & charm in succulent, rich-fruited & polished style. Similar to 11 ⑧⑦, which was 'Pictus III'.

★★★★☆ V ⓥ Complex, textured oaked blend of grenache blanc, chenin & roussanne, 16 ⑨① impresses with intensity of fruit, aromatic appeal & stony minerality on very long finish.

★★★★☆ VI ⓝⓔⓦ ⓐ 'Lycaon pictus' scientific name for Painted Wolf. Stellar white blend sibling to 'V' comprises 43% Agter Paarl grenache, 37% Stellenbosch chenin & organic Swartland viognier, all barrel fermented. 17 ⑨④ rich & concentrated yet fresh, elegant, layered & lingering.

Pack range

★★★★ Guillermo Swartland pinotage named after grower Billy 'Guillermo' Hughes, middleweight 15 ⑧⑨ packed with berries, subtle spice from 14 months oak, soft, slightly less elegant than 14 ★★★★★ ⑨①.

★★★★ Swartland Syrah ⓥ Black olive tapenade adds savoury intrigue to 15 ⑧⑦'s concentrated dark fruit, opulently full bodied yet not heavy, with hints of black pepper & allspice. No 14.

★★★★ Old Vine Chenin Blanc ⓥ Wild/barrel-fermented 17 ★★★★★ ⑨⓪ from two 30+ year old blocks in Paarl, creamy, complex with luscious melange melon, guava & stonefruit, touch vanilla from 15% new oak, zesty/pithy grapefruit finish, fresh acidity & pleasing 12.5% alcohol. Step up on 15 ⑧⑦. No 16.

★★★★ Paarl Roussanne ⓥ Ambient yeast ferment for mouthfilling & delicious 15 ⑧⑦, hay & waxy stonefruit, 10% new oak adds vanilla complexity to broad & expansive palate.

★★★★ Penny Viognier ⓥ Ex Swartland, organically grown, wild-yeast-fermented 14 ⑧⑦ shows exuberant fruit, creamy peach melba with supportive vanilla oak & textured mouthfeel.

In abeyance: Lycaon Grenache. Discontinued: Chenin Blanc, Roussanne.

Peloton range

★★★★ Blanc ⓥ Abundant ripe, tangy tropical fruit on balanced, focused 16 ⑧⑦, previewed multi-blend including viognier, chenin, roussanne & marsanne, deftly oaked for rich, creamy mouthfeel. No 15.

Rouge ⓥ ★★★★ Blending pinotage & Rhône grapes (also wine, wheels & wild dogs, as cyclists pedal for conservation), 15 ⑧④ very ripe, succulent red berry/cherry fruit, sweet vanilla appeal.

The Den Comfort Wines

Sauvignon Blanc ⓥ ★★★★ Nothing tart/green about tropical 17 ⑧④, blend Darling/Swartland fruit, fresh & dry but softly rounded from 15% oaked portion.

Cabernet Sauvignon ★★★ Soft, cocoa powder tannins from oak stave treatment in juicy 17 ⑧① , rounded off with soupçons malbec, merlot & cab franc. Pinotage ★★★ Calling for a partner of BBQ beef ribs or mole poblano-sauced chicken, juicy 17 ⑧② packed with ripe red cherry/berry fruit to handle spice. Shiraz ⓥ ★★★ Previewed 15 ⑧① has whiffs of smoke & mocha adding to dark fruit concentration; finishes a little abruptly. WO Paarl, as next. Pinotage Rosé ★★☆ Apricots & cranberries in 18 ⑦⑧, a little more acerbic than previous. Chenin Blanc ★★★★ Pre-bottling 18 ⑧④ tropical fruit salad flavours & leesy, creamy depth from 50% oak component. WO Swartland.

Black Pack range

In abeyance: Stellenbosch Pinotage. Discontinued: Merlot, Paarl Pinotage.

Discontinued: Cape 'Hunting' Blends, Painted Dog range. — JG

Location/map: Paarl ▪ Map grid reference: E5 ▪ WO: Coastal/Paarl/Swartland ▪ Est/1stB 2007 ▪ Tasting & sales Tue-Fri 11-4 Sat 10-2 ▪ Fee various ▪ Closed Sun/Mon, Easter Fri-Mon, Dec 25 & Jan 1 ▪ SIT Café ▪ Owner(s) Jeremy & Emma Borg, & 16 'pack members' ▪ Cellarmaster(s) Madre van der Walt ▪ Winemaker(s) Jeremy Borg ▪ 20ha (grenache, mourv, ptage, shiraz, viog) ▪ 30t/20,000cs own label 75% red 20% white 5% rosé ▪ Other export brands: Painted Dog, Jemma ▪ 125 Main Rd Paarl 7646 ▪ sales@paintedwolfwines.com ▪ www. paintedwolfwines.com ▪ S 33° 45' 9.34" E 018° 57' 44.06" ▪ ⒨ fish.graphic.chapters ▪ T +27 (0)21-863-2492

☐ Palesa Fairtrade see Daschbosch
☐ Pandora's Box see Nicholson Smith
☐ Pantére see Knorhoek Wines
☐ Papillon see Van Loveren Family Vineyards
☐ Par Excellence see David Frost Wines

Parow Brandy

Afrikaans rapper Jack Parow is a keen brandy drinker, like his 'fan demographic'. 'Brandy should be a fun and edgy drink' the thinking goes, so the packaging is wild and funny and brilliant, and the contents, developed by brandy master Kobus Gelderblom at Oude Molen, impressive for the category.

Parow Brandy (②) ★★★★ 30% potstill brandy from colombard & chenin, smooth, flavourful & unfiery enough for sipping solo - helped by dryness rare for this type. Mostly destined for mixing, however. — TJ

Location: Cape Town ▪ Closed to public ▪ Owner(s) Famous Liquors (Pty) Ltd ▪ Brandy master Kobus Gelderblom (Oude Molen Distillery) ▪ PO Box 369 Bonnievale 6730 ▪ info@parowbrandy.co.za ▪ www. parowbrandy.co.za ▪ **T** +27 (0)23-616-2010

Paserene

The name of this Franschhoek high-end boutique winery comes from Passeriformes, the order of 'travelling and free' birds that includes swallows, swifts and martins — very apt for co-owner and winemaker/viticulturist Martin Smith, who grew up in Worcester, studied at Elsenburg, then worked in California for a decade before coming home to make wine at US/SA-owned Vilafonté for six years. At Paserene, he and business partner Ndabe Mareda believe they have successfully laid the foundations. 'Now it is time to slowly but surely build the brand. Quality remains our main objective, followed closely by beautiful art and music.'

★★★★☆ **Union** (⊛) Expressive & voluptuous Rhône-style blend from Tulbagh fruit, **16** (93) red berry, violet & lavender, Xmas spice perfume from 22 months older oak, savoury truffle finish. Syrah (44%), carignan (34%) & mourvèdre.

★★★★☆ **Marathon** (⊛) Impressive three-way partnership cab (53%), petit verdot & splash rare-in-SA carmenère; **16** (94) blackcurrant, mulberry & cedar tones; like petit verdot-dominated **15** (93), tight-knit tannins for the long haul but with sufficient fruit, freshness to broach young. WO W Cape.

★★★★☆ **Chardonnay** (⊛) Multifaceted **16** (93), yellow stonefruit & citrus mélange gently accented by judicious 30% new oak. Like stellar **15** ★★★★★ (95), ex Elgin, vibrant & elegant with almond nuance & flinty minerality. — GM

Location/map: Franschhoek ▪ Map grid reference: C4 ▪ WO: Tulbagh/Elgin/Western Cape ▪ Est/1stB 2013 ▪ Tasting by appt Wed-Sun 10-5.30 ▪ Owner(s) Martin Smith & Ndabe Mareda ▪ Cellarmaster(s)/winemaker(s) Martin Smith (Jan 2013) ▪ Viticulturist(s) Martin Smith ▪ 60t/1,400cs own label 60% red 40% white ▪ Farm 1665, on R45 Franschhoek 7690 ▪ info@paserene.co.za ▪ www.paserene.co.za ▪ S 33° 52' 43.8" E 019° 3' 34.1" ▪ ⊠ endorsed.lifesavers.dunk ▪ **T** +27 (0)21-876-2714

☐ **Passions** see Cavalli Wine & Stud Farm
☐ **Patatsfontein** see Ron Burgundy Wines

Paul Cluver Estate Wines (②) (🍴) (◎) (⬤)

This fine, large estate in Elgin – or rather, its owner Paul Cluver, a neurosurgeon - pioneered commercial winefarming in the area in the late 1980s (though it remains a very substantial producer of apples too). Its success and prestige have been a vital stimulus to Elgin's development this century as a source of fine wines. Dr Cluver has long since pulled back, leaving the next generation of the family firmly ensconced, with four of the five siblings fully involved (Paul jnr energetically in charge), and son-in-law Andries Burger cellarmaster since 1996. Apart from pinot noir, only white wines are made on the estate, all of them tending to the classic in style, and all benchmarks of their varieties. Environmental and social sustainability remain a vital concern.

CWG Auction Reserve range

★★★★★ **The Wagon Trail Chardonnay** (⊛) Despite modest 12.9% alcohol, bone-dry palate & racy acidity (only 10% malo), sleek & pure **17** (93) offers opulent peach, nectarine, apple & almond complexity, richness. Bunch-pressed block selection, natural fermented in oak, 23% new.

Estate range

★★★★ **Pinot Noir** (⊛) Lively sour cherry & strawberry nuances, lacy spice & savoury edge. **17** (88) variety's elevated acidity, fine-grained tannin & subtle oak detail from year 32% new oak.

★★★★☆ **Seven Flags Pinot Noir** ⓐ Best barrels for flagship red, month less in oak than siblings, larger new component, 38% in vibrant **16** ⑨③. Old World allure of wet earth & truffles, beautifully polished tannins, delicious red-fruit farewell. Also in magnum.

★★★★☆ **Chardonnay** ⓐ Beguiling honey, nectarine & kumquat nuances on striking **17** ⑨④, gorgeous satin texture, richness from wild ferment in barrel, purity & vivacity enhanced by cool-climate acidity.

★★★★☆ **Seven Flags Chardonnay** ⓐ Fine mineral core & precise acid-fruit tension among hallmarks of this flagship white. Site & natural ferment in oak both contribute to **17** ⑨④'s richness, texture & complexity, judicious 8 months 31% new barrels roughly equal to sibling.

★★★★ **Dry Encounter Riesling** ⓠ Pure & linear **16** ★★★★★ ⑨② trumps **15** ⑧⑦ with exuberant lemon & lime zest, firm streak of minerality, 20% portion aged 15 months in older barrels for weight to marmalade-scented & creamy palate.

★★★★☆ **Riesling** ⓝⒺⓦ ⊘ ⓐ Hits the spot between former Close & Dry Encounter bottlings. Clean-cut **17** ⑨③ alluring blossom fragrance, racy acidity deftly underpinned by gentle sweetness & steely minerality. Small oaked portion plumps out light body (10.9% alcohol).

★★★★☆ **Sauvignon Blanc** ⊘ ⓐ Increased lees stirring regime, dash lightly oaked semillon, several different yeast strains (for the first time) all add depth, complexity, to streamlined **18** ⑨③. Cool notes accented by gooseberry, apple & lime.

★★★★☆ **Riesling Noble Late Harvest** ⓐ Study in effortless harmony & complexity, **17** ★★★★★ ⑨⑤'s 190 g/l sweetness, pineapple & yellow stonefruit succulence neatly tucked in by almost impossibly precise acidity, while honey, citrus blossom & jasmine lift the tropical tones. First tasted since **14** ⑨③.

- - - - - - - - - -

Village Pinot Noir ⊘ ⓣ ★★★★ Satisfying, well-priced 'everyday' pinot from younger vines, lively **17** ⑧④'s cherry & spice appeal topped by ripe, snappy tannin farewell.

- - - - - - - - - -

Discontinued: **Gewürztraminer**, **Close Encounter Riesling**. — GM

Location/map/WO: Elgin ▪ Map grid reference: C2 ▪ Est 1896 ▪ 1stB 1997 ▪ Tasting & sales Mon-Fri 9-5 Sat/Sun 9-4 (summer) & 10-4 (winter); tasting centre closed Sun for period of 12 weeks in winter (Jul-18 Sep), phone ahead to confirm ▪ Fee R50-60pp; groups by appt only ▪ Closed Easter weekend, Dec 25/26 & Jan 1 ▪ Conservation area (part of Kogelberg Biosphere UNESCO heritage site) ▪ MTB track & bike park open to public, fee payable ▪ Salt@Paul Cluver restaurant T +27 (0)21-844-0012, saltatpaulcluver@gmail.com, booking essential ▪ Owner(s) Cluver family ▪ Cellarmaster(s) Andries Burger (Nov 1996) ▪ Winemaker(s) Andries Burger (Nov 1996), with Anne van Heerden (Dec 2016) ▪ Viticulturist(s) Rudi Zandberg (Dec 2013) ▪ 80ha (pinot, chard, riesling, sauv) ▪ 20% red 80% white ▪ Brands for clients: Woolworths, ScruCap ▪ WWF-SA Conservation Champion ▪ PO Box 48 Grabouw 7160 ▪ info@cluver.com ▪ www.cluver.com ▪ S 34° 10' 7.25" E 019° 5' 9.35" ▪ 🖵 uphill.crested.strop ▪ T +27 (0)21-844-0605

☐ **Paul de Villiers** see Landskroon Wines
☐ **Paulina's Reserve** see Rickety Bridge Winery
☐ **Paul René** see Wonderfontein

Paul Roos Farming   ⓠ

Educational benevolence, as the wine names ('Philanthropist' and 'School Principal') suggest, is central to the 'empowerment' wine brand off Tjuks and Johan Roos's long-established Helderberg farm: 'Building South Africa one child at a time' is the evocative slogan. The name of their late relative, Paul Roos, is also attached to a renowned Stellenbosch school. But it is wine excellence that has led to local and international expansion of the brand, while the winemaking has now moved to a new, but adjacent cellar. A once-off red blend has been created as tribute to co-founder Susan Roos, who died in the year the grapes ripened.

★★★★☆ **Die Filantroop** ⓐ Shiraz-based blend as usual, with cab, merlot & pinotage in **16** ⑨①. Confident presence, with just 13% alcohol, & a touch lighter than previous, but still a ripe, sweet hint. Well balanced, firmly structured, supported by unobtrusive oak - 20% new. All these will benefit from keeping.

★★★★☆ **Susan** ⓝⒺⓦ This **16** ⑨① a once-off tribute to Susan Roos, with Filantroop's varieties but cab now in the lead (64%). Tobacco aromas & more obvious sweet fruit is the result - perhaps more immediately charming too, but still a very serious structure.

★★★★☆ **Die Skoolhoof** Chenin with 18% chardonnay adding a lemony note in **17** (92), but maintaining the distinctive earthy tinge to the good fruit. Lively & fresh, with good (natural) acidity, but also weight & texture; sweet-fruited elegance & dry, lingering finish. Native yeasts for all these.— TJ

Location/WO: Stellenbosch ▪ Map: Helderberg ▪ Map grid reference: C1 ▪ Est 2008 ▪ 1stB 2014 ▪ Tasting, sales & cellar tours by appt ▪ Owner(s) Tjuks & Johan Roos, Paul Roos Farming Trust ▪ Winemaker(s) Augustus Dale (Jun 2012), with Ricardo Adams (1998) ▪ Viticulturist(s) Piet Adams (1974), with Jan Julius ▪ 24ha/18ha (cab, merlot, ptage, shiraz, chard, chenin) ▪ 7t/±800cs own label 40% red 60% white ▪ IPW, GlobalGAP, WIETA ▪ PO Box 397 Stellenbosch 7599 ▪ info@paulrooswine.com ▪ www.paulrooswine.com ▪ S 34° 0' 57.5" E 018° 49' 2.6" ▪ keyboards.barometers.activates ▪ F +27 (0)86-645-6706 ▪ **T +27 (0)21-855-3628**

Paul Wallace Wines

Confinement to the veranda of the cool-climate family farm in Elgin after ankle surgery was no hindrance for top consultant viticulturist and boutique vintner Paul Wallace. Tasting room visitors were regaled with wine, charm and bonhomie, while Paul kept an eye on trellising of last year's vines and new malbec plantings. Ever-efficient and equally convivial wife and co-owner Nicky juggled marketing, business and weekend-cottage admin, and ensured their two winemaker sons were kept in the loop.

★★★★ **Black Dog Malbec** Plush black-fruit appeal of **16** (89) is true to form; subtle tannin grip & spice from 19 months French oak. Juicy & elegant.

★★★★ **Brave Heart Pinot Noir** Loamy earthiness keeps cherry tang from tartness on **16** (86), with seamless oak, 20% new, supple & pliant texture. Takes a step up on **15** ★★★☆ (84).

★★★★ **Crackerjack** Merlot-led Bordeaux blend last seen in **10** (87). **16** (88) typical fruitcake flavour lifted by fresh acid & subtly spicy, well-knit oak (22% new). Some non-estate fruit.

★★★★☆ **Reflection Chardonnay** Rounded citrus typicity on **17** (93). Soft-textured, silky cream notes from 20% new oak that cradles fruit elegantly, improving on **16** ★★★☆ (83). Grapes from nearby property.

Little Flirt Sauvignon Blanc ★★★☆ Keeps granadilla tropicality & zippy lemon lightness of previous. **17** (85) good character & length. **The Nix Noble Late Harvest** Await new vintage. — FM, CR

Location/map/WO: Elgin ▪ Map grid reference: C3 ▪ Est/1stB 2004 ▪ Tasting facility open Saturdays, other days by appt or when open sign is displayed ▪ Tasting fee R50, waived on purchase ▪ Chocolate & wine pairing ▪ Self-catering accommodation ▪ Owner(s) Paul & Nicky Wallace ▪ Winemaker(s) Paul Wallace, advised by various other winemakers ▪ Viticulturist(s) Paul Wallace ▪ 25ha/12.5ha (cab f, malbec, pinot, chard, sauv) ▪ 120t/6,000cs own label 60% red 40% white ▪ IPW ▪ PO Box 141 Elgin 7180 ▪ nicky@paulwallacewines.co.za ▪ www.paulwallacewines.co.za ▪ S 34° 12' 58.67" E 019° 03' 32.18 ▪ marigolds.ordinate.blondie ▪ F +27 (0)86-646-3694 ▪ **T +27 (0)21-848-9744/+27 (0)83-255-1884/+27 (0)82-572-1406**

☐ **Pavillion** *see* Boschendal Wines
☐ **Peacock Wild Ferment** *see* False Bay Vineyards
☐ **Pearce Predhomme** *see* Radford Dale

Pearl Mountain

Having established the family winery on Paarl Mountain's slopes, Graham Retief now has his three sons involved to 'keep the ball rolling'. A little tweaking of the line-up has been done, and the Retief range is now 'Pearl Mountain' with a new chenin added. The second, easy-drinking range continues, its name borrowed from the French rétif ('impatient, restless, stubborn'). David Retief extends a standing invitation to stop in: 'Along with the wines, the views from our farmyard and restaurant stoep make a visit worthwhile!'

Pearl Mountain range

★★★★ **Wagon Trail Shiraz** Brawny, meaty **16** (86) shows promise, with thick, powdery tannins well balanced by plum pudding fruit, tarry notes. Give it time to integrate. Also in magnum.

★★★★ **Avis Chardonnay** Fruit draped in heavy oak mantle (70% new), showing toasted nuts, vanilla & bready notes. Decent body & length suggest **16** ★★★ (82) will settle, knit, & match last **14** (87). Natural ferment, as next.

Witkaree Chenin Blanc ⑭ ★★★★ Barrel-fermented **17** ⑧⑤ shows bold oak spices, savouriness, good weight & subdued stonefruit. Not tasted: **Three Oaks Cabernet Sauvignon**, **Above The Mist Merlot**.

Stubborn Man range

Merlot ② ★★★ Rustic, meaty **15** ⑧⓪ has solid plummy fruit, faint minty leafiness & chalky tannins. **Rosé** ★★★ Refreshing **18** ⑦⑧ blends shiraz, cab & merlot, has Ribena berry juice character. **Chardonnay Unwooded** ★★★ Still showing fermentation notes mid-2018, **18** ⑦⑧ has understated pear drop fruit. **Chenin Blanc** ★★★ Fruity, unfussy **18** ⑧⓪ made for easy everyday drinking, with generous tropical notes, light body. **Sauvignon Blanc** ★★★ Dominant khaki bush aromatic edge to **18** ⑧②, with primary granadilla fruit. Unsubtle but striking. Durbanville grapes. — GdB

Location/map: Paarl ▪ Map grid reference: E4 ▪ WO: Paarl/Western Cape ▪ Est 1747 ▪ 1stB 2004 ▪ Tasting & sales Tue-Sun 11.30-4 ▪ Closed Mondays, Dec 25 & Jan 1 ▪ Blacksmith's Kitchen Tue-Sat 12-10 Sun 11.30-4 ▪ The Venue @ Pearl Mountain for weddings & functions ▪ Owner(s) Pearl Mountain Wines (Pty) Ltd ▪ Winemaker(s) Lisha Nelson (2016, Nelson Family Vineyards) ▪ Viticulturist(s) David & Graham Retief ▪ 14ha (cab, grenache, merlot, shiraz, chard, chenin, sauv) ▪ 120t/7,000cs own label 50% red 50% white ▪ PO Box 709 Northern Paarl 7623 ▪ info@pearlmountain.co.za ▪ www.pearlmountain.co.za ▪ S 33° 41' 44.4" E 018° 57' 11.1" ▪ 🎦 younger.vitamins.whispers ▪ **T 021-872-9507/+27 (0)21-870-1550 restaurant & tasting**

☐ **Pearly Bay** see KWV Wines

☐ **Pecan Stream** see Waterford Estate

☐ **Pegalle** see Govert Wines

☐ **Pella** see Super Single Vineyards

☐ **Peloton** see Painted Wolf Wines

☐ **Penhill** see Conradie Penhill Artisanal Wines

Perdeberg Wines   ⑨ ⑪ ⓞ ⑧

Gnarled old vines feature on the label of this dynamic winery in Paarl's increasingly acclaimed Dryland Collection. With thousands of hectares of vines to draw on, most unirrigated, and many venerable, they have long been talked about as a vinous treasure trove. Pocket-pleasing whites and reds remain the bedrock of the brand named for the wild quagga which roamed nearby. The upgraded visitor offering caters for casual tastings to conferences to weddings, and there's lots of room for children to play safely.

Perdeberg Speciality range

★★★★☆ **Red Blend** ② Elegant Cape Blend of pinotage, shiraz, malbec, grenache noir, **14** ⑨① youthful ruby colour; brooding black fruit, game, gunsmoke & violets saturate the palate for a full-bodied, smooth generous offering with definition & freshness.

★★★★ **Endura Chenin Blanc** ⑭ Serious intent apparent on rich, pithy, marmalade-packed palate of **17** ⑧⑧ from Swartland single block. Amphora & oak combo adds structure & palate weight.

The Dryland Collection

★★★★ **Conqueror Cabernet Sauvignon** ⊘ Inky cassis on **15** ⑧⑥ in leaner, less opulent style than **13** ⑧⑨. Taut, reined-in & tensile from 18 months French oak, just 10% new - as next two. Paarl WO. **14** untasted.

★★★★ **Resolve Pinotage** Powdery lightness to subtly coffee-tinged but abundantly red-berried **15** ★★★★ ⑧⑤, earlier approachable & not as plush as **14** ⑧⑦. WO Paarl, as next.

★★★★ **Tenacious Shiraz** ⊘ Lightly fruited **14** ⑧⑧, plum & brush of fynbos & lavender; medium body & gentle, subtle spice & dry tannin squeeze. 20% American oak.

★★★★ **Joseph's Legacy** Almost equal shiraz & cab lead 6-way blend, **15** ⑧⑦ black fruit compote & spice lift, supple & pliable texture with good length. 20% American oak.

★★★★★ **Courageous Barrel Fermented Chenin Blanc** ⊘ ⑯ Serious **17** ⑨④ is rich, oxidatively styled but livened by fresh acidity, creamy apple tarte tatin & stonefruit offset by harmonious oaking (all French, just 10% new, 10 months), rounded & lengthy. Over-delivers, like standout **16** ★★★★★ ⑨⑤.

★★★★☆ **Rossouw's Heritage** Chenin blanc leads grenache blanc & viognier in **17** ★★★★ ⑧⑨ blend. Vivid peach & pineapple tempered by chalky grip & vanilla of oak, 10 months, 10% new French. Sprightly & light. Follows exciting & simply delicious **15** ⑨④. WO W Cape. No **16**.

★★★★★ **Longevity Natural Sweet Chenin Blanc** Ambrosial sweetness of **17** ★★★★★ ⑨⓪ suffused with sun-ripened pineapple, mango & apricot flavours so typical of the grape. Acid freshness prevents syrupy cloy on defined tail. Light yet structured from 7 months French oak, only 10% new, like **16** ⑨⑤. 375 ml. Paarl WO.

Pioneer Pinot Noir-Chardonnay ★★★★ Hint of blush on **18** ⑧③, light, tangy & pleasant dry summer rosé. Discontinued: **Chenin Blanc**, **Expression Sauvignon Blanc**.

The Vineyard Collection

★★★★ **Grenache Blanc** ⊘ Tempting peach blossom subtlety to **17** ⑧⑥. Ripe, with stonefruit & honey overlay, but acid keeps it fresh. Good heft to mid-palate & well-resolved clean, dry tail. WO W Cape.

★★★★ **Méthode Cap Classique Pinot Noir Rosé** ⊘ Frothy dry sparkler, red-berry tang to **15** ★★★ ⑧⓪, good body & length. **13** ⑧⑦ savoury, more serious. No **14**.

★★★★ **Méthode Cap Classique Chenin Brut** ⊘ New disgorgement of **12** ⑧⑥ dry bubbly presents crunchy apple fruit over shortbread & brioche, fine, lingering creamy mousse.

Cinsault ★★★☆ Cheery & bright **17** ⑧④ has savoury depth on black-fruited palate. Succulence vies with gentle tannin grip from third oaked, all old, 10 months. Paarl WO, like Pinotage, Shiraz. **Malbec** ★★★ Supple, light-bodied **17** ⑧② inky blue & black fruit, supportive oak cradle from year 15% new French barrels. **Pinotage** ⊘ ★★★ Plummy **15** ⑧① preview is sweet-fruited, with a savoury end thanks to year in older oak. **Shiraz** ⊘ ★★★ Easy-sipping, light-bodied **15** ⑧① tank sample, bright fruit with spicy oak nuance (year in older barrels). **Cinsault Rosé** ⓃⒺⓌ ★★★ Vivid raspberry & strawberry on **18** ⑦⑨ fresh, light, dry summertime sipper. **Chenin Blanc** ⊘ ★★★☆ Ever-popular easy-drinker. Elderflower & melon on light, succulent **18** ⑧④; riper, richer honey tones on also-tasted **17** ⑧④. **Sauvignon Blanc** ★★★ Grapefruit tang on **18** ⑧② livened by hint of flint, bright & fresh.

Perdeberg Classic range

Cabernet Sauvignon ⊘ ★★★★ Ever-reliable, well-priced cab. Blue & black berry fruit appeal on part-oaked **17** ⑧③, medium bodied & easy to drink. **Merlot** ⊘ ★★★ Unfussy, red-fruited & succulent **17** ⑧① has backbone from oak-staved portion (40%), like next 2. Paarl WO. **Pinotage** ⊘ ★★★ Rounded & soft, **17** ⑧② is cheery & appealing in its blue- & red-berried simplicity. **Shiraz** ⊘ ★★★ Dried herb & smoke whiff to cherry-toned **17** ⑧②, eminently drinkable at braai or dinner table. **Chenin Blanc** ⊘ ★★★ Subtle melon & nectarine appeal on **18** ⑧⓪ staple. Light, fresh & ever popular. **Sauvignon Blanc** ★★★ Flint & lemon-zest typicity on light, juicy **18** ⑦⑧. **Sparkling Rosé** ⊘ ★★★ Fizzy raspberry & strawberry simplicity on **17** ⑦⑨ mainly shiraz semi-sweet sparkling. Low 9.57% alcohol. WO W Cape. Discontinued: **Cabernet Sauvignon-Merlot**, **Sparkling Chenin Blanc**.

Perdeberg Soft Smooth range

Rosé ⓃⒺⓌ ⊘ ★★★ Gently sweet berry appeal of **18** ⑧⓪ is kept fresh with balancing acid. Rounded & soft. **White** ⓃⒺⓌ ★★★ Semi-sweet but zippy, fresh & light, with guava, melon & peach appeal, **18** ⑦⑨ mostly chenin & colombard. WO W Cape. **Red** ★★★ Uncomplicated, sweetish & easy-drinking **16** ⑧① red-berry appeal from cab, merlot & shiraz.

Rooted range

Merlot ⊘ ★★★★ Fruitcake, spice & hints of chocolate, all in harmony with vanilla oak. **15** ⑧④ smooth & ever so drinkable. **Chardonnay** ⊘ ★★★★ Fresh & energetic apple flavours, creamy vanilla with a zippy acid in **16** ⑧④. Paarl WO.

Ploughman range

Shiraz-Cabernet Sauvignon ⊘ ★★★ Spice, pepper & dark plums abound on succulent, savoury **15** ⑧①, balanced & moreish. WO Swartland. **Sauvignon Blanc-Chenin Blanc** ⊘ ★★★ Bouncy tropical fruit flavours & a brisk acid farewell on **16** ⑧①. — FM

Location/map: Paarl ▪ Map grid reference: B2 ▪ WO: Coastal/Paarl/Western Cape/Swartland ▪ Est 1941 ▪ 1stB 1942 ▪ Tasting & sales Mon-Fri 8-5 Sat 9.30-3 ▪ Closed Good Fri & Dec 25 ▪ Cellar tours Mon-Fri by appt ▪ Light meals, book for groups of 10+ ▪ Child friendly ▪ Function venue (up to 200 pax) ▪ Weddings ▪ Conferences ▪ Tutored tastings ▪ Wine pairings ▪ Wine blending/bottle your own wine, to be pre-booked ▪ Craft beer brewery ▪ Owner(s) 37 shareholders ▪ Cellarmaster(s) Albertus Louw (Oct 2008) ▪ Winemaker(s) Daniel Slabber (Jan 2017), Natalie Kühne (Dec 2015), Lodewyk Botha (Oct 2017) & Arthur Basson (Dec 2017) ▪ Viticulturist(s) Heinie Nel (Jul 2013) ▪ 6,000ha/2,564ha (cab, cinsaut, merlot, ptage, shiraz, chard, chenin, sauv) ▪ 18,000t/300,000cs own label 60% red 40% white ▪ Fairtrade, HACCP, IPW, WIETA ▪ PO Box 214 Paarl 7620 ▪ info@perdeberg.co.za ▪ www.perdeberg.co.za ▪ S 33° 39′ 30.00″ E 018° 49′ 37.00″ ▪ intentional. popup.crewmen ▪ **T +27 (0)21-869-8244**

Peter Bayly Wines

At a bend in the Nel River just outside Calitzdorp lies Peter and Yvonne Bayly's homestead and the 1.2 ha of vines they have been nurturing for nearly two decades. Harvest is a friends-and-family affair in the small traditional cellar. Peter takes care of the winegrowing, and Yvonne suggests phoning ahead 'to make sure we're here' before you pop in to taste their mostly port-style wines.

★★★★ **Cape Vintage** ⓥ Attractive port-style **10** ⑧⑥ from touriga (44%) with tinta & souzão. Bright, concentrated fruit, leather & spicy warmth. Will benefit from few years keeping. Also in 375 ml.

Cape Late Bottled Vintage ⓥ ★★★ Ripe plum & malty berry compote, **08** ⑦⑧ chiefly souzão (58%) & tinta, dash touriga. Soft & accessible, as per the LBV style. **Cape White** ⓥ ★★★★ Satisfying **NV** ⑧④ white 'port' from chenin. Full of golden raisins, candied peel, with touches apricot & honey. Recommended served on ice with tonic, mint & lemon. Not tasted: III. In abeyance: **Tinta Barocca, Cape Pink**. — CM

Location/WO: Calitzdorp ▪ Map: Klein Karoo & Garden Route ▪ Map grid reference: B5 ▪ Est 2002 ▪ 1stB 2004 ▪ Tasting, sales & tours by appt ▪ Owner(s) Peter Bayly Wines (Pty) Ltd ▪ Winemaker(s)/viticulturist(s) Peter Bayly ▪ 6.6ha/1.2ha (tinta, touriga, souzão) ▪ ±8t/±1,320cs own label ▪ PO Box 187 Calitzdorp 6660 ▪ info@baylys.co.za ▪ www.peterbayly.co.za ▪ S 33° 27′16.70″ E 021° 45′ 34.86″ ▪ saddles.tortoise.satellite ▪ F +27 (0)86-513-2727 ▪ **T +27 (0)44-213-3702/+27 (0)83-457-5037**

☐ **Peter Clarke Collection** *see* PaardenKloof

Peter Falke Wines

German entrepreneur Franz-Peter Falke bought Groenvlei, with its stately Cape Dutch homestead, in 1995 — fulfilling his dream to own a farm. The vineyards on the lower slopes of the Helderberg have now grown to 9 hectares, and fruit is also brought in as necessary, to be vinified by Werner Schrenk and consultant Louis Nel.

Signature range

★★★★ **Syrah** ⓥ Forward dark-fruit aromas on **15** ⑧⑥, & some intensity of flavour. Opulent & softly textured, with acid dealing with the ripe richness, & decent tannic grip. Big alcohol, like all the reds.

★★★★ **Exclusive Blend** ⓥ Mostly cab with merlot in **14** ⑧⑦. Inviting berry & cedar aromas. Plenty of ripeness & extract, rounded & warm. Most satisfying red of the vintage & a tad drier, more savoury.

★★★★ **Muscat d'Alexandrie** Charming grapey, floral aromas on latest **NV** ⑧⑦ fortified; delicious apricot intensity. Balanced & uncloying, with 17.4% alcohol & 187 g/l RS. Old-oak maturation. 500 ml.

PF range

★★★★ **Méthode Cap Classique** ⓥ Oatmeal biscuit with citrus & red/green apple notes on **14** ⑧⑥ sparkling from chardonnay. Light, elegantly fresh balance & effortless charm.

Cabernet Sauvignon ★★★ Attractive varietal aromas on **15** ⑧③. Plush, with notable ripeness compensated for by big acidity & firm, smooth tannins. 30% new oak; 14.8% alcohol. **Pinot Noir** ★★★★ Fresh raspberry & cherry notes on juicy & flavourful **16** ⑧⑤, with a light tannic tug & structuring acidity. Better balanced than previous, drinking very well now. WO W Cape. **Ruby Blend** ★★★ Dark berries & a little tobacco spice on **15** ⑧② cab-shiraz blend. Sweet fruited, ripe & softly textured but firm acid & smooth tannins. Not tasted: **Blanc de Noir, Chardonnay, Sauvignon Blanc**. — TJ

Location/map: Stellenbosch ▪ Map grid reference: E8 ▪ WO: Stellenbosch/Western Cape ▪ 1stB 2003 ▪ Tasting & sales Tue-Sun 11-7 ▪ Fee R65 ▪ Closed Good Fri, Dec 25 & Jan 1 ▪ Cheese platters, charcuterie & salads ▪ Owner(s) Franz-Peter Falke ▪ GM Werner Schrenk ▪ Winemaker(s) Werner Schrenk (2007) & Louis Nel (2013, consultant) ▪ Viticulturist(s) Werner Schrenk (2007) ▪ 24ha/9ha under vine ▪ PO Box 12605 Stellenbosch 7613 ▪ marketing@peterfalkewines.co.za ▪ www.peterfalkewines.com ▪ S 34° 0′ 2.1″ E 018° 50′ 19.3″ ▪ 🖂 factorial. overheated.enticed ▪ F +27 (0)21-881-3667 ▪ **T +27 (0)21-881-3677**

☐ **Petit** *see* Ken Forrester Wines

Pfeifer's Boutique Wines ⓠ

Co-owner and winegrower Pascal Pfeifer advises that vintages '05 to '07, the last Caelum Syrah made, are still available from his family's Helderberg farm.

Location: Stellenbosch ▪ Map: Helderberg ▪ Map grid reference: B2 ▪ Est 2000 ▪ 1stB 2003 ▪ Tasting & sales by appt ▪ Closed Easter Fri/Sun, Dec 25 & Jan 1 ▪ Owner(s) Pascal & Maya Pfeifer ▪ Winemaker(s)/viticulturist(s) Pascal Pfeifer (Jun 2006) ▪ 1.675ha/1.4ha (shiraz) ▪ 14-16t/±150cs own label 100% red ▪ IPW ▪ PO Box 5238 Helderberg 7135 ▪ enquiries@pfeifersvineyard.co.za ▪ www.pfeifersvineyard.co.za ▪ S 34° 01' 10.98" E 018° 47' 17.06" ▪ 🖭 voyeurism.inwardness.tactile ▪ F +27 (0)86-616-8850 ▪ **T +27 (0)21-842-3396**

☐ **Philip Jonker** *see* Weltevrede Estate
☐ **Phizante Kraal** *see* Groot Phesantekraal
☐ **Phoenix** *see* Stellenbosch Family Wines
☐ **Phumla** *see* House of Mandela

Picardi ReBEL

This nationwide drinks chain offers shoppers affordable house wines (red, white and sweet rosé) in 3L and 5L packs under the Picardi ReBEL label, as well as sparkling wine and fortifieds under the Naked Truth brand.

Est 1994 ▪ PO Box 1868 Cape Town 8000 ▪ F +27 (0)21-469-3434 ▪ **T +27 (0)21-469-3301**

☐ **Pick's Pick** *see* The Butcher Shop & Grill
☐ **Pictus** *see* Painted Wolf Wines
☐ **Piekeniers** *see* Tierhoek

Piekenierskloof Wine Company ⓠ

Changes aplenty at this Citrusdal-based winery, sourcing much of its fruit from the in-demand Piekenierskloof upland. Jaco van Niekerk, previously with Lutzville Vineyards, joined as general manager/ cellarmaster in time for the 2018 harvest, while Van Zyl siblings, whose ancestors were among the first to plant vines in the area, acquired the majority shareholding. With some of the oldest chenin, grenache, cinsaut and muscat de Frontignan vines in SA, strong focuses will be on vinifying single sites for the top wines, and burnishing the area's reputation for high-quality grenache.

Reserve range

★★★★ **Top White Blend** ⓒ Lemon & stonefruit layered with oak spice & vanilla, **16** ⑧⑦ vibrant, pinpoint balance, impressive length at mere 12.6% alcohol. 65% chenin, palomino & 2 more.
Not tasted: **Red**.

Piekenierskloof range

★★★★ **Grenache Noir** Previewed **17** ⑧⑨ on track to improve on previous in its lithe tannins, lively acidity, pure cherry/strawberry fruit. Full of energy & on-trend with lighter styling (12.8% alcohol).

★★★★ **Bergendal Chenin Blanc** ⓒ ⊛ Oak (some American) quite evident on **16** ⑧⑦ but works very well, adds aromatic complexity to white peach & pear flavours, texture to zingy palate.

★★★★ **Straw Wine** ⑯⑭ Stylish dessert in matching 375-ml packaging from muscat de Frontignan. **17** ⑧⑦ unctuous & smooth, stem ginger, dried peach & apricot subtly accented by ferment/year older oak, vibrant acidity prepares palate for next delicious sip.

Cinsault ⓒ ⊛ ★★★★ Appealing strawberry, scrub & herb aromas, good grip & stemmy freshness on **16** ⑧⑤, old oak provides shape not flavour. **Grenache Rosé** ★★★ Dry pink loses oaked portion in **18** ⑧⓪ but none of its charm, drinkability abetted by invisible gram sugar, strawberries-&-cream character to match the delicate blush. **Chenin Blanc** ★★★★ Flavoursome glassful raises the bar in **17** ⑧⑤ with earthy note, depth (aided by 10% oaked component) & precision on the palate. **Grenache Blanc** ★★★ Creamy texture from few months on lees, soft acidity & hint of tannin, bone-dry **17** ⑧② has faint nuttiness in the fennel/aniseed flavour spectrum.

Stonedance range

Cabernet Sauvignon ★★★ Ex tank, **17** ⑧⓪ meaty nuance to juicy black plums, tannins softened by plump fruit & time in French/American oak, which also adds a vanilla tone. WO Swartland & Fairtrade certified, as all this range. **Shiraz ★★★** Partial oaking (French/American) gives vanilla kiss to plum-packed **17** (80), fresh & ready to drink. **Chenin Blanc ★★★** Appeals with white peach & nectarine, **18** (82) bone-dry & lightish (12.3% alcohol) for carefree quaffing. **Sauvignon Blanc ★★★** Fairly intense fig & grass accompanied by almost 14% alcohol, yet **18** (82) tank sample slips down easily thanks to zesty acidity.

Six Hats Fairtrade range

Pinotage ★★★☆ Smoky **17** (84) from Swartland needs a few swirls to fully reveal its charms, but worth waiting for the juicy dark fruit, bright acidity, shapely dry tannins. Fairtrade certified & for export, as next. **Chardonnay ★★★** Easygoing **18** (82) ex tank has palate weight & creamy texture from 2 months on lees, buttered toast aromas from light oaking. WO W Cape. Not tasted: **Cabernet Sauvignon, Shiraz, Chenin Blanc, Sauvignon Blanc.** — CvZ

Location: Citrusdal ▪ Map: Olifants River ▪ Map grid reference: D7 ▪ WO: Piekenierskloof/Swartland/Western Cape ▪ Est/1stB 2007 ▪ Tasting room at Hebron, Piekenierskloof Pass, N7 ▪ Winery tours by appt only ▪ Owner(s) Majority shareholding Oubaas & Potgieter van Zyl ▪ Cellarmaster(s) Jaco van Niekerk (Dec 2017) ▪ Winemaker(s) Jaco van Niekerk (Dec 2017), with Elroy Hartnick (Nov 2016) & Jaydee Strauss (Feb 2017) ▪ Viticulturist(s) Hanno van Schalkwyk (Nov 2017) ▪ 550ha (cab, cinsaut, grenache n/b, merlot, mourv, ptage, ruby cab, shiraz, tannat, chard, chenin, hanepoot, pinot grigio, sauv, viog) ▪ 5,000t/30,000cs own label 45% red 50% white 5% rosé ▪ Brands for clients: Fairtrade Original, Liberty ▪ Fairtrade, HACCP, IPW, WIETA ▪ PO Box 41 Citrusdal 7340 ▪ info@pkwc.co.za ▪ www.piekenierskloofwines.co.za ▪ S 32° 37' 05.17" E 018° 57' 21.66" ▪ F +27 (0)22-921-3937 ▪ **T +27 (0)22-921-2233**

☐ **Pierneef Collection** see La Motte
☐ **Pierre Jourdan** see Haute Cabrière
☐ **Pillar & Post** see Stellenrust
☐ **Pioneer** see Thandi Wines
☐ **PK Morkel** see Bellevue Estate Stellenbosch

Plaisir de Merle

This Distell-owned Simonsberg-Paarl mountain estate delivers consistently superior quality under the long and sure stewardship of Niel Bester, ensconced in a unique cellar where high-tech intersects with sculptural artistry and Cape Dutch heritage. The latter is celebrated in the Charles Marais blend debuting this edition, named for the 17th-century founder. The other new release is a Signature Blend marking Niel's 20th vintage here, so it's entirely appropriate that this tribute wine should receive the guide's maximum five stars.

★★★★ Cabernet Sauvignon Notably fresh leafy-earthy aromas woven into heady cassis fruit, **15** (87) with rather sombre tarry notes & ripe, supple tannins - all very appealing. Splashes petit verdot & shiraz. Also in magnum.

★★★★ Cabernet Franc Impressive return after 6-vintage break. Linear, focused **15** (89) ex single block captivating pencil shaving & leafy blackcurrant flavours; firm tannins bolster substantial body & structure, all elegantly balanced.

★★★★ Merlot Tense, leafy blackcurrant fruit drives **16** (87), backed up with fine tannins & earthy black core. 14-18 months in barrel, 25% new, lend spicy oak notes.

★★★★ Shiraz Concentrated black cherry fruit on blockbuster **16** (88), with appealing tobacco spices & smoked meat aromas. Plump & generous, with plush tannin texture.

★★★★☆ Charles Marais (NEW) (🎖) Statuesque offering debuts with **13** (93) 4-way Cape Bordeaux blend headed by cab (30%). Layers of blackcurrant fruit, intense forest floor scents, & earthy liquorice, all delivered with poise & grace. Very impressive. Paarl WO.

★★★★★ Grand Plaisir (🏆) Aristocratic **11** (94) 4-way Bordeaux blend - malbec, merlot, cab, petit verdot - 16 months in mostly new barrels. Pure, focused berry & currant fruit, fine supple tannins. Beautifully crafted, still fresh & vibrant. Fitting flag bearer for estate.

★★★★★ Signature Blend (NEW) (🎖) 'Anniversary edition', marking winemaker's 20th vintage here. Superb 5-way Bordeaux red, cab & petit verdot (33/25) leading. **12** (96) shows impeccable form & substance. Rich & earthy, with herbaceous notes to blackcurrant fruit core, elegantly rounded body & lengthy finish. Hefty oak regime (90% new French) in perfect harmony.

★★★★ **Chardonnay** Solid lemon curd fruit prevails over serious oak (65% new) in **17** ⑱. Supple & shapely, with fine balance, promising more harmony with cellaring.

★★★★ **Grand Brut Méthode Cap Classique** Near equal pinot noir & chardonnay sparkling, **16** ⑱ is lean & focused, showing green apple fruit & primary acid on generous, foamy mousse. WO W Cape.

Petit Plaisir ★★★★ Competent, fullish **16** ⑱ is shiraz with cab & merlot. Plush, juicy cherry fruit with savoury notes. WO W Cape. Not tasted: **Malbec, Petit Verdot.** — GdB

Location: Paarl = Map: Franschhoek = Map grid reference: C6 = WO: Simonsberg-Paarl/Western Cape/Paarl = Est/1stB 1993 = Tasting, sales & cellar tours Mon-Sun 10-6 (Sep-Apr) & 10-5 (May-Aug) pub hols 10-4; last tastings winter/pub hols half an hour before closing = Closed Good Fri, Dec 25 & Jan 1 = Tasting fee R60 = Cheese platters available during trading hours R140 or R180 = Children welcome = Gifts = Manor House (sleeps 8) can be booked for functions, conferences & weddings = Owner(s) Distell = Cellarmaster(s) Niel Bester (1993) = Viticulturist(s) Drikus Heyns & Morne Steyn = 974ha/400ha (cabs s/f, malbec, merlot, p verdot, pinot, shiraz, chard, sauv) = 800t/80,000cs own label 80% red 20% white = ISO 9001:2008, ISO 14001:2004, BRC, SGS, WIETA, WWF-SA Conservation Champion = PO Box 121 Simondium 7670 = info@plaisirdemerle.co.za = www.plaisirdemerle.co.za = S 33° 51' 0.0" E 018° 56' 36.2" = ▨ patrons.flooring.satchel = F +27 (0)21-874-1689 = **T +27 (0)21-874-1071**

Plettenvale Wines ⓠ

Indomitable Plettenberg Bay boutique vintner Gloria Strack van Schyndel's home was destroyed in June 2017 by drought-fuelled wildfires. Though her precious vines fortunately escaped the conflagration, their yields were substantially down. Undaunted, Gloria is hopeful of bringing in a normal crop this season and moving into a new, fire-resistant residence. Fans will be pleased that supplies of the current releases are unaffected.

Ruby Rush Our Blend ⓠ ★★ From pinot & shiraz in hearty, rustic style; **NV** ⑭ plentiful ripe fruit (though just 12.3% alcohol) with robust tannins. Older oak. **Dry Rosé** ⓠ ★★★ Attractive pinky rose brilliance on **NV** ⑱ from chardonnay, shiraz, drop pinot. Equally enticing fresh summer red-berry scents, lively fruity acids. **Chardonnay** ⓠ ★★★ Ripe & generous **NV** ⑱ from Robertson grapes, mouthfilling peachy, orange juiciness braced by firm acid. **Brut Rosé Méthode Cap Classique** ⓠ ★★★ Copper-toned **NV** ⑱ fizz from pinot noir & chardonnay. Developed leesy, saline features, very brisk & dry. — AL

Location: Plettenberg Bay = Map: Klein Karoo & Garden Route = Map grid reference: C1 = WO: Plettenberg Bay/Western Cape = Est 2008 = 1stB 2011 = Tasting & sales every Sat 10-1, all other times by appt = Short tour of cellar available with tasting = Owner(s)/winemaker(s) Gloria Strack van Schyndel = Viticulturist(s) Paul Wallace (Nov 2007, consultant) = 5.3ha/2.5ha (pinot, shiraz, chard, viog) = PO Box 2103 Plettenberg Bay 6600 = info@plettenvalewines.co.za = www.plettenvalewines.co.za = S 34° 04' 53.9" E 023° 19' 41.4" = ▨ endures.bronze.wing = **T +27 (0)44-533-9146/+27 (0)82-322-0765**

☐ **Ploughman** see Perdeberg Wines
☐ **Poetry** see Flagstone Winery
☐ **Poker Hill** see Somerbosch Wines
☐ **Polkadraai** see Stellenbosch Hills Wines
☐ **Polo Club** see Val de Vie & Polo Club Wines
☐ **Pomüla** see Imbuko Wines

Pongrácz

Two new celebrators join the line-up of fine méthode cap classiques under this specialist sparkling wine brand, named for the Hungarian nobleman and refugee, Desiderius Pongrácz, who settled in Stellenbosch in 1958 and became the inspirational chief viticultural adviser to Distell's precursor, Distillers Corporation.

★★★★ **Blanc de Blancs** ⑩ From chardonnay, extra dry, **NV** ⑲ appeals with smoky impression, focused apple & yeast flavours, clean & long from 77 months on lees & 5 in bottle. Fine food pairer.

★★★★ **Brut** Rich, balanced & versatile dry sparkle, pinot noir-led with chardonnay. **NV** ⑰ appealing brioche, honey & stonefruit flavours, surprisingly creamy for 'just' 2 years on lees. Step up on previous. Also in 375ml, 1.5L & 3L.

★★★★☆ **Desiderius** ⓐ Fine, pedigreed flagship bubbly, **11** ◯ 94 inverse blend to siblings, 55% chardonnay plus pinot noir. Wonderfully refined, with lengthy fresh focus, smoky toasted hazelnut & brioche tones from 77 months on lees - less than marginally more impressive **09** ★★★★★ ◯ 95 (90 months). No **10**.

★★★★ **Demi-Sec** ⓝⓔⓦ Semi-sweet bubbles from pinot noir & chardonnay, **NV** ⑧⑦ gentle, creamed honey flavours, 41.2 g/l sugar gracefully balanced, not cloying at all. A pâte & light desserts partner.

Brut Rosé ★★★★ Same pinot noir (55%) & chardonnay blend, winemaking & time on lees (24 months) as Brut & Demi-Sec, skin contact provides blush & savoury tang. **NV** ⑧⑤ dry, light & bright, shade less depth & character than previous, which saw 36 months sur lie. Also in magnum & 375 ml. — MW

Location: Stellenbosch • WO: Western Cape • Owner(s) Distell • Cellarmaster(s) Elunda Basson • Winemaker(s) Elunda Basson (2007), with John November (2011) • Viticulturist(s) Bennie Liebenberg (Jan 2000) • 27ha own vyds • 20% red 80% white • ISO 9200 • PO Box 184 Stellenbosch 7599 • www.pongracz.co.za

Porcupine Ridge

Named for the indigenous Franschhoek fauna, Boekenhoutskloof's original good-value range remains recognisably 'Boekenhoutskloof', with the 'svelte lady' emblem prominently featured on the bespoke bottle and tactile labels. We noted before that these wines are models of palate and pocket friendliness, with a dash of style, and the new vintages only underscore that welcome message for budget-conscious winelovers.

Syrah ⊘ 🏆 ★★★★ By no means 'hidden', but a 24-carat gem in **17** ⑧⑤, 133,000 cases of lekkerness from Swartland. Beguiling lavender, pepper-spiced mulberry, fleshy & rounded, palate-cleansing, food-friendly dusty olive grip on exit. **Chardonnay** ⊘ 🏆 ★★★★ Mum's baked apple pie aroma welcomes you to **17** ⑧⑤, touch of oak & few months on lees give palate versatility: creaminess for solo, subtle grip for food.

Cabernet Sauvignon ⊘ ★★★★ Red-fruited **17** ⑧④ soft & smooth for everyday. Tad higher wooded portion no impediment, only extends the enjoyment (up to 5 years, per winemakers, as all the reds). WO Coastal unless noted. **Merlot** ⊘ ★★★☆ Fruitcake, plum & warm spice on super-drinkable, any-occasion **17** ⑧③. Well balanced & creamy palate leads to choc-mint finish. **Rosé** ⊘ ★★★ Rosepetal pink **18** ⑧⓪ from syrah, splash cinsaut does not disappoint: vibrant crunchy red fruit with a nice tang. Bone-dry & thus weight-watcher friendly, too. **Chenin Blanc** ⊘ ★★★★ Tropical-toned **17** ⑧④ has touch more complexity, intensity & balance than previous, drinks as easily & well. Swartland fruit. **Sauvignon Blanc** ★★★ Salad of fruit flavours in **18** ⑧⓪ come together with salinity & twist of lemon on satisfyingly dry farewell. Widely sourced grapes, like Chardonnay. Discontinued: **Syrah-Viognier**, **Viognier-Grenache Blanc**. — WB

Porseleinberg

The stony hills, not far from Riebeek-Kasteel in the Swartland, which give this farm its name are now planted with some 90 hectares of vines. Only a few hectares pre-dated the purchase of Porseleinberg by Boekenhoutskloof in 2009, and they go into the single wine made, in a modest cellar on the property, by Callie Louw, who has also been responsible for all the vineyards from the start. The rest of the grapes go to the parent cellar in Franschhoek, some of them into the famous Boekenhoutskloof Syrah. Callie's own wine has also achieved international renown. It's made with infinite care but minimal intervention, according to the precepts of Swartland Independent Producers.

★★★★★ **Porseleinberg** ⓐ Sophisticated & cerebral syrah from a special Swartland site. **16** ⑨⑤'s piercing spice perfumes, toned fruit & same fine musculature as **15** ★★★★★ ⑨③ promise a decade+ of sheer drinking pleasure. Hands-off, whole-bunch natural vinification; year large old oak, 30% concrete 'egg'.— DS

Location: Malmesbury • WO: Swartland • Est 2009 • 1stB 2010 • Closed to public • Owner(s) Boekenhoutskloof Winery (Pty) Ltd • Winemaker(s)/viticulturist(s) Callie Louw (Jun 2009) • 130ha/90ha (cinsaut, grenache, shiraz) • 50t/1,000cs own label 100% red • PO Box 433 Franschhoek 7690 • callie@porseleinberg.com • www.porseleinberg.com • F +27 (0)86-566-9332 • **T +27 (0)79-884-2309**

☐ **Postcard Series** *see* Stark-Condé Wines

Post House Vineyards ⓘ ⌂ ⌂ ◎ ♿

It's been 21 years since boutique vintner Nick Gebers released his first wine, which we noted as a 'welcome newcomer to chenin revival'. The philatelic theme comes from being housed in an old Post Office building (extended and upgraded for the 2018 vintage) at Raithby in the Helderberg foothills. The stories behind the names and labels are engaging, even (especially?) for non stamp enthusiasts. The wine style remains unchanged, with outspoken personalities and flavours throughout.

★★★★ **Bulls Eye Cabernet Sauvignon** 🍇 Perfumed violet & berry fruit abundance of **16** ⑧⑧ is seductive. Intense, but restrained by tannic backbone from 18 months French oak, third new, long & rewarding. Alcohol is high at 15%, as several reds.

★★★★ **Black Mail Merlot** Concentrated & rounded dark fruit with cocoa & hint of mint on naturally fermented **16** ⑧⑦, fine dry tannins frame fruit well. Tad aloof at present, unlike full-throttle **15** ★★★★ ⑧③.

★★★★ **Missing Virgin** Interesting & unusual Cape Blend, 76% pinotage & petit verdot, **16** ⑧⑥ ripe cassis & raspberry vibrancy tempered by spicy flavour & dry oak tannin (20% new French, ±2 years).

★★★★ **Penny Black** 🍇 Flagship eclectic blend shiraz, 3 Bordeaux grapes & dab chenin blanc. Dried herb, choc & berry brightness smartly juggled on naturally fermented **16** ★★★★★ ⑨⓪. Pliable & plush, with layers of flavour. **14** ⑧⑦ poised if powerful. **15** untasted.

★★★★ **Stamp Of Chenin** Vibrant peach & tropical notes on **17** ⑧⑥ underpinned by broad creaminess from 10 months in oak, 10% new. On song after **16** ★★★★ ⑧⑤. Like all others, bar Blueish White, naturally fermented, minimally sulphured & unfiltered.

★★★★☆ **Treskilling Yellow** Like **14** ⑨③, this a Noble Late Harvest from chenin. Jasmine, honeyed apricots & marmalade on rich **15** ★★★★ ⑧⑥. Fresh acidity counters sweetness while 2 years older oak adds creamy cashew nuance. Focused & taut, not syrupy. 375 ml.

Merry Widow Shiraz ★★★★ Spicy star anise & vanilla on bold, plummy **16** ⑧⑤. Bright, fresh as well as lithe & supple, the chalky tannins from 18 months oak, 20% new & some American, need a bit of time. **Blueish Black** ★★★☆ Supple, soft berry appeal on **16** ⑧④ shiraz-led blend including 29% pinotage. Spice mingles with cocoa & cigarbox, with backbone from oak (25%, older barrels). WO W Cape. **Golden Monkey** ★★★★ Savoury Rhône blend, **17** ⑧⑤ gentle blue berry fruits & spice, supple & appealing. Shiraz just 45%, with mourvèdre & grenache nearly a third each. Follows handsome **16** ★★★★ ⑧⑨, with 60% shiraz. Coastal WO. **Blueish White** ★★★ Tangy citrus & grapefruit vivacity on **17** ⑧② mainly sauvignon & dab chenin. Light bodied, unoaked & appealing. WO Coastal. — FM

Location: Stellenbosch ▪ Map: Helderberg ▪ Map grid reference: C1 ▪ WO: Stellenbosch/Coastal/Western Cape ▪ Est/1stB 1997 ▪ Tasting, sales & cellar tours Mon-Fri 9-5 Sat by appt ▪ Fee R40 ▪ Closed all pub hols ▪ BYO picnic ▪ Guest house ▪ Function/wedding venue (up to 150 pax) ▪ Owner(s) Nicholas Gebers ▪ Cellarmaster(s) Nick Gebers ▪ Winemaker(s) Nick Gebers, with Madri Dreyer ▪ 70ha/39ha (cab, merlot, p verdot, ptage, shiraz, chenin, sauv) ▪ 200t/16,000cs own label 65% red 35% white ▪ PO Box 5635 Helderberg 7135 ▪ nick@posthousewines.co.za ▪ www.posthousewines.co.za ▪ S 34° 1' 8.1" E 018° 48' 41.6" ▪ 🖼 softest. materialistic.quickening ▪ F +27 (0)21-842-2409 ▪ **T +27 (0)21-842-2409**

☐ **Post Tree** see Valley Vineyards Wine Company
☐ **Potjie** see Mooiuitsig Wine Cellars
☐ **Pot Luck Club** see Almenkerk Wine Estate
☐ **Pride of Kings** see Stellenview Premium Wines
☐ **Prince** see Bayede!
☐ **Princess** see Bayede!
☐ **Printer's Devil** see Rickety Bridge Winery
☐ **Private Collection** see Saxenburg Wine Farm
☐ **Prohibition** see Camberley Wines
☐ **Protea** see Anthonij Rupert Wyne
☐ **Provenance** see Saronsberg Cellar
☐ **Provoyeur** see Devonvale Golf & Wine Estate

Pulpit Rock Winery

The Brink family's estate lies on the foothills of Swartland's Kasteelberg, and their wine brand is named for a distinctive outcrop on that mountain. They enter their fifteenth year of bottling under the family label with an expansion of the Louisa label (a tribute to patriarch Ernst's wife) and regrouping of some wines under a Brink Family Vineyards banner, as part of a wider brand update.

Brink Family Vineyards range

★★★★ **Barrel Fermented Chardonnay** ⊘ Subtle honeysuckle, citrus & oatmeal on **17** ⑧⑦, sumptuous courtesy oak ferment/ageing & regular bâtonnage but with focused seam of enlivening acidity.

★★★★ **Chenin Blanc** ⊘ Unwooded but complex thanks to tropical fruit spectrum from papaya to pineapple, aided by 2 months on lees. **18** ⑧⑧ deliciously dry, very long. Step up on **17** ★★★ ⑧①.

★★★★ **Sauvignon Blanc** ⊘ From Darling bushvines, **18** ⑧⑨ characterful & lengthy, fresh, good balance between tropical and green flavours. Improves on **17** ★★★ ⑧①.

Cabernet Sauvignon ★★★ Big, bold **16** ⑧②'s dry tannins underpin ripe blackberry & cassis fruit. At 15% alcohol, balance is shade off previous. **Merlot** ⊘ ★★★★ Velvet tannin & violet appeal in **16** ⑧④, herbal note, chocolate complexity from year French oak, satisfying length & dryness. **Pinotage** ★★★ Now bottled, inky **16** ⑧①'s full body of prune & blackberry fruit locked in a tannin cage for now, with 15% alcohol warmth. **Shiraz** ★★★ Smoky, savoury & intense, **16** ⑦⑧ fine tannin, true-to-variety red plum & pepper fruit. **Chardonnay** ★★★ Ripe yellow-fruit aromas accented by juicy citrus notes on unwooded **18** ⑧①, medium body, 3 months lees contact giving roundness, weight.

Louisa range

★★★★ **Petit Verdot** ⊘ Naturally fermented **16** ⑧⑨, typical inky depth & spicy black fruit, muscular but with some subtlety, tannic grip for food from 16 months French/American wood.

★★★★ **Cape Blend** Pinotage with shiraz & petit verdot, individually vinified & best barrels blended. **15** ⑧⑦ dense & packed with flavour, spicy fruit given form by nicely dry tannin. **14** untasted.

★★★★ **Méthode Cap Classique** ⑭ ⊘ Creamy blanc de blancs dry sparkling from chardonnay. **17** ⑧⑨ vivacious mousse, apple & lemon favours, persistent tail. Delicious now, should gain complexity with year/2 in bottle.

Swartland Stories

Shiraz-Pinotage-Grenache ★★★ Revisited **16** ⑧②, better knit than last time, crowd-pleasing blackberry flavours with caramel & smoky overtones. **Chenin Blanc-Viognier** ★★★ Melange of fruits in **18** ⑧①, cheerful summer quaffer with pithy mineral farewell. Not tasted: **Pinotage Rosé**. — HC

Location: Riebeek West ▪ Map: Swartland ▪ Map grid reference: D6 ▪ WO: Swartland/Coastal ▪ Est 2003 ▪ 1stB 2004 ▪ Tasting & sales Mon-Fri 9—5 Sat 10—2 ▪ Closed Easter Fri-Sun, Dec 25/26 & Jan 1 ▪ Cellar tours by appt ▪ BYO picnic ▪ Walks/hikes ▪ MTB trail ▪ Annual olive festival (May) ▪ Self-catering accommodation ▪ Owner(s) Brink family ▪ Winemaker(s) Dewald Huisamen (Dec 2016) ▪ 600ha/475ha (cab, grenache, merlot, mourv, p verdot, ptage, shiraz, chard, chenin) ▪ 650t/30,000cs own label 70% red 29% white 1% rosé + 3m L bulk ▪ Other export brands: Cape Haven, Cape Tranquility ▪ PO Box 1 Riebeek West 7306 ▪ info@pulpitrock. co.za ▪ www.pulpitrock.co.za ▪ S 33° 20′ 47.4″ E 018° 51′ 14.1″ ▪ 🖃 buds.exploration.jitters ▪ F +27 (0)22-461-2028 ▪ **T +27 (0)22-461-2025**

☐ **Purebred** *see* Excelsior Estate

Quando Vineyards & Winery

The Quando '18 wines weren't ready for tasting this edition, but previously reviewed vintages are still selling and 'drinking beautifully' per Fanus Bruwer, winemaker in this brothers-in-wine boutique venture. Martin Bruwer is responsible for the vines on their Bonnievale farm, where conditions have not been conducive to making another vintage of the popular Natural Sweet Sauvignon, currently out of stock ex cellar.

Mourvèdre ⓥ ★★★★ Bright mulberry flavours with loads of silk-textured, juicy drinkability on delightful **16** ⑧④. Older oak well hidden in exuberant single-block fruit. **Pinot Noir** ⓥ ★★★ Perfumed red fruit & damp earth notes soften the slightly brusque nature of **15** ⑧①. Appealingly fresh. **Mourvèdre Rosé** ⓥ ★★★ A hint of salmon pink from free-run juice, with tangy cranberry impression on **17** ⑧① dry sunset sipper. **Chenin Blanc-Viognier** ⓥ ★★★★ Richness from old-vine chenin, co-fermented with viognier

(29%), makes for creamy, aromatic, unoaked **17** (85). Fruit packed & accessible. Not tasted: **Sauvignon Blanc, Natural Sweet Sauvignon Blanc**. — MW

Location: Bonnievale ▪ Map/WO: Robertson ▪ Map grid reference: D4 ▪ Est/1stB 2001 ▪ Tasting & sales by appt ▪ Closed all pub hols ▪ Owner(s) FM Bruwer cc ▪ Cellarmaster(s)/winemaker(s) Fanus Bruwer (Jan 1991) ▪ Viticulturist(s) Martin Bruwer (Jan 1991) ▪ 190ha/80ha (mourv, chenin, sauv) ▪ 6,000cs own label 10% red 90% white ▪ PO Box 82 Bonnievale 6730 ▪ info@quando.co.za ▪ www.quando.co.za ▪ S 33° 56' 9.6" E 020° 1' 28.8" ▪ ⓐ articles.searchers.ducking ▪ F +27 (0)23-616-2752 ▪ **T +27 (0)23-616-2752**

☐ **Quartet** see Wine-of-the-Month Club
☐ **Queen of Africa** see Olivedale Private Vineyards
☐ **Quest** see Du Toitskloof Winery

Quoin Rock Wines   (Ⓠ)(Ⓜ)(ⓐ)(ⓞ)(Ⓐ)

This Simonsig-Stellenbosch property, developed in the early 2000s and under new ownership since 2011, has been ringing the changes. Revised pruning techniques and structural revamps of the cellar underpin a new range of wines 'paying tribute to Africa and the Ukraine', in tandem with a Quoin Rock label re-design. Visitors can look forward to a new reception, tasting room, events venue and 'exciting' restaurant.

Quoin Rock range

★★★★☆ Shiraz Wild fruit, morello cherries, peppery savouriness, **15** (92)'s palate shows masterly oaking (20 months French, just over half new, like Red Blend) which gives a scrub-toned dry finish, yet the texture is supple, polished. High alcohol, as all the reds, but masked by the fruit.

★★★★ Red Blend Cab (66%), with cab franc & merlot, liquorice-nuanced **15** (89) projects opulence in its creamy dark fruit, spice array, until you get to the palate, where it's all business. Firm, dry tannins guarantee a rewarding long life, no barrier to current enjoyment, pair it with rich dishes. WO Stellenbosch.

★★★★☆ Chardonnay ⓐ Classic buttered toast & citrus styling at first glance for **17** (93), but it's the other layers that are so seductive, pine nuts, grapefruit, lemon rind. Bone-dry without austerity, there's elegance & polish, precision. WO W Cape, as next.

★★★★ White Blend (NEW) Sauvignon with 15% semillon, nearly half the wine oaked, **17** (88)'s profile is tinned pea & fynbos, bolstered by a cedar-spiced seam that takes the edge off the green notes.

★★★★ Méthode Cap Classique Elgin pinot noir & chardonnay, 52 months on lees, trim-figured & bone-dry **13** (88) has toasted brioche & citrus richness in its perfume & flavours, then comes the unexpected racy acidity adding vigour & vitality, & a saline-mineral note to the finish.

★★★★☆ Vine Dried Sauvignon Blanc ⓐ Sumptuous expression of a vine-dried wine, lightly oaked **17** (93)'s sauvignon converted into glacé pineapple, pulpy stonefruit, peach/apricot, the high sugar revitalised by zesty acidity. Never-ending finish, the pleasure continues. 375 ml.

Tribute range (NEW)

★★★★ Namysto Shiraz-Cabernet Sauvignon Also a dab of merlot, cab franc in **15** (88), but shiraz dictates the styling: dark fruit, smoke, savoury spicing including black pepper. Oaked 20 months, 30% new, tannins a midden strength, the body curvaceous, silky.

★★★★ Namysto Sweet Similar intensity, concentration to **17** sibling, but vine-dried **14** (89) shows some development: honey, barley sugar, more dried than fresh fruit, especially apricots. Gorgeous. Nevertheless, drink soon. 375 ml.

Namysto Sauvignon Blanc-Semillon ★★★★ Just 5% semillon in **17** (84), that portion of wine oaked. Very distinctive, a nervy intensity that's more Old World than New, wild grasses & tinned pea, the semillon's role more evident on the palate texture, smooth & lightly savoury. WO W Cape. — CR, CvZ

Location/map: Stellenbosch ▪ Map grid reference: F3 ▪ WO: Simonsberg–Stellenbosch/Western Cape/ Stellenbosch/Elgin ▪ Est 1998 ▪ 1stB 2001 ▪ Tasting & sales Tue-Sat 10–4 ▪ Closed Easter Fri/Sun, Dec 25/26 & Jan 1 ▪ Meals/refreshments ▪ Function venue ▪ Child friendly ▪ Accommodation ▪ Owner(s) Quoin Rock Wines (Pty) Ltd ▪ Winemaker(s) Jacques Maree ▪ Viticulturist(s) Nico Walters ▪ PO Box 23 Elsenburg 7607 ▪ info@quoinrock.co.za ▪ www.quoinrock.com ▪ S 33° 52' 42.5" E 018° 52' 2.3" ▪ ⓐ avid.refuse.readily ▪ **T +27 (0)21-888-4740**

☐ **Route 43** *see* Aan de Doorns Cellar

Raats Family Wines

Bruwer Raats has been devoting himself full-time to his own label for some 15 years, though it was founded earlier, in 2000 - in the early years a partnership with brother Jasper. 2004 saw the label centred on a small property on the Polkadraai Hills. A tasting room was built (the wines are vinified in rented space elsewhere) and later a small vineyard was planted. Last year two brilliant first wines off this vineyard helped Raats Family Wines become our Winery of the Year. They were respectively from chenin blanc and cabernet franc, the varieties which have been Bruwer's focus from the outset. As for the 'family' bit of the name: Bruwer's cousin Gavin Slabbert works alongside him in vineyard and cellar (they also jointly established B Vintners, listed separately).

★★★★★ **Cabernet Franc** ⊛ Off low-yield decomposed granite soils; shows why Raats leads pack of cab franc exponents in SA. **16** ⑨ extremely expressive with black olive, fynbos, mulberry & a aromatic baking spices. Oak support, as in **15** ⑨, carefully judged (25% new).

★★★★★ **Dolomite Cabernet Franc** ⊘ ⊛ Exquisite **16** ★★★★★ ⑨ improves on complex & plush **15** ⑨. Dark fruit energised by variety's typical herbal edge, lingering & persistent. Approachable now but structured for the long haul; well priced, too.

★★★★★ **Eden High Density Single Vineyard Cabernet Franc** ⊛ Masterly **16** ★★★★★ ⑨ off 0.2 ha vineyard planted to 8,000 vines/ha. Typical varietal leafiness reined in, perfumed black fruit supported by 100% new oak (18 months). Follows stunning debut **15** ⑨.

★★★★☆ **Jasper Red Blend** ⊛ Bordeaux red - the full quintet - named for patriarch & viticulturist during the label's early years, mainly cab franc, malbec (60/31) in **16** ⑨. Pared back version of fruit-filled **15** ⑨ & the better for it, intense but well-structured.

★★★★★ **Eden High Density Single Vineyard Chenin Blanc** ⊛ From low-crop 0.6 ha Polkadraai parcel, **16** ★★★★★ ⑨ thrilling expression of delicate fruit, steely backbone, linear & fine texture from carefully judged new oak portion (50% new, 11 months). Just a shade off understated power & elegance of **15** ⑨.

★★★★☆ **Old Vine Chenin Blanc** ⊛ From 3 vineyard parcels, average age 40 years, **17** ⑨ pure-fruited with piercing seam of acidity tempered by barrel-fermented portion. Peach, pear & yellow apple complexity. Worthy successor to svelte **16** ★★★★★ ⑨.

★★★★☆ **Original Chenin Blanc** ⊛ Unoaked SA icon from decomposed granite & sandstone vineyards. **17** ⑨'s 6-month sojourn on lees adds texture, savoury note to yellow stonefruit & apple palate. Endless saline length, like standout **16** ★★★★★ ⑨.— HC

Location/map/WO: Stellenbosch ▪ Map grid reference: B6 ▪ Est/1stB 2000 ▪ Tasting & sales Mon-Fri 9-5 by appt only ▪ Fee R500 per group (2-10 pax) ▪ Closed all pub hols ▪ Owner(s) Bruwer Raats ▪ Cellarmaster(s) Bruwer Raats (Jan 2000) ▪ Winemaker(s) Gavin Bruwer Slabbert (Feb 2010) ▪ Viticulturist(s) Bruwer Raats (Jan 2000) & Gavin Bruwer Slabbert (Feb 2010) ▪ 30ha (cab f, chenin) ▪ 150t/20,000cs own label 40% red 60% white ▪ PO Box 2068 Dennesig Stellenbosch 7601 ▪ braats@mweb.co.za ▪ www.raats.co.za ▪ S 33° 58' 16.6" E 018° 44' 55.3" ▪ ⌨ shredded.balance.undefended ▪ F +27 (0)86-647-8500 ▪ **T +27 (0)21-881-3078**

☐ **Racetrack** *see* Damarakloof

Radford Dale

Broad-based and long-term recognition of the top-tier Radford Dale brand, synonymous with the success of this acclaimed multi-nation-owned Helderberg winery, has prompted the change of name from The Winery of Good Hope to Radford Dale. Slight tweaking of the tiers, but no change to the philosophy of non-interventionist vine- and wine-growing (wild ferments, lower alcohols, natural acidities, minimal additives), preference for lighter-style reds or innovative showcasing of heritage varieties. Or ingrained and tangible care for social and environmental well-being. Strong connections with Burgundy ensures the ranges remain nirvana for pinotphiles (and chardonnay fanciers).

Radford Dale range

★★★★ Thirst Cinsault ⓥ Thirst-quenchingly low in alcohol (10.5%), carbonic/bunch-fermented **17** ⑧⑥ brims with tangy, grippy cranberry fruit. Proudly geeky, & delicious, requires chilling. Unoaked, as next.

★★★★ The Antidote Gamay Noir ⑯④ Savoury **17** ⑧⑨ billows meat spice & raspberry fruit, is light-tripping on palate with bone-dry finish. Wholebunch carbonic fermentation with wild yeasts in 7,000L oak vessel.

★★★★ Thirst Gamay Noir Vibrant red cherry notes on light, fresh **18** ⑧⑥, fruity Beaujolais-style red made like Cinsault sibling &, like it, best served chilled. Just 10.5% alcohol for lunch. And beyond.

★★★★☆ AD Pinot Noir ⓥ ⓐ Curated under the hand of co-founder Alex Dale, the most fragrant, perhaps most delicate of the house's pinots. Elgin fruit destemmed & wholeberry fermented; **17** ⑨④ no lightweight given its black cherry intensity & serious structure, with grippy tannins. Bone-dry, naturally low 10.5% alcohol.

★★★★☆ Freedom Pinot Noir ⓥ ⓐ Best of the top 3 Elgin pinots, all 10 months in oak, this 10% new, rest only old barrels. Poised **17** ⑨③'s floral/violet bouquet leads to tangy black berry fruit, fresh acidity & fine-grained tannins, some smoked meat nuances, too. All the components harmonious.

★★★★☆ Frankenstein Pinotage ⓥ Handled like a pinot noir (50% bunch ferment, 10 months older oak), vibrant **16** ⑨① packed with bright, juicy red berry fruit; at 12.75% alcohol, no monster, actually rather poised & elegant; perfumed & fresh.

★★★★☆ Nudity Syrah ⓐ 'Natural wine' (no additives, not even sulphur) from organic Voor-Paardeberg site. Intensely aromatic **16** ⑨③; vibrant pepper tones, wild berries, hints of fynbos & smoked meat, a chalky minerality. Like **15** ⑨①, great complexity considering older oak imparts no spice.

★★★★☆ Syrah ⓐ Singular Stellenbosch rendition, more muscular, less fragrant than Nudity; **15** ⑨③'s scrub, fynbos & earthy profile heralds savoury intensity with beautiful balance in a long tail. Portion bunch-fermented, some post-ferment maceration. 20% new oak, 18 months.

★★★★★ Black Rock ⓥ **15** ⑨⑤ maintains fine form. Gorgeous fynbos perfume, brambly berries & spice from 40% syrah, 25% cinsaut, carignan, grenache & mourvèdre, co-fermented/aged in oak, 16 months, 20% new. Naturally fermented Swartland fruit, like **14** ⑨⑦, our 2017 Red Wine of the Year.

★★★★☆ Gravity ⓥ Forceful, forward **10** ⑨② from shiraz, cab, merlot offering spice & bright red & black berries on a firmly structured base. Successfully balances the claims of fresh fruitiness & savoury depths to give some early complexity supported by good oaking. Will benefit from cellaring.

★★★★☆ Chardonnay ⓐ Winemaker as chaperone rather than surgeon allows natural processes to yield balanced **17** ⑨④; fresh peachy fruit in firm but pliable support with remarkably low alcohol (11.5%). There's added allure of vanilla-spiced creaminess from 10 months in French oak, 15% new.

★★★★☆ The Renaissance of Chenin Blanc From dryland Helderberg bushvines, partial bunch-pressing, wild yeast ferment in older oak, bone-dry, modest 12.5% alcohol. Sensual **17** ⑨① has honeysuckle aromas & a velvety structure supporting fresh citrus & waxy lanolin. Exceptional refreshment.

★★★★ Vinum Chenin Blanc Partly barrel fermented with extended lees contact, **17** ◯87 has savoury 'umami' backbone, ripe melon fruit centre. Rich, with a balancing acidity, steely finish & pleasing 12.5% alcohol.

Thirst Clairette Blanche ⓣ **★★★★** Rare varietal bottling expressing 'integrity, energy, individuality'. **18** ⑧⑤ 'natural wine' refreshes with restrained alcohol (12.5%), as grapefruit on palate gives way to saline finish.

Not tasted: **Vine Dried Chenin Blanc**. Discontinued: **Vinum Cabernet Sauvignon**.

Labeye range

★★★★☆ Pinot Noir ⓥ ⓐ Like Freedom sibling, destemmed Elgin grapes are not crushed to allow semi-carbonic maceration. Reflecting the persona of the cellarmaster, **17** ⑨③ brawniest of the pinots with earthy wild strawberry & morello cherry fruit, enticing fynbos perfume & savoury truffle hints.

Pearce Predhomme range

★★★★ Cinsault-Syrah Duo for export customer. Pot-pourri on nose of 'whole-cluster, wild-ferment' **17** ★★★★☆ ⑨① fabulously expressive of red berry fruit from 65/35 blend. Lighter **16** ⑧⑨ 'Syrah-Cinsault' (55/45 blend) had tangy-sweet fruit against on backdrop. Lovely 12.5% alcohol.

★★★★☆ **Chenin Blanc** Made from 5 parcels in collaboration with 'like-minded' Canadian sommeliers, elegant old-vine, wild-ferment **17** ⑨① more vinous than fruity but balanced. Peachy **16** ⑨④ offered tangerine & melon fruit cut by very bright acidity. Touch of new oak, trademark moderate alcohol.

Land of Hope range

★★★★ **Reserve Cabernet Sauvignon** Plush but poised, ripe yet restrained **16** ⑧⑧ has earth, tobacco & leather notes to complement concentrated dark berry fruit. Now more new/longer French oak: 35%, 20 months.

★★★★ **Reserve Pinot Noir** ⊘ Wholeberry fermented, basket pressed, naturally fermented in tank & then briefly buffed in oak, **16** ⑧⑧ has grip with an earthy, savoury, mineral edge. WO W Cape.

★★★★ **Reserve Chenin Blanc** Part bunch-pressed, natural-yeast fermented in barrel. **17** ⑧⑧ fuller, tighter, more palate traction than siblings in the ranges, cling peach & yellow apple features with subtle oak spice.

Syrah (NEW) ★★★ Farmyard aromas spiral around streamlined fruit in austere **16** ⑧② from destemmed & crushed grapes. Year old oak. Not tasted: **Chardonnay**. Discontinued: **Cabernet Sauvignon**.

Winery of Good Hope range

★★★★ **Reserve Pinot Noir** ⊘ Fresh & bright, with tangy black berry fruit, soft & yielding. **17** ⑧⑦ Elgin grapes destemmed, crushed & naturally fermented in steel before year in older oak. Great value.

· ·

Oceanside Cabernet Sauvignon-Merlot ⍟ ★★★★ Charming & generous **16** ⑧⑤ blend (88/12) frames blackcurrant & mulberry fruit in soft-textured mouthful, brief lick of old oak. **Bush Vine Chenin Blanc** ⍟ ★★★★ Pre-bottling, **18** ⑧⑤ gushes tropical fruit unfettered by oak, but taut, bone-dry finish brings balance. Uncomplicated yet deep flavoured.

· ·

Whole Berry Pinotage ★★★★ Name adjusted to reflect cellar's choice of wholeberry maceration & fermentation. Unoaked **18** ⑧⑤ a pure-fruited expression that avoids jammy, astringent tones; bone-dry, with early-drinking appeal. Coastal WO. **Mountainside Syrah** ★★★★ Previewed **17** ⑧③ shows relative restraint; white pepper woven into somewhat stern texture. Year seasoned casks. **Granite Ridge Reserve** ★★★★ Back after hiatus of three years; syrah combo with cab & merlot rests 18 months in seasoned oak. **16** ⑧④ peppery nuance & firm tannin, for food. WO W Cape, as next. **Unoaked Chardonnay** ★★★★ Made for early & easy drinking, **18** ⑧⑤ brims with citrus fruit, fresh acidity & even some stony minerality. — DS

Location: Stellenbosch ▪ Map: Helderberg ▪ Map grid reference: C1 ▪ WO: Stellenbosch/Elgin/Western Cape/ Coastal/Swartland/Voor Paardeberg ▪ Est/1stB 1998 ▪ Tasting & sales Mon-Fri 9-5 ▪ Closed all pub hols ▪ Owner(s) Alex Dale, Andy Openshaw, Yalumba, Edouard Labeye, Cliff Roberson, Ben Radford, Heather Whitman, Kathleen Krone & Jacques de Klerk ▪ Cellarmaster(s) Edouard Labeye (1998) ▪ Winemaker(s) Jacques de Klerk (Oct 2009), with Gerhard Joubert (Jun 2016) ▪ Viticulturist(s) Edouard Labeye, Jacques de Klerk, Gus Dale & Gerhard Joubert ▪ ±100ha (cab, carignan, cinsaut, gamay, grenache, mourv, ptage, pinot, shiraz, chard, chenin, clairette, verdelho) ▪ 700t/40,000cs own label 50% red 50% white ▪ Level 2 BEE, IPW, WIETA ▪ Postnet Suite 124 Private Bag X15 Somerset West 7129 ▪ thirsty@radforddale.com ▪ www. radforddale.com ▪ S 34° 0′ 57.5″ E 018° 49′ 2.6″ ▪ ✉ dancing.lessened.carbonates ▪ F +27 (0)21-855-5529 ▪ **T +27 (0)21-855-5528**

Rainbow's End Wine Estate ⓥ ⓐ

South Africans are adept at 'making a plan', which is exactly what retired engineer Jacques Malan was advised to do by a French vigneron friend after planting vines on the steep slopes of Stellenbosch's Banhoek Valley in the 1990s. So, instead of spending money on erecting a cellar, Jacques repurposed the existing farm buildings and, there, sons Anton and Francois handcraft increasingly impressive, elegantly powerful reds with basket pressing and manual punchdowns in the traditional way.

Reserve range

★★★★☆ **Family Reserve** ⍟ Exceptional **15** ⑨④ sees flagship Bordeaux red upped from 4- to 5-way blend, cab franc & merlot in the lead. Elegant, refined & supple, has fruitcake, graphite, spice & tobacco harmoniously integrated with silky oak, 66% new. Powerful but gentle.

Estate range

★★★★☆ Cabernet Sauvignon ⓐ Solid core of ripe cassis fruit on **16** ⑨④. Seamless, velvety palate is rich, with beautifully assimilated oak, 45% new, for a year. Nuanced & complex, it had a further year of bottle maturation before release.

★★★★ Cabernet Franc Hedgerow fruit & brush of herb on typically inky, cocoa-toned **16** ⑧⑨. Good grip & firm tannin from year French oak, 40% new. Rich & long.

★★★★☆ Cabernet Franc Limited Release ⓐ Silky soft, textured & ripe **16** ⑨③ is dark, deep & concentrated. Rich & rewarding too, with blue/black fruit & trademark pencil shavings. Complex, layered with fine dry tannin from year in 45% new oak.

★★★★ Merlot Mulberry & inky blue fruits on **17** ★★★★★ ⑨②, fraction leaner than **16** ⑧⑥ but rich, succulent & effortlessly refined nonetheless. Firm core & chalky grip of tannin from year in oak, third new. Also in magnum.

★★★★ Shiraz Approachable **16** ⑧⑨ is rounded & plummy, with a smoky liquorice nuance. Palate is layered but soft, juicy & supple. Oak is restrained - just 30% new.

Mystical Corner ★★★★ Bright red-fruit cheer on **17** ⑧③ 4-way blend, half cab with petit verdot, shiraz & malbec. Easy, juicy & light. **Rosé ★★★** Smoky cranberry vibrancy to dry, tangy **17** ⑧①. Berry entry makes way for honeyed fantail. Balanced & easy cab franc-led 6-way mix. **Chenin Blanc** ⓠ **★★★★** Bold quince & pear notes, **16** ⑧③ fresh succulence countered by creamy breadth from one third oaking, all new. — FM

Location/map: Stellenbosch ▪ Map grid reference: H6 ▪ WO: Banghoek ▪ Est 1978 ▪ 1stB 2002 ▪ Tasting, sales & tours by appt ▪ Fees: R50 tasting/R80 tour, waived on purchase of R250+ ▪ Closed all pub hols ▪ Sales also via website, delivery free of charge ▪ Conservation area ▪ Owner(s) Malan family ▪ Cellarmaster(s) Anton Malan (Nov 2000) ▪ Winemaker(s) Anton Malan (Nov 2000) & Francois Malan (Jan 2005) ▪ Viticulturist(s) Francois Malan (Jan 2005) ▪ 42ha/19ha (cabs s/f, malbec, merlot, p verdot, shiraz) ▪ 120t/8,200cs own label 90% red 10% rosé ▪ IPW, WIETA ▪ PO Box 2253 Dennesig 7601 ▪ info@rainbowsend.co.za ▪ www.rainbowsend.co.za ▪ S 33° 56′ 25.8″ E 018° 56′ 42.6″ ▪ 🖼 tracking.either.dinosaur ▪ **T +27 (0)21-885-1719/+27 (0)83-411-0170/+27 (0)82-404-1085**

☐ **Raised By Wolves** see Yardstick Wines

Raka

⬤⬤⬤⬤

Paterfamilias Piet Dreyer gave up commercial squid fishing after 36 years and named his Stanford wine venture after his beloved black fishing vessel, Raka. Sons Josef (winemaker) and Pieter (viticulturist) work with sister Jorika Visser in handling the marketing and promotion of the family business. Though the Klein River meanders through the property, 2018 was difficult because of the drought, but a ray of light was the first harvest of 32 tons for their staff empowerment arm, Akkedisberg, and 'quality overall was good'.

★★★★☆ Cabernet Sauvignon ⊘ ⓐ Svelte, spicy & amply fruited, **16** ⑨⓪ everything a cab should be. Smart, nuanced, focused, with backbone of oak (25% new French) beautifully supporting core of ripe, supple black fruit. Long & rewarding.

★★★★☆ Cabernet Franc Floral & spicy, with tobacco leaf note, brisk acid, **16** ★★★★ ⑧⑨ marginally lighter & less expressive than **15** ⑨③. Dry, grippy tannins on the tail.

★★★★ Barrel Select Merlot Like Cab Franc, **16** ⑧⑨ bit more austere than **15** ★★★★★ ⑨①. Ample hedgerow fruit, leafy blackcurrant & spice but firm tannins make it lean. Selection of best 30 barrels.

★★★★ Petit Verdot After dense & forceful **13** ⑧⑦, **16** ★★★★ ⑧⑤ is leaner, its cranberry succulence & chalky tannin grip striking a gawky note. No **14**, **15**.

★★★★☆ Biography Shiraz ⊘ Blueberry succulence, herb brush & vanilla cream oak notes of **16** ⑨⓪ beautifully poised. Inky, complex & deep, with sympathetic barrelling (25% new French, as all the reds unless noted). Matches also-tasted **15** ⑨⓪ in elegance & refinement. Long, rich, defined finish. No **14**.

★★★★☆ Five Maidens ⓠ Knockout **11** ⑨⓪ 5-way cab-led Bordeaux-style commemorates 10 years of the Dreyer family in wine. Elegant intensity, without excess weight. Great vibrancy & persistence.

★★★★☆ Quinary ⊘ ⓐ Ever-reliable 5-way Bordeaux red, cab (45%) led in **16** ⑨①, with soft brambly appeal which lives up to **15** ⑨⓪ (also reviewed) & previous. Tealeaf, black cherry & star anise well balanced with oak, supple, textured & soft. Will reward patience. Also in 1.5L to 18L.

★★★★ **Figurehead Cape Blend** Ⓥ Pinotage with the 5 Bordeaux reds, **15** Ⓐ⑨ leans towards the latter, with leafy herbal notes, earthy minerality & spicy blackcurrant fruit. Sophisticated, showing restraint. **Malbec** ★★★★ Lively & succulent **16** ⑧④ appeals in its plum generosity. Oak (25% new) is harmonious & adds to overall poise. **Pinotage** ★★★★ Vivid generosity of bright spicy berries on **16** ⑧⑤, ably cradled by oak. Cheery & approachable, perfect spaghetti bolognese companion. Some American oak. **Sangiovese** Ⓥ ★★★★ Like a light & fresh Chianti, **15** ⑧⑤ shows the fruity charm of the variety without gravitas. Hints of tomato cocktail & raisins, with tanned leather. **Spliced** ★★★ Chunky **16** ⑧⓪ 5-way shiraz blend less well joined than name suggests. Rustic & meaty, it too shows influence of grippy wood. Cape South Coast WO. **Dry Rosé** ★★★ Tank sample **18** ⑦⑨ offers juicy brightness of strawberry & cherry. Dry & tangy, it's a poolside quaffer. **Sauvignon Blanc** ⊘ ★★★★ Elderflower & grapefruit tang to vivid **18** ⑧④. Long skin- & lees-ageing add extra nuance to succulent freshness. Discontinued: **Mourvèdre**. — FM

Location: Stanford ▪ Map: Walker Bay & Bot River ▪ Map grid reference: C8 ▪ WO: Klein River/Cape South Coast ▪ Est/1stB 2002 ▪ Tasting & sales Mon–Fri 9–5 Sat 10–2.30 ▪ Tasting fee: R15/6 wines on daily tasting list, or R85/whole range ▪ Closed Sun, Good Fri & Dec 25 ▪ Cellar tours & large groups by appt ▪ BYO picnic ▪ Conservation area ▪ Owner(s) Piet Dreyer ▪ Winemaker(s) Josef Dreyer (Jan 2007) ▪ Viticulturist(s) Pieter Dreyer (Jan 2007) ▪ 76ha/62ha (5 Bdx, mourv, ptage, sangio, shiraz, sauv, viog) ▪ 350t/30,000cs own label 75% red 17% white 8% rosé ▪ IPW ▪ PO Box 124 Caledon 7230 ▪ info@rakawine.co.za ▪ www.rakawine.co.za ▪ S 34° 23' 56.1" E 019° 37' 26.7" ▪ ⊠ captain.charmer.finders ▪ F +27 (0)86-606-5462 ▪ **T +27 (0)28-341-0676**

Rall Wines   Ⓥ

Two new wines from Donovan Rall illustrate his approach. A Syrah from the same source as Ava Chenin shows his fascination with the Swartland and his commitment to, above all, express origin. Many of his wines come from Swartland, conforming to the 'natural' precepts of the Swartland Independent Producers. And he's still looking to find a suitable small property there as a home for Rall Wines (at present his SIP wines are made in rented space). The new Wellington white, from the last few vines of cinsault blanc in SA, speaks of his exploration and experimentation (and his finesse), including his greater use of concrete and clay for fermentation and maturation. Donovan also makes wine for Clouds and Vuurberg in Stellenbosch.

★★★★★ **Cinsault** Perfumed red fruit with a deeper savoury tang on **17** ⑨② from Swartland & Darling grapes. Bunch fermented (for added brightness), foot-trodden, matured in concrete & old oak. Supple charm, with greater structure & seriousness than many local examples.

★★★★★ **Ava Syrah** ⓃⒺ Ⓖ Subtle spiciness, lilies & unshowy red fruit aromas on **17** ⑨⑤ from block beside Ava Chenin. Exciting, nervy palate, somewhat austerely tucking the pure fruit into the structure of stony, powdery dry tannins & fresh acid. Needs years in bottle to fulfil potential, but persistence suggests it.

★★★★☆ **Red** Ⓖ Appealing fragrance on **16** ⑨③ at least partly thanks to 15% cinsault; 70% syrah, adding spice & depth, plus carignan & grenache (all bunch pressed) for a convincing whole. Succulent acid & firm dry tannins beautifully control & guide the sweet, ripe fruit; elegant but not without oomph.

★★★★☆ **Ava Chenin Blanc** Ⓖ Last year **16** ⑨④ tasted, incorrectly vintaged. **17** ★★★★★ ⑨⑤ ex single vineyard a fine follow up, with similar intensity of pure, mineral-fruity aromas & flavours. Remarkable silky finesse & fresh subtlety, full of whispered sweet suggestiveness. 8-month ferment in old oak barrels.

★★★★ **Cinsault Blanc** ⓃⒺ From unique oak Wellington vines. After 4 days skin contact, into old barrel & clay pot. **17** ⑧⑨ aromas more leesy & savoury, but there's a core of sweet fruit to taste. Very clean & dry; bright, tight & light (11% alcohol), but well textured & with a gently lingering finish.

★★★★☆ **Grenache Blanc** Ⓖ From Piekenierskloof, bunch fermented in concrete 'egg'. **17** ⑨④ pure aromatic floral, lightly fruity charm, with a dry stony minerality giving a more austere elegance to the subtle depth & delicate generosity of the fresh palate. Riper richness than previously.

★★★★☆ **White** Ⓖ Delicately earth-tinged floral, peach aromas lead to a bright, refined palate replete with pervasive, persuasive ripe fruit & a thread of bright acid. Bunch pressed; older oak. **17** ★★★★★ ⑨⑤ mostly ex Swartland, as was **16** ⑨③, led by 71% chenin, with Stellenbosch verdelho (24%) & a little viognier.— TJ

Location: Malmesbury ▪ Map: Swartland ▪ Map grid reference: C7 ▪ WO: Swartland/Coastal/Wellington/ Piekenierskloof ▪ Est/1stB 2008 ▪ Tasting, sales & cellar tours by appt ▪ Owner(s)/winemaker(s)/viticulturist(s) Donovan Rall ▪ 30t/1,500cs own label 50% red 50% white ▪ info@rallwines.co.za ▪ www.rallwines.co.za ▪ S 33° 30' 39.1" E 018° 48' 22.5" ▪ **T +27 (0)72-182-7571**

Rannoch Farm

The lake and the scenery in general of Rory and Ricky Antrobus' Helderberg farm reminded them of the Scottish highlands, hence the name they chose. There's a tiny vineyard of cabernet, tended by Rory, whose wine is vinified at Avondale in Paarl.

★★★★ **Cabernet Sauvignon** Lovely, pure expression of blackcurrant fruit, subtle tobacco & cedar, **15** ⑧⑨'s seamless integration of new French oak, 18 months, aided by 3 years bottle ageing at cellar.— JG

Location/WO: Stellenbosch ▪ Est 1999 ▪ 1stB 2003 ▪ Closed to public ▪ Owner(s) Rory & Ricky Antrobus ▪ Winemaker(s) Corné Marais, with Ivan September (both Jan 2010, Avondale) ▪ Viticulturist(s) Rory Antrobus (Mar 1999) ▪ 8ha/1ha (cab) ▪ 6t/500cs own label 100% white ▪ PO Box 5667 Helderberg 7135 ▪ rory@gmint.co.za ▪ **T +27 (0)82-570-3106**

☐ **Raptor Post** see Fable Mountain Vineyards
☐ **Rare Sightings** see The Fledge & Co

Rascallion Wines ⓘ

The blends from this newer Stellenbosch negociant business owned by the Kretzmar family and marketing maven Ross Sleet should appeal to wine, word and music lovers alike. Off-beat labels for the Word Collection include Bombinate (hum, buzz), Susurrous (whisper, rustle) and Pandiculation (inhale, yawn). The Vinyl Collection evokes nostalgia for LP and single records. Acclaimed packaging for both.

Word Collection (NEW)

Bombinate ★★★★ Smooth, polished & long, **16** ⑧④ has a touch of style, exudes attractive dark fruit underpinned by judicious oak, 18 months, 25% new. Shiraz & grenache (85/15) from Stellenbosch.
Pandiculation ★★★ Dense & fairly serious **15** ⑧② needs year/2 or a meal for tannins/acid to meld. Shiraz (85%) & grenache noir fermented/aged separately (25% of shiraz in older oak). **Susurrous** ★★★ Attention to detail, as all these. **16** ⑧② barrel-fermented chenin (70%) & grenache blanc with 10% tank-fermented sauvignon for freshness. Still unknit mid-2018, should settle & improve over few years. **Aquiver** ★★★★ Complex & involving partnership 80% tank-fermented chenin, 10% each lees-fermented sauvignon & grenache blanc, latter in older barrels. **16** ⑧④ peach & white flowers, slightly smoky with nutty finish.

Vinyl Collection (NEW)

45 RPM ⓖ ★★★ Delicious everyday quaffing, unoaked **16** ⑦⑨ gets some complexity from mix grenache, cinsaut, mourvèdre & tannat. Like sibling, from Piekienierskloof vines. **33 1/3 RPM** ⓖ ★★★ Attractive **17** ⑧① white orchard fruit & spice, satisfying flavours & mouthfeel. Equal chenin/roussanne plus splashes grenache blanc, viognier & verdelho. — WB, CvZ

Location/map: Stellenbosch ▪ Map grid reference: E5 ▪ WO: Western Cape ▪ Est 2017 ▪ 1stB 2015 ▪ Tasting & sales Mon-Sun 10-6 (Nov-Apr) & Mon-Sat 10-5 (May-Oct) ▪ Owner(s) Ross Sleet, A Kretzmar Family Trust ▪ Winemaker(s) consultants ▪ 12,000cs own label 55% red 45% white ▪ PO Box 15176 Vlaeberg Cape Town 8018 ▪ ross@rascallionwines.co.za ▪ www.rascallionwines.co.za ▪ S 33° 56' 27.6" E 018° 50' 47.3" ▪ **T +27 (0)78-886-2246**

☐ **Ready Steady** see Southern Sky Wines
☐ **Rebourne Fairtrade** see Imbuko Wines
☐ **Rebus** see Romond Vineyards
☐ **Red Chair** see Rooiberg Winery
☐ **Red Falcon** see Middelvlei Estate

Redford Lane Wines ⓘ

The wine tourism element of this family winery on Redford Road in cool-climate Plettenberg Bay's The Crags area was being scaled down at press time, with the farm-style restaurant and deli closing. However, husband-and-wife team Brendan and Leanne Lane confirm that tastings and sales are still available by appointment. The current releases are '18 Sauvignon Blanc and NV Méthode Cap Classique Sauvignon Blanc.

Location: Plettenberg Bay ▪ Map: Klein Karoo & Garden Route ▪ Map grid reference: C1 ▪ Est 2008 ▪ 1stB 2013 ▪ Tasting & sales by appt only ▪ Closed Dec 25 ▪ Owner(s) Leanne & Brendan Lane ▪ Winemaker(s) Anton Smal (Bramon Wines) ▪ ±3ha (cab f, malbec, chenin, gewürtz, sauv, sem) ▪ 4-5t/200cs own label 100% white ▪ Postnet Suite 244 Private Bag X1006 Plettenberg Bay 6600 ▪ laneleanne1@gmail.com ▪ www.redfordlanewines.co.za ▪ S 33° 55' 58.32" E 023° 26' 21.40" ▪ 🗺 downtown.awaited.rocked ▪ **T +27 (0)83-708-0735**

☐ **Red Rhino** see Linton Park Wines

☐ **Releaf Organic** see Imbuko Wines

Remhoogte Wine Estate

A genuine family concern this – the Stellenbosch estate bought by Murray Boustred in 1994 (he was one of the early upcountry businessmen to move into Cape wine in the modern era), and his two sons now playing the dominant role: Chris in the cellar and amongst the vines, Rob marketing what he produces. Indoors, the tasting room expansion and upgrade is complete, and in the vineyards the planting programme continues, with Bordeaux red varieties in 2018 – grapes well suited, the team says, to these Simonsberg slopes, and the new plantings 'tying into the focus on these cultivars going forward'.

Reserve range

★★★★ Cabernet Sauvignon Plenty of oak character showing on **16** ⑧⑦ from 80% new barrels, adding to the big dry tannic structure. Dark berry fruit too, but not quite enough intensity to cope. Not unimpressive, though.

★★★★☆ Syrah ⓐ Attractive spicy, berry aromas on **16** ⑨④ lead to flavourful & powerful, muscular palate - though less massive than **15 ★★★★★** ⑨⑤. 30% wholebunch helps give lighter feeling than in other top reds here. 80% new oak under control. Intense fruit gives lingering dry finish. 14.5% alcohol.

★★★★☆ Sir Thomas Cullinan ⓐ Row selection from highest vineyards. Cedar, cigarbox & fruitcake aromas on handsome, intense **15** ⑨③ blend of merlot & 30% cab. Packed with fruit & savoury intensity, with tannins that need good few years to resolve, yet not untouched by finesse. Supportive oak, 40% new. 15% alcohol.

★★★★☆ Honeybunch Chenin Blanc Gleams mid-gold from 10 hours skin contact & oak (15% new). **17** ⑨② full-bodied, its richness enhanced by 5 g/l sugar - balanced acidity ensures no undue sweetness. Broad & deep, supple & silky, with plenty of flavour & characteristic honey note. Native yeast ferment, as both ranges.

Premium range

★★★★ Aspect Merlot Shows fruitcake, choc, with a herbal twist & oaky overlay. **15** ⑧⑥ lots of flavour, with big, dry tannic structure exacerbated by 2 years in barrel (30% new). Burly 14.8% alcohol.

★★★★ Vantage Pinotage Most appealing deep dark-fruit aromas on **16** ⑧⑦, the rich ripe flavours no less so. Juicy, chewy & fleshy, the dry tannins reined in for early approachability (but no hurry).

★★★★ Chronicle Cape Blend Forward ripe aromas on **15** ⑧⑦ from estate's 4 red grapes. Boldly flavourful though not very intense, the 14.8% alcohol & firm dry tannins in balance - & the oak should soon become so.

★★★★ First Light Chenin Blanc ⊘ Always a small oaked component (from Honeybunch) in fresh, fruit-driven style. Tasted very young, **18** ⑧⑥ exuberantly flavourful, with serious core of crisp acidity. **17** ⑧⑧ also reviewed: calmer, more spicy, some complexity gained; similar freshness & usual marmalade sweet-sour element. Stellenbosch WO.— TJ

Location/map: Stellenbosch ▪ Map grid reference: F3 ▪ WO: Simonsberg–Stellenbosch/Stellenbosch ▪ Est 1812 ▪ 1stB 1995 ▪ Tasting & sales Mon-Fri 9–5 Sat 10-4 ▪ Closed Easter Fri-Sun, Dec 25/26 & Jan 1 ▪ Cellar tours by appt ▪ Cheese platters, craft beer ▪ Functions ▪ Walks/hikes ▪ Game ▪ Guest cottage ▪ Wild Beast Craft Brewery ▪ Owner(s) Murray Boustred Trust ▪ Cellarmaster(s) Chris Boustred (Jan 2011) ▪ Winemaker(s)/viticulturist(s) Chris Boustred (Jan 2007) ▪ 55ha/25ha (cab, merlot, ptage, shiraz, chenin) ▪ 130t/10,000cs own label 80% red 20% white ▪ IPW ▪ PO Box 2032 Dennesig 7601 ▪ info@remhoogte.co.za ▪ www.

remhoogte.co.za ▪ S 33° 53' 4.2" E 018° 51' 4.6" ▪ ⬛ nobody.tweaked.whom ▪ F +27 (0)21-889-6907 ▪ **T +27 (0)21-889-5005**

☐ **ReMogo** *see* Walking Woods Wines
☐ **Renaissance Collection** *see* New Beginnings Wines
☐ **Renosterbos** *see* Hofstraat Kelder

Restless River ⓘ

For boutique vintners Craig and Anne Wessels, producing varietal wines exclusively from home-grown grapes in Upper Hemel-en-Aarde Valley has its challenges and temptations when both sell out pre-release. But their commitment is unwavering to site and restraint, realised in their ageworthy, classic pair (the long-awaited pinot noir is yet to arrive). New is a barrel cellar, an enclosed, south-facing lean-to cut into the clay dam wall to bolster temperature stability. All the wine is now fermented in old French oak, and a portion of the chardonnay in two 400L Italian terracotta pots. The latter, Craig is pleased to note, allows him to cut back on the wood component. An extra textural dimension is another benefit, though ultimately the Wessels acknowledge 'the magic is in the Ava Marie vineyard'.

★★★★☆ **Main Road & Dignity Cabernet Sauvignon** ⓐ Single-vineyard, classic style **15** ⑨③ shows cool-climate purity, vibrancy in its blackcurrant, herbal & cedar notes. Youthful tautness suggests 10+ year maturation. The fruit is perfectly ripe & persists with delicious savoury length. Stylish 20% new oak trim.

★★★★★ **Ava Marie Chardonnay** ⓐ Fine single-vineyard wine beautifully composed in classic style. **16** ⑨⑤ pure, expressive lime intensity, underlying nutty richness harmonised, endlessly lengthened by savoury tension. Oak enhanced, 5% new. Texture, structure & balance ensure future pleasure.— AL

Location: Hermanus ▪ Map: Walker Bay & Bot River ▪ Map grid reference: B4 ▪ WO: Upper Hemel-en-Aarde Valley ▪ Est 1999 ▪ 1stB 2005 ▪ Tasting & sales by appt ▪ Closed all pub hols ▪ Owner(s) Craig & Anne Wessels ▪ Winemaker(s) Craig Wessels (Jan 2005) ▪ Viticulturist(s) Kevin Watt (2012) ▪ 20ha/7ha (cab, pinot, chard) ▪ 20t/2,500cs own label 50% red 50% white ▪ PO Box 1739 Hermanus 7200 ▪ anne@restlessriver.com ▪ www.restlessriver.com ▪ S 34° 21' 26.11" E 19° 16' 32.80" ▪ ⬛ parental.earmark.inform ▪ **T +27 (0)28-313-2881/+27 (0)82-650-3544**

☐ **Retief Reserve** *see* Van Loveren Family Vineyards
☐ **Retief Wines** *see* Pearl Mountain
☐ **Retro Series** *see* Elemental Bob
☐ **Revenant** *see* False Bay Vineyards

Reverie ⓘ

Drought has brought 'serious challenges', especially for dry-farmed vines like these, planted in 1978, from which Radford Dale winemaker Jacques de Klerk produces soupçons of his own stellar chenin. But increasing sales through new distribution deals in Johannesburg and the UK have ensured rewards for his grower's efforts, and encouraged Jacques and French-born wife Amelie to introduce an 'exciting' red soon.

★★★★☆ **Chenin Blanc** ⓐ Finessed from tiny berries off 40+ year old Swartland dryland bushvines, 5 day skin contact, natural ferment in old oak. **17** ⑨③ is crisp & dry, with an intriguing oystershell minerality/salinity. Exceptionally elegant at 11% alcohol, as was sensational **16** ★★★★★ ⑨⑤.— DS

Location: Stellenbosch ▪ WO: Swartland ▪ Est 2011 ▪ 1stB 2012 ▪ Tasting & sales by appt ▪ Closed all pub hols ▪ Owner(s) Jacques de Klerk ▪ Cellarmaster(s)/viticulturist(s) Jacques de Klerk (Nov 2011) ▪ Winemaker(s) Jacques de Klerk (Nov 2011), with Amelie de Klerk (Nov 2011) ▪ 150cs own label 100% white ▪ 15 Seaview Rd Somerset West 7130 ▪ reveriechenin@gmail.com ▪ **T +27 (0)82-783-7647**

☐ **Rex Equus** *see* Perdeberg Wines

Reyneke Wines ⓘ ⓐ ⓑ

Co-owner and viticulturist Johan Reyneke's original family estate, Uitzicht, in Stellenbosch's Polkadraai has been farmed biodynamically since 2004, and currently is one of only two SA farms with official (Demeter) certification. A neighbour's property was acquired in 2016, giving cellarmaster Rudiger Gretschel a total of

60 ha of vineyards, and a range of soils, slopes and altitudes to work with. At press time the incorporated land was nearing the third and final year of conversion to organic and biodynamic viticulture. Adherence to nature-centric principles has enabled the Reyneke vineyards to fare remarkably well through three years of drought, with consistent yields and high natural acidity. The Organic range, from outsourced certified-organic fruit, has been expanded and packaging tweaked, including reverting to sustainable cork closures.

Biodynamic Reserve range

★★★★☆ **Cabernet Sauvignon** ◎ ⊛ Classic cassis & cedar, pencil shavings, tannins remarkably lithe, lovely core of sweet fruit, exceptional **15** ★★★★★ ⑨⑤ more streamlined & polished than **14** ⑨⓪, the result of stringent selection in the cellar - just 6 barrels chosen, 24 months in new oak after natural fermentation (as all here except Cornerstone) in concrete tanks.

★★★★☆ **Red** ◎ ⊛ 100% syrah, as always, from one vineyard, showing elegance as well as intensity in **16** ⑨④, white pepper, sweet spice & scrub, fine dry tannins. The elements well integrated if unevolved, deserving of cellaring or decanting in youth. Finer, more nuanced than Biodynamic sibling.

★★★★☆ **Natural Chenin Blanc** ◎ ⊛ A single clay amphora bottled for this old-vines label with no fining, filtration or added sulphur in **17** ⑨⓪. Lovely fruit purity though more demure in style, surprisingly so in fresher vintage, than more expressive, oaked **16** ⑨④. Quietly elegant & contemplative, with modest 12.5% alcohol. Needs some time to unfurl.

★★★★☆ **White** ◎ ⊛ Elegant expression of sauvignon in **17** ⑨③, mostly new oak vs older wood for Biodynamic sibling. This a much more outgoing personality, with white peach, florals & lime, developing more yeasty almond nuances on palate. Both vibrant & quite textural courtesy lees contact.

Biodynamic range

★★★★☆ **Syrah** ♡ Tenderly foot-trodden **16** ★★★★ ⑧⑨, supple, dry tannins & ample white pepper & savoury flavours. More approachable & riper, though less concentrated & impressive than **15** ⑨④.

★★★★ **Cornerstone** ⊗ ♡ Well-melded trio cab, merlot & cab franc spiced with 30% new oak. **15** ⑧⑧ classic dark-fruited aromas, creamy flesh & lively, fresh structure already happily absorbed.

★★★★ **Chenin Blanc** ⊛ Delicate florals & beeswax, some peach flavours from old vines. **17** ⑧⑥ fresh, balanced but very understated & just a shade off **16** ⑧⑦. Laudably light 11.5% alcohol.

★★★★ **Sauvignon Blanc** ♡ Fresh, flinty **17** ⑧⑥, stonefruit & lime, clean-cut & bright with gentle leesy undertone. Tad more freshness & less fruit than **16** ⑧⑦, but ready to enjoy.

Organic range

Chenin Blanc ⑭ ⑦ ♡ ★★★☆ Fruity appeal aplenty in **18** ⑧⑤, both fresh & creamy with tangy, clean farewell & echoes of ripe pear & peach. As enjoyable solo as with a meal. WO W Cape, like all these.

Cabernet Sauvignon-Merlot ⑭ ♡ ★★★ Previewed 60/40 blend reveals bright core of berry fruit, firm tannin framework still unknit in youth but **17** ⑧⓪ pleasingly fruit focused, the old oak a gentle support.
Shiraz-Cabernet Sauvignon ♡ ★★★ Shiraz is 90% of the duo in **17** ⑧②, smoky, savoury, supple, with juicy-spicy fruit & light oaking ready to braai, philosophise, warm wintry cockles. **Sauvignon Blanc-Semillon** ♡ ★★★☆ Same no-wood vinification & approachable, easy-drinking style for pair of vintages tasted. **17** ★★★ ⑧① fresher, lighter, oatmeal & some minerality; **18** ⑧④ riper & more expressive, creamy, with succulent stonefruit & honey. — MW

Location/map: Stellenbosch ▪ Map grid reference: B6 ▪ WO: Stellenbosch/Western Cape ▪ Est 1863 ▪ 1stB 1998 ▪ Tasting by appt only at R50/R150pp ▪ VIP tasting & vineyard walk with viticulturist and/or winemaker at R250pp (max 20), booking essential ▪ Sales Mon-Thu 9-5 Fri 9-3.30 ▪ Paintings by Mila Posthumus on display ▪ Owner(s) Reyneke Wines (Pty) Ltd ▪ Cellarmaster(s) Rudiger Gretschel ▪ Winemaker(s) Rudiger Gretschel, with Nuschka de Vos (Dec 2015) ▪ Viticulturist(s) Johan Reyneke, guided by Rosa Kruger ▪ 80ha/60ha (cabs s/f, merlot, ptage, shiraz, chenin, sauv) ▪ 70,000cs own label 70% red 30% white + 5,000cs for clients ▪ CERES (organic), Demeter (biodynamic), IPW ▪ PO Box 61 Vlottenburg 7604 ▪ lizanne@ reynekewines.co.za ▪ www.reynekewines.co.za ▪ S 33° 57′ 13.00 E 018° 44′ 26.50 ▪ ▦ railings.gingers. strategists ▪ T +27 (0)21-881-3451(main)/3517

Rhebokskloof Wine Estate

Tucked into a kloof of Paarl Mountain, the centuries-old estate has been converted into a modern multi-purpose leisure and business venue. But winegrowing is taken very seriously, the cellar duo of Rolanie Lotz and Karin Louw sharing over a decade here, their knowledge of the farm supplemented by the experience of new viticulturist André Rousseau (ex Constantia Uitsig). All concerned are enthused about the innovative new lightweight, easy-carry 187-ml pouches, 'for winelovers who cannot resist the call of the outdoors'.

Flagship range

★★★★★ **The Rhebok** ⓠ Powerful **14** ⑨⓪ blend shiraz (50%), pinotage & splash durif generously delivers dark fruit & Xmas spice, with a lovely freshness to counter substantial alcohol (±15%). Glycerol sweetness in sync with bold persona, as is all-new French oak, 2 years, which adds to authoritative tannin.

Mountain Vineyards Reserves

★★★★☆ **Black Marble Hill Syrah** ⓐ Classic varietal expression, complexity of blueberry, plum, pepper & violet in exceptional **15** ★★★★★ ⑨⑤. Assertive but polished tannins, mineral finish lift it above fine **14** ⑨⓪; both from best barrels selected to showcase Paarl.

★★★★☆ **Sandstone Grove Chardonnay** Hedonistic stonefruit, honeysuckle & butterscotch richness on **16** ⑨① in line with **15** ⑨②'s distinctive Paarl fruit profile & deft use of French oak. Slightly riper, more alcoholic, but no less charming.

Occasional release: **Design Shiraz**.

Vineyard Selections

★★★★ **Pinotage** Great purity & finesse in cherry-toned **16** ⑧⑨. Commendably savoury, with ripe tannin hold, floral farewell. A keeper but delicious now.

★★★★ **Shiraz** Vibrant red & dark fruit dusted with black pepper & spice in elegantly built **16** ⑧⑦. Well-judged oaking, as for all reds in line-up, 25-30% new, 15-18 months.

★★★★ **The MGS** As name suggests, trio mourvèdre, grenache & shiraz. Fine **16** ⑧⑨ weaves dark spices & earth with redcurrant, plum & violets. Bright & engaging, supple oak for food or solo enjoyment. Follows standout **15** ★★★★★ ⑨②. WO W Cape.

★★★★ **Chardonnay** ⓥ Vivid citrus, stonefruit & almond notes in smartly done barrel-fermented/aged **17** ⑧⑧. Creamy palate from frequent bâtonnage freshened by crisp acidity. Also in 187 ml pouch, as Shiraz.

Cellar Selections

....

Cabernet Sauvignon-Shiraz ⓥ ★★★★ No new oak, so generous fruitiness shines in **16** ⑧⑤. Cassis & blueberry, pepper & lavender, smooth enough to enjoy now.

....

The Flatrock ★★★ Was 'Flat Rock Red'. Cape Blend, **16** ⑧② predominantly shiraz, durif & pinotage, whiffs cocoa, spice & plum, zesty palate. WO Coastal, as next. **Bosstok Chenin Blanc** ★★★★ Chill-&-savour **18** ⑧④, crisp, enticing glassful tropical fruit, pineapple persistence. **Hillside White** ★★★ Aromatic **18** ⑧②, viognier & chenin, bursts with apricot & citrus fruit on the palate, finishes with a tangy lift. Not tasted: **Sauvignon Blanc**.

Sparkling Wines

Not tasted: **Méthode Cap Classique**. — GM

Location/map: Paarl ▪ Map grid reference: D3 ▪ WO: Paarl/Coastal/Western Cape ▪ 1stB 1975 ▪ Tasting & sales Mon-Fri 9-5 Sat/Sun 10-4 ▪ Fee R25/5 wines ▪ Cellar tours by appt ▪ Rhebokskloof Restaurant open daily for b'fast & lunch ▪ Facilities for children ▪ Tour groups ▪ Weddings, functions & conferences ▪ MTB & hiking trails ▪ Owner(s) Siebrits & Albie Laker, ASLA Group ▪ Winemaker(s) Rolanie Lotz (Jan 2007), with Karin Louw (2007) ▪ Viticulturist(s) Andre Rosseau (2017) ▪ 180ha/38ha (cab, carignan, durif, mourv, p verdot, ptage, shiraz, chard, chenin, marsanne, rouss, viog) ▪ 250t/30,000cs own label 75% red 25% white + 3,000cs for buyers own brands ▪ CVC member ▪ PO Box 2637 Paarl 7620 ▪ info@rhebokskloof.co.za ▪ www.rhebokskloof.co.za ▪ S 33° 41' 6.1" E 018° 55' 56.6" ▪ ⌘ labyrinths.overhauls.starfish ▪ F +27 (0)21-869-8386 ▪ **T +27 (0)21-869-8386**

☐ **Rhinofields** see Durbanville Hills

☐ **Rhino of Linton Park** see Linton Park Wines

☐ **Rhino Run** *see* Van Loveren Family Vineyards
☐ **Rhino Tears** *see* Mount Vernon Estate

Richard Hilton Vineyards

Richard Hilton describes the journey since his first harvest in 2003 as 'challenging'. The Stellenbosch boutique vintner has since specialised in syrah and viognier sourced locally and in Elgin, his new skin-fermented viognier a natural progression as 'orange' wine became fashionable and the variety's thick skin suited the style. Ancient winemaking gave rise to the name, but Richard says: 'It had to go beyond that, have true amber colour, richer flavours and high tannin; the consumer must sit up and say "Wow, it's actually orange!"

Richard Hilton range

★★★★ **Ironstone** Fruit purity spotlit in elegant, harmonious **15** (88) Stellenbosch syrah. Supple spice & black berry fruit well supported by ripe, freshening grape tannin. 19 months in older French oak.

★★★★☆ **The Dalmatian** Fuller-bodied style of Stellenbosch syrah, **15** (92) rich in flavour - dark spice, berry fruit & whiff of mint - but finely judged tannin extraction, balanced acidity, ensure easy flow, no heaviness. Oak, 20% new, 22 months, background enhancement.

★★★★ **Rose Quartz 17** (89) subtle viognier character; quiet apricot, spice notes, in tune with old-oak seasoning; palate has fruit-lifting acidity, a suggestion of tannin on dry conclusion. All-round food partner.

★★★★☆ **The Ancient** (NEW) A remarkable viognier, **17** (93) fermented & aged on skins in 500L barrel, further ageing in oak, all old. Rich in orange hue, dried apricot, peach scents & sweet-fruited silky waves; the freshening tannins, mineral thread bring all to life & allow for lengthy flavour intensity.

★★★★☆ **The Emperor Probus** (🏵) Compelling style of viognier, fits between Rose Quartz & The Ancient; **17** (93) rich, full yet unshowy, deep flavours focused, lengthened by cool mineral thread. Judicious oaking (20% new), rounded grip from 5% skin contact stylish accessories.

Husk Spirit range

★★★★ **Eau de Vie de Marc de Viognier** (𝒬) Very smooth & satisfying, with a lanolin texture. Delicate flavours of stonefruit & spice, warming grip on the finish. Harmonious & moreish. Ex Elgin; unusually, made from wine as well as husks.— AL, WB

Location: Stellenbosch • WO: Elgin/Stellenbosch • Est 2003 • Closed to public • Owner(s) Richard Hilton • Cellarmaster(s)/winemaker(s) Richard Hilton (2003) & Riaan Wassüng (2005) • Viticulturist(s) Francois Hanekom & Richard Rose • (shiraz, viog) • 30t/3,600cs own label 65% red 35% white • info@hiltonvineyards.co.za • www.hiltonvineyards.co.za • **T +27 (0)21-855-5244/+27 (0)83-650-5661**

Richard Kershaw Wines   (𝒬)

It's 20 years since British-born Master of Wine Richard Kershaw arrived in South Africa to make wine, rather less since he launched his own brand. At the centre of his internationally renowned offering are the blends from cool-climate Elgin, where he is based. His remarkable Deconstructed range of chardonnays and syrahs are small-volume bottlings to thrill the geeks (and other sensualists) by expressing the sometimes subtle, sometimes more overt clonal, site and soil differences between the grapes going into the blends. The GPS Series 'explores exemplary parcels of vines from outside the Elgin region', with a new Syrah featuring this year. Smuggler's Boot wines, originally intended for export only, are now also available locally. They explore 'innovative techniques, in particular ceramic and polymer eggs for fermentation'.

Kershaw Clonal Selection

★★★★☆ **Elgin Pinot Noir** (🏵) Recalls previous with floral scent, pure dark cherry, raspberry & hint of forest floor. **17** (94) gorgeously velvety, but a light grip of tannin & firmer freshening acidity guide to a long finish. Complexity & delicious now, but like **16** ★★★★★ (95) will benefit from a good few years ageing.

★★★★★ **Elgin Syrah** (🏵) Lightly perfumed **16** ★★★★★ (93) offers red & dark fruit, spice & pepper & hints of chocolate, good successor to **15** (97). Silky, supple tannins & subtle intensity. Fine balance, the 60% new oak supportive only. There's sweetness of fruit, but the finish properly dry. Magnums too, like Chardonnay.

★★★★☆ **Elgin Chardonnay** (🏵) Oatmeal, hazelnut, spice & orange peel part of the complexity on delicately powerful **17** (94) (especially after air-contact: decant in youth, preferably keep 5+ years).

Piercing, thrilling acidity, slippery satin texture, intense & persistent flavours. 45% new oak; 13.6% alcohol. **16** ★★★★★ ⑨⑤ also appealed greatly.

Kershaw Deconstructed range

★★★★☆ **Groenland Bokkeveld Shale SH9C Syrah** ⊛ One of clonal pair off varied soils, **16** ⑨④ delicately scented with dark fruit, chocolate, earthiness. Sweeter-fruited than partner, less austere, but tannins firm & dry, acidity fresh & succulent. 60% new oak; highest alcohol of these at 14.2%. Magnums too.

★★★★☆ **Lake District Cartref SH22 Syrah** ⊛ The most elegant & balanced of the deconstructed syrahs, & with the most forward fruit - despite the 100% new oak, which is fully absorbed. **16** ⑨③ fine acid, firm tannins, some richness of texture, density, all harmonious.

★★★★☆ **Lake District Cartref SH9C Syrah** ⊛ Second version of SH9C clone. This **16** ⑨③ has less obvious bright fruit in the balance with peppery savoury notes. Firm but supple structure, the net effect being rather austerely grand, powerful intense & linear. Just 30% new oak.

★★★★☆ **Groenland Bokkeveld Shale CY548 Chardonnay** ⊛ Broad aromas on **17** ⑨③, showing evidence of 100% new oaking. The fruit emerges gradually on the long finish, from a powerful structure, notably acidic. In youth at least, with less grace than the others, yet undeniably impressive.

★★★★★ **Lake District Bokkeveld Shale CY95 Chardonnay** ⊛ The most complete & harmonious of the deconstructions, as in **16** ⑨⑤ & earlier. Green-glinting **17** ★★★★★ ⑨③ aromatic, with peach standing out amidst the subtleties, while redder citrus (grapefruit) notable on the full-fruited, balanced palate along with a stony note. 41% new oak.

★★★★☆ **Lake District Cartref CY96 Chardonnay** ⊛ Expressive aromas of oatmeal & lemon-lime. **17** ⑨③ elegantly built & already rather delicious, with fine acidity underscoring the delicate fruitiness till the lingering, limy finish. 60% new oak. These small-quantity chardonnays all in magnum too.

Kershaw GPS Series

★★★★☆ **Klein River Syrah** ⑩Ⓔ ⊛ Expressive, generous red-fruit, cherry aromas on **16** ⑨③. Integrated, balanced structure with bright charm tethered by an earthy element & depth of flavour, & a lightness of feel despite 14.2% alcohol. Texture like flowing silk. 50% new oak.

★★★★☆ **Lower Duivenhoks River Chardonnay** ⊛ Was 'Vermaaklikheid', now named for the ward. Lovely & lively **17** ⑨④ has gorgeous aromas & full-fruited lemony grace & charm, with a softness of texture despite the finely penetrating acid. Persistent, bone-dry finish. 44% new oak.

Smuggler's Boot range ⑩Ⓔ

★★★★ **GSM Blend** Easygoing but not trivial **16** ⑧⑧ blend 55% grenache with mourvèdre & a little shiraz. Fresh & pure, with some wildness on the perfume; no great intensity & a modest tannic tug. Very light oaking.

★★★★ **SBS Blend** Equal blend sauvignon blanc & oaked semillon - both clearly contributing to the subtle lemon & blackcurrant fragrance & flavours. **17** ⑨⓪ vibrant freshness, lively & even exciting, but with some breadth & depth too. These both WO W Cape.— TJ

Location/map: Elgin • Map grid reference: B2 • WO: Elgin/Western Cape/Klein River/Lower Duivenhoks River • Est/1stB 2012 • Tasting by appt • Owner(s) Richard Kershaw • Winemaker(s) Richard Kershaw (2012) & Dudley Wilson (2016) • ±8,000cs own label 50% red 50% white • PO Box 77 Grabouw 7160 • info@richardkershawwines.co.za • www.richardkershawwines.co.za • S 34° 12' 12.07" E 19° 02' 35.10" • ⓦ rebranded. bareness.goal • F +27 (0)86-637-6202 • **T +27 (0)21-200-2589**

☐ **Richard's** see Richard Kershaw Wines

Richelieu

This famous Distell-owned brand pays tribute to the origins of brandy though its French name and distinctive French-inspired flavour profile. A sibling of the SA-produced brandies, multi-award-winning Richelieu XO Cognac Fine Champagne, is also available.

★★★★ **10 Year Vintage Brandy** ⊘ Fine example of rare category of SA brandy, with well-matured spirit & potstill (30% minimum) components. Lovely silkiness with elegant dry richness, the fruit not too fruity, floral notes sidling into the complexity. Nudges higher rating.

Richelieu International ⓥ ★★★ Blended brandy shows some nice complexity of aroma but the spiritous, slightly heavy body still calls for a mixer to dilute the force. — WB

Rickety Bridge Winery

ⓥ ⓨ ⌂ ⌾ ⓐ ⓖ

There's a sense of history and creativity here in Franschhoek. The rickety bridge leading to the property has long been restored, along with the farm buildings and cellar, and many luxury amenities added by British owner Duncan Spence. But the name and connection to the past remain. So too Paulina's range and the restaurant, referring to an early owner, the widow De Villiers. The creativity's evident in the range names and label designs, the latest being Printer's Devil, with playful references to the gremlin said to live in printing works and cause carefully composed typography to turn out horribly - sometimes hilariously - wrng.

Icon range

★★★★☆ **The Bridge** ⓐ So much more than Reserve Cab: longer skin contact, wild ferment, 25 months new oak. **15** ⑨③ rich, intense blackcurrant, dark plum, cocoa tones, underlying meatiness, & heaps of spice in the flavours, savoury rather than fruity. Will benefit from keeping.

★★★★ **The Crossover** ⓝⓔⓦ Takes ripeness (15% alcohol) & oak to another level (new French barriques, 15 months), **16** ⑧⑥ pinotage is opulent, deep, with dark fruit, liquorice & cocoa-rich chocolate styling.

★★★★ **The Sleeper** ⓝⓔⓦ Wonderfully aromatic shiraz, dark berries/cherries, violets, mocha chocolate, **15** ⑧⑦ is full-ripe (15% alcohol), tamed by compact tannins, firm but undaunting, ending dry. 20 months, half new barrels. WO W Cape.

★★★★☆ **Road to Santiago** ⓐ ⓥ 1905 Franschhoek vines, wholebunch, wild ferment in concrete tank & foudre. Pale yellow-gold, bruised apple, an earthy note, **16** ★★★★★ ⑨⑤ has waxy, pine nut richness yet is bone-dry. Semillon so well formed, so complete, has a long life ahead, like **14** ⑨① No **15**.

Paulina's Reserve range

★★★★ **Cabernet Sauvignon** ⓐ Long skin contact, 24 months in French barriques, 35% new, yet **15** ⑧⑧ is plush, deep fruited, has lovely curves. Power built in for cellaring, but tannins well-judged, supple.

★★★★ **Chenin Blanc** Wild ferment in barrel, 6 months on lees, aged 10 months: polished **17** ⑧⑦ citrus & tropical scents, melba toast, then the surprising palate, a fuller expression than sleek 12.5% alcohol would suggest. WO W Cape. No **16**.

★★★★ **Semillon** Wild ferment/11 months in oak, **16** ⑧⑧'s fruit jumps out of the glass, melon, green apple, whiff of green pea, lightly toasted nuts. Has elegance, freshness, in the prime of health. **15** untasted.

Foundation Stone range

★★★★ **White** ⓥ Food-friendly, chenin-based quintet in **16** ⑧⑧. Alluring subtle yellow peach, apricot complexities enhanced by texture & breadth from older oak ferment. WO Coastal. Also in 1.5L.

. . . .

Rosé ⓥ ⓥ ★★★★ Delicate pink hue for multi-variety **18** ⑧④, half shiraz with grenache, mourvèdre, dash viognier, touch of oak. Red berries, hint of scrub, lovely tangy flavours, fruity-fresh & long.

. . . .

Red ★★★★ Shiraz with grenache, cinsaut, dollops mourvèdre, tannat, 18 months seasoned oak. **15** ⑧④ dark hedgerow fruit, cloves, crystallised violets, captured in a juicy, smoothly textured body. WO W Cape.

Rickety Bridge range

★★★★ **Merlot** ⓥ Youthful, inky **16** ★★★★ ⑧④ has touch unripe red plum in its brisk, slightly austere frame. May settle with year/two but misses succulence of **15** ⑧⑦.

★★★★ **Shiraz** ⓐ Generously oaked, 22 months, but **15** ⑧⑦'s fruit is a match: glossy berries & plums coat the tannins, leaving the body smoothly curvaceous, seamed by savoury spice. Has grip for ageing. WO W Cape, as Chenin.

★★★★ **Chardonnay** ⓥ Wild ferment in French/Austrian oak, on lees 11 months, giving **17** ⑧⑦ a Lemon Cream biscuit profile, nothing overt, restrained richness ideal for fine dining. Elegant, ends fresh, some mineral notes.

★★★★ **Méthode Cap Classique Blanc de Blancs** ⓝⓔⓦ Bubbly from chardonnay, drier than non-vintage version, higher acid, also small portion oaked. **15** ⑧⑥ lemon preserve, toasty richness making the freshness less racy, more balanced. Creamy palate weight, a delicious mouthful.

★★★★ **Noble Late Harvest** ⊘ Barrel-fermented/aged but chenin's stonefruit dominates **16** ⑧⑧ honeyed botrytis dessert. Tangy-sweet, less concentrated than usual for this style; offers notable drinkability, sleek elegance. Improves on **15** ★★★★ ⑧④. 375 ml.

Pinotage ★★★ Fruit-driven & ripe **17** ⑧②, plump blueberries/cherries, sweet spicing from year older oak, an attractive thread throughout, smooth & juicy. Also-tasted **16** ⑧②, more blackberries, ripe & curvy, as succulent. Coastal WO. **Chenin Blanc** ★★★ Tropical styling on dry **18** ⑧① forthcoming, engaging, lees contact giving body, creamy mouthfeel. Touch of oak but fruit in charge. **Sauvignon Blanc** ⓥ ★★★ Plenty refreshing zest in **17** ⑧① with usual sweet fresh-cut grass notes. Lees ageing & tiny oaked portion lend comfortable breadth. **Méthode Cap Classique Blanc de Blancs** ⊘ ★★★ Sparkling from chardonnay, now **NV** ⑧②, 18 months on lees, small portion oaked. Appealing citrus & toasted brioche, but its most distinguishing feature is a steely bite of acid that invigorates. Lovely aperitif. Not tasted: **Méthode Cap Classique Brut Rosé**.

Printer's Devil range (NEW)

......

Red ⓥ ★★★★ Subtitled 'Belphegor', creative label showing printing error (see intro for backstory). From cinsaut (1955 vines), 5% wooded cab, **17** ⑧⑤ lots of ripeness, dark prune fruit, earthy notes, scrub. Palate plush, succulent, curvaceous. **Rosé** ⓥ ★★★ 'Titivillus' from grenache noir, pale copper hue, **17** ⑧② transports you to southern France; elegant, nothing overt, pristine fruit, freshly dry. Bring food! **White** ⓥ ⊛ ★★★★ 'The Gremlin' near-equal sauvignon, old-vine semillon, year concrete tanks. **17** ⑧③ mellow, touch of honey, stonefruit preserve, green figs, yet body trim, dry & zesty. — CR

......

Location/map: Franschhoek ▪ Map grid reference: C2 ▪ WO: Franschhoek/Western Cape/Coastal ▪ Est 1990 ▪ Tasting, sales & cellar tours Mon-Sat 9–6 (Dec-Apr)/9-5 (May-Nov) Sun 10-5 ▪ Closed Dec 25 & Jan 1 ▪ Fee R45/5 wines ▪ Panna cotta & wine pairing ▪ Paulina's at Rickety Bridge ▪ Facilities for children ▪ Gift shop ▪ Conferences ▪ Weddings ▪ Rickety Bridge Manor House ▪ Owner(s) Duncan Spence ▪ Cellarmaster(s)/winemaker(s) Wynand Grobler (Nov 2007) ▪ 50ha/25ha (cab, grenache n/b, merlot, mourv, shiraz, chard, chenin, marsanne, rouss, sauv, sem) ▪ 500t/60,000cs own label 60% red 30% white 10% rosé ▪ PO Box 455 Franschhoek 7690 ▪ info@ricketybridge.com ▪ www.ricketybridge.com ▪ S 33° 53' 58.5" E 019° 5' 27.6" ▪ ⫴ craved.informal.steeper ▪ F +27 (0)21-876-3486 ▪ **T +27 (0)21-876-2129**

Rico Suter Private Cellar ⓠ ⌂

The Swiss family Suter's Breedekloof winery is named for patriarch Rico, who vinifies with son Carlo, while other scion Bruno cares for the vines. Materfamilias Erika manages the guest house, blessed with views and other allures, and receives many repeat bookings, including wine-loving friends in Europe.

Location: Worcester ▪ Map: Breedekloof ▪ Map grid reference: B2 ▪ Est/1stB 2004 ▪ Tasting & sales by appt ▪ Guest house (bookings: erika@ricosuterwines.com) ▪ Owner(s) Suter Family Trust ▪ Winemaker(s) Rico & Carlo Suter ▪ Viticulturist(s) Bruno Suter (2004) ▪ 750ha/35ha (cab, cinsaut, p verdot, ptage, shiraz, sauv, viog) ▪ 8-10t/ha ▪ PO Box 38 Breerivier 6858 ▪ rico@ricosuterwines.com ▪ S 33° 31' 39.00" E 019° 15' 13.00" ▪ ⫴ divot.nutrition.countdown ▪ F +27 (0)86-642-6591 ▪ **T +27 (0)23-355-1822**

Ridgeback ⓠ ⓨ ⌂ ◎ ⓐ ⓹

The Zimbabwean founders of this mountainside Agter Paarl venture brought their Rhodesian Ridgebacks with them, African hunting dogs known for their tenacity, providing the inspiration for the winery name and label design - and they are still there in the flesh. A conducive setting, with many different aspects, is likely what attracted viticulture student Toit Wessels here 19 years ago, and he remains central to the operation as winemaker, viticulturist and GM. The largely red range offers interest, quality and ageing 'tenacity'. For visitors, the many attractions include a new tasting room, now separate from the restaurant.

His Master's Choice range

★★★★★ **Signature C** ⓐ Cab franc leads **16** ⑨⑤, with merlot, 2 other Bordeaux grapes; cocoa, meaty savoury notes from 18 months in barrel, two-thirds new. Fruit easily handles it, mixed berries, plums. Serious, worth cellaring, the best lies ahead.

★★★★☆ **Signature S** ⓐ Shiraz with 10% viognier from 'precision-selected' vineyards, **16** ⑨④ has vivid black plum/prune styling, oak-driven scrub & cigarbox notes. Sleek & polished, this is a keeper, the fine-grained tannins promising an illustrious future.

Ridgeback range

★★★★ **Cabernet Sauvignon** Third new barrels in **16** ⑧⑨ brings oak spice to the fore, partnering the molten dark plums, subtle element of fynbos. Nice expression of cab, plush, compact, balanced.

★★★★☆ **Cabernet Franc** ⊘ ⓐ Lovely typicity in **16** ⑨③, a sprinkle of herbs over red berries, even graphite shading, a complex, involving wine. There's enough succulence for immediate enjoyment but its true worth lies in the future, the dry finish attests to that.

★★★★ **Merlot** Expressive fruit & dark chocolate in **16** ⑧⑧, strikes the right oaking balance, enough for a future but no barrier to current enjoyment. Supple, streamlined, well made.

★★★★ **Shiraz** Savoury without austerity, **16** ⑧⑧ is built to age but the dark fruit is an equal partner, giving flesh to the tannins. More Old World style than New in its tobacco & black pepper tones.

★★★★ **Journey** Bordeaux-style blend, equal merlot/cab, & cab franc, petit verdot. Glossy fruit, cassis & plums throughout, cedar spiced, **16** ⑧⑧ very likable but firm ageworthy tannins demand respect.

★★★★ **Chenin Blanc** ⊘ ⓐ Dryland bushvines, partial whole-berry press & natural ferment, mixed barrels 8 months, then 3% Natural Sweet viognier blended in. Something different, **17** ★★★★★ ⑨③ improves on last-tasted **15** ⑧⑦: orange blossom & melon, oatmeal seamed, vibrant lemony acidity.

★★★★☆ **Viognier** ⊘ ⓐ Standout version of the variety, shows restraint without losing aromatic character. French/Hungarian barrels 10 months for an almond seam to **17** ⑨④'s stonefruit, ends long, limy-fresh. Good ageing potential but already irresistible.

★★★★ **Natural Sweet Viognier** ② **15** ⑧⑦ continues in piquantly fresh style. Lively, light (10.5% alcohol) & racy dessert wine that exudes pineapple & lime.

SGMV ★★★ Liquorice & coffee grounds savoury notes to **15** ⑧①'s dark fruit, lithe with juicy freshness. Shiraz-led with grenache, mourvèdre, dab viognier. **Sauvignon Blanc** ★★★ Lemon drops & Rose's Lime Cordial, **18** ⑧①'s freshness & sauvignon typicity not in doubt. Friendly 12.5% alcohol adds to the appeal. Not tasted: **Viognier Méthode Cap Classique**. — CR

Location/map/WO: Paarl ▪ Map grid reference: D3 ▪ Est 1997 ▪ 1stB 2001 ▪ Tasting & sales Mon-Sat 10-5 (summer)/10-4 (winter) Sun 10-4 ▪ Fee R30pp/6 wines, R50pp/6 premium wines ▪ Closed Good Fri, Dec 25 & Jan 1 ▪ Cellar tours by appt ▪ The Deck Restaurant Tue-Sun 9.30-3.30 ▪ 4-star/5-room Ridgeback Guest House ▪ Hiking trails ▪ Children's play area ▪ Owner(s) Kilimanjaro Investments ▪ Cellarmaster(s)/wine-maker(s) Toit Wessels (Jan 2007) ▪ Viticulturist(s) Toit Wessels (Mar 2000) ▪ 65ha/35ha (cabs s/f, grenache, merlot, mourv, p verdot, shiraz, sauv, viog) ▪ 300t/30,000cs own label 60% red 35% white 5% sweet ▪ WIETA ▪ PO Box 2076 Windmeul Paarl 7630 ▪ tasting@ridgeback.co.za ▪ www.ridgebackwines.co.za ▪ S 33° 40'24.9" E 018° 54' 53.5" ▪ 🌐 suddenly.zippy.unabridged ▪ F +27 (0)21-869-8146 ▪ **T +27 (0)21-869-8068**

Riebeek Cellars ⓥ ⓐ ⓑ

Hot, dry Swartland was hard hit by the third year of drought. 'Worst we've had in 84 years,' the Riebeek Cellars winemakers report from their base in Riebeek-Kasteel. Despite the challenging conditions and attendant drop in yields, the team at this large venture, going strong for nearly 80 years, pronounced themselves exceptionally happy with the quality, especially of pinotage, shiraz and chenin.

Kasteelberg range

★★★★ **Pinotage** Rounded, textured **16** ⑧⑨ is subtly alluring & rich, with deep black berry fruits & spice. Gentle oak (just 10% new, 14 months) frames bushvine fruit. Cohesive, focused & long.

★★★★ **Shiraz** Retains Xmas appeal in soft sweet spice & black fruit abundance. Lovely body & presence, oak well knit despite being all new. **16** ⑧⑨ supple & rounded to end.

★★★★ **Chenin Blanc** Serious intent on **17** ⑧⑧ from bushvines. Creamy & rich yet bright & lively, with peach, orange & vanilla complexity. Lovely balance of fresh acidity & oak, all-new Hungarian & French.

Not tasted: **Méthode Cap Classique**, **Soet Steen**.

Riebeek Cellars Collection

Cabernet Sauvignon ⊘ 🏵 ★★★★ Gentle & juicy **17** ㉘ ticks all the boxes: dark fruit, structured & balanced (60% new French oak) yet easy to drink, fresh, long & delicious. A charmer.

Merlot ⊘ ★★★★ Delivers fruitcake & spice, & tones down green notes of previous. **17** ㉘ light oak grip from combo 10% new barrels & staves. **Pinotage** ⊘ ★★★★ Cherry & raspberry vivacity on structured, appealing **17** ㉝. Fruity & friendly, but with firm core & balanced oaking, staves & barrel, quarter Hungarian. **Shiraz** ★★★ Vanilla, plum & spice on attractive **17** ㉑. Oak adds a subtle coffee nuance, is a bit grippy & prominent. **Pinotage Rosé** ⊘ ★★★ Strawberry & cherry liveliness on dry **18** ㉑. Bright, juicy & cheerful for summer sipping. **Chardonnay** ★★★ Gentle citrus & peach on succulent, light **17** ㉒. Unoaked & fresh, with ample charm & length. **Chenin Blanc** ★★★ Ultra-reliable quaffer, **18** ㉘ mingles kiwi & pineapple with bright acidity. Well made for everyday enjoyment. **Sauvignon Blanc** ★★★ Modern styling on fruit salad-, pear-toned **18** ㉘. Light bodied & refreshing, with good cleansing acidity. **Pieter Cruythoff Brut** ★★★ Hint of blush pink on NV ㉘ dry pinot noir & chardonnay sparkler. Fizzy, fresh & packed with red berry fruit, lemon sherbet vivacity. **Cape Ruby Port** ⊘ ★★★☆ Nutty, rich & redolent of spice, raisins & liquorice, NV ㉝ fortified is sweet but not cloying. Well matched with cooler weather.

Short Street range

SGM ⓥ ★★★★ Excellent depth of flavour lifts **16** ㉘ above other everyday reds, plenty of perfume & pepper added to ripe strawberry fruit. **CGV** ⓥ ★★★ Pretty pineapple bouquet on **16** ㉑ chenin, grenache blanc & viognier. Soft & juicy, though lacks some of the wow of previous.

Montino range

Petillant Light ★★★ Muscat florality & grapiness add interest to light NV ㉘ perlé Natural Sweet. Easy drinking & low 9.4% alcohol. **Petillant Natural Sweet Rosé** ★★ Unfussy simplicity of cherry & berry flavour, NV ㉔ Natural Sweet has pétillan zip & low 8% alcohol. — FM

Location: Riebeek-Kasteel ▪ Map: Swartland ▪ Map grid reference: D6 ▪ WO: Swartland/Western Cape ▪ Est 1941 ▪ Tasting & sales Mon-Fri 9-5 Sat 9-4 Sun 10.30-4 (wine boutique) ▪ Closed Good Fri, Dec 25 & Jan 1 ▪ Cellar tours by appt ▪ BYO picnic ▪ Owner(s) ±40 shareholders ▪ CEO Andre Engelbrecht ▪ Production manager Alecia Boshoff ▪ Winemaker(s) Eric Saayman (Jan 1997), Alecia Boshoff (Dec 2004) & Jacques Theron (Dec 2017), with Thembile Ntloko (2016) ▪ Viticulturist(s) Tharien Hansen (Jul 2013) ▪ 1,200ha (cab, carignan, merlot, mourv, ptage, shiraz, tinta amarela, chard, chenin, sauv, viog) ▪ 17,000t/300,000cs own label 50% red 40% white 10% rosé & ±80,000cs for clients ▪ Brands for clients: Royal ▪ Fairtrade ▪ PO Box 13 Riebeek-Kasteel 7307 ▪ info@riebeekcellars.co.za ▪ www.riebeekcellars.com ▪ S 33°22'58.0" E 018°54'54.5" ▪ ⊠ spades.tradition.partaking ▪ F +27 (0)22-448-1281 ▪ **T +27 (0)22-448-1213**

Rietvallei Wine Estate ⓥ 🍴 ◎ ♿

One of the oldest wine estates in Robertson, that of the Burger family, with owner/winemaker Kobus the 6th generation here. It boasts red muscadel vines planted by a 2nd-generation Burger in 1908, the oldest in SA, and the bottle label proudly carries that as part of its design. The up-market range offers many other delights, including creative blends, a highly rated cabernet franc and evocatively named cinsaut. The Burger Family Vineyards, John B and Stonedale brands untasted.

Heritage Collection

★★★★ **JMB Cabernet Franc** ⓐ Plush & streamlined **14** ㉗; blackcurrants, hint of graphite, chopped herbs, good freshness supplying a lift. All-new French oak 24 months. Tasted this edition out of vintage sequence. Like **15** ㉗, built for the future, but also current enjoyment

★★★★ **Dark Cin** ⓥ Certainly earns its name: **16** ㉗ darker, denser, more intense than many cinsauts; oak component adding spicing, chocolate, the dark berry fruit juicy, fresh-fruity. Unexpected & delicious.

★★★★ **JMB Chardonnay** Nice progression across the 3 chardonnays: unoaked to part-wooded to new-barrel-fermented **18** ★★★★★ ㉚ preview. Citrus themed, same admirable elegance & purity, here showing the most intensity. Oak well-judged, in progress but promises well. Improves on **17** ㉗.

★★★★ **Estéanna Chardonnay-Sauvignon Blanc-Chenin Blanc-Viognier-Nouvelle** ⓥ Portion barrel fermented/aged, rest tank; though chardonnay dominates at 40%, **17** ㉗ different profile to a varietal chard: green fig & melon, creamy palate with balancing freshness & length.

★★★★☆ **1908 Red Muscadel** Muscat de Frontignan bushvines planted 1908, fortified style passed down the Burger generations. Deeper colour than Classic sibling, graininess in the dried fruit, also barley sugar, fynbos honey. No oak, would have spoilt **15** (94). sweet but beautifully proportioned. No **14**. 375 ml.

Estéanna Cabernet Sauvignon-Cabernet Franc-Petit Verdot (2) ★★★★ Near equal cab & cab franc, touch petit verdot, 2 years new oak give **15** (84) cassis & plum richness, attractive structural elegance. Supple & smooth, tannins harmonious for immediate enjoyment or cellaring. **Estéanna Sauvignon Blanc** (NEW) ★★★★ Previewed from second-fill barrel & provisionally rated, **18** (83) combination citrus & leafy tobacco, racy saline acidity. Wine not finished, could still change, but what's there already admirable.

Classic Collection

. . . .

Natural Chardonnay (？) ★★★ No oak for **18** (82), this is about fruit, which it has in abundance: lemon, grapefruit, some green apple. Vibrant freshness, gets the taste buds going. **Sauvignon Blanc** (⊘) (？) ★★★★ Unwooded, unlike Heritage sibling. Fractional cropping gives **18** (84) its layers; capsicum & cut grass but also passionfruit, ending with grapefruit. More than fruit salad, the different elements stand out. **Red Muscadel** (？) ★★★★ Pale red colour but rest of fortified **17** (84) is a power trip: intense dried fruit richness, tantalising floral nuances, round & syrupy, mouthcoating. Packed with flavour, very long finish.

. . . .

Cabernet Sauvignon ★★★★ Fruitcake richness to **16** (84), loads of flavour, generously spiced by 14 months in barrel, half new, tannins approachable. Attractive, well put together. **Shiraz-Petit Verdot-Viognier** (2) ★★★★ Uncommon blend with shiraz (69%) providing the anchor. Smoky dark wild fruit in **16** (84), quite intense in flavour, appealing juiciness offsetting the tannins, giving accessibility. **Classic Chardonnay** ★★★ 60% of wine oaked, half new barrels, plays a prominent role in **18** (81)'s aromas of vanilla biscuit, yet flavours are similar to Natural (unwooded) version: zesty, appetising citrus. **Chenin Blanc** ★★★ Spent 6 months in older barrels, adding an oatmeal tone to **18** (81)'s appley fruit, sets it apart. Trim-figured but flavourful, zesty-fresh. — CR

Location/map/WO: Robertson ▪ Map grid reference: B4 ▪ Est 1864 ▪ 1stB 1975 ▪ Tasting & sales Mon-Fri 8–5 Sat 10–2 ▪ Tasting fee standard ▪ Closed Easter Fri/Sat, Dec 25 & Jan 1 ▪ Cheese platters, book ahead for groups of 6+ ▪ Function venue ▪ Owner(s) Kobus Burger ▪ Cellarmaster(s)/winemaker(s) Kobus Burger (2003) ▪ 215ha/100ha (cab, red muscadel, chard, sauv) ▪ 2,000/150,000cs own label 40% red 50% white 5% rosé 5% fortified + 800,000L bulk ▪ PO Box 386 Robertson 6705 ▪ info@rietvallei.co.za ▪ www. rietvallei.co.za ▪ S 33° 49′ 25.7″ E 019° 58′ 39.4″ ▪ ⌖ mountains.confederate.attended ▪ F +27 (0)23-626-4514 ▪ **T +27 (0)23-626-3596**

☐ **Riggton** *see* Bonnievale Wines

Rijk's

Keen focus is what owner Neville Dorrington brought to bear when planting vines on virgin soil at the Rijk's home-farm in then unfancied Tulbagh in the late 1990s, against expert advice. His brand's subsequent sustained success, notably with pinotage and chenin blanc (including Diners Club Winemaker of the Year prestige with the latter for Pierre Wahl, cellar chief since 2002) has borne out his faith. And faith was needed in 2018's extreme drought, Neville taking the drastic step of not even harvesting some vineyards.

Location/map: Tulbagh ▪ Map grid reference: F5 ▪ Est 1996 ▪ 1stB 2000 ▪ Tasting & sales Mon-Fri 10-4 Sat 10-2 ▪ Fee R85/7 wines ▪ Closed Easter Fri-Mon, Dec 25 & Jan 1 ▪ Cellar tours by appt ▪ Rijk's Guest House ▪ Conferences ▪ Owner(s)/viticulturist(s) Neville Dorrington ▪ Winemaker(s) Pierre Wahl (Jan 2002) ▪ 135ha/39ha (carignan, grenache, mourv, ptage, shiraz, tinta amarela, chard, chenin, viog) ▪ 210t/24,000cs own label 75% red 25% white ▪ IPW ▪ PO Box 400 Tulbagh 6820 ▪ wineclub@rijks.co.za ▪ www.rijkswine. com ▪ S 33° 16′ 1.5″ E 019° 8′ 42.0″ ▪ ⌖ rectangle.solve.brushed ▪ **T +27 (0)23-230-1622**

☐ **Rita Marques** *see* Conceito Vinhos

Rivendell Boutique Wine Farm

After falling in love with scenic Bot River Valley, Austrians Heimo and Maria Thalhammer have revived Rivendell farm's (and their own family's) winegrowing history. Since last edition there's been expansion of the wine range and hospitality, and a more organic approach in the viticulture and winemaking. Under new management, The Singing Cook restaurant complements the multifaceted function venues among the vines.

Reserve range (NEW)

★★★★ **Shiraz** Modern, suave **15** (89), opulent smoky fruit elevated by maritime influence, so 15% alcohol is less intrusive. Bigger, more interesting personality than Rivendell sibling, deserves a dinner date.

★★★★ **Sauvignon Blanc** Commendable addition to burgeoning category, **17** (88) part-fermented in 100% new wood, lending distinct sweet toasty nuance to passionfruit & pungent green-herb tones. Dry, tangy & fresh, with plenty of palate appeal.

Rivendell range

★★★★ **Sauvignon Blanc** Cool-grown herb & greengage flavours on **16** (86), though less acid zing this vintage. 6 months on lees add breadth, but there's shade less verve & intensity than in **15** ★★★★★ (93).

Shiraz ★★★★ Liquid berry jam character in **14** (85) but fresh, juicy & bright, uncloying. Smoky twist from well-integrated oak, supple tannins; a food-friendly wine also in magnum. **Shiraz Rosé** ★★★ Nixes sauvignon & viognier for 100% shiraz, **17** (79) gains savoury overtone to red fruit; dry & crisply balanced, creaminess from part oaking. — MW

Location/WO: Bot River ▪ Map: Walker Bay & Bot River ▪ Map grid reference: B2 ▪ Est 2008 ▪ 1stB 2011 ▪ Tasting & sales daily 9-5 ▪ Light meals & platters ▪ The Singing Cook T +27 (0)72-462-4271 (Antonio)/+27 (0)82-896-5106 (Louise) open for lunch & pre-booked dinners; cater for functions of various sizes ▪ Pre-booked picnics in summer ▪ Child friendly ▪ Tour groups ▪ Venue for weddings & corporate functions (in & outdoor; 80 pax inside) with fully equipped kitchen ▪ Large secured parking area ▪ Owner(s) Whales & Castle Investments (Pty) Ltd (shareholders Heimo & Maria Thalhammer) ▪ Winemaker(s) Kobie Viljoen (Mar 2010, Villion Family Wines) ▪ Viticulturist(s) John van Tonder (Aug 2018) ▪ ±8.3ha/±4.8ha (shiraz, sauv) ▪ 30t/3,000cs own label 33% red 67% white ▪ PO Box 570 Onrusrivier 7201 ▪ office@rivendell-estate. co.za ▪ www.rivendell-estate.co.za ▪ S 34° 18' 5.22" E 019° 8' 32.23" ▪ ⌖ rebates.ended.lampshades ▪ T +27 (0)28-284-9185

☐ **River Collection** see Bonnievale Wines

River Garden

Previously under Lourensford Wine Estate, and still made there and offered for tasting, the River Garden brand has acquired an own identity and positioning, hence this separate listing. Styled to be 'accessible and easy-drinking yet with a classic palate structure', the wines are targeted mostly at the on-trade.

Flower Collection

Cabernet Sauvignon-Merlot ⊘ ★★★★ Plush black berry spice highlights on **16** (83), generous & pliant, well balanced. Stellenbosch WO, as both ranges. **Shiraz-Cabernet Sauvignon** ⊘ ★★★★ Smoky edge to red- & blue-fruited **16** (84) shiraz-led (86%) mix. Fresh & juicy but with inky depths too. **Rosé** ★★★ Tangy cranberry cheer on **18** (80), dry, balanced & zippy. Undisclosed varieties. **Unwooded Chardonnay** ★★★ Unfussy, lively & refreshing **17** (81) is light bodied & fun.

Classique range

Merlot ★★★★ Supple plum appeal to **16** (85) which matches **15** (85) for density, poise & depth. Nice frame of oak, 21% new, 17 months. Two vintages tasted, as all this range. **Shiraz** ★★★★ Succulent yet dry **16** (84) shows signature plum notes just brushed with fynbos. Harmonious & refreshing, like **15** (84). **Chardonnay-Pinot Noir** ★★★ Tang of grapefruit adds interest to bright, light-bodied **18** (82) dry rosé. **17** (82) just as juicy & quaffable in its 51/49 mix. **Chardonnay** ★★★★ Peaches-&-cream charm on broad, rich yet fresh **17** (83). Like **16** (84), portion aged in older oak for 9 months. **Sauvignon Blanc** ★★★ **18** (82) lightly tangy & rounded, with tropical notes, where **17** (81) is taut, with grapefruit zing. — FM

☐ **River Grandeur** see Viljoensdrift Fine Wines & Cruises
☐ **Riverscape** see Viljoensdrift Fine Wines & Cruises
☐ **The River's End** see Stellar Winery
☐ **RNW** see Bizoe Wines
☐ **Robert Alexander** see Nico van der Merwe Wines

Robertson Winery

From modest beginnings, this enterprising winery on Robertson's main road, established in 1941, has grown into a global brand, exporting to over 60 countries. It goes without saying that production is enormous, the range of products wide, whether it's bag-in-box or bottle, sweet, sparkling or dry. 'We now have a portfolio of almost 100 products for the South African market, available at every price point and in every convenient pack size,' says marketing coordinator Annalize Cooper, adding that this is in keeping with RW's 'More to Share' positioning and propensity for innovation. 'We have even more new products being added to the portfolio over the next year, making this a very exciting time for the brand.'

Constitution Road range

★★★★☆ **Shiraz** Inky, opulent **15** ⑨1 flagship from two blocks on Wolfkloof estate, concentrated fruit pastille aroma, ripe almost jammy black berry & plum flavours; full body & fruit richness lifted by black pepper & allspice; dark chocolate nuance ex 36 months new French barrels.

★★★★ **Chardonnay** ⑦ An increasingly sophisticated wine, **16** ★★★★★ ⑨0 more elegant than also-tasted **15** ⑧7, having spent only 13 months in new & 2nd-fill French barrels compared to 18, slightly lower alcohol too (13.9%). Smooth, rich, creamy, citrusy, balanced.

Winery range

Cabernet Sauvignon ★★★ Smooth, approachable **17** ⑧1, Ribena-like blackcurrant intensity, subtle oak spice from staves, as most of these reds. **Merlot** ★★★ Soft, mediumweight **17** ⑧0 easy to drink, ripe plum & cherry fruit, chocolate notes adding to appeal. **Pinot Noir** ⑦ ★★★ Choc-dipped strawberries & red cherries in fruity, lightly wooded **17** ⑦8, made for early drinking. **Pinotage** ★★★ Juicy **17** ⑦9, tangy raspberry, cherry & strawberry fruit, fresh & accessible with powdery tannins. **Ruby Cabernet** ★★★ Medium-bodied **17** ⑦7 unwooded for maximum expression of cheerful cherry fruit. **Shiraz** ★★★ Along with black pepper & berry typicity, **17** choc-vanilla edge from 6-8 months on oak, 20% American. **Cabernet Sauvignon-Shiraz** ★★★ Carefree quaffing in **17** ⑧1, 49% shiraz bringing subtle pepper & sweet American oak spice to ripe black-fruit melange. **Lightly Sparkling Pinot Noir Rosé** ★★ Frothy strawberries-&-cream on zingy **18** ⑦4, semi-dry with mild 10.5% alcohol. **Chardonnay** ⑦ ★★★ Vanilla cream texture from partial wooding adds to fresh ripe citrus tastiness of **17** ⑧0. **Chenin Blanc** ★★★ At 12% alcohol, with ripe fruit-salad flavours & brisk acidity, **18** ⑦9 is summery & refreshing. **Lightly Sparkling Sauvignon Blanc** ★★★ More fruit & substance than usual for perlé wine, vibrant, dry **17** ⑦7 has light fizz, easy 11% alcohol, lemon-lime freshness. **Sauvignon Blanc** ★★★ Crisply dry **18** ⑦8 tangy green apple & zesty lime tones for uncomplicated poolside quaffing. **Beaukett** ★★★ Aromatic **18** ⑧0, semi-sweet equal blend colombard & muscadel with ripe apple & melon notes balanced by fresh acidity. **Gewürztraminer Special Late Harvest** ★★★ Honeyed both in taste & texture, **18** ⑧1's sweet litchi flavour doesn't cloy thanks to lively acidity & apricot tang. **Red Muscadel** ⑦ ★★★ Ginger & barley sugar nuances to sweet muscat richness of **15** ⑧2. Rich & rewarding yet uncloying thanks to well-judged fortification. **White Muscadel** ⑦ ★★★ Clean, sweet muscat seduction on well-balanced & -defined **12** ⑧1. **Cape Ruby** ⑦ ★★★★ Occasional release, ruby cab 'port' returns after 6-year gap with **14** ⑧3, aged 18 months in old oak. Delicious berry compote of a wine, with vanilla & Xmas spice. Occasional release: **Viognier.**

Chapel range

Red ⑦ ★★ Range named for chapel used as wine cellar since 1941. Unoaked **17** ⑦6 cab & merlot very sweet plum & black berry flavours, ripe & rounded. Restrained 13.3% alcohol. **Extra Light** ★★ Low-kilojoule & -alcohol (9.5%) NV ⑦2 crisp, dry & lemon-fresh. Equal sauvignon & chenin. **White** ★★ Peachy **18** ⑦6 chenin & colombard, refreshingly dry & nicely rounded. **Semi-Sweet** ★★ Honey-drizzled fruit salad flavours in NV ⑦2 chenin & colombard. **Sweet Rosé** ★★ Pink sweets & red berries, NV ⑦0 90% colombard & ruby cab adding pretty hue, alcohol under 7.5%. **Sweet Red** ★★ Very-berry NV ⑦3, combo pinotage, cab & shiraz, light tannins & sweet fruit, balancing burst of acidity.

Light Cultivar range

Extra Light Merlot ⑦ ★★ Blackcurrant simplicity to juicy, low-alcohol (10%) **16** ⑦4. **Chenin Blanc** ★★ Just-dry **17** ⑦3, pear blossom aroma, tropical fruit flavour, slips down easily at sub-9% alcohol. **Pinotage Rosé** ★★ Light-alcohol (9%) **18** ⑦4 technically dry but touch sugar adds smoothness to berry cordial & glacé cherry flavours. **Extra Light Sauvignon Blanc** ★★ Very crisp, dry **18** ⑦ overtly herbaceous in style. Alcohol below 10%.

Natural Sweet range

Red ★★ Tastes like liquid cherry lollipops, turning faintly metallic on finish. **NV** ⑫ low 7.5% alcohol, as others this range. **Rosé** ★★ Cheery **NV** ⑦ pink-sweet aroma, sweet strawberry flavour. Colombard with blush from ruby cab. **White** ★★ Sweetness of fragrant **NV** ⑦ lifted by fresh sweet-sour tang of pineapple & citrus.

Sparkling Wines

Sweet Red ★★ Cheerful sweet **NV** ⑦ red sparkler, carbonated berry cordial character, low ±7% alcohol, as next. **Sweet Rosé** ★★★ Clean-finishing sweet pink **NV** ⑦ fizz a versatile food partner, from smoked salmon to strawberry cheesecake. **Brut** ★★★ Tiny bubbles elevate fresh green-apple & flint notes in tangy, dry, refreshing **NV** ⑦ from sauvignon. **Sweet White** ★★ Yellow apples, ripe nectarines & spanspek on sweet, frothy **NV** ⑦. Alcohol below 7%.

One-Litre Combibloc range

Sauvignon Blanc ★★★ Dry, crisp & zesty **18** ⑦, green apples & squeeze of lime for uncomplicated summer refreshment. **Cabernet Sauvignon** ★★★ Concentrated blackcurrant fruit, subtle oak spice on **17** ⑧, very smooth & approachable. **Merlot** ★★★ Easy-drinking **17** ⑧ soft, medium bodied, chocolate notes adding to ripe plum & cherry attraction. **Smooth Dry Red** ★★ Brimming with juicy black fruit, **NV** ⑦ indeed smooth & dry, with comfortable 13% alcohol. **Chardonnay** ⓧ ★★★ Vanilla cream texture from partial wooding adds to fresh, ripe citrus appeal of **17** ⑧. **Crisp Dry White** ★★ Latest **NV** ⑦ delicately crisp & dry with squeeze of lemon. **Crisp Extra Light** ★★ Light in body with alcohol under 10.5%, **NV** ⑦ dry & herbaceous equal colombard & chenin. **Selected Stein** ★★ Semi-sweet **NV** ⑫, mostly chenin with muscadel, white- & cling-peach flavours, apricot tang to finish. Chenin & colombard, as next. **Fruity Late Harvest** ★★ Gently sweet **NV** ⑦, just 10% alcohol & almost overripe fruit salad flavours. **Natural Sweet Rosé** ★★ Pink-sweet & strawberry flavours on upbeat **NV** ⑦, with just 7.5% alcohol. **Natural Sweet White** ★★ Fragrantly sweet **NV** ⑦ with combo fresh citrus & tropical fruit flavours. **Smooth Sweet Red** ★★ Unwooded, low-alcohol (7.5%) **NV** ⑫ tastes like cherry candy.

Two-Litre Certified Cultivar Slimline range

Cabernet Sauvignon ★★★ Smooth **17** ⑧, fairly intense blackcurrant fruit, subtle vanilla-choc notes from 4 months on oak staves. **Merlot** ★★★ Hints of chocolate add to ripe plum charm of soft, medium-bodied **17** ⑧. **Ruby Cabernet** ★★★ Unwooded **17** ⑦ medium body & soft tannins, plenty of ripe cherry fruit on offer. **Shiraz** ★★★ Choc-vanilla undertones from American oak staves, **17** ⑧ also twist of pepper lifting ripe black berry fruit. **Chardonnay** ⓧ ★★★ Partial oaking adds creamy texture & vanilla to fresh ripe citrus in **17** ⑧. **Chenin Blanc** ★★★ For your beach cooler this summer, **18** ⑦ ripe fruit salad flavours & fresh acidity, tippleable 12% alcohol. **Sauvignon Blanc** ★★★ Uncomplicated **18** ⑦ crisp & dry, piquant green apple & zesty lime tones.

Three-Litre Cultivar Slimline range

Cabernet Sauvignon ★★★ Oak staves add subtle spice to typical blackcurrant fruit of suave **17** ⑧. **Merlot** ★★★ Soft, midweight **17** ⑧ very appealing, ripe plum & cherry fruit, hint of chocolate. **Shiraz** ★★★ Ripe black berries & black pepper pinch, **17** ⑧ choc-vanilla sweetness from American-oaked portion. **Chardonnay** ★★★ Cream texture & vanilla from oaked component adds to ripe citrus attraction of **17** ⑧. **Chenin Blanc** ★★★ Crisp acidity enlivens ripe fruit salad, **18** ⑦ easy al fresco drinking at 12% alcohol. **Extra Light Sauvignon Blanc** ★★ Made in keenly herbaceous style, **18** ⑦ is bracing, bone-dry, gets no padding from sub-10% alcohol. **Sauvignon Blanc** ★★★ Zesty lime & Granny Smith apple freshness on dry, crisp, unpretentious **18** ⑦. **Natural Sweet White** ★★ Fragrantly sweet **NV** ⑦, happy marriage of citrus & tropical fruit, blissfully low 7.5% alcohol.

Three-Litre Blended Slimline range

Smooth Dry Red ★★ Undaunting 13% alcohol & juicy black fruit, **NV** ⑦ blend mellowly dry for everyday drinking. **Crisp Dry White** ★★ For fridge door on summer holidays, **NV** ⑦ lemon-fresh, crisp & dry. **Refreshing Extra Light** ★ Ripe peach tone, but **NV** ⑥'s light palate (9.5% alcohol) verges on austere. Serve chilled but don't add ice. **Johannisberger Semi-Sweet White** ★★ Gently sweet **NV** ⑦, soft & smooth, pear & litchi fruit, clean finish & modest 11% alcohol. **Natural Sweet Red** ★★ Berry cordial

& cherry-candy sweetness in low-alcohol (7.5%) **NV** (72). **Natural Sweet Rosé** ★★ Sweet strawberry flavours follow confectionery store aromas of cheery pink, low-alcohol **NV** (70). **Johannisberger Semi-Sweet Red** ★★ Hints of pepper & spice enliven cherry cola sweetness of **NV** (72), a match for hot curry.

Five-Litre Blended Slimline range (NEW)

Chapel Red ★★ Equal cab & merlot in unoaked **17** (74), smooth & dry, plums & black berries, 12.5% alcohol adds to easiness.

Brandy range

★★★★ **William Robertson 7 Year Potstill** Ⓡ Smooth & refined, with more ripe fruit complexity (built around apricot) than the two blended versions - this 100% potstill - though recognisably family in stressing the less obviously fruity components. Lower 38% alcohol gives more elegance.

5 Year Ⓡ ★★★ Rather fresher aromas of prunes & dried peach on this version of 5 year matured blended brandy, though also a trifle idiosyncratic. Fairly smooth & not too fiery, dry conclusion. These brandies all from colombard & distilled at Oude Molen. **William Robertson 5 Year** Ⓡ ★★★ Prunes, dried peach & nuts, & hint of mustiness on this blended brandy, designed for mixing, but neither very heavy nor very fiery. Like other 5 year version, has 40% potstill component. — JG, TJ

Location/map/WO: Robertson ▪ Map grid reference: B5 ▪ Est 1941 ▪ 1stB 1987 ▪ Tasting & sales Mon-Fri 9-5.30 Sat/pub hols 9-3 Sun 9-1 ▪ Closed Good Fri, Dec 25/26 & Jan 1 ▪ Cellar tours by appt ▪ Conferences ▪ Cellarmaster(s) Bowen Botha (Jan 1982) ▪ Winemaker(s) Francois Weich (Sep 1997), Jacques Roux (Jan 2001) & Thys Loubser (Jan 2012) ▪ Viticulturist(s) Briaan Stipp (May 2005) ▪ 2,400ha under vine ▪ 42,000t ▪ BRC, FSSC 22000, WIETA ▪ PO Box 566 Robertson 6705 ▪ info@robertsonwinery.co.za, sales@robertsonwinery.co.za, customercare@robertsonwinery.co.za ▪ www.robertsonwinery.co.za ▪ S 33° 48' 36.8" E 019° 52' 51.4" ▪ jelly.conga.solve ▪ F +27 (0)23-626-6807/+27 (0)23-626-4788 (sales) ▪ **T +27 (0)23-626-3059/+27 (0)23-626-8817 (sales)**

Robert Stanford Estate

Named for a previous owner, as is the nearby Overberg village, hillside Robert Stanford Estate produced wine back in the 1890s. The boutique quantity available today is vinified by Christo Versfeld of Villiersdorp Cellar, and it joins an unusually wide variety of farm attractions, notably an amphitheatre for music, comedy and other performances, restaurant under new management, and distillery producing a husk spirit.

Sir Robert Stanford range

★★★★ **The Hansom** Now bottled, **15** (87) complex blackcurrant & dried black cherry notes, cigarbox & thyme, restrained 12.5% alcohol. Cab (60%) & equal merlot, cab franc give firm structure, should reward few years cellaring.

★★★★ **Chenin Blanc** Ⓡ Unoaked **17** (87) preview, lovely spicy lift to white peach & floral notes; fresh & persistent, gently gripping.

★★★★ **Sauvignon Blanc** Ⓡ Ex-tank **17** (87)'s maritime influence shows in cool/green tone, lively but not bracing acidity & passionfruit pithiness. Satisfying anytime companion.

Pinot Noir ★★★ Packed with youthful red fruit, **17** (78) finishes on delicate spicy note. Tasty now & for a few years. Not tasted: **Shiraz**, **Rosé**, **Méthode Cap Classique Brut**.

Cutters Cove range

Pinot Noir Ⓡ ★★★ Touch sweetness on **15** (78) palate but mostly succulent strawberry & red cherry fruit, neatly shaped by powdery tannins. **Chenin Blanc** ★★★ Appealing, well-priced summer chenin. **17** (80) subtle vanilla oak & creaminess in harmony with peach fruit & tangy acidity. WO Cape South Coast. Discontinued: **Shiraz-Viognier**. — GM

Location: Stanford ▪ Map: Walker Bay & Bot River ▪ Map grid reference: B6 ▪ WO: Walker Bay/Cape South Coast ▪ Est 1855 ▪ 1stB 2008 ▪ Tasting & sales Thu-Mon 9-4 ▪ Closed Good Fri, Dec 25 & Jan 1 ▪ The Zesty Lemon Restaurant Thu-Mon 9-4 ▪ Facilities for children ▪ Gift shop ▪ Farm produce ▪ Conservation area ▪ Tractor tours/vineyard walks by appt ▪ Amphitheatre ▪ Accommodation ▪ Distillery ▪ Owner(s) Robert Stanford Vineyards (Pty) Ltd ▪ Winemaker(s) Christo Versfeld (Villiersdorp Cellar) ▪ Viticulturist(s) Jan Malan (Jan 2003) ▪ 176ha/60ha (pinot, shiraz, chenin, sauv) ▪ 320t/2,500cs own label 40% red 30% white 15% rosé 15% MCC ▪ WWF-SA Conservation Champion ▪ wines@robertstanfordestate.co.za ▪ www.

robertstanfordestate.co.za ▪ S 34° 25' 49.41" E 019° 27' 49.98" ▪ 🔲 tending.yielding.flowerpots ▪ **T +27 (0)82-304-4849**

Robin Hood Legendary Wine Series

Elgin-based brand owner Mark Simpson describes himself light-heartedly as a 'Huguenot-blooded orchard-ist,' and in similar playful fashion, his Robin Hood wine quartet pairs a figure from Sherwood Forest legend with a course in a four-part meal, rosé Maid Marian the starter to port-style Friar Tuck the cheese. Available from Mark's Elgin wine shop; his more serious Arumdale wines are listed separately.

Robin Hood ② ★★★★ Cab & merlot has trademark sweet note but it's offset by toned fruitcake & spicy berry flavours. NV ⑧③ improves on previous in body & length. Elgin WO, as all. **Maid Marian** ② ★★★ Deep pink hues of NV ⑦⑨ off-dry rosé lead to juicy raspberry palate, pleasantly uncomplicated & easy. From shiraz & merlot. **Little John** ② ★★★ Stonefruit & flint on bright NV ⑦⑦ from sauvignon, sweetish edge to pithy grapefruit zest, light & touch short. **Friar Tuck** ② ★★ Semi-sweet merlot & shiraz, NV ⑦③ offers leathery plum fruit & gentle spice simplicity. — FM

☐ **Rocco Bay** *see* Govert Wines
☐ **Rockfield** *see* Du Preez Estate

Rogge Cloof

Winegrowing is rare in high-altitude Sutherland-Karoo, perhaps unsurprisingly when one reads of the history of this farm since 1756 and its various owners 'enduring lions, droughts, snow and freezing winds'. But there are plans for planting vineyards on the estate – the highest in South Africa, they say; and there's now a tasting room, together with a restaurant ('with sweeping views'), and accommodation.

Location: Sutherland ▪ Est 1756 ▪ 1stB 2006 ▪ Tasting, sales & cellar tours by appt ▪ Meals & picnics available ▪ Facilities for children ▪ Tour groups ▪ Gift shop ▪ Farm produce ▪ Walks/hikes ▪ Conservation area ▪ 4x4 trail ▪ MTB trail ▪ Museum ▪ Guest house ▪ Stargazing ▪ Nature reserve ▪ 95% red 4% white 1% fortified ▪ Other brands: Cape to Cairo, De Knolle Fonteyn, Ermineo, Fair Karoo, Joachim Scholtz, Oranjezicht, Salpeterkop, Sneeukop ▪ Off the R354, Roggeveld Karoo, Sutherland 6920 ▪ info@roggecloof.com ▪ www.roggecloof.com ▪ S 32° 31' 24.79" E 20° 38' 13.00" ▪ 🔲 modules.stipulate.fortify ▪ **T +27 (0)23-004-1161**

☐ **Romansrivier** *see* Mountain Ridge Wines

Romond Vineyards

André and Rhona Liebenberg face a not unpleasant problem with regard to the grapes off their Helderberg vineyards: continue selling off some, or keep them back for their own boutique range, to meet growing demand? Customers clearly appreciate not only the wines but also 'the conviviality of the informal but informative tastings on offer', as André says.

Rebus range

★★★★ **Fanfaronne** Blend 59% cab franc with cab. 15 ⑧⑦ ripe, rich & powerful (warming 15% alcohol), hints at oak influence - 30 months, 5% new. Firm & well-rounded, nicely succulent. Last-tasted 09 ★★★★★ ⑨② included merlot.

★★★★ **Cape Cuvée** Pinotage (60%) with merlot & the 2 cabs on charming 16 ⑧⑦. 15% alcohol, dry firmness ex 30 months in oak, yet easier, lighter-feeling than other reds. Last tasted was 11 ★★★★ ⑧④.

Cabernet Franc ★★★★ Ripe, dark-fruited & tobacco aromas & well-structured palate with a herbal twist on 15 ⑧⑤ (first tasted since 10 ⑧④). 15% alcohol adds warmth & a sweet note to the dry finish. **Merlot** ② ★★★★ Big, ripe 12 ⑧④ shows dark fruit, with hints of tobacco & chocolate. Both softly textured & drily lean; powerful & grippy. **Pinotage** ② ★★★★ 09 ⑧④ fruity but serious, balanced & juicy, with delicious grip to finish. Tasted a few years back. **Impromptu Merlot Rosé** ★★★★ Copper-pink gleams on 17 ⑧③ has ripe but fresh aromas, not too forward. Dry, substantial & textured, but succulent lightness belies 15% alcohol. 6 months in older oak. — TJ

Location/WO: Stellenbosch ▪ Map: Helderberg ▪ Map grid reference: C2 ▪ Est 1994 ▪ 1stB 2003 ▪ Tasting, sales & tours by appt Mon-Sat 10-5.30 Sun 11-5.30 ▪ Fee R75, waived on purchase ▪ Closed Easter Fri-Sun, Dec 25/26 & Jan 1 ▪ Olive oil ▪ The Vintner's Loft self-catering apartment ▪ Owner(s) André & Rhona Liebenberg

▪ Winemaker(s) André Liebenberg ▪ Viticulturist(s) Francois Hanekom (May 2007) ▪ 11.5ha/9.5ha (cabs s/f, merlot, ptage) ▪ PO Box 5634 Helderberg 7135 ▪ info@romond.co.za ▪ www.romond.co.za ▪ S 34° 1' 52.61" E 018° 49' 59.67" ▪ ⌨ herself.catchments.wonderful ▪ F +27 (0)21-855-0428 ▪ **T +27 (0)21-855-4566**

Ron Burgundy Wines

The connection of this exciting young wine venture and a buffoonish film character named Ron Burgundy testifies to the shared sense of humour of partners Fritz Schoon, Henk Kotze and Reenen Borman – the last being winemaker at Boschkloof (handily enough for vinifying this range). The humour carries through to some of the wine names and labels, but the wines – innovative, individual, fresh, excellent – are no joke. The farm in Montagu where the white grapes are sourced has a new owner, who, says Reenen, 'is keen to help the vineyards flourish'. A single-vineyard colombard was ageing in a large oak vat as we went to press.

★★★★★ **Sons of Sugarland Syrah** ⓐ Dark-fruited, fragrant **17** (94) is fresh & notably pure, beautifully balanced, understated & subtle. Light-feeling, but vinous (13.5% alcohol) & not without an elegant musculature. Good now, but will develop. Bunch press, natural ferment, older oak, as all these.

★★★★☆ **Patatsfontein Steen** ⓐ From a single-vineyard in Montagu, one of the least showy & assertive of the Cape's really fine chenins. **17** (93) all subtle, complex allusion, working through the gentle persuasion of its peachy, citric, floral finesse. Silky texture, with tenderly penetrative acidity.

★★★★★ **Patatsblanc** At 36%, the chenin part of this mostly colombard **17** (92) up on previous. Still a remarkable achievement with a generally unassuming variety. Beeswax, earth & stone, with a kernel of sweet fruit. Generous, but no pushover. Serious but very drinkable now.— TJ

Location: Stellenbosch ▪ WO: Montagu/Stellenbosch ▪ 1stB 2014 ▪ Closed to public ▪ Owner(s) Fritz Schoon, Reenen Borman & Henk Kotze ▪ Winemaker(s) Reenen Borman ▪ 800cs own label

☐ **Rondekop** *see* Oldenburg Vineyards
☐ **Roodeberg** *see* KWV Wines

Roodezandt Wines   Ⓠⓐ�headphones

Roodezandt focuses on bulk wine, producing well over 25 million litres annually for brand owners in SA and abroad. Having upgraded the grape receiving area of their cellar, Christie Steytler and his team are planting tannat and malbec to broaden their palette. This grower-owned venture also bottles a small volume under its proprietary label, and invites winelovers to taste and buy at the visitor centre in Robertson town.

Roodezandt range

Chenin Blanc ⊘ ⑦ ★★★ Bright, sunshiny orchard & tropical fruit delights on zippy & moreish **18** (81), offers excellent value. **Late Harvest** ⊘ ⑦ ★★★ Balanced, juicy sweetness & lively lemon fruit made **NV** (82) a good solo sip & equally amenable partner for spicy fare.

Cabernet Sauvignon ★★★ Steps up in **16** (80) with gentle black fruit & chocolate flavours, supple tannins, smooth & gluggable. **Syrah** ★★★ Spice & forthcoming dark fruit on easygoing **17** (79). **Sauvignon Blanc** ★★★ Enticing, vibrant greengage, capsicum & citrus flavours in **18** (82), summertime light & crisply dry. **Red Muscadel** ★★★★ Improved **17** (85), lovely luminescent ruby, pleasing raisin & muscat flavours in harmony with the warm alcohol.

Keizer's Creek range

The Red ★★ Uncomplicated, unoaked **NV** (74) pinotage, cab & merlot offers fresh berry fruit & chocolate.

Balthazar range

Not tasted: **Chardonnay Brut Méthode Cap Classique**. — WB

Location/map/WO: Robertson ▪ Map grid reference: B5 ▪ Est 1953 ▪ Tasting & sales Mon-Fri 9-5 ▪ Cellar tours by appt Mon-Fri 8-12 & 2-5 ▪ Closed all pub hols ▪ Sales (at cellar price) also from La Verne Wine Boutique Mon-Fri 9-5.30 Sat 9-5 ▪ Facilities for children ▪ Owner(s) 45 members ▪ Cellarmaster(s) Christie Steytler (May 1980) ▪ Winemaker(s) Jean du Plessis (2012), with Tiaan Blom (Oct 2005) ▪ Viticulturist(s) Jaco Lategan (Dec 2006) ▪ 1,700ha (cab, malbec, merlot, ptage, ruby cab, shiraz, tannat, chard, chenin, cbard, muscadel w, sauv) ▪ 34,000t/26.5m L bulk ▪ BSCI, HACCP, IPW, WIETA ▪ PO Box 164 Robertson 6705 ▪ info@roodezandt.

co.za ▪ www.roodezandt.co.za ▪ S 33° 48′ 33.2″ E 019° 52′ 47.3″ ▪ ⌑ gallons.immunity.sugar ▪ F +27 (0)23-626-5074 ▪ T +27 (0)23-626-1160

Rooiberg Winery

Established in 1964, this Robertson Valley landmark with its distinctive red land-art, modern tasting room, Bodega de Vinho restaurant and sincere value pledge represents a private company with 30 shareholders. Cultivating some 20 farms at the western end of the valley, along the Breede River and some tributaries, they believe their 'extraordinary terroir' gives rise to 'an exciting expression of wine diversity' within not only their signature Rooiberg ranges but also their many export labels and brands produced for clients.

Reserve range

★★★★ Cabernet Sauvignon ⊘ Abundant mocha, caramel notes to black fruit on **17** ⑧⑥ from year 50% new oak, some American (as next three reds).

★★★★☆ Pinotage ⊘ Intriguing rosemary on nose of **17** ⑨⓪, big & bold on palate with ripe bananas, mulberries & plums, hints of dark chocolate & liquorice. Balanced at just over 14% alcohol.

★★★★ Shiraz ⊘ Pushing higher rating, **17** ⑧⑨ rich & concentrated, packed with ripe dark fruit, savoury black pepper & BBQ smoke vying with sweet vanilla & cocoa wood spice.

★★★★ Cape Blend ⊘ Pinotage, shiraz, cab blend, **15** ⑧⑥ over-delivers & improves on **13 ★★★★** ⑧④. Fruit driven (older oak) with softening tannins. No **14**.

★★★★ Chardonnay ⊛ Tangy sweet-sour citrus on smooth, balanced **16** ⑧⑦, with vanilla from year on fine lees in French oak, 25% new; spicy ginger to finish on fresh, dry, food-friendly note.

Premium range

★★★★ Cabernet Sauvignon ⊘ Outshines Reserve sibling in **15** ⑧⑦ with juicy dark plum & berry fruit, chocolate richness, soft tannins after older oaking, 2 years in bottle. Sub-14% alcohol.

★★★★ Shiraz ⊛ Excellent food wine (think juicy steaks & meaty pastas), **14** ⑧⑥ ripe dark plums on spicy black pepper base; tangy cranberry finish lingers forever.

Merlot ⊛ **★★★** Mocha & savoury notes on **15** ⑧① plum & cranberry flavours with nicely managed tannin, juicy finish. **Pinotage** ⊛ **★★★★** Slightly high-toned red berry, plum & mulberry notes with savoury undertone, fruit-sweet exit. **14** ⑧④ ready & could age a bit. Not tasted: **Chenin Blanc**.

The Game Reserve range

Merlot ★★★ Conservation-minded range, Cape Clawless Otter on label of violet-scented **15** ⑧②, packed with ripe plum & chocolate, buffed tannins after year French barrels, 20% new. WO W Cape. **Chardonnay ★★★★** Lightly wooded **16** ⑧⑤ has creamy mouthfeel, slight nuttiness, chalky minerality as delicious backdrop to zesty citrus fruit. Not tasted: **Cabernet Sauvignon**, **Pinotage**, **Shiraz**, **Chenin Blanc**, **Sauvignon Blanc**.

AlexKia range

Not tasted: **Alexandra Cabernet Sauvignon**, **Merlot Reserve**, **Chiara Chardonnay**.

Rooiberg range

★★★★☆ Red Muscadel ⊛ Fortified **16** ⑨⓪ invites serious fireside contemplation. Smooth & lusciously rich (230 g/l sugar), it evokes sun-kissed raisins yet also has vitalising fresh acidity.

. . . .

Chardonnay ⊘ ⊛ **★★★★** Unwooded **18** ⑧③ bursts with ripe citrus & Golden Delicious apple, dry & fresh yet smooth, soft from lees contact.

. . . .

Cabernet Sauvignon ⊘ **★★★** Older barrels/tanks with staves for most of these reds. **17** ⑧② has a medium body, with bright black-berry fruit. **Merlot** ⊘ **★★★** Close to 15% alcohol, **17** ⑧⓪ is all ripe plum & dark chocolate, no green notes. **Pinotage** ⊘ **★★★** Less ripe, juicy, balanced than previous, slightly astringent, persistent coffee edge taking shine off red berry fruit in **17** ⑧①. **Shiraz** ⊘ **★★★** Hints of smoke & BBQ spice add plenty of interest to smooth, easy-drinking **17** ⑧②, good match for hearty game dishes. **Cabernet Sauvignon-Merlot (Roodewyn)** ⊘ **★★★** 10% petit verdot adds inky depth to **17** ⑧①'kui-erwyn', with dark fruit from 60% cab & merlot, cinnamon from oak staves. **Mountain Red** ⊘ **★★★** Juicy, unwooded **17** ⑦⑦ to match braaied red meat, mostly cab & shiraz, splashes pinotage & others. **Pinotage Rosé** ⊘ **★★★** Smooth, semi-dry **18** ⑧① good match for sweet-&-sour Asian fare, offers fresh red berry

& white peach fruit, clean finish. **Chenin Blanc** ⊘ ★★★ Plenty of flavour & texture in easy-drinking **18** ⑧⓪, packed with tropical fruit. **Cape White Colombar** ⊘ ★★★ Though unpretentious, light-bodied **18** ⑧⓪ ticks the right boxes with honeyed melon & guava notes, uncloying sweetness. **Sauvignon Blanc** ⊘ ★★★ From passionfruit to pineapple, tropical flavours abound in **18** ⑧①, fruity & refreshing at 12.5% alcohol. **Flamingo Sparkling** ★★★ From red muscadel, festive pink **NV** ⑦⑦ fizz is sweet, with ripe grape & berry flavours. Pairs well with different cheeses, say winemakers. **Brut Sparkling** ★★★ Fun times call for these **NV** ⑦⑨ bubbles from sauvignon, fresh & frothy with green apple & lime notes. **Red Natural Sweet** ★★★ Cherry cola & rhubarb add interest to sun-ripe cherry & blueberry appeal of **17** ⑦⑧ sweet red. **Rosé Natural Sweet** ★★★ Candyfloss & musk sweets on nose of low-alcohol **18** ⑦⑦ from red muscadel, leading to ripe strawberry fruit. **Blanc Natural Sweet** ★★★ Litchis, figs & tasty sweet muscat grapiness to the fore in **18** ⑦⑨, slipping down easily, also below 10% alcohol. Discontinued: **Cape Vintage**.

Red Chair range

Bean There Pinotage ⊘ ★★★ Intended as more delicate style of 'coffee' pinotage, **17** ⑧⓪ largely succeeds, soft & juicy flavours, plum pudding & subtle mocha. Not tasted: **De Lite Sauvignon Blanc**. — JG

Location/map: Robertson ▪ Map grid reference: A7 ▪ WO: Robertson/Western Cape ▪ Est 1964 ▪ 1stB 1974 ▪ Tasting & sales Mon-Fri 9–5.30 Sat 9–4 ▪ Fee R20pp for tour groups ▪ Closed Good Fri, Dec 25 & Jan 1 ▪ Bodega de Vinho restaurant & bakery Mon-Fri 8–5 Sat 9–4 ▪ Facilities for children ▪ Tour groups ▪ Gift shop ▪ Rooiberg Conservancy ▪ Owner(s) 25 shareholders ▪ Cellarmaster(s) André van Dyk (Oct 2002) ▪ Winemaker(s) André Scriven (Jan 2008), with Willie Conradie (2017) ▪ Viticulturist(s) Hennie Visser (2007, VinPro consultant) ▪ 743ha (cab, merlot, ptage, ruby cab, shiraz, chard, chenin, cbard, sauv) ▪ 12,000t/130,000cs own label 35% red 65% white ▪ Other export brands: African Dawn, Finch Mountain, Zebra Collection ▪ Brands for clients: AlexKia, Blue Bottle Rumours, Cape Dreams, Goederust (Protea Hotels), Headbutt, Lorelei, Woolworths, Zikomo ▪ ISO 9001:2008, HACCP (SANS 10330:2007), IPW, LACON Organic, WIETA ▪ PO Box 358 Robertson 6705 ▪ info@rooiberg.co.za ▪ www.rooiberg.co.za ▪ S 33° 46' 35.3" E 019° 45' 42.9" ▪ ⌖ undigested.domains.dripping ▪ F +27 (0)23-626-3295 ▪ **T +27 (0)23-626-1663**

☐ **Rooibos Ridge** *see* Fairview
☐ **Rooi Kalahari** *see* Die Mas van Kakamas

Roos Family Vineyards ⓠ

A dinnertime discussion with friends in New York provided the spark for the creation of this label, sibling to the Mooiplaas Estate range. Aimed at the younger market and sporting consumer-friendly labels, Roos Family has grown into a successful international brand. Expanded facilities on Mooiplaas farm in Stellenbosch have facilitated the stocking and tasting of the wines locally.

The Collection

The Coco ⊘ ⓣ ★★★☆ Clever use of old oak transforms merlot into vinous version of Chocolate Hug-In-A-Mug. **17** ⑧⑤ very supple tannins, creamy & approachable, drier but more flavoursome than last.

The Bean ★★★ Now all pinotage, drier & touch better than previous, **17** ⑧② fresh-brewed coffee, smoke & spicy red fruit, same winemaking as Coco but firmer, hint coffee bean bitterness. **The Strawberry** ★★ Dry rosé from pinotage. Advertised berry character, light & sherbetty freshness in **18** ⑦⑥ for al fresco or sunset sipping, with moderate 12.3% alcohol. **The Lemongrass** ⊘ ★★★☆ From sauvignon, **17** ⑧③ lively citrus-infused green herb flavours, piquantly fresh, unheavy 14.2% alcohol. Perfect with a light meal. **The Peach** ⊘ ★★★☆ Aptly named unoaked blend has viognier's fruit perfume billowing forth, chenin & semillon in support. **17** ⑧④ balanced, creamy, ticks all boxes for summer, solo or with food. WO W Cape for all. Not tasted: **The Mulberry**. — MW

☐ **Rooster** *see* Middelvlei Estate
☐ **Rooted** *see* Perdeberg Wines
☐ **Rose House** *see* The Bald Ibis

Rosendal Wines

Cellarmaster Therese de Beer sources parcels of grapes and wines from various top producers around the Cape for the discerning clients of this direct-to-customer business, whose base is the luxurious Rosendal Winery & Wellness Retreat near Robertson. Those unable to visit the cellardoor can have it come to them, by making use of the Private Home Tastings facility. Visit the online store for details or email the address below.

Reserve range

★★★★ **Hilltop Shiraz** ⓥ Cinnabun notes with meaty/earthy hints on aromatic **14** ⑧⑦ add depth to ripe black fruit. Juicy tannins, good acidity make for an enjoyable wine. Robertson fruit. No **13**.

★★★★ **Cape Francolin** ⓐ 5-way cab-led Bordeaux blend **15** ⑧⑨ improves on **13** ★★★★ ⑧④ with more complex perfumed dark berry flavours, dried herb & spicy oak notes (30% new, 18 months). Full & rounded, excellent grilled meat partner. No **14**.

★★★★ **Vexator** ⓥ Cab-dominated Bordeaux blend excites with ripe black cherries & plums hedged with sweet cinnamon & nutmeg. **15** ⑧⑨ bright & lively, firm ripe tannins & positive finish.

★★★★ **Cape Ruby** Vibrant ruby glints from mostly tinta (with touriga, souzão), **NV** ⑧⑥ poised, very moreish, delicious berry tang to finish. Fine example of style from 'port capital' Calitzdorp.

Hilltop Merlot ★★★★ Helderberg & Stellenbosch fruit for **16** ⑧④ is sweet, plummy, spice sprinkled, though the 20% new oak needs time to integrate fully. Not tasted: **Hilltop Cabernet Sauvignon, Hilltop Pinot Noir.** In abeyance: **Classic Cuvée, Red Rock, Black Eagle, Black Spice, Serenity Chardonnay.**

Rosendal range

★★★★ **Merlot** ⓐ Pristine ripe plum & blackberry fruit supported by supple tannins & 10% new oak, **16** ⑧⑦ fleshier & more complex than **15** ★★★★ ⑧④, broad flavours & extended spiced cherry echo.

Pinotage Rosé ★★★ Cheerful just-dry pink offers bouncy sweet plum flavours, **17** ⑧① accessible & juicy, with perfumed finish. Not tasted: **Sauvignon Blanc.** In abeyance: **Syrah, Chenin Blanc, HVIT.**

Barony range

★★★★ **Rosslyng Chardonnay** ⓐ Another thoroughly enjoyable vintage, **17** ⑧⑧ rich & ripe yet elegant courtesy 50% tank portion, the combo fresh & baked apple flavours joined by spice & roasted nuts on long satisfying finish. No wonder **16** sold out untasted.

★★★★ **Cecile Sauvignon Blanc** Spans the spectrum from green grass, greengage to passionfruit & ripe pineapple. **17** ⑧⑥ better balance, structure & length than last-made **13** ★★★★ ⑧④.

August Cabernet Sauvignon ★★★★ Step-up **16** ⑧⑤ from Helderberg grapes is voluptuous & smooth, adds some creaminess from older oak, 12 months, to well-expressed fruit. **Bønne Pinotage** ★★★ Seems vinified in a roastery, so intense is the dark toasty oak enveloping **17** ⑧① ripe fruit barely peeping out. In abeyance: **Candelabra, Heidi Shiraz, Sophie.**

Noble Nomad range

He Stole My Horse Shiraz-Cabernet Sauvignon ★★★★ All about dark berries & spice, **16** ⑧③ generous & juicy, a savoury coriander note in aftertaste of 60/40 blend. **He Was My Lover Pinotage Rosé** ★★★★ New to the guide though familiar to Rosendal customers. Dry, coral pink **17** ⑧⑤ succulent & generous, moreish watermelon & candyfloss flavours. Swartland WO. **He Slept Beneath The Stars Sauvignon Blanc** ★★★★ Pungent nose of tropical fruit tempered on palate by greengage & squeeze of lime. **17** ⑧④ vibrant & lengthy mineral conclusion. Breedekloof WO. — WB

Location/map: Robertson ▪ Map grid reference: B4 ▪ WO: Western Cape/Breedekloof/Swartland/Calitzdorp ▪ 1stB 2003 ▪ Tasting & sales Mon-Sat 10-5 Sun 10-2 ▪ R130 tasting fee only charged for groups of 6+ ▪ Wine & Lindt chocolate tastings ▪ Restaurant & guest house ▪ Spa & wellness centre ▪ Conferences ▪ Owner(s) Du Toit Britz, Mike Harvey & Geir Tellefsen ▪ Cellarmaster(s)/winemaker(s) Therese de Beer (Jan 2012) ▪ 18ha ▪ 80% red 15% white 5% rosé ▪ PO Box 3 Suite 128 Roggebaai 8012 ▪ info@rosendalwinery.com ▪ www.rosendalwines.com ▪ S 33° 48′ 7.8″ E 019° 59′ 19.0″ ▪ 🖃 unloaded.flatter.bulk ▪ F +27 (0)21-424-1570 ▪ **T +27 (0)21-424-4498 (sales)/+27 (0)23-626-1570 (farm)**

☐ **Rough Diamond Project** see Van der Merwe & Finlayson

Rousseau Wines

André Rousseau left Constantia Uitsig in 2015 to start his own label, after a long and distinguished career there, first as viticulturist, later as winemaker too. He's still based in Constantia, making his wines — in increasing quantities — in the Steenberg cellar. His first red has arrived, in style, the next (continuing the tributes to special women from the Rousseau family), Julianna Shiraz, due at press time. To follow, a yet unnamed sparkling. All wines are available only directly — they're not in stores.

★★★★☆ **Babette** (NEW) ⊘ Accomplished Bordeaux red, equal cabs sauvignon & franc, 10% merlot in **15** (90). Dark berries, supple palate & savoury persistence, lead pencil & cigarbox complexity from 50% new oak. Constantia plus Darling & Stellenbosch fruit.

★★★★ **Sacharia Wooded Sauvignon Blanc** 100% oaked & bigger bodied than sibling, **17** (86) more vanilla & toasty notes but in harmony with tropical fruit, creamy & full. Elgin grapes, like **16** ★★★★ (84), bunch pressed, older-barrel fermented.

Grace Sauvignon Blanc ★★★★ Exuberant tropical fruit salad with cooler blackcurrant counterweight. Rich & textured from skin maceration & 5% oaked portion. **18** (85) Constantia & 5% Elgin fruit. — WB

Location: Constantia ▪ Map: Cape Peninsula ▪ Map grid reference: B4 ▪ WO: Western Cape ▪ Est/1stB 2015 ▪ Tasting by appt ▪ Sales to the public via email/phone orders ▪ Owner(s) André Rousseau ▪ Winemaker(s) André Rousseau (2015) ▪ 2,000cs own label 30% red 70% white ▪ c/o Steenberg Wine Estate PO Box 224 Steenberg 7947 ▪ andre@rousseauwines.co.za ▪ S 34° 4' 17.0" E 018° 25' 31.1" ▪ **T +27 (0)21-713-2211/+27 (0)83-460-4037**

☐ **Royal** see Riebeek Cellars
☐ **Ruby Ridge** see Govert Wines

Rudera Wines

There are some particularly fine reds available under Riana Hall's Rudera brand. The grapes are sourced from Stellenbosch's Simonsberg area and vinified in an historic cellar in Jonkershoek Valley, on the other side of town. Exports, mostly to China and Canada, make up 95% of Riana's boutique production. The trained psychologist-turned-vintner remains confident and optimistic - justifiably so, as this quality brand continues to grow with forays now into the UK and America.

★★★★☆ **Cabernet Sauvignon** Riper than Platinum, & concentrated, with more of a compote character, firm but supple tannin framework. **14** ★★★★ (89) dark-fruited, brooding, give it time. 70% new French oak. Stellenbosch fruit, where **12** (90) had ex-Paarl portion. **13** untasted.

★★★★☆ **Platinum Cabernet Sauvignon** (Ⓐ) Simonsberg fruit, as for sibling, but a berry & barrel selection, which shows in brighter flavours & lovely dry cedary tannins. Layered, fresh & elegant, 80% new oak in sync. Though quality's a tiny fraction off **11** (93), **14** (92) richly deserves cellaring. No **12**, **13** untasted.

★★★★ **Syrah** Smooth textured, supple & balanced **14** (87), alcohol better integrated into opulent fruit profile, dark prune & sweet tobacco than last. Rounded & complete, a few years in store. **13** untasted.

★★★★ **De Tradisie Chenin Blanc** (Ⓟ) From old Piekenierskloof vines, **15** (86) subtly nuanced, drier than Robusto, pear & lime flavours peeping through obvious oak.

★★★★☆ **Robusto Chenin Blanc** (Ⓟ) 40 year old dryland Koelenhof vines, **13** ★★★★ (83) more oak, sugar & acidity than Tradisie, warm impression from fruit ripeness & 14.4% alcohol. Shade off **12** (90).

Not tasted: **Noble Late Harvest**. Occasional release: **Platinum Chenin Blanc**. — MW

Location/map: Stellenbosch ▪ Map grid reference: G6 ▪ WO: Stellenbosch/Piekenierskloof ▪ Est 1999 ▪ 1stB 2000 ▪ Tasting & cellar tours by appt only ▪ Fee R100pp/5 wines, waived on purchase ▪ Owner(s) Riana Hall ▪ Winemaker(s) Riana Hall (2017) ▪ 15ha/10ha (cab, shiraz, chenin) ▪ ±160t/20,000cs own label & BOB 70% red 30% white ▪ IPW ▪ PO Box 589 Stellenbosch 7599 ▪ riana@rudera.co.za ▪ www.rudera.co.za ▪ S 33° 56' 26.5" E 018° 54' 14.3" ▪ ▦ freed.starters.rotation ▪ **T +27 (0)21-882-8214**

☐ **Rudi Schultz Wines** see Schultz Family Wines

Ruitersvlei Wines

The first mention of this farm on the slopes of Paarl Mountain, originally known as Ruigtervallei, was in 1688. Fast forward to today, and there are wines and a range of options for visitors including boating, having a picnic or restaurant lunch – or even a wedding The white wines reviewed previously are still selling, recent vintages of the reds and rosé untasted.

Chenin Blanc Ⓡ ★★ Demure thatch & tropical tones, **16** (74) soft, fleeting finish. **Sauvignon Blanc** Ⓡ ★★★ Lively but unaggressive **16** (77) ex Durbanville, juicy tropical fruit, upbeat dry finish. — AL

Location/map: Paarl ▪ Map grid reference: D6 ▪ WO: Paarl/Durbanville ▪ Tasting, sales & cellar tours Mon-Sun 9-5; in season (from mid Sep) tastings continue till 10pm at restaurant ▪ Ruitersvlei Restaurant open daily for breakfast & lunch; refreshments & picnic baskets ▪ Child friendly ▪ MTB ▪ Weddings/functions & conferences (up to 200 pax) ▪ 12 guest rooms ▪ Owner(s).Ruitersvlei Holdings (Pty) Ltd ▪ Winemaker(s) Nico Vermeulen ▪ 120ha ▪ PO Box 532 Suider-Paarl 7624 ▪ sales@ruitersvlei.co.za, admin@ruitersvlei.co.za, reservations@ruitersvlei.co.za ▪ www.ruitersvlei.co.za ▪ S 33° 45′10.8″ E 018° 54′28.0″ ▪ furred.candlelit.excellence ▪ **T +27 (0)71-116-7445/+27 (0)71-491-6166**

☐ **Rumours** *see* Rooiberg Winery
☐ **Runner Duck** *see* Vergenoegd Löw Wine Estate
☐ **Running Duck** *see* Stellar Winery

Rupert & Rothschild Vignerons

The internationally acclaimed wines from this joint venture between the Rupert family and Baron Benjamin de Rothschild were not available for review, but the current releases are '15 Baron Edmond (Bordeaux red), '16 Classique (red blend) and '17 Baroness Nadine (wooded chardonnay).

Location: Paarl ▪ Map: Franschhoek ▪ Map grid reference: B7 ▪ Est 1997 ▪ 1stB 1998 ▪ Tasting & sales Tue-Fri 10-4.30 Sat/Sun 10-4 ▪ Seasonal menu and Wine & Food pairing menu Tue-Sun 12-3 ▪ Closed Christian religious holidays, Dec 26 & Jan 1 ▪ Owner(s) Rupert family & Baron Benjamin de Rothschild ▪ Head winemaker Yvonne Lester (Sep 2001), with winemaker André Roux (Oct 2013) ▪ 90ha (cabs s/f, merlot, p verdot) ▪ 2,200t/220,000cs own label 98% red 2% white ▪ ISO 14001, HACCP, IPW ▪ PO Box 412 Franschhoek Valley 7690 ▪ info@rupert-rothschildvignerons.com ▪ www.rupert-rothschildvignerons.com ▪ S 33° 50′14.5″ E 018° 56′51.1″ ▪ outsides.flood.thermos ▪ F +27 (0)21-874-1802 ▪ **T +27 (0)21-874-1648**

☐ **Rupert Wines** *see* Anthonij Rupert Wyne

Rustenberg Wines

One of the loveliest of Stellenbosch's estates, and among the most historic, Rustenberg is fittingly set against the splendid Simonsberg. Industrialist Peter Barlow bought the two farms into which Rustenberg had been split in 1810 (the other half called Schoongezicht) and reunited the property in 1945. His son Simon now owns it, and grandson Murray is cellarmaster – the latter (twice Diners Club Young Winemaker of the Year) has over recent years re-established the range of Rustenberg's wines as among Stellenbosch's finest, expressing a classic approach in warm-climate conditions. Fires before harvest in 2016 seriously affected some vineyards, and left a few gaps in the vintages listed below. But historic sites are being reinvigorated and replanted, with new blocks on the estate's varied slopes. Meanwhile the drought has increased focus on 'conservation and maximisation' of water.

Flagship range

★★★★☆ **Buzzard Kloof Syrah** Ⓡ From a specific cooler site, yet **15** (90) is a big, powerful wine, with a majestic structure of ripe tannin & acid. But it's the intensity & spicy complexity of the fruit that counts, & the appropriate oaking (40% new), & the balance, which doesn't reveal the 14.7% alcohol.

★★★★☆ **John X Merriman** Ⓡ 5-way Bordeaux blend with cab (56%) & merlot (38%) in the lead in classic **14** (92). Similar overall character to **15** (92) but lighter, less intense & a touch more sombre. Also well balanced.

★★★★ **Stellenbosch Chardonnay** Oak (25% new) still showing in youth on **17** ★★★★☆ (90), needing year/2 to harmonise with hazelnut, oatmeal, lime-lemon character, but fruit is intense enough for good development. Silky texture, as on **16** (87), with fine acid a forceful part of the balance. Stellenbosch WO.

Site Specific range

★★★★☆ **Peter Barlow** ⊛ Grandly gorgeous **15** ⑨④ must augment its reputation as one of the leading Cape cabs. Expensive oak notes mingle happily with dark fruit aromas & intense flavours. Well balanced & already winning, but very firm structure demands ageing. Long sweet-fruited finish. No **14**.

Not tasted: **Five Soldiers**.

Regional range

★★★★★ **Stellenbosch Cabernet Sauvignon** ⊘ ⊛ Plenty of dark berries plus tobacco notes in the savoury depths of impressive **16** ⑨③. Fine, firm tannins & succulent acidity already integrating deliciously; overall suggesting confident gracefulness rather than power. Restrained oaking (20% new) aids approachability.

★★★★ **Stellenbosch Grenache** ⓺ Light-toned **16** ⑧⑦ fresh, gently perfumed, friendly & outgoing. Delicious, but not trivial - though by Rustenberg standards modestly structured. Good dry finish.

★★★★ **Stellenbosch Merlot** ⊘ As usual, **16** ⑧⑥ with fruitcake, savoury/tobacco notes & herbal twist. Generous but serious; firm dry tannic grip, but approachable young thanks to fruit depth & good oak.

★★★★ **Stellenbosch Shiraz** ⊘ Softly textured, fleshy, fruit-filled & spicy **16** ⑧⑦; firm but unassertive tannin-acid. No pushover, though, even burly. Good length suggests enough concentration for ageing.

★★★★ **RM Nicholson** ⊘ Half shiraz with merlot & cab. **16** ⑧⑦ good combo of red/dark berries, spice, oak hints. Earlier approachable than other reds this vintage, with sweet fruit & firm build; balanced & moreish. Stellenbosch WO, as next.

★★★★ **Unwooded Chardonnay** ⊘ Tropical fruity charm on ripe but fresh, clean & dry **17** ⑧⑥ - **16** ★★★ ⑧① a little sweet. Creamy, but good acidity. Easygoing pleasure but certainly not trivial.

★★★★ **Stellenbosch Sauvignon Blanc** ⊘ Tropical fruit dominates character of **17** ⑧⑥, but there's also peach, plus greener notes. Unaggressively succulent acid freshness, though rather richly textured. At least as tasty as **16** ★★★★ ⑧④.

★★★★ **Straw Wine** ⊘ Decadently delicious but fresh air-dried **17** ★★★★☆ ⑨② from chenin with viognier & crouchen. Raisin, honey & apricot notes. Charming balance: sweet but not cloying or too soft - better acidic bite than on previous **15** ⑧⑦; 10% alcohol; old oak barrels. 375 ml. WO Stellenbosch.

★★★★ **Red Muscadel** ⓺ There's no denying the soft, sweet grapey & floral delights of this fresh, airy **15** ⑧⑦ fortified (16% alcohol) from Calitzdorp grapes. Lightly oaked & not quite trivial. 375 ml.

Stellenbosch Petit Verdot Rosé ⓺ ★★★ Forward, fruity aromas & flavours on richly soft, just-dry **17** ⑧①. Not tasted: **Stellenbosch Roussanne**. — TJ

Location/map: Stellenbosch ▪ Map grid reference: F4 ▪ WO: Simonsberg–Stellenbosch/Stellenbosch/ Western Cape ▪ Est 1682 ▪ 1stB 1892 ▪ Tasting & sales Mon-Fri 9–4.30 Sat 10–4 Sun 10-3 ▪ Closed Good Fri, Dec 25 & Jan 1 ▪ Gardens ▪ Filming ▪ Owner(s) Simon Barlow ▪ Cellarmaster(s) Murray Barlow (Nov 2011) ▪ Winemaker(s) Randolph Christians (Nov 1995), with Craig Christians (Jun 2012) & Nick van Zyl (Nov 2015) ▪ Viticulturist(s) Simon Barlow (Aug 1987), with Tessa Moffat (Nov 2013) ▪ 880ha/±110ha (cabs s/f, grenache n/b, malbec, merlot, p verdot, shiraz, chard, rouss, sauv) ▪ ±1,200t/120,000cs own label 51% red 47% white 2% other ▪ IPW ▪ PO Box 33 Stellenbosch 7599 ▪ wine@rustenberg.co.za ▪ www.rustenberg.co.za ▪ S 33° 53' 44.8" E 018° 53' 33.6" ▪ 🎧 tickles.usages.medium ▪ **T** +27 (0)21-809-1200

Rust en Vrede Wine Estate ⓺ 🍽 ◎

One of Stellenbosch's original wine properties, dating back to 1694, as the flagship blend recalls, Rust en Vrede's current custodian, Jean Engelbrecht, has taken the ball (passed by his father and former Springbok rugby star Jannie) and run with it. The elder Engelbrecht rescued the venerable Cape Dutch buildings and premium vine land on Helderberg mountain, and re-established Rust en Vrede's reputation for stylish reds in the latter half of the 1900s. Engelbrecht junior, ably assisted by winemaker Coenie Snyman, has gone one step further: fine-tuned the vineyards, added a barrel room specifically for the single-vineyard wines, and tapped into the romance of the much-loved estate with a world-class restaurant, plus, more recently, a refurbished underground cellar to accommodate winter lunch service and tastings.

Estate Vineyards range

★★★★☆ **Cabernet Sauvignon** Classically styled to endure, but **16** ⑨② shows well already. Heady rose fragrance woven into dense black fruit, earthy undertones & fine tannins. Follows form of imposing **15** ⑨②. 50% new oak, as next.

★★★★☆ **Single Vineyard Cabernet Sauvignon** ⓐ Sublime **15** ⑨④ with beguiling notes of earth, forest floor & iodine gently spicing formidable black fruit core. Emphasises form, intensity & structure, will only reveal its full potential in future years. **14** ★★★★★ ⑨⑤ was full of savoury delights.

★★★★ **Merlot** Distinct mulberry fruit, restrained leafy notes, hints of oak-spice. **16** ⑧⑧ generous & full, with bold tannins, impressively long finish, showing pedigree.

★★★★☆ **Single Vineyard Syrah** ⓐ Bold, intensely expressive **15** ★★★★★ ⑨⑤ gushes with aromas & nuances: tarry tobacco blended with maraschino cherries, roasted meat, plums & prunes, all borne on a robust tannin backbone. Approachable, but so much better in 6-10 years. **14** ⑨④ also en route to greatness.

★★★★☆ **Syrah** Deep, dark & brooding **15** ⑨① with fragrant highlights of rose & spices. Dense black cherry fruit, velvety tannins. Also-tasted **16** ★★★★ ⑧⑨ plusher, less floral, with savoury & baked fruit notes. Both finely crafted, for the long road.

★★★★☆ **1694 Classification** ⓐ Pricey flagship of an impressive fleet, **15** ⑨④ reins in some excesses of previous years to produce great balance & harmony. Richly ripe & rounded, subtle spicy nuances, velvet texture & endless finish. Syrah & cab (66/34), 22 months oaked, 50% new, as for **14** ★★★★★ ⑨⑤.

★★★★☆ **Estate** ⓐ Iconic cab-syrah since '88, still one of Cape's jewels. Dense, concentrated black fruit on **15** ★★★★★ ⑨⑤ (with 9% merlot) shows layers of complexity & detail: heady fynbos, taut earthiness, supple texture. Beautifully crafted for cellaring, like **14** ⑨② Larger formats up to 27L available.— GdB

Location/map/WO: Stellenbosch ▪ Map grid reference: E8 ▪ Est 1694 ▪ 1stB 1979 ▪ Tasting & sales Mon-Sat 9–5 Sun seasonal, call to enquire ▪ Fee R40/4 wines & R70/6 wines, waived on purchase ▪ Closed Easter Fri/Sun, Dec 25 & Jan 1 ▪ Rust en Vrede Restaurant (fine dining, evenings only) ▪ Rust en Vrede Winemaker's Lunch ▪ Merchandise available ▪ Owner(s) Jean Engelbrecht ▪ Winemaker(s) Coenie Snyman (Dec 2006), with Malie McGregor (Jan 2018) ▪ Viticulturist(s) Dirkie Mouton (Jun 2010) ▪ 50ha/34ha (cab, merlot, shiraz) ▪ ±250t/40,000cs own label 100% red ▪ IPW, WWF-SA Conservation Champion ▪ PO Box 473 Stellenbosch 7599 ▪ info@rustenvrede.com ▪ www.rustenvrede.com ▪ S 33° 59' 54.0" E 018° 51' 22.5" ▪ 🖳 snaps.proposes. years ▪ **T +27 (0)21-881-3881**

☐ **Rusthof** see Mooiuitsig Wine Cellars
☐ **Ruyter's Bin** see Stellenrust
☐ **Ryk Neethling** see Val de Vie & Polo Club Wines

Saam Mountain Vineyards ⓠ

Agter Paarl estate Eenzaamheid inspired the name of this brand, sourced from specific blocks on farms owned by 3rd-generation family growers, and vinified on behalf of SAAM Mountain Vineyards by the team at Perdeberg Wines, where tastings/sales are offered.

Cellar Selection

Chenin Blanc ⓠ ★★★ Easy-sipping **17** ⑦⑧ shows tropical flavours & a gentle acid. Paarl WO. Not tasted: **Cabernet Sauvignon**, **Pinotage**, **Sauvignon Blanc**. — WB

☐ **Saartjie Single Vineyard Selections** see Hillcrest Estate
☐ **Sabi Sabi** see Stellenrust

Sadie Family Wines ⓠ

It's been less than two decades since Eben Sadie sold his first wine, the '00 Columella, to UK wine merchant Richards Walford. He's since grown to be known and respected at the highest levels of world wide, as evidenced by him named

'Winemakers'Winemaker' by the Institute of Masters of Wine/The Drinks Business in 2017. His Paarderberg venture has twice been this guide's Winery of the Year (2010, 2015), and each year his compact but extraordinarily fine and consistent range passes the litmus test, selling out on allocation worldwide. Impressive as these achievements are, there's more to come, as Eben believes 'building a great wine is not the work of one generation'. So, with assistant Paul Jordaan assuming greater responsibility in the cellar, he's building the future in the vineyards, including establishing his family's first vines and working with growers up and down the Cape's West Coast to nurture small experimental blocks of varieties equipped to thrive in a warming climate. Another of his sayings is: 'What I learnt from the first 10 years is much more important than what I actually did in the first 10.' Sons Markus and Xander, who've shown an interest in emulating their father, are 'in training'. Both are keen, and well-tutored tasters, and clearly hands-on. Markus, for example, spent time in the Loire learning percheron-powered ploughing before completing the harvest there.

Signature Series

★★★★☆ **Columella** (Ⓐ) Standard bearer for SA reds, with smidgen carignan joining shiraz, mourvèdre, grenache, cinsaut & tinta in **16** (94). Powerful, almost austere, benefits from decanting & will reward decade+ cellaring. Despite ongoing drought, exhibits house's fruit authenticity & integrity, fine-grained tannin structure. Also in 1.5 & 3L, as next.

★★★★★ **Palladius** (Ⓐ) Step-change in **16** (96), tighter, tenser than previous, will unwind slowly over ±10 years. Steely & precise, with striking purity, umami nuance, tremendous presence. Chenin with 10 other varieties fermented/aged year on lees in concrete 'eggs' & clay amphora, then year older foudres.

Old Vine Series

★★★★★ **Soldaat** (Ⓐ) (Ⓥ) Ex venerable, high-altitude dryland vines in Piekenierskloof, arguably SA's top terroir for grenache. **17** ★★★★★ (95) intense strawberry & raspberry tones lifted by spice, given form by hallmark feisty grape tannin grip. Ethereal, treads as lightly as **16** (94) but no pushover, has legs for ageing.

★★★★☆ **Treinspoor** (Ⓥ) From 44 year old unirrigated bushvine tinta barocca beside old railway line (treinspoor), **17** (92) variety's signature orange zest & pot-pourri aromatics, bright acidity, lattice-like tannins. Uncompromisingly dry & totally captivating.

★★★★☆ **Pofadder** (Ⓥ) Cinsaut from old Riebeek-Kasteel vines; more than any in line-up, **17** (93) vintage at least, evocative of place rather than fruit, even drier, steelier than **16** ★★★★★ (95) (1.3 g/l sugar versus 1.9 g/l). Nuances of wild vegetation & earth, minimalistic yet reveals something new with each sip.

★★★★★ **Skurfberg** (Ⓐ) (Ⓥ) Distinguished old-bushvine chenin off 3 dryland parcels in Olifants River; **17** (97) one the purest expressions yet. White peach & nectarine notes on earthy, mineral & saline substrate. Markedly dry, with great depth but not the richness of **16** (95), compact & perfectly balanced.

★★★★☆ **Mev. Kirsten** (Ⓐ) (Ⓥ) Chenin from partly-100+ year old block in Stellenbosch, vinified differently to white siblings, initial carbonic maceration to protect oxidation-prone juice. **17** (94) less savoury & mineral than Skurfberg, opulent without cosmetic of oak or big alcohol; as always, precision personified.

★★★★☆ **Kokerboom** (Ⓐ) (Ⓥ) Semillon - both white & red variant - from Olifants River, 18 month on lees in large old oak 'stukvate' (foudres). Like smoky **16** (92), lemon-toned **17** (93) most fruit-filled in line-up, with variety's spirited acidity contrasting with its richness, driving persistent finish.

★★★★☆ **'T Voetpad** (Ⓐ) (Ⓥ) Field blend chenin, semillon, palomino, muscat from vineyard planted between 1900 & 1928. Slate-like leanness, effortless balance, **17** (93) as breathtaking as always. Cool white peach & nectarine, some citrus & semillon's waxiness a welcome detail. Co-fermented/year older vats.

★★★★☆ **Skerpioen** (Ⓥ) Interplanted chenin & palomino off unique chalky West Coast soils, co-fermented/year very old foudres. **17** (92) more expressive in youth than **16** (90), **15** (93), yellow stonefruit, white peach fruitedness; as saline & earthy, though; well-judged acidity brings focus & length.— CvZ

Location: Malmesbury • Map: Swartland • Map grid reference: C8 • WO: Swartland/Olifants River/Stellenbosch/Piekenierskloof • Est 1999 • 1stB 2000 • Only scheduled tastings - bookings essential, contact sales@thesadiefamily.com • Owner(s) The Sadie Family (Pty) Ltd • Winemaker(s)/viticulturist(s) Eben Sadie (1999) • 25ha (cinsaut, grenache n/b, mourv, shiraz, tinta barocca, chenin, clairette, palomino, rouss, sem, verdelho, viog) • 60t/8,000cs own label 50% red 50% white • PO Box 1019 Malmesbury 7299 • office@thesadiefamily.com • www.thesadiefamily.com • S 33° 31′ 31.0″ E 018° 48′ 18.1″ • 📧 broomstick.gargled. tomorrow • F +27 (0)86-692-2852 • **T +27 (0)76-151-7131**

☐ **Safari** see Frater Family Wines

☐ **Sailor's Selection** see La Couronne Wines

☐ **Sainsbury** see Bosman Family Vineyards

St Francis Point Vineyards

On the coastal dunes at St Francis Bay in the Eastern Cape, Jean Fynn's vineyards are exposed to fresh sea breezes, helping preserve the grapes' delicate flavours and acidity. The resultant wine is popular at her nearby function venues, catering for events ranging from weddings to conferences.

Sauvignon Blanc ★★★ Restrained but involving fig, grass & pear aromas & flavours, invigorating acidity extends the farewell. Light 12% alcohol adds to previewed **18** (82)'s cool, fresh personality. — CvZ

Location/WO: St Francis Bay ▪ Map: Eastern Cape ▪ Map grid reference: D6 ▪ Est 2009 ▪ Tasting by appt ▪ Owner(s)/viticulturist(s) Jean Fynn ▪ Winemaker(s) Jean Fynn & Albertus van Rensburg ▪ 3.5ha (chard, sauv, sem) ▪ PO Box 355 St Francis Bay 6312 ▪ sfpvineyard@gmail.com ▪ S 34° 11' 6.61" E 024° 50' 34.05" ▪ 🌐 flightless.octane.huddle ▪ **T** +27 (0)42-294-0548/+27 (0)82-491-3373

☐ **Saints** see DGB (Pty) Ltd
☐ **Salpeterkop** see Rogge Cloof

Saltare

Operating from central Stellenbosch (cellar and convivial tasting venue a stone's throw apart, on opposite banks of the Eerste River), winemaker and co-owner (with husband Christoff) Carla Pauw sources the fruit for her boutique label from various growers, and singles out Robertson chardonnay supplier Fritz Breytenbach for his years-long focus on soil health. 'Someday, hopefully, this visionary farmer will be recognised as a post-chemical pioneer of our industry.' Carla's quest in all her wines is ever more refined texture, her grail being champagne and its 'elusive lightness and indescribable deliciousness'. She also handcrafts soap from virgin olive oil and intends to create her own perfume brand.

★★★★☆ Syrah (②) Polished & integrated **14 ★★★★** (89) shade less intense than stellar **13** (94), nonetheless radiates black fruit charm with fragrant aromas backed up by well-formed tannins & balancing acidity. Swartland fruit, with 3% carignan.

★★★★ Specialis Occasional release. **15 ★★★★** (85) Bordeaux red from Paarl vines lighter than **12 ★★★★★** (93) & **08** (87), salty & iodine hints on supple blackcurrant fruit. Cab & merlot, dash cab franc.

★★★★ Old Vines Chenin Blanc Generously rounded body on **15** (88) spiced with subtle (old) oak, wild yeast. Bright yellow peach & apricot fruit has buttery malo notes, appealing savoury finish. Paardeberg fruit, like oakier **14 ★★★★** (84).

★★★★ Méthode Cap Classique Brut Rosé Enticing whiffs of stewed rhubarb, tobacco & spices on **NV** (88) pinot noir sparkler from Stellenbosch. Pale brassy pink, delicate bead. Elegantly fresh & crisp, appealing salty twist on finish. Magnums for all bubblies save Brut Nature.

★★★★☆ Méthode Cap Classique Brut Blanc de Blancs Delectable premium-priced sparkling, **NV** (92) from Robertson chardonnay reflects lime-rich soils, crisp salty bite & delicate but piercing acidity. Yeasty savouriness & bright lemon notes, borne on fine but full mousse. 15% portion oak-matured.

★★★★☆ Méthode Cap Classique Brut Nature Convincing zero-dosage **NV** (91) (20% reserve fraction) bubbles, 56% Robertson chardonnay with Helderberg pinot noir. Rich, creamy brioche & green apple, lingering, scented finish. Fullness from 15% oaked portion, 19 months on lees.

★★★★☆ Méthode Cap Classique Brut Reserve (⑭) Finely crafted **NV** (94) sparkling from Robertson chardonnay, Helderberg pinot noir, delivers on every level. Sumptuous palate weight with spicy baked apple, nutty brioche, all laced with perky acid tang. 20% oaked, 20% reserve wine, 100% spot-on.

In abeyance: **Single Vineyard Chenin Blanc**. — GdB

Location/map: Stellenbosch ▪ Map grid reference: F5 ▪ WO: Swartland/Western Cape/Robertson/Paarl/ Stellenbosch ▪ 1stB 2005 ▪ Tasting & cellar tour by appt ▪ Olive oil ▪ Owner(s) Christoff & Carla Pauw ▪ Cellarmaster(s)/winemaker(s) Carla Pauw (2005) ▪ 19t/2,200cs own label 15% red 15% white 70% MCC ▪ 30 Die Laan Stellenbosch 7600 ▪ info@saltare.co.za ▪ www.saltare.co.za ▪ S 33° 56' 18.4" E 018° 52' 05.7" ▪ 🌐 briefer.kebabs.fills ▪ **F** +27 (0)88-021-883-9568 ▪ **T** +27 (0)21-883-9568

☐ **Sandrivier** see Overgaauw Wine Estate
☐ **Sandveld** see Tierhoek
☐ **Sanniesrust** see Van der Merwe & Finlayson

Sarah's Creek

Stockwell, the Malherbe estate in Robertson Valley, has been in the family since 1888. Here, grapes for export brand Sarah's Creek are grown on the scenic slopes of the Langeberg mountains, and vinified by Marga Malherbe, daughter-in-law of current custodian Dirk. A different family member, whose fascination with a farm stream made her habitually late for school, is recalled in the branding.

Location: Robertson ▪ Closed to public ▪ Owner(s) Dirk C Malherbe ▪ Winemaker(s) Marga Malherbe ▪ 25ha (cab, ptage, ruby cab, shiraz, chenin) ▪ PO Box 6531 Welgemoed 7538 ▪ marga@scwines.co.za ▪ www. sarahscreek.co.za ▪ **T** +27 (0)21-300-1731/+27 (0)84-941-2526

Saronsberg Cellar

This Tulbagh estate was established by Pretoria businessman Nick van Huyssteen in 2002 (and named for the mountain rising above it), and has been central to the growth in the area's reputation for fine wine in the past decade or two. There are two farms, one on the lower mountain slopes, one stretching down the valley, giving veteran winemaker Dewaldt Heyns varied terroirs with which to work. Saronsberg is best known for its reds, especially those based on shiraz. They are substantial, rich and powerful, yet with a degree of finesse that eludes many similarly styled warm-country wines. Dewaldt welcomes the winery's many awards as highlighting 'Saronsberg's focus on quality and consistency'. Visitors will also find art, accommodation, and a wedding venue.

Saronsberg range

★★★★ **Grenache** Light on its feet, **16** ⑧⑧ more elegant than **15** ⑧⑥, but palate as measured, with smooth tannins & seasoned oak neatly sewn in.

★★★★ **Mourvèdre** ⑭ House's full-throttle styling evident in **16** ⑧⑨'s ripe mulberry fruit, plush tannins, 20-month oaking & 14.8% alcohol, the latter still apart mid-2018, needing further year to marry.

★★★★☆ **Shiraz** ⑧ As rich in local & international awards as in ripe, near-sweet power - expressed with usual refinement in **16** ⑨③. Lovely supple tannin, plenty of French oak (80% new, 20 months) & 14.4% alcohol continue the big, bold & rewarding styling.

★★★★☆ **Full Circle** ⑧ Depth, complexity & power combine in sensational **16** ★★★★★ ⑨⑤; shiraz with grenache, mourvèdre & 1% viognier - the last evident in peachy perfume & lingering finish. As **15** ⑨③, weighty but still agile, commanding but balanced, muscular but not chunky, the all-new oak unobtrusive.

★★★★ **Brut Méthode Cap Classique** Notes of oven-fresh biscuit & sweet citrus on **16** ⑧⑧ dry bubbly from chardonnay, plumped by 2 years on lees. Balanced & flavourful, pleasing steeliness behind the fruit.

Sauvignon Blanc ★★★★ Reductive handling makes for a juicy, fruity & fresh **18** ⑧③ glassful in which exuberant tropical aromas jostle with greener, grassier notes. WO Coastal. **Viognier** ★★★★ Decorous rather than blockbuster expression, thanks to winemaking (25% wild yeasts, 33% new barrels, no malo) which keeps **17** ⑧④'s apricot ebullience in check, preserves freshness. Not tasted: **Six Point Three Straw Wine**.

Provenance range

Shiraz ⑰ ★★★★ Scrumptious, savoury **16** ⑧⑤ is well balanced, with fresh acidity & modest tannic grip aided by 30% new oak. Utterly moreish. Ready, but will keep a few years. WO W Cape. **Seismic** ⑰ ★★★★ Bordeaux red from all 5 varieties, unpretentious **15** ⑧⑤ delivers cassis fruit in spades, backed by a good tannic structure, typically big alcohol (14.7%) not too obvious.

Shiraz Rosé ★★★ Light-hearted **18** ⑧② with overt red-fruit notes finishes bone-dry. Coastal WO. **Earth in Motion** ★★★ Chenin, mostly, & sauvignon in tasty **18** ⑧① with lingering summer salad charm. — DS

Location/map: Tulbagh ▪ Map grid reference: F4 ▪ WO: Tulbagh/Coastal/Western Cape ▪ Est 2002 ▪ 1stB 2004 ▪ Tasting & sales Mon-Fri 8.30-5 Sat 10-2 Sun 10-1 ▪ Fee R80pp ▪ Closed Good Fri, Ascension day & Dec 25 ▪ Cellar tours by appt ▪ Olive oil ▪ BYO picnic ▪ Artworks & sculptures on display ▪ Christmas in Winter Tulbagh festival (Jun) ▪ Self-catering guest cottages ▪ Wedding venue ▪ Owner(s) Saronsberg Cellar (Pty) Ltd ▪ Cellarmaster(s)/viticulturist(s) Dewaldt Heyns (2003) ▪ Winemaker(s) Dewaldt Heyns (2003), with Joshua van Blommestein ▪ 550ha/50ha (shiraz) ▪ 500t own label 70% red 30% white ▪ WIETA ▪ PO Box 361 Tulbagh 6820 ▪ info@saronsberg.com ▪ www.saronsberg.com ▪ S 33° 14' 48.2" E 019° 7' 2.0" ▪ 🗺 fishers.assets. cosmos ▪ F +27 (0)23-230-0709 ▪ **T** +27 (0)23-230-0707

Saurwein Wines

Jessica Saurwein dreams of having her own 'small set-up' one day, but meanwhile enjoys working alongside other winemakers at a host cellar in Stellenbosch. She's already expanding, though. In 2018 she made a second pinot, from Hemel-en-Aarde, and a riesling from Elgin. The winemaking is 'as hands-off as possible', but Jessica is getting increasingly more involved — and hands-on — in the vineyards she draws grapes from.

★★★★ **Nom Pinot Noir** Short for nombulelo, 'gratitude' in Xhosa. **17** ⑧⑨ more structured, even tad austere after charming, light-footed **16** ⑧⑧, but depth & intensity augur well for 3+ years cellaring. Elandskloof grapes, spontaneous ferment, 25% new oak (previous only older wood).— DS

Location: Stellenbosch ▪ WO: Elandskloof ▪ 1stB 2015 ▪ Tasting by appt ▪ Sales online only ▪ Owner(s)/winemaker(s) Jessica Saurwein ▪ 2.3t/330cs own label 100% red ▪ IPW ▪ c/o Cape Crush, Winery Rd Stellenbosch 7599 ▪ saurweinwines@gmail.com ▪ www.saurwein.co.za ▪ **T +27 (0)76-228-3116**

Sauvignon Wines

This satellite listing of the excellent and dynamic Diemersdal Estate this edition changes its name from 'Granger Bay' to accommodate a sibling brand, Leaf Plucker, which is for export.

Granger Bay range
Cabernet Sauvignon-Merlot ★★★ Plums, blackberries & sweet oak spice (all old) among **17** ⑧②'s enticements, smooth, friendly & eminently sippable solo or with, say, pasta. WO W Cape, as both ranges.
Sauvignon Blanc ★★★★ Fragrant **18** ⑧⑤, classic grass, green herbs, plus interesting white peach extra; amiable & vivacious, a saline seam ups the food compatibility.

Leaf Plucker range ⑭ⓔⓦ
Sauvignon Blanc ★★★★ Tropical toned, understated **18** ⑧③ brushed with older oak, giving depth & interest. — WB

Savage Wines

'Savage is finally starting to take shape.' Duncan Savage, winemaker/viticulturist of this exceptional small-scale, family-run venture, is referring to the range of wines on which he can concentrate now his Cape Town city cellar is fully operational. Regionality, the focus of his attention, sees two wines join the line-up: from Piekenierskloof, Thief In The Night, as someone once referred to Duncan; he didn't agree, but thought it a cracking name for a wine! The even quirkier Never Been Asked To Dance (would it be asked for by name in a restaurant?) memorialises an old clairette blanche vineyard, uprooted and never bottled. The wine under this moniker is actually chenin, mostly from an even older block in Paarl, and certainly no Cinderella.

★★★★☆ **Follow The Line** ⓐ New path for **17** ⑨④ sees cinsaut with just 7% syrah, both ex Darling. Fabulously scented, silky; a squeeze of supple substance offsetting overall lightfooted feel. Freshness, vibrancy extend spiced dark/red fruit medley. Delicious, moreish.
★★★★☆ **The Girl Next Door** ⓐ From syrah, delicious **17** ⑨④ with fynbos & pepper spice; richly fleshed & fuller bodied than previous but captures precision of cool Cape Peninsula source. Freshness, upbeat vitality in conclusion extend current peppery, savoury pleasure, lifespan. No **16**.
★★★★☆ **Are We There Yet?** ⓐ Equal shapely syrah & touriga ex Malgas. **17** ⑨③ has elegance & verve, though no shortage of dark fruit concentration, dry grainy tannins. All in balance to allow for greater harmony, complexity in future. Co-fermented, syrah wholebunch, touriga destemmed.
★★★★☆ **Red** ⓐ Released after **16** ⑨③, **15** ⑨③ held back for extended oak ageing (30 months) to allow for evolution. Still not short of power & structure in its syrah-led mix with touriga, cinsaut & grenache, whose sweetly spiced, elegant fruit will easily bide time needed to harmonise. Open fermenters for reds, 50% whole bunches unless noted. Old oak, various sizes. Unfined.
★★★★☆ **Thief In The Night** ⑭ⓔⓦ ⓐ Grenache, cinsaut, syrah (as formerly in Follow The Line). **17** ⑨③ ex Piekenierskloof showcases delicious layers of pure, dark, spicy concentration, with a nip of tannin. Elegance & freshness for immediate & future pleasure. 70% bunch ferment; old oak matured. Unfined.
★★★★★ **Never Been Asked To Dance** ⑭ⓔⓦ ⓐ Second white here, scintillating first from chenin in **17** ⑨⑤. In modern style, texture plays important role; 5 days bunch ferment, completed in old larger oak, gives lively grip to complex honeyed fruit. Fine acid seam provides length, assured future. Paarl & some Malgas fruit.

★★★★★ **White** ⊛ Same sauvignon, semillon, chenin mix, fermented, aged in older oak. **17** ⑨⑤ flavoursome white peach, apple blossom layered on well-textured waxy base. Enlivening natural acid adds length to delicious savoury tail. Whole greater than sum of its parts.— AL

Location: Cape Town • Map: Cape Peninsula • Map grid reference: C2 • WO: Western Cape/Darling/Malgas/ Piekenierskloof/Cape Peninsula • Est 2006 • 1stB 2011 • Tasting by appt only • Owner(s) Duncan Savage • Winemaker(s) Duncan Savage (Jan 2006), with Kiara Scott (Jan 2018) • 6ot/6,000cs own label 75% red 25% white • 6 Spencer Rd Salt River Cape Town 7925 • info@savagewines.com • www.savagewines.com • S 33° 55' 45.10" E 018° 27' 54.30" • ☒ evaporation.beacons.morals • **T +27 (0)21-785-4019**

Saxenburg Wine Farm ⓘ ⑪ ⌂ ◎

The tradition of making classically styled wines continues at the substantial Bührer-family-owned and -run estate in Stellenbosch's Polkadraai Hills. Edwin Grace, now in his third year at the winemaking helm, and further inspired by a recent visit to the Rhône, shares long-serving predecessor Nico van der Merwe's focus on maintaining the highest standards. He's ably partnered by viticulturist Donovan Diedericks, who has another 10 ha destined for planting this year as part of the farm's 5-year vine renewal plan. The hospitality side of the business is modern and on-trend, catering for every taste, with function venues and attractions ranging from dining to safari tastings.

Saxenburg Limited Release

★★★★☆ **Shiraz Select** ② Stunning depth & complexity of **09** ⑨② excites. Beautifully judged weight & structure underscore rich, complex fruit in a dry, concentrated package. Complete & integrated now, with great ageing potential. Just a shade off magnificent **07** ★★★★★. No **08**.

Private Collection

★★★★ **Cabernet Sauvignon** ⊛ Less new oak (30%, year, as for Merlot) for **15** ★★★★★ ⑨② than **13** ⑧⑨, aiding lovely cassis fruit purity, freshness & lithe tannin support. Already balanced, but deserves 3-5 years ageing, with further rewards in time. Seamless, elegant step up. No **14**.

★★★★ **Merlot** Alluring chocolate & dark berry fruit, quite mouthfilling, rich & warm-hearted (14.5% alcohol), well restrained by clean dry tannins. **13** ⑧⑥ riper & more voluptuous than previous.

★★★★☆ **Shiraz** Ripe & spicy berries from 2 weeks skin contact (no sulphur), mostly older oak (some American, absent in Merlot & Cab) well integrated. **16** ★★★★ ⑧⑧ succulently balanced, more modern-style than **15** ⑨③, vintage warmth contained, though, despite 14.5% alcohol.

★★★★☆ **Chardonnay** Rich toast & lime flavours on **17** ★★★★ ⑧⑧, all-oak ferment/ageing adds a creamy nuance (new barrels upped to 15%, previously 10%). Elegant & approachable, with potential to age, but shade off fresher, brighter **15** ⑨⓪. **16** untasted.

★★★★ **Sauvignon Blanc** Stellenbosch's signature fresh, grassy & passionfruit flavours again evident on **18** ⑧⑦ preview. Crunchy & crisp, plumped by a selection of yeasts & 3 months lees contact.

★★★★ **Méthode Cap Classique** Brut sparkling from chardonnay, **NV** ⑧⑨. Base wine 6 months in old oak & longer lees ageing (48 months) impart smoky, nutty nuance & creamy, broad feel. Less vibrant than last, still very appealing.

Not tasted: **Pinotage**.

Guinea Fowl range

Red ⊘ ⑦ ★★★★ Smoky red fruit & cedar on old-oak-matured **16** ⑧④ Bordeaux blend, takes juicy step up with lithe tannins & lovely freshness. Perfect table mate over next few years. **White** ⑦ ★★★ Pre-bottling, **18** ⑧② lightly oaked chenin tastes is apple pie in a glass - with the cream! Delicious, succulent yet fresh. — MW

Location: Kuils River • Map/WO: Stellenbosch • Map grid reference: A5 • Est 1693 • 1stB 1990 • Tasting & sales Mon-Fri 10-6 Sat/Sun 10-5 • Wine tasting fee R45/R75 • Chocolate & wine pairing R75/3 wines • Safari tasting R250pp (incl all wines, glass of MCC, cheese platter with biltong & nuts) - to book in advance, minimum 5 guests • Closed Good Fri, Dec 25 & Jan 1 • Cheese platters • Cattle Baron Grill Room restaurant T +27 (0)21-906-5232, www.cattlebaron.co.za • Gifts • Conservation area • Game park • Guest cottages • Owner(s) Adrian & Birgit Bührer • Cellarmaster(s) Edwin Grace (Jan 2005) • Viticulturist(s) Donovan Diedericks (Apr

2008) ▪ 195ha/85ha (cabs s/f, malbec, merlot, ptage, shiraz, chard, chenin, sauv) ▪ 650t/100,000cs own label
78% red 20% white 2% rosé ▪ PO Box 171 Kuils River 7580 ▪ info@saxenburg.co.za ▪ www.saxenburg.co.za ▪
S 33° 56′ 47.9″ E 018° 43′ 9.4″ ▪ visits.lively.waistband ▪ **T +27 (0)21-903-6113**

☐ **Say Lovey** *see* M'hudi Wines

Scali ⓠ ⓐ

Husband-and-wife team Willie and Tania de Waal rate 2018 as one of the most promising and healthiest
vintages of their two-decade custodianship of historic Schoone Oord estate in Voor Paardeberg, despite
the drought. Good news for fans of their Scali brand, and the prestigious producers who source from their
certified-organic vineyards. Equally positive is the recent refurbishment of the cellar and visitor facilities, as
they turn their focus to wine tourism.

Scali range

★★★★ Blanc ⓠ ⓢ Artisanal **15** ⑧⑦ from undisclosed variety/ies. Stonefruit & lemon bouquet has
slight ginger beer note; waxy texture, pleasing richness lifted by persistent acidity. Worth seeking out.
Pinotage ⓠ **★★★★** Subtle raspberry & mulberry notes, chalky tannin allure on light-bodied **15** ⑧④.
Elegant, with prominent acidity, enduring cherry finish. For current drinking. **Syrah** ⓠ **★★★★** Very
youthful **15** ⑧④ intense black fruit, black pepper & tar. Stylistically on the riper side; fruit density enlivened
by slight stemminess, fine powdery tannin. **Ancestor** ⓠ ⓢ **★★★★** Personality-packed méthode
ancestrale sparkling usually from chenin. **14** ⑧③ tad rustic but delicious. Bruised apple & honeysuckle notes,
frothy mousse & savoury conclusion.

Sirkel range

Pinotage ⓠ ⓢ **★★★☆** Turbid, cherry-toned **16** ⑦⑧ has variety's whiff of banana, is rather grippy. Not
tasted: **Syrah**, **Chenin Blanc**. — CvZ

Location/map: Paarl ▪ Map grid reference: C1 ▪ Est/1stB 1999 ▪ Tasting, sales & cellar tours Mon-Sat by
appt ▪ Closed all pub hols ▪ Self-catering cottages ▪ Owner(s) Willie & Tania de Waal ▪ Cellarmaster(s)/
winemaker(s) Willie & Tania de Waal (Aug 1999) ▪ Viticulturist(s) Willie de Waal (Feb 1991) ▪ 270ha/70ha
(cab, merlot, ptage, shiraz, chard, chenin, rouss, sauv, viog) ▪ 45t/6,000cs own label 67% red 33% white ▪
CERES (vyds, wines certified organic) ▪ PO Box 7143 Paarl 7620 ▪ info@scali.co.za ▪ www.scali.co.za ▪ S 33°
36′ 70.6″ E 018° 51′ 49.5″ ▪ safaris.visibly.equated ▪ F +27 (0)86-617-5040 ▪ **T +27 (0)82-854-9005/+27
(0)82-563-8304**

☐ **Schaap** *see* Skaap Wines
☐ **Schalk Burger & Sons** *see* Welbedacht Wine Estate

Schalkenbosch Wines ⓠ ⓐ ⓞ

This substantial estate in Tulbagh has a vastly greater area conserved for wildlife and indigenous vegetation
than dedicated to vineyards – whose fruit is vinified by consultant Suzanne Hartmann. There are extensive
walking, hiking and biking trails, as well as luxury cottages and function venues no doubt enjoying the
home-produced wine.

Schalkenbosch range

Grenache Noir ⓠ **★★★★** Light but ripe fruit mingles with savoury, oak-supported notes on **15** ⑧④.
Juicy berry flavours, & sour-sweet element on finish warmed by 15% alcohol. **Malbec** ⓠ **★★★** Quietly
luscious sweet berry fruit on **15** ⑧① but insufficiently fleshy to give real match to dry, extracted tannins.
Cumulus ⓠ **★★★★** Quintet of Bordeaux black grapes in ripe & burly **15** ⑧④. Solid, sweet fruit copes
well with muscular structure. Finishes with sweetish, warming glow from 15.1% alcohol. **Stratus** ⓠ
★★★★ Bold shiraz-led blend with grenache, mourvèdre & a little viognier. **12** ⑧④ sweet-fruited succulence
accompanying rather austere structure to substantial finish. Not tasted: **Pinotage**.

Edenhof range

Cabernet Sauvignon ⓠ **★★★** Very ripe, straightforward berry aromas lead to fairly flavourful palate
with extracted, rather tough tannins & a little sweetness on **15** ⑦⑧. **Shiraz** ⓠ **★★★★** A successful variety
here. **15** ⑧④ with spicy, darker aromas & bright flavour. Balanced, solid & well built, with well-judged
oaking. **Cabernet Sauvignon-Merlot** ⓠ **★★ 13** ⑦④ simple 56/44 blend with light & fleeting plum &

red berry features, brisk tail. **Nighthawk 409** ⓒ ★★★★ Mourvèdre leads satisfying **13** ⑧⑤ partnered by shiraz, viognier & grenache; smooth, dense but unheavy with well-paced spice, dark berry, meaty features & savoury length. **Rosé** ⓒ ★★★ Pleasant, zippy & fruity-savoury character on friendly dry **17** ⑦⑧ from mostly shiraz. **Chenin Blanc** ⓒ ★★★ Thatchy, melon notes on **17** ⑦⑧ with juicy, succulent, balanced appeal. **Sauvignon Blanc** ⓒ ★★ Light, grassy **17** ⑦④ has a little sweet fruit & a nice fresh grip. Not tasted: **Pinotage, Chardonnay, Viognier.** — TJ

Location/map/WO: Tulbagh ▪ Map grid reference: G5 ▪ Est 1792 ▪ 1stB 2002 ▪ Tasting, sales & tours by appt ▪ Closed all pub hols ▪ Tour groups ▪ Weddings/functions ▪ Walking/hiking & MTB trails ▪ Conservation area ▪ Self-catering cottages ▪ Owner(s) Platinum Mile Investments ▪ Winemaker(s) Suzanne Hartmann (consultant) ▪ Viticulturist(s) Johan Wiese & Andrew Teubes ▪ 1,800ha/37ha (cab, shiraz) ▪ 140t/20,000cs own label 80% red 18% white 2% rosé ▪ WWF-SA Conservation Champion ▪ PO Box 95 Tulbagh 6820 ▪ info@ schalkenbosch.co.za ▪ www.schalkenbosch.co.za ▪ S 33° 18′ 49.7″ E 019° 11′ 59.9″ ▪ 🌐 unlocks.kiosk.ornately ▪ F +27 (0)86-519-2605/+27 (0)86-654-8209 ▪ **T +27 (0)23-230-0654/1488**

Schenkfontein Kelders ⓒ

Sibling to separately listed Winkelshoek, 153-ha Schenkfontein farm north of Piketberg is named for an early 1900s Dutch schoolmaster who used the shade of an old pomegranate tree as his classroom in the sweltering Swartland summers. With only 23 ha of vines, winemaker/viticulturist Hendrik Hanekom sources some fruit from farmers in the area for his easygoing wines, now offered for tasting/sale on-site by appointment.

Merlot ★★ Plum & high-toned icing sugar tones; racy acidity on **17** ⑦④ early-drinker. Coastal WO, like Shiraz. **Pinotage** ⊘ ★★★ Standout in range, **17** ⑧⓪ appealing mulberry aromas & flavours, enough grip for food, good dry finish. Would rate higher but for prominent acid. WO W Cape. **Shiraz** ★★★ Faint fynbos & black pepper lift, ripe-fruit body, pleasing grape tannin squeeze. **17** ⑦⑨ shows house's bracing acidity. **Rosé** ⓒ ★★★ Perfumed, nutty **16** ⑧① from grenache is dry, with warmth from 13.9% alcohol needing to be served well chilled. **Chardonnay** ⓒ ★★★ Attractive **17** ⑦⑧, easy lemon & spice tones for uncomplicated enjoyment. **Chenin Blanc** ★★ Muted flavours but pleasing vinosity on zesty, just-dry **18** ⑦⑥. In abeyance: **Cabernet Sauvignon, Colombar, Sauvignon Blanc.** — CvZ

Location: Piketberg ▪ Map: Olifants River ▪ Map grid reference: C7 ▪ WO: Swartland/Coastal/Western Cape ▪ Est 2000 ▪ 1stB 2014 ▪ Tasting by appt ▪ Owner(s) Hennie Hanekom ▪ Cellarmaster(s)/winemaker(s)/viticulturist(s) Hendrik Hanekom (Nov 2010) ▪ 500ha/60ha (muscadel r/w, ptage, shiraz, chenin, cbard, grenache b, hanepoot) ▪ 800t/150,000L own label 30% red 70% white ▪ PO Box 2 Eendekuil 7335 ▪ hendrik@ winkelshoek.co.za ▪ www.winkelshoek.co.za ▪ S 32° 42′ 18.85″ E 018° 47′ 43.09″ ▪ F +27 (0)22-942-1488 ▪ **T +27 (0)22-942-1484**

Schultz Family Wines ⓒ

Thelema winemaker Rudi Schultz's personal project, a reflection of his relationship with cellarmaster Gyles Webb that he was able to branch out early on. Using Stellenbosch grapes made in the styles and varieties of particular interest to him, it was a red range until joined now by a chenin from 30-year-old vines. Worth buying for the label alone, it was named by surfing nut Rudi after the Jeffreys Bay road with closest access to the beach. The label text is pure surfing poetry. Rudi's used to awards, but a particular source of pride is that his cabernet was served at the Commonwealth Heads of Government Meeting banquet in London in 2018.

★★★★☆ **Cabernet Sauvignon** ⓐ Usual winemaking care, hand sort, wild ferment, 18 months oaking, 30% new, **15** ⑨④ follows string of exemplary vintages. Glossy fruit, supple tannins yet latent power for ageing; finishes long. Whole effect polished, assured. Bottelary vines, as usual, like next.

★★★★ **Syrah** Remarkable fruit concentration, maraschino cherry richness, notes of violets, Provençal herbs. **16** ★★★★★ ⑨① has a tannin backbone for ageing, but masterly handled, savoury toned, food-friendly dry, no barrier to enjoyment. More layered than **15** ⑧⑦.

★★★★ **Pepper Street Chenin Blanc** 🆕 30 year old vines, whole bunch, barrel fermented/aged, for smoky, almond savouriness to partner the quince & thatch. **17** ⑧⑨ sophisticated version of chenin.

Occasional release: **Reserve Syrah.** — CR

Location/WO: Stellenbosch ▪ Est 2002 ▪ Tasting by appt ▪ Closed all pub hols ▪ Owner(s) Rudi Schultz ▪ Cellarmaster(s)/winemaker(s) Rudi Schultz (Jan 2002) ▪ Viticulturist(s) Dirkie Morkel ▪ 12t/1,000cs own

454 · SCIONS OF SINAI

label 100% red ▪ 8 Fraser Rd Somerset West 7130 ▪ rudi@thelema.co.za ▪ F +27 (0)21-885-1800 ▪ **T +27 (0)82-928-1841**

Scions of Sinai

The 'scions' in the brand name are 7th-generation winemaker Bernhard Bredell and some precious old dryland bushvines, formerly part of his family's holdings in the Helderberg, centred around a hill colloquially known as Sinai. Now based on Klein Helderberg farm in a renovated cellar used by an earlier Bredell generation, Bernhard also works with vines in Voor Paardeberg and Langeberg-Garcia (see JP Bredell Wines listing).

Location: Stellenbosch ▪ Est 2016 ▪ 1stB 2017 ▪ Closed to public ▪ Owner(s) Bernhard Bredell ▪ Winemaker(s)/viticulturist(s) Bernhard Bredell (Jun 2016) ▪ 7t/850cs own label 70% red 15% white 15% orange ▪ info@scionsofsinai.com ▪ www.scionsofsinai.com ▪ **T +27 (0)82-772-8657**

Scrucap Wines

Consultant Kent Scheermeyer and a quartet of elite SA producers are behind this refreshingly modern selection of wines, designed to dovetail with the philosophy of LUX* Resorts & Hotels in the Indian Ocean, China and the Middle East to offer a lighter, brighter alternative to traditional five-star holidays.

★★★★ **Cabernet Sauvignon** Was 'Reserve'. Nuanced with tobacco & leather, **15** ⑧⑧ pleasingly dry, well-judged 30% new oak, 16 months, meshes nicely with the plush fruit. By Radford Dale, as Chenin.

★★★★ **Chardonnay** ⊘ Fragrant cool-climate **16** ⑧⑦, expressive baked apple & pear flavours, creamy vanilla oak on elegant, layered palate that refuses to budge. By Paul Cluver, as next 2.

★★★★ **Gewürztraminer** ⑲ⓔ ⊘ Oh-so-lovely **17** ⑧⑥, litchi, pineapple & pot-pourri perfumes are pure hedonism yet the palate is swept dry & made moreish by freshening grapefruit acidity. 375 ml.

★★★★ **Sauvignon Blanc** ⊘ Two vintages tasted, each with forthcoming gooseberry/granadilla aromas, more restrained kiwi fruit/lime palate. Both with satisfying mineral finish, **17** ⑧⑦ fuller while **18** ⑧⑧ lighter (13.3% alcohol) & racier.

★★★★ Also in 375 ml.

★★★★ **Popcap Méthode Cap Classique Rosé** Attractive salmon pink sparkler with pinot noir's vivacious strawberries & crunchy red apples. Now **NV** ⑧⑨, year on lees, shade off last edition's vintage-dated bottling but still delectable. By Steenberg, as next.

★★★★ **Popcap Méthode Cap Classique Brut** Bright & engaging celebratory bubbles, ample style & vibrancy, rather delicious segue from apple pie aromas to fresh apple flavours. **NV** ⑧⑨ from Robertson chardonnay, year on lees, 15% barrel fermented.

Pinot Noir ⊘ ⑦ ★★★★ Smooth & plush, becoming more expressive on finish, Paul Cluver's delightful **16** ⑧④ has earth & black tealeaf on platter of strawberries & raspberries. Second bottling, in 375 ml, tasted.

Shiraz ⑲ ★★★★ White pepper & savoury spice lead-in to elegant **15** ⑧④, light styled but flavourful, perfect for anytime sipping. By Lammershoek, as next. **Rosé** ★★★ Delicious take on Provence dry rosé: mostly syrah tweaked in old oak to make it savoury, food friendly. **18** ⑧① herby & sweet spicy nuance to vibrant cherries. **Chenin Blanc** ★★★★ Unoaked **17** ⑧⑤, peach & pear aromas, creamy texture from extended lees ageing, fresh acidity, dry pithy grapefruit finish. — Various tasters

WO: Various ▪ Est 2011 ▪ Closed to public ▪ Cellarmaster(s) Andries Burger (Paul Cluver), JD Pretorius (Steenberg), Edouard Labeye (Radford Dale), Schalk Opperman (Lammershoek) ▪ 20,000cs own label 40% red 40% white 10% rosé 10% MCC ▪ ksconsult@icloud.com ▪ www.luxresorts.com ▪ **T +27 (0)83-484-8781**

Seal Breeze Wines   ⑫ ⑪ ⑧ ⑤

Joan Wiggins bought back the family's West Coast winegrape farm over a decade ago and immersed herself in boutique winecrafting. The self-taught vintner believes her wines, whites included, have excellent longevity, noting that visitors who taste a range of vintages invariably buy the oldest one.

Location: Lutzville ▪ Map: Olifants River ▪ Map grid reference: A3 ▪ Est 2004 ▪ 1stB 2005 ▪ Tasting, sales & cellar tours Mon-Fri 9-4 Sat 9-12 ▪ Closed Easter Fri-Mon, Ascension day, Dec 25 & Jan 1 ▪ Meals/refreshments by prior arrangement ▪ Facilities for children ▪ Tour groups ▪ Owner(s)/viticulturist(s) Joan Wiggins ▪

Cellarmaster(s) Joan Wiggins (Feb 2004) ▪ Winemaker(s) Joan Wiggins (Feb 2004), with Tenday Chimhanda (2013) ▪ ±92ha/±70ha (cab, merlot, shiraz, chenin, cbard, hanepoot, sauv) ▪ 1,200t total ▪ 12t/15 barrels own label ▪ PO Box 316 Dagbreek Lutzville 8165 ▪ joan@sealbreeze.co.za ▪ www.sealbreezewine.co.za ▪ S 31° 34′ 50.1″ E 018° 19′ 9.8″ ▪ 🎥 themed.garnish.inspired ▪ F +27 (0)27-217-1458 ▪ **T +27 (0)84-505-1991**

☐ **Secateurs** see AA Badenhorst Family Wines
☐ **Secret Cellar** see Ultra Liquors

Sedgwick's Old Brown

Venerable Distell fortified brand, warming winters since 1916; today in bottle sizes from 200ml to 2L.

The Original Old Brown ⊘ ★★★ Jerepiko & dry 'sherry' blend, unchanging style (no need, lots of fans). **NV** ⑧① rich sherried aroma, raisins & molasses, not over-sweet - there's a delicious tanginess. — CR

☐ **Selection Vivante** see The House of JC le Roux
☐ **Selena** see Marianne Wine Estate
☐ **Selma** see Nordic Wines
☐ **Semara** see Wine-of-the-Month Club
☐ **Sentinel** see Wine-of-the-Month Club
☐ **Series Privée Unfiltered** see Fleur du Cap
☐ **SeriesRARE** see Artisanal Boutique Winery
☐ **Seriously Cool** see Waterkloof

Ses'Fikile

The brand name means 'we have arrived, in style', which is what former teacher and entrepreneurial vintner Nondumiso Pikashe does with her return to the guide, with a freshened and on-trend line-up made by Madré van der Walt, assistant winemaker at Leeuwenkuil. The white blend and a cabernet (untasted by us) feature in a prestigious new listing, under the name Sun Star Ses'Fikile, for selected Sun International hotels.

Cabernet Sauvignon-Merlot ★★★ Also has 20% cab franc, equal cab & merlot, so the cabs have it: **15** ⑦⑨ blackcurrant & smoky spice, firm grip at the end. **Shiraz-Cinsault** (NEW) ★★ Near-equal blend, **16** ⑦⑥ has earthy, leathery styling, the fruit more evident on palate than nose. Smooth, light, easy drinking. **Chenin Blanc-Roussanne** (NEW) ★★★ Partnership 83/17, so chenin dictates the style in light-textured **17** ⑦⑦, fresh apple & pear, crisply dry. — CR, CvZ

Location: Cape Town ▪ WO: Western Cape ▪ Est 2008 ▪ Tasting by arrangement in Gugulethu ▪ Owner(s) Ses'Fikile Wine Services ▪ Winemaker(s) Madré van der Walt ▪ 50,000c own label 70% red 30% white ▪ Ny 99 no 107 Gugulethu Cape Town 7750 ▪ sesfikile@gmail.com ▪ www.sesfikile.co.za ▪ **T +27 (0)83-431-0254**

☐ **7even** see Zevenwacht
☐ **7 Icon Wines** see Bayede!

Seven Sisters Vineyards   Ⓨ ⑪ ⓐ

The eponymous Brutus sisters (and brother John who recently made it on to a label too!) grew up in the West Coast village of Paternoster - with sister Vivian (Kleynhans) having led the formation of their African Roots company more than a decade back. Now they have a wine-base further south, on their farm in Stellenbosch.

Brutus Family Reserve range

Shiraz Ⓨ ★★★★ **15** ⑧④ starts with aromatic notes of smoked meat, spice & plums. Lightly oaked, with smooth tannic structure supporting the pleasantly juicy sweet fruit. **John Brutus** Ⓨ ★★★★ Tobacco notes with ripe fruit on aromas of **14** ⑧④ from petit verdot, cab, cab franc & merlot. Flavoursome, generous & rounded, with smooth but shaping tannins. Approachable young, to give substantial but easy satisfaction. **Chardonnay** Ⓨ ★★★★ **16** ⑧④ shows notes of toasty oak on aromas & flavours, but there's good ripe citrus & stonefruit in support & it's fairly well balanced. More intense & structured than standard version.

Seven Sisters range

Cabernet Sauvignon ⓥ ★★★ Easygoing **16** ⑦⑨ omits 'Carol' from name but does add a wooded component, giving typical dark berry notes. Soft texture, sweetish finish, but a little grip. **Shiraz** ⓥ ★★ Ripe fruity aromas on sampled **16** ⑦④ quaffer; gently smooth tannins don't disrupt the easiness. **Chardonnay** ⓥ ★★★ Ripe **16** ⑦⑧ from widely sourced grapes has an interesting liquorice note. Pleasing soft silkiness; acid a bit apart, leaving a slightly limy-sour finish. **Moscato** ⓥ ★★ Omits 'Yolanda' from name in sweet **16** ⑦① with light but balanced charm, the flavours as fleeting as the perlé bubbles. **Sauvignon Blanc** ⓥ ★★★ Light- & sweet-fruited **17** ⑦⑧ from Swartland grapes pleases from forward tropical aromas to passionfruit finish. Was 'Vivian'. — TJ

Location/map: Stellenbosch ▪ Map grid reference: C7 ▪ WO: Stellenbosch/Western Cape ▪ Call gate for entry +27 (0)60-696-9814 ▪ Wine tasting 9-4 daily ▪ The Village Table restaurant serving traditional South African cuisine open daily for breakfast, lunch & dinner ▪ Weddings/conferences/special functions ▪ Owner(s) African Roots Wine ▪ Winemaker(s) Vivian Kleynhans ▪ PO Box 4560 Tygervalley 7536 ▪ vivian@africanrootswines.com ▪ www.sevensisters.co.za ▪ S 33° 59′ 23.41″ E 018° 46′ 34.35″ ▪ 🌐 adornment.modern. escalating ▪ F +27 (0)86-514-5569 ▪ **T +27 (0)71-049-4109/+27 (0)79-162-8973**

Seven Springs Vineyards　　　　　　　　　　　　　　ⓥ

The plans British owners Tim and Vaughan Pearson outlined last year have been realised: harvest 2018 saw the first crush in their own cellar, a renovated building on a neighbour's property; Renico Botes joined as senior cellar assistant; and the new tasting venue - where the range, now boasting a rosé, may be sampled - was set to open at press time. After nine years helping the Pearsons establish this property in the Shaw's Mountain foothills between Caledon and Hermanus, winemaker Riana van der Merwe is moving on to explore new ventures.

Seven Springs range

★★★★ **Pinot Noir** ⓥ Older oak gives free rein to delicious redcurrant, cherry & spice whiffs in **14** ⑧⑦. Refreshing acidity, soft tannins & meaty undertones to enjoy now & over 3-5 years. Also in magnum.

★★★★ **Syrah** ⓥ Generous plum pudding fruit & savoury complexity (biltong, white pepper, forest floor), irresistible feathery tannins. **14** ⑧⑦ elegantly crafted, for satisfying sipping, like **13** ★★★★ ⑧⑤.

★★★★ **Chardonnay** Sweet lemon & orange fragrance with gentle oak spicing attractions on **16** ★★★★ ⑧⑤. A little creaminess from lees ageing adds weight but ends on sweet-&-sour note. Old oak, as was fresh & engaging **15** ⑧⑧.

★★★★ **Sauvignon Blanc** ⊘ ⓐ Glorious expression of cool-climate sauvignon, always released once youthful edginess has calmed but mineral thread, fruit clarity remain at their freshest best. **16** ★★★★★ ⑨④ has blackcurrant, tropical intensity, with a ripe farewell flourish. Even more attractive than **15** ⑧⑦.

Syrah Rosé (NEW) ★★★ Attractive peachy pink **18** ⑧① from variety much suited to this style: spicy fruit charm, dry, with gentle freshness for enjoyable summer sipping. **Unoaked Chardonnay** ★★★☆ **15** ⑧⑤ beneficiary of 2 years bottle maturation prior to release; evolving, with nutty, toasty lees attractions while remaining fresh & zestily dry.

Art Series

★★★★ **Syrah** ⓥ Tasted out of vintage sequence, **12** ⑧⑨ opens in glass to Xmas spice & tapenade, chewy tannins yet backed by juicy fruit, promising a good future. Limited release in magnum, only ex farm.

Occasional release: **Pinot Noir**. — AL

Location: Hermanus ▪ Map: Walker Bay & Bot River ▪ Map grid reference: C5 ▪ WO: Overberg ▪ Est 2007 ▪ 1stB 2010 ▪ Tasting & sales Mon-Fri 11-4 ▪ Owner(s) Tim & Vaughan Pearson ▪ Winemaker(s) Riana van der Merwe (Nov 2009), with Renico Botes (Nov 2017, snr cellar assistant) ▪ Vineyard manager(s) Peter Davison (Jul 2007) ▪ 12ha/±8ha (pinot, shiraz, chard, sauv) ▪ ±67t/10,000cs own label 55% red 40% white 5% rosé ▪ Other export brand: Over the Mountain ▪ Private Bag X15 Suite 162 Hermanus 7200 ▪ tim@7springs.co.za ▪ www.7springs.co.za ▪ S 34° 19′ 36.76″ E 019° 22′ 38.65″ ▪ 🌐 purchased.taillights.vowing ▪ F +27 (0)86-571-0623 ▪ **T +27 (0)28-316-4994 (office)/+27 (0)82-487-7572 (winemaker)**

☐ **1791** see Nederburg Wines

Shannon Vineyards ⓥ ⓖ

Grapes from the vineyards on the lovely Elgin farm of James and Stuart Downes go into the bottles of a handful of leading producers, but more and more of them are going into their own wines – the brand name deriving from the family's Irish ancestry. These are vinified in Hemel-en-Aarde by Gordon and Nadia Newton Johnson, giving the finesse that might be expected to result from James' meticulous viticulture (supported by eminent consultant Kevin Watt) and the Newton Johnson magic in the cellar. In fact, so successful has the Shannon label been that 'behind the scenes' they've been working on three new wines for the impressive portfolio. These were released in 2018, including the RocknRolla from the farm's oldest vineyard.

★★★★★ **Mount Bullet Merlot** ⓐ A Cape benchmark. **15** ★★★★★ ⑨④ violet perfume leads suave red/mulberry fruit to complex, persistent savoury conclusion. Stellar, with substance for decade-plus cellaring, like elegant **14** ⑨⑤. Natural ferment (as all), 22 months in barrel, 20% new. Magnums available.

★★★★★ **The Shannon Black** ⓃⒺⓌ ⓐ Aka 'Black Bullet', a serious, premium-priced barrel selection of a single Italian clone of merlot, in striking black livery with nary a name on the front label. **13** ⑨⑤ massive, meaty, brooding, but with balance & leavening savoury finish. 22 months in oak, half new.

★★★★☆ **RocknRolla** ⓃⒺⓌ ⓥ ⓐ Winemaker insisted on keeping separate a parcel from specific vines in the original (2000) pinot block. 'Let's rock'n'roll!' he said of breathtaking **16** ⑨③. Deeper, darker, more introverted than sibling, a sensual thrill to experience. Just 2 barrels.

★★★★☆ **Rockview Ridge Pinot Noir** ⓥ Iron fist in a velvet glove; **17** ⑨② black cherry & farmyard aromas followed by a mouthful of dense fruit, assertive tannins & tight acidity, powerful yet balanced, with lower alcohol (13.4%) than **16** ⑨③. 30% new barriques, year.

★★★★☆ **Sanctuary Peak Sauvignon Blanc** ⓥ Elegant & composed, sauvignon not reliant on acidity for presence or persistence. 10% new-oak-fermented semillon adds lanolin & vanilla nuances to **17** ⑨①'s white peach & citrus, gives weight & texture to its focused minerality. Even better with few years age.

★★★★★ **Triangle Block Semillon** ⓐ Adds vineyard name with perfectly poised **17** ★★★★★ ⑨③. Lambswool & hay on scintillating array of aromas & flavours, focused by rapier-like acidity. As with **16** ⑨⑤ & previous, ferment in 30% new oak, 9 months at 3℃ to retain freshness of lemon-toned fruit.

★★★★★ **Capall Bán** ⓐ Best semillon (70%) & sauvignon of **15** ⑨⑤, named for the London pub run by great-grandfather. Intense greengage & quince introduce complex, unfurling layers of concentrated spice & textured fruit, echoing finish. 30% new oak, 3 years in bottle for complete integration.

★★★★☆ **Macushla Pinot Noir Noble Late Harvest** 'My Darling' a deliciously idiosyncratic dessert. Ferment in older oak, then extended ageing at 3℃ à la Semillon to prevent malolactic fermentation & retain ample acidity to counter **17** ⑨⓪'s 163 g/l sugar. 375 ml. — DS

Location/map/WO: Elgin ▪ Map grid reference: A2 ▪ Est 2000 ▪ 1stB 2003 ▪ Tasting by appt Mon-Fri 10-3 ▪ Owner(s) Stuart & James Downes ▪ Winemaker(s) Gordon & Nadia Newton Johnson ▪ Viticulturist(s) Kevin Watt (consultant) ▪ 75ha/11.5ha (merlot, pinot, sauv, sem) ▪ 100t/10,000cs own label 66% red 34% white ▪ Global GAP, IPW, Tesco's Natures Choice ▪ PO Box 20 Elgin 7180 ▪ james@shannonwines.com ▪ www. shannonwines.com ▪ S 34° 11' 3.9" E 018° 59' 3.6" ▪ ⓦ beckons.lemon.decibel ▪ F +27 (0)21-859-5389 ▪ **T +27 (0)21-859-2491**

☐ **Sharks** *see* Wildekrans Wine Estate
☐ **Shepherd's Cottage** *see* Overgaauw Wine Estate

Sherwood Berriman Wines

Occasional bottlings of a cabernet blend from Constantia grapes are produced by SA-born, internationally schooled brothers Mark and Greg Sherwood and friend Mike Berriman. The latter two are UK-based, Greg (MW) senior buyer for Handford Wines in London, who markets the wine.

Location: Constantia ▪ Est/1stB 2003 ▪ Closed to public ▪ Owner(s) Mark Sherwood, Mike Berriman & Greg Sherwood MW ▪ Winemaker(s) Mark Sherwood, assisted by David van Niekerk (High Constantia) ▪ 500cs own label 100% red

Ship

Originally 'Ship Sherry', this Distell-owned piece of South African wine patrimony was launched in 1929.

Ship ⓦ ★★ Stalwart jerepiko in distinctive tall, flat bottle, **NV** ⑦④ curvaceous, sweet, very raisiny. — CR

- ☐ **Short Story** see Neethlingshof Estate
- ☐ **Short Street** see Riebeek Cellars
- ☐ **Shortwood** see Imbuko Wines
- ☐ **SHZ Cilliers/Kuün Wyne** see Stellendrift - SHZ Cilliers/Kuün Wyne
- ☐ **Signal Cannon** see Vondeling

Signal Gun Wines

ⓦ ⑪ ⊚

The Signal Gun home-farm is a high-lying Durbanville property with cool growing conditions ideally suited to sauvignon blanc, an area speciality, so no surprise that the variety features in four of the wines, solo and blended. The De Witt family have lived here for five generations, and current owner MJ occasionally fires the eponymous cannon, over 300 years old.

De Wit Family Reserves

★★★★ **Sea Smoke Sauvignon Blanc** ⊘ From misty/foggy single-vineyard, highest in Durbanville (455 m), yet **17** ⑧⑧ is ripe, gutsy, with melon & passionfruit flavours, tangy-fresh. Different style to **16** ⑧⑦ but works: the slender body now has curves.

Gun Smoke Merlot ★★★★ Was 'Merlot' in Signal Gun range. Expressive perfume, cassis, violets, tobacco, **16** ⑧⑤ spent 12 months in barrel, 45% new. Tannins supple, palate smooth, polished, finishes long. **B Loved Méthode Cap Classique** ⓦ ★★★★ Only 300 bottles of fresh, pink-tinged bubbly from chardonnay & pinot noir. Delightful **12** ⑧④ offers crunchy apple & lime frothiness.

Signal Gun range

★★★★ **Shiraz** Expressive fruit profile, hedgerow berries, piquant cherries, **16** ⑧⑧'s oak showing only in the flavours, espresso savouriness, the body succulent, curvaceous. **15** sold out untasted.

★★★★ **Blanc de Blanc** ⓦ Admirable **17** ⑧⑦, sauvignon & chenin; lemon drops & ripe apples, zinging fresh, ending on a saline note. With food or solo watching a sunset.

....

Chenin Blanc ⓝⒺⓦ ⊘ ⑨ ★★★ Crisp green apples, just-sliced pear, **18** ⑧② is crunchy freshness personified, zesty, appetising.

....

Pinotage ★★★ Blueberries & sweet spice, opulent liquorice tones, **16** ⑧② is proudly ripe, luscious, easy to like. **Blanc de Noir** ⓝⒺⓦ ⊘ ★★★ Pale pink, restrained berries, which is better for food, dry **18** ⑦⑨ from merlot has some herbaceous notes, adding to its personality. **Rosé** ⓦ ★★★ Change in **17** ⑧①, now 100% merlot, cherries/red berries, tangy-dry. Lacks the distinction of **15** ★★★★ ⑧⑦ from merlot/sauvignon. **16** untasted. **Sauvignon Blanc** ⊘ ★★★★ Attractive green notes in **18** ⑧④ alongside the gooseberries, palate showing mineral notes. Involving, lots on offer here. **Muy-Scattie** ⓦ ★★★ Charming name for unusual blend sauvignon, muscat d'Alexandrie. Graininess throughout **17** ⑧①, 60% sauvignon's influence in zesty touch to the sweetness. Not tasted: **Chardonnay**.

Tin Hill range

....

Cape Blend ⑨ ★★★ Was 'Red Blend'. Only half of **17** ⑧① oaked, pinotage/merlot duo designed for easy drinking, with character. Red & dark berries, sweet spice, smooth & juicy. — CR

....

Location: Durbanville ▪ Map: Durbanville, Philadelphia & Darling ▪ Map grid reference: C7 ▪ WO: Durbanville/ Western Cape ▪ Est/1stB 2006 ▪ Tasting & sales Tue-Sat 10-5 Sun 11-5 ▪ Fee depends on tasting R50-R70 ▪ Wine & food pairing ▪ Closed Good Fri, Dec 25 & Jan 1 ▪ Ke-Monate Restaurant ▪ Conferences ▪ Game drives ▪ Craft beer brewery ▪ Owner(s) WRM de Wit ▪ Cellarmaster(s)/winemaker(s) Riaan Oosthuizen (2011), MJ de Wit (Jan 2006) ▪ Viticulturist(s) Walter Smith ▪ 210ha/95ha (cab, merlot, ptage, shiraz, chard, sauv) ▪ 19t/3,000cs own label 50% red 50% white ▪ PO Box 364 Durbanville 7551 ▪ wine@signalgun.com ▪ www. signalgun.com ▪ S 33° 49' 13.26" E 018° 36' 40.32" ▪ ▦ seasoned.scholars.hallways ▪ F +27 (0)86-611-8747 ▪ **T +27 (0)21-976-7343**

Signal Hill Wines

French-born vigneron Jean-Vincent Ridon rents Stellenbosch cellar space for his trimmed range, after closing his Cape Town 'city winery' (named after a nearby landmark). The tiny suburban Clos d'Oranje shiraz vineyard remains his public 'hub', where he offers tastings and masterclasses in vine tending. Having obtained his Association de la Sommellerie International diploma, he also manages the new Sommeliers Academy in Cape Town, linking with local and overseas bodies to train wine waiters to world standards.

Signal Hill range

★★★★☆ **Clos d'Oranje** Named for & sourced from tiny shiraz single-vineyard in Cape Town's Oranjezicht on lower Table Mountain slopes. Polished, assured **13** ⑨⓪ scented with brambleberry & cherry, violets, wood char; bone-dry but fruit-padded, silky. Ready after 18 months old oak, 3 years bottle.

Not tasted: **Camps Bay Vineyard**, **Old Vines Semillon**, **Méthode Cap Classique Pinot Noir**, **Crème de Tête Muscat d'Alexandrie NLH**, **Eszencia**, **Straw Wine**, **Vin de l'Empereur Solera**.

Single Barrel range

★★★★ **Malbec** Ⓧ Loaded with personality & juiciness, **14** ⑧⑨ vibrant but not over the top; supple frame supports pristine Durbanville fruit to persistent finish. Only very old oak.

★★★★ **1771 Heritage Vine** Ⓧ One 240 year old city-centre chenin vine bore this intriguing curiosity, full of flavour, sweet impression despite low sugar & alcohol. Very limited **11** ⑧⑦ & untasted **12**, **13** selling.

Not tasted: **Pinot Noir**, **Pineau de Ludovic**. — CR, CvZ

Location: Cape Town ▪ WO: Durbanville/Cape Town ▪ 1stB 1997 ▪ Closed to public; only the city vineyard can be visited by appt ▪ Clos d'Oranje vineyard: tasting & visit by appt in season; masterclass for organic farming ▪ Owner(s) Signal Hill Wines cc ▪ Cellarmaster(s) Jean-Vincent Ridon ▪ 1ha ▪ PO Box 12481 Cape Town 8010 ▪ info@winery.co.za ▪ www.winery.co.za ▪ F +27 (0)21-422-5238 ▪ **T +27 (0)21-422-5206**

☐ **Signatures of Doolhof** see Doolhof Wine Estate

Sijnn

'We feel that our Malgas project has come of age,' says David Trafford (also of De Trafford), reflecting on the maturing vines at this farm near the mouth of the Breede River, and on the fact that it's had a cellar and resident winemaker (Charla Haasbroek) there since the 2015 vintage. His 'growing confidence' is being reinforced with a new-look label – debuting on the Red '15 and White '17. Focus will increasingly be on these two blends, with several vintages available concurrently, to highlight the value of ageing wine – a concept which the new Free Reign reinforces. All these characterful, fine wines, made with minimal intervention, are as unique as their origins: tasting them it is easy to imagine the uncompromising, dry and stony landscape from which they emerge.

★★★★ **Low Profile** A less concentrated, lighter-oaked version of Sijnn Red, but **16** ⑧⑦ no pushover, given a fairly severe structure. Similarly distinctive. Good juicy fruit, vibrant freshness, dry stony finish.

★★★★ **Sijnn Red** Ⓐ Two vintages tasted; both exciting but still youthful, needing bottle age - decant for drinking young. **13** ★★★★☆ ⑨① nearly half shiraz with touriga, mourvèdre, trincadeira. Rich dark spice, chocolate, sweet fruit character - some reminiscence of 'port'. Powerfully elegant, lively acidity, firm tannins. **15** ★★★★☆ ⑨③ (very limited release for now) less mourvèdre, some cab. Fuller fruit giving more balanced harmony with big structure. 20% new oak; 14% alcohol. Various bottle formats, as for White. Uniquely distinctive. **14** yet unreleased.

★★★★☆ **Free Reign** ⑨⑥④ Ⓐ Remarkable '1st edition' of **NV** ⑨③ blend: 2009/10 touriga, 2010/11 shiraz. Some early tertiary development adding complexity, though colour youthful. Serious acid/tannin structure gives austere note to full, sweet fruit; lingering dry finish. Fascinating 'meditation wine'. Also 1.5 & 3L.

★★★★ **Saignée** 'Bled' off fermenting skins - mourvèdre, trincadeira, shiraz in characterful **16** ⑧⑦ - for a lightish red (far from rosé this year). Full & rich flavours: meaty, spicy, earthy, sweet fruit. Balanced & firm.

★★★★☆ **Sijnn White** Ⓐ Individual & rather gorgeous, light gold **17** ⑨④ from 84% chenin with viognier (adding floral, apricot notes) & roussanne. Tending more to savoury than fruity, richly full of flavour, with texture & a lovely natural acidity. Good oak support, 10% new. 13.5% alcohol.

Occasional release: **Syrah**, **Touriga Nacional**. — TJ

Location: Malgas ▪ Map: Southern Cape ▪ Map grid reference: D1 ▪ WO: Malgas/Swellendam ▪ Est 2003 ▪ 1stB 2007 ▪ Tasting, sales & cellar tours at Sijnn Sat 10-3, or by appt ▪ Vintners platters ▪ Wines are also sold at De Trafford ▪ Owner(s) David & Rita Trafford, Simon Farr, Quentin Hurt ▪ Winemaker(s) David Trafford & Charla Haasbroek (Dec 2014) ▪ Viticulturist(s) Schalk du Toit (2002, consultant) ▪ 125ha/22ha (cab, grenache, mourv, shiraz, tempranillo, touriga nacional, trincadeira, chenin, rouss, viog) ▪ 60t/5,400cs own label 52% red 48% white ▪ 1.5ha olives ▪ PO Box 495 Stellenbosch 7599 ▪ info@sijnn.co.za ▪ www.sijnn.co.za ▪ S 34° 19' 0.27" E 020° 36' 41.37" ▪ 🗺 picturesque.consist.tenacious ▪ T +27 (0)21-880-1398

Silkbush Mountain Vineyards 🏠

Guarded by Breedekloof's Sybasberg (Silkbush Mountain), amidst wild fynbos, the high-elevation vines here supply quality grapes to some of SA's majors as well as Silkbush's own labels, vinified by Chris du Toit of nearby Bergsig. Overseeing California-owned Silkbush is Anton Roos, who developed most of the 80-plus hectares and also looks after the on-site accommodation, Kingsbury Cottage.

....

Shiraz 🍷 ★★★★ Herbal aromas & ripe red fruit to the fore on **16** (84). Elegant, with nice tannin grip.

....

Pinotage ★★★★ High-toned **17** (84), with generous mulberry & plum fruit, plush texture, good body & finish. **Altitude** 🍷 ★★★★ Piquant Cape Blend from farm's highest blocks, 20% pinotage & 4 others. **14** (88) hints of fynbos & blueberry in attractively lean structure with older oak well knit. **Rosé** 🍷 ★★★ Summer celebrator **17** (81) from shiraz is drier than previous, packed with strawberry flavour, bright acidity; savoury note pairs well with food. **Sauvignon Blanc** ★★★ Interesting floral scent with crisply fresh, forward kiwi fruit on **18** (82). Modest 12.5% alcohol. **Viognier** 🍷 ★★★ Alluring floral & cling peach bouquet, **17** (78) lime flavours, brisk acidity & pithy texture. Good match for curries. Not tasted: **Hillside Red**, **Summer White**. — GdB

Location: Wolseley ▪ WO: Breedekloof ▪ Est 2000 ▪ 1stB 2007 ▪ Closed to public ▪ Kingsbury Cottage (self-catering), www.silkbush.com/guest-house ▪ Owner(s) Silkbush Holdings LP ▪ Winemaker(s) Chris du Toit (2015, Bergsig Estate) ▪ Viticulturist(s) Anton Roos (2000) ▪ 143ha/87ha (cabs s/f, malbec, merlot, mourv, p verdot, ptage, shiraz, sauv, sem, viog) ▪ 1,200t/10,000cs own label 100% red ▪ Other export brand: Lion's Drift ▪ PO Box 91 Breërivier 6858 ▪ anton@silkbush.co.za ▪ www.silkbush.com ▪ F +27 (0)86-520-3261 ▪ T +27 (0)83-629-1735

☐ **Silverhurst** see High Constantia Wine Cellar

Silvermist Organic Wine Estate 🍷 🍴 🏠 ◎

If a tourist wish list included luxury accommodation in a mountaintop retreat with stunning views over False Bay, fine-dining, top-class wine, on-farm activities and conservation area, Silvermist would tick all of those boxes. This boutique wine estate is also the only one on the Cape Peninsula that's organically certified.

★★★★ **Sauvignon Blanc** 🍷 Feisty & brisk, with pungent wild herb, gooseberry flavours. Quite intense, hint of grapefruit pithiness, making **17** (87) a tablemate vs smoother **16** (86)'s solo sipper.

Not tasted: **Cabernet Sauvignon**, **Rocket Dog Red**. — MW

Location/WO: Constantia ▪ Map: Cape Peninsula ▪ Map grid reference: B3 ▪ Est 1984 ▪ 1stB 2010 ▪ Wine tasting & sales: plse see website for opening times ▪ The Green Vine (www. greenvineeatery.com): Mon-Sun 8-5 for breakfast, lunch & all-day foods ▪ Events: events@silvermistestate.co.za ▪ Silvermist Boutique Hotel: hotel@silvermistestate.co.za ▪ Walks & hikes ▪ Conservation area ▪ La Colombe Restaurant: www.lacolombe. co.za / reservations@lacolombe.co.za ▪ Owner(s) Constantia Ridge Estates (Pty) Ltd ▪ Cellarmaster(s)/ winemaker(s)/viticulturist(s) Gregory Brink Louw (Jan 2005) ▪ 22ha/6ha (cab, shiraz, sauv) ▪ 5.2t/580cs own label 30% red 70% white ▪ CERES organic ▪ PO Box 608 Constantia 7848 ▪ silvermistvineyards@gmail. com ▪ www.silvermistestate.co.za ▪ S 34° 0' 51.93" E 018° 24' 5.13" ▪ 🗺 refilling.diffidence.interests ▪ T +27 (0)21-794-7601

☐ **Silver Myn** see Zorgvliet Wines

Silverthorn Wines

Co-owner/winemaker John Loubser is relishing the joy of working for himself after many years at the helm of one of the Cape's top wineries. His acclaimed boutique brand of méthode cap classique bubblies is heading overseas for the first time, to Germany and Switzerland, while – as he puts it – he continues to hit 'hardcore leather on tar' throughout SA, cementing locals' love of his wines. Much work has been done in their vineyards in Robertson over the past year, combating the effects of the drought and preparing the soils to better cope with future water shortages.

Méthode Cap Classique range

★★★★ **The Genie** Earthy, salty notes on **NV** ⑧⑨ rosé bubbly from shiraz lead to cooked red fruit & floral spice. 15 months lees- & further 8 months bottle-ageing add pleasing weight.

★★★★☆ **CWG Auction Reserve Big Dog IV** ⓐ Rich, appetising flavours of grass, apple, hay & brioche balanced by racy acidity. **13** ⑨④ savoury edge courtesy of low sugar, creamy yoghurt note from 51 months on lees, deeply satisfying & complex. 60/40 old-oaked chardonnay & pinot. WO W Cape, as next.

★★★★☆ **Jewel Box** ⓐ Ups the chardonnay component in **14** ⑨③ sparkling to 70% (vs 60% in **13** ⑨②) to excellent effect, giving rich apple pie flavours & tangy oyster juice nuance. Pinot noir portion, 60% old oak, 42 months on lees add weight & length, balanced by lively acidity & persistent bubbles.

★★★★☆ **The Green Man** ⓐ Fruity blanc de blancs, **15** ⑨③ mixes crisp apples, lemon sherbet & fine notes of celery, yeast & fresh bread. Thrilling bubbles & good palate weight (sur lie 28 months) lead to satisfying finish. 100% chardonnay, 10% old oaked, like **14** ⑨③.— CM

Location: Robertson • WO: Robertson/Western Cape • Est 1998 • 1stB 2004 • Closed to public • Owner(s) Silverthorn Wines (Pty) Ltd • Cellarmaster(s)/winemaker(s)/viticulturist(s) John Loubser (1998) • 10.5ha/4ha (cab, shiraz, chard) • 75t/7,000cs own label 55% white 45% rosé • IPW • PO Box 381 Robertson 6705 • john@silverthornwines.co.za, karen@silverthornwines.co.za • www.silverthornwines.co.za • T +27 (0)21-788-1706

☐ **Silwervis** see Terracura Wines

Simelia Wines

A new generation is putting its stamp on Simelia home-farm Woestkloof, set on Wellington's Groenberg Mountain and dating back to the 1800s, and producing increasingly impressive wines from its vines. The brand combines the names of owners Simon and Celia Obholzer, and focuses on 'traditional wines according to Old World methods'. With venerable single blocks on the property, the Obholzers plan to join the Old Vine Project, and are excited about a new hectare of cabernet taking shape at press time.

Simelia range

★★★★ **Merlot** Though intense, rich & structured, **15** ⑧⑨ expresses its ripe red fruit elegantly, manages tannins better than **14** ★★★★ ⑧④, shows same attractive & chocolate note from obvious but integrated oak (70% new, 3 years). Magnums, too, for these.

★★★★ **Syrah** Seductive fragrances of ripe black cherry, black pepper & plum, whiff of oak (same regime as Merlot), subtle fine tannin & captivatingly dry finish take **15** ★★★★★ ⑨① up a level from **14** ⑧⑦.

Casa Simelia range Ⓝⓔⓦ

★★★★ **Syrah** A savoury, smoky bouquet welcomes & follows through to **17** ⑧⑨'s perfectly dry palate, showing pristine fruit sweetness & balanced ripe tannins, well-absorbed wood (15 months, 20% new).

★★★★ **Merlot-Cabernet Sauvignon** Cab's 30% contribution shows in intense - not unpleasant - grip, buffered by mouthwateringly luscious mulberry, cassis & plum. Pampering in 20% new oak, 15 months, aids finely etched texture & length in **17** ⑧⑧.— HC

Location/WO: Wellington • Est farm 1837/Simelia wine label 2012 • 1stB 2013 • Closed to public • Casa Simelia luxury self-catering guest house • Hiking/walking trails on farm • Owner(s) Simon A Obholzer & Celia Hoogenhout-Obholzer • Winemaker(s) Louis Nel (Nov 2012) & Simon A Obholzer • 42ha/4.3ha (cab, merlot, shiraz) • 8t/ha total • ±1,050cs/ha plus ±250 magnum btls/ha 100% red • PO Box 15587 Vlaeberg Cape Town 8018 • info@simelia.co.za • www.simelia.co.za • F +27 (0)21-300-5026 • T +27 (0)21-300-5025

☐ **Simonsbosch** see Koelenhof Winery

Simonsig Estate

Cause for celebration at the Malan family's substantial Stellenbosch estate is the 50th anniversary of its first wine, a chenin, marked by a limited-release Simonsig Steen in a magnum flute with the original (1968) label design. Late founder Frans Malan would have been proud, seeing sons Francois (CEO/viticulturist) and Johan (cellarmaster) build on his legacy, and grandson Michael officially joining the winemaking team. The elder Malan's innovations, from pioneering SA bottle-fermented bubbly to co-founding the first wine route, have been translated into four styles of award-winning MCC bubblies and a chic MCC-and-oyster bar in town, while Johan's CWG bottlings test new varieties and combinations - viz the (untasted by us) Roussanne-Marsanne for the 2018 auction) - for a portfolio of great depth and breadth.

Malan Family Selection

★★★★☆ The Garland ⓥ Single cab vineyard on Simonsberg belonging to Malan relatives. Stands apart in packaging & vintages, released only when ready. Deeply rich **10** ⑨① still in the prime of youth; 27 months new oak well partnered by fruit, but built for the long haul. Impressive.

★★★★☆ Redhill Pinotage ⓐ Single bushvine vineyard named for soil colour. Full & rich, suave tannin & oaking (80% new French/American, 15 months) seamlessly merge with smoky brambleberries & ripe plums on firm structure of **16** ⑨③.

★★★★☆ Merindol Syrah ⓐ Single-site **15** ⑨③ opulent & generous, with fine bramble & dark plum concentration. Judicious oaking (new, 15 months) provides cinnamon, spice & structured backbone for long ageing.

★★★★☆ Tiara ⓐ Cab-led Bordeaux blend with 15% merlot, 6% cab franc in **14** ⑨⓪ vs 5-part combo in **13** ⑨⓪, both ageworthy. Succulent blackcurrant fruit in harmony with serious oaking, 75% new, 15 months, giving accessibility plus the prospect of good ageing.

★★★★ Frans Malan Cape Blend Pinotage (70%), cab & merlot named for Malan patriarch, estate founder. Plush dark fruit coils around supple tannin spine, **16** ⑧⑨ glossy, & built to age but approachable in youth, too.

★★★★ Chenin Avec Chêne ⓐ Literally, 'With Oak', & in **17 ★★★★☆** ⑨⓪ the wood is all older, 12 months. Voluptuous Golden Delicious apple, nectarine, cinnamon-spiced quince & roasted nuts complexity. Similar refreshing conclusion to elegant **16** ⑧⑧, with more concentration in the flavours.

CWG Auction Reserves

★★★★☆ Heirloom Shiraz ⓐ Detailed & finely crafted for the long haul, with masterly tannin construction, dense core of fruit & savoury lift. **16** ⑨③'s bold 14.7% alcohol neatly wrapped in cloak of silky dark fruit & vanilla.

Cultivar Selection

Chenin Blanc ⓥ ⓣ **★★★★** Popular favourite since 1968 does not disappoint in its 50th vintage. **18** ⑧④ friendly & inviting, energetic & very flavoursome.

Labyrinth Cabernet Sauvignon ★★★★ Suave & fresh glassful with black fruit appeal, lipsmacking tannin nip. **16** ⑧⑤ benefits from no new oak & limited skin contact on some bunches to maximise fruit without losing acidity. **Pinotage ★★★★** Juicy **16** ⑧④ all about the fruit: dark plums & dates, Xmas pudding & spice. Friendly, with gentle tannins from light oak-staving. **Mr Borio's Shiraz ★★★★** Earthy & savoury **16** ⑧④ smooth dark fruit, cured meat notes & lifted spicy finish. 15 months older French/American oak add enough grip for meaty food. **Cabernet Sauvignon-Merlot ★★★** Medium-bodied **17** ⑦⑨ strikes good balance between fruit & gentle tannins, smidgen sugar gives extra drinkability. Export only. **Cabernet Sauvignon-Shiraz ★★★** Generous mouthful of many things nice in near-equal **17** ⑧① blend, including ripe fruit, vanilla & hint of spice. Juicy, smooth, perfect for hamburger with all trimmings. WO W Cape, like Gewürztraminer & Sunbird. **The GSM ★★★** Large portion of **17** ⑧①'s fruit picked early, given carbonic fermentation, delivering deliciously drinkable red-berry flavours. Grenache noir (24%), shiraz (30%) & mourvèdre. **Chardonnay ★★★★** Barrel-fermented **17** ⑧⑤ shines with pure stonefruit & baked apple aromas, flavours. Careful oaking & handling give crème brûlée texture, animated finish. **Gewürztraminer ★★★★** With splash morio muscat, aromatic Special Late Harvest-style **18** ⑧⑤ mingles Turkish delight with rosewater & litchi, balanced sweetness allows for spicy bobotie pairing or sipping solo. **Sunbird Sauvignon Blanc ★★★★** Veritable tropical fruit salad in **18** ⑧⑤, fresh & breezy, courtesy some cooler-climate grapes, satisfying body, lemon farewell. Bone-dry, modest 12.4% alcohol. **Sauvignon Blanc-Semillon** ⓧ ★★★★ Just 15% semillon in **17** ⑧④ but plays an important role. Rounds off sauvignon's edges, gives palate weight, adds melon notes without detracting from the core fruity-freshness. Export only. Not tasted: **Roussanne**.

Méthode Cap Classique Sparkling range

★★★★ **Kaapse Vonkel Brut Rosé** Palest pink **17** ⑧⑨ sparkler, perky cranberry & strawberry flavours, smooth fine mousse. Very dry, elegant & pleasurable. Pinot noir (72%) with pinotage (27%), meunier. These WO W Cape unless noted.

★★★★☆ **Cuvée Royale** ⓧ ⓐ Prestige blanc de blancs MCC from chardonnay, longest on lees of range (4-5 years). No oak portion in **12** ⑨③; apple scented, but lots more to beguile - creamy baked apple richness, toasted brioche, a steely acid backbone keeping it vital, focused. Stellenbosch WO.

★★★★ **Kaapse Vonkel Brut** First SA MCC in 1971, still a Cape classic. Pinot noir, barrel-fermented chardonnay (45/46) & touch meunier in vivacious **16** ⑧⑨. Creamy mousse, fresh apple & vanilla biscuit appeal, lingering dry nutty finish.

★★★★ **Kaapse Vonkel Demi Sec** More meunier than Vonkel siblings, it (8%) & pinot noir add palate weight, chardonnay freshness & citrus tones. **16** ⑧⑧ perfect accompaniment to chicken liver parfait: smooth, creamy mousse, sweet-fruit flavours, zesty citrus to counter 37 g/l sugar.

Dessert Wines

★★★★ **Vin de Liza** Light-footed & perfectly balanced **17** ⑧⑥ from wooded sauvignon & semillon delights with soft dried-apricot & roasted hazelnut flavours, tangerine zest finish. 375 ml.

★★★★☆ **Straw Wine** ⓧ Occasional release, last in guide was **11** ★★★★ ⑧④. From sun-dried muscat ottonel, **15** ⑨① is intense, with variety supplying a sublime grapiness. Savoury oak notes don't overshadow the essential character. Finishes drier than the 76 g/l sugar would suggest.

★★★★ **Cape Vintage Reserve** ⓧ From shiraz, port-style **14** ⑧⑧ shows brambleberry & fruitcake richness, 25 months older oak giving welcome tannic grip, adding to drinkability & appeal. No **10** - **13**.

Exclusive range

★★★★ **Gees Van Die Wingerd Husk Spirit Gewürztraminer** ⓥ Fragrant & aromatic **15** ⑧⑦, smooth & refreshing after dinner tipple or a shot in your espresso. Harmonious, with warm, clean farewell.— WB

Location/map: Stellenbosch ▪ Map grid reference: E2 ▪ WO: Stellenbosch/Western Cape ▪ Est 1953 ▪ 1stB 1968 ▪ Tasting Mon-Fri 8.30–4.30 Sat/pub hols 8.30–3.30 Sun 11-2.30 ▪ Sales Mon-Fri 9—5 Sat/pub hols 8.30–4 Sun 11-3 ▪ Fee R50-R75pp ▪ MCC tour & tasting ▪ Closed Good Fri, Dec 25 & Jan 1 ▪ Cellar tours daily at 11, booking advised ▪ Cuvée restaurant ▪ Facilities for children ▪ Tour groups ▪ Gifts ▪ Farm produce ▪ Conferences ▪ Labyrinth vineyard ▪ First Fizz day (every first Thu of the month: Oct-Apr) ▪ Music Saturdays (every second week: Oct-Mar) ▪ Owner(s) Malan Family Trusts ▪ Cellarmaster(s) Johan Malan (1981) ▪ Winemaker(s) Debbie Thompson (Nov 1999), Charl Schoeman (Dec 2012) & Michael Malan (Oct 2017) ▪ Viticulturist(s) Francois Malan (Jan 1981) & Tommie Corbett (Nov 2008), with Conrad Schutte (VinPro) ▪ 210ha (cab, merlot, ptage, pinot, shiraz, chard, chenin, sauv) ▪ 2,700t/340,000cs own label 27% red 43% white 30% MCC ▪ HACCP, IPW, SANAS, WIETA ▪ PO Box 6 Koelenhof 7605 ▪ wine@simonsig.co.za ▪ www.simonsig.co.za ▪ S 33° 52'12.1" E 018° 49'31.7" ▪ 🖃 gazette.stylist.wants ▪ F +27 (0)21-888-4909/4916 ▪ **T +27 (0)21-888-4900 (farm), +27 (0)21-888-4915 (tasting), +27 (0)21-888-4932/+27 (0)76-207-8930 (Cuvée)**

Simonsvlei International　ⓧ ⓟ ⓐ ⓑ ⓒ

It's difficult to miss this large winery, thanks to the landmark 'wine bottle' (a giant storage tank) just off the N1 motorway near Paarl. And, once here, numerous activities and facilities await, including wine-tasting and -sales, conference and function venue, restaurant and area to keep the youngsters amused. Wine-wise, the mantra is 'quality wines at affordable prices', and the annual crush — 60% of which is white — is vinified into a broad range tailored to satisfy all palates, locally and in expanding international markets.

Hercules Paragon range

★★★★ **SMCV** ⓥ Abundant red fruit, gentle spice from mostly older oak & fresh acidity, **16** ⑧⑥ successful quartet shiraz, mourvèdre, cinsaut & viognier, perennial cellardoor favourite.

★★★★ **Sauvignon Blanc** ⓥ 17 ⑧⑦ improves on 15 ★★★★ ⑧⑤, similar but more intense cool/green & tropical melange, full body & ripe flavours, long satisfying finish. **16** untasted.

Shiraz ⓥ ★★★ A little leaner, less juicy than last, oak (40% new French) adding perfume to simple spicy tones in **13** ⑧①. Not tasted: **Cabernet Sauvignon**, **Shiraz-Cabernet Sauvignon**.

New Generation range

Ja-Mocha Pinotage ★★★ Not quite delivering the expected coffee 'hit', yet **17** ⑧② packed with sweet mulberries & cream, hint oak char to wake up your taste buds. **Toffee Chunk Syrah** ⓥ ★★ More char, more black pepper spicing than toffee or caramel on - yes - chunky **16** ⑦④.

Premier range

Cabernet Sauvignon ⓥ ★★★ Attractive blackberry fruit, good vinosity & fair grip for food on easygoing **17** ⑦⑦. **Pinotage** ★★ Fresh, with sufficient tannic tug for a meal, **17** ⑦⑥ light red berries, smoky tail. **Shiraz** ⓥ ★★★ Unchallenging **17** ⑦⑦ offers some spice & cigar notes, not-too-obvious 14.5% alcohol. **Zenzela Pinotage Rosé** ★★ Palest of pinks, shyest of bouquets, gentlest sweetness, **18** ⑦① slips down easily. **Chardonnay** ⓥ ★★★ Most variety-true in the line-up, **17** ⑧⓪ lemon & orange notes, subtle vanilla overlay & complexity. **Chenin Blanc** ⓥ ★★★ Lightly flavoured but with satisfying vinosity, pleasing thatch/floral nuances on **18** ⑦⑨ poolside sipper. **Sauvignon Blanc** ★★ Delicate grass & capsicum zing, **18** ⑦③ zesty & fresh casual quaffer. **Humbro Red Jerepiko** ★★★ Grapey fortified pudding wine a Simonsvlei stalwart. **NV** ⑧⓪ rooibos honey & orange zest complexity, well-judged spirit for solo in winter, over ice in summer. Not tasted: **Shiraz Rosé**. Occasional release: **Cabernet Sauvignon-Merlot**.

Lifestyle range

Cabernet Sauvignon ⓥ ★★★ Berries-&-cream aromas on lightly flavoured **17** ⑦⑦, gently oaked so's not to overwhelm. **Merlot** ★★ Some plummy fruit, hint of sweetness, **17** ⑦⑥ soft, uncomplicated fun. **Pinotage** ⓥ ★★★ Good honest quaffing from SA's home-grown grape. **16** ⑦⑧ decent pinotage mulberry & banana tones, supple tannins. **Shiraz** ⓥ ★★★ Tug of grape tannin, cranberry tang give **16** ⑧① lift & vivacity, extend its finish. Plenty of varietal red fruit & black pepper, too. **Simonsrood** ⓥ ★★★ Perennial pocket-pleaser, **NV** ⑧⓪ exactly as per label: 'fruity & fun for smooth drinking'. Packs more flavour, character than siblings. **Chenin Blanc** ★★ At 13.5% alcohol, **18** ⑦② bit fuller than the other blanc, understated peach & floral appeal. **Sauvignon Blanc** ★★ Water-white & subtly grassy, **18** ⑦② balanced but shade less substance, flavour than usual. **Extra Light Natural Sweet Rosé** ⓥ ★★ Pearly pink **NV** ⑦④, strawberries & cream flavours, sweet but balanced, just 9% alcohol. Discontinued: **Simonsblanc**.

Simonsvlei range

Dry Red ★★ Dusty berries rounded out by touch sugar, **NV** ⑦① laudably light in alcohol (12%). 5L pack, as all these. **Dry White** ★ Delicate pear drop notes, **NV** ⑥⑨ easy drinkability from modest 11.5% alcohol, slight sweetness. **Natural Sweet Rosé** ★★ Party favourite **NV** ⑦④'s red berry flavours enhanced by the sweetness, brightened by perky acidity. Low 9% alcohol.

Villa Cape Kosher range

Pinotage ★★★ Unwooded **16** ⑦⑧ forthcoming strawberry & candyfloss aromas, few grams sugar up the drinkability. **Shiraz Rosé** ⒩⒠⒲ ★★ Pretty pink hue & inviting berry bouquet, **18** ⑦⑤ dry & soft, light alcohol for long lunches. **Chardonnay** ⒩⒠⒲ ★★ Unwooded, creamy **18** ⑦③, tropical fruit flavours & nice mouthfeel for solo sipping. **Chenin Blanc** ⒩⒠⒲ ★★★ Fresh **18** ⑦⑧'s white peach & dried pear flavours highlighted by bouncy acidity. Not tasted: **Cabernet Sauvignon**, **Merlot**. — CvZ

Location/map: Paarl ▪ Map grid reference: D7 ▪ WO: Western Cape ▪ Est/1stB 1945 ▪ Tasting & sales Mon-Fri 8–5 Sat 8.30–4.30 Sun 11–3 ▪ Fee R30pp/6 wines ▪ Cellar tours by prior arrangement/request ▪ Wine tasting closed Good Fri, Dec 25 & Jan 1 ▪ Eat@Simonsvlei, upmarket family restaurant serving slow cooked country fare; cellardoor wine prices ▪ Kids play area ▪ Conference & function venue (100 pax, depending on setup) ▪ Karoo Craft Breweries (www.kcbrew.co.za) ▪ Owner(s) 65 shareholders ▪ 33 active producers ▪ Cellarmaster(s) Helena Senekal (Oct 2016) ▪ Winemaker(s) NJ Steyn (Oct 2016, assistant) ▪ 5,200t 40% red 60% white ▪ Brands for clients: Kelvin Grove, Woolworths ▪ BRC, E-Mark, Fairtrade, IPW, WIETA ▪ PO Box 584 Suider-Paarl 7624 ▪ info@simonsvlei.co.za, steven@simonsvlei.co.za ▪ www.simonsvlei.co.za ▪ S 33° 47' 23.31" E 018° 55' 48.15" ▪ ⓜ luckier.metro.start ▪ F +27 (0)21-863-1240 ▪ **T +27 (0)21-863-3040**

☐ **Simplicity** *see* Weltevrede Estate

☐ **Since 1922** see Villiersdorp Cellar
☐ **Sir George** see Napier Vineyards
☐ **Sirkel** see Scali

Sir Lambert Wines
(symbols)

This 'story in a bottle' begins at Lamberts Bay on the West Coast, in a block of sauvignon blanc just 3 km from the cold Atlantic Ocean. Named for 19th-century seafarer Sir Robert Lambert, the venture involves Diemersdal cellar chief Thys Louw, two partners, and the local community who hand-harvest the grapes.

★★★★ **Sauvignon Blanc** Back to form in **18** ⑧⑥, complex tropical & citrus fruit wrapped around a fresh core of salty acidity. Balanced, with lengthy finish. **17** ★★★★ ⑧⑤ shade less persistent.— WB

Location/WO: Lamberts Bay ▪ Map: Olifants River ▪ Map grid reference: B5 ▪ Est 2004 ▪ 1stB 2007 ▪ Tasting by appt in Lamberts Bay or Mon-Sat/pub hols 9-5 Sun 10-3 at Diemersdal ▪ Closed Good Fri, Dec 25 & Jan 1 ▪ Xamarin Guest House & Restaurant ▪ BYO picnic ▪ Conference & function venue (up to 250 people) ▪ Game drives ▪ Golf course ▪ Tour groups ▪ Conservation area ▪ 4x4 trail ▪ Facilities for children ▪ Owner(s) John Hayes, Johan Teubes & Thys Louw ▪ Winemaker(s) Thys Louw & Mari Branders ▪ Viticulturist(s) John Hayes (2015) ▪ 10ha (shiraz, sauv) ▪ 60t/6,000cs own label 10% red 90% white ▪ PO Box 27 Durbanville 7551 ▪ info@sirlambert.co.za ▪ www.sirlambert.co.za ▪ S 32° 5' 52.40" E 018° 18' 19.50" ▪ ⎚ feathered.yearned.paid ▪ F +27 (0)21-979-1802 ▪ **T +27 (0)21-976-3361**

☐ **Sir Robert Stanford Estate** see Robert Stanford Estate
☐ **Six Hats** see Piekenierskloof Wine Company
☐ **Sixpence** see Opstal Estate
☐ **1685** see Boschendal Wines
☐ **Sixty 40** see Boland Kelder

Skaap Wines
(symbols)

There is certainly a sense of humour here: the winery name and 'woolly' front labels are a witty take on Dutch owner Thierry Schaap's surname (meaning 'sheep'), and the new rosé's name is a similar play on words. The wines, however, are serious. Made since inception by Riaan Oosthuizen (see Nomada), the sauvignon and shiraz fruit comes from the Sir Lowry's Pass home property, which includes the renowned Schapenberg Hill (kismet!), while the rest is outsourced.

★★★★ **Shiraz 45** Inky hue from long skin contact, with oaking gives character, good tannin structure. **16** ⑧⑧ white pepper & cloves, dark fruit, ending savoury. Drink now, will reward cellaring.

★★★★☆ **Sauvignon Blanc 46** ⊘ ⊛ Riper style than **16** ⑨⓪, with tropical fruit throughout, **17** ⑨③ still has intensity & verve, an acid backbone that keeps it tightly focused, vibrating with health. Can age, when mineral notes will surface, but already hard to resist.

Okuphinki 46 ⑩④ ★★★ Rosé (of course, it's in the Zulu name!) from sauvignon & merlot, **17** ⑧② shows both: red berry scents, liquorice nuances, sauvignon's influence found in the crisp dry citrus flavours. Not tasted: **Méthode Cap Classique Brut**. — CR

Location: Sir Lowry's Pass ▪ Map: Helderberg ▪ Map grid reference: H6 ▪ WO: Stellenbosch/Coastal ▪ Est/1stB 2011 ▪ Private functions/dinner by appt ▪ Local art on display & for sale ▪ Conferences (up to 16 pax) ▪ Walks/hikes ▪ Conservation area ▪ 5-bedroom guesthouse, dining room with chef & 2 self-catering lodges plus villa ▪ Swimming pool ▪ Owner(s) Thierry Schaap ▪ Cellarmaster(s)/winemaker(s) Riaan Oosthuizen (Jan 2011) ▪ 17ha/4ha (shiraz, sauv) ▪ 1,700cs own label 30% red 70% white ▪ IPW ▪ PO Box 3794 Somerset West 7130 ▪ info@skaapwines.com ▪ www.skaapwines.com ▪ S 34° 06' 11.35" E 018° 55' 05.87" ▪ ⎚ truce.product.freestyle ▪ **T +27 (0)21-858-1982**

☐ **Sketchbook** see Carrol Boyes Collection

Skilpadvlei Wines
(symbols)

This family farm on the Polkadraai Hills in Stellenbosch gets its name from the turtles found there in the 1800s – in advance of the Jouberts, who arrived in 1917. More recently (only this century) they started diverting some of their grapes into wines for their own label. There's also accommodation, a farm-style restaurant (with a new outdoors bar), and wedding and conference venues – but turtles go unmentioned.

★★★★ **ML Joubert** Equal blend cab-merlot, with classic fruitcake & cigarbox. **16** (86) rich, full flavoured, with grip to keep it from being too easy. Bit more happening than in **15** ★★★★ (84), with 80% cab.

Pinotage ★★★★ Clean, fresh fruity aromas on **17** (85) lead to juicy, fleshy palate, with balanced grip, supportive oaking. Happily easygoing. **Shiraz** (NEW) ★★★★ Good sweet fruit flavours on **16** (85), rounded but effective tannin-acid structure. Typical of the estate's engaging, unpretentious approach to giving pleasure. **Chenin Blanc** ★★★ Deftly made, balanced, fruity & fresh **18** (82) - not varietally typical, given the tropical notes, but satisfying. **Sauvignon Blanc** ★★★ Just what a straight-down-the-line sauvignon should be: **18** (81) aromatic, flavourful, dry & unaggressively crisp. Not tasted: **Grenache Rosé**. — TJ

Location/map/WO: Stellenbosch ▪ Map grid reference: C6 ▪ Est 2004 ▪ 1stB 2001 ▪ Tasting & sales Mon-Sat 8-5 Sun 8-4 ▪ Fee R25 ▪ Closed Dec 25/26 & Jan 1/2 ▪ Restaurant Mon-Sat 8-late Sun 8-4 ▪ Facilities for children ▪ Gift/decor shop ▪ Conferences ▪ Weddings & functions ▪ B&B guest house & self-catering cottages ▪ Owner(s) WD Joubert ▪ Cellarmaster(s) Kowie du Toit (consultant) ▪ Viticulturist(s) Johan Pienaar & Eben Archer (consultants) ▪ 78ha/55ha (cab, merlot, ptage, shiraz, chenin, sauv) ▪ 652t/12,000cs own label 80% red 20% white ▪ PO Box 17 Vlottenburg 7604 ▪ info@skilpadvlei.co.za ▪ www.skilpadvlei.co.za ▪ S 33° 57′ 31.5″ E 018° 45′ 52.4″ ▪ ⌖ ahead.both.budding ▪ F +27 (0)21-881-3538 ▪ **T +27 (0)21-881-3237**

☐ **Skipper's** see New Beginnings Wines
☐ **Skoon Vallei** see Eerste Hoop Wine Cellar

Slaley   ⓠ ⑪ ⓒ

The third generation has taken the wheel of the Hunting family's winery in prime Simonsberg-Stellenbosch, and there have been many changes as a result, including 'innovation in both the vineyard and cellar'. Unaltered are the welcome extended to visitors to the multifaceted cellardoor, and the 'long-held winemaking philosophy of producing classically styled wines made to age'.

Slaley range

★★★★ **Merlot** ⓠ Big & bold, but **08** (87) has aged gracefully, revealing plum compote & spice on well-integrated tannin frame. Serious oaking: 36 months in 50% new oak, as for Pinotage.

★★★★ **Shiraz** ⓠ Plush, plump & supple **07** (86) is ready to drink but still bright & perky. Expressive black plum & stewed prune fruit. Similar mint nuance as tannic **06** ★★★★ (84).

★★★★ **Merlot-Cabernet Sauvignon** ⓠ Brooding **08** (86) beginning to emerge from dense tannin cloak, revealing ripe damson & blackcurrant fruit, aromatic liquorice & tobacco. Well up on **07** ★★★ (81).

★★★★ **Chardonnay** ⓠ Improved **09** (87) leaner, more fruit-driven than **06** ★★★★; dry, lime & mineral nuances combining over a tight structure. 20% new oak. Good potential.

★★★★ **Reserve Noble Late Harvest Chardonnay** ⓠ Decadent & irresistible dessert, **07** (87) concentrated honey/raisin character (from vine-dried grapes) perfect match for strong cheeses.

Pinotage ⓠ ★★★★ Opulent ripe dark berry fruit & big alcohol (15%) have melded into engaging, smooth **08** (84) offering, ready to drink. WO W Cape, like Merlot.

Broken Stone range

★★★★ **Pinotage** Dark prune & pot-pourri nuances, **11** ★★★ (78) flagging somewhat, burly alcohol (16.2%) standing apart. Last tasted was polished & elegant **06** (87).

Cabernet Sauvignon ★★★ Supple **11** (82) showing its age in mature Christmas cake flavours, generous sprinkle of spice & some warmth (15.5%). Best to drink soon. **Chardonnay** ★★★ Now bottled, **17** (77) pronounced bruised apple & pear flavours, fleeting honeyed finish. Not tasted: **Shiraz, Cabernet Sauvignon-Shiraz-Pinotage**.

Social range

Lindsay's Whimsy Red ⓠ ★★★ Wholesome & robust **11** (82), pinotage, shiraz & cab, intense black fruit & plum pudding richness on solid tannins. **Lindsay's Whimsy Rosé** ⓠ ★★★ Dry **13** (79) from pinotage, deliberately weightier in style, says team, so wine will 'stay wine as opposed to water if you add ice'! **The Whimsy Sauvignon Blanc** ★★★ Pleasingly different fruit profile of citrus & orchard fruit, **17** (80) light & breezy for early drinking. — WB

Location/map: Stellenbosch ▪ Map grid reference: E2 ▪ WO: Simonsberg–Stellenbosch/Western Cape ▪ Est 1957 ▪ 1stB 1997 ▪ Tasting & sales Tue-Sun 10–4 ▪ Fee R40, waived on purchase ▪ Closed Good Fri, Dec 24/25

& Jan 1 ▪ Bistro: light meals during tasting hours ▪ Venue & conference facility with AV capacity ▪ Owner(s) Hunting family ▪ Winemaker(s)/viticulturist(s) Marjan Smit (Jan 2018) ▪ 183ha/30ha (cab, merlot, ptage, shiraz, chard, sauv) ▪ 220t/15–20,000cs own label 90% red 9% white 1% rosé ▪ IPW ▪ PO Box 119 Koelenhof 7605 ▪ venue@slaley.co.za, accounts@slaley.co.za ▪ www.slaley.co.za ▪ S 33° 51′ 53.7″ E 018° 50′ 51.1″ ▪ 🎞 paint.awesome.scoots ▪ **T +27 (0)21-865-2123**

Slanghoek Winery   ⓘ ⓒ ⓖ

Grower-owned Slanghoek Winery near Rawsonville, surrounded by spectacular mountains, is not just a winery but a destination, offering many activities for the adventurous. Wine of course is the first one, with diverse styles, including some specialities like a long-aged chenin, and well-priced ranges. On offer nearby are 4x4 trails, mountain biking, hiking, canoeing, fishing and frequent festivals geared to the time of year.

Legends range

★★★★ Barrel Fermented Chenin Blanc Like **15 ★★★★** ⑧⑤, **16** ⑧⑧ unashamedly bold, 26 months new French oak for the shortbread seam in lime marmalade, which intensifies on the palate, tangy-fresh. Enjoy on its own, it's good enough.

Private Selection

★★★★ Crème de Chenin ⓧ Bargain-priced Natural Sweet, **16** ⑧⑦ captures the essence of sweet chenin. Intense apricot & pear, piercing acidity cutting a swathe through 91 g/l sugar, keeping it vibrant.

★★★★ Noble Late Harvest ⓧ **16** ⑧⑨ retasted, extra year deepened, enriched the flavours. Crème caramel & honey, 60% oaking giving ginger biscuit overlay, ends racy-fresh, offsetting the sweetness. Chenin, dash muscat.

Merlot ⓦ **★★★** Again manages to get fruit intensity, a constant style through the vintages. Succulent & fresh drinkability adds to **17** ⑧⑦'s appeal. **Shiraz** ⓦ **★★★** Oldest of these reds, which is one of **15** ⑧⑦'s attractions: mellow dark fruit, sweet spice, a prosciutto note, succulent & smooth. **Sauvignon Blanc** ⓦ **★★★** Gooseberry at core, with crushed herbs, **18** ⑧⑦ ends on a mineral note: lots on offer in a light, zesty body.

Cabernet Sauvignon ★★★ Longer oaking than other range reds, 18 months, & lower alcohol (12.5%), **16** ⑧⑦ is elegant yet packed with flavour, plums & chocolate, with gentle tannin grip. **Pinotage ★★★** Blueberries & spice, some liquorice, **16** ⑧⑦ is made to give immediate pleasure, plus age a bit. French oaking, as rest of reds, already harmonious. **Camerca** ⓧ **★★★** Cab & merlot, touch of cab franc, lithe **16** ⑧⑦ isn't shy about its wooding, savoury tones to the fruit, a firm backbone & dry finish. Needs another year/2. **Chardonnay ★★★** Portion of **17** ⑧⑦ oaked, so expect a good savoury/fruit combination, citrus & vanilla. Attractive limy freshness. **Chenin Blanc ★★** Pear drops in a light-textured body (12.5%), zesty **18** ⑦④ is designed for easy, early drinking. **Special Late Harvest ★★★★** A celebration of fruit, **17** ⑧④'s highly aromatic styling from muscat d'Alexandrie goes well with a sweeter wine. Generous, hedonistic.

Slanghoek range

Cuvée Brut ★★ Chardonnay/chenin carbonated **NV** ⑦⑤ bubbly, reliable style: lemon sherbet with palate-cleansing freshness. **Vin Doux ★★★** Muscat d'Alexandrie fits well with the sweeter style of bubbly, there's grapey exuberance in **NV** ⑦⑧, zesty freshness that aids drinkability. **Hanepoot Jerepigo ★★★★** Distinctive (fortified) wine style of the area, **17** ⑧④ wonderfully grapey, as befits muscat d'Alexandrie. Full-sweet but in a tangy way, fresh sultanas & dried fruit vie for attention. **Red Muscadel ★★★** Sweetest of these fortified wines, but not by a big margin. **17** ⑧⑦ is raisiny, with enlivening red-fruit top notes, the flavours rich, mouthcoating. Chilly night fare. **Red Jerepigo ★★★** With red-berry fruit gum vibrancy, **17** ⑦⑧ from pinotage has jammy sweetness, rich, full & round. Great with cheese. **Cape Ruby ★★★** Unwooded **17** ⑧⑦ 'port' from touriga celebrates fruit, as style is supposed to, sweet yet fresh. Cranberry & plum flavours, eminently drinkable.

Vinay range

Smooth Blended Red ★★ Equal pinotage, malbec, petit verdot, **NV** ⑦④ lives up to its name: dark fruited, sleek & juicy. **Crispy White ★★** Bargain priced, as all these. Unwooded sauvignon & chenin with dollop colombard, **NV** ⑦⑤ has crunchy apple flavours, is well named. **Natural Sweet Rosé ★★★** From red muscadel, the grapiness in **NV** (77) jumps out the glass, tangy-sweet, some candyfloss notes. Just 8.5% alcohol but still packs a flavour punch. — CR

Location: Rawsonville ▪ Map: Breedekloof ▪ Map grid reference: A5 ▪ WO: Slanghoek ▪ Est 1951 ▪ 1stB 1970 ▪ Tasting & sales Mon-Fri 9–5 Sat 10–1 ▪ Closed Easter Fri/Sun, Dec 25 & Jan 1 ▪ Cellar tours by appt ▪ Slanghoek MTB Route, fee R20: 13km ride with optional extra, more challenging 4km ▪ Owner(s) 25 producers ▪ Cellarmaster(s) Pieter Carstens (Aug 2002) ▪ Winemaker(s) Nico Grundling (Dec 2002) & Werner du Plessis (Aug 2014), with Jacques de Goede (Dec 2001) & Elaine Conradie (Nov 2016) ▪ Viticulturist(s) Callie Coetzee (Nov 2010) ▪ 1,830ha ▪ 30,000t/80,000cs own label 25% red 55% white 10% rosé 10% fortified ▪ Other export brand: Zonneweelde ▪ ISO 22000, IPW, IPW ▪ PO Box 75 Rawsonville 6845 ▪ info@slanghoek.co.za ▪ www.slanghoek.co.za ▪ S 33° 39' 1.1" E 019° 13' 49.0" ▪ ⌨ equates.reflectors.booking ▪ F +27 (0)23-344-3157 ▪ **T +27 (0)23-344-3026**

☐ **Slent** *see* Ayama Wines

Slowine ⓠ ⓖ

'Quality takes time' is the motto, and the Common Padloper Tortoise is the logo of Slowine, a collection of flavourful wines for everyday. Villiersdorp, Beaumont and Luddite wineries are the partners, and vinification is by Villiersdorp's wine-and-vine man Christo Versfeld.

Pinotage ⓦ ★★★ Delicious raspberry notes on fresh, lively **17** (82). Hint of coffee, soft tannins, very nice to drink. WO W Cape. **Chenin Blanc** ⓦ ★★★ Oh-so-tasty **18** (82), oodles of ripe tropical fruit (pineapple, mango), bouncy acidity & lengthy lime cordial conclusion. **Chenin Blanc-Sauvignon Blanc** ⊘ ⓦ ★★★★ Vibrant 60/40 blend **18** (84) awash with fresh yellow fruit. Lime zest acidity, pungent herbal notes, juicy finish – what's not to like?

Cabernet Sauvignon ★★★ Black fruit & vanilla on pleasant **17** (80), chewy tannins should settle. Previewed, as all the reds. **Merlot** ★★★ Cheery mouthful of ripe black & red fruit on easy-drinking **17** (80). **Shiraz** ★★★ Menthol notes dominate on **17** (79) before dark fruit & leather come through at slightly bitter finish. **Rosé** ★★ Some red-fruit character on lean, bone-dry **18** (74). **Sauvignon Blanc** ★★★ Crowd-pleasing **18** (80) mixes grapefruit & guava with fresh acid backbone. Perfect for summer sipping. — CM

Location/map: Villiersdorp ▪ Map grid reference: C1 ▪ WO: Cape South Coast/Western Cape ▪ Est/1stB 2005 ▪ Tasting & sales Mon-Fri 8–5 Sat 9-1 ▪ Closed Easter Fri-Mon & Dec 25/26 ▪ Owner(s) Villiersdorp Cellar ▪ Shareholders Beaumont Family Wines & Luddite Wines ▪ Technical team: Sebastian Beaumont & Niels Verburg ▪ Winemaker(s)/viticulturist(s) Christo Versfeld ▪ 300ha (merlot, chenin, sauv) ▪ 3,600t/40,000cs own label 40% red 40% white 20% rosé ▪ IPW ▪ PO Box 151 Villiersdorp 6848 ▪ cellaradmin@villiers-dorpcellar.co.za ▪ www.slowine.co.za ▪ S 33° 59' 11.2" E 019° 17' 48.5" ▪ ⌨ custard.crackle.stretcher ▪ F +27 (0)28-840-0957 ▪ **T +27 (0)28-840-0083**

☐ **Smiley** *see* Terracura Wines
☐ **Smuggler's Boot** *see* Richard Kershaw Wines
☐ **Sneeukop** *see* Rogge Cloof

Snow Mountain Wines

Winter 2018 saw Sneeuberg, the large peak which towers over Wellington's Bovlei Valley, dusted with snow more than once. The landmark's name is anglicised for this range of small batches from unique, sometimes high-lying or even seafront vineyards, by James McKenzie, also cellar master at Wellington's Nabygelegen.

The Artisan Collection

Beulah ⓠ ★★★ Zesty citrus notes & light lees character on crisp & tangy **NV** (81) sparkling from equal parts chardonnay & pinot noir. Not tasted: **Kalk Bay**, **Steen**. Discontinued: **The Anvil**.

Snow Mountain range

Not tasted: **Pinot Noir**, **The Mistress**, **Syrah**, **Chardonnay-Pinot Noir**, **Chardonnay**. — FM

Location: Wellington ▪ WO: Coastal ▪ Est/1stB 2009 ▪ Closed to public ▪ Owner(s) Snow Mountain CC ▪ Cellarmaster(s)/winemaker(s) James McKenzie (2009) ▪ 60t ▪ own label 50% red 50% white ▪ PO Box 302 Wellington 7654 ▪ avalonwines@icon.co.za ▪ www.snowmountainwines.com ▪ **T +27 (0)82-829-1189**

☐ **Social** *see* Slaley
☐ **Soek Die Geluk** *see* Goedverwacht Wine Estate

SoetKaroo Wine Estate ⓐ ⓑ

Crafting sweet ('soet') wines from varieties that include a rare red-skinned mutation of hanepoot from their vineyard in the town centre of Groot Karoo's Prins Albert, winemaker Susan Perold and husband Herman see climate change affecting crop levels and wine character, and forcing fruit buy-in in 2019. Currently available from the '17 vintage are two unfortified desserts and a jerepigo (the Cape Vintage 'port' out of stock for now).

Location: Prince Albert ▪ Map: Klein Karoo & Garden Route ▪ Map grid reference: A4 ▪ Est 2000 ▪ 1stB 2004 ▪ Tasting & sales Mon-Sat 9-1; afternoons by appt ▪ Closed Dec 25 ▪ Owner(s) Herman & Susan Perold ▪ Cellarmaster(s)/winemaker(s) Susan Perold (Jan 2007) ▪ 2t ▪ 56 Church Str Prince Albert 6930 ▪ perold@ netactive.co.za ▪ www.soetkaroo.co.za ▪ S 33° 13' 21.9" E 022° 1' 48.0" ▪ ⌖ catching.hideouts.lapping ▪ T +27 (0)23-541-1768

Solara ⓐ

Small-scale winegrowing at certified-organic McGregor farm Houtbaai, bought in 2003 by former entrepreneur Pat Werdmuller von Elgg and son Otto as an animal rehabilitation centre, has been invigorated by a new partnership with Arendsig co-owner/winemaker Lourens van der Westhuizen. Nonagenarian Pat's strong-held views on sustainable farming are being married with Lourens' focus on single vineyards, an initial sauvignon to be followed by other varieties planted on the estate, which can be toured by appointment.

Location: McGregor ▪ Map: Robertson ▪ Map grid reference: D6 ▪ Est 2004 ▪ 1stB 2014 ▪ Tasting by appt at Arendsig Wines (see entry) & Grape De-Vine Wine Bar, McGregor ▪ Farm tour by prior arrangement ▪ Owner(s) Pat & Otto Werdmuller Von Elgg ▪ Winemaker(s) Lourens van der Westhuizen (Arendsig) ▪ 27.556ha/10.52ha (ptage, cbard, sauv) ▪ 8-10t/ha 1,100cs own label 100% white ▪ IPW, SGS/Lacon Organic, WIETA ▪ PO Box 181 McGregor 6708 ▪ houtbaai@breede.co.za ▪ www.solarawines.co.za ▪ S 33° 57' 37.17 E 019° 48' 57.79 ▪ ⌖ fanfare.choppers.ostensibly ▪ T +27 (0)23-625-1867

☐ **Soleil de Karoo** *see* Karusa Premium Wines & Craft Brewery
☐ **Solidus** *see* Claime d'Or

Solitary Wine (NEW)

After taking over family winegrowing farm Karibib in Stellenbosch's Polkadraai Hills in 2010, then Warwick winemaker Jozua Joubert minted his Solitary single-vineyard wines in 2014, currently comprising a small bottling of sauvignon and pinot noir he markets via social media. Having inherited some 52 ha of mature vines (including 32-year-old chenin), he strives for minimalist, intense wines from the farm's granitic soils. **Morning Bell Pinot Noir** ★★★★ Minimalist winemaking to reflect the granite soils, Polkadraai Hills climate, as next. Natural ferment, 10 months in barrel, **16** ⑧④ has lovely typicity, plush berries, some forest floor, lead pencils, briskly underpinned by acidity, giving freshness & ageability. **Owl House Sauvignon Blanc** ★★★★ Lees contact rather than oak infusion the objective in **17** ⑧⑤, just 30% barrel contact, gooseberry flavours, good palate weight & racy saline acidity keeping it fresh, on point. — CR, CvZ

Location/WO: Stellenbosch ▪ Est/1stB 2014 ▪ Closed to public ▪ Owner(s) Jozua Joubert ▪ Cellarmaster(s)/ winemaker(s) Jozua Joubert (Jun 2014) ▪ Viticulturist(s) Jozua Joubert (Oct 2010) ▪ 56ha/52ha (cab, pinot, chenin, sauv) ▪ 7t/ha 500cs own label 40% red 60% white ▪ PO Box 81 Kuils River 7579 ▪ jozua@solitary-wine.co.za ▪ www.solitarywine.co.za ▪ T +27 (0)82-336-3370

Solms-Delta ⓐ ⓑ

Sadly, this ground-breaking wine venture, a three-way collaboration between local neuroscientist Mark Solms, British philanthropist Richard Astor and staff on a trio of Franschhoek farms represented by the Wijn de Caab Trust was facing liquidation as this edition went to print, following withdrawal of state funding supporting a 50% personnel shareholding which failed to solve growing financial problems. No 2018 wines had been released, a handful of '15s were available and others discontinued, with new winemaker Gustav Fouche and viticulturist Joan Heatlie holding the fort. Mark's original vision saw derelict vineyards and buildings transformed, exciting wines launched in 2004, and the historic role of long-marginalised winelands workers celebrated at a cultural hub offering traditional cuisine, music, a museum and archaeological site.

Terroir Collection

★★★★ **Grenache** ⓥ Lovely red fruit purity in judiciously oaked **15** ⑧⑦ from Piekenierskloof, small tank-portion to preserve freshness. Has balance, elegance & grace, Old World subtlety. Fine example.

★★★★ **Verdelho-Roussanne** ⓥ Voor Paardeberg fruit, 14 months oak, **15** ⑧⑥ something different; green fruits & pear, slight stonefruit, brushed with oak's biscuit flavours. Everything deliciously in sync. Not tasted: **Syrah**.

Heritage Collection

★★★★☆ **Amalie** ⓥ Grenache blanc, chenin & 2 others fermented/aged combo barrel, concrete 'eggs', **15** ⑨③'s palate weight from year on lees. Bone-dry, complex layers stonefruit & thatch, toasted almonds. Classic, individual, assured.

Hiervandaan ⓥ ★★★☆ Grenache with shiraz, dab cinsaut in **15** ⑧③ preview. Wild berries, maraschino cherries in light texture, succulent, nice firm finish. Not tasted: **Africana**, **Gemoedsrus**. Discontinued: **Koloni**.

Lifestyle Collection

Cape Jazz Shiraz ⓥ ★★★ The name says it all, made for convivial occasions. Packaged as a bubbly, pétillant **NV** ⑦⑧ friendly alcohol (10%), bright red berry tones, the froth offsetting sweetness. Not tasted: **Shiraz**, **Rosé**, **Chenin Blanc**. — CR

Location/map: Franschhoek ▪ Map grid reference: C5 ▪ WO: Western Cape/Piekenierskloof ▪ 1stB 2004 ▪ Tasting & sales daily 9-5 ▪ Owner(s) Solms & Astor Family Trusts and Wijn de Caab Workers' Trust ▪ Winemaker(s) Gustav Fouche, with Joan Heatlie (Aug 2012) ▪ Viticulturist(s) Joan Heatlie (Apr 2016, consultant) ▪ 78ha/33ha (grenache n/b, mourv, ptage, shiraz, chenin, macabeo, muscat de F, rouss, viog) ▪ 370t/80,000cs own label 63% red 33% white 4% rosé ▪ IPW, WIETA ▪ PO Box 123 Groot Drakenstein 7680 ▪ info@solms-delta.co.za ▪ www.solms-delta.co.za ▪ S 33° 51' 51.0" E 018° 59' 23.8" ▪ ✉ redeemer.burners. riverside ▪ F +27 (0)21-874-1852 ▪ **T +27 (0)21-874-3937**

Somerbosch Wines   ⓥ 🍴 ⓞ Ⓐ ⓖ

The name reflects the location of the Roux family farm exactly halfway between Somerset West and Stellenbosch. 'We'd like customers to have as much fun drinking our wines as we have making them,' say brothers Marius and Japie, now also brewing craft beer in partnership with the Finest Hops Brewing Co.

Somerbosch range

★★★★ **Kylix** ⓥ Flagship blend has merlot's ripe plum/fruitcake notes, complexity from cab (cigarbox) & shiraz (pepper) with some oak-derived mocha. **13** ⑧⑥ alcohol almost 15%.
Cabernet Sauvignon ★★★ Sweet ripe black & red fruit on **15** ⑧⓪, only 50% wooded in older French oak, lusciously but not very persistent. **Merlot** ★★★ Youthful **16** ⑦⑦ needs time for tart fruit to integrate with sweeter wood notes (seasoned oak, 50% American, as most of the reds). **15** to be released later. **Shiraz** ★★★ Smooth **16** ⑧② full of ripe plum & blackberry fruit, hints of leather & baking spice, warmth from 15% alcohol at end. **Shiraz-Merlot** ★★★ Medium-bodied **17** ⑧⓪ an equal partnership, very fruity with berry cordial intensity & vanilla whiffs. **Rosé** ★★★ Creamy **17** ⑦⑧ less sweet than expected from cherry aroma & 16.5 g/l sugar. **Chardonnay** ★★★ Lovely freshness to unwooded **17** ⑧⓪, packed with lemon & lime flavour, dry grapefruit finish. Walker Bay vines. **Chenin Blanc** ★★★ Fruit salad flavours in **18** ⑦⑨ preview, promising easy drinking when bottled. **Sauvignon Blanc** ★★★ Granny Smith apple & lime on crisp, dry, zingy **18** ⑦⑨ tank sample. **Sauvignon Blanc-Semillon** ★★★ Pre-bottling, unoaked 50/50 blend refreshes, with lingering mineral tone on clean finish. **18** ⑧② quite smooth despite zestiness. **Méthode Cap Classique Brut** ★★★★ Underlying chalkiness to latest **NV** ⑧③ sparkling, 100% chardonnay from Elgin fruit gives sherbetty citrus & green apple profile. **Late Bottled Vintage Port** ★★★ From cab, aged 2 years in old barrels, latest **NV** ⑧① is decadently sweet with spiced fruitcake richness. Not tasted: **Pinotage**.

Poker Hill range

Not tasted: **Shiraz-Merlot**, **Semillon-Chenin Blanc**. — JG

Location: Stellenbosch ▪ Map: Helderberg ▪ Map grid reference: C1 ▪ WO: Stellenbosch/Western Cape ▪ Est 1950 ▪ 1stB 1995 ▪ Tasting & sales daily 9–5 ▪ Fee R30/6 wines, waived on purchase of any 3 btls; R55pp/ice cream & red wine tasting ▪ Closed Dec 25 ▪ Cellar tours by appt ▪ Somersbosch Bistro: breakfast & lunch daily ▪ Facilities for children ▪ Farm produce ▪ Conferences ▪ Craft beer ▪ Owner(s) Somersbosch Wines cc ▪ Cellarmaster(s)/winemaker(s)/viticulturist(s) Marius & Japie Roux (both 1995) ▪ 55ha/43ha (cab, merlot, shiraz, sauv) ▪ 350t 55% red 45% white ▪ PO Box 12181 Die Boord 7613 ▪ enquiries@somersbosch.co.za, sales@somersbosch.co.za ▪ www.somersbosch.co.za ▪ S 34° 0′ 28.6″ E 018° 49′ 6.9″ ▪ sayings.realists.clinic ▪ F +27 (0)21-855-4457 ▪ **T +27 (0)21-855-3615**

Somerset Wines

Owned by Boetie Rietoff, an industry stalwart with over 40 years' experience, Somerset Wines is a national sales, marketing and distribution company with a healthy selection of SA's best-loved wine, brandy, spirit and ready-to-drink labels. These are Boetie's own value-for-money ranges, made by Pieter-Niel Rossouw of Darling Cellars with another wine veteran, consultant Jeff Wedgwood.

Lord Somerset range

Merlot-Cabernet Sauvignon ⊘ ★★★ Equal blend in **17** ⑦ easy-drinker. Red berries & cream nuances, tiny tug of tannin for interest, food. **Sauvignon Blanc** ⊘ ★★★ Wallet-friendly **18** ⑦, grassy aroma, figgy flavour & lively acidity true to variety, but brief. **Soft Smooth Red** ★★ Relaxed summer quaffing delivered by light-textured **NV** ⑦, with medley lively red/black fruits, few grams smoothing sugar. Not tasted: **Cabernet Sauvignon**, **Shiraz**, **Chenin Blanc**.

Lady Somerset range

Sweet Red ⊘ ★★★ Attractive ripe plum perfume & sweetness, latest **NV** ⑦ greater vinosity than usual with 13.7% alcohol versus ±9%. **Sparkling Blush** ★★★ Pale pink **NV** ⑦ fizz is mostly chenin, frothy & light at under 8% alcohol, whispers of strawberry & raspberry. **Natural Sweet White** ★★ Grapey & fresh **NV** ⑦ has light 10.8% alcohol upping the appeal. Not tasted: **Stylish Elegant Red**, **Crisp Dry White**, **Natural Sweet Rosé**. — CvZ

Location: Somerset West ▪ Map: Helderberg ▪ Map grid reference: E6 ▪ WO: Western Cape ▪ Est 2010 ▪ 1stB 2011 ▪ Tasting & sales Mon-Fri 9-5 Sat 9-1 ▪ Closed all pub hols ▪ Tour groups ▪ Wine shop ▪ Owner(s) Boetie Rietoff ▪ Winemaker(s) Pieter-Niel Rossouw (Darling Cellars) & Jeff Wedgwood (consultant) ▪ 200,000cs 80% red 20% white ▪ PO Box 2240 Somerset West 7129 ▪ orders@swdirect.co.za ▪ www.swdirect.co.za ▪ S 34° 6′ 12.27″ E 018° 51′ 25.83″ ▪ believer.starting.actors ▪ **T +27 (0)21-851-0734/+27 (0)21-852-5473**

Somfula Wines

Swartland-based Bongi Somfula's dream of owning an oeno-brand recognised locally and overseas was kindled while working as a wine label designer in Cape Town. At press time she was sourcing new vintages for festive season release.

Location: Riebeek West ▪ Est/1stB 2009 ▪ Tasting by appt ▪ Closed Easter Fri/Sun/Mon, Dec 25/26 & Jan 1 ▪ Owner(s) Nokubonga Somfula ▪ 60% red 20% white 20% rosé ▪ c/o PO Box 1 Riebeek West 7306 ▪ info@somfulawine.co.za ▪ www.somfulawine.co.za ▪ F +27 (0)86-293-3443 ▪ **T +27 (0)79-464-0204**

☐ **Sonance** see United Nations of Wine

Sonklip Wine

Stellenbosch engineer and vintner Frik Kirsten produces just 200 cases of wine annually, which makes his artisan Sonklip among the Cape's smallest commercial labels. The focus is on red wine, and an old Frik favourite, malbec, features this edition in a new, creditable and different take on Cape Bordeaux.

★★★★ **Single Barrel Selection** ⓝ Liquorice detail, spice-infused plum & cherry on **16** ⑧⑥ malbec (80%) & petit verdot. Marked acidity but well-judged tannin, commendable dryness & satisfaction at just 12% alcohol. Also in magnum, as Special Red.

Special Red Blend ⓝ ★★★★ Polished Bordeaux trio cab, malbec, petit verdot (50/30/20) shows serious intent in **16** ⑧⑤. Vibrant, involving, vanilla overlay to dark berries & slightly elevated acidity. Bottelary grapes, like Single Barrel. **Shiraz-Mourvèdre** ⓥ ★★★★ Vanilla, milk chocolate notes from older oak on **14** ⑧④. Sleek, slips down easily, ends fresh. Not tasted: **Malbec-Cabernet Sauvignon**. — CvZ

Location/map: Stellenbosch ▪ Map grid reference: G5 ▪ WO: Coastal ▪ 1stB 2009 ▪ Tasting & cellar tours by appt ▪ Owner(s)/winemaker(s) Frik Kirsten ▪ 200cs own label 100% red ▪ PO Box 6198 Uniedal 7612 ▪ frik. kirsten@gmail.com ▪ S 33° 56′ 3.55″ E 018° 53′ 44.95″ ▪ ⦿ basin.dart.scooter ▪ F +27 (0)21-887-5869 ▪ **T +27 (0)21-887-5869**

☐ **Sonop** see Jacques Germanier

Sophie & Mr P

This range is from Iona – who take it very seriously, despite light-hearted labels on the screwcapped bottles. Mr P comes from pinot noir on an Elgin farm owned by Iona, while Sophie Te'blanche (a local nickname for sauvignon blanc) is partly from own grapes, but also draws more widely from the Cape South Coast.

★★★★ **Mr P Pinot Noir** ⊘ Charming **17** ⑧⑥, beguiling aromas of dark fruit with a little forest floor. Only old oak, so it's fresh, light & pure as well as silky - but far from frivolous. From Elgin.

Sophie Te'blanche ★★★★ Undemonstrative & unshowy by sauvignon blanc's standards, but **17** ⑧③ fresh & pleasing, with good stonefruit & citrus, if not long-lingering. — TJ

Location: Elgin ▪ WO: Cape South Coast/Elgin ▪ Est/1stB 2009 ▪ Closed to public ▪ Owner(s) Andrew Gunn ▪ Cellarmaster(s) Werner Muller (May 2011) ▪ (pinot, sauv) ▪ 150t/20,000cs own label 90% white 10% rosé ▪ PO Box 527 Grabouw 7160 ▪ orders@sophie.co.za ▪ www.sophie.co.za ▪ F +27 (0)86-627-8960 ▪ **T +27 (0)28-284-9678**

☐ **Southern Cape Vineyards** see Barrydale Winery & Distillery

---

Southern Right   ⓠ ◎ ♿

Co-owner Anthony Hamilton Russell reports little change as the Hemel-en-Aarde Valley-based Southern Right brand marks its 25th anniversary — still with just two wines in its portfolio. And why change, when the style is hitting all the marks both at home and overseas, particularly in the US, where the Sauvignon Blanc is capitalising on shortages experienced in other parts of the globe. Anthony and winemaker Emul Ross continue to dial back on overt oak for the Pinotage, creating a purer-fruit style much enjoyed by their customers. The only lament is: there's not enough grapes to keep up with demand!

★★★★ **Pinotage** Fabulously spicy **17** ⑧⑦ entices with pepper, clove, cinnamon & cumin adding piquancy to ripe black plum & cherry. Upright tannins & charry finish suggest time needed to settle, meld.

★★★★ **Sauvignon Blanc** Flinty **18** ⑧⑧ shimmers with tangy, lean green fruit - lime, some lemon - in clean, fresh mouthful. 4 months lees add touch of creamy confection. No splash semillon this year.— CM

Location: Hermanus ▪ Map: Walker Bay & Bot River ▪ Map grid reference: A3 ▪ WO: Walker Bay ▪ Est 1994 ▪ 1stB 1995 ▪ Tasting & sales Mon-Fri 9-5 Sat 10-2 ▪ Cellar tours by appt ▪ Closed Easter Fri/Mon, Dec 25/26 & Jan 1 ▪ Fynbos reserve, renosterveld reserve & 3 wetlands ▪ Quad bike route ▪ Owner(s) Mark Willcox, Mikki Xayiya & Anthony Hamilton Russell ▪ Winemaker(s) Emul Ross (2014) ▪ Viticulturist(s) Johan Montgomery (2005) ▪ 447ha/±36ha (ptage, sauv) ▪ 225-280t/30-40,000cs own label 20% red 80% white ▪ PO Box 158 Hermanus 7200 ▪ info@southernright.co.za ▪ www.southernright.co.za ▪ S 34° 24′ 3.2″ E 019° 13′ 0.4″ ▪ ⦿ unduly.energetics.steamy ▪ F +27 (0)28-312-1797 ▪ **T +27 (0)28-312-3595**

Southern Sky Wines   ⓠ

Paarl negociant Andrew Milne focuses on red wine in the various ranges he markets, including Hawk's Head, Imagine, Marimba, Ready Steady and Tara Hill. He also provides a range of services, such as custom wine packaging, bulk-wine sourcing, and brand development and positioning consulting.

Location/map: Paarl ▪ Map grid reference: E6 ▪ Est/1stB 2002 ▪ Tasting & sales by appt ▪ Owner(s) Andrew Milne ▪ Winemaker(s) Andrew Milne (Jan 2003) ▪ 10,000cs own label 95% red 5% white ▪ PO Box 1312 Paarl 7624 ▪ andrew@ssw.co.za ▪ www.ssw.co.za ▪ S 33° 45′ 8.78″ E 018° 57′ 42.55″ ▪ ⦿ elaborate.client.boating ▪ **T +27 (0)21-863-4440**

South Hill Vineyards   ⓠ ⑪ ⌂ ◎ ♿

This Elgin farm was converted from neglected apple and pear orchards to grapes (plus a whole range of other attractions) early this century. It's owned by Kevin King, whose family's names feature in the eponymous range. Sean Skibbe deftly crafts the rather elegant, dry wines. From the 2019 vintage ('if all goes well!'), he'll be taking the black grapes into the newly built on-site red-wine production and storage facility.

South Hill range

★★★★ Cabernet Sauvignon Ripe, pure varietal character with a herbal twist on **16** ⑧. Prominent tannins in youth. Warming 15.1% alcohol, but saved from over-boldness by modest oaking. **15** untasted.

★★★★ Syrah Spicy, bright aromas on **16** ⑧ lead to well-built, youthful palate. Only older oak maturation, leaving sweet fruit flavours clean & clear. Good dry finish.

★★★★ Sauvignon Blanc Reliably focused & fresh, **18** ⑧ crisp & dry, with pleasing mix of tropical & grassy character, modest intensity of flavour & palate weight, fine natural acidity. **17** untasted.

Rosé ★★★★ Spicy, fresh & fruity-savoury character on pale pink-red **18** ⑧ from undisclosed varieties. Bone-dry for crisp, light elegance. Not tasted: **Pinot Noir**.

Kevin King range

★★★★ BBK ⓥ From malbec, **15** ⑧ richly fruity (including typical loganberry), but retrained & not without elegance, thanks to a fresh acid succulence & dry finish. Older oak. Most attractive.

★★★★ Micah Unusual blend half shiraz with mourvèdre & barbera, **15** ⑧ with ripe, fairly fruity & pure aromas & palate. Firmly structured, touch of sweetness on finish abetted by 14.5% alcohol. A serious but friendly wine. Last tasted was **13** ⑧.

★★★★ Bassey ⓥ Sauvignon leads semillon in older-oaked **15** ⑧ blend, but latter's wax & lemon dominant in youth, though lifted by grass & blackcurrant notes. Fresh, softly silky & well balanced.— TJ

Location/map/WO: Elgin ▪ Map grid reference: C3 ▪ Est 2001 ▪ 1stB 2006 ▪ Tasting Mon-Sun 10-4 ▪ The Gallery @ South Hill (original artworks) ▪ South Hill Restaurant open daily for breakfast & lunch ▪ The Guest House & Pumphouse Cottage ▪ Function venue for conferences & weddings ▪ Conservation area ▪ Owner(s) South Hill Vineyards (Pty) Ltd ▪ Winemaker(s) Sean Skibbe (Jun 2005) ▪ Viticulturist(s) Kevin Watt (Jun 2015, consultant) ▪ 57ha/28ha (cab, pinot, shiraz, chard, riesling, sauv, sem, viog) ▪ 130t/7,000cs own label 20% red 80% white ▪ PO Box 120 Elgin 7180 ▪ info@southhill.co.za ▪ www.southhill.co.za ▪ S 34° 14' 6.22" E 019° 6'32.77" ▪ ⓜ bubbly.disbanding.unloading ▪ F +27 (0)86-530-4065 ▪ **T +27 (0)21-844-0888**

Spekulasie ⓥ ⑪

Swartland-based Johan and Linza Louw founded a boutique winemaking venture on their large dryland bushvine estate, Spekulasie, between Malmesbury and Darling, more than a decade ago, naming the wines after celebrated family members. Sadly, for economic reasons, the couple are no longer producing but do have stock of recent vintages of De Pieterzoon red blend, De Beatrix shiraz and The Elizabeth rosé for tasting and sale, and continue to welcome visits by appointment.

Location: Malmesbury ▪ Map: Swartland ▪ Map grid reference: A6 ▪ Est 2008 ▪ 1stB 2010 ▪ Tasting, sales & cellar tours Mon-Sat/pub hols by appt ▪ Fee R50pp ▪ Light meals & refreshments by appt only ▪ Owner(s)/ cellarmaster(s) Johan & Linza Louw ▪ Winemaker(s) Linza Louw ▪ Sensory specialist Leanie Louw ▪ PO Box 173 Malmesbury 7299 ▪ spekulasie@cornergate.com ▪ www.spekulasie-wines.co.za ▪ S 33° 23'23.43" E 018° 35'7.58" ▪ ⓜ bazaars.relative.bedsides ▪ **T +27 (0)82-559-6066/+27 (0)72-375-7078**

☐ **Spencer Bay** see Namaqua Wines
☐ **Spes Bona** see Mooiuitsig Wine Cellars

Spice Route Winery ⓥ ⑪ ◎ ⓖ

Creditworthy as catalyst for the Swartland as source of terroir-based, new-wave Mediterranean-style wines, and of stellar rehabilitated-old-vine vinifications, Fairview's Charles Back (and partners he later bought out) established Spice Route in the late 1990s. Originally homed in a derelict tobacco shed among vineyards on Klein Amoskuil farm, Spice Route now also has a public presence at the Spice Route Destination on Paarl Mountain. Long-standing winemaker Charl du Plessis' standout creations include a flor 'sherry' from very old sauvignon vines, and share space with delicacies and items of beauty crafted by fellow artisans.

★★★★ Terra de Bron Swartland Carignan ⓥ Winemaker Charl du Plessis' favourite grape, **14** ⑧'s enticing perfume of dried flower & spice nicely complemented by savoury & smoky notes, nimble tannins.

★★★★☆ **Grenache** (ⓐ) Strikingly pristine berry fruit, supple body on **16** (93) make for pure drinking pleasure. Poised & lithe, charmingly approachable, showcasing Swartland's affinity with Mediterranean varieties. 15 months older French oak.

★★★★ **Terra de Bron Swartland Grenache** (②) Limited release from single block of dryland bushvines. **15** (88) dark fruit & Xmas spice with hints of tobacco & salami, all encased in chewy tannins, herbs & white pepper on the farewell.

★★★★ **Mourvèdre** (②) **14** (87)'s savouriness reprised in **15** (87), along with dark fruit & spice; nice friendly tannins from 14 months seasoning in French & American barrels. From low-yield bushvines.

★★★★ **Terra de Bron Swartland Mourvèdre** (②) Dusty mulberry fruit on previewed **12** (88), great integration of supple tannins already, with touches of cured meat & lavender to add to complexity.

★★★★ **Pinotage** Impressively rounded & balanced, with sweet cherry fruit, **17** (88) from single home-farm bushvine vineyard is juicy, generous, yet restrained. Vanilla notes from year American oak.

★★★★☆ **Chakalaka** (ⓐ) Piquant & bold, as the name (a local blend of spices) suggests, eclectic 6-variety Rhône-leaning **15** (94) blend is opulently fruity, succulently supple. Shades of biltong, cloves & pepper add punch to dense plum pudding core.

★★★★☆ **Malabar** (ⓐ) Brilliant syrah-driven blend with mourvèdre, petite sirah & carignan has depth, detail & elegance in **15** (93). Supple & succulent, exemplifying its conducive terroir, unfurling layers of spice, cherry fruit, herbal scrub & tobacco.

★★★★☆ **Chenin Blanc** Enticing melon & peach on restrained **17** (92), with fruit to the fore, subtle minerality balancing & broadening the palate. Poised & measured, master-handled to express Swartland terroir. Portion fermented & 9 months in older barrels.

★★★★ **Sauvignon Blanc** Grassy, stony & unmistakeably West Coast, **17** (89) grippy & aromatic, offering ripe gooseberry fruit with harmonious acid, grassy notes & satisfying length. Darling WO. **16** untasted.

★★★★ **The Amos Block Sauvignon Blanc** (②) (❀) From oldest sauvignon block in SA, **17** (88) alluring greengage, apple & mineral freshness enhanced by brisk acidity & mineral-tropical tail. No **16**.

★★★★ **Viognier** Luscious yellow peach introduction to **17** (89), with sweet perfumed highlights & tingling acidity to balance the generously full, leesy body. Fermented & 10 months in old French barrels.

★★★★ **The Amos Block Perpetual Reserve Under Flor** (②) Sherry-style **NV** (87) ('14-'16) from sauvignon, matured under flor with gentle alcohol strength (15%). Signature nutty character with dried fig & apple accents, dry & elegant. Serve well-chilled.

Not tasted: **Terra de Bron Darling Syrah**, **Terra de Bron Swartland Syrah**, **Saffron Rosé**, **Terra de Bron Darling Semillon**. — GdB

Location: Malmesbury/Paarl ▪ Map: Paarl ▪ Map grid reference: D6 ▪ WO: Swartland/Darling ▪ Tasting & sales Mon-Sun 9-5, last tasting 30min before closing ▪ Standard/master tasting (applicable fees apply) ▪ Closed Dec 25 & Jan 1 ▪ Bertus Basson Restaurant ▪ Red Hot Glass Studio ▪ DV Artisan Chocolate Roastery & Espresso Bar ▪ Barley & Biltong Emporium ▪ Brenda's Deli ▪ Richard Bosman's ▪ The Trading Company ▪ The Barn Artist Studio ▪ Wilderer's Distillery & La Grapperia Restaurant ▪ Cape Brewing Company ▪ Owner(s) Charles Back ▪ Winemaker(s) Charl du Plessis (Dec 2001), with Licia Solomons (Jan 2006) ▪ 90ha (barbera, carignan, grenache, mourv, petite sirah, ptage, sangio, shiraz, tannat, chenin, rouss, sauv, sem, viog) ▪ 60% red 40% white ▪ Fairtrade, HACCP, IPW, WIETA ▪ PO Box 583 Suider-Paarl 7624 ▪ info@spiceroute.co.za ▪ www.spiceroutewines.co.za ▪ S 33° 45' 50.5" E 018° 55' 9.7" ▪ 🖷 jarring.chills.pavers ▪ **T +27 (0)21-863-5200**

Spier   (ⓟ)(🍴)(🏠)(◎)(🛇)(♿)

This Stellenbosch visitor mecca, among ancient oaks and 17th-century Cape Dutch architecture on the Enthoven family's riverside estate, combines winegrowing and eco-tourism with sustainable agriculture and community development. New attractions include the Artisan Studio, offering mosaic/ceramic apprentice training and retail opportunities, and Spier Farm Kitchen and Vadas Smokehouse & Bakery, both using organically grown, ethically sourced produce. On the wine side are the inaugural releases from the certified-organic boutique wine cellar (vinifying home-grown grapes only; the main cellar selects parcels far and wide for cellarmaster Frans Smit and his quality-driven team). Note, too, the new Growing for Good icon on all wine labels, alerting customers to Spier's staff and community empowerment initiatives.

Frans K. Smit range

★★★★★ **CWG Auction Reserve Frans K. Smit 20 Year Celebration** ⊛ Fine **15** ★★★★★ ⑨④ blend has great concentration, detailed fruit core with iodine & tarry liquorice, showing finesse & nobility. Equal parts cab, cab franc & merlot in harmony, as is 100% new oak & 15% alcohol. Natural ferment. Last CWG parcel was linear & lean **13** ⑨⑧.

★★★★☆ **Frans K. Smit Red** ⊛ Flagship maintains lofty standards in **13** ⑨③, with plush, silky texture, concentrated blackberry & black cherry core tinged with tobacco. Cab & merlot (49/35), cab franc, shiraz blend spent 29 months in new French oak. Like CWG version, good for decade or more.

★★★★☆ **Frans K. Smit White** ⊛ Quintessential Bordeaux styling on **16** ⑨④ sauvignon & semillon blend 70/30: dusty pebbles, lanolin, figs & salty notes on finish. Lean, lithe & focused, yet rounded & textural. Fermented & 11 months in various sized oak, 40% new. WO Coastal.

21 Gables range

★★★★☆ **Cabernet Sauvignon** ⊛ Aristocratic expression of variety, **15** ⑨④ benefits from fine vintage. Dense, intense & complex, with myriad mineral nuances, rich blackcurrant fruit & heady truffle notes. Muscular but supple, begging for time in cellar. Helderberg vines.

★★★★☆ **Pinotage** ⊛ Bold, assertive **16** ⑨① has massive black fruit, robust tannins & serious appeal. Tempered notes of mocha & mint, floral & roasted nut highlights. Impressive now, but promises bright future. Southern Stellenbosch vineyards. Also in 1.5L, like Cab.

★★★★☆ **Chenin Blanc** ⊛ Imposing fruit shines through oaking (60% new) on **17** ★★★★★ ⑨⑤, peach, apricot & pineapple among others. Sumptuously dense, richness from 12-14 months on lees; offers fine drinking now but promising more with time. One vineyard in Cape Town WO. **16** ⑨③ widely sourced.

★★★★☆ **Sauvignon Blanc** Power & subtlety in fine balance, ripe gooseberry & granadilla fruit on excellent **18** ⑨② tank sample from single WO Cape Town block. Dusty floral aromas, steely mineral notes, lengthy & focused finish.

Creative Block range

★★★★☆ **Five** ⊘ ⊛ Precise, sculpted **15** ⑨③ 5-way Bordeaux blend led by cab & merlot shows great form. Velvet tannins cosset dense blackcurrant core woven with iodine & anise, earthy minerality guiding the finish. WO Coastal, as all these.

★★★★ **Eight** Allsorts pinotage-led **16** ⑧⑨ Cape Blend is plush & charming, with gentle tannins, spicy berry fruit & richly aromatic highlights. Full & generous, ripe & accessible.

★★★★☆ **Three** ⊘ Mostly shiraz with dashes mourvèdre, viognier, **15** ⑨⓪ is generously ripe & expressive, with meaty, savoury & wild scrub, spiced with hints of pepper. Seductively smooth & rich. Fruit from Groeneloof & Stellenbosch. **14** ★★★★ ⑧⑨ was denser.

★★★★ **Two** Stylish sauvignon (88%) & semillon blend, **18** ⑧⑦ is virtually unwooded, big on flavour & aromatic lift. Appealingly full gooseberry fruit, lengthy finish.

Farm House Organic range

★★★★★ **Rosé** ⓃⒺⓌ ⊘ Seriously conceived, barrel-fermented dry **16** ⑨⓪ from shiraz has charm & gravitas - & stellar quality. Rich & leesy, with brioche notes & plush texture, evolved berry compote fruit profile lightly spiced by older oak. Light year from your usual party pink.

★★★★★ **Chenin Blanc** ⓃⒺⓌ ⊘ ⊛ Beautifully wrought small-batch offering from recent dedicated organic cellar in the historic farm cluster. Seasoned-barrel-fermented **16** ⑨⑤ shows artisanal touch with rich textural lees influence, layered complexity of fruit & minerality, subtly nuanced finish.

Occasional release: **Straw Wine**.

Organic range ⓃⒺⓌ

★★★★☆ **First Stone** ⊘ ⊛ Muscular but lithe **15** ⑨② merlot-cab is impossibly dense, with massive ripe tannins, inky opacity. Pure, concentrated blackcurrant fruit needs time to emerge & knit, but shows great potential.

Yellow Wood Red ⊘ ★★★★ Oak spices pervade juicy **16** ⑧⑤ merlot-cab blend, with cassis & tobacco underpin. Thick tannins, somewhat fleeting finish. Coastal WO. **Yellow Wood Rosé** ⊘ ★★★★ Weighty, seriously handled dry **18** ⑧④ has leesy richness, convincing redcurrant fruit. 5% barrel-fermented portion.

Ideology range

Merlot Rosé (NEW) ★★★★ Light, elegant, tinsel-pink 18 ⑧⑤ from Cape Agulhas vines avoids the clichés, offering oystershell salty-mineral tones with floral-imbued dry fruit flavours. Occasional release: **Wild Ferment Pinotage**, **Rhône Blend**, **Chardonnay-Pinot Noir**, **Chenin Blanc**, **Sauvignon Blanc**.

Signature range

★★★★ **Méthode Cap Classique** Classically shaped 15 ⑧⑥ sparkling from chardonnay (57%) & pinot noir has lime-mineral core with shortbread, brisk mousse & appealing spicy baked apple fruit. 10% barrel fermented. Stellenbosch WO, rest W Cape.

. . . .

Chenin Blanc ⊘ ⑦ ★★★★ Cheerfully fruit-driven, 18 ⑧④ delivers a feast of tropical flavours. Fine acid edge adds to easy-drinking appeal. **Sauvignon Blanc** ⊘ ⑦ ★★★★ Generous gooseberry & granadilla fruit on overtly ripe 18 ⑧⑤. Tempered acidity, good breadth of palate. 10% semillon.

. . . .

Cabernet Sauvignon ★★★ Supple, fruit-driven 17 ⑧② delivers well at the price, with plummy red fruit, hints of varietal earthiness. 20% barrel matured. **Merlot** ⊘ ★★★★ Precise, authentic & approachable budget offering, 17 ⑧③ is true to form, with cassis & plum fruit. **Pinotage** ★★★ Dependable, superior everyday quaffing, 17 ⑧② ripe red primary fruit, savoury spices, soft texture. **Shiraz** ★★★ Variety-true 17 ⑧②, with lightish body, pepper & scrub spicing, measured tannins. 20% barrel aged. **Cabernet Sauvignon-Merlot-Shiraz** ★★★ Juicy black fruit with cherries & smoky twist, 17 ⑧② is a delightful end-of-day unwinder. **Chardonnay-Pinot Noir** ★★★ Pale salmon hue, floral notes, refreshing raspberry fruit on appealing, well-focused 18 ⑧② dry rosé. **Chardonnay** ⊘ ★★★★ Previewed 18 ⑧③ follows form: mostly tank fermented with 5% oaked fraction, delivering satisfying heft & texture, bright citrus fruit. McGregor & Windmeul vines.

Vintage Selection range

Not tasted: **Weisser Riesling**.

Discontinued: **Collaborative Series**. — GdB

Location/map: Stellenbosch ▪ Map grid reference: C7 ▪ WO: Stellenbosch/Western Cape/Coastal/Cape Town/Cape Agulhas ▪ Est 1692 ▪ 1stB 1770 ▪ Tasting & sales Mon-Sat 9-5 Sun 11-6 ▪ Tasting from R40 ▪ Facilities for children ▪ Tour groups ▪ Farm produce ▪ Picnics ▪ Conferences ▪ Manor House & Heritage Walk ▪ Spier Artisan Studio Stellenbosch ▪ Conservation area ▪ 4-star Spier Hotel ▪ Eight Restaurant, Farm Kitchen & Spier Hotel Restaurant ▪ Vadas Smokehouse & Bakery ▪ Owner(s) Enthoven family ▪ Cellarmaster(s) Frans Smit (Dec 1995) ▪ Winemaker(s) Johan Jordaan (reds, Jul 2007), Jacques Erasmus (whites, Apr 2007) & Tania Kleintjes (organic wine, Jan 2016) ▪ Wine procurement/winemaker(s) Johan de Villiers, Anton Swarts & Lizanne Jordaan ▪ Viticulturist(s) Johann Smit (Dec 1999) ▪ 650ha (barbera, cabs s/f, malbec, merlot, mourv, p verdot, ptage, shiraz, chard, chenin, sauv, sem, viog) ▪ 3,850t own label 65% red 31% white 3% rosé 1% MCC ▪ Fairtrade, FSSC 22000, IPW, Organic, WIETA, WWF-SA Conservation Champion ▪ PO Box 99 Lynedoch 7603 ▪ info@spier.co.za ▪ www.spier.co.za ▪ S 33° 58' 24.63" E 018° 47' 2.23" ▪ 🚗 induce.breathe.mufflers ▪ F +27 (0)21-809-1930 ▪ **T +27 (0)21-809-1100 (wine tasting)**

Spioenkop Wines ⓠ

The estate of Koen and Hannelore Roose-Vandenbroucke is increasingly well known for producing fine, fresh and characterful wines off unirrigated vines - a rare choice in Elgin, but part of Koen's uncompromising determination to make 'pure, tight and elegant terroir wines from our unique Spioenkop hill'. Two single-vineyard chenins have replaced the former blend, and now comes the first of the single-vineyard pinots. Another 2 ha of pinotage have been planted – 'high density and extremely steep... to keep the adrenaline flowing in our veins', says Koen. The new tasting venue we reported on last year has had some delays – but should be a completed 'glass room in the sky' by press time.

1900 range

★★★★☆ **Pinotage** (🐝) As usual, 17 ⑨③ one of the freshest, most elegant pinotages around, while especially the Stellenbosch fruit component gives great fruit character - aromatic, pure & flavourful. Good structuring acidity, firm & tight tannins, good oak support (33% new).

Spioenkop range

★★★★ **Ghandi** (🆕) The first of the single-vineyard pinot noirs to be released. Light fruit, but deeper than the blend, along with fungal & freshly tilled earth notes on **16** (89); bigger structure, silkier texture, more lingering. Natural ferment, 15% wholebunch. A promising debut.

★★★★ **Pinot Noir** From 3 quite young vineyards. **16** (87) light-feeling & bright, the fruit also modest but emerging as the wine gets air. Good balance with 13% alcohol, supportive oaking (25% new), tannin touch. Also in magnum.

★★★★☆ **Pinotage** Both sweeter-fruited & more austere than 1900 version; **17** (90) also made in a refined style with good acidity, but a touch less harmoniously proportioned in youth, the tannins drier (abetted by a little more new oak). A few years will bring out more charm.

★★★★☆ **Johanna Brandt** (🍃) Of the pair of estate chenins, this off shale. **17** (94) offers generous fruit aromas with floral & citric notes; broader than Sarah (11 months on lees in older barrels), but with penetrating 'mineral' acidity, intense & focused flavours, firm & effectively dry finish.

★★★★☆ **Sarah Raal** (🍃) Chenin off ferricrete soils. **17** ★★★★★ (95) nervy, fine aromas, with earthy-nutty notes. Excellent balance - acidity & sugar (subtle 6.6 g/l) higher than Johanna, but poised & integrated, entwined with intense flavour, for exultant fantail finish. 9 months on lees, 3 in oak. **16** (93) focused & tense.

★★★★☆ **Riesling** Thrilling peach complexity on **17** (91), with an early aromatic note of kerosene. Bone-dry, with good balance & texture, the fresh acidity integrated with concentrated fruit to lively, moreish effect. Should develop a good few years. Natural ferment.

★★★★ **Sauvignon Blanc** Released unusually mature. Developing aromas on **15** (87), hints of green bean as well as fig. Green rather than tropical flavours dominate well-textured but rather severe, acidic palate.— TJ

Location/map: Elgin ▪ Map grid reference: C4 ▪ WO: Elgin/Western Cape ▪ Est 2008 ▪ 1stB 2010 ▪ Tasting & sales Tue-Sat 9-4 ▪ Tasting fee R50pp, waived on purchase ▪ Pre-booking required for: tasting & cellar tour R75pp; speciality tasting, exclusive vineyard walk with winemaker R150pp ▪ Closed all pub hols ▪ Owner(s) Valuline 119 (Pty) Ltd, 5 shareholders ▪ Cellarmaster(s)/winemaker(s)/viticulturist(s) Koen Roose-Vandenbroucke (2008) ▪ ±47ha/10ha (ptage, pinot, chenin, riesling, sauv) ▪ 60t/8,000cs own label 63% red 37% white ▪ PO Box 340 Grabouw 7160 ▪ info@spioenkopwines.co.za ▪ www.spioenkopwines.co.za ▪ S 34° 14'14" E 019° 3'50" ▪ 🗺 bidders.costume.achiever ▪ **T +27 (0)21-859-1458/+27 (0)79-491-6613/+27 (0)72-440-2944**

Splattered Toad ⓥ

Now with refreshed label design, this easy-drinking range by Cape Point Vineyards debuted in our 2011 edition to help raise awareness for the Western Leopard Toad, a legally protected species endemic to Cape Town. Due to increased urbanisation, the amphibian's habitat and breeding success rate are under threat.

Shiraz ★★★ Was 'Syrah'. Floral aroma adds to easy-drinking appeal of **17** (82), smooth & fresh, the ripe berry fruit subtly spiced. WO W Cape, as next. **Sauvignon Blanc** (✓) ★★★★ Reliable as ever for everyday drinking, zesty **18** (85) has 15% chenin to plump out tropical fruit, moderate 12.5% alcohol. — JG

☐ **Splendidior 150** *see* Welgevallen Wines - Splendidior 150

Spookfontein Wines ⓥ 🍴 🏠 📷

There's a ghost, or so it's said, in the spring flowing through Spookfontein, the ca 1840 farm and 'fynbos heaven' purchased by Mike Davis, founder of Ocean Eyewear and Dragons Sports, as a weekend retreat. There are only 12 ha of vines, their grapes vinified with advice from neighbour Hannes Storm (Storm Wines). Vistas of Upper Hemel-en-Aarde Valley are among the allures of the architect-designed cellardoor.

★★★★ **Syrah** (🆕) Pepper abounds on **16** (87) from Hemel-en-Aarde Valley, basket pressed, naturally fermented, lightly oaked, unfined/filtered to spotlight vibrant dark plum, cherry & blackcurrant fruit.

★★★★ **Phantom** (ⓥ) Merlot-led **16** (87) Bordeaux blend gets structure from cab & freshness from cab franc (25% each), framing succulent dark fruit. More interesting than last-tasted **14** ★★★ (81).

★★★★☆ **Chardonnay** Ambient yeast fermented, gently oaked (25% new), **17** ⑳ more intense, complex & elegant than **16** ★★★★ ㊐. Nuttiness complements peach, pear & citrus fruit on creamy, textured palate with dry, lingering, mineral finish.

★★★★ **Sauvignon Blanc** Definite seaside salinity to **18** ㊆ pre-bottling, crisply dry yet shapely from 3 months on lees, fruit quite restrained but should open up. Hemel-en-Aarde Valley WO.

★★★★ **Full Moon** Unwooded equal sauvignon & semillon ex Hemel-en-Aarde Ridge nudges higher rating. **18** ㊈ fruity yet flinty, mouthwatering natural acidity promising long future.

Cabernet Sauvignon ⓥ ★★★☆ After 6-year gap, cab returns in **15** ㊄ with cassis & other ripe black fruit, also dark chocolate & liquorice from 20% new French oak. Soft tannins & fresh finish. **Cabernet Franc** ★★★★ Mint & subtle spice frame fresh raspberry in taut **16** ㊂, 14 months in French oak, 20% new. **Merlot** ⓥ ★★★★ Velvety **15** ㊄, rich fruitcake & choc-dipped cherry notes supported by dry tannins, oak well meshed. **Pinot Noir** ⓥ ★★★☆ Slight stalkiness on nose gives way to fragrant violets, **16** ㊂ quite lean but intensely flavoured with cranberry, strawberry & redcurrant; fresh finish. **Merlot Rosé** ★★ Tentatively rated **18** ㊅ early preview promises red berry & glacé cherry fruit, dry finish. Not tasted: **Noble Late Harvest.** Discontinued: **Méthode Cap Classique.** — JG

Location: Hermanus ▪ Map: Walker Bay & Bot River ▪ Map grid reference: B4 ▪ WO: Upper Hemel-en-Aarde Valley/Hemel-en-Aarde Valley/Hemel-en-Aarde Ridge ▪ Est 2000 ▪ 1stB 2004 ▪ Tasting & sales Mon-Sat 10-4.30 Sun/pub hols 10-4 ▪ Closed Dec 25/26 & Jan 1 ▪ Restaurant @ Spookfontein open for lunch ▪ Functions T +27 (0)73-067-7936 Vaughan ▪ Two self-catering guest cottages ▪ Conservation area ▪ Owner(s) Spookfontein Wines cc (Mike Davis) ▪ Winemaker(s) advised by Hannes Storm (2014) ▪ Viticulturist(s) Andries Gotze (Jan 2000) ▪ 313ha/±12ha (cabs s/f, merlot, pinot, chard) ▪ 50t/2,000cs own label 85% red 5% white 10% rosé ▪ PO Box 12031 Mill Str Cape Town 8010 ▪ admin@spookfontein.co.za ▪ www.spookfontein.co.za ▪ S 34° 21' 19.5" E 019° 17' 20.8" ▪ ⓜ quarterfinals.pieced.avenging ▪ T +27 (0)72-199-8774

Spotswood Wines   ⓥ

The Spotswood family moved from Polokwane in the north to a boutique property in Stellenbosch's Blaauwklippen Valley and bottled the first wine under their name just over a decade ago. Former chocolate production engineer Bill and son Nick chose a road less travelled in planting durif, but the locally rare French variety (aka petite sirah) has been a hit for them, latterly innovatively also as a dry rosé.

Durif ⓥ ★★★☆ From the cultivar also known as petite sirah. Very ripe **12** ㊃, with dark fruit & meaty aromas. Big & forthright, packed with flavour, but quite juicy, reined-in enough for hearty drinkability. **Shiraz** ⓥ ★★★ New bottling of **12** ㊁ more restrained than previous, but still very ripe, leading to unfreshness, though succulent. Big tannins & acid make for balance, if not harmony. **Durif Dry Rosé** ⓥ ★★★ 2nd bottling of unusual pink from durif (aka petite sirah), dry **17** ㊂ an individual, piquant, pomegranate-toned alternative to the generic strawberry/candyfloss styling of many SA rosés. **Chardonnay** ⓥ ★★★ Easygoing, lightly oaked **16** ㊁ made for early, undemanding pleasure, shows clean-cut varietal citrus profile. **Viognier** ★★★★ Trumpets variety's apricot & peach features, spice & whisper older oak add dimension. **18** ㊄ juicy, fresh & bone-dry. — DS

Location/map/WO: Stellenbosch ▪ Map grid reference: F7 ▪ Est 2007 ▪ 1stB 2008 ▪ Tasting & sales by appt ▪ Owner(s) Spotswood family ▪ Winemaker(s) Guy Webber (Jan 2012, consultant) & Gunter Schultz (consultant) ▪ Viticulturist(s) Bill Spotswood (Sep 2007) ▪ 7.05ha/3ha (durif, shiraz, chard, viog) ▪ 28t/3,000cs own label 56% red 19% white 25% rosé ▪ Suite 200 Private Bag X4 Die Boord 7613 ▪ spotswoodwines@gmail.com ▪ www.spotswoodwines.com ▪ S 33° 59' 2.0" E 018° 51' 35.0" ▪ ⓜ carry.enlarge.bashed ▪ F +27 (0)21-880-2893 ▪ T +27 (0)21-880-2893

Springfield Estate   ⓥ ⓐ

Present custodians of this family estate in Robertson, brother and sister Abrie and Jeanette Bruwer, believe that a good farmer is an observant one, and that good wine is grown not made. The land they and a team of dedicated staff farm is so unyielding, it takes strength and extreme effort to plant the vines, erect trellising and work organic material into the soil. But no-one baulks. It's this determination, coupled with a long-held minimalist mindset, that allows them to handcraft wine true to their motto: Made on Honour.

★★★★ **Whole Berry Cabernet Sauvignon** ⓐ Hallmark lighter styling than many SA cabs, elegantly fruit-filled **16** ㊇'s distinctive cassis tones lightly dusted with spice courtesy judicious oaking, third new.

★★★★☆ **The Work of Time** 4-way Bordeaux blend from old vines, ready-now **11** ⑳ graceful & under-stated, classic pencil shavings, tobacco & blackberries, melded yet still-firm tannin, enlivening acidity. Like **10** ★★★★ ㉘ & previous, unhurried winemaking: natural ferment, 2 years in oak, 4 in bottle.

★★★★☆ **Méthode Ancienne Chardonnay** Worth waiting for these occasional releases. **16** ★★★★ ㉖ first since **12** ㉑, lengthy 55-day wild ferment in larger oak (30% new) creates wonderfully opulent wine with blue-orange bouquet, tangerine palate, vanilla finish. Unfiltered/fined/stabilised.

★★★★ **Wild Yeast Chardonnay** ⊘ Ethereal purity, subtle minerality in refined **17** ★★★★★ ㉑, fermented naturally 60 days in tank. As confident & assured as **16** ㉘, but fresher lemongrass undertone, less honeyed mellowness.

★★★★ **Life From Stone Sauvignon Blanc** From 16-22 year old vines, **18** ㉙ flintier, less obviously herbaceous than sibling. Passionfruit characters, including the pithiness, temper feisty acidity.

★★★★ **Special Cuvée Sauvignon Blanc** Uncompromising & thrilling **18** ㉙, not-for-everyone assertive pea shoot tone & acidity. Mimics **17** ★★★★★ ㉚'s greenness, unusual for this more tropical wine. 27 year old vines on sandier soils vs sibling's quartz-dominated site.

Pinot Noir ★★★ Steep rocky outcrop planted with extreme 9,000 vines/ha. Cherry-hued **15** ㉒ nicely dry with gentle cherry fruit, medicinal lift. **Miss Lucy** ★★★★ Nickname for threatened Red Stumpnose, raising awareness for conservation. **18** ㉓ house's least expressive white but fresh, tasty, deliberately seafood-friendly. Sauvignon & 2 others. Not tasted: **Méthode Ancienne Cabernet Sauvignon**. — CvZ

Location/map/WO: Robertson ▪ Map grid reference: B5 ▪ Est/1stB 1995 ▪ Tasting & sales Mon-Fri 8-5 Sat 9-3 ▪ Closed Easter Fri/Sun, Dec 25 & Jan 1 ▪ Cellar tours by appt ▪ BYO picnic ▪ Owner(s) Bruwer family ▪ Cellarmaster(s)/viticulturist(s) Abrie Bruwer ▪ Winemaker(s) Abrie Bruwer, with Johan van Zyl ▪ 150ha (cabs s/f, merlot, p verdot, chard, sauv) ▪ IPW ▪ PO Box 770 Robertson 6705 ▪ wine@springfieldestate.com ▪ www.springfieldestate.com ▪ S 33° 50' 12.1" E 019° 54' 54.0" ▪ ⌖ cross.layover.pancake ▪ F +27 (0)23-626-3664 ▪ **T +27 (0)23-626-3661**

Springfontein Wine Estate

⑳ ⑪ ⌂ ⌾

From vintage 2019, wines from the Stanford estate owned by German former mining engineer Johst Weber with partners, family and friends will be certified organic, both cellar (Tariro Masayiti's domain) and vineyards (tended by Tariro's wife Hildegard Witbooi) receiving Ecocert approval. This, after years of converting to organic growing (using aids like fertilisers from local seafood waste) in the area's distinctive limestone-rich soils. The latter inspired a collection of wines named for famous rock songs, chenin and pinotage seen as present and future stars of not only this but Springfontein's other ranges too.

Limestone Rocks range

★★★★ **Child in Time** Brooding & intense **15** ㉘ is 85% petit verdot partially tamed by 15% pinotage. Densely packed black fruit, leathery tannins, tarry overtones. Not for the faint-hearted.

★★★★☆ **Whole Lotta Love** ㉛ Sophisticated **15** ㉜ pinotage-led Cape Blend with petit verdot, shiraz, delivers on vintage's promise. Lashings of ripe black fruit on taut, densely formed body, thick ripe tannins. Built to last.

★★★★☆ **Dark Side of The Moon** Alchemy in the cellar produces offbeat but charming barrel-fermented chenin, pinotage, chardonnay blend, combining skin contact with controlled oxidation, natural yeasts. **16** ⑳ sherried, nutty notes, convincing fruit, wild savoury spiciness, plumply rounded body. Certified as 'Alternative white'.

Gadda da Vida ★★★★ Pinotage with 15% petit verdot, **14** ㉕ has typical high-toned acidity, mulberry fruit, sweet caramel notes. Robust, full bodied.

Single Vineyard range

★★★★☆ **Jonathan's Ridge Pinotage** Big & bold **15** ★★★★ ㉘ exudes ripeness & power, shows high-toned notes through intense black fruit. Balance is challenged by spiky oak, thick tannins. Less complete & lithe than **14** ㉑. Registered single-vineyard, as next.

Jil's Dune Chenin Blanc ★★★★ Labours under powerful oak (11 months, 40% new), gallant peachy fruit peeking through. **16** ㉔ step down from riper, richer **15** ★★★★ ㉗.

Daredevils' Drums range

★★★★ **Bunches Broken Shiraz** Vine-dried grapes produce raisin-prune fruit profile on **16** (87), with appealing spiciness, commendably reined-in body. Characterful, with good length, velvet tannins.

★★★★ **Juices Untamed Chardonnay** Dense, textural **16** ★★★★☆ (90) emerges from natural ferment, 6 days skin contact & extended barrel ageing (15 months, 50% new) intact & complex. Evolved but focused quince/baked apple fruit with chiselled acidity, lingering finish. Notch up on **15** (87). Certified as 'Skin-macerated white'.

★★★★ **Skins Agleam Sauvignon Blanc** Radical techniques produce quirky, characterful **17** (87) 'orange wine': carbonic maceration 4 weeks, on skins 8 days, giving appealingly musty fruit profile, big tannic body. Improves on debut **16** ★★★★☆ (84).

★★★★ **Blushes Inverse** Barrel-fermented blanc from pinotage, **17** (86) has very appealing apricot & citrus zest fruit with leesy fatness, restrained oak. Rung up on **16** ★★★★☆ (84).

Mashes Extreme Cabernet Sauvignon ★★★★ Least successful of these experimental wines. Extended (11-week) skin maceration for **16** (84) yields plush, dense fruit but also raw tannins & exaggerated oak.

Terroir Selection

★★★★ **Pinotage** Succulently juicy **14** (87) is a big improvement on **13** ★★★ (81), with vibrant red fruit spiced by prominent oak. Ripely rounded body wrapped in velvet tannins could be cellared few years.

★★★★ **Chenin Blanc** Fruit-driven, generous **17** (88) offers inviting peach & pear whiffs, fine palate texture. Half older barrels, rest concrete 'eggs' maintain purity & focus, express limestone soils. **16** ★★★★ (84) less structured, intense.

★★★★☆ **Ikhalezi Noble Late Harvest** ⓦ Highly unusual but fascinating **09** (90) botrytis dessert from chenin spent a remarkable 7 years in oak acquiring deep brown colour & complex flavours. Incredibly sweet (372 g/l sugar) but with savoury/umami notes coming through on lengthy finish.

Ulumbaza range

Red of Springfontein ★★★★ Generous fruit, silky texture on **15** (84) blend of pinotage, shiraz, cab & merlot, with charred oak & vanilla from lengthy stay in barrel. **Pink of Springfontein** ★★ Merlot-pinotage **17** (75) dry rosé has thick mouthfeel, rather low in fruit flavour. **White of Springfontein** ★★★★ Reworked (unoaked) blend of sauvignon (32%) with equal semillon, pinotage & chardonnay improves on previous. **17** (83) rounded body, pleasant apple & pear fruit. — GdB

Location: Stanford ▪ Map: Walker Bay & Bot River ▪ Map grid reference: B5 ▪ WO: Walker Bay ▪ Est 1996 ▪ 1stB 2004 ▪ Wine Bar(n) @ Springfontein open daily 11-9: wine tasting & sales; bits & bites (wine pairing with small warm/cold dishes); dry-aged steaks on selected evenings from 5 ▪ Springfontein Eats fine dining ▪ Cellar tours ▪ Walking/hiking trail ▪ Springfontein Sleeps lodging ▪ Olive oil ▪ Fynbos vermouth ▪ Owner(s) Johst Weber, with Tariro Masayiti, Hildegard Witbooi, family & friends ▪ Cellarmaster(s) Tariro Masayiti (Jan 2013) ▪ Winemaker(s) Tariro Masayiti, with Fikile Pike (Feb 2017) ▪ Viticulturist(s) Hildegard Witbooi (Oct 2013) ▪ 500ha/30ha (cab, merlot, p verdot, ptage, shiraz, chard, chenel, chenin, sauv, sem) ▪ 120t/15,000cs own label 75% red 23% white 2% rosé ▪ Certified organic by Ecocert (vyds & cellar) ▪ PO Box 71 Stanford 7210 ▪ info@springfontein.co.za ▪ www.springfontein.co.za ▪ S 34° 25′ 38.5″ E 019° 24′ 32.7″ ▪ 🆆 calories. restricts.brotherly ▪ **T +27 (0)28-341-0651 Office/+27 (0)28-341-0571 Eats/+27 (0)28-341-0651 Wine Bar(n)**

Spring Grove Wines ⓦ

Banhoek's Spring Grove, originally part of the Zorgvliet property, was purchased by David Parodi and family 14 years ago. After uprooting the vineyards, their Italian heritage encouraged them to include sangiovese and pinot grigio in the replant. The wines are made at Zorgvliet by Bernard le Roux.

★★★★ **Sangiovese** ⓦ Worth the 2-vintage wait for a new bottling. **16** (87) lighter styled yet not lacking savoury, meaty, dark cherry & floral enticements, unencumbered by new oak.

Pinot Grigio ⓦ ★★★★ Now-bottled **16** (84), unusually for variety shows delicate lemon, even tropical fruit flavours. Smooth, with citrus twist on finish. **Sauvignon Blanc** ⓦ ★★★ Gooseberry & floral wafts abound on now-bottled **16** (81). Balanced & smooth, with savoury dried lemon tail. — WB

Location/map: Stellenbosch ▪ Map grid reference: H4 ▪ WO: Banghoek ▪ 1stB 2005 ▪ Tasting & sales by appt ▪ Owner(s) Parodi family ▪ Winemaker(s) Bernard le roux (Dec 2013) ▪ Viticulturist(s) Hannes Jansen van

Vuuren (Mar 2008) ▪ 10ha/6.4ha (sangio, shiraz, pinot gris, sauv, viog) ▪ 41t/25,200L bulk ▪ PO Box 670 Vereeniging 1930 ▪ hannes@zorgvliet.com ▪ S 33° 54′ 46.50″ E 018° 56′ 13.6″ ▪ 🅦 smile.adopts.icon ▪ F +27 (0)86-697-3938 ▪ **T +27 (0)82-856-8717**

☐ **Springlights** *see* Kay & Monty Vineyards
☐ **Springvalley** *see* Old Vines Cellars
☐ **Spruitdrift** *see* Namaqua Wines
☐ **Stablemate** *see* Excelsior Estate

Stamboom

This project is about families, as the name (Family Tree) suggests. Firstly, it's 'a Vlok family wine', says Conrad Vlok, winemaker at Strandveld, which is the source of the grapes too, and the family's brief comments on the wine are all given on the back-label. Secondly: grapes also have relationships, and this blend is of pinotage and its parent varieties, pinot noir and cinsaut.

★★★★★ **Stamboom** Pinot noir dominates blend (50%) & cherry, raspberry notes on **17** ★★★★ (89); cinsaut shares credit for fragrance. Pinotage plumminess shows on quite easygoing palate, with modest dry tannins, & harmless bitter tinge on finish. Older oak only. Just a touch off quality of last-made **15** (90). — TJ

Location/WO: Elim ▪ 1stB 2004 ▪ Closed to public ▪ Winemaker(s) Conrad Vlok ▪ info@zush.co.za ▪ **T +27 (0)28-482-1755**

Stanford Hills Winery 🅠 🅟 🏠 📷 ♿

Peter and Jami Kastner's farm near charming Stanford town (not far inland from Hermanus) offers not only wine but also, amongst others, accommodation (including luxury 'glamping'), a restaurant, horse-riding and lovely valley views. Peter makes the wines, which are never less than characterful and are frequently more, in a cellar in the aircraft hangar, with sons Jack and Alex as 'winemakers-in-training'.

Stanford Hills range

★★★★ **Jacksons Pinotage** Perfumed fruit charm & more detracting sticking-plaster notes on **16** ★★★★ (83). Lightish flavours, fairly firm, supportive oak. Like **15** (86), big alcohol (14.5%) in balance.
★★★★ **Sauvignon Blanc** ⊘ Vibrant **18** (87) has tropicality together with customary delectable blackcurrant & savoury note. A rich, ripe fruitiness & weight too, well balanced 13.7% alcohol & fresh acidity.
★★★★ **Méthode Cap Classique** Pinotage adds red berry accent to brioche aromas on **15** (87) sparkling (& a slight, interesting twist of bitterness), with chardonnay upped to 66%. Flavourful, fresh & bone-dry.
Reserve Shiraz ⊘ ★★★★ Big & pleasantly rustic, the 15% alcohol balanced - but giving a hint of glow on the finish. **15** (84) juicy & succulent, savoury edge to the sweet ripe fruit, subtle oaking & lovely smooth tannins. **Rosé** ★★★ Pleasing, lightly fruity aromas touched with earthiness & boiled sweet notes on dry **18** (82) from shiraz. **Chardonnay** ★★★★ Returns to guide after extended break. Typical citrus & oatmeal on **18** (85). Fairly light (just 12.5% alcohol) but flavoursome, well balanced by fresh acid. Third fermented in oak, rest in concrete 'egg' to underline dry linearity.

Veldfire range

Pinotage ★★★ Attractive wild fruitiness on dry **17** (79), with the slightly funky twist also on Jacksons version. Light fruit. **Cape Blend** ⊘ ★★★★ Greater than sum of its parts (65% shiraz, 35% pinotage) **14** (83) has ripe red & black berries lifted by hints of fynbos, pepper & spice. Walker Bay WO. **Rosé** ★★★ From pinotage in **18** (80) (last was shiraz). Light-feeling & fresh, mildly fruity & dry. A little richer than other version. — TJ

Location: Stanford ▪ Map: Walker Bay & Bot River ▪ Map grid reference: B6 ▪ WO: Stanford Foothills/Walker Bay ▪ Est 1856 ▪ 1stB 2002 ▪ Tasting, sales & restaurant Mon-Sun 8.30-5 ▪ Grappa, preserves ▪ Restaurant: breakfast & lunch, chalkboard menu changes daily ▪ Functions & events (up to 180 pax) ▪ Hiking/MTB trails ▪ Horse riding ▪ Fishing ▪ Whale watching flights from own airfield ▪ 5 self-catering cottages & main farmhouse (sleeps up to 32 pax) plus AfriCamps at Stanford Hills (up to 25 guests) ▪ Owner(s) Stanford Hills Estate (Pty) Ltd ▪ Cellarmaster(s)/winemaker(s) Peter Kastner (Apr 2005) ▪ Viticulturist(s) Peter Kastner ▪ 131ha/12ha (ptage, shiraz, chard, sauv) ▪ 60t/4,000cs own label 66% red 34% white ▪ PO Box 1052 Stanford

7210 ▪ info@stanfordhills.co.za ▪ www.stanfordhills.co.za ▪ S 34° 25' 21.4" E 019° 28' 25.7" ▪ ⬚ pickling.
impacts.barnacle ▪ F +27 (0)28-341-0286 ▪ **T +27 (0)28-341-0841**

Star Hill   ⓠ ⑪ ⓐ ⓞ ⑧

The estate that is home to Star Hill is large (over 2,000 ha), in the Tradouw Highlands ward in the Klein
Karoo. Nearly half of it is set aside for conservation, and just 15 ha for high-lying vines. The mostly
single-vineyard wines are vinified by Lourens van der Westhuizen in Robertson.

Directors Reserve
★★★★ Fountainhead Attractive ripe berry & tobacco aromas on **16 ★★★★** ⑧⑤ from cab & merlot;
more herbaceous palate, despite sweet fruit. Firm tannin, acid. Last tasted was plusher **12** ⑧⑦ from 4
varieties. Robertson WO.

Star Hill range
★★★★ Sauvignon Blanc ⊘ Always an interesting, individual example; **17** ⑧⑥ savoury, earthy undertones to tropical aromas - with passionfruit more obvious on green-tinged palate. Integrated acidity.

Blanc de Noir ★★★ Nearly-dry & characterful **17** ⑦⑨ from shiraz with boiled-sweet fruity exuberance.
14.5% alcohol. **Viognier ★★★** Maturing herbal, floral & peach notes on lightly oaked **16** ⑧① but more
savoury than fruity; firm acid structure. Not tasted: **Shiraz, Chenin Blanc**. — TJ

Location: Montagu ▪ Map: Klein Karoo & Garden Route ▪ Map grid reference: C7 ▪ WO: Tradouw Highlands/
Robertson ▪ Est 2005 ▪ 1stB 2009 ▪ Tasting & sales daily 9-3 ▪ Closed Dec 25 ▪ Akkerboom farmstall &
restaurant ▪ Facilities for children ▪ Gifts ▪ Farm produce ▪ Conference facilities on Killarney Farm ▪ Walks/
hikes ▪ MTB ▪ Akkerboom self-catering cottages ▪ Owner(s) Grant Hatch & Christopher Palmer Tomkinson
▪ Winemaker(s)/viticulturist(s) Lourens van der Westhuizen (consultant) ▪ 15ha (shiraz, chenin, sauv, viog)
▪ 4,000cs own label 40% red 60% white ▪ PO Box 342 Montagu 6720 ▪ elzie@starhillwines.com, harry@
starhillwines.com ▪ www.starhillwines.com ▪ S 33° 54' 46.86" E 020° 29' 32.31" ▪ ⬚ attracts.midriff.distinct ▪
T +27 (0)28-050-0145

Stark-Condé Wines   ⓠ ⑪ ⓑ

Prime mover José Conde is a graphic designer by profession and boutique winemaker by choice - and
by way of New York City and Japan. His classic, restrained and elegant aesthetic has been applied to his
winecrafting the past two decades, and lately he's been delighted to 'take it up a notch' with the help of Cape
Winemakers Guild protégé Rudger van Wyk, who joined him at the impossibly scenic Jonkershoek Valley
cellar in 2017. 'Rudger's dedication to creating iconic cabernets has really focused our vision, and brings a
whole new energy.' The dynamism clearly is also going into the white wines, with the Sauvignon Blanc from
27-year-old vines and stellar Field Blend being joined by a Chenin Blanc from the same co-planted vineyard.

Three Pines range
★★★★☆ Cabernet Sauvignon ⧈ Floral, black-fruit seduction on superbly refined, restrained &
elegant **16** ⑨③. Harmonious too, with nothing dominating. Dabs petit verdot, malbec & cab franc merge
seamlessly with oak (70% new) & part natural ferment to add complexity, length. Old, high-lying vines,
as **15 ★★★★★** ⑨⑤.

★★★★☆ Syrah ⧈ Dry **16** ⑨③ vintage is rich & generous but also shows restraint, suppleness. Nuanced
black fruit, spice, cocoa & graphite. Basket pressed with portion wholebunch, supportively oaked (French,
40% new, 22 months). Like other reds, unfined/filtered.

Stark-Condé range
★★★★☆ Cabernet Sauvignon ⧈ Trademark elegance with light tannin grip on **16** ⑨③ with dabs
petit verdot, cab franc, malbec & petite sirah. Supple & sleek but with lean muscle & power. 40% naturally
fermented. Oak is French, third new, for 20 months. Composed & alluring. WO Stellenbosch, as next 2.

★★★★☆ Petite Sirah Shy inky blue fruit of **16** ⑨① with splashes malbec & cab franc unfurls slowly.
Subtle, silky & not as overtly generous as stablemates, touch lean in youth. **15** untasted. French oak,
quarter new, joined by 10% American for 22 months.

★★★★☆ Petit Verdot ⓧ Confident debut for **15** ⑨① variety used mainly for Bordeaux blend support.
Core of succulent fruit, with typical tannin intensity hinted at. Dry nutty tail from 30% new French oak.

★★★★★ **Syrah** ⓐ Intricate winemaking on **16** ⑨④: basket pressed with portion co-fermented viognier & roussanne added. Gently sexy, violet & lavender over plush black fruit & crack of pepper too. Complex, detailed & svelte, seamlessly wooded (20% new).

★★★★★ **Oude Nektar** ⓐ Only second release since fire wiped out farm's highest vineyard. **15** ⑨③ powerful yet restrained & fresh, with powdery violet perfume, gentle berry compote (20% petit verdot & dab merlot, joining cab) & seamless, silky texture despite 70% new French oak, 20 months.

★★★★★ **Jan Lui's Chenin Blanc** ⓝⓔⓦ ⓐ Bright pear & nectarine on **17** ⑨③ from co-planted vineyard. Textured, ripe yet fresh with vivid acid, it shows rapier precision. Complex winemaking & oaking (20% new French) with extended lees contact adding breadth & length. Integrated & harmonious.

★★★★ **Round Mountain Sauvignon Blanc** ⓐ Gooseberry, lime & melon on rounded **17** ★★★★★ ⑨③. Broad & rich with vivid, integrated acidity. Lovely freshness but with real palate weight & texture from time in old, neutral oak. Reined-in minerality on long, rewarding tail. Definite improvement on **16** ⑧⑨.

★★★★★ **The Field Blend** ⓐ Baked stonefruit & spice countered by vivacious acidity on **17** ★★★★★ ⑨⑤ mix of equal (36%) chenin & roussanne with viognier & verdelho, co-planted in unique vineyard named Jan Lui's Field after early owner. Same complex vinification as **16** ⑨③, involving concrete 'egg', tank & older oak. Focused, taut & long.

Postcard Series
Not tasted: **Pinot Noir, Chenin Blanc, Sauvignon Blanc.** — FM

Location/map: Stellenbosch ▪ Map grid reference: G6 ▪ WO: Jonkershoek Valley/Stellenbosch ▪ Est/1stB 1998 ▪ Tasting & sales Mon-Sun 9.30–4 ▪ Fee from R60pp ▪ Closed most pub hols (please call to confirm) ▪ Postcard Café open Wed-Sun 9.30–4 ▪ Owner(s) Jonkershoek Cellars (Pty) Ltd ▪ Cellarmaster(s) José Conde (1998) ▪ Winemaker(s) Rudger van Wyk (2017) ▪ Viticulturist(s) Andrew Klinck, with Kevin Watt ▪ 250ha/40ha (cabs s/f, merlot, p verdot, shiraz) ▪ 250t/12,000cs own label 80% red 20% white ▪ PO Box 389 Stellenbosch 7599 ▪ info@stark-conde.co.za ▪ www.stark-conde.co.za, www.postcardcafe.co.za ▪ S 33° 57' 13.83" E 018° 54' 37.59" ▪ ⓥ voices.monkeys.hangs ▪ **T +27 (0)21-861-7700**

☐ **Starlette** see Allée Bleue Wines

Steenberg Vineyards
In 1682 Catharina Ras was granted the land that was later to become Steenberg – her name is now recalled in the estate red blend and a restaurant. This is the most southerly of the Constantia farms and so more open to cooling and fungus-unfriendly (but sometimes violent and salt-laden) winds off False Bay. Its modern incarnation, with massive investment, as a 'leisure complex' including housing, hotel, restaurants and golf course – and of course a winery - dates from the mid 1990s. Since 2005 Steenberg has been owned by Graham Beck Enterprises. The large range of wines, some with a contribution from bought-in grapes, is made under the aegis of cellarmaster JD Pretorius, who this year celebrates his first decade here.

Icon range
★★★★★ **Magna Carta** ⓐ Perennially impressive white Bordeaux blend, sauvignon & semillon (60/40), 30% new oak in **17** ⑨④. Approachable in youth, with bountiful lemongrass, spice, citrus & melon succulence, yet also coiled & profound, crisp acid platform to carry it forward.

Flagship range
★★★★★ **Nebbiolo** Standout red in very smart lineup. **16** ⑨① raspberry & sour cherry on dry tannin bed, ably supported by older oak. Crystalline & fresh but hiding its true charm, needs year/2 to show at best.

★★★★★ **Catharina** ⓐ Flagship blend named for estate's original owner, usually merlot-led. Hallmark elegance, power & poise in **16** ⑨③, which lifts the bar on **15** ⑨① with greater concentration & form, 20% syrah & 5% petit verdot augmenting merlot's black fruit, bolstering structure & length.

★★★★★ **The Black Swan Sauvignon Blanc** ⓐ After explosive **16** ⑨④, **17** ★★★★★ ⑨⑤ subtler marriage of top 2 vineyards, but by no means less complex. Green fig & apple, nettle & grapefruit notes, & a vital seam of acidity. None of the usual (unwooded) semillon; breadth comes from 8 months on lees.

★★★★★ **Semillon** ⓐ Classic & refined **17** ⑨③, understated lanolin, tangerine & floral appeal, well-judged barrel ferment/ageing (35% new) adding just a hint of vanilla, smoothing the texture. Harmonious, will continue to thrill 5+ years. **16** ⑨③ similar, gentle but vibrant.

Super Premium range

★★★★ **Stately Red** Mostly cab (67%) from Constantia & Darling with Constantia syrah. **16** ⑧⑦ fruity but also nicely dry, older oak adding spice & depth.

Ruby Rosé ★★★★ Properly dry & lightish (12.5% alcohol), **18** ⑧④ pink from syrah & cinsaut, red-fruit flavours are vivacious yet not frivolous, enough depth & substance to stand with rest of range. WO W Cape, as next. **Sphynx Chardonnay** ★★★★ Half barrel-fermented portion (50% new oak) adds aroma, flavour & structure to nicely built **18** ⑧⑤. Expressive citrus perfume, bone-dry finish & friendly 12.5% alcohol.

Estate range

★★★★★ **Merlot** As serious as previous, **15** ⑨⓪ has 14% petit verdot adding extra depth & plushness, an iron fist in a velvet glove. Opulent blackberry fruit envelopes authoritative tannins while violet nuances mingle with oak-derived chocolate.

★★★★ **Syrah** White pepper, earthy notes adorn supple & graceful **16** ⑧⑨. Deft oak, some small barrels joining larger formats this time (33% new), fine-grained tannin for cellaring; drinks well now, too.

★★★★ **Rattlesnake Sauvignon Blanc** From select vineyards, **17** ⑧⑥ adds concrete 'egg' fermenters to the usual barrel vinification, goes up a notch on **16** ★★★★ ⑧③ with brilliant seam of acidity, greater finesse.

★★★★ **Sauvignon Blanc** From different blocks picked at varying ripeness levels to build complexity & manage acidity, **18** ⑧⑥ delightful airy freshness about it, flavour without weight, lighter-tripping than **17** ★★★★ ⑧⑤.

Sparkling Wines

★★★★ **1682 Pinot Noir Méthode Cap Classique** Salmon-hued rosé bubbly with abundant, lively strawberry & red apple flavours, year on lees. Now NV ⑧⑨, still attractive though slightly less profound than previous. WO W Cape.

★★★★ **1682 Chardonnay Méthode Cap Classique** Elegant celebrator from Robertson grapes, some barrel-fermented, year on lees plus 15% reserve-wine portion in latest NV ⑧⑨. Baked apple nuances, tightly wound & very fresh.

★★★★☆ **Lady R Méthode Cap Classique** ⓐ Charming & sophisticated sparkler, 70% pinot noir from Darling, old-oak-fermented chardonnay from Robertson in **13** ⑨③. Delicate & persistent bead, seamless & smooth glassful after 54 months on lees. Delicious now & will reward few years cellaring, like **12** ★★★★★ ⑨⑤.

Sparkling Sauvignon Blanc ⓥ ★★★★ Bottle-fermented with no extended lees ageing (a requirement for MCC). No hardship! NV ⑧④ fruity & engaging, whisper of sauvignon's grassiness. — HC

Location: Constantia ▪ Map: Cape Peninsula ▪ Map grid reference: B4 ▪ WO: Constantia/Western Cape/Coastal ▪ Est 1990 ▪ 1stB 1996 ▪ Tasting & sales Mon-Sun 10–6 ▪ Tasting from R50-R150pp subject to availability ▪ Closed Good Fri & Dec 25 ▪ Cellar tours Mon-Fri 11 & 3 ▪ Bistro Sixteen82; Catharina's Restaurant ▪ Steenberg Hotel & Spa; conferences; world-class golf course, walking trail ▪ Extensive merchandising area ▪ Annual festival: Constantia Fresh (Feb) ▪ Owner(s) Graham Beck Enterprises ▪ Cellarmaster(s) JD Pretorius (Mar 2009) ▪ 60ha (cab, malbec, merlot, nebbiolo, shiraz, sauv, sem) ▪ 312t/70,000cs own label 40% red 60% white ▪ WIETA ▪ PO Box 224 Steenberg 7947 ▪ info@steenbergfarm.com ▪ www.steenbergfarm.com ▪ S 34° 4'17.0" E 018° 25'31.1" ▪ ⚐ nominations.moonlit.lily ▪ F +27 (0)21-713-2201 ▪ **T +27 (0)21-713-2211**

☐ **Steenhuis** see Wine-of-the-Month Club

☐ **STELL** see Stellenrust

Stellar Winery ⓠ

A remarkable success story, the first wines were produced in 2003 but Stellar Winery, still largely family-owned (23% in an empowerment trust), has grown into the world's largest maker of no-sulphur-added wines, and SA's largest producer of certified-organic Fairtrade bottlings. Based near Vredendal, its Koekenaap terroir is part of the success: low rainfall, cool temperature, Atlantic terroir that is largely disease-free. Own vineyards are only one-third of the supply, however, the rest is from West Coast partners, reflecting the collective commitment to the organic vision. And they get the marketing right, with in-house design facilities and evocative range names telling stories that resonate locally and internationally.

The River's End range

★★★★ Chenin Blanc ⊘ ⊙ Cool origin yet riper style than other chenins. **17** ⑧⑧ aged older barrels, creates something special: melon & quince preserve, vanilla biscuit overlay, ends crisply dry.

Pinot Noir ⊘ ⊙ ★★★★ Light coloured & textured, as befits the variety, **16** ⑧⑧'s raspberry fruit has a piquant wild edge. Oak, 50% new, well integrated. Fairtrade certified, as all wines. WO Koekenaap, like Chenin.

The Sensory Collection

★★★★ Grande Reserve Shiraz ⊙ Handsome packaging, heavyweight bottle, as all these. Well-spiced dark fruit in **16** ⑧⑦, a good surprise in the flavours: scrub & white pepper, appealing freshness.

Grande Reserve Pinotage ⊙ ★★★★ Black plum/prune richness to **16** ⑧④'s perfume, flavours, savoury seam from 18 months in barrel, half new. Drinks well, good ageing potential. WO Koekenaap, as all. **Grande Reserve Chardonnay** ⊙ ★★★★ Offering dried peach & apricot richness, **16** ⑧④ is boldly styled, the oak component a shortbread seam throughout.

The Storyteller range

Viognier ⑰ ⊙ ★★★★ **18** ⑧⑤ is elegant (12% alcohol) & dry, its dab of oak a biscuit thread in the aromatic fruit. Nicely avoids the variety's excesses. WO Olifants River.

NSA Cabernet Sauvignon ⊙ ★★★ Cigarbox features in **17** ⑦⑧'s berry fruit, dry tannin structure, but still youthful, should smooth in time.

Running Duck range

Reserve Malbec ⑧ ⊙ ★★★ Lot packed into slender frame (12.5% alcohol), unoaked **15** ⑧① is meaty, dark fruited, the grape tannins adding firmness for food, some ageing. **Merlot** ⑭ᴱᵂ ⊙ ★★★ Blackcurrants & spice, the emphasis in **18** ⑦⑧ is on tasty, easy drinkability. **Shiraz** ⑭ᴱᵂ ⊙ ★★★ Bright fruited with red berries, **17** ⑧① has some oak-driven spicing, but the charm lies in its palate fruity freshness, smooth texture. **Reserve Cabernet Sauvignon-Pinotage** ⊙ ★★★ Only 50% oaked to allow greater fruit expression in **17** ⑦⑧. Fynbos/scrub notes, mulberry vibrancy, especially in the flavours. **Chardonnay** ⊙ ★★★ Unwooded **18** ⑦⑧'s orange & tangerine flavours perked up by zippy acidity. **Chenin Blanc** ⊙ ★★★ Always satisfies, an apple intensity & crispness in **18** ⑧① sleek & lively. **Sauvignon Blanc** ⊙ ★★★ Sliced pear freshness in **18** ⑧①, zesty & bright, mineral notes at the end. **Reserve Sauvignon Blanc-Semillon** ⊙ ★★★ Crunchy summer fruits, **18** ⑧①'s backing limy acidity & svelte lines make for ideal food accompaniment.

Stellar Organics range

Chardonnay-Pinot Noir Sparkling ⊙ ★★★ Very pale copper colour from just 5% pinot noir, which plays a surprisingly dominant role in **NV** ⑦⑧; red berries in perfume & flavours, offsetting the dryness. WO Koekenaap, as next. **Extra Dry Sparkling** ⊙ ★★★ From chenin, **18** ⑧①'s dryness & grapefruit flavours make it a good aperitif. Unheady 12% alcohol.

Stellar Organics No-Sulphur-Added range

Cabernet Sauvignon ⊙ ★★★ Mainly seasoned barrels, 30% new (previous unwooded), giving **18** ⑧① meaty tones to go with the cassis. Streamlined, tasty. **Merlot** ⊙ ★★ Offering juicy drinkability, **18** ⑦⑤ has blackcurrants, toasty oak, a herbal note. **Pinotage** ⊙ ★★ Blueberries, with a wood char note, **18** ⑦⑥ ends firmly dry, food friendly. **Shiraz** ⊙ ★★★ Expressive fruit in **18** ⑦⑨, some spice top notes, but the major part of the appeal is its lithe, smooth drinkability. **Rosé** ⑧ ⊙ ★★★ Mainly colombard, **17** ★★★ ⑧①'s light pink colour from dab pinotage; a basket of summer fruits, appetisingly fresh & dry. Olifants River WO. **Limited Release Blanc de Blanc** ⑧ ⊙ ★★★ From colombard, bright-fruited **17** ⑦⑧ is slender, bone-dry & nicely refreshing, will have you reaching for a second glass.

Heaven on Earth range

★★★★★ Muscat d'Alexandrie ⊘ ⊙ ⊛ Was 'Natural Sweet'. From grapes air-dried on bed of straw & organic rooibos, unoaked **NV** ⑨④ is a full-sweet marvel: apricots, fynbos honey & barley sugar. And yes, nuances of rooibos! 375 ml.— CR

Location: Vredendal ▪ Map: Olifants River ▪ Map grid reference: B4 ▪ WO: Western Cape/Koekenaap/Olifants River ▪ Est 2000 ▪ 1stB 2001 ▪ Tasting & sales Mon-Fri 8–5 ▪ Closed all pub hols ▪ Cellar tours by appt ▪

Owner(s) Rossouw family, Stellar Empowerment Trust & others ▪ Winemaker(s) Klaas Coetzee (Aug 2010) & Mauritius Naude ▪ Viticulturist(s) Klaas Coetzee ▪ ±68ha Stellar Farming, ±149ha independent organic producers (cab, merlot, ptage, pinot, ruby cab, shiraz, chenin, chard, muscat d'A, sauv) ▪ 11,900t ▪ Other export brands: Dig This!, Firefly, Live-A-Little, Moonlight Organics, Natural Star, No House Wine ▪ PO Box 308 Vredendal 8160 ▪ info@stellarorganics.co.za ▪ www.stellarorganics.co.za ▪ S 31° 42′ 24.70″ E 018° 33′ 33.70″ ▪ ⌖ legislate.contoured.arachnid ▪ F +27 (0)86-635-1968 ▪ **T +27 (0)27-216-1310**

Stellekaya Winery ⓠ

They're tightening up the all-red portfolio at Dave and Jane Lello's Stellenbosch winery, concentrating on the grapes drawn from their Blaauwklippen Valley farm (the cellar and visitor facilities are at Bosman's Crossing, on the edge of town). A notable advantage of the range is the comparative maturity of the wine: it's rare to have these older vintages available as current, thanks to unusually lengthy barrel maturation, helping to make the wine generally more savoury (and even classic) than upfront-fruity.

Limited Releases

★★★★ **Malbec** ⓥ Serious-minded single-vineyard bottling. **12** ⑧⑦'s generous mulberry & plum fruit in harmony with gripping yet ripe tannins, but will reward few years patience. Only 700 numbered bottles.

★★★★ **Orion Reserve** Cab with merlot plus drops cab franc, malbec. Retasted, **12** ⑧⑨ showing well mid-2018. Developed character, bringing more complex, oxidative, savoury, even sombre notes to the dark fruit. Fine tannins - rather dry thanks to 44 months in oak. Great food wine for a few more years.

Stellekaya range

★★★★ **Cabernet Sauvignon** Previewed last time, **14** ⑧⑦ classic notes cedar & tobacco on restrained fruit; herbal edge. Firmly, even austerely built, but survived 42 months oak. Benefits from decanting. No **13**.

★★★★ **Malbec** (NEW) By house's unshowy standards, **14** ⑧⑥ quite forward juicy fruit to complement the firm tannic structure, savoury element & long oaking. Nice loganberry finish.

★★★★ **Merlot** ⓥ Lovely rich red-fruited aromas & flavours on **14** ⑧⑦ preview. Properly ripe, supple tannins, balanced & fresh, oak well judged. Shows good potential.

★★★★ **Pinot Noir** ⓥ Sour cherry fruit & some earthiness, brisk acidity, quite high toned. **13**★★★ ⑦⑧ best enjoyed soon with a meal. Less beguiling than last **11**. WO W Cape.

★★★★ **Orion** 50% cab, with merlot, cab franc, malbec - **14** ⑧⑧ fleshier, less severe than Cab; quite elegant, good savoury balance & hints of sweet fruit. Also 44 months oak, but firm tannins not too dry. No **13**.

Hercules ★★★★ From 87% sangiovese with drops of Bordeaux varieties. **14** ⑧⑤ cherry & tomato leaf notes. Sweet fruit, even juicy, despite moderate dry tannins. **Cape Cross** ⓥ ★★★★ Cape Blend gets black/strawberry fruitiness from pinotage, structure from 11% cab, roundness from 38% merlot. **09** ⑧⑤ judicious oak (30% new) adds appealing choc/mocha effect. WO W Cape. — TJ

Location/map: Stellenbosch ▪ Map grid reference: E5 ▪ WO: Stellenbosch/Western Cape ▪ Est 1998 ▪1stB 1999 ▪ Tasting, sales & cellar tours by appt ▪ Closed all pub hols & Dec 16 to 2nd week of Jan ▪ Owner(s) Dave & Jane Lello ▪ Winemaker(s) Mark Carmichael-Green (2016, consultant) ▪ Viticulturist(s) Paul Wallace (Jan 2005, consultant) ▪ 23ha/15ha under vine ▪ 12,000cs own label ▪ IPW ▪ PO Box 12426 Die Boord Stellenbosch 7613 ▪ info@stellekaya.co.za ▪ www.stellekaya.co.za ▪ S 33° 56′ 27.6″ E 018° 50′ 47.3″ ▪ ⌖ circling.swan.sang ▪ F +27 (0)21-883-2536 ▪ **T +27 (0)21-883-3873**

Stellenbosch Family Wines ⓠ

The beautiful rising phoenix labels of the international range of this boutique Stellenbosch venture have been joined by a collection aimed at the local market, named Glorious, featuring equally creative packaging by artist Michelle-Lize van Wyk, a member of one of the three families behind the brand. Vinification is at Koelenhof Winery by the amazingly youthful Carlo de Vries, just 14 years old, and his father Andrew, a seasoned winemaker and Koelenhof's general manager.

Phoenix range

Cabernet Sauvignon (NEW) ★★★ Unusual **17** ⑧⓪ has medicinal nuance to ripe black fruit, fragrant notes of violets & mint, soft tannins despite 100% new oak. **Merlot** (NEW) ★★★ Wood dominates **17** ⑦⑦ though ripe chocolate-dipped cherry fruit suggests it may harmonise with time. **Pinot Noir** (NEW) ⓥ ★★★ Jammy red-fruit confection but **16** ⑦⑦ handles the spicy wood well, attractive earthy notes developing. **Pinotage**

(NEW) ★★★ Cherry fruit on ripe **17** (82), good balance & pleasant tannins. Less oak than others & the better for it. **Family Blend** (②) ★★ Merlot/cab show their compatibility in the plummy/berry character; gentle spice & structure from oak staves in **13** (75). **CMP Legacy Red** (②) ★★ Mostly cab with merlot & pinot noir. **13** (74) red berries & gentle savoury spice, slight herbaceous note but the palate is accessible, drinks easily. **Chardonnay** (NEW) ★★★★ Interesting citrus/tropical vibe on lively **17** (83) - orange, grapefruit, touch melon - good balance, judicious oak (50%, none new) adding clove & vanilla tweaks.

Glorious range
Cabernet Sauvignon (②) ★★★ Tar-tinted sweet cassis fruit still gripped by tannins, **15** (80) needs food or few years cellaring to soften. **Merlot** ★★ Same charry choc overlay on cherry fruit as previous, **17** (76) finishes on astringent note. **Pinot Noir** ★★ Revisited, **15** (71)'s oak dominates slight red-fruit aromas, shows as smoky & charry on palate. **Pinotage** (②) ★★★ Reined-in wooding lets appealing fresh-fruit profile shine, **15** (82) mulberries, strawberries, fair intensity, bold but unharsh tannins. **Family Blend** (②) ★★★★ Restrained hedgerow fruit, zippy acidity & friendly tannic hold, **15** (83) merlot (51%) & cab combo slips down easily. **CMP Legacy Red** (②) ★★★ Mainly cab with merlot & pinot noir, **15** (80) mouthcoating tannins & brisk acidity for beefy stews & potjies. **Chardonnay** (②) ★★★★ Aperitif-style **15** (83) will have broad appeal with its attractive nut, citrus & lemon thyme bouquet, toast & vanilla flavours. — CM

Location/map/WO: Stellenbosch ▪ Map grid reference: D1 ▪ Est/1stB 2013 ▪ Tasting by appt ▪ Fee R30/6 wines ▪ Sales Mon-Sat 8-6 by appt ▪ Owner(s) Renata de Vries, Michelle-Lize van Wyk & Christel Truter ▪ Winemaker(s) Carlo de Vries, with Andrew de Vries (both Jan 2013, consultants) ▪ 2,900cs own label 90% red 10% white ▪ c/o PO Box 1 Koelenhof 7605 ▪ info@stellenboschfamilywines.co.za ▪ www.stellenbos-chfamilywines.co.za ▪ S 33° 50′ 5.2″ E 018° 47′ 52.7″ ▪ 🌐 toolkit.sounds.junction ▪ **T** +27 (0)82-835-7107

Stellenbosch Hills Wines   (②) (⑤)
Heritage and innovation are recurring themes at Stellenbosch Hills Wines, among several collaborative ventures established in the 1940s and now a modern grower-owned company with cellar and easily-accessible visitor venue on the Polkadraai Hills. In a nod to tradition, one of the original member-farms, Viljee Carinus' Le Serena, is spotlit as the source of a new and collectible release of a seldom-seen muscat. Novelty comes in the form of their first MCC sparkling, in gestation at press time.

1707 Reserve range
★★★★ **Red** (②) Shiraz & 3 Bordeaux varieties, **15** (89) sets red-wine style here: ripe, plump fruit in often robust tannic frame, vanilla oak (60% new for this wine) adds sense of sweetness.

★★★★ **White** Seriously styled & -packaged chardonnay, semillon & viognier, **16** (87)'s obvious new French oak (though down to 50%) giving textured buttery/coconut seam to the fruit, just enough acidity in the finish to freshen.

Limited Releases (NEW)
★★★★☆ **La Serena** (⑥) Prestige limited bottling of rare muscat de Hambourg, long a signature grape of this winery, fortified with 7 year old brandy. **14** (93) pomegranate, nougat & nut packed into full-sweet explosion of flavour, the spirit smoothly integrated. Lightly chill for luxurious aperitif or serve with cheese.

Stellenbosch Hills range
★★★★ **Muscat de Hambourg** (②) Engagingly sweet & grapey **16** (88) preview, a balanced fortified wine for all seasons: on ice in summer, over ice cream in spring, solo when weather turns chilly. **Cabernet Sauvignon** (✓) ★★★★ Bramble & woodsmoke aromas lead out **16** (85), blackcurrant fruit under tight tannic mantle mid-2018, needs time to settle. 15% new oak, as all these reds. **Merlot** ★★★ Violet perfume & minty freshness to smoked bacon interest of **16** (82). Mix American & French wood, as next. **Bushvine Pinotage** ★★★ Red-wine partner for the dessert course: **16** (81) oozes fruitcake, coconut & mocha sweetness, contrasted by firm tannins. **Shiraz** ★★★ Succulent but nice & dry, **16** (80) suave dark fruits with hints of choc-coffee & vanilla. **Chenin Blanc** (✓) ★★★ Look no further than **18** (81) for juicy fruit in a snappy quaffer that doesn't cost the earth. **Sauvignon Blanc** ★★★ Crisply dry, uncomplicated tropical fruitiness of **18** (80) has refreshing grassy conclusion.

Polkadraai range
Pinotage-Merlot (✓) ★★★ Sweet red berry tones of **17** (78) in smooth harmony with spice from 8 months well-seasoned oak. Polkadraai Hills WO, as all these. 3L cask only, as next 2. **Merlot-Shiraz** ★★

Ripe mulberry features ushered into a toasty frame, **17** Ⓒ easy, succulent, good value. **Sauvignon Blanc** ★★ Tropical fruit & cut-grass note, tingling freshness to **18** Ⓒ, super-value year-round sipping. **Chenin Blanc-Sauvignon Blanc** ★★ Plump **18** Ⓒ chenin fruit trimmed by sauvignon's crisp dry freshness. Not tasted: **Pinot Noir Sparkling Rosé, Sauvignon Blanc Sparkling Brut**. — DS

Location/map: Stellenbosch ▪ Map grid reference: D6 ▪ WO: Stellenbosch/Polkadraai Hills ▪ Est 1945 ▪ 1stB 1972 ▪ Tasting & sales Mon-Fri 9-5 Sat 10-3 ▪ Fee R15; R65 wine, biltong & droëwors tasting ▪ Closed Sun & all pub hols ▪ Owner(s) 16 members ▪ Cellarmaster(s) PG Slabbert (Jan 1997) ▪ Winemaker(s) James Ochse (Sep 2016) ▪ Viticulturist(s) Johan Pienaar & Eben Archer (consultants) ▪ 715ha (cab, merlot, ptage, shiraz, chard, chenin, muscat de Hambourg, sauv) ▪ 6,000t/20,000cs own label 68% red 30% white 2% other ▪ IPW ▪ PO Box 40 Vlottenburg 7604 ▪ info@stellenbosch-hills.co.za ▪ www.stellenbosch-hills.co.za ▪ S 33° 57' 38.2" E 018° 48' 1.8" ▪ ⬚ pilots.brittle.withdrew ▪ F +27 (0)21-881-3357 ▪ **T +27 (0)21-881-3828**

☐ **Stellenbosch Manor** *see* Stellenrust

Stellenbosch Reserve ⓥ

With heritage names and charmingly rendered architectural landmarks on the front labels, Rust en Vrede proprietor Jean Engelbrecht pays homage to Stellenbosch, 'a unique town [and] birthplace, and home to many of South Africa's greatest leaders, intellectuals, artists, scientists, sportsmen and winemakers'.

★★★★★ **Ou Hoofgebou Cabernet Sauvignon** ⊘ ⓐ Precise, sophisticated **16** Ⓒ is a conspicuous over-performer, delivering rich cassis on a raft of earthy, mineral layers. Sublime structure, texture & balance with complex iodine & oak spices (20% new wood, as all), all finely integrated.

★★★★ **Kweekskool Merlot** Juicy & generous, with ripe, smooth tannins but **16** Ⓒ, excellent as it is, misses some of the depth & finesse of its impressive siblings.

★★★★☆ **Vanderstel** ⓐ Stately elegance persists in **16** Ⓒ, though less impressive than high-flying **15** ★★★★★ Ⓒ. Cab-led 4-way Bordeaux blend has poise, ripeness & complexity. **17** Ⓒ, also tasted, 5-way assemblage is deeper, fuller, with brooding cassis & forest floor notes.

★★★★ **Moederkerk Chardonnay** Modestly wooded (part-oaked, 9 months) **17** Ⓒ appeals with mineral-lime texture, shapely lemon fruit, layers of savoury & aromatic spices. Delightful saline finish.— GdB

Location/WO: Stellenbosch ▪ Est 2004 ▪ 1stB 2005 ▪ Tasting & sales at Guardian Peak (see entry) ▪ Owner(s) Jean Engelbrecht ▪ Winemaker(s) Roelof Lotriet (Sep 2014) ▪ ±160t/26,000cs own label 70% red 30% white ▪ IPW ▪ PO Box 473 Stellenbosch 7599 ▪ info@stellenboschreserve.com ▪ www.stellenboschreserve.com ▪ **T +27 (0)21-881-3881**

Stellenbosch University Welgevallen Cellar ⓥ

If you're wondering whether the university in the heart of SA's winelands, with a renowned oenology faculty, has its own wine brand, the answer is yes. Made (and offered for tasting/sale) in a cellar dating to the birth of its home town (1680), and poised to grow in both volume and diversity with the planting of a further 9ha of vines on the Welgevallen experimental farm, vinification of the first malbec ('18) and planned introduction of a wine marking Maties' founding on 2 April 1918.

Die Laan range

★★★★☆ **Rector's Reserve Pinotage** ⊘ Worthy flagship, uni's chief should be proud to serve delectably decadent, fulsome yet refined **15** Ⓒ. Supple, finely judged rush of ripe, dense berry fruit easily taming 100% new French oak.

★★★★ **Shiraz** ⓩ Delicious medley of red & dark fruit seasoned with vanilla, coriander & black pepper. Gently oaked, fresh lift, soft tannin & good length aid **15** Ⓒ as partner for hearty stews.

★★★★ **Chenin Blanc Reserve** ⊘ Big, brawny & generous, fruit-driven **17** Ⓒ is barrel fermented, showing oak spice & weight. Rich leesy texture, lengthy farewell. Great value.

★★★★ **Chardonnay Méthode Cap Classique** ⓩ Attractive blanc de blancs sparkling, **11** Ⓒ quince-soaked brioche & fresh lime notes, secondary fruit character neatly balanced by lively, mouthfilling mousse, salty tail & nutty aftertaste.

Cabernet Sauvignon ★★★★ Light-bodied but well-focused **16** Ⓒ shows typical varietal leafy-earthiness, blackcurrant fruit with nice herbal highlights. **Merlot** ★★★★ Distinctive herbal-leafy tones in **17** Ⓒ, underpinned by sweetly ripe blackcurrant & plum fruit. **Merlot Reserve** (NEW) ★★★★ Brawny, tannic 17 (84) shows good varietal fruit & leafy herbaceousness. Rather rough at the edges, chalky finish. **Chenin Blanc** (✓) ★★★★ Ripe melon & pear spiced with gentle oak on appealing 17 (84), with mineral twist at finish. **Sauvignon Blanc** ★★★ Highly aromatic, well-judged 18 (82) still showing fermentation tones. Bright fruit & acid, good weight, rather brief though. **Viognier** ★★★★ Ratcheted-up oak on 17 (85) does no favours to delicate floral-tinged peach fruit. Laudable body & weight, with vanilla-tinged finish. Elgin fruit. Not tasted: **Pinotage, Cape Fortified**.

Maties range

Rooiplein ★★★ Unpretentious but competent **NV** (82) pinotage-cab blend, showing cheerfully ripe red berries, smooth tannins. — GdB

Location/map: Stellenbosch ▪ Map grid reference: F5 ▪ WO: Stellenbosch/Elgin ▪ Est 2001 ▪ 1stB 2009 ▪ Tasting Mon-Fri 9-4 ▪ Fee R35pp ▪ Closed all pub hols & Dec 15-Jan 10 ▪ Owner(s) Stellenbosch University ▪ Cellarmaster(s)/winemaker(s) Riaan Wassüng (Jan 2004) ▪ Viticulturist(s) Emma Moffat (Jan 2018) ▪ 11ha/10ha (cab, ptage, shiraz, sauv) ▪ 4,600cs own label 68% red 32% white ▪ Department of Viticulture & Oenology Private Bag X1 Matieland 7602 ▪ winesales@sun.ac.za, rfw@sun.ac.za ▪ http://academic.sun.ac.za/viti_oenol/ ▪ S 33° 56′22.38″ E 018° 52′1.92″ ▪ anyone.crusher.likely ▪ **T +27 (0)21-808-2925/+27 (0)83-622-6394**

Stellenbosch Vineyards

(Ⓠ)(Ⓐ)(Ⓖ)

The only constant is change at this global wine business sited on 17th-century Stellenbosch farm Welmoed. Here, cellar capacity has been upgraded to 7,500 tons in line with planned production increases of the fine-wine offerings, mostly under the Flagship and Limited Release labels. New, in fact, in the latter line-up are a varietal cinsaut and therona — cinsaut previously an industry workhorse but now enjoying almost cult status, therona a cross of two blancs, chenin and crouchen, last featured in this guide as a solo bottling (by a Northern Cape producer) back in 2002. Boosting Stellenbosch Vineyards' already impressive international reach - more than 80% of output is exported - is the recent acquisition of the major share by French wine company, AdVini. See separate listing for the Welmoed range.

The Flagship range

★★★★½ **Petit Verdot** (Ⓐ) Assured & uncompromising yet unforced 12 (93), opulent plum fruit given near-perfect form by vibrant acidity, commanding tannins, emphatic dry finish & well-integrated oak (48 months, 80% new). WO Coastal.

★★★★½ **Right Bank** (NEW) (Ⓐ) Firm & linear interpretation of merlot-dominated (67%) Bordeaux, 15 (94) with equal splashes cab, cab franc & petit verdot; judicious spicing from 2 years in 50% new oak, beautiful dry end. Ideally structured to reward 10+ years cellaring.

Occasional release: **Cabernet Franc**.

Limited Release range

★★★★½ **Cinsault** (NEW) (Ⓐ) Highly attractive addition to SA's modern, lightly oaked, medium-intensity red pack. 17 (93) vivid cherry & berry aromas & flavours, impressive acid-tannin balance.

★★★★½ **Grenache** Single-parcel bottling on-trend for lighter-oaked &-styled reds. 17 (92) strawberry, white pepper & cured meat appeal, stemmy tone on nose & palate. Similar depth, weight to 16 (92), slightly warmer farewell.

★★★★½ **Verdelho** (Ⓐ) Vivacious & engaging glassful, with big bones (14.9% alcohol) smartly draped with layers of mandarin, honey, Asian spice & coconut. 17 (93) delightfully exotic, smooth & seamless too. Barrel-fermented single block.

Therona (NEW) ★★★★ Only varietal bottling in this edition of seldom-seen locally developed grape. Oaked 17 (85) subdued white peach & nectarine, honeyed, quite broad & chunky.

Credo range

★★★★ **Pinotage Reserve** (Ⓠ) Ex Helderberg bushvines, 15 (87) fruit-sweet from start to finish, soft, without much tannin, misses 14 (87)'s exotic spice but delivers typical pinotage mulberry & banana.

★★★★ **Shiraz** (Ⓠ) Shy 15 ★★★★★ (91) matches 14 (87)'s elegance but more poised, nuanced. Sophisticated floral fragrance to black fruit, well-judged acidity for a fresh, balanced mouthful that lingers.

★★★★ Chardonnay Almost a caricature of barrel-fermented chardonnay: obvious vanilla oak matched by generous lemon & orange flavours, vibrant citrus acidity. Almost! **17** ⑧'s just too well-crafted for that.

★★★★☆ Chenin Blanc Full-bore peach & nectarine, vanilla & crème caramel, **16** ★★★★ ⑧ good example of its style. Slightly sweeter than **15** ㉑, misses some acid ennoblement & thus longevity.

Shiraz-Merlot-Viognier ★★★★ This range for lovers of bold flavours. Intense white pepper, red & black fruit, charry oak livened by viognier's florals. **16** ⑧ involving & tasty red, now & for few years.

Infiniti range

★★★★ Methodé Cap Classique Brut ⊘ First tasted since delightful **08** ⑧, fine-beaded **14** ⑧ sparkling similarly rich & dry, with apple tart aromas, lengthy finish. From chardonnay (56%) & pinot noir, 48 months on lees. WO W Cape, as next.

★★★★ Noble Late Harvest ⊘ Botrytis dessert relies on complexity & flavour for its charm, not sugar which is both quite low & offset by penetrating acidity. Deliciousness from almonds, lemon-lime zest, apricots (fresh & dried). **16** ⑧ 100% (unoaked) chenin whereas last-tasted **12** ⑧ had drop muscat. 500 ml.

Stellenbosch Vineyards range

★★★★ Bushvine Pinotage ⊘ Strawberry & mulberry, hint banana, bright acidity - classic pinotage profile. **16** ⑧ level up from red siblings thanks to better-managed tannins, less fruit-sweetness.

Cabernet Sauvignon ★★★★ Spice & Italian herbs, dark plums & just enough grip for mealtimes; **16** ⑧'s moderate 13.4% alcohol a bonus. **Shiraz ★★★★** Laudably dry but varietally shy, **15** ⑧ is enjoyable nonetheless, fresh & lightly spiced. **Unwooded Chardonnay** (NEW) **★★★** Sleek & delicate **17** ⑧, subdued citrus wafts, creamy touches, slightly sweet impression in tail. Enjoy soon. **Bushvine Chenin Blanc ★★★** Barrel-fermented **17** ⑧ has lovely depth of peach & nectarine flavour, touch sugar to round out peppy acidity. **Sauvignon Blanc ★★★★** Too young to rate last time, **17** ⑧ grass, fig & obvious green/pyrazine notes, lean & precise, fresh & flavoursome with trenchant acidity. — CvZ

Location/map: Stellenbosch ▪ Map grid reference: C7 ▪ WO: Stellenbosch/Western Cape/Coastal ▪ Est 2004 ▪ Tasting & sales Mon–Fri 9–6 Sat/Sun & pub hols 10–5 ▪ Tasting fee R30pp/standard & R80pp/premium ▪ Closed Good Fri, Dec 25 & Jan 1 ▪ Facilities for children ▪ Owner(s) 12 shareholders ▪ Winemaker(s) Abraham de Villiers (Dec 2004) & Bernard Claassen (Feb 2005), with Petri de Beer (Jan 2015) & Stefan Erwee (Feb 2014) ▪ Viticulturist(s) Francois de Villiers (1998) ▪ 5,500t ▪ 55% red 35% white 10% rosé ▪ BEE, Fairtrade, IPW, WIETA ▪ PO Box 465 Stellenbosch 7599 ▪ info@stellvine.co.za ▪ www.stellenboschvineyards.co.za ▪ S 33° 59'26.06" E 018° 46'2.21" ▪ ▦ wingspans.sprinkler.hotspots ▪ F +27 (0)21-881-3102 ▪ **T +27 (0)21-881-3870**

Stellendrift – SHZ Cilliers/Kuün Wyne

The names of Fanie Cilliers' wines reflect his Huguenot grape-growing and wine-making family's history from their arrival at the Cape in 1700. Some of his wines are collaborations with other cellars and winemakers, and some are produced intermittently - the Cab Reserve was last vinified in 2005.

Stellendrift range

Cabernet Sauvignon Reserve ★★★ Good typicity, some herbaceous nuances in **14** ⑦'s berries, palate more serious, savoury & dry from 24 months oak. Pair with food. Occasional release. **Kruispad Pinotage ★★★** Oak (24 months) an equal partner in **13** ⑧'s flavour spectrum: dark berries, allspice, cloves, some freshness on the palate, ends savoury. **VOC Syrah ★★★** Full-ripe expression of the variety, **13** ⑧ dark plums/prunes, liquorice & mocha tones from 24 months in barrel. Savoury finish, match with rich dishes. Not tasted: **Cabernet Sauvignon, Josué Merlot, Cape Huguenot Merlot-Pinotage, Giant Sauvignon Blanc**. Occasional release: **Rosa Rosaceae Red Select, Cape White Savour**. In abeyance: **Merlot-Cabernet Sauvignon Blitz**.

Cilliers Cellars range

Not tasted: **Elizabeth Couvret Merlot, Jacko's Pinotage-Cabernet Sauvignon**. Occasional release: **De Reijgersdaal Cabernet Sauvignon**.

De Oude Opstal range

Not tasted: **Cabernet Sauvignon Reserve, Merlot-Cabernet Sauvignon**. — CR

Location/WO: Stellenbosch ▪ Est 1995 ▪ 1stB 1996 ▪ Closed to public ▪ Owner(s) Fanie Cilliers (SHZ Cilliers/ Kuün Wines) ▪ Winemaker(s)/viticulturist(s) Fanie Cilliers (Nov 1995) ▪ 2,200cs own label 90% red 10% white ▪ PO Box 6340 Uniedal 7612 ▪ fcilliers@vodamail.co.za ▪ www.stellendrift.co.za ▪ F +27 (0)21-887-6561 ▪ T +27 (0)21-887-6561/+27 (0)82-372-5180

Stellenrust   ⓠ ⑪ ⓜ ⊜ ⊚

Growth continues at this Stellenbosch family estate with vineyards in the Helderberg 'golden triangle', Devon Valley and Bottelary Hills. So well have their older dryland vineyards performed in the recent drought conditions (pinotage with a record crop in 2018), and in anticipation of new blocks coming on stream, an increase in production capacity was necessary. With confirmation by the Old Vine Project that vines are officially 'old' at 35, Stellenrust can boast that 10% of their vineyards, mainly chenin, cinsaut and pinotage, qualify. Vineyard health is of utmost importance, acknowledges cellarmaster Tertius Boshoff, and replacing virused vines, young or old, is a strict protocol. Regarding the varietal mix, Tertius and viticulturist Kobie van der Westhuizen plan to replant some of the Helderberg blocks with 'niche varieties' such as assyrtiko, roussanne, marsanne and grenache. Meanwhile, chenin blanc still leads the pack, the '52' awarded best chenin trophy at both the International Wine Challenge and International Wine & Spirit Competition.

Super Premium range

★★★★☆ **Barrel Selection Cabernet Franc** ⊘ ⊛ Distinguished **15** ⑨③ adds 'Barrel Selection'; reflects compatibility of variety with Helderberg. Spice, dried leaf & violet enticements are intense, richly fleshed; 30% new oak adds complexity. Freshness, lively tannins provide lingering memory. **14** ★★★★ ⑧⑦ less complex.

★★★★ **Old Bush Vine Cinsaut 17** ⑧⑨ back on form after quieter **16** ★★★★ ⑧④. Subtle but complex spice, raspberry interweave is lifted by bright natural acid. Oak, 20% new, fine grip add weight & structure without being intrusive.

★★★★ **Cornerstone Pinotage 15** ★★★★★ ⑨⓪ tops **14** ⑧⑨, has concentration, depth of flavour expected from 50 year old Bottelary bushvines. Earthy, dark cherry aromas still restrained, little sombre; palate more expressive, creamily rich but enlivened by perfectly managed tannins & oak, 35% new French.

★★★★ **Peppergrinder's Shiraz** From 40+ year old vineyard. **15** ★★★★★ ⑨⓪ back on expressive, fresh form after heartier **14** ★★★★ ⑧④. Lively spice & floral aromas mingle with savoury flavours, supple texture & ripe, well-padded tannins, offering youthful & future pleasure, like elegant **13** ⑧⑦.

★★★★☆ **Timeless** ⊘ ⊛ **15** ⑨③ cab-led Bordeaux-style blend reflects excellence of vintage; there's power, solid infrastructure & layers of spice & cedar-scented ripe dark fruit; all fused with sense of balance assuring longevity. **14** sold out untasted.

★★★★☆ **Barrel Fermented Chardonnay** ⊛ Oatmeal & pickled lime enhanced by subtle but important 32% new oak, natural ferment deliver delicious **17** ⑨③. Lively mouthwatering fruity acids balanced by underlying creaminess, lead to upbeat, sweet-fruited tail. Lovely now, great future.

★★★★★ **53 Barrel Fermented Chenin Blanc** ⊛ Venerable Bottelary Hills bushvines, now 53, yield glorious **17** ⑨⑤. Still tightly wound but elegant intensity of ripe fruit, complexing honeyed botrytis evident behind steely acidity, especially on endless fantail finish. Deserves time required to reach full potential.

★★★★☆ **Barrel Fermented Sauvignon Blanc** ⊛ Bushvine block celebrates its 4th decade with magnificent **17** ⑨④. Sophisticated & compelling; ferment/lees-ageing in old oak adds a dimension to blackcurrant & fig complexity without dimming fruit's focus, purity. Structure, intensity indicate lengthy future.

★★★★ **Chenin d'Muscat** ⓖ Dainty, amazingly fresh **15** ★★★★★ ⑨④ from chenin (67%) & muscat d'Alexandrie, latter vine dried. Hauntingly, subtly aromatic. Exhilarating acid carves through 118 g/l sugar leaving botrytis-laced echo. Natural ferment, year older oak. 11% alcohol. 375 ml. First tasted since **09** ⑧⑦.

Discontinued: **JJ Handmade Picalót.**

Premium range

★★★★ **Chenin Blanc** ⊘ One of Tertius Boshoff's favourite varieties, little brother to '53', from mature vines. **18** ⑧⑦ quiet red apple & honey features, currently restrained by bracing acidity; needs time to settle, reap enrichment benefits of 16% older-oak-fermented portion, 5 months on lees.

Cabernet Sauvignon ✓ ★★★★ 17 ⑧⑤ true to type & satisfying. Plentiful charm in its scented cassis blackberry ripeness, spiced with cedary oak (30% new), 7% cab franc for extra class. Properly firm but not impenetrable ripe grape tannins allow for current drinking & few years. **Merlot** ★★★ Straightforward spicy plum fruit in 17 ⑦⑧, hint of spicy oak too; zesty, with tight finishing grip. May settle after short ageing. **Pinotage** ✓ ★★★★ 17 ⑧④ in usual youthfully approachable style. Plentiful juicy berry fruit, lively freshness balanced by smooth frame. **Shiraz** ✓ ★★★★ From Helderberg & Bottelary fruit, 17 ⑧⑤ more serious style, still plenty ready enjoyment in its enticing dark spice, blackberry richness & concentration. Firm build, balanced freshness suggest warrants few years' ageing too. **Simplicity** ✓ ★★★★ 17 ⑧③ more restrained, fresher than previous. Mainly shiraz with cab, merlot showing dark, soft berry flavours, lively acidity & tannin trim. Also in 375 ml, like Sauvignon. **Chardonnay** ✓ ★★★★ Zesty, fruity style, given extra interest from small older-oak-fermented component. Generous & lively ripe citrus flavours on 18 ⑧④, gentle creamy backing for immediate drinking pleasure. **Sauvignon Blanc** ✓ ★★★★ Lots of youthful appeal in 18 ⑧⑤; forthright granadilla, tropical juicy flavours, lipsmacking acid & medium body adding to refreshing summer sipping.

Kleine Rust range

Pinotage-Shiraz ✓ ★★☆ Compatible, fruit-driven 17 ⑦⑧ partnership. Smooth juicy flavours, older oak rounded & lifted by few grams sugar. Also in 375ml, 1.5L, like Chenin-Sauvignon. This range Fairtrade certified. **Pinotage Rosé** ✓ ★★★ 18 ⑦⑧ eye-catching pink, lively strawberry & cream flavours extended on just-dry tail. **Chenin Blanc-Sauvignon Blanc** ★★★ 18 ⑦⑧ fulfils usual easy, tasty sipping; juicy mouthful of lively tropical fruit, lifted by few grams sugar. **Semi-Sweet** ★★★ Quiet grapey flavours, gentle fruity acids on chenin-based 18 ⑦⑧ provide more interest than 'semi-sweet' label. Coastal WO. — AL

Location/map: Stellenbosch ▪ Map grid reference: E7, C3 ▪ WO: Stellenbosch/Coastal ▪ Est/1stB 1928 ▪ Tasting & sales (Hberg & Bltlry) Mon-Fri 10—5 Sat 10-3 ▪ Closed Ash Wed, Easter Fri-Mon, Ascension day, Dec 25/26 & Jan 1 ▪ Cellar tours by appt ▪ Farm-style platters & pre-arranged lunches/dinners ▪ BYO picnic ▪ Tour groups ▪ Grape stomping/make your own wine ▪ Gifts ▪ Conferences ▪ Weddings/functions (300+ pax) ▪ Walking/ hiking & MTB trails ▪ Art exhibition ▪ Owner(s) Stellenrust Family Trust ▪ Cellarmaster(s) Tertius Boshoff (Jan 2004) ▪ Winemaker(s) Herman du Preez (2014) ▪ Viticulturist(s) Kobie van der Westhuizen (Jan 2000) ▪ 200ha (cabs s/f, carignan, cinsaut, grenache noir, merlot, ptage, shiraz, chard, chenin, muscat d'A, sauv) ▪ 2,000t/300,000cs own label 50% red 40% white 10% rosé + 40,000cs for clients ▪ Other export brands: Pillar & Post, STELL, Stellenbosch Manor, Steynsrust, Xaro ▪ Brands for clients: Embrace, Lion's Pride, Ruyter's Bin, Sabi Sabi Private Game Lodge ▪ Fairtrade, HACCP, WIETA ▪ PO Box 26 Koelenhof 7605 ▪ info@stellenrust. co.za ▪ www.stellenrust.co.za ▪ S 33° 59' 18.0" E 018° 50' 57.9" (Helderberg) S 33° 51' 44.41" E 018° 46' 34.11" (Bottelary) ▪ ▦ spark.sailor.pancake ▪ F +27 (0)21-880-2284 ▪ **T +27 (0)21-880-2283**

Stellenview Premium Wines ⓠ

Such has been the success at this Devon Valley venture that it's prompted an office move to Technopark outside Stellenbosch, and the wide buying in of grapes to address expanding sales needs. Driving force behind Stellenview is Reino Kruger, cellarmaster, entrepreneur and marketer. The ranges keep growing (not all featured in the guide), each carefully positioned to meet market requirements locally and internationally, with many African/wildlife-themed labels and names giving a clear sense of place abroad.

Stellenview Reserve range

Cabernet Sauvignon ★★★★ Smoky tones & liquorice alongside dark-fruit ripeness, 15 ⑧④ plush, with enough grip on finish for food, ageing. As Kruger sibling, 30% new oak, same time in barrel, similar style. **Shiraz** ★★★★ Oak vanilla attractive top note to 15 ⑧④'s lush dark fruit; palate juicy, smoothly round, tannins in support, supple. Ends savoury, good grip on finish to partner meat dishes. Stellenbosch WO this range & next.

Kruger Family Reserve range

Cabernet Sauvignon ★★★★ Longer oaking at this range level, 16 months. 15 ⑧④ deep & dark toned, whiffs of wood char & liquorice, adding some complexity around the cassis/plum core. Grip at the end speaks of latent power. **Shiraz** ★★★★ Savoury tones to 15 ⑧④'s plum/raspberry fruit, juicy, smooth body with lots of spice in the flavours, finishing dry. Good quality progression from Great Five & Cape Five ranges. **Chardonnay** ★★★ House-style elegance & racy acidity for these whites. 17 ⑧② essentially citrus with

Lemon Cream biscuit extras from lees contact & oak. Tasty, good fruit/wood balance. **Sauvignon Blanc** ★★★ Early picked **17** (81), just 12.5% alcohol; lemon purity & zesty-fresh, some pear & mineral notes making it more food friendly.

Cape Five Reserve range

Cabernet Sauvignon Ⓥ ★★★ Cab's typical blackcurrant styling for **14** (81), juicy-smooth & round, enough acidity to brighten. Amenable tannins, ending dry, food friendly. Year barrel, 10% new unless noted. **Merlot** ★★★ More oak than Great Five sibling (as all) gives **16** (81) a meaty scent, notes of cloves/allspice, but the red berries are there in the flavours. Streamlined, nice freshness. **Pinotage** ★★★ Blueberries & mulberries, well-spiced **17** (81) has variety's trademark juicy palate, fresh & fruity, but a serious note in the tannins, firm but ripe, promising a future. **Shiraz** ★★★ Dark toned, there's opulence & ripeness in **15** (81); curvaceous body, nicely smooth. Marriage of vanilla-spiced oak & plummy fruit adds to the appeal. **Red Reserve Organic** Ⓥ ★★★ Six-part blend of mainly shiraz, cab & merlot, **13** (82) is opulent, plush, red berries rather than dark, enough flesh for the tannins, now equal partners. Dry finish a food plus. 20% new oak, 36 months. **Cape Premier Red** ★★★ Shiraz 60% with merlot, small portion unwooded, **15** (81) has fruitcake richness with all the spices, vanilla showing strongly. Heaps of flavour, rounded body, tannins supple. Will make many friends.

Great Five Reserve range

Cabernet Sauvignon ★★★ Small portion unoaked, as all these. Appealing smokiness to **16** (78), fitting well with blackcurrant fruit. Balanced, smooth, drinks easily. **Merlot** ★★★ Merlot at its accessible, plummy best; **16** (78) gentle herbaceous note, smooth textured, with mintiness adding piquancy. **Pinotage** ★★★ Fruit shines in **16** (78), mulberries & plums, prominent vanilla spicing. Ends dry but tannins offset by succulence, nice smooth effect. **Shiraz** ★★★ Displays the spicy/dark fruit profile one expects from shiraz; **15** (78) ripe & smooth, good drinkability. **Cape Premier Red** Ⓥ ★★★ Shiraz/merlot in **15** (81), luscious red fruit supported by tailored tannins designed to give immediate access. — CR

Location/map: Stellenbosch ▪ Map grid reference: D4 ▪ WO: Coastal/Stellenbosch ▪ Est/1stB 2015 ▪ Tasting, sales & cellar tours Mon-Fri 8-5 Sat/Sun by appt ▪ Closed all pub hols ▪ Owner(s) Reino Kruger ▪ Cellarmaster(s) Reino Kruger (Apr 2015) ▪ Winemaker(s) Monique Fourie (Jan 2018), Skye Nolan (Jan 2017) ▪ 12ha (cabs s/f, merlot, p verdot) ▪ 450t/500,000cs own label 80% red 20% white ▪ Other export brands: Africa Five, Cape Discovery, KFK Reserve, Openers, Pride of Kings, Zulu 8 ▪ PO Box 7177 Stellenbosch 7599 ▪ info@stellenviewwines.com ▪ www.stellenviewwines.com ▪ S 33° 54'.0.61" E 018° 48'23.49" ▪ ⌨ unique. pencils.kite ▪ F +27 (0)86-240-7394 ▪ **T +27 (0)87-152-0997/+27 (0)76-248-4739**

Stellenzicht Wines

This Helderberg Mountain property, long hailed for top-quality wine, remains closed for major renovations, having been bought in 2017 by Baron Hans von Staff-Reitzenstein. The Bavarian wine collector and investor, and partner in nearby Ernie Els Wines, has handed control over the 218 ha estate and 1980s cellar to acclaimed Ernie Els cellarmaster Louis Strydom, who looks forward to 'breathing new life' into a 'wonderful old grande dame of the Cape winelands'. The vision is to develop a quintessential New World property in an area capable of wines of rare 'structure and fruit purity'.

Location/map: Stellenbosch ▪ Map grid reference: F8 ▪ Est 1982 ▪ 1stB 1989 ▪ Tasting room closed for renovations - please phone ahead ▪ Owner(s) Stellenzicht Wines ▪ Winemaker(s) L'Re Burger (Jul 2017) ▪ Viticulturist(s) Nico Nortjé ▪ 218ha/99ha (cabs s/f, malbec, merlot, p verdot, ptage, shiraz, chard, sauv, sem, viog) ▪ PO Box 7599 Stellenbosch 7599 ▪ info@stellenzichtwines.com ▪ S 33° 59' 50.0" E 018° 51' 59.8" ▪ ⌨ nozzles.drilling.pegged ▪ F +27 (0)21-880-1107 ▪ **T +27 (0)21-880-1103**

Stettyn Family Vineyards

Ⓥ ☕ ⓞ Ⓑ ♿

The name change, from 'Cellar' to 'Family Vineyards', better reflects that all but one of the farms growing grapes for this state-of-the-art production facility near Villiersdorp are family owned, and even the outlier is part of the original 18th-century farm Stettyn, home to eight generations of Bothas. A 'quality first' approach sees them continue as sought-after supplier to leading export brands, including FirstCape.

Stettyn range

The Guardian ② ★★★★ Cab & shiraz in **15** ⑧, fuller bodied than previous but still smooth, accessible; lots going on: pepper, smoke, leather, earth & vanilla oak, too. Not tasted: **Reserve Straw Wine**, **Reserve Cape Vintage**.

Griffin range

Cabernet Sauvignon ⊘ ★★★★ Offers good everyday drinking with its soft texture, ripe mulberry fruit, undaunting 13.6% alcohol. **16** ⑧ only 30% wooded, 6 months, like most of these reds. **Merlot** ★★★ Very approachable **16** ⑧, ripe, juicy plum & blueberry fruit, smoother than previous unwooded vintage. **Pinotage** ⑥ ★★★ Packed with ripe red fruit, **15** ⑧ also has savoury hints of mocha & smoked meat. **Shiraz** ★★★ Quite jammy in its blackcurrant intensity, **16** ⑦ a fruit bomb with a hint of earthiness. **Chardonnay** ② ★★★★ Light, unwooded **16** ⑧ redolent of citrus blossoms, quite pretty, sweet-sour tangerine & pineapple flavours, smooth & clean. **Chenin Blanc** ⑥ ⊘ ★★★★ At friendly 12.5% alcohol, **18** ⑧ slips down easily with peach, pear & zesty orange citrus, lingering on finish. This, Sauvignon & Stone duo first WO Stettyn wines in guide. **Sauvignon Blanc** ★★★ Refreshes with tangy green apple & lime flavours, smooth texture in **18** ⑧. Not tasted: **Pinot Grigio**, **Chardonnay-Pinot Noir**.

Stone range

Red ⊘ ★★★ Uncomplicated ripe dark-fruit appeal on **17** ⑦, unoaked 50/50 merlot & petit verdot, very quaffable, with modest alcohol. **White** ⊘ ★★★ Crisp, dry **18** ⑧ has 30% sauvignon adding zesty lime to chenin's soft ripe melon, grapefruit pith on finish. — JG

Location: Villiersdorp ▪ Map: Worcester ▪ Map grid reference: A6 ▪ WO: Western Cape/Stettyn ▪ Est 1964 ▪ 1stB 1984 ▪ Tasting & sales Mon-Thu 9–5 Fri 9-4.30 Sat (Oct-Mar) 10-1 ▪ Closed all pub hols ▪ Cellar tours from 1.30-4 by appt ▪ BYO picnic ▪ Facilities for children ▪ Vineyard tours R200pp ▪ Owner(s) 4 major producers (3 family owned) ▪ Cellarmaster(s) Albie Treurnicht (Nov 2000) ▪ Winemaker(s) Albie Treurnicht (Nov 2000), with JM Crafford (Nov 2012) ▪ Viticulturist(s) Pierre Snyman (VinPro) ▪ 400ha (cab, merlot, ptage, shiraz, chard, chenin, sauv) ▪ 7,500t/19,000cs own label 25% red 75% white + 6.1m L bulk ▪ Brands for clients: FirstCape, Felicité, The Griffin Range ▪ ARA, BEE, HACCP, IPW, WIETA ▪ PO Box 1520 Worcester 6849 ▪ info@stettynwines.co.za ▪ www.stettynwines.co.za ▪ S 33° 52′14.8″ E 019° 22′2.3″ ▪ ✉ exporting.trouble.solving ▪ F +27 (0)86-771-3568 ▪ **T +27 (0)23-340-4220**

☐ **Steynsrust** *see Stellenrust*
☐ **Steytler** *see Kaapzicht Wine Estate*
☐ **Stilfontein** *see Eerste Hoop Wine Cellar*

Stoep ②

Garagiste label Stoep is owned by SA asset manager Gerrit Mars and Swiss partners, and the blended Red produced under contract. After a decade's maturation in barrel and bottle, the '09 is about to be released.

Location: Stellenbosch ▪ Est/1stB 2001 ▪ Tasting, sales & tours by appt ▪ Owner(s) Zelpy 1023 (Pty) Ltd: 3 shareholders Gerrit Mars (SA), Sven Haefner (Swiss) & Daniel Hofer (Swiss) ▪ Cellarmaster(s)/winemaker(s) André Liebenberg (Romond) & Gerrit Mars ▪ 50% red 50% white ▪ gerritmars@mweb.co.za ▪ **T +27 (0)82-352-5583**

Stofberg Family Vineyards ② ⑪ ◎ ⑧

Third-generation Mariëtte Coetzee (née Stofberg) is the winegrower behind this Breedekloof family boutique venture with a very rare - and very good - pinot blanc in its top range. Also stellar is the new chardonnay, produced under Mariëtte's guidance by cellar assistant Israel Delport, whose dedication and effort earned him a place on a Franco-SA exchange programme, gaining priceless work experience in Burgundy.

Mariëtte range

★★★★ **Syrah** ② Leathery dark fruit on concentrated **14** ⑧, fruity palate in balance with firm tannin & 30 months French oak. Finish is long, with cocoa dusting. Deserves time to show best.

★★★★ **Chenin Blanc** Great care taken: only fruit from better performing of 2 interplanted clones harvested for this bold but well-balanced, flavourful wine. **17** ⑧ billows sweet tropical fruit, vanilla & spice from barrel ferment. No **16**.

★★★★☆ **Pinot Blanc** ⊛ Beautifully crafted; one of only 2 varietal bottlings in the guide. **17** ⑭ melange of orchard fruit, apricot kernel, exotic spice, roasted nuts & brush of vanilla from spontaneous ferment in old oak. Rich, broad layers of citrus on silky palate.

★★★★ **Méthode Cap Classique Chardonnay** ⊘ Rich & robust **13** ㊷ traditional-method dry bubbly has creamy lemon curd flavours & a contrasting fine, seamless mousse. Lovely complexity.

Cabernet Sauvignon ⑭ ★★★★ Bright ruby colour, **15** ㉟ ample ripe dark berries, firm tannin structure, warm finish from 15.5% alcohol. Serious intent evident in barrel ferment, 24 months ageing.

Special range ⑭

★★★★☆ **Israel Chardonnay** Delicate ripe apple, white blossom & orchard fruit aromas on barrel-fermented **17** ⑨⓪, made by a treasured member of staff. Just-dry but harmonious, with crème brûlée flavours, lengthy & elegant.

Mía range

Shiraz ★★★ Spicy & bright fruited, succulent & easy, hints of mocha on finish in **16** ㈧③. Good foil for tomato-based fare. **Pinot Noir Rosé** ⊘ ★★★ Vibrant blush on **17** ㉛ mirrored in riot of red-berry fruit, lemony acidity on dry exit is food friendly. **Chenin Blanc** ⊘ ★★★ Easygoing sipper **17** ㉗ unoaked, fresh stonefruit flavour & squeeze grapefruit at end. Breede River Valley WO. — WB

Location: Rawsonville ▪ Map: Breedekloof ▪ Map grid reference: C5 ▪ WO: Breedekloof/Breede River Valley ▪ Est 2011 ▪ 1stB 2012 ▪ Tasting, sales & restaurant Mon-Thu 11-9 Fri/Sat 11-10 Sun 11-3 ▪ Tasting R25/3 Mía wines, R45/4 Mariëtte wines or R65 for all 7; gin experience R55/2 gins & 2 tonics with dressings; beer tasting R45/4 craft beers ▪ Cellar tours by appt ▪ Closed Dec 25 & Jan 1 ▪ Ou Stokery Restaurant, admin@oustokery.co.za ▪ Play area for children ▪ Craft gin/brandy distillery ▪ Craft beer brewery ▪ Owner(s) PJD Stofberg, M Stofberg-Coetzee & GJN Coetzee ▪ Cellarmaster(s)/winemaker(s) Mariëtte Stofberg-Coetzee (Nov 2011) ▪ Viticulturist(s) Pieter Jacobus Daniël Stofberg (Jan 1981), Andries de Wet (Jun 2002, consultant) & Gideon Jacobus Nicolaas Coetzee (Nov 2011) ▪ ±102ha ▪ 42.5t 19% red 25% white 12% MCC 9% rosé 35% brandy ▪ PO Box 298 Rawsonville 6845 ▪ mariette@stofbergfamilyvineyards.co.za ▪ www.stofbergfamilyvineyards. co.za ▪ S 33° 40' 17.24" E 019° 18' 37.27" ▪ ▱ patterns.trumpeters.dragging ▪ F +27 (0)86-770-5138 ▪ **T +27 (0)82-867-6958 (cellar); +27 (0)82-511-0500 (restaurant)**

☐ **Stone** see Stettyn Family Vineyards

Stonebird Wines ⊘

The origin of the name of Gavin Patterson's brand is Zimbabwean (as is his own): 'a mythical birdlike creature' symbolising a connection to earth and nature. The second (2017) vintages of his wines, vinified and matured in Italian clay pots, were still resting as we went to press — allowing them 'to relax a bit more', as he feels this technique gives rise to layers of flavour that 'are not all initially apparent but are later revealed'. Gavin himself is clearly not resting: he's taken up a 'winemaking day job in the exciting UK industry'.

★★★★☆ **Pinot Noir** ⊘ There's raspberry, cherry & spice to be detected on **16** ㉙② from Hemel-enAarde, but beyond the fresh, flavourful presence it's serious, intense & savoury rather than merely pretty, with a little sweetness hovering over the lovely dryness. Fermented/10 months in clay pot. Good prospects.

★★★★☆ **Chardonnay** ⊘ The pleasing chalky dryness (it's rare to lack fruit sweetness on local ripe chardonnay) on **16** ㉙② perhaps prompted by ferment & maturation in 400-litre clay amphoras. Savoury succulence & fruit intensity on the palate, with a persistent finish. 12.6% alcohol.

★★★★ **Gonzo** ⊘ Why make, in a solera, fortified pinot noir with very ripe fruit & pinot husk spirit? Well, because it can interest like this **NV** ㈧⑨. It's bright, dry in effect (67 g/l sugar; 18% alcohol). Not complex (coffee-ground, orange peel, tealeaf notes) but a little strange & very moreish. 375 ml. — TJ, CvZ

Location: Elgin ▪ WO: Walker Bay ▪ Est/1stB 2016 ▪ Tasting by appt only ▪ Owner(s)/winemaker(s) Gavin Patterson ▪ 616cs own label 47% red 45% white 8% fortified ▪ c/o Farm No. 7 Viljoenshoop Rd Elgin 7180 ▪ gavin@stonebirdwines.com ▪ www.stonebirdwines.com

☐ **Stonedale** see Rietvallei Wine Estate
☐ **Stonedance** see Piekenierskloof Wine Company
☐ **Stonehaven** see Cape Point Vineyards

Stone Ridge Wines ⓠ

The Eksteens have been growing wine grapes on their 300-ha Voor Paardeberg property for 6 generations. Viticulturist Jan Eksteen keeps back prime red and white grapes to craft small parcels for the Stone Ridge and flagship Eksteen Family Vineyards labels with adviser Bernard Smuts.

Location/map: Paarl • Map grid reference: D1 • Est 2002 • 1stB 2003 • Tasting by appt only • Winemaker(s) Bernard Smuts (consultant) • Viticulturist(s) Jan Eksteen (2002) • 300ha (cab, ptage, shiraz, chard, chenin, sauv) • 20t/2,400cs own label 50% red 50% white • PO Box 7046 Northern Paarl 7623 • stoneridge@uitkijk. co.za • S 33° 34′ 19.72″ E 018° 52′ 45.48″ • ⓦ chamber.pleasant.grasshopper • F +27 (0)21-869-8071 • T +27 (0)82-324-8372

☐ **Stone Road** see Louisvale Wines
☐ **Stones in the Sun** see Dunstone Winery

Stonewall Wines ⓠ ⓘ ⓐ

Happy Vale, De Waal Koch's Stellenbosch farm, is almost 200 years old, its elegantly gabled cellar dating back to 1828. The boutique wine range is named for another standout architectural feature, the traditional, sturdy ringmuur. Consultant winemaker Ronell Wiid praises the soils, saying they're suited to cabs sauvignon and franc, and linear, focused wines rather than fruity, rich ones. 'For ageing,' she recommends.

★★★★ **Cabernet Sauvignon** ⊘ Fruit compote & cinnamon spice on **16** (86), somewhat 'old school' but attractive & sleek nonetheless, well-integrated oak (40% new) supporting the fruit.

★★★★ **Rubér** ⊘ Cab franc leads, as last, in elegant **16** (87) Bordeaux blend with merlot & dab cab. Firm, toned palate with graphite & inky blue & black fruit. Only older French oak, 18 months.

Chardonnay ⓠ ★★★ Oak-fermented & -aged **16** (81), ripe & rounded, ready to drink. — FM

Location/WO: Stellenbosch • Map: Helderberg • Map grid reference: C2 • Est 1828 • 1stB 1997 • Tasting & sales by appt Mon-Fri 10—5 Sat 10—1 • Closed Easter Fri-Sun, Dec 25/26 & Jan 1 • Refreshments by appt • Helderberg Wine Festival • Owner(s) De Waal Koch • Cellarmaster(s) Ronell Wiid (Jan 2000, consultant) • Winemaker(s) De Waal Koch (Jan 2000) • Viticulturist(s) De Waal Koch (Jun 1984) • 90ha/70ha (cabs s/f, merlot, ptage, shiraz, chard, pinot gris, sauv) • 300t/4,000cs own label 80% red 20% white • PO Box 5145 Helderberg 7135 • stonewall@mweb.co.za • www.stonewallwines.co.za • S 34° 1′ 59.0″ E 018° 49′ 14.6″ • ⓦ resting.approximates.qualifying • T +27 (0)21-855-3675/+27 (0)83-310-2407

Stony Brook ⓠ ⓐ ⓑ

Excitement is in the air at the Franschhoek vineyards and cellar owned by the McNaught family. There's the launch of their maiden cabernet franc, and release of its red siblings from the lauded 2015 vintage, 'among the best to be produced on Stony Brook' avers co-owner Nigel. The self-catering cottages, with magnificent views of Franschhoek Valley, remain the best place to enjoy the wide range of wines. One of these, The Max, has the name of the family's irrepressible Jack Russell, who sadly took off his collar for the last time in 2018.

★★★★☆ **Ghost Gum** ⓐ As always, 100% cabernet from rigorously sorted grapes. **14** (93) quintessential cassis, cedar & graphite notes, generous body encased in authoritative tannin. Bone-dry, structured for decade or more. Seriousness underscored by 34 months in new French oak.

★★★★ **Cabernet Franc** ⓃⒶ ⓐ Auspicious debut in **16** (89), meticulously crafted to preserve red-fruit character. Intensity leavened by mint & other herby notes, serious tannin structure for the long haul. 16 months older oak, only best 2 barrels bottled.

★★★★ **Pinot Noir** ⊘ Vibrant & alluring **16** (87)'s sour black cherry enveloped in fine-textured tannin, sympathetic oaking (18 months, older barrels) adds depth, richness, on bone-dry finish.

★★★★☆ **Syrah Reserve** Intense black-fruit character enlivened by white pepper & crisp acidity, helps disguise 15% alcohol though, overall, **15** ★★★★ (89) shade off unshowy & understated **14** (92).

★★★★☆ **Ovidius** ⓐ Big, bold (15.2% alcohol) **15** (93) from tempranillo, inky black fruit & oak-derived coconut & choc tones (26 months, 50% new). Plush, leathery & comforting - like a favourite armchair.

★★★★☆ **The Max** ⊘ ⓐ 4-way Bordeaux blend dominated by cab & merlot, opulent fruit beautifully supported by imposing tannin scaffold. **15** (93) will reward few years patience.

★★★★ **SMV** Succulent & harmonious **15** ⑧⑧ mix mourvèdre (43%), co-fermented shiraz (54%) & viognier; partial carbonic maceration/wild ferment, some stems included for freshness.

★★★★ **Heart of the Lees** Unusual winemaking technique for Elgin sauvignon: bunch pressed & settled, lees then fermented in older wood. Only 2 barrels of **16** ⑧⑨, leesy richness punctuated, lifted by zesty farewell. Excellent, involving, though not quite as impactful as **15** ★★★★☆ ⑨⓪.

★★★★ **Sauvignon Blanc** Incorrectly vintaged last time, **17** ⑧⑧ from Walker Bay an explosion of passionfruit & lime, glorious fusion zippy acidity & fruit intensity with satisfying palate weight from 8 months on lees plus regular bâtonnage.

★★★★☆ **Ghost Gum White** (Ⓐ) Continues fine form of previous vintages in **17** ⑨③. Mostly chardonnay (88%) with semillon for vivacity, intense but unshowy, delectable citrus flavours & generous creamy farewell. Clever, almost unobtrusive 50% new oak.

★★★★ **The 'J'** Multi-region blend led by viognier with chenin, semillon, chardonnay & sauvignon, part barrel fermented. Floral, spicy & fruity **17** ⑧⑦ light-tripping yet full of flavour.

★★★★☆ **Lyle** Accomplished MCC sparkler from chardonnay, tiny portion **13** ⑨② barrel fermented before second fermentation in bottle & 4 years on lees. Lively lemon & brioche appeal, creamy mouthfeel pepped up by oystershell minerality.

★★★★☆ **V on A** Unctuous, full-sweet yet vibrant **15** ⑧⑦, spicy apricot character perfect with a fruity dessert. Partly botrytised viognier, barrel fermented in 4th fill French oak, aged 30 months.

Occasional release: **Mourvèdre**, **Camissa**, **Snow Gum**. Discontinued: **Bailey**. — HC

Location/map: Franschhoek ▪ Map grid reference: D1 ▪ WO: Franschhoek/Walker Bay/Elgin/Western Cape ▪ Est 1995 ▪ 1stB 1996 ▪ Tasting by appt ▪ Fee R50 ▪ Sales Mon-Fri 10—5 Sat 10-1; enquire about pub hols ▪ Self-catering cottages ▪ Owner(s) Nigel & Joy McNaught ▪ Winemaker(s) Craig McNaught (2011), with Michael Blaauw (Jan 2008) ▪ Viticulturist(s) Paul Wallace (consultant) ▪ 23ha/14ha (cab, malbec, merlot, mourv, p verdot, pinot, shiraz, tempranillo, chard, sem, viog) ▪ 100t/6,500cs own label 65% red 35% white ▪ ISO 14001:2003 ▪ PO Box 22 Franschhoek 7690 ▪ info@stonybrook.co.za ▪ www.stonybrook.co.za ▪ S 33° 56' 28.7" E 019° 7' 4.1" ▪ ⬚ annual.offsets.bushes ▪ **T +27 (0)21-876-2182**

Stormfontein

Fred Huang and Gideon Joubert export various products, mostly to Taiwan, including wine under the brand Stormfontein. The labels reference SA's Bill of Rights (Love, Privacy, Life, Freedom, Dignity and Equality), feature designs by local artists, and support DICE, a KwaZulu-Natal charity for children and the elderly.

Location: Somerset West ▪ Est 2015 ▪ 1stB 2014 ▪ Closed to public ▪ Owner(s) G.D. Joubert & Fred Huang ▪ 500cs own label 33% red 33% white 33% rosé + 500cs for clients ▪ 39 Plein Str Somerset West 7140 ▪ donnie@stormfontein.co.za ▪ www.stormfontein.co.za ▪ F +27 (0)21-845-4089 ▪ **T +27 (0)21-845-4093**

Storm Wines   Ⓠ

With his 2016 pinot noirs, Hannes Storm celebrated the fifth release under his own label - he was still working at Hamilton Russell Vineyards in its earliest years, before going solo. Noting with pleasure that the wines are ageing 'graciously', he looks back at the years of intense focus ('with blood, sweat and tears') and feels, modestly, that 'we are finally beginning to understand the intricacies of the unique terroirs that we work with'. Hannes is, in fact, the only producer to offer single-parcel pinots from each of the three Hemel-en-Aarde wards. They're made in identical, hands-off fashion, so their identities come only from their vineyard origins. They are also among the Cape's most uncompromising in their classicism and seriousness. There's just one chardonnay, however - so far.

★★★★☆ **Ignis Pinot Noir** (Ⓐ) Lifted perfume & pure-fruited charm with forest floor undertone on **16** ⑨④ from Upper Hemel-en-Aarde. Like previous vintages, the easiest in youth, the least severely structured, of a range that needs years to start showing its best. Splendidly balanced, long-lingering.

★★★★☆ **Vrede Pinot Noir** (Ⓐ) Deeply intense, brooding **16** ⑨③ from Hemel-en-Aarde Valley, with a fruity-savoury density seething with pent-up energy. The most overt structure of acid &, especially, tannin of the 3 pinots, also the most complete-seeming. Needs many years to start delivering on its potential.

★★★★☆ **Ridge Pinot Noir** ⊛ Another brooder needing time. **16** ⑨③ deep, sweet perfumed fruit with savoury complexity, yet fairly austere in youth. Touch less mid-palate conviction than Vrede, & less tannic. These all 25% new oak. Pinots all natural ferment, 10-15% wholebunch, no fining/filtration.

★★★★☆ **Vrede Chardonnay** ⊛ Usual aromatic & flavour complexity on **17** ⑨③ from Hemel-en-Aarde Valley: floral, stonefruit, oatmeal, orange peel. Subtly powerful palate, stony & silky, with fine lemony acid; the 25% new oak only supportive. Enduring, deeply satisfying. Also in magnum, as all.— TJ

Location: Hermanus ▪ Map: Walker Bay & Bot River ▪ Map grid reference: B4 ▪ WO: Hemel-en-Aarde Valley/Upper Hemel-en-Aarde Valley/Hemel-en-Aarde Ridge ▪ Est 2011 ▪ 1stB 2012 ▪ Tasting by appt ▪ Closed Easter Fri/Sun, Ascension day, Dec 25/26 & Jan 1 ▪ Owner(s) Hannes Storm ▪ Winemaker(s)/viticulturist(s) Hannes Storm (Dec 2011) ▪ 5ha (pinot, chard) ▪ 18t/1,400cs own label 80% red 20% white ▪ IPW ▪ PO Box 431 Hermanus 7200 ▪ hannes@stormwines.co.za ▪ www.stormwines.co.za ▪ S 34° 21' 16.99" E 019° 16' 59.23" ▪ �░ excavating.vacuuming.flocked ▪ **T +27 (0)28-125-0073**

Stoumann's Wines   ⓟ ⍟ ◎

The Cape's 'Big Dry' hasn't been all bad for Vredendal boutique vintners and nature lovers Napoleon and Annalise Stoumann, who support conservation of the Cape Geometric Tortoise. Due to grape shortages, a large producer snapped up their entire crop. But clearly that meant nothing new to bottle under the family brand, so they hasten to add that stocks of some previous releases are available for always-welcome visitors.

Location: Vredendal ▪ Map: Olifants River ▪ Map grid reference: B4 ▪ Est 1998 ▪ 1stB 2008 ▪ Tasting, sales & cellar tours by appt only ▪ Closed all pub hols ▪ Cheese platters/meals/braai available on request ▪ Tour groups ▪ Farm produce ▪ Conferences ▪ Owner(s)/cellarmaster(s)/winemaker(s) Napoleon Stoumann ▪ Viticulturist(s) CG Stoumann (Jan 2010) ▪ 100ha (cab, merlot, muscadel r/w, ptage, ruby cab, shiraz, chard, chenin, cbard, hanepoot) ▪ 1,040t/4,000cs own label 50% red 40% white 10% rosé + 800,000L bulk ▪ IPW ▪ PO Box 307 Vredendal 8160 ▪ stoumanns@cybersmart.co.za ▪ www.stoumanns.co.za ▪ S 31° 41' 20.5" E 018° 30' 23.3" ▪ ⍟ unswerving.cloves.burrito ▪ **F +27 (0)27-213-1448 ▪ T +27 (0)27-213-2323/+27 (0)83-236-2794**

Strandveld Wines   ⓟ ⍟ ⌂ ◎

Inland from Cape Agulhas, Africa's most southerly point, at the continent's most southerly winery, vineyards are wind-bitten and cool. Conditions are not exactly easy here, then, but viticulturist Tienie Wentzel can give Conrad Vlok, winemaker at Strandveld from the start, the distinctive sort of grapes he wants. And the vineyards are expanding: recently planted grenache and viognier are now being followed by more shiraz and sauvignon blanc, on a newly broken part of the farm. The indigenous vegetation is not forgotten, with Strandveld Vineyards part of the Nuwejaars Wetland project, which sustainably oversees protection of the precious wetlands and their endemic populations.

Strandveld range

★★★★ **Anders Sparrman Pinot Noir** ⊘ Raspberry, cherry on **15** ⑧⑧ lead to ripe, rich, sweetly fruited palate, with firm tannins. Tight, youthful; less charm & generosity than power. Needs time.

★★★★☆ **Syrah** ⊛ Has a splash of viognier which adds subtly to the forceful ripe, spicy, dark fruit. **15** ⑨② firmly structured in a vigorous, muscular, lean style, serious & dry. Should go many years. Oaking (40% new) integrated much more than on **14** ★★★★ ⑧⑦.

★★★★☆ **The Navigator** ⊛ Adds grenache & a little viognier & mourvèdre to 58% shiraz in **15** ⑨③. More generous & rich in fruit character than Syrah, but also with powerfully 'masculine' effect of solidly firm structure. Toasty oak support (third new). Give it time. WO Cape S Coast. Also in magnum, as Adamastor.

★★★★☆ **Sauvignon Blanc Pofadderbos** ⊛ Broader, more complexly suggestive aromas & flavours on **17** ⑨③ than the First Sighting version. Ripe but fresh palate, rather elegant & with a lovely blackcurrant & stony intensity telling of the cool climate.

★★★★ **Adamastor** Sauvignon leads semillon as usual in **16** ⑧⑨. Less intense, softer & more serene than the straight sauvignons - partial oaking adds to breadth - but still lively, juicy & fresh.

Skaamgesiggie Méthode Cap Classique ★★★★ Name aptly suggests a shy blush for this rosé sparkling from pinot noir - though the fruity charm of berries & red apple is not held back. **16** ⑧⑤ dry, fresh, balanced & pleasing.

First Sighting range

★★★★ **Sauvignon Blanc** ⊘ As usual, semillon splash on **17** ⑧⑨ adds weight. Delightful mix of tropical, citrus, grassy & blackcurrant, with good flavour intensity & luscious, succulent acid.

Pinot Noir ⊘ ★★★ Fresh, modest aromas & lightish fruit on **15** ⑧②, with grippy acid, a tannic touch & some toasty oak notes. A little severe. WO Cape Agulhas, like Sauvignon. **Shiraz** ★★★★ Drops of mourvèdre & viognier & 12% grenache on rather elegant, balanced **16** ⑧④. Decent fruit depth, light spicing; herbal element & grippy acidity confirm cool-climate origin. WO Cape S Coast, as next. **Rosé** ★★★ Just-about-dry **18** ⑧①, from grenache & shiraz, is fruity & forward, with almost bubblegum aromas. — TJ

Location: Elim ▪ Map: Southern Cape ▪ Map grid reference: B3 ▪ WO: Elim/Cape South Coast/Cape Agulhas ▪ Est 2002 ▪ 1stB 2003 ▪ Tasting, sales & cellar tours Mon-Thu 8–5 Fri 8-4 Sat 10-3 ▪ Closed Good Fri & Dec 25 ▪ Farm produce ▪ BYO picnic ▪ Walks/hikes ▪ MTB ▪ Conservation area ▪ Two self-catering cottages ▪ Owner(s) Strandveld Vineyards & Rietfontein Trust ▪ Winemaker(s) Conrad Vlok (Dec 2004) ▪ Viticulturist(s) Tienie Wentzel (Oct 2009) ▪ 64ha (grenache, mourv, pinot, shiraz, sauv, sem, viog) ▪ 280t/27,000cs own label 45% red 55% white ▪ IPW ▪ PO Box 1020 Bredasdorp 7280 ▪ info@strandveld.co.za ▪ www.strandveld. co.za ▪ S 34° 39' 59.2" E 019° 47' 26.8" ▪ ⟲ logbook.resentful.promise ▪ F +27 (0)28-482-1902/6 ▪ **T +27 (0)28-482-1902/6**

☐ **String of Pearls** see Francois La Garde

Strydom Vintners

After many years of (rather famously) making wines for others, 'a moment arrived where opportunity and possibility collided' for Rianie and Louis Strydom. They 'took a leap into the great unknown' by buying land on the Simonsberg in Stellenbosch and planting vines for their own range. Louis, MD and cellarmaster at Ernie Els, cares for the vineyards; Rianie, until recently cellarmaster at Haskell/Dombeya, makes the wines, or, as she puts it, 'transforms his handiwork into wines that can capture their origins and the personality of where they are grown'.

★★★★☆ **Rex Cabernet Sauvignon** ⓧ Cab certainly is 'King' in Stellenbosch, & this portfolio. Cassis & pencil lead features are still coiled in taut, restrained **15** ⑨④, which had 30% new oak, 18 months. Like **14** ⑨②, will need time to unveil the generous, rich, dark-fruit filling. But well worth the wait.

★★★★ **Rock Star Syrah** From rocky, marginal land, svelte **15** ⑧⑨ shares **14** ⑧⑥'s dark spice richness, fine red-berry fruit & full body, but merits higher rating for superbly balanced, supple structure.

★★★★☆ **CWG Auction Reserve The Game Changer Cabernet Franc-Merlot** ⑩④ 🅐 Different take on the Strydoms' CWG Auction reds, cab sauvignon ceding control to franc (80%) for first time in **15** ⑨④. Fabulous violet & cedar aromas herald measured melange of red/cranberry fruit, tight acidity & polished tannins. 15% alcohol, but balanced, as is 40% new oak, 18 months.

★★★★ **Danièle Chenin Blanc** Wine named for daughter better be good... & is! Old oak- & amphora-aged **17** ⑧⑧ has a distinct personality: fresh pear & exotic rosemary in a compact structure threaded with zesty acidity.

Retro Red Blend ★★★★ #ThrowbackThursday could be hashtag here, given traditional cab & cinsaut composition - also thimble cab franc in **16** ⑧⑤, superior country wine, savoury & sinewy, excellent hearty food partner. WO W Cape. **The Freshman** ★★★☆ Previewed **18** ⑧④ sauvignon blanc; clean-cut lemongrass & greengage flavours, balanced & vivacious. — DS

Location: Stellenbosch ▪ WO: Stellenbosch/Western Cape ▪ Est 2012 ▪ 1stB 2009 ▪ Closed to public ▪ Owner(s) Louis & Rianie Strydom ▪ Cellarmaster(s) Rianie Strydom ▪ 8.5ha (cab, shiraz) ▪ 1,000cs own label 70% red 30% white ▪ IPW ▪ PO Box 1290 Stellenbosch 7599 ▪ rianie@strydomvineyards.com ▪ www.strydomvineyards.com ▪ **T +27 (0)21-889-8553/+27 (0)82-290-6399**

☐ **Stubborn Man** see Pearl Mountain
☐ **Stumble Vineyards** see Flagstone Winery
☐ **Suikerbossie Ek Wil Jou Hê** see Boer & Brit

Sumaridge Wines

（⚲）（🍴）（🏠）（◎）（⚇）（⚲）

British owners Simon Turner and wife Holly Bellingham are now in their second decade of ownership of this Upper Hemel-en-Aarde Valley farm, and can be proud of their achievements. The first Walker Bay-area producers to get WIETA ethical accreditation, their focus includes not only staff welfare but also the environment. They practice sustainable farming, and have set aside close to a third of the property for fynbos conservation, with diverse trails for visitors to explore. The maritime climate reflects in the wine styles - and in one wine name. The two new bottlings this edition show that quality and progress remain on the agenda.

★★★★ **Merlot** With full dark-fruited ripeness, **16** ⑧⑦ is curvaceous, confident, has much to give. Well spiced, some cocoa, rich chocolate notes from 18 months in barrel, tannins firm but accessible.

★★★★☆ **Pinot Noir** ⚲ Elegant & balanced **13** ⑨④, freshness, malleable tannins, spice & earthy notes adding to the drinking pleasure now & at least 5 years to come. Like **12** ★★★★★ ⑨⑦, needs time to develop. Also in 1.5 & 3L, like Pinotage & Maritimus.

★★★★ **Pinotage** Care lavished, half wild ferment, 18 months French barriques, 30% new, **15** ⑧⑧ shows ripe plum/prune ripeness, dusting of sweet spice, supple tannins. Handsome, loads of personality.

★★★★ **Syrah** ⚲ Complex savoury, white pepper & spice aromas, modest 12.6% alcohol, **13** ⑧⑧ ripe yet not jammy, tannins still chewy after 2 years 25% new oak, some Hungarian.

★★★★ **Bushell** (ⓃⒺⓌ) Merlot leads, with cab franc, malbec, **15** ⑧⑥'s 15 months French/Hungarian oak giving cocoa styling, allspice/clove savoury spicing, solid bed of tannin. Deep, dark & dense in an interesting way. Walker Bay WO, like Klip Kop.

★★★★ **Epitome** ⚲ Cape Blend **11** ⑧⑨, shiraz & 48% pinotage, the former dominates & gives opulent spice, merging well with the bramble fruit, elegant tannins. Fine follow-up to **10** ★★★★☆ ⑨①.

★★★★☆ **Chardonnay** ⚲ Opulent **15** ⑨② seduces with roasted almond, oatmeal & fresh honey, crisp acidity keeps creamy palate in check, sympathetic oak (30% new) allows flinty-fresh fruit to shine.

★★★★ **Sauvignon Blanc** ⚲ Bone-dry & crunchy **17** ⑧⑨ opens in glass to vibrant tropical fruit with citrus & mineral undertones.

★★★★ **Klip Kop** (ⓃⒺⓌ) ⊘ Only 16% semillon component is (old) oaked in **17** ⑧⑧ blend with sauvignon, so freshness reigns; gooseberry, passionfruit, distinctive minerality at the end courtesy of cool climate. Racy acidity keeps it vibrant.

★★★★ **Maritimus** ⚲ Intended for site expression & ageing, natural-ferment **13** ⑧⑨ is 45% sauvignon with chardonnay & semillon. Intriguing savoury seaweed nuance, zesty acidity, touch oak adds palate weight. Similar profile to **12** ★★★★★ ⑨⓪.

★★★★ **The Wayfarer** Not discontinued as we thought, cerise-coloured berry-rich **15** ★★★★ ⑧③ MCC sparkling also has herbal top notes, presenting variety-true character. Dry, elegant, touch of oak, could do with more freshness. From pinot noir, like last-tasted **10** ⑧⑦.

Tara Rosé ★★★★ Mainly merlot, with malbec, cab franc, **18** ⑧③ has expected red berries, but with an underlying seriousness; this is a food wine, elegant & crisply dry. Walker Bay WO. — CR

Location: Hermanus ▪ Map: Walker Bay & Bot River ▪ Map grid reference: B4 ▪ WO: Upper Hemel-en-Aarde Valley/Walker Bay ▪ Est 1997 ▪ 1stB 2000 ▪ Tasting & sales daily 11—5 ▪ Tasting fee applicable, waived on purchase ▪ Closed Dec 25 & Jan 1 ▪ Seasonal tasting platters and soups, kiddies platters ▪ Facilities for children ▪ Tour groups ▪ Conferences ▪ Weddings ▪ Luxury self-catering lodge ▪ Conservation area ▪ Extensive nature trails ▪ MTB ▪ Bass & fly fishing by arrangement ▪ Owner(s) Holly & Simon Bellingham-Turner ▪ Winemaker(s) Walter Pretorius (Jul 2013), with Reginald Maphumulo (Jun 2000) ▪ Viticulturist(s) Petrus Bothma (Jul 2017) ▪ 210ha/35ha (cab f, malbec, merlot, ptage, pinot, shiraz, chard, sauv, sem) ▪ 150t/20,000cs own label 45% red 50% white 5% rosé ▪ IPW, WIETA ▪ PO Box 1413 Hermanus 7200 ▪ info@sumaridge.co.za ▪ www.sumaridge.co.za ▪ S 34° 22′ 1.6″ E 019° 15′ 18.6″ ▪ 🖃 phrased.seating.incurring ▪ F +27 (0)86-623-4248 ▪ **T +27 (0)28-312-1097**

☐ **Sumerton** see Zidela Wines

Summerhill Wines

（⚲）（🍴）（◎）

The Stellenbosch vineyards owned by Charles Hunting and feeding his boutique wine brand are being entirely replanted with classic varieties and fashionable grenache. Vinification is still on-site by Malanot

Wines' Marius Malan, and the cellardoor remains on trend, with Sir Thomas Brewing Co handcrafting beer. Rumbling tummies aren't neglected, with the resident pizza maker using only authentic buffalo mozzarella.

Chenin Blanc ⊘ ⊛ ★★★★ Despite no oaking, **18** ⑧ is weighty & luscious, shows lemon, quince & apricot intensity that punches far above its price. The 750 cases guaranteed to fly out of the cellar.

Shiraz-Merlot ⓐ ★★★ Not a usual partnership but it works **13** ⑧ mocha spicing, dark fruit, tannins adding stiffening for food matching. **Rosé** ⓐ ★★★ Dry **17** ⑧ tank sample from shiraz has the requisite red berries & also an intriguing herbaceous note, improving its food compatibility. — WB

Location/map/WO: Stellenbosch ▪ Map grid reference: E3 ▪ 1stB 2008 ▪ Tasting & sales Mon-Thu 9-4.30 Fri 9-2 ▪ Private tastings in manor house by appt; or anytime at the brewery ▪ Closed all pub hols ▪ Pizzeria ▪ Craft beer & gin ▪ Owner(s) Summerhill Wines cc, Charles R Hunting ▪ Winemaker(s) Marius Malan CWM (Malanot Wines) ▪ Viticulturist(s) Paul Wallace (consultant) ▪ 15ha/3.5ha (merlot, shiraz, chenin) ▪ 24t/2,500cs own label 40% red 60% white ▪ PO Box 12448 Die Boord 7613 ▪ charles@summerhillwines. co.za, manager@summerhillwines.co.za ▪ www.summerhillwines.co.za ▪ S 33° 52' 57.71" E 018° 50' 49.39" ▪ ⌨ comfort.twist.veered ▪ F +27 (0)86-621-8047 ▪ **T +27 (0)21-889-5015**

Sumsaré Wines ⓠ ⓐ

Spell 'Sumsaré' backwards, and you get 'Erasmus', the family behind the brand. Patriarch Danie's idea of bottling a wine for the Robertson home farm's 200th anniversary has grown into a boutique wine and brandy business run by the 7th generation, daughters Francèl, Danielle and Janine, and son Johannes.

Location/map: Robertson ▪ Map grid reference: C8 ▪ Est 2008 ▪ 1stB 2007 ▪ Tasting, sales & tours by appt Mon-Fri 9-5 Sat 9-1 ▪ Closed Easter Fri-Mon, May 13, Pentecost, Dec 25/26 & Jan 1 ▪ Tour groups ▪ Facilities for children ▪ Potstill brandy ▪ Owner(s) Francèl Rabie, Johannes Erasmus, Danielle Jackson & Janine Joubert ▪ Winemaker(s) Lourens van der Westhuizen (Arendsig) ▪ Viticulturist(s) Briaan Stipp (Robertson Winery) ▪ 45ha/40ha (cab, ptage, ruby cab, shiraz, chard, chenin, sauv) ▪ 700t/±260cs own label 40% red 60% white ▪ PO Box 402 Robertson 6705 ▪ sumsare.wines@barvallei.co.za ▪ www.sumsarewines.co.za ▪ S 33° 54' 14.66" E 019° 40' 4.75" ▪ ⌨ abridged.jazz.hood ▪ F +27 (0)86-505-8590 ▪ **T +27 (0)72-779-4800/+27 (0)82-552-3486**

Sun International Wines ⓠ ⓔ ⓐ

As one of SA's foremost hotel groups, Sun International offers its guests a selection of wines from reputable producers, but the Food & Beverage team also works with Somerset West boutique vintner Rikus Neethling of Bizoe Wines to offer the pair of own-label wines listed below. This bespoke line-up is now being supplemented by a new label, Sun Star Ses'Fikile, featuring some of the wines in the portfolio of Cape Town entrepreneur Nondumiso Pikashe (see Ses'Fikile listing).

Dusk ★★★ Still subtitled 'Cape Blend' but no pinotage in **16** ⑦'s equal blend cab & shiraz from Robertson & Paarl. Soft, supple & gently spicy. Drink now, solo or with a meal. **Dawn** ★★★ Faint citrus tones, flinty edge on tangy **17** ⑦ sauvignon from Bot River & Stellenbosch; vivacious if brief easy-sipper. — FM, CvZ

WO: Western Cape ▪ Est 2004 ▪ 1stB 2010 ▪ Tasting & sales daily at Sun International hotel group ▪ Hotels ▪ Restaurants (à la carte/buffet) ▪ Casino bars ▪ Conference venues ▪ Facilities for children ▪ Tour groups ▪ Festivals ▪ Concerts ▪ Owner(s) Sun International Management Limited ▪ Winemaker(s) Rikus Neethling (Jul 2010, consultant) ▪ 24,000cs own label 50% red 50% white ▪ www.suninternational.com ▪ F +27 (0)11-780-7716 ▪ **T +27 (0)11-780-7000**

☐ **Suo** see Aslina Wines

Super Single Vineyards ⓠ

As the name suggests, Daniël de Waal's small-batch winery on the Canettevallei family farm in Stellenbosch seeks out special, older parcels around the Cape for the Pella range. And, more than 300 km away in Sutherland, at 1,500 metres in elevation, Daniël grows the Mount Sutherland range. Two different climates, Mediterranean and Continental respectively, each with their share of drought-induced challenges in harvest 2018. Daniël says, though, that by keeping canopies thin and small, and yields lower, they overcame the difficulties. In fact, he declares the Mount Sutherland harvest went really well: 'No black frost, so a crop of healthy fruit from every variety.'

Pella Coastal Wines

★★★★☆ Granietbult Cabernet Sauvignon ⓐ Svelte **14** ⑨⑬ announced by ripe dark berries judiciously scented with new French oak (40%). Sleek, sweet-fruited length with complementary tailored tannins for requisite ageing. Stellenbosch WO, as all these unless noted.

★★★★ Cinsaut ⓥ Perfumed & light of foot, **15** ⑧⑨ does justice to Swartland's old dryland bushvines. Sweet raspberry & spice succulence & grape tannins, in a style both serious & accessible. Year older oak.

★★★★ Oukliprant Malbec Deftly spiced (25% new oak) mulberry, wild herb scents on **14** ⑧⑨; juicy core enlivened by racy acidity, tightly bound by ripe grape tannin. Mouthwatering prospect in few years.

★★★★ Verlatenkloof Merlot Adds 'Verlatenkloof' to name in **13** ⑧⑨, from old dryland bushvines. Core gentle, silky elegance supports vibrant flavours, including tangy red berries & savoury length. Stiffened with 10% cab.

★★★★☆ Thomas Se Dolland Pinotage ⓥ Well-fruited but not fruity **14** ★★★★★ ⑨⓪, ripe, creamy texture held by layered fine tannin; finishes with impressive savoury length. French oak, 33% new, final polish to this modern classic. **13** ⑧⑨ sleek & nimble.

★★★★☆ Family Reserve ⓥ Bordeaux-style blend, 85% cab with splashes malbec, merlot which sweeten, add flesh to cab's fine but stern grape tannin. **13** ⑨⑬ accomplished, beautifully proportioned, all suggesting greater complexity with age. Oaked to enhance structure, 18 months older French barriques.

★★★★☆ Kanniedood Chenin Blanc ⓐ Ex Swartland, **16** ⑨⑬ reflects this rugged area; an openness of sun-filled dried peach aromas, richness of flavour, bound by firm yet unintimidating grip from 3 days skin contact, year French oak, 10% new. Immensely likeable & ageworthy.

Koueveld Petit Verdot ⓥ ★★★★ Well-structured **14** ⑧④, good acidity gives length to sound blueberry features. Properly dry, edgy tannins will benefit from further few years. 30% new oak. Coastal WO.

Mount Sutherland Continental Wines

★★★★ Nebbiolo ⓥ Maiden crop from high-lying vineyards, just 1 t/ha. **14** ⑧⑦ much to like, if unusually approachable in its attractive floral aromas, savoury fruit & close tannin weave. Older oak.

★★★★ Pinot Noir ⓥ Exciting **15** ⑧⑦ bunch-fermented for fruit focus, older French oak matured. **15** ⑧⑦ still harmonising mid-2017, needed time to reveal underlying dark fruit richness. No **14**.

★★★★☆ Ouberg Syrah ⓝⓔⓦ ⓐ From older of the two syrah blocks, planted 6,000 vines/ha. **13** ⑨⑬ has cool precision, lithe feel, if yet to reveal full array of its lifted spice & dark berry concentration. Judicious oaking, 20% new, adds a little plushness but not at expense of firm, emphatically dry conclusion.

★★★★☆ Syrah ⓐ Outstanding reflection of this high-altitude vineyard: **15** ⑨⑬ pure, complex blackberry, heady spice fragrance; supple, silky, but also core freshness, careful extraction. Restrained oaking, none new, enhances endless savoury length. Promises years of pleasure. No **14**.

★★★★☆ Tempranillo ⓐ Cool purity & depth of character in splendid **15** ⑨⑬. Full bodied yet unheavy, silky texture, spice & tobacco features lifted by fresh, fine tannins. Memorably long. French oak enhanced, 20% new. Straddles modern/traditional styling. **14** ★★★★ ⑧⑧ bigger, more tannic.

★★★★ Riesling Wooded ⓥ Delightful individual; unusual (spontaneous) barrel ferment. **14** ⑧⑦ lovely poise, taut feel & subtle varietal spice. 14 months on lees add weight, retain purity, zest.— AL

Location/map: Stellenbosch ▪ Map grid reference: C5 ▪ WO: Sutherland-Karoo/Stellenbosch/Coastal ▪ Est/1stB 2004 ▪ Tasting Mon-Sat 10-5 ▪ Closed all pub hols ▪ Owner(s)/viticulturist(s) Daniël de Waal ▪ Winemaker(s) Daniël de Waal, with Kyle Zulch (also marketing/sales) ▪ 60ha Canettevallei farm ▪ (cab, malbec, nebbiolo, p verdot, ptage, pinot, shiraz, tempranillo, chenin, riesling) ▪ 2,000cs own label 80% red 20% white ▪ PO Box 89 Vlottenburg 7604 ▪ marketing@ssvineyards.co.za ▪ www.supersinglevineyards.co.za ▪ S 33° 56′ 29.73″ E 018° 45′ 15.20″ ▪ ⓦ arrived.reply.master ▪ F +27 (0)21-881-3026 ▪ **T +27 (0)72-200-5552 (Daniël)/+27 (0)82-556-0205 (Kyle)**

Surfing Vintners

Wine-makers, -marketers and viticulturists gather for the annual Vintners Surf Classic to not only ride the waves but donate 50L of wine, blended at Grangehurst in Stellenbosch to create the 'benevolent causes' wine, Big Red. Proceeds go to ongoing fundraiser, Surf4Life, created by the late Taryn Pratt.

★★★★ **Big Red** New bottling of **15** ⑧⑥, red & black berry fruit & gentle squeeze of dry, fine tannin. Subtle density & body with long, rewarding tail. Near-equal cab, pinotage, shiraz in magnum only.— FM

Location: Stellenbosch ▪ WO: Coastal-Cape South Coast ▪ Est/1stB 2000 ▪ Closed to public ▪ Winemaker(s) various, led by Jeremy Walker, Gunter Schultz & Miles Mossop ▪ 700 magnums own label 100% red ▪ PO Box 206 Stellenbosch 7599 ▪ jeremy@grangehurst.co.za ▪ F +27 (0)86-710-6067 ▪ **T +27 (0)21-855-3625**

☐ **Survivor** see Overhex Wines International
☐ **Sutherland** see Thelema Mountain Vineyards
☐ **Sutherland Continental** see Super Single Vineyards
☐ **Swallow** see Natte Valleij Wines

Swallow Hill Single Vineyard Wine Estate

You can enjoy tapas and wine tasting on the stoep of Di and Brian Dawes' boutique winery in Greyton, looking across vines to the Riviersonderend mountains (but do book first). The vineyards, tended organically, are of viognier and tempranillo – with sadly minimal crop in 2018, the third year of the drought. A craft gin is planned for 2019, to accompany the vegan-friendly wines.

★★★★ **Tempranillo** Tomato leaf note on **17** ★★★★ ⑧⑤, but aromas less forward than on last-tasted **15** ⑧⑦. Big, dry tannins a touch out of balance with pleasing light, fresh fruit. 12.2% alcohol. Slight sweetness on sundried tomato finish.

★★★★ **Viognier** Previewed last year, **17** ★★★★ ⑧④ has nicely restrained peach perfume & flavour with spice & ginger from oak stave influence. Less elegant than **16** ⑧⑥, with rather heavy texture, but good balance of acidity.

The Natural Blonde ⑨ ★★★★ Oak vanilla the initial impression on **14** ⑧③ viognier, chenin, chardonnay from Greyton & Wellington, then come pleasing fruity fullness & nice dry end. Not tasted: **Tempranillo Rosé**. Discontinued: **The Red One**. — TJ

Location: Greyton ▪ Map: Southern Cape ▪ Map grid reference: A1 ▪ WO: Greyton/Western Cape ▪ Est 2009 ▪ 1stB 2013 ▪ Tasting, sales & cellar tours by prior arrangement ▪ Tapas & tasting R95pp ▪ Open between Oct to May (inclusive) for lunch R250pp (2 pax/more) & dinner R350pp (4 pax/more) - booking essential ▪ Conservation area ▪ Farm stay: en suite guest room (2 pax) ▪ Owner(s) Di & Brian Dawes ▪ Cellarmaster(s) John Brian Dawes ▪ Winemaker(s) Di Dawes, with John Brian Dawes ▪ Viticulturist(s) Di & John Brian Dawes ▪ 21ha/2ha (tempranillo, viog) ▪ 2t own label 50% red 50% white ▪ IPW, SAWIS ▪ PO Box 299 Greyton 7233 ▪ wine@swallowhill.co.za ▪ www.swallowhill.co.za ▪ S 34° 6′ 10.10″ E 019° 36′ 35.46″ ▪ 🗺 searchable.fortify. outsold ▪ **T +27 (0)82-423-9634**

☐ **Swallows' Tale** see Trizanne Signature Wines
☐ **Swanepoel** see Oude Compagnies Post Private Cellar
☐ **Swartland Stories** see Pulpit Rock Winery

Swartland Winery

Based outside Malmesbury in Swartland's heart, this substantial winery has 60 producer-owners and 2,689 ha of vineyards, many being unirrigated bushvines. In its eighth decade of production, the venture has a comprehensive range to meet all consumer tastes. The wines are widely distributed through major SA supermarket chains and liquor outlets, and exports under their own and other brand names now go to 35 countries. Social responsibility and sustainability are a focus, with local and international accreditation.

Idelia range

★★★★ **Cape Blend** From 40 year old dryland bushvines, a fine blend of 60% pinotage coupled with shiraz, cab, all-new oak. **15** ⑧⑧ dark smoky depths & complexity, good ageing potential. No **14**.

Bush Vine range

Chenin Blanc ⊕ ★★★☆ Oaking & bottle age pay respect to **16** ⑧③'s older vines, thereby intensifying the stonefruit & lime character, adding savoury notes. Nicely done.

Cabernet Sauvignon ★★★☆ Cassis & dark chocolate **15** ⑧④ well structured for ageing, thanks to 18 months in barrel, yet smoothly accessible. **Pinotage** ★★★☆ **15** ⑧④ full, ripe, packed with flavour, including oak-driven vanilla spicing. Bound to be popular. **Syrah** ★★★☆ Half new oak & 18 months maturation give **15** ⑧④ vanilla/sweet spicing to its plush dark fruit. Bold, ripe style.

Reserve range

Pinotage ⊘ ⊕ ★★★☆ Dark toned & intense, yet sleek & silky, unwooded **17** ⑧⑤ proudly showcases the variety.

Cabernet Sauvignon-Merlot ⓧ ★★★ Friendly brightness to unfussy **14** ⑧① blend with neither grape dominating in mix of equal parts. **Limited Selection Cabernet Sauvignon-Merlot** ★★★ Occasional release. Equal blend, half barrel matured, rest staves, **17** ⑧① nicely combines piquant berries & savoury notes. Drinks smoothly.

Winemakers Collection

Merlot ⊘ ⊕ ★★★ Vivid, mulberry-rich **17** ⑧① offers luscious drinkability. **Tinta Barocca** ⊘ ⊕ ★★★ Unadorned by oak, as rest of these reds, **17** ⑧①'s hedgerow fruit shines through, juicy, smooth, tasty. **White Jerepigo** ⊕ ★★★ Sultanas & apricot essence, hard to resist this sweet **NV** ⑧① fortified from chenin. Serve well-chilled.

Cabernet Sauvignon ⊘ ★★★ Succulent berries & plums, **17** ⑧① is cab at its friendly, early-drinking best. **Pinotage** ★★★ Medium bodied & dark fruit toned, **17** ⑦⑧ drinks easily & well. **Syrah** ⊘ ★★★ Smoky nuances in ripe dark fruit, **17** ⑧① is curvy, with attractive freshness. **Dry Red** ⓧ ★★★ Herb & fynbos sheen to dark-fruited **NV** ⑦⑨ merlot & cab blend. **Blanc de Noir** ⊘ ★★★ Touch of sweetness in sleek **18** ⑦⑨, fits well with red berry flavours ex pinotage; fresh finish. WO W Cape. **Chardonnay** ★★★ Stonefruit & citrus combo make dry **18** ⑦⑧ an ideal food wine. **Chenin Blanc** ⊘ ★★★ Pear drops & melon in softly fruity **18** ⑦⑧. **Sauvignon Blanc** ★★★ With green fig & gooseberry vibrancy, **18** ⑧⓪ is a light, tasty, versatile food wine. **Bouquett** ⓃⒺⓌ ⊘ ★★★ Aptly named, muscat d'Alexandrie perks up semi-sweet chenin-based **18** ⑦⑧ with aromatic grapey flavours. WO W Cape. **Natural Sweet Sparkling Rosé** ⓧ ★★★ Sweet berry & apple appeal to **NV** ⑦⑦ carbonated lower-alcohol sparkler from pinotage. WO W Cape, like next. **Cuvée Brut** ★★★ Tropical flavours in latest **NV** ⑦⑧ sparkling from sauvignon, touch of lemon gives requisite zip. **Hanepoot** ★★★ Sultana in **NV** ⑦⑦'s perfume & flavour, richly sweet. **Red Jerepigo** ★★★ Pinotage gives this **NV** ⑧① its red fruit character, medium-bodied structure. Full-sweet but tastes drier. **Cape Ruby** ★★★ Equal shiraz & tinta in plushly fruited **NV** ⑧①, sweetness offset by nice tannin grip at the end. WO W Cape. Discontinued: **Bukettraube**, **Red Muscadel**.

Contours Collection

Not tasted: **Merlot**, **Merlot-Cabernet Sauvignon**, **Chenin Blanc**, **Moscato**, **Sauvignon Blanc**.

D' Vine range

Not tasted: **Cabernet Sauvignon-Merlot**, **Rosé**, **Chenin Blanc-Sauvignon Blanc**. — CR

Location: Malmesbury ▪ Map: Swartland ▪ Map grid reference: C7 ▪ WO: Swartland/Western Cape ▪ Est/1stB 1948 ▪ Tasting & sales Mon-Thu 9-5 Fri 9–4 Sat 9–2 Sun closed ▪ Closed Mar 21, Easter Fri/Sun, Dec 25/26 & Jan 1 ▪ Facilities for children ▪ Tour groups ▪ Farm produce ▪ Owner(s) 60 producers ▪ Wine coordinator Christo Koch (Feb 2014) ▪ Viticulturist(s) Claude Uren (Nov 2010) ▪ 2,689ha (cab, malbec, merlot, ptage, shiraz, chard, chenin, sauv) ▪ 20,000t 38% red 55% white 5% rosé 2% sparkling ▪ BRC, IFS, IPW, WIETA ▪ PO Box 95 Malmesbury 7299 ▪ susan@swwines.co.za ▪ www.swartlandwinery.co.za ▪ S 33° 27′ 12.7″ E 018° 45′ 17.7″ ▪ 🅦 footfalls.purring.checking ▪ F +27 (0)22-482-1750 ▪ **T +27 (0)22-482-1134**

☐ **Swepie Selection** *see* Domein Doornkraal

☐ **Swerwer** *see* JC Wickens Wines

SylvanVale Vineyards

Wines under the SylvanVale label are made by consultants for guests of the Devon Valley Hotel outside Stellenbosch. The luxury establishment has its own young vineyards, carefully nurtured, with the potential to provide home-grown grapes for the wines in the future.

Ghost Tree range

Three Colours Red ⓥ ★★★ Switches from blend to solo pinotage, lightly oaked, **15** ⑧⓪ showing piquant wild berry juiciness & some earthy notes. Dry chalky tannins invite robust fare. **Three Colours White** ⓥ ★★★ Fragrant tropical chenin, balanced & friendly. Slightly creamy, warm centre means **16** ⑧⓪ is best served well chilled. WO W Cape. **Bristle White** ⓥ ★★★★ Viognier ageing gracefully, peach & tangy apricot flavours mellowing into creamy texture as oak-derived vanilla spice & hints of toasted nuts prevail. Drink **11** ⑧⑤ soon.

SylvanVale range

Cape Blend Rosé ★★★ Lovely vermilion hue, savoury red-fruit aromas & flavours from mostly pinotage & cab. **16** ⑧① supple, dry & eminently drinkable. Discontinued: **Sauvignon Blanc**. — MW

Location/map: Stellenbosch ▪ Map grid reference: D4 ▪ WO: Stellenbosch/Western Cape ▪ Est 1997 ▪ 1stB 1998 ▪ Tasting & sales daily 11–7 ▪ Open pub hols ▪ Flavours Restaurant: 120 seater; Vineyard Terrace; Cedarwood Bar & Lounge ▪ The Devon Valley Hotel: 50 rooms ▪ Facilities for children ▪ Tour groups ▪ Conferences ▪ 6 banqueting venues (max capacity 98 pax) ▪ Walking/hiking trails ▪ Gin, whisky & craft beer tastings ▪ Owner(s) Louis Group Hotels, Spas & Vineyards ▪ Viticulturist(s) Lorna Hughes (1997, consultant) ▪ 8ha/4.3ha (cab, ptage, chenin) ▪ PO Box 68 Stellenbosch 7599 ▪ info@sylvanvale.com ▪ www.sylvanvale.com ▪ S 33° 54'12.5" E 018° 48'57.7" ▪ ⚏ trails.square.recover ▪ T +27 (0)21-865-2012

Taillard Family Wines

Despite the possible sale of their grape source, family farm Kersfontein in Voor Paardeberg, father-and-daughter team Pieter and Anelise Taljaard intend continuing the Taillard and Lobola ranges, with the help of new winemaker Hugo Truter, using alternative fruit and cellar resources.

Taillard Premiere Collection

★★★★ **Pinotage Reserve** Whiffs of raspberry freshen **16** ⑧⑦'s dark fruit features, as do old oak & firm tannic structure though perhaps touch more acidity would bring real balance. **15** untasted.

★★★★ **Watershed** Toned Bordeaux blend cab (40%), equal cab franc & merlot. Like **14** ⑧⑦, **15** ★★★★★ ⑨⓪ least overt wine here. Classic cedar & graphite introduce svelte palate displaying precise balance, supple tannins, integrated oak.

★★★★ **Chenin Blanc Reserve** ⓥ Big, bold **16** ⑧⑦ has peaches-&-cream styling, oozes ripe quince preserve, vanilla oak from year 40% new barrels, all amplified by oxidative notes. Serious if not subtle.

Lobola range

★★★★ **Beau Rouge** Accessible **15** ⑧⑧ equal cab & shiraz. Dark-berried fruity aromas, full, rich flavour, juicy tannins in ripe house style, big 14.9% alcohol warms the finish. WO W Cape, as next two.

★★★★ **Belle Blanc** ⓥ With 80/20 chardonnay & chenin, **14** ⑧⑦ displays complexity & balance; succulent crispness, 40% new oak bringing depth & breadth.

Miner range

★★★★ **Cabernet Sauvignon** ⓥ With ample cassis fruit, **15** ⑧⑦ improves on **14** ★★★★ ⑧④; classic cab in big, ripe style, but shows more restraint, balance.

Bedrock Merlot ★★★★ Savoury meat-spice tones of **16** ⑧⑤ somewhat leaven rather stern, tarry tannins that mask more delicate fruit in youth. **Bullion Pinotage** ★★★★ Pleasingly less ebullient than some earlier versions, **16** ⑧⑤ is plum fruited, with measured tannins & alcohol. **Deep Level Shiraz** ⓥ ★★★★ Improved **15** ⑧③ is savoury & tasty, with leather notes, succulent flavourful palate & slightly dry tannins. **Gully Chenin Blanc** ★★★★ Returns after hiatus as solo chenin, hence name change from 'Blanc de Blanc'. **18** ⑧⑤ fresh & fruity, short sojourn in old oak adds breadth for more serious quaffing. **Prospectors Seekers Red** ⓥ ★★★★ Fortified dessert with relatively high sugar & low alcohol, from cabernet. Fruity **NV** ⑧④ will find many fans. — DS

Location/map: Paarl ▪ Map grid reference: C1 ▪ WO: Paarl/Western Cape ▪ Tasting, sales & tours by appt ▪ Closed all pub hols ▪ Owner(s) Pacas Winery (Pty) Ltd (Pieter Taljaard) ▪ Cellarmaster(s)/winemaker(s) Hugo Truter (2018) ▪ Viticulturist(s) Morné van Greunen (Feb 2009) ▪ ±44ha (cabs s/f, merlot, p verdot, ptage, shiraz, chenin) ▪ 1,000cs own label 80% red 20% white ▪ IPW ▪ PO Box 7274 Noorder-Paarl 7623 ▪ admin@taillardwines.com ▪ www.taillardwines.com ▪ S 33° 35'22.5" E 018° 52'45.0" (VP) ▪ ⌨ tofu.mobiles.interlaced ▪ **T +27 (0)21-869-8384**

☐ **Taillefert** see Erasmus Family Wines

Taillefert Wines

The brand name honours Huguenot Jean Taillefert, first owner of Paarl's Laborie estate, granted a charter in 1691. The considerable winemaking skills of Erlank Erasmus of separately listed Erasmus Family Wines are featured in this new-to-the-guide boutique venture, with a home and tasting area on Laborie, where visitors can sip the wines on the stoep overlooking the lawns and/or at one of the on-site restaurants.

Taillefert Wines range (NEW)

★★★★ **Chardonnay** Nicely integrated **16** (88) blends fresh peach, orange peel & jasmine with buttery/creamy oak (25% new), enticing spices add interest to soft, cooked apple finish.

★★★★☆ **Méthode Cap Classique Brut** ⊘ ⊛ Impressive **12** (94) sparkler mostly chardonnay, 20% pinot noir. Some oak (10% new) & malo add to richness of 65 months on lees, making for complex mouthful of Lemon Cream biscuit, cinnamon & salted brioche. Excellent length, persistent bubbles, satisfying celebrations all round.

Pinot Noir ⊘ ★★★ Primary fruit of **16** (80) - raspberry, blackberry - somewhat confected with eucalyptus note. Pleasant enough but no more. — CM

Location/map: Paarl ▪ Map grid reference: E6 ▪ WO: Western Cape ▪ Est/1stB 2010 ▪ Tasting & sales Wed-Thu 11-4 Fri/Sat 11-5 Sun/pub hols 11-2:30 ▪ Closed Good Fri, Dec 25 & Jan 1 ▪ Owner(s) La Concorde ▪ Winemaker(s) Erlank Erasmus ▪ 2,000cs own label 30% red 70% white ▪ BEE ▪ Taillerfer Str Paarl 7646 ▪ erlank@capewinecompany.co.za ▪ S 33° 45'55.2" E 018° 57'27.6" ▪ ⌨ deserved.eminent.edit ▪ **T +27 (0)21-863-0872**

☐ **Talent & Terroir** see Boland Kelder
☐ **Tall Horse** see DGB (Pty) Ltd

Tamboerskloof Wine – Kleinood Farm

Engineer and cutting-edge cellar designer Gerard de Villiers and wife Libby have transformed their Stellenbosch riverside estate, Kleinood (meaning 'small and precious'), into a model of country living and modern Cape boutique winegrowing. New wine man Reynie Oosthuizen, seasoned at Rust en Vrede nearby, inter alia, supported by Julio Engelbrecht will continue sustainably nurturing vineyards, olive orchards and wines. Solar power joins an aerobic sewage digestor and cellar wastewater reed bed filtration system, alleviating drought pressure and providing a paradise for bird lovers.

★★★★☆ **Syrah** Lilting whiffs of white pepper & pimento spice in savoury **15** (91); bold blackberry fruit folded into well-knit/judged tannic core. Svelte & suave, with dashes mourvèdre & viognier adding dimension. 15% gets 19 months in new oak, rest seasoned wood. Magnums available.

★★★★ **Viognier** Brush of older oak gives breadth & interest to **17** (86), splash roussanne adds to perfume. Variety's apricot/peach pip exuberance kept in check by silky, dry, lingering finish.

Katharien Syrah Rosé ★★★★☆ Charming straw/raspberry characters in dry, well-textured **18** (85), with hint of tannic grip & overall sophisticated appeal. 5% oaked. Not tasted: **John Spicer Syrah**. — DS

Location/map/WO: Stellenbosch ▪ Map grid reference: F7 ▪ Est 2000 ▪ 1stB 2002 ▪ Tasting, sales & cellar tours Mon-Thu by appt; Fri (except pub hols) open from 10-2; open first Sat of every month ▪ Closed all pub hols ▪ Olive oil ▪ Tree identification route ▪ Owner(s) Gerard & Libby de Villiers ▪ Winemaker(s) Reynie Oosthuizen (Oct 2018), with Julio Engelbrecht (Jan 2008) ▪ Viticulturist(s) Reynie Oosthuizen (Oct 2018) ▪ 22ha/10ha (mourv, shiraz, rouss, viog) ▪ 100t/8,500cs own label 70% red 7% white 23% rosé ▪ IPW ▪ PO Box 12584 Die Boord 7613 ▪ office@kleinood.com ▪ www.kleinood.com ▪ S 33° 59'42.6" E 018° 52'14.8" ▪ ⌨ stuns.lion.case ▪ **F +27 (0)21-880-2884 ▪ T +27 (0)21-880-2527**

Tanagra Winery & Distillery

Always something new from McGregor's boutique vintners/distillers, Robert and Anette Rosenbach – this edition a pair of special and delicious cask-aged spirits, joining the handcrafted portfolio of single-vineyard wines (an untasted 3-year-aged apricot eau de vie also introduced recently). In the repertoire, too, are luxury accommodation, fresh produce and proximity to the cheerfully named Vrolijkheid Nature Reserve.

Tanagra range

★★★★ **Cabernet Franc** Floral edge to refined, serious **16** (88), fermented naturally, as all the wines. Ample blue & black fruit well framed by integrated oak (14 months; none new). Matches also-tasted **15** (88) for structure & poise.

★★★★ **Shiraz** ⊘ Reined-in **16** (87), earthy spice & succulent ripeness, excellent structure & persistence of flavour. Notch up on also-reviewed **15** ★★★★ (85). Oak same as cabs; ex registered single-vineyard, as all except Carah.

★★★★ **Carah** ⊘ Equal cab & shiraz blend is savoury & rich, with dry fine tannin. **16** (88) pleasant interplay of fruit generosity & oak backbone from 14 months in older French oak.

Cabernet Sauvignon ★★★★ Approachable ease of **16** (83) cab. Medium body, with fruitcake & sweet spice, dry finish from 14 months in older oak. **Colombard** ★★★☆ Lively & zippy, with lipsmacking acid freshness, **17** (85) is charmingly vivacious. Natural ferment & 10 months on lees in tank add structure & interest. Not tasted: **Heavenly Chaos, Cabernet Franc Blanc de Noir.**

Husk Spirit range (NEW)

★★★★☆ **Cabernet Sauvignon Eau de Vie de Lie 5 Years Reserve** Gorgeous golden colour, with an enticing melange of dark berry, chocolate, liquorice & vanilla aromas. Intense on the palate but silky-smooth, light footed, with lifted spirit finish. Aged 5 years in old red-wine barrels. Well worth seeking out.

★★★★☆ **Marc de Hanepoot 3 Years Reserve** Vibrant amber hue, with fragrant muscat, exotic spice & roasted nut aromas. Rich, rounded & smooth, with raisin notes & candyfloss delicacy, long satisfying finish. Aged 3 years in old muscat barrels. Attractive packaging in 500 ml for both.— WB, FM

Location/WO: McGregor ▪ Map: Robertson ▪ Map grid reference: C6 ▪ Est/1stB 2003 ▪ Tasting (wine/grappa), sales & cellar/distillery tours daily by appt ▪ Fee R40pp, refunded on purchase of R200 ▪ Farm produce ▪ Luxury farm accommodation in 6 cottages (self-catering) ▪ Adjoining Vrolijkheid Nature Reserve ▪ Craft distillery ▪ Owner(s) Robert & Anette Rosenbach ▪ Distiller(s) Robert Rosenbach ▪ Cellarmaster(s)/wine-maker(s)/viticulturist(s) Lourens van der Westhuizen ▪ 78ha/12.5ha (cabs s/f, merlot, ptage, shiraz, cbard) ▪ 120t/3,500cs own label 70% red 15% white 15% blanc de noir; 600cs spirits ▪ IPW, WIETA ▪ PO Box 92 McGregor 6708 ▪ tanagra@tanagra-wines.co.za ▪ www.tanagra-wines.co.za ▪ S 33° 55′ 29.6″ E 019° 52′ 15.9″ ▪ 🌐 leaves.fruitfully.husky ▪ F +27 (0)23-625-1847 ▪ **T +27 (0)23-625-1780**

Tangled Tree

These eco-friendly wines from Robertson have entwined Karee trees on their labels, symbols of the bond between Van Loveren founders and passionate gardeners Hennie and Jean Retief. Packaged in light, robust, recyclable, low-carbon PET (plastic) bottles, they're perfect for active and outdoorsy winelovers.

Chocolate Cabernet Sauvignon ⊘ ★★☆ Cocoa-rich dark chocolate, thanks to **17** (77)'s oaking, accompanied by tasty plum flavours. **Spicy Shiraz** ★★ There is spice in **17** (74), with some woodsmoke tones, the whole effect more savoury than fruity. **Rose Petal Moscato Rosé** ⊘ ★★ Semi-sweet **17** (74) aptly named, rosepetal perfume & flavours, low 10% alcohol. **Butterscotch Chardonnay** ⊘ ★★☆ Exactly that! **17** (78)'s oak treatment gives butterscotch tones to the peachy fruit, finishes perky fresh. **Tropical Sauvignon Blanc** ⊘ ★★☆ Light & dry, **18** (77) has variety-true styling, litchi & gooseberries, appealing freshness. WO Robertson, as all. — CR

Tanzanite Wines

It was in 2001, after being appointed cellar manager and sparkling-wine maker at Distell, that Melanie van der Merwe realised bubbly production is her true passion. She honed her craft at the company and in Champagne for more than a decade before founding, with husband Wentzel, this widely acclaimed handcrafted MCC sparkling venture, based in Worcester. Her bubbles, from classic varieties in Robertson limestone soils, increasingly appear on wine lists overseas, notably in Belgium. Sadly and bravely, Melanie has 'declassified' the wines from harvest 2018, quality not being in line with the Tanzanite standard.

★★★★ **Méthode Cap Classique Brut Rosé** ⓦ Lovely depth, pinpoint acid balance in **NV** ⑧⑦ bubbly. Less pinot noir than last, hence less savoury but smoother, with chardonnay's elegance & freshness.

★★★★☆ **Méthode Cap Classique Brut** ⓦ Always-superb sparkler, **NV** ⑨④ chardonnay-led with 20% pinot noir. Richer, more brioche & creaminess than Rosé despite same 60 months on lees. Poised, pure & persistent, with nuanced Golden Delicious apple finish.— CvZ

Location/map: Worcester ▪ Map grid reference: A2 ▪ WO: Western Cape ▪ Est 2006 ▪ Tasting Mon-Sat by appt ▪ Owner(s) Wentzel & Melanie van der Merwe ▪ Cellarmaster(s) Melanie van der Merwe (Apr 2006) ▪ 2,500cs own label ▪ PO Box 5102 Worcester 6850 ▪ melanie@tanzanitewines.co.za ▪ www.tanzanitewines. co.za ▪ S 33° 36' 54.2" E 019° 26' 33.8" ▪ ⌨ layouts.guarantors.polishing ▪ F +27 (0)86-694-0654 ▪ **T +27 (0)82-555-8105**

☐ **Tara Hill** *see* Southern Sky Wines

Tassenberg

Perhaps *the* SA wine institution, Tassenberg is an affable dry red that since 1936 has launched millions on a wine journey. Affectionately known as 'Tassies', it's available in 750 ml, 2L & 5L. By Distell.

Tassenberg ⓥ ★★★ Entry-level favourite, **NV** ⑦⑧ perennially sound & pleasant. — GdB

☐ **Taste** *see* Truter Family Wines

Teddy Hall Wines

Cape Winemakers Guild member Teddy Hall's labels evoke colourful characters from 17th- and 18th-century Stellenbosch: 'All anti-heroes; I identify!' He left a finance career to study oenology, earning serious accolades for serious chenins while with Kanu and later co-owned Rudera, and now his eponymous proprietary label. Special parcels, vinified in rented cellar space, encompass select bottlings like his latest character, Oubaas Mark, and the Doreen duo, celebrating his wife and fellow Harley-Davidson fan.

Premium range

★★★★☆ **Nico Theunissen** ⓐ No-holds-barred Stellenbosch cabernet, **16** ⑨③ muscular, with cassis fruit in a fine-grained but authoritative tannic framework, 18 months all-new oak & 14.5% alcohol adding to the power. A big personality, needs cellar time. No **15**.

★★★★ **Hercùles van Loon Shiraz** ⓦ Bold (15% alcohol) **13** ⑧⑦ offers attractive ripe aromas with a little spicy perfume. Well knit; firm, supple, youthful tannins; subtle oaking; sweet fruit.

★★★★☆ **Oubaas Mark** ⓝⓔⓦ ⓐ Bold Bordeaux blend, third each cab, cab franc & merlot, plump berry fruit, ripe tannins, all-new wood & 15% alcohol shoe-horned into **16** ⑨③'s body. Balance comes via suave minty tones, pliable structure & lovely balance, suggesting much future pleasure.

★★★★☆ **Dr Jan Cats Chenin Blanc Reserve** Pretty mid-gold colour speaks of ferment/18 months in oak, some new, & oxidative touch adding bruised apple note to aromas of mature **13** ⑨⓪. Deep & intense, all components integrated & ready for pleasurable drinking.

★★★★ **Brut Méthode Cap Classique** ⓦ Pure & precise bottle-fermented sparkling from chardonnay. **NV** ⑧⑦ lemon & subtle brioche character, zippy acidity & lots of fine, long-lasting bubbles.

Sybrand Mankadan Chenin Blanc ★★★★ Whatever the real Sybrand's transgressions, this alter ego an exemplar of consistency, flavour (ripe melon in **17** ⑧⑤), freshness & character, restrained oaking. **Brut Rosé Méthode Cap Classique** ⓦ ★★★ Fresh, lean **NV** ⑦⑧ sparkling from pinotage offers light red fruit & bone-dry conclusion. **Blanc de Blancs Méthode Cap Classique** ⓦ ★★★★ Occasional release, **08** ⑧④ is champagne-method sparkling from chardonnay. Ripe citrus, liquorice & yeasty notes. Rich & full, soft mousse, tangy acidity. Discontinued: **Hercùles van Loon Cabernet Sauvignon**.

Doreen range

Shiraz ⓦ ★★★ Dark berry & tobacco notes on **15** ⑧①. Softly textured, serious tannins a little at odds with the touch of ripe sweetness. **Sauvignon Blanc** ★★★★ Full-throttle tropical fruit on **17** ⑧⑤, deftly moderated by fresh acidity. Forthright & very tasty.

Discontinued: **Moments Collection**. — DS

Location/WO: Stellenbosch ▪ Closed to public ▪ Owner(s)/cellarmaster(s)/winemaker(s)/viticulturist(s) Teddy Hall ▪ PO Box 2868 Somerset West 7129 ▪ teddy@teddyhallwines.com ▪ www.teddyhallwines.com ▪ F +27 (0)86-504-8178 ▪ **T +27 (0)83-461-8111**

Tempel Wines $\quad$ ⓅⓎⓐⓞⓑ

Midway between Paarl and Wellington, the boutique Tempel home-farm was once a Jewish place of worship. Pinotage bushvines were planted by the next-to-last owner, an English-speaking Catholic Afrikaner, to produce and market kosher wine. His successor continued with pinotage (latterly conventionally vinified) while bringing in other grapes. New owners Tom Heeremans and Tatjana Holkina are looking to extend the pinotage-only plantings with Mediterranean varieties, but the focus will remain on black grapes. Their approach is 'back to the roots', with as much as possible being 'handcrafted, completely natural'.

Location/map: Paarl ▪ Map grid reference: E3 ▪ Est 2000 ▪ 1stB 2003 ▪ Tasting, sales & cellar tours by appt ▪ Fee R50 ▪ Wine, beer, cocktails & tasting platters available ▪ Playground, jungle gym ▪ Guest house/B&B (5-star) ▪ Gin ▪ Owner(s) Tom Heeremans & Tatjana Holkina ▪ Winemaker(s) Neil Marais (Jan 2018, consultant) ▪ Viticulturist(s) Marko Roux (Mar 2018, consultant) ▪ 6ha/4ha (ptage) ▪ 24t own label 100% red ▪ Suite 12 Private Bag X3041 Paarl 7620 ▪ info@tempelwines.com ▪ www.tempelwines.com ▪ S 33° 40' 34.0" E 018° 58' 32.2" ▪ Ⓜ steroids.goodness.hatch ▪ **T +27 (0)79-833-9617**

Terracura Wines $\quad$ Ⓟ

Hands-off winemaking devotee Ryan Mostert crafts the wines in this boutique portfolio in rented space in Voor Paardeberg, just outside the Swartland region, where the fruit is sourced. Established in 2010 and now co-owned with financial whizz Michael Roets, Terracura recently joined the Old Vine Project, its 'ethos of taking care of the earth' in step with the growing movement to nurture and restore SA's old vineyards. Look out for the project's Certified Heritage Vineyard seal on bottlings of Silwervis Chenin Blanc.

Terracura Wines range

★★★★☆ **Syrah** Savoury-toned **16** ⑨②'s fruity richness overlaid with orange zest & floral complexity - violets, lilies & roses, lifted by surge of acidity. At 13.5% alcohol, somewhat punchier than last, yet with similar fine tannin firmness. Natural ferment, ±year older oak, & available in magnum, as next.

★★★★★ **White** ⑭Ⓐ Textural & weighty **17** ⑨③ from chenin unapologetically bone-dry & savoury, thrillingly unforgiving with taut acidity, penetrating saline seam. Not for the faint-hearted.

Silwervis range

★★★★☆ **Cinsault** Ⓐ As exuberant as the Terracura bottlings are uncompromising, but unoaked **16** ⑨④ also gains structure & length from by lively acidity & lacy tannins, so there's a cerebral element as well. Just 12.5% alcohol.

★★★★☆ **Chenin Blanc** Ⓟ Poised & confident **16** ⑨① whiteflowers, dried cling peaches & wet clay. More fruit-filled than either white sibling but also intense & generous. Like Cinsault, ex single Paardeberg vineyard, natural ferment & year on lees in concrete 'egg', then year in steel. Also in 1.5 & 3L, as next range.

Smiley range

★★★★ **Dry Red** Natural ferment (some co-), very lightly oaked **NV** ⑧⑧ from 2018-2016 vintages; equal portions cinsaut & mourvèdre, 15% tinta, 5% shiraz. Deliciously 'raw & unplugged', approachable yet fine & dry tannins.

★★★★ **Chenin Blanc** Idiosyncratic **NV** ⑧⑨ combining 'fresh' 2018 wine with skin-contact, 'sun wine' & flor-matured components from 3 previous vintages. Courtesy this complex technique, mouthfilling at only 13% alcohol & 1.7 g/l sugar, with umami savoury presence, tensile edge.— CvZ

Location/map: Paarl ▪ Map grid reference: C2 ▪ WO: Swartland ▪ Est 2010 ▪ 1stB 2011 ▪ Tasting, sales & cellar tours by appt only ▪ Closed all pub hols ▪ Owner(s) M. Roets & R.P. Mostert ▪ Winemaker(s) Ryan Mostert (Nov 2013) ▪ Viticulturist(s) various ▪ 45ha (cinsaut, mourv, shiraz, tinta barocca, chenin, sem) ▪ 40t 50% red 50% white ▪ Staart van die Paardeberg 7620 ▪ samantha@terracura.co.za ▪ www.terracura.co.za, www.silwervis.com ▪ S 33° 37' 47.1" E 018° 50' 08.4" ▪ Ⓜ reliant.clouding.trimmed ▪ **T +27 (0)76-392-4301**

☐ **Terra Del Capo** see Anthonij Rupert Wyne

☐ **Terra Madre** *see* High Constantia Wine Cellar
☐ **Terre de Papillon** *see* Baratok Wines

Tesselaarsdal Wines ⓥ

Tesselaarsdal owner Berene Sauls celebrated much personal success last year, winning not one but two ministerial awards (Best Female Entrepreneur and Youth In Agriculture) for her growing wine business. Her dream of owning a vineyard inches ever closer. In the mean time she intends adding a chardonnay to her label, and has increased production threefold to meet demand and allow her to enter new export markets. Hamilton Russell Vineyards winemaker Emul Ross continues to assist with sourcing fruit and vinifying, in between both his and Berene's day jobs at the Hemel-en-Aarde estate.

★★★★☆ **Pinot Noir** ⓐ Fresh & forthright **17** ⑨① mingles ripe red stonefruit, attractive charry, toasty notes (100% barrel aged, 30% new) & exotic spice. Very primary, will repay keeping few years.— CM

Location: Hermanus ▪ WO: Hemel-en-Aarde Ridge ▪ Est/1stB 2015 ▪ Tasting by appt ▪ Owner(s) Berene Sauls ▪ Winemaker(s) Emul Ross (Jan 2015, Hamilton Russell Vineyards) ▪ 645cs own label 100% red ▪ PO Box 158 Hermanus 7200 ▪ berene@tesselaarsdalwines.co.za ▪ www.tesselaarsdalwines.co.za ▪ F +27 (0)28-312-1797 ▪ **T +27 (0)28-312-3595/+27 (0)73-322-9499**

Teubes Family Wines ⓥ ⓜ ⓐ ⓒ ⓑ ⓖ

Three generations of Teubes farm on the family property near Vredendal on the Cape's northerly Atlantic Coast - practising organic grape-growing for two decades now (Johan Teubes is a well-known viticultural consultant). Winemaker Sybrand Teubes has a restaurant and tasting room in Lambert's Bay - where customers 'can look forward to a new heritage range of wines'.

Teubes Organic range

Pinotage Reserve ⓥ ★★★★ Offers a mix of dark, ripe fruit with pronounced herbal note. **16** ⑧⑤ effectively oaked, with good balance & texture. Hint of varietal bitterness on end. Needs a few years. WO Olifants River. **Barrel Fermented Chenin Blanc** ⓧ ★★★★ Shows oak-enhanced ripe melon, floral features. Few grams sugar lift fruit, smooth effects of 14.3% alcohol. **15** ⑧④ may benefit from short-term ageing. Not tasted: **Cabernet Sauvignon**, **Shiraz**, **Sauvignon Blanc**.

Karoobossie range ⓝ

★★★★ **Méthode Cap Classique Brut Rosé** Pale pink **16** ⑧⑧ from pinot noir, pinotage, meunier. Delightful aromas of brioche, light berry. Dry & rather elegant, with rich, full flavours & good freshness.

Malkopbaai range

Pinotage ⓧ ★★★ Clean, fruity, slightly perfumed aromas on pleasant **16** ⑦⑧. More structure than sweet fruit, but not forbiddingly so. Balanced oaking. **Lightly Wooded Chenin Blanc** ⓧ ★★ Faint floral & thatchy notes on **16** ⑦④, but some hardness & little real charm. **Sauvignon Blanc** ⓧ ★★ Slightly insipid green & tropical notes on **17** ⑦④, but zestily pleasant enough.

Limited Releases

Not tasted: **Cabernet Sauvignon**.

Discontinued: **Lambert's Bay's Finest range**. — TJ

Location: Vredendal ▪ Map: Olifants River ▪ Map grid reference: B4 B5 ▪ WO: Western Cape/Olifants River ▪ Est 2010 ▪ 1stB 2011 ▪ Tasting & sales Mon-Fri 8-5 Sat 9.30-5; Lambert's Bay tasting venue & Kreefhuis restaurant Mon-Sat 10-5 ▪ Tasting fee ▪ Cellar tours ▪ Tour groups ▪ Facilities for children ▪ Farm produce ▪ Cheese platters & pizza ▪ Conferences/functions ▪ Walks/hikes ▪ Bergkraal 4x4 trail ▪ MTB ▪ Conservation area ▪ Guest cottages ▪ Owner(s) Johan & Ella Teubes ▪ Cellarmaster(s) Sybrand Teubes ▪ Winemaker(s) Sybrand Teubes, with Mariska Teubes ▪ Viticulturist(s) Johan Teubes ▪ (cab, ptage, shiraz, chard, sauv) ▪ 300t ▪ Organic, WIETA ▪ PO Box 791 Vredendal 8160 ▪ info@teubeswines.co.za, sybrand@teubeswines.co.za ▪ www.teubeswines. co.za ▪ S 31° 43' 19.1" E 018° 30' 14.5" (Vredendal) S 32° 5' 35.35" E 018° 18' 10.12" (Lambert's Bay) ▪ ⓦ forever. passive.weirdly ▪ F +27 (0)27-213-3773 ▪ **T +27 (0)27-213-2377**

Thabani Wines

Jabulani Ntshangase started out in wine as a store assistant in New York City some four decades ago, going on to co-found seminal Spice Route Winery, and mentoring young black winemakers. His own brand, Thabani, is made to spec mostly for the on-trade. Highberry, listed separately, is a newer venture.

Location: Cape Town ▪ Closed to public ▪ Owner(s) Jabulani Ntshangase ▪ PO Box 1381 Stellenbosch 7599 ▪ jntshangase@aol.com ▪ www.thabani.co.za ▪ F +27 (0)86-648-3676 ▪ **T +27 (0)82-734-9409**

Thandi Wines

With HQ in Stellenbosch's Eersterivier cellar, Thandi is one of SA's original agricultural empowerment ventures (1995) and the world's first Fairtrade-accredited wine label (2003). The vision of being socially and ethically responsible has remained steadfast, and all profits go towards upliftment initiatives.

Private Collection (NEW)

Natural Sweet Rosé ★★★ Lovely pink glints, violet, jasmine & red cherry perfumes, full-sweet but a fresh flourish on finish ensures **17** ⑧① is balanced, moreish. From shiraz. **Natural Sweet White ★★★** Dew-fresh quality to ripe orchard fruit in **17** ⑧⓪ from chenin, intriguing Asian spice nuance. Full & sweet but poise maintained by zingy citrus cleanout.

Premium Selections

Chardonnay ⓠ **★★★** Easy-drinking **16** ⑧⓪ has ripe apple flavour, smooth creamy mouthfeel, hint of vanilla oak. Stellenbosch WO. Not tasted: **Merlot**, **Shiraz**, **Sauvignon Blanc**.

Pioneer range

Not tasted: **Shiraz-Cabernet Sauvignon**, **Shiraz Rosé**, **Chardonnay-Chenin Blanc**, **Shiraz Rosé Sparkling**. — WB

Location/map: Stellenbosch ▪ Map grid reference: D6 ▪ WO: Western Cape/Stellenbosch ▪ Est 1995 ▪ Tasting & sales Mon-Thu 10-4 Fri 10-3 ▪ Fee R30pp ▪ Closed all pub hols ▪ Tour groups ▪ Owner(s) Thandi Wines (Pty) Ltd ▪ Fairtrade ▪ PO Box 597 Stellenbosch 7599 ▪ info@thandiwines.co.za ▪ www.thandiwines.com ▪ S 33° 57′ 47.66″ E 018° 47′ 38.51″ ▪ 🗺 bubbles.river.human ▪ F +27 (0)86-561-0152 ▪ **T +27 (0)21-881-3290**

That Wine Demesne

On their small mountainous estate east of Plettenberg Bay, David and Joanna Butler locally pioneered planting pinot noir clones best suited for serious red wine rather than sparkling. The vineyard has now doubled in size... to just under 1 hectare! The life of 'peasant farmers' has proved difficult (think rot and ravening birds for starters), says Joanna – though they're now stronger, and ever more passionate about the pinot coming off their young vines. It's vinified for them by Anton Smal at Bramon.

That Wine range (NEW)

Pinot Noir ★★★★ Pretty & delicate strawberry, raspberry notes & soft spice on **17** ⑧⑤. Pure fruit flavours supported by oak, just 12% alcohol. Eminently drinkable, & one to watch, but for now lacks gravitas. — TJ, CvZ

Location/WO: Plettenberg Bay ▪ Est 2012 ▪ 1stB 2016 ▪ Wines available for purchase at Bramon Wines ▪ That Place: 3-bedroom house; Vine Cottage - both self-catering & pet-friendly ▪ Owner(s) David & Joanna Butler ▪ Winemaker(s) Anton Smal (Bramon Wines) ▪ 0.9ha (pinot) ▪ ±213cs own label 100% red ▪ PO Box 197 The Crags 6602 ▪ thatwine@thatplace.co.za ▪ www.thatplace.co.za ▪ **T +27 (0)82-578-1939**

The Ahrens Family

Albert Ahrens, working from a Paarl cellar, crafts a boutique range under this family label (see also The House of GM&Ahrens for a collaborative MCC sparkling). His intent is to reflect the essence not just of varieties and vineyards but also area of origin, hence the spread of WOs in the current collection.

★★★★ Swartland Black Adds origin to name in **16** ⑧⑧. Wild ferment, as all, long skin contact, 14 months old French oak, **16** ⑧⑧ is 70% syrah, rest carignan, grenache & cinsaut; appealing combo black fruit & savoury spice, woodsmoke nuances adding interest. Palate is smooth & savoury, supple, ending dry.

★★★★ **Bottelary Seventy** Cabernet & cinsaut (60/40), **16** ⑧⑥ a vivid spread of cassis, wonderfully perfumed, tannins in support, supple & savoury. Lithe structure but well-toned muscles, everything in place for current enjoyment, a rewarding future. Oak as above.

★★★★☆ **Bottelary OVC (Old Vine Chenin)** ⊛ Intensive block & fruit selection, as all, barrel aged 11 months; melon & bruised apple, olive oil, **16** ⑨⓪ has a distinctive profile, the palate showing flavour density, richness but muted fruit, very attractive texture. Will live a long time.

★★★★☆ **The White Black** Same winemaking as OVC for **16** ⑨⓪ equal blend roussanne, marsanne, grenache blanc, clairette blanche from Voor Paardeberg. Stonefruit, floral notes, highly aromatic, gentle biscuit tone in the flavours, acidity adding a citrus freshness & length. Lovely.

Discontinued: **Elgin Pinot Noir**. — GdB, CR

Location/map: Paarl ▪ Map grid reference: G6 ▪ WO: Bottelary/Swartland/Voor Paardeberg ▪ Est/1stB 2008 ▪ Tasting & sales by appt only ▪ Tastings with either lunch or dinner by appt only; private tastings for groups in Gauteng, Bloemfontein & KZN ▪ Owner(s) Albert Ahrens ▪ Cellarmaster(s)/winemaker(s)/viticulturist(s) Albert Ahrens (2008) ▪ 35t/4,000cs own label 50% red 50% white ▪ taste@theahrensfamily.co.za ▪ S 33° 45′ 11.30″ E 019° 1′ 48.19″ ▪ 🔲 openings.perkily.locked ▪ **T +27 (0)79-196-6887**

☐ **The Artisan Collection** see Snow Mountain Wines
☐ **Theater of Wine** see Val du Charron
☐ **The Auction Crossing** see Auction Crossing Private Cellar
☐ **The Back Roads** see Black Elephant Vintners

The Bald Ibis
⊘ 🍴 🏠 📷

Growing vines at 1,700 m above sea level within sight of the Maluti Mountains in the eastern Free State has its triumphs and tribulations, not least that boutique vintners John and Trish Critchley are on their own in this — no neighbours to compare notes. There's also the weather pattern, radically different to the Western Cape. 'Despite delaying pruning,' John says of challenging harvest 2018, 'late frosts in October and snow in November caused shoot damage and reduction in yield. Sugar levels were affected by rain in February and March.' The Critchleys are undaunted, thankfully, and the first crop of tempranillo is due this year, a decade after the couple indulged their love of wine by planting vines that would yield the first and still only Wine of Origin Free State wines. These, unfortunately, were not ready for tasting this time.

Location: Fouriesburg ▪ Est 2008/2009 ▪ 1stB 2013 ▪ Tasting & sales Mon-Sat 10-4 ▪ Fee 25, redeemable on purchase ▪ Closed Easter Sun, Dec 25/26 & Jan 1 ▪ Cellar tours by appt ▪ The Rose Hip lunch venue 11-3 ▪ Farm produce ▪ Walking/hiking trails ▪ The Rose House: 2 garden suites & 1 garden cottage (B&B); 2 barn cottages (self-catering) ▪ Owner(s)/cellarmaster(s)/winemaker(s) John & Trish Critchley ▪ Viticulturist(s) Johan Wiese (Aug 2008) ▪ ±46oha/1.5ha (ptage, pinot, shiraz) ▪ 6-8t/800cs own label 100% red ▪ PO Box 149 Fouriesburg 9725 ▪ critch@netactive.co.za ▪ www.therosehouse.co.za ▪ S 28° 37′ 34.76″ E 028° 15′ 32.51″ ▪ 🔲 jumbled.excerpts.shawl ▪ **T +27 (0)82-319-0722**

☐ **The Bare Facts** see CK Wines
☐ **The Beachhouse** see Douglas Green
☐ **The Bernard Series** see Bellingham

The Berrio Wines

It's more than 20 years since Francis Pratt established vineyards on virgin land at his windswept farm near the southernmost tip of Africa. Which means it's time to begin replanting the ground-breaking blocks, as part of an ongoing rejuvenation programme. Cederberg cellarmaster David Nieuwoudt makes the wines (alongside his own from the Elim ward) and remains highly enthusiastic about the quality of the shiraz, in particular, from these ancient viticultural soils, amongst the oldest in the world.

★★★★☆ **Shiraz** ⊘ Continuing an upward curve, **16** ⑨⓪ has many layers of flavour from cranberry, plum & cherry to tobacco, wild herbs, meat & mint. 20% new oak adds attractive smoky-charry notes to soft tannins. Delicious drinking.

★★★★☆ **Sauvignon Blanc** ⊘ Exuberant **18** ⑨⓪ preview leaps from the glass with pungent aromas of grass, pepper, guava & more. Lively acidity gives definition to slightly candied fruit before succulent & lengthy finish. One to watch for in future 5-star line-ups.

★★★★★ **Weather Girl** ⓧ Unoaked 54/46 mix sauvignon & semillon, **17** ⑨①'s rich layers of fragrant pear, honey & spicy orchard fruit brought to life by zesty minerality. Elegant, textured, like **15** ⑨③, **16** sold out untasted.— CM

Location/WO: Elim ▪ Est 1997 ▪ 1stB 2002 ▪ Closed to public ▪ Owner(s)/viticulturist(s) Francis Pratt ▪ Cellarmaster(s) David Nieuwoudt (Cederberg) ▪ Winemaker(s) David Nieuwoudt (2013, Cederberg) ▪ 2,276ha/±30ha (pinot, shiraz, sauv, sem) ▪ ±30t/3,000cs own label 20% red 80% white ▪ PO Box 622 Bredasdorp 7280 ▪ wine@theberrio.co.za ▪ www.theberrio.co.za ▪ T +27 (0)28-482-1880/+27 (0)27-482-2827

☐ **The Big 5** see Jacques Germanier

The Blacksmith

Fable Mountain Vineyards' winemaker Tremayne Smith's personal 'passion project' involves vinifying mostly Rhône varieties, which he believes are well-suited to the warming Cape climate. Production is small, but has grown from four to ten tons, most of which is exported to the US, Japan and Europe. The wines, none yet tasted by us, are made in accordance with a strictly minimal-interventionist approach at Fable in Tulbagh.

Location: Riebeek-Kasteel ▪ 1stB 2014 ▪ Closed to public ▪ Owner(s)/winemaker(s) Tremayne Smith ▪ 10t own label 54% red 46% white ▪ tremayne@theblacksmithwines.co.za

☐ **The Bonfire Hill Wine Company** see Bruce Jack Wines

The Bridge of Hope Wines   ⓧ

A research project for her Masters degree in Business Leadership piqued owner Rosemary Mosia's interest in the wine industry and encouraged her to 'bridge' the gap between her day job (advising new businesses on their growth) and her burgeoning wine brand. The cheerful, characterful wines are made at Linton Park.

Premium range

Cabernet Sauvignon ★★★ Attractive Xmas mince pie notes on ripe **16** ⑧②, dried fruit & peel spicing up jammy black fruit. For earlier drinking than last. **Café Cabernet** ★★★☆ In popular choc/coffee style, **17** ⑧③ balances ripe dark fruit & mocha notes well. Few grams sugar for easy drinkability. **Merlot** ⓧ ★★★ Plummy, almond features of **14** ⑦⑦ in the vanguard of promising debut. WO W Cape. **Chardonnay** ⓧ ★★★☆ Oak adds buttered toast & caramel nuance to **16** ⑧④'s citrus preserve, savoury finish is very food friendly. **Sauvignon Blanc** ★★★ Clean, zippy, fresh **17** ⑦⑨, light flavours of yellow & green fruit.

Classic range

Cabernet Sauvignon ⊘ ★★★ Soft, juicy **16** ⑧⓪ has bright black-fruit notes unhampered by oak. WO W Cape, like Natural Sweets. **Unwooded Chardonnay** ★★★ Characterful **17** ⑧⓪ has appealing yellow fruit & fresh, lively acidity - a crowd-pleaser, with modest alcohol. **Natural Sweet Red** ⓧ ★★★ Who needs dessert when it's already in the glass? **NV** ⑦⑦'s mocha-laden flavours glide down effortlessly. Mostly merlot, shiraz. **Natural Sweet Rosé** ⓧ ★★ As sweet as it is ruby in hue, **NV** ⑦⓪ will charm many. Discontinued: **Sauvignon Blanc**. — CM

Location: Cape Town ▪ WO: Wellington/Western Cape ▪ Est 2012 ▪ 1stB 2010 ▪ Pre-booked private tasting only ▪ Owner(s) Rosemary P Mosia ▪ Winemaker(s) JG Auret (2012, Linton Park) ▪ Viticulturist(s) Rudolf Jansen van Vuuren (2012, Linton Park) ▪ 70% red 30% white ▪ 66 Loch Rd Rondebosch 7700 ▪ rmosia@yahoo.com, rmosia@thebridgeofhopewines.co.za ▪ www.thebridgeofhopewines.co.za ▪ F +27 (0)86-594-1501 ▪ T +27 (0)21-686-2294/+27 (0)83-276-3759

☐ **The Bridge Wines** see The Bridge of Hope Wines

The Butcher Shop & Grill   ⑪

The Butcher Shop & Grill is a local restaurant industry institution with outlets in Sandton's Nelson Mandela Square and Cape Town's Mouille Point oceanfront. Proprietor Alan Pick is a prolific and high-profile buyer at the Cape Winemakers Guild auction, and his long relationships with guild members and other producers give rise to these cut-above house labels.

Limited Editions

★★★★☆ **Morgenster** Ⓧ Master-crafted Bordeaux blend dominated by cabs (sauvignon & franc, 70%) in **03** ⑨② , should be spectacular now. Followed merlot-driven **01**. No **02**.

★★★★ **The Natalie** Ⓧ Merlot-led 5-part Bordeaux-style blend, **13** ⑧⑧ handles half-new oaking with aplomb, that's how concentrated the fruit is. Enough tannin backbone for food, ageing. By Le Riche.

★★★★☆ **Niels Verburg Red Blend** Ⓐ Was 'Cab-Shiraz-Mourvèdre', now 77% shiraz, previous two, pinch cab franc. **15** ⑨④'s opulence & intensity mirrors **13** ⑨④: mulberries, molten black plums, sweetly spiced, supple tannins, finishing dry. Powerful, impressive, packed with flavour & interest. No **14**.

Pick's Pick Gold Label range

★★★★☆ **Cabernet Sauvignon** Ⓐ Smidgens petit verdot & shiraz help boost **16** ⑨③'s already commendable complexity. Classic dark fruit & cigarbox, cedar & dark spice wafts yield to dense graphite finish. Give plenty of air if broaching soon. By Ernie Els.

★★★★ **Merlot** Mulberries & hints tobacco & fynbos, enduring flavours in a supple body. **14** ★★★★ ⑧④ satisfying yet understated, like **13** ⑧⑦, will aid rather than stop the conversation. By Morgenster.

★★★★ **Reserve Pinot Noir** Fragrant, bright & expressive **17** ⑧⑦, Elgin grapes fermented wholeberry in steel for aroma & freshness, then 9 months in seasoned oak. Succulent, delicious. By Radford Dale.

Shiraz ★★★★ Medium body, with ample smoky blue fruit & cherry appeal on **15** ⑧④ by Montpellier. Succulent but firm grip of oak. **Selection Rouge** Ⓝⓔⓦ ★★★ Cabernet & merlot blend by Montpellier is tad brusque, with dry spicy oak (10% new) shading red cherry fruit on **15** ⑧①. **Sauvignon Blanc** ★★★★ Not as exuberant or persistent as some, but fresh & pleasing **17** ⑧③, with good stonefruit & citrus flavours. By Iona Vineyards. Not tasted: **Pinotage**.

Pick's Pick Platinum range Ⓝⓔⓦ

Cabernet Sauvignon ★★★★ Chunky black-fruited **12** ⑧④ from Montpellier shows grippy tannin despite only 10% new oak & 60 months maturation in bottle, but will stand up to a steak.

Pick's Pick range

★★★★ **Merlot** Jordan's **15** ⑧⑥ confident & settled, with pleasing dry finish, lively acidity, silky depth. On track after lighter-styled **14** ★★★★ ⑧④.

★★★★ **Shiraz** ⊘ Like sleek & smooth **15** ⑧⑦, **16** ⑧⑦ savoury toned, subtle & confident. Approachable dinner companion or solo sipper from Zevenwacht.

★★★★ **Shiraz-Cabernet Sauvignon** Youthful, fruit-filled **16** ⑧⑦, fragrant berries & spices, savoury tapenade tail from oaking (all older, 30% American). Excellent beef partner. 84/16 blend by Ernie Els.

★★★★ **Unoaked Chardonnay** By Jordan, **17** ⑧⑧ lemon-infused bouquet, generous palate & finish, citrus-fresh acidity rounded by 8 months lees ageing in tank.

★★★★ **Sauvignon Blanc** Attractive blackcurrant, tropical & granadilla tones on **18** ⑧⑨. Tasted ex tank, yet to settle, but showing same good weight & enlivening acidity as also-tasted **17** ⑧⑨, gentle phenolic tug for extra interest. By Jordan.

★★★★ **Bubbly** Restrained but rich NV ⑧⑥ sparkler, creamy, yet with refreshing zip. From pinot noir (48%), chardonnay & dab meunier. By Villiera.

Pinotage ★★★★ From pinotage specialist Beyerskloof, **17** ⑧③ plummy & very smooth, perfect with the spare ribs. **Rosé** ★★★★ Suave, dry & flavoursome, **17** ⑧③ from merlot & shiraz is sure to please. Ex Jordan. **Chardonnay** ★★★★ Restrained, & with a saltiness that pairs well with food, Radford Dale's unoaked **18** ⑧⑤ delivers appealing lemon tones, easy drinkability. — Various tasters

Location: Cape Town/Sandton ▪ WO: Various ▪ Owner(s) Alan Pick ▪ Beach Rd Mouille Point (opposite lighthouse) Cape Town 8005; Shop 30 Nelson Mandela Square Sandton 2196 ▪ thebutchershop@mweb.co.za ▪ F +27 (0)11-784-8674 ▪ **T +27 (0)11-784-8676/7**

☐ **The Cinsault Collective** *see* Natte Valleij Wines
☐ **The Cirrus Wine Company** *see* Cirrus Wines
☐ **The Colene** *see* David Frost Wines

☐ **The Collection** see Roos Family Vineyards
☐ **The Cooperative** see Bosman Family Vineyards
☐ **The Crags** see Bramon Wines
☐ **The Cross Collection** see Dieu Donné Vineyards
☐ **The Curator's Collection** see Glen Carlou
☐ **The Den** see Painted Wolf Wines
☐ **The Dome** see Lourensford Wine Estate
☐ **The Drift** see Bruce Jack Wines

Theescombe Estate Wine   Ⓠ Ⓟ �◎

On the outskirts of Port Elizabeth lies this tiny wine venture run by a husband and wife team. Roger Futter looks after the vineyard, comprising less than 2 ha, albeit planted with five varieties, while Sandy looks after vinification and visitors, including loyal locals. The expanded range includes a singular chenin.

Cabernet Sauvignon (ⓃⒺⓌ) ★ Light colour & texture, **17** ⑥⑦ very savoury, no fruit showing, pepper & forest floor the predominant flavours. **Pinotage** Ⓥ ★★★ Pleasing spicy fruitcake perfume on **13** ⑧①, but woody character of staves (over-)used in maturation dominates the fruit - though not unpleasantly. 14.5% alcohol not obvious. **Rosé** (ⓃⒺⓌ) ★ Pale copper-hued, off-dry **17** ⑥⑦ from cab shows no fruit, just light-textured (11% alcohol) freshness. **Chenin Blanc** (ⓃⒺⓌ) ★★★★ Deep yellow gold **13** ⑧⑤ has maturity, scents of preserved melon, baked apple, marzipan - & savoury bacon crackers (yet unoaked). Flavours the same: rich, full & tasty. Unusual, almost solera-style umami character but it works. **White Muscadel Dry** (ⓃⒺⓌ) ★★ Grapey, sultana aromas greet the nose, expectation of sweetness, richness, but (unfortified) **17** ⑦④ is dry & vibrantly fresh. Would have worked better with more fruit in the flavours. — CR

Location: Port Elizabeth ▪ Map/WO: Eastern Cape ▪ Map grid reference: D5 ▪ Est/1stB 2010 ▪ Tasting, sales & cellar tours by appt ▪ Fee R45 for tour ▪ Meals/platters (cheese, olives & biltong) to be pre-booked ▪ Functions ▪ Card facilities available ▪ Owner(s) Futter family ▪ Winemaker(s) Sandra Futter (Oct 2007) ▪ Viticulturist(s) Roger Futter (Jun 2006) ▪ 1.94ha/1ha (cab, ptage, chenin, sem, white muscadel) ▪ 1-4t ▪ PO Box 28642 Sunridge Park Port Elizabeth 6008 ▪ theescombewines@hotmail.co.za ▪ www.theescombewines. wix.com/theescombewines, www.theescombewines.yolasite.com ▪ S 33° 58' 44.82" E 025° 28' 27.46" ▪ ⒲ length.iceberg.vows ▪ **T +27 (0)41-379-4035/+27(0)73-889-6663**

☐ **The Fair Trade** see Koopmanskloof Vineyards
☐ **The Flagship** see Stellenbosch Vineyards

The Fledge & Co   Ⓠ

There's always plenty of news from Margaux Nel (also winemaker at Boplaas) and Leon Coetzee, the dynamic, creative duo behind this range of often unusual, invariably refined and excellent wines. The most significant, says Leon, is that 'after 13 years we finally decided to get married'. They also added to the wide range of vineyards they source from: 15 varieties now, and 34 parcels 'from Piketberg to Waboomskraal', working with 'really great farmers' and continually learning more about the blocks in order to improve the wines. In the cellar, 'we're doing more and more little things which are resulting in far greater refinements'.

Rare Sightings range

★★★★★ **Pinot Noir** (ⓃⒺⓌ) ⊘ ⓐ Much charm & elegance, beguiling cherry fragrance, **16** ⑨③ pure but also complex. Supple, flavoursome, with bright freshness that speaks of cool-climate Elgin fruit. Fine, firm tannins; well-structured for ageing. French oak, all older, 9 months. Unfined/filtered.

★★★★★ **Red Blend** ⓐ In best vintages only. **15** ⑨③ local take on Douro red table wines; mostly touriga, tinta with splash touriga franca; rich, earthy aromas brightened with fragrant florals. Quite powerful but well controlled; good acid thread avoids any heaviness & lengthens sweet fruit. Structured for ageability.

Not tasted: **Hatchi**.

Nest Egg range

★★★★ **KatVis Pinot Noir** Gently handled to show off fruit purity, **16** ★★★★ ⑧③ darker, forest floor spectrum than Rare Sighting, fine structure. Pleasingly fresh, if more straightforward. Elgin, Tradouw & small percentage Klein Karoo grapes, like **15** ⑧⑧.

★★★★ **Syrah** Brilliant translucent ruby, 16 ⑧⑥ lightish body, vibrant freshness highlighting dark berry, floral & light peachy flavours. A still-edgy finish should benefit from few years ageing. Tradouw grapes, older oak, unfined/filtered.

★★★★☆ **HoekSteen Chenin Blanc** ⓐ Stellenbosch dryland bushvines dating from 1970s/80s. 17 ⑨③ ripest of the chenins, but elegant, poised. Blossom, red apple fragrance, great breadth of crunchy flavours, crisp, clean finish. Subtle extra dimension from 50/50 older-oak ferment, tank ferment with lees ageing. 16 untasted.

★★★★ **Klipspringer Steen** Lightish, vibrant 17 ⑧⑧ from old Swartland dryland bushvines. Steely, with more mineral tension than expressive fruit, just glimpses of fragrant red apple. 60% barrel ferment, all older; 40% tank on lees adds substance. Sprightly, characterful. 16 untasted.

★★★★ **Fumé Blanc** Old-oak-fermented sauvignon with 5% semillon; 17 ⑧⑦ more vinous than fruity, a little citrus & earthy features. Sleek, dense satin texture, lemongrass, honey flavours lifted by firm acidity. Unfined/filtered. Better suited to food than aperitif. 16 not tasted.

★★★★ **Vagabond** Allsorts, widely sourced, barrel-fermented blend, chardonnay-led with viognier, grenache blanc, chenin, drop verdelho. Some evolution on quiet, citrus peachy nose of 16 ⑧⑧. Brighter plump juiciness but still treads lightly.

Not tasted: **Red**.

Jikken Bareru Experimental Barrels range
★★★★ **Sauvignon Blanc** ⓃⒺⓌ ⊘ Elgin & 2 high-lying Stellenbosch sites in 18 ⑧⑧. Pure yet unshowy tropical, citrus fruit with a cool, mineral line & tug of pithy grip on dry, lengthy finish. 'Fresh, fresh' winemakers aptly say.

Nel & Coetzee Steen ⓃⒺⓌ ★★★★ From 2 blocks Swartland dryland bushvines. 18 ⑧③ inviting red apple, floral freshness & light yeasty note. Characterful sipping, mouthwatering length courtesy sprightly fruity acids. **Riesling** ⓃⒺⓌ ★★★★ Ex Elgin, 17 ⑧⑤ spice, light terpene notes; has area's zing, bracingly fresh fruity acids slightly tempered by few grams sugar. Medium-bodied, hot-weather refreshment. Discontinued: **Straw Wine**. — AL, CvZ

Location: Calitzdorp/Riebeek West ▪ WO: Western Cape/Swartland/Stellenbosch/Elgin/Stellenbosch-Elgin ▪ Est 2007 ▪ 1stB 2010 ▪ Tasting & sales by appt at Boplaas ▪ Closed all pub hols ▪ Owner(s) Margaux Nel & Leon Coetzee ▪ Winemaker(s) Margaux Nel & Leon Coetzee (both Jan 2007) ▪ Viticulturist(s) Margaux Nel (Jan 2007) & Leon Coetzee (Jan 2015) ▪ 65t/7,000cs own label 45% red 55% white ▪ IPW ▪ wine@thefledge.co.za ▪ www.thefledge.co.za ▪ T +27 (0)82-828-8416/+27 (0)72-385-6503

The Foundry ⓠ

This own-brand venture of Meerlust cellarmaster Chris Williams - in partnership with James Reid, operations director at Accolade Wines - not only produced this guide's first 5-star viognier three editions back, but also last year's White Wine of the Year with the Grenache Blanc. Those wines indicate a continuing concern with less-mainstream varieties – or, as Chris puts it, 'following our noses in a quest for character and quality, irrespective of where that leads us'. It sometimes leads to vineyards in Voor Paardeberg, where James has a historic property with its own small cellar, though for now The Foundry wines are made at Meerlust.

★★★★ **Grenache Noir** ⓠ Pristine fruit on finessed 15 ★★★★☆ ⑨②, light tannic hold & freshness from 15% wholebunch & portion aged in older oak. Like 14 ⑧⑧, delivers great presence without obvious power.

★★★★☆ **Syrah** ⓠ ⓐ Only 10% new oak (15 months) for 12 ⑨③ from Faure vines. Beguiling cinnamon, clove & nutmeg top notes on plum fruit, structured velvety tannins, savoury conclusion.

★★★★☆ **Grenache Blanc** ⓐ Benchmark for variety in SA, ex Voor Paardeberg grapes. 17 ⑨④ refined, intense & generous. Overt yellow stonefruit, citrus & touch of sesame. Still tight, & year or so extra will benefit an already majestic wine. Delicate 15 ★★★★★ ⑨⑨ was our 2018 White Wine of the Year. No 16.

★★★★☆ **Roussanne** ⓐ A leader of the pack in this small but growing category. Delicate 17 ⑨③ is floral, stonefruit toned. 7 months older oak, few grams of sugar add palate weight. Finishes perfectly fresh.

★★★★☆ **Viognier** ⓠ Standout Cape bottling from maritime vineyard, always delivers excellent balance between expressiveness & subtlety. 16 ⑨②'s preserved lemon, citrus blossom & spicy apricot perfectly synced with creamy texture, silky acidity & subtle touch of old oak (5 months, 2nd fill).— HC

Location/map: Stellenbosch ▪ Map grid reference: C8 ▪ WO: Stellenbosch/Voor Paardeberg ▪ Est 2000 ▪ 1stB 2001 ▪ Tasting, sales & cellar tours by appt ▪ Closed all pub hols ▪ Owner(s) Chris Williams & James Reid ▪ Cellarmaster(s)/winemaker(s) Chris Williams (Nov 2000) ▪ Viticulturist(s) Chris Williams (Nov 2000), with growers ▪ 11ha (grenache, shiraz, rouss, viog) ▪ ±30t/4,000cs own label 40% red 60% white ▪ PO Box 12423 Die Boord 7613 ▪ thefoundry@mweb.co.za ▪ www.thefoundry.co.za ▪ S 34° 1' 1.7" E 018° 45' 24.7" ▪ ⌘ truffle. hilariously.onwards ▪ F +27 (0)21-843-3274 ▪ **T +27 (0)82-577-0491**

☐ **The Front Row** see Hirst Wines

☐ **The Game Reserve** see Rooiberg Winery

The Garajeest ⑨

The garagiste is Somerset West-based, Elgin-sourcing Callan Williams, not one for the conventional - in spelling or other things perhaps, a 'creative spirit' and 'playful composer of cultivars and counterculture' she calls herself. Her wines are named for favourite rock stars, with bold, award-winning labels; there are also 100 magnums named Jagger, untasted by us.

★★★★ Jim Semillon Like still-selling **16** ⑧⑦, **17** ⑧⑥ is 50% older-oaked for good texture & breadth, but less classic, more burly. Full, ripe stonefruit flavours, plus a bruised apple note, & big lemony acidity.

Bruce Cabernet Franc ★★★★ Big, bold & ripely rich **16** ⑧③ has soft but useful tannins, firm acidity & some warmth & sweetness on the finish. Only old oak barrels used. **17** available but untasted. — TJ

Location: Somerset West ▪ WO: Elgin ▪ Est 2014 ▪ 1stB 2015 ▪ Tasting by appt ▪ Owner(s) Callan Williams ▪ Cellarmaster(s)/winemaker(s) Callan Williams (May 2014) ▪ (cab f, sem) ▪ 12t/±1,800cs own label 70% red 30% white ▪ IPW ▪ Oudehuis Centre 122 Main Rd Somerset West 7130 ▪ callan@thegarajeest.co.za, c.williams@hotmail.co.za ▪ www.thegarajeest.co.za ▪ **T +27 (0)72-524-2921**

The Giant Periwinkle ⑨

A highlight of 2018 for Cape Town advocate Pierre Rabie and co-owners Robert Stelzner and Karen van Helden was making the first wines in the new cellar in the South Coast hamlet of Baardskeedersbos (tasting facilities were nearing completion at press time). Developments in the winemaking regime include using larger vessels and a modicum of new wood, while the new wines exercising the boutique vigneron's skills are all related to the Afrikaans 'baard' (beard) and Baardskeerder (aka Wind Scorpion), a big-jawed arachnid said to clip the beards of the unwary to line their nests! 'Sun Spider' will be a less hair-raising pinotage.

★★★★ Baardbek Like previous, delicious **17** ⑧⑧ out to please but not trivial. Headed by cinsaut with shiraz & malbec; aromatic exuberance matched by equally emphatic spice, wild red fruit encouraged by ±30% bunch ferment. WO W Cape, as next.

★★★★ Coenraad de Buys ⊘ Changes to grenache, malbec, shiraz blend in **17** ⑧⑦. Less exuberant than Baardbek, just 5% bunch ferment, still rich in flavour, lengthened by savoury acid. Should lose youthful edginess with further year/2. **16** untasted. **15** ★★★★ ⑧④ was Elim syrah.

★★★★☆ Blanc Fumé ⑧ A very grown-up sauvignon, both serious & delicious. Fruity acids in **17** ⑨③ still taut, intense, as many in this vintage, but all in balance with underlying waves of blackcurrant concentration to allow for future complexity. Old-oak ferment adds dimension & style.

★★★★☆ Wind Scorpion ⑭ ⊘ Unoaked sauvignon, **18** ⑨⓪ about structure, racy agile acid, mineral vitality; fruit an undercurrent. Heady freshness, saline length reflection of most southerly, maritime Cape Agulhas vineyards & winemaker's aim of expressing typicity & place. Interesting potential.

★★★★ The Bard ⑭ ⊘ Cool lemongrass-scented **18** ⑧⑨ mainly semillon with important herbal, delicate floral infusion from nouvelle, viognier, splash sauvignon. Old oak fermented, aged in Flexcube without wood to maintain fruit purity & persistence.

Not tasted: **Kelp Forest Syrah**. Occasional release: **Old Lady On The Corner Pinot Noir**. In abeyance: **Sea Witch Pinot Noir**. Discontinued: **Cinsaut**. — AL

Location: Baardskeedersbos ▪ Map: Southern Cape ▪ Map grid reference: A3 ▪ WO: Cape South Coast/Western Cape/Cape Agulhas ▪ Est 2009 ▪ 1stB 2012 ▪ Tasting by appt only T +27 (0)82-821-2301 ▪ Owner(s) Pierre Jacques Rabie, Robert Stelzner & Karen van Helden ▪ Winemaker(s) Pierre Jacques Rabie ▪ 2.46ha (Baardskeedersbos: ptage, albariño, sauv, sem; Bredasdorp: pinot) ▪ PO Box 415 Bredasdorp 7280 ▪ pjrabie@capebar.co.za ▪ S 34° 34' 31.25" E 019° 35' 39.74" ▪ trophy.physicists.trancelike ▪ F +27 (0)21-422-2142 ▪ **T +27 (0)21-426-2653**

The Goose Wines   ⓠ ⑪ ☺ ⑧

Yields from these lofty vineyards in the Outeniqua mountains near George are up, despite the drought. The wines are made by consultant Rocco de Villiers at the Lourensford cellars in Somerset West, but winetasting is at the refurbished visitor facility on home-farm Ganzekraal ('Goose Pen'), aptly named, as part-owner and professional golfer Retief Goosen's nickname is 'The Goose'.

★★★★ **Expression** ⓠ Plush, ripe-styled **09** ⑧⑦ from cab & shiraz. Dark plummy fruit has vibrant acid support, soft supple tannins. 30% new French oak.

★★★★ **Sauvignon Blanc** ⊘ Zesty citrus & herb flavours from a low crop (5T). Previewed **18** ⑧⑥ similar to previous: tangy, with good balance of ripe grapefruit & acidity. Ready for the festive season.

Cabernet Sauvignon ★★★ From low-yield (4T) Upper Langkloof vines, **16** ⑧⓪ warm spicy berry nuance in youth curtailed by brisk acidity & robust tannins. Misses fruit intensity, balance, of previewed **15** ★★★★ ⑧⑦. **Pinot Noir** ⓠ ★★★★ Alluring earth, spice & red berry aromas, turning more savoury on palate. **14** ⑧⑤ balanced & approachable, satisfying now, with potential for good few years. **Shiraz** ⓠ ★★★★ Cool provenance & vintage accentuate **15** ⑧⑤'s high acidity, conceal tightly coiled red fruit core in youth. Give it a few years. **Chardonnay** ⓠ ★★★★ Tangy lime & butterscotch (though unoaked) on feisty **16** ⑧④. More structure than previous, some real pithy grip. Needs a meal or some time to settle. WO W Cape. — MW

Location: George ▪ Map: Klein Karoo & Garden Route ▪ Map grid reference: C3 ▪ WO: Upper Langkloof/ Western Cape ▪ Est 2005 ▪ Tasting by appt ▪ Meals/refreshments by appt; or BYO picnic ▪ Family friendly ▪ Owner(s) Retief Goosen & Werner Roux ▪ GM Pieter Haasbroek (Jul 2015) ▪ Winemaker(s) Rocco de Villiers (2018 vintage, consultant) ▪ Viticulturist(s) Bennie Botha (Jan 2009) ▪ 500ha/21ha (cab, shiraz, sauv) ▪ 120t/18,666cs own label 66% red 34% white ▪ HACCP ▪ PO Box 2053 George 6530/The Goose Office 37 Mark Str Stellenbosch 7600 ▪ michele@thegoosewines.com ▪ www.thegoosewines.com ▪ S 33° 47′ 25.72″ E 022° 41′ 45.36″ ▪ ⓜ fancy.hyper.waistline ▪ F +27 (0)86-543-1808 ▪ **T +27 (0)82-610-2276**

The Grape Grinder

Paarl negociants Oliver Kirsten and Johan du Toit aim to showcase SA wine's creativity and energy, in terms of both winemaking (including sourcing old-vine fruit mostly from Swartland) and packaging (particularly celebrating the uniquely biodiverse Cape Floral Region). They've also diversified into spirits with an artisan fynbos-infused gin, and consumer response has been 'quite phenomenal'.

The Grinder range

Chenin Blanc ⊘ ⑦ ★★★ From old dryland Swartland vines, **18** ⑧② nudges higher rating with concentrated ripe peach & yellow apple fruit, fresh acidity & lustrous texture from over 6 months on lees.

Pinotage ⊘ ★★★★ 'Coffee' style **17** ⑧④ given 4 months oak staving/barrelling for chocolate, mocha & sweet spice shading to juicy berry & plum fruit. **Shiraz** ⊘ ★★★★ From Paarl & Swartland, **16** ⑧③ is soft & very approachable, with cherries galore, acidity accentuating spicy kick. Half wooded. Not tasted: **Rosé**.

Blue Moose range
Cabernet Sauvignon-Shiraz ⊘ ★★★★ Was 'Blue Moose'. Still from cab & shiraz, latter only 4% in inky **17** ⑧③, rich in ripe dark fruit with subtle choc-nut & baking spice from 10 months older oak. Swartland grapes. For cosy firesides.

Cape Fynbos range
Chenin Blanc ⊘ ★★★ Worth buying for the beautiful 3L-pack alone, **18** ⑧⓪ fresh & zesty, with tropical fruit salad flavours. Coastal WO.

Milkwood range
Shiraz-Viognier ⊘ ★★★★ **16** ⑧⑤ sees 4% viognier co-fermented with shiraz for fynbos perfume, red cherry/berry fruit, wild herbs & black pepper. Oak subtler than last.

Wild Olive range
Old Vines Chenin Blanc ⊘ ⑦ ★★★ Old vines showcased by concentrated tropical & stonefruit of **18** ⑧②, smooth after 6 months lees contact, enlivened by brisk acidity. Swartland WO.

Not tasted: **Rosé**. — JG

Location: Paarl ▪ WO: Western Cape/Swartland/Coastal ▪ Est/1stB 2010 ▪ Closed to public ▪ Owner(s) Oliver Kirsten & Johan du Toit ▪ Cellarmaster(s) Pieter Carstens (Dec 2010, consultant) ▪ Winemaker(s) Madré van der Walt (Jul 2015, consultant) ▪ Viticulturist(s) Koos van der Merwe (Dec 2010, consultant) ▪ 70,000cs own label 75% red 20% white 5% rosé ▪ ISO 2009, BRC, WIETA ▪ PO Box 606 Paarl 7624 ▪ oliver@grapegrinder. com ▪ www.grapegrinder.com ▪ F +27 (0)86-588-4338 ▪ **T +27 (0)21-863-3943**

The Great South African Wine Company

Carl van der Merwe and Wendy Appelbaum are respectively winemaker and owner of DeMorgenzon, but this ambitiously named project is a separate one for the partnership. Grapes are sourced from vineyards in higher-lying parts of Stellenbosch – 'inspiring places', Carl says. If the red blend looks back to Cape tradition, the striking and witty label design alludes to old medicine bottles. There's a vintage gap for both wines because Carl, for various reasons, decided not to make wine for the Company in 2016.

★★★★ **The Great Red** ⓐ Blends 60% cab, 24% cinsaut (half fermented with stems) with cab franc & petit verdot. **17** ★★★★★ ⑨③ heady light perfume; fresh, lively & light-feeling; gentle but firm structure. No new oak, unlike last-made **15** ⑧⑦, where it showed. This one altogether better balanced.

★★★★☆ **The Great White** ⓐ Semillon (42%), sauvignon (32%) & chenin blend seamlessly on **17** ⑨③ to give complex array of aromas & full flavours. Natural ferment & maturation in old oak, the varieties aged separately. Bright, vibrant lemony acidity well integrated. Should develop interestingly. No **16**.— TJ

Location/map/WO: Stellenbosch ▪ Map grid reference: C5 ▪ Est 2014 ▪ 1stB 2015 ▪ Tasting by appt only ▪ Owner(s) Wendy Appelbaum & Carl van der Merwe ▪ Cellarmaster(s)/winemaker(s) Carl van der Merwe (2014) ▪ 12-15t ▪ 1,000cs own label 50% red 50% white ▪ PO Box 1388 Stellenbosch 7599 ▪ carl@greatsaw-ineco.com ▪ www.greatsawineco.com ▪ S 33° 56'22.99" E 018° 45'0.17" ▪ ᵐ totals.pictures.buddy ▪ F +27 (0)21-881-3773 ▪ **T +27 (0)82-600-9457**

☐ **The Griffin** see Stettyn Family Vineyards
☐ **The Grinder** see The Grape Grinder
☐ **The Haven Collection** see Glen Carlou

The High Road

High-flying and in high demand, say partners and longtime friends Les Sweidan and Mike Church of their specialised Bordeaux-focused boutique operation located at Stellenbosch's Bosman's Crossing 'crushpad'. Sales have grown so substantially that they are planning for the foreseeable future when their wines might be available on allocation only.

★★★★ **Cabernet Sauvignon** Improving on **15** ★★★★ ⑧⑤ in its gentle, rounded black fruit appeal, **16** ⑧⑦ is balanced & long, with lovely cedar tail from oak staves & 14 months in bottle.

★★★★ **Classique** Supple, velvety & refined **15** ★★★★★ ⑨② merlot-led 5-part Bordeaux blend, a rung above **14** ⑧⑧. Nothing is overplayed: smooth, layered, rich, persistent, supportively oaked - all old. Soft but firm, & with copious fruitcake appeal.

★★★★☆ **Director's Reserve** ⓐ Reflects superb **15** ⑨④ vintage in classic cab-led Bordeaux red, dab malbec (5%) added to **14** ⑨④'s 4 components. Pliable, succulent yet structured, richly fruited, with firm core & backbone of all-new oak (16 months). Nuanced, subtly generous & lengthy. Also in 1.5L.— FM

Location/map/WO: Stellenbosch ▪ Map grid reference: E5 ▪ Est/1stB 2003 ▪ Tasting by appt only ▪ Closed all pub hols ▪ Boardroom facilities ▪ Owner(s) Les Sweidan & Mike Church ▪ Winemaker(s) Mark Carmichael-Green (2004, consultant) ▪ Viticulturist(s) Paul Wallace (2004, consultant) ▪ 50t/3,500cs own label 100% red ▪ 7D Lower Dorp Str Bosman's Crossing Stellenbosch 7600 ▪ wine@thehighroad.co.za ▪ www.thehighroad. co.za ▪ S 33° 56'27.1" E 018° 50'49.1" ▪ ᵐ myth.heats.uptown ▪ F +27 (0)21-886-4288 ▪ **T +27 (0)76-044-5020**

The Hills

Chimanimani is a smallholding in Stellenbosch's prime Devon Valley where Vic Hills, whose family has owned the property since 1964, oversees 5 ha of red-wine varieties and a block of old chenin. The harvest is mostly sold but since 2006 a smidgen has been made for the own label by consultants.

Cabernet Sauvignon ★★★☆ Appealing notes of forest floor, tar & liquorice spice up lively blackcurrant fruit, **15** (85) well-judged weight & tannins, expressing ripe fruit. **Pinot Noir** (②) ★★★ Spicy smoked meat notes to **15** (77), aged in old oak. Stellenbosch WO. **Dry Red** (②) ★★★★ From shiraz, **13** (84) delivers much more than its name, sleek & juicy with intense red berries, extended oaking fully assimilated. **Shiraz** ★★★ Freshness on spicy **15** (81) belies 2 years in barrel. Meaty, slight medicinal whiff, light body. **Ensemble** ★★★ Somewhat unsettled cab-shiraz, **15** (77) prominent oak spice & tannins, sour cherry fruit. Older vintages available, as for most of the reds. **Chenin Blanc** ★★★★ Generous body & fruit, buttery notes (though unoaked), **17** (85) well-structured & -balanced. Above-average everyday drinking. — GdB

Location/map: Stellenbosch ▪ Map grid reference: D4 ▪ WO: Devon Valley/Stellenbosch ▪ Est/1stB 2006 ▪ Tasting & sales by appt ▪ Owner(s) The Victor Hills Family Trust ▪ Winemaker(s) Nicky Claasens (2016, consultant) & Danie Steytler (consultant) ▪ Viticulturist(s) Vic Hills (Jan 1998) ▪ 6ha/5ha (cab, pinot, shiraz, chenin) ▪ 40t/600cs own label 80% red 20% white ▪ PO Box 12012 Die Board Stellenbosch 7613 ▪ vwhills@ iafrica.com ▪ www.thehillswine.co.za ▪ S 33° 55′ 04.1″ E 018° 48′ 47.1″ ▪ [≡] among.paper.darkest ▪ **T +27 (0)21-865-2939/+27 (0)82-493-6837**

The House of GM&AHRENS   (②) (¶¶)

Lawyer Gerrit Maritz and independent vintner Albert Ahrens co-own this Franschhoek-based boutique brand of ultra-premium bottled-fermented bubbly, uniquely presented in 5-bottle cases, complementing the winemaker's The Ahrens Family output (see entry), both with assistant winemaker Marinda Schabort.
★★★★☆ **Vintage Cuvée** Bone-dry MCC sparkling, **14** ★★★★ (88) displays richness - toasted brioche, citrus preserve - & character, finishes fresh. Near-equal chardonnay & pinot noir, 11 months in barrel, 34 months on lees vs 42 for last-tasted **11** (94). Limited magnums.— GdB, CR

Location/map: Franschhoek ▪ Map grid reference: C1 ▪ WO: Western Cape ▪ Est 2007 ▪ 1stB 2008 ▪ Tasting, sales & cellar tours by appt ▪ Closed all pub hols ▪ Meals/refreshments by appt ▪ Owner(s) Albert Ahrens & Gerrit Maritz ▪ Cellarmaster(s)/viticulturist(s) Albert Ahrens (Jan 2007) ▪ 15t/1,000 x 5-btl cs own label 100% MCC ▪ info@gmahrens.com ▪ www.gmahrens.co.za ▪ S 33° 54′ 14″ E 019° 07′ 08″ ▪ [≡] multilayer.shower.along ▪ **T +27 (0)79-196-6887 (Albert)/+27 (0)83-348-1230 (Gerrit)**

The House of JC le Roux   (②) (¶¶) (◎) (&)

Embracing the French 'champagne house' concept, Distell has created a multifaceted and stylish facility in Stellenbosch dedicated to sparkling wine, providing edutainment about every facet of its production and appreciation. The sparklers created here cover everything from the classic flagship, Scintilla, and sweeter dessert MCCs, to fun, pocket-friendly carbonated fizzes made from non-traditional varieties, to iced lollies and granitas. A new cocktail bar shows how versatile bubbly can be when combined with fruit and liqueurs, while the al fresco deck offers both food to pair with the bubbles and magnificent views across Devon Valley. This is a destination in its own right, delightful to locals and tourists alike.

Méthode Cap Classique range
★★★★ **Scintilla** Flag bearer, mostly chardonnay, attractive brioche & minerality in **14** (89), hint of saltiness too. Finer, more focused & drier than other sparklers from this house. Elegant oyster partner. **12** & **13** untasted.
La Vallée Rosé Demi-Sec ★★★ Identical varietal mix & composition to Demi-Sec sibling, with a blush of colour. **NV** (82) fizz gets the delicate sweet/fresh balance right. **Brut** ★★★★ Balanced, versatile & friendly sparkle for drier drinkers. Mostly pinot noir, some chardonnay, **NV** (85). Savoury brioche morphs into berries on palate, gentle creaminess from year on lees. **La Vallée Demi-Sec** ★★★ Light, balanced & charming **NV** (82) from pinot noir & chardonnay, sweetness delicately woven into fresh palate. Works well with spicy or smoked food. Or simply solo. Not tasted: **Pinot Noir Rosé**, **Pinot Noir**.

Vibrazio range
Rosé Demi-Sec ★★★ These bubblies are from non-traditional varieties. This blush **NV** (78) sauvignon & pinotage, splashes muscadel & shiraz, generous fizz & savoury nuance deftly balancing the sweetness. Low alcohol, like White. Carbonated, as all below. **Sauvignon Blanc** ★★ Uncomplicated fizzer is driest in this range, highest in alcohol (13%). **17** (75) loses splash colombard, gets tad leaner, less charming than last, her-

baceous & nettle notes in the mousse. **White Demi-Sec ★★★** Perfumed, grapey NV 79's sweetness lifted by delightful bubbles, very quaffable. Sauvignon & muscadel, appears touch fresher than Vibrazio cousin.

Sélection Vivante

La Chanson ★★ Light, sweet red fizz from pinotage, shiraz & cab franc, offering spice, smoky berries & plum compote in newest NV 76, sugar neatly balanced by zingy effervescence. Well chilled, real crowd pleaser for the sweet toothed, as all. **La Fleurette ★★** Fun rosé bubbles with rosepetal, strawberry & pineapple, NV 76 same fresh & cloy-free persona as last, added impression of savoury dryness from red cultivars & plenty lively foam. **Le Domaine ★★** Sauvignon's fresh herb, infused with muscadel's alluring grapey perfume in latest NV 74, light in alcohol (7.5%), as all these sparklers. — MW

Location/map: Stellenbosch ▪ Map grid reference: D4 ▪ WO: Western Cape/Stellenbosch ▪ 1stB 1983 ▪ Tasting & sales Mon-Fri 10–4 Sat/pub hols 10–3 Sun 10–2; booking essential ▪ Fee R80-R120 ▪ Closed Good Fri, Dec 25 & Jan 1 ▪ Nougat pairing, olive pairing ▪ Self-tour available during opening hrs ▪ Cocktails & platters ▪ Gifts ▪ Le Venue restaurant open for breakfast & lunch, booking essential ▪ Conference/wedding facilities ▪ Owner(s) Distell ▪ Cellarmaster(s) Elunda Basson ▪ Winemaker(s) Elunda Basson (2007), with John November (2011) ▪ Farm manager Graham Daniels (2015) ▪ Viticulturist(s) Bennie Liebenberg (Jan 2000) ▪ 27ha own vyds ▪ 20% red 80% white ▪ ISO 9200 ▪ PO Box 184 Stellenbosch 7599 ▪ info@jcleroux.co.za ▪ www.jcleroux.co.za ▪ S 33° 54' 16.6" E 018° 48' 37.4" ▪ 📖 running.shares.belong ▪ **T +27 (0)21-865-8200**

☐ **The House of Krone** see Krone

☐ **The House of Mandela** see House of Mandela

☐ **The Hypocrite** see Wazu Wine Merchants

☐ **The Innocent** see Lammershoek Winery

☐ **The Introduction** see Miles Mossop Wines

The Kitchen Sink   ⓠ

Originally a second label within the Metzer Family Wines portfolio, The Kitchen Sink has evolved into a standalone brand, hence this separate listing. 'Distinctive vineyard parcels' across the Western Cape are vinified in Stellenbosch by minimalist Wade Metzer 'to retain as much terroir and fruit character as possible'.

★★★★ Red Blend ⓖ Complex multi-region 16 89 led by shiraz, naturally fermented. Seductive choc-laced dark-berry depths without tannic edges, lower 14.5% alcohol after 15% in lush 15 87.

Not tasted: **White Blend**. — DS

Location: Somerset West ▪ WO: Western Cape ▪ Tasting by appt ▪ Owner(s) Wade Metzer & Barry Holfeld ▪ Winemaker(s) Wade Metzer ▪ info@kitchensinkwine.com ▪ www.kitchensinkwine.com ▪ **T +27 (0)72-279-7645**

☐ **The Legend** see Windmeul Cellar

Thelema Mountain Vineyards   ⓠ ♿

Looking at Thelema today, it's hard to believe it started as an old fruit farm at the crest of Stellenbosch's Helshoogte Pass. But, bought by the McLean and Webb families in 1983, the conversion turned it into a model wine farm and internationally hailed pioneer of modern SA wine. Thomas Webb handles day-to-day matters while his father and co-founder Gyles remains at the helm of winemaking, ably assisted by Rudi Schultz and Duncan Clarke. There are two strings to this bow, both cool-climate, Thelema itself and the Elgin property Sutherland, whose wines are made at the home farm. This edition sees some changes, a new Bucher press, two sales and marketing staff appointments, and the release of three new Sutherland wines, taking that range to new heights. All Reserve wines, the Petit Verdot is a first from Elgin.

Thelema range

★★★★☆ Cabernet Sauvignon ⓐ Impressive crafting & balance, 15 94 confirms why Stellenbosch is renowned for its cabs. Intensely flavoured & perfumed, cassis & spice, hint of graphite, supported by fine-grained tannins. Musculature for a long life. 14 untasted. Also in magnum.

★★★★ The Mint Cabernet Sauvignon Living up to its name with Mint Crisp chocolate perfume & flavours, 14 88 also appeals with its sleek polished lines, harmony between fruit & oak.

★★★★ **Merlot** Bright fruited, with dark chocolate notes, tobacco, **15** ⑧⑦ is smooth textured & elegant, offering current appeal as well as cellaring potential. Well crafted.

★★★★☆ **Merlot Reserve** ⑧ All-new oak in **15** ★★★★★ ⑨⑤, selection of special vineyard parcels, & it shows in the fruit intensity, layers of spicing, sleek structure. Like **14** ⑨②, impressive, involving, with a great future ahead.

★★★★ **Shiraz** Different styling to Sutherland, **15** ⑧⑨ is smoky, savoury, its dark fruit well matched to supple tannins, texture silky, curvaceous. But hidden strength here, good ageing potential.

★★★★☆ **Rabelais** ⑧ Cab-dominant 4-part Bordeaux-style blend, 20 months French oak, 80% new, **14** ⑨③'s compact body built for the long haul but already accessible. Dark fruit & scrub, some meaty notes, has complex depths, give it the time it deserves.

★★★★ **Chardonnay** ⑦ A great food wine, **15** ⑧⑦ is packed with flavour, citrus & buttered toast, zesty freshness brightening the palate, extending the flavours. Lovely balance, well-judged oaking.

★★★★ **Ed's Reserve Chardonnay** Ed was Gyles Webb's feisty, memorable late mother-in-law. From unusual 'muscat' clone of chardonnay, **16** ⑧⑧ barrel fermented/aged, gives aromatic zesty grapiness, it's one-of-a-kind, much like Ed.

★★★★ **Riesling** Distinctive **16** ⑧⑧ from estate's oldest block, planted 1984. Floral notes vie with pineapple, bottle age intensifying the flavours. Racy freshness & dry, sleek body, hard to resist.

★★★★☆ **Sauvignon Blanc** ⊘ ⑧ Different style to Sutherland, although both have cool growing conditions. Citrus with a mineral core to polished **18** ⑨④, tangy limy acidity giving it focus & incredible length.

★★★★ **Méthode Cap Classique Brut** Elgin-sourced sparkling, 32 months on lees, classic chardonnay/pinot noir blend, **14** ⑧⑨ ticks all boxes: lemon/lime & brioche, elegant yet great length. Has finesse & style.

★★★★ **Semillon Late Harvest** ⑦ Step up on **13** ★★★☆ ⑧⑤, **14** ⑧⑦ celebrates fruit, melon & citrus preserve, honey overlay. Doesn't prepare you for the flavour intensity, sweetness, perked by acidity. 375 ml.

★★★★ **Vin de Hel Late Harvest** Named for Helshoogte Pass where Thelema lies. Aromatic & grapey, with notes of candied citrus peel, **15** ⑧⑨ white muscat de Frontignan is richly sweet, a freshening acid lift giving length & delicious drinkability. 375 ml.

. . . .

Mountain Red ⑦ ★★★★ Creative 5-part blend, near equal grenache, petit verdot & shiraz, dark-toned **15** ⑧④ has wild berries, salty liquorice & peppery notes. Finishes food-friendly firm & dry. WO W Cape.

Muscat ⑦ ★★★★ Was 'Muscat de Frontignan'. Strikingly grapey, aromatic, **18** ⑧④ is lithe (12% alcohol), now dry, with zesty freshness, & a finish that goes on & on.

. . . .

Discontinued: **Sauvignon Blanc Reserve**, **Verdelho**, **Blanc de Blancs Méthode Cap Classique**.

Sutherland range

★★★★☆ **Reserve Grenache** ⑩ ⑧ An impressive maiden vintage, **16** ⑨③ shows scrub & red berries, violets, nails the variety by showing that intensity is possible with elegance & grace. Ripeness without excess; polished, harmonious, a long life ahead. Elgin WO, as all below.

★★★★★ **Reserve Petit Verdot** ⑩ ⑧ All-new French oak in **15** ⑨⑤, signalling its class & serious intent. Complex notes of wild berries & violets, beautifully threaded through with cigarbox & scrub. Cellarworthy, still an infant. Confirms why the variety is often welcomed into a Bordeaux blend.

★★★★ **Syrah** Ripe dark berries & cocoa, **14** ⑧⑨ is opulently perfumed but has a serious side, a savoury fine-grained tannin backbone that promises years of pleasure ahead.

★★★★★ **Chardonnay** Lemon cream & buttered toast, **17** ⑧⑧ wears its oaking with pride, the citrus core keeping it fresh & lively. Delicious food wine.

★★★★☆ **Reserve Chardonnay** ⑩ ⑧ Three chardonnays in the range, each worthy & different. This **16** ⑨③ a barrel selection, long lees contact & bottle age providing orange preserve richness & palate weight. Has latent power, belying its elegance (just 13% alcohol).

★★★★ **Unwooded Chardonnay** ⊘ Tangerine with a lemon underpin, there's lovely tangy freshness in **18** ⑧⑧; pure & focused, a mineral thread throughout.

★★★★ **Sauvignon Blanc** ⊘ ⑧ Zinging freshness in **18** ★★★★★ ⑨③, lime & nettles, reflecting the cool-climate terroir. Sleek, focused & pure. Improves on **17** ⑧⑧, more intense.

★★★★☆ **Viognier-Roussanne** ⊛ Viognier dominates in **15** ⑨④, fermented/matured in seasoned barrels, stonefruit given a savoury overlay. Elegant, a range trademark, without sacrificing flavour intensity. **Cabernet Sauvignon** ★★★★ Nice combo cassis & oak spice, the **14** ⑧④ tannins supple for immediate enjoyment, plus cellaring. **Pinot Noir** ★★★★ Mulberries & raspberries with firm tannin adding a serious note, **15** ⑧④ will reward cellaring, a pinot noir built to last. **Grenache Rosé** ★★★ Elegant, dry **18** ⑧①, red-fruited, tangy & fresh. Hits the right spot. **Riesling** ⓥ ★★★★ Always noteworthy for varietal elegance & refinement. Sample **17** ⑧④ doesn't disappoint, lovely aromatics, floral & spice, racy acidity offset by a dab of sweetness, adding to the appeal. — CR

Location/map: Stellenbosch ▪ Map grid reference: G4 ▪ WO: Stellenbosch/Elgin/Western Cape ▪ Est 1983 ▪ 1stB 1988 ▪ Tasting & sales Mon-Fri 9–5 Sat 10–3 ▪ Fee R80/6 wines, waived on purchase ▪ Owner(s) McLean & Webb family trusts ▪ Cellarmaster(s) Gyles Webb (1983) ▪ Winemaker(s) Rudi Schultz (Dec 2000), with Duncan Clarke (Jan 2009) ▪ 257ha/90ha (cab, grenache, merlot, p verdot, pinot, shiraz, chard, muscat, riesling, rouss, sauv, viog) ▪ 1,000t/60,000cs own label 40% red 60% white ▪ PO Box 2234 Dennesig Stellenbosch 7601 ▪ info@thelema.co.za ▪ www.thelema.co.za ▪ S 33° 54' 30.0" E 018° 55' 23.4" ▪ ⒨ slap. testing.march ▪ F +27 (0)21-885-1800 ▪ **T +27 (0)21-885-1924**

The Liberator

Richard Kelley MW, one of the UK's most respected authorities on SA wine, visits several times a year to 'liberate' experimental batches or interesting offcuts that might otherwise be blended away or sold in bulk. Each bottling is an 'episode', its story recounted on bottle and online.

★★★★ **The Francophile Syrah** Middleweight **16** ⑧⑥, attractive lavender aroma, juicy black cherry fruit, a pinch of white pepper. Older oak, as next.

★★★★ **The Francophile Chenin Blanc** First impression of **18** ⑧⑨ is crisp, lean & mineral, then peach & citrus fruit burst through. Charming, with satisfying breadth/texture from light wooding.

★★★★ **The Wendy House** ⓃⒺⓌ Richer, oaking more obvious (in viscous mouthfeel) than Francophile, **16** ⑧⑧ Helderberg chenin has aniseed adding intrigue to citrus & stonefruit.

★★★★ **Bunny Chow** ⓃⒺⓌ No furry animals harmed in the making of **17** ⑧⑦! Quirky name a reference to favourite local spicy fast food, with which this fragrant, full-bodied, wooded viognier would be delicious.

★★★★ **An Arrogance of Sommeliers** ⓥ Smooth, suave **15** ★★★★★ ⑨③ is mostly barrel-aged semillon (oak barely discernible) & 10% sauvignon; elegant & complex, with herbaceous notes as well as tangy lime & lanolin. Great breadth, depth & long finish. Last tasted was youthfully brusque **13** ⑧⑨.

In abeyance: **Midnight at the Lost & Found**. — JG

WO: Stellenbosch ▪ Est 2010 ▪ 1stB 2008 ▪ Closed to public ▪ Owner(s) Richard Kelley MW & Eduard Haumann ▪ 50% red 50% white ▪ richard@dreyfus-ashby.co.uk ▪ www.theliberatorwine.com ▪ **T +44 (0)1476-870717**

☐ **The Lion Hound** see Ridgeback

The Love Boat Wines

'The romance will continue,' confirm Duncan Savage and Adi Badenhorst, friends, winemakers and CWG members who shared some 'interesting' Airbnbs on a marketing trip to Norway, took a 'compromising' selfie in a one-bed studio, causing much hilarity when posted on Twitter. The upshot, a pair of joint-venture wines sold on the CWG's annual auction. So far a one-off. 'After the emotional intensity of the first vintage we decided to cool off for 2017.' Fans needn't fear; a commercial release is promised from the 'epic' 2018 vintage.

Location: Cape Town ▪ Est 2017 ▪ 1stB 2016 ▪ Closed to public ▪ Owner(s) Adi Badenhorst & Duncan Savage ▪ ±200cs own label 60% red 40% white ▪ info@savagewines.com ▪ **T +27 (0)21-785-4019**

☐ **The Marais Family** see Wonderfontein
☐ **The Mason's Winery** see Mason's Winery

Thembi & Co
ⓥ

Nursing assistant turned wine entrepreneur Thembi Tobie, previously Wellington based, now markets her eponymous Fairtrade range from Stellenbosch. Included are a chenin, sauvignon, shiraz and pinotage.

Location: Stellenbosch ▪ Tasting by appt only ▪ Owner(s) Thembi Tobie ▪ Bottelary Hills Stellenbosch 7605 ▪ thembi@thembiwines.co.za ▪ www.thembiwines.co.za ▪ **T** +27 (0)83-277-5117

☐ **Thembu Tribute** *see* House of Mandela
☐ **The Mentors** *see* KWV Wines

Themika

The 40-year-old chenin vines on Cape Town doctors Paul and Dagmar Whitaker's fruit, wine and olive farm in Tulbagh (named for daughters Kim and Thea) suffered badly during the 'disastrous' lingering drought but happily the gnarled veterans have been rescued with the help of neighbour and Theuniskraal viticulturist, Wagner Jordaan. 'We are back to our record production of 1.5 tons per hectare!' Paul chuckles.

Barrel Select range

★★★★☆ **Chenin Blanc** ⊛ From venerable low-yield single block, succulently delicious **17** ⑨³ is unfussy & focused, its complex layers of baked apple, stonefruit & beeswax interwoven with subtle (old) oak spices. Silky texture & lingering finish.

Not tasted: **White Blend**. — GdB

Location/map/WO: Tulbagh ▪ Map grid reference: F4 ▪ 1stB 2013 ▪ Tasting by appt only ▪ Themika guest house (farm house & 3 self-catering cottages) T +27 (0)78-472-0934 (Douglas) ▪ MTB routes ▪ Owner(s) Paul & Dagmar Whitaker ▪ Winemaker(s)/viticulturist(s) Paul Whitaker ▪ 56ha/2ha (chenin) ▪ 4.5t/220cs own label 100% white ▪ ansec166@docswhitaker.co.za ▪ www.themika.com ▪ S 33° 13' 4.14" E 019° 6' 35.44" ▪ ⌖ flowerbeds.redoubts.mossy

☐ **The Mysteries** *see* Lammershoek Winery
☐ **The Naked Truth** *see* Picardi ReBEL
☐ **The Nature Reserve** *see* Erasmus Family Wines
☐ **The Old Man's Blend** *see* Groote Post Vineyards
☐ **The Pactolus Collection** *see* Glen Carlou
☐ **The Pavillion** *see* Boschendal Wines
☐ **The Pierneef Collection** *see* La Motte
☐ **The Pledge** *see* Grand Domaine
☐ **The Ploughman** *see* Perdeberg Wines
☐ **The Raptor Post** *see* Fable Mountain Vineyards
☐ **The Rhino of Linton Park** *see* Linton Park Wines
☐ **The Rhino Run** *see* Van Loveren Family Vineyards
☐ **The Rhythm** *see* Wildekrans Wine Estate
☐ **The Rose House** *see* The Bald Ibis
☐ **The Royal** *see* Valley Vineyards Wine Company
☐ **The Rustler** *see* Flagstone Winery
☐ **The Sadie Family** *see* Sadie Family Wines
☐ **The Saints** *see* DGB (Pty) Ltd
☐ **The Search** *see* Trizanne Signature Wines
☐ **The Sensory Collection** *see* Stellar Winery
☐ **The Spice Route Winery** *see* Spice Route Winery
☐ **The Stellenbosch Reserve** *see* Stellenbosch Reserve
☐ **The Storyteller** *see* Stellar Winery
☐ **The Tin Mine** *see* Zevenwacht
☐ **The Township Winery** *see* Township Winery

Theuniskraal

Named for a son of one of the earliest families to settle in Tulbagh (circa 1699), Theuniskraal has been farmed by the Jordaan family since 1927. These paragons of continuity last year produced the 71st vintage of their consumer favourite, Cape Riesling. Floral-themed and -packaged Ixia is a more recent brand.

Theuniskraal range

Prestige Ⓥ ★★★ Bright, spicy red fruit on unoaked, easy-drinking **15** ⑦ previewed blend of ruby cab, cab & shiraz. **Moscato Rosé** Ⓥ ★★ From muscat ottonel & shiraz, **17** ⑦ ex tank is soft, sweet & fragranced with rosepetals. **Semillon-Chardonnay** Ⓥ ★★★ Previewed cheerful, sippable unwooded **16** ⑧. Generously fruity, nice leesy structure. **Bouquet Blanc** Ⓥ ★★★ From gewürztraminer & white muscadel, perfumed **17** ⑦ has Asian spice appeal, lovely balanced sweetness, perfect for Cape Malay fare. Not tasted: **Cape Riesling**.

Ixia range

Cabernet Sauvignon Ⓥ ★★★ Ruby **16** ⑧ shows choc-dipped raspberry aromas, light body & smooth vanilla-tinged flavours. **Shiraz** Ⓥ ★★ Inky purple **16** ⑦, dark berries overtaken by bushfire flavours. **Sauvignon Blanc** Ⓥ ★★★ Tank sample **17** ⑦ floral hints, lemon & lime tones, brisk farewell. — WB

Location/map/WO: Tulbagh • Map grid reference: F4 • Est 1705 • 1stB 1947 • Tasting & sales Mon-Fri 9–5 Sat 9–2 • Closed Easter Sat/Sun, Dec 25 & Jan 1 • Owner(s)/viticulturist(s) Jordaan family • Cellarmaster(s) Andries Jordaan (1991) • Winemaker(s) Andries Jordaan (1991) & Wagner Jordaan • 140ha total • PO Box 34 Tulbagh 6820 • admin@tkraal.co.za • www.theuniskraal.co.za • S 33° 13′ 41.3″ E 019° 8′ 7.1″ • seesaws. consulate.autobiography • F +27 (0)23-230-1504 • **T +27 (0)23-230-0689**

☐ **The Vine Guys** *see* Mischa Estate

The Vinoneers

A long working relationship between winemaker Etienne Louw of Altydgedacht Estate and graphic designer Brenden Schwartz of Bravo Design eventually led to this collaboration, creating small-batch, handcrafted wines with beautiful and artistic labels. The idea to combine wine and art has led to multiple awards for the intriguingly dressed bottles and their imaginative backstories. The grapes are sourced from both Durbanville, Etienne's home range, and around the Western Cape, allowing him to track down interesting old parcels.

Orpheus & The Raven range

★★★★★ **No. 42 Cape Blend** Unusual blend of pinotage & its parents cinsaut & pinot noir (42/16/42), **16** ⑨ ripe berry fruit with meaty/gamey notes & hints of rubber & tar. Deliciously bouncy texture & weight with appealing mineral edge makes excellent partner for charcuterie. Coastal WO.

★★★★ **No. 42 Old Bush Vine Chenin Blanc** From 40 year old Durbanville vines, **17** ⑧ very lovely example with concentrated cooked apples, pears & spice (100% wooded, none new), delightful texture & enlivening lemony acidity. Award-winning labels on all these a pleasure to behold.

★★★★★ **The Swansong** Ⓥ From 35 year old gewürztraminer vines uprooted after this harvest, hence the name. **16** ⑨ has pure litchi & rosepetal aromas, fresh & linear, just off-dry. Seductive & playful on nose, but so sophisticated on the palate: pristine & focused.— CM

Location: Durbanville • WO: Durbanville/Coastal • Est/1stB 2016 • Closed to public • Owner(s) Etienne Louw & Brenden Schwartz • Winemaker(s) Etienne Louw (2015) • 600cs own label 66% red 34% white • etienne@vinoneers.com • www.vinoneers.com • **T +27 (0)21-976-1295**

☐ **The W Collection** *see* Wellington Wines
☐ **The Winery of Good Hope** *see* Radford Dale

The Wine Thief

The name alludes to the pipette used for taking samples of wine through barrel bungholes; certainly not to brand owner Ewan Mackenzie. He's a sommelier-about-town, and about the winelands, where he works with established winemakers for generally one-off bottlings. But there's also the expanding Costa del Swart range, 'focusing on single-barrel creations with Swartland winemakers and Swartland fruit'.

Costa del Swart range 🆕

★★★★★ **Chenin Blanc** Made from Paardeberg fruit (so the witty allusion to Swartland), including drops of roussanne & grenache blanc. Fruitiness is not what interesting **17** ⑨ is most about, despite dried peach & lingering thatchy flavours - crucially, these go with stony minerality & fresh, succulent acid.

The Wine Thief range

Petit Verdot Blanc de Noir ★★★★ Naturally fermented in old oak, characterful, delightful **17** ⑧⑤ pink has a splash of roussanne. Modest but balanced acid gives dry, caressing softness. Restrained but full fruit, with a hint of umami. — TJ

Location: Cape Town ▪ WO: Swartland/Slanghoek ▪ Est 2015 ▪ 1stB 2013 ▪ Consultant sommelier, training initiatives, events & functions, private dinners & tours ▪ Owner(s) Ewan Mackenzie ▪ Cellarmaster(s)/winemaker(s)/viticulturist(s) Various ▪ 45-140cs own label 33% red 33% white 33% rosé ▪ Other export brand: Lavine & Mackenzie Limited (UK) ▪ ewan@winethief.co.za ▪ **T +27 (0)71-116-8129**

The Wolftrap

Modestly priced over-deliverers of note, the increasingly successful trio of Wolftrap wines benefits from the tender loving care of the eminent Boekenhoutskloof team, who source from Stellenbosch, Swartland and Robertson for this exceptional-value sibling brand to Porcupine Ridge (see entries).

★★★★ **White** ⊘ Best value on the shelf. Totally captivating white flower & dewy stonefruit character, **17** ⑧⑦ lively & delicious to last spice-laden drop. Great care taken, near-equal viognier/chenin with grenache blanc, components handled separately & partly oaked.

Red ⊘ ⊛ ★★★★ Shiraz, mourvèdre, viognier combine with supple tannins (two-thirds oaked) for **17** ⑧⑤ smooth, harmonious mouthful berries, tapenade & vanilla. Also in magnum. **Rosé** ⊘ ⊛ ★★★ Juicy, succulent **18** ⑧⓪, delightful dry easy-drinker from cinsaut, syrah, grenache. WO W Cape, as all. — WB

☐ **The Zahir** see Lateganskop Winery
☐ **Thierry & Guy** see Fat Bastard

Thistle & Weed

'Our search for interesting, unique sites continues,' note the friends behind a stellar micro-venture valuing old vines for the same tenacity and survival skills as their undesired vineyard counterparts (identified by their Afrikaans names). Brandnetel from Stellenbosch joins Paarl's star-studded Duwweltjie, and there are more chenins, a verdelho and a red on the bright horizon.

★★★★☆ **Brandnetel** ⑭ Subtle & understated bunch-pressed, barrel-fermented **17** ⑨⓪ from Stellenbosch chenin, made in artisan style, shows seductive lees creaminess, focused minerality & delicate, integrated fruit. Generously proportioned, lingering & persistent.

★★★★★ **Duwweltjie** ⑧ Sourced from 1956 Paarl bushvine chenin, **17** ⑨⑤ follows stellar form of maiden **16** ⑨⑦. Big & brawny, with intensity & pinpoint focus, showing yeasty brioche with subtle baked apple fruit, ending with elegant chalky twist. All fermented & matured in older barrels.

Not tasted: **Nastergal**. — GdB

Location: Stellenbosch ▪ WO: Paarl/Stellenbosch ▪ Est 2015 ▪ 1stB 2016 ▪ Closed to public ▪ Wines available online ▪ Owner(s) Etienne Terblanche & Stephanie Wiid ▪ Winemaker(s) Stephanie Wiid (Sep 2015) ▪ Viticulturist(s) Etienne Terblanche (Sep 2015) ▪ Less than 10t/450cs own label 30% red 70% white ▪ PO Box 62 Koelenhof 7605 ▪ info@thistleandweed.co.za ▪ www.thistleandweed.co.za

Thokozani Wines

⊚ ⊚ ⊚ ⊚

David Sonnenberg of Diemersfontein Wines was the wind beneath the wings of Thokozani, but the Wellington wine venture is now flying high, 80% owned by staff and so successful, international pundits are studying its rise and rise. Canada and China are newer export markets, and locally there's an office on Diemersfontein where visitors can 'engage with our business of transformation'.

Thokozani range

★★★★ **SMV** Big improvement in **17** ⑧⑧ shiraz-led (74%) Rhône blend on **16** ★★★ ⑧⓪. Added body & substance, pepper & cinnamon spicing to opulently ripe fruit, appealing roasted meat & tobacco notes. Not tasted: **Rosé**, **CCV**.

Ovation range

Merlot (NEW) ★★★ Juicy & supple **17** (82) from Robertson & Wellington grapes offers fair intensity, berry complexity for uncomplicated, early enjoyment. **Cabernet Sauvignon-Merlot** (NEW) ★★★ Sip-soon **16** (80) light bodied & fruity, blackcurrant & mulberry flavours, tarry oak farewell. **Sauvignon Blanc** (NEW) ★★★ Generous green & tropical fruit aromas & flavours of **17** reined in by fresh acidity, satisfying dryness. **Spumante** ★★ Brightly packaged, off-dry perlé sauvignon blanc from Robertson grapes. **NV** (75) fresh, light-hearted quaffer with a slight spritz. — GdB

Location/map: Wellington ▪ Map grid reference: B4 ▪ WO: Western Cape/Wellington ▪ Est/1stB 2005 ▪ Tasting & sales daily 10-5 ▪ Closed Dec 25 ▪ Cellar tours by appt ▪ Seasons Restaurant ▪ Tour groups ▪ Conferences ▪ Walks/hikes ▪ 4-star Thokozani Cottages ▪ Owner(s) Diemersfontein employees & Diemersfontein Wines ▪ Winemaker(s) Francois Roode (Sep 2003), with Lauren Hulsman (Nov 2011) ▪ Viticulturist(s) Waldo Kellerman (Aug 2007) ▪ 180ha/45ha (cabs s/f, grenache, malbec, mourv, p verdot, ptage, roobernet, shiraz, chenin, viog) ▪ 15,000cs own label 60% red 40% white ▪ WIETA ▪ PO Box 41 Wellington 7654 ▪ denisestubbs@thokozani.co.za ▪ www.thokozani.co.za ▪ S 33° 39' 41.1" E 019° 0' 31.1" ▪ [map] gates.cakes.mere ▪ F +27 (0)21-864-2095 ▪ T +27 (0)21-864-5050

Thorne & Daughters Wines

John Thorne Seccombe makes these wines in the Gabriëlskloof cellar in the Overberg, as part of a small, harmonious 'winemaking clan' (with Peter-Allan Finlayson of Gabriëlskloof and Marelise Niemann of Momento) that is a fine example of the comradeship and mutual help that has characterised the avant garde of SA winemaking in the remarkable last few decades. John's wine is also in that avant-garde spirit: fresh (and generally light), pure and untrammeled by new oak, non-interventionist. Two new single-site and small-volume wines join the range in the very successful 2017 vintage: a chenin from the Paardeberg in Swartland and, much more rare, a clairette blanche from Stellenbosch. Focus is the watchword, says John, 'as we build explorative with our compelling sites'.

★★★★ **Wanderer's Heart** (🏠) From widely sourced grapes: 59% grenache, 33% cinsaut giving bright, pure-fruited, aromatic power & charm, mourvèdre adding darker breadth & depth. **17** ★★★★★ (93) not just delicious - serious, with fine, powder-tannin grip, freshness & ageability. More substantial than **16** (87).

★★★★★ **Cat's Cradle Chenin Blanc** (NEW) (🏠) (🍇) Ethereal fragrant elegance & charm on **17** (93), & a slightly austere, withdrawn delicacy. A fresh, pure-fruited wine, its delights to be treasured more than most more effusive offerings. Old oak adds subtle breadth; wholebunch ferment adds a phenolic grip.

★★★★★ **Man In The Moon Clairette Blanche** (NEW) One of few SA wines from the variety, **17** (90) is fresh, delicately light (under 12% alcohol) & bone-dry; subtle aroma & flavour (salt-preserved lemon, suggests the winemaker) & gently severe, grippy succulence. Old oak maturation, like all. WO Stellenbosch.

★★★★ **Tin Soldier Semillon** The less expressive of the 2 semillons, from the red-skinned version: 7-10 days on skins gives old-gold colour. **17** ★★★★★ (92) all about elegance, refinement, tension. Fine powdery tannin suggestion, deeply satisfying pervasive acidic thread. 12.7% alcohol - a touch riper than **16** (89).

★★★★★ **Paper Kite Old Vine Semillon** (🏠) (🍇) **17** (93) the first entirely ex Swartland. A little more generous & easy than Tin Soldier version - & notably delicious, with depth of fruit allied with finesse, fine acid balance & stability promising many years of development. 12.6% alcohol. Simple, natural winemaking, as all these.

★★★★★ **Rocking Horse Cape White Blend** (🏠) Tweaked each year: roussanne, chenin, semillon, chardonnay & clairette in magical **17** (96). No primary fruitiness, but great aromatic & flavour depth & incipient complexity. More vinous & rich than other whites (13.7% alcohol), with a brilliantly poised acidity. — TJ

Location: Bot River ▪ WO: Swartland/Western Cape/Stellenbosch ▪ Est 2012 ▪ 1stB 2013 ▪ Closed to public ▪ Owner(s) John & Tasha Seccombe ▪ Cellarmaster(s)/winemaker(s)/viticulturist(s) John Seccombe (Dec 2012) ▪ 35t/2,000cs own label 25% red 75% white ▪ PO Box 96 Elgin 7180 ▪ john@thorneanddaughters.com ▪ www.thorneanddaughters.com ▪ F +27 (0)86-246-2923 ▪ T +27 (0)76-036-7116

Thor Vintners

Thor, the boutique winery of widely travelled and seasoned winemaker Emile Gentis, produces under its own labels, including export ranges Voyageur and Wind Song, and is the local partner to the Ghanaian owners of the Long Mountain, Gecko Ridge and Athena labels, after their recent sale by Pernod Ricard.

Location: Durbanville ▪ Est 2016 ▪ 1stB 2010 ▪ Closed to public ▪ Cellarmaster(s) Emile Gentis ▪ PO Box 46140 Durbanville 7550 ▪ info@thortrading.co.za ▪ www.thorvintners.com

☐ **1000 Miles** see Mulderbosch Vineyards
☐ **Three Graces** see Women in Wine
☐ **Three Peaks** see Mount Vernon Estate
☐ **Three Pines** see Stark-Condé Wines
☐ **Three Rivers** see Bon Courage Estate

Thunderchild

In 2003 Robertson farmers got together to plant vines on land owned by the community's children's home. The fruit is vinified, again pro bono, by sympathetic wineries and sold from their cellardoors. Profits go to Die Herberg's 'thunderchildren', helping them overcome 'dark and threatening clouds'.

Thunderchild ⓧ ★★★☆ Delightful, modestly oaked blend of merlot, cab & cab franc, **15** ⑧⑤ balanced, firmly but gently structured, & both juicy & rather elegant behind its attractive label. — DS

Location/WO: Robertson ▪ Est 2003 ▪ 1stB 2008 ▪ Wines available from Ashton Winery, Bon Courage Estate, De Wetshof Estate, Robertson Winery, Rooiberg Winery & Tanagra Winery (see entries for opening times); Ashton Wine Boutique, Affie Plaas Farmstall, Platform 62 & La Verne Wine Boutique ▪ Owner(s) Thunderchild Wingerd Trust ▪ Cellarmaster(s) Various Robertson winegrowers ▪ 5ha (cabs s/f, merlot) ▪ PO Box 770 Robertson 6705 ▪ info@thunderchild.co.za ▪ www.thunderchild.co.za ▪ F +27 (0)23-626-3664 ▪ **T +27 (0)23-626-3661**

Tierhoek

ⓧ 🍴 🏠 📷

Tierhoek, in the remote, high-lying and wild beauty of Piekenierskloof, is one of the oldest surviving farms on the West Coast Sandveld (the distinguishing soil and vegetation of the area). It was established in 1886 but was run down, the buildings derelict, when Shelley and the late Tony Sandell bought it in 2001. There were some fine old vineyards – still supplying grenache and chenin for the top wines – and others were planted. Wines are made as naturally as possible: no pesticides or herbicides in the vineyards, spontaneous fermentation, the aim always being freshness.

Tierhoek range

★★★★☆ **Grenache** Bright, clean, pure fruit aromas & flavours on **17** ⑨⓪ unobscured by the older oak barrel maturation. Forceful structure of both acid & dry tannins. Persistent finish. Old bushvines.

★★★★☆ **Grenache Private Reserve** 🆕 🐝 Deeper in colour, more intense, densely fruited & complex in aromas & flavour than standard version; rather rounder in structure. **17** ⑨③ similar natural ferment & maturation in older barrels. Should continue to develop in bottle a good few years. Also in magnum.

★★★★ **Grenache-Syrah-Mourvèdre** Name tweaked in response to blend - 49% grenache in attractive, warm-hearted **17** ★★★★ ⑧⑤. Aromatic, spicy & fruity, with a little tannic grip, but no great concentration. **16** ⑧⑧ was more complex.

★★★★ **Chardonnay** Orange peel & blossom on **17** ⑧⑥, with both savoury & fruity characters, latter enhanced by partial maturation in tank - older oak for the rest. Some richness of texture cut by firm, fresh acidity. Natural ferment, like most, in older oak. Single-vineyard, as Reserve Chenin.

★★★★ **Chenin Blanc** Characterful earthy, biscuity, savoury notes with varietal dried peach on serious-minded **17** ⑧⑨. Full flavour, good texture, with a balanced, slightly green acidity.

★★★★☆ **Chenin Blanc Reserve** ⓧ Differently vinified to its sibling, natural ferment in seasoned barrels, 9 months on lees. Lime cordial & unblanched almonds, rather than **14** ⑨② 's stonefruit, **15** ⑨③ has more intensity, is as tightly knit. Years off its peak.

★★★★ **Sauvignon Blanc** ⊘ Pre-bottling, **18** ⑧⑨ offers forward ripe aromas enhanced by 4% oaked viognier (rest unoaked on lees 6 months). Green notes on flavourful, intense palate; lively acid.

★★★★☆ **Méthode Cap Classique** ⓦ Natural ferment, 5 months on lees in tank, before 4 years bottle-ageing. From chardonnay, **NV** ⑨ sparkling arresting fruit purity, vivid citrus perfume & flavours, mouthwatering limy acidity.

★★★★☆ **Straw Wine** Latest **NV** ⑨ from air-dried chenin, matured in solera (older oak barrels) with wines from 2007 onwards. Clean & piercing fruit despite oxidative element & savoury depth. Intense, with fine acidity controlling the great sweetness. Fascinating & delicious. 11.6% alcohol. 375 ml.

Not tasted: **Mourvèdre**, **Old Blocks Chenin Blanc**.

Sandveld range

★★★★☆ **Sauvignon Blanc** ⊘ ⓐ Broader & more complex, characterful aromas & flavours on fine **17** ⑨ than its sibling, also with a little oaked viognier. Splendidly penetrative, enlivening acidity balances the 5.9 g/l sugar which adds to richness without sweetening.

Piekeniers range

Not tasted: **White**. — TJ

Location: Citrusdal ▪ Map: Olifants River ▪ Map grid reference: C6 ▪ WO: Piekenierskloof ▪ Est 2001 ▪ 1stB 2003 ▪ Tasting, sales & cellar tours on the farm Mon-Sun 8.30-4.30 by appt ▪ Tasting fee applicable, waived on purchase ▪ Closed all pub hols ▪ BYO picnic ▪ Walks/hikes ▪ Conservation area ▪ Guest house (sleeps 9) ▪ Owner(s) Shelley Sandell ▪ Winemaker(s) Roger Burton (Aug 2006, consultant), with Basie Snyers (Oct 2006) ▪ Viticulturist(s) Ryno Kellerman (Aug 2006) ▪ 700ha/16ha (grenache, mourv, shiraz, chard, chenin, sauv) ▪ 70t/6,000cs own label 40% red 60% white ▪ IPW ▪ PO Box 53372 Kenilworth 7745 ▪ info@tierhoek. com ▪ www.tierhoek.com ▪ S 32° 23′ 27.49″ E 018° 51′ 24.14″ ▪ ⓦ leagues.byways.radiate ▪ F +27 (0)86-731-6351 ▪ **T +27 (0)21-674-3041/+27 (0)82-536-7132 (owner), +27 (0)22-125-0249/0179 (farm)**

☐ **Timestone Vineyards** *see* Trizanne Signature Wines
☐ **Tin Cups** *see* Wineways Marketing
☐ **Tin Hill** *see* Signal Gun Wines
☐ **Tin Mine** *see* Zevenwacht
☐ **Titanic** *see* Louis
☐ **Title Deed** *see* Croydon Vineyard Residential Estate

Tokara   ⓦ ⑪ ⓒ ⓐ ⓖ

Worth visiting for the views alone, the Tokara winery lies at the crest of Stellenbosch's Helshoogte Pass with 360-degree panoramic views, including a fan of vineyards and olive groves spreading out on undulating slopes below. Owned by GT and Anne-Marie Ferreira, whose artworks are dotted around the buildings and gardens, the wines were made by Miles Mossop for 18 years before he handed the reins over to Stuart Botha, ex Eagles' Nest, in 2018. Continuity is supplied by viticulturist Aidan Morton, who has done extensive mapping of the vineyards with drones and has the knowledge to perfectly match variety to terroir. In the cellar, the renewing of the wooden open-top fermenters is taking place before the next vintage.

Reserve Collection

★★★★☆ **Cabernet Sauvignon** ⓐ Power in the full ripeness, but it's in their DNA to combine it with sleekness, a streamlined body. Lots of cellar care, including wild ferment, 22 months oaking (63% new) but **15** ⑨ projects pure pleasure: glossy fruit, tailored tannins. Long future.

★★★★ **Syrah** ⓦ Unashamedly bold & big, **14** ⑧ abundant ripe red fruit, spice & oak (& 15% alcohol). Fruit driven, modern, yet very polished & not overdone.

★★★★☆ **Director's Reserve Red** ⓐ Cab with merlot, dashes petit verdot & cab franc, **14** ⑨ less opulent than **13** ⑨ & better for it. Abundant cassis, with freshness, succulence; has polish & poise. Complexity from oak (22 months, 57% new) & blend partners; already delicious, great prospects.

★★★★☆ **Chardonnay** ⓐ Best vineyard blocks, **17** ⑨ barrel ferment/11 months, oak a big role in styling. Oat biscuit, buttered toast, but fruit intense enough to handle it - citrus, lemon/grapefruit, the finish very long. Anchored by acidity, vibrates with life.

★★★★☆ **Sauvignon Blanc** ⓦ ⓐ White pepper, papaya & other tropical flavours on enticing **17**
★★★★★ ⑨, textured, intense, lively lemon/lime acidity, fresh & linear. Excellent unwooded cool-climate Elgin sauvignon, like **16** ⑨.

★★★★☆ **Director's Reserve White** ⊛ **16** ㉔ has same sauvignon & semillon blend as **15** ★★★★★ ㉗ - 71:29. There's restraint, finesse, breeding (only best blocks used); minerality, fennel & greengage, the oaking subtle but adds savoury tones, some tension. Complete, everything fits perfectly.

Limited Release Collection

★★★★ **Grenache** ⓥ Fresh red fruit, perfumed & juicy, **15** ㊼ from Walker Bay lovely broad tannins on an extremely fresh backbone supported by 10 months older oak. Improves on last **12** ★★★★ ㉘.

★★★★☆ **Pinotage** ⊛ Sumptuous fruit & savoury spicing, **16** ㉝'s deep, lush styling draws you in. Complex, flavour packed, much to admire. Fruit concentration allows ambitious oaking, 22 months, half new, but tannins supple, finishing dry. Good ageing backbone.

★★★★☆ **Méthode Cap Classique** ⓥ Sensational blanc de blancs sparkling from Elgin, showing pristine, crystalline purity. Abundant honeysuckle perfume, brioche & Granny Smith apple borne on extremely elegant mousse. **11** ㊾ enticingly fresh yet 15 months in oak & 48 months on lees add richness.

★★★★☆ **Noble Late Harvest** ⓥ Exceptional botrytised dessert, **16** ★★★★★ ㊾ like last **14** ㊼, from Elgin sauvignon. Dried apricot & caramelised lemon succulence supported by hardly noticeable oak (25% new); magically light on its feet with a tangy, enchantingly long finish. 375 ml.

Not tasted: **Cabernet Franc**.

Tokara range

★★★★ **Cabernet Sauvignon** ⓥ Always serious & sturdily built. Standout **15** ★★★★★ ㊼ with dash merlot, lively, juicy & bright, elegant yet with ample cassis & graphite core, to which 25% new French oak, 18 months, adds lovely spice & structure. Improves on **14** ㊳.

★★★★ **Chardonnay** Admirable impression of richness, lemon preserve, vanilla biscuit, curvaceous, yet **16** ㊉ is dry, has modest alcohol. It's quality of fruit & expert cellar work that expands what's there. WO W Cape, as next.

★★★★ **Sauvignon Blanc** ⊘ Tropical fruit salad but in a fresh way, **18** ㊈'s acid seam holds everything in place, giving vigour, vitality & incredible length. The ultimate food wine but good enough to enjoy solo.

Shiraz ⓥ ★★★★☆ Saline, tarry entry with prominent strawberry jam note & fine tannins; savoury, fresh, lingering bone-dry farewell. **16** ㊄ with small portion mourvèdre & well-judged oak (9% new, 10 months). **Rosé** ⓥ ★★★ Appealing rose & cranberry aromas on sunset-hued **16** ㊂ from grenache. Dry, balanced, light-tripping & very versatile.

Brandy range

★★★★ **Potstill Brandy** ⓥ Modern, warming & luxurious yet subtle, with floral notes enhancing the smooth, velvety palate. **09** ㊇ from chenin, 33% new limousin oak, rest 20 year old cask.— CR, WB

Location/map: Stellenbosch ▪ Map grid reference: G4 ▪ WO: Stellenbosch/Elgin/Western Cape/Walker Bay ▪ 1stB 2001 ▪ Tasting & sales Mon-Sun 10–6 ▪ Closed Dec 25 & Jan 1 ▪ Tokara Restaurant Tue-Sun lunch 12.30-2.30 & dinner 7-9.30 ▪ Delicatessen Tue-Sun 10-4 ▪ Facilities for children ▪ Gift shop ▪ Art exhibitions ▪ Owner(s) GT & Anne-Marie Ferreira ▪ Winemaker(s) Stuart Botha (Sep 2017), with Timothy Whitfield (May 2018) ▪ Viticulturist(s) Aidan Morton (Nov 2000) ▪ 104ha (cabs s/f, grenache, malbec, merlot, mourv, p verdot, ptage, shiraz, chard, chenin, sauv, sem) ▪ 70st/100,000cs own label 40% red 59% white 1% rosé ▪ PO Box 662 Stellenbosch 7599 ▪ wine@tokara.com ▪ www.tokara.com ▪ S 33° 55′ 2.9″ E 018° 55′ 13.7″ ▪ ⬛ feeds.avid.curiosity ▪ F +27 (0)21-808-5911 ▪ **T +27 (0)21-808-5900**

☐ **Tooverberg** see Klein Parys Vineyards
☐ **Tooverberg Contour** see Klein Parys Vineyards

Topiary Wines

This hillside Franschhoek farm was bought in late 2014 by Burgundian vigneron Philippe Colin and sommelier and consultant Serge Jaczynski. Unsurprisingly, given Philippe's Chassagne-Montrachet background, there's a focus on chardonnay: apart from the ever-improving, elegant still version, the MCC reappears with further-extended lees contact. The flagship chardonnay vineyard now boasts 'an innovative trellising system'. Hikers and travellers wanting 'a little luxury on a working wine farm' are catered for too.

★★★★ **Chardonnay** (🍷) Improves year on year. 17 ★★★★★ (93) offers beguiling aromas - nut, oatmeal, a little citrus. Full & generous, sweetly ripe flavours (13.8% alcohol) yet graceful & fresh, silky & balanced. Like subtle 16 (87), has well integrated oak, 33% new.

★★★★☆ **Blanc de Blancs Brut** Méthode cap classique sparkling from chardonnay, 12 (91) has a developing bouquet of biscuit & brioche; red apple freshness also comes on the rich, well balanced palate, & a hint of lime on the lingering finish. 4 years on lees. 14.5 g/l sugar a touch sweeter than official Brut.

Cabernet Sauvignon ★★★ Clean, fresh & beautifully dry 16 (85) is less richly substantial than standout 15 ★★★★ (87), but the structure & restrained oaking are in balance, wine already drinks well. **Syrah** ★★★★ Was 'Shiraz'. Dark cherries & spice on attractive, understated yet notably ripe & sweet-fruited 16 (85). A little new oak, but nothing obvious. Spontaneous fermentation, as for Cab. **Rosé** ★★★ Salmon-hued 17 (81) from shiraz has muted berry fruit, stressing the savoury side. Rounded & soft, but bone-dry. — TJ

Location/map/WO: Franschhoek ▪ Map grid reference: C4 ▪ Est 2005 ▪ 1stB 2006 ▪ Tasting & sales Tue-Sat 9-5 Sun/Mon by appt only ▪ Fee R30, waived on purchase ▪ Closed Easter Sun, Dec 24/25 & Jan 1 ▪ Meals/refreshments & cellar tours on special request ▪ BYO picnic ▪ Small tour groups ▪ 1.7km fynbos hiking trail ▪ Conservation area ▪ Honeymoon suite plus 2 self-catering cottages ▪ Owner(s) Philippe Colin & Serge Jaczynski ▪ Cellarmaster(s)/winemaker(s) Philippe Colin (Aug 2014) ▪ Viticulturist(s) Dirk Wouter van der Merwe (Jan 2013) ▪ 63ha/20ha (cab, shiraz, chard) ▪ 44t/1,500cs own label 90% red 10% white ▪ PO Box 108 La Motte 7691 ▪ topiarysales@telkomsa.net ▪ www.topiaryvineyards.simplesite.com ▪ S 33° 51' 52.2" E 019° 2' 39.0" ▪ 🌐 spirals.pancake.therapy ▪ F +27 (0)86-750-1742 ▪ **T +27 (0)21-867-0258**

☐ **Topography** see David & Nadia

☐ **Top Secret** see Ultra Liquors

☐ **Totus** see Trajan Wines

☐ **Touch of Oak** see Rijk's

Township Winery (🍷)

This innovative community project encourages householders in the economically challenged areas of Philippi, Nyanga and Crossroads to plant backyard vines and supply grapes to a small Philippi Village cellar, where the resulting wines can also be tasted and bought. Original impetus came from low-income housing developer Kate Jambela, supported by Wellington entrepreneur and vintner Graham Knox, who made the current releases from wider-sourced fruit.

★★★★ **Philippi Merlot-Cabernet Sauvignon** Elegant & poised 14 (86), plum- & currant-infused mouthful laced with wood spice & crushed herbs. Helderberg merlot & Durbanville cab, ready now but with some years to go. Last 12 (87) was 'Cab-Merlot'.

Philippi Sauvignon Blanc ★★★★ Vivacious 15 (83) from West Coast vines within 10 km of Atlantic, hence cool lemongrass & lime tone; juicy, involving, lingering greengage & fig finish. WO W Cape. Not tasted: **The Flats Pinotage, The Flats Viognier.** — GM

Location: Philippi ▪ Map: Cape Peninsula ▪ Map grid reference: D3 ▪ WO: Coastal/Western Cape ▪ Est 2009 ▪ 1stB 2010 ▪ Tasting Mon-Fri 10-4 ▪ Owner(s) The Township Winery cc ▪ Cellarmaster(s) Graham Knox ▪ 800cs own label 50% red 50% white ▪ PO Box 1209 Wellington 7654 ▪ graham@townshipwinery.com ▪ S 34° 0' 1.02" E 018° 35' 37.71" ▪ 🌐 munched.cabin.elevate ▪ F +27 (0)21-447-4476 ▪ **T +27 (0)83-625-2865**

Trajan Wines

Established by winelovers wanting an own brand and a means of community service, Stellenbosch-based Trajan for many years worked on Fairtrade projects. Now, says viniculturist Mark van Schalkwyk, they are moving to introduce their own social responsibility projects 'where more people can benefit instead of focusing only on one specific group'.

Totus range

Cabernet Sauvignon ★★★ Ripe berries & vanilla oak aromas, flavours on 17 (82). Less sweet than Cab-Merlot, same 30% new oak; rounded, with balanced grip. **Limited Release Pinotage** (NEW) ★★★☆ Appealing mocha notes from plenty of toasted oak (60% new) dominate the dark berry fruit aromas on 17 (83) - but fruitier on the well-structured, just-dry palate. **Cabernet Sauvignon-Merlot** ★★★ Oaky, just-dry **17** ⑧ has dark, ripe fruit; juicy & easygoing, with some firming tannin. Not tasted: **Pinotage**, **Shiraz**, **Shiraz-Mourvèdre**, **Sauvignon Blanc**. Occasional release: **Chenin Blanc**. — TJ

Location/WO: Stellenbosch ▪ Est 2005 ▪ 1stB 2008 ▪ Closed to public ▪ Owner(s) Trajan Wines (Pty) Ltd ▪ Winemaker(s) Mark van Schalkwyk (Sep 2005) ▪ Viticulturist(s) Mark van Schalkwyk ▪ 10,000cs own label 70% red 30% white ▪ PO Box 1498 Stellenbosch 7599 ▪ info@trajanwines.co.za ▪ www.trajanwines.co.za ▪ F +27 (0)86-299-4281 ▪ **T +27 (0)83-505-2681**

☐ **Trans-Karoo** see Boer & Brit
☐ **Travino** see Klawer Wine Cellars
☐ **Tree of Knowledge** see Wijnskool
☐ **Tribal Skin** see Jacques Germanier
☐ **Tribal Sparkling** see Jacques Germanier
☐ **Tribal Spear** see Jacques Germanier

Trizanne Signature Wines

Now into the second decade of crafting elegant wines for her Trizanne Signature Wines label from Elim, Darling and Swartland grapes, Cape Town-based Trizanne Barnard also produces several bottled-wine labels for overseas markets as well as sizeable bulk-wine exports. And, with large distances to cover between grape sources, you'd expect there not to be much time for her other passion, surfing. But her new-design barcode labels depict a waverider either in the act, or looking to push out into the ocean, so there's no doubt she still manages to spread the love between vine and sea.

Reserve range

★★★★☆ **Darling Barbera** On upward trajectory as Darling bushvine vineyard matures. Italian variety's acidity prominent but pleasant on **17** ⑨②, its tannin equally well-modulated for early approachability. Sour cherry fruit & tealeaf note neatly presented in old-oaked package.

★★★★★ **Syrah** ⓐ Precise **17** ★★★★★ ⑨③, pure black & red fruits, fine peppery aromatics & Elim's cool-climate finesse all given a place in the spotlight by minimal-intervention, old-oak maturation. Like **16** ⑨⑤, truly lovely now but will reward cellaring.

★★★★ **Elim Semillon** ⓝⓔⓦ Mature (20 year old) vines adroitly handled to create smooth, almost slippery **17** ⑧⑨, showing textual richness alongside toasty nutty nuance which should develop interestingly given time. Old-oak ferment, 16 months on lees with stirring.

★★★★☆ **Semillon-Sauvignon Blanc** ⓐ Semillon (52%) just leads in impressive & very persistent **17** ⑨④, invigorating lemon nuance & acidity neatly complementing sauvignon's grass & fig tones, accenting smoky whiffs from old-barrel ferment.

Signature range

★★★★ **Swartland Syrah** ⊘ ⓐ Bone-dry, savoury glassful. **16** ⑧⑧ attractive scrub & pepper notes, similar berry character & deft touch of older oak as previous, splash grenache for complexity.

★★★★ **Elim Sauvignon Blanc** Vivacious **18** ⑧⑦ both cool-climate & excitingly different in its flavour profile, exotic cassis & pear added to green fig. Nicely dry, too, brief lees-ageing giving light grip. — CvZ

Location: Cape Town ▪ WO: Elim/Darling/Swartland ▪ Est 2008 ▪ 1stB 2009 ▪ Closed to public ▪ Wine sales via website ▪ Owner(s)/winemaker(s) Trizanne Barnard ▪ 25,000cs own label 45% red 65% white + 2.5m L bulk wine export ▪ Export-only brands: Clearsprings, Dawn Patrol, Indwe, Swallows'Tale, The Search, Timestone Vineyards ▪ 14 Van der Horst Ave Kommetjie 7975 ▪ info@trizanne.co.za ▪ www.trizanne.co.za ▪ F +27 (0)86-669-0913 ▪ **T +27 (0)21-783-0617/+27 (0)82-383-6664**

Truter Family Wines

Now into the second decade of their own-label boutique venture, Wellington husband-and-wife winemaking team Hugo and Celeste Truter maintain that consensus is key: if they don't agree stylistically, the wine isn't bottled. 'It maintains harmony at home too.' The focus remains on blends, but exciting things are expected from Piekenierskloof grenache blanc and Wellington chenin in the future.

Agaat range

John David ★★★★ Gentle ease to **16** (84) blend of equal pinotage & cab, dabs shiraz & petit verdot. Plum & raspberry, with twist of oak tannin, just 10% new. Widely sourced fruit, as next. **Christina** ★★★★ Sauvignon blanc leads on 4-way, unwooded **17** (83), nouvelle & chenin share equal billing (14%) & dab viognier. Pithy gooseberry zip & tang, flinty tail. Drinks well.

Cape Fern range (NEW)

Shiraz ⊘ ★★★★ Attractive coffee bean & smoky black fruit on **16** (84), supple palate from 6 months in mainly older oak, 10% new. Wellington grapes, as all following. **Sauvignon Blanc** ★★★ Light elderflower & lemon zest typicity on **17** (82), succulent & fresh, concludes on a gravel note.

Taste range (NEW)

Shiraz-Cabernet Sauvignon ⊘ ★★★ Varieties share top billing equally in **16** (82). Light bodied, juicy & fresh, ample dark-berried drinking pleasure. Oak staves, 10% new, add light frame. **Chenin Blanc** ★★★ Guava, melon & fruit salad on **18** (79), easy & quaffable. **Sauvignon Blanc** ★★★ Tropical-styled **18** (77), lemon zest piquancy & dry crispness, perfect for summer sipping. — FM

Location: Wellington ▪ WO: Western Cape ▪ Est 2008 ▪ 1stB 2010 ▪ Closed to public ▪ Owner(s) Hugo & Celeste Truter ▪ Winemaker(s) Hugo Truter ▪ 3,000cs own label 50% red 50% white ▪ hugo@truterfamilywines.co.za ▪ www.truterfamilywines.co.za ▪ **T +27 (0)83-639-6288**

TTT Cellar Calitzdorp   ⓥ ⑤

No wines were made last vintage at TTT (Things Take Time) winery in Calitzdorp town, but owner Pat Mason says stocks of the Vintage Port '08, '09 and '13 are still available for tasting and sale, and visitors are welcome to tour the cellar.

Location: Calitzdorp ▪ Map: Klein Karoo & Garden Route ▪ Map grid reference: B5 ▪ 1stB 2003 ▪ Tasting, sales & tours Mon-Fri 8-4 Sat 8-2 Sun by appt ▪ Closed Easter Fri-Mon, Apr 27, May 1, Dec 25 & Jan 1 ▪ Owner(s) Pat Mason ▪ 0.5ha (souzão, tinta, touriga, hanepoot) ▪ 4t/600cs own label 100% red ▪ PO Box 7067 Newton Park 6055 ▪ patmason11@gmail.com ▪ S 33° 31' 50.94" E 021° 41' 44.88" ▪ 𝑓 storyboard.tiled.chirpy ▪ F +27 (0)44-213-3114 ▪ **T +27 (0)44-213-3114**

Tulbagh Winery   ⓥ ⓒ ⑤

Tulbagh Winery's satellite cellar in Porterville has been shut and its winemaker, Marius Prins, redeployed to the original production facility near Tulbagh town. Carl Allen, veteran of 16 vintages, continues as chief vine nurturer, as does the grower-owned venture's focus on bulk wine, with smaller parcels bottled for select clients and the own labels listed below. 'Best quality at the best possible prices' remains the goal throughout.

Klein Tulbagh range

Cabernet Sauvignon ⑲ ★★★★ Lots going on in **14** (84), cassis, hint of mint, interwoven with oak-driven espresso. You'd expect sterner tannins but the texture is supple, flavours fruity-fresh. From official single-vineyard & Tulbagh WO, as all. **Merlot** ⑲ ★★★★ Cassis, dark chocolate, a spice array, seductively perfumed **14** (84) doesn't disappoint on the palate either. Vanilla & dark berries, curvaceous, & tannin backbone for a future. **Pinotage** ⑲ ★★★★ Expressive **15** (83) shows intense mulberries & sweet spice, more savoury on the palate. Oaking well handled, giving smooth tasty appeal plus ageability. **Shiraz** ⑲ ★★★★ **14** (84) received 18 months oaking, half new, as all these reds, intensifying the meaty dark fruit, spicy flavours. In perfect drinking condition but can still age.

Not tasted: **Port**.

Tulbagh range

Cabernet Sauvignon ★★★ Mocha, meaty overlay to **17** (78)'s berry fruit, tannins sturdy enough for food matching, ageing. **Merlot** ★★★ Red berries & chocolate savouriness, **17** (78) has appealing succulent freshness, smooth & round. **Pinotage** ★★★ Blueberries & gentle toastiness, some liquorice, **17** (81) has good typicity, smooth mouth appeal, is very easy to like. **Syrah** ★★★ Black plums & sweet spice from French/American oak treatment, **17** (81) has a supple texture, appealing juicy accessibility. **Shiraz-Pinotage** ★★★ Some barrel ageing in **NV** (78) but essentially designed for earlier drinking: dark fruit, savoury seamed, juicy accessibility. **Pinotage Rosé** ★★ Gentle red berries in **16** (74), light (13% alcohol), dry, goes down easily.

Chardonnay ★★★ Tangerine perfume/flavours in **17** (78), a biscuit seam from light oaking, finishes bone-dry. **Chenin Blanc** ⊘ ★★★ **18** (80) has guava & fresh apple flavours, crisply dry, sleek, ends on a mineral note. **Sauvignon Blanc** ★★ With lemon drops, **17** (76) has tasty, tangy flavours. Light (11.5% alcohol) & dry enough for summertime quaffing. **Blanc de Blancs Méthode Cap Classique** (NEW) ⊘ ★★★ **NV** (81) from chardonnay, 48 months on lees, giving brioche/barley sugar tones, ends crisply dry & long. For those who like more mature-style bubblies.

Paddagang range

Paddapoot Hanepoot ⊙ ★★★ Buy it for the frog-themed label alone, but **NV** (82) fortified is worth it in its own right. Intensely grapey, with melon, ginger & barley sugar notes, sweet but moreish. WO W Cape.

CCM ★★★ Cab-led with cab franc, merlot, **14** (81) is ready to drink: plush cassis with a mint chocolate nuance & softly textured body. Not tasted: **Sopkoppie Rooi Muskadel**.

Flippenice range

Cabernet Sauvignon-Merlot ★★★ Light oaking adds liquorice notes to **NV** (77)'s berries, the texture ultra smooth, nicely rounded. WO W Cape. **Xtra Lite** ★★★ Living up to its name, **NV** (78) is crisply dry, just 9% alcohol, mostly from unusual fernão pires, giving greengage flavours. **Chenin Blanc-Sauvignon Blanc** ★★ Freshly sliced apple, light texture (11.5% alcohol) & touch sugar, **NV** (74) is tasty summertime fare. **Sauvignon Blanc Brut** ★★★ Moved from Tulbagh range. Lemon drop freshness throughout, dry **17** (78) bubbly would be a good aperitif. **XLite Natural Sweet Rosé** ★★ From pinotage, **NV** (75) has a mere 9% alcohol, the 35 g/l sugar showing as fruity rather than sweet. Not tasted: **Pinotage Doux**. — CR

Location/map: Tulbagh ▪ Map grid reference: F5 ▪ WO: Coastal/Tulbagh/Western Cape ▪ Est 1906 ▪ 1stB 1910 ▪ Tasting & sales Mon-Fri 9–5 Sat & pub hols 9–1; closed Easter Fri-Sun, Dec 25/26 & Jan 1 ▪ Cellar tours by appt ▪ Gifts ▪ Farm produce ▪ MTB in the area ▪ Owner(s) 86 members ▪ Cellarmaster(s) / production manager(s) Naude Bruwer (Jan 2010) ▪ Winemaker(s) Marius Prins (Oct 2016) ▪ Viticulturist(s) Carl Allen (Aug 2003) ▪ 740ha (cab, merlot, ptage, shiraz, chenin, chard, sauv) ▪ 9,600t own label 65% red 30% white 5% rosé & 8m L bulk + 40,000cs for clients ▪ PO Box 85 Tulbagh 6820 ▪ info@tulbaghwine.co.za ▪ www.tulbaghwine.co.za ▪ S 33° 15′ 8.8″ E 019° 8′ 36.5″ ▪ ⌨ soldiers.incursions.waistband ▪ **T +27 (0)23-230-1001**

☐ **Tunnel** see Du Toitskloof Winery
☐ **Twee Jonge Gezellen** see Krone

Twelve Apostles Winery   ⓛ

Respectively civil engineer and full-time winemaker, Cape Town father-and-son Chris and Charles Lourens after hours are 'true garagistes', with old-school practices like minimum intervention from vine to bottle. Their small-batch wines were between bottlings and thus not available for review.

Location: Cape Town ▪ Est/1stB 2009 ▪ Tasting by appt only ▪ Owner(s)/winemaker(s) Chris & Charles Lourens ▪ 3-st/±650cs own label 50% red 50% white ▪ Brands for clients: Kanah Winery ▪ SAWIS ▪ PO Box 16007 Panorama 7506 ▪ info@twelveapostleswinery.co.za ▪ www.twelveapostleswinery.co.za ▪ F +27 (0)86-510-2431 ▪ **T +27 (0)82-375-2884**

☐ **24 Rivers** see Valley Vineyards Wine Company
☐ **21 Gables** see Spier
☐ **Twins** see Lateganskop Winery
☐ **TwoCenturies** see Nederburg Wines
☐ **Two Cubs** see Knorhoek Wines

Two Oceans

Distell's global brand Two Oceans, introduced in the early 1990s and now in some 80 countries, is styled for easy/early enjoyment and has a feel-good factor via its sustainability minded lightweight bottles. Keeping on-trend, the top-selling Cab-Merlot and Sauvignon Blanc are also offered in 3L bag-in-box.

Shiraz ⊘ ★★★ Middleweight **17** (79) has ripe plum & dark berry fruit, braai-compatible whiffs of smoke & pepper. WO W Cape, as all. **Cabernet Sauvignon-Merlot** ⊘ ★★★ Soft & approachable **18** (78), light dusting of cocoa on juicy plum & berry fruit. **Shiraz Rosé** ⊘ ★★★ Bright cherry-pink **18** (77) is semi-dry, like strawberry cordial for grown-ups (at 12.5% alcohol) with a clean, fresh finish. **Pinot Grigio** ⊘ ★★★ With a squeeze of zesty lime on greengage & honeydew melon, **18** ⑧⓪ is fresh & nicely balanced. **Sauvignon Blanc** ⊘ ★★★ Ripe tropical aroma leads to gooseberry, passionfruit & pineapple tang on the palate in dry, fresh **18** ⑦⑨. Not tasted: **Pinot Noir**, **Pinotage**, **Soft & Fruity Red**, **Shiraz-Cabernet Sauvignon**, **Chardonnay**, **Semillon-Chardonnay**, **Fresh & Fruity White**. — JG

☐ **221** *see* Alvi's Drift Private Cellar
☐ **Uitkyk Estate** *see* Warwick Estate
☐ **Ukuzala** *see* Mountain River Wines

Ultra Liquors

'A very dry year for grapes, a hugely fruitful vintage for Ultra,' quips Mark Norrish, MD for this nationwide drinks chain's wine division, who collaborates with various winemakers to source and blend wines for the house brands (anonymity guaranteed, as per the Top Secret and Secret Cellar range names). Listing 2018's array of awards to illustrate Ultra's commitment to quality, Mark highlights three of the top five spots for value-for-money red wines at a leading national wine show as endorsement of the 'small on pocket, big on palate' philosophy.

Top Secret range

★★★★ **Méthode Cap Classique Brut** Classically styled **NV** ⑧⑧ sparkler from Robertson chardonnay & pinot noir, both varieties contributing: freshness & citrus tones given aromatic addition, palate weight from the red berries.

Pinot Noir ⓥ ★★★☆ Smoky edge to typical forest fruit notes of light, pleasingly savoury **13** ⑧④ from Elgin, with earthy depth too. **Pinotage** ⓥ ★★★☆ Offers coconut-tinged red & blue berry fruit verve; **16** ⑧④ pliable & well framed, with good succulence and length. **Shiraz-Cabernet Sauvignon 1020** ⊘ ★★★☆ Rounded soft berry & plum abundance with supportive oak on **16** ⑧⑤. Cinnamon, liquorice & earthy nuances add interest. **Wooded Chenin Blanc** ⓥ ★★★ Hints of melon & tropical fruit, framed by noticeable creamy, well-integrated oak. **16** ⑧⓪ juicy & lively to end. Coastal WO. **Méthode Cap Classique Blanc de Blancs** ⓥ ★★★ Tangy citrus verve to **NV** ⑧② all-chardonnay bubbles. Broad & richly creamy but focused & taut succulence limits flab.

Secret Cellar range

★★★★ **Cabernet Sauvignon 259** ⓥ Structured elegance to **14** ⑧⑦, with fruitcake, cocoa & fynbos sheen. Confident step up on **13** ★★★★ ⑧④. Concentrated, broad, rich, layered & long. Coastal WO.

★★★★ **Pinotage 211** ⊘ With splashes shiraz & viognier, **16** ★★★★ ⑧⑤ offers vibrant plum characters, & feisty 14.6% alcohol. Not as deep & dense as last-tasted, cocoa-nuanced **14** ⑧⑦. Darling WO.

....

High Five 723 ⓝⒺⓌ ⊘ ⓣ ★★★★ Multi-vintage **NV** ⑧⑤ red blend from mostly cab & shiraz (45/35). Smoothly fruity, gentle tannins without hard edges are ready for enjoyment.

....

Merlot 747 ⓥ ★★★ Sappy, juicy, fruity **15** ⑧⓪ an easy crowd pleaser. Light, with fynbos nuance. **Shiraz 884** ⓝⒺⓌ ⊘ ★★★☆ Mature, leafy **13** ⑧④ from Stellenbosch vines is ready to drink, fireside or at table. **Merlot-Cabernet Sauvignon 143** ⓥ ★★★ Merlot leads boldly fruited, very ripe palate with light tannin grip on **13** ⑧①. **Merlot-Malbec-Cabernet Sauvignon 702** ⊘ ★★★ Meaty herb nuance to **16** ⑧②'s succulent blueberry & plum, uncomplicated & easy drinking. WO Stellenbosch. **Shiraz-Mourvèdre 822** ⓥ ★★★ Uncomplicated & light **15** ⑧⓪, raspberry & plum with vivid cinnamon highlights. **Syrah-Mourvèdre-Grenache 303** ⊘ ★★★ Easy plum & graphite styling on **NV** ⑧② blend from Stellenbosch. Gentle cocoa & spice nuances but short final flourish. **Red Blend 907** ⓝⒺⓌ ⊘ ★★★☆ Cab (42%) leads **13** ⑧③ petit verdot, shiraz, cab franc & merlot melange. Tealeaf & cedar aromas over fading red berry fruit, not for further keeping. **Chardonnay-Pinot Noir 955** ⊘ ★★★ Broad peach & lees breadth to copper-toned **17** ⑧② rosé off Robertson vines, light & unfussy. **Rosé 658** ⓥ ★★★ Cherry & melon tang on crisp, dry **17** ⑦⑨ from colombard & petit verdot. Bright, fresh acidity. Robertson WO. **Wooded Chardonnay 686** ⓥ ★★★ Grapefruit zest & marmalade framed by subtle creamy oak, **16** ⑧⓪ fresh, juicy & eminently drinkable. Breedekloof WO. **Chenin Blanc 235** ★★★★ Pineapple & nectarine on **17** ⑧④, lively & medium bodied, with concentrated length of flavour. Coastal WO. **Sauvignon Blanc 527** ★★★★ From Darling, **17** ⑧③ boasts capsicum pungency & dustiness, zesty succulence diminishing with bottle age.

Drink soon. **Sauvignon Blanc 600** ★★★ Gooseberries & green figs, nice typicity in **18** ⑧①, fresh & lively. **Chardonnay-Chenin Blanc-Grenache Blanc 808** ② ★★★ Appealing simplicity of peach & citrus tones on **NV** ⑦⑦ poolside quaffer. **Méthode Cap Classique Blanc de Blancs 428** ⊘ ★★★★ Old gold **NV** ⑧③ all-chardonnay sparkler shows broadening butterscotch features, for enjoyment now. **Méthode Cap Classique Brut 558** ② ★★★★ Yeast, toast & hint of oystershell on 50/50 chardonnay/pinot noir **NV** ⑧④ bubbly. Rounded from 2 years on lees.

What A Mouthful range

Red ② ★★ Easy, soft plum simplicity to **NV** ⑦④ sipper from mainly shiraz. **White** ② ★★ Cheerful tropicality to **NV** ⑦④ zesty summer quaffer from chenin. — DS

Location: Cape Town ▪ WO: Western Cape/Robertson/Coastal/Darling/Stellenbosch/Breedekloof/Elgin ▪ Owner(s) Colin Robinson ▪ Winemaker(s) various ▪ 426 Main Rd Wynberg Cape Town 7800 ▪ marknorrish@ ultraliquors.co.za, dale@ultraliquors.co.za ▪ F +27 (0)21-797-4351 ▪ **T +27 (0)21-797-4340**

☐ **Ulumbaza** *see* Springfontein Wine Estate

Under Oaks ⑨ ⑪ ⑯

After renovation in 2014 of the Britz family's 17th-century Paarl Mountain farm's old cellar came blocks of 'interesting' new varieties to the vineyard mix, the fruits of which feature in the new wines by consultant winemaker Bertus Fourie, famed for his 'coffee' pinotages, among others. Also passionate about food, Bertus is the creator of Under Oaks' wine-and-food pairings, and the pizzeria and four-star guest house menus.

Premium range (NEW)

★★★★☆ **Just B** Textured mouthful of olives, herbs & black fruit on **15** ⑨⓪ well-judged Bordeaux blend, mostly petit verdot with cab & merlot. Savoury, structured, with depth & concentration. Fine dry tannin, firm body & long finish.

★★★★ **Three Twenty** Lovely freshness, with cling peach & spice on one-off **15** ⑧⑧ grenache blanc, viognier & roussanne to mark 320 years of farming the land. Balanced, delicate, with creamy oak support.

French Flair ★★★★ Initial grip on **15** ⑧③ mix of equal grenache noir, mourvèdre, carignan with dab shiraz tempered by juicy freshness. Spicy & tangy.

Britz Brothers range (NEW)

The Secret ★★★★ 'Mystery' red **15** ⑧③ is soft, medium bodied but sweet fruited & spicy. Interplay of oregano & black fruit, overt oak on the finish.

Under Oaks range

Cabernet Sauvignon Reserve ★★★ Abundant commercial appeal to unfussy **15** ⑧①, boasting black fruit & spice. **Merlot** ★★★ Soft, gentle black-berried palate with ample succulence, **15** ⑧⓪ touch dry on the finish. **Pinotage Reserve** (NEW) ★★★ Coffee bean edge to light-bodied & uncomplicated **15** ⑧⓪, juicy & approachable. **Shiraz Reserve** ★★★★ Ripe **15** ⑧③ delivers heaps of spicy plum appeal & twist of dry tannin from 18 months in French oak. **Lightly Wooded Chardonnay** ★★★ Succulent & fresh mouthful of grapefruit with bright, zippy acidity on **17** ⑧② Easy, ideal for summer. Not tasted: **Chenin Blanc**, **Sauvignon Blanc**. Occasional release: **Cabernet Sauvignon-Syrah**. — WB, FM

Location/map: Paarl ▪ Map grid reference: E3 ▪ WO: Coastal ▪ 1stB 2003 ▪ Tasting & sales Tue-Sun 11-4 ▪ Fee R50pp standard tasting, various seasonal pairings ▪ Cellar tours/private tastings by appt only ▪ Pizzeria Sep-Mar: Tue-Sat 11.30-10 Sun 12-3.30; Apr-Aug: Wed-Sat 11.30-9.30 Sun 12-3.30 ▪ 4-star country house ▪ Winemaker(s) Bertus Fourie (2002, consultant) ▪ wine@underoaks.co.za ▪ www.underoaks.co.za ▪ S 33° 40' 30.0" E 018° 56' 32.2" ▪ 🗺 erosional.gongs.ropes ▪ F +27 (0)86-649-9307 ▪ **T +27 (0)21-869-8045**

United Nations of Wine

United Nations of Wine is the umbrella brand for Fairtrade, WIETA and CarbonNeutral labels Frisky Zebras, Luscious Hippos and newer Sonance, intended as 'fun, friendly and affordable' by their Canadian-born, locally resident creator David John Bate. His other line, Leopard Frog, is listed separately.

Location: Sandton ▪ Est/1stB 2005 ▪ Closed to public ▪ Owner(s) Dogwood Trust ▪ Cellarmaster(s)/wine-maker(s) David John Bate (Jun 2005) ▪ 60,000cs own label 50% red 50% white ▪ Fairtrade, CarbonNeutral,

WIETA ▪ 8 Royal Ascot Lane Sandown Sandton 2196 ▪ info@unitednationsofwine.com ▪ www.unitednation-
sofwine.com ▪ F +27 (0)11-883-0426 ▪ **T +27 (0)11-884-3304**

☐ **Unorthodox** *see* Zandwijk
☐ **Upington** *see* Orange River Cellars

Upland Organic Estate   ⓠ ⓞ

Veterinarian, winegrower and distiller Edmund Oettlé was ahead of his time in farming sustainably, gaining organic certification back in 1994, using recycled equipment and vinifying/distilling traditionally. The wines and spirits featured this edition typify his natural, unhurried approach, and the styling of the Ruby 'port'-aged a category-busting seven years! - reveals an iconoclastic element which is also de rigueur.

Estate range

★★★★ Intuition Pinot Noir ⓝⓔⓦ ⊘ ⊗ Farmyard styling leans toward rustic, but gentle, pliable frame for red berry fruit is elegant. **17** ⑧⑨ year in seasoned cask; just six months for also-tasted **15** ★★★★ ⑧⑤), no sulphur added, so shows development, not for keeping. Just 240 bottles each. No **16**.

★★★★☆ Earth Song Méthode Ancienne ⓝⓔⓦ ⊗ Méthode ancestrale (single-ferment) sparkling from chenin, splash pinot noir. **17** ⑨⓪ rain-on-parched-earth character leads to a most satisfying dry finish. No added sulphites. Also-tasted **18** too unformed to rate fairly.

★★★★ Tandem Cape Ruby ⊗ From cabernet, individual, less obviously fruity than many Ruby 'ports'. 3 years in oak & 4 in bottle give **NV** ⑧⑧ beautiful integration of clean spirit (18% alcohol), firm dry-tasting finish. Leap up on sterner previous.

Cabernet Sauvignon ⓠ ⊗ **★★★★** Restasted mid-2015, **09** ⑧④ had benefited from another year in bottle, showed suppler structure, mature dark-berry fruit. Succulent **08** ★★★ also still available.

Brandy range

★★★★☆ Drakenwijn ⓝⓔⓦ ⊗ Handsome packaging for 15 year old brandy from chenin & crouchen. Rich amber hue introduces fine floral & prune compote notes; on palate great intensity of fruit, warm spice & roasted nuts, creamy dark chocolate hints on long finish.

★★★★ Pure Potstill Brandy ⊗ 10 year old from chenin & crouchen. Jewel-bright amber glints, nuances of dried peach, prune & sandalwood; smooth, rich & full bodied, ginger spice aftertaste. 500 ml.

★★★★ Undiluted Cask Strength Potstill Brandy ⓠ ⊗ Only local cask-strength brandy (62% alcohol), 13 years in wood. Intense, perfumed aromas, smooth despite the power. For small sips!

Witblitz ⊘ ⊗ **★★★★** Fun retro 200-ml 'half-jack' packaging for unmatured brandy from chenin & colombard. Water-white, aromatic, subtle notes of florals, fynbos & fresh fruit. For mixing (50% alcohol), says distiller. New bottling tasted, as for Pure Potstill & Grapé.

Husk Spirit range

★★★★ Grapé ⊘ ⊗ Fragrant dried herbs, wildflower notes on 15 year old from pinot noir & cabernet husks. Smooth, with raisin & gentle nut notes, rounded & perfect for after a rich dinner. 375 ml.— DS, WB

Location/map/WO: Wellington ▪ Map grid reference: C4 ▪ Est 1990 ▪ 1stB 1996 ▪ Tasting, sales & tours by appt ▪ Closed Easter Fri-Mon & Dec 25 ▪ Organic olives, olive oil, dried fruit & nuts ▪ Craft workshop ▪ Distillery: brandy, grappa, witblits, limoncello, gin ▪ Owner(s) Edmund & Elsie Oettlé ▪ Cellarmaster(s) / brandy master(s) Edmund Oettlé ▪ Winemaker(s)/viticulturist(s) Edmund Oettlé ▪ 46ha/10ha (cab, pinot, chenin, cbard, crouchen) ▪ 20t/1,200cs own label 100% red & 2,000L brandy ▪ QCS organic certification ▪ PO Box 152 Wellington 7654 ▪ info@organicwine.co.za ▪ www.organicwine.co.za ▪ S 33° 40' 19.9" E 019° 2' 40.0" ▪ ⊞ corded.rejoin.tipping ▪ **T +27 (0)82-731-4774**

Usana   ⓠ ⓞ

Sweet sixteen this edition, Usana is based on a farm in Stellenbosch's Lynedoch area owned by the Winshaw family since the 1970s. Vinification takes place under contract a few kilometres away, at Longridge in the Hederberg. Brand owners and brothers JP and Pierre welcome phone-ahead tastings of their boutique wines, with permanent on-site visitor facilities still in the planning.

★★★★ The Fox Cabernet Sauvignon ⓥ Handsome **15 ★★★★★** ⑨⓪'s intense cassis & blueberry fruit supported by textured tannins & spicy oak from 22 months in 20% new barrels. Fine balance of power & freshness; step up on leafier **14** ⑧⑧.

★★★★ Barrel Fermented Chenin Blanc Enticing honeysuckle aromas before a platter of pure yellow stonefruit, honey & beeswax. Long & intense **16** ⑧⑥ helped by judicious old oak, natural ferment. Improves on **15 ★★★★** ⑧④, also from Elgin fruit.

★★★★ Pinot Gris ⊘ Yellow apple & bright acidity, **17** ⑧⑥ slightly riper than last & better for it. Tangy & lingering, some richness from partial barrel ageing. Delicious, & more serious than **16 ★★★★** ⑧③.

Sauvignon Blanc ★★★★ The full green monty - fig, pepper & grass - in **17** ⑧④, some creaminess from 4 months on lees in old barrels. Fresh & food-perfect. — HC

Location/map: Stellenbosch ▪ Map grid reference: C8 ▪ WO: Stellenbosch/Elgin ▪ Est/1stB 2003 ▪ Tasting & sales by appt ▪ Farm produce ▪ Weddings & functions ▪ Owner(s) JP & Pierre Winshaw ▪ Winemaker(s) Jasper Raats (2012, consultant), with Hendrien de Munck (2010, consultant) ▪ Viticulturist(s) Pierre Winshaw ▪ 300ha/45ha (cabs s/f, malbec, merlot, chard, pinot gris, sauv) ▪ 29t/4,000cs own label 40% red 60% white ▪ PO Box 68 Lynedoch 7603 ▪ jp@usana.co.za, pierre@usana.co.za ▪ www.usana.co.za ▪ S 34° 0' 14.42" E 018° 45' 36.97" ▪ *M* posterity.firestorm.mayonnaise ▪ **T +27 (0)83-650-9528**

Uva Mira Mountain Vineyards   ⓥ ⑪ ◎ ⓖ

The vineyards of Uva Mira are situated within Stellenbosch's 'golden triangle', up to 620 metres on the Helderberg. At this altitude the vines are often enveloped in cloud, and they also benefit from cooling breezes rising from nearby False Bay. Viticulture is both sustainable and precise, and it underpins the establishment of a further ten hectares, some using the echalas (staked vine) training system. The wine labels tell meaningful stories about the natural flora and fauna on the estate, and some pay tribute to those who helped shape the farm, including the previous owners and OT Venter, inspirational father of the proprietor. The wines are consistently excellent and thoroughly deserve their local and international acclaim.

★★★★ The Mira Cabernet Sauvignon ⓥ Sophisticated **15 ★★★★★** ⑨⑤ showcases its cool mountain provenance. Complexity, depth & varietal character without exaggeration. After OTV, the most oak of the reds (18 months, 60% new), but effortlessly integrated. Ageworthy classic that improves on **14** ⑧⑧.

★★★★☆ The Dance Cabernet Franc ⓐ Though less austere than **14 ★★★★** ⑧⑨, **15** ⑨② does show finer vintage's more reserved, compact structure. Fresh piquancy & core of good fruit, will unfurl with time. Name inspired by courtship display of farm's resident pair of Verreaux's eagles.

★★★★ The Mira Merlot 16 ★★★★ ⑧④ appears even more subdued & savoury than **15** ⑧⑥. Youthful & tightly buttoned, with food-friendly tannins still evolving. Cellar time or decanting will resolve.

★★★★☆ DW Syrah ⓐ Effortless sophistication in **15** ⑨④, with touch less new oak than previous, more expressive & greater fruit intensity than introverted Mira sibling. Creamy chocolate with a dusting of white pepper spice. Lovely balance, freshness & length, potential for graceful development.

★★★★ The Mira Shiraz Earthy red fruit on **16** ⑧⑦, quite tight, all elements in place, needing time to develop. Less oak (now 40% new) & fruit expression at this young stage than impressive **15 ★★★★★** ⑨③.

★★★★ OTV ⓐ Still cab franc-led, with 42% cab in **15 ★★★★★** ⑨④, a polished step up on **14** ⑧⑦. Confident structure streamlines savoury & perfumed dark fruit. Oak (65% new, 18 months) & alcohol unobtrusive, the whole inherently balanced. Destined to evolve with distinction.

★★★★ The Mira Chardonnay Piercing lemon & oystershell minerality on **17** ⑧⑧. Zesty acidity, bright clean style, also lowest alcohol (13.4%) & new oak of the trio. Youthful & compact table wine.

★★★★☆ The Single Tree Chardonnay From a single-vineyard, has the most new oak (60%) & highest acidity of the chardonnays but enough fruit intensity to carry it. **16** ⑨② more vivacious & creamy than focused Mira sibling, yet not lacking potential to age.

★★★★☆ Uva Mira Chardonnay ⓐ Ex 0.2 ha portion of the same single-vineyard as Single Tree. **16** ⑨③ lovely lime & toasted nut impression from 50% new oak (less than **14** ⑨③), & like siblings, aged 9 months, does not obscure fruit intensity or freshness. Deserves cellaring to show full potential. No **15**.

★★★★☆ Sing-a-Wing Sauvignon Blanc ⓐ Cool, racy refinement on **17** ⑨② from 470 m vineyard, lower alcohol (12.9%) & touch higher acidity than sibling. Grapefruit, tinned asparagus flavours, a creamy substrate interwoven with citrus & long, clean farewell. A fine-dining companion worth ageing.

★★★★ **The Mira Sauvignon Blanc** From the highest vineyards (620 m), **17** ⑧⑨ riper, more stonefruit richness but still beautifully fresh & crisp; creamy, bright & lingering. More sprightly than **16** ⑧⑦.— MW

Location/map/WO: Stellenbosch ▪ Map grid reference: E8 ▪ Est 1997 ▪ 1stB 1998 ▪ Tasting & sales Mon-Sun 10-6; last service at 5 (tasting & platters) ▪ Fee R60/3 wines, R100/5 wines, call to confirm ▪ Closed Easter Fri/Sun, Dec 25/26 & Jan 1 ▪ Artisan cheese platters & savoury meat platters ▪ Olive oil, honey ▪ Conservation area ▪ Owner(s) Toby Venter ▪ Winemaker(s) Christiaan Coetzee (2012) ▪ Viticulturist(s) Christo Crous (2014) ▪ 127ha/33ha (cabs s/f, merlot, shiraz, chard, sauv) ▪ 200t/20,000cs 60% red 40% white ▪ Off Annandale Rd Stellenbosch 7600 ▪ info@uvamira.co.za ▪ www.uvamira.co.za ▪ S 34° 1′ 31.3″ E 018° 51′ 26.1″ ▪ Ⓦ cofounder.transact.advertisement ▪ F +27 (0)21-880-1682 ▪ T +27 (0)21-880-1683

Vaalvlei Wines

Ⓠ ⌂ ⓒ

Conservationists as well as winegrowers, Naas Terblanche and family on moving to their Stanford-area farm in 2005 were delighted to discover the air thick with frog calls, hence the endangered Western Leopard Toad emblem on their labels. The focus remains on shiraz and sauvignon blanc, grown on sandstone and ferricrete, touched by what Naas describes as Walker Bay's 'unique four-seasons-in-a-day weather patterns'.

Sauvignon Blanc Ⓐ ★★★ Cool-climate styling, intense capsicum & green grass scents in bright & cheerful **17** ⑧⑴, pebbly minerality the last impression. **Cape Vintage** Ⓐ ★★★★ Deep & dark, intense cassis in **15** ⑧④ 'port' from shiraz; potpourri & orange aromas, savoury underpin from 18 months in barrique. Drier than most but still satisfies. Not tasted: **Shiraz**. — CR, CvZ

Location: Stanford ▪ Map: Walker Bay & Bot River ▪ Map grid reference: B7 ▪ WO: Walker Bay ▪ Est 2005 ▪ 1stB 2008 ▪ Tasting & sales Mon-Fri 9-5 Sat 9-1 ▪ Closed Good Fri & Dec 25 ▪ 2 self-catering cottages ▪ Fly-fishing ▪ Owner(s) Terblanche family ▪ Cellarmaster(s)/viticulturist(s) Naas Terblanche (Mar 2005) ▪ Winemaker(s) Naas Terblanche (Mar 2005) & Josef Dreyer (Aug 2005, Raka), advised by Charl van Teijlingen (Mar 2008) ▪ 50ha/3ha (shiraz, sauv) ▪ 19t/650cs own label 40% red 60% white ▪ PO Box 92 Stanford 7210 ▪ info@vaalvlei.co.za ▪ www.vaalvlei.co.za ▪ S 34° 26′ 56.11″ E 019° 33′ 07.05″ ▪ Ⓦ sprayed.redecorate.elongates ▪ T +27 (0)28-341-0170/+27 (0)72-782-3431

☐ **Val de Valley Life** *see* Val de Vie & Polo Club Wines

Val de Vie & Polo Club Wines

Ⓠ ⓒ ♿

This Paarl luxury residential and polo estate, in a nod to the land's 18th-century Huguenot winegrowing history, maintains vines and a modern boutique cellar for its Val de Vie range, recently expanded with new-look Val de Valley Life (Bordeaux-) and Ryk Neethling (Rhône-style) blends. Continuing the sport association is a limited bottling to mark the annual Absa Cape Epic MTB race finishing here for the next five years.

Location: Paarl ▪ Map: Franschhoek ▪ Map grid reference: A7 ▪ Est 2003 ▪ 1stB 2004 ▪ Tasting by appt ▪ Sales Mon-Fri 11-4 ▪ Closed weekends & pub hols ▪ L'Huguenot Venue & Vinoteque at Val de Vie ▪ Coffee roastery ▪ Owner(s) Val de Vie Wines (Pty) Ltd ▪ Jan van Riebeeck Drive Paarl 7646 ▪ barbara@lhuguenot.com ▪ www.valdevie.co.za ▪ S 33° 48′ 15.0″ E 018° 58′ 4.0″ ▪ Ⓦ quickened.diets.nightshade ▪ T +27 (0)21-876-8847

Val du Charron

Ⓠ ⒴ ⌂ ⓒ Ⓐ ♿

A semi-derelict fruit farm in 2006 when it was purchased by the Entwistle family, this Wellington 'wine and leisure estate' now boasts a guest house, spa, two restaurants (also offering craft beer and artisan gin) and 21 ha of vineyards planted with no fewer than 16 varieties - 'We strongly believe in blending,' explains director Catherine Entwistle.

Estate Reserve range

★★★★ **Merlot** Ⓐ Violets & smoked bacon aromas attract, **15** ⑧⑦'s velvety mouthful delivers in balanced interplay of mulberry fruit, supple tannins, freshness & 40% new oak. Wellington WO, as all these.

★★★★ **Chardonnay** Very rich, with leavening acidity, **18** ⑧⑦ has 6% viognier adding perfume & spice to intense citrus, cashew & vanilla cream from 3 months 50% new French oak. First since **15** ★★★★ ⑧③.

Cabernet Sauvignon Ⓐ ★★★★ Rich blackcurrant fruit woven into mediumweight body of **14** ⑧③, firm but smooth tannins in support. **Pinot Gris** Ⓐ ★★★★ Interesting take on fashionable grape, **17** ⑧⑤ with dashes viognier, chardonnay, brush new oak, none detracting from racy greengage freshness - perfect for food. Not tasted: **Malbec**, **Syrah**.

Theater of Wine range

★★★★ **Erasmus** ⊘ First since **12** ★★★★ ⑧④, cab-led **15** ⑧⑥ with shiraz, petit verdot, pinotage has soft plum fruit, pinch pepper, hints liquorice & allspice from year in 30% new French wood.

★★★★ **Four White Legs** ⊘ Smooth, lightly oaked **18** ⑧⑥, 6-way blend of 30% chardonnay for zesty citrus, viognier for floral perfume, pinot gris, chenin, roussanne & grenache blanc for green apple, pear & greengage fruit.

Black Countess ⓠ ★★★☆ Shiraz, mourvèdre & grenache, **15** ⑧⑤ plump juicy fruit & spice kept in order by 40% new oak.

Aphaea range

Aphaea Red ⓠ ★★★ Majestic solitary tree on home-farm celebrated in swirling front-label art & delicious contents of **16** ⑧① cab/Rhône blend, deftly wooded. **Silk Rosé** ⓝⓔⓦ ⊘ ★★★ Cherry-pink **18** ⑦⑨ an off-dry 8-way blend (25% shiraz) with watermelon & sweet red berry fruit. Serve chilled with spicy food. **Aphaea White** ⓝⓔⓦ ⊘ ★★★★ Fresh, easy-drinking **17** ⑧③ has white flower perfume, concentrated peach, apricot & green apple flavours. — JG

Location/map: Wellington ▪ Map grid reference: C3 ▪ WO: Western Cape/Wellington ▪ Est 2007 ▪ 1stB 2009 ▪ Tasting daily 10-4 ▪ Sales Mon-Fri 8-5 Sat/Sun 10-4 ▪ Cellar tours by appt ▪ The Grillroom; Pizz e Vino ▪ Children play area ▪ Tour groups ▪ Conferences (20 pax) ▪ Spa ▪ 4 & 5 star guest house (stay@vdcwines.com) ▪ Craft beer & artisan gin ▪ Owner(s) Val du Charron Wines (Pty) Ltd ▪ Winemaker(s) Bertus Fourie (Apr 2010, consultant) & Paul Engelbrecht (2017-2018 harvest) ▪ Viticulturist(s) Heinie Nel (Apr 2010, consultant) ▪ 43ha/21ha (cab, ptage, shiraz, chard, chenin) ▪ ±300t ▪ IPW, WIETA ▪ PO Box 890 Wellington 7654 ▪ ce@vdcwines.com ▪ www.vdcwines.com ▪ S 33° 37′ 28.14″ E 019° 2′ 55.32″ ▪ ⊞ precollege.aubergine.shrivels ▪ F +27 (0)86-509-4865 ▪ **T +27 (0)21-873-1256**

Valley Vineyards Wine Company

New World wine specialists Richard James and Richard Addison combine their knowledge and long experience to select SA wines for their substantial export brand portfolio, and private label business which includes the Huntersville, Hutton Ridge, Journeymaker, Lion Ridge, Mischief Maker, Post Tree, The Royal and 24 Rivers ranges sourced in the Swartland.

Location: Riebeek-Kasteel ▪ Est/1stB 2009 ▪ Closed to public ▪ Owner(s) Richard Addison & Richard James ▪ ±100,000cs own label 40% red 40% white 15% rosé 5% other ▪ PO Box 2175 Riebeek-Kasteel 7307 ▪ raddison@valleyvineyardswine.com ▪ www.valleyvineyardswine.com ▪ **T +27 (0)14-120-1211**

Van Biljon Wines   ⓠ ⌂

One quality wine, Cinq, is produced on Anton and Julia van Biljon's small Polkadraai Hills property outside Stellenbosch by red-wine maestro Chris Keet, from the five Bordeaux varieties planted there. Being classically styled, long-lived wines, the '15 and subsequent blends are still maturing. '13 and '14 are available ex cellar and in select fine-dining venues locally and in Europe, including Belgium's Michelin-starred Lijsterbes.

★★★★☆ **Cinq** ⓠ ⓐ 5 Bordeaux varieties in ripe but refined blend, **14** ⑨④ from 53% cab to 3% petit verdot. Powerful 14.5% alcohol balanced by juicy fruit, firm structure & modest, supportive oaking (20% new), a savoury dimension too & admirable dryness on the finish. Like **13** ⑨④, deserves time.— MW

Location/map/WO: Stellenbosch ▪ Map grid reference: B6 ▪ Est 2004 ▪ 1stB 2013 ▪ Tasting, sales & cellar tours Mon-Sat by appt ▪ Closed all pub hols ▪ Self-catering Tarentaal Cottage ▪ Owner(s) Anton & Julia van Biljon ▪ Winemaker(s) Christopher Keet (Oct 2008, consultant), with Anton van Biljon (Jan 2011) ▪ Viticulturist(s) Christopher Keet (Oct 2008, consultant) ▪ 5ha/4ha (cabs s/f, malbec, merlot, p verdot) ▪ 1st/500cs own label 100% red ▪ IPW ▪ PO Box 1292 Hermanus 7200 ▪ info@vanbiljonwines.co.za ▪ www.vanbiljonwines.co.za ▪ S 33° 58′ 4.98″ E 018° 45′ 8.39″ ▪ ⊞ pleasant.stockings.consorts ▪ F +27 (0)28-313-0435 ▪ **T +27 (0)21-882-8445**

☐ **Van Coller Family** see Fijndraai Estate

Van der Merwe & Finlayson

Pieter van der Merwe is David Finlayson's winemaker at Edgebaston, where he also makes these naturally fermented wines - previously listed separately - for his personal projects. The Sanniesrust label is named for Pieter's Free State family farm, with cultivars that he particularly enjoys drinking. A pinotage is set to join the range. Rough Diamond (with David as a supporting partner) 'is about finding vineyards with less fashionable or "forgotten" varieties that suit their sites exceptionally'.

Sanniesrust range

★★★★ Grenache ⓐ Variety's trademark earth, scrub & wild berries in **16** ⑧⑦, appeals from first to last. Harmoniously older oaked, invigorating acidity & fine grape tannin courtesy bunch fermentation.

Cinsaut ★★★★ Just-dry, light-footed & lively **17** ⑧④, crunchy cherry & cranberry fruit, earth & faint vanilla tones in a delicate body best enjoyed lightly chilled.

Rough Diamond range

Tempranillo ★★★★ Abundant sour cherries on vibrant & generous **17** ⑧⑤, dry, pleasantly gripping grape tannin for food partnering, older oak an invisible support. **Viognier ★★★★** Perfumed sweet flowers, peach melba & honey complexity, **17** ⑧③ light oaking & dash sugar add to voluptuousness on palate, touch more freshness would rate higher. — WB

Location/WO: Stellenbosch • Est/1stB 2016 • Tasting by appt only • Closed all pub hols • Owner(s) David Finlayson & Pieter van der Merwe • Winemaker(s) David Finlayson & Pieter van der Merwe (both Jan 2016) • 8t/390cs own label 94% red 6% white • PO Box 2033 Dennesig 7601 • pwavandermerwe@gmail.com, sanniesrust@gmail.com • **T +27 (0)21-300-1168/+27 (0)84-512-5266**

Van Loggerenberg Wines

Two new wines join the range in Lukas van Loggerenberg's second vintage since his 'great leap of faith' in going solo: a chenin blending grapes from different areas and a syrah-cinsaut from Stellenbosch. Quantities are also up — though still very small. Also new is Thomas, Lukas and Roxanne's first child, who was born during the early days of harvest 2018 - compensating for the drought-stricken Kameraderie dryland vineyard in Paarl. The wines are still made in the simple shed atop a Devon Valley hill (where he also crafts the Carinus Family wines in exchange for the hospitality) — but such 'very basic' conditions are fine for the rigorously non-interventionist approach behind these fresh, elegant wines.

★★★★☆ Breton ⓐ Darkly bright **17** ★★★★★ ⑨⑤ cab franc owes more to Loire inspiration than Bordeaux in its lightness (ripe, but sub 13% alcohol, as was **16** ⑨②), transparency & older oaking. A stern element from firm tannin & fresh acidity, but plenty of cherry & other fruit. Restrained, elegant & properly dry. WO Stellenbosch.

★★★★ Geronimo ⓐ One of SA's more serious, complex examples of fashionable cinsaut. **17** ★★★★☆ ⑨③ fragrant & pure fruited, with an earthy-savoury note & complexity. Vinous, flavourful with penetrating acidity & balanced tannic base. Dry, dry finish, but succulent. From Stellenbosch/Paarl fruit.

★★★★☆ Graft ⓝⓔⓦ ⓐ 55/45 blend of Stellenbosch cinsaut & syrah - **17** ⑨③ darker, riper & more expressive, interesting & complex than the straight cinsaut. Generously built (13.5% alcohol the highest in this range), with fine, powdery tannin & lipsmacking acidity. Really needs a good few years before broaching.

★★★★☆ Break a Leg Old-oaked blanc de noir from Paarl cinsaut, **17** ⑨⓪ the opposite of the insipid, off-dry style of rosé. Pale partridge eye in colour, light-feeling but with some seriousness, a restrained intensity & fine texture, with a tart cranberry freshness. Bone-dry.

★★★★☆ Kameradarie ⓐ Stony, complexly gorgeous aromas & flavours on **17** ⑨④ Paarl chenin. There's intense but subtle fruit, expressed in dried peach, herbs, fennel; a touch saline & a good grip from a brilliantly exciting acidity & even a tannic element. Should develop many years in bottle. Matured in old oak.

★★★★☆ Trust Your Gut ⓝⓔⓦ ⓐ Widely sourced **17** ⑨④ chenin more immediately charming, light-er-feeling in youth than Kameradarie, only a touch less complex & intense. Very fine, with stony angularity & notable lemony acidity. Like all, natural ferment, no additives, maturation in old barrels (5 months here). WO Cape.— TJ

Location: Stellenbosch ▪ WO: Paarl/Stellenbosch/Western Cape/Stellenbosch-Paarl ▪ Est/1stB 2016 ▪ Tasting by appt only ▪ Closed all pub hols ▪ Owner(s) Lukas & Roxanne van Loggerenberg ▪ Winemaker(s) Lukas van Loggerenberg (Jan 2016) ▪ 15t/2,200cs own label 57% red 27% white 16% rosé ▪ PO Box 94 Somerset Mall 7137 ▪ lukas@vanloggerenbergwines.co.za ▪ www.vanloggerenbergwines.co.za ▪ T +27 (0)82-093-8091

Van Loveren Family Vineyards

Established in 1937 on a modest 25 ha in Robertson owned by Wynand and Nico Retief's parents, supplying bulk wine to the industry, to the major player Van Loveren is today, is a story not only of hard work but also vision and focus. Cue in the sons of the founders, each qualified in a different field, who latterly added a dynamic complementary brand, Four Cousins, serving niche and younger markets, based in its own venue in Robertson town. There's also been expansion into African and international markets, as well as other liquor fields such as brandy and craft beer. In no way does this devalue the home-farm on the Breede River bank, still meeting core values of quality and hospitality, with well-priced wines for every taste in the ranges.

Christina Van Loveren Limited Releases

★★★★ **Cabernet Sauvignon** Designed for pleasure, without stinting on quality, **16** ⑧⑧ plush dark fruit, intriguing aromatic scrub/Provençal herb top note. Sleekly muscled for cellaring, already accessible.

★★★★ **Shiraz** Always beautifully constructed, glossy fruit, layers of interest & tailored tannins, **16** ⑧⑧ has all the attributes you expect from top shiraz, given polish & great drinkability.

★★★★☆ **Chardonnay** ⊘ ⊛ All-new French oak for **17** ⑨③, perfectly matched to the citrus intensity, lemon, tangerine, coating the fruit with buttered toast savouriness. Sleekly curvaceous, characterful, lots to admire. From a single block.

★★★★☆ **Sauvignon Blanc** ⊘ ⊛ Following standout **17 ★★★★★** ⑨⑤ & with the same focus, nervy intensity, **18** ⑨③ is mineral at core, graphite, wet slate, with grassy, meadow top notes. More Old World than New.

★★★★ **Méthode Cap Classique Brut** ⊘ Chardonnay leads pinot noir in classically styled **NV** ⑧⑧ bubbly, both varieties contributing. Freshness & citrus tones given aromatic addition, palate weight from the red berries.

★★★★ **10 Year Old Brandy** ⓧ Small release of 10 year potstill from chenin, only ex cellardoor. Delicate bouquet of caramel & nuts, with fresher peach & apricot, plus chocolate notes, on restrained palate.

- - -

Méthode Cap Classique Brut Rosé ⊘ ⊕ ★★★★ Expressive red berries, strawberries in pretty pink-hued **NV** ⑧④ sparkling from pinot noir. No pushover, asks to be taken seriously: elegant, dry, zesty finish, lovely purity.

Noble Late Harvest Chenin Blanc ⓧ ★★★★ Rich but not over-sweet **13** ⑧④, unwooded, with notes of honey nougat, hazelnuts & watermelon jam. Perfect match for blue cheese. 375 ml.

Retief Reserve range (NEW)

Retief Reserve ★★★★ Cape Blend, pinotage with cab, shiraz. Mixed berries & juicy freshness make **16** ⑧④ a treat; oak spicing a savoury thread, tannins supple. Lovely label shows famous roadside red cannas.

Five's Reserve range

- - -

Merlot Rosé ⊘ ⊕ ★★★ Upfront red berries, **18** ⑧② is rosé with personality, the dry finish giving versatility for food or enjoying solo.

Cabernet Sauvignon ⊘ ★★★ Cassis perfume & flavours, expressive & attractive, oak's vanilla adding appeal to **17** ⑧①. Smooth & round, a food-friendly toasty finish. **Pinotage** ⊘ ★★★ Unwooded, but dark berry-toned **17** ⑧① has some smoky, spicy notes; smooth textured & fresh, very easy to like. **Chenin Blanc** ⊘ ★★★ Apple & pear flavours, **18** ⑦⑧ is dry but ends appealingly fruity. New packaging for the range. **5 Year Old Brandy** ⓧ ★★★ Blended brandy from chenin with plenty of nuts & fruitiness (apple, pear, raisin). Enough sweetness to benefit from ice or a mixer, but sippable neat (in gingerly fashion!).

The Rhino Run range

- - -

Ian Player ⊕ ★★★ Named for the renowned international conservationist; sales contribute to rhino protection. Cab/merlot blend for **16** ⑧①, plush fruit, well spiced & savoury, enough grip for food.

- - -

Cabernet Sauvignon ⓦ ★★★ Like rest of range, fruit-filled & honest, for early enjoyment. Cassis-rich **15** ⑧①'s fruit good partner for oak, ends savoury, dry. **Pinotage** ⓦ ★★★ Palate- & wallet-pleasing, as are red siblings, **15** ⑦⑧ ticks variety's strawberry & supple tannin boxes, some sugar rounds the finish. **Chardonnay** ⓦ ★★★ Balanced oaking adds biscuit tone to **16** ⑧①'s citrus flavours, ends tangy-fresh.

Van Loveren range

River Red ⓥ ⓦ ★★★ Perennial favourite, unoaked **17** ⑧⓪ pairs shiraz & pinotage for succulence & loads of flavour. Also in 500ml, 1.5L. **Blanc de Noir Red Muscadel** ⓥ ⓦ ★★★ The expected scents & flavours are there, muscat grapiness, Turkish delight, floral notes, & just enough sweetness to fit **18** ⑧①'s aromatic style. **Daydream Chardonnay-Pinot Noir** ⓥ ⓦ ★★★ Delicate pink-hued **18** ⑧① dry rosé's 6% pinot noir contributes colour & a red berry seam. The citrus ending, though, is pure chardonnay. **Neil's Pick Colombar** ⓥ ⓦ ★★★ Just a touch of sugar, but **18** ⑧① is tangy-fresh rather than sweet, fits the litchi/guava flavours. Great drinkability. **Red Muscadel** ⓦ ★★★★ Liquidised raisins & stonefruit, bargain-priced **16** ⑧⑤ postprandial fortified has admirable concentration. Full-sweet, mouthcoatingly lusciously, demands respect. Sip slowly & speak of wise things.

Cabernet Sauvignon ★★★ Lovely cassis in **17** ⑧①, some delicate sweet spice, vibrantly appealing texture, fruity-fresh yet smooth. **Merlot** ★★★ Short oaking, 6 months, giving **17** ⑦⑧ some vanilla spicing to its red berries, no interference with the smooth texture. **Blue Velvet Pinot Noir** ⓥ ★★★ Combining fresh berries & scrub notes with savoury oak, **16** ⑧① has lots to give, layers of flavour, light-textured drinkability. **African Java Pinotage** ★★★ No doubt about the coffee styling, **17** ⑧⓪ delivers that in both perfume & flavours, the bit of sweetness fitting right in (coffee with sugar, right?). **Cabernet Sauvignon-Merlot** ⓦ ★★★ Red berries & sweet spice, **16** ⑧①'s fruit intensifies in the flavours, well balanced by supple tannins. **Blanc de Noir Shiraz** ⓦ ★★ Salmon-hued **17** ⑦① reflects shiraz in its strawberry flavours, is fresh, dry. **Chardonnay** ⓦ ★★★ Lightly oaked, with underlying grapefruit, **17** ⑦⑧ is fresh & dry, a good food match. **Chenin No 5** ⓥ ★★★ Bone-dry, appealing apple & quince styling, **18** ⑦⑧, is shot through with zesty freshness. **Pinot Grigio** ★★★ One of few on the market. Some mineral & pear notes in crisply dry **18** ⑦⑧, good seafood companion. **Sauvignon Blanc** ⓥ ★★★ Gooseberries & green figs, nice typicity in **18** ⑧①, fresh & lively. **Blanc de Blanc** ⓥ ★★★ Mainly colombard, some chenin, friendly alcohol as all whites & rosés (±12%), **18** ⑦⑧ has 'crisp white' on the label & fits that perfectly. **Special Late Harvest Gewürztraminer** ⓦ ★★★★ After showcasing the variety's floral/glacé pineapple aromas, **17** ⑧④ ups the appeal, delivers a spicy, honeyed richness. **Cape Ruby** ★★★ Xmas cake richness, latest **NV** ⑧② 'port' has ultra-smooth drinkability - as a good Ruby should. From touriga. Also in 500 ml. Discontinued: **Blackberry Cabernet Sauvignon-Shiraz**.

Four Cousins Skinny range

Red ★★ Weigh-Less endorsed, reduced kilojoule, low 9% alcohol (as all these), easy-drinking **NV** ⑦① from merlot has plummy flavours, touch of sweetness. **Sweet Rosé** ★★ Red muscadel gives **NV** ⑦④ an intense grapiness, the sweetness making it all go down so easily. **White** ★★ From semillon, **NV** ⑦⑤ has green melon, appley crispness; perfect summer fare. — CR, TJ

Location/map/WO: Robertson ▪ Map grid reference: B5 C4 ▪ Est 1937 ▪ 1stB 1980 ▪ Tasting & sales: Van Loveren wines (only at home-farm) Mon-Fri 8.30-5 Sat 9.30-3 Sun 11-2; Four Cousins wines (only at @ Four Cousins venue, Robertson) Mon-Fri 8.30-5 Sat 9.30-4 Sun 11-3 pub hols 9.30-4 ▪ Closed Easter Fri/Sun, Dec 25 & Jan 1 ▪ Cellar tours by appt ▪ Garden tours ▪ Food & wine tasting platters ▪ Fish Eagle hiking trail ▪ MTB trails ▪ Christina's @ Van Loveren bistro open daily ▪ Amenities @Four Cousins: Food & wine pairings; craft Boet Beer tasting; whiskey pairings ▪ Tasting platters R6opp; R2o/gin, R1o/1oyr brandy, any other 4 wines R2opp ▪ @Four Cousins restaurant open daily ▪ Owner(s) Nico, Wynand, Phillip, Hennie, Bussell & Neil Retief ▪ Cellarmaster(s) Bussell Retief ▪ Winemaker(s) Danelle Conradie (Jan 2007) & Chris Crafford (Nov 2014), with Jonas Cupido & Jakob Pieterse ▪ Viticulturist(s) Neil & Hennie Retief ▪ 750ha (cab, merlot, mourv, muscadel r/w, ptage, pinot noir/gris, ruby cab, shiraz, touriga nacional, chard, chenin, cbard, gewürz, irsai olivér, morio muscat, nouvelle, sauv, sem, viog) ▪ 10,600t/2m cs own label 33% red 33% white 34% rosé ▪ Brands for clients: Liquor City, Ultra Liquors, Woolworths ▪ Fairtrade, IPW, WIETA ▪ PO Box 19 Klaasvoogds 6707 ▪ info@vanloveren.co.za ▪ www.vanloveren.co.za ▪ S 33° 48' 17.36" E 019° 52' 26.62" (@Four Cousins) S 33° 52' 31.3" E 020° 0' 9.1" (home-farm) ▪ ⌨ pearls.severally.aubergine ▪ F +27 (0)23-615-1336 ▪ **T +27 (0)23-615-1505**

Van Ryn

Distell's flagship brandy range, named for its Dutch immigrant founder, garners much local and overseas praise for its premium potstill products. Best Brandy Worldwide and Distiller of the Year crowns at the International Wine & Spirit Competition are just some of the more recent plaudits. Also globally recognised is Van Ryn's century-old, visitor-friendly premises near Stellenbosch, offering tours (including rare on-site cooperage), exhibits and special events, and a line-up of tasting options such as Decadent Delight, pairing the 12, 15 and 20 YO brandies with bite-size confectionery.

★★★★★ **20 Year Old Potstill** ⓥ Concentrated nose of dark berries, dried fruit & spice. Spice, especially, repeated on the palate along with apricot & prune amidst the complexity. Reminiscences of oak but never intrusive. Mellow, silky & very rich, with forthright finish.

★★★★★ **15 Year Old Potstill** ⓥ Irresistible notes of fragrant flowers, orange zest & dark chocolate just part of the ethereal complexity of this exquisite glassful of sniffing & sipping delight. Like others, from chenin & colombard, widely sourced.

★★★★★ **12 Year Old Potstill** ⓥ Deep colour, with mahogany gleam. Fragrant, delicate aromas of fruit, herbs, flowers lead to full, richly powerful but gentle palate, then a long, sustained finish. Complete, balanced, triumphant.

★★★★ **10 Year Old Potstill** (NEW) Now entirely a blend from potstill brandy (previously the 10 Year had a matured non-potstill component). Less delicate, more forceful than senior siblings, but house style shows in combining flavourful richness with finesse.

Discontinued: **Au.Ra**, **Vintage 10 Year**. — WB, TJ

Location/map: Stellenbosch ▪ Map grid reference: D6 ▪ Est 1905 ▪ Tasting & sales Mon-Fri 9-5 (May-Sep) 9-6 (Oct-Apr) Sat 9-4 Sun (Oct-Apr only) 11-4 ▪ Tasting options: Cape Smoke, Brandy & Chocolate, Decadent Delight ▪ Closed Good Fri, Dec 25 & Jan 1 ▪ Cellar tours Mon-Fri 10, 11.30 & 3 Sat 10, 11.30 & 1 ▪ Tour groups ▪ Gift shop ▪ Conference & boardroom facilities ▪ Exhibitions & special events ▪ Museum collection of historical brandies on display ▪ Owner(s) Distell ▪ Brandy master(s) Marlene Bester (Jul 2009) ▪ ISO 9001:1995 ▪ Van Ryn Rd Vlottenburg Stellenbosch 7604 ▪ info@vanryns.co.za ▪ www.vanryn.co.za ▪ S 33° 57' 43.26" E 018° 48' 4.87" ▪ 🌐 successes.harps.mint ▪ F +27 (0)21-881-3127 ▪ **T +27 (0)21-881-3875**

☐ **Vansha** see Ridgeback

Van Wyk Family Wines

For this newer own label, Constantia Glen winemaker Justin van Wyk scours the Cape to find special sites and parcels to work with. 'I source grapes from old vineyards as much as possible — many of them planted before I was born, which was in 1984 — and strive to make elegant, honest wines that are expressive of nature, circumstance and my passion for the Cape's heritage grape varieties.'

★★★★ **Syrah** ⓥ Elegant **16** (87) from Elgin decidedly dry, cool-climate expression, with bright fruit, spice & tobacco, fresh tannic grip, persistent finish. Can cellar few years.

★★★★ **Rebecca May** Cinsaut (69%) from Slanghoek & Darling combines with Darling grenache, splash Elgin syrah in midweight **17** (86), fresher than **16** ★★★★ (85), with raspberries, rhubarb & red cherries.

★★★★ **Olivia Grace** Widely sourced, **17** (88) unusual combo chenin, riesling, chardonnay & viognier is floral, peachy, fresh & harmonious after 7 months in French oak (10% new) & 20% concrete 'eggs'.

Chenin Blanc ★★★★ From old Darling bushvines, barrel-fermented **17** (85) shows more complexity than previous, from white peach & orange peel to leesy umami. — JG

Location: Constantia ▪ WO: Western Cape/Darling/Elgin ▪ Est/1stB 2016 ▪ Wines available for tasting & sale from Constantia Glen tasting room ▪ Owner(s) Van Wyk Family Wines (Pty) Ltd ▪ Winemaker(s)/viticulturist(s) Justin van Wyk (Jan 2016) ▪ 12t/1,600cs own label 40% red 60% white ▪ PO Box 780 Constantia 7848 ▪ justin@vanwykfamilywines.co.za ▪ www.vanwykfamilywines.co.za ▪ **T +27 (0)84-582-0107**

☐ **Van Zijl Family Vintners** see Imbuko Wines

Van Zylshof Estate

Stellenbosch University-trained Andri van Zyl wears both hats, winemaker and viticulturist, at this small family estate on the banks of the Breede River near Bonnievale. Making these fresh, crowd-pleasing wines runs in his veins, being the third-generation winemaker after his father Chris and grandfather Andries, who built the cellar in 1940.

Chenin Blanc ⊘ ⑦ ★★★★ Flavoursome **18** ⑧ crunchy apple with feisty acidity to lift creamy centre. Attractive easy-drinking style at a low 12.9% alcohol, tailor-made for summer.

Cabernet Sauvignon-Merlot ⊛ ★★★ Appealing **15** ⑦ shows plummy fruit intensity, brims with spice & choc-dipped berry nuances. Delicious but tad unlingering. **Riverain Unwooded Chardonnay** ★★★ Angelica, pear & starfruit flavours, rounded, with brisk thread of acidity. **18** ⑧ is ready for carefree quaffing. **Sauvignon Blanc** ★★★ **18** ⑦ tart & sherbetty, with tropical guava overlay for crisp al fresco swigging. Discontinued: **Rosé**. — MW

Location: Bonnievale ▪ Map/WO: Robertson ▪ Map grid reference: D3 ▪ Est 1940 ▪ 1stB 1994 ▪ Tasting & sales Mon-Fri 9–5 Sat 9–1 ▪ Closed Good Fri, Ascension day, Dec 25 & Jan 1 ▪ Cellar tours by appt ▪ Owner(s) Van Zylshof Trust ▪ Cellarmaster(s)/winemaker(s)/viticulturist(s) Andri van Zyl (Mar 1993) ▪ 37ha/32ha under vine ▪ 450t/±8,000cs own label 15% red 80% white 5% rosé ▪ PO Box 64 Bonnievale 6730 ▪ vanzylshof@lando.co.za ▪ www.vanzylshof.co.za ▪ S 33° 56' 18.5" E 020° 6' 23.4" ▪ ⌖ undulates.automobiles.woods ▪ F +27 (0)23-616-3503 ▪ **T +27 (0)23-616-2401**

Varkenskraal   ⑨ ⌂

A casualty of the drought on André and Gail Cockcroft's boutique wine and guest farm near the Klein Karoo town of De Rust was the Chardonnay - none was produced in 2017. But, on the bright side, there are other wines to taste (by arrangement), extended lodgings to relax in, and 'a stunning view across the vineyards.'
Merlot ★★★ Mint, white chocolate flavours, brightened by hint oak spice. Some gentle flesh on **16** ⑦ dimmed by rather grippy tannins. **Chardonnay** ⊛ ★★★ Light oak-spice adds interest to ripe citrus flavours on tangy-dry **16** ⑦. **Chenin Blanc** ★★★ Ripe melon, red apple juiciness in **17** ⑦; brisk, just-dry. — AL

Location: De Rust ▪ Map: Klein Karoo & Garden Route ▪ Map grid reference: B3 ▪ WO: Klein Karoo ▪ Est 1995 ▪ 1stB 2014 ▪ Tasting by appt ▪ Guest house ▪ Owner(s) André & Gail Cockcroft ▪ Cellarmaster(s) Jacques Conradie (Feb 2017, Karusa) ▪ Viticulturist(s) Herman van der Walt & VinPro (Mar 2014, consultant) ▪ 82ha/7.18ha (merlot, chard, chenin) ▪ 28t/1,700cs own label 26% red 74% white ▪ PO Box 93 De Rust 6651 ▪ andre@varkenskraal.co.za ▪ www.varkenskraal.co.za ▪ S 33° 27' 19.21" E 022° 33' 29.70" ▪ ⌖ sways.quirkiness.stacked ▪ **T +27 (0)44-241-2352**

Vaughan Johnson's Wine & Cigar Shop

Retailing doyen Vaughan Johnson opened SA's first fine-wine shop in Johannesburg in 1985, and for the past 27 years has been purveying top local labels to winelovers from around the world at premises in Cape Town's V&A Waterfront. His own range is for those times when all you want is a tasty drop for a modest price.
Good Everyday Cape Red ⊛ ★★★ Mostly cab, with merlot, petit verdot. **NV** ⑦ bright, sweet cherry fruit seamed with savoury oak spiciness. Quaff soon. **Good Everyday Cape White** ⊛ ★★★ Chenin, sauvignon & chardonnay, **NV** ⑧ nicely rounded, fruity, with mineral salty twist to finish. — GdB

Location: Cape Town ▪ Map: Cape Peninsula ▪ Map grid reference: B1 ▪ WO: Wellington ▪ Est/1stB 1985 ▪ Sales Mon-Fri 9–6 Sat 9–5 Sun 10–5 ▪ Open pub hols ▪ Gifts, souvenirs, spirits & beer available ▪ Owner(s) Vaughan Johnson ▪ PO Box 50012 Waterfront 8002 ▪ vjohnson@mweb.co.za ▪ www.vaughanjohnson.co.za ▪ S 33° 54' 19.15" E 018° 25' 10.68" ▪ ⌖ pampered.motorboats.extinguish ▪ F +27 (0)86-509-6401 ▪ **T +27 (0)21-419-2121**

☐ **Veldfire** *see* Stanford Hills Winery
☐ **Velo** *see* Wildehurst Wines

Vendôme   ⑨ ⑪ ◎ ⑤

Farmed by the Le Roux family for 10 generations, Vendôme on the Berg River banks in Paarl was named for their ancestral home in central France. They are part of the marketing venture Kaapse Familie Wingerde, with the family owners of Oude Denneboom and Kuyperskraal (see entries).

Location/map: Paarl ▪ Map grid reference: E6 ▪ Est 1692 ▪ 1stB 1999 ▪ Tasting & sales by appt ▪ Closed all pub hols ▪ Restaurant Mon-Fri 8-5 Sat 8-2 ▪ Functions ▪ Owner(s)/winemaker(s)/viticulturist(s) Jannie le Roux ▪ 20ha (cab, merlot, shiraz, chard, chenin, cbard, sauv, sem) ▪ 5t/600cs own label 50% red 50% white ▪ PO Box 36 Paarl 7645 ▪ lerouxjg@icon.co.za ▪ www.vendome.co.za, www.kaapsefamiliewingerde.com ▪ S 33° 45′27.8″ E 018° 58′42.4″ ▪ 🗺 panels.minus.clauses ▪ F +27 (0)21-863-0094 ▪ **T +27 (0)21-863-3905**

☐ **Vera Cruz Estate** *see* Delheim Wines

Véraison Vineyards

A boutique property of just 2.5 ha in Franschhoek, owned by a couple who fell in love with it and bought it on a visit from their London base in 2006. Originally from New York, Steve and Marisa Drew focus on cabernet, with personalised labels, each vintage featuring a local artist's work, whose details appear on the back label so that he/she could be contacted.

Artist Series

Cabernet Sauvignon ⓥ ★★★ Pleasant mellow aromas introduce **08** ⑧①, ripely sweet with touches of sour & savoury too, tannins still firm though acid starting to show, best enjoyed soon. — TJ, CvZ

Location: Franschhoek ▪ WO: Western Cape ▪ Est/1stB 2006 ▪ Owner(s) Marisa & Steve Drew ▪ 2.5ha/1ha (cab) ▪ 3t/500cs own label 100% red ▪ Erf 1271 Franschhoek 7690 ▪ LoveYourWine@veraison.co.za ▪ www. veraison.co.za ▪ **T +27 (0)72-920-0208**

Vergelegen Wines ⓥ ⑪ ◎ ⑧ ⑤

Like most things on global mining giant Anglo American's meticulously restored and -run property, conceived by a late 17th-century Cape governor as a model architectural and agricultural estate, the stellar wine portfolio is a standard bearer of authentic, consistent quality. Vines occupy expert-identified sites on a total of ± 160 ha, with most of the remainder of the 3,000 ha on the Hottentots Holland mountains devoted to vast tracts of restored indigenous fynbos vegetation. Wines are vinified by long-time winemaker André van Rensburg in consultation with leading French oenologist Michel Rolland. The multi-level, partly-underground, gravity-fed cellar-in-the-round is a local showpiece, as are many of the other historic, cultural, gastronomic and horticultural facets of the property.

Flagship range

★★★★★ **Vergelegen V** ⓥ Premium-priced flagship. 100% cabernet, taut **12** ⑨⓪ is designed for ageing but so well crafted, power is latent rather than overt. Cassis at core, expected complex nuances to beguile collectors, but plenty more to unfold over time. Worth the wait.

★★★★★ **Vergelegen GVB Red** ⑧ Cab leads merlot with splashes cab franc & petit verdot in **13** ⑨③, showing its dominant role with earthy blackcurrants, iodine & liquorice. Big, serious & forceful but not intimidating, showing integration from 4 years in bottle.

★★★★★ **Vergelegen GVB White** ⑧ Expressive, elegant Bordeaux blend, 60/40 semillon/sauvignon, **15** ★★★★★ ⑨⑤ reflects fine vintage, with poise & balance, power & purity; luscious spiced fruit with herbal notes. Built to last, like **14** ⑨③. Fermented & 10 months in French oak.

Reserve range

★★★★★ **Cabernet Sauvignon** ⑧ Quintessential New World cab, **13** ⑨③ ticks the boxes: big & muscular, tending towards fruit ripeness & beguiling generosity. But also purity & restraint. Still youthful, promising many years of development.

★★★★★ **Merlot** ⓥ Consistently one of the Cape's finest. Layered plums & cherries enriched by chocolate & savoury spice, **13** ⑨②'s fruit/tannin balance finely tuned. Svelte, supple, an iron fist in a velvet glove.

★★★★★ **Shiraz** ⑧ Reflects the exceptional quality of the vintage. **15** ⑨③ concentrated yet finely nuanced, with plum pudding, tobacco & delicate herbs in perfect harmony. Silky & approachable in youth, but worth laying down.

★★★★★ **DNA** ⓥ Uncompromising Bordeaux blend with cab franc in the spotlight (70%), **13** ⑨⓪ struts its taut, focused stuff. Pencil shavings with tar & ink, jet-black fruit & dark mineral tones. Linearity is fleshed out with merlot, cab & petit verdot.

★★★★☆ **Chardonnay** (❀) Understated, subtly complex **16** (93) has finely detailed citrus, showing zest, marmalade & blossom notes. Also-tasted **17** (93) follows form, less butter & oak spice emphasis. Both elegantly weighted, with lingering finish. Bunch pressed, barrel fermented, matured 9 months.

★★★★☆ **Sauvignon Blanc SV Schaapenberg** (❀) Adds 'SV' to name. Heady, pungent herbaceousness laced with flint is the hallmark of this celebrated single-vineyard reserve. **17** (93) true to form, layered & voluptuous, with fruit & minerality in sublime balance. 9 months in 2,500L Austrian seasoned-oak vats.

★★★★☆ **Semillon** (❀) Refined, finely focused **17** (93) upholds Cape benchmark standard. Exquisite layers of minerality, dusty lanolin & floral scents, with subtle oak highlights. Sumptuous texture & lingering, fragrant finish. Bunch pressed, 25% new-barrel fermented. Excellent potential.

★★★★☆ **Sauvignon Blanc-Semillon Straw Wine** (①) Dessert wine from dried grapes fermented on skins/stems & aged 15 months older barrels. A symphony of stonefruit, pineapple & orange marmalade, **13** (92)'s oak an almond infusion. Sweet, but enough acidity to lengthen the palate, give a future.

Not tasted: **MMV**.

Premium range

★★★★ **Shiraz** 2 vintages tasted. **16** (88) has tarry, black-fruit character, with hints of tobacco. Ripe, plush & smoothly textured. **15** ★★★★★ (90) similar, with added purity of fruit, firmer tannins. Both impressive lower-tier offerings.

★★★★ **Cabernet Sauvignon-Merlot** (①) To enjoy earlier than the other Bordeaux reds, but **12** (88) still has a good future thanks to concentration & structure, intense cassis, a seam of fine tannins.

★★★★ **Chardonnay** Stylish **17** (88) has emphatic whack of citrus fruit still not fully knit with buttery oak (80% French barriques, 20% new). Promises more elegance with time in bottle. No **16**.

★★★★ **Sauvignon Blanc** Precise & lean, **17** (88) follows tried & trusted formula, offers pungent nettles, flint & passionfruit in finely balanced harmony. 13 different own vineyards, now with oaked (15%) & wholebunch components.— GdB

Location: Somerset West ▪ Map: Helderberg ▪ Map grid reference: F5 ▪ WO: Stellenbosch ▪ Est 1987 ▪ 1stB 1991 ▪ Tasting & sales daily 9–4.30 (gate closes at 4) ▪ Estate closed Good Fri, May 1 & Dec 25 ▪ Daily heritage & gardens tour at 9.30; cellar tours at 11 & 3 ▪ All tours R50pp (reservations advised) ▪ Tastings from R30pp ▪ Camphors Restaurant ▪ Stables Bistro & Forest Picnic (child-friendly) ▪ Gift shop ▪ Historic Cape Dutch homestead ▪ Library ▪ Exhibition corridor ▪ Ancient camphor trees (National Monuments since 1942) ▪ Conservation area ▪ 17 gardens including Camellia garden of excellence & children's adventure garden & maze ▪ Owner(s) Anglo American plc ▪ Winemaker(s) André van Rensburg (Jan 1998) ▪ Viticulturist(s) Dwayne Lottering (Nov 2003) ▪ 3,000ha/158ha (cab, merlot, sauv) ▪ 900t/120,000cs own label 58% red 42% white ▪ ISO 9001, ISO 14001, ISO 22000, OSHAS 18000, WIETA, WWF-SA Conservation Champion ▪ PO Box 17 Somerset West 7129 ▪ info@vergelegen.co.za ▪ www.vergelegen.co.za ▪ S 34° 4' 38.33" E 018° 53' 30.03" ▪ ⫴ bottle.locating.cobbles ▪ **T +27 (0)21-847-2100**

Vergenoegd Löw Wine Estate   (①)(📷)(🍴)(♿)

Adopting the name of proprietor Peter Löw, of German investment group Livia, reflects a new era for this centuries-old Stellenbosch farm. Renowned for reds, Vergenoegd is increasing white plantings (chardonnay, chenin, sauvignon and viognier), renovating its cellar and initiating waterbird habitat research, inspired by its huge flock of Indian runner ducks used as pest control (and one of many visitor drawcards).

Premium range

★★★★ **Cabernet Sauvignon** Big, assertive **13** (87) has dense cassis fruit with appealing savoury farmyard/earthy tones, tarry core & herbal aromas. Chewy tannins showing signs of yielding.

★★★★ **Estate Blend** Reflecting fine vintage, **09** (89) shows more staying power than **08** (88). Cab-led 5-way Bordeaux red has weight & focus, with bold savoury notes, complex stewed fruit. Drinking well now.

★★★★ **Cape Vintage** (❀) Intense black plum fruit & grippy spirit (20%) on convincing, naturally fermented **11** (86) 'port', preview from equal tinta & touriga, tobacco & roasted nuts on lingering finish. Ageworthy.

Mid-Tier range

★★★★ **Little Flower Brut** Accomplished & appealing **NV** ⑧ MCC sparkling is 75% chardonnay, pinot noir. Grippy acid, lively mousse & rich, yeasty brioche, with spicy apple fruit.

Merlot ★★★ Earthy & leafy notes, quite austere black fruit, big tannins, tarry backbone on **15** ⑧. Rather angular & ungenerous mid-2018, might just need more time. **Shiraz** ★★★ Lightish body with reticent fruit & minty-leafy notes on **15** ⑧. Full tannins, brief finish. **Terrace Bay** ★★★★ Quirky 5-way blend leading with shiraz & merlot, part-oaked **15** ⑧ full & fruity, with beefy 15% alcohol.

Runner Duck range

Red ★★★ Eclectic 5-way blend **15** ⑧ offers salty liquorice core with dark fruitcake. Juicy, easy to quaff (but note 15% alcohol). **Rosé** ★★★ Light, fresh **18** ⑦ is from gently pressed malbec & merlot, showing modest strawberry fruit, tangy & dry finish. **Sauvignon Blanc** ★★★ Crisply refreshing **18** ⑧ preview ex Robertson has tingling acidity, glacé fruit notes. Occasional release: **Reserve White**.

Limited Edition range

Occasional release: **Cabernet Franc**, **Malbec**, **Petit Verdot**. — GdB

Location/map: Stellenbosch ▪ Map grid reference: B8 ▪ WO: Stellenbosch/Western Cape ▪ Est 1696 ▪ 1stB 1972 ▪ Tasting & sales Mon-Sun 9–5 ▪ Open 365 days a year ▪ Tasting R55/6 wines ▪ Wine experiences ▪ Wine club ▪ Cellar tours by appt ▪ Facilities for children ▪ Tour groups ▪ Wine-related gifts ▪ Lawn games available ▪ Duck parades 3 x daily ▪ Duck tours ▪ Waterbird habitat project ▪ Bird hides ▪ Market every Saturday ▪ Live concerts in summer ▪ Owner(s) Livia Winery ▪ Winemaker(s) Marlize Jacobs (Dec 2007) ▪ Viticultural manager Louis Horn (Jun 2017) ▪ 161ha/57ha (cabs s/f, malbec, merlot, p verdot, shiraz, tinta, touriga) ▪ 300t 90% red 7% white 3% rosé ▪ IPW, WIETA ▪ PO Box 1 Faure 7131 ▪ info@vergenoegd.co.za ▪ www.vergenoegd.co.za ▪ S 34° 2'2.8" E 018° 44'20.1" ▪ 🌐 online.spoiler.themes ▪ F +27 (0)21-843-3118 ▪ **T +27 (0)21-843-3248**

Versailles   ⓘ ◎

Based on Versailles farm, owner Annareen de Reuck is a scion of the Malan family which helped establish the Wellington grower-owned cellars now merged into Wellington Wines. She's added a Pinotage to her Malan de Versailles Merlot and Sauvignon Blanc, intended as 'nice, easy-drinking, value-for-money wines'.

Location/map: Wellington ▪ Map grid reference: B3 ▪ Est/1stB 2004 ▪ Tasting, sales & tours by appt ▪ Conservation area ▪ Owner(s) Annareen de Reuck (Malan) ▪ PO Box 597 Wellington 7654 ▪ adereuck@ezinet. co.za, orders@versailleswines.co.za ▪ www.versailleswines.co.za ▪ S 33° 37'34.98" E 018° 59'37.11" ▪ 🌐 briskly.outlast.staging ▪ F +27 (0)86-502-1482 ▪ **T +27 (0)21-873-2618/+27 (0)82-898-9314**

☐ **Vet Rooi Olifant** see Kaapzicht Wine Estate

☐ **Vibrazio** see The House of JC le Roux

Viceroy

Among SA's most enduring blended brandies, with mid-1800s ties to the Van Ryn Wine & Spirit Company (both labels now owned by Distell). Today Viceroy, with five years' barrel maturation upping the ante in its category, is sold throughout Africa — in fact, it's becoming one of the biggest brandy export labels there. In addition, it's the leading brandy marque by volume in SA.

5 Year ⓥ ★★★★ A more serious blended brandy. More complex than 5 year category would imply; though touch obviously fiery & sweet on the finish, still sippable unmixed. **Makoya** ⓥ ★★★★ Brilliant amber colour on this newer blended brandy. Rich peach crème brûlée, roasted nuts & pear drop flavours, sweet & smooth - made for mixing. — WB

Vierkoppen

A mutual love of wine between two business associates in the medical supplies industry and their wives led to the establishment of this boutique winery, the name a reference to the 'four heads' involved, and the hilly terrain in Robertson's northerly ward, Klaasvoogds. Latterly, UK-based David and Daphne Briscoe forged ahead on their own, with increasingly impressive results, but sadly David passed away in early 2018, and Daphne, reluctantly, has decided to close the venture after current stocks sell out.

★★★★☆ **Cabernet Sauvignon** ⓥ Cool-toned **12** ⑨ 100% cab (**11** ⑨ has dash cab franc); cassis & coconut spicing from 2 years French oak (30% new) but shows other interesting layers too: a bit of scrub, forest floor. Polished, silky, with aristocratic elegance.

The Basket Case Merlot ⓥ ★★★★ Primary flavours - berries, violets, smoked meat - to the fore in just-bottled **15** ㊙, accessible & moreish. Klaasvoogds WO. **Pinotage** ⓥ ★★★★ Quintessential pinotage - chunky banana, clove & glossy blueberry features before sweet vanilla, but **13** ㊙ saved from rusticity by fine tannins. 100% oaked, half each French & American, 18 months. **Weavers Nest Reserve** ⓥ ★★★★ Classic cab & merlot blend (60/40) launches the Reserve label; **13** ㊙ brambly cassis, tobacco & cedar lead out a soft & supple ensemble, easy to drink but worthy of contemplation too. — DS

Location: Robertson ▪ WO: Robertson/Klaasvoogds ▪ Est 2008 ▪ 1stB 2009 ▪ Owner(s) Daphne Briscoe ▪ PO Box 950 Robertson 6705 ▪ info@vierkoppen.com ▪ www.vierkoppen.com ▪ 🖼 cuter.montage.notches ▪ **T +27 (0)78-413-1733**

Vilafonté ⓥ

This top-end wine collaboration between eminent US viticulturist Phil Freese, his highly acclaimed winemaker wife Zelma Long and SA marketing supremo Mike Ratcliffe is named after the vilafontes soils of their Simonsberg-Paarl vineyards. It's 'seriously old dirt' (the phrase now also the name of a third wine, reviewed here for the first time). On the estate, construction of a dam is underway ('a necessity with the ongoing drought… to secure future vintages'), and new plantings are planned. In charge of day-to-day operations at the Bosman's Crossing cellar in Stellenbosch is resident winemaker Chris de Vries, who shares their 'uncompromising determination to produce wines which stand shoulder-to-shoulder with the great wines of the world. Nothing less'.

★★★★☆ **Series C** ⓥ Dense yet refined cab-led Bordeaux blend with merlot, cab franc & malbec (19/15/9), **15** ㊚ deserves lengthy cellaring, 22 months in French oak (67% new) adding to structure, poise & persistent cedarwood perfume.

★★★★☆ **Series M** ⓐ More succulent, velvety blend of 40% merlot, near-equal cab & malbec, **15** ㊙'s deep-piled black & blue fruit is fine textured & already accessible, seamed with delicious subtle earthiness. Cocoa powder & vanilla spicing after 22 months in oak, 18% new.

★★★★☆ **Seriously Old Dirt** New to the guide, 3rd Bordeaux blend has malbec ahead of merlot & cab (29/28). Youthfully approachable, only lightly oaked (22 months older barrels) & lusciously soft. **15** ㊙ seductive ripe black fruit & baking spices, moderate 13.5% alcohol. Vegan friendly, as all. — JG

Location/map: Stellenbosch ▪ Map grid reference: E5 ▪ WO: Paarl ▪ Est 1996 ▪ 1stB 2003 ▪ Tasting, sales & tours by appt only ▪ Owner(s) Mike Ratcliffe, Zelma Long & Phil Freese ▪ Winemaker(s) Zelma Long & Chris de Vries (Oct 2016) ▪ Viticulturist(s) Phil Freese & Edward Pietersen (2006) ▪ 17ha (cabs s/f, malbec, merlot) ▪ 70t/4,000cs own label 100% red ▪ Unit 7C Lower Dorp Str Bosman's Crossing Stellenbosch 7600 ▪ info@ vilafonte.com ▪ www.vilafonte.com ▪ S 33° 56' 26.8" E 018° 50' 49.8" ▪ 🖼 abacus.blizzard.rather ▪ F +27 (0)21-883-8231 ▪ **T +27 (0)21-886-4083**

Viljoensdrift Fine Wines & Cruises ⓥ ⑪ ⊚

The 5th generation to grow and make wine in Robertson (historically for sale in bulk), incumbent Viljoen brothers Manie and Fred started bottling under their own label in 1998 and have steadily increased quantities over the years. Their visitor facilities are among the most unusual in the winelands, and deservedly popular, with river cruises and, on the banks, a self-help deli for leisurely picnics.

River Grandeur range

Cabernet Sauvignon ⓥ ★★★ Juicy ripe plums with a cocoa dusting, **16** ㊛ is smooth & lifted by a berry finish. **Pinotage Single Vineyard** ★★★★ Big & bold, in house style, yet **17** ㊙ balanced, too, its ripe plum fruit checked by a raspberry freshness, firm grip of oak & nice savoury finish. **Shiraz** ★★★ Generous hedgerow fruit, cured meat & exotic spice mingle with savoury oak in **17** ⑳ pleasant everyday red. **Cape Blend** ★★★★ Equal pinotage & cab in muscular **17** ㊙, upfront dark berry flavours & hints of violets & dried herbs. Appealing but robust, needs time to show at best. **Crispy Sauvignon Blanc** ★★★ As the name says, **18** ㊐ is crisp & zippy (if a tad brief), offers apple & lemon flavours, quite a steely acidity. Not tasted: **Merlot**, **Chardonnay**.

Viljoensdrift range

★★★★ **Villion** ② Refreshingly dry sparkling from chardonnay, with 2 years on lees. **09** ⑧⑧ expressive citrus, biscuit aromas, lively bubble & creamy undertones, the nutty/leesy flavours linger pleasurably.

Muskapino Sweet Pink Sparkling Wine ★★ Sweet fragrance on **18** ⑦⑥ vibrant pink bubbly from muscadel & pinotage, low alcohol to get the party started. **Cape Vintage Reserve** ★★★★ Spicy, lively red fruit & plum pudding on **15** ⑧③ 'port' from tinta. Gentle vanilla spice ex 3 years in oak, good spirity farewell.

Anchor Drift range

Dry White ★★★ Easy-sipping **NV** ⑦⑦ from semillon has a medium body, pleasing balance & mouthfeel, waxy finish. Not tasted: **Dry Red**. — WB

Location/map/WO: Robertson ▪ Map grid reference: C5 ▪ Est/1stB 1998 ▪ Tasting, sales & river cruises at riverside venue Mon-Fri 10—5 Sat 10-4 & 1st Sun/month 10-3; open 7 days/week Dec-Feb ▪ Closed Good Fri, Dec 25 & Jan 1 ▪ Self-help deli - create your own picnic basket ▪ Tour groups ▪ Conferences ▪ Owner(s) Fred & Manie Viljoen ▪ Winemaker(s) Fred Viljoen, with Zonia Lategan ▪ Viticulturist(s) Manie Viljoen ▪ 240ha/120ha (cab, merlot, ptage, shiraz, chard, sauv) ▪ 2,000t/±160,000cs own label 55% red 40% white 4% rosé 1% port + 15,000L for clients ▪ Other export brands: Elandsberg, Riverscape, Vuurgloed ▪ IPW, WIETA ▪ PO Box 653 Robertson 6705 ▪ rivercruises@viljoensdrift.co.za ▪ www.viljoensdrift.co.za ▪ S 33° 52' 8.4" E 019° 59' 13.6" ▪ ⊠ cucumber.toothless.logo ▪ F +27 (0)23-615-3417 ▪ **T +27 (0)23-615-1901 (cellar)/+27 (0)23-615-1017 (tasting/cruises)**

☐ **Villa Cape Kosher** *see* Simonsvlei International

☐ **Villa Esposto** *see* Klawer Wine Cellars

☐ **Village Walk** *see* Franschhoek Cellar

Villiera Wines   ⑨ ⑪ ⑩ ⑤

A family concern since inception in 1983, Villiera continues to innovate, and in typical low-key fashion does so without shouting it from the rooftops — which, inventively, now harvest roughly 6 million litres of rainfall! Jeff Grier's steady hand on the winemaking helm keeps a true course, while cousin Simon splits his time between vineyard and conservancy. Next-generation Xander (son of Great Wall of China-running chef/philanthropist David Grier) is in the cellar now, too. From helping take MCC sparkling production to new heights, to providing a home for the worthy Pebbles Project charity, to an on-site clinic for own and neighbours' staff, to covering the cellar roof in solar panels, this has to be one of Stellenbosch's most respected estates for quality and environmental/social concern. Power generation has been ramped up, the Old Vine Project joined and amphoras used in the cellar... Villiera keeps it fresh, too!

Villiera Wines range

★★★★ **Cabernet Sauvignon** ⊘ ⊛ Effortless ease to **16** ⑧⑥. Supple, smooth, black fruited & spicy, with well-knit oak (25% new), including 10% dab American. Confident & structured for the long haul.

★★★★ **Monro** Switches from 3-way Bordeaux blend in **15** ⑧⑦ to 100% merlot in **16** ★★★★★ ⑨①. Hedgerow fruit, ink & graphite mingle with cigarbox, framed by 50% new French oak for 18 months. Supple as a gymnast; rich, rewarding, yet restrained & elegant.

★★★★ **Stand Alone Pinot Noir** ⊛ ⊘ Lithe, pliant yet powerful **15** ⑧⑨ from Hemel-en-Aarde Ridge grapes. Solid core of lively red fruit vies with deeper, inky nuance. Natural ferment, 20% wholebunch & older oak.

★★★★★ **The Clan** ⊛ Drops 'Special Reserve Red' from name. **16** ⑨④ picks up where **15** ⑨③ left off: a superb, unusual blend of cab franc & 10% carignan. Muscular but silky, complex & nuanced. Rich & powerful yet controlled, spent 18 months in oak, 60% new.

★★★★ **Traditional Bush Vine Blanc Fumé** Name & style change sees portion of low-crop bushvine fruit skin-fermented in 'egg', then all briefly oaked in half-new barrels. **17** ⑧⑧ fresh & zesty, textured & long.

★★★★ **Antithesis** ② Pleasing chenin blend (75%) with chardonnay & muscat, lightly wooded **15** ⑧⑦ bright gold glassful with pear, peach & floral complexity, creamy layered palate & lingering spicy farewell.

★★★★☆ **Inspiration** ② Botrytised chenin, riesling dessert. Bronze-hued **10** ⑨② shows unctuous dried fruit flavours with citrus twist. Delightful fresh acidity ably controls richness.

Merlot ★★★☆ Textural **16** ⑧⑤ offers tealeaf subtext to bright berry fruit. Cedar spice nuance from integrated oak, quarter new. Long, rich cocoa-tinged finish. **Pinotage** ★★★☆ Instant appeal of juicy raspberry & plum tones on **17** ⑧⑤. Concentration & depth belie vivacity. Lithe & persistent. Like previous, 25% new oak. **Chenin Blanc** ⊘ ★★★☆ Bold tropical styling on **18** ⑧⑤ offers enjoyment & value in spades. Vibrant yet rich from dabs oak ferment & lees contact. Summertime staple. **Sauvignon Blanc** ★★★☆ Gentle lemon verbena notes on vibrant, juicy **18** ⑧③ which, like previous, has some Elgin fruit. Refreshing & fun for warm-weather sipping. **Jasmine** ★★★☆ Heady rosepetal notes from **18** ⑧③ semi-sweet muscat-led blend with gewürztraminer & riesling. Bright, rounded & uncloyingly juicy, with clean finish. Not tasted: **Traditional Barrel Fermented Chenin Blanc**.

Méthode Cap Classique range

★★★★☆ **Brut Natural** Nutty brioche & green apple piquancy from **14** ★★★★ ⑧⑨ all-chardonnay bubbly boasting zero dosage & 42 months on lees. Complex, bright, rich & broad with beautiful mouthfeel & dry, crisp finish. Follows fine & harmonious **12** ⑨①. **13** untasted.

★★★★☆ **Monro Brut** ⊘ ⊛ Distinct oystershell nuance to flagship **12** ★★★★★ ⑨⑤ sparkler, mostly chardonnay (some old-barrel fermented) for citrus vivacity. Complexity & length added by pinot noir (30%) & meunier. Fresh vibrancy belies 72 months on lees. Elegant & rich. **11** ⑨③ was 5 years on lees.

★★★★ **Tradition Brut** ⊘ Restrained but rich **NV** ⑧⑥ sparkler which helped establish house reputation. Pinot noir (48%) just ahead of chardonnay & dab meunier. Creamy, but light zip from 18 months on lees & 6 months in bottle. Also in 1.5L & 375ml.

Tradition Brut Rosé ⊘ ★★★☆ Pinot noir just leads pinotage & chardonnay in **NV** ⑧⑤ pink-hued sparkler with dash meunier. Red berries, lees & crunchy dryness on bright yet lengthy, creamy palate. Also in magnum. **Starlight Brut** ⊘ ★★★☆ Marmalade tang to low-alcohol chardonnay-led (50%) **NV** ⑧④ fizz with pinot noir & pinotage. Zesty citrus with light toast note. Crisp & dry.

Down to Earth range

Red ⊘ ★★★☆ Ample spice & berry charm on **16** ⑧④ mix of touriga & shiraz. Plush, juicy & downy, with medium body & length. **White** ★★★ Vivid & zippy, as befits **18** ⑧② mix of predominantly sauvignon (82%) & semillon. Ideal summer quaffer. — FM

Location/map: Stellenbosch ▪ Map grid reference: D1 ▪ WO: Stellenbosch/Hemel-en-Aarde Ridge/ Stellenbosch-Elgin ▪ Est/1stB 1983 ▪ Tasting, sales & self-guided cellar tours Mon-Fri 9—5 Sat 9—3 ▪ Closed Good Fri, Dec 25 & Jan 1 ▪ MCC & nougat pairing; cheese platters ▪ Wildlife sanctuary ▪ Game drive safaris & birding (incl tasting & self-guided tour of cellar), phone for cost and to book ahead ▪ Owner(s) Grier family ▪ Cellarmaster(s) Jeff Grier (1983) ▪ Winemaker(s) Nathan Valentine (reds/whites) & Xander Grier (MCC/ reserve wines) ▪ Viticulturist(s) Simon Grier ▪ 180ha (cab, merlot, ptage, pinot, shiraz, chard, chenin, sauv) ▪ 1,600t/110,000cs own label 25% red 30% white 45% MCC ▪ Brands for clients: Woolworths (local); Marks & Spencer (export) ▪ B-BBEE, HACCP, IPW, WIETA ▪ PO Box 66 Koelenhof 7605 ▪ wine@villiera.com ▪ www. villiera.com ▪ S 33° 50′14.4″ E 018° 47′34.4″ ▪ ▥ concoct.launchpad.layouts ▪ F +27 (0)21-865-2314 ▪ **T +27 (0)21-865-2002/3**

Villiersdorp Cellar ⓠ ⑪ ◎ ⓑ

The farms of Villiersdorp Cellar's 40 grower-owners are situated in distinct geographical regions around Villiersdorp town, and some of these terroirs are recognised in the names of the Since 1922 range. The visitor offering includes something unique in the winelands: a tractor museum, open by appointment.

Since 1922 range

Van Der Stel Sauvignon Blanc-Semillon ⊘ ★★★ Grapey & grapefruity **18** ⑧⓪, 70/30 blend makes for easy summer sipping. Just-dry, will be good friends with fishy foods. Also in 3L cask. Cape South Coast WO. Not tasted: **Bossieveld Cabernet Sauvignon-Merlot**.

Villiersdorp Cellar range

Treintjiewyn ★★★ Flowers, grapes, perfume & peaches all vie for attention on **NV** ⑧⓪ hanepoot jerepiko, well-managed sweetness & fire. Add tonic, lemon slice & ice for a lovely summer drink. **Cape Ruby** ★★★ Attractive spiced coffee notes on **NV** ⑧⓪ 'port' add to chewy black fruit, gritty, tarry texture & pleasing soft tannins. From tinta & splash pontac. — CM

Location/map: Villiersdorp ▪ Map grid reference: C1 ▪ WO: Western Cape/Cape South Coast ▪ Est 1922 ▪ 1stB 1974 ▪ Tasting & sales Mon-Fri 8–5 Sat 9-1 ▪ Fee R10 for groups of 7+ ▪ Closed Easter Fri-Mon & Dec 25/26 ▪ Cellar tours by appt ▪ Kelkiewyn Restaurant ▪ Farm produce ▪ Tractor museum open on request ▪ Owner(s) 40 growers ▪ Winemaker(s)/viticulturist(s) Christo Versfeld ▪ 300ha (merlot, chenin, sauv) ▪ 3,600t/19,000cs own label 30% red 30% white 30% rosé 10% fortified ▪ IPW ▪ PO Box 151 Villiersdorp 6848 ▪ cellaradmin@ villiersdorpcellar.co.za ▪ www.villiersdorpcellar.co.za ▪ S 33° 59' 11.2" E 019° 17' 48.5" ▪ ⬚ custard.crackle. stretcher ▪ F +27 (0)28-840-0957 ▪ **T +27 (0)28-840-0083**

Villion Family Wines

Kobie Viljoen had more than 20 years' winemaking experience before deciding to go solo (with wife Elnette) in 2015 under a banner recalling ancestor Francois Villion, a Huguenot who settled in the Cape in 1671. Selecting fruit from the Cape South Coast region, his focus is on eco-friendly and traditional methods (native/open-top ferments, inter alia) in the cellar. Commercial and critical success means the Viljoens are 'ready to take the next step' - opening a tasting room on Barton farm near Bot River, where the cellar is.

★★★★☆ **Cabernet Sauvignon** ⑭ 🍇 Impressive **15** ㊛ a classic expression of variety: cassis, blueberry fruit interwoven with graphite, athletic tannins. Full body, with enlivening acidity, judicious 25% new oak adding chocolate & spice lift. WO Bot River.

★★★★ **Syrah** Supple, spicy & savoury **15** ★★★★ ㊄ mixes mostly Elgin syrah with 20% from Bot River, splashes grenache & viognier. Generous berry fruit, jasmine & black pepper accents. Also-tasted **16** ㊅ likewise mainly Elgin syrah (70%), dashes mourvèdre & viognier & some Bot River syrah. Similar vibrancy, violet & lavender perfume but meatier & more defined, bigger tannic structure. Both mostly older oak.

★★★★ **Henning Chenin Blanc** From 30+ year old Bot River vines, wild ferment on skins. Retasted **16** ★★★★ ㊃ combo oak & tank portions with faint apple & honey whiffs, wet wool & quince farewell. **17** ㊆, 100% oaked, more generous & complex, with layered peach, nectarine, quince, vanilla & cream. Benefits, too, from better sugar/total acid balance.

Blanc de l'Atlantique 🍃 ★★★★ Viognier (68%), chardonnay (22%) & skin-fermented chenin in harmony in lightly oaked **16** ㊃. Retasted, exuberant white peach, lemon & nectarine supported by delicate oak-derived vanilla.

Pinot Noir ★★★ Strawberry, redcurrant, spice & dust on revisited **15** ㊘ from Bot River, Overberg & Elgin fruit. Gentle oak tannin grip from mainly older barrels, earthy farewell. **Chardonnay** ★★★★ French-oak-matured & revisited **16** ㊃'s rich & evolved caramelised stonefruit & marmalade lifted by Elgin's bracing acidity; pure citrus from unwooded portion. Medium body, with elegant 13.3% alcohol. — GM

Location: Bot River ▪ Map: Walker Bay & Bot River ▪ Map grid reference: B2 ▪ WO: Cape South Coast/Bot River/Elgin ▪ Est 2015 ▪ 1stB 2012 ▪ Tasting Mon-Fri 9-5 Sat 10-4 ▪ Owner(s)/winemaker(s) Kobie Viljoen ▪ 15t/3,000cs own label 48% red 52% white ▪ R43/Hermanus Rd Bot River 7185 ▪ elnette@villionwines.com, kobie@villionwines.com ▪ www.villionwines.com ▪ S 34° 15' 43.8" E 019° 10' 29.2" ▪ **T +27 (0)28-284-9248**

☐ **Vinay** see Slanghoek Winery

VinGlo Wines

VinGlo selects, produces, blends and exports its own wines as well as bespoke labels for clients to China, Ghana, Madagascar, Nigeria and the US, in partnership with winemakers from the leading production areas. At press time, a public tasting venue at Simondium Guild Business Park, accessible via the Franschhoek Wine Tram, was set to open.

8th Wonder range

Lively Grove Pinotage ⓥ ★★★ Intense berry bouquet dusted with oak vanilla, **11** ㊑ supple & fruit-filled, so could be broached now but possibly better in year/2 once oak tannins knit. **Silver Tree Red** ⓥ ★★★ Merlot & cab franc (49/38) dominate Bordeaux red **13** ㊑, labelled 'Meritage' in Californian tradition. Homely & easygoing, plum fruit, malleable tannin from 4 years older oak, mainly French, smidgen American. Not tasted: **Cape Cauldron**, **Silver Tree Reserve**, **Good Hope Chardonnay**.

Amy range

Not tasted: **Merlot**, **Sauvignon Blanc**. — TJ, CvZ

Location: Simondium ▪ WO: Stellenbosch ▪ Est/1stB 2012 ▪ Tasting by appt ▪ Winemaker(s) Therese de Beer (2012) ▪ 7-10t/ha ▪ 8,000cs own label 80% red 20% white ▪ 50 Esme Rd Newlands Cape Town 7700 ▪ grant@vinglo.co.za ▪ www.vinglowines.co.za ▪ F +27 (0)86-548-3343 ▪ **T +27 (0)21-671-7905**

Vinimark

The largest independent wine-specialist company in SA, distributing and marketing more than 50 well-known brands, including wholly owned ones, many listed in these pages.

Location: Stellenbosch ▪ Closed to public ▪ Directors Gys Naudé, Cindy Jordaan, Geoff Harvey, Eckhardt Gerber, Rudiger Gretschel & Guy Pause ▪ Exports: Geoff Harvey ▪ PO Box 441 Stellenbosch 7599 ▪ geoff@vinimark.co.za ▪ www.vinimark.co.za ▪ F +27 (0)21-886-4708 ▪ **T +27 (0)21-883-8043/4**

☐ **Vinography** see Benguela Cove Lagoon Wine Estate
☐ **Vinoneers** see The Vinoneers
☐ **Vino Pronto** see Hirst Wines
☐ **Vino Sacci** see Klawer Wine Cellars
☐ **Vins de Balise** see La Couronne Wines

Vintales Wines International ⓠ ⓟ

It's been a busy year for Paarl-based Anneli Karsten, marketing director and co-owner (with a large SA winery) of this lifestyle brand. She's added two sparkling wines to the portfolio, and opened markets in the Maldives, Lithuania and Uganda. The year ahead puts the United Kingdom in her sights and; with competition success in her quiver, she's aiming at local market expansion too.

Crowded Café Cabernet Sauvignon ★★ With some chocolate & cassis, few grams sugar & light tannin, **17** (73) slips down effortlessly. **Road Trip Pinotage** ★★ Mulberries & cream flavours, hint of baking spice, **17** (75) is like dessert in a glass. **Last Call Shiraz** ★★ Smoke & char notes, fresh & fruity flavours plumped out by few grams sugar in **17** (75). **Sunset Rosé** ★★ Gently sweet **18** (76) pink, packed with cherry fruit to get the party started. **Serenade Chardonnay** ★★ Offers sherbet & Lemon Cream tones, but unwooded **18** (73) waves goodbye all too soon. **Lazy Days Chenin Blanc** ★★ Demure **18** (74), faint gooseberry appeal, suggestion of vinosity & sweetness. **Sea Breeze Sauvignon Blanc** ★★ Water-white **18** (75), understated grass & gooseberry, feisty acidity to partner creamy food. **Espontaneo Sparkling Sweet Rosé** ★★ Plenty of racy bubbles in pink **NV** (75) fizz with red-boiled-sweet character, dab sugar for drinkability. **Espontaneo Sparkling Brut** (NEW) ★ Dry **NV** (67) sparkler is smooth & vinous, with quickly dissipating bubbles. **Espontaneo Sparkling Moscato** (NEW) ★★ Gets vinosity from 12.5% alcohol, aside from which latest softly dry **NV** (73) is all grapey charm & zingy bubbles to chill well before serving. **Bloomin' Late Moscato** ★★ Engaging spice nuance on **18** (76)'s grapey nose & palate; to enjoy well-chilled. **Sugar & Spice Natural Sweet Red** ★★ Forthright red berries & spice, sweetness curbed by nudge tannin, lowish 11% alcohol on **NV** (75) casual sipper. **Best Of Both Natural Sweet Rosé** ★★ Appealing sunset hue, sweet berries & cherries on **NV** (74) carefree quaffer. **Head Over Heels Natural Sweet White** ★☆ Full-sweet **NV** (72) grape juice for adults. — CvZ

Location: Paarl ▪ WO: Western Cape ▪ Est 2012 ▪ 1stB 2015 ▪ Tasting & tours/excursions by appt ▪ Sales via website or by appt ▪ Meals/refreshments by prior arrangement ▪ Owner(s) 2 shareholders ▪ WIETA ▪ 13 Constantia Str Paarl 7646 ▪ story@vintaleswine.com, anneli@vintaleswine.com ▪ www.vintaleswine.com ▪ **T +27 (0)82-783-9935**

☐ **Vinum Africa** see Radford Dale
☐ **Vinyl Collection** see Rascallion Wines

Virgin Earth

Just a tiny proportion of Kobus du Plessis's vast property in the rugged, remote and beautiful foothills of the Langeberg range is planted to vines – entitled to take the name of the Langeberg-Garcia ward. They were planted on virgin soils (whence the name) and always farmed organically. No wines tasted this edition, but winemaker consultant Nico Vermeulen promises new vintages for next year.

★★★★☆ **Kobus du Plessis Chardonnay** Resonates cool-climate elegance from the first fresh citrus sniffs to the lingering green-tinged succulence of the finish, **14** ⑨③ not lacking flavour & intensity in the harmonious balance, oak influences well absorbed. WO W Cape.

Pinot Noir ② ★★★☆ Light-footed, savoury **13** ⑧⑤ shows lovely fruit/oak balance. Cherry, plum flavours in a charming body. Wallet friendly for a pinot. Not tasted: **Cabernet Franc**, **Lost Barrel Shiraz**, **High 5**, **Shiraz-Viognier**, **Chenin Blanc**, **Pepper Tree Sauvignon Blanc**, **Succulent**, **Sauvignon Blanc-Semillon**, **Viognier MCC**. Occasional release: **Noble Late Harvest**. — TJ

Location: Riversdale ▪ WO: Philadelphia/Western Cape ▪ Est 2002 ▪ 1stB 2003 ▪ Closed to public ▪ Owner(s) Kobus du Plessis ▪ Winemaker(s) Kobus du Plessis & Nico Vermeulen (Jan 2018, consultant) ▪ Viticulturist(s) Hendrik Otto (2004) ▪ 13,000ha/25ha (cabs s/f, merlot, p verdot, pinot, shiraz, chard, chenin, sauv, sem, verdelho, viog) ▪ 8,000cs own label 40% red 60% white ▪ IPW, organic in conversion, WIETA ▪ PO Box 701 Riversdale 6670 ▪ info@virginearthwine.co.za ▪ www.virginearthwine.co.za ▪ **T +27 (0)78-099-1111**

Viva Africa Wines

Walter Bader was literally born into the wine industry — at Koopmanskloof, where his winemaker father, Walter Bader Snr, worked before moving to Riebeek Cellars. In 1998 Walter Jnr founded Viva Africa Wines, which is jointly owned with brother John and now introduces its own label. The range of easy-drinking wines, made for affordable enjoyment, has women as a 'target market', says Walter. He hopes to have a fully fledged wine estate in the near future.

Bader & Walters range

Cabernet Sauvignon ★★★ Fresh & fruity **16** ⑧⓪ doesn't have a strong cab character, gentle blackcurrants & plums, but enough curves & grip for uncomplicated early enjoyment solo or with food. **Pinotage** ★★★ Appealing varietal aromas of plums, mulberries & banana; zesty acidity, juicy tannins a hidden strength; **16** ⑧② ticks all the year-round drinking boxes. **Shiraz** ★★★ Red fruits & subtle spice, **15** ⑦⑧ lightly oaked, like red siblings, smooth textured to slip down easily. **Shiraz Rosé** ★★ Lightish 13% alcohol, smoothing few grams sugar in the tail, **17** ⑦④ deep pink poolside sipper. **Sauvignon Blanc** ★★★ Trim-figured (13% alcohol) **17** ⑦⑧ is understated, with grassy, nettly tones & sauvignon's racy acidity. — CR, CvZ

Location: Moorreesburg ▪ WO: Western Cape ▪ Est 1998 ▪ 1stB 2017 ▪ Closed to public ▪ Owner(s) Viva Africa Wines cc (members: Walter Bader, John Bader) ▪ Cellarmaster(s) Walter Bader ▪ Winemaker(s)/viticulturist(s) Johan Joubert (consultant) ▪ 100,000 L own label 60% red 25% white 15% rosé + 2,000cs for clients ▪ PO Box 548 Moorreesburg 7310 ▪ admin@vivaafricawine.co.za, walter@bwine.co.za ▪ www.bwines.co.za ▪ F +27 (0)22-433-3058 ▪ **T +27 (0)22-433-3050**

☐ **Voetspore** *see* Arendskloof-New Cape Wines

Vondeling

Conservation is one of the important focuses at Vondeling farm in Voor Paardeberg, richly endowed in botanical species, so it's no surprise that the team are very proud of their WWF-SA Conservation Champion status. Sustainability informs both viticultural and winemaking practices, and management of the extensive area of fynbos. Further 'green' investment in solar technology has enabled them to work 'off the grid' during daylight hours for most of the year. Vondeling was the first in SA to produce a certified méthode ancestrale sparkling, and winemaker Matthew Copeland is particularly upbeat about mastering more of the intricate techniques involved and increasing production for Vondeling to become the leading local maker of this style.

Flagship Wines

★★★★☆ **Monsonia** Shiraz-led Rhône blend was 'Erica', now recognises different rare fynbos species on home-farm. **15** ⑨⓪ savoury tobacco & spice, restrained & tightly woven in fine vintage. Balanced, with development potential & track record to grow into rating.

★★★★☆ **Babiana** Bunch-pressed, naturally fermented chenin, with part tank/oak-fermented viognier, roussanne & grenache blanc. **17** ⑨⓪ gently scented bouquet of tropical fruit, spice & citrus on creamy substrate. Well-integrated & flavoursome, though touch less intense than **16** ⑨②.

★★★★☆ **Sweet Carolyn** Vine-dried white muscat de Frontignan, unoaked, wholeberry fermented on skins to enhance alluring varietal flavours. Zesty, fresh citrus ensures balance, uncloying despite decadent 203 grams sugar. Welcomely light 10.5% alcohol. **17** ㉒ stylish dessert though shade off **16** ㉔. 500 ml.

Limited Releases

★★★★☆ **Bowwood Pinotage** Best 5 barrels from single block yield deep core of concentrated, spice-laden (clove & coconut) fruit. **15** ★★★★ ㊾'s all-American oak (2nd fill) centre stage mid-2018, masking more of fruit than **14** ㉒. Needs time to reveal the beauty within.

★★★★☆ **Philosophie** ⊛ Low yields, careful barrel selection & fine **15** ㉔ vintage align in rich, concentrated cab-led Bordeaux blend. Seamless & polished, with fine dry tannins, 100% French oak in sync with fruit intensity. Like **14** ㉓, deserves ageing.

★★★★ **Rurale** Yeast, brioche & apple flavours, richness from riper-picked chardonnay but no sugar added in **15** ㉙ creamy méthode ancestrale sparkling (28 months sur lie), with a fresh citrus thread.

Rurale Blanc de Noir ⊗ ★★★★ Rosé méthode ancestrale bubbly from organically grown pinotage, **15** ㉔ lovely sunrise orange hue, fine mousse, dry & savoury, delicate cranberry hint & creaminess.

Vondeling range

★★★★ **Cabernet Sauvignon** From some of highest, most temperate vineyards, **16** ㉘ exudes cassis & cedar, with fine dry tannins. Riper than **15** ㉗ but retains freshness & balance, palate weight & dry finish add gravitas.

★★★★ **Baldrick Shiraz** ⊘ Spice, white pepper, floral & plummy tones on **17** ㊱, 100% shiraz (no mourvèdre). Supple tannins, (older) oak secondary, bright fruit is the star, finishes respectably dry. More earnest intent than **16** ★★★★ ㉔.

★★★★ **Chardonnay** Bunch pressed, naturally fermented & oak matured, attractive spice, ginger & spring blossom flavours, deft wooding. **17** ㉙ succulent, fresh & well-crafted tablemate. **16** untasted.

Sauvignon Blanc ★★★★ Stonefruit & some tropical nuances, **18** ㊳ creamy undertone from 4 months on lees, fresh but plump & rounded, good food partner, now unoaked.

Lifestyle range
. . . .

Petit Rouge ⊘ ⊛ ★★★★ Bright as a button, with berry & cherry flavours, supple & juicy, raring to entertain solo or with meaty meals. **18** ㉔ 100% merlot, still pocket friendly.
. . . .

Rosé ★★★ Mostly merlot, **18** ㉗ fresh berries & rosepetals, dry, easy to drink with some fatness from lees contact. **Petit Blanc** ★★★ From old chenin on granite slopes, **18** ㉗ gentle, ripe Golden Delicious apple flavour, fresh, balanced if understated. — MW

Location/map: Paarl ▪ Map grid reference: C1 ▪ WO: Voor Paardeberg ▪ Est 2001 ▪ 1stB 2005 ▪ Tasting & sales Mon–Fri 10–5 Sat/pub hols by appt ▪ Wedding/function/conference venue ▪ St Clement's Chapel ▪ Owner(s) Richard Gower, Julian Johnsen & Anthony Ward ▪ Winemaker(s) Matthew Copeland (Jul 2007), with Emile van der Merwe (Dec 2011) ▪ Viticulturist(s) Magnus Joubert (Jul 2012) ▪ 100ha (cabs s/f, carignan, grenache r/w, malbec, merlot, mourv, p verdot, shiraz, chard, chenin, muscat de F, sauv, viog) ▪ 900t/100,000cs own label 40% red 40% white 20% rosé ▪ Other export brand: Signal Cannon ▪ WWF-SA Conservation Champion ▪ PO Box 57 Wellington 7654 ▪ admin@vondelingwines.co.za ▪ www.vondelingwines.co.za ▪ S 33° 35'22.50" E 018° 52'45.00" ▪ ⌨ closest.each.cruised ▪ F +27 (0)21-869-8219 ▪ **T +27 (0)21-869-8595**

☐ **Voyageur** see Thor Vintners

Vrede en Lust Wine Farm   ⊗ ⊗ ⌂ ⊚ ⊗ ♿

The Buys family continues refreshing its home-farm and ancillary properties. Joining the team's vine and visitor-friendly mix are more cabernet and chardonnay plantings (here and in Elgin, now with its own viticulturist), children's play area and a weekly fun run.

Location: Paarl ▪ Map: Franschhoek ▪ Map grid reference: B7 ▪ Est 1688 ▪ 1stB 2002 ▪ Tasting & sales daily 10–5 ▪ Closed Good Fri & Dec 25 ▪ Tours 10–4 by appt ▪ Lust Bistro & Bakery ▪ Guest accommodation in deluxe suites & manor house ▪ Tour groups by appt ▪ Conferences, functions & weddings ▪ Play area for children ▪ Pétanque courts ▪ Run2Wine (5km fun run) ▪ Owner(s) Buys family ▪ Cellarmaster(s) Karlin Nel (Sep 2017) ▪ Winemaker(s) Karlin Nel (Sep 2017), with Duan Engelbrecht (May 2017) ▪ Viticulturist(s) Etienne Buys (Jun 1998) & Annette

Davel (Oct 2017, Casey's Ridge) ▪ 275ha total ▪ Vrede en Lust: 66ha (cab, grenache, malbec, merlot, p verdot, shiraz, chard, viog); Casey's Ridge, Elgin: 88.9ha (cabs s/f, merlot, shiraz, chard, chenin, pinots g/n, riesling, sauv, sem, viog); Ricton: 127ha (cab, cinsaut, ptage, shiraz, chard) ▪ 800t/45,000cs own label ▪ WIETA ▪ PO Box 171 Groot Drakenstein 7680 ▪ info@vnl.co.za ▪ www.vnl.co.za ▪ S 33° 50' 15.9" E 018° 57' 13.4" ▪ �⌉ houseplant. dedicating.reached ▪ F +27 (0)21-874-1859 ▪ **T +27 (0)21-874-1611**

Vredenheim Wines ⓆⓀⓎⓐⓔⓕ

Family-owned Vredenheim estate in Stellenbosch is recognised and frequented for its smorgasbord of visitor amenities. Matriarch and 'gracious lady' Rikie Bezuidenhout and late husband 'M'Lord' Coen moved here from a KwaZulu-Natal game farm in 1986, hence the large antelope enclosure and popular Big Cats Park. To note, however, the Jaguars for hire are of the four-wheeled sort.

Pinotage ⓥ ★★★ Only older oak used here - to good effect, allows the wild berries to run riot on nose & palate, also adds savoury touch at the end. **17** ⑧⓪ juicy & food friendly.

Cabernet Sauvignon ★★★★ Dark chocolate & blackcurrant mingle with dusty, firm but not harsh tannins, **16** ⑧③'s fruit well-balanced with the oak (30% new French, 22 months). **Merlot** ★★★ Improved **15** ⑧⓪ has more presence but remains easy to drink thanks to soft, plump plums & spice sprinkle from 25% new oak. **Shiraz** Ⓩ ★★★★ Somewhat old-style but satisfying, well executed. **14** ⑧③ meat & leather, fruit plushness reined in by firm tannins, savoury finish. **Gracious Lady** Ⓩ ★★★★ Vanilla-toned **15** ⑧④ flagship is unshowy & elegant, ready now. Cab & merlot's dusty plum/tobacco notes, shiraz's red fruit & malleable tannins. **Rosé** ★★★ Off-dry NV ⑦⑨ pink from sauvignon & splash cab, gentle, with wafts of dried flowers & crushed herbs. **Sauvignon Blanc** ★★ Somewhat less companionable than last, **17** ⑦⑤ is lean, with green/grassy flavours & assertive zingy farewell. **Vredenvonkel** ★★★ Was 'Sparkling Wine Off-Dry', & still is - shows appealing touch of sweetness & suggestion of pink hue. **NV** ⑦⑨ from sauvignon & cab. In abeyance: **M'Lord Chardonnay**. — WB

Location/map/WO: Stellenbosch ▪ Map grid reference: D6 ▪ Tasting & sales Mon-Sat 9-4.30 ▪ Closed Good Fri & Dec 25 ▪ Restaurant Barrique T +27 (0)21-881-3001 ▪ Hudson's Coffee Shop T +27 (0)21-881-3590 ▪ Conferences/functions ▪ Vredenheim Angus Stud ▪ Big Cats Park ▪ Jaguar cars for hire ▪ Curio shop ▪ Guesthouse ▪ Craft beer brewery & gin distillery: tasting Tue-Sun 10-5 ▪ Owner(s) Bezuidenhout family ▪ Winemaker(s) Kowie du Toit ▪ Viticulturist(s) Kalie Kirsten ▪ 80ha under vine ▪ 20,000cs own label 60% red 40% white ▪ PO Box 369 Stellenbosch 7599 ▪ wine@vredenheim.co.za ▪ www.vredenheim.co.za ▪ S 33° 57' 38.2" E 018° 48' 29.4" ▪ ⌉⌉ premiums.widgets.cover ▪ F +27 (0)21-881-3296 ▪ **T +27 (0)21-881-3637**

Vriesenhof Vineyards Ⓠ

'If the grapes feel at home in the land, they will tell the story the land has written with a clear voice.' Manager Eddie Smit speaks for all at Vriesenhof, not least vintner Jan 'Boland' Coetzee, who bought this Stellenbosch Mountain land almost 40 years ago (while at Kanonkop). He's explored it ever since, establishing a home for himself and his classic Bordeaux red blend components, beloved Burgundian chardonnay and pinot, 'proudly SA' pinotage and, more recently, grenache, opening a fresh path to explore, along with winemaker Nicky Claasens, who's been part of the journey for more than a quarter of those 40 years.

★★★★ **Grenache** Juicy rush of red berries on barrel sample **17** ⑧⑦, with gentle tannin texture. Fragrant floral & spicy aromatic notes, sweetly focused finish. Piekenierskloof vines. Limited quantities also in magnum, as next 2. **16** untasted.

★★★★ **Pinot Noir** Muted raspberry fruit & perfume on previewed **16** ★★★★ ⑧⑤, still showing primary barrel influence. Tad off fine **15** ⑧⑧ though nicely rounded body, fresh acid & tannins should knit with time.

★★★★ **Kallista** Darkly serious **15** ⑧⑨ cab, merlot, cab franc blend, pre-bottling has richly ripe black fruit, forest floor earthiness & tarry/meaty centre. Dense & full bodied, with tannins to match. Should reward cellaring. No **14**.

★★★★ **Chardonnay** Heavy oak (40% new) prevails over **16** ★★★★ ⑧④, cloaking solid citrus fruit with nutty nuances. Big bodied, spicy & robust, less balanced than **15** ⑧⑦.

Pinotage Ⓩ ★★★★ Typical varietal 'wild' aromas on **16** ⑧⑤, convincing mulberry-bramble fruit. Full & ripe, with pleasant tannin grip. **Grenache-Shiraz-Mourvèdre** Ⓩ ★★★★ Appealing Rhône blend, **16** ⑧④ abundant red berry fruit, medium-light body well rounded from year in older barrels. **Ongehoute**

Chardonnay ⓧ ★★★ Unoaked **16** light bodied, fresh & lean, tending towards mineral, with candied fruit. Also-tasted **17** ⑧ fresher, with appealing lemon notes. Not tasted: **Cabernet Sauvignon**. — GdB

Location/map: Stellenbosch ▪ Map grid reference: F7 ▪ WO: Stellenbosch/Piekenierskloof ▪ Est 1980 ▪ 1stB 1981 ▪ Tasting & sales Mon-Thu 10–4 Fri 10–3.30 Sat by appt ▪ Fee R25 ▪ Closed all pub hols ▪ Cellar tours by appt ▪ Owner(s) Landgoed Vriesenhof (Pty) Ltd ▪ Cellarmaster(s) Jan Coetzee ▪ Winemaker(s) Nicky Claasens (2008), with Richard Phillips (2001) ▪ 60ha/45ha (cabs s/f, grenache, merlot, ptage, pinot, chard) ▪ 300t 90% red 10% white ▪ PO Box 155 Stellenbosch 7599 ▪ info@vriesenhof.co.za ▪ www.vriesenhof.co.za ▪ S 33° 58'16.7" E 018° 52'2.8" ▪ ⬚ manager.ports.cactus ▪ F +27 (0)21-880-1503 ▪ **T +27 (0)21-880-0284**

☐ **Vry Burger** *see* Group CDV
☐ **King Vusani** *see* House of Mandela

Vuurberg ⓠ

The character of the wines made off this small Banhoek estate has changed substantially since the early days after it was bought by Netherlander Sebastiaan Klaassen (he was seduced by beautiful Stellenbosch while visiting the Cape on a kite-surfing holiday in 2000). Donovan Rall, who also has his own 'new wave' label and makes wine for nearby Clouds, has been here since 2010 and has more recently shifted the wine-making approach 'by decreasing the new oak component, working with bigger oak vessels, and replacing the merlot component in the Red with cinsault.'

★★★★★ **Reserve Red** ⓐ Radical blend shift in **15** ⑨. Petit verdot was largest variety, now 25% with 62% cab. These give much of the ripe flavour & big tannic structure, but 13% Swartland cinsaut adds vital perfume & lightness. Only older oak. 15.5% alcohol not warming, but adds some sweetness. Approachable, but really needs few years.

★★★★☆ **White** Blends 6 varieties (chenin in the lead) from 3 regions. Wholebunch, natural ferment & maturation in old oak. **17** ⑨ rich & ripe, packed with a range of flavours. Reasonable acidity, but 4 g/l sugar adds obvious charm & sweetness as well as enhancing the velvet texture.— TJ

Location/map: Stellenbosch ▪ Map grid reference: H4 ▪ WO: Coastal/Western Cape ▪ Tasting, sales & cellar tours by appt ▪ Closed all pub hols ▪ Owner(s) Sebastiaan Klaassen ▪ Cellarmaster(s) Donovan Rall ▪ Winemaker(s) Donovan Rall (Oct 2010) ▪ 8ha (cabs s/f, malbec, merlot, p verdot, chenin, viog) ▪ 2,000cs own label 50% red 50% white ▪ PO Box 449 Stellenbosch 7599 ▪ info@vuurberg.com ▪ www.vuurberg.com ▪ S 33° 54'28.9" E 018° 56'52.7" ▪ ⬚ princes.projects.defender ▪ **T +27 (0)72-182-7571**

☐ **Vuurgloed** *see* Viljoensdrift Fine Wines & Cruises

Waboomsrivier Winery ⓠ

'Fresh and fruity, that's our mission,' says Bennie Wannenburg, long the cellarmaster at modern, mostly bulk-wine-producing, grower-owned Waboomsrivier in northern Breedekloof, between Worcester and Ceres. Beside vines and wine, trees are a thing here: the traditionally preferred wood for wagon wheel production gives the winery its name, and one of the popular own-labels is a Cape Blend named Arborea.

Wagenboom range

Chenin Blanc ⓧ ⓣ ★★★ Pear & guava fruit abound in fragrant **18** ⑧, nicely rounded for everyday appeal, with fresh acidity & a dry finish.

Shiraz-Pinotage ⓝⓔⓦ ★★★ Dark berries, slightly caramelised, in juicy 50/50 NV ⑦ blend. **Sauvignon Blanc** ⓧ ★★★ A steal with its granadilla & green apple tang, **18** ⑦ just 11.5% alcohol. **Hanepoot** ⓧ ★★★☆ Well-handled, freshening spirit gives **13** ⑧ fortified dessert extra warmth & charm, lifts its tropical pineapple & papaya flavours. **Cape Vintage** ⓧ ★★★ More Ruby than Vintage 'port' in style, with fairly low alcohol, highish sugar, yet **14** ⑧ very drinkable, like all under this wallet-friendly label. Attractive Xmas cake & tangerine nuances. Not tasted: **Pinotage**, **Arborea**. — JG

Location: Worcester ▪ Map/WO: Breedekloof ▪ Map grid reference: A3 ▪ Est 1949 ▪ Tasting & sales Mon-Fri 8-5 ▪ Closed all pub hols ▪ Cellar tours by appt during harvest ▪ Cellarmaster(s) Bennie Wannenburg (Sep 2005) ▪ Winemaker(s) Charl Myburgh (Oct 2016), with Lara Prins (Nov 2016) ▪ Viticulturist(s) Pierre Snyman (VinPro) ▪ ±998.90ha ▪ 16,340t ▪ ISO 22000:2011 ▪ PO Box 24 Breërivier 6858 ▪ sales@waboms.co.za ▪ www.

waboomsrivier.com ▪ S 33° 31′ 43.08″ E 019° 12′ 35.24″ ▪ ⌨ catalytic.shimmy.pizzerias ▪ F +27 (0)23-355-1731 ▪ **T +27 (0)23-355-1730**

Wade Bales Fine Wines & Spirits ⓠ

Long-established, Constantia-based Wade Bales is a specialist merchant sourcing fine-wine from producers and selling directly to private clients. Wade is also a negociant, bottling and marketing exclusive and limited-release wines under his Reserve, Bales Choice and Wade Bales Winemaker Selection labels.

Location: Constantia ▪ Map: Cape Peninsula ▪ Map grid reference: B3 ▪ Est 1992 ▪ Tasting & sales Mon-Fri 8.30-5 ▪ Closed all pub hols ▪ Owner(s) Wade Bales ▪ 10,000c own label ▪ Private Bag X2 Constantia 7848 ▪ info@wadebales.co.za ▪ www.wadebales.co.za ▪ S 34° 2′ 5.43″ E018° 25′ 32.98″ ▪ ⌨ reposed.unpaged. picnicked ▪ F +27 (0)21-794-2821 ▪ **T +27 (0)21-794-2151**

☐ **Wade Bales Winemaker Selection** *see* Wade Bales Fine Wines & Spirits

☐ **Wagenboom** *see* Waboomsrivier Winery

☐ **Waghuis** *see* Org de Rac

Walker Bay Estate ⓠ ⓘ ⓞ ⓐ ⓖ

Recent appointee Marinda Kruger brings considerable knowledge and experience to this small winery outside Stanford, now registered as a 'unit for the production of estate wine' (and the established home of Birkenhead Brewery). Marinda is a PhD student, specialising in fermentation, and has worked in various cellars locally and overseas (latterly for Boutinot SA). Her focus is now on fine-tuning the 24 hectares of vines and realising the potential of the cool-location farm, just 9 km from the sea.

★★★★ **Cabernet Sauvignon** ⊘ Smoky cassis, chocolate flavours & supple tannins on **16** ⑧⑦ ensure satisfying drinkability. Fresh, creamy texture & long fruit-laden finish. Trumps last-tasted **11**★★★ ⑦⑧.

★★★★ **Barrel Fermented Sauvignon Blanc** ⒩ Natural ferment in 90% old oak adds creamy, rich dimension to tangy stonefruit flavours on **18** ⑧⑥ preview. Brief skin contact, as for Limestone version.

Merlot ★★★ Successful NV ⑧② blend of vintages, balanced, with smoky black cherry flavours & fresh finish. Ready to entertain. **Petit Verdot** ⒩ ★★★★ Appealing black cherry, blueberry seamed with supple chalky tannins. **16** ⑧④'s freshness & balance render 14.8% alcohol unobtrusive. **Shiraz** ⓠ ★★ Dark spice & a raisin note on **15** ⑦④. Softish, with sweet fruit, but finishes with grip of 15.3% alcohol. **Amesteca** ⓠ ★★★★ Bordeaux-style blend; merlot's sweet red-fruit fragrance/flesh in command on **15** ⑧③. Fresh acid, modicum grip allow good drinking now, further year/2. **Chardonnay** ★★ Lemony, lemony impression on **17** ⑦⑥. Dry, subtle oak in leaner style. **Limestone Sauvignon Blanc** ⒩ ★★★★ Limestone soils & part natural ferment impart minerality & mid-palate weight on pre-bottled **18** ⑧⑤. Juicy grapefruit nuance adds food-friendly appeal. Ex single block, as all the sauvignons. **Sauvignon Blanc** ★★★ Fresh herb & tropical flavours on **18** ⑧⓪ from sandy soils. Tank sample is attractive, easy drinking, improves on previous. Not tasted: **Rosé, Chardonnay Unoaked**. — MW

Location: Stanford ▪ Map: Walker Bay & Bot River ▪ Map grid reference: B6 ▪ WO: Walker Bay ▪ Est 1997 ▪ 1stB 2007 ▪ Tasting & sales Mon-Sat 10-5 Sun 11-4 ▪ Tasting fee applicable ▪ Closed Dec 25 ▪ Cellar tours by appt ▪ Restaurant ▪ Facilities for children ▪ Tour groups ▪ Craft beer brewery ▪ Winemaker(s)/viticulturist(s) Marinda Kruger (Oct 2017) ▪ 300ha/24ha (cab, merlot, p verdot, pinot, shiraz, chard, sauv, sem) ▪ 100t/14,000c own label 40% red 60% white ▪ PO Box 530 Stanford 7210 ▪ walkerbayvineyards@birkenhead.co.za ▪ www. walkerbayestate.com ▪ S 34° 26′ 30.5″ E 019° 27′ 40.5″ ▪ ⌨ compactly.pomegranates.unanswered ▪ F +27 (0)28-341-0196 ▪ **T +27 (0)28-341-0013**

Walking Woods Wines

Founded in 2004 as 'Re'Mogo' by a group of black entrepreneurs exploring business interests in wine, among other sectors, this now renamed and Pretoria-based venture is fronted by Thamsanqa Hombana, and sources wines mainly from Olifants River and latterly also Stellenbosch.

Location: Pretoria ▪ WO: Western Cape ▪ Est 2004, Trust est 2011 ▪ Sales Mon-Fri & pub hols 9-3 by appt only ▪ Online shop ▪ Owner(s) Simatule Trust ▪ Winemaker(s) Stellar Winery & Koopmanskloof Wingerde ▪ 50% red 50% white ▪ 1 Meiring Naude Rd Brummeria Pretoria 0184 ▪ woods.southafrica@gmail.com ▪ www. walkingwoods.co.za ▪ F +27 (0)86-610-7047 ▪ **T +27 (0)82-638-6774**

Warwick Estate

A new era began with the sale end 2017 of the Stellenbosch family farm where matriarch Norma Ratcliffe made the first Warwick wines in the early 1980s, to Charles Marston and Kishore Bopardikar of San Francisco investment company Eileses Capital. Next came the duo's acquisition of neighbouring Distell-owned Uitkyk (with its rare Cape Georgian homestead). Sharing an 18th-century history, the properties combine some 700 hectares of prime Simonsberg-Stellenbosch terroir under the Warwick brand name. Warwick viticulturists Ronald Spies and Marko Roux and Uitkyk's Rudi Buys are replanting some 170ha on Uitkyk and Warwick with cabernet, cabernet franc and merlot, recognising the area's suitability for classic Bordeaux varieties.

★★★★☆ **The Blue Lady** ⓐ Intricate & focused cabernet, **15** ★★★★★ ⑨⑤ a barrel selection with plethora of primary fruit, mainly dark berries, fusing well with graphite & cedarwood spice from 38% new oak. Solid tannins in support guarantee drinking pleasure for many years to come; like **14** ⑨①.

★★★★☆ **Cabernet Franc** ⓐ As statuesque as **14** ⑨③, **15** ⑨④ hangs taut tannins from a beam of pure, sleek blackcurrant fruit, has bright acidity, violet & dried thyme accents.

★★★★☆ **The Black Lady** ⓐ Single-site shiraz. Flamboyant **15** ⑨③'s solid tannin structure is well balanced, ends with plum & tapenade persistence. Lifts bar on softer, less structured **14** ★★★★ ⑧⑧.

★★★★ **Three Cape Ladies** ⊘ ⓐ Much-improved **15** ★★★★★ ⑨④ from Bordeaux varieties only, unlike **14** ⑧⑦'s Cape Blend cab, pinotage, shiraz. Opulent & multifaceted, showing authoritative tannins well matched with fruit & acidity. To keep 10+ years. WO Stellenbosch.

★★★★☆ **Trilogy** ⓐ Invariably excellent trio of red Bordeaux varieties; cab franc leading pack for first time in plush **15** ⑨④. Blackcurrant fruit nuanced by graphite minerality & wood spice ex 44% new oak. Supple & smooth, delicious now but will reward keeping decade+. Also in 1.5, 5 & 12L. WO Simonsberg-Stellenbosch, as Blue Lady, Cabernet Franc, Black Lady.

★★★★★ **The White Lady** ⓐ Vibrant & pure expression of chardonnay, focused by subtle oaking in classic **17** ⑨⑤. Apple, pear & nectarine fruit nuances interwoven with chamomile, honey & mineral notes. Natural ferment; 10 months 33% new oak. WO Stellenbosch.

★★★★★ **Professor Black** ⓐ Metamorphosis for this label: up to **15** ★★★★ ⑧⑤ unoaked sauvignon blanc as per original name, but **17** ⑨⑤ a (older) wooded Bordeaux blend sauvignon & semillon. Scented fig, lime & gooseberry notes, full bodied & slightly creamy with mouthwatering acidity. No 20167.

. . . .

The First Lady Cabernet Sauvignon ⓥ ★★★★ Redcurrant, cassis & cigarbox complexity on youthful **16** ⑧④. Noticeable tannin grip for meaty companions, dark-fruit handshake. Also in magnum.

. . . .

The First Lady Dry Rosé ★★★ Red berries accented by pomegranate, watermelon & rosepetal in **18** ⑧② from pinotage. Dry & zesty for everyday summer enjoyment. **The First Lady Chardonnay** ★★★★ Easygoing, likeable **18** ⑧④, lemon, melon & floral tones, zesty acidity & light texture. No oak but good palate weight & fresh citrus persistence. **The First Lady Sauvignon Blanc** ★★★★ Vibrant **18** ⑧③, with dash semillon, displays a peacock's tail of cool- & warm-climate fruits - citrus, kiwi & greengage, pineapple & papaya. Not tasted: **Méthode Cap Classique**. — GM

Location/map: Stellenbosch ▪ Map grid reference: F1 ▪ WO: Western Cape/Simonsberg–Stellenbosch/ Stellenbosch ▪ Est 1964 ▪ 1stB 1983 ▪ Tasting & sales daily 9–5 ▪ Cellar tours by appt ▪ 'Big 5' vineyard safari ▪ Gourmet picnics in summer; à la carte winter menu ▪ Facilities for children ▪ Gifts ▪ Conferences ▪ Weddings ▪ Owner(s) Charles Marston & Kishore Bopardikar ▪ CEO Christiane von Arnim ▪ Winemaker(s) Carami van der Merwe (Jun 2015) & Estelle Lourens (May 2018) ▪ Viticulturist(s) Ronald Spies (Nov 2001) & Rudi Buys (May 2018) ▪ 700ha/105ha (cabs s/f, merlot, chard, sauv) ▪ 1200t/46,380cs own label 60% red 40% white ▪ WIETA ▪ IPW ▪ ▪ PO Box 2 Elsenburg 7607 ▪ info@warwickwine.com ▪ www.warwickwine.com ▪ S 33° 50' 27" E 018° 51' 54.0" ▪ ▦ outdone.reader.graphics ▪ **T +27 (0)21-884-4410**

Waterford Estate

After this handsome estate in Stellenbosch's Blaauwklippen Valley was bought by Jeremy and Leigh Ord late last century, it was rejuvenated and developed with the crucial help of accomplished cellarmaster and business partner Kevin Arnold. Ten red grape varieties were established to add to the existing cabernet sauvignon, chardonnay and sauvignon blanc vineyards. The farm's diversity is well expressed in the flagship red blend, The Jem, while the Library Collection is a shifting collection of mostly experimental wines. The cellardoor experience extends beyond the Italianate buildings and courtyard to include a pre-booked vineyard safari wine-drive and guided wine-walk for tasting the single vineyard wines where they were born. A more recent estate development, olive oil production (for sale at cellardoor only), is being expanded.

Waterford Estate range

★★★★☆ **Cabernet Sauvignon** ⊛ Elegant & complex Stellenbosch cabernet with real poise. Rich, unfolding **15** ⑨ dark black fruit & spice with fynbos nuance, subtle & generously silky, dabs merlot, petit verdot & 2% cab franc adding to the layers. Receives house's wholeberry ferment, 18 months oak, 35% new. In magnum too, as next 3.

★★★★★ **The Jem** ⊛ Flagship from selection of estate's 11 black grapes - Italian, Spanish & French - most planted since 1999. Cab-led **14** ⑨⑤ is tall, dark & handsome; packed with juicy berry fruit & savoury spice, 32% new oak in harmonious support. Rich, lithe & deeply alluring, a wine for the long haul.

★★★★ **Single Vineyard Chardonnay** Peach kernel & lime intensity from 30+ year old vines; hot & dry **16** ⑧⑧ low in acid vigour but full in body. Like previous, pleasingly restrained oak (±20% new).

....

Rose-Mary ⑦ ★★★★ Salmon glints match the vibrant red-berry fruit in low-alcohol **18** ⑧⑤. Zesty & fun, but this bone-dry rosé is more serious than most.

....

Grenache Noir ★★★★ Characterful & individual **16** ⑧⑤ combines farmyard & game meat whiffs, cranberry fruit & tense tannins; old oak is unobtrusive; portion finished in porcelain jars. Discontinued: **Sauvignon Blanc**.

Library Collection

★★★★☆ **Cabernet Sauvignon** ⊛ Athletic, elegant, impressive **16** ⑨⓪, ex unusual block with 3 distinct soils - sandstone, granite & schist. Buffed 18 months in oak, 25% new, more structural/textural than fruit-driven, firm tannins shroud the berries for now.

★★★★☆ **Cabernet Franc** 🆕 ⊛ Idea is to bottle components of The Jem separately & eventually present them all alongside the blend. Hence the Cab above & this exceptional **15** ⑨③ ex single Helderberg block, classic pencil shavings, cigarbox & vibrant red fruit on textured, balanced tannic base. Wholeberry ferment, 18 months seasoned oak.

★★★★ **2BB** ⊛ Bordeaux blend centres on interplay between the 2 cabs (merlot, petit verdot also feature). Serious **12** ⑧⑦'s brambly fruit gripped by fine but authoritative tannins, sappy savoury tail.

★★★★☆ **Antique Chenin** 🆕 ⊛ From one-barrel 'solera' started 2002; each year half bottled, topped with wine of the harvest, so NV ⑨④ is irresistible combo of amazingly fresh melon fruit, touch oxidative oatmeal/butterscotch, extraordinary texture & resounding length of flavour. Great balance too. All of 118 bottles.

★★★★☆ **Chenin Blanc** 🆕 ⊕ 3 old Helderberg, Bottelary & Klipheuwel blocks. Seasoned oak & concrete 'egg' maturation adds limpid, oxidative oatmeal layers to ripe melon fruit; **17** ◯90 rich, round & delicious.

Edition: Riesling ⊘ ★★★★ Vibrant apple & lime curd on dry **13** ⑧⑤ from Elgin, fresh acidity & focus. Needs time to develop & show true potential. These are small parcels, some mature one-offs, reflecting ongoing experimentation with grape varieties, sites & styles. Earlier releases, not repeated here, may still be available; only from the cellardoor.

Waterford range

★★★★ **Elgin Pinot Noir** Expressive bright cherry fruit from 11 year old single block. Delicate, lacy tannin of **17** ⑧⑨ shows poise, but tad lean for higher rating. 100% wholeberry ferment, as next.

★★★★☆ **Kevin Arnold Shiraz** Subtitled 'Michael Ian', the Ords' only son, **14** ⑨① straddles flavour spectrum from peppery spice to earthy leather; deep, dark & concentrated fruit in velvety frame, dash mourvèdre adding panache. 20 months old oak. Also in 1.5, 3 & 5L.

★★★★ **Méthode Cap Classique Brut** ⊘ **09** ★★★★★ ⑨③ bubbly continues recent uptick; pure chardonnay remarkably long 7 years on lees, then year under cork. Rich brioche aromas & creamy gloss to surprisingly lively fruit. **07** ⑧⑦, equal chardonnay & pinot noir, improved on **06** ★★★★ ⑧④. No **08**.

★★★★ **Heatherleigh** Solera-aged Natural Sweet dessert of muscat d'Alexandrie with chardonnay, chenin & viognier. NV ⑧⑧ beautifully balanced; piquant marmalade, brûlée delicacy, dry-ish tail. WO W Cape. 375 ml.

Elgin Sauvignon Blanc ★★★★ Penetrating, pure-fruited lemongrass & nettle to **18** (85) tank sample, good body & length, lipsmacking tang in tail.

Pecan Stream range

Pebble Hill (Ⓥ) ★★★★ 'Mini Jem' - shiraz, mourvèdre, tempranillo, sangiovese & merlot made as if for flagship - punches way above its weight. **15** (85) has juicy, supple plum-fruit allure. WO W Cape, as all these.
Chenin Blanc (✓) (Ⓥ) ★★★★ Pre-bottling, **18** (85) refreshing tangy stonefruit, splashes oak-touched chardonnay & viognier adding to bright, juicy & unfussy appeal. Limited magnums.

Sauvignon Blanc ★★★ Plump passionfruit profile to full & satisfying **18** (81). — DS

Location/map: Stellenbosch ▪ Map grid reference: F8 ▪ WO: Stellenbosch/Western Cape/Elgin ▪ Est/1stB 1998 ▪ Tasting, sales & cellar tours Mon-Fri 9–5 Sat 10–5 ▪ Tasting fees: R80/portfolio; R85/chocolate; R115/Estate; R95/The Jem (current vintage only); R210/Library; R295/reserve; R450/wine walk & R1,150/wine drive, pre-booking essential ▪ Closed Good Fri, Dec 25 & Jan 1 ▪ Tea/coffee/soft drinks & chocolates ▪ Olive oil ▪ Owner(s) Jeremy & Leigh Ord; Kevin Arnold (partner) ▪ Cellarmaster(s) Kevin Arnold (1998) ▪ Winemaker(s) Mark le Roux (Jul 2009) ▪ Viticulturist(s) David van Schalkwyk (Jun 2014) ▪ 120ha/60ha (barbera, cabs s/f, grenache, malbec, merlot, mourv, p verdot, sangio, shiraz, tempranillo, chard) ▪ 550t/54,000cs own label 70% red 30% white ▪ 27.3ha conserved land ▪ WWF-SA Conservation Champion ▪ PO Box 635 Stellenbosch 7599 ▪ info@waterfordestate.co.za ▪ www.waterfordestate.co.za ▪ S 33° 59' 54.6" E 018° 52' 12.7" ▪ 🎥 shots. slipping.traffic ▪ F +27 (0)21-880-1007 ▪ **T +27 (0)21-880-5300**

Waterkloof   Ⓠ Ⓜ ⓐ ⓑ

Paul Boutinot's 150-ha estate, in a natural amphitheatre on Schapenberg Hill, has breathtaking views over False Bay. Since acquisition in 2003, Waterkloof has been radically transformed, with a world-class restaurant, WWF-SA Conservation Champion status and 60 ha of biodynamically farmed vineyards. Recent purchase of 20 ha of neighbouring land for future vines resulted in them having to forgo their official certification with Demeter. They remain unwavering in their commitment to farming biodynamically, however. There's a real sense of natural rhythms at work, all staff and creatures on the farm playing a part in the life cycle and contributing to the greater sustainable whole. Winemaker Nadia Barnard, however, has the benefit of an modern cellar, and celebrated her vinous successes as well as her marriage last year.

Waterkloof range

★★★★☆ **Sauvignon Blanc** (🐝) The flagship, biodynamically produced from two low-yield Schapenberg blocks. Barrel-vinified **17** (93) lovely depth & intensity, richly textured, creamy starfruit, nectarine flavours, some clean minerality too. Balanced freshness & length. This & all wines from Waterkloof undergo natural, slow ferments, lees ageing & are unfined.

Circle of Life range

★★★★ **Red** (✓) (🐝) **15** ★★★★★ (94) trumps **14** (88), with savoury, white pepper from syrah in leading role, merlot & petit verdot the structured support cast. Layers of flavour, lively dry tannins, rich, creamy texture, real depth & intensity. Bordeaux varieties destemmed, others bunch pressed, as all reds.
★★★★☆ **White** (🐝) Understated yet layered & complex **15** (94) is from co-fermented, oak-aged sauvignon & chenin (61/39). Stony minerality, lime & lanolin, almondy nuance & creamy lees undertone. Follows stellar **13** ★★★★★ (95); **14** untasted. Range named for journey to biodynamic farming.

Seriously Cool range

Cinsault (Ⓥ) ★★★★ Old (40+ years) Helderberg bushvines deliver gentle, clean, scented fynbos flavours. **17** (85) balanced & engaging meal mate or as label directs, to serve chilled & enjoy!

Chenin Blanc ★★★★ Aptly named **17** (84), cool stonefruit & apple flavours, smooth textured courtesy lees contact. Balanced for summer quaffing. Ex 30-40 year Helderberg & Stellenbosch bushvines, fermented in barrel and concrete 'egg'.

Circumstance range

★★★★ **Cabernet Sauvignon** (Ⓠ) Fuller bodied than other reds, but retains elegance & balance. **15** (89) showcases gentle fruit handling, as for all their grapes. Remarkably accessible, but will reward ageing.

★★★★☆ **Mourvèdre** Savoury dark fruit, with the most supple tannins of the Circumstance reds from foot treading of grapes. Good fruit intensity at lowish 12.5%. All elements in sync, **16** ★★★★ (89) just needs time, though shade off debut **15** (93).

★★★★☆ **Syrah** Appealing white pepper, clove & savouriness. Dry tannins, more supple than Cab Franc but less intensity & balance than **15** (93). Cellar time will allow **16** ★★★★ (87)'s fruit to shine.

★★★★ **Chardonnay** Lime & scented pear/starfruit from low-crop fruit, partly new-oak fermented, balance concrete 'eggs', hence **17** (86)'s lovely freshness, lightness, long tangy-creamy farewell. Pleasing 12% alcohol. Big improvement on **16** ★★★ (82).

★★★★ **Sauvignon Blanc** Different vineyards to flagship, 90% old-oak fermented & longer time on lees. **17** (89) yeasty, rich lime & piquant fruit, good length & freshness. Brighter than **16** (88).

★★★★ **Viognier** More elegant than last-tasted **15** (86), **17** (88) has graceful balance, more in sync with other whites even at 14% alcohol. Good typicity from low (2T) yield vines, creamy texture ex barrels/lees.

Cabernet Franc ★★★★ Scented herb & floral aromas/flavours restrained by very firm chalky tannins from smaller, tougher-skinned grapes. Like previous, **16** (85) slow evolving, needs time. **Merlot** ⓥ ★★★★ Firm tannins envelop tightly coiled dark fruit in **15** (84). Needs cellar time, unlike last-tasted **13** ★★★★ (87), which more velvety & flavoursome. **Cape Coral Mourvèdre Rosé** ⓥ ★★★ Dry, crisp & savoury, **17** (81) touch more alcohol (12.5%) but less serious intent & bright berry flavours than last. Good with a charcuterie platter. **Chenin Blanc** ★★★★ Understated, graceful & textural, more a fine-dining wine than Seriously sibling. Barrel-fermented **17** (85) gentle lemon & crunchy apple, some minerality from cool-grown bushvines, elegant 12% alcohol.

Astraeus range

★★★★ **Méthode Cap Classique Reserve Pinot Noir** Dry rosé sparkling from organically grown Elgin fruit. Smoky berry flavours, touch more sugar & fruitier than Chardonnay sibling but not as intense, notch below previous **NV** (87). Base wine oak-fermented & 18 months bottle matured.

★★★★☆ **Méthode Cap Classique Reserve Chardonnay Brut** Flinty apple & brioche with smoky undertone on **NV** (90) dry sparkler from organically grown Elgin grapes & dash 2009 reserve. Fine, under-stated, 2 years on lees vs 3 last time, thus not quite as rich; more elegant, nuanced than Pinot. — MW

Location: Somerset West ▪ Map: Helderberg ▪ Map grid reference: F6 ▪ WO: Stellenbosch/Elgin ▪ Est 2004 ▪ 1stB 2005 ▪ Tasting & sales daily 10-5 ▪ Fee: standard R40/6 wines, premium R50/6 wines ▪ Closed Dec 25 & Jan 1 ▪ Healey's cheese tasting ▪ Waterkloof platters R150 with selection of cheese, olives, meat terrine, gherkins, pickles, chutney & bread ▪ Cellar tours by appt ▪ The Restaurant at Waterkloof ▪ Walking/hiking/horse riding trails ▪ Conservation area ▪ Art collection on display ▪ Tutored horse riding & biodynamic walking tours with ploughman's platter & wine tasting ▪ Healey's Cheesery & Deli open Mon-Sat 10-5 Sun 10-2 ▪ Owner(s) Paul Boutinot ▪ Cellarmaster(s)/winemaker(s) Nadia Barnard (Jan 2013) ▪ Viticulturist(s) Christiaan Loots (Jan 2010) ▪ 149ha/61ha (cabs s/f, grenache, merlot, mourv, p verdot, shiraz, chard, chenin, sauv, sem, viog) ▪ 450t/20,000cs own label 50% red 45% white 5% rosé ▪ Ecocert organic, IPW, WIETA, WWF-SA Conservation Champion ▪ PO Box 2093 Somerset West 7129 ▪ info@waterkloofwines.co.za ▪ www.waterkloofwines.co.za ▪ S 34° 5' 55.4" E 018° 53' 22.8" ▪ ⎙ lush.wagers.slippers ▪ F +27 (0)21-858-1293 ▪ **T +27 (0)21-858-1292**

☐ **Waterlily** *see Bloemendal Wine Estate*

Waverley Hills Organic Wines & Olives   ⓥ ⑪ ◎ ⓑ ⓖ

Attractive new labels are being phased in at the certified-organic and WWF-SA Conservation Champion winery near Tulbagh, owned by the Du Toit family via their recycling company, Brenn-O-Kem. The new livery is fynbos-themed, cellarmaster Johan Delport says, 'to tell more of a story about the organic approach and environmental conservation initiatives on the farm, as well as the underlying scrub undertones of the wines'.

Premium range

★★★★ **Grenache** ⊘ Earthy & fragrant **17** (89) charms with lively red fruit, herbs & spice, smooth gentle tannins from year large older barrels. 10% wholebunch.

★★★★ **CW Reserve Shiraz** ⊘ Pre-bottling, **15** ★★★★★ ⑨⓪ steps up from **14** ⑧⑨, shows good promise & more elegance with aromas of dark berries, scrub & exotic spice. Palate meaty & full, fruit wrapping serious yet supple tannins & 100% new oak, 3 years.

★★★★ **De Huijsbosch** ⊘ Was 'Cabernet Sauvignon-Cabernet Franc-Merlot', **16** ⑧⑧ still from those varieties. Sweet fruit in a frame of dried herbs & spices. Succulent & mouthfilling pleasure. Coastal WO.

★★★★ **Shiraz-Mourvèdre-Viognier** ⊘ Perfumes of hedgerow fruit on **14** ⑧⑦ merging with blackcurrant, ripe cherries, hint of mocha, seductive spice - vibrant & fine structural balance, fresh, juicy finish.

★★★★ **Chardonnay** ⊘ ⊘ Apple blossom, citrus & orchard fruit aromas abound on **16** ⑧⑧. Harmonious & complex, a dash of co-fermented semillon giving breadth & depth. Textured, layered, superb oak management evident in smooth, long vanilla finish. Will age well. Tank sample **17** ★★★★☆ ⑨⓪ has drop viognier, needs time to meld & show true character.

Not tasted: **Méthode Cap Classique Brut**. Discontinued: **Viognier-Semillon-Chardonnay**.

Estate range

Shiraz ⊘ ★★★★ Previewed **17** ⑧④ sweet dark berries, energetic spice, dark chocolate & earthy tones leaping from glass. Touch mourvèdre adds complexity. Balanced. Long savoury finish. **Cabernet Sauvignon-Shiraz** ⊘ ★★★ Dark-fruited near-equal blend with appealing spiciness, **17** ⑧① mellow, juicy & gentle for everyday enjoyment. **Pinot Grigio** ⊘ ★★☆ Light floral wafts on easy **18** ⑦⑦, perky acid to finish. **Sauvignon Blanc-Semillon** ⊘ ★★★★ Unoaked **18** ⑧④ brims with bright orchard & tropical fruit, poised, succulent & harmonious. Perfect for flame-roast chicken. **Red Jerepigo** ⓧ ⊘ ★★★ Dessert from cab, fortified with organic in-house-distilled merlot. **NV** ⑧① grape & plum compote flavours, very sweet.

No Sulphites Added range

Cabernet Sauvignon ⊘ ★★★ Unoaked; vibrant red fruit & hint chocolate on **17** ⑦⑧ carefree everyday sipper. — WB

Location/map: Tulbagh ▪ Map grid reference: G6 ▪ WO: Tulbagh/Coastal ▪ Est 2006 ▪ 1stB 2004 ▪ Tasting, sales & cellar tours Mon-Sat 10-4 Sun 11-3 ▪ Closed Easter Fri/Mon & Dec 25 ▪ Restaurant Tue-Sat 10-4 Sun 11-3 & Wed/Fri evenings ▪ Picnic baskets by appt ▪ Facilities for children ▪ Tour groups ▪ Conferences ▪ Wedding venue & chapel ▪ Walks/hikes ▪ Conservation area ▪ Owner(s) Brenn-O-Kem (Pty) Ltd ▪ Cellarmaster(s) Johan Delport (Oct 2008) ▪ Winemaker(s) Eric Frieslaar (May 2017) ▪ Viticulturist(s) Johan Greeff (May 2012) ▪ 80ha/30ha (cab, grenache, merlot, mourv, ptage, shiraz, chard, pinot gris, sauv, sem, viog) ▪ 230t/20,000cs own label 80% red 15% white 5% MCC ▪ Cape Nature Stewardship, WIETA, WWF-SA Conservation Champion ▪ PO Box 71 Wolseley 6830 ▪ info@waverleyhills.co.za ▪ www.waverleyhills.co.za ▪ S 33° 24' 21.2" E 019° 14' 19.6" ▪ ⓜ nominally.innovating.humble ▪ F +27 (0)23-231-0004 ▪ **T +27 (0)23-231-0002**

Wavescape Wines

'Taste the Stoke' is the upbeat slogan of the joint-venture between Jeremy Walker of Grangehurst (who handles the wines at his Stellenbosch cellar) and fellow wave-rider and -reporter Steve Pike, aimed at creating 'vibrant blends of surfing and winemaking'. Sourced, of course, from Coastal vineyards.

Red Barrel ⓧ ★★★★ Balanced, ready **09** ⑧⑤, cab-shiraz & drop mourvèdre unobstructed by oak, with good fruit complexity. Mid-wave between serious & fun. Not tasted: **White Curl**. — FM

Location: Stellenbosch ▪ WO: Coastal ▪ Est 2014 ▪ 1stB 2009 ▪ Closed to public ▪ Sales by telephone or websites ▪ Owner(s) Grangehurst Winery (Jeremy Walker) & Wavescape (Steve Pike) ▪ Cellarmaster(s) Jeremy Walker ▪ 1,700cs own label 70% red 30% white ▪ PO Box 206 Stellenbosch 7599 ▪ jeremy@grangehurst. co.za, spike@wavescape.co.za ▪ www.wavescape.co.za, www.grangehurst.co.za ▪ F +27 (0)86-710-6067 ▪ **T +27 (0)21-855-3625**

Wazu Wine Merchants

Supplier to a number of retailers and restaurants, Cape Town's Wazu Wine Merchants also has its own wines under labels like Hypocrite, intended as good-value offerings.

Location: Cape Town ▪ Est 2015 ▪ 1stB 2014 ▪ Sales Mon-Fri 9-5 ▪ Price's Park, Nelson Rd Observatory Cape Town 7925 ▪ info@wazu.co.za ▪ www.wazu.co.za ▪ **T +27 (0)76-838-6507**

☐ **Weathered Hands** *see* Dewaldt Heyns Family Wines

Webersburg Wines   ⓥ ⑪ 🏠 ◎ ♿

A showpiece 230-year-old Helderberg heritage property which has been sympathetically restored by owner Fred Weber, Webersburg could easily tick over purely as a wedding, conference and functions venue — but the local wine scene would be poorer without its classic, ageworthy reds, in particular, skilfully vinified by cellar chief (and son-in-law) Matthew van Heerden, and released only when deemed ready to drink.

★★★★☆ **Cabernet Sauvignon** ⓥ Regal **14** (91) as restrained & understated as ever. Cake & spicy fruit notes seamlessly meshed with oak, 70% new. Subtle but powerful. A Stellenbosch classic.

★★★★ **Webersburg** ⓥ Merlot (60%) leads cab on soft-textured **14** (87) blend. Ripe cherry tobacco brightness & nutty oak from 22 months in 70% new French. First tasted since **11** (88).

Sauvignon Blanc ★★★ Lemon vivacity of **18** (81) tempered by light smokiness. Crisp, zesty & fresh, it features some Elgin grapes. **Webersburg MCC Brut Rosé** ⓥ ★★★★ Creamy lees & red fruit notes characterise **NV** (83) pink bubbly. Light citrus tang but a touch sweet. 60 months on lees. **Webersburg MCC Brut** ⓥ ★★★★ Lemon sherbet zip on **NV** (83) bubbly vies with biscuit & yeast fullness. Dry & crisp, with long toasty tail. Five years on lees. WO W Cape. — FM

Location/map: Stellenbosch ▪ Map grid reference: E8 ▪ WO: Western Cape/Stellenbosch ▪ Est 1995 ▪ 1stB 1996 ▪ Tasting, sales & cellar tours Mon-Fri 10–5 Sat/Sun 10-4 ▪ Closed for lunch on Mondays ▪ Bistro ▪ Tour groups ▪ Historic buildings: manor house 1786; cellar & jonkershuis 1796 ▪ 5-star Cape Dutch guest house ▪ Conferences ▪ Weddings/functions ▪ Owner(s) Fred Weber ▪ Winemaker(s) Matthew van Heerden (2009-2015; 2018) ▪ 20ha/5ha under vine ▪ 30t/4,000cs own label 80% red 20% white ▪ PO Box 3428 Somerset West 7129 ▪ info@webersburg.co.za ▪ www.webersburg.co.za ▪ S 34° 0′ 22.1″ E 018° 50′ 34.5″ ▪ ▦ flatland. smokers.standouts ▪ F +27 (0)21-881-3217 ▪ **T +27 (0)21-881-3636**

Wederom Boutique Winery   ⓥ ⑪ 🏠 ◎

There are only 3 ha of vines on the farm Wederom, recently acquired by the Viljoen and Meyer families. The 2018 crop was vinified by Ferdie Viljoen with help from seasoned AB Krige and, despite the vintage challenges, they produced 'great-tasting wines'. These weren't ready for us to review this edition, but will doubtless be enjoyed by guests who come to enjoy the on-site hospitality. The 'tribute' shiraz below is still selling, and thematically links to the Italian Prisoners of War Museum on the Robertson property.

Giovanni Salvadori Shiraz ⓥ ★★★★ A whole palette of spiced red-fruit flavours, ripe, rounded & rich, clean dry conclusion. **15** (85) delicious, & an amazing bargain. — MW

Location/map/WO: Robertson ▪ Map grid reference: B7 ▪ Est 2002 ▪ Tasting, sales & cellar tours by appt ▪ Fee R60pp tasting/tour ▪ Meals by appt ▪ Weddings, conferences, tours ▪ Italian Prisoners of War Museum ▪ Hanepoot Huisies guest house ▪ Owner(s) Meyer & Viljoen Family ▪ Cellarmaster(s) Ferdie Viljoen ▪ Winemaker(s) Ferdie Viljoen, assisted by AB Krige ▪ Viticulturist(s) Ferdie Viljoen, assisted by R. Hugo ▪ 3ha (merlot, shiraz) ▪ IPW ▪ Goree Rd Robertson 6705 ▪ info@wederom.co.za, bookings@wederom.co.za ▪ www. wederom.co.za ▪ S 33° 49′ 5.5″ E 019° 47′ 15.8″ ▪ ▦ shelving.captaincy.imposition ▪ **T +27 (0)23-626-4139**

☐ **Wedgewood** *see* Nordic Wines

Welbedacht Wine Estate   ⓥ ⑪ 🏠 ◎ ⑧ ♿

Owned by the Burgers, a famous rugby family, Wellington's Welbedacht has a strong sports focus, down to the on-site cricket oval. However, wine is what draws crowds these days. 'The old tasting room got a bit cramped, so we have moved into the original 1800s cellar,' says marketing manager Tiaan Burger. 'You can see the old cement fermenters and underground tanks - a must visit!' The good-value Meerkat label has had a revamp, and a chenin block, nearly 50 years old, has prompted membership of the Old Vine Project.

Schalk Burger & Sons Proprietors Reserve range

★★★★ **Myra** ⓥ Old bushvine chenin & 4 others in (unwooded) **15** (88), more focused, less oxidative than previous. Stonefruit & citrus, nicely layered, becoming more mineral on the palate.

Mon René ⓥ ★★★★ Chardonnay MCC sparkling; current **NV** (84) nicely captures variety's citrus tones, enriched by lees ageing. Though elegantly dry, has almost honeyed flavours. Occasional release: **No. 6**.

Welbedacht Estate range

★★★★ Old Bush Vine Pinotage Was 'Pinotage' (though from 30 year old vines). In sleek **16** (86), 5% cinsaut enhances sweet tangy red fruit, pleasant earthiness, fresh fynbos notes. No obvious oak from 20 months old barrels (some Hungarian). Improves on **15** ★★★★ (84).

★★★★ Bohemian Syrah (ⓐ) With splash petite sirah, 20 months older oak, **16** (89) has violets & five-spice adding layers to lush dark fruit. With ample tannic staying power.

★★★★ Cricket Pitch (②) Merlot-led 4-part Bordeaux blend, **13** (86) is beautifully scented, cedar-nuanced cassis & violets. Palate more serious, firm but ripe tannins promise a long future. **11**, **12** untasted.

★★★★ Hat Trick Alcohol over 15% but in balance on **15** (86) Cape Blend, 58% pinotage with equal grenache & merlot, showing red & dark fruit with hints of tobacco, velvet tannic grip. No **13**, **14**.

★★★★ Patriot Where **12** ★★★★ (84) was a showy cab-led blend with 30% new wood, **14** (88) mostly pinotage with 25% grenache, 12.5% each malbec & cab, more deftly oaked & harmonious. No **13**.

★★★★ Old Bush Vine Chenin Blanc (❀) Plenty of oxidative richness (marmalade, almond, lemon crème brûlée) on **15** (86), aged year in old oak (10% American), further year in tank. **13**, **14** not made.

Cabernet Sauvignon Barrique Select ★★★★ Aged 20 months in older oak (5% Hungarian), **16** (85) has velvet texture with upfront, ripe macerated black fruit. **Merlot Barrique Select** ★★★★ Fairly lush **16** (83) has dark plum & cherry fruit, chocolate nuance after 18 months in older oak, quite chewy tannins. **Barrel Fermented Chardonnay** ★★★★ **15** (83) citrus & melon fruit, lively acidity, medium body with biscuit nuances from 10-12 months on lees in older wood.

Meerkat range

Chenin Blanc (⑰) ★★★ Tastebud-tingling **18** (81) has tangy pineapple & tart green apple notes for uncomplicated but vibrant refreshment.

Pinotage (②) ★★★ Unwooded style for earlier drinking, **15** (78) offers plush fruit & gentle grip from grape tannins. **Burrow Blend** (②) ★★★ Well-priced (as rest of range) blend of pinotage & 7 others, lightly oaked **16** (78) offers tasty early drinking. **Pinotage Rosé** (②) ★★ Red-fruited semi-sweet **17** (74) offers uncomplicated easy drinking. **Unwooded Chardonnay** ★★★ Fresh & citrusy **16** (80), well rounded from 6 months on lees. **Sauvignon Blanc** ★★★ Redolent of lemongrass & Granny Smith apples, **17** (79) is crisp & dry. First WO Groenberg wine in the guide. **Sun Angel Semi-Sweet** (②) ★★ Unspecified blend, melon-flavoured **NV** (75) has enough freshening acidity to offset its sweetness, tastes drier than it is. — JG
Location/map: Wellington ▪ Map grid reference: B1 ▪ WO: Wellington/Groenberg ▪ Est/1stB 2005 ▪ Tasting, sales & cellar tours Mon-Fri 9-5 Sat 10-2 Sun by appt 10-2 ▪ Fee R15 ▪ Closed Easter Fri & Mon, Dec 25 & Jan 1 ▪ No. 6 Restaurant @ Welbedacht ▪ Picnics ▪ Facilities for children ▪ Tour groups ▪ Gifts ▪ Conferences ▪ Functions ▪ Welbedacht cricket oval ▪ Bradgate manor house ▪ Owner(s) Schalk Burger Family Trust ▪ Winemaker(s) Hardus van Heerden (Jan 2015) ▪ 140ha/110ha (19 varieties r/w) ▪ 1,000t ▪ 75% red 20% white 5% rosé ▪ CVC, IPW, OVP, WIETA ▪ PO Box 51 Wellington 7654 ▪ info@welbedacht.co.za ▪ www.meerkat-wines.co.za, www.schalkburgerandsons.co.za, www.welbedacht.co.za ▪ S 33° 34'39.8" E 019° 1'12.8" ▪ ⟨☰⟩ victors.will.trout ▪ F +27 (0)86-669-5641 ▪ **T +27 (0)21-873-1877**

Welgegund Heritage Wines   (ⓟ) (◎)

A member of the Old Vine Project, with three parcels older than the qualifying 35 years, Welgegund proudly displays the new Certified Heritage Vineyard seal on both wines featured this edition. The venerable Wellington estate was acquired in 2014 by the Brimacombe family who, in addition to nurturing the vinous patrimony, are lovingly restoring a heritage building into a guest house.

★★★★ Providence (②) (❀) Red fruit melange, lovely freshness & supple tannins, **15** (86) shiraz with 30% old-vine (41 years) cinsaut, dash carignan, adroitly oaked (30% new) for extra appeal.

★★★★ Chenin Blanc (❀) Shows serious intent at modest 12.5% alcohol, good depth & dryness, **17** (86) subtly saline & earthy, well-handled partial oaking, 33% new. Similar attractive unfruity styling to last **15** ★★★★ (85). 44 year old dryland vines. Coastal WO. — CvZ

Location/map: Wellington ▪ Map grid reference: C4 ▪ WO: Coastal/Wellington ▪ Est 1777 ▪ 1stB 1997 ▪ Tasting & sales by appt ▪ Olive oil ▪ Owner(s) Brimacombe family ▪ Winemaker & vineyard manager Friedrich Kühne ▪ 35ha/13ha (carignan, cinsaut, grenache, shiraz, chard, chenin) ▪ 1,550cs 50% red 50% white ▪ PO Box 683

Wellington 7654 ▪ sales@welgegund.co.za ▪ www.welgegund.co.za ▪ S 33° 39′ 38.3″ E 019° 2′ 13.6″ ▪ 🗺 taker.
chef.blurred ▪ **T +27 (0)21-873-2123**

☐ **Welgevallen Cellar-Stellenbosch University** *see* Stellenbosch University Welgevallen Cellar

Welgevallen Wines - Splendidior 150 ⓠ

Named for the farm on which Stellenbosch's prestigious Paul Roos Gymnasium was built in 1866,
Welgevallen wines are donated by old boys who are now winemakers and estate owners. Sales generate
funds enabling talented youngsters from economically disadvantaged families to attend the school.

★★★★ Splendidior 150 Cabernet Sauvignon ⓠ **13** ⑧⑦ magnum commemorating Paul Roos
Gymnasium's 150th anniversary, barrel each from 12 past students - a who's who of Stellenbosch wine.
Enough pride at stake, there's cassis & cedar, silky smooth body, a long life ahead. Splendid indeed.

Not tasted: **Pinotage, Cabernet Sauvignon-Merlot, Sauvignon Blanc**. — CR

Location/map: Stellenbosch ▪ Map grid reference: F5 ▪ WO: Bottelary ▪ Est/1stB 2000 ▪ Visits Mon-Fri 10—2 ▪
Closed pub & school hols ▪ Owner(s) Paul Roos Gymnasium Old Boys Union ▪ Winemaker(s)/viticulturist(s)
Wouter Pienaar, Tinnie Momberg, Danie Steytler & Coenie Snyman (consultants) ▪ 800cs own label 75% red
25% white ▪ c/o Paul Roos Gymnasium Old Boys Union Suidwal Stellenbosch 7600 ▪ oldboys@paulroos.
co.za ▪ www.paulroos.co.za ▪ S 33° 56′ 31.2″ E 018° 51′ 41.1″ ▪ 🗺 animated.wiggly.spark ▪ F +27 (0)21-883-
8627 ▪ **T +27 (0)21-883-8627**

Wellington VO

'The brandy for the regular South African guy', according to brand owner Edward Snell & Co. A blend of
3- and 5-year-old barrel-matured brandies, distilled in 1,000L copper potstills at Oude Molen in Elgin by
consultant brandy master Kobus Gelderblom, Wellington VO is notable for being one of the few 'natural'
local blended brandies: without bonificateurs, natural flavouring agents allowed by law.

Wellington VO ⓠ ★★★ Designed for mixing, for which purpose it has plenty of oak-tinged apricotty
flavour & power. A touch too sweet & fiery for solo sipping. — TJ

Wellington Wines ⓠ 🍷 ◎ ♿

A substantial and significant producer, with roots in SA's two oldest grower-owned wineries and today
operating from three cellars in Wellington town, Wellington Wines' labels (slightly tweaked this edition)
cover many preferences and styles: La Cave, serious and long lived; Duke of Wellington (previously True to
Terroir), single varieties, now with a blanc de noir from pinotage; and The W Collection, sweet, low-alcohol
perlé wines. All are offered to winelovers with this exhortation: 'Live a great story'.

La Cave range

★★★★ Cabernet Sauvignon ⓠ Powerful **16** ⑧⑥, like cellar siblings, shows its all-new oak & strong
tannin platform but currant fruit promises pleasure given time, more so than slightly lean **15** ★★★★ ⑧④.

★★★★ Pinotage Generous plump berries are laced with spice & lavished with new barrels 18 months;
tropical fruit & plum vie with heady vanilla in riot of **17** ★★★★★ ⑨⓪ flavour, but stern tannins keep the
gates of hedonism shut in youth. Allow time to settle, soften, like ambitious but tad more austere **16** ⑧⑥.

★★★★ Shiraz ⓠ Under **16** ⑧⑥'s enthusiastic tannin extraction & new small-oaking lies succulent ripe
cherry fruit waiting for time to bring harmony. Be patient or team with country food.

★★★★ Cape Blend ⓠ Apparently divergent components (half pinotage, equal cab & shiraz, 16
months in new oak) in fact harmonise well in **16** ⑧⑥, show spicy dark blackcurrant fruit. Fine but still
dense tannic core needs food or a cellar.

★★★★ Chenin Blanc ⓠ Oxidative, oaky (all-new barrels, year), **16** ⑧⑥'s baked custard styling has
immediate & considerable appeal, perhaps best enjoyed soon while still at peak.

Discontinued: **Méthode Cap Classique Pinot Noir, Méthode Cap Classique Chardonnay**.

Duke of Wellington range

Cabernet Sauvignon ⊘ ★★★★ Herb-toned **17** ⑧③ cements uptick of recent vintages; juicy bramble
fruit with pliable tannin support, savoury tail. Decent drinking, not at all trivial. **Merlot** ★★★ Lavender
& violet aromas lift, & firm tannic structure anchors the ripe berry features of **17** ⑧②; oak in harmony.

Pinotage ★★☆ Vibrant plum, banana & clove flavours on **17** (79), fleshy yet firm, with 14% alcohol in balance. **Chenin Blanc ★★★** Clean, fresh & uncluttered ripe-fruit profile to crisp, unoaked **18** (80). **Sauvignon Blanc ★★★** Cut grass freshness of **18** (78) adds zing to riper summer fruit salad flavours, brisk acid tempered by lick of sugar. **White Pinotage** (NEW) **★★★** Free-run juice of black grape made as a dry white wine. Wild scrub notes add interest to red berry fruits of unoaked **18** (81). Not tasted: **Shiraz**. Discontinued: **Pinotage 10.5% Alcohol**, **Chardonnay**, **Chenin Blanc 10% Alcohol**.

The W Collection

Blushing Pino Frizzante ★★ Lightly sparkling Natural Sweet rosé. Carnival pink **NV** (70) is hanepoot with chenin, dash pinotage. Low 9% alcohol & WO W Cape, as next. **Moscato Frizzante ★★** Pétillant Natural Sweet from hanepoot & chenin. **NV** (70) is frothy & grapey, to kick-start a party. Discontinued: **Brut**. — DS

Location/map: Wellington ▪ Map grid reference: B3 C3 ▪ WO: Wellington/Western Cape ▪ Est 1941 ▪ Tasting & sales Mon-Fri 9-5; Sat 9–5 Sun/pub hols 11-3 (only Bovlei tasting room) ▪ Fee R40/5 wines ▪ BYO picnic ▪ Gift shop ▪ Seasonal wine pairing menu ▪ Venue for private functions ▪ Owner(s) ▪ Production team: Francois van Niekerk, Chris Smit (Nov 2005), Reon Richter (Oct 2013), Erik van Wyk (Jan 2015) ▪ Viticulturist(s) Nikey van Zyl (2017) ▪ 2,400ha ▪ 27,000t 60% red 40% white ▪ BRC, Fairtrade, HACCP, IPW, WIETA ▪ PO Box 509 Wellington 7654 ▪ marketing@wellingtonwines.com ▪ www.wellingtonwines.com ▪ S 33° 38' 17.7" E 018° 59' 20.6" (Wellington), S 33° 38' 18.4" E 019° 1' 54.2" (Bovlei) ▪ [map] lemons.songs.then ▪ F +27 (0)21-873-3194/+27 (0)21-864-1483 ▪ **T +27 (0)21-873-1582**

Welmoed

Well-priced easy-drinking range named for the property whose 17th-century owner, Jacobus van der Heyden, resisted government corruption and earned the people's admiration for his 'moed' (courage). The site is now home to brand owner Stellenbosch Vineyards.

Pinotage (⊕) **★★★** Appealing icing sugar & plum aromas, variety's zippy acidity; **17** (78) enough grip for food. Stellenbosch WO, as all unless noted. **Gewürztraminer** (⊕) **★★★** Litchi & rosewater fragrances, engaging balance between few grams sugar, firm acidity & modest 12.5% alcohol; **18** (82) a crowd pleaser. WO W Cape.

Cabernet Sauvignon (②) **★★★** Previewed **16** (80) packed with sweet berry & plum fruit, pleasant leafy note adds appeal, firm tannic bite for food. **Merlot ★★☆** Red plum, chocolate & smoke, like all in this good-value range, **17** (78) for easy, uncomplicated enjoyment. **Shiraz** (✓) **★★★ 16** (80) ups the ante with a drier impression, spicy complexity & savoury note not found on red siblings. **Rosé ★★** From shiraz, **18** (76) paler, less flavoursome than usual; lighter 11.5% alcohol & hint sweetness for easy sipping. **Chardonnay ★★★** As always, brief oaking adds extra appeal to this wallet-friendly white. Citrus, grassy top notes, whiff vanilla; **18** (79) doesn't disappoint. WO W Cape. **Chenin Blanc ★★★** Very understated **18** (79), some peach & khaki bush notes, rounded mouthfeel. **Pinot Grigio ★★** Cassis & wine gum aromas the allure in crisp, lightish (12.5% alcohol) **18** (74). WO W Cape. **Sauvignon Blanc ★★★** Figgy aromas & flavours, pleasant slightly gravelly texture; **18** (79) for solo enjoyment or with seafood. **Sparkling Brut ★★★** Frothy **NV** (77) celebratory sipper with lemon, orange & Granny Smith apple whiffs. Usually from chenin & chardonnay - winemaking team keeping mum this year! WO W Cape. — CvZ

Weltevrede Estate

(②)(⑪)(⌂)(◎)(⑤)

This estate near Bonnievale in Robertson Valley dates back to 1912 – the year celebrated in the name of the top range – though the first wines bottled under the Weltevrede label only came in the mid-1970s. Cellarmaster Philip Jonker is the (notably creative and market-savvy) fourth generation of his family here; his father Lourens is owner and 'free consultant', with half a century behind him in the wine industry, including a period as chair of KWV. It was Lourens who built the estate to its present size. While the vineyards are extensive, unspoilt nature occupies more than 150 hectares.

Weltevrede 1912 Collection

Cabernet Sauvignon (②) **★★★☆** Clean berry aromas & flavours on **16** (84). Juicy sweet fruit, with undominating firm structure. Oak well integrated. Should develop well a good few years. **Merlot-Cabernet Sauvignon** (②) **★★★** Choc-mint & tobacco mingle with fruit on the aroma of **15** (78), but herbaceousness more obvious on the flavour, with an edgy acidity too. **Chardonnay** ⓧ ★★★ Oak dominates the oatmeal & citrus on **16** ⑧⓪ & gives tough rasp to the finish. Soft texture, the sweetness matched by bright, lemony acidity for easygoing effect. Not tasted: **Malbec**, **Pinotage**.

Estate range

★★★★ **Poet's Prayer Chardonnay** Occasional release. Deepish colour of **16** ⑧⑥ tells of oxidative making & 2 years new oak. Rich texture, bright acidity, some intensity of citrus flavour, lemon-sweet conclusion.

Hardrock Cabernet Sauvignon ★★★☆ Ripe, just-about-dry **16** ⑧④ combines berry aromas & flavours with dry tannins & tobacco-vanilla notes from serious oaking (year, all new). **Bedrock Black Syrah** ★★★★ Deep-coloured **16** ⑧④ has spicy, oaky character, firm tannic grip & acidic bite balancing the sweet fruit. Might knit in year or two. **Place of Rocks Chardonnay** ⓧ ★★★★ Lightish, well-balanced **16** ⑧④ less oaky than wooded siblings but a pleasant toasted oatmeal note. Fresh, succulent, just 12% alcohol.

Philip Jonker Brut Cap Classique Collection

★★★★ **The Ring** ⓧ Refined **10** ★★★★★ ⑨⓪ sparkling from chardonnay. Thrillingly tight-knit courtesy lower sugar, longer lees-ageing than **09** ⑧⑦. Romantic backstory on label explains the name.

Entheos ⓧ ★★★★ Appley, easy & fresh chardonnay, pinot noir (60/40) **NV** ⑧④ sparkler, the flavours not intense but the whole well balanced & pleasing. Robertson WO for this & Estate range.

Simplicity range

Chocmint Cabernet Sauvignon ★★ A really easy sipper, this **16** ⑦⑥, with a pleasing touch of tobacco with the announced flavour. Off dry, but balanced. **Cherrychoc Merlot** ★★ As usual, some herbaceousness too on **17** ⑦⑥. Soft, flavourful, very easy, just-dry. **Cigarbox Shiraz** ⓧ ★★★ Spicy, ripe fruit & tobacco notes on neatly balanced **16** ⑦⑧; a little structure, but sugar-sweetness adds to easygoing tastiness. **Turkish Delight Rosé** ⓝⓔⓦ ★★ Gewürztraminer adds the rosepetal notes, pinot noir the colour to charming, soft, sweetish **18** ⑦⑥. **Vanilla Chardonnay** ★★★ Butterscotch as well as the oak-derived vanilla on **17** ⑦⑦, with sweet toffee finish. **Lemon Zest Chardonnay** ⓝⓔⓦ ★★★ More flavour interest on elegantly dry & light (10.5% alcohol), unwooded **18** ⑧⓪ than on Vanilla version. A clever achievement. **Trop!co Sauvignon Blanc** ★★★ Plenty of passionfruit character on balanced **17** ⑦⑨ with a good fresh bite; unusually dry for this range.

Heritage range

★★★★ **Ouma se Wyn** ⓧ Ageworthy 'Granny's Wine' from fortified white muscat de Frontignan. **15** ⑧⑥ scented Turkish delight, smooth, gentle yet intense. Uncloyingly sweet - just like Ouma.

Oupa se Wyn ★★★ Grandpa's **17** ⑧① tipple is fortified red muscadel. Forthright grapiness, slippery-sweet & quite fiery, with a resin edge to the aftertaste. 375 ml & Robertson WO for both. — TJ

Location: Bonnievale ▪ Map: Robertson ▪ Map grid reference: D3 ▪ WO: Western Cape/Robertson ▪ Est 1912 ▪ 1stB 1945 ▪ Tasting & sales Mon-Fri 8—5 Sat 9—3.30 ▪ Closed Easter Fri/Sun, Dec 25/26 & Jan 1 ▪ Cellar tours & underground tasting by appt ▪ Restaurant Tue-Sat 9-3 ▪ Walks/hikes ▪ Conservation area ▪ Weddings/functions ▪ 4 self-catering guest cottages ▪ Owner(s) Lourens Jonker ▪ Cellarmaster(s) Philip Jonker (Jan 1997) ▪ Viticulturist(s) Francois Viljoen (consultant) ▪ 360ha/106ha (cab, merlot, pinot, shiraz, chard, cbard, gewürz, sauv) ▪ 1,300t/50,000cs own label 15% red 75% white 10% other ▪ Brands for clients: Woolworths ▪ PO Box 6 Bonnievale 6730 ▪ info@weltevrede.com ▪ www.weltevrede.com ▪ S 33° 56′ 30.9″ E 020° 3′ 4.4″ ▪ ⓦ dangles.shires.unicorn ▪ F +27 (0)23-616-2460 ▪ **T +27 (0)23-616-2141**

Welvanpas   ⓧ ⓝ ⓒ ⓐ

Dan Retief, owner, winemaker and viticulturist of Wellington estate Welvanpas, is the custodian of a heritage spanning more than 300 years and 10 generations. Yet even if he lacked a sturdy family tree, including Voortrekker leader Piet Retief, or the farm a long backstory, which Dan shares during the pre-booked History Package lunch and talk, both would still be admired by lovers of heartfelt, handcrafted wines, and the scores of MTB riders, trail runners and hikers using some 60 km of mountain foothill paths made available to them.

Daniel Pinotage ⓧ ★★★ Adds 3 year old son to wine's name in unwooded **16** ⑦⑧. Nice typicity: blueberries, succulence, a bit of grape tannin giving definition. **De Krakeelhoek Rood** ⓧ ★★★★ **14** ⑧① merlot (71%) with shiraz, relaxed & confident & ready now, cassis sharing the limelight with smoked meat tones, supple tannins. **Revival Red** ⓧ ★★ Cab-led with merlot & shiraz, good dark-fruit expression,

ANNO 1941

PERDEBERG WINES

DRY LAND INFLUENCED WINES

*UNDER EXTREME CONDITIONS
MOTHER NATURE PRODUCES HER BEST FRUIT*

WINE TASTING • WINE PAIRING
TAPAS PICNICS • KIDDIES PAIRING
FUNCTION VENUE • CHEESE PLATTERS

OPEN: Monday – Saturday

📞 021 869 8244 ✉ info@perdeberg.co.za
📍 Vryguns Farm, Windmeul, Paarl, SOUTH AFRICA, 7630
📍 S 33° 39' 30.00", E 18° 49' 37.00" f PerdebergWinery
🐦 @perdebergWinery 🌐 www.perdeberg.co.za

clean leather & forest floor in **14** (74); juicy tannins for early drinking but a gentle grip at the end says it can age a bit. **Suzanne Pinotage Rosé** (②) ★★★ Returns to guide after a break (like Sauvignon). **16** (78) elegant & dry, packed with red berries, a vibrant patio sipper. **Chardonnay** (②) ★★ Savoury notes dominate **16** (74)'s buttered toast, whiffs of olive oil, shy stonefruit; portion American oak adds a sweet vanilla farewell. **Sauvignon Blanc** (②) ★★ Green melon, whiffs of capsicum in ready-now **16** (74) following through to the palate. Dry, light textured (12% alcohol), slips down easily. — CR, CvZ

Location/map/WO: Wellington ▪ Map grid reference: C3 ▪ Est 1704 ▪ 1stB 1994 ▪ Tasting & sales Tue-Fri 8–5 Sat/Sun 8–3 ▪ Fee R30pp ▪ Closed Easter Fri-Mon, Dec 16-Jan 2 ▪ Die Ou Meul coffee shop Tue-Fri 8-5 Sat/Sun 8-3 ▪ Facilities for children ▪ Tour groups ▪ History Package incl lunch & talk on Piet Retief family, booking required ▪ Farm produce ▪ Walks/hikes ▪ Bains MTB trails ▪ Craft beer ▪ Owner(s)/viticulturist(s) Dan Retief ▪ Cellarmaster(s) Dan Retief (Jan 1993) ▪ Winemaker(s) Dan Retief (Jan 1990), with Neels Kruger (Jan 1999) ▪ 260ha/50ha (11 varieties r/w) ▪ 25t own label 80% red 15% white 5% rosé ▪ PO Box 75 Wellington 7654 ▪ welvanpas@gmail.com ▪ S 33° 37′ 59.9″ E 019° 4′ 12.5″ ▪ brunt.stating.ultrahigh ▪ F +27 (0)21-864-1239 ▪ **T +27 (0)21-864-1239**

☐ **Weskus** see Winkelshoek Wine Cellar

Whalehaven Wines   (②) (◎)

This artisanal winery's Hermanus home was recently revamped by the Italian Bottega family, also the driving force behind Sir Lowry's Pass-based Idiom. The two brands share a winemaker (Reino Thiart) and main fruit source (the family's mountain vineyards in the Helderberg), but grapes for Whalehaven are also sourced around Walker Bay and elsewhere in the Coastal region.

Conservation Coast range
★★★★ **Pinot Noir** Vibrantly aromatic **16** (87) is big-boned & forceful, with scented red berry fruit & meaty savouriness. Prominent oak spicing on lingering finish suggests cellaring to fully knit.

★★★★ **Chardonnay** Seriously conceived, barrel-fermented **16** ★★★★☆ (90) shows oaky spices on solid citrus & butter core. Plush & satin textured, with charming marmalade/grapefruit highlights, showing more refinement than **15** (87). Upper Hemel-en-Aarde WO for these.

Classic range
★★★★ **Pinot Noir** (⊘) Subtle, fragrant berry & cherry fruit with faint floral scents, **16** (86) lighter than **15** (87) but charmingly supple & silky. Hemel-en-Aarde Ridge vines.

★★★★ **Unwooded Viognier** Less opulent than **15** (87), but still displaying variety's signature peach fruit & viscous texture, **17** ★★★★ (84) tends to tangy & lean. 15% chardonnay. Coastal WO. No **16**.

Not tasted: **Cabernet Franc, Merlot, Pinotage, Sauvignon Blanc**.

Abalone range
Not tasted: **Pinotage-Merlot, Chenin Blanc-Viognier**.

Old Harbour range
Not tasted: **Red, Pinotage Rosé, White**. — GdB

Location: Hermanus ▪ Map: Walker Bay & Bot River ▪ Map grid reference: A3 ▪ WO: Upper Hemel-en-Aarde Valley/Coastal/Hemel-en-Aarde Ridge ▪ Est/1stB 1995 ▪ Tasting & sales Mon-Fri 9.30-5 Sat/Sun 10.30-4.30 ▪ Wine tasting R40pp/R80pp for paired tastings with fine floral chocolates & aromatic jams ▪ Tour groups (up to 40 pax) ▪ Private tasting room can be booked for small functions/corporate events (up to 14 pax) ▪ Owner(s) Bottega family ▪ Winemaker(s) Reino Thiart ▪ 120t capacity ▪ Private Bag X14 Hermanus 7200 ▪ experience@whalehaven.co.za, info@bottegafamilywine.co.za ▪ www.whalehaven.co.za, www.bottegafamilywine.co.za ▪ S 34° 24′ 36.9″ E 019° 11′ 60.0″ ▪ lineage.disappearance.hooks ▪ **T +27 (0)28-316-1633**

☐ **What A Mouthful** see Ultra Liquors
☐ **Whispering Jack** see Flagstone Winery
☐ **White Rhino** see Linton Park Wines
☐ **White River** see Bergsig Estate

Wightman, Gouws & Clarke

In reverse order: David and Jeanette Clarke (of Ex Animo wine distributors) own this small, Swartland-based project, Jurgen Gouws (Intellego Wines) makes the fresh, light-styled Dry Red, and Andrew Wightman (Môrelig Vineyards) grows the pinotage grapes on the Paardeberg. A sizeable proportion of the small production goes to David's native Australia.

Location: Cape Town ▪ Closed to public ▪ Owner(s) Ex Animo Wine Co ▪ Winemaker(s) Jurgen Gouws ▪ Viticulturist(s) Andrew Wightman ▪ 1t/135cs ▪ PO Box 386 Newlands Cape Town 7725 ▪ david@exanimo.co.za ▪ **T** +27 (0)81-011-8505

Wijnskool

A Diners Club Winemaker of the Year, Bartho Eksteen started his wine academy to introduce high school students to different styles, vinification techniques, industry-related career options and responsible use of alcohol ('the respect that this noble product deserves'). Part of the hands-on educational process is to produce these two wines, the proceeds of which go towards operational costs. 'Until now, Wijnskool has only been offered through Boland Agricultural High School for boys, where we have a satellite cellar. But the new facility on our farm in Hemel-en-Aarde will enable us to draw boys and girls from the local community, too.'

★★★★ Tree of Knowledge Sauvignon Blanc Zesty **17** ⑧⑨ sees intense citrus & sherbety green apple flavours contained by soft mouthfeel from 7 months on lees. A polished wine, very nicely integrated.

Tree of Knowledge SMGV ★★★★ Was 'Shiraz' but, like **16** ⑧⑤, got support from mourvèdre & grenache, smidgen viognier. Fragrant & tangy, well knit & balanced at 14.5% alcohol. — JG

Location: Paarl/Hermanus ▪ Map: Paarl ▪ Map grid reference: C3 ▪ WO: Western Cape ▪ Est/1stB 2011 ▪ Tasting, sales & cellar tours by appt ▪ Nature reserve ▪ Owner(s) Bartho & Suné Eksteen ▪ Winemaker(s) Bartho Eksteen (Feb 2011), with Pieter Willem Eksteen (Jan 2012) & learners at Boland Agricultural High School & other schools ▪ Viticulturist(s) Gerhard Bruwer (De Bos Estate, Hermanus); Jaco Mouton (Benguela Cove, Hermanus) - bought in grapes ▪ 30t/3,680cs own label 50% red 50% white ▪ PO Box 1999 Hermanus 7200 ▪ wijnskool@hermanus.co.za, sune@hermanus.co.za ▪ www.wijnskool-academy.co.za ▪ S 33° 39′ 11.45″ E 018° 52′ 59.77″ ▪ ✉ sergeants.cockpit.loveable ▪ F +27 (0)86-554-0896 ▪ **T** +27 (0)82-920-7108 (Bartho), +27 (0)72-323-5060 (Suné)

☐ **Wild Card** see Le Sueur Wines

Wildeberg Wines ⓥ

A change of name for UK-based wine company Boutinot, now operating under the name of their Franschhoek Valley farm. While they wait for new vineyards to come online, winemakers Ryno Booysen and JD Rossouw source grapes from their wide network of growers, many of whom have worked with the company for up to 20 years. Unusual varieties and intriguing blends are their aim, crafting wines which are infinitely more interesting than the sum of their parts.

★★★★ Underworld Grenache Blanc (NEW) ⊘ Unwooded **17** ⑧⑥ balances candied lemon peel with light floral aromas & touch of aniseed. Nice weight from gram sugar, excellent partner for spicy, aromatic foods. WO W Cape.

★★★★ Tea Leaf Chenin Blanc-Grenache Blanc-Palomino Aromatic **17** ★★★★ ⑧④ a fruity treat of pineapple chunks & peach iced tea, with zippy acidity. Delightful, but lacks precision of **16** ⑧⑦. Piekenierskloof WO.

Mantlepiece Cinsault (NEW) ★★★★ Delicious ripe red fruit (strawberry & raspberry) on light & perfumed **17** ⑧④. Softest of tannins, zippy acidity, perfect summer red. **Wandering Beeste Syrah ★★★** Appetising & enjoyable **17** ⑧② ex Swartland, bright black fruit, supportive tannins, slight bitter twist at finish.

On Reflection Chenin Blanc (NEW) ⊘ ★★★★ Creamy texture, persistent length & some pleasing development (hints of wax & wool) all make **17** ⑧④ an excellent wine to pair with roast pork & apple sauce.

Chrome Yellow Semillon (NEW) ★★★★ Great varietal character on unoaked **17** ⑧④, mixing fresh herbs & grass with aromatic fynbos honey. Zesty acidity & good length. **Filigree Blanc de Blancs ★★★★** Bone-dry **NV** ⑧⑤ sparkler from chardonnay sports soft bubbles & creamy texture from old oak & year on lees. Crisp yellow apple & yeasty, buttery finish. Less complex than last. WO Banghoek. — CM

Location/map: Franschhoek ▪ Map grid reference: D1 ▪ WO: Coastal/Swartland/Banghoek/Piekenierskloof/Western Cape ▪ Est/1stB 2016 ▪ Tasting, sales & cellar tours by invitation ▪ Closed all pub hols ▪ Owner(s) Dennis Whitely & Michael Moriaty ▪ Winemaker(s) Ryno Booysen (2016) & JD Rossouw (Sep 2017) ▪ 150t ▪ own label 50% red 50% white ▪ henrietteh@boutinot.com ▪ S 33° 56′ 13″ E 019° 08′ 03″ ▪ clubs.cheering.dust ▪ T +27 (0)82-895-4111

Wildehurst Wines

A decade on since the first bottling, interesting, creative things continue to happen at Joanne Hurst's small but expanding winery in Swartland hamlet Koringberg, including a varietal cinsaut. When the tiny home vineyard can't provide the grapes, they're brought in, mostly from Swartland – Wildehurst has long been a member of Swartland Independent Producers, meeting their strict hands-off winemaking criteria.

Wildehurst range

★★★★ **Cinsaut** (NEW) Creamy & rich **17** ⑧⑧, fine tannic structure supporting lengthy sour cherry, herb & spice flavours. Wild fermented/10 months in old oak. Minuscule production, as all.

★★★★ **The Wilde** Witty name for winemaker's experimental space. Improved **17** ⑧⑨ playful early-drinking take on serious, long-lived nebbiolo. Tasty cherry, liquorice & spice from Breedekloof vines. **15** ★★★ ⑧① a shiraz blend; no **16**.

★★★★ **Red** Balances elegance & power in **14** ★★★★★ ⑨⓪ Rhône blend, improves on **13** ⑧⑧ with generous, spice-laden mouthful of redcurrant fruit pastilles. Wild-fermented syrah, mourvèdre, viognier, splash cinsaut, old-oaked 18 months.

★★★★☆ **Chenin Blanc** Ⓐ Sunshine-in-a-glass styling but **17** ⑨③'s ripe tropical fruit melange is finessed with a textural element. Effect is serious enough to contemplate, easy enough to want to quaff. Quintessential pure-fruited Swartland chenin, fermented/6 months older oak.

★★★★ **Méthode Cap Classique Chenin Blanc-Chardonnay** Interesting **16** ⑧⑥ chenin-led (56%) dry sparkler with creamy citrus & apple notes from chardonnay, mouthwatering acidity. Intricate, with better composure, more complexity than **15** ★★★★ ⑧④.

Not tasted: **Petit Wilde**, **Viognier**. Occasional release: **Méthode Cap Classique**, **Méthode Cap Classique Chardonnay**.

Unlabelled range

★★★★ **Red Blend** Ⓥ Franco-SA allsorts mix headed by cinsaut & featuring dash pinotage. **16** ⑧⑧ spice box aroma focused by old oak, joined on palate by generous red berries & pepper. Structured yet easy.

Velo range

★★★★ **Red** More refined **15** ⑧⑥ improves on already delicious **14** ★★★★ ⑧⑤, fruity & fresh with exceptional length. Near-equal grenache & shiraz, soupçon viognier.

★★★★ **Blanc** Ⓥ White-pear-perfumed **17** ⑧⑦, delectable medley of colombard, chenin & viognier, naturally fermented in tank. A great summer white, & well-priced step up on **16** ★★★★ ⑧⑤.

Rosé ★★★★ Fruity, friendly & light (11.5% alcohol) **18** ⑧⑤, fresh dry strawberry flavour from cinsaut, textured farewell from part barrel ferment. — HC

Location: Koringberg ▪ Map: Swartland ▪ Map grid reference: B2 ▪ WO: Swartland/Breedekloof ▪ Est 2006 ▪ 1stB 2009 ▪ Cellar tours & tasting by appt at 1 Main Rd, Koringberg ▪ Guest accommodation ▪ Owner(s) Joanne Hurst ▪ Winemaker(s) Sheree Nothnagel (Dec 2013) ▪ Viticulturist(s) John Loxton (2006, consultant) ▪ 1.1ha (carignan, cinsaut, grenache, mourv, shiraz, viog) ▪ 24t ▪ own label 45% red 45% white 10% rosé ▪ PO Box 103 Koringberg 7312 ▪ info@wildehurst.com ▪ www.wildehurst.com ▪ S 33° 01′ 10.10″ E 018° 40′ 26.42″ ▪ eruptions.intervals.invoice ▪ T +27 (0)22-423-8396 (winery)/+27 (0)60-374-9267

Wildekrans Wine Estate

The Harlow family, owners the past decade, have renovated, renewed and extensively invested in their large Wildekrans estate at Bot River to realise its potential. Among their focuses has been hospitality, and ensuring visitors of a warm welcome with many cellardoor amenities. The Harlows have proudly seen their concerted efforts validated through an invitation to join the Cape Vintner Classification (CVC), the independent producer association aimed at promoting terroir-specific winegrowing and excellence in cellar practice, environmental care and visitor experience.

Barrel Select Reserve range

★★★★ Pinot Noir ⊘ Beautiful ruby colour on elegant **14** ⑧⑦, perfumed berry & pomegranate followed by tangy, spicy finish, well-judged oak rounding (older barrels, 18 months).

★★★★★ Pinotage ⊘ Reveals serious intent in **15** ⑨④, with prominent tannins, generous dark berry fruit, touches of spice & coconut from 70% new French oak, 22 months. Intense, lingering finish.

★★★★ Shiraz ⊘ Fynbos, herbs & hint of mint support a melange of berries (blue & blackcurrant); top notes of baking spice & olive complete the **15** ⑧⑦ package. Fresh, intense & lively.

★★★★ Cape Blend ⊘ Intense berry & cherry announce **15** ★★★★★ ⑨③ pinotage (44%) blend, with shiraz, pinot noir & cab adding complexity. Elegant yet rich & vibrant, less sweet than **14** ⑧⑦.

★★★★ Chenin Blanc ⊘ ✦ From 35 year old, cooler, south-facing vines, bunch-pressed **16** ★★★★★ ⑨② with delicate lemon blossom, yellow apple fruit & hints of ginger. Subtle oaking (30% new, year) supports, few grams sugar round the mouthfeel. Step above **15** ⑧⑦.

Estate range

★★★★ Sauvignon Blanc ⊘ Outgoing as always, **18** ⑧⑦'s lemon & nettle underpinned by crisp texture & excellent acid/fruit balance. Great tension & purity, rewarding & delicious.

Pinotage ★★★★ More expressive than previous, **16** ⑧③ chocolate & red-berry fruit, firm & pleasingly dry tannin supported by spicy oak, 14 months, seasoned French. Not tasted: **Shiraz, Cabernet Franc-Merlot.**

Méthode Cap Classique range

★★★★ Brut Rosé ⊘ Delicious **15** ★★★★★ ⑨⓪ dry sparkling, 18 months on lees leave a creamy, lively texture with red apple in the flavours. Beautiful salmon hue & fine chains of bubbles from equal pinot noir & chardonnay. Distinctly more celebratory than **13** ⑧⑦ & very well priced. No **14.**

Chenin Blanc ★★★★ Chenin MCC bubbly growing but still rare in SA. **14** ⑧④'s sweetish entry balanced by fresh, mouthcoating acidity; very attractive oak touch, creamy yellow fruit & fragrant farewell. — HC

Location/WO: Bot River ▪ Map: Walker Bay & Bot River ▪ Map grid reference: B1 ▪ Est/1stB 1993 ▪ Tasting, sales & cellar tours Mon-Fri 8.30–5 Sat 11-5 Sun 11-4 ▪ Restaurant ▪ Picnics to order ▪ Olive oil ▪ Tour groups ▪ Conferences/functions ▪ Self-catering cottages ▪ Walks/hikes ▪ MTB ▪ Birding ▪ Horseback riding ▪ Conservation area ▪ Grappa still, tour/tasting to be pre-booked ▪ Owner(s) Gary & Amanda Harlow ▪ Winemaker(s) Braam Gericke (2017), with Andre Olkers ▪ Viticulturist(s) Braam Gericke (2008) ▪ 1,015ha/71.8ha (cabs s/f, merlot, ptage, pinot, shiraz, chard, chenin, grenache b, hanepoot, riesling, sauv, sem) ▪ 350t own label 55% red 40% white 5% rosé; ±13,200cs for clients ▪ CVC, WIETA, WWF-SA Conservation Champion ▪ PO Box 31 Botrivier 7185 ▪ wines@wildekrans.com ▪ www.wildekrans.com ▪ S 34° 14'23.50" E 019° 11'54.42" (home farm, Bot River) ▪ ⌂ unlocking.heartless.dealmakers ▪ F +27 (0)21-413-0967 ▪ T +27 (0)28-284-9902

☐ **Wildflower** see Darling Cellars
☐ **Wild Olive** see The Grape Grinder

William Everson Wines ⓠ ⌂

With a cellar in his Grabouw home, William Everson is a literal garagiste albeit occupied full-time in recent vintages by his artisan apple and pear ciders. Previous releases of his wines are available from the Everson's Cider Tasting facility at nearby Peregrine Farm Stall.

Location: Grabouw ▪ Map: Elgin ▪ Map grid reference: B2 ▪ Est/1stB 2001 ▪ Tasting, sales & tours by appt ▪ Self-catering accommodation (www.mentmor.co.za) ▪ Owner(s)/winemaker(s) William Everson ▪ 4t/800cs own label 60% red 40% white ▪ 2281 Essenhout Ave Klipkop Grabouw 7160 ▪ william@eversonwine.co.za, william@eversonscider.com ▪ www.eversonwine.co.za, www.eversonscider.com ▪ S 34° 9'52.06" E 019° 2' 6.19" ▪ ⌂ mini.laying.primary ▪ F +27 (0)86-662-4045 ▪ T +27 (0)82-554-6357

☐ **Willowbrook** see Wine-of-the-Month Club

Windfall Wine Farm ⓠ ⌂

Steady growth, while maintaining a keen eye on quality, is the philosophy guiding this family-owned boutique winery in Robertson's scenic Agterkliphoogte Valley. Poetically named by former owner and cricketing legend Eddie Barlow for the mist cascading down the mountains, Windfall also offers a fine potstill brandy, extra virgin olive oil and accommodation in five colourful cottages, each named for one of the wines.

Windfall Wine range

Pinotage (NEW) (♥) ★★★ Cardamom- & clove-nuanced **17** (82)'s attractive strawberry/mulberry fruit & lively acidity well framed by complementary all-new oak. Smooth vanilla tail for easy enjoyment.

Cabernet Sauvignon (♀) ★★★ **15** (81) offers great drinkability with supple tannins, ample blackberries & brush vanilla oak plus few grams unobtrusive, fruit-lifting sugar. **Pinot Noir** (♀) ★★★ Cherry- & earth-toned **17** (81) provisionally rated preview quite shy but true to variety, with focus on acidity rather than tannin. **Shiraz** (♀) ★★★ Riper black berry notes on **14** (78) than 13% alcohol would suggest. Balanced freshness, with hint of oak tannin, spice & sweetish conclusion. **Barrel 41** (♀) ★★★ Ex-tank **15** (81) lifts the bar substantially, rings the changes, too, with merlot & the 2 cabs joining shiraz (previous a Rhône blend); well rounded & vibrant. **Kibali** (♀) ★★★ Tasty shiraz, cab, mourvèdre, grenache combo, **14** (81) has good spicy berry fruit richness in firm frame. Would rate higher but for prominent acid. **Grenache Rosé** ★★ Soft red fruits & boiled sweets (from 15% pinot noir component), low 10.8% alcohol; dry **18** (73) for anytime enjoyment. **Chenin Blanc** ★★★ Refreshing **18** (77) with subtle peach & more intense guava aromas, pleasant grip from ageing on lees, small oaked portion. **Sauvignon Blanc** ★★ Partly wooded, 2 months on lees, **18** (73) is delicate, with muted varietal character. **Mendola** ★★★ First since **08** (81), frothy **15** (80) MCC sparkler from chardonnay with candy apple aromas & flavours, quite dry (9 g/l sugar) & salty finish.

Brandy range

★★★★ **The Hunter** (♀) Turn up the Mozart & enjoy this 6 year old potstill from chenin. Bright hues, sweet peach, apricot & pear drop tones, vibrant floral & spice finish. 500 ml.— CvZ, WB

Location/map/WO: Robertson ▪ Map grid reference: C8 ▪ Est 1998 ▪ 1stB 2006 ▪ Tasting, sales & tours by appt ▪ Closed all pub hols ▪ 5 self-catering cottages (sleeps between 2 & 4 people) R450pp/n ▪ Owner(s) Bianca Weingartz, Sarah Alexander & Jaco de Wet ▪ Cellarmaster(s) Kobus van der Merwe (Jan 2006, consultant) & Jaco de Wet ▪ Winemaker(s) Kobus van der Merwe (Jan 2006, consultant), with Van Zyl de Wet (Jan 2009, consultant) ▪ Viticulturist(s) Jaco de Wet (Jan 2003) ▪ 300ha/63ha (cab, merlot, pinot, ruby cab, chard, chenin, sauv) ▪ 1,100t/1,250cs own label 75% red 25% white ▪ PO Box 22 Robertson 6705 ▪ info@ windfallwine.co.za ▪ www.windfallwine.co.za ▪ S 33° 56' 33.37" E 019° 38' 42.98" ▪ ⒲ greatness.chronicle. trainee ▪ F +27 (0)86-743-4162 ▪ **T +27 (0)83-320-8473**

Windmeul Cellar   (♀) (♔) (◎) (♨) (♿)

Two significant milestones this edition for the grower-owned Agter Paarl venture named after Blake's Mill, an engineering wonder of its day: cellarmaster Danie Marais marks 20 years' service at the winery, and their popular monthly farmers' market celebrates a decade of attracting visitors in search of quality farm produce and local specialities. The enterprising Windmeul team have since added the Parskuip market, open daily and on Saturdays, and KontreiKombuis for meals with a regional flavour. Meanwhile Danie and his crew have expansion plans of their own, with new wines to be added to The Legend series.

Reserve range

★★★★ **Cabernet Sauvignon** Pot-pourri & tangerine notes on dark-fruited **16** (86). More generous than **15** (89), lovely balance & freshness from well-judged oak, acidity.

★★★★☆ **Cape Blend** (✓) (♨) Repeats successful formula of recent years: 55% pinotage with mostly cab, smidgens merlot, petit verdot. Lead variety's inherent bright acidity key to **16** (90)'s structure but doesn't detract from impressively tight-packed fruit, muscular tannins. Will reward many years patience.

Chardonnay ★★★★ Lightly oaked **17** (85) takes time to reveal scented bouquet of lemon, lemongrass & lemon thyme, fruit-sweet tail in which oak provides form not flavour. **VSOP Brandy** (♀) ★★★★☆ Delightfully different, light-feeling - no doubt due to the rare sauvignon blanc component giving more apple & pear notes than apricot & peach. Sweetly smooth, with no need of mixer or ice. 40.5% alcohol. Aged 5-6 years in oak. Not tasted: **Pinotage**, **Shiraz**.

The Legend Collection

★★★★ **Left Wing** (🐝) Was 'The Legend'. Confident **16** ★★★★★ (90) cab (57%) blend with equal merlot, petit verdot, 5% cab franc. Classic walnut, cigarbox & lead pencil complexity, plush but not sweet cassis tones throughout, precise tannin structure for 5+ years ageing. More restrained than bold, earthy **15** (89).

★★★★ **Chenin Blanc** (🌸) Nicely dry **17** (87)'s nuttiness & palate breadth from year in barrel add extra dimension to ripe white peach, floral & earth aromas, rich & lengthy palate.

Windmeul range

Pinotage (🍇) ★★★ Good everyday enjoyment delivered by **16** (80)'s vibrant strawberry aromas & flavours, bright acidity & kiss of oak.

Cabernet Sauvignon ★★★ Less convincing than previous, **16** (79) brief but not easy, with astringent tannins. **Shiraz** ★★★ Attractive meaty tobacco aromas but **16** (78) is more about choc & coffee flavours. 14.5% alcohol a touch warming. **Cabernet Sauvignon-Merlot** ★★★ Well-upholstered with cassis, plum & mulberry to counter its slightly bitter lift, **16** (77) commendably also retains a savoury appeal. **Chardonnay** (🍇) ★★★ Characterful quaffer, unwooded **17** (82) has bright, forward fruit, good acid balance, chalky lees texture. **Chenin Blanc** ★★★ Shy **18** (78) has pear drop & white peach nuances, fair vinosity for relaxed enjoyment. **Sauvignon Blanc** ★★★ Water-white, lean **18** (78), dusty grass & blackcurrant flavours with lemon conclusion. **Port** (🍇) ★★★ Lightish & juicy-sweet berry fruit, touch of spice on **09** (81). Not tasted: **Merlot, White Muscadel**.

Mill range

Cinsaut-Shiraz (🍇) ★★★ Budget range offers pleasant everyday drinking. Charming sweet red-berry fruit on **NV** (81) from 80% cinsaut, unwooded. **Rosé** ★★ Palest pink **NV** (73), just-dry, with faint strawberry notes. From pinotage. **Chenin Blanc** (NEW) ★★★ Tad brief but flavoursome, **NV** (78) tank sample has peach & khaki bush charm. — CvZ, TJ

Location/map: Paarl ▪ Map grid reference: D3 ▪ WO: Coastal ▪ Est 1944 ▪ 1stB 1945 ▪ Tasting & sales Mon-Fri 9–5 Sat 9–3 ▪ Closed all pub hols ▪ Cellar tours by appt ▪ Parskuip Neighbourhood Marketplace Mon-Fri 8-5 Sat 9-3 & KontreiKombuis Sat 9-3 with focus on regional products ▪ Farmers' market every 1st Sat of each month (excl Jan) ▪ Function/tasting area ▪ Facilities for children ▪ Owner(s) 30 members ▪ Cellarmaster(s) Danie Marais (Oct 1999) ▪ Winemaker(s) Abraham van Heerden (Nov 2014), with Berto Dippenaar (Dec 2016) ▪ Viticulturist(s) Anton Laas (Oct 2007) ▪ 1,700ha ▪ 11,000t/20,000cs own label 54% red 44% white 1% rosé 1% fortified + 800cs for clients ▪ PO Box 2013 Paarl 7620 ▪ windmeul@iafrica.com ▪ www.windmeul. com ▪ S 33° 40' 18.1" E 018° 54' 30.6" ▪ 🌐 educational.riffraff.megawatt ▪ F +27 (0)21-869-8614 ▪ **T +27 (0)21-869-8100/8043**

☐ **Winds of Change** *see* Jacques Germanier
☐ **Wind Song** *see* Thor Vintners
☐ **Wine Boutique l'Aghulhas** *see* Breëland Winery
☐ **Winemaster's Reserve** *see* Nederburg Wines

Wine-of-the-Month Club

Wine-of-the-Month is SA's longest-standing and largest wine club, offering members the best-scoring wines in blind tastings by an independent panel of eleven judges. The club also has several proprietary labels, including Berg en Dal, Boschenheuwel, Jakkalskloof, Klaasenbosch, Lakehurst, Martindale, Mortons, Quartet, Semara, Sentinel, Steenhuis and Willowbrook.

Location: Cape Town ▪ Est 1986 ▪ MD Cliff Collard ▪ Private Bag X2 Glosderry 7702 ▪ cheers@wineofthemonth. co.za ▪ www.wineofthemonth.co.za ▪ **T +27 (0)21-492-4100**

☐ **Winery of Good Hope** *see* Radford Dale
☐ **Wine Thief** *see* The Wine Thief

Wine Village-Hermanus   ⓠ ⓖ

Wine Village at the entrance to Hemel-en-Aarde Valley is the realisation of retailers Paul and Cathy du Toit's dream to bring together the fine wines of South Africa under one roof. Daughter Ulla manages events and the popular annual Hermanus Wine & Food Festival. Their house brand is Are We Having Fun Yet?

Location: Hermanus ▪ Map: Walker Bay & Bot River ▪ Map grid reference: A3 ▪ Est 1998 ▪ 1stB 2004 ▪ Open Mon-Fri 9-6 Sat 9-5 Sun 10-3 ▪ Closed Good Fri & Dec 25 ▪ Tasting of wine, craft beer, gin, brandy & olive oil ▪ Owner(s) Paul & Cathy du Toit ▪ ±2,000cs 50% red 50% white ▪ PO Box 465 Hermanus 7200 ▪ winevillage@ hermanus.co.za ▪ www.winevillage.co.za ▪ S 34° 24' 40.7" E 019° 12' 1.9" ▪ ⛶ kilos.amendment.graduating ▪ F +27 (0)86-509-4931 ▪ T +27 (0)28-316-3988

Wineways Marketing

Headquartered in Blackheath near Kuils River, substantial negociant business Wineways Marketing buys grapes across the winelands for vinification at Leeuwenkuil and Stellenbosch Vineyards, and marketing under a variety of brand names. The wines, some in bag-in-box and some low-alcohol, are available locally and in many export markets.

Black Box range

Merlot ⓥ ★★★ Soft & shy red-fruit aromas, NV ⑦⑦ pleasant savoury flavours & finish. 5L pack, as all this range. **Pinotage** ★★ Plum & touch oak on uncomplicated, light-bodied NV ⑦④. Lubricating few grams sugar, as next. **Shiraz** ★★ Bright berry fun, NV ⑦③ for everyday enjoyment. **Merlot-Cabernet Sauvignon** ⓥ ★★★ Juicy, fresh red & black berries, plus appealing sweet spiciness for BBQ ribs. NV ⑦⑦ unwooded, as all ranges unless noted.

Black Tie range

Cabernet Sauvignon ⓐ ★★★ A savoury note & chocolate flavours add extra appeal to 17 ⑦⑧'s ripe black fruit. **Merlot** ⓐ ★★ No hard edges, just soft black cherries on 17 ⑦④ curvaceous sipper. **Pinotage** ★★ Soft brambleberries & hint of spice, 17 ⑦④ slips down easily. **Merlot-Cabernet Sauvignon** ⓐ ★★★ Ticks all the party boxes: 17 ⑦⑧ plummy flavours, subtle spice & smooth fruity finish. **Sauvignon Blanc** ⓥ ★★★ Light-bodied, dry 18 ⑦⑦ shows fruit salad flavours, wafts of green herbs. **Shiraz Natural Sweet** ★★ Rounded, bouncy & fresh 17 ⑦④, dark berry fruit mingled with variety's subtle spice.

Coral Reef range

Cabernet Sauvignon ⓥ ★★★ Rich berries & dark chocolate flavours on gentle 17 ⑦⑦. **Merlot** ⓐ ★★ Friendly tannins, cheerful fruit & slight sour plum nuance, 17 ⑦④ ready for any occasion. **Pinotage** ★★ Soft brambleberries & hint of spice, 17 ⑦④ tasty & easy to drink. **Merlot-Cabernet Sauvignon** ⓐ ★★★ With red & black plums, & just enough tannin grip, 17 ⑦⑧ a tasty meaty meal mate. **Sauvignon Blanc** ⓥ ★★★ Light & dry 18 ⑦⑦ has green herb notes seaming the fruit salad flavours. **Shiraz Natural Sweet** ★★ Controlled sweetness in 17 ⑦④, meaning the subtly spiced dark berries taste lively & fresh.

De Villiers Wines range

Pinotage ⓥ ⓣ ★★★ Juicy & round, a satisfying creaminess underlies 17 ⑧①'s plums, smoke & hit of espresso. Could convince many pino-sceptics.

Cabernet Sauvignon ⓥ ★★★ Raspberry toned, with variety's gripping fruit tannins in 17 ⑦⑦, tad short, as last vintage. **Merlot** ⓐ ★★★ Unfettered by oak, 17 ⑦⑧'s bright plum aromas & flavours shine. Piquant, with good fruit definition.

Fabulous! range

Sweet Red ★★ Reticent aromas, then the berry riot starts, then warm spice joins in. NV ⑦④ welcomely modest alcohol, as all this range. **Sweet Rosé** ★★ Coral-shaded NV ⑦③, wispy sweet candyfloss flavours, brief & light (9% alcohol). **Sweet White** ★★ Tropical-toned party wine, NV ⑦③ very delicate & unassuming. Discontinued: **Dry White**.

Leipoldt 1880 range

Merlot-Cabernet Sauvignon ⓐ ★★★ 50/50 blend in fruity yet streamlined 17 ⑦⑧. Plum & cassis, enough grip to hold interest & make it a good everyday glassful. **Sauvignon Blanc** ⓥ ★★★ Light-bodied, dry **18** (77) shows fruit salad flavours, wafts of green herbs. **Shiraz Natural Sweet ★★** Vivacious black fruit & dried herb nuance, **17** (74) sweet but poised, nice spicy undercurrent.

Mountain Shadows range

Cabernet Sauvignon ⊘ ⊛ **★★★** Not the highest scorer here, but **17** (77) is generous & satisfying, a mini festival of plum, chocolate & leafy herbs.

Merlot ⊘ **★★★** Cherries & warm Christmas spice in **17** (78), for easy sipping. Also in 3L cask. **Pinotage** ⊘ **★★★** Dense plum & mulberry fruit nuanced with liquorice, **17** (81) well-crafted for everyday enjoyment. **Shiraz** (ℚ) **★★★** Light-footed **16** (81)'s liquorice-tinged red berries & plums, cranberry acidity a good match for rich food. **Sauvignon Blanc ★★** Touch leaner than last, **18** (74) lemon & apple flavours, best to serve well-chilled.

Tin Cups Screw Cap range

Merlot-Cabernet Sauvignon (ℚ) **★★ 17** (74) offers soft, easy if unlingering red & black berries on nose & palate. **Sauvignon Blanc ★★** Greenpepper & crunchy apple on light & fleeting **18** (72). **Sweet Rosé ★★** Low-alcohol pink Natural Sweet, **NV** (74) strawberry flavours, racy & piquant acidity neutralise the sugar. **Smooth Red ★★** Smooth as advertised, **17** (71) light & easy mouthful of spicy berry flavours. Softly dry this time vs noticeably sweet previous. — WB

Location: Kuils River ▪ WO: Western Cape ▪ Est 2000 ▪ Closed to public ▪ Owner(s) Carl Schmidt, Stephen Vermeulen & Fanie Marais ▪ Winemaker(s) Pieter Carstens (Leeuwenkuil) & Bernard Claassen (Stellenbosch Vineyards) ▪ 400,000cs own label 80% red 20% white ▪ Plot 689 Zinfandel Str Saxenburg Park 2 Blackheath 7580 ▪ info@wine-ways.co.za ▪ www.wine-ways.co.za ▪ F +27 (0)86-509-9587 ▪ **T +27 (0)21-905-7713/6/9**

Winkelshoek Wine Cellar Ⓠ

Front labels redolent of sandcastles and crayfish on the braai underline the West Coast domicile of Hennie Hanekom's Winkelshoek portfolio, which covers all the prandial possibilities, pre- to -post, especially -post, with six sweet fortifieds on offer. The tasting venue on sibling property Schenkfontein, mooted last edition, has materialised, and the small-batch Schenkfontein wines (see listing) can be sampled there too.

Weskus range

Rooigety (NEW) ⊛ **★★★** Need a change from white or rosé during the day? 'Red Tide' might do nicely: unwooded **17** (79) merlot/cab with juicy fruit, crunchy acidity, satisfying tannin & lowish 12.5% alcohol.

Pinotage ★★★ Mulberry & plum bouquet, enlivening acidity, decent grip & friendly price: unwooded **17** (78) ticks all the everyday red boxes - but note 15% alcohol. **Sweet Rosé ★★** Wild strawberries & spice, **17** (71) pink's perky acidity lifts its 52 g/l sweetness for casual, uncomplicated sipping. **Chenin Blanc ★★** Bone-dry, light **18** (73) fleeting apricot aromas & flavours. **Sauvignon Blanc** (ℚ) **★★** Restrained grassiness, fresh acidity & granadilla finish on **17** (74) preview. **Natural Sweet White ★★** Peaches & florals on **17** (74), pleasing sweetness best enjoyed well chilled.

Winkelshoek range

Hanepoot ★★★ Fortified **17** (80) marries grapes from white & rare red muscat d'Alexandrie for interesting litchi, cherry, spice mouthful energised by bite of 18% alcohol. **Red Muscadel** (ℚ) **★★★★** Unctuous **15** (84) fortified dessert has a pink-tinged tawny appearance, flavours of honey & raisin, gentle alcohol grip. **White Muscadel** (ℚ) **★★★** Bright gold in hue, **16** (78) fortified dessert has high-toned talcum powder aroma, very sweet raisin flavours. **Red Jerepigo** (ℚ) **★★★** Provisionally rated **17** (81) fortified, youthful orange-flecked pink, unusual tomato juice nuance to more classic tealeaf, decidedly sweet yet light footed. **White Jerepigo** (ℚ) **★★★★** Tank sample shows some complexity in dried sultana, Golden Delicious apple, campfire ash characters; vibrant acidity & alcohol fire keep **17** (84) lively. **Cape Vintage** (ℚ) **★★★** 'Port' from undisclosed varieties, **15** (78) older style, with lots of sugar, less alcohol enlivenment, yet not unbalanced; might just need time to perk up. — CvZ

Location: Piketberg ▪ WO: Western Cape ▪ Tasting by appt at Schenkfontein Kelders ▪ Owner(s)/cellarmaster(s) Hennie Hanekom ▪ Winemaker(s) Hendrik Hanekom (2011) ▪ PO Box 395 Piketberg 7320 ▪ info@winkelshoek.co.za ▪ www.winkelshoek.co.za ▪ F +27 (0)22-913-1095 ▪ **T +27 (0)22-913-1092**

☐ **Witch** *see* Mother Rock Wines

Withington   ⓠ ⓑ

Charles Withington's wines — easygoing but with claims to modest seriousness and elegance, and smartly labelled — are sourced from Darling district, where he's based. Charles is particularly pleased about export successes in tough markets: like Malbec in London and Voorkamer Brandy in Canada.

Withington range

Malbec ⓠ ★★★★ Tobacco note (but only old oak), good fruit presence on **15** ⑧④, hints of varietal loganberry. Firmly structured & not without seriousness despite tasty drinkability. **Roan Ranger** ⓠ ★★★☆ Expected lightish colour & bright red fruit on lightly oaked **15** ⑧④ from cinsaut with grenache & dash mourvèdre. Balanced & buoyant, grippier than many in this modish style. **NBC Chardonnay** ⓠ ★★★☆ Bold citrus & pineapple on unwooded **13** ⑧④, refreshing squeeze of limy acidity, clean dry finish.

Brandy range

★★★★ **Voorkamer** ⓠ 7-year potstilled colombard is gentle, with a smooth creamy texture, spiced orchard fruit & lingering balanced citrus conclusion. A delight. Also in 50 ml 'miniatures'.

★★★★ Discontinued: **Darlington range**. — TJ, WB

Location/WO: Darling ▪ Map: Durbanville, Philadelphia & Darling ▪ Map grid reference: A1 ▪ Est 2001 ▪ 1stB 2003 ▪ Tasting & sales at Darling Wine Shop Mon-Sat 10-6 (10-7 in summer) Sun 11-2 ▪ Closed Mar 21, Easter Fri/Sun & Dec 25/26 ▪ Fresh West Coast mussels on order every Friday ▪ Owner(s) Withington family ▪ 2,000cs own label 85% red 10% white 5% potstill brandy ▪ PO Box 236 Darling 7345 ▪ taste@withington. co.za ▪ www.withington.co.za ▪ S 33° 22′ 28″ E 018° 22′ 38″ ▪ ⬚ nudge.excluder.lionesses ▪ **T +27 (0)22-492-3971/+27 (0)74-194-1711**

Withoek   ⓠ ⌂ ◉

In the red hills on the fringe of Calitzdorp village, the Geyser family vineyards share space with fruit orchards, self-catering cottages and a cellar dating from the 1940s, where Fanie Geyser makes his wine, keeping things simple and traditional. The tiny batches, including sweet fortifieds, sell out in no time.

Location: Calitzdorp ▪ Map: Klein Karoo & Garden Route ▪ Map grid reference: B5 ▪ Est/1stB 1996 ▪ Tasting, sales & cellar tours by appt ▪ Self-catering cottages ▪ Walks ▪ Conservation area ▪ Owner(s) Geyser family ▪ Winemaker(s) Fanie Geyser ▪ Viticulturist(s) Johannes Mellet ▪ 454ha/30ha (cab, p verdot, ruby cab, shiraz, tinta, touriga, chenin, cbard, hanepoot, muscadel) ▪ ±300t/800cs own label 50% red 50% fortified ▪ PO Box 181 Calitzdorp 6660 ▪ withoek@telkomsa.net ▪ www.withoek.blogspot.com ▪ S 33° 32′ 24.1″ E 021° 40′ 59.8″ ▪ ⬚ forms.meditator.catchments ▪ **F +27 (0)86-628-7853 ▪ T +27 (0)44-213-3639**

☐ **Witklip** *see* Eerste Hoop Wine Cellar
☐ **Woestkloof** *see* Simelia Wines
☐ **Wolftrap** *see* The Wolftrap

Wolvendrift Private Cellar   ⓠ ◉ ⓑ ⓑ

Robertson's Wolvendrift farm has been in the Klue family for more than 100 years, and 4 generations have made wine in its cellar - fortified muscat a speciality since inception. Hospitality is another focus, and the facilities and attractions include a spacious deck with vineyard and mountain views.

Location/map: Robertson ▪ Map grid reference: C4 ▪ Est 1903 ▪ Tasting & sales Mon-Fri 8.30-4.30 Sat by appt ▪ Closed Easter Fri-Mon, May 1, Dec 25/26 & Jan 1 ▪ Cellar tours by appt ▪ Facilities for children ▪ Tour groups ▪ Walking/hiking trails ▪ Owner(s) Josef Klue & Seun (Pty) Ltd ▪ Winemaker(s) Jan Klue (Jan 2003) ▪ Viticulturist(s) Michael Klue jnr (Apr 2015) ▪ 120ha (cab, merlot, chard, chenin, sauv) ▪ 45% red 45% white 10% fortified ▪ PO Box 24 Robertson 6705 ▪ info@wolvendriftwines.co.za ▪ www.wolvendriftwines. co.za ▪ S 33° 55′ 0.1″ E 020° 0′ 9.0″ ▪ ⬚ circling.unimportant.plight ▪ **F +27 (0)23-616-2396 ▪ T +27 (0)23-616-2890**

Women in Wine

One of the first entirely women-owned and -run enfranchisement ventures in the winelands, Women in Wine was established just over a decade ago. The founders, all black female professionals, were inspired by quality wines, and aimed to recognise the immense contribution of women to the industry, and afford them business opportunities and an overdue share in the profits - laudable goals that inform an expanded range.

Women in Wine range

Shiraz ⓃⒺⓌ ★★★ Bonfire smokiness to firm, bramble-fruited **17** ⑧①. **Rosé** ⓃⒺⓌ ★★★ Notably sweet palate of **17** ⑦⑧ is well balanced by the cherry/berry fruit, lively acidity, making it ideal for summer. **Chenin Blanc** ⓃⒺⓌ ★★★ Fig & guava appeal on light & easy **17** ⑧⓪, acidity is gentle but juicy. Not tasted: **Cabernet Sauvignon, Chardonnay, Sauvignon Blanc**.

Three Graces Reserve range

Not tasted: **Euphrosyne Cabernet Sauvignon, Thalia Merlot, Aglaia Chardonnay**. — WB, FM

Location: Paarl ▪ WO: Western Cape ▪ Closed to public ▪ PO Box 12869 Die Boord Stellenbosch 7613 ▪ info@ womeninwine.co.za ▪ www.womeninwine.co.za ▪ F +27 (0)21-872-8967 ▪ **T +27 (0)21-872-8967**

Wonderfontein   ⓆⒼ ⓐ

A warm welcome awaits at family boutique bubbly specialist Wonderfontein, based in Robertson and now open five days a week, enticing visitors with handcrafted wines and innovative packaging. The still wines offer affordability and everyday enjoyment, while the MCC's sales are taking off, necessitating new plantings of pinot noir to cope with the demand.

Paul René Méthode Cap Classique range

★★★★ **Brut Rosé** Delicious step up from **14** ★★★★ ⑧④ to **15** ⑧⑦ for this dry sparkling, pinot noir & 25% chardonnay. Refreshing salty savouriness from 2 years on lees, balancing delicate fresh red fruit.

★★★★ **Brut** Softly fruity nose on **15** ⑧⑦ bubbly comes into focus on palate with fresh citrus, biscuit & almond combining for very satisfactory & lengthy finish. From chardonnay, 24 months on lees.

Wonderfontein range

★★★★ **Wonderfontein Red Muscadel** Perfume & flowers on **16** ★★★★ ⑧③ give way to toffee, coffee hints with warm alcohol & just enough acid. Should improve. Last-tasted **11** ⑧⑦ also fragrant, fresh. **La Bonne Vigne Merlot** Ⓠ ★★ Wallet-friendly **15** ⑦④ everyday red is light bodied, with gentle grip. **La Bonne Vigne Shiraz** Ⓠ ★★★ Ready-now **13** ⑦⑧ has sweet strawberry fruit, malleable tannins & soft acidity for uncomplicated sipping. **La Bonne Vigne Sauvignon Blanc** ★★★ Candied citrus peel enlivened by zesty acidity on **18** ⑦⑨ for uncomplicated sipping. **Wonderfontein White Muscadel** ★★★ Appealing floral notes, **16** ⑧⓪'s alcohol still fiery, needs time to integrate, tad more acid would improve.

The Marais Family range

Merlot Ⓠ ★★ Anytime companion **15** ⑦④ has subtle nudge of tannin, light plummy fruit. — CM

Location/map/WO: Robertson ▪ Map grid reference: B6 ▪ Est ca 1884 ▪ Tasting Mon-Fri 9-4 Sat/Sun & pub hols by appt only ▪ Sales Mon-Fri 9–5.30 Sat 9–1 ▪ Tour groups ▪ Conferences/events (40-80 pax) ▪ Owner(s) Paul René Marais ▪ Winemaker(s) Stefan Bruwer ▪ Viticulturist(s) Gert Visser & Gerald Stemmet ▪ (merlot, muscadel r/w, pinot, shiraz, chard, sauv) ▪ PO Box 4 Robertson 6705 ▪ henk@wonderfonteinestate. co.za ▪ www.wonderfonteinestate.co.za, www.paulrenemcc.co.za ▪ S 33° 49′ 3.5″ E 019° 52′ 2.1″ ▪ 🄸 selling. cross.soloist ▪ F +27 (0)23-626-2669 ▪ **T +27 (0)23-626-2212**

Woolworths

This upmarket, nationwide retail giant's wine department offers an all-encompassing selection of unimpeachable quality and good value, invariably reflecting the latest in styles and taste trends, courtesy of long-time wine selector and Cape Wine Master Allan Mullins, working alongside white wine and bubbly buyer Rebecca Constable, and sourcer of reds and imports Rob Gower. The nearly 250 labels featured below, including over 20 newcomers, are made, blended or selected especially for 'Woollies', and producers behind the labels - a who's who of quality-wine making - range from one-person boutiques to some of SA's largest wineries. Often ahead of the pack, Allan and the team have introduced a (untasted by us) de-alcoholised wine, Lautus Savvy White, by ex-Delheim and newly independent young gun Reg Holder.

Cabernet Sauvignon range

★★★★ **Diemersdal Cabernet Sauvignon** Velvet-textured **17** (88)'s appealing cassis & green herbs wrapped in a vanilla cloak created by 20% new oak. Succulent, accessible, freshening cranberry farewell.

★★★★ **Diemersfontein Reserve Collection Cabernet Sauvignon** Serious, deftly crafted **16** (89) has structure & presence. Earthy blackcurrant & liquorice, with solid velvety tannins.

★★★★☆ **Grangehurst Cabernet Sauvignon** ⊘ Smooth & refined **13** (90), fruitcake richness & brush of herbs, lovely integration & depth on long, nuanced palate. Follows improved **11** (92). No **12**.

★★★★☆ **Signature Series Cabernet Sauvignon** ⊘ ⊛ From Thelema, combining fruit intensity with polished elegance, **16** (91) displays classic cab styling: cassis, whiff of mint, French oak (18 months, 45% new) adding spice & suave tannins. Confirms Stellenbosch's cab fame.

★★★★ **Spier Private Collection Cabernet Sauvignon** Big & bold **16** (86) has sweetly ripe black fruit, soft tannins & aromatic spices from 50% new oak. Appealing earthy underbelly, with salty liquorice notes.

★★★★☆ **Thelema Cabernet Sauvignon** ⊘ ⊛ Elgin fruit in **16** (93), no new oak, 18 months French, terroir intensifying the fruit, giving floral notes. Tannins firm, ripe, promising a future.

★★★★ **Villiera Cabernet Sauvignon** ⊛ Cassis, fruitcake & spice mingle with subtle violet notes on accomplished **16** (86). Lovely density & concentration. Structured, full & rewarding, will age well.

Cape Town Wine Co Cabernet Sauvignon (NEW) ★★★★ Medium-bodied **17** (84) for early enjoyment with sweet dark-berry fruit, light vanilla/mocha oak spice kiss. **Diemersfontein Blackberry Cabernet Sauvignon** ★★★ Lives up to its name: **17** (80) pure berry fruit, light tannins, pleasant quaffing. **Fairview Cabernet Sauvignon** ★★★★ Lighter, easy-drinking **16** (83) has savoury tone with expressive black fruit, suede tannins. **Longmarket Cabernet Sauvignon** ★★ Dark fruit, hints of chocolate & vanilla on easy-going, just-dry **17** (75) from Weltevrede. **Organic NSA Cabernet Sauvignon** ⊘ ⊛ ★★★ From Stellar Winery. Previously unwooded, **18** (81) gains from ageing in mainly seasoned barrels. Meaty savoury tones to accompany cassis; streamlined, tasty. Fairtrade certified. **Warwick Cape Lady Cabernet Sauvignon** ★★★★ Ripe redcurrants & cassis, cigarbox aroma from 10% new oak, noticeable tannin grip on youthful **16** (85). **Woolworths Cabernet Sauvignon** ⊘ ★★★ Translucent **17** (80), light tannic grip, packed with juicy berries & plums, ticks the boxes for easy everyday enjoyment. By Bergsig. Not tasted: **Single Vineyard The Hutton Cabernet Sauvignon**, **Spier Vintage Selection Cabernet Sauvignon**.

Merlot range

★★★★ **Jordan Reserve Collection Merlot** ⊛ Bright & juicy **15** (87), with similar elegant balance, supple structure as **14** ★★★★ (85), greater complexity & nuance, attractive ferrous tones, savoury end.

★★★★ **Organic Merlot** ⊘ ⊛ From Laibach, always gets the fruit/structure balance right. **17** (87) is wonderfully perfumed, cassis & violets, sweet spice, the palate's supple tannins are food friendly.

★★★★ **Shannon Merlot** Voluptuous, with hint of oak & enough tannic grip to extend meaty finish. Naturally fermented **17** (89) delightfully accessible, will reward from the get-go. Light the barbecue fire!

★★★★ **Signature Series Merlot** Deep & intense **16** (88) from Spier, inviting plum & choc notes, sweet fruit overlaid with vanilla & oak spice. Smooth & rounded now, structure for ±5 years.

★★★★ **Vergelegen Merlot** ⊛ Mainly older oak for **15** (87), less forthcoming than last, well composed & restrained, with ripe tannins that promise a future but don't hinder immediate enjoyment.

Origami NSA Merlot ⊛ ★★★★ Vivacious & fruit-filled, with oak (70% American) in support. **17** (83) from Jordan, flavoursome, dry & ready for everyday enjoyment. **Woolworths Merlot** ⊛ ★★★ Wellington Wines' **17** (81) offers choc-berry flavours, juicy drinking above the price point.

Blackcherry Merlot ★★ Herbal-tinged, very soft, easy (& just-off-dry) **17** (76) from Weltevrede. Undeniably tasty! **De Wetshof Merlot** ⊛ ★★★★ Soft, plummy **16** (85) epitomises what fans want merlot to be; feathery tannins, plush fruit soaking up 100% new oak, sweet fruit lingering in aftertaste. **Hartenberg Merlot Reserve Collection** ★★★★ Riper yet piquant red fruit on **16** (85). Lively acidity tempers alcohol & vintage warmth. A juicy, flavoursome food pairer, but shade off more balanced **15** ★★★★ (87). **La Motte Platinum Merlot** ★★★★ Cherry appeal to **16** (84), improves on previous with layered, rich palate. Firm but supple. **Light Merlot** ★★ Mostly unoaked **17** (73) by Spier has upfront mulberry fruit, dusty & nutty notes, just 9% alcohol. **Longmarket Merlot** ★★ Entry-level **17** (73) from Spier offers pleasant drinking at the price, with solid, oak-brushed black fruit. **Oakleaf Merlot Delheim** ★★★★

Plums & prunes, dark cherries & touch of jam, **16** ⑧⑤ hits the merlot spot, attractive herbaceous note freshens palate through to pleasing finish. **Organic NSA Merlot** ⊘ ★★ Offering varietal typicity, blackcurrants with a herbal note, **18** ⑦⑤'s oak spice adds to the juicy drinkability. Fairtrade certified, from Stellar Winery. **Ovation Merlot** ★★★ Juicy **17** ⑧② by Thokozani, from Robertson & Wellington grapes. Robust dark fruit with supple body, for early drinking. **Villiera Merlot** ★★★★ Supple & juicy **16** ⑧⑤ is light, soft & plummy. Gentle, with a good centre of fruit & long tail. Not tasted: **Durbanville Hills Merlot**.

Pinot Noir range

★★★★ Catherine Marshall Pinot Noir ⊘ Cheerily fruited with black cherries, **17** ⑧⑨ also has earthy & savoury nuances in dry but supple build, with Marshall's signature elegance.

★★★★ Ferricrete Pinot Noir Generous cherry fruit, coupled with a graceful bearing & vivacious acid/tannin structure make **17** ⑧⑧ a delicious drink now & for the next few years. By Paul Cluver.

★★★★ Shannon Pinot Noir ⊘ Was 'Le Petit Shannon'. Hint of mushroom adds allure to smooth **17** ⑧⑧'s good varietal character. Meaty flavours, fair grip, like **16** ★★★★ ⑧⑤, but more intensity.

DMZ Pinot Noir ⊘ ★★★☆ Pure cherry, raspberry aromas on **17** ⑧⑤ from DeMorgenzon. Charming in its fresh, soft light elegance. Like **16** ★★★★ ⑧⑦, scarcely oaked.

Pinotage range

★★★★ Diemersfontein Pinotage (NEW) ⊘ Honest, vibrant fruit to the fore, borne on silky tannins, **17** ⑧⑦ provides genuine drinking pleasure.

★★★★ Diemersfontein Pinotage Reserve Focused black berry core on **16** ⑧⑧, elegantly oak spiced. Robust, big-bodied, with silky tannins & satisfying finish.

Bellevue Reserve Collection Pinotage ★★★★ Lovely mouthfeel & freshness in **15** ⑧④, the red fruit in harmony with oak vanilla & wild herb undertones. **Beyerskloof Reserve Collection Pinotage** ★★★★ Few months on French oak staves give concentrated black berry & ripe plum fruit of **17** ⑧④ a vanilla sweetness, also evident last vintage. **Coffee Pinotage** (⊗) ★★★ Powerful coffee/toffee on Diemersfontein's **16** ⑧② masks otherwise sound, well-structured wine. **Longmarket Pinotage** ★★★ Juicy **17** ⑧⓪ from Rooiberg has tangy red berry & plum fruit, subtle vanilla & mocha from mostly older oak barrels & staves. **Organic NSA Pinotage** ⊘ ★★ Savoury wood char note to **18** ⑦⑥'s blueberry flavours, the firm dry finish, while not harsh, creating a food-friendly style. From Stellar Winery. Fairtrade certified. **Woolworths Pinotage** ⊘ ★★★★ Cheery, soft, plump **17** ⑧③ from Ken Forrester. Cherry packed, unwooded & smooth. Not tasted: **Signature Series**.

Shiraz range

★★★★ Hartenberg Shiraz Reserve Collection Blend of different vineyards, **16** ⑧⑥ aged in old oak. Savoury meaty tones with core of dark fruit encased in firm, creamy tannins. A food partner.

★★★★ Neil Ellis Groenekloof Bush Vine Shiraz ⊘ Aroma of polished leather & flavours of smoky cured meat, tangy berries & spice on **16** ⑧⑥, made even smoother by splash cinsaut.

★★★★ Reserve Radford Dale Syrah (⊗) Stunner from Radford Dale. Natural ferment, only 15% new oak enhance immediate appeal of pepper- & scrub-toned **15** ★★★★★ ⑨⓪; pristine red fruit, linear tannins, a sense of weightless intensity. Decant now or cellar 5+ years. **14** ⑧⑦ also very fine.

★★★★ Saronsberg Life is Fine Shiraz Powerful, with fruit sweetness on the finish. **16** ⑧⑥ touch unsophisticated perhaps but not lacking interest, drinkability or structure, firm oak, 30% new, bracing the ripe mulberries. **15** untasted.

★★★★ Signature Shiraz Opulent **16** ⑧⑧ from Hartenberg, deep core of spicy dark fruit & black pepper; supple dry tannins, partly from serious oaking (50% new, 18 months); ripe & succulent, already tempting.

Chocolate Shiraz ★★★ More coffee & vanilla than chocolate, **17** ⑧⓪ from Diemersfontein will appeal to fans of the aromatised style. Generously full bodied, densely fruity. **Fairview Shiraz** (NEW) ★★★★ Satisfyingly earthy, herbaceous **16** ⑧③ has tarry-tobacco core with meaty, savoury notes, full ripe tannins. **Kleine Zalze Shiraz** ★★★★ Red-fruited, spicy, with dusting of dried herbs. **16** ⑧⑤ rounded & savoury with succulent fruit, good dry finish. Perfect for meaty dishes. **Organic NSA Shiraz** ⊘ ★★★ Nothing shy about **18** ⑦⑨ from Stellar Winery: expressive morello cherry piquancy, oak spice & smooth drinkability. Fairtrade approved. **Woolworths Shiraz** ⊘ ★★★★ Appealing choc-cherry liqueur aroma, very ripe plummy notes, hint oak spice, **17** ⑧③ good solo, & just enough tannin for food partnering. Ex Darling Cellars. Not tasted: **Longmarket Shiraz**.

Niche Red Cultivars

★★★★ **Granite Blocks Cabernet Franc** ⓥ Spicy & leafy, exuberant **14** ⑧⑨ showing plush, powerful black berry fruit, lively acid & firm integrated tannin. Satisfyingly structured. No **13**. By Raats Family.

★★★★ **Ken Forrester Reserve Collection Grenache** Bright & refreshing cranberry-hued **16** ★★★★ ⑧④, light & lithe; like **15** ⑧⑥, shows subtle tannin grip from 18 months older oak.

★★★★ **Bellevue Reserve Collection Malbec** ⓥ Brims with plum, spice & fynbos in **15** ⑧⑥; there's plenty of fruit cushioning for the firm structure & 50% new oak. Excellent grilled meat partner.

★★★★ **Diemersfontein Malbec Reserve** Bright, juicy example of variety, **16** ⑧⑦ expressive & characterful, with reined-in tannins & alcohol. Ready to enjoy now, but showing potential.

Terra del Capo Reserve Collection Sangiovese ⓥ ★★★★ Cherries & violets, sleek & silky, very true to variety, **15** ⑧⑤ from Anthonij Rupert Wyne handled with finesse, delicacy. Lovely purity.

Boplaas Tinta Barocca ★★★★ Eminently drinkable **17** ⑧④ shows black fruit & leather, with lively acid & soft tannins. Not tasted: **Marras Piekenierskloof Grenache**.

Red Blends

★★★★☆ **Jordan Cobblers Hill** Complex, high-end Bordeaux blend (cab, merlot, cab franc). **14** ⑨① exceptional purity of fruit, fine tannins & elegant balance; deserves few years cellaring to show at best.

★★★★ **Neil Ellis Reserve Cabernet Sauvignon-Merlot** ⓥ Vibrant ruby **16** ⑧⑦, good freshness & bright berry appeal, dab cab franc adding leafy complexity. Balanced, smooth tannins for early drinking.

★★★★ **Organic Ladybird Red** ⓩ ⓥ 5-way Bordeaux blend by Laibach. Youthful **15** ⑧⑦ dominated by cab & merlot; more classic than **14** ★★★★ ⑧④, fruitcake enveloped in firm chalky tannins. Ageworthy.

★★★★ **Warwick Cape Lady Cape Blend** ⓥ Spiced plums & cherries in **16** ⑧⑦ pinotage (69%), shiraz & cabernet, 18 months French oak, 10% new. Meaty & spicy, white pepper nuance & cherry finish.

★★★★ **La Motte Platinum Shiraz-Grenache** Refined yet muscular **16** ⑧⑥, deep flavoured spice & plum fruit on 50/50 blend. Textured & layered, with dry, fine tannin from seasoned oak. Walker Bay fruit.

★★★★ **Reserve Collection Shiraz-Grenache-Mourvèdre** ⓥ Ken Forrester's **15** ⑧⑦, with dabs more grenache (26%) & mourvèdre (16%), improves on **14** ★★★★ ⑧⑤ with spicy blue & black fruit appeal, balanced fruit & oak, none new, 18 months.

★★★★ **Saronsberg SGM** Enticing **16** ⑧⑨ mostly shiraz (72%), with grenache & a little mourvèdre; ripely rich, with structure from 35% new oak & good tannic grip; finishes tad sweet, as last vintage.

Fairview Roaming Goat ⓝⓔⓦ ⓥ ★★★★ Very appealing 5-way, shiraz-based Rhône blend, **17** ⑧④ leather, meat & scrub on medium body.

Delaire Redstone ⓩ ★★★★ Cab-based blend with 4 other red Bordeaux varieties. **15** ⑧④ herbal & tobacco notes along with dark berry fruit. Fairly easygoing tannins allied with juiciness & integrated oak allow for early approachability. **Delheim Reserve Collection Cabernet Sauvignon-Merlot** ★★★☆ Very enjoyable everyday drinking in **16** ⑧⑤, mixing plenty of blackcurrants & cassis with juicy red plums & cherries. **Diemersdal Reserve Collection Merlot-Malbec** ★★★★ Graceful & smooth **17** ⑧④, charming blackberries & cherries, chocolate & smoke from 14 months 20% new oak. **Grand Rouge** ⓥ ★★★☆ Ample supple velvety fruitcake appeal on **16** ⑧⑤ cab/merlot mix from La Motte. Juicy, easy & plush, with nice frame from year in old oak. **La Motte Platinum Cabernet Sauvignon-Merlot** ★★★☆ Cab shades 40% merlot on cocoa- & cherry-toned **16** ⑧④ blend. Subtly spicy yet rich & gentle textured. **Longmarket Cabernet Sauvignon-Merlot** ★★ Blackberry & plum flavours on juicy **17** ⑦⑥, tasty & undemanding. By Wellington Wines. **Origami Bordeaux Blend** ⓩ ★★★ No added sulphur for **16** ⑧①, has fresh leafy note from cab franc (41%), dark plum & berry fruit from equal merlot & cab, firm nudge tannin for food. By Jordan. **Ovation Cabernet Sauvignon-Merlot** ⓝⓔⓦ ★★★ Tarry blackcurrants with mulberry notes on cheerful **16** ⑧⓪ by Thokozani. Light bodied, fruit driven, for early drinking. **Porcupine Ridge Cabernet Sauvignon-Merlot** ⓩ ★★★ Bouncy blackberry & cassis fruit, **16** ⑧① slightly leafy lift & firm tannins for mealtimes. **Pinopasso** ⓝⓔⓦ ★★★ Inspired by the Ripasso technique, **17** ⑧② remembers Italian WW2 POWs billeted at Bellingham. Mostly pinotage, off-dry, fresh black fruit layered with attractive coffee/choc notes. **Alto 1693** ⓝⓔⓦ ★★★★ Shiraz-led blend with the 2 cabs, merlot, dash petit verdot, from same stable as SA stalwart Alto Rouge. **16** ⑧⑤ fruit filled, with firm tannins, bright acidity for food or few years ageing.

DMZ Concerto Red ★★★★ Ripe, generous, warm-hearted shiraz blend from DeMorgenzon. 17 ⑧⑤ Full of flavour, easygoing, with just enough grip. Last-made 14 ★★★★ ⑧⑦ was more structured. **Longmarket Shiraz-Cabernet Sauvignon** ★★★ Produced by Rooiberg, smooth 17 ⑧⓪ also has dash petit verdot adding to ripe black berry intensity, pepper upfront & mocha to finish. **Cape Red** ★★ Light, smooth & quaffable NV ⑦⑥ from Wellington Wines, for easy drinking. **Diemersfontein Cabernet Sauvignon-Shiraz** ★★★★ 64/40 cab-led 16 ⑧⑤ offers satisfying drinking, with meaty red & black berry fruit, toasty oak notes, good finish. **Juicy Red** ★★ Easygoing, generous NV ⑦⑥ by Wellington Wines, sweetish berry fruitiness & just a little tannic grip. **Light Red** ★★ Nutty, pippy & brief, 17 ⑦④ shiraz-cinsaut from Spier has black cherry fruit, hints of oak, low 9% alcohol. **Portuguese Connection** ⓥ ★★★★ Inviting & fruit-forward 15 ⑧③, juicy rounded fruit, soft brush of oak very easy to like. By Boplaas, from mostly tinta. **Natural Sweet Red** ★★ Tastes like red grape juice with 9% dash of alcohol. Spier's 18 ⑦⓪ from ruby cab has no oak but plenty plumping sugar. **Cape Sweet Red** ★ Sweet plum pudding in a glass. NV ⑥⑧ by Wellington Wines. Not tasted: **Boschendal Nicolas De Lanoy Red Blend**.

Rosé Wines

Bellingham Strawberry Rosé ★★★ Pretty dry pink from mainly pinotage 18 ⑧② is fragrant & perfumed, with lovely strawberry & lemon flavours. **Delheim Pinotage-Shiraz Rosé** ★★★ Cheerful & pretty 18 ⑧① gains from tiny touch of muscat. Technically dry, but few grams sugar add delicious confected note to jammy red fruit. **Diemersdal Rosé** ★★★ Rosepetal pink, dry 18 ⑦⑦ from grenache. Easy to love the candyfloss & strawberry flavours. **Organic Ladybird Rosé** ⓥ ★★★ From Laibach, 18 ⑧① equal merlot/chenin, with cab, dollop petit verdot. The red berries shine but there's elegance, friendly 13% alcohol & fresh dryness that will appeal widely. **Steenberg Rosé** NEW ★★★★ Lovely dryness & freshness on 18 ⑧⑤, strawberry, raspberry & herbal fragrance & flavours but subtly presented, to not overwhelm food. Good on its own, too. From shiraz & cinsaut. **Tranquille Blush** ★★★★ Reliable, likeable dry pink from pinot noir & chardonnay. NV ⑧⑤ packed with berry fruit, finishing with a salty-mineral twist. By Haute Cabriere. **Villiera Pinot Noir Rosé** ⓥ ★★★ Fruit basket & floral whiffs, 17 ⑦⑧ a light, dry & zesty easy-sipper. **Warwick Cape Lady Rosé** NEW ★★★ From pinotage, pomegranate, watermelon & rosepetal appeal in 18 ⑧②, dry, zesty palate & spiced berry farewell. **Longmarket Pinotage Rosé** ⓥ ★★★ Cherry & strawberry ease & approachability to semi-dry 17 ⑧② pink from Villiera. Bright, light & refreshing, just 11.3% alcohol. **Cape Rosé** ★★ Baked plum nuance to NV ⑦⓪ Natural Sweet pink by Wellington Wines. Just 10% alcohol. **Natural Sweet Rosé** ★★ Spier's cinsaut 18 ⑦② is full-sweet, uncomplicated, with boiled sweet fruitiness & low 9.5% alcohol.

Chardonnay range

★★★★ **Hartenberg Reserve Collection Chardonnay** From different parcels of fruit, oak-fermented/matured 17 ⑧⑦ smooth-textured pear & citrus, lovely clean acidity & tangy flavour.

★★★★★ **Ladybird Chardonnay** ⓥ ⓐ ⓑ By Laibach. Similar to 16 ⑨③'s profile, 17 ⑨③ individual & striking, sophisticated: lemon preserve, wax, an oatmeal/almond seam focusing the elements, giving length. Naturally made, combo older barrels, concrete 'eggs' & stainless steel; splash chenin.

★★★★★ **Neil Ellis Barrel Fermented Elgin Chardonnay** ⓥ ⓑ Baked apple pie & cinnamon allure on long, intense & ageworthy 17 ⑨②. Elegant but mouthfilling, with citrus, quince & vanilla spice on palate; refreshing lemon tail.

★★★★ **Signature Chardonnay** By De Wetshof, 17 ⑧⑥'s opulent lime & lemon palate swathed in 60% new oak (fermented/aged year), luxurious feel enhanced by sweetly ripe Robertson fruit.

★★★★ **Danie de Wet Limestone Hill Chardonnay** 18 ⑧⑥ similar lemon & lime features as 17 ★★★★ ⑧③, but fresher. Well-executed unoaked style, lees aged for creamy smoothness. By De Wetshof.

★★★★ **Reserve Collection Unoaked Chardonnay** Jordan's 17 ⑧⑦ impresses most on palate: full fruited & creamy from 4 months on lees, zesty acid lift & taut, steely finish. 16 ★★★★ ⑧④ more muted.

DMZ Chardonnay NEW ★★★★ Easygoing 17 ⑧⑤ with pleasing, modest notes of peach & pear, some breadth & a lively acid thread for freshness. With all the usual flair of DeMorgenzon. **Longmarket Chardonnay** ⓥ ★★★ Pale lemon hue, lemon & clove smells & tastes: 18 ⑧⓪ from Robertson Winery unchallenging refreshment at the end of a long day. **Vanilla Chardonnay** ★★ Butterscotch & citrus join the vanilla on forthright, just-dry 17 ⑦⑥ from Weltevrede. **Warwick Cape Lady Chardonnay** ★★★★ Rich & ripe with blue-orange nuances, good length. 17 ⑧④ less crisp than last but easy to drink.

Boschendal Jean Garde Chardonnay (NEW) ★★★ Attractive tropical & stonefruit aromas on unoaked **17** (82), well balanced, dry & easygoing, though the lemony acid is a touch sourly green. **Light Chardonnay** ★★ Quaffably likeable **18** (76) from Spier has oak-free lemon/citrus fruit, zippy acid, low 9% alcohol. **Organic Chardonnay** (organic) ★★★ No oak used in Stellar Winery's Fairtrade-certified **18** (78); racy acidity adds vibrancy to the orange/tangerine flavours. **Woolworths Chardonnay** ★★★ Lemon & lime on straightforward, fruit-filled **18** (77), with a nice fresh bite & dry finish. Unwooded, from Weltevrede.

Chenin Blanc range

★★★★ **Bosman Chenin Blanc** (NEW) (organic) Just-bottled **18** (86) youthfully crisp & fresh yet nicely textured from skin-fermented component, with layers of white peach & pear, pithy grapefruit conclusion. Partly wooded. Some air-dried grapes.

★★★★ **Ken Forrester Reserve Collection Chenin Blanc** (organic) True to form, oak-touched **17** (86) offers rich stonefruit with lightly creamy frame & balancing acidity. Poised, nuanced & long.

★★★★ **Spier Private Collection Chenin Blanc** Over-delivering, barrel-fermented **17** (86) shows ripeness & lees richness, with tropical & stonefruit to the fore, oak in supporting role.

★★★★ **Noble Late Harvest Chenin Blanc** Ambrosial **17** (87) by Ken Forrester sets sweetness against tangy, freshening acidity. Rich concentration of marmalade zest & honeyed appeal, long tail is clean, dry-seeming. Year oaked. Last-made **14** also still available. 375 ml.

....

Kleine Zalze Chenin Blanc (symbol) ★★★★ Skin/lees contact has given **18** (84) a voluptuous, creamy body, packed with tropical fruit & baked apple flavours, zesty lemon twist to finish. **Reserve Collection Unwooded Chenin Blanc** (symbol) ★★★★ Fragrant stonefruit in **18** (85), a dew-fresh & fruity delight for everyday drinking on its own or with food. From Simonsig.

....

DMZ Chenin Blanc ★★★ Exuberant, ripely opulent **17** (85) from DeMorgenzon. Very lightly oaked. Packed with delicious flavour, tethered by good acidic structure. **Villiera Chenin Blanc** ★★★★ **18** (85) vibrant yet rich from dabs oak ferment, lees contact. Bold tropical styling for summer enjoyment solo or with food. **Fairview Chenin Blanc** (NEW) ★★★★ Fresh-&-fruity style **18** (83) has substance & charm. Ripe tropical fruit, crisp acidity. **Light Chenin Blanc** ★★ Low-alcohol (±9%), neutral, just-dry **18** (72) by Spier. **Longmarket Chenin Blanc** (symbol) ★★★ Granadilla & tangy lime brightness on unwooded **16** ★★★ (82) from Ken Forrester, unfussy & refreshing. **Organic Chenin Blanc** (organic) ★★★ Lovely typicity in Stellar Winery's vibrant **18** (81), apple-fresh, elegant, with zesty dryness. Backed by Fairtrade. **Peachy Chenin Blanc** (organic) ★★★★ Fruit-driven (yes, peach) **18** (83) is deliciously fresh, roundly dry, moreish in an uncomplicated way. By Spier. **Woolworths Chenin Blanc** ★★★ At under 12.5% alcohol, friendly **18** (82) from Rooiberg is dry, fruit driven, with crisp apple & tropical flavours. Not tasted: **Marras Piekenierskloof Chenin Blanc**.

Sauvignon Blanc range

★★★★ **Ferricrete Sauvignon Blanc** **17** ★★★★☆ (92) vibrant, complex & complete; sleek body, depth aided by lightly oaked 12% semillon. Improves on **16** (87), also by Paul Cluver.

★★★★☆ **Shannon Sauvignon Blanc** (organic) Gaining structure, concentration & flavour depth as vines mature. Intense grass & citrus notes of **17** (91) tempered by savoury touch from old oak (5%); delicious now, long finish invites cellaring a few years.

★★★★ **Cape Point Vineyards Cape Town Sauvignon Blanc** Flinty **18** (89) from own (Noordhoek) & WO Cape Town fruit has gooseberry, lime & grapefruit freshness, enhanced by 7.5% waxy semillon, which adds to smooth mouthfeel from 3 months lees contact.

★★★★ **Cape Town Wine Co Sauvignon Blanc** (NEW) Perfumed **17** (86), with green apple & lime, zesty acid lift but smooth conclusion from 3 months on lees, clean flinty finish.

★★★★ **Delaire White Rock** (organic) Step up **18** (88) less flamboyant than **17** ★★★★ (85) preview, more refined & subtle showing distinct wet-pebble mineral character.

★★★★ **Diemersdal Sauvignon Blanc** More serious sibling of 'Passionfruit'. Elegant & well-crafted **18** (86), delicate floral & orchard perfumes, concentrated citrus flavours & fresh mineral farewell.

★★★★ **Neil Ellis Cool Climate Sauvignon Blanc** (symbol) Tank sample **17** (87) improves on **16** ★★★★ (84) with intense tropical flavours, focused & firm, with a good acid backbone & super lemon tang to finish.

★★★★☆ **Neil Ellis Elgin Sauvignon Blanc** ⊘ Aperitif-styled **18 ★★★★** ⑧⑨'s forthcoming tropical fruit flavours matched by cool, crisp greengage, apple & citrus. Vibrant & fresh, long mineral aftertaste. Follows **15** ⑨②, which showed fine presence. No **16**; **17** untasted.

★★★★ **Reserve Collection Nitida Sauvignon Blanc** ⑧ Zippy yet rounded **17** ⑧⑨ offers gooseberry & lime with tropical nuances & flint overtone. Structured, with good body & acidity.

★★★★ **Steenberg Sauvignon Blanc** With its focus on mouthfeel & texture, **18** ⑧⑦ food friendly; extended lees contact, dash semillon adding breadth & silkiness to the grassy, gooseberry fruit.

★★★★ **Vergelegen Sauvignon Blanc** Shows Vergelegen's distinctive flinty, khaki bush aromas. **17** ⑧⑦ vibrant & finely balanced, elegant weight with generous gooseberry fruit. Splash (unoaked) semillon.

Durbanville Hills Sauvignon Blanc ★★★★ Durbanville's signature 'dusty' nuance, Granny Smith apple acidity & grapefruit pith character/texture on lively but not too dry **18** ⑧③. **Fairview Sauvignon Blanc** ★★★ Characterful, aromatic **17** ⑧② has nettle & khaki bush, dry grass & piquant passionfruit. **Kleine Zalze Sauvignon Blanc** ★★★★ Vibrates with freshness, **18** ⑧③ sleek & satisfying, with tinned pea & grassy tones, wet stone mineral finish. **Light Sauvignon Blanc** ★★★ Pleasantly crisp, flavourful **18** ⑦⑦ from Spier has dusty grassy notes, low 9% alcohol. **Longmarket Sauvignon Blanc** ★★★ No edgy acidity, just carefree sipping in gooseberry-toned, well-balanced **18** ⑦⑧ from Darling Cellars. **Organic Sauvignon Blanc** ⑦ ★★★ Crisp & lively, Stellar Winery's **18** ⑧① has fresh pear flavours, ends on a mineral note. Fairtrade endorsed. **Ovation Sauvignon Blanc** ★★★ By Thokozani, **17** ⑧⓪ from Robertson fruit offers satisfying tautness & generous fruit. **Passionfruit Sauvignon Blanc** ★★★ Fresh & forthright **18** ⑧① from Diemersdal, overt passionfruit tone plus grass & citrus - all in delicious harmony, slips down easily. **Warwick Cape Lady Sauvignon Blanc** ⑲ ★★★★ Combines cool-climate & warmer-area fruit for complexity in **18** ⑧③ while retaining acidity to brighten the citrus, kiwi & gooseberry flavours. **Woolworths Sauvignon Blanc** ★★★ Muted grassy aromas, some white pepper notes on zesty & bright **18** ⑧② wallet-friendly summer cooler from Bergsig. Not tasted: **Signature Series Sauvignon Blanc, Ghost Corner Reserve Collection Sauvignon Blanc, Thelema Cool Climate Sauvignon Blanc.**

Niche White Cultivars

★★★★ **Ferricrete Gewürztraminer** ⑧ Rosepetal & Turkish delight aromas leap out the glass while litchi & lemon freshen the palate. **16** ⑧⑦ excellent partner for Asian fare. By Paul Cluver.

★★★★ **Ken Forrester Reserve Collection Viognier** ⊘ Unwooded **17** ⑧⑦ creamy, long & well-structured, ripe peach & nectarine with light lemon brightness & fresh acid. Raises bar on **16 ★★★★** ⑧⑤.

Woolworths Moscato ★★★ Honeysuckle grapiness to sweet **18** ⑧⓪ from rare morio muscat. Easy, fresh & tangy, with unchallenging 11.9% alcohol. By Villiera. **Woolworths Pinot Grigio** ★★★ From Van Loveren, one of only a few on the market. Some mineral & pear notes in crisply dry **18** ⑦⑧, good seafood companion. Not tasted: **Ferricrete Riesling**.

White Blends

★★★★ **Chardonnay-Pinot Noir** ⊘ Previewed **18** ⑧⑥ offers fat & generous peach & pear fruit gently cosseted by acid, gratifying smooth finish. By Haute Cabrière.

★★★★ **Reserve Collection Nitida Sauvignon Blanc-Semillon** Switches to unwooded **17 ★★★★** ⑧⑤ ex Darling fruit. Tad less smooth than creamy **16** ⑧⑨, though nice flint & lemon zest typicity.

Woolworths Spier Chardonnay-Pinot Noir ⑲ ★★★ Pleasing dry blush **18** ⑧② is balanced, refreshing & characterful. Floral scents, reined-in raspberry fruit. **Light White** ★★ Colombard by Spier from Slanghoek vines. **18** ⑦④ just-dry, crisp & clean, light in fruit & alcohol (9%). **Allure Chardonnay-Pinot Noir** ⑧ ★★★ By Graham Beck, **17** ⑧① palest of blushes, ample sweet strawberry fruit from 40% pinot, lively acidity & light 10.5% alcohol for long patio lunches. **Cape White** ★★ Flavoursome sweet fruitiness on soft but fresh enough **NV** ⑦⑤ from Wellington Wines. **Chenin Blanc-Pinotage Reserve Collection** ★★★ Palest blush on creative blend by Simonsig, **18** ⑧① delectable berry freshness, hint of spice, fresh fruity finish. Undemanding in the best sense. **Longmarket Sauvignon Blanc-Chenin Blanc** ★★★ Easy summer sipper by Villiera. **18** ⑧⓪ ratio is 60/40, with light stonefruit & lemon typicity livened by fresh acid. **Natural White** ★★★★ Villiera's **18** ⑧③ unusual blend of riesling & chardonnay has rounded pear & pineapple, & honey note from natural ferment. Bright & fresh, with nothing added. **Porcupine Ridge Sauvignon Blanc-Semillon** ⑧ ★★★ Mostly sauvignon (89%) in **17** ⑧① everyday sipper & it shows: expressive green grass & granadilla, semillon adding extra zip. **Vintage Selection Sauvignon Blanc-Semillon ★★★☆** Dusty/grassy profile with sweetly ripe fruit on unwooded **18** (84) from Spier. Commendable body & length. **Zesty White ★★** Mildly fruity **NV** (75) blend from Wellington Wines, crisp & easy. **Cape Sweet White ★** Wellington Wines' charming **NV** (69) for the sweet tooth, but doesn't cloy. **Natural Sweet White ★★** Spier's **18** (75) from chenin has has tartly crisp acidity to balance substantial sweetness, muscat-like fruit profile, low 9% alcohol. Discontinued: **Grand Blanc**.

Méthode Cap Classique Sparkling range

★★★★ NSA Pinot Noir Rosé ⊘ No-sulphur-added palely blushing sparkler, **17** (87) gentle berry flavours, smooth bubbles & hints of spice on dry, lingering finish. By Simonsig, all below by Villiera.

★★★★ Brut Crisp **NV** (86) dry bubbly shows restraint, elegance & balanced apple & lime vivacity. Structured & long, with creamy breadth from 18 months on lees. From chardonnay, pinot noir & meunier.

★★★★☆ Brut Natural Top-notch **14 ★★★★** (89) sparkler has zero dosage or sulphur added, like excellent **12** (91), also all-chardonnay. Sourdough, apple & lemon vie with richly evolved (42 months on lees) notes. Complex yet crisply balanced. **13** untasted.

★★★★☆ Vintage Reserve Brut (🍋) Complex, rich & elegant bubbly from chardonnay with pinot noir & meunier. **12 ★★★★★** (95) broad & creamy thanks to 6 years lees aging, impressive verve & acid freshness. Impressive **11** (93) spent about a year less sur lie.

Brut Rosé ★★★★ Bright **NV** (85) dry pink sparkler with red-fruit notes & subtle mousse. Good yeast richness from 18 months on lees. **Light Brut ★★★★** Lemon-toned, low-alcohol (9.4%) **NV** (83) bubbly, lean & light, from chardonnay, pinot noir & pinotage. **Demi Sec ★★★** Golden Delicious appeal to off-dry **NV** (81) bubbly. Gentle sweetness well balanced by acidity & yeasty lees complexity. Not tasted: **Ladybird Brut Méthode Cap Classique**.

Sparkling Wines

Organic Pinotage Rosé Brut ⊘ **★★★** Coral-pink, dry **17** (78) sparkles with strawberry & ruby grapefruit notes, not only refreshing & low-alcohol but planet-friendly too. By Rooiberg unless noted. **Spumante Rosé ★★★** Pops with cotton candy, grape & strawberry flavours, **NV** (77) fizzer is sweet yet slightly bitter on finish. **Avivado Sec-Si** (NEW) **★★★** Innovative crown-capped fizz intended as a perk-me-up, & touch sweeter, fruitier than Brut. From chardonnay & chenin, **NV** (82) has bright peach & citrus appeal. By Villiera. **Organic Sauvignon Blanc Brut** ⊘ **★★★** Less 'green' in taste than how it was grown, **18** (79) bubbly has ripe melon & Golden Delicious apple flavours, leaving fresh yet off-dry impression. **Spumante Brut ★★★** Tiny, zippy bubbles in fresh, peachy **NV** (79), perfect for Buck's Fizz or Bellini cocktail. **Steenberg Sparkling Sauvignon Blanc** (NEW) **★★★★** Characterful **NV** (84) sparkler, tiny racy bubbles tasting of grass, blackcurrant & wet pebbles, lively & immensely drinkable. **Spumante Doux ★★☆** With under 9% alcohol, unpretentious **NV** (77) has musky, floral aromas, grape & peach flavours, sweet but clean aftertaste.

1L Box range

Dry Red ★★ NV (75) with red berry medley, slight leafy lift & satisfying tannic tug for food. By Simonsvlei & from undisclosed varieties, as all below. **Light Red** (NEW) **★★★** Appealing translucent cherry hue, cherry & red berry perfumes, lemon-toned acidity. **NV** (77) is light (9% alcohol) & pleasantly plump from few grams sugar. **Crisp White ★★** With Granny Smith apple charm, **NV** (76) is light in body yet fruit-rich, with friendly acidity. **Light White** ⊘ **★★★** Grass & thatch notes, crisp acidity & low 9% alcohol make **NV** (77) easy to drink. **Sweet Red ★★** Satisfying berries-&-cream flavour at just 10% alcohol, **NV** (75) Natural Sweet also has nicely balanced sugar. **Natural Sweet Rosé ★★** Attractive orange-pink hue, soft rose & berry aromas & flavours, just 9% alcohol, **NV** (76) is easy & fun.

2L Box range

Woolworths Merlot ⊘ **★★★** Amicable companion **17** (77) treads lightly with 12.9% alcohol, fruit-filled nose & palate, slight tannic tug. **Woolworths Sauvignon Blanc ★★★** Bone-dry, lightish (12.5% alcohol) with tropical & grass tones, **17** (79) lively dry white for lunchtime.

3L Box range

Dry Red ★★ Juicy & fresh, with a nudge of tannin, **NV** (75) slips down easily. **Light Red** ⊘ **★★★** Light cherry hue, vivid berry aroma, brisk acidity & just 9% alcohol, **NV** (77) has a lot going for it - plus a mellowing touch of sugar. **Crisp White ★★** Appley **NV** (76) just 11% alcohol, for all-day fun. **Light White** ⊘ **★★★** Zesty lemon acidity adds lift, extends the finish on low-alcohol, grass- & thatch-toned **NV** (77).

Natural Sweet Red ★★ Smooth & silky **NV** ⑦ has enlivening touch of tannin, uncloying sweetness.
Natural Sweet Rosé ★★ Aromas of berries & soft candy on low-alcohol **NV** ⑦, joined on palate by light sprinkle of herbs. Appealing, not over-sweet. **Sweet White** (NEW) **★★** Baked apple & biscuit whiffs on round & mouthfilling **NV** ⑦ Natural Sweet, with low 9.5% alcohol.

5L Box range

Dry Red ★★ Party/braai-perfect **NV** ⑦ has bright red & black berry flavour, bouncy freshness & just the right amount of tannin for food. **Crisp White ★★** Lightish & easy to drink, **NV** ⑦ offers Granny Smith apple aromas & flavours with the advertised crispness. **Sweet Red** (NEW) **★★** Easygoing & uncomplicated **NV** ⑦ Natural Sweet has creamy berry nuances, balanced sugar. **Natural Sweet Rosé ★★** Herbal lift to **NV** ⑦'s delicate tones, satin texture from well-managed sweetness. — Various tasters

WO: Various ▪ Buyer Rob Gower T +27 (0)21-407-7644 RobGower@woolworths.co.za ▪ Buyer Rebecca Constable T +27 (0)21-407-3162 RebeccaConstable@woolworths.co.za ▪ Selector Allan Mullins T +27 (0)21-407-7443 AllanMullins@woolworths.co.za ▪ Owner(s) Woolworths Holdings ▪ Woolworths House 93 Longmarket Str Cape Town 8000 ▪ www.woolworths.co.za ▪ F +27 (0)21-407-3958 ▪ **T +27 (0)21-407-9111**

☐ **#WOPrieska** see Lowerland
☐ **Word Collection** see Rascallion Wines
☐ **Workhorse** see Ken Forrester Wines
☐ **Xaro** see Stellenrust
☐ **Xenna** see Annex Kloof Wines
☐ **Y** see Yonder Hill

Yardstick Wines ⓟ

This is Adam Mason's personal project, which he owns in partnership with Stellenbosch's Mulderbosch, where he is winemaker and crafts the small-batch Yardstick wines. Over the years, Adam says, he's had the benefit of working with 'many amazing vineyards', and for his original Yardstick and Marvelous ranges, he combined the fruit from those blocks. Latterly, however, he's introduced Raised by Wolves as a platform 'to give these sites their just dues' by vinifying and bottling them as single vineyards or, in the case of Old School, as a blend with a single 'message'. The results invariably are both fascinating and delicious.

Raised By Wolves range

★★★★ Bonniemile Cabernet Sauvignon (NEW) From 1986 enclosed vineyard on koffieklip (ferricrete) soils. **16** ⑧⑧ savoury fruit encased in dry chalky tannins, shows house's restraint & elegance (12.9% alcohol).

★★★★ Newlands Meunier Piquant cranberry impression on old-oak-matured **17 ★★★★** ⑧⑤. Refined, light (12.7% alcohol) solo or light meal partner with clean dry farewell. More demure than **16** ⑧⑦.

★★★★ Limestone Pinot Noir ⓟ Natural freshness, restrained 13% alcohol lift & lengthen **15** ⑧⑨'s dark cherry flavours. From Vermaaklikheid (Cape South Coast) block, built for medium-term ageing.

★★★★ Old School Riper **16** ⑧⑥ has smoky berry nuance from old-vine cinsaut's lead (75%) in traditional blend with cab. Achieves succulent balance, with gentle savoury tone. Commendably modest (12.7%) alcohol, a common thread in all these wines, all naturally fermented except Cab.

★★★★ Karibib Chardonnay ⓟ Softish, tempered 12.8% alcohol, yet **16** ⑧⑦ shows bright peachy, nutty fruit, depth in the creamy layers. Polkadraai vines, older 500L barrels; some maceration carbonique.

★★★★☆ 777 Chardonnay (NEW) 🐝 Name refers to lofty altitude of Piekenierskloof vines. **17** ⑨③ has a lovely purity & concentration; deft oaking (only wine here using new barrels: 31%) adds complementary spice. Balanced & fresh, despite going though malolactic ferment, elegant & focused.

★★★★ Driehoek Chenin Blanc Restrained, quietly confident & balanced **17** ⑧⑧. Subtle dried peach, nutty tone from old Montpellier clone. Freshness woven into creamy lees substrate.

★★★★☆ La Colline Semillon Different parts of same 1930s Franschhoek block as sibling, neutral-oak aged. **17** ⑨② lanolin & honey, silky texture & clean fresh vein. Graceful intensity & moderate 12.9% alcohol, understated yet insistent.

★★★★ **La Colline 'Semillon Gris'** Orange hue reflects a possibly unique 'rooi groendruif' mutation of semillon, from old Franschhoek vines. Part carbonic macerated, part old-oak fermented/aged. **17** ⑧⑥'s tangy red fruit has brush of tannin, making a great food wine, especially at 11.8% alcohol.

★★★★ **Bonniemile Muscat Blanc** ⑭ⓔⓦ (White) muscat de Frontignan's scented, grapey allure in bone-dry, creamy **17** ⑧⑦. Early picked fruit is part carbonic, part old-oak fermented/aged. Soft but balanced acidity, pleasing 10.8% alcohol. Delicious food pairer.

Yardstick range

★★★★ **Pinot Noir** ⓐ **15** ★★★★ ⑧⑷ ex Elgin, Agter Witzenberg, riper, more robust than **14** ⑧⑦. Quite plush dark berry fruit lifted by 20% new French oak. Ends a little heavy, sweet (though technically dry).

★★★★ **Chardonnay** ⓐ Classically styled **15** ⑧⑨ has oatmeal, citrus introduction; lees ageing adds complexity, creaminess but no heaviness thanks to natural/clean feel of cool-climate fruit.

Marvelous range

★★★★ **Blue** ⓐ Cab franc (33%) brings fragrant note of distinction to **15** ⑧⑧. Nice flesh for current drinking, firmness for few years from merlot, cab, drops malbec, petit verdot. Older French oak.

★★★★ **Red** ⓐ Freshness & savoury depths add to delicious drinkability of **15** ⑧⑦. Well-assembled cinsaut, shiraz/syrah partnership with 3 others, older oak rounded. **14** ★★★★ ⑧⑷ lacked similar punch.

★★★★ **Yellow** ⓐ Chenin, backed by muscat de Frontignan, semillon, clairette & chardonnay, all fused in older 500L French oak. **16** ⑧⑥ tasty if perhaps lacking intrigue of **15** ⑧⑦. — MW

Location/map: Stellenbosch ▪ Map grid reference: C5 ▪ WO: Stellenbosch/Western Cape/Franschhoek/Cape South Coast/Piekenierskloof ▪ Est/1stB 2009 ▪ Tasting by appt ▪ Owner(s) Adam Mason in partnership with Mulderbosch Vineyards ▪ Winemaker(s) Adam Mason ▪ Raised By Wolves 1,000cs 25% red 75% white ▪ adam@yardstickwines.com ▪ www.yardstickwines.com, www.marvelouswines.com ▪ S 33° 53' 22.8" E 018° 49' 8.3" ▪ ⓦ jacket.panels.dwelled ▪ F +27 (0)21-881-3372 ▪ **T +27 (0)82-924-3286**

Yonder Hill

The Naudé family's estate at the foot of yonder Helderberg has 5 ha of vines, straw-mulched by consultant viticulturist/winemaker Abé Beukes and team for much-needed moisture retention; a cellar and visitor centre with brand-new, fully equipped function and conference facility — and a pasture-ful of enormous horns! Attached, it must be said, to the heads of an Ankole cattle herd, so imposing and extraordinary, they just had to be featured in the name and on the label of the newest addition to the product range, craft beer.

Premium range

★★★★ **Merlot** ⓐ Seductive nose of dark berries, spicy fruitcake & vanilla oak, **14** ⑧⑥ creamy & full, supple tannins & fresh grip on the finish. Perfect for grilled meat.

★★★★ **Inanda** ⓐ More complexity on cab franc-led Bordeaux blend **15** ⑧⑦ than **14** ★★★☆ ⑧⑷. Floral aromas, a good black-fruit flavour punch balanced by silky tannins.

★★★★ **Nicola** ⓐ Sibling 4-way Bordeaux blend is majority cab (37%), & it shows in deep cassis fruit, firm tannins that will aid ageing. Cedar nuance from 80% new oak on **15** ⑧⑦.

Danilo Rosé ★★★★ Attractive copper hue, **18** ⑧⑷ merlot/grenache tank sample's abundant red bouquet layered with cinnamon & flowers. Dry, zesty & balanced.

Y range

Merlot ★★★ Friendly **17** ⑧① soft & juicy, unfettered by oak for immediate enjoyment. Wallet-pleasing price, too. WO W Cape. **Sauvignon Blanc** ⓥ ★★★★ Crisp **18** ⑧③ preview, kiwi fruit, apple & gooseberry appeal, lingering tropical finish & sense of lightness despite 13.9% alcohol. — GM

Location: Stellenbosch ▪ Map: Helderberg ▪ Map grid reference: C3 ▪ WO: Stellenbosch/Western Cape ▪ Est 1989 ▪ 1stB 1993 ▪ Tasting & sales Mon-Fri 9–4 Sat (Nov-Feb) 10-4 ▪ Closed all pub hols ▪ Cellar tours by appt only ▪ Function & conference venue: functions@yonderhill.co.za ▪ Tour groups ▪ Gift shop ▪ Olives & olive oil tasting ▪ Ankole craft beer ▪ Owner(s) Naudé family ▪ Cellarmaster(s)/winemaker(s) Abé Beukes (2014) ▪ Viticulturist(s) Abé Beukes ▪ 14ha/5ha (cabs s/f, merlot, p verdot) ▪ 50t/15,000cs own label 80% red 20% white ▪ PO Box 914 Stellenbosch 7599 ▪ wines@yonderhill.co.za ▪ www.yonderhill.co.za ▪ S 34° 2' 22.5" E 018° 49' 40.2" ▪ ⓦ superstore.rekindling.handwritten ▪ F +27 (0)21-855-1006 ▪ **T +27 (0)21-855-1008**

☐ **Zahir** see Lateganskop Winery

☐ **Zakkie Bester** see Bester Family Wines

☐ **Zalze** see Kleine Zalze Wines

Zanddrift Vineyards - Chapel Cellar ⓠ ⑪ ⓐ ⓑ

Owned by retired Singapore architect Koh Seow Chuan, Zanddrift boutique winery's mostly exported Chapel Cellar range - semi-sweet Rosé and blends Myrna and Lost - is named for the chapel-like visitor locale near Paarl, catering for all members of the family.

Location/map: Paarl ▪ Map grid reference: E6 ▪ Est 1995 ▪ Tasting & sales Mon-Fri 9-5 ▪ Restaurant & function venue T +27 (0)60-802-2933 (Hennie) ▪ Kids play area with jungle gym ▪ Special menu for kids ▪ Small weddings (70-80 pax) ▪ Private functions ▪ Live entertainment ▪ Owner(s) Windsharp Trading 23, Koh Seow Chuan (Singapore) ▪ Winemaker(s)/viticulturist(s) Christo Jacobs ▪ 8.5ha (cab, shiraz) ▪ PO Box 1302 Suider-Paarl 7624 ▪ zanddrift@telkomsa.net ▪ S 33° 45' 39.20" E 018° 59' 11.41" ▪ ⓦ lookout.speeds.from ▪ F +27 (0)86-530-1892 ▪ **T +27 (0)21-863-2076/+27 (0)82-256-5006**

Zandvliet Wine Estate ⓠ ⓐ ⓑ

Known as a 'home of shiraz', because of not only the current range but also plantings dating back to the 1870s, Zandvliet is enjoying a renaissance under the ownership of ANB Investments, perhaps best known for its ClemenGold mandarin brand. Some vines on the Robertson estate have given way to citrus; heightened focus on the remainder is yielding results, though GM/winemaker Jacques Cilliers also emphasises the importance of terroir: 'The magical key to our success lies within our kalkveld or calcareous Karoo soils.'

Hill of Enon range

★★★★ **Small Berry Pick Shiraz** Basket-pressed **16** ★★★★★ (90), 2 years in equal French/American oak, 50% new, has dense, luscious, ripe yet tangy forest fruit flavours & sweet wood spice. Rich yet elegantly fresh at under 13% alcohol. A step up on last-tasted **12** (88).

Occasional release: **Terroir Chardonnay**.

Kalkveld range

★★★★ **Shiraz** Billowing berry aromas on **15** (89), lusciously intense fruit on palate, spice from 2 years French oak, 30% new, well-judged tannins/acidity, as in **14** ★★★★ (84). Poised & refined at 13.5% alcohol.

Zandvliet Estate range

★★★★ **Shiraz** ⊘ Retasted **15** (88) has acquired smoky, leathery, herbal complexity over past year. Enjoyable young, thanks to juicy red fruit, can age. Like **14** ★★★ (81), also in bottle sizes from 375ml to 27L.

★★★★ **Chardonnay** Evoking lemon-drizzled almond cake with its tangy citrus freshness & nut nuances from 7 months in older oak, wild-fermented **17** (87) is dry, with hint marmalade from ±5% botrytis.

★★★★ **Sauvignon Blanc** Brief lees contact gives some weight & mineral smoothness to **18** (86), redolent of lime & passionfruit, focused & refreshing at under 13% alcohol. **17** sold out untasted.

White Muscat Natural Sweet ⊘ ⑰ ★★★★ Fresh mandarin & tangy dried apricot on **18** (85), high acid & low alcohol (±7%) provide vibrant balance to muscadel's sweetness.

VLW Cape Vintage Shiraz ⑫ ★★★★ Estate's signature grape inspanned for 'port'; **13** (83)'s smoky molasses tones & curvaceous body have serious tannin seam from 3 years in barrel, finishes dry, savoury.

My Best Friend range

Cape Red ★★★ Touch of oak on juicy **NV** (77), equal parts shiraz/cab with 10% merlot. Pizza wine. **Semi-Sweet** ★★★ Lemon-drop tangy sweetness on light **18** (78), a good Asian food match. **Cape White** ★★★ Fruity, easy-drinking **18** (77) mostly chenin, with partners sauvignon & chardonnay. — JG

Location: Ashton ▪ Map/WO: Robertson ▪ Map grid reference: C4 ▪ Est 1867 ▪ 1stB 1975 ▪ Tasting, sales & cellar tours Mon-Fri 9—5 Sat 10-4 ▪ Closed Easter Fri/Sun, Dec 25/26 & Jan 1 ▪ Tour groups ▪ Private tastings by appt ▪ Art exhibition ▪ Winemaker(s) / GM Jacques Cilliers (Dec 2011) ▪ PO Box 36 Ashton 6715 ▪ info@zandvliet. co.za ▪ www.zandvliet.co.za ▪ S 33° 50' 50.7" E 020° 2' 13.7" ▪ ⓦ stringency.spasmed.senator ▪ F +27 (0)23-615-1327 ▪ **T +27 (0)23-615-1146**

Zandwijk

This small winery is the sole kosher-only producer in SA, based at the Zandwijk farm on Paarl Mountain. Winemaker Jean van Rooyen makes quality wines that are Orthodox Union certified under the supervision of the Cape Town Beth Din. The Unorthodox range, intended as 'kosher wines that defy convention', are doing particularly well in the US and Canada, acclaimed for both their refreshingly quirky labels and the wine.

Unorthodox range

Merlot-Cabernet Sauvignon ⓥ ★★★★ Mevushal & kosher for Passover (as both ranges) blend aimed at the fine-wine market, **14** (83) suitably careful oaking (French only for cab, some American for merlot) adds attractive spicing to concentrated fruit. WO Paarl. **Chenin Blanc** (NEW) ★★★ Pineapple & baked apple pie flavours with a viscous texture, some plumpness from lees contact & alcohol, just enough acidity to balance smooth & affable **18** (82). **Sauvignon Blanc** ⓥ ★★★★ Widely sourced **17** (83) good varietal character & acidity, significantly improves on winery's previous sauvignon bottlings.

Kleine Draken range

Vin Doux ⓥ ★★ Watermelon notes on **NV** (73) sweet sparkler from sauvignon & riesling. Low-alcohol for all these (7-9%). **Natural Sweet Red** ★★ Now from merlot, **NV** (71) is gently sweet, with very slight dark cherry & berry flavour. **Natural Sweet White** ★★ Delicate jasmine-scented sweetness, light, with a hint of lime sherbet. **NV** (72) from riesling. **Kiddush** ★★ Sacramental wine, **NV** (74) with cherry, grapey tones from 15% red muscadel & merlot, cloying sweetness. — MW, GdB

Location/map: Paarl ▪ Map grid reference: D6 ▪ WO: Coastal/Paarl ▪ Est 1983 ▪ 1stB 1988 ▪ Tasting & sales Mon-Fri 8–4 ▪ Closed all pub hols & Jewish holy days ▪ Cellar tours by appt ▪ Pre-booked kosher picnics available ▪ Owner(s) Cape Gate (Pty) Ltd ▪ Winemaker(s) Jean van Rooyen (Dec 2007) ▪ Viticulturist(s) Frank Pietersen (1984) ▪ 12.5ha/8ha under vine ▪ 55t/20,000cs own label 60% red 40% white ▪ IPW, OU certified ▪ PO Box 2674 Paarl 7620 ▪ zandwijk@capegate.co.za ▪ www.zandwijk.co.za ▪ S 33° 46' 33.3" E 018° 56' 50.4" ▪ 🗺 stole.retrial.secrets ▪ **T +27 (0)21-863-2368**

☐ **Zaràfa** see Mountain River Wines
☐ **Z-Collection** see Zevenwacht
☐ **Zebra Collection** see Rooiberg Winery
☐ **Zellerhof** see Huguenot Wine Farmers
☐ **Zenith** see Kumala

Zevenwacht

With the ambitious soil study project spanning Zevenwacht and Zevenrivieren, respectively the Johnson family's home-farm just outside Stellenbosch and their second property in Banhoek, already informing a vineyard rejuvenation programme, the focus has shifted to individual vines and cellar techniques. More specifically, the establishment of a nursery where bought-in vines will be nurtured ahead of being planted in the hope that the opportunity to develop a bigger root system will result in more robust growth. In the cellar, new winemaker Hagen Viljoen is picking up on various experiments designed to enhance blend component options, including spontaneous primary ferments, spontaneous malolactic ferments in white-wine barrels and wholebunch ferments.

Flagship range

★★★★ **Cabernet Sauvignon** ⓥ Slightly less plush than last, as expected in structured **15** (87) vintage, firmer tannins, livelier acidity & brighter fruit; equal harmony & polished oaking, 30% new, 18 months.

★★★★ **Syrah** ⓥ Generous savoury red & black fruit overlaid with smoked meat, subtle oak spice (30% new), **16** (87) really vibrant, balanced & not over-worked. Enough grip for food but terrific solo too.

★★★★ **Chardonnay Barrel Fermented** With pure lemon fruit masked by oak (30% new) mid-2018, **17** ★★★★ (84) doesn't quite hit same notes as well-judged **16** (86). Less rich & knit, but bone-dry, may show better with time.

★★★★ **Chenin Blanc** ⓦ From 36 year old vines, engaging **17** (86) white & yellow peaches & pine-apples, judicious barrel ferment/ageing (20% new) gives sweet vanilla note but retains variety's vibrant acidity, bone-dry finish enhances appeal.

★★★★☆ **Sauvignon Blanc** Cool-climate fruit & soft acidity the focus of **18** (90), tasted newly bottled yet already poised & delicious. From highest, sea-facing vines, with usual unoaked semillon (13%) for extra depth & breadth. Also in 375 ml, like Cabernet.

Merlot ★★★★ No new oak for vivacious **15** (85), chocolate- & plum-toned, as usual, with sappy, food-friendly tannins.

Z-Collection

★★★★ **Reserve** (②) Bordeaux-style quintet led by cab (74%), plump logan- & blueberries, leathery note in **14** (87). Good grip from grape tannin & 40% new oak, sweet-fruit finish. Benefits from decanting but ideally should be cellared to settle, show complexity.

★★★★ **Gewürztraminer** (②) (④) Oak adds sophistication, as in **15** (89), but doesn't temper blowsier features or food-inviting pithiness of variety in dry **16** ★★★★ (84).

★★★★☆ **360° Sauvignon Blanc** (④) Assured & polished **17** (93) from south-facing 18 year old vines on coolest site. Similar leafy blackcurrant & ruby grapefruit tones as Flagship but richer, weightier, thanks to 15% oaked semillon. Elevated acidity gives more zing. No **16**.

Not tasted: **Grenache**.

The Tin Mine Collection

★★★★ **Red** (✓) Serious but friendly Rhône blend, **15** (86) mostly shiraz (57%) with lovely pepperiness from grenache. Approachable, but tannins have legs for a few years. Well-priced, especially in 1.5L format.

White ★★★★ Rounded & rich, gently oaked to preserve ample ripe fruit, **17** (85) has all ingredients for a cut-above everyday white. Chenin & chardonnay, splashes viognier, roussanne, mostly older oaked.

7even range

Pinotage ★★★ Dash sugar for enhanced drinkability, **16** (80) mulberry & smoke attractions, friendly tannins from clever oak-staving. **Rood** ★★★ Attractive easy-drinking red with no rough edges. **16** (80) mainly shiraz (86%), splashes grenache & mourvèdre, few months older barrels. **Rosé** ★★★ Slightly drier, more serious & intense than most lunchtime pinks, **18** (80) berries-&-cream character from cab franc. **Sauvignon Blanc** ★★★ Perfumed & well-flavoured, **18** (80)'s daub of sweetness heightens the appeal. **Bouquet** ★★★ Usual trio aromatic varieties deliver the pretty bouquet in **18** (80), noticeably sweet this time, needs to be chilled well. Mostly viognier, dashes gewürztraminer, muscat de Frontignan. — CvZ

Location: Kuils River ▪ Map/WO: Stellenbosch ▪ Map grid reference: B5 ▪ Est 1980 ▪ 1stB 1983 ▪ Tasting & sales Mon-Fri 8.30–5 Sat/Sun 9.30–5 ▪ Fee R35 ▪ Closed Dec 25 ▪ Cellar tours by appt ▪ Restaurant ▪ Picnics in summer ▪ Facilities for children ▪ Conferences ▪ Weddings/banqueting ▪ Walking & MTB trails ▪ Conservation area ▪ Bakwena Spa ▪ 4-star Country Inn ▪ Owner(s) Harold Johnson ▪ Winemaker(s) Hagen Viljoen (Aug 2018), with Charles Lourens (Jun 2014) ▪ Viticulturist(s) Eduard van den Berg (Jan 2001) ▪ 473ha/100ha (cabs s/f, grenache, merlot, mourv, ptage, primitivo, shiraz, chard, chenin, gewürz, muscat de F, rouss, sauv, sem, viog) ▪ 657t/100,000cs own label 48% red 48% white 4% rosé ▪ IPW ▪ PO Box 387 Kuils River 7579 ▪ info@zevenwacht.co.za ▪ www.zevenwacht.co.za ▪ S 33° 55' 46.0" E 018° 43' 38.2" ▪ ⓘ hearse.postings.fending ▪ F +27 (0)21-903-3373 ▪ **T +27 (0)21-900-5700**

Zidela Wines

Stellenbosch family negociant Zidela, its owners well versed in wine buying, production and marketing, provides bulk and bottled wine for buyers' own brands as well as proprietary marques African King, Boschheuvel, Mbali, Mooiberg, Sumerton and Zidela to markets around the globe.

Location: Stellenbosch ▪ Est 2001 ▪ 1stB 2002 ▪ Closed to public ▪ Owner(s) Danie, Erik & Jaco Kritzinger ▪ 60% red 30% white 10% rosé ▪ 13-million litres for clients ▪ PO Box 3021 Matieland 7602 ▪ info@zidelawines.co.za ▪ www.zidelawines.co.za, www.privatewinelabel.co.za ▪ F +27 (0)21-880-2937 ▪ **T +27 (0)21-880-2936**

Zonnebloem

For many decades now, an exemplar of consistency and value, Distell's Zonnebloem label balances this heritage with a thoroughly modern approach to the wines and the people entrusted with making them. Hence the largely female viti-vini team producing the popular favourites and hidden gems, and the new player, Dumisani Mathonsi, with 14 years' seasoning at top-flight Tokara, running on as white-wine maker.

Zonnebloem range

★★★★ **Shiraz-Mourvèdre-Viognier** ⊘ Most demure but most beguiling of cellar's shiraz-dominant trio. **16** ⑧⑨ savoury pepper & black olives, dark fruit & Asian spice make for a really good drink.

★★★★ **Lauréat** ⊘ Cab/merlot with shiraz & petit verdot. Super-smooth & -stylish **15** ★★★★★ ⑨⓪ adds spice to polished black fruit on sleek body. Well-balanced, achieves more with less alcohol force than **14** ⑧⑨. Serious oaking (70% new barrels, 2 years) effortlessly assimilated.

. . . .

Shiraz ⊘ 🍷 ★★★★ Juicy **16** ⑧⑤ offers ripe dark berries & smoky bacon, medium body & supple tannins; satisfying anytime wine. **Blanc de Blanc** ⊘ 🍷 ★★★ Perennial favourite. Chenin & sauvignon **18** ⑧② is charming, offers unexpected concentration, flavour variety (lime, papaya, crunchy apple) & smile-inducing price.

. . . .

Cabernet Sauvignon ⊘ ★★★★ Solid, dependable, & like red siblings, enough fruit, not too much wood, medium weight. Good varietal definition makes **16** ⑧⑤ a gratifying drop. **Merlot** ★★★ A standard dry red with respectable vinosity, violet aromas & plum & liquorice flavours on **16** ⑧②. **Pinotage** ★★★ Undemanding **16** ⑧① out of the textbook: generous fruit presence (cherries, plums) & grippy tannins for above-average everyday quaffing. **Chardonnay** ⊘ ★★★★ Uncomplicatedly tasty **17** ⑧④ offers pleasant fruit medley, creaminess from lees & support of aromatic vanilla oak. **Sauvignon Blanc** ★★★ **18** ⑧② delivers interest, refreshment with flavours/textures from grass through fresh lime to plump gooseberry.

Limited Editions

Not tasted: **Cabernet Sauvignon**, **Pinotage**, **Shiraz**, **Chenin Blanc**, **Sauvignon Blanc**. — DS

Location/WO: Stellenbosch ▪ Est 1893 ▪ Wine sales at Die Bergkelder Wine Centre ▪ Owner(s) Distell ▪ Cellarmaster(s) Elize Coetzee (Nov 2015) ▪ Winemaker(s) Bonny van Niekerk (reds, Oct 2007) & Dumisani Mathonsi (whites, 2018), with Kelly Jacobs & Ulrich Hohns ▪ Viticulturist(s) Isabel Habets ▪ (cab, merlot, shiraz, chard, sauv, sem) ▪ 9,500t/±109,000cs own label 60% red 40% white ▪ ISO 9002, Fairtrade ▪ PO Box 184 Stellenbosch 7599 ▪ info@zonnebloem.co.za ▪ www.zonnebloem.co.za ▪ F +27 (0)21-886-4879 ▪ T +27 (0)21-809-7000

☐ **Zonneweelde** see Slanghoek Winery

Zorgvliet Wines   🍷 🍴 🏠 📷 🛏 ♿

Occupying prime sites on the southern Simonsberg slopes, the vineyards on Stephan and Izelle van der Merwe's estate are gradually being converted to a classic Bordeaux mix as other varieties are replaced, most recently with cab, cab franc and semillon. Add a new sorter/destemmer in the cellar and it's little wonder that winemaker Bernard le Roux is excited about the estate's wine quality, matching attractive visitor and guest amenities, and wraparound mountain scenery in this corner of Banhoek Valley.

Grand Cuvée range

★★★★★ **Richelle** 🐝 Authoritative cab-led Bordeaux blend, lavish blue berry, cassis & floral-herbal tone in **16** ⑨③, stylish cigarbox note from 60% new oak. Like stellar **15** ★★★★★ ⑨⑤, has structure & flesh to reward cellaring decade/more. Also in magnum, as next.

★★★★★ **Simoné** 🐝 Fine & elegant barrel-fermented sauvignon & semillon showcases fruit purity, freshness & length in **17** ⑨③. (Old) oak in support, subtly adding vanilla nuances, breadth & weight. As sharply focused as previous, with apple & citrus tones.

Zorgvliet range

★★★★★ **Cabernet Sauvignon** ⊘ 🐝 Though bone-dry, **16** ⑨③ shows house's fruit generosity, dense mulberry & cassis complemented by mountain herbs & cedar spice, tamed by variety's firm tannin grip, graphite minerality. 37% new oak, less than in **15** ⑨③; both for good few years cellaring.

★★★★ **Cabernet Franc** Helping build Banhoek's reputation for superior cab franc, **16** ⑧⑦ vibrant raspberry & blackcurrant fruit, herbal touches, judicious 32% new oak.

★★★★ **Malbec** Red-fruit bouquet scented with violet & rooibos, **16** ⑧⑥ mulberry & plum palate framed by nimble tannins, edged with cool minerality.

★★★★ **Merlot** Accessible **16** ⑧⑦, delightful savoury-fruity contrast: heady plum, blueberry & dark chocolate followed by spice from well-judged 17% new oak, limber tannins supportive.

★★★★ **Petit Verdot** Wild berry & coriander attractions, **16** (88) dense fruit centre, compact tannins, mineral conclusion to an impressive package. 36% new oak.

★★★★ **Cabernet Franc Rosé** (✷) First under Zorgvliet label, salmon-hued **17** (87) very delicate, dry & crisp, pinpoint red berry fruit & attractive crushed herb undertone. Refined summer party pink.

★★★★ **Single Vineyard Sauvignon Blanc** (✷) Trademark tropical fruit, fig & citrus array on **17** ★★★★★ (94), delivered with greater breadth, depth & concentration than in last-tasted **15** (87). Exceptional. Zesty lemon cleanout sets up the next sip.

Silver Myn range

Argentum (✓) (✷) ★★★★ Youthful, nimble & juicy **17** (84), 5-way Bordeaux red mostly merlot & cab, older oak for pure fruit expression, hint spice. Very well priced, for early enjoyment. WO Stellenbosch, as all.

Rosé ★★★ Pink from sauvignon, semillon & cab franc; acidity holds cherry & strawberry aromas/flavours in check, giving bracingly dry effect in **18** (81). **Sauvignon Blanc** ★★★ Dash semillon adds extra freshness to zesty, tropical-toned **18** (81). — GM

Location/map: Stellenbosch ▪ Map grid reference: H4 ▪ WO: Banghoek/Stellenbosch ▪ Est/1stB 2000 ▪ Tasting & sales Mon-Fri 9—5 Sat 10-5 Sun/pub hols 11—5 ▪ Closed Good Fri, Dec 25 & Jan 1 ▪ Fee R10/wine, waived on purchase ▪ Cellar tours by appt ▪ Zorgvliet picnic Sep-Apr ▪ Facilities for children ▪ Tour groups ▪ Gifts ▪ Conferences ▪ Walks/hikes ▪ Zorgvliet Country Lodge (17 rooms) ▪ Owner(s) Stephan & Izelle van der Merwe ▪ Winemaker(s) Bernard le Roux (Dec 2013), with Ruben Adams ▪ Viticulturist(s) Hannes Jansen van Vuuren ▪ 58ha/25ha (cabs s/f, merlot, p verdot, sauv, sem) ▪ 300t/35,000cs own label 32% red 64% white 4% rosé + 200t for clients ▪ PO Box 1595 Stellenbosch 7599 ▪ winecellar@zorgvliet.com ▪ www.zorgvlietwines.com ▪ S 33° 54' 41.7" E 018° 56' 32.0" ▪ (⌨) instant.spreads.averts ▪ F +27 (0)21-885-1318 ▪ **T +27 (0)21-885-1399**

☐ **Zulu 8** *see* Stellenview Premium Wines

VIVAT BACCHUS

Restaurant, Wine Bar & Cheese Room

Home from home
...in London

South African co-owner Gerrie came over from Johannesburg in 2003; known for the *Roxy Rhythm Bar* in the 1980s and later on *Browns of Rivonia*, he was determined to bring a taste of SA to London and so Vivat Bacchus came into being.

A celebration of rustic robust food, particularly steaks, artisan cheeses and a focus on great SA wines, it's the place to visit in London.

Cellars full of SA wines

Great steaks and SA smiles

Visit our walk-in Cheese Rooms

BRINGING
HOME **GOLD**
SINCE 2010

RIO LARGO

GOLD

EXTRA
VIRGIN
OLIVE
OIL

Cold Extracted

PRODUCT OF SOUTH AFRICA

RIO LARGO

OLIVE ESTATE

TRY IT. YOU'LL LOVE IT!

Breede River Valley, Western Cape
Tel.: +27 23 340 4776
info@riolargo.co.za | www.riolargo.co.za

This Year's Ratings Summarised

Here we summarise the wines featured in the A–Z section, with their ratings, sorted first by wine style, in alphabetical order, and then by producer or brand. New wines in **bolder type**. **NS** = no star; **NT** = not tasted; **NR** = tasted but not rated; **D** = discontinued. Where wineries produce more than one version of a particular style, the number of versions is indicated in brackets after the name. A number of wines were tasted as pre-bottling barrel or tank samples, and therefore ratings are provisional. Refer to the A–Z for details.

Albariño
★★★★☆ Newton Johnson

★★★ Nederburg

Alternative white/red
★★★★☆ Springfontein (White blends, wooded, dry), **Neil Ellis** (White blends, wooded, dry), Maanschijn (Grenache gris)

★★★★ Maanschijn (Verdelho)

★★★★ Dragonridge (2) (Chenin blanc unwooded dry, White blends, wooded, dry) ★★★ Dragonridge (2) (Red blends, with pinotage, Chardonnay wooded)

Barbera
★★★★☆ Trizanne

★★★★ Fairview, Idiom, Merwida

★★★★ Altydgedacht, Bester ★★ Hofstraat **NT** BruceJack, Idiom, Jakkalsvlei

Biodynamic
★★★★★ Reyneke (Cabernet sauvignon)

★★★★☆ Reyneke (3) (Shiraz/syrah, Chenin blanc unwooded dry, Sauvignon blanc wooded), Elgin Ridge (2) (Chardonnay wooded, White blends, wooded, dry)

★★★★ Elgin Ridge (Pinot noir)

★★★★ Elgin Ridge (Sauvignon blanc unwooded)

Blanc de noir
★★★★☆ Van Loggerenberg

★★★★ Olifantsberg

★★★★ Blaauwklippen, Buitenverwachting, Lemberg, Maison (2), The Wine Thief ★★★ Altydgedacht, Arra, Esona, Landskroon, Lynx, Meerendal, Van Loveren ★★★ **Bezalel**, Calitzdorp, Deux Frères, Lovane, Nieuwedrift, **Signal Gun**, Star Hill, Swartland ★★ Niel Joubert ★★ Van Loveren **NT** Abingdon, Ameera, Boschendal, Brenaissance, Doolhof, Packwood, Peter Falke, Tanagra

Brandy
★★★★★ Boplaas, KWV Brandies (5), Oude Meester, Van Ryn (3)

★★★★★ Barrydale, Blaauwklippen, **Boplaas** (2), Diemersfontein, Klipdrift, Oude Meester (2), Oude Molen, Upland

★★★★ Avontuur, Backsberg (3), Barrydale (2), Bezalel, Boplaas, Boschendal, **Copeland**, D'Aria, **Dalla Cia**, Flight of the Fish Eagle, Groot Constantia, Kaapzicht, Kingna, KWV Brandies (2), Louiesenhof, Mimosa, Napier, Nuy, Oude Molen, Richelieu, Robertson, Tokara, Upland (2) (Organic), Van Loveren, **Van Ryn**, Windfall, Withington

★★★★ 100 Reserve, Barrydale, Die Mas, Grundheim (2), Klipdrift (2), KWV Brandies, Oude Meester, Oude Molen, Parow, Upland (Organic), Viceroy (2), Windmeul ★★★ Die Mas, Douglas, Grundheim, Kingna, Louiesenhof, Olof Bergh, Richelieu, Robertson, Van Loveren ★★★ Grundheim, Robertson, Wellington VO **NT AA Badenhorst**, Anthonij Rupert, Aufwaerts, Bezalel, Boplaas, Huguenot (2), Louiesenhof, Mooiuitsig (2), Sumsaré, Wonderfontein (2) **D** Louiesenhof, Mimosa, Van Ryn

Bukettraube
★★★★ Cederberg **D** Swartland

Cabernet franc
★★★★★ Raats (2), Van Loggerenberg

★★★★☆ Anthology, Anthonij Rupert, Buitenverwachting, Cape Chamonix, Edgebaston, Eikendal, Gabriëlskloof, Hermanuspietersfontein, Holden Manz, Keermont, Mitre's Edge, Môreson, Mulderbosch, Nelson, Oldenburg, Raats, Rainbow's End, Ridgeback, Stellenrust, Uva Mira, Warwick, Waterford

★★★★ Botanica, CK Wines, De Kleine Wijn Koöp, Druk My Niet, Glenelly, Hannay, Hillcrest, Jakob's Vineyards, Joubert-Tradauw, Knorhoek, Lynx, Mont du Toit, Morgenster, Ormonde, Plaisir de Merle, Rainbow's End, Raka, Rietvallei, **Stony Brook**, Tanagra (2), Woolworths, Zorgvliet

★★★★ Morgenhof, Romond, Spookfontein, The Garajeest, Waterkloof ★★★ Avontuur, Bushmanspad, Hawksmoor ★★★ Camberley **NT** Annandale, Audacia, Benguela Cove, Brugman, CK Wines, De Trafford, Doolhof, Gentleman's Reserve, Haut Espoir, High Constantia, Idiom, Jakkalsvlei, Kleinhoekkloof,

Lovane, My Wyn, Nomada, Snow Mountain, Stellenbosch Vineyards, Tokara, Vergenoegd, Virgin Earth, Vrede en Lust, Whalehaven **D** Blaauwklippen, Claime d'Or, Glen Carlou, Kaapzicht

Cabernet sauvignon

★★★★★ Bartinney, **Erika Obermeyer**, Le Riche, Reyneke (Biodynamic), Stellenbosch Reserve, Uva Mira, Warwick

★★★★☆ Anthonij Rupert, Bartinney, Bayede!, Boekenhoutskloof (2), Bon Courage, Buitenverwachting, Cederberg (2), Dalla Cia, De Trafford, Delaire Graff, Delheim, DeWaal, Diemersdal, Dornier, **Durbanville Hills**, Edgebaston (2), Eikendal, Ernie Els (2), Flagstone, Fleur du Cap, Glen Carlou, Glenelly, **Grangehurst** (2), Groot Constantia, Guardian Peak, Hartenberg, Johan Joubert, Jordan, Journey's End, Kanonkop, Kleine Zalze (2), Knorhoek, KWV, La Bri, La Petite Ferme, Laibach, Le Riche (2), **Louisvale**, Marianne, Meerlust, Mooiplaas, Môreson (2), Muratie (2), Nederburg (2), Neil Ellis, Nitida, **Oldenburg** (2), Org de Rac (Organic), PaardenKloof, Rainbow's End, Raka, Restless River, Rickety Bridge, Rudera, Rust en Vrede (2), Rustenberg (2), Saxenburg, Schultz Family, Simonsig, Spier, Stark-Condé (2), Stony Brook, Strydom, Super Single Vineyards, Teddy Hall, The Butcher Shop, Thelema, Tokara (2), Usana, Vergelegen (2), Vierkoppen, **Villion**, Waterford (2), Webersburg, Woolworths (3), Zorgvliet

★★★★ Alto, **Anura** (2), Avontuur, Backsberg (2), Beau Joubert, Belfield, Boland, Bon Courage, Boplaas, Bosman, Botanica, Brenaissance, Cloof, **Collatio**, Croydon, De Meye, De Wetshof, Domaine Coutelier, Durbanville Hills, Edgebaston, Eerste Hoop, Excelsior, Fairview, Glen Carlou (2), Glenelly, Goedverwacht, Graceland, Groenland, Groot Phesantekraal, Guardian Peak, Hartenberg, Haskell, Haut Espoir, Havana Hills, Holden Manz, Imbuko, Jacobsdal, Jakob's Vineyards, Jason's Hill, Joostenberg (Organic), Joubert-Tradauw, Journey's End, Kaapzicht, Katbakkies, **Keermont**, Knorhoek, KWV, L'Avenir, La Motte, Landskroon, Lanzerac, Le Bonheur, Leopard's Leap, **Lomond**, Lutzville (2), Lynx, Marklew, McGregor, Meinert, Mellasat, Middelvlei, Mimosa, Mischa, Mitre's Edge, Mooiplaas, Muratie, Nederburg, Neil Ellis, Niel Joubert, Noble Hill, Nuy, Oldenburg, Org de Rac (Organic, Fairtrade), Ormonde, Overhex, PaardenKloof, Perdeberg (Alternative white/red), Plaisir de Merle, Post House, Radford Dale, Rannoch, Remhoogte, Rickety Bridge, Ridgeback, Rooiberg (2), Rudera, Scrucap, South Hill, Springfield, Stellekaya, Stonewall, Taillard, The

High Road, Thelema, Ultra Liquors, Van Loveren, Vergenoegd, Villiera, Vondeling, Walker Bay Estate, Waterkloof, Welgevallen, Wellington Winery, Windmeul, Woolworths (4), **Yardstick**, Zevenwacht

★★★☆ Akkerdraai, Allesverloren, Ameera, Annandale, Anthonij Rupert, Arendskloof, Arra, Asara, Audacia, Benguela Cove, Bonnievale, Boplaas, **Bosman**, Cape Rock, **Cape Town Wine Company**, Cavalli, Chennells, CK Wines, Cloof (2), **Collatio**, De Krans, Diemersfontein, Domaine Brahms, Dormershire (2), Druk My Niet, Du Preez, Ernie Els, Fat Bastard, Fleur du Cap, Glen Carlou, Grande Provence, Highberry, House of Mandela, Jacques Smit, Jan Harmsgat (Fairtrade), KWV, Kyburg, La Petite Provence, La Petite Vigne, Laibach, Landskroon, Le Pommier, Linton Park (2), Longridge, Lovane, Maastricht, MAN Family, Miravel, Mischa, MolenVliet, Mont du Toit, Morgenhof, Morgenster, Mountain Ridge (2), Namaqua, Nederburg, Neethlingshof, Ormonde, Perdeberg (Alternative white/red), Peter Falke, Porcupine Ridge, Riebeek, Rietvallei, Rosendal, Simonsig, Spookfontein, Springfontein, Stellenbosch Hills, Stellenbosch University, Stellenbosch Vineyards, Stellenrust, Stellenview (2), Stettyn, **Stofberg**, Swartland, Tanagra, The Bridge of Hope, **The Butcher Shop**, The Hills, Thelema, Topiary, Tulbagh Winery, Upland (Organic), Val du Charron, Vredenheim, Warwick, Welbedacht, Wellington Winery, Weltevrede (2), **Woolworths** (3), Zonnebloem ★★★ Alexanderfontein, Alvi's Drift, Asara, **Barnardt Boyes**, Bayede!, Bloemendal, Boschendal, Boschrivier, Botha, Brampton, Breëland, Bushmanspad, Cape Classics, Cape Dreams, Carrol Boyes, **Cilmor**, Clairvaux, Darling Cellars, **Daschbosch**, Dragonridge, Excelsior, FirstCape, Fort Simon, Hoopenburg (2), Imbuko, Ken Forrester, Klawer, Klein Parys, Kleine Zalze (2) (Fairtrade), Koopmanskloof (Fairtrade), Kranskop, Le Manoir de Brendel, Leopard's Leap, Libby's Pride, Linton Park, Louisvale, Major's Hill, Merwida, Miravel, Mostertsdrift, Mountain River, Napier, Nederburg, Niel Joubert, Nuy, **Osbloed**, Oude Compagnies Post, **Overhex** (2), Painted Wolf, Piekenierskloof, Pulpit Rock, Robertson (4), Roodezandt, Rooiberg, Slaley, Slanghoek, Slowine, Somersbosch, Spier, Stellar (Organic, Fairtrade), **Stellenbosch Family Wines** (2), Stellenview, Swartland, The Bridge of Hope (2), The Goose, Theuniskraal, Trajan, Under Oaks, Van Loveren (3), Véraison, Viljoensdrift, **Viva Africa**, Welmoed, Windfall, Woolworths (3) (Organic, Fairtrade) ★★☆ Aan de Doorns, Bergsig, **Bizoe**, Brandvlei, Calais, Calitzdorp, David Frost,

Desert Rose, Douglas Green, Du Preez, Du Toitskloof, FirstCape, Flagstone, **Highgate** (2), Hofstraat, Imbuko, KWV (2), Louis, **Lyngrove**, Namaqua, Orange River, Schalkenbosch (Fairtrade), Seven Sisters, Simonsvlei (2), Stellar (Organic, Fairtrade), Stellendrift, Stellenview, Tangled Tree, Tulbagh Winery, Waverley Hills (Organic), Windmeul, Wineways (4) ★★ Audacia, De Breede (Organic), Douglas, House of Mandela, Klein Roosboom, Montagu Wine Cellar, **Namaqua**, Nicholson Smith, Vintales, Weltevrede, Woolworths ★★ Lutzville ★ **Theescombe NT** Abingdon, Anthology, Arendsig (2), Arra (2), Ashton, Aslina, Ayama, Beau Joubert, Bergsig, Black Pearl, Blue Crane, **Boschheim** (2), Boschkloof, Botha, Brothers, Brugman, Camberley (2), Cape Dreams, Cape Point, Charla Haasbroek, Claime d'Or, Conradie, Cronier (2), De Doorns, De Kleine Wijn Koöp, De Villiers (3), De Wet, Delaire Graff, Devonvale, Die Mas, Dieu Donné, Doolhof, Douglas, Drostdy-Hof, DuVon, Edgebaston, Eikehof, Entre Nous, False Bay, Fernskloof (Organic), FirstCape (3), Franschhoek Cellar, Goede Hoop, Goedvertrouw, Groenland, Group CDV, Hazendal, High Constantia (2), Hildenbrand, Hunneyball, Jakkalsvlei, Kaapse Familie Wingerde, La Chaumiere, La Kavayan, Langverwacht, Leipzig, Leopard Frog, Linton Park, Louis, M'hudi, **Maison de Teijger**, MAN Family, Manley, Maske, Meerendal, Mitre's Edge, Mont Rochelle, Montpellier, Mooi Bly, Mount Vernon, Mountain River, Nabygelegen, Napier, Nederburg, New Beginnings, Olsen, Oneiric (2), Pearl Mountain, Piekenierskloof, Rico Suter, Rooiberg (2), Rosendal, Ruitersvlei, Saam, Sarah's, Schenkfontein, Seal Breeze, Silvermist, Simonsvlei (2) (Kosher), Somerset Wines, Southern Sky (3), Springfield, Stellendrift (3), Stone Ridge, Stoumann's, Sumsaré, Teubes (2), United Nations, VinGlo, Vriesenhof, Wazu, William Everson, Women in Wine (2), Woolworths (2), Zidela, Zonnebloem **D** Altydgedacht, Asara, Blaauwklippen (2), Darling Cellars, Du Preez, Fairvalley (Fairtrade), Fairview, Goudini, House of Mandela, Huguenot, Kloovenburg, Koelenhof, Linton Park (2), Lyngrove, Namaqua, Opstal, Overgaauw, Radford Dale (2), Stellenzicht, Teddy Hall, The Bridge of Hope, The Butcher Shop, Zanddrift

Cape Riesling
★★★★ Osbloed **NT** Hildenbrand, Theuniskraal

Carignan
★★★★☆ Artisanal Boutique, Blackwater
★★★★ Spice Route
★★★★ Kloovenburg ★★★ Anura **NT** Cape Rock **D** Signal Hill

Carmenère
NT Dagbreek, Lozärn

Chardonnay unwooded
★★★★☆ Benguela Cove, Eikendal, Springfield, Stonebird
★★★★ Bouchard Finlayson, Cape Chamonix, Constantia Uitsig, De Wetshof (2), Diemersdal, Glenelly, GlenWood, Jordan, Meerendal, Môreson, Rustenberg, The Butcher Shop, Thelema, Woolworths (2)
★★★★ Blue Owl, Bonnievale, Canto, **Elemental Bob**, False Bay, Fram, Glen Carlou, Groote Post, Kleine Zalze, Kruger Family, La Bourgogne, Neethlingshof, Newstead, Radford Dale, Rooiberg, Seven Springs, Stettyn, The Butcher Shop, The Goose, Warwick, Withington ★★★ Backsberg (Kosher), Barrydale, Bellpost, Boland, Bon Courage, **Cloof**, Compagniesdrift, De Meye, **Du Toitskloof** (Fairtrade), False Bay, Felicité, Glen Carlou, Goudini, Hill & Dale, Hoopenburg, Ken Forrester, Klein Roosboom, Le Grand Chasseur, Leopard's Leap, Louisvale, **Maison de Teijger**, Middelvlei, Overhex, Pulpit Rock, Riebeek, Rietvallei, River Garden, Somersbosch, **Stellenbosch Vineyards**, The Bridge of Hope, Van Zylshof, Vriesenhof, Welbedacht, **Weltevrede**, Windmeul, **Woolworths**★★★ Alexanderfontein, Bellevue, Brampton, Klawer, Klein Parys, Koopmanskloof (Fairtrade), Landskroon, Libby's Pride, **Linton Park** (2), Lutzville, McGregor, Pearl Mountain, Plettenvale, Schenkfontein, Slaley, Stellar (Organic, Fairtrade), Swartland, Woolworths (2) (Organic, Fairtrade), Zandvliet ★★ Ashton, Calais, Darling Cellars, De Krans, Flagstone, Simonsvlei (Kosher), Vintales, Woolworths **NT** Boucheron, Brunia, Buffalo Creek, Claime d'Or, De Villiers, Dieu Donné, Doolhof, Franschhoek Cellar, Frater, Group CDV (3), Hartenberg, Hildenbrand, **Idun**, Jakkalsvlei, Karusa, Kloovenburg, La Petite Ferme, Leeuwenberg, Mount Vernon, Mountain River, Oneiric, Rooiberg, Signal Gun, Stone Ridge, Sumsaré, United Nations, Vendôme, Vrede en Lust, Walker Bay Estate, Wolvendrift, Women in Wine **D** Asara (Fairtrade), Fairview, La Couronne, Ultra Liquors, Wellington Winery

Chardonnay wooded
★★★★★ Haskell, Leeu Passant, Oak Valley, Restless River, Warwick
★★★★☆ Almenkerk, Alvi's Drift, Anthology, Anthonij Rupert, B Vintners, Bartinney (2), Bouchard Finlayson (2), Buitenverwachting, **Cap Maritime**, Cape Chamonix (2), Cape Point, Capensis, Creation (3), Crystallum (2), De Grendel,

De Wetshof (2), Delaire Graff (2), Delheim, DeMorgenzon, **Die Kat**, Dorrance, **Eikendal** (3), Elgin Ridge (Biodynamic), Glen Carlou, Glenelly, GlenWood (2), Groot Constantia, Groote Post, Hamilton Russell, Hannay, Hartenberg, Highlands Road, Hoopenburg, Iona, JH Meyer, Jordan (3), Julien Schaal (2), Kleine Zalze, **Kruger Family** (2), La Bri, Laibach (Organic), Lanzerac, Le Riche, Longridge (Organic), Lourensford, Maison, Malanot, Mont Blois, Mont Rochelle, Môreson (2), MVH Signature Wines, Neil Ellis, Newton Johnson (2), Oak Valley, Paserene, Paul Cluver (3), Paul Wallace, Quoin Rock, Radford Dale, Rhebokskloof (Alternative white/red), Richard Kershaw (5), Rietvallei, Robertson, Rustenberg, Spookfontein, Springfontein (Skin-macerated white), Stellenrust, **Stofberg**, Storm, Sumaridge, **Thelema**, Tokara, Topiary, Uva Mira (2), Van Loveren, Vergelegen (2), Virgin Earth, Waverley Hills (Organic), Whalehaven, Woolworths (2) (Organic), **Yardstick**

★★★★ Anura, Avontuur, Babylonstoren, Backsberg, Bayede!, Benguela Cove, **Bergsig**, Bizoe, Bloemendal, Bon Courage, Boschkloof, Bosman, **Canto**, Clouds, Constantia Uitsig, Corder, Dalla Cia, De Wet, De Wetshof, Delaire Graff, DeMorgenzon, Domaine Coutelier, **Durbanville Hills** (2), Edgebaston, Elgin Vintners (2), Ernst Gouws, Esona (4), Fairview, Flagstone, Fleur du Cap, **Glen Carlou** (3), Grande Provence, Hartenberg, Haskell, Haut Espoir, Havana Hills, Holden Manz, **House of Mandela**, Houw Hoek, Jan Harmsgat (Fairtrade), Joubert-Tradauw, Journey's End (3), Kloovenburg, **Kruger Family**, KWV (2), La Bri, La Couronne, La Petite Ferme, La Vierge, **Laarman**, Lanzerac, **Linton Park**, Longridge (Organic), Lord's, Lothian, Louisvale, Lourensford (3), Marklew, Meerlust, Migliarina (2), Mimosa, Mont Blois, Mulderbosch, Muratie, Napier, Nitida, Oldenburg, Org de Rac (Organic), Ormonde (2), Overhex, Plaisir de Merle, Pulpit Rock, Rhebokskloof (Alternative white/red), Rickety Bridge, Rooiberg, Rosendal, Saxenburg, Scrucap, Slaley, Springfield, Stellenbosch Reserve, Stellenbosch Vineyards, **Taillefert**, Thelema (3), Tierhoek, Tokara, Uva Mira, Val du Charron, Vergelegen, Vondeling, Waterford, Waterkloof, Waverley Hills (Organic), Weltevrede, Woolworths (2), Yardstick (2), Zandvliet

★★★★ Backsberg, Badsberg, Baleia, Bellingham, Bergsig, Bon Courage, Boschendal, Cape Classics, Cape Dreams, Clos Malverne, Dâbar, Douglas Green, Durbanville Hills, Eerste Hoop, Fat Bastard, Fleur du Cap, Fort Simon, Freedom Hill, Goedverwacht, Groot Parys, **Kruger Family**, La Motte, Le Bonheur, Linton Park, Louisvale, Lyngrove, **Maison de Teijger**, MAN Family, Mellasat, Merwida, Mont Rochelle, Morgenhof, Mountain River, Muratie, Namaqua, Niel Joubert, Nuy, Olsen, Org de Rac (Organic), Perdeberg, Porcupine Ridge, River Garden (2), Rooiberg, Seven Sisters, Seven Springs, Simonsig, Spier, Stanford Hills, Steenberg, Stellar (Organic, Fairtrade), **Stellenbosch Family Wines** (2), Stellenrust, The Bridge of Hope, Villion, Vriesenhof, Welbedacht, Weltevrede, Windmeul, **Woolworths** (2), Zevenwacht, Zonnebloem

★★★ Alvi's Drift, Anthonij Rupert, Anura, Asara, Ashton, Brandvlei, Burgershof, Carrol Boyes, Cavalli, Dragonridge (Alternative white/red), Eerste Hoop, Excelsior, Fairvalley (Fairtrade), Hildenbrand, Journey's End, Koelfontein, Kranskop, KWV, **Le Grand Chasseur**, Middelvlei, Nederburg, Nelson, Niel Joubert, Olivedale, Orange River, **Packwood**, Pearl Mountain, Piekenierskloof, Rietvallei, Robertson (4), Simonsvlei, Slanghoek, Spotswood, Stellenview, Stonewall, Thandi (Fairtrade), Ultra Liquors, Under Oaks, Van Loveren, Weltevrede, Woolworths

★★★ Carmen Stevens, **Cilmor**, Du Toitskloof, Du'SwaRoo, Goede Hoop, Goedverwacht, Highgate, KWV, **Meerhof** (Fairtrade), Seven Sisters, Tangled Tree, Tulbagh Winery, Van Loveren, Varkenskraal, Welmoed, Weltevrede

★★ Le Manoir de Brendel, New Beginnings, Walker Bay Estate, Welvanpas, Woolworths

NT Abingdon, Arendsig, Arendskloof, Aslina, Ataraxia, Boland, Boschendal, Botha, Brenaissance, Brothers, Calitzdorp, Capelands, Die Mas, Dieu Donné (2), Domaine des Dieux, Drostdy-Hof, Eikehof, Elgin Heights, Entre Nous, Fairvalley (Fairtrade), Flagstone, Foothills, Four Paws, Goedvertrouw, Groot Parys (Organic), Haute Cabrière, **Hildenbrand**, Hillock, Imbuko, Klein Constantia, Klein Parys, Kumala (2), La Chaumiere, La Vierge, Langverwacht, Lazanou (Organic), Le Grand Chasseur, Leeu Passant, Leipzig, Leopard Frog, Lismore, Lodestone, Louiesenhof, Lutzville, Major's Hill, Meinert, Montpellier, Mooi Bly, Mount Vernon, Mulderbosch, Nederburg, Oneiric, Peter Falke, Radford Dale, Rosendal, Rupert & Rothschild, Rustenberg, Sarah's, Schalkenbosch, Snow Mountain, Stoumann's, Thembi & Co, Two Oceans, Viljoensdrift, VinGlo, Vrede en Lust, Vredenheim, Walking Woods (Organic, Fairtrade), Women in Wine, Zandvliet

D B Vintners, Barista, Bouchard Finlayson, Claime d'Or, House of Mandela (2) (Fairtrade), Linton Park, Neil Ellis, Overgaauw, Riebeek, Withington

Chenin blanc off-dry/semi-sweet (w & u/w)

★★★★☆ Longridge

★★★★ Kanu, Slanghoek

★★★★ False Bay ★★★ Landskroon ★★★ Douglas ★★ Ashton (Perlé), Fleur du Cap ★★ Seven Sisters **NT** Beaumont, Bonnievale (Perlé, Light & low-alcohol), Dagbreek, Hazendal, Hillock, Katbakkies, Ken Forrester, Rijk's, Trajan, Valley Vineyards **D** Huguenot, Joostenberg

Chenin blanc unwooded dry

★★★★★ Alheit, Clouds, De Trafford, Grande Provence, Leeuwenkuil, Namaqua, Raats, Reyneke (Biodynamic), Sadie, Terracura

★★★★ Bayede!, Beaumont, Black Pearl, Blackwater, Boland, Bosman (2), Cederberg, **Elemental Bob**, Glen Carlou, Huis van Chevallerie, Kyburg, Maison, Neethlingshof, Noble Savage, Pulpit Rock

★★★★ **Allesverloren**, Annex Kloof, Ayama, Babylon's Peak, Babylonstoren, Barton, Bester, Boland (2), **Bonnievale**, **Boschendal**, Carrol Boyes, **Cilmor**, **Croydon**, De Meye, Diemersfontein, Dragonridge (Alternative white/red), Ernie Els, Ernst Gouws, Fairview, **Grande Provence**, Groot Phesantekraal, Hawksmoor, **J9**, Joostenberg, **Jordan**, Kaapzicht, Kleine Zalze, Knorhoek, Malanot, MAN Family, **Meerhof** (Fairtrade), Merwida, Mooiplaas, Nick & Forti's, Nieuwedrift, Olsen, **Ormonde** (2), Oude Denneboom, Overhex, Perdeberg (2), Radford Dale, Rhebokskloof (Alternative white/red), Scrucap, Simonsig, Spier, **Stettyn**, Summerhill, **The Fledge**, The Hills, **Theescombe**, Ultra Liquors, Van Zylshof, **Wildeberg**, Woolworths (4) ★★★ Alexanderfontein, Alvi's Drift, Anthonij Rupert, Ayama, Backsberg, Badsberg, Barrydale, **Bayede!**, Bergsig, Brandvlei, Cape Dreams, Croydon, Daschbosch (Fairtrade), De Wet, DeWaal, Domaine Brahms, Dornier, Douglas Green, Du Toitskloof, Du'SwaRoo, Freedom Hill, Goudini, Groot Parys, Groote Post, Hoopenburg, Kanu, Ken Forrester, Klawer, Kleine Zalze (2), La Chataigne, Laibach, Landskroon, Leeuwenkuil, Leopard's Leap, **Lovane**, Lyngrove, Pearl Mountain, Perdeberg, Piekenierskloof (Fairtrade), Riebeek, Roodezandt, Rooiberg, Saxenburg, **Signal Gun**, Skilpadvlei, Slowine, Stellar (Organic, Fairtrade), Stellenbosch Hills, Stettyn, SylvanVale, The Grape Grinder (3), Tulbagh Winery, Waboomsrivier, Welbedacht, Wellington Winery, **Women in Wine**, Woolworths (3) (Organic, Fairtrade), **Zandwijk**★★★ Aan de Doorns, Ashton, Bon Courage, Boschendal, **Cilmor**, **Cloof** (2), Darling Cellars, De Krans, Eagle's Cliff, Fairvalley (Fairtrade), Fish Hoek (Fairtrade), Groenland, Hildenbrand, Imbuko, Klein Parys, Knorhoek (2), Koopmanskloof (Fairtrade), KWV, Linton Park, Nederburg, Nelson, Niel Joubert, Nuy, Orange River,

Robertson (3), Saam, Schalkenbosch, **Simonsvlei** (2) (Kosher), Somerbosch, Stofberg, Swartland, **Truter Family**, Van Loveren (2), Varkenskraal, Vondeling, Welmoed, **Windmeul** (2) ★★ Ashton, Botha, Daschbosch, Domein Doornkraal, **Gerakaris**, Imbuko, Koelenhof, **Kunjani**, **KWV**, La Couronne, Lutzville, McGregor, Mountain Ridge, Robertson (Light & low-alcohol), Ruitersvlei, Schenkfontein, Slanghoek, Ultra Liquors, Vintales, Winkelshoek ★★ **Klawer**, Simonsvlei, Woolworths **NT** Arendsig, Arra, Ayama, Boschendal, Calitzdorp, Cape Venture, Capelands, Charla Haasbroek, CK Wines, Cronier, De Villiers (2), Doolhof, Drostdy-Hof, DuVon, Fairview, Flagstone, Franschhoek Cellar, Goede Hoop, Groot Parys (Organic), **Jordan**, L'Avenir, Langverwacht, Maske, Mitre's Edge, Montagu Wine Cellar, Montpellier, Mooi Bly, Mountain River, Namaqua, **Natte Valleij**, Nederburg (2), New Beginnings, Old Vines, Piekenierskloof, Rosendal, Scali (Organic), Somerset Wines, Spier, Stoumann's, Swartland, The Blacksmith, Thembi & Co, Tierhoek, Under Oaks, United Nations, Valley Vineyards (2), Virgin Earth, Vrede en Lust, Walking Woods (Organic, Fairtrade), Wine Village-Hermanus, Wolvendrift, Woolworths, Zidela (2), Zonnebloem **D** Asara (Fairtrade), Blaauwklippen (2), House of Mandela (Fairtrade), Huguenot, Jordan, Painted Wolf, Perdeberg, Teddy Hall, Wellington Winery (Light & low-alcohol)

Chenin blanc wooded, dry

★★★★★ Beaumont, Botanica, Cederberg, **City on a Hill**, David & Nadia (3), DeMorgenzon (2), Metzer, Rall, Sadie, **Savage**, **Spier** (2) (Organic), Spioenkop, Stellenrust, Thistle & Weed

★★★★★ Alheit (5), Alvi's Drift (2), Anthonij Rupert (2), Bellingham, **Blackwater**, Bosman (Fairtrade), Botanica, Carinus Family (2), Catherine Marshall, Charla Haasbroek, **Creation**, Darling Cellars, De Trafford, DewaldtHeyns, Donkiesbaai, Doran, **Dornier**, Dorrance (Fairtrade), Edgebaston, **Elemental Bob** (2), Flagstone, Fram, Gabriëlskloof, Hogan, **Huis van Chevallerie**, Illimis, JC Wickens, Jean Daneel, Jordan, Kaapzicht, Keermont, Ken Forrester (2), Kleine Zalze (2), KWV, L'Avenir, **Lourens Family** (2), Matzikama (Organic, Fairtrade), **Metzer**, **Michaella**, Mimosa, Mont Blois, Mother Rock, Mulderbosch (2), Mullineux (2), Naudé, Nuy, Opstal, Painted Wolf, Perdeberg (Alternative white/red), Raats (2) (Alternative white/red), Radford Dale (2), Remhoogte, Reverie, Ridgeback, Ron Burgundy, Simonsig, Spice Route, Spioenkop, **Stark-Condé**, Super Single Vineyards, Teddy Hall, **Terracura**, The Ahrens Family, The Fledge, **The Wine Thief**, Themika, **Thistle &**

Weed, Thorne & Daughters, Tierhoek, Van Loggerenberg (2), Waterford (2), Wildehurst, Wildekrans

★★★★ Allée Bleue, **Alvi's Drift**, Bellingham, Bergsig, Boland, Cape Classics, Catherine Marshall, **Collatio**, Daschbosch, De Wet, Delaire Graff, Delheim, DeMorgenzon, Dornier, Druk My Niet, **Durbanville Hills**, Eenzaamheid, **Esona**, Fleur du Cap, Flotsam & Jetsam, **Gabriëlskloof**, Glen Heatlie, Groot Phesantekraal, Hirst, Holden Manz, Hornbill, Jan Harmsgat, **Jason's Hill**, **Joostenberg** (2) (Organic), Kaapzicht, Klawer, Knorhoek, **Kottabos**, L'Avenir, **Laibach** (Organic, Skin-macerated white), Le Sueur, Leeuwenkuil, Leopard's Leap, Longridge (Organic), Lyngrove, Merwida, Migliarina, Miles Mossop, **Mont du Toit**, Mooiplaas, **Mother Rock**, Mulderbosch (2), Mullineux, Nederburg, Oldenburg, **Olifantsberg** (2), Overhex, **Perdeberg** (Alternative white/red), Piekenierskloof, Post House, Radford Dale (2), Remhoogte (2), Reyneke, Rickety Bridge, Riebeek, Robert Stanford, Rudera, Saltare, **Schultz Family**, Signal Hill, Slanghoek, Springfontein, Stellar (Organic, Fairtrade), Stellenbosch University, Stellenbosch Vineyards, Stellenrust, Stofberg, Strydom, Taillard, Terracura, The Fledge, **The Liberator** (2), The Vinoneers, Tierhoek, Usana, Villion, Welbedacht, Welgegund, Wellington Winery, Windmeul, **Woolworths** (3), Yardstick, Zevenwacht

★★★★ Anura, Asara, Badsberg, Beau Joubert, Blake, Botha, Breëland, **Brookdale**, **Collatio**, **Deux Frères**, Fairview, False Bay, Kleine Zalze, **Kranskop**, Landskroon, Lateganskop, Leipzig, Lutzville, **Môrelig**, Morgenhof, **Nico Vermeulen**, Opstal, Painted Wolf, **Pearl Mountain**, Piekenierskloof, Porcupine Ridge, Rainbow's End, **Reyneke** (Organic), Rudera, Springfontein, Stellenbosch University, Stellenbosch Vineyards, Swartland, Taillard, Teddy Hall, Teubes, Van Wyk, Villiera, Villion, Waterford, Waterkloof (2), Woolworths (2) ★★★ Arendskloof, Axe Hill, **Cavalli**, **DA Hanekom**, Damaraloof, Dragonridge, Durbanville Hills, **Erasmus Family Wines**, Fleur du Cap, Fort Simon, Groot Parys, **House of Mandela**, Lanzerac, Rickety Bridge, Rietvallei, Robert Stanford, Ultra Liquors★★★ Blue Crane, Kumala, **Mountain Ridge**, Windfall ★★ Botha, **Gerakaris**, Teubes **NT** AA Badenhorst (3), Andy Mitchell, Avondale (Organic), Beaumont, Bellevue, Craven, Dagbreek, Diemersfontein, Domaine Brahms, Doolhof, Groot Parys (3) (Organic), Hawksmoor, Hazendal, Hermit on the Hill, Hildenbrand, Hofstraat, Intellego (3), Jean Daneel, Koelenhof, Lammershoek,

Luddite, M'hudi, Maison, MAN Family, Mother Rock, Mount Abora, Mullineux (2), Nabygelegen, Rijk's (2), Rooiberg (3), Rudera, Saltare, Snow Mountain, Solms-Delta, Star Hill, Stark-Condé, Stone Ridge, Sumsaré, The Blacksmith, The Kitchen Sink, Villiera **D** Boer & Brit, Grande Provence, Linton Park, Napier, Painted Wolf, Spier (Organic), Val de Vie

Cinsaut

★★★★☆ Bosman, Eenzaamheid, **Elemental Bob**, Jasper Raats, Kaapzicht, **Laarman**, Naudé, Neil Ellis, Rall, Savage, **Stellenbosch Vineyards**, Terracura, Van Loggerenberg

★★★★ AD Wines, Blackwater, **Die Kat**, Enfin, Erasmus Family Wines, Fairview, Flotsam & Jetsam, Fram, Illimis, Kruger Family, **Metzer**, Mount Abora (Alternative white/red), **Myburgh Bros**, Radford Dale, Rietvallei, Stellenrust, Super Single Vineyards, **Wildehurst**

★★★☆ Bellevue, De Kleine Wijn Koöp, Dorrance, **Erika Obermeyer**, **Le Bonheur**, Leeuwenkuil, **Osbloed**, Perdeberg, Piekenierskloof, **Rickety Bridge**, Van der Merwe & Finlayson, Waterkloof, **Wildeberg** ★★★ Bemind, Darling Cellars, Kleine Zalze, Overhex★★★ Landskroon **NT** AA Badenhorst, Craven, **Maison de Teijger**, MAN Family, Natte Valleij (5), Nederburg, Rico Suter **D** Kaapzicht, Signal Hill, The Giant Periwinkle

Cinsaut blanc
★★★★ Rall

Clairette blanche
★★★★☆ Thorne & Daughters
★★★★ Radford Dale **NT** Craven

Colombard
★★★★☆ Micu Narunsky
★★★★ Lowerland
★★★☆ Tanagra ★★★ Bon Courage, Cape Dreams, Goedverwacht, McGregor, Orange River, Rooiberg, Van Loveren★★★ Aan de Doorns, Bezalel, Stellar ★★ Nuy, Woolworths **NT** Langverwacht, Schenkfontein

Fairtrade
★★★★☆ Bosman (Chenin blanc wooded, dry), Stellar (Vin de paille/straw wine, Organic), Dorrance (Chenin blanc wooded, dry), Matzikama (Chenin blanc wooded, dry)

★★★★ Stellar (2) (Chenin blanc wooded, dry, Shiraz/syrah, Organic), Bosman (2) (Red blends, shiraz/syrah-based, White blends, wooded, dry), Asara (Red blends, Cape Bordeaux), Org de Rac (2) (Shiraz/syrah, Cabernet sauvignon, Organic),

Fairview (Pinotage), Rivendell (Sauvignon blanc unwooded, dry), Jan Harmsgat (2) (Chardonnay wooded, Sauvignon blanc unwooded), Spice Route (2) (Mourvèdre, Mourvèdre)

★★★★ Stellar (3) (Pinot noir, Chardonnay wooded, Viognier, Organic), Org de Rac (2) (Merlot, White blends, unwooded, dry, Organic), Fish Hoek (Rosé dry), Jan Harmsgat (3) (Cabernet sauvignon, Pinotage, Shiraz/syrah), **Meerhof** (3) (Rosé dry, Chenin blanc unwooded dry, White blends, wooded, dry), Virgin Earth (Pinot noir), **Matzikama** (Petite sirah/durif, Organic), Schalkenbosch (Shiraz/syrah)

★★★ Woolworths (3) (Cabernet sauvignon, Chenin blanc unwooded dry, Sauvignon blanc unwooded, Organic), **Stellar** (8) (Malbec, Shiraz/syrah, Chenin blanc unwooded dry, Sauvignon blanc unwooded, White blends, unwooded, dry, Sparkling, Non-MCC, white, dry, Cabernet sauvignon, Rosé dry, Organic), **Du Toitskloof** (2) (Red blends, with pinotage, Chardonnay unwooded), Thandi (Chardonnay wooded), Daschbosch (Chenin blanc unwooded dry), Piekenierskloof (2) (Shiraz/syrah, Chenin blanc unwooded dry), Kleine Zalze (Cabernet sauvignon), Fairvalley (3) (Pinotage, Chardonnay wooded, Sauvignon blanc unwooded), Fish Hoek (3) (Merlot, Merlot, Shiraz/syrah), Koopmanskloof (4) (Cabernet sauvignon, Pinotage, Rosé dry, Sauvignon blanc unwooded), **Meerhof** (Shiraz/syrah), Jacques Germanier (2) (Red blends, Cape Bordeaux, White blends, unwooded, dry, Organic) ★★★ Woolworths (2) (Shiraz/syrah, Chardonnay unwooded, Organic), **Stellar** (5) (Cabernet sauvignon, Merlot, Red blends, with pinotage, Chardonnay unwooded, Sparkling, Non-MCC, rosé, dry, Organic), Asara (White from red/black grapes (not Blanc de noir)), Stellar (2) (Shiraz/syrah, Colombard, Organic), **Du Toitskloof** (Rosé dry), Daschbosch (Pinotage), Stellenrust (4) (Red blends, with pinotage, Rosé dry, White blends, unwooded, dry, White blends, off-dry/semi-sweet (w & u/w)), Rivendell (Rosé dry), Fairvalley (Chenin blanc unwooded dry), Fish Hoek (3) (Pinotage, Chenin blanc unwooded dry, Sauvignon blanc unwooded), **Koopmanskloof** (5) (Merlot, Pinotage, Shiraz/syrah, Chardonnay unwooded, Chenin blanc unwooded dry), **Meerhof** (2) (Chardonnay wooded, Sauvignon blanc unwooded), Schalkenbosch (Cabernet sauvignon) ★★ Woolworths (2) (Merlot, Pinotage, Organic), Stellar (2) (Merlot, Pinotage, Organic), Daschbosch (2) (Merlot, Sauvignon blanc unwooded), House of Mandela (Sauvignon blanc unwooded) **NT** Stellar (2) (Red blends, shiraz/syrah-based, White blends, unwooded, dry, Organic), Stellar (2) (Shiraz/syrah, White blends,

unwooded, dry, Organic), Thandi (3) (Merlot, Shiraz/syrah, Sauvignon blanc unwooded), Stellar (6) (Red blends, shiraz/syrah-based, Rosé dry, White blends, unwooded, dry, White blends, off-dry/semi-sweet (w & u/w), Sparkling, Non-MCC, rosé, off-dry/semi-sweet, Sweet red, Organic), Township Winery (2) (Pinotage, Viognier), Thandi (4) (Red blends, shiraz/syrah-based, Rosé dry, White blends, unwooded, dry, Sparkling, Non-MCC, rosé, dry), Fairvalley (Chardonnay wooded), Fish Hoek (Malbec), United Nations (2) (Shiraz/syrah, Sauvignon blanc unwooded), Spice Route (3) (Shiraz/syrah, Shiraz/syrah, Semillon wooded), Virgin Earth (2) (Red blends, Cape Bordeaux, Sauvignon blanc unwooded), Walking Woods (7) (Pinotage, Red blends, with pinotage, Rosé dry, Chardonnay wooded, Chenin blanc unwooded dry, Sparkling, Méthode cap classique, white, dry, Sparkling, Non-MCC, rosé, off-dry/semi-sweet, Organic), Havana Hills (Rosé dry), Jacques Germanier (2) (Red blends, other, White blends, unwooded, dry, Organic) **D** House of Mandela (4) (Merlot, Pinotage, Chardonnay wooded, Chenin blanc unwooded dry), Fairvalley (Cabernet sauvignon), Asara (4) (Red blends, other, Chardonnay unwooded, Chenin blanc unwooded dry, Sauvignon blanc unwooded)

Gamay noir
★★★★ Radford Dale (2)

Gewürztraminer
★★★★★ The Vinoneers

★★★★ Altydgedacht, Nederburg, Neethlingshof, Scrucap, Woolworths

★★★★ Bergsig, **Buitenverwachting**, Delheim, Simonsig, Zevenwacht ★★★ Bon Courage, Welmoed **NT** Montpellier, Nederburg, New Beginnings **D** Paul Cluver

Grenache blanc
★★★★☆ Bellingham, Bosman, DeMorgenzon, KWV, **Olifantsberg**, Rall, The Foundry

★★★★ Mont Blois, Perdeberg (Alternative white/red), **Wildeberg**

★★★★ KWV, Leeuwenkuil ★★★ Piekenierskloof **NT** Elemental Bob, Glen Heatlie, Hermit on the Hill **D** Signal Hill

Grenache gris
★★★★☆ Maanschijn

★★★★ Momento ★★★ Fram

Grenache noir
★★★★★ Sadie

★★★★☆ Anysbos, Artisanal Boutique, **Blackwater**, Creation, David & Nadia, Fairview, Migliarina, **Mischa**, Mother Rock, Naudé, Neil Ellis, Spice Route, Stellenbosch Vineyards, The Foundry, Thelema, Tierhoek (2)

★★★★ DeMorgenzon, **Donkiesbaai**, **Elemental Bob**, Erasmus Family Wines, **Fable**, Fairview, Fraai Uitzicht 1798, Franki's, Kloovenburg, Lammershoek, Leeuwenkuil, **Olifantsberg**, Piekenierskloof, Rustenberg, Saronsberg, Solms-Delta, Spice Route, Tokara, Van der Merwe & Finlayson, Vriesenhof, Waverley Hills

★★★★ Anura, Four Paws, Lynx, Oldenburg (2), Ormonde, Schalkenbosch, Waterford, Woolworths ★★★ Anura, Oude Compagnies Post **NT** Badenhorst, Arendsig, Black Elephant, De Kleine Wijn Koöp, Momento, Nederburg, Painted Wolf (Organic), Woolworths, Zevenwacht **D** Diemersdal, Signal Hill

Grüner veltliner

★★★★☆ Diemersdal

Hanepoot fortified

★★★★★ Boplaas, Daschbosch, Du Preez

★★★★ Aan de Doorns, Calitzdorp, Constantia Uitsig, Kaapzicht, Klawer, Muratie, Opstal, Orange River, Peter Falke

★★★★ Badsberg, Domein Doornkraal, Du Toitskloof, Slanghoek, Waboomsrivier ★★★ Boplaas, Clairvaux, De Wet, JMA Louw, Tulbagh Winery, Villiersdorp, Winkelshoek★★★ Douglas, Swartland **NT** Calitzdorp, Die Mas, Huguenot (2) (Sacramental), Jakkalsvlei, Mooiuitsig, Signal Hill, Stoumann's **D** Grande Provence, JMA Louw, Koelenhof

Hanepoot unfortified

★★★★★ B Vintners

★★★★ City on a Hill

★★★ Bellevue, KWV★★★ Cape Classics, Overhex, Riebeek **NT** Hofstraat (Light & low-alcohol), Swartland (Light & low-alcohol), Zidela

Hárslevelü

★★★★ Lammershoek

NT Lemberg

Husk spirit/grappa-styles

★★★★★ Dalla Cia

★★★★☆ Gentleman Spirits, Tanagra (2)

★★★★ Dalla Cia (3) (Organic), **Delaire Graff**, Gentleman Spirits (2), Org de Rac (Organic), Richard Hilton, Simonsig, Upland

★★★☆ Dalla Cia, Kaapzicht ★★★ Iona **NT** Dalla Cia, Gentleman Spirits (2), **Robert Stanford D** Klein Constantia

Icewine

D Kaapzicht

Jerepigo red

★★★★ Catherine Marshall, Stonebird

★★★★ Badsberg, Domein Doornkraal, KWV, Orange River, Taillard ★★★ Blaauwklippen, Domein Doornkraal, Simonsvlei, Swartland, Waverley Hills (Organic), Winkelshoek★★★ Botha, Douglas, JMA Louw, Slanghoek **NT** Camberley, Grundheim, Huguenot, Jakkalsvlei, SoetKaroo, Solms-Delta, Stoumann's **D** Daschbosch

Jerepigo white

★★★★ Backsberg, Haute Cabrière

★★★★ Botha, Calitzdorp, Lateganskop, Niel Joubert, Orange River, Winkelshoek ★★★ Sedgwick's Old Brown, Swartland★★★ Namaqua ★★ Ship **NT** Bezalel, Brandvlei, Huguenot, **Karusa**, Picardi ReBEL, Riebeek, Signal Hill, SoetKaroo **D** Daschbosch, Opstal

Kosher

★★★★ Zandwijk (2) (Red blends, Cape Bordeaux, Sauvignon blanc unwooded), Dragonridge (Pinotage) ★★★ Backsberg (3) (Pinotage, Chardonnay unwooded, Sparkling, Méthode cap classique, white, dry), **Zandwijk** (Chenin blanc unwooded dry)★★★ Backsberg (Merlot), **Simonsvlei** (2) (Pinotage, Chenin blanc unwooded dry) ★★ Backsberg (Sweet red, Sacramental), Zandwijk (2) (Sparkling, Non-MCC, white, off-dry/ semi-sweet, Sweet red, Sacramental, Light & low-alcohol), **Simonsvlei** (2) (Rosé dry, Chardonnay unwooded) ★★ Zandwijk (2) (Natural Sweet, red, Natural Sweet, white, Light & low-alcohol) **NT** Simonsvlei (2) (Cabernet sauvignon, Merlot)

Late Harvest

★★★★☆ Gabriëlskloof

★★★★ Thelema (2) (Light & low-alcohol)

★★★★ Bergsig ★★★ Highlands Road, Roodezandt ★★★ Drosdy-Hof ★★ Vintales ★★ Kellerprinz, Overmeer Cellars, Robertson **NT** Drosdy-Hof, Gabriëlskloof, Landau du Val, Mooiuitsig

Light & low-alcohol

★★★★★ Paul Cluver (Noble Late Harvest), Mullineux (Vin de paille/straw wine)

★★★★☆ Fleur du Cap (Noble Late Harvest), La Motte (Vin de paille/straw wine), Laibach (Natural Sweet, white, Alternative white/red), De Wetshof (Noble Late Harvest), Donkiesbaai (Vin de paille/ straw wine)

★★★★ Glen Carlou (Noble Late Harvest), Druk My Niet (Vin de paille/straw wine), Durbanville Hills (Noble Late Harvest), De Grendel (Noble Late

Harvest), Mimosa (Natural Sweet, white), Thelema (Late Harvest)

★★★★ Woolworths (Sparkling, Méthode cap classique, white, dry), Villiera (Sparkling, Méthode cap classique, white, dry), Zandvliet (Natural Sweet, white) ★★★ Namaqua (Noble Late Harvest), Blaauwklippen (Noble Late Harvest), **Darling Cellars** (Sparkling, Méthode cap classique, white, off-dry/semi-sweet)★★★ Woolworths (Sauvignon blanc unwooded), Robertson (Sparkling, Non-MCC, rosé, off-dry/semi-sweet), **Woolworths** (3) (Sparkling, Non-MCC, white, off-dry/semi-sweet, Red blends, other, White blends, unwooded, dry), Lutzville (2) (Natural Sweet, red, Natural Sweet, white), Perdeberg (Sparkling, Non-MCC, rosé, off-dry/semi-sweet), Klawer (Sparkling, Non-MCC, rosé, off-dry/semi-sweet), Daschbosch (Natural Sweet, white, Perlé), Rooiberg (Natural Sweet, rosé), Woolworths (2) (Red blends, other, White blends, unwooded, dry), Tulbagh Winery (White blends, unwooded, dry), Riebeek (Hanepoot unfortified, Perlé), Orange River (Sparkling, Non-MCC, rosé, off-dry/semi-sweet), Imbuko (Muscadel, white, unfortified, Perlé), Slanghoek (Natural Sweet, rosé), Badsberg (Sparkling, Non-MCC, white, off-dry/semi-sweet), Domein Doornkraal (Natural Sweet, white), Somerset Wines (Sparkling, Non-MCC, rosé, dry) ★★ Robertson (2) (Merlot, Chenin blanc unwooded dry), Woolworths (3) (Merlot, Red blends, other, Chardonnay unwooded), Robertson (5) (Sweet red, Rosé dry, Natural Sweet, white, Sparkling, Non-MCC, red, off-dry/semi-sweet, Sparkling, Non-MCC, white, off-dry/semi-sweet), Woolworths (2) (Colombard, Natural Sweet, white), Robertson (Natural Sweet, white), Woolworths (Natural Sweet, rosé), Simonsvlei (Natural Sweet, rosé), Lutzville (Natural Sweet, red), Robertson (Natural Sweet, white), Du Toitskloof (2) (Rosé off-dry/semi-sweet, Sweet red), Conradie (Rosé off-dry/semi-sweet, Perlé), Daschbosch (Natural Sweet, rosé, Perlé), Simonsvlei (Natural Sweet, rosé), Woolworths (Natural Sweet, rosé), Overhex (Sparkling, Non-MCC, rosé, off-dry/semi-sweet), **De Krans** (Sweet red, Perlé), Tulbagh Winery (Natural Sweet, rosé), Douglas (2) (Natural Sweet, rosé, Natural Sweet, white), Du Toitskloof (Sparkling, Non-MCC, red, off-dry/semi-sweet), Viljoensdrift (Sparkling, Non-MCC, rosé, off-dry/semi-sweet), Zandwijk (2) (Sparkling, Non-MCC, white, off-dry/semi-sweet, Sweet red, Sacramental, Kosher), Woolworths (Natural Sweet, rosé), Fleur du Cap (2) (Rosé dry, Chenin blanc off-dry/semi-sweet (w & u/w)), Van Loveren (2) (Rosé off-dry/semi-sweet,

Semillon unwooded), Riebeek (Natural Sweet, rosé, Perlé), The House of JC le Roux (3) (Sparkling, Non-MCC, red, dry, Sparkling, Non-MCC, rosé, off-dry/semi-sweet, Sparkling, Non-MCC, white, off-dry/semi-sweet), Badsberg (Rosé off-dry/semi-sweet, Perlé), De Wet (Muscadel, white, unfortified, Perlé), Tangled Tree (Rosé off-dry/semi-sweet), Wineways (Natural Sweet, rosé), Drostdy-Hof (5) (Rosé dry, White blends, unwooded, dry, Natural Sweet, red, Natural Sweet, rosé, Natural Sweet, white), **Theescombe** (Muscadel, white, unfortified) ★★ Woolworths (2) (Natural Sweet, red, Natural Sweet, rosé), Robertson (2) (White blends, unwooded, dry, Natural Sweet, rosé), Woolworths (Chenin blanc unwooded dry), Robertson (6) (Sauvignon blanc unwooded, Natural Sweet, red, Natural Sweet, rosé, Natural Sweet, rosé, Sauvignon blanc unwooded, Natural Sweet, rosé), 4th Street (2) (Natural Sweet, red, Natural Sweet, white), **Woolworths** (Natural Sweet, white), Zandwijk (2) (Natural Sweet, red, Natural Sweet, white, Kosher), Van Loveren (Merlot), Audacia (Shiraz/syrah), Wellington Winery (2) (Natural Sweet, rosé, Natural Sweet, white, Perlé) ★ Woolworths (2) (Sweet red, Natural Sweet, white), 4th Street (Natural Sweet, rosé), De Krans (White blends, off-dry/semi-sweet (w & u/w), Perlé), Bonnievale (Ruby cabernet, Perlé), **Theescombe** (Cabernet sauvignon) **NT** Woolworths (Rosé dry), Group CDV (Natural Sweet, white), Kumala (2) (Sparkling, Non-MCC, rosé, off-dry/semi-sweet, Sparkling, Non-MCC, white, off-dry/semi-sweet), Swartland (Hanepoot unfortified), Mullineux (Vin de paille/straw wine), Swartland (Rosé off-dry/semi-sweet), Overhex (3) (Rosé off-dry/semi-sweet, White blends, off-dry/semi-sweet (w & u/w), Sweet red), Bonnievale (2) (Chenin blanc off-dry/semi-sweet (w & u/w), White blends, off-dry/semi-sweet (w & u/w), Perlé), Quando (Natural Sweet, white), Hofstraat (Hanepoot unfortified), Somerset Wines (Natural Sweet, rosé) **D** Paul Cluver (Riesling), Wellington Winery (2) (Pinotage, Chenin blanc unwooded dry), 4th Street (3) (Natural Sweet, red, Natural Sweet, rosé, Natural Sweet, white, Perlé), Alvi's Drift (2) (Sparkling, Non-MCC, rosé, off-dry/semi-sweet, Sparkling, Non-MCC, white, off-dry/semi-sweet)

Malbec

★★★★☆ Lanzerac, Morgenhof

★★★★ Akkerdal, Annex Kloof, Bellevue, Diemersfontein, Enfin, Glen Carlou, Hillcrest, **Idiom**, La Couronne, **Linton Park**, Mitre's Edge, Niel Joubert, Paul Wallace, Signal Hill, South Hill,

Stellekaya (2), Super Single Vineyards, Woolworths (2), Zorgvliet

★★★★ Bizoe, Blake, Bloemendal, Bushmanspad, Diemersdal, Druk My Niet, Le Pommier, Neethlingshof, Ormonde, Overhex, Raka, Withington ★★★ Dornier, **Idiom**, La Bourgogne, **La Couronne**, **Linton Park**, Maison de Teijger, Perdeberg, Schalkenbosch, Stellar **NT** Anura, Black Elephant, Buitenverwachting, Doolhof, FirstCape, Fish Hoek (Fairtrade), Flagstone, Hildenbrand, Kumala, Mooi Bly, Mount Vernon, Nederburg, Plaisir de Merle, Southern Sky, Val du Charron, Vergenoegd, Vrede en Lust, Weltevrede **D** Blaauwklippen, Fairview, Flat Roof Manor, Withington

Marsanne

★★★★ Leeuwenkuil

NT Maanschijn

Merlot

★★★★★ Oldenburg, **Shannon**, Thelema
★★★★☆ Almenkerk, Anthonij Rupert, Bein (2), Creation, De Trafford, Delaire Graff, Eagles' Nest, Eikendal, Fleur du Cap, Groot Constantia, Hartenberg, Keermont, Laibach (Organic), Lourensford (2), Meerlust, Rainbow's End, Shannon, Steenberg, Vergelegen, Villiera

★★★★ Anthonij Rupert, Arendskloof, Audacia, Barton, Bayede!, Belfield, Bon Courage, Botanica, Buitenverwachting, Bushmanspad, Canto, Catherine Marshall, Clos Malverne, Creation, De Wetshof, Domaine Coutelier (2), Dornier, Dunstone, **Durbanville Hills** (2), Ernie Els, Ernst Gouws, Excelsior, Freedom Hill, Glenelly, GlenWood, Graceland, Groenland, Haskell, Hillcrest, **Holden Manz**, Jordan, Journey's End, Kaapzicht, Kings Kloof, Kloovenburg, La Bri, La Petite Ferme, Laibach, Landskroon, Lanzerac, Linton Park, Longridge, Meerendal, Meinert, Mischa (2), Mitre's Edge, Muratie, Nederburg, **Nitida**, Overgaauw, Plaisir de Merle, Post House, Raka, Remhoogte, Ridgeback, Rosendal, Rust en Vrede, Rustenberg, Saxenburg, Simelia, Slaley, Stellekaya, Stellenbosch Reserve, Sumaridge, Super Single Vineyards, The Butcher Shop, Thelema, Township Winery, Val du Charron, Woolworths (5) (Organic), Yonder Hill, Zorgvliet

★★★☆ Anura, Asara, Audacia, **Bemind**, Blue Owl, Boschkloof, Bosman, CK Wines, **Cloof** (2), **Croydon**, De Breede (Organic), De Grendel, DeWaal, Diemersdal, Diemersfontein, Durbanville Hills, Elgin Vintners, Fairview, False Bay, Fleur du Cap, Fort Simon, Glen Carlou, Groote Post, Guardian Peak, Hartenberg, Havana Hills, Jordan, JP Bredell, Kranskop, Kyburg, La Couronne, La Petite Provence,

Lomond, Lyngrove, Maastricht, **MAN Family**, Marianne, Marklew, Mont du Toit, Morgenhof, Morgenster, **Namaqua**, New Beginnings, Noble Hill, Org de Rac (2) (Organic, Fairtrade), Ormonde (2), Perdeberg, Porcupine Ridge, Pulpit Rock, Rickety Bridge, Riebeek, River Garden (2), Romond, Roos Family, Rosendal, Signal Gun, Spier, Spookfontein, **Stellenbosch University** (2), Taillard, The Butcher Shop, Tulbagh Winery, Uva Mira, Vierkoppen, Villiera, Vondeling, Waterkloof, Welbedacht, Woolworths (6), Zevenwacht ★★★ Alvi's Drift, Anthonij Rupert, Anura, Backsberg, Bein, Bellpost, Bloemendal, Bon Courage, Bonnievale, Boschendal, Botha, Cape Classics, Cape Dreams, **Cloof**, Darling Cellars, **Daschbosch**, De Meye, Delheim, DeWaal, Domein Doornkraal, Du Preez, Excelsior, Fat Bastard, Fish Hoek (2) (Fairtrade), Glenview, Goede Hoop (2), Hill & Dale, Hillcrest, Hoopenburg, Hout Bay, **J9**, Kanu, Klein Parys, Klein Roosboom, Kleine Zalze, Koelenhof, Kruger Family, Landskroon, Leopard's Leap, Libby's Pride, Linton Park, **Louis 57**, Major's Hill, Miravel, MolenVliet, Nederburg, Neethlingshof, Overhex, Pearl Mountain, Perdeberg (Alternative white/red), Robertson (4), Rooiberg (3), Slanghoek, Slowine, Stellenbosch Hills, Stellenview, Stettyn, Swartland, **Thokozani**, Ultra Liquors, Under Oaks, Vergenoegd, Vredenheim, Walker Bay Estate, Wellington Winery, Woolworths (2), Yonder Hill, Zonnebloem ★★★ Alexanderfontein, **Ashton**, Audacia (2), Backsberg (Kosher), Bayede!, Botha, Burgershof, Calitzdorp, Carrol Boyes, **Cathedral Peak**, D'Aria, Douglas Green, Du Toitskloof, Flagstone, Fort Simon (2), Fraai Uitzicht 1798, Goedverwacht, Goudini, **Highgate**, Hoopenburg, Imbuko, Jason's Hill, Klein Parys, Koopmanskloof (Fairtrade), KWV (2), Le Manoir de Brendel, Louisvale, Lutzville, Middelvlei, Namaqua, Niel Joubert, Somersbosch, **Stellar** (Organic, Fairtrade), **Stellenbosch Family Wines**, Stellenrust, Stellenview, The Bridge of Hope, Tulbagh Winery, Van Loveren, Varkenskraal, Welmoed, Wineways (3), Woolworths ★★ Daschbosch (Fairtrade), Douglas, Klawer, Klein Parys, Mountain Ridge, **Namaqua**, Nicholson Smith, Robertson (Light & low-alcohol), Schenkfontein, Simonsvlei, Stellar (Organic, Fairtrade), Stellenbosch Family Wines, Weltevrede, Wineways (2), Wonderfontein (2), Woolworths (4) (Organic, Light & low-alcohol, Fairtrade) ★★ Van Loveren ★ **Klawer NT** Annandale, Arra, Audacia, Ayama, Badsberg, Bein, Boland, Boplaas, Brenaissance, Buffalo Creek, Camberley, **Cilmor**, Cronier (2), De Villiers (2), Die Mas, Dieu Donné, Doolhof, Douglas, Drostdy-Hof, Eikehof, Fairview,

Fernskloof (Organic), FirstCape (2), Flagstone, Franschhoek Cellar, Group CDV (3), High Constantia (2), Hillock, Hofstraat, Hornbill, **Idun**, Ken Forrester, Kirabo, Kleinhoekkloof, Knorhoek, L'Avenir, **Le Sueur**, Leeuwenberg, Lievland, Linton Park, **Maison de Teijger**, Maske, Meerendal (2), Mischa, Mount Vernon, Nabygelegen, Nederburg (2), Nico van der Merwe, Niel Joubert, Old Vines, Olsen, Oneiric, Pearl Mountain, Rooiberg, Ruitersvlei, Sarah's, Seal Breeze, Simonsvlei (Kosher), Stellendrift (2), Stone Ridge, Swartland, Thandi (Fairtrade), United Nations, Val de Vie, Versailles, Viljoensdrift (2), VinGlo, Vrede en Lust, Wazu, Whalehaven, Windmeul, Women in Wine, Woolworths **D** Akkerdal, Alte Neffen, Asara, Blaauwklippen (2), Du Preez, Flat Roof Manor, House of Mandela (Fairtrade), Linton Park, Lourensford, Mont Rochelle, Oude Compagnies Post, Painted Wolf, Spier

Meunier/pinot meunier
★★★★ Yardstick

Morio Muscat unfortified
★★★ Woolworths

Mourvèdre
★★★★★ Beaumont (2)
★★★★ Deux Frères, Fairview, Glen Carlou, **Saronsberg**, Spice Route (2) (Fairtrade), Waterkloof
★★★★ Arra, **Fable**, Hawksmoor, Quando
★★★ Dragonridge, Oude Compagnies Post
★★★ Leeurivier **NT** Arendsig, Arra, Black Pearl, Boschheim, Hermit on the Hill, Idiom, Joostenberg (Organic), MAN Family, Signal Hill, Stony Brook, Tierhoek **D** Hirst, Mother Rock, Raka

Muscadel, red, fortified
★★★★★ Nuy (2), Rietvallei, Rooiberg
★★★★ Aan de Doorns, Allesverloren, Badsberg, Boplaas, Burgershof, Calitzdorp, Clairvaux, Dagbreek, De Wet, Domein Doornkraal, Montagu Wine Cellar, **Olivedale**, Orange River, Rustenberg
★★★★ Bon Courage, Du Toitskloof, Excelsior Vlakteplaas, Klawer (2), KWV, Namaqua, Rietvallei, Roodezandt, Van Loveren, Winkelshoek, Wonderfontein ★★★ Ashton, **Darling Cellars**, Douglas, Robertson, Slanghoek★★★ McGregor **NT** Conradie, De Doorns, Die Mas, Grundheim, Jakkalsvlei, Karusa, Klein Parys, Mooiuitsig, Tulbagh Winery, Wolvendrift **D** Boplaas (2), Fairview, Swartland

Muscadel, red, unfortified
★★★ Douglas

Muscadel, white, fortified
★★★★★ Alvi's Drift, Bon Courage, Boplaas, Calitzdorp, De Krans, Lutzville, Monis, **Mont Blois** (2), Orange River
★★★★ De Wet, Klawer, Nuy, Weltevrede
★★★★ Boplaas, Douglas, **Le Grand Chasseur**, Merwida, Namaqua, **Nico Vermeulen** ★★★ Clairvaux, Excelsior Vlakteplaas, McGregor, Montagu Wine Cellar, Robertson, Wonderfontein★★★ Winkelshoek **NT** Die Mas, Grundheim, La Couronne, Mooiuitsig, Windmeul, Withoek **D** Boplaas

Muscadel, white, unfortified
★★★★ Yardstick
★★★★ Thelema★★★ Imbuko ★★ De Wet (Perlé, Light & low-alcohol), **Theescombe NT** Karusa (2), The Fledge

Muscat de Hambourg fortified
★★★★★ Stellenbosch Hills
★★★★ Stellenbosch Hills
★★★ Weltevrede

Natural Sweet, red
★★★★ Darling Cellars
★★★ Arra, Cape Dreams, Libby's Pride, Lutzville (Light & low-alcohol), Rooiberg, The Bridge of Hope ★★ Bonnievale, Cellar Cask, Drostdy-Hof (Light & low-alcohol), Nicholson Smith, Vintales, Wineways (4), Woolworths (3) ★★ 4th Street (Light & low-alcohol), Kanu, Robertson (2) (Light & low-alcohol), Woolworths (Light & low-alcohol), Zandwijk **D** 4th Street (Perlé, Light & low-alcohol)

Natural Sweet, rosé
★★★★★ Groot Constantia
★★★ Thandi ★★★ Orange River, Rooiberg (Light & low-alcohol), Slanghoek ★★ Cellar Cask, Daschbosch (Perlé, Light & low-alcohol), Douglas (Light & low-alcohol), Drostdy-Hof (Light & low-alcohol), Lutzville (Light & low-alcohol), **Nelson**, Nicholson Smith, Riebeek (Perlé, Light & low-alcohol), Simonsvlei (2) (Light & low-alcohol), Tulbagh Winery (Light & low-alcohol), Vintales, Wineways (2) (Light & low-alcohol), Woolworths (3) (Light & low-alcohol) ★★ Robertson (4) (Light & low-alcohol), The Bridge of Hope, Wellington Winery (Perlé, Light & low-alcohol), Woolworths (2) (Light & low-alcohol) ★ 4th Street **NT** Cronier, Linton Park, Picardi ReBEL, Somerset Wines (Light & low-alcohol), Versailles **D** 4th Street (Perlé, Light & low-alcohol), Nelson

Natural Sweet, white
★★★★★ Klein Constantia

★★★★☆ Badsberg, Bartho Eksteen, **Constantia Nectar**, Dornier, Jordan, Laibach (Light & low-alcohol, Alternative white/red), Perdeberg, Quoin Rock, Stellenrust

★★★★ Delheim, **La Bourgogne**, Mimosa (Light & low-alcohol), **Quoin Rock**, Ridgeback, Stony Brook, Waterford

★★★☆ Avontuur, Zandvliet ★★★ Arra, **Thandi** ★★☆ Daschbosch (Perlé, Light & low-alcohol), Domein Doornkraal (Light & low-alcohol), Lutzville (Light & low-alcohol), Rooiberg, Theuniskraal ★★ Cellar Cask, Douglas (Light & low-alcohol), Drostdy-Hof (Light & low-alcohol), Nicholson Smith, Orange River, Robertson (3) (Light & low-alcohol), Somerset Wines, Wineways, Winkelshoek, Woolworths ★★☆ 4th Street (Light & low-alcohol), Vintales, Wellington Winery (Perlé, Light & low-alcohol), **Woolworths** (Light & low-alcohol), Zandwijk ★ Woolworths **NT Black Elephant**, Cape Dreams, Cronier, Group CDV (Light & low-alcohol), Herold, Lynx, Nederburg, Quando **D** 4th Street (Perlé, Light & low-alcohol)

Nebbiolo

★★★★★ Idiom (2), Steenberg

★★★★ **Anura**, Arcangeli, Dagbreek, Morgenster, Super Single Vineyards, Wildehurst

★★★☆ Du Toitskloof ★★★ Hofstraat **NT** Abingdon, Idiom

Nero d'Avola

★★★★ Bosman

Noble Late Harvest

★★★★★ Paul Cluver (Light & low-alcohol), Tokara

★★★★☆ Badsberg, Benguela Cove, Boekenhoutskloof, Bon Courage, Boschendal, Buitenverwachting, De Wetshof (Light & low-alcohol), Delheim, Diemersdal, Fleur du Cap (Light & low-alcohol), GlenWood, Highlands Road, Joostenberg, Ken Forrester, L'illa, **Lomond**, **Lothian**, **Lourensford**, Lutzville, Miles Mossop, Neethlingshof, Neil Ellis, Shannon, Springfontein, Villiera

★★★★ Asara, Beaumont, Bergsig, D'Aria, De Grendel (Light & low-alcohol), Delaire Graff, Durbanville Hills (Light & low-alcohol), Fort Simon, Glen Carlou (Light & low-alcohol), Kranskop, Longridge (**Organic**), Mooiplaas, Post House, Rickety Bridge, Simonsig, Slaley, Slanghoek, Stellenbosch Vineyards, Woolworths

★★★☆ **Darling Cellars**, Nelson, Van Loveren ★★★ Blaauwklippen (Light & low-alcohol), Namaqua **NT** Bizoe, Black Oystercatcher, Bloemendal, Cape Point,

Dieu Donné, Fryer's Cove, Hartenberg, Hildenbrand, Nederburg (2), Nitida, Olivedale, Paul Wallace, Rudera, Signal Hill (2), Spookfontein, Virgin Earth **D** Badsberg, Blaauwklippen, Darling Cellars, Kanu, Morgenhof, Mulderbosch, Spier

Nouveau

★★★★ Org de Rac (Sparkling, Méthode cap classique, white, dry)

NT Groot Parys (Pinotage)

Organic

★★★★★ **Spier** (Chenin blanc wooded, dry)

★★★★☆ Woolworths (Chardonnay wooded), Org de Rac (Red blends, shiraz/syrah-based), **Spier** (2) (Rosé dry, Red blends, Cape Bordeaux), Org de Rac (Cabernet sauvignon), Longridge (2) (Chardonnay wooded, Chenin blanc off-dry/semi-sweet (w & u/w)), Joostenberg (Red blends, other), Laibach (Merlot), Waverley Hills (2) (Shiraz/syrah, Chardonnay wooded), Laibach (Chardonnay wooded), Stellar (Vin de paille/straw wine, Fairtrade), **Upland** (Sparkling, Méthode ancestrale, Méthode ancestrale), **JAN Wines** (Red blends, shiraz/syrah-based), Hughes Family (White blends, wooded, dry), **Upland** (Brandy), Matzikama (Chenin blanc wooded, dry)

★★★★ Woolworths (2) (Merlot, Red blends, Cape Bordeaux), Stellar (2) (Chenin blanc wooded, dry, Shiraz/syrah, Fairtrade), Org de Rac (2) (Shiraz/syrah, Chardonnay wooded, Fairtrade), Joostenberg (4) (Cabernet sauvignon, Shiraz/syrah, Chenin blanc wooded, dry, White blends, wooded, dry), **Laibach** (2) (Pinotage, Chenin blanc wooded, dry, Skin-macerated white), **Org de Rac** (5) (Cabernet sauvignon, Shiraz/syrah, Roussanne, Sauvignon blanc wooded, Sparkling, Méthode cap classique, white, dry, Nouveau, Fairtrade), Waverley Hills (3) (Grenache noir, Red blends, Cape Bordeaux, Red blends, shiraz/syrah-based), Longridge (Chardonnay wooded), Waverley Hills (Chardonnay wooded), Longridge (2) (Chenin blanc wooded, dry, Noble Late Harvest), Reyneke (3) (Shiraz/syrah, Red blends, Cape Bordeaux, Sauvignon blanc wooded), Dalla Cia (Husk spirit/grappa-styles), **Joostenberg** (3) (Shiraz/syrah, Touriga nacional, Chenin blanc wooded, dry), Org de Rac (Husk spirit/grappa-styles), Constantia Mist (Sauvignon blanc unwooded), De Breede (Shiraz/syrah), **Upland** (2) (Pinot noir, Port-style, red), **Lowerland** (2) (Tannat, Colombard), **Myburgh Bros** (Viognier), Scali (White blends, wooded, dry), Silvermist (Sauvignon blanc unwooded), Upland (3) (Brandy, Brandy, Husk spirit/grappa-styles)

★★★★ Stellar (4) (Pinot noir, Pinotage, Chardonnay wooded, Viognier, Fairtrade), Org de Rac (White blends, wooded, dry), Teubes (Pinotage), **Spier** (2) (Red blends, Cape Bordeaux, Rosé dry), **Org de Rac** (4) (Merlot, Red blends, shiraz/syrah-based, Chardonnay wooded, Verdelho), Waverley Hills (2) (Shiraz/syrah, White blends, unwooded, dry), Joostenberg (Red blends, shiraz/syrah-based), Org de Rac (White blends, unwooded, dry, Fairtrade), Laibach (Red blends, Cape Bordeaux), **Reyneke** (2) (Chenin blanc wooded, dry, White blends, unwooded, dry), De Breede (Merlot), Upland (Cabernet sauvignon), **JAN Wines** (White blends, wooded, dry), Scali (Sparkling, Méthode ancestrale), Upland (Brandy), **Matzikama** (Petite sirah/durif)

★★★ Woolworths (4) (Cabernet sauvignon, Rosé dry, Chenin blanc unwooded dry, Sauvignon blanc unwooded, Fairtrade), **Stellar** (6) (Malbec, Shiraz/ syrah, Chenin blanc unwooded, dry, Sauvignon blanc unwooded, White blends, unwooded, dry, Sparkling, Non-MCC, white, dry, Fairtrade), Org de Rac (Port-style, red), Stellar (2) (Cabernet sauvignon, Rosé dry, Fairtrade), Waverley Hills (2) (Red blends, other, Jerepigo red), Org de Rac (Red blends, Cape Bordeaux), Stellenview (Red blends, shiraz/syrah-based), **Reyneke** (3) (Red blends, Cape Bordeaux, Red blends, shiraz/syrah-based, White blends, unwooded, dry), Jacques Germanier (2) (Red blends, Cape Bordeaux, White blends, unwooded, dry, Fairtrade) ★★★ Woolworths (2) (Shiraz/syrah, Chardonnay unwooded, Fairtrade), **Stellar** (5) (Cabernet sauvignon, Merlot, Red blends, with pinotage, Chardonnay unwooded, Sparkling, Non-MCC, rosé, dry, Fairtrade), Woolworths (2) (Sparkling, Non-MCC, rosé, dry, Sparkling, Non-MCC, white, dry), Stellar (2) (Shiraz/syrah, Colombard, Fairtrade), Waverley Hills (2) (Pinot gris/grigio, Cabernet sauvignon), De Breede (2) (Red blends, Cape Bordeaux, Red blends, Cape Bordeaux), Scali (Pinotage) ★★ Woolworths (2) (Merlot, Pinotage, Fairtrade), Stellar (2) (Merlot, Pinotage, Fairtrade), De Breede (Cabernet sauvignon) ★☆ De Breede (Red blends, Cape Bordeaux) **NT** Avondale (7) (Shiraz/ syrah, Red blends, Cape Bordeaux, Red blends, shiraz/syrah-based, Rosé dry, Chenin blanc wooded, dry, White blends, wooded, dry, Sparkling, Méthode cap classique, white, dry), Spier (Vin de paille/ straw wine), Woolworths (Sparkling, Méthode cap classique, rosé, dry), Painted Wolf (Grenache noir), Stellar (2) (Red blends, shiraz/syrah-based, White blends, unwooded, dry, Fairtrade), Waverley Hills (Sparkling, Méthode cap classique, white, dry), Stellar (2) (Shiraz/syrah, White blends, unwooded,

dry, Fairtrade), Klein Constantia (Sauvignon blanc unwooded), Stellar (6) (Red blends, shiraz/ syrah-based, Rosé dry, White blends, unwooded, dry, White blends, off-dry/semi-sweet (w & u/w), Sparkling, Non-MCC, rosé, off-dry/semi-sweet, Sweet red, Fairtrade), Joostenberg (Mourvèdre), Groot Parys (8) (Pinotage, Rosé dry, Chardonnay wooded, Chenin blanc wooded, dry, Chenin blanc wooded, dry, Chenin blanc wooded, dry, Chenin blanc unwooded dry, Vin de paille/straw wine, Nouveau), Fernskloof (5) (Cabernet sauvignon, Merlot, Pinotage, Red blends, shiraz/syrah-based, Rosé dry), Lazanou (4) (Chardonnay wooded, Chenin blanc unwooded dry, Viognier, White blends, unwooded, dry), Silvermist (Red blends, other), Solara (Sparkling, Non-MCC, white, dry), Walking Woods (7) (Pinotage, Red blends, with pinotage, Rosé dry, Chardonnay wooded, Chenin blanc unwooded dry, Sparkling, Méthode cap classique, white, dry, Sparkling, Non-MCC, rosé, off-dry/ semi-sweet, Fairtrade), Jacques Germanier (2) (Red blends, other, White blends, unwooded, dry, Fairtrade), Scali (Chenin blanc unwooded dry), Groot Parys (Red blends, with pinotage) **D** Joostenberg (Viognier), Spier (Chenin blanc wooded, dry), Waverley Hills (White blends, wooded, dry), Laibach (Sauvignon blanc wooded), Matzikama (Pinot noir)

Other fortified

★★★★ JMA Louw

Palomino/malvasia rei

★★★★★☆ Elemental Bob

★★★★ Blackwater

NT AA Badenhorst

Perlé Wines

★★★ Louiesenhof (Rosé off-dry/semi-sweet) ★★★ Robertson (Sauvignon blanc unwooded, Perlé), Solms-Delta (Shiraz/syrah, Perlé), Daschbosch (Natural Sweet, white, Perlé, Light & low-alcohol), Riebeek (Hanepoot unfortified, Perlé, Light & low-alcohol), Imbuko (Muscadel, white, unfortified, Perlé, Light & low-alcohol), Autumn Harvest Crackling (Sweet red, Perlé), De Wet (Rosé off-dry/ semi-sweet, Perlé), Calitzdorp (White blends, off-dry/semi-sweet (w & u/w)) ★★ Robertson (Rosé off-dry/semi-sweet, Perlé), Conradie (Rosé off-dry/semi-sweet, Perlé, Light & low-alcohol), Daschbosch (Natural Sweet, rosé, Perlé, Light & low-alcohol), **De Krans** (Sweet red, Perlé, Light & low-alcohol), Ashton (Chenin blanc off-dry/ semi-sweet (w & u/w), Perlé), Riebeek (Natural Sweet, rosé, Perlé, Light & low-alcohol), Autumn Harvest Crackling (Rosé off-dry/semi-sweet, Perlé),

Badsberg (Rosé off-dry/semi-sweet, Perlé, Light &
low-alcohol), Capenheimer (White blends, off-dry/
semi-sweet (w & u/w), Perlé), De Wet (Muscadel,
white, unfortified, Perlé, Light & low-alcohol),
Paarl Perlé (White blends, off-dry/semi-sweet
(w & u/w), Perlé), Thokozani (Sauvignon blanc
unwooded) ★★ Seven Sisters (Chenin blanc off-dry/
semi-sweet (w & u/w), Perlé), Autumn Harvest
Crackling (White blends, off-dry/semi-sweet (w
& u/w), Perlé), Wellington Winery (2) (Natural
Sweet, rosé, Natural Sweet, white, Perlé, Light &
low-alcohol) ★ De Krans (White blends, off-dry/
semi-sweet (w & u/w), Perlé, Light & low-alcohol),
Bonnievale (Ruby cabernet) NT Group CDV (White
blends, off-dry/semi-sweet (w & u/w), Perlé),
Bonnievale (2) (Chenin blanc off-dry/semi-sweet
(w & u/w), White blends, off-dry/semi-sweet (w
& u/w), Perlé, Light & low-alcohol), Blaauwklippen
(Sparkling, Non-MCC, rosé, dry, Perlé), Jakkalsvlei
(Rosé off-dry/semi-sweet) D Bergsig (White blends,
off-dry/semi-sweet (w & u/w), Perlé), 4th Street
(3) (Natural Sweet, red, Natural Sweet, rosé, Natural
Sweet, white, Perlé, Light & low-alcohol)

Petit verdot

★★★★★ Thelema

★★★★☆ KWV, Stark-Condé, Stellenbosch
Vineyards

★★★★ Anura, Definitum, Du Preez, Hillcrest,
Mitre's Edge, **Montegray**, Pulpit Rock, Zorgvliet

★★★☆ **Dornier**, **Leeurivier**, Lovane, Maison de
Teijger, Miravel, Raka, Super Single Vineyards,
Walker Bay Estate ★★★ **Du'SwaRoo**, KWV,
Leeurivier NT Bellevue, Botanica, Douglas,
Du'SwaRoo, High Constantia, Kirabo, Kleinhoekkloof,
Leeuwenberg, My Wyn, Nederburg, Plaisir de Merle,
Rico Suter, Vergenoegd **D** Asara, Die Mas

Petite sirah/durif

★★★★★ Arendskloof, Fairview, Stark-Condé

★★★★ Black Elephant

★★★☆ Ayama, **Matzikama** (Organic, Fairtrade),
Spotswood **NT** Karusa, The Blacksmith, Wildehurst

Pinot blanc

★★★★★ Stofberg

★★★★ Lanzerac

Pinot gris/grigio

★★★★★ Migliarina, Usana

★★★★ Arendskloof, Idiom, Nederburg, Spring
Grove, Val du Charron ★★★ Anthonij Rupert (2),
Anura, Leipzig, Merwida, Overhex, Two Oceans★★★
Van Loveren, Waverley Hills (Organic), Woolworths
★★ Nederburg, Welmoed **NT** Craven, Flat Roof

Manor, Stellekaya, Stettyn, United Nations **D**
Fairview, Overhex

Pinot noir

★★★★★ Crystallum, Newton Johnson

★★★★☆ B Vintners, Blackwater, Botanica,
Bouchard Finlayson (2), BruceJack, **Cap Maritime**,
Cape Chamonix (2), Catherine Marshall (2),
Cederberg, Clouds, **Creation** (4), Crystallum (3),
De Grendel, Driehoek, Euphoria, Hamilton Russell,
Herold, Iona, JH Meyer (2), La Vierge, Litigo,
Meerlust, Moya's, MVH Signature Wines, Newton
Johnson (3), Nitida, Oak Valley, Paul Cluver, Radford
Dale (3), Richard Kershaw, **Shannon** (2), Stonebird,
Storm (3), Sumaridge, Tesselaarsdal, **The Fledge**

★★★★ Anthonij Rupert, Baleia, Benguela
Cove, Black Block, Brunia, Catherine Marshall,
Dalla Cia, De Wetshof, **Die Kat**, Domaine des
Dieux, Donkiesbaai, Edgebaston, Elgin Ridge
(Biodynamic), Elgin Vintners, Garden Route,
Groote Post, Haute Cabrière, Herold, Highlands
Road, Hoopenburg, Jasper Raats, **JH Meyer**,
Joubert-Tradauw, Kaapzicht, Kleine Zalze, La
Vierge (2), Leopard's Leap, Lothian, **Lourensford**
(2), Miss Molly, Muratie, Newton Johnson, Oak
Valley, **PaardenKloof**, Paul Cluver, Paul Wallace,
Radford Dale (2), Saurwein, Seven Springs, Sophie
& Mr P, **Spioenkop** (2), Stony Brook, Strandveld,
Super Single Vineyards, The Butcher Shop, **Upland**
(Organic), **Villiera**, Waterford, Whalehaven (2),
Wildekrans, Woolworths (3), Yardstick

★★★☆ Andy Mitchell, Arendskloof, Blackwater,
Bon Courage, Bosman, **Bouchard Finlayson**, Cape
Elevation, Dâbar, Elemental Bob, Enfin, FirstCape,
Flagstone, Foothills, Fryer's Cove, Glen Carlou,
Havana Hills, Herold, Klein Constantia, Kruger Family,
La Vierge, Lemberg, **Lodestone**, Lomond, Lynx,
Maastricht, Namaqua, Ormonde (2), Paul Cluver,
Peter Falke, Scrucap, **Solitary**, Spookfontein, Stellar
(Organic, Fairtrade), **That Wine Demesne**, The
Fledge, The Goose, Thelema, Ultra Liquors, Upland,
Virgin Earth (Fairtrade), Vriesenhof, Woolworths,
Yardstick ★★★ Avontuur, Eerste Hoop, Ernst Gouws,
Felicité, Lord's, Nederburg, Overhex, Quando,
Springfield, Strandveld, **Taillefert**, Van Loveren,
Villion, Windfall★★★ Kranskop, Robert Stanford
(2), Robertson, Stellekaya, **Stellenbosch Family
Wines**, The Hills ★★ Haute Cabrière ★★ **Leeurivier**,
Stellenbosch Family Wines **NT** Andy Mitchell,
Arendsig (2), Ataraxia, Bellevue, Bezalel, Boschendal,
Botanica, Buitenverwachting, Claime d'Or, Corder,
Craven, Crystallum, Edgebaston, Elemental Bob,
Esona, Goedvertrouw, Herold, JH Meyer (2), Karusa,
Kleinhoekkloof, La Chaumiere, Leopard Frog,

Lismore, Meerendal, Meinert, Nederburg, Newstead, Packwood, Rosendal, Seven Springs, Signal Hill, Snow Mountain (2), South Hill, Stark-Condé, The Giant Periwinkle (2), The Liberator, Two Oceans, Vrede en Lust **D** B Vintners, Boschheim, Fat Bastard, Glen Carlou, Laibach, Lord's, Matzikama (Organic), Newton Johnson, The Ahrens Family

Pinotage

★★★★★ Beeslaar, Beyerskloof, Kanonkop
★★★★☆ Allée Bleue, Alvi's Drift (2), Arendskloof, Ashbourne, B Vintners, Bellingham, **Beyerskloof**, Cape Chamonix, David & Nadia, Delheim, DeWaal (2), **Diemersdal** (2), Diemersfontein, Eenzaamheid, Eikendal, Flagstone (2), Fram, Grangehurst, Kaapzicht, Kanonkop, Kleine Zalze, KWV, L'Avenir, La Couronne, Lanzerac, Lemberg, Meerendal, Môreson (2), Neethlingshof, Neil Ellis, Radford Dale, Rooiberg, Simonsig, Spier, Spioenkop (2), Stellenbosch University, Stellenrust, Super Single Vineyards, Tokara, Wellington Winery, Wildekrans

★★★★ Alkmaar, **Allée Bleue**, Altydgedacht, Anthonij Rupert, Anura, Arendskloof, **Asara**, Babylon's Peak, Badsberg, Bayede!, Beaumont, Bellevue, Bellingham, Beyerskloof, Bosman, **Canto**, Cloof, Clos Malverne (2), DewaltHeyns, Diemersdal, **Durbanville Hills**, Eenzaamheid, Fairview (2) (Fairtrade), Fleur du Cap, Four Paws, Grangehurst, Groot Constantia, Groot Phesantekraal, Kaapzicht, Kanonkop, L'Avenir, **Laibach** (Organic), Lanzerac, **Linton Park**, Longridge, Lutzville, Lyngrove, Marianne, Marklew, Mimosa, Olifantsberg, Overhex, Painted Wolf, Remhoogte, Rhebokskloof (Alternative white/red), **Rickety Bridge**, Riebeek, Southern Right, Spice Route, Springfontein (2), Stellenbosch Vineyards (2), Sumaridge, Taillard, Vondeling, Welbedacht, **Woolworths** (2)

★★★★ Allée Bleue, **Anura** (2), **Asara**, Ayama, Backsberg, Badsberg, Barista, Bellevue, Bergsig, Beyerskloof, Bloemendal, Blue Crane, Brampton, Camberley, Croydon, D'Aria, **DA Hanekom**, Darling Cellars (2), De Grendel, Delheim, DeWaal, Diemersfontein, Dornier, Dragonridge (Kosher), Durbanville Hills, Eagle's Cliff, **Erasmus Family Wines**, Ernst Gouws, Flagstone, Fort Simon, Frater, Freedom Hill, Goede Hoop, Jan Harmsgat (Fairtrade), **Kanu**, Ken Forrester, **Klawer**, Kleine Zalze, Kruger Family, Laibach, Lammershoek, **Le Grand Chasseur**, Leipzig, **Leopard's Leap**, Louis 57, Maastricht, Meinert, Middelvlei, Miravel, Morgenhof, Mountain River, Namaqua, Neethlingshof, Nuy, Olsen, Perdeberg (Alternative white/red), Piekenierskloof, Radford Dale, Raka, Riebeek, Romond, Rooiberg,

Scali, Silkbush, Simonsig, Skilpadvlei, Slaley, Springfontein, Stanford Hills, Stellar (Organic), Stellenrust, Swartland (2), Taillard, Teubes (Organic), The Butcher Shop, The Grape Grinder, **Trajan**, Tulbagh Winery, Ultra Liquors (2), Vierkoppen, Viljoensdrift, Villiera, Vriesenhof, Wildekrans (Alternative white/red), Woolworths (3) ★★★
Aan de Doorns, Arra, Avontuur, Ayama, Backsberg (Kosher), Bayede!, Bergsig, Bon Courage, Bonnievale, Boplaas, Boschendal, Brandvlei, Cape Dreams, Carmen Stevens, **Cathedral Peak** (2), Darling Cellars (2), **Daschbosch**, David Frost, Domaine Brahms, Doran, Douglas Green, Du Toitskloof, Du'SwaRoo, Durbanville Hills, Fairvalley (Fairtrade), False Bay, **Fat Bastard** (2), FirstCape, Fleur du Cap, Freedom Hill, Hawksmoor, **Highate** (2), Hill & Dale, Hoopenburg, Hornbill, **House of Mandela**, Imbuko (2), Jacobsdal, Klawer, Knorhoek, Koelenhof, Koopmanskloof (Fairtrade), Kuyperskraal, KWV, Lemberg, Major's Hill, Malanot, MAN Family, Meerendal, Merwida, Morgenhof, Nederburg (2), **Niel Joubert**, Nuy, Orange River, Painted Wolf, Perdeberg (2) (Alternative white/red), Pulpit Rock, Rickety Bridge (2), Rooiberg (2), Roos Family, Rosendal, Schenkfontein, Signal Gun, Simonsvlei, Slanghoek, Slowine, Spier, **Stellenbosch Family Wines** (2), Stellenbosch Hills, Stellendrift, Stellenview, **Stettyn**, SylvanVale, Theescombe, Tulbagh Winery, **Under Oaks**, Van Loveren (2), VinGlo, **Viva Africa**, Vredenheim, **Windfall**, Windmeul, Wineways (2), Woolworths (5), Zevenwacht, Zonnebloem
★★★ Alvi's Drift, Ashton, **Bayede!**, Botha, Burgershof, Calitzdorp, **Cilmor**, **Cloof**, Daschbosch (Fairtrade), Fish Hoek (Fairtrade), **Grande Provence**, Hawksmoor, Imbuko (2), Knorhoek, **Koopmanskloof** (Fairtrade), Le Manoir de Brendel, Lyngrove, McGregor, Mooiplaas, Robertson, Scali (Organic), Simonsvlei (2) (Kosher), Slaley, Stanford Hills, Stellenview, Swartland, Teubes, Van Loveren, Welbedacht, Wellington Winery, Welmoed, Welvanpas, Winkelshoek ★★ Breëland, Landskroon, Linton Park, Lutzville, Namaqua, **Nicholson Smith**, Simonsvlei, Stellar (Organic, Fairtrade), Vintales, Wineways (3), Woolworths ★★ Oude Compagnies Post **NT** Arendsig (2), Arendskloof, Arra, Beyerskloof, **Black Elephant**, Boer & Brit, Boland, Buffalo Creek, Cadequin, Cape Dreams, Chateau Naudé, Conradie, Cronier, Dagbreek, De Villiers, Die Mas, Doolhof (2), Doran, Drostdy-Hof, Escapades, Fairview, Fernskloof (Organic), FirstCape (3), Flagstone, Franschhoek Cellar, Groot Parys (Organic, Nouveau), Group CDV (3), Hofstraat, Jakkalsvlei, Karusa, Klein Parys, Kleine Zalze, Koelenhof, KWV, L'Avenir, Louiesenhof, M'hudi,

Maison de Teijger, MAN Family, Manley, Mount Vernon, Mountain River (2), Namaqua, Nederburg (2), New Beginnings, Old Vines, Overhex, Painted Wolf, Rico Suter, Rijk's (4), Rooiberg (2), Saam, Saxenburg, Schalkenbosch (2), Somerbosch, Spier, Stellekaya, Stellenbosch University, The Bald Ibis (2), The Butcher Shop, Thembi & Co, Township Winery (Fairtrade), Trajan, Two Oceans, United Nations, Valley Vineyards, Versailles, Waboomsrivier, Walking Woods (Organic, Fairtrade), Welgevallen, Weltevrede, Whalehaven, Wightman, Windmeul, **Woolworths**, Zidela, Zonnebloem **D** Annex Kloof, Darling Cellars, Hidden Valley, House of Mandela (2) (Fairtrade), KWV, La Couronne, Neil Ellis, Oude Compagnies Post, Painted Wolf, Spier, Stellenzicht (2), Tempel (2), Wellington Winery (Light & low-alcohol)

Port-style, pink
★★ De Krans **NT** Peter Bayly

Port-style, red
★★★★★ Beaumont, De Krans, JP Bredell, Overgaauw

★★★★★ Beaumont, Boplaas (4), De Krans, Delaire Graff, KWV, Landskroon, Muratie

★★★★ Allesverloren, Axe Hill (2), Bergsig, Beyerskloof, Bezalel, Boplaas, De Krans (2), Hout Bay, JP Bredell, Monis, Morgenhof, Muratie (2), Peter Bayly, Rosendal, Simonsig, Upland (Organic), Vergenoegd

★★★★ Aan de Doorns, Alto, Annandale, **Arra**, Backsberg, Beau Joubert, Bergsig, Boplaas, Calitzdorp (2), **CK Wines**, De Krans, De Wet, **Du'SwaRoo** (2), Fairview, Flagstone, Groot Constantia, Grundheim, Jacques Smit, **Klawer**, Koelenhof, KWV, Louiesenhof, Monis, Riebeek, Robertson, Vaalvlei, Viljoensdrift, Zandvliet ★★★ Anthonij Rupert, Axe Hill, Bon Courage, Botha, Domein Doornkraal, Du Toitskloof, **Du'SwaRoo**, Holden Manz, Louiesenhof, Org de Rac (Organic), Slanghoek, Somerbosch, Swartland, Van Loveren, Villiersdorp, Waboomsrivier, Windmeul ★★★ Clairvaux, **Darling Cellars**, Douglas, Jacques Smit, Lovane, Orange River, Peter Bayly, Winkelshoek ★★ **Namaqua**, Robin Hood **NT** Allée Bleue, Badsberg, Bergsig, Boplaas (2), Dagbreek, Die Mas, Domein Doornkraal, **Eikehof**, Entre Nous, Grundheim (2), Hofstraat, Karusa, Kloovenburg, McGregor, My Wyn, SoetKaroo, Stellenbosch University, Stettyn, TTT Cellar, Tulbagh Winery, Withoek (4) **D** Anura, Kaapzicht, Klawer, Namaqua, Rooiberg

Port-style, white
★★★★ Axe Hill, Peter Bayly ★★★ Grundheim, Haut Espoir **NT** My Wyn

Red blends, Cape Bordeaux
★★★★★ Allée Bleue, Kanonkop, Muratie, **Plaisir de Merle**, Ridgeback

★★★★★ Babylonstoren, Backsberg (2), Bartinney, Beaumont, Beyerskloof, Boschkloof, Buitenverwachting, Cape Chamonix, Capelands, Catherine Marshall, **Clouds**, Constantia Glen (2), Dalla Cia, De Toren (2), **De Trafford**, Delaire Graff, DeMorgenzon, Diemersdal, Dornier, Du Toitskloof, Durbanville Hills, Eikendal, Epicurean, Ernie Els, Fleur du Cap, **Franschhoek Cellar**, **Glen Carlou**, Grangehurst, **Groenland**, Groot Constantia, Hartenberg, Haskell, Havana Hills, Hermanuspietersfontein, Hidden Valley, Hillcrest, Idiom, Jean Daneel, Jordan (2), Kaapzicht, Keet, La Vierge, Laibach, Leipzig (2), **Lourensford**, Lynx, Meerlust, Miles Mossop, Mitre's Edge, Mont du Toit, Morgenhof, Morgenster (2), Mulderbosch, Mvemve Raats, Nederburg, Neethlingshof, Nitida, Oldenburg, Overgaauw, **Plaisir de Merle** (2), Raats, Rainbow's End, Raka (3), Remhoogte, **Rousseau**, Rustenberg, Simonsig, **Spier** (3) (Organic), Springfield, Stark-Condé, Stellenbosch Reserve (2), **Stellenbosch Vineyards**, Stellenrust, Stony Brook, **Strydom**, Super Single Vineyards, Taillard, **Teddy Hall**, The Butcher Shop, The High Road (2), Thelema, Tokara, **Under Oaks**, Uva Mira, Van Biljon, Vergelegen (2), Vilafonté (3), Vondeling, Warwick (2), Windmeul, Woolworths, Zorgvliet

★★★★ Allée Bleue, Alto, Anthonij Rupert (2), Asara (Fairtrade), Avontuur, Babylon's Peak, Barton, Beau Constantia, Beau Joubert, Benguela Cove, **Blaauwklippen**, Boschkloof, Botanica, Buitenverwachting, Camberley, Capaia, Cape Chamonix, Constantia Uitsig, Creation, Darling Cellars, De Grendel, De Toren, Dornier (2), Druk My Niet, Flagstone, Frater, Gabriëlskloof, Glen Carlou, Grande Provence, Grangehurst (2), Haut Espoir, Hermanuspietersfontein, Hirst, Holden Manz, **Hoopenburg**, Jason's Hill, JP Bredell, Kanu, Knorhoek, KWV, La Bri, La Motte, La Vierge, Landskroon, **Lanzerac**, Le Pommier, **Leopard's Leap** (2), Linton Park, Louis 57, Louisvale, Lynx, Marianne, **Marklew**, Miles Mossop, **Mischa**, Mitre's Edge, Mooiplaas, Namaqua, Napier, Nederburg, Neil Ellis, Nelson (2), Nico van der Merwe, Noble Hill, Noble Savage, Paul Wallace, Peter Falke, **Quoin Rock**, Reyneke (Organic), Ridgeback, Robert Stanford, Romond, Rosendal (2), **Simelia**, Skilpadvlei, Slaley, **Sonklip**, Spookfontein,

Stellekaya (2), Stonewall, **Sumaridge**, The Butcher Shop, Vergelegen, Vergenoegd, Vriesenhof, Waterford, Waverley Hills (Organic), Webersburg, Welbedacht, Woolworths (2) (Organic), Yardstick, Yonder Hill (2), Zevenwacht

★★★★ Aden's Star, Alkmaar, Andy Mitchell, Arcangeli, Black Oystercatcher, Buitenverwachting, Cape Chamonix, Cape Classics, Carmen Stevens, Cavalli, Cloof (2), Clos Malverne, Damarakloof, Definitum, Deux Frères, Domaine Brahms, Domaine Coutelier, Edgebaston, Grande Provence, Havana Hills, Hillcrest, Journey's End, Kaapzicht, Klein Constantia, Kruger Family, L'Avenir, La Petite Provence, Laibach (Organic), Le Bonheur, Leopard's Leap, Lovane, Meinert, Mimosa, Miravel, MolenVliet (3), Neethlingshof, Nick & Forti's, Nico Vermeulen, Overgaauw, Radford Dale, Rietvallei, River Garden, Robin Hood, Saltare, Saronsberg, Saxenburg, Schalkenbosch, Seven Sisters, **Sonklip**, **Spier** (Organic), Star Hill, Stellenbosch Family Wines, Thunderchild, Vierkoppen, Walker Bay Estate, Woolworths (5), Zandwijk (Kosher), Zorgvliet ★★★ Audacia, Avontuur, Barry Gould, Bayede!, Beau Joubert, Beyerskloof (2), **Bushmanspad**, Camberley, Carrol Boyes, Compagniesdrift, Conradie, De Wet, Fort Simon, Goedverwacht, **Grand Domaine**, Hartenberg, Hoopenburg, **J9**, Jacques Germanier (Organic, Fairtrade), **Jordan** (2), Kleine Zalze, **Koni**, Landskroon, **Le Grand Chasseur**, Leopard's Leap, Louiesenhof, MolenVliet, Morgenhof, Mostertsdrift, Opstal, Org de Rac (Organic), **Reyneke** (Organic), Rooiberg, Sauvignon Wines, Slanghoek, Swartland (2), **The Butcher Shop**, **Thokozani**, Trajan, Tulbagh Winery, Ultra Liquors (2), Van Loveren (2), VinGlo, **Woolworths** (3) ★★★ Ashton, Bon Courage, Bonnievale, Darling Cellars, De Breede (2) (Organic), Diemersdal, FirstCape, Klein Roosboom, **Kunjani**, KWV, La Couronne, Nicholson Smith, Overhex, Ses'Fikile, Simonsig, Somerset Wines, Stettyn, Swartland, Tulbagh Winery, Two Oceans, Van Zylshof, Vaughan Johnson, Weltevrede, Windmeul, Wineways (4), **Winkelshoek** ★★ Fort Simon, McGregor, Mountain Ridge, Oude Compagnies Post, **Robertson** (2), Schalkenbosch, Stellenbosch Family Wines, Wineways, Woolworths ★★ De Breede **NT** Akkerdraai, Anura, Arra, Aslina, Avondale (Organic), Beau Constantia, Bellevue, Boer & Brit, Boschendal, Brothers, Camberley, Cape Dreams, Capelands, CK Wines, Claime d'Or, Cronier (4), D'Aria, Dieu Donné, Doolhof (2), Doran (2), Eagle's Cliff, Equitania, Fernskloof, Fort Simon, High Constantia, Imbuko, Jordan, Leopard Frog, Longridge, Lowerland, **Lozärn**, Marklew, Meerlust, Montpellier, Mooiplaas,

Nabygelegen, Natte Valleij, Nederburg, Nomada, Old Vines, Oneiric, Ormonde, Rogge Cloof, Rosendal (3), Ruitersvlei (2), Rupert & Rothschild, Saxenburg, Sherwood, Simonsvlei, Somfula, Sonklip, Stellendrift (3), Stoep, Stony Brook, Swartland (2), Villiersdorp, VinGlo, Virgin Earth (Fairtrade), Vrede en Lust, Welgevallen, Wildekrans, **Woolworths D** Akkerdal (2), Cavalli, Daschbosch, Elgin Vintners, Gabriëlskloof, Jordan, Morgenhof, Oak Valley, Overhex, Perdeberg, Tempel, Ultra Liquors (3), Val de Vie, Wolvendrift

Red blends, other

★★★★★ Ernie Els, Le Sueur, Rust en Vrede, Waterford

★★★★☆ Arendskloof, Axe Hill, Black Pearl, Boplaas (2), Bouchard Finlayson, **BruceJack** (2), Dalla Cia, Darling Cellars, De Krans, **Donkiesbaai**, Erasmus Family Wines, Ernie Els, Fable, Fairview (3), Glenelly, Hogan, JC Wickens, Joostenberg (Organic), Keermont, Ken Forrester (2), Kottobos, Leeu Passant (2), Lingen, **Lourens Family**, Maanschijn, Mont du Toit, **Mother Rock**, Mount Abora, Nederburg (2), Nico van der Merwe, Paserene, Radford Dale (2), Sadie, **Savage**, **Sijnn**, Spier, Steenberg, The Fledge, The Great SA Wine Co, Thorne & Daughters, **Van Loggerenberg**, Villiera, Vuurberg, Zonnebloem

★★★★ Akkerdal (2), Arumdale, Bergsig, Bushmanspad, Capaia, Cederberg, De Meye, DeMorgenzon, Dragonridge, Druk My Niet, Fairview, Fraai Uitzicht 1798, Groenland, Holden Manz, Jean Daneel, Kyburg, Lanzerac, Le Riche, Micu Narunsky, **Mischa**, Mont du Toit, Morgenster, Nabygelegen, Rhebokskloof (Alternative white/ red), **Richard Kershaw**, Sijnn, Somersbosch, Stamboom, Steenberg, Taillard, Tanagra, Terracura, The Ahrens Family, The Giant Periwinkle (2), The Goose, Van Wyk, Wildehurst, Yardstick (2)

★★★☆ Alphabetical, Alto, Axe Hill, Black Door, Bon Courage, Brampton, Calais, Capaia, Cape Rock, Cloof, De Krans, Desert Rose, Dornier, Du Toitskloof, FirstCape, Franki's, Glen Carlou, Goats do Roam, Groenland, Groote Post, Hartenberg, Hermanuspietersfontein, Herold, Hidden Valley, Idiom (2), Jacques Smit, Klein Parys, Konkelberg, Malanot, Marianne, Mitre's Edge, Mont du Toit (2), Mont Rochelle, Nederburg, Neil Ellis, Nietgegund, **Opstal**, Orange River, Osbloed, Rainbow's End, Rhebokskloof (Alternative white/red), Schalkenbosch, Solms-Delta, Stettyn, Strydom, The Grape Grinder, Thelema, Tierhoek, **Ultra Liquors** (2), **Under Oaks** (2), Villiera, Vredenheim, Vriesenhof, Wavescape, Withington, Woolworths (2) ★★★ Allée Bleue, Allesverloren, Arra, Audacia, **Axe Hill**, Backsberg, Badsberg, Barton, Bushmanspad, Calais,

Calitzdorp, Chennells, Clos Malverne, Du Toitskloof, **Du'SwaRoo** (2), **Fable**, Hermit on the Hill, Hill & Dale, KWV, Landskroon, Louis 57, Napier, Osbloed (2), Perdeberg, Peter Falke, Robertson, Simonsig (2), Spier, Stellenbosch Family Wines, Stellenview, Val du Charron, Waverley Hills (Organic), Welvanpas, Windmeul★★★ Aan de Doorns, Botha, Camberley, Chateau Libertas, Drostdy-Hof, Kanu, La Couronne, Mitre's Edge, Montagu Wine Cellar, **Rascallion**, Somerset Wines, Sun International Wines, Tassenberg, The Hills, Theuniskraal, **Woolworths** (2) (Light & low-alcohol), Zandvliet ★★ Audacia, Barrydale, Brandvlei, Burgershof, Landskroon, Nicholson Smith, Overmeer Cellars, Plettenvale, Robertson (2), Stellenbosch Family Wines, Stellenbosch Hills, Welvanpas, Woolworths (6) (Light & low-alcohol) ★★ Mooiplaas, Simonsvlei **NT** 4G Wine Estate (2), Allesverloren, Ameera, Annandale, Ataraxia, Baleia, Black Pearl, Blue Crane, Boer & Brit, Boschheim (2), Boucheron, Buffalo Creek, Capaia, Carmen Stevens, Casa Mori, Cranefields (2), Cronier, De Trafford, Dieu Donné, Du'SwaRoo, Elemental Bob, Escapades, Four Paws, Gilga, Graceland (2), Havana Hills, Hazendal, Herold, High Constantia, Jacques Germanier (Organic, Fairtrade), Karusa, Kay & Monty, Kirabo (2), Klein Constantia, Kumala (4), KWV (2), Kyburg, La Chataigne, La Chaumiere, La Kavayan, Leeuwenberg (4), Leopard Frog (2), Leopard's Leap, Lowerland, M'hudi, Maiden, Marianne, Mooiuitsig, Mount Vernon, Mountain River, My Wyn, Natte Valleij, Nederburg (3), Oneiric, Peter Bayly, Picardi ReBEL, Rico Suter, Silvermist (Organic), Somerset Wines, Southern Sky, Spier, Stony Brook, Stoumann's, Tanagra, The Blacksmith, The Fledge, Thistle & Weed, TTT Cellar, Under Oaks, **Van Loveren**, Versailles, Zanddrift, Zidela **D** Akkerdal, Asara (Fairtrade), Axe Hill, Bayede!, Blaauwklippen (2), Bonnievale (2), Conradie, Huguenot (2), Kanu, Le Bonheur, Linton Park, Lourensford, Mont Destin, Mother Rock, Oude Compagnies Post, Snow Mountain, Swallow Hill, Tempel, Van Loveren

Red blends, shiraz/syrah-based

★★★★★ Boekenhoutskloof, **Erika Obermeyer**, Radford Dale, Saronsberg

★★★★☆ Akkerdal, Annex Kloof, Anthonij Rupert (2), Anwilka, Artisanal Boutique, Babylon's Peak, Bartho Eksteen, Bellingham, Black Pearl, BruceJack, Cape Rock, De Grendel, Eikendal, **Flagstone**, Groote Post, Haskell, Hermanuspietersfontein, Hidden Valley, Hoopenburg, Iona, **JAN Wines** (Organic), Ken Forrester, Kronendal, KWV (2), Lomond, Lourensford, Luddite, **Migliarina**, Mörelig, Neil Ellis, Olifantsberg, Org de Rac (Organic),

Paserene, Post House, Rall, Ridgeback, Rust en Vrede, Sadie, Savage (2), Sijnn (2), Spice Route (2), Spier, Strandveld, The Butcher Shop, Vondeling, Waterkloof, Wildehurst

★★★★ Alkmaar, Annandale, Anura, Anwilka, Arcangeli, Arendskloof, Bartho Eksteen, Beau Constantia, Biodynamix, Black Oystercatcher, Blackwater, **Boland**, Bosman (Fairtrade), Cape Rock, Creation, **De Kleine Wijn Koöp**, Deux Frères, Diemersfontein, Du Toitskloof, Eerste Hoop, Ernie Els, Goats do Roam, Graceland, Guardian Peak, Hartenberg, Hawksmoor (2), Hermanuspietersfontein, Holden Manz, Hout Bay, **Kanu**, Klein Parys, Kleine Zalze, Kloovenburg, **Leeuwenkuil**, Lemberg (2), Lourensford, Lynx, **Metzer**, Migliarina, Mullineux, Newton Johnson, Painted Wolf, Perdeberg (Alternative white/ red), **Quoin Rock**, Rustenberg, Sijnn, Simonsvlei, South Hill, Stellenbosch Hills, Stony Brook, The Ahrens Family, The Butcher Shop, The Kitchen Sink, Thokozani, Trizanne, Waverley Hills (Organic), Welgegund, Woolworths (3), Zevenwacht, Zonnebloem

★★★★ Ashton, Babylon's Peak, Barton, Beaumont, **Bezuidenhout Family**, Blaauwklippen, Brampton, BruceJack, D'Aria, **Darling Cellars** (2), Delheim, Domaine des Dieux, Edgebaston, Frater, Glen Heatlie, Goats do Roam, **Grand Domaine**, Grangehurst, Hartenberg, Idiom, Joostenberg (Organic), Journey's End, Kaapzicht, Kleine Zalze, **Kruger Family**, **Lammershoek**, Leipzig, Louis, Nico van der Merwe, Old Vines, Org de Rac (Organic), Plaisir de Merle, Post House, Radford Dale, Rickety Bridge, Riebeek, Rietvallei, River Garden, Rosendal, Schalkenbosch, Sonklip, Stellenbosch Vineyards, Stellenrust, The Grape Grinder, The Wolftrap, Ultra Liquors, Val du Charron, Vergenoegd, Waterford, Wijnskool, **Woolworths** (3) ★★★ Anura, Arra, Beau Joubert, Boschendal, Desert Rose, Dormershire, Eagle's Cliff, Flagstone, Hartenberg, Havana Hills, **Klawer**, Kleine Zalze, Knorhoek, **La Bourgogne**, Olivedale, Oude Compagnies Post, **Overhex**, Raka, Reyneke (Organic), Ridgeback, Simonsvlei, Somersbosch, Stellenview (2) (Organic), Summerhill, **Truter Family**, Ultra Liquors (2), Vergenoegd, Windfall (2), Woolworths, Zevenwacht ★★★ Darling Cellars, Excelsior, Groenland, Imbuko, Lynx, Maske ★★ **Cilmor**, Domaine Brahms, Kumala, **Ses'Fikile**, Ultra Liquors ★★ Klawer **NT** AA Badenhorst (2), Andy Mitchell, Arra, Avondale (Organic), Blaauwklippen, Black Elephant, Blue Crane, Boschendal (3), Brenaissance, Cape Venture, Cecilia, Cronier, De Villiers, Dieu Donné, Doran, Drostdy-Hof

(2), Fernskloof (Organic), Fijndraai, Four Paws, Gentleman's Reserve, Group CDV, **Hildenbrand**, Hunneyball, Intellego (2), Joostenberg, Karusa (2), Kleinhoekkloof, Kumala, Lammershoek (2), Leopard Frog, Lievland, Lodestone, Louis, MAN Family (2), Marianne, Mellasat, Mother Rock, Muratie, My Wyn, Naughton's, Nederburg, Newton Johnson, Ormonde, Overhex, Piekenierskloof, Rico Suter, Rogge Cloof, Rosendal (2), Ruitersvlei, Simonsvlei, Somerbosch, Spekulasie, Stellar (2) (Organic, Fairtrade), Thandi (Fairtrade), Trajan, Two Oceans, United Nations, Val de Vie, Valley Vineyards (3), Vendôme, Virgin Earth, Vrede en Lust (2), Welbedacht, Wine Village-Hermanus, Zidela **D** Cavalli, Daschbosch, Freedom Hill, Klawer, Knorhoek, Mont Destin, Noble Hill, Oude Compagnies Post (2), Porcupine Ridge, Riebeek, Robert Stanford, Teddy Hall

Red blends, with pinotage

★★★★★ Beyerskloof

★★★★☆ Alvi's Drift (4), Beaumont, **Bellevue**, Bosman, Clos Malverne, David & Nadia, Hughes Family, Kaapzicht, KWV (2), Meerendal, Meinert, Môreson, Nuiba, Opstal, **Paul Roos** (2), Perdeberg, Rhebokskloof (Alternative white/red), Springfontein, The Vinoneers, Wildekrans, Windmeul

★★★★ Altydgedacht, **Alvi's Drift**, Anura, Asara, **Ashbourne**, Babylonstoren, **Bartho Eksteen**, Beyerskloof (2), Blake, Boland, Cecilia, Clos Malverne, Darling Cellars, **Daschbosch**, David Frost, DeWaal, Flagstone, **Grangehurst** (2), Groot Constantia, Hornbill, Idiom, Kanonkop, La Petite Ferme, Lanzerac, Lateganskop, Leipzig, Lutzville, Lyngrove, Middelvlei, Nuy, Post House, Pulpit Rock, Raka, Remhoogte, Romond, Rooiberg, Simonsig, Spier, Springfontein, Sumaridge, Surfing Vintners, Swartland, Val du Charron, Welbedacht (2), Wellington Winery, Wildehurst, Woolworths

★★★☆ Arra, Asara, Carrol Boyes, Cloof, Croydon, Darling Cellars, Eenzaamheid, Kaapzicht, Klein Parys, Koelenhof, Kruger Family, Lyngrove, Maske, Meerendal, Olsen, Painted Wolf, Post House, Silkbush, Springfontein, Stanford Hills, Stellekaya, Truter Family, **Van Loveren**, Viljoensdrift ★★★ Anura, Ayama, Bellevue, Bergsig, Cloof, Clos Malverne, De Wet, Definitum, Diemersfontein, Dragonridge (2) (Alternative white/red), Du Preez, **Du Toitskloof** (2) (Fairtrade), Freedom Hill (2), Middelvlei, Namaqua (4), Nuy, Overhex, Pulpit Rock, Rhebokskloof (Alternative white/red), Signal Gun, Slaley, Stellenbosch University, Van Loveren, **Woolworths**★★★☆ Aan de Doorns, Cape Dreams, **Cathedral Peak**, Conradie, Nederburg,

Rooiberg, Stellar (Organic, Fairtrade), Stellenbosch Hills, Stellenrust (Fairtrade), Tulbagh Winery, **Waboomsrivier**, Welbedacht ★★ De Doorns, Du Toitskloof, Roodezandt, Slanghoek **NT** Ashton, Beaumont, Boer & Brit, Clos Malverne, Croydon, David Frost, Doolhof (2), Fernskloof, Flagstone, Goede Hoop, Groot Parys (Organic), Hawksmoor (2), Hillock, Jakkalsvlei, Jason's Hill, Koelenhof (2), Kumala (7), L'Avenir, Lemberg, Leopard Frog, Louiesenhof, Manley, Marianne, Meerendal, Miss Molly, Mount Vernon, New Beginnings, Overhex, Rijk's, Rogge Cloof, Ruitersvlei, Rupert & Rothschild, Silkbush, Slaley, Spekulasie, Stellendrift (2), Two Oceans, Valley Vineyards, Waboomsrivier, Walking Woods (Organic, Fairtrade), Whalehaven (2), Zidela **D** Anura, D'Aria, Darling Cellars, Diemersfontein, Doolhof, Kaapzicht, Oude Compagnies Post, Painted Wolf, Stellenrust, Stellenzicht

Riesling

★★★★☆ Catherine Marshall, **Hartenberg**, Iona, Oak Valley, **Paul Cluver** (2), Spioenkop

★★★★ De Wetshof, Fairview, Groote Post, Hartenberg, Illimis, Jordan (2), Meinert, Migliarina, Nitida, Super Single Vineyards, Thelema

★★★☆ Bergsig, **Blackwater**, La Vierge, Lothian, **The Fledge**, Thelema, Waterford ★★★ Groote Post, Herold **NT** Hartenberg, Klein Constantia, Nederburg (2), Spier, Vrede en Lust, Woolworths **D** Paul Cluver

Rosé dry

★★★★☆ Bartho Eksteen, Spier

★★★★ Anthonij Rupert, Bramon, BruceJack, Clouds, Haute Cabrière, Hermanuspietersfontein, Zorgvliet

★★★☆ Alkmaar, Allée Bleue, Allesverloren, **Ashbourne**, Bein, **Bezuidenhout Family**, Black Elephant, Black Oystercatcher, Boschendal, **Bosman**, Botanica, Capaia, Cederberg, Delaire Graff, DeMorgenzon, Desert Rose, Diemersdal, Dorrance, Fable, Fish Hoek (Fairtrade), Foothills, Goats do Roam, Grande Provence, Grangehurst, **Groot Constantia**, Haute Cabrière, Hawksmoor, Herold, Highlands Road, Jordan, Kanonkop, Klein Constantia, L'Avenir, La Bourgogne, **La Bri**, **Leeuwenkuil**, Leopard's Leap, Longridge, Lothian, **Meerhof** (Fairtrade), Morgenster, Mulderbosch, **Nuiba**, Opstal, Perdeberg (Alternative white/red), Rickety Bridge, Romond, Rosendal, South Hill, **Spier** (2) (Organic), Steenberg, Sumaridge, Tamboerskloof, The Butcher Shop, Waterford, Wildehurst, **Woolworths** (2), Yonder Hill ★★★ **Alphabetical**, Anthonij Rupert, Anura, Arumdale, Asara, Babylonstoren, Backsberg, Barton, Bayede!,

Benguela Cove, Beyerskloof, **Bonnievale**, Bushmanspad, Compagniesdrift, Croydon, D'Aria, De Grendel, Delheim, Diemersfontein, Dornier, Dunstone, Durbanville Hills, Elgin Vintners, Ernie Els, **Fable**, Felicité, Flagstone, Franki's, Gabriëlskloof, Glen Carlou, Goedverwacht, Groote Post, Haut Espoir, Havana Hills, Hill & Dale, Ken Forrester, Klein Roosboom, **Kleine Zalze**, Knorhoek, Koopmanskloof (Fairtrade), **Kranskop**, Krone, KWV, La Couronne, Lammershoek, Lanzerac, Le Pommier, Leopard's Leap, **Lomond** (2), Lord's, **LuKa**, Malanot, Marianne, Mellasat, Merwida, Muratie, Nederburg, Noble Savage, **Overhex**, Piekenierskloof, Plettenvale, Porcupine Ridge, Quando, Rainbow's End, **Rickety Bridge**, Riebeek, River Garden (3), Rosendal, Rustenberg, Saronsberg, Schenkfontein, Scrucap, **Seven Springs**, Signal Gun, Silkbush, **Skaap**, Spier, Spotswood, Stanford Hills (2), Stellar (Organic, Fairtrade), Stofberg, Strandveld, Summerhill, SylvanVale, The Wolftrap, Thelema, Tokara, Topiary, Ultra Liquors, Van Loveren (2), Warwick, Waterkloof, **Woolworths** (5) (Organic), Zevenwacht, Zorgvliet★★★ Bergsig, **Cloof** (2), Clos Malverne, De Meye, **Du Toitskloof** (2) (Fairtrade), **Du'SwaRoo**, **Eerste Hoop** (2), Excelsior, False Bay, Fat Bastard, Freedom Hill, Grande Provence, Holden Manz, Hout Bay, Klawer, **KWV**, La Petite Ferme, Lutzville, **Misty Mountains**, Morgenhof, **Napier**, Nelson, Overhex, Painted Wolf, Pearl Mountain, **Perdeberg** (Alternative white/red), Raka, Rivendell (Fairtrade), Schalkenbosch, Slaley, Stellenrust (Fairtrade), Two Oceans, Ultra Liquors, Vergenoegd, Vondeling, Welvanpas, Woolworths (2) ★★ Alvi's Drift, Boschrivier, Darling Cellars (2), De Krans, Drostdy-Hof (Light & low-alcohol), Fleur du Cap (Light & low-alcohol), **Highgate**, Kunjani, KWV, Louis 57, Louisvale, Mooiplaas, **Oude Compagnies Post**, Robertson (Light & low-alcohol), Roos Family, **Simonsvlei** (Kosher), Slowine, Spookfontein, Springfontein, Tulbagh Winery, **Viva Africa**, Welmoed, Windfall, Windmeul ★★ Koelenhof **NT** AA Badenhorst, Akkerdal, Andy Mitchell, Arendskloof, Avondale (Organic), Avontuur, Baleia, Belfield, Bloemendal, Boschendal, Brampton, Cape Rock, Carrol Boyes, **Cilmor**, Claime d'Or, David Frost, De Villiers, Domaine des Dieux, Doran, Dragonridge, Drostdy-Hof, Du'SwaRoo, Eagle's Cliff, Escapades, Fernskloof (Organic), Four Paws, Franschhoek Cellar, Fryer's Cove, Graceland, Groot Parys (Organic), Group CDV, Havana Hills (Fairtrade), Hazendal, Hildenbrand, Hillcrest, Kaapse Familie Wingerde, Kaapzicht, Klein Parys, Kleinhoekkloof, L'Avenir, La Chataigne, Leeuwenberg, Leeuwenkuil, Leopard Frog, Leopard's Leap, Lodestone, Lozärn, Mitre's Edge, Montpellier, Mother Rock, Mount Vernon, Mountain River, Niemandsrivier, Noble Hill, Olivedale, **Oneiric**, Packwood, Piekenierskloof, Pulpit Rock, Robert Stanford, Ruitersvlei, Simonsvlei, Snow Mountain, Solms-Delta, Spekulasie, Spice Route, Spier, Stellar (Organic, Fairtrade), Swallow Hill, Thandi (Fairtrade), The Grape Grinder (2), Thokozani, United Nations, Vrede en Lust, Walker Bay Estate, Walking Woods (Organic, Fairtrade), Whalehaven, **Woolworths D** Blaauwklippen (2), Doran, Glen Carlou, Kanu, Kleine Zalze (2), Konkelberg, New Beginnings (2), Oude Compagnies Post, Van Zylshof

Rosé off-dry/semi-sweet

★★★ Calitzdorp, Cape Dreams, Hoopenburg, Louiesenhof (Perlé), **Perdeberg** (Alternative white/red), Rooiberg, Woolworths★★★ Backsberg, De Wet (Perlé), Libby's Pride, Nederburg, Robin Hood, Somersbosch, **Val du Charron**, Vredenheim, **Women in Wine** ★★ Ashton, Autumn Harvest Crackling (Perlé), Badsberg (Perlé, Light & low-alcohol), Bezalel, Bon Courage, Botha, Conradie (Perlé, Light & low-alcohol), Dormershire, Du Toitskloof (Light & low-alcohol), Graça, Overmeer Cellars, Robertson (Perlé), Tangled Tree (Light & low-alcohol), Van Loveren (Light & low-alcohol), Vintales, Welbedacht, **Weltevrede** ★★ Darling Cellars, Simonsvlei, Theuniskraal, Winkelshoek ★ Klawer, **Theescombe NT** Breëland, Buffalo Creek, **Cilmor**, Dieu Donné, Domein Doornkraal, Jakkalsvlei (Perlé), Karusa, Kumala (5), KWV, Leopard's Leap, Linton Park, Mooiuitsig, Overhex (Light & low-alcohol), Skilpadvlei, Stoumann's, Swartland (Light & low-alcohol), Zanddrift, Zidela **D** Kanu, Koelenhof, Kumala, Overhex

Roussanne

★★★★☆ Bellingham, DeMorgenzon, Ken Forrester, The Foundry
★★★★ Fairview, Mischa, **Org de Rac** (Organic), Painted Wolf
NT Hermit on the Hill, Rustenberg, Simonsig **D** Painted Wolf

Ruby cabernet

★★★ Bellpost, Orange River★★★ Robertson (2) ★ Bonnievale **NT** Langverwacht

Sacramental Wines

★★★ Douglas (Muscadel, red, unfortified) ★★ Backsberg (Sweet red, Sacramental, Kosher), Zandwijk (Sweet red) **NT** Huguenot (Hanepoot fortified)

Sangiovese

★★★★ Idiom, La Vierge, Spring Grove

★★★★ Anthonij Rupert, Havana Hills, Morgenster, Raka, Stellekaya, Woolworths ★★★ **Leeurivier**

★★★ Bezalel, Dragonridge **NT** Anura, Casa Mori, Idiom, Koelenhof **D** Fairview

Sauvignon blanc unwooded

★★★★★ Steenberg, Tokara

★★★★☆ Almenkerk, **Benguela Cove**, Bosman, Bouchard Finlayson, Bramon, Buitenverwachting, Cape Point (2), Cederberg, Clouds, Constantia Glen, Constantia Uitsig, D'Aria, Diemersdal (3), Driehoek, Flagstone, Fryer's Cove, Groote Post, Hannay, Highlands Road, Iona, Kleine Zalze (2), KWV, Moya's, Neethlingshof, Neil Ellis, Nicky Versfeld, Nitida, Seven Springs, Skaap, Spier, Strandveld, The Berrio, **The Giant Periwinkle**, Thelema (2), Uva Mira, Van Loveren, Zevenwacht, Zorgvliet

★★★★ Akkerdal, Allée Bleue, Altydgedacht, Anthonij Rupert, Anura, Boplaas, Bouchard Finlayson, **Cape Point**, **Cape Town Wine Company**, Cederberg, Constantia Mist (Organic), Constantia Royale, Corder, **David Frost**, De Wetshof, Delaire Graff, DeMorgenzon, Diemersdal, **Durbanville Hills** (2), Eikendal, **Erika Obermeyer**, Esona, Fairview, Fleur du Cap, Gabriëlskloof, **Grand Domaine** (2), Groot Phesantekraal, Groote Post, Hermanuspietersfontein, Herold, Hidden Valley, Izak van der Vyver, Jan Harmsgat (Fairtrade), Jordan, Kings Kloof, Klein Constantia, KWV, La Motte, Lanzerac, Le Grand Chasseur, Le Pommier, **Le Sueur**, Lomond (4), Maastricht, Meerendal, Merwida, **Mischa**, Morgenster, Nederburg (2), Nico Vermeulen (2), Nitida, Ormonde (3), PaardenKloof, Packwood, Pulpit Rock, Rivendell (Fairtrade), Robert Stanford, Rosendal, Rustenberg, Saxenburg, Scrucap (2), Signal Gun, Silvermist (Organic), Simonsvlei, Sir Lambert, South Hill, Southern Right, Spice Route (2), Spioenkop, Spookfontein, Springfield (2), Stanford Hills, Star Hill, Stony Brook, Strandveld, Sumaridge, The Butcher Shop (2), **The Fledge**, The Goose, Tokara, Trizanne, Uva Mira, Wijnskool, Wildekrans (Alternative white/red), **Woolworths** (9), Zandvliet

★★★★ Arendskloof, Asara, Bartinney, Bayede!, Bellingham, **Blaauwklippen**, Black Oystercatcher, Blue Crane, **Boland**, **Boplaas**, Boschendal, Boschkloof, Boschrivier, Breëland, Buitenverwachting, **Canto**, Capaia, **Cilmor**, Clos Malverne, Creation, D'Aria, Dalla Cia, **Daschbosch**, De Grendel, Diemersdal, Domaine des Dieux, Du Toitskloof, Durbanville Hills, Eagles' Nest,. Edgebaston, Elgin Ridge (Biodynamic), Elgin Vintners, Ernie Els, Esona (2), False Bay, Foothills (Alternative white/red), Fryer's Cove, Garden Route, Glen Carlou, Grande Provence, Hartenberg, Haskell, Hout Bay, Journey's End, Kaapzicht, Ken Forrester, Klein Constantia, **Klein Roosboom**, Kleine Zalze, Konkelberg (2), Kuyperskraal, KWV, La Motte, La Petite Ferme, Leipzig, Lemberg, Lomond, Louis 57, LuKa, Lutzville, Malanot, MAN Family, Midgard, Mimosa, Miravel, Misty Mountains, Mooiplaas, Noble Savage, Nuy, **PaardenKloof**, Paul Wallace, Raka, Rietvallei, Roos Family, Rosendal, Saronsberg, Sauvignon Wines, Signal Gun, Simonsig, Sophie & Mr P, Spier, Splattered Toad, Stellenbosch Vineyards, Stellenrust, Strydom, The Butcher Shop, Township Winery, Ultra Liquors, Villiera, Vondeling, **Walker Bay Estate**, Warwick, Waterford, **Woolworths** (3), Yonder Hill, Zandwijk ★★★ Alexanderfontein, Ameera, Anthonij Rupert, Arumdale, Barrydale, Barton, Bayede!, Bellevue, **Benguela Cove**, Bergsig, Bon Courage, Cape Classics, Cape Dreams, **Cilmor**, **Cloof** (2), Clos Malverne, Conradie, **Croydon**, D'Aria, **Darling Cellars**, David Frost, De Wet, Delheim, DeWaal, Diemersfontein, Dornier, Douglas, Du Preez, Ernst Gouws, Esona, Excelsior, Fairvalley (Fairtrade), Fleur du Cap, Fort Simon (2), Freedom Hill, Glen Carlou, Glenview, Goedverwacht, Grande Provence, Groenland, Havana Hills, Hill & Dale, Hoopenburg, Hout Bay, **Idun**, Imbuko, **J9**, Ken Forrester, Klein Parys, Kloovenburg, Koopmanskloof (Fairtrade), Kranskop, **Kunjani**, La Chataigne, Le Grand Chasseur, Lodestone, Louisvale, Lyngrove, Maison de Teijger, Marklew, **MolenVliet**, Morgenhof, Muratie, Nederburg, Neethlingshof, Nelson, Newstead, Nico van der Merwe, Nuy, Orange River, Overgaauw, PaardenKloof (2), Pearl Mountain, Perdeberg (Alternative white/red), Piekenierskloof, Porcupine Ridge, Ridgeback, Riebeek, River Garden (2), Roodezandt, Rooiberg, Silkbush, Skilpadvlei, Slaley, Slanghoek, Slowine, Spring Grove, St Francis Point, Stellar (Organic), Stellenbosch Hills, Stellenbosch University, Stellenview (Skin-macerated white), Stettyn, Swartland, **Thokozani**, **Truter Family**, Ultra Liquors, Vaalvlei, Van Loveren, Vergenoegd, Walker Bay Estate, Waterford, Webersburg, Woolworths (5) (Organic, Fairtrade), Zevenwacht, Zonnebloem, Zorgvliet ★★★ Ashton, Avontuur, Backsberg, Badsberg, **Bizoe**, Bonnievale, Brampton, Burgershof, Clairvaux, Darling Cellars, De Doorns, Douglas Green, Eagle's Cliff, Excelsior, Fat Bastard, Fish Hoek (Fairtrade), Flagstone, Fort Simon, Goede Hoop, Guardian Peak, Hoopenburg, Kanu, Klein Roosboom, Knorhoek, Koelenhof, KWV (2), La Couronne, Landskroon, Le Manoir de Brendel, Leopard's Leap, Libby's Pride, Linton Park (2), Lord's, Louiesenhof, Lutzville, **Meerhof** (Fairtrade), **Namaqua**, Nederburg, Niel Joubert, **Overhex** (2), Perdeberg (Alternative white/red), Robertson (5) (Perlé), Robin Hood, Ruitersvlei, Seven Sisters, Somerbosch, Somerset Wines, Tangled Tree, The Bridge of Hope, Theuniskraal, **Truter Family**, Two Oceans, Van Zylshof, Viljoensdrift, **Viva Africa**, Waboomsrivier, Welbedacht, Wellington Winery, Welmoed, Weltevrede, Windmeul, Wineways (3), Wonderfonteyn, Woolworths (3) (Light & low-alcohol) ★★ Aan de Doorns, Calais, Daschbosch (Fairtrade), Devonvale, Goudini, House of Mandela (Fairtrade), Imbuko (2), Klawer, Koelenhof, **Koni**, McGregor, Mountain Ridge, Mountain River (2), Nicholson Smith (2), Schalkenbosch, Simonsvlei, Stellenbosch Hills, Teubes, Thokozani (Perlé), Tulbagh Winery, Vintales, Vredenheim, Welvanpas, Wineways, Winkelshoek ★★ Brandvlei, Robertson (2) (Light & low-alcohol), Simonsvlei, Wineways **NT** Abingdon, Aden's Star, Anura, Arendsig (2), Aslina, Ataraxia, Beau Joubert, Bemind, Bezalel, Bitou, Black Elephant, Black Oystercatcher, Blackwater, Boer & Brit, Boland, Boplaas, Boschendal, Bramon, Brenaissance, Brothers, Brugman, Brunia, Buffalo Creek, Calitzdorp, Camberley, Cape Elevation, CK Wines, Conradie, Cronier, Dâbar, De Villiers, Die Mas, Dieu Donné, Domein Doornkraal, Doolhof, Dormershire, Drostdy-Hof, Du Toitskloof, Dunstone, DuVon, Eikehof, Elgin Heights, Fairview, False Bay, Flagstone, Four Paws, Franschhoek Cellar, Freedom Hill, Fryer's Cove, Goedvertrouw, High Constantia (2), Hillcrest (2), Hillock, Imbuko, Jakkalsvlei, Kaapse Familie Wingerde, Karusa, Kay & Monty, Klein Constantia (Organic), Klein Roosboom, Kleinhoekkloof, Knorhoek, L'Avenir, Langverwacht, Lateganskop, Leeuwenberg, Lievland, Louis, Lovane, Lozärn, M'hudi, Major's Hill, Misty Mountains, Mont du Toit, Montpellier, Mooiuitsig, Mount Vernon, Nabygelegen, Namaqua, Nederburg, Noble Hill, Nomada (2), Old Vines, Oneiric, Peter Falke, Piekenierskloof, Quando, Redford Lane, Rhebokskloof (Alternative white/red), Rooiberg (3), Rosendal, Saam, Sarah's, Schenkfontein, Seal Breeze, Stellendrift, Stoumann's, Sumsaré, Thandi (Fairtrade), Trajan, Under Oaks, United Nations (Fairtrade), Val de Vie, Valley Vineyards, Versailles, VinGlo, Virgin Earth (Fairtrade), Vrede en Lust, Wazu, Welgevallen, Whalehaven, Women in Wine, **Woolworths** (2), Zidela (2), Zonnebloem **D** Asara (Fairtrade), Blaauwklippen, Claime d'Or, Du Preez, Excelsior, KWV, Le Bonheur, Linton Park, Perdeberg,

Stellenzicht, SylvanVale, Teubes, The Bridge of Hope, Thelema, Waterford, Wolvendrift

Sauvignon blanc wooded

★★★★★ Bartho Eksteen, Bloemendal, Highlands Road

★★★★☆ Bartho Eksteen, Buitenverwachting, Cape Point, Catherine Marshall, Cederberg, D'Aria, De Grendel, Delaire Graff, Diemersdal (2), **Erika Obermeyer**, Groot Constantia, Hermanuspietersfontein, **Iona**, Jordan, Klein Constantia (4), Mulderbosch, Nederburg (2), Neil Ellis, Oak Valley, Paul Cluver, Reyneke (Biodynamic), Shannon, Stark-Condé, Stellenrust, The Giant Periwinkle, Tierhoek, Vergelegen, Waterkloof, Woolworths (2), Zevenwacht

★★★★ Avontuur, Backsberg, Bartho Eksteen, Benguela Cove, Black Oystercatcher, Cape Chamonix, Fryer's Cove, Highberry, Jasper Raats, Jordan, La Vierge, Marianne, **Namaqua**, Newton Johnson, Nitida, **Org de Rac** (Organic), Overhex, Reyneke (Organic), **Rivendell**, Rousseau, Spier, Springfontein, Steenberg (2), Stony Brook, The Fledge, Tierhoek, Vergelegen, Villiera, **Walker Bay Estate**, Waterkloof

★★★☆ Carmen Stevens, Enfin, **Fortes** (2), Le Bonheur, **Meinert**, Miravel, Mont Rochelle, Mulderbosch, Painted Wolf, **Quoin Rock**, **Rietvallei**, Rousseau, **Sauvignon Wines**, **Solitary**, Teddy Hall, Usana ★★★ Bloemendal, Botha, Bushmanspad, Namaqua, Rickety Bridge ★★ **Barnardt Boyes** (2), Kumala, Windfall **NT** Alvi's Drift, Baleia, Escapades, Hazendal, High Constantia, Jean Daneel, Klein Constantia (3), Lismore, Louis, Miss Molly, Spier, Stark-Condé, Stone Ridge, Swartland, Teubes, Vrede en Lust, Woolworths **D** CK Wines, Darling Cellars, Laibach (Organic)

Semillon gris

★★★★☆ Mullineux, Thorne & Daughters

Semillon unwooded

★★★★★ Benguela Cove

★★★★ Kings Kloof

★★★☆ **Wildeberg** ★★★ Viljoensdrift ★★ Van Loveren **NT** Brunia

Semillon wooded

★★★★★ Alheit, Rickety Bridge

★★★★☆ Anthonij Rupert, Arcangeli, Bloemendal, Boekenhoutskloof, Botanica, Cederberg, David & Nadia, Hermanuspietersfontein, Naudé, Opstal, Sadie, Shannon, Steenberg (2), Thorne & Daughters, Vergelegen, Yardstick

★★★★ Constantia Uitsig, Dornier, **Foothills**, Groote Post, Hermit on the Hill, **Highlands Road**, **Idiom**, KWV, La Bourgogne, **La Bri**, Nicky Versfeld, Nitida, **Olivedale**, Rickety Bridge, The Garajeest, **Trizanne**, Yardstick

★★★★ Haut Espoir, **Idiom**, Meinert ★★★ Hildenbrand **NT** Black Elephant, Cape Point, Eikehof, Escapades (2), Hillcrest, La Chataigne, Landau du Val, My Wyn, Signal Hill, Spice Route (Fairtrade), Vrede en Lust **D** David & Nadia

Sherry-style wines

★★★★ KWV Sherry-Style Wines (3), Monis, Spice Route

★★★★ Monis (2) ★★★ Douglas **NT** Huguenot (2), Karusa, Picardi ReBEL

Shiraz/syrah

★★★★★ Dorrance, Hartenberg, Leeuwenkuil, Luddite, Mullineux (2), Nico van der Merwe, Porseleinberg, **Rall**, Rhebokskloof (Alternative white/red), Rust en Vrede

★★★★☆ Almenkerk, Alto (2), Annandale, Anthonij Rupert, Arra, Artisanal Boutique, Beau Constantia, Beaumont, Bellingham, Bizoe, Blackwater, Boekenhoutskloof (2), Boschkloof (2), Brunia, Cederberg, Cirrus, Cloof, Clouds, D'Aria, **De Grendel** (2), De Trafford (3), Delheim, DeMorgenzon, DewaldtHeyns, Driehoek, Eagles' Nest, Eenzaamheid (2), Erasmus Family Wines, Ernie Els, **Fable** (2), Fairview (3), Flagstone, Gabriëlskloof (2), GlenWood, Groot Constantia, Hartenberg (2), Haskell (2), Highlands Road, Holden Manz, Jasper Raats, Jordan, Keermont (2), Kleine Zalze, Kloovenburg, KWV, La Bri, La Motte, Lomond (2), Metzer, **Michaella**, Mont Destin, Mont Rochelle, Mullineux (2), Muratie, Quoin Rock, Radford Dale (2), Raka (2), Remhoogte, Reyneke (Biodynamic), Richard Hilton, **Richard Kershaw** (5), Robertson, Ron Burgundy, Rust en Vrede, Rustenberg, Saronsberg, Savage, Saxenburg, Schultz Family, Signal Hill, Simelia, Simonsig (2), Stark-Condé (2), Stellenbosch Vineyards, Stellenrust, Strandveld, **Super Single Vineyards** (2), Tamboerskloof, Terracura, The Berrio, The Foundry, Trizanne, Uva Mira, Vergelegen (2), Warwick, Waterford, Waverley Hills (Organic), Woolworths, Zandvliet

★★★★ Akkerdal, **Allée Bleue**, Alte Neffen, Andreas, **Anura**, Arra, Avontuur, Babylonstoren, Backsberg, Bayede!, Beau Joubert, Benguela Cove, Bloemendal (2), Boland, Bon Courage, Bonnievale, Camberley, Carinus Family, Cloof (2), **Collatio**, Conceito, Croydon, D'Aria, Dâbar, De

Breede (Organic), DeMorgenzon, Diemersfontein, Domaine Brahms, Doran, Dornier, **Durbanville Hills**, Edgebaston, Eerste Hoop, Elgin Vintners, Enfin (2), Esona (4), Excelsior, **Fable** (2), Fairview, Flying Cloud, **Foothills**, Fram, Gabriëlskloof, **Glen Carlou** (2), Glenelly, GlenWood, Grande Provence, Groenland, Groote Post, Guardian Peak, Hartenberg (2), Haskell (2), Haut Espoir, Havana Hills, Hirst, House of Mandela, Hout Bay, Joostenberg (2) (Organic), Joubert-Tradauw, Journey's End (2), JP Bredell, Kaapzicht, Keermont, Kings Kloof, Kleine Zalze, Kloovenburg, Koelfontein, KWV, La Bri, La Motte, La Petite Ferme, La Vierge, Landskroon, Lanzerac, Linton Park, Lomond, Lord's, Lyngrove, Lynx, Maison, Malanot, MAN Family, Marklew, Middelvlei, Migliarina, Mimosa, Mont Rochelle, **Montegray**, Mooiplaas, Môrelig, Mountain Ridge, Nederburg (2), Neil Ellis, Nelson, Nico van der Merwe, Niel Joubert, Nitida, Noble Hill, Nuy, **Oldenburg** (2), Olifantsberg, Org de Rac (2) (Organic, Fairtrade), Ormonde, Oude Denneboom, PaardenKloof, Painted Wolf, Pearl Mountain, Perdeberg (Alternative white/red), Peter Falke, Plaisir de Merle, Rainbow's End, Reyneke (Organic), Rhebokskloof (Alternative white/red), Richard Hilton, **Rickety Bridge** (2), Ridgeback, Riebeek, **Rivendell**, Rooiberg (2), Rosendal, Rudera, Rust en Vrede, Rustenberg, Saltare, Saxenburg, Seven Springs (2), Signal Gun, **Simelia**, Skaap, Slaley, South Hill, **Spookfontein**, Springfontein, Steenberg, Stellar (Organic, Fairtrade), Stellenbosch University, Stofberg, Stony Brook, Strydom, Sumaridge, Tanagra, Teddy Hall, The Butcher Shop, The Fledge, The Liberator, Thelema (2), Tokara, Uva Mira, Van Loveren, Van Wyk, Vergelegen, Villion, Vondeling, Waterkloof, Welbedacht, Wellington Winery, Wildekrans, **Woolworths** (5), Zandvliet (2), Zevenwacht

★★★★ Allée Bleue, Allesverloren, Ameera, Anthonij Rupert, Arendskloof, Arra, Asara, Audacia, Bellingham, Blue Crane, Boland, Bon Courage, Boschendal, Boschrivier, **Bosman**, Botha, Bushmanspad, Cape Dreams, Carmen Stevens, Carrol Boyes, **Cloof**, **Collatio**, Darling Cellars (2), De Meye, Delheim, Diemersdal, Dragonridge, Druk My Niet, Du Toitskloof, Dunstone, Durbanville Hills, Eagle's Cliff, Elgin Vintners, Enfin, Ernst Gouws, False Bay, Foothills, Fort Simon (2), Fraai Uitzicht 1798, Glen Carlou, Groot Phesantekraal, Hartenberg, Hawksmoor, Hermit on the Hill, Herold, Hofstraat, Hoopenburg, **Hornbill**, Imbuko, Jan Harmsgat (Fairtrade), Jean Daneel, Katbakkies, Klein Parys, **Kleine Schuur**, Knorhoek, **Koni**, Kyburg, La

Couronne, Lammershoek, **Le Grand Chasseur**, Leeuwenkuil, Leipzig, Leopard's Leap, Louiesenhof, Louis 57 (2), Lutzville, Major's Hill, MAN Family, Marianne, Meerendal, **Meinert**, Mellasat, Mischa, Mitre's Edge (2), Mont du Toit, Mother Rock, **Mountain Ridge** (2), Namaqua, Naughton's, Nederburg, Neethlingshof, Nick & Forti's, Nico Vermeulen, Niel Joubert, Niemandsrivier, Nuiba, Nuy, **Olivedale**, Orange River, PaardenKloof, Porcupine Ridge, Post House, Radford Dale, **Rascallion**, Rivendell, River Garden (2), Saronsberg, Scali, Schalkenbosch (Fairtrade), Scrucap, Seven Sisters, Silkbush, Simonsig, **Skilpadvlei**, Stanford Hills, Stellenbosch Vineyards, Stellenrust, Stellenview (2), Stofberg, Strandveld, Swartland, Taillard, Tanagra, The Butcher Shop, The Goose, The Grape Grinder, The Hills, Tokara, Topiary, **Truter Family**, Tulbagh Winery, **Ultra Liquors**, Under Oaks, Villion, Vredenheim, Waverley Hills (Organic), Wederom, Weltevrede, **Woolworths** (3), Zonnebloem ★★★ Alexanderfontein, Alvi's Drift, Anura, Ashton, Audacia, Barrydale, Bayede!, Bellpost, Bernind, Black Elephant, Brampton, Brandvlei, Calitzdorp, **Camberley**, Chennells, Clairvaux, De Wet, Delaire Graff, Devonvale, DeWaal, Dormershire, Douglas Green, Du'SwaRoo (2), Eerste Hoop, Excelsior, False Bay, Fat Bastard, Fish Hoek (Fairtrade), Fort Simon, **Frater**, Freedom Hill, **Gerakaris** (2), Goedverwacht, Graceland, Groenland, **Highgate**, **Houw Hoek**, Jason's Hill, Klein Roosboom, Kleine Zalze, Kranskop, Kumala, KWV, La Bourgogne, La Terre La Mer, Landskroon, Le Manoir de Brendel, **Leeurivier** (2), Linton Park, Lord's, Louisvale, Lovane, Lyngrove, **Meerhof** (Fairtrade), Nelson, Nieuwedrift, Ormonde, Oude Compagnies Post (2), Overhex, Painted Wolf, Perdeberg (2) (Alternative white/red), Pfeifer's, Piekenierskloof (Fairtrade), **Radford Dale**, **Rascallion**, Riebeek, Robertson (2), Rooiberg, Simonsvlei (2), Slanghoek, Somerbosch, Spier, Splattered Toad, Spotswood, **Stellar** (Organic, Fairtrade), Stellenbosch Hills, Stellendrift, Stellenview, Swartland, Teddy Hall, The Hills, Tulbagh Winery, Vergenoegd, Viljoensdrift, Welmoed, Wildeberg, Wineways, **Women in Wine**, Woolworths ★★★ Aan de Doorns, Annex Kloof, Bellevue, Botha, Carrol Boyes, **Cilmor**, David Frost, Devonvale, Du Toitskloof, Fleur du Cap, Goudini, Hawksmoor, House of Mandela, Koelenhof, Koopmanskloof (Fairtrade), **Kunjani**, KWV, Le Manoir de Brendel, Mountain River, Namaqua, Nicholson Smith, Orange River, Pulpit Rock, Roodezandt, Schenkfontein, Simonsvlei, Slowine, Solms-Delta (Perlé), Stellar (Organic, Fairtrade),

Stellenview, Stettyn, Two Oceans, **Viva Africa**, Weltevrede, Windfall, Windmeul, Wonderfontein, Woolworths ★★ Bonnievale, Daschbosch, FirstCape, Klawer, KWV, Lutzville, Middelvlei, Nederburg, Seven Sisters, Simonsvlei, Tangled Tree, Vintales, Walker Bay Estate, Wineways ★★ Audacia (Light & low-alcohol), McGregor, Theuniskraal **NT** Abingdon, Andy Mitchell, Arendsig, Arumdale, Auction Crossing, Avondale (Organic), Axe Hill, Ayama (2), Baleia, Belfield, Bergheim, Bezalel, Boer & Brit, **Boschheim** (2), Brothers, Capaia, Cape Dreams, Claime d'Or, Corder, Craven (2), Creation, Cronier (2), De Villiers, Desert Rose, Devonvale, Die Mas, Dieu Donné, Doran, Dormershire, Drostdy-Hof, Du Preez, Dunstone, Durbanville Hills, DuVon, Eikehof, Elgin Heights, Fairview, Fernskloof, FirstCape, Four Paws, Franschhoek Cellar, Fryer's Cove, Gabriëlskloof, Garden Route, Gilga, Goede Hoop, Grundheim, Havana Hills, High Constantia, Hildenbrand (2), Hillock, **Idun**, Imbuko, Intellego (2), Iona, Jacques Smit, JC Wickens, Kanu, Karusa, Katbakkies, Kirabo, Kleinhoekkloof, Kumala, La Chaumiere, Lammershoek, Langverwacht (2), Lemberg, Libby's Pride, Lievland, Linton Park, Lismore, **Lozärn**, M'hudi, Maastricht, Manley, Marianne (2), Mason's Winery, Meerendal, Misty Mountains, Montpellier, Mooi Bly, Mount Pleasant, Mount Vernon, Mountain River, Nederburg (2), New Beginnings, Olsen, Oneiric (2), Piekenierskloof, Rhebokskloof (Alternative white/red), Rijk's (3), Robert Stanford, Robertson, Rogge Cloof, Rooiberg (2), Rosendal (3), Sarah's, Scali, Schultz Family, Seal Breeze, Sijnn, Slaley, Snow Mountain, Solms-Delta (3), Somerset Wines, Spice Route (2) (Fairtrade), Star Hill, Stellar (Organic, Fairtrade), Stellekaya, Stone Ridge (2), Stoumann's, Sumsaré, Tamboerskloof, Teubes, Thandi (Fairtrade), The Bald Ibis, The Giant Periwinkle, Thembi & Co, Trajan, United Nations (Fairtrade), Vaalvlei, Val du Charron, Valley Vineyards, Virgin Earth, Vrede en Lust (2), Wellington Winery, Wildekrans, William Everson, Windmeul, Wolvendrift, Woolworths, Zonnebloem **D** AA Badenhorst, Anura, Blaauwklippen (3), Darling Cellars, Du Preez, Fairview, Hermit on the Hill (2), Hill & Dale, House of Mandela, Jordan, Konkelberg, La Couronne, Libby's Pride, Linton Park (2), Oak Valley, Stellenzicht (2), Ultra Liquors, Zanddrift

Skin-macerated white

★★★★☆ Springfontein (Chardonnay wooded)

★★★★ Laibach (Chenin blanc wooded, dry)

★★★ Stellenview (Sauvignon blanc unwooded)

Sparkling, Méthode ancestrale

★★★★☆ Upland

★★★★ Dragonridge, Vondeling

★★★★ Scali (Organic), Vondeling **NT** AA Badenhorst, Groot Parys, The Blacksmith

Sparkling, Méthode cap classique, red, dry
★★★★ Camberley **NT** Mount Babylon

Sparkling, Méthode cap classique, rosé, dry
★★★★☆ Amberloui, Anthonij Rupert, Bon Courage, **Charles Fox** (2), De Wetshof, Graham Beck, Newstead, Wildekrans

★★★★ Anthonij Rupert, **Canto**, Clos Malverne, Colmant, Dainty Bess, Graham Beck, Groot Constantia, Haute Cabrière, Kleine Zalze, Krone, KWV, Longridge, Lourensford, Miss Molly, Môreson, Saltare, Scrucap, Silverthorn, Simonsig, Steenberg, Tanzanite, **Teubes**, Waterkloof, Wonderfontein, Woolworths

★★★★ Allée Bleue, Arendskloof, Bayede!, Boschendal, **BruceJack**, **Canto**, **Cape Town Wine Company**, **Carrol Boyes**, Elgin Ridge, **Grande Provence**, Groote Post, L'Avenir, Lodestone, Lourensford, Namaqua, Pongrácz, Signal Gun, Strandveld, Sumaridge, Van Loveren, Villiera, Webersburg, Woolworths ★★★ Aurelia, Black Oystercatcher, **Darling Cellars**, Franschhoek Cellar, Koelenhof, **Linton Park**, Lord's, Louisvale, Lovane, **Misty Mountains**, Perdeberg, The House of JC le Roux★★★ Plettenvale, Teddy Hall **NT** Ayama, Chabivin, Dieu Donné, Domaine des Dieux, Francois La Garde (2), Gentleman's Reserve, Hillock, Karusa, Le Lude, Leopard Frog, Lyngrove, Montpellier, My Wyn, Packwood, Rickety Bridge, The House of JC le Roux, Woolworths (2) (Organic) **D** Boplaas, Stony Brook, Ultra Liquors, Wellington Winery

Sparkling, Méthode cap classique, rosé, off-dry/semi-sweet
★★★★ Krone
NT Tulbagh Winery

Sparkling, Méthode cap classique, white, dry
★★★★★ Colmant, Villiera, Woolworths

★★★★☆ Babylonstoren, Bartho Eksteen, Bon Courage (2), Cederberg, Charles Fox (3), CK Wines, Colmant (2), Graham Beck (3), Haute Cabrière, Hoopenburg, **Klein Constantia**, Krone, KWV, La Bri, Longridge, Pongrácz, Saltare (3), Silverthorn (3), Simonsig, Steenberg, Stony Brook, **Taillefert**, Tanzanite, Tierhoek, Tokara, Topiary, Waterford, Waterkloof, Weltevrede

★★★★ Allée Bleue, Ambeloui, Anthonij Rupert (2), Anura, Benguela Cove, Black Elephant, Boschendal (2), **Bosman**, Bramon (2), Canto, **Charles Fox**, Clouds, Constantia Uitsig, Darling

Cellars, De Grendel, De Wet, De Wetshof, Delaire Graff, Delheim, DeMorgenzon, Durbanville Hills, Fairview, **Foothills**, Graham Beck, Grande Provence, Groot Phesantekraal, Haute Cabrière, Hoopenburg, Hout Bay, **Jordan**, Kleine Zalze, Krone, KWV, L'Avenir, La Motte, Longridge, Lord's, Lourensford (2), **Lowerland**, Miss Molly, Mooiplaas, Môreson, Morgenhof, Newstead, Nico van der Merwe, Nieuwedrift, Noble Hill, Nuy, Org de Rac (Organic, Nouveau), Perdeberg, Peter Falke, Plaisir de Merle, **Pongrácz** (2), **Pulpit Rock**, Quoin Rock, **Rickety Bridge**, Saronsberg, Saxenburg, Scrucap, Simonsig, Spier, Stanford Hills, Steenberg, Stellenbosch University, Stellenbosch Vineyards, Stofberg, Teddy Hall, The Butcher Shop, The House of GM&AHRENS, The House of JC le Roux, Thelema, Ultra Liquors, Van Loveren, Vergenoegd, Viljoensdrift, Villiera (2), Wildehurst, Wonderfontein, Woolworths (2)

★★★★ Asara, Aurelia, Backsberg, Boschendal, Buitenverwachting, **Canto**, **Cavalli**, De Krans, Du Preez, Franschhoek Cellar, Genevieve, **Huis van Chevallerie**, Kanu, Ken Forrester, Klein Constantia, Klein Parys, Koelenhof, Lanzerac, Lateganskop, Leopard's Leap, Louisvale, MAN Family, Mulderbosch, Muratie, Nitida, Somerbosch, Teddy Hall, The House of JC le Roux, Ultra Liquors (2), Villiera (Light & low-alcohol), Webersburg, Welbedacht, Weltevrede, Wildeberg, Wildekrans, Woolworths ★★★ **Alkmaar**, Avontuur, Backsberg (Kosher), Bemind, Blaauwklippen, Bloemendal, Cloof, **Croydon**, Dâbar, Du Toitskloof, **Goede Hoop**, **Grande Provence**, **Linton Park**, Maison, Morgenster, Niel Joubert, Rickety Bridge, Snow Mountain, **Tulbagh Winery**, Ultra Liquors, Windfall **NT** Altydgedacht, Alvi's Drift, Andy Mitchell, Avondale (Organic), Ayama (2), Beau Joubert, Boer & Brit, Cape Chamonix, Carrol Boyes (3), Chabivin (2), Conradie, Dieu Donné, Domaine Coutelier, Domaine des Dieux, Elgin Heights (2), **Esona**, Francois La Garde (2), Gabriëlskloof, Genevieve, Gentleman's Reserve, High Constantia, Hildenbrand, Hillock, Jean Daneel, Karusa, Kay & Monty (2), Klein Roosboom, Kleine Zalze, La Chaumiere, Laibach, Le Lude (4), Leopard Frog (2), **Lourensford**, **Maison de Teijger** (3), Meerendal, Mimosa (2), Montpellier (2), Mount Babylon, My Wyn (2), Old Vines, Overhex, Redford Lane, Rhebokskloof (Alternative white/red), Ridgeback, Riebeek, Rijk's, Robert Stanford, Roodezandt, Saxenburg, Signal Hill, Skaap, Tanzanite, The House of JC le Roux, Val de Vie (2), Vergelegen, Virgin Earth, Walking Woods (Organic, Fairtrade), Warwick, Waverley Hills (Organic), Wildehurst (2) **D**

Bosman, Krone, Longridge, Perdeberg, Spookfontein, Thelema, Wellington Winery

Sparkling, Méthode cap classique, white, off-dry/semi-sweet
★★★★ Graham Beck, **Pongrácz**, Simonsig
★★★☆ New Beginnings ★★★ Boschendal, **Darling Cellars** (Light & low-alcohol), The House of JC le Roux, Woolworths

Sparkling, Non-MCC, red, dry
★★★ D'Aria ★★ The House of JC le Roux **NT** M'hudi

Sparkling, Non-MCC, red, off-dry/semi-sweet
★★ Du Toitskloof (Light & low-alcohol), Robertson

Sparkling, Non-MCC, rosé, dry
★★★★ Huis van Chevallerie, Kloovenburg ★★★ Boplaas, D'Aria, Riebeek★★★ Somerset Wines (Light & low-alcohol), Stellar (Organic, Fairtrade), Woolworths **NT** Blaauwklippen (Perlé), Thandi **D** Knorhoek

Sparkling, Non-MCC, rosé, off-dry/semi-sweet
★★★ Bon Courage, Domein Doornkraal, Klawer (Light & low-alcohol), Nuy, Orange River (Light & low-alcohol), Perdeberg (Light & low-alcohol), Robertson (Light & low-alcohol), Rooiberg, Swartland, The House of JC le Roux, Vredenheim, Woolworths ★★ Aan de Doorns, Goedverwacht, Overhex (Light & low-alcohol), The House of JC le Roux (Light & low-alcohol), Viljoensdrift (Light & low-alcohol), Vintales ★★ Ashton **NT** Koelenhof, Kumala (Light & low-alcohol), Woolworths ★★ Mountain Ridge, Stellar (Organic, Fairtrade), Stellenbosch Hills, Walking Woods **D** Alvi's Drift

Sparkling, Non-MCC, white, dry
★★★★ Colmant, Darling Cellars, Hermit on the Hill
★★★☆ Steenberg, **Woolworths** ★★★ Clos Malverne, Durbanville Hills, Goudini, **Leopard's Leap**, Nederburg, Orange River, Stellar (Organic, Fairtrade), **Woolworths**★★☆ Botha, **Brandvlei**, D'Aria, Du Toitskloof, **Havana Hills**, Klein Parys, KWV, Overhex, Robertson, Rooiberg, Swartland, Tulbagh Winery, Welmoed, Woolworths (2) (Organic) ★★ Ashton, Merwida, Slanghoek, The House of JC le Roux ★ **Vintales NT** Bonnievale, Cronier (2), Lyngrove, Solara (Organic), Stellenbosch Hills **D** Alvi's Drift, Wellington Winery

Sparkling, Non-MCC, white, off-dry/semi-sweet
★★★★ Krone

★★★☆ Badsberg (Light & low-alcohol), Koelenhof, Nuy, Opstal, Orange River, Slanghoek, The House of JC le Roux, Woolworths ★★ De Doorns, KWV, Robertson (Light & low-alcohol), The House of JC le Roux (Light & low-alcohol), **Vintales**, Zandwijk **NT** Kumala **D** Alvi's Drift

Special Late Harvest
★★★★ Bon Courage, Nederburg
★★★☆ Backsberg, Slanghoek, Van Loveren ★★★ Robertson★★★ De Wet **D** Bergsig

Sweet red
★★★★ Dormershire ★★★ **Fat Bastard**, Perdeberg ★★★ Autumn Harvest Crackling (Perlé), Darling Cellars ★★ Backsberg (Sacramental, Kosher), **De Krans** (Perlé, Light & low-alcohol), Du Toitskloof (Light & low-alcohol), **Nicholson Smith**, Robertson (Light & low-alcohol), Somerset Wines, Zandwijk ★★ Cape Classics, Robertson (2), Wineways ★ Woolworths **NT** Imbuko, Kumala (2), Mooiuitsig, Overhex (Light & low-alcohol), Roos Family, SoetKaroo (2), Stellar (Organic, Fairtrade), Versailles **D** Louiesenhof

Sylvaner
★★★★ Overgaauw

Tannat
★★★★ Arendskloof, Fairview, FirstCape, Lowerland
★★★★ Kranskop★★★ **Du'SwaRoo NT** Mooi Bly **D** Glen Carlou

Tempranillo/tinta roriz
★★★★★ Stony Brook, Super Single Vineyards
★★★★ Baleia, De Krans, Mellasat
★★★★ Olivedale, Swallow Hill, Van der Merwe & Finlayson ★★★ Dornier **NT** Anura

Therona
★★★★ Stellenbosch Vineyards

Tinta barocca
★★★★★ Elemental Bob
★★★★★ Sadie
★★★★ Allesverloren, Lammershoek
★★★★ Micu Narunsky, Momento, Woolworths ★★★ Boplaas, **Hofstraat**, Swartland★★★ Du'SwaRoo **NT** Dagbreek, Peter Bayly **D** Boplaas

Touriga franca
★★★★ Boplaas

Touriga nacional
★★★★☆ Boplaas
★★★★ Axe Hill, De Krans, Joostenberg

★★★★ Boplaas, Dagbreek, Overgaauw ★★★ Bergsig, Du'SwaRoo★★★ Du'SwaRoo NT Allesverloren, Calitzdorp, MAN Family, Sijnn

Trincadeira/tinta amarela
NT Dagbreek

Verdelho
★★★★☆ Arcangeli, Stellenbosch Vineyards

★★★★ Fairview, Maanschijn

★★★★ Org de Rac ★★★ Cavalli **NT** Alphabetical, Flagstone **D** Thelema

Vermentino
★★★★☆ Morgenster

★★★★ Ayama

Vin de paille/straw wine
★★★★★ Mullineux

★★★★☆ Botanica, De Trafford, DeMorgenzon, Donkiesbaai (Light & low-alcohol), Fairview, Foothills, Keermont, Klawer, La Motte (Light & low-alcohol), Orange River, Rustenberg, Simonsig, Stellar (Organic, Fairtrade), Tierhoek, Vergelegen, Vondeling

★★★★ Boplaas, Druk My Niet (Light & low-alcohol), Fairview, Maison, Meinert, Môreson, **Piekenierskloof**

★★★★ Asara, Bosman, Dagbreek ★★★ Dragonridge **NT** Brugman, Goede Hoop, Groot Parys (Organic), Hazendal, Lammershoek, Mellasat, Mullineux (2) (Light & low-alcohol), Naughton's, Radford Dale, Saronsberg, Signal Hill, Spier (Organic), Stettyn **D** JMA Louw, The Fledge

Viognier
★★★★☆ Creation, Eagles' Nest, **Richard Hilton** (2), Ridgeback, The Foundry

★★★★ Backsberg, Beau Constantia, Bellingham, De Grendel, Diemersfontein, Flagstone, Franki's, Idiom, Kanu, **La Couronne**, Lourensford (2), Lowerland, Lynx, Maison, Mellasat, **Myburgh Bros** (Organic), Oldenburg, Painted Wolf, Richard Hilton, Spice Route, Tamboerskloof, **The Liberator**, Waterkloof, Woolworths

★★★★ Alkmaar, Anura, Arra, Babylonstoren, Black Elephant, Blue Crane, Chennells (2), Dorrance, Fairview, Fraai Uitzicht 1798, La Petite Ferme, Nitida, Noble Hill, Saronsberg, Spotswood, Stellar (Organic, Fairtrade), Stellenbosch University, Swallow Hill, SylvanVale, Van der Merwe & Finlayson, Whalehaven ★★★ Alvi's Drift, Axe Hill, Ayama, Calais, Dunstone, Elgin Vintners, Excelsior, **Foothills**, Fort Simon, Klawer, Kranskop, Leipzig, Star Hill★★★ **Entre Nous**, Lynx, Silkbush ★★ Bezalel **NT** Abingdon,

Arendsig (2), Arra (2), Buitenverwachting, Casa Mori, Eerste Hoop, Karusa, Katbakkies (2), La Bri, Lismore (2), Mitre's Edge, Montpellier, My Wyn, Robertson, Schalkenbosch, Township Winery (Fairtrade), Vergenoegd, Vrede en Lust, Whalehaven, Wildehurst **D** Dieu Donné, Franki's, Glen Carlou, Grande Provence, Hermit on the Hill, Hidden Valley, Joostenberg (Organic), Riebeek, Spier

White blends, off-dry/semi-sweet (w & u/w)
★★★★ Four Paws

★★★★☆ Altydgedacht, Villiera ★★★ Grande Provence, Ken Forrester, Robertson, Signal Gun, Zevenwacht★★★ Brandvlei, Calitzdorp (Perlé), Koelenhof, Nederburg, **Perdeberg** (Alternative white/red), Stellenrust (Fairtrade), **Swartland** ★★ Capenheimer (Perlé), Darling Cellars, Du Toitskloof, Graça, **Nicholson Smith**, Overmeer Cellars, Paarl Perlé (Perlé), Tulbagh Winery, Welbedacht ★★ Autumn Harvest Crackling (Perlé), Robertson (3) ★ De Krans **NT** Bonnievale (Perlé, Light & low-alcohol), Boschendal, Drostdy-Hof (2), Group CDV (Perlé), Imbuko, Kumala (2), KWV, Leopard's Leap, Mooiuitsig (2), Overhex (Light & low-alcohol), Stellar (Organic, Fairtrade), Swartland, Two Oceans, Virgin Earth **D** Bergsig (Perlé), Bonnievale, Fairview, Kanu, Solms-Delta

White blends, unwooded, dry
★★★★☆ The Berrio

★★★★ Elgin Vintners, GlenWood, KWV, Nico Vermeulen, Signal Gun, Spookfontein, Welbedacht, Wildehurst, Woolworths

★★★★ Alkmaar, Allée Bleue, Ashbourne, Bouchard Finlayson, Buitenverwachting, Doran, Foothills, Goats do Roam, Groote Post, Kaapzicht, Kruger Family, Lynx, MAN Family, Old Vines, Org de Rac (Organic, Fairtrade), **Overhex** (2), Quando, Reyneke (Organic), **Rickety Bridge**, Roos Family, Simonsig, Slowine, Springfield, Springfontein, Truter Family, **Val du Charron**, Waverley Hills (Organic), Woolworths (3) ★★★ Alvi's Drift, Beyerskloof, Bon Courage, **Cilmor**, Flagstone, Frater, Hartenberg, Imbuko (2), Jacques Germanier (Organic, Fairtrade), Jordan, McGregor, Mellasat, Napier, Opstal, Perdeberg, Post House, Pulpit Rock, **Rascallion**, Reyneke (Organic), Rhebokskloof (Alternative white/red), Riebeek, Saronsberg, Somerbosch, Stellar (Organic, Fairtrade), Theuniskraal, Vaughan Johnson, Villiera, Villiersdorp, Woolworths (4), Zonnebloem ★★★ Aan de Doorns, Beau Joubert, Boschendal, Darling Cellars, Drostdy-Hof, Landskroon, Mooiplaas, Nederburg, Niel Joubert, Nuy, **Ses'Fikile**, Stellenrust (Fairtrade), Sun International Wines, Tulbagh Winery

(Light & low-alcohol), Ultra Liquors, Van Loveren, Woolworths (2) (Light & low-alcohol), Zandvliet ★★ Drostdy-Hof (Light & low-alcohol), Du Toitskloof, Klawer, Overhex, Robertson (3), Slanghoek, Stellenbosch Hills, Woolworths (5) ★★ Kanu, Le Manoir de Brendel, Overmeer Cellars, Robertson (2) (Light & low-alcohol) ★ Robertson, Simonsvlei ☆ Oom Tas **NT** Boer & Brit, Boplaas, Boschendal, Cranefields, Doran, Eikehof, Four Paws, Group CDV (2), Jacques Germanier (Organic, Fairtrade), Jakkalsvlei, Joostenberg, Karusa, Kleinhoekkloof, Kumala (6), KWV (2), Leeuwenberg, Leopard's Leap, Mount Vernon, Mountain River, My Wyn, Nabygelegen, Namaqua, New Beginnings, Overhex, Picardi ReBEL, Rosendal, Saxenburg, Silkbush, Somerbosch, Somerset Wines, Stellar (3) (Organic, Fairtrade), Stellendrift, Stettyn, Thandi (Fairtrade), Thokozani, United Nations (2), Versailles, Vrede en Lust (2), Wavescape, Whalehaven, Zanddrift, Zidela (2) **D** Asara, Barton, Bonnievale, Conradie (2), Diemersfontein (2), Grande Provence, Knorhoek, Konkelberg, Linton Park, Morgenhof, Noble Hill, Opstal, Simonsvlei, Wineways

White blends, wooded, dry

★★★★★ B Vintners, Cape Point, **Lourens Family**, Mullineux, Rall, Sadie, Savage, **Shannon**, Stark-Condé, Thorne & Daughters, Vergelegen, Warwick

★★★★☆ Alheit, Alvi's Drift, Anthonij Rupert, **Anysbos**, Backsberg, Beau Constantia, Beaumont, Bergsig, Bizoe, Black Oystercatcher, Blackwater, Bloemendal, Boplaas, Cape Chamonix, Cape Rock, Cederberg, Celestina, City on a Hill, Constantia Glen, Darling Cellars, David & Nadia, De Grendel, Délaire Graff, **DeMorgenzon** (2), Doran, Durbanville Hills, Elemental Bob, Elgin Ridge (Biodynamic), Fable, Fairview, Flagstone, Flying Cloud, Gabriëlskloof, GlenWood, Grande Provence, Groot Constantia, Highlands Road, Hughes Family (Organic), Iona, Keermont, **Lammershoek**, Lemberg, **Lourensford**, Luddite, Miles Mossop, Momento, Morgenster, **Mullineux**, Naudé, Nederburg, Neethlingshof, **Neil Ellis** (Alternative white/red), Newton Johnson, Nico van der Merwe, Olifantsberg, **Opstal**, **Painted Wolf** (2), Paul Roos, **Richard Kershaw**, Ron Burgundy, Sadie (2), Sijnn, Solms-Delta, Spier, Springfontein (Alternative white/red), Steenberg, Stony Brook, The Ahrens Family, The Great SA Wine Co, The

Liberator, Thelema, Tokara, Trizanne, Vondeling, Vuurberg, Waterkloof, Zorgvliet

★★★★ Allée Bleue, Altydgedacht, Arendskloof, Babylon's Peak, **Babylonstoren**, Benguela Cove, **Bezuidenhout Family**, Blake, Boland, Bosman (Fairtrade), Cavalli, Constantia Uitsig, Creation, Darling Cellars, De Krans, Dornier, Ernst Gouws, Fram, **Glen Carlou**, Hermanuspietersfontein, Joostenberg (Organic), Kloovenburg, La Bourgogne, **La Bri**, Leipzig, Lomond (2), Miss Molly, **Montegray**, Mother Rock, Muratie, Nabygelegen, Nuiba, Painted Wolf, Perdeberg, Piekenierskloof, **Quoin Rock**, Rickety Bridge, Rietvallei, Scali (Organic), Solms-Delta, South Hill, Stellenbosch Hills, Stony Brook, Strandveld, **Sumaridge** (2), Taillard, The Fledge, **The Giant Periwinkle**, The Wolftrap, **Under Oaks**, Val du Charron, Van Wyk, Villiera, Yardstick

★★★☆ Alphabetical, Blue Crane, BruceJack, Dragonridge (Alternative white/red), Edgebaston, Eerste Hoop, **False Bay**, Fijndraai, Haut Espoir, Hermit on the Hill, **JAN Wines** (Organic), **Lanzerac**, Le Pommier, Malanot, **Meerhof** (Fairtrade), Org de Rac (Organic), Swallow Hill, Villion, Wildeberg, Zevenwacht ★★★ Bellpost, Black Elephant, Eenzaamheid, **Grand Domaine**, Hidden Valley, Hildenbrand, Mont Rochelle **NT** AA Badenhorst, Avondale (Organic), Beau Constantia, Bergheim, Doolhof, Doran, Elemental Bob, Escapades, Fairview, Groote Post, Hazendal, Hildenbrand, Karusa, Kumala (4), **Lammershoek** (3), Leeuwenberg, Leopard Frog (2), Lodestone, My Wyn, Nederburg (2), Nitida, Nomada, **Rascallion** (2) Themika, Tierhoek, Two Oceans, Virgin Earth, Vrede en Lust **D** AA Badenhorst (2), Cavalli, Daschbosch, Kanu, Kumala, Mulderbosch, Porcupine Ridge, Stellenzicht, Waverley Hills (Organic)

White from red/black grapes (not Blanc de noir)

★★★★☆ Artisanal Boutique
★★★★ Meinert, Mellasat, Springfontein
★★★ **Wellington Winery** ★★★ Asara **NT** Boucheron, Flagstone **D** Tempel

Zinfandel/Primitivo

★★★★ Grande Provence ★★★ Blaauwklippen **NT** Idiom **D** Blaauwklippen

The Industry

Overview

South Africa is the 8th-largest wine-producing nation by volume, according to the latest available data (2017), down from 7th largest the year before. Italy, with 15.9% of global production, remains number one, followed by France (13.8%), Spain (12%) and the US (8.7%). SA, with 1,080 m litres (excluding grape juice and grape juice concentrate), in 2017 contributed 4.1% to global volume, up from 3.9% the previous year and equal with China.

The number of SA wine-grape growers continued to decline (3,029 compared with 3,145 in 2016), along with the hectares under vine (94,545 vs 95,775) and the overall number of wine cellars crushing grapes (546 vs 568). Total private cellars also dipped, from 493 to 472, as did producing wholesalers crushing grapes, to 26. Co-operatives – 'producer cellars' in officialese – were steady at 48. Producers vinifying less than 100 tons fell from 248 to 224, yet at ±41% of the total, these micro-cellars remained a major force in the industry.

Vineyards

After inching up to 2,095 in 2016, vineyard establishment slumped to a new low of 1,211 ha. Planting for white wine again outstripped that for red (766 ha vs 445), albeit by a smaller margin, while white-wine grape chenin blanc retained its entrenched position as most-planted variety (220 ha added). Sauvignon blanc (177) surpassed colombard (138) as second-most-planted white-wine variety, followed by chardonnay (125). Cabernet sauvignon

2007 56% 44%   **2017** 55% 45%

Red ⬤ and white ◯ grape varieties as % of total area

(121) remained the most-planted red-wine variety, followed by shiraz (101), pinotage (54), pinot noir and durif/petite sirah (27) which, surprisingly, edged out merlot (26).

Also unexpectedly, chenin (600) was replaced as most-uprooted variety overall by colombard (601) in 2017, but the former still led the overall hectareage table, with 18.6% of the total 94,545 ha (279 m vines). Cabernet sauvignon, with ±11%, remained the leading red. The percentage of very young vines (under 4 years) dipped to ±6%, while the portion older than 20 again rose, to ±24%.

Exports

Exports in 2017 of 448 m litres, almost 49% of SA's total wine production, represented the third year of growth. Chenin, sauvignon and chardonnay topped the list of most-exported varietal wines (bottled and bulk), with pinks, cabernet, shiraz, pinotage and merlot also in demand. The UK, Germany, surging US, France and Canada were the top five

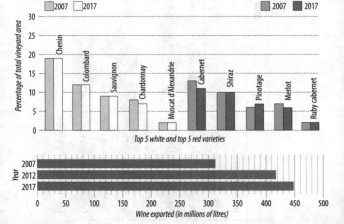

South African Wine Industry – Ten-Year Overview

	2008	2009	2010	2011	2012	2013	2014	2015	2016	2017
Number of wineries	585	604	573	582	582	564	559	566	568	546
Total vine area (excl sultana) (hectares)	101 312	101 259	101 016	100 568	100 097	99 687	99 472	98 594	95 775	94 545
Producing area 4 yrs & older (excl sultana) (hectares)	92 439	93 220	93 119	92 594	91 810	91 958	92 010	91 453	88 747	88 624
Avg yield (tons/hectare)	15.42	14.46	13.55	14.07	15.41	16.29	16.52	16.15	15.84	16.22
Grapes crushed (millions of tons)	1.43	1.35	1.26	1.30	1.41	1.50	1.52	1.48	1.41	1.44
Total production (millions of litres)	1 089.0	1 033.4	984.8	1 012.8	1 097.0	1 156.9	1 181.1	1 154.0	1 089.0	1 118.0
Domestic sales (millions of litres)	355.8	338.3	346.4	353.3	361.4	368.3	395.3	425.1	436.9	449.7
Consumption per capita (litres SA wine)	7.19	6.75	6.81	6.85	6.90	6.93	7.33	7.76	7.86	7.96
Export volume (millions of litres)	411.7	395.6	378.5	357.4	417.2	525.6	422.7	420.0	428.4	448.4

markets for SA wine (packaged and bulk) in 2017. For packaged wine only, the UK, Germany, the Netherlands, Sweden and the US remained the five biggest outlets.

Local wine consumption

SA's per-capita wine consumption continued rising, to 7.9L in 2017, the highest mark since 2002.

While wine's combined market share (natural, fortified and sparkling) also kept growing, to 18.7%, it remained substantially lower than beer (55.5%). Brandy's share continued a long-term decline, to 4.7%, while whisky's was static at 5.9%.

Of natural wine sold domestically (including locally bottled imports), 44% was in glass (unchanged from 2016), and of that ±63% was in the standard 750-ml bottle. Wine in bag-in-box, after rapid rises, was steady at 37% of total sales. Plastic containers accounted for ±15% and Tetra packs ±3%. Foil bags — the notorious papsakke, now carefully regulated — were a minuscule 0.1%.

Note

Statistical data was provided by SA Wine Industry Information & Systems.

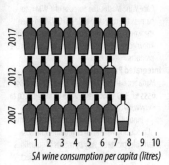

SA wine consumption per capita (litres)

Percentage market share (based on alcohol content)

Beverage

Industry Organisations

Agricultural Ethical Trade Initiative See Wine & Agricultural Ethical Trade Association.

ARC Infruitec-Nietvoorbij Senior manager, research: prof Bongani Ndimba ▪ Public relations officer: Derusha Crank ▪ **T +27 (0)21-809-3100** ▪ F +27 (0)21-809-3400 ▪ infocape@arc.agric.za ▪ www.arc.agric.za

Internationally regarded one-stop research institute, committed to providing sustainable technologies to the agricultural sector in SA. ARC's mandate is research and development as well as technology transfer on the breeding, cultivation and post-harvest technology of deciduous fruit, grape vines, alternative crops and indigenous herbal teas. Nietvoorbij, an ARC farm, is synonymous with quality research in oenology and viticulture. Annually, 1,000 small-batch wines are made for research purposes, along with commercial wines for sale to the public.

Biodiversity & Wine Initiative (BWI) See WWF-SA Conservation Champion Programme

Biodynamic & Organic Wines of South Africa (BOWSA) Chair: Marion Smith ▪ marion@ elginridge.com ▪ **T +27 (0)79-433-9400** ▪ www. biodynamicorganicwine.co.za

Recently formed association aiming to help consumers and media easily see which local wine producers and grape growers are officially certified as biodynamic and organic.

Cape Brandy Distillers Guild Patron: Dave Hughes ▪ Trustees: Kobus Gelderblom (kobus@ capebrandy.org) & Alastair Coombe (alastair@ capebrandy.org) ▪ www.capebrandy.org

Opt-in communication and promotion platform for the Cape Brandy (100% potstill) segment within the SA brandy category. Members enjoy access to skills and expertise, and benefit from collective marketing and attendance at local/ international trade shows.

Cape Port Producers' Association (CAPPA) Chair: Mike Neebe ▪ **T +27 (0)44-213-3326** ▪ F +27 (0)44-213-3750 ▪ boplaas@mweb.co.za

Cape Vintner Classification (CVC) CEO Charl Theron ▪ **T** +27(0)83-269-0577 ▪ F +27(0)86-275-8887 ▪ info@cvc1659.co.za ▪ www.cvc1659.co.za

Independent body committed to the accreditation, governance, representation and promotion of distinctive site-specific wines. Through a system of certification and classification, CVC endorsement underscores its members' commitment to terroir-specific winemaking as well as excellence in cellar practices, environmental championing and cellardoor experience.

Cape Winemakers Guild (CWG) Chair: Boela Gerber ▪ General manager: Kate Jonker ▪ **T** +27 (0)21-852-0408 ▪ F +27 (0)21-852-0409 ▪ info@capewinemakersguild.com ▪ www.capewinemakersguild.com

Independent, invitation-only association, founded in 1982 to promote winemaking excellence among its members. Since 1985, the CWG has held an annual public auction of rare and unique wines, produced by its members exclusively for the auction. The Nedbank CWG Development Trust, established in 1999, supports social development in the winelands through its oenology and viticulture protégé programmes, Billy Hofmeyr AgriSeta bursaries and support of Wine Training South Africa.

Chardonnay Forum of South Africa Chair: Johann de Wet ▪ johanndewet@dewetshof.com ▪ **T** +27 (0)23-615-1853 ▪ F +27 (0)23-615-1915

Chenin Blanc Association (CBA) Chair: Ken Forrester ▪ **T** +27 (0)21-855-2374 / +27 (0)82-783-7203 ▪ F +27 (0)21-855-2373 ▪ ken@kenforresterwines.com ▪ www.chenin.co.za ▪ Manager: Ina Smith ▪ **T** +27 (0)82-467-4331 ▪ F +27 (0)86-672-8549 ▪ ina.smith@iafrica.com ▪ @CheninBlancAsso

Fairtrade Africa - Southern Africa Network (FTA-SAN) Regional head: Zachary Kiarie ▪ **T** +27 (0)21-447-3486 ▪ z.kiarie@fairtradeafrica.net ▪ www.fairtradeafrica.net

Fairtrade Africa (FTA) is the independent non-profit umbrella organisation representing all Fairtrade-certified producers in Africa. FTA is owned by its members, who are African producer organisations certified against international Fairtrade standards. The Southern Africa Network (SAN), located in Cape Town, is one of four FTA regional networks which represent Fairtrade-certified producers (smallholder farmers, farm-workers and -owners) in southern Africa. SAN provides technical support on Fairtrade

standards; facilitates trade linkages and markets access opportunities; advocates on behalf of and with its producers on relevant issues; and enhances knowledge and capacity around social and environmental issues.

Garagiste Movement of South Africa See under Make Your Own Wine or Brandy

Institute of Cape Wine Masters National chair: Conrad Louw ▪ **T** +27 (0)83-326-1844 ▪ National vice-chair: Kristina Beuthner ▪ +27 (0)82-900-7238 ▪ Secretary: Raymond Noppé ▪ **T** +27 (0)82-335-2020 ▪ info@icwm.co.za ▪ www.icwm.co.za

Cape Wine Master, instituted in 1983, is one of the most sought-after formal qualifications in SA wine. To date 98 candidates have qualified, and a further 3 have been awarded the title Honorary Cape Wine Master. The purpose of ICWM is to harness the collective ability of CWMs to open the world of wine and brandy to others through knowledge, deep understanding and love for the products.

Integrated Production of Wine (IPW) Manager: Daniël Schietekat ▪ **T** +27 (0)21-889-6555 ▪ F +27 (0)866-903-224 ▪ daniel@ipw.co.za ▪ www.ipw.co.za

Innovative, widely supported initiative aimed at producing wine in an environmentally sustainable, profitable way by means of guidelines for both farm and cellar, embracing all aspects of grape production, winemaking and biodiversity conservation. See also Sustainable Wine South Africa.

Méthode Cap Classique Producers' Association Chair: Pieter Ferreira ▪ bubblesferreira@gmail.com ▪ Admin: Elsabé Ferreira ▪ **T** +27(0)21-863-1599 ▪ F +27 (0)21-863-1552 ▪ info@capclassique.co.za

Muscadel SA Chair: Henri Swiegers ▪ **T** +27 (0)23-344-3021 ▪ henri@badsberg.co.za ▪ Vice-chair: André Scriven ▪ **T** +27 (0)23-626-1664 ▪ andres@rooiberg.co.za

Old Vine Project (OVP) Marketing & communications consultant: André Morgenthal ▪ **T** +27 (0)82-658-3883 ▪ andre@oldvineproject.co.za ▪ www.oldvineproject.co.za

Believing that old vines produce wines with a unique character – pure and delicate yet powerful – OVP strives to preserve as many of SA's 3,200 gnarled-vine hectares as possible, while creating a culture of helping young vineyards mature into stellar seniors. OVP recently launched the Certified Heritage Vineyards seal which, affixed to a bottle, not only assures winelovers the content is from genuinely venerable vines (35+ years) but also displays the actual establishment date of the vineyard. See also Editor's Note.

Pinotage Association Chair: Beyers Truter ▪ T +27 (0)21-865-1235 ▪ F +27 ()21-865-2683 ▪ reception@beyerskloof.co.za ▪ Manager: Elsabé Ferreira T +27 (0)21-863-1599 ▪ F +27 (0)21-863-1552 ▪ admin@pinotage.co.za ▪ www. pinotage.co.za

Sauvignon Blanc Interest Group of South Africa (SBIG) Chair: JD Pretorius ▪ T +27 (0)21-713 2211 ▪ jd@steenbergfarm.com ▪ Admin: Elsabé Ferreira ▪ T +27 (0)21-863-1599 ▪ F +27 (0)21-863-1552 ▪ elsabe@efpromosies.co.za

Shiraz South Africa Chair: Edmund Terblanche ▪ T +27 (0)82-770-2929 ▪ F +27 (0)21-876-3446 ▪ et.cellar@la-motte.co.za ▪ Secretary: Sandra Lotz ▪ T +27 (0)82-924-7254 ▪ F +27 (0)86-267-4333 ▪ info@shirazsa.co.za

South African Brandy Foundation (SABF) Director: Christelle Reade-Jahn ▪ T +27 (0)64-754-6552 ▪ christelle@sabrandy.co.za ▪ www. sabrandy.co.za

A registered non-profit organisation representing more than 95% of local brandy producers, SABF facilitates long-term growth and helps preserve the integrity and heritage of the SA brandy industry.

South African Pinot Noir Association Chair: Emul Ross ▪ emul@hamiltonrussellvineyards.com ▪ T +27 (0)28-312-3595 ▪ F +27 (0)28-312-1797 ▪ Admin: Vanessa Hoek ▪ vanessa@winemachin-erygroup.com

Producer group aiming to further improve the general quality of local pinot noir still-wines by sharing ideas, and ultimately finding an identity for the variety in SA.

South African Sommelier Association (SASA) Chair: Higgo Jacobs ▪ Vice-chair: David Clarke ▪ info@sommeliers.org.za ▪ www.sommeliers.org.za

Membership-driven, non-profit, voluntary private organisation established in 2012 to promote a culture of fine wine, food and service excellence in South Africa; formalise the profession of sommelier; and provide a forum for dialogue, exchange of ideas, knowledge and skills.

South African Wine Industry Information & Systems NPC (SAWIS) Executive manager: Yvette van der Merwe ▪ T +27 (0)21-807-5703 ▪ F +27 (0)86-559-0274 ▪ info@sawis.co.za

Responsible for the collection, processing and dissemination of industry information.

Administers the Wine of Origin (WO) system and manages the Information Centre, a comprehensive information resource base for the SA wine and brandy industry.

Southern Africa Fairtrade Network (SAFN) See Fairtrade Africa-Southern Africa Network

Sustainable Wine South Africa (SWSA) www. swsa.co.za ▪ Contact details as for individual organisations.

Alliance between the Wine & Spirit Board (WSB), Integrated Production of Wine (IPW), WWF-SA Conservation Champion Programme (CCP) and Wines of South Africa (WOSA), driving the industry's commitment to sustainable, eco-friendly production.

Swartland Independent Producers (SIP) Chair: Craig Hawkins ▪ T +27 (0)22-001-0001 / +27 (0)72-601-6475 ▪ swartlandindependent@gmail. com, swartlandsocialmedia@gmail.com ▪ www. swartlandindependent.co.za

Alliance of like-minded Swartland producers seeking to make wines that are a true expression of their Swartland origin. SIP members share a number of core values, such as natural vinification and minimal intervention, and follow an evolving set of guidelines covering vineyard and cellar practices.

Wine & Agricultural Ethical Trade Association (WIETA) CEO: Linda Lipparoni ▪ T +27 (0)21-880-0580 ▪ F +27 (0)21-880-0580 ▪ linda@ wieta.org.za, info@wieta.org.za ▪ www.wieta. org.za

Multi-stakeholder, non-profit, voluntary organisation established in 2002 to promote ethical trade in wine and general agriculture. WIETA has adopted a code of labour standards for the wine industry, and its main task is to support, enhance and promote members' ethical performance, encourage best practice and promote improved working conditions on farm and at the cellar through training, capacity building and ethical auditing. WIETA also issues a Fair Labour Certification seal on individual wines, which has been endorsed by the wine industry in recognition of wine supply chains' ethical commitment to good working conditions on farms and in cellars.

Wine & Spirit Board Chair: Matome Mbatha ▪ Secretary: Olivia Poonah ▪ T +27 (0)21-889-6555 ▪ F +27 (0)21-889-5823 ▪ olivia@wsb.org.za

Administers the Wine of Origin, Estate Brandy and Integrated Production of Wine (IPW) schemes.

Wines of South Africa (WOSA) CEO: Siobhan Thompson ▪ Non-executive chair: Carina Gous ▪ info@wosa.co.za ▪ **T +27 (0)21-883-3860** ▪ F +27 (0)21-883-3861 ▪ www.wosa.co.za

Generic marketing organisation, responsible for raising the profile of SA wine in key export markets.

Wine Industry Development Association (WIDA) Executive manager: Henry Petersen ▪ **T +27 (0)82-658-2386** ▪ henry@wida.co.za ▪ www.wida.co.za

Promotes transformation through social development, human resource development and training, economic empowerment and industrial relations, and protects the interests of vulnerable communities in the industry.

Wine Industry Network of Expertise & Technology (WINETECH) Executive manager: Gerard Martin ▪ **T +27 (0)21-276 0498** ▪ F +27 (0)86-611-7846 ▪ marting@winetech.co.za

Coordinates research, development, innovation and knowledge transfer in the SA wine industry, to strengthen both local and international competitiveness and profitability.

WWF-SA Biodiversity & Wine Initiative See WWF-SA Conservation Champion Programme.

WWF-SA Conservation Champion Programme manager: Shelly Fuller ▪ **T +27 (0)21-881-3086** ▪ sfuller@wwf.org.za ▪ Head of extension: Joan Isham ▪ **T +27 (0) 21-881-3086** ▪ jisham@wwf.org.za

In 2005 the Biodiversity & Wine Initiative (BWI) started as a world-leading partnership between the SA wine industry and the conservation sector to minimise further loss of threatened natural habitat within the Cape Floral Kingdom (CFK), and contribute to sustainable wine production through better environmental management practices on farm and in the cellar. After 10 years of successful implementation, the needs of the membership base are now shifting to a more holistic approach of managing environmental risk and thus the programme has moved into a new phase. The BWI name has fallen away, and consumers can support WWF-SA Conservation Champions by buying wines displaying the colourful sugarbird and protea logo, recognising industry leaders who have strengthened their commitment to biodiversity conservation and show continual improvement of production practices, energy-efficiency measures and water stewardship.

Winegrowing Areas

From modest beginnings in the Dutch East India Company's 17th-century gardens below Table Mountain, South Africa's vineyards now cover 94,545 ha and more than 100 official appellations. Changes to the Wine of Origin (WO) scheme of 1972/3 saw 'geographical units' incorporated into the WO classification alongside 'regions', 'districts' and 'wards' (the latter have the smallest footprint of the WO areas, following earlier amendments to the 'estate' legislation). Below are brief notes

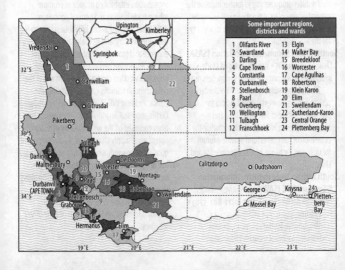

Some important regions, districts and wards	
1 Olifants River	13 Elgin
2 Swartland	14 Walker Bay
3 Darling	15 Breedekloof
4 Cape Town	16 Worcester
5 Constantia	17 Cape Agulhas
6 Durbanville	18 Robertson
7 Stellenbosch	19 Klein Karoo
8 Paarl	20 Elim
9 Overberg	21 Swellendam
10 Wellington	22 Sutherland-Karoo
11 Tulbagh	23 Central Orange
12 Franschhoek	24 Plettenberg Bay

1 Philadelphia 3 Cape Town 5 Constantia
2 Durbanville 4 Hout Bay

on the most noteworthy grape cultivation zones. Information supplied by Wines of South Africa (WOSA) and SA Wine Industry Information & Systems NPC (SAWIS), and reflects 2016 data for the WO areas. Note: Area maps are not to the same scale.

Breedekloof Large (12,941 ha) Breede River Valley district producing mainly for brandy industry and merchant trade, but also featuring some quality-focused boutiques and family estates with reputations for pinotage, chenin, chardonnay and semillon. Major varieties (ha): chenin (2,872), colombard (1,992), sauvignon (1,129), pinotage (946), chardonnay (842). See under Robertson for climate, geology etc.

Cape South Coast 'Umbrella' region (2,601 ha) for Cape Agulhas, Elgin, Overberg, Plettenberg Bay, Swellendam and Walker Bay districts, and Herbertsdale, Lower Duivenhoks River, Napier and Stilbaai East wards.

Cape Town Maritime district (2,735 ha) incorporating Constantia, Durbanville, Hout Bay and Philadelphia wards, and vines in Cape Town city.

Cederberg 101-ha ward in the Cederberg Mountain range, with some of SA's remotest and highest vineyards (950-1,100 m). Best known for shiraz (18 ha), chenin (17) and sauvignon (16). Also cab (12) and bukettraube (11).

Central Orange River This ward along the Orange River (Gariep) is a production zone within the Northern Cape Geographical Unit. Altitude: 500-1,000 m; Mean February Temperature (MFT) 25.3°C; rain total/summer: 250/208 mm; geology: granite, dolorite, shale, alluvial. Overwhelmingly a white-grape area but red plantings are increasing. Sultana (5,757), colombard (1,962), chenin (923), villard blanc (201), muscat d'Alexandrie (108).

Constantia Premium viticultural ward on the eastern slopes of the Cape Peninsula, cooled by south-easterly sea breezes. Recognised for whites generally, notably sauvignon, semillon and muscat. Altitude: 100-300 m; temp 20.6°C; rain: 1,056/335 mm; geology: granite (sandstone). Major varieties: sauvignon (186), cab (37), merlot (35), shiraz (28), muscat de Frontignan (26).

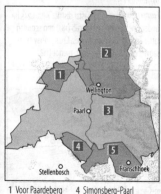

1 Voor Paardeberg 4 Simonsberg-Paarl
2 Wellington 5 Franschhoek
3 Paarl

1 Polkadraai Hills 5 Stellenbosch
2 Bottelary 6 Simonsberg-Stellenbosch
3 Devon Valley 7 Jonkershoek Valley
4 Papegaaiberg 8 Banghoek

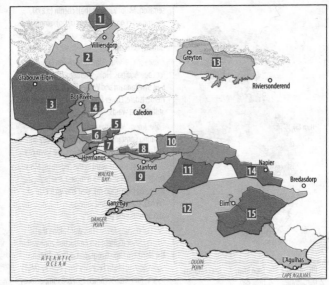

1 Elandskloof	4 Bot River	7 Hemel-en-Aarde Valley	10 Klein River	13 Greyton
2 Theewater	5 Hemel-en-Aarde Ridge	8 Stanford Foothills	11 Sunday's Glen	14 Napier
3 Elgin	6 Upper Hemel-en-Aarde	9 Walker Bay	12 Cape Agulhas	15 Elim

Darling District (2,784 ha) encircling the eponymous West Coast town, best known for the wines from higher-lying ward Groenekloof, long the source of top sauvignon; growing reputation for reds, especially shiraz. Groenekloof: cab (405), shiraz (343), sauvignon (332), pinotage (181), merlot (170).

Durbanville Ocean-tempered hilly ward in Cape Town district with reputation for sauvignon (445) and merlot (211). Cab (187), shiraz (170) and pinotage (89). Altitude: 150–350 m; temp 22.4°C; rain: 481/140 mm; geology: shale.

Elgin Cool upland district (756 ha) in Cape South Coast region yielding aromatic whites and elegant reds. Altitude: 200–250 m; temp 19.7°C; rain: 1,011/366 mm; geology: shale (sandstone). Sauvignon (277), pinot noir and chardonnay (109), shiraz (67), cab (51).

Elim Maritime ward in Cape Agulhas district, its 141 ha of vineyards arrayed around the old mission village of Elim near Africa's most southerly point. Sauvignon (81), shiraz (29), semillon (14), pinot noir (9), merlot (3).

Franschhoek Valley Coastal district with 1,245 ha under vine, recognised for cab (181) and semillon, latter among SA's oldest vines. Chardonnay (197), sauvignon (189), shiraz (157), merlot (118).

1 Montagu	5 Malgas	9 Langeberg-Garcia	13 Prince Albert Valley	16 Swartberg
2 Stormsvlei	6 Buffeljags	10 Still Bay East	14 Cango Valley	17 Upper Langkloof
3 Swellendam	7 Tradouw	11 Herbertsdale	15 Outeniqua	18 Plettenberg Bay
4 Tradouw Highlands	8 Klein Karoo	12 Calitzdorp		

Hemel-en-Aarde See Walker Bay.

Klein Karoo Scrubby semi-arid region (2,229 ha), reliant on irrigation. Recognised for 'ports' and fortifieds generally. Calitzdorp district: muscat d'Alexandrie (77), colombard (65), chenin (48), touriga and cab (17). Tradouw ward: merlot (7), colombard (6), chardonnay, sauvignon and shiraz (5). Boutique-scale plantings in Langeberg-Garcia district (46), and Cango Valley (9), Tradouw Highlands (10) and Upper Langkloof (47) wards.

Northern Cape Quality moves afoot in this geographical unit, particularly Sutherland-Karoo, high-altitude (1,450 m) semi-arid area around SA's coldest town, Sutherland. SA's smallest district (5 ha, mostly pinot noir, shiraz, chardonnay) by far, but big on character, quality. Also-exciting recent ward Prieska (neighbour of Central Orange River - see separate entry), with 13 ha of mostly reds, including rare tannat.

Olifants River Grapes for SA's highest-rated wines increasingly originate from this north-westerly region (9,695 ha), particularly the Citrusdal Mountain district (579), cool upland ward of Piekenierskloof (466), Bamboes Bay 'micro-ward' (6 ha) and, near the coast, Lutzville Valley district (3,035). Inland, a climate conducive to organic cultivation is being exploited to that end. Altitude: 20-100 m; temp 23°C; rain: 139/47 mm; geology: mainly schist and alluvial deposits. Koekenaap ward (Lutzville Valley): chenin (298), colombard (213), sauvignon (147), cab (57), pinotage (45).

Piekenierskloof: pinotage (72), grenache noir (57), chenin (49), palomino (41), sauvignon (38). Citrusdal Mountain: chenin (90), pinotage (82), grenache noir (57) sauvignon (47), palomino (42).

Orange River See Central Orange River.

Paarl This district has many mesoclimates, soils and aspects, and thus succeeds with a variety of styles and grapes. Altitude: 100-300 m; temp 23.2°C; rain: 945/273 mm; geology: granite and shale. Paarl proper is recognised for shiraz and, more recently, viognier and mourvèdre grown on warmer slopes. Chenin (1,362), shiraz (841), cab (825), pinotage (586), cinsaut (356). The following are wards: Simonsberg-Paarl, on the warmer slopes of the Simonsberg, recognised for red blends, shiraz and chardonnay. Cab (259), chardonnay (201), sauvignon (175), shiraz (160), chenin (133); and Voor Paardeberg, long an uncredited source of top-quality grapes, now a star in own right. Cab (390), shiraz (322), chenin (235), merlot (194), pinotage (182).

Robertson Traditionally a white-wine district (12,910), latterly also recognised for shiraz and cab though chardonnay, sauvignon and sparkling remain standouts. Altitude: 150-250 m; temp 23°C; rain: 280/116 mm; geology: shale and alluvial. Colombard (2,013), chardonnay (1,714), chenin (1,577), sauvignon (1,525), cab (1,272).

Stellenbosch To many, this intensively farmed district (12,511) is the wine capital of SA. Key

| 1 Swartland | 3 Malmesbury | 5 Riebeekberg |
| 2 Darling | 4 Riebeeksrivier | 6 Tulbagh |

1 Lutzville Valley	6 Olifants River
2 Bamboes Bay	7 Citrusdal Mountain
3 Lamberts Bay	8 Citrusdal Valley
4 Vredendal	9 Piekenierskloof
5 Spruitdrift	10 Cederberg

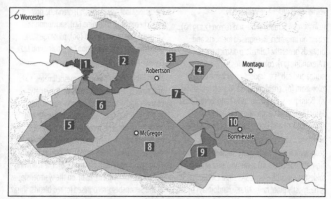

1 Eilandia	3 Hoopsrivier	5 Agterkliphoogte	7 Robertson	9 Boesmansrivier
2 Vinkrivier	4 Klaasvoogds	6 Le Chasseur	8 McGregor	10 Bonnievale

contributors to quality are the cooler mountain slopes, varied soil types and breezes off False Bay which moderate summer temperatures. Altitude: 200-400 m; temp 21.5°C; rain: 713/229 mm; geology: granite (sandstone). Jonkershoek Valley, a ward east of Stellenbosch town, is recognised for cab

and cab blends. Cab (55), chardonnay and pinotage (20), sauvignon and merlot (19). Simonsberg-Stellenbosch, in the south-western foothills of the Simonsberg Mountain, especially recognised for cab, cab blends and pinotage, and reds generally. Cab (312), merlot (169), sauvignon (167), shiraz (141),

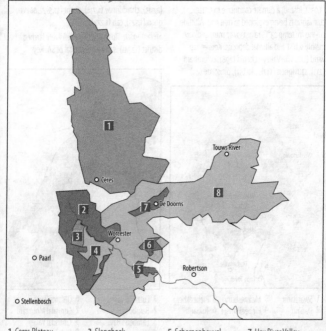

1 Ceres Plateau	3 Slanghoek	5 Scherpenheuvel	7 Hex River Valley
2 Breedekloof	4 Goudini	6 Nuy	8 Worcester

chardonnay (131). North-west of Stellenbosch town are four adjoining wards: Papegaaiberg - sauvignon (22), chenin (21), pinotage (11), chardonnay (8), cab (8); Devon Valley, recognised mainly for red blends - merlot (102), sauvignon (97), cab (89), shiraz (57), pinotage (46); Bottelary, noted for chenin, pinotage, shiraz and warm-blooded blends - chenin (387), cab (347), pinotage (264), shiraz (258), sauvignon (247); the most westerly ward, Polkadraai Hills - sauvignon (149), cab (145), shiraz (117), merlot (84), chenin (67); and Banghoek, the mountain amphitheatre above the village of Pniel - cab (61), shiraz (42), merlot (29), sauvignon and chardonnay (24). The remainder of the Stellenbosch district, as yet officially undemarcated, includes Stellenboschberg, Helderberg and Faure, recognised for red blends, chenin and sauvignon. Cab (1,519), shiraz (1,134), sauvignon (958), merlot (796), chenin (711).

Sutherland-Karoo See Northen Cape.

Swartland Traditionally associated with hearty wines, but latterly with elegant, personality-packed chenins, Mediterranean-style reds and whites, and revived heirloom varieties, this fashionable district (10,087) north of Cape Town has three wards, Malmesbury, Riebeekberg and newer St Helena Bay, plus a large unappellated area. Riebeekberg: chenin (202), shiraz (161), pinotage (155), cab (75), chardonnay (72); Malmesbury: cab (663), shiraz (578), chenin (482), pinotage (476), sauvignon (306); St Helena Bay: sauvignon (13), chenin (7), semillon (4), shiraz and muscat d'Alexandrie (3).

'Swartland': chenin (1,641), shiraz (880), cab (642), pinotage (637), chardonnay (332). Altitude: 100-300 m; temp 23.3°C; rain: 523/154 mm; geology: mostly granite and shale.

Tulbagh Inland district (1,045) traditionally known for sparkling and lightish whites, more recently also for quality reds and serious white blends. Altitude: 160-400 m; temp 24°C; rain: 551/175 mm; geology: sandstone boulderbeds and shale. Chenin (202), shiraz (127), colombard (122), cab (91), chardonnay (78).

Walker Bay Highly regarded maritime district (1,004) south-east of Cape Town, recognised for pinot noir, pinotage, sauvignon and chardonnay. Altitude: 100-250 m; temp 20.3°C; rain: 722/322 mm; geology: shale, granite and sandstone. Sauvignon (260), shiraz (143), pinot noir (138), chardonnay (102), cab (73). Bot River, Hemel-en-Aarde Ridge, Hemel-en-Aarde Valley, Stanford Foothills, Sunday's Glen and Upper Hemel-en-Aarde Valley are wards.

Wellington District (4,015) in the Coastal region increasingly reputed for shiraz and gutsy red blends. Chenin (833), cab (656), shiraz (593), pinotage (417), chardonnay (313).

Worcester District (6,360) producing chiefly for the brandy industry and merchant trade, but small quantities bottled under own labels are increasingly impressive. Recognised for red and white blends, chenin and fortifieds. Chenin (1,877), colombard (1,209), sauvignon (465), chardonnay (399), shiraz (391). See under Robertson for climate, geology etc.

Grape Varieties

Below are brief notes on the grape varieties mentioned in the guide, and their contribution to the national vineyard (statistics from SA Wine Industry Information & Systems NPC – SAWIS). See under Winegrowing Areas for details of the most widely planted and best-performing varieties in the major vine cultivation zones.

Red-wine varieties

Barbera Piedmont's second grape (after nebbiolo), its natural high acidity suiting warm climates; sought after, too, for low tannins, good colour. 0.03% of total vineyard area.

Cabernet franc Like its descendant cabernet sauvignon, with which it is often partnered, a classic part of the Bordeaux blend, but in SA and elsewhere – particularly in the Loire – also used for varietal wines. (0.87%)

Cabernet sauvignon Adaptable and internationally planted black grape making some of the world's finest and longest-lasting wines. And retaining some of its inherent qualities even when

overcropped in less suitable soils and climates. Can stand alone triumphantly, but frequently blended with a wide range of other varieties: traditionally, as in Bordeaux, with cab franc, merlot and a few minor others, but also in SA sometimes partnering varieties such as shiraz and pinotage. Number of different clones, with differing characteristics. (10.96%)

Carignan Hugely planted in the south of France, where it is not much respected. But there, as in SA, older, low-yielding vines can produce pleasant surprises. (0.12%)

Carmenère Dark-skinned, late-ripening parent of cabernet franc; once important in Bordeaux, today

– To page 638 –

Wine of Origin-defined production areas
(New appellation/s in **bold**.)

Geographical Unit	Region	District	Ward
Eastern Cape	—	—	St Francis Bay
Free State	—	—	Rietrivier
KwaZulu-Natal	—	Central Drakensberg	—
		Lions River	
Limpopo	—	—	—
Northern Cape	—	Douglas	—
	—		Central Orange River
	—		Hartswater
	—		Prieska
	—	Sutherland-Karoo	—
Western Cape	Breede River Valley	Breedekloof	Goudini
			Slanghoek
		Robertson	Agterkliphoogte
			Boesmansrivier
			Bonnievale
			Eilandia
			Hoopsrivier
			Klaasvoogds
			Le Chasseur
			McGregor
			Vinkrivier
		Worcester	Hex River Valley
			Nuy
			Scherpenheuvel
			Stettyn
	Cape South Coast	Cape Agulhas	Elim
		Elgin	—
		Overberg	Elandskloof
			Greyton
			Klein River
			Theewater
		Plettenberg Bay	—
		Swellendam	Buffeljags
			Malgas
			Stormsvlei
		Walker Bay	Bot River
			Hemel-en-Aarde Ridge
			Hemel-en-Aarde Valley
			Stanford Foothills
			SundaAy's Glen
			Upper Hemel-en-Aarde Valley
		—	Herbertsdale
		—	Lower Duivenhoks River
		—	Napier
		—	Stilbaai East

Geographical Unit	Region	District	Ward
Western Cape *(continued)*	Coastal	Cape Town	Constantia
			Durbanville
			Hout Bay
			Philadelphia
			Groenekloof
		Darling	—
		Franschhoek Valley	
		Paarl	**Agter Paarl**
			Simonsberg-Paarl
			Voor Paardeberg
		Stellenbosch	Banghoek
			Bottelary
			Devon Valley
			Jonkershoek Valley
			Papegaaiberg
			Polkadraai Hills
			Simonsberg– Stellenbosch
		Swartland	Malmesbury
			Paardeberg
			Paardeberg South
			Riebeekberg
			Riebeeksrivier
			St Helena Bay
		Tulbagh	—
		Wellington	Blouvlei
			Bovlei
			Groenberg
			Limietberg
			Mid-Berg River
		—	Lamberts Bay
	Klein Karoo	Calitzdorp	—
		Langeberg-Garcia	—
		—	Cango Valley
		—	Montagu
		—	Outeniqua
		—	Tradouw
		—	Tradouw Highlands
		—	Upper Langkloof
	Olifants River	Citrusdal Mountain	Piekenierskloof
		Citrusdal Valley	—
		Lutzville Valley	Koekenaap
		—	Bamboes Bay
		—	Spruitdrift
		—	Vredendal
	—	—	Cederberg
	—	Ceres Plateau	Ceres
	—	—	Prince Albert Valley
	—	—	Swartberg

Source: SAWIS NPC

most significant in Chile. Deep-hued/flavoured wines if picked fully ripe. Handful of bottlings in SA - varietals as well as blends. (0.01%)

Cinsaut (noir) 'Cinsault' in France. Another of the mass, undistinguished plantings of southern France, which only occasionally comes up trumps. Used to be known locally as hermitage, the name reflected in its offspring (with pinot noir), pinotage. (1.86%)

Durif See Petite sirah.

Gamay noir Although it produces some serious long-lived wines in Beaujolais, its use for (mainly) early- and easy-drinking 'nouveau' wines there, often using carbonic maceration, is the model mostly copied in SA. (0.01%)

Grenache (noir) The international (ie French) name for the Spanish grape garnacha. Widespread in Spain and southern France, generally used in blends (as in Rioja and Châteauneuf), but occasionally solo. A favourite for rosés. When vigour restrained, capable of greatness, but this is rare. (0.38%) White/ pink versions also occur.

Malbec Once a significant part of Bordeaux's blend, now most important in Cahors in western France (where it is known as cot), and as Argentina's signature variety. In SA a small but rising number of varietal and some blended examples. (0.49%)

Mataro See Mourvèdre.

Merlot Classic blending partner (as in Bordeaux) for cabernet, fashionable around the world, where it tends to be seen as an 'easier' version of cab – although this is perhaps because it is often made in a less ambitious manner. Merlot varietal wines increasingly common in SA too. (5.77%)

Meunier See Pinot meunier.

Mourvèdre Internationally known by its French name, though originally Spanish (monastrell). In Australia and California also called mataro. Particularly successful in some serious southern French blends, and increasingly modish internationally. (0.51%)

Nebbiolo Perhaps the greatest red grape to have scarcely ventured from its home — Piedmont in this case, where it makes massive, tannic, long-lived wines. (0.03%)

Nero d'Avola Sicily's major red grape, aka calabrese, of interest to SA because of heat tolerance and ability to produce full-flavoured/coloured wines. Locally, only one, single-varietal bottling.

Petite sirah/durif Originally from southern France, a cross of peloursin and syrah/shiraz. Produces tannic, densely fruited wines. (0.16%)

Petit verdot Use of this excellent variety in the Médoc limited by its late ripening. Recently appearing in some local blends, and a few varietals. (0.79%)

Pinotage A 1920s cross between pinot noir and cinsaut ('hermitage'). Made in a range of styles, from simply fruity to ambitious, well-oaked examples. (7.38%)

Pinot meunier Aka meunier, a mutation of pinot noir and, like pinot noir and chardonnay, significant in France's Champagne region where it adds fruitiness to blended sparklings. Rare in SA; also mostly for bubbly, lone varietal bottling. (0.02%)

Pinot noir Notoriously difficult grape to succeed with outside its native Burgundy, but SA, along with the rest of the New World, now produces some excellent examples. (1.25%)

Roobernet Relatively recent local crossing of cabernet sauvignon and what was thought to be pontac, in fact alicante bouschet. Mostly blended. (0.28%)

Ruby cabernet US cross between cabernet sauvignon and carignan, designed for heat tolerance. Rather rustic, used mostly in cheaper blends. (2.35%)

Sangiovese Tuscany's signature black grape, producing light or big wines, depending on how it is grown. Can be unacceptably acidic and tannic with little colour unless well managed in the vineyard. (0.07%)

Shiraz Better known as syrah outside SA and Australia (and on some local labels too). Internationally increasing in popularity, with northern Rhône and now also Australia as its major

Approximate ripening dates in the Stellenbosch area for some important grape varieties

domiciles. Made here in a variety of styles – generally wooded. (10.30%)

Syrah See Shiraz.

Tannat From France's Basque region, recently Uruguay's calling card but still little more than a curiosity in SA. Known for deep colour and high tannin. (0.13%)

Tempranillo Aka tinta roriz. The soul of Spain's storied Rioja and Ribera del Duero. Low tannin, balanced acidity and plush fruit; suited to warm climates but hardly on the SA radar – yet. (0.10%)

Tinta amarela See Trincadeira.

Tinta barocca Elsewhere spelt 'barroca'. One of the important Portuguese port-making grapes, which is its primary role in SA, usually blended. Also used for some varietal unfortified wines, and namelessly in some 'dry reds'. (0.20%)

Touriga franca Formerly known as touriga francesa. Most-planted grape in Portugal's Douro Valley, used for port as well as unfortified reds. Only a few hectares in SA.

Touriga francesa See Touriga franca.

Touriga nacional Important Portuguese port-making grape, usefully grown here for similar ends, along with tinta barocca, tinta roriz (tempranillo) and souzão. (0.11%)

Trincadeira Also 'tinta amarela'; from Portugal, deep coloured with good black fruit and big tannins. (0.01%)

Zinfandel The quintessential Californian grape (of European origin, and the same as Italy's primitivo), used here in a small way for some big wines. (0.03%)

White-wine varieties

Albariño Aromatic, high-acid white grape from Spain's damp north-west (also grown in Portugal, as alvarinho), recently fashionable in New World. Mostly varietals, occasionally oaked, potentially ageworthy. Just one bottling - varietal - in SA. (0.02%)

Bukettraube Light and acidic variety, mostly used to add zing to white blends. (0.05%)

Chardonnay In SA, as elsewhere, many new vineyards of this grape have come on-stream, with wines showing a wide range of styles, quality and price. Generally used varietally, but also in blends, and for sparkling. Wooded, lately with a lighter touch, in more ambitious wines. (7.14%)

Cape Riesling See Riesling

Chenin blanc SA has more chenin (locally also called steen) than even France's Loire Valley, the variety's home. Used here for everything from generic 'dry white' to ambitious sweet wines, to brandy. Increasing numbers of table-wine successes in recent years, as well as inexpensive but flavoursome easy-drinkers. (18.56%)

Clairette blanche High-alcohol, low-acid, musky component of southern Rhône white blends; bottled as single variety only off superior sites. In SA, also mainly used in blends. (0.21%)

Colombar(d) One of the mainstays of brandy production in SA, colombard (usually without the 'd' in SA) is also used for numerous varietal and blended wines, ranging from dry to sweet – seldom wooded. (11.93%)

Crouchen Blanc See Riesling

Fernão pires Aromatic workhorse from Portugal; can be used for wide range of wine styles. (0.07%)

Gewürztraminer Readily identifiable from its rosepetal fragrance, best known in its Alsatian guise. In SA usually made off-dry. (0.11%)

Grenache blanc Staple of Rhône white blends, finding adherents in SA, particularly when given skin contact, oak fermentation/ageing. Needs careful handling. (0.13%) Also very rare gris plantings/vinifications.

Grüner veltliner Austria's no. 1 white grape (by hectare and repute) venturing west (to America), east (Australasia) and south to SA, where plantings are still tiny and vinification follows dry, full, aromatic style of home country's top examples. (0.01%)

Hanepoot Traditional Afrikaans name for muscat d'Alexandrie, SA's most common muscat variety (see also muscadel below). (1.83%, some for raisins and table grapes). Also minuscule red plantings.

Hárslevelü From Tokaj, Hungary; delicate when fermented dry, fat and smoky in sweeter styles. Only 24 ha in SA (0.02%).

Marsanne Rhône grape, more widely planted than 'twin' roussanne. Dependable, but flabby in too-warm terroir, bland in too-cool. (0.02%)

Muscadel Name used here for both muscat de Frontignan and muscat blanc à petits grains (both red and white versions). The grape associated with the famous Constantia dessert wines of the 18th century today is used chiefly for dessert and fortified wines and for touching up blends. (1.28% red and white). Morio muscat, muscat de Hambourg and muscat Ottonel also bottled on small scale, mostly as fortifieds.

Muscat See Hanepoot and Muscadel.

Nouvelle Local crossing of semillon and neutral ugni blanc/trebbiano, produces intense grass and greenpepper characters. Typically blended. (0.46%)

Palomino Aka malvasia rei, fransdruif, white french. Once important in Spain's sherry industry and locally for distilling, palomino fino is now just 0.13% of the total vineholding. Roles in some hipster bottlings may help raise the profile.

Pinot blanc Import from north-east Italy; very few serious examples locally. (0.01%)

Pinot gris/grigio In north-east Italy prized for acidity, France's Alsace for plump richness. Tiny quantities in SA, named 'gris' or 'grigio' depending on style. (0.39%)

Riesling The name by itself now refers to the great German grape (as it does in this guide). Previously, the grape by law had to carry the prefix 'Rhine' or 'weisser', and the 'riesling' was an official SA synonym for the inferior crouchen blanc, also known as Cape riesling and mostly used anonymously in blends, occasionally varietally. Rhine riesling often off-dry here, in blends or varietally, some excellent botrytised dessert examples. (Rhine: 0.15%, crouchen: 0.26%)

Roussanne Like frequent blending partner marsanne, from the northern Rhône. Also aromatic component of Châteauneuf du Pape. Gaining a following in SA. (0.09%)

Sauvignon blanc Prestigious vine most associated with eastern Loire regions, Bordeaux and New Zealand — whose wines have helped restore fashionability to the grape. The SA version no longer a poor relation of these. Usually dry, but some sweet wines; sometimes wooded (and occasionally called fumé blanc/blanc fumé), more often not. (9.81%)

Semillon Spelt sémillon in French. Sometimes heavily wooded, sometimes sweet, more often in blends. (1.18%, including rare red-skinned version)

Sylvaner Native of Germany's Franken, more about style and texture than flavour. Just 1 ha and one varietal bottling in SA.

Verdelho From Portugal (not to be confused with Spain's verdejo). Both a grape and a (sweet) fortified style in Madeira; mostly dry in the southern hemisphere.

Vermentino Sardinia and Corsica's premier white grape is new in SA but holds potential to deliver aroma, flavour and verve in a warming climate. Sole local version made, appropriately, by Italians.

Viognier Increasingly fashionable variety internationally, spreading out from its home in the northern Rhône, now showing promise here. Usually wooded. (0.85%)

Competitions, Challenges & Awards

An increasing number of wine competitions, awards and challenges are run by liquor industry bodies, independent companies, publishing houses and individuals. Below are the main national events:

Absa Top 10 Pinotage Competition Run annually by the Pinotage Association and a major financial institution to help set international quality targets for growers of pinotage. Local/overseas judges. See under Industry Organisations for contact details.

Amorim Cap Classique Challenge Annual competition to appoint SA's top bottle-fermented sparkling wines. Mostly local judges. ▪ admin@capclassique.co.za ▪ www.capclassique.co.za ▪ **T +27 (0)21-863-1599** ▪ F +27 (0)21-863-1552

Cabernet Franc Challenge Recent annual event aimed at raising public awareness and rewarding quality in the production of cabernet franc varietals and blends. 'Museum' category spotlights maturation potential. Local judges. ▪ cobie@cvomarketing.co.za ▪ **T +27 (0)21-981-0216 / +27 (0)83-556-3740**

CAPPA Cape Port & Wine Challenge Organised by the Cape Port Producers' Association to award best in class and gold medals in each of the port categories, and select the Top 10 Portuguese-style wines. Local judges. ▪ info@boplaas.co.za ▪ www.capeportproducers.co.za ▪ **T +27 (0)44-213-3326** ▪ F +27 (0)44-213-3750

Chenin Blanc Top 10 Challenge See Standard Bank Chenin Blanc Top 10 Challenge.

Diners Club Winemaker of the Year Inaugurated in 1981, this prestigious competition features a different category each year. The Young Winemaker of the Year recognises the winning entrant aged 30 years or younger. Local panel with some overseas representation.

Winemaker of the Year since inception

1981 Walter Finlayson, Blaauwklippen Zinfandel 1980

1982 Walter Finlayson, Blaauwklippen Cabernet Sauvignon 1980

1983 Günter Brözel, Nederburg Rhine Riesling 1983

1984 Manie Rossouw, Eersterivier Sauvignon Blanc 1984

1985 Günter Brözel, Nederburg Gewürztraminer 1985

1986 Sydney Back, Backsberg Chardonnay 1985

1987 Beyers Truter, Kanonkop Pinotage 1985

1988 Wilhelm Linde, Nuy White Muscadel 1985

1989 Peter Finlayson, Hamilton Russell Pinot Noir 1986

1990 André Bruwer, Bon Courage Gewürztraminer Special Late Harvest 1989

1991 Wilhelm Linde, Nuy Riesling 1991

1992 Jean Daneel, Buitenverwachting Reserve Merlot 1991

1993 Danie de Wet, De Wetshof Finesse Chardonnay 1993

1994 Gyles Webb, Thelema Cabernet Sauvignon-Merlot 1992

1995 Nicky Krone, Twee Jonge Gezellen Krone Borealis Brut 1993 **1996** Gyles Webb, Thelema Cabernet Sauvignon 1994

1997 Jeff Grier, Villiera Bush Vine Sauvignon Blanc 1997

1998 Danie Malan, Allesverloren Shiraz 1996

1999 Ronell Wiid, Hazendal Shiraz-Cabernet Sauvignon 1998

2000 Paul de Villiers, Landskroon Port 1997

2001 Teddy Hall, Kanu Chenin Blanc 2001

2002 Danie de Waal, Uiterwyk De Waal Top of the Hill 2001

2003 John Loubser, Constantia Uitsig Reserve Semillon 2002

2004 Pieter Ferreira, Graham Beck Brut Blanc de Blancs 1999

2005 Carl Schultz, Hartenberg Merlot 2004

2006 Gottfried Möcke, Chamonix Reserve Chardonnay 2005

2007 Marc Kent, Boekenhoutskloof Syrah 2005

2008 Not awarded

2009 Coenie Snyman, Rust en Vrede Cabernet Sauvignon 2007

2010 Bartho Eksteen, Hermanuspietersfontein Nr. 5 Sauvignon Blanc 2009

2011 Johan Jordaan, Spier Creative Block 5 2009

2012 Razvan Macici, Nederburg Private Bin Eminence 2007

2013 Christiaan Groenewald, Arendskloof Voetspoere Tannat-Syrah 2011

2014 Jacques Erasmus, Spier Creative Block 2 2014

2015 Johann Fourie, KWV The Mentors Pinotage 2013

2016 Pierre Wahl, Rijk's Chenin Blanc 2014

2017 Christiaan Groenewald, Eagle's Cliff Pinotage 2017

Young Winemaker of the Year since inception

2001 Henri Swiegers, Slanghoek Noble Late Harvest 2001

2002 Boela Gerber, Groot Constantia Merlot 2001

2003 Ivy du Toit, Jason's Hill Sauvignon Blanc 2003

2004 Johan Nesenberend, For My Friends Shiraz 2002

2005 Johan Kruger, Sterhuis Chardonnay 2004

2006 Francois Agenbag, Mountain Ridge Seven Oaks 6+1 Reserve Cabernet Sauvignon-Shiraz 2004

2007 Ruth Penfold, Steenberg Semillon 2007

2008 Ossie Sauermann, La Vigne Single Vineyard Shiraz 2007

2009 Clayton Reabow, Môreson Premium Chardonnay 2007

2010 RJ Botha, Nitida Calligraphy 2009

2011 Matthew van Heerden, Uva Mira Chardonnay 2009

2012 Anri Truter, Beyerskloof Diesel Pinotage 2010

2013 Murray Barlow, Rustenberg Stellenbosch Chardonnay 2012

2014 JD Pretorius, Steenberg Merlot 2012

2015 Philip Viljoen, Bon Courage Noble Late Harvest 2015

2016 Murray Barlow, Rustenberg RM Nicholson 2015

2017 Wade Roger-Lund, Jordan Blanc de Blancs Méthode Cap Classique 2015

▪ winemaker@dinersclub.co.za ▪ www.dinersclub.co.za ▪ T +27 (0)21- 795-5400 ▪ F +27 (0)21-794-8185

Michelangelo International Wine & Spirits Awards sponsored by Multi-Color Corp, SA Airlink & Tsogo Sun, partnered by Checkers & SA Airways Run in SA since 1997, Michelangelo is said to be the largest international drinks competition in the southern hemisphere, with a record 2,255 entries from 16 countries received in 2018. 30 internationally accredited experts sit on specialist panels, judging wines and spirits. Entries are judged under OIV guidelines and awarded trophies as well as Platinum, Gran d'Or, Gold and Silver medals. Bespoke QR codes on award stickers add value for consumers. ▪ llorraine@michelangeloawards.com ▪ www.michelangeloawards.com ▪ T +27 (0)82-556-8679 / +27 (0)21-856-0059

Muscadel Award for Excellence Annual competition aimed at raising consumer awareness and recognising quality in the creation, packaging and promotion of SA's muscadel wines. Local judges. ▪ henri@badsberg.co.za, andres@rooiberg.co.za ▪ T +27 (0)23-344-3021 / +27 (0)23-626-1664

National Wine Challenge Fine-wine competition incorporating Top 100 SA Wines. Uses key international and local judges with a focus on MW qualifications. Blind-tasted audited results yield Double Platinum/Top 100 status for the top-scoring 100 wines, National Champion 'Grand Cru' status for best-in-class wines, and either Double Gold or Double Silver awards for high-scoring wines. Winning wines are showcased via a free Android/iOS app and at tasting events around the world. ▪ operations@buybetterwine.com ▪ www.

buybetterwine.com, www.thenationalwinechallenge.
com

Novare South African Terroir Wine Awards
Only wines that truly portray a specific terroir can
enter, making this a highly exclusive competition. The
best wines certified as from single vineyards, units
registered for the production of estate wine, wards
in SA's officially recognised winegrowing areas, and
small districts that are not divided into more than
one ward, are awarded. SA's top 5 estate wines are
also honoured. Novare Trophies for SA Terroir Top Wine
Area, Top Wine Estate, Top Single Vineyard Wine and
Top Producer are also awarded. Seven local judges ▪
mlab@iafrica.com ▪ www.terroirwineawards.co.za ▪
T +27 (0)21-975-8166

Old Mutual Trophy Wine Show Convened by
Michael Fridjhon and sponsored by Old Mutual. Seeks
to identify the best wines in SA and award trophies
to the top gold medal winner in the major classes,
as well as the top producer overall. Local and international judges. ▪ alex@outsorceress.co.za ▪ www.
trophywineshow.co.za ▪ T +27 (0)11-482-5936 ▪
F +27 (0)86-532-5177

Perold Absa Cape Blend Competition Launched
in 2011 and aimed at creating a signature style for Cape
Blends (see SA Wine Styles section). Local judges.
Contacts as for Absa Top Ten Pinotage.

Shiraz SA Wine Challenge Annual competition to
identify the 12 best varietal shirazes and 3 best shiraz
blends across all regions and styles. Local/international
judges. ▪ info@shirazsa.co.za ▪ www.shirazsa.co.za ▪
T +27 (0)82 924 7254 ▪ F +27 (0)86-267 4333

**South African Airways (SAA) Wine
Awards** Annual selection of wines to fly with
the national carrier (drinkability in flight conditions
an important consideration). Local and overseas
palates. ▪ NompumeleloSambo@flysaa.com T
+27(0)11-978-9301 ▪ MotshabiPaile@flysaa.com ▪
T +27(0)11-978-9305 ▪ MelindaUys@flysaa.com T

+27(0)11-978-6482 ▪ YolandeSchutte@flysaa.com ▪
T +27 (0)11-978-3982

SA National Bottled Wine Show See Veritas.

South African Terroir Wine Awards See Novare
South African Terroir Wine Awards.

**South African Wine Tasting Championship
(SAWTC)** In the spirit of ongoing education, and
in an attempt to encourage new converts to wine,
SAWTC offers all winelovers the chance to put their
talents to the test and be the centre of a local wine
event, with an opportunity to compete internationally.
▪ sawtc@wine.co.za ▪ www.sawtc.co.za ▪ T +27
(0)21-422-5206 ▪ F +27 (0)21-422-5238

South African Young Wine Show Inaugurated
1975 to gauge the quality of embryo wines, prior
to finishing and bottling, thereby also recognising
wineries which sell their products in bulk. The grand
champion receives the General Smuts Trophy. Local
judges. ▪ info@veritas.co.za ▪ www.youngwineshow.
co.za ▪ T +27 (0)21-863 1599 ▪ F +27 (0)21-863-1552

**Standard Bank Chenin Blanc Top 10
Challenge** Annual event in which varietal chenins
and chenin-dominated (85%) blends in the drier
spectrum (max 12 g/L sugar) are assessed by a panel
of five judges (one from abroad) and an associate. The
ten winners each receive R25,000, to be used to rein-
force economic and social benefits in the workplace.
▪ ina.smith@iafrica.com ▪ www.chenin.co.za ▪ T +27
(0)82-467-4331

Top 100 South African Wines See National Wine
Challenge.

Trophy Wine Show See Old Mutual Trophy Wine
Show.

Veritas SA's biggest competition for market-ready
wines, awarding double-gold, gold, silver and bronze
medals across a wide range of categories. Local palates
with some overseas input. ▪ info@veritas.co.za ▪
www.veritas.co.za ▪ T +27 (0)21-863 1599 ▪ F +27
(0)21-863-1552

Wine & Brandy Education

Academy of Wine & Spirits Established in 2015 by
SA wine professionals, the Academy is a platform to
provide wine-and-spirit education and qualifications
to fellow professionals and enthusiasts in the tertiary,
hospitality, retail, tourism and corporate sectors
countrywide. The Academy is an official provider for
WSET courses. ▪ info@academyofwineandspirits.co.za
▪ www.academyofwineandspirits.co.za ▪ Stellenbosch:
T +27 (0)21-889-8844 ▪ F +27 (0)21-889-7391;

Johannesburg: T +27 (0)11-024-3616 ▪ F +27
(0)86-559-7329

**Brandy Course for Hospitality
Staff** Underwritten by the Cape Wine Academy
(CWA) and subsidised by the SA Brandy Foundation,
this quarterly training programme is aimed specifically
at tasting room and other hospitality staff. Topics
covered include the history of brandy, brandy production and conducting a brandy tasting. Successful

students receive a CWA certificate. danie@sabrandy. co.za ▪ T +27 (0)21-880-1686

Cape Wine Academy Recognised leader in the education of wine appreciation in SA, CWA focuses on the transfer of knowledge and skills to wine enthusiasts generally, as well as front-of-house personnel of wine producers, employees in retail wine divisions, staff of hotel groups and wine-industry corporate staff. Courses are held in public venues and tertiary institutions in various provinces, and presented by wine-industry experts, winemakers and Cape Wine Masters, inter alia. ▪ info@capewineacademy. co.za ▪ www.capewineacademy.co.za ▪ Stellenbosch: T +27 (0)21-889-8844 ▪ F +27 (0)21-889-7391 ▪ Johannesburg: T +27 (0)11-024-3616 ▪ F +27 (0)86-559-7329

The School of Fine Wine Three interactive, excursion-based wine courses specifically designed for the hospitality industry. Students are taken to wine farms and experience winemaking, meet winemakers, walk in vineyards and taste wines, and acquire a practical understanding of the production of wine. The day courses, each on a different level, are presented by qualified winemaker and teacher Lieze Norval, and available in Cape Town and Johannesburg, in association with Caroline's Fine

Wine Cellar. ▪ carowine6@mweb.co.za ▪ T +27 (0)21-419-8984

University of Stellenbosch Garagiste Winemaking Course See under Make Your Own Wine or Brandy

Wine Judging Academy Run by Michael Fridjhon in association with the University of Cape Town's Graduate School of Business, this intensive 3-day tasting and wine judging course aims to increase the number of competent wine judges at work in the local industry. ▪ crossley@reciprocal.co.za

WSET in South Africa with the International Wine Education Centre Led by WSET Educator of the Year, Cathy Marston, IWEC was the first provider of the UK-based Wine & Spirit Education Trust's (WSET) courses in SA, catering for enthusiastic amateurs and wine industry professionals alike. WSET wine and spirit qualifications are recognised as the industry standard in over 70 countries. The IWEC offers all WSET wine and spirit courses, and is the only provider of the flagship qualification, WSET Level 4, in Africa and the Middle East. In-house training and ad hoc courses are also offered, and for those wanting to take their wine education to the highest level, WSET is the direct path to Master of Wine (MW) and Master Sommelier (MS). ▪ info@thewinecentre.co.za ▪ www.thewinecentre. co.za ▪ T +27 (0)82-764-0680

Make Your Own Wine or Brandy

BuytheBarrel at Mooi Bly Winery Sign up and buy a barrel, choose your grapes and decide which style of wine you want to make. Either pick and press the grapes — the hard part — or fast-forward to taste and blend your wine with the help of the qualified resident winemaker. Then design your label, bottle your wine (you get 300 bottles!) and sip, ship, sell or share it as you see fit. ▪ alex@icloud.com ▪ www. buythebarrel.co.za ▪ T +27 (0)84-582-6376

Craft distilling with Roger Jorgensen (Jorgensen's Distillery) Stellenbosch-based master distiller Roger Jorgensen's popular one-day workshops cater for up to 12 delegates and cover three basic modules: introduction to spirits and distillation, for enthusiasts or novices; advanced general distilling, for commercial winemakers and home distillers who want to add a spirit to their portfolio or sharpen their skills; and specialist courses in the theory and practice of producing a specific product. The course fee includes lunch and refreshments. ▪ roger@jd7.co.za ▪ www.jd7.co.za ▪ T +27 (0)82-564-2512

Cape Crush Winemaking Services Located in the Helderberg, Cape Crush offers individual clients

the opportunity to make their own wine, and supplies a winemaking service to farm owners and other wineries. Cape Crush's cellar is equipped with a variety of tank volumes, and also has a storage facility for bottled wine. ▪ rocco@capecrush.co.za ▪ www. capecrush.co.za ▪ T +27 (0)82-821-4625

Garagiste Movement of South Africa
Formally constituted association, providing a platform for small-scale winegrowers to connect with like-minded producers, obtain advice and market their wines. ▪ communications@garagistemovement.co.za

Hofstraat Kelder See listing in A–Z directory.

Sign Your Name in Wine at Stellenrust Stellenrust wine farm near Stellenbosch offers groups of 20 or more the oppor-tunity to pick grapes, crush them in 3-ton open-tank fermenters and put a personal signature on their very own wine. Packages include a full-day excursion followed by traditional braai lunch and bottles of participants' handcrafted wine (after proper barrel maturation in the boutique cellar). info@stellenrust. co.za ▪ www.stellenrust.co.za ▪ T +27 (0)21-880-2283 ▪ F +27 (0)21-880-2284

University of Stellenbosch Garagiste Winemaking Course The premium short course for people interested in producing quality small-scale wines at home or simply expanding their wine knowledge. Attendees receive a set of notes; observe the use of garagiste winemaking equipment; taste different vinifications; bottle their own wine; and receive a certificate from Stellenbosch University. A follow-on, advanced course was introduced in 2016. ▪ wdutoit@sun.ac.za ▪ T +27 (0)21-808-2022 ▪ F +27 (0)21-808-4781

A-Code Numbers & Certification Codes

Many wines appear on the market under brand names, with, at first glance, no reference to their producers or purveyors. However, consumers need not buy 'blind', and may trace a wine's provenance by checking the official 'A-number' which appears on the bottle or pack. This identity code tells you either who produced the wine, or who sourced it for resale. In the latter case, an enquiry to the merchant should elicit the source. The list keeps growing and being revised, and is too lengthy to reproduce in this guide. Via the SAWIS NPC web page **www.sawis.co.za/ sealsearch.php**, it is possible however to search the list of A-codes, as well as the certification codes issued for each wine by the Wine & Spirit Board, for details about the production area, variety and vintage.

Styles & Vintages

Recent South African Vintages

South African wines do not exhibit the major vintage variations seen in some other winegrowing areas. There are, nevertheless, perceptible differences from year to year. Dry, hot summers are the norm but a variety of factors make generalisations difficult and possibly misleading.

2018 Challenging year for reds and whites, lingering drought requiring particular focus on optimal picking times, conserving vine resources and managing extractions. Generally healthy, smaller berries yielded sound, concentrated if perhaps earlier-peaking wines.

2017 Growers expecting a worsening of 2016's drought and extreme heat were pleasantly surprised when the latter failed to materialise, resulting in a smaller but excellent crop with freshness and fine flavour concentration on reds as well as whites.

2016 Exceptionally hot, dry and challenging, with later-ripening varieties benefiting from lower temperatures. In cool climates, disease-free conditions could yield some stellar wines.

2015 Near-perfect conditions produced a smaller but pristine crop displaying exceptional quality across the style spectrum. One of the great vintages, possibly surpassing 2009.

2014 Later, slightly smaller and unusually cool, among wettest pre-seasons in years. Seemingly lighter, less powerful wines; potential for fine concentration and elegance if picked judiciously.

2013 Biggest crop to date; moderate conditions yielded good to very good reds and whites, lighter alcohol levels.

2012 Unusually dry, hot January strained unirrigated vineyards; otherwise good to very good vintage for both reds and whites; moderate alcohol levels.

2011 Yet more variable than the last, impossible to generalise. As in 2010, producer's track record should guide the buying/cellaring decision.

2010 A real test of the winegrower's savvy, and one of the toughest recent harvests to call. Be guided by producer's track record.

2009 Perhaps one of the greatest vintages. Late, gruelling, but whites and reds both stellar.

2008 Long, wet, late and challenging but also unusually cool, favouring elegance in reds and whites.

2007 Elegant, structured whites; smaller red-grape berries gave intense colour and fruit concentration.

2006 Perhaps the best white-wine vintage in a decade – particularly expressive sauvignon and chenin. Fleshy, mild-tannined reds, with lower alcohols.

Older Vintages

2005 Concentrated if alcoholic reds; mostly average whites, some exceptions. **2004** Cooler dry conditions yielded elegant, often ageworthy wines with lower alcohols, softer tannins. **2003** Outstanding, especially for reds – concentrated and structured, and often slow to show their best. **2002** Challenging and patchy, but top producers show fine concentration and moderate alcohols. **2001** Some excellent reds – fruity and concentrated, best are long lived. Flavourful if alcoholic whites. **2000** Powerful, concentrated reds, befitting a hot year; the best have kept very well. Whites generally less impressive, not for long ageing. **1999** Fat, alcoholic reds with ripe fruit for earlier drinking. Generally not too much excitement among the whites. **1998** Excellent red vintage with enough fruit for extended cellaring; whites generally not for keeping. **1997** Among coolest and latest vintages on record. Supple, elegant reds; some excellent and stylish whites. **1996** Generally awkward reds, not for

keeping; whites, except for top NLHs, best drunk up. **1995** For many, the vintage of the 90s. Concentrated reds, some still maturing spectacularly. **1994** Hottest, driest vintage in decades; variable quality; new-clone cabs and early ripening reds fared well. **1993** Without serious mishaps; some excellent sauvignons; above-average reds. **1992** Coolish season, favouring whites, especially sauvignon; the reds (notably pinotage) very good; **1991** Dry, warm to hot, favouring early to mid-season ripeners; some long-lasting reds. **1990** Uneven year, alternately cool and warm; average whites and reds; not for further ageing. **1980s**: even years ('82, '84, '86) usually more favourable for reds; uneven years, marginally cooler, favoured whites, but 'white' years '87 and, especially, '89 produced remarkable reds. **1970s**: again, even years generally favoured reds. Best was '74; but top wines from some other vintages are still delicious. **1960s** and earlier yielded some astonishingly long-lived wines.

South African Wine Styles

Agrafe/agraffe See Sparkling wine.

Air-dried See Straw wine.

Alternative white/red Intended to allow for greater flexibility within the official certification framework, this recent category provides for dry (≤4 g/L), lower-sulphur wines with colours ranging from light gold to amber (white) and light red to purple (red). Certification is mandatory.

Amber wine See Orange wine.

Biodynamic See Winemaking Terms section.

Blanc de blancs White wine made from white grapes only; also used for champagne and cap classique. Alternative name is 'vin gris'.

Blanc de noir A pink wine (shades range from off-white through peach to pink) made from red grapes. See also Rosé.

Blanc fumé or **fumé blanc** Dry white from sauvignon, usually but not necessarily wooded (nor smoked, smoky).

Blend See Varietal wine, and Cape Blend.

Brut See Sugar or sweetness, and Sparkling wine.

Cap classique See Sparkling wine.

Cape Blend Usually denotes a (red) blend with pinotage, the 'local' grape making up a significant part of the assemblage; sometimes simply a blend showing a distinct 'Cape' character; occasionally used for chenin-based blends.

Carbonated See Sparkling wine.

Cultivar Grape variety (a contraction of 'cultivated variety').

Cuvée French term for the blend of a wine.

Demi-sec See Sugar or sweetness.

Dessert wine A sweet wine, often to accompany the dessert but sometimes pleasurably prior, as in the famous Sauternes/foie gras combo.

Dry to sweet See Sugar or sweetness.

Estate wine Term now reserved for wine originating from an officially registered 'unit for the production of estate wine' (see www.sawis.co.za/cert/about.php for current list).

Extended barrel-aged white/gris Newer category of vintage-dated, dry (≤4 g/L) wine from white/gris grapes, light gold to amber in colour, matured in oak for at least 2 years and showing a nutty/oxidative character.

Fortified wines Increased in alcoholic strength by the addition of spirit, by SA law to minimum 15% alcohol by volume.

Grand cru See Premier Grand Cru.

Ice wine Intensely sweet wine from ripe grapes picked and pressed while frozen. Not an official category.

Jerepiko or **jerepigo** Red or white wine, produced without fermentation; grape juice is fortified with grape spirit, preventing fermentation; very sweet, with considerable unfermented grape flavours.

Kosher See Winemaking Terms section.

Late Harvest Unfortified wine from late-harvested and therefore sweeter grapes. Alcohol by volume (ABV) must exceed 10%. See also Sugar or sweetness.

Méthode ancestrale See Sparkling wine.

Méthode cap classique (MCC) See Sparkling wine.

Natural pale/non-fortified pale Recently gazetted class of oak-matured (under a film of flor yeast, for minimum of 2 years) white wines with discernible almond, flor yeast and wood characters.

Natural Sweet Aka Sweet Natural. Unfortified wine with residual sugar greater than 20 g/L. See also Sugar or sweetness.

Noble Late Harvest (NLH) Sweet dessert wine (still, perlé or sparkling) exhibiting a noble rot (botrytis) character, from grapes infected by the botrytis cinerea fungus. This mould, in warm, misty autumn weather, attacks the skins of ripe grapes, causing much of the juice to evaporate. As the berries wither, their sweetness and flavour become powerfully concentrated. SA law dictates that grapes for NLH must be harvested at a minimum of 28° Balling and residual sugar must exceed 50 g/L.

Nouveau Term originated in Beaujolais for fruity young and light red, usually from gamay and made by the carbonic maceration method. Bottled soon after vintage to capture the youthful, fresh flavour of fruit and yeasty fermentation.

Orange wine Unofficial name for fashionable style of white-wine making using extended skin contact (see Winemaking Terms section), as for red wine, resulting in darker hues and greater flavour/aroma intensity, sometimes with an (attractive) oxidative character and/or noticeable tannins. See also Skin-macerated white.

Organic See Winemaking Terms section.

Perlant, perlé, pétillant Lightly sparkling, usually carbonated wine.

Port Fortified dessert with excellent quality record in SA since late 1980s, partly through efforts of Cape Port Producers' Association which has adopted 'Cape' to identify the local product. Following are CAPPA-defined styles: **Cape White**: non-muscat grapes, oak-aged min 6 months, any size vessel, drier to full-sweet; **Cape Pink**: non-muscat varieties, pink hue, barrel/tank-aged min 6 months; **Cape Ruby**: full bodied, fruity; min 50% barrel/tank-aged 6-36 months; can be vintage dated; **Cape Vintage**: fruit of one harvest; dark, full-bodied; tank/cask-aged min 1 year; must be certified, sold in glass, vintage dated; **Cape Vintage Reserve**: as for Vintage, but 'superior quality'; **Cape Late Bottled Vintage** (LBV): fruit of single year, full-bodied, slightly tawny colour, barrel/bottle aged min 3 years (of which min 2 years in oak); **Cape Tawny**: min 80% wood matured, amber-orange (tawny) colour, smooth, slightly nutty taste; **Cape Dated Tawny**: single-vintage tawny.

Premier Grand Cru Unlike in France, not a quality rating in SA – usually an austerely dry white.

Residual sugar See Sugar or sweetness.

Rosé Pink wine, made from red or a blend of red and white grapes. The red grape skins are removed before the wine takes up too much colour.

Single-vineyard wine Classification for wines from officially registered vineyards, no larger than 6ha in size and planted with a single variety.

Skin-macerated white Newer official classification for a dry (≤4 g/L) white wine, light gold to deep orange in colour, macerated on-skin for at least 96 hours.

Sparkling wine Bubbly, or 'champagne', usually white but sometimes rosé and even red, given its effervescence by carbon dioxide – allowed to escape in the normal winemaking process. **Champagne** undergoes its second fermentation in the bottle. Under an agreement with France, SA does not use the term, which describes the sparkling wines from the Champagne area. Instead, **méthode cap classique** (MCC) is the SA term to describe sparkling wines made by the classic method. **Méthode ancestrale** results from a spontaneous ferment initiated in tank and completed in bottle. **Charmat** undergoes its second, bubble-forming fermentation in a tank and is bottled under pressure. **Carbonated** sparklers are made by the injection of carbon dioxide bubbles (as in fizzy soft drinks). **Agrafe** (or agraffe) bubblies undergo bottle-fermentation under cork instead of the usual metal crown cap. See also Sugar or sweetness.

Special Late Harvest (SLH) SA designation for a lighter dessert-style wine. There is no legal stipulation for residual sugar content, but if the RS is below 20 g/L, the label must state 'extra dry',

'dry', 'semi-dry' or 'sweet', as the case may be. The minimum alcohol content is 11% by volume.

Stein Semi-sweet white wine, usually a blend and often confused with steen, a grape variety (chenin blanc), though most steins are at least made partly from steen grapes.

Straw wine Vin de paille in French; sweet, unfortified wine from ripe grapes that are 'naturally dried' (optionally on straw mats). Minimum ABV is 16%.

Sugar or sweetness In still wines: extra-dry or bone-dry wines have less than 2.5 g/L residual sugar, undetectable to the taster. A wine legally is dry up to 5 g/L*. Taste buds will begin picking up a slight sweetness, or softness, in a wine – depending on its acidity – at about 6 g/L, when it is still off-dry. By about 8–9 g/L a definite sweetness can usually be noticed. However, an acidity of 8–9 g/L can render a sweet wine fairly crisp even with a sugar content of 20 g/L plus. Official sweetness levels in SA wine are listed in the table below.

Wine	Sugar (g/L)
Still wines	
Extra-dry	≤ 2.5
Dry*	≤ 5
Semi-dry*	> 5 ≤ 12
Semi-sweet	> 5 <30
Late Harvest	≥ 20
Special Late Harvest (SLH)	—
Natural Sweet (or Sweet Natural)	> 20
Noble Late Harvest (NLH)	> 50
Naturally dried grape wine (straw).	> 30
Sparkling wines	
Brut nature	<3
Extra brut	<6
Brut	<12
Extra-dry	12–17
Dry	17–32
Semi-sweet	32–50
Sweet	> 50

* Recent amendments allow for higher sugar levels for dry (9 g/L) and semi-dry (18 g/L) if the total acidity is within 2 g/L or 10 g/L respectively of the sugar level.

Sun wine Bottlings in this recent fortified category must be from white grapes, pale to deep gold in colour and show a maderised character (see under Winetasting Terms section). Must be certified and vintage dated.

Sweet Natural See Natural Sweet.

Varietal wine From a single variety of grape. Legislation requires the presence in the wine of 85% of the stated variety or vintage. Blends may name component parts only if those components were vinified separately, prior to blending; then they are listed with the larger contributor(s) named first. If any one of the blend partners is less than 20%, percentages for all the varieties must be given. Blends may be vinified separately in any recognised WO area; component areas may be named, as above except the threshold is 30%.

Vin de paille See Straw wine.

Vine-dried wine Often — but not necessarily — sweet, from grapes desiccated on the vine.

Vintage In SA primarily used to denote year of harvest. Not a quality classification (a 'vintage' port in Europe means one from an officially declared great port-grape year).

South African Brandy, Husk Spirit & Sherry-Style Wines

Brandy and Husk Spirit

SA brandy is divided into three main stylistic categories. Put simply and reductively, these are as follows:

- **Blended brandy** must by law contain at least 30% brandy distilled in a potstill and aged for at least three years in oak barrels. The remaining component will be of unmatured wine spirit (made in a continuous still). More often than not, these brandies are intended to partner mixers or to play a role in cocktails. The alcohol by volume (ABV) must be at least 43% (in practice it usually is 43%).
- **Vintage brandy** (a small category) must have at least 30% potstill brandy aged minimum eight years. Up to 70% wine spirit is permitted but it too must be matured at least eight years.
- **Potstill brandy** must be 100% potstilled and matured at least three years in oak barrels. The ABV is a minimum of 38%, as for Vintage brandy. Increasingly labelled 'Cape Brandy'.

Sherry-Style Fortified Wines

There are eight classes of sherry-style wines described in South Africa's Liquor Products Act. The colour of these wines must range — depending on the class — from pale straw to amber. Their aromas and flavours must be 'nutty' and 'woody'. Five of the eight classes must have a discernible flor yeast and/or wood character. In addition:

- In the case of **Fino**, the residual sugar shall not exceed 20 g/L, and the alcohol content must not exceed 16%. It should have an almond flavour.
- The alcohol content of an **Amontillado** must be at least 16%, and it should have a flavour of hazelnuts.
- **Oloroso** must have rich, nutty flavours, a minimum of 50 g/L residual sugar, and at least 16% alcohol by volume.
- The residual sugar content of a **Pale Dry** wine cannot exceed 30 g/L, and its alcohol content should exceed 16%.

Estate brandy is brandy in any of the above categories in which all stages of production, from vineyard to maturation, took place on one property (as for 'estate' wine).

Not (yet) regulated locally, these official French (cognac) designations are increasingly used here, with minimum age adjustments for VS to comply with local legislation:

- **VS (Very Special)** - youngest component is at least 3 years old (2 for cognac).
- **VSOP (Very Superior Old Pale)** - youngest component is at least 4 years old.
- **XO (Extra Old)** - youngest component is at least 10 years old.

Husk Spirit will have an ABV level of at least 43% and not be matured; **Premium Husk Spirit** must be at least 40% ABV, and be matured in oak for between three and six months.

- Similarly, the alcohol content of a **Pale Cream** must exceed 16%, but its residual sugar can only range between 30 g/L and 80 g/L.
- The remaining three classes need only exhibit a discernible wood character.
- In addition, the residual sugar and alcohol content of a **Medium Cream** must be between 80 g/L and 115 g/L, and above 16% respectively.
- A **Full Cream** wine must have at least 115 g/L residual sugar, and an alcohol content above 16%.
- A muscat character and an aldehyde content of at least 80 mg/L, a residual sugar content of at least 100 g/L, and at least 16% alcohol by volume is necessary for an **Old Brown**. This may also only be sweetened with concentrated must, or with fortified wine with a residual sugar content of at least 180 g/L.

Words & Phrases

Winetasting Terms

Short of a ready description? Here are a few frequently used words, phrases and explanations that may be helpful. See also Winemaking Terms, and SA Wine Styles.

Accessible, approachable Flavours and feel of the wine are harmonious, easily recognised; it is ready to drink.

Aftertaste The lingering flavours and impressions of a wine; its persistence – the longer, the better.

Alcoholic 'Hot' or, in excess, burning character caused by imbalanced or excessive alcohol. Also simply spiritous.

Astringent Mouth-puckering sensation, associated with high tannin (and sometimes acid); also bitter, sharp.

Aroma Smells in the bouquet, or nose, especially the odours associated with the grape rather than the winemaking process.

Attack First sensations on palate/nose – pungent, aggressive, quiet etc.

Austere Usually meaning unyielding, sometimes harsh. Sometimes, more favourably, to imply a notable restraint/refinement.

Backbone The wine is well formed, firm, not flabby or insipid.

Baked 'Hot', earthy quality. Usually from scorched/ shrivelled grapes which have been exposed too long to the sun, or from too warm a barrel fermentation, especially in some whites.

Balance Desirable attribute. The wine's chief constituents – alcohol, acid, tannin, fruit and wood (where used) – are in harmony.

Bead Bubbles in sparkling wine; a fine, long-lasting bead is the most desirable. See also Mousse.

Big Expansive in the mouth, weighty, full-bodied, as a result of high alcohol or fruit concentration.

Bite or **grip** Imparted by tannin, acid and/or alcohol, important in young wines designed for ageing. If overdone can impart undesirable bitterness, harshness or spirity 'glow'.

Bitter Sensation perceived mainly on the back of the tongue, and in the finish of the wine. Usually unpleasant, though an accepted if not immediately admired character of certain Italian wines. Sometimes more positively associated with the taste of a specific fruit or nut, such as cherry-kernel or almond.

Body Fullness on the palate.

Botrytis/ed Exhibits a noble rot/botrytis character, from grapes infected by the *botrytis cinerea* fungus.

Bottle-age Negative or positive, depending on context. Positively describes development of aromas/flavours (ie complexity) as wine moves from youth to maturity. Much-prized attribute in fine whites and reds. Negatively, bottle age results in a wine with stale, empty or even off odours.

Buttery Flavour and texture associated with barrel-fermented white wines, especially chardonnays; rich, creamy smoothness.

Claret Another name for a dry red Bordeaux or Bordeaux-like red.

Classic Showing characteristics of the classics of Bordeaux, Burgundy etc; usually implying balance, elegance, subtlety.

Coarse Rough, unbalanced tannins, acid, alcohol or oak.

Complexity Strong recommendation. A complex wine has several layers of flavour, usually developing with age/maturation. See Bottle-age.

Concentration See Intensity.

Confected Over-elaborately constructed, artificial, forced; sometimes overly sweet.

Corked, corky Wine is faulty; its flavours have been tainted by yeast, fungal or bacterial infections, often but not necessarily from the cork. It smells damp and mouldy in its worst stages – but sometimes it's barely detectable. In a restaurant, a corked wine should be rejected and returned immediately; producers are honour-bound to replace corked wine.

Creamy Not literally creamy, of course; more a silky, buttery feel and texture.

Crisp Refers to acidity. Positively, means fresh, clean; negatively, too tart, sharp.

Deep and **depth** Having many layers; intense; also descriptive of a serious wine.

Dense Well-padded texture, flavour packed.

Deposits (also sediment or crust) Tasteless and harmless tartrates, acid crystals or tannin in older red wines. Evidence that wine has not been harshly fined, filtered or cold-stabilised.

Dried out Bereft of fruit, harder constituents remaining; tired.

Earthy Usually positive, wine showing its origins from soil, minerals, damp leaves, mushrooms etc.

Easy Undemanding (and hopefully inexpensive).

Elegant Stylish, refined, 'classic'.

Esters Scents and smells usually generated by alcohols and acids in wine. A wine may be 'estery' when these characteristics are prominent.

Extract An indication of the 'substance' of a wine, expressed as sugar-free or total extract (which would include some sugars). 18g/L would be low, light; anything much above 23g/L in whites is significant; the corresponding threshold for reds is around 30g/L.

Fat Big, full, ample in the mouth.

Finesse Graceful, polished. Nothing excessive.

Finish The residual sensations – tastes and textures – after swallowing. Should be pleasant (crisp, lively) and enduring, not short, dull or flat. See also Aftertaste and Length.

Firm Compact, has good backbone.

Flabby Usually, lacking backbone, especially acid.

Flat Characterless, unexciting, lacks acid. Or bubbly which has lost its fizz.

Fleshy Very positive, meaning a wine is well fleshed out with texture and grape flavours.

Flowery, floral Flower-like (ie the smell of rose, honeysuckle, jasmine etc). Distinct from 'fruity' (ie smell/taste of papaya, cantaloupe, grape! etc).

Forward rather than shy; advancing in age too; mature.

Fresh Lively, youthful, invigorating. Closely related to the amount of acid in the wine and absence of oxidative character: a big, intensely sweet dessert without a backbone of acidity will taste flat and sickly; enough acid and the taste is fresh and uncloying.

Fruity See Flowery.

Full High in alcohol and extract.

Gamey Overripe, decadent, not universally unattractive; also meaty, 'wild'.

Gravel/ly With suggestions of mineral, earthy quality; also firm texture.

Green Usually unripe, sour; also herbaceous; sometimes simply youthful.

Grip Gripping, firm on palate, in finish. Acid, tannin, alcohol are contributors.

Heady Usually refers to the smell of a wine. High in alcohol; intense, high-toned.

Herbaceous Grassy, hay-like, heathery; can also indicate under-ripeness.

Hollow Lacking substance, flavours.

Honey or **honeyed** Sometimes literally a honey/beeswax taste or flavour; a sign of developing maturity in some varieties or more generally a sign of bottle age.

Hot Burning sensation of alcohol in finish.

Intensity No flab, plenty of driving flavour; also deep colour.

Lean Thin, mean, lacking charm of ample fruit; also, more positively, compact, sinewy.

Lees/leesy Taste-imparting dead yeast cells (with grape skins and other solid matter) remaining with wine in tank/barrel (or bottle in the case of méthode champenoise sparkling wines) after fermentation. The longer the wine is 'on its lees' (sur lie) the more richness and flavour it should absorb.

Light/lite Officially wines under 10% alcohol by volume; also light in body (and often short on taste); a health-conscious trend in both reds and whites.

Lively Bouncy, fresh flavours.

Long or **length** Enduring; wine's flavours reverberate on the palate long after swallowing.

Maderised Oxidised and flat; colour is often brownish. Over-mature. More positively, a madeira-like oxidative quality, with 'cooked'/caramelised flavours.

Meaty Sometimes suggesting a general savouriness; but also literally the aroma of meat – raw, smoked etc.

Mousse Fizz in sparkling wines; usually refers also to quality, size and effervescence of the bubbles. See also Bead.

Mouthfeel, mouthfilling Texture, feel; racy, crispness (fine with appropriate dishes) or generous, supple, smooth.

Neutral What it says, neither here nor there.

New World Generally implies accessible, bold, often extrovert (in terms of fruit and use of oak). **Old World** embraces terms like subtle, complex, less oaky, more varied and generally more vinous (than fruity). See also Classic.

Oaky Having exaggerated oak aromas/flavours (vanilla, spice, char, woodsmoke etc). Oak balanced by fruit in young wines may lessen with age, but over-oaked young wines (where fruit is not in balance) will become over-oaked old wines.

Palate Combination of flavour, taste and texture of a wine.

Pebbly See Gravelly.

Perfumed or **scented** Strong fragrances (fruity, flowery, animal etc)

Phenolic Astringency or bitterness, usually in white wine, attributed to excessive phenolic compounds.

Plump Well fleshed in a charming, cherubic way.

Porty Heavy, over-ripe, stewed; a negative in unfortified wine.

Rich Flavourful, intense, generous. Not necessarily sweet.

Robust Strapping, full-bodied (but not aggressive).

Rough Bull-in-a-china-shop wine, or throat sand-papering quality.

Round Well balanced, without gawkiness or jagged edges.

Sharp or **tart** All about acid, usually unbalanced. But occasionally sharpish, fresh wine is right for the occasion.

Short or **quick** Insubstantial wine, leaving little impression.

Simple One-dimensional or no flavour excitement.

Stalky Unripe, bitter, stemmy.

Stewed Over-ripe, cooked, soft, soggy fruit.

Structure The wine's make up (fruit, acid, tannin, alcohol etc), also in relation to its ageing ability; if a wine is deemed to have 'the structure to age' it suggests these principal elements are in place.

Stylish Classy, distinguished; also voguish.

Supple Very desirable (not necessarily subtle), yielding, refined texture and flavours. See also Mouthfeel.

Tannic Tannins are prominent in the wine, imparting, positively, a mouth-puckering, grippy, tangy quality; negatively, a harsh, unyielding character.

Tension Racy, nervy fruit-acid play on the palate.

Terpene(s)/terpenoid Strong, floral compounds influencing the aromas of especially riesling, gewürztraminer and the muscats; with bottle-age, terpenes can develop a pungent resinous oiliness.

Texture Tactile 'feel' in the mouth: hard, acidic, coarse and alcoholic; or, smooth, velvety, 'warm'.

Toasty Often used for barrel-fermented or -aged wines showing a pleasant biscuity, charry character.

Vegetal Grassy, leafy, herby – in contrast to fruity, flowery, oaky. Overdone, a no-no.

Yeasty Warm bakery smells, often evident in barrel-fermented whites and méthode champenoise sparkling wines, where yeasts stay in contact with the wine after fermentation.

Winemaking Terms

A few brief reference explanations. See also sections on Winetasting Terms and SA Wine Styles.

Acid and **acidity** The fresh – or, in excess, sharp or tart – taste of wine. Too little acid and the wine tastes dull and flat. In SA, winemakers are permitted to adjust acidity either by adding acid – at any stage before bottling – or by lowering the acid level with a de-acidifier. See also Volatile acid and Malolactic.

Alcohol Essential component of wine, providing fullness, richness and, at higher levels, sometimes an impression of sweetness. Also a preservative, helping keep wines in good condition. Produced by yeasts fermenting the sugars in the grape. Measured by volume of the total liquid. Most unfortified table wines in SA have between 11% and 14.5% alc by vol; fortifieds range from ±15% to 21%. A variation of up to 1% between the strength stated on the label and the laboratory analysis is permitted by local law. Various techniques (such as reverse osmosis and 'spinning cone', also the addition of water) exist to address the increasingly important issue of high alcohol levels in wine, and some are legal in SA (though not for export to, eg, Europe).

Barrels (**barrel-aged**; **barrel-fermented**) Wines are transferred to barrels to age, pick up oaky flavours etc. When must or fermenting must is put into barrels, the resulting wine is called barrel-fermented. A barrel or cask is generally a 225–500L oak container; barrique is a French word for a 225-L barrel; pipe, adapted from the Portuguese

pipa, usually indicates a vessel of 530–630L; vat and foudre are terms generally used for larger (2,000–5,000L) wooden vessels.

Bâtonnage See Lees.

Biodynamic See Organic.

Blend A wine made from two or more different grape varieties, vintages, vineyards or containers. Some of the world's finest wines are blends.

Bottles While the 750-ml (75-cl) bottle is now the most widely used size of container for wine, it is by no means the only one. Smaller bottles (375 and 500 ml) are popular with restaurants and airlines, and larger sizes are prized by collectors because of their novelty value and/or their tendency to promote slower wine ageing. The following are the larger bottle sizes (note: some no longer in production):

Capacity		Bordeaux	Champagne/Burgundy
litres	bottles		
1.5	2	Magnum	Magnum
3	4	Double magnum	Jéroboam
4.5	6	Jéroboam	Rehoboam
6	8	Impériale	Methuselah
9	12	—	Salmanazar
12	16	—	Balthazar

Capacity		Bordeaux	Champagne/ Burgundy
litres	bottles		
15	20	—	Nebuchadnezzar

Brettanomyces or **'brett'** Naturally occurring yeast, usually associated with red wine and regarded as a spoilage factor, because its growth triggers the formation of volatile acids, phenols and other compounds which, in sufficient concentration, impart a range of unpleasant characters, from barnyard to sweat to cheese. At low concentrations, can enhance complexity and character.

Carbonic maceration or **maceration carbonique** Method of fermenting wine without first crushing the grapes. Whole clusters with stalks etc are put into closed vat; intracellular fermentation occurs within the grape berries, which then burst.

Chaptalisation Originally French term for the addition of sugar to grape must to raise the alcohol of a wine. Selectively legal in northern Europe, where acid adjustments are not allowed as they are in SA.

Charmat Method of making sparkling wine in a sealed tank (cuvée close) under pressure. Easier, cheaper than méthode champenoise.

Chips See Oak chips.

Cold ferment 'Cold' is a relative term; applied to fermentation of mainly white wines in temperature-controlled tanks, it refers to a temperature around usually 13–16°C. The benefits, especially important in a warm country, include conserving the primary fruit aromas and ensuring fermentation is carried out steadily and thoroughly.

Cold soak or **cold maceration** Red-wine making method carried out prior to fermentation. Skins and juice are held, usually for a few days, at a sufficiently cool temperature to prevent fermentation. The theory is that this extracts more favourable colour and aromas than after fermentation.

Cold stabilisation Keeping a wine at about -4°C for a week or more to precipitate tartaric acid and 'clean up' the wine, preventing later formation of (harmless) tartrate crystals in bottle. Some winemakers believe this process damages flavour and prefer to avoid it.

Concrete Traditionally the preferred construction material for larger fermentation and storage containers, largely superseded since the 1970s by stainless steel. More recently concrete 'eggs', their shape reminiscent of the amphoras of antiquity, have found favour for reasons varying from more-uniform fermentations to improved wine structure, texture and flavour.

Disgorgement (dégorgement in French) Important stage in the production of traditionally fermented sparkling where accumulated sediment (or lees), which could cloud the finished wine, is removed from the neck of the bottle.

Dosage The sugar added to sparkling wine after the second fermentation.

Fermentation The conversion of sugar in grapes into alcohol and carbon dioxide, a function of enzymes secreted by yeasts. In modern Cape winemaking, cultured yeasts are normally added to secure the process, but along with the growth of the natural winemaking movement, ferments using wild yeasts (which occur both in vineyard and cellar) are increasing. Beyond about 15% of alcohol, yeasts are overwhelmed and fermentation ceases, although it usually is stopped (for instance by cooling, filtration or the addition of alcohol) before this stage. See also Malolactic.

Filtration Removes last impurities including yeast cells. Done excessively, can thin a wine. Some traditionalists bottle without cold- or protein-stabilisation or filtration.

Fining and **protein stabilisation** Fining is ridding wine of suspended particles by adding substances that attract and draw the particles from the wine.

Flash-pasteurisation See Kosher.

Free run After grapes have been de-stalked and crushed, juice runs freely.

Garage wine Generic term for wine made in minuscule quantities, sometimes literally in a garage; a grower of such wine is sometimes called a garagiste.

Glycerol Minor product of alcoholic fermentation; from the Greek for sweet. Has an apparent sweetening effect on even dry wines and also gives a viscous, mouthfilling character.

Icewine Sweet, concentrated wine from grapes picked and pressed while frozen. Not a recognised category for SA wine production.

Kosher Wine made 'correctly', ie under rabbinical supervision, to be suitable for use by religious Jews. Vinification and any initial movement of the wine must be done by an observant Jew. Flash-pasteurisation, increasingly by means of flavour-preserving processes such as Thermoflash, renders the resulting meshuval wine (literally 'boiled' or 'cooked') fit for handling by non-Jews.

Leafroll virus Virus (or complex of viruses), widespread throughout the winegrowing world, which causes the vine to perform below its potential and thereby produce wine which is lower in colour, body and flavour than that derived from virus-free or 'cleaned-up' plants.

Lees Spent yeast cells and other matter which collect at the bottom of any container in winemaking. Yeast autolysis, or decomposition, can impart richness and flavour to a wine, sometimes referred to as leesy. Lees stirring or bâtonnage involves mixing the bed of lees in a barrel or tank through the wine, which is said to be sur lie; it is employed primarily on barrel-fermented white wines. The main effects of mixing lees and wine are to prevent off-odours developing from lack of oxygen, to limit the amount of wood tannin and oak character extracted, and to increase flavour.

Malolactic fermentation (malo) Occurs when bacteria convert malic into lactic acids. This reduces the acidity of a wine, a normal and healthy process, especially in reds — provided, of course, it occurs before bottling.

Maturation Ageing properties are closely related to tannin and/or fixed acid content of a wine. A relatively full red wine with tannin has lasting power. With age, it may develop complexity, subtlety and smooth mellowness. Lighter wines with lower tannins are drinkable sooner but probably will not reach the same level of complexity. A rising number of Cape whites mature well over several years, but most are best drunk in their fruity youth, up to 18 months.

Méthode champenoise Classic method of making champagne by inducing secondary fermentation in the bottle and producing fine bubbles. Due to French restrictions on terminology, Cape sparkling wines made in this way are called méthode cap classique (MCC).

Micro-oxygenation Technique enabling introduction of precise, controlled doses of oxygen to must/ wine. Advocates claim softer tannins, more stable colours and other advantages.

Oak chips, either in older barrels or stainless steel tanks, are widely used in SA, as are oak **staves**. Still frowned on by some purists, the 'additives' approximate the flavour effects of a new barrel, far more cheaply, more easily handled.

Oak-matured See Barrels.

Organic viticulture/winemaking Increasingly popular alternative to 'conventional' or 'industrialised' winegrowing, emphasising natural and sustainable farming methods and cellar techniques. A variant is biodynamic viticulture, influenced by anthroposophy, focused on improving wine quality through harmony with nature and its rhythms.

Oxidation Change (usually for the worse) due to exposure to air, in whites often producing dark yellow or yellowish colour (called maderisation), altering, 'ageing' the taste. Controlled oxidation can be used to produce positive development in wine (see next entry).

Oxidative winemaking Intentional exposure to oxygen during vinification, imparting in a nutty/ biscuity quality to the wine. Contrast with protective winemaking, where contact with oxygen is avoided as much as possible.

Pasteurisation See Kosher.

pH A chemical notation, used in winemaking and evaluation. The pH of a wine is its effective, active acidity — not in volume but by strength or degree. The reading provides a guide to a wine's keepability. The optimum pH in a wine is somewhere between 3.1 and 3.4 — which significantly improves a wine's protection from bacterial spoilage, so permitting it to mature and develop if properly stored.

Racking Drawing or pumping wine off from one cask or tank to another, to leave behind the deposit or lees.

Reductive Wine in an unevolved, unoxidised state is said to be 'reductive'; usually with a tight, sometimes unyielding character. The absence of air (in a bottled wine) or the presence of substantial sulphur dioxide (anti-oxidant) levels, will inhibit both oxidation and reduction processes, which are linked and complementary.

Reverse osmosis A specialised filtration technique, permitted in SA for various purposes, including the removal of water from wine. See also Alcohol.

Skin contact After crushing and de-stemming, white grapes may be left for a period with the juice, remaining in contact with skins (before being moved into the press, from which the grape juice is squeezed). Some winemakers believe the colours and flavours in and under the grape skins should be maximised in this way; others believe extended (or any) contact can lead to coarseness, even bitterness.

Sulphur dioxide (SO$_2$) Sterilising agent and preservative, near-ubiquitous in winemaking since antiquity, now strictly controlled. In SA, max total SO$_2$ level for dry wines is 150–160 mg/L; for wines with 5+ g/L sugar it is 200 mg/L; and botrytis-style wines 300 mg/L. Any wine with more than 10 mg/L total SO$_2$ must carry the warning 'Contains sulphites' (or 'sulfites') on the label.

Sur lie See Lees.

Tannin Vital preservative in wine, derives primarily from the grape skins. Necessary for a red wine's longevity. A young wine's raw tannin can give it a harshness, but no red wine matures into a great one without tannin, which itself undergoes change, combines with other substances and mellows. Tannin leaves a mouth-puckering dryness about the gums, gives 'grip' to a wine. A wooded wine will usually also contain some wood tannin.

Tartrates Harmless crystals formed by tartaric acid precipitating in non-cold-stabilised wine. Because of lack of public acceptance, usually avoided through cold stabilisation.

Terroir Important, controversial (and in SA over-used) French term embracing soil, climate, topography and other elements which constitute the natural environment of a vineyard site and give it a unique character.

Thermovinification/Thermoflash See Kosher.
Unfiltered See Filtration.

Virus or **virused** See Leafroll.
Volatile acid (VA) The part of the acidity which can become volatile. A high reading indicates a wine is prone to spoilage. Recognised at high levels by a sharp, 'hot', vinegary smell. In SA, most wines must by law be below 1.2 g/L of VA; in practice, the majority are well below 1 g/L.

Whole-bunch pressing or **cluster pressing** Some SA cellars use this age-old process of placing whole bunches directly in the press and gently squeezing. The more usual method is to de-stem and crush the berries before pressing. Whole-bunch pressing is said to yield fresher, cleaner must, and wine lower in polyphenols which, in excess, tend to age wines faster and render them coarser.

Wood-fermented/matured See Barrels.
Yeasts Micro-organisms that secrete enzymes which convert or ferment sugar into alcohol. See Fermentation.

Touring Wine Country

Wine Routes, Trusts & Associations

For localised information about regional official wine routes and wineries, contact these organisations:

Breedekloof Wine & Tourism ▪ T +27 (0)23-349-1791 ▪ F +27 (0)23-349-1720 ▪ info@breedekloof.com ▪ www.breedekloof.com

Constantia Wine Route ▪ T +27 (0)83-679-4495 (Carryn Wiltshire) ▪ info@constantiawineroute.com ▪ www.constantiawineroute.com

Darling Wine & Food Experience ▪ +27 (0)22-492-3971 ▪ taste@darlingwine.co.za ▪ www.darlingtourism.co.za

Durbanville Wine Valley Association ▪ T +27 (0)83-310-1228 (Angela Fourie) ▪ valleyconnect@durbanvillewine.co.za ▪ www.durbanvillewine.co.za

Wines of Elgin ▪ T +27 (0)71-267-9785 ▪ info@winesofelgin.co.za ▪ www.winesofelgin.co.za

Elim Winegrowers ▪ T +27 (0)28-482-1902 / +27 (0)82-376-8498 (Jackie Rabe) ▪ jackie@strandveld.co.za

Franschhoek See Vignerons de Franschhoek.

Helderberg See Stellenbosch.

Hemel-en-Aarde Wines ▪ T +27 (0)28-313-2881 (Craig Wessels) ▪ craig@hemelenaardewines.com ▪ www.hemelenaardewines.com

Klein Karoo Wine Route ▪ T +27(0)44-272-7492 / +27 (0)82-214-5910 ▪ F +27 (0)86-528-4055 (Ellen Marais) ▪ info@kleinkaroowines.co.za ▪ www.kleinkaroowines.co.za

Northern Cape Wine Association See Orange River Wine Route

Olifants River Vodacom Wine Route See West Coast Wine Route

Orange River Wine Route ▪ T +27 (0)54-337-8800 (Jorine Viviers) ▪ F +27 (0)54-332-4408 ▪ info@orangeriverwines.com

Paarl Wine Tourism Office ▪ T +27 (0)21-872-4842 ▪ paarlwineroute@dlta.co.za ▪ www.paarlonline.com

Plett Winelands (Plettenberg Bay) ▪ T +27 (0)44-553-4065 ▪ info@plettwinelands.com ▪ www.plettwinelands.com

Robertson Wine Valley ▪ T +27 (0)23-626-3167 / +27 (0)83-701-5404 ▪ manager@robertsonwinevalley.com ▪ www.robertsonwinevalley.com

Santam Swartland Wine & Olive Route ▪ T +27 (0)22-487-1133 ▪ F +27 (0)22-487-2063 ▪ swartlandinfo@westc.co.za ▪ www.swartland-wineandolives.co.za

Stanford Wine Route ▪ T +27 (0)82-572-5856 / +27 (0)82-927-0979 ▪ stanfordwr@gmail.com

Stellenbosch Wine Routes ▪ T +27 (0)21-886-4310 ▪ info@wineroute.co.za ▪ www.wineroute.co.za

Tulbagh Wine Route ▪ T/F +27 (0)23-230-1348/75 ▪ info@tulbaghtourism.co.za ▪ www.tulbaghwineroute.com ▪ www.tulbaghtourism.co.za

Vignerons de Franschhoek ▪ T +27 (0)21-876-2861 ▪ F +27 (0)21-876-2768 ▪ info@franschhoek.org.za ▪ www.franschhoek.org.za

Walker Bay Wine Wander ▪ T +27 (0)28-316-3988 ▪ F +27 (0)86-509-4931 ▪ wine@hermanus.co.za

Wellington Wine Tourism Office ▪ T +27 (0)21-864-1378 ▪ wellingtoninfo@dlta.co.za ▪ www.wellington.co.za

West Coast Wine Route ▪ T +27 (0)83-446-6930 / +27 (0)27-201-3376 ▪ F +27 (0)27-213-4819 ▪ wine@visitnwc.com ▪ www.visitnwc.com

Worcester Wine & Olive Route ▪ T +27 (0)84-245-3922 ▪ info@worcesterwineroute.co.za ▪ www.worcesterwineroute.co.za

Winelands Tourism Offices

For additional accommodation options, brochures and local advice, contact the information offices and/or publicity associations of the wine areas you plan to visit.

Breedekloof Wine & Tourism ▪ T +27 (0)23-349-1791 ▪ F +27 (0)23-349-1720 ▪ info@breedekloof.com ▪ www.breedekloof.com

Calitzdorp Tourism ▪ T +27 (0)44-213-3775 ▪ tourism@calitzdorp.org.za ▪ www.calitzdorp.org.za

Cape Town Tourism ▪ Contact centre: T +27 (0)86-132-2223

Cape Town Tourism (Head office) ▪ T +27 (0)21-487-6800 ▪ F +27 (0)21-487-6859 ▪ capetown@capetown.travel, info@capetown.travel

Somerset West ▪ T +27 (0)21-840-1400 ▪ F +27 (0)21-840-1410 ▪ somersetwest@capetown.travel

Elgin Valley Tourism ▪ T +27 (0)21-848-9838 ▪ F +27 (0)86-660-0398 ▪ info@elginvalley.co.za ▪ www.elginvalley.co.za

Franschhoek Wine Valley ▪ T +27 (0)21-876-2861 ▪ F +27 (0)21-876-2768 ▪ info@franschhoek.org.za ▪ www.franschhoek.org.za

Hermanus Tourism Bureau ▪ T +27 (0)28-312-2629 ▪ hermanustourism2@hermanus.co.za ▪ www.hermanustourism.info

McGregor Tourism ▪ T +27 (0)23-625-1954 ▪ info@tourismmcgregor.co.za ▪ www.tourism-mcgregor.co.za

Northern Cape Tourism ▪ T +27 (0)53-832-2657 ▪ F +27 (0)53-831-2937 ▪ marketing@experiencenortherncape.com ▪ www.experiencenortherncape.com

Paarl Visitor Information Centre ▪ T +27 (0)21-872-4842 ▪ paarlinfo@dlta.co.za ▪ www.paarlonline.com

Robertson Tourism Association ▪ T +27 (0)23-626-4437 ▪ info@robertson.org.za ▪ www.robertsontourism.co.za

Route 62 ▪ info@route62.co.za ▪ www.route62.co.za

Stellenbosch 360 ▪ T +27 (0)21-883-3584 ▪ F +27 (0)21-882-9550 ▪ info@stellenbosch360.co.za ▪ www.stellenbosch.travel

Tulbagh Tourism ▪ T/F +27 (0)23-230-1348/75 ▪ info@tulbaghtourism.co.za ▪ www.tulbaghwineroute.com ▪ www.tulbaghtourism.co.za

Wellington Visitor Information Centre ▪ T +27 (0)21-864-1378 ▪ wellingtoninfo@dlta.co.za ▪ www.wellington.co.za

Worcester Tourism Association ▪ T +27 (0)23-342-6244 / +27 (0)76-200-8742 ▪ info@worcestertourism.com ▪ www.worcestertourism.com

---

Specialist Wine Tours

Below are some specialist wine tour guides operating in Cape Town and the winelands. These are paid entries. The guides supplied information on their services, which was then edited for consistency of style.

African Story Wine Tours Contact Bruce Storey ▪ info@africanstorytours.com ▪ www.africanstorytours.com ▪ English ▪ T +27 (0)73-755-0444 / +27 (0)79-694-7915 ▪ Tour times: about 8.30am-5.30pm daily, pick-up/drop-off in Cape Town city centre ▪ Closed Christmas & New Year ▪ Facebook/Twitter/Flickr/YouTube: African Story Tours ▪ 109 Son Vida Flats, 79 Somerset Rd, Green Point ▪ PO Box 15039, Vlaeberg 8018 ▪ Special/unique facilities & features: private and group tours also offered.

The scheduled tour leaves from Cape Town city centre and is fun but informative, visiting Paarl, Franschhoek and Stellenbosch wine regions. The day includes four wineries and a delicious gourmet lunch, plus pairings of cheese, chocolate and wine. Cellar tours are included. Private and group tours are also offered.

Cape Fine Wine Tours Contact John Lawrence ▪ john@capefinewinetours.com ▪ www.capefinewinetours.com ▪ English, German, Italian ▪ T +27 (0)82-258-2951 ▪ 41 Loresta, St Andrews Rd, Rondebosch, Cape Town ▪ Special/unique facilities & features: introductions to winemakers.

Cape Fine Wine Tours' winelands excursions are private and customised, and include cellar tours, vineyard walks, barrel tastings and library tastings. Overnight tours are a speciality, and feature fine wines and fine dining.

Caroline's Fine Wine Tours Contact Lieze Norval ▪ carowine6@mweb.co.za ▪ www.carolineswine.com ▪ English, Afrikaans, Spanish, Italian ▪ T +27 (0)21-419-8984 / +27 (0)82-828-5249 ▪ 62 Strand Str, Cape Town ▪ Special/unique facilities & features: winemaker-led wine tours.

Caroline's Fine Wine Tours takes novice or connoisseur winelovers through the greater Cape winelands to discover hidden gems, travelling routes based on clients' particular preferences, interests and tastes. Guide Lieze Norval is a winemaker herself, and thus the tours are extraordinarily informative, as well as enjoyable and memorable. Private tours are a focus, and special interest groups are catered for.

Explore Sideways info@exploresideways.com ▪ www.exploresideways.com ▪ English, French, German, Italian, Dutch, Spanish, Portuguese ▪ T +27 (0)79-607-1978 ▪ Facebook/Twitter: @ExploreSideways ▪ 401A, 66 Albert Rd, Woodstock Exchange, Woodstock, Cape Town ▪ Special/unique facilities & features: insider access, exclusive experiences, expert wine guides, highly curated, flexible itineraries using industry connections and long-standing relationships.

Explore Sideways is the leader in highly curated, private gourmet food, wine and cultural day tours in the winelands involving industry experts, specialist guides and handcrafted itineraries. Each unique tour offers off-the-beaten track access and can be personalised to suit your interests and palate. Visit the Explore Sideways TripAdvisor page to see our Certificate of Excellence and 5-star reviews.

Gourmet Wine Tours Contact Stephen Flesch ▪ sflesch@iafrica.com ▪ www.gourmetwinetours.co.za ▪ English, Afrikaans ▪ T +27 (0)21-710-5454

/ +27 (0)83-229-3581 ▪ F +27 (0)86-241-1685 ▪ 213 Fernbridge, Alnwick Rd, Diep River, Cape Town ▪ Special/unique facilities & features: tours are led personally by Stephen Flesch, who is passionate and knowledgeable about the Cape winelands.

Explore the scenically stunning winelands of the Western Cape – an epicurean's dream – and experience the best of South African wine and food. Private tours are offered for individuals or small groups, covering the principal wine areas and estates, combined with meals in selected leading restaurants.

Jeanette Bosman Wine Tours Contact Jeanette Bosman ▪ jbosman@polka.co.za ▪ English, Afrikaans, German ▪ T +27 (0)23-626-5775 / +27 (0)82-520-0882 ▪ Facebook: jeanette.bosman.35 ▪ 6 Victoria Street, Robertson ▪ Special/unique facilities & features: private and customised tours by experienced tourism and communications consultant.

Jeanette Bosman offers private and bespoke wine tours in Robertson Wine Valley. From individuals to large groups, fun, interactive or educational excursions can be arranged, with additional activities such as olive and olive oil tastings and lavender farm visits optionally included. Cellar tours and boat cruises can add to the ultimate Robertson wine experience.

La Rochelle Wine & Gourmet Tours Contact Johan Barnard ▪ info@larochelletours.com ▪ www.larochelletours.com ▪ English, Afrikaans ▪ T +27 (0)83-301-6774 / +27 (0)82-256-1606 ▪ Twitter/Instagram: @capewinetours ▪ Franschhoek, Paarl, Stellenbosch

Established in 2000 and ranked #1 on TripAdvisor, La Rochelle Wine & Gourmet Tours strive to offer a once-in-a-lifetime experience. Specialist wine guides provide personalised scheduled/private wine tours with collections from Franschhoek, Stellenbosch and Paarl. Tours cater for everyone from novices who wish to learn more about wine in a relaxed manner, to connoisseurs with more specific requests. Non-guided driver services are available for repeat visitors who prefer to follow their own itinerary.

Luhambo Tours Contact Cedric Jones ▪ bookings@luhambotours.com ▪ www.luhambo-tours.com ▪ English, Afrikaans, German ▪ T +27 (0)21-551-0467 / +27 (0)82-306-4141 ▪ Twitter: @CapeTownWine ▪ Facebook: @LuhamboTours ▪ 31B Platinum Junction, School Str, Milnerton 7441 ▪ Special/unique facilities & features: specialist wine guides, air-conditioned seven- and ten-seater vehicles, private and customised tours.

Luhambo Tours offers high-quality wine tours in Cape Town, Stellenbosch, Franschhoek, Paarl and the greater Cape winelands. Small, personalised groups with a maximum of seven participants enable Luhambo Tours to provide guests with the ultimate winelands experience. Tours depart daily from Cape Town.

Nine Yards Travel Contact Maria Steyn ▪ info@nineyardstravel.com ▪ www.nineyardstravel.com ▪ English ▪ T +27 (0)21-881-3441 / +27 (0)60-998-8426 ▪ F +27 (0)21-881-3426 ▪ Facebook/Twitter/LinkedIn: Nine Yards Travel ▪ Stellenboschkloof Rd, Stellenbosch ▪ Special/unique facilities & features: with strong links to the winelands, via Jordan Wine Estate, Nine Yards Travel places an emphasis on promoting wine tourism and supporting the wine industry.

Nine Yards Travel, derived from the famous Jordan Nine Yards Chardonnay, is a destination management business founded by Gary and Kathy Jordan, also proud owners of Jordan Wine Estate. As the company name implies, Nine Yards Travel covers the full spectrum of client requests and preferences, including guided winelands excursions in partnership with select, experienced and knowledgeable local tour operators. For self-drive visitors, Nine Yards Travel joins with leading wine estates, restaurants and guest lodges to offer customised itineraries in wine-country and beyond. The extensive offering encompasses international and domestic flights, accommodation, transfers, car rental and activities – in short, the whole nine yards.

Percy Tours Hermanus Contact Percy Heywood ▪ travel@percytours.com ▪ www.percytours.com ▪ www.hermanuswinetours.com ▪ English, Afrikaans, some French ▪ T +27 (0)72-062-8500 ▪ WhatsApp/Instagram/Facebook/Twitter: Percy Tours Hermanus ▪ PO Box 488, Hermanus 7200 ▪ Special/unique facilities & features: registered and accredited with Cape Wine Academy; Cape Town and Hermanus & Overberg tourism boards; tour guides registered with CATHSSETA and PDP professional chauffeurs; insured to the highest levels (Passenger Liability and General Liability policies); first aid trained.

Percy Tours specialise in fully tailor-made, personalised and individualised tours of Hermanus and Cape Town regions, with a fleet of spacious and luxurious minibuses (and cars) with highly knowledgeable chauffeur wine tour guides who will collect you from your accommodation and supply many comforts on board. The tour guides have completed Cape Wine Academy courses, so they will discuss many wine topics - and much more - while you sip delicious wines. Restaurant lunches at wineries are highly recommended and Percy Tours can easily arrange these too. Visit Percy Tours' TripAdvisor page to view wine tour reviews from their many very happy clients.

Sunswept Tours   Contact Glynis van Rooyen ▪ glynis@hermanus.co.za ▪ www.sunswept.co.za ▪ English, Afrikaans ▪ **T +27 (0)82-775-8843** ▪ Facebook: Sunswept Tours ▪ PO Box 1216, Hermanus 7200 ▪ Special/unique facilities & features: wine and olive oil tasting specialist, registered tour guide with luxury vehicle.

Sunswept Tours immerse you in the taste, feel, look, sound and smell of the Cape, with explorations of less-travelled roads leading to cellars and dining rooms of wine-makers and -lovers revealing hidden gems and creating indelible memories. Day excursions and longer tours are tailor-made for discerning visitors who wish to savour the winelands' sensuous delights.

Taste The Cape Travel & Tours   Contact Ann-Marie Breen ▪ info@tastethecape.co.za ▪ www. tastethecape.co.za ▪ English ▪ **T +27 (0)21-788-1649 / +27 (0)79-812-0220** ▪ Special/unique facilities & features: owner-operated tour-guiding company offering wine and culinary excursions tailored to clients' particular interests.

Owner Ann-Marie Breen is a qualified and registered tour guide, and Cape Town resident for the past 25 years. Passionate about good food and wine, she has an excellent knowledge of the vast possibilities of 'foodie' experiences that Cape Town and surrounds have to offer, and is able to create bespoke tours covering all the bases, including hotels and car hire. Where possible, tours are woven into culinary events taking place in the Mother City and winelands.

Tsiba Tsiba Wine Tours & Travel   Contact Willem Swanepoel ▪ info@tsibatsiba.co.za ▪ www.tsibatsiba. co.za ▪ Dutch, English, French, German, Spanish ▪ **T +27 (0)82-956-8104** ▪ F +27 (0)86-568-1756 ▪ Facebook: Tsiba Tsiba Wine Tours & Travel ▪ Twitter: Tsiba Tsiba Tours ▪ PO Box 3192, Matieland 7602 ▪ Special/unique facilities & features: tours tailored to clients' wine preferences.

Tsiba Tsiba Wine Tours & Travel is based in the heart of SA's winelands and specialises in bespoke wine experiences for connoisseurs, winelovers and wine novices alike. Clients enjoy a day of award-winning wines and spectacular scenery in the company of guides whose expertise has garnered TripAdvisor's Certificate of Excellence in 2013, 2014, 2015 and 2016; and African Corporate Excellence Awards' Luxury Travel Guides Award in 2016 and 2017, as well as Best SA Wine Tour Company in 2016. Private tours and larger groups are also catered for.

Vineyard Ventures (Glen Christie)   Contact Glen Christie ▪ vinven@iafrica.com ▪ www.vineyard-ventures.co.za ▪ English, Afrikaans, German; other languages on request ▪ **T +27 (0)21-434-8888 / +27 (0)82-920-2825** ▪ F +27 (0)86-579-9430 ▪ A82 Punta Del Mar, Milton Rd, Sea Point ▪ PO Box 554, Sea Point 8060

Private and individually tailored tours woven around personal interests and preferences. Vineyard Ventures' approach, based on professional expertise, more than 20 years of extensive contacts with estates and winemakers in every region, personal attention and flexibility, ensures an enjoyable and unforgettable adventure in wine and food, and an experience beyond the expected.

Restaurants in the Winelands and Cape Town

Below are some dining out options in Cape Town and the winelands. These are paid entries. The venues supplied information on their cuisine, menus and attractions, which was then edited for consistency of style. For more restaurants among the vines, consult the A–Z section of the guide for wineries that offer light lunches, picnics etc. Look for the f symbol beside the individual entries. Unless stated to the contrary, all allow you to bring your own (BYO) wine – the corkage fee is indicated at the start of each entry. Should you wish to know about wheelchair access, please discuss with the relevant restaurant.

INDEX OF RESTAURANTS

Aubergine Restaurant	Cape Town Central	Flavours Restaurant	Stellenbosch
Auslese Function Venue	Cape Town Central	Guardian Peak Winery & Grill	Stellenbosch
Azure	Camps Bay	Indochine	Stellenbosch
Bergsig Bistro	Breedekloof	Jonkershuis Constantia	Constantia
B's Stro@Lavierge	Hermanus	Jordan Restaurant	Stellenbosch
Delaire Graff Restaurant	Stellenbosch	Lanzerac Wine Estate – Dining	Stellenbosch
Eight	Stellenbosch	Longtable Restaurant	Stellenbosch

Marigold. . . . . Franschhoek
Moody Lagoon . . . . .Hermanus
Nom Nom . . . . Somerset West
Nuy On The Hill . . . . Worcester
Orangerie @ Le Lude . . . . Franschhoek
Readers Restaurant. . . . . Tulbagh
Restaurant @ Glen Carlou . . . . .Paarl
Rust en Rede Restaurant . . . . Stellenbosch
Rust en Rede Winemaker's Lunch . . . Stellenbosch
Sotano . . . . Cape Town Central
South Hill Vineyards . . . . .Elgin
The Franschhoek Cellar Restaurant . . . Franschhoek
The Pool Room at Oak Valley . . . . .Elgin
The Restaurant at La Petite Ferme . . . Franschhoek
The Restaurant @ Misty Mountains . . . . .Stanford
The Restaurant at Neethlingshof . . . . Stellenbosch
The Restaurant at Waterkloof . . . . Somerset West
The Royal Restaurant. . . . . Riebeek-Kasteel
Tuk Tuk Microbrewery . . . . Franschhoek
Vergelegen . . . . Somerset West
Warwick Estate - Gourmet Picnics . . . Stellenbosch
Zevenwacht Restaurant . . . . .Kuils River

BREEDEKLOOF

Bergsig Bistro Bergsig Estate, Route 43, Breërivier ▪ Bistro ▪ Open Mon-Fri 8am-4pm, Sat & pub hols 9am-3pm ▪ Closed Sun, Christmas Day & Good Friday ▪ Booking advised ▪ Children welcome ▪ Major credit cards accepted ▪ No BYO ▪ Owner De Wet Lategan ▪ wine@bergsig.co.za ▪ www.bergsig.co.za ▪ **T +27 (0)23-355-1603**

The Bistro on Bergsig Wine Estate is stylishly decorated and offers a friendly, relaxed dining atmosphere for up to 36 guests. In summer, request a table in the Balcony Room on the terrace and enjoy sweeping views of vineyards and the Bainskloof mountain range; in winter, especially when those peaks become snowcapped, a log fire will keep you cosy. Functions and special occasions can be catered for by prior arrangement. (See also Bergsig Estate in A-Z section.)

CAMPS BAY

Azure The Twelve Apostles Hotel & Spa, Victoria Rd, Camps Bay, Cape Town ▪ Contemporary South African cuisine with global culinary influences ▪ Open daily for breakfast 7am-10.30am, lunch 12.30pm-3.30pm & dinner 6pm-10pm ▪ Booking advised ▪ Children welcome ▪ No BYO ▪ Major credit cards accepted ▪ Owners Tollman family/Red Carnation Hotels ▪ Executive chef Christo Pretorius ▪ restaurants@12apostles.co.za ▪ www.12apostleshotel.com ▪ **T +27 (0)21-437-9000** ▪ F +27 (0)21-437-9062

Azure is the fine-dining restaurant at Cape Town's Twelve Apostles Hotel & Spa, where mesmerising ocean views vie for attention with executive chef Christo Pretorius' creations, some of them taken from internationally honoured owner Bea Tollman's cookbook. Azure offers leisurely breakfasts including fresh oysters and sparkling wine, à la carte lunches and dinners, special vegetarian, vegan and piscatorial tasting menus, and Sunday buffet lunches on the Atlantic-facing terrace — the perfect spot for spectacular sunsets and cocktails. (See also The Twelve Apostles Hotel & Spa in Accommodation section.)

CAPE TOWN CENTRAL

Aubergine Restaurant 39 Barnet Str, Gardens, Cape Town ▪ Classical cuisine with innovative twists & Asian influence ▪ Outdoor terrace ▪ Lunch Wed-Fri 12pm-2pm in summer, dinner Mon-Sat 6pm-10pm ▪ Closed Sun & alternate Mon ▪ Booking advised ▪ Children 5+ welcome ▪ Major credit cards accepted ▪ No BYO ▪ Owner/chef Harald Bresselschmidt ▪ info@ aubergine.co.za ▪ www.aubergine.co.za ▪ **T +27 (0)21-465-0000** ▪ F +27 (0)86-671-0835

At this warmly sophisticated restaurant revolving around wine pairing, a 15,000-bottle cellar gives chef/patron Harald Bresselschmidt's keen palate and culinary skills free rein to accent flavour, aroma and texture, whether preparing seafood, prime aged meat or produce from the restaurant's own garden. Degustation menu taste teasers include duck breast with lentils and duck liver emulsion, seafood pot-pourri with crayfish clouds, venison loin with cocoa tortellini, and lime gastrique with fennel parfait, pineapple and coconut. (See also Auslese Function Venue under Restaurants.)

Auslese Function Venue 115 Hope Str, Gardens, Cape Town ▪ Wines paired with sophisticated menus in classic yet innovative style ▪ Booking advised ▪ Open for pre-booked functions only ▪ Closed Sun & alternate Mon ▪ Children welcome ▪ Major credit cards accepted ▪ BYO by arrangement ▪ Owner/ chef Harald Bresselschmidt ▪ info@auslese.co.za ▪ www.auslese.co.za ▪ **T +27 (0)21-461-9727** (reservations/enquiries **T+27 (0)21-465-0000)** ▪ F +27 (0)86-671-0835

At this sister venue to elegant Aubergine, chef/patron Harald Bresselschmidt can tailor any occasion for you, from a private birthday party to a corporate event — or simply when you want the perfect pairing for your wine gems but don't feel like cooking. Custom designed for functions, whether cocktail events with canapés and tapas or sit-down wine-pairing dinners, Auslese also hosts regular music evenings and winemaker events. (See also Aubergine Restaurant under Restaurants.)

Sotano 121 Beach Rd, Mouille Point & 199 Bree Str, Cape Town ▪ Mediterranean, classic tapas ▪ Open daily 7am-10.30pm ▪ Booking advised ▪ Children welcome ▪ Major credit cards accepted ▪ No BYO ▪ Owner Brendon Crew ▪ Executive chef Russel Jalil ▪ info@sotano.co.za ▪ www.sotano.co.za ▪ **T +27 (0)21-433-1757** (Mouille Point) **+27 (0)21-422-0567** (Bree Str)

Mediterranean-inspired food is the star at this vibey eatery, now with a city-centre outlet in addition to the original seaside venue. Sip bubbly watching the sunset from the outside deck or nibble an array of tapas like calamari a la plancha, halloumi and patatas bravas while overlooking the city. Hearty mains feature signature paella; tempting lighter options include salads and flat breads with creative toppings. Try spicy Lebanese shakshouka for something different, and don't miss delicious Eggs Benedict at brunch. The winelist is well curated.

CONSTANTIA

Jonkershuis Constantia Groot Constantia Wine Estate, Groot Constantia Rd, Constantia, Cape Town ▪ Cape Malay/global cuisine ▪ Summer trading (Sep-Apr) Mon-Sat 9am-9pm & Sun 9am-5pm ▪ Reduced winter trading hours ▪ Breakfast daily 9am-11.30am ▪ Booking essential ▪ Children welcome ▪ Function facilities ▪ Major credit cards & Zapper accepted ▪ No BYO ▪ Owners Chris Coetzee, Tammy Botbyl & Angelina Moepana ▪ info@jonkershuisconstantia. co.za ▪ www.jonkershuisconstantia.co.za ▪ **T +27 (0)21-794-6255** ▪ F +27 (0)86-532-6961

Nestled in the historic core of the Groot Constantia Estate, with sweeping views over the oldest wine-producing vineyards in SA and across the coastline of False Bay, Jonkershuis Constantia offers intimate fireside and al fresco dining on the front lawns, main restaurant or courtyard areas. The menu reflects sustainability and a rich Cape Malay heritage. (See also Groot Constantia Estate in A-Z section.)

ELGIN

South Hill Vineyards 113 Valley Rd, Elgin ▪ Contemporary, bistro, country-style tapas & platters ▪ Open 7 days a week for breakfast & lunch 8am-4pm ▪ Open pub hols ▪ Closed 25/26 December & 1 Jan ▪ Winetasting Mon-Sun 10am-5pm ▪ Booking advised ▪ Children welcome ▪ BYO allowed but not encouraged ▪ Corkage R50/bottle ▪ VISA & MasterCard accepted ▪ Conferences ▪ Weddings/ functions ▪ Owners Kevin & Sandra King ▪ info@

southhill.co.za ▪ www.southhill.co.za ▪ **T +27 (0)21-844-0888**

The restaurant in South Hill's gallery space serves breakfasts and lunches of country platters, tapas and a selection of daily specials, with homemade breads and deli items also available. Produce is sourced from the kitchen garden and local suppliers. A variety of artworks is on display, including paintings, small- and large-scale sculptures, photographs, ceramics and mixed-medium works, as well as conceptual work. (See also South Hill Vineyards under Accommodation and in A-Z section.)

The Pool Room at Oak Valley by Gordon Manuel Oak Valley Estate, R321, Oak Ave, Elgin ▪ French/country cuisine ▪ Breakfast Tue-Sun 9am-11am, lunch Tue-Sun 12pm-3pm, dinner Fri 6.30pm-9pm ▪ Picnics available by pre-order 1 Nov-30 Apr ▪ Closed 24 Jun-17 Jul 2019 (re-opening 19 Jul 2019) & 1 Jan ▪ Booking advised ▪ Children welcome ▪ Wheelchair friendly ▪ Major credit cards accepted (no Amex) ▪ No BYO ▪ No pets ▪ Owners AG Rawbone-Viljoen ▪ poolroom@oak-valley.co.za ▪ www.oakvalley.co.za ▪ **T +27 (0)21-859-4111** ▪ F +27 (0)21-859-3405

When visiting Oak Valley Estate in Elgin, relax on The Pool Room terrace relishing country-inspired cuisine, using ingredients sourced from the farm where possible. Feast on free-range beef, acorn-fed pork, charcuterie platters, locally grown vegetables and freshly baked artisanal breads from the wood-burning oven. (See also Oak Valley Estate in A-Z section.)

FRANSCHHOEK

Marigold 9 Huguenot Str, Franschhoek ▪ Indian cuisine ▪ Open for lunch daily; May-Oct: 12pm-2.30pm & 6pm-9pm; Nov-Apr: 12pm-2.30pm & 6pm-10pm ▪ Bookings advised ▪ Children welcome ▪ Major credit cards accepted ▪ Owner Leeu Collection ▪ Head chef Vanie Padayachee ▪ marigoldfhk@leeucollection.com ▪ www.marigold-franschhoek.com ▪ **T +27 (0)21-876-8970**

The first classic Indian cuisine restaurant in Franschhoek, Marigold is another element of the Leeu Collection of fine accommodation and dining establishments. Situated on the village main road, the restaurant evokes the exotic with its small-plates menu inspired by aromatic and spicy north Indian cuisine. Sit indoors and enjoy the exposed brickwork, original timber ceiling, subtle geometric wallpaper and mid-century furniture design; or al fresco in the courtyard, which is the social hub of Heritage Square. (See also Leeu Estates/Leeu House/

Le Quartier Français under Accommodation, and Tuk Tuk Microbrewery in Restaurants section.)

Orangerie @ Le Lude Le Lude Méthode Cap Classique, Bowling Green Ave (Lambrechts Rd), Franschhoek ▪ Contemporary cuisine ▪ Open daily for tastings & canapés 10am-6pm ▪ Tue-Sun for lunch 12pm-4pm & high tea 3pm-6pm ▪ Booking advised ▪ Major credit cards accepted ▪ Owners Nic & Ferda Barrow ▪ Chef Nicolene Barrow ▪ info@lelude.co.za ▪ www.lelude.co.za ▪ **T +27 (0)21-100-3464**

Orangerie @ Le Lude is a grape throw away from the iconic Huguenot Monument. The interior is spacious and light, with a French flair, while outdoors there is a gorgeous terrace with a magnificent view of the Franschhoek mountains. Fresh herbs and vegetables from the kitchen garden are transformed into dishes that reflect the seasonal abundance. Enjoy a lazy lunch or high tea, or try the carefully paired canapés with Le Lude méthode cap classique sparklings or Le Mesnil champagne. (See also Lily Pond House under Accommodation and Le Lude Méthode Cap Classique in A-Z section.)

The Franschhoek Cellar Restaurant The Franschhoek Cellar, R45/Franschhoek Main Rd, Franschhoek ▪ Bistro cuisine ▪ Open Mon-Sat 10am-6pm & Sun 10am-5pm ▪ Open pub hols ▪ Closed Good Friday, Easter Monday & 25 Dec ▪ Booking advised ▪ Children welcome ▪ VISA & MasterCard accepted ▪ No BYO ▪ Chef Jerry Kennedy ▪ fhcellardoor@dgb.co.za ▪ www.thefranschhoekcellar.co.za ▪ **T +27 (0)21-876-2086**

The kitchen opens at 11am and serves light snacks, lunches and cakes throughout the day. Expect hearty and delicious artisanal food using home-grown ingredients and fresh produce from local markets and suppliers in Franschhoek Valley. Chef Jerry Kennedy garners inspiration from the natural goodness of farm life, and expertly combines modern and traditional techniques to produce a menu that is as exciting as it is wholesome. (See also The Franschhoek Cellar – Rose & Protea Cottages under Accommodation and Franschhoek Cellar in A-Z section.)

The Restaurant at La Petite Ferme Pass Rd, Franschhoek ▪ Rustic contemporary cuisine ▪ Open daily 12pm-3.30pm, dinners in season 7pm-9.30pm (Nov-Apr), winter 6.30pm-9pm (Fri & Sat) ▪ Booking advised ▪ Children welcome ▪ No BYO ▪ Major credit cards accepted ▪ Owners The Nest Estate ▪ reception@lapetiteferme.co.za ▪ www.lapetiteferme.co.za ▪ **T +27 (0)21-876-3016**

The Restaurant at La Petite Ferme Boutique Hotel & Winery offers a culinary experience like no other.

The best and freshest ingredients are sourced locally in Franschhoek and a combination of international methods are used to deliver flavours in a unique rustic contemporary style. (See also La Petite Ferme under Accommodation and La Petite Ferme Winery in A-Z section.)

Tuk Tuk Microbrewery 14 Huguenot Str, Franschhoek ▪ Mexican-inspired cuisine ▪ Open Mon-Sun 11am-11pm ▪ No reservations ▪ Children welcome ▪ Major credit cards accepted ▪ No BYO ▪ Owner Leeu Collection ▪ Head chef Martin Senekal ▪ info.tuktuk@leeucollection.com ▪ www.tuktukbrew.com ▪ **T +27 (0)21-492-2207**

The first and only microbrewery in Franschhoek's town centre, Leeu Collection's intimate and authentic Tuk Tuk offers the highest level of quality and variety. Sit indoors and watch fine beer being handcrafted in a German-designed industrial-chic facility, or relax outdoors on the bustling village main street. Tuk Tuk's 'taqueria' offers fresh and authentic Mexican-inspired dishes (think nachos, ceviche and tacos) by head chef Martin Senekal and the culinary team. (See also Leeu Estates/Leeu House/Le Quartier Français under Accommodation and Marigold in Restaurants section.)

HERMANUS

B's Stro@Lavierge R320, Hemel-en-Aarde Valley, Hermanus ▪ Traditional South African steak & local twists to popular cuisines ▪ Lunch Tue-Sun, dinner Sat ▪ Open pub hols ▪ Closed Mon, 15 May-10 June 2019 ▪ Booking advised ▪ Children welcome ▪ Major credit cards accepted ▪ No BYO ▪ Owner/head chef Bruce Henderson ▪ bruce@lavierge.co.za ▪ www.lavierge.co.za ▪ **T +27 (0)28-313-2007**

At the summit of an infamous cycling hill, with a superb view over Hemel-en-Aarde Valley, B's Stro@Lavierge continues where local legend B's Steakhouse left off, serving exceptional grain-fed South African beef, game in season and plenty of other traditional - and different - fare to please all palates (speciality dish: 350g sirloin with foraged mushroom sauce). Acclaimed La Vierge and Domaine des Dieux wines complement the experience. Excellent venue for weddings, corporate functions, private parties, product launches and more. (See also La Vierge Private Cellar in A-Z section.)

Moody Lagoon Benguela Cove Lagoon Wine Estate, R43, Bot River Lagoon, Hermanus ▪ South African-style menu ▪ Open for breakfast Sat 8am-10:30am; brunch Sun 10am-12pm; lunch Mon-Sun 12pm-3pm; dinner Thu-Sat 6pm-9pm ▪ Booking advised ▪ Children welcome ▪ Major credit cards accepted ▪ Corkage R150/bottle ▪ Owner Penny Streeter OBE ▪ Head chef Annie Badenhorst ▪ dine@benguelacove.co.za ▪ www.benguelacove.co.za ▪ **T +27 (0)87-357-0637**

Moody Lagoon is set in the heart of the Benguela Cove Lagoon Wine Estate. The restaurant has an elevated setting with expansive views of the lagoon and the Atlantic Ocean. Namibian-born chef Annie Badenhorst heads up the kitchen. She is a talented young woman with a passion for using only the best fresh produce. Badenhorst and her team create simple yet creative menu items. Guests can expect a choice of delicious dishes, paired with sensational Benguela Cove wines. (See also Nom Nom under Restaurants, Lakeside Lodge & Spa under Accommodation and Benguela Cove Lagoon Wine Estate in A-Z section.)

KUILS RIVER

Zevenwacht Restaurant Zevenwacht Wine Estate, Langverwacht Rd, Kuils River, Cape Town ▪ Contemporary country cuisine ▪ Breakfast Mon-Fri 7am-10am, Sat/Sun & pub hols 8am-11am, lunch 12pm-3pm & dinner 6pm-10pm daily ▪ Booking advised ▪ Children welcome ▪ Major credit cards accepted ▪ No BYO ▪ Executive chef Henna von Wielligh ▪ restaurant@zevenwacht.co.za ▪ www.zevenwacht.co.za ▪ **T +27 (0)21-900-5800** ▪ F +27 (0)21-903-5257

Decorated with finesse and charm, Zevenwacht Restaurant is located within a turn-of-the-19th century Cape Dutch manor house with views of a tranquil lake and park-like gardens. Open for breakfast, lunch and dinner seven days a week, the restaurant offers contemporary country cuisine, perfectly prepared, as well as a range of picnic baskets (including a braai basket) served on tree-shaded lawns sloping down to the lake. (See also Zevenwacht Country Inn under Accommodation and Zevenwacht in A-Z section.)

PAARL

Restaurant @ Glen Carlou Simondium Rd, Klapmuts ▪ South African contemporary cuisine ▪ Open Mon-Sun 12pm-4pm incl pub hols ▪ Closed 25 Dec, 1 Jan & Good Friday ▪ Booking advised ▪ Children welcome ▪ Major credit cards accepted ▪ Corkage R60/bottle ▪ Owner Pactolus Consortium ▪ Head chef Johan Stander ▪ restaurant@glencarlou.co.za ▪ www.glencarlou.co.za ▪ **T +27 (0)21-875-5528**

Consistency, expertise and a commitment to always deliver beyond expectations is what Glen Carlou strives for - not just with every bottle of wine but also every plate of food. Guests enjoy innovative dishes while taking in the breathtaking landscape from inside the architect-designed building or the shaded terrace deck. Chef Johan Stander uses the rhythm of the seasons, panoramic views and selection of awarded wines to produce a classic menu with a contemporary twist. (See also Glen Carlou in A-Z section.)

RIEBEEK-KASTEEL

The Royal Restaurant 33 Main Str, Riebeek-Kasteel ▪ Modern South African cuisine ▪ Open daily 7.30am-9.30pm ▪ Booking advised ▪ Children welcome ▪ BYO allowed ▪ Corkage R50 (wine), R75 (sparkling) ▪ Major credit cards & EFT accepted ▪ info@royalinriebeek.com ▪ www.royalinriebeek.com ▪ **T +27 (0)22-448-1378** ▪ F +27 (0)86-545-3559

'More than anything, food should satisfy.' Set in the oldest Hotel in the Cape, The Royal Restaurant uses the latest techniques and best produce, yet remains faithful to its rich heritage and diverse influences. Enjoy lunch or dinner imbued with the flavours of the Swartland and paired with some of the best wines from the region and beyond. Stroll down memory lane with a world-famous gin & tonic from the 150-year-old bar. Life doesn't get much better. 2017 Eat Out Top 500 Award. (See also The Royal Hotel under Accommodation.)

SOMERSET WEST

Nom Nom C/o Main Rd & Coronation Ave, Somerset West ▪ South African cuisine ▪ Open Mon-Sat 10am-8pm ▪ Closed Sun ▪ Children welcome ▪ Major credit cards accepted ▪ Corkage R150/bottle ▪ Owner Penny Streeter OBE ▪ Head chef Sebastian Smith ▪ nomnom@benguelacove.co.za ▪ www.nomnom.co.za ▪ **T +27 (0)21-851-6197**

Nom Nom is an everyday eatery with a modern menu that helps guests create their own experience. Choose between six different categories: Brunch, Nibbles, Bread, Light, Hungry or Sweets. The Petit Nom Nom menu caters for little ones. On offer is everything from snacks to full meals, coffee to cocktails, or simply enjoying Benguela Cove wines. Nom Nom is the perfect place for a quick brunch, work meeting or an after-work drink with friends at the Wine Bar upstairs. (See also Moody Lagoon under Restaurants, Lakeside Lodge & Spa under Accommodation and Benguela Cove Lagoon Wine Estate in A-Z section.)

The Restaurant at Waterkloof Waterkloof Estate, Sir Lowry's Pass Village Rd, Somerset West ▪ Classic French cuisine with a modern twist ▪ Open daily Mon-Sat 12pm-2pm & 7pm-9pm & Sun 12pm-2pm ▪ Closed Mon & Tue in winter ▪ Closed mid-Jun to mid-July, 25 Dec & 1 Jan ▪ Booking advised ▪

Major credit cards accepted ▪ No BYO ▪ Owner Paul Boutinot ▪ Executive chef Grégory Czarnecki ▪ restaurant@waterkloofwines.co.za ▪ www.waterkloofwines.co.za ▪ **T +27 (0)21-858-1491** ▪ F +27 (0)21-858-1293

High on the slopes of the Schapenberg, Waterkloof's 'restaurant in the sky' is stylishly appointed in a 10-meter-high, all-glass promontory flowing from a slick tasting lounge and gravitational cellar. Here chef Grégory Czarnecki, 2016 Eat Out San Pellegrino Chef of the Year, gives sophisticated contemporary classics a whimsical and polished edge. Showcasing confidence and immense skill, his dishes are not only consistently beautiful to look at, they also beg to be eaten. (See also Waterkloof in A-Z section.)

Vergelegen Vergelegen Wine Estate, Lourensford Rd, Somerset West ▪ **Camphors at Vergelegen** (à la carte/contemporary/global) lunch Wed-Sun 12pm-3pm, dinner Fri & Sat 6.30pm-9pm; **Stables at Vergelegen** (bistro) open Mon-Sun for breakfast 9am-11.30am, lunch 11.30am-3.30pm, tea/coffee & cakes 9am-4pm; **Picnic at Vergelegen** (luxury/elegant picnic) pre-booked baskets Nov-Apr 12.15pm-1.30pm ▪ Estate closed Good Friday, 1 May & 25 Dec ▪ Bookings essential ▪ Picnic & Stables specifically child friendly ▪ Major credit cards accepted ▪ No BYO ▪ Owners Anglo American plc ▪ info@vergelegen.co.za ▪ www.vergelegen.co.za ▪ Camphors Restaurant/Picnic at Vergelegen **T +27 (0)21-847-2131** ▪ Stables **T +27 (0)21-847-2156**

Experience the world of Vergelegen first-hand – from spectacular gardens to arts and culture, historic homestead and ancient camphor trees, winetasting and cellar tours, and restaurants to suit all tastes. The Camphors at Vergelegen signature restaurant, Stables at Vergelegen bistro restaurant and the seasonal luxury Picnic at Vergelegen are only a few of many enjoyable activities at Vergelegen. (See also Vergelegen in A-Z section.)

STANFORD

The Restaurant @ Misty Mountains R43 between Hermanus & Stanford ▪ Pizza & pasta ▪ Open Mon-Sun 10am-5pm ▪ Open pub hols ▪ Closed Christmas Day & New Year's Day ▪ Booking advised ▪ Children welcome ▪ Major credit cards accepted ▪ No BYO ▪ Owner André van Vuuren ▪ bookings@mistymountains.co.za ▪ www.mistymountains.co.za ▪ **T +27 (0)82-973-5943**

Set in the cellar, The Restaurant @ Misty Mountains Wine Estate offers authentic pizza and a few speciality items made from quality ingredients to tempt your taste buds. With a modern industrial design, the restaurant has renowned South African artist Bastiaan van Stenis' artwork showcased on the exposed brick walls. (See also Misty Mountains Self-catering under Accommodation and Misty Mountains Estate in A-Z section.)

STELLENBOSCH

Delaire Graff Restaurant Delaire Graff Estate, Helshoogte Pass, Stellenbosch ▪ Bistro-chic cuisine ▪ Open daily (times change according to the season) ▪ Booking advised ▪ Children welcome during lunch only ▪ Major credit cards accepted ▪ Corkage fee ▪ Owner Laurence Graff ▪ reservations@delaire.co.za ▪ www.delaire.co.za ▪ **T +27 (0)21-885-8160**

The dining experience here on the exquisite Delaire Graff Estate is an expression of the seasons, underpinned by the belief that the best food starts with the best ingredients. Classic bistro favourites are served with the finest South African touches, enriched by the restaurant's high-altitude location, affording unique views from the terrace of Simonsberg Mountain and its mantle of vines and olives, down into the steep-sloped Banhoek Valley. Inside, the David Collins Studio designed interiors include curving orange leather banquettes and handpicked art. (See also Indochine under Restaurants, Delaire Graff Lodges & Spa under Accommodation and Delaire Graff Estate in A-Z section.)

Eight Spier Wine Farm, R310, Baden Powell Rd, Stellenbosch ▪ Farm-to-table South African fare ▪ Open Thu-Tue (call ahead for opening hours) ▪ Closed for dinner in winter ▪ Booking advised ▪ Children welcome ▪ Major credit cards accepted ▪ No BYO ▪ eight@spier.co.za ▪ www.spier.co.za ▪ **T +27 (0)21-809-1188** ▪ F +27 (0)21-881-3087

Eight is Spier's farm-to-table eating experience. Like its name, the restaurant is an expression of balance, cycles, harmony, infinity and abundance. The produce used at Eight is either grown on the farm or sourced from nearby farmers. Natural and organic ingredients are preferred and combined to create nourishing, healthy and delicious food. (See also Spier Hotel under Accommodation and Spier in A-Z section.)

Flavours Restaurant The Devon Valley Hotel, Devon Valley Rd, Devon Valley, Stellenbosch ▪ Contemporary Cape cuisine ▪ Open daily 7am-10.30pm ▪ Booking advised ▪ Children welcome ▪ Major credit cards accepted ▪ Executive chef Markus Schwemberger ▪ Owner HS&V Hospitality ▪ info@devonvalleyhotel.com ▪ www.devonvalleyhotel.com ▪ **T +27 (0)21-865-2012**

Flavours Restaurant at the Devon Valley Hotel offers an elegant dining experience in a picturesque setting. With breakfast, lunch and dinner daily, the restaurant's focus is on contemporary Cape cuisine: classic dishes with bold flavours and fresh, clean tastes, perfectly paired with wines from an award-winning list. The Vineyard Terrace offers unique gourmet tasting pairings with SylvanVale wine, single malt Scotch whisky, craft beer and indigenous gin. (See also The Devon Valley Hotel under Accommodation and SylvanVale Vineyards in A-Z section.)

Guardian Peak Winery & Grill Guardian Peak Wines, Annandale Rd (off R44), Stellenbosch ▪ Grill house ▪ Open Mon-Sun 12pm-3.30pm, Wed-Sat 6pm-10pm ▪ Closed Good Friday, Easter Sunday, Christmas Day, New Year's Day ▪ Reservations advised ▪ Children welcome ▪ Major credit cards accepted ▪ No BYO ▪ Owner Jean Engelbrecht ▪ Executive chef Willie Mostert ▪ info@guardian-peak.com ▪ www.guardianpeak.com ▪ **T +27 (0)21-881-3899**

A relaxed Stellenbosch winelands experience with vineyard and mountain vistas, appreciated from a wide veranda and adjacent deck. Generous lunches and dinners, with focus on prime-quality beef and venison, enjoyed with Guardian Peak wines, as well as other family wine brands Stellenbosch Reserve, Donkiesbaai and Cirrus. (See also Rust en Vrede Restaurant (Dinner Only)/Winemaker's Lunch under Restaurants, and Guardian Peak Wines and Rust en Vrede Estate in A-Z section.)

Indochine Restaurant Delaire Graff Estate, Helshoogte Pass, Stellenbosch ▪ Asian-influenced cuisine ▪ Open daily for lunch 12pm-2.30pm & dinner 6.30pm-9pm ▪ Booking advised ▪ Children welcome ▪ Major credit cards accepted ▪ Corkage fee ▪ Owner Laurence Graff ▪ Head chef Virgil Kahn ▪ guest.relations@delaire.co.za ▪ www.delaire.co.za ▪ **T +27 (0)21-885-8160**

Indochine is more than a restaurant: it's a fine-dining food theatre, where delicate Asian-inspired flavours come alive and exquisitely balanced dishes are synonymous with vitality, wellness and healthy living. Discover tapas turned into an art form, experience a tea ceremony, savour signature dishes like pork belly and duck. You'll find that all elements are finely crafted to create a multi-sensory dining experience, including the intimate setting, featuring a calming blue and copper colour palette and stunning aerial art installation by Lionel Smit and André Stead, with over 1,000 swallows becoming part of the panoramic views stretching to Table Mountain. (See also Delaire Graff under Restaurants, Delaire Graff Lodges & Spa under Accommodation and Delaire Graff Estate in A-Z section.)

Jordan Restaurant Jordan Wine Estate, Stellenbosch Kloof Rd, Stellenbosch ▪ Continental cuisine ▪ Open for lunch Mon-Sun 12pm-2pm & dinner Thu, Fri & Sat 6.30pm-8pm (Nov-Apr) ▪ Closed Mon & Sat dinner (May-Oct) ▪ Open pub hols ▪ Booking advised ▪ No under 12s at dinner ▪ Major credit cards accepted ▪ BYO allowed if not on winelist (corkage R100, 1 bottle/table) ▪ Owners George & Louise Jardine ▪ Chefs George Jardine and Kyle Burn ▪ restaurant@jordanwines.com ▪ www.jordanwines.com ▪ **T +27 (0)21-881-3612**

Jordan Restaurant has been open for 8 years and continues to serve modern continental food in a relaxed outdoor setting. The menu changes daily according to the best seasonal produce available. (See also Jordan Luxury Suites under Accommodation and Jordan Wine Estate in A-Z section.)

Lanzerac Wine Estate – Dining No.1 Lanzerac Rd, Stellenbosch ▪ Culinary classics reimagined ▪ Open daily from 7am-midnight ▪ Booking advised ▪ Children welcome ▪ Corkage R80 ▪ Major credit cards accepted ▪ Executive chef Stephen Fraser ▪ fandb@lanzerac.co.za ▪ www.lanzerac.co.za ▪ **T +27 (0)21-887-1132** ▪ F +27 (0)21-887-2310

The Manor Kitchen, the main à la carte restaurant at Lanzerac, opens daily to welcome guests with contemporary and seasonal dishes, served with the estate's own award-winning wines. Generous buffet-style breakfasts, and appetising lunches and dinners are served daily on the estate, with al fresco meals offered on the outdoor terrace, overlooking the historic manor house. Light meals and platters are served at the Lanzerac Deli. (See also Lanzerac Wine Estate – Hotel under Accommodation and Lanzerac Wine Estate in A-Z section.)

Longtable Restaurant Haskell Vineyards, Annandale Rd, Lynedoch, Stellenbosch ▪ Continental small-plates menu ▪ Open Tue-Sun & pub hols 11:30am-6pm ▪ Closed Mon, Christmas Day & New Years' Day ▪ Booking advised ▪ Children welcome ▪ VISA, MasterCard & Diners Club accepted ▪ No BYO ▪ Owner Haskell Vineyards ▪ Head chef Charles N Joubert ▪ longtable@haskellvineyards.co.za ▪ www.haskellvineyards.com ▪ **T +27 (0)21-881-3746**

The culinary team on Haskell Vineyards estate has created the relaxing and convivial Longtable venue among the vines, where you can take time to savour unpretentious yet mouthwatering food and wine. The idea of a small-plates menu is to allow you to experience a kaleidoscope of flavours and sensations, and share these with fellow diners at your leisure. Each dish is a fitting match for the multi-award-winning Haskell and Dombeya wines. (See also The Residence at Haskell Vineyards under Accommodation and Haskell Vineyards in A-Z section.)

Rust en Vrede Restaurant (Dinner Only) Rust en Vrede Wine Estate, Annandale Rd (off R44), Stellenbosch ▪ Fine dining ▪ Tue-Sat 6.30pm till late ▪ Closed Good Friday, Christmas Day, New Year's Day ▪ Reservations essential ▪ Major credit cards accepted ▪ No BYO ▪ Owner Jean Engelbrecht ▪ Executive chef Fabio Daniel ▪ dining@rustenvrede.com ▪ www.rustenvrede.com ▪ **T +27 (0)21-881-3757**

Contemporary fine dining within Rust en Vrede Wine Estate's historic former cellar (also a national monument), where the front-and-centre kitchen, fine stemware and bespoke crockery enhance creative four- and six-course menus. A comprehensive winelist carries wide local and international selections, leaving little to be desired. (See also Guardian Peak Winery & Grill and Rust en Vrede Restaurant Winemaker's Lunch under Restaurants, and Guardian Peak Wines and Rust en Vrede Estate in A-Z section.)

Rust en Vrede Winemaker's Lunch Rust en Vrede Wine Estate, Annandale Road (off R44), Stellenbosch ▪ Set menu ▪ Mon-Sat 12pm-3pm, Sun seasonal - call to enquire ▪ Closed Good Friday, Easter Sunday, Christmas Day, New Year's Day ▪ No reservations; first come, first served ▪ Major credit cards accepted ▪ No BYO ▪ Owner Jean Engelbrecht ▪ Executive chef Rommel Rodriguez ▪ sales@rustenvrede.com ▪ www.rustenvrede.com ▪ **T +27 (0)21-881-3881**

Comprising a two-item set menu, salmon and steak, historic Stellenbosch estate Rust en Vrede's lunch experience is a no-fuss version of its celebrated fine-dining dinner. Tables set under ancient oaks suggest a laid-back approach, yet the linen is classily crisp and white, the cookery flawless and the service impeccable. Enjoy your choice of meal with a glass of red or white. (See also Guardian Peak Winery & Grill and Rust en Vrede Restaurant (Dinner Only) under Restaurants, and Guardian Peak Wines and Rust en Vrede Estate in A-Z section.)

The Restaurant at Neethlingshof Neethlingshof Wine Estate, Polkadraai Rd, Stellenbosch ▪ Contemporary bistro-style South African cuisine & light meals ▪ Open Mon, Tue & Thu 9am-5pm; Wed, Fri & Sat 9am-9pm; Sun 12pm-4pm ▪ Open pub hols & Christmas lunch ▪ Closed Christmas Eve & Good Friday ▪ Booking advised ▪ Children welcome ▪ Major credit cards accepted ▪ No BYO except for bubbly (R55 per bottle corkage) ▪ Owner Stone Pine Wines (Pty) Ltd ▪ Head chef Brendan Stein ▪ restaurant@neethlingshof.co.za ▪ www.neethlingshof.co.za ▪ **T +27 (0)21-883-8966 / +27 (0)81-353-2039**

The Restaurant at Neethlingshof Wine Estate is situated in the original manor house, built in 1814. The history-steeped setting, complete with ancient oaks, is mirrored in the menu, with its emphasis on long-time-favourite South African ingredients and dishes, presented bistro-style with contemporary touches. Springbok shank, ostrich fillet, grilled miso aubergine and gourmet burgers are among the choices, served (weather permitting) on the terrace with vistas of manicured gardens, vineyards and mountains. The Restaurant proudly supports StreetSmart SA. (See also Neethlingshof Estate in A-Z section.)

Warwick Wine Estate - Gourmet Picnics Warwick Wine Estate, R44 between Stellenbosch & Paarl ▪ Gourmet picnics ▪ Open Mon-Sun 9am-5pm ▪ Booking advised ▪ Children welcome ▪ Major credit cards accepted ▪ No BYO ▪ Owners Mike & Norma Ratcliffe ▪ Executive chef Shaun Dampies ▪ visit@warwickwine.com ▪ www.warwickwine.com ▪ **T +27 (0)21-884-4410**

Warwick has a well-deserved reputation for its gourmet picnics. Executive chef Shaun Dampies combines the highest-quality ingredients from locally sourced artisan suppliers. The delicious picnics are perfect for that special occasion or just a lazy day out in wine country. Gourmands rave about the picnics and keep coming back — you will too. For families, there are delicious children's picnics designed by parents who 'get it'. (See also Warwick Estate in A-Z section.)

TULBAGH

Readers Restaurant 12 Church Str, Tulbagh ▪ Global contemporary, fusion of flavours ▪ Open Wed-Mon 9am-9.30pm ▪ Closed Tue ▪ Booking advised ▪ Children welcome ▪ Major credit cards, SnapScan & Zapper accepted (no Amex) ▪ Corkage R30 ▪ Owner Carol Collins ▪ readers@iafrica.com ▪ www.readersrestaurant.co.za ▪ **T +27 (0)23-230-0087 / +27 (0)82-894-0932**

Built in 1754, the oldest house on Tulbagh's colourful Church Street was revitalised in 1997 as this charming restaurant under Silwood-trained chef Carol Collins. Since then Carol has maintained her excellent reputation for 'home-cooked meals with a difference', from game steak served with gooseberry and Amarula sauce, to homemade ice cream in unusual flavours. The menu changes daily depending on the availability of fresh produce. Food-and-wine pairing dinners can be arranged, as well as murder mystery dinners and theme evenings. Order a picnic basket to enjoy after tasting wine at a venue of your choice. (See also Wittedrift Manor House under Accommodation.)

WORCESTER

Nuy On The Hill Nuy Winery, R60 between Worcester & Robertson, 6858 Nuy, Western Cape ▪ Al fresco style ▪ Mon-Fri 9am-5pm, Sat & Sun 9am-4pm; kitchen closes 4pm daily ▪ Closed Good Friday, 25 Dec & 1 Jan ▪ Booking advised ▪ Functions & weddings catered for ▪ Children welcome ▪ No BYO ▪ Major credit cards (except Amex) & Zapper accepted ▪ Wheelchair friendly ▪ Deli ▪ Playground ▪ Pet-friendly outside area ▪ Owners Danette Thompson & Wilna van der Westhuizen ▪ Executive chef Wilna van der Westhuizen ▪ onthehill@nuywinery.co.za ▪ www.nuywinery.co.za ▪ **T +27 (0)23-347-0272** ▪ F +27 (0)86-520-1782

Overlooking mountains and vines, Nuy On The Hill offers al fresco style dining with jaw-dropping views. The menu ranges from pizzas, burgers and gourmet milkshakes to perennial favourites like roosterkoek and gemmerbier (griddle bread and ginger beer). A traditional cake table is available daily. Other child- and wheelchair-friendly amenities include craft beer and winetasting. (See also Nuy Winery in A-Z section.)

Accommodation in the Winelands and Cape Town

Featured below are some guest lodges, hotels, country inns, B&Bs and self-catering cottages in the winelands, many of them on wine farms (look for the ⓐ symbol beside the individual entries in the A–Z section of this guide). These are paid entries. The venues supplied information on their facilities and attractions, which was then edited for consistency of style. Unless stated to the contrary, all speak English and Afrikaans, have parking and gardens/terraces. Rates are for standard double rooms unless otherwise specified – for example per person (pp) or breakfast included (B&B). Tourism Grading Council of South Africa (TGCSA) ratings where provided. Should you wish to know about wheelchair access, please discuss with the relevant venue.

INDEX OF ACCOMMODATION

Delaire Graff Lodges & Spa	Stellenbosch
Hemel-en-Aarde Village Acc	Hermanus
Jordan Luxury Suites	Stellenbosch
Laibach Vineyards Lodge	Stellenbosch
Lakeside Lodge & Spa	Sedgefield
Lanzerac Wine Estate – Hotel	Stellenbosch
La Petite Ferme	Franschhoek
Leeu Estates	Franschhoek
Leeu House	Franschhoek
Le Quartier Français	Franschhoek
Lily Pond House	Franschhoek
Misty Mountains Self-catering	Stanford
South Hill Vineyards	Elgin
Spier Hotel	Stellenbosch
The Devon Valley Hotel	Stellenbosch
The Franschhoek Cellar	Franschhoek
The Homestead at Oldenburg	Stellenbosch
The Residence at Haskell Vineyards	Stellenbosch
The Retreat at Groenfontein	Calitzdorp
The Royal Hotel	Riebeek-Kasteel
The Twelve Apostles Hotel	Camps Bay
Wittedrift Manor House	Tulbagh
Zevenwacht Country Inn	Kuils River

CALITZDORP

The Retreat at Groenfontein Groenfontein Rd, district Calitzdorp (20km from Calitzdorp, off Route 62) ▪ TGCSA 3 & 4-star guest house; AA Quality Assured highly recommended ▪ Rates on request ▪ VISA & MasterCard accepted ▪ Restaurant (problem diets catered for - advise when booking) ▪ Pool ▪ Children & pets welcome ▪ Mountain biking ▪ Walking trails ▪ Birding ▪ River with rock pools ▪ Secure parking ▪ Laundry service ▪ Safe ▪ Wifi in lounge ▪ French, German, Italian & Swedish spoken ▪ Owner Marie Holstensson ▪ info@groenfontein.com ▪ www.groenfontein.com ▪ **T +27 (0)44-213-3880** ▪ F +27 (0)86-271-5373

A consistent award winner, this welcoming, personally run, 3- and 4-star Victorian farmhouse offers both standard and garden rooms. You'll enjoy personal pampering, hearty breakfasts and tasty dinners. The inviting lounge and dining room overlook sweeping lawns and the majestic Swartberg. Take leisurely walks, challenging trails, explore the rock pools in the river, bird-watch or simply laze at the pool, soaking up the peace and silence.

CAMPS BAY

The Twelve Apostles Hotel & Spa Victoria Rd, Camps Bay, Cape Town ▪ TGCSA 5-star hotel ▪ 70 rooms ▪ Best available seasonal rates B&B ▪ Major credit cards accepted ▪ Azure and Café Grill Restaurants ▪ Conferences ▪ Weddings/functions ▪ Spa ▪ Gym ▪ Hydrotherapy pools ▪ Walks/hikes ▪ Birding ▪ Wine, gin & craft beer tasting ▪ Secure parking ▪ Shuttle service ▪ Laundry service ▪ Air-conditioning ▪ TV ▪ DStv ▪ DVD player ▪ Wifi ▪ Safe ▪ French, Mandarin & Dutch spoken ▪ Owners Tollman family/Red Carnation Hotels ▪ reservations1@12apostles.co.za ▪ www.12apostleshotel.com ▪ **T +27 (0)21-437-9000** ▪ F +27 (0)21-437-9062

Award-winning Twelve Apostles Hotel & Spa is situated on Cape Town's most scenic route, flanking Table Mountain National Park and overlooking the Atlantic Ocean. Part of the family-run Red Carnation Hotel Collection, it offers 55 deluxe guest rooms and 15 luxurious suites, not to mention a holistic spa and private cinema, with Azure Restaurant serving up breathtaking views in addition to legendary local cuisine. (See also Azure under Restaurants.)

ELGIN

South Hill Vineyards 113 Valley Rd, Elgin ▪ TGCSA 4-star self-catering (Exclusive Category) ▪ Rates from R1,210 per room B&B, exclusive use of the Guest House (6 rooms, self-catering) from R6,070 per night, Pumphouse Cottage (sleeps 2) from R1,570 per night B&B ▪ Major credit cards accepted ▪ Restaurant ▪ Conferences ▪ Weddings/functions ▪ Jacuzzi (Pumphouse Cottage) ▪ Pool (Guest House) ▪ Fireplace ▪ Mountain biking ▪ Walks/hikes ▪ Birding ▪ Fishing ▪ Boule court ▪ Winetasting ▪ TV (Guest House) ▪ DStv ▪ Wifi ▪ stay@southhill.co.za ▪ www.southhill.co.za ▪ **T +27 (0)21-844-0888**

South Hill Guest House is a six-bedroom, en suite luxury villa with full guest amenities. Rooms have vineyard, orchard or garden views, with mountain ranges in the distance. The secluded, self-contained Pumphouse Cottage has a private courtyard, overlooks one of the farm dams and is surrounded by indigenous fynbos gardens and vineyards. Whether you are visiting for a wedding, weekend, holiday or just a complete chill-out in the week, South Hill has much to offer! (See also South Hill Vineyards under Restaurants and in A-Z section.)

FRANSCHHOEK

La Petite Ferme Pass Road, Franschhoek ▪ TGCSA 4-star boutique hotel ▪ 9 rooms ▪ Rates from R3,465-R8,717 per room ▪ Breakfast included ▪ Major credit cards accepted ▪ Restaurant ▪ Cellar tours ▪ Winetasting ▪ Secure parking ▪ Air-conditioning ▪ Ceiling fans ▪ Fireplace ▪ Under-floor heating ▪ Safe ▪ TV ▪ DStv ▪ Wifi ▪ Some rooms have plunge pools ▪ Owners The Nest Estate ▪ accommodation@lapetiteferme.co.za ▪ www.lapetiteferme.co.za ▪ **T +27 (0)21-876-3016**

La Petite Ferme Boutique Hotel & Winery offers the perfect combination of private, traditional country-style accommodation, luxury amenities and heart-warming hospitality. Situated on the Oliphants Pass high on the Middagkrans Mountain slopes, the Manor House and Vineyard Suites each have all the creature comforts you'd expect plus spectacular views of Franschhoek Valley – a picture-perfect paradise in which to relax. (See also The Restaurant at La Petite Ferme under Restaurants and La Petite Ferme Winery in A-Z section.)

Leeu Estates Dassenberg Rd, Franschhoek ▪ TGCSA 5-star boutique hotel ▪ 17 rooms ▪ Rates from R8,827 per room per night ▪ Breakfast included ▪ All major credit cards accepted ▪ 1 hour from Cape Town ▪ Restaurant ▪ Spa ▪ Gym ▪ Swimming pool ▪ Walks/hikes ▪ Winetasting ▪ Shuttle service ▪ Secure parking ▪ Laundry service ▪ Fully air-conditioned ▪ Ceiling fans & fireplaces (selected rooms) ▪ Under-floor heating ▪ TV ▪ DStv ▪ Safe ▪ Wifi ▪ Owner Leeu Collection ▪ reservations@leeucollection.com ▪ www.leeucollection.com ▪ **T +27 (0)21-492-2222**

One of three properties in Leeu Collection Franschhoek, Leeu Estates is an exclusive boutique hotel and winery in scenic Franschhoek Valley, just an hour from Cape Town. The focal point of this elegant and sophisticated private hideaway is the refurbished 19th-century manor house with its six guest rooms, dining room, reading room and living room. Adjacent is Leeu Spa & Gym, plus five spacious cottages scattered among gardens, oak trees and vineyards. (See also Tuk Tuk Microbrewery/Marigold under Restaurants, and Leeu House/Le Quartier Français in Accommodation section.)

Leeu House 12 Huguenot Str, Franschhoek ▪ TGCSA 5-star boutique hotel ▪ 12 rooms ▪ Rates from R7,061 per room per night ▪ Breakfast included ▪ All major credit cards accepted ▪ 1 hour from Cape Town ▪ Restaurant ▪ Swimming pool ▪ Winetasting ▪ Shuttle service ▪ Secure parking ▪ Laundry service ▪ Fully air-conditioned ▪ Ceiling fans (selected rooms) ▪ Under-floor heating ▪ TV ▪ DStv ▪ Safe ▪ Wifi ▪ Owners Leeu Collection ▪ reservations@leeucollection.com ▪ www.leeucollection.com ▪ **T +27 (0)21-492-2221**

Leeu House is an oasis of tranquillity and comfort in the heart of Franschhoek, one of the world's great food and wine destinations, a mere hour from Cape

Town. Leeu House's special appeal is its country ambience despite being located on the village's vibrant main street, very near award-winning restaurants, art galleries and boutiques. The House's stylish interiors are a contemporary take on Franschhoek's Cape Dutch heritage, with its strong French influences. (See also Tuk Tuk Microbrewery/Marigold under Restaurants, and Leeu Estates/Le Quartier Français in Accommodation section.)

Le Quartier Français 16 Huguenot Str, Franschhoek ▪ TGCSA 5-star ▪ 32 rooms ▪ Rates from R7,616 per room per night ▪ All major credit cards accepted ▪ 1 hour from Cape Town ▪ Restaurant ▪ Spa ▪ Gym ▪ Swimming pool ▪ Winetasting ▪ Shuttle service ▪ Laundry service ▪ Fully air-conditioned ▪ Ceiling fans & fireplaces (selected rooms) ▪ Under-floor heating ▪ TV ▪ DStv ▪ Safe ▪ Wifi ▪ Owner Leeu Collection ▪ reservations@leeucollection.com ▪ www.leeucollection.com ▪ T +27 (0)21-492-2222

Tucked away in the heart of Franschhoek, just an hour from Cape Town, Le Quartier Français is an exclusive and romantic 32-room boutique hotel with two separate villas, revered culinary landmark and member of Leeu Collection. This peaceful auberge's ideal location makes it easy to wander out from its scented gardens to explore the quaint charms of the village and the wonders of the winelands beyond. (See also Tuk Tuk Microbrewery/Marigold under Restaurants, and Leeu House/Leeu Estates in Accommodation section.)

Lily Pond House Le Lude Méthode Cap Classique, Bowling Green Ave (Lambrechts Rd), Franschhoek ▪ Luxury guest villa ▪ Two en suite rooms ▪ Rates from R4,660 per night ▪ Major credit cards accepted ▪ Restaurant ▪ Pool ▪ Cellar tours ▪ Méthode cap classique tasting ▪ Fully air-conditioned ▪ Under-floor heating ▪ Secure parking ▪ Fully equipped kitchen ▪ Braai area ▪ TV ▪ DStv ▪ Safe ▪ Wifi ▪ Owners Nic & Ferda Barrow ▪ info@lelude.co.za ▪ www.lelude.co.za ▪ T +27 (0)21-100-3464

Your own private cottage with 5-star luxury is situated between vineyards and lily ponds. The Lily Pond House is fully equipped, with a modern kitchen, dining/sitting room, private pool and sheltered braai area. Maximum of 4 persons. (See also Orangerie @ Le Lude under Restaurants and Le Lude Méthode Cap Classique in A-Z section.)

The Franschhoek Cellar – Rose & Protea Cottages The Franschhoek Cellar, R45, Franschhoek Main Rd, Franschhoek ▪ 2 cottages sleeping 4 pax per cottage ▪ R2,000-R2,500 per cottage ▪ VISA & MasterCard accepted ▪ Restaurant ▪ Conference facilities ▪ Weddings/functions ▪ Winetasting ▪ Secure parking ▪ Air-conditioning ▪ Fireplace ▪ Safe ▪ TV ▪ DStv ▪ Wifi ▪ accommodation@thefranschhoekcellar.co.za ▪ www.thefranschhoekcellar.co.za ▪ T +27 (0)21-876-2086

Ideal for winelovers wanting to be close to the action, Rose and Protea cottages are situated beside the production cellar on the premises in the heart of Franschhoek. Both cottages have been remodelled to match the contemporary-chic styling of the visitor venue, which is also on the property. The self-catering homes each sleep four adults and have been fitted with all modern conveniences to ensure you have a relaxing stay in one of South Africa's food capitals. (See also The Franschhoek Cellar Restaurant under Restaurants and Franschhoek Cellar in A-Z section.)

HERMANUS
Hemel-en-Aarde Village

Accommodation 19 Village Lane, Hemel-en-Aarde Village, Hermanus ▪ TGCSA 4-star self-catering ▪ Rates from R600-R1,250 per night ▪ Major credit cards accepted ▪ TV ▪ DStv ▪ Wifi ▪ Safe ▪ Owner Christine Henderson ▪ christine@hemelenaardeaccommodation.co.za ▪ www.hemelenaardeaccommodation.co.za ▪ T +27 (0)82-922-3815

An easy drive from Cape Town, these four exclusive self-catering rooms offer peace, quiet, supreme comfort and proximity to the seaside town of Hermanus, the internationally reputed Hemel-en-Aarde wine valley as well as three spectacular Blue Flag beaches, playgrounds of migrating Southern Right whales. Within walking distance of all Hemel-en-Aarde Village facilities, including restaurants, jewellery manufacturers, art galleries, wine shop, wineries, beauty and hair salons, and one of the busiest markets in the area. Newly completed Whale Coast Mall is ten minutes away on foot.

KUILS RIVER

Zevenwacht Country Inn Zevenwacht Wine Estate, Langverwacht Rd, Kuils River ▪ TGCSA 4-star country house (Country Inn honeymoon and luxury suites only) ▪ Total 38 rooms: 1 honeymoon suite (deluxe), 12 Country Inn luxury suites, 7 x 3-bedroom cottages, 1 x 4-bedroom self-catering chalet ▪ Low season from R825 pps B&B, high season from R1,040 pps B&B ▪ Major credit cards accepted ▪ Restaurant ▪ Conferences ▪ Weddings/functions ▪ Spa ▪ Sauna ▪ Pool ▪ Tennis court ▪ Mountain biking ▪ Walks/hikes ▪ Birding ▪ Cellar tours ▪ Winetasting ▪ Secure parking ▪ Shuttle service ▪ Laundry service ▪ Air-conditioning ▪ TV ▪ DStv ▪ Wifi ▪ Safe ▪ Owners Harold & Denise Johnson ▪ reservations@zevenwacht.co.za ▪ www.

zevenwacht.co.za ▪ **T +27 (0)21-900-5700** ▪ F +27 (0)21-906-1570

Meaning 'Seven Expectations', the name Zevenwacht encapsulates several delights that await visitors at this historic estate. Choose between the Country Inn, offering four-star accommodation in luxuriously appointed, air-conditioned suites; three-bedroom Vineyard Cottages; or self-catering four-bedroom chalet. (See also Zevenwacht Restaurant under Restaurants and Zevenwacht in A-Z section.)

RIEBEEK-KASTEEL

The Royal Hotel 33 Main Str, Riebeek-Kasteel ▪ AA Superior Hotel ▪ 1 Grand Garden room: low season (16 May-30 Sep) R995pp-R1,990pp, high season (1 Oct-15 May) R1,295 pp-R2,590 B&B; 9 Standard rooms: low season from R845-R1,690 pps B&B, high season R1,095 pp-R2,190 B&B; 4 King suites: low season R1,495 pp-R2,990, high season R1,995 pp-R3,990 B&B ▪ Major credit cards & EFT accepted ▪ The Royal Restaurant ▪ Conferences ▪ Weddings/functions ▪ Pool ▪ Laundry service ▪ Air-conditioning ▪ Under-floor heating ▪ Safe ▪ TV ▪ DStv ▪ DVD player ▪ Free wifi ▪ Owner Robert Brendel ▪ info@royalinriebeek.com ▪ www.royalinriebeek.com ▪ **T +27 (0)22-448-1378** ▪ F +27 (0)86-545-3559

Located in Riebeek-Kasteel, the Royal Hotel is the Western Cape's oldest and most colonial hotel. It offers beautiful and luxurious accommodation with great valley and Kasteelberg views from the garden, swimming pool and pool deck. Listed in 2006 among the government's 50 most fabulous places to visit in South Africa, the hotel boasts a 150-year-old bar and the longest stoep south of the Limpopo. (See also The Royal Restaurant under Restaurants.)

SEDGEFIELD

Lakeside Lodge & Spa 3 Lakeside Dr, Swartrivier, Sedgefield ▪ TGCSA 5-star boutique hotel ▪ Rates on request ▪ 9 bedroom suites ▪ VISA & MasterCard accepted ▪ Benguela Brasserie & Restaurant ▪ Weddings/functions ▪ Spa ▪ Pool ▪ Jacuzzi ▪ Children welcome ▪ Walks/hikes ▪ Birding ▪ Fishing ▪ Winetasting ▪ Secure parking ▪ Pontoon cruises ▪ Air-conditioning ▪ In-room safe ▪ DStv ▪ iPod docking station ▪ Wifi ▪ 2016 Sanlam Top Destination and 2017 LTG Africa & Middle East awards ▪ Owner Penny Streeter OBE ▪ info@lakesidelodge.co.za ▪ www.lakesidelodge.co.za ▪ **T +27 (0)44-343-1844**

Lakeside Lodge & Spa is a 5-star boutique hotel with the highest rating from the TGCSA (Tourism Grading Council of South Africa). The lodge has nine luxurious bedroom suites, all with breathtaking views of the Swartvlei Lagoon. Guests can look forward to divine food at the Benguela Brasserie whilst overlooking the lakeside setting. Breakfast, lunch or dinner - Benguela Brasserie & Restaurant is the perfect choice! (See also Moody Lagoon and Nom Nom under Restaurants and Benguela Cove Lagoon Wine Estate in A-Z section.)

STANFORD

Misty Mountains Self-catering Accommodation R43 between Hermanus & Stanford ▪ 4 self-catering cottages ▪ Rates from R750-R900 per night ▪ VISA & MasterCard accepted ▪ Restaurant ▪ Weddings/functions ▪ Children welcome ▪ Walks/hikes ▪ Cellar tours ▪ Winetasting ▪ Secure parking ▪ Ceiling fans ▪ Fireplace ▪ Owner Misty Mountains Estate ▪ bookings@mistymountains.co.za ▪ www.mistymountains.co.za ▪ **T +27 (0)82-973-5943**

Tranquil, modern, comfortable and set in pristine natural beauty, Misty Mountains Wine Estate offers four newly renovated self-catering cottages with breathtaking views of Hermanus Lagoon. All bedrooms are furnished with luxurious and spacious beds to whisk you away into pleasant dreams. En-suite bathrooms are fully equipped with beautifully finished and spacious showers, soft white towels and abundant natural light. Kitchens are extensively stocked to satisfy the needs of every chef, cook or avid food lover, including an outside BBQ facility that would bring a tear to any braai aficionado. (See also The Restaurant @ Misty Mountains under Restaurants and Misty Mountains Estate in A-Z section.)

STELLENBOSCH

Delaire Graff Lodges & Spa Helshoogte Pass, Stellenbosch ▪ Villa, Owners, Presidential, Superior, Luxury & Deluxe lodges ▪ Rates from R7,275 pps ▪ Breakfast included ▪ VISA, MasterCard & international money transfer accepted ▪ Delaire Graff & Indochine restaurants ▪ Weddings/functions ▪ Spa ▪ Sauna ▪ Gym ▪ Pool ▪ Jacuzzi ▪ Mountain biking ▪ Walks/hikes ▪ Cellar tours ▪ Winetasting ▪ Secure parking ▪ Shuttle service ▪ Air-conditioning ▪ Fireplace ▪ Under-floor heating ▪ Safe ▪ TV ▪ DStv ▪ DVD player ▪ iPod docking station ▪ Wifi ▪ Condé Nast Traveller Gold List - Top 20 Best Hotels in the World (Feb 2018) ▪ guest.relations@delaire.co.za, lodge.reservations@delaire.co.za ▪ www.delaire.co.za ▪ **T +27 (0)21-885-8160**

Nestled between majestic mountains, Delaire Graff Estate is a unique destination offering exceptional experiences. A magnificent Cape winelands property, it boasts two outstanding restaurants, a state-of-the-art winery and wine lounge, exclusive lodges, a destination spa and luxury boutiques. Designed by master craftsmen, with walls adorned with inspirational works of art, the estate captivates and enchants you from the moment you arrive. (See also Delaire Graff Restaurant and Indochine under Restaurants and Delaire Graff Estate in A-Z section.)

Jordan Luxury Suites Jordan Wine Estate, Stellenbosch Kloof Rd, Stellenbosch ▪ Klink Award best accommodation on a wine estate ▪ 13 rooms ▪ Rates on request (breakfast included) ▪ Major credit cards accepted ▪ Restaurant ▪ Conference facilities ▪ Weddings/functions ▪ Cellar tours ▪ Winetasting ▪ Secure parking ▪ Laundry service ▪ Air-conditioning ▪ Fireplace ▪ Safe ▪ TV ▪ DStv ▪ Wifi ▪ English & Afrikaans spoken ▪ Owners Jordan family ▪ accommodation@jordanwines.com ▪ www.jordanwines. com ▪ **T +27 (0)21-881-3048**

Tucked away close to the wine cellar, restaurant and bakery, the new luxury suites on Jordan Wine Estate offer panoramic views of the vineyards and Stellenbosch mountains. Each suite has spacious interiors that are individually designed and uniquely decorated, making Jordan Luxury Suites an ideal choice for a perfect winelands getaway. (See also Jordan Restaurant under Restaurants and Jordan Wine Estate in A-Z section.)

Laibach Vineyards Lodge Laibach Vineyards, R44, Klapmuts Rd, Stellenbosch ▪ TGCSA 4-star self-catering apartments ▪ 5 apartments ▪ R800 pps, single R1,350 ▪ Major credit cards accepted ▪ Pool ▪ Walks/hikes ▪ Winetasting ▪ Secure parking ▪ Ceiling fans ▪ TV ▪ DStv ▪ Wifi ▪ Safe ▪ Owners Laibach family from Germany ▪ info@laibachwines.com ▪ www. laibachwines.com ▪ **T +27 (0)21-884-4511** ▪ F +27 (0)86-665-2839

Laibach Vineyards invites you to its lodge in the middle of a sea of organic vines. At this 50-hectare working wine farm, just a few kilometres north of Stellenbosch, five spacious and comfortable self-catering apartments are offered, each with a private en suite bathroom, small but fully furnished kitchen, LCD satellite TV and wifi, and deck with magnificent Table Mountain views. (See also Laibach Vineyards in A-Z section.)

Lanzerac Wine Estate – Hotel No.1 Lanzerac Rd, Stellenbosch ▪ TGCSA 5-star boutique hotel ▪ 53 rooms & suites ▪ Seasonal rates on request ▪ Major credit cards accepted ▪ Main restaurant & casual deli ▪ Conferences ▪ Weddings/functions ▪ Day spa ▪ Sauna ▪ Gym ▪ Pool ▪ Jacuzzi ▪ Helipad ▪ Horse riding ▪ Mountain biking ▪ Walks/hikes ▪ Birding ▪ Cellar tours ▪ Winetasting on-site ▪ Secure parking ▪ Shuttle service ▪ Laundry service ▪ Air-conditioning ▪ Under-floor heating ▪ TV ▪ DStv ▪ Wifi ▪ In-room tea & coffee facilities ▪ Safe ▪ info@lanzerac.co.za ▪ www.lanzerac.co.za ▪ **T +27 (0)21-887-1132** ▪ F +27 (0)21-887-2310

Steeped in history, and nestled in Stellenbosch's idyllic Jonkershoek Valley, 327-year-old Lanzerac is synonymous with Old World charm and rich Cape heritage. Staying in exquisitely styled rooms and suites, blending period grandeur with contemporary style, guests are indulged with warm and passionate service, and the best wine and cuisine – in short, the finest hospitality the Cape winelands has to offer. (See also Lanzerac Wine Estate - Dining under Restaurants and Lanzerac Wine Estate in A-Z section.)

Spier Hotel R310, Baden Powell Rd, Stellenbosch ▪ 4-star hotel ▪ 153 rooms ▪ From R2,020 per room B&B ▪ Major credit cards accepted ▪ Eight restaurant ▪ Conferences ▪ Weddings/functions ▪ Spa ▪ Pool ▪ Mountain biking ▪ Walks/hikes ▪ Segway tours, Eagle Encounters & self-guided VoiceMap walks ▪ Birding ▪ Winetasting ▪ Secure parking ▪ Shuttle service ▪ Laundry service ▪ Air-conditioning ▪ Ceiling fans ▪ TV ▪ DStv ▪ Wifi ▪ Safe ▪ TripAdvisor Hall of Fame ▪ Dutch & French spoken ▪ Hoghouse Bakery & Café ▪ Spier Shop ▪ info@spier.co.za ▪ www.spier.co.za ▪ **T +27 (0)21-809-1100** ▪ F +27 (0)21-881-3087

Village-style buildings, lush green lawns and spacious rooms beside the calming Eerste River are the defining characteristics of the 4-star Spier Hotel. The rooms are clustered around six courtyards, each with its own swimming pool. The design is reminiscent of the Bo-Kaap or Mediterranean villages where pedestrians have right of way. The hotel is situated on the historic Spier wine farm in the heart of the Stellenbosch winelands, just 20 minutes from Cape Town International Airport. (See also Eight under Restaurants and Spier in A-Z section.)

The Devon Valley Hotel Devon Valley Rd, Devon Valley, Stellenbosch ▪ TGCSA 4-star hotel ▪ 50 suites ▪ Seasonal rates from R1,250-R1,600 pps B&B ▪ Major credit cards accepted ▪ Flavours Restaurant ▪ Conferences ▪ Weddings/functions ▪ 2 pools ▪ Mountain biking ▪ Walks/hikes ▪ Birding ▪ Boule court ▪ Winetasting ▪ Secure parking ▪ Shuttle service ▪ Laundry service ▪ Air-conditioning ▪ Fireplaces (some) ▪ TV ▪ DStv & DVD player ▪ Free wifi ▪ Safe ▪ German spoken ▪ Owner HS&V Hospitality ▪ info@

devonvalleyhotel.com ▪ www.devonvalleyhotel.com ▪ T +27 (0)21-865-2012

The award-winning Devon Valley Hotel is hidden away in a shady, green and peaceful corner of the Stellenbosch winelands. Nestling among its own SylvanVale vineyards, the hotel showcases breathtaking views of olive groves, vineyards and majestic Helderberg mountains while offering the finest in authentic handmade hospitality. The hotel offers 50 stylishly furnished bedrooms and six air-conditioned conference venues with an abundance of natural light. (See also Flavours Restaurant under Restaurants and SylvanVale Vineyards in A-Z section.)

The Homestead at Oldenburg Vineyards

Zevenrivieren Rd, Banghoek, Stellenbosch ▪ Guest villa sleeping max 12 pax ▪ Rates from R24,530-R41,030 (breakfast included) ▪ Guests staying min 3 nights treated to signature SA braai or 3-course dinner (included in rate) ▪ 6 bedrooms ▪ Major credit cards accepted ▪ Gym ▪ Pool ▪ Mobile spa (extra cost) ▪ Mountain biking (extra cost for hiring bikes) ▪ Walks/hikes ▪ Birding ▪ Cellar tours ▪ Winetasting ▪ Secure parking ▪ Shuttle service available (extra cost) ▪ Laundry service ▪ Safe ▪ Air-conditioning ▪ Fireplace in common areas ▪ Under-floor heating in bathrooms ▪ TV ▪ DStv ▪ Wifi ▪ homestead@oldenburgvineyards.com ▪ www.oldenburgvineyards.com ▪ T +27 (0)87-095-1139 / +27 (0)21-885-1618

Spacious and elegantly proportioned, the 200-year-old Oldenburg homestead has been meticulously restored and modernised to create a seamless flow of indoor and outdoor spaces for relaxed family living and sophisticated entertaining. Sleeping up to 12 in six bedrooms, this luxury guest villa is well suited to a multi-generational family, party of friends or corporate team in need of a discreet setting for high-powered meetings. Fringed by a well-established garden, olive groves and vineyards, the two-level house has deep verandas, large swimming pool and glass-walled gym from which to appreciate the dramatic Groot Drakenstein mountains. It comes with resident manager/butler/concierge and two housekeepers; additional staff can be arranged. (See also Oldenburg Vineyards in A-Z section.)

The Residence at Haskell Vineyards

Annandale Rd, Lynedoch, Stellenbosch ▪ Luxury country house ▪ Rates from R1,500-R3,700 per night ▪ 2-bedroom house & 1-bedroom cottage ▪ Major cards, EFT & cash accepted ▪ Restaurant ▪ Conference facilities ▪ Weddings/functions ▪ Children welcome ▪ Walks/hikes ▪ Winetasting ▪ Secure parking ▪ Laundry service ▪ Safe ▪ Air-conditioning ▪ Fireplace ▪ TV ▪ DStv ▪ Wifi ▪ German spoken ▪ Owner Haskell Vineyards ▪ theresidence@haskellvineyards.co.za ▪ www.haskellvineyards.com ▪ T +27 (0)21-881-3895

The Residence and the Cottage are set in the foothills of Helderberg Mountain, within 9 km of De Zalze Golf Estate. Secluded and fringed by vines, both homes offer tranquillity and stunning mountain views. The historic town of Stellenbosch is a 15-minute drive, and the surrounding countryside offers nature lovers outstanding hiking and walking opportunities in a beautiful part of South Africa. (See also Longtable Restaurant under Restaurants and Haskell Vineyards in A-Z section.)

TULBAGH

Wittedrift Manor House 5 Vos Str, Tulbagh ▪ 6-bedroomed Manor House (communal self-catering facilities; can sleep up to 15) ▪ Garden cottages ▪ Seasonal rates from R1,000 to R2,000 per room/cottage ▪ Nearby restaurants ▪ Conferences ▪ Weddings/functions ▪ Pool ▪ Secure parking ▪ Laundry service ▪ TV, DStv & DVD player in living room, plus fireplace ▪ Wifi ▪ Safe ▪ Manager Carol Collins ▪ info@wittedriftmanorhouse.com ▪ www.wittedriftmanorhouse.com ▪ T +27 (0)82-894-0932 / +27 (0)82-970-3703

Boasting a remarkable art collection, Wittedrift in Tulbagh's historic town centre offers comfortable, fully equipped self-catering accommodation for up to 15 in the Manor House and eight in three garden cottages. The stately Manor House has two queen rooms en suite, two twin rooms with private bathroom, and one family suite. The large dining room is ideal for private parties, soirees, small conferences and wine-and-food pairing evenings, while the large stoep leads to beautiful gardens with a pool, braai area and lapa. A great venue for a celebration. (See also Readers Restaurant under Restaurants.)

Disabled Access in SA Wineries

The Accessibility for All initiative, launched in conjunction with Guy Davies' Disability Solutions team in the 2002 guide, has been funded by Platter's in the interests of inclusive wine tourism.

The aim is to verify that venues which are open to the public at set times, and claim to be disabled friendly, are in fact accessible. Accessibility for All means that any person with a special need, not only wheelchair users (as the international wheelchair icon seems to suggest) is provided safe access at venues where the icon is displayed in the guide.

Here are some key points to note about the assessments to date:

- Jeremy Hazell, Disability Solutions' leg-man, visited only wineries that considered their facilities to be disabled friendly. The evaluations covered both new and recently upgraded venues, and the results were incorporated into the relevant producer entries in the A-Z section of the book, in the form of the universally recognisable 'wheelchair' icon, as well as in the look-up tables which accompany the maps.

- Wineries open only by appointment were excluded, as it was felt that in these cases visitors could ascertain their individual requirements when making an appointment.

- The assessments covered four aspects: parking, the tasting area, toilet facilities and cellar tours, if offered. The focus was on the tasting area, however, and in the A-Z we displayed the icon for wineries whose tasting area was considered accessible.

- All assessments were concluded with suggestions to wineries on how to improve access, where necessary, in all four of the above aspects.

- Many wineries had perfectly accessible toilet facilities but others had toilets that were either in the process of renovation or not spacious enough for all wheelchair users. We suggest that wineries are phoned in advance to determine if their toilet facilities are adequate.

- Bear in mind that wineries which are not flagged as accessible in the A-Z or the map tables do not necessarily have deficient or non-existent facilities for people with disabilities; it might simply be that we were not in a position to comment on them.

- While the assessments were based on the principles of Universal Design (making things safer, easier and more convenient for everyone), they tried to be sensitive to the practical implications for each winery. In agricultural, rural and historical settings it is often a real challenge for wineries to ensure that access conforms to international standards.

The project is an on-going one and we invite readers who have any comments and suggestions about the project to contact our offices directly.

Winelands Maps

The maps in this section show locales where wine is available for tasting/sale either at set times or by appointment. The larger-scale map below shows the areas covered by the maps, and the table starting on the next page lists some details for prospective visitors.

Areas covered by the maps

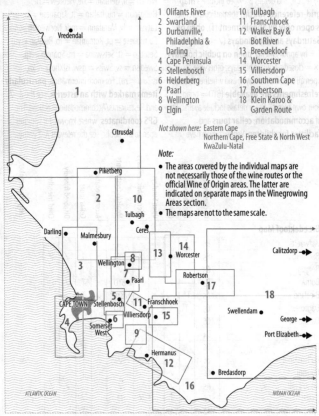

1 Olifants River
2 Swartland
3 Durbanville, Philadelphia & Darling
4 Cape Peninsula
5 Stellenbosch
6 Helderberg
7 Paarl
8 Wellington
9 Elgin

10 Tulbagh
11 Franschhoek
12 Walker Bay & Bot River
13 Breedekloof
14 Worcester
15 Villiersdorp
16 Southern Cape
17 Robertson
18 Klein Karoo & Garden Route

Not shown here: Eastern Cape
Northern Cape, Free State & North West
KwaZulu-Natal

Note:

- The areas covered by the individual maps are not necessarily those of the wine routes or the official Wine of Origin areas. The latter are indicated on separate maps in the Winegrowing Areas section.
- The maps are not to the same scale.

Some distances from Cape Town (kilometres)

Calitzdorp	370	Paarl	60	Tulbagh	125
Franschhoek	80	Plettenberg Bay	520	Upington	800
Hermanus	120	Robertson	160	Vredendal	300
Malmesbury	70	Stellenbosch	50	Worcester	110

Key for maps

—— Main access roads	R62 R60 Road numbers
—— Roads	⬟ ● Towns
······ Gravel roads	

Details of Locales Shown on Maps

The tables below are intended to facilitate winery visits by providing summary information about all the winetasting venues which are open to the public, either at set times or by appointment, and appear on our winelands maps. Venues are listed by region, and details provided include a **map grid-reference**; whether the particular venue is **open only by appointment** (T); **open on Saturdays and/or Sundays** (✓ = at set times; T = by appointment); **open on public holidays** (✗ = closed all public holidays; otherwise assume open all or some holidays); and whether **meals/refreshments are available** (BYO = bring your own picnic). Other details include availability of **accommodation**, **cellar tours** and **facilities for children**. Venues which have

tasting facilities **friendly to individuals with reduced mobility**, as audited by our disability consultants, are highlighted. **Other languages spoken** (besides English and Afrikaans) are also noted (Danish = da, Dutch/Flemish = nl, French = fr, German = de, Hebrew = he, Hungarian = hu, Italian = it, Japanese = ja, Latvian = lv, Mandarin = mdr, Norwegian = nn, Portuguese = pt, Romanian = ro, Russian = ru, Sesotho = st, Setswana = tn, Spanish = sp, Swedish = sv, Swiss = gsw, isiXhosa = xh, isiZulu = zu). For more information, **particularly items marked with an asterisk**, see the A–Z and Restaurants/Accommodation sections. For **GPS coordinates**, where known, for wineries open to the public, see the relevant A-Z entries.

	Grid reference	Open by appt. only	Open Saturdays	Open Sundays	Open public holidays	Meals/refreshments	Accommodation	Cellar tours	Disabled friendly	Child friendly	Languages spoken
Breedekloof Map											
Aufwaerts	B6	T									
Badsberg	B5		✓		✗	BYO		T	✓	✓	
Bergsig	A3		✓			✓		T	✓	✓	
Botha	B3		✓			BYO		T	✓		
Breëland	A5	T*				T/BYO*	✓	T			
Dagbreek	C5	T			✗	BYO		T			
Daschbosch	C6		✓						✓		
De Breede	D4	T									
Du Preez	B6		✓		✗			T*	✓		
Du Toitskloof	B6		✓			✓		T	✓		de
Goudini	C6		✓					T			
Jason's Hill	A5		✓			✓			✓	✓	
Kirabo	C6		T		✗	T*		✓		✓	
Lateganskop	A2							T			
Merwida	C6		✓				✓		✓		
Mountain Ridge	A2		✓		✗	BYO		T	✓		
Olifantsberg	C4	T*									
Opstal	A5		✓	T		✓*	✓	✓*	✓	✓	
Rico Suter	B2	T					✓				de/fr/it
Slanghoek	A5		✓					T	✓		
Stofberg	C5		✓	✓		✓*		T		✓	
Waboomsrivier	A3				✗			T*			

	Grid reference	Open by appt. only	Open Saturdays	Open Sundays	Open public holidays	Meals/refreshments	Accommodation	Cellar tours	Disabled friendly	Child friendly	Languages spoken
Cape Peninsula Map											
Ambeloui	B3	T									
Beau Constantia	B3		✓	✓		✓					
Buitenverwachting	B3		✓		×	✓		T	✓		
Cape Point	A4		✓	✓		✓*			✓	✓	
Constantia Glen	B3		✓	✓		✓*					
Constantia Royale	B3	T			×						
Constantia Uitsig	B3		✓*	✓*		✓					
Dorrance	B1					✓		✓			fr
Eagles' Nest	B3		✓	✓		✓*			✓		
Groot Constantia	B3		✓	✓		✓		✓	✓	✓	fr
High Constantia	B3		✓			T/BYO		✓			
Hout Bay	A3	T						T		✓	de
Klein Constantia	B3		✓	✓*		✓*			✓		fr/sv
New Beginnings	B1	T									fr
Rousseau	B4	T									
Savage	C2	T									
Silvermist	B3		✓	✓		✓*	✓				
Steenberg	B4		✓	✓		✓	✓	✓	✓	✓	
Township Winery	D3										
Vaughan Johnson	B1										
Wade Bales	B3				×						
Durbanville, Philadelphia & Darling Map											
Altydgedacht	C7		✓	✓		✓		T		✓	
Blake	A1		✓	✓							
Bloemendal	C7		✓	✓		✓			✓		
Canto	C7		✓			✓*				✓	
Capaia	C5		✓*	✓*		✓		✓		✓	de
Cloof	B3		✓		×*			T	✓	✓	
DA Hanekom	C7	T			×						
D'Aria	C7		✓	✓		✓	✓			✓	nl
Darling Cellars	B2		✓			✓*		T	✓	✓	xh
David Frost	C7	T									
De Grendel	C8		✓	✓		✓		T	✓		
Diemersdal	D7		✓	✓		✓		T			
Durbanville Hills	C7		✓	✓		✓*		T	✓	✓	
Groot Phesantekraal	D7		✓			✓					
Groote Post	A3		✓	✓		✓*		✓	✓	✓	
Hillcrest	C7		✓	✓		✓		T			
House of Mandela	C7	T									
JMA Louw	A3		✓	✓		✓		✓	✓	✓	
Klein Roosboom	C7		✓	✓		✓*		✓	✓	✓	
Kronendal	C7	T				✓*		T	✓		
Maastricht	C7	T									
Maison de Teijger	D7	T*									

	Grid reference	Open by appt. only	Open Saturdays	Open Sundays	Open public holidays	Meals/refreshments	Accommodation	Cellar tours	Disabled friendly	Child friendly	Languages spoken
Meerendal	C7		√	√		√	√	T	√	√	xh/zu
Nitida	C7		√	√		√			√	√	
Ormonde	A1		√							√	
Signal Gun	C7		√	√		√					
Withington	A1		√	√					√		
Eastern Cape Map											
La Terre La Mer	B2	T						T			
St Francis Point	D6	T									
Theescombe	D5					T*		T			
Elgin Map											
Almenkerk	B2		√	√		√/BYO*		√*			nl/fr
Arumdale	B1		T	T	T						
Barry Gould	D2	T				T*	√			√	
Belfield	B2	T					√	T			
Charles Fox	C3		√	√				√		√	
Elgin Ridge	B3		√	√		BYO		√			fr
Elgin Vintners	B2		T	T			*				
Hannay	B2	T				T/BYO		T			
Highlands Road	C3		√	√		√*		√	√	√	
Houw Hoek	D3		√			√				√	
Iona	C4		T		X			√			
Lothian	A2	T					√				sp
Oak Valley	B1		√	√		√	√		√	√	it/fr
Oneiric	C4	T*				T*					
Oude Molen	B1				X						
Paul Cluver	C2		√	√*		√*			√		
Paul Wallace	C3	T*	√				√				
Richard Kershaw	B2	T									fr
Shannon	A2	T*							√		de/sp
South Hill	C3		√	√		√*	√		√		
Spioenkop	C4		√		X			√*			fr/nl
William Everson	B2	T						√	T		
Franschhoek Map											
Akkerdal	C4	T*			X		√				
Allée Bleue	C6		√	√		√	√	T	√	√	de
Anthonij Rupert	C5	T				√		√			
Babylonstoren	B8		√	√		√*	√	√	√		
Backsberg	B8		√	√		√*		T*	√	√	
Bellingham	C2		√	√		√*				√	
Black Elephant	C1	T						T			
Boekenhoutskloof	D1	T			X				√		xh
Boschendal	D6		√	√		√	√	√	√	√	
Cape Chamonix	C1		√	√		√	√	T			
Colmant	C1							√*	√		fr
Dieu Donné	C1		√	√		√		T*			

	Grid reference	Open by appt. only	Open Saturdays	Open Sundays	Open public holidays	Meals/refreshments	Accommodation	Cellar tours	Disabled friendly	Child friendly	Languages spoken
Eikehof	C3		✓	✓		✓*					
Enfin	C1	T									
Four Paws	C3	T			x						
Franschhoek Cellar	C2		✓	✓		✓*	✓		✓	✓	
Freedom Hill	B5				x				✓	✓	
GlenWood	C2		✓*	✓*		✓		✓*	✓		
Grande Provence	C2		✓	✓		✓	✓	✓*	✓	✓	
Haut Espoir	D1		T	T	x			T	✓		
Haute Cabrière	C1		✓	✓		✓		✓*	✓		fr/de
Holden Manz	D1		✓	✓		✓	✓	T	✓		de
La Bourgogne	D1		✓	✓		✓*				✓	
La Bri	C1		✓	✓		✓*		✓			
La Chataigne	C4		T	T	T			✓		✓	sv
La Chaumiere	C2	T						T			
La Couronne	C1		✓	✓*		✓*	✓			✓	
La Motte	C3		✓			✓			✓	✓	xh
La Petite Ferme	C1	T*				✓	✓				
La Petite Vigne	C1	T						T			
Landau du Val	D2	T*									
Le Lude	C1		✓	✓		✓	✓	✓			
Le Manoir de Brendel	C3		✓	✓						✓	
Leeu Passant	C2		✓	✓							
Leopard's Leap	C3		✓	✓		✓				✓	
Lynx	C4		✓	T	T			✓			de/sp
Maison	C3		✓	✓		✓					
Mont Rochelle	C2		✓	✓		✓	✓	✓*			
Môreson	C3		✓	✓		✓		✓			
Mullineux	C2		✓	✓							
My Wyn	B1	T*			T	T/BYO*		T			
Noble Hill	B7		✓	✓		✓		T	✓		fr
Old Road	C2		✓			✓					
Paserene	C4	T*									
Plaisir de Merle	C6		✓	✓		✓*	*	✓	✓	✓	de
Rickety Bridge	C2		✓	✓		✓	✓	✓	✓	✓	
Rupert & Rothschild	B7		✓	✓		✓*		✓			
Solms-Delta	C5		✓	✓				✓			
Stony Brook	D1	T*					✓	✓			
The House of GM&AHRENS	C1	T			x	T		T			
Topiary	C4		✓	T		T/BYO	✓	T	✓		fr
Val de Vie	A7	T*			x				✓		
Vrede en Lust	B7		✓	✓		✓	✓	T*	✓	✓	
Wildeberg	D1	T*			x			T*			
Helderberg Map											
Avontuur	C2		✓	✓		✓		T	✓		de/pt
Cadequin	H8	T*					✓			✓	nl

	Grid reference	Open by appt. only	Open Saturdays	Open Sundays	Open public holidays	Meals/refreshments	Accommodation	Cellar tours	Disabled friendly	Child friendly	Languages spoken
Cape Classics	F4	T									
Capelands	F7					✓*	✓				
Catherine Marshall	D1	T						T			
Cavalli	C1		✓	✓		✓*			✓		
Chennells	C2	T*			×			T			de/sp
Collatio	A3	T			×						
Croydon	A3				×			T	✓	✓	
Eikendal	C1		✓*	✓		✓*	✓	✓	✓	✓	de
Equitania	C3	T*			×	BYO					
Flagstone	B6		✓					T	✓		
Foothills	B1	T				T	✓				
Grangehurst	C1		T*	T*	T		✓				
Highberry	F6	T									
Idiom	H7		✓	✓		✓*					it
Jasper Raats	C1		✓								
Journey's End	G7	T*				T/BYO*					
Ken Forrester	C2 B2		✓	✓*		✓*			✓		
Kings Kloof	E4	T									
Konkelberg	C1		✓								
Le Riche	B1		T		×			✓			de
Lithos	H6	T*			×			T			
Longridge	C1		✓			✓		T	✓		
Lourensford	F4		✓	✓		✓		✓	✓	✓	
Lyngrove	B1	T					✓				
Miravel	A3	T			T	T					nl/fr
Morgenster	F5		✓	✓		✓					
Nomada	D2	T									
Osbloed	E6	T*						T*			
Paul Roos	C1	T						T			fr
Pfeifer's	B2	T									gsw/de
Post House	C1		T		×	BYO	✓	✓	✓		
Radford Dale	C1				×						fr/sv
Romond	C2	T*					✓	T*			
Skaap	H6					T*	✓			✓	nl
Somerbosch	C1		✓	✓		✓		T	✓	✓	
Somerset Wines	E6		✓	×							
Stonewall	C2	T*				T					
Vergelegen	F5		✓	✓		✓		✓*	✓	✓	
Waterkloof	F6		✓	✓		✓*		T	✓		
Yonder Hill	C3		✓*		×			T	✓		
Klein Karoo & Garden Route Map											
Axe Hill	B5	T						T			
Baleia	C6		✓			✓/BYO	✓	✓		✓	
Barrydale	C7		✓	✓		✓					
Bitou	C1	T			×						

	Grid reference	Open by appt. only	Open Saturdays	Open Sundays	Open public holidays	Meals/refreshments	Accommodation	Cellar tours	Disabled friendly	Child friendly	Languages spoken
Boplaas	B5 C4		✓	✓		✓		T		✓	
Bramon	C1		✓	✓		✓	✓	T	✓	✓	
Calitzdorp	B5		✓			BYO		T	✓		
De Krans	B5		✓	✓		✓*			✓	✓	
Domein Doornkraal	B3		✓	✓*		✓*	✓				
Du'SwaRoo	B5		✓		✗			✓			
Excelsior Vlakteplaas	B3	T									
Fernskloof	A3		✓	T*		BYO	✓	✓			sp
Flying Cloud	C3										
Garden Route	C3 B5		✓*						✓		
Grundheim	B4		✓						✓		
Herold	C3					✓*	✓	✓	✓	✓	
Hillock	B6		✓	✓		✓	✓	✓			
Jakkalsvlei	C5		✓	✓		✓				✓	
Joubert-Tradauw	C7		✓			✓	✓	✓		✓	
JP Bredell	C5	T									
Karusa	B3		✓			✓		✓			
Kay & Monty	C1		✓	✓		✓	✓				
Kingna	C8		T	T				✓*			de
Lodestone	C1		✓	✓		✓					
Louis BYOT	C4		✓								
LuKa	C1										
Mimosa	B8		✓	✓		✓	✓		✓		de/gsw
Montagu Wine Cellar	B8				✗				✓		
Newstead	C1		✓			T*	✓				zu
Packwood	-C1		✓	✓	T	✓*	✓				
Peter Bayly	B5	T						T			
Plettenvale	C1	T*						T*			
Redford Lane	C1	T									
SoetKaroo	A4		✓*						✓		de
Star Hill	C7		✓	✓		✓	✓			✓	
The Goose	C3	T				T/BYO				✓	
TTT Cellar	B5		✓	T				✓	✓		
Varkenskraal	B3	T					✓				
Withoek	B5	T					✓	T			
KwaZulu-Natal Map											
Abingdon	B2	T*	✓	✓		✓*					
Cathedral Peak	A1		✓*	✓*							zu
Highgate	B2		✓	✓		✓		✓*		✓	de
Northern Cape, Free State & North West Map											
Bezalel	B8		✓			✓*	✓	✓		✓	nl
Die Mas	B8		✓			T/BYO*	✓	✓		✓	
Douglas	C5				✗			T			
Lowerland	C6	T						T			
Orange River	B8		✓					✓*	✓		

	Grid reference	Open by appt. only	Open Saturdays	Open Sundays	Open public holidays	Meals/refreshments	Accommodation	Cellar tours	Disabled friendly	Child friendly	Languages spoken
Olifants River Map											
Bellpost	B3	T*						T			
Boer & Brit	A1		✓	✓							de/fr/nl/sp/xh
Cape Rock	B4	T				BYO					
Cecilia	D7		✓								
Cederberg	D7		✓	✓*		BYO	✓				
Driehoek	D6		✓				✓			✓	
Fryer's Cove	A4		✓			✓*		✓	✓	✓	
Klawer	B4		✓			BYO			✓	✓	
Lutzville	B3		✓			✓		T	✓		
Namaqua	B4		✓			✓*		✓*			
Piekenierskloof	D7	T*						T			
Schenkfontein	C7	T									
Seal Breeze	A3		✓			T*		✓	✓	✓	
Sir Lambert	B5	T*				✓/BYO*	✓			✓	
Stellar	B4				x			T			
Stoumann's	B4	T			x	T*					
Teubes	B4 B5		✓			✓*	✓	✓	✓	✓	
Tierhoek	C6	T*			x	BYO	✓	T*			
Paarl Map											
Anura	C7		✓	✓		✓*		✓	✓		de
Arra	C8		✓	✓							
Avondale	F6		✓	✓		✓		T	✓	✓	
Ayama	B2		✓	✓		T/BYO*	✓			✓	it
Baratok	F3	T			x						
Bayede!	E6		T	T	x						
Bergheim	E6	T									
Bezuidenhout Family	E6		✓	✓						✓	
Black Pearl	D5	T*					✓	T*	✓		
Boland	E4		✓			✓		T			
Calais	G4	T*					✓				
Damarakloof	A7	T*									
De Villiers	E6	T									
Domaine Brahms	C3	T			T	✓		T			
Doran	C1	T*	✓	✓					✓		
Druk My Niet	G4	T			x	T/BYO		T			de
Eenzaamheid	B5	T									
Erasmus Family Wines	E6		✓	✓							
Fairview	D6		✓	✓		✓			✓		
Glen Carlou	D7		✓	✓		✓		T	✓	✓	de
Groot Parys	E5	T									nl
Hawksmoor	A7	T*				T*	✓				fr/de/ja
Jacques Germanier	C1	T				✓*	✓	T			fr
Joostenberg	A7	T*				✓	✓	T		✓	

	Grid reference	Open by appt. only	Open Saturdays	Open Sundays	Open public holidays	Meals/refreshments	Accommodation	Cellar tours	Disabled friendly	Child friendly	Languages spoken
Klein Parys	E5		✓			✓		✓	✓	✓	
KWV	E6		✓	✓		✓*		✓	✓		de
Landskroon	D6		✓*			BYO	✓	T*		✓	
Mason's Winery	E6	T				✓*					
Mellasat	G5		✓	✓		T*		T	✓		
Mitre's Edge	C8	T*					✓	T			
Mooi Bly	F4	T				BYO	✓	T			nl
Myburgh Bros	A7	T						T			de
Nederburg	F5		✓	✓		✓*		✓	✓		de
Nelson	D3				x		✓	T	✓	✓	
Niel Joubert	C8	T*			x						
Olsen	G5	T									
Oude Denneboom	C2							✓			
Painted Wolf	E5		✓			✓					fr
Pearl Mountain	E4		✓	✓		✓					
Perdeberg	B2		✓			✓*		T*		✓	
Rhebokskloof	D3		✓	✓		✓		T	✓	✓	
Ridgeback	D3		✓	✓		✓	✓	T	✓	✓	
Ruitersvlei	D6		✓	✓		✓			✓	✓	
Scali	C1	T*			x		✓	T			
Simonsvlei	D7		✓	✓		✓		T	✓	✓	
Southern Sky	E6	T									
Spice Route	D6		✓	✓		✓			✓		
Stone Ridge	D1	T									
Taillard	C1	T			x			T	✓		
Taillefert	E6		✓	✓							
Tempel	E3	T				T*	✓	T		✓	fr/lv/nl/ru
Terracura	C2	T			x						
The Ahrens Family	G6	T				T*					
Under Oaks	E3		✓	✓		✓	✓	T			
Vendôme	E6	T			x	✓			✓		
Vondeling	C1		T		T				✓		
Wijnskool	C3	T						T			
Windmeul	D3		✓		x	✓*		T	✓	✓	
Zanddrift	E6					✓				✓	
Zandwijk	D6				x	T*		T	✓		
Robertson Map											
Arendsig	C4	T				T/BYO	✓	T			
Ashton	B4		✓			T*		T	✓	✓	
Bemind	D6		✓			T*		✓			
Bon Courage	B5		✓			✓			✓	✓	
Bonnievale	D3		✓						✓	✓	
Buffalo Creek	D6		✓	T				✓*			
Bushmanspad	C1					T/BYO*	✓				nl
Cape Dreams	A6	T						T			

	Grid reference	Open by appt. only	Open Saturdays	Open Sundays	Open public holidays	Meals/refreshments	Accommodation	Cellar tours	Disabled friendly	Child friendly	Languages spoken
Clairvaux	B6				x	BYO		T	✓		
Cloverfield	B5								✓		
De Wetshof	C4		✓					T*	✓		
DuVon	B7	T					✓	T			
Esona	C4		✓			✓*					
Excelsior	C4		✓			✓*	✓			✓	
Fraai Uitzicht 1798	B4	T*				✓	✓				de
Goedverwacht	C4		✓			✓/BYO*		✓			
Graham Beck	B6		✓	✓				T	✓		
Jan Harmsgat	C2		✓	✓		✓	✓				
Kleinhoekkloof	B4	T*									
Kranskop	B4		✓			BYO		✓			de
Langverwacht	D4				x			✓	✓		
Le Grand Chasseur	B6	T			x			✓			
Lord's	D7		✓	T	T	✓*		✓			
Lozärn	D3							T			
McGregor	D6		✓						✓		
Mont Blois	A5	T*						T*			fr
Quando	D4	T			x						de
Rietvallei	B4		✓			✓*			✓		
Robertson	B5		✓	✓				T	✓		
Roodezandt	B5				x			T*	✓	✓	
Rooiberg	A7		✓			✓			✓	✓	
Rosendal	B4		✓	✓		✓	✓		✓		nn
Solara	D6	T*									
Springfield	B5					BYO		T			
Sumsaré	C8	T*						T*		✓	
Tanagra	C6	T*					✓	T			de
Van Loveren	C4 B5		✓	✓		✓		T	✓		
Van Zylshof	D3		✓					T	✓		
Viljoensdrift	C5		✓	✓*		✓*					fr
Wederom	B7	T			T	T	✓	T			de
Weltevrede	D3		✓			✓*	✓	T	✓		
Windfall	C8	T			x		✓	T			
Wolvendrift	C4		T					T	✓	✓	
Wonderfontein	B6		T*	T	T						
Zandvliet	C4		✓					✓	✓		
Southern Cape Map											
Andy Mitchell	A1	T						T			
Black Oystercatcher	B3		✓			✓*	✓	✓	✓	✓	
BruceJack	B2	T									
Brunia	B2	T			x						
Fortes	B2	T			x	BYO		T			
Jean Daneel	B2	T				✓		T			de
Lismore	A1	T									

	Grid reference	Open by appt. only	Open Saturdays	Open Sundays	Open public holidays	Meals/refreshments	Accommodation	Cellar tours	Disabled friendly	Child friendly	Languages spoken
Lomond	A3		✓	✓		✓*					
Olivedale	D1	T			×						
Sijnn	D1		✓*			✓*		✓*			
Strandveld	B3		✓			BYO	✓	✓			
Swallow Hill	A1	T				T*	✓	T			de/fr/sp
The Drift	B2	T					✓				
The Giant Periwinkle	A3	T									
Stellenbosch Map											
Akkerdraai	E8	T									de
Alto	E8		✓	✓							
Ameera	D7	T									nl/fr/de
Annandale	E8		✓			BYO			✓		
Artisanal Boutique	C3	T			×			T			
Asara	D6		✓	✓		✓	✓	T*		✓	de
Audacia	E8	T*	✓	✓	×	✓*			✓	✓	
B Vintners	B6	T*			×						
Bartinney	H5		✓*			✓*	✓	T	✓		
Bein	B6	T						T			de/fr
Bellevue	C3		✓	✓		✓*				✓	
Beyerskloof	E3		✓	✓		✓		T	✓		
Blaauwklippen	E7		✓	✓		✓		✓*	✓	✓	de
Blackwater	E1	T									
Boschheim	E5	T									de
Boschkloof	C6		✓			✓/BYO		✓			
Botanica	D4	T*				✓*	✓				
Brampton	F5		✓	✓		✓*					
Brenaissance	D4		✓	✓		✓	✓			✓	
Camberley	H4		✓	✓		✓*	✓	T			
Carmen Stevens	B6	T						T			
Casa Mori	D3	T					✓	T			it/fr
Chabivin	E7		✓	✓							fr
Clos Malverne	D4		✓	✓		✓	✓	✓*	✓		
Clouds	H5		✓	✓		✓*	✓				
Dalla Cia	E5		✓			✓		T*	✓		it
De Meye	E1		✓	✓		✓*		T*	✓		
De Toren	B6	T*			×			T*			
De Trafford	G8	T*	✓		×			T*			
Delaire Graff	H5		✓	✓		✓	✓	T*	✓		
Delheim	F2		✓	✓		✓		✓	✓		de
DeMorgenzon	C5		✓	✓				T			
Deux Frères	E3		✓*			T*		✓			
Devonvale	D3	T*				✓	✓		✓		de/fr
DeWaal	C5		✓			✓*					de
Die Bergkelder	E5		✓					✓	✓		
Domaine Coutelier	D4	T			×		✓	T			fr

	Grid reference	Open by appt. only	Open Saturdays	Open Sundays	Open public holidays	Meals/refreshments	Accommodation	Cellar tours	Disabled friendly	Child friendly	Languages spoken
Dormershire	A5	T*									
Dornier	F7		✓	✓		✓*	✓	T	✓		
Edgebaston	E3	T									
Entre Nous	H5	T			T	BYO		T			
Ernie Els	E8	T*							✓		
Ernst Gouws	D1		✓						✓	✓	de
Escapades	B4										
Fort Simon	C4		✓		X			T	✓		
Francois La Garde	E5	T									
Gentleman Spirits	E7		✓*	✓*				T			de
Gentleman's Reserve	E4	T				T*	✓				
Gilga	D5	T					✓				
Glenelly	F4		✓	✓		✓		T	✓		de/fr
Goede Hoop	C3		✓			T*		✓			
Graceland	E7	T*			X						
Grand Domaine	D4	T									
Groenland	B3		✓					T	✓		
Guardian Peak	E8		✓	✓		✓		✓			
Hartenberg	C4		✓	✓*		✓*		T	✓	✓	de
Haskell	F8		✓	✓*		✓*	✓	T	✓	✓	
Hazendal	B3		✓	✓		✓		✓*	✓	✓	de/ru
Hidden Valley	E8		✓	✓		✓*		T	✓		
Hoopenburg	E1				X	BYO	✓	✓			
Hunneyball	F5	T					✓				
J9	E1		✓			✓*					
Jacobsdal	B6	T*									
Jordan	C5		✓	✓		✓*	✓	T*	✓		
Kaapzicht	B4		✓				✓				de
Kanonkop	F2		✓			T/BYO*		✓			
Kanu	E3		✓	✓		✓		✓			
Kap Vino Estate	D3	T					*				
Katbakkies	D5	T*			X						
Keermont	G8	T*					✓	T			
Klein DasBosch	F7	T*				✓					
Kleine Zalze	E7		✓	✓		✓	✓				
Knorhoek	F3		✓	✓		✓*	✓	✓	✓	✓	
Koelenhof	D1		✓			✓*		✓	✓	✓	de
Koni	E1		T		T			✓			st/xh/zu
Kunjani	D3		✓	✓		✓	✓				de
Kyburg	D4	T					✓				fr/de
La RicMal	C3	T*									
Laibach	F1		✓*				✓	T			
Lanzerac	G5		✓	✓		✓	✓	✓*	✓		
L'Avenir	E3		✓	✓		✓	✓	T	✓	✓	fr
Le Bonheur	F1	T									
Le Pommier	H4		✓	✓		✓	✓			✓	

	Grid reference	Open by appt. only	Open Saturdays	Open Sundays	Open public holidays	Meals/refreshments	Accommodation	Cellar tours	Disabled friendly	Child friendly	Languages spoken
Lievland	F1		✓	✓					✓		
Louiesenhof	E4		✓	✓			✓		✓	✓	de
Louisvale	D4		✓						✓		
Lovane	D6		✓	✓			✓	✓			
Malanot	E3	T						T*	✓		
Marianne	G1		✓	✓		✓	✓	✓	✓	✓	de/fr
Marklew	F1	T						T			
Meerlust	C8		✓		✕	✓		T			
Meinert	D4	T*			✕						de
Middelvlei	E4		✓	✓		✓*	✓	T	✓	✓	
MolenVliet	H4	T*					✓				
Montegray	F5		✓			✓*					
Mooiplaas	B4		✓	✓*		T*				✓	
Morgenhof	F3		✓*	✓*		✓		T	✓	✓	de
Mostertsdrift	E4	T				T*		T		✓	
Mulderbosch	C5		✓	✓		✓*			✓		fr
Muratie	F3		✓	✓		✓*		T			
Mvemve Raats	B6	T*			✕						
Natte Valleij	F1	T*			✕		✓	T*		✓	
Neethlingshof	D5		✓	✓		✓*		T	✓	✓	de
Neil Ellis	G5		✓			✓*			✓		
Nico van der Merwe	B6		✓								fr/de
Nietvoorbij	F4	T*			✕						
Noble Savage	F5		✓								
Oldenburg	H5		✓				*		✓		
Origin	D3	T									fr/de
Overgaauw	D5	T*				✓*			✓		
Peter Falke	E8		✓	✓		✓*					
Quoin Rock	F3		✓			✓	T			✓	
Raats	B6	T*			✕						
Rainbow's End	H6	T			✕			T			
Rascallion	E5		✓	✓*							
Remhoogte	F3		✓			✓*	✓	T	✓		
Reyneke	B6	T*						T	✓		
Roos Family	B4	T									
Rudera	G6	T						T			
Rust en Vrede	E8		✓	✓*		✓*					
Rustenberg	F4		✓	✓					✓		
Saltare	F5	T						T			
Saxenburg	A5		✓	✓		✓	✓				
Seven Sisters	C7		✓	✓		✓					
Simonsig	E2		✓	✓		✓		✓*	✓	✓	
Skilpadvlei	C6		✓	✓		✓	✓		✓	✓	
Slaley	E2		✓	✓		✓					
Sonklip	G5	T						T			
Spier	C7		✓	✓		✓	✓		✓	✓	de/xh

	Grid reference	Open by appt. only	Open Saturdays	Open Sundays	Open public holidays	Meals/refreshments	Accommodation	Cellar tours	Disabled friendly	Child friendly	Languages spoken
Spotswood	F7	T									
Spring Grove	H4	T									
Stark-Condé	G6		✓	✓	x*	✓			✓		ja
Stellekaya	E5	T			x			T			zu
Stellenbosch Family Wines	D1	T									
Stellenbosch Hills	D6		✓		x				✓		
Stellenbosch University	F5				x						
Stellenbosch Vineyards	C7		✓	✓					✓	✓	xh
Stellenrust	E7, C3		✓		x*	✓/BYO*		T			xh
Stellenview	D4		T	T	x			✓*			
Stellenzicht	F8	T*									
Summerhill	E3				x	✓					
Super Single Vineyards	C5		✓		x						
SylvanVale	D4		✓	✓		✓	✓		✓	✓	de/xh
Tamboerskloof	F7	T*			x			T			de/fr
Thandi	D6				x						
The Foundry	C8	T			x			T			
The Great SA Wine Co	C5	T									
The High Road	E5	T			x				✓		
The Hills	D4	T									
The House of JC le Roux	D4		✓	✓		✓*		✓*	✓		
Thelema	G4		✓						✓		
Tokara	G4		✓	✓		✓			✓	✓	
Usana	C8	T									
Uva Mira	E8		✓	✓		✓*					
Van Biljon	B6	T			x		✓	T			
Van Ryn	D6		✓	✓*				✓*			
Vergenoegd	B8		✓					T	✓	✓	xh
Vilafonté	E5							T			
Villiera	D1		✓			✓*		✓	✓		fr
Vredenheim	D6		✓			✓	✓		✓		
Vriesenhof	F7		T		x			T			
Vuurberg	H4	T			x			T			
Warwick	F1		✓	✓		✓*		T	✓	✓	
Waterford	F8		✓					✓	✓		
Webersburg	E8		✓	✓		✓	✓	✓	✓		
Welgevallen	F5				x						
Yardstick	C5	T									
Zevenwacht	B5		✓	✓		✓	✓	T	✓	✓	xh
Zorgvliet	H4		✓	✓		T*	✓	T	✓	✓	
Swartland Map											
AA Badenhorst	C8	T			x		T	T			
Allesverloren	D6		✓			✓*		T	✓	✓	
Annex Kloof	C7	T*			x*		✓	T	✓		
Babylon's Peak	C8	T					✓		✓		

	Grid reference	Open by appt. only	Open Saturdays	Open Sundays	Open public holidays	Meals/refreshments	Accommodation	Cellar tours	Disabled friendly	Child friendly	Languages spoken
City on a Hill	C8	T									
David & Nadia	C8	T									
Dragonridge	C8	T				T*	✓	T		✓	
Franki's	A6	T*			x	BYO*	✓	T*			
Hofstraat	C7	T*				✓*		T			
Hughes Family	C6	T									sp
Huis van Chevallerie	C8	T			x*						de/fr/it
JC Wickens	C8	T									
Kloovenburg	D6		✓			BYO				✓	
Lammershoek	C8	T						T			
Meerhof	D6		✓	✓		✓					
Môrelig	C8	T									
Mullineux	D6	T									
Nieuwedrift	C2		✓			✓*		✓		✓	
Org de Rac	C2		✓			✓*		✓	✓	✓	de
Pulpit Rock	D6		✓			BYO	✓	T			
Rall	C7	T						T			
Riebeek	D6		✓	✓		BYO		T	✓		
Sadie	C8	T*									
Spekulasie	A6	T			T	T		T			
Swartland	C7		✓						✓	✓	
Wildehurst	B2	T*					✓	T*			
Tulbagh Map											
Koelfontein	H5		✓		x		✓				
Krone	F4		✓		x			✓			pt/sp
Lemberg	F5		✓	✓		T/BYO*	✓	✓	✓		
Manley	F5	T*	✓	✓		✓*	✓	T			
Montpellier	F5		✓	✓		✓*	✓	✓		✓	
Oude Compagnies Post	F4	T					✓	T			
Oudekloof	F5		✓	✓		✓*	✓			✓	
Rijk's	F5		✓				✓	T	✓		
Saronsberg	F4		✓	✓		BYO	✓	T			
Schalkenbosch	G5	T			x		✓	T			de
Thernika	F4	T					✓				
Theuniskraal	F4		✓						✓		
Tulbagh Winery	F5		✓					T	✓		
Waverley Hills	G6		✓	✓		✓*		✓	✓	✓	
Villiersdorp Map											
Cranefields	B2	T									
Eerste Hoop	A2	T						T			
Slowine	C1		✓						✓		
Villiersdorp	C1		✓			✓		T	✓		
Walker Bay & Bot River Map											
Alheit	B4	T*									
Anysbos	C3	T						T			

	Grid reference	Open by appt. only	Open Saturdays	Open Sundays	Open public holidays	Meals/refreshments	Accommodation	Cellar tours	Disabled friendly	Child friendly	Languages spoken
Arcangeli	C3	T				✓	✓				
Ataraxia	C4		✓	✓*							
Bartho Eksteen	A3		✓			T*		T			fr/xh
Barton	B2		✓				✓	✓	✓		
Beaumont	C2		✓			✓*	✓		✓		
Benguela Cove	B2		✓	✓		✓*		✓	✓	✓	
Boschrivier	C8		✓			✓/BYO	✓		✓		
Bosman	B3	T*				T*					
Bouchard Finlayson	B4		✓		×	✓/BYO*		✓	✓		de/fr
Creation	C4		✓	✓		✓		✓	✓	✓	de/fr
Domaine des Dieux	C4		✓	✓		✓*			✓		
Gabriëlskloof	C3		✓			✓		✓	✓	✓	
Genevieve	C2	T									
Goedvertrouw	D2	T				T	T			✓	
Hamilton Russell	B4		✓					T			tn/xh
Hermanuspietersfontein	A3		✓	✓*		✓*	✓	✓*	✓		
Hornbill	A3		✓			✓	✓		✓		
Jakob's Vineyards	C4	T									
La Vierge	B4		✓	✓		✓			✓		
Leeurivier	C3	T									
Luddite	D2		T	T		T*		T	✓		nl
Misty Mountains	B5		✓	✓		✓	✓	T			
Mount Babylon	C4	T*									
Moya's	B4	T*									
Newton Johnson	B4		✓		×	✓					
PaardenKloof	C3 C2		✓	✓*		✓*				✓	xh
Raka	C8		✓			BYO		T	✓		
Restless River	B4	T			×						
Rivendell	B2		✓	✓		✓*				✓	
Robert Stanford	B6		✓	✓		✓*				✓	
Seven Springs	C5										
Southern Right	A3		✓					T	✓		
Spookfontein	B4		✓	✓		✓	✓				
Springfontein	B5		✓	✓		✓*	✓	✓			
Stanford Hills	B6		✓	✓		✓	✓		✓		
Storm	B4	T									
Sumaridge	B4		✓			✓*		✓	✓		
Vaalvlei	B7		✓				✓				
Villion	B2		✓								
Walker Bay Estate	B6		✓	✓		✓		T	✓	✓	
Whalehaven	A3		✓	✓							
Wildekrans	B1		✓	✓		✓	✓	✓	✓		
Wine Village-Hermanus	A3		✓	✓				✓			

	Grid reference	Open by appt. only	Open Saturdays	Open Sundays	Open public holidays	Meals/refreshments	Accommodation	Cellar tours	Disabled friendly	Child friendly	Languages spoken
Wellington Map											
Alkmaar	C4		✓		T			T			
Andreas	C3	T*			×		✓	T			sv
Blouvlei Wyne	C4		T		×			✓*	✓		de
Bosman	C3	T*						T			
Diemersfontein	B4		✓	✓		✓	✓	T			
Doolhof	D3		✓	✓		✓*	✓	T	✓		
Dunstone	C3		✓	✓		✓	✓	✓*	✓		
Hildenbrand	B4		T*	T*		T*	✓		✓		de
Imbuko	B4		✓			T*		T			
Jacques Smit	B3	T						T		✓	
Lazanou	B2	T*				T*	✓				
Linton Park	C2		✓			✓		T			
Maske	C4	T									de
Mischa	B2	T			T	T		T*			
Mont du Toit	C4	T			×			T	✓		de
Nabygelegen	C3	T*			×		✓	T			
Napier	C3				×			T	✓		
Thokozani	B4		✓	✓		✓	✓	T			
Upland	C4	T			T			T			de
Val du Charron	C3		✓	✓		✓	✓	T	✓	✓	
Versailles	B3	T						T			
Welbedacht	B1		✓	T*		✓	✓	✓	✓	✓	de
Welgegund	C4	T									
Wellington Winery	B3 C3		✓	✓		BYO			✓		
Welvanpas	C3		✓	✓		✓*				✓	nl
Worcester Map											
Aan de Doorns	B4		✓		×			T*	✓		
Alvi's Drift	B5	T			×			T			
Auction Crossing	C1	T			×			T			
Brandvlei	B5		✓		×			T	✓		
Cilmor	B4		T	T	×						
Conradie	C3		✓				✓	✓		✓	
De Doorns	D1		✓						✓		
De Wet	B3		✓		×	✓/BYO*		T	✓		
Eagle's Cliff	A6				×	✓*			✓	✓	
Leipzig	C3		✓			T*	✓	✓*		✓	ru
Major's Hill	D1		✓			✓*	✓			✓	
Nuy	C4		✓	✓		✓				✓	
Overhex	B3		✓	✓		✓*		T	✓	✓	
Stettyn	A6		✓*		×	BYO		T*	✓	✓	
Tanzanite	A2	T*									

Olifants River & West Coast

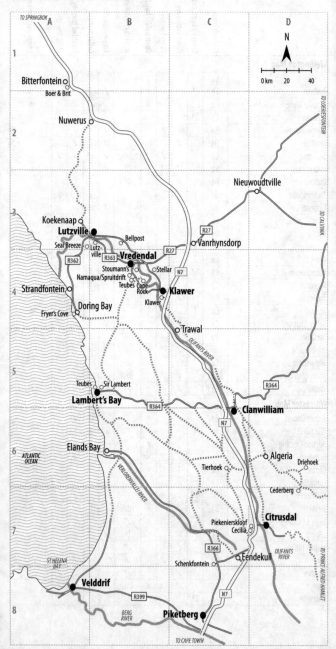

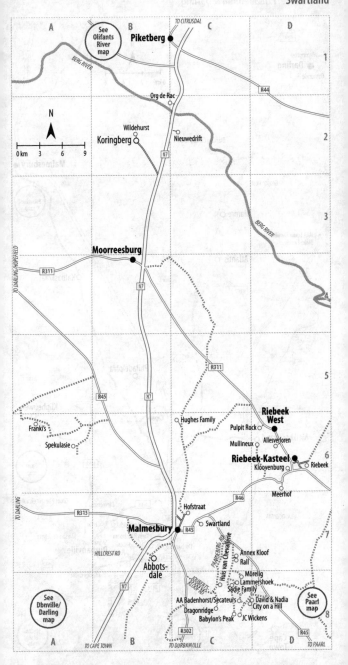

Durbanville, Philadelphia & Darling

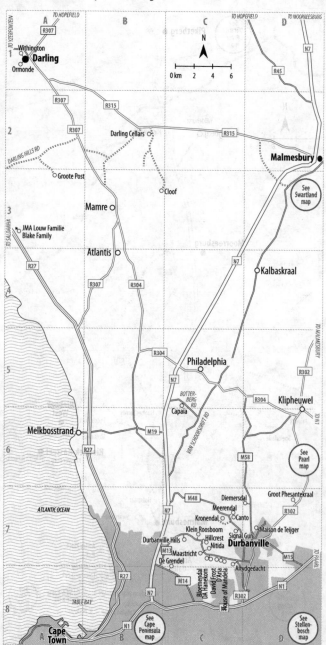

Cape Peninsula

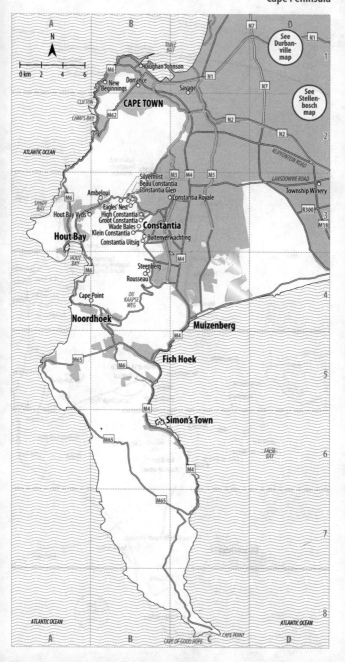

Stellenbosch

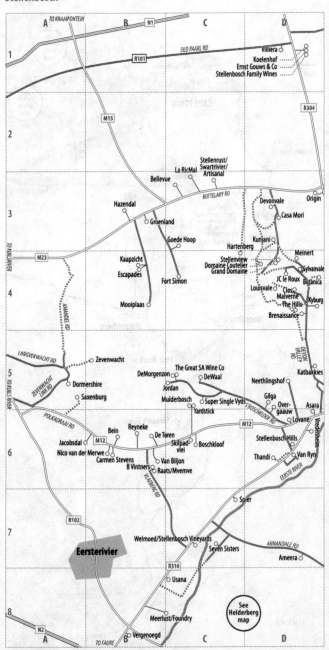

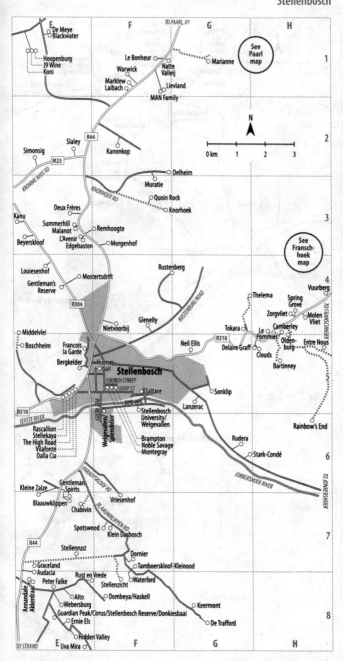

E
De Meye
Blackwater

Hoopenburg
J9 Wine
Koni

F
Le Bonheur
Warwick
Natte Valleij
Marklew
Laibach
Lievland
MAN Family

G
TO PAARL, N1
Marianne

See Paarl map

H

1

N

0 km   1   2   3

2

R44
Slaley
Simonsig
Kanonkop
M23
KROMME RIVER RD

Delheim
Muratie
KNORHOEK RD
Quoin Rock
Knorhoek

3

See Franschhoek map

Kanu
Deux Frères
Summerhill
Malanot
L'Avenir
Edgebaston
Remhoogte
Morgenhof
Beyerskloof

4

Vuurberg
Thelema
Spring Grove
Zorgvliet
Molen Vliet
Camberley
Le Pommier
Oldenburg
Entre Nous

Louiesenhof
Gentleman's Reserve
Mostertsdrift
R304
Rustenberg
RUSTENBURG ROAD
Glenelly
Nietvoorbij
Tokara
Delaire Graff
Clouds
Bartinney

Middelvlei
Boschheim
Francois la Garde
Bergkelder
Hunneyball
Neil Ellis
R310

5

Stellenbosch
CHURCH STREET
DORP ST
Saltare
DWO WALL
Sonklip
Lanzerac

Rainbow's End

R310
EERSTE RIVER
PIET RETIEF
Welgevallen
Splendido
Stellenbosch University/Welgevallen
Brampton
Noble Savage
Montegray

Rascallion
Steliekaya
The High Road
Vilafonté
Dalla Cia

Rudera
Stark-Condé
JONKERSHOEK RIVER
TO JONKERSHOEK

6

Kleine Zalze
Gentleman Spirits
PARADYSKLOOF RD
Blaauwklippen
Chabivin
Vriesenhof
BLAAUWKLIPPEN RD

7

R44
Spotswood
Klein Dasbosch
Stellenrust
Dornier
Graceland
Tamboerskloof-Kleinood
Audacia
Peter Falke
Rust en Vrede
Stellenzicht
Waterford
Alto
Weberburg
Dombeya/Haskell
Keermont
Annandale
Akkerdraal
Guardian Peak/Cirrus/Stellenbosch Reserve/Donkiesbaai
Ernie Els
De Trafford
TO STRAND
Hidden Valley
Uva Mira

8

E   F   G   H

Helderberg

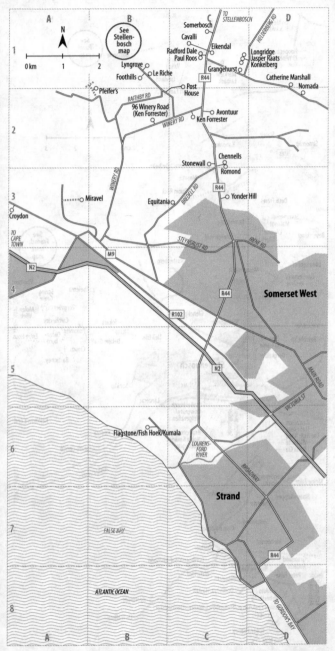

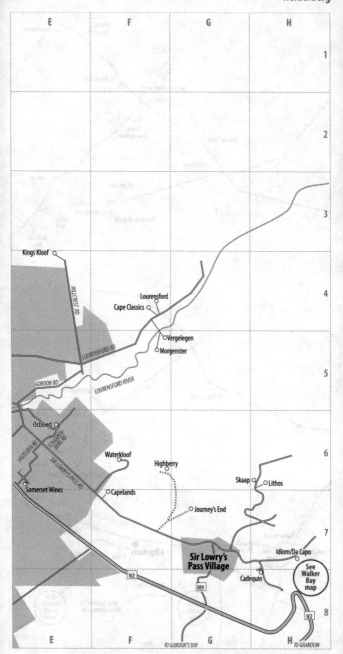

Paarl

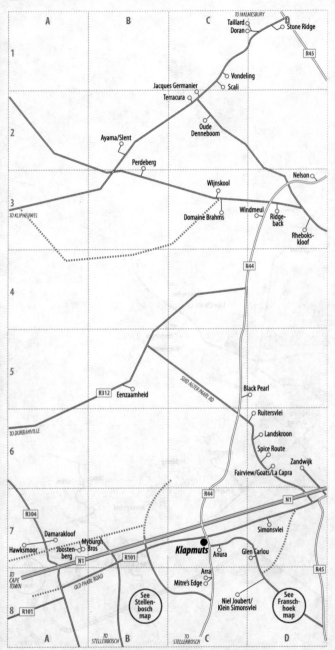

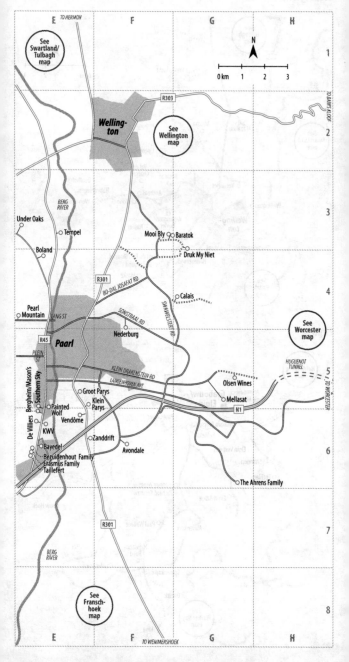

Wellington

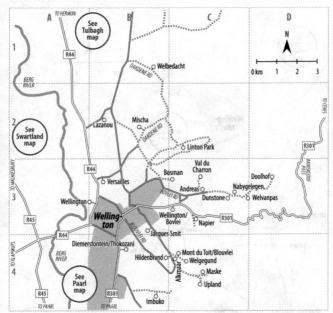

Elgin

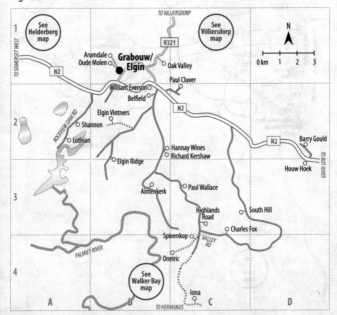

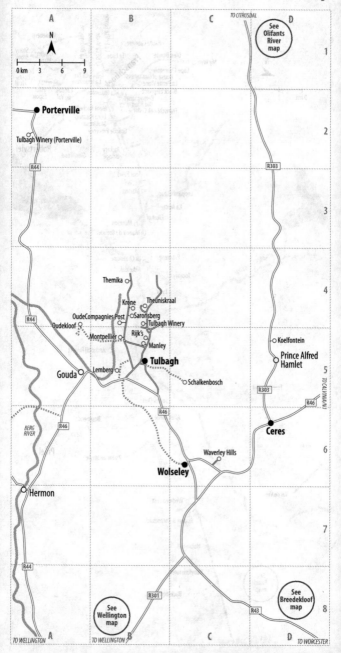

TO CITRUSDAL

See
Olifants
River
map

Porterville

Tulbagh Winery (Porterville)

R44

R303

Themika

Krone
Theuniskraal
OudeCompagnies Post
Saronsberg
Oudekloof
Tulbagh Winery
Montpellier
Rijk's

Koelfontein

Manley
Tulbagh

Prince Alfred
Hamlet

Gouda
Lemberg

Schalkenbosch

R303

R46

TO CALVINIA?

BERG
RIVER

R46

Ceres

Waverley Hills

Hermon

Wolseley

R44

See
Wellington
map

R301

See
Breedekloof
map

R43

TO WELLINGTON

TO WELLINGTON

TO WORCESTER

N

0 km   3   6   9

Franschhoek

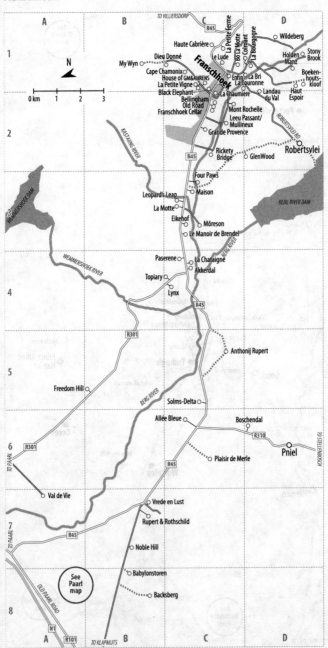

R45

Haute Cabrière
Le Lude
La Petite Ferme
Colmant
B50 La Motte
La Bourgogne
Wildeberg

Dieu Donné
My Wyn
Holden
Manz
Stony Brook

Cape Chamonix
House of GM&AHRENS
La Petite Vigne
Black Elephant
Bellingham
Old Road
Franschhoek Cellar

Franschhoek

Enfin
La Bri
La Couronne
Boeken-
houts-
kloof

La Chaumière
Landau
du Val
Haut
Espoir

Mont Rochelle
Leeu Passant/
Mullineux

Grande Provence

ROBERTSVLEI RD

Rickety
Bridge
GlenWood
Robertsvlei

R45

KASTLING RIVER

WEMMERSHOEK DAM

Four Paws

BERG RIVER DAM

Leopard's Leap
Maison

La Motte

Eikehof
Môreson

Le Manoir de Brendel

Paserene
La Chataigne

Topiary
Akkerdal

Lynx

R45

WEMMERSHOEK RIVER

BERG RIVER

R301

Anthonij Rupert

Freedom Hill

BERG RIVER

Solms-Delta

Allée Bleue
Boschendal

R310

Pniel

TO PAARL

R301

Plaisir de Merle

R45

TO STELLENBOSCH

Val de Vie

Vrede en Lust

R45

Rupert & Rothschild

Noble Hill

TO PAARL

Babylonstoren

See Paarl
map

Backsberg

OLD PAARL ROAD

N1

R101

TO KLAPMUTS

0 km   1   2   3

N

Walker Bay & Bot River

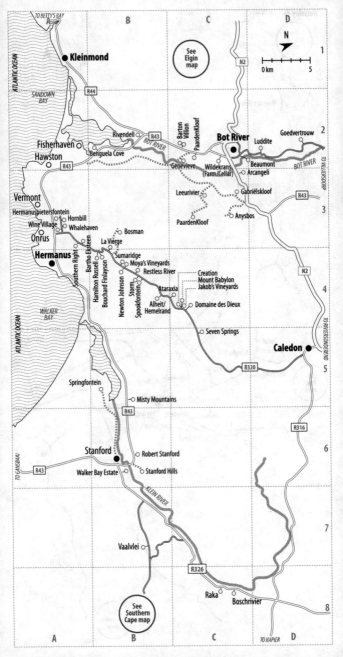

Breedekloof

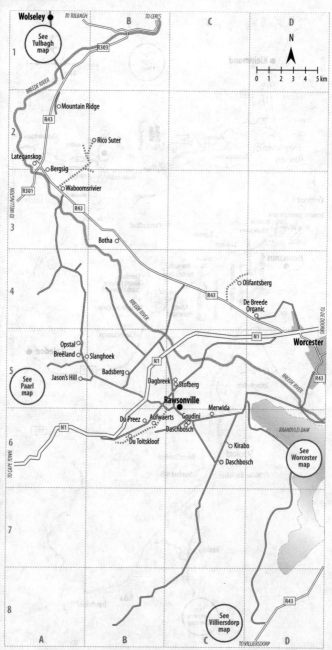

Worcester

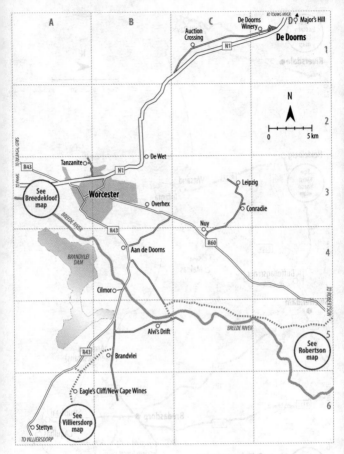

Villiersdorp

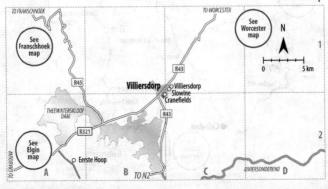

Southern Cape

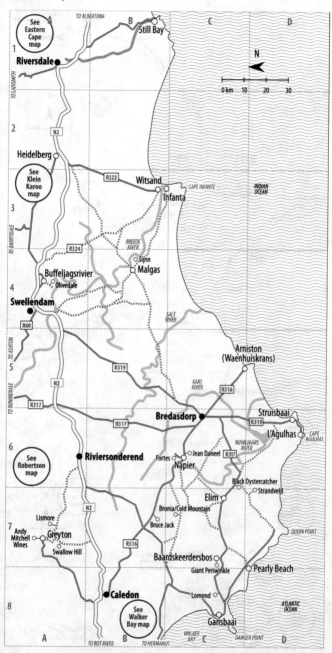

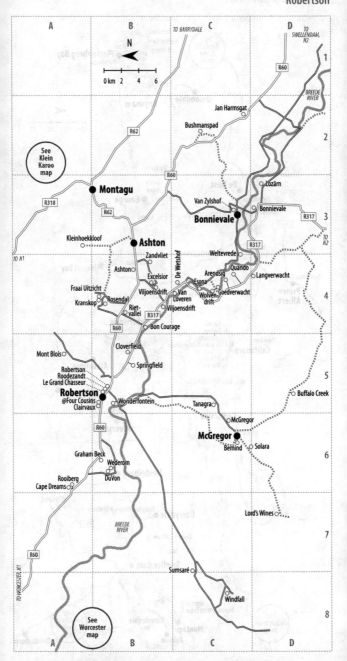

Klein Karoo & Garden Route

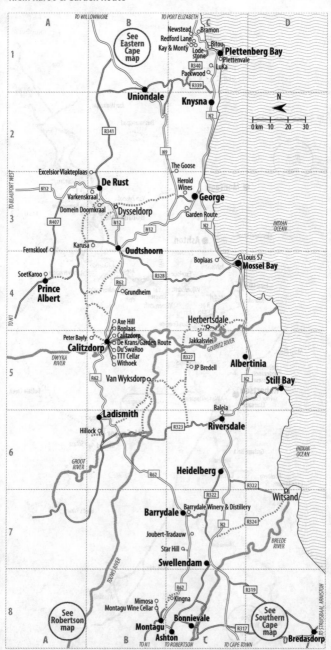

Northern Cape, Free State & North West

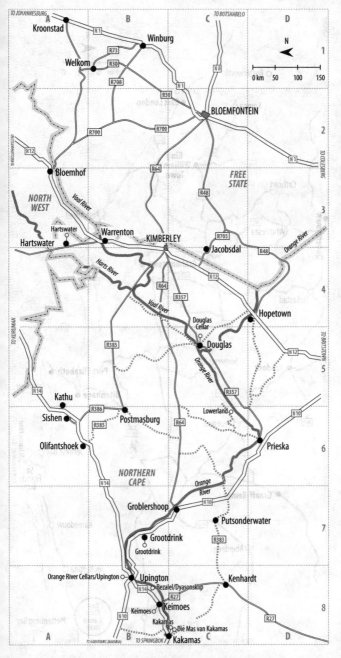

Eastern Cape

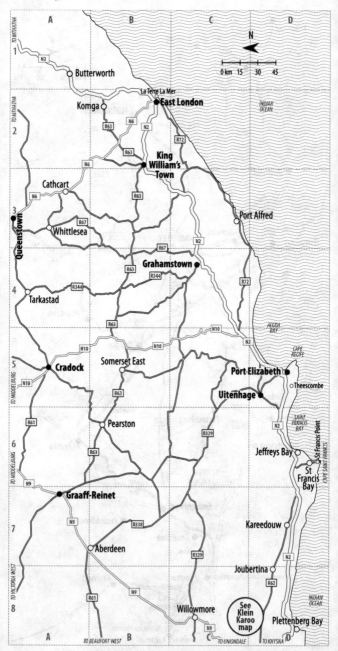

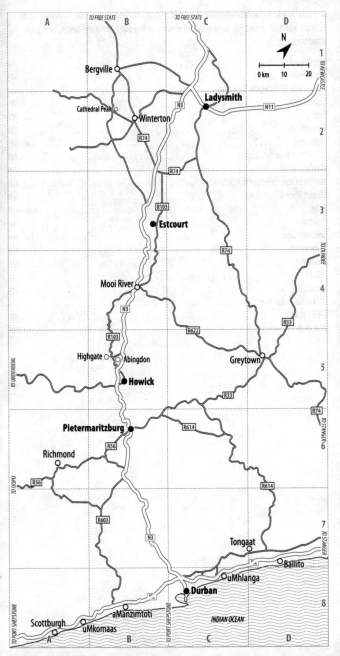

Index of Maps

The order in which the maps are placed has been changed this edition, and now reads from north to south and west to east. For convenience, the maps are listed alphabetically below, with page references.

Breedekloof 704
Cape Peninsula 693
Durbanville, Philadelphia & Darling 692
Eastern Cape 710
Elgin 700
Franschhoek 702
Helderberg 696–697
Klein Karoo & Garden Route 708
KwaZulu-Natal 711
Northern Cape, Free State & North West 709
Olifants River & West Coast 690
Paarl 698–699
Robertson 707
Southern Cape 706
Stellenbosch 694–695
Swartland 691
Tulbagh 701
Villiersdorp 705
Walker Bay & Bot River 703
Wellington 700
Worcester 705